The New Penguin Thesaurus

THE NEW
PENGUIN
THESAURUS

Edited by
Rosalind Fergusson
Martin Manser
David Pickering

PENGUIN BOOKS

PENGUIN BOOKS

Published by the Penguin Group
Penguin Books Ltd, 27 Wrights Lane, London w8 5TZ, England
Penguin Putnam Inc., 375 Hudson Street, New York, New York 10014, USA
Penguin Books Australia Ltd, Ringwood, Victoria, Australia
Penguin Books Canada Ltd, 10 Alcorn Avenue, Toronto, Ontario, Canada M4V 3B2
Penguin Books India (P) Ltd, 11, Community Centre, Panchsheel Park, New Delhi – 110 017, India
Penguin Books (NZ) Ltd, Private Bag 102902, NSMC, Auckland, New Zealand
Penguin Books (South Africa) (Pty) Ltd, 5 Watkins Street, Denver Ext 4, Johannesburg 2094, South Africa

Penguin Books Ltd, Registered Offices: Harmondsworth, Middlesex, England

First published 2000
7

Typeset in Linotype ITC Stone
Typeset by Rowland Phototypesetting Ltd, Bury St Edmunds, Suffolk
Printed in Finland by WS Bookwell Ltd

ISBN 0140-29311-6

Contents

Preface

The aim of the *New Penguin Thesaurus* is to collect groups of words of similar meaning, enabling users to avoid repetition in writing and speaking, and to find quickly and easily the most appropriate word for any occasion. English has a prolific vocabulary reflecting the multiplicity of its sources – the Anglo-Saxon of its early inhabitants, the enrichment provided by its Roman, Viking and Norman invaders, and borrowings from languages throughout the world. The result is a language stock that has an enormous range of precise shades and nuances of meaning. For the users of such a language, a dictionary of synonyms becomes a necessity.

While it is probable that there are no true synonyms – that few words can really be interchanged in all contexts without any difference in connotations – on many occasions memories need to be nudged for the appropriate synonym to complete a sentence or paragraph without repetition. To achieve this, this dictionary consists of a single alphabetical list of headwords, each followed by a selection of synonyms arranged under numbered senses. Within each sense an example of the word's use in context is given to pin-point the precise meaning that is required. The example is followed by synonyms grouped together according to the different shades of meaning.

Two markers are used to distinguish words that suggest a particular style: (*inf*) (for 'informal') for words used especially in relaxed conversation and casual writing (e.g. used between friends) rather than in formal writing; (*sl*) (for 'slang') for very informal words that refer to subjects traditionally thought to be shocking or vulgar or for words that are sometimes restricted to a particular group in society.

At the end of certain headwords, fixed expressions or phrases (e.g. *in abeyance, at large, last word*) have their own lists of synonyms.

In addition to the synonym lists, for many of the entries the word that is opposite in meaning (an antonym) is given after the word OPPOSITE at the end of the sense division or entry.

Part-of-speech markers are given where necessary to distinguish between the different senses or between headwords with identical spelling. They are as follows:

adj (adjective)	*pl noun* (plural noun)
adv (adverb)	*prep* (preposition)
conj (conjunction)	*pronoun*
interj (interjection)	*verb*
noun	

The *New Penguin Thesaurus* is a complete reworking of the dictionary that was originally published as the *Nuttal Dictionary of English Synonyms and Antonyms*, with its last revised edition in 1986. In recent years many words and senses have changed their meaning and many new ones have appeared, so for this entirely new edition the dictionary has been thoroughly updated and significantly enlarged, both in the selection of words covered and in the range of synonyms and opposites offered.

Acknowledgements

We would like to thank Gloria Wren and Catherine Wren for their assistance in compiling parts of the text and also Commander F. Val Jones, who, with his late wife, made many helpful suggestions for revising the text.

Rosalind Fergusson
Martin Manser
David Pickering

The Thesaurus

aback *adv* **taken aback** surprised, startled, amazed, astonished, dumbfounded, speechless, gobsmacked (*inf*), flabbergasted (*inf*), nonplussed, disconcerted.

abandon *verb* **1** (*abandon a friend*) desert, leave, strand, maroon, leave high and dry (*inf*), leave in the lurch (*inf*), forsake, cast aside, cast away, discard, get rid of, ditch (*inf*), drop, jilt, chuck (*inf*), run out on (*inf*). OPPOSITE: support. **2** (*abandon ship*) leave, quit, depart from, vacate, evacuate, withdraw from. **3** (*abandon a habit*) give up, stop, cease, abort, scrap (*inf*), pack in (*inf*), desist from, kick (*inf*), forgo, renounce, abdicate, resign, jack in (*inf*). OPPOSITE: continue. **4** (*abandon a claim*) yield, surrender, give up, cede, waive, relinquish. OPPOSITE: retain.
≫ *noun* recklessness, carelessness, unrestraint, immoderation, wildness, lawlessness, dash, verve, impulsiveness, impetuosity, wantonness. OPPOSITE: restraint.

abandoned *adj* **1** (*an abandoned car*) left, discarded, cast away, cast aside, rejected, unused, unoccupied, deserted, vacant, empty, derelict, stranded, marooned, forsaken, forlorn. OPPOSITE: occupied. **2** (*abandoned behaviour*) unrestrained, uninhibited, immoderate, reckless, wild, mad, wanton, immoral, shameless, impenitent, dissolute, debauched, licentious, depraved, corrupt. OPPOSITE: restrained.

abase *verb* lower, reduce, disgrace, dishonour, humiliate, mortify, humble, demean, degrade, debase, disparage, belittle, malign, demote. OPPOSITE: exalt.

abasement *noun* lowering, reduction, disgrace, dishonour, ignominy, shame, humiliation, mortification, degradation, disparagement, demotion. OPPOSITE: exaltation.

abashed *adj* embarrassed, ashamed, shamefaced, disconcerted, discomposed, discomfited, discountenanced, humiliated, humbled, daunted, overawed, intimidated, confused, confounded, floored (*inf*), bewildered, taken aback, dumbfounded, nonplussed. OPPOSITE: composed.

abashment *noun* embarrassment, shame, chagrin, discomposure, discomfiture, humiliation, intimidation, confusion, bewilderment. OPPOSITE: composure.

abate *verb* **1** (*waiting for the storm to abate*) subside, let up, die down, remit, moderate, lessen, reduce, decrease, diminish, decline, wane, ebb, ease, slacken. OPPOSITE: increase. **2** (*abate the pain*) relieve, alleviate, ease, assuage, soothe, palliate, calm, pacify, appease, quell, mitigate, moderate, lessen, reduce, decrease, diminish, attenuate, weaken. OPPOSITE: intensify.

abatement *noun* **1** (*abatement of the storm*) remission, moderation, easing, lessening, reduction, decrease, diminution, decline, wane. OPPOSITE: increase. **2** (*abatement of the pain*) relief, alleviation, assuagement, palliation, appeasement, mitigation, moderation, reduction. OPPOSITE: intensification. **3** (*noise abatement*) lowering, decrease, suppression, control, restraint, limitation, termination.

abbey *noun* monastery, friary, priory, nunnery, convent, cloister, church, minster, cathedral.

abbreviate *verb* shorten, curtail, truncate, clip, trim, cut, abridge, cut down, reduce, condense, contract, shrink, compress, paraphrase, summarize, précis, abstract, digest. OPPOSITE: lengthen.

abbreviation *noun* **1** (*an abbreviation of a company name*) short form, truncated form, contraction, acronym, initialism. OPPOSITE: expansion. **2** (*an abbreviation of the text*) shortening, curtailment, truncation, abridgment, reduction, condensation, contraction, compression, paraphrase, summary, précis, résumé, synopsis, abstract, digest. OPPOSITE: extension.

abdicate *verb* **1** (*when a monarch abdicates*) resign, retire, stand down, quit, vacate, give up the throne. **2** (*abdicate responsibility*) refuse, give up, relinquish, renounce, forgo, abandon, turn one's back on, disown, repudiate, abjure, reject, cast aside, wash one's hands of (*inf*), yield, surrender, cede, waive. OPPOSITE: accept.

abdication *noun* **1** (*abdication from the throne*) resignation, retirement, renunciation, standing down. **2** (*abdication of responsibility*) refusal, relinquishment, abandonment, repudiation, abjuration, abnegation, rejection, surrender, cession, waiver. OPPOSITE: acceptance.

abdomen *noun* belly, paunch (*inf*), stomach, tummy (*inf*), tum (*inf*), midriff, gut, intestines, viscera, guts (*inf*), insides (*inf*), corporation (*inf*), potbelly (*inf*), beer gut (*inf*).

abdominal *adj* intestinal, visceral, coeliac, gastric, stomachic, ventral.

abduct *verb* kidnap, carry off, run away with, run off with, make off with, snatch, seize, appropriate, remove, hold to ransom, hold hostage, seduce, spirit away. OPPOSITE: restore.

abduction *noun* kidnapping, snatching, seizure, appropriation, removal, seduction. OPPOSITE: restoration.

aberrant *adj* irregular, abnormal, atypical, anomalous, freakish, rogue, unusual, singular, eccentric, peculiar, odd, deviant, deviating, divergent, wandering, rambling, erroneous, wrong, perverted, corrupt. OPPOSITE: regular.

aberration *noun* **1** (*aberration in behaviour*) deviation, divergence, wandering, straying, irregularity, abnormality, anomaly, freak, eccentricity, peculiarity, oddity, variation, mistake. OPPOSITE: regularity. **2** (*mental aberration*) delusion, vagary, hallucination, instability, derangement, disorder, disease.

abet *verb* aid, assist, help, back, endorse, second, support, sustain, succour, advocate, promote, favour, condone, sanction, encourage, incite, spur, urge, egg on (*inf*). OPPOSITE: hinder.

abettor *noun* accomplice, accessory, partner in crime, assistant, helper, associate, confederate, instigator, adviser. OPPOSITE: opponent.

abeyance *noun* suspension, deferment, postponement, dormancy, latency, remission. OPPOSITE: revival.
in abeyance suspended, deferred, postponed, set aside, pending, hanging fire (*inf*), shelved (*inf*), on the back burner (*inf*), on ice (*inf*).

abhor *verb* loathe, detest, execrate, abominate, shrink from, recoil from, spurn, hate, dislike, despise. OPPOSITE: adore.

abhorrence *noun* loathing, detestation, execration, abomination, odium, repugnance, repulsion, disgust, horror, aversion, antipathy, hate, hatred, dislike. OPPOSITE: love.

abhorrent *adj* loathsome, detestable, execrable, abominable, odious, heinous, obnoxious, repugnant, repulsive, repellent, revolting, disgusting, offensive, hateful, horrid. OPPOSITE: delightful.

abide *verb* **1** (*can't abide noisy children*) stand, bear, tolerate, put up with, take, suffer, brook, endure, sustain, accept. **2** (*feelings that abide*) last, endure, persist, remain, continue, survive. OPPOSITE: perish. **3** (*wherever such people abide*) live, dwell, reside, lodge, sojourn, settle, rest, tarry, stay. OPPOSITE: depart.

abide by comply with, conform to, observe, obey, keep, keep to, submit to, hold to, adhere to, stick to, stand by, fulfil, carry out, go along with, agree to, accept. OPPOSITE: break.

abiding *adj* lasting, enduring, persisting, continuing, continual, persistent, chronic, long-term, long-lasting, durable, permanent, eternal, everlasting, unending, changeless, unchanging, immutable, steadfast, constant, stable, firm. OPPOSITE: short-lived.

ability *noun* **1** (*the ability to adapt*) capacity, capability, power, potential, propensity, facility, faculty. OPPOSITE: inability. **2** (*her ability as a teacher*) competence, proficiency, aptitude, qualification, skill, expertise, prowess, genius (*inf*), talent, gift, knack, flair, touch (*inf*), savoir-faire, know-how (*inf*), adeptness, adroitness, deftness, dexterity, cleverness. OPPOSITE: incompetence.

abject *adj* **1** (*abject cowardice*) contemptible, despicable, ignoble, ignominious, mean, low, base, worthless, vile, degraded, debased. OPPOSITE: honourable. **2** (*abject poverty*) miserable, wretched, pitiable, pathetic, hopeless, forlorn, destitute, humiliating, shameful. **3** (*an abject apology*) grovelling, servile, sycophantic, obsequious, ingratiating, cringing, snivelling, slavish, submissive.

abjure *verb* **1** (*abjure an opinion*) retract, recant, withdraw, deny, disclaim, disavow, forswear, abandon, renege on. OPPOSITE: acknowledge. **2** (*abjure extravagance*) renounce, give up, abstain from, refrain from, eschew, forgo, relinquish, abandon, discard, reject, repudiate, disown, forsake.

ablaze *adj* **1** (*the car was ablaze*) blazing, burning, on fire, alight, ignited, in flames, flaming, aflame, afire OPPOSITE: extinguished. **2** (*ablaze with lights*) illuminated, lit up, alight, incandescent, brilliant, radiant, shining, gleaming, glowing, sparkling, shimmering, flashing. **3** (*ablaze with anger*) aroused, impassioned, passionate, inflamed, ardent, fervent, fiery, animated, excited, stimulated, exhilarated, furious, raging, frenzied.

able *adj* capable, competent, efficient, fit, apt, qualified, adept, proficient, adroit, skilful, clever, talented, gifted, accomplished, skilled, expert, masterly, powerful, strong. OPPOSITE: incapable.

able-bodied *adj* fit, healthy, hale and hearty, in good shape (*inf*), robust, hardy, sturdy, strong, sound, tough, rugged, strapping, powerful, vigorous, lusty, muscular, burly. OPPOSITE: infirm.

ablution *noun* washing, bathing, showering, cleansing, purification.

abnegate *verb* renounce, deny, abjure, reject, relinquish, surrender, abstain from, eschew, forgo.

abnegation *noun* **1** (*the abnegation of a belief*) renunciation, denial, abjuration, rejection, relinquishment, surrender. **2** (*a life of abnegation*) abstinence, temperance, self-denial, self-sacrifice, resignation.

abnormal *adj* irregular, unusual, uncommon, extraordinary, aberrant, deviant, divergent, different, atypical, anomalous, exceptional, unnatural, freakish, monstrous, singular, peculiar, strange, odd, curious, weird, queer, eccentric, idiosyncratic, oddball (*inf*). OPPOSITE: normal.

abnormality *noun* anomaly, irregularity, aberration, deviation, divergence, difference, exception, deformity, malformation, flaw, dysfunction, monstrosity, peculiarity, strangeness, oddity, eccentricity, idiosyncrasy. OPPOSITE: normality.

abode *noun* dwelling, home, residence, domicile, habitation, habitat, lodging, quarters, accommodation, house, flat, pad (*inf*).

abolish *verb* destroy, do away with, annihilate, eradicate, get rid of, eliminate, stamp out, wipe out, expunge, extirpate, erase, obliterate, terminate, discontinue, stop, end, put an end to, scrap (*inf*), axe (*inf*), cancel, suppress, revoke, rescind, repeal, overturn, annul, quash, abrogate, nullify, invalidate, vitiate. OPPOSITE: retain.

abolition *noun* destruction, annihilation, eradication, elimination, extirpation, obliteration, termination, ending, end, cancellation, suppression, revocation, repeal, annulment, abrogation, invalidation, vitiation. OPPOSITE: introduction.

abominable *adj* detestable, loathsome, abhorrent, hateful, execrable, odious, obnoxious, foul, vile, repulsive, repellent, repugnant, revolting, disgusting, offensive, hellish, damnable, cursed, accursed, wretched, terrible, atrocious, god-awful (*inf*), horrible, unpleasant, disagreeable, nasty. OPPOSITE: lovable.

abominate *verb* abhor, detest, loathe, execrate, recoil from, hate, dislike, condemn, despise. OPPOSITE: adore.

abomination *noun* **1** (*feelings of abomination*) abhorrence, detestation, loathing, execration, odium, antipathy, aversion, hatred, repugnance, repulsion, disgust, distaste. OPPOSITE: love. **2** (*murder is an abomination*) evil, villainy, wickedness, atrocity, obscenity, disgrace, offence. **3** (*the task is an abomination*) nuisance, annoyance, pest, plague, torment, bugbear, curse, anathema. OPPOSITE: blessing.

aboriginal *adj* native, indigenous, autochthonous, original, first, earliest, primary, primitive, primeval, primordial, ancient.

abort *verb* **1** (*abort a pregnancy*) terminate, miscarry. **2** (*abort a mission*) abandon, call off, stop, arrest, check, halt, suspend, terminate, end, axe (*inf*), pull the plug on (*inf*). OPPOSITE: accomplish. **3** (*the mission aborted*) fail, go wrong, miscarry, terminate, come to an end.

abortion *noun* **1** (*have an abortion*) miscarriage, termination of pregnancy, foeticide, stillbirth. **2** (*the abortion of a mission*) failure, termination, end, disappointment, mishap, misadventure, fiasco. OPPOSITE: accomplishment.

abortive *adj* failed, unsuccessful, futile, useless, vain, idle, fruitless, unavailing, unproductive, ineffectual, worthless. OPPOSITE: successful.

abound *verb* be plentiful, proliferate, superabound, flourish, thrive, luxuriate, teem, be thronged, swarm, be crawling (*inf*), be full, overflow, brim over. OPPOSITE: lack.

about *prep* **1** (*a book about gardening*) concerning, relating to, pertaining to, connected with, concerned with, to do with, on, re, apropos of, touching, regarding, with regard to, respecting, with respect to, referring to, with reference to. **2** (*scattered about the room*) over, all over, throughout, round, around. **3** (*her arms about his waist*) around, round, encircling, surrounding, on all sides. **4** (*live somewhere about here*) near, nearby, close to, around, round, by, beside, adjacent to.
➤ *adv* **1** (*about six years*) approximately, roughly, almost, nearly, well-nigh, more or less, in the region of, in the neighbourhood of, circa. OPPOSITE: precisely. **2** (*walking about*) around, round, here and there, to and fro, from place to place, hither and thither. **3** (*hiding somewhere about*) near, nearby, in the vicinity, around.

about to on the point of, on the verge of, on the brink of, soon to, ready to, preparing to, going to, intending to.

above *prep* **1** (*above the mantelpiece*) over, on top of, higher than, atop. OPPOSITE: below. **2** (*above our expectations*) exceeding, surpassing, superior to, over, higher than, beyond, greater than, more than, in excess of. OPPOSITE: below. **3** (*above criticism*) beyond, not open to, not liable to, not subject to. OPPOSITE: beneath. **4** (*value happiness above success*) rather than, in preference to, in favour of, before, more than, instead of.
➤ *adv* **1** (*the sky above*) overhead, aloft, higher, high up, on high, on the top, at the top. OPPOSITE: below. **2** (*mentioned above*) earlier, before, previously, formerly. OPPOSITE: below.
➤ *adj* above-mentioned, aforementioned, aforesaid, preceding, foregoing, earlier, prior, previous, former.

aboveboard *adj* honest, legitimate, straight, on the level (*inf*), open, frank, candid, forthright, truthful, honourable, reputable, trustworthy. OPPOSITE: dishonest.

abrasion *noun* **1** (*worn away by abrasion*) erosion, friction, rubbing, scraping, scouring, chafing, excoriation, attrition, grinding, wearing down. **2** (*a few minor abrasions*) graze, scratch, scrape, cut, sore, chafe.

abrasive *adj* **1** (*abrasive cleaning products*) rough, coarse, harsh, scratching, scraping, chafing, grating, frictional, erosive, corrosive. OPPOSITE: smooth. **2** (*abrasive remarks*) biting, caustic, cutting, sharp, hurtful, nasty, unpleasant, irritating, annoying.
➤ *noun* abradant, scourer, rasp, file, emery board, sandpaper, grindstone, pumice stone.

abreast *adv* **1** (*marching three abreast*) alongside, beside, side by side, shoulder to shoulder, aligned, level. **2** (*keep abreast of developments*) acquainted, familiar, informed, knowledgeable, conversant, up to date, au courant, au fait, in touch. OPPOSITE: out of touch.

abridge *verb* shorten, condense, compress, contract, cut, reduce, cut down, prune, truncate, curtail, abbreviate, summarize, synopsize, précis, abstract, digest, lessen, diminish, decrease. OPPOSITE: expand.

abridgment *noun* **1** (*an abridgment of the story*) short version, summary, résumé, synopsis, précis, abstract, digest, outline, compendium, epitome. **2** (*in the process of abridgment*) shortening, condensation, compression, contraction, cutting, reduction, pruning, truncation, abbreviation, summarization, abstraction, lessening, diminution. OPPOSITE: expansion.

abroad *adv* **1** (*travel abroad*) overseas, in foreign parts, to foreign parts, out of the country, away, elsewhere, far and wide. OPPOSITE: at home. **2** (*spread news abroad*) about, around, forth, at large, widely, extensively, far and wide, everywhere, publicly, in circulation.

abrogate *verb* repeal, revoke, rescind, countermand, reverse, annul, nullify, cancel, expunge, quash, overrule, invalidate, void, abolish, do away with, scrap (*inf*), axe (*inf*), terminate, end. OPPOSITE: enact.

abrupt *adj* **1** (*an abrupt change*) sudden, unexpected, unanticipated, unforeseen, surprising, quick, swift, rapid, headlong, hurried, hasty, precipitate, rash. OPPOSITE: gradual. **2** (*an abrupt slope*) steep, sheer, precipitous, sharp, declivitous. OPPOSITE: gentle. **3** (*an abrupt refusal*) curt, brusque, terse, short, unceremonious, gruff, snappish, blunt, impolite, rude. OPPOSITE: courteous. **4** (*an abrupt style*) uneven, jerky, disconnected, discontinuous, broken, rough. OPPOSITE: flowing.

abscess *noun* sore, pustule, boil, pimple, ulcer, inflammation.

abscond *verb* run away, run off, do a runner (*inf*), do a bunk (*inf*), skedaddle (*inf*), vamoose (*inf*), decamp, bolt, beat it (*inf*), clear off (*inf*), cut and run (*inf*), escape, flee, fly, take flight, make off, leave, withdraw, slip away, sneak off, disappear, vanish. OPPOSITE: appear.

absence *noun* **1** (*absence from work*) nonattendance, nonappearance, absenteeism, truancy. OPPOSITE: attendance. **2** (*in the absence of evidence*) lack, want, need, default, deficiency, dearth, scarcity, paucity, unavailability, nonexistence. OPPOSITE: presence.

absent *adj* **1** (*absent from school*) away, off, missing, truant, not here, not there, elsewhere, out, abroad, gone. OPPOSITE: present. **2** (*absent from the menu*) missing, lacking, wanting, unavailable, nonexistent. OPPOSITE: available. **3** (*an absent look*) blank, empty, vacant, inattentive, abstracted, absentminded, in a world of one's own (*inf*), absorbed, preoccupied, distracted, oblivious, unaware, unheeding, dreaming, daydreaming, woolgathering, faraway, miles away (*inf*), elsewhere, in a brown study, distrait, vague. OPPOSITE: attentive.

absent oneself stay away, keep away, play truant, leave, depart, withdraw, abscond. OPPOSITE: attend.

absentminded *adj* forgetful, scatterbrained, scatty (*inf*), with a mind like a sieve (*inf*), inattentive, distracted, preoccupied, absorbed, abstracted, absent, dreaming, daydreaming, faraway, oblivious, unaware, unconscious, unheeding, unthinking. OPPOSITE: attentive.

absolute *adj* **1** (*an absolute disaster*) complete, utter, total, entire, full, unlimited, unrestricted, unconditional, unqualified, out and out, outright, downright, thorough, sheer, rank, consummate, perfect, pure, unadulterated, undiluted, unalloyed, unmixed. OPPOSITE: partial. **2** (*absolute certainty*) positive, definite, categorical, undoubted, unquestionable, indubitable, unambiguous, real, genuine, actual, veritable, sure, certain, confirmed, conclusive, decisive. **3** (*absolute rule*) despotic, autocratic, tyrannical, dictatorial, totalitarian, arbitrary, authoritative, supreme, plenary, omnipotent, sovereign, autonomous, unlimited, unrestricted, unbounded, boundless.

absolutely *adv* **1** (*absolutely ruined*) completely, utterly, totally, entirely, fully, wholly, in every way, downright, thoroughly, perfectly. OPPOSITE: partially. **2** (*absolutely certain*) positively, definitely, categorically, undoubtedly, unquestionably, indubitably, without a doubt, dead (*inf*), really, genuinely, actually, veritably, certainly, indeed, conclusively, decisively. OPPOSITE: possibly.

absolution *noun* forgiveness, pardon, exoneration, exculpation, vindication, acquittal, dispensation, amnesty, remission, reprieve, discharge, release, liberation, deliverance, freedom, emancipation. OPPOSITE: condemnation.

absolve *verb* forgive, pardon, exonerate, exculpate, clear, vindicate, acquit, remit, reprieve, excuse, let off, release, discharge, release, liberate, free, set free, emancipate. OPPOSITE: condemn.

absorb *verb* **1** (*absorb liquid*) soak up, suck up, take in, draw in, blot up, mop up. OPPOSITE: exude. **2** (*absorb nutrients*) assimilate, incorporate, imbibe, swallow, consume, ingest, devour, engulf. **3** (*absorb information*) take in, assimilate, incorporate, digest, hold, retain. **4** (*absorb her attention*) engross, preoccupy, monopolize, engage, occupy, rivet, captivate, fascinate, enthral.

absorbed *adj* engrossed, preoccupied, immersed, wrapped up, engaged, occupied, riveted, captivated, fascinated, enthralled, spellbound. OPPOSITE: bored.

absorbent *adj* porous, permeable, pervious, spongy, spongelike, blotting, absorptive, sorbefacient, receptive, assimilative. OPPOSITE: impermeable.

absorbing *adj* engrossing, engaging, interesting, entertaining, riveting, captivating, fascinating, enthralling, spellbinding, gripping, unputdownable (*inf*), intriguing. OPPOSITE: dull.

absorption *noun* **1** (*absorption of liquid*) soaking up, sucking up, osmosis. **2** (*absorption of nutrients*) assimilation, incorporation, consumption, ingestion, digestion. **3** (*absorption in a task*) engrossment, preoccupation, concentration, intentness, involvement, engagement, occupation, captivation, fascination, enthralment.

abstain *verb* refrain, forbear, desist, keep from, decline, refuse, forgo, renounce, give up, shun, eschew, avoid, resist, hold back. OPPOSITE: indulge.

abstemious *adj* abstinent, temperate, moderate, sober, teetotal, continent, self-restrained, self-disciplined, self-denying, self-abnegating, ascetic, austere, sparing, frugal. OPPOSITE: intemperate.

abstention *noun* abstaining, refraining, forbearing, desisting, declining, refusal, avoidance, resistance.

abstinence *noun* teetotalism, sobriety, temperance, moderation, abstemiousness, continence, self-restraint, self-discipline, self-denial, self-abnegation, asceticism, austerity. OPPOSITE: self-indulgence.

abstract *adj* theoretical, hypothetical, unreal, conceptual, imaginary, notional, vague, indefinite, general, generalized, abstruse, recondite, profound, deep, academic, intellectual, philosophical, metaphysical, spiritual. OPPOSITE: concrete.
➤ *noun* summary, synopsis, outline, précis, résumé, digest, epitome, condensation, abridgment.
➤ *verb* **1** (*abstract water from the river*) remove, extract, take out, draw off, separate, detach, isolate, dissociate.

OPPOSITE: insert. **2** (*abstract a thesis*) summarize, synopsize, outline, précis, digest, epitomize, condense, shorten, abridge, abbreviate. OPPOSITE: expand.

abstracted *adj* preoccupied, absorbed, engrossed, inattentive, distracted, distrait, absentminded, faraway, daydreaming, dreaming, woolgathering, musing, thoughtful, pensive, oblivious, unaware, unheeding. OPPOSITE: attentive.

abstraction *noun* **1** (*in a moment of abstraction*) preoccupation, absorption, inattention, distraction, absentmindedness, absence, dream, reverie, brown study, thoughtfulness. OPPOSITE: attention. **2** (*talking in abstractions*) idea, concept, notion, theory, hypothesis, generality, supposition, presumption. **3** (*the abstraction of ore*) removal, extraction, separation, detachment, isolation, withdrawal. OPPOSITE: insertion.

abstruse *adj* obscure, recondite, esoteric, arcane, occult, cryptic, enigmatic, mysterious, perplexing, puzzling, incomprehensible, unfathomable, inscrutable, profound, deep, abstract, vague, nebulous, remote, subtle. OPPOSITE: clear.

absurd *adj* ridiculous, ludicrous, preposterous, crazy, nonsensical, senseless, irrational, incongruous, unreasonable, stupid, foolish, idiotic, silly, daft (*inf*), asinine, inane, laughable, risible, derisory, farcical, comical, funny. OPPOSITE: sensible.

absurdity *noun* ridiculousness, ludicrousness, craziness, senselessness, irrationality, incongruity, stupidity, foolishness, folly, idiocy, silliness, daftness (*inf*), inanity, nonsense, rubbish, balderdash, twaddle, gibberish, drivel, claptrap (*inf*), farce, comedy, humour. OPPOSITE: sense.

abundance *noun* plenty, plentifulness, copiousness, lavishness, profusion, exuberance, luxuriance, ampleness, amplitude, fullness, wealth, affluence, richness, bounty, flood, overflow, surfeit, glut, excess, plethora, lots (*inf*), heaps (*inf*), piles (*inf*), masses (*inf*), loads (*inf*), bags (*inf*), oodles (*inf*), lashings (*inf*). OPPOSITE: scarcity.

abundant *adj* plentiful, copious, lavish, profuse, exuberant, luxuriant, ample, full, large, great, rich, bountiful, replete, overflowing, teeming, galore. OPPOSITE: scarce.

abuse *verb* **1** (*abuse power*) misuse, misapply, misemploy, pervert, exploit, take advantage of. **2** (*abuse a child*) ill-treat, maltreat, mistreat, harm, injure, hurt, beat, molest, wrong, persecute, oppress. OPPOSITE: cherish. **3** (*abuse a police officer*) insult, swear at, curse, call names, revile, disparage, defame, libel, slander, calumniate, denigrate, malign, vilify, reproach, upbraid, castigate. OPPOSITE: praise.
» *noun* **1** (*drug abuse*) misuse, misapplication, misemployment, exploitation. **2** (*the abuse of animals*) ill-treatment, maltreatment, mistreatment, ill-use, damage, harm, injury, hurt, cruelty, beating, molestation, persecution, oppression. OPPOSITE: care. **3** (*shouting abuse*) insults, curses, swearwords, expletives, obscenities, blasphemy, invective, slander, calumny, libel, defamation, disparagement, denigration, vilification, revilement, vituperation, tirade, diatribe, upbraiding, castigation. OPPOSITE: praise.

abusive *adj* insulting, offensive, rude, vulgar, blasphemous, defamatory, libellous, slanderous, calumnious, derogatory, pejorative, derisive, scornful, scathing, hurtful, injurious, vituperative, opprobrious. OPPOSITE: complimentary.

abut *verb* adjoin, touch, meet, join, border, verge, impinge, end at.

abutting *adj* adjacent, neighbouring, next to, adjoining, touching, meeting, bordering, verging.

abysmal *adj* **1** (*abysmal ignorance*) utter, complete, thorough, profound, extreme, shocking, appalling, awful, dreadful, disgraceful. **2** (*an abysmal pit*) deep, unfathomable, immeasurable, incalculable, bottomless, endless.

abyss *noun* gulf, gorge, chasm, crevasse, ravine, canyon, hole, cavity, crater, pit, bottomless pit, abysm, void, depths.

academic *adj* **1** (*academic journals*) scholarly, learned, erudite, intellectual, highbrow, cerebral, scholastic, literary, collegiate, educational, pedagogical, instructional. **2** (*less academic than her brother*) intellectual, learned, well-read, bookish, studious, donnish, brainy (*inf*). **2** (*the question is purely academic*) abstract, theoretical, hypothetical, notional, conjectural, speculative, artificial, unreal, irrelevant, unimportant. OPPOSITE: real.
» *noun* scholar, professor, lecturer, don, master, fellow, tutor, teacher, intellectual, highbrow, bluestocking, egghead (*inf*), bookworm, pedant.

academy *noun* school, college, university, institution, institute, seminary.

accede *verb* **1** (*accede to a request*) agree, concur, assent, acquiesce, consent, grant, concede, accept, comply. OPPOSITE: disagree. **2** (*accede to an office*) attain, come to, inherit, assume, succeed, ascend, enter upon.

accelerate *verb* **1** (*the driver accelerated*) speed up, go faster, hurry, hasten, put one's foot down (*inf*), step on it (*inf*), open up (*inf*), give it some welly (*sl*). OPPOSITE: decelerate. **2** (*accelerate the process*) quicken, speed up, hurry, hasten, expedite, precipitate, step up, further, advance, forward, promote, urge on, spur on, stimulate. OPPOSITE: retard.

accent *noun* **1** (*speak with a French accent*) pronunciation, enunciation, articulation, diction, inflection, modulation, intonation, tone, pitch, brogue, twang (*inf*). **2** (*put the accent on the last syllable*) stress, emphasis, accentuation, force, beat, rhythm, cadence, pitch, tone. **3** (*with the accent on style*) priority, importance, prominence, highlighting, underlining.
» *verb* accentuate, stress, emphasize, highlight, underline.

accentuate *verb* **1** (*accentuate the first syllable*) accent, stress, emphasize, put the stress on, put the emphasis on. **2** (*accentuate the difference*) highlight, underline, underscore, draw attention to, point up, heighten, intensify, strengthen, deepen. OPPOSITE: play down.

accept *verb* **1** (*accept an offer*) take, say yes to, jump at (*inf*), receive, gain, acquire, obtain, get. OPPOSITE: refuse. **2** (*accept responsibility*) take on, assume, bear, undertake, tackle. OPPOSITE: deny. **3** (*accept their decision*) agree to, concur with, accede to, assent to, comply with, go along with, acquiesce, acknowledge, recognize, admit, allow, affirm, avow. OPPOSITE: reject. **4** (*accept their excuse*) believe, credit, buy (*inf*), swallow (*inf*), trust, have faith in. OPPOSITE: disbelieve. **5** (*can't accept such behaviour*) tolerate, put up with, bear, stand, suffer, abide. **6** (*be accepted into the family*) welcome, receive, integrate, embrace.

acceptable *adj* **1** (*reach an acceptable standard*) satisfactory, adequate, passable, admissible, tolerable, all right, OK (*inf*), not bad, so-so (*inf*). OPPOSITE: unsatisfactory. **2** (*such behaviour is not acceptable*) tolerable, bearable, supportable, allowable, permissible, admissible. OPPOSITE: unacceptable. **3** (*a very acceptable gift*) welcome, desirable, agreeable, pleasant, pleasing, delightful, gratifying. OPPOSITE: undesirable.

acceptance *noun* **1** (*acceptance of an award*) taking, receipt, reception, accepting, acquiring, obtaining. OPPOSITE: refusal. **2** (*nod to signify acceptance*) agreement, assent, approval, approbation, favour, sanction, ratification, affirmation, acquiescence, acknowledgment, recognition, admission. OPPOSITE: rejection. **3** (*acceptance of our explanation*) belief, credit, credence, faith, trust, reliance. OPPOSITE: disbelief. **4** (*acceptance into the community*) welcome, reception, integration, adoption.

accepted *adj* approved, authorized, sanctioned, ratified, recognized, received, standard, established, traditional, conventional, orthodox, customary, usual, normal, regular, correct, appropriate. OPPOSITE: unconventional.

access *noun* **1** (*a garage with rear access*) approach, way in, entrance, entry, passage, door, gate, way, road, path, drive. **2** (*gain access to the building*) admission, admittance, entrance, entry. **3** (*an access of rage*) attack, fit, paroxysm, spasm, onset, outburst.

accessible *adj* **1** (*accessible by boat*) approachable, reachable, attainable, getatable (*inf*). OPPOSITE: inaccessible. **2** (*aid that is readily accessible*) obtainable, available, to hand, nearby. OPPOSITE: unavailable. **3** (*an accessible explanation*) understandable, intelligible, comprehensible, fathomable. OPPOSITE: incomprehensible. **4** (*a manager with an accessible manner*) affable, cordial, genial, friendly, approachable, informal, easygoing, obliging. OPPOSITE: unapproachable.

accession *noun* **1** (*accession to the title*) succession, inheritance, assumption, attainment, inauguration, investiture, installation. **2** (*a new accession to the collection*) acquisition, addition, augmentation, increase, gain, extension, expansion.

accessory *noun* **1** (*car accessories*) supplement, addition, adjunct, component, part, element, detail, appendage, attachment, fitting, fitment, extra, ornament, adornment, embellishment, trimming. OPPOSITE: essential. **2** (*an accessory to the crime*) accomplice, abettor, confederate, associate, partner, helper, assistant. ➤ *adj* supplementary, additional, extra, auxiliary, ancillary, subsidiary, subordinate, secondary, minor. OPPOSITE: chief.

accident *noun* **1** (*have an accident*) mishap, misadventure, mischance, misfortune, blow, casualty,

calamity, disaster, tragedy, injury, crash, collision, shunt (*inf*), prang (*inf*), smash-up (*inf*) pile-up (*inf*). **2** (*by accident*) chance, hazard, fortune, luck, fluke (*inf*), fortuity, serendipity, contingency, coincidence. OPPOSITE: intention.

accidental *adj* chance, fortuitous, contingent, casual, random, haphazard, adventitious, serendipitous, unintentional, inadvertent, unwitting, unintended, unplanned, unpremeditated, unforeseen, unexpected. OPPOSITE: deliberate.

accidentally *adv* by accident, by mistake, unintentionally, inadvertently, unwittingly, by chance, without design, fortuitously, adventitiously. OPPOSITE: deliberately.

acclaim *verb* applaud, clap, cheer, celebrate, praise, commend, extol, laud, exalt, honour, salute, hail, welcome. OPPOSITE: denounce.
➤ *noun* praise, commendation, homage, tribute, acclamation, applause, ovation, cheers, plaudits, bouquets, congratulations. OPPOSITE: criticism.

acclamation *noun* applause, ovation, cheers, shouting, acclaim, praise, commendation, tribute, homage, salutation, welcome. OPPOSITE: denunciation.

acclimatize *verb* habituate, familiarize, accustom, adjust, adapt, accommodate, naturalize, inure, season.

acclivity *noun* ascent, upward slope, rising ground, elevation, incline, hill. OPPOSITE: declivity.

accommodate *verb* **1** (*couldn't accommodate all the visitors*) house, lodge, board, put up, quarter, billet, shelter, harbour, receive, take, hold, contain. **2** (*accommodate our needs*) oblige, help, aid, assist, serve, provide, supply, indulge. **3** (*accommodate oneself to new surroundings*) adapt, adjust, modify, fit, suit, settle, compose, reconcile, harmonize.

accommodating *adj* obliging, helpful, cooperative, adaptable, yielding, pliable, compliant, willing, indulgent, conciliatory, considerate, kind, friendly, hospitable, unselfish, polite. OPPOSITE: disobliging.

accommodation *noun* **1** (*rented accommodation*) housing, board, lodgings, digs (*inf*), quarters, billet, shelter. **2** (*reach an accommodation*) agreement, settlement, harmony, compromise, reconciliation, negotiation. **3** (*accommodation to the environment*) adaptation, adjustment, modification, conformity, harmonization.

accompaniment *noun* **1** (*musical accompaniment*) backing, backup, support, obbligato. **2** (*serve as an accompaniment to spicy food*) complement, supplement, addition, adjunct, attendant, accessory, appendage, attachment.

accompany *verb* **1** (*accompanied her to the theatre*) escort, go with, attend, wait on, usher, conduct, chaperon, partner, squire, convoy, follow. OPPOSITE: desert. **2** (*the notes that accompanied the lecture*) supplement, go with, belong to, complement, coincide with, coexist with. **3** (*accompanied him on the guitar*) back, back up, support, play with.

accomplice *noun* accessory, abettor, collaborator, conspirator, associate, confederate, ally, partner, henchman, right-hand man, sidekick (*inf*), helper, assistant, mate. OPPOSITE: opponent.

accomplish *verb* complete, finish, achieve, attain, effect, carry out, execute, perform, do, discharge, fulfil, realize, succeed, bring off, perfect, consummate.

accomplished *adj* **1** (*an accomplished performer*) talented, gifted, skilled, expert, masterly, consummate, experienced, practised, proficient, competent, able, skilful, adept, deft, qualified, professional, educated, refined, polished. OPPOSITE: unskilled. **2** (*an accomplished task*) finished, done, completed, executed. OPPOSITE: unfinished.

accomplishment *noun* **1** (*a list of their accomplishments*) achievement, attainment, exploit, feat, success, triumph, coup, ability, capability, proficiency, talent, gift, skill. OPPOSITE: failure. **2** (*the accomplishment of the task*) completion, execution, performance, achievement, attainment, fulfilment, realization, perfection, consummation.

accord *verb* **1** (*accord them special privileges*) give, grant, confer, bestow, award, present, offer, tender, yield, concede, allow, vouchsafe. OPPOSITE: deny. **2** (*does not accord with the evidence*) agree, correspond, tally, match, fit, suit, conform, concur, harmonize, be in unison. OPPOSITE: contrast.
➣ *noun* harmony, concord, sympathy, rapport, agreement, unanimity, consensus, unison, accordance. OPPOSITE: discord.
of one's own accord voluntarily, freely, willingly, without being asked.
with one accord unanimously, concertedly, unitedly, of one mind, in unison, with one voice.

accordance *noun* accord, agreement, conformity, compliance, harmony, unison. OPPOSITE: difference.
in accordance with in agreement with, in compliance with, in line with, in keeping with, consistent with, according to, following, after.

according *adj* **according to 1** (*according to the author*) as stated by, as claimed by, on the authority of, on the report of. **2** (*acted according to her principles*) in accordance with, in compliance with, obeying, following, in line with, in keeping with, in harmony with, in agreement with, conforming to. OPPOSITE: against. **3** (*paid according to experience*) commensurate with, in proportion to, in relation to, depending on.

accordingly *adv* **1** (*behave accordingly*) correspondingly, consistently, appropriately, suitably, properly. **2** (*accordingly he lost his job*) consequently, therefore, as a result, in consequence, so, thus, hence, ergo.

accost *verb* confront, approach, greet, address, hail, stop, waylay, assail, solicit, importune, buttonhole (*inf*). OPPOSITE: avoid.

account *noun* **1** (*a detailed account of the incident*) narrative, narration, tale, story, description, version, relation, report, statement, explanation, exposition, record, chronicle. **2** (*business accounts*) bill, invoice, statement, ledger, book, balance sheet, calculation, reckoning, tally, score, count. **3** (*of no account*) consideration, importance, significance, note, consequence, import, repute, worth, profit, advantage.
➣ *verb* judge, adjudge, esteem, deem, regard, look upon, consider, think, reckon, count.
account for 1 (*this accounts for his reluctance*) explain,

elucidate, clear up, justify, vindicate, answer for. **2** (*exports account for most of their profits*) provide, supply, make up, be responsible for.
on account of because of, owing to.
on no account under no circumstances, certainly not.

accountable *adj* responsible, answerable, liable, amenable, chargeable.

accoutrements *pl noun* equipment, gear, tackle, apparatus, kit, outfit, paraphernalia, bits and pieces (*inf*), trappings, appurtenances, fixtures, fittings, trimmings, adornments, dress, apparel, attire.

accredit *verb* attribute, credit, ascribe, assign.

accredited *adj* licensed, certified, legal, official, authorized, appointed, commissioned, delegated, recognized, approved, sanctioned, endorsed. OPPOSITE: unofficial.

accretion *noun* growth, increase, enlargement, accumulation, agglomeration. OPPOSITE: dispersion.

accrue *verb* **1** (*interest accruing on investments*) accumulate, amass, build up, increase, grow. OPPOSITE: diminish. **2** (*technological advances accruing from this discovery*) result, ensue, arise, come, proceed, issue.

accumulate *verb* gather, collect, assemble, amass, heap up, pile up, hoard, stash (*inf*), store, stockpile, increase, grow, build up, snowball (*inf*), cumulate, aggregate, accrue, multiply. OPPOSITE: disperse.

accumulation *noun* heap, pile, hoard, store, stockpile, mass, accretion, increase, build-up, collection, assembly, cumulation, aggregation. OPPOSITE: dispersion.

accuracy *noun* accurateness, exactness, exactitude, precision, correctness, truth, authenticity, veracity, faithfulness, strictness. OPPOSITE: inaccuracy.

accurate *adj* exact, precise, spot on (*inf*), bang on (*inf*), correct, right, unerring, faultless, perfect, true, authentic, truthful, veracious, faithful, close, strict, literal, word-for-word, careful, scrupulous, rigorous. OPPOSITE: inaccurate.

accursed *adj* damned, wretched, despicable, detestable, abominable, execrable, obnoxious, odious, hateful. OPPOSITE: blessed.

accusation *noun* charge, allegation, imputation, blame, indictment, impeachment, incrimination, inculpation, arraignment, denunciation, recrimination, complaint. OPPOSITE: vindication.

accuse *verb* charge, impute, blame, indict, impeach, arraign, denounce, point the finger at (*inf*), censure, summon, cite, prosecute, incriminate, inculpate. OPPOSITE: exculpate.

accustom *verb* familiarize, acquaint, habituate, make used, acclimatize, inure, adjust, adapt, train, drill.

accustomed *adj* **1** (*my accustomed route home*) customary, habitual, routine, usual, normal, regular, fixed, set, established, traditional, conventional. OPPOSITE: unusual. **2** (*not accustomed to getting up early*) used, habituated, inured, acquainted, familiar, adapted, adjusted, given, wont. OPPOSITE: unused.

ace *noun* expert, master, virtuoso, genius, adept, dab hand (*inf*), wizard, whiz (*inf*), professional, pro (*inf*), champion, winner, hotshot (*inf*). OPPOSITE: loser.
➣ *adj* excellent, first-rate, first-class, crack (*inf*),

outstanding, superb, great, brilliant. OPPOSITE: terrible.

acerbic *adj* **1** (*an acerbic taste*) bitter, sour, tart, acid, acidulous, acrid, pungent, astringent, sharp. OPPOSITE: sweet. **2** (*acerbic remarks*) harsh, sharp, stinging, caustic, biting, mordant, cutting, trenchant, bitter, vitriolic, acrimonious, rancorous. OPPOSITE: mild.

ache *verb* **1** (*my back aches*) hurt, pain, be sore, throb, pound, twinge, sting, smart. **2** (*with aching hearts*) suffer, agonize, sorrow, grieve, mourn. **3** (*ached to return*) long, yearn, pine, crave, hanker, desire, hunger, thirst, itch.
➤ *noun* **1** (*the ache in her shoulder*) pain, agony, soreness, hurt, discomfort, throb, pang, twinge. **2** (*the ache in his heart*) suffering, anguish, distress, grief, sorrow, misery, woe. **3** (*an ache for the past*) longing, yearning, craving, hankering, desire, hunger, thirst.

achieve *verb* accomplish, complete, finish, conclude, perfect, consummate, do, perform, execute, carry out, fulfil, realize, effect, reach, attain, gain, earn, win, get, obtain, acquire, procure. OPPOSITE: miss.

achievement *noun* **1** (*proud of her achievements*) accomplishment, attainment, exploit, feat, deed, act, effort. **2** (*the achievement of our aims*) fulfilment, realization, accomplishment, attainment, execution, performance, completion, perfection, consummation. OPPOSITE: failure.

acid *adj* **1** (*an acid taste*) sour, bitter, tart, sharp, pungent, acerbic, acidulous, vinegary. OPPOSITE: sweet. **2** (*acid wit*) biting, cutting, sharp, trenchant, mordant, caustic, incisive, sarcastic, acerbic, vitriolic. OPPOSITE: mild.

acknowledge *verb* **1** (*acknowledge defeat*) recognize, admit, grant, own, confess, concede, allow, accept, acquiesce, declare, profess. OPPOSITE: deny.
2 (*acknowledge a letter*) answer, reply to, respond to, give thanks for. **3** (*acknowledge an acquaintance*) greet, address, hail, salute, recognize, notice. OPPOSITE: ignore.

acknowledged *adj* recognized, attested, accredited, accepted, approved, admitted, declared, professed, confirmed, avowed.

acknowledgment *noun* **1** (*acknowledgment of a mistake*) recognition, admission, confession, acceptance, declaration, avowal. OPPOSITE: denial. **2** (*acknowledgment of a letter*) answer, reply, response, reaction, thanks, tribute.

acme *noun* top, summit, peak, pinnacle, apex, vertex, zenith, apogee, crown, height, climax, culmination. OPPOSITE: nadir.

acolyte *noun* follower, adherent, admirer, attendant, assistant, helper.

acquaint *verb* familiarize, inform, tell, advise, notify, let know, apprise, enlighten, teach, instruct.

acquaintance *noun* **1** (*friends and acquaintances*) associate, companion, contact, colleague, friend. **2** (*acquaintance with the rules*) familiarity, awareness, knowledge, cognizance, understanding, experience. OPPOSITE: ignorance.

acquainted *adj* familiar, conversant, knowledgeable, well-versed, aware, informed, apprised, cognizant, privy, abreast, au fait. OPPOSITE: ignorant.

acquiesce *verb* assent, agree, concur, consent, accept, approve, accede, conform, comply, concede, submit, yield, give in. OPPOSITE: object.

acquiescence *noun* assent, agreement, concurrence, consent, acceptance, approval, compliance, concession, submission, yielding. OPPOSITE: objection.

acquiescent *adj* consenting, compliant, obedient, submissive, servile, obsequious, ingratiating, subservient, self-effacing. OPPOSITE: resistant.

acquire *verb* obtain, get, pick up, come by, procure, buy, purchase, gain, secure, win, earn, achieve, attain, collect, gather, receive, appropriate. OPPOSITE: lose.

acquisition *noun* **1** (*our latest acquisitions*) purchase, buy, possession, property, prize, gain, addition. **2** (*the acquisition of wealth*) acquirement, achievement, attainment, gaining, securing, obtaining, procurement, collection, appropriation. OPPOSITE: loss.

acquisitive *adj* greedy, avid, voracious, grasping, rapacious, predatory, covetous, avaricious, mercenary.

acquit *verb* exonerate, exculpate, clear, absolve, pardon, forgive, excuse, discharge, free, release, liberate, deliver. OPPOSITE: condemn.

acquit oneself act, behave, conduct oneself, comport oneself, bear oneself, perform, do.

acquittal *noun* exoneration, exculpation, absolution, pardon, discharge, release, liberation, deliverance.

acrid *adj* **1** (*an acrid smell*) pungent, sharp, harsh, bitter, sour, tart, acid, caustic. OPPOSITE: sweet. **2** (*an acrid remark*) biting, cutting, trenchant, astringent, sarcastic, sardonic, acerbic, vitriolic, acrimonious. OPPOSITE: mild.

acrimonious *adj* bitter, sour, sharp, harsh, severe, acerbic, biting, cutting, trenchant, mordant, caustic, astringent, sarcastic, sardonic, spiteful, malignant, virulent, venomous, vitriolic, petulant, peevish, testy, crabbed, waspish, cross, irascible, resentful. OPPOSITE: amicable.

acrimony *noun* bitterness, sourness, harshness, severity, asperity, trenchancy, sarcasm, spite, spitefulness, virulence, vitriol, venom, petulance, peevishness, spleen, gall, resentment. OPPOSITE: goodwill.

acrobatics *noun* agility, gymnastics, skill.

across *prep* crosswise, transversely, athwart, astride, over. OPPOSITE: along.

act *verb* **1** (*act normally*) do, perform, operate, work, function, behave, move, take action, react. **2** (*act a role*) play, represent, portray, characterize, impersonate, mimic, imitate, assume, affect, put on, feign, counterfeit, simulate, dissimulate, pose, pretend, perform, enact, stage.
➤ *noun* **1** (*acts of courage*) action, deed, feat, exploit, undertaking, enterprise, achievement, accomplishment. **2** (*caught in the act*) performance, execution, operation. **3** (*act of parliament*) bill, measure, statute, law, ordinance, edict, decree, judgment, ruling, resolution, enactment. **4** (*a variety act*) show, performance, turn, item, routine, sketch. **5** (*putting on an act*) pretence, show, front, pose, affectation, dissimulation, counterfeit, fake.

act for represent, replace, deputize for, cover for, stand in for, fill in for.

act on 1 (*act on orders*) follow, obey, carry out, fulfil,

comply with, conform to, heed. **2** (*drugs that act on the brain*) affect, influence, modify, alter, change, transform.
act up misbehave, cause trouble, mess around (*inf*), play up (*inf*), malfunction.

acting *adj* substitute, surrogate, temporary, interim, provisional, deputy, relief, supply, standby, reserve. OPPOSITE: permanent.
➤ *noun* drama, theatre, the stage, the performing arts, stagecraft, playacting, dramatics, theatricals, histrionics.

action *noun* **1** (*noble actions*) act, deed, feat, exploit, enterprise, undertaking, endeavour, effort, exertion, move, step, measure, proceeding, process. **2** (*using actions instead of words*) movement, motion, gesture, gesticulation. **3** (*put a plan into action*) operation, exercise, performance, activity, work. **4** (*a man of action*) activity, energy, force, spirit, liveliness, vitality, vigour, vim, get-up-and-go (*inf*). OPPOSITE: inaction. **5** (*the action of a chemical*) effect, influence, power, function, result, consequence. **6** (*killed in action*) battle, fight, engagement, skirmish, encounter, fighting, conflict, warfare. **7** (*legal action*) lawsuit, case, litigation, prosecution, proceedings.

activate *verb* trigger, set off, start, switch on, turn on, trip, fire, energize, mobilize, actuate, stimulate, motivate, drive, propel, prompt, initiate. OPPOSITE: stop.

active *adj* **1** (*an active lifestyle*) busy, bustling, industrious, diligent, hard-working, occupied, on the go (*inf*). OPPOSITE: lazy. **2** (*very active for her age*) agile, nimble, sprightly, quick, alert, prompt, ready, energetic, lively, vigorous, spirited. OPPOSITE: sluggish. **3** (*while the machine is active*) operative, functioning, working, running, in action. OPPOSITE: inactive. **4** (*active ingredients*) effective, effectual, potent, powerful. **5** (*active members*) devoted, enthusiastic, involved, committed, engaged, militant. OPPOSITE: apathetic.

activity *noun* **1** (*the activity of the city*) bustle, movement, motion, stir, action, life, animation, industry, business, commotion, tumult. OPPOSITE: inactivity. **2** (*leisure activities*) pursuit, hobby, pastime, interest, undertaking, enterprise, endeavour, venture, project, scheme, act, deed, task, occupation.

actor *noun* player, trouper, performer, entertainer, comedian, tragedian, thespian, star, leading man.

actress *noun* player, trouper, performer, entertainer, comedienne, tragedienne, thespian, star, leading lady.

actual *adj* real, true, veritable, genuine, authentic, positive, absolute, certain, definite, confirmed, indisputable, factual, physical, material, substantial, tangible, concrete, present, existent. OPPOSITE: apparent.

actually *adv* really, truly, indeed, in fact, in reality, in truth, veritably.

actuate *verb* motivate, stimulate, move, stir, prompt, instigate, incite, urge, impel, drive, encourage, spur, goad, inspire, rouse, awaken, kindle, activate, trigger, set off. OPPOSITE: deter.

acumen *noun* keenness, sharpness, acuteness, shrewdness, astuteness, insight, perspicacity, perspicuity, perception, discernment, judgment, discrimination, penetration, sense, wit, cleverness, smartness, ingenuity, sagacity, wisdom. OPPOSITE: stupidity.

acute *adj* **1** (*an acute mind*) keen, sharp, quick, shrewd, astute, perspicacious, perspicuous, perceptive, discerning, discriminating, penetrating, incisive, clever, smart, sagacious, wise. OPPOSITE: obtuse. **2** (*an acute pain*) intense, severe, sharp, cutting, stabbing, piercing, shooting, excruciating, exquisite, agonizing, violent, fierce. OPPOSITE: dull. **3** (*an acute shortage*) severe, extreme, grave, serious, critical, crucial, urgent, pressing, dangerous. OPPOSITE: mild.

acutely *adv* very, extremely, strongly, intensely, keenly, sharply, deeply, profoundly. OPPOSITE: slightly.

adage *noun* saying, proverb, aphorism, truism, maxim, precept, axiom, dictum, byword, apophthegm, saw.

adamant *adj* determined, resolute, unyielding, inflexible, unbending, rigid, firm, tough, hard, unrelenting, intransigent, immovable, unshakeable, stubborn, obdurate. OPPOSITE: flexible.

adapt *verb* **1** (*adapt to new surroundings*) adjust, accommodate, familiarize, habituate, acclimatize, conform, match, harmonize, coordinate. **2** (*adapt a novel for the stage*) alter, modify, change, convert, transform, remodel, tailor, customize, fit, prepare.

adaptable *adj* adjustable, convertible, alterable, modifiable, variable, versatile, flexible, pliant, malleable, amenable, compliant, easygoing. OPPOSITE: inflexible.

adaptation *noun* **1** (*adaptation to the environment*) adjustment, accommodation, familiarization, habituation, acclimatization, conformity. **2** (*the adaptation of the novel*) alteration, modification, change, conversion, transformation, remodelling, reworking, revision.

add *verb* **1** (*add an extra line*) append, annex, put on, put in, throw in (*inf*), include, attach, affix, adjoin, join, connect, combine. OPPOSITE: remove. **2** (*add the figures together*) sum, total, add up, tot up (*inf*), reckon, tally, compute, calculate. OPPOSITE: subtract.
add to increase, enlarge, augment, supplement, aggravate, intensify, magnify, amplify. OPPOSITE: reduce.
add up 1 (*add up the scores*) sum up, total, tot up (*inf*), add. **2** (*it adds up to a good day's work*) constitute, comprise, amount to, come to, signify, indicate, mean, spell (*inf*). **3** (*the evidence doesn't add up*) make sense, stand to reason, ring true, hang together, hold water (*inf*).

added *adj* additional, extra, more, further, supplementary.

addendum *noun* addition, adjunct, appendage, appendix, supplement, codicil, postscript, afterthought, rider, tag.

addict *noun* **1** (*drug addict*) user, junkie (*inf*), druggie (*inf*) dope fiend (*inf*), pothead (*sl*), acid head (*sl*). **2** (*television addict*) enthusiast, devotee, fan, buff (*inf*), freak (*inf*), fiend (*inf*).
➤ *verb* accustom, habituate, devote, dedicate.

addicted *adj* dependent, hooked (*inf*), habituated, inclined, devoted, dedicated, obsessed.

addiction *noun* dependence, craving, habit, monkey (*sl*), obsession, mania, enslavement, devotion, dedication.

addition *noun* **1** (*the addition of a new chapter*) adding,

inclusion, attachment, joining. OPPOSITE: removal. **2** (*an addition to the family*) adjunct, extra, supplement, increase, increment, extension, annex, appendage, addendum, augmentation, enlargement. OPPOSITE: deduction. **3** (*a mistake in the addition*) adding up, summing, totalling, computation, calculation. OPPOSITE: subtraction.
in addition also, as well, too, besides, moreover, additionally.

additional *adj* supplementary, extra, added, further, more, new, fresh.

additionally *adv* also, as well, in addition, into the bargain, besides, moreover, furthermore, to boot.

address *noun* **1** (*name and address*) home, residence, domicile, abode, dwelling, lodging, location, place, whereabouts, directions. **2** (*gave an address to the assembly*) speech, discourse, talk, lecture, presentation, oration, harangue, diatribe, philippic, sermon, homily, monologue, soliloquy.
➤ *verb* **1** (*address the crowd*) speak to, talk to, lecture, harangue, preach to, sermonize. **2** (*addressed me in the street*) greet, hail, accost, approach. OPPOSITE: ignore. **3** (*address your complaints to the manager*) communicate, direct, send, convey. **4** (*how to address a duchess*) call, name, designate, denominate.
address oneself to attend to, turn to, get down to, apply oneself to, engage in, undertake, concentrate on, focus on.

adduce *verb* cite, quote, name, mention, point out, give, offer, proffer, present, put forward, advance.

adept *adj* proficient, competent, skilled, expert, masterly, ace (*inf*), brilliant (*inf*), versed, practised, accomplished, experienced, good, skilful, adroit, deft, able, clever, talented, gifted. OPPOSITE: incompetent.
➤ *noun* expert, master, dab hand (*inf*), genius, ace (*inf*), wizard (*inf*), professional, specialist. OPPOSITE: bungler.

adequacy *noun* **1** (*the adequacy of our resources*) sufficiency, adequateness, ampleness. OPPOSITE: insufficiency. **2** (*the adequacy of their work*) acceptability, reasonableness, fairness, mediocrity. OPPOSITE: excellence. **3** (*his adequacy to the job*) fitness, suitability, ability, capability, competence. OPPOSITE: inadequacy.

adequate *adj* **1** (*adequate resources*) enough, sufficient, ample, requisite. OPPOSITE: inadequate. **2** (*an adequate performance*) satisfactory, acceptable, passable, reasonable, fair, not bad, mediocre, average, run-of-the-mill, so-so (*inf*), all right, OK (*inf*), unexceptional, indifferent, nothing to write home about (*inf*), no great shakes (*inf*). OPPOSITE: exceptional. **3** (*be adequate to the job*) fit, suitable, equal, able, capable, qualified, competent. OPPOSITE: incompetent.

adhere *verb* stick, cohere, glue, paste, hold fast, cling, cleave, fix, attach, unite. OPPOSITE: separate.
adhere to follow, observe, heed, keep, respect, comply with, fulfil, abide by, be faithful to, stand by. OPPOSITE: break with.

adherent *noun* disciple, follower, hanger-on (*inf*), supporter, upholder, advocate, admirer, fan, devotee, aficionado, votary, partisan, ally. OPPOSITE: opponent.
➤ *adj* adhering, sticking, clinging, attached, adhesive.

adhesion *noun* adherence, sticking, adhesiveness, stickiness, cohesion, bond, attachment.

adhesive *noun* glue, gum, paste, cement, fixative, mucilage.
➤ *adj* sticky, gummed, stick-on, self-adhesive, tacky, gummy, gluey, viscous, glutinous, mucilaginous, tenacious, clinging, adherent.

adieu *interj* goodbye, farewell, au revoir, bye (*inf*), cheerio (*inf*), so long (*inf*). OPPOSITE: hello.
➤ *noun* farewell, valediction, parting, leave-taking. OPPOSITE: greeting.

adjacent *adj* adjoining, contiguous, touching, abutting, juxtaposed, bordering, conterminous, connecting, linking, attached, neighbouring, next-door, alongside, near, close, proximate. OPPOSITE: distant.

adjoin *verb* abut, touch, border, verge, neighbour, be next to, juxtapose, connect, link, join, attach, unite, combine, add, annex. OPPOSITE: separate.

adjourn *verb* **1** (*adjourn a meeting*) suspend, interrupt, discontinue, postpone, put off, defer, shelve, delay, procrastinate, prorogue. **2** (*adjourn for lunch*) stop, break, pause. OPPOSITE: continue. **3** (*adjourn to the lounge*) withdraw, retire, repair.

adjournment *noun* suspension, interruption, discontinuation, break, pause, interval, intermission, postponement, deferral, delay, procrastination, prorogation. OPPOSITE: continuation.

adjudge *verb* pronounce, declare, judge, adjudicate, decide, award, allot, assign.

adjudicate *verb* judge, adjudge, arbitrate, determine, decide, settle, umpire, referee.

adjudication *noun* judgment, judging, arbitration, settlement, decision, verdict, ruling, sentence, award.

adjunct *noun* addition, extra, addendum, appendage, attachment, appurtenance, accessory, supplement, auxiliary. OPPOSITE: essential.

adjure *verb* charge, command, enjoin, invoke, appeal to, entreat, implore, beseech, beg, pray, supplicate.

adjust *verb* **1** (*adjust the settings*) alter, change, adapt, modify, amend, revise, convert, fix, rectify, regulate, set, trim, tune, tweak (*inf*), arrange, dispose, fit, suit, tailor, shape. **2** (*adjust to a change of climate*) adapt, harmonize, conform, accommodate, acclimatize, habituate, get used, become accustomed, reconcile oneself.

adjustable *adj* changeable, adaptable, modifiable, movable. OPPOSITE: fixed.

adjustment *noun* **1** (*make a few adjustments*) alteration, change, adaptation, modification, amendment, revision, regulation, tuning, arrangement, fitting. **2** (*adjustment to a different environment*) acclimatization, habituation, adaptation, harmonization, accommodation, naturalization, assimilation, integration.

ad-lib *verb* improvise, extemporize, make up, invent.
➤ *adj* improvised, impromptu, extempore, extemporaneous, off-the-cuff (*inf*), unrehearsed, spontaneous. OPPOSITE: prepared.
➤ *adv* impromptu, extempore, extemporaneously, off the cuff (*inf*), off the top of one's head (*inf*), without preparation, spontaneously, freely.

administer *verb* **1** (*administer a company's affairs*) manage, run, organize, operate, control, regulate, conduct, direct, govern, superintend, supervise, oversee, head, preside over. **2** (*administer medicine*) give, bestow, supply, provide, distribute, dispense, measure out, mete out, hand out, apply, impose, perform, execute, discharge.

administration *noun* **1** (*the administration of a company*) management, executive, running, organization, operation, control, direction, government, superintendence, supervision, bureaucracy, red tape (*inf*). **2** (*during the Labour administration*) government, ministry, executive, regime, term of office. **2** (*the administration of medicine*) supply, provision, distribution, dispensing, application, imposition, execution.

administrative *adj* managerial, directorial, management, executive, governmental, ministerial, legislative, authoritative, controlling, regulatory, supervisory.

administrator *noun* manager, director, executive, head, chief, leader, organizer, controller, governor, superintendent, supervisor, overseer, bureaucrat.

admirable *adj* praiseworthy, commendable, laudable, worthy, estimable, meritorious, good, fine, excellent, superb, wonderful, marvellous, brilliant, first-class, first-rate, masterly, great. OPPOSITE: despicable.

admiration *noun* esteem, regard, respect, reverence, veneration, awe, wonder, approval, approbation, praise, appreciation, liking, love, adoration. OPPOSITE: contempt.

admire *verb* esteem, regard, think highly of, respect, look up to, value, prize, appreciate, revere, venerate, worship, idolize, put on a pedestal, adore, love, like, approve, praise, laud, commend, compliment, applaud, extol. OPPOSITE: despise.

admirer *noun* **1** (*admirers of modern art*) devotee, aficionado, enthusiast, fan, buff (*inf*), supporter, advocate, follower, disciple, adherent, worshipper, idolater. OPPOSITE: critic. **2** (*one of her many admirers*) suitor, beau, boyfriend, girlfriend, lover, sweetheart.

admissible *adj* acceptable, allowable, permissible, allowed, permitted, lawful, legitimate, just, fair, right, proper, reasonable, justifiable. OPPOSITE: inadmissible.

admission *noun* **1** (*admission of guilt*) acknowledgment, recognition, acceptance, allowance, concession, confession, avowal, declaration, affirmation, profession, divulgence, disclosure, revelation. OPPOSITE: denial. **2** (*admission to the club*) admittance, access, entrance, ingress, entry, entrée, introduction. OPPOSITE: exclusion.

admit *verb* **1** (*admit an error*) acknowledge, recognize, accept, allow, concede, grant, own, confess, avow, declare, affirm, profess, divulge, disclose, reveal. OPPOSITE: deny. **2** (*admit people to a building*) let in, give access to, allow to enter, accept, receive, welcome. OPPOSITE: exclude.

admittance *noun* admission, right of entry, entry, entrance, access, passage, reception, welcome, introduction, initiation. OPPOSITE: exclusion.

admonish *verb* **1** (*admonished her for breaking the rules*) reprimand, rebuke, reprove, scold, tell off (*inf*), chide, upbraid, berate, censure. OPPOSITE: commend.

2 (*admonished him to work harder*) warn, caution, advise, counsel, instruct, urge, enjoin, exhort.

admonition *noun* **1** (*admonition for wrongdoing*) reprimand, rebuke, reproof, remonstrance, scolding, telling-off (*inf*), upbraiding, censure. OPPOSITE: praise. **2** (*admonition to work harder*) warning, caution, advice, counsel, instruction, exhortation.

ado *noun* fuss, bother, trouble, to-do, bustle, flurry, commotion, hubbub, stir, upset, tumult, turmoil, excitement. OPPOSITE: tranquillity.

adolescence *noun* youth, teens, teenage years, minority, pubescence, boyhood, girlhood, immaturity, development, youthfulness, boyishness, girlishness. OPPOSITE: maturity.

adolescent *adj* **1** (*an adolescent girl*) teenage, teenaged, young, youthful, pubescent, growing, developing, immature, juvenile. OPPOSITE: adult. **2** (*adolescent behaviour*) immature, juvenile, puerile, childish, boyish, girlish. OPPOSITE: mature.
➤ *noun* teenager, youth, young person, youngster, minor, juvenile, boy, girl. OPPOSITE: adult.

adopt *verb* **1** (*adopt a child*) take in, foster, parent, father, mother. OPPOSITE: abandon. **2** (*adopt an approach*) take on, assume, affect, appropriate, take over, embrace, espouse, choose, select, accept, approve, endorse, ratify, sanction, support. OPPOSITE: reject.

adoption *noun* **1** (*give a child for adoption*) taking in, fostering, parenting. OPPOSITE: abandonment. **2** (*the adoption of an approach*) assumption, appropriation, embracing, espousal, choice, selection, acceptance, approval, endorsement, ratification, sanction. OPPOSITE: rejection.

adorable *adj* lovable, charming, appealing, winsome, sweet, dear, darling, divine, delightful, wonderful, lovely, captivating, enchanting, winning, fetching, attractive. OPPOSITE: abominable.

adoration *noun* **1** (*a look of adoration*) love, devotion, worship, idolization, admiration, esteem, passion. OPPOSITE: abomination. **2** (*adoration of God*) worship, veneration, reverence, homage, praise, extolment, exaltation, magnification, glorification.

adore *verb* **1** (*adore a person*) love, cherish, hold dear, dote on, think the world of (*inf*), worship, idolize, venerate, revere, esteem, admire. OPPOSITE: despise. **2** (*adore chocolate*) love, like, be fond of, relish, enjoy, delight in. OPPOSITE: abhor.

adorn *verb* decorate, ornament, embellish, garnish, trim, deck, festoon, beautify, enhance, grace, enrich, emblazon, gild. OPPOSITE: strip.

adornment *noun* **1** (*without any adornments*) decoration, ornament, embellishment, garnish, trimming, frill, furbelow, accessory. **2** (*the adornment of the table*) decoration, ornamentation, embellishment, beautification, enhancement, enrichment.

adrift *adj* **1** (*adrift on the ocean*) drifting, floating, afloat, unanchored, unmoored, loose. OPPOSITE: anchored. **2** (*adrift in the big city*) rootless, unsettled, aimless, purposeless, directionless **3** (*the wire came adrift*) loose, unfastened, untied, detached, separated. OPPOSITE: secure. **4** (*their plans went adrift*) astray, off course, amiss, awry, wrong.

adroit *adj* dexterous, skilful, adept, able, clever, skilled, expert, proficient, masterly, deft, ingenious, resourceful. OPPOSITE: clumsy.

adroitness *adj* dexterity, skilfulness, skill, expertise, proficiency, mastery, adeptness, ability, cleverness, deftness, ingenuity, resourcefulness. OPPOSITE: ineptitude.

adulation *noun* worship, idolization, adoration, praise, flattery, blandishment, compliment, sycophancy, fawning, servility, obsequiousness. OPPOSITE: obloquy.

adulatory *adj* flattering, blandishing, unctuous, fawning, sycophantic, servile, obsequious.

adult *noun* grown-up, man, woman. OPPOSITE: child.
➤ *adj* **1** (*in adult life*) grown-up, of age, mature, fully grown, fully developed. OPPOSITE: immature. **2** (*adult magazines*) pornographic, obscene, salacious, dirty, smutty.

adulterate *verb* debase, degrade, vitiate, alloy, dilute, water down, weaken, attenuate, tamper with, doctor, contaminate, pollute, corrupt, taint, spoil. OPPOSITE: purify.

adulterated *adj* debased, vitiated, diluted, watered down, impure, contaminated, polluted, tainted. OPPOSITE: pure.

adultery *noun* infidelity, unfaithfulness, extramarital sex, extramarital relationship, affair, flirtation, bit on the side (*inf*). OPPOSITE: fidelity.

adumbrate *verb* **1** (*adumbrate a plan*) outline, sketch, delineate, silhouette. **2** (*adumbrate a future event*) foreshadow, presage, forecast, predict, denote, represent, indicate, hint, suggest.

advance *verb* **1** (*the advancing army*) go on, go forward, move forward, progress, make headway, gain ground, forge ahead, proceed, continue. OPPOSITE: retreat.
2 (*medical knowledge has advanced*) progress, go ahead, proceed, move on, improve, develop, thrive, flourish, prosper. **3** (*advance the process*) hasten, expedite, push forward, spur, propel, speed up, accelerate, step up. OPPOSITE: retard. **4** (*advance a cause*) promote, further, help, assist, strengthen, boost, increase, augment, foster, support. OPPOSITE: hamper. **5** (*advance an idea*) suggest, put forward, propose, propound, submit, offer, proffer, present. OPPOSITE: withdraw. **6** (*advance a sum of money*) lend, loan, pay, give.
➤ *noun* **1** (*the advance of the army*) advancement, progress, headway, forward movement. **2** (*technological advances*) development, progress, headway, improvement, breakthrough, innovation, invention, discovery. OPPOSITE: retrogression. **3** (*an advance of money*) loan, retainer, deposit, down payment, credit. **4** (*made an advance to her*) proposal, offer, proposition, approach, overture, move.
in advance ahead, beforehand, earlier, previously.

advanced *adj* forward, ahead, avant-garde, progressive, ahead of its time, modern, ultramodern, sophisticated, complex, high-level, high-tech, state-of-the-art, leading-edge. OPPOSITE: backward.

advancement *noun* advance, progress, development, improvement, betterment, amelioration, furtherance, growth, rise, promotion, preferment.

advantage *noun* **1** (*the advantage of this method*) benefit, gain, profit, good, good point, asset, plus, help, assistance, avail, use, usefulness, convenience, boon, blessing, beauty (*inf*). OPPOSITE: disadvantage. **2** (*have the advantage over another*) superiority, ascendancy, supremacy, dominance, mastery, power, edge, lead, upper hand, trump card.

advantageous *adj* **1** (*previous experience is advantageous*) beneficial, profitable, good, helpful, useful, worthwhile, valuable, of service, convenient. OPPOSITE: prejudicial. **2** (*in an advantageous position*) favourable, superior, ascendant, dominant, powerful.

advent *noun* arrival, coming, approach, appearance, occurrence, onset, beginning, dawn, birth. OPPOSITE: departure.

adventitious *adj* accidental, fortuitous, unexpected, incidental, casual, extrinsic, extraneous, superfluous.

adventure *noun* **1** (*exciting adventures*) venture, undertaking, enterprise, exploit, feat, incident, event, occurrence. **2** (*spirit of adventure*) risk, hazard, danger, peril, gamble, uncertainty, chance, speculation.

adventurous *adj* **1** (*go on, be adventurous!*) daring, audacious, bold, brave, intrepid, fearless, enterprising, venturesome, daredevil, foolhardy, rash, reckless. OPPOSITE: timid. **2** (*an adventurous expedition*) dangerous, perilous, risky, hazardous. OPPOSITE: safe.

adversary *noun* opponent, antagonist, enemy, foe, rival, competitor. OPPOSITE: ally.

adverse *adj* unfavourable, disadvantageous, hostile, unfriendly, inimical, antipathetic, antagonistic, opposing, contrary, conflicting, negative, harmful, hurtful, injurious, detrimental, untoward, inauspicious, unpropitious, unfortunate, unlucky. OPPOSITE: favourable.

adversity *noun* misfortune, ill luck, bad luck, affliction, trouble, setback, reverse, hardship, hard times, bad times, trial, tribulation, suffering, woe, misery, sorrow, distress, calamity, disaster, catastrophe. OPPOSITE: prosperity.

advertise *verb* **1** (*advertise a product*) publicize, promote, push (*inf*), tout, plug (*inf*), praise, puff, hype (*inf*). **2** (*advertise a concert*) make known, announce, declare, proclaim, publish, broadcast, promulgate.

advertisement *noun* commercial, advert (*inf*), ad (*inf*), publicity, promotion, plug (*inf*), puff, blurb, announcement, notice, placard, poster, bill, circular, handout, propaganda, trailer.

advice *noun* **1** (*giving advice to young people*) guidance, counsel, counselling, direction, instruction, caution, warning, admonition, recommendation, suggestion, hint, tip, idea, opinion, view. **2** (*advice of a change to the timetable*) notification, news, word, communication, intelligence, information, data.

advisable *adj* prudent, sensible, judicious, wise, politic, recommended, suggested, expedient, advantageous, beneficial, desirable, best, proper, appropriate, fitting, suitable. OPPOSITE: inadvisable.

advise *verb* **1** (*advise them to wait*) counsel, recommend, suggest, guide, direct, instruct, persuade, urge, enjoin, admonish, caution, warn. OPPOSITE: deter. **2** (*advise us of your decision*) inform, tell, notify, apprise, acquaint.

adviser *noun* counsellor, mentor, confidant, confidante, consultant, tutor, teacher, instructor, guide, guru, therapist, aide, helper.

advisory *adj* consultative, advising, counselling, guiding, helping, assisting.

advocacy *noun* recommendation, support, endorsement, backing, sponsorship, promotion, defence, campaigning. OPPOSITE: opposition.

advocate *verb* recommend, advise, urge, encourage, support, subscribe to, endorse, back, champion, promote, favour, countenance, maintain, uphold, defend, plead for, campaign for, press for, lobby for. OPPOSITE: oppose.
➤ *noun* **1** (*an advocate of electoral reform*) supporter, backer, sponsor, patron, promoter, champion, defender, upholder, campaigner, apologist, spokesperson, proponent, exponent. OPPOSITE: opponent. **2** (*a legal advocate*) lawyer, counsel, barrister, solicitor, attorney.

aegis *noun* support, patronage, sponsorship, auspices, protection, guardianship, wing, defence, championship, favour.

aerial *adj* high, lofty, airy, ethereal, empyrean.

aeronautics *noun* aviation, flying, flight, acrobatics.

aeroplane *noun* plane, aircraft, airliner, jet, glider, microlight.

aesthetic *adj* tasteful, classic, artistic, beautiful, cultured, refined. OPPOSITE: ugly.

afar *adv* far off, far away, yonder, away, abroad. OPPOSITE: nearby.

affable *adj* amicable, friendly, congenial, amiable, cordial, genial, pleasant, agreeable, complaisant, approachable, easygoing, open, sociable, mild, kind, kindly, good-natured, good-humoured, benign, benevolent, obliging, gracious, civil, urbane, suave, polite, courteous. OPPOSITE: aloof.

affair *noun* **1** (*that's not your affair*) business, concern, interest, duty, responsibility, matter, subject, topic, issue, question. **2** (*the affair of the missing necklace*) incident, event, episode, occurrence, happening, circumstance. **3** (*having an affair with her friend's husband*) liaison, intrigue, romance, fling (*inf*), amour, relationship, love affair. **4** (*an affair at the town hall*) party, reception, function, do (*inf*), get-together (*inf*).

affairs *pl noun* business, concerns, matters, finances, transactions, operations, ventures, undertakings, proceedings, activities, interests.

affect *verb* **1** (*affect the results*) influence, have an effect on, alter, modify, change, transform, act on, work on, attack, strike. **2** (*it doesn't affect you*) relate to, apply to, concern, regard, interest, involve. **3** (*deeply affected by the tragedy*) move, touch, impress, stir, upset, disturb, trouble, distress. **4** (*affect a foreign accent*) put on, adopt, assume, pretend, feign, simulate, sham, fake, counterfeit.

affectation *noun* pretence, sham, show, facade, appearance, display, posturing, posing, artificiality, insincerity, hypocrisy, affectedness, pretension, mannerism, airs, airs and graces. OPPOSITE: naturalness.

affected *adj* unnatural, insincere, artificial, sham, fake, counterfeit, put-on, feigned, studied, contrived, mannered, pretentious, pompous, ostentatious, high-flown. OPPOSITE: natural.

affecting *adj* moving, touching, stirring, impressive, poignant, pathetic, upsetting, distressing.

affection *noun* love, devotion, attachment, caring, fondness, liking, inclination, partiality, predilection, favour, kindness, warmth, friendship, amity, goodwill, tenderness, feeling, passion, desire. OPPOSITE: dislike.

affectionate *adj* loving, devoted, attached, caring, doting, fond, warm, friendly, tender, passionate. OPPOSITE: cold.

affiance *verb* betroth, engage, bind, pledge, promise.

affidavit *noun* declaration, statement, deposition, testimony, evidence.

affiliate *verb* join, unite, combine, merge, coalesce, amalgamate, incorporate, associate, ally, annex, adopt. OPPOSITE: sever.

affiliation *noun* amalgamation, incorporation, merger, alliance, league, coalition, union, association, relationship, link, bond, tie, annexation, adoption. OPPOSITE: severance.

affinity *noun* **1** (*have an affinity for someone*) attraction, liking, fondness, inclination, partiality, predilection, rapport, sympathy. OPPOSITE: antipathy. **2** (*an affinity between the two concepts*) relationship, kinship, connection, correspondence, correlation, analogy, resemblance, similarity, likeness.

affirm *verb* assert, declare, state, pronounce, profess, aver, swear, maintain, attest, ratify, confirm, corroborate, uphold, certify, endorse, vouch for. OPPOSITE: deny.

affirmation *noun* assertion, declaration, statement, pronouncement, profession, avowal, asseveration, testimony, deposition, attestation, ratification, confirmation, corroboration. OPPOSITE: denial.

affirmative *adj* positive, assertive, declaratory, confirming, corroborative, agreeing, concurring, assenting, approving, favourable. OPPOSITE: negative.

affix *verb* attach, fasten, pin, tack, stick, glue, paste, join, connect, subjoin, adjoin, add, append, annex. OPPOSITE: detach.
➤ *noun* appendage, addition, prefix, suffix.

afflict *verb* trouble, burden, distress, wound, hurt, pain, grieve, sorrow, torment, rack, smite, beset, try, harass, vex, plague, persecute, oppress. OPPOSITE: console.

affliction *noun* trouble, distress, suffering, pain, torment, agony, anguish, grief, sorrow, misery, woe, trial, tribulation, adversity, misfortune, hardship, ordeal, scourge, plague, sickness, illness, disease, disorder. OPPOSITE: comfort.

afflictive *adj* troublesome, burdensome, oppressive, grievous, sorrowful, wretched, miserable, painful, distressing, harrowing, piteous, deplorable, tragic, dire.

affluence *noun* wealthiness, richness, wealth, fortune, prosperity, riches, opulence, abundance, plenty, profusion. OPPOSITE: poverty.

affluent *adj* **1** (*the affluent society*) wealthy, rich, opulent, prosperous, moneyed, well-off, flush (*inf*), rolling in it (*inf*), in the money (*inf*), well-heeled (*inf*), loaded (*sl*). OPPOSITE: poor. **2** (*an affluent supply*) abundant, plentiful, profuse, copious, luxuriant, exuberant. OPPOSITE: scarce.

afford *verb* **1** (*I can't afford the expense*) spare, allow, sustain, bear, support, pay for. **2** (*the fence affords some protection*) give, bestow, supply, provide, furnish, offer, produce, yield, generate. OPPOSITE: deny.

affray *noun* fight, fray, brawl, mêlée, free-for-all (*inf*), scrap, scuffle, tussle, set-to, clash, conflict, battle, strife, quarrel, altercation, squabble, row, fracas, rumpus, disturbance, commotion, breach of the peace. OPPOSITE: order.

affront *verb* insult, outrage, slight, hurt, injure, offend, annoy, vex, irritate, provoke, pique, anger, incense. OPPOSITE: pacify.
➤ *noun* insult, outrage, aspersion, slight, snub, offence, indignity, wrong, injury, provocation, slap in the face (*inf*). OPPOSITE: compliment.

afire *adj* **1** (*the house was afire*) ablaze, aflame, alight, burning, blazing, on fire, ignited. OPPOSITE: extinguished. **2** (*afire with enthusiasm*) aglow, aroused, passionate, ardent, fervent. OPPOSITE: indifferent.

afloat *adj* floating, drifting, loose, at sea. OPPOSITE: aground.

afoot *adj* going on, up, about, around, abroad, in circulation, in the air, astir, in motion, in operation.

aforesaid *adj* aforementioned, above-mentioned, above-named, described above, preceding, foregoing, previous, earlier.

afraid *adj* **1** (*afraid of the dark*) frightened, scared, fearful, alarmed, terrified, petrified, anxious, nervous, uneasy, apprehensive, timid, timorous, cowardly, craven, daunted, intimidated. OPPOSITE: bold. **2** (*I'm afraid I don't know*) sorry, apologetic, regretful, unhappy, concerned.

afresh *adv* again, anew, newly, once more, once again, over again.

after *prep* **1** (*run after the dog*) following, behind, in pursuit of, in search of. **2** (*page after page of notes*) succeeding, later than, subsequent to, below. OPPOSITE: before. **3** (*after all I've done for you*) despite, in spite of, regardless of, notwithstanding. **4** (*he despised her after what she said*) because of, on account of, owing to, in view of. **5** (*ask after someone's health*) about, regarding, concerning, with reference to. **6** (*a painting after Titian*) imitating, in the style of, on the model of.
➤ *adv* afterwards, later, subsequently, behind.

aftermath *noun* results, consequences, after-effects, repercussions, wake, issue, outcome, upshot, end.

afterthought *noun* postscript, addition, appendix, reflection, second thought, hindsight, retrospect.

afterwards *adv* after, subsequently, next, thereupon, later, thereafter. OPPOSITE: before.

again *adv* **1** (*try again*) anew, afresh, once more, another time. **2** (*and again, we need the money*) besides, moreover, furthermore, also. **3** (*then again, she may be lying*) on the other hand, conversely, on the contrary.

again and again repeatedly, over and over again, time and time again, frequently, often, continually, persistently.

against *prep* **1** (*vote against the motion*) opposing, versus,

opposed to, counter to, resisting, hostile to, at odds with, anti (*inf*), in defiance of, confronting, facing, opposite to. OPPOSITE: for. **2** (*lean against the wall*) touching, on, in contact with, up against, abutting.

agape *adj* **1** (*with mouths agape*) gaping, yawning, wide open. **2** (*agape with horror*) open-mouthed, dumbfounded, thunderstruck, astonished, amazed, stupefied.

age *noun* **1** (*the space age*) period, time, era, epoch, eon, span, duration, date, years, generation. **2** (*mental powers decline with age*) maturity, seniority, advancing years, elderliness, oldness, old age, dotage, senility, senescence. OPPOSITE: youth.
➤ *verb* grow old, mature, ripen, season, decline, fade.

aged *adj* old, elderly, getting on (*inf*), past it (*inf*), over the hill (*inf*), senescent, senile, doting, geriatric, superannuated, antiquated, ancient. OPPOSITE: young.

agency *noun* **1** (*an employment agency*) organization, business, bureau, office, company, firm, concern. **2** (*through the agency of the wind*) action, operation, effect, influence, power, force, means, medium, instrumentality, intervention, mediation, intercession.

agenda *noun* list, schedule, programme, plan, timetable, calendar.

agent *noun* **1** (*a literary agent*) representative, delegate, deputy, substitute, proxy, factor, broker, middleman, intermediary, go-between, negotiator, envoy, emissary. **2** (*the agent of her success*) author, executor, doer, perpetrator, mover, operator, performer. **3** (*an agent of change*) instrument, cause, force, power, means, vehicle, medium, agency.

ages *noun* a long time, hours on end, days on end, weeks on end, months, years, an eternity.

agglomerate *verb* gather, collect, cluster, accumulate, aggregate, conglomerate, mass, heap. OPPOSITE: disperse.

agglomeration *noun* mass, lump, heap, pile, cluster, clump, accumulation, build-up, aggregation, conglomeration, gathering, collection, miscellany, hotchpotch.

agglutinate *verb* adhere, stick, glue, paste, cement, bond, fuse, unite, weld, solder, attach, cling. OPPOSITE: detach.

agglutination *noun* adhesion, bonding, fusion, union, attachment, accumulation, agglomeration, conglomeration, mass, group.

aggrandize *verb* magnify, enlarge, augment, amplify, inflate, exaggerate, exalt, glorify, glamorize, elevate, upgrade, promote, advance, ennoble, dignify. OPPOSITE: debase.

aggravate *verb* **1** (*aggravate the pain*) worsen, make worse, exacerbate, compound, increase, heighten, intensify, inflame, magnify, exaggerate. OPPOSITE: mitigate. **2** (*an aggravating noise*) irritate, annoy, get on one's nerves (*inf*), provoke, rub up the wrong way (*inf*), vex, irk, nettle, needle (*inf*), exasperate, infuriate. OPPOSITE: soothe.

aggravation *noun* **1** (*aggravation of the situation*) worsening, exacerbation, increase, heightening, intensification, magnification. OPPOSITE: mitigation. **2** (*a minor aggravation*) irritant, pest, nuisance, hassle (*inf*), pain (*inf*), thorn in the flesh, irritation, annoyance, provocation, vexation.

aggregate *noun* total, sum, sum total, whole, totality, entirety, gross amount, collection, assemblage, agglomeration, conglomeration. OPPOSITE: unit.
» *adj* total, whole, combined, added, collected, massed, composite, compound, collective, corporate. OPPOSITE: individual.
» *verb* collect, gather, accumulate, amass, heap, pile, agglomerate, conglomerate, cluster. OPPOSITE: disperse.

aggregation *noun* collection, gathering, assemblage, accumulation, agglomeration, cluster, clump, heap, pile, mass. OPPOSITE: distribution.

aggression *noun* **1** (*an act of aggression*) attack, assault, offensive, raid, foray, onslaught, invasion, intrusion, encroachment, infringement, offence, provocation. OPPOSITE: resistance. **2** (*aggression in the workplace*) aggressiveness, hostility, belligerence, bellicosity, pugnacity, militancy. OPPOSITE: passivity.

aggressive *adj* **1** (*became aggressive when asked to leave*) hostile, attacking, offensive, pugnacious, belligerent, bellicose, warring, militant, quarrelsome, argumentative, contentious, provocative. OPPOSITE: peaceful. **2** (*an aggressive sales campaign*) assertive, bold, vigorous, energetic, forceful, dynamic, enterprising, go-ahead, insistent, pushy (*inf*), in-your-face (*sl*). OPPOSITE: passive.

aggressor *noun* attacker, assailant, assaulter, invader, intruder, instigator, initiator, provoker, offender, enemy, foe.

aggrieved *adj* annoyed, vexed, piqued, angry, indignant, resentful, bitter, distressed, afflicted, hurt, injured, wounded, harmed, wronged, abused, ill-used, maltreated. OPPOSITE: pleased.

aghast *adj* horrified, appalled, shocked, dismayed, stunned, thunderstruck, dumbfounded, gobsmacked (*inf*), flabbergasted (*inf*), stupefied, astounded, astonished, amazed. OPPOSITE: relieved

agile *adj* **1** (*agile movements*) nimble, active, spry, sprightly, lively, brisk, quick, swift, lithe, supple, limber, fit. OPPOSITE: clumsy. **2** (*an agile mind*) alert, smart, clever, sharp, acute, quick-witted, prompt, ready. OPPOSITE: dull.

agility *noun* **1** (*agility in movement*) nimbleness, activity, sprightliness, liveliness, briskness, quickness, litheness, suppleness, fitness, mobility. OPPOSITE: clumsiness. **2** (*mental agility*) acumen, sharpness, alertness, smartness, cleverness. OPPOSITE: dullness.

agitate *verb* **1** (*agitate the mixture*) stir, beat, whisk, shake, churn, toss. **2** (*try not to agitate her*) excite, work up, arouse, provoke, incite, disturb, trouble, upset, ruffle, fluster, flurry, disconcert, disquiet, alarm, perturb, worry. OPPOSITE: calm. **3** (*agitating for better working conditions*) campaign, fight, argue, debate, stir.

agitated *adj* worried, anxious, uneasy, nervous, jumpy, unsettled, fidgety, ruffled, flustered, in a state (*inf*), troubled, upset, alarmed, perturbed. OPPOSITE: calm.

agitation *noun* (*in his agitation he dropped the key*) trouble, upheaval, commotion, upset, disquiet, discomposure, flurry, fluster, excitement,

arousal. OPPOSITE: calmness. **2** (*agitation for reform*) campaigning, fighting, argument, discussion, debate.

agitator *noun* troublemaker, stirrer (*inf*), instigator, inciter, agent provocateur, subversive, revolutionary, firebrand, demagogue, rabble-rouser, activist, militant.

agnostic *noun* sceptic, doubter, doubting Thomas, unbeliever, disbeliever, cynic, freethinker, pagan, heathen. OPPOSITE: believer.

ago *adv* past, gone by, earlier, before now, in the past, formerly, previously, since.

agog *adj* eager, avid, keen, impatient, excited, expectant, on tenterhooks, in suspense, on the edge of one's seat (*inf*), curious, interested. OPPOSITE: cool.

agonize *verb* worry, labour, struggle, strive, strain, suffer, be in agony.

agonized *adj* tortured, tormented, suffering, pained, afflicted, distressed.

agonizing *adj* excruciating, racking, searing, exquisite, piercing, acute, intolerable, insufferable, harrowing, distressing, painful. OPPOSITE: mild.

agony *noun* torment, torture, pain, pangs, throes, suffering, anguish, affliction, distress, misery, woe. OPPOSITE: ecstasy.

agree *verb* **1** (*I agree with you*) concur, accord, see eye to eye, be of the same mind. OPPOSITE: disagree. **2** (*agree to our proposal*) assent, consent, give the go-ahead (*inf*), give the green light (*inf*), acquiesce, accede, comply, accept, concede, yield, grant, allow, permit, promise, engage. OPPOSITE: refuse. **3** (*the statements don't agree*) correspond, tally, match, harmonize, accord, concur, coincide, conform, fit. OPPOSITE: differ. **4** (*agree a time for the meeting*) settle, fix, arrange, decide on.

agreeable *adj* **1** (*an agreeable place to live*) pleasant, pleasing, attractive, charming, delightful, nice, acceptable. OPPOSITE: unpleasant. **2** (*an agreeable young man*) likeable, pleasant, charming, friendly, amiable, good-natured. OPPOSITE: obnoxious. **3** (*if you are agreeable to our plan*) assenting, consenting, in agreement, in accord, compliant, willing, amenable, accommodating.

agreement *noun* **1** (*they are in agreement*) accord, assent, consent, concurrence, concord, harmony, unison, unanimity, consensus, correspondence, conformity, congruity, accordance. OPPOSITE: disagreement. **2** (*sign an agreement*) contract, undertaking, treaty, pact, compact, covenant, bond, transaction, deal, bargain, settlement.

agricultural *adj* farmed, cultivated, tilled, farming, agrarian, agronomic, rural, pastoral, bucolic.

agriculture *noun* farming, husbandry, cultivation, tillage, agronomy, agronomics, agribusiness, agroscience.

aground *adj* grounded, stuck, ashore, beached, stranded, marooned, high and dry, foundered, shipwrecked, on the rocks. OPPOSITE: afloat.

ahead *adv* **1** (*go ahead*) in front, leading, before, in advance, further on, forward, onward. OPPOSITE: behind. **2** (*plan ahead*) in advance, beforehand, earlier on. OPPOSITE: afterwards. **3** (*we were ahead at halftime*) winning, in the lead, superior, in the forefront.

ahead of in front of, in advance of, before, earlier than.

aid *verb* **1** (*aid us in our work*) help, assist, abet, lend a hand, support, back, second, serve, oblige, relieve, sustain, succour, rally round. OPPOSITE: hinder. **2** (*aid recovery*) facilitate, ease, encourage, promote, boost, expedite, hasten, speed up. OPPOSITE: retard.
➤ *noun* **1** (*with the aid of my friends*) help, assistance, succour, helping hand, support, backing, encouragement, service. OPPOSITE: hindrance. **2** (*financial aid*) relief, benefit, subsidy, grant, donation, gift, contribution, alms, charity, sponsorship, patronage.

aide *noun* helper, assistant, aider, abettor, adviser, aide-de-camp, attaché, adjutant, right-hand man, supporter, second, colleague, associate, ally. OPPOSITE: opponent.

ail *verb* **1** (*what ails you?*) afflict, trouble, pain, hurt, distress, upset, bother, worry. OPPOSITE: comfort. **2** (*she never ailed*) suffer, sicken, be ill, be unwell.

ailing *adj* suffering, sick, ill, unwell, indisposed, poorly, off colour, under the weather (*inf*), out of sorts (*inf*), sickly, diseased, infirm, unfit, weak, feeble, frail. OPPOSITE: healthy.

ailment *noun* illness, sickness, indisposition, complaint, malady, infection, disease, disorder, affliction, infirmity, disability.

aim *verb* **1** (*aim a gun*) point, direct, level, focus, train, sight, target, zero in on (*inf*). **2** (*we aim to please*) mean, intend, purpose, propose, plan, design, aspire, set one's sights on, strive, try, endeavour, seek.
➤ *noun* **1** (*the main aim of the mission*) intention, purpose, plan, design, end, object, target, objective, mark, goal, aspiration, ambition, desire, wish. **2** (*take aim and fire*) pointing, sighting, direction, bearing.

aimless *adj* purposeless, pointless, useless, futile, random, chance, haphazard, erratic, unpredictable, wayward, stray, wandering, rambling, drifting, goalless, directionless, undirected, unfocused. OPPOSITE: purposeful.

air *noun* **1** (*fly through the air*) atmosphere, aerospace, sky, heavens, ether. **2** (*a breath of air*) breeze, draught, puff of wind, zephyr. **3** (*an air of indifference*) aspect, look, appearance, manner, demeanour, bearing, mien, attitude, aura, ambience, impression, effect, character, quality, feeling, tone. **4** (*playing a traditional air*) tune, melody, strain, theme, song, lay.
➤ *verb* **1** (*air a room*) ventilate, freshen, cool, fan, aerate. **2** (*air a grievance*) display, show, exhibit, expose, reveal, make known, publicize, broadcast, publish, communicate, express, vent, voice, utter. OPPOSITE: conceal.

aircraft *noun* aeroplane, plane, airliner, jet, fighter, bomber, glider, seaplane, helicopter, chopper (*inf*), balloon, airship, zeppelin, rocket.

airiness *noun* **1** (*the airiness of the room*) openness, ventilation, spaciousness. OPPOSITE: airlessness. **2** (*with airiness in his step*) lightness, buoyancy, jauntiness, sprightliness, liveliness, vivacity, levity, gaiety, blitheness, nonchalance.

airing *noun* **1** (*give the room an airing*) ventilation, aeration, freshening, drying. **2** (*go for an airing in the park*) stroll, walk, promenade, constitutional, outing, excursion, jaunt, drive, ride. **3** (*give one's views an airing*) expression, venting, communication, publication, dissemination, broadcast, declaration, statement, disclosure, revelation.

airless *adj* close, heavy, muggy, oppressive, sultry, stifling, suffocating, stuffy, unventilated, stale, musty. OPPOSITE: airy.

airs *pl noun* affectation, affectedness, posing, swank (*inf*), pretensions, pretentiousness, superciliousness, haughtiness, hauteur, pomposity. OPPOSITE: humility.

airtight *adj* **1** (*an airtight container*) sealed, closed, impermeable, impenetrable. **2** (*an airtight alibi*) unassailable, invulnerable, indisputable, incontrovertible.

airy *adj* **1** (*an airy building*) open, well-ventilated, spacious, roomy, uncluttered. OPPOSITE: airless. **2** (*in an airy position*) ventilated, exposed, draughty, breezy, windy, blowy. **3** (*an airy manner*) blithe, light-hearted, nonchalant, offhand, flippant, breezy, jaunty, lively, vivacious, sprightly, nimble, graceful, supple, lithe. **4** (*an airy being*) ethereal, incorporeal, flimsy, delicate, insubstantial, weightless, light, buoyant.

aisle *noun* passageway, gangway, corridor, passage, path, lane, alley.

ajar *adj* unclosed, half open, gaping, open, unfastened, unlatched. OPPOSITE: shut.

akin *adj* related, kindred, cognate, consanguineous, analogous, allied, connected, similar, like, corresponding. OPPOSITE: unrelated.

alacrity *noun* quickness, swiftness, speed, haste, promptness, readiness, willingness, eagerness, zeal, enthusiasm, alertness, agility, liveliness. OPPOSITE: reluctance.

alarm *verb* frighten, scare, startle, put the wind up (*inf*), terrify, horrify, shock, dismay, distress, daunt, intimidate, unnerve, perturb, rattle (*inf*). OPPOSITE: reassure.
➤ *noun* **1** (*caused alarm among the residents*) fear, fright, scare, shock, terror, panic, horror, dread, apprehension, trepidation, dismay, distress, anxiety, unease, consternation, disquiet. OPPOSITE: reassurance. **2** (*fire alarm*) siren, bell, alert, tocsin, danger signal, warning sound.

alarming *adj* worrying, disturbing, distressing, unnerving, daunting, intimidating, frightening, scary, terrifying, horrifying, appalling, shocking, terrible, dreadful, ominous, threatening. OPPOSITE: reassuring.

alarmist *noun* scaremonger, doomster, doom merchant, pessimist.

albeit *conj* although, even though, notwithstanding that.

album *noun* **1** (*photograph album*) book, folder, scrapbook, file, collection. **2** (*the band's latest album*) record, disc, CD, LP.

alcohol *noun* drink, liquor, spirits, intoxicant, Dutch courage, booze (*inf*), tipple (*inf*), the bottle (*inf*), the hard stuff (*inf*).

alcoholic *adj* intoxicating, inebriating, hard, strong, distilled, brewed, spirituous, vinous. OPPOSITE: soft.
➤ *noun* drunk, drunkard, inebriate, dipsomaniac, tippler, imbiber, boozer (*inf*), wino (*inf*), lush (*inf*), soak

(*inf*), alkie (*inf*), dipso (*inf*), tosspot (*inf*), piss artist (*sl*). OPPOSITE: teetotaller.

alcove *noun* recess, niche, nook, corner, cubbyhole, cubicle, compartment, opening, bay, bower, arbour, retreat.

alert *adj* **1** (*alert to danger*) watchful, vigilant, attentive, observant, on the lookout, on the qui vive, wide-awake, with one's eyes open, heedful, wary, cautious, circumspect, on one's guard, ready, prepared. OPPOSITE: oblivious. **2** (*an alert mind*) smart, quick, brisk, prompt, on the ball (*inf*), sharp, keen, agile, nimble, active, lively, on one's toes (*inf*). OPPOSITE: lethargic.
≫ *noun* alarm, warning, signal, siren.
≫ *verb* signal, warn, notify, inform, tip off (*inf*), tell.

alertness *noun* **1** (*alertness to danger*) watchfulness, vigilance, attention, wariness, caution, circumspection. OPPOSITE: oblivion. **2** (*mental alertness*) quickness, briskness, sharpness, keenness, agility, nimbleness, activity, liveliness. OPPOSITE: lethargy.

alias *adv* also called, also known as, a.k.a. (*inf*), otherwise, formerly, née.
≫ *noun* pseudonym, assumed name, false name, nom de guerre, pen name, nom de plume, stage name, sobriquet, nickname.

alibi *noun* defence, excuse, pretext, reason, explanation, justification, vindication, plea, story.

alien *adj* **1** (*an alien language*) foreign, nonnative, exotic, remote, extraterrestrial. OPPOSITE: native. **2** (*in alien surroundings*) strange, unfamiliar, unknown, incongruous, outlandish. OPPOSITE: familiar. **3** (*alien to my principles*) contrary, conflicting, differing, adverse, opposed, incompatible, antagonistic, hostile, inimical, repugnant, unacceptable. OPPOSITE: harmonious.
≫ *noun* foreigner, immigrant, stranger, outsider, newcomer. OPPOSITE: native.

alienate *verb* estrange, disaffect, set against, divert, turn away, sever, separate, divorce, cut off, break off, withdraw. OPPOSITE: conciliate.

alienation *noun* estrangement, disaffection, withdrawal, remoteness, isolation, separation, divorce, severance, rupture, breach, division. OPPOSITE: conciliation.

alight[1] *verb* **1** (*alight from a train*) get off, disembark, debark, dismount, descend. OPPOSITE: board. **2** (*alight on a branch*) land, touch down, settle, perch, come to rest, light.

alight[2] *adj* **1** (*set the wood alight*) lit, ignited, burning, on fire, blazing, ablaze. OPPOSITE: extinguished. **2** (*with eyes alight*) bright, shining, lit up, illuminated.

align *verb* **1** (*align the columns*) straighten, range, rank, line up, even up, make parallel, adjust, regulate, arrange, put in order. **2** (*politically aligned with neighbouring countries*) affiliate, associate, ally, unite, join, combine, side, sympathize, agree, cooperate.

alignment *noun* **1** (*out of alignment*) straightness, ranking, line, evenness, adjustment, arrangement, order. **2** (*political alignment*) affiliation, association, alliance, union, sympathy, agreement, cooperation.

alike *adj* similar, resembling, like, comparable, allied, related, akin, cognate, analogous, corresponding,

equivalent, the same, identical, indistinguishable, interchangeable, equal, even. OPPOSITE: unlike.
≫ *adv* the same, in the same way, similarly, correspondingly, identically, equally.

alimony *noun* maintenance, support, keep, livelihood.

alive *adj* **1** (*while my grandparents were alive*) living, live, breathing, animate, in the land of the living (*inf*), alive and kicking (*inf*), still going strong (*inf*), existent, extant, active. OPPOSITE: dead. **2** (*I don't feel very alive this morning*) alert, quick, smart, sharp, lively, sprightly, animated, vivacious, full of life, active, energetic, vigorous, spirited, vital, zestful. OPPOSITE: sluggish. **3** (*alive with ants*) crawling, teeming, swarming, bristling, crowded, packed, overflowing, full.
alive to aware of, heedful of, cognizant of, alert to, awake to, sensitive to.

all *adj* **1** (*not all cats hate water*) each, every, every single, each and every. OPPOSITE: no. **2** (*with all our strength*) the whole of, the entirety of, the totality of, every bit of. OPPOSITE: some. **3** (*in all fairness*) complete, total, entire, utter, full, perfect. OPPOSITE: partial.
≫ *adv* wholly, entirely, completely, totally, altogether, utterly, quite, fully. OPPOSITE: partly.
≫ *noun* **1** (*all were sold*) whole, total, sum, aggregate, entirety, totality, everything, the lot (*inf*), the whole lot (*inf*). OPPOSITE: nothing. **2** (*signed by all present*) everybody, everyone, each person. OPPOSITE: nobody.

allay *verb* soothe, alleviate, ease, relieve, lessen, diminish, reduce, mitigate, moderate, abate, restrain, subdue, quiet, still, calm, appease, pacify, mollify, assuage, repress, quell, check. OPPOSITE: aggravate.

allegation *noun* assertion, statement, declaration, testimony, affirmation, avowal, averment, asseveration, deposition, accusation, charge, claim. OPPOSITE: denial.

allege *verb* assert, state, declare, maintain, affirm, avow, aver, asseverate, profess, claim, plead, put forward, advance. OPPOSITE: deny.

alleged *adj* supposed, assumed, professed, claimed, declared, stated, doubtful, unlikely, dubious, so-called.

allegiance *noun* loyalty, faithfulness, fidelity, constancy, devotion, support, adherence, obedience, duty, fealty, homage. OPPOSITE: disloyalty.

allegorical *adj* metaphorical, figurative, parabolic, symbolic, emblematic, representative, typical. OPPOSITE: literal.

allegory *noun* fable, parable, apologue, story, tale, myth, legend, symbol, symbolism, metaphor, analogy.

allergic *adj* **1** (*allergic to cats*) sensitive, hypersensitive, susceptible, affected. **2** (*allergic to work*) disinclined, loath, averse, opposed, hostile, antagonistic. OPPOSITE: fond.

allergy *noun* **1** (*an allergy to dairy products*) sensitivity, hypersensitivity, susceptibility. **2** (*an allergy to work*) disinclination, dislike, aversion, opposition, antipathy, hostility, antagonism. OPPOSITE: liking.

alleviate *verb* allay, soothe, relieve, ease, palliate, assuage, mitigate, lessen, diminish, reduce, moderate, temper, mollify, soften, quell, abate, dull, deaden, numb. OPPOSITE: intensify.

alleviation *noun* soothing, relief, easing, palliation, mitigation, moderation, abatement, dulling, deadening. OPPOSITE: intensification.

alley *noun* alleyway, passage, passageway, path, pathway, footpath, way, walk, lane, back street.

alliance *noun* **1** (*the parties formed an alliance*) treaty, pact, compact, agreement, contract, bond, union, coalition, league, confederacy, confederation, federation, affiliation, partnership, merger, association, bloc, cartel, consortium, syndicate. **2** (*the alliance between the two disciplines*) affinity, correspondence, association, relationship, similarity, resemblance, connection, link.

allied *adj* **1** (*allied forces*) united, joined, confederate, affiliated, amalgamated, combined, joint, cooperating, in league, hand in glove (*inf*). OPPOSITE: separate. **2** (*geography and allied subjects*) related, akin, kindred, cognate, alike, similar, analogous, connected, linked. OPPOSITE: unrelated.

allocate *verb* assign, designate, earmark, set aside, allot, apportion, divide, distribute, give out, share out, parcel out, mete out, dispense, ration.

allocation *noun* **1** (*this is your allocation*) portion, share, cut (*inf*), slice of the cake (*inf*), quota, ration, allowance, lot, measure. **2** (*the allocation of funds*) allotment, apportionment, division, distribution, assignment, designation.

allot *verb* assign, designate, earmark, set aside, allocate, apportion, divide, distribute, give out, deal out, mete out, dispense, grant, administer. OPPOSITE: withhold.

allotment *noun* **1** (*the allotment of resources*) allocation, apportionment, division, distribution, assignment, designation. **2** (*spent her allotment on books*) portion, quota, share, ration, allowance, grant. **3** (*vegetables grown on his allotment*) plot, patch, strip of land, garden.

all-out *adj* complete, total, full, comprehensive, thorough, thoroughgoing, exhaustive, intensive, wholesale, full-scale, no-holds-barred (*inf*), vigorous, powerful, unrestrained, unlimited, maximum, utmost, determined, resolute. OPPOSITE: half-hearted.

allow *verb* **1** (*allow her to leave*) permit, let, authorize, sanction, approve, agree to, consent to, give the green light to (*inf*), give the go-ahead to (*inf*), OK (*inf*), suffer, bear, tolerate, put up with, endure. OPPOSITE: forbid. **2** (*allow three hours to get there*) allot, allocate, apportion, assign, set aside, deduct, give, grant, spare, afford, provide. OPPOSITE: withhold. **3** (*allowed that he might be mistaken*) acknowledge, concede, grant, admit, confess, own, agree. OPPOSITE: deny.

allow for consider, take into consideration, take into account, keep in mind, provide for, make provision for, plan for, foresee.

allowable *adj* permissible, admissible, authorized, sanctioned, lawful, legal, licit, legitimate, legit (*inf*), proper, right, acceptable, justifiable, warrantable. OPPOSITE: inadmissible.

allowance *noun* **1** (*exceed the baggage allowance*) ration, quota, share, portion, allocation, allotment. **2** (*a monthly clothing allowance*) payment, remittance, grant, pension, pocket money, expenses, maintenance, subsidy, contribution, benefit, weighting. **3** (*increase tax allowances*) deduction, reduction, discount, rebate, concession.

make allowances for take into consideration, take into account, bear in mind, keep in mind, consider, allow for, excuse, forgive, pardon.

alloy *noun* compound, mixture, blend, amalgam, composite, combination, admixture.
➤ *verb* **1** (*alloy metals*) mix, blend, combine, amalgamate, compound. OPPOSITE: separate. **2** (*pleasure alloyed by guilt*) adulterate, debase, impair, diminish, depreciate. OPPOSITE: purify.

all right *adj* **1** (*was the meal all right?*) acceptable, satisfactory, OK (*inf*), adequate, passable, unobjectionable, reasonable, fair, average. OPPOSITE: unacceptable. **2** (*make sure the children are all right*) well, healthy, sound, right as rain (*inf*), safe, safe and sound, secure, OK (*inf*), unharmed, unhurt, uninjured, unimpaired, undamaged, unbroken.
➤ *adv* satisfactorily, well enough, OK (*inf*), acceptably, adequately, passably, unobjectionably, reasonably. OPPOSITE: unsatisfactorily.
➤ *interj* yes, very well, OK (*inf*).

allude *verb* refer, mention, cite, speak of, touch on, suggest, hint, intimate, insinuate, imply.

allure *verb* tempt, entice, lead on, lure, bait, seduce, attract, beguile, bewitch, fascinate, captivate, enchant, charm, cajole, coax, inveigle, persuade. OPPOSITE: repel.
➤ *noun* attraction, appeal, charm, fascination, enchantment, lure, temptation, enticement, seduction.

alluring *adj* tempting, enticing, seductive, attractive, beguiling, fascinating, captivating, enchanting, charming. OPPOSITE: repulsive.

allusion *noun* reference, mention, citation, suggestion, hint, intimation, insinuation, innuendo, implication.

allusive *adj* suggestive, hinting, insinuating, referential, indicative, symbolic, figurative.

ally *verb* unite, unify, join, combine, collaborate, go into partnership, join forces, band together, team up, league, affiliate, confederate, federate, associate, merge, marry. OPPOSITE: separate.
➤ *noun* confederate, associate, partner, colleague, friend, accomplice, abettor, accessory, assistant, helper. OPPOSITE: enemy.

almanac *noun* yearbook, annual, calendar, register, annals, ephemeris.

almighty *adj* **1** (*Almighty God*) all-powerful, omnipotent, supreme, absolute. OPPOSITE: impotent. **2** (*an almighty crash*) great, terrible, awful, dreadful, severe, intense.

almost *adv* nearly, well-nigh, approaching, verging on, virtually, practically, as good as, to all intents and purposes, pretty well (*inf*), just about, all but, not quite.

alms *pl noun* charity, bounty, gift, donation, handout, gratuity.

aloft *adv* above, overhead, high up, on high, skyward, up. OPPOSITE: below.

alone *adj* **1** (*live alone*) solitary, by oneself, one one's own, on one's tod (*inf*), lonely, lonesome. OPPOSITE: together. **2** (*the house stood alone*) isolated, apart, detached, separate, single, sole, lone, unique. **3** (*he alone* *knows the answer)* only, solely, exclusively, uniquely. **4** *(left her all alone)* lonely, forsaken, abandoned, deserted. **5** *(do it alone)* solo, unaided, unassisted, single-handed, unaccompanied, by oneself, on one's own. OPPOSITE: accompanied.

along *prep* alongside, beside, by, through, during. OPPOSITE: across.
➤ *adv* **1** *(move along)* forward, onward, on, ahead. **2** *(took his daughter along)* together, in company, simultaneously.

along with together with, accompanied by, in addition to, plus.

aloof *adj* distant, detached, apart, separate, remote, unapproachable, cold, cool, chilly, haughty, supercilious, standoffish, unsociable, unfriendly, unresponsive, reserved, uninterested, indifferent. OPPOSITE: friendly.

aloud *adj* audibly, distinctly, clearly, plainly, out loud, loudly, noisily. OPPOSITE: silently.

already *adv* by now, by this time, before now, before, hitherto, heretofore, previously.

also *adv* as well, too, in addition, additionally, into the bargain, to boot, besides, furthermore, moreover, and, plus.

altar *noun* shrine, sanctuary, holy of holies.

alter *verb* change, modify, adjust, adapt, amend, revise, reshape, remodel, vary, diversify, transform, transfigure, metamorphose, convert, turn, transmute. OPPOSITE: maintain.

alteration *noun* change, modification, adjustment, adaptation, amendment, revision, variation, difference, transformation, transfiguration, metamorphosis, conversion. OPPOSITE: conservation.

altercation *noun* quarrel, argument, dispute, row, wrangle, squabble, disagreement, difference, dissension, controversy, contention, strife. OPPOSITE: agreement.

alternate *verb* rotate, interchange, take turns, reciprocate, substitute, replace, oscillate, fluctuate, chop and change *(inf)*.
➤ *adj* **1** *(on alternate Saturdays)* alternating, every other, every second. **2** *(alternate rain and sunshine)* rotating, in rotation, interchanging, reciprocal, successive, sequential.

alternative *noun* choice, option, recourse, substitute, backup, plan B *(inf)*.
➤ *adj* **1** *(an alternative plan)* different, other, another, second, substitute, backup. **2** *(alternative medicine)* unorthodox, unconventional, fringe. OPPOSITE: conventional.

alternatively *adv* or, on the other hand, instead, as an alternative, otherwise, if not.

although *conj* though, even though, even if, notwithstanding, despite the fact that, while, albeit.

altitude *noun* height, elevation, loftiness, tallness, stature. OPPOSITE: depth.

altogether *adv* **1** *(an altogether different problem)* completely, entirely, wholly, fully, utterly, totally, quite, perfectly, thoroughly, absolutely. OPPOSITE: partially. **2** *(£50 altogether)* in all, in sum, all told, in toto, with everything included. **3** *(altogether the mission was a*

success) all things considered, all in all, collectively, on the whole, in general, in the main, by and large.

altruistic *adj* unselfish, selfless, philanthropic, public-spirited, charitable, benevolent, generous, open-handed. OPPOSITE: selfish.

always *adv* **1** *(she always leaves early)* every time, without exception, unfailingly, invariably, consistently, regularly, habitually. OPPOSITE: never. **2** *(he's always criticizing me)* continually, incessantly, unceasingly, perpetually, forever, constantly, repeatedly, again and again. OPPOSITE: seldom. **3** *(I'll always remember that day)* eternally, everlastingly, for ever, evermore.

amalgam *noun* compound, alloy, composite, mixture, compound, combination, blend, synthesis.

amalgamate *verb* unite, join, fuse, combine, mix, blend, mingle, commingle, intermingle, compound, alloy, incorporate, integrate, unify, merge, consolidate, coalesce, synthesize, homogenize. OPPOSITE: separate.

amalgamation *noun* mixture, combination, blend, compound, merger, synthesis, union, fusion, incorporation, integration, unification, consolidation. OPPOSITE: separation.

amanuensis *noun* copyist, transcriber, scribe, clerk, secretary.

amass *verb* gather, collect, garner, accumulate, accrue, heap up, pile up, hoard, store, stash away *(inf)*, assemble, aggregate, agglomerate. OPPOSITE: scatter.

amateur *noun* nonprofessional, layman, laywoman, layperson, dilettante, dabbler, ham *(inf)*, novice, learner, beginner, tyro. OPPOSITE: expert.
➤ *adj* nonprofessional, lay, unqualified, untrained, unpaid. OPPOSITE: professional.

amateurish *adj* unprofessional, inexpert, unskilled, incompetent, inept, bungling, clumsy, crude, inferior, second-rate. OPPOSITE: skilled.

amatory *adj* amorous, loving, romantic, tender, passionate, sensual, erotic.

amaze *verb* astonish, astound, stagger, surprise, startle, shock, stun, stupefy, flabbergast *(inf)*, dumbfound, gobsmack *(inf)*, take one's breath away *(inf)*, bowl over *(inf)*, knock for six *(inf)*, daze, nonplus, bewilder, confound, disconcert, floor *(inf)*.

amazement *noun* astonishment, incredulity, surprise, shock, wonder, awe, stupefaction, bewilderment, perplexity.

amazing *adj* astonishing, astounding, staggering, surprising, startling, remarkable, striking, stunning, prodigious, extraordinary, stupendous, marvellous, wonderful. OPPOSITE: ordinary.

ambassador *noun* diplomat, envoy, emissary, plenipotentiary, consul, legate, attaché, deputy, representative, delegate, minister.

ambience *noun* atmosphere, surroundings, environment, setting, milieu, air, aura, mood, feeling, vibrations, vibes *(inf)*, tone, tenor, spirit.

ambient *adj* surrounding, encircling, encompassing, enfolding.

ambiguity *noun* equivocacy, double meaning, double entendre, equivocation, double talk, paradox, enigma, puzzle, uncertainty, imprecision, vagueness, obscurity, abstruseness, doubt, doubtfulness, dubiety. OPPOSITE: clarity.

ambiguous *adj* equivocal, two-edged, double-edged, paradoxical, unclear, uncertain, indefinite, indeterminate, inconclusive, imprecise, vague, obscure, cryptic, enigmatic, abstruse, puzzling, doubtful, dubious. OPPOSITE: clear.

ambition *noun* **1** (*achieve their ambitions*) goal, objective, target, aim, purpose, intent, design, desire, wish, hope, dream, aspiration. **2** (*full of ambition*) aspiration, desire, yearning, longing, striving, enterprise, initiative, drive, thrust, push, force, energy, get-up-and-go (*inf*), eagerness, zeal, commitment. OPPOSITE: apathy.

ambitious *adj* **1** (*an ambitious young woman*) aspiring, desirous, intent, striving, eager, avid, zealous, committed, enterprising, go-ahead, forceful, assertive, pushy (*inf*). OPPOSITE: lethargic. **2** (*an ambitious project*) challenging, demanding, exacting, difficult, arduous, strenuous, formidable, bold, elaborate, grandiose. OPPOSITE: easy.

ambivalence *noun* uncertainty, doubt, hesitation, irresolution, indecision, wavering, vacillation, confusion, conflict, clash, contradiction, opposition. OPPOSITE: certainty.

ambivalent *adj* uncertain, unsure, doubtful, hesitant, in two minds, irresolute, indecisive, wavering, vacillating, fluctuating, mixed, confused, conflicting, clashing, contradictory, opposing, equivocal. OPPOSITE: certain.

amble *verb* saunter, stroll, dawdle, toddle (*inf*), walk, meander, ramble, wander, mosey (*inf*). OPPOSITE: hurry.

ambush *noun* **1** (*lay an ambush*) ambuscade, surprise attack, waylaying, trap, snare, lure, pitfall. **2** (*lie in ambush*) hiding, concealment, cover, shelter, retreat.
» *verb* lie in wait for, lurk, hide, ambuscade, surprise, pounce on, waylay, trap, ensnare, lure, decoy.

ameliorate *verb* improve, better, enhance, amend, advance, promote, raise, elevate, ease, alleviate. OPPOSITE: deteriorate.

amelioration *noun* improvement, betterment, enhancement, amendment, advancement, promotion, alleviation. OPPOSITE: deterioration.

amenable *adj* **1** (*amenable to the idea*) agreeable, acquiescent, willing, accommodating, persuadable, flexible, pliant, tractable, susceptible, manageable, docile, submissive. OPPOSITE: obstinate. **2** (*amenable to the law*) liable, subject, accountable, answerable, responsible.

amend *verb* alter, change, modify, adjust, revise, improve, ameliorate, better, enhance, correct, put right, rectify, remedy, fix, repair. OPPOSITE: mar.

amendment *noun* **1** (*an amendment to the text*) alteration, change, modification, adjustment, revision, correction, reform, improvement, amelioration, remedy, repair. **2** (*an amendment to the constitution*) addition, appendage, attachment, addendum.

amends *noun* recompense, compensation, atonement, requital, reparation, restitution, satisfaction, indemnity, redress, apology. OPPOSITE: injury.

make amends compensate, recompense, conciliate, atone, make good, repair, indemnify, repay, requite, redress, apologize.

amenity *noun* **1** (*all the amenities of the leisure centre*) facility, utility, convenience, service, resource, advantage. **2** (*the amenity of our surroundings*) pleasantness, agreeableness, niceness. OPPOSITE: austerity. **3** (*social amenities*) politeness, courtesy, suavity, graciousness, amiability, affability. OPPOSITE: rudeness.

amiable *adj* friendly, affable, pleasant, agreeable, likeable, hearty, genial, amicable, good-tempered, good-natured, kind, kindly, warm, benign, benevolent, outgoing, unreserved, sociable, companionable, attractive, charming, polite, cordial, congenial. OPPOSITE: unfriendly.

amicable *adj* friendly, good-natured, cordial, congenial, amiable, neighbourly, sociable, harmonious, peaceable, peaceful, civilized, civil, polite, courteous. OPPOSITE: hostile.

amid *prep* amidst, among, amongst, between, with, surrounded by, in the middle of, in the midst of, in the thick of.

amiss *adj* wrong, incorrect, inaccurate, erroneous, false, untrue, unsatisfactory, improper, untoward, unsuitable, inappropriate, out of order, faulty, defective, awry, wonky (*inf*). OPPOSITE: right.
» *adv* wrongly, incorrectly, inaccurately, erroneously, falsely, badly, improperly, wrong, awry, astray.

amity *noun* friendship, friendliness, amicableness, cordiality, comity, accord, concord, harmony, understanding, sympathy, goodwill, peace, peacefulness, comradeship, fellowship, fraternity. OPPOSITE: hostility.

ammunition *noun* munitions, armaments, shells, cartridges, bullets, rounds, shot, gunpowder, explosives, missiles, rockets, bombs, grenades.

amnesty *noun* pardon, forgiveness, absolution, remission, acquittal, reprieve, immunity, dispensation, clemency, indulgence. OPPOSITE: condemnation.

amok *adv* berserk, in a frenzy, wildly, uncontrollably, madly, insanely, like a lunatic, violently, destructively.

among *prep* amongst, between, amid, amidst, with, surrounded by, in the middle of, in the thick of.
among themselves together, jointly, mutually, reciprocally, with one another, with each other.

amorous *adj* fond, affectionate, loving, tender, romantic, amatory, passionate, impassioned, ardent, lustful, randy (*inf*), erotic, sensual, sexual. OPPOSITE: cold.

amorphous *adj* shapeless, formless, unformed, unstructured, inchoate, irregular, indeterminate, vague, nebulous, confused, chaotic. OPPOSITE: definite.

amount *noun* quantity, number, measure, magnitude, extent, expanse, mass, bulk, volume, total, sum, aggregate, whole, lot, quota.
amount to 1 (*the bill amounts to £500*) add up to, come to, total, reach, run to, equal, make. **2** (*it amounts to the same thing*) correspond to, be equivalent to, be tantamount to, mean, come down to, boil down to.

3 (*the storm didn't amount to anything*) become, develop into, progress to.

ample *adj* **1** (*ample opportunity*) enough, sufficient, adequate, plenty of, substantial, considerable. OPPOSITE: inadequate. **2** (*an ample supply*) abundant, plentiful, copious, profuse, rich, lavish, generous, bountiful, liberal, unrestricted, unlimited. OPPOSITE: scanty. **3** (*ample proportions*) large, big, great, broad, wide, extensive, spacious, roomy, voluminous, capacious, commodious. OPPOSITE: small.

amplification *noun* **1** (*amplification of sound*) increase, augmentation, intensification, heightening. OPPOSITE: reduction. **2** (*amplification of a statement*) expansion, enlargement, development, fleshing out, expatiation, elaboration, addition, supplement, extension, broadening, widening. OPPOSITE: contraction.

amplify *verb* **1** (*amplify sound*) increase, raise, augment, boost, intensify, heighten, strengthen. OPPOSITE: decrease. **2** (*amplify a statement*) expand, enlarge on, develop, fill out, flesh out, expatiate on, elaborate on, add to, supplement, extend, broaden, widen, lengthen. OPPOSITE: condense.

amplitude *noun* ampleness, abundance, plenty, plenitude, profusion, copiousness, magnitude, dimensions, proportions, size, bulk, mass, volume, capacity, capaciousness, spaciousness, bigness, largeness, width, breadth, extent, range, scope, sweep, compass.

amputate *verb* cut off, sever, lop, dock, clip, prune, remove, separate, curtail, truncate.

amulet *noun* charm, lucky charm, talisman, fetish, protector.

amuse *verb* **1** (*a story that amused him*) please, charm, delight, regale, entertain, divert, enliven, cheer, gladden, gratify, tickle (*inf*), crease (*inf*). OPPOSITE: depress. **2** (*amuse yourselves while I'm away*) occupy, absorb, engross, interest, distract, divert, entertain. OPPOSITE: bore.

amusement *noun* **1** (*a look of amusement on her face*) mirth, laughter, hilarity, merriment, gaiety, delight. OPPOSITE: displeasure. **2** (*make your own amusement*) entertainment, diversion, distraction, pastime, hobby, game, sport, recreation, fun, enjoyment, pleasure. OPPOSITE: boredom.

amusing *adj* funny, droll, comical, humorous, witty, jocular, facetious, hilarious, pleasing, pleasant, delightful, charming, entertaining, diverting, interesting, absorbing. OPPOSITE: boring.

anaemic *adj* **1** (*an anaemic complexion*) bloodless, colourless, pale, pallid, wan, ashen, livid, chalky, pasty, sickly. OPPOSITE: ruddy. **2** (*an anaemic performance*) weak, feeble, insipid, ineffectual, ineffective, impotent, powerless, enervated, languid. OPPOSITE: powerful.

anaesthetic *noun* painkiller, analgesic, anodyne, sedative, narcotic, opiate, soporific, stupefacient.
➤ *adj* numbing, deadening, painkilling, analgesic, anodyne, sedative, narcotic, soporific.

anaesthetize *verb* dull, deaden, numb, desensitize, drug, dope, stupefy.

analogous *adj* similar, like, alike, resembling, corresponding, matching, homologous, parallel, equivalent, comparable, related, kindred. OPPOSITE: different.

analogy *noun* similarity, likeness, resemblance, correspondence, correlation, agreement, homology, parallel, equivalence, relation, comparison, simile. OPPOSITE: difference.

analyse *verb* **1** (*analyse a chemical compound*) break down, decompose, separate, fractionate, dissect, take apart, anatomize, assay, reduce, resolve. OPPOSITE: synthesize. **2** (*analyse the problem*) examine, scrutinize, study, investigate, inquire into, interpret, explain, evaluate, review, consider, sift.

analysis *noun* **1** (*scientific analysis*) breakdown, decomposition, fractionate, dissection, partition, separation, reduction, resolution. OPPOSITE: synthesis. **2** (*political analysis*) examination, scrutiny, study, investigation, inquiry, interpretation, explanation, evaluation, review.

analytic *adj* analytical, investigative, inquiring, questioning, searching, in-depth, detailed, logical, systematic, methodical, organized, problem-solving, diagnostic, interpretative, explanatory, critical, evaluative.

anarchic *adj* lawless, ungoverned, nihilistic, libertarian, riotous, disorderly, disorganized, confused, chaotic, revolutionary, rebellious, mutinous. OPPOSITE: ordered.

anarchist *noun* rebel, insurgent, revolutionary, revolutionist, rabble-rouser, agitator, terrorist, nihilist, libertarian.

anarchy *noun* lawlessness, misrule, anarchism, nihilism, mobocracy, riot, disorder, confusion, chaos, mayhem, pandemonium, revolution, rebellion, insurgence, insurrection, mutiny. OPPOSITE: order.

anathema *noun* **1** (*the idea is anathema to her*) abomination, bane, bugbear, bête noire, aversion, antipathy, abhorrence. **2** (*an ecclesiastical anathema*) curse, imprecation, malediction, denunciation, excommunication, ban, proscription. OPPOSITE: blessing.

anatomize *verb* dissect, dismember, cut up, vivisect, analyse, examine, scrutinize, study, investigate, probe, sift.

anatomy *noun* **1** (*the anatomy of the cockroach*) skeleton, structure, framework, frame, build, composition, make-up. **2** (*study anatomy at medical school*) dissection, dismemberment, vivisection, zootomy, analysis, examination, scrutiny, investigation.

ancestor *noun* forebear, forefather, progenitor, parent, predecessor, forerunner, precursor, antecedent, prototype. OPPOSITE: descendant.

ancestral *adj* inherited, hereditary, patrimonial, familial, parental, lineal, genealogical.

ancestry *noun* ancestors, forebears, forefathers, progenitors, family, house, line, lineage, pedigree, race, stock, blood, roots, descent, parentage, extraction, genealogy, family tree, origin, derivation, heritage, background. OPPOSITE: posterity.

anchor *noun* **1** (*drop the anchor*) kedge, grapnel, hook (*inf*), mooring. **2** (*he was my anchor*) security, stay, mainstay, defence, support, protection.

➤ *verb* fasten, secure, make fast, fix, attach, bind. OPPOSITE: release.

anchorage *noun* mooring, wharf, quay, harbour, dock, port, refuge, shelter.

ancient *adj* **1** (*an ancient chest*) old, aged, antique, archaic. OPPOSITE: new. **2** (*ancient civilizations*) primitive, primeval, primordial, prehistoric, antediluvian, early, earliest, olden, bygone. OPPOSITE: contemporary. **3** (*ancient ideas*) archaic, obsolete, antiquated, superannuated, outmoded, old-fashioned, out-of-date, passé. OPPOSITE: modern. **4** (*an ancient tradition*) age-old, timeworn, long-lived, old as the hills (*inf*). OPPOSITE: recent.

ancillary *adj* subsidiary, auxiliary, accessory, secondary, additional, supplementary, extra, contributory, helping, attendant, supporting, subordinate, subservient. OPPOSITE: essential.

and *conj* plus, in addition, including, along with, together with, also, besides, furthermore, what's more (*inf*).

androgynous *adj* hermaphrodite, hermaphroditic, epicene, bisexual, gynandrous.

anecdote *noun* story, tale, yarn, sketch, illustration, narrative, account, memoir, reminiscence, incident, occurrence.

anew *adv* afresh, again, newly, once more, once again, over again.

anfractuous *adj* winding, sinuous, tortuous, devious, meandering, circuitous, roundabout, intricate, convoluted. OPPOSITE: straight.

angel *noun* (*the angels in heaven*) seraph, cherub, archangel, principality, power, spirit, divine messenger, heavenly messenger, guardian angel. OPPOSITE: devil. **2** (*you're an angel!*) saint, darling, dear, treasure, gem, paragon, ideal, beauty.

angelic *adj* **1** (*angelic choirs*) seraphic, cherubic, divine, heavenly, celestial, ethereal, empyrean. OPPOSITE: diabolic. **2** (*an angelic smile*) adorable, delightful, charming, entrancing, beautiful, lovely, pure, innocent, virtuous, saintly, beatific, holy, pious. OPPOSITE: fiendish.

anger *noun* rage, wrath, ire, fury, choler, exasperation, annoyance, irritation, vexation, displeasure, outrage, indignation, dudgeon, resentment, rancour, passion, temper, spleen, gall, ill humour, pique, chagrin. OPPOSITE: composure.
➤ *verb* enrage, infuriate, incense, outrage, madden, exasperate, annoy, irritate, aggravate (*inf*), provoke, rouse, wind up (*inf*), antagonize, rile, nettle, vex, irk, displease, piss off (*sl*), gall, needle, pique, miff (*inf*), offend, affront. OPPOSITE: appease.

angle[1] *noun* **1** (*the angles of the building*) corner, intersection, fork, bend, flexure, crook, hook, elbow, knee, nook, niche, recess. **2** (*placed at an angle*) inclination, gradient, slope, slant, obliquity. **3** (*considered from a different angle*) viewpoint, point of view, position, standpoint, aspect, outlook, slant, perspective, approach, direction, side, facet.
➤ *verb* **1** (*angle the lens*) slope, slant, incline, lean, tilt, turn, point, direct, face. **2** (*angle the report*) slant, distort, skew, bias.

angle[2] *verb* (*go angling*) fish, cast, hook, catch.
angle for fish for, look for, invite, solicit, seek, be after (*inf*), scheme for, contrive to get.

angry *adj* furious, irate, enraged, infuriated, incensed, mad (*inf*), livid, fuming, seething, on the warpath (*inf*), wrathful, vexed, irked, exasperated, annoyed, irritated, aggravated (*inf*), roused, provoked, riled, uptight (*inf*), wound up (*inf*), hot under the collar (*inf*), in a rage, in a temper, in a paddy (*inf*), indignant, outraged, up in arms (*inf*), displeased, pissed off (*sl*), piqued, miffed (*inf*), offended, affronted, chafed, inflamed, heated, hot, passionate, cross, irritable, moody, bad-tempered, ill-humoured, irascible, splenetic, choleric. OPPOSITE: calm.

angst *noun* anxiety, worry, fear, apprehension, foreboding, disquiet, unease.

anguish *noun* agony, torture, torment, pain, pangs, throes, suffering, distress, woe, misery, grief, sorrow, heartache, heartbreak, desolation. OPPOSITE: ecstasy.

anguished *adj* afflicted, stricken, suffering, distressed, harrowed, miserable, wretched, tortured, tormented, agonized, dolorous, hurt, pained, wounded, injured. OPPOSITE: soothed.

angular *adj* bony, gaunt, thin, lean, spare, skinny, scrawny, rangy, lanky, gawky, awkward, ungainly, stiff, austere. OPPOSITE: plump.

animadversion *noun* censure, rebuke, reproof, blame, condemnation, aspersion, criticism, disapproval, stricture. OPPOSITE: praise.

animal *noun* **1** (*animals at the zoo*) creature, beast, brute, mammal. **2** (*behaved like an animal*) beast, brute, swine (*inf*), pig (*inf*), monster, barbarian, savage.
➤ *adj* animalistic, bestial, brutish, savage, wild, carnal, fleshly, bodily, physical, sensual. OPPOSITE: spiritual.

animate *verb* enliven, liven up, vitalize, invigorate, pep up (*inf*), vivify, stimulate, activate, energize, galvanize, fire, spark, waken, arouse, rouse, stir, quicken, excite, goad, provoke, encourage, hearten, gladden, buck up (*inf*), inspire, incite, urge, move. OPPOSITE: depress.
➤ *adj* alive, living, live, breathing, moving. OPPOSITE: inanimate.

animated *adj* lively, spirited, full of beans (*inf*), vigorous, energetic, brisk, active, dynamic, forceful, vital, vivacious, blithe, buoyant, elated, excited, ebullient, enthusiastic, zestful, fervent, ardent, fiery, aroused, impassioned, passionate, vehement. OPPOSITE: lethargic.

animation *noun* liveliness, life, activity, spirit, vitality, energy, vigour, forcefulness, dynamism, pep (*inf*), vivacity, verve, sparkle, zing (*inf*), zest, buoyancy, elation, excitement, ebullience, enthusiasm, ardour, fervour, zeal, passion. OPPOSITE: apathy.

animosity *noun* hatred, hate, aversion, loathing, abhorrence, dislike, ill feeling, bad blood, antagonism, animus, antipathy, hostility, enmity, malice, spite, ill will, spleen, malignity, bitterness, acrimony, rancour, resentment, grudge. OPPOSITE: love.

annals *pl noun* archives, records, chronicles, accounts, reports, registers, rolls, journals, memoirs, history.

annex *verb* **1** (*annex a clause to the contract*) add, append, adjoin, attach, affix, fasten, join, subjoin, connect, unite. OPPOSITE: detach. **2** (*annex neighbouring territory*) occupy, conquer, seize, appropriate, expropriate, arrogate, confiscate, take over, acquire.

annexation *noun* **1** (*the annexation of a clause*) addition, appending, attachment, union. OPPOSITE: separation. **2** (*the annexation of territory*) occupation, conquest, seizure, appropriation, expropriation, arrogation, confiscation, takeover, acquisition.

annexe *noun* **1** (*housed in the annexe*) extension, wing. **2** (*an annexe to the document*) addition, appendage, attachment, supplement, postscript, codicil.

annihilate *verb* **1** (*annihilate the human race*) abolish, exterminate, wipe out, eradicate, extirpate, uproot, root out, obliterate, efface, erase, extinguish, blast, raze, destroy, kill, decimate, liquidate, nullify, annul. OPPOSITE: preserve. **2** (*annihilate the opposition*) conquer, defeat, rout, beat, thrash (*inf*), trounce (*inf*).

annihilation *noun* abolition, extermination, extinction, eradication, extirpation, obliteration, destruction, decimation, liquidation, nullification. OPPOSITE: creation.

annotate *verb* comment on, gloss, explain, explicate, interpret, elucidate, illustrate.

annotation *noun* note, footnote, comment, remark, observation, gloss, explanation, exegesis, explication, interpretation, elucidation, illustration, commentary.

announce *verb* **1** (*announce their engagement*) declare, proclaim, make known, give out, publish, broadcast, blazon, publicize, advertise, promulgate, propound, report, reveal, disclose, divulge, intimate. OPPOSITE: conceal. **2** (*announce the arrival of winter*) herald, presage, portend, augur, foretell, signal, betoken, signify, indicate.

announcement *noun* **1** (*make an announcement*) declaration, proclamation, bulletin, communiqué, notice, statement, report, broadcast, advertisement, revelation, disclosure. **2** (*the announcement of their engagement*) publication, broadcast, promulgation, declaration, proclamation, revelation, disclosure, divulgence, intimation. OPPOSITE: suppression.

announcer *noun* presenter, broadcaster, commentator, reporter, newsreader, newscaster, linkman, linkwoman, anchorman, anchorwoman, host, compere, master of ceremonies, MC, herald, town crier, messenger, harbinger.

annoy *verb* irritate, vex, irk, nettle, get on someone's nerves (*inf*), get up someone's nose (*inf*), exasperate, enrage, anger, infuriate, drive up the wall (*inf*), drive round the bend (*inf*), bother, trouble, disturb, get to (*inf*), harass, hassle (*inf*), pester, hector, badger, nag, harry, plague, torment, tease, provoke, needle, rub up the wrong way (*inf*), get someone's back up (*inf*), rile, madden, bug (*inf*). OPPOSITE: please.

annoyance *noun* **1** (*a gesture of annoyance*) irritation, vexation, exasperation, displeasure, anger, ire, pique. OPPOSITE: pleasure. **2** (*the noise is an annoyance*) nuisance, pest, pain (*inf*), pain in the neck (*inf*), irritant, affliction, bore, drag (*inf*), bother, trouble, hassle (*inf*), bind (*inf*).

annoyed *adj* irritated, cross, vexed, exasperated, angry, irate, upset, displeased, piqued, indignant, peeved (*inf*),

miffed (*inf*), fed up (*inf*), cheesed off (*inf*). OPPOSITE: pleased.

annoying *adj* irritating, vexatious, irksome, exasperating, infuriating, aggravating (*inf*), bothersome, nagging, niggling, troublesome, provoking, maddening, galling. OPPOSITE: pleasing.

annual *adj* yearly, every year, once a year.
➤ *noun* yearbook, almanac, calendar.

annually *adv* yearly, per annum, by the year, each year, every year, once a year.

annul *verb* nullify, invalidate, void, render null and void, declare null and void, abolish, repeal, revoke, abrogate, cancel, countermand, overrule, quash, rescind, reverse, negate, eliminate, annihilate, extinguish, obliterate. OPPOSITE: confirm.

annular *adj* circular, ring-shaped, round.

annulment *noun* nullification, invalidation, abolition, repeal, revocation, abrogation, rescindment, cancellation, negation, elimination, annihilation, obliteration. OPPOSITE: confirmation.

anodyne *adj* **1** (*anodyne drugs*) painkilling, analgesic, anaesthetic, numbing, deadening, narcotic, palliative, lenitive, sedative. **2** (*anodyne music*) bland, inoffensive, innocuous, neutral.
noun painkiller, analgesic, narcotic, opiate, palliative, sedative.

anoint *verb* **1** (*anoint a priest*) ordain, consecrate, sanctify, hallow, bless. **2** (*anointed with lotion*) rub, smear, spread, daub, oil, embrocate, grease, lubricate.

anomalous *adj* abnormal, irregular, atypical, unusual, rare, singular, exceptional, unnatural, freakish, incongruous, inconsistent, aberrant, deviating, deviant, eccentric, peculiar, odd, bizarre. OPPOSITE: normal.

anomaly *noun* abnormality, irregularity, rarity, exception, freak, incongruity, inconsistency, aberration, deviation, eccentricity, peculiarity, quirk, oddity.

anon *adv* soon, shortly, presently, before long, by and by, in a little while.

anonymous *adj* **1** (*an anonymous benefactor*) nameless, unnamed, innominate, unidentified, unspecified, unknown, incognito, unsigned, unacknowledged, uncredited. OPPOSITE: named. **2** (*an anonymous facade*) featureless, nondescript, undistinguished, unexceptional, faceless, impersonal. OPPOSITE: distinctive.

another *adj* **1** (*another slice of cake*) a second, a further, an additional, an extra, a spare. **2** (*use another pen*) a different, an alternative, some other, not the same.

answer *verb* **1** (*answer a question*) reply, respond, acknowledge, retort, riposte, rejoin, react, retaliate. **2** (*answer a need*) satisfy, fulfil, fill, meet, serve, suit, fit, measure up to, conform to, correspond to, match.
➤ *noun* reply, response, acknowledgment, retort, riposte, rejoinder, comeback (*inf*), reaction, retaliation, solution, resolution, key, explanation, defence, plea. OPPOSITE: question.

answer back contradict, disagree, argue, dispute, talk back, be cheeky, be impertinent.

answer for **1** (*I cannot answer for my colleagues*) speak for, vouch for, be responsible for, be accountable for.

2 (*answer for your wrongdoing*) be punished for, pay for, suffer for, take the blame for, be accountable for, be liable for.

answerable *adj* liable, responsible, accountable, amenable.

antagonism *noun* hostility, animosity, antipathy, enmity, opposition, rivalry, competition, contention, conflict, friction, discord, disharmony, dissension, contradiction. OPPOSITE: accord.

antagonist *noun* opponent, adversary, enemy, foe, rival, competitor, contender. OPPOSITE: ally.

antagonistic *adj* opposed, opposing, opposite, adverse, hostile, unfriendly, inimical, antipathetic, conflicting, rival, at odds, at variance, dissonant, disharmonious, incompatible. OPPOSITE: friendly.

antagonize *verb* anger, enrage, annoy, provoke, offend, alienate, estrange, disaffect, repel.

antecedence *noun* precedence, priority, anteriority.

antecedent *adj* preceding, prior, previous, earlier, anterior, foregoing, precursory. OPPOSITE: following.
➤ *noun* precedent, precursor, forerunner, harbinger, herald.

antecedents *pl noun* ancestors, forebears, forefathers, predecessors, ancestry, extraction, genealogy, history, past, background.

antedate *verb* predate, precede, forego, come before, forestall, anticipate. OPPOSITE: follow.

antediluvian *adj* antiquated, old-fashioned, outmoded, out of the ark (*inf*), out-of-date, obsolete, archaic, ancient, age-old, prehistoric, primeval, primordial. OPPOSITE: modern.

anterior *adj* **1** (*anterior lobe*) front, fore, forward. OPPOSITE: posterior. **2** (*anterior in time*) prior, preceding, earlier, previous, former, foregoing, introductory. OPPOSITE: following.

anteroom *noun* antechamber, vestibule, foyer, lobby, reception area, waiting room.

anthem *noun* hymn, song, psalm, canticle, chorale, chant, paean, song of praise.

anthology *noun* collection, compilation, compendium, digest, treasury, miscellany, selection, excerpts, extracts.

anticipate *verb* **1** (*I don't anticipate any problems*) expect, foresee, forecast, predict, contemplate, look for, await, prepare for, reckon on, count on, bank on. **2** (*they anticipated our every move*) forestall, intercept, prevent, pre-empt, beat to it (*inf*). **3** (*eagerly anticipating her arrival*) await, prepare for, look forward to, hope for. **4** (*anticipate the discovery of antibiotics*) predate, antedate, precede, come before. OPPOSITE: follow.

anticipation *noun* expectation, prospect, contemplation, prediction, forecast, preparation, foresight, presentiment, premonition, foretaste, expectancy, hope, apprehension.

anticlimax *noun* comedown, letdown, disappointment, disillusionment, bathos.

antics *pl noun* pranks, tricks, capers, jokes, mischief, skylarking, larks, romps, frolics, horseplay, tomfoolery, buffoonery.

antidote *noun* remedy, cure, corrective, restorative, countermeasure, counteragent, neutralizer, antivenin, antitoxin, antibody. OPPOSITE: poison.

antipathy *noun* dislike, aversion, loathing, hate, hatred, abhorrence, detestation, repugnance, disgust, distaste, hostility, opposition, antagonism, animosity, enmity, bad blood, ill feeling. OPPOSITE: sympathy.

antiquated *adj* old-fashioned, dated, out-of-date, outmoded, passé, old hat (*inf*), superannuated, obsolete, archaic, ancient, antique, antediluvian, fossilized, bygone. OPPOSITE: modern.

antique *adj* **1** (*antique furniture*) old, ancient, vintage, veteran, antiquarian, early, primitive, primordial, primeval. OPPOSITE: modern. **2** (*antique ideas*) archaic, antiquated, old-fashioned, out-of-date, outmoded, superannuated, obsolete.
➤ *noun* curio, objet d'art, rarity, heirloom, relic, museum piece, fossil, antiquity.

antiseptic *adj* **1** (*antiseptic cream*) germicidal, bactericidal, disinfectant, medicated. **2** (*in an antiseptic environment*) aseptic, sterile, germ-free, clinical, hygienic, sanitary, clean, pure, uncontaminated, unpolluted. OPPOSITE: polluted.
➤ *noun* disinfectant, germicide, bactericide.

antisocial *adj* **1** (*an antisocial child*) unsociable, uncommunicative, withdrawn, reserved, retiring, unapproachable, unfriendly, misanthropic, hostile, antagonistic. OPPOSITE: gregarious. **2** (*antisocial behaviour*) asocial, unacceptable, lawless, rebellious, disruptive, disorderly. OPPOSITE: acceptable.

antithesis *noun* opposite, reverse, inverse, converse, contrary, contradiction, contrast, opposition, reversal.

anxiety *noun* **1** (*anxiety about their welfare*) worry, concern, disquiet, uneasiness, misgiving, foreboding, apprehension, fear, dread, nervousness, tension, suspense, stress, strain, angst, trouble, care, solicitude, distress, anguish. OPPOSITE: tranquillity. **2** (*anxiety to please*) eagerness, keenness, avidity, desire, longing, yearning, impatience.

anxious *adj* **1** (*anxious about the future*) worried, concerned, troubled, fretful, restless, uneasy, on edge, nervous, tense, in suspense, on tenterhooks, apprehensive, fearful, afraid. OPPOSITE: calm. **2** (*anxious to succeed*) eager, keen, avid, longing, yearning, impatient.

any *adj* some, several, a few, one, whichever, whatever.
➤ *adv* at all, in the least, somewhat, to some extent.

anyhow *adv* **1** (*anyhow, I don't care*) anyway, in any case, at any rate, in any event. **2** (*scattered anyhow*) haphazardly, at random, carelessly, negligently.

anyway *adv* in any case, at any rate, in any event, anyhow, however, nevertheless, nonetheless.

apace *adv* quickly, rapidly, swiftly, fast, speedily, hastily, hurriedly, without delay. OPPOSITE: slowly.

apart *adv* **1** (*stand apart*) aside, to one side, away, afar, aloof, isolated, alone, by itself, separately, at a distance, on its own, on one's own, independently. **2** (*take it apart*) asunder, to pieces, to bits, in pieces, in bits, piecemeal. OPPOSITE: together.
apart from except, but, save, besides, other than, excluding, not counting.

apartment *noun* flat, suite, rooms, room, chamber, quarters, accommodation, lodging.

apathetic *adj* indifferent, unconcerned, uninterested, impassive, unfeeling, unresponsive, unmoved, insensible, cold, cool, callous, soulless, dull, listless, lethargic, passive, languid, torpid, sluggish. OPPOSITE: enthusiastic.

apathy *noun* indifference, unconcern, lack of interest, impassivity, lack of feeling, unresponsiveness, insensibility, coldness, coolness, callousness, listlessness, lethargy, passivity, inertia, languor, torpor, sluggishness. OPPOSITE: enthusiasm.

ape *noun* anthropoid, monkey, gorilla, baboon, gibbon, chimpanzee.
➣ *verb* imitate, mimic, copy, mirror, echo, parrot, take off, parody, caricature, counterfeit, affect.

aperture *noun* opening, hole, orifice, gap, space, interstice, breach, chink, cleft, crack, fissure, rift, rent, slit, slot, mouth, eye, eyelet, perforation, passage, vent, window.

apex *noun* top, summit, pinnacle, peak, vertex, apogee, acme, zenith, height, high point, climax, culmination, tip, point, crown, crest, brow. OPPOSITE: base.

aphorism *noun* proverb, saying, maxim, dictum, axiom, adage, apophthegm, gnome, saw, byword, precept.

aphrodisiac *adj* stimulant, erotic, erogenous, erotogenous, titillating.

apiece *adv* each, individually, separately, respectively. OPPOSITE: collectively.

aplomb *noun* poise, self-possession, assurance, self-assurance, confidence, self-confidence, composure, collectedness, calmness, coolness, sangfroid, equanimity. OPPOSITE: agitation.

apocalyptic *adj* revelatory, prophetic, oracular, predictive, ominous, warning, threatening, dire, terrible.

apocryphal *adj* unsubstantiated, unauthenticated, unverified, dubious, doubtful, debatable, questionable, spurious, false, untrue, fictitious, imaginary, legendary, mythical. OPPOSITE: authentic.

apologetic *adj* **1** (*apologetic about the delay*) sorry, regretful, rueful, remorseful, contrite, penitent, repentant. OPPOSITE: unrepentant. **2** (*apologetic writings*) defensive, vindicatory, justificatory, exculpatory.

apologist *noun* supporter, advocate, champion, defender, vindicator. OPPOSITE: adversary.

apologize *verb* beg pardon, say sorry, eat humble pie (*inf*), be sorry, regret.

apologue *noun* allegory, fable, parable, story, tale.

apology *noun* **1** (*apologies for absence*) explanation, excuse, justification, vindication, defence, plea, confession, acknowledgment, expression of regret. **2** (*wrote an apology for the doctrine*) defence, vindication, justification, argument, apologia. **3** (*served up an apology for a meal*) travesty, mockery, imitation, caricature, substitute, excuse.

apophthegm *noun* proverb, saying, maxim, dictum, axiom, adage, aphorism, gnome, saw, byword, precept.

apostasy *noun* desertion, abandonment, dereliction, defection, backsliding, recidivism, disloyalty, perfidy, treason, treachery, heresy, infidelity, unfaithfulness, faithlessness. OPPOSITE: loyalty.

apostate *noun* deserter, renegade, turncoat, backslider, recidivist, recreant, defector, traitor, heretic. OPPOSITE: loyalist.
➣ *adj* disloyal, perfidious, treacherous, traitorous, unfaithful, false, heretical. OPPOSITE: loyal.

apostle *noun* missionary, preacher, evangelist, proselytizer, crusader, pioneer, champion, advocate, supporter, campaigner, propagandist, proponent.

apotheosis *noun* deification, elevation, exaltation, glorification, idealization, quintessence.

appal *verb* horrify, outrage, shock, stun, astound, dismay, disconcert, daunt, intimidate, unnerve, alarm, frighten, terrify, petrify. OPPOSITE: reassure.

appalling *adj* dreadful, frightful, awful, terrible, dire, horrific, horrifying, shocking, outrageous, atrocious, ghastly, hideous, harrowing, daunting, intimidating, alarming, frightening, nightmarish. OPPOSITE: wonderful.

apparatus *noun* **1** (*laboratory apparatus*) equipment, gear, tackle, tools, implements, utensils, instruments, appliances, materials, machinery, plant. **2** (*an apparatus for lifting boxes*) device, contrivance, contraption, gadget, appliance, tool, implement, mechanism. **3** (*the apparatus of government*) structure, framework, system, organization, set-up, network.

apparel *noun* clothes, clothing, garments, wear, attire, dress, garb, gear (*inf*), wardrobe, outfit, costume, habit, robes, vestments, trappings.

apparent *adj* **1** (*for no apparent reason*) obvious, evident, patent, plain, clear, distinct, conspicuous, manifest, visible, perceptible, discernible. OPPOSITE: hidden. **2** (*his apparent indifference*) seeming, ostensible, external, outward, superficial. OPPOSITE: actual.

apparently *adv* **1** (*apparently you don't need a ticket*) seemingly, ostensibly, outwardly, on the face of it, allegedly, supposedly, reputedly. OPPOSITE: actually. **2** (*she was apparently concerned*) obviously, evidently, patently, plainly, clearly, distinctly, visibly, perceptibly.

apparition *noun* **1** (*strange apparitions in the courtyard*) ghost, spectre, phantom, spook (*inf*), spirit, wraith, shade, visitant, vision, illusion, hallucination, chimera. **2** (*the apparition of the mark*) appearance, manifestation, materialization, emergence, presence.

appeal *noun* **1** (*an appeal for money*) request, call, entreaty, plea, prayer, supplication, petition, suit, application, claim. **2** (*the appeal of the cinema*) attraction, temptation, allure, attractiveness, beauty, charm, charisma, fascination, enchantment, interest. OPPOSITE: unattractiveness.
➣ *verb* **1** (*appeal for help*) ask, request, call, solicit, entreat, implore, beg, beseech, pray, invoke, plead, petition, address, apply, claim. **2** (*it doesn't appeal to me*) attract, engage, interest, fascinate, captivate, charm, entice, tempt, invite. OPPOSITE: repel.

appear *verb* **1** (*a face appeared at the window*) come into view, come into sight, loom, arrive, turn up, show up, emerge, surface, arise, dawn, materialize, occur, crop up, be present, attend. OPPOSITE: disappear. **2** (*he appeared upset*) seem, look, come across as. **3** (*appear in *pantomime*) act, perform, play, take part, be on stage. **4** (*when the new model appears*) come out, come on the market, become available, go on sale.

appearance *noun* **1** (*the sudden appearance of a stranger*) arrival, advent, coming, emergence, materialization, manifestation, occurrence, presence, attendance, debut, publication. OPPOSITE: disappearance. **2** (*a change in her appearance*) look, expression, aspect, demeanour, manner, air, bearing, mien, looks, image. **3** (*give the appearance of self-confidence*) impression, semblance, illusion, pretence, show, front, facade.

appease *verb* pacify, placate, propitiate, conciliate, reconcile, mollify, soften, satisfy, quench, quell, assuage, moderate, mitigate, lull, still, calm, soothe, allay, tranquillize, alleviate, relieve, ease, lessen, reduce, diminish, abate. OPPOSITE: aggravate.

appeasement *noun* placation, propitiation, conciliation, peacemaking, compromise, concession, accommodation, assuagement, mitigation, alleviation, relief, reduction, diminution, abatement.

appellation *noun* name, title, designation, cognomen, sobriquet, epithet, term, denomination.

append *verb* add, attach, affix, adjoin, annex, join, fasten, hang, subjoin, tag on, tack on. OPPOSITE: detach.

appendage *noun* **1** (*an appendage to the document*) attachment, adjunct, addition, addendum, appendix, supplement, accessory, appurtenance. OPPOSITE: essential. **2** (*an appendage used for locomotion*) part, organ, projection, protuberance, limb, member, leg, foot, arm, wing, feeler, tail.

appendix *noun* addition, adjunct, supplement, addendum, postscript, epilogue, codicil, rider, extension, annexe, appendage.

appertain *verb* belong, pertain, refer, relate, touch, concern, bear, apply, be connected, be relevant, be pertinent, have reference.

appetite *noun* **1** (*have a good appetite*) hunger, relish, zest, taste, palate, stomach. **2** (*an appetite for adventure*) desire, want, need, lust, craving, longing, yearning, hankering, hunger, thirst, passion, relish, taste, liking, affinity, appetence, inclination, propensity, proclivity. OPPOSITE: indifference.

appetizer *noun* apéritif, canapé, hors d'oeuvre, antipasto, starter.

appetizing *adj* **1** (*an appetizing smell*) savoury, palatable, mouth-watering, delicious, tasty, scrumptious (*inf*), succulent, piquant. OPPOSITE: unappetizing. **2** (*an appetizing prospect*) tempting, inviting, appealing, enticing, alluring.

applaud *verb* **1** (*applaud the soloist*) clap, cheer, give a standing ovation to, put one's hands together for, give a big hand to (*inf*). OPPOSITE: boo. **2** (*applaud the decision*) praise, acclaim, laud, extol, approve, commend, encourage, congratulate, compliment. OPPOSITE: denounce.

applause *noun* clapping, ovation, standing ovation, a big hand (*inf*), cheers, cheering, bravos, encores, praise, acclamation, acclaim, eulogy, approbation, approval, commendation, encouragement, congratulations,

compliments, plaudits, accolades. OPPOSITE: denunciation.

appliance *noun* **1** (*domestic appliances*) device, machine, mechanism, contrivance, gadget, instrument, tool, implement, utensil, apparatus, piece of equipment. **2** (*the appliance of common sense*) application, use, exercise, practice.

applicable *adj* appropriate, apt, suitable, fitting, suited, fit, proper, apposite, apropos, germane, relevant, pertinent, useful, convenient. OPPOSITE: inappropriate.

applicant *noun* candidate, interviewee, aspirant, suitor, petitioner, claimant, enquirer, contestant, contender, competitor.

application *noun* **1** (*an application for a job*) request, demand, requisition, claim, petition, appeal, suit, enquiry. **2** (*the application of force*) appliance, administration, use, employment, exercise, practice. **3** (*little application to the subject under discussion*) relevance, pertinence, bearing, significance, germaneness, aptness, appropriateness. OPPOSITE: irrelevance. **4** (*a tool with various applications*) purpose, function, use, value. **5** (*students who show application*) dedication, commitment, diligence, industry, assiduity, sedulousness, effort, perseverance, persistence. OPPOSITE: indolence.

apply *verb* **1** (*apply pressure*) use, utilize, employ, put to use, exercise, put into practice, bring into play, execute, administer, exert, bring to bear, wield, ply. OPPOSITE: withhold. **2** (*apply for a job*) ask, request, put in, demand, claim, appeal, petition, solicit, seek, enquire. **3** (*apply yourself to the problem*) dedicate, devote, commit, direct, address. OPPOSITE: divert. **4** (*does not apply in this case*) refer, be relevant, be appropriate, relate, pertain, appertain, fit, suit, have a bearing. **5** (*apply ointment*) spread, smear, daub, rub in, put on, cover with, treat with.

apply oneself work hard, make an effort, buckle down, concentrate, pay attention, persevere, persist, study.

appoint *verb* **1** (*appoint a secretary*) name, nominate, designate, assign, elect, select, choose, pick, install, employ, take on, hire, engage, commission, recruit. OPPOSITE: dismiss. **2** (*at the appointed time*) fix, set, arrange, choose, settle, decide, determine, establish, ordain, prescribe, decree, designate, assign, allot. OPPOSITE: cancel.

appointment *noun* **1** (*an appointment with the manager*) meeting, interview, consultation, date, rendezvous, tryst, assignation, engagement, arrangement. **2** (*her appointment as headmistress*) office, post, position, job, situation, place. **3** (*the appointment of a safety officer*) appointing, nomination, designation, assignment, election, selection, choice, installation, employment, engagement, recruitment. OPPOSITE: dismissal.

apportion *verb* divide, share, ration, allot, assign, allocate, administer, dispense, distribute, deal out, mete out, hand out, dole out (*inf*). OPPOSITE: retain.

apportionment *noun* division, sharing, rationing, allocation, allotment, distribution, dispensation.

apposite *adj* apt, appropriate, fitting, fit, suitable, suited, proper, applicable, relevant, pertinent, germane, apropos, to the point. OPPOSITE: inappropriate.

appraisal *noun* appraisement, evaluation, assessment, inspection, review, survey, valuation, estimation, estimate, judgment.

appraise *verb* evaluate, assess, sum up, size up (*inf*), inspect, review, survey, value, price, rate, estimate, gauge, judge.

appreciable *adj* noticeable, perceptible, detectable, discernible, marked, obvious, evident, significant, substantial, considerable, goodly, sizeable. OPPOSITE: imperceptible.

appreciate *verb* **1** (*I appreciate your honesty*) value, prize, cherish, treasure, rate highly, think highly of, esteem, respect, acknowledge, be grateful for, be thankful for, be indebted to. OPPOSITE: scorn. **2** (*they don't appreciate the problem*) recognize, acknowledge, perceive, see, comprehend, understand, grasp, realize, be aware of, be conscious of, be sensitive to, sympathize with. OPPOSITE: ignore. **3** (*appreciate in value*) rise, mount, go up, increase, grow, gain, multiply, intensify, escalate, inflate. OPPOSITE: depreciate.

appreciation *noun* **1** (*express your appreciation*) value, esteem, regard, respect, admiration, acknowledgment, gratitude, gratefulness, thanks, thankfulness, indebtedness, obligation. OPPOSITE: scorn. **2** (*appreciation of the problem*) recognition, acknowledgment, perception, comprehension, understanding, grasp, realization, awareness, consciousness, sensitivity, sympathy. **3** (*appreciation in value*) rise, increase, growth, gain, intensification, escalation, inflation. OPPOSITE: depreciation. **4** (*write an appreciation of the poem*) review, critique, evaluation, assessment, analysis, commentary, notice.

appreciative *adj* **1** (*appreciative of your assistance*) grateful, thankful, indebted, obliged, beholden. OPPOSITE: scornful. **2** (*an appreciative audience*) enthusiastic, admiring, encouraging, supportive, responsive, sensitive, sympathetic. OPPOSITE: unappreciative.

apprehend *verb* **1** (*apprehend a criminal*) seize, catch, nab (*inf*), collar (*inf*), capture, take prisoner, arrest, detain, take into custody, nick (*inf*), bust (*inf*), run in (*inf*). OPPOSITE: release. **2** (*apprehend the problem*) understand, comprehend, grasp, perceive, see, recognize, realize, appreciate, conceive, imagine.

apprehension *noun* **1** (*apprehension about going into hospital*) fear, alarm, dread, trepidation, anxiety, worry, concern, qualm, nervousness, nerves, butterflies in the stomach (*inf*), misgiving, foreboding, disquiet, uneasiness, mistrust, suspicion. OPPOSITE: composure. **2** (*the apprehension of criminals*) seizure, capture, arrest, detention. OPPOSITE: release. **3** (*apprehension of the problem*) understanding, comprehension, grasp, perception, recognition, realization, appreciation, conception, concept, notion, belief. OPPOSITE: misapprehension.

apprehensive *adj* anxious, worried, nervous, fearful, frightened, afraid, scared, alarmed, concerned, troubled, uneasy, suspicious, mistrustful. OPPOSITE: composed.

apprentice *noun* trainee, student, pupil, probationer, learner, novice, beginner, tyro, neophyte, greenhorn, rookie (*inf*). OPPOSITE: expert.

apprise *verb* inform, tell, notify, acquaint, enlighten, make aware, brief, fill in (*inf*), advise, warn, tip off (*inf*).

approach *verb* **1** (*approach the town*) near, come near, draw near, advance, move towards, catch up, gain on, reach, arrive. OPPOSITE: withdraw. **2** (*approach a stranger*) accost, address, speak to, talk to, greet, salute, hail. OPPOSITE: avoid. **3** (*approach a task*) tackle, undertake, set about, embark on, start, begin, commence, broach. **4** (*something approaching what we need*) come close to, border on, verge on, approximate, resemble, compare with. **5** (*approached me for a loan*) appeal to, apply to, contact, get in touch with, make advances to, make overtures to, proposition, solicit.
⯈ *noun* **1** (*the approach of winter*) advent, coming, nearing, advance, arrival. OPPOSITE: departure. **2** (*the approach to the castle*) access, entrance, passage, way, road, path, avenue, drive, driveway. OPPOSITE: exit. **3** (*a different approach to the problem*) method, means, procedure, technique, modus operandi, way, style, manner, attitude, strategy, tactics, course of action. **4** (*make an approach to the bank*) appeal, application, request, proposition, proposal, advances, overtures, invitation.

approachable *adj* **1** (*approachable from the east*) accessible, reachable, attainable, getatable (*inf*). OPPOSITE: inaccessible. **2** (*a more approachable boss*) friendly, sociable, affable, congenial, easygoing, informal, communicative, talkative. OPPOSITE: aloof.

approbation *noun* approval, sanction, assent, consent, recognition, acclaim, praise, commendation, encouragement, support. OPPOSITE: censure.

appropriate *adj* apt, fitting, suitable, right, proper, seemly, becoming, befitting, timely, opportune, apposite, pertinent, relevant, germane, appurtenant. OPPOSITE: inappropriate.
⯈ *verb* **1** (*appropriate a vehicle*) seize, take, requisition, commandeer, annex, arrogate, expropriate, confiscate, impound. OPPOSITE: return. **2** (*money appropriated for new projects*) assign, allot, allocate, apportion, earmark, set aside, set apart, ring-fence. **3** (*appropriate company funds*) embezzle, misappropriate, peculate, steal, purloin, pilfer, filch, pocket, nick (*inf*), pinch (*inf*).

appropriateness *noun* aptness, suitability, fitness, propriety, timeliness, relevance, pertinence.

appropriation *noun* **1** (*appropriation of property*) seizure, capture, expropriation, arrogation, confiscation, impounding. OPPOSITE: return. **2** (*appropriation of money*) assignment, allotment, allocation, apportionment. **3** (*appropriation of company funds*) embezzlement, misappropriation, peculation, stealing, pilfering.

approval *noun* **1** (*hoping to win the audience's approval*) approbation, admiration, regard, respect, esteem, appreciation, favour, liking, praise, commendation, acclaim, acclamation, applause. OPPOSITE: censure. **2** (*get approval for our plan*) sanction, authorization, ratification, validation, OK (*inf*), assent, consent, agreement, acquiescence, acceptance, nod (*inf*), thumbs-up (*inf*), endorsement, blessing, green light (*inf*), go-ahead (*inf*), support, encouragement, recommendation. OPPOSITE: disapproval.

approve *verb* **1** (*approve of your choice*) admire, regard, esteem, value, prize, appreciate, favour, like, be pleased with, think well of, praise, commend, acclaim, applaud. OPPOSITE: disapprove. **2** (*approve our plan*) sanction, authorize, ratify, validate, OK (*inf*), rubber-stamp (*inf*), assent to, consent to, agree to, acquiesce in, accept, endorse, bless, countenance, give the green light to (*inf*), give the go-ahead to (*inf*), uphold, support, encourage, recommend. OPPOSITE: oppose.

approved *adj* authorized, official, orthodox, proper, accepted, recognized, preferred, favoured, recommended, permitted, sanctioned. OPPOSITE: unorthodox.

approximate *adj* rough, estimated, guessed, inexact, imprecise, loose, similar, near, close, ballpark (*inf*). OPPOSITE: exact.
➤ *verb* approach, come close to, come near to, border on, verge on, resemble, be similar to, compare with.

approximately *adv* roughly, about, around, circa, in the region of, in the neighbourhood of, more or less, nearly, almost, approaching, not far off. OPPOSITE: precisely.

approximation *noun* **1** (*an approximation of the cost*) estimate, rough calculation, guess, conjecture, guesstimate (*inf*), rough idea. **2** (*an approximation to the truth*) semblance, similarity, likeness, resemblance, correspondence.

appurtenance *noun* appendage, adjunct, accessory, attachment, addition, supplement, incidental, concomitant. OPPOSITE: essential.

appurtenances *pl noun* equipment, paraphernalia, impedimenta, trappings, accoutrements, belongings.

apropos *adj* appropriate, apt, apposite, relevant, pertinent, germane, timely, opportune, suitable, fit, proper, seemly, fitting, becoming. OPPOSITE: inappropriate.
➤ *adv* appropriately, aptly, pertinently, to the purpose.
➤ *prep* regarding, with regard to, with reference to, respecting, with respect to, in connection with, on the subject of, re.

apt *adj* **1** (*an apt description*) appropriate, suitable, fitting, proper, accurate, spot-on (*inf*), felicitous, opportune, timely, apropos, apposite, pertinent, relevant, germane. OPPOSITE: inappropriate. **2** (*apt to forget*) disposed, inclined, prone, liable, subject, given, likely. OPPOSITE: unlikely. **3** (*an apt student*) able, clever, smart, bright, intelligent, quick, sharp, astute, gifted, talented, adroit, dexterous, expert, adept. OPPOSITE: slow.

aptitude *noun* ability, faculty, capacity, proficiency, competence, skill, gift, talent, knack, flair, cleverness, intelligence, disposition, inclination, leaning. OPPOSITE: incompetence.

aptness *noun* **1** (*the aptness of the description*) appropriateness, suitability, fitness, accuracy, timeliness, appositeness, pertinence, relevance. OPPOSITE: unsuitability. **2** (*aptness to forget*) aptitude, disposition, inclination, liability, tendency.

aquatic *adj* water, sea, marine, maritime, nautical, river, fluvial.

aquiline *adj* eagle-like, hooked, bent, curved, Roman. OPPOSITE: straight.

arable *adj* cultivable, farmable, ploughable, tillable, fertile, fecund, fruitful, productive.

arbiter *noun* **1** (*the arbiter of the dispute*) judge, adjudicator, arbitrator, referee, umpire. **2** (*an arbiter of fashion*) authority, expert, pundit, master, lord, director, controller, governor, ruler, sovereign.

arbitrary *adj* (*an arbitrary choice*) random, chance, capricious, whimsical, subjective, personal, discretionary, unreasoned, unreasonable, irrational, illogical, erratic, inconsistent. OPPOSITE: reasoned. **2** (*an arbitrary ruler*) despotic, dictatorial, autocratic, tyrannical, absolute, imperious, magisterial, domineering, overbearing, high-handed.

arbitrate *verb* judge, adjudicate, referee, umpire, pass judgment, decide, determine, settle, mediate, intervene, negotiate, conciliate.

arbitration *noun* judgment, adjudication, arbitrament, decision, determination, settlement, mediation, intervention, negotiation, conciliation.

arbitrator *noun* judge, adjudicator, arbiter, referee, umpire, mediator, negotiator, intermediary, peacemaker, go-between.

arbour *noun* bower, pergola, gazebo, shelter, retreat, recess, alcove.

arc *noun* bend, curve, arch, bow, crescent, semicircle.

arcade *noun* colonnade, peristyle, portico, loggia, cloister, gallery, passageway, precinct, mall.

arcane *adj* mysterious, cryptic, enigmatic, abstruse, occult, esoteric, recondite, secret, hidden, concealed, covert.

arch[1] *noun* curve, bend, bow, arc, archway, vault, span, bridge, dome.
➤ *verb* curve, bend, bow, arc, vault, camber.

arch[2] *adj* **1** (*her arch rival*) chief, main, principal, leading, first, foremost, greatest. OPPOSITE: minor. **2** (*an arch smile*) shrewd, knowing, cunning, artful, roguish, waggish, mischievous, playful, frolicsome, saucy.

archaic *adj* ancient, old, bygone, antiquated, obsolete, obsolescent, superannuated, dated, outmoded, old-fashioned, out-of-date, old hat (*inf*), primitive, antediluvian. OPPOSITE: modern.

arched *adj* curved, bowed, domed, vaulted, concave. OPPOSITE: straight.

archetypal *adj* typical, standard, stock, characteristic, representative, original, classic, model, ideal, exemplary.

archetype *noun* original, prototype, precursor, type, form, standard, model, pattern, paradigm, example, exemplar, paragon, ideal, epitome, stereotype.

architect *noun* **1** (*the architect's drawings for the building*) designer, planner, draughtsman, draughtswoman, builder, constructor, maker. **2** (*the architect of the welfare state*) creator, originator, instigator, founder, author, engineer, prime mover, mastermind.

architecture *noun* **1** (*the architecture of the city*) design, planning, building, construction, architectonics, style. **2** (*the architecture of the system*) structure, framework, composition, make-up, design, arrangement.

archives *pl noun* records, annals, chronicles, registers, rolls, documents, papers.

arctic *adj* **1** (*arctic regions*) polar, northern, boreal, hyperborean. OPPOSITE: antarctic. **2** (*arctic weather*) cold, freezing, frozen, glacial, icy, frosty, wintry, chilly, bitter, bleak. OPPOSITE: hot.

ardent *adj* fervent, fervid, passionate, impassioned, burning, hot, fiery, keen, eager, avid, enthusiastic, zealous, devoted, dedicated, earnest, spirited, vehement, fierce, intense. OPPOSITE: apathetic.

ardour *noun* fervour, passion, feeling, emotion, warmth, heat, fire, keenness, eagerness, avidity, enthusiasm, zeal, devotion, dedication, earnestness, spirit, vehemence, intensity. OPPOSITE: apathy.

arduous *adj* difficult, hard, tough, taxing, laborious, onerous, burdensome, toilsome, tiring, wearying, exhausting, backbreaking, strenuous, rigorous, gruelling, punishing, formidable, Herculean, harsh, severe, steep, uphill. OPPOSITE: easy.

area *noun* **1** (*living in the same area*) district, region, quarter, parish, zone, sector, locality, neighbourhood, territory, patch, realm, domain. **2** (*area of expertise*) sphere, field, realm, domain, province, department, branch, scope, compass, range. **3** (*calculate the area of the room*) extent, size, surface, space, measurements, dimensions. **4** (*an area of land*) expanse, stretch, tract, part, section, portion, plot, enclosure.

arena *noun* **1** (*competing in the arena*) stadium, ground, field, track, ring, stage, enclosure, amphitheatre, coliseum, hippodrome. **2** (*enter the political arena*) area, scene, battlefield, battleground, sphere, world, realm, domain, province, department

argue *verb* **1** (*arguing with her parents*) dispute, disagree, fall out (*inf*), quarrel, wrangle, squabble, bicker, row, altercate, fight, feud, cross swords (*inf*), be at each other's throats (*inf*). OPPOSITE: agree. **2** (*argue that smoking should be banned*) debate, discuss, moot, reason, contend, maintain, hold, insist, assert, declare, claim, plead, persuade, convince. **3** (*argues a need for reform*) denote, indicate, show, demonstrate, exhibit, evince, betoken, suggest, imply.

argument *noun* **1** (*had an argument with his neighbour*) dispute, disagreement, difference of opinion, falling out (*inf*), quarrel, wrangle, squabble, tiff (*inf*), barney (*inf*), row, altercation, fight, conflict, clash, set-to (*inf*), dust-up (*inf*). OPPOSITE: agreement. **2** (*a cause of much argument*) discussion, debate, polemic, controversy. **3** (*the argument against corporal punishment*) defence, case, evidence, proof, reasoning, rationale, logic, reasons, grounds, contention, plea, claim, assertion, declaration. **4** (*the argument of the book*) summary, outline, synopsis, abstract, gist, plot, theme, subject, topic.

argumentative *adj* contentious, quarrelsome, disputatious, litigious, contrary, perverse, stroppy (*inf*), belligerent, combative. OPPOSITE: conciliatory.

arid *adj* **1** (*an arid landscape*) dry, parched, baked, scorched, dehydrated, desiccated, desert, waterless, barren, sterile. OPPOSITE: fertile. **2** (*an arid discussion*) dull, uninteresting, boring, tedious, monotonous, flat, dry, uninspiring, jejune, dreary, drab, colourless, insipid, vapid, lifeless. OPPOSITE: lively.

aright *adv* rightly, correctly, properly, accurately, exactly, truly.

arise *verb* **1** (*problems arising from cultural differences*) originate, derive, spring, issue, flow, stem, begin, proceed, emanate, result, ensue, follow. OPPOSITE: end. **2** (*if the need arises*) appear, come to light, emerge, occur, happen, crop up, turn up. **3** (*arise at dawn*) get up, rise, stand up. **4** (*smoke arose from the ashes*) rise, ascend, go up, climb, mount, soar. OPPOSITE: sink.

aristocracy *noun* nobility, gentry, peerage, ruling class, upper class, upper crust (*inf*), high society, haut monde, élite, patriciate. OPPOSITE: proletariat.

aristocrat *noun* noble, nobleman, noblewoman, gentleman, lady, nob (*inf*), toff (*inf*), patrician, lord, grandee, peer, peeress, earl, baron. OPPOSITE: plebeian.

aristocratic *adj* noble, titled, upper class, patrician, blue-blooded, highborn, élite, genteel, dignified, elegant, stylish, refined, sophisticated, well-bred, gentlemanly, ladylike, haughty, snobbish, arrogant. OPPOSITE: vulgar.

arm[1] *noun* **1** (*raise your left arm*) limb, forelimb, member, appendage. **2** (*the political arm of the organization*) branch, offshoot, wing, division, department, section, detachment. **3** (*an arm of the sea*) inlet, channel, strait, sound, estuary, firth, bay, cove. **4** (*the arm of the law*) power, force, authority, might, strength.

arm[2] *verb* **1** (*armed with rifles*) equip, provide, supply, issue, furnish, fit out. OPPOSITE: disarm. **2** (*armed against attack*) fortify, strengthen, reinforce, guard, protect, prepare, forearm, brace, steel.

armada *noun* fleet, flotilla, squadron, navy.

armaments *pl noun* arms, weapons, weaponry, munitions, ordnance, matériel.

armistice *noun* truce, cease-fire, peace, reprieve, suspension, intermission.

armour *noun* covering, protection, mail, chain mail, armour plate.

armoured *adj* protected, reinforced, ironclad, armour-plated, bulletproof, bombproof.

armoury *noun* arsenal, magazine, ammunition dump, ordnance depot, arms depot, warehouse, depository, stockpile.

arms *pl noun* **1** (*selling arms to terrorists*) weapons, weaponry, munitions, armaments, ordnance, matériel, firearms, guns, artillery, ammunition. **2** (*heraldic arms*) shield, escutcheon, insignia, blazonry, armorial bearings, coat of arms, heraldic device, emblem, crest.

army *noun* **1** (*the defeated army*) soldiers, troops, armed forces, military. **2** (*an army of sightseers*) multitude, host, crowd, throng, mob, horde, pack, swarm.

aroma *noun* odour, smell, scent, fragrance, perfume, bouquet, redolence, savour.

aromatic *adj* fragrant, scented, perfumed, balmy, sweet-smelling, redolent, odoriferous, spicy, pungent, savoury.

around *prep* **1** (*around his waist*) round, surrounding, encircling, encompassing, about. **2** (*around four hours*) roughly, approximately, about, circa, more or less, close to, nearly. **3** (*scattered around the room*) all over, throughout, about.

≫ adv **1** (*run around*) on all sides, in all directions, everywhere, about, here and there, to and fro. **2** (*somewhere around*) near, nearby, at hand, close, close by.

arouse verb **1** (*arouse the sleeping children*) wake, wake up, waken, awaken, rouse. **2** (*arouse their curiosity*) cause, prompt, provoke, stimulate, whet, sharpen, stir, excite, rouse, animate, instigate, kindle, spark, trigger. OPPOSITE: quell. **3** (*aroused to anger*) agitate, animate, spur, goad, urge, egg on, incite, inflame. OPPOSITE: calm. **4** (*sexually aroused*) stimulate, excite, turn on (*inf*).

arraign verb summon, prosecute, accuse, charge, indict, impeach, incriminate, denounce, censure, upbraid, reprove, reproach, rebuke, take to task. OPPOSITE: acquit.

arraignment noun summons, prosecution, accusation, charge, indictment, impeachment, incrimination, denunciation, censure, reproof.

arrange verb **1** (*arrange the books*) order, array, dispose, distribute, group, sort, rank, classify, class, categorize, file, marshal, organize, systematize, codify, range, place, position, lay out, tidy, align, adjust, regulate. OPPOSITE: disarrange. **2** (*arrange a meeting*) settle, decide, fix, agree to, prepare, plan, organize, coordinate, set up, contrive, devise. **3** (*arrange music*) adapt, set, orchestrate, score, instrument.

arrangement noun **1** (*flower arrangement*) order, array, disposition, distribution, grouping, positioning, layout, format, design, pattern, plan, scheme, alignment, ranking, classification, categorization, filing, organization, system, structure. OPPOSITE: disarray. **2** (*a change in the arrangements*) plan, preparation, provision, measure, schedule, timetable. **3** (*have an arrangement with the bank*) agreement, settlement, understanding, compact, contract. **4** (*an arrangement for string quartet*) adaptation, setting, interpretation, version, orchestration, score, instrumentation.

arrant adj **1** (*arrant nonsense*) utter, total, absolute, downright, outright, out-and-out, thorough, thoroughgoing, veritable, blatant, flagrant, brazen, barefaced, rank, gross. **2** (*an arrant knave*) infamous, notorious, vile, atrocious, monstrous.

array verb **1** (*ornaments arrayed on the shelf*) arrange, dispose, display, exhibit, marshal, muster, assemble, amass, line up, draw up, range, rank, order, place, position. OPPOSITE: disarrange. **2** (*arrayed in velvet robes*) dress, clothe, attire, garb, apparel, accoutre, adorn, deck, bedeck, equip, fit out, supply. OPPOSITE: strip.
≫ noun **1** (*a fine array of artefacts*) display, collection, show, exhibition, parade, arrangement, disposition, order, line-up, formation, muster, assemblage, aggregation. OPPOSITE: disarray. **2** (*the queen's attendants in colourful array*) dress, clothing, garments, attire, apparel, garb, finery, regalia.

arrears pl noun debt, debts, liabilities, amount overdue, outstanding payment, balance, deficit.
in arrears behind, behindhand, late, in debt, in the red, in default, overdue, outstanding, owing, owed.

arrest verb **1** (*arrest a criminal*) seize, catch, pick up (*inf*), nab (*inf*), collar (*inf*), capture, take prisoner, apprehend, take into custody, detain, nick (*inf*), run in (*inf*), bust (*inf*). OPPOSITE: release. **2** (*arrest the bleeding*) check,

restrain, stop, end, stem, halt, interrupt, inhibit, slow, delay, retard, hold back, hinder, impede, obstruct, block, prevent. OPPOSITE: stimulate. **3** (*arrested my attention*) attract, catch, capture, engage, occupy, absorb, engross, rivet, grip, hold, fascinate, intrigue. OPPOSITE: bore.
≫ noun **1** (*the arrest of the murderer*) seizure, capture, apprehension, detention. OPPOSITE: release. **2** (*cardiac arrest*) check, restraint, stoppage, cessation, halt, interruption, inhibition, suppression, delay, retardation, obstruction, blockage. OPPOSITE: stimulation.
under arrest detained, in custody, helping police with their enquiries.

arresting adj striking, stunning, amazing, impressive, remarkable, outstanding, extraordinary, noteworthy, conspicuous, noticeable. OPPOSITE: unremarkable.

arrival noun **1** (*the arrival of the train*) appearance, entrance, entry, advent, coming, occurrence, approach. OPPOSITE: departure. **2** (*greeting the latest arrivals*) newcomer, visitor, caller, guest, incomer, immigrant.

arrive verb **1** (*when the doctor arrives*) come, come on the scene, get there, get here, enter, check in, clock in, land, touch down, dock, pull in, appear, put in an appearance, turn up, show up, roll up (*inf*), blow in (*inf*), materialize, occur, happen, befall. OPPOSITE: depart. **2** (*a singer who's really arrived*) succeed, make it (*inf*), make the grade (*inf*), reach the top, prosper, thrive, flourish. OPPOSITE: fail.
arrive at reach, get to, come to, attain, realize.

arrogance noun pride, haughtiness, loftiness, hauteur, self-importance, conceit, egotism, superciliousness, condescension, snobbishness, snobbery, disdain, contempt, scorn, lordliness, imperiousness, pomposity, pretentiousness, presumption, insolence, self-assurance, self-assertion. OPPOSITE: humility.

arrogant adj proud, haughty, lofty, self-important, conceited, egotistic, full of oneself (*inf*), supercilious, uppity (*inf*), condescending, patronizing, snobbish, stuck-up (*inf*), disdainful, contemptuous, scornful, overbearing, high and mighty (*inf*), lordly, imperious, pompous, pretentious, presumptuous, insolent, boastful, blustering, swaggering, self-assured. OPPOSITE: modest.

arrogate verb appropriate, seize, claim, assume, usurp, commandeer, demand. OPPOSITE: waive.

arrow noun **1** (*bow and arrows*) shaft, dart, bolt. **2** (*follow the arrows*) pointer, marker, indicator.

arsenal noun armoury, magazine, ammunition dump, arms depot, ordnance depot, warehouse, depository, store, stockpile, stock, supply.

arson noun fire-raising, incendiarism, pyromania.

art noun **1** (*study art at university*) painting, drawing, sculpture, architecture, craft, design, draughtsmanship, fine arts, visual arts. **2** (*the art of conversation*) skill, technique, craft, aptitude, facility, gift, talent, knack, flair, expertise, mastery, virtuosity, finesse, dexterity, adroitness, address, cleverness, ingenuity. **3** (*the art of the fox*) artfulness, shrewdness, astuteness, slyness, wiliness, cunning, guile, deceit, duplicity, artifice, craft, trickery. OPPOSITE: honesty.

artful adj cunning, sly, wily, foxy, subtle, insidious, shrewd, astute, sharp, knowing, crafty, deceitful, tricky, clever, ingenious, resourceful, skilful, dexterous, adroit. OPPOSITE: artless.

article *noun* **1** (*articles of value*) item, thing, object, commodity, thingamajig (*inf*), thingummy (*inf*), whatsit (*inf*), unit, part, component, constituent. **2** (*a magazine article*) story, report, piece, feature, column, essay, composition, paper, treatise, review, write-up, commentary. **3** (*an article of the contract*) section, division, clause, point, paragraph, passage, part, portion, piece.

articulate *verb* **1** (*articulate a word*) pronounce, enunciate, utter, speak, say, state, voice, vocalize, express, verbalize. **2** (*articulated parts*) join, unite, connect, link, couple, hinge, joint, interlock. OPPOSITE: separate.
≫ *adj* clear, distinct, coherent, intelligible, comprehensible, understandable, lucid, eloquent, well-spoken, fluent, communicative, vocal, expressive, meaningful. OPPOSITE: inarticulate.

articulation *noun* **1** (*the speaker's articulation*) pronunciation, enunciation, elocution, diction, speech, delivery, presentation, utterance, vocalization, expression, verbalization. **2** (*the articulation of the parts*) connection, joint, linkage, coupling, hinge.

artifice *noun* **1** (*an artifice used to win*) trick, stratagem, wile, subterfuge, deception, fraud, machination, contrivance, device, tactic, manoeuvre, ruse, scheme, dodge. **2** (*the use of artifice*) cunning, artfulness, slyness, wiliness, deceit, duplicity, chicanery, trickery, guile, craftiness, craft, strategy, skill, art, cleverness, ingenuity. OPPOSITE: honesty.

artificial *adj* **1** (*artificial fibres*) synthetic, man-made, manufactured, unnatural, simulated, imitation, mock, ersatz, fake, counterfeit, sham, bogus, phoney (*inf*), spurious. OPPOSITE: natural. **2** (*an artificial smile*) affected, insincere, unnatural, forced, laboured, strained, contrived, studied, mannered, assumed, feigned, pretended, put on, false, fake, sham, phoney (*inf*). OPPOSITE: sincere.

artillery *noun* guns, gunnery, cannon, cannonry, ordnance, battery.

artisan *noun* craftsman, craftswoman, master, expert, artificer, skilled worker, technician, mechanic.

artist *noun* **1** (*a picture signed by the artist*) painter, sculptor, designer, draughtsman, draughtswoman. **2** (*an artist at his trade*) master, expert, adept, genius. **3** (*artists performing for charity*) artiste, performer, entertainer, singer, musician, dancer, comedian, actor, actress, player, trouper.

artistic *adj* creative, tasteful, exquisite, beautiful, attractive, decorative, ornamental, stylish, elegant, refined, cultured, cultivated, aesthetic, sensitive, imaginative. OPPOSITE: tasteless.

artistry *noun* art, craft, craftsmanship, workmanship, skill, talent, gift, flair, genius, brilliance, virtuosity, expertise, mastery, touch, finesse, sensitivity, creativity. OPPOSITE: incompetence.

artless *adj* **1** (*an artless remark*) simple, plain, natural, unaffected, unpretentious, guileless, honest, truthful, straightforward, sincere, open, frank, candid, forthright, naive, unsophisticated, unworldly, ingenuous,

innocent, childlike. OPPOSITE: artful. **2** (*an artless performance*) awkward, clumsy, inept, inexpert, untaught, ignorant, crude, primitive. OPPOSITE: refined.

as *conj* **1** (*as I opened the door*) while, when, just as. **2** (*as it was raining*) because, since, seeing that, considering that. **3** (*dress as the local people do*) like, in the manner that, in the way that, in the same way that. **4** (*wild animals, as lions and tigers*) for example, for instance, such as, like.
≫ *prep* like, being, in the role of, in the guise of, acting as, functioning as.

as for as to, as regards, with regard to, with reference to, with respect to, on the subject of, in relation to, in connection with.

as it were so to speak, in a manner of speaking, in a way, in some way.

as yet up to now, until now.

ascend *verb* go up, climb, scale, mount, rise, arise, soar, fly up, slope upwards. OPPOSITE: descend.

ascendancy *noun* superiority, dominance, advantage, edge, authority, upper hand, control, domination, power, sway, influence, mastery, supremacy, dominion, command, sovereignty, rule. OPPOSITE: servitude.

ascendant *noun* ascendancy, superiority, dominance, authority, control, power, supremacy, dominion, command, sovereignty, rule.
≫ *adj* **1** (*the ascendant party*) dominant, prevailing, superior, powerful, influential, commanding, ruling, authoritative. OPPOSITE: subordinate. **2** (*ascendant branches*) rising, ascending, climbing, mounting, soaring. OPPOSITE: descending.

in the ascendant rising, ascending, mounting, growing, increasing, flourishing, thriving, up-and-coming, on the up and up (*inf*).

ascent *noun* **1** (*the ascent of Everest*) ascension, ascending, rise, rising, climb, climbing, scaling, mounting. OPPOSITE: descent. **2** (*a steep ascent*) gradient, incline, slope, acclivity, rising ground, ramp, elevation, height, eminence.

ascertain *verb* discover, find out, learn, get to know, suss out (*inf*), determine, identify, pin down (*inf*), verify, make certain, confirm, establish, settle, resolve. OPPOSITE: surmise.

ascetic *noun* abstainer, self-denier, recluse, solitary, hermit, anchorite, stylite, monk, nun, fakir, dervish.
≫ *adj* abstemious, abstinent, self-denying, self-disciplined, continent, celibate, temperate, moderate, puritanical, frugal, austere, spartan, severe, rigorous, harsh, strict. OPPOSITE: luxurious.

ascribe *verb* attribute, assign, credit, accredit, impute, blame, charge, put down, refer.

ashamed *adj* **1** (*ashamed of himself*) abashed, shamefaced, mortified, embarrassed, blushing, red-faced, humiliated, sheepish, with one's tail between one's legs (*inf*), guilty, conscience-stricken, remorseful, contrite, sorry, apologetic, chagrined, distressed, crestfallen, bashful, shy. OPPOSITE: proud. **2** (*ashamed to admit she was wrong*) hesitant, reluctant, unwilling, self-conscious, modest.

ashen *adj* ashy, pale, pallid, pale-faced, wan, pasty,

livid, ghastly, white, blanched, colourless, anaemic, washed out, grey, leaden. OPPOSITE: ruddy.

ashore *adv* to the shore, shoreward, landward, on shore, on land, on dry land, on the shore, on the beach, aground, beached, stranded.

aside *adv* away, out of the way, apart, aloof, separately, detached, in isolation, to the side, alongside, on one side, in reserve.
➤ *noun* whisper, stage whisper, digression, departure, soliloquy, monologue.

asinine *adj* stupid, foolish, idiotic, moronic, imbecilic, silly, daft (*inf*), barmy (*inf*), potty (*inf*), batty (*inf*), senseless, nonsensical, absurd, inane, fatuous, doltish, thick-headed, half-witted, brainless, dumb (*inf*), dopey (*inf*), gormless (*inf*). OPPOSITE: intelligent.

ask *verb* **1** (*I don't know, ask your teacher*) question, quiz, interrogate, cross-examine, grill (*inf*), pump (*inf*), interview, poll, canvass. **2** (*'What's the time?' she asked*) inquire, query. OPPOSITE: reply. **3** (*ask a question*) put, pose, posit, postulate, propose, suggest. OPPOSITE: answer. **4** (*ask for help*) request, seek, demand, order, expect, require, desire, crave, petition, sue, solicit, approach, apply to, appeal to, entreat, beg, implore, beseech, supplicate. **5** (*ask him to dinner*) invite, bid, summon, have round, have over.

askance *adv* **1** (*looked askance at the man beside her*) obliquely, aslant, sideways, indirectly, out of the corner of one's eye. OPPOSITE: directly. **2** (*looked askance at their suggestion*) disapprovingly, contemptuously, scornfully, disdainfully, sceptically, dubiously, suspiciously, mistrustfully.

askew *adj* awry, crooked, aslant, oblique, askance, lopsided, off-centre, out of line, skew-whiff (*inf*). OPPOSITE: straight.

asleep *adj* sleeping, slumbering, in the arms of Morpheus, dozing, napping, snoozing (*inf*), having forty winks (*inf*), fast asleep, sound asleep, dead to the world (*inf*), out like a light (*inf*), resting, reposing, dormant, inactive, inert, comatose, numb, insensible. OPPOSITE: awake.

aspect *noun* **1** (*all aspects of modern life*) side, angle, point, feature, facet, factor, part, phase. **2** (*consider it from a different aspect*) side, angle, slant, direction, light, view, viewpoint, standpoint, outlook. **3** (*a bungalow with a southern aspect*) direction, orientation, situation, position, view, outlook, prospect. **4** (*the gloomy aspect of her companions*) look, appearance, bearing, manner, demeanour, mien, attitude, air, expression.

asperity *noun* harshness, roughness, ruggedness, sharpness, acerbity, tartness, bitterness, acrimony, sourness, moroseness, sullenness, churlishness, crabbedness, peevishness, irascibility, irritability, severity, virulence. OPPOSITE: mildness.

aspersion *noun* slander, calumny, defamation, abuse, vilification, denigration, disparagement, deprecation, censure, obloquy, slur, smear, mudslinging (*inf*). OPPOSITE: commendation.

asphyxiate *verb* suffocate, smother, stifle, choke, strangulate, strangle, throttle.

aspirant *noun* aspirer, seeker, hopeful, postulant,

claimant, applicant, candidate, competitor, contestant, contender, suitor.

aspiration *noun* desire, longing, yearning, craving, hope, dream, ambition, goal, aim, object, objective, target. OPPOSITE: apathy.

aspire *verb* desire, long, yearn, hanker, hunger, crave, hope, dream, seek, aim.

aspiring *adj* hopeful, expectant, would-be, aspirant, ambitious, enterprising, striving, budding, eager, keen. OPPOSITE: apathetic.

ass *noun* donkey, jackass, dolt, ninny, nincompoop, fathead (*inf*), chump (*inf*), wally (*sl*), simpleton, halfwit, fool, idiot, imbecile, moron, dickhead (*sl*), blockhead, dunce, dope (*inf*), nitwit (*inf*), twit (*inf*), twerp (*inf*), nerd (*sl*).

assail *verb* **1** (*assailed by an angry crowd*) attack, assault, set about, lay into, fall upon, accost, mug, jump (*inf*), charge, strike, invade. OPPOSITE: resist. **2** (*assailed by doubts*) beset, attack, strike, plague, bedevil, prey upon, worry, trouble, torment. **2** (*assailed by the critics*) abuse, slander, calumniate, defame, vilify, denigrate, malign, impugn, revile, attack, berate, lambaste, lash, bombard, criticize, deride, ridicule. OPPOSITE: vindicate.

assailable *adj* vulnerable, susceptible, sensitive, unprotected, defenceless, lame, weak. OPPOSITE: unassailable.

assailant *noun* attacker, assaulter, assailer, accoster, mugger, aggressor, invader, enemy, antagonist, opponent. OPPOSITE: protector.

assassin *noun* killer, murderer, slayer, liquidator, executioner, gunman, hitman (*inf*), hatchet man (*inf*), cut-throat.

assassinate *verb* kill, murder, slay, bump off (*inf*), do in (*inf*), liquidate, eliminate (*inf*), dispatch, execute, hit (*inf*).

assassination *noun* killing, murder, liquidation, elimination (*inf*), dispatch, execution.

assault *verb* **1** (*assault a police officer*) attack, assail, set about, fall upon, lay into, strike, hit, mug, beat up (*inf*), do over (*inf*). OPPOSITE: protect. **2** (*assault the citadel*) charge, invade, attack, storm, beset. OPPOSITE: defend. **3** (*sexually assaulted*) molest, interfere with, abuse, rape.
➤ *noun* **1** (*an assault on the enemy*) attack, onslaught, onset, charge, strike, invasion, storming, offensive, aggression. OPPOSITE: defence. **2** (*arrested for assault*) violence, battery, mugging, actual bodily harm, grievous bodily harm, GBH (*inf*). **3** (*sexual assault*) molestation, interference, abuse, rape.

assay *verb* test, try, prove, analyse, examine, scrutinize, inspect, check, investigate, probe, assess, evaluate, appraise.
➤ *noun* test, trial, analysis, examination, scrutiny, inspection, check, investigation, probe, assessment, evaluation, appraisal.

assemblage *noun* assembly, gathering, crowd, throng, group, body, collection, combination, medley, accumulation, aggregation, conglomeration, mass, cluster.

assemble *verb* **1** (*assemble in the hall*) collect, gather, muster, congregate, meet, get together, convene, rally, come together, flock together, mass, cluster. OPPOSITE: disperse. **2** (*assemble the evidence*) bring together, collect, gather, accumulate, amass, marshal, round up, muster, convoke, summon, call. **3** (*assemble a computer*) construct, fabricate, make, manufacture, put together, piece together, join, connect, build, erect. OPPOSITE: dismantle.

assembly *noun* **1** (*address the assembly*) gathering, meeting, rally, conference, convention, convocation, congress, council, conclave, congregation, group, body, crowd, throng, multitude, throng. **2** (*the assembly of motor vehicles*) construction, putting together, fabrication, manufacture, building, erection. OPPOSITE: demolition.

assent *verb* agree, acquiesce, concur, accept, go along with, approve, consent, allow, accord, grant. OPPOSITE: dissent.
➤ *noun* agreement, acquiescence, concurrence, acceptance, approval, approbation, sanction, consent, permission, compliance, accord. OPPOSITE: opposition.

assert *verb* **1** (*assert that it will work*) declare, affirm, attest, asseverate, aver, avow, swear, maintain, state, announce, proclaim, pronounce, predicate, postulate, argue, allege, claim. OPPOSITE: deny. **2** (*asserting his rights*) insist upon, push for, emphasize, stress, uphold, support, defend, stand up for.
assert oneself make one's presence felt, exert one's influence.

assertion *noun* declaration, statement, pronouncement, affirmation, attestation, asseveration, averment, avowal, announcement, proclamation, predication, allegation, claim. OPPOSITE: denial.

assertive *adj* positive, confident, self-confident, self-assured, not backward in coming forward (*inf*), dogmatic, opinionated, emphatic, insistent, strong-willed, firm, forceful, aggressive, overbearing, domineering, self-assertive, pushy (*inf*). OPPOSITE: hesitant.

assess *verb* **1** (*assess her ability*) estimate, gauge, weigh up, size up, judge, appraise, evaluate, value, rate. **2** (*assess property values*) calculate, compute, determine, fix, impose, levy, tax.

assessment *noun* **1** (*their assessment of the situation*) evaluation, appraisal, review, judgment, opinion, estimation, valuation, rating. **2** (*tax assessment*) charge, levy, tax, duty, toll, tariff, rate, demand, fee.

asset *noun* advantage, benefit, plus (*inf*), boon, blessing, virtue, resource, help, aid, strong point, strength, forte. OPPOSITE: disadvantage.

assets *pl noun* property, estate, possessions, belongings, effects, chattels, goods, capital, funds, wealth, money, valuables, securities, holdings, reserves, resources. OPPOSITE: liabilities.

asseverate *verb* declare, affirm, attest, avow, aver, assert, state, maintain, predicate. OPPOSITE: deny.

asseveration *noun* declaration, affirmation, attestation, avowal, averment, assertion, statement, predication. OPPOSITE: denial.

assiduity *noun* assiduousness, industry, diligence, sedulousness, application, devotion, persistence, perseverance, effort, exertion, labour, pains, care,

attention, conscientiousness, tirelessness, constancy. OPPOSITE: indolence.

assiduous *adj* industrious, hard-working, diligent, sedulous, zealous, persistent, persevering, studious, laborious, painstaking, attentive, conscientious, untiring, tireless, unflagging, indefatigable, constant, steady. OPPOSITE: indolent.

assign *verb* **1** (*assigned him to the task*) appoint, designate, nominate, name, select, choose, delegate, detail, charge, commission. OPPOSITE: dismiss. **2** (*assign funds*) allot, allocate, apportion, distribute, dispense, give, grant, designate, earmark, set aside. **3** (*assign a limit*) fix, set, determine, decide, specify, stipulate. **4** (*assigned their fear to ignorance*) attribute, ascribe, put down, chalk up (*inf*), accredit, impute. **5** (*assign property*) transfer, convey, consign, make over.

assignation *noun* meeting, rendezvous, tryst, appointment, date.

assignment *noun* **1** (*set an assignment*) task, job, project, mission, errand, duty, obligation, post, appointment, commission, charge, responsibility. **2** (*his assignment to the task*) appointment, nomination, selection, delegation, commissioning. **3** (*the assignment of funds*) allotment, allocation, apportionment, distribution, dispensation, designation. **4** (*the assignment of a limit*) determination, specification, stipulation. **5** (*the assignment of property*) transfer, conveyance, consignment.

assimilate *verb* **1** (*assimilate new information*) absorb, take in, digest, incorporate, learn. OPPOSITE: reject. **2** (*assimilate into the community*) adapt, adjust, accommodate, acclimatize, accustom, naturalize, blend, mingle, merge, integrate, conform, fit.

assist *verb* **1** (*assist your colleagues*) help, aid, abet, lend a hand, give a leg up (*inf*), support, back, second, reinforce, work with, cooperate, collaborate, do one's bit (*inf*), rally round, relieve, succour. OPPOSITE: hinder. **2** (*assist his recovery*) promote, advance, further, expedite, facilitate, enable, serve. OPPOSITE: retard.

assistance *noun* help, aid, service, helping hand (*inf*), support, backing, reinforcement, cooperation, collaboration, relief, succour. OPPOSITE: hindrance.

assistant *noun* **1** (*with the help of my assistants*) helper, helpmate, aider, aide, accomplice, abettor, ally, confederate, collaborator, partner, colleague, second, supporter. OPPOSITE: opponent. **2** (*the manager's assistant*) auxiliary, subordinate, right-hand man, man Friday, girl Friday, deputy, second in command. **3** (*an assistant in a shop*) salesperson, salesman, saleswoman, server, checkout operator.

associate *verb* **1** (*associate snow with Christmas*) relate, link, connect, couple, pair. OPPOSITE: dissociate. **2** (*an associated organization*) affiliate, incorporate, amalgamate, merge, unite, join, attach, combine, ally, league. OPPOSITE: separate. **3** (*associating with the wrong sort of people*) consort, fraternize, socialize, hobnob (*inf*), mix, mingle, rub shoulders (*inf*), befriend, pal up (*inf*), keep company, go around, hang out (*inf*).
➤ *noun* colleague, co-worker, partner, confederate, ally, accomplice, helper, assistant, fellow, mate, peer,

comrade, friend, companion, sidekick (*inf*). OPPOSITE: enemy.

association *noun* **1** (*join an association*) society, organization, union, guild, league, federation, confederation, alliance, consortium, syndicate, cartel, company, partnership, corporation, body, club, fellowship, lodge, fraternity, sorority, group, band, clique. **2** (*association of ideas*) relation, relationship, correlation, connection, link, bond, tie, union. OPPOSITE: dissociation. **3** (*association with criminals*) fraternization, socialization, friendship, intimacy.

assort *verb* sort, group, classify, rank, distribute, dispose, arrange, array.

assorted *adj* mixed, varied, various, miscellaneous, multifarious, heterogeneous, diverse, different, motley, sundry, several. OPPOSITE: homogeneous.

assortment *noun* mixture, variety, miscellany, medley, pot-pourri, hotchpotch, salmagundi, farrago, jumble, mishmash, selection, range, collection, set, batch, lot, array, arrangement.

assuage *verb* **1** (*assuage suffering*) ease, relieve, alleviate, allay, soothe, mitigate, moderate, temper, lessen, reduce, diminish, abate, mollify, soften, dull, blunt. OPPOSITE: aggravate. **2** (*assuage their guilt*) calm, pacify, appease, tranquillize, lull. **3** (*assuage our hunger*) quell, quench, slake, satisfy, take the edge off.

assuagement *noun* relief, alleviation, mitigation, moderation, reduction, abatement. OPPOSITE: aggravation.

assume *verb* **1** (*I assumed you would wait*) presume, suppose, presuppose, surmise, deduce, infer, understand, gather, accept, take for granted, take it (*inf*), expect, believe, think, imagine, fancy, postulate, hypothesize. OPPOSITE: know. **2** (*assume an air of indifference*) affect, feign, put on, pretend, counterfeit, sham, simulate. **3** (*assume command*) take, accept, take on, adopt, undertake, embark on, set about, shoulder, embrace, acquire, appropriate, seize, take over, commandeer, usurp, arrogate. OPPOSITE: discard.

assumed *adj* false, fake, bogus, phoney (*inf*), made-up, fictitious, counterfeit, sham, spurious, pseudo (*inf*), feigned, pretended, affected, simulated. OPPOSITE: genuine.

assuming *adj* presumptuous, arrogant, imperious, overbearing, haughty, forward, brazen, bold, audacious. OPPOSITE: modest.

assumption *noun* **1** (*make an assumption*) presumption, supposition, presupposition, conjecture, guess, hypothesis, theory, postulate, premise, surmise, deduction, inference, belief, idea, notion, fancy. OPPOSITE: knowledge. **2** (*the assumption of power*) assuming, taking, acceptance, adoption, undertaking, appropriation, seizure, usurpation, arrogation. **3** (*astounded at her assumption*) presumptuousness, presumption, arrogance, conceit, self-importance, forwardness, impertinence, boldness, audacity. OPPOSITE: modesty.

assurance *noun* **1** (*gave them my assurance*) promise, word, word of honour, guarantee, pledge, vow, oath, assertion, affirmation, attestation, declaration, undertaking, security. **2** (*with an air of assurance*)

assuredness, self-assurance, confidence, self-confidence, self-possession, poise, nerve, courage, boldness, effrontery, presumption, arrogance, conceit. OPPOSITE: timidity. **3** (*his assurance of her innocence*) certainty, sureness, conviction, persuasion, confidence, belief. OPPOSITE: doubt.

assure *verb* **1** (*assured them it was correct*) promise, give one's word, guarantee, warrant, pledge, vow, swear, attest, certify, aver, affirm, confirm. **2** (*assured me of her competence*) convince, persuade, reassure, comfort, encourage, hearten. **3** (*in order to assure success*) ensure, make certain, guarantee, secure, clinch, seal.

assured *adj* **1** (*an assured manner*) self-assured, self-confident, self-possessed, poised, confident, complacent, positive, assertive, pushy (*inf*), audacious, bold, presumptuous, arrogant. OPPOSITE: timid. **2** (*success is assured*) certain, sure, guaranteed, secure, reliable, dependable, indubitable, unquestionable. OPPOSITE: doubtful.

astir *adj* active, on the move, in motion, stirring, roused, awake, alert, up and about, afoot. OPPOSITE: idle.

astonish *verb* amaze, astound, stagger, flabbergast (*inf*), dumbfound, gobsmack (*inf*), take one's breath away (*inf*), bowl over (*inf*), knock for six (*inf*), daze, stun, stupefy, startle, surprise, take aback, confound, nonplus, floor (*inf*).

astonished *adj* amazed, astounded, staggered, flabbergasted (*inf*), dumbfounded, speechless, open-mouthed, bowled over (*inf*), knocked for six (*inf*), dazed, stunned, stupefied, startled, surprised, taken aback, nonplussed, floored (*inf*).

astonishing *adj* amazing, astounding, staggering, startling, surprising, stunning, impressive, breathtaking. OPPOSITE: ordinary.

astonishment *noun* amazement, stupefaction, surprise, shock, disbelief, awe, wonder, bewilderment, confusion.

astound *verb* amaze, astonish, stagger, flabbergast (*inf*), dumbfound, gobsmack (*inf*), take one's breath away (*inf*), bowl over (*inf*), knock for six (*inf*), daze, stun, stupefy, shock, dismay, startle, surprise, take aback, confound, nonplus, floor (*inf*).

astounding *adj* amazing, astonishing, staggering, startling, surprising, shocking, overwhelming, stunning, impressive, breathtaking. OPPOSITE: ordinary.

astral *adj* stellar, sidereal, starry, starlike.

astray *adv* wrong, amiss, off course, off the right track, off the rails (*inf*), straying, wandering, loose, adrift, abroad, lost, missing, absent.

astringent *adj* **1** (*an astringent lotion*) styptic, constricting, constrictive, contracting, contractive. **2** (*an astringent remark*) sharp, acerbic, caustic, mordant, trenchant, harsh, austere, stern, severe, rigorous, strict, stringent. OPPOSITE: mild.

astronaut *noun* spaceman, spacewoman, cosmonaut.

astute *adj* shrewd, sharp, acute, quick, quick-witted, intelligent, keen, penetrating, discerning, perceptive, perspicacious, knowing, canny, subtle, artful, cunning, crafty, wily, clever, ingenious. OPPOSITE: stupid.

astuteness *noun* shrewdness, sharpness, acumen, quick-wittedness, intelligence, discernment, perception, insight, subtlety, artfulness, guile, cunning, craftiness, cleverness, ingenuity. OPPOSITE: stupidity.

asunder *adv* apart, to pieces, to bits. OPPOSITE: together.

asylum *noun* **1** (*seek asylum*) sanctuary, refuge, haven, retreat, shelter, protection, safety. **2** (*put him in an asylum*) institution, home, hospital, mental hospital, psychiatric hospital, madhouse (*inf*), loony bin (*inf*), funny farm (*inf*).

asymmetrical *adj* unbalanced, lopsided, uneven, irregular, disproportionate, distorted, malformed, crooked, awry. OPPOSITE: symmetrical.

atavism *noun* recurrence, resurgence, reversion, throwback.

atheism *noun* irreligion, godlessness, unbelief, nonbelief, nihilism, disbelief, scepticism, doubt, freethinking, rationalism, heresy, heathenism, paganism. OPPOSITE: belief.

atheist *noun* unbeliever, nonbeliever, nihilist, disbeliever, sceptic, doubter, freethinker, heretic, infidel, heathen, pagan. OPPOSITE: believer.

athlete *noun* sportsman, sportswoman, sportsperson, runner, gymnast, player, contestant, competitor, contender.

athletic *adj* **1** (*of athletic build*) muscular, sinewy, brawny, strapping, well-built, strong, robust, sturdy, stalwart, powerful, lusty, husky (*inf*). OPPOSITE: weak. **2** (*I'm not very athletic*) sporty, energetic, vigorous, active, fit, able-bodied. **3** (*athletic events*) sporting, sports, games.

athletics *noun* sports, games, track and field events, races, gymnastics.

athwart *adv* across, crosswise, transversely, obliquely. OPPOSITE: straight.
≫ *prep* across, over. OPPOSITE: along.

atmosphere *noun* **1** (*the earth's atmosphere*) air, aerospace, sky, heavens. **2** (*the atmosphere at work*) environment, milieu, surroundings, background, setting, ambience, aura, climate, mood, tone, tenor, character, quality, feeling, spirit, vibrations, vibes (*inf*).

atom *noun* molecule, particle, scrap, bit, jot, iota, whit, mite, scintilla, shred, crumb, grain, morsel, trace, hint, spot, speck.

atone *verb* expiate, redeem, make good, compensate, make up, recompense, pay, make amends, make reparation, redress, do penance. OPPOSITE: offend.

atonement *noun* expiation, redemption, compensation, recompense, payment, indemnity, amends, reparation, restitution, satisfaction, propitiation, redress, penance. OPPOSITE: offence.

atrocious *adj* **1** (*atrocious crimes*) monstrous, abominable, detestable, horrible, horrifying, shocking, infamous, nefarious, villainous, wicked, evil, outrageous, heinous, vile, hideous, infernal, diabolical, fiendish, cruel, vicious, brutal, inhuman, savage, barbaric, barbarous, ruthless, merciless. OPPOSITE: noble. **2** (*an atrocious performance*) appalling, terrible, dreadful, awful, shocking, disgraceful, abysmal. OPPOSITE: excellent.

atrocity *noun* **1** (*wartime atrocities*) outrage, brutality, barbarity, monstrosity, enormity, horror, crime,

violation, act of cruelty, act of savagery. **2** (*the atrocity of their crimes*) atrociousness, monstrousness, infamy, villainy, wickedness, evil, outrageousness, heinousness, vileness, fiendishness, cruelty, viciousness, brutality, inhumanity, savagery, barbarity, ruthlessness, mercilessness. OPPOSITE: nobility.

atrophy *noun* decline, degeneration, decay, wasting, emaciation, shrivelling, withering, diminution, dwindling.
≫ *verb* decline, degenerate, decay, waste away, shrivel, dry up, wither, wilt, diminish, dwindle. OPPOSITE: flourish.

attach *verb* **1** (*attach the wires to the battery*) fasten, join, connect, tie, secure, bind, pin, tack, hitch, couple, clamp, fix, affix, stick, adhere, bond, append, add, annex, subjoin. OPPOSITE: detach. **2** (*attached himself to our group*) affiliate, associate, ally, unite, join, combine. OPPOSITE: dissociate. **3** (*temporarily attached to the sales department*) assign, second, detail, appoint, allot, allocate. **4** (*attach great importance to the survey*) attribute, ascribe, associate, accredit, impute, assign, apply, put, place, lay.

attached *adj* **1** (*very attached to her pets*) fond, loving, affectionate, devoted, enamoured, infatuated. **2** (*are you attached?*) married, engaged, spoken for, in a relationship, going steady (*inf*). OPPOSITE: unattached.

attachment *noun* **1** (*power tools and their attachments*) accessory, fitting, extension, part, appendage, appurtenance, adjunct, addition, extra, supplement, appendix, codicil. **2** (*deep attachment to her pets*) fondness, tenderness, love, affection, liking, partiality, regard, affinity, attraction, bond, fidelity, devotion. OPPOSITE: hatred. **3** (*an attachment from head office*) assignment, secondment, detail, appointment. **4** (*the attachment of the wires*) fastening, junction, connection, bond, tie, coupling, link.

attack *verb* **1** (*attacked by a violent criminal*) assault, assail, set about, go for, ambush, fall upon, mug, beat up (*inf*), do over (*inf*), strike, hit, lay into, knock into the middle of next week (*inf*), let someone have it (*inf*). OPPOSITE: protect. **2** (*the army attacked at dawn*) invade, raid, charge, storm, rush, beset, besiege, assault, assail, strike. OPPOSITE: defend. **3** (*attacked by the critics*) reprove, rebuke, revile, criticize, find fault with, pick holes in (*inf*), knock (*inf*), have a go at (*inf*), run down (*inf*), censure, slate (*inf*), pan (*inf*), slam (*inf*), pull to pieces (*inf*), slander, calumniate, abuse, berate, harangue, fulminate against, vilify, malign, impugn, blame. OPPOSITE: praise. **4** (*a disease that attacks the lungs*) affect, infect, infest, destroy. **5** (*attack the project with enthusiasm*) embark on, undertake, tackle, set about, begin, start.
≫ *noun* **1** (*an attack on enemy territory*) invasion, incursion, aggression, offensive, assault, raid, foray, sortie, sally, charge, rush, onslaught, onset, strike, bombardment, blitz. OPPOSITE: defence. **2** (*a vicious attack on a tourist*) assault, ambush, mugging, beating up (*inf*). **3** (*an attack on modern art*) criticism, knocking (*inf*), censure, slating (*inf*), slander, abuse, invective, flak (*inf*), fulmination, vilification, impugnment, blame. **4** (*an attack of rheumatism*) bout, spasm, access, fit, convulsion, paroxysm, seizure.

attacker *noun* assailant, mugger, aggressor, invader, intruder, raider. OPPOSITE: defender.

attain *verb* achieve, realize, accomplish, fulfil, complete, effect, succeed in, bring off, reach, arrive at, get to, grasp, secure, get, obtain, acquire, procure, gain, win, earn. OPPOSITE: lose.

attainable *adj* achievable, realizable, reachable, within reach, accessible, at hand, obtainable, winnable, possible, potential, likely, feasible, viable, practicable, realistic. OPPOSITE: unattainable.

attainment *noun* **1** (*a list of my attainments*) accomplishment, achievement, exploit, feat, success, qualification, ability, skill, proficiency, talent, gift. **2** (*the attainment of his ambitions*) fulfilment, realization, accomplishment, achievement, consummation, success, procurement, acquisition. OPPOSITE: failure.

attempt *verb* try, endeavour, essay, have a go at, try one's hand at (*inf*), give it a whirl (*inf*), strive, do one's best, seek, venture, set out, undertake, tackle.
➤ *noun* try, effort, endeavour, bid, go, stab (*inf*), crack (*inf*), bash (*inf*), shot (*inf*), undertaking, venture, experiment, trial.

attend *verb* **1** (*attend school*) be present, go, appear, turn up, show up (*inf*), visit, frequent, haunt. **2** (*officers attending the king*) accompany, escort, usher, chaperon, guard, serve, wait on, follow. **3** (*attend the sick*) minister to, tend, nurse, look after, mind, care for, take care of. OPPOSITE: desert. **4** (*attend to what I say*) listen, pay attention, concentrate, heed, mark, mind, observe, watch, note. OPPOSITE: ignore. **5** (*problems that attended the mission*) go with, accompany, coexist with, be associated with, result from, arise from.
attend to deal with, see to, handle, take care of, look after, manage, direct, process, follow up.

attendance *noun* **1** (*your attendance is requested*) presence, appearance, attending, being there. OPPOSITE: absence. **2** (*attendances have increased*) audience, turnout, house, gate, number present.
in attendance present, serving, helping, assisting, on duty, on guard.

attendant *noun* escort, companion, chaperon, usher, guide, marshal, servant, retainer, steward, maid, valet, footman, lackey, menial, guard, follower, aide, assistant, helper.
➤ *adj* accompanying, concomitant, associated, related, incidental, consequent, resultant.

attention *noun* **1** (*my attention wandered*) attentiveness, heedfulness, mind, alertness, awareness, vigilance, observation, notice, thought, consideration, concentration, application, intentness. OPPOSITE: inattention. **2** (*attract their attention*) notice, recognition, awareness, consciousness, heed, regard. OPPOSITE: disregard. **3** (*medical attention*) care, ministration, treatment, therapy, service, help, aid. OPPOSITE: neglect. **4** (*matters requiring attention*) action, thought, consideration, handling, processing. **5** (*flattered by his attentions*) respect, deference, courtesy, politeness, civility, gallantry, compliment, address.

attentive *adj* **1** (*attentive students*) heedful, alert, aware, all ears (*inf*), conscious, mindful, careful, observant, watchful, vigilant, concentrating, intent, diligent, sedulous. OPPOSITE: inattentive. **2** (*attentive to her guests*) considerate, thoughtful, kind, obliging, accommodating, gracious, gallant, chivalrous, civil, polite, courteous. OPPOSITE: neglectful.

attenuate *verb* thin, rarefy, extend, draw out, diminish, reduce, lessen, weaken, dilute.

attenuated *adj* thin, slender, fine, elongated, drawn out.

attenuation *noun* thinning, rarefaction, diminution, reduction, lessening, weakening, dilution.

attest *verb* affirm, aver, asseverate, confirm, corroborate, verify, authenticate, testify to, bear witness to, certify, ratify, endorse, support, back up, vouch for. OPPOSITE: deny.
attest to show, exhibit, manifest, display, demonstrate, prove, evidence, evince, bear out, substantiate.

attestation *noun* testimony, statement, affirmation, averment, confirmation, corroboration, ratification, endorsement, support, backing, evidence, proof. OPPOSITE: denial.

attic *noun* loft, garret. OPPOSITE: basement.

attire *noun* dress, clothing, clothes, garments, wear, garb, gear (*inf*), togs (*inf*), wardrobe, outfit, costume, rigout (*inf*), habit, robes, vestments, apparel, finery, glad rags (*inf*), trappings, accoutrements.
➤ *verb* dress, clothe, garb, robe, array, apparel, fit out, rig out. OPPOSITE: strip.

attitude *noun* **1** (*attitude of mind*) opinion, point of view, view, viewpoint, stance, position, outlook, perspective, approach, disposition, mood, frame of mind, mentality, way of thinking. **2** (*attitude of the body*) pose, posture, position, stance, air, manner, demeanour, bearing, carriage, deportment.

attorney *noun* agent, deputy, substitute, proxy, factor.

attract *verb* draw, pull, bring in, allure, entice, tempt, induce, seduce, engage, interest, charm, fascinate, enchant, bewitch, captivate, win. OPPOSITE: repel.

attraction *noun* **1** (*the attraction of a magnet*) draw, pull, magnetism. OPPOSITE: repulsion. **2** (*the attraction of early retirement*) charm, appeal, allure, lure, enticement, temptation, inducement, interest, fascination, attractiveness, glamour. **3** (*tourist attractions*) feature, activity, diversion, entertainment. **4** (*their attraction to each other*) affinity, liking, fascination, captivation.

attractive *adj* **1** (*attractive to look at*) pleasing, lovely, good-looking, beautiful, handsome, striking, stunning, gorgeous, fair, pretty, comely, fetching, prepossessing, winsome, charming, enchanting, picturesque, sweet, cute, appealing, engaging, captivating, winning, seductive, alluring, desirable, sexy. OPPOSITE: ugly. **2** (*an attractive offer*) tempting, inviting, appealing, desirable, interesting, fascinating, pleasant, agreeable. OPPOSITE: unattractive.

attributable *adj* ascribable, assignable, imputable, chargeable.

attribute *verb* ascribe, assign, credit, accredit, impute, blame, charge, put down, chalk up (*inf*).

➢ *noun* **1** (*intelligence is one of her attributes*) property, quality, virtue, characteristic, trait, feature, peculiarity, quirk, idiosyncrasy. **2** (*the sceptre is an attribute of power*) mark, note, sign, symbol, indicator, indication.

attrition *noun* **1** (*made smooth by attrition*) abrasion, friction, wear, rubbing, chafing, scraping, grinding, erosion, detrition. OPPOSITE: accretion. **2** (*war of attrition*) weakening, enfeebling, debilitation, enervation, attenuation, sapping, wearing down, wearing away.

attune *verb* harmonize, accord, coordinate, adjust, regulate, set, adapt, tailor, fit, accustom, assimilate, acclimatize, familiarize.

atypical *adj* unusual, exceptional, uncharacteristic, abnormal, anomalous, aberrant, deviant, freakish, eccentric. OPPOSITE: typical.

auburn *adj* reddish-brown, copper-coloured, chestnut, russet, rust-coloured, henna, Titian, bronze, tawny.

audacious *adj* **1** (*an audacious plan*) bold, daring, fearless, dauntless, intrepid, venturesome, adventurous, courageous, brave, valiant, plucky, rash, reckless, foolhardy, risky. OPPOSITE: cautious. **2** (*an audacious young woman*) forward, brazen, impertinent, impudent, insolent, cheeky, pert, saucy, rude, arrogant, presumptuous, assuming. OPPOSITE: modest.

audacity *noun* **1** (*the audacity of a circus performer*) boldness, daring, fearlessness, intrepidity, nerve, guts (*inf*), courage, bravery, valiance, pluck, rashness, recklessness, foolhardiness, risk. OPPOSITE: caution. **2** (*had the audacity to correct me*) forwardness, shamelessness, brazenness, effrontery, gall, cheek, nerve, impertinence, impudence, insolence, pertness, sauce, rudeness, arrogance, presumption. OPPOSITE: humility.

audible *adj* perceptible, discernible, detectable, distinct, clear, hearable, heard. OPPOSITE: inaudible.

audience *noun* **1** (*a member of the audience*) assembly, congregation, gathering, crowd, turnout, house, gate, onlookers, spectators, viewers, listeners, patrons, regulars, public, market, following, fans, devotees, buffs (*inf*). **2** (*an audience with the pope*) interview, hearing, reception, meeting, consultation, conference.

audit *verb* inspect, examine, scrutinize, go through, check, verify, go over, analyse, review.
➢ *noun* inspection, examination, scrutiny, checking, verification, analysis, review.

audition *noun* hearing, test, trial, tryout.

augment *verb* **1** (*augment my income*) add to, increase, multiply, enlarge, magnify, amplify, expand, swell, inflate, extend, boost, strengthen, enhance, raise, heighten, intensify. OPPOSITE: decrease. **2** (*public interest has augmented*) grow, increase, multiply, enlarge, expand, swell, extend, rise, intensify, escalate. OPPOSITE: diminish.

augmentation *noun* addition, growth, increase, enlargement, magnification, amplification, expansion, inflation, extension, boost, rise, intensification, escalation. OPPOSITE: decrease.

augur *verb* predict, forecast, foretell, prophesy, portend, presage, bode, foreshadow, herald, signify, betoken, promise.

➢ *noun* prophet, soothsayer, seer, oracle.

augury *noun* **1** (*practise augury*) divination, soothsaying, prophecy, prediction, prognostication. **2** (*an augury for a successful mission*) omen, portent, presage, prophecy, harbinger, herald, sign, token, auspice.

august *adj* dignified, imposing, impressive, grand, magnificent, stately, majestic, regal, noble, venerable, lofty, exalted, illustrious, awe-inspiring, solemn. OPPOSITE: humble.

aura *noun* air, atmosphere, ambience, feeling, mood, vibrations, vibes (*inf*), quality, character, tone, emanation, hint, suggestion.

auspices *pl noun* aegis, patronage, sponsorship, backing, support, favour, influence, protection, guidance, control, supervision.

auspicious *adj* favourable, bright, rosy, promising, encouraging, hopeful, optimistic, propitious, opportune, timely, successful, fortunate, lucky, happy, felicitous. OPPOSITE: inauspicious.

austere *adj* **1** (*austere in manner*) stern, severe, harsh, strict, stringent, firm, inflexible, unbending, rigid, stiff, grim, forbidding, grave, serious, unsmiling, solemn, formal, distant, aloof, cold, unfeeling. OPPOSITE: genial. **2** (*an austere lifestyle*) abstemious, self-denying, self-abnegating, Spartan, economical, frugal, ascetic, self-disciplined, sober, abstinent, puritanical, celibate, chaste, pure. OPPOSITE: luxurious. **3** (*austere design*) plain, simple, unadorned, unornamented, basic, bleak, stark. OPPOSITE: ornate.

austerity *noun* **1** (*the austerity of his manner*) sternness, severity, harshness, strictness, firmness, inflexibility, rigidity, seriousness, solemnity, formality, aloofness, coldness. OPPOSITE: geniality. **2** (*the austerity of monastery life*) abstemiousness, self-denial, self-abnegation, economy, frugality, privation, hardship, asceticism, self-discipline, sobriety, abstinence, puritanism, celibacy, chastity, purity. OPPOSITE: luxury.

authentic *adj* **1** (*an authentic document*) genuine, true, veritable, real, the real McCoy (*inf*), legitimate, legal, lawful, valid, bona fide, kosher (*inf*). OPPOSITE: spurious. **2** (*an authentic account*) truthful, honest, reliable, dependable, trustworthy, accurate, correct, factual, true, faithful, credible, authoritative, straight from the horse's mouth (*inf*). OPPOSITE: inaccurate.

authenticate *verb* verify, prove, substantiate, evidence, validate, certify, seal, confirm, ratify, endorse, guarantee, warrant, underwrite, attest, vouch for. OPPOSITE: disprove.

authenticity *noun* **1** (*the authenticity of the document*) genuineness, legitimacy, legality, lawfulness, validity. OPPOSITE: spuriousness. **2** (*the authenticity of the account*) truth, veracity, honesty, reliability, dependability, accuracy, fidelity, credibility, authority. OPPOSITE: inaccuracy.

author *noun* **1** (*the author of the book*) writer, novelist, storyteller, biographer, essayist, poet, playwright, dramatist, screenwriter, journalist, reporter, contributor, composer, songwriter, lyricist, librettist. **2** (*the author of the plan*) creator, originator, initiator, founder, prime mover, mastermind, parent, inventor, designer, planner, architect, producer, perpetrator.

authoritarian *adj* strict, harsh, tough, severe, draconian, disciplinarian, despotic, autocratic, tyrannical, dictatorial, absolute, dogmatic, imperious, domineering, overbearing, oppressive. OPPOSITE: lenient.
➤ *noun* disciplinarian, despot, autocrat, tyrant, dictator.

authoritative *adj* **1** (*from an authoritative source*) official, legitimate, valid, approved, sanctioned, authentic, genuine, certified, reliable, dependable, trustworthy, true, factual, learned, scholarly, definitive, decisive, conclusive, certain, sure, positive. OPPOSITE: unofficial. **2** (*in an authoritative manner*) assertive, confident, self-confident, assured, self-assured, commanding, masterful, peremptory, dogmatic, authoritarian, dictatorial, imperious, overbearing, arrogant, imposing. OPPOSITE: subordinate.

authorities *pl noun* establishment, administration, management, government, state, council, powers that be (*inf*), officialdom, bureaucracy, red tape (*inf*).

authority *noun* **1** (*people in authority*) power, control, command, jurisdiction, charge, management, direction, government, sovereignty, rule, dominion, supremacy, ascendancy, influence, sway, force, clout (*inf*), might, muscle (*inf*). OPPOSITE: subordination. **2** (*acting with authority*) authorization, sanction, permission, consent, leave, say-so (*inf*), right, prerogative, credentials, warrant, licence, permit. OPPOSITE: ban. **3** (*an authority on the subject*) expert, consultant, specialist, professional, master, scholar, pundit, connoisseur, buff (*inf*). OPPOSITE: novice. **4** (*information from a reliable authority*) source, reference, documentation, bibliography, bible (*inf*). **5** (*the authority of eyewitnesses*) evidence, testimony, deposition, statement, declaration, attestation, avowal, word, say-so (*inf*).

authorization *noun* empowerment, accreditation, licence, commission, warrant, permit, validation, legalization, sanction, approval, ratification, endorsement, permission, consent, green light (*inf*), go-ahead (*inf*), OK (*inf*). OPPOSITE: prohibition.

authorize *verb* empower, enable, accredit, entitle, license, commission, certify, validate, legalize, sanction, approve, rubber-stamp (*inf*), ratify, endorse, warrant, permit, allow, consent to, agree to, give the green light to (*inf*), give the go-ahead to (*inf*). OPPOSITE: forbid.

autobiography *noun* life story, memoirs, diary, journal.

autocracy *noun* dictatorship, despotism, tyranny, absolutism, totalitarianism. OPPOSITE: democracy.

autocrat *noun* dictator, despot, tyrant, absolute ruler, totalitarian, little Hitler (*inf*).

autocratic *adj* dictatorial, despotic, tyrannical, absolute, totalitarian, unlimited, omnipotent, all-powerful, domineering, imperious, overbearing, oppressive, high-handed, bossy (*inf*). OPPOSITE: democratic.

autograph *noun* signature, name, initials, mark, cross.
➤ *verb* sign, initial, make one's mark, countersign.

automatic *adj* **1** (*an automatic machine*) automated, mechanized, self-activating, self-regulating, programmed, unmanned, mechanical, robotic, push-button. OPPOSITE: manual. **2** (*an automatic response*) involuntary, unconscious, instinctive, reflex, knee-jerk (*inf*), spontaneous, natural, mechanical, uncontrolled. OPPOSITE: deliberate. **3** (*an automatic fine*) inevitable, unavoidable, certain, assured, necessary, routine. OPPOSITE: discretionary.

autonomous *adj* self-governing, self-ruling, autarchic, self-reliant, self-sufficient, independent, free, unfettered. OPPOSITE: dependent.

autonomy *noun* self-government, self-rule, home rule, autarchy, self-reliance, self-sufficiency, independence, freedom. OPPOSITE: dependence.

autopsy *noun* post mortem, necropsy, dissection.

auxiliary *adj* supplementary, accessory, additional, extra, spare, reserve, back-up, ancillary, subsidiary, secondary, subordinate, supporting, assisting, helping. OPPOSITE: essential.
➤ *noun* ancillary, accessory, subordinate, assistant, aide, helper, right-hand man, second, backer, supporter, partner, ally, confederate, associate. OPPOSITE: opponent.

avail *noun* use, benefit, good, profit, advantage, help, service.
➤ *verb* be of use, benefit, profit, help, serve. OPPOSITE: hinder.

avail oneself of use, exploit, make use of, take advantage of. OPPOSITE: waste.

available *adj* obtainable, accessible, to hand, within reach, handy, convenient, ready, at one's disposal, on tap (*inf*), free, unoccupied, vacant, usable, up for grabs (*inf*). OPPOSITE: unavailable.

avalanche *noun* landslide, landslip, cascade, deluge, flood, inundation.

avant-garde *adj* experimental, innovative, pioneering, progressive, unconventional, way-out (*sl*), modernistic, futuristic, modern, contemporary, advanced, forward-looking. OPPOSITE: old-fashioned.

avarice *noun* greed, greediness, rapacity, cupidity, materialism, acquisitiveness, covetousness, miserliness, parsimony, close-fistedness, meanness, selfishness. OPPOSITE: generosity.

avaricious *adj* greedy, rapacious, grasping, materialistic, mercenary, acquisitive, covetous, miserly, niggardly, parsimonious, close-fisted, mean, stingy (*inf*), tight (*inf*). OPPOSITE: liberal.

avenge *verb* revenge, retaliate, requite, repay, punish, get even (*inf*), get one's own back (*inf*). OPPOSITE: pardon.

avenue *noun* approach, access, entrance, entry, way, path, course, route, passage, alley, drive, road, street, boulevard.

aver *verb* assert, affirm, asseverate, avow, state, declare, proclaim, pronounce, say, allege, maintain, claim. OPPOSITE: deny.

average *noun* mean, medium, median, midpoint, centre, norm, standard, par, rule, yardstick. OPPOSITE: extreme.
➤ *adj* **1** (*calculate the average height*) mean, median, medial, medium, middle, intermediate. **2** (*the average British summer*) normal, standard, typical, ordinary, usual, common, everyday, routine. **3** (*an average*

performance) middling, mediocre, passable, acceptable, satisfactory, adequate, not bad, fair, fair to middling, indifferent, moderate, tolerable, all right, OK (*inf*), so-so (*inf*), unexceptional, undistinguished, nothing special (*inf*), run-of-the-mill (*inf*), second-rate, not up to much (*inf*), no great shakes (*inf*), not much to write home about (*inf*). OPPOSITE: exceptional.
➤ *verb* equate, even out, balance out, proportion.

averment *noun* assertion, affirmation, asseveration, avowal, statement, declaration, proclamation, pronouncement, allegation, claim. OPPOSITE: denial.

averse *adj* reluctant, unwilling, indisposed, disinclined, loath, opposed, hostile, inimical, antagonistic, antipathetic. OPPOSITE: keen.

aversion *noun* loathing, repugnance, abhorrence, detestation, hate, hatred, phobia, antipathy, dislike, distaste, disgust, horror, revulsion, opposition, hostility, antagonism, reluctance, indisposition, unwillingness, avoidance, evasion. OPPOSITE: love.

avert *verb* turn away, turn aside, divert, deflect, ward off, fend off, parry, avoid, evade, forestall, thwart, frustrate, prevent, preclude, obviate. OPPOSITE: direct.

aviation *noun* flight, flying, aeronautics.

aviator *noun* airman, airwoman, aviatrix, flier, pilot, aeronaut.

avid *adj* **1** (*an avid reader*) keen, eager, enthusiastic, fervent, ardent, passionate, zealous, fanatical, devoted, dedicated. OPPOSITE: apathetic. **2** (*avid for publicity*) greedy, hungry, thirsty, ravenous, insatiable, rapacious, grasping, avaricious, covetous, acquisitive.

avidity *noun* **1** (*the avidity of his fans*) keenness, eagerness, impatience, longing, enthusiasm, fervour, ardour, passion, zeal, devotion, dedication. OPPOSITE: apathy. **2** (*punished for her avidity*) greed, greediness, rapacity, avarice, acquisitiveness, cupidity.

avoid *verb* evade, elude, dodge, shirk, get out of (*inf*), shun, refrain from, abstain from, eschew, escape, avert, circumvent, sidestep, bypass, get round, steer clear of, keep away from, give a wide berth to (*inf*). OPPOSITE: confront.

avow *verb* affirm, assert, asseverate, aver, state, declare, proclaim, swear, admit, acknowledge, recognize, confess. OPPOSITE: deny.

avowal *noun* affirmation, assertion, asseveration, averment, statement, declaration, proclamation, oath, admission, acknowledgment, confession, profession, testimony, deposition. OPPOSITE: denial.

await *verb* wait for, expect, anticipate, look forward to, be ready for, be in store for.

awake *adj* wakeful, waking, aroused, conscious, aware, alert, attentive, vigilant, watchful, lively, active. OPPOSITE: asleep.
➤ *verb* wake up, awaken, stir, rouse. OPPOSITE: sleep.

awaken *verb* arouse, rouse, excite, stimulate, kindle, provoke, incite, stir up, activate, animate, enliven, revive. OPPOSITE: lull.

award *verb* give, present, grant, endow, bestow, confer, assign, appoint, allot, apportion, adjudge, determine. OPPOSITE: withdraw.
➤ *noun* prize, trophy, medal, decoration, grant,

endowment, bestowal, conferment, presentation, judgment, verdict.

aware *adj* mindful, conscious, cognizant, sensitive, appreciative, enlightened, apprised, informed, au courant, knowledgeable, in the know (*inf*), clued up (*inf*), acquainted, familiar, conversant, alert, on the ball (*inf*), awake, vigilant, watchful, attentive, observant. OPPOSITE: unaware.

awareness *noun* consciousness, cognizance, appreciation, recognition, perception, understanding, enlightenment, knowledge, acquaintance, familiarity, alertness, vigilance. OPPOSITE: ignorance.

away *adv* **1** (*away from home*) absent, out, elsewhere, abroad, gone, far, distant, remote. OPPOSITE: present. **2** (*move away*) off, aside, apart, at a distance. OPPOSITE: near. **3** (*chattering away*) continuously, incessantly, endlessly, interminably, relentlessly, persistently.

awe *noun* admiration, wonder, respect, honour, reverence, veneration, amazement, astonishment, dread, fear, terror. OPPOSITE: contempt.
➤ *verb* impress, amaze, astonish, astound, overwhelm, daunt, intimidate, cow, subdue, frighten, alarm, dismay. OPPOSITE: reassure.

awesome *adj* **1** (*an awesome sight*) awe-inspiring, impressive, breathtaking, spectacular, stunning, majestic, sublime, magnificent, splendid, wonderful, marvellous, excellent. OPPOSITE: contemptible. **2** (*an awesome responsibility*) formidable, daunting, intimidating, frightening, alarming, dreadful, fearsome, overwhelming.

awful *adj* dreadful, terrible, fearful, frightful, dire, abominable, abysmal, appalling, atrocious, ghastly, horrendous, nasty, horrid, unpleasant, bad, horrible, hideous, ugly, foul, disgusting. OPPOSITE: wonderful.

awhile *adv* briefly, for a moment, for a while, for a time.

awkward *adj* **1** (*an awkward gesture*) ungainly, graceless, clumsy, maladroit, inept, unskilful, bungling, ham-fisted, gauche, lumbering, uncoordinated, oafish, uncouth, coarse, rough, crude, unpolished, unrefined. OPPOSITE: dexterous. **2** (*an awkward shape*) unwieldy, unmanageable, cumbersome. **3** (*arrived at an awkward moment*) inconvenient, inopportune, untimely, embarrassing, delicate, difficult, tricky, problematic. OPPOSITE: convenient. **4** (*don't be awkward!*) perverse, contrary, trying, vexatious, annoying, stubborn, obstinate, bloody-minded (*inf*), unhelpful, uncooperative, obstructive. OPPOSITE: obliging. **5** (*he felt awkward in her presence*) uncomfortable, ill at ease, embarrassed, shy, bashful.

awning *noun* canopy, tarpaulin, covering, shelter.

awry *adj* askew, askance, oblique, slanting, crooked, distorted, lopsided, uneven, cockeyed (*inf*), skew-whiff (*inf*), wrong, amiss. OPPOSITE: straight.
➤ *adv* askew, askance, obliquely, off-centre, to one side, crookedly, lopsidedly, wrongly, amiss.

axe *noun* chopper, hatchet, cleaver, tomahawk.
➤ *verb* **1** (*trees to be axed*) cut, chop, fell, hew, cleave, split. **2** (*axe the programme*) cancel, terminate, end, discontinue, get rid of, dismiss, discharge, sack (*inf*), fire (*inf*).

axiom *noun* truism, truth, principle, precept, maxim, adage, aphorism, dictum.

axiomatic *adj* self-evident, true, unquestionable, incontestable, indubitable, absolute, certain, manifest, fundamental, given, presupposed, assumed, understood.

axis *noun* pivot, hinge, vertical, horizontal.

axle *noun* shaft, rod, spindle, pin.

azure *adj* blue, sky-blue, cerulean.

babble *verb* **1** (*babble on thoughtlessly*) prattle, gibber, blab, gossip, mutter, chatter, gabble, jabber, prate, mumble, murmur, waffle (*inf*), rabbit (*inf*). **2** (*a babbling stream*) ripple, burble, murmur, gurgle.
➤ *noun* chatter, prattle, gabble, gibberish, drivel, nonsense, murmur, whisper.

babbler *noun* chatterbox, prattler, gabbler, gossip, blabber, blabbermouth.

babe *noun* **1** (*a newborn babe*) baby, babe in arms, infant, nurseling, suckling. OPPOSITE: adult. **2** (*merely a babe in the big wide world*) child, innocent, ingenue, novice, beginner, greenhorn.

babel *noun* hubbub, din, clamour, uproar, tumult, commotion, confusion, disorder, pandemonium, hullabaloo. OPPOSITE: quiet.

baby *noun* infant, babe, newborn, suckling, nurseling, child, toddler, tot, youngest. OPPOSITE: adult.
➤ *adj* tiny, miniature, minute, diminutive, mini, dwarf, midget, small, little, wee. OPPOSITE: giant.
➤ *verb* coddle, mollycoddle, pamper, spoil, pet, cosset, indulge, overindulge, spoon-feed.

babyish *adj* childish, infantile, puerile, immature, silly, foolish, inane. OPPOSITE: adult.

bacchanalia *noun* revelry, revel, orgy, saturnalia, carousal, debauch, spree, merrymaking, festival.

bacchanalian *adj* riotous, wild, drunken, orgiastic, debauched, licentious, unrestrained, merry, festive. OPPOSITE: sober.

back *noun* **1** (*at the back of the building*) rear, stem, reverse, posterior, end, backside, hindquarters. OPPOSITE: front. **2** (*injured his back*) backbone, spine, dorsum.
➤ *adj* **1** (*in the back seat*) rear, hind, hindmost, end, last. OPPOSITE: front. **2** (*back issues*) earlier, former, past, bygone, previous, elapsed, overdue.
➤ *adv* backwards, rearwards, to the rear, behind. OPPOSITE: forwards.
➤ *verb* **1** (*the lorry backed out*) go back, move back,

reverse, retreat, retire, recoil, withdraw. OPPOSITE: advance. **2** (*back the project*) support, encourage, second, stand by, sustain, help, aid, assist, abet, finance, sponsor, champion, subsidize, underwrite, advocate, endorse, favour, countenance. OPPOSITE: obstruct. **3** (*back a horse*) bet on, wager on, gamble on.

back away retreat, withdraw, retire, recede, recoil, step back.

back down withdraw, yield, submit, give in, concede, backpedal, backtrack.

back out abandon, give up, withdraw, retreat, renege, chicken out (*inf*).

back up support, stand by, side with, help, aid, assist, endorse, advocate, vouch for.

behind someone's back secretly, deceitfully, covertly, slyly, sneakily, surreptitiously.

backbite *verb* malign, revile, defame, vilify, asperse, denigrate, run down, slander, calumniate, traduce, attack, abuse. OPPOSITE: praise.

backbiting *noun* defamation, denigration, aspersion, slander, libel, calumny, malice, spitefulness, bitchiness (*inf*), vilification, mudslinging, slagging off (*inf*), gossip, scandalmongering. OPPOSITE: praise.

backbone *noun* **1** (*hurt his backbone*) spine, spinal column, vertebral column, vertebrae. **2** (*the backbone of the organization*) foundation, basis, structure, mainstay, core. **3** (*lack backbone*) stamina, fortitude, mettle, courage, nerve, grit, pluck, determination, resolution, firmness, character, moral fibre, bottle (*inf*). OPPOSITE: weakness.

backer *noun* patron, sponsor, benefactor, promoter, supporter, advocate, champion, seconder, angel (*inf*), well-wisher. OPPOSITE: opponent.

backfire *verb* **1** (*the car backfired*) detonate, explode, discharge, blow up. **2** (*the project backfired*) fail, rebound, recoil, boomerang, blow up in someone's face (*inf*).

background *noun* **1** (*the background to a situation*) setting, context, environment, milieu, circumstances.

2 (*from a working-class background*) upbringing, family, education, qualifications, experience, grounding, preparation, breeding.
in the background unobtrusive, inconspicuous, behind the scenes, unnoticed, out of sight.

backhanded *adj* indirect, oblique, equivocal, ambiguous, double-edged, two-edged, ironic, sarcastic.

backing *noun* **1** (*with the backing of the government*) support, endorsement, aid, help, assistance, commendation, sponsorship, patronage, finance, subsidy, grant, advocacy, approval. OPPOSITE: opposition. **2** (*musical backing*) accompaniment, support, backup, harmony.

backlash *noun* response, reaction, reprisal, retaliation, kickback.

backlog *noun* accumulation, supply, stockpile, reserves, arrears.

backpedal *verb* take back, withdraw, back down, climb down, change your mind, have second thoughts, do a U-turn (*inf*).

backslide *verb* relapse, regress, revert, lapse, go wrong, go astray, sin, leave the straight and narrow, fall from grace.

backslider *noun* apostate, renegade, deserter, fallen angel, recreant, recidivist. OPPOSITE: adherent.

backup *noun* support, reinforcements, help, aid, assistance, encouragement, endorsement, favour.

backward *adj* **1** (*a backward movement*) rearward, reverse, regressive, retrograde. **2** (*a backward child*) slow, retarded, undeveloped, underdeveloped, dull, stupid, behind, tardy, late. OPPOSITE: advanced. **3** (*not backward in volunteering himself*) reluctant, hesitant, unwilling, averse, disinclined, loath, bashful, shy. OPPOSITE: bold.
≫ *adv* backwards, rearwards, behind, in reverse, retrogressively, back to front. OPPOSITE: forwards.

backwash *noun* **1** (*the backwash of a ship*) wash, wake, flow, swell. **2** (*the backwash of an event*) repercussions, aftereffects, aftermath, result, results, consequence, consequences.

backwoods *pl noun* bush, outback, back of beyond (*inf*), middle of nowhere (*inf*), the sticks (*inf*).

bacteria *pl noun* germs, viruses, microorganisms, microbes, bugs (*inf*).

bad *adj* **1** (*a bad person*) wicked, evil, villainous, immoral, depraved, corrupt, sinful, dishonest, criminal, crooked, reprobate. OPPOSITE: virtuous. **2** (*too much drinking is bad for you*) harmful, injurious, pernicious, detrimental, hurtful, destructive, deleterious, unwholesome, noxious, poisonous, vile. OPPOSITE: good. **3** (*bad management*) inferior, poor, defective, inadequate, imperfect, substandard, faulty, unsatisfactory, useless, ropy (*inf*), lousy (*inf*), crappy (*sl*). **4** (*a bad child*) naughty, mischievous, disobedient, unruly, wayward. OPPOSITE: well-behaved. **5** (*bad news*) unpleasant, disagreeable, distressing, discouraging, unwelcome, unfortunate, adverse, serious, grave, severe, harsh. OPPOSITE: splendid. **6** (*a bad accident*) serious, critical, severe, terrible. **7** (*a bad time to ring*) inconvenient, unfortunate, difficult, unsuitable, inappropriate, inauspicious. OPPOSITE: convenient. **8** (*the fish is bad*) decayed, rotten, mouldy, putrid, rancid, off, spoiled, tainted, contaminated, putrescent. **9** (*feel bad*) sick, ill, unwell, poorly, miserable, wretched, under the weather (*inf*). OPPOSITE: well.
not bad fair, average, all right, passable, tolerable, so-so (*inf*), OK (*inf*).

badge *noun* **1** (*a school blazer with a badge*) emblem, device, insignia, shield. **2** (*a badge of shame*) sign, mark, token, stamp, emblem, brand.

badger *verb* harass, torment, plague, harry, bother, provoke, persecute, worry, trouble, tease, bait, vex, annoy, try, hector, pester, nag, hassle (*inf*).

badinage *noun* banter, raillery, teasing, chaff, repartee, persiflage.

badly *adv* **1** (*play badly*) poorly, inadequately, unsatisfactorily, imperfectly, defectively, uselessly. OPPOSITE: well. **2** (*badly hurt*) seriously, severely, critically, greatly, intensely, extremely, acutely, painfully, desperately. OPPOSITE: slightly. **3** (*need something badly*) much, very much, extremely, greatly, exceedingly, enormously, deeply. **4** (*behave badly*) naughtily, mischievously, disobediently, waywardly. OPPOSITE: well.

bad-tempered *adj* cross, irritable, ill-tempered, quick-tempered, short-tempered, grumpy, snappy, short, touchy, edgy, prickly, crabby, ratty (*inf*), stroppy (*inf*).

baffle *verb* **1** (*the question baffled me*) perplex, bewilder, confuse, confound, puzzle, mystify. OPPOSITE: enlighten. **2** (*baffled his efforts*) frustrate, foil, balk, check, thwart, block, deflect, hinder, defeat. OPPOSITE: abet.

bag *noun* sack, pouch, container, receptacle, satchel, shoulder bag, handbag, case, suitcase, rucksack, haversack, knapsack, duffel bag, purse.

baggage *noun* luggage, suitcases, bags, belongings, effects, paraphernalia, things, gear, equipment, accoutrements.

baggy *adj* loose, ill-fitting, billowing, puffed out, roomy, sagging, bulging, slack, floppy, shapeless, lumpish. OPPOSITE: tight.

bail *noun* surety, security, bond, guarantee, warranty, collateral, pledge.

bail out **1** (*bailed him out of a difficulty*) release, rescue, aid, assist, help, relieve. **2** (*bailed out before the crash*) escape, withdraw, get out, break free, leave, quit.

bait *noun* **1** (*bait for fish*) lure, decoy, snare. **2** (*customers taking the bait*) attraction, incentive, lure, enticement, allurement, temptation, inducement, incentive, bribe.
≫ *verb* **1** (*bait a hook*) lure, entice, tempt, seduce, beguile. OPPOSITE: repel. **2** (*baited their younger sister*) badger, tease, persecute, torment, harry, harass, hector, plague, worry, try, vex, annoy, bother, hassle (*inf*), needle (*inf*), wind up (*inf*).

bake *verb* cook, braise, roast, scorch, sear, burn, dry, parch, harden.

balance *verb* **1** (*balance on one foot*) steady, poise, stabilize, level, adjust, square, match. **2** (*balance the different needs*) counterweigh, equalize, counterbalance, offset, counteract, neutralize, compensate, make up for. **3** (*balance the costs against the benefits*) weigh, estimate, compare, evaluate, consider, ponder.

❯ *noun* **1** (*lost his balance*) steadiness, stability, poise, equipoise. OPPOSITE: instability. **2** (*the balance of power*) equilibrium, equipoise, evenness, symmetry, parity, equivalence, correspondence. **3** (*pay the balance of the money*) remainder, rest, surplus, excess, residue, difference. **4** (*kept her balance even in crises*) equanimity, composure, self-possession, self-control, poise, aplomb, stability. OPPOSITE: agitation.
in the balance uncertain, unpredictable, unknown, unclear, vague, iffy (*inf*), up in the air (*inf*).
on balance all things considered, all in all.

balcony *noun* terrace, veranda, loggia, portico, gallery, upper circle.

bald *adj* **1** (*his bald head*) hairless, bald-headed, depilated. **2** (*bald moors*) bare, uncovered, barren, bleak. **3** (*a bald statement*) plain, unadorned, simple, unvarnished, undisguised, unembellished, outright, stark, severe, straightforward, blunt.

balderdash *noun* rubbish, nonsense, drivel, rot, trash, humbug, poppycock (*inf*), claptrap (*inf*), piffle (*inf*), bilge (*inf*), cobblers (*inf*), rot (*inf*), balls (*sl*), crap (*sl*), shit (*sl*), bombast, verbiage. OPPOSITE: wisdom.

bale *noun* bundle, package, pack, parcel, truss, bunch.
bale out escape, withdraw, get out, break free, leave, quit.

baleful *adj* harmful, injurious, ruinous, disastrous, pernicious, deadly, dangerous, noxious, malevolent, menacing, threatening, ominous, sinister, wicked, evil. OPPOSITE: benign.

balk *verb* **1** (*the horse balked at the fence*) hesitate, shrink from, recoil, flinch, jib, stop, refuse, demur. **2** (*balked in his plans*) thwart, frustrate, baffle, hinder, confound, defeat, foil, check, prevent, disappoint. OPPOSITE: abet.

ball[1] *noun* **1** (*a tennis ball*) sphere, orb, globe, globule, drop. **2** (*a cannon ball*) bullet, pellet, shot, projectile.

ball[2] *noun* dance, hop (*inf*), party, soiree, social.

ballad *noun* song, folk song, poem, shanty.

ballast *noun* weight, packing, filling, stabilizer, balance, counterweight, equilibrium, stability.

balloon *noun* airship, dirigible, blimp, zeppelin.
❯ *verb* swell, dilate, inflate, puff out, fill out, billow, distend, bag, belly.

ballot *noun* poll, vote, election, referendum, plebiscite.

ballyhoo *noun* fuss, excitement, commotion, brouhaha, to-do (*inf*), racket, hue and cry, song and dance (*inf*), hype.

balm *noun* **1** (*balm for a wound*) ointment, unguent, lotion, salve, cream, oil, liniment, embrocation. OPPOSITE: irritant. **2** (*balm for an anxious soul*) comfort, consolation, solace, remedy, cure.

balmy *adj* calm, mild, pleasant, clement, temperate, sweet, fragrant, scented, aromatic, soothing, mitigating, assuasive, sedative, healing. OPPOSITE: harsh.

bamboozle *verb* cheat, defraud, deceive, mislead, trick, hoax, dupe, hoodwink, con (*inf*), gull (*inf*), confuse, baffle, perplex, puzzle, bewilder, stump, mystify.

ban *verb* prohibit, forbid, veto, suppress, restrict, proscribe, interdict, outlaw, disallow, exclude, bar. OPPOSITE: permit.
❯ *noun* prohibition, embargo, bar, veto, suppression, restriction, boycott, interdiction, proscription, taboo, proclamation, edict, decree. OPPOSITE: permission.

banal *adj* trite, commonplace, everyday, clichéd, hackneyed, unoriginal, humdrum, ordinary, platitudinous, uninspired, corny (*inf*), old hat (*inf*), stereotyped. OPPOSITE: original.

banality *noun* platitude, commonplace, cliché, truism, bromide.

band[1] *noun* **1** (*a band of enthusiasts*) group, company, body, troop, gang, crew, party, society, association, club, horde, crowd. OPPOSITE: individual. **2** (*a musical band*) group, ensemble, combo.
❯ *verb* join, unite, combine, merge, affiliate, ally, associate, confederate, gather, group. OPPOSITE: separate.

band[2] *noun* **1** (*a silk band*) strip, belt, girdle, ribbon, bandage, tie, cord, ligament, ligature, strap, bond, binding. **2** (*a band of blue*) strip, bar, line, stripe.

bandage *noun* ligature, dressing, compress, tourniquet, gauze, plaster, band, fillet, Elastoplast®, Band-Aid®.
❯ *verb* dress, bind up, bind, cover, swathe, wrap.

bandit *noun* brigand, outlaw, robber, thief, marauder, pirate, hijacker, gangster, desperado, highwayman, highway robber, footpad.

bandy *verb* exchange, reciprocate, swap, trade, interchange, toss, throw, pass.
❯ *adj* bent, curved, crooked, bowed, bow-legged. OPPOSITE: straight.

bane *noun* **1** (*weeds are the bane of gardeners*) woe, misery, affliction, curse, plague, scourge, torment, pest, nuisance, blight, ruin, ruination, calamity, disaster, injury, destruction, harm. OPPOSITE: delight. **2** (*leopard's bane*) poison, venom, toxin.

bang *noun* **1** (*a loud bang*) explosion, boom, detonation, shot, report, burst, thud, thump, crash, clap, peal, clash, clang. **2** (*a bang on the head*) blow, knock, stroke, hit, bump, thump, whack, slap, bash (*inf*), wallop (*inf*), sock (*inf*).
❯ *verb* **1** (*banging on the door*) knock, hit, beat, bump, strike, bash (*inf*), thump, rap, hammer, pound. **2** (*the engine banged*) boom, explode, burst, detonate, blow up, crash, thump, clatter, echo, resound, ring, peal.
❯ *adv* **1** (*arrive bang on time*) precisely, exactly, right, directly, straight, headlong, smack (*inf*). **2** (*bang went my holiday*) suddenly, abruptly.

bangle *noun* band, bracelet, armlet, wristlet.

banish *verb* **1** (*banished from their country*) expel, eject, exile, deport, expatriate, transport, exclude, ostracize, outlaw, cast out. **2** (*banished from his mind*) dismiss, repudiate, spurn, abandon, dispel, drive away, get rid of. OPPOSITE: harbour.

banishment *noun* exile, deportation, expatriation, expulsion, repudiation, transportation, exclusion.

banisters *pl noun* rail, railing, handrail, balustrade.

bank[1] *noun* **1** (*on the banks of a river*) side, shore, margin, border, edge, embankment, brink. **2** (*a bank of ground*) heap, pile, mound, rise, slope, incline, knoll, ridge, embankment.
❯ *verb* incline, slope, slant, pitch, tilt.
bank up 1 (*snow banked up*) form, accumulate, pile,

amass, gather. **2** (*bank up a fire*) stifle, smother, damp down.

bank² *noun* **1** (*a savings bank*) commercial bank, high-street bank, clearing bank, merchant bank, savings bank, building society, financial institution, finance house. **2** (*a blood bank*) store, stock, fund, reserve, savings, accumulation, depository, storehouse, hoard.
➤ *verb* deposit, keep, save, save up, put by, put aside, lay by, lay aside, store, stash away (*inf*).
bank on depend on, count on, rely on, lean on, trust, expect, believe in, pin one's hopes on, pin one's faith in.

bank³ *noun* (*a bank of switches*) row, series, line, array, panel.

bankrupt *adj* **1** (*a bankrupt company*) insolvent, broke (*inf*), in debt, failed, bust (*inf*), hard up (*inf*), gone to the wall (*inf*), on the rocks (*inf*), on one's uppers (*inf*), ruined, destitute, impoverished, depleted, lacking, deficient. OPPOSITE: affluent. **2** (*spiritually bankrupt*) empty, lacking, deficient, exhausted, deprived, depleted.
➤ *verb* cripple, ruin, impoverish.

bankruptcy *noun* insolvency, liquidation, ruin, failure, disaster, depletion, deficiency. OPPOSITE: affluence.

banner *noun* standard, flag, colours, ensign, streamer, pennant, pennon, gonfalon, gonfanon, banderole.

banquet *noun* feast, dinner, repast, revel, celebration, entertainment, regalement, treat, spread (*inf*).

banter *verb* chaff, tease, rib (*inf*), rag (*inf*), kid (*inf*), pull someone's leg (*inf*), ridicule, mock, jeer, deride, make fun of, twit.
➤ *noun* badinage, raillery, chaff, repartee, teasing, jesting, ribbing (*inf*), kidding (*inf*), joking, mockery, ridicule, derision.

baptism *noun* **1** (*a child's baptism*) christening, sprinkling, immersion, naming, dedication, purification, initiation, aspersion. **2** (*a baptism of fire*) initiation, inauguration, beginning, launch, debut.

baptize *verb* christen, sprinkle, immerse, name, dedicate, purify, initiate.

bar *noun* **1** (*a metal bar*) rod, rail, pole, shaft, crosspiece. **2** (*a bar of chocolate*) block, slab, cake, chunk, lump, nugget, wedge, ingot. **3** (*a bar to getting a job*) barrier, obstacle, barricade, hindrance, obstruction, deterrent, impediment, ban, prohibition, injunction, embargo, boycott. OPPOSITE: aid. **4** (*order a drink from the bar*) counter, saloon, lounge, pub (*inf*), public house, inn, tavern, hotel. **5** (*a snack bar*) counter, buffet, stall, table. **6** (*a bar of light*) band, strip, line, stripe, streak. **7** (*called to the bar*) tribunal, bench, court, barristers, advocates.
➤ *verb* **1** (*bar the door*) lock, bolt, secure, padlock, barricade. **2** (*barred from the country*) prohibit, forbid, ban, hinder, obstruct, impede, stop, prevent, deter, restrain, exclude, ostracize. OPPOSITE: allow.
➤ *prep* except, but for, apart from, excluding, barring, with the exception of.

barb *noun* **1** (*the barb on a fishhook*) point, bristle, spine, quill, thorn, needle, spike, prickle. **2** (*critical barbs*) gibe, insult, rebuff, sneer, taunting, mocking, dig (*inf*).

barbarian *noun* savage, brute, ruffian, boor, lout, ignoramus, philistine.
➤ *adj* primitive, savage, barbarous, wild, brutish,

uncivilized, unsophisticated, uncouth, boorish, rough, vulgar. OPPOSITE: civilized.

barbaric *adj* savage, brutal, cruel, vicious, ruthless, inhuman, barbarous, uncivilized, wild, primitive, barbarian. OPPOSITE: humane.

barbarism *noun* cruelty, harshness, savagery, brutality, inhumanity, barbarity.

barbarity *noun* **1** (*the barbarity of war*) cruelty, brutality, savagery, inhumanity, ruthlessness, viciousness, barbarism, outrage, atrocity, enormity. OPPOSITE: humanity. **2** (*barbarities against good taste*) coarseness, vulgarity, crudity, rudeness. OPPOSITE: refinement.

barbarous *adj* **1** (*barbarous people*) uncivilized, primitive, barbarian, uncouth, ignorant, uncultured, unsophisticated, uncultivated, unrefined, rough, rude, coarse, vulgar, crude. OPPOSITE: civilized. **2** (*a barbarous attack*) brutal, savage, barbaric, cruel, inhuman, ferocious, vicious, ruthless. OPPOSITE: humane.

barbed *adj* **1** (*barbed thorns*) prickly, thorny, spiked, spiny, pointed. **2** (*barbed comments*) snide, hostile, nasty, critical, cutting, caustic, acid.

bare *adj* **1** (*walk in bare feet*) naked, nude, unclothed, undressed, stripped, denuded, uncovered, exposed, unprotected. OPPOSITE: clothed. **2** (*a bare hillside*) bleak, desolate, barren, treeless, exposed, unprotected. **3** (*the room looks bare*) unfurnished, empty, barren, austere. OPPOSITE: ornamented. **4** (*the bare truth*) plain, simple, stark, cold, hard, bald, unadorned, unembellished. OPPOSITE: embellished. **5** (*the bare minimum*) basic, least, mere, inadequate, insufficient, meagre, scant, scanty.

barefaced *adj* impudent, brazen, shameless, audacious, bold, undisguised, unconcealed, patent, manifest, glaring, blatant, palpable, flagrant. OPPOSITE: concealed.

barely *adv* scarcely, only just, no more than, hardly, merely, just, by the skin of one's teeth (*inf*), by a whisker (*inf*).

bargain *noun* **1** (*make a bargain with you*) agreement, arrangement, pact, contract, compact, stipulation, deal, transaction, understanding, promise, pledge. **2** (*bargains at the supermarket*) discount, reduction, giveaway (*inf*), snip (*inf*), steal (*inf*), good buy.
➤ *verb* **1** (*bargain at the market*) negotiate, haggle, barter, deal, trade, traffic. **2** (*bargain for land*) agree, arrange, contract, pledge, promise.
bargain for anticipate, expect, foresee, contemplate, imagine, allow for, take into account, take into consideration.
bargain on depend on, rely on, count on, expect, anticipate.
into the bargain in addition, additionally, as well, besides.

barge *noun* canalboat, houseboat, narrow boat, flatboat, lighter.
➤ *verb* push, push your way, shove, press, jostle, elbow, bump, collide.
barge in interrupt, butt in, burst in, break in, intrude.

bark¹ *verb* **1** (*the dog barked*) yelp, yap, bay, woof, howl, snap, snarl, growl. **2** (*the sergeant major barked orders*) shout, yell, bawl, scream, shriek.
➤ *noun* yelp, yap, howl, woof, snarl.

bark[2] *noun* (*tree bark*) covering, casing, crust, rind, skin, peel, hull, integument, cortex.

barmy *adj* crazy, idiotic, mad, insane, daft, nuts (*inf*), dippy (*inf*), batty (*inf*), dotty, loony (*inf*), loopy (*inf*), off one's head (*inf*), off one's trolley (*inf*), round the bend (*inf*), round the twist (*inf*), silly, foolish, stupid. OPPOSITE: sensible.

barn *noun* shed, shelter, stables, mews, outhouse.

baron *noun* **1** (*the baron's stately home*) noble, nobleman, lord, peer, earl, aristocrat. **2** (*a press baron*) tycoon, magnate, mogul, entrepreneur, financier, captain of industry.

baroque *adj* elaborate, ornate, decorated, embellished, flamboyant, florid, fussy, extravagant, convoluted, fanciful, fantastic, overelaborate. OPPOSITE: plain.

barracks *pl noun* camp, billet, garrison, fort, quarters, encampment.

barrage *noun* **1** (*artillery barrage*) bombardment, battery, volley, hail, cannonade, shelling. **2** (*a barrage of complaints*) deluge, storm, stream, onslaught, avalanche, torrent, profusion, plethora.

barrel *noun* cask, keg, vat, butt, tun, firkin, hogshead, tank, vessel, container.

barren *adj* **1** (*a barren woman*) infertile, sterile, infecund, childless. **2** (*barren land*) unfruitful, unproductive, infertile, bare, arid, waste, desolate, empty. OPPOSITE: fertile. **3** (*barren arguments*) futile, useless, fruitless, unprofitable, dull, boring, uninteresting, ineffectual, unavailing, vain. OPPOSITE: useful.

barricade *noun* barrier, obstruction, blockade, roadblock, bulwark, obstacle, hindrance.
» *verb* obstruct, block, blockade, bar, fortify, protect, defend, fence in, shut in.

barrier *noun* **1** (*a crash barrier*) barricade, obstacle, obstruction, bar, blockade, fence, railing, wall, rampart, ditch, moat. **2** (*barriers to increased trade*) hindrance, impediment, stumbling block, block, obstruction, obstacle, hurdle, limitation, restriction, restraint, difficulty. OPPOSITE: aid.

barrister *noun* lawyer, counsel, solicitor, advocate, attorney.

barrow *noun* handcart, truck, wheelbarrow, handbarrow.

barter *verb* exchange, trade, swap, deal, traffic, haggle, bargain.
» *noun* trade, trading, traffic, trafficking, exchange, swapping, dealing, negotiation.

base[1] *noun* **1** (*the base of a triangle*) bottom, foot, foundation, support, rest, prop, stand, pedestal. OPPOSITE: top. **2** (*establish a good research base*) basis, foundation, core, heart, source, essence, root, principal. **3** (*a military base*) home, settlement, camp, headquarters, centre, post, starting point.
» *verb* **1** (*based on firm evidence*) establish, found, build, rest, ground, hinge, depend. **2** (*based in Paris*) station, locate, situate, position, post.

base[2] *adj* **1** (*base behaviour*) low, mean, despicable, vile, wicked, bad, evil, contemptible, abject, ignoble, dishonourable, disgraceful, shameful, depraved, immoral, worthless, wretched, miserable, pitiful, sorry, menial, lowly. OPPOSITE: noble. **2** (*base coin*) false, fake, spurious, counterfeit, alloyed, adulterated, impure, debased, cheap, inferior, poor. OPPOSITE: refined.

baseless *adj* groundless, unfounded, unconfirmed, unsupported, uncorroborated, unsubstantiated, unreasonable, unjustifiable. OPPOSITE: reasonable.

basement *noun* cellar, crypt, vault.

bashful *adj* shy, timid, timorous, coy, diffident, modest, reserved, reticent, shrinking, sheepish, demure, self-effacing, abashed, shamefaced. OPPOSITE: bold.

bashfulness *noun* shyness, timidity, demureness, coyness, self-effacement, diffidence, modesty, reserve, reticence, constraint. OPPOSITE: boldness.

basic *adj* **1** (*basic requirements*) fundamental, essential, central, intrinsic, inherent, rudimentary, underlying, primary, elementary. OPPOSITE: subsidiary. **2** (*a basic rate of pay*) standard, starting, lowest, minimum. **3** (*basic cooking facilities*) simple, plain, spartan, stark, austere, unadorned, undeveloped.

basically *adv* fundamentally, essentially, primarily, centrally, firstly, intrinsically.

basics *pl noun* fundamentals, essentials, rudiments, brass tacks (*inf*), hard facts, practicalities, nitty-gritty (*inf*), nuts and bolts (*inf*).

basin *noun* **1** (*a pudding basin*) container, vessel, receptacle, bowl, dish. **2** (*a river basin*) channel, bed, depression, dip.

basis *noun* **1** (*form the basis of a discussion*) starting point, premise, base, foundation, bottom, ground, cause, reason, principle, fundamental, essence, core, root. **2** (*provides income on a regular basis*) arrangement, system, method, manner, way, term, approach, procedure.

bask *verb* **1** (*bask in the sunshine*) bathe, wallow, indulge oneself, lounge, lie, relax, laze. **2** (*basked in their approval*) revel, luxuriate, enjoy, delight, savour, relish.

basket *noun* container, hamper, pannier, bassinet, punnet, creel.

bass *adj* deep, low, deep-pitched, low-pitched, grave, sonorous, resonant. OPPOSITE: treble.

bastard *adj* (*a bastard son*) illegitimate, natural, baseborn. OPPOSITE: legitimate. **2** (*a bastard style*) abnormal, irregular, imperfect, inferior, impure, debased, corrupt, contaminated, adulterated, counterfeit, fake, spurious.
» *noun* **1** (*the monarch's bastard*) illegitimate child, love child, natural child. **2** (*some nasty bastard*) villain, rogue, scoundrel, rascal, wretch, cad, rotter (*inf*).

bastardize *verb* adulterate, debase, degrade, corrupt, defile, contaminate, pervert.

bastion *noun* **1** (*attack the enemy's bastion*) citadel, fortress, fort, stronghold, bulwark, garrison. **2** (*a bastion of male privilege*) protection, defence, protector, defender, support, supporter, prop, mainstay.

bat *noun* stick, club, mallet, racquet, cudgel.

batch *noun* set, lot, quantity, amount, group, bunch, cluster, collection, crowd, accumulation, mass, assemblage, conglomeration, aggregate, aggregation.

bath *noun* **1** (*install a new bath*) tub, bathtub,

steambath, sauna, Jacuzzi®, whirlpool, sitz bath. **2** (*have a bath*) wash, washing, bathing, soak, dip, scrub, shower, ablution, douche.

➤ *verb* wash, bathe, scrub, soak, shower, douche.

bathe *verb* **1** (*bathe a wound*) wash, cleanse, clean, rinse, immerse, soak, steep, wet, moisten, suffuse. **2** (*bathe in the lake*) swim, go for a swim, float, go for a dip, paddle. **3** (*bathed in moonlight*) suffuse, envelop, flood, engulf, imbue, infuse.

➤ *noun* swim, float, dip, paddle.

bathing suit *noun* swimming costume, bathing costume, swimming trunks, trunks, bikini, swimsuit, cossie (*inf*).

bathos *noun* anticlimax, letdown, comedown, triteness, superficiality, shallowness, sentimentality, mawkishness.

baton *noun* stick, wand, bar, rod, staff, mace, club, truncheon.

battalion *noun* **1** (*battalions of soldiers*) company, force, brigade, regiment, squadron, division, platoon, legion, unit, section, contingent. **2** (*battalions of people*) throng, crowd, mass, horde, multitude, herd.

batten[1] *noun* (*fastened on to a batten*) bar, strip, support bar.

➤ *verb* fix, fasten, secure, tighten, nail down.

batten[2] *verb* **batten on** (*batten on others' hard work*) prosper on, flourish on, thrive on, gain at the expense of.

batter *verb* **1** (*waves battering against the sea wall*) beat, pound, pummel, thrash, lash, buffet, deface, mar, shatter, damage, smash, demolish, destroy. **2** (*battered his wife*) hit, smite, strike, abuse, beat, assault, attack, hurt, thrash, injure, wear, bruise.

battered *adj* abused, beaten, assaulted, attacked, injured, bruised.

battery *noun* **1** (*a battery of telephones*) series, group, set, sequence, cycle, progression. **2** (*assault and battery*) attack, grievous bodily harm, GBH, beating, striking, thrashing, violence, mugging (*inf*). **3** (*anti-aircraft batteries*) cannons, guns, artillery, cannonry.

battle *noun* **1** (*killed in battle*) fight, war, conflict, armed conflict, confrontation, combat, engagement, skirmish, encounter, contest, action, hostilities. OPPOSITE: peace. **2** (*a legal battle*) conflict, campaign, struggle, disagreement, argument, controversy, strife, clash, feud, dispute, debate, altercation.

➤ *verb* **1** (*battle against the wind*) fight, struggle, contest, combat, contend, feud, war. **2** (*battle against the authorities*) quarrel, argue, dispute, disagree, wrangle, bicker. OPPOSITE: agree.

battle-axe *noun* dragon, virago, harridan, termagant, tartar, martinet, fury, shrew.

battle cry *noun* war cry, rallying call, motto, slogan, watchword.

battlefield *noun* battleground, field of battle, field of operations, front, arena, war zone, combat zone, theatre of operations.

battlement *noun* parapet, balustrade, embankment, bulwark, wall, fortification, rampart, bastion, outwork.

battleship *noun* warship, man-of-war, battle cruiser, dreadnought, corvette, ram.

batty *adj* eccentric, odd, peculiar, crazy, mad, insane, foolish, stupid, idiotic, daft (*inf*), nutty (*inf*), barmy (*inf*), bonkers (*inf*), loony (*inf*), round the bend (*inf*).

bauble *noun* trinket, trifle, toy, plaything, gewgaw, bagatelle, knick-knack, ornament.

bawdy *adj* obscene, blue, lewd, indecent, coarse, pornographic, vulgar, rude, risqué, salacious, filthy, dirty, crude, racy, suggestive, smutty.

bawl *verb* **1** (*bawl an order*) yell, shout, cry, cry out, call out, vociferate, roar, bellow, screech, holler (*inf*), howl. OPPOSITE: whisper. **2** (*a baby bawling*) cry, weep, sob, wail, lament, blubber.

bay[1] *noun* (*a ship anchored in the bay*) cove, inlet, gulf, bight, sound, basin, arm, firth, estuary.

bay[2] *noun* (*a loading bay*) recess, alcove, niche, opening, compartment.

bay[3] *verb* (*a dog baying*) bark, yelp, howl, cry.

bazaar *noun* **1** (*an eastern bazaar*) market, marketplace, mart, exchange, souk. **2** (*a church bazaar*) fete, fair, sale, bring and buy sale.

be *verb* **1** (*to be or not to be*) exist, live, breathe. **2** (*the pen is on the table*) be situated, be located, be positioned. **3** (*the film is on tonight*) occur, happen, take place, come about, come to pass, arise, develop, transpire. **4** (*I have always been there*) survive, persist, remain, stay, continue, endure, prevail, last.

beach *noun* shore, seashore, seaside, strand, sands, shingle, coast, coastline, littoral, margin, brink, rim.

beachcomber *noun* forager, scavenger, gatherer, wanderer, scrounger, loafer, bum (*inf*).

beached *adj* aground, ashore, wrecked, grounded, stranded, marooned, high and dry, stuck fast, deserted, forsaken, abandoned.

beacon *noun* signal, flare, rocket, smoke signal, beam, lighthouse, bonfire, warning, sign, mark, landmark, guidepost.

bead *noun* **1** (*a necklace of beads*) spherule, pellet, pill, spheroid, ball. **2** (*beads of sweat*) drop, droplet, globule, bubble, blob.

beads *pl noun* necklace, necklet, pearls, choker, pendant, chaplet, rosary.

beak *noun* **1** (*a bird's beak*) bill, mandible, nib, rostrum. **2** (*the beak on a ship*) prow, bow, stem, rostrum.

beaker *noun* cup, glass, mug, goblet, tankard.

beam *noun* **1** (*a wooden beam*) plank, board, timber, rafter, girder, support, joist, stanchion, scantling. **2** (*a beam of light*) ray, streak, shaft, flash, gleam, glint, glimmer.

➤ *verb* **1** (*the sun beamed down on them*) shine, gleam, glitter, glisten, radiate. **2** (*beam a tv signal*) emit, transmit, send, direct. **3** (*beam with satisfaction*) smile, grin. OPPOSITE: frown.

beaming *adj* bright, brilliant, gleaming, shining, radiant, sunny, smiling, grinning, cheerful, joyful. OPPOSITE: dull.

bear *verb* **1** (*bear gifts*) carry, convey, transport, take, bring, fetch, move, waft. OPPOSITE: drop. **2** (*bear his* *weight*) support, sustain, hold up, lift, shoulder, uphold. **3** (*can't bear selfishness*) endure, stand, tolerate, suffer, abide, brook, stomach, allow, permit, admit, submit to, put up with. OPPOSITE: resist. **4** (*bear pain*) endure, go through, suffer, experience. **5** (*bear a child*) give birth to, bring forth, beget, engender, breed, produce, generate, yield. **6** (*bear a good crop*) produce, yield, provide, generate. **7** (*bear scars from the fight*) display, show, exhibit, have, show signs of. **8** (*bear a grudge*) harbour, cherish, hold, have, possess, maintain, keep, entertain. OPPOSITE: discard. **9** (*bear the cost*) accept, take, support, sustain, shoulder. **10** (*bear right at the junction*) turn, veer, go, curve, fork.

bear on affect, concern, regard, relate to, pertain to.

bear out confirm, substantiate, corroborate, support, uphold, verify, prove, justify, vindicate.

bear up cope, persevere, carry on, endure, survive, withstand, grin and bear it (*inf*).

bear with tolerate, put up with, endure, stand, suffer, make allowances for, be patient with.

bearable *adj* tolerable, supportable, endurable, admissible, passable, sufferable, sustainable. OPPOSITE: unbearable.

beard *noun* facial hair, whiskers, stubble, bristle, bristles, goatee, Vandyke, imperial, sideburns, sideboards, sidewhiskers, muttonchops, moustache, five o'clock shadow.
    » *verb* confront, face, defy, oppose, brave, challenge, stand up to, resist.

bearded *adj* unshaven, whiskered, bewhiskered, bristly, stubbly, hairy, bushy, shaggy, hirsute. OPPOSITE: smooth.

bearer *noun* **1** (*a flag bearer*) carrier, porter, conveyor. **2** (*a bearer of bad news*) messenger, agent, courier, runner. **3** (*pay the bearer of the document*) holder, incumbent, beneficiary, payee, consignee.

bearing *noun* **1** (*his erect, assertive bearing*) behaviour, conduct, deportment, carriage, manner, attitude, posture, mien, demeanour, air, aspect. **2** (*have no bearing on the policy*) relevance, connection, relation, pertinence. **3** (*lose your bearings*) orientation, direction, course, aim, whereabouts, position, location, situation, way.

bearish *adj* surly, gruff, bad-tempered, churlish, boorish, clumsy, rough, coarse, uncouth, rude. OPPOSITE: polite.

beast *noun* **1** (*birds and beasts*) brute, animal, creature. **2** (*you're such a beast!*) savage, monster, brute, ogre, barbarian, pig, swine.

beastly *adj* **1** (*beastly weather*) unpleasant, vile, nasty, mean, rotten, foul, loathsome, abominable, terrible, awful, disagreeable. OPPOSITE: splendid. **2** (*beastly behaviour*) brutal, bestial, cruel, inhuman, savage, coarse, depraved. OPPOSITE: humane.

beat *verb* **1** (*beat a dusty carpet*) strike, hit, thrash, whip, flog, lash, spank, cane, whack (*inf*), batter, bash, pound, pummel, hammer, knock, smack, thwack, thump, cudgel, belt (*inf*), clout (*inf*), fill in (*inf*), maul. OPPOSITE: caress. **2** (*beat a drum*) strike, hit, bang, pound. **3** (*beat an opponent*) defeat, overcome, subdue, quell, vanquish, trounce, rout, conquer, lick (*inf*), overpower, hammer (*inf*), slaughter (*inf*). **4** (*his heart was beating*) throb,

pulsate, pound, thump, palpitate, tremble, vibrate. **5** (*beat the eggs*) whisk, whip, blend, stir, mix. **6** (*the waves beating against the sea wall*) strike, pound, dash, break, wash, lap. **7** (*a bird beating its wings*) flap, swing, shake, flutter, quiver, vibrate, tremble. **8** (*beat metal*) hit, forge, hammer, work, fashion, shape, form, model. **9** (*beat a record*) surpass, exceed, top, transcend, outdo, outstrip.
    » *noun* **1** (*the beat of her heart*) throb, pulsation, pulse, vibration. **2** (*the beat of a drum*) stroke, hit, blow, punch, lash, thump. **3** (*musical beat*) accent, rhythm, stress, metre, cadence, time, tempo. **4** (*a police officer's beat*) round, circuit, course, route, zone, area.
    » *adj* tired out, worn out, exhausted, wearied, spent.

beat up attack, assault, batter, mug (*inf*), do over (*inf*), rough up (*inf*), duff up (*inf*), knock about (*inf*), knock into the middle of next week, knock the living daylights out of.

beaten *adj* **1** (*beaten soldiers*) defeated, conquered, subdued, baffled, vanquished, thwarted. OPPOSITE: victorious. **2** (*a beaten path*) trampled, trodden, worn, well-used, well-trodden, well-worn. OPPOSITE: untrodden. **3** (*beaten metal*) hammered, forged, fashioned, shaped, worked. **4** (*beaten eggs*) whisked, whipped, stirred, mixed, blended.

beatific *adj* ecstatic, glorious, joyful, blessed, blissful, serene, heavenly, enchanting, rapturous. OPPOSITE: woeful.

beating *noun* **1** (*gave the boy a beating*) striking, hitting, thrashing, spanking, flogging, whipping, caning, pasting (*inf*), punishment. **2** (*plans took a beating*) defeat, conquest, rout, overthrow, setback, downfall, ruin. OPPOSITE: success. **3** (*beating of the heart*) throbbing, pulsation, vibration.

beatitude *noun* blessing, ecstasy, delight, joy, happiness, rapture, bliss, blissfulness, felicity, blessedness, saintliness, beatification.

beau *noun* **1** (*a woman's beau*) admirer, suitor, escort, sweetheart, boyfriend, lover, fiancé, partner. **2** (*a well-dressed beau*) dandy, fop, ladies' man, popinjay, man about town.

beautiful *adj* attractive, lovely, fair, gorgeous, charming, elegant, graceful, seemly, becoming, handsome, pretty, comely, good-looking, ravishing, alluring, stunning, pulchritudinous. OPPOSITE: ugly.

beautify *verb* adorn, embellish, titivate, ornament, prettify, glamorize, bedeck, array, enhance, garnish, gild, embroider, decorate, doll up (*inf*), tart up (*inf*), glam up (*inf*). OPPOSITE: disfigure.

beauty *noun* **1** (*the woman's beauty*) attractiveness, fairness, loveliness, prettiness, comeliness, elegance, grace, glamour, charm, pulchritude. OPPOSITE: ugliness. **2** (*she's a real beauty*) belle, Venus, goddess, charmer, picture, good-looker (*inf*), stunner (*inf*), knockout (*inf*), peach (*inf*), smasher (*inf*), corker (*inf*). **3** (*the beauty of the plan*) advantage, benefit, attraction, boon, asset, blessing. OPPOSITE: disadvantage.

beaver *verb* **beaver away** work hard, persist, persevere, slog (*inf*), plug away (*inf*), graft (*inf*).

becalmed *adj* motionless, still, unmoving, immobile, immovable, stuck, stranded, marooned.

because *conj* as, since, for, seeing that.
 because of owing to, on account of, thanks to, by reason of, by virtue of, as a result of.

beckon *verb* **1** (*beckon to the child*) summon, invite, bid, signal, call, wave, gesture, gesticulate, nod. **2** (*the mountains beckoned him*) attract, call, draw, pull, entice, lure, allure, coax, persuade, tempt.

becloud *verb* dim, bedim, darken, obscure, befog, cloud, veil, confuse, obfuscate. OPPOSITE: illuminate.

become *verb* **1** (*the sky became cloudy*) grow, turn, get, develop into, change into, evolve into, pass into, transform into, come to be. **2** (*the dress becomes her*) suit, grace, enhance, embellish, flatter, ornament, look good on, set off, befit.
 become of happen to, befall.

becoming *adj* **1** (*a becoming dress*) attractive, comely, pretty, pleasing, flattering, lovely, elegant, stylish, tasteful. **2** (*behaviour that is not becoming*) suitable, appropriate, fitting, apt, decent, right, worthy, decorous, seemly, in keeping. OPPOSITE: unbecoming.

bed *noun* **1** (*sleep in a bed*) bunk, couch, divan, berth, cot, cradle, hammock, kip (*inf*), sack (*inf*), hay (*inf*). **2** (*the sea bed*) bottom, base, floor, foundation, layer, stratum, substratum, seam. **3** (*a bed of flowers*) area, plot, patch, border, row, strip.
 ➤ *verb* embed, establish, fix, set, base.
 bed down go to bed, settle down, sleep, turn in (*inf*), hit the hay (*inf*), hit the sack (*inf*), kip down (*inf*).
 go to bed with sleep with, have sex with, seduce, spend the night with, make love to, have sexual intercourse with, be intimate with, make out with (*inf*), have it off with (*sl*), hump (*sl*), screw (*sl*), shag (*sl*), fuck (*sl*), bed (*sl*), lay (*sl*), bang (*sl*).

bedaub *verb* daub, smear, plaster, besmear, bespatter, splash, stain, smirch, deface, mar.

bedclothes *pl noun* sheets, covers, linen, bed linen, pillowcases, blankets, bedding, duvets, quilts, eiderdowns.

bedding *noun* **1** (*air the bedding*) bedclothes, covers, sheets, linen, bed linen, blankets, duvets, quilts, eiderdowns. **2** (*bedding for animals*) litter, straw, hay.

bedeck *verb* decorate, array, adorn, deck, festoon, ornament, embellish, garnish. OPPOSITE: strip.

bedevil *verb* afflict, beset, distress, harass, torment, pester, plague, annoy, irritate, irk, vex, confuse, muddle, confound.

bedew *verb* moisten, dampen, sprinkle, spray, wet.

bedim *verb* dim, darken, cloud, becloud, shadow, obscure, befog. OPPOSITE: illuminate.

bedlam *noun* uproar, pandemonium, hubbub, furore, clamour, chaos, confusion, disorder, tumult, turmoil, commotion. OPPOSITE: quiet.

bedraggled *adj* untidy, unkempt, dishevelled, dirty, muddy, stained, soiled, grimy, wet, soaking, soaked, sodden, drenched, dripping. OPPOSITE: neat.

bedridden *adj* incapacitated, confined, housebound, flat on one's back (*inf*), laid up (*inf*).

bedrock *noun* **1** (*the bedrock of the earth*) rock bed, foundation, substratum. **2** (*the bedrock of his beliefs*) foundation, basis, core, fundamentals, basics, essentials, nitty-gritty (*inf*).

beef *noun* **1** (*put all his beef into the job*) flesh, brawn, bulk, strength, muscle, physique, power, effort. **2** (*what's the beef now?*) complaint, grumble, criticism, grievance, moan, gripe, grouse, nit-picking (*inf*).
 ➤ *verb* complain, grumble, criticize, moan, object, gripe, grouse.
 beef up strengthen, consolidate, develop, reinforce, toughen, substantiate.

beefy *adj* brawny, muscular, strong, big, hefty, stocky, bulky, burly, fat, fleshy, heavy, stocky, corpulent. OPPOSITE: slight.

beetling *adj* overhanging, jutting, projecting, protruding, sticking out, prominent.

befall *verb* **1** (*see that no evil befalls him*) happen to, overtake, betide. **2** (*before great things befall*) happen, occur, take place, supervene, chance, transpire, ensue.

befitting *adj* suitable, appropriate, fitting, fit, apt, right, proper, seemly, becoming. OPPOSITE: unsuitable.

befog *verb* obscure, confuse, muddle, perplex, obfuscate, blur. OPPOSITE: clarify.

befool *verb* fool, dupe, trick, hoodwink, deceive, cheat, beguile, bamboozle, mislead, delude.

before *prep* **1** (*before lunch*) prior to, earlier than, previous to, sooner than. OPPOSITE: after. **2** (*stand before the throne*) in front of, in advance of. OPPOSITE: behind. **3** (*perform before the monarch*) in the presence of, in front of, in the sight of. **4** (*put family before work*) in preference to, sooner than, rather than.
 ➤ *adv* **1** (*not met before*) earlier, previously, formerly, already, beforehand, sooner. OPPOSITE: afterwards. **2** (*walk before*) ahead, in advance. OPPOSITE: behind.

beforehand *adv* before, in advance, previously, earlier, already, sooner.

befriend *verb* make friends with, assist, help, aid, defend, protect, look after, take care of, keep an eye on, stand by, support, encourage, patronize, favour, advocate. OPPOSITE: oppose.

befuddle *verb* **1** (*befuddled by modern life*) confuse, muddle, perplex, bewilder, daze, stun, stupefy, numb. **2** (*befuddled by drink*) intoxicate, inebriate, daze, stupefy.

beg *verb* **1** (*begged to come with us*) ask, request, entreat, beseech, pray, desire, plead, supplicate, implore, crave, solicit, petition. **2** (*beg for money*) cadge, scrounge (*inf*), sponge off (*inf*), solicit alms, seek charity, mooch (*inf*).

beget *verb* **1** (*beget children*) father, sire, breed, generate, procreate. **2** (*unemployment begets crime*) engender, create, produce, cause, effect, result in, give rise to.

beggar *noun* **1** (*beggars asking for money*) pauper, down-and-out, mendicant, tramp, vagrant, cadger, scrounger (*inf*), bum (*inf*), sponger (*inf*), moocher (*inf*), parasite. **2** (*he's a lazy beggar!*) fellow, chap, person, bloke (*inf*), guy (*inf*).
 ➤ *verb* **1** (*return home beggared*) impoverish, ruin, bankrupt, pauperize. OPPOSITE: assist. **2** (*beggar description*) surpass, exceed, challenge, defy.

beggarly *adj* impoverished, poor, indigent, needy, wretched, destitute, miserable, pitiful, contemptible, abject, paltry, inadequate, scant, petty, slight, meagre, mean, shabby, vile.

beggary *noun* poverty, impoverishment, ruin, bankruptcy, insolvency, penury, destitution, wretchedness, pitifulness, pauperism, indigence, mendicancy.

begin *verb* **1** (*begin work*) start, commence, originate, inaugurate, institute, initiate, embark on, set about, set in motion, kick off (*inf*), fire away (*inf*), get cracking (*inf*), get moving (*inf*), set the ball rolling (*inf*), take the plunge (*inf*). OPPOSITE: end. **2** (*since records began*) start, commence, arise, happen, crop up, appear, emerge, come into being, come into existence.

beginner *noun* novice, learner, tyro, neophyte, recruit, initiate, pupil, apprentice, trainee, student, amateur, fledgling, tenderfoot, fresher, greenhorn (*inf*), rookie (*inf*). OPPOSITE: expert.

beginning *noun* **1** (*the beginning of his career*) start, starting point, commencement, opening, outset, dawn, birth, origin, source, creation, onset, inception, initiation, inauguration, the word go (*inf*), kickoff (*inf*), day one (*inf*), square one (*inf*). OPPOSITE: end. **2** (*had its beginnings in the 3rd century*) origin, source, birth, creation, starting point, spring, root, roots, seed, seeds, genesis. **3** (*the beginning of a book*) start, opening, chapter one, first chapter, part one, first part, preface, foreword, introduction.

begrime *verb* soil, dirty, foul, sully, defile, tarnish, besmirch, blacken, bedaub, smear, spatter. OPPOSITE: cleanse.

begrudge *verb* envy, grudge, resent, be jealous of.

beguile *verb* **1** (*beguiled by her good looks*) delude, deceive, cheat, trick, hoodwink, mislead, dupe, fool. **2** (*beguiled by the exotic atmosphere*) charm, delight, enchant, amuse, entertain, divert, cheer, attract, please, solace. **3** (*beguile the time*) pass, spend, while away, absorb, occupy.

beguiling *adj* deceptive, misleading, seductive, bewitching, charming, attractive, delightful.

behalf *noun* interest, benefit, advantage, good, part, side, sake.
on behalf of for, acting for, representing, on account of, in support of, in the interests of, for the benefit of, for the good of, for the sake of, to the advantage of, to the profit of.

behave *verb* **1** (*behave well*) act, perform, conduct oneself, acquit oneself, comport oneself, deport oneself. **2** (*the children behaved themselves*) be good, be well-behaved, act politely, show one's manners, mind one's manners, mind one's p's and q's (*inf*), toe the line, not put a foot wrong (*inf*), keep one's nose clean (*inf*). OPPOSITE: misbehave. **3** (*atoms behave like this*) act, function, operate, perform, react, work.

behaviour *noun* **1** (*the children's behaviour*) conduct, bearing, deportment, comportment, demeanour, manners, actions, habits, ways. **2** (*the behaviour of the virus*) operation, functioning, action, reaction, response.

behead *verb* decapitate, guillotine, execute, decollate.

behest *noun* injunction, command, order, decree, edict, ruling, direction, directive, injunction, instruction, mandate, precept, demand, bidding, request, wish.

behind *prep* **1** (*behind the door*) at the back of, at the rear of, on the further side of, on the other side of. **2** (*ran behind us*) after, following, at the back of, in the wake of, close upon. **3** (*behind schedule*) later than, after, slower than. **4** (*the reason behind the change of plan*) explaining, accounting for, responsible for, giving rise to, at the back of, at the bottom of. **5** (*we're behind your proposals*) supporting, backing, for, endorsing, on the side of. OPPOSITE: against.
➤ *adv* **1** (*running behind*) in the rear, following, after, afterwards, at the back, next. OPPOSITE: ahead. **2** (*be behind with payment*) behindhand, late, slow, behind schedule, in arrears, overdue, in debt.

behindhand *adv* late, slow, behind, behind schedule, overdue, in arrears, in debt.

behold *verb* see, look at, observe, eye, contemplate, view, regard, survey, scan, gaze at, stare at, watch, witness, discern, mark, perceive. OPPOSITE: miss.
➤ *interj* look, see, mark, watch, observe.

beholden *adj* obliged, indebted, bound, obligated, under obligation, thankful, grateful. OPPOSITE: ungrateful.

behove *verb* befit, become, be fitting, be proper, be seemly, be decorous, be necessary, be incumbent upon.

beige *adj* buff, fawn, sandy, sand, neutral, ecru, biscuit, coffee, oatmeal, mushroom.

being *noun* **1** (*the science of being*) existence, actuality, reality, living, life, animation, presence. OPPOSITE: nonexistence. **2** (*to the core of her being*) essence, substance, soul, spirit, nature. **3** (*a living being*) creature, animal, thing, individual, person, human, mortal, body.

belabour *verb* **1** (*belabour the obvious*) flog (*inf*), emphasize too much, discuss at length. **2** (*belabour the author*) attack, criticize, censure, berate, lay into. OPPOSITE: praise. **3** (*belaboured his back*) pummel, beat, strike, hit, thrash, batter, pound, whip.

belated *adj* late, overdue, behindhand, tardy, delayed, postponed. OPPOSITE: prompt.

belch *verb* **1** (*belch after eating food*) burp (*inf*), eruct, eructate, hiccup, break wind, bring up wind. **2** (*smoke belching from the chimney*) emit, discharge, eject, spew, gush, give out, give off, issue, vent, vomit, disgorge, expel.

beleaguer *verb* **1** (*beleaguer a city*) besiege, lay siege to, surround, encompass, encircle, hem in, blockade, beset, assail. OPPOSITE: relieve. **2** (*beleaguer parents*) harass, badger, plague, pester, bother, annoy, vex.

belie *verb* **1** (*the evidence belies his testimony*) disprove, contradict, deny, give the lie to, negate, gainsay. OPPOSITE: confirm. **2** (*pleasantness belying his resentment*) misrepresent, falsify, disguise, distort, conceal, hide, gloss over.

belief *noun* **1** (*belief in his own ability*) faith, believing, conviction, confidence, assurance, trust, credence. OPPOSITE: disbelief. **2** (*it is my belief that racism is still widespread*) view, viewpoint, point of view, opinion, conviction, judgment, notion, theory, feeling, impression. **3** (*political belief*) creed, doctrine, dogma, teaching, principles, tenets, ideology, faith, religion.

believable *adj* credible, conceivable, imaginable, likely, possible, probable, plausible, within the realms of possibility, not beyond the realms of possibility.

believe *verb* **1** (*believe he's telling the truth*) be convinced, have faith, have confidence, trust, credit, accept, rely on, depend on, swallow (*inf*), fall for (*inf*) buy (*inf*). OPPOSITE: doubt. **2** (*I believe we've met before*) think, reckon, maintain, hold, opine, suppose, presume, conjecture, assume, imagine, gather, understand.

believe in 1 (*believe in God*) be sure of the existence of, be sure of the reality of, be convinced of. **2** (*believe in taxing the wealthy*) support, favour, approve of, set store by, set great store by, swear by, rate (*inf*).

believer *noun* convert, disciple, follower, adherent, supporter, upholder. OPPOSITE: sceptic.

belittle *verb* disparage, decry, deprecate, depreciate, underestimate, undervalue, underrate, deride, scorn, sneer at, detract, play down, diminish, make light of, minimize. OPPOSITE: extol.

bellicose *adj* aggressive, belligerent, pugnacious, warlike, militant, combative, contentious, quarrelsome. OPPOSITE: genial.

belligerent *adj* **1** (*a belligerent attitude*) aggressive, antagonistic, pugnacious, argumentative, quarrelsome. OPPOSITE: peaceful. **2** (*belligerent nations*) at war, warring, battling, warlike, martial, militant.

bellow *verb* roar, bawl, yell, cry, shout, blare, trumpet, howl, shriek, scream, screech. OPPOSITE: whisper.

belly *noun* abdomen, paunch, stomach, tummy (*inf*), corporation (*inf*), potbelly (*inf*), beer gut (*inf*), breadbasket (*inf*), gut.

belong *verb* **belong to 1** (*this book belongs to me*) be owned by, be the property of, be the possession of, be one's. **2** (*belong to a cycling club*) be a member of, be associated with, be affiliated to, be an adherent of. **3** (*belongs to the Victorian era*) relate to, go with, fit, be part of, be connected with.

belongings *pl noun* possessions, property, effects, personal effects, chattels, things (*inf*), stuff (*inf*), gear (*inf*), paraphernalia, accoutrements, appurtenances.

beloved *adj* dear, dearest, darling, favourite, pet, cherished, treasured, precious, loved, adored, idolized, worshipped. OPPOSITE: hated.
➤ *noun* sweetheart, dear, dearest, darling, favourite, precious, sweet, pet, fiancé, fiancée, boyfriend, girlfriend, inamorato, inamorata.

below *prep* **1** (*below the surface*) under, underneath, beneath, lower than. OPPOSITE: above. **2** (*below a certain level*) less than, lower than, inferior to, subordinate to. **3** (*thought that talking to ordinary people was below him*) unbefitting, unworthy of, unbecoming, degrading to.
➤ *adv* **1** (*to the valley below*) under, underneath, beneath, down, lower, lower down. OPPOSITE: above. **2** (*see page 100 below*) later, further on.

belt *noun* **1** (*a leather belt*) band, girdle, sash, cummerbund, waistband. baldric, cestus, cincture. **2** (*the commuter belt*) zone, region, area, district, tract. **3** (*a fan belt*) band, conveyor belt, fan belt. **4** (*gave him a belt over

the head*) blow, thump, punch, swipe, wallop (*inf*), whack (*inf*), bash (*inf*), clout (*inf*).
➤ *verb* **1** (*belted him round the ears*) hit, strike, thump, punch, swipe, pound, wallop (*inf*), whack (*inf*), bash (*inf*), clout (*inf*), biff (*inf*). **2** (*belt down the road*) dash, rush, hurry, tear, run, speed.

bemire *verb* soil, dirty, muddy, bedaub, begrime, spatter, smear, sully, defile. OPPOSITE: cleanse.

bemoan *verb* lament, mourn, grieve over, sorrow, weep over, bewail, deplore, regret, moan. OPPOSITE: rejoice.

bemuse *verb* bewilder, baffle, confuse, muddle, perplex, puzzle, daze, stupefy, stun, disconcert, discomfit, overwhelm, astonish, astound, amaze.

bench *noun* **1** (*sit on a bench*) form, pew, stall, seat, settle. **2** (*work at a bench*) workbench, worktable, trestle table, board, counter. **3** (*be questioned by the bench*) court, tribunal, judiciary, judicature, judge, magistrate.

benchmark *noun* criterion, standard, point of reference, model, pattern, norm, touchstone, guideline, yardstick.

bend *verb* **1** (*try to bend the iron bar*) curve, bow, crook, twist, contort, flex. OPPOSITE: straighten. **2** (*the road bends here*) curve, incline, deviate, diverge, veer, swerve, twist, turn. **3** (*she bent towards me*) stoop, crouch, squat, bow, incline, hunch, lean. **4** (*bent them to our will*) mould, influence, dispose, sway, subdue, overwhelm. **5** (*they bent to our will*) yield, submit, give way, bow, concede, agree.
➤ *noun* curve, bow, arc, angle, turn, twist, corner, swerve, divergence, deflection, deviation, zigzag, crook, hook.

beneath *prep* **1** (*beneath the surface*) below, under, underneath. OPPOSITE: above. **2** (*beneath a certain level*) lower than, inferior to, subordinate to, less than. **3** (*thought that talking to ordinary people was beneath him*) unworthy of, unbefitting, undignified for, degrading to.
➤ *adv* below, under, underneath, down, lower. OPPOSITE: above.

benediction *noun* blessing, grace, favour, consecration, prayer, invocation, thanksgiving. OPPOSITE: curse.

benefaction *noun* **1** (*generous in their benefactions*) donation, contribution, gift, present, bequest, legacy, endowment, grant, bounty, alms, boon. **2** (*no signs of his benefaction*) generosity, philanthropy, charity, beneficence, benevolence. OPPOSITE: avarice.

benefactor *noun* patron, sponsor, donor, backer, supporter, philanthropist, promoter, contributor, subsidizer, angel (*inf*), helper, friend, well-wisher.

benefice *noun* living, office, sinecure, stipend, emolument.

beneficence *noun* **1** (*signs of his beneficence*) generosity, liberality, bounty, charity, benevolence, kindness, unselfishness, altruism. OPPOSITE: avarice. **2** (*a generous beneficence*) gift, donation, benefaction, aid, relief.

beneficent *adj* generous, liberal, munificent, charitable, benevolent, benign, kind, helpful. OPPOSITE: hard.

beneficial *adj* helpful, useful, valuable, advantageous, profitable, favourable, good, wholesome, serviceable, propitious, accommodating, salutary, salubrious, healthy. OPPOSITE: unwholesome.

benefit *noun* **1** (*reap the benefits of modernization*) advantage, good, dividend, profit, gain, boon, blessing. OPPOSITE: disadvantage. **2** (*for her benefit*) good, sake, interest, use, service, help, aid, assistance, avail, welfare, well-being. OPPOSITE: detriment. **3** (*child benefit*) allowance, income, payment, credit, money.
 ≫ *verb* help, aid, assist, gain, avail, serve, profit, improve, promote, further, advance, advantage. OPPOSITE: damage.

benevolence *noun* kindness, generosity, goodness, kindheartedness, compassion, goodwill, humanity, humanitarianism, philanthropy, altruism, magnanimousness, charity, beneficence, liberality. OPPOSITE: malevolence.

benevolent *adj* **1** (*a benevolent uncle*) kind, kindly, benign, compassionate, humane, kindhearted, good, magnanimous, unselfish, charitable, philanthropic, altruistic, humanitarian, beneficent, bountiful, liberal. OPPOSITE: malevolent. **2** (*a benevolent institution*) non-profit-making, charitable, almsgiving, eleemosynary.

benighted *adj* unenlightened, uncivilized, uneducated, uncultured, illiterate, primitive, ignorant, backward. OPPOSITE: sophisticated.

benign *adj* **1** (*a benign attitude*) kind, kindly, benevolent, sympathetic, gentle, compassionate, genial, amiable, friendly, obliging, gracious. OPPOSITE: cold. **2** (*benign conditions*) favourable, encouraging, helpful, opportune, propitious, beneficial, advantageous, good, lucky. OPPOSITE: unfavourable. **3** (*a benign tumour*) treatable, curable, harmless. OPPOSITE: malignant.

bent *adj* **1** (*a bent wire*) crooked, twisted, curved, bowed, contorted. OPPOSITE: straight. **2** (*her bent figure*) arched, hunched, stooped. **3** (*a bent police officer*) corrupt, crooked, dishonest, fraudulent.
 ≫ *noun* inclination, tendency, disposition, leaning, aptitude, forte, flair, faculty, talent, gift, penchant, predilection, partiality, liking, fondness, predisposition.
bent on determined to, set on, resolved to, decided on, fixed on, inclined to, disposed to.

benumb *verb* deaden, numb, anaesthetize, blunt, stupefy, paralyse. OPPOSITE: stimulate.

bequeath *verb* **1** (*money bequeathed to his wife*) leave, will, bestow, endow, make over, grant, entrust, give. **2** (*bequeath a tradition to future generations*) pass on, pass down, hand on, hand down, transmit, impart.

bequest *noun* legacy, inheritance, endowment, bestowal, settlement, trust, gift.

berate *verb* reprove, reprimand, chide, scold, rebuke, upbraid, castigate, tell off (*inf*), dress down (*inf*), blast (*inf*), slate (*inf*), bawl out (*inf*), read the riot act to (*inf*), tear a strip off (*inf*), censure, vituperate, revile. OPPOSITE: commend.

bereave *verb* deprive, rob, dispossess, strip, divest, despoil. OPPOSITE: restore.

bereavement *noun* loss, deprivation, dispossession, distress, affliction, misfortune, tribulation. OPPOSITE: consolation.

bereft *adj* **bereft of** deprived of, cut off from, parted from, lacking, minus, devoid of, stripped of, destitute of.

berserk *adj* frenzied, insane, mad, enraged, violent, raging, rabid, wild, crazy, out of one's mind, off one's head (*inf*), maniacal, unrestrainable, uncontrollable. OPPOSITE: subdued.

berth *noun* **1** (*a berth on a ship*) bed, bunk, billet. **2** (*a berth in a harbour*) mooring, anchorage, harbour, dock, docking, quay, wharf. **3** (*got me a good berth*) post, position, appointment, situation, job, employment.
 ≫ *verb* dock, anchor, drop anchor, moor, land, tie up.

beseech *verb* implore, beg, entreat, pray, plead, call upon, appeal to, invoke, supplicate, petition, adjure, crave, solicit, ask.

beset *verb* beleaguer, surround, encircle, besiege, encompass, assail, attack, harass, trouble, bother, torment, pester, badger, plague, perplex. OPPOSITE: relieve.

besetting *adj* habitual, persistent, compulsive, constant inveterate, harassing, troublesome.

beside *prep* **1** (*sat beside me*) next to, alongside, adjacent to, near, close to, cheek by jowl with. **2** (*this year's income looks bad beside last year's*) compared with, next to, in contrast with.
beside oneself frenzied, frantic, distraught, mad, crazed, insane, unbalanced, deranged, demented, hysterical, unhinged.
beside the point irrelevant, immaterial, unrelated, inapplicable.

besides *prep* apart from, other than, except, excepting, excluding, in addition to, over and above.
 ≫ *adv* moreover, further, furthermore, in addition, additionally, as well, too, also, what's more.

besiege *verb* **1** (*besiege a city*) surround, encompass, hem in, blockade, lay siege to. **2** (*besieged by reporters*) surround, enclose, beleaguer, beset, harass, importune, plague, hound.

besmear *verb* besmirch, smear, daub, bedaub, soil, dirty, spatter, begrime, defile, sully, stain, tarnish.

besmirch *verb* sully, defame, stain, damage, taint, tarnish, slander.

besotted *adj* **1** (*besotted with her*) infatuated, doting, smitten, obsessed. **2** (*besotted with drink*) intoxicated, befuddled, stupefied, foolish, confused, muddled, blotto (*inf*), smashed (*inf*), sozzled (*inf*), plastered (*inf*), pissed (*sl*).

bespatter *verb* splash, spatter, daub, bedaub, splatter, soil, dirty, muddy, begrime, besmear, besmirch, defile, sully.

bespeak *verb* **1** (*his tone bespeaks profound thoughts*) denote, signify, indicate, betoken, suggest, imply, reveal, show, demonstrate, exhibit, display. **2** (*bespeak goods*) order, engage, solicit, request, ask for.

besprinkle *verb* sprinkle, scatter, strew, dust, dredge, bedew, moisten, spray, spatter.

best *adj* finest, outstanding, excellent, foremost, chief, top, first-rate, first-class, highest, supreme, leading, unsurpassed, perfect, superlative, second to none (*inf*), ace (*inf*), number one (*inf*), tops (*inf*), the tops (*inf*). OPPOSITE: worst.
 ≫ *adv* **1** (*it works best this way*) excellently, perfectly,

superlatively, supremely, unsurpassedly, outstandingly. **2** (*you know her best*) greatly, extremely, to the greatest extent, to the greatest degree.
➤ *noun* **1** (*pupils who are the best in their class*) choice, pick, flower, élite, cream, prime. **2** (*did their best*) hardest, utmost, damnedest (*inf*). **3** (*not at his best in the mornings*) peak, prime, height, top form. **4** (*that's the best of living in the country*) advantage, asset, benefit, blessing, boon.
➤ *verb* defeat, beat, conquer, thrash, trounce, overwhelm, overcome, overpower, lick (*inf*), slaughter (*inf*), hammer (*inf*).

bestial *adj* brutish, beastly, brutal, savage, wild, barbaric, inhuman, depraved, degraded, degenerate, carnal, sensual, vile, sordid, low.

bestir *verb* stir, rouse, awaken, animate, get going (*inf*), activate, stimulate, exert, bustle, hasten, hurry. OPPOSITE: restrain.

bestow *verb* confer, give, grant, accord, present, hand over, distribute, award, impart, entrust, bequeath, endow. OPPOSITE: withhold.

bestrew *verb* strew, scatter, sprinkle, spread, sow, disseminate, broadcast. OPPOSITE: gather.

bestride *verb* straddle, bridge, span, extend across, cross, step over, dominate, tower over.

bet *verb* **1** (*bet money on a horse*) wager, stake, put money on, pledge, gamble, risk, speculate, venture, hazard. **2** (*I bet they'll be late*) be sure, be certain, be convinced, expect, predict.
➤ *noun* **1** (*place a bet*) wager, gamble, ante, stake, pledge, flutter (*inf*), speculation, venture, lottery, sweepstake. **2** (*my bet is that it will rain*) opinion, belief, expectation, prediction, feeling, view, point of view, viewpoint. **3** (*your best bet*) choice, option, alternative, course of action.

bête noire *noun* bane, bugbear, anathema, aversion, pet aversion, pet hate.

betide *verb* befall, chance, happen, occur, crop up, supervene, come to pass, ensue, transpire.

betoken *verb* denote, indicate, signify, represent, show, manifest, betray, proclaim, declare, bespeak, presage, augur, portend, bode. OPPOSITE: hide.

betray *verb* **1** (*betray a friend*) inform on, double-cross, break faith with, be disloyal, be treacherous, shop (*inf*), rat on (*inf*), squeal on (*inf*), blow the whistle on (*inf*), sell out (*inf*), sell down the river (*inf*), stab in the back (*inf*). **2** (*betrayed his nervousness*) disclose, reveal, divulge, expose, tell, blab, blurt out, give away, lay bare, let slip, show, exhibit, manifest, display. OPPOSITE: conceal. **3** (*betrayed him into doing wrong*) deceive, conceive, mislead, delude, beguile, ensnare, trap, lure, seduce, lead astray, corrupt, undo. **4** (*betrayed his wife and family*) abandon, desert, walk out on, forsake, jilt.

betrayal *noun* **1** (*betrayal of his country*) disloyalty, treachery, double-crossing, breaking faith, perfidy. **2** (*betrayal of a secret*) revelation, disclosure, divulgence, giving away, blabbing, blurting out.

betroth *verb* engage, affiance, pledge, promise, contract, covenant, espouse, plight.

betrothal *noun* engagement, marriage contract, plighting, troth, promise, pledge, vow, vows, espousal.

better *adj* **1** (*produce better work*) superior, finer, surpassing, greater, higher, preferable, more desirable. OPPOSITE: worse. **2** (*feel better*) improving, recovering, progressing, on the mend (*inf*), fitter, well, healthier, healthy, recovered, cured. OPPOSITE: ill.
➤ *verb* **1** (*bettered his situation*) improve, ameliorate, advance, raise, promote, further, amend, correct, rectify, relieve, enhance, reform. OPPOSITE: worsen. **2** (*better the previous record*) surpass, exceed, excel, outdo, outstrip, beat, improve on.

betterment *noun* improvement, amelioration, enhancement, reform, edification. OPPOSITE: deterioration.

between *prep* **1** (*sitting between them*) mid, amidst, in the middle of, in the midst of, betwixt, among. **2** (*a new railway between the north and the south*) connecting, joining, linking, uniting.

bevel *noun* angle, cant, chamfer, oblique, slant, tilt, slope, incline.

beverage *noun* drink, liquid, refreshment, potable, potation, libation, draught, bevvy.

bevy *noun* flock, swarm, flight, pack, troop, group, assembly, gathering, company, throng, bunch, collection, band, troupe, party.

bewail *verb* lament, mourn, bemoan, grieve for, grieve over, cry for, weep over, deplore, regret, sorrow over, wail, moan. OPPOSITE: rejoice.

beware *verb* take care, watch out, look out, be careful, mind, be wary, be cautious, watch out for, be on the look out for, take heed, avoid, steer clear of, guard against, be on one's guard.

bewilder *verb* confuse, puzzle, perplex, confound, muddle, distract, bemuse, baffle, nonplus, mystify, daze, stupefy, faze (*inf*), stump (*inf*), bamboozle (*inf*). OPPOSITE: enlighten.

bewildered *adj* confused, puzzled, perplexed, baffled, muddled, nonplussed, speechless, fazed (*inf*), bamboozled (*inf*), all at sea (*inf*).

bewilderment *noun* confusion, perplexity, puzzle, muddle, bafflement, mystification, stupefaction. OPPOSITE: enlightenment.

bewitch *verb* enchant, spellbind, fascinate, captivate, entrance, mesmerize, hypnotize, transfix, charm, beguile, allure, enrapture, transport. OPPOSITE: repel.

bewitched *adj* spellbound, fascinated, charmed, beguiled, captivated, entranced, mesmerized, hypnotized.

beyond *prep* **1** (*beyond the river*) further than, farther than, on the far side of, past, above, over, apart from. **2** (*beyond the age of 12*) over, above, greater than, past, later than. **3** (*beyond my understanding*) out of reach of, beyond the range of, more than, over and above, surpassing.
➤ *adv* farther, further, farther on, further on, afar, yonder.

bias *noun* **1** (*a bias against homosexuals*) tendency, inclination, proclivity, predisposition, bent, propensity, leaning, predilection, partiality, prejudice, bigotry, intolerance, narrow-mindedness, favouritism, one-sidedness. OPPOSITE: impartiality. **2** (*a cut on the bias*) diagonal, oblique, slant, angle, cross.

≫ *verb* influence, predispose, incline, sway, distort, weight, twist, prejudice.

biased *adj* prejudiced, partial, influenced, bigoted, intolerant, one-sided, narrow-minded.

Bible *noun* **1** (*study the Holy Bible*) Scriptures, Scripture, Holy Bible, Holy Writ, the Good Book, Old Testament, New Testament, Apocrypha, deuterocanonical books, writings, law, Pentateuch, prophets, Gospels, letters, epistles. **2** (*the angler's bible*) handbook, authority, manual, directory, companion, textbook, guide, guidebook.

bibliography *noun* catalogue, book list, record.

bibulous *adj* alcoholic, boozy (*inf*), intemperate. OPPOSITE: teetotal.

bicker *verb* quarrel, squabble, wrangle, row, fight, spar, argue, dispute, disagree, fall out, have a row, scrap (*inf*). OPPOSITE: agree.

bicycle *noun* cycle, bike, two-wheeler, mountain bike, racer, tandem, unicycle, tricycle, push-bike (*inf*).

bid *verb* **1** (*bid £800 for the chair*) offer, tender, put forward, advance, proffer, propose, submit. **2** (*she bade us enter*) command, order, demand, require, direct, instruct, summon, enjoin, invite, request, ask. OPPOSITE: forbid. **3** (*bid us goodnight*) say, wish, tell, call, greet.

≫ *noun* **1** (*accept the highest bid*) offer, tender, proposal, submission, proposition, price, amount, sum. **2** (*a bid for power*) attempt, try, endeavour.

biddable *adj* willing, amenable, obedient, cooperative, persuadable, pliant, teachable, tractable.

bidding *noun* **1** (*bidding at the auction*) offers, tenders, submissions, proposals, prices, tendering, auction. **2** (*acted on her bidding*) order, command, behest, injunction, instruction, summons, invitation, request.

big *adj* **1** (*a big house*) large, great, huge, massive, enormous, immense, colossal, gigantic, vast, spacious, extensive, substantial, voluminous, sizeable, mammoth. OPPOSITE: small. **2** (*a big man*) large, tall, burly, hulking, bulky, brawny, solid, heavy, well-built, stout, obese, fat, gross. OPPOSITE: little. **3** (*your big sister*) older, elder, grown-up, adult. OPPOSITE: younger. **4** (*a big commitment*) important, significant, momentous, serious, major, weighty. OPPOSITE: minor. **5** (*she's big in the City*) important, significant, prominent, influential, powerful, eminent, notable, famous, well-known, principal, main. OPPOSITE: insignificant. **6** (*that's big of you*) generous, kind, kindhearted, kindly, magnanimous, unselfish, altruistic, gracious, benevolent. OPPOSITE: mean. **7** (*big talk*) arrogant, boastful, pompous, proud, haughty, conceited, inflated, pretentious. OPPOSITE: humble.

bigot *noun* fanatic, zealot, dogmatist, sectarian, racialist, sexist, jingoist, chauvinist.

bigoted *adj* intolerant, narrow-minded, illiberal, one-sided, dogmatic, opinionated, obstinate, prejudiced, biased, racist, sexist, chauvinist. OPPOSITE: tolerant.

bigotry *noun* prejudice, one-sidedness, bias, partiality, discrimination, narrow-mindedness, intolerance,

dogmatism, obstinacy, racism, sexism, chauvinism. OPPOSITE: tolerance.

bigwig *noun* VIP, notable, celebrity, dignitary, heavyweight (*inf*), nob (*inf*), big gun (*inf*), big noise (*inf*), big shot (*inf*), big cheese (*inf*), panjandrum.

bile *noun* anger, spleen, ill humour, irritability, irascibility, peevishness, rancour, bitterness, resentment, indignation.

bilge *noun* nonsense, rubbish, gibberish, bunkum, drivel, twaddle, piffle (*inf*), rot (*inf*), poppycock (*inf*), claptrap (*inf*).

bilious *adj* **1** (*feel bilious*) queasy, sick, nauseated, liverish. **2** (*a bilious attack on the media*) bad-tempered, ill-tempered, crotchety, irritable, peevish, cross, grumpy, ratty (*inf*), testy, touchy. OPPOSITE: affable. **3** (*bilious colours*) garish, nauseating, sickly, disgusting, unpleasant.

bilk *verb* **1** (*bilked their hopes*) thwart, balk, frustrate, foil. **2** (*bilk investors*) deceive, cheat, defraud, trick, bamboozle, elude, dodge, escape.

bill[1] *noun* **1** (*pay a bill*) account, statement, invoice, reckoning, tally, score, charge, fee. **2** (*post no bills*) poster, notice, placard, advertisement, bulletin, flier, announcement, handbill, handout, circular, leaflet, brochure, ad (*inf*). **3** (*top the bill*) list, listing, agenda, programme, playbill, card, schedule. **4** (*a parliamentary bill*) measure, proposal, proposed law, legislation, piece of legislation.

≫ *verb* **1** (*will bill you monthly*) charge, invoice, debit, send a statement, send an invoice. **2** (*be billed to play at the concert*) advertise, announce, post, give notice, present, arrange, describe.

bill[2] *noun* beak, nib, mandible.

billet *noun* **1** (*assign soldiers to billets*) quarters, accommodation, lodgings, rooms, barracks. **2** (*a well-paid billet*) job, position, post, office, appointment, situation.

≫ *verb* quarter, put up, house, accommodate, lodge, assign, station.

billow *verb* roll, surge, swell, heave, puff out, puff up, belly, balloon, ebb and flow.

≫ *noun* wave, breaker, roller, surge, swell, flood, deluge, rush, outpouring, tide.

billowy *adj* rolling, heaving, surging, swelling, tossing, rising, rippling, undulating, swirling. OPPOSITE: smooth.

bin *noun* receptacle, container, box, can, case, crate.

bind *verb* **1** (*bound his arms together*) tie, tie up, truss, secure, fasten, attach, strap, rope, tether, fetter, lace, lash, wrap, bandage, encircle, gird. OPPOSITE: loose. **2** (*bind around*) bandage, wrap, dress, cover. **3** (*communities bound by a common grief*) unite, join, pull together, cooperate, close ranks. OPPOSITE: divide. **4** (*bound to keep the law*) oblige, force, compel, impel, constrain, obligate, require, prescribe. **5** (*bound by regulations*) restrict, confine, restrain, hamper, inhibit, hinder, yoke, encumber. OPPOSITE: liberate. **6** (*bind the mixture*) stick, glue, paste, cement. OPPOSITE: separate. **7** (*bind a cloth with ribbon*) edge, hem, trim, border, finish.

≫ *noun* **1** (*commuting is a real bind*) nuisance, bore, drag (*inf*), irritation, inconvenience. **2** (*be in a bind*) predicament, quandary, dilemma, spot (*inf*), tight spot (*inf*), pickle (*inf*).

binding *adj* obligatory, compulsory, necessary, mandatory, imperative, irrevocable.
➤ *noun* cover, covering, fastening, band.

binge *noun* spree, orgy, bout, fling, jag (*inf*), bender (*inf*), blinder (*inf*).

biography *noun* life, history, life story, memoir, profile, account, bio (*inf*).

birth *noun* **1** (*the birth of a child*) childbirth, parturition, delivery, confinement, nativity. **2** (*the birth of a nation*) genesis, origin, beginning, beginnings, source, start, creation, emergence, appearance. OPPOSITE: death. **3** (*of noble birth*) ancestry, descent, extraction, line, lineage, derivation, house, family, blood, race, stock, strain, pedigree, parentage, background, breeding.

birthmark *noun* blemish, mole, patch, discoloration, naevus.

birthright *noun* prerogative, privilege, right, inheritance, due, legacy.

bisect *verb* halve, cut in two, divide, split, bifurcate, cleave, intersect, cross. OPPOSITE: unite.

bisexual *adj* androgynous, hermaphrodite, hermaphroditic, epicene, gynandrous, monoclinous, AC/DC (*inf*), bi (*inf*).

bishop *noun* prelate, patriarch, suffragan, overseer, elder.

bishopric *noun* diocese, see, episcopacy, episcopate.

bit[1] *noun* **1** (*bits of broken glass*) scrap, sliver, fragment, piece, morsel, crumb, particle, jot, iota, atom, mite, whit, tittle, speck, grain, drop, trace, hint. OPPOSITE: lot. **2** (*wait a bit*) moment, minute, little while, while, second, instant, flash, jiffy (*inf*), tick (*inf*), two shakes of a lamb's tail (*inf*).

bit[2] *noun* (*a horse's bit*) restraint, restrainer, bar, check, curb, snaffle.

bitch *noun* **1** (*that woman's a real bitch*) shrew, vixen, virago, cow (*sl*). **2** (*this job's a bitch*) difficulty, problem, dilemma, nuisance, bind (*inf*).
➤ *verb* complain, grumble, moan, gripe, grouse, beef (*inf*), whinge (*inf*).

bitchy *adj* mean, nasty, cruel, snide, malicious, vindictive, backbiting, catty.

bite *verb* **1** (*bite an apple*) chew, gnaw, champ, munch, crunch, eat, masticate, nibble. **2** (*bit the postman*) nip, snap, tear, rend, pierce, wound. **3** (*insects bite*) smart, sting, puncture, tingle. **4** (*acids biting into metal*) burn, corrode, eat into, dissolve. **5** (*bite into the snow*) grip, hold, grasp, clutch, clasp. **6** (*taxes beginning to bite*) have an effect, take effect, work, produce results, grip.
➤ *noun* **1** (*the dog gave him a bite*) nip, snap. **2** (*an insect bite*) sting, wound, puncture. **3** (*have a bite to eat*) morsel, mouthful, piece, taste, snack, refreshment. **4** (*cheese with a bite to it*) piquancy, sharpness, spiciness, pungency, kick (*inf*), punch (*inf*).

biting *adj* **1** (*a biting wind*) piercing, keen, nipping, sharp, stinging, piquant, pungent, penetrating, cold, freezing. OPPOSITE: mild. **2** (*biting criticism*) stinging, caustic, cutting, incisive, mordant, trenchant, sarcastic, withering, scathing. OPPOSITE: genial.

bitter *adj* **1** (*a bitter taste*) acrid, pungent, biting, harsh, sharp, sour, acid, tart, vinegary. OPPOSITE: sweet. **2** (*a bitter old man*) acrimonious, resentful, embittered, sour, rancorous, indignant, morose, hostile, sullen, crabbed, with a chip on one's shoulder (*inf*). **3** (*a bitter argument*) intense, severe, harsh, fierce, virulent, angry, cruel, acrimonious, vindictive, rancorous, malicious, spiteful, malevolent, venomous. **4** (*a bitter disappointment*) distressing, sore, sad, painful, grievous, poignant, tragic, harrowing, heartbreaking, heartrending. OPPOSITE: cheery. **5** (*a bitter wind*) intense, severe, harsh, fierce, virulent, piercing, sharp, penetrating, biting, stinging, cruel. OPPOSITE: mild.

bitterness *noun* **1** (*a taste of bitterness*) acridity, pungency, harshness, sharpness, sourness, tartness. OPPOSITE: sweetness. **2** (*feelings of bitterness*) acrimony, resentment, antagonism, spite, spitefulness, malice, rancour, spleen, pique, grudge, hostility, animosity, asperity. **3** (*the bitterness of the wind*) intensity, severity, harshness, fierceness, cruelty, virulence. OPPOSITE: mildness.

bizarre *adj* strange, odd, weird, extraordinary, grotesque, peculiar, unusual, curious, abnormal, unconventional, fantastic, outlandish, ridiculous, ludicrous, eccentric. OPPOSITE: normal.

blab *verb* divulge, reveal, let slip, blurt out, squeal (*inf*), tell, tattle, prate, prattle, gossip.

black *adj* **1** (*black hair*) dark, inky, sooty, swarthy, dusky, ebony, jet, pitchy, pitch-black, jet-black. OPPOSITE: white. **2** (*black skin*) dark, dark-skinned, Negro, Negroid, swarthy, coloured, melanistic. OPPOSITE: white. **3** (*black skies*) dark, moonless, starless, dingy, dusky, dim, unlit, unilluminated, overcast, gloomy, sombre, crepuscular, tenebrous, Cimmerian, stygian. OPPOSITE: light. **4** (*the future looks black*) dark, sombre, gloomy, dismal, distressing, depressing, mournful, forbidding, ominous, lugubrious, funereal. OPPOSITE: bright. **5** (*black hands*) dirty, filthy, soiled, stained, grubby, grimy, muddy, sooty. OPPOSITE: clean. **6** (*in a black mood*) angry, hostile, furious, belligerent, aggressive, menacing, threatening. OPPOSITE: cheerful. **7** (*black deeds*) bad, vile, evil, villainous, heinous, nefarious, wicked, sinful, foul, atrocious, horrible. OPPOSITE: good. **8** (*black comedy*) macabre, grim, sickening, sick, cynical.
➤ *verb* **1** (*black goods*) bar, ban, embargo, boycott, blacklist. **2** (*black someone's eye*) bruise, punch, hit, injure.

black out **1** (*black out after the accident*) faint, collapse, pass out, lose consciousness, flake out (*inf*) swoon. **2** (*black out all the lights*) cover, cover up, darken. **3** (*black out news*) suppress, censor, conceal, withhold, cover up.

in black and white **1** (*read the details in black and white*) in print, printed, written, written down, clearly stated. **2** (*a black and white opinion*) clear-cut, absolute, categorical, unambiguous, unequivocal, uncompromising.

in the black solvent, in credit, with one's head above water (*inf*).

blackball *verb* vote against, ban, bar, exclude, expel, throw out, shut out, blacklist, ostracize, snub, give the cold shoulder to (*inf*).

blacken *verb* **1** (*blacken a ceiling*) soil, begrime, dirty, darken, cloud, obscure. **2** (*blackened his reputation*) defame, slander, libel, sully, defile, vilify, malign, traduce, run down, drag through the mud, denigrate, calumniate, besmear, besmirch. OPPOSITE: vindicate.

blackguard *noun* scoundrel, rogue, rascal, villain, wretch, knave, bounder (*inf*), blighter (*inf*), rotter (*inf*), swine (*inf*), scumbag (*inf*). OPPOSITE: gentleman.

blacklist *verb* exclude, ban, bar, black, boycott, shut out, throw out, reject, repudiate, proscribe, ostracize, snub, give the cold shoulder to (*inf*), send to Coventry (*inf*). OPPOSITE: accept.

blackmail *noun* extortion, exaction, intimidation, hush money (*inf*), bribe, bribery, ransom, protection money (*inf*).
 ≫ *verb* extort, exact, bribe, milk, squeeze, wrest, bleed (*inf*), lean on (*inf*), coerce, compel, force.

blackout *noun* **1** (*suffer a blackout*) fainting, passing-out, loss of consciousness, coma, syncope, flaking-out (*inf*). **2** (*an electricity blackout*) power failure, power cut, electricity failure. **3** (*a news blackout*) embargo, suppression, censorship, withholding, cover-up.

blameable *adj* answerable, responsible, blameworthy, in the wrong, guilty, liable, culpable. OPPOSITE: blameless.

blame *verb* **1** (*blame them for the accident*) hold responsible, find guilty, censure, condemn, criticize, find fault with, disapprove, reproach, reprove, chide, rebuke. OPPOSITE: praise. **2** (*blame the crime on him*) accuse, charge, hold responsible, ascribe, pin on (*inf*), attribute. OPPOSITE: vindicate.
 ≫ *noun* **1** (*accepted the blame for the explosion*) accusation, charge, incrimination, responsibility, culpability, fault, guilt, accountability, rap (*inf*). OPPOSITE: vindication. **2** (*I always get the blame*) censure, condemnation, disapproval, criticism, reproach, reproof. OPPOSITE: approval.

blameless *adj* innocent, guiltless, in the clear, above suspicion, unimpeachable, above reproach, irreproachable, unsullied, unblemished, spotless, immaculate, inculpable, perfect, faultless, virtuous. OPPOSITE: blameworthy.

blameworthy *adj* to blame, at fault, guilty, responsible, culpable, reprehensible, inexcusable, indefensible, discreditable, shameful, blameable. OPPOSITE: blameless.

blanch *verb* **1** (*his face blanched*) whiten, wash out, bleach, fade, pale, blench. OPPOSITE: colour. **2** (*blanched the vegetables*) scald, boil.

bland *adj* **1** (*bland food*) tasteless, insipid, flavourless, weak, mild. OPPOSITE: tasty. **2** (*a bland story*) dull, boring, uninteresting, insipid, nondescript, mediocre, weak, unexciting. OPPOSITE: stimulating. **3** (*a bland manner*) mild, gentle, soft, soothing, benign, suave, affable, amiable, agreeable. OPPOSITE: harsh.

blandishments *pl noun* flattery, compliments, cajolery, coaxing, wheedling, fawning, blarney, ingratiation, soft soap (*inf*), sweet talk (*inf*).

blank *adj* **1** (*a blank piece of paper*) empty, void, vacant, unfilled, bleak, plain, clear, white, unadorned, bare, unmarked, spotless. OPPOSITE: filled. **2** (*gave her a blank stare*) expressionless, deadpan, vacant, empty, vacuous,

poker-faced, impassive, uninterested, emotionless, indifferent, apathetic. OPPOSITE: alert. **3** (*a blank look*) confused, confounded, at a loss, perplexed, dazed, disconcerted, dumbfounded, uncomprehending, nonplussed, floored (*inf*). **4** (*a blank refusal*) outright, absolute, utter, complete, unqualified, unmitigated. OPPOSITE: partial.
 ≫ *noun* void, emptiness, vacuum, space, empty space, vacancy, nothingness, gap, vacuity.

blanket *noun* **1** (*a blanket on a bed*) cover, covering, coverlet, bedding, bedcover, bedspread, afghan, shawl, rug, throw. **2** (*a blanket of mist*) cover, carpet, cloak, mantle, sheet, wrapping, mass, envelope, coating, layer, film.
 ≫ *verb* cover, overlay, envelop, coat, cloak, carpet, cloud, shroud, veil, mask, conceal. OPPOSITE: uncover.
 ≫ *adj* all-inclusive, inclusive, all-embracing, comprehensive, general, wide-ranging, sweeping, across-the-board.

blare *verb* proclaim, broadcast, trumpet, blast, roar, boom, bellow, resound, peel, ring, clang, clamour, sound, blow, toot.

blarney *noun* flattery, blandishments, compliments, cajolery, coaxing, soft soap (*inf*), sweet talk (*inf*), fawning, adulation. OPPOSITE: bluntness.

blasé *adj* apathetic, indifferent, offhand, nonchalant, uncaring, emotionless, phlegmatic, unmoved, satiated, surfeited, cloyed, jaded, hardened, bored, weary. OPPOSITE: excited.

blaspheme *verb* swear, curse, execrate, damn, cuss (*inf*), revile, abuse, profane, desecrate. OPPOSITE: worship.

blasphemous *adj* impious, profane, sacrilegious, irreligious, irreverent, godless, ungodly. OPPOSITE: reverent.

blasphemy *noun* impiety, profanity, swearing, cursing, oaths, execration, sacrilege, irreligiousness, ungodliness, irreverence. OPPOSITE: reverence.

blast *noun* **1** (*be killed in the blast*) explosion, discharge, burst, eruption, boom, bang. **2** (*a blast of cold air*) gust, squall, draught, rush, flurry, gale, storm. **3** (*a blast on a whistle*) blare, thunder, boom, roar, honk, toot, bellow, trumpeting, peal, clamour, clang. **4** (*the blast of an epidemic*) blight, pestilence, infestation, affliction.
 ≫ *verb* **1** (*blasted a hole in the wall*) explode, blow up, burst, shatter, demolish, destroy, annihilate, ruin. **2** (*the music blasted out*) blare, blare out, roar, boom, boom out, blow, thunder, bellow, trumpet. **3** (*minister blasts new report*) criticize, denounce, attack, reprimand, rebuke, upbraid, castigate, tell off. **4** (*frost blasted the flowers*) blight, wither, shrivel, kill.

blast off lift, lift off, take off, launch, be launched.

blatant *adj* **1** (*blatant discrimination*) conspicuous, obvious, glaring, flagrant, brazen, bald, naked, shameless, overt, unmitigated, sheer, outright. OPPOSITE: concealed. **2** (*blatant protesters*) clamorous, noisy, obstreperous, vociferous, loud, deafening. OPPOSITE: quiet.

blaze *verb* **1** (*a fire blazing*) flame, burn, flare up, burst into flames. **2** (*blazing with lights*) shine, glitter, glow, glimmer, gleam, beam, flash, flare, glare. **3** (*blazing with *anger*) flare up, explode, erupt, burst, rage, fume, boil, seethe, see red (*inf*).

➤ *noun* **1** (*destroyed in the blaze*) flame, fire, inferno, conflagration, holocaust. **2** (*a blaze of flowers*) glow, glimmer, flash, flare, glare, light, beam, glitter, radiance, brilliance. **3** (*a blaze of anger*) outburst, burst, outbreak, explosion, eruption, storm, blast, torrent, flare-up.

blazon *verb* proclaim, make known, broadcast, advertise, publish, publicize, blaze, herald, trumpet. OPPOSITE: suppress.

bleach *verb* blanch, whiten, fade, lighten, pale, wash out, decolorize, etiolate. OPPOSITE: darken.

bleak *adj* **1** (*a bleak landscape*) bare, exposed, open, unsheltered, barren, desolate, windswept, cold, raw, chilly. OPPOSITE: sheltered. **2** (*bleak news*) gloomy, dismal, dreary, cheerless, depressing, miserable, sombre, hopeless, discouraging, disheartening. OPPOSITE: cheerful.

bleary *adj* blurred, hazy, cloudy, dim, indistinct, unclear, watery, rheumy.

bleed *verb* **1** (*his head was bleeding*) lose blood, shed blood, haemorrhage, exude, ooze, trickle, flow, spurt, run, seep, weep, gush. **2** (*bleed a patient*) draw blood from, let blood from, drain, exhaust, suck dry, phlebotomize. **3** (*bleed money*) extort, extract, milk, fleece, squeeze.

blemish *noun* **1** (*a blemish on her skin*) spot, mark, speck, stain, scratch, blotch, discoloration, birthmark, naevus. **2** (*a blemish in his character*) defect, fault, imperfection, taint, stain.

➤ *verb* tarnish, taint, blot, sully, spoil, mar, flaw, impair, deface, disfigure, mark, spot, stain.

blench *verb* shrink, recoil, flinch, wince, tremble, shy, shudder, quail, cower, hesitate, falter, shirk, avoid, evade, shun. OPPOSITE: face.

blend *verb* **1** (*blend ingredients*) mix, mingle, intermingle, combine, amalgamate, fuse, coalesce, merge, unite, homogenize, admix, commix. OPPOSITE: separate. **2** (*styles blending with each other*) harmonize, go with, suit, fit, combine, come together, complement. OPPOSITE: clash.

➤ *noun* mixture, mix, combination, compound, fusion, alloy, amalgamation, union, unity, synthesis, admixture, composite.

bless *verb* **1** (*bless God*) praise, extol, glorify, exalt, laud, magnify, hallow. OPPOSITE: curse. **2** (*bless a married couple*) pray for, ask God's grace for, sanctify, consecrate, dedicate, anoint. **3** (*blessed with four children*) bestow, endow, grant, give, grace, favour.

blessed *adj* **1** (*a blessed sacrament*) sacred, holy, hallowed, divine, revered, consecrated, adored, glorified, beatified. **2** (*a blessed relief*) happy, cheerful, glad, blissful, joyful, joyous, contented. OPPOSITE: sad. **3** (*blessed with a good memory*) favoured, fortunate, lucky, endowed, graced.

blessing *noun* **1** (*the priest gave a blessing*) benediction, grace, thanksgiving, dedication, invocation, prayer, praise, honour, glory. OPPOSITE: curse. **2** (*gave the idea her blessing*) approval, backing, support, sanction, consent, assent, permission, favour, good wishes. **3** (*the blessings of prosperity*) boon, advantage, help, gift, benefit,

godsend, bounty, gain, profit, favour, good fortune. OPPOSITE: disadvantage.

blight *noun* **1** (*potato blight*) disease, infestation, pestilence, canker, fungus. **2** (*the blight of poverty*) scourge, plague, bane, misfortune, calamity, adversity, curse, woe, affliction.

➤ *verb* destroy, crush, ruin, wreck, dash, frustrate, disappoint, damage, spoil, mar, kill, blast, wither, shrivel.

blind *adj* **1** (*blind in one eye*) sightless, unseeing, unsighted, visually impaired, partially sighted, purblind, half blind, eyeless. OPPOSITE: seeing. **2** (*love is blind*) unreasoned, injudicious, unreasoning, unthinking, uncritical, rash, reckless, hasty, impetuous, careless, mindless. OPPOSITE: careful. **3** (*a blind alley*) closed, shut, blocked, impassable, without exit. OPPOSITE: open. **4** (*a blind entrance*) concealed, hidden, out of sight.

➤ *verb* **1** (*blinded in the explosion*) make blind, deprive of sight, render sightless, render unsighted. **2** (*blinded by the car's headlights*) dazzle, obscure one's vision, block one's vision, block one's line of vision. **3** (*blind with science*) confuse, bewilder, overwhelm, deceive, mislead, trick.

➤ *noun* **1** (*a roller blind*) shade, screen, curtain, shutter, cover. **2** (*a blind for selling drugs*) mask, cloak, camouflage, disguise, feint, facade, stratagem, ruse, cover-up.

blind to indifferent to, ignorant of, unaware of, unconscious of, uninformed about, unenlightened about, oblivious to, neglectful of, thoughtless of, inconsiderate to, heedless to, inattentive to. OPPOSITE: aware of.

blindly *adv* **1** (*blindly fumbled his way*) without sight, sightlessly, unseeingly. **2** (*don't just blindly follow your brother*) unthinkingly, uncritically, mindlessly, carelessly, undiscerningly, hastily, rashly, recklessly, heedlessly.

blink *verb* **1** (*eyes blinking*) wink, nictitate, flutter, bat, squint, peer. **2** (*lights blinking*) flicker, twinkle, glitter, glimmer, gleam, sparkle.

➤ *noun* **1** (*gave her a quick blink*) glance, glimpse, wink, flutter. **2** (*the blink of lights*) twinkle, gleam, flash, flicker, glimmer.

blink at ignore, disregard, overlook, turn a blind eye to, condone.

bliss *noun* blissfulness, ecstasy, happiness, joy, delight, pleasure, euphoria, rapture, elation, felicity, gladness, seventh heaven, paradise, utopia, Eden, Arcadia. OPPOSITE: misery.

blissful *adj* happy, joyful, ecstatic, euphoric, delightful, glad, elated. OPPOSITE: miserable.

blister *noun* pustule, vesicle, bleb, boil, carbuncle, pimple, blain, abscess, ulcer, cyst, wen, sore, bubble, swelling.

blistering *adj* **1** (*blistering heat*) extreme, intense, great, greatest, maximum. **2** (*a blistering attack*) critical, scathing, angry, fierce, harsh, savage, severe, searing, trenchant, mordant.

blithe *adj* **1** (*in a blithe mood*) merry, jolly, cheerful, carefree, joyful, happy, vivacious, lively, animated, buoyant, sprightly, jaunty. OPPOSITE: dejected. **2** (*with* *blithe indifference*) heedless, indifferent, casual, nonchalant, thoughtless.

blitz *noun* **1** (*bombed in the blitz*) attack, assault, strike, bombardment, onslaught, offensive, blitzkrieg. **2** (*have a blitz on the garden*) all-out effort, attack, exertion, set-to, campaign, attempt, endeavour.

blizzard *noun* snowstorm, squall, storm.

bloat *verb* swell, puff up, puff out, expand, inflate, balloon, distend, dilate, enlarge. OPPOSITE: shrink.

blob *noun* drop, globule, glob, pellet, pill, bead, ball, bubble, pearl, lump, mass, spot, dab, splash, daub, blotch.

bloc *noun* alliance, group, federation, coalition, union, group, syndicate, ring, axis.

block *noun* **1** (*a block of ice*) lump, mass, chunk, hunk, wedge, piece, cake, bar, brick. **2** (*a tower block*) building, complex, development, structure. **3** (*a block of shares*) set, group, cluster, batch, quantity. **4** (*a block in the pipe*) blockage, obstruction, hindrance, impediment, bottleneck, jam, stoppage, obstacle, barrier, blockade. OPPOSITE: passage.
➤ *verb* **1** (*block the road*) obstruct, blockade, check, stop, clog, plug. OPPOSITE: clear. **2** (*block progress*) obstruct, impede, hinder, thwart, deter, frustrate, check, stop, halt, bar.

blockade *noun* barrier, obstacle, impediment, restriction, closure, siege.
➤ *verb* block, obstruct, close, besiege.

blockage *noun* block, obstruction, hindrance, impediment, jam, stoppage, obstacle, barrier.

blockhead *noun* dunce, simpleton, dolt, idiot, fool, numskull, nitwit, noodle, dope, halfwit, ignoramus, dickhead (*inf*), jerk (*inf*), dork (*inf*), wally (*inf*), geek (*inf*).

bloke *noun* fellow, man, boy, male, chap (*inf*), guy (*inf*), bod (*inf*).

blond *adj* light, fair, flaxen, fair-haired.

blonde *adj* light, fair, flaxen, fair-haired. OPPOSITE: brunette.

blood *noun* **1** (*lose blood*) gore, lifeblood, life fluid, vital fluid, plasma. **2** (*of Danish blood*) ancestry, descent, family, extraction, lineage, line, pedigree, race, stock, kinship, kindred, relations, consanguinity. **3** (*bad blood between people*) feeling, temper, spirit, temperament, nature, disposition, humour.

bloodcurdling *adj* terrifying, horrifying, horrific, fearful, hair-raising, spine-chilling, chilling, appalling, frightening.

bloodless *adj* **1** (*bloodless hands*) pale, wan, colourless, pallid, pasty, chalky, sickly, anaemic, ashen. OPPOSITE: ruddy. **2** (*his bloodless form*) lifeless, listless, languid, sluggish, torpid, unfeeling, feeble, cold, indifferent. **3** (*a bloodless coup*) peaceful, nonviolent, unwarlike, strifefree. OPPOSITE: violent.

bloodshed *noun* killing, carnage, slaughter, butchery, bloodbath, murder, massacre.

bloodthirsty *adj* murderous, savage, ferocious, vicious, cruel, inhuman, sadistic, brutal, barbaric, barbarous, bloody, ruthless.

bloody *adj* **1** (*a bloody nose*) gory, sanguinary, bleeding, bloodstained. **2** (*bloody thoughts*) bloodthirsty, murderous, savage, ferocious, vicious, brutal, ruthless, cruel.

bloom *noun* **1** (*lovely red blooms*) blossom, flower, inflorescence, bud, efflorescence, flowering. **2** (*the bloom of youth*) freshness, beauty, radiance, flush, lustre, glow, sheen, blush, prime, perfection, heyday, health, vigour. OPPOSITE: decadence.
➤ *verb* **1** (*flowers blooming*) blossom, flower, bud, burgeon, blow, open, open out. OPPOSITE: wither. **2** (*bloomed since getting a new job*) flourish, prosper, succeed, progress, get on, thrive, grow, wax. OPPOSITE: fade.

blossom *noun* bloom, flower, flowers, bud, floret, efflorescence.
➤ *verb* **1** (*trees blossoming*) bloom, flower, burgeon, bud, blow. OPPOSITE: wither. **2** (*blossomed in a new school*) develop, mature, grow, bloom, thrive, flourish, prosper, succeed, progress, get on. OPPOSITE: decline.

blot *noun* **1** (*a blot of ink*) spot, stain, smudge, mark, dot, patch, speck, blotch, splodge. **2** (*a blot on his reputation*) blemish, taint, stain, flaw, blur, disgrace, fault, defect, imperfection.
➤ *verb* **1** (*blot up the ink*) absorb, dry, dry up, soak up. **2** (*paper blotted with ink*) spot, stain, spatter, blotch, splodge. **3** (*blotted his character*) sully, spot, soil, mar, spoil, disfigure, tarnish, stain, taint, blacken, disgrace, dishonour. OPPOSITE: clear.

blot out **1** (*clouds blotting out the sun*) obscure, hide, conceal, obliterate, darken, dim. **2** (*blot out bad memories*) destroy, erase, expunge, obliterate, wipe out, dispel. OPPOSITE: perpetuate.

blotch *noun* patch, spot, splodge, smudge, blot, speck, smear, mark, stain, blemish.

blow[1] *verb* **1** (*the wind was blowing*) gust, flurry, puff, blast, bluster. **2** (*the wind blew the leaves away*) waft, fan, drive, move, sweep, drift, toss, whisk, buffet, blast, whirl. **3** (*blow air from your mouth*) breathe, exhale, expel, pant, puff, gasp. **4** (*blow a musical instrument*) sound, blast, blare, whistle, toot, play. **5** (*blow a lot of money*) squander, lavish, misspend, fritter away. **6** (*blow a chance*) spoil, bungle, ruin, waste, wreck, screw up (*inf*).

blow out extinguish, snuff, douse, put out, smother, stifle.

blow over subside, die down, pass away, pass, vanish, disappear, cease.

blow up **1** (*the plane blew up*) explode, go off, detonate, burst, shatter, bomb, blast, smash. **2** (*blow up a tyre*) pump, pump up, puff up, balloon, swell, enlarge, expand, inflate, distend. **3** (*blow up a storm*) exaggerate, amplify, magnify, embroider, overelaborate, add colour to. **4** (*blow up a photograph*) enlarge, make bigger, make larger. **5** (*I blew up at the decision*) lose one's temper, become angry, fly into a rage, boil over, flip (*inf*), blow one's top (*inf*), blow a fuse (*inf*), blow one's cool (*inf*), hit the roof (*inf*), fly off the handle (*inf*), go off the deep end (*inf*).
➤ *noun* blast, gust, gale, storm, flurry, puff, breath.

blow[2] *noun* **1** (*a blow on the head*) hit, stroke, knock, thump, buffet, slap, punch, rap, smack, whack, bang, bash (*inf*), wallop (*inf*), belt (*inf*), slosh (*inf*). **2** (*his death was a terrible blow*) shock, upset, calamity, disaster, bombshell, catastrophe, disappointment, setback, reversal, misfortune, affliction.

blowout *noun* **1** (*have a blowout on the motorway*) puncture, burst tyre, flat tyre, flat (*inf*). **2** (*have a blowout at Christmas*) feast, party, celebration, binge, spree, bash (*inf*), rave (*inf*), rave-up (*inf*), knees-up (*inf*).

blubber *verb* sob, cry, weep, wail, whine.

bludgeon *noun* cudgel, club, stick, truncheon.
‣ *verb* **1** (*bludgeoned to death*) hit, strike, club, beat, cudgel. **2** (*bludgeoned into paying*) coerce, force, compel, intimidate, pressurize, bully, hector, browbeat, dragoon, bulldoze, steamroller.

blue *adj* **1** (*a blue sky*) azure, sapphire, cobalt, turquoise, aquamarine, ultramarine, navy, cyan, cerulean. **2** (*feel blue*) dejected, depressed, unhappy, sad, low, miserable, melancholy, gloomy, glum, downcast, downhearted, despondent, down in the dumps (*inf*). OPPOSITE: cheerful. **3** (*blue jokes*) obscene, dirty, indecent, improper, lewd, coarse, risqué, bawdy, smutty, steamy (*inf*), near the knuckle (*inf*), near the bone (*inf*).

blueprint *noun* design, pattern, model, template, prototype, layout, representation, plan, sketch, draft.

blues *pl noun* sadness, unhappiness, depression, dejection, gloom, gloominess, melancholy, despondency, low spirits, doldrums, dumps (*inf*). OPPOSITE: elation.

bluff¹ *verb* (*I was only bluffing*) mislead, deceive, delude, lie, pretend, fake, put it on, sham, feign.
‣ *noun* deceit, deception, fraud, pretence, feint, sham, hoax, delusion, show, bravado, bluster.

bluff² *adj* (*his bluff manner*) open, blunt, frank, direct, candid, outspoken, straightforward, hearty, genial, good-natured. OPPOSITE: reserved.
‣ *noun* cliff, ridge, crag, peak, slope, scarp, headland, promontory, bank, escarpment.

blunder *noun* error, mistake, oversight, slip, gaffe, faux pas, inaccuracy, clanger (*inf*), slip-up (*inf*), boo-boo (*inf*), boob (*inf*), indiscretion.
‣ *verb* **1** (*the government has blundered again*) err, botch, bungle, misjudge, mismanage, slip up (*inf*), mess up (*inf*), foul up (*inf*), screw up (*sl*). **2** (*heard someone blundering around downstairs*) stumble, flounder, falter, lurch, stagger.

blunt *adj* **1** (*a blunt knife*) dull, unsharpened, rounded, worn, dulled, pointless. OPPOSITE: sharp. **2** (*her blunt manner*) bluff, unceremonious, plain, plainspoken, direct, frank, open, candid, straightforward, to the point, tactless, outspoken, rude, impolite, abrupt, brusque, curt. OPPOSITE: tactful.
‣ *verb* dull, deaden, numb, weaken, soften, dampen, alleviate, take the edge off. OPPOSITE: sharpen.

blur *verb* **1** (*low cloud blurred the view*) dim, obscure, becloud, befog, fog, cloud, veil, mask, make indistinct. OPPOSITE: clarify. **2** (*a window blurred by rain*) blot, blotch, stain, spot, smear, besmear, besmirch, smudge, sully, tarnish, mar. **3** (*blur a distinction*) dull, obscure, dim, make indistinct, make unclear, make less sharp.
‣ *noun* **1** (*a faint blur on the horizon*) haze, fog, haziness, fogginess, confusion, obscurity, dimness, cloudiness, indistinctness. OPPOSITE: clarity. **2** (*a blur on the window*) blot, stain, spot, smear, smudge, blotch, blemish.

blurred *adj* hazy, fuzzy, blurry, indistinct, vague, foggy, unclear, out of focus, nebulous. OPPOSITE: clear.

blurt *verb* **blurt out** cry, cry out, exclaim, come out with, blab, reveal, divulge, disclose, let slip, let the cat out of the bag (*inf*), give the game away, spill the beans (*inf*).

blush *verb* redden, flush, colour, turn red, go red, go pink, glow, crimson. OPPOSITE: blanch.
‣ *noun* flush, reddening, colour, rosiness, ruddiness, pinkness, glow. OPPOSITE: pallor.

bluster *verb* **1** (*the wind blustered*) gust, blast, blow, roar, storm. **2** (*he blustered noisily*) swagger, boast, vaunt, brag, roar, rant, storm, bully, threaten, domineer, hector, harangue, throw one's weight about.
‣ *noun* **1** (*the bluster of the storm*) roar, roaring, gusting, blast, tumult, storming. **2** (*their empty bluster*) boasting, bravado, swaggering, bluff, bragging, ranting, boisterousness, tumult, commotion, bombast, braggadocio. OPPOSITE: reticence.

blustery *adj* windy, gusty, squally, stormy, tempestuous, wild, blusterous, boisterous. OPPOSITE: quiet.

board *noun* **1** (*a board of wood*) plank, panel, beam, slat, lath, timber. **2** (*board and lodging*) food, meals, provisions, victuals, nosh (*inf*), grub (*inf*). **3** (*the board of directors*) committee, council, panel, group, directors, directorate.
‣ *verb* **1** (*board a bus*) get on, embark, mount, enter, go aboard. OPPOSITE: alight. **2** (*board lodgers*) lodge, house, put up, accommodate, feed. **3** (*the students board there*) stay, live, lodge, have rooms, be housed.

board up cover, cover up, cover over, close, close up, shut, shut up, seal.

boast *verb* **1** (*boast about his success*) brag, vaunt, crow, exaggerate, swagger, bluster, flaunt, show off, congratulate oneself, blow one's own trumpet, pat oneself on the back, swank (*inf*). **2** (*the cathedral boasts the world's tallest spire*) possess, have, enjoy, own, pride oneself in.
‣ *noun* **1** (*his proudest boast*) brag, vaunt, exaggeration, bragging, crowing, blustering, bluster, fanfaronade, gasconade, rodomontade. OPPOSITE: modesty. **2** (*the main boast of the ancient city*) pride, treasure, gem, pearl, pride and joy.

boastful *adj* bragging, vaunting, vain, crowing, swaggering, blustering, vainglorious, conceited, egotistical, cocky, swollen-headed, big-headed (*inf*), swanky (*inf*), swanking (*inf*). OPPOSITE: modest.

boat *noun* vessel, craft, yacht, dinghy, canoe, barge, ferry, ship.

bob *verb* **1** (*bob up and down*) float, move, bounce, shake, quiver, wobble. **2** (*bob down behind the wall*) jump, leap, spring, jerk, skip, duck.

bob up emerge, pop up, appear, arrive, rise, arise, materialize, show up (*inf*).

bode *verb* presage, portend, betoken, signify, augur, import, predict, foretell, foreshadow.

bodily *adj* physical, corporeal, material, carnal, fleshly, sensual, actual, tangible. OPPOSITE: spiritual.
‣ *adv* wholly, entirely, completely, totally, altogether, collectively, as a group, as one, en masse.

body *noun* **1** (*her beautiful body*) trunk, torso, skeleton, physique, build, frame, form, shape, figure. **2** (*a dead body*) corpse, cadaver, carcass, stiff (*inf*). **3** (*a governing body*) organization, group, collection, party, company, band, crowd, throng, multitude, association, corporation, bloc, congress, society, confederation. OPPOSITE: individual. **4** (*a body of data*) substance, mass, whole, bulk, essence, majority. OPPOSITE: part. **5** (*in the body of the plane*) main part, central part, principal part, core, centre, substance. **6** (*the substance lacks body*) density, solidity, firmness, substance, consistency.

bog *noun* swamp, marsh, marshland, mire, quagmire, fen, morass, slough.

bog down obstruct, halt, stop, impede, encumber, trap, entrap, ensnare, entangle, delay, slow down, stall.

bogey *noun* **1** (*nightmares about bogeys*) ghost, spirit, evil spirit, bogeyman, hobgoblin, gremlin, phantom, spectre, spook (*inf*). **2** (*put that bogey to rest*) anxiety, worry, dread, pet hate, bugbear, bête noire.

boggle *verb* **1** (*the mind boggles at the amount of work involved*) start, take fright, shy, be alarmed, be surprised, be amazed, be astounded. **2** (*boggle at paying such a high price*) hesitate, falter, vacillate, waver, shrink from, flinch from, hang back, demur.

bogus *adj* false, counterfeit, sham, fraudulent, forged, artificial, fake, phoney (*inf*), spurious. OPPOSITE: genuine

bohemian *adj* unconventional, unorthodox, original, avant-garde, nonconformist, bizarre, exotic, offbeat, oddball (*inf*), arty (*inf*). OPPOSITE: conventional.
» *noun* hippy, dropout, beatnik, nonconformist.

boil[1] *verb* **1** (*the water is boiling*) seethe, bubble, foam, froth, simmer, cook, heat, stew. OPPOSITE: cool. **2** (*boil with anger*) fume, rage, storm, be angry, seethe, rant, rave, explode, lose one's temper, blow one's top (*inf*), blow a fuse (*inf*), blow one's cool (*inf*), hit the roof (*inf*), fly off the handle (*inf*)

boil[2] *noun* (*a boil on one's skin*) furuncle, carbuncle, tumour, ulcer, pustule, blister, gathering, sore.

boiling *adj* **1** (*boiling hot*) scorching, roasting, baking, sweltering, blistering, searing, torrid. **2** (*boiling with rage*) furiously angry, seething, fuming, flaming, incensed, enraged, infuriated, mad (*inf*).

boisterous *adj* **1** (*boisterous children*) lively, unruly, unrestrained, rowdy, noisy, loud, vociferous, high-spirited, exuberant, obstreperous, clamorous, riotous, uproarious. OPPOSITE: quiet. **2** (*boisterous weather*) stormy, blustery, gusting, wild, raging, turbulent, tumultuous, tempestuous. OPPOSITE: calm.

bold *adj* **1** (*a bold leader*) brave, fearless, valiant, lion-hearted, daring, gallant, undaunted, dauntless, courageous, intrepid, heroic, audacious, adventurous, valorous. OPPOSITE: timid. **2** (*a bold, shameless young man*) insolent, rude, brazen, brash, shameless, impudent, pert, cheeky, forward, overconfident. OPPOSITE: modest. **3** (*bold colours*) prominent, striking, vivid, conspicuous, eye-catching. OPPOSITE: faint.

boldness *noun* **1** (*boldness of the government's reforms*) bravery, valiance, courage, fearlessness, audacity, bravura. OPPOSITE: timidity. **2** (*boldness of the pupil towards the teacher*) insolence, rudeness, shamelessness, impudence, brazenness, cheek, forwardness,

overconfidence. OPPOSITE: modesty. **3** (*boldness of the designs*) vividness, prominence, conspicuousness. OPPOSITE: faintness.

bolshie *adj* awkward, perverse, stroppy (*inf*), bloody-minded (*inf*), stubborn, disobliging, uncooperative, unhelpful, difficult.

bolster *verb* support, prop up, brace, hold up, shore up, buoy up, buttress, maintain, reinforce, strengthen, boost, aid, help, assist.
» *noun* pillow, cushion, support, pad.

bolt *noun* **1** (*a bolt on a door*) bar, latch, catch, lock, fastening, fastener, rod, rivet, pin, peg. **2** (*a bolt of lightning*) flash, blaze, burst. **3** (*fire a bolt*) arrow, dart, shaft, missile, projectile. **4** (*a bolt of cloth*) roll, drum, reel.
» *verb* **1** (*bolt the door*) fasten, secure, latch, lock, bar. OPPOSITE: unbolt. **2** (*bolted the food*) gulp, devour, wolf, gobble, cram, stuff. **3** (*bolt through the open window*) escape, run away, abscond, flee, fly, dash, dart, leap, spring, rush. OPPOSITE: stay.

bolt upright straight, very straight, erect, stiff, rigid.

bomb *noun* explosive, torpedo, mine, shell, grenade, incendiary, missile, charge, rocket, projectile.
» *verb* shell, bombard, blow up, blitz, torpedo, strafe.

bombard *verb* **1** (*bombard the airport*) attack, assail, raid, bomb, shell, blow up, blitz, torpedo, pound. **2** (*bombarded her with questions*) attack, besiege, hound, bother, pester, harass.

bombardment *noun* attack, raid, air raid, assault, shelling, bombing, blitz, blitzkrieg, fusillade, cannonade.

bombast *noun* pomposity, verbosity, grandiloquence, magniloquence, rant, ranting, bluster, bravado, braggadocio, rodomontade, fustian.

bombastic *adj* pompous, grandiloquent, magniloquent, grandiose, fustian, pretentious, high-flown, turgid, flatulent, verbose, ranting, declamatory.

bona fide *adj* genuine, sincere, real, true, authentic, actual, valid, lawful, legal, legitimate.

bonanza *noun* windfall, stroke of luck, blessing, godsend.

bond *noun* **1** (*released from bonds*) cord, band, ligament, ligature, tie, fastening, chain, fetter, manacle, shackle. **2** (*bonds of friendship*) link, tie, connection, affinity, attachment, union. **3** (*agree to a bond*) contract, compact, agreement, obligation, pledge, guarantee, promise, pact, covenant, concordat.
» *verb* bind, fasten, connect, join, stick, unite, attach, fuse, weld, glue, cement. OPPOSITE: separate.

bondage *noun* slavery, servitude, captivity, imprisonment, confinement, duress, enslavement, serfdom, thraldom, thrall, subjugation. OPPOSITE: freedom.

bonny *adj* fair, pretty, comely, beautiful, handsome, sweet, lovely, fine, healthy. OPPOSITE: ugly.

bonus *noun* **1** (*thrown in as an added bonus*) award, reward, gift, bounty, premium, extra, dividend. **2** (*pay a bonus at Christmas*) tip, gratuity, commission, gift, reward, honorarium, perquisite, perk (*inf*).

bony *adj* lean, thin, skinny, emaciated, angular, lanky, gawky, gangling, gaunt, scraggy, scrawny, skeletal, rawboned.

booby *noun* dunce, fool, simpleton, idiot, blockhead.

book *noun* **1** (*publish a book*) volume, tome, tract, text, novel, manual, handbook, directory, work, guidebook, publication, title. **2** (*wrote it down in a book*) notebook, exercise book, jotter, pad.
➤ *verb* reserve, engage, charter, schedule, programme, arrange, line up.

book in register, enter, record, log, enrol.

bookish *adj* studious, learned, erudite, scholarly, intellectual, academic, literary, highbrow, pedantic, bluestocking. OPPOSITE: illiterate.

books *pl noun* accounts, records, ledgers, finances, financial statement.

boom *verb* **1** (*drums booming*) resound, reverberate, roar, thunder, explode, bang, blast, bellow. **2** (*business is booming*) prosper, thrive, flourish, succeed, develop, grow, increase, gain, burgeon. OPPOSITE: decline.
➤ *noun* **1** (*the boom of a cannon*) roar, thunder, crash, blast, bang, explosion, resounding, reverberation. **2** (*a boom in the economy*) rise, increase, development, growth, advance, progress, upsurge, upturn, spurt, boost. OPPOSITE: decline.

boomerang *verb* bounce back, come back, spring back, rebound, recoil, ricochet, backfire.

boon *noun* blessing, benefit, advantage, godsend, plus, bonus, gain, grant, favour, gift, present. OPPOSITE: drawback.

boor *noun* lout, oaf, churl, bumpkin, rustic, clodhopper, peasant, barbarian, philistine.

boorish *adj* rough, crude, rude, loutish, oafish, clumsy, awkward, rustic, uncouth, coarse, ill-bred, vulgar, uncivilized, unrefined, churlish, gruff, yobbish (*inf*). OPPOSITE: refined.

boost *verb* **1** (*boost production*) increase, expand, develop, further, help, aid, assist, amplify, enlarge, jack up (*inf*), hike up (*inf*). **2** (*boosted his confidence*) raise, encourage, improve, increase, inspire, uplift. **3** (*boost a new product*) promote, advertise, publicize, market, plug (*inf*).
➤ *noun* **1** (*a boost to morale*) uplift, encouragement, inspiration, increase, improvement, stimulus, shot in the arm. **2** (*a boost to sales*) increase, expansion, development, rise, growth, hike (*inf*). **3** (*give a boost to the product*) promotion, advertisement, publicity, write-up, plug (*inf*), hype (*inf*), puff (*inf*).

boot *verb* **boot out** kick out, expel, throw out, dismiss, sack (*inf*), give someone their cards (*inf*).

booth *noun* stall, stand, cubicle, compartment, enclosure, carrel.

bootless *adj* unavailing, useless, unsuccessful, pointless, futile, vain, fruitless, ineffective, worthless, abortive. OPPOSITE: useful.

booty *noun* spoils, plunder, pillage, loot, haul, swag (*inf*), takings, profits, pickings.

booze *noun* drink, alcohol, liquor, beer, wine, spirits.

border *noun* **1** (*the border between two countries*) boundary, frontier, marches. **2** (*plant flowers in the border*) edge, margin, fringe, rim, hem, skirt, verge, brink, limit, bound. OPPOSITE: centre.
➤ *verb* adjoin, abut, impinge on, be next to, touch, join, connect.

border on verge on, approach, resemble, come close to.

bore[1] *verb* (*bore a hole*) drill, mine, pierce, perforate, penetrate, puncture, tunnel, burrow, dig out.
➤ *noun* **1** (*sink a bore*) hole, tunnel, shaft, cavity. **2** (*the bore of a gun*) calibre, diameter.

bore[2] *verb* (*bored by the long speech*) tire, weary, wear out, exhaust, fatigue, jade, vex, annoy, bother. OPPOSITE: excite.
➤ *noun* pest, nuisance, bother, drag (*inf*), pain (*inf*).

bored *adj* weary, wearied, tired, exhausted, uninterested, unexcited, cheesed off (*inf*), sick and tired (*inf*), fed up (*inf*), browned off (*inf*), brassed off (*inf*). OPPOSITE: excited.

boredom *noun* weariness, dullness, tedium, monotony, sameness, dreariness, languor, malaise, ennui, apathy. OPPOSITE: excitement.

boring *adj* dull, tedious, monotonous, uninteresting, samey (*inf*), repetitious, routine, humdrum, flat, unvaried, tiresome, wearisome. OPPOSITE: exciting.

borough *noun* town, township, municipality.

borrow *verb* **1** (*borrow some money*) take, cadge, scrounge, sponge (*inf*). OPPOSITE: lend. **2** (*borrow ideas from another author*) take, appropriate, copy, plagiarize, imitate, pirate, steal, filch. **3** (*words borrowed from English*) appropriate, adopt, acquire, take in, take over.

bosh *noun* nonsense, balderdash, rubbish, rot.

bosom *noun* **1** (*a woman of ample bosom*) chest, breasts, breast, bust, boobs (*inf*), tits (*inf*), knockers (*sl*), bristols (*sl*). **2** (*harboured resentment in his bosom*) heart, soul, mind, spirit, being, emotions, feelings. **3** (*in the bosom of the family*) centre, heart, core, depths, recesses, midst, protection, shelter.
➤ *adj* close, intimate, dear, confidential, loving, devoted, faithful, boon.

boss[1] *noun* (*ask the boss for time off*) employer, supervisor, superintendent, overseer, manager, director, foreman, master, leader, chief, head, executive, administrator, controller, governor (*inf*), gaffer (*inf*), honcho (*inf*). OPPOSITE: employee.
➤ *verb* employ, supervise, direct, manage, head, head up, command, control, administer.

boss around order about, push around, bully, domineer, oppress, tyrannize, throw one's weight about.

boss[2] *noun* (*a boss on a ceiling*) stud, knob, protuberance, umbo.

bossy *adj* domineering, overbearing, authoritarian, dominating, dictatorial, high-handed, autocratic, imperious, arrogant. OPPOSITE: meek.

botch *verb* bungle, spoil, mar, muff, mismanage, mess up, make a hash of, screw up (*sl*), foul up (*inf*), louse up (*inf*), cock up (*sl*), balls up (*sl*), blunder. OPPOSITE: accomplish.
➤ *noun* mess, hash, miscarriage, failure, blunder, bungle. OPPOSITE: success.

both *adj* the two. OPPOSITE: neither.

bother *verb* **1** (*stop bothering me*) disturb,

inconvenience, trouble, hassle (*inf*), annoy, irritate, vex, pester, harass, plague, worry, disturb, upset, perplex, disconcert, fret, perturb. OPPOSITE: comfort. **2** (*not bother to check*) make an effort, make the effort, concern oneself, take the time, go to the trouble.

➤ *noun* **1** (*caused a lot of bother*) trouble, nuisance, hassle (*inf*), annoyance, vexation, irritation, inconvenience, upset, problem, difficulty, fuss, flurry. **2** (*get into a spot of bother with the law*) trouble, fighting, disturbance, disorder, commotion, uproar.

bottle *verb* **bottle up** suppress, keep back, restrain, keep in check, hide, conceal, curb.

bottleneck *noun* holdup, congestion, blockage, block, obstruction, restriction, constriction, narrowing.

bottom *noun* **1** (*the bottom of the stairs*) base, foot, ground, basis, foundation, support, pedestal, substructure, underpinning. OPPOSITE: top. **2** (*the bottom of the lake*) bed, floor, depths. OPPOSITE: surface. **3** (*the bottom of a boat*) underside, underpart, underneath, undersurface, belly, sole. OPPOSITE: topside. **4** (*sat on his bottom*) seat, rump, buttocks, rear, tail, posterior, backside (*inf*), behind (*inf*), bum (*inf*), arse (*sl*), butt (*inf*), ass (*inf*), fundament. **5** (*at the bottom of the street*) end, far end, furthest end, farthest end. **6** (*bottom of the league*) lowest level, lowest position, least successful position, least important part. **7** (*get to the bottom of a problem*) origin, root, source, root, essence, core, heart.

➤ *adj* lowest, last, basic, fundamental. OPPOSITE: top.

bottomless *adj* unfathomable, abysmal, deep, fathomless, unfathomed, immeasurable, infinite, boundless, unlimited.

bough *noun* branch, limb, stem, stalk, shoot, twig. OPPOSITE: trunk.

boulder *noun* rock, stone.

boulevard *noun* avenue, road, drive, mall, parade, promenade, thoroughfare.

bounce *verb* **1** (*the ball bounced*) rebound, recoil, spring, spring back, bob, ricochet. **2** (*bounce on a trampoline*) jump, leap, bound, bob, spring.

➤ *noun* **1** (*a ball with not much bounce*) springiness, spring, elasticity, give, resilience. **2** (*with a bounce in the air*) spring, leap, jump, bound. **3** (*a dog full of bounce*) vitality, energy, liveliness, life, vigour, animation, spirit, go (*inf*), get-up-and-go (*inf*), zip (*inf*), zing (*inf*), pep. OPPOSITE: lethargy.

bouncing *adj* healthy, strong, fit, robust, thriving, flourishing, blooming, vigorous.

bound[1] *adj* **1** (*boxes bound with ropes*) tied, fastened, secured, strapped, roped, shackled, fettered. OPPOSITE: free. **2** (*bound by an agreement*) obliged, forced, compelled, constrained, obligated, required, beholden. **bound to** certain to, sure to, likely to, destined to. OPPOSITE: unlikely to.

bound up with tied up with, associated with, connected with, linked with, related to.

bound[2] *verb* (*bound across a wall*) spring, leap, jump, vault, bounce, hurdle, skip, hop, prance, romp, frisk, caper.

➤ *noun* spring, leap, jump, vault, bounce, hop, hurdle, skip, prance, romp, frisk, caper.

bound[3] *verb* (*a garden bounded by a fence*) limit, restrict, confine, restrain, border, enclose, surround, hem in, wall in, circumscribe, demarcate.

bound[4] *adj* **bound for** (*be bound for home*) heading for, headed for, travelling to, off to.

boundary *noun* **1** (*the boundary between two countries*) border, perimeter, barrier, pale, frontier, partition. **2** (*push back the boundaries of science*) limit, confine, bound, margin, edge, extremity, perimeter, termination.

boundless *adj* unlimited, infinite, endless, unending, unbounded, immense, vast, immeasurable, measureless, inexhaustible, infinite, interminable, untold. OPPOSITE: limited.

bounds *pl noun* restrictions, limits, limitations, confines, extremities.

out of bounds off limits, forbidden, prohibited. OPPOSITE: allowed.

bountiful *adj* **1** (*bountiful harvests*) plentiful, abundant, ample, copious, profuse, lavish, prolific, luxuriant. OPPOSITE: meagre. **2** (*our bountiful God*) generous, kind, liberal, giving, open-handed, unsparing, unstinting, bounteous, princely, beneficent, munificent, magnanimous, benevolent. OPPOSITE: miserly.

bounty *noun* **1** (*summer's bounty of fruits*) generosity, liberality, charity, beneficence, philanthropy, almsgiving. OPPOSITE: meanness. **2** (*pay a bounty*) gift, present, donation, grant, award, bonus, premium, reward, recompense, largess.

bouquet *noun* **1** (*a bouquet of flowers*) bunch, posy, nosegay, spray, corsage, garland, wreath, buttonhole, boutonniere. **2** (*a fruity bouquet*) aroma, fragrance, scent, perfume, smell, redolence.

bourgeois *adj* middle class, conservative, conventional, traditional, ordinary, uncreative, unimaginative, materialistic, capitalistic. OPPOSITE: unconventional.

bout *noun* **1** (*won the bout*) fight, contest, conflict, encounter, match. **2** (*a drinking bout*) spell, period, session, time, stretch, spree, turn. **3** (*a bout of flu*) attack, spell, fit, turn.

bovine *adj* **1** (*a bovine animal*) cattlelike, cowlike. **2** (*bovine behaviour*) stupid, dull, slow, slow-witted, dim, dim-witted.

bow[1] *verb* **1** (*bow before the king*) bend the knee, salaam, kowtow, bob, curtsy, genuflect, kneel, prostrate oneself, make obeisance, nod. **2** (*bow your head*) incline, stoop, bend, curve, flex, arch, warp, droop. OPPOSITE: straighten. **3** (*bowed down by the bad news*) subdue, crush, conquer, vanquish, depress, humble, weigh down.

➤ *noun* salaam, bob, curtsy, genuflection, prostration, obeisance, nod.

bow out withdraw, leave, retire, step down, resign, give up, quit, pull out, back out.

bow to submit to, yield to, surrender to, give into, accept, give way to, comply with. OPPOSITE: resist.

bow[2] *noun* (*the bow of a ship*) prow, beak, stern, front, rostrum.

bowdlerize *verb* edit, cut, censor, expunge, expurgate, blue-pencil.

bowels *pl noun* **1** (*irritation of the bowels*) intestines, colon, entrails, guts, viscera, innards (*inf*), insides (*inf*).

2 (*in the bowels of the building*) depths, interior, inside, belly, core. OPPOSITE: surface.

bower *noun* arbour, alcove, recess, grotto, shelter, summerhouse, pergola, gazebo, conservatory.

bowl[1] *noun* **1** (*a bowl of food*) basin, container, receptacle, vessel, dish, plate, saucer. **2** (*the bowl of a pipe*) hollow, dip, depression. **3** (*the Hollywood bowl*) stadium, arena, coliseum, amphitheatre.

bowl[2] *verb* (*bowl a ball*) throw, pitch, spin, hurl, fling, send, deliver, roll.

bowl over 1 (*bowled over by the mob*) knock down, floor, fell, topple, unbalance. **2** (*bowled over by her charm*) overwhelm, surprise, dumbfound, astound, flabbergast, stun, amaze.

box[1] *noun* **1** (*boxes of fruit*) carton, package, pack, case, chest, trunk, casket, receptacle, container, crate. **2** (*a theatre box*) enclosure, area, cubicle, compartment.
➤ *verb* encase, pack, package, wrap, confine.

box in shut in, confine, enclose, block in, fence in, corner, trap, constrain.

box[2] *verb* **1** (*know how to box*) spar, fight. **2** (*boxed his ears*) cuff, buffet, strike, hit, thump, slap, wallop, belt (*inf*), clout (*inf*), sock (*inf*).
➤ *noun* cuff, buffet, stroke, blow, thump, slap, wallop, belt (*inf*), clout (*inf*), sock (*inf*).

boxer *noun* fighter, prizefighter, sparring partner, pugilist.

boy *noun* lad, youth, youngster, kid, junior, stripling. OPPOSITE: man.

boycott *verb* ostracize, shun, refuse, avoid, eschew, spurn, send to Coventry, reject, black, blacklist, blackball, ban, prohibit, proscribe, embargo, bar, exclude.

boyfriend *noun* date, young man, lover, sweetheart, suitor, admirer, beau.

boyish *adj* young, youthful, juvenile, childlike, childish, immature, puerile. OPPOSITE: adult.

brace *verb* **1** (*beams bracing the roof*) support, prop, steady, reinforce, strengthen, hold up, shore up, fortify, bind, fasten, secure, tie, tighten. **2** (*braced himself for the shock*) prepare, make ready, fortify, strengthen, steel.
➤ *noun* **1** (*a brace for a wall*) support, prop, strut, spar, truss, beam, bracket, reinforcement, buttress, shoring, stanchion, clamp, vice, fastener. **2** (*braces of quail*) pair, couple.

bracelet *noun* bangle, circlet, band, wristlet.

bracing *adj* invigorating, stimulating, reviving, strengthening, restorative, healthy, tonic, refreshing, exhilarating, crisp, brisk. OPPOSITE: relaxing.

bracket *noun* **1** (*fit a bracket on a wall*) support, prop, brace, buttress, corbel, console, shelf. **2** (*an income bracket*) group, grouping, category, categorization, division, order, class, classification, status.

brackish *adj* salty, briny, saline, impure.

brag *verb* boast, vaunt, crow, swagger, bluster, show off, blow one's own trumpet, talk big (*inf*), gasconade, flaunt, flourish.
➤ *noun* boast, boasting, crowing, showing-off, vaunt, bluster, gasconade. OPPOSITE: modesty.

braggart *noun* brag, braggadocio, boaster, show-off, big

mouth (*inf*), windbag (*inf*), loudmouth (*inf*), blusterer, swaggerer.

braid *verb* weave, interweave, plait, twine, entwine, intertwine, twist, wind, lace, interlace. OPPOSITE: unravel.
➤ *noun* thread, cord, twine, yarn, tape, plait.

brain *noun* **1** (*messages to and from the brain*) encephalon, grey matter, cerebral matter. **2** (*use your brain*) mind, head, intellect, intelligence, wit, understanding, grey matter. **3** (*the country's best brains*) thinker, scholar, expert, mastermind, intellectual, egghead (*inf*), boffin (*inf*).

brainless *adj* stupid, foolish, thoughtless, witless, senseless, idiotic. OPPOSITE: wise.

brains *pl noun* mind, sense, head, intellect, reason, intelligence, understanding, cleverness, shrewdness, common sense, nous (*inf*), savvy (*inf*). OPPOSITE: stupidity.

brainwashing *noun* indoctrination, pressurizing, conditioning, persuasion, re-education.

brainy *adj* clever, intelligent, brilliant, gifted, smart, bright. OPPOSITE: stupid.

brake *noun* curb, rein, restraint, control, check, damper.
➤ *verb* slow down, slow, decelerate, moderate, check, halt, stop. OPPOSITE: accelerate.

branch *noun* **1** (*branches on a tree*) limb, bough, arm, shoot, stem, twig, sprig, offshoot, ramification, spray. **2** (*the branch of a river*) tributary, feeder, affluent, channel. **3** (*branches of an organization*) office, department, division, subdivision, section, part, wing.
➤ *verb* diverge, divide, separate, ramify, bifurcate, fork. OPPOSITE: converge.

branch off turn off, turn aside from, leave, depart from, diverge from, deviate from.

branch out expand, extend, develop, increase, diversify, widen, spread out, enlarge, multiply, proliferate.

brand *noun* **1** (*a brand of detergent*) kind, sort, type, make, variety, mark, stamp, emblem, label, trademark, symbol. **2** (*his brand of politics*) strain, kind, sort, type, grade, quality, variety. **3** (*identify a sheep by its brand*) tag, marker, mark, identification. **4** (*the brand of that day's disgrace*) stigma, disgrace, infamy, blot, stain, taint. OPPOSITE: honour.
➤ *verb* **1** (*brand cattle*) mark, label, stamp, burn, burn in, scorch, sear. **2** (*branded as a liar*) stigmatize, mark, denounce, disgrace, taint, discredit.

brandish *verb* flourish, wield, swing, wave, raise, shake, flaunt, exhibit, show, show off, display.

brash *adj* **1** (*brash behaviour*) rash, hasty, precipitate, reckless, foolhardy, impulsive, impetuous. OPPOSITE: cautious. **2** (*a brash young woman*) insolent, impudent, rude, audacious, bold, self-confident, self-assertive, forward, brassy, brazen, cheeky, cocky, pushy (*inf*), saucy. OPPOSITE: modest.

brass *noun* audacity, cheek, gall, nerve (*inf*), boldness, effrontery, impertinence, impudence, assurance, presumption.

brassy *adj* **1** (*brassy music*) harsh, loud, bold, blaring, deafening, raucous, cacophonous, jarring, strident.

2 (*brassy confidence*) cheeky, brazen, shameless, insolent, impertinent, impudent, presumptuous, bold, pushy (*inf*).

brat *noun* urchin, guttersnipe, child, kid, youngster, rascal, imp, whippersnapper.

bravado *noun* bragging, boast, boasting, showing-off, boldness, swagger, vaunting, bluster, bombast, braggadocio, fanfaronade. OPPOSITE: modesty.

brave *adj* courageous, valiant, heroic, gallant, audacious, dauntless, undaunted, daring, fearless, intrepid, bold, valorous, resolute, plucky, gutsy (*inf*), spunky (*inf*), gritty (*inf*). OPPOSITE: cowardly.
» *verb* confront, face, defy, endure, bear, suffer, stand up to, put up with, challenge, dare.

bravery *noun* courage, valour, heroism, gallantry, daring, fearlessness, dauntlessness, audacity, boldness, mettle, pluck, spirit, grit, guts (*inf*), spunk (*inf*). OPPOSITE: cowardice.

brawl *verb* fight, wrangle, tussle, scuffle, wrestle, scrap (*inf*), dispute, argue, quarrel, bicker, clash, disagree, squabble, row (*inf*). OPPOSITE: agree.
» *noun* fight, wrangle, scrap (*inf*), punch-up (*inf*), fracas, fray, mêlée, scuffle, affray, broil, row, rumpus, uproar, tumult, disagreement, clash, tussle, quarrel, dispute, altercation.

brawn *noun* muscle, strength, might, heftiness, burliness, bulkiness, bulk, robustness, beef (*inf*), beefiness (*inf*).

brawny *adj* strong, powerful, muscular, sinewy, strapping, hefty, burly, mighty, well-built, lusty, sturdy, robust, stalwart, athletic, herculean. OPPOSITE: weak.

bray *verb* hee-haw, neigh, whinny, call, roar, blare, hoot, bellow.

brazen *adj* bold, audacious, forward, brassy, brash, barefaced, shameless, defiant, presumptuous, immodest, impudent, insolent, saucy, pushy (*inf*), pert, impertinent. OPPOSITE: modest.

brazen it out defy, be defiant, be unashamed, be impenitent, be unrepentant, stand one's ground, put a brave face on it, put a bold face on it.

breach *noun* **1** (*repair the breach in the sea wall*) rupture, fracture, break, crack, rent, cleft, fissure, rift, hole, gap, opening, gulf, chasm. **2** (*breach of a law*) violation, infringement, breaking, neglect, infraction, contravention, transgression, trespass. OPPOSITE: observance. **3** (*a breach in a relationship*) separation, schism, alienation, breakup, estrangement, dissension, severance, division, falling-out, difference, variance, disagreement, quarrel. OPPOSITE: reconciliation.
» *verb* **1** (*breach an agreement*) violate, break, disobey, infringe, contravene, transgress against. **2** (*breach a barrier*) rupture, burst through, break through, split, open, open up.

bread *noun* **1** (*our daily bread*) nourishment, nutriment, sustenance, subsistence, food, fare, provisions, aliment. **2** (*earned his daily bread*) money, cash, funds, finance, dough (*inf*), dosh (*inf*).

breadth *noun* **1** (*the breadth of the room*) width, broadness, wideness, span, spread. OPPOSITE: length. **2** (*her breadth of experience*) magnitude, amplitude, vastness, expanse, extent, range, scope, scale, sweep,

spread, volume, size, measure, dimensions. OPPOSITE: narrowness. **3** (*breadth of feeling*) latitude, liberality, freedom, openness, broad-mindedness.

break *verb* **1** (*break a window*) smash, shatter, fracture, snap, crack, rend, sever, split, tear, divide, separate, shiver, splinter, disintegrate, fragment, demolish, destroy, wreck. OPPOSITE: mend. **2** (*break a law*) violate, infringe, disobey, breach, contravene, defy, transgress against. OPPOSITE: obey. **3** (*the machine has broken*) fail, malfunction, stop working, stop operating, stop functioning, seize up, pack up (*inf*), go on the blink (*inf*), conk out (*inf*), go kaput (*inf*). **4** (*break for a rest*) pause, stop, rest, break off, halt, knock off (*inf*) OPPOSITE: continue. **5** (*break the silence*) interrupt, suspend, disturb, discontinue, cut, bring to an end. **6** (*break the skin*) rupture, pierce, puncture, perforate. **7** (*break a record*) surpass, excel, beat, exceed, surpass, outdo, cap (*inf*). **8** (*break the news gently*) reveal, disclose, divulge, let out, betray, tell, inform, impart, make known, release. **9** (*broke his spirit*) crush, destroy, weaken, overcome, defeat, enervate, enfeeble, tame, cow, subdue, impair, cripple. OPPOSITE: strengthen. **10** (*break a secret code*) decipher, crack, solve, discover, find out, work out, figure out. **11** (*the weather broke*) change, alter, vary, change for the worse, change for the better. **12** (*break the force of a blow*) weaken, soften, reduce, cushion, diminish. **13** (*morning has broken*) appear, come into being, begin, emerge, erupt, dawn, burst forth, burst out.
» *noun* **1** (*a break in the defences*) fracture, crack, split, gap, breach, rupture, rift, opening, hole, gash, chink, rent, cleft, chasm, fissure. **2** (*a break for a rest*) pause, stop, interval, interlude, interruption, recess, respite, rest, halt, breathing space, breather (*inf*), letup (*inf*), time-out (*inf*), suspension, intermission, hiatus, discontinuation. **3** (*a weekend break*) holiday, vacation, time off. **4** (*a lucky break*) opportunity, advantage, chance, opening, stroke of luck.

break away 1 (*the prisoners broke away*) escape, run away, quit, flee, fly, make a run for it (*inf*), leg it (*inf*). **2** (*break away from the main political party*) leave, part company, secede, separate, split off, detach.

break down 1 (*the machine broke down*) fail, malfunction, stop working, pack up (*inf*), conk out (*inf*), go on the blink (*inf*), go kaput (*inf*). OPPOSITE: work. **2** (*negotiations broke down*) collapse, fail, fall through, come to nothing, founder. OPPOSITE: succeed. **3** (*break down the figures*) analyse, separate, categorize, classify, dissect, detail. **4** (*broke down his resistance*) overcome, weaken, overwhelm, defeat, crush, subdue. **5** (*break down in tears*) collapse, lose control, crack up (*inf*), go to pieces (*inf*).

break in 1 (*broke in when I was talking*) interrupt, intervene, intrude, interfere, butt in, cut in, barge in, put one's oar in (*inf*), put one's spoke in (*inf*). **2** (*broke in and stole £500*) burgle, rob, break and enter, enter illegally. **3** (*break in the new worker*) initiate, prepare, train, accustom, settle in, induct, show someone the ropes, tame. **4** (*break in a new pair of boots*) get used to, wear, begin to use, condition.

break into 1 (*broke into our conversation*) interrupt, intrude on, interfere in, butt in on, cut into. **2** (*break into a building*) rob, burgle, enter illegally. **3** (*break into song*) burst into, launch into, begin suddenly, start suddenly, commence. **4** (*broke into his savings*) dip into, start to spend, use part of.

break off 1 (*break off a branch*) detach, sever, cut off, separate, snap off, remove. OPPOSITE: attach. **2** (*break off in mid-sentence*) stop, stop talking, suddenly stop. **3** (*break off a relationship*) end, finish, bring to an end, stop, halt, cease, terminate, discontinue, suspend. OPPOSITE: start.

break out 1 (*fighting broke out*) start, begin, commence, arise, occur, erupt, burst out. **2** (*break out of prison*) escape, run away, abscond, bolt, flee, get free, break loose. **3** ('*Hold on,' she broke out*) exclaim, burst out, cry out, cry, shout, call out.

break through overcome, penetrate, pass, get past, progress, succeed, achieve.

break up 1 (*break up a large organization*) separate, dismantle, divide, disband, scatter, split up. OPPOSITE: unite. **2** (*the couple broke up*) split up, divorce, separate, finish, dissolve, go one's separate ways, come to an end. **3** (*the meeting broke up*) adjourn, finish, stop, discontinue, terminate, disperse, come to an end. OPPOSITE: start.

breakable *adj* fragile, brittle, delicate, flimsy, insubstantial, frail, jerry-built, frangible, friable.

breakdown *noun* **1** (*the breakdown of a machine*) stopping, failure, malfunction, packing-up (*inf*), conking-out (*inf*). **2** (*breakdown of the negotiations*) collapse, failure, foundering, falling-through, ruin. OPPOSITE: restoration. **3** (*a nervous breakdown*) collapse, cracking-up (*inf*), going to pieces (*inf*). **4** (*a breakdown of the data*) analysis, itemization, separation, classification, categorization, dissection, review, summary.

breaker *noun* wave, comber, billow, roller, white horses.

break-in *noun* illegal entry, breaking and entering, burglary, housebreaking, theft, robbery.

breakneck *adj* very fast, speedy, rapid, reckless, dangerous.

breakthrough *noun* advance, development, success, improvement, progress, step forward, leap, quantum leap, discovery, invention.

breakup *noun* **1** (*the breakup of their marriage*) dissolution, splitting-up, collapse, failure, ending, termination, divorce, separation, parting, parting of the ways. **2** (*the breakup of the large organization*) dismantling, division, disbanding, disintegration.

breakwater *noun* mole, groyne, jetty, embankment, barrier, sea wall.

breast *noun* **1** (*a woman's breasts*) bust, chest, front, thorax, bosom, udder, teat, tit (*inf*), boob (*inf*), knocker (*sl*), bristol (*sl*). **2** (*emotions in his breast*) heart, soul, core, being, emotions, feelings, affections.

breath *noun* **1** (*take deep breaths*) respiration, breathing, inhalation, inspiration, exhalation, air, gasp, pant, wheeze. **2** (*a breath of air*) breeze, gust, puff, waft, flurry, draught, zephyr. **3** (*a breath of summer*) odour, aroma, whiff, smell, vapour. **4** (*pause for breathe*) pause, respite, rest, breather, breathing space, break, interval, lull. **5** (*a breath of scandal*) hint, suggestion, whisper, murmur, trace, touch, sigh, gust, puff, waft. **6** (*the breath of life*)

animation, life, life force, vitality, vital force, existence.

breathe *verb* **1** (*breathe deeply*) respire, inhale, exhale, gasp, expire, wheeze, pant, puff, sigh. **2** (*no finer fellow has ever breathed*) exist, live, be alive. **3** (*don't breathe a word about it*) say, utter, articulate, express, voice, whisper, murmur. **4** (*breathe new life into an ailing club*) imbue, instil, infuse, inject, impart.

breather *noun* rest, break, pause, recess, respite, interval, breathing space, time-out (*inf*).

breathless *adj* **1** (*breathless after the climb*) gasping, panting, winded, out of breath, wheezing, puffing, exhausted, spent. **2** (*breathless tension*) eager, excited, open-mouthed, amazed, thunderstruck, anxious, in suspense, with bated breath, on tenter hooks.

breathtaking *adj* awesome, awe-inspiring, impressive, magnificent, amazing, astounding, astonishing, stunning, exciting, thrilling. OPPOSITE: uninspiring.

breed *verb* **1** (*breed dogs*) rear, raise, nurture, bring up, bear, produce, give birth to, multiply, bring forth, engender, beget, procreate, propagate, reproduce, generate. **2** (*I was bred in the city*) rear, raise, bring up, nurture, foster, educate, train, teach, school, instruct, discipline. **3** (*breed resentment*) create, produce, generate, originate, cause, bring about, give rise to, occasion, arouse.
➤ *noun* **1** (*a breed of horses*) race, stock, strain, variety, kind, sort, type, species, pedigree, line, lineage, progeny, family, extraction. **2** (*a new breed of manager*) kind, sort, type, class, strain.

breeding *noun* **1** (*the breeding of cattle*) reproduction, propagation, procreation, generation, bearing, begetting, training, education, upbringing, development, rearing, nurture. **2** (*ladies of breeding*) background, ancestry, manners, bearing, conduct, refinement, culture, cultivation, polish, civility, courtesy, politeness.

breeze *noun* light wind, zephyr, gust, flurry, waft, puff, breath of air, breath of wind, draught. OPPOSITE: hurricane.
➤ *verb* drift, glide, sweep, wander, sail, sally, flit.

breezy *adj* (*breezy weather*) windy, fresh, airy, blustery, blowy. OPPOSITE: calm. **2** (*her breezy personality*) carefree, casual, light-hearted, cheerful, cheery, confident, easygoing, relaxed, sparkling, blithe, buoyant, sprightly, lively, vivacious, jaunty.

brevity *noun* **1** (*the brevity of the report*) briefness, conciseness, terseness, succinctness, compactness, pithiness. OPPOSITE: prolixity. **2** (*the brevity of life*) briefness, shortness, transience, transitoriness, impermanence, ephemerality.

brew *verb* **1** (*brew tea*) infuse, boil, stew, steep, soak, ferment, prepare, make. **2** (*trouble is brewing*) gather, develop, build up, form, threaten. **3** (*brew trouble*) foment, bring about, plot, hatch, contrive, devise, concoct, design, plan.
➤ *noun* **1** (*make a strong brew*) drink, beverage, infusion, potion, preparation, fermentation. **2** (*a powerful brew of drugs and violence*) mixture, blend, concoction, preparation, cocktail.

bribe *verb* buy, buy off, pay off (*inf*), suborn, corrupt, square, tempt, entice, lure, reward, fix (*inf*), grease someone's palm (*inf*).

➤ *noun* inducement, enticement, reward, backhander (*inf*), lure, graft, hush money (*inf*), sweetener, carrot (*inf*), payoff (*inf*), protection money (*inf*), payola (*inf*).

bric-a-brac *pl noun* knick-knacks, trinkets, ornaments, baubles, gewgaws, antiques.

bridal *adj* nuptial, conjugal, matrimonial, marital, connubial, wedding, marriage.

bride *noun* newlywed, wife, honeymooner, spouse, marriage partner.

bridegroom *noun* groom, newlywed, husband, honeymooner, spouse, marriage partner.

bridge *noun* **1** (*a railway bridge*) span, arch, flyover, viaduct, overpass. **2** (*act as a bridge between the two groups*) link, tie, connection, bond.
➤ *verb* **1** (*bridge the river*) span, traverse, cross, cross over, pass over, go over. **2** (*bridge the gap between rich and poor*) connect, unite, join, link. OPPOSITE: divide.

bridle *noun* curb, restraint, check, control, halter.
➤ *verb* **1** (*bridled his temper*) curb, restrain, check, keep in check, hold back, control, keep control of, subdue, govern, master. OPPOSITE: release. **2** (*bridled at his autocratic tone*) bristle, be indignant, raise one's hackles, get angry.

brief *adj* **1** (*a brief visit*) short, fleeting, transitory, transient, ephemeral, momentary, temporary, evanescent, fugacious. OPPOSITE: long. **2** (*a brief report*) concise, short, terse, succinct, compact, to the point, pointed, compressed, economic, sparing, pithy, laconic. OPPOSITE: lengthy. **3** (*his brief manner*) curt, abrupt, short, sharp, brusque, blunt.
➤ *noun* **1** (*a brief of what happened*) abstract, synopsis, outline, summary, précis, résumé, sketch, epitome, digest. **2** (*with a brief to inform the government*) responsibility, remit, instructions, directions, directive, mandate, guidance. **3** (*a legal brief*) case, argument, evidence, proof, defence, data.
➤ *verb* instruct, inform, fill in (*inf*), enlighten, guide, direct, explain, prepare, advise, give someone the rundown, put in the picture.

briefing *noun* **1** (*call a briefing*) meeting, conference, discussion, seminar, forum. **2** (*give a briefing to the candidates*) information, guidance, advice, instructions, directions, gen (*inf*), filling-in (*inf*), rundown (*inf*).

briefly *adv* **1** (*answer briefly*) in brief, in short, tersely, pithily, concisely, succinctly, to the point, in a nutshell. **2** (*we live briefly*) momentarily, in passing, fleetingly, hurriedly, transitorily, transiently, ephemerally.

brigade *noun* group, party, troop, squad, unit, team, band, body, association, force, section, crew, corps, contingent, organization, company.

brigand *noun* bandit, robber, outlaw, ruffian, thug, desperado, gangster, marauder, plunderer, highwayman.

bright *adj* **1** (*bright lights*) luminous, shining, brilliant, radiant, gleaming, glittering, sparkling, flashing, blazing, beaming, glowing, glossy, lustrous, resplendent, glorious, dazzling, vivid, intense. OPPOSITE: dull. **2** (*bright colours*) strong, vivid, intense, bold, brilliant, rich, glowing. OPPOSITE: dull. **3** (*a bright day*) sunny, fine, pleasant, cloudless, unclouded. OPPOSITE: overcast.

4 (*she's a bright child*) intelligent, clever, smart, acute, keen, sharp, brainy, astute, quick, quick-witted. OPPOSITE: stupid. **5** (*eyes bright with excitement*) cheerful, happy, merry, jolly, genial, lively, lighthearted, vivacious. OPPOSITE: miserable. **6** (*a bright future*) favourable, promising, good, optimistic, fortunate, encouraging, rosy, auspicious, propitious.

brighten *verb* **1** (*brighten a room*) illuminate, lighten, light up, clear, grow bright, shine, polish, enhance, illumine, irradiate. OPPOSITE: darken. **2** (*brightened his spirits*) enliven, cheer, cheer up, gladden, hearten, encourage, perk up, buck up (*inf*), pep up (*inf*). OPPOSITE: dishearten.

brilliance *noun* **1** (*the brilliance of the sun*) brightness, radiance, vividness, intensity, lustre, sheen, glitter, sparkle, dazzle, effulgence, pomp, splendour, magnificence, resplendence, refulgence. OPPOSITE: dullness. **2** (*her brilliance as a pianist*) excellence, distinction, talent, genius, virtuosity, greatness, wisdom, cleverness. OPPOSITE: mediocrity.

brilliant *adj* **1** (*a brilliant light*) bright, radiant, shining, sparkling, beaming, luminous, glittering, lustrous, intense, vivid, dazzling, splendid, magnificent, effulgent, resplendent, refulgent. OPPOSITE: dull. **2** (*has a brilliant mind*) intelligent, clever, bright, brainy, smart, excellent, outstanding, exceptional, distinguished, illustrious, learned, scholarly, erudite, eminent, famous, accomplished, expert, talented, gifted. OPPOSITE: mediocre. **3** (*a brilliant career*) successful, exceptional, outstanding, flourishing, prosperous. OPPOSITE: unsuccessful **4** (*what a brilliant idea!*) great, superb, wonderful, fantastic, excellent, marvellous. OPPOSITE: awful.

brim *noun* rim, lip, edge, brink, margin, verge. OPPOSITE: centre.
➤ *verb* be full with, be filled with, overflow with.

brindled *adj* mottled, speckled, patched, spotted, dappled, streaked, tabby.

brine *noun* salt water, seawater, sea, saline solution, pickle.

bring *verb* **1** (*bring her a present*) bear, carry, convey, conduct, lead, usher, escort, accompany. OPPOSITE: remove. **2** (*war brings suffering*) cause, engender, produce, result in, prompt, provoke. **3** (*bring a legal case*) initiate, propose, lay. **4** (*the car should bring £900*) fetch, make, produce, yield, net, gross.

bring about cause, effect, occasion, result in, create, produce, bring to pass, accomplish, achieve, realize.

bring down 1 (*bring down costs*) reduce, decrease, lower, cut. OPPOSITE: increase. **2** (*bring down the president*) overthrow, unseat, defeat, oust, depose, topple.

bring forward 1 (*bring forward a proposal*) introduce, raise, propose, suggest. **2** (*bring forward a date*) advance, make earlier. OPPOSITE: put back.

bring in 1 (*bring in a profit*) earn, yield, fetch, return, produce, profit, gross, net, realize. **2** (*bring in a new law*) introduce, initiate, establish, inaugurate, institute, begin, launch.

bring off achieve, pull off, accomplish, carry out, execute, fulfil, perform.

bring on 1 (*bring on fresh growth*) help, encourage,

advance, accelerate, expedite. **2** (*bring on indigestion*) produce, cause, lead to, result in, prompt, provoke, give rise to.

bring out **1** (*bring out a new book*) publish, issue, launch, release, present, bring on to the market. **2** (*bring out small details*) reveal, convey, make known, draw out, emphasize, highlight.

bring round **1** (*bring round someone who is unconscious*) revive, resuscitate, awaken, bring to. **2** (*brought round to my opinion*) win over, persuade, convince, convert.

bring up **1** (*bring up a child*) raise, rear, nurture, train, educate, teach, develop, foster. **2** (*bring up a subject*) propose, put forward, raise, mention, introduce, broach. **3** (*bring up food*) vomit, regurgitate, spew up, throw up (*inf*), puke (*inf*), barf (*inf*).

brink *noun* **1** (*the brink of a cliff*) border, edge, rim, margin, verge, threshold, bank, shore, boundary, limit. OPPOSITE: centre. **2** (*on the brink of a catastrophe*) verge, edge, extremity, threshold.

brisk *adj* **1** (*go for a brisk walk*) energetic, lively, active, animated, vigorous, agile, nimble, spry, quick, fast, speedy, rapid, swift, alert. OPPOSITE: sluggish. **2** (*business is brisk*) busy, active, rapid, hectic. OPPOSITE: quiet. **3** (*a brisk manner*) businesslike, efficient, lively, no-nonsense, well-ordered. **4** (*brisk weather*) sharp, keen, crisp, fresh, invigorating, bracing, biting, exhilarating, refreshing. OPPOSITE: oppressive.

bristle *noun* hair, whisker, barb, spine, prickle, thorn, quill.
≫ *verb* **1** (*hair bristling*) stand up, rise, prickle, stand on end. **2** (*bristle with anger*) be indignant, be angry, bridle, seethe, flare up. **3** (*bristling with tourists*) swarm, teem, crawl, be alive, abound, be thick (*inf*).

bristly *adj* hairy, whiskered, whiskery, bearded, unshaven, stubbly, rough, prickly, thorny, spiky.

brittle *adj* **1** (*brittle material*) fragile, frail, delicate, crisp, breakable, frangible, crumbly, friable. **2** (*a brittle relationship*) delicate, fragile, weak, frail, unstable. **3** (*a brittle personality*) sharp, insensitive, tense, curt, irritable, on edge, uptight (*inf*). **4** (*a brittle laugh*) short, sharp, hard, harsh, grating, strident.

broach *verb* **1** (*broach a subject*) introduce, suggest, mention, bring up, raise, submit, open, propose, advance. **2** (*broach a barrel*) open, tap, pierce, uncork, break into, draw off. OPPOSITE: seal.

broad *adj* **1** (*a broad passage*) wide, ample, vast, large, extensive, spacious, roomy, capacious. OPPOSITE: narrow. **2** (*a broad range of interests*) extensive, wide, wide-ranging, full, comprehensive, inclusive, vast, sweeping, all-embracing, unlimited, boundless, universal, general. OPPOSITE: limited. **3** (*received broad support*) widespread, general, common, extensive. OPPOSITE: limited. **4** (*in broad terms*) general, rough, loose, vague, inexact, imprecise. OPPOSITE: detailed. **5** (*a broad hint*) clear, explicit, obvious, direct, plain, straightforward, undisguised, unconcealed. **6** (*in broad daylight*) full, complete, clear, total, perfect, absolute. **7** (*a broad accent*) strong, noticeable, marked, distinct, definite, dialectal. **8** (*broad humour*) vulgar, coarse, indecent, blue, gross, indelicate.

broadcast *verb* **1** (*broadcast a TV programme*) transmit,

relay, show, air, beam, send out, televise, radio. **2** (*broadcast a message*) publish, make known, declare, disseminate, proclaim, announce, advertise, promulgate. **3** (*broadcast seed*) disseminate, spread.
≫ *noun* show, programme, transmission.

broaden *verb* widen, enlarge, amplify, expand, fill out, open up, swell, develop, increase, augment. OPPOSITE: restrict.

broad-minded *adj* liberal, tolerant, indulgent, forbearing, permissive, unprejudiced, unbiased, unbigoted, dispassionate, open-minded, catholic, free-thinking, progressive. OPPOSITE: narrow-minded.

broadside *noun* **1** (*fire a broadside at a ship*) attack, assault, bombardment, salvo, volley. **2** (*a broadside against the government*) attack, criticism, censure, abuse, diatribe, philippic, fulmination, harangue, invective, slating (*inf*), flak (*inf*), stick (*inf*), brickbats (*inf*).

brochure *noun* leaflet, pamphlet, booklet, folder, handout, flyer, handbill, notice, circular, advertisement.

broil¹ *verb* (*broil a chicken*) grill, cook, fry, roast, barbecue.

broil² *noun* (*turned into a nasty broil*) quarrel, dispute, row, brawl, scuffle, wrangle, fray, fracas.
≫ *verb* quarrel, dispute, brawl, wrangle.

broiling *adj* hot, scorching, roasting, baking, sweltering, blistering, searing.

broke *adj* penniless, insolvent, bankrupt, ruined, impoverished, poverty-stricken, impecunious, indigent, penurious, skint (*inf*), bust (*inf*), stony-broke (*inf*), cleaned out (*inf*), strapped for cash (*inf*), on one's beam ends (*inf*), on one's uppers (*inf*), without two pennies to rub together (*inf*). OPPOSITE: rich.

broken *adj* **1** (*a broken window*) shattered, smashed, fractured, ruptured, torn, split, burst, rent, separated, fragmented, demolished, destroyed. OPPOSITE: mended. **2** (*a broken machine*) broken-down, faulty, defective, out of order, out of action, inoperative, bust (*inf*), kaput (*inf*), wonky (*inf*), on the blink (*inf*). OPPOSITE: working. **3** (*broken sleep*) disturbed, disrupted, discontinuous, interrupted, disconnected, incomplete, fragmentary, intermittent, spasmodic. OPPOSITE: continuous. **4** (*a broken man*) defeated, beaten, weakened, spent, exhausted, run-down, demoralized, crushed, humbled, discouraged, dispirited, feeble. **5** (*speak broken German*) halting, imperfect, hesitant, hesitating, disjointed, faltering, stumbling, stammering. OPPOSITE: fluent.

brokenhearted *adj* inconsolable, desolate, sorrowful, grief-stricken, miserable, wretched, heartbroken, crestfallen, disappointed, despairing, devastated. OPPOSITE: delighted.

broker *noun* agent, middleman, intermediary, negotiator, factor, dealer, go-between, third party.

brooch *noun* pin, clasp, clip.

brood *verb* **1** (*brood over a problem*) think, ponder, muse, meditate, reflect, ruminate, dwell on, worry, fret. **2** (*hens brooding*) sit on eggs, incubate eggs, hatch eggs.
≫ *noun* **1** (*a brood of ducklings*) litter, clutch, offspring, family, young, progeny, issue. **2** (*a brood of children*) children, family, youngsters, offspring, kids (*inf*).

brook[1] *noun* (*a babbling brook*) stream, beck, rivulet, rill, burn, runnel, gill.

brook[2] *verb* (*brook no interruptions*) bear, endure, suffer, stand, abide, tolerate, put up with (*inf*), allow.

brothel *noun* house of ill repute, bordello, bawdy house, whorehouse, knocking shop (*inf*).

brother *noun* **1** (*my elder brother*) sibling, kinsman, blood brother, bro (*inf*). OPPOSITE: sister. **2** (*brothers in the fight against racism*) comrade, partner, companion, friend, colleague, associate, chum (*inf*), mate (*inf*), pal (*inf*). **3** (*brothers worshipping*) monk, friar.

brotherhood *noun* **1** (*a secret brotherhood*) fraternity, society, association, alliance, club, league, union, guild, lodge. **2** (*feelings of peace and brotherhood*) brotherliness, fraternalism, friendship, companionship, comradeship, friendliness, fellowship, camaraderie.

brotherly *adj* fraternal, friendly, affectionate, amicable, cordial, kind, kindly, charitable, sympathetic, benevolent, altruistic, philanthropic. OPPOSITE: unkind.

brow *noun* **1** (*mopped his brow*) forehead, temple, front, eyebrow, face, countenance, appearance. **2** (*the brow of a hill*) crown, summit, peak, top, brink, verge, edge, rim.

browbeat *verb* bully, compel, force, coerce, intimidate, cow, overbear, domineer, badger, hector, dragoon, bulldoze (*inf*).

brown *adj* **1** (*a brown colour*) chestnut, bronze, copper, rust, auburn, ginger, tan, tawny, chocolate, coffee, cocoa, hazel, walnut, bay, henna, umber, brunette, fuscous, sorrel, roan. **2** (*brown from lying in the sun*) tanned, bronzed, sunburnt. OPPOSITE: pale.
➤ *verb* grill, fry, toast, cook.

browned off *adj* discontented, fed up, discouraged, disgruntled, bored, brassed off (*inf*), cheesed off (*inf*), hacked off (*inf*).

browse *verb* **1** (*browse through a magazine*) scan, glance, skim, dip, thumb, leaf, look through, peruse, look around. **2** (*deer browsing*) nibble, crop, feed, graze.

bruise *verb* **1** (*bruised his arm*) injure, damage, hurt, batter, pound, crush, mark, blemish, discolour, blacken, contuse. **2** (*bruised my feelings*) offend, upset, crush, injure, wound. **3** (*bruised fruit*) mark, spoil, blemish, discolour.
➤ *noun* discoloration, mark, blemish, blackening, black eye, shiner (*inf*), injury, contusion, ecchymosis.

brunette *adj* dark, dark-brown, darkish, dark-haired, brown-haired OPPOSITE: blonde.

brunt *noun* shock, force, full force, impact, thrust, burden, violence, stress, strain, pressure.

brush[1] *noun* **1** (*use a brush for cleaning*) broom, besom, sweeper, hairbrush, paintbrush. **2** (*a brush with the law*) skirmish, clash, encounter, confrontation, conflict, engagement, contest, fight, battle, tussle, scrap (*inf*). **3** (*felt the brush of her silk dress*) touch, stroke, contact.
➤ *verb* **1** (*brush the room*) sweep, wipe, clean, dust, groom. **2** (*brushed my arm*) touch, graze, stroke, kiss, scrape.

brush aside dismiss, sweep aside, disregard, ignore, think no more of, have no time for.

brush off reject, spurn, slight, snub, rebuff, scorn, dismiss, cold-shoulder.

brush up 1 (*brush up your German*) revise, read up, go over, study, cram, relearn, polish, bone up on (*inf*). **2** (*brush up before going out*) clean up, freshen up, refresh oneself, tidy up.

brush[2] *noun* (*got lost in the brush*) scrub, thicket, wood, undergrowth, bushes, copse.

brush-off *noun* rejection, snub, slight, rebuff, cold shoulder.

brusque *adj* curt, abrupt, short, gruff, bluff, blunt, sharp, terse, rude, impolite, discourteous, unceremonious. OPPOSITE: polite.

brutal *adj* **1** (*a brutal murder*) cruel, savage, ferocious, vicious, barbarous, ruthless, inhuman, pitiless, merciless, remorseless. OPPOSITE: humane. **2** (*brutal honesty*) harsh, severe, gruff, rude, uncivil, callous, heartless, unfeeling. OPPOSITE: gentle. **3** (*brutal instincts*) coarse, crude, gross, vulgar, brutish, bestial, animal, uncouth, carnal, sensual. OPPOSITE: refined.

brutality *noun* cruelty, inhumanity, savagery, ferocity, harshness, severity, barbarism, atrocity, pitilessness, ruthlessness. OPPOSITE: humanity.

brute *noun* **1** (*brutes of the forest*) animal, beast, creature. **2** (*what a brute he is!*) beast, savage, monster, ogre, devil, fiend, barbarian, swine.
➤ *adj* **1** (*brute force*) physical, bodily, carnal, sensual, bestial, savage. **2** (*brute feelings*) instinctive, mindless, unthinking.

bubble *noun* **1** (*soap bubbles*) blob, drop, bead, globule, glob, blister, vesicle. **2** (*the bubble of optimism burst*) delusion, illusion, fantasy, dream, vanity.
➤ *verb* **1** (*cola bubbling*) sparkle, foam, froth, seethe, boil, fizz, effervesce. **2** (*water bubbling*) gurgle, burble, babble, murmur. **3** (*bubble with enthusiasm*) be excited, be full, be filled, sparkle.

bubbly *adj* **1** (*a bubbly drink*) effervescent, sparkling, fizzy, carbonated, foaming, frothy. **2** (*a bubbly personality*) lively, sparkling, vivacious, animated, buoyant, happy, merry, exuberant, ebullient.

buccaneer *noun* pirate, corsair, freebooter, privateer, sea rover.

buck *verb* spring, jump, leap, prance, jerk, throw, unseat.

buck up 1 (*bucked up his spirits*) cheer up, encourage, brighten, perk up, gladden, enliven, hearten. **2** (*buck up or you'll miss the bus*) hurry, speed up, get a move on, hasten.

bucket *noun* pail, can, scuttle, pitcher, vessel, container.

buckle *noun* **1** (*a buckle on a belt*) clasp, clip, fastener, catch, hasp. **2** (*a buckle in metal*) distortion, warp, bulge, twisting, crumpling.
➤ *verb* **1** (*metal buckling under pressure*) bow, bend, warp, distort, contort, twist, bulge, crumple, collapse, cave in. **2** (*buckled her belt*) fasten, secure, close, clasp, catch, clip, tie, strap, hook.

bucolic *adj* agricultural, rural, rustic, pastoral, agrarian.

bud *noun* shoot, germ, sprout, floret, burgeon.
➤ *verb* sprout, shoot, burgeon, germinate, grow, develop, burst forth. OPPOSITE: wither.

budding *adj* promising, developing, growing,

flowering, fledgling, promising, embryonic, incipient, nascent.

budge *verb* **1** (*the door wouldn't budge*) move, stir, go, shift, dislodge, give way. **2** (*he's so stubborn he won't budge*) change one's mind, be swayed, give in, give way, yield.

budget *noun* estimate, statement, plan, cost, funds, resources, allocation, allowance, quota, ration.
➤ *verb* plan, schedule, cost, estimate, allocate, apportion, set aside.

buff[1] *adj* (*buff envelopes*) yellowish-brown, brownish-yellow, beige, sandy, straw-coloured.
➤ *verb* polish, shine, burnish, rub, smooth.

buff[2] *noun* (*a movie buff*) enthusiast, fan, expert, devotee, addict, admirer, aficionado, expert, freak (*inf*), fiend (*inf*).

buffer *noun* bumper, shock absorber, cushion, fender, screen, shield, guard, bulwark.

buffet[1] *noun* **1** (*a station buffet*) café, cafeteria, snack bar, counter, bar. **2** (*a cold buffet*) table, meal, self-service, smorgasbord. **3** (*a buffet for displaying china*) sideboard, cabinet, cupboard.

buffet[2] *verb* (*buffeted by strong winds*) knock, bump, batter, pound, strike, hit, beat, bang, push, box, thump, slap.
➤ *noun* knock, bump, stroke, slap, cuff, hit, blow, bang, box, battering, thump.

buffoon *noun* jester, clown, harlequin, fool, comic, comedian, wit, joker, wag, droll.

buffoonery *noun* clowning, jesting, drollery, tomfoolery, silliness, nonsense. OPPOSITE: wisdom.

bug *noun* **1** (*bugs in the grass*) insect, flea, creepy-crawly. **2** (*pick up a tummy bug*) germ, virus, bacterium, microorganism, infection, disease. **3** (*got the travel bug*) craze, obsession, fad, passion, fixation, mania, thing (*inf*). **4** (*a bug in computer software*) flaw, defect, error, fault, imperfection, gremlin. **5** (*put a bug in a room*) listening device, microphone, tap, phone-tap, wire-tap.
➤ *verb* **1** (*it really bugs me*) irritate, annoy, anger, vex, bother, pester, harass, exasperate, irk, plague, wind up (*inf*), needle (*inf*), get one's back up. **2** (*bug an office*) eavesdrop, tap, phone-tap, wire-tap, listen in.

bugbear *noun* bogey, dread, nightmare, bane, pet hate, bête noire, anathema, abomination.

build *verb* **1** (*build a new shopping centre*) erect, put up, raise, construct, make, manufacture, fabricate, assemble, put together, form. OPPOSITE: demolish. **2** (*build a career*) establish, found, originate, begin, set up, inaugurate, institute.
➤ *noun* physique, body, figure, form, frame, structure, shape.

build up **1** (*build up an army*) assemble, extend, enlarge, put together. **2** (*built up his strength*) reinforce, develop, increase, expand, intensify, improve, escalate, fortify. **3** (*built up my confidence*) boost, strengthen, increase, heighten, enhance. **4** (*build up a new product*) advertise, publicize, promote, market, plug (*inf*), hype (*inf*).

building *noun* edifice, erection, construction, structure, house, pile.

buildup *noun* **1** (*the buildup of traffic*) increase, growth, expansion, enlargement, development, amplification, intensification, accumulation, amassing, stockpile. OPPOSITE: reduction. **2** (*the buildup to the film's première*) publicity, promotion, marketing, plugging (*inf*), hype (*inf*).

built-in *adj* **1** (*built-in wardrobes*) integral, fitted. **2** (*built-in productivity clauses*) inherent, included, incorporated, essential.

bulbous *adj* rounded, swollen, bloated, bulging.

bulge *verb* swell, bloat, enlarge, balloon, balloon out, puff out, protrude, project, stick out, expand, dilate, distend.
➤ *noun* **1** (*a bulge in his pocket*) swelling, lump, bump, protuberance, protrusion, projection, prominence. OPPOSITE: hollow. **2** (*a bulge in the birthrate*) increase, rise, growth, expansion, intensification, surge, upsurge.

bulk *noun* **1** (*the powerful bulk of his chest*) size, volume, mass, weight, extent, magnitude, dimensions, substance, largeness, bigness, immensity, hugeness, bulkiness. **2** (*the bulk of the workforce*) majority, preponderance, greater part, lion's share, body, mass, most. OPPOSITE: minority.

bulk out expand, fill out, pad out, augment.

bulky *adj* **1** (*a bulky package*) large, big, massive, huge, enormous, substantial, immense, colossal, unwieldy, cumbersome, unmanageable, awkward, unwieldy. OPPOSITE: small. **2** (*his bulky body*) plump, heavy, big, large, solid, stout, chubby, portly.

bulldoze *verb* **1** (*bulldoze buildings*) destroy, knock down, level, flatten, raze, clear. **2** (*bulldozed into giving money*) force, compel, pressurize, coerce, bully, browbeat, dragoon, railroad.

bulletin *noun* **1** (*a news bulletin*) announcement, newsflash, news update, statement, report, message, communication, communiqué, dispatch. **2** (*the office's in-house bulletin*) newsletter, newspaper, broadsheet, leaflet, pamphlet.

bullish *adj* confident, optimistic, positive, hopeful, assured, sanguine, upbeat (*inf*).

bully *noun* intimidator, browbeater, ruffian, tough, thug, hector, tormentor, persecutor, oppressor.
➤ *verb* browbeat, intimidate, force, compel, pressure, pressurize, overbear, domineer, hector, coerce, terrorize, torment, persecute, harass, tyrannize, push around (*inf*), strong-arm (*inf*).

bulwark *noun* **1** (*the fort's bulwark*) rampart, fortification, embankment, redoubt, bastion, outwork, buttress. **2** (*a bulwark against the decay in morals*) defence, support, buffer, mainstay, guard, safeguard, security, protection.

bum[1] *noun* (*sat on his bum*) bottom, seat, buttocks, posterior, backside, behind (*inf*), butt (*inf*), ass (*inf*), arse (*sl*).

bum[2] *noun* **1** (*a bum begging on the street*) tramp, vagrant, scrounger (*inf*), sponger (*inf*), hobo. **2** (*a lazy bum*) idler, loafer, good-for-nothing, layabout.

bum around laze around, lounge around, loaf around, idle.

bumbling *adj* awkward, clumsy, blundering, incompetent, inefficient, inept, bungling, botching.

bump *verb* **1** (*bump into a tree*) knock, bang, strike, hit, collide, crash, slam (*inf*). **2** (*bump along the road*) jostle, bounce, jolt, jar, jerk, shake, rattle.
➤ *noun* **1** (*have a bump in the car*) blow, knock, bang, crash, collision, impact, shock, jar, jolt. **2** (*hear a bump*) bang, crash, thud, thump, knock. **3** (*a bump on his forehead*) swelling, lump, protuberance, injury, protrusion, tumescence, papilla, nodule. **4** (*bumps on the road surface*) hump, lump, bulge, protrusion, projection, sleeping policeman.
bump into come across, meet, encounter, run into, chance upon.

bumper *adj* big, large, generous, abundant, plentiful, excellent, exceptional, huge, immense, jumbo (*inf*), whopping (*inf*), massive. OPPOSITE: meagre.

bumpkin *noun* rustic, peasant, yokel, oaf, lout, boor, lubber, clod, clodhopper.

bumptious *adj* conceited, vain, arrogant, self-important, self-assertive, self-opinionated, pushy (*inf*), overbearing, cocky, puffed up. OPPOSITE: modest.

bumpy *adj* **1** (*a bumpy road*) rough, uneven, rutted, potholed, irregular, knobbly. OPPOSITE: level. **2** (*a bumpy ride*) rough, jerky, uneven, bouncy, jolting, choppy. OPPOSITE: smooth.

bunch *noun* **1** (*a bunch of flowers*) bouquet, posy, spray, corsage, garland, nosegay. **2** (*a bunch of papers*) cluster, clump, collection, assortment, group, bundle, sheaf, batch, lot, heap, pile, mass. **3** (*a bunch of people*) collection, group, company, crowd, mob, gathering, crew, team, party, flock.
➤ *verb* cluster, gather, bundle, pack, mass, batch, herd, huddle.

bundle *noun* bunch, sheaf, collection, batch, parcel, package, pack, packet, bale, heap, pile, accumulation, stack.
➤ *verb* **1** (*bundle clothes together*) pack, wrap, tie, tie up, package, parcel, fasten together, gather, pile, stack. **2** (*bundled into a van*) hurry, push, rush, thrust, shove.

bungle *verb* botch, mismanage, mess up, make a mess of, mishandle, spoil, mar, muff, foul up (*inf*), louse up (*inf*), cock up (*sl*), screw up (*sl*). OPPOSITE: accomplish.

bungler *noun* botcher, fumbler, incompetent, dunce, duffer (*inf*), butterfingers (*inf*). OPPOSITE: expert.

bungling *adj* awkward, clumsy, blundering, unskilful, botching, maladroit, gauche, incompetent, inept, cack-handed (*inf*), ham-fisted (*inf*). OPPOSITE: expert.

bunker *noun* **1** (*a coal bunker*) container, bin, chest, tank. **2** (*a bunker on a golf course*) obstacle, hazard.

bunkum *noun* nonsense, claptrap, balderdash, rubbish, twaddle, bunk (*inf*), rot (*inf*), poppycock (*inf*), baloney (*inf*), bilge (*inf*), bosh (*inf*), piffle (*inf*), balls (*sl*).

buoy *noun* float, marker, signal, beacon, guide.
➤ *verb* cheer, cheer up, hearten, encourage, sustain, support, boost, raise the spirits of. OPPOSITE: depress.

buoyancy *noun* **1** (*the buoyancy of light wood*) lightness, weightlessness, floatability. OPPOSITE: heaviness. **2** (*the buoyancy of his mood*) cheerfulness, joy, high spirits,

breeziness, lightheartedness, liveliness, vivacity, sparkle, animation. OPPOSITE: despondency.

buoyant *adj* **1** (*buoyant material*) light, weightless, floating, floatable. OPPOSITE: heavy. **2** (*in a buoyant mood*) cheerful, bright, breezy, lighthearted, sparkling, lively, vivacious, animated, carefree, bouncy (*inf*), peppy (*inf*), blithe. OPPOSITE: despondent.

burden *noun* **1** (*place a considerable burden on the manager*) duty, responsibility, charge, encumbrance, impediment, weight, millstone, onus, trouble, affliction, trial, worry, strain, stress, sorrow. **2** (*beasts carrying burdens*) cargo, freight, load, weight, capacity, tonnage.
➤ *verb* load, weigh down, charge, saddle, oppress, overload, afflict, trouble, distress, worry, stress, overwhelm, encumber, tax. OPPOSITE: relieve.

burdensome *adj* onerous, heavy, difficult, taxing, troublesome, trying, exacting, weighty. OPPOSITE: easy.

bureau *noun* **1** (*drawers in a bureau*) desk, writing desk, chest, dresser. **2** (*an information bureau*) department, office, agency, branch, division.

bureaucracy *noun* **1** (*reduce the bureaucracy*) red tape, administration, rules and regulations, procedures, officialdom. **2** (*administrative bureaucracies*) civil service, government, the system, the authorities.

bureaucrat *noun* official, officeholder, civil servant, minister, functionary, mandarin, apparatchik.

bureaucratic *adj* official, administrative, ministerial, governmental, procedural, complex, complicated, rigid, by the book, inflexible.

burgeon *verb* grow, develop, bud, flourish, thrive, prosper, escalate, multiply, expand, proliferate, mushroom, snowball.

burglar *noun* housebreaker, robber, thief, cat burglar, pilferer, picklock, safecracker.

burglary *noun* housebreaking, breaking and entering, illegal entry, theft, robbery.

burial *noun* burying, interment, inhumation, entombment, sepulture, funeral, obsequies, exequies. OPPOSITE: exhumation.

burial ground *noun* graveyard, cemetery, burial place, churchyard, God's acre, necropolis, mausoleum, catacomb.

burlesque *noun* caricature, parody, satire, lampoon, travesty, takeoff (*inf*), send-up (*inf*), spoof (*inf*).
➤ *adj* caricatural, parodic, ludicrous, comic, mocking, satirical, ironical, mock-heroic, hudibrastic.

burly *adj* sturdy, stout, stocky, thickset, well-built, big, strong, powerful, muscular, brawny, beefy, hefty, strapping. OPPOSITE: frail.

burn *verb* **1** (*the fire is burning*) be ablaze, be on fire, go up, smoke, flame, blaze, flare, flicker, glow, smoulder. **2** (*burn old letters*) ignite, light, set on fire, set alight, kindle, reduce to ashes, incinerate. OPPOSITE: extinguish. **3** (*burned his fingers on the hot hob*) scorch, char, singe, sear, toast, parch, scald. **4** (*my throat is burning*) smart, sting, prick, hurt, bite, tingle. **5** (*burn with rage*) seethe, fume, simmer, smoulder. **6** (*burning to know the result*) yearn, long, desire, itch, pant, lust, be eager, be consumed.

burning *adj* **1** (*a burning house*) ablaze, aflame, flaming, blazing, fiery, hot, glowing, smouldering, scorching, flickering. **2** (*burning hot*) scalding, hot, scorching, boiling, roasting, baking. OPPOSITE: cold. **3** (*a burning sensation*) smarting, stinging, tingling, prickling, caustic. **4** (*a burning ambition*) ardent, fervent, intense, passionate, vehement, eager, earnest. OPPOSITE: cool. **5** (*a burning question*) urgent, important, critical, pressing, crucial, vital, acute, essential. OPPOSITE: unimportant.

burnish *verb* polish, polish up, shine, rub, buff, furbish, glaze, brighten. OPPOSITE: dull.

burp *verb* belch, bring up wind, eruct, eructate.

burrow *noun* tunnel, hollow, hole, excavation, den, lair, retreat.
≫ *verb* **1** (*burrow a hole*) dig, excavate, delve, gorge, hollow out, scoop out, tunnel. **2** (*burrow through papers*) search, hunt, delve, rummage, ferret.

bursar *noun* treasurer, cashier.

burst *verb* **1** (*the tyre burst*) puncture, blow up, rupture, crack, break, break open, shatter, shiver, fracture, fragment. **2** (*the dam burst*) erupt, rush, gush, break, pour, spout, surge. **3** (*the missile burst*) blow up, explode, detonate. **4** (*burst into my bedroom*) rush, hurry, run, break in, barge, push one's way. **5** (*burst into laughter*) break, break out, begin suddenly, start suddenly.
≫ *noun* **1** (*have a burst in the car*) puncture, blowout. **2** (*a burst in the pipe*) explosion, blast, blasting, break, split, rupture, breach. **3** (*a burst of activity*) eruption, outburst, torrent, gush, outbreak, spate, fit.

burst out **1** ('*Wait for me!*' *he burst out*) exclaim, cry, cry out, call, call out, blurt out. **2** (*burst out laughing*) break out, begin suddenly, start suddenly.

bury *verb* **1** (*bury a dead body*) inter, inhume, entomb, lay to rest, sepulchre. OPPOSITE: exhume. **2** (*buried her head in her hands*) cover, conceal, hide, submerge, put out of sight, secrete. **3** (*the bullet buried deep into his flesh*) sink, embed, implant, submerge. **4** (*buried himself in his work*) occupy, absorb, engulf, immerse, engross.

bush *noun* **1** (*a rose bush*) shrub, hedge, thicket, undergrowth. **2** (*lost in the bush*) brush, scrub, scrubland, wilds, backwoods.

bushy *adj* rough, thick, shaggy, luxuriant, fuzzy, bristly.

business *noun* **1** (*what's her line of business*) occupation, trade, craft, profession, line, employment, work, job, vocation, calling, pursuit, career, métier. OPPOSITE: leisure. **2** (*set up a business*) company, firm, organization, concern, partnership, industry, enterprise, consortium, conglomerate, multinational. **3** (*do business*) commerce, trade, buying and selling, dealings, industry, transaction, trafficking. **4** (*that is not your business*) affair, concern, problem, matter, issue, responsibility, duty, function. **5** (*the business of the meeting*) subject, issue, matter, question, theme, task, work.

businesslike *adj* efficient, effective, organized, well-ordered, orderly, methodical, systematic, thorough, meticulous, painstaking, assiduous, correct, professional.

bust[1] *noun* **1** (*a woman's bust*) chest, bosom, breast, boobs (*inf*), tits (*inf*), knockers (*sl*). **2** (*a bust of the king*) sculpture, head, statue, torso.

bust[2] *verb* **1** (*bust the door down*) break, damage, smash,

tear, burst, crack. **2** (*busted for possession of drugs*) arrest, catch, capture, seize, nab (*inf*), nick (*inf*), book (*inf*), collar (*inf*).
≫ *adj* bankrupt, insolvent, ruined, broke (*inf*), gone to the wall (*inf*), on the rocks (*inf*).

bustle *verb* hurry, dash, rush, scamper, scurry, scuttle, stir, fuss, flutter.
≫ *noun* fuss, flurry, activity, commotion, stir, ado, hurly-burly, tumult, to-do, hurry, haste. OPPOSITE: calm.

busy *adj* **1** (*be busy at the moment*) occupied, engaged, employed, at work, engrossed, involved. OPPOSITE: free. **2** (*a busy person*) active, energetic, lively, on the go (*inf*), bustling, astir, industrious, diligent, sedulous, assiduous. OPPOSITE: idle. **3** (*they're busy working*) occupied, engrossed, absorbed, involved, preoccupied, working, toiling. **4** (*a busy time of year*) full, eventful, hectic, frantic, exacting, strenuous, tiring. **5** (*his busy nature*) nosy, inquisitive, fussy, officious, interfering, meddling, meddlesome.

busybody *noun* meddler, snooper, interferer, pry, nosy parker (*inf*), eavesdropper, gossip, scandalmonger.

but *conj* yet, still, on the contrary, however, nevertheless, on the other hand.
≫ *prep* except, save, other than, bar, barring, notwithstanding.
≫ *adv* only, merely, just, simply.

butch *adj* mannish, masculine, male.

butcher *noun* **1** (*meat from the butcher*) meat counter, meat seller, supermarket, superstore. **2** (*a butcher of thousands of innocent people*) slaughterer, killer, murderer, assassin, slayer, homicide, destroyer.
≫ *verb* slaughter, massacre, kill, slay, murder, assassinate, mutilate, destroy, cut down, put to death, put to the sword.

butchery *noun* slaughter, massacre, carnage, bloodbath, murder, slaying, homicide, bloodshed.

butt[1] *noun* **1** (*the butt of a gun*) stock, shaft, handle, hilt, end. **2** (*a cigarette butt*) stub, end, tip, tail end, fag end (*inf*), dog-end (*inf*). **3** (*sitting on his butt*) bottom, buttocks, posterior, behind (*inf*), ass (*inf*), arse (*sl*).

butt[2] *noun* (*the butt of many jokes*) target, object, subject, victim, scapegoat, dupe, laughingstock.

butt[3] *verb* (*butted him with its horns*) push, shove, ram, thrust, buffet, jab, poke, prod, bump, knock.
butt in interfere, meddle, intrude, interrupt, chip in (*inf*), stick one's nose in (*inf*), put one's oar in (*inf*).

butt[4] *noun* (*a butt of cider*) cask, barrel.

buttocks *noun* rump, hindquarters, rear, posterior, seat, behind (*inf*), bottom, bum (*inf*), butt (*inf*), ass (*inf*), arse (*sl*).

button *noun* **1** (*buttons on a dress*) fastener, clasp, catch. **2** (*the buttons on a machine*) knob, disc, switch.

buttonhole *verb* accost, waylay, catch, grab, detain, importune.

buttress *noun* support, stay, prop, strut, brace, shore, reinforcement, abutment, stanchion.
≫ *verb* support, strengthen, reinforce, prop up, back up, back, defend, uphold, help, aid, assist.

buxom *adj* plump, healthy, lusty, ample, full-bosomed,

voluptuous, hearty, lively, jolly, attractive, comely, bonny. OPPOSITE: thin.

buy *verb* **1** (*buy a camera*) purchase, pay for, procure, obtain, acquire, invest in, get. OPPOSITE: sell. **2** (*try to buy the judge*) bribe, corrupt, suborn, pay off (*inf*), fix (*inf*), grease someone's palm (*inf*).
➤ *noun* purchase, acquisition, investment, bargain, deal.

buzz *verb* **1** (*bees buzzing*) hum, murmur, drone, whirr, purr, whisper, hiss, bombinate. **2** (*buzzing with excitement*) hum, pulse, throb, be busy. **3** (*buzzing around in his car*) rush, dash, hurry, bustle.
➤ *noun* **1** (*the buzz of bees*) humming, droning, whirring, purring, hissing, murmur, whisper, bombination. **2** (*I'll give you a buzz later*) ring, call, phone call. **3** (*driving fast gives him a real buzz*) thrill, excitement, kick (*inf*). **4** (*the latest buzz*) rumour, gossip, latest report, news, hearsay, whisper, scandal.

by *prep* **1** (*sit by the window*) near, next to, close to, alongside, beside. **2** (*enter by the front door*) through, by way of, over, via. **3** (*she succeeded by hard work*) by means of, through, through the means of, under the aegis of. **4** (*be home by midnight*) before, at, no later than, not later than.
➤ *adv* near, aside, past, beyond.

bygone *adj* past, previous, gone by, departed, former, one-time, forgotten, lost, dead, extinct, obsolete, antiquated, erstwhile, ancient, of old. OPPOSITE: future.

bylaw *noun* local law, local regulation, statute, rule.

bypass *noun* ring road, detour, alternative route, diversion.
➤ *verb* **1** (*bypass the city*) drive round, go round, pass round. **2** (*bypass the normal procedures*) avoid, get round, evade, go over the head of, circumvent, overlook, neglect, pass over, ignore.

bystander *noun* onlooker, spectator, observer, looker-on, eyewitness, witness, watcher, viewer, passer-by, rubberneck (*inf*).

byword *noun* **1** (*a byword for quality*) slogan, catchword, embodiment, motto. **2** (*traditional bywords*) proverb, epithet, saying, maxim, adage, aphorism, precept, apophthegm.

cab *noun* **1** (*call a cab*) taxi, taxicab, minicab, hackney, hackney carriage. **2** (*a truck driver's cab*) compartment, cabin, quarters, cubicle.

cabal *noun* **1** (*members of the cabal*) clique, coterie, set, ring, gang, band, camp, faction, party, junta, league, coalition, confederacy. **2** (*details of the cabal*) plot, intrigue, conspiracy, scheme, plan.

cabalistic *adj* mystic, occult, arcane, esoteric, secret, mysterious, cryptic, obscure, vague, impenetrable, inscrutable.

cabaret *noun* **1** (*take part in the cabaret*) show, floor show, entertainment. **2** (*a singer in a cabaret*) club, nightclub, nightspot, discotheque, disco (*inf*).

cabin *noun* **1** (*a cabin in the forest*) hut, shed, chalet, cottage, lodge, shack, shanty, hovel, shelter, refuge. **2** (*a cabin on the ship*) compartment, berth, sleeping quarters, room, stateroom, apartment.

cabinet *noun* **1** (*a display cabinet*) case, dresser, cupboard, closet, chest, locker. **2** (*ministers of the cabinet*) council, committee, assembly, senate, administration, executive, government, ministry, advisers, counsellors.

cable *noun* **1** (*cut the cable*) line, wire, flex, lead, rope, cord, chain. **2** (*send a cable*) cablegram, wire, telegram, telegraph, message, telex, fax, facsimile.
➤ *verb* wire, telegraph, radio, telex, fax.

cache *noun* **1** (*a cache for the loot*) hiding place, hidey-hole (*inf*), repository, storehouse. **2** (*an arms cache*) stockpile, store, hoard, stash (*inf*), supply, reserve, fund, collection, accumulation.

cachet *noun* prestige, eminence, distinction, reputation, renown, regard, esteem, respect, admiration, approval, approbation, seal of approval, stamp of approval.

cackle *verb* **1** (*hens cackle*) cluck, squawk, crow, quack. **2** (*cackle in derision*) chuckle, giggle, chortle, snigger, titter, laugh. **3** (*cackling with her neighbours*) chatter, gabble, jabber, blather, prattle, prate, babble.

cacophonous *adj* discordant, dissonant, inharmonious, jarring, harsh, strident, raucous, grating. OPPOSITE: harmonious.

cacophony *noun* discord, dissonance, disharmony, jarring, harshness, stridency, raucousness, grating, caterwauling. OPPOSITE: concord.

cad *noun* scoundrel, rogue, rascal, knave, blackguard, wretch, rotter (*inf*), heel (*inf*), bounder (*inf*), rat (*inf*), swine (*inf*).

cadaver *noun* corpse, body, dead body, stiff (*inf*), remains, carcass.

cadaverous *adj* deathly, deathlike, corpselike, ghastly, pallid, pale, ashen, wan, like death warmed up (*inf*), haggard, gaunt, emaciated, skeletal. OPPOSITE: ruddy.

cadence *noun* intonation, tone, modulation, inflection, accent, lilt, swing, rhythm, beat, pulse, tempo, metre.

cadge *verb* scrounge, beg, sponge (*inf*), bum (*inf*), bludge (*inf*), freeload (*inf*), lig (*sl*).

café *noun* cafeteria, snack bar, brasserie, buffet, bistro, restaurant, tea shop, tearoom, coffee bar, coffee shop.

cafeteria *noun* canteen, buffet, self-service restaurant, café.

cage *noun* enclosure, pen, pound, box, hutch, coop, aviary.
➤ *verb* confine, shut in, lock up, imprison, incarcerate, impound, corral, coop up, pen in, fence in, hem in, restrain, restrict. OPPOSITE: release.

cagey *adj* secretive, guarded, cautious, wary, chary, careful, circumspect, discreet, noncommittal, evasive, equivocal, wily, shrewd. OPPOSITE: frank.

cajole *verb* coax, wheedle, persuade, get round, beguile, tempt, entice, lure, entrap, dupe, inveigle, flatter, blandish, soft-soap (*inf*), sweet-talk (*inf*), butter up (*inf*). OPPOSITE: bully.

cajolery *noun* coaxing, wheedling, persuasion, beguilement, temptation, enticement, flattery, blandishments, blarney, soft soap (*inf*), sweet talk (*inf*). OPPOSITE: force.

cake *noun* **1** (*tea and cakes*) pastry, bun, patisserie, gateau, tart, pie, flan. **2** (*a cake of soap*) lump, chunk, block, bar, slab, loaf, piece, mass.
» *verb* **1** (*blood cakes around the wound*) solidify, harden, thicken, congeal, coagulate, dry, bake. **2** (*caked with mud*) encrust, plaster, cover, coat.

calamitous *adj* disastrous, catastrophic, cataclysmic, ruinous, devastating, fatal, dire, ill-starred, ill-fated, unfortunate, unlucky, adverse, deplorable, dreadful, tragic, woeful, grievous, wretched. OPPOSITE: fortunate.

calamity *noun* disaster, catastrophe, cataclysm, ruin, devastation, tragedy, misfortune, mishap, setback, reverse, blow, trouble, adversity, hardship, affliction, trial, tribulation, distress, woe. OPPOSITE: blessing.

calculate *verb* **1** (*calculate the cost*) compute, work out, reckon, figure, count, enumerate, measure, determine, value, assess. **2** (*calculate the likelihood of success*) estimate, gauge, judge, weigh up, rate, consider. **3** (*calculated on her accepting the offer*) rely, depend, count, bank.

calculated *adj* **1** (*a statement calculated to win votes*) aimed, intended, designed, planned. OPPOSITE: unintended. **2** (*a calculated insult*) intentional, deliberate, purposeful, intended, planned, premeditated, considered. OPPOSITE: unintentional.

calculating *adj* scheming, devious, crafty, cunning, sly, Machiavellian, shrewd, sharp, designing, manipulative. OPPOSITE: artless.

calculation *noun* **1** (*an error in my calculations*) computation, working out, reckoning, figuring, enumeration, valuation, assessment, answer, result. **2** (*calculation of the risk*) estimation, estimate, judgment, forecast, consideration, deliberation. **3** (*get what you want by calculation*) planning, design, foresight, forethought, care, caution, discretion, circumspection, wariness, shrewdness, craft, cunning, deviousness.

calendar *noun* almanac, chronology, list, register, agenda, schedule, timetable, diary.

calibre *noun* **1** (*the calibre of a gun*) diameter, bore, gauge, size, measure. **2** (*a candidate of this calibre*) quality, worth, merit, distinction, excellence, capacity, ability, capability, talent, gifts, endowments.

call *noun* **1** (*a warning call*) cry, shout, yell, scream, shriek, exclamation, signal. **2** (*I'll give you a call*) telephone call, phone call, ring, buzz (*inf*), bell (*inf*), tinkle (*inf*). **3** (*a call for reform*) request, appeal, plea, demand, claim, order, command, summons, invitation, announcement, notice. **4** (*no call for such rudeness*) need, occasion, cause, reason, grounds, excuse, justification. **5** (*not much call for such skills these days*) demand, requirement, want, need. **6** (*the call of the wild*) attraction, appeal, lure, allurement, fascination.
» *verb* **1** (*called to his friend*) shout, cry, yell, scream, shriek, roar, bellow, exclaim, hail. OPPOSITE: whisper. **2** (*called Sam for short*) name, christen, baptize, nickname, dub, entitle, denominate, designate, label, term, style, brand. **3** (*call a strike*) declare, proclaim, announce, decree, order, convene, convoke, muster, assemble. OPPOSITE: dismiss. **4** (*called to the manager's office*) summon, invite, send for, order, bid. **5** (*I'll call you tomorrow*) ring, ring up, telephone, phone, contact, give

someone a ring, give someone a buzz (*inf*), give someone a bell (*inf*), give someone a tinkle (*inf*). **6** (*call me at six*) rouse, arouse, wake up, waken, awaken. **7** (*called at every house*) visit, pay a visit, pay a call, stop by, drop in, pop in (*inf*). OPPOSITE: leave.

call for **1** (*this calls for a celebration*) necessitate, need, demand, require, involve, entail, occasion, warrant, justify. **2** (*call for better working conditions*) demand, push for, press for, campaign for, agitate for. **3** (*I'll call for you at nine*) fetch, pick up, collect, go for.

call off **1** (*call off the meeting*) cancel, abandon, postpone, defer, shelve (*inf*), countermand, revoke. **2** (*call off the dogs*) check, stop, hold back, order away.

call on **1** (*a doctor calling on her patients*) visit, go and see, drop in on, look in on, look up (*inf*). **2** (*call on them to help*) appeal to, invoke, ask, request, urge, entreat.

call up **1** (*call up happy memories*) evoke, recall, bring to mind, summon up. **2** (*called up to fight*) enlist, recruit, draft, sign up. OPPOSITE: demobilize.

on call on duty, standing by, ready.

calling *noun* vocation, mission, career, profession, occupation, métier, craft, trade, business, job, work, employment, line, field, province.

callous *adj* unfeeling, insensitive, cold, cold-hearted, unsympathetic, indifferent, uncaring, apathetic, hard, hardened, obdurate, indurate, thick-skinned, unsusceptible, tough, harsh, hard-hearted, stony-hearted, heartless, soulless. OPPOSITE: tender.

callow *adj* inexperienced, naive, ingenuous, innocent, immature, raw, green, simple, unsophisticated, guileless. OPPOSITE: experienced.

calm *adj* **1** (*calm water*) smooth, waveless, still, motionless, undisturbed, like a millpond. OPPOSITE: rough. **2** (*calm weather*) still, windless, serene, tranquil, peaceful, quiet, mild, balmy, equable. OPPOSITE: stormy. **3** (*remained calm throughout his ordeal*) placid, composed, self-possessed, self-controlled, collected, unruffled, unflustered, unexcited, unmoved, cool, impassive, unemotional, dispassionate, relaxed, laid back (*inf*), tranquil, serene, sedate, poised, cool-headed, imperturbable, unflappable (*inf*). OPPOSITE: agitated.
» *noun* calmness, serenity, tranquillity, stillness, smoothness, peace, peacefulness, quiet, quietness, hush, lull. OPPOSITE: storm.
» *verb* pacify, placate, appease, mollify, still, quiet, hush, lull, allay, assuage, soothe, alleviate, compose, relax, sedate, tranquillize. OPPOSITE: agitate.

calm down compose oneself, relax, settle down, quieten, cool down (*inf*), simmer down (*inf*).

calmness *noun* **1** (*the calmness of the evening*) calm, serenity, tranquillity, stillness, smoothness, peacefulness, quietness. OPPOSITE: disturbance. **2** (*the calmness of her manner*) composure, self-possession, self-control, cool (*inf*), placidity, sedateness, coolness, impassivity, dispassionateness, sang-froid, equanimity, poise, serenity, tranquillity. OPPOSITE: agitation.

calumniate *verb* slander, libel, defame, vilify, malign, disparage, denigrate, blacken, traduce, detract, asperse, revile, abuse, insult, slag off (*inf*). OPPOSITE: eulogize.

calumnious *adj* slanderous, libellous, defamatory,

derogatory, aspersive, abusive, scurrilous, insulting, vituperative. OPPOSITE: complimentary.

calumny *noun* slander, calumniation, libel, misrepresentation, defamation, vilification, disparagement, denigration, mudslinging, backbiting, aspersion, slur, smear, abuse, insult, vituperation, obloquy, revilement. OPPOSITE: eulogy.

camaraderie *noun* comradeship, companionship, fellowship, brotherhood, fraternity, brotherliness, friendliness, esprit de corps, affinity, closeness, sociability. OPPOSITE: enmity.

camber *noun* curve, arch, curvature, convexity.

camouflage *noun* disguise, mask, cloak, screen, veil, blind, guise, front, facade, covering, protective colouring, concealment, masquerade, subterfuge, deception.
➤ *verb* disguise, mask, cloak, screen, veil, cover, conceal, hide, obscure. OPPOSITE: expose.

camp[1] *noun* **1** (*an army camp*) encampment, cantonment, bivouac, campsite, camping ground, tents. **2** (*members of the opposite camp*) faction, clique, coterie, set, party, group, sect, cabal.
➤ *verb* encamp, pitch camp, pitch one's tent, settle, lodge, sleep out, rough it (*inf*).

camp[2] *adj* effeminate, limp-wristed (*inf*), homosexual, gay, queer (*sl*), mannered, affected, artificial, studied, exaggerated, theatrical, over the top (*inf*), extravagant, flamboyant, ostentatious, posing, posturing.

camp it up overact, ham it, overdo it, spread it on thick, posture, behave affectedly.

campaign *noun* **1** (*a military campaign*) battle, fight, war, operation, exercise, manoeuvre, expedition, crusade, attack, offensive. **2** (*a sales campaign*) drive, push, promotion, movement, operation, exercise, strategy, tactics, course of action.
➤ *verb* fight, battle, crusade, push, press, strive, struggle, agitate, work.

can *noun* tin, jar, container, receptacle.
➤ *verb* tin, preserve.

canal *noun* **1** (*a boat on the canal*) channel, waterway, watercourse. **2** (*the alimentary canal*) tube, duct, pipe, passage.

cancel *verb* **1** (*cancel the wedding*) call off, abandon, abort, stop, discontinue, drop, scrap (*inf*), axe (*inf*), postpone, defer, shelve (*inf*). **2** (*cancel an order*) annul, nullify, revoke, repeal, rescind, retract, countermand, negate, abrogate, repudiate, quash, abolish. OPPOSITE: confirm. **3** (*cancel that last remark*) obliterate, erase, expunge, delete, cross out, efface, eliminate, get rid of, do away with. OPPOSITE: retain.

cancel out neutralize, counteract, counterbalance, balance, offset, compensate for, make up for, redeem.

cancellation *noun* abandonment, postponement, annulment, nullification, revocation, repeal, rescindment, retraction, negation, abrogation, abolition, obliteration, deletion, elimination. OPPOSITE: confirmation.

cancer *noun* **1** (*lung cancer*) tumour, carcinoma, malignancy, growth. **2** (*a cancer of modern society*) canker, blight, bane, evil, curse, scourge, rot, corruption, pestilence, plague, disease, sickness.

candid *adj* frank, open, straightforward, direct, honest, truthful, sincere, blunt, forthright, outspoken, unreserved, plain, simple, guileless, artless, naive, ingenuous. OPPOSITE: devious.

candidate *noun* applicant, aspirant, claimant, nominee, contestant, competitor, contender, entrant, runner, possibility.

candle *noun* taper, light.

candour *noun* frankness, openness, straightforwardness, directness, honesty, truthfulness, sincerity, bluntness, forthrightness, plainness, simplicity, artlessness, naivety, ingenuousness. OPPOSITE: deviousness.

cane *noun* stick, staff, crook, rod, stem, stalk.
➤ *verb* beat, thrash, flog, whip, lash, scourge, strike, hit.

canker *noun* (*a canker in the ear*) abscess, ulcer, ulceration, infection, lesion, sore, chancre, boil, blister. **2** (*a canker of modern society*) blight, bane, evil, curse, scourge, rot, corruption, pestilence, plague, disease, sickness, cancer.

cannabis *noun* marijuana, hemp, hashish, grass (*inf*), pot (*inf*), hash (*inf*), ganja, bhang, dope (*inf*), kef (*inf*), joint (*inf*), reefer (*inf*), spliff (*inf*).

cannibal *noun* anthropophagite, man-eater, people-eater, savage, barbarian.

cannon *noun* gun, field gun, big gun (*inf*), howitzer.

cannonade *noun* bombardment, shelling, battery, barrage, assault, attack, broadside, volley, salvo.

canny *adj* astute, shrewd, knowing, perspicacious, discerning, penetrating, sharp, acute, subtle, clever, artful, wise, sagacious, judicious, prudent, cautious, careful, circumspect. OPPOSITE: foolish.

canon *noun* **1** (*the canons of good taste*) law, statute, rule, regulation, convention, decree, edict, precept, formula, norm, standard, principle, criterion, yardstick, benchmark, model, pattern. **2** (*the Shakespearean canon*) catalogue, list, roll, enumeration, litany.

canonical *adj* authorized, official, accepted, approved, recognized, orthodox, conventional, standard, regular. OPPOSITE: unorthodox.

canopy *noun* awning, shade, cover, shelter, tarpaulin, baldachin, tester, tilt.

cant[1] *noun* **1** (*politicians' cant*) hypocrisy, insincerity, humbug, lip service, sanctimoniousness, platitudes. **2** (*underworld cant*) jargon, lingo, patter, argot, slang, vernacular.

cant[2] *noun* **1** (*the floor is on a cant*) inclination, slope, slant, tilt, angle.
➤ *verb* incline, lean, slope, slant, tilt, tip.

cantankerous *adj* irritable, irascible, testy, crabbed, crabby, bad-tempered, grumpy, grouchy (*inf*), crotchety (*inf*), crusty, peppery, choleric, ill-humoured, peevish, touchy, captious, difficult, cranky (*inf*), perverse, contrary, quarrelsome, argumentative. OPPOSITE: affable.

canteen *noun* cafeteria, snack bar, restaurant, dining room.

canter *verb* amble, trot, jog, lope, gallop.

canticle *noun* hymn, song, psalm, poem.

canvas *noun* sailcloth, tarpaulin, ticking, drill.

canvass *verb* **1** (*canvassing for the Conservatives*) electioneer, campaign, solicit votes, drum up support. **2** (*canvass 500 of our readers*) poll, survey, ask, inquire. **3** (*canvass public opinion*) examine, scrutinize, analyse, sift, study, investigate, look into, inquire into, explore. **4** (*ideas canvassed at the conference*) debate, discuss, dispute, air.
➤ *noun* poll, survey, study, investigation, examination, scrutiny.

canyon *noun* ravine, gully, gulch, gorge, valley, chasm, abyss, gulf.

cap *noun* **1** (*with a cap on his head*) hat, headgear, bonnet, skullcap, baseball cap, beret, tam-o'-shanter. **2** (*put the cap on the bottle*) lid, top, cover, stopper. **3** (*snow on the mountain caps*) top, peak, pinnacle, summit, apex, acme, crest. OPPOSITE: foot.
➤ *verb* **1** (*mountains capped with snow*) top, crown, surmount, overspread, cover, coat, blanket. **2** (*cap her previous record*) surpass, exceed, excel, transcend, outshine, eclipse, outdo, outstrip, beat, better. **3** (*the rates have been capped*) restrict, limit, curb, restrain. **4** (*a treaty that capped months of negotiations*) complete, perfect, consummate, round off.
to cap it all as a finishing touch, as the last straw, on top of everything else.

capability *noun* ability, capacity, faculty, means, potential, power, competence, proficiency, adeptness, skilfulness, skill, facility, aptitude, qualification, experience, talent, gift, knack, flair, cleverness, intelligence, efficiency, effectiveness. OPPOSITE: inability.

capable *adj* able, competent, proficient, accomplished, adept, skilful, practised, experienced, qualified, talented, gifted, clever, intelligent, efficient, effective, adequate. OPPOSITE: incompetent.
capable of inclined to, disposed to, prone to, apt to, likely to, liable to, fitted to, suited to.

capacious *adj* spacious, roomy, commodious, ample, wide, broad, big, large, substantial, huge, vast, immense, voluminous, extensive, comprehensive, generous, liberal. OPPOSITE: small.

capacitate *verb* enable, empower, qualify, entitle, authorize, sanction. OPPOSITE: prevent.

capacity *noun* **1** (*the capacity of the tank*) volume, dimensions, proportions, size, magnitude, amplitude, space, room, scope, extent, range, compass. **2** (*her capacity to work under pressure*) ability, capability, faculty, power, potential, facility, aptitude, talent, gift, skill, intelligence, cleverness, competence, proficiency. OPPOSITE: inability. **3** (*in my capacity as head of department*) position, office, post, appointment, function, role, job, sphere, province, duty, service.

cape[1] *noun* (*wearing a fur-trimmed cape*) cloak, mantle, shawl, wrap, poncho, pelerine, pelisse.

cape[2] *noun* (*sailed round the cape*) headland, head, ness, mull, promontory, point, tongue, peninsula.

caper *verb* frolic, frisk, gambol, romp, hop, skip, jump, leap, bound, spring, dance, cavort, prance.
➤ *noun* **1** (*have a caper in the field*) frolic, romp, gambol, hop, skip, jump, leap, bound, spring, prance. **2** (*another of his little capers*) prank, practical joke, trick, stunt, antic, escapade, sport, game, jest, jape, lark.

capital *adj* **1** (*of capital importance*) principal, chief, main, key, leading, first, primary, foremost, cardinal, paramount, prime, major, crucial, vital, central, pivotal. OPPOSITE: minor. **2** (*a capital offence*) serious, grave, fatal. **3** (*a capital idea*) excellent, first rate, first class, super (*inf*), splendid, fine, superb, outstanding. OPPOSITE: poor.
➤ *noun* **1** (*capital to set up a business*) money, cash, finance, funds, assets, resources, reserves, investments, savings, stock, principal, wherewithal, means, wealth, property. **2** (*written in capitals*) capital letter, block letter, upper-case letter, majuscule, uncial. **3** (*the capital of Spain*) seat of government, administrative centre.

capitalism *noun* private enterprise, private ownership, free enterprise, laissez-faire.

capitalist *noun* financier, investor, banker, tycoon, mogul, plutocrat, fat cat (*sl*).

capitalize *verb* finance, fund, back, sponsor.
capitalize on take advantage of, profit from, turn to account, cash in on (*inf*), exploit, make the most of, realize.

capitulate *verb* surrender, yield, submit, succumb, give in, give up, throw in the towel (*inf*), throw in the sponge (*inf*), back down, relent, accede, acquiesce. OPPOSITE: resist.

capitulation *noun* surrender, yielding, submission, acquiescence. OPPOSITE: resistance.

caprice *noun* whim, whimsy, vagary, impulse, fancy, notion, humour, fad, crotchet, freak, quirk, fickleness, inconstancy.

capricious *adj* fickle, inconstant, unstable, changeable, variable, unpredictable, mercurial, volatile, impulsive, whimsical, fanciful, faddish, freakish, wayward, odd, quirky, erratic, fitful, irresolute, uncertain. OPPOSITE: steady.

capsize *verb* overturn, upturn, upend, invert, upset, knock over, tip over, turn over, keel over, turn turtle.

capsule *noun* **1** (*drugs in capsule form*) lozenge, tablet, pill, bolus. **2** (*seed capsules*) case, sheath, covering, shell, pod, vessel, receptacle. **3** (*a space capsule*) craft, probe, compartment, section.

captain *noun* commander, leader, head, chief, pilot, skipper, master, boss (*inf*), number one (*inf*).

caption *noun* title, heading, head, legend, inscription, explanation, gloss, note, comment.

captious *adj* carping, cavilling, quibbling, censorious, fault-finding, critical, hypercritical, nit-picking (*inf*). OPPOSITE: appreciative.

captivate *verb* fascinate, charm, enchant, bewitch, beguile, enthral, entrance, attract, allure, seduce, win, enamour, infatuate, delight, enrapture, ravish, transport, dazzle, hypnotize, mesmerize. OPPOSITE: repel.

captivating *adj* fascinating, charming, enchanting, enthralling, attractive, alluring, seductive, winning, delightful, ravishing, dazzling. OPPOSITE: repulsive.

captive *noun* prisoner, hostage, convict, jailbird, detainee, internee, slave, bondsman.
➤ *adj* captured, in captivity, imprisoned, incarcerated, locked up, detained, interned, confined, restricted, restrained, caged, penned up, enslaved, in bondage. OPPOSITE: free.

captivity *noun* imprisonment, incarceration, confinement, custody, detention, internment, restraint, constraint, duress, bondage, slavery, enslavement, servitude, subjection, thraldom. OPPOSITE: freedom.

capture *verb* catch, take, seize, nab (*inf*), collar (*inf*), arrest, apprehend, nick (*inf*), detain, take into custody, take prisoner, trap, entrap, ensnare, net, bag (*inf*). OPPOSITE: release.
➤ *noun* catching, taking, seizure, arrest, apprehension, detention, imprisonment, incarceration. OPPOSITE: release.

car *noun* automobile, motor car, motor, jalopy (*inf*), banger (*inf*), vehicle, wheels (*inf*), limousine, limo (*inf*).

carafe *noun* flask, decanter, bottle, flagon, jug, pitcher.

caravan *noun* **1** (*a car towing a caravan*) mobile home, camper, trailer, van, wagon, cart. **2** (*a caravan crossing the desert*) convoy, procession, cavalcade, troop, band, group, company.

carcass *noun* **1** (*the carcass of a deer*) corpse, body, dead body, cadaver, remains. **2** (*the carcass of the ship*) structure, framework, skeleton, hulk, shell.

card *noun* **1** (*made of thin card*) cardboard, pasteboard. **2** (*send him a card*) postcard, greetings card. **3** (*she gave me her card*) business card, calling card, identification card.
on the cards possible, likely, probable, in the air, in the wind.

cardinal *adj* principal, chief, main, key, capital, vital, crucial, essential, fundamental, basic, central, pivotal, primary, first, leading, foremost, prime, paramount, major, important. OPPOSITE: secondary.

care *noun* **1** (*help him forget his cares*) concern, anxiety, worry, disquiet, unease, trouble, affliction, distress, sorrow, grief, woe, hardship, tribulation, pressure, stress, strain, burden, responsibility. OPPOSITE: joy. **2** (*handle the china with care*) carefulness, attention, heed, regard, consideration, thought, conscientiousness, diligence, pains, meticulousness, accuracy, precision. OPPOSITE: carelessness. **3** (*take care on the icy roads*) caution, wariness, prudence, circumspection, forethought, watchfulness, vigilance, heedfulness, mindfulness, attention, alertness, awareness. **4** (*in the care of my aunt*) custody, guardianship, wardship, protection, safekeeping, keeping, charge, management, control, supervision. **5** (*showed no care for our feelings*) regard, consideration, thoughtfulness, interest, concern, solicitude, sympathy, understanding. OPPOSITE: disregard. **6** (*the care of young children*) looking after, tending, attention, minding, supervision. OPPOSITE: neglect.
➤ *verb* worry, be concerned, be interested, bother, trouble, mind, give a damn (*sl*), give a hang (*inf*), give a toss (*inf*), give a monkey's (*sl*).

care for 1 (*caring for the sick*) tend, nurse, minister to, attend to, mind, look after, watch, supervise, take care of, protect. OPPOSITE: neglect. **2** (*I don't care for jazz*) like, enjoy, be fond of, love, cherish, treasure. OPPOSITE: hate. **3** (*would you care for a drink?*) want, desire, wish for, long for, like, fancy.

career *noun* **1** (*a career in medicine*) calling, vocation, profession, work, occupation, job, trade, métier, business, livelihood. **2** (*the next stage in his military career*) progress, progression, path, course, passage. **3** (*a wild career through the streets*) rush, dash, run, race, bolt.
➤ *verb* rush, dash, hurtle, run, speed, race, tear, bolt, shoot. OPPOSITE: dawdle.

carefree *adj* cheerful, light-hearted, happy, merry, cheery, unworried, untroubled, unconcerned, happy-go-lucky, easygoing (*inf*), laid back (*inf*), nonchalant, insouciant, breezy, airy, blithe, buoyant, jaunty, upbeat (*inf*). OPPOSITE: anxious.

careful *adj* **1** (*be careful on the icy roads*) cautious, wary, chary, prudent, circumspect, judicious, vigilant, watchful, heedful, mindful, alert, aware. OPPOSITE: reckless. **2** (*after careful consideration*) attentive, thoughtful, conscientious, diligent, assiduous, painstaking, meticulous, scrupulous, punctilious, thorough, methodical, systematic, precise, accurate. OPPOSITE: careless. **3** (*people who need careful handling*) tactful, discreet, thoughtful, considerate, solicitous, attentive, concerned. OPPOSITE: thoughtless. **4** (*careful with her money*) thrifty, economical, frugal, sparing. OPPOSITE: extravagant.

careless *adj* **1** (*a careless driver*) negligent, remiss, irresponsible, heedless, unmindful, thoughtless, unthinking, forgetful, absentminded, inattentive, imprudent, foolish, rash, reckless. OPPOSITE: prudent. **2** (*careless work*) neglectful, slipshod, slapdash, hasty, cursory, perfunctory, untidy, disorderly, slovenly, sloppy (*inf*), messy (*inf*), disorganized, unsystematic, inaccurate. OPPOSITE: careful. **3** (*a careless remark*) tactless, indiscreet, insensitive, thoughtless, unthinking, unguarded, offhand, throwaway. **4** (*careless of the consequences*) indifferent, uncaring, unconcerned, untroubled, unworried, nonchalant, insouciant, casual, lackadaisical. OPPOSITE: concerned. **5** (*with careless grace*) artless, unstudied, natural, simple, spontaneous, carefree, happy-go-lucky. OPPOSITE: studied.

carelessness *noun* **1** (*accidents caused by carelessness*) inattention, neglect, negligence, heedlessness, thoughtlessness, imprudence, rashness, recklessness. OPPOSITE: care. **2** (*carelessness in their work*) untidiness, slovenliness, sloppiness (*inf*), disorganization, inaccuracy. OPPOSITE: carefulness.

caress *noun* stroke, fondle, pat, touch, slap and tickle (*inf*), cuddle, hug, embrace, kiss.
➤ *verb* stroke, fondle, pet, pat, touch, grope (*inf*), cuddle, hug, embrace, kiss.

caretaker *noun* janitor, curator, custodian, keeper, warden, porter, doorkeeper, concierge, steward.

careworn *adj* tired, weary, worn out, gaunt, haggard, troubled, anxious.

cargo *noun* load, lading, freight, consignment, shipment, goods, merchandise, contents, shipload, truckload.

caricature *noun* cartoon, lampoon, burlesque, satire, parody, take-off (*inf*), send-up (*inf*), spoof (*inf*), travesty, distortion, exaggeration, representation, imitation, mimicry.
➤ *verb* lampoon, burlesque, satirize, parody, mock, ridicule, take off (*inf*), send up (*inf*), distort, exaggerate, represent, mimic.

carnage *noun* slaughter, massacre, butchery, bloodbath, bloodshed, mass murder, holocaust, pogrom.

carnal *adj* sexual, sensual, voluptuous, erotic, licentious, lascivious, prurient, salacious, lubricious, lewd, lecherous, lustful, libidinous, wanton, impure, base, coarse, gross, fleshly, physical, bodily, corporeal, human, animal, natural. OPPOSITE: spiritual.

carnality *noun* sexuality, sensuality, voluptuousness, licentiousness, lasciviousness, prurience, salaciousness, lewdness, lechery, lust, baseness, coarseness, physicality, corporeality. OPPOSITE: chastity.

carnival *noun* festival, fête, fair, gala, jamboree, fiesta, masquerade, Mardi Gras, celebration, festivity, revel, merrymaking, revelry.

carol *noun* song, hymn, canticle, Christmas song, noel, chorus, ditty, lay.
➤ *verb* sing, chant, wassail, troll, chorus, warble, trill.

carousal *noun* revel, revelry, party, rave-up (*inf*), celebration, merrymaking, spree, binge (*inf*), bacchanalia, booze-up (*inf*), bender (*inf*), debauch, orgy, saturnalia.

carouse *verb* revel, roister, wassail, party, celebrate, make merry, live it up (*inf*), go on a spree, paint the town red (*inf*), drink, imbibe, booze (*inf*), go on a bender (*inf*).

carp *verb* complain, cavil, censure, criticize, find fault, pick holes, quibble, nit-pick (*inf*), nag, reproach. OPPOSITE: praise.

carpenter *noun* joiner, woodworker, cabinetmaker.

carpet *noun* 1 (*a carpet for the lounge*) rug, mat, runner, fitted carpet, carpeting, matting. 2 (*a carpet of bluebells*) covering, layer, blanket, mantle, expanse.
➤ *verb* cover, blanket, mantle, overlay, overspread.

carping *adj* cavilling, critical, fault-finding, captious, censorious, hypercritical, quibbling, nit-picking (*inf*), hard to please. OPPOSITE: appreciative.

carriage *noun* 1 (*horse and carriage*) vehicle, conveyance, coach, cab, car, gig, fly, landau, phaeton, trap, chariot, wagon, dray. 2 (*the upright carriage of a soldier*) posture, bearing, demeanour, mien, air, deportment, conduct, behaviour. 3 (*the price includes carriage*) carrying, conveyance, transport, transportation, freight, delivery.

carrier *noun* 1 (*the carrier of the goods*) bearer, porter, transporter, haulier, messenger, runner, courier, delivery service. 2 (*carriers of the disease*) vector, transmitter, bearer, conveyor, vehicle.

carry *verb* 1 (*carry a bag*) bear, take, transport, convey, haul, lug (*inf*), hump (*inf*), cart (*inf*), tote (*inf*), transmit, conduct, relay, transfer, move, shift, bring, fetch. OPPOSITE: drop. 2 (*will it carry our weight?*) support, sustain, hold up, bear, shoulder, maintain, uphold. 3 (*they carry a good range of wines*) sell, stock, have, offer. 4 (*carry the day*) win, secure, gain, accomplish, effect. OPPOSITE: lose. 5 (*sound carries a long way*) extend, reach, spread. 6 (*a speech that carried the crowd*) affect, influence, spur, stimulate, motivate, impel, drive, urge, propel. 7 (*the motion was carried*) pass, accept, adopt, ratify. 8 (*newspapers that carried the story*) print, publish, release, broadcast, communicate, contain, cover.

carry on 1 (*carry on working*) continue, go on, keep on, persist, persevere, keep going, restart, resume. OPPOSITE: stop. 2 (*carry on a business*) conduct, run, administer, manage, operate. 3 (*carrying on with his wife's best friend*) have an affair, commit adultery, be involved. 4 (*stop carrying on!*) make a fuss, create (*inf*), misbehave, play up (*inf*), mess around (*inf*).

carry oneself hold oneself, bear oneself, deport oneself, comport oneself, conduct oneself

carry out 1 (*carry out a threat*) effect, implement, discharge, fulfil, complete, accomplish, achieve, realize. 2 (*carry out an investigation*) conduct, perform, execute, make, do.

cart *noun* barrow, wheelbarrow, handcart, wagon, dray, vehicle, carriage.
➤ *verb* carry, transport, convey, haul, lug (*inf*), hump (*inf*), tote (*inf*), bear, move, shift.

carton *noun* box, packet, pack, case, container, package.

cartoon *noun* 1 (*children's cartoons*) animation, animated film, comic strip. 2 (*a political cartoon*) caricature, lampoon, burlesque, parody, satire, spoof (*inf*). 3 (*cartoons for famous paintings*) sketch, drawing, draft, plan.

cartridge *noun* case, container, cassette, magazine, shell, capsule, cylinder, tube.

carve *verb* 1 (*carve wood*) cut, chisel, whittle, hew, sculpt, sculpture, fashion, shape, form, mould. 2 (*carve an inscription*) incise, engrave, etch, cut in. 3 (*carve meat*) slice, cut up, divide, chop.

carve up divide, subdivide, partition, share out, parcel out, split up, separate.

carving *noun* sculpture, statue, model, relief, etching, engraving, incision.

cascade *noun* waterfall, falls, cataract, chute, fountain, shower, torrent, deluge, flood, avalanche, outpouring, rush, gush.
➤ *verb* fall, tumble, descend, plunge, pour, shower, spill, overflow, gush, rush, surge.

case[1] *noun* 1 (*the case in point*) instance, occurrence, occasion, example, illustration, specimen. 2 (*if this is the case*) situation, state, circumstance, condition, position, predicament, plight. 3 (*in any case*) event, occurrence, contingency, situation, circumstance, context. 4 (*hear a case in court*) action, suit, lawsuit, dispute, cause, trial, process, proceedings, statement, testimony, evidence, claim, plea. 5 (*made out a good case for reform*) argument, presentation, exposition, thesis. 6 (*treatment for more serious cases*) patient, invalid, sufferer, victim.

case[2] *noun* 1 (*a case of books*) box, crate, trunk, carton, pack, chest, casket, coffer, cabinet, cupboard. 2 (*pack your cases*) suitcase, valise, portmanteau, holdall, grip, bag, item of luggage, piece of baggage, trunk, briefcase, portfolio. 3 (*a pencil case*) container, receptacle, holder. 4 (*in a protective case*) casing, housing, covering, sheath, integument, husk, shell, pod, capsule, cartridge, envelope, wrapper, jacket, cover.

cash *noun* 1 (*pay in cash*) coin, specie, currency, legal tender, change, coins, banknotes, ready money, ready cash, readies (*inf*). 2 (*short of cash*) money, dosh (*sl*), dough (*sl*), bread (*sl*), lolly (*inf*), brass (*inf*), funds, finance, capital, resources, means, wherewithal.

⮞ *verb* encash, change, exchange, liquidate, realize.

cashier[1] *noun* (*pay the cashier*) clerk, bank clerk, teller, bursar, purser, treasurer, accountant, banker.

cashier[2] *verb* (*cashiered from the army*) dismiss, discharge, expel, drum out, throw out, kick out (*inf*), boot out (*inf*), reject, discard, get rid of.

casino *noun* gaming house, gambling club, gambling den.

cask *noun* barrel, tun, keg, vat, firkin, hogshead, butt, vessel, container.

casket *noun* **1** (*a jewel casket*) box, chest, coffer, case, receptacle, container. **2** (*a burial casket*) coffin, sarcophagus, box (*inf*), wooden overcoat (*sl*).

cast *verb* **1** (*cast a stone*) throw, fling, toss, pitch, sling, hurl, shy, chuck, lob, launch, send, drive, thrust, impel. **2** (*cast light*) emit, give off, radiate, diffuse, spread, scatter, distribute, direct, project, send out. OPPOSITE: absorb. **3** (*cast doubt*) put, place, bestow, confer, impart. **4** (*cast in bronze*) mould, found, shape, form, fashion, model, sculpt. **5** (*snakes cast their skin*) shed, drop, throw off, slough off, discard, get rid of. OPPOSITE: retain. **6** (*cast a vote*) enter, record, register. **7** (*cast a set of figures*) compute, calculate, reckon, add, sum, total.
⮞ *noun* **1** (*the cast of the film*) actors, players, performers, characters, dramatis personae, company, troupe. **2** (*a plaster cast*) casting, mould, shape, form, figure. **3** (*the cast of his features*) turn, stamp, kind, sort, style, look, air, manner, bearing, mien, demeanour. **4** (*the cast of the dice*) throw, fling, toss, pitch, lob, launch, thrust. **5** (*with a silvery cast*) tinge, shade, tone, touch, trace, suggestion, hint.

cast about hunt, look, search, grope.

cast down depress, deject, sadden, dispirit, dishearten, discourage, crush. OPPOSITE: cheer up.

castaway *noun* outcast, exile, discard, cast-off.
⮞ *adj* shipwrecked, marooned, stranded, adrift, discarded, rejected.

caste *noun* class, group, order, rank, grade, status, position, station, place, estate, race.

castigate *verb* chastise, rebuke, reprimand, chide, scold, admonish, take to task, upbraid, berate, reprove, reproach, censure, dress down (*inf*), tear a strip off (*inf*), haul over the coals (*inf*), correct, chasten, discipline, punish, beat, thrash. OPPOSITE: praise.

castigation *noun* chastisement, rebuke, reprimand, scolding, upbraiding, censure, dressing-down (*inf*), bollocking (*sl*), correction, discipline, punishment, beating, thrashing. OPPOSITE: praise.

castle *noun* citadel, fortress, stronghold, keep, palace, mansion, château, stately home.

castrate *verb* geld, emasculate, neuter, spay.

castration *noun* gelding, emasculation, orchidectomy, oophorectomy.

casual *adj* **1** (*a casual occurrence*) accidental, chance, fortuitous, serendipitous, unexpected, unforeseen, unplanned, incidental, contingent, haphazard, random. OPPOSITE: deliberate. **2** (*casual clothes*) informal, unceremonious, relaxed, comfortable, leisure. OPPOSITE: formal. **3** (*a casual remark*) offhand, throwaway, spontaneous, impromptu. **4** (*a casual attitude*) nonchalant, insouciant, happy-go-lucky, easygoing (*inf*), laid back (*inf*), blasé, offhand, lackadaisical, indifferent, unconcerned, uncaring, couldn't-care-less (*inf*), apathetic, lukewarm. **5** (*a casual glance at the letter*) cursory, perfunctory, desultory, superficial, hasty. OPPOSITE: thorough. **6** (*casual work*) part-time, short-term, temporary, provisional, occasional, intermittent, irregular. OPPOSITE: permanent.

casualty *noun* victim, sufferer, loser, injury, fatality, death, loss, injured person, wounded person, missing person, dead person.

casuistry *noun* sophistry, sophism, speciousness, quibbling, equivocation, subtlety, chicanery.

cat *noun* feline, tabby, tom, puss (*inf*), pussy (*inf*), moggy (*inf*), mouser, kitten.

cataclysm *noun* upheaval, convulsion, catastrophe, disaster, calamity, debacle, deluge, flood, avalanche, earthquake.

catacomb *noun* crypt, vault, tomb, sepulchre, ossuary, underground cemetery, tunnel, passage, underground labyrinth.

catalogue *noun* list, inventory, schedule, register, roll, record, table, classification, file, index, directory, guide, brochure, prospectus.
⮞ *verb* list, index, record, register, classify, categorize, file, alphabetize.

catapult *noun* sling, ballista, trebuchet.
⮞ *verb* propel, shoot, launch, hurl, pitch, fling.

cataract *noun* cascade, waterfall, falls, rapids, torrent, downpour, deluge, flood.

catastrophe *noun* disaster, calamity, cataclysm, blow, reverse, mishap, misfortune, affliction, adversity, trouble, distress, tragedy, trial, tribulation, failure, ruin, fiasco, flop (*inf*). OPPOSITE: triumph.

catastrophic *adj* disastrous, calamitous, cataclysmic, devastating, ruinous, dire, terrible, dreadful, awful, distressing, tragic, fatal.

catcall *noun* boo, hiss, whistle, jeer, raspberry (*inf*), the bird (*inf*).

catch *verb* **1** (*catch a ball*) take, seize, snatch, grab, grasp, grip, clutch, hold, intercept, receive, acquire. OPPOSITE: drop. **2** (*catch a bird*) capture, snare, ensnare, trap, entrap, entangle, hook, net, corner, round up, arrest, apprehend, nab (*inf*), collar (*inf*). OPPOSITE: release. **3** (*catch the culprit*) discover, find out, detect, expose, unmask, surprise, startle. **4** (*catch a disease*) contract, develop, get, pick up, go down with (*inf*), come down with (*inf*), succumb to. **5** (*I didn't catch that last remark*) hear, discern, perceive, make out, take in, grasp, understand, comprehend, fathom, twig (*inf*), follow, get the drift of (*inf*). OPPOSITE: miss. **6** (*it caught their attention*) attract, draw, hold, grasp, captivate, fascinate, charm, enchant, bewitch. OPPOSITE: repel.
⮞ *noun* **1** (*undo the catch*) clasp, fastener, fastening, clip, hook, hasp, bolt, lock, latch, snib. **2** (*what's the catch?*) snag, drawback, disadvantage, fly in the ointment (*inf*), stumbling block, obstacle, hitch, problem, trap, trick. **3** (*today's catch of fish*) take, haul (*inf*), bag, net, trophy, prize.

catch on 1 (*the craze didn't catch on*) become popular, become fashionable, become trendy (*inf*), become all the rage (*inf*). **2** (*she caught on at last*) understand, comprehend, see the light, get the picture (*inf*), latch on (*inf*), twig (*inf*).

catch up gain on, reach, draw level with, overtake, pass.

catching *adj* **1** (*the disease is not catching*) infectious, contagious, communicable, transmittable, transmissible. **2** (*a catching smile*) charming, enchanting, captivating, fascinating, bewitching, alluring, attractive, appealing, fetching, taking, winning. OPPOSITE: repulsive.

catchword *noun* slogan, motto, byword, watchword, password, shibboleth, formula, catchphrase, cliché, saying, refrain.

catchy *adj* haunting, memorable, unforgettable, tuneful, melodious, melodic, singable, popular, attractive, appealing. OPPOSITE: forgettable.

catechism *noun* interrogation, questioning, examination, drill, instruction.

catechize *verb* interrogate, question, quiz, pump (*inf*), cross-examine, grill (*inf*), give the third degree (*inf*), examine, test, drill.

categorical *adj* positive, definite, emphatic, unqualified, unconditional, unreserved, absolute, total, utter, downright, direct, express, explicit, plain, unequivocal, unambiguous. OPPOSITE: tentative.

categorize *verb* class, classify, group, break down, pigeonhole, stereotype, sort, rank, grade, order, list, catalogue, tabulate, arrange.

category *noun* class, classification, grouping, group, division, section, heading, title, list, listing, order, grade, rank, sort, kind, type, genre, variety.

cater *verb* provision, victual, feed.
cater for serve, provide for, supply, satisfy.
cater to indulge, humour, gratify, oblige, pander to.

caterwaul *verb* yell, howl, yowl, scream, screech, shriek, bawl, wail, cry.

catharsis *noun* purification, cleansing, depuration, lustration, purging, purgation, release, abreaction.

cathartic *adj* purifying, cleansing, purgative, abreactive.

catholic *adj* **1** (*of catholic appeal*) general, universal, worldwide, global, comprehensive, all-inclusive, all-embracing, all-encompassing, eclectic, broad, wide. OPPOSITE: narrow. **2** (*with catholic views*) liberal, tolerant, broad-minded, open-minded, unbiased, unbigoted. OPPOSITE: bigoted.

cattle *pl noun* cows, bulls, livestock, stock, animals, beasts.

catty *adj* spiteful, malicious, nasty, snide, bitchy (*inf*), venomous, malevolent, mean, ill-natured. OPPOSITE: kind.

caucus *noun* **1** (*a right-wing caucus*) group, faction, cabal, set, clique, coterie. **2** (*attending the caucus*) meeting, gathering, assembly, conference, convention, conclave, parley.

cauldron *noun* pot, kettle, boiler, copper, vat.

cause *noun* **1** (*the cause of our problems*) source, origin, root, spring, beginning, genesis, originator, prime mover, agent, factor, creator, maker, producer, author. OPPOSITE: effect. **2** (*no cause for concern*) reason, basis,

justification, grounds, occasion, call, motive, inducement, incentive. **3** (*a worthy cause*) principle, ideal, conviction, belief, movement, enterprise, undertaking, purpose, object, objective, aim, end. **4** (*pleading her cause*) case, suit, lawsuit, action.
» *verb* **1** (*cause a riot*) occasion, bring about, engender, generate, originate, create, produce, effect, precipitate, provoke, trigger off, start, begin, give rise to, lead to, result in. **2** (*cause them to retreat*) force, compel, constrain, induce, make.

caustic *adj* **1** (*caustic chemicals*) corrosive, burning, mordant, acid, pungent, acrid, astringent. **2** (*caustic remarks*) biting, cutting, trenchant, mordant, sharp, keen, stinging, scathing, sarcastic, acrimonious, bitter, virulent. OPPOSITE: mild.

cauterize *verb* burn, sear, scorch, singe.

caution *noun* **1** (*proceed with caution*) care, carefulness, wariness, vigilance, watchfulness, attention, heed, heedfulness, prudence, circumspection, discretion. OPPOSITE: rashness. **2** (*let them off with a caution*) admonition, warning, advice, counsel, injunction.
» *verb* warn, forewarn, alert, tip off (*inf*), admonish, advise, counsel, urge, enjoin.

cautious *adj* careful, wary, chary, softly-softly (*inf*), vigilant, watchful, alert, heedful, prudent, circumspect, judicious, discreet, guarded, cagey (*inf*). OPPOSITE: rash.

cavalcade *noun* procession, parade, march, cortege, retinue, train, column, file, caravan.

cavalier *noun* **1** (*ladies with their cavaliers*) courtier, gentleman, gallant, escort, beau. **2** (*riding with the cavaliers*) knight, horseman, equestrian, chevalier.
» *adj* arrogant, haughty, lofty, proud, supercilious, patronizing, condescending, disdainful, contemptuous, insolent, offhand, casual. OPPOSITE: meek.

cavalry *noun* mounted soldiers, horsemen, horse, dragoons, lancers, hussars.

cave *noun* cavern, grotto, hollow, cavity, pothole, tunnel, dugout, den, cellar.

caveat *noun* warning, caution, admonition, alarm.

cavern *noun* cave, grotto, underground chamber.

cavernous *adj* hollow, concave, sunken, depressed, gaping, yawning, huge, vast, deep, unfathomable, echoing, resonant.

cavil *verb* carp, object, complain, quibble, nit-pick (*inf*), criticize, find fault, censure. OPPOSITE: praise.
» *noun* objection, complaint, quibble, criticism, censure.

cavilling *adj* carping, captious, quibbling, hypercritical, nit-picking (*inf*), critical, fault-finding, censorious. OPPOSITE: appreciative.

cavity *noun* hole, hollow, pit, crater, gap, orifice, aperture.

cease *verb* **1** (*cease fighting*) stop, end, finish, terminate, conclude, discontinue, break off, suspend, halt, desist from, refrain from, leave off, quit (*inf*), pack in (*inf*). OPPOSITE: start. **2** (*the noise finally ceased*) stop, end, finish, terminate, conclude, halt, let up, abate, peter out (*inf*), fizzle out (*inf*). OPPOSITE: begin.

ceaseless *adj* unceasing, incessant, constant, unremitting, continuous, uninterrupted, nonstop, endless, unending, never-ending, interminable, continual, perpetual, eternal, everlasting. OPPOSITE: intermittent.

cede *verb* yield, surrender, give up, relinquish, renounce, abandon, abdicate, resign, transfer, hand over, turn over, make over, convey, give, grant, allow, concede. OPPOSITE: retain.

ceiling *noun* **1** (*the ceiling of the chapel*) roof, vault, dome, rafters, awning, canopy. OPPOSITE: floor. **2** (*a ceiling on pay rises*) limit, upper limit, maximum, cut-off point.

celebrate *verb* **1** (*celebrate Christmas*) observe, keep, mark, remember, commemorate, honour, toast, drink to. OPPOSITE: ignore. **2** (*celebrating after their victory*) rejoice, exult, put the flags out (*inf*), make merry, party, revel, have a ball (*inf*), whoop it up (*inf*), go on a spree, go on the razzle (*inf*), paint the town red (*inf*). **3** (*celebrate the Eucharist*) perform, solemnize, bless. **4** (*celebrating the glory of nature*) praise, laud, extol, eulogize, exalt, glorify, proclaim, announce, make known, broadcast, advertise.

celebrated *adj* famous, famed, well-known, distinguished, eminent, illustrious, notable, noted, acclaimed, renowned, prominent, outstanding, great, legendary, revered, popular. OPPOSITE: unknown.

celebration *noun* **1** (*celebrations at the end of term*) festivity, party, bash (*inf*), rave-up (*inf*), revelry, merrymaking, jollification, junketing, carousal, festival, fête, gala, carnival. **2** (*the celebration of Christmas*) commemoration, remembrance, observance, anniversary. **3** (*the celebration of the Eucharist*) ceremony, rite, performance, solemnization.

celebrity *noun* **1** (*visiting celebrities*) star, superstar, personality, famous person, somebody, personage, dignitary, VIP, bigwig (*inf*), big shot (*inf*), notable, worthy, luminary, name, big name (*inf*), household name, living legend, legend in one's own lifetime, hero, heroine, idol, lion. OPPOSITE: nobody. **2** (*achieve celebrity*) fame, renown, note, distinction, eminence, illustriousness, glory, honour, acclaim, reputation, repute, prestige, prominence, popularity, stardom. OPPOSITE: ignominy.

celerity *noun* speed, swiftness, fleetness, rapidity, quickness, promptness, haste, dispatch, expedition, velocity, pace. OPPOSITE: slowness.

celestial *adj* **1** (*celestial beings*) ethereal, empyrean, heavenly, divine, godly, godlike, angelic, seraphic, cherubic, immortal, eternal, spiritual, transcendental, supernatural. OPPOSITE: earthly. **2** (*celestial bodies*) heavenly, astral, stellar, extraterrestrial. OPPOSITE: terrestrial.

celibacy *noun* abstinence, self-denial, self-restraint, continence, chastity, purity, virginity, singleness, bachelorhood, spinsterhood, asceticism, monasticism.

celibate *adj* abstinent, continent, chaste, pure, virginal, single, unmarried.
➤ *noun* virgin, ascetic, monk, nun, bachelor, spinster, single person.

cell *noun* **1** (*a prison cell*) room, chamber, cubicle, compartment, stall, dungeon, lock-up. **2** (*the cells of a honeycomb*) recess, cavity, hole, compartment. **3** (*a*

terrorist cell) nucleus, unit, section, group, faction, clique, coterie, set.

cellar *noun* basement, vault, crypt, storeroom. OPPOSITE: attic.

cement *verb* unite, join, connect, attach, affix, cleave, cohere, bind, stick, glue, gum, paste, bond, solder, weld. OPPOSITE: separate.
➤ *noun* mortar, plaster, grouting, concrete, adhesive, glue, gum, paste, sealant, bonding.

cemetery *noun* graveyard, burial ground, necropolis, churchyard, God's acre.

cenotaph *noun* monument, memorial, shrine.

censor *verb* cut, delete, expurgate, bowdlerize, edit, blue-pencil.
➤ *noun* inspector, examiner, editor, expurgator, bowdlerizer.

censorious *adj* critical, fault-finding, captious, carping, cavilling, disapproving, disparaging, deprecatory, condemnatory, denunciatory. OPPOSITE: complimentary.

censurable *adj* blamable, blameworthy, at fault, guilty, culpable, reproachable, reprehensible. OPPOSITE: blameless.

censure *noun* criticize, blame, condemn, denounce, disapprove, reprehend, reprove, rebuke, reproach, reprimand, admonish, chide, scold, castigate, upbraid, berate, haul over the coals (*inf*). OPPOSITE: praise.
➤ *noun* criticism, blame, condemnation, denunciation, stricture, obloquy, disapproval, disapprobation, reprehension, reproof, rebuke, reproach, reprimand, admonition, chiding, scolding, castigation. OPPOSITE: approval.

central *adj* **1** (*a central line*) middle, mid, median, medial, inner, interior. OPPOSITE: outer. **2** (*of central importance*) focal, pivotal, core, crucial, key, chief, cardinal, principal, main, essential, fundamental, basic, primary, foremost, prime, major. OPPOSITE: peripheral.

centralize *verb* concentrate, focus, centre, converge, collect, consolidate, amalgamate, compact, condense, unify, rationalize, streamline. OPPOSITE: decentralize.

centre *adj* middle, midpoint, focus, focal point, hub, pivot, linchpin, midst, core, heart, kernel, nucleus. OPPOSITE: edge.
➤ *verb* focus, converge, gravitate, concentrate, hinge, pivot, revolve.

century *noun* hundred years, centenary, centennial, era, period, age.

ceramics *noun* pottery, earthenware, faience, china, porcelain, ware.

cereal *noun* grain, corn, crop, seed, meal.

ceremonial *adj* formal, official, ritual, ritualistic, solemn, stately, imposing, dignified, majestic, liturgical, sacramental. OPPOSITE: informal.
➤ *noun* ceremony, ritual, rite, liturgy, sacrament, solemnity, formality, protocol, etiquette, custom, tradition.

ceremonious *adj* precise, punctilious, scrupulous, exact, just-so (*inf*), formal, stiff, starchy (*inf*), courteous, deferential, civil, polite. OPPOSITE: unceremonious.

ceremony *noun* **1** (*during the ceremony*) ritual, rite, ceremonial, observance, commemoration, service, liturgy, sacrament, festival, celebration, parade, pageant, show. **2** (*behave with ceremony*) formality, pomp, pageantry, stateliness, protocol, etiquette, form, decorum, propriety, punctilio. OPPOSITE: informality.

certain *adj* **1** (*are you certain?*) sure, positive, convinced, confident, assured, unwavering, unshaken, persuaded, satisfied. OPPOSITE: doubtful. **2** (*it's certain that she's innocent*) unquestionable, indubitable, undoubted, indisputable, incontestable, incontrovertible, irrefutable, open-and-shut (*inf*), absolute, conclusive, definite, positive, manifest, plain, clear, evident, obvious. OPPOSITE: uncertain. **3** (*certain to win*) bound, destined, fated, sure, assured, in the bag (*inf*), inevitable, unavoidable, inescapable, inexorable, ineluctable. OPPOSITE: unlikely. **4** (*no certain remedy*) infallible, unfailing, reliable, dependable, sound, foolproof, sure-fire (*inf*), definite, positive. OPPOSITE: unreliable. **5** (*the date is not yet certain*) definite, decided, settled, determined, fixed, established, cut-and-dried (*inf*). **6** (*has a certain charm*) particular, specific, special, especial, precise, express, individual. **7** (*to a certain degree*) moderate, fair, reasonable, partial, indeterminate.

certainly *adv* **1** (*it's certainly going to rain*) undoubtedly, without doubt, unquestionably, indisputably, absolutely, positively, surely, assuredly, definitely, plainly, clearly, obviously. OPPOSITE: possibly. **2** (*'May I come too?' 'Certainly!'*) yes, of course, by all means, naturally, willingly, surely, definitely.

certainty *noun* **1** (*he said it with certainty*) conviction, sureness, positiveness, confidence, assurance, certitude, trust, faith, reliability. OPPOSITE: doubt. **2** (*the certainty of death*) fact, truth, validity, reality, actuality. OPPOSITE: possibility. **3** (*the certainty of the evidence*) unquestionableness, indubitableness, incontestability, incontrovertibility, irrefutability, conclusiveness, positiveness, plainness, obviousness. OPPOSITE: uncertainty. **4** (*it's a certainty that they'll lose*) inevitability, inescapability, foregone conclusion, sure thing (*inf*), safe bet (*inf*) **5** (*a certainty for the next race*) certain winner, cert (*inf*), dead cert (*inf*), cinch (*inf*).

certificate *noun* document, credential, testimonial, diploma, voucher, certification, licence, warrant, authorization.

certified *adj* qualified, professional, licensed, chartered, accredited, recognized, official.

certify *verb* attest, testify, avow, aver, confirm, corroborate, substantiate, verify, validate, authenticate, document, declare, pronounce, guarantee, vouch for, warrant, endorse, prove, show. OPPOSITE: deny.

certitude *noun* certainty, sureness, positiveness, confidence, assurance, conviction. OPPOSITE: doubt.

cessation *noun* ceasing, end, ending, stop, stoppage, termination, conclusion, discontinuation, arrest, halt, pause, break, recess, stay, suspension, intermission, interval, abeyance, respite, remission, let-up. OPPOSITE: continuance.

cession *noun* surrender, yielding, capitulation, submission, abandonment, relinquishment, renunciation, transfer, conveyance, grant, concession. OPPOSITE: retention.

chafe *verb* **1** (*the collar chafes my neck*) rub, abrade,

scrape, scratch, excoriate, rasp, grate, inflame, wear, fray, erode. **2** (*chafing her frozen hands*) warm, rub. **3** (*chafed by the restrictions*) irritate, annoy, vex, irk, anger, incense, exasperate, infuriate, gall, offend, provoke, worry, ruffle, trouble. OPPOSITE: soothe. **4** (*chafing at the delay*) fume, rage, blow one's top (*inf*), fret, be impatient.

chaff[1] *noun* (*separate the chaff from the grain*) husks, hulls, shells, pods, cases, waste, rubbish, refuse, debris, detritus, remains, dregs.

chaff[2] *noun* (*the chaff of his colleagues*) banter, badinage, persiflage, joking, jesting, kidding (*inf*), teasing, raillery, ribbing (*inf*), ragging (*inf*).
» *verb* banter, joke, jest, kid (*inf*), tease, josh, rib (*inf*), rag (*inf*), mock, ridicule, taunt, deride.

chagrin *noun* irritation, annoyance, vexation, anger, exasperation, indignation, displeasure, dissatisfaction, discomfiture, disquiet, discomposure, mortification, embarrassment, humiliation, shame. OPPOSITE: pleasure.
verb irritate, annoy, vex, irk, anger, enrage, infuriate, exasperate, aggrieve, peeve (*inf*), miff (*inf*), displease, dissatisfy, discomfit, discompose, mortify, embarrass, humiliate. OPPOSITE: please.

chain *noun* **1** (*in chains*) bond, fetter, shackle, manacle, restraint. **2** (*a chain of events*) series, succession, sequence, string, train, progression, course, cycle, set, row, line, concatenation.
» *verb* tether, tie, hitch, moor, fasten, secure, bind, fetter, shackle, trammel, manacle, handcuff, enslave, imprison, restrain, confine. OPPOSITE: loose.

chair *noun* **1** (*sitting on chairs*) seat, stool, bench, pew, stall, throne. **2** (*the chair of economics*) professorship, professorate. **3** (*the chair of the committee*) chairperson, chairman, chairwoman, president, director, master of ceremonies, MC, speaker, toastmaster.
» *verb* preside over, lead, direct, manage, control, supervise, oversee.

chalk *verb* **chalk up 1** (*chalk it up to lack of confidence*) attribute, ascribe, accredit, credit, put down, charge, impute. **2** (*chalk up another victory*) achieve, attain, register, record, enter, log, score.

chalky *adj* **1** (*a chalky complexion*) white, ashy, ashen, pale, pallid, wan, pasty, colourless. **2** (*chalky consistency*) powdery, dusty, crumbly, cretaceous. **3** (*chalky soil*) calcareous, limy.

challenge *verb* **1** (*challenged him to a duel*) dare, defy, summon, invite, throw down the gauntlet (*inf*), confront, accost, provoke, brave, beard. **2** (*a challenging job*) stretch, tax, test, try, arouse, stimulate, excite, inspire. **3** (*challenge the decision*) question, query, dispute, disagree with, oppose, object to, take exception to, protest against. OPPOSITE: accept.
» *noun* **1** (*accept a challenge*) dare, defiance, ultimatum, confrontation, provocation, summons, call, bidding, invitation. **2** (*face a challenge*) test, trial, difficulty, problem, obstacle, hurdle, hazard, risk. **3** (*a challenge to their authority*) question, disputation, dissension, opposition, stand, objection, protest.

chamber *noun* **1** (*retired to her chamber*) room, bedroom, boudoir, cell, cubicle, compartment, hall, apartment. **2** (*a chamber in the rock*) cavity, hollow, cell, compartment, recess. **3** (*the lower chamber of the* *parliament*) assembly, council, judicature, legislature, house.

champ *verb* chew, gnaw, bite, munch, crunch.

champion *noun* **1** (*the reigning champion*) winner, title-holder, champ (*inf*), victor, conqueror, hero, heroine. **2** (*champions of the cause*) defender, protector, guardian, upholder, supporter, advocate, backer, sponsor, patron.
≫ *verb* defend, protect, fight for, stand up for, espouse, uphold, support, advocate, back, promote, sponsor. OPPOSITE: oppose.

chance *noun* **1** (*leave it to chance*) luck, fortune, providence, fate, destiny, accident, coincidence, fluke (*inf*), fortuity, serendipity. OPPOSITE: design. **2** (*a chance to escape*) opportunity, opening, break (*inf*), occasion, time. **3** (*no chance of success*) possibility, likelihood, likeliness, probability, prospect, odds. OPPOSITE: certainty. **4** (*take a chance*) risk, gamble, hazard, venture, speculation, peril, jeopardy, uncertainty.
≫ *verb* **1** (*it chanced that the bus was late*) happen, occur, take place, befall, betide, come about, come to pass. **2** (*I'll chance it*) risk, hazard, venture, gamble, speculate, stake, jeopardize.
≫ *adj* accidental, unintentional, coincidental, fortuitous, serendipitous, unforeseen, unexpected, unanticipated, unplanned, unpremeditated, incidental, casual, random, arbitrary, haphazard. OPPOSITE: deliberate.

chance on find, discover, stumble on, come across, come upon, meet, encounter, bump into (*inf*), run into (*inf*).

chancy *adj* risky, hazardous, dangerous, perilous, tricky, speculative, uncertain, dicey (*inf*), iffy (*inf*), dodgy (*inf*).

change *verb* **1** (*change the spelling*) alter, vary, modify, transform, convert, transmute, transfigure, remodel, restyle, reshape, reform, reorganize, revise, amend, adjust, adapt. OPPOSITE: retain. **2** (*the weather changed*) alter, vary, develop, evolve, mutate, metamorphose, move, shift, veer, alternate, fluctuate, vacillate. OPPOSITE: remain. **3** (*change seats*) replace, substitute, exchange, interchange, transpose, switch, swap, trade, barter, commute.
≫ *noun* **1** (*a change in appearance*) alteration, modification, difference, variation, conversion, transmutation, transformation, transfiguration, mutation, metamorphosis, reform, reorganization, reconstruction, revision, amendment, adjustment, move, shift, about-turn (*inf*), U-turn (*inf*). OPPOSITE: conservation. **2** (*changes in temperature*) alternation, fluctuation, vacillation, vicissitude, difference, variation. OPPOSITE: constancy. **3** (*a period of change*) transition, development, evolution, adjustment, adaptation, revolution, flux. **4** (*a change of jobs*) exchange, interchange, switch, swap, replacement, substitution. **5** (*go by coach for a change*) variety, innovation, novelty. **6** (*a pocketful of change*) coins, silver, coppers, cash.

changeable *adj* **1** (*changeable weather*) variable, varying, changeful, changing, inconstant, unsettled, unpredictable, unreliable, erratic, irregular, fickle, capricious, fitful, fluctuating, wavering, vacillating, unsteady, unstable, shifting, mobile, fluid, mercurial, volatile, chameleonic, protean, kaleidoscopic, chequered, mutable, vicissitudinous. OPPOSITE: constant.

2 (*changeable settings*) alterable, modifiable, convertible, mutable, adjustable, adaptable. OPPOSITE: immutable.

changeless *adj* constant, steadfast, unchanging, unvarying, consistent, predictable, reliable, fixed, regular, steady, immutable, unalterable, permanent, abiding, perpetual, everlasting, eternal. OPPOSITE: changeable.

channel *noun* **1** (*drainage channels*) duct, conduit, passage, main, gutter, groove, furrow, trough, ditch, culvert, watercourse, waterway, canal, strait, sound. **2** (*channels of communication*) approach, avenue, route, course, path, way, means, medium, agency, vehicle.
≫ *verb* (*channel your energy into work*) direct, guide, conduct, convey, transport, transmit. **2** (*channelling the rocks*) groove, furrow, flute, carve, cut.

chant *noun* **1** (*Gregorian chant*) song, cantata, carol, psalm, canticle, plainsong, intonation, melody, tune, chorus, incantation, mantra. **2** (*the chant of the crowd*) shout, cry, chorus, slogan, motto, watchword.
≫ *verb* sing, carol, intone, chorus, recite.

chaos *noun* disorder, confusion, shambles (*inf*), turmoil, tumult, upheaval, upset, disruption, havoc, pandemonium, bedlam, uproar, riot, anarchy, lawlessness. OPPOSITE: order.

chaotic *adj* disordered, confused, upset, awry, in disarray, topsy-turvy, disorganized, shambolic (*inf*), tumultuous, riotous, anarchic, lawless. OPPOSITE: ordered.

chap *noun* boy, man, fellow, bloke (*inf*), guy (*inf*), person, individual, character, type, sort, customer (*inf*).

chaperon *noun* escort, companion, duenna, governess, attendant, protector.
≫ *verb* escort, accompany, shepherd, attend, guard, protect, look after, mind, watch over, supervise, keep an eye on.

chaplet *noun* wreath, garland, coronal, circlet.

chapped *adj* sore, raw, red, rough, cracked, split, open.

chapter *noun* **1** (*the last chapter of the book*) part, division, section, episode. **2** (*an eventful chapter in the company's history*) phase, period, time, stage. **3** (*a chapter of accidents*) series, succession, sequence, chain, set. **4** (*the local chapter of the society*) branch, lodge, wing, section, division.

char *verb* burn, scorch, singe, sear, carbonize, cauterize.

character *noun* **1** (*a change of character*) personality, temperament, disposition, nature, individuality, identity, attributes, ethos, quality, calibre, constitution, make-up, cast, complexion. **2** (*a stain on her character*) reputation, repute, name, status, standing, position. **3** (*a man of character*) honour, integrity, uprightness, rectitude, moral fibre. OPPOSITE: disrepute. **4** (*a likeable character*) person, individual, sort, type, customer (*inf*), fellow, chap. **5** (*she's quite a character*) eccentric, original, individual, oddity, oddball (*inf*), card (*inf*), case (*inf*). **6** (*the character of Hamlet*) role, part, persona, portrayal, representation, characterization. **7** (*characters used in Japanese*) letter, figure, symbol, sign, type, mark, device, emblem, rune, hieroglyph, cipher.

characteristic *adj* distinctive, distinguishing, peculiar, singular, individual, idiosyncratic, special, particular, specific, typical, representative, symbolic, symptomatic. OPPOSITE: general.

➤ *noun* peculiarity, idiosyncrasy, mannerism, quirk, trait, feature, quality, attribute, property, mark, sign, symptom.

characterize *verb* **1** (*the atonality that characterizes his music*) typify, distinguish, mark, brand, stamp, label, identify, designate, denote, indicate, specify. **2** (*characterized her as a psychopath*) represent, describe, portray, depict, delineate.

charade *noun* travesty, pretence, sham, pantomime, farce, parody.

charge *verb* **1** (*charged with dangerous driving*) accuse, arraign, impeach, indict, incriminate, impute, blame. OPPOSITE: acquit. **2** (*charge £10 for admission*) ask, demand, levy, impose, bill, invoice, debit, put down. **3** (*the army charged the gates*) attack, assault, assail, rush, storm, fall on, lay into (*inf*). **4** (*charged her with too much responsibility*) entrust, commit, load, burden, encumber, saddle, weigh down, afflict. OPPOSITE: relieve. **5** (*charged him to drop his gun*) command, order, direct, instruct, bid, enjoin, exhort, require. **6** (*charged with emotion*) suffuse, imbue, permeate, pervade, fill, load.

➤ *noun* **1** (*a charge of murder*) accusation, indictment, imputation, allegation. OPPOSITE: plea. **2** (*no extra charge for delivery*) fee, levy, toll, dues, payment, price, cost, rate, tariff, outlay, expense, expenditure. **3** (*a cavalry charge*) attack, assault, onset, onslaught, sortie, raid, incursion. OPPOSITE: retreat. **4** (*damaged while in your charge*) custody, care, keeping, safekeeping, protection, guardianship, ward, trust, responsibility, duty, office, commission. **5** (*a charge to the jury*) command, order, injunction, direction, instruction, mandate.

in charge responsible, in control, in command, managing, directing, supervising, overseeing.

charger *noun* horse, war-horse, mount, steed.

charitable *adj* **1** (*charitable acts*) philanthropic, humanitarian, kind, benevolent, beneficent, unselfish, selfless, altruistic, generous, liberal, bountiful, munificent, open handed, almsgiving, eleemosynary. OPPOSITE: mean. **2** (*take a charitable view*) considerate, understanding, compassionate, sympathetic, kindly, humane, gracious, magnanimous, big-hearted, indulgent, tolerant, broad-minded, lenient, forgiving. OPPOSITE: harsh.

charity *noun* **1** (*dependent on charity*) alms, almsgiving, benefaction, philanthropy, relief, aid, assistance, donations, contributions, handouts, gifts, endowments. **2** (*supporting local charities*) trust, foundation, fund. **3** (*her charity knew no bounds*) kindness, benevolence, goodwill, compassion, thoughtfulness, sympathy, love, humanity, generosity, bounty, unselfishness, selflessness, altruism, indulgence, tolerance. OPPOSITE: selfishness.

charlatan *noun* fake, fraud, phoney (*inf*), impostor, pretender, quack, mountebank, cheat, deceiver, swindler, confidence trickster, conman (*inf*).

charm *verb* delight, please, enchant, fascinate, captivate, bewitch, beguile, mesmerize, hypnotize, entrance, transport, enrapture, enamour, seduce, allure, attract, draw, win, win over, cajole. OPPOSITE: repel.

➤ *noun* **1** (*the charms of country life*) attraction, attractiveness, appeal, allure, desirability, fascination, captivation, delightfulness. **2** (*personal charm*) pleasantness, attractiveness, suavity, charisma. **3** (*a magic charm*) spell, enchantment, sorcery, magic. **4** (*a lucky charm*) amulet, talisman, trinket, bauble.

charming *adj* delightful, pleasing, lovely, attractive, fetching, appealing, alluring, seductive, enchanting, fascinating, bewitching, captivating, engaging, winning, suave, urbane, courteous, polite. OPPOSITE: repulsive.

chart *noun* **1** (*draw a chart*) plan, diagram, graph, table, tabulation, blueprint, map. **2** (*at the top of the charts*) list, listing, league, hit parade, top twenty.

➤ *verb* **1** (*chart a course*) map, map out, plot, sketch, draft, draw, delineate, outline. **2** (*chart the effects*) record, register, document, note, observe, monitor, follow.

charter *noun* **1** (*by royal charter*) licence, warrant, permit, franchise, concession, authority, authorization, sanction, privilege, right, prerogative, document, deed, bond, contract. **2** (*the United Nations charter*) code, canon, constitution, laws, rules, principles.

➤ *verb* **1** (*charter a boat*) hire, rent, lease, commission, engage. **2** (*a chartered surveyor*) certify, accredit, license, warrant, sanction, authorize.

chary *adj* cautious, careful, prudent, circumspect, heedful, guarded, wary, leery, distrustful, suspicious, slow, reluctant, unwilling. OPPOSITE: reckless.

chase *verb* **1** (*chase the thief*) pursue, follow, run after, hunt, track, trail, hound, shadow, tail, be hot on the heels of (*inf*). **2** (*chased them from the garden*) drive, expel, send away, send packing, put to flight. **3** (*chasing around all morning*) rush, hurry.

➤ *noun* pursuit, hunt, hunting, trail, rush, race.

chasm *noun* **1** (*a bridge across the chasm*) abyss, gorge, canyon, crevasse, ravine, gulf, rift, cleft, fissure, crevice, crack, split, breach, gap, crater, cavity, hollow, hole, opening. **2** (*a chasm between the two parties*) gulf, rift, breach, gap, separation, alienation, estrangement.

chassis *noun* frame, framework, skeleton, structure, substructure, mounting, support.

chaste *adj* **1** (*a chaste young woman*) pure, undefiled, unsullied, immaculate, vestal, virginal, celibate, continent, abstinent, virtuous, good, decent, wholesome, decorous, modest, innocent, uncorrupted, moral, upright. OPPOSITE: corrupt. **2** (*a chaste style*) simple, unaffected, plain, unadorned, austere, severe. OPPOSITE: ornate.

chasten *verb* **1** (*a chastening experience*) humble, humiliate, subdue, repress, cow, tame, curb, restrain. OPPOSITE: encourage. **2** (*chasten the culprits*) punish, penalize, correct, discipline, chastise, castigate, reprimand, upbraid, scold, chide, reprove, take to task, haul over the coals (*inf*). OPPOSITE: praise.

chastise *verb* punish, correct, discipline, castigate, beat, flog, lash, whip, scourge, cane, birch, tan the hide of (*inf*), smack, spank, thrash, thump (*inf*), wallop (*inf*), berate, upbraid, scold, chide, reprimand, reprove, take to task, dress down (*inf*), haul over the coals (*inf*). OPPOSITE: reward.

chastisement *noun* punishment, correction, discipline, castigation, beating, flogging, whipping, caning,

spanking, thrashing, censure, scolding, reproof.
OPPOSITE: reward.

chastity noun **1** (*preserve her chastity*) purity, virginity, maidenhood, celibacy, continence, abstinence, virtue, modesty, decency, innocence. OPPOSITE: corruption.
2 (*chastity of style*) simplicity, plainness, austerity.
OPPOSITE: ornateness.

chat verb talk, converse, gossip, tittle-tattle, natter (*inf*), gas (*inf*), jaw (*inf*), have a chin-wag (*inf*), chew the fat (*inf*), chew the rag (*inf*), chatter, prattle, prate, jabber, gab (*inf*), rabbit (*inf*).
≫ noun talk, conversation, confab (*inf*), gossip, natter (*inf*), chin-wag (*inf*), heart-to-heart, tête-à-tête, chatter, gab (*inf*), chitchat, small talk.

chattels pl noun goods, belongings, property, effects, movables.

chatter verb prattle, prate, babble, blather, jabber, gab (*inf*), witter (*inf*), rabbit (*inf*), talk the hind legs off a donkey (*inf*), talk, chat, gossip, tittle-tattle, natter (*inf*), gas (*inf*).
≫ noun prattle, prating, babble, blathering, jabber, gab (*inf*), talk, conversation, chitchat, gossip, nattering (*inf*).

chatterbox noun chatterer, babbler, gossip, blabbermouth (*inf*), loudmouth (*inf*), tittle-tattler, prattler, windbag (*inf*), gasbag (*inf*), motormouth (*inf*).

chatty adj **1** (*a chatty person*) talkative, loquacious, voluble, garrulous, mouthy (*inf*), babbling, prating, gabby (*inf*), glib, gushing, effusive. OPPOSITE: reserved.
2 (*a chatty letter*) gossipy, conversational, informal, colloquial, familiar, friendly, newsy (*inf*). OPPOSITE: formal.

chauvinism noun jingoism, flag-waving, nationalism, partisanship, bias, prejudice.

cheap adj **1** (*cheap petrol*) inexpensive, low-priced, low-cost, reasonable, affordable, economical, reduced, discounted, marked down, cut-price, going for a song (*inf*), bargain, sale, budget, economy, no-frills, rock-bottom, giveaway. OPPOSITE: expensive. **2** (*cheap wine*) shoddy, inferior, second-rate, poor, indifferent, paltry, two-bit (*inf*), worthless, trashy, cheap and nasty, cheapjack, cheapo (*inf*), common, vulgar, tatty, tawdry, tacky (*inf*). OPPOSITE: superior. **3** (*a cheap trick*) mean, shabby, contemptible, despicable, low, base. OPPOSITE: noble. **4** (*he felt cheap*) degraded, debased, humiliated, shameful, ashamed, embarrassed, mortified.

cheapen verb **1** (*don't cheapen yourself*) degrade, debase, demean, lower, devalue, depreciate, belittle, denigrate, disparage, derogate. OPPOSITE: appreciate. **2** (*cheapen the cost*) reduce, lower, cut, slash, discount, mark down.

cheat verb **1** (*cheating his customers*) deceive, delude, trick, hoax, con (*inf*), take for a ride (*inf*), dupe, fool, beguile, hoodwink, bamboozle, double-cross, two-time (*inf*), defraud, swindle, bilk (*inf*), diddle (*inf*), do (*inf*), rip off (*inf*), fleece (*inf*), take to the cleaners (*inf*). **2** (*cheated of victory*) deprive, deny, prevent, thwart, frustrate, baulk, foil. **3** (*cheat death*) escape, dodge, elude, avoid, evade, shun, eschew.
≫ noun **1** (*you're a cheat!*) swindler, conman (*inf*), trickster, sharper, rogue, crook, shark, fraud, impostor, charlatan, liar, deceiver, double-crosser. **2** (*a cheat used to*

win) trick, artifice, imposture, deception, hoax, con (*inf*), fraud, swindle, rip-off (*inf*).

check verb **1** (*check the figures*) inspect, examine, test, screen, vet, scrutinize, look at, scan, look over, give the once-over (*inf*), study, investigate, inquire into, probe, monitor, compare, cross-check, verify, confirm, make sure, ascertain. **2** (*check the flow*) halt, arrest, stop, stem, staunch, slow, retard, delay, hinder, impede, obstruct, block, inhibit, repress, curb, restrain, limit, control, contain, nip in the bud (*inf*), bridle, rein in. **3** (*she never checks the children*) chide, scold, rebuke, reprove, reprimand, tell off (*inf*), correct, discipline, punish.
≫ noun **1** (*a baggage check*) inspection, examination, scrutiny, once-over (*inf*), test, trial, screening, study, investigation, inquiry, probe, comparison, verification, confirmation, audit. **2** (*a check on spending*) curb, restraint, limitation, control, inhibition, deterrent. **3** (*a check on progress*) hindrance, impediment, obstruction, barrier, stoppage, stop, arrest, halt, pause, retardation, delay.

checkmate noun defeat, rout, conquest, victory, stoppage, stop, arrest, halt.
≫ verb frustrate, thwart, foil, stop, block, overcome, conquer, vanquish, defeat, beat.

checkup noun examination, inspection, scrutiny, analysis, investigation, probe, assessment, appraisal, evaluation.

cheek noun impertinence, impudence, effrontery, brazenness, sauce (*inf*), insolence, disrespect, lip (*inf*), audacity, temerity, nerve, gall (*inf*), brass neck (*inf*). OPPOSITE: respect.

cheeky adj impertinent, impudent, bold, audacious, forward, brazen, pert, saucy (*inf*), insolent, disrespectful, lippy (*inf*). OPPOSITE: respectful.

cheep verb chirp, chirrup, tweet, twitter, chatter, pipe, peep.

cheer verb **1** (*cheer the winner*) applaud, clap, acclaim, hail, salute, welcome, shout, yell, encourage, spur, urge, root for (*inf*). OPPOSITE: boo. **2** (*cheered by the news*) gladden, hearten, encourage, buoy up, buck up (*inf*), comfort, console, solace, cheer up, perk up, enliven, animate, elate, exhilarate, inspirit, uplift. OPPOSITE: depress.
≫ noun **1** (*the cheers of the spectators*) shout, yell, cry, hurrah, applause, acclamation. OPPOSITE: boo. **2** (*a time of cheer*) cheerfulness, gladness, happiness, joy, gaiety, merriment, comfort, solace, hope, hopefulness, optimism, buoyancy, blitheness, good spirits, animation, liveliness, high spirits, jubilation, revelry, merrymaking. OPPOSITE: dejection.

cheer up brighten, perk up, liven up, rally, take heart, buck up (*inf*).

cheerful noun happy, glad, contented, joyful, bright, merry, jolly, gay, buoyant, blithe, good-humoured, sunny, cheery, breezy, carefree, light-hearted, chirpy, bright-eyed and bushy-tailed (*inf*), sparkling, lively, animated, hopeful, optimistic, positive, smiling, laughing, friendly, obliging, willing. OPPOSITE: dejected.

cheerio interj goodbye, bye (*inf*), so long (*inf*), ta-ta (*inf*), see you later (*inf*), farewell, adieu, au revoir, auf Wiedersehen, ciao. OPPOSITE: hello.

cheerless *adj* dreary, dull, gloomy, dismal, dark, sombre, bleak, barren, depressing, melancholy, mournful, doleful, morose, pessimistic, glum, dejected, depressed, despondent, miserable, sad, disconsolate, forlorn, desolate, comfortless, uninviting. OPPOSITE: cheerful.

cheers *interj* here's to you, here's mud in your eye (*inf*), your good health, all the best, skol, prosit, slainte, bottoms up (*inf*), down the hatch (*inf*).

cheery *adj* hearty, jovial, genial, cheerful, happy, joyous, blithe, merry, jolly, lively, sprightly, jaunty, sunny, breezy, carefree, happy-go-lucky. OPPOSITE: glum.

chemist *noun* pharmacist, apothecary.

chequered *adj* **1** (*a chequered career*) varied, diverse, mixed, eventful, full of ups and downs. **2** (*chequered cloth*) checked, tartan.

cherish *verb* **1** (*cherish your children*) treasure, prize, hold dear, love, adore, dote on, idolize, cosset, pamper, indulge, look after, tend, nurture, nourish, shelter, protect. OPPOSITE: neglect. **2** (*cherish hopes*) harbour, entertain, cling to, foster, nurse. OPPOSITE: abandon.

cherub *noun* **1** (*cherubs painted on the ceiling*) angel, seraph. **2** (*cherubs smiling at the camera*) child, infant, baby, babe, innocent, darling, dear.

chest *noun* **1** (*a pain in my chest*) breast, thorax, sternum, bosom, bust. **2** (*a treasure chest*) box, case, trunk, crate, coffer, casket.

chew *verb* masticate, munch, crunch, champ, grind, gnaw, bite, nibble.

    chew over ponder, consider, deliberate about, cogitate about, ruminate on, meditate on, reflect on, weigh up, mull over.

chic *adj* fashionable, modish, voguish, trendy (*inf*), stylish, smart, elegant, dressy (*inf*). OPPOSITE: unfashionable.

chicanery *noun* trickery, dishonesty, fraud, sharp practice, deception, deceitfulness, duplicity, guile, wiles, stratagems, artifice, subterfuge, underhandedness, jiggery-pokery (*inf*), sophistry, intrigue. OPPOSITE: honesty.

chide *verb* scold, reprimand, admonish, tell off (*inf*), tick off (*inf*), rebuke, reprove, reproach, upbraid, berate, take to task, dress down (*inf*), criticize, censure, blame. OPPOSITE: praise.

chief *noun* leader, head, chieftain, ruler, overlord, captain, commander, master, supremo, governor, principal, president, director, manager, boss (*inf*), gaffer (*inf*). OPPOSITE: subordinate.

    » *adj* **1** (*the chief accountant*) principal, head, leading, prime, supreme, grand, arch. **2** (*the chief reason*) main, principal, first, foremost, primary, cardinal, capital, key, essential, vital, paramount, prevailing, predominant, major. OPPOSITE: minor.

chiefly *adv* especially, above all, principally, mainly, in the main, mostly, for the most part, predominantly, on the whole, primarily.

child *noun* **1** (*when I was still a child*) boy, girl, kid (*inf*), nipper (*inf*), bairn, sprog (*inf*), shaver (*inf*), brat (*inf*), baby, infant, toddler, tot (*inf*), youngster, youth, juvenile, adolescent, teenager, minor. OPPOSITE: adult.

2 (*they have four children*) son, daughter, offspring, progeny, issue, descendant. OPPOSITE: parent.

childbirth *noun* labour, delivery, parturition, confinement, accouchement, lying-in.

childhood *noun* boyhood, girlhood, babyhood, infancy, youth, adolescence, minority, immaturity. OPPOSITE: adulthood.

childish *adj* babyish, infantile, puerile, juvenile, immature, young, youthful, adolescent, boyish, girlish, silly, foolish, trivial, trifling, simple. OPPOSITE: mature.

childlike *adj* innocent, artless, guileless, naive, ingenuous, credulous, gullible, trustful, trusting.

chill *noun* **1** (*a chill in the air*) cold, coldness, chilliness, coolness, crispness, rawness, nip, bite, frost, iciness, frigidity, gelidity. OPPOSITE: warmth. **2** (*catch a chill*) cold, flu, influenza, fever. **3** (*the chill of his stare*) frostiness, coldness, coolness, frigidity, aloofness, distance, hostility, unfriendliness. **4** (*sent a chill down my spine*) shiver, shudder, tremor, dread, fear. **5** (*cast a chill over the gathering*) cloud, damper, gloom, depression.

    » *verb* **1** (*chill the wine*) cool, ice, refrigerate, freeze. OPPOSITE: heat. **2** (*chilled our hopes*) depress, discourage, dishearten, dispirit, dampen. OPPOSITE: encourage. **3** (*a chilling account of the murder*) frighten, scare, terrify, horrify. OPPOSITE: reassure.

    » *adj* chilly, cool, cold, raw, biting, wintry, bleak, depressing. OPPOSITE: warm.

chill out calm down, relax, take it easy (*inf*).

chilly *adj* **1** (*a chilly morning*) cold, cool, chill, fresh, crisp, nippy (*inf*), parky (*inf*), raw, biting, frosty, icy, freezing, frigid, gelid, wintry, bleak. OPPOSITE: warm. **2** (*a chilly response*) frosty, cool, frigid, aloof, distant, hostile, unfriendly, unwelcoming, unsympathetic. OPPOSITE: friendly.

chime *verb* **1** (*the bells were chiming*) toll, sound, strike, peal, ring, clang, ding, dong, tinkle, jingle, reverberate, resound. **2** (*the clock chimed three*) strike, indicate, show, mark. **3** (*their ideas chimed with ours*) harmonize, accord, agree, fit in, blend, coordinate, complement. OPPOSITE: clash.

    chime in interrupt, interpose, break in, cut in, chip in (*inf*), butt in (*inf*).

chimera *noun* hallucination, fantasy, dream, delusion, fancy, illusion, figment of the imagination, phantom, spectre, will-o'-the-wisp.

chimerical *adj* illusory, unreal, fanciful, imaginary, hallucinatory, visionary, fantastic. OPPOSITE: real.

chimney *noun* shaft, vent, flue, lum.

china *noun* **1** (*made of china*) porcelain, pottery, earthenware, ceramics. **2** (*use the best china on special occasions*) crockery, tableware, service, dishes.

chink[1] *noun* (*a chink in the curtains*) gap, opening, aperture, slit, crack, fissure, cleft, rift, crevice, cranny.

chink[2] *noun* (*the chink of coins*) clink, jingle, jangle, tinkle, ring.

    » *verb* clink, jingle, jangle, tinkle, ring.

chip *noun* **1** (*chips of wood*) piece, fragment, flake, sliver, splinter, shard, shaving, paring, bit, shred, scrap, snippet. **2** (*a chip in the paintwork*) nick, notch, dent, scratch, crack, flaw, defect, fault. **3** (*gambling chips*)

token, counter, disc. **4** (*fish and chips*) fry, French fry, fried potato.
➤ *verb* chisel, whittle, cut, hew, nick, notch, dent, scratch, gash, crack, break off.

chip in 1 (*we should have enough if everyone chips in*) contribute, donate, subscribe, pay. **2** (*keeps chipping in with irrelevant remarks*) interrupt, interpose, chime in, break in, cut in, butt in (*inf*).

chirp *verb* chirrup, cheep, tweet, twitter, chatter, sing, warble, trill, pipe, peep.

chirpy *adj* bright, cheerful, jaunty, perky (*inf*), happy, merry, blithe, light-hearted. OPPOSITE: downcast.

chisel *verb* carve, sculpt, cut, hew, whittle, engrave, incise, chase, shape, model.

chit *noun* note, slip, voucher, receipt.

chitchat *noun* chat, conversation, small talk, gossip, tittle-tattle, chatter, talk.

chivalrous *adj* knightly, heroic, valiant, courageous, brave, bold, intrepid, gallant, protective, courtly, gentlemanly, courteous, well-mannered, gracious, generous, magnanimous, noble, high-minded, honourable, loyal, constant, true. OPPOSITE: boorish.

chivalry *noun* knighthood, heroism, valour, courage, bravery, boldness, gallantry, courtesy, graciousness, generosity, magnanimity, nobility, honour, integrity, loyalty, constancy. OPPOSITE: cowardice.

chivvy *verb* urge, goad, prod, spur, badger, hound, nag, pester, harass, hassle (*inf*), pressure, pressurize, hurry, hasten.

choice *noun* **1** (*make a choice*) selection, pick, adoption, election, preference, decision. **2** (*no choice but to go*) option, alternative, possibility, solution, answer. **3** (*a wide choice of jobs*) range, selection, variety, array, display, stock, supply.
➤ *adj* select, hand-picked, élite, best, plum, prize, excellent, first-rate, first-class, prime, superior, rare, uncommon, unusual, fine, exquisite, dainty, exclusive, special, valuable, precious. OPPOSITE: inferior.

choke *verb* **1** (*choked to death*) strangle, throttle, stifle, suffocate, smother, asphyxiate. **2** (*the fumes made us choke*) gag, retch, gasp, cough. **3** (*leaves choking the gutter*) block, obstruct, congest, clog, dam, plug, stop.

choke back suppress, hold back, fight back, restrain, control, contain, curb, bridle, repress, inhibit, overcome, overpower.

choleric *adj* irritable, irascible, bad-tempered, testy, touchy, crotchety, crabby, peevish, petulant, angry, fiery, hot-tempered, quick-tempered. OPPOSITE: placid.

choose *verb* **1** (*choose a car*) select, pick, opt for, go for, plump for (*inf*), take, settle on, decide on, fix on, single out, elect, appoint, designate, adopt, espouse. OPPOSITE: reject. **2** (*let them do as they choose*) prefer, favour, like, fancy, desire, wish, want, see fit.

choosy *adj* discriminating, selective, picky (*inf*), particular, fussy, faddy, finicky, pernickety, fastidious, exacting.

chop *verb* cut, hack, hew, fell, axe, lop, sever, cleave, carve, slice, dice, cube, mince, cut up, chop up.

choppy *adj* rough, bumpy, turbulent, stormy, squally, blustery, tempestuous, ruffled, broken, wavy, uneven.

chore *noun* job, task, piece of work, duty, routine, burden, bother, drag (*inf*), fag (*inf*).

chortle *verb* laugh, chuckle, snigger, cackle, crow, guffaw, roar.

chorus *noun* **1** (*members of the chorus*) choir, choristers, singers, vocalists, choral group, ensemble. **2** (*sing the chorus*) refrain, burden, response. OPPOSITE: verse. **3** (*reply in chorus*) unison, harmony, concert, unity, accord, concord.

christen *verb* baptize, name, call, dub, style, term, designate, denominate, entitle.

Christian name *noun* first name, forename, given name.

Christmas *noun* Xmas, Yule, Noel, Christmastide, Yuletide, festive season.

chronic *adj* **1** (*chronic illness*) recurring, perennial, deep-seated, deep-rooted, long-lasting, long-standing, lingering, persistent, constant, incessant, permanent, incurable. **2** (*a chronic gambler*) inveterate, habitual, confirmed, hardened, ingrained. **3** (*chronic weather*) appalling, dreadful, terrible, awful, atrocious. OPPOSITE: excellent.

chronicle *noun* journal, diary, log, record, register, history, annals, archive, account, narrative, story, saga.
➤ *verb* record, register, enter, set down, document, report, relate, tell, recount, narrate.

chronicler *noun* historian, historiographer, annalist, archivist, diarist, recorder, narrator, reporter.

chronological *adj* consecutive, sequential, in sequence, serial, ordered, in order, progressive, historical.

chubby *adj* plump, tubby, podgy, round, rotund, portly, stout, fat, flabby, fleshy. OPPOSITE: lean.

chuck *verb* **1** (*chuck a stone*) throw, toss, hurl, cast, pitch, sling, **2** (*he chucked his job*) give up, quit, abandon, pack in (*inf*), discard, reject, drop (*inf*), dump (*inf*), give the elbow (*inf*).

chuckle *verb* giggle, titter, chortle, snigger, laugh, crow, cackle, grin, smile.

chum *noun* friend, pal (*inf*), mate (*inf*), buddy (*inf*), companion, comrade, crony.

chummy *adj* friendly, close, intimate, pally (*inf*), matey (*inf*), thick as thieves (*inf*).

chunk *noun* lump, hunk, block, slab, wedge, wodge (*inf*), mass, piece, portion.

church *noun* **1** (*lives near the church*) chapel, kirk, cathedral, abbey, minster, temple, tabernacle, mosque, synagogue, house of God, place of worship. **2** (*the Roman Catholic Church*) denomination, faith, sect, cult. **3** (*members of the church*) congregation, parish, clergy.

churchyard *noun* graveyard, cemetery, burial ground, necropolis, God's acre.

churl *noun* boor, lout, oaf, rustic, peasant, bumpkin, yokel. OPPOSITE: gentleman.

churlish *adj* uncouth, boorish, loutish, oafish, vulgar, rude, impolite, discourteous, uncivil, ill-mannered, ill-bred, brusque, curt, surly, waspish, crabbed, ill-tempered, sullen, morose, unsociable, unfriendly, unneighbourly, mean. OPPOSITE: polite.

churlishness noun uncouthness, boorishness, vulgarity, rudeness, impoliteness, discourtesy, lack of breeding, brusqueness, surliness, sullenness, moroseness, unfriendliness, meanness. OPPOSITE: politeness.

churn verb 1 (churn the milk) beat, whip, stir, agitate, shake, disturb. 2 (the churning waters) foam, froth, boil, seethe, convulse, writhe, toss, shake, turn, swirl.

chute noun slide, slope, incline, ramp, channel, trough, groove, gutter, shaft, funnel.

cigarette noun filter-tip, roll-up, cigar, cig (inf), ciggy (inf), fag (inf), smoke (inf), gasper (inf), coffin nail (inf), cancer stick (inf), joint (inf), reefer (inf), spliff (inf), fag end (inf), dog end (inf).

cinch noun child's play, doddle (inf), piece of cake (inf), piece of piss (sl), walkover (inf), pushover (inf).

cinder noun ash, ember, charcoal, coal, clinker, coke.

cinema noun 1 (go to the cinema) pictures, movies, flicks (inf), film theatre, multiplex, picture house, picture palace, fleapit (inf). 2 (a career in cinema) films, motion pictures, big screen (inf), silver screen (inf).

cipher noun 1 (written in cipher) code, cryptograph, cryptogram, symbol, character, figure, device. 2 (a mere cipher) nonentity, nobody, nothing, nil, zero, nought.

circle noun 1 (draw a circle) ring, round, hoop, wreath, loop, coil, spiral, disc, sphere, ball, globe, orb, cycle, revolution, rotation, gyration, circumference, periphery. 2 (circle of friends) set, clique, coterie, club, society, fraternity, sorority, fellowship, company, group, band, gang, crowd. 3 (in academic circles) domain, province, realm, sphere, orbit, range, compass, field, area, region, circuit, bounds.
 ⟩ verb 1 (circling overhead) revolve, rotate, turn, pivot, swivel, gyrate, whirl, wheel, circulate, swirl, loop, coil, spiral. 2 (circle the town) ring, encircle, surround, gird, belt, circumscribe, enclose, hem in. 3 (circle the earth) orbit, circumnavigate.

circuit noun 1 (another circuit of the track) revolution, round, lap, orbit, turn, loop, circle, tour. 2 (on the lecture circuit) tour, journey, trip, excursion, perambulation, peregrination, round, beat. 3 (the circuit of the estate) boundary, bounds, limits, compass, ambit, circumference, perimeter, periphery. 4 (a racing circuit) track, course, racetrack, racecourse.

circuitous adj roundabout, indirect, oblique, devious, tortuous, winding, twisting, serpentine, meandering, rambling, labyrinthine. OPPOSITE: direct.

circular adj round, annular, ring-shaped, hoop-shaped, discoid, spherical, globular. OPPOSITE: square.
 ⟩ noun notice, advertisement, flier, handbill, leaflet, pamphlet, brochure.

circulate verb 1 (circulate information) spread, disseminate, diffuse, propagate, promulgate, publicize, advertise, publish, broadcast, transmit, issue, distribute, give out, pass round, send round. OPPOSITE: withhold. 2 (blood circulates) move round, go round, flow, radiate, circle, rotate, revolve, gyrate, whirl. OPPOSITE: stagnate.

circulation noun 1 (the circulation of information) spread, spreading, dissemination, diffusion, propagation, promulgation, publication, broadcast, transmission, issue, distribution. OPPOSITE: retention. 2 (the circulation of traffic) flow, movement, motion, circling, rotation. OPPOSITE: stagnation.

circumference noun periphery, perimeter, circuit, girth, outline, border, edge, rim, margin, verge, fringe, skirt, boundary, bounds, limits, confines, outside, extremity. OPPOSITE: diameter.

circumlocution noun periphrasis, verbosity, wordiness, long-windedness, prolixity, discursiveness, tautology, pleonasm, redundancy, convolution, indirectness, euphemism, equivocation, ambiguity. OPPOSITE: terseness.

circumlocutory adj periphrastic, verbose, wordy, long-winded, prolix, discursive, tautologous, tautological, pleonastic, redundant, convoluted, indirect, roundabout, circuitous, euphemistic, equivocal, ambiguous. OPPOSITE: terse.

circumscribe verb 1 (circumscribing the area) surround, encircle, encompass, enclose, bound, limit, confine, hem in, define, outline, demarcate, delineate, mark off. 2 (circumscribed by habit) restrict, restrain, confine, limit, bound, curb, curtail, hamper.

circumspect adj cautious, wary, careful, chary, vigilant, watchful, alert, heedful, attentive, guarded, discreet, prudent, judicious, politic, sagacious, wise. OPPOSITE: rash.

circumspection noun caution, wariness, care, vigilance, alertness, heed, attention, discretion, prudence, sagacity. OPPOSITE: rashness.

circumstance noun 1 (a similar circumstance) incident, event, occurrence, happening, case, element, factor, detail, particular, respect, point, item, thing. 2 (a victim of circumstance) fate, destiny, lot, fortune.

circumstances pl noun 1 (only in exceptional circumstances) situation, condition, position, state, state of affairs, event, occurrence, background. 2 (living in reduced circumstances) means, resources, status, station, surroundings, environment, times, lifestyle, plight, predicament.

circumstantial adj 1 (circumstantial evidence) inferential, conjectural, presumed, implied, indirect, hearsay, incidental, contingent. OPPOSITE: positive 2 (a circumstantial report) detailed, elaborate, particular, specific, minute, precise, accurate, exact. OPPOSITE: vague.

circumvent verb bypass, get round, get out of, dodge, sidestep, avoid, evade, elude, foil, frustrate, thwart, outwit. OPPOSITE: confront.

circumvention noun bypassing, dodging, sidestepping, avoidance, evasion, frustration, outwitting. OPPOSITE: confrontation.

cistern noun tank, reservoir, well, vat, sink, tub.

citadel noun fortress, stronghold, castle, keep, tower, bastion.

citation noun 1 (citations from the Bible) quotation, quote, passage, excerpt, extract, illustration, allusion, reference, source. 2 (a citation for bravery) commendation, award, mention, honour.

cite verb 1 (cited as an example) quote, name, mention, allude to, refer to, adduce, enumerate. 2 (cited to appear in court) summon, call, subpoena, arraign.

citizen *noun* townsman, townswoman, inhabitant, dweller, denizen, local, resident, householder, voter, taxpayer, burgher, freeman, subject. OPPOSITE: outsider.

city *noun* metropolis, municipality, town, burgh, conurbation, megalopolis, urban sprawl, concrete jungle, big smoke (*inf*).

civic *adj* municipal, community, communal, public, borough, town, city, metropolitan, urban. OPPOSITE: rural.

civil *adj* **1** (*civil war*) domestic, home, internal, interior, national, local. OPPOSITE: international. **2** (*civil authorities*) national, state, civilian, nonmilitary, secular, lay, nonreligious, civic, municipal, public, local. **3** (*be civil to your mother-in-law*) polite, courteous, well-mannered, well-bred, ladylike, gentlemanly, respectful, civilized, refined, urbane, suave, gracious, complaisant, obliging, accommodating, pleasant, cordial, genial, affable. OPPOSITE: churlish.

civilian *adj* civil, nonmilitary, lay, ordinary, private.

civilities *pl noun* etiquette, protocol, proprieties, decorum.

civility *noun* politeness, courtesy, manners, breeding, respect, refinement, urbanity, graciousness, complaisance, pleasantness, cordiality, geniality. OPPOSITE: churlishness.

civilization *noun* **1** (*modern civilization*) development, advancement, progress, refinement, sophistication, cultivation, culture. OPPOSITE: barbarism. **2** (*ancient civilizations*) society, nation, people, community, way of life. **3** (*the civilization of the inhabitants*) improvement, education, instruction, edification, enlightenment, humanization, socialization.

civilize *verb* refine, sophisticate, cultivate, polish, improve, educate, instruct, teach, edify, enlighten, humanize, socialize, domesticate, tame. OPPOSITE: barbarize.

civilized *adj* **1** (*civilized nations*) advanced, developed, cultivated, cultured, educated, enlightened, humanized, socialized. OPPOSITE: barbarous. **2** (*a civilized dinner party*) refined, sophisticated, cultivated, urbane, polite, gracious, sociable. OPPOSITE: uncouth. **3** (*behave in a civilized manner*) reasonable, sensible, polite, courteous. OPPOSITE: uncivilized.

clack *verb* **1** (*clacking typewriters*) clatter, click, rap, tap, rattle. **2** (*set tongues clacking*) chatter, prattle, prate, jabber, gabble, babble.

clad *adj* dressed, clothed, wearing, attired, apparelled, covered.

claim *verb* **1** (*claim the reward*) ask for, request, put in for, lay claim to, demand, call for, require, requisition, commandeer, appropriate, usurp, take, exact. OPPOSITE: waive. **2** (*claimed that she was a doctor*) assert, insist, maintain, hold, contend, allege, profess, declare, state, avow, aver, affirm.
  ➤ *noun* **1** (*a claim for compensation*) demand, call, requirement, requisition, request, appeal, petition, application. **2** (*his claim to the throne*) right, title, entitlement, privilege, prerogative, inheritance, heritage. **3** (*refuted their claims*) assertion, contention, allegation, profession, declaration, avowal, averment, affirmation.

claimant *noun* applicant, candidate, pretender, supplicant, petitioner, plaintiff, litigant, suitor.

clairvoyance *noun* extrasensory perception, ESP, sixth sense, second sight, telepathy, fortune-telling.

clairvoyant *adj* psychic, extrasensory, second-sighted, telepathic, fortune-telling, prescient, visionary, prophetic, oracular.
  ➤ *noun* psychic, telepathist, fortune-teller, soothsayer, seer, visionary, prophet, prophetess, augur, diviner, oracle.

clamber *verb* climb, scramble, crawl, scale, ascend, mount, shin.

clammy *adj* damp, moist, wet, sticky, viscous, slimy, sweaty, dank, close, humid, muggy. OPPOSITE: dry.

clamorous *adj* vociferous, noisy, loud, deafening, blaring, uproarious, riotous, tumultuous, boisterous, unruly, obstreperous, demanding, insistent, vehement. OPPOSITE: quiet.

clamour *noun* **1** (*the clamour of children at play*) noise, din, racket, hullabaloo, uproar, shouting, yelling, vociferation, hubbub, brouhaha, commotion, fuss. **2** (*the clamour for reform*) demand, call, insistence, request, petition, protest, complaint, outcry. OPPOSITE: quiet.
  ➤ *verb* **1** (*clamouring for reform*) demand, call, insist, press, urge. **2** (*children clamouring in the playground*) shout, cry, yell, shriek, vociferate.

clamp *noun* vice, brace, clasp, grip, bracket.
  ➤ *verb* secure, fasten, fix, brace, hold, clasp, grip, clench, press, squeeze.

clamp down on restrict, limit, control, restrain, curb, suppress, crack down on, prevent, stop, put a stop to.

clamp-down *noun* restriction, limitation, control, restraint, suppression, crack-down, prevention.

clan *noun* **1** (*the Scottish clans*) family, sept, tribe, race, line, house. **2** (*join their clan*) group, company, band, gang, crowd, set, circle, clique, coterie, fraternity, brotherhood, sect, faction.

clandestine *adj* furtive, surreptitious, furtive, stealthy, underhand, sly, cloak-and-dagger, secret, undercover, underground, private, hidden, concealed, covert. OPPOSITE: open.

clang *verb* ring, resound, reverberate, toll, chime, peal, clank, clash, jangle.
  noun clank, clash, jangle, clangour, ringing, resounding, reverberation, toll, chime, peal.

clanger *noun* mistake, error, fault, slip, blunder, gaffe, faux pas, bloomer (*inf*), howler (*inf*), boob (*inf*) boo-boo (*inf*).

clangour *noun* clang, clash, ringing, resounding, reverberation, clamour, din, uproar, racket.

clank *noun* clash, clang, clangour, jangle, clunk, clink, chink, rattle, clatter.
  verb clash, clang, jangle, ring, clunk, clink, chink, rattle, clatter.

clannish *adj* cliquish, exclusive, select, insular, provincial, parochial, sectarian, narrow. OPPOSITE: open.

clap *verb* **1** (*the spectators clapped*) applaud, put one's hands together, cheer, acclaim. OPPOSITE: boo. **2** (*clapped her on the back*) slap, smack, strike, hit, pat, bang, whack,

wallop (*inf*). **3** (*clap them in prison*) throw, cast, toss, push, thrust.
➤ *noun* **1** (*give him a clap*) applause, ovation, cheer, acclaim. **2** (*a clap on the back*) slap, smack, blow, pat, bang, whack, wallop (*inf*). **3** (*a clap of thunder*) burst, peal, explosion, bang.

claptrap *noun* nonsense, rubbish, trash, drivel, twaddle, bunk (*inf*), bunkum (*inf*), guff (*inf*), piffle (*inf*), rot (*inf*), bilge (*inf*), codswallop (*inf*), cobblers (*inf*), bombast, cant, humbug, blarney, flannel (*inf*), insincerity, hypocrisy.

clarification *noun* explanation, exposition, elaboration, elucidation, illumination, simplification, resolution. OPPOSITE: mystification.

clarify *verb* **1** (*clarify the situation*) explain, elaborate, make clear, elucidate, illuminate, throw light on, shed light on, simplify, demystify, clear up, resolve. OPPOSITE: obscure. **2** (*clarified butter*) purify, refine, filter, strain, clear, cleanse.

clarity *noun* **1** (*the clarity of the water*) clearness, transparency, limpidity, pellucidity, purity. OPPOSITE: murkiness. **2** (*the clarity of her account*) lucidity, clearness, comprehensibility, intelligibility, obviousness, explicitness, plainness, simplicity. OPPOSITE: obscurity. **3** (*clarity of thought*) sharpness, keenness, definition, distinctness, precision, perspicacity. OPPOSITE: dullness.

clash *noun* **1** (*a clash with the police*) conflict, disagreement, discord, opposition, collision, crash, brush, confrontation, fight, quarrel, struggle, showdown. OPPOSITE: harmony. **2** (*the clash of the cymbals*) clang, clank, crash, bang, clatter, jangle.
➤ *verb* **1** (*clashed with our neighbours*) disagree, differ, quarrel, feud, fight, contend, battle, war, wrangle, grapple, struggle, cross swords, lock horns, conflict, collide, crash. OPPOSITE: agree. **2** (*the dates clashed*) coincide, conflict. **3** (*orange clashes with red*) jar, scream (*inf*), be discordant, be incompatible, not match, not go. **4** (*the cymbals clashed*) clang, clank, crash, bang, clatter, jangle.

clasp *verb* **1** (*clasping her purse*) hold, grip, clutch, grasp, seize, press, squeeze, hug, embrace, enfold. OPPOSITE: release. **2** (*clasped together*) fasten, clip, pin, hook, attach, join, connect, link, unite. OPPOSITE: detach.
➤ *noun* **1** (*undo the clasp*) fastener, fastening, hook, catch, hasp, buckle, clip, pin, brooch. **2** (*in his clasp*) grasp, clutch, grip, hold, hug, embrace.

class *noun* **1** (*sorted into classes*) set, collection, group, grouping, classification, category, section, division, grade, rank, league, degree, order, kind, sort, type, genre, species, genus, phylum. **2** (*people of a lower class*) status, standing, caste, stratum, level, grade, rank, quality, sphere. **3** (*in the same class at school*) form, year, grade, set, study group. **4** (*go to evening classes*) lesson, seminar, tutorial, lecture, workshop, course. **5** (*she has class*) excellence, distinction, quality, style, stylishness, elegance, chic, sophistication, refinement.
➤ *verb* classify, rank, grade, sort, order, dispose, arrange, group, categorize, file, designate, brand, pigeonhole.

classic *adj* **1** (*a classic film*) excellent, first-class, first-rate, brilliant, masterly, consummate, outstanding, exemplary, ideal, best, finest. OPPOSITE: inferior. **2** (*a

classic example*) typical, archetypal, stereotypical, stock, standard, model, definitive, quintessential, paradigmatic, characteristic, representative. OPPOSITE: atypical. **3** (*a classic design*) traditional, time-honoured, enduring, abiding, timeless, ageless, immortal.
➤ *noun* masterpiece, exemplar, paradigm, prototype, model, standard.

classical *adj* **1** (*classical architecture*) Greek, Grecian, Hellenic, Attic, Roman, Latin. **2** (*classical style*) pure, chaste, simple, understated, refined, polished, elegant, aesthetic, harmonious, symmetrical, balanced, well-proportioned. OPPOSITE: vulgar.

classification *noun* **1** (*the classification of plants*) categorization, grouping, ranking, sorting, arrangement, tabulation, codification, systematization, organization, taxonomy. **2** (*in a different classification*) category, group, class, division, set, collection.

classify *verb* sort, group, class, rank, order, rate, grade, categorize, pigeonhole, designate, dispose, arrange, distribute, tabulate, codify, systematize, catalogue, index, file.

classy *adj* stylish, elegant, chic, sophisticated, refined, excellent, fine, select, exclusive, high-class, upmarket, posh (*inf*), ritzy (*inf*). OPPOSITE: vulgar.

clatter *verb* rattle, crash, bang, clash, clank, clang, jangle.
noun rattle, crash, bang, clash, clank, clang, jangle.

clause *noun* **1** (*in clause 4 of the contract*) section, subsection, division, passage, paragraph, part, chapter, heading, item, point. **2** (*a confidentiality clause*) provision, proviso, stipulation, specification, condition, term, rider, addendum, codicil.

claw *noun* nail, talon, unguis, pincer, nipper, chela.
➤ *verb* scratch, tear, rip, lacerate, maul, gouge, dig, scrape, scrabble.

clean *adj* **1** (*a clean floor*) spotless, immaculate, unsullied, unsoiled, cleaned, cleansed, washed, laundered, scrubbed, dusted, sterilized, decontaminated, sterile, aseptic, hygienic, sanitary. OPPOSITE: dirty. **2** (*a clean record*) unblemished, unspotted, unstained, untarnished, spotless, immaculate, flawless, faultless, perfect. OPPOSITE: blemished. **3** (*clean air*) pure, unadulterated, uncontaminated, unpolluted, untainted, clear, fresh, natural. OPPOSITE: contaminated. **4** (*a clean break*) perfect, whole, entire, total, complete, utter, conclusive, decisive, final. **5** (*clean lines*) neat, tidy, elegant, graceful, shapely, streamlined, smooth, clean-cut, simple, uncluttered. OPPOSITE: untidy. **6** (*leading a clean life*) innocent, guiltless, moral, virtuous, pure, chaste, undefiled, virginal, decent, respectable, honourable, reputable, upright, honest, squeaky-clean (*inf*). OPPOSITE: immoral. **7** (*a clean fight*) fair, just, proper, legal, according to the rules. **8** (*a clean sheet of paper*) blank, empty, vacant, unused, unmarked.
➤ *verb* cleanse, purify, wash, launder, rinse, scrub, scour, dust, vacuum, sweep, mop, wipe, swab, tidy, valet. OPPOSITE: soil.
➤ *adv* completely, absolutely, totally, utterly, altogether, entirely, fully, quite.

cleanse *verb* **1** (*cleanse the wound*) clean, wash, scrub, rinse, bathe, disinfect, sterilize, decontaminate, purify. OPPOSITE: pollute. **2** (*cleansed of sin*) clear, absolve, purify, purge, lustrate.

cleanser *noun* soap, detergent, cleaner, solvent, scourer, disinfectant, purifier.

clear *adj* **1** (*on a clear day*) fine, fair, cloudless, sunny, bright, light, luminous, undimmed. OPPOSITE: dull. **2** (*clear glass*) transparent, see-through, crystalline, glassy, unclouded, limpid, pellucid, translucent, diaphanous, colourless. OPPOSITE: opaque. **3** (*a clear voice*) plain, distinct, audible, perceptible. OPPOSITE: indistinct. **4** (*a clear explanation*) lucid, explicit, distinct, crystal-clear, coherent, intelligible, understandable, comprehensible. OPPOSITE: unclear. **5** (*a clear outline*) distinct, well-defined, sharp, plain, conspicuous, visible, apparent. OPPOSITE: vague. **6** (*a clear case of mistaken identity*) obvious, evident, plain, apparent, patent, manifest, palpable, clear-cut, unquestionable, indisputable, incontrovertible, irrefutable, unmistakable, definite, positive, unequivocal, unambiguous. OPPOSITE: debatable. **7** (*keep the path clear*) open, free, empty, unobstructed, unimpeded, unhindered, unencumbered, unhampered. OPPOSITE: blocked. **8** (*a clear conscience*) innocent, guiltless, untroubled, undisturbed, tranquil, serene. OPPOSITE: guilty. **9** (*a clear record*) clean, pure, spotless, immaculate, unsullied, unblemished, untarnished, faultless, flawless, perfect. OPPOSITE: tarnished. **10** (*clear thinking*) sharp, keen, penetrating, perspicacious, quick, sensible, logical, rational, reasonable. OPPOSITE: muddled. **11** (*I'm quite clear about what I saw*) certain, sure, convinced, confident, positive. OPPOSITE: unsure. **12** (*three clear days*) whole, complete, full, entire. ≫ *adv* **1** (*loud and clear*) clearly, plainly, distinctly, audibly. **2** (*stand clear*) aside, apart, away, at a distance. ≫ *verb* **1** (*if the weather clears*) brighten, lighten, clear up, improve. OPPOSITE: darken. **2** (*cleared of all charges*) acquit, exonerate, exculpate, vindicate, absolve, pardon, discharge, release, let go, liberate, free, emancipate. OPPOSITE: condemn. **3** (*clear a space*) empty, vacate, evacuate, unload, sweep, wipe, erase, free, rid, disencumber, disentangle. **4** (*clear the drains*) unblock, unclog, decongest, clean, cleanse. OPPOSITE: block. **5** (*clear the dishes away*) remove, take, tidy, move, shift. **6** (*clear the air*) filter, refine, purify, clean. OPPOSITE: pollute. **7** (*clear your debts*) settle, square, pay off, discharge. **8** (*clear £500 a week*) earn, make, net, take home, gain, acquire, secure. **9** (*the horse cleared the fence*) jump, leap, vault, pass over, miss. OPPOSITE: hit. **10** (*the aircraft was cleared for takeoff*) authorize, sanction, permit, allow, pass, approve, give the green light (*inf*), give the go-ahead (*inf*). OPPOSITE: ban.

clear out **1** (*they cleared out without paying the bill*) leave, depart, go, decamp, withdraw, retire, go away, make oneself scarce, get out, beat it (*inf*), hop it (*inf*), clear off (*inf*), push off (*inf*), piss off (*inf*). **2** (*clear out the attic*) empty, vacate, evacuate, clean, tidy. **3** (*clear out the rubbish*) eject, throw away, throw out, get rid of, eliminate.

clear up **1** (*clear up the mystery*) clarify, elucidate, explain, solve, crack (*inf*), resolve, iron out, straighten out, untangle, unravel. **2** (*clear up the mess*) remove, take

away, tidy up, clean up. **3** (*it may clear up this afternoon*) brighten, lighten, clear, improve.

clearance *noun* **1** (*clearance for takeoff*) authorization, sanction, permission, leave, consent, green light (*inf*), go-ahead (*inf*), OK (*inf*). **2** (*clearance under the bridge*) headroom, leeway, margin, allowance, gap, space, room. **3** (*slum clearance*) emptying, vacation, evacuation, eviction, clearing, cleansing, removal, withdrawal, demolition.

clear-cut *adj* plain, distinct, specific, precise, explicit, unambiguous, clear, definite. OPPOSITE: vague.

clearing *noun* gap, space, glade, dell.

clearly *adv* plainly, obviously, evidently, patently, manifestly, palpably, unquestionably, indisputably, undoubtedly, without doubt, definitely, positively, surely, certainly. OPPOSITE: possibly.

cleave[1] *verb* (*cleave the rock*) split, divide, separate, part, open, sunder, rend, crack, cut, hack, chop, slash, hew, sever. OPPOSITE: unite.

cleave[2] *verb* (*cleave to their ideals*) cling, stick, adhere, cohere, attach, hold, hold fast, remain faithful, be devoted. OPPOSITE: disunite.

cleaver *noun* chopper, hatchet, axe, knife.

cleft *noun* rift, crack, split, fissure, crevice, chink, cranny, fracture, break, breach, chasm, gap, opening. ≫ *adj* split, divided, separated, parted, rent, torn, cloven, branched, forked.

clemency *noun* **1** (*treated with clemency*) mercy, pity, leniency, forgiveness, pardon, indulgence, tolerance, forbearance, compassion, sympathy, tenderness, kindness, humanity, benevolence, magnanimity, generosity. OPPOSITE: harshness. **2** (*the clemency of the weather*) mildness, temperateness, balminess, warmth, fairness. OPPOSITE: inclemency.

clement *adj* **1** (*a clement judge*) merciful, lenient, forgiving, indulgent, tolerant, forbearing, compassionate, tender, soft-hearted, kind, kind-hearted, benevolent, magnanimous, generous. OPPOSITE: harsh. **2** (*clement weather*) mild, temperate, moderate, balmy, warm, fair, fine. OPPOSITE: inclement.

clench *verb* close, shut, grit, double, tighten, grip, grasp, hold, clutch. OPPOSITE: relax.

clergy *pl noun* clergymen, clergywomen, churchmen, churchwomen, clerics, ecclesiastics, ministry, priesthood, the church, the cloth, holy orders.

cleric *noun* clergyman, clergywoman, churchman, churchwoman, ecclesiastic, divine, man of God, woman of God, preacher, minister, vicar, parson, pastor, rector, curate, priest, padre, chaplain, dean, canon, rabbi, imam. OPPOSITE: layperson.

clerical *adj* **1** (*clerical work*) administrative, office, white-collar, secretarial, typing, filing, bookkeeping. OPPOSITE: manual. **2** (*clerical vestments*) ecclesiastical, priestly, sacerdotal, canonical, pastoral, ministerial. OPPOSITE: lay.

clerk *noun* office worker, pen pusher (*inf*), secretary, typist, bookkeeper, receptionist, junior, assistant, official, recorder, registrar, scribe, copyist.

clever *adj* **1** (*a clever student*) bright, smart, intelligent, brainy (*inf*), quick-witted, astute, sharp, knowledgeable, educated, gifted, talented, able, capable, adroit, dexterous, adept, skilful, expert, masterly. OPPOSITE: stupid. **2** (*a clever idea*) ingenious, resourceful, inventive, shrewd, canny, cunning, sly. OPPOSITE: foolish.

cleverness *noun* brightness, smartness, intelligence, brains, astuteness, sharpness, gift, talent, ability, adroitness, dexterity, skill, ingenuity, resourcefulness, shrewdness, cunning. OPPOSITE: stupidity.

cliché *noun* platitude, commonplace, truism, banality, bromide, old chestnut (*inf*).

click *verb* **1** (*the mechanism clicked*) clack, snap, crack, clink, chink, tick, beat, clap. **2** (*he really clicked with the audience*) get on, hit it off, be on the same wavelength, be popular, be successful, go down well. **3** (*I was puzzled, then it suddenly clicked*) make sense, fall into place.
➤ *noun* clack, snap, crack, clink, chink, tick, beat, clap.

client *noun* customer, patron, regular, habitué, buyer, purchaser, shopper, consumer, user, patient, protégé, dependant.

clientele *noun* clients, customers, patrons, regulars, market, business, trade, following.

cliff *noun* crag, tor, bluff, face, precipice, scar, scarp, escarpment, headland, promontory.

climate *noun* **1** (*a change of climate*) weather, temperature, clime, place, country, region, area, zone. **2** (*the current political climate*) feeling, mood, aura, ethos, atmosphere, ambience, setting, environment, trend, tendency.

climax *noun* culmination, acme, zenith, apogee, peak, pinnacle, summit, apex, top, head, height, high point, high spot, crisis, turning point. OPPOSITE: nadir.

climb *verb* **1** (*climb a tree*) ascend, mount, scale, go up, shin up, clamber up, scramble up. OPPOSITE: descend. **2** (*as the aircraft climbed*) rise, ascend, go up, soar, bank. **3** (*the temperature was climbing*) increase, rise, go up, soar, shoot up.

climb down back down, retract, eat one's words, retreat, withdraw.

clinch *verb* **1** (*clinch the deal*) conclude, complete, close, sew up (*inf*), settle, decide, confirm, assure, seal, cap. **2** (*clinch a nail*) fix, secure, fasten, rivet, bolt, clamp. **3** (*clinching each other*) hold, grip, grasp, clutch, hug, embrace.
➤ *noun* hold, grip, clasp, clutch, hug, embrace, cuddle.

cling *verb* **1** (*cling on with both hands*) hang, hold, grip, grasp, clutch, clasp. **2** (*the pages clung together*) stick, adhere, cleave, hug, embrace.

cling to stick to, adhere to, hold fast to, abide by, stand by, defend, remain faithful to, be devoted to.

clinic *noun* health centre, medical centre, hospital, outpatients' department.

clinical *adj* **1** (*a clinical approach*) cold, unfeeling, unemotional, dispassionate, disinterested, detached, objective, impersonal, scientific, analytic. OPPOSITE: subjective. **2** (*clinical decor*) plain, simple, basic, unadorned, stark, severe, austere, spartan. OPPOSITE: ornate.

clink *verb* ring, jingle, tinkle, chink, clank.
➤ *noun* ring, jingle, tinkle, chink, clank.

clip[1] *verb* **1** (*clip the hedge*) cut, snip, trim, prune, pare,

shear, crop, dock, shorten, curtail, truncate, abridge. OPPOSITE: lengthen. **2** (*clip him round the ear*) strike, hit, cuff, box, punch, smack, thump, wallop (*inf*), whack (*inf*), clout (*inf*).
➤ *noun* **1** (*a clip round the ear*) blow, hit, cuff, box, punch, smack, thump, wallop (*inf*), whack (*inf*), clout (*inf*). **2** (*a film clip*) extract, excerpt, trailer, clipping, cutting, snippet, passage, section, piece, fragment. **3** (*the hedge needs a clip*) cut, trim, pruning, shearing, cropping, shortening, truncation. **4** (*going at a fair clip*) speed, velocity, pace, rate, lick (*inf*).

clip[2] *verb* (*clip the cheque to the letter*) fasten, fix, pin, staple, attach, hold. OPPOSITE: detach.
➤ *noun* fastener, pin, staple, grip, clasp.

clipping *noun* cutting, snippet, passage, section, piece, fragment, excerpt, extract, clip.

clique *noun* set, circle, crowd, in-crowd, coterie, gang, clan, band, bunch, group, party, faction, ring, fraternity, sorority, society, club.

cloak *verb* hide, conceal, cover, shroud, veil, screen, mask, disguise, camouflage. OPPOSITE: expose.
➤ *noun* **1** (*wearing a cloak*) cape, mantle, wrap, shawl, robe, coat. **2** (*a cloak of secrecy*) cover, mantle, shroud, veil, screen, blind, mask, front, pretext, disguise, camouflage.

clock *noun* timepiece, chronometer, chronograph, timer, dial, speedometer, taximeter, mileometer.

clock up record, register, chalk up (*inf*), reach, attain, achieve, do (*inf*).

clod *noun* **1** (*a clod of earth*) lump, mass, sod, turf. **2** (*you stupid clod!*) fool, idiot, blockhead, dunce, dolt, fathead (*inf*), chump (*inf*), wally (*sl*).

clog *verb* block, obstruct, choke, congest, jam, dam, occlude, hinder, hamper, impede, encumber, burden, load, restrain, shackle, fetter. OPPOSITE: free.
➤ *noun* block, obstruction, congestion, jam, hindrance, impediment, encumbrance, burden, drag, restraint, handicap.

cloister *noun* **1** (*a stroll through the cloisters*) colonnade, arcade, gallery, covered walk, ambulatory, corridor, aisle. **2** (*living in a cloister*) monastery, friary, priory, abbey, convent, nunnery.

cloistered *adj* secluded, sequestered, restricted, confined, enclosed, sheltered, shielded, protected, reclusive, withdrawn, solitary, hermitic, monastic, cloistral. OPPOSITE: sociable.

close[1] *verb* **1** (*close the window*) shut, slam, fasten, secure, lock, latch, bolt, bar. OPPOSITE: open. **2** (*close the gap*) stop, plug, cork, block, clog, choke, obstruct, seal, narrow, lessen, reduce. **3** (*close the conversation*) finish, conclude, end, cease, stop, terminate, discontinue, adjourn, complete, round off, wind up (*inf*). OPPOSITE: begin. **4** (*close a deal*) conclude, complete, clinch, sew up (*inf*), settle, decide, fix, agree, seal. **5** (*as the curtains closed*) come together, join, connect, unite, merge, fuse. **6** (*close with the enemy*) grapple, grip, clutch, come together.
➤ *noun* end, finish, conclusion, cessation, termination, completion, culmination, finale. OPPOSITE: beginning.

close down close, shut, shut down, cease trading, cease operating, fail, fold (*inf*), go bankrupt, go bust (*inf*).

close in approach, draw near, encircle, surround, hem in.

close[2] *adj* **1** (*close to the station*) near, near by, adjacent, adjoining, neighbouring, close by, hard by. OPPOSITE: distant. **2** (*Christmas is close*) imminent, impending, near, at hand. **3** (*a close translation*) accurate, precise, exact, faithful, conscientious, true, strict, literal. OPPOSITE: rough. **4** (*they were close in age*) similar, alike, like, akin, comparable, corresponding. **5** (*a close friend*) dear, intimate, familiar, bosom, devoted, loving, attached, inseparable. **6** (*my brother and I are very close*) devoted, inseparable, friendly, chummy (*inf*), matey (*inf*), pally (*inf*). **7** (*in close formation*) dense, solid, compact, condensed, compressed, tight, packed, squeezed, crowded, congested, cramped. OPPOSITE: loose. **8** (*it's very close today*) oppressive, heavy, muggy, humid, sultry, sticky, stifling, suffocating, airless, unventilated, stuffy, fuggy, musty, stale, stagnant. OPPOSITE: fresh. **9** (*a close contest*) well-matched, hard-fought, neck-and-neck. **10** (*pay close attention*) fixed, concentrated, keen, earnest, intent, dogged, careful, assiduous, thorough, painstaking, rigorous, detailed, minute. OPPOSITE: cursory. **11** (*close with her money*) mean, miserly, tight-fisted, tight (*inf*), niggardly, near, parsimonious, stingy, illiberal, ungenerous. OPPOSITE: generous. **12** (*close about their plans*) secretive, uncommunicative, unforthcoming, reticent, reserved, taciturn, quiet, private, secret. OPPOSITE: open.

close[3] *noun* (*walk across the close*) courtyard, quadrangle, enclosure, square, place, piazza, mews, cul-de-sac.

closet *noun* cupboard, wardrobe, cabinet, locker, room. ≫ *adj* secret, private, hidden, concealed, undisclosed, unrevealed, covert, furtive, surreptitious. OPPOSITE: open. ≫ *verb* shut away, confine, sequester, cloister.

closure *noun* close, closing, closedown, shutting, shutdown, end, finish, conclusion, cessation, termination, stoppage, obstruction. OPPOSITE: start.

clot *noun* **1** (*clot of blood*) lump, mass, clump, glob, coagulation, thrombus. **2** (*you silly clot!*) fool, ass, blockhead, dolt, dope (*inf*), buffoon, ninny, nincompoop, nitwit (*inf*). ≫ *verb* coagulate, congeal, thicken, curdle, set, solidify, cake.

cloth *noun* **1** (*a length of cloth*) fabric, textile, material, stuff. **2** (*wipe it with a cloth*) rag, duster, flannel.

clothe *verb* dress, attire, garb, robe, deck, array, apparel, accoutre, habit, fit out, rig out, turn out, cover, wrap, drape, swathe, endow, invest. OPPOSITE: strip.

clothing *pl noun* clothes, garments, dress, attire, wear, garb, gear (*inf*), clobber (*inf*), togs (*inf*), wardrobe, outfit, costume, rigout (*inf*), getup (*inf*), habit, robes, vestments, raiment, finery, glad rags (*inf*).

cloud *noun* **1** (*a cloud of spray*) haze, mist, fog, vapour, nebulosity. **2** (*a cloud of dust*) pall, shroud, cloak, mantle. **3** (*a cloud of insects*) swarm, flock, crowd, throng, horde, host, multitude. **4** (*cast a cloud over the celebrations*) shadow, gloom, darkness, obscurity. ≫ *verb* dim, dull, darken, obscure, shade, shadow, overshadow, eclipse, conceal, cover, veil, shroud, blur, mist, fog, confuse, muddle. OPPOSITE: clear.

cloudy *adj* **1** (*a cloudy day*) overcast, dull, grey, sunless, dark, gloomy, lowering, leaden, murky, hazy, misty, foggy. OPPOSITE: bright. **2** (*cloudy water*) opaque, milky, murky, muddy, turbid. OPPOSITE: clear. **3** (*a cloudy recollection*) dim, obscure, confused, muddled, blurred, hazy, indistinct, nebulous, vague, indefinite. OPPOSITE: distinct.

clout *verb* hit, strike, thump, wallop (*inf*), clobber (*inf*), smack, slap, whack (*inf*), cuff, box, punch, sock (*inf*). ≫ *noun* **1** (*a clout on the head*) blow, thump, wallop (*inf*), smack, slap, whack (*inf*), cuff, punch, sock (*inf*). **2** (*political clout*) influence, pull (*inf*), power, muscle (*inf*), authority, prestige, standing, weight.

clown *noun* **1** (*circus clowns*) buffoon, jester, fool, harlequin, pierrot. **2** (*the office clown*) joker, comic, comedian, wag, wit. **3** (*some clown pressed the wrong switch*) fool, idiot, imbecile, dolt, dope (*inf*), nitwit (*inf*), twit (*inf*), wally (*sl*).

clown around fool around, mess around (*inf*), muck around (*inf*), joke, jest, act the fool, act the goat (*inf*).

clownish *adj* foolish, silly, awkward, clumsy, ungainly, coarse, rough, loutish, oafish.

cloy *verb* surfeit, satiate, sate, glut, sicken, nauseate.

cloying *adj* sickly, sickening, nauseating, sugary, saccharine, fulsome, excessive.

club *noun* **1** (*join the club*) society, association, organization, company, group, circle, clique, coterie, set, fraternity, sorority, brotherhood, sisterhood, guild, league, union. **2** (*armed with clubs*) cudgel, truncheon, bludgeon, cosh, stick, bat, staff, mace. ≫ *verb* beat, batter, bash, cudgel, bludgeon, cosh, hit, strike, clobber (*inf*), clout (*inf*).

club together unite, combine, amalgamate, join forces, pool resources, share the cost, contribute, have a whip-round (*inf*).

clue *noun* hint, tip, guide, indication, lead, pointer, sign, evidence, key, tip-off, suggestion, intimation, inkling, suspicion.

clump *noun* bunch, cluster, bundle, tuft, mass, lump, group, collection, accumulation, agglomeration, gathering, assembly. ≫ *verb* **1** (*clumped across the stage*) clomp, stump, stomp, stamp, thump, thud, tramp, plod, trudge, lumber. **2** (*buildings clumped together*) bunch, cluster, bundle, mass, group, collect, accumulate, gather, congregate, assemble. OPPOSITE: disperse.

clumsy *adj* **1** (*a clumsy person*) awkward, maladroit, bungling, blundering, bumbling, unskilful, inexpert, ham-fisted (*inf*), cack-handed (*inf*), all thumbs (*inf*), uncoordinated, ungainly, ungraceful, gauche, accident-prone, butter-fingered (*inf*), lumbering, ponderous, like a bull in a china shop (*inf*). OPPOSITE: adroit. **2** (*a clumsy desk*) bulky, heavy, cumbersome, unwieldy, unmanoeuvrable, awkward. **3** (*a clumsy remark*) gauche, tactless, insensitive, crass, graceless, uncouth, rough, crude. OPPOSITE: tactful.

cluster *noun* clump, bunch, bundle, knot, huddle, group, company, gathering, assembly, collection, accumulation, aggregation, agglomeration. ≫ *verb* clump, bunch, bundle, gather, assemble, collect, flock, throng, crowd, accumulate, aggregate, agglomerate. OPPOSITE: disperse.

clutch *verb* hold, grip, hang on to, cling to, clasp, clench, grasp, seize, snatch, grab, catch at, reach for.
➤ *noun* hold, grip, clasp, grasp.

clutches *pl noun* power, control, keeping, custody, possession, hands, claws, talons, grip, grasp.

clutter *verb* litter, strew, scatter, disorder, disarrange, mess up, make untidy, fill, encumber.
➤ *noun* litter, mess, rubbish, lumber, jumble, muddle, hotchpotch, disorder, disarray, confusion, chaos.

coach *noun* **1** (*travel by coach*) bus, charabanc. **2** (*a railway coach*) carriage, wagon, car. **3** (*a horse-drawn coach*) carriage, chariot. **4** (*a tennis coach*) tutor, instructor, trainer, teacher, mentor, manager.
➤ *verb* train, drill, exercise, instruct, teach, tutor, cram (*inf*).

coagulate *verb* clot, thicken, curdle, congeal, gel, harden, solidify, set.

coalesce *verb* unite, combine, join, incorporate, integrate, amalgamate, blend, mix, commingle, merge, fuse, consolidate. OPPOSITE: separate.

coalition *noun* alliance, confederation, confederacy, federation, affiliation, association, league, bloc, compact, union, amalgamation, merger, fusion, combination.

coarse *adj* **1** (*coarse texture*) rough, uneven, scaly, bristly, prickly, lumpy, thick, crude, impure, unrefined, unpolished, unfinished. OPPOSITE: fine. **2** (*coarse humour*) rude, impolite, vulgar, indecent, obscene, blue (*inf*), earthy, dirty, smutty, crude, gross, offensive, indelicate, immodest, prurient, lewd, ribald, bawdy, raunchy (*inf*). OPPOSITE: polite. **3** (*coarse behaviour*) boorish, loutish, churlish, rude, ill-mannered, uncivil, uncouth, unsophisticated. OPPOSITE: refined.

coarsen *verb* roughen, thicken, toughen, harden. OPPOSITE: soften.

coast *noun* seaside, shore, seashore, beach, strand, littoral, shoreline, seaboard.
➤ *verb* sail, glide, cruise, drift, taxi, freewheel.

coat *noun* **1** (*buy a new coat*) overcoat, jacket, blazer, anorak, parka, raincoat, mackintosh, fur, cape, cloak, mantle. **2** (*animals with thick coats*) fur, hair, pelt, hide, skin, fleece, wool. **3** (*another coat of paint*) covering, coating, layer, overlay, film, glaze, varnish, veneer, finish.
➤ *verb* cover, overlay, apply, spread, smear, daub, paint, glaze, finish.

coating *noun* coat, layer, dusting, film, sheet, blanket, cover, covering, glaze, varnish, veneer, finish, patina, overlay, membrane, lamination.

coax *verb* cajole, wheedle, persuade, talk into, prevail upon, induce, entice, lure, tempt, beguile, flatter, inveigle, soft-soap (*inf*), sweet-talk (*inf*), urge, implore. OPPOSITE: coerce.

cobble *verb* mend, repair, patch, botch.
cobble together make, improvise, knock up, put together.

cock *noun* rooster, cockerel, chanticleer, male bird. OPPOSITE: hen.

➤ *verb* **1** (*the dog cocked its ears*) raise, lift, prick up, stick up. **2** (*with her hat cocked at jaunty angle*) tilt, tip, slant, incline.

cockeyed *adj* **1** (*the picture is cockeyed*) crooked, askew, awry, lopsided, aslant, oblique, skew-whiff (*inf*). **2** (*a cockeyed plan*) crazy, absurd, ludicrous, preposterous, barmy (*inf*), mad, insane.

cocksure *adj* confident, assured, overconfident, arrogant, cocky, presumptuous, bumptious, self-important, pushy (*inf*). OPPOSITE: humble.

cocky *adj* overconfident, cocksure, arrogant, proud, egotistical, vain, conceited, swollen-headed. OPPOSITE: modest.

cocoon *verb* envelop, wrap, cover, protect, overprotect, isolate, insulate, cushion. OPPOSITE: expose.

coddle *verb* pamper, indulge, humour, cosset, mollycoddle, overprotect, baby, spoil, pet. OPPOSITE: harden.

code *noun* **1** (*a code of conduct*) system, canon, laws, rules, regulations, guidelines, principles, ethics, morals, morality, custom, convention, etiquette, manners. **2** (*written in code*) cipher, cryptograph, cryptogram, secret writing, secret language. **3** (*a dialling code*) numbers, letters, characters, symbols.

codicil *noun* supplement, appendix, addendum, addition, rider, postscript.

codify *verb* systematize, organize, classify, catalogue, order, tabulate, collect.

coerce *verb* force, constrain, compel, oblige, twist someone's arm (*inf*), press, pressure, pressurize, lean on (*inf*), put the screws on (*inf*), drive, impel, bulldoze (*inf*), browbeat, bully, intimidate, dragoon, press-gang. OPPOSITE: coax.

coercion *noun* force, constraint, compulsion, pressure, duress, browbeating, bullying, intimidation, strongarm tactics. OPPOSITE: coaxing.

coexistent *adj* coeval, coetaneous, contemporary, contemporaneous, simultaneous, synchronous, concurrent.

coffee *noun* espresso, cappuccino, filter coffee, instant coffee, decaffeinated coffee, decaf (*inf*).

coffer *noun* chest, trunk, case, box, casket, repository, treasury, safe, strongbox, moneybox.

coffin *noun* casket, sarcophagus, box, wooden overcoat (*inf*).

cogency *noun* force, strength, conviction, power, potency, weight, authority, effectiveness, conclusiveness. OPPOSITE: weakness.

cogent *adj* forceful, strong, convincing, persuasive, potent, powerful, weighty, influential, authoritative, telling, effective, compelling, irresistible, conclusive. OPPOSITE: weak.

cogitate *verb* think, ponder, ruminate, meditate, reflect, muse, contemplate, consider, deliberate, mull over.

cogitation *noun* thought, rumination, meditation, reflection, contemplation, consideration, deliberation.

cognate *adj* related, akin, kindred, consanguine,

connected, allied, affiliated, associated, analogous, corresponding, alike, similar. OPPOSITE: unrelated.

cognition noun perception, awareness, discernment, intuition, insight, reasoning, rationality, intelligence, enlightenment, comprehension, understanding, apprehension, knowledge, cognizance.

cognizance noun awareness, consciousness, knowledge, acquaintance, familiarity, cognition, perception, comprehension, understanding, recognition. OPPOSITE: ignorance.
take cognizance of recognize, acknowledge, accept, notice, note, heed.

cognizant adj aware, conscious, informed, knowledgeable, versed, acquainted, familiar, conversant. OPPOSITE: ignorant.

cognomen noun surname, title, name, nickname, sobriquet.

cohabit verb live together, live in sin (inf), shack up together (sl), sleep together.

cohere verb 1 (cohering parts) stick, adhere, cling, cleave, join, unite, fuse, coalesce, consolidate. OPPOSITE: part. 2 (the arguments don't cohere) be consistent, be connected, follow, make sense, hang together, correspond, agree, harmonize.

coherence noun consistency, connection, correspondence, congruity, agreement, harmony, concordance, unity, logic, rationality, reason, sense, lucidity, articulateness, intelligibility, comprehension. OPPOSITE: incoherence.

coherent adj consistent, connected, systematic, orderly, organized, logical, rational, reasoned, lucid, articulate, intelligible, comprehensible. OPPOSITE: incoherent.

cohesion noun adhesion, adherence, union, fusion, coalescence, accretion, consolidation. OPPOSITE: disintegration.

cohort noun 1 (Roman cohorts) troop, division, squad, squadron, brigade, regiment, legion, company, band, body, group. 2 (the president and his cohorts) friend, companion, associate, crony, mate (inf), buddy (inf), supporter, follower, assistant, accomplice.

coil noun spiral, helix, corkscrew, convolution, curl, loop, ring, twist, whorl, roll.
➤ verb wind, twine, twist, snake, curl, loop, spiral, convolute, wreathe, entwine. OPPOSITE: uncoil.

coin verb 1 (coin a phrase) formulate, make up, devise, conceive, think up, dream up, invent, create, originate, fabricate, make, produce. 2 (coin money) mint, mould, stamp, forge, counterfeit.
➤ noun 1 (a handful of coins) piece, bit, copper. 2 (paid in coin) money, specie, cash, change, silver, gold.

coincide verb 1 (his account coincides with hers) agree, concur, correspond, tally, harmonize, accord, match, square. OPPOSITE: conflict. 2 (their visit coincided with the carnival) happen together, occur simultaneously, be concurrent, clash, synchronize, coexist.

coincidence noun 1 (by sheer coincidence) chance, fluke, accident, fortuity, serendipity, stroke of luck. OPPOSITE: design. 2 (the coincidence of ideas) correspondence, harmony, agreement, concurrence. OPPOSITE: difference.

3 (the coincidence of events) synchronism, simultaneity, concurrence, concomitance, coexistence.

coincident adj 1 (coincident with the facts) corresponding, agreeing, concurring, harmonious, in accordance, matching. OPPOSITE: differing. 2 (coincident events) synchronous, simultaneous, concurrent, concomitant, contemporaneous, coexistent.

coincidental adj chance, fortuitous, serendipitous, casual, accidental, unintentional, unplanned. OPPOSITE: planned.

coitus noun coition, copulation, mating, coupling, sexual intercourse, lovemaking, carnal knowledge, sex, having it off (sl), having it away (sl), bonking (sl), shagging (sl), screwing (sl), fucking (sl).

cold adj 1 (cold weather) cool, chill, chilly, fresh, nippy (inf), parky (inf), frosty, icy, freezing, frozen, frigid, gelid, arctic, polar, glacial, wintry, raw, bitter, biting. OPPOSITE: hot. 2 (turn the heating up if you're cold) chilly, shivery, chilled to the marrow, freezing, frozen, numb. OPPOSITE: warm. 3 (a cold manner) unfeeling, uncaring, unsympathetic, unresponsive, insensitive, heartless, callous, impassive, indifferent, unmoved, unconcerned, phlegmatic, unemotional, distant, remote, standoffish, aloof, cool, frigid, glacial, stony, flinty, cold-hearted, unfriendly, inhospitable, hostile. OPPOSITE: warm-hearted. 4 (it leaves me cold) unresponsive, indifferent, unmoved, apathetic, lukewarm, uninterested. OPPOSITE: passionate.
➤ noun coldness, coolness, chill, chilliness, frost, frostiness, ice, iciness, frigidity, wintriness, rawness, bitterness. OPPOSITE: heat.

cold-blooded adj cruel, inhuman, barbarous, barbaric, brutal, savage, vicious, ruthless, merciless, pitiless, heartless, callous, unfeeling. OPPOSITE: humane.

collaborate verb 1 (collaborate on a project) cooperate, work together, join forces, team up, unite, combine. OPPOSITE: compete. 2 (collaborate with the enemy) conspire, collude, connive, intrigue, fraternize, associate.

collaboration noun 1 (working in collaboration) cooperation, partnership, alliance, association, teamwork, union, combined effort. 2 (collaboration with the enemy) conspiracy, collusion, intrigue, fraternization, treachery, betrayal.

collaborator noun 1 (my collaborator on the project) partner, associate, confederate, colleague, co-worker, teammate, contributor, participant. OPPOSITE: rival. 2 (executed as a collaborator) conspirator, colluder, collaborationist, fraternizer, traitor, turncoat, renegade, quisling. OPPOSITE: patriot.

collapse verb 1 (the wall collapsed) subside, fall in, cave in, give way, crumble, disintegrate, fall to pieces, come apart, break down, sink, founder. 2 (the deal collapsed) founder, fold (inf), fail, flop (inf), break down, come to nothing, fall through. OPPOSITE: recover. 3 (he collapsed at work) faint, pass out, swoon, keel over, black out, lose consciousness. OPPOSITE: revive. 4 (she collapsed into an armchair) fall, drop, flop, slump.
➤ noun 1 (the collapse of the bridge) subsidence, cave-in, crumbling, disintegration, fall, breakdown. 2 (the collapse of the business) failure, flop (inf), fall, breakdown,

downfall, ruin. OPPOSITE: recovery. **3** (*recovered from his collapse*) faint, swoon, blackout, loss of consciousness. OPPOSITE: resuscitation. **4** (*she was in a state of collapse*) exhaustion, prostration.

collar *noun* neckband, ruff, ruche, gorget.
≫ *verb* grab, seize, nab (*inf*), catch, capture, apprehend, arrest, nick (*inf*). OPPOSITE: release.

collate *verb* collect, gather, sort, order, arrange, organize, compare, contrast, check, verify.

collateral *noun* security, surety, deposit, pledge, assurance, guarantee.
≫ *adj* indirect, related, allied, connected, subordinate, secondary, supporting.

collation *noun* **1** (*the collation of information*) collection, gathering, sorting, organization, comparison, verification. **2** (*a cold collation*) snack, light meal.

colleague *noun* partner, associate, co-worker, fellow-worker, workmate, teammate, collaborator, helper, assistant, auxiliary, ally, confederate, companion, comrade, confrère. OPPOSITE: opponent.

collect *verb* **1** (*collect stamps*) amass, accumulate, gather, glean, assemble, aggregate, agglomerate, save, hoard, stockpile, pile up, heap up. OPPOSITE: scatter. **2** (*a crowd collected outside*) congregate, gather, muster, rally, assemble, convene, cluster, flock together. OPPOSITE: disperse. **3** (*I'll collect the car tomorrow*) fetch, pick up, call for, go and get. OPPOSITE: deliver. **4** (*collect money for charity*) solicit, raise, gather, obtain, acquire, secure. **5** (*paused to collect her thoughts*) gather, muster, rally, assemble, compose.

collected *adj* calm, composed, poised, self-possessed, serene, tranquil, cool, unruffled, unperturbed. OPPOSITE: agitated.

collection *noun* **1** (*a collection of old photographs*) set, series, group, assortment, miscellany, job lot, cluster, mass, accumulation, heap, pile, stockpile, hoard, store, stock, display, array. **2** (*a collection of people*) gathering, muster, assembly, congregation, crowd, throng, flock, cluster, group, body, company. **3** (*a collection of love poems*) anthology, compilation, ana, corpus. **4** (*a collection for charity*) alms, donation, contribution, whip-round (*inf*). **5** (*take the collection in church*) offering, offertory.

collective *adj* joint, combined, united, concerted, collaborative, cooperative, shared, common, mutual, communal, corporate, aggregate, cumulative.

college *noun* **1** (*study at college*) educational establishment, school, university, academy, institution, institute, department, faculty. **2** (*an electoral college*) association, society, company, corporation, guild, union, league, fellowship.

collide *verb* **1** (*the cars collided head-on*) crash, smash, bump, bang, meet, encounter. **2** (*their views collided*) clash, conflict, differ, disagree, be at variance. OPPOSITE: accord.

collision *noun* **1** (*injured in a head-on collision*) crash, smash, impact, bump, prang (*inf*), accident, pile-up. **2** (*a collision between the two factions*) clash, conflict, difference, disagreement, variance, opposition, confrontation, brush, fight, battle. OPPOSITE: agreement.

collocate *verb* arrange, order, dispose, group, put together, combine, juxtapose.

collocation *noun* grouping, arrangement, order, combination, juxtaposition, phrase, expression.

colloquial *adj* informal, casual, conversational, chatty, familiar, everyday, idiomatic, vernacular, popular, demotic. OPPOSITE: formal.

colloquy *noun* conversation, discourse, talk, dialogue, debate, discussion, conference.

collude *verb* connive, conspire, intrigue, plot, scheme, machinate, collaborate.

collusion *noun* connivance, complicity, collaboration, cahoots (*inf*), conspiracy, intrigue, plot, scheme, machination.

collusive *adj* conniving, conspiring, plotting, scheming, deceitful, fraudulent, dishonest. OPPOSITE: honest.

colonist *noun* settler, pioneer, colonial, expatriate, migrant, emigrant, immigrant.

colonize *verb* settle, occupy, populate, people, found, pioneer.

colonnade *noun* arcade, portico, peristyle, cloister, gallery, covered walk.

colony *noun* **1** (*one of Spain's former colonies*) settlement, community, province, dominion, territory, possession, dependency, protectorate, outpost, satellite state. **2** (*a colony of artists*) group, association, community, commune, settlement, district, quarter, ghetto.

colossal *adj* enormous, huge, immense, vast, massive, whopping (*inf*), gigantic, giant, gargantuan, Brobdingnagian, mammoth, elephantine, herculean, titanic, mountainous, prodigious, tremendous, monumental, mega (*inf*). OPPOSITE: tiny.

colour *noun* **1** (*paint it a different colour*) tint, hue, shade, tinge, tone, colouring, coloration. **2** (*an artist's colours*) paint, pigment, colorant, dye, tint, tincture. **3** (*bring some colour to their cheeks*) rosiness, ruddiness, redness, pinkness, flush, blush, glow, bloom. OPPOSITE: pallor. **4** (*races of different colours*) complexion, pigmentation, colouring, coloration. **5** (*add colour to the story*) life, liveliness, animation, vividness, richness. **6** (*under the colour of religion*) front, facade, appearance, show, pretext, excuse, disguise, pretence, guise, semblance.
≫ *verb* **1** (*colour the fabrics*) dye, tint, paint, stain, tinge. **2** (*she coloured at the mention of his name*) blush, flush, redden, go crimson. OPPOSITE: blanch. **3** (*colour an account*) distort, pervert, garble, falsify, misrepresent, varnish, embroider, exaggerate, overstate. **4** (*opinions coloured by propaganda*) influence, affect, bias, prejudice, slant, warp, distort, pervert, taint.

colourful *adj* **1** (*colourful clothing*) bright, gaudy, multicoloured, motley, variegated, psychedelic, kaleidoscopic, brilliant, vivid, rich, vibrant. OPPOSITE: colourless. **2** (*a colourful account*) vivid, graphic, rich, vibrant, lively, animated, interesting, exciting. OPPOSITE: dull.

colourless *adj* **1** (*colourless plastic*) uncoloured, achromatic, hueless, blanched, bleached, neutral, monochrome, transparent, clear. OPPOSITE: coloured.

2 (*children with colourless faces*) pale, wan, washed-out, anaemic, sickly, pasty, pallid, ashen, livid. OPPOSITE: ruddy. **3** (*a colourless existence*) dull, dreary, drab, lacklustre, dry, insipid, vapid, tame, monotonous, boring, uninteresting, characterless, unmemorable. OPPOSITE: colourful.

colours *pl noun* **1** (*a nation's colours*) flag, pennant, ensign, standard, banner, emblem, insignia, badge, uniform. **2** (*saw him in his true colours*) nature, character, personality, identity.

coltish *adj* frisky, frolicsome, playful, sportive, lively, spirited, unruly. OPPOSITE: lethargic.

column *noun* **1** (*supported by columns*) pillar, post, shaft, upright, support, pier, pilaster, caryatid, obelisk, monolith. **2** (*a column of soldiers*) line, file, queue, row, rank, string, procession, train, cavalcade. **3** (*a newspaper column*) article, feature, piece, item, editorial, review, report, story.

columnist *noun* journalist, reporter, correspondent, writer, editor, critic, reviewer.

coma *noun* unconsciousness, insensibility, oblivion, blackout, stupor, trance, torpor, lethargy, somnolence. OPPOSITE: consciousness.

comatose *adj* unconscious, insensible, in a coma, out, out cold, drugged, stupefied, torpid, lethargic, sluggish, drowsy, sleepy, somnolent. OPPOSITE: conscious.

comb *verb* **1** (*comb your hair*) disentangle, untangle, smooth, neaten, tidy, groom, arrange, dress, curry. **2** (*combed the wreckage*) search, sift, rake, rummage, ransack, scour, go over with a fine-tooth comb.

combat *verb* fight, oppose, resist, withstand, defy, take up arms, battle, do battle, war, wage war, contest, contend, struggle, strive. OPPOSITE: surrender.
≫ *noun* war, battle, action, hostilities, fight, fighting, conflict, encounter, clash, skirmish, engagement, struggle, strife, contest, bout, duel. OPPOSITE: peace.

combatant *noun* fighter, soldier, serviceman, servicewoman, warrior, enemy, foe, adversary, opponent, contender, contestant, competitor, rival.
≫ *adj* fighting, warring, belligerent, opposing, conflicting, rival. OPPOSITE: neutral.

combative *adj* aggressive, militant, warlike, belligerent, bellicose, pugnacious, argumentative, quarrelsome, contentious, antagonistic, hostile. OPPOSITE: pacific.

combination *noun* **1** (*a combination of sorrow and anger*) mixture, mix, blend, compound, synthesis, amalgamation, amalgam, composite, alloy, solution. **2** (*the combination of the ingredients*) mixing, blending, mingling, amalgamation, incorporation, integration, fusion, coalescence. OPPOSITE: separation. **3** (*businesses working in combination*) association, union, alliance, coalition, confederacy, confederation, federation, league, consortium, syndicate, synergy, cooperation, coordination, conjunction.

combine *verb* mix, blend, mingle, compound, synthesize, amalgamate, alloy, put together, incorporate, integrate, homogenize, unite, join, fuse, bond, marry, link, connect, pool, merge, ally, join forces, team up, cooperate. OPPOSITE: separate.
≫ *noun* association, union, alliance, coalition, confederacy, league, consortium, syndicate.

combustible *adj* inflammable, flammable, ignitable, incendiary, explosive. OPPOSITE: incombustible.

combustion *noun* burning, incineration, cremation, ignition, igniting, kindling, firing.

come *verb* **1** (*come here*) approach, advance, near, draw near, move towards. OPPOSITE: go. **2** (*I invited her but she didn't come*) arrive, enter, attend, appear, put in an appearance, materialize, turn up, show up (*inf*). OPPOSITE: depart. **3** (*what comes next*) occur, happen, take place, befall, come about, come to pass, transpire. **4** (*he comes from Australia*) originate, hail, issue, emanate, proceed, flow, spring. **5** (*skill comes from practice*) result, ensue, arise, stem, develop, evolve. **6** (*the skirt comes to my knees*) reach, extend, stretch. **7** (*it comes in various colours*) be available, be made, be produced. **8** (*don't come the innocent with me*) act, play, imitate.

come about occur, happen, take place, befall, come to pass, transpire, result, ensue, arise.

come across find, discover, stumble upon, happen upon, chance upon, hit upon, meet, encounter, run into, bump into (*inf*).

come along 1 (*his work is coming along*) progress, advance, develop, improve, get better, pick up, recover, rally, mend. OPPOSITE: deteriorate. **2** (*come along, we're late!*) hurry, hurry up, make haste, get a move on (*inf*), speed up, step on it (*inf*).

come apart break, crumble, disintegrate, collapse, fall to pieces, fall to bits, separate, split, tear.

come at attack, assault, assail, charge, rush, fall upon. OPPOSITE: resist.

come between separate, divide, part, split up, alienate, estrange.

come by get, obtain, acquire, procure, secure, get hold of (*inf*), get one's hands on (*inf*).

come clean own up, confess, admit, acknowledge, make a clean breast of it (*inf*).

come down fall, drop, descend, decline, decrease, reduce, deteriorate, worsen. OPPOSITE: go up.

come down on criticize, slate (*inf*), censure, blame, rebuke, reproach, reprimand, jump on (*inf*), berate, upbraid. OPPOSITE: praise.

come down to mean, amount to, boil down to, end up as.

come down with catch, contract, sicken for, fall ill with.

come in enter, penetrate, cross the threshold, arrive, appear, turn up, show up (*inf*). OPPOSITE: leave.

come in for suffer, endure, undergo, experience, get, receive.

come into inherit, be left, succeed to, receive.

come off succeed, work, happen, occur, end up.

come on progress, advance, develop, come along, improve, get better, thrive, flourish.

come out 1 (*when her book comes out*) become available, be published, be issued, be launched, appear. **2** (*the truth came out*) become known, be revealed, be disclosed, be divulged, be released. **3** (*the daffodils are coming out*) flower, bloom, blossom. **4** (*it came out all right*) end, finish, conclude, terminate.

come out with say, speak, utter, state, declare, exclaim, blurt out.

come round 1 (*coming round from the anaesthetic*)

regain consciousness, revive, recover, come to, awaken, wake up. **2** (*come round to our way of thinking*) submit, yield, give way, relent, mellow, soften, acquiesce, concede, grant, allow. **3** (*come round for a cup of tea*) visit, call, drop in (*inf*), pop in (*inf*).

come through survive, endure, withstand, succeed, triumph.

come to 1 (*I came to at the foot of the stairs*) regain consciousness, revive, recover, come round, awaken, wake up. OPPOSITE: faint. **2** (*the bill came to £500*) total, add up to, amount to, equal. **3** (*come to the end*) arrive at, reach, attain, achieve. **4** (*the answer suddenly came to me*) strike, occur to, dawn on.

come up arise, crop up, happen, occur, present itself.

come up to meet, reach, match, measure up to, bear comparison with, hold a candle to (*inf*).

come up with advance, put forward, propose, suggest, submit, present, offer, produce, provide, supply.

comeback *noun* **1** (*a singer making a comeback*) return, reappearance, resurgence, revival, recovery, rally. **2** (*a witty comeback*) reply, answer, response, rejoinder, retort, riposte.

comedian *noun* comic, wit, wag, humorist, entertainer, clown, buffoon, jester, joker, card (*inf*).

comedown *noun* decline, degradation, demotion, downgrading, humiliation, descent, reverse, setback, blow, disappointment, letdown, anticlimax, deflation.

comedy *noun* **1** (*made her name in comedy*) farce, slapstick, satire, burlesque, pantomime, vaudeville, revue, light entertainment, sitcom (*inf*). OPPOSITE: tragedy. **2** (*the comedy of the situation*) humour, fun, wit, drollery, joking, badinage, levity, hilarity, funniness. OPPOSITE: gravity.

comely *adj* pretty, attractive, good-looking, beautiful, handsome, fair, bonny, lovely, pleasing, charming, engaging, fetching, appealing, winsome, elegant, graceful. OPPOSITE: ugly.

come-on *noun* attraction, enticement, lure, inducement, temptation, encouragement, invitation.

come-uppance *noun* just deserts, due reward, retribution, nemesis, punishment, requital, recompense.

comfort *verb* console, solace, sympathize with, empathize with, cheer, gladden, hearten, encourage, support, help, strengthen, invigorate, revive, refresh, reassure, relieve, ease, alleviate, soothe, assuage, calm. OPPOSITE: trouble.
≫ *noun* **1** (*words of comfort*) consolation, solace, sympathy, commiseration, condolence, cheer, encouragement, support, help, aid, succour, compensation, reassurance, relief, ease, alleviation. OPPOSITE: distress. **2** (*a life of comfort*) ease, repose, relaxation, well-being, contentment, content, satisfaction, peace, tranquillity, snugness, cosiness, luxury, opulence, plenty, sufficiency. OPPOSITE: discomfort.

comfortable *adj* **1** (*comfortable furniture*) snug, cosy, homely, comfy (*inf*), agreeable, pleasant, easy, relaxing, restful, convenient, commodious, ample, roomy. OPPOSITE: uncomfortable. **2** (*a comfortable lifestyle*) luxurious, opulent, well-off, well-to-do, prosperous, affluent. OPPOSITE: deprived. **3** (*I don't feel comfortable*

about it) relaxed, at ease, satisfied, contented, happy, cheerful, serene, tranquil. OPPOSITE: uneasy.

comforting *adj* consoling, consolatory, sympathetic, cheering, heartening, encouraging, supportive, helpful, refreshing, reassuring, soothing, calming. OPPOSITE: disturbing.

comic *adj* funny, humorous, amusing, entertaining, diverting, light, witty, droll, facetious, jocular, comical, zany, farcical, slapstick. OPPOSITE: serious.
≫ *noun* comedian, wit, wag, humorist, entertainer, clown, buffoon, jester, joker, card (*inf*).

comical *adj* **1** (*a comical dance*) funny, amusing, entertaining, diverting, comic, droll, hilarious, sidesplitting, priceless (*inf*). OPPOSITE: serious. **2** (*a comical idea*) ludicrous, ridiculous, absurd, silly, laughable, risible. OPPOSITE: sensible.

coming *adj* approaching, advancing, near, at hand, imminent, impending, in store, forthcoming, future, next, due. OPPOSITE: past.
≫ *noun* advent, approach, advance, arrival, appearance, birth, dawn. OPPOSITE: departure.

comity *noun* civility, courtesy, politeness, friendliness, affability, harmony, accord. OPPOSITE: incivility.

command *verb* **1** (*commanded them to stop*) order, bid, enjoin, direct, charge, instruct, prescribe, compel, require, demand. OPPOSITE: beg. **2** (*command an army*) lead, head, govern, rule, control, direct, manage, supervise, superintend, preside over, dominate. OPPOSITE: obey.
≫ *noun* **1** (*obey his commands*) order, bidding, behest, injunction, direction, directive, charge, instruction, commandment, decree, edict, dictate, precept, mandate, requirement, demand. OPPOSITE: entreaty. **2** (*under her command*) leadership, government, rule, control, direction, management, administration, supervision, superintendence, charge, authority, power, sway, mastery, ascendancy, dominion, domination.

commandeer *verb* seize, take, usurp, arrogate, hijack, appropriate, requisition, expropriate, confiscate, sequester, sequestrate, impound. OPPOSITE: surrender.

commander *noun* captain, commanding officer, number one (*inf*), chief, leader, head, governor, ruler, director, boss (*inf*).

commanding *adj* **1** (*in a commanding position*) leading, controlling, directing, dominant, superior, advantageous, strong, powerful, dominating, overlooking. OPPOSITE: subordinate. **2** (*a commanding personality*) forceful, assertive, compelling, impressive, imposing, authoritative, masterful, imperious, peremptory. OPPOSITE: meek.

commemorate *verb* celebrate, observe, keep, mark, honour, pay tribute to, salute, solemnize, immortalize, perpetuate, memorialize, remember. OPPOSITE: forget.

commemoration *noun* celebration, observance, ceremony, memorial service, honour, tribute, salute, remembrance, memory, memorialization, perpetuation, immortalization.

commemorative *adj* memorial, celebratory, dedicatory, marking, in honour, in tribute, in remembrance, in memory.

commence *verb* **1** (*commence work*) begin, start, make a start on, embark on, set about, open, launch, inaugurate, institute, found, initiate, originate, instigate. OPPOSITE: end. **2** (*ready to commence*) go ahead, begin, start, set the ball rolling (*inf*), get the show on the road (*inf*). OPPOSITE: stop.

commencement *noun* beginning, start, opening, outset, launch, inauguration, institution, initiation, origin, dawn, birth. OPPOSITE: end.

commend *verb* **1** (*commended their performance*) praise, extol, laud, eulogize, applaud, acclaim, speak highly of, compliment, approve. OPPOSITE: condemn. **2** (*has little to commend it*) recommend, advocate, endorse, promote, put in a good word for. **3** (*commended him to her care*) entrust, commit, hand over, give, yield, deliver, consign.

commendable *adj* praiseworthy, laudable, admirable, estimable, worthy, deserving, meritorious, creditable, excellent, exemplary, noble. OPPOSITE: deplorable.

commendation *noun* praise, extolment, compliment, tribute, credit, acclaim, acclamation, applause, accolade, eulogy, panegyric, encomium, approval, approbation, encouragement, recommendation. OPPOSITE: condemnation.

commensurate *adj* corresponding, proportional, proportionate, commensurable, to scale, equivalent, comparable, equal, appropriate, due, fitting, in accordance, compatible, consistent, adequate, sufficient. OPPOSITE: disproportionate.

comment *noun* **1** (*a comment about the weather*) remark, observation, statement, note, opinion, view. **2** (*comments on the text*) annotation, note, footnote, gloss, explanation, interpretation, elucidation, illustration, exposition, commentary, criticism.
➤ *verb* remark, observe, say, state, point out, note, mention, interpose, interject.
comment on annotate, gloss, explain, interpret, elucidate, clarify, illustrate, criticize.

commentary *noun* **1** (*a sports commentary*) narration, voice-over, comments, remarks, observations, description, account, report, analysis, review. **2** (*a commentary on a text*) annotation, notes, exposition, explanation, interpretation, elucidation, analysis, exegesis, critique, criticism, review, treatise, dissertation, essay.

commentator *noun* **1** (*a TV commentator*) reporter, correspondent, broadcaster, sportscaster, narrator, commenter. **2** (*commentators on the text*) annotator, expositor, interpreter, critic.

commerce *noun* **1** (*international commerce*) business, trade, buying and selling, traffic, barter, exchange, trafficking, dealing, dealings, transactions, merchandising, marketing, industry, enterprise. **2** (*social commerce*) communication, intercourse, relations, dealings, interchange, communion.

commercial *adj* **1** (*commercial traffic*) business, trade, trading, mercantile, merchant, sales, marketing. **2** (*a commercial proposition*) profitable, profit-making, saleable, marketable, entrepreneurial, financial, mercenary, materialistic.
➤ *noun* advertisement, advert (*inf*), ad (*inf*), promotion,

publicity, plug (*inf*), announcement, poster, bill, leaflet, jingle, blurb.

commiserate *verb* **commiserate with** sympathize with, empathize with, condole with, pity, feel sorry for, feel for, console, comfort, solace.

commiseration *noun* sympathy, condolence, pity, compassion, fellow feeling, consolation, comfort, solace.

commission *noun* **1** (*a commission to write her biography*) assignment, task, job, appointment, employment, work, duty, charge, errand, mission, mandate, authority, warrant, permit, licence. **2** (*set up a commission to investigate the problem*) committee, board, council, advisory body, delegation, deputation. **3** (*the agent takes 20% commission*) share, dividend, percentage, cut (*inf*), rake-off (*inf*), allowance, fee, brokerage, royalty. **4** (*the commission of a crime*) perpetration, committal, execution, performance.
➤ *verb* authorize, empower, nominate, appoint, delegate, depute, assign, detail, engage, employ, contract, order.

commissioner *noun* agent, deputy, delegate, representative, envoy, ambassador, official, officer.

commit *verb* **1** (*commit a crime*) do, perform, perpetrate, enact, effect, execute, carry out. **2** (*it was committed to her care*) entrust, trust, confide, consign, hand over, deliver, charge, commend, give, assign. **3** (*reluctant to commit himself*) pledge, promise, covenant, bind, obligate, engage, involve, align, devote, dedicate. **4** (*commit a psychopath*) confine, put away, lock up, detain, imprison, jail, intern, incarcerate, hospitalize, institutionalize. OPPOSITE: release.

commitment *noun* **1** (*make a commitment*) pledge, promise, covenant, vow, undertaking, assurance, guarantee. **2** (*have other commitments*) obligation, duty, task, responsibility, liability, engagement, tie. **3** (*show commitment*) dedication, devotion, involvement, loyalty, allegiance.

committal *noun* **1** (*committal to her care*) consignment, delivery, entrustment, charge, assignment. **2** (*the committal of a crime*) perpetration, commission, execution, performance. **3** (*the committal of a psychopath*) confinement, imprisonment, custody, detention, internment, incarceration, hospitalization, institutionalization.

committed *adj* engaged, involved, devoted, dedicated, loyal, card-carrying (*inf*), zealous, fervent, ardent, active, diligent, industrious, assiduous. OPPOSITE: apathethic.

committee *noun* board, council, commission, panel, jury, working party, task force, think tank (*inf*).

commodious *noun* spacious, roomy, capacious, ample, large, extensive, vast, expansive, comfortable, convenient. OPPOSITE: narrow.

commodities *pl noun* goods, wares, merchandise, products, produce, output, stock.

commodity *noun* thing, item, article, product.

common *adj* **1** (*common interests*) joint, shared, mutual, collective, universal, general. OPPOSITE: individual. **2** (*common land*) public, communal, community, shared, collective, popular. OPPOSITE: private. **3** (*a common misconception*) widespread, prevalent, general, universal, familiar, popular, accepted, conventional, traditional, commonplace, stock. OPPOSITE: rare. **4** (*a common cause of accidents*) frequent, regular, routine, daily, everyday, ordinary, usual, customary, habitual, normal, average, standard, typical, stock, plain, simple, workaday, run-of-the-mill, common-or-garden, two a penny (*inf*), ten a penny (*inf*), unexceptional, undistinguished, familiar, popular. OPPOSITE: unusual. **5** (*written in common style*) trite, banal, pedestrian, hackneyed, stale, commonplace, inferior, mediocre, unexceptional, undistinguished. OPPOSITE: high-flown. **6** (*his new girlfriend's rather common*) vulgar, ill-bred, low, coarse, uncouth. OPPOSITE: refined.

commonplace *adj* **1** (*a commonplace occurrence*) ordinary, everyday, common, usual, normal, regular, frequent, widespread, prevalent. OPPOSITE: special. **2** (*commonplace language*) undistinguished, unexceptional, unremarkable, humdrum, mundane, dull, trite, banal, pedestrian, hackneyed, stale, threadbare, worn-out. OPPOSITE: distinctive.
➤ *noun* cliché, platitude, truism, banality.

commonsense *adj* sensible, reasonable, rational, sane, sound, wise, practical, commonsensical, pragmatic, realistic, hard-headed, shrewd, astute, prudent, judicious, level-headed, down-to-earth, matter-of-fact. OPPOSITE: foolish.

common sense *noun* sense, good sense, horse sense (*inf*), wit, native wit (*inf*), mother wit (*inf*), intelligence, wisdom, discernment, gumption (*inf*), nous (*inf*), practicality, pragmatism, realism, hard-headedness, prudence, judiciousness, shrewdness. OPPOSITE: folly.

commotion *noun* turmoil, tumult, upheaval, disorder, disruption, disturbance, fuss, ado, to-do (*inf*), riot, rumpus, ferment, agitation, perturbation, bustle, hurly-burly, uproar, clamour, noise, din, row, racket, furore, hullabaloo, brouhaha, hubbub. OPPOSITE: calm.

communal *adj* public, community, common, shared, joint, collective, general. OPPOSITE: private.

commune[1] *verb* **1** (*commune with friends*) communicate, converse, talk, chat, speak, discourse, discuss, confer, confide. **2** (*commune with nature*) feel at one, relate, empathize, identify.

commune[2] *noun* community, collective, cooperative, kibbutz, colony, settlement.

communicable *adj* infectious, contagious, catching, transferable, transmittable, transmissible.

communicate *verb* **1** (*communicate news*) impart, tell, make known, publish, broadcast, declare, announce, proclaim, divulge, disclose, reveal, disseminate, spread, transmit, pass on, relay, transfer, convey, bestow, confer. OPPOSITE: withhold. **2** (*communicate with his parents*) converse, talk, speak, commune, correspond, write, telephone, phone, call, ring, fax, e-mail, contact, get in touch, have dealings, interface. **3** (*communicating rooms*) connect, adjoin, abut.

communication *noun* **1** (*the communication of information*) intimation, publication, broadcasting, announcement, proclamation, divulgence, disclosure, revelation, dissemination, spreading, transmission, transfer, conveyance. **2** (*a communication from head office*) message, note, memorandum, letter, call, fax, e-mail, announcement, declaration, proclamation, report, bulletin, communiqué, dispatch, news, word, information, intelligence, account, statement. **3** (*a breakdown in communication*) conversation, discourse, intercourse, correspondence, contact, touch, link, connection.

communicative *adj* open, unreserved, forthcoming, expansive, frank, candid, talkative, voluble, loquacious, chatty, sociable, friendly, outgoing, extrovert. OPPOSITE: reserved.

communion *noun* **1** (*communion with others*) intercourse, exchange, communication, conversation, dialogue, rapport, affinity, sympathy, empathy, intimacy, closeness, togetherness, fellowship, harmony, accord, concord, agreement, unity. OPPOSITE: estrangement. **2** (*Holy Communion*) Eucharist, Lord's Supper, Mass.

communiqué *noun* bulletin, dispatch, announcement, communication, report, statement.

communism *noun* Marxism, Leninism, Bolshevism, sovietism, socialism, collectivism. OPPOSITE: fascism.

communist *noun* Marxist, Leninist, Bolshevik, Red (*inf*), socialist, collectivist, leftist, radical. OPPOSITE: fascist.

community *noun* **1** (*the local community*) neighbourhood, district, parish, locality, colony, settlement, village, township, residents, inhabitants, populace, population, people, public, nation, state, society. **2** (*a community of artists*) group, body, company, association, society, brotherhood, sisterhood, fellowship, colony, ghetto. **3** (*community of interests*) similarity, likeness, affinity, agreement.

commute *verb* **1** (*commute by train*) travel, journey, travel back and forth, shuttle. **2** (*the sentence was commuted to life imprisonment*) change, alter, adjust, modify, exchange, switch, swap, trade, barter, substitute, replace, reduce, lessen, shorten, curtail, remit, mitigate, alleviate.

commuter *noun* traveller, passenger, straphanger (*inf*), driver, suburbanite.

compact[1] *adj* **1** (*a compact mass*) close, dense, thick, impenetrable, solid, firm, compressed, condensed, packed, tight. OPPOSITE: loose. **2** (*a compact machine*) small, neat, portable, pocket. OPPOSITE: unwieldy. **3** (*a compact style*) short, brief, terse, concise, succinct, pithy, laconic. OPPOSITE: rambling.
➤ *verb* compress, condense, press, pack, cram, stuff, ram, tamp, consolidate, fuse, bind.

compact[2] *noun* contract, covenant, treaty, concordat, alliance, pact, bond, entente, understanding, agreement, settlement, arrangement, bargain, deal, transaction.

companion *noun* **1** (*separated from her companions*) associate, comrade, acquaintance, friend, crony, intimate, mate (*inf*), buddy (*inf*), chum (*inf*), pal (*inf*), accomplice, ally, colleague, partner, consort, escort, squire, attendant, aide, chaperon, duenna. OPPOSITE: enemy. **2** (*the companion to this glove*) fellow, counterpart, match, mate, twin. **3** (*wrote a companion to sailing*) guide, handbook, manual, vade mecum.

companionable *adj* friendly, affable, amiable, approachable, outgoing, extrovert, gregarious, sociable, genial, convivial, congenial, informal, familiar. OPPOSITE: hostile.

companionship *noun* fellowship, friendship, amity, brotherhood, sisterhood, comradeship, camaraderie, esprit de corps, rapport, conviviality, togetherness, intimacy, company, society, association. OPPOSITE: loneliness.

company *noun* **1** (*an insurance company*) business, firm, concern, outfit (*inf*), establishment, house, corporation, association, partnership, syndicate, cartel, consortium, conglomerate, multinational. **2** (*address the company*) assembly, assemblage, gathering, meeting, concourse, convention, congregation, crowd, throng. **3** (*a company of actors*) group, body, band, ensemble, troupe, troop, party, gang, crew, team, set, circle, association, collection, unit, detachment. **4** (*I'd be glad of the company*) companionship, fellowship, society, friendship, support, contact, togetherness, conviviality. **5** (*are you expecting company?*) visitors, guests, callers.

comparable *adj* like, similar, resembling, alike, akin, related, analogous, corresponding, equivalent, commensurate, proportional, proportionate, tantamount, as good, equal, on a par, in the same league, in the same class. OPPOSITE: incomparable.

comparative *adj* relative, by comparison, in comparison, qualified, approximate, near. OPPOSITE: absolute.

compare *verb* **1** (*compare the two accounts*) correlate, collate, juxtapose, contrast, balance, weigh. **2** (*compared the animal to an elephant*) liken, equate, link, relate, analogize, parallel.

compare with resemble, equal, correspond to, approximate to, come up to, approach, compete with, vie with, be on a par with, be in the same class as, be in the same league as, hold a candle to (*inf*).

comparison *noun* **1** (*there's no comparison*) likeness, resemblance, similarity, relation, analogy, parallel, correlation, comparability. **2** (*make a comparison*) likening, analogy, simile, correlation, collation, juxtaposition, contrast, distinction.

compartment *noun* **1** (*a secret compartment in the desk*) cubbyhole, pigeonhole, booth, stall, cubicle, cell, chamber, locker, alcove, niche, bay. **2** (*a separate compartment of my life*) part, section, division, partition, area, department. OPPOSITE: whole.

compass *noun* range, scope, extent, reach, span, stretch, circumference, circuit, boundary, bounds, limits, sphere, realm, field, area, zone.
  ➤ *verb* encircle, encompass, surround, circumscribe, gird, circle, ring, enclose, hem in, besiege, beset.

compassion *noun* sympathy, pity, fellow feeling, commiseration, condolence, soft-heartedness, tender-heartedness, tenderness, gentleness, care, concern, consideration, understanding, kindness, kindliness, kind-heartedness, humanity, charity, benevolence, magnanimity, leniency, indulgence, clemency, mercy. OPPOSITE: cruelty.

compassionate *adj* kind, kindly, kind-hearted, tender, gentle, sympathetic, understanding, soft-hearted, tender-hearted, humane, benign, charitable, benevolent, magnanimous, indulgent, lenient, clement, merciful. OPPOSITE: cruel.

compatible *adj* **1** (*projects that are compatible with our principles*) congruous, consistent, reconcilable, in keeping, consonant, accordant, harmonious, in harmony, in tune, agreeable. OPPOSITE: antagonistic. **2** (*the couple are not compatible*) well-suited, well-matched, like-minded, at one, in harmony. OPPOSITE: incompatible.

compatriot *noun* fellow countryman, fellow countrywoman, fellow national, fellow citizen.

compel *verb* **1** (*compelled us to go*) force, coerce, dragoon, drive, impel, urge, twist someone's arm (*inf*), put the screws on (*inf*), pressure, pressurize, bulldoze (*inf*), railroad (*inf*), make, oblige, constrain, require, necessitate. OPPOSITE: coax. **2** (*compel attention*) exact, insist on, force, necessitate.

compelling *adj* **1** (*a compelling tale*) absorbing, fascinating, enthralling, gripping, riveting, spellbinding, hypnotic, mesmeric, compulsive, unputdownable (*inf*). OPPOSITE: boring. **2** (*compelling evidence*) forceful, convincing, irrefutable, conclusive, cogent, telling, weighty, powerful. OPPOSITE: weak.

compendious *adj* comprehensive, summary, abridged, condensed, compressed, compact, concise, succinct, pithy, brief, short, terse. OPPOSITE: wordy.

compendium *noun* synopsis, summary, digest, abstract, abridgment, condensation, résumé, précis. OPPOSITE: amplification.

compensate *verb* **1** (*compensated him for loss of earnings*) recompense, reimburse, repay, refund, remunerate, reward, indemnify, requite, satisfy. **2** (*compensate for her crimes*) atone, make amends, make up, make good, redress, redeem. **3** (*their hearing compensates for their poor vision*) offset, balance, counterbalance, cancel out, neutralize, nullify.

compensation *noun* **1** (*refused to pay compensation*) recompense, reimbursement, repayment, refund, remuneration, reward, indemnity, indemnification, reparation, damages, requital, satisfaction. **2** (*compensation for past misdeeds*) atonement, expiation, amends, redress, restoration, restitution. **3** (*one of the compensations of being unemployed*) consolation, comfort.

compere *noun* host, presenter, master of ceremonies, MC.

compete *verb* **1** (*compete in a race*) enter, take part, participate, go in for, be in the running (*inf*), run, race. **2** (*compete for a contract*) contest, contend, vie, rival, challenge, oppose, pit oneself, struggle, strive, fight, battle. OPPOSITE: ally.

competence *noun* **1** (*the competence of the staff*) ability, capability, capacity, qualification, experience, proficiency, expertise, mastery, skill, aptitude, adeptness, efficiency. OPPOSITE: incompetence. **2** (*the competence of their work*) adequacy, sufficiency, acceptability, fitness, suitability. OPPOSITE: inadequacy.

competent *adj* **1** (*competent staff*) able, capable, trained, qualified, experienced, proficient, expert, masterful, masterly, skilled, skilful, accomplished, adept, efficient, knowledgeable. OPPOSITE: incompetent. **2** (*not* *competent to answer that question*) fit, fitted, suitable, suited, equal, qualified. OPPOSITE: unfit. **3** (*competent work*) adequate, sufficient, satisfactory, acceptable, passable, fit, suitable, appropriate. OPPOSITE: unacceptable.

competition *noun* **1** (*enter a competition*) contest, tournament, championship, event, bout, race, match, game, quiz. **2** (*set up in competition*) rivalry, opposition, challenge, contention, strife, conflict, contest. OPPOSITE: alliance. **3** (*beat the competition*) rivals, opposition, opponents, challengers, competitors, contestants, contenders, field. OPPOSITE: allies. **4** (*a spirit of competition*) competitiveness, combativeness, aggression, rivalry, challenge, survival of the fittest.

competitive *adj* **1** (*a competitive industry*) rival, competing, vying, aggressive, cutthroat, dog-eat-dog (*inf*). **2** (*a competitive person*) combative, aggressive, striving, ambitious, assertive, pushy (*inf*).

competitor *noun* **1** (*losing trade to our competitors*) rival, opponent, adversary, antagonist, opposition, competition. OPPOSITE: ally. **2** (*a competitor in the race*) contestant, contender, challenger, entrant, participant, player, runner, candidate, aspirant.

compilation *noun* **1** (*a compilation of songs*) collection, anthology, treasury, album, assortment, miscellany, selection, compendium, omnibus, corpus. **2** (*the compilation of reference books*) compiling, composition, preparation, collection, gathering, accumulation, assembly, collation, organization, arrangement.

compile *verb* collect, gather, garner, cull, amass, accumulate, assemble, put together, collate, compose, prepare, organize, arrange.

complacency *noun* smugness, self-satisfaction, triumph, contentment, pleasure, satisfaction, gratification, serenity, tranquillity, ease, placidity. OPPOSITE: uneasiness.

complacent *adj* smug, self-satisfied, gloating, triumphant, contented, pleased, satisfied, gratified, serene, tranquil, at ease, placid, unconcerned. OPPOSITE: uneasy.

complain *verb* grumble, moan, whine, whinge (*inf*), bleat (*inf*), grouse, grouch, gripe (*inf*), bellyache (*inf*), beef (*inf*), bewail, bemoan, lament, deplore, murmur, mutter, carp, cavil, criticize, find fault, protest, object, lodge a complaint, make a fuss. OPPOSITE: rejoice.

complaint *noun* **1** (*make a complaint*) grumble, grievance, moan, whine, lament, grouse, gripe (*inf*), beef (*inf*), quibble, cavil, criticism, protest, objection, charge, accusation, remonstrance. **2** (*a hereditary skin complaint*) disorder, disease, sickness, illness, ailment, malady, indisposition, affliction, trouble.

complaisance *noun* acquiescence, agreeableness, compliance, graciousness, civility, politeness, courtesy, deference. OPPOSITE: obstinacy.

complaisant *adj* acquiescent, agreeable, amenable, accommodating, obliging, compliant, biddable, gracious, civil, polite, courteous, deferential. OPPOSITE: obstinate.

complement *noun* **1** (*the full complement*) quota, allowance, total, sum, aggregate, totality, entirety, whole, capacity, load. OPPOSITE: part. **2** (*the perfect complement to curry*) companion, counterpart, match, coordinate, supplement, addition, accessory, finishing touch.

➤ *verb* complete, round off, crown, set off, go well with, match, coordinate with, supplement, add to, make up. OPPOSITE: clash.

complementary *adj* completing, finishing, perfecting, consummating, matching, coordinating, corresponding, reciprocal, correlative, interdependent. OPPOSITE: conflicting.

complete *adj* **1** (*a complete set*) entire, whole, total, full, integral, intact, plenary, unabridged, unexpurgated, undivided, unbroken, unimpaired, perfect. OPPOSITE: incomplete. **2** (*when the work is complete*) finished, completed, ended, concluded, terminated, finalized, fulfilled, accomplished, achieved, done, over. OPPOSITE: unfinished. **3** (*in complete ignorance*) absolute, utter, total, thorough, downright, outright, out-and-out, perfect, consummate, unqualified, unconditional. OPPOSITE: partial.

➤ *verb* finish, end, conclude, settle, terminate, finalize, wind up (*inf*), wrap up (*inf*), fulfil, realize, achieve, attain, accomplish, do, perform, execute, discharge, effect, perfect, consummate, crown, cap, round off. OPPOSITE: begin.

completely *adv* absolutely, utterly, totally, fully, wholly, entirely, lock stock and barrel (*inf*), hook line and sinker (*inf*), quite, altogether, in every respect, thoroughly, through and through (*inf*), perfectly.

completion *noun* finish, end, conclusion, termination, close, finalization, fulfilment, realization, fruition, achievement, accomplishment, performance, execution, discharge, perfection, consummation. OPPOSITE: beginning.

complex *adj* **1** (*a complex business*) complicated, intricate, involved, elaborate, difficult, knotty, tangled, tortuous, convoluted, labyrinthine. OPPOSITE: straightforward. **2** (*a complex structure*) composite, compound, multiple, manifold, mixed, heterogeneous, varied, diverse. OPPOSITE: simple.

➤ *noun* **1** (*a leisure complex*) structure, network, system, scheme, development, establishment, organization, synthesis, composite. **2** (*a complex about his weight*) obsession, fixation, hang-up (*inf*), preoccupation, thing (*inf*), phobia, neurosis.

complexion *noun* **1** (*her pale complexion*) skin, skin tone, colour, colouring, pigmentation. **2** (*put a different complexion on things*) appearance, aspect, look, countenance, cast, stamp, character, nature, angle, light.

complexity *noun* intricacy, complication, difficulty, problem, ramification, convolution, involvement, entanglement, multiplicity, heterogeneity, variety, diversity. OPPOSITE: simplicity.

compliance *noun* **1** (*in compliance with the rules*) obedience, conformity, accordance, observance, respect, adherence, satisfaction, fulfilment, discharge, performance, execution. OPPOSITE: defiance. **2** (*counting on her compliance*) acquiescence, agreement, consent, assent, concurrence, submission, yielding, docility, passivity, deference, subservience, complaisance, cooperation, obedience, conformity. OPPOSITE: resistance.

compliant *adj* acquiescent, agreeable, submissive, yielding, tractable, biddable, docile, passive, deferential, subservient, obliging, accommodating, complaisant, cooperative, obedient. OPPOSITE: obstinate.

complicate *verb* confuse, involve, entangle, jumble, muddle, confound, make difficult, compound. OPPOSITE: simplify.

complicated *adj* confused, involved, complex, intricate, fiddly (*inf*), elaborate, convoluted, tortuous, labyrinthine, difficult, problematic, tangled, knotty, perplexing, cryptic. OPPOSITE: simple.

complication *noun* **1** (*the complication of the issue*) complexity, intricacy, confusion, muddle, involvement, entanglement, tangle, web, network. OPPOSITE: simplicity. **2** (*a series of complications*) difficulty, problem, obstacle, drawback, snag, repercussion, ramification.

complicity *noun* collusion, conspiracy, connivance, collaboration, abetment, involvement.

compliment *noun* praise, commendation, eulogy, tribute, honour, accolade, bouquet, congratulation, felicitation, flattery, admiration, favour, approval. OPPOSITE: abuse.
➤ *verb* flatter, admire, congratulate, felicitate, praise, commend, speak highly of, sing the praises of, extol, laud, eulogize, acclaim, salute, pay tribute to, pay homage to. OPPOSITE: insult.

complimentary *adj* **1** (*a complimentary remark*) flattering, admiring, congratulatory, appreciative, approving, favourable, commendatory, adulatory, laudatory, eulogistic. OPPOSITE: insulting. **2** (*a complimentary ticket*) free, free of charge, gratis, courtesy, on the house (*inf*).

compliments *pl noun* greetings, salutations, respects, regards, good wishes, best wishes.

comply *verb* submit, yield, defer, acquiesce, agree, consent, assent, accede, obey, conform, oblige, accommodate. OPPOSITE: resist.
comply with obey, conform to, observe, respect, follow, abide by, adhere to, meet, satisfy, fulfil, discharge, perform, execute. OPPOSITE: defy.

component *noun* part, section, piece, bit, constituent, element, ingredient, factor, unit, module, item. OPPOSITE: whole.
➤ *adj* constituent, integral, intrinsic.

comport *verb* agree, tally, correspond, coincide, accord, harmonize, match, suit. OPPOSITE: differ.
comport oneself act, behave, conduct oneself, deport oneself, carry oneself, bear oneself, acquit oneself.

compose *verb* **1** (*composed of assorted ingredients*) form, make, produce, put together, assemble, collate, construct, build, comprise, constitute, make up. **2** (*compose a song*) write, make up, compile, formulate, invent, concoct, think up, create, contrive, devise, produce. **3** (*she managed to compose herself*) calm, pacify, appease, quiet, still, steady, soothe, assuage, quell, control, collect. OPPOSITE: disturb. **4** (*he composed his thoughts*) adjust, arrange, align, put in order, organize,

systematize. **5** (*they have composed their differences*) settle, resolve, reconcile.

composed *adj* calm, tranquil, serene, cool, collected, together (*inf*), poised, self-possessed, self-controlled, unruffled, unworried, untroubled, unperturbed, imperturbable, unflappable (*inf*), placid, sedate, relaxed, at ease. OPPOSITE: agitated.

composite *adj* compound, complex, intricate, manifold, multiple, conglomerate, heterogeneous, mixed, combined, blended, synthesized, hybrid, patchwork. OPPOSITE: simple.
➤ *noun* compound, amalgam, alloy, mixture, combination, blend, synthesis, conglomerate, complex, patchwork.

composition *noun* **1** (*the chemical composition of the substance*) formation, make-up, structure, configuration, organization, arrangement, layout, form, character, constitution. **2** (*the composition of poetry*) writing, making up, compilation, formulation, invention, creation, production. **3** (*one of her earlier compositions*) work, opus, piece, creation, study, exercise. **4** (*write a composition for homework*) essay, story. **5** (*the composition of a photograph*) balance, symmetry, harmony, arrangement.

compost *noun* fertilizer, manure, muck, mulch, humus, dressing.

composure *noun* calm, calmness, tranquillity, serenity, coolness, collectedness, poise, aplomb, sang-froid, self-possession, self-control, imperturbability, unflappability (*inf*), placidity, ease, equanimity, equilibrium. OPPOSITE: agitation.

compound *noun* mixture, blend, alloy, combination, amalgam, synthesis, composite, complex, medley, hybrid.
➤ *adj* composite, complex, complicated, intricate, multiple, mixed, blended, combined, hybrid. OPPOSITE: simple.
➤ *verb* **1** (*compound the ingredients*) mix, blend, mingle, intermingle, alloy, combine, amalgamate, unite, synthesize, fuse. OPPOSITE: separate. **2** (*compound the problem*) intensify, heighten, magnify, augment, add to, worsen, make worse, aggravate, exacerbate, complicate. OPPOSITE: ameliorate.

comprehend *verb* **1** (*failed to comprehend what I meant*) understand, fathom, grasp, apprehend, see, perceive, discern, make out, assimilate, take in. OPPOSITE: misunderstand. **2** (*comprehending the whole estate*) include, encompass, embrace, take in, cover, involve, comprise, contain. OPPOSITE: exclude.

comprehensible *adj* understandable, intelligible, fathomable, graspable, accessible, clear, plain, simple, explicit, lucid, coherent, distinct, articulate. OPPOSITE: incomprehensible.

comprehension *noun* understanding, grasp, apprehension, conception, perception, discernment, awareness, realization, sense, intelligence, intellect, knowledge, ken (*inf*). OPPOSITE: incomprehension.

comprehensive *adj* wide, broad, large, extensive, sweeping, general, universal, inclusive, all-inclusive, all-embracing, overall, blanket, umbrella, exhaustive, thorough, full, encyclopedic, catholic. OPPOSITE: limited.

compress *verb* **1** (*compressed into a solid block*) compact, concentrate, condense, pressurize, press, squeeze, squash, cram, pack, tamp, crush, flatten, constrict, contract. OPPOSITE: expand. **2** (*compress the narrative*) condense, reduce, shorten, abbreviate, abridge, summarize, synopsize, précis. OPPOSITE: lengthen.

compression *noun* **1** (*the compression of gases*) contraction, constriction, pressure, squeezing, crushing, flattening, concentration, pressurization. OPPOSITE: expansion. **2** (the compression of text) condensation, reduction, shortening, abbreviation, abridgment. OPPOSITE: lengthening.

comprise *verb* **1** (*the set comprises twelve pieces*) consist of, be composed of, contain, include, embrace, encompass, comprehend, take in. OPPOSITE: exclude. **2** (*the players that comprise the team*) form, compose, constitute, make up.

compromise *verb* **1** (*compromise on a price*) meet halfway, give and take, strike a balance, reach an understanding, come to terms, make a deal, bargain, negotiate, agree, settle, concede, adjust, adapt, accommodate. OPPOSITE: disagree. **2** (*without compromising his principles*) discredit, dishonour, bring into disrepute, shame, embarrass. **3** (*compromised her chances of success*) endanger, imperil, jeopardize, risk, expose, prejudice, weaken, harm, damage. OPPOSITE: protect.
➤ *noun* concession, give-and-take, adjustment, accommodation, middle ground, happy medium, balance, understanding, terms, agreement, settlement, deal, trade-off, bargain, negotiation. OPPOSITE: disagreement.

compulsion *noun* **1** (*not under any compulsion to stay*) obligation, duress, pressure, force, constraint, coercion, insistence. OPPOSITE: coaxing. **2** (*a compulsion to lose weight*) urge, drive, impulse, need, necessity, desire, longing, obsession, preoccupation.

compulsive *adj* **1** (*the article is compulsive reading*) absorbing, fascinating, enthralling, gripping, riveting, spellbinding, hypnotic, mesmeric, compelling, unputdownable (*inf*). OPPOSITE: boring. **2** (*a compulsive desire to spend*) obsessive, obsessional, overwhelming, overpowering, uncontrollable, ungovernable, irresistible, urgent, driving, compelling, addictive. **3** (*a compulsive gambler*) habitual, inveterate, hardened, incurable, pathological (*inf*), addicted, dependent, hooked (*inf*).

compulsory *adj* obligatory, binding, imperative, mandatory, de rigueur, necessary, essential, requisite, required, set, contractual, enforced, unavoidable. OPPOSITE: voluntary.

compunction *noun* remorse, regret, contrition, repentance, penitence, qualm, scruple, misgiving, unease, hesitation, reluctance, sorrow, guilt, embarrassment, shame.

computation *noun* calculation, reckoning, adding up, counting, enumeration, estimation, assessment, valuation, measurement.

compute *verb* calculate, work out, reckon, figure, total, add up, count, enumerate, estimate, assess, rate, measure. OPPOSITE: guess.

computer *noun* processor, database, terminal, workstation, PC, laptop, palmtop.

computing *noun* data processing, programming, information technology, IT.

comrade *noun* companion, associate, fellow, peer, colleague, team-mate, partner, confederate, ally, friend, crony, mate (*inf*), buddy (*inf*), chum (*inf*), pal (*inf*). OPPOSITE: enemy.

con *verb* swindle, defraud, rip off (*inf*), do (*inf*), cheat, deceive, dupe, hoodwink, bamboozle, mislead, delude.
➤ *noun* swindle, fraud, rip-off (*inf*), racket, fiddle (*inf*), scam (*inf*), confidence trick, con trick (*inf*), trick, hoax, bluff, cheat, deception.

concatenation *noun* chain, series, succession, sequence, string, thread, train, progression, continuity, connection, link, linking, coupling, interlocking.

concave *adj* hollow, curved in, incurvate, sunken, depressed, indented, cupped, hollowed, scooped, excavated. OPPOSITE: convex.

conceal *verb* **1** (*conceal the body*) hide, keep out of sight, cover, obscure, screen, cloak, mask, veil, shroud, camouflage, disguise, bury, submerge, secrete, tuck away. OPPOSITE: reveal. **2** (*conceal the truth*) suppress, dissemble, keep secret, keep dark, keep the lid on (*inf*), keep quiet, hush up (*inf*), hide, cover up, whitewash (*inf*). OPPOSITE: divulge.

concealed *adj* hidden, unseen, invisible, covered, obscured, screened, veiled, camouflaged, disguised, secret, covert. OPPOSITE: conspicuous.

concealment *noun* **1** (*a place of concealment*) hiding, shelter, retreat, privacy, secrecy, cover, blind, screening, masking, camouflage, disguise, secretion. OPPOSITE: revelation. **2** (*concealment of the truth*) suppression, dissembling, cover-up, whitewash (*inf*), smokescreen (*inf*). OPPOSITE: divulgence.

concede *verb* **1** (*conceded that I was right*) admit, acknowledge, confess, own, grant, allow, recognize, accept. OPPOSITE: deny. **2** (*concede territory*) yield, surrender, cede, relinquish, give up, hand over, deliver. OPPOSITE: retain.

conceit *noun* **1** (*a player full of conceit*) vanity, conceitedness, immodesty, pride, arrogance, egotism, vainglory, self-esteem, self-admiration, self-adulation, self-love, narcissism, boastfulness, big-headedness (*inf*), boasting, swagger, cockiness, smugness, complacency. OPPOSITE: modesty. **2** (*literary conceits*) simile, comparison, metaphor, image, figure, ornament, decoration. **3** (*strange conceits*) idea, notion, fancy, whim, caprice, thought, belief, concept, fantasy, imagination.

conceited *adj* vain, immodest, proud, arrogant, egotistical, vainglorious, self-important, narcissistic, big-headed (*inf*), swollen-headed (*inf*), full of oneself (*inf*), too big for one's boots (*inf*), boastful, swaggering, cocky, smug, complacent, haughty, supercilious, stuck-up (*inf*). OPPOSITE: modest.

conceivable *adj* possible, likely, imaginable, thinkable, believable, credible. OPPOSITE: inconceivable.

conceive *verb* **1** (*conceive an idea*) devise, contrive, invent, originate, think up, come up with, formulate,

draw up, design, plan, project, create, produce, develop.
2 (*can't conceive how they must feel*) understand,
comprehend, perceive, apprehend, grasp, fathom, see,
realize, appreciate, imagine, picture, visualize, envisage,
think, believe, fancy, suppose. **3** (*women trying to
conceive*) become pregnant, become impregnated,
become inseminated, reproduce.

concentrate *verb* **1** (*concentrate our efforts*) focus,
converge, centre, bring to bear, muster, gather, collect,
amass, consolidate, intensify. **2** (*industry is concentrated
in the north*) centre, centralize, localize, focus, converge,
cluster, conglomerate, amass, congregate, assemble,
muster, gather, collect. OPPOSITE: disperse. **3** (*concentrate
a liquid*) condense, evaporate, reduce, boil down, distil,
purify, thicken, compress, compact. OPPOSITE: dilute.
4 (*finding it hard to concentrate*) pay attention, apply
oneself, be engrossed, be absorbed, think, meditate,
ponder, ruminate.

concentrated *adj* **1** (*concentrated efforts*) focused,
single-minded, concerted, consolidated, intense,
intensive, vigorous, all-out (*inf*). OPPOSITE: half-hearted.
2 (*concentrated liquid*) condensed, evaporated, reduced,
distilled, pure, thick, dense, strong, undiluted. OPPOSITE:
diluted.

concentration *noun* **1** (*I lost my concentration*)
attention, application, engrossment, absorption, heed,
thought, mind. OPPOSITE: distraction. **2** (*the concentration
of power*) centralization, focus, convergence,
consolidation, intensification, collection, gathering,
conglomeration, aggregation, accumulation. OPPOSITE:
dispersal. **3** (*a concentration of troops*) cluster,
conglomeration, accumulation, mass. **4** (*the
concentration of liquid*) condensation, evaporation,
reduction, distillation, purification, compression.
OPPOSITE: dilution.

concept *noun* idea, notion, thought, abstraction,
conception, conceptualization, impression, image,
picture, visualization, view, hypothesis, theory.

conception *noun* **1** (*no conception of what it is like*) idea,
notion, concept, impression, image, picture,
visualization, perception, understanding,
comprehension, knowledge, appreciation, inkling, clue.
2 (*an interesting conception*) plan, design, scheme, project,
proposal, idea, notion, concept, thought, theory,
hypothesis, abstraction. **3** (*since the conception of the
project*) beginning, outset, inception, origin, birth,
genesis, origination, invention, creation, initiation,
inauguration, launch. OPPOSITE: termination. **4** (*methods
of preventing conception*) fertilization, fecundation,
impregnation, insemination, reproduction.

concern *verb* **1** (*laws that concern small businesses*) affect,
involve, interest, regard, relate to, pertain to, appertain
to, apply to, touch, bear on. **2** (*the article concerns
unemployment*) be about, deal with, regard, relate to, be
connected with, have to do with. **3** (*her loss of appetite
concerned me*) worry, perturb, alarm, bother, prey on
one's mind, disturb, trouble, distress, upset. **4** (*he
concerned himself with administration*) occupy, busy,
devote, interest, involve.
➤ *noun* **1** (*it is not your concern*) affair, business, duty,
responsibility, job, task, field, domain, department,
discipline, subject, matter, problem. **2** (*an issue of concern

to motorists*) interest, importance, consequence, bearing,
relevance, applicability. **3** (*showed little concern for others*)
care, solicitude, thought, consideration, regard, heed,
attention. OPPOSITE: indifference. **4** (*a cause for concern*)
anxiety, worry, care, disquiet, perturbation,
apprehension, unease, alarm, trouble, distress, sorrow,
grief. OPPOSITE: relief. **5** (*a multinational concern*)
company, firm, business, enterprise, corporation,
organization, establishment, house.

concerned *adj* **1** (*inquiries from concerned parents*)
anxious, worried, perturbed, apprehensive, uneasy,
alarmed, bothered, disturbed, troubled, distressed, upset,
unhappy. OPPOSITE: relieved. **2** (*a concerned attitude to
their patients*) caring, solicitous, thoughtful, considerate,
attentive. OPPOSITE: indifferent. **3** (*notify all concerned
parties*) affected, interested, involved, implicated,
connected.

concerning *prep* about, re, relating to, with reference
to, regarding, with regard to, respecting, with respect to,
as to, apropos of, in the matter of, touching, connected
with, to do with. OPPOSITE: disregarding.

concert *noun* performance, recital, entertainment,
show, festival, engagement, gig (*inf*).
in concert together, jointly, collectively, concertedly,
unanimously, in agreement, in accord, in concord, in
harmony, in unison, cooperatively, in collaboration,
shoulder to shoulder, side by side. OPPOSITE: separately.

concerted *adj* combined, united, joint, collective,
shared, mutual, cooperative, collaborative, coordinated,
synchronized, synergetic, concentrated, intense,
intensive. OPPOSITE: individual.

concession *noun* **1** (*as a special concession*) right,
privilege, favour, exemption, exception, dispensation,
indulgence, allowance, grant, licence, permit, discount,
reduction, cut. **2** (*make concessions*) allowance,
adjustment, modification, compromise. **3** (*their
concession that I might be right*) admission,
acknowledgment, recognition, acceptance. **4** (*the
concession of territory*) yielding, surrender,
relinquishment, handover.

conciliate *verb* mediate, negotiate, reconcile, reunite,
placate, appease, propitiate, pacify, mollify, soothe,
disarm, win, win over. OPPOSITE: alienate.

conciliation *noun* mediation, negotiation,
reconciliation, peacemaking, placation, appeasement,
propitiation, pacification, mollification. OPPOSITE:
estrangement.

conciliatory *adj* reconciliatory, peacemaking, irenic,
placatory, appeasing, propitiative, pacificatory,
mollifying, soothing, disarming, winning, friendly.
OPPOSITE: antagonistic.

concise *adj* brief, short, terse, to the point, compact,
pithy, succinct, laconic, condensed, compressed,
summary, compendious, synoptic, epigrammatic.
OPPOSITE: lengthy.

conclave *noun* council, assembly, meeting, session,
cabinet, synod, convention, conference, parley.

conclude *verb* **1** (*conclude a meeting*) close, end,
terminate, discontinue, finish, complete, round off,
wind up (*inf*), wrap up (*inf*). OPPOSITE: begin. **2** (*conclude
a deal*) settle, resolve, decide, determine, fix, work out,

negotiate, effect, accomplish, pull off (*inf*), close, complete, clinch, sew up (*inf*). **3** (*concluded that she had left*) infer, deduce, construe, assume, presume, guess, suppose, surmise, conjecture, gather, reckon, judge, decide, come to the conclusion.

conclusion *noun* **1** (*the conclusion of a meeting*) close, end, ending, termination, finish, completion. OPPOSITE: beginning. **2** (*the conclusion of a deal*) settlement, resolution, negotiation, accomplishment, completion, clinching. **3** (*jump to conclusions*) inference, deduction, assumption, presumption, guess, supposition, surmise, conjecture, opinion, judgment, decision, resolution, verdict. **4** (*a foregone conclusion*) outcome, issue, result, consequence, upshot.

conclusive *adj* final, definitive, ultimate, decisive, convincing, clinching, indisputable, incontrovertible, irrefutable, incontestable, unarguable, unanswerable, categorical, definite, positive. OPPOSITE: inconclusive.

concoct *verb* **1** (*concoct an excuse*) contrive, devise, invent, think up, cook up (*inf*), brew, hatch, plot, plan, design, formulate, make up, fabricate. **2** (*concoct a potion*) prepare, mix, blend, brew, make, put together, rustle up (*inf*).

concoction *noun* mixture, blend, compound, brew, preparation, creation.

concomitant *adj* attendant, accompanying, accessory, incidental, associated, related, affiliated, connected, linked, concurrent, synchronous, coincident, coexistent, contemporaneous. OPPOSITE: independent.

concord *noun* agreement, harmony, accord, concert, unity, unanimity, consensus, concordance, consonance, peace, rapport, entente, amity, friendship, goodwill. OPPOSITE: discord.

concordant *adj* harmonious, accordant, consonant, in agreement, in concert, unanimous, at one. OPPOSITE: discordant.

concordat *noun* covenant, treaty, compact, pact, convention, settlement, agreement, bond.

concourse *noun* assembly, meeting, gathering, collection, crowd, throng, mob, multitude, horde, swarm, crush, press, cluster, convergence, confluence.

concrete *adj* **1** (*concrete objects*) material, physical, real, actual, substantial, tangible. OPPOSITE: abstract. **2** (*concrete evidence*) specific, particular, precise, explicit, definite, positive, real, actual, genuine, factual. OPPOSITE: vague. **3** (*a concrete substance*) firm, solid, solidified, consolidated, compressed, compact, dense, petrified, calcified. OPPOSITE: fluid.

concubine *noun* mistress, lover, paramour, kept woman, courtesan, odalisque.

concupiscence *noun* desire, passion, libido, sexual appetite, lust, lechery, lasciviousness, lustfulness, libidinousness, lubricity, prurience, randiness (*inf*), horniness (*inf*). OPPOSITE: continence.

concur *verb* **1** (*the judges concurred*) agree, assent, acquiesce, accede, accord, be in harmony. OPPOSITE: disagree. **2** (*their visits concurred*) coincide, happen together, occur simultaneously, clash, synchronize, coexist. **3** (*concurring to produce the desired effect*) combine, unite, work together, cooperate, collaborate, join forces.

concurrence *noun* **1** (*concurrence with the ruling*) agreement, assent, acquiescence, accord, harmony. OPPOSITE: disagreement. **2** (*concurrence of events*) coincidence, simultaneity, contemporaneity, synchronism, coexistence, concomitance. **3** (*acting in concurrence*) combination, cooperation, collaboration, alliance, union.

concurrent *adj* **1** (*concurrent phenomena*) simultaneous, synchronous, contemporaneous, parallel, coincident, coexistent, concomitant, attendant. **2** (*concurrent lines*) convergent, confluent, meeting, joining, intersecting. OPPOSITE: divergent. **3** (*opinions concurrent with my own*) agreeing, accordant, harmonious, in agreement, in harmony, unanimous, at one. OPPOSITE: discordant.

concussion *noun* collision, crash, impact, shock, clash, blow, jolt, jar, jolting, jarring, shaking, agitation.

condemn *verb* **1** (*condemn their antisocial behaviour*) disapprove, criticize, censure, blame, rebuke, upbraid, reproach, reprove, deplore, deprecate, slam (*inf*), slate (*inf*), denounce, proscribe, prohibit, ban, bar. OPPOSITE: praise. **2** (*criminals condemned to death*) sentence, punish, convict, judge, find guilty. OPPOSITE: acquit. **3** (*condemned to a life of poverty*) doom, damn, force, compel. **4** (*her reply condemned her*) incriminate, inculpate, accuse, indict.

condemnation *noun* **1** (*condemnation of their action*) disapproval, disapprobation, criticism, censure, blame, reproach, reproof, reprobation, deprecation, disparagement, denunciation, proscription, prohibition. OPPOSITE: praise. **2** (*the condemnation of the criminals*) judgment, conviction, punishment, sentence. OPPOSITE: acquittal.

condemnatory *adj* accusatory, incriminating, damning, disapproving, critical, censorious, reproachful, reprobatory, defamatory, deprecatory, denunciatory, proscriptive. OPPOSITE: laudatory.

condensation *noun* **1** (*the condensation of liquid*) concentration, reduction, distillation, consolidation, solidification, coagulation, evaporation, precipitation, crystallization. OPPOSITE: dilution. **2** (*the condensation of steam*) liquefaction, deliquescence. **3** (*wipe the condensation off the glass*) mist, fog, droplets, liquid. **4** (*the condensation of text*) shortening, abridgment, abbreviation, summarization, encapsulation, compression, contraction, reduction. OPPOSITE: amplification. **5** (*a condensation of the report*) abridgment, summary, synopsis, précis, résumé, abstract, digest, epitome.

condense *verb* **1** (*condense text*) shorten, cut, abridge, abbreviate, summarize, synopsize, précis, epitomize, encapsulate, compress, compact, contract, reduce. OPPOSITE: amplify. **2** (*condense liquid*) concentrate, reduce, boil down, distil, consolidate, solidify, coagulate, thicken, evaporate, precipitate, crystallize. OPPOSITE: dilute. **3** (*steam condenses on the glass*) liquefy, deliquesce.

condescend *verb* **1** (*she condescended to wash up*) deign, see fit, vouchsafe, stoop, descend, lower oneself, demean oneself, humble oneself, vouchsafe **2** (*doctors who condescend to their patients*) patronize, talk down.

condescending *adj* patronizing, disdainful, supercilious, pompous, lofty, superior, haughty, lordly, imperious, snobbish, snooty (*inf*), toffee-nosed (*inf*). OPPOSITE: humble.

condescension *noun* stooping, patronage, disdain, superciliousness, pomposity, loftiness, airs, haughtiness, imperiousness, snobbery, snootiness (*inf*). OPPOSITE: humility.

condign *adj* fitting, suitable, appropriate, apt, just, fair, deserved, merited. OPPOSITE: undeserved.

condiment *noun* sauce, relish, dressing, seasoning, flavouring, spice.

condition *noun* **1** (*one of the conditions of the contract*) stipulation, provision, proviso, term, clause, qualification, restriction, limitation, requirement, prerequisite, necessity, essential, demand. **2** (*used cars in good condition*) shape, form, order, state, nick (*inf*). **3** (*players who are out of condition*) fitness, health, fettle, shape, form, trim. **4** (*suffering from a heart condition*) disorder, complaint, problem, disease, illness, ailment, weakness, infirmity, disability, defect. **5** (*the condition of the unemployed*) state, situation, position, circumstance, plight, predicament, quandary. **6** (*rise above his condition*) estate, rank, status, station, position, footing, standing, class, caste, grade, stratum.
➤ *verb* **1** (*animals conditioned to respond in this way*) accustom, habituate, inure, adapt, adjust, prepare, groom, equip, prime, educate, train, teach, coach, indoctrinate, brainwash. **2** (*behaviour conditioned by past experience*) influence, affect, determine, govern. **3** (*shampoos that condition the hair*) improve, tone up, make healthy, treat, restore, revive.

conditional *adj* provisional, qualified, restricted, limited, relative, dependent, subject, contingent, based, tied. OPPOSITE: absolute.

conditions *pl noun* circumstances, situation, state, surroundings, environment, milieu, setting, background, context, atmosphere, climate.

condolence *noun* commiseration, sympathy, pity, fellow feeling, compassion, consolation, comfort, solace.

condom *noun* sheath, contraceptive, protective, prophylactic, Durex®, French letter (*inf*), rubber (*inf*), johnny (*inf*).

condonation *noun* pardon, forgiveness, amnesty, dispensation, excusing, overlooking, ignoring, disregarding. OPPOSITE: punishment.

condone *verb* pardon, forgive, excuse, make allowances for, overlook, ignore, disregard, let pass, wink at, turn a blind eye to. OPPOSITE: punish.

conduce *verb* lead, tend, contribute, aid, assist, help, advance, promote, forward. OPPOSITE: hinder.

conducive *adj* leading, tending, contributory, instrumental, helpful, useful, favourable, beneficial, advantageous, productive, encouraging, promoting. OPPOSITE: detrimental.

conduct *noun* **1** (*good conduct*) behaviour, bearing, mien, demeanour, attitude, deportment, comportment, carriage, manners, ways, habits, actions, practices. **2** (*the*

conduct of the operation) management, administration, running, control, handling, leadership, direction, guidance, supervision.
➤ *verb* **1** (*conducted them to the door*) guide, lead, direct, steer, pilot, usher, escort, accompany, take, bring. **2** (*conduct electricity*) convey, transmit, carry, bear. **3** (*conduct an experiment*) carry out, perform, execute, do. **4** (*conduct negotiations*) lead, preside over, chair, direct, supervise, manage, administer, run, control, regulate, handle.

conduct oneself act, behave, comport oneself, deport oneself, carry oneself, bear oneself, acquit oneself.

conduit *noun* duct, passage, pipe, tube, channel, canal, main, trough, gutter.

confab *noun* confabulation, conversation, talk, chat, gossip, natter (*inf*), discussion, debate.

confabulate *verb* talk, converse, chat, gossip, natter (*inf*), gas (*inf*), jaw (*inf*), have a chin-wag (*inf*), chatter, gab (*inf*).

confection *noun* making, manufacture, production, composition.

confectionery *noun* sweets, sweetmeats, candy, preserves, confections.

confederacy *noun* alliance, league, confederation, federation, coalition, bloc, union.

confederate *adj* allied, associated, combined, united, federal, federate, federated, confederated. OPPOSITE: opposed.
➤ *noun* ally, associate, partner, colleague, collaborator, abettor, accomplice, accessory. OPPOSITE: opponent.
➤ *verb* ally, associate, combine, unite, merge, amalgamate, federate. OPPOSITE: separate.

confederation *noun* federation, confederacy, association, alliance, league, coalition, union.

confer *verb* **1** (*confer a title*) bestow, award, present, grant, accord, vouchsafe, give. OPPOSITE: withdraw. **2** (*confer with my advisers*) discuss, debate, deliberate, consult, talk, converse, parley.

conference *noun* **1** (*address a conference*) meeting, congress, convention, convocation, summit, forum, symposium, colloquium, seminar, discussion, debate. **2** (*the judges are in conference*) consultation, discussion, debate, deliberation, talk, conversation, parley, dialogue, communication.

confess *verb* **1** (*confessed her ignorance*) acknowledge, admit, own, grant, concede, recognize, aver, assert, affirm, avow, declare, profess, divulge, disclose, reveal, make known, expose. OPPOSITE: deny. **2** (*forced the culprit to confess*) own up, admit guilt, accept blame, come clean (*inf*), tell all (*inf*), spill the beans (*inf*), unburden oneself, unbosom oneself, make a clean breast of it (*inf*), get it off one's chest (*inf*).

confession *noun* acknowledgment, admission, recognition, assertion, affirmation, avowal, declaration, profession, disclosure, revelation, exposure. OPPOSITE: denial.

confidant *noun* intimate, close friend, friend, crony, pal (*inf*), mate (*inf*), buddy (*inf*).

confidante *noun* intimate, close friend, bosom friend, friend, crony, pal (*inf*), mate (*inf*).

confide verb 1 (*confided that he was nervous*) disclose, reveal, divulge, tell, impart, whisper, breathe, confess, admit. OPPOSITE: conceal. 2 (*confided her valuables to their custody*) entrust, commit, commend, consign, assign, hand over, turn over, make over, give.

confide in 1 (*can't confide in my staff*) trust, depend on, rely on, have faith in, believe in. OPPOSITE: distrust. 2 (*he confided in his sister*) open one's heart to, unburden oneself to, unbosom oneself to.

confidence noun 1 (*have lost confidence in the system*) trust, dependence, reliance, faith, belief, credence, assurance, conviction. OPPOSITE: doubt. 2 (*an air of confidence*) self-confidence, self-assurance, self-possession, poise, aplomb, self-reliance, courage, nerve, mettle, boldness, audacity. OPPOSITE: timidity. 3 (*took me into her confidence*) confidentiality, intimacy, secrecy, privacy.

in confidence confidentially, secretly, in secret, privately, in private, between ourselves, between you and me, off the record, behind closed doors, in camera, sub rosa. OPPOSITE: publicly.

confident adj 1 (*confident that we would win*) sure, certain, positive, assured, convinced, satisfied, optimistic. OPPOSITE: doubtful. 2 (*a confident young man*) self-confident, assured, self-assured, sure of oneself, self-possessed, cool, calm, composed, unselfconscious, self-reliant, assertive, positive, bold, courageous, fearless, dauntless. OPPOSITE: timid.

confidential adj 1 (*confidential information*) private, secret, personal, intimate, sensitive, off-the-record, classified, restricted, hush-hush (*inf*). OPPOSITE: public. 2 (*a confidential friend*) trustworthy, trusty, trusted, dependable, reliable, faithful, close, bosom, intimate, familiar. OPPOSITE: unreliable.

confidentially adv in confidence, secretly, in secret, privately, in private, between ourselves, between you and me, off the record, behind closed doors, in camera, sub rosa. OPPOSITE: publicly.

configuration noun figure, form, shape, outline, contour, formation, conformation, structure, arrangement, disposition.

confine verb 1 (*confined to a cell*) imprison, incarcerate, immure, intern, lock up, cage, pen, coop up, keep in, enclose, shut up. OPPOSITE: free. 2 (*confined by regulations*) restrict, limit, circumscribe, hem in, bound, bind, constrain, restrain, hold back, control, shackle, trammel, repress, inhibit. OPPOSITE: derestrict.
≫ noun limit, bound, boundary, border, frontier, edge, circumference, perimeter, scope, limitation, restriction.

confinement noun 1 (*the confinement of criminals*) imprisonment, incarceration, internment, detention, custody, captivity, duress, constraint, restraint, restriction, limitation. OPPOSITE: liberation. 2 (*during her last confinement*) childbirth, lying-in, accouchement, labour, parturition, delivery.

confirm verb 1 (*confirmed his story*) verify, corroborate, substantiate, validate, authenticate, bear out, prove, evidence, endorse, back up. OPPOSITE: refute.
2 (*confirming my suspicions*) strengthen, reinforce, fortify, support, uphold, back up. 3 (*confirm a booking*) fix, establish, settle, affirm, assert, aver, assure, pledge,

promise, guarantee. OPPOSITE: cancel. 4 (*confirm her appointment*) authorize, ratify, sanction, approve, endorse, underwrite.

confirmation noun 1 (*confirmation of his story*) verification, corroboration, substantiation, validation, proof, evidence, endorsement. OPPOSITE: refutation. 2 (*confirmation of my suspicions*) strengthening, reinforcement, fortification, support. 3 (*confirmation of a booking*) affirmation, assertion, assurance, pledge. OPPOSITE: cancellation. 4 (*confirmation of her appointment*) authorization, ratification, sanction, approval.

confirmed adj habitual, chronic, incurable, inveterate, ingrained, dyed-in-the-wool, hardened, seasoned, established, set, fixed, entrenched.

confiscate verb seize, take, sequester, sequestrate, dispossess, distrain, impound, appropriate, arrogate, commandeer, expropriate. OPPOSITE: restore.

conflagration noun fire, blaze, inferno, holocaust.

conflict noun 1 (*military conflict*) battle, war, warfare, hostilities, action, fight, combat, strife, struggle, contest, contention, clash, encounter, engagement, skirmish, scuffle, tussle, scrap. 2 (*conflict between neighbours*) disagreement, discord, dispute, dissension, friction, antagonism, hostility, antipathy, bad blood, feud, quarrel, row. OPPOSITE: agreement. 3 (*conflict of interests*) clash, collision, difference, variance, friction, opposition, antagonism.
≫ verb clash, collide, disagree, differ, be at variance, interfere, oppose, fight, combat, contest, contend. OPPOSITE: agree.

conflicting adj opposed, antagonistic, at odds, at variance, clashing, different, incompatible, inconsistent, contradictory, paradoxical, contrary, opposing. OPPOSITE: accordant.

confluence noun conflux, convergence, junction, meeting, union, concurrence. OPPOSITE: divergence.

confluent adj converging, meeting, joining, merging, mingling, blending. OPPOSITE: divergent.

conform verb 1 (*those who refuse to conform*) comply, yield, submit, obey, toe the line (*inf*), be conventional, follow the crowd (*inf*), run with the pack (*inf*), go with the flow (*inf*), swim with the stream (*inf*), adapt, adjust, accommodate, reconcile. OPPOSITE: rebel. 2 (*conforms with our expectations*) agree, correspond, tally, match, accord, harmonize, suit, square, fit. OPPOSITE: disagree.

conform to obey, follow, observe, comply with, fall in with, adapt to, adjust to. OPPOSITE: disobey.

conformist noun conventionalist, traditionalist, yes-man (*inf*). OPPOSITE: nonconformist.

conformity noun 1 (*conformity among the young*) conventionality, traditionalism, orthodoxy, yielding, submission, adaptation, adjustment, accommodation. OPPOSITE: nonconformity. 2 (*in conformity with your request*) obedience, observance, compliance. OPPOSITE: disregard. 3 (*in conformity with our expectations*) agreement, correspondence, likeness, resemblance, similarity, affinity, accord, harmony, consonance, congruity, compatibility. OPPOSITE: discord.

confound verb 1 (*the results confounded the experts*) astound, astonish, amaze, surprise, startle, stun, dumbfound, flabbergast (*inf*), perplex, puzzle, confuse, mystify, baffle, flummox (*inf*), bewilder, bemuse, nonplus, disconcert, discomfit, dismay. **2** (*confound the enemy*) defeat, beat, trounce, annihilate, destroy, overwhelm, overthrow. **3** (*confounded our plans*) upset, thwart, frustrate, spoil, ruin. **4** (*confound a theory*) contradict, refute, quash, annihilate, demolish, destroy, explode. OPPOSITE: confirm.

confounded *adj* wretched, accursed, damned, blasted, abominable, execrable, detestable, odious. OPPOSITE: blessed.

confront *verb* **1** (*confront the enemy*) face up to, challenge, defy, brave, beard, tackle, accost, waylay, oppose, resist, withstand, stand up to. **2** (*confront a problem*) face, encounter, tackle, deal with, address, get to grips with (*inf*), face up to, meet head on (*inf*). OPPOSITE: evade. **3** (*problems that confront us*) threaten, trouble, harass, face.

confrontation *noun* clash, collision, encounter, showdown, conflict, contest, battle, fight, quarrel, set-to (*inf*).

confuse *verb* **1** (*their instructions confused me*) bewilder, perplex, puzzle, confound, mystify, baffle, flummox (*inf*), tie in knots (*inf*), bemuse, nonplus, muddle, disorientate, throw (*inf*), upset, discompose, disconcert, discomfit, fluster, abash, embarrass, mortify. OPPOSITE: enlighten. **2** (*don't confuse the issue*) complicate, involve, muddle, mix up, jumble, disorder, disarrange, derange, tangle, garble. OPPOSITE: simplify. **3** (*confuse left and right*) mistake, muddle, jumble, mix up, mingle. OPPOSITE: distinguish.

confused *adj* **1** (*she looked confused*) bewildered, perplexed, puzzled, mystified, baffled, flummoxed (*inf*), all at sea (*inf*), bemused, nonplussed, muddled, mixed-up, disorientated, dazed, upset, discomposed, flustered, not knowing whether one is coming or going (*inf*), abashed, embarrassed, mortified. **2** (*a confused mess*) muddled, jumbled, disorderly, untidy, chaotic, disorganized, topsy-turvy (*inf*), higgledy-piggledy (*inf*). OPPOSITE: tidy. **3** (*a confused account*) unclear, indistinct, obscure, muddled, garbled, hazy, foggy. OPPOSITE: distinct.

confusing *adj* puzzling, baffling, muddling, complicated, involved, unclear, obscure, ambiguous, misleading. OPPOSITE: clear.

confusion *noun* **1** (*trying to hide his confusion*) bewilderment, perplexity, puzzlement, mystification, bafflement, muddle, disorientation, discomposure, discomfiture, chagrin, abashment, embarrassment, mortification. OPPOSITE: enlightenment. **2** (*a state of confusion in my study*) mess, disorder, disarray, muddle, jumble, untidiness, shambles (*inf*). OPPOSITE: order. **3** (*in the confusion following the explosion*) commotion, upheaval, tumult, turmoil, chaos, anarchy.

confute *verb* refute, disprove, rebut, invalidate, belie, contradict, controvert, overthrow, overcome. OPPOSITE: prove.

congeal *verb* coagulate, clot, cake, curdle, thicken, set, gel, stiffen, harden, solidify, freeze.

congenial *adj* pleasant, agreeable, pleasing, nice, friendly, genial, affable, amiable, companionable, kindly, sympathetic, compatible, like-minded, well-suited, well-matched, suitable, fit, favourable, comfortable, cosy, homely. OPPOSITE: disagreeable.

congenital *adj* **1** (*a congenital disease*) inborn, inbred, inherent, innate, inherited, hereditary, connate, natural. **2** (*a congenital liar*) habitual, chronic, incurable, inveterate, ingrained, dyed-in-the-wool, hardened, seasoned, confirmed, utter, complete, thorough, thoroughgoing.

congested *adj* **1** (*congested roads*) full, crowded, packed, crammed, stuffed, overflowing, teeming, blocked, obstructed, clogged, jammed. OPPOSITE: clear. **2** (*congested lungs*) blocked, clogged, stopped up, choked.

congestion *noun* crowding, overcrowding, jam, bottleneck, gridlock, snarl-up (*inf*), block, blockage, obstruction, blocking, clogging, choking, surfeit, repletion. OPPOSITE: clearance.

conglomerate *verb* cluster, gather, collect, amass, accumulate, aggregate, agglomerate. OPPOSITE: disperse. ➤ *noun* **1** (*works for a large conglomerate*) multinational, corporation, cartel, consortium, merger, firm, concern, company, bustiness. **2** (*a conglomerate of rock fragments*) conglomeration, cluster, mass, aggregate, agglomerate. ➤ *adj* clustered, gathered, collected, amassed, accumulated, aggregate, agglomerate.

conglomeration *noun* cluster, mass, aggregation, agglomeration, accumulation, assortment, medley, miscellany, hotchpotch.

congratulate *verb* compliment, felicitate, pat on the back (*inf*), acclaim, praise, take one's hat off to (*inf*).

congratulations *pl noun* **1** (*offered our congratulations*) compliments, felicitations, bouquets, best wishes, good wishes, greetings. **2** (*you've won, congratulations!*) well done, bravo, congrats (*inf*).

congregate *verb* collect, gather, assemble, meet, convene, rendezvous, muster, rally, mass, throng, flock, crowd, converge, accumulate. OPPOSITE: disperse.

congregation *noun* **1** (*a congregation of people*) gathering, assembly, muster, meeting, convention, convocation, rally, crowd, throng, host, flock, mass, cluster, group. **2** (*the congregation of the church*) parish, parishioners, flock, laity.

congress *noun* assembly, meeting, gathering, conference, convention, convocation, conclave, synod, council, legislature, parliament, senate, diet.

congruity *noun* agreement, accord, concord, correspondence, congruence, consonance, consistency, harmony, compatibility, suitability, fitness, appropriateness. OPPOSITE: incongruity.

congruous *adj* agreeing, accordant, concordant, corresponding, congruent, consonant, consistent, harmonious, compatible, suitable, fit, appropriate. OPPOSITE: incongruous.

conical *adj* conic, cone-shaped, pyramidal, funnel-shaped, infundibular, tapering, pointed.

conjectural *adj* hypothetical, theoretical, academic, speculative, postulated, posited, supposed, assumed, suspected, putative, surmised, guessed, tentative. OPPOSITE: proven.

conjecture *verb* guess, surmise, suppose, assume,

presume, infer, suspect, imagine, fancy, theorize, hypothesize, postulate. OPPOSITE: prove.

➤ *noun* guess, surmise, supposition, assumption, presumption, inference, suspicion, speculation, theory, hypothesis, imagination, fancy, notion, belief, judgment, conclusion. OPPOSITE: proof.

conjoin *verb* join, connect, link, unite, tie, bind, fasten, hitch, combine, associate, league, merge, confederate. OPPOSITE: sever.

conjugal *adj* connubial, matrimonial, married, wedded, marital, nuptial, bridal, hymeneal, epithalamic. OPPOSITE: celibate.

conjunction *noun* **1** (*conjunction of efforts*) joining, connection, link, union, combination, association, alliance, collaboration, cooperation. OPPOSITE: separation. **2** (*conjunction of events*) coincidence, concurrence, co-occurrence, coexistence, contemporaneousness, simultaneity, juxtaposition. **in conjunction with** with, together with, along with, alongside, in association with, in partnership with, in combination with, combined with.

conjuncture *noun* juncture, stage, point, turning point, crossroads, crisis, emergency, exigency, predicament, dilemma, quandary.

conjuration *noun* **1** (*the witch's conjurations*) incantation, chant, invocation, spell, charm, magic, sorcery, enchantment. **2** (*ignored their conjurations*) appeal, entreaty, adjuration, plea, prayer, supplication.

conjure *verb* **1** (*telling jokes and conjuring*) perform magic, do tricks, juggle. **2** (*conjure spirits*) invoke, call up, summon, rouse. **3** (*conjured them to desist*) appeal to, beseech, implore, entreat, adjure, crave, beg, pray, supplicate.
conjure up evoke, call to mind, bring to mind, recall, recollect, imagine, create, produce, make appear.

conjuror *noun* magician, illusionist, prestidigitator, juggler, sorcerer, wizard.

conjuring *noun* magic, tricks, illusions, sleight of hand, prestidigitation, juggling, sorcery, wizardry.

conk *verb* **conk out** break down, fail, pack up (*inf*), go on the blink (*inf*).

conman *noun* confidence trickster, swindler, cheat, fraud, impostor, deceiver.

connate *adj* inborn, innate, congenital, natural, inherent.

connect *verb* **1** (*connect the two wires*) join, attach, fasten, tie, bind, unite, link, couple, affix, adhere, secure, clamp, combine, fuse, weld, solder. OPPOSITE: disconnect. **2** (*he connects fire with pain*) link, relate, associate, ally, identify, equate, bracket. **3** (*connecting passages*) communicate, adjoin, abut, border, neighbour.

connected *adj* **1** (*connected pipes*) joined, attached, fastened, bound, united, linked, coupled, clamped, combined, fused, welded. OPPOSITE: disconnected. **2** (*problems connected with unemployment*) linked, related, akin, associated, allied. OPPOSITE: unconnected. **3** (*connected thoughts*) coherent, intelligible, comprehensible, fluent, consecutive, sequential, uninterrupted, unbroken. OPPOSITE: incoherent.

4 (*connected rooms*) communicating, adjoining, adjacent, neighbouring. OPPOSITE: separate.

connection *noun* **1** (*a loose connection*) joint, junction, union, link, coupling, tie, bond, attachment, fastening. **2** (*no connection between the two crimes*) link, relation, relationship, liaison, association, alliance, correspondence, correlation, parallel, analogy. **3** (*its meaning in this connection*) context, reference, relation. **4** (*one of my connections at head office*) contact, acquaintance, friend, associate, ally, patron, sponsor. **5** (*she's Welsh with Irish connections*) relative, relation, kin, kindred, family, ancestry.

connivance *noun* conspiracy, intrigue, plotting, scheming, collusion, collaboration, complicity, abetment, consent, approval.

connive *verb* conspire, intrigue, plot, scheme, collude, collaborate.
connive at overlook, disregard, ignore, blink at, wink at, turn a blind eye to, let pass, gloss over, condone, allow. OPPOSITE: oppose.

conniving *adj* scheming, plotting, conspiring, colluding, nasty, unscrupulous, unprincipled, corrupt.

connoisseur *noun* expert, authority, pundit, specialist, savant, cognoscente, devotee, aficionado, fan, buff (*inf*), judge, arbiter, critic, epicure, gourmet, gastronome, aesthete.

connotation *noun* implication, significance, meaning, nuance, undertone, overtone, association, suggestion, hint, intimation, insinuation, inference, allusion, reference.

connote *verb* imply, signify, mean, betoken, indicate, suggest, hint at, infer, intimate, insinuate, involve, implicate.

connubial *adj* conjugal, matrimonial, married, wedded, marital, nuptial, bridal, hymeneal, epithalamic. OPPOSITE: celibate.

conquer *verb* **1** (*conquer the enemy*) defeat, vanquish, beat, trounce, best, worst, overcome, overpower, overthrow, master, subdue, crush, quell, subjugate, rout, checkmate, humble, humiliate. OPPOSITE: surrender to. **2** (*conquer land*) seize, appropriate, take, possess, annex, occupy, invade, overrun, win, gain, obtain, acquire. OPPOSITE: lose. **3** (*conquer fear*) overcome, surmount, rise above, master, crush, suppress, triumph over, prevail over, vanquish. OPPOSITE: yield to.

conqueror *noun* victor, winner, champion, defeater, vanquisher, master, lord, conquistador, hero. OPPOSITE: victim.

conquest *noun* **1** (*celebrating their conquest*) victory, win, triumph, success. **2** (*conquest of the enemy*) defeat, vanquishment, trouncing, overpowering, overthrow, mastery, subjugation, rout, humiliation. OPPOSITE: surrender. **3** (*the conquest of land*) invasion, occupation, annexation, possession, appropriation, seizure, capture. OPPOSITE: loss. **4** (*the conquest of their hearts*) captivation, enchantment, seduction, allurement, enticement. OPPOSITE: repulsion. **5** (*his latest conquest*) catch, captive, prize, acquisition, trophy, booty, plunder, loot, spoils.

consanguinity *noun* relationship, kinship, blood tie, family tie, common ancestry, affinity, association, connection.

conscience *noun* scruples, principles, morals, ethics, moral sense, still small voice, integrity, honesty.

conscience-stricken *adj* guilt-ridden, guilty, ashamed, troubled, sorry, regretful, remorseful, contrite, penitent, repentant. OPPOSITE: unrepentant.

conscientious *adj* **1** (*a conscientious worker*) diligent, assiduous, industrious, hardworking, dedicated, devoted, attentive, careful, painstaking, scrupulous, meticulous, punctilious, particular, thorough, exact, precise, accurate, strict, faithful. OPPOSITE: careless. **2** (*a conscientious citizen*) honest, upright, just, fair, scrupulous, principled, moral, high-minded, incorruptible, responsible, good, honourable. OPPOSITE: unprincipled.

conscious *adj* **1** (*conscious of the problem*) aware, awake, alert, cognizant, mindful, heedful, sensible, knowing, percipient. OPPOSITE: unaware. **2** (*make a conscious effort*) deliberate, intentional, planned, premeditated, calculated, studied, wilful, volitional, voluntary. OPPOSITE: unintentional. **3** (*the conscious mind*) thinking, reasoning, rational, sensible. OPPOSITE: subconscious. **4** (*remained conscious during the operation*) awake, aware, alert, responsive, sentient, alive. OPPOSITE: unconscious.

consciousness *noun* **1** (*consciousness of the problem*) awareness, alertness, realization, recognition, cognizance, mindfulness, heedfulness, knowledge, perception, apprehension. OPPOSITE: ignorance. **2** (*when she regained consciousness*) wakefulness, awareness, alertness, responsiveness, sentience.

conscript *verb* recruit, enlist, draft, call up, mobilize, muster.
➤ *noun* recruit, enlistee, draftee. OPPOSITE: volunteer.

consecrate *verb* **1** (*consecrate a building*) sanctify, bless, anoint, hallow, make holy, dedicate. OPPOSITE: desecrate. **2** (*consecrate a bishop*) ordain, bless, anoint, venerate, revere, honour, exalt. **3** (*consecrated her life to helping the needy*) dedicate, devote, commit, assign, pledge, vow.

consecutive *adj* successive, sequential, serial, following, succeeding, continuous, uninterrupted, unbroken, progressive, step-by-step, orderly, logical, chronological. OPPOSITE: discontinuous.

consecutively *adv* sequentially, in turn, successively, continuously, one after the other, back to back (*inf*), on the trot (*inf*).

consensus *noun* agreement, concurrence, unanimity, common consent, harmony, concord, accord, unity. OPPOSITE: dissension.

consent *verb* agree, concur, assent, accede, acquiesce, concede, submit, yield, give in, comply, go along with, permit, allow, give the go-ahead (*inf*), give the green light (*inf*), approve, grant, authorize, rubber-stamp (*inf*). OPPOSITE: refuse.
➤ *noun* **1** (*without their parents' consent*) agreement, concurrence, assent, acquiescence, permission, clearance, go-ahead (*inf*), green light (*inf*), thumbs-up (*inf*), OK (*inf*), approval, sanction, authorization. OPPOSITE: refusal. **2** (*by common consent*) accord, harmony, unanimity, consensus, agreement, concurrence. OPPOSITE: dissension.

consequence *noun* **1** (*the consequences of your actions*) result, outcome, issue, effect, end, event, upshot, aftermath, repercussion, reverberation. OPPOSITE: cause. **2** (*a matter of little consequence*) importance, significance, concern, moment, import, weight, substance, note, value. OPPOSITE: insignificance. **3** (*a woman of consequence*) distinction, standing, status, rank, repute, esteem, notability, eminence, prominence, importance, influence, prestige.

consequent *adj* resultant, resulting, consequential, ensuing, following, subsequent, successive, sequential. OPPOSITE: preceding.

consequential *adj* **1** (*a consequential decision*) important, significant, momentous, weighty, substantial, noteworthy, serious. OPPOSITE: insignificant. **2** (*a consequential official*) self-important, pompous, bumptious, pretentious, conceited, vain, proud, arrogant, supercilious. OPPOSITE: modest. **3** (*consequential loss of earnings*) resultant, resulting, consequent, ensuing, following, subsequent.

consequently *adv* therefore, ergo, thus, hence, as a result, subsequently.

conservation *noun* preservation, maintenance, upkeep, protection, custody, care, safekeeping, saving, husbandry, economy. OPPOSITE: destruction.

conservative *adj* **1** (*a conservative attitude*) moderate, middle-of-the-road, cautious, prudent, temperate, sober, stable, unchanging, conventional, traditional, orthodox, unprogressive, old-fashioned, hidebound, reactionary, diehard, set in one's ways. OPPOSITE: liberal. **2** (*the Conservative Party*) Tory, right-wing, reactionary, traditionalist, establishmentarian.
➤ *noun* Tory, right-winger, reactionary, traditionalist, establishmentarian.

conservatory *noun* **1** (*grown in a conservatory*) greenhouse, glasshouse, hothouse. **2** (*studying at the conservatory*) conservatoire, academy, music school, drama school.

conserve *verb* preserve, maintain, keep, protect, take care of, safeguard, save, spare, go easy on (*inf*), store, hoard, reserve, keep back. OPPOSITE: squander.

consider *verb* **1** (*need time to consider*) reflect, ponder, deliberate, contemplate, meditate, ruminate, cogitate, muse, think. **2** (*consider his proposal*) think about, give thought to, study, examine, weigh up, mull over, chew over, ponder, contemplate. **3** (*consider her a fool*) regard, deem, think, believe, judge, rate, estimate, count, hold. **4** (*consider their feelings*) respect, have regard for, care for, heed, mark, note, remember, bear in mind, take into account, take into consideration. OPPOSITE: ignore.

considerable *adj* **1** (*a considerable sum*) great, large, big, substantial, sizeable, ample, abundant, plentiful, lavish, decent, respectable, goodly, tidy (*inf*). OPPOSITE: trifling. **2** (*with considerable effort*) much, a lot of, a good deal of, great, marked, noticeable, appreciable. OPPOSITE: little. **3** (*a considerable player*) important, significant, noteworthy, remarkable, great, illustrious, distinguished, renowned, influential, venerable. OPPOSITE: insignificant.

considerably *adv* much, a lot, a good deal, greatly, substantially, noticeably, significantly.

considerate *adj* thoughtful, kind, kindly, benevolent,

compassionate, sympathetic, caring, attentive, solicitous, concerned, obliging, accommodating, mindful, sensitive, tactful, discreet, patient, forbearing, charitable, unselfish, selfless. OPPOSITE: inconsiderate.

consideration *noun* **1** (*after some consideration*) reflection, deliberation, contemplation, meditation, rumination, cogitation, thought, study, examination, scrutiny, analysis, notice, attention, regard, heed. OPPOSITE: disregard. **2** (*they showed us little consideration*) thoughtfulness, kindness, kindliness, benevolence, compassion, sympathy, care, attentiveness, solicitude, concern, sensitivity, tact, discretion, patience, forbearance, charity, unselfishness, selflessness. OPPOSITE: thoughtlessness. **3** (*taking her inexperience into consideration*) account, reckoning. **4** (*went up in my consideration*) esteem, estimation, respect, regard, admiration. **5** (*several other important considerations*) issue, factor, circumstance, concern, point. **6** (*for a small consideration*) payment, fee, recompense, reward, remuneration, perquisite, emolument, tip, gratuity.

considering *prep* **1** (*considering her inexperience*) in view of, in the light of, bearing in mind, taking into account, taking into consideration. **2** (*he did very well, considering*) all things considered, all in all.

consign *verb* **1** (*consigned to my care*) commit, entrust, hand over, deliver, transfer, bequeath. **2** (*consigned to the scrap heap*) assign, banish, relegate, deposit. **3** (*consign a package*) send, dispatch, ship, convey, transmit, post, mail.

consignment *noun* **1** (*consignment to my care*) committal, entrusting, handing over, delivery, transfer. **2** (*the consignment of goods*) sending, dispatch, shipping, conveyance. **3** (*a consignment of books*) load, shipment, delivery, batch.

consist *verb* **consist in** lie in, reside in, be contained in. **consist of** comprise, be composed of, be made up of, contain, include, incorporate, embody, involve, amount to.

consistency *noun* **1** (*a semisolid consistency*) thickness, density, viscosity, firmness, coherence, cohesion. **2** (*consistency with the evidence*) accordance, agreement, correspondence, conformity, consonance, correlation, congruity, compatibility. OPPOSITE: inconsistency. **3** (*consistency in performance*) regularity, constancy, uniformity, steadiness, dependability, reliability. OPPOSITE: irregularity.

consistent *adj* **1** (*consistent with the evidence*) accordant, agreeing, corresponding, matching, conforming, consonant, congruous, compatible. OPPOSITE: inconsistent. **2** (*consistent performance*) regular, constant, unchanging, uniform, steady, dependable, reliable, unfailing, faithful, loyal. OPPOSITE: erratic.

consolation *noun* comfort, solace, sympathy, commiseration, cheer, encouragement, ease, alleviation, reassurance, relief, support, help. OPPOSITE: distress.

console[1] *verb* (*console the bereaved relatives*) comfort, solace, sympathize with, commiserate with, cheer, encourage, hearten, soothe, calm, reassure, relieve, support, help. OPPOSITE: upset.

console[2] *noun* (*turn a knob on the console*) panel, control

panel, instrument panel, board, dashboard, keyboard, controls, instruments, switches, buttons, keys, dials.

consolidate *verb* **1** (*consolidate the businesses*) unite, join, combine, amalgamate, merge, fuse. OPPOSITE: separate. **2** (*consolidate our position*) strengthen, fortify, reinforce, stabilize, secure. OPPOSITE: weaken. **3** (*consolidated into a stony mass*) compact, compress, fuse, coalesce, congeal, harden, solidify. OPPOSITE: disintegrate.

consolidate *verb* **1** (*consolidation of the businesses*) amalgamation, merger, fusion, association, federation, confederation, affiliation, unification, alliance, combination. OPPOSITE: separation. **2** (*consolidation of our position*) strengthening, fortificaiton, reinforcement, stabilization, securing. OPPOSITE: weakening. **3** (*consolidation into a stony mass*) compaction, compression, fusion, coalescence, congelation, hardening, solidification. OPPOSITE: disintegration.

consonance *noun* consistency, compatibility, congruity, accord, harmony, agreement, concord, conformity, accordance, correspondence, suitability. OPPOSITE: discord.

consonant *adj* consistent, compatible, congruous, accordant, harmonious, in harmony, agreeing, in agreement, concordant, conforming, in accordance, correspondent, appropriate, suitable. OPPOSITE: discordant.

consort *noun* companion, partner, mate, spouse, husband, wife, associate, fellow, friend, comrade.
➤ *verb* associate, fraternize, mix, mingle, keep company, spend time, go around, hang around.

consortium *noun* syndicate, cartel, bloc, federation, confederation, league, alliance, partnership, association, organization, guild, union, combination, agreement.

conspicuous *adj* **1** (*a conspicuous error*) obvious, evident, plain, clear, patent, manifest, visible, apparent, marked, prominent, standing out a mile (*inf*), glaring, flagrant, blatant, noticeable, discernible, perceptible, observable. OPPOSITE: inconspicuous. **2** (*conspicuous colouring*) showy, ostentatious, flashy, garish, loud, bold, striking. OPPOSITE: subdued. **3** (*a conspicuous success*) remarkable, outstanding, striking, impressive, eminent, notable, distinguished, celebrated, famous, renowned, illustrious, great. OPPOSITE: insignificant.

conspiracy *noun* **1** (*a conspiracy to kill the king*) plot, intrigue, scheme, stratagem, machination. **2** (*accused of conspiracy*) plotting, intrigue, machination, collaboration, collusion, connivance, treason, treachery. **3** (*members of the conspiracy*) cabal, league, conspirators.

conspirator *noun* conspirer, plotter, intriguer, schemer, collaborator, colluder, traitor.

conspire *verb* **1** (*conspiring against the government*) plot, intrigue, plan, scheme, machinate, collaborate, collude, connive, be in cahoots (*inf*). **2** (*everything was conspiring against us*) combine, unite, concur, act together, cooperate, work together, join forces, gang up.

constancy *noun* **1** (*the constancy of his supporters*) faithfulness, fidelity, loyalty, devotion, steadfastness, staunchness. OPPOSITE: inconstancy. **2** (*constancy of purpose*) doggedness, determination, resolution, firmness, perseverance, tenacity. **3** (*the constancy of the* *temperature*) regularity, uniformity, evenness, permanence, stability, steadiness. OPPOSITE: irregularity.

constant *adj* **1** (*at a constant speed*) regular, uniform, even, unchanging, unvarying, invariable, fixed, permanent, stable, steady. OPPOSITE: changeable. **2** (*in constant pain*) perpetual, continuous, incessant, unceasing, ceaseless, unending, never-ending, endless, interminable, nonstop, uninterrupted, unbroken, unrelenting, unremitting, sustained, persistent. OPPOSITE: intermittent. **3** (*a constant friend*) faithful, loyal, devoted, steadfast, staunch, dependable, trustworthy, trusty, true. OPPOSITE: fickle. **4** (*constant effort*) dogged, determined, resolute, firm, persevering, tenacious, unflagging, unwavering, unshaken.

constantly *adv* always, forever, continually, perpetually, continuously, nonstop, incessantly, ceaselessly, interminably, ad nauseam, relentlessly. OPPOSITE: occasionally.

constellation *noun* galaxy, cluster, collection, group, assemblage.

consternation *noun* dismay, distress, shock, alarm, fear, terror, fright, horror, dread, trepidation, panic, anxiety, perturbation, confusion, bewilderment, surprise, astonishment, amazement. OPPOSITE: relief.

constituent *adj* component, integral, intrinsic, elemental, basic, essential.
➤ *noun* **1** (*the constituents of the mixture*) component, ingredient, element, part, unit, factor. OPPOSITE: whole. **2** (*a meeting with her constituents*) voter, elector.

constitute *verb* **1** (*the parties that constitute the alliance*) compose, make up, comprise, form. **2** (*behaviour that constitutes a violation of the rules*) be, represent, add up to, amount to, be tantamount to, be equivalent to, be regarded as. **3** (*constituted himself their representative*) appoint, nominate, depute, ordain, invest, empower, authorize, commission, charter. **4** (*constitute a charitable organization*) found, establish, set up, create, institute. OPPOSITE: abolish.

constitution *noun* **1** (*the constitution of the committee*) composition, make-up, structure, organization, formation, foundation, establishment, creation, institution. **2** (*the American constitution*) code, charter, canon, bill of rights, laws, statutes, rules. **3** (*a woman with a strong constitution*) health, physique, build, make-up, disposition, temper, temperament, character, nature, spirit.

constitutional *adj* **1** (*constitutional rights*) lawful, legitimate, legal, statutory, authorized, ratified, chartered, vested. OPPOSITE: unconstitutional. **2** (*a constitutional weakness*) inherent, intrinsic, innate, inborn, inbred, congenital, natural, organic.
➤ *noun* stroll, walk, turn, airing, promenade, saunter, amble.

constrain *verb* **1** (*not constrained to reply*) compel, force, oblige, make, coerce, drive, impel, urge, press, pressurize, railroad. **2** (*constrained by her clothing*) restrain, hold back, curb, check, hamper, hinder, impede, restrict, limit, confine, hem in, cage, imprison, bind, chain. OPPOSITE: free.

constrained *adj* unnatural, forced, stiff, uneasy, inhibited, reserved, guarded. OPPOSITE: relaxed.

constraint *noun* **1** (*I felt under constraint*) compulsion, force, obligation, coercion, duress, pressure. **2** (*constraints on spending*) restraint, curb, check, hindrance, obstruction, restriction, limitation, confinement. OPPOSITE: freedom. **3** (*constraint of manner*) unnaturalness, inhibition, repression, suppression, reservedness, guardedness. OPPOSITE: relaxation.

constrict *verb* **1** (*constrict the tube*) squeeze, tighten, narrow, contract, shrink, compress, cramp, pinch, strangle, strangulate. OPPOSITE: expand. **2** (*constrict the flow*) choke, obstruct, impede, hinder, hamper, restrict, limit, check, curb, restrain, inhibit.

constriction *noun* **1** (*a constriction in her throat*) tightness, narrowing, stricture, pressure, cramp, strangulation, knot, lump, blockage, obstruction, impediment. **2** (*constriction of choice*) restriction, limitation, check, curb, restraint, inhibition.

construct *verb* **1** (*construct a bridge*) build, erect, raise, elevate, put up, establish, set up, assemble, put together, make, fabricate, manufacture. OPPOSITE: destroy. **2** (*construct a theory*) formulate, compose, frame, put together, form, fashion, shape, model, create, design, invent, devise.

construction *noun* **1** (*the construction of a bridge*) building, erection, elevation, assembly, fabrication, manufacture. OPPOSITE: demolition. **2** (*analyse the construction*) formation, composition, structure, framework, fabric. **3** (*skyscrapers and similar constructions*) building, edifice, erection, structure, shape, figure. **4** (*the construction of a theory*) formulation, composition, formation, creation, design, invention. **5** (*put a different construction on the remark*) interpretation, explanation, rendering, reading, meaning, inference, deduction.

constructive *adj* positive, useful, helpful, practical, productive, valuable. OPPOSITE: destructive.

construe *verb* interpret, explain, expound, translate, render, analyse, parse, read, take, infer, deduce.

consult *verb* **1** (*consult a specialist*) ask, refer to, turn to, seek advice from. **2** (*consult a dictionary*) refer to, turn to, look up. **3** (*consulted local residents about the plans*) canvass, ask, question, interrogate. **4** (*after consulting with my colleagues*) confer, talk, discuss, debate, deliberate. **5** (*consult the tastes of your guests*) consider, regard, respect, take into account. OPPOSITE: ignore.

consultant *noun* specialist, expert, authority, adviser, guru.

consultation *noun* meeting, conference, forum, session, interview, hearing, audience, examination, talk, discussion, debate, deliberation, consideration, council, parley, powwow, dialogue, colloquy, tête-à-tête.

consume *verb* **1** (*consume a meal*) devour, eat, drink, swallow, ingest, take, tuck into (*inf*), scoff (*inf*), guzzle (*inf*), down (*inf*), put away (*inf*), polish off (*inf*). OPPOSITE: refuse. **2** (*consume resources*) use, utilize, use up, exhaust, drain, devour, eat up, swallow up, deplete, spend, expend, go through, get through, dissipate, waste, squander, lavish, fritter away. OPPOSITE: conserve. **3** (*consumed by fire*) destroy, demolish, devastate, lay waste, ravage, raze, gut. **4** (*consumed by passion*) absorb, engross, preoccupy, obsess, devour, eat up, monopolize, rivet, grip.

consumer *noun* buyer, purchaser, shopper, user, customer, client, patron. OPPOSITE: producer.

consuming *adj* absorbing, engrossing, compelling, overwhelming, preoccupying, obsessive, riveting, gripping.

consummate *verb* accomplish, achieve, fulfil, realize, perform, execute, carry out, complete, finish, conclude, end, perfect, crown, cap. OPPOSITE: abort.
» *adj* accomplished, skilled, expert, masterly, proficient, practised, polished, perfect, excellent, superb, matchless, supreme, ultimate, utter, complete, absolute, total, unqualified. OPPOSITE: imperfect.

consummation *noun* accomplishment, achievement, fulfilment, realization, performance, execution, completion, finish, conclusion, end, perfection, crown, cap, culmination.

consumption *noun* **1** (*the consumption of alcohol*) ingestion, swallowing, eating, drinking. **2** (*the consumption of fuel*) use, utilization, exhaustion, depletion, spending, expenditure, dissipation, waste. OPPOSITE: conservation. **3** (*consumption by fire*) destruction, demolition, devastation, ravaging.

contact *noun* **1** (*the surfaces are not in contact*) touch, union, junction, contiguity, juxtaposition, tangency. OPPOSITE: isolation. **2** (*after contact with toxic substances*) touching, exposure, proximity, association. **3** (*lost contact with my old schoolfriends*) communication, connection, correspondence, association. **4** (*one of his contacts at the ministry*) connection, acquaintance, associate, ally.
» *verb* get in touch with, get hold of, reach, get through to, approach, speak to, communicate with, notify, telephone, phone, ring, call, write to, fax, e-mail.

contagion *noun* infection, communication, transmission, spread, contamination, corruption, pollution.

contagious *adj* infectious, catching, communicable, transmissible, transferable, spreading, epidemic, pandemic, pestilential.

contain *verb* **1** (*the film contains strong language*) include, incorporate, involve, embrace. **2** (*the set contains six glasses*) comprise, consist of, incorporate, embody. **3** (*a tank containing 40 litres*) hold, carry, accommodate, admit, enclose. **4** (*could not contain their curiosity*) restrain, hold back, keep back, check, curb, control, repress, suppress, stifle. OPPOSITE: release.

container *noun* receptacle, holder, vessel, repository.

contaminate *verb* pollute, adulterate, debase, infect, poison, corrupt, vitiate, deprave, soil, foul, defile, sully, stain, tarnish, taint. OPPOSITE: cleanse.

contaminated *adj* impure, polluted, infected, poisonous, toxic, corrupt, depraved, soiled, dirty, foul, sullied, tarnished, tainted. OPPOSITE: pure.

contamination *noun* impurity, pollution, adulteration, debasement, infection, contagion, poisoning, toxicity, corruption, vitiation, defilement, dirtiness, foulness. OPPOSITE: purification.

contemplate *verb* **1** (*contemplate the problem*) consider, ponder, think about, reflect on, meditate on, mull over, study, examine. **2** (*left her to contemplate*) think, ponder, deliberate, meditate, ruminate, muse, cogitate. **3** (*contemplate the scene*) look at, stare at, gaze at, view, survey, behold, regard, observe, watch, eye, scan, scrutinize, examine, inspect. OPPOSITE: ignore. **4** (*what do you contemplate doing about it?*) intend, plan, mean, propose, envisage, have in mind, foresee, expect to.

contemplation *noun* **1** (*lost in contemplation*) thought, consideration, deliberation, reflection, meditation, rumination, cogitation, reverie, brown study (*inf*). **2** (*contemplation of the scene*) observation, scrutiny, examination, inspection, viewing, surveying. **3** (*in contemplation of marriage*) prospect, anticipation, expectation, intention, plan.

contemplative *adj* thoughtful, pensive, reflective, meditative, ruminative, introspective, intent, rapt, lost in thought, in a brown study (*inf*).

contemporary *adj* **1** (*artists contemporary with Picasso*) contemporaneous, coexistent, coexisting, coeval, coetaneous, concurrent, synchronous, simultaneous. **2** (*contemporary architecture*) modern, up-to-date, up-to-the-minute, fashionable, trendy (*inf*), with it (*inf*), latest, recent, current, present, present-day, newfangled, avant-garde, futuristic. OPPOSITE: ancient.

contempt *noun* **1** (*view them with contempt*) scorn, derision, mockery, disrespect, disdain, condescension, superciliousness, contemptuousness, dislike, hatred, loathing, disgust, abhorrence. OPPOSITE: admiration. **2** (*contempt of court*) disrespect, disregard, neglect. OPPOSITE: respect.

contemptible *adj* despicable, base, mean, low, vile, abject, shameful, cheap, paltry, worthless, derisory, pitiful, pathetic, lamentable, miserable, wretched, disreputable, shabby, ignominious, detestable, loathsome, abhorrent. OPPOSITE: noble.

contemptuous *adj* scornful, derisive, mocking, jeering, sneering, cynical, disrespectful, insulting, insolent, disdainful, withering, condescending, patronizing, supercilious, haughty, arrogant, high and mighty. OPPOSITE: respectful.

contend *verb* **1** (*contending for the trophy*) compete, vie, contest, dispute, challenge, oppose, clash, fight, combat, battle, war, grapple, wrestle, tussle, struggle, strive. OPPOSITE: surrender. **2** (*contended that the man was innocent*) argue, maintain, hold, aver, assert, affirm, claim, allege, declare, state. OPPOSITE: disclaim.

contend with face, take on, tackle, address, deal with, cope with, get to grips with, grapple with, wrestle with, struggle with.

content[1] *noun* (*a smile of content*) contentment, contentedness, satisfaction, gratification, fulfilment, ease, comfort, tranquillity, serenity, peace of mind, pleasure, happiness, gladness, cheerfulness. OPPOSITE: discontent.
» *adj* contented, satisfied, gratified, fulfilled, at ease, comfortable, tranquil, serene, untroubled, unworried, pleased, happy, glad, cheerful, willing, agreeable. OPPOSITE: dissatisfied.
» *verb* satisfy, gratify, appease, pacify, placate, mollify, humour, indulge, please, gladden, delight. OPPOSITE: displease.

content[2] *noun* **1** (*the content of the letter*) matter, substance, essence, pith, gist, burden, meaning, significance, text, material, subject matter, topic, theme, idea. **2** (*the content of the tank*) capacity, volume, size, dimensions, measure, magnitude. **3** (*with a low fat content*) amount, quantity, proportion.

contented *adj* content, satisfied, gratified, fulfilled, at ease, comfortable, relaxed, complacent, tranquil, serene, pleased, happy, glad. OPPOSITE: discontented.

contention *noun* **1** (*in contention for the trophy*) competition, rivalry, contest, opposition, clash, conflict, fight, combat, battle, war, struggle, strife. **2** (*a matter of contention between them*) conflict, discord, dissension, disagreement, dispute, debate, controversy, wrangle, squabble, altercation, quarrel, argument, feud, strife, antagonism, hostility, enmity. OPPOSITE: agreement. **3** (*her contention that he was innocent*) assertion, affirmation, claim, allegation, declaration, statement, belief, conviction, opinion, view, viewpoint, stand, position, thesis, argument, point.

contentious *adj* **1** (*dealing with contentious people*) quarrelsome, argumentative, disputatious, bickering, wrangling, belligerent, pugnacious, combative, litigious, querulous, peevish, petulant, captious, contrary, perverse. OPPOSITE: peaceable. **2** (*a contentious issue*) controversial, polemical, debatable, disputable. OPPOSITE: incontrovertible.

contentment *noun* content, contentedness, satisfaction, gratification, ease, comfort, complacency, equanimity, tranquillity, serenity, peace of mind, pleasure, happiness, gladness. OPPOSITE: dissatisfaction.

contents *pl noun* **1** (*the contents of the package*) load, content, filling, items, constituents, components, parts, elements, ingredients. **2** (*a table of contents*) chapters, sections, divisions, parts, topics, subjects.

contest *noun* **1** (*an archery contest*) competition, tournament, championship, match, game, race, event. **2** (*the contest for the leadership*) struggle, battle, fight, combat, skirmish, tussle, fray, conflict, dispute, debate, contention.
➤ *verb* **1** (*contest the decision*) dispute, argue, litigate, object to, oppose, challenge, question, call into question, doubt. OPPOSITE: accept. **2** (*contest the championship*) compete for, contend for, vie for, fight over, battle over, struggle for, strive for. OPPOSITE: surrender.

contestant *noun* competitor, contender, aspirant, candidate, entrant, participant, player, runner, opponent, adversary, rival, antagonist.

context *noun* **1** (*the meaning changes according to context*) frame of reference, connection, relation, subject, topic. **2** (*in their cultural context*) background, setting, surroundings, environment, situation, conditions, circumstances, state of affairs.

contiguity *noun* contiguousness, contact, adjacency, juxtaposition, nearness, proximity. OPPOSITE: remoteness.

contiguous *adj* meeting, joining, touching, in contact, abutting, adjoining, adjacent, juxtaposed, beside, next to, conterminous, bordering, neighbouring, near, close. OPPOSITE: remote.

continence *noun* self-restraint, self-control,

moderation, temperance, sobriety, abstinence, abstemiousness, self-denial, asceticism, austerity, chastity, celibacy, purity. OPPOSITE: licentiousness.

continent *adj* self-restrained, self-controlled, moderate, temperate, sober, abstinent, abstemious, self-denying, ascetic, austere, chaste, celibate, pure, virginal. OPPOSITE: licentious.

contingency *noun* possibility, eventuality, event, occurrence, incident, happening, occasion, juncture, chance, fortuity, uncertainty, accident, casualty, emergency, situation, circumstance, case, factor, aspect, detail.

contingent *adj* **1** (*bonuses contingent on productivity*) dependent, depending, subject, based, conditional, provisional. **2** (*contingent events*) accidental, incidental, casual, chance, fortuitous, random, haphazard, unforeseen, unpredictable, possible, uncertain.
➤ *noun* group, body, band, party, company, faction, deputation, detachment, section, division, batch, quota, complement, portion.

continual *adj* recurrent, repeated, regular, frequent, constant, persistent, perpetual, sustained, nonstop, incessant, interminable, endless, unremitting, continuous. OPPOSITE: intermittent.

continually *adv* constantly, perpetually, persistently, incessantly, forever, always, all the time, repeatedly, recurrently, frequently, regularly. OPPOSITE: occasionally.

continuance *noun* continuation, constancy, permanence, persistence, perseverance, endurance, survival.

continuation *noun* **1** (*a continuation of the story*) sequel, addition, supplement, postscript, epilogue, appendix. **2** (*a continuation of the bypass*) extension, prolongation. **3** (*continuation long into the night*) continuance, maintenance, furtherance, extension, protraction, prolongation. OPPOSITE: cessation. **4** (*continuation after an adjournment*) resumption, recommencement, renewal.

continue *verb* **1** (*continue working during the power cut*) carry on, go on, keep on, press on, pursue, persist, persevere, stick at (*inf*). OPPOSITE: stop. **2** (*continue after lunch*) resume, recommence, start again, begin again, carry on, go on, proceed, advance. OPPOSITE: interrupt. **3** (*continue the talks into the evening*) prolong, extend, lengthen, draw out, protract. OPPOSITE: curtail. **4** (*if this weather continues*) last, endure, survive, hold out, abide, stay, remain, persist, carry on. OPPOSITE: cease. **5** (*continue the tradition*) sustain, keep up, maintain, carry on, perpetuate. OPPOSITE: abandon.

continuity *noun* connection, linkage, interrelationship, cohesion, coherence, flow, progression, sequence, succession, continuousness, uninterruptedness. OPPOSITE: interruption.

continuous *adj* unbroken, uninterrupted, solid, consecutive, constant, nonstop, endless, unending, never-ending, incessant, ceaseless, unceasing, eternal, everlasting, sustained, prolonged, extended, unremitting, perpetual, continual. OPPOSITE: broken.

contort *verb* deform, misshape, twist, warp, distort,

gnarl, knot, convolute, writhe, squirm. OPPOSITE: straighten.

contortion *noun* deformity, twist, warp, distortion, convolution, convulsion, grimace.

contour *noun* outline, silhouette, profile, relief, shape, form, figure, line, curve.

contraband *noun* smuggling, trafficking, bootlegging, gunrunning.
≫ *adj* smuggled, illegal, illicit, unlawful, banned, prohibited, proscribed, black-market, bootleg, hot (*inf*). OPPOSITE: lawful.

contraception *noun* birth control, family planning, safe sex, contraceptives, barrier methods, prophylactics.

contract *verb* **1** (*the metal contracts*) shrink, reduce, lessen, diminish, decrease, compress, compact, shorten, narrow, constrict, tighten, shrivel, wrinkle. OPPOSITE: expand. **2** (*contract a muscle*) tighten, tense, narrow, constrict, squeeze, draw in, purse. OPPOSITE: extend. **3** (*contract the text*) shorten, condense, compress, abbreviate, abridge, curtail, epitomize, synopsize, summarize, précis. **4** (*contracted to work on Sundays*) agree, arrange, engage, undertake, commit oneself, pledge, promise, covenant, stipulate, bargain, negotiate, come to terms. **5** (*contract measles*) catch, get, pick up, develop, succumb to, go down with (*inf*). **6** (*contract a debt*) incur, acquire.
≫ *noun* agreement, pact, compact, treaty, convention, concordat, covenant, bond, pledge, commitment, undertaking, engagement, settlement, arrangement, understanding, bargain, transaction, deal.

contraction *noun* **1** (*the contraction of the metal*) shrinkage, reduction, lessening, diminution, decrease, compression, shortening, narrowing, constriction, tightening, shrivelling. OPPOSITE: expansion. **2** (*muscle contraction*) tightening, tensing, narrowing, constriction. OPPOSITE: extension. **3** (*'can't' is a contraction*) shortening, short form, elision, abbreviation, abridgment.

contradict *verb* **1** (*he contradicted my statement*) deny, gainsay, dispute, controvert, impugn, oppose, challenge, contest, disprove, refute, rebut, confute. OPPOSITE: confirm. **2** (*she contradicted me*) oppose, challenge, counter, go against, disagree with, be at variance with. OPPOSITE: agree with. **3** (*two accounts that contradict each other*) negate, belie, clash with, conflict with, disagree with, be at odds with, be at variance with, contravene, fly in the face of (*inf*). OPPOSITE: correspond with.

contradiction *noun* **1** (*contradiction of my statement*) denial, opposition, challenge, dissension, refutation, rebuttal, confutation, negation, contravention. OPPOSITE: confirmation. **2** (*contradiction between the accounts*) inconsistency, incongruity, variance, discrepancy, disagreement, conflict, clash. OPPOSITE: correspondence.

contradictory *adj* contrary, opposing, opposite, at variance, at odds, disagreeing, conflicting, clashing, contrasting, antagonistic, irreconcilable, incompatible, inconsistent, incongruous, paradoxical, antithetical. OPPOSITE: affirmative.

contraption *noun* contrivance, device, gadget, gizmo

(*inf*), thingamajig (*inf*), whatsit (*inf*), rig, gear, apparatus, machine, mechanism, appliance.

contrariety *noun* opposition, contrast, conflict, disagreement, discord, antagonism, hostility, contradiction, incompatibility, inconsistency. OPPOSITE: harmony.

contrary *adj* **1** (*contrary opinions*) opposed, opposing, opposite, counter, adverse, antagonistic, hostile, inimical, contradictory, discordant, disagreeing, conflicting, clashing, contrasting, incompatible, inconsistent, at variance, at odds. OPPOSITE: like. **2** (*a contrary child*) perverse, awkward, difficult, stroppy (*inf*), obstinate, stubborn, pig-headed, intractable, refractory, recalcitrant, wayward, wilful, self-willed, headstrong. OPPOSITE: obliging.
≫ *noun* opposite, reverse, converse, antithesis.

contrary to against, in opposition to, counter to, at variance with.

on the contrary in contrast, quite the opposite, quite the reverse.

contrast *verb* **1** (*contrast his work with hers*) compare, juxtapose, differentiate, distinguish, discriminate. OPPOSITE: liken. **2** (*painted in a contrasting colour*) stand out, set off, differ, oppose, clash, conflict. OPPOSITE: match. **3** (*his explanation contrasts with hers*) differ, oppose, be at variance, be at odds, clash, conflict, contradict, go against. OPPOSITE: agree.
≫ *noun* difference, dissimilarity, disparity, distinction, differentiation, opposition, antithesis, polarity. OPPOSITE: similarity.

in contrast to in comparison with, as distinct from, as opposed to, rather than.

contravene *verb* **1** (*contravene the regulations*) break, infringe, violate, disobey, flout, transgress. OPPOSITE: keep. **2** (*the facts contravene this proposition*) contradict, refute, rebut, oppose, challenge, dispute, run counter to, nullify, annul, abrogate. OPPOSITE: validate

contravention *noun* **1** (*contravention of the rules*) infringement, violation, disobedience, breach, transgression, trespass. **2** (*contravention of the theory*) contradiction, refutation, rebuttal, opposition, antagonism, nullification, abrogation.

contretemps *noun* **1** (*a slight contretemps on the way home*) mishap, misadventure, accident, mistake, blunder, gaffe, difficulty, predicament, hitch, setback. **2** (*a little contretemps with my neighbour*) argument, dispute, quarrel, altercation, squabble, row, tiff (*inf*), clash, brush, confrontation.

contribute *verb* **1** (*contribute money*) supply, provide, furnish, give, donate, present, bestow, confer, grant, endow, subscribe, chip in (*inf*). OPPOSITE: withhold. **2** (*contributed to their success*) lead, conduce, be conducive, tend, add, help, promote, advance, play a part, be instrumental, cause, occasion. OPPOSITE: hinder. **3** (*contributing articles to journals*) write, compose, compile, prepare, supply, provide.

contribution *noun* **1** (*a contribution of £500*) donation, gift, present, offering, grant, subsidy, endowment, subscription. **2** (*made little contribution to the project*) help, assistance, participation, input, addition.

3 (*contributions for the magazine*) article, piece, item, feature, column, story, report.

contributor *noun* **1** (*contributors to the fund*) donor, giver, subscriber, sponsor, patron, benfactor, backer, supporter. **2** (*contributors to the newspaper*) writer, correspondent, reporter, journalist, columnist, critic, reviewer, freelance.

contributory *adj* instrumental, accessory, conducive, helpful, participatory, responsible.

contrite *adj* penitent, repentant, sorry, regretful, remorseful, conscience-stricken, guilt-ridden, chastened, humble, embarrassed, shamefaced, ashamed. OPPOSITE: unrepentant.

contrition *noun* penitence, repentance, sackcloth and ashes, sorrow, regret, remorse, self-reproach, compunction, shame, embarrassment, humiliation. OPPOSITE: impenitence.

contrivance *noun* **1** (*a contrivance for cleaning the windows*) device, invention, contraption, gadget, gizmo (*inf*), machine, mechanism, apparatus, appliance, piece of equipment, implement, tool, instrument. **2** (*a contrivance to avoid paying*) scheme, plan, plot, ruse, ploy, stratagem, artifice, trick, dodge, expedient.

contrive *verb* **1** (*contrive a makeshift ladder*) devise, invent, design, create, make, fabricate, construct, improvise. **2** (*contrive a plan*) frame, formulate, think up, devise, concoct, create, originate. **3** (*contrive a meeting*) engineer, manoeuvre, wangle (*inf*), arrange, set up, orchestrate, stage-manage, effect, bring about. **4** (*contrive to oust the president*) scheme, plot, conspire, intrigue, machinate, manage, succeed, find a way.

contrived *adj* artificial, forced, unnatural, strained, laboured, overdone, elaborate, mannered, affected, recherché. OPPOSITE: spontaneous.

control *verb* **1** (*control the company*) direct, lead, command, head, preside over, govern, rule, reign over, manage, run, conduct, supervise, superintend, oversee. **2** (*can't control the children*) manage, handle, discipline, dominate, master, boss (*inf*). **3** (*control an impulse*) restrain, curb, check, subdue, bridle, hold back, repress, suppress, contain, confine, limit, restrict, constrain, keep a tight rein on (*inf*). **4** (*control the temperature*) regulate, monitor, verify, adjust. **5** (*control the machine*) operate, work, drive, steer, pilot, guide.
» *noun* **1** (*the company is under her control*) direction, leadership, command, government, rule, authority, jurisdiction, charge, management, supervision, superintendence, power, sway, supremacy, dominance. **2** (*lost control of himself*) mastery, dominance, discipline, power, influence, hold, self-control, self-restraint. **3** (*arms control*) restraint, curb, check, brake, restriction, limitation, constraint, regulation. **4** (*quality control*) regulation, monitoring, verification. **5** (*adjust the controls*) lever, switch, knob, button, instrument, dial. **6** (*mission control*) base, headquarters, centre of operations.
be in control have authority, be the boss (*inf*), wear the trousers (*inf*), be in charge, be in the driving seat (*inf*), be in the saddle (*inf*), rule the roost (*inf*), run the show (*inf*), pull the strings (*inf*), call the shots (*inf*), call the tune (*inf*).

controversial *adj* contentious, disputed, at issue, under discussion, open to question, disputable, debatable, questionable, controvertible, polemic, dialectical. OPPOSITE: indisputable.

controversy *noun* dispute, argument, debate, polemic, war of words, discussion, wrangle, quarrel, altercation, disagreement, contention, dissension, strife, discord, friction. OPPOSITE: agreement.

controvert *verb* deny, refute, rebut, counter, oppose, challenge, contest, dispute, contradict. OPPOSITE: affirm.

contumacious *adj* stubborn, obstinate, perverse, contrary, refractory, recalcitrant, rebellious, insubordinate, obdurate, intractable, headstrong, tenacious, wilful, self-willed. OPPOSITE: docile.

contumely *noun* insult, affront, abuse, invective, obloquy, opprobrium, reproach, reproof, contempt, scorn, derision, disdain, arrogance, superciliousness, insolence, rudeness, discourtesy. OPPOSITE: respect.

contusion *noun* bruise, discoloration, ecchymosis, mark, blemish, injury, knock, bump, lump, swelling.

conundrum *noun* riddle, puzzle, poser, brainteaser (*inf*), enigma, mystery, problem.

convalesce *verb* recover, recuperate, improve, get better, mend, get well. OPPOSITE: deteriorate.

convalescence *noun* recovery, recuperation, improvement, amelioration, cure, restoration, rehabilitation. OPPOSITE: deterioration.

convalescent *adj* recovering, recuperating, improving, getting better, on the mend. OPPOSITE: deteriorating.

convene *verb* **1** (*convene a meeting*) call, summon, convoke, rally, round up, muster, assemble. OPPOSITE: disband. **2** (*convene in the hall*) meet, collect, gather, congregate, assemble, muster. OPPOSITE: disperse.

convenience *noun* **1** (*the convenience of the moment*) suitability, fitness, appropriateness, appositeness, timeliness, opportuneness, propitiousness. OPPOSITE: unsuitability. **2** (*the convenience of the arrangement*) expedience, utility, usefulness, handiness. OPPOSITE: inconvenience. **3** (*the convenience of the shops*) availability, accessibility, handiness, nearness, closeness, proximity. OPPOSITE: inaccessibility. **4** (*for your convenience*) advantage, benefit, aid, help, assistance, service, use, comfort, ease, accommodation. OPPOSITE: hindrance. **5** (*at your convenience*) leisure, spare time, free time. **6** (*modern conveniences*) facility, amenity, appliance, device, contrivance, gadget.

convenient *adj* **1** (*at a convenient time*) suitable, fit, fitting, appropriate, apposite, timely, well-timed, seasonable, opportune, propitious, favourable, beneficial, advantageous. OPPOSITE: inconvenient. **2** (*a convenient excuse*) handy, expedient, useful, helpful, serviceable, suited, fitted, adapted. **3** (*in a convenient location*) accessible, available, handy, to hand, at hand, close at hand, near by, just around the corner (*inf*), within reach, at one's fingertips (*inf*). OPPOSITE: inaccessible.

convent *noun* nunnery, cloister, abbey, priory, religious community.

convention *noun* **1** (*attend a convention*) meeting, gathering, assembly, conference, convocation, congress, council, synod, conclave. **2** (*sign a convention*) agreement, treaty, pact, entente, concordat, arrangement, compact, contract, transaction, bargain, deal. **3** (*observe the conventions*) custom, tradition, practice, usage, protocol, etiquette, code, formality, conventionality, propriety, punctilio. **4** (*literary conventions*) method, technique, practice, style.

conventional *adj* **1** (*conventional behaviour*) accepted, received, approved, expected, proper, correct, decorous, formal, official, orthodox, traditional, customary, prevailing, prevalent, conservative, conformist, mainstream. OPPOSITE: unconventional. **2** (*the conventional method*) standard, regular, normal, usual, habitual, routine, everyday, ordinary, common. OPPOSITE: alternative. **3** (*conventional design*) commonplace, common-or-garden, run-of-the-mill, stereotypical, trite, banal, prosaic, hackneyed, pedestrian, unoriginal, conservative, hidebound. OPPOSITE: original.

converge *verb* meet, intersect, join, unite, merge, blend, mingle, become one, focus, concentrate, centre, coincide, concur, come together, gather, flock, mass. OPPOSITE: diverge.
converge on approach, move towards, tend towards, flock towards, close in on, gather around.

convergence *noun* meeting, intersection, junction, union, merging, mingling, confluence, conflux, focus, concentration, coincidence, concurrence. OPPOSITE: divergence.

conversant *adj* familiar, acquainted, informed, apprised, au fait, versed, knowledgeable, well up (*inf*), experienced, practised, skilled, proficient. OPPOSITE: unfamiliar.

conversation *noun* **1** (*have a conversation*) talk, discussion, dialogue, exchange, discourse, conference, parley, powwow, confabulation, confab (*inf*), chat, gossip, natter (*inf*), chin-wag (*inf*), heart-to-heart, tête-à-tête. **2** (*in the course of conversation*) communication, talk, discussion, dialogue, discourse, intercourse, colloquy, converse, chat, gossip, chitchat, small talk.

conversational *adj* **1** (*a conversational style*) colloquial, informal, casual, chatty. OPPOSITE: formal. **2** (*a conversational person*) chatty, communicative, talkative, loquacious, garrulous, voluble, expansive, open, unreserved. OPPOSITE: taciturn.

converse¹ *verb* (*conversing with his colleagues*) talk, speak, communicate, commune, discuss, confer, confabulate, chat, gossip, natter (*inf*), gas (*inf*), chew the fat (*inf*), chew the rag (*inf*).
➤ *noun* conversation, communication, talk, discussion, dialogue, discourse, chat, gossip.

converse² *noun* (*the converse is true*) opposite, reverse, contrary, antithesis, obverse, other side of the coin (*inf*). OPPOSITE: same.
➤ *adj* opposite, opposing, reverse, contrary, counter, antithetical, obverse.

conversion *noun* **1** (*the conversion of the loft*) change, transformation, transfiguration, transmutation, metamorphosis, alteration, modification, adaptation, reshaping, remodelling, reorganization, reconstruction. **2** (*the conversion of currency*) exchange, transposition,

switch, swap, substitution, change. **3** (*conversion to Christianity*) conviction, persuasion, reformation, rebirth, regeneration, proselytization, baptism.

convert *verb* **1** (*convert the garage into a study*) change, transform, transfigure, transmute, metamorphose, make, turn, alter, modify, adapt, reshape, remodel, restyle, reorganize, rebuild, reconstruct. **2** (*convert dollars into pounds*) exchange, transpose, switch, swap, change, turn. **3** (*converted to Christianity*) convince, persuade, win over, reform, regenerate, proselytize, baptize.

convex *adj* bulging, rounded, humped, curved out, swelling, swollen, gibbous, protuberant. OPPOSITE: concave.

convey *verb* **1** (*convey goods*) carry, bear, transfer, transport, move, shift, take, bring, fetch, conduct, transmit, channel, pipe, send, dispatch, deliver. **2** (*convey information*) transmit, pass on, hand on, communicate, impart, make known, express, tell, relate, reveal, disclose. **3** (*convey property*) transfer, transmit, grant, cede, devolve, demise, bequeath, will.

conveyance *noun* **1** (*public conveyances*) vehicle, means of transport, car, carriage, wagon, van, lorry, truck, bus, coach. **2** (*the conveyance of goods*) carriage, transport, transportation, shipping, haulage, movement, dispatch, delivery. **3** (*the conveyance of information*) transmission, communication, imparting, expression, telling, revelation, disclosure. **4** (*the conveyance of property*) transfer, transmission, granting, cession, devolution, demise.

convict *verb* condemn, find guilty, sentence, imprison. OPPOSITE: acquit.
➤ *noun* criminal, felon, offender, lawbreaker, crook (*inf*), culprit, malefactor, wrongdoer, villain, prisoner, jailbird, con (*inf*), old lag (*inf*).

conviction *noun* **1** (*the conviction of criminals*) condemnation, judgment, sentence, punishment, imprisonment. OPPOSITE: acquittal. **2** (*he replied with conviction*) assurance, confidence, certainty, certitude, firmness, fervour, earnestness, persuasion, trust, belief, faith. OPPOSITE: doubt. **3** (*her political convictions*) opinion, view, idea, belief, faith, creed, principle, tenet.

convince *verb* **1** (*convince him it is correct*) persuade, satisfy, assure, reassure, prove to. **2** (*convince her to accept their offer*) prevail upon, bring round, talk round, persuade, sway, win over.

convinced *adj* sure, certain, positive, confident, assured, persuaded, satisfied. OPPOSITE: doubtful.

convincing *adj* plausible, credible, probable, likely, cogent, persuasive, powerful, forceful, impressive, telling, conclusive, decisive. OPPOSITE: unconvincing.

convivial *adj* sociable, congenial, jovial, jolly, merry, festive, cheerful, hearty, cordial, genial, affable, amiable, friendly. OPPOSITE: unsociable.

conviviality *noun* jollity, merriment, mirth, merrymaking, festivity, gaiety, cheer, cordiality, geniality, friendliness, bonhomie. OPPOSITE: gloom.

convocation *noun* assembly, gathering, congregation, meeting, convention, conference, congress, council, synod, conclave.

convoke *verb* call, summon, convene, muster, assemble, gather, rally. OPPOSITE: disband.

convoluted *adj* intricate, complex, complicated, involved, tortuous, twisting, turning, winding, meandering. OPPOSITE: straightforward.

convolution *noun* **1** (*the convolutions of the intestines*) coil, curl, kink, twist, turn, loop, whorl, spiral, helix, roll, fold, undulation. **2** (*the convolutions of the story*) intricacy, complexity, complication, involvement, entanglement, tortuousness.

convoy *noun* **1** (*under police convoy*) escort, guard, protection, defence, attendance, entourage. **2** (*trucks travelling in convoy*) fleet, group, company, line, file, train, procession, cortège, caravan.
➤ *verb* escort, accompany, attend, chaperon, guard, protect, defend, usher, shepherd, pilot, lead, direct, guide.

convulse *verb* agitate, shake, churn, heave, discompose, unsettle, disturb, derange. OPPOSITE: compose.

convulsion *noun* **1** (*patients suffering convulsions*) seizure, fit, paroxysm, spasm, contraction, cramp, tic, tremor. **2** (*political convulsions following the coup*) agitation, disturbance, upheaval, disruption, upset, commotion, turbulence, tumult, turmoil, disorder. OPPOSITE: calm.

cook *verb* **1** (*cook a meal*) prepare, put together, rustle up (*inf*), bake, stew, boil, fry, roast, grill. **2** (*cook the books*) falsify, forge. **3** (*what's cooking?*) happen, occur, take place, go on.
cook up concoct, devise, invent, contrive, think up, make up, prepare, create, fabricate, improvise, plan, plot, scheme.

cool *adj* **1** (*a cool wind*) chilly, chill, cold, coldish, nippy, breezy, draughty, fresh, crisp, refreshing, bracing. OPPOSITE: warm. **2** (*keep the wine cool*) cold, unheated, chilled, refrigerated, iced, ice-cold. OPPOSITE: hot. **3** (*remain cool in a crisis*) composed, calm, collected, unruffled, unperturbed, unflappable (*inf*), relaxed, laid back (*inf*), placid, quiet, tranquil, serene, self-possessed, self-controlled, poised, level-headed, cool as a cucumber (*inf*), unemotional, dispassionate, impassive. OPPOSITE: agitated. **4** (*a cool response*) unfriendly, cold, frigid, frosty, chilly, uninviting, unwelcoming, unresponsive, uncommunicative, undemonstrative, reserved, aloof, distant, standoffish, indifferent, unconcerned, lukewarm, unenthusiastic, apathetic. OPPOSITE: friendly. **5** (*you look really cool in that jacket*) smart, elegant, stylish, fashionable, trendy (*inf*). **6** (*kids who think they're cool*) sophisticated, urbane, streetwise (*inf*). **7** (*a cool new game*) excellent, marvellous, wonderful, great.
➤ *verb* **1** (*cool the wine*) make cold, chill, refrigerate, ice, freeze. OPPOSITE: heat. **2** (*leave the mixture to cool*) cool down, become cold, get cold, lose heat. OPPOSITE: warm up. **3** (*cool her passion*) dampen, quench, calm, quiet, assuage, allay, moderate, temper, abate, lessen, diminish, reduce. OPPOSITE: excite. **4** (*his enthusiasm cooled*) abate, lessen, diminish, moderate, cool off.
➤ *noun* **1** (*in the cool of the evening*) coolness, chill, coldness, freshness, crispness. OPPOSITE: warmth. **2** (*don't lose your cool*) composure, calmness, self-possession, self-control, poise, tranquillity, serenity.

coop *noun* cage, pen, enclosure, pound, box, hutch.
coop up cage, pen, confine, shut up, hem in, enclose, imprison, lock up, incarcerate, immure. OPPOSITE: liberate.

cooperate *verb* help, aid, assist, lend a hand, abet, conspire, connive, collaborate, work together, pull together, coact, coordinate, combine, unite, team up, join forces, pool resources, contribute, participate, pitch in (*inf*), go along, play ball (*inf*). OPPOSITE: oppose.

cooperation *noun* help, aid, assistance, support, contribution, participation, collaboration, interaction, coordination, teamwork, combined effort, synergy, give and take. OPPOSITE: opposition.

cooperative *adj* **1** (*they were not very cooperative*) helpful, helping, assisting, of assistance, supportive, obliging, accommodating, willing, responsive. OPPOSITE: uncooperative. **2** (*a cooperative venture*) collective, combined, joint, united, concerted, shared, collaborative, interactive, coactive, coordinated. OPPOSITE: individual.

coordinate *verb* **1** (*coordinate a search party*) organize, systematize, categorize, arrange, order, integrate, mesh, synchronize. **2** (*coordinating colours*) harmonize, match, correspond, correlate. **3** (*coordinating parts*) work together, act together, collaborate, cooperate.

cope *verb* manage, succeed, come through, get by, get along, get on, make out (*inf*), survive, subsist, hold one's own.
cope with handle, treat, deal with, weather, hack (*inf*), contend with, grapple with, struggle with, wrestle with, dispatch, take care of.

copious *adj* abundant, plentiful, plenteous, ample, profuse, lavish, exuberant, luxuriant, rich, overflowing, full, bountiful, bounteous, liberal, generous. OPPOSITE: scanty.

copiousness *noun* abundance, plenty, amplitude, profusion, lavishness, exuberance, luxuriance, richness, fullness, bounty. OPPOSITE: sparseness.

copse *noun* coppice, thicket, grove, wood, brush, bush.

copulate *verb* mate, couple, have sex, make love, go to bed, have it off (*sl*), have it away (*sl*), bonk (*sl*), shag (*sl*), screw (*sl*), fuck (*sl*).

copulation *noun* mating, coupling, coition, coitus, sexual intercourse, sex, lovemaking, carnal knowledge, having it off (*sl*), having it away (*sl*), bonking (*sl*), shagging (*sl*), screwing (*sl*), fucking (*sl*).

copy *verb* **1** (*copy the document*) duplicate, replicate, reproduce, photocopy, scan, transcribe, plagiarize, crib, pirate, forge, fake, counterfeit. OPPOSITE: originate. **2** (*copy what she does*) imitate, mimic, ape, parrot, echo, mirror, simulate, follow, emulate, repeat.
➤ *noun* **1** (*a copy of the document*) duplicate, replica, facsimile, reproduction, photocopy, Photostat®, Xerox®, print, carbon, transcription, plagiarism, crib, representation, model, forgery, fake, counterfeit, likeness, image, imitation, simulation. OPPOSITE: original. **2** (*unsold copies of the newspaper*) issue, example, sample, specimen.

coquetry *noun* flirtation, philandering, dalliance, trifling, teasing, ogling.

coquettish *adj* flirtatious, come-hither (*inf*), seductive, vampish, flighty, philandering, dallying, teasing.

cord *noun* **1** (*a length of cord*) line, string, twine, rope, cable, flex, wire. **2** (*the cords of love*) bond, tie, link, connection.

cordial *adj* friendly, warm, pleasant, affectionate, courteous, gracious, sociable, genial, amiable, affable, hearty, sincere, earnest, ardent, heartfelt, wholehearted. OPPOSITE: unfriendly.

cordiality *noun* friendliness, warmth, affection, courtesy, graciousness, geniality, amiability, affability, heartiness, sincerity, earnestness, wholeheartedness. OPPOSITE: hostility.

cordon *noun* line, chain, ring, barrier.
cordon off close off, shut off, fence off, isolate, separate, enclose, surround, encircle, picket.

core *noun* centre, heart, kernel, nucleus, nub, crux, essence, quintessence, substance, gist, pith, nitty-gritty (*inf*). OPPOSITE: exterior.

cork *noun* stopper, plug, bung.

corn *noun* **1** (*fields of corn*) cereal, grain, arable crop. **2** (*served with peas and corn*) maize, sweet corn, corn on the cob.

corner *noun* **1** (*go round the corner*) angle, bend, crook, knee, elbow, joint, junction, intersection, convergence, turn, turning. **2** (*hidden in a corner*) niche, recess, nook, cranny, crevice, cavity, hole, hidey-hole (*inf*), hideout, hideaway, retreat. **3** (*found myself in a corner*) predicament, plight, hole (*inf*), spot (*inf*), pickle (*inf*), jam (*inf*). **4** (*in our corner of the country*) part, region, area, district, quarter, neck of the woods (*inf*)
⯈ *verb* **1** (*cornered the animal*) trap, bring to bay, run to earth, block off. **2** (*corner the market*) monopolize, control, dominate, hog (*inf*).

corny *adj* trite, banal, hackneyed, stale, commonplace, platitudinous, old-fashioned, old hat (*inf*), mawkish, sentimental, weak, feeble. OPPOSITE: original.

corollary *noun* inference, deduction, conclusion, consequence, result, upshot.

coronation *noun* crowning, enthronement, accession, investiture.

coronet *noun* crown, diadem, circlet, tiara, wreath, garland.

corporal *adj* bodily, fleshly, physical, carnal, somatic, corporeal. OPPOSITE: mental.

corporate *adj* combined, joint, shared, communal, collective, united, allied, merged, pooled.

corporation *noun* **1** (*a commercial corporation*) company, firm, concern, establishment, trust, partnership, association, organization, combine, conglomerate, consortium, cartel. **2** (*the city corporation*) council, authority, authorities, governing body. **3** (*a man with a corporation*) paunch, potbelly, beer belly, spare tyre (*inf*).

corporeal *adj* physical, material, actual, real, tangible, substantial, corporal. OPPOSITE: spiritual.

corps *noun* company, troupe, body, group, band, crew, team, gang, party, squad, unit, detachment, contingent, troop, regiment, squadron, platoon, division.

corpse *noun* cadaver, body, dead body, stiff (*inf*), carcass, remains, skeleton, mummy.

corpulence *noun* fatness, stoutness, plumpness, tubbiness, rotundity, portliness, embonpoint, obesity, heaviness, burliness. OPPOSITE: thinness.

corpulent *adj* fat, stout, plump, tubby, rotund, roly-poly, portly, large, big, obese, overweight, podgy, chubby, bulky, heavy, burly, beefy, thickset, strapping. OPPOSITE: thin.

correct *adj* **1** (*the correct answer*) accurate, true, right, faultless, flawless, unerring, exact, precise, spot on (*inf*), strict, faithful. OPPOSITE: incorrect. **2** (*the correct way to behave*) proper, fitting, suitable, appropriate, seemly, decorous, accepted, approved, conventional, standard, regular, usual. OPPOSITE: improper.
⯈ *verb* **1** (*correct a mistake*) put right, set right, right, rectify, redress, amend, emend, alter, adjust, improve, ameliorate, remedy, cure. **2** (*correct a deficiency*) counteract, neutralize, offset, counterbalance, compensate for, make up for, rectify. **3** (*correct an instrument*) adjust, regulate, set, standardize. **4** (*correct badly-behaved children*) discipline, punish, chastise, castigate, admonish, reprove, reprimand, chide, scold, rebuke. OPPOSITE: indulge.

correction *noun* **1** (*make a few corrections*) rectification, amendment, emendation, alteration, change, modification, adjustment, improvement, amelioration, remedy, reparation, repair. **2** (*the correction of wrongdoers*) discipline, punishment, chastisement, castigation, admonition, reproof, reprimand, scolding, reformation. OPPOSITE: indulgence.

corrective *adj* **1** (*faults needing corrective treatment*) remedial, therapeutic, restorative, curative, rectifying, improving, reparatory. OPPOSITE: detrimental. **2** (*corrective action against offenders*) disciplinary, punitive, penal, castigatory, reformatory.

correctness *noun* **1** (*the correctness of the translation*) accuracy, truth, rightness, faultlessness, flawlessness, exactness, exactitude, precision, strictness, fidelity. OPPOSITE: incorrectness. **2** (*behave with correctness*) propriety, correctitude, suitability, appropriateness, seemliness, decorum, etiquette, protocol, civility, good manners. OPPOSITE: impropriety.

correlate *verb* compare, equate, relate, tie in, connect, associate, correspond, agree, coordinate, interact.

correlation *noun* correspondence, equivalence, interrelationship, reciprocity, mutuality, interdependence, connection, association, relationship. OPPOSITE: independence.

correlative *noun* corresponding, equivalent, interrelated, reciprocal, mutual, complementary. OPPOSITE: independent.

correspond *verb* **1** (*the two accounts do not correspond*) agree, concur, accord, harmonize, conform, tally, match, square, fit, dovetail, coincide, correlate, be similar, be comparable, be equivalent, be analogous. OPPOSITE: differ. **2** (*correspond with the author*) communicate, write, exchange letters, keep in touch.

correspondence *noun* **1** (*correspondence between the accounts*) agreement, concurrence, accord, harmony, conformity, match, coincidence, correlation, similarity,

resemblance, comparison, congruity, consonance, equivalence, analogy. OPPOSITE: difference.
2 (*correspondence from readers*) letters, mail, post, communication, writing.

correspondent *noun* **1** (*a newspaper correspondent*) journalist, reporter, stringer (*inf*), columnist, contributor, writer. **2** (*replying to my correspondents*) letter writer, pen-friend, pen pal (*inf*).

corresponding *adj* correspondent, analogous, equivalent, comparable, similar, like, reciprocal, complementary, parallel, matching, accordant. OPPOSITE: different.

corridor *noun* passage, passageway, hall, hallway, aisle, gallery, cloister.

corroborate *verb* confirm, substantiate, verify, validate, bear out, support, back up, endorse, ratify, uphold, sustain, document, certify, authenticate, establish, prove, evidence. OPPOSITE: invalidate.

corroboration *noun* confirmation, substantiation, verification, validation, support, endorsement, ratification, documentation, authentication, proof, evidence. OPPOSITE: invalidation.

corrode *verb* rust, oxidize, erode, wear away, abrade, eat away, consume, gnaw, impair, destroy, ruin, disintegrate, crumble, rot, waste away. OPPOSITE: restore.

corrosion *noun* rust, oxidation, erosion, attrition, wearing away, deterioration, destruction, disintegration. OPPOSITE: restoration.

corrosive *adj* corroding, erosive, abrasive, wearing, consuming, destructive, acid, acrid, caustic, mordant, trenchant, biting, cutting, incisive.

corrugated *adj* wrinkled, crinkled, furrowed, grooved, ridged, fluted, puckered, ruffled, crumpled, creased. OPPOSITE: smooth.

corrupt *adj* **1** (*a corrupt politician*) dishonest, unscrupulous, unprincipled, dishonourable, bribable, venal, fraudulent, crooked, bent (*inf*), shady (*inf*). OPPOSITE: honest. **2** (*corrupt sexual practices*) immoral, depraved, perverted, warped, degenerate, debauched, abandoned, decadent, dissolute, profligate, sinful, wicked, evil. OPPOSITE: moral. **3** (*a corrupt substance*) impure, adulterated, contaminated, infected, polluted, tainted, defiled, rotten, putrid. OPPOSITE: pure.
➤ *verb* **1** (*officials who are easily corrupted*) bribe, suborn, buy, buy off, pay off, square (*inf*), grease the palm of (*inf*). **2** (*corrupting our children*) deprave, pervert, warp, debauch, lead astray, lure, entice, seduce. OPPOSITE: edify. **3** (*corrupt the water supply*) contaminate, infect, pollute, taint, defile, debase, vitiate, spoil, mar, blight, adulterate, doctor, tamper with. OPPOSITE: purify.

corruption *noun* **1** (*corruption in high places*) dishonesty, unscrupulousness, bribery, subornation, venality, fraud, fraudulence, crookedness, sharp practice, deception, deceit. OPPOSITE: honesty. **2** (*moral corruption*) immorality, depravity, perversion, vice, wickedness, evil, sin, iniquity, turpitude, degeneracy, debauchery, abandonment, decadence, dissolution, profligacy. OPPOSITE: virtue. **3** (*corruption of the material*) contamination, pollution, defilement, debasement, vitiation, adulteration, spoiling, rot, decay, putrefaction. OPPOSITE: purification.

corsair *noun* pirate, buccaneer, freebooter, privateer, raider, marauder.

corset *noun* girdle, foundation, belt, stays, corselet, bodice.

cortege *noun* procession, parade, cavalcade, line, file, column, train, suite, retinue, entourage.

coruscate *verb* sparkle, flash, glint, gleam, scintillate, glitter, twinkle, glisten, glimmer, shimmer.

coruscation *noun* sparkle, flash, glint, gleam, scintillation, glitter, twinkle, glimmer, ray, beam.

cosmetic *adj* **1** (*cosmetic surgery*) beautifying, improving. **2** (*a purely cosmetic change*) surface, superficial, external, peripheral.

cosmetics *pl noun* make-up, war paint (*inf*), beauty products.

cosmic *adj* **1** (*cosmic forces*) universal, of space. **2** (*of cosmic proportions*) great, huge, immense, enormous, vast, immeasurable, limitless, infinite. OPPOSITE: tiny.

cosmonaut *noun* astronaut, spaceman, spacewoman.

cosmopolitan *adj* **1** (*of cosmopolitan significance*) universal, global, worldwide, international. **2** (*a cosmopolitan city*) international, multiracial, multicultural. **3** (*a cosmopolitan outlook*) broad-minded, liberal, urbane, sophisticated, cultured, worldly, worldly-wise, well-travelled, globe-trotting, jet-setting. OPPOSITE: insular.

cosmos *noun* world, universe, solar system, nature, creation, macrocosm.

cosset *verb* pamper, coddle, mollycoddle, baby, indulge, spoil, pet, caress, fondle, hug, cuddle. OPPOSITE: neglect.

cost *noun* **1** (*the cost of a new car*) price, charge, rate, fee, expense, expenditure, outlay, payment, amount, figure, damage (*inf*), worth, value, valuation, quotation, estimate. **2** (*the war was won, but at great cost*) loss, sacrifice, penalty, price, expense, damage, detriment, harm, injury, hurt, pain, suffering. OPPOSITE: gain.
➤ *verb* **1** (*a book that costs £50*) sell for, retail at, be priced at, be worth, fetch, go for, amount to, come to, set one back (*inf*), knock one back (*inf*). **2** (*cost a project*) price, value, evaluate, estimate, quote for. **3** (*it cost him his health*) lose, sacrifice, damage, harm, injure, hurt. **4** (*it will cost a lot of effort*) involve, need, necessitate, require, lead to, result in.

costly *adj* **1** (*a costly lifestyle*) dear, expensive, valuable, priceless, precious, fine, sumptuous, splendid, luxurious, rich, opulent, lavish, extravagant, extortionate, excessive, exorbitant, steep (*inf*). OPPOSITE: cheap. **2** (*a costly error*) damaging, harmful, injurious, detrimental, deleterious, destructive, ruinous, disastrous, catastrophic.

costs *pl noun* expenses, outgoings, expenditure, outlay, spending, budget.

costume *noun* dress, apparel, garb, attire, clothes, clothing, gear (*inf*), get-up (*inf*), outfit, uniform, livery, robes, vestments, habit, fashion.

cosy *adj* snug, comfortable, comfy (*inf*), warm, sheltered, secure, safe, homely, intimate, congenial, easy, relaxed. OPPOSITE: uncomfortable.

coterie *noun* set, circle, crowd, in-crowd, clique, gang, bunch, group, cabal, faction, camp, fraternity, sorority, club, society, association, company.

cottage *noun* lodge, chalet, cabin, hut, shack, shanty.

couch *noun* sofa, settee, chesterfield, chaise longue, divan, bed.
➤ *verb* utter, say, state, express, phrase, word, frame, style.

cough *noun* hack, bark, hem, tickle (*inf*), frog in one's throat (*inf*).
➤ *verb* hack, hawk, bark, hem, clear one's throat.

cough up pay, pay up, stump up (*inf*), pay out, shell out (*inf*), fork out (*inf*).

council *noun* **1** (*the county council*) authority, governing body, cabinet, chamber, ministry, parliament, congress, senate, diet. **2** (*the sports council*) board, panel, jury, committee, commission, advisory body, advisory group, working party. **3** (*hold a council*) meeting, gathering, assembly, rally, conference, convention, convocation, conclave, synod.

counsel *noun* **1** (*heed her counsel*) advice, guidance, instruction, direction, warning, caution, admonition, suggestion, recommendation, opinion. **2** (*in counsel with his colleagues*) consultation, deliberation, discussion, conference. **3** (*counsel for the prosecution*) advocate, attorney, lawyer, solicitor, barrister.
➤ *verb* advise, guide, urge, exhort, instruct, direct, warn, caution, admonish, suggest, recommend, advocate. OPPOSITE: discourage.

counsellor *noun* adviser, mentor, confidant, confidante, guide, director.

count *verb* **1** (*count the pages*) add up, total, sum up, tot up (*inf*), number, enumerate, calculate, compute, reckon, tally, tell. **2** (*not counting the children*) include, take into account, take into consideration, allow for, number among, embrace, embody. **3** (*I count it an honour*) consider, regard, esteem, deem, judge, rate, think, reckon, hold, look upon. **4** (*experience counts in this job*) matter, signify, be important, tell, weigh, carry weight, cut ice (*inf*).
➤ *noun* **1** (*keep a count*) enumeration, calculation, computation, reckoning, tally, score, poll. **2** (*the pollen count*) sum, total, aggregate, whole, amount, proportion.

count on depend on, rely on, bank on, lean on, trust, believe in, swear by, take for granted.

count out exclude, except, leave out, omit, ignore, disregard, pass over, neglect. OPPOSITE: include.

countenance *noun* **1** (*their gloomy countenances*) face, features, physiognomy, visage, expression, aspect, appearance, look, mien, air. **2** (*gave countenance to the project*) approval, approbation, sanction, favour, support, endorsement, backing, encouragement, aid, assistance. OPPOSITE: disapproval. **3** (*a loss of countenance*) calmness, coolness, composure, poise, self-control, self-possession, equanimity.
➤ *verb* **1** (*countenanced our plans*) approve, sanction, favour, support, endorse, back, encourage, aid, assist, help, advocate, promote, champion. OPPOSITE: oppose. **2** (*cannot countenance such behaviour*) accept, condone, tolerate, endure, brook, put up with, stand for (*inf*), permit, allow. OPPOSITE: forbid.

counter[1] *adv* (*running counter to predictions*) against, versus, in opposition, at variance, in defiance, contrarily, conversely.
➤ *adj* contrary, adverse, opposite, opposed, opposing, contradictory, conflicting, contrasting. OPPOSITE: like.
➤ *verb* retaliate, hit back, respond, answer, oppose, resist, offset, parry, ward off, dispute, combat, contradict, rebut.

counter[2] *noun* **1** (*serve at the counter*) table, board, worktop, bar, stand, stall, checkout. **2** (*move your counter around the board*) disc, token, marker, piece, man.

counteract *verb* neutralize, annul, nullify, counterbalance, offset, negate, invalidate, undo, act against, oppose, resist, check, frustrate, thwart, foil, defeat. OPPOSITE: assist.

counteraction *noun* neutralization, annulment, nullification, negation, invalidation, opposition, resistance, check, frustration, defeat.

counterbalance *verb* balance, equilibrate, equalize, offset, neutralize, counteract, undo, compensate, make up for, counterpoise, countervail.

counterfeit *verb* forge, fake, pretend, sham, feign, simulate, copy, reproduce, pirate, imitate, impersonate.
➤ *adj* forged, fake, false, sham, spurious, feigned, simulated, imitation, mock, ersatz, pirate, bogus, fraudulent, phoney (*inf*). OPPOSITE: genuine.
➤ *noun* forgery, fake, copy, reproduction, imitation, sham, fraud, phoney (*inf*).

countermand *verb* revoke, rescind, repeal, quash, annul, abrogate, cancel, retract, withdraw, reverse, override. OPPOSITE: confirm.

counterpart *noun* equivalent, equal, opposite number, partner, mate, fellow, match, double, twin, complement, supplement, analogue, correlative, parallel, copy, duplicate, likeness.

counterpoise *verb* counterbalance, balance, equilibrate, equalize, offset, neutralize, counteract, countervail.
➤ *noun* counterweight, counterbalance, balance, equilibrium.

countless *adj* innumerable, numberless, myriad, legion, incalculable, untold, immeasurable, measureless, infinite, endless, boundless, limitless, no end of, umpteen (*inf*). OPPOSITE: few.

country *noun* **1** (*a neighbouring country*) nation, state, republic, kingdom, realm, people. **2** (*fighting for their country*) homeland, native land, fatherland, motherland, roots. **3** (*supported by most of the country*) people, populace, population, inhabitants, residents, citizens, community, electorate, voters. **4** (*rough country*) land, terrain, territory, area, part, region, district, neighbourhood, locality. **5** (*moved to the country*) countryside, farmland, moorland, green belt, provinces, rural areas, outback, backwoods, bush, wilds, sticks (*inf*), back of beyond (*inf*), middle of nowhere (*inf*). OPPOSITE: town.
➤ *adj* rural, rustic, pastoral, bucolic, countrified, provincial, agricultural, agrarian, idyllic, Arcadian, georgic, sylvan. OPPOSITE: urban.

countryman *noun* **1** (*local countrymen*) rustic, provincial, yokel, bumpkin, hick (*inf*), hillbilly (*inf*), peasant, farmer. OPPOSITE: townsman. **2** (*fellow* *countrymen*) compatriot, citizen, national, native, indigene. OPPOSITE: foreigner.

countryside *noun* (*living in the countryside*) country, farmland, moorland, green belt, provinces, rural areas, great outdoors (*inf*). **2** (*admiring the countryside*) landscape, scenery, panorama, view, vista. OPPOSITE: town.

county *noun* province, shire, region, area, district, territory, administrative unit.

coup *noun* **1** (*a real coup for the club*) feat, exploit, masterstroke, tour de force, accomplishment, achievement, deed, action, manoeuvre, stunt. OPPOSITE: failure. **2** (*a military coup*) coup d'état, putsch, rebellion, revolution, revolt, uprising, insurgence, takeover, overthrow.

couple *noun* pair, brace, team, duo, twosome, partners, lovers, husband and wife, newlyweds.
➤ *verb* **1** (*coupled together*) connect, link, join, unite, attach, hitch, fasten, bind, yoke, bracket, pair, marry, wed, match, associate, ally. OPPOSITE: separate.
2 (*animals coupling*) mate, copulate, have sex, make love.
a couple of two, two or three, a few.

coupon *noun* voucher, token, certificate, ticket, slip, card, form.

courage *noun* bravery, valour, fearlessness, boldness, audacity, pluck, nerve, mettle, intrepidity, dauntlessness, daring, grit, spunk (*inf*), guts (*inf*), bottle (*inf*), heroism, gallantry, fortitude, resolution, determination, tenacity, hardihood, lion-heartedness, stout-heartedness. OPPOSITE: cowardice.

courageous *adj* brave, valiant, valorous, fearless, unafraid, bold, audacious, plucky, mettlesome, intrepid, dauntless, daring, spunky (*inf*), gutsy (*inf*), heroic, gallant, resolute, determined, tenacious, hardy, indomitable, lion-hearted, stout-hearted. OPPOSITE: cowardly.

courier *noun* **1** (*delivered by courier*) messenger, bearer, carrier, dispatch rider, runner, herald, harbinger, envoy, emissary, representative, legate. **2** (*the courier leading the tour*) guide, escort.

course *noun* **1** (*the course of events*) progression, series, succession, sequence, order, progress, proceeding, advance, furtherance, march, flow, continuity, development. **2** (*in the course of my career*) duration, period, time, term, span, season, spell, lapse, passage. **3** (*wander off course*) route, path, road, track, way, channel, direction, line, tack, trajectory, circuit, orbit, ambit, round, beat. **4** (*a different course of action*) policy, plan, programme, procedure, system, regimen, mode, method, manner, way, approach, line, tack, conduct, behaviour. **5** (*a university course*) classes, lectures, lessons, studies, curriculum, syllabus, programme, schedule. **6** (*the first course of the meal*) dish, part, stage.
➤ *verb* **1** (*blood courses through the veins*) run, flow, pour, gush, surge, rush, race, dash, hurry, speed, bolt, charge. **2** (*course hares*) chase, pursue, run after, follow, hunt, track.
of course naturally, needless to say, certainly, by all means, surely, obviously, undoubtedly, indubitably, definitely. OPPOSITE: maybe.

court *noun* **1** (*a court of law*) lawcourt, bar, bench, tribunal, trial, session, assize. **2** (*the court of Louis XVI*) retinue, train, suite, entourage, cortège, attendants, royal household, palace, castle, château. **3** (*in the court outside*) courtyard, yard, quadrangle, square, plaza, piazza, cloister. **4** (*a tennis court*) enclosure, arena, ground, playing area. **5** (*paid court to my sister*) homage, deference, attention, addresses, respects, civilities, suit, wooing, courtship.
➤ *verb* **1** (*courted my sister*) woo, pay court to, chase, run after, date, take out, go out with, go steady with (*inf*). **2** (*while we were courting*) date, see each other, go out, go steady (*inf*). **3** (*court danger*) invite, solicit, seek, ask for, provoke, bring on, prompt, attract. OPPOSITE: avoid. **4** (*courting the shareholders*) cultivate, curry favour with, butter up (*inf*), flatter, blandish, soft-soap (*inf*), sweet-talk (*inf*), wheedle, cajole, fawn on, toady to, pander to.

courteous *adj* polite, civil, well-mannered, mannerly, well-bred, gentlemanly, ladylike, refined, polished, urbane, debonair, gallant, chivalrous, courtly, ceremonious, respectful, deferential, gracious, complaisant, affable, genial, cordial, obliging, attentive, kind, considerate, tactful, diplomatic. OPPOSITE: impolite.

courtesan *noun* prostitute, whore, harlot, strumpet, woman of ill repute, fille de joie, demimondaine, mistress, kept woman, paramour.

courtesy *noun* **1** (*have the courtesy to apologize*) politeness, civility, manners, breeding, refinement, polish, urbanity, gallantry, chivalry, courtliness, respect, deference, graciousness, complaisance, affability, cordiality, tact, diplomacy. OPPOSITE: rudeness. **2** (*by courtesy of my employers*) generosity, benevolence, kindness, indulgence, favour, consent, permission.

courtier *noun* noble, lord, lady, attendant, steward, follower, henchman, liegeman, squire, page, cupbearer, lady-in-waiting.

courtly *adj* refined, polished, well-bred, dignified, decorous, formal, ceremonious, stately, gallant, chivalrous, gentlemanly, ladylike, noble, aristocratic, elegant, polite, well-mannered, respectful, deferential, gracious, affable. OPPOSITE: churlish.

courtship *noun* wooing, suit, romance, affair, dating, going steady (*inf*).

courtyard *noun* court, quadrangle, quad (*inf*), yard, enclosure, area, square, cloister.

cove *noun* bay, bight, inlet, creek, firth, sound.

covenant *noun* agreement, contract, compact, pact, treaty, convention, concordat, promise, pledge, bond, commitment, undertaking, warranty, guarantee, deed, transaction, bargain, deal.
➤ *verb* agree, contract, promise, pledge, undertake, guarantee.

cover *verb* **1** (*covered her face with her hands*) hide, conceal, obscure, mask, screen, cloak, veil, shroud, disguise, camouflage, secrete, bury. OPPOSITE: uncover. **2** (*covered with mud*) coat, spread, plaster, cake, daub, spatter, overlay, overspread, blanket, mantle, carpet, clothe, robe, envelop, wrap, invest, encase. OPPOSITE: strip. **3** (*cover the plants at night*) shelter, protect, shield, guard, house, sheathe. OPPOSITE: expose. **4** (*cover all the exits*) defend, guard, watch over, protect, fortify. **5** (*topics*

covered in the syllabus) include, embrace, incorporate, embody, contain, comprise, comprehend, take in, encompass, involve, deal with, treat, consider, examine, study, review. OPPOSITE: exclude. **6** (covered the ground swiftly) cross, traverse, pass through, travel over. **7** (covered for fire and theft) insure, indemnify, protect.
➤ **noun 1** (a protective cover) covering, lid, top, cap, case, sheath, jacket, wrapper, wrapping, envelope, blanket, shield, guard. **2** (a cover of dust) coating, coat, layer, covering, film, crust, blanket, mantle, carpet. **3** (under cover of darkness) cloak, veil, mask, screen, shroud. **4** (a cover for a smuggling operation) disguise, camouflage, facade, front, pretence, pretext, cover-up, smokescreen. **5** (the woods provide cover) defence, protection, shield, guard, shelter, refuge, sanctuary, haven, camouflage, hiding place. **6** (chase the game out of cover) covert, undergrowth, thicket, bushes, shrubbery, woodland. **7** (new covers for the beds) bedspread, bedcover, coverlet, sheet, blanket, bedclothes. **8** (cover against fire and theft) insurance, assurance, indemnification, indemnity, protection.
cover for replace, substitute for, deputize for, stand in for, fill in for, relieve, take over from.
cover up conceal, hide, whitewash (inf), suppress, repress, keep secret, keep dark, hush up (inf). OPPOSITE: disclose.

coverage noun reporting, reportage, articles, stories, accounts.

covering noun **1** (a protective covering) cover, lid, top, cap, case, casing, housing, sheath, jacket, wrapper, wrapping, envelope, blanket, shield, guard, shell, skin. **2** (a covering of dust) coating, coat, layer, cover, overlay, film, veneer, crust, blanket, mantle, carpet.
➤ adj accompanying, explanatory, descriptive, introductory.

covert adj clandestine, secret, private, concealed, hidden, disguised, underground, surreptitious, furtive, stealthy, sidelong, underhand, sly, insidious. OPPOSITE: open.

cover-up noun concealment, smokescreen, whitewash (inf), pretence, front, suppression, secrecy, complicity, conspiracy. OPPOSITE: disclosure.

covet verb desire, wish for, long for, hanker after, crave, hunger for, thirst for, lust for, yearn for, set one's heart on, aspire to, dream of, fancy (inf), envy, begrudge. OPPOSITE: despise.

covetous adj envious, jealous, desirous, acquisitive, grasping, greedy, avaricious, rapacious, eager, avid, craving, yearning, longing, hankering.

covetousness noun envy, jealousy, desire, greed, cupidity, avarice, rapacity, avidity, craving, hunger, thirst, lust, yearning.

covey noun brood, flight, flock, bevy, group, party, set, company.

cow verb frighten, unnerve, awe, overawe, daunt, intimidate, browbeat, bully, domineer, terrorize, oppress, subdue, break, discourage, dishearten, dismay. OPPOSITE: encourage.

coward noun craven, poltroon, dastard, recreant, renegade, chicken (inf), scaredy-cat (inf), yellow-belly

(inf), baby, sissy (inf), weakling, wimp (inf). OPPOSITE: hero.

cowardice noun cowardliness, timidity, timorousness, fear, pusillanimity, faint-heartedness, spinelessness, cold feet (inf). OPPOSITE: bravery.

cowardly adj timid, timorous, fearful, scared, craven, dastardly, pusillanimous, chicken (inf), yellow (inf), faint-hearted, lily-livered, yellow-bellied (inf), spineless, gutless (inf), weak, weak-kneed (inf), wimpish (inf). OPPOSITE: brave.

cowboy noun **1** (cowboys working on the ranch) cowhand, cowherd, herder, drover, cattleman, stockman, rancher. **2** (the cowboys who built our extension) scoundrel, rogue, rascal, bungler, incompetent, amateur. OPPOSITE: professional.

cower verb cringe, shrink, recoil, draw back, flinch, wince, blench, quail, tremble, quake, quiver, crouch, stoop, fawn, grovel, skulk, slink. OPPOSITE: confront.

coy adj shy, bashful, diffident, reserved, reticent, retiring, backward, timid, shrinking, modest, self-effacing, demure, prudish, arch, coquettish, flirtatious, kittenish, skittish. OPPOSITE: forward.

cozen verb cheat, trick, dupe, deceive, swindle, defraud, con (inf), take for a ride (inf), beguile, inveigle, hoodwink, bamboozle.

crabbed adj **1** (a crabbed old man) crabby, irritable, irascible, bad-tempered, ill-humoured, testy, touchy, snappish, waspish, crusty, cantankerous, crotchety (inf), grouchy (inf), captious, perverse, peevish, petulant, surly, morose, sour, tart, acrid, acrimonious. OPPOSITE: genial. **2** (crabbed handwriting) cramped, illegible, unreadable, indecipherable.

crabbedness noun crabbiness, ill humour, bad temper, irascibility, irritability, spleen, testiness, crustiness, captiousness, peevishness, petulance, surliness, moroseness, sourness, acrimony. OPPOSITE: geniality.

crack verb **1** (crack the window) break, fracture, split, cleave, burst, shatter, chip, splinter, craze, chap. OPPOSITE: mend. **2** (twigs cracking underfoot) snap, break, pop, crackle, clap, crash, boom, bang, burst, explode, detonate. **3** (cracked my head on the roof) bang, hit, strike, knock, bump, bash, clout (inf), wallop (inf). **4** (crack under pressure) yield, succumb, give way, break down, collapse, go to pieces, crack up (inf). OPPOSITE: resist. **5** (crack the puzzle) solve, work out, figure out, fathom, decipher, decode, unravel.
➤ **noun 1** (a crack in the wall) break, fracture, rupture, chip, split, cleft, rift, breach, fissure, gap, crevice, chink, cranny, slit, hole, aperture. **2** (the crack of a pistol) snap, pop, clap, crash, bang, boom, burst, explosion, detonation, report. **3** (a crack on the head) bang, hit, blow, knock, bump, bash, clout (inf), wallop (inf). **4** (have another crack at it) try, attempt, bid, go, stab (inf), bash (inf), shot (inf). **5** (making cracks about her age) joke, gag (inf), quip, wisecrack, witticism, jibe, dig (inf).
➤ adj expert, ace (inf), first-class, first-rate, brilliant, excellent, outstanding, elite, top-notch (inf).
crack down on restrict, limit, control, restrain, curb, suppress, clamp down on, prevent, stop, put a stop to.
crack up break down, collapse, go to pieces, fall apart at the seams (inf), lose control, go mad, go crazy.

cracked adj **1** (*cracked glass*) broken, fractured, chipped, splintered, split, crazed, chapped, damaged, defective, flawed, imperfect, faulty. **2** (*you must be cracked!*) mad, crazy, insane, out of one's mind, off one's head (*inf*), crackers (*inf*), nuts (*inf*), bats (*inf*), nutty (*inf*), batty (*inf*), round the bend (*inf*), round the twist (*inf*). OPPOSITE: sane.

crackers adj mad, crazy, insane, out of one's mind, nuts (*inf*), nutty (*inf*), round the bend (*inf*), round the twist (*inf*).

crackle verb snap, crack, pop, crepitate.

cradle noun **1** (*babies in their cradles*) cot, crib, bassinet, Moses' basket, bed. **2** (*the cradle of democracy*) birthplace, origin, source, fountainhead, wellspring, fount, spring.
➤ verb hold, support, nestle, shelter, rock, lull, nurse, nurture, foster, tend.

craft noun **1** (*the craft of the designer*) art, skill, ability, technique, skilfulness, dexterity, aptitude, talent, knack, flair, cleverness, expertness, expertise, mastery, artistry, workmanship, handiwork, handicraft. OPPOSITE: incompetence. **2** (*win by craft*) craftiness, cunning, artfulness, guile, subtlety, slyness, wiliness, deceit, deceitfulness, duplicity, trickery, artifice, subterfuge, wiles, ruses, stratagems. OPPOSITE: artlessness. **3** (*learn a craft*) trade, vocation, calling, occupation, business, line of work, work, employment, job, pursuit, handicraft, art. **4** (*the person steering the craft*) vessel, boat, ship, aircraft, spacecraft.

craftsman noun artisan, artist, artificer, expert, master, skilled worker, technician, maker, smith, wright.

craftsmanship noun artistry, art, skill, technique, expertise, master, workmanship.

craftswoman noun artisan, artist, artificer, expert, skilled worker, technician, maker.

crafty adj cunning, artful, guileful, subtle, sly, wily, foxy, sharp, shrewd, astute, canny, calculating, designing, scheming, tricky, devious, deceitful, duplicitous, fraudulent, crooked, underhand, insidious, treacherous. OPPOSITE: artless.

crag noun rock, tor, cliff, bluff, escarpment, scarp, ridge, peak, pinnacle.

craggy noun **1** (*craggy slopes*) rugged, rough, uneven, broken, jagged, rocky, stony, steep, precipitous. OPPOSITE: even. **2** (*a craggy face*) rough, rugged, lined, furrowed. OPPOSITE: smooth.

cram verb **1** (*cramming apples into their pockets*) stuff, press, ram, push, shove, force, pack, jam, squeeze, crush, compress, compact. **2** (*cramming their pockets with apples*) fill, overfill, stuff, pack, crowd, overcrowd, jam, choke. **3** (*cram for an exam*) study, revise, grind, swot (*inf*), mug up (*inf*), bone up (*inf*).

cramp[1] verb (*cramped my style*) hinder, hamper, obstruct, impede, encumber, hamstring, handicap, check, restrain, restrict, limit, confine, constrain, shackle, bridle, inhibit, thwart, frustrate. OPPOSITE: free.

cramp[2] noun (*muscle cramp*) spasm, contraction, twinge, pang, stitch, crick, ache, pain, stiffness.

cramped adj small, narrow, poky (*inf*), tight, uncomfortable, restricted, limited, confined, hemmed in, packed, crowded, overcrowded, congested, no room to swing a cat (*inf*).

crane noun derrick, davit, winch, hoist, tackle.

crank noun **1** (*turn the crank*) lever, bar, arm, shaft, spindle, handle. **2** (*regarded as a bit of a crank*) eccentric, oddity, character, crackpot (*inf*), weirdo (*inf*), oddball (*inf*), loony (*sl*), maniac, fanatic, zealot, enthusiast, devotee, fan, buff (*inf*), nut (*inf*).
➤ verb start, turn over, rev (*inf*), turn, rotate, spin.
crank up increase, improve, accelerate, speed up, hasten, hurry up.

cranky adj **1** (*cranky behaviour*) eccentric, odd, strange, peculiar, bizarre, weird, queer, funny (*inf*), wacky (*inf*), idiosyncratic, unconventional, quirky, obsessive, fanatical. OPPOSITE: normal. **2** (*cranky children*) bad-tempered, ill-humoured, cross, irritable, crabbed, crabby, crotchety (*inf*), awkward, difficult. OPPOSITE: placid.

cranny noun chink, crevice, fissure, rift, cleft, crack, split, breach, gap, opening, aperture, interstice.

crash verb **1** (*crashed against the rocks*) break, smash, shatter, shiver, splinter, fragment, disintegrate, dash, batter. **2** (*crashed her car*) smash up, prang (*inf*), wreck, write off (*inf*). **3** (*crashed into a tree*) collide, hit, knock, bump, bang, drive, run, hurtle, rush, smash, plough. **4** (*crashed to the ground*) fall, topple, tumble, plunge, pitch. OPPOSITE: soar. **5** (*the cymbals crashed*) clatter, clash, clang, bang, boom, roar, thunder. **6** (*the business crashed*) fail, fold (*inf*), founder, go under, go bankrupt, go bust (*inf*), go to the wall (*inf*), collapse, flop (*inf*). OPPOSITE: flourish. **7** (*the computer crashed*) go down, fail, malfunction, pack up.
➤ noun **1** (*fell with a crash*) clatter, clash, clang, bang, thud, boom, roar, thunder, racket, din, clangour. **2** (*a car crash*) collision, accident, bump, knock, shunt (*inf*), prang (*inf*), accident, smash, wreck, pile-up (*inf*). **3** (*a stock-market crash*) collapse, failure, fall, downfall, ruin, bankruptcy.
➤ adj intensive, rapid, accelerated, concentrated, urgent, emergency.

crass adj stupid, dense, thick, obtuse, asinine, doltish, oafish, boorish, indelicate, insensitive, tactless, rude, gross, vulgar, crude, coarse, unrefined, uncouth. OPPOSITE: sensitive.

crate noun case, box, chest, basket, hamper, container, receptacle.

crater noun hole, cavity, pit, hollow, depression, dip, chasm, abyss.

crave verb **1** (*crave a cigarette*) want, desire, wish for, long for, yearn for, hanker after, fancy (*inf*), hunger for, thirst for, be dying for (*inf*), covet, lust after, pant for, need, require, cry out for. OPPOSITE: spurn. **2** (*crave forgiveness*) ask, beg, beseech, entreat, implore, plead, pray, supplicate, petition, solicit.

craven adj cowardly, dastardly, pusillanimous, timid, timorous, fearful, scared, chicken (*inf*), yellow (*inf*), faint-hearted, lily-livered, yellow-bellied (*inf*), spineless, gutless (*inf*). OPPOSITE: brave.
➤ noun coward, poltroon, dastard, recreant, renegade, chicken (*inf*), scaredy-cat (*inf*), yellow-belly (*inf*), weakling, wimp (*inf*). OPPOSITE: hero.

craving noun desire, longing, yearning, yen (*inf*),

hankering, fancy (*inf*), hunger, thirst, appetite, lust, urge, need, addiction.

crawl *verb* **1** (*crawl across the floor*) creep, inch, steal, sneak, slink, worm, slither, move slowly, go on all fours. OPPOSITE: race. **2** (*the place was crawling with photographers*) swarm, teem, seethe, bristle. **3** (*crawl to the boss*) grovel, cringe, fawn, toady, bow and scrape, curry favour, suck up (*inf*).

craze *noun* fashion, trend, vogue, fad, rage, thing (*inf*), novelty, whim, fancy, mania, enthusiasm, obsession, preoccupation, passion, infatuation.

crazed *adj* mad, crazy, insane, deranged, unbalanced, unhinged, demented, wild, berserk, enraged, inflamed. OPPOSITE: calm.

crazy *adj* **1** (*they thought I was crazy*) mad, insane, demented, deranged, unbalanced, unhinged, crazed, mental, lunatic, daft (*inf*), barmy (*inf*), potty (*inf*), nutty (*inf*), nuts (*inf*), crackers (*inf*), bonkers (*inf*), round the bend (*inf*), round the twist (*inf*), out of one's mind (*inf*), off one's head (*inf*), off one's rocker (*inf*), not all there (*inf*), one sandwich short of a picnic (*inf*). OPPOSITE: sane. **2** (*a crazy idea*) silly, stupid, foolish, absurd, ludicrous, ridiculous, preposterous, outrageous, idiotic, senseless, inane, asinine, ill-conceived, half-baked (*inf*), impractical, unworkable, unrealistic, unwise, imprudent, reckless, foolhardy, harebrained (*inf*). OPPOSITE: sensible. **3** (*crazy stories*) strange, odd, peculiar, bizarre, weird, fantastic. OPPOSITE: normal. **4** (*crazy about cars*) infatuated, enamoured, smitten, wild, mad, passionate, ardent, fervent, enthusiastic, fanatical, zealous, keen, avid. OPPOSITE: indifferent.

creak *verb* squeak, grate, rasp, scrape, grind, squeal, groan, screech.

cream *noun* **1** (*face cream*) paste, emulsion, lotion, ointment, unguent, salve, liniment. **2** (*the cream of the students*) best, pick, prime, flower, elite, crème de la crème.
▶ *adj* creamy, cream-coloured, off-white, buff, ivory, yellowish-white, whitish-yellow.

crease *noun* fold, pleat, tuck, line, wrinkle, crinkle, pucker, ridge, furrow, groove, corrugation.
▶ *verb* fold, pleat, tuck, line, wrinkle, crinkle, crimp, pucker, crumple, rumple, ruck, ridge, furrow, groove, corrugate.

crease up amuse, entertain, make laugh, make fall about (*inf*), have rolling in the aisles (*inf*).

create *verb* **1** (*create an artificial language*) invent, originate, initiate, coin, formulate, devise, concoct, design, make, fashion, forge, shape, form, produce, develop, build, construct, generate, engender, beget, father, sire, procreate, spawn, hatch. OPPOSITE: destroy. **2** (*he was created Duke of York*) appoint, install, invest, ordain. **3** (*create a charitable trust*) constitute, establish, found, set up, institute, inaugurate. OPPOSITE: abolish. **4** (*create a disturbance*) cause, occasion, bring about, start, begin, lead to, give rise to, result in.

creation *noun* **1** (*the creation of an artificial language*) invention, origination, conception, formulation, concoction, design, making, formation, production, development, construction, generation, procreation. OPPOSITE: destruction. **2** (*since its creation*) start,

beginning, origin, genesis, birth, inception, establishment, foundation, institution, inauguration. **3** (*all the species in creation*) the universe, the cosmos, the world, the earth, nature, life. **4** (*her latest creation*) work, opus, production, invention, design, concept, brainchild, work of art, masterpiece, chef-d'oeuvre, pièce de résistance.

creative *adj* artistic, inventive, imaginative, inspired, visionary, original, innovative, ingenious, resourceful, clever, talented, gifted, skilled, productive, fertile. OPPOSITE: unimaginative.

creator *noun* maker, producer, inventor, originator, author, architect, designer, founder, father, mother, begetter, prime mover, first cause, God.

creature *noun* **1** (*creatures from outer space*) being, living thing, animal, beast, organism, monster, person, individual. **2** (*a creature of habit*) person, human being, human, mortal, individual, soul, body, character. **3** (*just one of the president's creatures*) minion, lackey, parasite, hanger-on, dependant, puppet, tool, hireling, vassal, sycophant, toady.

credence *noun* belief, credit, acceptance, faith, trust, reliance, confidence, assurance. OPPOSITE: disbelief.

credentials *pl noun* certificate, diploma, licence, warrant, permit, authorization, authority, pass, passport, identity card, testimonial, reference, letter of introduction, deed, title, documentation.

credibility *noun* **1** (*the credibility of the story*) plausibility, tenability, probability, likelihood. OPPOSITE: incredibility. **2** (*damaging the government's credibility*) trust, faith, reliability, dependability, honesty, integrity, sincerity. OPPOSITE: unreliability.

credible *adj* **1** (*a credible story*) believable, plausible, conceivable, imaginable, thinkable, tenable, probable, likely, convincing, persuasive. OPPOSITE: incredible. **2** (*a credible witness*) trustworthy, reliable, dependable, trusty, honest, truthful, sincere. OPPOSITE: unreliable.

credit *noun* **1** (*deserves more credit for her achievements*) praise, commendation, recognition, acknowledgment, honour, glory, kudos, acclaim, tribute, homage, merit. OPPOSITE: blame. **2** (*gained credit in the town*) reputation, standing, status, influence, prestige, respect, regard, esteem, name, character. OPPOSITE: discredit. **3** (*he's a credit to the team*) asset, gem, source of pride, pride and joy (*inf*), boast, feather in the cap (*inf*). OPPOSITE: shame. **4** (*give credit to their story*) credence, belief, acceptance, faith, trust, reliance, confidence. OPPOSITE: disbelief. **5** (*their story lacks credit*) credibility, plausibility, trustworthiness, reliability, honesty, integrity, probity. OPPOSITE: implausibility.
▶ *verb* **1** (*credited with the invention*) ascribe, attribute, accredit, assign, impute, charge, put down, chalk up. **2** (*couldn't credit her excuse*) believe, accept, buy (*inf*), swallow (*inf*), fall for (*inf*), trust, have faith in, rely on, depend on. OPPOSITE: disbelieve.

in credit solvent, in the black (*inf*). OPPOSITE: insolvent.

on credit on account, on the slate (*inf*), by instalments, by deferred payment, by hire purchase, on tick (*inf*), on the never-never (*inf*).

creditable *adj* praiseworthy, laudable, commendable, exemplary, excellent, admirable, estimable, meritorious, deserving, worthy, honourable, reputable, respectable. OPPOSITE: shameful.

credulity *noun* credulousness, gullibility, naivety, blind faith, trustfulness, simplicity. OPPOSITE: scepticism.

credulous *adj* gullible, naive, green, wet behind the ears (*inf*), trustful, trusting, unsuspicious, unsuspecting, deceivable, dupable, simple. OPPOSITE: suspicious.

creed *noun* belief, faith, credo, dogma, doctrine, teaching, tenet, canon, catechism, principles, rules, articles of faith.

creek *noun* **1** (*sailed up the creek*) inlet, firth, sound, estuary, bay, bight, cove. **2** (*fishing in the creek*) stream, brook, river, watercourse.

creep *verb* **1** (*creep into the room*) steal, sneak, tiptoe, skulk, slink, slither, wriggle, glide, worm, insinuate, crawl, inch, edge. OPPOSITE: rush. **2** (*creep to the boss*) grovel, cringe, fawn, crawl, toady, kowtow, bow and scrape, bootlick (*inf*), curry favour, suck up (*inf*).
➤ *noun* sycophant, toady, bootlicker (*inf*).

creeper *noun* climber, climbing plant, rambler, trailing plant, runner, vine, liana.

creeps *pl noun* fear, terror, horror, disgust, revulsion, repulsion, unease, disquiet.

creepy *adj* eerie, weird, ghostly, ghoulish, macabre, frightening, scary (*inf*), terrifying, hair-raising, horrifying, spine-chilling, gruesome, nightmarish, sinister, ominous, threatening, menacing, disturbing.

crest *noun* **1** (*the crest of the hill*) top, apex, summit, pinnacle, peak, ridge, crown, head. OPPOSITE: foot. **2** (*a bird with a colourful crest*) tuft, comb, topknot, plume, panache, aigrette, tassel, mane. **3** (*the family crest*) bearings, arms, badge, emblem, symbol, device, insignia, regalia, charge.

crestfallen *adj* disappointed, discouraged, dispirited, disheartened, dejected, depressed, downcast, downhearted, despondent, sad, melancholy, disconsolate, gloomy, in the doldrums (*inf*), down in the dumps (*inf*). OPPOSITE: elated.

crevasse *noun* chasm, abyss, ravine, gorge, fissure, cleft.

crevice *noun* chink, cranny, crack, slit, cleft, rift, split, fissure, gap, breach, hole, opening, interstice.

crew *noun* company, team, squad, unit, corps, troop, gang, party, band, group, troupe, crowd, horde, throng, mob, pack, bunch, set, lot.

crib *noun* **1** (*babies in their cribs*) cot, cradle, bassinet, Moses' basket, bed. **2** (*animals feeding at the crib*) rack, manger, box, bin, stall, pen, enclosure. **3** (*a crib of my poem*) copy, reproduction, duplication, replica, plagiarization, plagiarism, piracy.
➤ *verb* **1** (*cribbed our ideas*) steal, pilfer, purloin, pinch (*inf*), copy, reproduce, duplicate, replicate, plagiarize, pirate, lift (*inf*). **2** (*cribbed animals*) pen, enclose, corral, cage, coop up, shut in, restrict, confine, imprison. OPPOSITE: free.

crick *noun* cramp, spasm, twinge, pang, pain, stiffness.

crime *noun* **1** (*the victim of his latest crime*) felony, offence, misdemeanour, misdeed, violation, transgression, trespass, fault, wrong, tort. **2** (*a reduction in violent crime*) lawbreaking, illegality, wrongdoing, misconduct, malefaction, delinquency, villainy,

wickedness, evil, vice, corruption. **3** (*a crime against humanity*) offence, atrocity, outrage, wrong, sin, iniquity.

criminal *noun* felon, offender, lawbreaker, wrongdoer, malefactor, miscreant, delinquent, recidivist, villain, gangster, crook (*inf*), culprit, transgressor, sinner, convict, con (*inf*), jailbird, prisoner.
➤ *adj* **1** (*criminal activities*) unlawful, illegal, illicit, dishonest, crooked (*inf*), bent (*inf*), wrong, felonious, indictable, culpable, guilty, corrupt, wicked, evil, nefarious, villainous, delinquent. OPPOSITE: lawful. **2** (*a criminal waste of talent*) deplorable, scandalous, shameful, reprehensible, wicked, iniquitous, sinful, senseless, preposterous, ridiculous.

crimp *verb* **1** (*crimp hair*) curl, wave, frizz. **2** (*crimp paper*) crinkle, wrinkle, pucker, ruffle, gather, smock, pleat, tuck, fold, crease, ridge, flute, corrugate, groove, furrow.

cringe *verb* **1** (*cringed at the sound*) flinch, wince, shrink, recoil, draw back, cower, duck, start, shy, quail, tremble, quake, quiver, blench. **2** (*cringing to her superiors*) fawn, grovel, toady, crawl (*inf*), creep (*inf*), kowtow, bow and scrape, bootlick (*inf*).

cringing *adj* servile, obsequious, fawning, sycophantic, toadying, kowtowing, bootlicking (*inf*).

crinkle *verb* crimp, rumple, crumple, wrinkle, crease, pucker, furrow, flute, corrugate, fold, curl. OPPOSITE: smooth.

crinkly *adj* crimped, crumpled, wrinkled, wrinkly, creased, puckered, furrowed, grooved, fluted, ridged, corrugated, curly, wavy, kinky, frizzy. OPPOSITE: smooth.

cripple *verb* **1** (*the fall crippled him*) lame, disable, handicap, paralyse, incapacitate, injure, maim, mutilate, hamstring, enfeeble, weaken, debilitate. **2** (*the strike crippled trade*) paralyse, hamstring, hamper, impede, impair, damage, harm, injure, mar, spoil, ruin, destroy.

crippled *adj* lame, disabled, handicapped, paralysed, paraplegic, incapacitated, bedridden, laid up (*inf*).

crisis *noun* **1** (*keep calm in a crisis*) emergency, exigency, dilemma, quandary, plight, predicament, strait, extremity, fix (*inf*), hole (*inf*), hot water (*inf*), disaster, catastrophe, calamity. **2** (*reach a crisis*) turning point, crux, climacteric, climax, height, culmination, juncture, moment of truth.

crisp *adj* **1** (*a crisp biscuit*) crunchy, brittle, friable, crumbly, breakable, crispy, dry, firm, fresh. OPPOSITE: pliable. **2** (*a crisp winter's day*) fresh, cool, chilly, cold, brisk, bracing, invigorating, stimulating, refreshing. OPPOSITE: sultry. **3** (*a crisp reply*) brief, short, terse, succinct, concise, pithy, snappy (*inf*), brusque, curt, abrupt, clear, incisive. OPPOSITE: lengthy.

criterion *noun* standard, norm, test, measure, gauge, scale, touchstone, benchmark, yardstick, rule, law, principle, canon, guide, model, example, exemplar.

critic *noun* **1** (*a drama critic*) reviewer, commentator, analyst, authority, expert, pundit, specialist, connoisseur, arbiter, judge. **2** (*critics of her work*) censurer, attacker, detractor, knocker (*inf*), faultfinder, carper, caviller, nit-picker (*inf*).

critical *adj* **1** (*critical of the government*) censorious, captious, disparaging, derogatory, disapproving, judgmental, fault-finding, carping, cavilling, niggling, quibbling, nit-picking (*inf*). OPPOSITE: complimentary. **2** (*a critical study*) analytical, diagnostic, evaluative, interpretative, expository, explanatory, perceptive, discerning, penetrating, probing. **3** (*at the critical moment*) crucial, decisive, pivotal, climacteric, vital, essential, momentous, all-important, high-priority, urgent, exigent, pressing, serious, grave. OPPOSITE: unimportant. **4** (*in a critical condition*) serious, grave, dangerous, perilous, risky, precarious, touch-and-go. OPPOSITE: safe.

criticism *noun* **1** (*literary criticism*) judgment, evaluation, assessment, appraisal, appreciation, analysis, commentary, interpretation, exposition, explication, examination, review, critique, notice, write-up (*inf*). **2** (*criticism of their decision*) censure, blame, animadversion, condemnation, denunciation, disapproval, objection, stricture, reproof, fault-finding, carping, cavilling, nit-picking (*inf*), disparagement, knocking (*inf*), slating (*inf*), panning (*inf*), slamming (*inf*), bad press (*inf*), bad notices (*inf*), brickbats (*inf*), flak (*inf*). OPPOSITE: praise.

criticize *verb* **1** (*criticize their decision*) censure, blame, condemn, denounce, disapprove, object to, find fault with, carp at, cavil at, pick holes in (*inf*), disparage, denigrate, knock (*inf*), slate (*inf*), pan (*inf*), slam (*inf*), rubbish (*inf*), pull to pieces (*inf*), tear to shreds (*inf*). OPPOSITE: praise. **2** (*criticize literature*) judge, evaluate, assess, appraise, analyse, comment on, interpret, expound, examine, review.

critique *noun* evaluation, assessment, appraisal, analysis, commentary, interpretation, exposition, explication, essay, review, notice, write-up (*inf*).

croak *verb* grunt, squawk, caw, rasp, wheeze, gasp, groan, murmur.

croaky *adj* hoarse, husky, throaty, harsh, rough, rasping, low, deep.

crockery *noun* pottery, earthenware, china, porcelain, tableware, dishes, crocks, pots.

crone *noun* hag, witch, old woman, old bag (*inf*), old bat (*inf*).

crony *noun* friend, chum (*inf*), pal (*inf*), mate (*inf*), buddy (*inf*), companion, comrade, associate, confederate, ally, sidekick (*inf*). OPPOSITE: enemy.

crook *noun* **1** (*arrested the crook who sold it to me*) criminal, lawbreaker, rogue, villain, thief, robber, swindler, fraud, cheat, shark (*inf*). **2** (*in the crook of his arm*) bend, angle, hook, bow, curve, turn.
➤ *verb* bend, flex, angle, hook, bow, curve, turn, twist, warp, distort, deform. OPPOSITE: straighten.

crooked *adj* **1** (*a crooked line*) bent, hooked, bowed, curved, twisting, winding, tortuous, anfractuous, sinuous, serpentine, zigzag, twisted, warped, distorted, deformed, misshapen, irregular, uneven, asymmetric, lopsided, off-centre, awry, askew, skew-whiff (*inf*), oblique, slanting, angled. OPPOSITE: straight. **2** (*a crooked dealer*) dishonest, fraudulent, bent (*inf*), criminal, illegal, unlawful, underhand, questionable, dubious, shady (*inf*), deceitful, dishonourable, unscrupulous, unprincipled, corrupt. OPPOSITE: honest.

croon *verb* sing, warble, lilt, hum.

crop *noun* **1** (*a good crop of potatoes*) yield, produce, fruits, harvest, vintage, gathering, garner. **2** (*the usual crop of problems*) assortment, collection, batch, lot, group. **3** (*a bird's crop*) gullet, throat, craw, maw.
➤ *verb* cut, trim, clip, shear, mow, lop, pare, prune, shorten, curtail.

crop up happen, occur, take place, come to pass, arise, turn up, appear, emerge.

cross *noun* **1** (*marked with a cross*) crucifix, rood, X. **2** (*a cross to bear*) burden, affliction, suffering, trial, tribulation, trouble, worry, woe, misery, misfortune, adversity, disaster, calamity, catastrophe. **3** (*a cross between a lion and a tiger*) hybrid, mongrel, crossbreed, blend, amalgam, combination, mixture.
➤ *verb* **1** (*cross the river*) go across, pass over, traverse, ford, span, bridge. **2** (*where the lines cross*) meet, join, converge, intersect, crisscross, interweave, entwine, lace. **3** (*cross a lion with a tiger*) hybridize, interbreed, crossbreed, mongrelize, cross-fertilize, cross-pollinate, mix, blend. **4** (*he doesn't like to be crossed*) hinder, impede, block, obstruct, frustrate, foil, thwart, oppose, resist, deny, contradict. OPPOSITE: help.
➤ *adj* **1** (*your mother will be cross with you*) angry, annoyed, irritated, vexed, upset, put out, short, shirty (*inf*). OPPOSITE: pleased. **2** (*a cross old man*) bad-tempered, ill-humoured, irritable, irascible, testy, touchy, fractious, peevish, petulant, crusty, crotchety (*inf*), cantankerous, grumpy, grouchy (*inf*), snappish, waspish. OPPOSITE: affable. **3** (*cross fire*) transverse, crosswise, oblique, diagonal, intersecting, reciprocal. OPPOSITE: parallel. **4** (*at cross purposes*) contrary, adverse, unfavourable, opposing, opposite. OPPOSITE: favourable.

cross out delete, obliterate, strike out, blue-pencil, cancel, eliminate. OPPOSITE: stet.

cross-examine *verb* interrogate, question, cross-question, quiz, catechize, grill (*inf*), pump (*inf*).

crossing *noun* **1** (*stop at the crossing*) junction, intersection, crossroads. **2** (*a pedestrian crossing*) zebra crossing, pelican crossing, subway, underpass. **3** (*a calm crossing*) journey, trip, sail, passage, voyage.

crosswise *adv* crossways, diagonally, obliquely, aslant, athwart, transversely, across, over.

crotch *noun* crutch, groin, angle, fork.

crotchet *noun* notion, fancy, whim, whimsy, caprice, vagary, fad, quirk, eccentricity.

crotchety *adj* cross, irritable, peevish, fractious, touchy, prickly, grumpy, grouchy (*inf*), crabbed, crabby, bad-tempered, ill-humoured, irascible, crusty, testy, cantankerous, contrary, awkward, difficult. OPPOSITE: affable.

crouch *verb* squat, kneel, stoop, hunker down, bend, bow, hunch, duck, cower, cringe.

crow *verb* boast, brag, blow one's own trumpet (*inf*), vaunt, parade, show off, swagger, strut, gloat, bluster, exult, triumph, rejoice.

crowd *noun* **1** (*got lost in the crowd*) throng, mob, host, multitude, horde, rabble, herd, drove, flock, swarm, pack, press, crush, assembly, gathering, company, congregation, concourse. **2** (*follow the crowd*) majority, masses, multitude, mob, populace, general public, common people, proletariat, hoi polloi, riff-raff, rabble.

3 (*the crowd at the golf club*) group, bunch, gang, lot, set, circle, coterie, clique. **4** (*the crowd at the football match*) spectators, audience, turnout, attendance, gate, house.
➤ *verb* **1** (*crowding around the singer*) gather, assemble, congregate, cluster, huddle, mass, throng, herd, flock, swarm, stream. OPPOSITE: disperse. **2** (*they crowded into the room*) push, shove, jostle, elbow, pack, squeeze. **3** (*we were crowded into the lift*) cram, pack, stuff, jam, press, squeeze, compress, pile, bundle. **4** (*onlookers crowded the square*) fill, pack, congest, throng. **5** (*don't crowd me!*) pester, badger, hound, nag, harass, hassle (*inf*), pressure, pressurize.

crowded *adj* full, overflowing, packed, jam-packed (*inf*), crammed, congested, cramped, crushed, busy, teeming, swarming, thronged, populous. OPPOSITE: deserted.

crown *noun* **1** (*wearing a golden crown*) diadem, coronet, coronal, circlet, tiara, chaplet, wreath, garland. **2** (*competing for the champion's crown*) award, reward, prize, trophy, laurels, bays, kudos, honour, glory, distinction. **3** (*lands owned by the Crown*) sovereign, monarch, ruler, king, queen, emperor, empress, monarchy, royalty, royals (*inf*). **4** (*the crown of the hill*) top, apex, brow, crest, head, tip, cap, summit, pinnacle, peak, acme, zenith, culmination, height, climax. OPPOSITE: foot.
➤ *verb* **1** (*crown the new king*) invest, induct, install, enthrone, anoint, adorn, decorate, honour, dignify, reward. **2** (*crowning her career*) complete, finish, conclude, round off, consummate, fulfil, perfect, cap, top. OPPOSITE: begin. **3** (*crowned with a dome*) top, cap, surmount.

crucial *adj* critical, decisive, determining, central, key, pivotal, vital, essential, all-important, imperative, momentous, high-priority, urgent, exigent, pressing, compelling. OPPOSITE: trivial.

crucify *verb* **1** (*wrongdoers were crucified*) execute, put to death, nail to a cross. **2** (*crucified by the media*) persecute, torture, torment, harrow, mock, ridicule, attack, tear to pieces (*inf*), criticize, slate (*inf*), slam (*inf*).

crude *adj* **1** (*crude jokes*) rude, vulgar, ribald, lewd, bawdy, risqué, raunchy (*inf*), dirty, smutty, earthy, blue (*inf*), tasteless, gross, offensive, obscene, indecent, coarse, uncouth, crass, boorish. OPPOSITE: polite. **2** (*crude oil*) raw, natural, unrefined, unprocessed, coarse, rough, unfinished, unpolished. OPPOSITE: refined. **3** (*a crude dwelling*) primitive, rudimentary, basic, simple, makeshift, rough-and-ready, sketchy, incomplete. OPPOSITE: sophisticated.

crudity *noun* crudeness, rudeness, vulgarity, ribaldry, lewdness, raunchiness (*inf*), tastelessness, grossness, obscenity, indecency, indelicacy, impropriety, coarseness, crassness. OPPOSITE: refinement.

cruel *adj* **1** (*a cruel tyrant*) savage, barbarous, barbaric, brutal, inhuman, ferocious, vicious, bloodthirsty, cold-blooded, sadistic, merciless, pitiless, unrelenting, ruthless, remorseless, harsh, severe, heartless, unfeeling, inhumane, unkind, callous, hard-hearted, stony-hearted, implacable, malicious, malevolent, evil, wicked. OPPOSITE: kind. **2** (*a cruel blow*) unpleasant, painful, distressing, harrowing, unkind, unfair, hard, harsh, severe, bitter.

cruelty *noun* savagery, barbarousness, barbarity, barbarism, brutality, inhumanity, ferocity, viciousness, sadism, mercilessness, pitilessness, ruthlessness, remorselessness, harshness, severity, heartlessness, unkindness, callousness, hard-heartedness, malice, malevolence, evil, wickedness. OPPOSITE: compassion.

cruise *noun* sail, voyage, trip, holiday.
➤ *verb* sail, travel, journey, voyage, coast, drift.

crumb *noun* scrap, morsel, bit, fragment, piece, shred, sliver, snippet, particle, speck, grain, atom, mite, jot, iota.

crumble *verb* **1** (*crumble the bread*) crush, pound, grind, pulverize, triturate, comminute, powder, granulate, break up, fragment. OPPOSITE: consolidate. **2** (*the organization is crumbling*) collapse, fail, break down, disintegrate, fall apart, fall to pieces, break up, fragment, decay, deteriorate, degenerate, decompose, rot, perish, fade away. OPPOSITE: endure.

crumbly *adj* brittle, friable, powdery.

crummy *adj* inferior, second-rate, third-rate, poor, worthless, contemptible, pathetic (*inf*), cheap, shoddy, trashy, grotty (*inf*). OPPOSITE: excellent.

crumple *verb* **1** (*crumple the paper*) rumple, ruffle, wrinkle, crease, crush, screw up, pucker, crinkle. OPPOSITE: smooth. **2** (*their resistance crumpled*) collapse, fail, fall, break down, crumble, go to pieces, cave in, give way, shrivel, shrink. OPPOSITE: endure.

crunch *verb* munch, gnaw, bite, chew, champ, chomp, masticate, grind, crush, pound, scrunch.
➤ *noun* crisis, crux, test, moment of truth, emergency, pinch (*inf*).

crusade *noun* campaign, movement, cause, struggle, drive, push.
➤ *verb* campaign, fight, battle, struggle, strive, drive, push, promote, advocate.

crusader *noun* campaigner, fighter, champion, advocate, enthusiast, zealot, reformer, missionary.

crush *verb* **1** (*crush the fruit*) squeeze, press, squash, compress, pulp, mash, pound. **2** (*crushing the rock*) smash, shatter, shiver, splinter, fragment, break up, crumble, grind, pulverize, triturate, comminute, powder, granulate. **3** (*crushed her dress*) crumple, rumple, wrinkle, crinkle, crease, squash. **4** (*crushed my fingers in the door*) pinch, compress, squeeze, squash, bruise, contuse. **5** (*crush the opposition*) overpower, overwhelm, overcome, subdue, quell, suppress, quash, put down, stamp out, defeat, vanquish, conquer. OPPOSITE: resist. **6** (*crushed by his remarks*) abash, shame, humiliate, mortify, chagrin, put down (*inf*).
➤ *noun* **1** (*the crush outside the theatre*) crowd, throng, pack, press, congestion, jam. **2** (*had a crush on her teacher*) infatuation, passion, pash (*inf*), love, fancy, liking.

crust *noun* topping, covering, coating, layer, film, incrustation, scab, surface, exterior, outside, skin, rind, shell, husk, casing.

crusty *adj* bad-tempered, ill-humoured, irritable, irascible, touchy, testy, crabbed, crabby, peevish, fractious, captious, snappish, waspish, cantankerous, crotchety (*inf*), grumpy, grouchy (*inf*), surly, curt, gruff, brusque. OPPOSITE: affable.

crux *noun* centre, heart, core, kernel, nucleus, nub, essence, quintessence.

cry *verb* **1** (*the baby is crying*) sob, weep, burst into tears, wail, bawl, howl, whine, whimper, snivel, blubber, lament, keen. OPPOSITE: laugh. **2** (*crying for help*) call, shout, yell, scream, shriek, screech, roar, bellow, bawl, holler (*inf*), exclaim, ejaculate. OPPOSITE: whisper. **3** (*crying their wares*) proclaim, announce, broadcast, trumpet, blazon, advertise, hawk.
➤ *noun* **1** (*have a good cry*) sob, weep, wail, bawl, howl, whimper, blubber, lament, crying, sobbing, weeping, tears, lamentation. OPPOSITE: laugh. **2** (*a cry of pain*) call, shout, yell, scream, shriek, screech, roar, bellow, howl, exclamation, ejaculation. OPPOSITE: whisper. **3** (*a cry for mercy*) plea, entreaty, supplication, prayer, petition, appeal, request, demand, call.

cry down disparage, belittle, decry, denigrate, run down.

cry off cancel, withdraw, back out, excuse oneself, change one's mind.

cry out for need, require, want, demand, call for.

crypt *noun* vault, tomb, catacomb, burial chamber, sepulchre, mausoleum.

cryptic *adj* enigmatic, mysterious, puzzling, perplexing, secret, hidden, occult, esoteric, arcane, abstruse, recondite, obscure, vague, ambiguous, equivocal. OPPOSITE: clear.

cub *noun* **1** (*wolf cubs*) offspring, young, pup, whelp. **2** (*cub reporters*) trainee, apprentice, probationer, student, learner, beginner, novice, tyro, neophyte, tenderfoot, greenhorn (*inf*), rookie (*inf*).

cubbyhole *noun* compartment, pigeonhole, slot, recess, niche, den.

cube *noun* dice, hexahedron.

cuddle *verb* hug, embrace, clasp, hold, fondle, caress, pet, smooch (*inf*), canoodle (*inf*), snuggle, nestle.

cuddly *adj* cuddlesome, huggable, lovable, soft, plump, warm, cosy.

cudgel *noun* club, bludgeon, cosh, truncheon, stick, baton, bastinado, shillelagh.
➤ *verb* beat, batter, pound, baste, drub, club, bludgeon, cosh.

cue *noun* signal, sign, indication, nod, wink, hint, suggestion, intimation, reminder, prompt, catchword, keyword.

cuff *verb* hit, strike, thump, belt (*inf*), clobber (*inf*), box, slap, smack, buffet, knock.
➤ *noun* hit, blow, thump, box, slap, smack, buffet, knock.

off the cuff impromptu, extempore, ad lib, improvised, unrehearsed, unscripted, off the top of one's head (*inf*), spontaneous, on the spur of the moment (*inf*).

cuisine *noun* cookery, cooking, menu, food, fare.

cul-de-sac *noun* dead end, blind alley, no through road, close.

cull *verb* **1** (*cull information*) pick, choose, select, single out, pluck, gather, collect, glean. **2** (*cull animals*) kill, slaughter, destroy, thin out.

culminate *verb* end, finish, close, conclude, terminate, wind up (*inf*), climax, peak, come to a head. OPPOSITE: start.

culmination *noun* climax, zenith, meridian, acme, height, top, cap, summit, peak, pinnacle, apex, crown, crest, consummation, completion, end, finish, close, conclusion, termination, finishing touch, finale. OPPOSITE: beginning.

culpable *adj* blameworthy, blamable, to blame, censurable, reproachable, reprehensible, wrong, in the wrong, at fault, guilty, answerable, accountable, responsible, liable, offending, sinful, peccant. OPPOSITE: innocent.

culprit *noun* offender, guilty party, wrongdoer, malefactor, miscreant, transgressor, criminal, felon, lawbreaker, delinquent, sinner, villain, baddie (*inf*).

cult *noun* **1** (*join a cult*) sect, clique, faction, party, school, belief, faith, persuasion, religion, denomination. **2** (*the cult of the Virgin Mary*) worship, homage, veneration, reverence, adoration, devotion, idolization. **3** (*the cult of self-improvement*) craze, fashion, trend, vogue, fad, rage, thing (*inf*), mania, obsession, preoccupation.

cultivate *verb* **1** (*cultivate land*) farm, till, work, dig, plough, prepare, fertilize, plant, sow. **2** (*cultivate crops*) plant, sow, grow, raise, produce, tend, bring on, harvest. **3** (*cultivating their minds*) improve, better, ameliorate, develop, civilize, culture, refine, polish, enrich, enlighten, educate, train. **4** (*cultivate a friendship*) promote, further, advance, forward, foster, nurture, encourage, support, back, help, aid, assist. OPPOSITE: neglect. **5** (*cultivating influential people*) court, woo, dance attendance on, curry favour with, butter up (*inf*), suck up to (*inf*), pursue, run after, associate with, get in with (*inf*).

cultivated *adj* cultured, refined, polished, genteel, well-bred, civilized, enlightened, educated, well-read, erudite, scholarly, knowledgeable, sophisticated, urbane, discerning, discriminating. OPPOSITE: uncouth.

cultivation *noun* **1** (*methods of cultivation in dry countries*) agriculture, agronomy, farming, husbandry, tillage, gardening. **2** (*the cultivation of the people*) culture, civilization, development, refinement, polish, improvement, amelioration, enlightenment, education, training. **3** (*the cultivation of talent*) promotion, furtherance, advancement, fostering, nurture, encouragement, support, backing, patronage, help, aid, assistance. OPPOSITE: neglect.

cultural *adj* **1** (*cultural activities*) artistic, intellectual, elevating, enriching, improving, educational, instructive, edifying, enlightening, civilizing. **2** (*cultural heritage*) national, traditional, ethnic, folk.

culture *noun* **1** (*people of culture*) refinement, polish, cultivation, sophistication, urbanity, gentility, breeding, taste, discernment, discrimination, education, erudition, enlightenment, edification. OPPOSITE: barbarity. **2** (*people of a different culture*) civilization, society, way of life, lifestyle, customs, traditions, habits, mores. **3** (*a centre of culture*) arts, humanities, literature, drama, music, painting, sculpture, intellectual pursuits. **4** (*the culture of soft fruits*) growing, production, cultivation, farming.

cultured *adj* cultivated, refined, polished, genteel, well-bred, civilized, enlightened, educated, well-read, erudite, scholarly, intellectual, highbrow, artistic, sophisticated, urbane. OPPOSITE: ignorant.

culvert *noun* channel, conduit, duct, passage, drain, sewer, gutter, watercourse.

cumbersome *adj* **1** (*cumbersome pieces of furniture*) awkward, clumsy, unwieldy, bulky, heavy, weighty, burdensome, cumbrous, large, unmanageable, inconvenient, incommodious. OPPOSITE: convenient. **2** (*a cumbersome process*) slow, lengthy, difficult, complicated, complex, unwieldy, inefficient. OPPOSITE: efficient.

cumulative *adj* accumulative, collective, aggregate, increasing, accruing, multiplying, snowballing (*inf*), growing, mounting, swelling. OPPOSITE: decreasing.

cunning *adj* **1** (*a cunning rogue*) artful, crafty, sly, wily, foxy, guileful, tricky, sharp, shrewd, astute, canny, knowing, arch, subtle, devious, calculating, designing, deceitful, dishonest, shifty. OPPOSITE: artless. **2** (*a cunning plan*) ingenious, resourceful, inventive, imaginative, clever, skilful, deft, adroit, dexterous.
➤ *noun* **1** (*the cunning of the thief*) artfulness, craft, craftiness, slyness, wiliness, guile, trickery, sharpness, shrewdness, astuteness, subtlety, deviousness, deceitfulness, deception, dishonesty. OPPOSITE: artlessness. **2** (*the cunning of the designer*) ingenuity, resourcefulness, inventiveness, imaginativeness, cleverness, skill, art, finesse, deftness, adroitness, dexterity.

cup *noun* mug, beaker, tankard, chalice, goblet, trophy.

cupboard *noun* cabinet, locker, closet, sideboard, wardrobe.

cupidity *noun* greed, avarice, avariciousness, acquisitiveness, rapacity, rapaciousness, covetousness, lust, desire, longing, yearning, hankering, itch, thirst, hunger, voracity, voraciousness, eagerness, avidity.

cur *noun* **1** (*the landlord and his cur*) dog, hound, mongrel, mutt (*inf*). **2** (*she married a cur*) scoundrel, rogue, blackguard, villain, cad, bounder (*inf*), rotter (*inf*), rat (*inf*), louse (*inf*), wastrel, ne'er-do-well, wretch, creep (*inf*).

curative *adj* healing, restorative, remedial, therapeutic, medicinal, sanative, tonic, salutary, healthful. OPPOSITE: noxious.

curator *noun* custodian, keeper, caretaker, conservator, guardian, warden, steward, attendant.

curb *verb* restrain, hold back, check, control, bridle, muzzle, suppress, repress, contain, restrict, moderate, impede, retard. OPPOSITE: encourage.
➤ *noun* restraint, check, control, bridle, rein, limit, limitation, restriction, moderation, damper, brake, constraint, deterrent. OPPOSITE: incentive.

curdle *verb* coagulate, congeal, clot, solidify, thicken, go sour, turn.

cure *verb* **1** (*cure the sick*) heal, restore, make better, make well, treat, help. OPPOSITE: aggravate. **2** (*cure a*

disease) remedy, correct, rectify, heal, treat, ease, alleviate, relieve. **3** (*cure fish*) preserve, dry, salt, pickle, smoke, kipper.
➤ *noun* remedy, antidote, curative, restorative, corrective, treatment, therapy, medicine, drug, specific, panacea, cure-all, healing, restoration, recovery.

curio *noun* curiosity, antique, novelty, objet d'art, trinket, bibelot, knick-knack.

curiosity *noun* **1** (*to satisfy my curiosity*) inquisitiveness, questioning, interest, prying, snooping, nosiness (*inf*), meddling, interference. OPPOSITE: indifference. **2** (*a collection of curiosities*) curio, antique, novelty, objet d'art, oddity, rarity, phenomenon, freak, spectacle, sight, marvel, wonder.

curious *adj* **1** (*curious about his background*) inquisitive, inquiring, questioning, querying, interested, searching, probing, prying, snooping, nosy (*inf*), meddlesome, meddling, interfering. OPPOSITE: uninterested. **2** (*a curious noise*) odd, strange, queer, funny, weird, bizarre, peculiar, singular, extraordinary, remarkable, mysterious, puzzling, unusual, uncommon, rare, exotic, novel, unorthodox, unconventional, unexpected. OPPOSITE: ordinary.

curl *verb* twist, wind, coil, spiral, snake, meander, twine, wreathe, convolute, loop, curve, bend, kink, wave, crimp, frizz. OPPOSITE: straighten.
➤ *noun* coil, spiral, helix, whorl, curlicue, convolution, loop, kink, wave, ringlet, lock, tress.

curly *adj* **1** (*curly hair*) curled, curling, wavy, kinky, permed, crimped, frizzy, fuzzy. **2** (*a curly design*) twisting, winding, coiling, spiralling, convoluted, looped, curved, curving.

currency *noun* **1** (*foreign currency*) money, legal tender, cash, notes, coins, coinage, specie. **2** (*the idea gained currency*) acceptance, popularity, vogue, prevalence, circulation, dissemination, communication, transmission, publicity, exposure.

current *adj* **1** (*current trends*) present, present-day, ongoing, in progress, existing, extant, latest, up-to-date, up-to-the-minute, modern, contemporary, fashionable, in (*inf*). OPPOSITE: obsolete. **2** (*when the practice was current*) accepted, widespread, rife, general, common, popular, prevalent, prevailing, in circulation, circulating, going around (*inf*).
➤ *noun* flow, stream, tide, wind, drift, trend, tendency, course, progression, movement.

curriculum *noun* syllabus, course, course of study, programme.

curse *noun* **1** (*uttering curses under his breath*) oath, expletive, swearword, four-letter word (*inf*), blasphemy, profanity, obscenity, imprecation, bad language. **2** (*put a curse on her*) charm, spell, jinx, voodoo, evil eye, incantation, execration, imprecation, anathema, malediction, denunciation, excommunication, damnation. OPPOSITE: benediction. **3** (*the curse of environmental pollution*) scourge, bane, blight, evil, affliction, cross, burden, ordeal, trouble, torment, plague, vexation, misfortune, disaster, calamity. OPPOSITE: blessing.
➤ *verb* **1** (*cursing under his breath*) swear, blaspheme, use bad language, cuss (*inf*). **2** (*cursed by the witch doctor*) put

a curse on, jinx, voodoo, put the evil eye on, execrate, imprecate, anathematize, denounce, excommunicate, damn, blast (*inf*). OPPOSITE: bless. **3** (*she was cursed by ill health*) scourge, blight, afflict, trouble, torment, plague, beset, vex, destroy, ruin.

cursed *adj* accursed, confounded, wretched, damnable, blasted (*inf*), hateful, detestable, loathsome, odious, abominable, execrable, vile, fiendish, devilish, infernal. OPPOSITE: blessed.

cursory *adj* superficial, perfunctory, summary, hasty, hurried, rapid, quick, brief, desultory, passing, fleeting, careless, slapdash. OPPOSITE: thorough.

curt *adj* brusque, abrupt, terse, short, brief, concise, succinct, laconic, offhand, blunt, rude, unceremonious, uncivil, gruff, tart, sharp, snappish. OPPOSITE: polite.

curtail *verb* shorten, cut short, truncate, abridge, abbreviate, cut, lop, dock, trim, pare, prune, cut back, retrench, reduce, decrease, diminish, lessen, contract, shrink, slim down, compress. OPPOSITE: lengthen.

curtailment *noun* shortening, truncation, abridgment, abbreviation, cutting, docking, pruning, retrenchment, reduction, decrease, diminution, contraction, compression. OPPOSITE: extension.

curtain *noun* **1** (*draw the curtains*) hanging, screen, blind, drape. **2** (*a curtain of secrecy*) veil, cloak, mantle, screen, cover, shield.
➤ *verb* conceal, hide, separate, screen, veil, cloak, shroud, shield. OPPOSITE: expose.

curtsy *noun* bob, genuflection.

curvaceous *adj* shapely, well-proportioned, well-rounded, buxom, bosomy, voluptuous.

curvature *noun* curve, curving, concavity, convexity, flexure, bend, bending. OPPOSITE: straightness.

curve *verb* bend, arc, arch, hook, bow, turn, twist, wind, curl, loop, coil, spiral. OPPOSITE: straighten.
➤ *noun* bend, arc, arch, camber, vault, hook, bow, turn, twist, kink, curl, loop, crescent, curvature.

curved *adj* bent, rounded, arched, vaulted, bowed, humped, convex, concave, crooked, twisted, warped, winding, sinuous, serpentine. OPPOSITE: straight.

cushion *noun* pad, squab, bolster, pillow, hassock, beanbag, headrest, buffer, shock absorber.
➤ *verb* **1** (*cushioned his head*) support, cradle, bolster, brace. **2** (*cushioning the blow*) lessen, reduce, diminish, soften, deaden, muffle, dampen, absorb, stifle, suppress. **3** (*cushioned from reality*) protect, shield, guard. OPPOSITE: expose.

cushy *adj* easy, undemanding, soft, comfortable. OPPOSITE: hard.

cusp *noun* point, tip, apex, angle.

custodian *noun* guardian, protector, keeper, warden, warder, curator, conservator, caretaker.

custody *noun* **1** (*in the custody of his parents*) care, protection, keeping, safekeeping, charge, ward, tutelage, guardianship, trusteeship, supervision, superintendence, surveillance, watch, auspices, aegis. **2** (*in custody at the police station*) arrest, confinement, imprisonment, incarceration, captivity, detention, duress, restraint. OPPOSITE: release.

custom *noun* **1** (*as was her custom*) habit, routine, wont, use, practice, policy, rule, way, manner, fashion, style. **2** (*an old Irish custom*) convention, tradition, institution, usage, practice, way, procedure, formality, ritual, rite, ceremony, observance. **3** (*losing valuable custom*) trade, business, patronage, goodwill.

customarily *adv* usually, as a rule, generally, normally, ordinarily, commonly, conventionally, traditionally. OPPOSITE: rarely.

customary *adj* usual, habitual, wonted, accustomed, regular, routine, conventional, traditional, fixed, set, established, normal, ordinary, common, familiar, popular, favourite, stock. OPPOSITE: unusual.

customer *noun* client, patron, regular (*inf*), buyer, purchaser, shopper, consumer. OPPOSITE: seller.

customize *verb* adapt, modify, convert, alter, adjust, tailor, fit, suit.

customs *pl noun* duty, tariff, toll, levy, tax.

cut *verb* **1** (*cut the meat*) slice, carve, hack, chop, cut up, dissect, divide, cleave, sever. **2** (*I've cut my finger*) gash, slash, slit, nick, pierce, penetrate, incise, lance, lacerate, wound. **3** (*get her hair cut*) snip, trim, clip, crop, dock, shear, mow, prune, lop, pare, shave. **4** (*cut glass*) score, engrave, incise, carve. **5** (*cut stone*) chip, whittle, hew, sculpt, sculpture, carve, chisel, shape, form, fashion. **6** (*cut some flowers*) reap, harvest, pick, gather. **7** (*cut spending*) reduce, lessen, lower, decrease, retrench, economize on, cut back, cut down, prune, slash. OPPOSITE: increase. **8** (*cut the text*) shorten, abridge, abbreviate, curtail, truncate, edit, reduce, cut down, condense, summarize, epitomize, précis. OPPOSITE: lengthen. **9** (*cut the reference to his wife*) delete, omit, exclude, edit out, excise, cut out, expurgate, bowdlerize. OPPOSITE: insert. **10** (*I waved, but he cut me*) snub, ignore, shun, cold shoulder, avoid, spurn, slight, rebuff, cut dead (*inf*), look right through (*inf*) OPPOSITE: acknowledge. **11** (*where the line cuts the circumference*) cross, intersect, bisect, meet, join.
➤ *noun* **1** (*a cut on my leg*) wound, gash, laceration, slash, nick, incision. **2** (*a cut and blow-dry*) trim, clip, crop. **3** (*a cut in wages*) reduction, decrease, fall, drop, cutback, retrenchment, economy, saving. **4** (*a cut of the profits*) share, percentage, proportion, slice, piece, portion, ration, quota. **5** (*a power cut*) breakdown, failure, fault. **6** (*the cut of the jacket*) style, shape, form, fashion.

cut back reduce spending, retrench, economize, cut down, rationalize, downsize.

cut down **1** (*cut down a tree*) fell, hew, lop, chop down, level, raze. **2** (*cut down on chocolate*) reduce, lessen, lower, decrease, cut back, curb, curtail.

cut in interpose, interrupt, butt in, intervene.

cut off **1** (*cut off supplies*) intercept, obstruct, block, interrupt, discontinue, stop, halt, suspend, disconnect. **2** (*cut off from her friends*) isolate, seclude, separate, insulate. **3** (*cut off his leg*) amputate, sever, chop off, detach, remove.

cut out **1** (*cut out the tumour*) remove, excise, extract, eliminate. **2** (*cut out any offensive words*) delete, edit out, blue-pencil, omit, leave out, exclude, drop. **3** (*cut it out!*) stop, cease, desist, abstain from, refrain from, quit (*inf*), leave off (*inf*), pack in (*inf*). **4** (*I'm not cut out for this job*) suit, fit, qualify, equip.

cut short curtail, truncate, break off, halt, stop, discontinue, suspend, interrupt, abort, terminate, end.

cut up chop, dice, mince, grind, slice, carve, dissect, dismember.

cute *adj* sweet, appealing, winsome, attractive, pretty, delightful, charming. OPPOSITE: repulsive.

cut-price *adj* reduced, discount, bargain, cheap.

cutthroat *adj* ruthless, relentless, fierce, keen, competitive, dog-eat-dog (*inf*).

cutting *adj* **1** (*a cutting remark*) sharp, keen, trenchant, mordant, biting, incisive, caustic, acid, acerbic, barbed, scathing, sardonic, sarcastic, cruel, vicious, bitter, acrimonious, hurtful, wounding, stinging. OPPOSITE: kind. **2** (*a cutting wind*) keen, piercing, penetrating, biting, bitter, stinging, raw, cold, chill, icy. OPPOSITE: mild.

➤ *noun* clipping, clip, excerpt, extract, piece, bit, slip, snippet.

cycle *noun* circle, revolution, rotation, round, run, series, succession, sequence, order, rota.

cyclone *noun* tornado, typhoon, whirlwind, hurricane, tempest, storm, gale, squall.

cynic *noun* pessimist, sceptic, doubter, misanthrope, doomster, killjoy, wet blanket (*inf*), scoffer, mocker.

cynical *adj* pessimistic, sceptical, unbelieving, distrustful, suspicious, misanthropic, contemptuous, scornful, derisive, sardonic, sarcastic, ironic, mocking, sneering.

cynicism *noun* pessimism, scepticism, doubt, unbelief, distrust, suspicion, misanthropy, contempt, scorn, derision, sarcasm, irony.

cyst *noun* blister, sac, vesicle, bladder, bleb, wen.

dab *verb* pat, tap, touch, daub, bedaub, spot, press, blot.
➤ *noun* **1** (*a dab of butter*) spot, drop, speck, touch, bit, dash, soupçon, hint, suggestion, trace. **2** (*wiped tears with a dab of tissue*) pat, tap, stroke, blow, press, touch.

dab hand *noun* expert, master, adept, ace (*inf*), wizard, dabster.

dabble *verb* dip, paddle, splash, spatter, spray, sprinkle, moisten, wet.

dabble in tinker with, trifle with, dally with, toy with, flirt with, potter about with, play at, dip into.

dabbler *noun* trifler, dallier, amateur, lay person, dilettante. OPPOSITE: professional.

daft *adj* **1** (*what a daft idea!*) silly, foolish, stupid, idiotic, crazy, absurd, nonsensical, senseless, lunatic, insane, potty (*inf*), crackpot (*inf*), dotty (*inf*). OPPOSITE: sensible. **2** (*he's going daft*) crazy, mad, insane, lunatic, crackers (*inf*), nuts (*inf*), nutty (*inf*), loony (*inf*), loopy (*inf*), bonkers (*inf*), cuckoo (*inf*), not all there (*inf*).

daft about infatuated with, enthusiastic about, obsessed about, fanatical about, nuts (*inf*), potty (*inf*), sweet on (*inf*).

dagger *noun* dirk, stiletto, poniard, skean, knife, blade.

daily *adj* (*daily life*) routine, everyday, regular, common, commonplace, ordinary, customary, habitual. **2** (*a daily broadcast*) everyday, diurnal, quotidian, circadian.
➤ *adv* every day, day by day, day after day.

dainty *adj* **1** (*a dainty handkerchief*) delicate, fine, elegant, refined, exquisite, charming, pretty, beautiful, graceful, petite, neat, trim. OPPOSITE: clumsy. **2** (*a dainty morsel*) delicious, tasty, tender, choice, appetizing, savoury, luscious, delectable, flavoursome, juicy, succulent, toothsome, palatable. OPPOSITE: loathsome. **3** (*very dainty about what he eats*) scrupulous, fastidious, discriminating, refined, squeamish, particular, fussy, finicky, choosy.
➤ *noun* delicacy, titbit, fancy, sweetmeat, bonne bouche.

dais *noun* platform, rostrum, stage, podium, stand, pulpit.

dale *noun* valley, vale, dell, dingle, glen. OPPOSITE: hill.

dalliance *noun* trifling, playing, flirting, fooling around.

dally *verb* dawdle, loiter, linger, dillydally, tarry, delay, waste time, hang around. OPPOSITE: hurry.

dally with trifle with, toy with, play with, flirt with, fool around with.

dam *noun* barrier, barricade, barrage, embankment, wall, blockage, hindrance.
➤ *verb* block, restrict, confine, obstruct, staunch, stem.

damage *noun* harm, injury, hurt, suffering, mischief, impairment, abuse, defacement, defilement, vandalism, detriment, loss, destruction, devastation, ruin. OPPOSITE: reparation.
➤ *verb* harm, hurt, injure, impair, tamper with, mar, spoil, abuse, defile, vandalize, devastate, ruin, wreck, deface, mutilate. OPPOSITE: repair.

damages *pl noun* compensation, reparation, indemnity, reimbursement, restitution, satisfaction, costs, expenses, penalty, fine.

dame *noun* lady, noblewoman, aristocrat, peeress, baroness, matron, dowager.

damn *verb* **1** (*critics damning the play*) condemn, denounce, censure, criticize, berate, reprimand, rebuke, abuse, vituperate, vilify, castigate, inveigh against, excoriate, slate (*inf*), slam (*inf*), knock (*inf*), pan (*inf*), pick holes in (*inf*), tear to pieces (*inf*). OPPOSITE: extol. **2** (*constantly damning*) curse, swear, blaspheme, blast, cuss (*inf*), anathematize, imprecate, maledict. OPPOSITE: bless. **3** (*damned to hell*) doom, sentence, condemn, convict, execrate, excommunicate, proscribe. OPPOSITE: acquit.
➤ *noun* trifle, jot, whit, iota, hoot (*inf*), brass farthing (*inf*), tinker's cuss (*inf*).

give a damn care, mind, be concerned.

damnable *adj* abominable, vile, odious, detestable,

cursed, accursed, despicable, revolting, repulsive, foul, horrible, atrocious. OPPOSITE: splendid.

damnation noun condemnation, denunciation, punishment, perdition, doom, objurgation, excommunication, proscription, exile, ban, doom, anathema, curse. OPPOSITE: blessing.

damned adj **1** (a damned nuisance) abominable, confounded, infernal, odious, vile, fiendish, annoying nasty, detestable, blasted (inf), darned (inf). **2** (damned to hell) cursed, doomed, condemned, lost, execrated, excommunicated, proscribed, anathematized, reprobate.

damning adj incriminating, condemning, accusatorial, implicating, inculpatory.

damp adj moist, dewy, wet, wettish, dank, humid, muggy, clammy, soggy, sodden, misty, vaporous, drizzly. OPPOSITE: dry.
➤ noun dampness, moisture, humidity, wetness, mugginess, clamminess, fog, mist, vapour, dankness, dew. OPPOSITE: dryness.
➤ verb **1** (damp a cloth) moisten, dampen, wet, bedew, humidify. OPPOSITE: dry. **2** (damp a fire) extinguish, stifle, smother, bank.

damp down discourage, dampen, check, curb, restrain, moderate, abate, allay, temper, dull, deaden, blunt, cool, inhibit, stifle, muffle, dishearten, depress, dispirit, deject. OPPOSITE: encourage.

dampen verb **1** (dampen a cloth) damp, wet, moisten, bedew, humidify. OPPOSITE: dry. **2** (dampened his competitive spirit) moderate, restrain, temper, dull, blunt, deaden, stifle, discourage, depress, damp, damp down, put a damper on. OPPOSITE: encourage.

damper noun obstacle, hindrance, impediment, hitch, check, restraint, depression, gloom, discouragement, pall, cloud, wet blanket (inf), killjoy.

dampness noun moisture, moistness, wetness, damp, dankness, humidity, clamminess, mugginess, mist, vapour, drizzle, rain.

damsel noun girl, lass, maiden, maid, young lady, young woman.

dance verb **1** (danced with her boyfriend) sway, rock, jig, hop, whirl, pirouette, shake a leg (inf), hoof it (inf). **2** (dance with excitement) caper, skip, hop, jig, swing, rock, whirl, spin, prance, frolic, gambol. **3** (lights dancing over the surface of the lake) play, leap, sway, move, flicker, twinkle, shimmer, sparkle.
➤ noun ball, social, hop (inf), knees-up (inf), disco (inf).

dandle verb caress, pet, fondle, dance, bounce, ride, rock, cradle, amuse.

dandy noun beau, fop, coxcomb, swell (inf), popinjay, ladies' man, man about town.
➤ adj fine, excellent, splendid, great, first-rate.

danger noun **1** (his life is in danger) peril, risk, jeopardy, hazard, vulnerability, endangerment, insecurity, precariousness. OPPOSITE: safety. **2** (a danger to public health) threat, menace, risk, peril.

dangerous adj perilous, risky, hazardous, unsafe, unsound, treacherous, chancy, hairy (inf), vulnerable, insecure, precarious, ominous, alarming, threatening, menacing, minatory, minacious. OPPOSITE: safe.

dangle verb **1** (clothes dangling from pegs) hang,

suspend, swing, droop, trail, sway, oscillate, flaunt, brandish, wave, flourish. **2** (dangle a reward in front of someone) entice, tempt, lure, hold out, flourish.

dank adj damp, clammy, moist, dewy, humid, wet, chilly. OPPOSITE: dry.

dapper adj **1** (a dapper young man) smart, spruce, neat, trim, chic, elegant, well-groomed, well-turned-out, natty (inf). OPPOSITE: slovenly. **2** (a dapper little bird) alert, nimble, spry, brisk, agile, lively, sprightly, active, quick. OPPOSITE: slow.

dappled adj mottled, variegated, marked, dotted, flecked, spotted, speckled, piebald, pied, blotched, parti-coloured, brindled.

dare verb **1** (dare you to ask her out) challenge, provoke, goad, taunt, throw down the gauntlet. **2** (dare to do a parachute jump) risk, hazard, venture, be brave enough to, endanger, gamble, stake, attempt, presume. OPPOSITE: quail. **3** (dared her family's anger) defy, brave, meet, confront, face, face up to, stand up to.
➤ noun challenge, provocation, ultimatum, gauntlet.

daredevil noun desperado, madcap, adventurer, stunt man, stunt woman, stunt performer.
➤ adj adventurous, bold, brave, intrepid, dauntless, fearless, reckless, foolhardy, death-defying.

daring adj bold, brave, adventurous, venturesome, audacious, valiant, intrepid, dauntless, fearless, courageous, plucky, unshrinking, rash, reckless, daredevil, foolhardy, desperate, death-defying. OPPOSITE: cautious.
➤ noun boldness, audacity, bravery, intrepidity, courage, valour, nerve, mettle, pluck, guts (inf), bottle (inf), spunk (inf), temerity, rashness, recklessness. OPPOSITE: caution.

dark adj **1** (gets dark early in autumn) dim, unlit, shadowy, dingy, sunless, murky, cloudy, overcast, dusky. OPPOSITE: light. **2** (have a dark skin) black, swarthy, sallow, ebony, sable, pitchy. OPPOSITE: light. **3** (feel bad in dark moments) sombre, drab, dismal, gloomy, cheerless, bleak, mournful, grim, grave, morose, discouraging. OPPOSITE: bright. **4** (in a dark state of mind) dour, sullen, morose, threatening, forbidding, glowering, ominous, menacing, sinister. OPPOSITE: cheerful. **5** (dark ages of history) ignorant, unenlightened, uncultured, uncultivated, benighted, uneducated. OPPOSITE: enlightened. **6** (dark secrets) secret, hidden, concealed, veiled, abstruse, recondite, profound, unfathomable, esoteric, cryptic, incomprehensible, unintelligible, obscure, mysterious, enigmatic, occult, arcane. OPPOSITE: plain. **7** (dark deeds) evil, wicked, vile, atrocious, horrible, base, sinful, sinister, infernal, hellish, satanic, nefarious, infamous. OPPOSITE: good.
➤ noun **1** (in the dark of night) darkness, dimness, blackness, gloom, obscurity, murkiness, dusk, shade, shadowiness, twilight, tenebrosity, evening, night. OPPOSITE: light. **2** (kept in the dark about the affair) ignorance, blindness, secrecy, privacy, obscurity, concealment. OPPOSITE: enlightenment.

darken verb **1** (the skies darkened) dim, obscure, eclipse, shade, shadow, overshadow, cloud, cloud over, blacken, make dark, go dark. OPPOSITE: lighten. **2** (darkened her *spirits*) deject, depress, dishearten, discourage, oppress, sadden, dispirit, make gloomy. OPPOSITE: brighten.

darkness *noun* **1** (*the darkness of night*) dark, gloom, blackness, murkiness, murk, dimness, obscurity, shadows, dusk, twilight, evening, night, tenebrosity. OPPOSITE: brightness. **2** (*in the darkness of their minds*) ignorance, blindness, secrecy, obscurity, mystery, concealment. OPPOSITE: enlightenment.

darling *noun* **1** (*love you, darling*) dear, dearest, sweetheart, beloved, pet, love, favourite, honey, angel, treasure, sweetie (*inf*), poppet (*inf*). **2** (*the darling of the fashion world*) favourite, pet, apple of one's eye, blue-eyed boy (*inf*).
» *adj* **1** (*my darling wife*) dear, dearest, beloved, precious, cherished, adored, loved, treasured, prized, valued, pet, favourite. **2** (*what a darling movie!*) charming, lovely, sweet, adorable, captivating, enchanting. OPPOSITE: repulsive.

darn *verb* mend, repair, stitch, sew, sew up, patch.
» *noun* mend, patch, repair.

dart *verb* **1** (*darted across the room*) dash, rush, race, sprint, shoot, flash, fly, rim, scoot, tear. OPPOSITE: amble. **2** (*dart a scornful glance*) hurl, throw, send, fling, cast, pitch, toss, sling, propel.
» *noun* **1** (*throw a dart*) arrow, barb, bolt. **2** (*made a dart for the door*) rush, dash, run, race, bolt, sprint.

dash *verb* **1** (*dashed out of the door*) rush, run, race, dart, hurry, tear, speed, hasten, fly, bolt, sprint. OPPOSITE: amble. **2** (*waves dashing against the sea wall*) beat, smash, strike, crash, break, hurl, throw, cast, fling, shatter, splinter. **3** (*dashed all his hopes*) frustrate, thwart, foil, ruin, destroy, shatter, check, balk.
» *noun* **1** (*made a dash for it*) bolt, run, flight, dart, rush, spurt, sprint, onset. **2** (*add a dash of salt*) tinge, touch, trace, soupçon, hint, suspicion, suggestion, drop, bit, pinch, grain, smack, sprinkling. **3** (*an orchestra playing with great dash*) élan, flair, style, flourish, verve, liveliness, vivacity, panache, vigour, gusto, spirit, pizzazz (*inf*), oomph (*inf*), zing (*inf*), zip (*inf*).

dashing *adj* **1** (*a dashing young soldier*) lively, spirited, energetic, animated, exuberant, impetuous, dynamic, gallant, valiant, daring, plucky. OPPOSITE: lethargic. **2** (*a dashing style*) smart, showy, flamboyant, brilliant, dazzling, elegant, debonair, sporty, chic, stylish, dapper, jaunty.

dastard *noun* coward, craven, poltroon, cur, worm, mouse.

dastardly *adj* **1** (*a dastardly traitor*) cowardly, craven, faint-hearted, timorous, chicken-livered, lily-livered, pusillanimous, yellow (*inf*). OPPOSITE: brave. **2** (*dastardly deeds*) base, mean, despicable, low, underhand. OPPOSITE: noble.

data *pl noun* facts, figures, information, input, material, statistics.

date *noun* **1** (*the date of these old coins*) age, period, stage, era, epoch, time, day, month, year, decade, century, millennium. **2** (*make a date*) appointment, engagement, meeting, assignation, tryst, rendezvous. **3** (*he brought his date to the party*) partner, escort, boyfriend, girlfriend, lover, steady (*inf*).
» *verb* **1** (*clothes that have hardly dated*) become dated,

become old-fashioned, become obsolete, go out of date, obsolesce. **2** (*date an old college friend*) go out with, take out, court, go steady with.

date from originate in, come from, go back to, exist from.

out of date **1** (*wear out of date clothes*) old-fashioned, outdated, archaic, outmoded, dated, passé, obsolete, antiquated, superannuated, old hat (*inf*). OPPOSITE: modern. **2** (*the food is out of date*) past its sell-by date, expired, invalid, lapsed. OPPOSITE: current.

to date until now, up to now, so far, up to the present.

up to date modern, fashionable, trendy (*inf*), up-to-the-minute, current, contemporary. OPPOSITE: dated.

dated *adj* out of date, old-fashioned, outdated, outmoded, passé, old hat (*inf*), antiquated, obsolescent. OPPOSITE: modern.

daub *verb* **1** (*daub paint on walls*) smear, paint, plaster, cover, bedaub, spatter, splatter. **2** (*daub the walls with mud*) soil, begrime, deface, sully, stain, smudge.
» *noun* smear, smudge, spot, patch, blotch, blot, smirch.

daunt *verb* intimidate, unnerve, dismay, disconcert, alarm, scare, frighten, terrify, appal, cow, overawe, unman, discourage, dispirit, deter, put off, stop, check, thwart. OPPOSITE: encourage.

dauntless *adj* undaunted, bold, daring, brave, fearless, intrepid, valiant, doughty, indomitable, courageous, stouthearted, heroic. OPPOSITE: cowardly.

dawdle *verb* lag, lag behind, loiter, dilly-dally (*inf*), dally, waste time, take one's time, idle, trifle, potter. OPPOSITE: hurry.

dawdler *noun* laggard, loiterer, snail, slowcoach (*inf*), idler.

dawn *noun* **1** (*stay up till dawn*) daybreak, break of day, sunrise, sunup, first light, cockcrow, aurora, daylight, morning. OPPOSITE: sunset. **2** (*since the dawn of time*) beginning, start, commencement, outset, origin, rise, appearance, arrival, birth, genesis, inception, advent, onset, emergence. OPPOSITE: end.
» *verb* **1** (*morning dawned*) break, gleam, grow light, brighten. **2** (*a new civilization dawned*) begin, start, commence, arrive, appear, emerge, rise, open, originate, come into being. OPPOSITE: close.

dawn on occur to, come to, strike, hit, sink in, register.

day *noun* **1** (*at the start of the day*) daylight, daytime, sunshine. OPPOSITE: night. **2** (*in my day we walked to school*) generation, age, period, epoch, era, time, lifetime.

day after day continually, endlessly, relentlessly, persistently, without respite.

day by day progressively, gradually, steadily, slowly but surely.

have had its day be past its prime, have had its heyday, be out of date, be past it (*inf*), be past its sell-by date (*inf*).

daybreak *noun* dawn, sunrise, sunup, cockcrow, first light, morning. OPPOSITE: nightfall.

daydream *noun* dream, reverie, musing, imagining, woolgathering, fancy, vision, pipe dream, figment of the imagination, fantasy, hallucination, castle in the air.

➤ *verb* dream, muse, fantasize, stargaze, imagine, hallucinate.

daylight *noun* **1** (*work in the daylight*) sunshine, sunlight, day, daytime, light of day. OPPOSITE: night. **2** (*get up at daylight*) dawn, daybreak, break of day, sunrise, sunup, cockcrow, morning.

daze *verb* stun, stupefy, shock, dumbfound, amaze, astonish, astound, flabbergast (*inf*), floor (*inf*), faze (*inf*), bewilder, confuse, take aback, dismay, disconcert, unnerve, blind, dazzle.
➤ *noun* stupor, trance, shock, confusion, distraction, bewilderment.

dazzle *verb* **1** (*dazzled by the light*) blind, bedazzle, daze. **2** (*dazzled by her charm*) stun, stagger, amaze, astonish, astound, dumbfound, strike dumb, impress, overawe, overwhelm, overpower, bowl over (*inf*), knock out (*inf*), fascinate. OPPOSITE: bore.
➤ *noun* brilliance, splendour, magnificence, sparkle, flash, gleam, glitter. OPPOSITE: dullness.

dead *adj* **1** (*a dead body*) lifeless, defunct, deceased, late, departed, perished, gone, passed away, passed on, extinct, inanimate, exanimate. OPPOSITE: alive. **2** (*fall on dead ears*) insensitive, unresponsive, unfeeling, unsympathetic, cold, frigid, lukewarm, indifferent, apathetic, spiritless, torpid, dull, numb. OPPOSITE: sensitive. **3** (*my arm has gone dead*) numb, paralysed, gone to sleep, not feeling anything. **4** (*feel dead*) tired, tired out, exhausted, worn out, dead beat (*inf*), knackered (*inf*). OPPOSITE: refreshed. **5** (*a dead language*) extinct, obsolete, lapsed, disused. OPPOSITE: living. **6** (*that issue is now dead*) obsolete, lapsed, outdated, outmoded, passé, ineffective. **7** (*the line is dead*) inactive, inert, still, inoperative, not working. **8** (*a dead town with no night life*) dull, boring, uninteresting, tedious, quiet, tiresome, wearisome. OPPOSITE: exciting. **9** (*dead centre*) absolute, exact, perfect, precise. **10** (*a dead loss*) complete, utter, downright, total, entire, outright, absolute, thorough, out and out, unmitigated.
➤ *noun* midst, depth, darkness, coldness, stillness.
➤ *adv* completely, utterly, totally, exactly, absolutely, entirely, thoroughly, categorically.

deaden *verb* damp, damp down, dampen, muffle, blunt, subdue, suppress, weaken, moderate, reduce, diminish, lessen, abate, alleviate, assuage, mitigate, dull, numb, incapacitate, anaesthetize, paralyse. OPPOSITE: intensify.

deadlock *noun* stalemate, checkmate, impasse, standstill, halt, stop, stoppage, cessation, tie, draw, dead heat.

deadly *adj* **1** (*a deadly poison*) mortal, fatal, lethal, death-dealing, malignant, dangerous, harmful, virulent, poisonous, pernicious, noxious, venomous, destructive, baleful. OPPOSITE: harmless. **2** (*deadly enemy*) implacable, mortal, hated, murderous, savage, remorseless, unrelenting, sanguinary. **3** (*a deadly paleness*) pale, ashen, deathly, deathlike, wan, white, pallid, ghastly, ghostly, livid. OPPOSITE: ruddy. **4** (*in deadly earnest*) intense, serious, extreme, great, marked. **5** (*with deadly accuracy*) accurate, precise, exact, sure, true, unerring, unfailing. **6** (*a deadly party*) boring, dull, tedious,

monotonous, wearisome, tiresome. OPPOSITE: enthralling.
➤ *adv* completely, utterly, totally, absolutely, entirely.

deaf *adj* unhearing, stone deaf, hard of hearing, with impaired hearing.
deaf to heedless of, oblivious to, insensitive to, unmoved by, indifferent to. OPPOSITE: aware of.

deafen *verb* make deaf, din, drown out, muffle.

deafening *adj* earsplitting, earpiercing, piercing, thunderous, booming, ringing, resounding, overwhelming, intense. OPPOSITE: quiet.

deal *verb* **1** (*deal cards*) distribute, hand out, dispense, mete, dole, bestow, give, give out, divide, divide up, share, share out, allot, allocate, apportion. **2** (*deal in antiques*) trade, traffic, buy and sell, bargain, negotiate, do business. **3** (*deal a blow*) give, direct, aim, deliver, administer. **4** (*deal with people*) act, behave, conduct oneself.
➤ *noun* **1** (*come to a deal*) agreement, bargain, transaction, negotiation, contract, pact, understanding. **2** (*a great deal of money*) quantity, amount, degree, extent.
deal with 1 (*deal with a problem*) handle, manage, cope with, sort out, tackle, see to, take care of, attend to. **2** (*the issues are dealt with on page 100*) be about, discuss, concern, treat, treat of.

dealer *noun* merchant, salesman, saleswoman, salesperson, trader, tradesman, tradeswoman, tradesperson, wholesaler, retailer, vendor, trafficker.

dealings *pl noun* **1** (*business dealings*) business, commerce, trade, transactions, negotiations, traffic, trafficking. **2** (*my dealings with the family*) action, behaviour, relations, practices, methods, policy.

dear *adj* **1** (*a dear friend*) beloved, loved, adored, intimate, close, darling, precious, cherished, treasured, valued, prized, favoured, favourite, attractive. OPPOSITE: loathsome. **2** (*the camera is too dear*) expensive, high-priced, high-cost, overpriced, exorbitant, costly, pricey (*inf*), steep (*inf*). OPPOSITE: cheap.
➤ *noun* darling, beloved, treasure, love, loved one, sweetheart, precious, pet, angel.
➤ *adv* at a great cost, at a heavy cost, at a high price, with great loss.

dearly *adv* **1** (*loved him dearly*) greatly, deeply, fondly, lovingly, devotedly, affectionately, intimately. **2** (*paid dearly for his folly*) at a great cost, at a heavy cost, at a high price, with great loss.

dearth *noun* lack, deficiency, scarcity, shortage, insufficiency, want, need, famine, poverty, meagreness, sparseness, scantiness, absence, paucity, exiguity. OPPOSITE: abundance.

death *noun* **1** (*the death of my father*) decease, demise, expiration, dying, passing, passing on, passing away, departure, quietus, exit, end, cessation, dissolution, curtains (*inf*). OPPOSITE: birth. **2** (*the death of modern art*) end, finish, cessation, termination, destruction, annihilation, extermination, extinction, eradication, extirpation.

deathless *adj* immortal, undying, imperishable, everlasting, eternal, perpetual, unceasing, timeless. OPPOSITE: mortal.

deathly *adj* **1** (*look deathly pale*) deathlike, ghastly, livid, pale, wan, gaunt, haggard, cadaverous. **2** (*a deathly hush*) intense, great, extreme, utmost, complete, utter.

debacle *noun* ruin, collapse, downfall, breakup, disintegration, failure, fiasco, wreck, havoc, devastation, catastrophe, rout, defeat, overthrow.

debar *verb* bar, exclude, shut out, keep out, blackball, forbid, prevent, preclude, disallow, veto, proscribe, prohibit, restrain, impede, hinder, obstruct, thwart, stop. OPPOSITE: admit.

debase *verb* **1** (*debased himself in public*) degrade, lower, abase, reduce, humble, humiliate, shame, drag down, disgrace, dishonour, demean, discredit, bring shame on, devalue, depreciate, deteriorate. OPPOSITE: raise. **2** (*debase a coin*) adulterate, contaminate, dilute, deprave, corrupt, taint, defile, pollute, sully, alloy, vitiate, impair. OPPOSITE: purify.

debasement *noun* degradation, lowering, abasement, humiliation, disgrace, dishonour, depreciation, reduction, deterioration, adulteration, contamination, pollution, corruption, depravation.

debatable *adj* disputable, questionable, arguable, unsettled, undecided, moot, contestable, controversial, doubtful, open to doubt, dubious, uncertain. OPPOSITE: certain.

debate *verb* **1** (debate an issue) discuss, dispute, argue, contend, contest, question, moot, wrangle, controvert, altercate, kick around (inf). OPPOSITE: agree. **2** (debate where to go on holiday) deliberate, consider, ponder, reflect, think over, meditate, contemplate, muse, cogitate, mull over. OPPOSITE: decide.
⟩ *noun* discussion, argument, dispute, disputation, polemic, controversy, wrangle, altercation, war of words, contention, contest. OPPOSITE: agreement.

debauch *verb* deprave, corrupt, debase, demoralize, pervert, vitiate, defile, deflower, violate, seduce, lead astray. OPPOSITE: purify.
⟩ *noun* spree, orgy, fling, revel, carousal, saturnalia, binge (inf), bout.

debauched *adj* depraved, corrupt, licentious, degenerate, dissolute, dissipated, immoral, profligate, intemperate, promiscuous, abandoned, wanton. OPPOSITE: ascetic.

debauchery *noun* depravity, immorality, corruption, dissipation, dissoluteness, lust, licentiousness, degeneracy, perversion, promiscuity, intemperance, profligacy, rakishness, incontinence, indulgence, excess, revelry, wantonness, debauch. OPPOSITE: restraint.

debilitate *verb* enfeeble, weaken, wear out, enervate, sap, exhaust, impair, cripple, prostrate, incapacitate, undermine. OPPOSITE: strengthen.

debility *noun* feebleness, weakness, enfeeblement, fatigue, enervation, prostration, exhaustion, infirmity, decrepitude, impairment, frailty, sickliness, languor, lassitude, incapacity. OPPOSITE: strength.

debonair *adj* affable, gracious, courteous, polite, suave, urbane, refined, elegant, smart, self-assured, confident, dashing, jaunty, carefree, sprightly, buoyant, cheery, sunny, breezy, lighthearted.

debris *noun* remains, ruins, wreckage, detritus, fragments, pieces, rubble, rubbish, litter.

debt *noun* **1** (*debts of thousands of pounds*) liability, obligation, due, duty, debit, arrears, deficit, bill, tally, account, score. OPPOSITE: asset. **2** (*our debt to our ancestors*) indebtedness, obligation, thankfulness.
in debt owing, owing money, liable, accountable, in arrears, in the red (inf).

debunk *verb* expose, unmask, mock, ridicule, puncture, deflate, show up, show in one's true colours.

debut *noun* beginning, launch, premiere, coming-out, introduction, presentation, entrance, first appearance, first performance.

decadence *noun* corruption, dissipation, dissolution, debauchery, immorality, depravity, corruption, licentiousness, decay, decline, degeneration, deterioration, wane, fall, retrogression, degradation, debasement.

decadent *adj* depraved, dissolute, dissipated, self-indulgent, immoral, corrupt, debauched, licentious, profligate, intemperate, promiscuous, degenerate, debased, decaying, declining, waning, deteriorating.

decamp *verb* **1** (*decamp with the club's money*) abscond, bolt, fly, flee, run away, run off, take off, make off, escape, scarper (inf), skedaddle (inf), vamoose (inf), do a runner (inf), do a bunk (inf), do a moonlight flit (inf). **2** (*the army decamped*) break camp, strike camp, move on.

decant *verb* pour, pour out, draw off, tap, drain, pump off.

decapitate *verb* behead, guillotine, execute.

decay *verb* **1** (*food decaying*) rot, decompose, spoil, perish, go bad, putrefy. **2** (*institutions decaying*) decline, fail, collapse, sink, deteriorate, waste away, wither, crumble, die, wear away, atrophy, degenerate, wane, ebb, decrease, dwindle. OPPOSITE: flourish.
⟩ *noun* **1** (*tooth decay*) rot, decomposition, spoilage, putrefaction, caries, gangrene, mould. **2** (*the decay in educational standards*) decline, deterioration, disintegration, crumbling, decadence, wasting, wasting away, atrophy, degeneration, wane, ebbing, collapse, failure, downfall. OPPOSITE: growth.

decease *noun* death, demise, dying, expiration, passing, passing on, passing away, departure, exit, release, curtains (inf). OPPOSITE: birth.

deceased *adj* dead, lifeless, defunct, departed, gone, late, passed away, passed on, former, expired. OPPOSITE: alive.

deceit *noun* **1** (*speak deceit*) fraud, fraudulence, deception, deceitfulness, guile, duplicity, cheating, trickery, double-dealing, treachery, chicanery, underhandedness, artifice, craftiness, wiliness, dishonesty, dissimulation. OPPOSITE: honesty. **2** (*invented deceits*) trick, ruse, stratagem, wile, subterfuge, pretence, imposture, fraud, swindle, lie, dodge, hoax, misrepresentation, falsehood.

deceitful *adj* dishonest, untruthful, deceptive, hollow, false, insincere, hypocritical, two-faced, double-dealing, underhand, cheating, fraudulent, crooked, treacherous, sly, wily, cunning, crafty, scheming, tricky, guileful, artful, mendacious, perfidious. OPPOSITE: honest.

deceive *verb* mislead, cheat, trick, fool, beguile, dupe, hoodwink, cozen, lead on, delude, hoax, swindle, con (*inf*), bamboozle (*inf*), double-cross (*inf*), take in (*inf*), take for a ride (*inf*), pull someone's leg (*inf*), pull the wool over someone's eyes (*inf*), pull a fast one on (*inf*), lead up the garden path (*inf*).

deceiver *noun* cheat, fraud, impostor, swindler, sharper, conman (*inf*), con artist (*inf*), hypocrite, liar, charlatan.

decelerate *verb* slow, slow down, brake, reduce speed, put the brakes on, put one's foot on the brake. OPPOSITE: accelerate.

decency *noun* propriety, modesty, decorum, delicacy, good taste, fitness, correctness, respectability, seemliness, etiquette. OPPOSITE: impropriety.

decent *adj* **1** (*decent behaviour*) respectable, proper, seemly, fitting, appropriate, becoming, decorous, nice, polite, pure, dignified, delicate, modest. OPPOSITE: indecent. **2** (*decent citizens*) upright, honest, worthy, respectable, trustworthy, obliging, accommodating, kind, helpful, generous, thoughtful, courteous. OPPOSITE: dishonest. **3** (*a decent sized garden*) adequate, passable, fair, reasonable, not bad, acceptable, sufficient, ample, tolerable. OPPOSITE: inadequate.

deception *noun* **1** (*obtain the goods by deception*) deceit, fraud, fraudulence, cheating, guile, artifice, duplicity, double-dealing, chicanery, hypocrisy, trickery, cunning, treachery, deceitfulness, dishonesty, dissimulation. OPPOSITE: honesty. **2** (*a cruel deception*) trick, ruse, wile, fraud, stratagem, dodge, artifice, subterfuge, pretence, imposture, swindle, hoax, lie, bluff, sham, misrepresentation, illusion.

deceptive *adj* misleading, deceiving, unreliable, illusory, illusive, specious, spurious, mock, pseudo (*inf*), delusive, fallacious, ambiguous, fraudulent, underhand, crooked, cunning, crafty, false, fake, counterfeit, dishonest, deceitful. OPPOSITE: true.

decide *verb* **1** (*decide to go to Paris*) make up one's mind, come to a decision, make a decision, reach a decision, resolve, come to a conclusion. **2** (*decide an issue*) determine, settle, adjudicate, judge, rule, decree, referee, umpire.

decide on pick, select, choose, elect, opt for, go for, plump for (*inf*).

decided *adj* **1** (*a decided change for the better*) definite, certain, unquestionable, indisputable, unmistakable, unequivocal, unambiguous, undeniable, positive, obvious, pronounced, absolute, distinct, clear, clear-cut, categorical. OPPOSITE: doubtful. **2** (*a decided effort*) determined, resolute, unwavering, firm, decisive, strong-minded, unswerving, unfaltering, unhesitating. OPPOSITE: irresolute.

decidedly *adv* clearly, definitely, distinctly, obviously, certainly, positively, markedly, unmistakably, unambiguously, undeniably.

deciding *adj* decisive, conclusive, categorical, final, crucial, critical, determining, main, chief, prime, crunch (*inf*).

decipher *verb* solve, unravel, unfold, decode, translate, interpret, explain, understand, comprehend, construe,

read, make out, work out, crack (*inf*). OPPOSITE: encode.

decision *noun* **1** (*reach a decision*) resolution, conclusion, verdict, judgment, ruling, pronouncement, adjudication, settlement, finding. **2** (*a person of decision*) determination, resolution, resolve, resoluteness, doggedness, firmness, decisiveness, strong-mindedness, purposefulness, purpose. OPPOSITE: indecision.

decisive *adj* **1** (*a decisive victory*) conclusive, deciding, definitive, absolute, categorical, final, emphatic, momentous, significant, determinate, critical, crucial, influential. OPPOSITE: inconclusive. **2** (*a decisive person*) resolute, decided, determined, dogged, purposeful, firm, unwavering, unhesitating, unswerving, unfaltering. OPPOSITE: indecisive.

deck *verb* adorn, decorate, clothe, dress, attire, trim, festoon, garnish, garland, ornament, embellish, enhance, beautify, dress up, tart up (*inf*), bedeck, array. OPPOSITE: strip.

declaim *verb* orate, harangue, make a speech, lecture, pronounce, sermonize, hold forth, rant, proclaim, speak, enunciate, recite, perorate, spout, sound off (*inf*).

declaim against criticize, attack, speak out against, protest at, denounce, decry, inveigh against, rail at.

declamation *noun* harangue, tirade, recitation, oration, speech, address, lecture, discourse, sermon, oratory, grandiloquence.

declamatory *adj* rhetorical, bombastic, oratorical, high-flown, grandiloquent, magniloquent, fustian, turgid, orotund, pompous, theatrical, pretentious, stilted.

declaration *noun* **1** (*a declaration of war*) proclamation, announcement, notice, publication, statement, broadcast, promulgation, decree, edict, manifesto, pronouncement, notification, pronunciamento. **2** (*a declaration of his innocence*) statement, affirmation, maintaining, avowal, assertion, claim, swearing, asseveration, averment, acknowledgment, testimony, confirmation, proof, validation, attestation, deposition, profession. OPPOSITE: denial.

declare *verb* **1** (*declare war*) proclaim, announce, broadcast, make known, publish, promulgate, trumpet, pronounce, decree. **2** (*declared that he was innocent*) state, affirm, avow, assert, attest, aver, say, maintain, claim, contend, profess, allege, swear, testify, certify. OPPOSITE: deny.

declension *noun* decline, fall, deterioration, decay, decadence, degeneracy. OPPOSITE: rise.

declination *noun* inclination, slope, descent, declivity, deviation, divergence, departure.

decline *verb* **1** (*decline to discuss the matter*) refuse, turn down, reject, forgo, deny, say no to, rebuff, repudiate, give the thumbs down to (*inf*). OPPOSITE: accept. **2** (*the industry has declined*) decrease, diminish, lessen, get less, fade, dwindle, wane, ebb, sink, fall, fall off, taper off, fail, deteriorate, weaken, droop, flag, abate, languish, pine, degenerate, decay, waste away. OPPOSITE: flourish. **3** (*the land declines*) descend, sink, dip, slope, incline. OPPOSITE: ascend.

➤ *noun* **1** (*economic decline*) decrease, diminution, lessening, recession, wane, waning, deterioration, downturn, dwindling, falling, fall, slump, recession, weakening, degeneration, failure, decay, senility, decrepitude. **2** (*the decline of the land*) declivity, slope, incline, descent. OPPOSITE: ascent.

declivity *noun* descent, declination, downward slope, decline, incline, hill. OPPOSITE: acclivity.

decompose *verb* **1** (*dead plants decomposing*) rot, go bad, putrefy, decay, crumble, fall apart, break up. **2** (*decompose light into the colours of the spectrum*) disintegrate, dissolve, break down, break up, divide, analyse, dissect, atomize, distil, separate, resolve.

decomposition *noun* **1** (*decomposition of the dead plants*) rotting, putrefaction, putrescence, decay, corruption. **2** (*decomposition of light*) disintegration, analysis, breakdown, breakup, division, atomization, dissection, dissolution, separation, resolution. OPPOSITE: synthesis.

decor *noun* decoration, ornamentation, furnishing, furniture, colour scheme.

decorate *verb* **1** (*decorate a birthday card*) ornament, embellish, adorn, deck, bedeck, trim, garnish, garland, festoon, beautify, enhance, prettify. OPPOSITE: mar. **2** (*decorate the bathroom*) paint, wallpaper, paper, refurbish, renovate, furbish, do up (*inf*), tart up (*inf*). **3** (*decorated for services to the community*) cite, honour, give an award to.

decoration *noun* **1** (*the decoration took months*) embellishment, ornament, ornamentation, enhancement. **2** (*the simple decoration of the room*) decor, ornamentation, furnishing, furniture, colour scheme. **3** (*decorations on the Christmas tree*) adornment, trimming, garnish, ornament, flourish, frill, flounce, frippery, bauble, trinket, knick-knack, tinsel. **4** (*given a decoration for bravery*) medal, order, award, honour, citation, badge, ribbon, crown, star, laurel, garland.

decorous *adj* proper, seemly, decent, becoming, fitting, tasteful, comme il faut, apt, appropriate, suitable, correct, mannerly, dignified, sedate, demure, refined, well-behaved, genteel, respectable, elegant, polite. OPPOSITE: unseemly.

decorum *noun* propriety, correctness, appropriateness, seemliness, decency, etiquette, protocol, refinement, breeding, good taste, good manners, courtesy, politeness, dignity, respectability. OPPOSITE: impropriety.

decoy *verb* lure, allure, entice, tempt, induce, bait, inveigle, seduce, deceive, mislead, trap, ensnare, entrap. ➤ *noun* lure, enticement, inducement, temptation, attraction, bait, snare, trap, ensnarement, entrapment, pretence, fake.

decrease *verb* lessen, diminish, reduce, dwindle, decline, lower, wane, subside, ebb, fall, fall off, drop, abate, let up, slacken, ease, cut down, cut back, cut back on, curtail, taper off, peter out, shrink, contract. OPPOSITE: increase. ➤ *noun* lessening, diminution, reduction, decline, lowering, slackening, ebb, recession, wane, fall, falling-off, abatement, letting-up, cutback, retrenchment, curtailment, shrinkage, contraction. OPPOSITE: increase.

decree *noun* **1** (*the president's decree*) edict, order, command, precept, law, act, enactment, statute, mandate, rule, regulation, injunction, fiat, manifesto,

dictum, ordinance. **2** (*the decree of a court*) judgment, decision, ruling, verdict, finding, findings. ➤ *verb* order, command, adjudge, ordain, rule, enact, dictate, lay down, direct, appoint, proclaim, pronounce, decide, prescribe, enjoin, determine.

decrement *noun* decrease, diminution, decline, reduction. OPPOSITE: increment.

decrepit *adj* **1** (*decrepit old people*) infirm, enfeebled, feeble, weak, frail, crippled, incapacitated, debilitated, disabled, old, elderly, aged, doddering, tottering, senescent. OPPOSITE: youthful. **2** (*a decrepit building*) dilapidated, ramshackle, broken-down, run-down, tumbledown, rickety, worn-out, in bad condition, antiquated, superannuated.

decry *verb* disparage, belittle, deprecate, depreciate, underrate, underestimate, undervalue, diminish, detract, devalue, undervalue, play down, discredit, run down, abuse, criticize, condemn, denounce, rail against, defame, vilify, knock (*inf*), slate (*inf*), pull to pieces (*inf*), tear to shreds (*inf*). OPPOSITE: appreciate.

dedicate *verb* **1** (*dedicated himself to voluntary work*) devote, pledge, commit, assign, give, give over. **2** (*dedicate a church*) consecrate, sanctify, hallow, bless, make holy, set apart. OPPOSITE: desecrate. **3** (*dedicate the book to her*) inscribe, address, name.

dedicated *adj* **1** (*a dedicated musician*) committed, devoted, wholehearted, single-minded, enthusiastic, zealous, hard-working. OPPOSITE: apathetic. **2** (*a dedicated phone line*) customized, custom-built.

dedication *noun* **1** (*teach with dedication*) devotion, commitment, wholeheartedness, allegiance, single-mindedness, enthusiasm, zeal, loyalty, fidelity. **2** (*dedication of the church*) consecration, sanctification, hallowing, ordination, blessing. OPPOSITE: desecration. **3** (*a dedication in a book*) inscription, address, message.

deduce *verb* conclude, infer, gather, understand, derive, come to the conclusion, reason, presume, surmise.

deduct *verb* subtract, take away, withdraw, remove, take off, dock. OPPOSITE: add.

deduction *noun* **1** (*draw an obvious deduction*) conclusion, inference, corollary, finding, reasoning, result, assumption. **2** (*the deduction of tax and insurance*) subtraction, reduction, decrease, withdrawal, removal, taking-off, allowance, discount. OPPOSITE: addition.

deed *noun* **1** (*good deeds*) action, act, feat, exploit, achievement, accomplishment, enterprise, undertaking, performance, doing. **2** (*deeds to the land*) title, document, contract, agreement, indenture, instrument.

deem *verb* consider, judge, hold, feel, see, regard, think, imagine, believe, estimate, calculate, account, suppose.

deep *adj* **1** (*a deep hole*) profound, bottomless, fathomless, unfathomable, immeasurable, broad, wide, extensive, cavernous, yawning. OPPOSITE: shallow. **2** (*a deep roar*) low, low-pitched, bass, sonorous, resonant, rich, powerful, resounding, booming rumbling. OPPOSITE: high. **3** (*a deep blue*) dark, rich, intense, vivid, strong, full, rich. OPPOSITE: light. **4** (*regarded with deep suspicion*) grave, great, intense, extreme, profound, heartfelt, ardent, fervent, deep-rooted, deep-seated. **5** (*deep in thought*) engrossed, absorbed, preoccupied, intent, engaged, rapt, immersed, involved. **6** (*a deep*

secret) abstruse, obscure, difficult, unclear, mysterious, enigmatic, impenetrable, unfathomable, arcane, recondite, esoteric, incomprehensible. OPPOSITE: plain. **7** (*a deep thinker*) learned, intellectual, astute, perceptive, penetrating, shrewd, knowing, discerning, intelligent, wise, sagacious.
➤ *adv* a long way, far.
➤ *noun* **1** (*sea creatures of the deep*) sea, ocean, main, briny (*inf*). **2** (*in the deep of the night*) depth, bottom, vastness, middle, midst, dead, still.

deepen *verb* **1** (*deepen a channel*) dig, hollow, hollow out, excavate, scoop out, dredge, mine, sink. **2** (*deepened his knowledge*) intensify, increase, grow, amplify, augment, add to, magnify, heighten, strengthen, enhance. OPPOSITE: lessen.

deeply *adv* profoundly, extremely, very, intensely, greatly, strongly, thoroughly, seriously, earnestly.

deface *verb* disfigure, mar, spoil, ruin, damage, deform, blemish, flaw, mutilate, injure, vandalize, sully, tarnish. OPPOSITE: beautify.

defacement *noun* disfigurement, injury, ruin, damage, mutilation, vandalism, blemish, flaw. OPPOSITE: beautification.

de facto *adj* real, actual, existing, existent.
➤ *adv* in fact, in reality, in effect, actually, really, in actuality.

defalcation *noun* misappropriation, embezzlement, deficit, shortage, deficiency, default.

defamation *noun* aspersion, abuse, slander, libel, scandal, slur, smear, smear campaign, insult, backbiting, vilification, denigration, malediction, disparagement, calumny, traducement, obloquy, contumely, mudslinging (*inf*). OPPOSITE: praise.

defamatory *adj* abusive, slanderous, libellous, injurious, scandalous, insulting, backbiting, vilifying, malicious, denigrating, disparaging, traducing, contumelious, calumnious, maledictory, mudslinging (*inf*). OPPOSITE: complimentary.

defame *verb* cast aspersions on, insult, slander, libel, denigrate, run down, vilify, discredit, dishonour, malign, speak ill of, abuse, smear, asperse, besmirch, calumniate, traduce, disparage, belittle, throw mud at (*inf*), drag through the mud (*inf*). OPPOSITE: praise.

default *noun* failure, omission, neglect, lapse, oversight, want, lack, absence, deficiency, deficit, nonpayment.
➤ *verb* fail, neglect, dodge, evade, cheat, bilk, welsh (*inf*).

defaulter *noun* offender, delinquent, absentee, nonpayer, embezzler, cheat, bilker, welsher (*inf*).

defeat *verb* **1** (*defeat the enemy*) beat, conquer, vanquish, overcome, get the better of, rout, worst, overpower, overthrow, overwhelm, subdue, subjugate, quell, crush, quash, thrash, trounce, clobber (*inf*), lick (*inf*), run rings around (*inf*), make mincemeat of (*inf*), wipe the floor with (*inf*). OPPOSITE: surrender. **2** (*defeat a plan*) thwart, foil, frustrate, prevent, hinder, ruin, discomfit, impede, hamper, checkmate, balk, check, baffle, puzzle, perplex, confound.
➤ *noun* **1** (*the defeat of the enemy*) conquest, overthrow, overpowering, overwhelming, thrashing, beating, rout, quelling, crushing, quashing, vanquishment,

subjugation, trouncing. OPPOSITE: victory. **2** (*defeat of their plans*) frustration, reverse, setback, discomfiture, checkmate, failure, confounding, thwarting, prevention, hindrance, ruin, disappointment.

defeatist *noun* quitter, yielder, pessimist, doomwatcher, prophet of doom.

defecate *verb* **1** (*defecate after eating*) excrete, evacuate, empty one's bowels, move one's bowels, pass a motion, egest, do a poo (*inf*), do number two (*inf*), shit (*sl*), crap (*sl*). **2** (*defecated sewage*) purge, cleanse, purify, clarify, refine. OPPOSITE: pollute.

defecation *noun* **1** (*vomiting and defecation*) excretion, evacuation, bowel movement, egestion. **2** (*defecation of sewage*) purification, cleansing, clarification, purge. OPPOSITE: pollution.

defect *noun* imperfection, flaw, fault, blemish, weak spot, error, failing, weakness, deformity, shortcoming, deficiency, omission, default, lack, inadequacy, insufficiency, want. OPPOSITE: perfection.
➤ *verb* desert, abandon, forsake, change sides, turn traitor, apostatize, tergiversate, go over to the other side, rebel, renounce, repudiate, mutiny.

defection *noun* desertion, abandonment, dereliction, backsliding, apostasy, disloyalty, mutiny, rebellion, betrayal, treason, perfidy, tergiversation.

defective *adj* faulty, imperfect, flawed, impaired, broken, out of order, not working, deformed, inadequate, insufficient, incomplete, deficient, weak, lacking, wanting, low, short. OPPOSITE: perfect.

defector *noun* deserter, traitor, rebel, turncoat, betrayer, Judas, apostate, renegade, tergiversator, rat (*inf*).

defence *noun* **1** (*defence against enemy attack*) resistance, protection, guard, safeguard, security, shelter, cover, shield, screen, fortification, bulwark, rampart, buttress, fortress, bastion, keep, barricade. OPPOSITE: attack. **2** (*the city's defences*) resources, forces, weapons, armaments. **3** (*speak in defence of the proposal*) vindication, justification, excuse, explanation, extenuation, rebuttal, exoneration, plea, apology, apologia, argument. OPPOSITE: accusation.

defenceless *adj* unprotected, unguarded, unfortified, unarmed, exposed, vulnerable, wide open, weak, powerless, impotent, helpless. OPPOSITE: protected.

defend *verb* **1** (*defend a border*) resist, protect, guard, watch over, safeguard, shield, screen, shelter, secure, garrison, preserve, fortify, arm. OPPOSITE: attack. **2** (*defend the police's action*) support, endorse, uphold, maintain, sustain, vindicate, justify, plead, argue for, make a case for, champion, stand by, stick up for, represent, speak for, speak on behalf of. OPPOSITE: accuse.

defendant *noun* accused, offender, litigant, prisoner, respondent, appellant. OPPOSITE: plaintiff.

defender *noun* **1** (*defender of the castle*) protector, guard, escort, bodyguard, keeper, preserver, guardian. OPPOSITE: assailant. **2** (*a defender of the poor*) champion, advocate, supporter, guardian, endorser, upholder, backer, vindicator. OPPOSITE: accuser.

defensible *adj* **1** (*a defensible theory*) tenable, justifiable, plausible, vindicable, valid, secure, safe, maintainable, permissible, pardonable, excusable, unassailable. **2** (*a defensible building*) impregnable, impenetrable, safe, secure, fortified, invulnerable, unassailable.

defensive *adj* **1** (*defensive measures against attack*) defending, protective, protecting, resisting, shielding, opposing, watchful, on the defensive, on guard. OPPOSITE: attacking. **2** (*defensive about his own ideas*) oversensitive, self-justifying, self-defensive, prickly (*inf*).

defer[1] *verb* (*defer a decision*) delay, postpone, put off, adjourn, shelve, suspend, hold over, procrastinate, hold in abeyance, temporize, prorogue, put on ice (*inf*), put on the back burner (*inf*). OPPOSITE: hasten.

defer[2] *verb* **defer to** (*I defer to your wishes*) comply with, yield to, submit to, bow to, accede to, surrender to, capitulate to, give in to, give way to. OPPOSITE: resist.

deference *noun* **1** (*deference to one's elders*) respect, regard, esteem, honour, attention, thoughtfulness, reverence, homage, veneration, consideration, courtesy, politeness, courteousness. OPPOSITE: disrespect. **2** (*deference to the experts*) compliance, submission, yielding, capitulation, acquiescence, complaisance, obedience, nonresistance. OPPOSITE: resistance.

deferential *adj* obedient, respectful, considerate, attentive, thoughtful, reverential, courteous, polite, submissive, compliant, obeisant, obsequious, complaisant, yielding, acquiescent. OPPOSITE: defiant.

deferment *noun* deferral, delay, postponement, suspension, shelving, adjournment, moratorium, stay, respite, abeyance, procrastination.

defiance *noun* resistance, opposition, confrontation, challenge, insubordination, disobedience, insolence, scorn, rebelliousness, disregard, contempt, recalcitrance, contumacy. OPPOSITE: compliance.

defiant *adj* antagonistic, resistant, aggressive, belligerent, challenging, rebellious, provocative, audacious, bold, daring, insolent, disobedient, insubordinate, mutinous, stubborn, unyielding, recalcitrant, contumacious, refractory, truculent. OPPOSITE: compliant.

deficiency *noun* **1** (*vitamin deficiency*) lack, shortage, want, insufficiency, dearth, deficit, scantiness, scarcity, inadequacy, absence, paucity. OPPOSITE: abundance. **2** (*deficiencies in the process*) weakness, weak point, failing, shortcoming, imperfection, fault, defect, flaw. OPPOSITE: perfection.

deficient *adj* **1** (*deficient in proteins*) lacking, short, short of, wanting, insufficient, inadequate, scarce, scant, skimpy, scanty, exiguous. OPPOSITE: abundant. **2** (*a deficient process*) defective, imperfect, incomplete, flawed, faulty, infirm, weak. OPPOSITE: perfect.

deficit *noun* shortage, shortfall, deficiency, loss, arrears, debt. OPPOSITE: surplus.

defile *verb* **1** (*defile the minds of young people*) pollute, soil, dirty, pervert, infect, befoul, contaminate, sully, taint, tarnish, corrupt, poison, vitiate, besmirch, disgrace, degrade, debase. OPPOSITE: purify. **2** (*defile a sanctuary*) profane, desecrate, pollute, contaminate, treat sacrilegiously. OPPOSITE: hallow. **3** (*defile a woman*) deflower, ravish, violate, rape, molest.

definable *adj* specific, exact, determinable, ascertainable, perceptible, describable, fixed, definite, precise. OPPOSITE: indefinable.

define **1** (*define a word*) describe, explain, interpret, clarify, spell out, specify, determine, designate, fix, lay down. **2** (*define a boundary*) delineate, outline, demarcate, limit, specify, determine, establish, fix, bound, circumscribe.

definite *adj* **1** (*definite arrangements*) certain, fixed, settled, positive, sure, decided, guaranteed, final, conclusive, determined. OPPOSITE: possible. **2** (*a definite change in her behaviour*) clear, clear-cut, explicit, exact, precise, specific, marked, particular, plain, obvious, unambiguous. OPPOSITE: vague.

definitely *adv* surely, certainly, positively, absolutely, plainly, unmistakably, unquestionably, without question, without doubt, beyond doubt, undeniably, doubtless.

definition *noun* **1** (*the definition of words*) description, explanation, meaning, interpretation, exposition, clarification, elucidation. **2** (*the photograph lacks definition*) distinctness, clarity, sharpness, precision, contrast, focus. OPPOSITE: blurredness. **3** (*definition of boundaries*) demarcation, delineation, delimitation, determination, specification, fixing, settling.

definitive *adj* **1** (*a definitive statement*) final, conclusive, decisive, ultimate, authoritative, complete, perfect, categorical, absolute, positive. **2** (*a definitive book*) authoritative, exhaustive, approved, best, most reliable, authorized.

deflate **1** (*deflate a tyre*) collapse, let down, flatten, empty, shrink, contract, void, puncture. OPPOSITE: inflate. **2** (*feel deflated after the failure*) chasten, humble, humiliate, subdue, mortify, squash, dash, discourage, dispirit, put down (*inf*). OPPOSITE: boost. **3** (*deflate prices*) reduce, lower, diminish, devalue, depreciate, depress.

deflect *verb* deviate, diverge, veer, swerve, bend, curve, turn, change course, change direction, twist, divert, sidetrack, switch, shy, turn aside, turn away, glance off, ricochet.

deflection *noun* deviation, divergence, declination, refraction, aberration, diversion, bend, curve, turn, twist, swerve, switch.

deflower *verb* rape, ravish, violate, despoil, defile, mar, harm, spoil, molest, assault, debauch, corrupt, seduce, desecrate.

deform *verb* distort, misshape, contort, twist, warp, malform, disfigure, deface, mar, injure, maim, cripple, mutilate, mangle.

deformed *adj* misshapen, malformed, disfigured, ugly, injured, maimed, crippled, twisted, crooked, bent, contorted, warped, gnarled.

deformity *noun* malformation, abnormality, misshapenness, distortion, disfigurement, crookedness, ugliness, monstrosity.

defraud *verb* cheat, swindle, fleece, rook (*inf*), cozen, dupe, deceive, take in, rob, bilk, beguile, trick, hoodwink, bamboozle (*inf*), rip off (*inf*), diddle (*inf*), do (*inf*), con (*inf*), sting (*inf*), take for a ride, (*inf*), pull a fast one on (*inf*).

defray *verb* meet, pay, cover, clear, repay, recompense, reimburse, refund, discharge, settle, liquidate.

deft *adj* adept, dextrous, adroit, skilful, clever, able, expert, proficient, handy, neat, agile, nimble, brisk. OPPOSITE: clumsy.

defunct *adj* **1** (*his defunct predecessors*) dead, gone, deceased, departed, extinct. OPPOSITE: living. **2** (*a long defunct tv programme*) obsolete, old-fashioned, outmoded, passé, expired, invalid, inoperative, not functioning.

defy *verb* **1** (*defied his parents' wishes*) flout, disregard, ignore, scorn, scoff at, deride, spurn, slight, disobey, challenge, brave, dare, confront, provoke, resist, withstand, stand up to, defeat, repel, oppose, thumb one's nose at. OPPOSITE: obey. **2** (*defies description*) elude, frustrate, avoid, foil, baffle, withstand.

degeneracy *noun* dissoluteness, dissipation, depravity, decadence, corruption, immorality, debasement, degradation, profligacy, decline, deterioration, degeneration, decay, meanness, lowness, inferiority, turpitude, baseness. OPPOSITE: refinement.

degenerate *verb* decline, deteriorate, decay, retrogress, sink, lapse, slip, worsen, fail, fall, fall away, go downhill (*inf*), go the dogs (*inf*), go to pot (*inf*). OPPOSITE: improve.
➤ *adj* dissolute, debauched, depraved, corrupt, decadent, fallen, immoral, low, mean, base, wicked, vile, sinful, sordid, debased, degraded, degenerated, inferior. OPPOSITE: superior.
➤ *noun* deviant, pervert, rake, decadent, reprobate, profligate.

degeneration *noun* decline, deterioration, degeneracy, decay, drop, slide, lapse, sinking, descent, decrease, retrogression, depravation, debasement, failure, worsening, degradation, dissolution. OPPOSITE: improvement.

degradation *noun* **1** (*a life of misery and degradation*) poverty, misery, shame, disgrace, ignominy, deprivation, squalor, dirtiness, immorality, corruption, decadence, depravity, vice, dissoluteness, debauchery. OPPOSITE: honour. **2** (*the degradation of democracy*) degeneration, abasement, decline, deterioration, decadence, debasement.

degrade *verb* **1** (*pornography degrades women*) dishonour, humiliate, demean, disgrace, discredit, belittle, lower, abase, cheapen, debase, corrupt, pervert, vitiate, deprave, defame, disparage, depreciate, deteriorate. OPPOSITE: exalt. **2** (*degraded to a lower rank*) demote, downgrade, cashier, depose, reduce in rank, lower in rank, dethrone, unseat, drum out (*inf*), kick upstairs (*inf*). OPPOSITE: promote.

degrading *adj* dishonouring, demeaning, debasing, belittling, cheapening, dishonourable, disgraceful, shameful, humiliating.

degree *noun* **1** (*a high degree of accuracy*) extent, measure, amount, intensity, strength, magnitude, range, scope, level, standard, proportion, rate, ratio. **2** (*change by slow degree*) stage, step, rung, gradation, level, grade, point, measure, mark, notch, division, interval. **3** (*people of high degree*) grade, rank, class, order, standing, status, station, position.

by degrees gradually, step by step, little by little, bit by bit, slowly, by stages.

dehydrate *verb* dry, dry out, dry up, parch, desiccate, exsiccate, sear, drain, evaporate. OPPOSITE: moisten.

deify *verb* worship, adore, revere, aggrandize, elevate, exalt, ennoble, glorify, idolize, apotheosize, immortalize, pay homage to, venerate, idolize. OPPOSITE: debase.

deign *verb* condescend, stoop, lower oneself, demean oneself, see fit, consent. OPPOSITE: refuse.

deity *noun* God, god, goddess, immortal, divine being, supreme being, divinity, godhead. OPPOSITE: mortal.

deject *verb* dishearten, depress, cast down, sadden, demoralize, dismay, discourage, dispirit. OPPOSITE: cheer.

dejected *adj* downcast, despondent, disconsolate, downhearted, dispirited, disheartened, crestfallen, cast down, down, depressed, sad, unhappy, miserable, forlorn, doleful, woebegone, gloomy, glum, melancholy, blue, down in the dumps (*inf*). OPPOSITE: cheerful.

dejection *noun* despondency, downheartedness, misery, wretchedness, depression, unhappiness, sadness, gloom, low spirits, dispiritedness, disconsolateness, despair, melancholy, sorrow, blues, the dumps (*inf*). OPPOSITE: cheerfulness.

delay *verb* **1** (*delayed my departure*) defer, postpone, put off, adjourn, suspend, shelve, hold over, procrastinate, temporize, stall, put on ice (*inf*), put on the back burner (*inf*). OPPOSITE: advance. **2** (*delayed by an accident*) hold up, obstruct, hinder, impede, hold back, slow down, retard, set back, bog down, detain, arrest, stop, halt, restrain. OPPOSITE: hasten. **3** (*don't delay*) dawdle, linger, loiter, lag, hang on, dilly-dally (*inf*). OPPOSITE: hurry.
➤ *noun* **1** (*send the letter without delay*) deferment, postponement, suspension, procrastination, lull, interlude, pause, wait, break, breather, hiatus, interval. OPPOSITE: continuation. **2** (*delays caused by fog*) holdup, obstruction, hindrance, impediment, stoppage, setback, check, interruption. **3** (*their delay left us behind schedule*) dawdling, lingering, loitering, dalliance, hesitation. OPPOSITE: haste.

delectable *adj* **1** (*delectable food*) delicious, choice, luscious, palatable, savoury, flavoursome, toothsome, ambrosial, scrumptious (*inf*), yummy (*inf*), tasty, dainty, appetizing. **2** (*a delectable voice*) delightful, attractive, inviting, adorable, ravishing, charming, agreeable, pleasing, pleasant. OPPOSITE: repulsive.

delectation *noun* delight, enjoyment, pleasure, gratification, joy, satisfaction, excitement, amusement, entertainment, refreshment, relish, ecstasy, rapture.

delegate *noun* representative, envoy, ambassador, spokesman, spokeswoman, spokesperson, messenger, agent, go-between, deputy, commissioner.
➤ *verb* **1** (*delegate work to others*) give, commit, transfer, handover, entrust, assign, devolve. **2** (*the army was delegated to protect the citizens*) depute, appoint, commission, authorize, empower, mandate, nominate, name, select, choose, elect, ordain, charge.

delegation *noun* **1** (*send a delegation to investigate the alleged atrocities*) deputation, contingent, committee, embassy, legation, mission. **2** (*the delegation of authority*) assignment, devolvement, devolution, authorization, transference, committal, commissioning.

delete *verb* cross out, strike out, obliterate, efface, cancel, expunge, remove, take out, rub out, erase, cut out, edit, edit out, blue-pencil, eradicate. OPPOSITE: insert.

deleterious *adj* harmful, noxious, injurious, hurtful, pernicious, ruinous, disadvantageous, destructive, damaging, detrimental, unwholesome, bad, noisome. OPPOSITE: beneficial.

deliberate *verb* consider, ponder, ruminate, reflect, think, cogitate, meditate, muse, mull over, weigh, evaluate, debate.
➤ *adj* **1** (*a deliberate act of disobedience*) intentional, premeditated, calculated, planned, designed, purposeful, conscious, meant, considered, painstaking, wilful, studied, preplanned, preconceived, predetermined. OPPOSITE: accidental. **2** (*walk with slow deliberate steps*) cautious, careful, circumspect, thoughtful, methodical, unhurried, slow, steady, ponderous, laborious, leisurely, measured. OPPOSITE: hasty.

deliberately *adv* **1** (*the fire was started deliberately*) intentionally, on purpose, wilfully, knowingly, purposefully, consciously, wittingly, calculatedly. OPPOSITE: accidentally. **2** (*move slowly and deliberately*) cautiously, carefully, circumspectly, thoughtfully, methodically, unhurriedly, slowly, leisurely. OPPOSITE: hastily.

deliberation *noun* **1** (*after an hour's deliberation*) consideration, rumination, reflection, thought, cogitation, meditation, pondering, mulling, study, scrutiny. **2** (*the result of their deliberations*) discussion, debate, consultation, conference. **3** (*speak with great deliberation*) care, caution, circumspection, wariness, thoughtfulness, steadiness, laboriousness, prudence. OPPOSITE: rashness.

delicacy *noun* **1** (*the delicacy of her features*) fineness, daintiness, fragility, flimsiness, slightness, slenderness, lightness, exquisiteness, grace, gracefulness, elegance, subtlety. OPPOSITE: coarseness. **2** (*the delicacy of her health*) frailty, weakness, debility, infirmity, sickness. OPPOSITE: robustness. **3** (*deal with the matter with delicacy*) tact, sensitivity, sensibility, scrupulousness, care, consideration. OPPOSITE: tactlessness. **4** (*delicacy of taste*) fastidiousness, discrimination, refinement, finesse, elegance, nicety, purity, precision, accuracy. OPPOSITE: indelicacy. **5** (*a sweet delicacy*) morsel, titbit, dainty, sweetmeat, luxury, treat, appetizer, savoury, bonne bouche.

delicate *adj* **1** (*a delicate glass vase*) fine, dainty, exquisite, choice, elegant, graceful, flimsy, slender, slight, fragile, tender. OPPOSITE: robust. **2** (*delicate in health*) weak, frail, infirm, ailing, sickly. OPPOSITE: healthy. **3** (*a delicate shade of yellow*) faint, muted, pale, understated, subdued, soft, subtle, pastel. OPPOSITE: garish. **4** (*deal with a delicate issue*) sensitive, tricky, critical, precarious, difficult, ticklish. **5** (*needs delicate treatment*) sensitive, tactful, diplomatic, careful, considerate, discreet. **6** (*delicate taste*) fastidious, discriminating, refined, finicky, choosy, pure. **7** (*a delicate mechanism*) sensitive, accurate, exact, precise.

delicious *adj* **1** (*delicious food*) tasty, appetizing, luscious, scrumptious (*inf*), yummy (*inf*), ambrosial, toothsome, succulent, mouth-watering, savoury, palatable, delectable, dainty, choice. OPPOSITE: unpalatable. **2** (*a delicious sensation*) delightful, exquisite, charming, enchanting, agreeable, nice, pleasant, enjoyable. OPPOSITE: loathsome.

delight *verb* gladden, excite, entrance, captivate, charm, enchant, ravish, thrill, transport, enrapture, please, gratify, cheer, bowl over (*inf*), send (*inf*), tickle pink (*inf*). OPPOSITE: disappoint.
➤ *noun* charm, enchantment, happiness, excitement, bliss, ecstasy, rapture, transport, elation, felicity, joy, jubilation, delectation, pleasure, gratification, enjoyment. OPPOSITE: disgust.

delight in enjoy, love, like, relish, savour, take pleasure in, glory in, revel in. OPPOSITE: dislike.

delighted *adj* happy, glad, pleased, joyful, excited, enchanted, elated, overjoyed, ecstatic, gratified, enraptured, blissful, transported, thrilled, jubilant, joyous, over the moon (*inf*), tickled pink (*inf*), pleased as Punch (*inf*), happy as Larry (*inf*). OPPOSITE: disappointed.

delightful *adj* pleasing, pleasant, fascinating, charming, enchanting, ravishing, captivating, thrilling, rapturous, engaging, attractive, heavenly, lovely, pretty, beautiful, delectable, agreeable, enjoyable, entertaining, amusing, diverting, gratifying, out of this world (*inf*), top-notch (*inf*), terrific (*inf*), smashing (*inf*). OPPOSITE: nasty.

delineate *verb* describe, depict, portray, set forth, picture, draw, sketch, outline, draft, trace, design, chart, map, map out.

delineation *noun* description, representation, depiction, portrayal, portrait, picture, drawing, sketch, draft, outline, profile, diagram, chart, map, account, narration.

delinquency *noun* crime, offence, misdeed, misdemeanour, misconduct, wrongdoing, transgression, dereliction, failure, omission, negligence.

delinquent *noun* offender, wrongdoer, criminal, malefactor, miscreant, transgressor, vandal, ruffian, young offender, lawbreaker, culprit.
➤ *adj* offending, criminal, miscreant, lawbreaking, culpable.

delirious *adj* **1** (*delirious with fever*) raving, incoherent, demented, deranged, irrational, babbling, insane, mad, crazy, out of one's mind. OPPOSITE: sane. **2** (*delirious with excitement*) frenzied, frantic, wild, ecstatic, carried away, euphoric, beside oneself, hysterical.

delirium *noun* **1** (*suffer from delirium*) madness, insanity, derangement, raving, incoherence, hallucination, fever. OPPOSITE: sanity. **2** (*a delirium of joy*) frenzy, passion, hysteria, ecstasy, euphoria, excitement, rapture.

deliver **1** (*deliver the post*) take, send, transmit, convey, transport, dispatch, bear, carry, bring. **2** (*deliver a speech*) voice, utter, speak, present, give, read, declare, announce, proclaim, broadcast, promulgate, enunciate, pronounce. **3** (*delivered into his care*) transfer, entrust, commit, hand over, turn over, make over, consign, give, give up, grant, surrender, relinquish, yield, cede.

OPPOSITE: appropriate. **4** (*delivered from suffering*) release, liberate, free, set free, loose, set loose, emancipate, acquit, discharge, rescue, save, redeem, manumit. OPPOSITE: capture. **5** (*deliver a blow*) direct, deal, administer, inflict, aim, throw, strike, launch. **6** (*deliver better services*) fulfil, achieve, supply, provide, come up with, carry out, do, implement.

deliverance *noun* release, liberation, emancipation, freedom, discharge, acquittal, rescue, salvation, redemption. OPPOSITE: capture.

delivery *noun* **1** (*delivery of the goods*) transport, transportation, conveyance, carriage, distribution, transmission, consignment, dispatch, shipment, transfer, surrender, handing over. **2** (*have a clear delivery*) articulation, enunciation, elocution, intonation, diction, utterance, speech. **3** (*the mother had an easy delivery*) childbirth, confinement, labour, parturition, accouchement.

delude *verb* deceive, mislead, misguide, dupe, beguile, defraud, cheat, fool, trick, outwit, cozen, take in, hoodwink, bamboozle (*inf*), con (*inf*), take for a ride (*inf*), lead up the garden path (*inf*), pull a fast one on (*inf*), pull someone's leg (*inf*), pull the wool over someone's eyes (*inf*).

deluge *noun* **1** (*homes damaged in the deluge*) flood, inundation, cataclysm, downpour, cloudburst, overflow, rush, torrent, spate, flash flood. OPPOSITE: drought. **2** (*a deluge of letters*) flood, inundation, rush, torrent, spate, avalanche.
➤ *verb* **1** (*rain deluging a village*) flood, inundate, soak, drench, overrun, overwhelm, engulf, drown, submerge. **2** (*deluged with complaints*) flood, inundate, overwhelm, swamp, engulf, drown, submerge.

delusion *noun* **1** (*under the delusion that people are basically selfless*) illusion, hallucination, fancy, mirage, vision, dream, misapprehension, misconception, misunderstanding, fool's paradise, error, mistake, fallacy, deception, self-deception. OPPOSITE: reality. **2** (*tricked by a delusion*) artifice, trick, ruse, deception, deceit, imposture, fraud, hoax.

delusive *adj* misleading, deceptive, fallacious, illusive, illusory, imaginary. OPPOSITE: real.

de luxe *adj* luxurious, luxury, choice, select, superior, exclusive, expensive, costly, rich, lavish, sumptuous, grand, palatial, elegant, plush (*inf*).

delve *verb* **1** (*delved into a rucksack*) dig, burrow, ferret out, unearth, probe, search, rummage, ransack, hunt through. **2** (*delved into his past*) examine, investigate, research, look into, probe.

demagogue *noun* orator, agitator, firebrand, rabble-rouser, haranguer, troublemaker.

demand *verb* **1** (*demanded action now*) request, call for, ask for, press for, solicit, claim, lay claim to, insist on, order, exact. OPPOSITE: waive. **2** (*the task demands a lot of hard work*) require, need, necessitate, call for, involve. OPPOSITE: obviate. **3** (*'Can I go now?' he demanded*) ask, question, interrogate, inquire, query. OPPOSITE: reply.
➤ *noun* **1** (*children making constant demands*) request, claim, entreaty, order, requisition, command, clamour, direction, charge, bidding, behest. **2** (*the demands of the work*) requirement, need, want, claim, necessity,

exigency. **3** (*respond to a demand*) question, query, inquiry, interrogation. OPPOSITE: answer.
in demand sought-after, asked for, requested, required, popular, fashionable, trendy (*inf*).

demanding *adj* **1** (*a demanding task*) challenging, trying, difficult, hard, tough, exacting, taxing, tiring, trying, exigent. OPPOSITE: easy. **2** (*a demanding child*) insistent, nagging, harassing, clamorous, trying. OPPOSITE: easygoing.

demarcation *noun* distinction, differentiation, division, separation, delimitation, marking off, definition, boundary, border, limit, margin, bound, confine.

demean *verb* lower, humble, abase, belittle, devalue, demote, descend, stoop, debase, degrade. OPPOSITE: exalt.

demeanour *noun* behaviour, conduct, bearing, manner, air, appearance, mien, carriage, deportment.

demented *adj* insane, deranged, unhinged, unbalanced, mad, crazy, out of one's mind, of unsound mind, touched, idiotic, lunatic, non compos mentis, daft (*inf*), barmy (*inf*), nuts (*inf*), loopy (*inf*), dotty (*inf*), batty (*inf*), bonkers (*inf*), off one's rocker (*inf*), off one's nutter (*inf*), round the bend (*inf*), round the twist (*inf*), need one's head examining (*inf*), out to lunch (*inf*).

demerit *noun* fault, misdeed, crime, offence, delinquency.

demesne *noun* estate, land, property, realm, domain.

demise *noun* **1** (*since his demise*) death, dying, decease, expiration, passing, passing on, passing away. OPPOSITE: birth. **2** (*the demise of communism*) collapse, cessation, downfall, failure, ruin, end, termination. **3** (*the demise of lands*) transfer, conveyance, transmission, alienation.
➤ *verb* bequeath, leave, will, transfer, convey.

democracy *noun* self-government, autonomy, representative government, popular government, republic, commonwealth.

democratic *adj* egalitarian, republican, autonomous, self-governing, popular, representative. OPPOSITE: autocratic.

demolish *verb* **1** (*demolish buildings*) knock down, destroy, raze, level, flatten, bulldoze, tear down, break down, pull down, dismantle, take down. OPPOSITE: build. **2** (*demolish someone's ideas*) destroy, wreck, ruin, devastate, shatter. **3** (*demolish one's opponents*) defeat, conquer, overwhelm, crush, overthrow, quash, suppress, annihilate, vanquish, wipe out, trounce, rout, drub, slaughter (*inf*), hammer (*inf*), clobber (*inf*), lick (*inf*), thrash (*inf*), wipe with floor with (*inf*).

demolition *noun* **1** (*the demolition of a building*) knocking down, destruction, razing, flattening, pulling down, bulldozing, devastation, ruin, wrecking. OPPOSITE: building. **2** (*the demolition of the opposition*) defeat, annihilation, conquest, overthrow, crushing, routing, slaughter (*inf*), hammering (*inf*), clobbering (*inf*), thrashing (*inf*).

demon *noun* **1** (*possessed by a demon*) fiend, devil, goblin, imp, evil spirit, cacodemon, afreet, incubus, succubus. OPPOSITE: angel. **2** (*the despot is an absolute demon*) rogue, villain, scoundrel, knave, fiend, brute, beast, savage, barbarian, monster, ogre. **3** (*a demon dancer*) fiend, addict, fanatic, wizard, master, ace (*inf*), freak (*inf*).

demonic *adj* **1** (*demonic forces*) demoniac, demoniacal, evil, wicked, fiendish, diabolic, diabolical, devilish, satanic, hellish, infernal. OPPOSITE: angelic. **2** (*with demonic intensity*) frenzied, frenetic, frantic, hectic, maniacal, rabid, feverish, delirious, mad, crazed, demented, hysterical.

demonstrable *adj* verifiable, provable, attestable, arguable, evident, obvious, self-evident, confirmable, evincible.

demonstrate *verb* **1** (*demonstrate a link between smoking and cancer*) show, prove, substantiate, establish, display, manifest, evince, indicate. OPPOSITE: disprove. **2** (*demonstrated her musical talent*) show, display, exhibit, express, indicate, manifest. **3** (*demonstrate how to do a job*) explain, illustrate, describe, show, teach, make clear. **4** (*demonstrate against cuts in finance*) protest, march, rally, strike, picket, parade, sit in.

demonstration *noun* **1** (*a demonstration of his commitment*) display, exhibition, manifestation, showing, show, evidence, proof, substantiation, indication, verification, affirmation, testimony, confirmation. OPPOSITE: concealment. **2** (*give a demonstration of new products*) explanation, exposition, presentation, experiment, trial, illustration, example. **3** (*students staged a mass demonstration*) march, protest march, rally, mass rally, parade, protest, sit-in, demo (*inf*).

demonstrative *adj* **1** (*demonstrative in welcoming us*) open, unreserved, unrestrained, expressive, communicative, emotional, loving, warm, affectionate, effusive. OPPOSITE: reserved. **2** (*demonstrative diagrams*) illustrative, indicative, symptomatic, explanatory. **3** (*demonstrative proof*) indisputable, convincing, telling, conclusive, absolute, certain, sure, incontrovertible, irrefutable. OPPOSITE: debatable.

demoralize *verb* **1** (*teachers demoralized by yet more paperwork*) dishearten, dispirit, discourage, depress, deject, daunt, cast down, unnerve, unman, weaken, enfeeble, cripple, crush, subdue. OPPOSITE: encourage. **2** (*demoralize human nature*) corrupt, deprave, pervert, debase, defile, contaminate, debauch, vitiate. OPPOSITE: improve.

demote *verb* downgrade, degrade, cashier, depose, relegate, reduce in rank, strip of rank, humble, declass, disrate. OPPOSITE: promote.

demulcent *adj* soothing, lenitive, mild, calming, sedative, emollient, softening, mollifying. OPPOSITE: irritant.

demur *verb* object, raise objections, protest, dispute, take exception, be reluctant, be unwilling, scruple, hesitate, refuse, dissent, balk, cavil. OPPOSITE: consent. ➤ *noun* demurral, objection, protest, dispute, dissent, hesitation, qualm, misgivings, reservation, reluctance, scruple.

demure *adj* modest, diffident, shy, bashful, retiring, reserved, meek, unassuming, sedate, staid, sober, grave, discreet, decorous, prudish, straitlaced, priggish, puritanical, prim. OPPOSITE: wanton.

den *noun* **1** (*a lion's den*) lair, hole, cavern, cave, hollow, hideout, hideaway, haunt, shelter. **2** (*a den of thieves*) haunt, meeting place, dive (*inf*), joint (*inf*). **3** (*shut himself in his den*) study, retreat, hideaway, sanctuary, cloister, snuggery, sanctum, sanctum sanctorum.

denial *noun* **1** (*a denial of the rumours*) contradiction, negation, refutation, disavowal, disclaimer, repudiation, retraction, disaffirmation, dissent, renunciation, abjuration. OPPOSITE: confirmation. **2** (*the denial of justice to all*) refusal, rejection, rebuff, veto, declination, proscription, prohibition. OPPOSITE: consent. **3** (*denial of one's friends*) disowning, renunciation, repudiation, rejection, forsaking, disavowal.

denigrate *verb* disparage, belittle, defame, run down, diminish, detract from, slander, libel, besmirch, blacken, deprecate, traduce, vilify, calumniate, malign, cast aspersions on, speak ill of, throw mud at (*inf*). OPPOSITE: praise.

denizen *noun* citizen, resident, occupier, occupant, inhabitant, dweller, habitant.

denominate *verb* designate, name, style, entitle, dub, christen, call, term.

denomination *noun* **1** (*religious denominations*) church, school, creed, faith, persuasion, order, religion, sect, tradition, communion. **2** (*stamps of different denominations*) grade, unit, value. **3** (*animals grouped under different denominations*) class, classification, grouping, group, kind, sort, type, category. **4** (*known under various denominations*) designation, appellation, name, term, label, tag, style, title, handle (*inf*), moniker (*inf*).

denote *verb* **1** (*a wildcard is denoted by an asterisk*) indicate, betoken, signify, be a sign of, symbolize, mean, imply, stand for, represent, typify, designate, mark. **2** (*this prefix denotes 'again'*) mean, refer to, signify, indicate, connote, imply, allude to.

denouement *noun* climax, culmination, conclusion, finale, final act, last act, termination, resolution, solution, outcome, issue, result, upshot.

denounce *verb* **1** (*denounce the government*) condemn, criticize, decry, denunciate, deplore, arraign, attack, censure, revile, impugn, upbraid, rebuke, castigate, rail against, inveigh against, fulminate against. OPPOSITE: extol. **2** (*denounced him to the police*) accuse, charge, inform against, incriminate, indict, bring charges against, take to court, impeach, vilify, defame, brand, stigmatize.

dense *adj* **1** (*a dense forest*) compacted, solid, thick, compact, close, compressed, condensed, concentrated, packed, crammed, crowded. OPPOSITE: sparse. **2** (*dense fog*) thick, impenetrable, concentrated, opaque. **3** (*stop being so dense!*) stupid, obtuse, dull, dull-witted, slow, slow-witted, thick (*inf*), dim (*inf*), dim-witted, stolid, crass, blockish. OPPOSITE: clever.

density *noun* **1** (*density of housing*) denseness, thickness, solidity, bulk, mass, closeness, compactness, impenetrability. **2** (*his density of mind*) stupidity, obtuseness, dullness, slowness, stolidity, crassness, crassitude. OPPOSITE: cleverness.

dent *verb* gouge, depress, indent, dint, press in, chip, notch, groove, hollow.

≫ *noun* hollow, depression, dint, pit, concavity, hole, impression, indentation, notch, chip.

denude *verb* strip, divest, bare, expose, uncover, denudate. OPPOSITE: clothe.

denunciation *noun* condemnation, criticism, denouncement, censure, reproof, castigation, vituperation, accusation, arraignment, fulmination, animadversion, obloquy. OPPOSITE: eulogy.

deny *verb* **1** (*deny an accusation*) contradict, dispute, disprove, oppose, disagree with, dissent from, disclaim, retract, controvert, negate, refute, nullify, repudiate, gainsay. OPPOSITE: confirm. **2** (*he was denied access to the children*) refuse, withhold, reject, turn down, prohibit, forbid, veto, proscribe. OPPOSITE: allow. **3** (*deny one's friends*) disown, renounce, disavow, turn one's back on, abjure, disclaim, recant, repudiate.

deodorant *noun* antiperspirant, air-freshener, deodorizer, fumigant, disinfectant.

depart *verb* go, leave, start, set out, set off, decamp, abscond, escape, go away, go off, take one's leave, get going, disappear, vanish, exit, make an exit, make oneself scarce, quit, withdraw, retreat, retire, make tracks (*inf*), skive (*inf*), clear off (*inf*), shove off (*inf*), push off (*inf*), skedaddle (*inf*), vamoose (*inf*), split (*inf*), scarper (*inf*), do a runner (*inf*), hit the road (*inf*), hightail it (*inf*), make a bolt for it (*inf*). OPPOSITE: arrive.

depart from deviate from, diverge from, digress from, veer from, swerve from, differ from, vary from, branch off from.

departed *adj* dead, deceased, late, gone, passed away, passed on, expired.

department *noun* **1** (*the research department*) branch, division, subdivision, section, office, agency, bureau, unit. **2** (*that's not my department*) sphere, realm, domain, province, area, responsibility, area of responsibility, authority, line, station, function, specialty, speciality.

departure *noun* **1** (*his departure for France*) exit, going, going away, going off, leaving, leave-taking, setting out, setting off, disappearance, withdrawal, exodus, retreat, retirement. OPPOSITE: arrival. **2** (*a radical departure from the norm*) deviation, divergence, digression, veering, variation, difference, branching off, novelty, innovation.

depend *verb* **depend on** **1** (*he depended on us for support*) rely on, count on, bank on, lean on, cling to, trust in, have confidence in, confide in, put one's faith in. **2** (*the economy depends on tourism*) be dependent, hang on, hinge on, turn on, rest on, be influenced by, be determined by, be based on, be contingent on, be subject to.

dependable *adj* reliable, trusty, trustworthy, responsible, sure, steady, steadfast, stable, unfailing, faithful, true. OPPOSITE: unreliable.

dependant *noun* child, minor, relative, charge, hanger-on, protégé, protégée, parasite, minion, retainer, subordinate, henchman.

dependence *noun* **1** (*place dependence in someone*) reliance, trust, faith, confidence. **2** (*dependence on alcohol*) addiction, attachment, habit, weakness, subordination, subjection, subservience, abuse,

helplessness, vulnerability, defencelessness. OPPOSITE: independence. **3** (*the economy's dependence on tourism*) reliance, bearing, relevance, influence, connection, relationship.

dependency *noun* **1** (*try to reduce dependency on his mother*) reliance, dependence, trust, faith, confidence. **2** (*European countries and their dependencies*) colony, province, protectorate. **3** (*alcohol dependency*) addiction, dependence, attachment, habit, weakness, subservience, abuse.

dependent *adj* relying, reliant, counting, clinging, helpless, weak, defenceless, vulnerable, immature, subordinate, supported, sustained, subject. OPPOSITE: independent.

dependent on contingent on, depending on, determined by, conditioned by, conditional on, subject to.

depict *verb* **1** (*depict in a work of art*) portray, sketch, delineate, draw, paint, outline, picture, illustrate, represent, chart, trace, characterize, detail. **2** (*the story depicts events before the war*) portray, describe, narrate, relate, recount, tell, record, set forth, represent, outline, sketch, illustrate.

deplete *verb* empty, drain, evacuate, exhaust, use up, expend, spend, consume, reduce, decrease, lessen, diminish, lower, impoverish. OPPOSITE: fill.

depletion *noun* emptying, evacuation, draining, expenditure, exhaustion, using up, consumption, reduction, decrease, lessening, lowering, diminution.

deplorable *adj* **1** (*live in deplorable conditions*) lamentable, miserable, unfortunate, disastrous, sad, dire, tragic, grievous, regrettable, pitiable, wretched, pathetic, distressing, calamitous. OPPOSITE: auspicious. **2** (*their deplorable behaviour*) scandalous, disgraceful, shameful, contemptible, dishonourable, disreputable, despicable, reprehensible, abominable, base, vile, sordid, opprobrious. OPPOSITE: commendable.

deplore *verb* **1** (*deplore violence*) condemn, denounce, criticize, censure, decry, abhor, disapprove of, slam (*inf*), slate (*inf*). OPPOSITE: extol. **2** (*deplore their death*) lament, mourn, regret, bemoan, bewail, rue, grieve for, weep over, sorrow over. OPPOSITE: welcome.

deploy *verb* arrange, position, dispose, station, extend, spread out, distribute, use, utilize.

deport *verb* **1** (*deport illegal immigrants*) expel, banish, exile, evict, expatriate, extradite, transport, remove. **2** (*deport oneself well*) conduct, behave, comport, bear, hold, carry, acquit.

deportation *noun* expulsion, exile, banishment, eviction, removal, expatriation, extradition, transportation.

deportment *noun* carriage, bearing, posture, air, mien, appearance, demeanour, behaviour, conduct, comportment, manner, stance, attitude.

depose *verb* **1** (*depose a ruler*) dethrone, oust, displace, remove, remove from office, unseat, dismiss, cashier, demote, degrade, fire (*inf*), sack (*inf*). OPPOSITE: enthrone. **2** (*depose that the accused was at the scene of the crime*) declare, testify, swear, attest to, asseverate.

deposit *verb* **1** (*deposit the cargo at the quay*) lay, lay down, drop, place, put, put down, set, set down. **2** (*deposit money in a bank*) save, store, hoard, bank, lodge, consign, entrust, put away, put by, stow. OPPOSITE: withdraw. **3** (*sediment deposited on the surface*) settle, set down, precipitate.
➤ *noun* **1** (*left a chemical deposit*) sediment, precipitate, precipitation, layer, accumulation, deposition, silt, alluvium, dregs, lees. **2** (*pay a deposit now and the balance later*) down payment, part payment, security, pledge, stake, warranty, retainer, instalment.

depositary *noun* trustee, guardian, steward, fiduciary.

deposition *noun* **1** (*the deposition of a witness*) affidavit, statement, sworn statement, attestation, declaration, testimony, evidence. **2** (*the deposition of the ruler*) dethronement, displacement, dismissal, demotion, ousting, removal, unseating, demotion, degrading. OPPOSITE: enthronement.

depository *noun* depot, store, storehouse, warehouse, repository, bank, safe, safe deposit.

depot *noun* **1** (*an arms depot*) storehouse, warehouse, depository, repository, magazine, arsenal, cache. **2** (*a bus depot*) station, terminus, garage, terminal.

deprave *verb* corrupt, debauch, subvert, demoralize, pervert, lead astray, seduce, debase, degrade, pollute, defile, contaminate, degenerate, vitiate. OPPOSITE: improve.

depraved *adj* corrupt, immoral, debauched, demoralized, reprobate, debased, degraded, degenerate, dissolute, corrupted, unprincipled, abandoned, licentious, lascivious, lecherous, profligate, perverted, warped, wicked, evil, vicious, vile, sinful, shameless, iniquitous, base, wanton. OPPOSITE: virtuous.

depravity *noun* corruption, corruptness, immorality, debauchery, abandonment, degeneracy, dissoluteness, degradation, profligacy, turpitude, depravation, demoralization, profligacy, perversion, lewdness, licentiousness, lasciviousness, lechery, vice, evil, iniquity, wickedness, vileness, baseness, sin. OPPOSITE: virtue.

deprecate *verb* **1** (*deprecate the amount of violence on television*) deplore, condemn, criticize, denounce, censure, inveigh against, frown on, disapprove of, object to, protest against, rail against, inveigh against, slam (*inf*), slate (*inf*), knock (*inf*). OPPOSITE: commend. **2** (*deprecated her own accomplishments*) belittle, disparage, denigrate, discredit, diminish, depreciate. OPPOSITE: praise.

deprecatory *adj* **1** (*admitted her mistakes in a deprecatory tone*) apologetic, sorry, regretful, rueful, remorseful, penitent, contrite, compunctious. **2** (*deprecatory comments about his leadership*) disapproving, deploring, condemnatory, disparaging, critical, censorious, reproachful, protesting, admonishing.

depreciate *verb* **1** (*prices have depreciated considerably*) devalue, devaluate, deflate, reduce, lower, lose value, decrease in value, fall, decline. OPPOSITE: appreciate. **2** (*depreciated their achievements*) disparage, belittle, deprecate, denigrate, diminish, malign, traduce,

underrate, undervalue, underestimate, make light of, minimize, decry, deride, slight. OPPOSITE: praise.

depreciation *noun* (*depreciation of the dollar*) devaluation, cheapening, markdown, deflation, depression, decline, fall, drop, slump. OPPOSITE: appreciation. **2** (*depreciation of their achievements*) disparagement, belittlement, deprecation, detraction, denigration, discrediting, derogation, undervaluing, underestimation. OPPOSITE: praise.

depredation *noun* plunder, pillage, laying waste, spoliation, despoliation, rapine, robbery, theft, marauding, raid, devastation.

depredator *noun* robber, thief, plunderer, looter, pillager, marauder, raider, despoiler.

depress *verb* **1** (*sure to depress her*) deject, sadden, dishearten, discourage, dispirit, daunt, get down (*inf*), cast down, bring down, weigh down, oppress, burden, overburden, desolate, upset, damp, chill. OPPOSITE: cheer. **2** (*depress trade*) weaken, debilitate, enfeeble, exhaust, drain, sap, tire, weary, enervate, devitalize, impair, reduce, lessen, slow down. OPPOSITE: fortify. **3** (*may depress share prices*) depreciate, devalue, devaluate, cheapen, reduce, slash (*inf*), bring down, lower, cut, diminish, downgrade. OPPOSITE: raise. **4** (*depress the pedal*) press down, push down, flatten, lower, level.

depressant *noun* sedative, tranquillizer, sleeping pill, soporific, opiate, hypnotic, downer (*inf*), relaxant, calmant, calmative. OPPOSITE: stimulant.

depressed *adj* **1** (*depressed at the prospect*) dejected, dispirited, discouraged, disheartened, unhappy, blue (*inf*), fed up (*inf*), glum, low, low-spirited, despondent, down, downcast, down in the dumps (*inf*), cast down, downhearted, moody, morose, gloomy, pessimistic, miserable, sad, saddened, melancholy, crestfallen, distressed. OPPOSITE: elated. **2** (*a depressed area*) poor, needy, disadvantaged, deprived, distressed, run-down, down-at-heel, destitute, poverty-stricken, grey. OPPOSITE: affluent. **3** (*a depressed market*) weak, weakened, enervated, debilitated, devitalized, impaired, devalued, depreciated, discounted. **4** (*depressed by her thumb*) pushed in, pressed in, sunken, recessed, set back, indented, dented, concave, hollow.

depressing *adj* dejecting, saddening, sad, dismal, bleak, gloomy, cheerless, dreary, disheartening, unhappy, melancholy, sombre, grey, black, daunting, discouraging, dispiriting, depressive, harrowing, heartbreaking, distressing, painful, hopeless, grave, funereal. OPPOSITE: cheering.

depression *noun* **1** (*cast into depression*) dejection, gloom, gloominess, despondency, melancholy, melancholia, sadness, unhappiness, glumness, low spirits, despair, blues (*inf*), dumps (*inf*), dolefulness, downheartedness, hopelessness, desolation, discouragement, moodiness, moroseness, pessimism, the hump (*inf*), doldrums. OPPOSITE: elation. **2** (*a depression in the surface*) indentation, impression, concavity, hollow, pit, dent, dint, dimple, hole, excavation, cavity, sink, basin, bowl, dish, valley. OPPOSITE: mound. **3** (*economic depression*) recession, slump, crash, decline, slowdown, standstill, hard times, stagnation, paralysis, inactivity. OPPOSITE: boom.

deprivation *noun* **1** (*deprivation of his freedom*) denial, deprival, loss, lack, withdrawal, withholding, removal, stripping, expropriation, confiscation, appropriation, dispossession, robbing, wresting, divestment, bereavement. OPPOSITE: endowment. **2** (*living in conditions of deprivation*) hardship, destitution, privation, penury, need, neediness, want, distress, disadvantage.

deprive *verb* take away, strip, divest, dispossess, rob, wrest, confiscate, deny, refuse, withhold, despoil, bereave, expropriate. OPPOSITE: endow.

deprived *adj* poor, destitute, impoverished, needy, in need, in want, necessitous, underprivileged, disadvantaged, distressed, lacking, bereft, forlorn, denuded. OPPOSITE: prosperous.

depth *noun* **1** (*the depth of the well*) deepness, profoundness, profundity, extent, measure, drop. OPPOSITE: shallowness. **2** (*a man of considerable depth*) wisdom, insight, sagacity, understanding, profundity, penetration, discernment, astuteness, acumen, shrewdness, perception, perspicacity, awareness, intuition, acuity, cleverness. **3** (*depth of feeling*) intensity, strength, thoroughness, earnestness, passion, fervour, vigour, gravity, seriousness, severity. **4** (*depth of tone*) intensity, vividness, richness, strength, brilliance, warmth, glow, darkness. **5** (*ocean depths*) deep, bowels, bed, pit, floor, bottom, abyss, chasm, gulf, middle, midst. OPPOSITE: surface. **6** (*depth of their expertise*) extent, extensiveness, scope, amount, compass, profundity.

in depth thoroughly, comprehensively, exhaustively, extensively, intensively, in detail. OPPOSITE: superficially.

deputation *noun* **1** (*received the deputation*) delegation, delegates, envoys, deputies, embassy, legation, commission, committee, mission, representatives. **2** (*by official deputation*) appointment, designation, nomination, commission, authorization, assignment, installation, induction, investiture, ordination.

depute *verb* **1** (*deputed to head the commission*) appoint, nominate, designate, commission, second, deputize, authorize, empower, entrust, charge, accredit, mandate. OPPOSITE: dismiss. **2** (*depute responsibility*) delegate, transfer, assign, hand over, pass on, consign.

deputize *verb* stand in for, replace, take over, substitute, sub for (*inf*), represent, act for, take the place of, understudy, relieve, double, cover.

deputy *noun* substitute, stand-in, agent, representative, delegate, envoy, ambassador, commissioner, legate, surrogate, proxy, locum, spokesperson, lieutenant, assistant, subordinate, second-in-command, vice (*inf*), nuncio.
➤ *adj* assistant, representative, substitute, stand-in, surrogate, subordinate, proxy, suffragan.

deranged *adj* disordered, confused, delirious, demented, distracted, distraught, disturbed, irrational, berserk, frantic, frenzied, unhinged, unbalanced, maddened, crazy, crazed, insane, loony (*inf*), lunatic, loopy (*inf*), barking (*inf*), barmy (*inf*), bats (*inf*), batty (*inf*), bonkers (*inf*), cracked (*inf*), crackpot (*inf*), cuckoo

(*inf*), dippy (*inf*), dotty (*inf*), nutty (*inf*), nuts (*inf*), potty (*inf*), round the bend (*inf*), round the twist (*inf*), out to lunch (*inf*), screwy (*inf*), up the pole (*inf*), mad, touched, non compos mentis. OPPOSITE: lucid.

derelict *adj* **1** (*a derelict building*) abandoned, forsaken, desolate, deserted, discarded, neglected, dilapidated, crumbling, ruined, ramshackle, rickety, tumbledown, run-down, in disrepair. **2** (*derelict in their duties*) remiss, negligent, neglectful, irresponsible, lax, slack, delinquent, careless, sloppy, slipshod.
➤ *noun* tramp, vagrant, beggar, down-and-out, bum (*inf*), bag lady, outcast, drifter, hobo, wastrel, ne'er-do-well, no-good, good-for-nothing, wretch, dosser (*inf*).

dereliction *noun* **1** (*in a state of dereliction*) dilapidation, ruin, disrepair, abandonment, desolation, desertion, forsaking, relinquishment, abdication, renunciation, rejection. **2** (*gross dereliction of duty*) neglect, negligence, neglectfulness, carelessness, sloppiness, slackness, irresponsibility, laxity, relinquishment, delinquency, remissness, abdication, abandonment, desertion, evasion, renunciation, omission, nonperformance, fault, failure, betrayal, default. OPPOSITE: observance.

deride *verb* mock, ridicule, scoff, jeer, laugh at, taunt, chaff, scorn, disdain, sneer at, poke fun at, make fun of, lampoon, satirize, disparage, denigrate, belittle, pooh-pooh (*inf*), knock (*inf*), insult, slight, abuse, gibe, vilify, contemn, rag, tease, torment. OPPOSITE: respect.

derision *noun* mockery, ridicule, scoffing, jeer, taunt, raillery, scorn, sneering, contempt, taunting, hissing, teasing, ragging, laughter, raillery, disdain, disparagement, denigration, disrespect, satire, lampoon, irony, abuse, insult, vilification, contumely. OPPOSITE: respect.

derisive *adj* scornful, contemptuous, disdainful, disparaging, denigratory, derisory, mocking, scoffing, jeering, sarcastic, satirical, disrespectful, insulting, irreverent, taunting. OPPOSITE: respectful.

derisory *adj* **1** (*a derisory offer*) laughable, ludicrous, absurd, ridiculous, contemptible, insulting, outrageous, preposterous, tiny, inadequate, minimal, paltry, risible. **2** (*a derisory speech*) contemptuous, derisive, mocking, jeering, ridiculing, insulting, scoffing, scornful, taunting.

derivation *noun* **1** (*the derivation of this belief*) source, origin, etymology, root, spring, foundation, beginning, basis, cause, rise, ancestry, genealogy, descent, extraction. **2** (*derivation of much satisfaction*) deriving, acquisition, extraction. **3** (*the derivation of information*) deriving, collection, getting, obtaining, gathering, gleaning, drawing out, eliciting, deduction, inference, eduction.

derivative *adj* **1** (*derivative theories*) derived, acquired, borrowed, obtained, procured, collected, elicited, deduced, inferred, educed. **2** (*a derivative essay*) unoriginal, hackneyed, secondhand, secondary, trite, uninventive, imitative, borrowed, copied, cribbed (*inf*), plagiaristic, plagiarized, rehashed (*inf*). OPPOSITE: original.
➤ *noun* derivation, offshoot, by-product, product, spin-off, development, outgrowth, branch, descendant.

derive *verb* **1** (*derived huge enjoyment*) draw, extract, get, obtain, gain, acquire, procure, receive, elicit, glean, collect, gather, borrow. **2** (*derived from this observation*) deduce, infer, trace, track, follow. **3** (*from which the custom derives*) originate, arise, spring, flow, proceed, emanate, issue, come, descend, stem, develop, evolve.

derogatory *adj* disparaging, belittling, diminishing, critical, detracting, deflating, depreciative, deprecatory, defamatory, discrediting, discreditable, insulting, denigratory, vilifying, offensive, abusive, slighting, injurious, damaging, disapproving, uncomplimentary, unfavourable, unflattering, dishonouring, opprobrious, pejorative. OPPOSITE: flattering.

descend *verb* **1** (*the leaf descended*) go down, sink, fall, drop, plummet, plunge, tumble, swoop, sink, subside, slope downwards, slump. OPPOSITE: ascend. **2** (*descend from the train*) dismount, alight, disembark, detrain, deplane, get off, get down, climb down. OPPOSITE: embark. **3** (*the plain descends to the sea*) dip, incline, slope, slant, gravitate, subside. **4** (*the cavalry descended upon the camp*) attack, assault, swoop, pounce, assail, raid, charge, overwhelm, invade, take over. **5** (*descended from apes*) originate, issue, spring, stem, proceed, emanate. **6** (*she descended to accept his hand*) condescend, deign, lower oneself, sink, stoop. **7** (*descended into misery*) degenerate, deteriorate, decline, sink, go downhill (*inf*), go to pot (*inf*), go to the dogs (*inf*).

descendants *pl noun* offspring, issue, progeny, seed, successors, lineage, line, posterity, scions, family, children. OPPOSITE: ancestors.

descent *noun* **1** (*the descent of the aircraft*) fall, drop, plunge, plummet, dip, sinking, subsiding. **2** (*the path down the descent*) slope, slant, gradient, decline, declivity, incline, drop, declination. OPPOSITE: ascent. **3** (*of noble descent*) ancestry, parentage, extraction, stock, heredity, genealogy, succession, lineage, line, pedigree, blood, strain, origin, derivation. **4** (*a descent in reputation*) decline, deterioration, degeneration, degeneracy, decadence, degradation, comedown, debasement, dip. **5** (*the descent of the cohorts*) attack, assault, onslaught, incursion, raid, charge, invasion, foray, sortie, pounce, swoop.

describe *verb* **1** (*describe the scene*) portray, depict, delineate, draw, picture, illustrate, characterize, detail, elucidate, explain, express, tell, talk, narrate, relate, recount, report, outline, define, specify, set out, present, represent. **2** (*I would not describe her as bright*) call, depict, portray, consider, think, style, label, designate, pronounce, brand, hail. **3** (*the smoke described a circle*) mark out, delineate, trace, outline, draw, sketch.

description *noun* **1** (*a description of events*) delineation, portrayal, depiction, characterization, elucidation, explanation, exposition, illustration, account, narration, narrative, relation, commentary, chronicle, report, statement, explanation, detail, outline, profile, sketch, portrait, presentation, representation. **2** (*goods of this description*) sort, kind, type, variety, category, species, specification, class, order, designation, brand, breed, genre, genus, ilk, kidney, grain, make, mould, stamp.

descriptive *adj* illustrative, explanatory, expressive, detailed, graphic, colourful, pictorial, picturesque, striking, vivid, detailed, depictive, circumstantial, elucidatory.

descry *verb* discern, make out, distinguish, behold, espy, catch sight of, glimpse, detect, perceive, discover, see, spot, sight, observe, discover, recognize, mark, notice. OPPOSITE: miss.

desecrate *verb* profane, defile, violate, pollute, contaminate, infect, befoul, pervert, debase, degrade, abuse, insult, misuse, blaspheme, despoil, violate, vandalize, dishonour, dishallow, vitiate. OPPOSITE: consecrate.

desecration *noun* profanation, defilement, sacrilege, blasphemy, impiety, violation, outrage, insult, abuse, debasement, dishonouring, pollution. OPPOSITE: consecration.

desert[1] *noun* (*the Sahara desert*) wilderness, waste, wasteland, wilds, dust bowl, barrenness, solitude, void.
➤ *adj* barren, bare, infertile, sterile, arid, dry, dried up, parched, scorched, burnt, torrid, moistureless, uncultivated, untilled, unproductive, desolate, bare, desolate, empty, wild, lonely, uninhabited, waste, solitary. OPPOSITE: fertile.

desert[2] *verb* **1** (*she deserted them*) abandon, leave, cast off, maroon, walk out on, run out on (*inf*), quit (*inf*), jilt, rat on (*inf*), strand, give up, forsake, leave in the lurch (*inf*), leave high and dry (*inf*), relinquish, renounce, neglect, shun. **2** (*deserted from the army*) run away, abscond, go AWOL, go over the hill (*inf*), defect, decamp, flee, fly, do a runner (*inf*). **3** (*desert the cause*) renounce, relinquish, abandon, give up, forsake, turn one's back on, deny, betray, recant, renege, apostatize.

desert[3] *noun* **1** (*received his just deserts*) due, right, reward, recompense, remuneration, payment, retribution, return, come-uppance (*inf*). **2** (*of great desert*) worth, value, merit, virtue, excellence.

deserted *adj* **1** (*deserted by her husband*) abandoned, left, cast off, forsaken, jilted, stranded, marooned, bereft, neglected, renounced, relinquished, shunned, left in the lurch. **2** (*deserted streets*) empty, vacant, unoccupied, uninhabited, underpopulated, untenanted, tenantless, abandoned, godforsaken, forsaken, unfrequented, lonely, secluded, solitary, isolated, forlorn, desolate, neglected, derelict. OPPOSITE: populous.

deserter *noun* runaway, truant, absconder, fugitive, defector, escapee, renegade, apostate, delinquent, turncoat, backslider, traitor, betrayer, rat (*inf*).

desertion *noun* **1** (*desertion of her family*) abandonment, forsaking, betrayal, relinquishment, renunciation, leaving, casting-off, giving up, jilting, quitting (*inf*). **2** (*desertion from the ranks*) defection, absconding, decamping, running-away, dereliction, French leave, flight, going AWOL, truancy, escape. **3** (*desertion from these high ideals*) abandonment, denial, defection, departure, betrayal, renunciation, forsaking, relinquishment, apostasy, renegation.

deserve *verb* earn, win, merit, be worthy of, be entitled to, rate, justify, warrant, incur, qualify for.

deserved *adj* merited, due, earned, well-earned, right, rightful, just, fair, fitting, reasonable, suitable, proper, appropriate, apt, justified, justifiable, legitimate, warranted, apposite, meet, condign. OPPOSITE: undeserved.

deserving *adj* worthy, meritorious, estimable, exemplary, admirable, creditable, commendable, laudable, praiseworthy, good, upright, righteous, virtuous, meritorious. OPPOSITE: undeserving.

desiccated *adj* dried, dry, arid, parched, dehydrated, drained, evaporated, powdered, sterile, dead, lifeless. OPPOSITE: moist.

design *verb* **1** (*design a new cinema*) plan, plot, scheme, devise, contrive, draw up, draw, sketch, outline, map out, block out, delineate, draft, depict, trace. **2** (*designed in the latest style*) invent, originate, conceive, hatch, think up, create, develop, construct, make, fashion, form, model, fabricate, tailor, innovate. **3** (*a book designed for intermediate students*) intend, plan, purpose, mean, aim.
➤ *noun* **1** (*a design for a boat*) sketch, draft, drawing, diagram, outline, pattern, map, plan, plot, scheme, model, guide, blueprint, delineation, depiction, prototype. **2** (*fashion design*) style, form, shape, figure, format, configuration, arrangement, organization, composition, construction, make-up, structure, motif, pattern, device, emblem, logo, monogram, cipher. **3** (*a design to win the day*) plan, plot, scheme, enterprise, project, undertaking, intrigue, stratagem, artifice, device. **4** (*with the design of winning them over*) proposal, aim, end, goal, intent, intention, object, objective, target, purpose, purport, point, view, meaning, wish, desire, hope, aspiration, ambition, dream.

designate *verb* **1** (*they were designated volunteers*) call, name, title, entitle, term, dub, style, christen. **2** (*at the designated time*) state, appoint, indicate, denote, specify, particularize, pinpoint, earmark, stipulate, set aside, define. **3** (*designated by the government*) appoint, assign, nominate, choose, depute, delegate, allot, select, elect, ordain, induct. **4** (*designating the way to go*) indicate, mark, point, denote, show.

designation *noun* **1** (*known by the following designation*) name, title, term, denomination, description, appellation, tag (*inf*), epithet, label, nickname, style, sobriquet, cognomen. **2** (*the designation of the date and time*) indication, specification, particularization, stipulation, description, definition, denoting, earmarking, marking. **3** (*their designation to the committee*) appointment, nomination, delegation, selection, election, induction. **4** (*designation of the route*) marking, indication, denoting.

designer *noun* **1** (*designer of aircraft*) inventor, deviser, planner, architect, artificer, creator, fashioner, originator, producer, author, contriver. **2** (*designer of fabrics*) couturier, stylist, fashioner. **3** (*designer of many intrigues*) originator, plotter, schemer, intriguer, conspirator, machinator, conniver.

designing *adj* artful, crafty, wily, foxy, sly, scheming, tricky, cunning, guileful, Machiavellian, intriguing, sharp, shrewd, underhand, unscrupulous, calculating, conspiring, plotting, astute, treacherous, insidious, crooked (*inf*), dishonest, devious, deceitful. OPPOSITE: artless.

desirability *noun* **1** (*a house of considerable desirability*) attractiveness, appeal, allure, marketability, popularity, eligibility, agreeableness, excellence, worth. **2** (*the desirability of confidence*) advantageousness, advantage, usefulness, advisability, preferableness, value, benefit, merit, profit, expedience. **3** (*she was conscious of her own desirability*) attractiveness, sexuality, voluptuousness, seductiveness, sexiness (*inf*), allure, allurement, eroticism, fascination.

desirable *adj* **1** (*a desirable outcome*) profitable, advantageous, beneficial, advisable, admirable, agreeable, appealing, attractive, enviable, sought-after, worthwhile, covetable, popular, good, excellent, pleasing, pleasant. **2** (*it is desirable that she should not know*) preferable, advisable, beneficial, expedient, recommendable, advantageous, sensible. **3** (*his desirable daughter*) attractive, adorable, captivating, alluring, glamorous, erotic, seductive, sexy (*inf*), fetching, fascinating, beguiling, tantalizing, tempting. OPPOSITE: undesirable.

desire *verb* **1** (*desire to go home*) wish for, want, long for, covet, crave, hanker after, yearn for, hunger for, thirst for, fancy, have designs of, hope for, like, need, aspire to. OPPOSITE: abhor. **2** (*I desire an answer*) ask, request, solicit, petition, entreat, demand, expect. **3** (*he desired her*) want, lust after, burn for, take to, fancy (*inf*), have a crush on (*inf*), have the hots for (*inf*), take a shine to (*inf*), letch after (*inf*).
➤ *noun* **1** (*a desire to see her*) longing, craving, yearning, yen (*inf*), hankering, itch (*inf*), wish, want, need, eagerness, fancy, inclination, predilection, aspiration, appetite, thirst, proclivity, predisposition. OPPOSITE: aversion. **2** (*hear my desire*) wish, hope, appeal, request, solicitation, petition, entreaty, importunity, supplication. **3** (*overcome with his desire for her*) lust, lustfulness, passion, ardour, the hots (*inf*), libido, lechery, lasciviousness, salaciousness, libidinousness, sensuality, sexuality, concupiscence, prurience.

desired *adj* **1** (*the desired shape*) required, necessary, right, correct, proper, exact, accurate, precise, specific, particular, appropriate, suitable, fitting, preferred, expected, ordained, express. **2** (*the desired result*) wished for, longed for, yearned for, aimed for, intended, craved, coveted.

desirous *adj* desiring, eager, avid, burning, enthusiastic, keen, longing, willing, wishing, yearning, craving, itching, wishing, hopeful, hoping, anxious, ambitious, aspiring, impatient, ready. OPPOSITE: apathetic.

desist *verb* stop, cease, break off, discontinue, end, halt, pause, suspend, abstain, refrain from, remit, forbear, give up, give over (*inf*), kick (*inf*), leave off, have done with. OPPOSITE: persist.

desolate *adj* **1** (*a desolate place*) deserted, abandoned, uninhabited, unoccupied, unfrequented, unvisited, desert, wild, waste, arid, barren, bare, bleak, dreary, gloomy, depressing, dismal, empty, lonely, godforsaken, forsaken, isolated, solitary. OPPOSITE: populous. **2** (*desolate when she left*) forlorn, forsaken, abandoned, bereft, lonely, friendless, depressed, dejected, disheartened, downhearted, despondent, dismal, gloomy, sad, cheerless, brokenhearted, comfortless, distressed, downcast, cast down, unhappy, grieving, wretched, melancholy, miserable. OPPOSITE: cheerful.

≫ *verb* **1** (*the village had been desolated*) destroy, devastate, lay waste, lay low, pillage, plunder, ravage, ruin, despoil, depopulate. **2** (*we were desolated at the news*) devastate, shatter (*inf*), floor (*inf*), overwhelm, upset, disconcert, deject, depress, dismay, distress, get down, daunt, discourage, dishearten, grieve, sadden, take aback, confound, nonplus, discomfit. OPPOSITE: cheer.

desolation *noun* **1** (*desolation of the city*) destruction, devastation, ruin, ruination, despoliation, ravaging, laying waste, pillage, depopulation. OPPOSITE: cultivation. **2** (*desolation of the mountains*) barrenness, bareness, bleakness, desolateness, emptiness, forlornness, remoteness, wildness, loneliness, isolation, solitude, solitariness. **3** (*such was the desolation she felt*) despondency, dejection, depression, despair, sadness, grief, brokenheartedness, downheartedness, anguish, sorrow, distress, gloom, gloominess, misery, melancholy, unhappiness, woe, wretchedness. OPPOSITE: joy.

despair *noun* hopelessness, desperation, despondency, gloom, dejection, depression, distress, misery, wretchedness, anguish, discouragement, disheartenment, melancholy, melancholia, defeatism, pessimism, resignation, disconsolateness, inconsolableness OPPOSITE: hope.
≫ *verb* lose hope, lose heart, resign oneself, give up, give in, throw in the towel (*inf*), throw in the sponge (*inf*), surrender, collapse, despond.

despairing *adj* hopeless, distraught, inconsolable, desolate, desperate, frantic, heartbroken, brokenhearted, griefstricken, miserable, anguished, wretched, suicidal, anxious, despondent, depressed, disconsolate, discouraged, disheartened, dejected, forlorn, gloomy, sorrowful, sorrowing, pessimistic, dismayed, downcast, cast down, resigned. OPPOSITE: hopeful.

desperado *noun* ruffian, thug, gangster, criminal, heavy (*inf*), cutthroat, gunman, hoodlum (*inf*), lawbreaker, villain, mugger (*inf*), bandit, outlaw, brigand, terrorist.

desperate *adj* **1** (*a desperate character*) rash, reckless, bold, daring, audacious, determined, headstrong, impetuous, mad, madcap, foolhardy, frantic, frenzied, hasty, precipitate, wild, violent, lawless. OPPOSITE: cautious. **2** (*a desperate remedy*) rash, reckless, bold, daring, foolhardy, harebrained, imprudent, incautious, injudicious, indiscreet, ill-conceived, risky, hazardous, precipitate, wild. **3** (*a desperate situation*) grave, serious, critical, urgent, pressing, dire, acute, severe, drastic, compelling, crucial, extreme, appalling, despairing, hopeless, deplorable, intolerable, lamentable, irretrievable, irrecoverable, irredeemable. OPPOSITE: hopeful. **4** (*she felt quite desperate*) despairing, despondent, forlorn, hopeless, anguished, distraught, desolate, miserable, wretched, griefstricken, heartbroken, inconsolable, abandoned, disconsolate, discouraged, dismayed, disheartened, dejected, depressed, downcast, pessimistic, sorrowful, suicidal.

desperately *adv* critically, gravely, acutely, hopelessly, seriously, severely, badly, dangerously, perilously, urgently, greatly, extremely, appallingly, dreadfully, fearfully, frightfully, shockingly.

desperation *noun* **1** (*the desperation of his decision*) recklessness, rashness, panic, impetuosity, madness, foolhardiness, frenzy, frenziedness, fury, rage, defiance. OPPOSITE: coolness. **2** (*a state of desperation*) despair, hopelessness, despondency, anxiety, agony, anguish, misery, distress, wretchedness, dejection, depression, gloom, melancholy, forlornness, disconsolateness, sorrow, heartache, torture, pain, distraction, worry, trouble. OPPOSITE: hope.

despicable *adj* contemptible, low, mean, base, degrading, cheap, shabby, abject, ignominious, ignoble, abominable, hateful, loathsome, reprobate, odious, vile, sordid, disreputable, reprehensible, detestable, disgusting, disgraceful, infamous, shameful, pitiful, miserable, sorry, wretched, worthless, villainous. OPPOSITE: admirable.

despise *verb* scorn, disdain, look down on, spurn, slight, disregard, flout, undervalue, mock, sneer, scoff at, jeer at, deride, dislike, deplore, detest, hate, loathe, shun, abominate, abhor, revile, execrate, contemn. OPPOSITE: admire.

despite *prep* in spite of, notwithstanding, in the face of, in the teeth of (*inf*), even with, regardless of, against, undeterred by, defying, in defiance of.

despoil *verb* pillage, plunder, loot, ravage, ransack, rifle, sack, total (*inf*), trash (*inf*), rob, deprive, strip, dispossess, denude, divest, devastate, desolate, destroy, ruin, wreck, lay waste, ravish, rape, raid, forage, harry, maraud, depredate, vandalize.

despondency *noun* depression, dejection, gloom, glumness, the blues (*inf*), heartache (*inf*), the hump (*inf*), melancholy, melancholia, misery, sadness, sorrow, downheartedness, low spirits, the doldrums, defeatism, discouragement, disheartenment, hopelessness, despair, desperation, distress, dispiritedness, disconsolateness, inconsolability, wretchedness, grief. OPPOSITE: cheerfulness.

despondent *adj* depressed, dejected, gloomy, miserable, doleful, low, down, down in the dumps (*inf*), downcast, cast down, downhearted, low-spirited, dismal, dispirited, discouraged, disheartened, heartbroken, inconsolable, defeatist, despairing, distressed, glum, morose, mournful, sad, sorrowful, melancholy, blue (*inf*), sick as a parrot (*inf*), woebegone, wretched. OPPOSITE: cheerful.

despot *noun* tyrant, autocrat, dictator, oppressor, ruler, monocrat, absolutist, boss. OPPOSITE: democrat.

despotic *adj* tyrannical, tyrannous, autocratic, dictatorial, totalitarian, monocratic, overbearing, oppressive, imperious, high-handed, arrogant, domineering, absolute, arbitrary, authoritarian, unconstitutional. OPPOSITE: democratic.

despotism *noun* tyranny, autocracy, dictatorship, absolutism, totalitarianism, autarchy, monocracy, oppression, repression. OPPOSITE: democracy.

dessert *noun* sweet, pudding, pud (*inf*), afters (*inf*).

destination *noun* **1** (*soon reached their destination*) terminus, stop, station, harbour, haven, landing place, stopping-place, port of call, journey's end. OPPOSITE: start. **2** (*the destination of these efforts*) goal, objective, object, end, target, ambition, aspiration, design, aim, purpose, intention.

destined adj **1** (*a ship destined for the east*) bound, heading, en route, directed, scheduled, booked, assigned. **2** (*destined to end unhappily*) fated, doomed, foredoomed, ordained, foreordained, preordained, predestined, predetermined, certain, sure, unavoidable, inescapable, bound, inevitable, ineluctable. **3** (*destined for his master*) meant, designed, intended, set, set apart, appointed, allotted, designated.

destiny noun **1** (*his destiny was written in the stars*) fate, fortune, future, doom, lot, portion, cup, due. **2** (*ordained by destiny*) fate, fortune, chance, luck, the stars, karma, kismet, predestination, predestiny.

destitute adj **1** (*destitute families*) poor, impoverished, poverty-stricken, impecunious, penniless, broke (*inf*), flat broke (*inf*), stony-broke (*inf*), insolvent, bankrupt, beggarly, indigent, penurious, necessitous, needy, short, down-and-out, hard-pressed, distressed, pauperized, ruined, badly off, hard up (*inf*), skint (*inf*), strapped (*inf*), cleaned out (*inf*). OPPOSITE: rich. **2** (*destitute of inspiration*) devoid, bereft, without, deficient, lacking, needy, wanting, deprived, drained, empty.

destitution noun poverty, impoverishment, impecuniousness, bankruptcy, insolvency, penury, pennilessness, beggary, indigence, need, neediness, want, privation, starvation, distress, dire straits, pauperdom. OPPOSITE: wealth.

destroy verb **1** (*destroy the defences*) demolish, raze, gut, ruin, wreck, devastate, blow up, explode, annihilate, smash, shatter, overthrow, overturn, dismantle, knock down, pull down, tear down, flatten, obliterate, total (*inf*), trash (*inf*), undermine, waste, level, spoil, ravage, ransack, break, crush, fell, sabotage, undo. OPPOSITE: build up. **2** (*destroy his enemies*) beat, defeat, vanquish, conquer, subdue, put down, rout, lick (*inf*), thrash (*inf*), trounce, drub, kill, slay, slaughter, murder, assassinate, massacre, extinguish, wipe out, annihilate, decimate, eliminate, liquidate, dispatch, eradicate, stamp out.

destruction noun **1** (*the destruction of the city centre*) annihilation, demolition, dismantling, knocking-down, pulling-down, tearing-down, blowing-up, ruin, ruination, razing, levelling, devastation, desolation, havoc, wreckage, crushing, smashing, shattering, vandalism. OPPOSITE: creation. **2** (*the destruction of their opponents*) defeat, beating, conquest, vanquishing, rout, downfall, nullification, overthrow, ruination, undoing, annihilation, eradication, elimination, end, extinction, extermination, liquidation, killing, massacre, slaughter, murder, assassination.

destructive adj **1** (*a destructive fire*) damaging, devastating, disastrous, ruinous, catastrophic, cataclysmic, calamitous, detrimental, deleterious, disruptive, ravaging, hurtful, injurious, dangerous, deadly, fatal, lethal, malignant, pernicious, mischievous, noxious, baneful, harmful, disadvantageous. OPPOSITE: beneficial. **2** (*destructive opinions*) negative, adverse, contrary, unfavourable, hostile, antagonistic, unfriendly, vicious, discouraging, disparaging, discrediting, derogatory, denigrating, disapproving, undermining, subversive. OPPOSITE: constructive.

desultory adj random, haphazard, irregular, unmethodical, unsystematic, unconnected, disconnected, inconsistent, inconstant, spasmodic, fitful, discursive, aimless, rambling, loose, roving, erratic, maundering, vague, undirected, uncoordinated, capricious, chaotic, disorderly, cursory, halfhearted. OPPOSITE: methodical.

detach verb **1** (*detach the two sheets*) separate, undo, disconnect, uncouple, unfasten, unfix, unhitch, remove, tear off, take off, disengage, disjoin, disunite, dissociate, cut off, sever, divide, segregate, isolate, loosen, free, disentangle. OPPOSITE: attach. **2** (*took care to detach himself from the party*) dissociate, separate, sever, split, cut off, free, loosen, isolate, estrange, segregate.

detached adj **1** (*the sole became detached*) separate, unconnected, unfastened, disconnected, unhitched, loosened, dissociated, discrete, divided, severed, free, loose, isolated. OPPOSITE: attached. **2** (*she remained detached*) aloof, remote, uninvolved, objective, impartial, unbiased, unprejudiced, uncommitted, nonpartisan, impersonal, indifferent, cool, cold, clinical, reserved, disinterested, unconcerned, dispassionate, unemotional, neutral, fair, independent. OPPOSITE: involved.

detachment noun **1** (*detachment of the two parts*) separation, disconnection, uncoupling, undoing, unfastening, unhitching, loosening, disentangling, severance, disunion, disengagement, division, removal, withdrawal, isolation. OPPOSITE: connection. **2** (*a sense of detachment*) aloofness, remoteness, reserve, indifference, unconcern, objectivity, fairness, impartiality, nonpartisanship, impassivity, disinterestedness, neutrality, coolness, dispassion, dispassionateness. OPPOSITE: involvement. **3** (*sent two detachments in*) squad, patrol, unit, party, group, detail, force, task force, corps.

detail noun **1** (*went over every detail*) particular, item, fact, component, ingredient, part, element, member, accessory, unit, nuts and bolts (*inf*), nitty-gritty (*inf*), factor, point, count, feature, aspect, respect, attribute, circumstance, specific, intricacy, complexity, technicality, minutiae, nicety, triviality. **2** (*an additional detail of troops*) detachment, body, group, party, force, patrol, fatigue, duty, assignment.

➤ verb **1** (*she detailed her requirements*) list, catalogue, enumerate, set out, set forth, recount, relate, narrate, recite, rehearse, describe, portray, depict, cite, particularize, itemize, specify, spell out, point out, delineate, tabulate. OPPOSITE: summarize. **2** (*detailed to work on the project*) appoint, assign, choose, allocate, delegate, elect, commission, charge, send, name, nominate.

in detail point by point, item by item, blow by blow, in depth, at length, comprehensively, carefully, fully, thoroughly, exhaustively, inside out.

detailed adj **1** (*a detailed plan*) comprehensive, exhaustive, thorough, all-inclusive, full, in-depth, minute, meticulous, circumstantial, exact, precise, specific, particular, itemized, particularized, blow-by-blow. OPPOSITE: cursory. **2** (*a detailed pattern*) complicated, complex, elaborate, intricate, involved, convoluted, entangled.

detain *verb* **1** (*detained by the weather*) delay, hold up, hold back, retard, slow, slow down, slow up, hinder, impede, inhibit, stay, keep, keep back, stop, check. **2** (*detain all suspects*) hold, confine, imprison, lock up, incarcerate, impound, intern, arrest, collar (*inf*), restrain. OPPOSITE: free.

detect *verb* **1** (*detect a change*) discover, perceive, discern, make out, see, sight, spot, spy, observe, notice, note, descry, sense, scent, smell, identify, ascertain. **2** (*detect the culprit*) discover, disclose, expose, reveal, identify, uncover, unearth, unmask, catch, find, trace, sniff out, track down, turn up, bring to light.

detection *noun* **1** (*the detection of radio signals*) discovery, observation, ascertaining, distinguishing, sighting, perception, recognition, discernment, identification. **2** (*the detection of crime*) uncovering, unearthing, unmasking, discovery, exposure, exposé, disclosure, revelation, tracking-down, sniffing-out, smelling-out, ferreting-out, investigating, sleuthing, probing.

detective *noun* investigator, private investigator, private eye (*int*), sleuth (*inf*), gumshoe (*inf*), dick (*inf*), private dick (*inf*), tec (*inf*), plain-clothes officer, policeman, policewoman, police officer, copper (*inf*), bizzy (*inf*).

detention *noun* custody, confinement, imprisonment, captivity, incarceration, internment, quarantine, porridge (*inf*), duress, restraint, constraint, detainment, arrest, punishment. OPPOSITE: release.

deter *verb* discourage, put off, turn off (*inf*), dissuade, caution, warn, daunt, intimidate, scare off, frighten, disincline, talk out of, damp, inhibit, restrain, prevent, prohibit, stop, check, hold back, hinder, impede, obstruct, block, thwart, debar. OPPOSITE: encourage.

detergent *noun* cleaner, cleanser, soap, soap powder, washing powder, washing-up liquid, solvent.
➤ *adj* cleaning, cleansing, purifying, detersive, abstergent.

deteriorate *verb* **1** (*its condition may deteriorate*) decline, degenerate, worsen, get worse, depreciate, debase, degrade, vitiate, drop, fail, fall off, lower, lapse, slide, relapse, slump, slip, ebb, wane, go downhill (*inf*), go to pot (*inf*), go to the dogs (*inf*), go down the tube (*inf*), go to seed (*inf*), retrograde, retrogress, weaken. OPPOSITE: improve. **2** (*the food will deteriorate*) decay, disintegrate, decompose, corrupt, spoil, taint, go bad, crumble, break up, fall apart, fall to pieces.

deterioration *noun* **1** (*deterioration in standards*) decline, degeneration, worsening, depreciation, debasement, degradation, vitiation, drop, failure, fall, falling off, lowering, lapse, slide, relapse, slump, slipping, ebb, waning, atrophy, corrosion, erosion, retrogression, downturn, weakening. OPPOSITE: improvement. **2** (*deterioration of the contents*) decay, disintegration, decomposition, corruption, spoiling, tainting, crumbling, erosion.

determination *noun* **1** (*began with determination*) resolution, resolve, resoluteness, firmness, constancy, conviction, single-mindedness, insistence, persistence, perseverance, purpose, conviction, dedication, drive, push, thrust, backbone, doggedness, stubbornness,

obduracy, intransigence, indomitability, fortitude, guts (*inf*), mettle, stamina, tenacity, pertinacity, grit (*inf*), steadfastness, will, willpower. OPPOSITE: irresolution. **2** (*the determination of the court*) decision, judgment, settlement, conclusion, solution, resolution, resolve, decree, verdict, ruling, opinion, result.

determine *verb* **1** (*determine the matter*) settle, decide, resolve, conclude, terminate, decree, judge, ordain, arbitrate, agree on, clinch (*inf*), establish, fix, finish, end, regulate. **2** (*determine the truth*) ascertain, detect, find out, identify, discover, learn, check, establish, calculate, verify, work out. **3** (*determine to show them*) decide, resolve, purpose, choose, elect, make up one's mind. OPPOSITE: waver. **4** (*determine the course of events*) influence, affect, shape, modify, condition, lead, incline, govern, rule, control, dictate, direct, guide, prompt, impel, induce, sway.

determined *adj* **1** (*a determined charge*) resolute, resolved, firm, single-minded, set, fixed, constant, intent, dogged, persevering, persistent, pertinacious, insistent, steadfast, unflinching, unwavering, uncompromising, stubborn, obdurate, intransigent, indomitable, inflexible, immovable, stalwart, tenacious, convinced, dedicated, decided, purposeful, strong, strong-willed, strong-minded, mettlesome, plucky. OPPOSITE: irresolute. **2** (*determined to win*) bent on, set on, intent on, hell-bent (*inf*).

deterrent *noun* impediment, hindrance, obstacle, discouragement, disincentive, inhibition, repellent, restraint, curb, check, bar, barrier, block, obstruction. OPPOSITE: encouragement.

detest *verb* abhor, loathe, abominate, execrate, hate, deplore, despise, dislike, shrink from, recoil from. OPPOSITE: love.

detestable *adj* abhorrent, loathsome, abominable, execrable, hateful, odious, repugnant, repulsive, repellent, revolting, obnoxious, contemptible, despicable, vile, accursed, offensive, obscene, disgusting, distasteful, heinous, reprehensible, sordid, shocking. OPPOSITE: adorable.

detestation *noun* abhorrence, loathing, abomination, execration, odium, repugnance, revulsion, hate, hatred, animosity, aversion, antipathy, dislike, disgust. OPPOSITE: love.

dethrone *verb* depose, uncrown, unthrone, unseat, oust, topple. OPPOSITE: enthrone.

detonate *verb* **1** (*the bomb did not detonate*) explode, go off, blow up, burst, ignite, discharge, blast. **2** (*they detonated the device*) explode, discharge, trigger, set off, let off, touch off, ignite, light, spark, kindle.

detour *noun* diversion, deviation, digression, bypass, byway, roundabout way, scenic route, circuitous route, indirect course.

detract *verb* diminish, lessen, lower, reduce, subtract from, take away from, devaluate, devalue, belittle, disparage, depreciate, spoil, mar. OPPOSITE: enhance.

detractor *noun* enemy, opponent, critic, backbiter, belittler, denigrator, disparager, traducer, vilifier, defamer, slanderer, muckraker, reviler, scandalmonger. OPPOSITE: supporter.

detriment *noun* damage, harm, injury, ill, hurt, loss,

impairment, mischief, wrong, evil, disservice, disadvantage, prejudice. OPPOSITE: benefit.

detrimental *adj* damaging, harmful, injurious, hurtful, destructive, deleterious, inimical, mischievous, pernicious, baleful, prejudicial, disadvantageous, adverse, unfavourable. OPPOSITE: beneficial.

detritus *noun* rubbish, garbage, junk, litter, scum, waste, remains, debris, rubble, fragments, shards, ruins, wreckage.

devastate *verb* **1** (*devastate the town*) desolate, despoil, spoil, ravage, lay waste, waste, destroy, demolish, level, flatten, raze, wreck, total (*inf*), trash (*inf*), ruin, pillage, plunder, ransack, sack, annihilate. **2** (*devastated at the result*) overwhelm, shatter (*inf*), overcome, overpower, confound, disconcert, discompose, shock, take aback, bewilder, nonplus, stun, floor (*inf*), perturb, discomfit, traumatize.

devastating *adj* **1** (*a devastating bombardment*) destructive, disastrous, damaging, deleterious, harmful, deadly, ruinous, wrecking, catastrophic, savage, fierce. **2** (*a devastating development*) shattering (*inf*), effective, incisive, overwhelming, bewildering, disconcerting, confounding, shocking, stunning, traumatic. **3** (*a devastating beauty*) stunning, dazzling, glamorous, ravishing, lovely, gorgeous, beautiful. **4** (*a devastating satire*) incisive, biting, caustic, cutting, keen, savage, effective, satirical, sardonic, deadly, vitriolic, withering, mordant, trenchant.

devastation *noun* desolation, destruction, demolition, havoc, ravages, damage, ruin, waste, wreckage, annihilation, pillage, plunder, despoliation, spoliation.

develop *verb* **1** (*develop into a major centre*) advance, grow, expand, branch out, spread, enlarge, evolve, improve, mature, blossom, ripen, progress, flourish, prosper, foster, nurture, cultivate, turn. OPPOSITE: stunt. **2** (*began to develop his argument*) elaborate, amplify, augment, expand, broaden, enlarge, magnify, supplement, reinforce, dilate, enhance, unfold, disclose, work out. OPPOSITE: abridge. **3** (*develop new theories*) begin, commence, start, set about, set in motion, found, institute, establish, invent, fashion, form, create, generate, breed, produce, originate. **4** (*how things will develop*) result, come about, grow, ensue, arise, follow, happen. **5** (*develop a cold*) catch, get, go down with, pick up, contract, succumb to, acquire.

development *noun* **1** (*the development of the town*) growth, evolution, advance, advancement, headway, progress, progression, increase, expansion, extension, spread, improvement, maturation, maturity. OPPOSITE: retrogression. **2** (*the development of a new theory*) generation, institution, invention, establishment. **3** (*a development of this argument*) amplification, expansion, enlargement, elaboration, augmentation. OPPOSITE: abridgment. **4** (*a new development in the story*) incident, occurrence, event, happening, circumstance, situation, change, outcome, result, issue, upshot. **5** (*build a new industrial development*) centre, block, complex, estate, land, area.

deviant *adj* divergent, aberrant, digressive, anomalous, abnormal, irregular, variant, odd, bizarre, peculiar, curious, eccentric, freakish, bent (*inf*), kinky (*inf*),

perverse, perverted, pervy (*inf*), sick (*inf*), warped, devious, twisted, queer, quirky, idiosyncratic, unorthodox, offbeat, wayward. OPPOSITE: normal.
➤ *noun* freak, oddity, misfit, pervert, oddball (*inf*), crank (*inf*), weirdo (*inf*), weirdie (*inf*).

deviate *verb* veer, diverge, wander, stray, err, go astray, drift, meander, depart, digress, swerve, bend, slew, avert, turn aside, deflect, differ, vary, change.

deviation *noun* divergence, aberration, departure, abnormality, anomaly, irregularity, eccentricity, digression, deflection, detour, alteration, fluctuation, inconsistency, change, shift, drift, variation, variance, variableness, difference, declination, disparity, discrepancy, quirk, freak.

device *noun* **1** (*a mechanical device*) contrivance, contraption (*inf*), gadget, gimmick, gizmo (*inf*), tool, machine, mechanism, instrument, implement, utensil, appliance, apparatus, invention. **2** (*the plan was a device to deceive the opposition*) ruse, wile, stratagem, strategy, artifice, plan, plot, project, design, scheme, subterfuge, blind, intrigue, conspiracy, deception, fraud, imposture, sleight, trick, ploy, dodge (*inf*), expedient, stunt, manoeuvre, gambit, machination, shift. **3** (*the device on his tunic*) emblem, symbol, mark, design, motif, figure, motto, legend, slogan, crest, coat of arms, badge, shield, seal, logo, insignia, token, colophon.

devil *noun* **1** (*the Devil himself*) Satan, Lucifer, Beelzebub, Mephistopheles, Belial, Old Nick (*inf*), Old Harry (*inf*), Prince of Darkness, Evil One, Lord of the Flies, Archfiend. **2** (*claimed she saw a devil*) demon, fiend, imp, evil spirit. OPPOSITE: angel. **3** (*he's a real devil*) rogue, scoundrel, rascal, wretch, thug, bully, knave, villain, beast, brute, fiend, ghoul, monster, ogre, barbarian, savage. **4** (*behaved like a little devil*) rascal, scamp, mischief, monkey (*inf*), pickle (*inf*), terror, troublemaker, demon, imp. **5** (*feel sorry for the poor devil*) wretch, creature, unfortunate, thing, beggar.

devilish *adj* **1** (*a devilish character*) diabolic, diabolical, demonic, demoniac, demoniacal, evil, fiendish, infernal, satanic, sinister, villainous, wicked, nefarious. OPPOSITE: angelic. **2** (*a devilish night*) fiendish, diabolical, hellish, infernal, evil, vile, wicked, accursed, damnable, atrocious, disastrous, dreadful, execrable, excruciating, outrageous, shocking.

devil-may-care *adj* careless, rash, reckless, wanton, impetuous, impulsive, casual, cavalier, easygoing, flippant, frivolous, happy-go-lucky, heedless, nonchalant, insouciant, jaunty, indifferent, unconcerned, unworried, audacious, swaggering, swashbuckling.

devious *adj* **1** (*devious behaviour*) underhand, deceitful, dishonest, surreptitious, artful, crafty, cunning, sly, slippery (*inf*), furtive, tricky (*inf*), wily, scheming, secretive, guileful, subtle, crooked (*inf*), calculating, designing, double-dealing, treacherous, unscrupulous, evasive, shifty, insidious, insincere, misleading, disingenuous. OPPOSITE: straightforward. **2** (*a devious route*) rambling, circuitous, roundabout, indirect, tortuous, crooked, meandering, wandering, excursive, winding, deviating, erratic, tortuous, digressive, confusing. OPPOSITE: direct.

devise *verb* invent, contrive, scheme, plan, plot, project, design, conceive, concoct, come up with, compose, create, forge, fabricate, hatch, frame, project, shape, form, originate, think up, dream up, cook up (*inf*), imagine, invent, formulate, work out, arrange, order, prepare, put together.

devoid *adj* lacking, wanting, deficient, without, destitute, bereft, bare, barren, void, empty, vacant, free, deprived, denuded. OPPOSITE: full.

devolve *verb* delegate, depute, transfer, commission, hand down, consign, convey, deliver, entrust, fall to, fall upon, rest with.

devote *verb* dedicate, consecrate, give, offer, pledge, assign, allot, allocate, consign, reserve, set apart, set aside, commit, sacrifice, enshrine, surrender, give oneself, apply, put in. OPPOSITE: withhold.

devoted *adj* **1** (*devoted to the cause*) ardent, zealous, dedicated, committed, devout, faithful, loyal, true, true blue, staunch, steadfast, constant, tireless, unswerving. OPPOSITE: indifferent. **2** (*your devoted admirer*) loving, affectionate, fond, admiring, caring, attentive, warm. **3** (*devoted to God*) dedicated, blessed, consecrated, sanctified, hallowed.

devotee *noun* enthusiast, fanatic, fan, admirer, aficionado, addict, fiend (*inf*), merchant (*inf*), buff (*inf*), freak (*inf*), hound (*inf*), zealot, follower, supporter, champion, adherent, advocate, disciple, votary.

devotion *noun* **1** (*his devotion to her*) dedication, commitment, loyalty, constancy, allegiance, adherence, faithfulness, fidelity, support, trueness, fervour, passion, staunchness, steadfastness, solidarity, zeal, ardour, earnestness, enthusiasm, admiration, adoration, regard, attachment, affection, love, fondness, care, caring, closeness, warmness, attentiveness. OPPOSITE: apathy. **2** (*the devotion of the priests*) devoutness, piety, saintliness, godliness, reverence, faith, holiness, spirituality, sanctity, religiousness **3** (*knelt for his devotions*) prayer, worship, religious observance.

devotional *adj* devout, pious, holy, sacred, religious, spiritual, reverential, dutiful, pietistic, solemn. OPPOSITE: profane.

devour *verb* **1** (*devour everything set before him*) consume, eat, eat up, gorge, gobble, guzzle, bolt, cram, stuff (*inf*), wolf (*inf*), gulp, swallow, feast on, pig out (*inf*), scoff (*inf*), tuck into (*inf*), put away (*inf*), knock back (*inf*), polish off (*inf*), finish off, relish, gormandize. **2** (*devour by fire*) destroy, demolish, devastate, dispatch, consume, ravage, annihilate, ruin, waste, lay waste, wreck, wipe out, absorb, engulf, envelop, overwhelm, absorb. **3** (*devour the book*) take in, drink in, feast on, relish, revel in, delight in, enjoy, appreciate. **4** (*devoured all her energy*) use up, consume, swallow up, spend, waste, cost.

devout *adj* **1** (*a devout clergyman*) pious, godly, saintly, pure, holy, religious, righteous, reverent, devotional, committed, prayerful, practising, church-going, orthodox. OPPOSITE: impious. **2** (*devout admiration*) sincere, genuine, heartfelt, earnest, devoted, faithful, staunch, constant, steadfast, unswerving, fervent, ardent, passionate, vehement, zealous, intense, serious, deep, profound, wholehearted. OPPOSITE: insincere.

dexterity *noun* **1** (*the dexterity of the performers*) skill, skilfulness, adroitness, handiness, cleverness, ability, aptitude, expertise, proficiency, mastery, readiness, ingenuity, facility, finesse, deftness, knack, felicity, art, artistry, craft, talent, agility, effortlessness, nimbleness, neatness, smoothness, legerdemain, address. OPPOSITE: clumsiness. **2** (*the dexterity of the negotiators*) skilfulness, tact, cunning, sagacity, ingenuity, inventiveness, resourcefulness, shrewdness, smartness, sharp-wittedness, acuteness, astuteness.

dexterous *adj* **1** (*with dexterous movements*) deft, adroit, adept, skilled, skilful, apt, able, clever, expert, accomplished, artistic, proficient, masterly, agile, nimble, nimble-fingered, neat, nifty (*inf*), nippy, quick, handy, facile. OPPOSITE: clumsy. **2** (*a dexterous politician*) clever, shrewd, astute, smart, sharp-witted, acute, cunning, crafty, artful, wily, ingenious, inventive, resourceful, sagacious.

diabolical *adj* **1** (*the diabolical creature*) diabolic, devilish, demonic, demoniacal, satanic, fiendish, infernal, hellish, nefarious, evil, wicked, monstrous. OPPOSITE: angelic. **2** (*diabolical behaviour*) outrageous, appalling, atrocious, disastrous, barbaric, brutish, monstrous, dreadful, execrable, shocking, excruciating, hateful, nasty, awful, unpleasant, vile, abominable, damnable, sinful, malevolent, malicious. **3** (*took diabolical liberties*) extreme, very great, excessive, inordinate, undue, uncalled-for, unpardonable.

diadem *noun* crown, coronet, circlet, tiara, headband, chaplet, mitre, wreath, fillet.

diagnose *verb* identify, determine, recognize, distinguish, pinpoint, analyse, explain, pronounce, isolate, detect, interpret, investigate.

diagnosis *noun* **1** (*diagnosis of disease*) analysis, identification, recognition, pinpointing, investigation, detection, examination, scrutiny, interpretation. **2** (*questioned her diagnosis*) opinion, judgment, verdict, pronouncement, conclusion, answer, explanation, interpretation.

diagonal *adj* slanting, slanted, cross, crossing, crossways, crosswise, sloping, oblique, crooked, angled, cornerways, cornerwise.

diagonally *adv* slantwise, aslant, on the slant, crossways, crosswise, on the cross, obliquely, at an angle, cornerways, cornerwise.

diagram *noun* plan, chart, drawing, sketch, illustration, picture, draft, representation, outline, cutaway, figure, layout, table, graph, bar chart, pie chart, flow chart, delineation, schema.

dial *verb* telephone, phone, ring, call.

dialect *noun* language, idiom, vernacular, patois, argot, jargon, lingo (*inf*), localism, provincialism, regionalism, accent, speech, diction, tongue, variety.

dialectic *adj* dialectical, logical, logistic, rational, rationalistic, analytic, analytical, polemic, polemical, inductive, deductive, argumentative, contentious, disputatious.
➤ *noun* argument, argumentation, analysis, debate, contention, dialogue, discussion, disputation, polemics, logic, deduction, induction, reasoning, rationale, ratiocination.

dialogue *noun* **1** (*engaged in dialogue*) conversation, confabulation, colloquy, interlocution, discourse, converse, talk, chat, chitchat, gossip, communication, exchange, interchange, argument, debate, discussion, tête-à-tête, parley, crack (*inf*), powwow (*inf*), rap (*inf*), duologue, conference. **2** (*the dialogue of the play*) lines, script, conversation.

diametrically *adv* directly, completely, absolutely, entirely, utterly, exactly, extremely, antithetically, contrastingly.

diaphanous *adj* translucent, pellucid, gauzy, gossamer, gossamery, cobwebby, silken, chiffony, fine, delicate, light, filmy, sheer, see-through, thin, transparent, veily, clear. OPPOSITE: opaque.

diarrhoea *noun* loose motions, the runs (*inf*), the trots (*inf*), the shits (*sl*), gippy tummy, holiday tummy, Montezuma's revenge, Tutankhamen's revenge, Delhi belly, Spanish tummy, dysentery.

diary *noun* journal, log, logbook, annal, chronicle, daybook, yearbook, personal organizer, record, appointment book.

diatribe *noun* tirade, harangue, tongue-lashing (*inf*), slamming (*inf*), running-down (*inf*), slating (*inf*), knocking (*inf*), philippic, castigation, invective, insult, abuse, criticism, attack, onslaught, denunciation, reproof, reprimand, rebuke, upbraiding, stricture, vituperation. OPPOSITE: eulogy.

dicey *adj* risky, chancy, iffy (*inf*), dodgy (*inf*), hairy (*inf*), unpredictable, uncertain, tricky, dangerous, difficult, problematic, ticklish, dubious.

dicky *adj* unsound, unsteady, unstable, unreliable, weak, ailing, frail, infirm, queer, shaky, fluttery.

dictate *verb* **1** (*dictate a letter*) say, speak, utter, announce, pronounce, recite, transmit, read, read aloud, read out. **2** (*dictate what was to happen*) command, order, demand, ordain, lay down, set down, direct, enjoin, insist, decree, bid, instruct, prescribe, rule, impose, promulgate.
➤ *noun* **1** (*the dictate of the emperor*) command, order, decree, injunction, ordinance, bidding, behest, charge, direction, mandate, injunction, edict, ruling, requirement, ultimatum, word, promulgation. **2** (*follow the dictates of reason*) rule, precept, principle, canon, law, code, statute, dictum.

dictator *noun* tyrant, despot, autocrat, oppressor, absolute ruler, supremo, Big Brother (*inf*), autarchist.

dictatorial *adj* **1** (*dictatorial leadership*) tyrannical, tyrannous, despotic, autocratic, totalitarian, authoritarian, autarchic, absolute, unlimited, unrestricted, arbitrary, all-powerful, imperious, omnipotent. OPPOSITE: democratic. **2** (*dictatorial attitude*) oppressive, repressive, overbearing, domineering, authoritarian, magisterial, tyrannical, despotic, imperious, ironhanded, bossy (*inf*), high-handed, high and mighty, peremptory, dogmatic.

dictatorship *noun* tyranny, despotism, totalitarianism, authoritarianism, autocracy, autarchy, absolute rule, absolutism, fascism, police state, reign of terror.

diction *noun* **1** (*her diction was unclear*) speech, language, enunciation, elocution, articulation, intonation, expression, inflection, pronunciation,

delivery, eloquence, fluency, oratory, rhetoric. **2** (*admired for the diction of his prose*) style, vocabulary, language, phraseology, phrasing, expression, wording, terminology, idiom, usage.

dictionary *noun* lexicon, wordbook, glossary, thesaurus, vocabulary, encyclopedia, concordance.

dictum *noun* **1** (*the dictum of the court*) ruling, decree, command, order, pronouncement, direction, injunction, dictate, canon, edict, precept, statement, assertion, fiat. **2** (*a favourite dictum of hers*) saying, maxim, adage, proverb, saw, axiom, aphorism, homily, platitude, truism, cliché, utterance.

didactic *adj* instructive, informative, educational, educative, pedagogic, prescriptive, preceptive, pedantic, moralistic, moralizing, moral, edifying, homiletic.

die *verb* **1** (*he did not want to die*) expire, decease, perish, depart, depart this life, pass away, pass on, peg out (*inf*), snuff it (*inf*), bite the dust (*inf*), buy it (*inf*), croak (*inf*), check out (*inf*), give up the ghost (*inf*), kick the bucket (*inf*), pop off (*inf*), meet one's maker (*inf*), meet one's end (*inf*), cash in one's chips (*inf*), push up the daisies (*inf*), turn up one's toes (*inf*), breathe one's last, draw one's last breath. OPPOSITE: live. **2** (*the light slowly died*) dwindle, fade, ebb, subside, pass, abate, die down, wane, decline, sink, wilt, wither, decline, decay, decrease, fail, peter out, dissolve, disappear, melt away, vanish, lapse, finish, end, stop. OPPOSITE: grow. **3** (*the outboard motor died*) break down, conk out (*inf*), stop, halt, fail, run down, fizzle out, lose power. **4** (*die for some attention*) long, yearn, pine, ache, desire, hunger.

diehard *adj* reactionary, hardline, conservative, ultraconservative, unreconstructed, rightist, fanatical, inflexible, immovable, unchanging, uncompromising, unyielding, adamant, rigid, intransigent, dyed in the wool, stick-in-the-mud (*inf*).

diet[1] *noun* **1** (*a healthy diet*) food, fare, nourishment, nutrition, nutriment, sustenance, subsistence, aliment, comestibles, edibles, foodstuffs, provisions, rations, victuals, commons, viands. **2** (*need to go on a diet*) fast, regimen, regime, abstinence.
➤ *verb* slim, lose weight, weightwatch (*inf*), fast, abstain, reduce.

diet[2] *noun* (*decisions of the diet*) parliament, congress, council, assembly, chamber, legislature, senate, synod.

differ *verb* **1** (*versions differ*) vary, diverge, contrast, contradict, stand apart. OPPOSITE: coincide. **2** (*the two sides agreed to differ*) argue, disagree, demur, dissent, conflict, oppose, take issue, dispute, be at odds with, clash, quarrel, squabble, wrangle, fall out, debate, contend, altercate. OPPOSITE: agree.

difference *noun* **1** (*the difference between the two*) dissimilarity, dissimilitude, unlikeness, contrast, contradiction, contradistinction, distinction, distinctness, contrariety, disparity, discrepancy, divergence, imbalance, diversity, deviation, variation, variance, variety, differentiation, nonconformity, incongruity, antithesis. OPPOSITE: similarity. **2** (*art with a difference*) distinction, distinctness, individuality, singularity, incongruity, idiosyncrasy, eccentricity, peculiarity, oddity. **3** (*a difference of opinion between father and son*) disagreement, argument, contention, wrangle, dispute, disputation, strife, misunderstanding, discord, conflict, variance, altercation, clash, feud, quarrel, row, set-to, vendetta, contretemps, tiff, controversy, bickering. OPPOSITE: agreement. **4** (*pay the difference*) balance, remainder, residue, residuum, rest, excess.

different *adj* **1** (*different from each other*) dissimilar, unlike, contrasting, disparate, discrepant, divergent, incompatible, inconsistent, deviating, clashing, conflicting, opposed, at odds, at variance, poles apart (*inf*), worlds apart (*inf*). OPPOSITE: similar. **2** (*suddenly different in appearance*) altered, changed, modified, transformed, metamorphosed. **3** (*attempted by different people*) varied, various, varying, diverse, separate, miscellaneous, certain, assorted, motley, variegated, sundry, some, several, manifold, multifarious, numerous, many. **4** (*something very different*) unusual, unique, individual, original, distinct, distinctive, special, extraordinary, out of the ordinary, noteworthy, new, novel, unconventional, atypical, anomalous, bizarre, strange, odd, rare, singular, uncommon, remarkable, peculiar. OPPOSITE: ordinary.

differentiate *verb* distinguish, discern, set apart, set off, separate, tell apart, discriminate, contrast, tell the difference, mark off, individualize, particularize.

difficult *adj* **1** (*a difficult climb*) hard, arduous, demanding, uphill, laborious, tough, backbreaking, strenuous, burdensome, onerous, painful, gruelling, tiring, exacting, exhausting, wearisome, formidable. OPPOSITE: easy. **2** (*a difficult case*) intricate, involved, complex, complicated, hard, abstract, abstruse, obscure, dark, baffling, perplexing, intractable, knotty, thorny, puzzling, ticklish, problematical, arcane, recondite, esoteric, enigmatic, deep, profound. OPPOSITE: simple. **3** (*a difficult character*) awkward, unaccommodating, unamenable, intractable, unmanageable, fractious, recalcitrant, refractory, obstreperous, perverse, obstinate, stubborn, tiresome, troublesome, trying, demanding, critical, fastidious, fussy, finicky, perfectionist, particular, rigid, unyielding, uncooperative. OPPOSITE: tractable. **4** (*experienced difficult times*) hard, bad, tough, trying, grim, dark, straitened.

difficulty *noun* **1** (*lift with difficulty*) difficultness, arduousness, hardship, labour, laboriousness, strenuousness, strain, struggle, struggling, awkwardness, painfulness. OPPOSITE: ease. **2** (*the difficulty of the task*) difficultness, hardness, complexity, complicatedness, intricacy, delicacy, perplexity, knottiness, obscurity, abstruseness, challenge. OPPOSITE: simplicity. **3** (*got into difficulty*) trouble, hole (*inf*), fix (*inf*), mess (*inf*), spot (*inf*), tight spot (*inf*), jam (*inf*), pickle (*inf*), pretty pass (*inf*), dire straits (*inf*), how-d'you-do (*inf*), hot water (*inf*), deep water (*inf*). **4** (*her intransigence represented a difficulty*) obstacle, hitch, barrier, hurdle, pitfall, stumbling-block, hindrance, impediment, objection, problem, complication, dilemma, quandary, predicament, snag, hang-up, fly in the ointment (*inf*), hiccup (*inf*), bugger (*sl*), bitch (*inf*), pain in the arse (*sl*). **5** (*times of difficulty*) hardship, trouble, trial, tribulation, struggle, ordeal, exigency.

in difficulty in trouble, up against it (*inf*), stumped (*inf*), out of one's depth (*inf*), in the soup (*inf*), in a fix

(*inf*), in a mess (*inf*), in a jam (*inf*), in a hole (*inf*), in dire straits (*inf*), in a scrape (*inf*), in hot water (*inf*), in deep water (*inf*), in a spot (*inf*), in a tight spot (*inf*), up shit creek (*sl*), embarrassed.

diffidence *noun* shyness, bashfulness, timidity, timidness, timorousness, backwardness, hesitancy, hesitation, apprehension, reluctance, sheepishness, meekness, modesty, humility, self-consciousness, self-effacement, self-doubt, doubt, inhibition, unassertiveness, constraint, reserve, insecurity, distrust, suspicion. OPPOSITE: confidence.

diffident *adj* shy, bashful, abashed, timid, timorous, nervous, backward, hesitant, apprehensive, reluctant, sheepish, meek, modest, humble, shrinking, tentative, self-conscious, self-effacing, shamefaced, self-doubting, doubting, unsure, inhibited, unassertive, unassuming, constrained, reserved, withdrawn, insecure, distrusting, suspicious. OPPOSITE: confident.

diffuse *verb* spread, scatter, disperse, send out, disseminate, propagate, promulgate, broadcast, circulate, effuse, permeate, dispense, distribute, dissipate, dispel. OPPOSITE: gather.
  ➤ *adj* **1** (*a diffuse community*) scattered, disconnected, dispersed, spread out, unconcentrated. OPPOSITE: concentrated. **2** (*a diffuse letter*) wordy, verbose, long-winded, waffling (*inf*), loquacious, rambling, wandering, meandering, maundering, copious, profuse, digressive, discursive, circumlocutory, roundabout, circuitous, periphrastic, prolix, imprecise, vague, loose. OPPOSITE: concise.

diffusion *noun* **1** (*the diffusion of light*) dispersion, scattering, spread, spreading, dissemination, radiation, propagation, promulgation, broadcasting, circulation, effusion, distribution, dispensation, dispelling. OPPOSITE: agglomeration. **2** (*the diffusion of his prose style*) verbosity, verbiage, prolixity, wordiness, diffuseness, rambling, wandering, waffling (*inf*), long-windedness, loquaciousness, loquacity, periphrasis, digressiveness, discursiveness, profuseness, circumlocution, circuitousness. OPPOSITE: terseness.

dig *verb* **1** (*dig a hole*) excavate, scoop, spade, gouge, delve, probe, penetrate, pierce, grub, burrow, hollow, hole, tunnel, channel, quarry, mine. **2** (*dig the soil*) turn over, break up, work, hoe, till, cultivate, harrow, plough. **3** (*dig his neighbour in the ribs*) poke, prod, jab, punch, thrust, drive, push. **4** (*dig into his employer's affairs*) investigate, delve, probe, go into, research, search, come across, come up with.
  ➤ *noun* **1** (*a dig in the ribs*) poke, prod, jab, punch, thrust. **2** (*a last dig at her expense*) gibe, taunt, jeer, sneer, insult, insinuation, slur, quip, barb, wisecrack (*inf*), crack (*inf*).

dig up 1 (*see what you can dig up*) discover, find, retrieve, track down, expose, uncover, root out, extricate, bring to light, unearth. **2** (*dig up the coffin*) disinter, exhume, unearth.

digest *verb* **1** (*digest a meal*) assimilate, absorb, ingest, incorporate, process, convert, dissolve, break down, macerate. **2** (*digest the news*) take in, absorb, grasp, assimilate, master, comprehend, understand, ponder, contemplate, meditate, think about, mull over, reflect, consider, weigh up, study. **3** (*digest all the material*) systematize, codify, classify, catalogue, arrange, order, dispose, methodize, tabulate. **4** (*digest his thesis*) abridge, condense, compress, summarize, précis, shorten, reduce. OPPOSITE: amplify.

➤ *noun* abridgment, summary, outline, compendium, abstract, synopsis, résumé, précis, review, epitome.

digestion *noun* **1** (*digestion of the meal*) assimilation, absorption, ingestion, conversion, breaking down, dissolution, maceration. **2** (*digestion of information*) assimilation, absorption, understanding, comprehension, mastery, consideration, contemplation.

dignified *adj* stately, grand, majestic, august, noble, lordly, regal, honourable, distinguished, lofty, exalted, imposing, impressive, solemn, grave, staid, upright, formal, ceremonious, decorous, reserved, courtly. OPPOSITE: lowly.

dignify *verb* ennoble, honour, exalt, elevate, raise, advance, promote, aggrandize, glorify, distinguish, adorn, grace, enhance. OPPOSITE: degrade.

dignitary *noun* notable, notability, worthy, personage, celebrity, celeb (*inf*), luminary, leading light, public figure, pillar of society, high-up (*inf*), somebody, star, lion, VIP (*inf*), bigwig (*inf*), big name (*inf*), big noise (*inf*), big shot (*inf*), big gun (*inf*), big wheel (*inf*), top brass (*inf*).

dignity *noun* **1** (*acted with dignity*) nobility, nobleness, stateliness, majesty, grandeur, augustness, lordliness, regalness, regality, impressiveness, exaltedness, hauteur, loftiness, eminence, elevation, greatness, importance, excellence, standing, rank, status, station, honour, honourability, respectability, solemnity, reserve, gravity, poise, propriety, decorum, ceremoniousness, self-possession, courtliness, formality. OPPOSITE: lowliness. **2** (*mindful of her dignity*) pride, self-respect, self-importance, self-esteem, self-regard, self-conceit, amour propre.

digress *verb* deviate, diverge, wander, stray, depart, drift, ramble, meander, maunder, turn aside, go off at a tangent, get off the subject, expatiate.

digression *noun* **1** (*digression from the main theme*) deviation, divergence, diversion, departure, wandering, drifting, rambling, straying, detour. **2** (*a speech with many digressions*) aside, footnote, parenthesis, obiter dictum, apostrophe.

dilapidated *adj* ramshackle, tumbledown, rickety, shaky, ruined, ruinous, broken-down, run-down, beat-up (*inf*), fallen in, decrepit, shabby, battered, neglected, uncared-for, decayed, decaying, crumbling, worn-out. OPPOSITE: restored.

dilapidation *noun* ruin, decay, deterioration, disintegration, destruction, disrepair, wear and tear, downfall, collapse, demolition, dissolution, waste. OPPOSITE: renovation.

dilate *verb* expand, extend, stretch, enlarge, widen, broaden, spread, increase, swell, bloat, distend, inflate, puff out. OPPOSITE: contract.

dilate on develop, amplify, enlarge on, expound, elaborate on, expatiate on, dwell on, detail, spin out. OPPOSITE: abridge.

dilation *noun* dilatation, expansion, extension, enlargement, increase, spread, widening, broadening,

distension, inflation, amplification. OPPOSITE: contraction.

dilatory *adj* dawdling, lagging, lingering, slow, sluggish, slack, lazy, lackadaisical, loitering, indolent, tardy, dallying, dilly-dallying, tarrying, behindhand, procrastinating, delaying, postponing, stalling, deferring, shelving, temporizing, time-wasting, backward. OPPOSITE: prompt.

dilemma *noun* quandary, conflict, predicament, embarrassment, plight, fix (*inf*), jam (*inf*), spot (*inf*), mess (*inf*), tight corner (*inf*), pickle (*inf*), difficulty, problem, puzzle, perplexity, strait, vicious circle, no-win situation (*inf*), catch 22 (*inf*).

dilettante *noun* **1** (*the enthusiasm of the dilettante*) dabbler, amateur, nonprofessional, trifler, dallier, potterer. **2** (*an audience of dilettantes*) aesthete, art lover, connoisseur.

diligence *noun* assiduity, assiduousness, application, industry, industriousness, laboriousness, intentness, care, conscientiousness, attention, attentiveness, heedfulness, doggedness, perseverance, thoroughness, persistence, constancy, concentration, dedication, pertinacity, tenacity, earnestness, sedulousness. OPPOSITE: carelessness.

diligent *adj* assiduous, industrious, hardworking, sedulous, painstaking, meticulous, thorough, attentive, careful, studious, earnest, heedful, intent, constant, dogged, slogging, laborious, persistent, persevering, conscientious, dedicated, indefatigable, tenacious, pertinacious, zealous, tireless, untiring, busy. OPPOSITE: lazy.

dilly-dally *verb* loiter, lag, dawdle, dally, linger, delay, procrastinate, shilly-shally (*inf*), tarry, potter, trifle, falter, hem and haw, hesitate, hover, waver, dither, vacillate, waste time. OPPOSITE: hurry.

dilute *verb* **1** (*dilute the mixture*) adulterate, attenuate, water down, cut, thin, weaken, reduce, diffuse. OPPOSITE: concentrate. **2** (*dilute the impact*) diminish, decrease, lessen, attenuate, reduce, temper, mitigate, moderate, tone down, soften, weaken.

dim *adj* **1** (*the dim twilight*) dark, dusky, shadowy, sombre, tenebrous, crepuscular, gloomy, dismal, dingy, dull, grey, cloudy, overcast, muted, lacklustre, feeble, leaden, lowering. OPPOSITE: bright. **2** (*a dim outline*) obscure, indistinct, vague, blurred, blurry, bleary, unclear, foggy, hazy, misty, nebulous, fuzzy, faint, weak, feeble, ill-defined, confused, imperfect, pale, shadowy, obfuscated. OPPOSITE: clear. **3** (*rather a dim boy*) stupid, dense, obtuse, slow, slow-witted, dim-witted, dumb (*inf*), thick (*inf*), dozy, gormless (*inf*), doltish. OPPOSITE: clever. **4** (*dim prospect*) unpromising, inauspicious, unfavourable, gloomy, sombre, bleak, discouraging, disheartening, depressing, dispiriting, adverse. OPPOSITE: encouraging.

➤ *verb* **1** (*dim the lights*) lower, dip, turn down, shade, obscure, darken, dull. OPPOSITE: brighten. **2** (*the glow dimmed*) weaken, cloud, cloud over, blur, fade, pale, tarnish, darken.

dimension *noun* **1** (*dimensions of the craft*) extent, size, scope, magnitude, proportions, measurement, measure, capacity, volume, bulk, mass, largeness, amplitude, length, width, breadth, height, depth, area. **2** (*the dimensions of the problem*) size, extent, bigness, greatness, magnitude, range, importance, scope, scale. **3** (*this adds a whole new dimension*) aspect, side, facet, element, factor, feature.

diminish *verb* **1** (*her chances diminished*) lessen, decrease, reduce, lower, shrink, contract, shrivel, shorten, cut, curtail, truncate, abate, weaken, subside, deflate, sink, decline, wane, die away, die out, fade, dwindle, peter out (*inf*), taper off, ebb, slacken, recede, narrow, constrict, retrench. OPPOSITE: increase. **2** (*attempts to diminish his achievements*) disparage, belittle, devalue, defame, deprecate, denigrate, derogate, demean, cheapen, vilify. OPPOSITE: appreciate.

diminution *noun* decrease, reduction, deduction, lessening, lowering, contraction, constriction, shrinkage, shortening, retrenchment, cut, cutback, curtailment, truncating, abatement, slackening, weakening, failing, decay, decline, dying away, ebb, wane, subsidence. OPPOSITE: increase.

diminutive *adj* tiny, minute, small, small-scale, little, miniature, wee, compact, pocket, pocket-sized, pygmy, midget, dwarfish, elfin, mini (*inf*), baby (*inf*), teeny (*inf*), teeny-weeny (*inf*), dinky (*inf*), Lilliputian, undersized, pint-sized (*inf*), slight, petite, microscopic, infinitesimal, bantam, puny, homuncular. OPPOSITE: large.

din *noun* noise, clamour, clangour, uproar, racket, row, crash, clatter, commotion, tumult, outcry, shout, shouting, yelling, hullabaloo, brouhaha, babble, hubbub, bedlam, pandemonium. OPPOSITE: silence. **din into** instil, drive home, reiterate, harp on, drum into, hammer, inculcate, reiterate.

dine *verb* eat, feed, sup, feast, banquet, lunch.

dingy *adj* dull, dark, dim, dusky, sombre, gloomy, murky, hazy, smoggy, smoky, obscure, drab, dreary, dismal, cheerless, colourless, faded, discoloured, shabby, run-down, worn, seedy, tacky (*inf*), dirty, grimy, soiled, sooty. OPPOSITE: bright.

dinky *adj* dainty, fine, small, cute, petite, neat, natty (*inf*), trim, diminutive, miniature, mini (*inf*).

dinner *noun* supper, lunch, tea, main meal, evening meal, meal, repast, collation, spread (*inf*), blowout (*inf*), feast, banquet, refection.

dint *noun* dent, impression, indentation, pit, hollow, depression.
by dint of by means of, by the agency of, by virtue of, by use of, by means of, by force of, through the power of.

dip *verb* **1** (*dipped her toes into the sea*) plunge, duck, submerge, immerse, souse, douse, dunk, lower, sink, bathe, dive, soak, drench, steep, rinse. **2** (*the sun dipped behind the hills*) set, descend, lower, sink, drop, fade, disappear, subside. **3** (*prices are sure to dip*) descend, sink, go down, lower, drop, fall, decrease, decline, slump, droop, sag, subside. OPPOSITE: rise. **4** (*where the land dips to the sea*) slope, descend, go down, fall, drop, sink, slant down, incline.
➤ *noun* **1** (*the dip between the hills*) incline, decline, descent, slope, slant. **2** (*a dip in the surface*) hollow, hole, depression, dent, indentation, concavity, basin. **3** (*a dip in popularity*) decline, fall, drop, slump, decrease,

lowering. **4** (*took a dip in the pool*) plunge, dive, ducking, dunking, soaking, drenching, sousing, dousing, bathe, swim, paddle, douche, immersion, infusion. **5** (*offered dips to the guests*) sauce, cream, dressing, mixture, concoction. **6** (*sheep dip*) disinfectant, preservative, solution, mixture, preparation, dilution, infusion, suspension.

dip into 1 (*a book to dip into*) skim, browse, peruse, look at, leaf through, look through, run through, glance at, flick through, thumb through. **2** (*dip into science*) dabble in, scratch the surface of, play at, sample, try. **3** (*dip into her savings*) spend, draw on, use.

diplomacy *noun* **1** (*international diplomacy*) statecraft, statesmanship, negotiations, politics, international relations. **2** (*showed great diplomacy in the matter*) tact, tactfulness, discretion, cleverness, cunning, subtlety, delicacy, finesse, care, sensitivity, politeness, judiciousness, prudence, skill, craft, artfulness, savoir faire. OPPOSITE: tactlessness.

diplomat *noun* **1** (*a diplomat representing his country*) ambassador, envoy, emissary, plenipotentiary, consul, attaché, chargé d'affaires, legate. **2** (*a reputation as a diplomat*) diplomatist, mediator, moderator, conciliator, reconciler, go-between, intermediary, middleman, arbitrator, negotiator, peacemaker, tactician, politician, statesman, stateswoman.

diplomatic *adj* **1** (*adopted a diplomatic approach*) tactful, discreet, sensitive, judicious, prudent, clever, careful, polite, politic, delicate, subtle, skilful, adept, artful. OPPOSITE: tactless. **2** (*a diplomatic mission*) consular, ambassadorial, foreign office.

dire *adj* **1** (*a dire situation*) direful, dreadful, terrible, frightful, fearful, alarming, distressing, shocking, harrowing, outrageous, unspeakable, appalling, awful, atrocious, cruel, grievous, grim, horrible, horrid, disastrous, calamitous, catastrophic, cataclysmic, ruinous, miserable, wretched, woeful. OPPOSITE: splendid. **2** (*a dire warning*) grave, dreadful, ominous, portentous, sinister, dismal, gloomy, grim, pessimistic, unfavourable, inauspicious, unpropitious. **3** (*a dire shortage*) desperate, urgent, pressing, drastic, crying, grave, critical, crucial, extreme, vital, compelling, exigent.

direct *adj* **1** (*took the direct route*) straight, unswerving, undeviating, uninterrupted, unbroken, nonstop, through, shortest. OPPOSITE: circuitous. **2** (*a direct manner*) straightforward, honest, frank, candid, blunt, bluff, outspoken, open, forthright, up-front (*inf*), downright, sincere, plain, plainspoken, matter-of-fact, point-blank, straight, unambiguous, unequivocal, explicit, clear, categorical. OPPOSITE: equivocal. **3** (*the direct opposite*) absolute, complete, exact, downright, diametrical, thorough. **4** (*direct contact*) immediate, firsthand, face-to-face, head-on, personal. OPPOSITE: indirect. **5** (*a direct copy*) precise, accurate, exact, correct, verbatim.
➤ *verb* **1** (*direct the project*) manage, control, run, organize, orchestrate, govern, lead, command, rule, conduct, guide, regulate, administer, superintend, preside over, oversee, supervise, call the shots (*inf*), run the show (*inf*), dominate, domineer, engineer, advise, handle, mastermind, dispose. **2** (*directed to hand over their*

weapons) command, order, charge, enjoin, bid, instruct, dictate, adjure. **3** (*direct the party*) guide, lead, conduct, point, show, steer, navigate, pilot, accompany, escort, usher. OPPOSITE: mislead. **4** (*directed at his enemies*) aim, point, level, fix, focus, train, steer, turn, destine, address, intend, mean. **5** (*directed to head office*) address, post, send, mail, route, label, superscribe.

direction *noun* **1** (*showed them the direction*) way, course, route, road, path, track, line, run, bearing, orientation. **2** (*direction of his affairs*) management, control, command, conduct, administration, government, regulation, orchestration, running, disposal, handling, leadership, supervision, superintendency, overseeing, masterminding, guidance, charge, rule. **3** (*the direction of her life*) course, trend, tendency, aim, current, drift, end, tack, tenor, bent, scope, bias, orientation, inclination, leaning, proclivity. **4** (*heard the direction*) order, command, instruction, charge, dictate, bidding, prescription, enjoinment. **5** (*scribbled down the direction*) address, label, mark, superscription.

directions *pl noun* instructions, guidelines, orders, commands, plan, recommendations, indications, injunctions, directives, rules, regulations, guidance, briefing.

directive *noun* direction, command, instruction, order, regulation, ruling, charge, imperative, dictate, decree, mandate, injunction, prescription, ordinance, bidding, edict, notice, enjoinment, fiat.

directly *adv* **1** (*I shall be with you directly*) immediately, straightaway, right away, at once, without delay, without hesitation, instantly, instantaneously, quickly, speedily, pronto (*inf*), promptly, forthwith, shortly, soon, as soon as possible, in a moment, presently, posthaste. OPPOSITE: later. **2** (*spoke directly to her*) bluntly, frankly, candidly, plainly, clearly, explicitly, forthrightly, honestly, point-blank, face-to-face, categorically, straightforwardly, unequivocally, unambiguously, sincerely, truthfully. **3** (*directly opposite*) exactly, diametrically, absolutely, completely, downright.

director *noun* manager, managing director, chairman, chairwoman, chairperson, chair, executive, chief executive, administrator, governor, head, chief, boss (*inf*), gaffer (*inf*), principal, president, superintendent, supervisor, overseer, controller, organizer, conductor, leader, producer, top dog (*inf*), kingpin (*inf*), honcho (*inf*).

dirge *noun* requiem, elegy, lament, keen, funeral song, dead march, burial hymn, threnody, monody, coronach.

dirt *noun* **1** (*bring dirt into the house*) filth, grime, gunge (*inf*), gunk (*inf*), crap (*inf*), crud (*inf*), yuck (*inf*), grot (*inf*), grunge (*inf*), muck, shit (*sl*), excrement, mire, mud, ooze, sludge, slime, dust, soot, dross, waste, stain, tarnish, smudge, pollution, impurity, dirtiness, foulness. OPPOSITE: cleanness. **2** (*digging in the dirt*) earth, soil, clay, mud, silt, loam, dust. **3** (*the dirt in this story*) indecency, impurity, smut (*inf*), sleaze (*inf*), sleaziness (*inf*), obscenity, pornography, lewdness, sordidness, coarseness, bawdiness, ribaldry, salaciousness. **4** (*dished*

the dirt about his background) gossip, scandal, rumour, talk, slander, libel, revelations.

dirty *adj* **1** (*dirty dishes*) filthy, grimy, begrimed, grotty (*inf*), soiled, mucky, messy, bedraggled, scruffy, shabby, dusty, sooty, unclean, unhygienic, grubby, greasy, miry, slimy, nasty, yucky (*inf*), cruddy (*inf*), unwashed, foul, contaminated, polluted, stained, spotted, smudged, sullied, defiled, tarnished, clouded, cloudy, dull, dark, muddy, murky. OPPOSITE: clean. **2** (*dirty magazines*) obscene, indecent, blue, sleazy (*inf*), coarse, filthy, smutty, raunchy (*inf*), lascivious, licentious, salacious, prurient, lewd, bawdy, ribald, risqué, sordid, vulgar, suggestive, pornographic, corrupt, improper. **3** (*a dirty liar*) mean, low, contemptible, abject, base, vile, nasty, despicable, cowardly, shabby, sordid, squalid, ignominious, unscrupulous, unsporting, crooked, deceitful, fraudulent, double-dealing, unfair, corrupt, dishonest, treacherous. OPPOSITE: honourable. **4** (*a dirty look*) malevolent, threatening, angry, resentful, bitter, smouldering, indignant, annoyed, offended, peeved. **5** (*ran into dirty weather*) stormy, bad, nasty, foul, gloomy, murky, overcast, lowering, misty, gusty, squally, rainy, unpleasant.

➣ *verb* soil, begrime, befoul, stain, smear, smirch, besmirch, smudge, splash, spatter, spot, mess up, spoil, muddy, blacken, foul, contaminate, pollute, sully, tarnish, defile, adulterate. OPPOSITE: clean.

disability *noun* **1** (*treatment of his disability*) handicap, defect, disablement, impairment, infirmity, affliction, disorder, affliction, ailment, complaint, illness, malady, weakness. **2** (*reduced to a state of disability*) incapacity, inability, incapability, infirmity, impotency, unfitness, weakness, powerlessness, incompetence, ineptitude, disqualification. OPPOSITE: fitness.

disable *verb* **1** (*disabled at birth*) cripple, lame, incapacitate, debilitate, paralyse, prostrate, immobilize, handicap, enfeeble, impair, damage, hamstring, weaken. **2** (*disable the lorry*) immobilize, deactivate, put out of action, render inoperative, stop, paralyse. OPPOSITE: activate.

disabled *adj* physically challenged, handicapped, incapacitated, immobilized, infirm, impaired, unfit, crippled, lame, maimed, paralysed, bedridden, enfeebled, weak, weakened, debilitated, indisposed, out of action. OPPOSITE: able-bodied.

disabuse *verb* undeceive, enlighten, correct, set right, set straight, disenchant, disillusion. OPPOSITE: deceive.

disadvantage *noun* **1** (*his lameness proved a disadvantage*) drawback, burden, snag, flaw, fault, defect, hindrance, liability, impediment, handicap, hang-up, fly in the ointment (*inf*), limitation, inconvenience, trouble, nuisance, penalty, privation, weakness, weak point, weak link, Achilles' heel (*inf*), minus, downside. OPPOSITE: advantage. **2** (*worked to her disadvantage*) detriment, harm, prejudice, disservice, hardship, lack, damage, injury, hurt, mischief, loss. OPPOSITE: benefit.

disadvantaged *adj* deprived, poor, poverty-stricken, handicapped, underprivileged, impoverished, discriminated against, struggling, in need, in want, in distress.

disadvantageous *adj* detrimental, prejudicial,

deleterious, injurious, damaging, destructive, harmful, hurtful, adverse, unfavourable, unfortunate, unlucky, inconvenient, ill-timed, inexpedient, inadvisable, inopportune, troublesome, hapless. OPPOSITE: advantageous.

disaffected *adj* disloyal, unfaithful, estranged, alienated, antagonistic, hostile, unfriendly, dissatisfied, discontented, disgruntled, uncompliant, unsubmissive, mutinous, rebellious, seditious. OPPOSITE: loyal.

disaffection *noun* estrangement, alienation, breach, disagreement, disloyalty, antagonism, antipathy, hostility, unfriendliness, animosity, ill will, resentment, bad blood, disharmony, discord, dissatisfaction, discontentment, coolness, dislike, repugnance, aversion. OPPOSITE: loyalty.

disagree *verb* **1** (*they often disagree*) dissent, debate, dispute, contend, take issue, contest, fight, object, differ, argue, squabble, wrangle, quarrel, have words (*inf*), bicker, spar, altercate, fall out (*inf*), oppose. OPPOSITE: agree. **2** (*their tastes disagree*) conflict, clash, differ, vary, contradict, diverge, deviate, be at variance. OPPOSITE: correspond. **3** (*the food disagreed with her*) upset, make unwell, bother, discomfort, distress, trouble, nauseate, sicken.

disagreeable *adj* **1** (*a disagreeable task*) unpleasant, displeasing, offensive, nasty, horrible, horrid, dreadful, hateful, detestable, obnoxious, objectionable, odious, repugnant, repulsive, repellent, revolting, uninviting, abominable, disgusting, distasteful, nauseating, yucky (*inf*), unsavoury, unpalatable. OPPOSITE: pleasant. **2** (*a disagreeable character*) unfriendly, brusque, abrupt, churlish, surly, awkward, difficult, contrary, disobliging, unhelpful, bad-tempered, ill-tempered, ill-natured, grouchy (*inf*), ratty (*inf*), tetchy (*inf*), peevish, irritable, cross, rude, impolite, discourteous, ungracious, nasty, unpleasant, unlikable. OPPOSITE: agreeable.

disagreement *noun* **1** (*a public disagreement*) argument, dispute, disputation, squabble, wrangle, falling-out (*inf*), bickering, quarrel, row, tiff (*inf*), sparring, altercation, conflict, clash, debate, controversy, misunderstanding, dissension, dissent, disharmony, contention, friction, discord, strife, division. OPPOSITE: harmony. **2** (*a marked disagreement between the figures*) discrepancy, difference, contrast, variation, variance, disparity, divergence, diversity, incompatibility, inconsistency, contradiction, conflict, nonconformity, clash, deviation, dissimilarity, dissimilitude, discord, incongruity, unlikeness. OPPOSITE: similarity.

disallow *verb* **1** (*disallowed from entry*) forbid, prohibit, ban, proscribe, bar, debar, cancel, veto, boycott, embargo. OPPOSITE: sanction. **2** (*his argument was disallowed*) reject, repudiate, disclaim, disaffirm, disavow, abjure, disown, dismiss, refuse, rebuff, repel, repulse, shun. OPPOSITE: accept.

disappear *verb* **1** (*disappear from view*) vanish, fade, melt away, dissolve, evaporate, evanesce, dematerialize, ebb, recede, wane. OPPOSITE: appear. **2** (*disappear from the scene*) go, depart, exit, retire, retreat, withdraw, flee, fly, scarper (*inf*), vamoose (*inf*), abscond, escape, hide, make tracks (*inf*). **3** (*such practices disappeared years ago*) vanish,

end, cease, fade, pass, die out, die away, expire, die, perish.

disappearance *noun* **1** (*his sudden disappearance*) vanishing, passing from sight, fading, evaporation, dematerialization, melting away, departure, withdrawal, exit, retreat, loss, going, passing, desertion, flight, ebb, wane, eclipse. OPPOSITE: appearance. **2** (*the disappearance of this tradition*) end, passing, vanishing, dying-out, death, perishing, extinction, expiry, eclipse, evanescence.

disappoint *verb* **1** (*had to disappoint her*) fail, let down, dissatisfy, disillusion, disenchant, delude, deceive, vex, depress, dispirit, disgruntle, discourage, dishearten, dismay, sadden, upset. OPPOSITE: satisfy. **2** (*disappoint his hopes*) frustrate, foil, thwart, defeat, confound, baffle, balk, hamper, hinder, impede, interfere with, obstruct, disconcert. OPPOSITE: gratify.

disappointed *adj* **1** (*disappointed fans*) let down, upset, saddened, deflated, disheartened, downhearted, downcast, cast down, depressed, dispirited, despondent, distressed, discontented, disgruntled, chagrined, miffed (*inf*), disenchanted, disillusioned, dissatisfied, vexed. OPPOSITE: pleased. **2** (*disappointed hopes*) frustrated, thwarted, baffled, foiled, balked, defeated, failed. OPPOSITE: satisfied.

disappointing *adj* **1** (*a disappointing result*) upsetting, saddening, sorry, unhappy, disagreeable, disheartening, discouraging, depressing, dispiriting, distressing, disenchanting, dissatisfying, anticlimactic, disconcerting, vexing. OPPOSITE: encouraging. **2** (*a disappointing response*) unsatisfactory, inadequate, insufficient, sorry, unworthy, underwhelming, inferior, second-rate, pathetic, lame. OPPOSITE: satisfactory.

disappointment *noun* **1** (*the children's disappointment*) sadness, disenchantment, disillusionment, chagrin, despondency, regret, dissatisfaction, discontent, disgruntlement, distress, discouragement, dispiritedness, displeasure, mortification, vexation. OPPOSITE: satisfaction. **2** (*the disappointment of his hopes*) frustration, thwarting, foiling, dashing, balking, defeat, failure. **3** (*the results are a disappointment*) letdown, setback, comedown, failure, defeat, miscarriage, misfortune, blow, disaster, calamity, fiasco, washout (*inf*), wipeout (*inf*), nonevent, anticlimax, damp squib (*inf*).

disapprobation *noun* disapproval, displeasure, disfavour, dislike, censure, blame, condemnation, denunciation, criticism, stricture, reproof, reproach, objection, exception. OPPOSITE: approbation.

disapproval *noun* disapprobation, displeasure, dissatisfaction, blame, censure, criticism, stick (*inf*), condemnation, denunciation, deprecation, disparagement, rebuke, rejection, veto, remonstration, reproof, reproach, objection, exception, dislike, animadversion. OPPOSITE: approval.

disapprove *verb* **1** (*disapprove of his tactics*) censure, blame, condemn, frown on, look down on, take a dim view of, discountenance, deplore, hold in contempt, denounce, deprecate, disparage, think little of, find unacceptable, reproach, rebuke, reprove, object to, take exception to, remonstrate against, criticize, dislike.

OPPOSITE: approve. **2** (*disapprove the suggestion*) reject, spurn, disallow, veto, turn down, refuse, set aside. OPPOSITE: sanction.

disarm *verb* **1** (*disarm the prisoners*) disable, unman, unarm, immobilize, put out of action. OPPOSITE: arm. **2** (*both sides are to disarm*) lay down arms, demilitarize, demobilize, disband, deactivate. **3** (*disarmed by his charm*) win over, charm, persuade, convert, set at ease, mollify, placate, appease, conciliate, propitiate.

disarmament *noun* demilitarization, demobilization, deactivation, arms control, weapons control, arms reduction, arms limitation.

disarming *adj* charming, winning, persuasive, irresistible, likable, conciliatory, mollifying.

disarrange *verb* derange, disorder, confuse, disorganize, disturb, unsettle, upset, discompose, untidy, mess up, mix up, muddle, dishevel, rumple, tousle, jumble, shuffle, shake up, dislocate, scatter. OPPOSITE: arrange.

disarray *noun* **1** (*the house is in disarray*) disorder, confusion, muddle, clutter, jumble, tangle, derangement, discomposure, dishevelment, untidiness, mess, mix-up, chaos, shambles, state. OPPOSITE: order. **2** (*the team was in a state of disarray*) disorder, disorderliness, confusion, disharmony, disunity, indiscipline, disorganization, disarrangement, discomposure, unruliness, unsettledness, upset.

disaster *noun* **1** (*a national disaster*) calamity, catastrophe, cataclysm, tragedy, stroke, blow, misfortune, accident, mishap, misadventure, mischance, reverse, reversal, setback, adversity, ruin, ruination, shock, trouble, affliction, act of God. OPPOSITE: blessing. **2** (*the campaign was a disaster*) fiasco, failure, debacle, flop (*inf*), dud (*inf*), washout (*inf*).

disastrous *adj* calamitous, catastrophic, dire, ruinous, destructive, cataclysmic, devastating, ravaging, detrimental, harmful, injurious, ruinous, terrible, appalling, black, dreadful, shocking, tragic, adverse, unfortunate, untoward, unlucky, unpropitious, ill-fated, ill-starred, fatal, hapless, miserable. OPPOSITE: auspicious.

disavowal *noun* denial, repudiation, contradiction, renunciation, gainsaying, disowning, disclaimer, recantation, retraction, rejection, dissent, disaffirmation, abjuration.

disband *verb* **1** (*the party disbanded*) disperse, break up, dissolve, scatter, separate, part company. OPPOSITE: gather. **2** (*we will disband the unit*) break up, dismiss, disperse, let go, send home, demobilize, demob (*inf*). OPPOSITE: muster.

disbelief *noun* unbelief, incredulity, doubt, scepticism, distrust, mistrust, suspicion, questioning, rejection, discredit, dubiety. OPPOSITE: belief.

disbelieve *verb* discredit, reject, repudiate, discount, distrust, mistrust, suspect, doubt, question, challenge, scoff at. OPPOSITE: believe.

disbeliever *noun* unbeliever, doubter, agnostic, atheist, questioner, challenger, sceptic, scoffer, doubting Thomas, nihilist, nullifidian. OPPOSITE: believer.

disburse *verb* spend, pay out, expend, fork out (*inf*),

cough up (*inf*), lay out, dish out (*inf*), shell out (*inf*). OPPOSITE: save.

disc *noun* **1** (*a metal disc*) circle, ring, plate, counter, saucer, discus. **2** (*collection of discs*) record, recording, single, LP, vinyl, album.

discard *verb* reject, abandon, cast aside, ditch (*inf*), dump (*inf*), relinquish, forsake, shed, chuck away (*inf*), chuck out (*inf*), throw away, throw out, toss out, get rid of, drop, dispose of, dispense with, jettison, junk (*inf*), scrap, repudiate, axe (*inf*), remove. OPPOSITE: retain.

discern *verb* perceive, descry, make out, see, observe, notice, behold, catch sight of, espy, pick out, detect, ascertain, determine, discover, discriminate, distinguish, differentiate, judge, recognize. OPPOSITE: miss.

discernible *adj* visible, perceptible, perceivable, noticeable, detectable, appreciable, distinct, distinguishable, observable, recognizable, apparent, obvious, clear, manifest, plain, conspicuous, palpable, patent, discoverable. OPPOSITE: imperceptible.

discerning *adj* discriminating, critical, judicious, wise, perceptive, percipient, perspicacious, clear-sighted, eagle-eyed, sensitive, astute, quick, sharp, penetrating, piercing, shrewd, intelligent, clever, knowing, ingenious, subtle, prudent, sagacious. OPPOSITE: dull.

discernment *noun* discrimination, perspicacity, perception, perceptiveness, percipience, judgment, sagacity, acuteness, astuteness, shrewdness, wisdom, acumen, keenness, sharpness, penetration, insight, ingenuity, intelligence, cleverness, understanding, awareness, clear-sightedness, taste. OPPOSITE: dullness.

discharge *verb* **1** (*discharge from prison*) release, free, set free, let go, liberate, emancipate, loose, pardon, absolve, acquit, clear, relieve, reprieve, dismiss, exonerate, exculpate, manumit. OPPOSITE: detain. **2** (*discharge from employment*) expel, eject, oust, dismiss, fire (*inf*), sack (*inf*), give someone the sack (*inf*), get rid of, axe (*inf*), boot out (*inf*), give someone the elbow (*inf*), turf out (*inf*), cashier, remove, discard. OPPOSITE: appoint. **3** (*discharge fumes*) emit, exude, give off, let off, let out, eject, excrete, release, gush, ooze, leak, empty, disgorge. OPPOSITE: absorb. **4** (*discharge your weapons*) fire, shoot, detonate, explode, set off, let off. **5** (*discharge a load*) unload, off-load, unburden, disburden, lighten, relieve, remove. OPPOSITE: load. **6** (*discharge your duty*) perform, execute, carry out, fulfil, accomplish, do. OPPOSITE: neglect. **7** (*discharged all his debts*) settle, clear, pay, honour, meet, satisfy, liquidate, square (*inf*).

➤ *noun* **1** (*on his discharge from prison*) liberation, release, acquittal, reprieve, emancipation, exoneration, clearance, dismissal, absolution, exculpation, manumission. OPPOSITE: detention. **2** (*discharge from employment*) dismissal, removal, sack (*inf*), firing (*inf*), the boot (*inf*), the elbow (*inf*), ejection, expulsion, ousting, cashiering, axeing (*inf*). OPPOSITE: recruitment. **3** (*a noxious discharge*) emission, secretion, suppuration, pus, flow, release, excretion, exudation, leak, ooze, seepage, voidance, ejection. OPPOSITE: absorption. **4** (*the discharge of the cannon*) blast, volley, salvo, fusillade, shot, report, explosion, detonation. **5** (*the discharge of his duties*) performance, execution, carrying out, fulfilment, accomplishment, achievement, doing, observance.

OPPOSITE: neglect. **6** (*the discharge of all his debts*) settling, clearance, payment, honouring, meeting, satisfaction, liquidation.

disciple *noun* follower, adherent, partisan, votary, devotee, advocate, supporter, believer, upholder, student, scholar, learner, pupil, convert, proselyte, apostle.

disciplinarian *noun* authoritarian, hard taskmaster, stickler, martinet, despot, tyrant, autocrat.

discipline *noun* **1** (*physical discipline*) training, routine, drill, exercise, instruction, schooling, coaching, practice, regimen, method. **2** (*strict discipline*) regulation, control, self-control, order, orderliness, rule, direction, government, restraint, self-restraint, check, curb, limitation, restriction, strictness. OPPOSITE: indiscipline. **3** (*discipline by the court*) punishment, chastisement, castigation, correction, reprimand, rebuke, reproof, penalty. OPPOSITE: indulgence. **4** (*an expert in several disciplines*) subject, area, field, course, branch, speciality, specialty.
≫ *verb* **1** (*discipline the squad*) train, drill, break in, exercise, coach, teach, educate, instruct, school, tutor, inculcate, inure, indoctrinate, prepare, ground. **2** (*discipline the class*) control, restrain, restrict, limit, check, curb, govern, regulate. **3** (*discipline the culprits*) punish, castigate, chastise, chasten, correct, rebuke, reprimand, reprove, penalize. OPPOSITE: indulge.

disclaim *verb* deny, abjure, abnegate, renounce, disown, abandon, forswear, disavow, disaffirm, retract, rebut, disallow, reject, repudiate, decline, refuse, discard, cast off. OPPOSITE: confess.

disclaimer *noun* denial, abjuration, abnegation, repudiation, retraction, disavowal, disaffirmation, retraction, renunciation, disowning, rejection. OPPOSITE: confession.

disclose *verb* **1** (*disclose the news*) divulge, confess, release, reveal, leak, let slip, blurt out, make known, tell, relate, blab, spill the beans (*inf*), blow the gaff (*inf*), blow the lid (*inf*), spill one's guts (*inf*), squeal about (*inf*), impart, communicate, broadcast, publish, avow, make public. OPPOSITE: suppress. **2** (*disclose the truth*) expose, lay bare, reveal, uncover, unveil, exhibit, show, discover, bring to light. OPPOSITE: conceal.

disclosure *noun* **1** (*disclosures of internal communications*) divulgence, revelation, exposé, leak, communication, confession, admission, avowal. **2** (*public disclosure*) announcement, declaration, release, broadcast, broadcasting, exposure, acknowledgment, discovery, publishing, uncovering, laying bare, unveiling, revelation, revealing, divulging, divulgence. OPPOSITE: suppression.

discoloration *noun* blemish, stain, soiling, spot, streak, mark, flaw, patch, blot, blotch, splotch, smirch, smear, tarnishing.

discolour *verb* stain, soil, tarnish, taint, tinge, mark, streak, bruise, fade, bleach, wash out, weather, mar, rust, disfigure.

discomfit *verb* **1** (*his speech discomfited his superiors*) embarrass, fluster, ruffle, abash, unsettle, perturb, rattle (*inf*), unnerve, flurry, worry, discompose, discomfort, disconcert, take aback, confuse, baffle, perplex,

confound, nonplus, faze (*inf*), demoralize. **2** (*discomfit her plans*) thwart, frustrate, foil, baffle, balk, defeat, obstruct, hinder, hamper, check, upset, outwit, trump, worst. OPPOSITE: assist.

discomfiture *noun* **1** (*caused her colleagues considerable discomfiture*) embarrassment, humiliation, shame, abashment, chagrin, unease, uneasiness, discomposure, disconcertion, confusion, demoralization. OPPOSITE: ease. **2** (*discomfiture of their plans*) frustration, undoing, failure, disappointment, defeat, overthrow, rout, ruin, ruination.

discomfort *noun* **1** (*discomfort in his elbow*) pain, soreness, ache, hurt, twinge, pang, throb, smart, irritation, affliction, malaise. OPPOSITE: ease. **2** (*felt discomfort at her persistence*) unease, uneasiness, embarrassment, discomfiture, discomposure, disquietude, anxiety, disquiet, disconcertment, apprehension, worry, restlessness, vexation, irritation, annoyance, gall. **3** (*conditions of discomfort*) hardship, trouble, distress, unpleasantness. **4** (*the discomforts of overcrowding*) inconvenience, difficulty, trouble, trial, tribulation, disadvantage, drawback, problem, worry, nuisance, bother, irritation, annoyance, vexation.

discomposure *noun* unease, uneasiness, discomfort, discomfiture, embarrassment, perturbation, trepidation, agitation, fluster, restlessness, anxiety, disquiet, disquietude, disconcertment, inquietude, nervousness, vexation, annoyance, irritation, perplexity, confusion, disturbance, malaise, upset. OPPOSITE: ease.

disconcert *verb* **1** (*his stare disconcerted her*) discompose, ruffle, discomfit, discompose, embarrass, flummox, fluster, unsettle, disturb, confuse, bewilder, alarm, perturb, rattle (*inf*), startle, surprise, perplex, bewilder, confound, distract, nonplus, take aback, faze (*inf*), put off, put out, throw (*inf*), unbalance, unnerve, abash, daunt, dismay, worry, agitate, shake, trouble, upset. OPPOSITE: reassure. **2** (*disconcert her plans*) frustrate, thwart, foil, balk, baffle, obstruct, hinder, hamper, baffle, confuse, defeat, undo. OPPOSITE: assist.

disconcerting *adj* disturbing, upsetting, off-putting (*inf*), perturbing, unnerving, daunting, alarming, worrying, bewildering, discomfiting, distracting, unsettling, embarrassing, awkward, baffling, confusing, perplexing, dismaying, bothering, bothersome.

disconnect *verb* **1** (*disconnect the two parts*) disengage, uncouple, undo, separate, part, take apart, divide, split up, sever, detach, disentangle, disjoin, dissociate, disunite, unhook, unhitch, unlink, cut off, unplug. OPPOSITE: connect. **2** (*disconnect all links*) discontinue, interrupt, break, suspend, halt, stop.

disconnected *adj* **1** (*disconnected parts*) unconnected, separate, separated, unattached, dissociated. **2** (*disconnected conversation*) confused, garbled, disjointed, disordered, jumbled, mixed-up, incoherent, rambling, wandering, illogical, irrational, uncoordinated, unintelligible, abrupt, staccato. OPPOSITE: coherent.

disconsolate *adj* forlorn, unhappy, sad, desolate, despondent, dejected, dismal, heartbroken, crushed, inconsolable, griefstricken, woeful, woebegone, wretched, blue, miserable, melancholy, gloomy, downcast, down, depressed, low, low-spirited, dispirited, heavyhearted, despairing, hopeless. OPPOSITE: joyful.

discontent *noun* discontentment, dissatisfaction, displeasure, uneasiness, disquiet, impatience, exasperation, irritation, chagrin, pique, envy, disaffection, misery, regret, unhappiness, wretchedness, fretfulness, vexation, restlessness, unrest. OPPOSITE: content.

discontented *adj* discontent, dissatisfied, disgruntled, fed up (*inf*), pissed off (*inf*), disaffected, hacked off (*inf*), brassed off (*inf*), browned off (*inf*), cheesed off (*inf*), vexed, complaining, querulous, fretful, irritated, annoyed, chagrined, peeved, piqued, exasperated, envious, restless, impatient, regretful, unhappy, miserable, displeased, wretched. OPPOSITE: contented.

discontinue *verb* **1** (*discontinued the lessons*) stop, terminate, end, finish, cease, break off, halt, suspend, interrupt, abandon, scrap (*inf*), axe (*inf*), drop, give up, quit (*inf*), kick (*inf*), refrain from, cut out (*inf*), cancel. OPPOSITE: continue. **2** (*the laughter discontinued*) cease, stop, halt, terminate, leave off, pause.

discontinuous *adj* broken, interrupted, intermittent, irregular, fitful, spasmodic, periodic, disjointed, disconnected, punctuated. OPPOSITE: continuous.

discord *noun* **1** (*discord between the two sides*) discordance, dissension, dissent, quarrelling, strife, war, contention, friction, conflict, argument, dispute, row, disagreement, variance, difference, wrangling, opposition, disunity, division, breach, rupture, split, incompatibility, hostility. OPPOSITE: accord. **2** (*discord of their voices*) dissonance, disharmony, cacophony, din, racket, tumult, harshness, jarring, jangle, jangling. OPPOSITE: harmony.

discordant *adj* **1** (*discordant views*) conflicting, incompatible, incongruous, contrary, contradictory, different, differing, divergent, disagreeing, dissenting, contentious, disputatious, clashing, opposing, hostile, inconsistent, at odds, at variance. OPPOSITE: concordant. **2** (*discordant voices*) dissonant, inharmonious, cacophonous, unmelodious, atonal, sharp, flat, harsh, jangling, jarring, grating, shrill, strident. OPPOSITE: harmonious.

discount *noun* reduction, rebate, allowance, concession, deduction, reduction, markdown, concession, cut, cut price. OPPOSITE: premium.
➤ *verb* **1** (*discount the possibility*) disregard, ignore, overlook, pass over, gloss over, brush off, disbelieve. **2** (*discount the price*) deduct, take off, cut, reduce, lower, lessen, mark down, slash (*inf*), rebate, take off, knock off (*inf*), knock down (*inf*).

discourage *verb* **1** (*she was not discouraged by his attitude*) damp, dampen, dishearten, dispirit, cow, abash, awe, overawe, daunt, put off, intimidate, frighten, scare, demoralize, unnerve, unman, psych out (*inf*), dismay, disappoint, deject, cast down, depress. OPPOSITE: inspire. **2** (*discourage him from entering*) deter, dissuade, talk out of, advise against, urge against, caution against, put off, restrain, check, curb, hold back, prevent, inhibit, hinder, obstruct, suppress. OPPOSITE: encourage. **3** (*discourage the notion*) disapprove of, disfavour, discountenance, frown on, deprecate, oppose, repress. OPPOSITE: sanction.

discouraged *adj* disheartened, dispirited, depressed, demoralized, dejected, dismayed, disappointed, downcast, cast down, despondent, glum, pessimistic, daunted, dashed, crestfallen, let-down, deflated, put off, deterred. OPPOSITE: encouraged.

discouragement *noun* **1** (*prey to discouragement*) downheartedness, dispiritedness, dejection, depression, demoralization, disappointment, despondency, hopelessness, pessimism, dismay, discomfiture, despair, gloom, melancholy, low spirits, cold feet (*inf*). **2** (*official discouragement*) opposition, disapproval, repression, deprecation. **3** (*overcame various discouragements*) deterrent, impediment, hindrance, barrier, obstacle, curb, check, restraint, constraint, restriction, damper, disincentive, setback, rebuff, put-down (*inf*).

discouraging *adj* disheartening, dispiriting, depressing, demoralizing, disappointing, off-putting, dissuasive, unfavourable, inauspicious, unpropitious, dampening, daunting, gloomy.

discourse *noun* **1** (*friendly discourse*) conversation, talk, chat, chitchat, discussion, dialogue, rap (*inf*), colloquy, converse, conference, confabulation, confab (*inf*), palaver, communication. **2** (*a discourse on religious matters*) speech, talk, sermon, homily, lecture, address, seminar, dissertation, paper, essay, study, treatise, oration, disquisition.
➤ *verb* **1** (*discourse with his family*) converse, talk, speak, chat, discuss, confer, chew the fat (*inf*), chinwag (*inf*), rap (*inf*), confabulate, debate. **2** (*discourse on politics*) talk, speak, hold forth, lecture, declaim, sermonize, preach, spout (*inf*), expatiate.

discourteous *adj* rude, bad-mannered, ill-mannered, unmannerly, ungracious, ungentlemanly, unladylike, impolite, uncivil, unceremonious, ill-bred, ungallant, boorish, churlish, uncouth, disrespectful, insolent, impertinent, impudent, curt, short, abrupt, brusque, gruff, offhand. OPPOSITE: courteous.

discourtesy *noun* **1** (*showed considerable discourtesy*) rudeness, bad manners, unmannerliness, ungraciousness, impoliteness, indecorousness, indecorum, incivility, ill-breeding, uncouthness, disrespect, disrespectfulness, impertinence, insolence, abruptness, curtness, brusqueness. OPPOSITE: courtesy. **2** (*one of many discourtesies*) rebuff, slight, snub, insult, affront.

discover *verb* **1** (*discover treasure*) find, come across, happen upon, stumble across, chance upon, light upon, unearth, dig up, ferret out, turn up, locate, bring to light, light on, uncover, disclose, reveal. OPPOSITE: conceal. **2** (*discover the truth*) find out, learn, fathom, determine, ascertain, establish, realize, understand, twig (*inf*), suss out (*inf*), rumble (*inf*), see, spot, discern, perceive, notice, recognize, descry, detect. OPPOSITE: miss. **3** (*discover the process*) invent, pioneer, devise, create, design, contrive, originate, conceive, think up, work out, compose.

discoverer *noun* **1** (*the discoverer of a new continent*) explorer, finder, pioneer. **2** (*the discoverer of the process*) founder, originator, pioneer, initiator, inventor, author, deviser, designer, creator.

discovery *noun* **1** (*the discovery of a masterpiece*) find, finding, location, locating, uncovering. **2** (*her discovery of the truth*) learning, finding out, realization, perception, discernment, recognition, revelation, disclosure, detection, determination, ascertainment. **3** (*the discovery of new lands*) exploration, pioneering. **4** (*the latest scientific discovery*) find, finding, invention, breakthrough, coup, innovation, research. **5** (*the discovery of new techniques*) invention, origination, devising, pioneering, introduction.

discredit verb **1** (*discredit the opposition*) dishonour, disgrace, degrade, belittle, devalue, devaluate, defame, decry, vilify, smear, tarnish, denigrate, deprecate, censure, slur, slander, blame, disparage, detract from, reproach, damage. OPPOSITE: honour. **2** (*discredit his character*) disbelieve, discount, doubt, question, challenge, distrust, mistrust. OPPOSITE: believe. **3** (*served to discredit the theory*) invalidate, refute, reject, deny, disprove, dispute, challenge, explode, debunk. OPPOSITE: prove.
➤ noun **1** (*brought discredit on his name*) dishonour, disgrace, disrepute, ill repute, censure, blame, shame, reproach, aspersion, slur, stigma, smear, scandal, infamy, ignominy, odium, opprobrium, obloquy, humiliation, damage, harm. OPPOSITE: credit. **2** (*the theory was regarded with discredit*) disbelief, doubt, question, incredulity, scepticism, distrust, mistrust, suspicion. OPPOSITE: belief.

discreditable adj dishonourable, disgraceful, disreputable, shameful, ignoble, degrading, ignominious, infamous, scandalous, blameworthy, reprehensible, improper, unworthy. OPPOSITE: honourable.

discreet adj careful, tactful, diplomatic, cautious, delicate, reserved, guarded, politic, strategic, wary, sensible, judicious, circumspect, prudent, wary, wise, thoughtful, sagacious, discerning, considerate, chary. OPPOSITE: indiscreet.

discrepancy noun inconsistency, difference, gap, variance, variation, dissimilarity, disparity, incongruity, inconsistency, deviation, divergence, disagreement, discordance, dissonance, conflict, contradiction, contrariety, inequality. OPPOSITE: correspondence.

discrete adj separate, distinct, detached, unattached, disconnected, individual, discontinuous, disjoined, disjunct.

discretion noun **1** (*approached the subject with discretion*) tact, tactfulness, diplomacy, caution, sense, wisdom, sagacity, acumen, forethought, discernment, discrimination, judgment, judiciousness, prudence, heedfulness, circumspection, care, carefulness, reserve, guardedness, consideration, wariness, chariness, strategy. OPPOSITE: rashness. **2** (*he had no discretion in the matter*) choice, option, liberty, freedom, preference, will, wish, desire, inclination, predilection, disposition, liking, pleasure, mind, volition.

discretionary adj discretional, optional, elective, arbitrary, voluntary, nonmandatory, unrestricted, open, volitional. OPPOSITE: mandatory.

discriminate verb **1** (*discriminate between the two*) distinguish, differentiate, discern, tell apart, separate, segregate, sift, isolate, judge, assess, evaluate.

2 (*discriminate against them*) show bias, be biased, be prejudiced, single out, victimize, disfavour.

discriminating adj discerning, cultivated, cultured, tasteful, refined, artistic, aesthetic, selective, critical, particular, fastidious, perceptive, sensitive, astute, keen, shrewd.

discrimination noun **1** (*discrimination is rife*) bias, prejudice, bigotry, intolerance, unfairness, favouritism, narrow-mindedness, inequity, segregation, racism, sexism, chauvinism, ageism, homophobia, distinction, differentiation. **2** (*showed considerable discrimination*) discernment, judgment, selectivity, fastidiousness, acumen, wisdom, sagacity, perspicacity, perception, acuteness, insight, shrewdness, astuteness, penetration, subtlety, keenness, sensitivity, refinement, taste, culture, cultivation, artistry, aestheticism.

discriminatory adj **1** (*discriminatory behaviour*) discriminative, biased, prejudiced, prejudicial, partial, inequitable, loaded, one-sided, weighted, partisan, unfair, unjust, preferential, racist, sexist. OPPOSITE: unbiased. **2** (*discriminatory art lovers*) discriminating, differentiating, discerning, astute, perceptive, perspicacious, critical, analytical.

discursive adj rambling, wandering, meandering, roving, desultory, erratic, episodic, digressive, prolix, wordy, circuitous, roundabout, circumlocutory, long-winded, verbose, diffuse, loose, wide-ranging. OPPOSITE: terse.

discuss verb debate, talk about, talk over, chat, confer, converse, confabulate, consult, argue, dispute, thrash out, kick around (*inf*), get together, consider, deliberate, examine, go into, analyse, scrutinize, weigh up, review, study, sift, air, ventilate.

discussion noun debate, argument, dispute, conference, talk, conversation, parley, powwow (*inf*), dialogue, discourse, confabulation, confab (*inf*), colloquy, consultation, exchange, forum, negotiation, consideration, deliberation, examination, review, ventilation, analysis, scrutiny, symposium, seminar.

disdain noun scorn, scornfulness, contempt, contemptuousness, contumely, superciliousness, haughtiness, hauteur, aloofness, arrogance, snobbishness, indifference, derision, deprecation, denigration, disparagement, sneering, dislike, abhorrence, opprobrium. OPPOSITE: admiration.
➤ verb scorn, spurn, snub, rebuff, contemn, despise, deride, sneer at, pooh-pooh (*inf*), belittle, undervalue, look down on, slight, cold-shoulder (*inf*), ignore, disregard, reject, turn down, disavow. OPPOSITE: respect.

disdainful adj scornful, contemptuous, supercilious, haughty, aloof, proud, pompous, lordly, arrogant, snobbish, high and mighty (*inf*), hoity-toity (*inf*), superior, indifferent, sneering, derisive, disparaging, slighting, insolent, contumelious. OPPOSITE: respectful.

disease noun sickness, illness, complaint, malady, ailment, affliction, disorder, disability, condition, upset, ill health, indisposition, infirmity, infection, bug (*inf*), virus (*inf*), contagion, epidemic, plague, pestilence, blight, cancer, canker. OPPOSITE: health.

diseased adj infected, contaminated, blighted, rotten, sick, ill, sickly, ailing, unwell, unhealthy, infirm, tainted, unsound, unwholesome, abnormal. OPPOSITE: healthy.

disembark verb land, arrive, go ashore, alight, get off, pile out (inf), step off, dismount, detrain, deplane, debark, leave. OPPOSITE: embark.

disembodied adj bodiless, incorporeal, immaterial, insubstantial, intangible, impalpable, ghostly, phantom, wraithlike, spectral, spiritual.

disembowel verb eviscerate, gut, draw, exenterate.

disenchanted adj disillusioned, undeceived, disabused, disappointed, let down, fed up (inf), discouraged, jaundiced, cynical, sick, soured, blasé, indifferent.

disenchantment noun disillusionment, disillusion, disappointment, cynicism.

disengage verb 1 (disengage the ropes) disentangle, ease, release, free, set free, extricate, liberate, loose, loosen, unloose, unbridle, unclasp, unfasten, untie, unfetter, unhitch, unhook. OPPOSITE: engage. 2 (disengage a coupling) detach, sever, separate, disjoin, divide, undo, disunite, disconnect, uncouple, withdraw. OPPOSITE: join.

disengaged adj free, loose, separate, apart, detached, released, liberated, disentangled, unattached, unconnected, uncoupled, unhitched. OPPOSITE: engaged.

disentangle verb 1 (disentangle the knot) untangle, undo, unravel, unfasten, unknot, unsnarl, untwist, unwind, unfold, loose, release, free, separate, detach, disengage, disconnect, straighten, straighten out, smooth out, unkink, extricate, disembroil. OPPOSITE: entangle. 2 (disentangle the problem) resolve, work out, sort out, clarify, clear up, simplify. OPPOSITE: embroil. 3 (disentangled herself from the mess) extricate, detach, separate, disconnect, distance.

disfavour noun 1 (viewed them with disfavour) disapproval, disapprobation, displeasure, dissatisfaction, dislike, distaste, disrespect, disesteem, disregard, discredit, disgrace. OPPOSITE: approval. 2 (fell into disfavour) unpopularity, discredit, disgrace, disrepute, ill repute, ignominy, shame, opprobrium, bad books (inf), doghouse (inf). 3 (did him a disfavour) disservice, bad turn, affront, discourtesy, offence. OPPOSITE: favour.

disfigure verb deface, mutilate, maim, scar, deface, blemish, distort, deform, disfeature, uglify, spoil, flaw, mar, damage, injure, ruin, vandalize. OPPOSITE: embellish.

disfigurement noun 1 (disfigurement of the countryside) defacement, vandalization, mutilation, scarring, damaging, ruin. 2 (facial disfigurement) blemish, defect, imperfection, scar, spot, blotch, stain, malformation, mutilation, deformity, injury, impairment, distortion, ugliness. OPPOSITE: embellishment.

disgorge verb 1 (disgorge the contents) discharge, empty, eject, emit, expel, spout, spit out, throw up (inf), regurgitate, vomit, spew out, chuck (inf), belch. 2 (disgorge their possession of the city) surrender, yield, relinquish, resign, cede, give up, renounce, hand over, abandon. OPPOSITE: retain.

disgrace noun 1 (living in disgrace) shame, dishonour, humiliation, ignominy, infamy, discredit, scandal, degradation, debasement, vitiation. 2 (brought them further disgrace) discredit, disapproval, disfavour, disrepute, disrespect, disapprobation, contempt, obloquy, loss of face, opprobrium, ignominy, infamy, odium, disesteem. OPPOSITE: esteem. 3 (the incident was a disgrace) slur, blot, stain, blemish, smear, smirch, stigma, scandal, dishonour, aspersion, defamation.

➤ verb dishonour, discredit, shame, humiliate, degrade, defame, debase, demean, sully, taint, stain, tarnish, besmirch, slur, stigmatize, brand. OPPOSITE: honour.

disgraceful adj 1 (disgraceful behaviour) shameful, shameless, scandalous, ignominious, infamous, blameworthy, culpable, discreditable, dishonourable, infamous, opprobrious, low, degrading, disreputable, contemptible, despicable, reprehensible, shocking, improper, outrageous, unseemly, unworthy. 2 (a disgraceful effort) bad, appalling, awful, dreadful, shocking, intolerable, terrible. OPPOSITE: honourable.

disgruntled adj discontented, malcontent, displeased, dissatisfied, disappointed, sulky, sullen, peeved, peevish, petulant, put out, resentful, annoyed, exasperated, irritated, grumpy, pissed off (sl), fed up (inf), hacked off (inf), brassed off (inf), huffy, cheesed off (inf), browned off (inf), testy, churlish, vexed, unhappy. OPPOSITE: contented.

disguise noun 1 (adopted a disguise) concealment, camouflage, guise, blind, cloak, costume, getup (inf), cover, screen, shroud, veil, mask. 2 (a disguise for her ambition) front, facade, veneer, semblance, masquerade, pretence, deception, misrepresentation, travesty, dissimulation, trickery.

➤ verb 1 (disguised as a tree) camouflage, conceal, hide, screen, cover, mask, veil, shroud, cloak, dress up, muffle. 2 (disguise the truth) cover up, falsify, deceive, pretend, misrepresent, gloss over, varnish, whitewash (inf), fake, feign, fudge, dissemble, dissimulate. OPPOSITE: reveal.

disgust verb 1 (the conditions disgusted us) sicken, nauseate, revolt, repel, turn off (inf), put off. 2 (disgusted by the idea) offend, displease, appal, shock, scandalize, annoy, anger, outrage. OPPOSITE: please.

➤ noun 1 (the state of the kitchen filled us with disgust) distaste, nausea, repulsion, revulsion, repugnance, disrelish, loathing, odium, abhorrence, dislike, detestation, displeasure, aversion, hatred, hatefulness, antipathy, abomination. OPPOSITE: relish. 2 (disgust at their language) offence, outrage, shock, disapproval, displeasure, dissatisfaction, annoyance, anger.

disgusting adj 1 (the sink was disgusting) sickening, nauseating, nauseous, noisome, foul, nasty, revolting, repulsive, repellent, repugnant, gross (inf), grotty (inf), yucky (inf), off-putting, offensive, obnoxious, vile, odious, abhorrent, loathsome, unappetizing, unpalatable, distasteful, detestable. 2 (disgusting language) bad, detestable, foul, abominable, offensive, gross, objectionable, unpleasant, outrageous, disgraceful, appalling, shocking, shameful, shameless, scandalous, obscene, vile, vulgar. OPPOSITE: delightful.

dish noun 1 (put the dishes on the table) plate, saucer, platter, bowl, vessel, salver, container, receptacle. 2 (a choice of dishes) food, fare, recipe, serving, helping, course, delicacy, speciality.

➤ verb ruin, muck up (inf), spoil, wreck, torpedo, end, finish.

dish out distribute, dole out, deal out, give out, hand out, share out, allocate, mete out, inflict.

dish up serve, present, ladle, scoop, spoon, offer, dispense.

dishearten *verb* discourage, dispirit, depress, cast down, sadden, deject, crush, dash, weigh down, damp, dampen, dismay, disappoint, daunt, deter, disconcert. OPPOSITE: encourage.

dishevelled *adj* unkempt, uncombed, bedraggled, blowsy, slovenly, messy, untidy, disarranged, disarrayed, disordered, ruffled, rumpled, tousled. OPPOSITE: tidy.

dishonest *adj* untruthful, fraudulent, deceitful, deceiving, deceptive, lying, mendacious, false, crooked (*inf*), perfidious, cheating, double-dealing, duplicitous, guileful, rascally, swindling, disreputable, bent (*inf*), shady (*inf*), iffy (*inf*), fishy (*inf*), dishonourable, crafty, cunning, designing, knavish, roguish, sly, devious, tricky, unfair, unscrupulous, unprincipled, treacherous, underhand, corrupt, unfair, unlawful, untrustworthy, untruthful, faithless. OPPOSITE: honest.

dishonesty *noun* untruthfulness, fraudulence, cheating, deceit, deception, lying, mendacity, double-dealing, duplicity, falseness, falsehood, falsity, perfidy, trickery, guile, wiliness, cunning, craft, unscrupulousness, treachery, corruption, crime, criminality, chicanery, fraud, criminality, crookedness, shadiness, underhandedness, untrustworthiness, irregularity, insincerity. OPPOSITE: honesty.

dishonour *noun* **1** (*brought dishonour on the family name*) disgrace, shame, humiliation, loss of face, disrepute, ill repute, discredit, ignominy, infamy, scandal, obloquy, odium, opprobrium, reproach, degradation, abasement, debasement, disesteem, disfavour. OPPOSITE: esteem. **2** (*considered it a dishonour*) disgrace, indignity, insult, affront, offence, abuse, outrage, slight, aspersion, blot, blemish, stigma, discourtesy.
≫ *verb* **1** (*dishonoured his country*) disgrace, discredit, humiliate, demean, shame, defile, degrade, debase, abase, lower, defame, stain, sully, blacken. OPPOSITE: honour. **2** (*dishonour a cheque*) refuse, reject, turn down. **3** (*dishonour the princess*) deflower, rape, seduce, ravish, molest, violate, defile, pollute, debauch.

dishonourable *adj* **1** (*a dishonourable episode*) discreditable, disgraceful, shameful, shaming, scandalous, infamous, despicable, degrading, ignominious, ignoble, despicable, contemptible, low, base, debasing, disreputable, shameless, reprehensible, blameworthy. OPPOSITE: honourable. **2** (*a dishonourable character*) unscrupulous, unprincipled, corrupt, untrustworthy, treacherous, perfidious, traitorous, shady (*inf*), disreputable, discreditable, unethical, unworthy.

disillusion *verb* disenchant, disabuse, undeceive, enlighten, disappoint.

disincentive *noun* deterrent, discouragement, hindrance, impediment, obstacle, barrier, constraint, damper, determent, dissuasion, repellent, restriction.

disinclination *noun* reluctance, unwillingness, hesitation, hesitancy, dislike, antipathy, loathness, distaste, repugnance, objection, opposition, resistance, recalcitrance, alienation, averseness, aversion.

disinclined *adj* reluctant, unwilling, hesitant, indisposed, averse, loath, opposed, resistant, unenthusiastic, antipathetic. OPPOSITE: willing.

disinfect *verb* sterilize, sanitize, decontaminate, purify, purge, clean, cleanse, fumigate, deodorize. OPPOSITE: contaminate.

disinfectant *noun* antiseptic, sterilizer, sanitizer, cleanser, decontaminant, bactericide, germicide, fumigant.

disingenuous *adj* insincere, deceitful, dishonest, devious, lying, two-faced, false, feigned, insidious, artful, designing, guileful, sly, shifty, crafty, cunning, duplicitous, wily, scheming, calculating, underhand, unfair. OPPOSITE: ingenuous.

disinherit *verb* dispossess, deprive, cut off, impoverish, disown, reject, renounce, repudiate, oust, abandon.

disintegrate *verb* crumble, break up, break apart, fall apart, separate, shatter, smash, splinter, decompose, erode, dissolve, decay, rot, moulder.

disinterested *adj* impartial, unbiased, unprejudiced, objective, dispassionate, neutral, open-minded, even-handed, impersonal, uninvolved, detached, equitable, fair, just, unselfish, honest, candid. OPPOSITE: biased.

disjointed *adj* **1** (*a disjointed narrative*) rambling, wandering, incoherent, desultory, fitful, spasmodic, bitty, loose, aimless, directionless, disordered, confused, disorganized, unconnected, disconnected, discontinuous. OPPOSITE: coherent. **2** (*disjointed parts*) disconnected, unconnected, dislocated, dismembered, severed, divided, separated, disunited, displaced, broken, split, disarticulated, torn apart.

dislike *verb* hate, detest, loathe, abhor, abominate, disapprove, distavour, disrelish, object to, mind, shun, despise, scorn, execrate. OPPOSITE: like.
≫ *noun* hate, hatred, detestation, loathing, abhorrence, aversion, antipathy, disgust, distaste, repugnance, animosity, antagonism, enmity, hostility, distavour, disapproval, disrelish, animus, disinclination, disapprobation, displeasure, disesteem, resentment. OPPOSITE: liking.

dislocate *verb* **1** (*dislocate a hip*) disjoint, displace, disarticulate, put out, misplace, twist, sprain, strain, disengage, unhinge, disconnect, disunite. **2** (*dislocated their arrangements*) disorder, disrupt, disorganize, derange, disarrange, mess up, confuse.

dislocation *noun* displacement, disarticulation, disconnection, derangement, disorder, disarray, disorganization, disruption, disturbance.

dislodge *verb* remove, displace, uproot, extricate, oust, expel, force out, eject, evict, sack (*inf*), move, shift, unseat. OPPOSITE: place.

disloyal *adj* unfaithful, faithless, perfidious, deceitful, double-dealing, treacherous, traitorous, treasonable, unpatriotic, seditious, subversive, dissident, false, two-faced, untrue, apostate, inconstant, recreant, disaffected. OPPOSITE: loyal.

disloyalty *noun* unfaithfulness, faithlessness, infidelity, perfidy, perfidiousness, deceit, double-dealing, treachery, treason, sedition, subversion, dissidence, falseness, falsity, falseheartedness, inconstancy, infidelity, adultery, betrayal, apostasy, inconstancy, untrustworthiness, disaffection. OPPOSITE: loyalty.

dismal adj **1** (a dismal location) gloomy, dreary, desolate, melancholy, depressing, sombre, dull, drab, bleak, dark, dingy, grim, gruesome, cheerless, comfortless, wretched, miserable, inhospitable, uninviting, forlorn, lonesome, funereal, dolorous. **2** (felt very dismal about it) gloomy, sad, doleful, miserable, unhappy, low-spirited, wretched, despondent, disconsolate, melancholy, morose, sorrowful, solemn, blue, woebegone, forlorn, black, joyless, lugubrious. OPPOSITE: cheerful. **3** (a dismal effort) bad, poor, feeble, inept, inadequate, bungling, disgraceful.

dismantle verb disassemble, take apart, pull apart, tear down, demolish, destroy, raze, strip, divest. OPPOSITE: assemble.

dismay verb **1** (dismayed her parents) alarm, frighten, scare, disturb, perturb, jolt, shock, unnerve, unsettle, upset, distress, bother, concern, worry, disconcert, startle, surprise, take aback, daunt, intimidate, terrify, horrify, appal. **2** (dismayed by the prospect) discourage, dishearten, depress, sadden, dispirit, cast down, disappoint, chagrin, abash, put off. OPPOSITE: reassure.
» **noun** **1** (the announcement provoked considerable dismay) consternation, alarm, distress, apprehension, dread, fear, fright, terror, horror, panic, anxiety, trepidation, agitation, misgiving. OPPOSITE: reassurance. **2** (filled with dismay at the news) discouragement, depression, unhappiness, disappointment, upset, disillusionment, chagrin.

dismember verb dissect, cut up, anatomize, disjoint, separate, dislocate, divide, sever, rend, amputate, mutilate, break up.

dismiss verb **1** (dismiss the squad) send away, discharge, release, disband, disperse, demobilize, free, remove, dissolve. **2** (all the staff were dismissed) lay off, let go, sack (inf), fire (inf), axe (inf), boot out (inf), turf out (inf), give someone the sack (inf), give someone the boot (inf), give someone their marching orders (inf), give someone their cards (inf), give someone the shove (inf), give someone the bum's rush (sl), show someone the door (inf), cashier, discharge, release, suspend, deselect. OPPOSITE: retain. **3** (dismiss the idea) banish, discount, disregard, discard, reject, repudiate, dispel, abandon, set aside, shelve, drop, spurn, put away, oust.

dismissal noun **1** (the dismissal of the class) discharge, disbandment, dispersal, dissolution, release, removal. **2** (dismissal from the service) notice, redundancy, sack (inf), sacking (inf), firing (inf), push (inf), elbow (inf), boot (inf), marching orders (inf), shove (inf), bum's rush (sl), heave-ho (inf), discharge, rejection, expulsion, laying-off.

dismount verb descend, alight, get off, get down, disembark. OPPOSITE: mount.

disobedience noun insubordination, noncompliance, contrariness, wilfulness, waywardness, unruliness, contumacy, contumacity, recalcitrance, defiance, indiscipline, mutiny, rebellion, revolt, delinquency, infraction, mischief. OPPOSITE: obedience.

disobedient adj insubordinate, contrary, wayward, defiant, noncompliant, refractory, intractable,

recalcitrant, undisciplined, naughty, mischievous, perverse, delinquent, disorderly, unruly, obstreperous, wilful, mutinous, rebellious, contumacious, recusant. OPPOSITE: obedient.

disobey verb infringe, violate, contravene, transgress, break, disregard, ignore, defy, flout, resist, rebel, overstep. OPPOSITE: obey.

disobliging adj unaccommodating, uncooperative, awkward, bloodyminded, unhelpful, unsympathetic, unwilling, ill-disposed, unpleasant, disagreeable, rude, discourteous, uncivil, offensive, unkind, unfriendly. OPPOSITE: obliging.

disorder noun **1** (the room was in disorder) confusion, chaos, disarray, clutter, muddle, jumble, mess, shambles (inf), disarrangement, derangement, disorderliness, untidiness, disorganization, turmoil, tumult, riot, commotion, disturbance. OPPOSITE: order. **2** (the town was in disorder) confusion, upheaval, uproar, commotion, shambles, disruption, disturbance, clamour, tumult, turmoil, rout, brouhaha, riot, rumpus, hubbub, hullabaloo, fracas, unrest, state, fight, brawl. **3** (suffering from a rare disorder) ailment, complaint, condition, indisposition, malady, illness, disease, disability, affliction, indisposition, sickness.
» **verb** disarrange, derange, discompose, disorganize, disturb, upset, confuse, confound, muddle, jumble, mess up, mix up, clutter, scatter, turn upside down, discompose, unsettle. OPPOSITE: arrange.

disorderly adj **1** (a disorderly home) untidy, messy, jumbled, muddled, cluttered, disordered, out of order, disorganized, disarranged, deranged, confused, chaotic, indiscriminate, shambolic, upside-down, higgledy-piggledy (inf), irregular, unsystematic. OPPOSITE: neat. **2** (disorderly behaviour) unruly, undisciplined, disobedient, unmanageable, uncontrollable, ungovernable, lawless, riotous, boisterous, rowdy, disruptive, tumultuous, turbulent, obstreperous, refractory, rebellious, mutinous, rough, stormy, wild. OPPOSITE: orderly.

disorganized adj **1** (a disorganized collection) disordered, disorderly, disarranged, deranged, unsorted, unsystematized, disrupted, disturbed, topsy-turvy, upset, confused, muddled, jumbled, haphazard, random, chaotic, shambolic, irregular. OPPOSITE: organized. **2** (a disorganized young woman) unorganized, muddled, careless, unmethodical, unstructured, unsystematic.

disorientated adj disoriented, confused, perplexed, puzzled, bewildered, muddled, lost, adrift, all at sea, astray, unsettled, upset, mixed up, unbalanced, unstable, unhinged.

disown verb repudiate, disclaim, abandon, reject, rebut, retract, cast off, forsake, renounce, deny, disavow, disallow, abnegate, ignore, disinherit, cut off. OPPOSITE: acknowledge.

disparage verb **1** (disparage their work) belittle, depreciate, underrate, undervalue, devalue, devaluate, underestimate, decry, derogate, minimize, deflate, run down, play down, downgrade, deprecate, denigrate, dishonour, ridicule, deride, mock, scorn, slight, lambaste, lampoon, disdain, dismiss, blast. OPPOSITE: extol. **2** (disparage his opponent) defame, rubbish (inf), run down, bad-mouth (inf), slag off (inf), slander, libel, traduce, malign, impugn, discredit, degrade, debase, asperse, criticize, vilify, calumniate.

disparagement noun belittlement, criticism, depreciation, denunciation, underestimation, debasement, degradation, derogation, deprecation, denigration, detraction, vilification, condemnation, defamation, discredit, disdain, contempt, ridicule, derision, scorn, aspersion, slander, decrial, contumely. OPPOSITE: appreciation.

disparate adj distinct, different, contrasting, contrary, unlike, dissimilar, diverse, at odds, at variance, discrepant, unequal. OPPOSITE: identical.

disparity noun difference, distinction, inequality, inequity, discrepancy, imbalance, unevenness, incongruity, disproportion, gap, gulf, contrast, dissimilarity, dissimilitude, discrepancy, unlikeness, unfairness, bias. OPPOSITE: equality.

dispassionate adj 1 (a dispassionate opinion) objective, impartial, unbiased, unprejudiced, disinterested, uninvolved, neutral, detached, impersonal, indifferent, candid, evenhanded, open-minded, fair, just, equitable. OPPOSITE: biased. 2 (a dispassionate manner) composed, calm, collected, cool, unemotional, emotionless, laid back (inf), unruffled, unflappable, unperturbed, imperturbable, self-controlled, self-possessed, nonchalant, serene, tranquil, poised, impassive, unmoved, placid, equable, sober, unexcited, unexcitable, levelheaded, temperate. OPPOSITE: excitable.

dispatch verb 1 (dispatch a letter) send, post, mail, transmit, express, remit, consign, convey, ship, forward. OPPOSITE: retain. 2 (dispatched his chores) conclude, finish, complete, discharge, perform, dispose of, settle, expedite, push through, hasten, hurry, accelerate. 3 (dispatched by firing squad) kill, execute, slay, murder, put to death, bump off (inf), knock off (inf), waste (inf), blow away (inf), take out (inf), do in (inf), eliminate, erase, slaughter, butcher, assassinate.
➤ noun 1 (worked with great dispatch) promptness, speed, rapidity, expedition, expeditiousness, haste, hurry, swiftness, quickness, promptitude, alacrity, celerity. OPPOSITE: slowness. 2 (a dispatch to the general) communication, message, report, bulletin, communiqué, document, missive, instruction, note, news, letter, epistle, story, account, article, item, piece.

dispel verb disperse, scatter, dismiss, banish, expel, allay, dissipate, disseminate, dissolve, melt away, eliminate, rout, drive away, drive off, chase away, get rid of, rid. OPPOSITE: collect.

dispensable adj expendable, disposable, unnecessary, nonessential, inessential, replaceable, superfluous, unrequired, needless, gratuitous, redundant, useless. OPPOSITE: essential.

dispensation noun 1 (special dispensation from the authorities) exemption, immunity, indulgence, licence, permission, privilege, exception, relaxation, release, relief, reprieve, remission, absolution. 2 (the dispensation of supplies) distribution, issue, handing out, sharing out, dealing out, apportionment, division, allotment, assignment, allocation, bestowal, endowment, conferment, disbursement. OPPOSITE: withholding. 3 (a

radically new political dispensation) authority, direction, regulation, control, arrangement, organization, administration, management, stewardship, disposal, system, order, scheme, plan. 4 (received his dispensation of goodies) quota, share, part, portion, award, dole. 5 (the dispensation of justice) administration, discharge, execution, application, implementation, operation, direction, enforcement, effectuation.

dispense verb 1 (dispense presents to the servants) distribute, give out, apportion, divide out, share, share out, parcel out, allot, assign, allocate, deal out, dole out, hand out, mete out, confer, supply, disburse. OPPOSITE: withhold. 2 (dispense justice) administer, carry out, apply, implement, operate, enforce, direct, discharge, execute, effectuate, undertake. 3 (dispense from payment) exempt, excuse, release, except, relieve, reprieve, absolve, exonerate, let off (inf).

dispense with 1 (dispense with the formalities) pass over, brush aside, disregard, ignore, waive, dispose of, get rid of, do away with, omit, discard, abolish, cancel, rescind, revoke. OPPOSITE: retain. 2 (dispense with tobacco) do without, abstain from, forgo, give up, renounce, relinquish.

disperse verb 1 (the party dispersed) separate, break up, scatter, disband, dismiss, rout, disappear, vanish, melt away, thin out, dissolve. OPPOSITE: gather. 2 (dispersing the news) broadcast, circulate, publish, diffuse, disseminate, distribute, scatter, spread, strew.

dispirit verb dishearten, discourage, damp, dampen, dash, crush, depress, deject, sadden, cast down, disappoint, deter, disincline. OPPOSITE: encourage.

dispirited adj downhearted, downcast, disheartened, discouraged, depressed, dejected, sad, cast down, crestfallen, despondent, down (inf), glum, gloomy, low, morose, fed up (inf), brassed off (inf), browned off (inf), cheesed off (inf). OPPOSITE: cheerful.

displace verb 1 (displace the contents) move, shift, disturb, derange, disarrange, disorder, transpose, relocate, dislodge, misplace, dislocate. OPPOSITE: fix. 2 (displace from her post) remove, dismiss, discharge, depose, eject, expel, cashier, sack (inf), fire (inf), boot out (inf). OPPOSITE: retain. 3 (displace the old order) replace, supplant, supersede, succeed, eject, oust, expel, evict, force out, exile, banish, crowd out.

display verb 1 (display his work) show, exhibit, demonstrate, expose, unveil, present, set forth, arrange, dispose, array, advertise, publicize, promote. OPPOSITE: disguise. 2 (display their real feelings) betray, disclose, reveal, show, expose, manifest, evince. OPPOSITE: conceal. 3 (display her wealth) parade, flaunt, show off, flourish, flash (inf), vaunt, blazon. 4 (display its wings) unfold, unfurl, spread out, open out, extend, expand.
➤ noun 1 (an acrobatic display) show, exhibition, exhibit, demonstration, exposition, presentation, array. 2 (a display of emotion) revelation, betrayal, disclosure, manifestation, exposure, evidence, evincement. 3 (a ceremonial display) parade, spectacle, show, pageant, pomp, ceremony, ostentation, flourish, splash (inf).

displease verb offend, annoy, irritate, vex, irk, anger, incense, provoke, exasperate, aggravate (inf), infuriate, piss off (sl), bug (inf), nettle, pique, rile, peeve, gall, dissatisfy, offend, disgust, disturb, hassle (*inf*), perturb, discompose, put out (*inf*), upset, hurt. OPPOSITE: please.

displeasure *noun* offence, annoyance, irritation, anger, exasperation, indignation, vexation, wrath, disgruntlement, disgust, distaste, disfavour, disapproval, disapprobation, dislike, dissatisfaction, resentment, discontentment, perturbation, chagrin, ire, pique, rancour.

disport *verb* **1** (*disport his audience with tales*) amuse, entertain, divert, cheer, beguile, delight. OPPOSITE: bore. **2** (*disporting themselves in the sunshine*) frolic, gambol, caper, cavort, frisk, romp, play, revel, sport. OPPOSITE: work.

disposable *adj* **1** (*disposable towels*) expendable, throwaway, paper, plastic, nonreturnable, decomposable, biodegradable. **2** (*disposable wealth*) available, usable, consumable, expendable, spendable, accessible, obtainable.

disposal *noun* **1** (*rubbish disposal*) removal, clearance, scrapping, dumping, discarding, jettisoning, ejection, destruction. **2** (*the disposal of allied forces*) arrangement, array, disposition, distribution, order, ordering, marshalling, grouping, placing, positioning, lining-up. **3** (*disposal of the property*) conveyance, transfer, transference, settlement, distribution, allotment, allocation, bestowal, bequest, consignment, assignment. **4** (*at our disposal*) control, command, discretion, conduct, direction, determination, regulation, government, management, power, authority, responsibility. **5** (*the disposal of her affairs*) settlement, determination, conclusion.

dispose *verb* **1** (*disposing his forces*) arrange, group, place, position, set up, put, situate, array, stand, align, order, marshal, range, rank, line up, organize, categorize, systematize, regulate, settle, adjust, fix. OPPOSITE: derange. **2** (*disposing her to give up hope*) incline, lead, make, move, prompt, tempt, induce, predispose, bias, influence, motivate, actuate, direct, adapt, condition.

dispose of 1 (*dispose of the rubbish*) get rid of, discard, throw away, throw out, clear out, scrap, bin (*inf*), dump (*inf*), junk (*inf*), chuck out (*inf*), get shot of (*inf*), shed, jettison, unload, destroy. OPPOSITE: retain. **2** (*dispose of the matter*) settle, determine, decide, deal with, attend to, see to, handle, tackle, look after, take care of, sort out, conclude, end, finish. **3** (*dispose of the property*) distribute, allocate, allot, assign, transfer, give out, bestow, make over, part with, sell, auction. **4** (*dispose of his enemies*) kill, murder, bump off (*inf*), knock off (*inf*), do away with, do in (*inf*), destroy, put to death, slay, slaughter.

disposed *adj* **1** (*disposed to violence*) prone, inclined, apt, liable, subject, likely, given. **2** (*disposed to listen*) inclined, willing, minded, predisposed, eager, ready, prepared.

disposition *noun* **1** (*a violent disposition*) character, nature, temperament, constitution, make-up, temper, humour, spirit. **2** (*a disposition towards cruelty*) inclination, tendency, bias, bent, leaning, proneness, weakness, habit, predisposition, predilection, proclivity, propensity, readiness, turn. **3** (*disposition of government forces*) disposal, arrangement, distribution, grouping,

marshalling, order, ordering, positioning, organization, placement, placing, setting-up, lining-up, alignment, pattern, system. **4** (*the disposition of property*) disposal, distribution, transfer, transference, conveyance, allocation, bestowal. **5** (*at the disposition of the court*) disposal, control, direction, management, authority, power, regulation.

dispossess *verb* **1** (*dispossess of his wealth*) deprive, divest, strip, take away, confiscate, expropriate, rob, bereave. **2** (*dispossess the squatters*) evict, expel, eject, oust, turn out, drive out, dislodge. OPPOSITE: house.

disproportion *noun* disparity, inequality, discrepancy, difference, imbalance, lopsidedness, unevenness, asymmetry. OPPOSITE: equality.

disproportionate *adj* unequal, uneven, unbalanced, out of proportion, irregular, top-heavy, excessive, extreme, inordinate, unreasonable, incommensurate. OPPOSITE: commensurate.

disprove *verb* confute, refute, rebut, deny, negate, invalidate, controvert, contradict, discredit, debunk (*inf*), expose, overturn. OPPOSITE: prove.

disputable *adj* debatable, arguable, contestable, moot, controversial, controvertible, questionable, doubtful, dubious, iffy (*inf*), uncertain. OPPOSITE: indisputable.

disputation *noun* argument, argumentation, debate, dispute, altercation, controversy, dissension, deliberation, polemics.

disputatious *adj* argumentative, contentious, controversial, quarrelsome, irascible, pugnacious, cantankerous, disputative, litigious, captious, polemical, cavilling. OPPOSITE: genial.

dispute *verb* **1** (*dispute with one another*) argue, debate, discuss, disagree, quarrel, wrangle, squabble, brawl, clash, bicker, altercate, contend, spar. OPPOSITE: agree. **2** (*dispute a theory*) question, challenge, contest, controvert, contradict, doubt, deny, oppose, impugn, gainsay, object to, resist. OPPOSITE: uphold.
⪢ *noun* argument, debate, discussion, disputation, controversy, contention, contest, conflict, friction, strife, discord, squabble, wrangle, quarrel, altercation, clash, dissension, feud, fracas, brawl, row, shindig (*inf*), disagreement, litigation. OPPOSITE: agreement.

disqualify *verb* eliminate, debar, preclude, prohibit, exclude, rule out, suspend, disable, disentitle. OPPOSITE: qualify.

disquiet *noun* disquietude, inquietude, anxiety, anxiousness, nervousness, worry, concern, foreboding, unease, uneasiness, restlessness, unrest, fear, dread, alarm, distress, perturbation, trepidation, anguish, angst, trouble, fretfulness, agitation, disturbance, upset, discomposure. OPPOSITE: calm.
⪢ *verb* worry, concern, unsettle, unnerve, frighten, fret, perturb, agitate, discompose, incommode, distress, shake, ruffle, upset, disturb, annoy, irritate, hassle (*inf*), bother, trouble, harass, pester, plague, vex, incommode. OPPOSITE: appease.

disquisition *noun* dissertation, essay, treatise, thesis, paper, lecture, monograph, discourse, discussion, exposition, sermon, explanation, exposé.

disregard *verb* **1** (*impossible to disregard it*) ignore, overlook, neglect, pass over, gloss over, discount, take no notice of, make light of, play down (inf), disobey, flout, forget, laugh off, set aside, brush aside, brush off. OPPOSITE: heed. **2** (*pointedly disregarded him*) slight, snub, shun, cold-shoulder (inf), disdain, insult, affront, disparage, denigrate, contemn.

➤ *noun* **1** (*with little disregard for his future*) inattention, neglect, negligence, carelessness, inattention, oversight, heedlessness, indifference. **2** (*treated her with total disregard*) indifference, disrespect, despise, disdain, contempt, scorn, disparagement, denigration, disesteem.

disrepair *noun* dilapidation, decay, deterioration, collapse, ruin, ruination, rack and ruin, decrepitude, shabbiness.

disreputable *adj* **1** (*disreputable behaviour*) discreditable, shameful, disgraceful, opprobrious, ignominious, reprehensible, base, abject, vile, dishonourable, dishonest, despicable, contemptible, mean, corrupt, low, notorious, outrageous, shocking, scandalous, infamous, shady (inf), dodgy (inf), shifty (inf), suspicious, questionable, dubious, unscrupulous, unprincipled, unrespectable, unworthy, unsavoury, rascally, crooked (inf), villainous. OPPOSITE: respectable. **2** (*of disreputable appearance*) scruffy (inf), shabby, bedraggled, dishevelled, unkempt, disorderly, untidy, seedy, dingy, slovenly, threadbare, worn OPPOSITE: smart.

disrepute *noun* disgrace, dishonour, discredit, shame, infamy, ignominy, odium, opprobrium, obloquy, notoriety, ill repute, ill favour, disfavour, disesteem, unpopularity. OPPOSITE: esteem.

disrespect *noun* impoliteness, incivility, rudeness, discourtesy, ungraciousness, churlishness, unmannerliness, irreverence, insolence, impertinence, impudence, cheek (inf), dishonour, disregard, neglect, contempt, scorn. OPPOSITE: respect.

disrespectful *adj* rude, discourteous, impolite, uncivil, bad-mannered, unmannerly, cheeky, insolent, insulting, impudent, impertinent, sassy (inf), churlish, ill-bred, irreverent, inconsiderate, contemptuous, scornful. OPPOSITE: polite.

disrobe *verb* undress, unclothe, take off, remove, strip, doff, shed, divest, denude, bare, uncover. OPPOSITE: dress.

disrupt *verb* disturb, upset, disorganize, disarrange, disorder, unsettle, agitate, confuse, break up, sabotage, interrupt, discontinue, butt in, intrude, interfere with, obstruct, impede, hamper, suspend, spoil.

disruption *noun* disturbance, disorder, disorderliness, confusion, disorganization, disarrangement, disarray, turmoil, upheaval, upset, interruption, interference, stoppage, suspension, discontinuation.

disruptive *adj* troublesome, unruly, divisive, undisciplined, disorderly, obstreperous, boisterous, noisy, turbulent, disturbing, upsetting, unsettling, distracting.

dissatisfaction *noun* discontent, discontentment, displeasure, dislike, unhappiness, malaise, discomfort, uneasiness, restlessness, disquiet, disappointment, dismay, distress, regret, chagrin, anger, annoyance, exasperation, irritation, frustration, disapproval, disapprobation, resentment, vexation. OPPOSITE: satisfaction.

dissatisfied *adj* discontented, displeased, disgruntled, put out, unhappy, annoyed, angry, vexed, frustrated, exasperated, fed up (inf), pissed off (sl), brassed off (inf), browned off (inf), cheesed off (inf), irritated, disappointed, disillusioned, disenchanted, disapproving, regretful, unfulfilled, unsatisfied, uneasy, restless. OPPOSITE: satisfied.

dissect *verb* **1** (*dissect a dead body*) anatomize, cut up, cut open, dismember, vivisect. **2** (*dissect the facts*) analyse, break down, scrutinize, examine, inspect, investigate, study, explore, sift, probe, pore over.

dissection *noun* **1** (*dissection of the dead bodies*) dismemberment, cutting up, cutting open, vivisection, anatomization, autopsy, postmortem, necropsy. **2** (*dissection of the facts*) analysis, breakdown, scrutiny, examination, inspection, investigation, study, exploration, sifting, probing, research.

dissemble *verb* pretend, feign, simulate, affect, sham, fake, falsify, counterfeit, dissimulate.

disseminate *verb* disperse, diffuse, spread, scatter, sow, distribute, circulate, broadcast, promulgate, dissipate, propagate, publish, proclaim, publicize, preach. OPPOSITE: suppress.

dissemination *noun* dispersion, diffusion, spread, distribution, circulation, broadcasting, promulgation, propagation, publication, publishing. OPPOSITE: suppression.

dissension *noun* disagreement, discord, friction, strife, conflict, argument, quarrel, contention, dispute, dissent, wrangling, bickering, variance, difference. OPPOSITE: agreement.

dissent *verb* disagree, differ, dispute, object, protest, decline, reject, repudiate, renounce, refuse, quibble, abjure, secede from. OPPOSITE: assent.

➤ *noun* disagreement, discord, friction, dissidence, dissension, objection, refusal, protest, dispute, controversy, difference, opposition, resistance, disaffection, nonconformity.

dissenter *noun* dissident, nonconformist, objector, protester, demonstrator, disputant, rebel, protestant, apostate, recusant, heretic, sectarian, revolutionary. OPPOSITE: conformist.

dissentient *adj* dissenting, disagreeing, dissident, differing, conflicting, opposing, protesting, objecting, rebellious, revolutionary, recusant, schismatic, apostate, heretical, heterodox, unorthodox, nonconformist, noncompliant. OPPOSITE: compliant.

dissertation *noun* discourse, treatise, essay, thesis, paper, monograph, exposition, critique, disquisition.

disservice *noun* disfavour, wrong, bad turn, ill turn, dirty trick (inf), con trick (inf), kick in the teeth (inf), damage, injury, harm, hurt, injustice, unkindness. OPPOSITE: favour.

dissident *adj* dissenting, dissentient, disagreeing, differing, discordant, nonconformist, heterodox, opposing, protesting, conflicting, rebellious, heretical, revolutionary, recusant, apostate, schismatic.

➤ *noun* dissenter, protester, objector, rebel,

revolutionary, agitator, heretic, nonconformist, schismatic, apostate, recusant.

dissimilar *adj* unlike, unalike, different, divergent, deviating, distinct, disparate, unrelated, heterogeneous, contrasting, diverse, incompatible, mismatched, manifold, various, variant, varying. OPPOSITE: alike.

dissimilarity *noun* dissimilitude, difference, unlikeness, incompatibility, distinction, deviation, divergence, incomparability, discrepancy, disparity, heterogeneity, nonuniformity, contrast, diversity, variance, variation, variety, unrelatedness. OPPOSITE: similarity.

dissimulate *verb* feign, fake, sham, pretend, affect, dissemble, lie, cover up (*inf*), conceal, disguise, mask, cloak, hide, camouflage.

dissipate *verb* 1 (*dissipate a fortune*) spend, expend, consume, drain, deplete, burn up, use up, exhaust, run through, get through, waste, squander, fritter away, lavish, misspend. OPPOSITE: hoard. 2 (*watched the cloud dissipating*) scatter, drive away, disperse, diffuse, break up, dispel, disappear, vanish, evaporate, dissolve, melt away. OPPOSITE: collect.

dissipated *adj* debauched, dissolute, corrupt, depraved, licentious, promiscuous, rakish, degenerate, profligate, abandoned, intemperate, unrestrained, wild, self-indulgent, wanton.

dissipation *noun* 1 (*led a life of drink and dissipation*) debauchery, profligacy, licence, licentiousness, dissoluteness, abandonment, corruption, depravity, immorality, self-indulgence, intemperance, excess, prodigality. 2 (*the dissipation of funds*) expenditure, consumption, depletion, squandering, wastefulness, waste, extravagance, excess, lavishness, prodigality. OPPOSITE: frugality. 3 (*dissipation of the gas*) dispersion, dispersal, diffusion, scattering, dissemination, dissolution, evaporation, disappearance, vanishing, disintegration. OPPOSITE: accumulation.

dissociate *verb* 1 (*dissociate cause and effect*) separate, disunite, disassociate, sever, detach, break off, disconnect, disjoin, disrupt, divorce, set apart, isolate, segregate. OPPOSITE: join. 2 (*dissociated himself from the movement*) distance, disconnect, cut off, withdraw, quit (*inf*), separate, secede.

dissociation *noun* separation, disunion, severance, severing, dissevering, detachment, division, disconnection, disjunction, disengagement, divorce, split, parting, break, distancing, setting apart, isolation, segregation. OPPOSITE: union.

dissolute *adj* dissipated, debauched, wanton, depraved, loose, lax, profligate, abandoned, libertine, licentious, lewd, corrupt, immoral, degenerate, rakish, intemperate, unrestrained, promiscuous, self-indulgent, wild. OPPOSITE: austere.

dissolution *noun* 1 (*dissolution of the empire*) disintegration, breakup, collapse, decay, parting, division, dispersion, dispersal, destruction, overthrow, ruin, annihilation, extinction, death, demise. OPPOSITE: consolidation. 2 (*dissolution of the marriage*) annulment, termination, discontinuation, end, ending, conclusion, finish, resolution, breakup, divorce, separation, dismissal, suspension, adjournment, disbandment, winding-up. 3 (*the dissolution of her dreams*) dispersal,

dissipation, disappearance, evaporation, vanishing, dwindling. 4 (*dissolution of the material*) decomposition, disintegration, dissolving, liquefaction, melting, solution, evaporation, deliquescence. 5 (*the dissolution of youth today*) dissipation, debauchery, profligacy, depravity, degeneracy, corruption, intemperance, abandonment, licentiousness, promiscuity, self-indulgence, wantonness, wildness.

dissolve *verb* 1 (*until the butter dissolves*) liquefy, melt, soften, thaw, deliquesce, fuse. OPPOSITE: solidify. 2 (*her hopes dissolved*) disintegrate, crumble, collapse, perish, die, decompose, disperse, diffuse, dissipate, evaporate, fade, dwindle, melt away, vanish, disappear, evanesce. OPPOSITE: endure. 3 (*watched his marriage dissolve*) break up, disintegrate, end, finish, terminate. 4 (*dissolve the partnership*) end, terminate, axe (*inf*), sever, break up, discontinue, wind up, disband, dismiss, suspend. OPPOSITE: unite. 5 (*the party dissolved*) break up, disband, split up, separate, disperse, scatter, disunite. 6 (*dissolve into tears*) break, burst, collapse.

dissonance *noun* 1 (*the dissonance of the composition*) discordance, cacophony, inharmoniousness, unmelodiousness, harshness, stridency, jarring, jangle, grating. OPPOSITE: harmony. 2 (*dissonance between the two parties*) discord, disagreement, dissension, disharmony, difference, discrepancy, disparity, incongruity, clash, quarrelling, wrangling, feuding, incompatibility, inconsistency, variance. OPPOSITE: accord.

dissonant *adj* 1 (*a dissonant passage of music*) discordant, inharmonious, unmelodious, unmusical, tuneless, cacophonous, harsh, strident, jangling, jarring, grating, raucous. OPPOSITE: harmonious. 2 (*a dissonant element*) inconsistent, incongruous, incompatible, irreconcilable, discrepant, anomalous, at variance, disagreeing, different, differing, divergent, clashing, irregular. OPPOSITE: congruous.

dissuade *verb* deter, discourage, disincline, put off, divert, turn aside, stop, talk out of, persuade against, advise against, warn, expostulate, remonstrate. OPPOSITE: urge.

distance *noun* 1 (*the distance between the two*) space, interval, gap, remove, separation, extent, range, stretch, span, reach, length, width, breadth, depth, height. 2 (*deterred by the distance*) remoteness, farness, inaccessibility. 3 (*a certain distance in his manner*) reserve, remoteness, coolness, coldness, frigidity, aloofness, constraint, restraint, stiffness, reticence, formality, unfriendliness, unresponsiveness. OPPOSITE: cordiality.
➤ *verb* separate, cut off, dissociate, remove, withdraw, break, secede.
in the distance far away, far off, afar, yonder, on the horizon.

distant *adj* 1 (*a distant shore*) far, remote, outlying, faraway, far-off, far-flung, afar, out-of-the-way, isolated, abroad, removed, separate, apart. OPPOSITE: near. 2 (*a distant manner*) reserved, cool, cold, frigid, aloof, stiff, ceremonious, formal, haughty, condescending, antisocial, standoffish, detached, withdrawn, reticent, restrained, unfriendly, unapproachable, uncommunicative, unresponsive. OPPOSITE: affable. 3 (*a* *distant possibility*) remote, faint, slight, indistinct, obscure, uncertain. OPPOSITE: clear.

distaste *noun* dislike, disgust, repugnance, disinclination, aversion, abhorrence, horror, loathing, revulsion, detestation, antipathy, displeasure, dissatisfaction, disfavour, disrelish. OPPOSITE: relish.

distasteful *adj* **1** (*a distasteful experience*) unpleasant, displeasing, disagreeable, undesirable, offensive, revolting, repellent, repugnant, obnoxious, disgusting, loathsome, objectionable, hateful, abhorrent, detestable, repulsive, obscene, off-putting, uninviting. OPPOSITE: pleasant. **2** (*distasteful food*) disgusting, revolting, unappetizing, unpalatable, unsavoury, nauseating. OPPOSITE: delightful.

distended *adj* dilated, enlarged, expanded, swollen, inflated, ballooning, bloated, puffed-out, puffy, stretched, extended, tumescent. OPPOSITE: deflated.

distension *noun* dilation, dilatation, enlargement, expansion, extension, spread, swelling, bloating, inflation, intumescence. OPPOSITE: contraction.

distil *verb* **1** (*distilled from salt water*) condense, vaporize, evaporate, purify, refine, separate, concentrate. **2** (*to distil the very essence of music*) extract, draw out, press out, express, derive. **3** (*to distil droplets*) drip, drop, dribble, trickle, leak, flow, exude, give out.

distillation *noun* extract, extraction, elixir, condensation, evaporation, essence, quintessence, spirit.

distinct *adj* **1** (*a distinct quality*) clear, sharp, clear-cut, well-defined, defined, plain, obvious, apparent, evident, definite, unmistakable, marked, conspicuous, noticeable, recognizable, palpable, patent, manifest, blatant, lucid, unambiguous, decided, unequivocal. OPPOSITE: indistinct. **2** (*distinct elements*) separate, detached, individual, discrete, disparate, unconnected, unassociated, different, dissimilar, unlike, unalike.

distinction *noun* **1** (*the distinction of right from wrong*) differentiation, discernment, discrimination, separation, penetration, perception. **2** (*the distinction between amateur and professional*) difference, division, dissimilarity, contrast, contradistinction, dissimilitude. **3** (*several important distinctions*) characteristic, peculiarity, individuality, feature, subtlety, nuance. **4** (*a family of some distinction*) fame, renown, repute, reputation, eminence, prestige, mark, note, prominence, celebrity, importance, significance, consequence, account, worth, superiority, name, rank, greatness, glory, quality. OPPOSITE: insignificance. **5** (*passed with distinction*) honour, credit, merit, excellence.

distinctive *adj* distinguishing, characteristic, individual, particular, peculiar, unique, original, special, singular, idiosyncratic, notable, noteworthy, remarkable, extraordinary, different, uncommon, unusual, typical.

distinctly *adv* **1** (*I distinctly remembered telling you*) clearly, plainly, evidently, apparently, decidedly, definitely, obviously, manifestly, patently, palpably, markedly, noticeably, sharply, unmistakably, unambiguously. **2** (*she spoke distinctly*) clearly, plainly, precisely, intelligibly.

distinguish *verb* **1** (*distinguish one thing from another*) differentiate, tell apart, tell between, discriminate,

separate, divide, determine, judge. **2** (*distinguished by his bearing*) single out, set apart, separate, characterize, individualize, particularize, mark off, stamp, categorize, classify. **3** (*difficult to distinguish in the gloom*) discern, perceive, see, observe, notice, pick out, descry, espy, ascertain, make out, identify, detect, apprehend, recognize. **4** (*distinguish herself at sport*) excel, do well, glorify, dignify, honour, ennoble, celebrate, immortalize, make famous, lionize.

distinguishable *adj* recognizable, discernible, clear, plain, evident, manifest, marked, well-defined, noticeable, conspicuous, obvious, observable, perceptible, appreciable. OPPOSITE: indistinguishable.

distinguished *adj* **1** (*a distinguished soldier*) eminent, illustrious, notable, renowned, famous, famed, well-known, prominent, noted, celebrated, acclaimed, honoured, respected, esteemed, legendary. OPPOSITE: unknown. **2** (*a distinguished manner*) dignified, refined, august, stately, majestic, lordly, aristocratic, noble. **3** (*a distinguished achievement*) marked, conspicuous, striking, outstanding, extraordinary, signal.

distinguishing *adj* distinctive, individual, individualistic, differentiating, different, marked, peculiar, singular, typical, characteristic, unique, discriminative, discriminatory.

distort *verb* **1** (*distort the shape*) deform, twist, contort, buckle, warp, misshape, disfigure, bend, turn, mangle, wrench, wrest, wring. OPPOSITE: straighten. **2** (*distort the truth*) falsify, misrepresent, pervert, colour, bias, slant, twist, alter, change, tamper with, torture, misinterpret, garble.

distortion *noun* **1** (*a distortion in the straight line*) deformation, deformity, contortion, crookedness, twist, bend, buckle, slant, warp, curvature, skew, malformation. **2** (*distortion of the truth*) falsification, misrepresentation, perversion, misinterpretation, alteration, change, garbling, colouring, slant, bias, twisting.

distract *verb* **1** (*distract from the matter in hand*) divert, deflect, sidetrack, turn aside, turn away, draw away, put off. OPPOSITE: focus. **2** (*distract the children*) amuse, divert, entertain, occupy, engage, engross, absorb, beguile. OPPOSITE: bore. **3** (*distracted by his appearance*) confuse, perplex, puzzle, bewilder, confound, disturb, discompose, disconcert, fluster, agitate, annoy, harass, hassle (*inf*), trouble, worry, torment. OPPOSITE: compose. **4** (*distracted by jealousy*) derange, madden, craze.

distracted *adj* **1** (*he appeared distracted*) confused, perplexed, bewildered, confounded, hassled (*inf*), troubled, perplexed, puzzled, bemused, abstracted, agitated, anxious, flustered, harassed, worried. OPPOSITE: composed. **2** (*distracted by grief*) overwrought, upset, distraught, desperate, griefstricken, distressed, frantic, frenzied, hysterical, wild, mad, maddened, deranged, raving, crazy, insane.

distraction *noun* **1** (*distraction from the matter in hand*) diversion, interference, disruption, interruption, disturbance, obstruction. **2** (*driven to distraction*) madness, insanity, frenzy, desperation, derangement, hysteria, delirium, mania, lunacy. **3** (*in a state of distraction*) confusion, bewilderment, befuddlement, perplexity, discomposure, perturbation, disturbance, disorder, agitation, turmoil, abstraction. OPPOSITE: composure. **4** (*a variety of distractions*) amusement, entertainment, diversion, pastime, occupation, recreation, game, sport, hobby, beguilement, divertissement.

distraught *adj* agitated, anxious, upset, overwrought, distracted, distressed, worked up, wrought up, beside oneself, desperate, frantic, hysterical, wild, raving, crazy, mad. OPPOSITE: calm.

distress *noun* **1** (*his death caused great distress*) grief, sorrow, heartache, heartbreak, anguish, misery, wretchedness, suffering, affliction, discomfort, pain, ache, agony, torture, trouble, perturbation, worry, unease, uneasiness, anxiety, sadness, angst, desolation, torment, tribulation, woe. OPPOSITE: joy. **2** (*a population living in distress*) adversity, hardship, privation, need, lack, poverty, destitution, penury, beggary, indigence, misfortune, disaster, calamity, trouble, trial. OPPOSITE: relief. **3** (*a yacht in distress*) danger, trouble, difficulty.
➤ *verb* upset, grieve, sadden, afflict, pain, hurt, wound, harrow, distress, disturb, perturb, trouble, cut up (*inf*), worry, bother, perplex, torment, agonize, vex, harass. OPPOSITE: please.

distribute *verb* **1** (*distribute food to the mob*) dispense, dole out, give out, hand out, deal out, dish out, pass round, mete out, allocate, allot, share, divide, apportion, measure out, parcel out, administer, assign, dispose, issue. OPPOSITE: withhold. **2** (*distribute copies*) deliver, convey, supply, hand out, issue, pass round, circulate, spread, transmit. **3** (*distribute grass seed*) scatter, spread, strew, sow, disperse, diffuse, disseminate. OPPOSITE: collect. **4** (*distributed into different classes*) classify, sort, assort, order, categorize, arrange, organize, class, file, group, place, position, locate, dispose.

distribution *noun* **1** (*the distribution of gifts*) dispensation, dole, giving-out, handing-out, sharing, division, apportionment, allotment, allocation, assignment, administration. **2** (*got a job in distribution*) delivery, supply, transport, transportation, marketing, trading, mailing, dealing, handling, conveyance. **3** (*distribution of seed*) circulation, spread, spreading, dissemination, dispersal, dispersion, diffusion, propagation, scattering. **4** (*distribution of the books into categories*) classification, grouping, arrangement, assortment, organization, location, disposition, position, placement, situation.

district *noun* **1** (*a rough district*) area, region, quarter, section, place, locality, locale, vicinity, territory, domain, community, neighbourhood, sector. **2** (*a representative from each district*) ward, borough, parish, department, canton, block, precinct, zone, division, community, constituency.

distrust *verb* doubt, mistrust, disbelieve, question, suspect, wonder about, discredit, be wary of. OPPOSITE: believe.
➤ *noun* doubt, doubtfulness, mistrust, disbelief, dubiety, unbelief, incredulity, incredulousness, suspicion, wariness, chariness, misgiving, qualm, question, questioning, scepticism. OPPOSITE: trust.

distrustful *adj* suspicious, mistrustful, distrusting, untrustful, untrusting, doubtful, doubting, dubious, sceptical, cynical, disbelieving, chary, wary, uneasy. OPPOSITE: trustful.

disturb *verb* **1** (*don't disturb them*) disrupt, interrupt, butt in on, intrude on, interfere with, hinder, hassle (*inf*), pester, bother, trouble, plague, harass, molest, rouse, inconvenience, put out, put off, distract, annoy, vex. **2** (*disturb the arrangements*) disarrange, disorganize, derange, upset, disorder, unsettle, muddle, confuse. OPPOSITE: arrange. **3** (*disturbed by the news*) worry, concern, trouble, agitate, excite, upset, distress, alarm, frighten, dismay, startle, perturb, unsettle, unnerve, discompose, throw (*inf*), discomfit, disconcert, fluster, ruffle, shake, stir. OPPOSITE: calm. **4** (*disturb the solution*) agitate, mix up, churn up, convulse.

disturbance *noun* **1** (*disturbance during working hours*) disruption, interruption, distraction, intrusion, interference, inconvenience, hindrance, bother, harassment, molestation, nuisance, upheaval. **2** (*resented the disturbance of his things*) muddling, confusion, confusing, disarrangement, disordering, disorganization. **3** (*a disturbance during the night*) commotion, disorder, turmoil, tumult, riot, brawl, affray, fray, fracas, uproar, hubbub, hullabaloo, noise, racket, row, ruction (*inf*), rumpus (*inf*), shindig (*inf*). OPPOSITE: peace. **4** (*mental disturbance*) agitation, confusion, bewilderment, discomposure, discomfiture, perturbation, derangement, trouble, alarm, distress, upset, worry. OPPOSITE: calm. **5** (*disturbance of the surface*) agitation, churning, convulsion.

disturbed *adj* **1** (*disturbed by his threats*) worried, anxious, apprehensive, uneasy, concerned, troubled, bothered, upset, confused, discomposed, flustered, nervous. **2** (*disturbed patients*) unbalanced, disordered, maladjusted, neurotic, psychotic, paranoid, upset, screwed-up (*inf*), hung-up (*inf*).

disturbing *adj* alarming, troubling, upsetting, unsettling, distressing, worrying, perturbing, disquieting, disconcerting, bewildering, confusing, dismaying, harrowing, discouraging, frightening, startling, agitating, threatening.

disunited *adj* separated, parted, divided, disjoined, disconnected, disrupted, severed, split, sundered, detached, disengaged, dissociated, estranged. OPPOSITE: joined.

disuse *noun* neglect, nonuse, abandonment, cessation, discontinuance, obsolescence, decay, desuetude. OPPOSITE: use.

disused *adj* unused, neglected, abandoned, discontinued, obsolete, decayed.

ditch *noun* trench, dyke, channel, canal, drain, gully, gutter, watercourse, rut, level, furrow, moat.
➤ *verb* discard, dispose of, get rid of, scrap, throw away (*inf*), throw out (*inf*), jettison, abandon, axe (*inf*), drop, dump (*inf*), junk (*inf*), chuck (*inf*), bin (*inf*).

dither *verb* waver, vacillate, hesitate, falter, hang back, delay, procrastinate, oscillate, teeter, faff about (*inf*), dilly-dally (*inf*), shilly-shally (*inf*). OPPOSITE: decide.
➤ *noun* bother, flap (*inf*), flutter, fluster, panic, stew (*inf*), tizzy (*inf*), twitter (*inf*), pother (*inf*).

diurnal *adj* daily, daytime, day-to-day, everyday, quotidian, circadian.

divan *noun* sofa, settee, couch, chaise longue, daybed, lounger, ottoman, chesterfield, davenport.

dive *verb* **1** (*dive into the water*) nosedive, plunge, jump, leap, bound, spring, bellyflop, submerge, dip, duck, plummet, descend, go down, fall, drop, swoop, pitch, disappear. **2** (*dive for the gun*) lunge, dart, jump, leap, rush, dash, bolt, duck, dodge, hurry, tear, fly.
➤ *noun* **1** (*the splash from her dive*) nosedive, plunge, jump, leap, bound, spring, bellyflop, dip, plummet, descent, fall, drop, swoop. **2** (*his dive for the glass*) lunge, dart, jump, leap, rush, dash, bolt, duck, dodge, header. **3** (*followed her into a dive*) bar, nightclub, club, pub, den, joint (*inf*), dump (*inf*), hole (*inf*), saloon, speakeasy, honky-tonk (*inf*).

diverge *verb* **1** (*where the paths diverge*) divide, subdivide, separate, split, fork, branch, bifurcate, divaricate, part, spread out, radiate, open. OPPOSITE: converge. **2** (*diverge from the original intention*) deviate, digress, wander, meander, stray, swerve, depart, veer, drift, divagate. **3** (*explanations diverge*) differ, vary, conflict, clash, disagree, contradict, dissent. OPPOSITE: agree.

divergence *noun* **1** (*at the divergence of the paths*) divide, division, separation, fork, forking, branch, branching-out, divarication, parting, spreading. OPPOSITE: convergence. **2** (*divergence from the original intention*) deviation, digression, wandering, meandering, straying, departure, deflection, divagation. **3** (*divergence of the two explanations*) difference, variance, varying, variation, conflict, disagreement, contradiction, disparity.

divergent *adj* **1** (*divergent views*) diverging, differing, different, diverse, dissimilar, disagreeing, variant, varying, conflicting, clashing, dissenting, separate. OPPOSITE: concordant. **2** (*divergent figures*) deviating, digressing, tangential, abnormal, aberrant.

divers *adj* sundry, various, varying, varied, different, manifold, multifarious, some, several, numerous, many, miscellaneous.

diverse *adj* different, differing, varied, various, assorted, mixed, miscellaneous, manifold, sundry, several, separate, distinct, discrete, unlike, heterogeneous, contrasting, conflicting, dissimilar, divergent, diversified, varying, variegated. OPPOSITE: similar.

diversify *verb* **1** (*diversify the programme*) vary, variegate, chequer, assort, mix, change, alter, transform, modify. **2** (*the need to diversify*) branch out, expand, extend, spread out.

diversion *noun* **1** (*diversion of attention*) deflection, redirection, turning aside, deviation, digression, divergence, alteration, change, variation, division, departure. **2** (*follow the diversion*) detour, redirection, deviation, alternative. **3** (*various diversions on offer*) amusement, entertainment, distraction, sport, play, recreation, pastime, game, hobby, relaxation, fun, pleasure, delight, enjoyment, enchantment, beguilement, divertissement. OPPOSITE: work.

diversity *noun* variety, assortment, mixture, medley, miscellany, multiplicity, difference, range, variance, variation, variegation, contrast, conflict, distinctiveness, divergence, diverseness, diversification, dissimilarity, dissimilitude, heterogeneity, unlikeness. OPPOSITE: similarity.

divert *verb* **1** (*divert the traffic*) redirect, reroute, deflect, switch, turn aside. **2** (*divert his attention*) deflect, turn aside, avert, sidetrack, distract, draw away, switch, shift, change. **3** (*divert the children*) amuse, entertain, distract, interest, occupy, absorb, engross, intrigue, beguile, delight, enchant, gratify, regale. OPPOSITE: bore.

diverting *adj* amusing, entertaining, enjoyable, absorbing, beguiling, interesting, pleasant, pleasurable, recreational, fun, funny, humorous, witty.

divest *verb* **1** (*divest himself of his armour*) take off, remove, unclothe, undress, strip, denude, disrobe, doff, shed. OPPOSITE: clothe. **2** (*divested of all his wealth*) dispossess, strip, deprive, relieve, despoil, bereave.

divide *verb* **1** (*divide it into two halves*) separate, split, part, partition, sever, shear, cleave, rend, subdivide, sunder, disunite, cut up, break up, bisect, halve, quarter, disjoin, detach, disconnect. **2** (*where the paths divide*) diverge, branch, fork, divert, separate, part, split. OPPOSITE: join. **3** (*divide her property*) share, apportion, portion out, distribute, dispense, deal out, allot, allocate, hand out, dole out, measure out, parcel out. OPPOSITE: collect. **4** (*their conflicting interests divided them*) alienate, estrange, come between, disunite, break up, separate, split up, set at odds. OPPOSITE: unite. **5** (*divide into classes*) classify, categorize, group, grade, rank, order, arrange, sort, dispose, separate, segregate.

dividend *noun* **1** (*dividends payable to investors*) share, portion, cut (*inf*), divvy (*inf*), surplus, gain. **2** (*the plan brought a dividend*) bonus, extra, plus, benefit, perk (*inf*), perquisite.

divination *noun* prophecy, prediction, foretelling, prognostication, presage, augury, divining, soothsaying, fortune-telling, sortilege, clairvoyance, second sight.

divine *adj* **1** (*a divine entity*) godlike, godly, supernatural, superhuman, ethereal, spiritual, angelic, seraphic, saintly, heavenly, celestial, transcendent, mystical. OPPOSITE: earthly. **2** (*divine scripture*) holy, sacred, religious, consecrated, hallowed, sanctified. OPPOSITE: profane. **3** (*divine heights*) lofty, exalted, supreme, rapturous, ecstatic, blissful, beatific. **4** (*a divine smile*) splendid, delightful, marvellous, wonderful, excellent, admirable, charming, stunning (*inf*), glorious, heavenly, gorgeous, lovely, beautiful, perfect, super (*inf*), superlative. OPPOSITE: dreadful.
➤ *verb* **1** (*divine the future*) predict, foretell, foresee, forecast, prophesy, prognosticate, augur, portend. **2** (*divine what was meant*) deduce, infer, suspect, intuit, apprehend, comprehend, understand, grasp, discern, perceive, surmise, guess, conjecture, speculate, suppose, assume, presume.
➤ *noun* cleric, ecclesiastic, theologian, clergyman, clergywoman, churchman, churchwoman, minister, priest, pastor, parson, reverend, prelate.

diviner *noun* prophet, seer, soothsayer, clairvoyant, fortune-teller, augur, oracle, astrologer, sibyl.

divinity *noun* **1** (*praise a divinity*) god, goddess, deity, spirit, angel, godhead, guardian, genius. **2** (*questioned his divinity*) godliness, godhood, holiness, sanctity. **3** (*the* *field of divinity*) theology, religion, religious education, religious instruction, religious studies, religious knowledge, scripture.

division *noun* **1** (*division of the whole*) separation, parting, partition, dividing, disunion, disconnection, detachment, detaching, severance, cutting up, splitting, bisection. OPPOSITE: union. **2** (*division of the spoils*) distribution, sharing out, apportionment, allotment, allocation. OPPOSITE: collection. **3** (*took home his division of the haul*) share, part, segment, slice, portion, section, piece, bit, chunk, fragment, component. **4** (*reports from each division*) section, group, grade, class, family, category, branch, arm, department, sector, compartment. **5** (*as far as the division between the two territories*) divide, dividing-line, demarcation line, partition, border, frontier, boundary. **6** (*a division between the two friends*) breach, rupture, rift, split, schism, feud, conflict, discord, variance, disagreement, dissension, disunion, alienation, estrangement. OPPOSITE: agreement.

divisive *adj* alienating, damaging, injurious, detrimental, pernicious, disruptive, troublesome, troublemaking, inharmonious, unsettling, discordant, estranging.

divorce *noun* **1** (*her first divorce*) annulment, dissolution, breakup, split-up, bust-up (*inf*), separation, disunion. OPPOSITE: marriage. **2** (*the divorce between the two parties*) separation, division, split, partition, severance, breach, rupture.

➤ *verb* **1** (*they have agreed to divorce*) break up, split up, split, part, separate. **2** (*divorced from reality*) separate, detach, disconnect, divide, disunite, split, sever, dissociate, part, disjoin, sunder. OPPOSITE: join.

divulge *verb* disclose, reveal, make known, communicate, tell, impart, leak (*inf*), spill (*inf*), spill the beans about (*inf*), blow wide open (*inf*), betray, let slip, confess, declare, proclaim, utter, expose, uncover, publish, broadcast, promulgate. OPPOSITE: conceal.

dizzy *adj* **1** (*the motion made them dizzy*) giddy, light-headed, unbalanced, off-balance, reeling, staggering, wobbly, vertiginous, shaky, unsteady, faint, woozy (*inf*). **2** (*dizzy at the speed of events*) confused, bewildered, bemused, dazed, muddled, befuddled, puzzled, perplexed. OPPOSITE: clearheaded. **3** (*a dizzy young woman*) giddy, foolish, silly, scatterbrained, featherbrained, irresponsible, fickle, flighty, frivolous, capricious, inconstant. OPPOSITE: reliable.

do *verb* **1** (*do everything on the list*) perform, execute, carry out, fulfil, attain, accomplish, achieve, bring about, implement, effect, effectuate, engineer, realize, complete, discharge, undertake, deal with, sort out, tackle, conclude, finish, end, work at, put into practice. OPPOSITE: neglect. **2** (*do as your mother would wish*) act, behave, conduct oneself, comport oneself. **3** (*that should do*) suffice, serve, be adequate, satisfy, suit, answer, measure up, fit the bill, pass muster. **4** (*I'll do the meal*) prepare, get ready, make, fix, arrange, manage, organize, see to, deal with, look after, take care of, produce, create, cause. **5** (*what does she do?*) work as, earn a living as. **6** (*are you doing all right?*) manage, get along, get on, come along, come on, proceed, progress, fare, develop, make out. **7** (*could not do the calculation*) figure out, solve,

resolve, work out, puzzle out, decipher. **8** (*I'm worried they'll do us*) cheat, swindle, trick, defraud, fleece (*inf*), diddle (*inf*), con (*inf*), rip off (*inf*), have (*inf*), dupe, deceive, hoax, stiff (*inf*), hoodwink. **9** (*do a business course at college*) take, read, study, learn, master. **10** (*the car will do one hundred miles per hour*) go at, reach, achieve, travel at.

➤ *noun* party, function, gathering, event, affair, occasion, soirée, celebration, bash (*inf*), knees-up (*inf*), rave-up (*inf*), thrash (*inf*).

do away with 1 (*do away with capital punishment*) get rid of, dispose of, dispense with, discard, abolish, annul, nullify, axe (*inf*), chuck (*inf*), junk (*inf*), repeal, revoke, rescind, discontinue, remove, eliminate. **2** (*do away with his wife*) destroy, exterminate, put to death, kill, murder, do in (*inf*), knock off (*inf*), bump off (*inf*), blow away (*inf*), take out (*inf*), liquidate, execute, assassinate, slaughter, slay, dispatch.

do in 1 (*the task did him in*) tire out, exhaust, weary, fatigue, shatter (*inf*), fag out (*inf*). **2** (*did he do in his uncle?*) kill, murder, eliminate (*inf*), exterminate, put to death, bump off (*inf*), knock off (*inf*), do away with (*inf*), assassinate, slay, slaughter.

do out of deprive of, cheat out of, trick out of, swindle out of, con out of (*inf*), fleece (*inf*), diddle out of (*inf*).

dos and don'ts rules, regulations, standards, instructions, customs, etiquette, code, policy.

do up 1 (*stooped to do up his laces*) tie, lace, button, zip up. **2** (*do up the parcel*) fasten, wrap, pack, enclose. **3** (*do up the family home*) renovate, restore, modernize, decorate, redecorate, repair, recondition, refurbish, adorn, beautify.

do without forgo, go without, manage without, abstain from, deny oneself, give up, refrain from, relinquish, dispense with, eschew.

docile *adj* tractable, manageable, amenable, obliging, compliant, cooperative, accommodating, submissive, yielding, ductile, malleable, manipulable, pliant, obedient, dutiful, biddable, controllable, controlled, meek, passive. OPPOSITE: obstinate.

docility *noun* tractability, manageability, amenability, compliance, submissiveness, ductility, pliability, pliancy, obedience, meekness, passiveness, biddableness, complaisance. OPPOSITE: obstinacy.

dock[1] *verb* **1** (*dock the sheep's tail*) clip, crop, cut off, lop, shorten, curtail, truncate. **2** (*dock their pay*) reduce, diminish, decrease, lessen, deduct, subtract, remove, withhold. OPPOSITE: increase.

dock[2] *noun* (*fit out a ship in the dock*) wharf, pier, quay, jetty, harbour, marina, boatyard, waterfront.

➤ *verb* **1** (*the ship will dock at noon*) moor, berth, anchor, drop anchor, tie up, put in, land. **2** (*the space shuttles will dock shortly*) couple, link up, hook up, join, rendezvous, unite.

docket *noun* document, documentation, paperwork, certificate, chit, chitty, ticket, label, receipt, tag, tab, bill, counterfoil, tally.

➤ *verb* document, label, tag, tab, ticket, mark, register, catalogue, file, index.

doctor *noun* doc (*inf*), physician, medical officer, medic (*inf*), quack (*inf*), general practitioner, GP, locum, surgeon, clinician, specialist, consultant.

> **verb 1** (*the memo had been doctored*) alter, tamper with, interfere with, change, falsify, misrepresent, pervert, distort, disguise, fudge. **2** (*doctor the engine*) fix, repair, mend, patch up, do up (*inf*), cobble, botch. **3** (*suspected of doctoring the drinks*) adulterate, contaminate, drug, lace, spike (*inf*), mix, dilute, weaken, water down. **4** (*doctor both dogs*) neuter, spay, castrate, sterilize.

doctrinaire *adj* **1** (*a doctrinaire attitude*) dogmatic, rigid, insistent, opinionated, narrow, hidebound, overbearing, inflexible, intolerant, pedantic, biased, fanatical. OPPOSITE: amenable. **2** (*doctrinaire plans*) theoretical, hypothetical, speculative, ideological, visionary, unrealistic, impractical, unpragmatic. OPPOSITE: realistic.

doctrine *noun* dogma, creed, credo, tenet, principle, precept, concept, teaching, canon, maxim, article, belief, opinion, conviction.

document *noun* paper, certificate, instrument, record, report, form, charter, deed, affidavit, credential, voucher, proof, evidence.
> **verb 1** (*document the claim*) support, back up, substantiate, corroborate, authenticate, prove, validate, verify. **2** (*document the episode*) record, report, chronicle, list, detail, particularize, register, cite, instance, chart, tabulate.

documentary *adj* documented, recorded, registered, chronicled, detailed, charted, tabulated, written.

doddering *adj* doddery, weak, feeble, shaky, frail, infirm, unsteady, staggering, tottering, tottery, trembling, trembly, quivering, shuffling, shambling, faltering, floundering, decrepit, aged, elderly, senile. OPPOSITE: robust.

dodge *verb* **1** (*dodge out of the way*) dart, duck (*inf*), dive, sidestep, swerve, veer. **2** (*dodge his enemies*) evade, elude, avoid, escape, fend off, steer clear of. **3** (*dodge difficult questions*) avoid, evade, shirk, shun, hedge, equivocate, fudge, parry, fend off, duck (*inf*), bypass, get round. OPPOSITE: face.
> **noun 1** (*a quick dodge to the side*) dart, duck (*inf*), dive, jump, lunge, sidestep, swerve, body-swerve. **2** (*a clever insurance dodge*) artifice, trick, ruse, wile, scheme, stratagem, manoeuvre, ploy, subterfuge, wheeze (*inf*), deception, machination, contrivance, device.

dodgy *adj* **1** (*a dodgy manoeuvre*) risky, dangerous, unsafe, delicate, chancy, dicey (*inf*), difficult, tricky, problematical, ticklish, uncertain, unreliable. OPPOSITE: safe. **2** (*a dodgy outfit*) disreputable, dubious, suspect, shifty (*inf*), dishonest. OPPOSITE: honest.

doer *noun* performer, agent, operator, executor, achiever, accomplisher, effectuator, entrepreneur, live wire (*inf*), go-getter (*inf*), dynamo (*inf*), wheeler-dealer (*inf*), whizz kid (*inf*), hustler, worker, organizer. OPPOSITE: idler.

doff *verb* **1** (*doff his cap*) raise, lift, tip, take off, remove, touch. **2** (*doff his jacket*) shed, cast off, slip off, slip out of, take off, throw off, remove, disrobe, undress, strip off, divest. OPPOSITE: don.

dog *noun* **1** (*the barking of a dog*) hound, cur, mongrel, whelp, pup, puppy, bitch, canine, mutt (*inf*), pooch (*inf*), tyke. **2** (*you dirty dog*) scoundrel, rascal, rogue,

villain, bastard, wretch, cur, beast, blackguard, heel (*inf*), knave, cad.
> **verb** follow, pursue, trail, track, tail (*inf*), hound, harry, plague, haunt, shadow, trouble, worry.

dogged *adj* determined, resolute, intent, tenacious, firm, steadfast, staunch, persevering, persistent, pertinacious, single-minded, relentless, enduring, unflagging, unfaltering, unwavering, indefatigable, indomitable, tireless, set, steady, wilful, headstrong, obdurate, stubborn, obstinate, stiff-necked, immovable, inflexible, unshakeable, unyielding. OPPOSITE: apathetic.

doggedness *noun* determination, resolution, intentness, tenaciousness, tenacity, firmness, steadfastness, steadiness, staunchness, perseverance, persistence, pertinacity, single-mindedness, relentlessness, endurance, indefatigability, tirelessness, steadiness, wilfulness, obduracy, stubbornness, obstinacy, immovability, inflexibility, unshakeability.

dogma *noun* doctrine, creed, credo, principle, tenet, maxim, code, precept, teaching, belief, conviction, opinion, article of faith.

dogmatic *adj* assertive, opinionated, obdurate, downright, emphatic, positive, insistent, pushy (*inf*), doctrinaire, doctrinal, arbitrary, domineering, overbearing, imperious, magisterial, authoritarian, authoritative, categorical, peremptory, dictatorial, unquestionable, unchallengeable, arrogant, intolerant, biased, prejudiced. OPPOSITE: amenable.

dogsbody *noun* menial, drudge, skivvy (*inf*), slave, general servant, general factotum, lackey, doormat, gofer, maid-of-all-work, man-of-all-work.

doing *noun* **1** (*the doing of the work*) performance, accomplishment, achievement, implementation, realization, execution, carrying out, discharging, effectuation. **2** (*all her various doings*) deed, action, act, activity, feat, exploit, adventure, achievement, accomplishment, work, handiwork, enterprise, proceeding, transaction, dealing, concern, affair. **3** (*persuading them took some doing*) effort, exertion, struggle, activity, work, application, concentration.

doldrums *pl noun* **1** (*stuck in the doldrums*) inactivity, inertia, lassitude, stagnation, dullness, sluggishness, torpor, flatness. **2** (*suffering the doldrums*) depression, dejection, melancholy, blues (*inf*), downheartedness, low spirits, gloom, inertia, apathy, listlessness, boredom, tedium, ennui, malaise.

dole *noun* **1** (*millions on the dole*) social security, unemployment benefit, benefit, welfare. OPPOSITE: wage. **2** (*a dole for the poor*) charity, alms, handout, donation, gift, allowance, grant, gratuity, subsidy, payment, income, credit, support.

dole out distribute, give out, hand out, dish out, dispense, apportion, allocate, allot, assign, share out, divide up, deal out, issue, ration, mete out, administer. OPPOSITE: withhold.

doleful *adj* gloomy, melancholy, sad, miserable, blue (*inf*), down (*inf*), unhappy, sorrowful, disconsolate, woeful, woebegone, sombre, dejected, depressed, depressing, distressing, dismal, dreary, cheerless, forlorn, rueful, lugubrious, funereal, mournful, painful, wretched, dolorous, pitiful, pathetic. OPPOSITE: joyful.

doll *noun* dolly (*inf*), puppet, marionette, moppet, figure, figurine, model, toy, plaything.

dolorous *adj* painful, harrowing, grievous, distressing, heartrending, doleful, dismal, melancholy, mournful, sad, sorrowful, miserable, anguished, woebegone, sombre, rueful, wretched. OPPOSITE: happy.

dolour *noun* sorrow, sadness, misery, grief, anguish, distress, heartache, heartbreak, suffering, lamentation, mourning.

dolt *noun* fool, idiot, imbecile, ignoramus, thickhead (*inf*), wally (*inf*), jerk (*inf*), dipstick (*inf*), nerd (*inf*), prat (*inf*), plonker (*inf*), prick (*sl*), geek (*inf*), airhead (*inf*), schmuck (*inf*), berk (*inf*), simpleton, dimwit (*inf*), dunderhead (*inf*), nutcase (*inf*), blockhead (*inf*), ass (*inf*), dunce, dullard, clot (*inf*), dope (*inf*), nitwit (*inf*), numskull (*inf*), nincompoop (*inf*), ninny (*inf*), chump (*inf*), twerp (*inf*), twit (*inf*). OPPOSITE: genius.

domain *noun* **1** (*throughout the royal domain*) dominion, kingdom, realm, empire, land, territory, demesne, estate, province, region. **2** (*that's out of my domain*) area, field, sphere, orbit, realm, world, scope, sway, department, province, region, bailiwick, section, concern, specialty, speciality, discipline, jurisdiction, authority.

dome *noun* cupola, rotunda, vault, mound, hemisphere.

domestic *adj* **1** (*her domestic life*) home, family, household, domiciliary, private, personal. OPPOSITE: public. **2** (*domestic in character*) home-loving, stay-at-home, homely, domesticated. **3** (*domestic pets*) domesticated, house-trained, trained, tame, pet. **4** (*domestic politics*) internal, home. OPPOSITE: international. **5** (*domestic produce*) native, indigenous, home-grown, home-bred.
➤ *noun* daily, daily help, domestic help, hired help, help, housekeeper, servant, menial, skivvy (*inf*), charwoman, char (*inf*), maid, au pair.

domesticate *verb* **1** (*hard to domesticate wild birds*) tame, break in, train, housetrain, gentle. **2** (*risky to domesticate a foreign species*) naturalize, assimilate, acclimatize, habituate, accustom, familiarize.

domesticated *adj* **1** (*domesticated animals*) tame, tamed, pet, house-trained, broken, broken-in. OPPOSITE: wild. **2** (*a domesticated soul*) domestic, home-loving, homely, house-proud, housewifely. **3** (*domesticated species*) naturalized, acclimatized, habituated. OPPOSITE: foreign.

domicile *noun* abode, home, dwelling, residence, pad (*inf*), house, mansion, habitation, quarters, lodgings, accommodation, address.
➤ *verb* settle, live, make one's home, establish, put down roots, ensconce oneself.

dominant *adj* **1** (*the dominant power in the country*) dominating, authoritative, commanding, controlling, ruling, governing, presiding, superior, supreme, powerful, all-powerful, strong, domineering, influential. OPPOSITE: subordinate. **2** (*the dominant factor*) principal, chief, major, main, primary, prime, key, outstanding, leading, commanding, important, paramount, predominant, preeminent, prominent, prevailing, prevalent, ascendant, supreme.

dominate *verb* **1** (*dominate the meeting*) control, rule, govern, reign, preside over, command, direct, boss (*inf*), monopolize, predominate, master, lead, domineer, overrule, prevail over, overbear, intimidate, subdue, tyrannize, subjugate, crush, suppress, override, overshadow. **2** (*the tower dominated the valley*) overlook, overshadow, eclipse, dwarf, bestride, tower above, survey, loom over, hang over, stand over.

domination *noun* **1** (*a challenge to their domination*) power, authority, dominion, ascendancy, superiority, supremacy, sway, rule, command, leadership, control, influence, mastery. **2** (*under the domination of the invaders*) tyranny, despotism, dictatorship, oppression, repression, suppression, subjugation, subjection, subordination. OPPOSITE: submission.

domineer *verb* tyrannize, oppress, overbear, dominate, subjugate, browbeat, intimidate, bully, hector, boss around (*inf*), swagger, trample, menace, threaten, terrorize. OPPOSITE: submit.

domineering *adj* overbearing, imperious, tyrannical, authoritarian, autocratic, dictatorial, despotic, lordly, magisterial, high-handed, ironhanded, ironfisted, forceful, oppressive, masterful, bossy (*inf*), pushy (*inf*), aggressive, coercive, peremptory, haughty, arrogant. OPPOSITE: meek.

dominion *noun* **1** (*her dominion over the empire*) power, authority, domination, ascendancy, sovereignty, suzerainty, supremacy, sway, rule, control, mastery, lordship, command, direction, government, jurisdiction. **2** (*throughout the dominion*) domain, country, territory, province, colony, realm, kingdom, empire, region, estate, patch (*inf*), turf (*inf*).

don *verb* put on, get into, slip on, slip into, pull on, dress in, clothe oneself, wear. OPPOSITE: doff.
➤ *noun* lecturer, tutor, academic, professor, scholar, teacher, pedagogue.

donate *verb* give, give away, gift, hand out, bestow, bequeath, grant, confer, present, contribute, subscribe, pledge, cough up (*inf*), fork out (*inf*), chip in (*inf*), shell out (*inf*). OPPOSITE: receive.

donation *noun* gift, present, grant, bequest, handout, contribution, offering, subscription, benefaction, boon, presentation, gratuity, stipend, largess, alms, charity.

done *adj* **1** (*get the job done*) finished, over, through, ended, complete, completed, concluded, terminated, fulfilled, executed, settled, realized, accomplished, consummated, perfected. OPPOSITE: unfinished. **2** (*tea's done*) cooked, ready, prepared, finished, well-done. **3** (*that gas can's done*) finished, used up, exhausted, spent, drained, depleted. **4** (*done after a day's work*) done in, exhausted, tired out, wearied, worn out, spent, drained. **5** (*the done thing*) conventional, acceptable, proper, right, correct, suitable, appropriate, fitting, seemly, decorous. **6** (*we've been done!*) tricked, swindled, conned (*inf*), cheated, duped, deceived, hoodwinked.
➤ *interj* agreed, OK (*inf*), accepted, settled, arranged, decided, right, absolutely.

done for ruined, wrecked, broken, destroyed, lost, foiled, dashed, beaten, defeated, vanquished, undone, finished, frustrated, thwarted, doomed.

done in done, tired out, exhausted, fatigued, worn out, wearied, weary, all in (*inf*), played out, clapped out (*inf*), shattered (*inf*), dead beat (*inf*), fagged out (*inf*), flaked out (*inf*), knackered (*inf*), bushed (*inf*), pooped (*inf*), zonked (*inf*).

have done with finish with, give up, throw over, desist, wash one's hands of.

donkey *noun* **1** (*donkey in the field*) ass, mule, jackass, burro, jenny, hinny. **2** (*the man's a donkey*) dunce, fool, idiot, blockhead, dolt, simpleton, dullard, dope (*inf*), ass (*inf*), nincompoop (*inf*), nitwit (*inf*), nerd (*inf*). OPPOSITE: genius.

donnish *adj* academic, intellectual, bookish, scholarly, scholastic, erudite, learned, pedagogic, pedantic, serious.

donor *noun* giver, donator, grantor, provider, benefactor, benefactress, philanthropist, contributor, backer, supporter, fairy godmother (*inf*), angel (*inf*). OPPOSITE: recipient.

doom *noun* **1** (*revealed his eventual doom*) fate, destiny, fortune, lot, portion. **2** (*the project met its doom*) ruin, ruination, rack and ruin, destruction, extinction, annihilation, termination, catastrophe, downfall, disaster, death. **3** (*the victim waiting to hear his doom*) judgment, verdict, decision, decree, sentence, condemnation, damnation, pronouncement.
➤ *verb* **1** (*doomed to an early death*) destine, predestine, ordain, foreordain, preordain, fate, damn, condemn, consign **2** (*doomed to hang*) condemn, sentence, judge, damn, decree, pronounce.

doomed *adj* fated, destined, ill-fated, condemned, damned, cursed, star-crossed, ill-starred, ill-omened, unlucky, luckless, bedevilled, bewitched, hopeless.

door *noun* **1** (*went through the door*) entrance, entry, exit, doorway, opening, hatch, gate, portal, barrier. **2** (*door to a new life*) entrance, entry, entrée, opening, opportunity, access, gateway, way, path, road, route.

dope *noun* **1** (*caught with some dope on him*) drug, narcotic, opiate, barbiturate, amphetamine, sedative, stimulant, hallucinogen. **2** (*he's a dope*) dolt, blockhead, fool, idiot, simpleton, dunce, thickhead, jerk (*inf*), wally (*inf*), nerd (*inf*), dipstick (*inf*), dickhead (*inf*), plonker (*inf*), prat (*inf*), prick (*sl*), geek (*inf*), schmuck (*inf*), berk (*inf*), charlie (*inf*), dimwit (*inf*), half-wit (*inf*), numskull (*inf*), clot (*inf*), nincompoop (*inf*), ninny (*inf*), nitwit (*inf*), twerp (*inf*), twit (*inf*). OPPOSITE: genius. **3** (*give us the dope*) facts, information, details, specifics, news, gen (*inf*), info (*inf*), lowdown (*inf*).
➤ *verb* sedate, drug, narcotize, anaesthetize, doctor, medicate, stupefy, spike (*inf*), knock out, inject.

dormant *adj* **1** (*dormant through the winter*) sleeping, asleep, hibernating, resting, quiescent, comatose, fallow, latent, inactive, immobile, motionless, inert, stagnant, inoperative, sluggish, lethargic, slumbering, torpid, passive, suspended. OPPOSITE: active. **2** (*dormant possibilities*) latent, potential, hidden, unrealized, undeveloped, undisclosed.

dose *noun* **1** (*a dose of medicine*) draught, measure, amount, portion, quantity, dosage, prescription, shot. **2** (*a dose of malaria*) bout, attack, spell, episode.
➤ *verb* medicate, prescribe, dispense, administer, treat.

dot *noun* point, spot, speck, pinpoint, mark, fleck, circle, dab, jot, mite, iota, atom, particle.

➤ *verb* spot, speckle, fleck, bespeckle, mark, dab, stud, pepper, pock, sprinkle, stipple, scatter.
on the dot punctually, promptly, precisely, exactly, sharp, on time.

dotage *noun* senility, old age, decrepitude, feebleness, infirmity, weakness, second childhood. OPPOSITE: youth.

dote *verb* idolize, adore, worship, love, admire, prize, treasure, cherish, hold dear, indulge, pamper, spoil. OPPOSITE: loathe.

doting *adj* adoring, devoted, loving, fond, affectionate, tender, soft, indulgent.

double *adj* **1** (*a double room*) twice, twofold, dual, duplex, duplicate, coupled, paired, twin. OPPOSITE: single. **2** (*a double helping*) doubled, twofold, large. **3** (*leading a double life*) dual, deceitful, false, insincere, hypocritical, two-faced, treacherous, perfidious, dishonest. OPPOSITE: honest. **4** (*a double meaning*) dual, double-edged, two-edged, ambiguous, ambivalent, equivocal, paradoxical.
➤ *verb* **1** (*double in size*) duplicate, enlarge, magnify, increase, repeat, multiply. OPPOSITE: halve. **2** (*double for the lead actor*) understudy, substitute, stand in. **3** (*double the sheets*) fold, bend over.
➤ *noun* twin, duplicate, match, copy, facsimile, counterpart, image, mate, fellow, replica, clone, lookalike, impersonator, doppelgänger, ringer (*inf*), dead ringer (*inf*), dead spit (*inf*), spitting image (*inf*).
at the double quickly, rapidly, briskly, posthaste, without delay, right away, straightaway, immediately, at once. OPPOSITE: slowly.

double-cross *verb* cheat, hoodwink, trick, con (*inf*), swindle, two-time (*inf*), defraud, betray, mislead, deceive.

double dealing *noun* cheating, swindling, betrayal, treachery, defrauding, fraud, fraudulence, double-crossing, perfidy, foul play, hypocrisy, deceit, deception, duplicity, trickery, hoodwinking, misleading, crookedness (*inf*), dishonesty, untrustworthiness, mendacity, underhandedness, two-facedness, two-timing (*inf*).

double entendre *noun* innuendo, double meaning, suggestiveness, ambiguity, wordplay, pun.

doubt *verb* **1** (*doubt her version of events*) suspect, question, query, mistrust, distrust, fear, disbelieve, discredit. OPPOSITE: trust. **2** (*reported to be doubting*) waver, vacillate, hesitate, demur, scruple, lack conviction, be uncertain. OPPOSITE: resolve.
➤ *noun* **1** (*doubts about her innocence*) suspicion, mistrust, distrust, disquiet, scepticism, misgiving, qualm, reservation, incredulity, apprehension, hesitation, uneasiness. **2** (*consumed with doubt*) uncertainty, confusion, indecision, hesitancy, hesitation, perplexity, vacillation, irresolution, doubtfulness, dubiety, disbelief. OPPOSITE: trust.
in doubt doubtful, uncertain, undecided, unresolved, unsettled, unreliable, ambiguous, confused, in question, questionable, debatable, problematic.
no doubt doubtless, doubtlessly, undoubtedly, definitely, unquestionably, certainly, surely, assuredly, of course, probably, most likely, presumably, admittedly.

doubter *noun* questioner, sceptic, cynic, scoffer, disbeliever, unbeliever, dissenter, pessimist, agnostic, doubting Thomas.

doubtful *adj* **1** (*doubtful about the outcome*) uncertain, unsure, unconvinced, undecided, indecisive, unresolved, irresolute, uneasy, wavering, vacillating, distrustful, apprehensive, tentative, hesitant, suspicious, sceptical. OPPOSITE: certain. **2** (*doubtful they will cooperate*) unlikely, improbable, questionable. **3** (*a doubtful conclusion*) unclear, vague, obscure, ambiguous, nebulous, equivocal, unsettled, inconclusive, dubious, problematic, difficult. OPPOSITE: definite. **4** (*of doubtful quality*) dubious, questionable, suspicious, suspect, disreputable, iffy (*inf*), dodgy (*inf*), fishy (*inf*), shady (*inf*), unreliable, debatable.

doubtless *adv* **1** (*doubtless want a rest*) certainly, surely, indisputably, unquestionably, undoubtedly, no doubt, truly, assuredly, precisely, clearly, of course, without doubt. OPPOSITE: maybe. **2** (*doubtless a friend of hers*) probably, most likely, apparently, ostensibly, seemingly, supposedly, presumably.

dour *adj* **1** (*a dour expression*) sullen, morose, sour, churlish, gruff, dismal, dreary, gloomy, grim, austere, forbidding, unsmiling, unfriendly. **2** (*a dour personality*) hard, inflexible, stern, austere, rigorous, harsh, strict, severe, rigid, unyielding, uncompromising, obstinate, uncommunicative.

douse *verb* **1** (*douse in vinegar*) souse, dip, plunge, duck, dunk, immerse, immerge, flood, deluge, submerge, soak, saturate, steep, drench, splash, wet, hose down. **2** (*douse the light*) extinguish, smother, snuff, put out, blow out, quench. OPPOSITE: light.

dovetail *verb* **1** (*dovetail the two planks*) fit, fit together, splice, join, unite, interlock, link, mortise, tenon. **2** (*the two projects dovetail nicely*) fit together, go together, correspond, match, coincide, fall in, conform, agree, concur, tally, harmonize, accord.

dowdy *adj* shabby, untidy, slovenly, scrubby (*inf*), tatty (*inf*), tacky (*inf*), drab, dull, dingy, frumpish, frumpy, frowsy, ill-dressed, inelegant, unfashionable, old-fashioned. OPPOSITE: smart.

down[1] *adv* (*down to the bottom*) to the ground, to the floor, downwards, low, below, beneath, under. OPPOSITE: up.
➤ *prep* **1** (*go down the path*) along, through. **2** (*down the years*) through, throughout.
➤ *adj* **1** (*feeling pretty down*) depressed, dejected, downcast, downhearted, disheartened, discouraged, dispirited, crestfallen, despondent, sad, miserable, unhappy, dismal, gloomy, melancholy, low, blue (*inf*), wretched. OPPOSITE: cheerful. **2** (*the system's down*) out of order, out of action, not working, crashed, inoperative, conked out (*inf*), bust (*inf*). OPPOSITE: working.
➤ *verb* **1** (*down his rival*) knock down, bring down, floor, fell, prostrate, topple, throw, overthrow, trip up, subdue, tackle. **2** (*down several pints*) drink, swallow, consume, knock back (*inf*), put away (*inf*), drain, gulp, swig (*inf*), swill (*inf*), toss off (*inf*).

down[2] *noun* (*filled the pillow with down*) feathers, fluff, fur, fuzz, floss, wool.

down-and-out *adj* destitute, impoverished, penniless, broke (*inf*), short, ruined, derelict. OPPOSITE: wealthy.
➤ *noun* tramp, vagrant, vagabond, beggar, outcast, pauper, dosser (*inf*), bum (*inf*), loser (*inf*).

down-at-heel *adj* shabby, poor, ill-dressed, frayed, tattered, tatty (*inf*), tacky (*inf*), ragged, drab, frowzy, dowdy, dingy, run-down, seedy (*inf*), slovenly, slipshod.

downbeat *adj* **1** (*sounded very downbeat*) down, downcast, low, gloomy, miserable, pessimistic, negative, depressed, despondent, cheerless, cynical. OPPOSITE: optimistic. **2** (*a downbeat attitude*) relaxed, calm, informal, casual, laid-back (*inf*), nonchalant, blasé, unhurried, unworried, insouciant. OPPOSITE: upbeat.

downcast *adj* dejected, depressed, despondent, sad, sorrowful, unhappy, doleful, mournful, wretched, miserable, down, blue (*inf*), low, melancholy, disheartened, downhearted, dispirited, fed up (*inf*), discouraged, disconsolate, disappointed, crestfallen, daunted, dismayed, glum, gloomy, cheerless. OPPOSITE: happy.

downfall *noun* **1** (*the downfall of the government*) fall, ruin, ruination, destruction, collapse, defeat, breakdown, failure, debacle, overthrow, undoing, debasement, degradation, disgrace. OPPOSITE: rise. **2** (*caught in a sudden downfall*) deluge, rainstorm, shower, downpour, cloudburst.

downgrade *verb* **1** (*his superiors will downgrade him*) degrade, demote, humble, debase, lower, relegate, reduce in rank. OPPOSITE: upgrade. **2** (*tried to downgrade their claims*) minimize, denigrate, disparage, belittle, defame, depreciate, detract from, run down (*inf*), do down (*inf*), bad-mouth (*inf*), sell short (*inf*), decry. OPPOSITE: praise.

downhearted *adj* discouraged, disheartened, dispirited, low-spirited, despondent, disconsolate, depressed, dejected, downcast, daunted, crestfallen, chapfallen, disappointed, dismayed, sad, sorrowful, unhappy, blue (*inf*), miserable, gloomy, glum. OPPOSITE: cheerful.

downpour *noun* cloudburst, deluge, torrent, flood, inundation, rainstorm, downfall.

downright *adj* **1** (*a downright lie*) absolute, positive, simple, utter, categorical, outright, complete, total, thorough, thoroughgoing, sheer, unmitigated, unqualified, out-and-out, arrant, rank, wholesale, blatant, clear, plain, explicit, undisguised, unequivocal. **2** (*a downright manner*) candid, frank, open, up-front (*inf*), honest, blunt, bluff, brusque, matter-of-fact, straightforward, forthright, plainspoken, outspoken, sincere. OPPOSITE: evasive.
➤ *adv* absolutely, plainly, utterly, clearly, completely, totally, thoroughly, profoundly, positively, categorically.

down-to-earth *adj* practical, realistic, commonsense, commonsensical, hardheaded, matter-of-fact, mundane, no-nonsense, sane, sensible, unsentimental, unromantic, unidealistic, plainspoken.

downtrodden *adj* oppressed, exploited, subservient, subjugated, trampled on, ground down, under the heel, burdened, overwhelmed, weighed-down, tyrannized, victimized, abused, bullied, helpless, powerless, prostrate, distressed, poor, miserable, wretched.

downward *adj* descending, declining, slipping, sliding, down, downhill, earthbound. OPPOSITE: upward.

dowry *noun* marriage portion, marriage settlement, portion, dower.

doze *verb* drowse, nap, catnap, snooze (*inf*), sleep, slumber, drift off, drop off (*inf*), nod, nod off (*inf*), go off. OPPOSITE: wake.
➤ *noun* nap, light sleep, short sleep, catnap, forty winks (*inf*), snooze (*inf*), kip (*inf*), shut-eye (*inf*), siesta.

drab *adj* dull, dingy, dreary, shabby, flat, colourless, featureless, grey, greyish, lacklustre, dark, sombre, gloomy, cheerless, depressing, lifeless, dismal, tedious, boring. OPPOSITE: bright.

draft *noun* **1** (*a rough draft*) sketch, outline, plan, rough, abstract, drawing, diagram, blueprint, delineation, skeleton. **2** (*bank draft*) bill of exchange, cheque, money order, postal order, letter of credit.
➤ *verb* draw, sketch, outline, delineate, draw up, put together, prepare, frame, design, plan, compose, formulate, write.

drag *verb* **1** (*drag the log*) draw, pull, haul, heave, lug, tug, tow, trail, yank. OPPOSITE: push. **2** (*the hours dragged by*) crawl, shuffle, shamble, creep, inch, plod, trudge, lag, linger, loiter, dawdle, limp, inch. OPPOSITE: hurry.
➤ *noun* bore, nuisance, bother, pest, trouble, annoyance, pain (*inf*), pain in the neck (*inf*), pain in the arse (*sl*), bind (*inf*), headache (*inf*).

drag out prolong, protract, spin out, draw out, lengthen, stretch out, extend.

dragoon *verb* force, compel, coerce, drive, impel, constrain, bully, harass, intimidate, browbeat, railroad (*inf*), strong-arm (*inf*). OPPOSITE: coax.

drain *verb* **1** (*drain the bottle*) empty, finish, down (*inf*), draw off, pump out, pump off, extract, remove, withdraw, evacuate, void, dry, strain, tap, bleed, milk. OPPOSITE: fill. **2** (*drain the batteries*) exhaust, sap, deplete, consume, expend, use up, dissipate, discharge, bleed, drink up, swallow, strain, tax, empty. **3** (*the last water drained from the lake*) drip, trickle, seep, leak, ooze, exude, effuse, discharge, flow out, well out.
➤ *noun* **1** (*a blocked drain*) channel, culvert, duct, conduit, pipe, gutter, ditch, culvert, dyke, sewer, outlet, trench, watercourse. **2** (*a drain on our resources*) depletion, exhaustion, drag, sap, strain, tax, reduction, consumption, expenditure, outflow.

drama *noun* **1** (*an entertaining new drama*) play, show, piece, spectacle, show, work, dramatization. **2** (*a lecturer on drama*) theatre, dramaturgy, stagecraft, acting, histrionics, dramatics, theatrics, scene. **3** (*hostage drama*) crisis, dilemma, sensation, excitement, thrill, tension, turmoil.

dramatic *adj* **1** (*a dramatic entertainment*) theatrical, stage, Thespian, histrionic, dramaturgic, dramaturgical. **2** (*a dramatic development*) exciting, electrifying, tense, sensational, significant, sudden, abrupt, startling, thrilling, breathtaking, suspenseful, unexpected, striking, distinct, marked, noticeable. **3** (*a dramatic effect*) striking, vivid, expressive, graphic, effective, impressive, spectacular, powerful, melodramatic,

stirring, affecting, emotive, emotional. OPPOSITE: unimpressive. **4** (*a dramatic gesture*) theatrical, histrionic, stagy, melodramatic, exaggerated, flamboyant, overdone, artificial.

dramatist *noun* playwright, scriptwriter, screenwriter, dramaturge, dramaturgist.

dramatize *verb* **1** (*dramatize three short stories*) adapt, stage, put on. **2** (*a tendency to dramatize*) exaggerate, playact, ham up (*inf*), act, overdo, overstate, lay it on thick (*inf*), play to the gallery.

drape *verb* **1** (*drape the furniture with sheets*) cover, envelop, swathe, wrap, blanket, overlay, cloak, veil, shroud, decorate, adorn, dress, clothe, array, deck, festoon. OPPOSITE: divest. **2** (*drape a coat around her shoulders*) hang, arrange, place, wrap. **3** (*draped his arm over her shoulder*) dangle, droop, hang, suspend, drop, let fall.

drastic *adj* extreme, far-reaching, radical, violent, forceful, powerful, strong, severe, sharp, harsh, intensive, rigorous, desperate, dire. OPPOSITE: moderate.

draught *noun* **1** (*a draught of fresh air*) breath, puff, current, movement, flow, breeze, influx. **2** (*a long draught of wine*) drink, potion, dose, drench, quantity, cup. **3** (*a draught of fifty tons*) pulling, drawing, dragging, haulage, traction.

draw *verb* **1** (*draw several sketches*) sketch, pencil, doodle, scribble, paint, delineate, design, map out, chart, outline, trace, depict, portray, represent. **2** (*draw up a chair*) pull, drag, haul, tow, tug, lug, heave, yank, trail. OPPOSITE: push. **3** (*draw the curtains*) pull together, close, shut. **4** (*draw closer*) come, advance, approach, move, proceed, progress, go, travel. OPPOSITE: repel. **5** (*draw his revolver*) extract, pull out, take out, bring out, unsheathe, produce, withdraw, remove. **6** (*draw breath*) inhale, breathe in, inspire, respire, suck in. **7** (*draw a big crowd*) attract, allure, lure, entice, invite, tempt, seduce, induce, prompt, persuade, influence, elicit, call forth, evoke, interest, engage, win, capture, captivate, fascinate. **8** (*draw this conclusion*) deduce, infer, conclude, gather, derive, glean, come to, reason. **9** (*draw lots*) pick, choose, decide on, select, opt for, go for, single out, plump for (*inf*), take. **10** (*draw the last pint from the barrel*) draw off, drain, siphon off, pump off, tap, bleed, milk. **11** (*draw a huge salary*) get, take, receive, obtain, procure, earn. **12** (*the two players are expected to draw*) tie, finish together.
➤ *noun* **1** (*proved an irresistible draw*) attraction, enticement, pull (*inf*), allure, lure, bait, interest, influence, magnetism, charisma, appeal. **2** (*could only manage a draw*) tie, stalemate, dead heat, deadlock, impasse. **3** (*won third prize in the draw*) raffle, lottery, sweepstake.

draw back recoil, start back, shrink, wince, flinch, retreat, withdraw, retract.

draw on use, put to use, utilize, rely on, exploit, apply, employ, quarry.

draw out 1 (*the lorry drew out of the lay-by*) pull out, move out, leave, depart, set out, start. **2** (*draw out the process*) protract, extend, prolong, drag out, spin out, stretch, elongate, lengthen, attenuate.

draw up 1 (*draw up the document*) draft, compose, formulate, prepare, frame, write out. **2** (*draw up at the* *station*) halt, stop, pull up, rein in. **3** (*draw up the two armies*) arrange, order, position, marshal, range, rank.

drawback noun disadvantage, snag, hitch, hindrance, impediment, obstacle, barrier, hurdle, flaw, fault, imperfection, defect, fly in the ointment (*inf*), weakness, weak spot, difficulty, trouble, problem, catch, stumbling block, nuisance, handicap, detriment, shortcoming, inconvenience, limitation, deficiency, downside, liability, deterrent, damper, discouragement. OPPOSITE: advantage.

drawing noun sketch, picture, delineation, outline, diagram, plan, illustration, cartoon, representation, depiction, portrait, portrayal, composition, study.

drawl verb drone, twang, whine, linger over, draw out. OPPOSITE: gabble.

drawn adj tired, drained, wan, washed out, fraught, fatigued, sapped, worn, haggard, gaunt, hollow-cheeked, pinched, strained, stressed, taut, tense, hassled (*inf*), harassed.

dread verb fear, quail, flinch, shy, cringe at, shrink from, cower, tremble, shudder, apprehend, anticipate, worry about.
➤ noun fear, terror, horror, fright, alarm, panic, anxiety, concern, apprehension, foreboding, perturbation, trepidation, misgiving, disquiet, qualm, worry, dismay. OPPOSITE: confidence.
➤ adj dreaded, dreadful, feared, fearful, awful, terrifying, terrible, alarming, frightening, frightful, dire, ghastly, grisly, gruesome, horrible.

dreadful adj **1** (*a dreadful disaster*) awful, terrible, fearful, frightful, horrific, horrible, dire, grim, appalling, shocking, alarming, frightening, terrifying, ghastly, hideous, horrendous, monstrous, gruesome, atrocious, distressing, harrowing, grievous, calamitous, tragic. OPPOSITE: wonderful. **2** (*that dreadful woman*) awful, appalling, nasty, disagreeable, unpleasant, horrible, hideous, repugnant, odious. **3** (*a dreadful waste*) appalling, shocking, outrageous, great, inordinate, terrific, formidable, tremendous.

dream noun **1** (*tried to describe her dream*) vision, illusion, delusion, hallucination, fantasy, trance, imagination, fancy, notion, nightmare. OPPOSITE: reality. **2** (*cherished a dream*) pipe dream, ambition, goal, target, aspiration, ideal, design, notion, plan, aim, hope, wish, desire, thirst, yearning, daydream, castle in the air. **3** (*seemed to be in a permanent dream*) reverie, trance, daze, stupor, fantasy, daydream. **4** (*a dream of a ob*) delight, gem, treasure, ideal, beauty, perfection, joy, marvel.
➤ verb **1** (*dream about being rich*) fantasize, hallucinate, imagine, envisage, visualize, fancy. **2** (*we would not dream of it*) think, consider, imagine, conceive, suppose. **3** (*she dreams all day long*) daydream, fantasize, imagine, muse, fancy, switch off (*inf*). **4** (*I dream of such a day*) long, desire, yearn, crave.
dream up invent, create, devise, conceive, envisage, concoct, cook up (*inf*), contrive, think up, imagine, conjure up, hatch, spin, fabricate.

dreamer noun visionary, idealist, utopian, daydreamer, romantic, romancer, fantasist, fantasizer, stargazer, theorizer. OPPOSITE: realist.

dreamy adj **1** (*a dreamy quality*) dreamlike, surreal, unreal, fantastic, imaginary, shadowy, unclear, indistinct, intangible, vague, dim, misty, hazy, faint, ethereal, phantasmagorical. **2** (*a dreamy personality*) impractical, unrealistic, fanciful, daydreaming, fantasizing, romantic, quixotic, idealistic, visionary, faraway, absent, absentminded, abstracted, preoccupied, abstracted, musing, pensive, thoughtful. **3** (*a dreamy atmosphere*) romantic, relaxing, soothing, lulling, calming, tranquil, peaceful, gentle, soft. **4** (*he was just dreamy*) gorgeous, marvellous, wonderful, fabulous, terrific, heavenly.

dreary adj **1** (*a dreary existence*) dull, flat, drab, colourless, featureless, lifeless, monotonous, boring, tedious, uninteresting, uneventful, unvaried, wearisome, routine, humdrum, run-of-the-mill, commonplace, solitary. OPPOSITE: exciting. **2** (*dreary surroundings*) gloomy, sombre, overcast, dark, cheerless, comfortless, bleak, dismal, uninviting, depressing, chilling. OPPOSITE: bright. **3** (*a dreary mood*) gloomy, glum, miserable, sad, doleful, forlorn, funereal, joyless, lonesome, mournful, melancholic, downcast, dejected, despondent, oppressed, depressed, wretched.

dregs pl noun **1** (*dregs left on the bottom*) sediment, residue, residuum, precipitate, lees, grounds, dross, refuse, waste, trash, deposit, detritus, debris, scum, leavings, scourings, remains, sublimate. **2** (*the dregs of humanity*) rabble, riff-raff, good-for-nothings, down-and-outs, outcasts, deadbeats, scum, refuse, vagrants, tramps, dossers (*inf*).

drench verb soak, wet, saturate, steep, douse, souse, immerse, duck, submerge, inundate, flood, swamp, drown, permeate. OPPOSITE: dry.

dress noun **1** (*spilt gravy on her dress*) frock, gown, robe, costume, garment, suit, outfit. **2** (*in the dress of a priest*) clothes, clothing, attire, garb, apparel, garments, wardrobe, costume, guise, habit, ensemble, vestments, getup (*inf*), gear (*inf*), togs (*inf*), duds (*inf*), habiliment.
➤ verb **1** (*dress in dry clothing*) clothe, put on, get into, slip into, throw on (*inf*), don, garb, rig, fit, turn out, attire, accoutre, wear, robe, drape, cover. OPPOSITE: strip. **2** (*dress her hair*) arrange, dispose, adjust, straighten, tidy, fix (*inf*), prepare, groom, comb, do, primp, preen. OPPOSITE: disarrange. **3** (*dress the wagon*) array, deck, adorn, decorate, deck, bedeck, embellish, garnish, trim, furbish. **4** (*dress the wound*) treat, tend, clean, cover, bandage, swathe, plaster, bind up, strap up, attend to. OPPOSITE: neglect. **5** (*dress meat*) prepare, get ready, clean.
dress down tell off (*inf*), bawl out (*inf*), reprimand, rebuke, reprove, scold, carpet (*inf*), haul over the coals (*inf*), tear off a strip (*inf*), chide, berate, castigate, upbraid.
dress up decorate, adorn, ornament, trim, embellish, festoon, beautify, prettify, improve, titivate, doll up (*inf*), tart up (*inf*), deck, gild, disguise.

dressing noun **1** (*dressing for the salad*) sauce, relish, condiment, garnish. **2** (*put a new dressing on the wound*) bandage, plaster, compress, poultice, ligature, covering. **3** (*put plenty of dressing round the roots*) manure, fertilizer, compost, dung, muck.

dressmaker *noun* seamstress, needlewoman, tailor, tailoress, couturier.

dribble *verb* **1** (*rain dribbled off his hat*) trickle, drip, drop, ooze, seep, leak, run, exude. **2** (*the dog dribbled*) drool, slaver, slobber, drivel.
➤ *noun* drip, trickle, droplet, leak, seepage, sprinkling.

drift *verb* **1** (*drift on the tide*) wander, meander, stray, roam, rove, digress, float, freewheel, coast, waft. **2** (*the snow began to drift*) accumulate, pile up, amass, gather, drive, bank.
➤ *noun* **1** (*the drift of the water*) flow, movement, course, direction, bearing, current, rush, sweep, impulse. **2** (*a drift in public opinion*) trend, tendency, movement, drive, deviation, digression, variation. **3** (*the drift of his message*) meaning, intention, purpose, aim, object, point, design, scope, tenor, gist, thrust, vein, implication, significance, substance, import, purport, essence, core. **4** (*a drift of snow*) bank, mound, pile, heap, mass, accumulation.

drill *verb* **1** (*drill the squad*) teach, instruct, train, coach, school, practise, rehearse, exercise, discipline, ground, inculcate. **2** (*drill two holes*) bore, pierce, perforate, puncture, punch, penetrate, prick.
➤ *noun* **1** (*attended drill*) instruction, training, coaching, tuition, grounding, preparation, exercise, practice, repetition, discipline, indoctrination. **2** (*you know the drill*) procedure, routine. **3** (*picked up the drill*) borer, awl, bit, gimlet, rotary tool.

drink *verb* **1** (*drink your tea*) imbibe, swallow, down, polish off (*inf*), quaff, sup, gulp down, swig (*inf*), knock back (*inf*), swill, sip, drain, absorb. **2** (*she's been drinking again*) booze (*inf*), hit the bottle (*inf*), tipple, tank up (*inf*), indulge, carouse, revel, tope.
➤ *noun* **1** (*I could do with a drink*) beverage, brew, potion, infusion, liquid, refreshment. **2** (*he took a last drink*) swallow, sip, swig (*inf*), gulp, slug (*inf*), snifter (*inf*), nip, spot, draught, glass, cup, mug. **3** (*drink got the better of him*) alcohol, booze (*inf*), liquor, spirits, hooch (*inf*), the bottle (*inf*), hard stuff (*inf*).

drink to toast, pledge, salute, drink the health of.

drinkable *adj* safe, clean, potable, fit to drink.

drinker *noun* drunk, drunkard, inebriate, alcoholic, alkie (*inf*), piss artist (*sl*), wino (*inf*), soak (*inf*), boozer (*inf*), tippler (*inf*), lush (*inf*), dipso (*inf*), dipsomaniac, imbiber. OPPOSITE: teetotaller.

drip *verb* drop, dribble, trickle, plop, splash, leak, exude, filter, percolate, seep, weep, ooze, sprinkle, drizzle.
➤ *noun* **1** (*drip of water*) drop, splash, plop, bead, tear, trickle, dribble. **2** (*he's such a drip*) wimp (*inf*), wally (*inf*), weakling, milksop, weed (*inf*), wet (*inf*), softy (*inf*), ninny (*inf*), namby-pamby (*inf*), mummy's boy (*inf*), bore.

drive *verb* **1** (*I will drive the car*) steer, direct, guide, control, handle, operate, pilot, propel. **2** (*let me drive you there*) take, run, transport, convey, carry, move, send. **3** (*drive the nail home*) strike, hammer, bang, ram, hit, knock, thump, dash, stab, dig, sink, thrust, plunge. **4** (*drive her to do something*) force, push, constrain, coerce, persuade, incite, oblige, press, compel, impel, pressure, pressurize, motivate, goad, spur, prod, prick, provoke, lead, prompt. OPPOSITE: deter. **5** (*drive the ball over the stands*) hit, send, hurl, direct. **6** (*drive the sheep to the shed*) herd, round up, shepherd, move, urge, impel, propel, guide, push. **7** (*drives his staff too hard*) burden, overburden, tax, overtax, overwork.
➤ *noun* **1** (*go out for a drive*) ride, jaunt, outing, excursion, joyride, journey, tour, trip, run, spin (*inf*). **2** (*he has lots of drive*) energy, vigour, verve, effort, enterprise, initiative, push, ambition, motivation, determination, will, resolve, spirit, tenacity, pep, get-up-and-go (*inf*), pizzazz (*inf*), zip (*inf*), vim (*inf*). OPPOSITE: apathy. **3** (*the drive to survive*) instinct, impulse, urge, pressure, need, desire. **4** (*the drive for change*) campaign, crusade, fight, battle, struggle, effort, push (*inf*), appeal, action. **5** (*walked up the drive*) driveway, avenue, road, roadway. **6** (*the drive from the engines*) thrust, surge, pressure, power, propulsion.

drive at imply, allude to, get at (*inf*), mean, suggest, hint at, intimate, have in mind, intend, insinuate, indicate, aim at, signify, refer to.

drivel *noun* **1** (*spouting drivel*) nonsense, gibberish, crap (*sl*), balls (*sl*), bullshit (*sl*), shit (*sl*), cobblers (*inf*), bunkum (*inf*), balderdash, rubbish, garbage, tosh (*inf*), tripe (*inf*), rot (*inf*), bilge (*inf*), claptrap (*inf*), waffle (*inf*), twaddle (*inf*), gobbledygook (*inf*), mumbo-jumbo (*inf*), eyewash (*inf*), hogwash (*inf*), poppycock (*inf*), bosh (*inf*). OPPOSITE: sense. **2** (*left drivel on his sleeve*) slaver, slobber, dribble, saliva.
➤ *verb* **1** (*drivel all over him*) dribble, slaver, slobber, drool. **2** (*drivel on and on*) prate, babble, jabber, chatter, ramble, maunder, blather, blether, gibber, gas (*inf*), witter (*inf*), gabble (*inf*), waffle (*inf*).

driver *noun* motorist, rider, motorcyclist, chauffeur, cabbie, trucker.

drizzle *noun* mist, spray, shower, mizzle, light rain.
➤ *verb* spit, spot, rain, sprinkle, shower, spray, mizzle.

droll *adj* **1** (*a droll play*) comic, comical, amusing, funny, humorous, entertaining, diverting, witty, whimsical, waggish, clownish, ridiculous, ludicrous, laughable, risible, facetious, farcical, jocular, zany. OPPOSITE: serious. **2** (*a droll character*) whimsical, quaint, eccentric, odd, oddball (*inf*), outlandish, bizarre, peculiar, strange, queer.

drone[1] *verb* **1** (*the bees droning*) hum, buzz, whirr, purr, drawl, murmur, thrum, chant, vibrate. **2** (*he droned on and on*) intone, spout (*inf*), drivel (*inf*), prattle.
➤ *noun* hum, buzz, buzzing, whirr, whirring, purring, drawling, murmuring, chant, vibration.

drone[2] *noun* (*a drone in society*) parasite, leech, sponger (*inf*), hanger-on, shirker, skiver (*inf*), idler, loafer, layabout, lazybones (*inf*), scrounger (*inf*), slacker, sluggard, lounger, couch potato (*inf*), dreamer. OPPOSITE: worker.

drool *verb* **1** (*drooling at the mouth*) dribble, slaver, slobber, drivel, salivate. **2** (*he drooled at the prospect*) dote, gush, slobber, gloat, enthuse.

droop *verb* **1** (*the flower drooped*) sag, sink, drop, bow, bend, hang down, dangle, wilt, stoop, fall, slump. **2** (*his spirits drooped*) wilt, fade, wither, shrivel, languish, weaken, faint, flag, falter, decline, diminish, slump, slouch, drop, fall down, lose heart, give way, deteriorate. OPPOSITE: flourish.

drop *verb* **1** (*the stone will drop*) fall, sink, droop, decline, descend, dive, plummet, plunge, tumble. OPPOSITE: rise. **2** (*water dropped down her neck*) drip, trickle, dribble, leak, plop, fall. **3** (*drop the gun*) lower, let fall, let go. **4** (*they dropped to their knees*) sink, fall, drop, slump, collapse, faint, swoon. **5** (*interest in the project is dropping*) lower, decrease, diminish, depreciate, dwindle, lessen, subside, decline, fall, sink, plummet, plunge, slacken off, weaken. **6** (*drop his acquaintance*) abandon, desert, forsake, discard, reject, jilt, relinquish, repudiate, renounce, chuck (*inf*), ditch (*inf*), give up, disown, run out on (*inf*), throw over (*inf*). OPPOSITE: continue. **7** (*drop what you are doing*) stop, end, cease, finish, terminate, give up, leave out, miss out, omit, exclude, dispense with, discontinue, forbear, forgo, abandon, quit (*inf*), kick (*inf*), relinquish, repudiate, renounce, throw up (*inf*). **8** (*drop hundreds of employees*) discharge, dismiss, let go, sack (*inf*), fire (*inf*), axe (*inf*), boot out (*inf*), turf out (*inf*).
➤ *noun* **1** (*a drop of blood*) bead, pearl, globule, drip, droplet, bubble, blob, driblet, tear, spheroid, oval. **2** (*give them a drop each*) sip, tot, draught, nip, shot (*inf*), dribble, splash, dash (*inf*), mouthful, spot (*inf*), sprinkle, trickle, taste, bit, little, pinch, dab, smidgen (*inf*), trace, tad (*inf*), speck, particle, modicum. **3** (*the car went over a steep drop*) fall, descent, incline, precipice, cliff, slope, chasm, abyss, plunge, declivity. **4** (*a drop in business*) decline, slump, plunge, fall-off, falling-off, decrease, downturn, lowering, reduction, cutback, diminution, depreciation, deterioration, devaluation. OPPOSITE: rise.
drop off 1 (*business is expected to drop off*) decline, drop, fall, fall off, decrease, lessen, diminish, dwindle, slacken off, plummet, plunge. **2** (*she usually drops off after tea*) fall asleep, doze, doze off, catnap, nod off (*inf*), drift off, go off, snooze (*inf*), drowse. **3** (*I shall drop off the package*) deposit, set down, unload, let off, put off, hand in, deliver, leave.
drop out give up, withdraw, back out (*inf*), cop out (*inf*), cry off (*inf*), leave, abandon, pull out, quit (*inf*), forsake, renounce, opt out, renege on.

dross *noun* scum, debris, waste, dregs, lees, slag, remains, refuse, rubbish, trash.

drought *noun* **1** (*the long summer drought*) dry spell, dryness, aridity, parchedness, dehydration, desiccation. OPPOSITE: deluge. **2** (*experiencing a drought in supplies*) shortage, deficiency, insufficiency, dearth, scarcity, lack, need, want. OPPOSITE: glut.

drove *noun* **1** (*a drove of sheep*) herd, flock, pack. **2** (*droves of football fans*) gathering, swarm, crowd, mob, herd, horde, press, crush, host, multitude, rabble, throng, assembly, company, collection.

drown *verb* **1** (*the village was drowned by the sea*) submerge, immerse, engulf, inundate, flood, deluge, swamp, drench, sink, go under. **2** (*the announcement was drowned out*) drown out, overwhelm, overpower, overcome, engulf, swallow up, swamp, muffle, stifle, deaden. **3** (*drown her disappointment in drink*) suppress, stifle, quench, deaden, silence, extinguish, obliterate, quash, wipe out.

drowsy *adj* **1** (*felt drowsy after his exertions*) sleepy, tired, weary, dreamy, dozy, dozing, nodding, somnolent, half-asleep, yawning, comatose, lethargic, sluggish, torpid, heavy, heavy-eyed, dull, dazed, dopey (*inf*), groggy (*inf*), drugged. OPPOSITE: alert. **2** (*a drowsy afternoon*) sleepy, soporific, somniferous, hypnotic, dreamy, soothing, lulling, restful.

drubbing *noun* defeat, clobbering (*inf*), beating, flogging, licking (*inf*), battering, bludgeoning, pasting (*inf*), pounding, pummelling, thrashing (*inf*), trouncing, walloping, whipping, working-over, hammering.

drudge *verb* toil, slave, labour, plod, grind (*inf*), slog away (*inf*), plug away (*inf*), work. OPPOSITE: idle.
➤ *noun* menial, worker, toiler, plodder, labourer, servant, slave, galley slave, general factotum, hack, lackey, skivvy (*inf*), char, charwoman, dogsbody (*inf*). OPPOSITE: idler.

drudgery *noun* toil, hard work, labour, donkeywork (*inf*), chore, skivvying, slog (*inf*), fag (*inf*), grind (*inf*), sweat (*inf*), slavery.

drug *noun* **1** (*pharmaceutical drug*) medicine, medication, medicament, remedy, potion, cure, physic, panacea. **2** (*illegal drug*) narcotic, opiate, barbiturate, amphetamine, sedative, stimulant, downer (*inf*), upper (*inf*), dope (*inf*).
➤ *verb* medicate, dose, treat, sedate, tranquillize, dope (*inf*), knock out (*inf*), narcotize, anaesthetize, stupefy, deaden, numb, befuddle, dull.

drugged *adj* high (*inf*), stoned (*inf*), bombed (*inf*), doped up (*inf*), spaced out (*inf*), smashed (*inf*), wasted (*inf*), stupefied, comatose, insensible.

drum *noun* tambour, tabor, kettledrum, bass drum, snare drum, tympanum, tom-tom.
➤ *verb* beat, tap, rap, knock, strike, thrum, throb, pulsate, reverberate, hammer, tattoo.
drum into instil, drive home, reiterate, harp on, din into, hammer, inculcate, reiterate.
drum out cashier, discharge, expel, dismiss, throw out (*inf*), drive out, oust, outlaw.
drum up obtain, get, collect, gather, round up, attract, canvass, solicit, petition, summon.

drunk *adj* drunken, pissed (*sl*), stoned (*inf*), wasted (*inf*), sloshed (*inf*), loaded (*inf*), smashed (*inf*), wrecked (*inf*), boozy (*inf*), inebriated, intoxicated, paralytic (*inf*), tipsy (*inf*), tiddly (*inf*), merry (*inf*), happy (*inf*), tight (*inf*), legless (*inf*), plastered (*inf*), stewed (*inf*), canned (*inf*), pickled (*inf*), sozzled (*inf*), tanked up (*inf*), lit up (*inf*), squiffy (*inf*), well-oiled (*inf*), blotto (*inf*), pie-eyed, woozy (*inf*), out of it (*inf*), soused (*inf*), bevvied (*inf*), blitzed (*inf*), bombed (*inf*), tired and emotional (*inf*), under the influence, under the table (*inf*), bibulous, crapulent. OPPOSITE: sober.
➤ *noun* drunkard, alcoholic, alkie (*inf*), boozer (*inf*), soak (*inf*), tippler (*inf*), drinker, inebriate, dipsomaniac, dipso (*inf*), wino (*inf*), piss artist (*sl*), lush (*inf*), sot (*inf*), toper (*inf*). OPPOSITE: teetotaller.

drunken *adj* **1** (*drunken soldiers*) drunk, pissed (*sl*), stoned (*inf*), wasted (*inf*), sloshed (*inf*), loaded (*inf*), smashed (*inf*), wrecked (*inf*), boozy (*inf*), inebriated, intoxicated, paralytic (*inf*), tipsy (*inf*), tiddly (*inf*), merry (*inf*), happy (*inf*), tight (*inf*), legless (*inf*), plastered (*inf*), stewed (*inf*), canned (*inf*), pickled (*inf*), sozzled (*inf*), tanked up (*inf*), lit up (*inf*), squiffy (*inf*), well-oiled (*inf*), blotto (*inf*), pie-eyed, woozy (*inf*), out of it (*inf*), soused (*inf*), bevvied (*inf*), blitzed (*inf*), bombed (*inf*), tired and emotional (*inf*), under the influence, under the table (*inf*), bibulous, crapulent. **2** (*drunken carrying-on*) debauched, dissipated, riotous, carousing, intemperate, revelling, roistering, wassailing, orgiastic, bacchanalian, bacchic, saturnalian, Dionysian.

drunkenness *noun* inebriation, inebriety, intoxication, tipsiness, insobriety, intemperance, overindulgence, alcoholism, dipsomania, debauchery, bibulousness, crapulence. OPPOSITE: temperance.

dry *adj* **1** (*a dry region*) dried up, arid, desiccated, parched, scorched, moistureless, waterless, unwatered, rainless, barren, thirsty, dehydrated, torrid, sterile. OPPOSITE: wet. **2** (*dry twigs*) dried, shrivelled, withered, wilted, desiccated, dehydrated. **3** (*dry bread*) dried out, hard, stale. **4** (*a dry account*) dull, flat, boring, tedious, humdrum, tiresome, wearisome, monotonous, uninteresting, unimaginative, prosaic, commonplace, run-of-the-mill, plain, dreary, vapid, insipid. OPPOSITE: interesting. **5** (*dry sense of humour*) witty, droll, waggish, sharp, keen, cutting, sly, ironic, laconic, cynical, sarcastic, satirical, deadpan, subtle, low-key. **6** (*a dry personality*) cool, cold, aloof, unemotional, indifferent, impersonal, remote.
≫ *verb* **1** (*dried by the sun*) parch, scorch, sear, desiccate, dehydrate, drain. **2** (*the seaweed dried quickly*) dry out, dry up, shrivel, harden, wither, wilt, dehydrate, desiccate, wizen, mummify. OPPOSITE: soak. **3** (*dry the fish*) dehydrate, desiccate, preserve, cure. **4** (*dry the rugs*) sponge, towel, wipe, blot, mop. OPPOSITE: wet.
dry up 1 (*the supply soon dried up*) run out, fail, stop, end, disappear, fade, die out. **2** (*he dried up when he realized nobody was listening*) fall silent, shut up, stop, forget one's lines, forget one's words.

dual *adj* double, twofold, duplicate, duplex, binary, twin, two-piece, matched, paired, coupled, combined. OPPOSITE: single.

dub *verb* name, christen, entitle, label, designate, denominate, nominate, nickname, style, call, tag, term.

dubiety *noun* doubt, doubtfulness, dubiosity, indecision, uncertainty, unsureness, misgiving, scepticism, suspicion, mistrust, qualm, hesitation, hesitancy, incertitude.

dubious *adj* **1** (*dubious about the right choice*) doubtful, uncertain, unsure, hesitant, irresolute, wavering, vacillating, undecided, unsettled, sceptical, suspicious. OPPOSITE: certain. **2** (*of dubious attribution*) doubtful, undecided, unsure, unsettled, undetermined, indeterminate, indefinite, unclear, imprecise, unresolved, open, equivocal, obscure, ambiguous, debatable, questionable, hazy, puzzling, enigmatic, cryptic, vague. **3** (*a dubious type*) questionable, debatable, suspect, suspicious, unreliable, undependable, untrustworthy, shady (*inf*), dodgy (*inf*), fishy (*inf*), iffy (*inf*), shifty (*inf*). OPPOSITE: trustworthy.

duck *verb* **1** (*duck under the wire*) bob, crouch, stoop, bow, bend, drop, squat, hunch down. OPPOSITE: straighten. **2** (*duck under the water*) dip, dunk, immerse, plunge, dive, submerge, douse, souse, wet, lower. **3** (*duck his duty*) dodge, avoid, evade, escape, shirk, shun, parry, elude, sidestep, wriggle out of. OPPOSITE: face.

duct *noun* conduit, pipe, tube, canal, channel, culvert, passage, funnel, vessel.

ductile *adj* **1** (*ductile material*) malleable, plastic, flexible, pliable, pliant, tensile, extensible. **2** (*a ductile character*) compliant, biddable, malleable, yielding, gullible, tractable, manageable, manipulable, docile, amenable, accommodating, cooperative, passive. OPPOSITE: obdurate.

dud *noun* failure, flop (*inf*), washout (*inf*), loser.
≫ *adj* broken, defective, inoperative, ineffectual, bust (*inf*), duff (*inf*), kaput (*inf*), failed, worthless, valueless.

due *adj* **1** (*pay the amount due*) owing, owed, payable, unpaid, outstanding, in arrears. OPPOSITE: paid. **2** (*his due reward*) rightful, right, fit, fitting, correct, right and proper, proper, apposite, appropriate, apt, suitable, becoming, justified, merited, deserved, requisite, obligatory, bounden. OPPOSITE: undue. **3** (*dished up a due amount of pudding*) adequate, sufficient, enough, ample, plenty, satisfactory, requisite. OPPOSITE: insufficient. **4** (*due next week*) scheduled, expected, anticipated, awaited, required.
≫ *adv* exactly, directly, precisely, dead (*inf*), straight, undeviatingly.
≫ *noun* right, birthright, prerogative, privilege, deserts, just deserts, merit, come-uppance (*inf*).
due to caused by, owing to, because of, as a result of, attributable to, ascribable to, ascribed to, assignable to.

duel *noun* **1** (*killed in a duel*) single combat, affair of honour. **2** (*a duel between the two sides*) contest, competition, rivalry, fight, clash, struggle, engagement, encounter.

dues *pl noun* fee, membership, charge, contribution, subscription, levy.

duffer *noun* bungler, blunderer, idiot, fool, wally (*inf*), nerd (*inf*), jerk (*inf*), clot (*inf*), clod (*inf*), booby (*inf*), bonehead (*inf*), dimwit (*inf*), dolt (*inf*), lummox (*inf*), dunce, ignoramus, oaf, numskull.

dulcet *adj* sweet, pleasant, pleasing, agreeable, delightful, charming, melodious, harmonious, musical, lyrical, sweet-sounding, euphonious, gentle, honeyed, mellow, mellifluous, mellifluent, soothing, soft, silver-toned. OPPOSITE: raucous.

dull *adj* **1** (*a dull day*) gloomy, sombre, dark, drab, colourless, murky, grey, overcast, cloudy, indistinct, opaque, faded, dim, dismal, dreary, leaden, cheerless, lacklustre, lustreless, matt. OPPOSITE: bright. **2** (*a dull ache*) blunt, dulled, muted, subdued, indistinct, muffled, mild, faint, feeble, weak. OPPOSITE: sharp. **3** (*a dull child*) dull-witted, obtuse, stolid, stupid, thick (*inf*), slow, slow-witted, dozy (*inf*), dense, dumb, dim, dim-witted (*inf*), witless, unintelligent, vacuous. OPPOSITE: clever. **4** (*a dull book*) boring, uninteresting, unexciting, unimaginative, uneventful, lifeless, dry, dreary, dismal, monotonous, vapid, plain, flat, heavy, ponderous, humdrum, tedious, tiresome, wearisome, pedestrian, prosaic, banal, bland, insipid, mind-numbing, stultifying, stereotyped. OPPOSITE: interesting. **5** (*dull towards the sufferings of others*) insensitive, numb, callous, dead, unfeeling, uncaring, apathetic, indifferent, unsympathetic, unemotional, passionless, unresponsive, blank, insensible. **6** (*dull after months of inactivity*) apathetic, idle, languid, listless, sluggish, lethargic, stagnant, torpid, vegetative, slow, heavy, inactive, inert, sleepy, drowsy. OPPOSITE: lively. **7** (*a dull blade*) dulled, blunt, blunted, edgeless, unsharpened. OPPOSITE: sharp. **8** (*a dull day on the markets*) quiet, slow, slack, sluggish, stagnant, depressed.

➤ *verb* **1** (*tried to dull the blow*) blunt, alleviate, assuage, relieve, mitigate, allay, lessen, reduce, decrease, diminish, soften, moderate, mute, tone down, ease. OPPOSITE: aggravate. **2** (*sleep had dulled his senses*) numb, benumb, deaden, paralyse, stupefy, sedate, tranquillize, drug. **3** (*dulled by the news*) depress, deject, dispirit, dishearten, discourage, cast down, sadden, dampen, subdue. OPPOSITE: cheer. **4** (*dulled by time and neglect*) dim, fade, bleach, wash out, cloud, obscure, tarnish, stain, sully, darken. OPPOSITE: brighten.

duly *adv* rightly, rightfully, correctly, properly, suitably, fittingly, befittingly, fitly, appropriately, deservedly, decorously, accordingly. OPPOSITE: unduly.

dumb *adj* **1** (*I was struck dumb*) silent, mute, mum (*inf*), speechless, voiceless, wordless, soundless, inarticulate, tongue-tied, taciturn, uncommunicative. OPPOSITE: articulate. **2** (*just a dumb kid*) stupid, foolish, unintelligent, dull, dull-witted, dim, dim-witted, dozy (*inf*), slow, slow-witted, thick (*inf*), dense, brainless (*inf*), doltish, gormless (*inf*), ignorant, obtuse. OPPOSITE: intelligent.

dumbfound *verb* astonish, astound, amaze, stun, shock, stagger, take aback, bowl over (*inf*), knock for six (*inf*), knock sideways, throw (*inf*), shake, floor (*inf*), overwhelm, surprise, startle, overcome, paralyse, flabbergast (*inf*), gobsmack (*inf*), confound, disconcert, nonplus, confuse, baffle, bewilder, perplex.

dummy *noun* **1** (*shop dummy*) figure, model, mannequin. **2** (*a dummy for practice*) sham, counterfeit, substitute, imitation, copy, duplicate, reproduction, sample, representation. **3** (*he's a real dummy*) dolt, blockhead (*inf*), fool, idiot, imbecile, wally (*inf*), jerk (*inf*), berk (*inf*), dipstick (*inf*), nerd (*inf*), plonker (*inf*), prick (*sl*), dimwit (*inf*), nitwit (*inf*), dope (*inf*), numskull (*inf*), oaf, charlie (*inf*), simpleton, dunce, ass, donkey, dullard, chump (*inf*), clot (*inf*), nincompoop, ninny.

➤ *adj* **1** (*dummy wall*) artificial, fake, imitation, false, bogus, phoney (*inf*), mock, sham. **2** (*dummy run*) simulated, mock, practice, trial.

dump *verb* **1** (*dump the bag on the floor*) drop, deposit, put, put down, place, lay down, throw down, fling down. **2** (*dumped the contents all over the desk*) discharge, unload, empty out, tip out, pour out, park, plonk (*inf*), bung (*inf*). **3** (*dump that old chair*) scrap, jettison, get rid of, discard, dispose of, ditch, tip, offload, throw away, throw out, chuck away (*inf*). OPPOSITE: keep. **4** (*she dumped him*) drop, chuck (*inf*), ditch (*inf*), leave, walk out on, desert, abandon, forsake.

➤ *noun* **1** (*took the rubbish to the tip*) tip, rubbish heap, junkyard, scrapyard. **2** (*she lives in a right dump*) hovel, pigsty (*inf*), slum, hole (*inf*), joint (*inf*), mess, shanty. **in the dumps** low, depressed, unhappy, blue (*inf*), gloomy, despondent, sad, melancholy, miserable, downhearted, disconsolate, dejected, downcast, dispirited.

dun *adj* brownish, greyish-brown, dull, dingy, khaki, mud-coloured, muddy, mouse-coloured, umber.

dunce *noun* ignoramus, dullard, simpleton, dummy, idiot, fool, imbecile, moron, wally (*inf*), jerk (*inf*), nerd (*inf*), dipstick (*inf*), blockhead (*inf*), thickhead, ass, dolt, halfwit, dimwit (*inf*), nincompoop (*inf*), ninny (*inf*), nitwit (*inf*), numskull (*inf*), twit (*inf*), twerp (*inf*), bonehead (*inf*). OPPOSITE: genius.

dung *noun* muck, excrement, faeces, droppings, ordure, manure, fertilizer, waste.

dungeon *noun* cell, cage, oubliette, prison, gaol, jail, lockup, vault, keep.

dupe *verb* cheat, deceive, hoax, hoodwink, trick, fool, swindle, take in, defraud, cozen, beguile, kid (*inf*), delude, outwit, overreach, humbug, bamboozle (*inf*), con (*inf*), rip off (*inf*).

➤ *noun* victim, fool, simpleton, sucker (*inf*), mug (*inf*), fall guy (*inf*), sap (*inf*), stooge (*inf*), pushover (*inf*), pawn, puppet, instrument, tool, gull.

duplicate *verb* **1** (*duplicated his signature*) copy, replicate, clone, reproduce, double, repeat, echo. **2** (*duplicate each document*) copy, photocopy, reproduce, fax, facsimile.

➤ *adj* identical, twin, matching, matched, paired, corresponding, double, duplex, twofold.

➤ *noun* **1** (*a duplicate of the real thing*) copy, replica, transcript, reproduction, imitation, clone, ringer (*inf*), dead ringer (*inf*), match, mate, twin, fellow, counterpart, double, lookalike, spitting image (*inf*). OPPOSITE: original. **2** (*a sheaf of duplicates*) copy, fax, facsimile, carbon copy, photocopy, reproduction.

duplicity *noun* deceit, deceitfulness, deception, double-dealing, treachery, betrayal, guile, falsehood, trickery, fraud, artifice, chicanery, hypocrisy, dissimulation, dishonesty, mendacity, perfidy. OPPOSITE: honesty.

durable *adj* **1** (*a durable friendship*) lasting, enduring, abiding, constant, continuing, persistent, persisting, unfading, long-lasting, permanent, firm, fixed, stable, fast, unchanging, changeless, invariable, dependable, resistant. **2** (*durable material*) long-lasting, hard-wearing, heavy-duty, strong, stout, robust, sturdy, substantial, reinforced, sound, resistant, imperishable, tough. OPPOSITE: perishable.

duration *noun* continuance, term, spell, period, time, span, stretch, length, extent, course, fullness.

duress *noun* **1** (*came under duress*) constraint, coercion, arm-twisting (*inf*), compulsion, pressure, pressurization, force, enforcement, exaction. **2** (*placed in duress*) imprisonment, detention, confinement, incarceration, captivity, custody, restraint, constraint, bondage. OPPOSITE: freedom.

during *conj* throughout, in, within, through.

dusk *noun* twilight, nightfall, sunset, evening, eventide, sundown, gloaming, gloom, murk, shade, shadows, darkness, dark, obscurity. OPPOSITE: dawn.

dusky *adj* **1** (*dusky evening*) shadowy, shady, dim, dark, darkish, gloomy, overcast, murky, obscure, cloudy, foggy, misty, hazy, twilit, crepuscular, tenebrous. OPPOSITE: light. **2** (*dusky skin*) swarthy, dark, dark-skinned, dark-coloured, dark-complexioned, black, brown, olive-skinned, tawny, sable. OPPOSITE: pale.

dust *noun* **1** (*dust filled the air*) powder, grit, grime, dirt, soot, smut, particles. **2** (*dead bodies returning to the dust of the ground*) earth, soil, ground, clay.
➤ *verb* **1** (*dust the furniture*) clean, wipe, flick clean, sweep, brush, mop, polish, burnish. **2** (*dust the cake*) sprinkle, powder, dredge, sift, scatter, strew, spray, spread, cover.

dusty *adj* **1** (*a dusty book*) dust-covered, dust-filled, undusted, unswept, dirty, grubby, grimy, filthy, unclean, sooty. **2** (*a dusty texture*) powdery, chalky, granular, crumbly, sandy, friable.

dutiful *adj* obedient, respectful, deferential, reverent, reverential, filial, conscientious, thoughtful, considerate, punctilious, faithful, devoted, submissive, docile, compliant, pliant, obliging. OPPOSITE: disobedient.

duty *noun* **1** (*busy fulfilling his many duties*) task, job, chore, assignment, mission, commission, office, obligation, responsibility, function, onus, burden, trust, charge, role, part, business, work, requirement, calling, service. **2** (*duty owed to one's employers*) respect, deference, reverence, obedience, allegiance, loyalty, faithfulness, fidelity. **3** (*duty is payable on that*) tax, excise, customs, toll, dues, fees, tariff, levy.
off duty on holiday, off, off work, at leisure, free, resting, inactive.
on duty working, at work, on call, engaged, busy, active, occupied, tied up (*inf*).

dwarf *noun* **1** (*circus dwarf*) midget, pygmy, manikin, homunculus, person of restricted growth. OPPOSITE: giant. **2** (*a wicked dwarf*) gnome, goblin.
➤ *adj* miniature, mini (*inf*), tiny, small, diminutive, pocket, petite, bantam, baby, pygmy, undersized, stunted, Lilliputian. OPPOSITE: giant.
➤ *verb* **1** (*the mountain dwarfs the foothills*) dominate, overshadow, bestride, tower over, rise above, diminish, minimize. **2** (*a plant dwarfed by lack of nutrients*) stunt, retard, check, arrest, atrophy.

dwell *verb* live, reside, inhabit, lodge, abide, rest, hang on (*inf*), sojourn, tarry, stay, remain, settle, stop, populate, people. OPPOSITE: move.
dwell on brood on, mull over, harp on, think about, meditate on, turn over, reflect on, ruminate on, linger over, elaborate, expound on, expatiate on.

dwelling *noun* dwelling-house, abode, residence, house, home, pad (*inf*), lodgings, lodge, quarters, domicile, habitation, establishment.

dwindle *verb* diminish, decrease, lessen, shrink, contract, fall, abate, wane, ebb, subside, decline, fade, peter out, taper off, tail off, weaken, shrivel, wither, waste away, vanish, disappear, die out. OPPOSITE: increase.

dye *noun* colour, colourant, colouring agent, pigment, tint, stain, wash, tinge, hue, shade.
➤ *verb* stain, tint, colour, shade, pigment, tincture, tinge, imbue.

dyed-in-the-wool *adj* entrenched, established, deep-rooted, inveterate, long-standing, settled, fixed, die-hard, hard-core, hardened, inflexible, unchangeable, uncompromising, unshakeable, through and through, thorough, complete, absolute, utter, confirmed, card-carrying.

dying *adj* **1** (*the dying queen*) at death's door, in extremis, expiring, perishing, passing away, sinking, moribund. **2** (*a dying practice*) moribund, passing, failing, ebbing, waning, fading, vanishing, disappearing. **3** (*his dying wish*) last, final.

dynamic *adj* forceful, powerful, energetic, vigorous, strong, active, lively, alive, spirited, potent, vital, driving, high-powered, go-ahead (*inf*), magnetic (*inf*), electric, aggressive, go-getting (*inf*), effective, effectual. OPPOSITE: lethargic.

dynasty *noun* house, line, succession, empire, ascendancy, dominion, reign, rule, jurisdiction, authority, sway, regime, administration, government, sovereignty.

each *pronoun* each one, every one, one and all.
➤ *adj* every, every single, each and every, individual, separate.
➤ *adv* apiece, per person, per capita, respectively, individually, separately, singly.

eager *adj* **1** (*eager students*) enthusiastic, keen, avid, ardent, fervent, intent, earnest, zealous, diligent, wholehearted, passionate, vehement. OPPOSITE: indifferent. **2** (*eager to leave*) impatient, anxious, agog, keen, wishing, desirous, longing, yearning, itching, hungry, thirsty. OPPOSITE: reluctant.

eagerness *noun* **1** (*the eagerness of the students*) enthusiasm, keenness, avidity, ardour, fervour, intentness, earnestness, zeal, diligence, passion, vehemence. OPPOSITE: indifference. **2** (*in her eagerness to leave*) impatience, anxiety, keenness, wish, desire, longing, yearning, itch, hunger, thirst. OPPOSITE: reluctance.

ear *noun* **1** (*have the ear of the president*) attention, notice, heed, regard, consideration. **2** (*have an ear for music*) sensitivity, discrimination, perception, appreciation, taste, flair, talent, gift, skill.

early *adj* **1** (*in the early stages*) initial, first, primary, opening, introductory. OPPOSITE: late. **2** (*his early death from cancer*) premature, untimely, forward, advanced, precocious. OPPOSITE: belated. **3** (*early civilizations*) primitive, primordial, primeval, ancient, prehistoric, autochthonous. OPPOSITE: modern.
➤ *adv* in advance, beforehand, too soon, prematurely, in good time, ahead of schedule, with time to spare. OPPOSITE: late.

earmark *verb* set aside, put aside, keep back, reserve, designate, label, tag, allocate, ring-fence.

earn *verb* **1** (*earn £500 a week*) make, get, receive, be paid, draw, collect, gross, net, clear, pocket, take home, yield, bring in, pull in. OPPOSITE: pay. **2** (*earn a reputation*) get, gain, obtain, procure, acquire, achieve,

attain, win, deserve, merit, warrant, rate, be entitled to, have a right to. OPPOSITE: forfeit.

earnest[1] *adj* **1** (*an earnest young woman*) serious, solemn, grave, intense, determined, resolute, passionate, wholehearted, fervent, ardent, eager, avid, keen, dedicated, committed, diligent, assiduous, zealous. OPPOSITE: apathetic. **2** (*his earnest hope*) sincere, deep, profound, heartfelt, wholehearted, passionate, warm, fervent, ardent, intent, fixed, set, determined, resolute, solemn. OPPOSITE: flippant.
in earnest 1 (*are you in earnest about this?*) sincere, genuine, serious, not joking. **2** (*we began digging in earnest*) earnestly, seriously, determinedly, resolutely, passionately, fervently, ardently, eagerly, avidly, diligently, assiduously, zealously. OPPOSITE: half-heartedly.

earnest[2] *noun* (*an earnest of my commitment*) pledge, promise, assurance, security, deposit, token, guarantee.

earnings *pl noun* pay, wages, salary, remuneration, emolument, stipend, honorarium, fee, income, profit, revenue, return, yield, receipts, proceeds. OPPOSITE: expenditure.

earth *noun* **1** (*orbiting the earth*) world, globe, planet, sphere, orb. **2** (*fell to earth*) land, ground. **3** (*a heap of earth*) soil, dirt, clay, loam, turf, sod.

earthenware *noun* pottery, ceramics, crockery, stoneware.

earthly *adj* **1** (*earthly existence*) terrestrial, tellurian, telluric, worldly, mundane, temporal, secular, profane, material, physical, fleshly, carnal, sensual, corporeal, mortal, human. OPPOSITE: spiritual. **2** (*no earthly reason*) possible, likely, feasible, conceivable, imaginable.

earthquake *noun* seism, quake (*inf*), tremor, aftershock.

earthy *adj* coarse, crude, lusty, robust, uninhibited, ribald, bawdy, raunchy (*inf*), blue (*inf*), vulgar, rude, rough, unsophisticated, unrefined, down-to-earth, plain, simple, natural. OPPOSITE: refined.

ease verb **1** (*ease the pain*) alleviate, allay, assuage, soothe, mitigate, palliate, relieve, comfort, appease, mollify, lessen, reduce, diminish, moderate, lighten, ameliorate. OPPOSITE: aggravate. **2** (*the storm is easing*) abate, moderate, subside, let up, ease off, calm, still, quieten, reduce, diminish, decrease, die down. OPPOSITE: intensify. **3** (*ease our progress*) facilitate, help, assist, aid, simplify, smooth, expedite, speed up, advance, further, forward. OPPOSITE: hinder. **4** (*eased it into place*) slide, slip, guide, steer, manoeuvre, inch, edge.
➤ noun **1** (*they won with ease*) facility, effortlessness, readiness, dexterity, deftness, adroitness, proficiency, mastery. OPPOSITE: difficulty. **2** (*for ease of use*) easiness, simplicity, straightforwardness, convenience, user-friendliness. OPPOSITE: awkwardness. **3** (*ease of mind*) peace, calmness, tranquillity, serenity, composure, quiet, repose, comfort, relief, security. OPPOSITE: disquiet. **4** (*a life of ease*) comfort, contentment, complacency, relaxation, rest, repose, leisure, freedom, liberty, wealth, affluence, prosperity, luxury, opulence, bed of roses (*inf*), life of Riley (*inf*). OPPOSITE: hardship.
at ease relaxed, comfortable, at home, secure, calm, composed. OPPOSITE: uneasy.

easily adv **1** (*they won easily*) with ease, without difficulty, effortlessly, comfortably, simply, readily, fluently, smoothly. **2** (*easily the best*) by far, far and away, indisputably, undeniably, undoubtedly, without a doubt, definitely, certainly, clearly, plainly, obviously. OPPOSITE: possibly.

easy adj **1** (*an easy job*) simple, effortless, straightforward, uncomplicated, child's play (*inf*), easy-peasy (*inf*), a piece of cake (*inf*), a doddle (*inf*), a cinch (*inf*), like falling off a log (*inf*), facile, light, undemanding, smooth, trouble-free, painless, foolproof, idiot-proof, user-friendly. OPPOSITE: difficult. **2** (*with an easy mind*) peaceful, calm, tranquil, serene, untroubled, unworried, quiet, relaxed, comfortable, secure. OPPOSITE: uneasy. **3** (*an easy victim*) gullible, trusting, susceptible, compliant, biddable, amenable, obliging, accommodating, flexible, yielding, submissive, docile, tractable. **4** (*too easy with the children*) tolerant, lenient, indulgent, permissive, mild, gentle. OPPOSITE: strict. **5** (*an easy manner*) natural, unaffected, unforced, casual, informal, unceremonious, relaxed, easygoing (*inf*), laid back (*inf*), carefree, nonchalant, insouciant, suave, urbane. OPPOSITE: formal. **6** (*at an easy pace*) leisurely, unhurried, moderate, gentle, undemanding, comfortable, relaxed, even, steady, regular. OPPOSITE: strenuous. **7** (*an easy life*) comfortable, contented, happy, relaxed, restful, leisured, wealthy, affluent, prosperous, luxurious, opulent. OPPOSITE: hardship.

easygoing adj calm, placid, serene, even-tempered, tolerant, understanding, flexible, amenable, casual, informal, easy, relaxed, laid back (*inf*), nonchalant, insouciant, carefree, happy-go-lucky. OPPOSITE: strict.

eat verb **1** (*eat a meal*) consume, devour, scoff (*inf*), tuck into (*inf*), guzzle (*inf*), put away (*inf*), bolt, wolf down (*inf*), eat up, polish off (*inf*), chew, munch, masticate, gnaw, nibble, take, swallow, ingest. **2** (*eat at a restaurant*) feed, dine, lunch, breakfast, feast, banquet, snack (*inf*), graze (*inf*).
eat away erode, corrode, wear away, gnaw away, rot, decay, dissolve, undermine, destroy.
eat into consume, use, deplete, spend, waste, use up, exhaust, drain.

eatable adj edible, comestible, esculent, digestible, wholesome, good, palatable. OPPOSITE: uneatable.

eavesdrop verb listen in, overhear, pry, snoop (*inf*), spy, monitor, tap (*inf*), bug (*inf*).

ebb verb **1** (*the tide is ebbing*) go out, flow back, recede, retrocede, regress, retreat, fall back, retire, withdraw. OPPOSITE: flow. **2** (*their enthusiasm ebbed*) subside, abate, sink, fall, decline, weaken, flag, fade, wane, lessen, decrease, diminish, dwindle, peter out, die away. OPPOSITE: grow.
➤ noun **1** (*the ebb of the tide*) reflux, recession, retrocession, regression, retreat. OPPOSITE: flow. **2** (*their enthusiasm is on the ebb*) decline, fall, drop, wane, abatement, decrease, diminution, dwindling, weakening, degeneration, deterioration. OPPOSITE: increase.

ebony adj black, jet black, sable, pitch black, inky, coal black, sooty.

ebullience noun exuberance, enthusiasm, excitement, animation, vivacity, chirpiness (*inf*), effusiveness, effervescence, sparkle, exhilaration, buoyancy, elation, euphoria, high spirits. OPPOSITE: lethargy.

ebullient adj exuberant, enthusiastic, excited, animated, vivacious, bubbly, chirpy (*inf*), irrepressible, effusive, gushing, effervescent, sparkling, exhilarated, buoyant, elated, euphoric. OPPOSITE: lethargic.

ebullition noun boiling, seething, bubbling, effervescence.

eccentric adj irregular, abnormal, anomalous, aberrant, strange, odd, queer, funny (*inf*), peculiar, singular, bizarre, weird, freakish, quirky, whimsical, capricious, unconventional, idiosyncratic, way-out (*inf*), offbeat (*inf*), wacky (*inf*), cranky (*inf*), dotty (*inf*), screwy (*inf*). OPPOSITE: normal.
➤ noun character, case (*inf*), oddity, original, nonconformist, weirdo (*inf*), oddball (*inf*), queer fish (*inf*), freak (*inf*), crank (*inf*), nutter (*inf*), crackpot (*inf*), loony (*sl*).

eccentricity noun irregularity, abnormality, strangeness, oddity, peculiarity, singularity, bizarreness, weirdness, unconventionality, idiosyncrasy, quirk, whim, caprice. OPPOSITE: normality.

ecclesiastic noun cleric, clergyman, clergywoman, churchman, churchwoman, man of the cloth, woman of the cloth, divine, reverend, priest, minister, preacher. OPPOSITE: lay-person.
➤ adj ecclesiastical, clerical, sacerdotal, church, churchly, religious, holy, spiritual, divine, priestly, ministerial, pastoral. OPPOSITE: secular.

echelon noun grade, rank, level, tier, step, rung, degree, status.

echo verb **1** (*echoing around the cave*) resound, reverberate, ring, repeat, reflect. **2** (*echoing her predecessor*) copy, imitate, ape, parrot, mimic, repeat, reiterate, reproduce, mirror, reflect, parallel, resemble.

≫ *noun* **1** (*hear an echo*) resonance, reverberation, repetition, reiteration, reflection. **2** (*an echo of her predecessor*) copy, imitation, reproduction, replica, clone, duplicate, parallel, counterpart, reflection, image, semblance, likeness. **3** (*echoes of the past*) reminder, memory, remembrance, reminiscence, evocation, allusion, suggestion, hint, trace, repercussion.

éclat *noun* **1** (*performed with éclat*) splendour, brilliance, lustre, pomp, pageantry, show, display, ostentation, effect. **2** (*greeted with éclat*) acclaim, acclamation, applause, glory, fame, renown, celebrity. OPPOSITE: obloquy.

eclectic *adj* diverse, varied, heterogeneous, multifarious, multifaceted, many-sided, complex, comprehensive, all-embracing, catholic, liberal, broad, wide-ranging, general. OPPOSITE: narrow.

eclipse *verb* **1** (*eclipse the sun*) obscure, block, hide, conceal, blot out, cover, veil, shroud, mask, shade, shadow, darken, dim, extinguish. **2** (*eclipsing his rivals*) surpass, transcend, excel, outdo, outstrip, run rings round (*inf*), dwarf, overshadow, outshine, put in the shade.
≫ *noun* **1** (*an eclipse of the sun*) obscuration, occultation, adumbration, hiding, concealment, obliteration, masking, shading, darkening, extinction. **2** (*the eclipse of his rivals*) surpassing, transcending, overshadowing, outshining. **3** (*the eclipse of the steelmaking industry*) decline, fall, failure, loss, deterioration, degeneration, wane, ebb.

economic *adj* **1** (*the current economic climate*) monetary, financial, fiscal, pecuniary, budgetary, commercial, business, industrial, trade, mercantile. **2** (*not an economic proposition*) profitable, viable, cost-effective, productive, remunerative, money-making, profit-making. OPPOSITE: uneconomic.

economical *adj* **1** (*economical with money*) thrifty, saving, provident, prudent, careful, sparing, frugal, scrimping, mean, niggardly, parsimonious. OPPOSITE: extravagant. **2** (*economical on fuel*) efficient, money-saving. OPPOSITE: wasteful. **3** (*an economical meal*) cheap, inexpensive, low-priced, low-cost, reasonable, budget. OPPOSITE: expensive.

economize *verb* save, conserve, husband, budget, cut back, retrench, tighten one's belt (*inf*), draw in one's horns (*inf*), scrimp, scrimp and save, cut corners (*inf*). OPPOSITE: squander.

economy *noun* **1** (*the nation's economy*) financial state, financial system, wealth, resources. **2** (*the need for economy*) thrift, thriftiness, saving, conservation, husbandry, providence, prudence, care, restraint, frugality, parsimony, cut, cutback, retrenchment. OPPOSITE: extravagance.

ecstasy *noun* rapture, bliss, joy, delight, elation, euphoria, seventh heaven (*inf*), cloud nine (*inf*), exhilaration, thrill, exultation, jubilation. OPPOSITE: misery.

ecstatic *adj* overjoyed, enraptured, blissful, joyful, delighted, tickled pink (*inf*), elated, euphoric, in seventh heaven (*inf*), on cloud nine (*inf*), exhilarated, thrilled, over the moon (*inf*), exultant, jubilant, rapturous, fervent, enthusiastic, delirious with happiness. OPPOSITE: indifferent.

ecumenical *adj* universal, worldwide, general, catholic, eclectic. OPPOSITE: sectarian.

eddy *noun* whirlpool, vortex, maelstrom, swirl, twist.
≫ *verb* whirl, swirl, twist, turn.

edge *noun* **1** (*the edge of the table*) border, rim, lip, margin, periphery, fringe, verge, brink, threshold, side, outline, contour, boundary, perimeter, limit, extremity. OPPOSITE: centre. **2** (*have the edge over the opposition*) advantage, superiority, dominance, ascendancy, upper hand (*inf*), whip hand (*inf*), lead, head start. OPPOSITE: disadvantage. **3** (*take the edge off the pain*) sharpness, acuteness, keenness, intensity, severity, virulence, force, zest, bite, sting, trenchancy, mordancy, pungency, acerbity, acrimony. OPPOSITE: dullness.
≫ *verb* **1** (*edged with braid*) trim, bind, border, fringe. **2** (*edging towards the door*) creep, inch, steal, sidle, slink, worm. OPPOSITE: dash. **3** (*edge the blade*) sharpen, whet, hone, strop. OPPOSITE: blunt.

on edge nervous, anxious, nervy (*inf*), twitchy (*inf*), tense, keyed up, uptight (*inf*), on tenterhooks, eager, impatient, edgy, touchy, irritable, uneasy, ill at ease, apprehensive. OPPOSITE: calm.

edging *noun* border, fringe, frill, trimming.

edgy *adj* nervous, anxious, nervy (*inf*), twitchy (*inf*), tense, on edge, sensitive, touchy, testy, irritable, irascible, uneasy, ill at ease, apprehensive. OPPOSITE: placid.

edible *adj* eatable, comestible, esculent, digestible, wholesome, good, palatable. OPPOSITE: inedible.

edict *noun* decree, ordinance, mandate, ruling, proclamation, declaration, pronouncement, fiat, command, order, injunction, dictate, statute, law, rule, regulation.

edification *noun* improvement, uplifting, elevation, enlightenment, information, instruction, education, schooling, teaching, instruction, tuition, coaching, guidance. OPPOSITE: corruption.

edifice *noun* building, erection, structure, construction, pile.

edify *verb* improve, uplift, elevate, enlighten, inform, educate, school, teach, instruct, tutor, coach, guide. OPPOSITE: corrupt.

edit *verb* correct, emend, revise, rewrite, modify, adapt, annotate, polish, redact, check, censor, expurgate, compile, prepare, compose, assemble.

edit out delete, blue-pencil, cut, remove, exclude, omit.

edition *noun* copy, issue, number, volume, impression, version, printing, publication.

editor *noun* reviser, redactor, compiler, writer, journalist.

educate *verb* school, instruct, teach, train, coach, tutor, exercise, drill, prime, inculcate, indoctrinate, edify, inform, enlighten, civilize, cultivate, develop, nurture, foster, rear, discipline.

educated *adj* scholarly, learned, erudite, intellectual, highbrow, brainy (*inf*), literate, lettered, well-read, knowledgeable, versed, schooled, cultivated, cultured, refined, enlightened, informed. OPPOSITE: ignorant.

education noun **1** (*the education of our children*) schooling, instruction, teaching, training, coaching, tuition, inculcation, indoctrination, edification, enlightenment, civilization, cultivation, intellectual development. **2** (*the value of education*) learning, knowledge, scholarship, erudition, literacy, letters, culture, refinement. OPPOSITE: ignorance.

educational adj **1** (*an educational film*) educative, informative, instructive, edifying, didactic, heuristic. **2** (*educational establishments*) academic, scholastic, learning, teaching, pedagogic, pedagogical.

educator noun educationalist, teacher, schoolmaster, schoolmistress, instructor, coach, tutor, pedagogue, academic, professor, lecturer.

educe verb elicit, evoke, bring out, draw forth.

eerie adj weird, uncanny, strange, mysterious, frightening, scary (*inf*), chilling, bloodcurdling, unnatural, unearthly, ghostly, creepy (*inf*), spooky (*inf*).

efface verb erase, rub out, obliterate, wipe out, eradicate, extirpate, cancel, expunge, remove, excise, delete, cross out, blot out, annihilate, destroy. OPPOSITE: imprint.
efface oneself withdraw, keep out of the limelight, be retiring, be modest.

effect noun **1** (*the effect of these reforms*) result, consequence, outcome, upshot, issue, fruit, event, conclusion, aftermath, repercussion. OPPOSITE: cause. **2** (*to little effect*) power, force, effectiveness, efficacy, efficiency, success, impact, impression, influence, strength, weight, cogency, validity. **3** (*with immediate effect*) action, operation, implementation, enforcement, execution, performance. **4** (*words to that effect*) meaning, significance, sense, import, drift, tenor.
▸ verb cause, bring about, initiate, create, produce, make, procure, actuate, effectuate, achieve, accomplish, fulfil, carry out, perform, execute, implement. OPPOSITE: prevent.
in effect in fact, actually, in reality, really, effectively, for all practical purposes, essentially, virtually, to all intents and purposes.
take effect act, work, function, be effective, come into effect, come into force, come into operation, begin, start.

effective adj **1** (*an effective method*) successful, productive, effectual, efficacious, efficient, competent, adequate, capable, able, useful. OPPOSITE: ineffective. **2** (*effective from next month*) active, operative, functioning, current, valid, in force, in effect, actual, effectual. OPPOSITE: inoperative. **3** (*an effective advertisement*) striking, impressive, powerful, potent, forceful, influential, telling, cogent, convincing, persuasive, moving. OPPOSITE: unimpressive. **4** (*the effective leader of the party*) actual, real, practical, essential, virtual.

effectiveness noun **1** (*the effectiveness of the method*) success, productivity, effectuality, efficacy, efficiency, competence, adequacy, use, usefulness. OPPOSITE: inefficacy. **2** (*the effectiveness of the advertisement*) power, potency, force, strength, weight, influence, cogency, conviction, persuasion. OPPOSITE: weakness.

effects pl noun goods, chattels, movables, property, belongings, possessions, baggage, trappings, accoutrements, paraphernalia, things (*inf*), stuff (*inf*), bits and pieces (*inf*).

effectual adj **1** (*an effectual action*) successful, productive, effective, efficacious, efficient, competent, capable, powerful, potent, forceful, influential, useful, functional. OPPOSITE: ineffectual. **2** (*an effectual document*) legal, lawful, licit, binding, in force, valid. OPPOSITE: invalid.

effectuate verb effect, actuate, cause, bring about, initiate, create, produce, make, procure, achieve, accomplish, fulfil, carry out, perform, execute, implement. OPPOSITE: thwart.

effeminate adj unmanly, womanish, womanly, feminine, effete, camp, soft, sissy (*inf*). OPPOSITE: virile.

effervesce verb bubble, fizz, sparkle, foam, froth, ferment, boil.

effervescence noun **1** (*the effervescence of the wine*) sparkle, fizz, bubbles, foam, froth, carbonation, fizziness, bubbliness, foaminess, frothiness, fermentation. OPPOSITE: flatness. **2** (*the effervescence of the partygoers*) ebullience, sparkle, exuberance, enthusiasm, excitement, animation, liveliness, vivacity, chirpiness (*inf*), exhilaration, buoyancy, elation, euphoria, merriment, high spirits. OPPOSITE: listlessness.

effervescent adj **1** (*effervescent drinks*) sparkling, carbonated, fizzy, fizzing, bubbly, bubbling, foaming, foamy, frothy, fermenting. OPPOSITE: flat. **2** (*effervescent children*) ebullient, sparkling, exuberant, enthusiastic, excited, animated, lively, vivacious, bubbly, chirpy (*inf*), irrepressible, exhilarated, buoyant, elated, euphoric. OPPOSITE: listless.

effete adj **1** (*an effete civilization*) weak, feeble, decrepit, drained, spent, exhausted, worn out, burnt out, barren, sterile, weakened, enfeebled, enervated, decadent, degenerate, dissipated. OPPOSITE: vigorous. **2** (*an effete young man*) effeminate, unmanly, womanish, feminine, camp, sissy (*inf*). OPPOSITE: virile.

efficacious adj effective, effectual, powerful, potent, active, vigorous, successful, productive, efficient, competent, capable, able, adequate, functional, useful. OPPOSITE: useless.

efficacy noun effectiveness, effectuality, effect, power, potency, force, success, productivity, efficiency, competence, ability, adequacy, usefulness. OPPOSITE: inefficacy.

efficiency noun **1** (*admired her efficiency*) competence, proficiency, skill, expertise, ability, capability, effectiveness, effectuality, productivity, organization. OPPOSITE: incompetence. **2** (*the efficiency of the method*) success, productivity, effectiveness, effectuality, efficacy, power. OPPOSITE: inefficiency.

efficient adj **1** (*an efficient secretary*) competent, proficient, skilled, skilful, expert, adept, able, capable, effective, effectual, powerful, productive, organized, businesslike. OPPOSITE: incompetent. **2** (*an efficient system*) effective, effectual, efficacious, successful, productive, economical, labour-saving, streamlined, rationalized, well-run, well-organized. OPPOSITE: inefficient.

effigy *noun* image, likeness, representation, icon, idol, figure, statue, model, dummy, guy.

efflorescence *noun* flowering, blooming, blossoming.

effluent *noun* outflow, efflux, effluence, discharge, waste, sewage, pollutant, pollution, emission, emanation, exhalation, effluvium. OPPOSITE: influx.

effluvium *noun* exhalation, emanation, emission, fumes, gas, vapour, miasma, odour, smell, stench, reek, stink, pong (*inf*).

effort *noun* **1** (*put a lot of effort into it*) exertion, energy, power, force, elbow grease (*inf*), struggle, striving, strain, application, pains, work, labour, toil. OPPOSITE: idleness. **2** (*made an effort to be polite*) attempt, try, endeavour, bid, go (*inf*), stab (*inf*), crack (*inf*), bash (*inf*), shot (*inf*). **3** (*praise for his latest effort*) achievement, accomplishment, exploit, feat, creation, production, work, opus.

effortless *adj* easy, simple, facile, straightforward, uncomplicated, smooth, trouble-free, painless, light, undemanding, unexacting. OPPOSITE: difficult.

effrontery *noun* audacity, temerity, boldness, nerve, gall, brass (*inf*), face (*inf*), impudence, impertinence, insolence, cheek, cheekiness, sauce, sauciness, forwardness, shamelessness, brazenness, presumption, assurance, arrogance. OPPOSITE: timidity.

effulgence *noun* brilliance, radiance, brightness, shine, dazzle, blaze, splendour, resplendence, lustre, sheen, sparkle, glow, incandescence. OPPOSITE: dullness.

effulgent *adj* brilliant, radiant, bright, shining, dazzling, blazing, fiery, splendid, resplendent, refulgent, lustrous, sparkling, luminous, glowing, incandescent, fluorescent. OPPOSITE: dull.

effuse *verb* gush, pour out, spill, emanate, issue, diffuse.

effusion *noun* outflow, outpouring, outburst, gush, stream, efflux, effluence, emission, discharge, voidance.

effusive *adj* gushing, unreserved, unrestrained, lavish, profuse, extravagant, fulsome, over the top (*inf*), demonstrative, exuberant, ebullient, enthusiastic, lyrical, rhapsodic, expansive, voluble, talkative. OPPOSITE: reserved.

egg *verb* **egg on** urge, encourage, drive, press, push, spur, goad, prod, incite, provoke, stimulate, prompt. OPPOSITE: deter.

egghead *noun* intellectual, highbrow, academic, scholar, boffin, brain, genius, know-all (*inf*). OPPOSITE: dunce.

ego *noun* self, oneself, identity, self-image, self-esteem, amour propre, self-confidence, self-importance.

egoism *noun* selfishness, self-interest, self-centredness, egocentricity, self-absorption, egomania, self-seeking, looking after number one (*inf*), egotism, self-regard, self-esteem, self-importance, conceit, vanity, narcissism, self-love. OPPOSITE: altruism.

egoist *noun* egomaniac, self-seeker, egotist. OPPOSITE: altruist.

egoistic *adj* selfish, self-interested, self-centred, egocentric, self-absorbed, self-seeking, egotistic, self-important, conceited, vain, narcissistic. OPPOSITE: altruistic.

egotism *noun* conceit, vanity, pride, arrogance, self-praise, boastfulness, braggadocio, blowing one's own trumpet (*inf*), narcissism, self-love, self-admiration, self-regard, self-esteem, self-importance, egoism, self-centredness, egocentricity, egomania. OPPOSITE: modesty.

egotist *noun* boaster, bragger, braggart, bighead (*inf*), egoist, egomaniac.

egotistic *adj* conceited, vain, proud, arrogant, boastful, bigheaded (*inf*), swollen-headed (*inf*), narcissistic, self-loving, self-admiring, self-important, egoistic, self-centred, egocentric. OPPOSITE: modest.

egregious *adj* flagrant, blatant, glaring, striking, gross, rank, arrant, scandalous, shocking, appalling, outrageous, notorious, infamous, heinous, monstrous, intolerable, insufferable.

egress *noun* exit, way out, outlet, vent, emergence, issue, departure, exodus, withdrawal, escape. OPPOSITE: entrance.

ejaculate *verb* **1** ('*I protest!*' *he ejaculated*) exclaim, cry, call, shout, yell, blurt out, utter, say. **2** (*ejaculate fluid*) discharge, emit, release, eject, expel, spurt, spout.

ejaculation *noun* **1** (*ejaculations of protest*) exclamation, cry, call, shout, yell, utterance. **2** (*the ejaculation of fluid*) discharge, emission, release, ejection, expulsion, spurt. **3** (*premature ejaculation*) discharge of semen, emission of semen, climax, orgasm, coming (*inf*).

eject *verb* **1** (*eject venom*) emit, discharge, secrete, exude, ejaculate, throw out, cast out, expel, spout, spew, disgorge, vomit, excrete. **2** (*ejected from the club*) remove, evict, dispossess, turn out, turf out (*inf*), show the door (*inf*), expel, throw out, chuck out (*inf*), kick out (*inf*), boot out (*inf*), dismiss, discharge, cashier, sack, fire (*inf*), banish, exile, deport, oust, get rid of, drive out. OPPOSITE: retain. **3** (*ejected from the aircraft*) propel, thrust out, throw out, expel.

ejection *noun* **1** (*the ejection of venom*) emission, discharge, secretion, exudation, ejaculation, spouting, spewing, vomiting, excretion. **2** (*her ejection from the club*) removal, eviction, dispossession, expulsion, throwing out, dismissal, discharge, sacking, firing (*inf*), banishment, exile, deportation, ouster. OPPOSITE: retention.

eke *verb* **eke out 1** (*trying to eke out his pension*) economize on, be frugal with, go easy on (*inf*), save, husband, stretch out, extend, supplement, add to, augment, increase. **2** (*eke out a living*) scrimp, scrape, scratch.

elaborate *adj* **1** (*an elaborate design*) ornate, fancy, fussy, showy, ostentatious, extravagant, baroque, rococo, complex, complicated, intricate, detailed. OPPOSITE: plain. **2** (*elaborate preparations*) thorough, painstaking, exact, precise, minute, detailed, studied, laboured, intricate, complicated, complex. OPPOSITE: simple.
➤ *verb* devise, work out, develop, amplify, expand, expatiate, flesh out, improve, refine, polish, enhance, embellish, embroider, decorate, ornament. OPPOSITE: précis.

élan *noun* flair, style, panache, flourish, dash, verve, pizzazz (*inf*), spirit, vivacity, vitality, vigour, zest, oomph (*inf*). OPPOSITE: apathy.

elapse *verb* pass, pass by, go by, go on, slip by, slip away, roll on, lapse, intervene, transpire.

elastic *adj* **1** (*an elastic material*) stretchy, stretchable, extensible, ductile, flexible, pliable, pliant, supple, yielding, resilient, springy, bouncy, rubbery, plastic. OPPOSITE: rigid. **2** (*the schedule is fairly elastic*) adaptable, adjustable, flexible, accommodating, yielding, fluid, variable. OPPOSITE: inflexible.

elasticity *noun* **1** (*the elasticity of the material*) stretch, give (*inf*), stretchiness, ductility, flexibility, pliability, pliancy, suppleness, resilience, springiness, bounce, rubberiness, plasticity. OPPOSITE: rigidity. **2** (*the elasticity of the schedule*) adaptability, adjustability, flexibility, fluidity, variability. OPPOSITE: inflexibility.

elated *adj* exhilarated, euphoric, ecstatic, blissful, rapturous, overjoyed, delighted, over the moon (*inf*), in seventh heaven (*inf*), on cloud nine (*inf*), joyful, gleeful, happy, glad, jubilant, exultant, animated, excited, ebullient. OPPOSITE: dejected.

elation *noun* exhilaration, euphoria, ecstasy, bliss, rapture, joy, delight, glee, happiness, jubilation, exultation, animation, excitement, ebullience, high spirits. OPPOSITE: dejection.

elbow *noun* angle, corner, bend, crook, joint, flexure. ⟫ *verb* jostle, push, shove, nudge, bump, knock, shoulder, hustle, bulldoze, barge (*inf*).

elbow-room *noun* space, room, scope, leeway, latitude, freedom.

elder *adj* older, senior, firstborn, earlier, former, superior. OPPOSITE: younger.
⟫ *noun* senior, superior, patriarch, chief.

elderly *adj* old, ageing, aged, advanced in years, senescent, hoary, past one's prime, past it (*inf*), over the hill (*inf*), long in the tooth (*inf*). OPPOSITE: young.
⟫ *pl noun* old people, senior citizens, retired people, pensioners, old-age pensioners, OAPs, wrinklies (*inf*).

elect *verb* choose, select, pick, appoint, designate, vote for, decide on, opt for, plump for (*inf*). OPPOSITE: reject.
⟫ *adj* élite, choice, select, hand-picked, appointed, designated, chosen, selected. OPPOSITE: rejected.

election *noun* **1** (*hold an election*) vote, voting, ballot, poll, referendum. **2** (*the election of a new captain*) appointment, choosing, selection, choice, preference. OPPOSITE: rejection.

elector *noun* voter, constituent, chooser, selector.

electric *adj* **1** (*electric appliances*) electrical, powered, mains-operated, battery-operated, rechargeable, cordless. **2** (*the atmosphere was electric*) electrifying, exciting, thrilling, stirring, rousing, stimulating, dynamic, galvanizing, charged, tense.

electrify *verb* excite, thrill, stir, rouse, charge, fire, stimulate, animate, invigorate, galvanize, jolt, shock, startle, amaze, astound. OPPOSITE: bore.

elegance *noun* style, stylishness, smartness, neatness, grace, dignity, refinement, polish, cultivation, culture, taste, tastefulness, beauty, charm, loveliness, grandeur, luxury, splendour, opulence, gentility, sophistication, politeness, propriety. OPPOSITE: coarseness.

elegant *adj* stylish, fashionable, modish, chic, smart, neat, graceful, dignified, refined, polished, cultivated, tasteful, aesthetic, classic, fine, beautiful, lovely, exquisite, choice, luxurious, sumptuous, opulent, genteel, sophisticated, polite, courtly, suave, debonair. OPPOSITE: coarse.

elegiac *adj* plaintive, mournful, lamenting, sorrowful, sad, melancholy, funereal, valedictory, dirgelike, threnodic. OPPOSITE: merry.

elegy *noun* lament, dirge, threnody, coronach, requiem.

element *noun* **1** (*other elements of the design*) component, constituent, member, unit, module, part, section, piece, segment, strand, ingredient, factor, feature, detail, particular. OPPOSITE: whole. **2** (*an element of doubt*) trace, grain, hint, suggestion, suspicion, soupçon. **3** (*out of its natural element*) medium, habitat, domain, realm, sphere, field, milieu, environment, surroundings.

elemental *adj* elementary, basic, fundamental, essential, radical, rudimentary, simple, natural, primitive, primary.

elementary *adj* basic, fundamental, essential, rudimentary, introductory, preparatory, preliminary, primary, simple, uncomplicated, straightforward. OPPOSITE: advanced.

elements *pl noun* **1** (*exposed to the elements*) weather, climate, atmospheric conditions, wind, rain. **2** (*the elements of algebra*) basics, fundamentals, essentials, rudiments, principles.

elephantine *adj* huge, immense, enormous, massive, giant, gigantic, colossal, mammoth, gargantuan, ponderous, heavy, hulking, lumbering, clumsy. OPPOSITE: tiny.

elevate *verb* **1** (*elevate the injured leg*) lift, raise, hoist, erect. OPPOSITE: lower. **2** (*elevated to the peerage*) exalt, ennoble, dignify, aggrandize, advance, promote, prefer, upgrade, kick upstairs (*inf*). OPPOSITE: downgrade. **3** (*elevated their spirits*) elate, exhilarate, gladden, brighten, cheer, hearten, perk up, buoy up, boost, uplift, rouse, animate. OPPOSITE: depress.

elevated *adj* **1** (*in an elevated position*) high, lofty, raised, hoisted, upraised, uplifted, exalted, noble, dignified, grand, great, sublime. OPPOSITE: low. **2** (*feeling elevated by the news*) elated, exhilarated, bright, cheerful, happy, glad, excited, animated, in high spirits. OPPOSITE: depressed. **3** (*in elevated style*) high-flown, lofty, exalted, pompous, bombastic. **4** (*elevated cholesterol levels*) raised, increased, high, heightened, intensified.

elevation *noun* **1** (*at an elevation of 200 metres*) height, altitude. OPPOSITE: depth. **2** (*built on an elevation*) hill, hillock, mound, eminence, rise, acclivity. OPPOSITE: dip. **3** (*elevation of the injured leg*) lifting, raising, hoisting, erection. OPPOSITE: lowering. **4** (*elevation to the peerage*) ennoblement, aggrandizement, promotion, advancement, preferment, upgrading, step up the ladder (*inf*). OPPOSITE: downgrading. **5** (*elevation of style*) exaltation, loftiness, nobility, dignity, grandeur, greatness, sublimity.

elf *noun* pixie, imp, sprite, puck, brownie, leprechaun, fairy, gnome, dwarf, goblin.

elfin *adj* **1** (*her elfin face*) small, little, tiny, petite, dainty, delicate, elflike, elfish, elvish. **2** (*elfin tricks*) impish, puckish, elfish, elvish, mischievous, arch, playful, frolicsome, sprightly.

elicit *verb* evoke, educe, call forth, bring forth, bring out, draw out, extract, extort, exact, derive, cause, give rise to.

eligible *adj* qualified, fit, appropriate, suitable, acceptable, worthy, desirable. OPPOSITE: ineligible.

eliminate *verb* **1** (*eliminate any possibility of error*) remove, get rid of, dispose of, discard, reject, dismiss, expel, oust, eject, throw out, exclude, omit, leave out, drop, do away with, eradicate, exterminate, annihilate, stamp out. OPPOSITE: include. **2** (*eliminated in the second round*) defeat, beat, knock out (*inf*), conquer, overwhelm, thrash (*inf*), hammer (*inf*). **3** (*eliminated by the gang*) kill, do in (*inf*), bump off (*inf*), rub out (*inf*), exterminate, liquidate (*inf*).

elimination *noun* **1** (*the elimination of heart disease*) removal, disposal, rejection, dismissal, expulsion, ejection, exclusion, omission, eradication, extermination, annihilation. OPPOSITE: inclusion. **2** (*the elimination of enemies*) killing, murder, extermination, liquidation (*inf*).

élite *noun* best, flower, pick, cream, crème de la crème, elect, meritocracy, aristocracy, nobility, gentry, upper class, high society, haut monde, jet set (*inf*). OPPOSITE: rabble.
≫ *adj* select, exclusive, choice, first-class, best, top, aristocratic, noble, upper-class. OPPOSITE: inferior.

elixir *noun* cure, remedy, cure-all, panacea, universal remedy, nostrum, solution, tincture, potion, mixture, extract, essence, concentrate, syrup.

elliptical *adj* **1** (*an elliptical orbit*) oval, ovate, ovoid, egg-shaped. **2** (*an elliptical remark*) ambiguous, cryptic, obscure, abstruse, recondite, incomprehensible, unfathomable. OPPOSITE: clear. **3** (*an elliptical style*) compact, concise, terse, laconic, succinct.

elocution *noun* delivery, diction, articulation, enunciation, pronunciation, eloquence, speech, oratory, rhetoric, declamation, public speaking.

elongate *verb* lengthen, extend, stretch, prolong, draw out, protract. OPPOSITE: shorten.

elope *verb* run away, run off, abscond, decamp, flee, bolt, escape, do a bunk (*inf*), slip off, slip away, sneak off, steal away, disappear, leave.

eloquence *noun* **1** (*the eloquence of the speaker*) oratory, rhetoric, delivery, diction, elocution, fluency, articulacy, cogency, forcefulness, expressiveness, way with words, command of language, gift of the gab (*inf*). OPPOSITE: inarticulateness. **2** (*the eloquence of the glance*) meaningfulness, significance, suggestiveness, expressiveness

eloquent *adj* **1** (*an eloquent speaker*) fluent, articulate, well-spoken, persuasive, glib, silver-tongued, smooth-tongued, cogent, forceful, impressive, effective, stirring, moving. OPPOSITE: inarticulate. **2** (*an eloquent glance*) meaningful, significant, pregnant, suggestive, expressive, telling, revealing.

else *adv* other, different, besides, more, in addition.

elsewhere *adv* somewhere else, not here, not there, absent, away.

elucidate *verb* explain, expound, explicate, clarify, clear up, illuminate, throw light on, shed light on, simplify, spell out, illustrate, exemplify, interpret, annotate, comment on, gloss. OPPOSITE: mystify.

elucidation *noun* explanation, exposition, explication, clarification, illumination, illustration, exemplification, interpretation, annotation, commentary, gloss, footnote. OPPOSITE: mystification.

elude *verb* **1** (*eluded her pursuers*) evade, avoid, escape, get away from, lose, shake off, give the slip, throw off the scent, dodge, duck, shun, shirk, circumvent, sidestep. OPPOSITE: face. **2** (*the solution eluded him*) confound, frustrate, thwart, foil, baffle, puzzle, stump.

elusive *adj* **1** (*their elusive prey*) hard to find, hard to catch, slippery, tricky, deceptive, shifty, evasive. **2** (*an elusive aroma*) intangible, fugitive, fleeting, transient, transitory, subtle, indefinable, indescribable. **3** (*an elusive concept*) difficult, baffling, puzzling, ambiguous, equivocal, fallacious, deceptive, misleading.

elysian *adj* blissful, happy, heavenly, paradisiacal, celestial, blessed, delightful, enchanting, charming, glorious. OPPOSITE: abominable.

emaciated *adj* lean, thin, gaunt, haggard, drawn, pinched, attenuated, scrawny, skinny, thin as a rake (*inf*), all skin and bone (*inf*), anorexic, skeletal, cadaverous, wizened, withered, wasted, atrophied. OPPOSITE: obese.

emaciation *noun* leanness, thinness, gauntness, haggardness, attenuation, scrawniness, wasting, atrophy, marasmus. OPPOSITE: obesity.

emanate *verb* **1** (*fear emanating from ignorance*) proceed, originate, derive, stem, arise, issue, spring, flow, emerge. OPPOSITE: culminate. **2** (*emanating dangerous radiation*) emit, send forth, send out, give off, discharge, radiate, exhale. OPPOSITE: absorb.

emanation *noun* **1** (*the emanation of rumours*) proceeding, origination, derivation, arising, springing, emergence. **2** (*emanations from the factory*) emission, discharge, effluent, effluence, efflux, effusion, radiation, exhalation.

emancipate *verb* liberate, free, release, deliver, discharge, loose, unshackle, unfetter, unchain, unyoke, manumit, disenthral, enfranchise, affranchise. OPPOSITE: enslave.

emancipation *noun* liberation, release, deliverance, discharge, release, manumission, freedom, liberty, enfranchisement, affranchisement, right to vote. OPPOSITE: enslavement.

emasculate *verb* **1** (*emasculating domestic animals*) castrate, geld, neuter, spay, unman. **2** (*emasculated the committee's recommendations*) weaken, debilitate, enfeeble, enervate, soften, dilute, water down, pull the teeth of (*inf*). OPPOSITE: strengthen.

emasculation *noun* **1** (*the emasculation of animals*) castration, gelding, neutering, spaying **2** (*the emasculation of their recommendations*) weakening, debilitation, enervation, dilution. OPPOSITE: strengthening.

embalm *verb* **1** (*embalm a dead body*) mummify, preserve, lay out. **2** (*embalm the memory*) cherish, treasure, enshrine, consecrate, immortalize, store, keep, conserve. **3** (*embalm the air*) perfume, scent, make fragrant.

embargo *noun* ban, prohibition, proscription, interdiction, bar, barrier, stoppage, check, restraint, restriction, obstruction, impediment, hindrance. OPPOSITE: licence.
≫ *verb* ban, prohibit, proscribe, interdict, bar, debar, stop, check, restrain, restrict, block, obstruct, impede, hinder. OPPOSITE: permit.

embark *verb* board, get on, go aboard. OPPOSITE: disembark.

embark on begin, start, commence, set about, undertake, take up, turn one's hand to, enter on, engage in, launch into, broach, initiate, institute. OPPOSITE: complete.

embarrass *verb* discomfit, disconcert, abash, shame, show up, humiliate, mortify, chagrin, distress, upset, fluster, confuse, confound, perplex, nonplus.

embarrassed *adj* awkward, uncomfortable, self-conscious, sensitive, discomfited, disconcerted, abashed, ashamed, sheepish, guilty, humiliated, mortified, chagrined, distressed, upset, flustered, confused, confounded, perplexed, nonplussed. OPPOSITE: unembarrassed.

embarrassing *adj* awkward, uncomfortable, tricky, sensitive, disconcerting, humiliating, mortifying, compromising, distressing, upsetting, confusing, perplexing.

embarrassment *noun* **1** (*blushing with embarrassment*) awkwardness, self-consciousness, discomfort, discomfiture, abashment, shame, guilt, humiliation, mortification, chagrin, distress, confusion, perplexity. OPPOSITE: ease. **2** (*financial embarrassment*) predicament, plight, difficulty, scrape (*inf*), pickle (*inf*), fix (*inf*), dilemma, quandary. **3** (*an embarrassment of riches*) abundance, profusion, deluge, overabundance, excess, surplus, plethora, superfluity, surfeit, glut. OPPOSITE: shortage.

embassy *noun* consulate, legation, ministry, mission, delegation, deputation.

embed *verb* fix, set, implant, plant, root, sink, insert, drive, hammer, ram.

embellish *verb* **1** (*embellish the archway*) ornament, decorate, adorn, deck, bedeck, festoon, garnish, trim, beautify, enhance, enrich, gild, emblazon. OPPOSITE: disfigure. **2** (*embellish the story*) varnish, embroider, colour, dress up, elaborate, exaggerate.

embellishment *noun* **1** (*carvings added for embellishment*) ornamentation, ornament, decoration, adornment, garnish, trimming, beautification, enhancement, enrichment, gilding, emblazonment. OPPOSITE: disfigurement. **2** (*a few extra embellishments*) ornament, decoration, festoon, trimming, enhancement. **3** (*the embellishment of the truth*) varnishing, embroidery, exaggeration, elaboration.

embers *pl noun* cinders, ashes, remains, residue.

embezzle *verb* steal, rob, thieve, purloin, pilfer, filch (*inf*), pinch (*inf*), nick (*inf*), appropriate, misappropriate, peculate, defalcate, have one's hand in the till (*inf*), defraud, swindle, cheat.

embezzlement *noun* stealing, robbery, theft, pilfering, larceny, appropriation, misappropriation, peculation, defalcation, fraud.

embitter *verb* sour, poison, envenom, disillusion, disenchant, disaffect, anger, madden, infuriate, exasperate, irritate, aggravate (*inf*).

emblazon *verb* **1** (*emblazon a shield*) adorn, decorate, ornament, embellish, blazon, paint, colour, illuminate. **2** (*emblazoned their deeds*) proclaim, publicize, herald, trumpet, glorify, extol, praise, laud.

emblem *noun* symbol, token, representation, sign, mark, badge, device, figure, insignia, logo.

emblematic *adj* symbolic, representative, figurative.

embodiment *noun* **1** (*she was the embodiment of virtue*) personification, incarnation, incorporation, reification, manifestation, realization, expression, representation, symbol, example, exemplification, epitome, model, type. **2** (*the embodiment of these features in the design*) incorporation, inclusion, comprehension, assimilation, integration, fusion, amalgamation, combination, unification, consolidation.

embody *verb* **1** (*he embodied the ideals of the movement*) personify, incarnate, incorporate, reify, manifest, express, represent, stand for, symbolize, exemplify, epitomize, typify. **2** (*laws that embody their requirements*) incorporate, embrace, encompass, include, comprise, comprehend, contain, collect, bring together, assimilate, integrate, amalgamate, combine, unite, consolidate.

embolden *verb* encourage, hearten, inspirit, rouse, stir, animate, stimulate, spur, impel, fire, invigorate, strengthen, rally, cheer, reassure. OPPOSITE: discourage.

embrace *verb* **1** (*embraced his sister*) clasp, hold, hug, enfold, cuddle, squeeze. **2** (*the lovers embraced*) hug, cuddle, neck (*inf*), pet (*inf*), smooch (*inf*), canoodle (*inf*). **3** (*embrace the idea*) adopt, espouse, take up, take on board (*inf*), seize, grasp, accept, welcome. OPPOSITE: reject. **4** (*the course embraces all aspects of theology*) include, comprise, comprehend, encompass, embody, incorporate, cover, take in, contain, subsume, involve. OPPOSITE: exclude.
≫ *noun* hug, cuddle, squeeze, clasp, hold, clinch (*inf*).

embroider *verb* **1** (*embroider a handkerchief*) sew, stitch, decorate, ornament. **2** (*embroider the truth*) embellish, elaborate, exaggerate, colour, varnish, gild, dress up, invent, fabricate.

embroidery *noun* **1** (*take up embroidery as a hobby*) needlework, sewing, cross stitch, crewelwork, needlepoint, tapestry. **2** (*tell the truth without embroidery*) embellishment, elaboration, exaggeration, varnishing, gilding, invention, fabrication.

embroil *verb* **1** (*embroiled in litigation*) involve, implicate, compromise, incriminate, entangle, enmesh, mix up. OPPOSITE: extricate. **2** (*embroiling the situation*) complicate, confuse, disorder, muddle, disturb, discompose, trouble.

embryo *noun* germ, nucleus, seed, root, beginning, rudiments.

embryonic *adj* rudimentary, undeveloped, unformed, early, immature, elementary, primary, inchoate, incipient, beginning, germinal, seminal. OPPOSITE: mature.

emend *verb* correct, rectify, amend, alter, improve, polish, rewrite, revise, edit, redact.

emendation *noun* correction, rectification, amendment, alteration, improvement, refinement, rewriting, revision, editing, redaction.

emerge *verb* **1** (*new buds emerged*) appear, materialize, come out, rise, surface, come up, proceed, issue, arise, emanate, come forth. OPPOSITE: disappear. **2** (*the truth emerged*) become known, come out, come to light, transpire, turn out.

emergence *noun* **1** (*the emergence of new buds*) appearance, apparition, materialization, rise, coming, advent, arrival, issue, emanation, evolution, development. OPPOSITE: disappearance. **2** (*the emergence of the truth*) disclosure, exposure, publication, broadcasting.

emergency *noun* crisis, accident, disaster, catastrophe, exigency, urgency, dire straits, juncture, extremity, pinch, crunch, necessity, contingency, unforeseen circumstances, predicament, difficulty, plight, quandary, fix (*inf*), scrape (*inf*).
≫ *adj* **1** (*the emergency services*) urgent, accident, danger. **2** (*emergency supplies*) reserve, backup, fallback, alternative, substitute, spare, extra.

emergent *adj* emerging, coming out, arising, beginning, dawning, budding, developing, embryonic.

emigrate *verb* migrate, move abroad, resettle, move, relocate, depart, leave, quit. OPPOSITE: immigrate.

emigration *noun* migration, expatriation, moving abroad, resettlement, moving, relocation, exodus, departure. OPPOSITE: immigration.

eminence *noun* **1** (*writers of eminence*) distinction, illustriousness, celebrity, fame, renown, mark, note, notability, prominence, conspicuousness, esteem, reputation, repute, importance, prestige, rank, standing, greatness, grandeur, dignity, loftiness, superiority. OPPOSITE: obscurity. **2** (*built on an eminence*) hill, mound, height, elevation.

eminent *adj* distinguished, illustrious, celebrated, well-known, famous, renowned, noted, notable, noteworthy, prominent, conspicuous, esteemed, revered, venerable, important, high-ranking, great, grand, lofty, exalted, superior, outstanding, paramount. OPPOSITE: unknown.

eminently *adv* highly, greatly, extremely, exceedingly, exceptionally, remarkably, strikingly, notably, very, well, quite, perfectly. OPPOSITE: moderately.

emissary *noun* agent, ambassador, envoy, delegate, representative, deputy, legate, intermediary, go-between, messenger, courier, herald, scout, spy.

emission *noun* discharge, release, issue, ejection, expulsion, ejaculation, emanation, exhalation, radiation, diffusion, secretion, exudation, leak.

emit *verb* **1** (*emit harmful gases*) discharge, give off, throw out, send forth, release, issue, eject, expel, ejaculate, emanate, exhale, radiate, diffuse, secrete, exude, ooze, leak. **2** (*emit a groan*) utter, let out, give vent to, express, voice, vocalize, articulate, pronounce.

emollient *adj* soothing, lenitive, assuasive, palliative, demulcent, softening, relaxing. OPPOSITE: astringent.
≫ *noun* ointment, liniment, embrocation, lotion, salve, balm, cream, oil, unguent.

emolument *noun* remuneration, pay, earnings, salary, wages, fee, stipend, honorarium, profit, gain, return, revenue, income, living, compensation, recompense, reward, benefit, allowance.

emotion *noun* feeling, sentiment, sensation, reaction, response, passion, ardour, fervour. OPPOSITE: indifference.

emotional *adj* **1** (*her sister is more emotional*) sensitive, susceptible, feeling, sentimental, responsive, demonstrative, warm, loving, tender. OPPOSITE: emotionless. **2** (*don't get so emotional about it*) passionate, ardent, fervent, excitable, temperamental, heated, impassioned, hot-blooded, fiery, melodramatic, hysterical, overwrought. OPPOSITE: calm. **3** (*an emotional scene*) touching, moving, affecting, heart-warming, soul-stirring, poignant, tear-jerking, pathetic. **4** (*an emotional issue*) emotive, rousing, stirring, controversial, sensitive, touchy, delicate, awkward.

emotionless *adj* cool, cold, cold-blooded, unemotional, unfeeling, impassive, indifferent, distant, remote, detached, clinical. OPPOSITE: emotional.

emotive *adj* emotional, rousing, stirring, controversial, sensitive, touchy, delicate, awkward.

empathize *verb* **empathize with** identify with, understand, talk the same language as (*inf*), be on the same wavelength as (*inf*), sympathize with, feel for.

emperor *noun* ruler, sovereign, monarch, imperator, tsar, kaiser, mikado, khan, shah.

emphasis *noun* **1** (*the emphasis is on practical experience*) weight, significance, importance, force, power, strength, stress, accent, underlining, underscoring, insistence, urgency, priority, pre-eminence, attention, prominence. **2** (*with the emphasis on the last syllable*) stress, accent, accentuation.

emphasize *verb* stress, accent, accentuate, underline, underscore, highlight, spotlight, point up, mark, feature, heighten, intensify, strengthen, press home, insist on. OPPOSITE: understate.

emphatic *adj* **1** (*an emphatic success*) positive, certain, definite, absolute, categorical, unequivocal, unmistakable, marked, striking, pronounced, strong, telling, important, significant, momentous. OPPOSITE: insignificant. **2** (*an emphatic refusal*) forceful, insistent, stressed, accented, earnest, energetic, vigorous, positive, definite, decided, determined, absolute, categorical, unequivocal. OPPOSITE: tentative.

empire *noun* **1** (*peace throughout the empire*) domain, dominion, realm, kingdom, commonwealth, province, territory. **2** (*held empire over the people*) sovereignty, dominion, supremacy, power, sway, authority, control, command, rule, government.

empirical *adj* experimental, experiential, observed, practical, pragmatic. OPPOSITE: theoretical.

employ *verb* **1** (*need to employ more staff*) engage, appoint, hire, recruit, enlist, enrol, take on, sign up, retain, commission, apprentice, indenture. OPPOSITE:

dismiss. **2** (*without employing force*) use, make use of, utilize, exploit, exercise, exert, apply, wield, ply, bring to bear. **3** (*employed too much of my time*) occupy, take up, engage, engross.

employed *adj* **1** (*has never been employed*) working, in work, in employment, earning, waged, salaried. OPPOSITE: unemployed. **2** (*employed in writing letters*) busy, occupied, active, engaged, engrossed, preoccupied. OPPOSITE: idle.

employee *noun* worker, member of staff, job-holder, wage-earner, hand, assistant, labourer, operative. OPPOSITE: employer.

employer *noun* director, manager, boss, gaffer (*inf*), governor (*inf*), contractor, proprietor, owner, company, firm, business. OPPOSITE: employee.

employment *noun* **1** (*seeking full-time employment*) situation, appointment, post, job, occupation, work, service, business, trade, craft, métier, profession, vocation. OPPOSITE: unemployment. **2** (*the employment of more staff*) engagement, appointment, hire, recruitment, enlisting, enrolment, commissioning. OPPOSITE: dismissal. **3** (*the employment of force*) use, utilization, exploitation, exercise, exertion, application.

emporium *noun* store, shop, market, mart, bazaar, fair.

empower *verb* authorize, warrant, license, commission, accredit, entitle, sanction, permit, allow, enable, equip, qualify. OPPOSITE: disqualify.

emptiness *adj* **1** (*the emptiness of the space*) void, vacuum, vacancy, bareness, blankness, clearness. OPPOSITE: fullness. **2** (*the emptiness of their promises*) worthlessness, meaninglessness, senselessness, insignificance, triviality, idleness, vanity, futility, uselessness, ineffectiveness, hollowness, insincerity. OPPOSITE: meaningfulness. **3** (*the emptiness of her existence*) aimlessness, purposelessness, meaninglessness, worthlessness, insignificance, triviality, frivolousness, futility, uselessness. OPPOSITE: purposefulness. **4** (*the emptiness of his gaze*) expressionlessness, blankness, vacantness, vacuousness.

empty *adj* **1** (*an empty space*) void, unfilled, hollow, vacant, unoccupied, deserted, uninhabited, devoid, destitute, bare, blank, clear, free. OPPOSITE: full. **2** (*their empty promises*) worthless, meaningless, senseless, insignificant, trivial, idle, vain, futile, useless, ineffective, ineffectual, hollow, insincere, unsubstantial. OPPOSITE: meaningful. **3** (*her empty existence*) aimless, purposeless, meaningless, worthless, insignificant, trivial, frivolous, futile, useless. OPPOSITE: purposeful. **4** (*his empty gaze*) expressionless, deadpan, blank, vacant, vacuous, silly, inane.
≫ *verb* drain, exhaust, deplete, void, evacuate, vacate, clear, discharge, unload, pour out. OPPOSITE: fill.

empyreal *adj* empyrean, aerial, ethereal, celestial, heavenly, sublime, unworldly. OPPOSITE: earthly.

emulate *verb* imitate, copy, mimic, echo, follow, take after, rival, compete with, vie with, equal, match.

emulation *noun* imitation, mimicry, rivalry, competition, contention, strife.

enable *verb* **1** (*glasses enabling them to see in the dark*) permit, allow, facilitate, assist, help, capacitate, empower, arm, equip, fit, prepare. OPPOSITE: prevent.

2 (*a pass enabling us to enter the building*) authorize, sanction, license, warrant, permit, allow, empower, capacitate, qualify, entitle. OPPOSITE: prohibit.

enact *verb* **1** (*enact a bill in parliament*) decree, ordain, pronounce, rule, pass, establish, make law, legislate, ratify, sanction, authorize. OPPOSITE: repeal. **2** (*enact a drama*) perform, act, act out, play, represent, portray, depict, stage.

enactment *noun* **1** (*the enactment of a bill*) decreeing, ordaining, pronouncement, ruling, passing, establishment, legislation, ratification, authorization. OPPOSITE: abrogation. **2** (*recent parliamentary enactments*) decree, ordinance, edict, dictate, pronouncement, proclamation, commandment, rule, ruling, law, statute, act, legislation, bill, measure. **3** (*the enactment of a drama*) performance, acting, representation, portrayal, depiction, staging.

enamoured *adj* fond, liking, loving, in love, infatuated, smitten (*inf*), charmed, enchanted, bewitched, taken, captivated, fascinated, enthralled, mad (*inf*), crazy (*inf*), wild (*inf*). OPPOSITE: repelled.

encamp *verb* camp, pitch camp, bivouac, lodge, settle.

encampment *noun* camp, campsite, bivouac, base, quarters.

encapsulate *verb* summarize, sum up, epitomize, condense, compress, précis, digest, include, contain, embrace, capture.

encase *verb* enclose, wrap, sheathe, pack, box, crate.

enchant *verb* attract, allure, captivate, win, charm, delight, enrapture, fascinate, beguile, entrance, enthral, bewitch, spellbind, hypnotize, mesmerize. OPPOSITE: repel.

enchanted *adj* **1** (*an enchanted forest*) magic, bewitched, spellbound. **2** (*enchanted by their performance*) captivated, charmed, delighted, pleased, fascinated, enthralled, spellbound, mesmerized. OPPOSITE: repelled.

enchanter *noun* magician, sorcerer, sorceress, magus, witch, wizard, warlock, necromancer, conjuror, hypnotist, mesmerist.

enchanting *adj* attractive, alluring, captivating, winning, charming, delightful, lovely, winsome, appealing, endearing, engaging, fascinating, beguiling, enthralling, bewitching, spellbinding, irresistible, hypnotic, mesmeric. OPPOSITE: repulsive.

enchantment *noun* **1** (*powers of enchantment*) magic, sorcery, witchcraft, wizardry, necromancy, conjuration, hypnotism, mesmerism, spell, charm, incantation. **2** (*cries of enchantment*) delight, charm, captivation, rapture, bliss, ecstasy, fascination, appeal, allure, entrancement, enthralment. OPPOSITE: repulsion.

enchantress *noun* **1** (*bewitched by an enchantress*) magician, sorceress, witch, necromancer, conjuror, hypnotist, mesmerist, siren. **2** (*seduced by an enchantress*) seductress, temptress, siren, vamp, femme fatale.

encircle *verb* surround, encompass, gird, circumscribe, ring, environ, enclose, shut in, fence in, hem in, confine.

enclose *verb* **1** (*the wall enclosing the grounds*) surround, encircle, gird, encompass, circumscribe, shut in, fence in, hem in, confine, cage, pen, contain, hold, encase, envelop, wrap, cocoon. **2** (*enclose a stamped addressed envelope*) include, insert, put in.

enclosure *noun* **1** (*standing in the enclosure*) pen, fold, pound, compound, paddock, corral, yard, area, arena, ring, court, close, cloister. **2** (*rebuilt the enclosure*) fence, railings, palisade, hedge, wall, barricade, enceinte. **3** (*the enclosure of a cheque*) inclusion, insertion.

encomium *noun* eulogy, panegyric, praise, acclaim, laudation, homage, tribute. OPPOSITE: vituperation.

encompass *verb* **1** (*encompassed by a high wall*) surround, encircle, gird, circumscribe, ring, environ, enclose, shut in, fence in, hem in, confine. **2** (*encompassing all aspects of the subject*) include, contain, embrace, envelop, cover, span, take in, deal with, comprise, comprehend, incorporate, embody. OPPOSITE: exclude.

encounter *verb* **1** (*encountered a few setbacks*) confront, face, be faced with, come up against, experience, undergo. OPPOSITE: avoid. **2** (*encountered a former employee*) meet, happen upon, come across, stumble across, run into (*inf*), bump into (*inf*). **3** (*encountered enemy troops*) accost, confront, fight, combat, engage with, clash with, contend with, grapple with, struggle with, tussle with, do battle with, cross swords with (*inf*). ➤ *noun* **1** (*since our last encounter*) meeting, contact, rendezvous. **2** (*injured in the encounter*) confrontation, clash, conflict, brush (*inf*), run-in (*inf*), fight, combat, battle, action, engagement, skirmish, scuffle, tussle, set-to (*inf*).

encourage *verb* **1** (*encouraged by the news*) cheer, hearten, rally, buoy up, buck up (*inf*), reassure, comfort, inspirit, embolden, rouse, stir, animate, stimulate, motivate. OPPOSITE: depress. **2** (*encouraging them to go faster*) persuade, influence, urge, exhort, egg on, spur, goad, incite, prompt, stimulate, motivate. OPPOSITE: discourage. **3** (*encourage foreign trade*) support, advocate, back, help, assist, aid, abet, foster, promote, advance, further, boost. OPPOSITE: deter.

encouragement *verb* **1** (*words of encouragement*) cheer, heartening, rallying, reassurance, comfort, inspiration, animation, stimulation, motivation. OPPOSITE: discouragement. **2** (*needed little encouragement*) persuasion, influence, urging, exhortation, spur, goad, incitement, prompting, stimulation, motivation. OPPOSITE: dissuasion. **3** (*the encouragement of foreign trade*) support, advocacy, backing, help, assistance, aid, abetment, fostering, promotion, advance, furtherance, boost. OPPOSITE: deterrence.

encouraging *adj* promising, hopeful, optimistic, bright, rosy, cheerful, heartening, reassuring, comforting, uplifting. OPPOSITE: discouraging.

encroach *verb* intrude, trespass, invade, infiltrate, overrun, infringe, impinge, entrench, muscle in (*inf*), overstep, arrogate, usurp, tread on someone's toes.

encroachment *verb* intrusion, trespassing, invasion, incursion, infiltration, infringement, impingement, arrogation, usurpation.

encrust *verb* plaster, coat, cover, overlay.

encumber *verb* hamper, hinder, impede, handicap, inconvenience, constrain, cramp, restrain, check,

obstruct, block, clog, congest, burden, load, weigh down, oppress, saddle, tax, strain. OPPOSITE: relieve.

encumbrance *noun* hindrance, impediment, handicap, inconvenience, constraint, restraint, obstacle, obstruction, block, congestion, burden, load, weight, millstone, cross, onus, responsibility, obligation, tax, strain, stress.

encyclopedic *adj* comprehensive, complete, all-inclusive, all-embracing, all-encompassing, universal, wide-ranging, thorough, exhaustive, broad, vast, compendious. OPPOSITE: narrow.

end *noun* **1** (*the end of the story*) ending, finish, conclusion, termination, close, cessation, stoppage, completion, resolution, finale, climax, denouement, culmination. OPPOSITE: beginning. **2** (*the end of the rope*) extremity, tip, point, edge, terminus, limit, bound, boundary, border, margin. **3** (*cigarette ends*) stub, butt, remnant, remainder, scrap, fragment. **4** (*working towards the same end*) aim, object, purpose, intention, reason, motive, design, goal, target, objective. **5** (*met his end in battle*) death, demise, doom, downfall, ruin, destruction, annihilation, extermination, extinction, finishing stroke, coup de grâce. OPPOSITE: birth. **6** (*the end justifies the means*) result, consequence, event, outcome, issue, upshot. **7** (*the sales end of the operation*) part, section, side, aspect, area, field, province, department. **8** (*keep their end of the bargain*) share, portion, part, side, responsibility. ➤ *verb* **1** (*end the story*) finish, conclude, terminate, close, cease, stop, discontinue, break off, complete, resolve, round off, wind up (*inf*). OPPOSITE: start. **2** (*ended her chances of winning*) ruin, destroy, annihilate, exterminate, extinguish, kill, eradicate, abolish, dissolve.

endanger *verb* imperil, jeopardize, hazard, risk, expose, threaten, compromise. OPPOSITE: protect.

endearing *adj* attractive, appealing, enchanting, engaging, charming, delightful, winning, captivating, adorable, lovable, sweet, winsome. OPPOSITE: repulsive.

endearment *noun* **1** (*a term of endearment*) love, affection, tenderness, fondness, liking, attachment. OPPOSITE: hatred. **2** (*whispered endearments*) loving word, soft word, sweet nothing, blandishment, pet name, diminutive, hypocorism. OPPOSITE: insult.

endeavour *verb* try, attempt, have a go (*inf*), strive, struggle, labour, essay, do one's best, aspire, aim, undertake, venture. ➤ *noun* try, attempt, bid, go (*inf*), stab (*inf*), crack (*inf*), bash (*inf*), shot (*inf*), struggle, effort, essay, aspiration, aim, undertaking, venture, enterprise.

ending *noun* end, finish, conclusion, termination, close, cessation, stoppage, completion, resolution, finale, climax, denouement, culmination. OPPOSITE: beginning.

endless *adj* **1** (*an endless supply*) unlimited, limitless, boundless, immeasurable, measureless, infinite, unending, interminable, unceasing, ceaseless, incessant, constant, perpetual, continuous, uninterrupted, unbroken. OPPOSITE: finite. **2** (*an endless lecture*) interminable, never-ending, nonstop, incessant, unremitting, monotonous, boring. **3** (*endless love*) eternal, everlasting, immortal, undying, unfading, constant, perpetual. OPPOSITE: transient. **4** (*an endless belt*) continuous, never-ending, unending, unbroken, uninterrupted, whole, entire.

endorse *verb* **1** (*endorse their proposals*) approve, sanction, ratify, confirm, authorize, support, back, second, be behind, advocate, champion, vouch for, corroborate, sustain, uphold. **2** (*endorse a cheque*) countersign, superscribe, underwrite, validate.

endorsement *noun* **1** (*endorsement of their proposals*) approval, sanction, ratification, confirmation, authorization, support, backing, advocacy, corroboration. **2** (*the endorsement on the cheque*) countersignature, superscription.

endow *verb* **1** (*endow a charitable trust*) bestow, bequeath, will, leave, give, present, grant, award, confer, fund, finance. **2** (*endowed with intelligence*) give, present, bless, provide, supply, furnish, equip, invest, endue. OPPOSITE: divest.

endowment *noun* **1** (*an endowment for the hospital*) bequest, legacy, settlement, inheritance, grant, award, gift, present, donation, benefaction, provision, fund, finance, revenue, inheritance. **2** (*among his endowments*) talent, gift, flair, faculty, attribute, quality, property, characteristic, feature, aptitude, ability, capability, capacity, facility, skill.

endurance *noun* **1** (*tested her endurance*) fortitude, stamina, strength, tenacity, staying power, persistence, perseverance, patience, resignation, stoicism, acceptance, tolerance, forbearance. OPPOSITE: weakness. **2** (*the endurance of our love*) permanence, durability, stability, immutability, duration, continuance, longevity, immortality. OPPOSITE: impermanence.

endure *verb* **1** (*can't endure the noise*) bear, stand, brook, tolerate, permit, allow, put up with, abide, stomach (*inf*), swallow (*inf*). **2** (*endured years of civil strife*) undergo, experience, go through, suffer, submit to, take, face, brave, cope with, weather, sustain, withstand. **3** (*built to endure*) last, persist, remain, stay, abide, continue, hold, prevail, survive. OPPOSITE: perish.

enduring *adj* lasting, long-lasting, durable, continuing, remaining, abiding, prevailing, stable, unwavering, unfaltering, immutable, changeless, permanent, eternal, everlasting, immortal. OPPOSITE: fleeting.

enemy *noun* **1** (*one of their enemies*) foe, adversary, opponent, antagonist, rival, competitor. OPPOSITE: ally. **2** (*defeat the enemy*) opposition, other side, competition.

energetic *adj* **1** (*an energetic worker*) vigorous, active, lively, full of beans (*inf*), dynamic, spirited, animated, brisk, sprightly, zippy (*inf*), bright-eyed and bushy-tailed (*inf*), tireless, indefatigable, busy, strenuous. OPPOSITE: lethargic. **2** (*an energetic attack*) forceful, powerful, potent, strong, aggressive, driving, effective, effectual. OPPOSITE: feeble.

energize *verb* invigorate, vitalize, animate, enliven, pep up (*inf*), stimulate, motivate, rouse, stir, goad, spur, galvanize, electrify, activate. OPPOSITE: enervate.

energy *noun* vigour, activity, liveliness, life, vitality, vivacity, dynamism, spirit, animation, pep (*inf*), zip (*inf*), get-up-and-go (*inf*), stamina, strength, power, might, force, drive, push, zeal, ardour, fervour, fire, zest,

verve, dash, élan, brio, exuberance, buoyancy, effervescence, sparkle. OPPOSITE: lethargy.

enervated *verb* weak, feeble, weakened, debilitated, enfeebled, devitalized, sapped, washed out (*inf*), tired, weary, fatigued, worn out, exhausted, done in (*inf*), prostrate, disabled, incapacitated, paralysed. OPPOSITE: invigorated.

enfeeble *verb* weaken, debilitate, enervate, devitalize, unman, unnerve, sap, tire, weary, wear out, exhaust, deplete, reduce, diminish. OPPOSITE: strengthen.

enfold *verb* **1** (*enfolded in mist*) envelop, wrap, swathe, shroud, enclose, encompass, surround. **2** (*enfolded him in her arms*) embrace, hug, clasp, hold.

enforce *verb* **1** (*enforce the law*) apply, administer, implement, execute, carry out, discharge, impose, bring to bear. OPPOSITE: waive. **2** (*enforce obedience*) force, compel, oblige, urge, constrain, require, insist on, impose, exact, extort, coerce, pressure, pressurize, dragoon.

enforced *adj* compulsory, obligatory, forced, compelled, required, necessary, imposed, prescribed, ordained, unavoidable, involuntary. OPPOSITE: optional.

enforcement *verb* **1** (*law enforcement*) application, administration, implementation, execution, discharge, imposition. OPPOSITE: waiver. **2** (*enforcement of obedience*) compulsion, obligation, constraint, requirement, insistence, imposition, coercion, pressure.

enfranchise *verb* **1** (*enfranchise immigrants*) give suffrage to, give the vote to, give citizenship to, naturalize. **2** (*enfranchise slaves*) emancipate, liberate, free, release, manumit, disenthral. OPPOSITE: enslave.

engage *verb* **1** (*engage a chauffeur*) hire, employ, appoint, take on, enlist, enrol, recruit, sign up, commission, retain. OPPOSITE: dismiss. **2** (*engage their interest*) engross, absorb, grip, hold, fill, occupy, busy, involve, tie up. **3** (*engaging her affection*) attract, draw, catch, win, captivate, charm. OPPOSITE: repel. **4** (*engaged to marry him*) pledge, promise, vow, undertake, contract, covenant, agree, commit, bind, oblige. **5** (*engage the enemy*) fight, battle, combat, attack, take on, encounter, meet. OPPOSITE: retreat. **6** (*engage third gear*) activate, apply, interconnect, interlock, mesh, join. OPPOSITE: disengage.

engage in participate in, take part in, join in, enter, undertake, tackle, embark on, set about, take up, practise.

engaged *adj* **1** (*the engaged couple*) betrothed, affianced, pledged, plighted, promised, spoken for (*inf*). OPPOSITE: unattached. **2** (*all the clerks were engaged*) busy, active, occupied, tied up, involved, engrossed, absorbed, immersed. OPPOSITE: free. **3** (*the line is engaged*) unavailable, in use, busy, occupied, taken, reserved, booked. OPPOSITE: available.

engagement *noun* **1** (*the couple announced their engagement*) betrothal, pledge. **2** (*a binding engagement*) pledge, promise, vow, oath, contract, pact, covenant, bond, obligation, commitment. **3** (*have a prior engagement*) appointment, meeting, rendezvous, date, assignation, arrangement, commitment. **4** (*in my last engagement*) employment, appointment, job, post, situation, work, business. **5** (*engagement in leisure* *pursuits*) occupation, involvement, absorption, immersion. **6** (*soldiers killed in the engagement*) fight, battle, skirmish, strife, combat, action, conflict, clash, encounter, attack, assault, offensive. OPPOSITE: retreat.

engaging *adj* charming, delightful, enchanting, captivating, winning, taking, appealing, winsome, attractive, fetching, pleasing, pleasant, agreeable, likable, lovable, adorable. OPPOSITE: repulsive.

engender *verb* **1** (*engender hatred*) produce, cause, occasion, bring about, lead to, effect, create, generate, give rise to, provoke, arouse, rouse, foment. OPPOSITE: suppress. **2** (*engender sons*) beget, breed, procreate, propagate, spawn, sire, father, conceive, give birth to.

engine *noun* locomotive, motor, generator, machine, mechanism, appliance, apparatus, device, contrivance, implement, tool, instrument, agent, means.

engineer *noun* **1** (*chartered engineers*) designer, planner, deviser, inventor, architect, originator, mastermind. **2** (*the engineer couldn't repair it*) mechanic, technician, operator, controller, driver.
➤ *verb* plan, devise, contrive, manoeuvre, manipulate, cause, bring about, arrange, orchestrate, direct, control, manage, superintend, mastermind.

engrave *verb* **1** (*engrave the glass*) inscribe, etch, cut, incise, carve, chisel, chase, mark, print, imprint, impress. **2** (*engraved on my memory*) stamp, imprint, impress, brand, fix, set, lodge, embed, ingrain. OPPOSITE: erase.

engraving *noun* **1** (*an engraving of the church*) print, impression, inscription, etching, woodcut, lithograph, carving, intaglio, plate, block. **2** (*the engraving of glass*) etching, cutting, carving, chiselling, printing, impression, lithography, intaglio.

engross *verb* absorb, preoccupy, occupy, engage, involve, interest, fascinate, captivate, grip, rivet, hold, fix, arrest, engulf, monopolize, corner. OPPOSITE: bore.

engrossed *adj* absorbed, immersed, preoccupied, intent, occupied, engaged, involved, caught up, interested, fascinated, captivated, riveted, fixated, rapt. OPPOSITE: bored.

engrossing *adj* absorbing, interesting, fascinating, enthralling, gripping, riveting, compelling, intriguing, unputdownable (*inf*). OPPOSITE: boring.

engulf *verb* consume, swallow up, overwhelm, swamp, flood, deluge, inundate, bury, immerse, submerge, plunge, absorb, engross, envelop.

enhance *verb* improve, embellish, enrich, increase, raise, augment, add to, heighten, intensify, boost, swell, magnify, amplify, lift, elevate, strengthen, reinforce, emphasize, stress. OPPOSITE: reduce.

enhancement *noun* improvement, embellishment, enrichment, increase, rise, augmentation, intensification, boost, magnification, amplification, elevation, reinforcement, emphasis, stress. OPPOSITE: reduction.

enigma *noun* mystery, riddle, conundrum, puzzle, poser (*inf*), teaser (*inf*), paradox, problem, dilemma, quandary. OPPOSITE: solution.

enigmatic *adj* puzzling, perplexing, mystifying, mysterious, cryptic, obscure, recondite, occult, arcane, esoteric, abstruse, incomprehensible, unfathomable,

unintelligible, inscrutable, inexplicable, paradoxical, ambiguous, equivocal. OPPOSITE: simple.

enjoin *verb* **1** (*enjoined her to leave*) order, command, direct, instruct, decree, ordain, require, charge, bid, urge, advise, counsel, admonish, warn. **2** (*enjoined him from entering the premises*) ban, bar, forbid, prohibit, proscribe, disallow, interdict. OPPOSITE: permit.

enjoy *verb* **1** (*enjoyed the meal*) like, love, appreciate, relish, savour, luxuriate in, take pleasure in, delight in, revel in, be amused by, be entertained by. OPPOSITE: detest. **2** (*enjoy freedom of speech*) have, possess, own, benefit from, be blessed with, be endowed with, experience, use, avail oneself of. OPPOSITE: lose.

enjoy oneself have fun, have a good time, have a whale of a time (*inf*), have the time of one's life (*inf*), have a ball (*inf*), party, revel, make merry, live it up (*inf*), let one's hair down (*inf*).

enjoyable *adj* pleasant, agreeable, nice, lovely, delightful, good, great (*inf*), fun, amusing, entertaining, diverting, delicious, delectable. OPPOSITE: unpleasant.

enjoyment *noun* **1** (*cries of enjoyment*) fun, jollity, pleasure, delight, joy, happiness, amusement, entertainment, recreation, diversion, delectation, gratification, appreciation, relish, gusto. OPPOSITE: displeasure. **2** (*the enjoyment of good health*) possession, ownership, use, exercise, benefit, advantage, favour, blessing.

enkindle *verb* kindle, ignite, inflame, excite, arouse, stir, provoke, stimulate. OPPOSITE: damp.

enlarge *verb* expand, amplify, magnify, swell, grow, increase, augment, add to, multiply, develop, extend, stretch, elongate, lengthen, heighten, deepen, widen, broaden, thicken, distend, bloat, dilate, inflate, blow up. OPPOSITE: diminish.

enlarge on expatiate on, descant on, dilate on, expound, develop, elaborate on, expand on, amplify, flesh out. OPPOSITE: summarize.

enlargement *noun* **1** (*enlargement of the garden*) expansion, amplification, magnification, increase, augmentation, multiplication, development, extension, elongation, widening, broadening, thickening. OPPOSITE: contraction. **2** (*enlargement of the diseased organ*) swelling, tumescence, tumefaction, bloating, distension, dilation.

enlighten *verb* instruct, edify, teach, educate, inform, make aware, apprise, illuminate, civilize, cultivate. OPPOSITE: confuse.

enlightened *adj* aware, informed, knowledgeable, educated, literate, wise, learned, erudite, civilized, cultivated, refined, sophisticated, broad-minded, open-minded, liberal. OPPOSITE: ignorant.

enlightenment *noun* understanding, awareness, insight, education, teaching, instruction, edification, information, learning, knowledge, wisdom, erudition, refinement, sophistication, civilization, cultivation, broad-mindedness, open-mindedness, liberalism. OPPOSITE: ignorance.

enlist *verb* **1** (*enlist soldiers*) recruit, enrol, sign up, register, draft, conscript, engage, hire, take on, employ. **2** (*enlist in the army*) volunteer, join up, sign up, enter. **3** (*enlisted our help*) secure, obtain, procure.

enliven *verb* animate, invigorate, vitalize, stimulate, inspirit, excite, rouse, wake up, liven up, brighten up, jazz up (*inf*), refresh, exhilarate, gladden, hearten, cheer up, buoy up, perk up (*inf*). OPPOSITE: damp.

en masse *adv* together, all together, as one, as a group, in a body, in a mass, ensemble, en bloc. OPPOSITE: individually.

enmesh *verb* entangle, snarl, catch, ensnare, trap, embroil, involve. OPPOSITE: extricate.

enmity *noun* hostility, animosity, antagonism, strife, discord, hate, hatred, antipathy, aversion, bad blood, ill will, rancour, bitterness, acrimony, spite, malice. OPPOSITE: friendship.

ennoble *verb* elevate, raise, uplift, aggrandize, magnify, exalt, glorify, dignify, honour. OPPOSITE: degrade.

ennui *noun* boredom, tedium, dissatisfaction, languor, lassitude, listlessness, lethargy, sluggishness. OPPOSITE: energy.

enormity *noun* **1** (*commit enormities*) atrocity, outrage, scandal, disgrace, horror, monstrosity, abomination, evil, villainy, violation, transgression, iniquity, crime. **2** (*the enormity of the crime*) outrageousness, evilness, wickedness, vileness, heinousness, cruelty, brutality, hideousness, monstrousness, depravity.

enormous *adj* huge, immense, vast, massive, whopping (*inf*), colossal, gigantic, giant, gargantuan, Brobdingnagian, mammoth, elephantine, jumbo (*inf*), herculean, titanic, mountainous, prodigious, stupendous, tremendous, monumental, astronomic, mega (*inf*). OPPOSITE: tiny.

enormously *adv* extremely, exceedingly, hugely, immensely, massively, stupendously, tremendously. OPPOSITE: slightly.

enough *adj* sufficient, adequate, ample, abundant, plentiful. OPPOSITE: insufficient.
  ⪼ *noun* sufficiency, adequacy, abundance, plenty. OPPOSITE: insufficiency.
  ⪼ *adv* sufficiently, adequately, tolerably, passably, reasonably, moderately, abundantly, amply. OPPOSITE: insufficiently.

en passant *adv* in passing, by the way, incidentally, apropos.

enquire *verb* ask, question, query, interrogate, quiz, examine, inquire, investigate, look into, study, research, probe, explore. OPPOSITE: respond.

enquiry *noun* question, query, interrogation, inquiry, inquest, investigation, study, survey, probe. OPPOSITE: response.

enrage *verb* incense, infuriate, madden, exasperate, make someone's blood boil (*inf*), anger, vex, irk, needle (*inf*), bug (*inf*), rouse, provoke, inflame, incite, make someone's hackles rise (*inf*), get someone's back up (*inf*), irritate, annoy, aggravate (*inf*), drive round the bend (*inf*). OPPOSITE: pacify.

enraged *adj* incensed, infuriated, exasperated, furious, livid, fuming, raging, mad (*inf*), angry, irate, roused, inflamed, irritated, annoyed. OPPOSITE: calm.

enrapture *verb* delight, enchant, entrance, fascinate, captivate, bewitch, charm, beguile, enthral, thrill, ravish, transport. OPPOSITE: repel.

enrich *verb* **1** (*enrich their lives*) make rich, make richer, enhance, improve, ameliorate, upgrade, refine, polish, uplift, augment, supplement, develop, aggrandize. OPPOSITE: impoverish. **2** (*enriched with carvings*) adorn, deck, decorate, ornament, trim, garnish, embellish, beautify, gild, grace. OPPOSITE: disfigure.

enrol *verb* **1** (*enrol for evening classes*) register, put one's name down, sign on, sign up, matriculate, enlist, join up. **2** (*enrol new students*) recruit, admit, accept, register, sign on, sign up. **3** (*enrol the results*) record, note, register, list, catalogue, chronicle.

enrolment *noun* registration, matriculation, recruitment, enlistment, admission, acceptance.

en route *adv* on the way, in transit.

ensconce *verb* nestle, snuggle up, curl up, settle, lodge, install, locate, place.

ensemble *noun* **1** (*viewed as an ensemble*) whole, totality, entirety, aggregate, sum, total, collection, set, assemblage, combination, composite. OPPOSITE: element. **2** (*wearing a stylish new ensemble*) outfit, costume, suit, coordinates, attire, getup (*inf*), rigout (*inf*). **3** (*a woodwind ensemble*) band, group, trio, quartet, quintet, sextet, septet, octet, company, troupe, cast, choir, chorus.
  ⪼ *adv* together, all together, en masse, as a group, in concert, at the same time, all at once. OPPOSITE: individually.

enshrine *verb* dedicate, consecrate, hallow, sanctify, revere, venerate, idolize, immortalize, cherish, treasure, preserve, embalm, protect, guard.

enshroud *verb* shroud, veil, cloak, mask, envelop, enfold, wrap, cover, obscure, conceal, hide.

ensign *noun* flag, pennant, banner, standard, colours, insignia, badge, emblem, device, crest, shield, escutcheon, coat of arms, bearings.

enslave *verb* subjugate, master, dominate, oppress, bind, chain, fetter, manacle, yoke. OPPOSITE: liberate.

enslavement *noun* slavery, servitude, bondage, captivity, subjugation, oppression, thraldom, serfdom, vassalage. OPPOSITE: freedom.

ensnare *verb* snare, trap, entrap, catch, capture, net, enmesh, entangle, embroil, inveigle, allure. OPPOSITE: loose.

ensue *verb* follow, come next, succeed, proceed, arise, issue, result, derive, stem, happen, occur, transpire, befall. OPPOSITE: precede.

ensure *verb* guarantee, warrant, assure, make sure, make certain, confirm, certify, secure, protect, guard, safeguard. OPPOSITE: jeopardize.

entail *verb* involve, necessitate, call for, demand, require, impose, occasion, cause, bring about, produce, result in, lead to, give rise to.

entangle *verb* **1** (*entangle the thread*) tangle, ravel, knot, mat, twist, intertwine. OPPOSITE: disentangle. **2** (*entangled in a net*) catch, snarl, enmesh, snare, ensnare, trap, entrap. **3** (*entangle the question*) complicate, confuse, muddle, jumble. **4** (*entangled in litigation*) embroil, enmesh, involve, implicate, mix up. OPPOSITE: extricate.

entanglement *noun* **1** (*an entanglement of barbed wire*) tangle, knot, intertwining. **2** (*business entanglements*) complication, involvement, affair, difficulty, predicament, confusion, muddle, jumble, mix-up. **3** (*the entanglement of the legal process*) complexity, intricacy, confusion, muddle, complication, involvement.

entente *noun* understanding, arrangement, agreement, deal, pact, compact, treaty.

enter *verb* **1** (*a stranger entered*) go in, come in, arrive, cross the threshold. OPPOSITE: leave. **2** (*enter a room*) go into, come into, move into, pass into, arrive in, penetrate, pierce, invade, infiltrate. OPPOSITE: exit. **3** (*entered her name on the list*) record, note, register, log, put down, take down, write, inscribe, keyboard, input, introduce, insert. OPPOSITE: expunge. **4** (*enter the armed forces*) join, enrol in, enlist in, sign up for, commit oneself to, take up, engage in. **5** (*enter a race*) put one's name down for, go in for, participate in, take part in, engage in. **6** (*enter a plea of not guilty*) put forward, submit, tender, offer, proffer, present. OPPOSITE: withdraw.

enter into begin, start, commence, embark on, set about, undertake. OPPOSITE: conclude.

enterprise *noun* **1** (*a new enterprise*) undertaking, venture, operation, project, plan, scheme, programme, campaign, effort, endeavour, attempt. **2** (*a profitable enterprise*) business, company, firm, establishment, house, concern, operation, industry. **3** (*lacking in enterprise*) initiative, resourcefulness, imagination, gumption, ambition, drive, push (*inf*), energy, vigour, get-up-and-go (*inf*), courage, boldness, audacity, daring, adventurousness, spirit, oomph (*inf*), enthusiasm, zest. OPPOSITE: apathy.

enterprising *adj* resourceful, inventive, imaginative, entrepreneurial, go-ahead (*inf*), self-starting (*inf*), adventurous, bold, daring, courageous, ambitious, aspiring, up-and-coming (*inf*), pushy (*inf*), keen, eager, ready, energetic, vigorous, strenuous, zealous, spirited, enthusiastic. OPPOSITE: apathetic.

entertain *verb* **1** (*entertain the spectators*) amuse, divert, interest, occupy, engage, engross, please, charm, enchant, delight, regale, cheer. OPPOSITE: bore. **2** (*entertain guests*) receive, welcome, accommodate, lodge, put up, host, have round, wine and dine, treat, regale. **3** (*we rarely entertain these days*) receive guests, have company, provide hospitality, keep open house, throw a party. **4** (*entertain suspicions*) harbour, foster, nurture, cherish, hold, have. OPPOSITE: banish. **5** (*wouldn't entertain the suggestion*) consider, contemplate, ponder, weigh up, think about, bear in mind. OPPOSITE: reject.

entertaining *adj* amusing, diverting, recreational, fun, interesting, engaging, pleasing, charming, delightful, enchanting, funny, comical, humorous, witty. OPPOSITE: boring.

entertainment *noun* **1** (*did it for entertainment*) amusement, diversion, recreation, pastime, hobby, play, sport, fun, pleasure, enjoyment. **2** (*put on an entertainment*) show, performance, presentation, play, concert, carnival, festival, gala, spectacle, extravaganza.

enthral *verb* captivate, charm, enchant, fascinate, spellbind, entrance, beguile, hypnotize, mesmerize,

rivet, grip, thrill, transport, enrapture, delight. OPPOSITE: bore.

enthralling *adj* riveting, gripping, thrilling, fascinating, intriguing, spellbinding, hypnotic, mesmerizing, captivating, charming, enchanting, delightful. OPPOSITE: boring.

enthrone *verb* crown, install, invest, induct, ordain, exalt, glorify, honour, ennoble, elevate, aggrandize, idolize. OPPOSITE: dethrone.

enthuse *verb* **1** (*enthusing about the decor*) be enthusiastic, rave, wax lyrical, gush, effervesce, bubble over. **2** (*enthused her students*) make enthusiastic, excite, inspire, motivate, fire.

enthusiasm *noun* **1** (*their enthusiasm about the project*) eagerness, keenness, avidity, earnestness, ardour, fervour, warmth, passion, vehemence, excitement, exuberance, wholeheartedness, devotion, commitment, zeal, fanaticism. OPPOSITE: apathy. **2** (*his latest enthusiasm is coin-collecting*) pastime, hobby, interest, passion, mania, craze, rage, fad.

enthusiast *noun* zealot, fanatic, devotee, admirer, supporter, fan, aficionado, buff (*inf*), fiend (*inf*), freak (*inf*).

enthusiastic *adj* eager, keen, avid, earnest, ardent, fervent, fervid, warm, passionate, vehement, excited, exuberant, ebullient, spirited, wholehearted, devoted, committed, zealous, fanatical, crazy (*inf*), wild (*inf*). OPPOSITE: indifferent.

entice *verb* tempt, lure, bait, draw, attract, allure, seduce, lead on, inveigle, cajole, wheedle, coax, persuade. OPPOSITE: deter.

enticement *noun* temptation, lure, bait, decoy, draw, attraction, come-on (*inf*), allurement, seduction, inveiglement, cajolery, coaxing, persuasion. OPPOSITE: deterrent.

entire *adj* complete, whole, total, full, undivided, intact, unbroken, sound, unharmed, perfect, unimpaired, unblemished, pure, unalloyed, thorough, absolute, outright, utter, unmitigated, unqualified, unreserved, unrestricted. OPPOSITE: partial.

entirely *adv* **1** (*an entirely different matter*) completely, wholly, totally, fully, altogether, perfectly, absolutely, utterly, in every respect, in every way, unreservedly, without reservation, without exception. OPPOSITE: slightly. **2** (*it's your fault entirely*) only, solely, exclusively.

entirety *noun* **1** (*broadcast in its entirety*) completeness, wholeness, totality, fullness, unity. **2** (*the entirety of his fortune*) whole, total, sum total, aggregate. OPPOSITE: part.

entitle *verb* **1** (*not entitled to vote*) qualify, make eligible, authorize, sanction, empower, enable, capacitate, permit, allow, license, warrant, accredit. OPPOSITE: disqualify. **2** (*a poem entitled 'Remembrance'*) call, name, style, dub, christen, designate, denominate, term.

entity *noun* **1** (*separate entities*) thing, object, article, individual, unit, body, creature, organism, being. **2** (*the entity of the organization*) being, existence, substance, essence, quintessence, quiddity.

entomb *verb* bury, inter, inhume. OPPOSITE: exhume.

entourage *noun* **1** (*the king and his entourage*) attendants, staff, retinue, suite, train, cortege, escort, bodyguard, followers, following, companions, company. **2** (*a pleasant entourage*) surroundings, environment, milieu, ambience.

entrails *pl noun* intestines, bowels, guts (*inf*), viscera, offal, giblets, internal organs, insides (*inf*), innards (*inf*).

entrance[1] *noun* **1** (*I'll meet you at the entrance*) way in, ingress, means of access, approach, drive, driveway, threshold, door, doorway, gate, gateway, portal, porch, entrance hall, lobby, vestibule, foyer, anteroom, passage, passageway, entry, opening, inlet. OPPOSITE: exit. **2** (*gained entrance to the palace*) entry, admission, admittance, entrée, access, ingress. **3** (*before making her entrance*) appearance, arrival, introduction, debut, beginning, start. OPPOSITE: departure.

entrance[2] *verb* enrapture, charm, enchant, delight, captivate, ravish, transport, fascinate, enthral, bewitch, beguile, spellbind, hypnotize, mesmerize. OPPOSITE: repel.

entrant *noun* **1** (*entrants to the profession*) newcomer, novice, learner, beginner, starter, fresher, tyro, neophyte, cub, tenderfoot, greenhorn (*inf*), rookie (*inf*), trainee, apprentice, probationer, new member, initiate, convert **2** (*the winning entrant*) competitor, contestant, contender, entry, candidate, applicant, player, participant, rival, opponent.

entrap *verb* **1** (*entrap their prey*) catch, capture, trap, snare, ensnare, net, bag, entangle, enmesh, involve, implicate, embroil. OPPOSITE: loose. **2** (*entrapped him into confessing*) trick, deceive, lure, entice, inveigle, seduce, lead on.

entreat *verb* beg, implore, beseech, plead, crave, solicit, petition, pray, supplicate, importune, enjoin, ask, request, exhort. OPPOSITE: command.

entreaty *noun* appeal, plea, suit, petition, solicitation, prayer, supplication, invocation, cry, request, exhortation. OPPOSITE: order.

entrench *verb* **1** (*the troops entrenched themselves*) establish, fix, lodge, settle, install, ensconce, dig in (*inf*), plant, implant, embed, root. OPPOSITE: dislodge. **2** (*entrenching on her privacy*) encroach, trespass, infringe, impinge, intrude, invade, infiltrate.

entrenched *adj* established, fixed, set, deep-rooted, deep-seated, firm, unshakeable, diehard, ingrained, dyed-in-the-wool.

entrepreneur *noun* businessman, businesswoman, executive, industrialist, tycoon, magnate, financier, impresario, broker, intermediary, middleman, agent.

entrust *verb* commit, consign, hand over, make over, turn over, deliver, commend, confide, give custody of, assign, delegate, depute, invest.

entry *noun* **1** (*we were refused entry*) admission, admittance, entrance, entrée, access, ingress, right of entry, permission to enter. **2** (*blocking the entry*) entrance, way in, ingress, means of access, approach, drive, driveway, door, doorway, gate, gateway, portal, porch, entrance hall, lobby, vestibule, foyer, passage, passageway, opening, inlet. OPPOSITE: exit. **3** (*the entry of the gladiators*) appearance, arrival, entrance, introduction. OPPOSITE: departure. **4** (*an entry in her diary*) item, note, jotting, record, minute, memorandum, statement, account, listing. **5** (*another entry for the competition*) submission, effort, attempt, entrant, competitor, contestant, contender, candidate, applicant, player, participant.

entwine *verb* twine, intertwine, weave, interweave, lace, interlace, twist, wind, braid, plait, knit, splice, knot, ravel, entangle. OPPOSITE: separate.

enumerate *verb* list, name, cite, quote, detail, specify, itemize, recount, recite, relate, tell, number, count, reckon, calculate, tally, sum up, add up, total.

enumeration *noun* list, listing, catalogue, specification, itemization, recapitulation, narration, counting, reckoning, calculation.

enunciate *verb* **1** (*enunciating his vowels*) articulate, pronounce, vocalize, voice, utter, say, speak. **2** (*enunciated their demands*) state, utter, express, propound, put forward, assert, affirm, declare, proclaim, pronounce, announce, promulgate, publish, broadcast. OPPOSITE: suppress.

enunciation *noun* **1** (*the enunciation of his vowels*) articulation, pronunciation, delivery, presentation, intonation, modulation, inflection, vocalization, voicing, utterance, speech. **2** (*the enunciation of their demands*) statement, utterance, expression, assertion, affirmation, declaration, proclamation, pronouncement, announcement, promulgation, publication. OPPOSITE: suppress.

envelop *verb* wrap, enwrap, swathe, swaddle, enfold, sheathe, encase, cover, shroud, cloak, veil, blanket, obscure, hide, conceal, engulf, surround, encompass, encircle, enclose. OPPOSITE: expose.

envelope *noun* wrapper, wrapping, case, casing, sheath, skin, shell, capsule, cover, jacket, coating, covering, holder, container.

envenom *verb* **1** (*envenomed arrows*) poison, contaminate, pollute, taint. **2** (*jealousy envenomed her mind*) embitter, sour, provoke, inflame, irritate, anger, enrage, incense, madden. OPPOSITE: appease.

enviable *adj* desirable, covetable, tempting, worth having, sought-after, excellent, favoured, privileged, blessed, lucky, fortunate. OPPOSITE: unenviable.

envious *adj* covetous, desirous, jealous, green, green-eyed, green with envy, resentful, grudging, begrudging, jaundiced, discontented, dissatisfied. OPPOSITE: content.

environ *verb* encircle, surround, encompass, circumscribe, gird, ring, enclose, hem in.

environment *noun* surroundings, milieu, circumstances, conditions, element, medium, habitat, territory, domain, background, setting, context, situation, location, atmosphere, ambience, mood.

environmentalist *noun* conservationist, preservationist, green, ecologist, ecofreak (*inf*).

environs *pl noun* surroundings, vicinity, neighbourhood, locality, district, precincts, purlieus, suburbs, outskirts.

envisage *verb* visualize, imagine, picture, conceive, think of, contemplate, envision, foresee, predict, see coming, anticipate.

envoy *noun* agent, representative, delegate, deputy,

diplomat, ambassador, consul, attaché, minister, plenipotentiary, legate, emissary, messenger, courier, intermediary, go-between.

envy *verb* covet, desire, crave, be jealous of, be envious of, resent, grudge, begrudge.
> *noun* enviousness, covetousness, desire, craving, jealousy, resentment, grudge, malice, spite, discontent, dissatisfaction. OPPOSITE: contentment.

ephemeral *adj* transitory, transient, fleeting, passing, brief, momentary, short, short-lived, fugacious, evanescent, impermanent, temporary. OPPOSITE: permanent.

epic *adj* heroic, legendary, historic, impressive, ambitious, grand, lofty, elevated, exalted, great, vast, huge, large-scale, long.
> *noun* saga, narrative, story, legend, myth, long poem, epopee.

epicure *noun* gourmet, gastronome, foodie (*inf*), bon vivant, bon viveur, connoisseur, epicurean, voluptuary, sensualist, hedonist, sybarite, gourmand, glutton.

epicurean *adj* gourmet, gastronomic, voluptuous, sensual, pleasure-seeking, hedonistic, sybaritic, self-indulgent, gourmandizing, gluttonous. OPPOSITE: ascetic.

epidemic *adj* widespread, extensive, prevalent, predominant, rampant, rife, wide-ranging, sweeping, pandemic, endemic.
> *noun* **1** (a flu epidemic) outbreak, plague, scourge. **2** (an epidemic of petty theft) upsurge, increase, rise, growth, outbreak, rash, wave, spate.

epigram *noun* witticism, quip, bon mot, jeu d'esprit, pun, double entendre, saying, adage, maxim, aphorism.

epigrammatic *adj* laconic, terse, brief, short, concise, compact, succinct, pithy, sharp, pointed, incisive, pungent, piquant, witty, ironic, satirical, aphoristic. OPPOSITE: verbose.

epilogue *noun* afterword, coda, tailpiece, appendix, codicil, postscript, PS, conclusion, swan song. OPPOSITE: prologue.

episode *noun* **1** (an embarrassing episode) incident, event, occurrence, happening, occasion, circumstance, affair, business, matter, adventure, experience, interlude. **2** (the next episode of the serial) instalment, part, chapter, section, passage, scene.

episodic *adj* **1** (episodic attacks of nausea) intermittent, irregular, spasmodic, sporadic, occasional, periodic. OPPOSITE: continual. **2** (an episodic narrative) rambling, wandering, digressive, anecdotal, discursive, picaresque, disconnected, disjointed.

epistle *noun* letter, missive, communication, message, note, bulletin.

epitaph *noun* inscription, commemoration, obituary, elegy.

epithet *noun* **1** (her epithet was 'the Virgin Queen') nickname, sobriquet, name, title, appellation, designation, label, tag, description. **2** (mouthing epithets behind his back) insult, term of abuse, oath, curse, swearword, obscenity, expletive, four-letter word (*inf*).

epitome *noun* **1** (the epitome of good taste) archetype, exemplar, prototype, model, type, example,

representation, embodiment, personification, incarnation, essence, quintessence. **2** (an epitome of her writings) summary, synopsis, précis, résumé, abridgment, digest, abstract, outline, compendium, conspectus. OPPOSITE: amplification.

epitomize *verb* **1** (epitomizing the decline in standards) typify, exemplify, illustrate, embody, personify, incarnate, symbolize, represent. **2** (epitomized his life's work) summarize, synopsize, précis, abridge, shorten, contract, condense, digest, abstract, outline. OPPOSITE: amplify.

epoch *noun* age, era, period, time, date.

equable *adj* **1** (an equable temperament) placid, composed, collected, unruffled, level-headed, unexcitable, cool, unemotional, dispassionate, even-tempered, easygoing (*inf*), relaxed, laid back (*inf*), tranquil, serene, imperturbable, unflappable (*inf*). OPPOSITE: excitable. **2** (an equable climate) moderate, temperate, even, uniform, unvarying, unchanging, constant, stable, steady, regular, consistent. OPPOSITE: variable.

equal *adj* **1** (an equal sum) identical, the same, like, alike, comparable, equivalent, commensurate, proportionate, tantamount, on a par. OPPOSITE: different. **2** (an equal temperature) uniform, even, unvarying, unchanging, constant, steady, regular. OPPOSITE: varying. **3** (at equal heights) level, even, balanced, matched, symmetrical. OPPOSITE: unequal. **4** (the contestants were equal) even, evenly matched, on an equal footing, level pegging (*inf*), neck and neck (*inf*), fifty-fifty (*inf*). OPPOSITE: uneven. **5** (equal treatment) egalitarian, fair, just, impartial, unbiased, even-handed, neutral, identical, the same, like. OPPOSITE: partisan. **6** (not equal to the task) adequate, sufficient, good enough, suitable, suited, fit, competent, capable, able. OPPOSITE: inadequate.
> *noun* peer, compeer, fellow, partner, mate, match, twin, counterpart, equivalent.
> *verb* **1** (one plus two equals three) add up to, come to, amount to, total, make, be equal to. **2** (supply equals demand) correspond to, balance, match, coincide with, equate to, be equivalent to, be tantamount to. **3** (equalled the world record) match, parallel, reach, achieve, come up to, measure up to, equalize, rival, emulate.

equality *noun* **1** (equality of value) uniformity, evenness, levelness, equivalence, parity, par, symmetry, balance, proportion, parallelism, identity, sameness, correspondence, similarity, likeness, comparability. OPPOSITE: difference. **2** (treated with equality) egalitarianism, fairness, justice, impartiality, even-handedness, neutrality. OPPOSITE: inequality.

equalize *verb* make equal, level, even up, square, match, balance, regularize, standardize, smooth, even out, make uniform.

equanimity *noun* composure, self-possession, self-control, level-headedness, presence of mind, calmness, tranquillity, serenity, placidity, imperturbability, unflappability (*inf*), coolness, cool (*inf*), sangfroid, phlegm, aplomb, poise, equilibrium. OPPOSITE: agitation.

equate *verb* **1** (equate ambition with greed) compare, liken, identify, associate, pair, bracket together, connect, link. **2** (*income equating to expenditure*) equal, match, square, tally, balance, correspond, parallel, equalize.

equation *noun* comparison, identification, association, agreement, equality, identity, sameness, likeness, matching, balance, correspondence.

equestrian *noun* rider, jockey, horseman, horsewoman, knight, cavalryman, hussar, dragoon.
➤ *adj* riding, mounted, on horseback, in the saddle.

equilibrium *noun* **1** (*forces in equilibrium*) balance, stability, steadiness, stasis, equipoise, equipollence, parity, symmetry, evenness, equality. OPPOSITE: imbalance. **2** (*maintained her equilibrium throughout the crisis*) equanimity, poise, aplomb, sangfroid, coolness, cool (*inf*), composure, self-possession, self-control, level-headedness, calmness, tranquillity, imperturbability, unflappability (*inf*). OPPOSITE: anxiety.

equip *verb* supply, provide, furnish, fit out, rig out, kit out, prepare, stock, arm, endow, dress, array, attire, accoutre. OPPOSITE: divest.

equipment *noun* apparatus, tackle, rig, gear, kit, outfit, tools, supplies, belongings, effects, things, stuff, baggage, paraphernalia, accoutrements, furnishings.

equipoise *noun* balance, stability, steadiness, equilibrium, counterbalance, counterpoise, ballast, stabilizer.

equitable *adj* just, fair, even-handed, unbiased, unprejudiced, impartial, disinterested, dispassionate, objective, right, rightful, proper, reasonable. OPPOSITE: unjust.

equity *noun* justice, fairness, fair play, even-handedness, equitableness, lack of bias, lack of prejudice, impartiality, disinterestedness, objectivity, rightfulness, propriety, reasonableness, rectitude, honesty, integrity, uprightness. OPPOSITE: injustice.

equivalence *noun* parity, equality, identity, sameness, correlation, comparability, correspondence, similarity, likeness, analogy, parallel. OPPOSITE: difference.

equivalent *adj* commensurate, tantamount, on a par, comparable, correspondent, corresponding, homologous, similar, alike, the same, identical, interchangeable, substitutable, synonymous, equal, equipollent. OPPOSITE: different.
➤ *noun* equal, parallel, homologue, match, twin, double, counterpart, opposite number, peer. OPPOSITE: opposite.

equivocal *adj* **1** (*an equivocal statement*) ambiguous, ambivalent, two-edged, vague, obscure, unclear, uncertain, indefinite, hazy, oblique, evasive, roundabout, circuitous, misleading. OPPOSITE: clear. **2** (*an equivocal character*) suspicious, suspect, shady (*inf*), doubtful, dubious, questionable.

equivocate *verb* prevaricate, fence, hedge, dodge, evade, tergiversate, quibble, shuffle, shift, fudge, waffle (*inf*), flannel (*inf*), beat about the bush (*inf*), hesitate, shilly-shally, sit on the fence (*inf*), vacillate, hum and haw, chop and change (*inf*).

equivocation *noun* prevarication, fencing, hedging, dodging, evasion, tergiversation, ambiguity, vagueness, double talk, weasel words (*inf*), waffle (*inf*), flannel (*inf*), hesitation, vacillation. OPPOSITE: directness.

era *noun* age, period, epoch, aeon, time, times, day, days, date, cycle, generation, season.

eradicate *verb* annihilate, extirpate, destroy, exterminate, wipe out, obliterate, efface, erase, expunge, uproot, deracinate, root out, weed out, remove, get rid of, do away with, abolish, eliminate, stamp out, extinguish. OPPOSITE: restore.

eradication *noun* annihilation, extirpation, destruction, extermination, obliteration, effacement, erasure, expunction, deracination, removal, riddance, abolition, elimination, extinction. OPPOSITE: restoration.

erase *verb* rub out, wipe off, expunge, efface, obliterate, blot out, eradicate, remove, excise, delete, cancel, cross out, strike out. OPPOSITE: engrave.

erasure *noun* rubbing out, expunction, effacement, obliteration, eradication, removal, excision, deletion, cancellation, crossing out. OPPOSITE: inscription.

erect *verb* **1** (*erect a monument*) build, construct, put up, raise, elevate, lift, rear, set upright, stand up. OPPOSITE: demolish. **2** (*erect a bookcase*) assemble, put together, construct, build. OPPOSITE: dismantle. **3** (*erect an institution*) establish, set up, found, initiate, institute, create. OPPOSITE: abolish.
➤ *adj* **1** (*an erect pole*) upright, vertical, perpendicular, straight, standing, raised. OPPOSITE: flat. **2** (*erect nipples*) hard, firm, stiff, rigid, tumid, tumescent. OPPOSITE: flaccid.

erection *noun* **1** (*an ugly new erection in the city centre*) building, construction, structure, edifice, pile (*inf*). **2** (*the erection of a monument*) raising, elevation, building, construction, fabrication, assembly. OPPOSITE: demolition. **3** (*the erection of an institution*) establishment, setting up, foundation, initiation, institution, creation, formation. **4** (*erection of the penis*) rigidity, stiffness, tumidity, tumescence, hard-on (*sl*).

ergo *adv* therefore, hence, consequently, then, so, thus.

eristic *adj* polemic, polemical, controversial, disputative, disputatious, argumentative.

erode *verb* wear, wear away, wear down, abrade, excoriate, grind down, corrode, eat into, eat away, gnaw away at, consume, devour, destroy, disintegrate, fragment, deteriorate, weaken, undermine.

erosion *noun* wear, wearing away, attrition, abrasion, excoriation, denudation, corrosion, eating away, consumption, destruction, disintegration, deterioration.

erotic *adj* titillating, sexually stimulating, sexually arousing, erogenous, aphrodisiac, sexy (*inf*), sensual, voluptuous, carnal, amatory, amorous, seductive, suggestive, pornographic, adult, dirty (*inf*), steamy (*inf*).

err *verb* **1** (*erred in my assessment of the situation*) be wrong, be incorrect, be in error, make a mistake, slip up (*inf*), blunder, boob (*inf*), miscalculate, misjudge, misunderstand, misconstrue, get hold of the wrong end of the stick (*inf*), bark up the wrong tree (*inf*). **2** (*God forgives those who err*) sin, transgress, do wrong, misbehave, go astray, lapse, fall from grace, wander, stray, deviate.

errand *noun* commission, mission, assignment, task, job, charge, undertaking, chore, message.

errant *adj* **1** (*her errant husband*) erring, wrong, incorrect, misbehaving, delinquent, sinful, peccant, straying, deviant, aberrant, wayward. **2** (*errant minstrels*) wandering, roving, roaming, rambling, travelling, itinerant, peripatetic, nomadic.

erratic *adj* changeable, variable, irregular, inconsistent, fitful, sporadic, unstable, volatile, unreliable, unpredictable, capricious, whimsical, eccentric, abnormal, aberrant, deviant, wayward, desultory, wandering, meandering. OPPOSITE: steady.

erratum *noun* error, mistake, misprint, literal, typo (*inf*), corrigendum, correction, amendment, omission.

erring *adj* errant, wrong, sinning, transgressing, offending, misbehaving, delinquent, criminal, lawless, straying, deviant.

erroneous *adj* wrong, incorrect, mistaken, untrue, false, inexact, inaccurate, unfounded, unsound, faulty, flawed, fallacious, spurious, specious. OPPOSITE: right.

error *noun* **1** (*the text is full of errors*) mistake, inaccuracy, miscalculation, slip, slip-up (*inf*), blunder, gaffe, boob (*inf*), booboo (*inf*), cock-up (*sl*), balls-up (*sl*), misprint, literal, typo (*inf*), solecism, howler (*inf*), erratum, corrigendum, oversight, omission, misapprehension, misjudgment, misunderstanding, misconception, fault, flaw, fallacy. **2** (*the error of her ways*) wrong, wrongdoing, misdeed, offence, transgression, trespass, sin, fault, crime, delinquency, misbehaviour, misconduct.

ersatz *adj* substitute, imitation, simulated, artificial, synthetic, man-made, fake, counterfeit, sham, bogus, phoney (*inf*), pretend, pseudo (*inf*), false, spurious. OPPOSITE: genuine.

erudite *adj* learned, scholarly, academic, knowledgeable, well-read, educated, literate, lettered, cultivated, cultured, refined, intellectual, highbrow. OPPOSITE: illiterate.

erudition *noun* learning, scholarship, knowledge, lore, education, literacy, letters, cultivation, culture, refinement. OPPOSITE: illiteracy.

erupt *verb* **1** (*the volcano erupted*) explode, blow up, burst open. **2** (*lava erupted from the volcano*) pour forth, gush, spout, spew, belch, be ejected, be emitted, be expelled, be discharged. **3** (*violence may erupt*) burst forth, break out, flare up, explode, blow up, go off.

eruption *noun* **1** (*the eruption of the volcano*) explosion, blowing up. **2** (*the eruption of lava*) ejection, emission, expulsion, discharge. **3** (*the eruption of violence*) outburst, outbreak, flare-up, explosion. **4** (*an eruption on the face*) rash, inflammation, spots, pimples.

escalate *verb* increase, grow, mushroom, snowball, expand, be magnified, be amplified, intensify, heighten, accelerate, be stepped up, rise, mount, climb, soar, spiral, rocket (*inf*), go through the roof (*inf*). OPPOSITE: diminish.

escapade *noun* adventure, exploit, scrape (*inf*), prank, frolic, caper, stunt, trick, antics, shenanigans (*inf*), romp, lark (*inf*), spree.

escape *verb* **1** (*escape from prison*) get away, break out, break free, flee, fly, fly the coop (*inf*), run away, run off, bolt, skedaddle (*inf*), scarper (*inf*), steal away, decamp, abscond, do a bunk (*inf*), do a runner (*inf*), make one's escape, make one's getaway. OPPOSITE: stay. **2** (*escape detection*) avoid, evade, dodge, sidestep, circumvent, steer clear of, shirk, duck (*inf*), elude, shake off, give the slip to. OPPOSITE: face. **3** (*gas escaped through the crack*) leak, seep, ooze, trickle, issue, discharge, flow, gush, spurt, drain.
➤ *noun* **1** (*escape from prison*) getaway, breakout, flight, bolt, decampment, absconding. **2** (*escape from detection*) avoidance, evasion, dodging, sidestepping, circumvention, shirking, ducking (*inf*), elusion. **3** (*a gas escape*) leak, leakage, seepage, discharge, emission, emanation, outflow, gush, spurt. **4** (*took up painting as a form of escape*) escapism, getting away from it all (*inf*), recreation, leisure, relaxation, diversion, distraction, pastime.

escapee *noun* fugitive, runaway, jailbreaker, absconder, deserter, defector, truant, refugee. OPPOSITE: captive.

escapism *noun* fantasy, dreaming, daydreaming, woolgathering, wishful thinking, escape, getting away from it all (*inf*), recreation, diversion, distraction. OPPOSITE: realism.

eschew *verb* shun, avoid, abstain from, forgo, refrain from, shrink from, steer clear of, give a wide berth to, renounce, abjure, forswear, give up, kick (*inf*), pack in (*inf*). OPPOSITE: embrace.

escort *noun* **1** (*her escort for the ball*) partner, companion, date (*inf*), beau, squire, gigolo. **2** (*the prisoner and his escort*) chaperon, attendant, guide, protector, guard, bodyguard. **3** (*a police escort*) cortège, retinue, train, entourage, convoy, company, guard, protection, defence.
➤ *verb* accompany, conduct, usher, shepherd, guide, lead, take, see, go with, partner, attend, chaperon, protect, guard, defend.

escutcheon *noun* shield, scutcheon, coat of arms, arms.

esoteric *adj* abstruse, recondite, arcane, occult, mystic, magical, cryptic, obscure, hidden, arcane, private, secret, inscrutable, unfathomable, incomprehensible, mysterious, enigmatic. OPPOSITE: exoteric.

especial *adj* **1** (*with especial care*) special, exceptional, extraordinary, unusual, uncommon, outstanding, notable, noteworthy, striking, remarkable, distinguished, eminent, marked, signal. OPPOSITE: ordinary. **2** (*my especial preference*) particular, individual, personal, own, specific, express, exclusive, distinctive, unique, singular, peculiar. OPPOSITE: general.

especially *adv* **1** (*especially difficult*) exceptionally, extraordinarily, unusually, uncommonly, notably, remarkably, eminently, markedly, signally, particularly, very, extremely. **2** (*especially when it rains*) particularly, in particular, above all, chiefly, mainly, principally, primarily. **3** (*especially for you*) specially, specifically, expressly, exclusively, uniquely.

espionage *noun* spying, intelligence, counterintelligence, counterespionage, secret service, undercover work, infiltration, reconnaissance, snooping (*inf*), surveillance, bugging (*inf*).

espousal *noun* adoption, embracing, support, backing,

maintenance, defence, championship, advocacy, promotion. OPPOSITE: rejection.

espouse *verb* adopt, embrace, take up, support, back, uphold, maintain, defend, champion, advocate, promote. OPPOSITE: reject.

espy *verb* spot, catch sight of, glimpse, spy, see, behold, observe, notice, perceive, descry, make out, discern, distinguish, detect. OPPOSITE: miss.

essay *noun* **1** (*write an essay*) composition, dissertation, thesis, treatise, paper, article, piece (*inf*), discourse, tract, commentary, critique. **2** (*make an essay*) attempt, try, endeavour, effort, bid, go, stab (*inf*), shot (*inf*), venture, experiment, test, trial.
» *verb* attempt, endeavour, try, have a go at, have a crack at (*inf*), have a bash at (*inf*), strive, seek, venture, undertake, tackle, take on.

essence *noun* **1** (*the essence of the individual*) nature, character, entity, being, quintessence, quiddity, substance, heart, core, kernel, marrow, spirit, soul, life, reality, actuality. **2** (*the essence of their argument*) crux, substance, pith, gist, significance, meaning, point, principle. **3** (*vanilla essence*) concentrate, extract, distillate, spirits, tincture, elixir.
in essence essentially, basically, fundamentally, in effect, to all intents and purposes, in the main, virtually.
of the essence crucial, essential, vital, indispensable, of the utmost importance.

essential *adj* **1** (*essential supplies*) vital, indispensable, necessary, requisite, required, needed, crucial, important. OPPOSITE: dispensable. **2** (*its essential character*) basic, fundamental, inherent, intrinsic, innate, elemental, principal, main, key, cardinal. OPPOSITE: incidental.
» *noun* necessity, requisite, prerequisite, must (*inf*), basic, fundamental, rudiment, sine qua non.

establish *verb* **1** (*establish a company*) found, start, begin, institute, set up, form, create, inaugurate, organize, build, construct. OPPOSITE: destroy.
2 (*established themselves in power*) settle, install, entrench, ensconce, lodge, secure, fix, plant. OPPOSITE: uproot. **3** (*establish our innocence*) prove, verify, confirm, substantiate, corroborate, support, show, demonstrate, validate, authenticate, certify, ratify. OPPOSITE: refute.

established *adj* accepted, official, conventional, traditional, orthodox, proven, tried and tested, settled, fixed.

establishment *noun* **1** (*the establishment of the club*) foundation, institution, setting up, formation, creation, inception, inauguration, organization, construction. OPPOSITE: destruction. **2** (*a profitable establishment*) business, concern, enterprise, company, firm, corporation, house, emporium, organization, institute, institution. **3** (*a private establishment*) household, house, home, abode, dwelling, domicile, residence. **4** (*rebelling against the Establishment*) authorities, powers that be, system, ruling class, bureaucracy, officialdom.

estate *noun* **1** (*an industrial estate*) development, area, region, tract, piece of land, park, centre. **2** (*a tour of the duke's estate*) land, lands, property, demesne, manor. **3** (*her estate was divided between her children*) property, assets, effects, belongings, possessions, holdings, wealth,

fortune. **4** (*people of low estate*) status, standing, position, station, condition, rank, class.

esteem *verb* **1** (*esteemed for her wisdom*) respect, admire, think highly of, look up to, honour, revere, venerate, value, prize, treasure, hold dear, cherish, love, like, appreciate, approve of. OPPOSITE: scorn. **2** (*I would esteem it an honour*) deem, regard, consider, judge, adjudge, think, believe, hold, estimate, rate, reckon, count, account.
» *noun* respect, admiration, estimation, regard, consideration, honour, deference, reverence, veneration, appreciation, approval, approbation, favour. OPPOSITE: contempt.

estimable *adj* admirable, respected, esteemed, valued, honourable, distinguished, worthy, meritorious, deserving, commendable, praiseworthy, creditable, good, excellent. OPPOSITE: despicable.

estimate *verb* reckon, gauge, assess, evaluate, value, appraise, rate, rank, judge, think, believe, guess, conjecture, surmise.
» *noun* **1** (*an estimate of the cost*) reckoning, rough calculation, approximation, educated guess, guesstimate (*inf*), assessment, evaluation, valuation, appraisal, judgment, guess, conjecture, surmise. **2** (*in my estimate he is the best*) judgment, opinion, view, belief, estimation, consideration, reckoning, thinking.

estimation *noun* **1** (*your estimation of the situation*) judgment, opinion, view, belief, estimate, evaluation, assessment, reckoning. **2** (*she went up in my estimation*) esteem, respect, admiration, regard, consideration, honour, reverence, appreciation, approval, favour. OPPOSITE: contempt.

estrange *verb* alienate, disaffect, separate, part, split up, divorce, divide, disunite, set apart, drive apart, drive a wedge between (*inf*), antagonize, set against, set at odds. OPPOSITE: reconcile.

estrangement *noun* alienation, disaffection, separation, parting, split, breach, divorce, breakup, division, disunity, antagonism, antipathy, hostility.

estuary *noun* inlet, mouth, arm, firth, fjord, creek, cove, bay.

et cetera *adv* and so on, and so forth, and the rest, and the like, and what have you (*inf*).

etch *verb* engrave, carve, cut, incise, inscribe, burn, corrode, eat into, stamp, impress, imprint, ingrain, infix. OPPOSITE: erase.

etching *noun* engraving, cut, print, impression, stamp, imprint, carving, inscription.

eternal *adj* **1** (*eternal life*) everlasting, immortal, deathless, undying, imperishable, indestructible, enduring, abiding, timeless, unchanging, immutable, infinite, unending, never-ending, endless. OPPOSITE: ephemeral. **2** (*eternal arguments*) interminable, incessant, ceaseless, nonstop, never-ending, endless, continuous, constant, perpetual, continual, unremitting. OPPOSITE: intermittent.

eternally *adv* **1** (*eternally grateful*) everlastingly, immortally, for ever, for all time, evermore, infinitely, endlessly. OPPOSITE: temporarily. **2** (*eternally arguing*) always, forever, morning noon and night (*inf*), interminably, incessantly, ceaselessly, endlessly, continuously, constantly, perpetually, continually. OPPOSITE: intermittently.

eternity *noun* **1** (*preserved for all eternity*) perpetuity, infinity, evermore. **2** (*belief in eternity*) immortality, imperishability, indestructibility, timelessness, endlessness, world without end, afterlife, life after death, hereafter, next world, heaven, paradise. **3** (*waited an eternity*) age, ages, long time, donkey's years.

ethereal *adj* **1** (*ethereal beauty*) light, airy, impalpable, delicate, fragile, dainty, insubstantial, fine, diaphanous, tenuous, subtle, rarefied. OPPOSITE: solid. **2** (*ethereal music*) heavenly, celestial, empyreal, unearthly, other-worldly, spiritual, paradisiacal, elysian. OPPOSITE: earthly.

ethical *adj* moral, right, correct, proper, seemly, decent, just, fair, righteous, good, virtuous, honest, upright, conscientious, honourable, high-minded, principled. OPPOSITE: unethical.

ethics *pl noun* morals, morality, moral code, standards, principles, scruples.

ethnic *adj* racial, native, indigenous, autochthonous, national, tribal, cultural, traditional, folk.

ethos *noun* beliefs, attitudes, principles, standards, ethics, code, spirit, character, tenor.

etiolated *adj* bleached, blanched, whitened, white, chalky, colourless, achromatic, pale, wan, faded, washed out.

etiquette *noun* propriety, decorum, manners, politeness, courtesy, civility, code of conduct, protocol, form, formality, ceremony, convention, code of practice, usage, custom. OPPOSITE: impropriety.

etymology *noun* origin, derivation, source, word history.

Eucharist *noun* Communion, Lord's Supper, Mass.

eulogize *verb* praise, praise to the skies, extol, laud, panegyrize, wax lyrical about, rave about (*inf*), hype (*inf*), exalt, glorify, acclaim, applaud, pay tribute to, commend, compliment. OPPOSITE: censure.

eulogy *noun* panegyric, encomium, paean, accolade, plaudit, bouquet, compliment, praise, extolment, laudation, exaltation, glorification, acclaim, acclamation, applause, tribute, commendation. OPPOSITE: obloquy.

euphemism *noun* polite term, inoffensive expression, genteelism, hypocorism, understatement, substitute.

euphemistic *adj* polite, inoffensive, genteel, hypocoristic, vague, indirect, neutral.

euphonious *adj* euphonic, melodious, tuneful, harmonious, symphonious, musical, dulcet, canorous, mellifluous, mellow, sweet, soft, clear, silvery. OPPOSITE: cacophonous.

euphony *noun* melody, tunefulness, harmony, music, sweetness, softness, smoothness, mellowness. OPPOSITE: harshness.

euphoria *noun* ecstasy, bliss, elation, joy, glee, jubilation, exultation, rapture, transport, exhilaration, intoxication, exaltation, high (*inf*). OPPOSITE: despondency.

euphoric *noun* ecstatic, blissful, elated, joyful, gleeful, in seventh heaven (*inf*), on cloud nine (*inf*), overjoyed,

thrilled, over the moon (*inf*), jubilant, exultant, enraptured, exhilarated, intoxicated, high (*inf*). OPPOSITE: despondent.

evacuate *verb* **1** (*evacuated their homes*) leave, depart from, quit, withdraw from, move out of, flee, vacate, clear, empty, abandon, desert, forsake. OPPOSITE: occupy. **2** (*evacuate waste from the body*) empty, void, purge, eject, expel, discharge, eliminate, excrete, defecate, urinate.

evacuation *noun* **1** (*the evacuation of the village*) departure, exodus, withdrawal, retreat, flight, vacating, clearance, emptying, abandonment, desertion. OPPOSITE: occupation. **2** (*the evacuation of waste*) voidance, purging, ejection, expulsion, discharge, elimination, excretion, defecation, urination.

evade *noun* **1** (*evading his responsibilities*) avoid, escape, get away from, elude, dodge, duck (*inf*), shirk, get out of (*inf*), circumvent, sidestep, get round (*inf*), shun, steer clear of. OPPOSITE: face. **2** (*evade the question*) quibble, prevaricate, equivocate, tergiversate, beat about the bush (*inf*), fence, hedge, avoid, fend off, parry.

evaluate *noun* appraise, assess, value, estimate, gauge, weigh, size up, judge, rate, calculate, compute, reckon, measure, determine.

evaluation *noun* appraisal, assessment, valuation, estimate, judgment, calculation, reckoning, measurement.

evanesce *verb* fade, dissipate, disperse, evaporate, dissolve, melt, disappear, vanish. OPPOSITE: appear.

evanescent *adj* fading, disappearing, vanishing, brief, short-lived, ephemeral, momentary, fleeting, fugitive, passing, transient, transitory. OPPOSITE: permanent.

evangelical *adj* **1** (*evangelical doctrine*) biblical, scriptural, canonical, orthodox. **2** (*evangelical preachers*) evangelistic, missionary, crusading, campaigning, converting, reforming, enthusiastic, zealous, Bible-bashing (*inf*), Bible-thumping (*inf*).

evangelist *noun* preacher, gospeller, missionary, crusader, reformer, revivalist, propagandist, Bible-basher (*inf*), Bible-thumper (*inf*).

evangelize *verb* preach, spread the word, crusade, campaign, convert, proselytize, reform.

evaporate *verb* **1** (*water evaporates*) vaporize, dry, dry up, dehydrate, desiccate. OPPOSITE: condense. **2** (*their hopes evaporated*) disappear, vanish, dematerialize, fade, evanesce, dissolve, melt away, dissipate, disperse. OPPOSITE: materialize.

evaporation *noun* **1** (*the evaporation of water*) vaporization, drying, drying up, dehydration, desiccation. OPPOSITE: condensation. **2** (*the evaporation of their hopes*) disappearance, vanishing, dematerialization, fading, evanescence, dissipation, dispersion. OPPOSITE: materialization.

evasion *noun* **1** (*evasion of responsibilities*) avoidance, escape, dodging, shirking, circumvention, sidestepping. **2** (*a reply full of evasion*) quibbling, prevarication, equivocation, tergiversation, fencing, hedging, flannel (*inf*), waffle (*inf*), sophistry, trickery, deception, subterfuge.

evasive *adj* **1** (*an evasive reply*) quibbling, prevaricating, equivocating, indirect, oblique, roundabout, circuitous, devious, misleading, deceptive, deceitful, tricky, slippery (*inf*), unforthcoming, cagey (*inf*). OPPOSITE: straightforward. **2** (*evasive tactics*) avoiding, escaping, elusive, dodging, sidestepping.

eve *noun* day before, night before, time before, threshold, brink, verge.

even *adj* **1** (*even ground*) level, flat, horizontal, plane, flush, smooth, uniform, equal, parallel, square, aligned. OPPOSITE: uneven. **2** (*an even temperature*) uniform, consistent, regular, stable, steady, constant, unvarying, unchanging, equable. OPPOSITE: variable. **3** (*an even chance*) same, identical, equal, similar, like, comparable, equivalent, symmetrical, balanced. OPPOSITE: unequal. **4** (*an even contest*) equal, evenly matched, level, level pegging, abreast, neck and neck, drawn, tied. **5** (*an even disposition*) calm, placid, serene, tranquil, well-balanced, even-tempered, cool, composed, unruffled, imperturbable, unflappable (*inf*). OPPOSITE: nervous.
≫ *adv* **1** (*even less enthusiastic*) yet, still, all the more, to a greater degree. **2** (*even as I speak*) just, exactly, precisely, at the same time, at the very moment. **3** (*it may be unpleasant, even painful*) indeed, more exactly, more precisely. **4** (*she didn't even apologize*) so much as, at all.
≫ *verb* level, flatten, plane, smooth, square, align, balance, equalize, regularize, standardize.

even so nevertheless, nonetheless, all the same, yet, still, notwithstanding that, in spite of that.

even-handed *adj* fair, just, equitable, balanced, impartial, unbiased, unprejudiced, neutral, dispassionate, disinterested. OPPOSITE: unfair.

evening *noun* dusk, twilight, sunset, sundown, night, nightfall, close of day, eve, eventide. OPPOSITE: morning.

event *verb* **1** (*the events of the day*) happening, occurrence, incident, affair, business, matter, occasion, episode, circumstance, fact, phenomenon. **2** (*track and field events*) contest, competition, fixture, meeting, engagement, race, game. **3** (*in the event of failure*) case, contingency, eventuality, possibility.

in any event come what may, whatever happens, regardless, irrespective, at all events, at any rate, in any case, anyway, anyhow.

eventful *adj* busy, action-packed (*inf*), lively, full, memorable, notable, remarkable, signal, momentous, significant, important, historic, crucial, critical, decisive. OPPOSITE: uneventful.

eventual *adj* final, ultimate, closing, concluding, consequent, resulting, ensuing, subsequent, prospective, future, impending, inevitable.

eventuality *noun* contingency, event, occurrence, happening, case, chance, likelihood, possibility, probability, emergency, crisis.

eventually *adv* finally, ultimately, at last, in the end, in the long run, in the fullness of time, at the end of the day, sooner or later, sometime.

eventuate *verb* result, end, follow, ensue, happen, occur, come about, take place. OPPOSITE: begin.

ever *adv* **1** (*ever complaining*) always, at all times, continually, perpetually, continuously, constantly, incessantly, endlessly, forever, eternally, evermore, to the end of time, till doomsday, till the cows come home

(*inf*). OPPOSITE: never. **2** (*have you ever been there?*) at any time, on any occasion, in any circumstances, by any chance, at all. **3** (*as happy as ever*) before, until now.

ever so very, extremely, really.

everlasting *adj* **1** (*everlasting love*) eternal, immortal, deathless, undying, imperishable, indestructible, enduring, abiding, timeless, unchanging, immutable, infinite, unending, never-ending, endless. OPPOSITE: ephemeral. **2** (*everlasting complaints*) interminable, incessant, ceaseless, nonstop, never-ending, endless, continuous, constant, perpetual, continual, unremitting. OPPOSITE: intermittent.

evermore *adv* always, ever, for ever, for all time, till the end of time, eternally, perpetually, ceaselessly, endlessly.

every *adj* each, every single, all, all possible. OPPOSITE: no.

everyday *adj* ordinary, common, commonplace, usual, familiar, habitual, routine, day-to-day, daily, quotidian, regular, accustomed, customary, conventional, stock, standard, plain, mundane, workaday, run-of-the-mill. OPPOSITE: unusual.

everyone *pronoun* everybody, all, one and all, all and sundry, every Tom Dick and Harry (*inf*), every man jack (*inf*), the whole world, all the world and his wife (*inf*). OPPOSITE: nobody.

everything *pronoun* all the lot, the whole lot, the whole shooting match (*inf*), the whole shebang (*inf*), the works (*inf*). OPPOSITE: nothing.

everywhere *adv* all around, all over, the world over, throughout, near and far, far and wide, high and low, left right and centre (*inf*). OPPOSITE: nowhere.

evict *noun* expel, eject, turn out, turn out of house and home (*inf*), throw out, throw out on the streets (*inf*), throw out on their ear (*inf*), chuck out (*inf*), turf out (*inf*), kick out (*inf*), show the door (*inf*), give the bum's rush to (*inf*), remove, oust, dislodge, dispossess. OPPOSITE: house.

evidence *noun* **1** (*produce evidence of his adultery*) proof, verification, confirmation, substantiation, corroboration, documentation, data, grounds, support. **2** (*evidence given in court*) testimony, deposition, attestation, declaration, statement, affidavit. **3** (*there was evidence of a break-in*) indication, sign, token, mark, trace, demonstration, manifestation.
≫ *verb* evince, indicate, show, demonstrate, manifest, display, exhibit, denote, signify.

in evidence evident, obvious, conspicuous, visible, noticeable.

evident *adj* apparent, plain, clear, obvious, patent, visible, palpable, tangible, perceptible, manifest, conspicuous, noticeable, unmistakable, indisputable, incontrovertible, incontestable.

evidently *adv* **1** (*evidently she doesn't mind*) apparently, seemingly, it seems, it appears, to all appearances, outwardly, ostensibly. **2** (*they were evidently distressed*) plainly, clearly, obviously, patently, visibly, perceptibly, manifestly, conspicuously, noticeably, unmistakably, indisputably.

evil *adj* **1** (*his evil master*) wicked, villainous, bad, wrong, sinful, iniquitous, base, vile, immoral, corrupt, depraved, vicious, malevolent, malignant, malicious,

nefarious, heinous, atrocious. OPPOSITE: virtuous. **2** (*evil spirits*) devilish, demonic, diabolic. OPPOSITE: good.
3 (*evil effects*) harmful, hurtful, injurious, detrimental, deleterious, pernicious, baleful, baneful, noxious, bad, mischievous, destructive, ruinous. OPPOSITE: beneficial.
4 (*an evil smell*) foul, vile, offensive, noisome, unpleasant, disagreeable, nasty, horrible. OPPOSITE: pleasant. **5** (*evil times*) disastrous, calamitous, catastrophic, dire, ill, adverse, unfortunate, unlucky, unpropitious, inauspicious. OPPOSITE: lucky.
➤ *noun* **1** (*the struggle between good and evil*) bad, badness, wrong, sin, iniquity, vice, immorality, corruption, depravity, baseness, vileness, wickedness, villainy, malevolence, maleficence. OPPOSITE: good.
2 (*social evils*) harm, hurt, injury, ill, bane, mischief, adversity, misfortune, pain, affliction, suffering, sorrow, misery, woe, ruin, disaster, calamity, catastrophe. OPPOSITE: benefit.

evince *verb* evidence, indicate, show, reveal, demonstrate, manifest, display, exhibit, denote, signify, betoken. OPPOSITE: conceal.

eviscerate *verb* disembowel, exenterate, gut, draw.

evocative *adj* suggestive, expressive, reminiscent, redolent.

evoke *verb* summon, call, call forth, conjure up, invoke, raise, stir, awaken, rouse, provoke, stimulate, excite, kindle, elicit, educe, recall, reawaken, rekindle. OPPOSITE: suppress.

evolution *noun* development, unfolding, progression, maturation, ripening, growth, increase, expansion, elaboration, derivation, descent, natural selection, Darwinism. OPPOSITE: retrogression.

evolve *verb* develop, unfold, unroll, progress, mature, ripen, grow, increase, expand, elaborate, result, emerge, derive, descend. OPPOSITE: retrogress.

exacerbate *verb* aggravate, make worse, worsen, intensify, inflame, irritate, provoke, infuriate, exasperate, enrage, madden, add fuel to the fire (*inf*), fan the flames (*inf*), add insult to injury (*inf*), rub salt in the wound (*inf*). OPPOSITE: soothe.

exacerbation *noun* aggravation, intensification, irritation, provocation, infuriation, exasperation. OPPOSITE: appeasement.

exact *adj* **1** (*the exact figure*) precise, accurate, spot on (*inf*), on the nail (*inf*), right, correct, faultless, unerring, true, faithful, literal, strict, rigid, specific, explicit, express, definite. OPPOSITE: inaccurate. **2** (*very exact in her habits*) careful, meticulous, scrupulous, punctilious, particular, conscientious, painstaking, methodical, orderly, rigorous, severe. OPPOSITE: slapdash.
➤ *verb* extort, extract, wring, wrest, force, compel, impose, levy, claim, demand, require, insist on, call for, elicit, request.

exacting *adj* difficult, hard, arduous, onerous, demanding, challenging, taxing, rigorous, stringent, strict, severe, harsh, stern, tough, firm, imperious, unsparing. OPPOSITE: easy.

exaction *noun* extortion, extraction, imposition, levy, demand, requisition.

exactitude *noun* exactness, precision, accuracy, correctness, faultlessness, faithfulness, fidelity,

strictness, rigour, scrupulousness, meticulousness, care, pains, perfectionism. OPPOSITE: inexactitude.

exactly *adv* precisely, accurately, spot on (*inf*), on the dot (*inf*), correctly, faultlessly, faithfully, literally, to the letter, word for word, strictly, rigidly, specifically, explicitly, absolutely, just, in every respect, to a T (*inf*).
➤ *interj* quite, quite so, just so, absolutely, indeed, precisely, truly, certainly, definitely, of course.

exaggerate *verb* overstate, hyperbolize, inflate, magnify, blow up out of all proportion (*inf*), amplify, aggrandize, stretch, embroider, embellish, colour, overdo, lay it on with a trowel (*inf*), emphasize, stress, overemphasize, overstress, overestimate, make a mountain out of a molehill (*inf*). OPPOSITE: understate.

exaggerated *adj* overstated, hyperbolic, inflated, overdone, excessive, extravagant, pretentious, bombastic, theatrical. OPPOSITE: understated.

exaggeration *noun* overstatement, hyperbole, inflation, magnification, amplification, aggrandizement, embroidery, embellishment, overemphasis, overestimation, excess, extravagance, pretentiousness. OPPOSITE: understatement.

exalt *verb* **1** (*exalt him to the peerage*) elevate, raise, upgrade, promote, advance, aggrandize, ennoble, dignify, honour. OPPOSITE: downgrade. **2** (*exalt her achievements*) praise, laud, extol, glorify, magnify, worship, revere, acclaim, applaud, commend. OPPOSITE: disparage. **3** (*exalt the imagination*) excite, stimulate, inspire, animate, exhilarate, thrill, elate, uplift. OPPOSITE: depress.

exaltation *noun* **1** (*exaltation to the peerage*) elevation, promotion, advancement, aggrandizement, ennoblement. OPPOSITE: demotion. **2** (*the exaltation of his position*) loftiness, eminence, prestige, grandeur, dignity, honour. OPPOSITE: lowliness. **3** (*the exaltation of her achievements*) praise, laudation, extolment, eulogy, glorification, magnification, worship, reverence, homage, tribute, acclaim, acclamation, applause, plaudits. OPPOSITE: disparagement. **4** (*the exaltation of the imagination*) stimulation, inspiration, animation, exhilaration. **5** (*filled with exaltation*) excitement, animation, exhilaration, elation, joy, rapture, jubilation, exultation.

exalted *adj* **1** (*an exalted position*) elevated, high, lofty, eminent, prestigious, grand, dignified, noble, lordly. OPPOSITE: lowly. **2** (*their exalted mood*) excited, animated, exhilarated, elated, happy, joyful, blissful, ecstatic, euphoric, jubilant, exultant. OPPOSITE: depressed.

examination *noun* **1** (*examination of the evidence*) inspection, scrutiny, observation, study, perusal, analysis, survey, research, investigation, exploration, probe, review, assessment, audit, check-up, once-over (*inf*). **2** (*the examination of witnesses*) questioning, interrogation, cross-examination, third degree (*inf*).
3 (*pass an examination*) exam, test, paper, practical, oral, viva, quiz.

examine *verb* **1** (*examine the evidence*) look at, scrutinize, observe, scan, study, peruse, pore over, analyse, inspect, vet, check, survey, research, investigate, look into, explore, probe, sift, review, consider, weigh up, assess, audit. OPPOSITE: disregard. **2** (*examine the* *witness*) question, interrogate, cross-examine, pump (*inf*), grill (*inf*), quiz, test.

example *noun* **1** (*an example of usage*) sample, specimen, illustration, exemplification, instance, case, precedent, exemplar, paradigm. **2** (*she is an example to us all*) ideal, paragon, model, pattern, standard, criterion. **3** (*as an example to discourage others*) warning, caution, admonition, lesson.
for example for instance, say, e.g., by way of illustration.

exasperate *verb* anger, incense, infuriate, enrage, madden, make someone's blood boil (*inf*), vex, irk, nettle, needle (*inf*), bug (*inf*), get to (*inf*), annoy, irritate, provoke, goad, wind up (*inf*). OPPOSITE: appease.

exasperation *noun* anger, fury, rage, vexation, annoyance, irritation, provocation. OPPOSITE: appeasement.

excavate *verb* dig, delve, burrow, tunnel, scoop, gouge, hollow, hollow out, dig out, quarry, mine, cut out, dig up, unearth, disinter, exhume, uncover, reveal.

excavation *noun* hole, cavity, trench, trough, hollow, crater, pit, quarry, mine, burrow, tunnel, dugout, cutting, dig.

exceed *verb* surpass, outstrip, outdo, beat, better, outclass, transcend, surmount, outshine, eclipse, overshadow, cap, top, pass, go beyond, go over, overstep.

exceedingly *adv* very, extremely, especially, inordinately, exceptionally, extraordinarily, greatly, highly, supremely, vastly, enormously, hugely, tremendously. OPPOSITE: slightly.

excel *verb* **1** (*she excelled at athletics*) shine, lead, predominate, be outstanding, be talented, be skilful, be proficient, succeed. **2** (*the chef has excelled himself*) surpass, outdo, beat, better, outclass, transcend, outshine, eclipse, overshadow, cap, top.

excellent *adj* superior, first rate, first-class, A1 (*inf*), top-notch (*inf*), exceptional, outstanding, superlative, superb, prime, choice, select, supreme, matchless, sterling, fine, admirable, estimable, worthy, eminent, distinguished, great, splendid, brilliant, wonderful, marvellous, super (*inf*), ace (*inf*), brill (*inf*), smashing (*inf*), terrific (*inf*), fantastic (*inf*), mega (*sl*), wicked (*sl*). OPPOSITE: inferior.

except *prep* but, excepting, with the exception of, save, saving, other than, apart from, besides, excluding, bar, barring. OPPOSITE: including.
» *verb* omit, exclude, leave out, pass over, reject, bar, ban, rule out. OPPOSITE: include.

exception *noun* **1** (*without exception*) omission, exclusion, rejection, debarment. OPPOSITE: inclusion.
2 (*the exception proves the rule*) anomaly, oddity, odd one out, freak, quirk, irregularity, peculiarity, special case. OPPOSITE: rule.
take exception object, demur, disagree, be offended, take offence, take umbrage.

exceptionable *adj* objectionable, unpleasant, disagreeable, offensive, obnoxious, disgusting, repugnant. OPPOSITE: acceptable.

exceptional *adj* **1** (*an exceptional occurrence*) abnormal,

anomalous, aberrant, deviant, irregular, special, unusual, rare, uncommon, atypical, out of the ordinary, odd, strange, peculiar, singular. OPPOSITE: normal.
2 (*with exceptional skill*) outstanding, remarkable, extraordinary, excellent, prodigious, phenomenal, superior, above average. OPPOSITE: average.

excerpt *noun* extract, passage, quotation, citation, selection, pericope, section, part, fragment, piece, clip, snippet.
» *verb* extract, take, quote, cite, select, pick out.

excess *noun* **1** (*an excess of zeal*) surfeit, overabundance, superabundance, glut, plethora, profusion, surplus, superfluity, overkill. OPPOSITE: dearth. **2** (*trim off the excess*) remainder, balance, residue, leftovers, overflow, backlog. **3** (*a life of excess*) immoderation, intemperance, overindulgence, unrestraint, extravagance, dissipation, debauchery, dissoluteness. OPPOSITE: restraint.
» *adj* extra, additional, surplus, superfluous, redundant, supernumerary, spare, residual, leftover. OPPOSITE: insufficient.

excessive *adj* extreme, immoderate, inordinate, undue, disproportionate, unreasonable, unwarranted, uncalled-for, unnecessary, needless, superfluous, superabundant, extravagant, exorbitant, steep (*inf*), too much, overmuch, over the top (*inf*), OTT (*inf*). OPPOSITE: moderate.

exchange *verb* trade, barter, swap, change, interchange, commute, transpose, switch, substitute, replace, reciprocate, bandy.
» *noun* **1** (*receive food in exchange for vouchers*) trade, traffic, barter, swap, substitution, replacement. **2** (*the exchange of ideas*) trading, swapping, interchange, commutation, transposition, switch, reciprocation. **3** (*a brief exchange with the manager*) conversation, chat, discussion, argument. **4** (*the corn exchange*) market, fair.

excise[1] *noun* (*pay excise on the goods*) duty, tax, levy, tariff, toll, impost, customs.

excise[2] *verb* (*excise offensive material*) cut out, remove, extract, delete, cross out, blue-pencil, expurgate, bowdlerize, expunge, erase, eradicate, eliminate. OPPOSITE: replace.

excitable *adj* volatile, mercurial, nervous, highly-strung, emotional, sensitive, passionate, fiery, temperamental, choleric, quick-tempered, hot-tempered, irascible, touchy, edgy (*inf*). OPPOSITE: imperturbable.

excite *verb* **1** (*excite the spectators*) rouse, arouse, animate, move, agitate, disturb, inflame, inspire, galvanize, electrify, thrill, exhilarate, titillate, turn on (*inf*). OPPOSITE: calm. **2** (*excite interest*) stimulate, provoke, arouse, awaken, stir up, kindle, evoke, elicit, cause, bring about, instigate, incite, spur, foment. OPPOSITE: deter.

excited *adj* animated, in high spirits, eager, enthusiastic, fired up (*inf*), thrilled, on the edge of one's seat (*inf*), exhilarated, elated, high (*inf*), agitated, disturbed, restless, worked up, overwrought, wild, frenzied, roused, aroused, titillated, turned on (*inf*). OPPOSITE: bored.

excitement *noun* **1** (*the excitement of the chase*) animation, enthusiasm, passion, thrill, exhilaration, elation, agitation, restlessness, commotion, tumult, ferment, fever. OPPOSITE: calmness. **2** (*sexual excitement*) stimulation, arousal, titillation. **3** (*the excitements of the holiday*) adventure, pleasure, thrill, kick (*inf*).

exciting *adj* stimulating, inspiring, rousing, moving, stirring, thrilling, enthralling, action-packed (*inf*), exhilarating, electrifying, breathtaking, hair-raising, nail-biting (*inf*), white-knuckle (*inf*), sensational, provocative, titillating, sexy (*inf*). OPPOSITE: boring.

exclaim *verb* cry, shout, yell, roar, bellow, scream, shriek, call, call out, declare, ejaculate, vociferate.

exclamation *noun* cry, shout, yell, roar, bellow, scream, shriek, call, ejaculation, interjection, vociferation, clamour, outcry.

exclude *verb* **1** (*excluded from the list*) omit, leave out, count out, miss out, pass over, ignore, skip (*inf*), except, preclude, rule out, eliminate, reject, repudiate, drop (*inf*). OPPOSITE: include. **2** (*excluded from membership*) ban, bar, debar, blackball, keep out, shut out, ostracize, proscribe, interdict, prohibit, forbid, veto, disallow. OPPOSITE: admit. **3** (*excluded from the meeting*) expel, eject, throw out, chuck out (*inf*), oust, evict, remove.

exclusion *noun* **1** (*exclusion from the list*) omission, exception, preclusion, elimination, rejection, repudiation. OPPOSITE: inclusion. **2** (*exclusion from membership*) ban, bar, proscription, interdiction, prohibition, veto, embargo, boycott. OPPOSITE: admission. **3** (*exclusion from the meeting*) expulsion, ejection, eviction, removal.

exclusive *adj* **1** (*exclusive rights*) individual, single, sole, only, unique, unshared. OPPOSITE: shared. **2** (*her exclusive attention*) undivided, total, full, complete, whole, absolute. OPPOSITE: partial. **3** (*exclusive membership*) limited, restricted, restrictive, closed, selective, select, choice. **4** (*an exclusive resort*) private, cliquish, clannish, snobbish, elegant, fashionable, chic, up-market, posh (*inf*), classy (*inf*), ritzy (*inf*), swish (*inf*).

exclusive of excluding, not including, not counting, omitting, excepting, barring. OPPOSITE: including.

excommunicate *verb* exclude, bar, debar, remove, banish, expel, eject, cast out, unchurch, anathematize, denounce, execrate, proscribe, interdict. OPPOSITE: admit.

excoriate *verb* **1** (*excoriated by the critics*) denounce, condemn, censure, blame, reprove, rebuke, reproach, upbraid, berate, castigate, chastise, bawl out (*inf*), tear off a strip (*inf*), attack, revile, vilify, criticize, knock (*inf*), run down (*inf*), slate (*inf*), slam (*inf*), pan (*inf*). OPPOSITE: extol. **2** (*excoriate an animal*) skin, flay. **3** (*excoriate the skin*) strip, peel, scrape, abrade, scratch, scarify.

excrement *noun* excretion, excreta, faeces, stools, crap (*sl*), shit (*sl*), ordure, dung, droppings, guano.

excrescence *noun* **1** (*its body covered with excrescences*) lump, growth, swelling, tumour, protuberance, protrusion, prominence, projection, outgrowth. **2** (*an excrescence on the skyline*) eyesore, monstrosity, disfigurement, blot.

excrete *verb* discharge, eject, expel, eliminate, pass, evacuate, void, defecate, urinate, egest, exude.

excruciating *adj* agonizing, racking, harrowing, distressing, painful, severe, intense, acute, sharp,

exquisite, searing, piercing, unbearable, insufferable, intolerable. OPPOSITE: soothing.

exculpate *verb* exonerate, vindicate, clear, absolve, pardon, excuse, let off, acquit, free, release, discharge. OPPOSITE: condemn.

excursion *noun* **1** (*an excursion to the seaside*) trip, outing, jaunt (*inf*), expedition, journey, tour, walk, drive, ride. **2** (*an excursion from the subject*) digression, deviation, diversion, detour.

excusable *adj* pardonable, forgivable, justifiable, defensible, understandable. OPPOSITE: inexcusable.

excuse *verb* **1** (*please excuse my ignorance*) pardon, forgive, overlook, condone, tolerate, indulge, bear with, make allowances for, remit, absolve. OPPOSITE: condemn. **2** (*nothing can excuse such rudeness*) vindicate, justify, explain, mitigate, defend. **3** (*excuse the offenders*) exonerate, exculpate, clear, pardon, let off, acquit. OPPOSITE: punish. **4** (*excuse him from work*) exempt, spare, relieve, let off, free, liberate, release, discharge, dismiss.

➤ *noun* **1** (*no excuse for the delay*) explanation, reason, grounds, justification, vindication, mitigation, defence, plea, alibi, apology. **2** (*just an excuse to stay in bed*) pretext, pretence, front, cover-up (*inf*), feint, shift, subterfuge, evasion, cop-out (*inf*).

excuse me pardon, sorry.

execrable *adj* abominable, abhorrent, detestable, loathsome, odious, hateful, horrible, vile, obnoxious, repulsive, disgusting, damnable, accursed, bad, appalling, atrocious. OPPOSITE: delightful.

execrate *verb* abominate, abhor, detest, loathe, hate, despise, revile, deplore, condemn, denounce, excoriate, curse, damn, imprecate. OPPOSITE: love.

execute *verb* **1** (*execute a criminal*) kill, put to death, hang, string up (*inf*), behead, guillotine, electrocute, send to the chair (*inf*), shoot, crucify. **2** (*execute a task*) perform, do, carry out, fulfil, complete, finish, accomplish, achieve, discharge, implement, effect, enforce, enact, administer.

execution *noun* **1** (*the execution of criminals*) capital punishment, death sentence, killing, hanging, beheading, electrocution, shooting, crucifixion. **2** (*the execution of a task*) performance, fulfilment, completion, accomplishment, achievement, discharge, implementation, enforcement, enactment, administration. **3** (*the player's execution of the piece*) style, technique, manner, mode, delivery, rendition, interpretation, presentation, staging, performance.

executive *noun* **1** (*members of the executive*) administration, management, directorate, top brass (*inf*), leadership, government, hierarchy. **2** (*a senior executive*) administrator, official, manager, director, leader, VIP, bigwig (*inf*), big shot (*inf*), big wheel (*inf*), big cheese (*inf*).

➤ *adj* administrative, managerial, directorial, governing, controlling, decision-making.

exegesis *adj* explanation, explication, clarification, exposition, interpretation.

exemplar *noun* example, sample, specimen, type, exemplification, illustration, instance, model, pattern, standard, criterion, ideal, paragon, epitome, embodiment.

exemplary adj 1 (exemplary conduct) model, ideal, perfect, faultless, admirable, estimable, commendable, praiseworthy, laudable, meritorious, good, fine, excellent, worthy, honourable. OPPOSITE: despicable. 2 (an exemplary punishment) cautionary, warning, admonitory. 3 (an exemplary specimen) typical, characteristic, representative, illustrative.

exemplify verb illustrate, instance, demonstrate, show, exhibit, display, manifest, represent, characterize, typify, epitomize, embody.

exempt verb excuse, release, free, liberate, relieve, except, exclude, spare, let off, absolve, exonerate, discharge, dismiss.
➤ adj exempted, excused, released, free, excepted, excluded, immune, privileged, not liable, not subject, spared, absolved, discharged. OPPOSITE: liable.

exemption noun exception, exclusion, immunity, indemnity, privilege, special treatment, dispensation, relief, freedom, release, absolution, discharge. OPPOSITE: liability.

exercise verb 1 (exercising in the yard) drill, train, work out, keep fit, limber up, warm up, practise. OPPOSITE: relax. 2 (exercise your rights) use, utilize, employ, exert, apply, bring to bear, implement, wield, practise. 3 (greatly exercised by the problem) worry, trouble, disturb, perturb, annoy, vex, upset, distress, afflict, burden, tax, preoccupy.
➤ noun 1 (physical exercise) exertion, activity, effort, work, labour, drill, training, workout, warm-up, keep fit, aerobics, callisthenics, walking, jogging, running, sports, PE, PT. OPPOSITE: rest. 2 (a translation exercise) task, lesson, problem, piece of work, practice, discipline, development. 3 (the exercise of influence) use, employment, exertion, application, implementation, accomplishment, discharge, performance, practice. 4 (a military exercise) drill, manoeuvre, operation, assignment, mission.

exert verb use, utilize, employ, exercise, apply, bring to bear, wield, expend, spend.
exert oneself struggle, strive, toil, labour, work, strain, push, make an effort, put oneself out, apply oneself, try hard, do one's best, give one's all. OPPOSITE: idle.

exertion noun 1 (physical exertion) effort, work, labour, toil, struggle, strain, exercise, activity, action, industry, endeavour, attempt, pains, perseverance. OPPOSITE: idleness. 2 (the exertion of influence) use, employment, exercise, application, expenditure.

exhalation noun breath, expiration, emission, emanation, vapour, steam, exhaust, fumes, effluvium. OPPOSITE: inhalation.

exhale verb breathe out, expire, emit, expel, emanate, give off. OPPOSITE: inhale.

exhaust verb 1 (exhausted our resources) consume, use up, finish, empty, drain, expend, spend, deplete, dissipate, squander, waste, fritter away, blow (inf). OPPOSITE: replenish. 2 (exhausted the climbers) tire, weary, fatigue, tire out, wear out, knock out (inf), prostrate, weaken, debilitate, enfeeble, enervate, sap, drain, take it out of (inf). OPPOSITE: refresh.

exhausted adj 1 (exhausted workers) tired, weary, fatigued, tired out, worn out, dead beat (inf), all in (inf), done in (inf), ready to drop (inf), knackered (inf), pooped (inf), whacked (inf), bushed (inf), prostrate, weak, debilitated, enfeebled, drained, jaded. OPPOSITE: refreshed. 2 (an exhausted mine) consumed, used up, finished, gone, at an end, empty, bare, dry, drained, spent, depleted. OPPOSITE: untouched.

exhausting adj tiring, wearing, hard, difficult, arduous, strenuous, backbreaking, laborious, taxing, debilitating, enervating, gruelling, punishing. OPPOSITE: easy.

exhaustion noun 1 (dropping with exhaustion) tiredness, weariness, fatigue, collapse, prostration, weakness, debility, enervation, lassitude. OPPOSITE: energy. 2 (the exhaustion of supplies) consumption, using up, expenditure, depletion, dissipation. OPPOSITE: replenishment.

exhaustive adj comprehensive, all-embracing, all-inclusive, full, total, thorough, detailed, extensive, wide-ranging, far-reaching, encyclopedic, intensive, all-out, in-depth. OPPOSITE: restricted.

exhibit verb 1 (exhibiting their wares) display, show, set out, array, present, demonstrate, model, parade, flaunt, air, expose. 2 (exhibiting her fear) show, demonstrate, indicate, manifest, evince, evidence, betray, give away, reveal, disclose, express. OPPOSITE: conceal.
➤ noun display, show, array, presentation, demonstration, model.

exhibition noun 1 (an art exhibition) display, show, fair, exposition, presentation, demonstration, parade, performance, spectacle. 2 (an exhibition of rudeness) indication, manifestation, revelation, disclosure, expression, airing, display, show. 3 (awarded an exhibition) scholarship, grant, bursary, allowance.

exhilarate verb elate, delight, gladden, cheer, brighten, excite, thrill, animate, enliven, invigorate, stimulate, exalt, inspirit. OPPOSITE: depress.

exhilaration noun elation, delight, joy, happiness, glee, mirth, merriment, gaiety, high spirits, excitement, thrill, animation, invigoration, liveliness, vivacity, exaltation, euphoria. OPPOSITE: depression.

exhort verb urge, enjoin, bid, implore, entreat, beseech, press, prevail upon, persuade, induce, advise, counsel, encourage, prompt, incite, spur, goad. OPPOSITE: deter.

exhortation noun urging, injunction, bidding, entreaty, beseeching, persuasion, encouragement, advice, counsel, warning, lecture, sermon, homily. OPPOSITE: discouragement.

exhume verb disinter, dig up, unearth, unbury, disentomb. OPPOSITE: inter.

exigency noun 1 (free to act in any exigency) urgency, emergency, crisis, extremity, strait, pass, predicament, plight, quandary, dilemma. 2 (the exigencies of the situation) need, necessity, demand, requirement, pressure, constraint.

exigent adj 1 (an exigent situation) urgent, pressing, critical, crucial, pivotal, imperative, importunate, insistent. OPPOSITE: unimportant. 2 (an exigent task) demanding, taxing, exacting, arduous, difficult, hard, harsh, severe, rigorous, stringent. OPPOSITE: easy.

exiguous *adj* scanty, meagre, paltry, small, tiny, diminutive, thin, slender, slight, trifling, negligible. OPPOSITE: ample.

exile *verb* expel, banish, expatriate, deport, drive out, eject, cast out, throw out, oust, ostracize, excommunicate, proscribe, outlaw, bar, ban. OPPOSITE: welcome.

➤ *noun* **1** (*living in exile*) expulsion, banishment, expatriation, deportation, ejection, ostracism, excommunication, proscription. **2** (*exiles in a foreign land*) deportee, refugee, émigré, emigrant, expatriate, displaced person, outlaw, outcast, pariah.

exist *verb* **1** (*unicorns do not exist*) be, live, breathe, be real, be present, occur, subsist, be extant. **2** (*the tradition has existed for centuries*) survive, be extant, remain, endure, last, continue, abide, prevail, obtain, be present, occur. **3** (*existing on bread and water*) subsist, survive, live, stay alive, eke out an existence.

existence *noun* **1** (*be in existence*) being, life, breath, animation, reality, actuality, presence, subsistence, survival, continuance. OPPOSITE: nonexistence. **2** (*a miserable existence*) life, way of life, lifestyle, mode of being, manner of survival.

existent *adj* existing, in existence, being, alive, living, breathing, animate, real, actual, present, current, prevailing, abiding, remaining, surviving, extant. OPPOSITE: nonexistent.

exit *noun* **1** (*an emergency exit*) way out, egress, door, gate, outlet, vent. OPPOSITE: entrance. **2** (*his exit from the competition*) departure, leaving, going, withdrawal, retirement, retreat, flight, exodus, farewell, leave-taking. OPPOSITE: arrival.

➤ *verb* depart, leave, go, withdraw, retire, retreat, flee, issue, emerge. OPPOSITE: enter.

exodus *noun* exit, departure, withdrawal, retirement, retreat, escape, flight, migration, emigration, evacuation, hegira. OPPOSITE: arrival.

exonerate *verb* **1** (*the accused was exonerated*) absolve, acquit, clear, exculpate, vindicate, justify, excuse, pardon, let off, discharge, free, release. OPPOSITE: charge. **2** (*exonerated from duty*) exempt, excuse, let off, spare, release, free, discharge, relieve.

exorbitant *adj* excessive, immoderate, inordinate, disproportionate, unreasonable, unwarranted, undue, extreme, extravagant, preposterous, outrageous, extortionate, prohibitive, steep (*inf*). OPPOSITE: moderate.

exorcise *verb* **1** (*exorcise a ghost*) expel, drive out, cast out. **2** (*exorcise a haunted house*) free, rid, deliver, purify.

exorcism *noun* expulsion, casting out, deliverance, purification.

exordium *noun* preamble, introduction, preface, foreword, prologue, prelude, opening, beginning. OPPOSITE: epilogue.

exotic *adj* **1** (*exotic plants*) foreign, alien, nonnative, tropical, imported, introduced, extraneous, extrinsic, external. OPPOSITE: native. **2** (*an exotic lifestyle*) strange, unusual, unfamiliar, extraordinary, outlandish, bizarre, curious, remarkable, striking, colourful, impressive, glamorous, exciting, fascinating, mysterious. OPPOSITE: ordinary.

expand *verb* enlarge, stretch, extend, lengthen, prolong, spread, broaden, widen, thicken, grow, increase, augment, add to, multiply, amplify, swell, distend, inflate, blow up, magnify, dilate, open, unfold, unroll, unfurl, develop, branch out, diversify. OPPOSITE: contract.

expand on elaborate on, expatiate on, dilate on, flesh out, amplify, develop, embellish, embroider.

expanse *noun* stretch, extent, spread, space, area, field, scope, range, sweep, breadth.

expansion *noun* enlargement, extension, prolongation, spread, growth, increase, augmentation, multiplication, amplification, swelling, distension, inflation, magnification, dilation, opening, unfolding, unrolling, development, diversification, elaboration, expatiation. OPPOSITE: contraction.

expansive *adj* **1** (*the expansive qualities of the material*) expandable, extendable, elastic, stretchy, spreading, swelling. OPPOSITE: contractile. **2** (*an expansive plain*) large, vast, wide, broad, extensive. OPPOSITE: small. **3** (*expansive coverage*) extensive, wide, broad, vast, comprehensive, far-reaching, wide-ranging, universal, global. OPPOSITE: narrow. **4** (*became more expansive after a few drinks*) talkative, loquacious, garrulous, communicative, outgoing, extrovert, sociable, affable, friendly, unreserved, uninhibited, frank, open. OPPOSITE: reserved.

expatiate *verb* enlarge, expand, dilate, elaborate, descant, discourse, dissertate.

expatriate *verb* exile, deport, banish, expel, proscribe, outlaw, ostracize.

➤ *noun* exile, deportee, émigré, emigrant, expat (*inf*), refugee, displaced person, gastarbeiter.

➤ *adj* exiled, deported, banished, expelled, emigrant, living abroad.

expatriation *noun* exile, deportation, banishment, expulsion, emigration.

expect *verb* **1** (*I expect you already know*) suppose, presume, assume, surmise, believe, think, imagine, reckon, guess (*inf*). **2** (*the police expected trouble*) anticipate, foresee, predict, forecast, envisage, contemplate, await, look forward to, hope for, bargain for, count on. **3** (*the general expected loyalty*) require, demand, exact, insist on, call for, count on, rely on, want, wish for, hope for.

expectant *adj* **1** (*their expectant faces*) expecting, anticipating, awaiting, hopeful, eager, apprehensive, anxious, ready, curious, in suspense, on tenterhooks. **2** (*expectant mothers*) pregnant, gravid, with child, expecting (*inf*), in the family way (*inf*), in the club (*inf*).

expectation *noun* **1** (*in expectation of bad weather*) anticipation, readiness, preparation, expectancy, contemplation, apprehension. **2** (*little expectation of success*) prospect, outlook, expectancy, hope, probability, likelihood, possibility. **3** (*the expectation that he would come*) trust, reliance, assurance, confidence, belief, supposition, presumption, assumption, surmise, conjecture. **4** (*lived up to our expectations*) prediction, forecast, requirement, demand.

expediency *noun* expedience, appropriateness, suitability, fitness, aptness, propriety, usefulness, helpfulness, advantage, benefit, worth, value, profit, gain, convenience, utility, practicality, pragmatism, desirability, advisability, wisdom, prudence, judiciousness.

expedient *adj* appropriate, suitable, fitting, apt, seemly, proper, right, useful, helpful, advantageous, beneficial, worthwhile, valuable, profitable, gainful, convenient, practical, pragmatic, desirable, advisable, sensible, wise, prudent, judicious, politic, timely, opportune. OPPOSITE: unwise.
➤ *noun* means, method, contrivance, device, shift, resource, resort, makeshift, stopgap, plan, scheme, stratagem, tactic, manoeuvre, ploy, ruse, trick, dodge (*inf*).

expedite *verb* accelerate, precipitate, speed up, step up, hasten, hurry, promote, advance, forward, further, assist, facilitate, dispatch. OPPOSITE: delay.

expedition *noun* 1 (*an expedition to the North Pole*) journey, voyage, trip, excursion, tour, safari, trek, hike, march, pilgrimage, exploration, enterprise, undertaking, project, mission, quest, crusade, campaign, raid. 2 (*an expedition to the shops*) trip, excursion, outing, jaunt. 3 (*a member of the expedition*) team, crew, company, party, group. 4 (*completed the task with expedition*) haste, speed, dispatch, swiftness, celerity, rapidity, alacrity, promptness. OPPOSITE: tardiness

expeditious *adj* prompt, punctual, instant, immediate, speedy, hasty, quick, fast, rapid, swift, brisk, efficient, nimble. OPPOSITE: slow.

expel *verb* 1 (*expelled from school*) eject, evict, throw out, chuck out (*inf*), turf out (*inf*), kick out (*inf*), send packing (*inf*), exile, banish, expatriate, deport, drive out, remove, oust, dismiss, discharge, drum out, proscribe, exclude, ostracize, blackball. OPPOSITE: welcome. 2 (*expelling exhaust gases*) discharge, eject, cast out, evacuate, void, eliminate, spew, belch.

expend *verb* 1 (*expend money*) spend, disburse, pay out, lay out, fork out (*inf*), shell out (*inf*), squander, waste, fritter away. OPPOSITE: save. 2 (*expend energy*) use, utilize, consume, use up, exhaust, deplete, dissipate, sap, drain. OPPOSITE: conserve.

expendable *adj* dispensable, replaceable, disposable, nonessential, unnecessary, unimportant. OPPOSITE: indispensable.

expenditure *noun* 1 (*expenditure on clothing*) spending, disbursement, expense, payment, outlay, outgoings, expenses, costs. OPPOSITE: income. 2 (*expenditure of energy*) use, utilization, consumption, exhaustion, depletion, dissipation. OPPOSITE: conservation.

expense *noun* 1 (*the expense of relocation*) cost, price, charge, fee, payment, expenditure, disbursement, outlay. 2 (*at the expense of his career*) sacrifice, cost, loss, detriment.

expenses *pl noun* spending, expenditure, costs, outgoings, incidentals, overheads, out-of-pocket expenses. OPPOSITE: receipts.

expensive *adj* dear, costly, high-priced, pricey (*inf*), exorbitant, extortionate, overpriced, steep (*inf*), extravagant, lavish, rich, valuable. OPPOSITE: cheap.

experience *verb* undergo, feel, suffer, sustain, go through, live through, endure, encounter, meet, face,

try, participate in, know, become familiar with. OPPOSITE: miss.
➤ *noun* 1 (*a traumatic experience*) event, occurrence, happening, incident, episode, adventure, encounter, affair, ordeal, trial. 2 (*experience of manufacturing industry*) knowledge, understanding, familiarity, acquaintance, contact, exposure, involvement, participation, practice, observation, impression. OPPOSITE: inexperience.

experienced *adj* knowledgeable, familiar, acquainted, expert, skilled, trained, qualified, practised, well-versed, accomplished, adept, able, competent, proficient, professional, master, veteran, mature, seasoned, worldly wise, sophisticated. OPPOSITE: inexperienced.

experiment *noun* 1 (*the results of the experiment*) trial, test, investigation, examination, research, study, observation, demonstration. 2 (*an experiment in community policing*) try, attempt, essay, venture, undertaking, enterprise, trial run, pilot study. 3 (*find out by experiment*) experimentation, research, analysis, trial and error, trying, testing.
➤ *verb* try, test, investigate, examine, research, study, observe, attempt, venture, explore.

experimental *adj* empirical, tentative, speculative, exploratory, provisional, preliminary, test, trial, pilot.

expert *noun* specialist, consultant, authority, pundit, connoisseur, buff (*inf*), professional, master, virtuoso, adept, dab hand (*inf*), ace (*inf*), pro (*inf*), past master, old hand (*inf*). OPPOSITE: novice.
➤ *adj* proficient, adept, skilful, skilled, adroit, dexterous, practised, experienced, well-versed, knowledgeable, masterly, brilliant, ace (*inf*), crack (*inf*), professional, specialist, qualified, accomplished. OPPOSITE: amateur.

expertise *noun* skill, proficiency, mastery, command, skilfulness, dexterity, ability, capability, facility, knack, professionalism, experience, knowledge, know-how (*inf*). OPPOSITE: incompetence.

expiate *verb* atone for, make amends for, redress, redeem, do penance for, pay for.

expiation *noun* atonement, amends, redress, reparation, satisfaction, redemption, penance.

expiration *noun* exhalation, breathing out. OPPOSITE: inhalation.

expire *verb* 1 (*my passport has expired*) lapse, run out, end, finish, cease, close, terminate, stop. OPPOSITE: begin. 2 (*the king expired at the age of ninety*) die, perish, pass away, pass on, breathe one's last, depart this life, give up the ghost (*inf*), kick the bucket (*inf*). 3 (*expire slowly and relax*) exhale, breathe out. OPPOSITE: inhale.

expiry *noun* end, finish, close, cessation, termination, expiration. OPPOSITE: beginning.

explain *verb* 1 (*explain what you must do*) define, describe, spell out, interpret, expound, explicate, clarify, make clear, elucidate, throw light on, illuminate, solve, decipher, decode, resolve, unravel, unfold, illustrate, demonstrate. 2 (*that explains why she was angry*) account for, justify, warrant, excuse, mitigate, vindicate, defend, rationalize.

explanation *noun* 1 (*no scientific explanation for the phenomenon*) definition, description, interpretation, exposition, explication, exegesis, clarification, elucidation, illumination, solution, answer, key, theory, illustration, demonstration. **2** (*demand an explanation for their behaviour*) reason, motive, account, justification, warrant, excuse, mitigation, vindication, defence, apologia, rationalization, meaning.

explanatory *adj* descriptive, illustrative, demonstrative, interpretative, expository, explicative, exegetic, elucidative, justificatory, vindicatory.

expletive *noun* oath, curse, swearword, four-letter word (*inf*), obscenity, blasphemy, profanity, imprecation, exclamation, ejaculation, epithet.

explicable *adj* explainable, accountable, justifiable, understandable, intelligible, definable, interpretable, solvable, resolvable. OPPOSITE: inexplicable.

explication *noun* **1** (*explication of a text*) explanation, exposition, interpretation, clarification, elucidation, illumination, illustration, analysis, exegesis, commentary. **2** (*explication of an idea*) formulation, development, evolution, construction.

explicit *adj* **1** (*an explicit warning*) plain, clear, distinct, unambiguous, unequivocal, precise, exact, specific, full, detailed, express, definite, positive, categorical, absolute. OPPOSITE: implicit. **2** (*explicit language*) direct, straightforward, forthright, blunt, frank, candid, open, unreserved, uninhibited, unrestrained, outspoken. OPPOSITE: restrained.

explode *noun* **1** (*the bomb exploded*) blow up, detonate, go off, go bang (*inf*), burst, fly apart, erupt, go up. **2** (*explode a bomb*) detonate, set off, let off, fire, discharge, blast, blow up. OPPOSITE: defuse. **3** (*explode with rage*) burst, erupt, flare up, blow up, blow a fuse (*inf*), blow one's top (*inf*), flip one's lid (*inf*), fly off the handle (*inf*), hit the roof (*inf*), lose one's rag (*inf*), freak out (*inf*). OPPOSITE: calm down. **4** (*explode a myth*) discredit, invalidate, refute, disprove, debunk, belie, give the lie to, reject, repudiate, blow sky-high (*inf*), knock the bottom out of (*inf*). OPPOSITE: confirm. **5** (*the population exploded*) grow rapidly, boom, mushroom, increase suddenly, escalate, rocket.

exploit *verb* **1** (*exploit mineral resources*) use, utilize, make use of, put to use, tap, draw on, milk (*inf*), take advantage of, capitalize on, turn to account, profit from, cash in on (*inf*). **2** (*accused of exploiting their workers*) take advantage of, misuse, abuse, manipulate, use, play on, impose on, oppress, walk all over (*inf*).
➤ *noun* feat, deed, act, achievement, accomplishment, attainment, adventure, stunt.

exploration *noun* **1** (*an exploration of the island*) tour, expedition, search, survey, reconnaissance. **2** (*an exploration of all the possibilities*) examination, study, analysis, investigation, inquiry, search, probe, inspection, scrutiny, research, survey, review.

exploratory *adj* investigative, fact-finding, searching, probing, tentative, experimental.

explore *verb* **1** (*explore the island*) travel, tour, traverse, range over, search, prospect, survey, reconnoitre, scout. **2** (*explore every possibility*) examine, study, analyse, investigate, look into, inquire into, search, probe, plumb, inspect, scrutinize, research, survey, consider, review, take stock of.

explorer *noun* traveller, discoverer, navigator, adventurer, prospector, surveyor, scout.

explosion *noun* **1** (*heard an explosion*) blast, detonation, burst, eruption, discharge, report, bang, boom, thunder, clap, crack, pop. **2** (*an explosion of rage*) outburst, eruption, outbreak, fit, paroxysm. **3** (*a population explosion*) boom, mushrooming, escalation, rocketing.

explosive *noun* bomb, mine, charge, gunpowder, dynamite, gelignite, nitroglycerine, TNT, Semtex®.
➤ *adj* **1** (*an explosive gas*) volatile, unstable, flammable, inflammable. **2** (*an explosive temper*) violent, wild, fiery, stormy, touchy, sensitive, volatile. **3** (*an explosive situation*) tense, charged, fraught, dangerous, hazardous, volatile, unstable, sensitive. **4** (*explosive growth*) rapid, sudden, booming, mushrooming, rocketing, meteoric (*inf*).

exponent *noun* **1** (*an exponent of this controversial theory*) advocate, supporter, backer, defender, champion, spokesperson, promoter, proponent, interpreter, commentator, expounder, expositor. **2** (*an acclaimed exponent of the technique*) practitioner, performer, player, interpreter, presenter.

export *verb* ship, send abroad, sell overseas. OPPOSITE: import.
➤ *noun* foreign trade, international trade.

expose *verb* **1** (*exposed his ignorance*) show, exhibit, display, reveal, disclose, divulge, betray, air, make known, bring out into the open, unveil, lay bare. OPPOSITE: hide. **2** (*expose corrupt practices*) denounce, blow the whistle on (*inf*), detect, unmask, uncover, take the lid off (*inf*), unearth, bring to light. OPPOSITE: cover up. **3** (*expose the wood to the elements*) uncover, bare, lay bare, strip, denude. **4** (*expose the children to danger*) lay open, put at risk, leave unprotected, make vulnerable, endanger, jeopardize, imperil. OPPOSITE: protect. **5** (*expose her to new experiences*) introduce, bring into contact, acquaint, familiarize.

expose oneself display one's genitals, flash (*inf*).

exposé *noun* exposure, revelation, disclosure, divulgence.

exposed *adj* **1** (*exposed areas of the body*) uncovered, bare, naked, stripped, denuded. **2** (*an exposed hillside*) unsheltered, unprotected, open. **3** (*exposed to criticism*) vulnerable, susceptible, subject, liable.

exposition *noun* **1** (*an exposition of the theory*) explanation, explication, interpretation, commentary, exegesis, critique, dissertation, treatise, study, analysis, description, account, presentation, elucidation, illustration. **2** (*an international trade exposition*) display, show, exhibition, demonstration, presentation, fair, market.

expostulate *verb* object, protest, argue, remonstrate, exhort, reason.

expostulation *noun* objection, protest, argument, remonstrance, exhortation, reasoning.

exposure *noun* **1** (*the exposure of his talent*) showing, exhibition, display, revelation, disclosure, divulgence, betrayal, airing, publication, unveiling, presentation. OPPOSITE: concealment. **2** (*exposure in the media*) publicity, advertising, hype (*inf*), broadcasting, airing. **3** (*the exposure of criminals*) unmasking, denunciation, whistle-blowing (*inf*), detection, discovery. **4** (*exposure to light*) uncovering, baring, laying open. **5** (*exposure to danger*) vulnerability, susceptibility, risk, hazard, jeopardy. OPPOSITE: protection. **6** (*exposure to new experiences*) introduction, contact, acquaintance, familiarity, experience.

expound *verb* explain, define, describe, set forth, spell out, detail, unfold, develop, interpret, explicate, elucidate, illustrate.

express *verb* **1** (*express my opinions*) utter, say, speak, voice, verbalize, articulate, word, phrase, communicate, put across, convey, state, declare, assert, proclaim, announce, air, vent. OPPOSITE: suppress. **2** (*expressed her feelings through music*) show, reveal, demonstrate, exhibit, manifest, evince, evidence, indicate, denote, depict, represent, symbolize.
≫ *adj* **1** (*express delivery*) fast, quick, rapid, swift, speedy, high-speed, direct, nonstop, through. OPPOSITE: slow. **2** (*his express instructions*) explicit, specific, precise, exact, plain, clear, distinct, unambiguous, unequivocal, unmistakable, definite, positive, categorical, particular, special. OPPOSITE: vague.

expression *noun* **1** (*a puzzled expression*) look, appearance, face, countenance, air, aspect. **2** (*a foreign expression*) phrase, locution, word, term, saying, idiom, turn of phrase, choice of words, phrasing, wording. **3** (*the expression of my opinions*) utterance, verbalization, articulation, communication, statement, declaration, assertion, proclamation, announcement, airing, venting. OPPOSITE: suppression. **4** (*the expression of his love*) manifestation, exhibition, demonstration, revelation, show, evidence, indication, sign, symbol, token. **5** (*performed with expression*) feeling, emotion, passion, spirit, force, power, depth, modulation, intonation.

expressionless *adj* blank, deadpan, straight-faced, inscrutable, poker-faced (*inf*), empty, vacuous, emotionless, unimpassioned.

expressive *adj* **1** (*an expressive gesture*) eloquent, meaningful, significant, pregnant, pointed, telling, vivid, graphic, striking, strong, forceful, emphatic. **2** (*expressive music*) moving, poignant, emotional, passionate, powerful, evocative, suggestive. **3** (*expressive of their patriotism*) showing, indicative, demonstrative, revealing.

expropriate *verb* seize, take, appropriate, requisition, commandeer, impound, confiscate, sequester, take over, usurp, assume, arrogate.

expulsion *noun* **1** (*expulsion from school*) ejection, eviction, exile, banishment, expatriation, deportation, dismissal, discharge, proscription, exclusion. OPPOSITE: welcome. **2** (*the expulsion of exhaust gases*) discharge, ejection, evacuation, elimination.

expunge *verb* erase, rub out, efface, obliterate, wipe out, blot out, delete, cross out, strike out, cancel, remove, eradicate, extirpate, annihilate, destroy, exterminate.

expurgate *verb* bowdlerize, censor, purge, purify, sanitize, clean up, cut, edit, blue-pencil.

exquisite *adj* **1** (*exquisite craftsmanship*) fine, delicate, dainty, beautiful, lovely, attractive, elegant. OPPOSITE: ugly. **2** (*exquisite wines*) choice, select, excellent, fine, outstanding, superb, rare, matchless, unique, valuable, precious. OPPOSITE: ordinary. **3** (*exquisite manners*) refined, cultured, cultivated, sophisticated, sensitive, appreciative, discriminating, selective, fastidious, impeccable, perfect. OPPOSITE: coarse. **4** (*exquisite pain*) intense, sharp, keen, acute, piercing, excruciating. OPPOSITE: dull.

extant *adj* existing, existent, present, living, surviving, subsisting, remaining, undestroyed. OPPOSITE: extinct.

extemporaneous *adj* extemporary, extempore, spontaneous, impromptu, ad-lib, improvised, unrehearsed, unprepared, off-the-cuff (*inf*). OPPOSITE: prepared.

extempore *adv* extemporaneously, spontaneously, on the spur of the moment (*inf*), ad lib, off the cuff (*inf*), off the top of one's head (*inf*).

extemporize *verb* ad-lib, improvise, make up, play it by ear (*inf*), think on one's feet (*inf*).

extend *verb* **1** (*extend across the plain*) spread, stretch, stretch out, reach, range, continue, run. **2** (*extend the building*) enlarge, lengthen, broaden, widen, add to. **3** (*extend the telescope*) lengthen, elongate, pull out, draw out, unfold, unfurl, unroll, unwind. OPPOSITE: shorten. **4** (*extend the contract*) prolong, lengthen, elongate, protract, draw out, spin out, continue. OPPOSITE: curtail. **5** (*extend our responsibilities*) expand, enlarge, increase, amplify, widen, broaden, develop, augment, supplement, add to. OPPOSITE: reduce. **6** (*extend a warm welcome*) offer, proffer, tender, hold out, advance, give, present, bestow, impart, confer. OPPOSITE: withhold.

extended *adj* long, longer, elongated, lengthy, prolonged, protracted, expanded, enlarged, increased.

extension *noun* **1** (*the extension of their territory*) enlargement, lengthening, broadening, widening, continuation. OPPOSITE: contraction. **2** (*the extension of the telescope*) stretching, lengthening, elongation, unfolding, unfurling, unrolling, unwinding. OPPOSITE: shortening. **3** (*the extension of our responsibilities*) expansion, enlargement, increase, amplification, widening, broadening, development, augmentation. OPPOSITE: reduction. **4** (*an extension of the deadline*) prolongation, protraction, continuation, delay, postponement, deferment. OPPOSITE: curtailment. **5** (*an extension to the will*) addition, addendum, adjunct, supplement, appendix, codicil. **6** (*build an extension*) annexe, wing.

extensive *adj* **1** (*extensive investigations*) broad, wide, widespread, universal, wide-ranging, all-embracing, all-inclusive, exhaustive, thorough, comprehensive, long, lengthy, protracted. OPPOSITE: limited. **2** (*extensive grounds*) large, huge, vast, sweeping, spacious, capacious, roomy, substantial, sizeable, broad, wide. OPPOSITE: small.

extent *noun* amount, quantity, measure, degree, size, magnitude, dimensions, length, breadth, width, height, depth, volume, capacity, area, expanse, coverage, range, scope, reach, compass, limit, bounds.

extenuate *verb* mitigate, palliate, lessen, diminish, reduce, temper, moderate, qualify, play down, minimize, excuse, justify. OPPOSITE: exaggerate.

exterior *noun* outside, surface, face, shell, skin,

covering, facade, front, appearance, aspect. OPPOSITE: interior.

> *adj* outer, external, outside, outward, superficial, surface. OPPOSITE: inner.

exterminate *verb* kill, destroy, annihilate, eradicate, extirpate, wipe out, eliminate, abolish.

extermination *noun* killing, destruction, annihilation, eradication, extirpation, elimination, abolition, extinction, slaughter, massacre, genocide, ethnic cleansing.

external *adj* **1** (*the external surface*) outer, exterior, outside, outward, superficial, apparent, visible. OPPOSITE: internal. **2** (*external influences*) extraneous, extrinsic, alien, foreign. **3** (*an external examiner*) visiting, nonresident, extramural.

extinct *adj* **1** (*extinct species*) dead, defunct, wiped out, vanished, gone, lost. OPPOSITE: extant. **2** (*an extinct volcano*) inactive, extinguished, quenched, put out. OPPOSITE: active. **3** (*extinct traditions*) obsolete, archaic, antiquated, outmoded, passé, defunct, finished, ended, terminated. OPPOSITE: living.

extinction *noun* annihilation, eradication, extirpation, destruction, termination, abolition, suppression, extermination, death, dying out. OPPOSITE: survival.

extinguish *verb* **1** (*extinguish a flame*) quench, put out, snuff, douse, blow out, smother, stifle, suffocate, choke. OPPOSITE: light. **2** (*extinguish their hopes*) annihilate, eradicate, extirpate, eliminate, kill, destroy, end, terminate, abolish, suppress, quash, erase, expunge, remove. OPPOSITE: kindle.

extirpate *verb* destroy, wipe out, annihilate, exterminate, eradicate, uproot, stamp out, abolish, extinguish. OPPOSITE: establish.

extirpation *noun* destruction, annihilation, extermination, eradication, abolition, extinction. OPPOSITE: establishment.

extol *noun* praise, laud, eulogize, panegyrize, sing the praises of, praise to the skies, wax lyrical about, rave about (*inf*), hype (*inf*), cry up (*inf*), exalt, glorify, magnify, celebrate, acclaim, applaud, commend, compliment. OPPOSITE: decry.

extort *verb* extract, wring, wrest, squeeze, coerce, force, exact, milk, bleed (*inf*).

extortion *noun* coercion, force, compulsion, exaction, blackmail, racketeering.

extortionate *adj* exorbitant, excessive, immoderate, unreasonable, steep (*inf*), sky-high (*inf*), preposterous, outrageous, inflated, usurious, exacting, hard, severe, harsh, grasping, rapacious. OPPOSITE: moderate.

extra *adj* **1** (*need extra help*) additional, supplementary, more, further, other, new, fresh. **2** (*carry an extra battery*) spare, reserve, accessory, ancillary, auxiliary, subsidiary. **3** (*if you have any extra cash*) surplus, excess, superfluous, redundant, supernumerary, leftover, unused.

> *noun* **1** (*optional extras*) addition, adjunct, accessory, attachment, supplement, bonus. OPPOSITE: essential. **2** (*an extra in the film*) supernumerary, bit-part player, walk-on, spear-carrier.

> *adv* **1** (*work extra hard*) especially, exceptionally, particularly, unusually. **2** (*delivery costs extra*) in

addition, over and above, on top, as well, besides, into the bargain (*inf*).

extract *verb* **1** (*extract the splinter*) remove, pull out, draw out, pluck out, take out, withdraw, wrench, uproot, tear out. OPPOSITE: insert. **2** (*extract the goodness from the vegetables*) derive, draw, distil, separate, squeeze, press, get, obtain. **3** (*extract a confession from them*) get, obtain, elicit, educe, glean, worm, wrest, wring, exact, extort, force. **4** (*extract a relevant passage*) select, choose, excerpt, abstract, cite, quote, copy, reproduce.

> *noun* **1** (*extracts from the play*) excerpt, abstract, quotation, citation, passage, clipping, snippet, selection. **2** (*malt extract*) essence, concentrate, distillate, juice.

extraction *noun* **1** (*the extraction of teeth*) removal, pulling, drawing, withdrawal, uprooting. OPPOSITE: insertion. **2** (*the extraction of nutrients*) derivation, distillation, separation, obtaining. **3** (*of noble extraction*) parentage, descent, ancestry, lineage, family, stock, blood, birth, origin.

extradition *noun* surrender, delivery, handing over, sending back, repatriation, deportation, expulsion, banishment, exile.

extraneous *adj* **1** (*extraneous noises*) extrinsic, external, exterior, alien, foreign, adventitious. OPPOSITE: intrinsic. **2** (*extraneous details*) irrelevant, immaterial, beside the point, unconnected, unrelated, incidental, peripheral, nonessential, unnecessary, superfluous, redundant. OPPOSITE: relevant.

extraordinary *adj* **1** (*an extraordinary sight*) strange, peculiar, singular, odd, curious, bizarre, weird, unusual, uncommon, rare, unprecedented. OPPOSITE: ordinary. **2** (*extraordinary talent*) outstanding, exceptional, striking, remarkable, phenomenal, wonderful, marvellous, fantastic (*inf*). **3** (*an extraordinary coincidence*) surprising, amazing, astonishing, astounding, strange, remarkable.

extravagance *noun* **1** (*extravagance with money*) lavishness, wastefulness, profligacy, prodigality, overspending, recklessness, imprudence, improvidence, thriftlessness. OPPOSITE: thrift. **2** (*the extravagance of their claims*) immoderation, unrestraint, excess, exaggeration, outrageousness, preposterousness, wildness, absurdity, folly. OPPOSITE: moderation. **3** (*allow myself a few extravagances*) luxury, indulgence, treat, extra, nonessential.

extravagant *adj* **1** (*extravagant with money*) lavish, wasteful, profligate, prodigal, spendthrift, reckless, imprudent, improvident, thriftless. OPPOSITE: thrifty. **2** (*extravagant claims*) immoderate, unrestrained, inordinate, excessive, exaggerated, outrageous, preposterous, wild, absurd, foolish. OPPOSITE: moderate. **3** (*an extravagant holiday*) expensive, dear, costly, overpriced, exorbitant, extortionate, steep (*inf*). OPPOSITE: economical. **4** (*extravagant behaviour*) flamboyant, ostentatious, pretentious, flashy (*inf*), over the top (*inf*), OTT (*inf*). OPPOSITE: subdued.

extreme *adj* **1** (*in extreme pain*) great, intense, severe, acute, ultimate, maximum, greatest, supreme, highest, utmost. OPPOSITE: slight. **2** (*extreme folly*) utter, downright, out-and-out, exceptional, remarkable, extraordinary. **3** (*extreme socialism*) radical, fanatical, zealous, overzealous, immoderate, unreasonable, excessive, inordinate. OPPOSITE: moderate. **4** (*extreme measures*) drastic, dire, draconian, radical, hard-line, uncompromising, unyielding, rigid, severe, strict, harsh, stringent. OPPOSITE: mild. **5** (*the extreme north*) farthest, outermost, most distant, most remote, last, final, ultimate, endmost. OPPOSITE: near.

➤ *noun* extremity, top, bottom, height, depth, maximum, minimum, zenith, nadir, peak, climax, end, termination, edge, limit, pole, opposite, contrary. OPPOSITE: median.

in the extreme extremely, exceptionally, exceedingly, excessively, inordinately.

extremely *adv* very, greatly, highly, intensely, severely, exceptionally, remarkably, extraordinarily, awfully (*inf*), terribly (*inf*), excessively, inordinately. OPPOSITE: slightly.

extremist *noun* radical, militant, fanatic, zealot, ultra, fundamentalist, diehard. OPPOSITE: moderate.

extremity *noun* **1** (*the southern extremity of the forest*) extreme, limit, boundary, border, edge, margin, verge, end, termination. **2** (*helped us in our extremity*) emergency, crisis, exigency, plight, predicament, hardship, adversity, misfortune, trouble.

extricate *verb* disentangle, disengage, detach, clear, free, liberate, release, deliver, rescue, save, relieve, remove, extract, withdraw, get out. OPPOSITE: involve.

extrinsic *adj* extraneous, external, exterior, outside, foreign, alien, exotic, unrelated, unconnected. OPPOSITE: intrinsic.

extrovert *adj* extroverted, outgoing, sociable, gregarious, clubbable, friendly, lively, effervescent, bubbly. OPPOSITE: introverted.

➤ *noun* socializer, mixer, mingler, joiner, life and soul of the party. OPPOSITE: introvert.

extrude *verb* eject, force out, squeeze out, press out, expel, discharge.

exuberance *noun* **1** (*dancing with exuberance*) liveliness, vivacity, vitality, animation, ebullience, effervescence, buoyancy, elation, exultation, vigour, enthusiasm. OPPOSITE: lethargy. **2** (*growing in exuberance*) abundance, plenty, copiousness, profusion, superabundance, richness, luxuriance, lavishness, rankness. OPPOSITE: scarcity.

exuberant *adj* **1** (*exuberant children*) lively, vivacious, animated, spirited, ebullient, effervescent, sparkling, bubbly, chirpy (*inf*), cheerful, buoyant, bouncy (*inf*), elated, high-spirited, exultant, energetic, enthusiastic, irrepressible. OPPOSITE: lethargic. **2** (*exuberant vegetation*) abundant, plentiful, copious, profuse, superabundant, rich, luxuriant, lavish, rank, prolific, thriving. OPPOSITE: scarce. **3** (*an exuberant display of affection*) unreserved, unrestrained, effusive, extravagant, exaggerated, excessive, prodigal, lavish. OPPOSITE: restrained.

exude *verb* **1** (*resin exudes from the wood*) ooze, seep, leak, filter, trickle, drip, flow out, discharge, issue. **2** (*exude venom*) secrete, excrete, ooze, leak, discharge, emit, emanate, give out. OPPOSITE: absorb. **3** (*exude confidence*) display, exhibit, send out, ooze, emanate, emit, give out.

exult *verb* rejoice, triumph, crow, gloat, glory, revel, be jubilant, be joyful, jump for joy. OPPOSITE: mourn.

exultant *adj* triumphant, jubilant, exulting, rejoicing, cock-a-hoop (*inf*), joyful, gleeful, delighted, elated, overjoyed, ecstatic, over the moon (*inf*). OPPOSITE: disappointed.

eye *noun* **1** (*cast an eye over the figures*) look, glimpse, glance, gaze. **2** (*an eye for design*) appreciation, taste, judgment, discernment, discrimination, sensitivity, perception, awareness. **3** (*in my eye she is innocent*) opinion, view, point of view, viewpoint, judgment, estimation, mind, belief. **4** (*under the eye of the teacher*) surveillance, observation, vigilance, watch, lookout, view, attention, notice.

➤ *verb* look at, peruse, scrutinize, scan, survey, watch, observe, gaze at, stare at, ogle, leer at, make eyes at.

keep an eye on watch, observe, mind, look after, take care of, attend to, supervise, monitor. OPPOSITE: ignore.

see eye to eye agree, concur, get on, get along, be on the same wavelength (*inf*), speak the same language (*inf*). OPPOSITE: disagree.

up to one's eyes busy, occupied, engrossed, wrapped up, overwhelmed, inundated, snowed under (*inf*). OPPOSITE: idle.

eye-catching *adj* striking, arresting, noticeable, prominent, conspicuous, showy, attractive, beautiful, stunning, captivating.

eyesight *noun* sight, vision, eyes, observation, perception.

eyesore *noun* monstrosity, sight (*inf*), scar, blemish, blight, excrescence, carbuncle, blot on the landscape, horror, disgrace, atrocity, disfigurement, defacement.

fable *noun* **1** (*a fable about a tortoise*) allegory, parable, apologue, tale, story, myth, legend, saga, epic. **2** (*is entirely fable*) untruth, lie, falsehood, fib, fiction, fabrication, invention, fantasy, romance, story, yarn (*inf*), tall story (*inf*). OPPOSITE: truth.

fabric *noun* **1** (*the shirt was of manmade fabric*) cotton, cloth, material, stuff, textile, texture, weave. **2** (*the fabric of society*) structure, framework, frame, organization, makeup, constitution, construction, essence.

fabricate *verb* **1** (*fabricate components*) build, construct, make, assemble, manufacture, produce, put together, form, fashion, shape, frame, erect. OPPOSITE: destroy. **2** (*fabricate an excuse*) make up, concoct, hatch, trump up, devise, invent, coin, think up, formulate. **3** (*fabricate evidence*) concoct, fake, forge, counterfeit, falsify.

fabrication *noun* **1** (*fabrication of the aeroplane*) building, construction, manufacture, production, assembly, erection. OPPOSITE: destruction. **2** (*fabrication of information*) invention, formulation, concoction. **3** (*fabrication of a document*) fake, forgery, fable, lie, falsehood, fiction.

fabulous *adj* **1** (*a fabulous party*) wonderful, amazing, astounding, marvellous, superb, great, incredible, unbelievable, out of this world (*inf*), super (*inf*), cool (*inf*), wicked (*sl*), way-out (*sl*). **2** (*fabulous creatures*) legendary, mythical, fantastic, fantastical, unreal, imaginary, fictitious, invented.

facade *noun* **1** (*the facade of a building*) front, appearance, exterior, frontage, outside. **2** (*a facade of respectability*) mask, disguise, veneer, show, appearance, guise, masquerade, pretence, semblance, illusion.

face *noun* **1** (*a pretty face*) countenance, visage, physiognomy, features, mug (*inf*), phiz (*inf*), kisser (*inf*). **2** (*a serious face*) appearance, look, expression, aspect, air, demeanour. **3** (*pull a face*) grimace, scowl, pout. **4** (*put on a brave face*) facade, front, surface, exterior, veneer, pretence, semblance. **5** (*the changing face of the countryside*) appearance, look, aspect, form. **6** (*lose face*) dignity, honour, respect, repute, prestige, standing, status, image. **7** (*have the face to answer back*) boldness, audacity, effrontery, brass, gall, impudence, cheek (*inf*), nerve (*inf*), brass (*inf*). OPPOSITE: timidity.
➤ *verb* **1** (*face opposition*) confront, brave, beard, defy, oppose, meet, encounter, come up against, deal with, face up to, come to terms with, get to grips with, cope with. OPPOSITE: avoid. **2** (*facing the harbour*) overlook, front on, be opposite. **3** (*face a stone*) cover, coat, surface, veneer, encrust, dress, line, finish, level, smooth.

face to face opposite, facing, confronting.

face up to confront, encounter, come up against, deal with, come to terms with, get to grips with, cope with. OPPOSITE: avoid.

facet *noun* **1** (*every facet of life*) aspect, angle, slant, element, detail, characteristic. **2** (*the facets of a diamond*) face, plane, surface, side.

facetious *adj* joking, jesting, jocular, witty, droll, waggish, frivolous, flippant, tongue-in-cheek, funny, playful, light-hearted, humorous, amusing, comic, comical. OPPOSITE: serious.

facile *adj* **1** (*a facile suggestion*) glib, superficial, shallow, slick. **2** (*a facile victory*) easy, simple, effortless, unchallenging. OPPOSITE: difficult.

facilitate *verb* assist, aid, help, forward, accelerate, further, advance, promote, expedite, speed up, ease, smooth, make easy, simplify. OPPOSITE: hinder.

facility *noun* **1** (*a facility for languages*) ease, easiness, effortlessness, smoothness, fluency, eloquence, articulateness, readiness, skill, dexterity, proficiency, ability, knack, talent, aptitude, adroitness, bent. OPPOSITE: awkwardness. **2** (*recreational facilities*) amenity, convenience, advantage, resource, aid, means, benefit.

facing *noun* covering, reinforcement, coating, lining, cladding, surface.

facsimile *noun* copy, reproduction, replica, duplicate, carbon, carbon copy, fax, photocopy, transcript. OPPOSITE: original.

fact *noun* **1** (*space travel is now a fact*) actuality, truth, reality, certainty. OPPOSITE: fiction. **2** (*an accessory before the fact*) event, happening, occurrence, incident, circumstance, deed, act.
in fact actually, in reality, indeed, really, truly, in truth, in point of fact.

faction *noun* **1** (*the country's warring factions*) group, party, gang, band, clique, set, junta, confederacy, cabal, contingent, division, splinter group, bloc, caucus, camp, ginger group, minority. **2** (*a spirit of faction*) disagreement, discord, dissension, strife, conflict, rebellion, sedition, upheaval, tumult, rupture, division, disunity, infighting. OPPOSITE: unanimity.

factious *adj* discordant, disagreeing, at variance, quarrelsome, disputatious, argumentative, dissenting, conflicting, warring, mutinous, insurrectionary, rebellious, seditious, dissident, refractory, divisive, schismatic, partisan, disruptive, at loggerheads.

factitious *adj* artificial, false, unnatural, contrived, affected, simulated, insincere, sham, mock, unreal, fake. OPPOSITE: genuine.

factor *noun* **1** (*the factors determining inflation*) element, part, component, feature, characteristic, ingredient, constituent, detail, item, facet, point, aspect, circumstance, cause, influence, determinant. **2** (*a factor in the car trade*) agent, middleman, middle party, go-between, intermediary, deputy, proxy, representative, broker, facilitator.

factory *noun* plant, shop, works, workshop, shop floor, assembly line, mill, foundry.

factotum *noun* odd job man, odd job woman, odd jobber, odd job worker, general jobber, maintenance worker, jack of all trades, man Friday, girl Friday, man of all work, maid of all work, fixer-upper (*inf*).

facts *pl noun* information, elements, details, points, particulars, features, info (*inf*), gen (*inf*), low-down (*inf*), items, factors.

factual *adj* authentic, genuine, true, true to life, real, realistic, actual, accurate, precise, correct, certain, sure, veritable, unbiased, objective, literal, exact, faithful, strict, unexaggerated. OPPOSITE: false.

faculties *pl noun* powers, capacities, capabilities, senses.

faculty *noun* **1** (*the faculty of hearing*) ability, aptitude, facility, gift, knack, talent, skill, dexterity, flair, proficiency, power, capacity, disposition, attribute, feature, property. OPPOSITE: inability. **2** (*the Faculty of Engineering*) department, school, discipline, division, profession. **3** (*conferred the faculty by law*) right, licence, power, authority, authorization, permission, sanction, prerogative, privilege.

fad *noun* fashion, vogue, trend, craze, rage, mode, mania, whim, enthusiasm, fancy.

faddy *adj* fussy, finicky, fastidious, particular, over-particular, hard to please, choosy (*inf*), picky (*inf*), pernickety (*inf*).

fade *verb* **1** (*colours fading*) pale, dim, dull, bleach, blanch, blench, discolour, decolorize, etiolate, wash out. OPPOSITE: darken. **2** (*her health is fading*) diminish,

decrease, dwindle, wane, ebb, fall, decline, fail, languish, wither, perish, faint, peter out, dissolve, disperse, evanesce, vanish, disappear, die, die away. OPPOSITE: grow.

faeces *pl noun* stool, excreta, excrement, bodily waste, droppings, ordure, crap (*sl*), shit (*sl*).

fag *verb* fatigue, weary, tire out, exhaust, jade, wear out, prostrate. OPPOSITE: refresh.
➤ *noun* **1** (*smoke a fag*) cigarette, smoke, roll-your-own, cig (*inf*), joint (*inf*). **2** (*work is a real fag*) chore, drag (*inf*), bother, nuisance, inconvenience, irritation, pain in the neck (*inf*), bind (*inf*).

fail *verb* **1** (*our plans failed*) miscarry, fall through, go wrong, be unsuccessful, flop (*inf*), founder, collapse, fall short, miss, be in vain, come to nothing, come to grief, fizzle out (*inf*), blow it (*inf*), go pear-shaped (*inf*), disappoint, let down. OPPOSITE: succeed. **2** (*fail to shut the door*) omit, neglect, forget, leave, desert, forsake, abandon. **3** (*his health failed*) decline, decay, wane, dwindle, fade, grow less, sink, weaken, flag, collapse, diminish, deteriorate, crumble, cease, die, disappear. OPPOSITE: flourish. **4** (*the business failed*) go bankrupt, crash (*inf*), collapse, go to the wall (*inf*), go under, fold (*inf*), flop (*inf*). OPPOSITE: succeed. **5** (*the engine failed*) break down, stop, cut out, malfunction, pack up (*inf*), conk out (*inf*), crash (*inf*). OPPOSITE: work.
➤ *noun* defeat, flop (*inf*), collapse, disappointment, letdown. OPPOSITE: success.

failing *noun* flaw, fault, defect, weakness, weak spot, blemish, frailty, imperfection, deficiency, shortcoming, drawback, foible, failure. OPPOSITE: strength.

failure *noun* **1** (*the failure of the plan*) miscarriage, abortion, lack of success, frustration, defeat, foundering, breakdown, collapse, fiasco, washout (*inf*), disappointment, letdown, flop (*inf*), dud (*inf*), loser, also-ran (*inf*). OPPOSITE: success. **2** (*his failure to appear*) omission, neglect, negligence, dereliction, delinquency, default, nonperformance. **3** (*felt he was a failure*) loser, write-off (*inf*), no-hoper (*inf*), also-ran (*inf*), has-been (*inf*), dead loss, nonstarter (*inf*). **4** (*failure in his health*) decline, decay, failing, deterioration, collapse, weakening, breakdown. **5** (*failure of a business*) collapse, bankruptcy, insolvency, ruin, folding (*inf*), flop (*inf*). **6** (*the failure of the machine*) breakdown, malfunctioning, stopping, crash (*inf*).

faint *adj* **1** (*a faint light*) weak, feeble, dim, pale, faded, indistinct, unclear, obscure, imperceptible, soft, subdued, low, muffled. OPPOSITE: strong. **2** (*feel faint*) dizzy, giddy, unsteady, light-headed, weak, weak-headed, woozy (*inf*), drooping, languid, exhausted, weary. **3** (*a faint chance*) slight, small, little, remote, minimal, vague.
➤ *verb* collapse, pass out, lose consciousness, black out, swoon, keel over (*inf*), flake out (*inf*).
➤ *noun* blackout, collapse, unconsciousness, swoon, syncope.

faint-hearted *adj* timid, diffident, weak, spiritless, timorous, cowardly, fearful, chicken (*inf*), yellow (*inf*). OPPOSITE: brave.

faintly *adv* slightly, remotely, vaguely, somewhat, a little, a bit.

fair[1] *adj* **1** (*a fair trial*) just, equitable, impartial, dispassionate, even-handed, unbiased, disinterested, objective, square, legitimate, right, proper, above board, honest, trustworthy, honourable, upright. OPPOSITE: unfair. **2** (*fair hair*) blond, blonde, flaxen, light. OPPOSITE: dark. **3** (*fair skin*) light, pale, white. OPPOSITE: dark. **4** (*a fair lass*) attractive, beautiful, handsome, pretty, lovely, bonny, comely, good-looking. OPPOSITE: ugly. **5** (*fair weather*) sunny, clear, bright, cloudless, fine, dry, favourable. OPPOSITE: stormy. **6** (*travel a fair distance*) reasonable, moderate, respectable, decent, goodish. **7** (*their work is fair*) adequate, satisfactory, passable, average, reasonable, moderate, middling, mediocre, so-so (*inf*), all right, OK (*inf*), not bad. OPPOSITE: excellent.

fair[2] *noun* (*a summer fair*) fete, gala, festival, carnival, bazaar, show, exhibition, exposition, expo (*inf*), market, trade fair.

fairly *adv* **1** (*fairly well*) quite, rather, reasonably, somewhat, pretty (*inf*). **2** (*fairly bursting with energy*) positively, absolutely, really, veritably. **3** (*treated them fairly*) justly, equitably, honestly, rightly, properly, legally, lawfully.

fairness *noun* justice, justness, impartiality, objectivity, even-handedness, equity, equitableness, disinterest.

fairy *noun* elf, sprite, pixie, brownie, imp, gnome, goblin, hobgoblin, leprechaun, fay, peri, puck, kelpie.

fairy tale *noun* **1** (*children's fairy tales*) fairy story, myth, legend, story, folktale. **2** (*not believe his fairy tales*) lie, untruth, falsehood, fib, tall story (*inf*), yarn (*inf*).

faith *noun* **1** (*lost faith in doctors*) belief, confidence, assurance, trust, reliance, dependence, credence, conviction. OPPOSITE: doubt. **2** (*the Christian faith*) religion, creed, teaching, doctrine, dogma, belief, persuasion, church, denomination, sect. **3** (*keep faith*) faithfulness, fidelity, loyalty, allegiance, devotion, steadfastness, constancy, truthfulness, truth. OPPOSITE: faithlessness.

faithful *adj* **1** (*a faithful friend*) loyal, true, devoted, steadfast, constant, committed, dedicated, staunch, trusty, trustworthy, true, reliable, dependable, unswerving. OPPOSITE: unfaithful. **2** (*a faithful translation*) accurate, exact, precise, close, strict, just, true, literal, factual. OPPOSITE: inaccurate.
➤ *noun* followers, believers, adherents.

faithfulness *noun* **1** (*faithfulness to a friend*) loyalty, devotion, constancy, commitment, dedication, reliability, dependability. OPPOSITE: disloyalty.
2 (*faithfulness to the original text*) accuracy, exactness, precision, closeness, correspondence, strictness. OPPOSITE: inaccuracy.

faithless *adj* **1** (*a faithless partner*) unfaithful, disloyal, untrue, false, treacherous, traitorous, untrustworthy, unreliable, fickle, inconstant, perfidious, dishonest, two-faced. OPPOSITE: faithful. **2** (*faithless people*) unbelieving, doubting, disbelieving, sceptical, agnostic.

fake *adj* counterfeit, forged, false, bogus, sham, spurious, phoney (*inf*), artificial, ersatz, reproduction, synthetic, pseudo (*inf*). OPPOSITE: genuine.
➤ *verb* counterfeit, forge, fabricate, copy, imitate, pirate, falsify, pretend, feign, affect, put on, sham, dissemble.
➤ *noun* **1** (*this money is fake*) counterfeit, forgery, imitation, reproduction, copy, sham, hoax. **2** (*the doctor is a fake*) fraud, impostor, charlatan, quack (*inf*), pseud (*inf*), phoney (*inf*).

fall *verb* **1** (*fall from a horse*) drop, descend, sink, go down, come down, slope, incline, plunge, dive, plummet, fall, fall down, trip, tumble, come a cropper (*inf*), keel over, topple. **2** (*prices have fallen*) slide, decline, go down, lower, sink, subside, abate, decrease, lessen, fall off, dwindle, diminish, ebb, slump, crash, collapse, plummet, dive, nosedive. OPPOSITE: rise. **3** (*fall asleep*) become, grow, turn, pass into. **4** (*fall to the enemy*) yield, surrender, submit, capitulate, give in, give up, be defeated, be taken. OPPOSITE: triumph. **5** (*fall in battle*) be killed, be lost, be slain, perish, die. OPPOSITE: survive. **6** (*the regime fell*) fade, fail, die, lose power. **7** (*fall to temptation*) lapse, err, sin, transgress, go astray. **8** (*Christmas falls on a Tuesday*) happen, occur, befall, chance, come to pass, take place.
➤ *noun* **1** (*a fall from a horse*) drop, plunge, dive, trip, collapse, tumble, descent, slope, declivity, incline. **2** (*a fall in prices*) decline, decrease, dwindling, reduction, ebb, slump, collapse, abatement. OPPOSITE: rise. **3** (*the fall of Troy*) surrender, yielding, capitulation, failure, defeat, overthrow, capture, downfall, ruin, destruction, demise, death. OPPOSITE: triumph. **4** (*the fall of humanity*) lapse, sin, original sin, transgression, offence.

fall apart crumble, disintegrate, come to pieces, break up, fall to pieces, fall to bits.

fall back withdraw, retreat, draw back, disengage.

fall back on resort to, have recourse to, turn to, call on, look to, use, make use of, employ.

fall behind drop back, lag, lag behind, trail. OPPOSITE: keep up.

fall for **1** (*fell for his sister*) fall in love with, take to, desire, fancy (*inf*) **2** (*fall for a lie*) accept, swallow (*inf*), be fooled by.

fall in collapse, cave in, subside.

fall in with **1** (*fall in with a group of friends*) meet, get involved with, associate with, go around with. **2** (*fall in with their arrangements*) agree to, accept, go along with, support.

fall off decrease, lessen, decline, go down, slump.

fall on fall upon, attack, assail, descend on, set upon, lay into.

fall out quarrel, argue, disagree, clash, differ, fight, wrangle, squabble.

fall through fail, come to nothing, collapse, go wrong, flop (*inf*), fizzle out (*inf*).

fallacious *adj* wrong, erroneous, mistaken, incorrect, inaccurate, imprecise, inexact, misleading, deceptive, delusive, illusory, false, untrue, fictitious, spurious, illogical, unsound, invalid, sophistic. OPPOSITE: true.

fallacy *noun* misconception, misbelief, misjudgment, misapprehension, mistake, error, inconsistency, illusion, delusion, chimera, falsehood, untruth, deception, sophistry, casuistry. OPPOSITE: truth.

fallen *adj* **1** (*fallen in battle*) dead, killed, perished, slaughtered, slain. **2** (*fallen women*) immoral, loose, promiscuous, shamed.

fallible *adj* imperfect, erring, flawed, weak, frail, mortal, human, unreliable. OPPOSITE: infallible.

fallow *adj* unploughed, uncultivated, unused, untilled, unsown, undeveloped, dormant, barren, inactive, idle, neglected, inert, resting. OPPOSITE: cultivated.

falls *pl noun* waterfall, cascade, cataract, rapids, torrent.

false *adj* **1** (*false information*) untrue, misleading, inaccurate, erroneous, wrong, incorrect, mistaken, faulty, invalid, untruthful, unreliable, unsound, fallacious, fictitious, mendacious, lying, deceitful, deceptive, delusive. OPPOSITE: true. **2** (*false to his country*) treacherous, disloyal, traitorous, untrue, faithless, unfaithful, hypocritical, two-faced, untrustworthy, duplicitous, dishonest, dishonourable, perfidious. OPPOSITE: faithful. **3** (*false enthusiasm*) fake, imitation, spurious, counterfeit, forged, ersatz, artificial, synthetic, unreal, mock, feigned, sham, bogus, phoney (*inf*), pseudo (*inf*). OPPOSITE: genuine.

falsehood *noun* **1** (*tell falsehoods*) lie, fib, untruth, fabrication, exaggeration, fiction, perjury, falsity, mendacity, untruthfulness. OPPOSITE: truth. **2** (*falsehood to his friends*) deceit, deception, treachery, disloyalty, faithlessness, unfaithfulness, duplicity. OPPOSITE: loyalty.

falsify *verb* misrepresent, belie, distort, pervert, tamper with, doctor, alter, adulterate, counterfeit, forge, fake, cook (*inf*), manipulate, fiddle (*inf*).

falter *verb* **1** (*falter in your opinion*) hesitate, waver, vacillate, delay, be unsure. OPPOSITE: decide. **2** (*faltered in his movements*) stumble, totter, dodder, tremble, shake. **3** (*her voice faltered*) stammer, stutter, speak haltingly.

fame *noun* renown, celebrity, name, distinction, note, notability, reputation, repute, credit, honour, glory, acclaim, eminence, illustriousness, stardom. OPPOSITE: oblivion.

familiar *adj* **1** (*a familiar face*) well-known, recognizable, recognized, known, usual, common, household, domestic, everyday, ordinary, accustomed, customary, routine, frequent. OPPOSITE: unfamiliar. **2** (*could not be familiar with him*) intimate, close, confidential, friendly, amicable, sociable. **3** (*too familiar with the manager*) forward, bold, presumptuous, overfamiliar, impudent, disrespectful. **4** (*written in a familiar style*) informal, unceremonious, easy, relaxed, casual, unconstrained, open, free. OPPOSITE: formal.

familiar with conversant with, acquainted with, well up in, versed in, conscious of, aware of, no stranger to.

familiarity *noun* **1** (*familiarity with the landscape*) knowledge, acquaintance, grasp, understanding, comprehension, experience, awareness. OPPOSITE: ignorance. **2** (*familiarity with royalty*) intimacy, closeness, friendliness. **3** (*familiarity with his wife*) boldness, presumption, liberty, overfamiliarity, impudence, disrespect, impertinence. **4** (*familiarity of atmosphere*) sociability, informality, openness, naturalness, ease. OPPOSITE: formality.

familiarize *verb* acquaint, accustom, habituate, inure, acclimatize, break in, train, teach, instruct, school.

family *noun* **1** (*the nuclear family*) relatives, relations, kin, folk, people, next of kin, children, offspring, progeny, household, ménage, flesh and blood. **2** (*start a family*) children, offspring, little ones (*inf*), kids (*inf*). **3** (*come from an aristocratic family*) ancestry, ancestors, forefathers, lineage, parentage, extraction, blood, race, strain, stock, background, roots, pedigree, clan, tribe, house, dynasty. **4** (*the cabbage family*) group, class, subdivision, genus, species, kind, type, system.

famine *noun* starvation, hunger, malnutrition, deprivation, want, lack, dearth, scarcity, shortage, deficiency. OPPOSITE: plenty.

famished *adj* starving, ravenous, hungry, empty, undernourished, voracious. OPPOSITE: full.

famous *adj* well-known, renowned, celebrated, famed, illustrious, prominent, respected, eminent, distinguished, notable, noted, great, acclaimed, legendary, memorable. OPPOSITE: unknown.

fan[1] *verb* **1** (*fanning oneself to cool down*) ventilate, air, air-condition, freshen, blow, cool, refresh. **2** (*fan the mob's fury*) agitate, excite, arouse, increase, stimulate, stir up, whip up, inflame, incite, work up, provoke. OPPOSITE: quell.
➤ *noun* ventilator, air conditioner, aerator, blower.

fan[2] *noun* (*a fan of radio comedy*) devotee, enthusiast, aficionado, addict, freak (*inf*), buff (*inf*), fiend (*inf*), admirer, follower, supporter, fanatic.

fanatic *noun* zealot, bigot, extremist, radical, militant, visionary, enthusiast, activist, addict, devotee, fan. OPPOSITE: moderate.

fanatical *adj* zealous, bigoted, immoderate, extreme, dogmatic, extremist, sectarian, radical, visionary, enthusiastic, fervent, passionate, frenzied, wild, mad, obsessive. OPPOSITE: restrained.

fanciful *adj* **1** (*fanciful ideas*) capricious, flighty, whimsical, wild, fantastic, fabulous, fancied, chimerical, imaginary, unreal, visionary, extravagant, impractical, romantic, mythical, imaginative, inventive. OPPOSITE: realistic. **2** (*fanciful designs*) elaborate, ornate, decorated, extravagant, creative, imaginative, curious, bizarre.

fancy *verb* **1** (*fancy something to eat*) want, desire, wish for, crave, long for, feel like, hanker after, like, prefer, favour. **2** (*he fancies blondes*) find attractive, go for, lech after (*inf*), have a crush on (*inf*), have the hots for (*sl*). **3** (*fancy that I could hear a cuckoo*) imagine, conceive, think, reckon, believe, suppose, conjecture, surmise, guess, picture, visualize, envisage.
➤ *noun* **1** (*a passing fancy*) caprice, whim, vagary, eccentricity, quirk, notion, idea, conception, image, picture, impression, vision, dream, fantasy. **2** (*took a fancy to the cat*) desire, urge, wish, want, impulse, hankering, yearning, inclination, tendency, liking, predilection, fondness, partiality. OPPOSITE: aversion.
➤ *adj* **1** (*fancy designs*) ornate, ornamental, decorative, ornamented, decorated, elaborate, showy, ostentatious. OPPOSITE: plain. **2** (*fancy ideas*) capricious, whimsical, fanciful, extravagant, imaginative, fantastic. OPPOSITE: practical.

fanfare *noun* **1** (*a fanfare of trumpets*) flourish, fanfaronade. **2** (*with a fanfare of publicity*) show, showiness, ostentation, display, razzmatazz, hype (*inf*).

fang *noun* tooth, tusk, prong.

fantasize *verb* imagine, dream, daydream, hallucinate.

fantastic *adj* **1** (*a fantastic party*) wonderful, splendid, marvellous, excellent, first-rate, great, superb, tremendous, cool (*inf*), brill (*inf*). **2** (*a fantastic amount of money*) tremendous, immense, vast, great, enormous, formidable. **3** (*fantastic ideas*) fanciful, imaginary, unreal, weird, odd, strange, grotesque, chimerical, bizarre, outlandish, ridiculous, absurd, wild, extravagant, capricious, whimsical, far-fetched, unrealistic, preposterous, incredible, mad, crazy, irrational. OPPOSITE: realistic.

fantasy *noun* fancy, imagination, invention, image, romance, dream, nightmare, illusion, hallucination, mirage, phantom, vision, daydream, flight of fancy, castle in the air, reverie. OPPOSITE: reality.

far *adj* distant, remote, removed, faraway, far-off, far-flung, outlying, out of the way, godforsaken. OPPOSITE: near.
➤ *adv* **1** (*not far away*) a long way, afar, miles. **2** (*far too hot*) greatly, considerably, to a great extent, much, very much, extremely, decidedly.
far and away easily, greatly, decidedly, markedly.
far and wide widely, extensively, everywhere.
far out extreme, radical, weird, outlandish, way out (*inf*).
so far up to this point, up to now, until now, to date.

farce *noun* **1** (*a bedroom farce*) comedy, burlesque, slapstick, buffoonery, satire. OPPOSITE: tragedy. **2** (*the election was a complete farce*) shambles, mockery, travesty, sham, absurdity, nonsense, joke.

farcical *adj* **1** (*farcical to suppose he'll come*) ludicrous, ridiculous, absurd, preposterous, laughable. **2** (*farcical drama*) comic, funny, humorous, amusing, slapstick, droll. OPPOSITE: tragic.

fare *noun* **1** (*the train fare*) charge, fee, price, cost. **2** (*the region's staple fare*) food, diet, meals, menu, provisions, victuals, nourishment, sustenance, eats (*inf*), nosh (*inf*).
➤ *verb* manage, get along, get on, do, make out, progress.

farewell *interj* goodbye, au revoir, adieu, bye (*inf*), cheers (*inf*), cheerio (*inf*), so long (*inf*), all the best (*inf*), ta-ta (*inf*).
➤ *noun* departure, leave-taking, valediction, goodbye, parting.

far-fetched *adj* improbable, implausible, unlikely, unbelievable, incredible, unconvincing, preposterous, fantastic, doubtful, dubious. OPPOSITE: probable.

farm *noun* farmstead, farmland, land, grange, homestead, smallholding, holding, croft, ranch, plantation.
➤ *verb* till, cultivate, work.
farm out contract out, subcontract, delegate.

farmer *noun* agriculturalist, agronomist, smallholder, crofter, rancher, husbandman, herdsman, herder, grazier, sower, reaper, breeder, nurseryman.

farming *noun* agriculture, agronomy, husbandry, cultivation, tilling.

farrago *noun* hotchpotch, miscellany, jumble, mixture, medley, potpourri, mishmash, salmagundi.

far-reaching *adj* sweeping, extensive, broad, thorough, widespread, wide-ranging. OPPOSITE: restricted.

farsighted *adj* forward-looking, discerning, wise, shrewd, prudent, circumspect. OPPOSITE: imprudent.

farther *adj* further, beyond, past, longer. OPPOSITE: nearer.

farthest *adj* furthest, longest, last, utmost, remotest, most distant, extreme. OPPOSITE: nearest.

fascinate *verb* charm, captivate, intrigue, beguile, enchant, delight, attract, allure, enthral, enrapture, entrance, spellbind, hypnotize, mesmerize, rivet, transfix, engross, absorb. OPPOSITE: bore.

fascinating *adj* intriguing, exciting, gripping, riveting, spellbinding, interesting, absorbing, delightful, attractive. OPPOSITE: boring.

fascination *noun* charm, appeal, allure, attraction, draw, pull, magnetism, enchantment, entrancement, captivation, hypnotism, mesmerism. OPPOSITE: repulsion.

fashion *noun* **1** (*the latest fashion*) vogue, mode, look, style, trend, craze, fad, custom, convention, practice, usage. **2** (*in an orderly fashion*) way, method, manner, style, approach, sort, kind, type.
➤ *verb* make, form, mould, shape, design, create, forge, construct, adapt, accommodate, suit, fit, adjust, tailor.
after a fashion approximately, roughly, in a rough way, to some extent.

fashionable *adj* stylish, modish, in fashion, in vogue, à la mode, chic, elegant, smart, trendy (*inf*), all the rage (*inf*), modern, up-to-date, current, in (*inf*), popular, with it (*inf*), snazzy (*inf*), ritzy (*inf*), swish (*inf*), trendy (*inf*), cool (*inf*). OPPOSITE: unfashionable.

fast *adj* **1** (*a fast train*) rapid, swift, quick, speedy, express, accelerated, brisk, fleet. OPPOSITE: slow. **2** (*the doors are fast*) secure, fixed, firm, immovable, tight, fastened. **3** (*fast friends*) firm, loyal, staunch, constant, steadfast, sound, lasting. **4** (*live a fast life*) dissolute, dissipated, rakish, loose, wild, reckless, immoral, promiscuous, extravagant, self-indulgent. OPPOSITE: restrained.
➤ *adv* **1** (*travel fast*) rapidly, swiftly, quickly, speedily, briskly, in haste, like a shot (*inf*), as fast as your legs will carry you (*inf*), lickety-split (*inf*). OPPOSITE: slowly.
2 (*held fast*) securely, firmly, tightly, immovably. OPPOSITE: loosely. **3** (*fast asleep*) deeply, soundly. **4** (*live fast*) wildly, recklessly, extravagantly, loosely, promiscuously, wantonly.

fasten *verb* **1** (*fasten a seat belt*) secure, fix, make fast, bind, tie, tether, attach, join, unite, connect, link, couple, bolt, chain, strap, lace, buckle, button, do up, hook, pin, clip, tack, latch, lock. OPPOSITE: unfasten.
2 (*fastened his attention*) aim, direct, focus, point, bend, fix, concentrate.

fastidious *adj* critical, hard to please, particular, overparticular, fussy, finicky, pernickety, hypercritical, meticulous, dainty, delicate, squeamish, choosy (*inf*), picky (*inf*).

fat *adj* **1** (*a fat man*) stout, overweight, large, solid, big, broad, heavy, plump, obese, flabby, podgy, chubby, rotund, tubby, potbellied, portly, corpulent, gross. OPPOSITE: thin. **2** (*low fat content*) fatty, greasy, oily. **3** (*a fat book*) wide, thick, substantial. OPPOSITE: slim. **4** (*a fat profit*) large, substantial, considerable, lucrative,

profitable. **5** (*fat fields*) rich, fertile, fruitful, productive, abundant, plentiful, wealthy, affluent. OPPOSITE: poor.
➤ *noun* **1** (*get your fat down*) plumpness, obesity, flabbiness, corpulence, overweight, paunch, pot belly, flab (*inf*). **2** (*animal fat*) fatty tissue, blubber, grease, oil, margarine, butter, lard, cream.

fatal *adj* **1** (*a fatal illness*) deadly, lethal, mortal, destructive, ruinous, calamitous, disastrous, incurable, terminal, final, malignant, harmful, pernicious, baleful, baneful. OPPOSITE: beneficial. **2** (*a fatal meeting*) critical, crucial, decisive, fateful, inevitable, destined, fated.

fatalism *noun* resignation, stoicism, acceptance, predeterminism, predestination, foreordination.

fatality *noun* death, disaster, catastrophe, casualty, mortality, accident, fate, destiny.

fate *noun* destiny, providence, chance, fortune, lot, portion, doom, kismet, predestination, destination, future, end, death, destruction, downfall, defeat, ruin.

fated *adj* destined, doomed, predestined, preordained, foreordained, sure, certain, inevitable, inescapable.

fateful *adj* **1** (*a fateful decision*) crucial, critical, decisive, pivotal, momentous, portentous, important, significant. **2** (*that fateful night*) disastrous, ruinous, fatal, deadly, catastrophic.

father *noun* **1** (*he's a good father*) dad (*inf*), daddy (*inf*), pop (*inf*), papa, pa (*inf*), old man (*inf*), pater. OPPOSITE: mother. **2** (*the traditions of our fathers*) parent, progenitor, sire, ancestor, forefather, forebear, predecessor, primogenitor. OPPOSITE: offspring. **3** (*the fathers of modern science*) creator, originator, initiator, maker, author, inventor, architect, founder, prime mover. **4** (*a spiritual father*) priest, minister, padre, clergyman.
➤ *verb* **1** (*father a child*) sire, beget, procreate, generate, engender. **2** (*father a plan*) create, make, invent, originate, initiate, establish, found.

fatherland *noun* homeland, home, native land, motherland.

fatherly *adj* paternal, kind, benevolent, benign, caring, tender, affectionate, sympathetic, understanding, protective, supportive, parental.

fathom *verb* **1** (*fathom the depths*) measure, sound, gauge, plumb, estimate. **2** (*can't fathom the problem*) probe, penetrate, understand, comprehend, grasp, see, get to the bottom of.

fathomless *adj* unfathomable, impenetrable, incomprehensible, immeasurable, bottomless, deep, profound. OPPOSITE: shallow.

fatigue *verb* exhaust, weary, tire out, tire, jade, fag, drain, weaken, enervate, debilitate, take it out of (*inf*). OPPOSITE: refresh.
➤ *noun* exhaustion, weariness, tiredness, lassitude, lethargy, listlessness, debility, enervation. OPPOSITE: vigour.

fatness *noun* plumpness, obesity, portliness, corpulence, stoutness, largeness, heaviness, tubbiness, rotundity, flabbiness. OPPOSITE: thinness.

fatten *verb* stuff, cram, feed, build up, bloat, make fat, get fat, swell, broaden, spread, put on weight. OPPOSITE: slim.

fatty *adj* fat, oily, greasy, fleshy, unctuous, adipose, sebaceous, oleaginous.

fatuity *noun* fatuousness, foolishness, folly, silliness, absurdity, inanity, stupidity, idiocy, pointlessness, imbecility, madness, lunacy. OPPOSITE: sense.

fatuous *adj* foolish, silly, absurd, inane, stupid, idiotic, senseless, pointless, nonsensical, asinine, witless, vacuous, moronic. OPPOSITE: sensible.

fault *noun* **1** (*a design fault*) flaw, blemish, defect, imperfection, failing, weakness, deficiency, frailty, shortcoming. OPPOSITE: virtue. **2** (*a fault in the calculation*) error, mistake, slip, lapse, offence, misdeed, crime, wrong, sin, transgression, misdemeanour. **3** (*the crash was their fault*) culpability, responsibility, accountability, blameworthiness, answerability.
➤ *verb* find fault with, criticize, blame, pick holes in (*inf*).
at fault to blame, culpable, blameable, responsible, accountable, guilty, in the wrong.
find fault complain, carp, cavil, quibble, criticize.
to a fault exceedingly, excessively, extremely, unduly, over the top (*inf*).

faultfinding *adj* critical, carping, hypercritical, overcritical, grumbling, querulous, nit-picking (*inf*).

faultless *adj* perfect, flawless, model, exemplary, impeccable, unblemished, immaculate, spotless, pure, blameless, irreproachable, guiltless, innocent. OPPOSITE: imperfect.

faulty *adj* **1** (*a faulty machine*) defective, imperfect, broken, damaged, impaired, not working, out of order. **2** (*a faulty argument*) unsound, weak, incorrect, erroneous, wrong, fallacious, invalid, inaccurate, imprecise, flawed. OPPOSITE: perfect.

faux pas *noun* blunder, gaffe, indiscretion, mistake, boob (*inf*), booboo (*inf*), goof (*inf*).

favour *noun* **1** (*look with favour on the project*) approval, approbation, countenance, sanction, backing, support, patronage, preference, partiality, bias, favouritism, good will, kindness, friendliness, graciousness, good books (*inf*). OPPOSITE: disapproval. **2** (*did them a favour*) good turn, good deed, benefaction, boon, service, courtesy, kindness. **3** (*gave him a favour*) gift, present, souvenir, memento, keepsake, token, badge, rosette, decoration.
➤ *verb* **1** (*favour a decrease in taxes*) approve, countenance, sanction, back, support, patronize, befriend, recommend, prefer, champion, advocate, encourage, oblige, help, assist, facilitate, ease, advance. OPPOSITE: oppose. **2** (*favours men with beards*) prefer, side with, choose, select, like, go in for, fancy, be partial to, esteem, value, indulge, spoil, pamper. **3** (*favours her mother*) resemble, take after, look like.
in favour of for, pro, approving, supporting, backing, behind, on the side of, for the sake of.

favourable *adj* **1** (*favourable conditions*) encouraging, promising, propitious, auspicious, advantageous, good, fair, hopeful, beneficial, helpful, suitable, fit, opportune, timely. OPPOSITE: unfavourable. **2** (*make a favourable impression*) approving, agreeable, amicable, well-disposed, kind, friendly, understanding, sympathetic, positive, pleasing, congenial, encouraging, enthusiastic. OPPOSITE: disapproving.

favourite noun pet, darling, dearest, beloved, preference, choice, blue-eyed boy (inf), apple of one's eye.
➤ adj dearest, best-loved, most-loved, special, preferred, chosen, pet.

favouritism noun nepotism, unfairness, partiality, partisanship, prejudice, inequality. OPPOSITE impartiality.

fawn[1] adj (a fawn carpet) beige, buff, yellowish-brown, sandy.

fawn[2] verb (fawn on the boss) grovel, cringe, crawl, creep, kowtow, bow and scrape, toady, truckle, flatter, court, curry favour.

fawning adj servile, obsequious, sycophantic, bootlicking (inf), grovelling, cringing, crawling (inf), creeping (inf), flattering. OPPOSITE: independent.

fealty noun loyalty, allegiance, fidelity, faithfulness, devotion, homage.

fear noun 1 (feel fear at the danger) terror, horror, panic, alarm, fright, cowardice, timidity, trepidation, dread, the creeps (inf), apprehension. 2 (a fear of failure) anxiety, worry, distress, concern, solicitude, unease, uneasiness, apprehension, disquiet, misgiving, qualm, foreboding. OPPOSITE: reassurance. 3 (a fear of dentists) phobia, bogey, bugbear, bête noire, dread, aversion, nightmare. 4 (fear of God) awe, reverence, wonder, veneration, respect. OPPOSITE: disrespect.
➤ verb 1 (fear the terror of night) dread, be afraid of, be frightened of, shudder at, be scared of, have cold feet about (inf), sweat blood over (inf), run a mile from (inf), spook (inf). 2 (fear for the worst) worry, be anxious, feel concern. 3 (fear God) revere, reverence, venerate, respect. 4 (fear I can't help) be afraid, anticipate, expect, suspect.

fearful adj 1 (fearful of death) terrified, afraid, frightened, scared, alarmed, uneasy, apprehensive, anxious, nervous, hesitant, jumpy, timid, timorous, diffident. OPPOSITE: bold. 2 (a fearful storm) dreadful, terrible, horrendous, awful, frightful, dire, grim, formidable, horrible, ghastly, distressing, harrowing, appalling, hideous, shocking, atrocious. OPPOSITE: wonderful.

fearless adj bold, brave, courageous, dauntless, undaunted, intrepid, plucky, confident, lionhearted, heroic, gallant, valiant, valorous, daring, unflinching, unafraid, gutsy (inf), spunky (inf). OPPOSITE: afraid.

fearsome adj formidable, daunting, frightening, terrific, fearful, awesome, dreadful, scary (inf), huge, colossal.

feasibility noun practicability, workability, viability, possibility, likelihood, attainability. OPPOSITE: impossibility.

feasible adj practicable, workable, viable, possible, likely, reasonable, practical, realistic, realizable, attainable, accomplishable, obtainable. OPPOSITE: impossible.

feast noun 1 (a feast in the President's honour) banquet, spread (inf), dinner, barbecue, blowout (inf), slap-up meal (inf), repast, treat, junket, festivities. 2 (the Feast of the Passover) festival, celebration, holy day, saint's day,

fête. 3 (a feast for the eyes) wealth, abundance, profusion, bounty, copiousness, cornucopia.
➤ verb 1 (feast on rich food) dine, banquet, eat one's fill, gorge, indulge, overindulge, stuff, regale, treat, wine and dine, entertain. 2 (feasted their eyes on her prettiness) delight, please, gladden, gratify, thrill, treat.

feat noun deed, act, exploit, achievement, accomplishment, performance, attainment, stroke, coup.

feather noun plume, quill, penna, plumule, aigrette, tuft, down, crest.

feathery adj 1 (a feathery bird) feathered, fleecy, fluffy, downy, plumose, plumulose. 2 (feathery tissue) soft, light, delicate, flimsy, insubstantial, wispy.

feature noun 1 (important features of city life) characteristic, peculiarity, trait, mark, hallmark, attribute, property, quality, aspect, facet. 2 (a garden feature) highlight, speciality, main item, attraction, display, focal point. 3 (a feature in a magazine) article, story, item, piece, column, report.
➤ verb 1 (special effects are featured in the film) highlight, emphasize, accentuate, play up, spotlight, give prominence to, promote, star. 2 (violence features prominently in his works) play a part, participate, appear, have a place.

features pl noun face, countenance, physiognomy, visage, lineaments, mug (inf), kisser (inf).

feculence noun scum, sediment, residue, dregs, lees, muck, filth, mud, dirt.

fecund adj fruitful, productive, fertile, rich, potent, prolific, abundant. OPPOSITE: barren.

federal adj confederated, federated, associated, allied, combined, united, integrated.

federate verb confederate, federate, ally, combine, unite, integrate.

federation noun confederation, confederacy, union, league, alliance, coalition, syndicate, combination, amalgamation.

fee noun cost, price, payment, remuneration, reward, recompense, pay, hire, emolument, honorarium, allowance, charge, toll, bill, account.

feeble adj 1 (a feeble old person) weak, frail, infirm, delicate, sickly, puny, debilitated, enervated, doddering, doddery, languid, drooping, failing, faint, slight, thin. OPPOSITE: strong. 2 (feeble government) ineffectual, powerless, unavailing, inefficient, incompetent, inadequate, unsuccessful. OPPOSITE: powerful. 3 (a feeble excuse) inadequate, poor, weak, tame, lame, flimsy, unconvincing.

feeble-minded adj retarded, simple, foolish, stupid, silly, slow.

feed verb 1 (to feed children) nourish, sustain, satisfy, provide for, supply, cater for, provision, suckle. OPPOSITE: starve. 2 (cattle feeding) graze, pasture, eat, devour, dine, fare, subsist. 3 (feed her self-esteem) support, strengthen, gratify, encourage. 4 (feed data to headquarters) supply, provide, give, furnish, introduce.
➤ noun fodder, forage, food, provender.

feel verb 1 (felt her hand) touch, handle, finger, stroke, caress, fondle, rub, paw, maul. 2 (feel pain) sense,

experience, perceive, observe, notice, be aware of, know, undergo, suffer, enjoy. **3** (*felt his way*) fumble, grope, explore. **4** (*feel that I should go*) think, consider, believe, judge, hold, sense. **5** (*the material feels soft*) seem, appear.
≫ *noun* **1** (*the feel of the material*) texture, surface, finish. **2** (*the feel of the place*) atmosphere, quality, air, mood, ambience, aura, vibes (*inf*). **3** (*have a feel for the piano*) knack, touch, ability, talent, gift, skill.
feel for sympathize with, commiserate with, empathize with, bleed for, be sorry for, weep for, grieve for.
feel like want, desire, fancy, wish, like.

feeler *noun* **1** (*an animal's feelers*) antenna, tentacle, palp. **2** (*put out feelers*) approach, advance, overture, probe.

feeling *noun* **1** (*a feeling of dizziness*) sense, sensation, impression, perception, consciousness, awareness, touch, contact, feel. **2** (*my personal feeling*) hunch, inkling, suspicion, idea, impression, notion, premonition, presentiment, opinion, viewpoint, point of view, thought. **3** (*a person of great feeling*) emotion, sentiment, sensibility, sensitivity, understanding, sympathy, empathy, fellow feeling, compassion, affection, tenderness, passion, warmth, ardour, fervour. OPPOSITE: insensitivity. **4** (*the feeling of a place*) atmosphere, quality, air, mood, ambience, aura, vibes (*inf*).
≫ *adj* sentient, sensible, sensitive, emotional, sympathetic, caring, compassionate, tender, warm, passionate, intense, ardent, fervent. OPPOSITE: unfeeling.

feelings *pl noun* sensitivities, ego, self-esteem, susceptibilities.

feign *verb* affect, put on, assume, pretend, make believe, play act, act, sham, simulate, fake, counterfeit, forge, fabricate, copy, imitate, dissemble.

feint *noun* dodge, trick, stratagem, ruse, artifice, pretext, expedient, blind, bluff, sham, hoax, pretence, show, dodge (*inf*).

felicitate *verb* congratulate, compliment.

felicitations *pl noun* congratulations, compliments, best wishes, greetings.

felicitous *adj* **1** (*a felicitous coincidence*) apt, appropriate, well-chosen, suitable, pertinent, apposite, opportune, timely, to the point, propitious, seasonable. OPPOSITE: inappropriate. **2** (*a felicitous occasion*) happy, fortunate, lucky, delightful, successful.

felicity *noun* **1** (*the felicity of the remark*) aptness, appropriateness, suitability, pertinence, propitiousness. OPPOSITE: inappropriateness. **2** (*the felicity of the occasion*) happiness, joy, bliss, ecstasy, rapture, delight. OPPOSITE: misery.

feline *adj* catlike, sleek, graceful, smooth, slinky, stealthy.

fell *verb* hew, cut down, knock down, strike down, prostrate, level, flatten, floor, raze, demolish.

fellow *noun* **1** (*a friendly fellow*) man, male, boy, person, chap (*inf*), bloke (*inf*), guy (*inf*). **2** (*his school fellows*) companion, comrade, friend, colleague, partner, equal, peer, compeer, mate, associate, counterpart, match, twin, chum (*inf*), crony (*inf*), pal (*inf*), buddy (*inf*).

fellowship *noun* **1** (*a sense of fellowship*)

companionship, comradeship, camaraderie, friendship, amiability, amity, brotherhood, sisterhood, intimacy, familiarity, sociability, chumminess (*inf*), palliness (*inf*), company, communion, social intercourse. OPPOSITE: enmity. **2** (*a Christian fellowship*) association, society, club, fraternity, sorority, guild, league.

felon *noun* criminal, offender, malefactor, wrongdoer, culprit, convict.

felony *noun* crime, offence, misdemeanour.

female *noun* **1** (*a pretty female*) woman, lady, girl, lass. OPPOSITE: male. **2** (*the female of a dog*) bitch, cow, duck, ewe, doe, sow, hen, mare, vixen.
≫ *adj* feminine, womanly, ladylike. OPPOSITE: male.

feminine *adj* **1** (*feminine hands*) womanly, girlish, ladylike, pretty, soft, gentle, tender, delicate, graceful. OPPOSITE: masculine. **2** (*a feminine young man*) effeminate, womanish, unmanly, sissy, weak, effete. OPPOSITE: manly.

femininity *noun* feminineness, womanhood, womanliness, girlishness, prettiness, gentleness, tenderness, delicacy, gracefulness.

feminism *noun* women's rights, women's lib, women's movement, suffragism.

fen *noun* bog, marsh, swamp, morass, quagmire.

fence *noun* railing, paling, hedge, wall, barrier, barricade, enclosure, stockade, palisade, defence, guard.
≫ *verb* **1** (*fence an area*) enclose, shut in, surround, encircle, circumscribe, bound, confine, secure, defend, protect, guard. OPPOSITE: expose. **2** (*fenced to avoid a decision*) hedge, quibble, prevaricate, equivocate, fudge, evade, dodge, dodge the issue, shilly-shally, parry, shuffle, tergiversate.
sit on the fence hedge, prevaricate, equivocate, fudge, dodge, dodge the issue, shilly-shally.

fend *verb* **fend for** provide for, support, look after, take care of.
fend off ward off, avert, forestall, deflect, turn aside, parry, stave off, beat off, repel, repulse, drive back.

feral *adj* **1** (*feral animals*) ferine, wild, untamed, unbroken, uncultivated. OPPOSITE: domesticated. **2** (*feral people*) savage, fierce, ferocious, vicious, brutal, cruel. OPPOSITE: gentle.

ferment *verb* **1** (*grapes fermenting*) foam, froth, bubble, effervesce, boil, seethe, brew, rise, work, leaven. **2** (*ferment a crowd*) rouse, arouse, stir up, excite, inflame, agitate, incite, foment, provoke. OPPOSITE: calm.
≫ *noun* **1** (*chemical ferment*) yeast, leaven, leavening, enzyme, bacteria. **2** (*political ferment*) excitement, commotion, tumult, stir, furore, uproar, turmoil, agitation, unrest, stew, heat, fever, frenzy, imbroglio. OPPOSITE: peace.

ferocious *adj* **1** (*a ferocious animal*) fierce, savage, vicious, wild, feral, bestial, cruel, brutal, barbarous, violent, inhuman, bloodthirsty, sanguinary, ruthless, merciless, pitiless, relentless. OPPOSITE: gentle. **2** (*ferocious heat*) intense, severe, harsh, extreme, acute, deep, wild. OPPOSITE: mild.

ferret *verb* search, rummage, scour, forage.
ferret out discover, find, track down, unearth, elicit.

ferry *noun* ferryboat, boat, vessel, shuttle, packet-boat, packet.
➤ *verb* transport, carry, convey, ship, shuttle, shift.

fertile *adj* **1** (*fertile soil*) fecund, productive, fruitful, prolific, teeming, abundant, profuse, plentiful, rich, luxuriant. OPPOSITE: barren. **2** (*a fertile mind*) creative, original, imaginative, resourceful, productive.

fertilize *verb* **1** (*fertilize a cow*) impregnate, inseminate, fecundate, pollinate. **2** (*fertilize land*) enrich, dress, feed, manure, marl, mulch, top-dress, compost.

fertilizer *noun* manure, mulch, feed, dress, dressing, topdressing.

fervent *adj* ardent, passionate, eager, enthusiastic, keen, earnest, zealous, animated, intense, vehement, excited, impassioned, heartfelt, emotional, spirited, burning, glowing, warm, fervid. OPPOSITE: apathetic.

fervour *noun* ardour, passion, fervency, eagerness, keenness, enthusiasm, earnestness, excitement, emotion, spirit, zeal, animation, intensity, vehemence. OPPOSITE: apathy.

fester *verb* **1** (*the wound is festering*) suppurate, ulcerate, infect, gather. **2** (*food festering*) putrefy, rot, decay, corrupt, decompose. **3** (*resentment festering*) rankle, irk, gall, rile, inflame, chafe, irritate.
➤ *noun* abscess, ulcer, boil, pustule, gathering.

festival *noun* gala, carnival, celebration, commemoration, anniversary, jubilee, fair, fête, banquet, feast, feast day, saint's day, holiday.

festive *adj* happy, cheerful, merry, jovial, jolly, convivial, hearty, joyful, joyous, mirthful, cheery, celebratory, jubilant. OPPOSITE: mournful.

festivity *noun* **1** (*the festivity of the event*) merriment, happiness, cheerfulness, joviality, conviviality, joyfulness, mirth, gaiety, jubilation, revelry, fun. OPPOSITE: mourning. **2** (*join in the festivities*) festival, carnival, celebration, party, entertainment, carousal, sport.

festoon *verb* decorate, adorn, array, deck, bedeck, wreathe, garland, drape, hang. OPPOSITE: strip.
➤ *noun* garland, wreath, chaplet.

fetch *verb* **1** (*fetch a pail of water*) bring, carry, convey, deliver, get, obtain, retrieve, go for. **2** (*the painting fetched £500*) realize, yield, bring in, make, sell for.

fetching *adj* attractive, sweet, taking, winsome, fascinating, charming, enchanting, alluring. OPPOSITE: repulsive.

fête *noun* **1** (*a summer fête*) fair, bazaar, gala, festival, carnival, garden party. **2** (*the fête of St Patrick*) holiday, feast day, saint's day, festival.

fetid *adj* foul, rank, malodorous, stinking, noisome, offensive, mephitic, rancid, corrupt, foul. OPPOSITE: fragrant.

fetish *noun* **1** (*a leather fetish*) obsession, mania, fixation, compulsion, thing (*inf*). **2** (*always carrying a fetish*) charm, talisman, amulet.

fetter *verb* chain, shackle, manacle, tie, bind, trammel, encumber, hamper, hinder, restrain, restrict, confine. OPPOSITE: loose.

fetters *pl noun* chains, shackles, manacles, bonds, trammels, irons.

fettle *noun* condition, shape, order, kilter.

feud *noun* vendetta, hostility, antagonism, rivalry, animosity, enmity, bad blood, discord, strife, conflict, dissension, contention, quarrel, row, argument, rupture, bickering, breach, faction. OPPOSITE: agreement.

fever *noun* **1** (*have a high fever*) feverishness, pyrexia, high temperature, temperature (*inf*). **2** (*a fever of excitement*) agitation, excitement, heat, flush, passion, fervour, frenzy, ferment, furore, turmoil. OPPOSITE: composure.

feverish *adj* **1** (*the child is feverish*) burning, fevered, delirious. **2** (*feverish impatience*) excited, heated, passionate, frenzied, restless, overwrought, nervous, hot and bothered (*inf*), in a tizzy (*inf*).

few *adj* rare, scarce, scanty, meagre, hardly any, not many, infrequent, sporadic. OPPOSITE: many.
➤ *pronoun* not many, hardly any, one or two, a handful.

fiancé *noun* betrothed, intended, prospective spouse, future husband, prospective husband.

fiancée *noun* betrothed, intended, prospective spouse, future wife, prospective wife.

fiasco *noun* failure, disaster, catastrophe, mess, flop (*inf*), washout (*inf*). OPPOSITE: success.

fiat *noun* **1** (*government by fiat*) order, command, decree, edict, proclamation, ordinance, law, dictum. **2** (*give a fiat*) permission, sanction, authorization, warrant. OPPOSITE: ban.

fib *noun* lie, untruth, falsehood, fiction, fabrication, story, fairy story, fairy tale, whopper (*inf*). OPPOSITE: truth.
➤ *verb* lie, misrepresent, falsify, prevaricate, equivocate.

fibre *noun* **1** (*the fibres of the fabric*) thread, strand, filament, fibril, staple, texture. **2** (*a person of great moral fibre*) spirit, nature, constitution, make-up, temperament, disposition, strength, stamina, toughness.

fickle *adj* changeable, variable, capricious, mercurial, volatile, flighty, unpredictable, fitful, erratic, irresolute, vacillating, wavering, inconstant, unstable, unsteady, unreliable. OPPOSITE: constant.

fiction *noun* **1** (*science fiction*) story, tale, novel, fable, legend, fantasy, romance, invention, fabrication, fancy, imagination. OPPOSITE: fact. **2** (*that excuse is pure fiction*) lie, falsehood, untruth, concoction, cock-and-bull story (*inf*).

fictional *adj* literary, unreal, invented, fabricated, made-up. OPPOSITE: real.

fictitious *adj* false, untrue, invented, imaginary, fanciful, make-believe, mythical, unreal, bogus, spurious, sham, counterfeit, artificial, feigned, assumed. OPPOSITE: true.

fiddle *verb* **1** (*fiddle with a pen*) play, tinker, tamper, toy, trifle, mess about, mess around, idle, fidget. **2** (*fiddled his expenses*) swindle, cheat, falsify, cook (*inf*), manoeuvre, finagle (*inf*), wangle (*inf*), diddle (*inf*), cook the books (*inf*).
➤ *noun* swindle, fix (*inf*), fraud, racket, wangle, con (*inf*).

fiddling *adj* trifling, trivial, small, insignificant, petty. OPPOSITE: important.

fidelity *noun* **1** (*fidelity to the Queen*) faithfulness, loyalty, devotion, allegiance, staunchness, constancy, steadfastness, trustworthiness, fealty, reliability, dependability. OPPOSITE: infidelity. **2** (*fidelity of the reproduction*) closeness, faithfulness, exactness, accuracy, precision, correspondence, conformity, accordance.

fidget *verb* squirm, twitch, wriggle, fiddle, twiddle, move about, jitter (*inf*), worry, upset, fret.

fidgety *adj* restless, restive, impatient, nervous, fretful, uneasy, jumpy, jittery (*inf*). OPPOSITE: still.

field *noun* **1** (*cattle grazing in the field*) meadow, pasture, green, grassland, common, ground, pitch. **2** (*an expert in the field of metallurgy*) domain, province, realm, sphere, department, discipline, speciality, territory, area. **3** (*a field of vision*) range, scope, extent, limits, bounds. **4** (*all the competitors in the field*) competitors, participants, contestants, competition, candidates, applicants.
» *verb* **1** (*field a ball*) catch, stop, return, throw back. **2** (*field questions*) deal with, answer, handle, parry, deflect.

fiend *noun* **1** (*Satan's fiends*) demon, devil, evil spirit, monster, brute, beast, savage, ogre. OPPOSITE: angel. **2** (*a computer fiend*) addict, enthusiast, fan, devotee, maniac, fanatic, aficionado, buff (*inf*), freak (*inf*).

fiendish *adj* **1** (*a fiendish plot*) demonic, devilish, diabolical, infernal, wicked, evil, malicious, malignant, malevolent, cruel, inhuman, savage, monstrous. OPPOSITE: angelic. **2** (*a fiendish task*) complex, intricate, difficult, involved, obscure. OPPOSITE: simple.

fierce *adj* **1** (*a fierce animal*) savage, ferocious, vicious, dangerous, menacing, threatening, wild, feral, brutal, barbarous, bloodthirsty, sanguinary, cruel, ruthless. OPPOSITE: harmless. **2** (*fierce competition*) wild, intense, keen, powerful, strong, violent, raging, furious, relentless, stormy, tempestuous, uncontrollable, passionate, ardent, fervent. OPPOSITE: gentle.

fiery *adj* **1** (*a fiery temper*) hot, burning, blazing, flaming, glowing, heated, ardent, fervent, vehement, passionate, excitable, temperamental, violent, fierce. OPPOSITE: cool. **2** (*fiery food*) spicy, hot, pungent, piquant.

fight *verb* **1** (*fight in a battle*) battle, combat, war, contend, strive, struggle, oppose, contest, clash, resist, defy, attack, assault, grapple, scuffle, wrestle, spar, box, brawl. **2** (*fighting over whose turn it is*) quarrel, dispute, argue, bicker, wrangle, fall out (*inf*). **3** (*fight poverty*) oppose, campaign against, dispute, take issue with.
» *noun* **1** (*the soldiers in the fight*) battle, combat, strife, conflict, war, fighting, hostilities, action, engagement, encounter, bout, duel. OPPOSITE: peace. **2** (*a fight outside the club*) scrap (*inf*), struggle, brawl, fray, fracas, riot, dispute, row, set-to (*inf*), punch-up (*inf*), aggro (*inf*). **3** (*a verbal fight*) dispute, argument, bickering, quarrel, row, difference of opinion. **4** (*the fight against racism*) campaign, battle, opposition, drive, crusade. **5** (*gave up all fight*) spirit, drive, determination, resoluteness, resolve, willpower, will to live.

fight back **1** (*the men fought back*) retaliate, resist, defend oneself. **2** (*fight back tears*) hold back, suppress, repress, contain, check, bottle up.

fight off beat off, stave off, hold at bay, repel, resist, rebuff.

fighter *noun* attacker, warrior, soldier, boxer, pugilist.

figment *noun* invention, fabrication, creation, illusion, fancy, notion, fiction, fable, story, falsehood. OPPOSITE: fact.

figurative *adj* metaphorical, emblematic, symbolic, allegorical, representative, typical, illustrative. OPPOSITE: literal.

figure *noun* **1** (*add up the figures*) number, numeral, digit, cipher, symbol, character. **2** (*see figures through the fog*) outline, shape, silhouette, form. **3** (*have a rounded figure*) body, build, physique, frame, torso, structure. **4** (*the book contains several figures*) diagram, drawing, picture, illustration, representation, chart, sketch. **5** (*a figure of speech*) image, design, pattern, device, motif, symbol, sign, emblem. **6** (*a public figure*) personage, character, notable, dignitary, celebrity, somebody, worthy, big shot (*inf*). OPPOSITE: nobody.
» *verb* **1** (*figure up the numbers*) calculate, reckon, compute, work out, add up, count. **2** (*he figures in the film*) feature, appear, represent, symbolize, depict, portray. **3** (*I figure he'll be late*) imagine, think, believe, picture, conceive. **4** (*figured with a special design*) decorate, adorn, ornament, embellish, mark, variegate.

figure out work out, solve, calculate, understand, comprehend, grasp, see, fathom.

figurehead *noun* **1** (*a figurehead on a ship*) bust, carving, sculpture. **2** (*he is merely a figurehead*) nominal head, token, mouthpiece, cipher, puppet.

figures *pl noun* numbers, arithmetic, calculations.

filament *noun* strand, thread, fibre, fibril, staple, cable, hair, wire, string.

filch *verb* steal, pilfer, rob, purloin, thieve, take, abstract, nick (*inf*), lift (*inf*), pinch (*inf*), swipe (*inf*), snaffle (*inf*), rip off (*inf*), knock off (*inf*). OPPOSITE: return.

file[1] *noun* **1** (*a manila file*) folder, portfolio, dossier, documents, information. **2** (*a file of people*) line, row, rank, queue, column, list, string, chain.
» *verb* **1** (*file the data*) record, register, place, classify, put in order, arrange, pigeonhole. **2** (*people filing by*) march, troop, parade, pass.

file[2] *verb* (*filed her nails*) rasp, scrape, grind, abrade, rub down, smooth, polish, shape.

fill *verb* **1** (*fill a container*) stuff, cram, pack, fill up, satisfy, content, satiate, glut, sate, swell, inflate, fill out, stock, load, supply, furnish, restock, replenish. OPPOSITE: empty. **2** (*sadness filled the air*) pervade, suffuse, imbue, impregnate, infuse, overspread, cover. **3** (*fill a hole*) plug, cork, bung, stop, stop up, close, block. **4** (*fill a post*) occupy, hold, take up, discharge, execute, perform, carry out, do, fulfil.
» *noun* enough, sufficiency, ampleness, plenty, abundance.

fill in **1** (*fill in a form*) complete, fill out, answer. **2** (*fill in for the boss*) replace, substitute, stand in, deputize. **3** (*filled us in on the details*) inform, advise, notify, apprise, acquaint, bring up to date.

fill out **1** (*fill out a form*) complete, fill in, answer. **2** (*the children filled out*) become fatter, put on weight, become plumper, become chubbier.

fillip *noun* boost, stimulus, incentive, inducement, motivation, impetus, push, prod, shove (*inf*).

film *noun* **1** (*saw the film at the cinema*) picture, movie (*inf*), flick (*inf*), video, videotape, motion picture. **2** (*a film of oil on the water*) covering, coat, coating, layer, sheet, skin, blanket, tissue, membrane, pellicle, veil, haze, blur, cloud, mist.
➤ *verb* photograph, record, shoot, video, videotape, televise.

film over blur, cloud over, mist over, become blurred.

filmy *adj* see-through, transparent, sheer, gossamery, cobwebby, fine, delicate, light, flimsy, translucent, diaphanous. OPPOSITE: opaque.

filter *verb* **1** (*filter the water*) strain, clarify, filtrate, purify, refine, screen, sieve, sift. **2** (*the liquid filtered out*) exude, ooze, seep, leak, trickle, dribble, leach, percolate, transude.
➤ *noun* strainer, screen, sieve, sifter, colander, riddle, net, netting, mesh, gauze.

filth *noun* **1** (*live in filth*) dirt, muck, grime, sewage, refuse, pollution, foulness, defilement, decay, corruption, squalor, filthiness, uncleanness, excrement, dung, ordure. OPPOSITE: cleanness. **2** (*read filth*) obscenity, pornography, smut, grossness, indecency, vulgarity, porn (*inf*), sleaze (*inf*).

filthy *adj* **1** (*a filthy room*) dirty, mucky, grimy, grubby, unwashed, decaying, foul, unclean, smelling, polluted, defiled, corrupt, squalid. OPPOSITE: spotless. **2** (*filthy language*) obscene, vulgar, pornographic, smutty, lewd, indecent, ribald, bawdy, blue (*inf*). **3** (*a filthy trick*) mean, despicable, contemptible, nasty, vile.

final *adj* **1** (*the final stage*) ultimate, last, terminal, ending, concluding, terminating, closing, eventual. OPPOSITE: first. **2** (*the decision is final*) conclusive, decisive, absolute, definitive, irrevocable, indisputable, incontrovertible.

finale *noun* end, conclusion, finish, close, termination, climax, culmination, denouement, finis. OPPOSITE: beginning.

finality *noun* conclusiveness, decisiveness, absoluteness, completeness, definitiveness, irrevocability, irrefutability, unavoidability, inevitability.

finalize *verb* conclude, complete, decide, settle, clinch (*inf*), wrap up (*inf*), sew up (*inf*).

finally *adv* **1** (*finally, after the delay*) ultimately, eventually, at last, in the end, in the long run, lastly. OPPOSITE: initially. **2** (*settled finally*) conclusively, decisively, irrevocably, definitively, definitely, absolutely, completely, for ever, once and for all.

finance *noun* banking, economics, accounting, commerce, investment, money, funds, accounts.
➤ *verb* fund, pay for, back, support, subsidize, underwrite, guarantee, capitalize, float.

finances *pl noun* resources, assets, wealth, means, funds, money, cash, capital, wherewithal.

financial *adj* monetary, money, fiscal, economic, commercial, budgetary, pecuniary.

find *verb* **1** (*find the key*) discover, come across, stumble on, happen upon, uncover, unearth, locate, track down, ferret out, encounter, meet, notice, observe, descry, perceive, detect. **2** (*find happiness*) attain, achieve, obtain, acquire, get. **3** (*find that the work gets easier*)

realize, discover, learn, conclude, observe, perceive. **4** (*find it easy*) think, consider, regard, judge, feel.
➤ *noun* discovery, finding, strike, catch, bargain, boon.

find out **1** (*find out something*) ascertain, learn, discover, realize, determine. **2** (*find out someone*) unmask, expose, uncover, reveal, suss out (*inf*).

finding *noun* verdict, judgment, decision, conclusion, award, sentence, order, decree, pronouncement.

fine[1] *adj* **1** (*a fine performance*) excellent, choice, select, superior, outstanding, exceptional, first-rate, first-class, splendid, great, superior, magnificent, ornate, showy, beautiful, lovely. OPPOSITE: inferior. **2** (*fine clothes*) expensive, smart, stylish, fashionable, elegant, tasteful, grand, exquisite. OPPOSITE: shabby. **3** (*feel fine*) healthy, fit, well, strong. OPPOSITE: ill. **4** (*the work is fine*) acceptable, satisfactory, good, all right, OK (*inf*). **5** (*fine weather*) sunny, cloudless, dry, bright, clear, fair, clement. OPPOSITE: cloudy. **6** (*fine gold*) pure, clear, unadulterated, refined, unalloyed. **7** (*fine sand*) powdery, ground, crushed, fine-grained. OPPOSITE: coarse. **8** (*fine thread*) thin, slender, attenuated, tenuous, slight, small, little, dainty, delicate, frail, fragile, flimsy, sheer, light. OPPOSITE: coarse. **9** (*a fine point of law*) subtle, precise, minute, nice. **10** (*a fine mind*) clever, brilliant, keen, acute, sharp, quick.

fine[2] *noun* (*a fine for speeding*) penalty, punishment, mulct, forfeit, damages.
➤ *verb* penalize, punish, mulct.

finery *noun* trappings, trinkets, showiness, decorations, ornaments, splendour, frippery, Sunday best, glad rags (*inf*), best bib and tucker (*inf*).

finesse *noun* **1** (*handled with finesse*) subtlety, tact, diplomacy, discretion, refinement, delicacy, grace, elegance, polish, skill, adroitness, mastery, craft. OPPOSITE: clumsiness. **2** (*a cunning finesse*) artifice, trick, ruse, wile, scheme, stratagem.

finger *verb* feel, touch, handle, manipulate, caress, fondle, play about with, toy with, fiddle with.

finicky *adj* fussy, particular, overparticular, meticulous, fastidious, dainty, squeamish, choosy (*inf*), difficult, hard to please, critical, overcritical.

finish *verb* **1** (*finish your work*) complete, conclude, close, terminate, end, stop, cease, fulfil, achieve, accomplish, do, discharge, execute, perform, settle, finalize, perfect, consummate, culminate, round off, polish off (*inf*), wrap up (*inf*). OPPOSITE: start. **2** (*finish your food*) consume, use, use up, eat, drink, devour, drain, empty, dispatch, dispose of, get rid of, deplete. **3** (*the race nearly finished me*) destroy, kill, ruin, defeat, overcome, overpower, overwhelm, finish off, do away with, wipe out (*inf*). **4** (*finish the table with varnish*) polish, varnish, face, dress, gild, veneer, lacquer, burnish, glaze, coat.
➤ *noun* **1** (*the finish of the race*) completion, conclusion, close, termination, end, cessation, perfection, consummation, culmination, accomplishment, execution, achievement, fulfilment. OPPOSITE: beginning. **2** (*a veneer finish*) surface, polish, varnish, lustre, shine, texture, grain, lacquer, veneer, appearance, coating. **3** (*ladies with finish*) refinement, polish, culture, suavity, urbanity.

finished *adj* **1** (*finished work*) complete, done, over, through, completed, ended, achieved, accomplished, discharged, fulfilled, wrapped up (*inf*), sewn up (*inf*). OPPOSITE: unfinished. **2** (*a finished performance*) accomplished, masterly, proficient, skilful, gifted, expert, skilled, consummate, polished, refined, elegant, perfect, impeccable. **3** (*plans that are finished*) ruined, lost, gone, over with, wrecked, done for (*inf*), doomed, bankrupt, defeated.

finite *adj* limited, restricted, bounded, circumscribed, demarcated, terminable, measurable. OPPOSITE: infinite.

fire *noun* **1** (*destroyed by fire*) burning, combustion, spark, flame, flames, blaze, conflagration, inferno, holocaust. **2** (*enemy fire*) bombardment, sniping, gunfire, barrage, salvo, volley, fusillade, cannonade, flak, shelling. **3** (*switch on the fire*) heater, radiator, convector. **4** (*the fire of fanaticism*) ardour, fervour, heat, passion, enthusiasm, eagerness, spirit, élan, vigour, energy, force, intensity, animation, light, radiance, lustre, splendour, glow, sparkle, excitement, inspiration, life, vivacity. OPPOSITE: coldness.
≫ *verb* **1** (*fire an engine*) ignite, kindle, light, set fire to, set on fire, set alight. OPPOSITE: extinguish. **2** (*fire a gun*) discharge, let off, trigger, shoot, detonate, explode, shell, hurl, launch. **3** (*fired with ambition*) animate, rouse, stir, stir up, stimulate, inspire, invigorate, excite, arouse, enliven, motivate, electrify, galvanize, inspirit, inflame. OPPOSITE: dampen. **4** (*fired from the job*) dismiss, discharge, cashier, sack (*inf*), give someone the sack (*inf*), give someone the push (*inf*). OPPOSITE: appoint.
on fire 1 (*buildings on fire*) alight, ablaze, burning, blazing, in flames. OPPOSITE: extinguished. **2** (*on fire with enthusiasm*) eager, keen, enthusiastic, passionate, ardent, spirited, excited, inspirited.

firearm *noun* weapon, gun, handgun, revolver, pistol.

firebrand *noun* agitator, troublemaker, rabble-rouser, revolutionary, demagogue, agent provocateur.

fireworks *pl noun* **1** (*fireworks on bonfire night*) firework display, pyrotechnics, illuminations, *feux d'artifice*. **2** (*there'll be fireworks when the boss finds out*) uproar, trouble, outburst, rage, row.

firm¹ *adj* **1** (*a firm mattress*) hard, compact, dense, stiff, rigid, inflexible, inelastic, unyielding, solid, set, congealed, frozen. OPPOSITE: soft. **2** (*the ladder is firm*) secure, fixed, fast, immovable, rooted, anchored, steady, stable, set, embedded, constant, enduring, sturdy, strong. OPPOSITE: unstable. **3** (*a firm grip*) strong, vigorous, secure, steady, tight, close. **4** (*be firm with someone*) resolute, determined, steadfast, resolved, decided, staunch, unwavering, unshakeable, dogged, tenacious, fixed, obdurate, adamant, unyielding, unswerving, inflexible, strict, unbending. **5** (*a firm decision*) definite, settled, fixed, established, unchangeable, unalterable. OPPOSITE: changeable. **6** (*firm friendship*) constant, loyal, steady, enduring, unchanging, long-standing. **7** (*firm evidence*) hard, solid, concrete, substantial, actual, real, sound, reasonable, valid. OPPOSITE: weak.

firm² *noun* (*a firm of accountants*) company, business, concern, establishment, organization, corporation, house, partnership.

firmament *noun* sky, skies, heaven, heavens, empyrean, vault, space, universe. OPPOSITE: earth.

firmness *noun* **1** (*the firmness of the mattress*) hardness, stiffness, rigidity, inflexibility, inelasticity. OPPOSITE: softness. **2** (*firmness in their opinions*) determination, resolution, resolve, doggedness, inflexibility, strictness. **3** (*the firmness of the grip*) strength, vigour, tightness, closeness.

first *adj* **1** (*the first period*) earliest, primeval, primordial, primitive, original, initial, opening, introductory. OPPOSITE: last. **2** (*first principles*) primary, rudimentary, elementary, basic, fundamental, introductory. **3** (*first priority*) foremost, chief, main, leading, greatest, principal, head, highest, top, supreme. OPPOSITE: lowest.
≫ *adv* beforehand, firstly, initially, to begin with, in the first place, at first, at the outset. OPPOSITE: last.
≫ *noun* start, beginning, outset, opening, introduction.

firsthand *adj* direct, immediate.
≫ *adv* directly, straight from the horse's mouth (*inf*).

first-rate *adj* excellent, superb, outstanding, exceptional, peerless, matchless, second to none, supreme, premier, fine, splendid, A1 (*inf*), top-notch (*inf*), ace (*inf*). OPPOSITE: inferior.

fiscal *adj* financial, monetary, money, economic, budgetary, pecuniary.

fish *verb* angle, trawl, cast, net.
fish for seek, solicit, invite, angle for, look for, search for, hunt for.
fish out take out, pull out, find, retrieve, extract, produce.

fishy *adj* odd, queer, strange, peculiar, suspicious, suspect, dubious, doubtful, questionable, unlikely, improbable.

fission *noun* splitting, parting, division, rupture, cleavage.

fissure *noun* opening, rift, cleft, crevice, cranny, chasm, crack, break, fracture, breach, fault, rupture, split, gap, interstice.

fit¹ *adj* **1** (*feel fit*) healthy, robust, sturdy, strong, hale, well, in shape, in good shape, in fine fettle. OPPOSITE: unfit. **2** (*not fit to look after children*) able, capable, competent, trained, qualified, eligible, ready, prepared, adequate, worthy, deserving. OPPOSITE: ineligible. **3** (*food fit to eat*) suitable, fitting, appropriate, well-suited, apt, right, correct, proper, seemly, due, becoming. OPPOSITE: inappropriate.
≫ *verb* **1** (*the lid doesn't fit*) be the right size for, be the right shape for. **2** (*the theory fits the facts*) match, tally with, correspond to, conform to, agree with, suit, go with, belong to, dovetail with, harmonize with, meet. **3** (*fit a washing machine*) install, insert, position, place. **4** (*fit a ship*) equip, rig, furnish, supply, provide, qualify, prepare, arm, accoutre. **5** (*fitted to the new situation*) adapt, adjust, accommodate, alter, modify, fashion, shape.
fit in 1 (*fit in some exercise*) slot in, find time for, find room for, pack in, squeeze in. **2** (*feels he doesn't fit in*) conform, live in harmony, agree.
fit out equip, supply, provide with, furnish, prepare, accoutre.
fit up equip, supply, provide with, furnish.

fit² *noun* **1** (*have a fit*) convulsion, paroxysm, spasm, seizure, attack, turn. **2** (*a fit of temper*) attack, tantrum, bout, spell, outburst, outbreak.
in fits and starts fitfully, spasmodically, irregularly, intermittently.

fitful *adj* irregular, intermittent, broken, disturbed, spasmodic, erratic, variable, inconstant, unstable, fluctuating, uneven, desultory, impulsive. OPPOSITE: regular.

fitness *noun* **1** (*physical fitness*) health, vigour, strength, fine fettle, good shape, condition. OPPOSITE: unfitness. **2** (*the candidates' fitness for the job*) competence, qualifications, eligibility, capability, readiness. OPPOSITE: ineligibility. **3** (*question the fitness of the remarks*) suitability, appropriateness, aptness, propriety, seemliness. OPPOSITE: impropriety.

fitted *adj* **1** (*fitted furniture*) built-in, fixed, permanent. **2** (*fitted to play the part*) suited, suitable, appropriate, right, qualified, cut out for.

fitting *adj* appropriate, apt, suitable, proper, correct, seemly, due, becoming.
➤ *noun* component, part, accessory, attachment, piece, unit.

fittings *pl noun* accessories, equipment, furnishings, fixtures, units, accoutrements.

fix *verb* **1** (*fix a handle to the door*) secure, make fast, anchor, cement, root, plant, place, locate, install, position, fasten, attach, connect, join, tie, bind, stick, glue, rivet, nail, pin. OPPOSITE: move. **2** (*fix a date*) settle, resolve, establish, decide, decide on, determine, limit, define, specify, arrange, appoint, name, set. **3** (*fix a clock*) mend, repair, patch up, restore, regulate, correct, adjust, rectify. OPPOSITE: damage. **4** (*fixed his eyes on the audience*) direct, focus, level, rivet. **5** (*fix your hair*) arrange, dress, tidy, groom, straighten, comb. **6** (*fix a meal*) prepare, make, get ready, cook. **7** (*fix a competition*) rig, falsify, tamper with, manipulate, fiddle (*inf*).
➤ *noun* dilemma, predicament, difficulty, quandary, plight, mess, spot (*inf*), pickle (*inf*), bind (*inf*).
fix up 1 (*fixed me up with a job*) provide, supply, furnish, sort out, lay on. **2** (*fix up a meeting*) arrange, settle, decide, plan, agree on, organize.

fixation *noun* obsession, idée fixe, compulsion, complex, mania, fetish, preoccupation, thing (*inf*), hang-up (*inf*).

fixed *adj* established, stable, firm, secure, fast, steady, constant, unchanging, immovable, rooted, set, intent, resolute, unwavering. OPPOSITE: variable.

fixture *noun* **1** (*fixtures and fittings*) equipment, installation, furnishing, appliance. **2** (*a sports fixture*) event, competition, match, race, contest, meet.

fizz *verb* sparkle, effervesce, bubble, froth, ferment, fizzle, foam, hiss.

fizzle *verb* **fizzle out** come to nothing, fall through, collapse, die away, peter away, fold (*inf*), flop (*inf*).

fizzy *adj* effervescent, sparkling, bubbling, carbonated, gassy.

flabbergasted *adj* amazed, astounded, dumbfounded, astonished, stunned, confounded, dazed, overcome, staggered, bowled over (*inf*), speechless, nonplussed.

flabby *adj* flaccid, limp, drooping, floppy, loose, slack, yielding, soft. OPPOSITE: firm.

flaccid *adj* limp, drooping, floppy, flabby, soft, yielding. OPPOSITE: firm.

flag¹ *noun* (*a flag flying in the wind*) standard, ensign, colours, banner, pennant, pennon, streamer, banderole, gonfalon, gonfanon, bunting, jack.
➤ *verb* **1** (*flag the important points*) mark, mark out, indicate, tag, label. **2** (*flagged the car down*) wave down, signal, signal to stop.

flag² *verb* (*their spirits were flagging*) droop, languish, faint, fail, fade, tire, weary, weaken, wilt, sag, drop, sink, decline, fall.

flagellate *verb* scourge, flog, lash, whip, beat, thrash, cane, birch, castigate, chastise.

flagitious *adj* monstrous, atrocious, outrageous, scandalous, shocking, heinous, villainous, wicked, notorious, infamous. OPPOSITE: honourable.

flagon *noun* bottle, decanter, carafe, flask, jug, pitcher.

flagrant *adj* blatant, glaring, bold, barefaced, arrant, conspicuous, open, obvious, ostentatious, outrageous, scandalous, shameless, disgraceful, shocking, atrocious, monstrous, egregious. OPPOSITE: disguised.

flail *verb* wave, thresh, thrash, strike, beat, whip.

flair *noun* **1** (*a flair for business*) talent, gift, knack, faculty, facility, capability, aptitude, disposition, skill, ability, genius, bent. **2** (*done with real flair*) style, dash, panache, elegance, élan, discernment, discrimination, taste.

flake *noun* scale, chip, sliver, shaving, peeling, fragment, particle, wafer.
➤ *verb* scale, peel, peel off, chip, desquamate, exfoliate.
flake out faint, pass out, collapse, keel over, swoon.

flamboyant *adj* showy, ostentatious, gaudy, flashy, dazzling, glamorous, brilliant, colourful, resplendent, florid, ornate, elaborate, fancy, extravagant, flashy (*inf*). OPPOSITE: plain.

flame *noun* **1** (*burst into flames*) fire, blaze, spark, flash, light, brightness, glow. **2** (*flame of desire*) ardour, fervour, passion, zeal, eagerness, keenness, enthusiasm, warmth, heat, intensity. OPPOSITE: coldness. **3** (*an old flame*) sweetheart, lover, partner, boyfriend, girlfriend, beau.
➤ *verb* burn, blaze, flare, flash, glow, shine, sparkle, beam.

flaming *adj* **1** (*flaming torches*) burning, blazing, glowing, ignited, ablaze, on fire. **2** (*flaming red*) bright, brilliant, blazing, intense, vivid. **3** (*a flaming row*) furious, angry, violent, raging, passionate.

flammable *adj* inflammable, combustible, ignitable. OPPOSITE: nonflammable.

flank *noun* **1** (*an animal's flank*) side, wing, loin, haunch, thigh, hip. **2** (*attack on both flanks*) side, wing, sector.
➤ *verb* border, edge, fringe, skirt, limit, bound.

flannel *noun* nonsense, rubbish, blarney, prevarication, waffle (*inf*), baloney (*inf*), rot (*inf*), sweet talk (*inf*).

➤ *verb* prevaricate, equivocate, hedge (*inf*), waffle (*inf*), sweet-talk (*inf*).

flap *verb* wave, swing, wag, flutter, shake, agitate, vibrate, beat, flail, thrash, thresh.
➤ *noun* **1** (*flaps on a tent*) fold, tab, overlap, fly, skirt, cover. **2** (*the flap of the sails*) waving, fluttering, swinging, vibrating. **3** (*get into a flap*) commotion, fuss, panic, agitation, fluster, tizzy (*inf*), state (*inf*), stew (*inf*).

flare *verb* **1** (*the light flared*) blaze, flash, gleam, sparkle, flicker, flutter, glitter, glare. **2** (*trousers flaring*) widen, broaden, splay, spread out, expand. OPPOSITE: taper.
➤ *noun* **1** (*the flare of lights*) blaze, gleam, flash, sparkle, flicker, flutter, glitter, glare. **2** (*a distress flare*) signal, light, beacon, rocket. **3** (*trousers with wide flares*) widening, spread, broadening, splay.
flare up 1 (*the fire flared up*) blaze, flash, flame. **2** (*fighting flared up*) explode, blow one's top (*inf*), blow up (*inf*), lose control, boil over, fly off the handle (*inf*), lose one's cool (*inf*).

flash *verb* **1** (*lights flashing*) flare, flame, light, shine, beam, glare, blaze, sparkle, scintillate, gleam, glint, twinkle, glitter, glisten, coruscate. **2** (*cars flashing past*) dash, tear, shoot, zoom, dart, streak, fly, race, bolt, speed. OPPOSITE: crawl. **3** (*flashed his wallet*) show, show off, display, flaunt, flourish, brandish. OPPOSITE: conceal.
➤ *noun* **1** (*flashes of light*) beam, ray, flare, blaze, burst, glare, glint, gleam, spark, twinkle, glitter, glimmer, streak, patch. **2** (*be back in a flash*) instant, moment, second, minute, trice, twinkling, split second, jiffy (*inf*), two shakes of a lamb's tail (*inf*). **3** (*a flash of inspiration*) burst, outbreak, display, show, showing, demonstration, manifestation.
➤ *adj* showy, ostentatious, gaudy, flamboyant, loud, garish, tasteless, cheap, tawdry.

flashy *adj* showy, ostentatious, gaudy, flamboyant, flash (*inf*), loud, garish, pretentious, tasteless, cheap, tawdry. OPPOSITE: plain.

flask *noun* bottle, carafe, flagon, jug, pitcher.

flat[1] *adj* **1** (*a flat surface*) level, even, smooth, unbroken, plane, low. **2** (*lie down flat*) horizontal, prostrate, recumbent, supine. **3** (*a flat dish*) shallow. OPPOSITE: deep. **4** (*a flat performance*) vapid, uninteresting, dull, insipid, bland, boring, tedious, monotonous, prosaic, lifeless, spiritless. OPPOSITE: exciting. **5** (*business is flat*) inactive, idle, sluggish, slack. OPPOSITE: busy. **6** (*a flat price*) fixed, set, standard, firm. OPPOSITE: variable. **7** (*a flat tyre*) punctured, burst, deflated, blown out, collapsed. **8** (*a flat refusal*) outright, direct, plain, straight, firm, downright, out-and-out, positive, absolute, categorical, final, unconditional. **9** (*feel flat after the party*) low, downcast, depressed, dispirited. OPPOSITE: cheerful.
➤ *adv* outright, directly, absolutely, categorically, straight, plainly, explicitly.
➤ *noun* lowland, plain, marsh, swamp, shallow, shoal, sandbank.
flat out at top speed, at full speed, all out.

flat[2] *noun* (*live in a flat*) apartment, digs, penthouse, maisonette, rooms, bed-sitter.

flatten *verb* **1** (*flatten a surface*) level, level off, smooth,

even out, iron, press, press down, roll, crush, squash. **2** (*flatten a building*) demolish, knock down, tear down, raze. **3** (*got flattened in the match*) beat, overwhelm, crush, knock down.

flatter *verb* **1** (*flattered me on my cooking*) praise, compliment, fawn, court, butter up (*inf*), humour, adulate, eulogize, blandish, cajole, wheedle, coax, play up to (*inf*), soft-soap (*inf*), sweet-talk (*inf*). OPPOSITE: insult. **2** (*dresses that flatter the fuller figure*) suit, become, enhance, show to advantage.

flattering *adj* complimentary, praising, blandishing, adulatory, fulsome, ingratiating, fawning, servile, unctuous.

flattery *noun* praise, compliments, fawning, sycophancy, servility, adulation, eulogy, blandishments, blarney, cajolery, sweet-talk (*inf*), soft-soap (*inf*), flannel (*inf*). OPPOSITE: abuse.

flatulent *adj* **1** (*flatulent foods*) windy, gassy, farting (*sl*). **2** (*flatulent prose*) wordy, verbose, long-winded, bombastic, pompous, pretentious, inflated, turgid. OPPOSITE: terse.

flaunt *verb* display, show off, parade, exhibit, sport, flash, brandish, flourish, vaunt, boast. OPPOSITE: hide.

flavour *noun* **1** (*the flavour of the food*) taste, savour, tang, smack, zest, piquancy, relish, seasoning, flavouring. **2** (*a strong political flavour*) essence, spirit, tone, character, quality, aspect, suggestion, style, taste, touch.
➤ *verb* season, spice, add flavouring to, ginger up.

flavouring *noun* seasoning, relish, flavour, extract, essence, additive.

flaw *noun* **1** (*flaws in his character*) defect, fault, blemish, imperfection, spot, mark, weakness, foible, failing. **2** (*a flaw in the glass*) crack, rift, cleft, fissure, split, rent, fault, defect, break, fracture, breach.

flawless *adj* perfect, faultless, unblemished, whole, intact, sound, undamaged, spotless, impeccable. OPPOSITE: flawed.

flay *verb* **1** (*flayed the animal alive*) skin, excoriate, peel, strip. **2** (*the newspapers flayed the play mercilessly*) attack, criticize, pan (*inf*), castigate, berate, pull to pieces (*inf*), tear a strip off (*inf*). OPPOSITE: praise.

fleck *verb* streak, speckle, spot, dot, sprinkle, spatter, dapple, variegate, mottle, mark.
➤ *noun* streak, spot, dot, speck, mark.

flee *verb* fly, run away, run off, abscond, take flight, make off, escape, run for it, bolt, decamp, scarper (*inf*), beat it (*inf*), scram (*inf*), take off (*inf*), leave, depart. OPPOSITE: stay.

fleece *noun* coat, wool, down.
➤ *verb* **1** (*fleece a sheep*) shear, clip, strip. **2** (*be fleeced by an expensive restaurant*) swindle, defraud, cheat, diddle (*inf*), overcharge, rip off (*inf*), rob, taken for a ride (*inf*), taken to the cleaners (*inf*), plunder, rifle.

fleet[1] *noun* (*a peace-keeping fleet*) armada, squadron, task force, navy, flotilla, argosy.

fleet[2] *adj* (*fleet of foot*) rapid, swift, fast, quick, speedy, nimble, agile. OPPOSITE: slow.

fleeting *adj* transitory, transient, ephemeral,

evanescent, passing, brief, short, short-lived, momentary, temporary, fugacious. OPPOSITE: lasting.

fleetness *noun* rapidity, swiftness, quickness, speed, velocity, celerity, nimbleness, agility. OPPOSITE: slowness.

flesh *noun* 1 (*animal flesh*) tissue, fat, meat, body, muscle. 2 (*pleasures of the flesh*) carnality, physicality, sensuality, corporeality. 3 (*all flesh will perish*) mankind, humanity, humankind, people, mortality, human race. 4 (*my own flesh and blood*) family, relatives, relations, folks (*inf*), kin, kindred, blood.
➤ *verb* make fuller, fill out, expand, add substance, give more details.
in the flesh in person, in real life, in bodily form.

fleshly *adj* carnal, sensual, lustful, lascivious, lecherous, animal, physical, bodily, corporeal, material, earthly, worldly. OPPOSITE: spiritual.

fleshy *adj* fat, plump, corpulent, stout, rotund, podgy, chubby, tubby, obese, overweight. OPPOSITE: thin.

flex *noun* wire, cable, cord, lead.
➤ *verb* bend, curve, bow, crook, move, stretch, tighten, contract.

flexible *adj* 1 (*flexible copper wire*) pliable, pliant, bendable, ductile, elastic, tensile, malleable, mouldable, plastic, supple, lithe, yielding. OPPOSITE: rigid. 2 (*flexible working practices*) adaptable, adjustable, variable, compliant, docile, biddable, amenable, tractable, complaisant. OPPOSITE: inflexible.

flexuous *adj* winding, serpentine, sinuous, tortuous, twisting, turning, bending, curving. OPPOSITE: straight.

flexure *noun* bending, flexing, incurvation, curvature, bend, turn, fold.

flick *verb* flip, rap, tap, dab, touch, snap, click, swish.
flick through scan, skim, browse, glance over, flip through, thumb through.

flicker *verb* flash, twinkle, glimmer, sparkle, shimmer, blink, flutter, waver, fluctuate, vibrate, quiver, tremble.
➤ *noun* flash, gleam, glimmer, spark, trace, vestige.

flight[1] *noun* 1 (*the flight of a bird*) flying, soaring, mounting, gliding. 2 (*principles of flight*) aviation, aeronautics, flying. 3 (*all flights are delayed*) journey, trip, run, shuttle. 4 (*a flight of birds*) swarm, flock, migration, squadron, unit, formation. 5 (*a flight of stairs*) staircase, stairs, set, steps.

flight[2] *noun* (*their flight from the army*) fleeing, escape, getaway, stampede, exodus, departure, retreat, rout, migration. OPPOSITE: return.
take flight flee, run away, escape, abscond, make off, decamp. OPPOSITE: stay.

flighty *adj* frivolous, capricious, fickle, volatile, mercurial, inconstant, changeable, irresponsible, scatterbrained, harebrained, giddy, wild, impulsive, thoughtless, unstable, erratic. OPPOSITE: constant.

flimsy *adj* 1 (*flimsy material*) frail, fragile, delicate, thin, sheer, light, insubstantial, slight, poor, inadequate, unsubstantial, rickety, shaky. OPPOSITE: strong. 2 (*a flimsy excuse*) weak, feeble, superficial, trivial, frivolous, poor, inadequate, unbelievable, unconvincing, implausible. OPPOSITE: convincing.

flinch *verb* wince, shrink, cower, quail, blench, recoil,

draw back, shy away, start, balk, withdraw, retreat, dodge, shirk, flee.

fling *verb* hurl, toss, throw, shy, pitch, cast, sling, lob (*inf*), chuck (*inf*).
➤ *noun* 1 (*with a fling of its limbs*) toss, throw, pitch, lob (*inf*), chuck (*inf*). 2 (*have a final fling*) spree, binge, debauch, fun, whirl (*inf*).

flip *verb* flick, jerk, toss, pitch, throw, spin, turn, twist, rap, tap, snap.
flip through skim, flick through, scan, thumb through, browse, glance at. OPPOSITE: study.

flippancy *noun* frivolity, levity, superficiality, shallowness, glibness, irreverence, impudence, pertness, impertinence, sauce (*inf*), sauciness (*inf*), cheek (*inf*). OPPOSITE: respect.

flippant *adj* frivolous, offhand, superficial, shallow, irreverent, glib, disrespectful, rude, impudent, pert, impertinent, cheeky (*inf*), saucy (*inf*). OPPOSITE: serious.

flirt *verb* philander, coquet, tease, lead on, make advances, ogle, chat up (*inf*).
➤ *noun* philanderer, playboy, coquette, vamp, tease.
firt with toy with, dally with, trifle with, entertain, consider.

flirtatious *adj* coquettish, teasing, amorous, provocative, philandering, come-hither.

flit *verb* fly, dart, skim, flash, speed, dash, hop, flutter, flitter.

float *verb* 1 (*floating on the water*) sail, drift, waft, glide, slide, ride, swim, bob, hover, hang. OPPOSITE: sink. 2 (*float an idea*) suggest, put forward, propose, present. 3 (*float a company*) launch, start, get going, establish, initiate, set up, promote.

floating *adj* 1 (*floating logs*) buoyant, afloat, drifting, gliding, bobbing, sailing, swimming. OPPOSITE: sinking. 2 (*floating voters*) uncommitted, unattached, unsettled, fluctuating. 3 (*a floating population*) unsettled, wandering, transitory, migratory, variable. OPPOSITE: fixed.

flock *noun* herd, pack, flight, swarm, bevy, host, crowd, throng, mass, group, company, collection, gathering, assembly, congregation.
➤ *verb* congregate, gather, collect, assemble, come together, converge, herd, swarm, throng, crowd, cluster. OPPOSITE: disperse.

flog *verb* 1 (*flog horses*) whip, lash, beat, scourge, flay, birch, belt, whack, flagellate, thrash, castigate, chastise, cane. 2 (*flog cheap goods*) sell, handle, trade in, offer for sale, put on sale.

flogging *noun* whipping, lashing, beating, scourging, belting, caning, whacking.

flood *verb* 1 (*rivers flooding the town*) inundate, deluge, submerge, immerse, drown, swamp, engulf, overwhelm, overflow, brim over, pour forth, swell. OPPOSITE: drain. 2 (*offers of help flooding in*) pour, surge, rush, gush, flow. 3 (*flood the market with cheap goods*) saturate, inundate, swamp, glut, overwhelm.
➤ *noun* 1 (*winter floods*) inundation, deluge, overflow, outpouring, torrent, downpour, spate, freshet, flow, stream. OPPOSITE: drought. 2 (*a flood of complaints*) abundance, profusion, excess, glut, torrent, plethora.

floor *noun* **1** (*the floor of a room*) ground, bottom, base, flooring. OPPOSITE: ceiling. **2** (*on the second floor*) storey, level, stage.
➤ *verb* **1** (*floored his opponent*) knock down, fell, overthrow, prostrate, beat, defeat. **2** (*floored by the question*) defeat, beat, confound, nonplus, stump, disconcert, perplex, puzzle, baffle, throw (*inf*).

flop *verb* **1** (*flop into a chair*) collapse, fall, slump. **2** (*hair flopping over her eyes*) droop, sag, drop, fall, hang, dangle. **3** (*the film flopped*) fail, founder, fall flat, crash (*inf*), bomb (*inf*). OPPOSITE: succeed.
➤ *noun* failure, fiasco, disaster, debacle, shambles, washout (*inf*). OPPOSITE: success.

floppy *adj* droopy, drooping, sagging, hanging, dangling, limp, loose.

flora *noun* plants, vegetation, botany, fauna, herbage.

florid *adj* **1** (*florid cheeks*) ruddy, red, reddish, flushed, rosy, rubicund. OPPOSITE: pale. **2** (*florid language*) flowery, ornate, elaborate, overelaborate, fussy, flamboyant, showy, embellished, high-flown, euphuistic. OPPOSITE: plain.

flotsam *noun* wreckage, rubbish, debris, junk.

flounce[1] *verb* (*flounced out of the room*) stamp, storm, fling, toss, jerk, bounce, spring.

flounce[2] *noun* (*a flounce round the dress*) frill, ruffle, trimming, fringe, valance, falbala.

flounder *verb* wallow, struggle, thrash, toss, stumble, blunder, falter, grope, fumble.

flourish *verb* **1** (*business is flourishing*) thrive, prosper, succeed, do well, get on, grow, increase, wax, boom, burgeon, bloom, blossom. OPPOSITE: decline. **2** (*came in, flourishing a job offer*) brandish, wield, wave, swing, shake, flaunt, parade, vaunt, display.
➤ *noun* **1** (*dance with a flourish*) show, display, ostentation, parade, wave, twirl, dash, panache, fanfare. **2** (*a flourish in handwriting*) ornament, decoration, embellishment, swirl, curlicue.

flout *verb* mock, jeer, scoff at, laugh at, ridicule, deride, sneer, scorn, disdain, contemn, spurn, defy. OPPOSITE: respect.

flow *verb* **1** (*a stream flowing in the valley*) run, pour, stream, course, roll, sweep, drift, glide, move, proceed, circulate, ooze, seep, surge, rush, gush, well, spout, spurt, cascade, abound, teem. OPPOSITE: stop.
2 (*improvements flowing from the changes*) originate, issue, proceed, arise, derive, emerge, spring, emanate, result.
➤ *noun* stream, course, drift, movement, circulation, progression, current, tide, surge, rush, spate, gush, outpouring, discharge, flood, excess, deluge, abundance, plethora.

flower *noun* **1** (*spring flowers*) bloom, blossom, bud, floret, inflorescence. **2** (*in the flower of youth*) prime, peak, height, acme, zenith, cream, pick, best, finest, élite, crème de la crème.
➤ *verb* bloom, blossom, bud, blow, effloresce, come out, open, unfold, develop, mature, thrive, succeed. OPPOSITE: wither.

flowery *adj* florid, ornate, fancy, elaborate, high-flown, rhetorical, figurative, grandiloquent, verbose, bombastic, euphuistic. OPPOSITE: plain.

flowing *adj* **1** (*flowing rivers*) running, streaming, rolling, sweeping, drifting, gliding, surging, rushing, oozing. **2** (*flowing speech*) fluent, smooth, easy, graceful, unbroken, continuous. OPPOSITE: stilted. **3** (*flowing robes*) hanging, falling, rolling, loose. **4** (*a land flowing with milk and honey*) rich, prolific, teeming, abounding. OPPOSITE: lacking.

fluctuate *verb* vacillate, waver, vary, change, alter, undulate, shift, veer, swing, seesaw, oscillate. OPPOSITE: stabilize.

fluctuation *noun* vacillation, wavering, instability, unsteadiness, inconstancy, change, variation, shift, undulation, oscillation. OPPOSITE: stability.

flue *noun* chimney, passage, channel, pipe, duct, vent, shaft.

fluency *noun* smoothness, ease, facility, control, command, eloquence, articulateness, gracefulness, naturalness, flow.

fluent *adj* smooth, flowing, fluid, easy, effortless, natural, articulate, eloquent, graceful, elegant, ready, voluble. OPPOSITE: stilted.

fluff[1] *noun* (*brush off the fluff*) down, floss, pile, nap, lint, dust.

fluff[2] *verb* (*fluff an exam*) botch, bungle, muck up, mess up, boob (*inf*), screw up (*sl*).

fluffy *adj* furry, fuzzy, fleecy, woolly, downy, flossy, silky, soft, light.

fluid *noun* liquid, solution, gas, vapour. OPPOSITE: solid
➤ *adj* **1** (*a fluid stream*) liquid, gaseous, molten, flowing, running, fluent. **2** (*fluid plans*) flexible, changeable, adjustable, adaptable, shifting, mobile, protean. OPPOSITE: fixed. **3** (*in her usual fluid style*) smooth, flowing, fluent, easy, effortless, natural, graceful, elegant.

fluke *noun* accident, chance, coincidence, stroke of luck, windfall, blessing, lucky break.

flummery *noun* nonsense, rubbish, trash, balderdash, humbug, poppycock (*inf*), flattery, blandishments, adulation.

flunkey *noun* **1** (*the king's flunkeys*) footman, lackey, servant, valet, underling, menial, minion, drudge. **2** (*the pop star's flunkeys*) sycophant, toady, yes-man, bootlicker (*inf*), puppet, stooge, hanger-on.

flurry *noun* **1** (*a flurry of activity*) bustle, stir, commotion, ado, excitement, agitation, whirl, hubbub, to-do (*inf*), flap (*inf*), fuss, fluster, hurry, haste. OPPOSITE: calm. **2** (*snow flurries*) squall, gust, outbreak, burst, shower, spell.
➤ *verb* fluster, agitate, bother, ruffle, disconcert, upset, unsettle, unnerve, disturb, rattle (*inf*), faze (*inf*), perturb, confuse, bewilder, perplex, confound. OPPOSITE: compose.

flush[1] *verb* **1** (*flushed with embarrassment*) blush, colour, redden, go red, turn red, glow, burn, suffuse. OPPOSITE: blanch. **2** (*flush a toilet*) clean out, rinse, drain, empty, flood, drench, douse, cleanse, wash. **3** (*flushed with victory*) excite, elate, elevate, exhilarate, thrill, inflame, delight, animate, stir, rouse, cheer, encourage. OPPOSITE: dampen.
➤ *noun* **1** (*a flush on her cheeks*) blush, colour, redness,

rosiness, colouring, bloom, glow, radiance. OPPOSITE: pallor. **2** (*a flush of excitement*) thrill, excitement, elation, exhilaration, animation.
➤ *adj* wealthy, rich, affluent, well-off, abundant, generous, lavish. OPPOSITE: poor.

flush[2] *adj* (*the doors flush with the wall*) even, level, flat, plane, smooth. OPPOSITE: uneven.

flush[3] *verb* **flush out** (*flushed out the enemy*) chase out, force out, drive out, expel, eject, expose.

fluster *verb* flurry, agitate, ruffle, disconcert, perturb, bother, disturb, upset, unsettle, unnerve, panic, rattle (*inf*), excite, confuse, faze (*inf*), bustle, hurry. OPPOSITE: compose.
➤ *noun* agitation, flutter, flap (*inf*), panic, bustle, flurry, turmoil, confusion, dither (*inf*), tizzy (*inf*), tizz (*inf*). OPPOSITE: composure.

fluted *adj* grooved, furrowed, corrugated, channelled.

flutter *verb* flap, wave, vibrate, shake, agitate, quiver, tremble, shiver, ripple, waver, fluctuate, oscillate, flicker, bat, beat, palpitate.
➤ *noun* **1** (*the flutter of a bird's wings*) vibration, quiver, shudder, tremble, shake, wavering, batting, tremor, palpitation. **2** (*their sudden arrival has put me all in a flutter*) fluster, flurry, stir, commotion, agitation, excitement, confusion, perturbation. OPPOSITE: composure. **3** (*have a flutter on a horse*) bet, gamble, wager, risk, speculation.

flux *noun* flow, fluidity, motion, transition, change, alteration, mutation, fluctuation, instability. OPPOSITE: stagnation.

fly[1] *verb* **1** (*birds flying high*) mount, soar, wing, hover, flutter, flap, flit, glide, float, sail. **2** (*fly a plane*) pilot, control, operate, aviate, manoeuvre. **3** (*fly a flag*) show, display, present, wave, brandish, flourish. **4** (*he flew down the street*) dash, dart, bolt, shoot, tear, rush, hurry, race, speed, career, zoom, hare (*inf*). OPPOSITE: amble. **5** (*time flew by*) pass, elapse, go by, slip away, race, rush, glide, roll on. **6** (*forced to fly the country*) escape, abscond, decamp, run, take flight. OPPOSITE: remain. **fly at** attack, strike, hit, lay into, charge, go for, fall upon, assail.

fly[2] *adj* artful, shrewd, astute, canny, cunning, sharp.

flying *adj* **1** (*flying insects*) airborne, hovering, soaring, flitting, gliding. **2** (*a flying visit*) brief, quick, short, hasty, rushed, fleeting.

foam *noun* froth, spume, spray, bubbles, fizz, effervescence, suds, lather.
➤ *verb* froth, lather, bubble, fizz, effervesce.

fob *verb* **fob off 1** (*fobbed off with an excuse*) deceive, trick, mislead, take for a ride. **2** (*fobbed the shoddy goods off on to them*) dump, get rid of, unload, palm off (*inf*), foist off (*inf*).

focus *noun* centre, core, heart, pivot, hub, nucleus, focal point, centre of attention, cynosure.
➤ *verb* **1** (*focus your attention on the schedule*) aim, direct, fix, concentrate, centre, zoom in on (*inf*). **2** (*the lines focused*) line up, converge, meet.

fodder *noun* feed, food, forage, silage, hay, provender, rations.

foe *noun* enemy, opponent, adversary, antagonist, rival, competitor, combatant. OPPOSITE: friend.

fog *noun* **1** (*a crash in thick fog*) mist, haze, smog, pea-souper (*inf*), gloom, murk, murkiness, brume. **2** (*in an intellectual fog*) obscurity, vagueness, haziness, haze, daze, stupor, confusion, perplexity, bewilderment.
➤ *verb* **1** (*the windows fogged*) cloud, mist, steam up, obscure, veil, shroud, dim. **2** (*fogged their understanding*) darken, confuse, bewilder, mystify, perplex, obfuscate. OPPOSITE: clarify.

foggy *adj* **1** (*a foggy morning*) misty, hazy, murky, cloudy, dark, smoggy. **2** (*foggy understanding*) obscure, dim, vague, blurred, indistinct, confused, unclear. OPPOSITE: clear.

foible *noun* weakness, failing, infirmity, fault, shortcoming, flaw, defect, imperfection, quirk, peculiarity, idiosyncrasy. OPPOSITE: forte.

foil[1] *verb* (*foil a plan*) frustrate, thwart, baffle, balk, outwit, defeat, check, checkmate, counter, circumvent, hamper, impede. OPPOSITE: assist.

foil[2] *noun* **1** (*the perfect foil for the comedian*) contrast, antithesis, complement, background, setting. **2** (*tin foil*) leaf, lamina, sheet, film.

foist *verb* **1** (*foist the shoddy goods on to them*) pass, palm, fob, force, dump, unload, get rid of, impose, thrust. **2** (*foist a paragraph into the contract*) insert, sneak, introduce, interpolate.

fold[1] *verb* **1** (*fold the paper*) bend, double, overlap, turn under, crease, pleat, tuck, crumple, gather. OPPOSITE: flatten. **2** (*fold someone in your arms*) enfold, envelop, wrap, enclose, clasp, embrace, entwine, intertwine. **3** (*the business folded*) collapse, fail, go under (*inf*), go bust (*inf*), go to the wall (*inf*), flop (*inf*), close, shut down. OPPOSITE: prosper.
➤ *noun* crease, wrinkle, pleat, tuck, bend, turn, overlap, layer.

fold[2] *noun* **1** (*a fold for the sheep*) enclosure, pen, compound, yard, court, stockade, corral, kraal. **2** (*return to the fold*) assembly, congregation, flock, gathering, church.

folder *noun* binder, file, portfolio, wallet, envelope, pocket.

foliage *noun* leaves, greenery, vegetation.

folk *noun* **1** (*country folk*) people, public, nation, race, tribe, clan. **2** (*took her to meet my folks*) relations, relatives, family, kin, kindred.

folklore *noun* myth, myths, mythology, legends, stories, lore, customs, traditions, beliefs.

follow *verb* **1** (*the years that followed the war*) succeed, come next, come after, go after, replace. OPPOSITE: precede. **2** (*police following a criminal*) pursue, chase, run after, shadow, dog, hound, hunt, track, stalk, trail. **3** (*followed her into the room*) attend, accompany, escort, go with, go along with, tag along. OPPOSITE: desert. **4** (*follow the rules*) obey, observe, note, heed, accept, pay attention to, conform to, comply with. OPPOSITE: break. **5** (*the consequence follows from his actions*) ensue, result, arise, spring, issue, develop, flow, proceed. **6** (*not follow your reasoning*) understand, comprehend, grasp, see, appreciate, take in, latch on to (*inf*). **7** (*follow someone's* style) copy, imitate, ape, emulate, adopt. **8** (*follow the latest developments*) keep up with, keep up to date with, keep abreast of, support, be interested in, be a fan of.

follow through continue, finish, complete, conclude, pursue, see through.

follow up investigate, look into, research, check out.

follower *noun* disciple, adherent, partisan, convert, supporter, backer, pupil, student, attendant, companion, escort, enthusiast, devotee, fan, admirer, hanger-on, buff (*inf*), freak (*inf*).

following *adj* next, subsequent, successive, ensuing, consequent, resulting, coming, later. OPPOSITE: preceding.

➤ *noun* entourage, train, suite, clientele, circle, public, supporters, backing, advocates, patrons, admirers, audience, coterie.

folly *noun* foolishness, stupidity, silliness, absurdity, nonsense, ludicrousness, illogicality, madness, craziness, idiocy, lunacy, rashness, recklessness, irrationality, indiscretion, imprudence. OPPOSITE: wisdom.

foment *verb* encourage, stimulate, instigate, incite, provoke, stir up, arouse, brew, agitate, excite, goad, spur, promote, foster. OPPOSITE: quell.

fomentation *noun* encouragement, stimulation, instigation, incitement, provocation, arousal, agitation, excitement.

fond *adj* **1** (*her fond husband*) loving, tender, warm, caring, affectionate, amorous, adoring, devoted, doting. OPPOSITE: cold. **2** (*fond expectations*) foolish, absurd, empty, vain, deluded, optimistic, overoptimistic, naive, credulous. OPPOSITE: sensible.

fond of partial to, attached to, keen on, enamoured of, having a liking for, hooked on (*inf*). OPPOSITE: averse to.

fondle *verb* caress, stroke, pet, pat, hug, cuddle.

fondness *noun* **1** (*fondness for food*) liking, love, partiality, penchant, predilection, fancy, soft spot, weakness. OPPOSITE: aversion. **2** (*fondness for his wife*) love, affection, warmth, tenderness, devotion, kindness, attachment, care. OPPOSITE: coldness.

food *noun* **1** (*food and drink*) nourishment, sustenance, nutriment, aliment, subsistence, fare, diet, meals, board, refreshments, foodstuffs, provisions, victuals, comestibles, eats (*inf*), eatables (*inf*), grub (*inf*), nosh (*inf*), commons, rations. **2** (*food for the cattle*) fodder, feed, provender, forage. **3** (*food for thought*) stimulation, stimulus, nourishment, sustenance, pabulum.

fool *noun* **1** (*what a fool I've been!*) blockhead, dunce, dolt, ninny, nincompoop, simpleton, idiot, numskull, half-wit, ass, donkey, chump (*inf*), twit (*inf*), clot (*inf*), dope (*inf*), birdbrain (*inf*), bonehead (*inf*), prat (*inf*), nerd (*inf*), plonker (*inf*). **2** (*a fool entertaining the court*) jester, clown, buffoon, comic, harlequin, pierrot.

➤ *verb* **1** (*fooled by his promises*) deceive, dupe, trick, hoodwink, beguile, cheat, delude, mislead, hoax, bamboozle, cozen, take in, con (*inf*), kid (*inf*), have on (*inf*). **2** (*children fooling about*) jest, joke, pretend, play, play tricks, trifle, toy, meddle, fiddle, tamper.

foolery *noun* clowning, antics, capers, mischief, pranks, tricks, high jinks, monkey tricks, shenanigans, buffoonery, tomfoolery, horseplay.

foolhardy *adj* reckless, rash, incautious, irresponsible,

daredevil, madcap, temerarious, bold, daring, adventurous, heedless, wild, impetuous, precipitate, desperate. OPPOSITE: cautious.

foolish *adj* silly, unwise, injudicious, imprudent, ill-advised, absurd, ridiculous, laughable, derisible, fatuous, senseless, unreasonable, inane, pointless, irrational, brainless, witless, stupid, unintelligent, simple, puerile, mad, crazy, idiotic, daft (*inf*), dotty (*inf*), barmy (*inf*), nutty (*inf*), wacky (*inf*). OPPOSITE: sensible.

foolishness *noun* folly, stupidity, imprudence, senselessness, absurdity, silliness, inanity, madness, craziness, lunacy, foolery, nonsense, rubbish, claptrap (*inf*), poppycock (*inf*), piffle (*inf*), hogwash (*inf*), crap (*sl*), balls (*sl*). OPPOSITE: sense.

foolproof *adj* safe, fail-safe, idiot-proof, guaranteed, never-failing.

foot *noun* **1** (*the animal's foot*) paw, hoof, trotter, pad. **2** (*at the foot of the stairs*) bottom, base, end, foundation, pedestal, support. OPPOSITE: top.

➤ *verb* pay, settle, discharge, meet.

foothold *noun* **1** (*a firm foothold for the business*) basis, foundation, settlement, position, standing, status. **2** (*lose your foothold*) footing, support, grip.

footing *noun* **1** (*put on a proper footing*) basis, foundation, establishment, settlement, groundwork, foothold. **2** (*on an equal footing*) standing, status, position, condition, basis, rank, grade, relationship, terms.

footstep *noun* **1** (*see his footsteps*) footprint, footmark, track, trace. **2** (*hear the footsteps*) footfall, step, tread.

fop *noun* dandy, coxcomb, beau, popinjay, toff (*inf*), swell (*inf*).

foppery *noun* foppishness, dandyism, vanity, affectation.

foppish *adj* dandyish, dandified, vain, conceited, affected, spruce, dapper. OPPOSITE: slovenly.

for *prep* **1** (*head for home*) towards, to, in order to. OPPOSITE: from. **2** (*a present for you*) belonging to, appropriate to, intended. **3** (*away for a month*) during, through, throughout. **4** (*vote for them*) in favour of, pro, with, in support of, on behalf of. OPPOSITE: against. **5** (*for this reason*) because of, owing to, due to. **6** (*green for go*) representing, in place of, standing for.

➤ *conj* since, as, because.

forage *noun* fodder, food, foodstuff, feed, provender, herbage.

➤ *verb* search, hunt, seek, scour, scavenge, scratch around, rummage, ransack, plunder, pillage, raid.

foray *noun* raid, incursion, inroad, invasion, sally, sortie, attack, assault, plundering. OPPOSITE: retreat.

forbear *verb* refrain, abstain, desist, cease, stop, pause, hold back, withhold, restrain oneself, avoid, keep, cease, shun, eschew, decline. OPPOSITE: indulge.

forbearance *noun* abstinence, restraint, self-control, moderation, temperance, patience, endurance, long-suffering, tolerance, leniency, clemency.

forbid *verb* **1** (*forbid her to go*) prohibit, ban, interdict, bar, preclude, proscribe, outlaw, taboo, veto, disallow. OPPOSITE: permit. **2** (*forbid a course of action*) impede, hinder, inhibit, prevent, exclude, rule out. OPPOSITE: allow.

forbidden *adj* **1** (*smoking is forbidden*) prohibited, banned, debarred, proscribed, outlawed, vetoed, taboo. **2** (*a forbidden place*) out of bounds, off limits.

forbidding *adj* menacing, threatening, ominous, foreboding, sinister, hostile, unfriendly, grim, severe, harsh, tough, stern, daunting, off-putting (*inf*), repulsive, repellent, unpleasant. OPPOSITE: attractive.

force *verb* **1** (*forced to resign*) compel, constrain, oblige, necessitate, make, drive, impel, coerce, press, pressurize, pressure, press-gang, urge, put the screws on (*inf*), twist someone's arm (*inf*). OPPOSITE: coax. **2** (*force the door open*) prise, strain, wrench, break open, blast, push, thrust. OPPOSITE: ease.
  ➤ *noun* **1** (*use force against the protesters*) compulsion, constraint, coercion, duress, pressure, violence. **2** (*the force of the explosion*) power, might, strength, vigour, drive, energy, dynamism, exertion, pressure. **3** (*military forces*) army, host, legion, squadron, troop, regiment, unit, division, detachment, corps, patrol, battalion. **4** (*the force of the argument*) cogency, weight, significance, meaning, thrust, stress, emphasis, impact. OPPOSITE: weakness. **5** (*a powerful force for good*) influence, power, authority, dominance, pull, clout (*inf*).

forced *adj* **1** (*a forced march*) compulsory, obligatory, mandatory, involuntary, enforced, compelled, constrained. OPPOSITE: voluntary. **2** (*a forced smile*) unnatural, strained, artificial, false, self-conscious, affected, mannered, laboured, stiff. OPPOSITE: natural.

forceful *adj* strong, powerful, compelling, persuasive, impressive, weighty, dynamic, vigorous, energetic. OPPOSITE; weak.

forcible *adj* **1** (*a forcible argument*) forceful, compelling, powerful, mighty, strong, potent, cogent, pithy, effective, weighty, vigorous, impressive. OPPOSITE: weak. **2** (*forcible action*) forced, compulsory, obligatory, violent, aggressive, coercive.

forcibly *adv* by force, violently, powerfully, vigorously, energetically, aggressively, compulsorily, against one's will.

fore *noun* front, lead, head, top, bow, forefront, foreground. OPPOSITE: rear.

forebear *noun* ancestor, forefather, progenitor, predecessor, forerunner. OPPOSITE: descendant.

forebode *verb* augur, portend, presage, foretell, predict, prophesy, prefigure, foreshadow, betoken, indicate, mean, signify, promise, warn, forewarn.

foreboding *noun* **1** (*a feeling of foreboding*) apprehension, misgiving, dread, fear, anxiety. OPPOSITE: reassurance. **2** (*a foreboding that the plane would crash*) premonition, presentiment, dread, fear, omen, portent, token, augury, prediction, prophecy, warning.

forecast *verb* predict, foretell, prophesy, divine, foresee, prognosticate, augur, anticipate, speculate, estimate, guess, conjecture, calculate, plan, project.
  ➤ *noun* prediction, prophecy, divination, prognosis, augury, anticipation, conjecture, guess, speculation, projection, outlook.

foreclose *verb* exclude, shut out, preclude, debar, block, hinder, prevent, stop.

forefather *noun* ancestor, forebear, progenitor, procreator, father. OPPOSITE: offspring.

forefront *noun* front, front line, fore, foreground, vanguard, spearhead,

foregoing *adj* preceding, prior, previous, former, antecedent, aforesaid, anterior. OPPOSITE: following.

foregone *adj* **1** (*in foregone times*) past, previous, former, earlier, bygone. OPPOSITE: future. **2** (*a foregone conclusion*) predetermined, predestined, preordained, fixed, inevitable.

foreground *noun* fore, front, forefront, prominence, limelight. OPPOSITE: background.

foreign *adj* **1** (*foreign countries*) overseas, remote, distant, exotic. OPPOSITE: native. **2** (*foreign policy*) international, overseas, external, exterior. OPPOSITE: home. **3** (*a foreign object*) external, exterior, extrinsic, extraneous. **4** (*foreign to his nature*) strange, unfamiliar, irrelevant, unrelated. OPPOSITE: relevant.

foreigner *noun* alien, immigrant, stranger, outsider, newcomer. OPPOSITE: native.

foreknowledge *noun* prescience, foresight, precognition, premonition, clairvoyance.

foreland *noun* cape, headland, promontory, spur, point.

foreman *noun* supervisor, overseer, superintendent, chargehand, manager, boss (*inf*).

foremost *adj* chief, leading, front, head, first, primary, principal, main, premier, advanced, highest, supreme, paramount, prime.

forerunner *noun* **1** (*a forerunner of the modern computer*) precursor, harbinger, herald, predecessor, ancestor, forebear, forefather. OPPOSITE: successor. **2** (*a forerunner of spring*) omen, portent, sign, token, indication, forewarning, premonition.

foresee *verb* anticipate, expect, envisage, forecast, predict, prophesy, divine, augur, foretell, forebode.

foreshadow *verb* augur, presage, predict, promise, prophesy, prefigure, portend, bode, forebode, betoken, indicate, mean, signal, signify.

foresight *noun* forethought, anticipation, provision, precaution, prudence, discernment, judiciousness, caution, care, circumspection, farsightedness. OPPOSITE: improvidence.

forest *noun* wood, woodland, woods, trees, grove, copse, plantation.

forestall *verb* anticipate, thwart, frustrate, pre-empt, intercept, ward off, fend off, stave off, parry, prevent, hinder, impede, obstruct, obviate, preclude.

foretaste *noun* indication, warning, premonition, preview, sample, appetizer.

foretell *verb* predict, prophesy, augur, divine, forecast, prognosticate, presage, foreshadow, forewarn, forebode, indicate, prefigure, betoken.

forethought *noun* anticipation, foresight, provision, precaution, prudence, discernment, judiciousness, caution, farsightedness. OPPOSITE: improvidence.

forever *adv* **1** (*will love you forever*) evermore, always, till

the end of time, eternally, constantly, perpetually, incessantly, all the time. OPPOSITE: temporarily.
2 (*forever changing his mind*) continually, constantly, incessantly, endlessly, all the time.

forewarn *verb* warn, alert, put on guard, caution, admonish, advise, tip off.

foreword *noun* preface, introduction, preamble, prologue. OPPOSITE: epilogue.

forfeit *verb* lose, surrender, relinquish, hand over, give up, renounce. OPPOSITE: earn.
➤ *noun* loss, penalty, fine, mulct, forfeiture, damages, confiscation, sequestration. OPPOSITE: reward.

forge[1] *verb* **1** (*forge rivets*) make, shape, form, mould, work, hammer out, beat, create, fabricate, manufacture, construct, devise, invent, frame, coin. **2** (*forge bank notes*) fake, counterfeit, falsify, copy, imitate.
➤ *noun* smithy, foundry, furnace, hearth.

forge[2] *verb* **forge ahead** (*forged ahead with reforms*) advance, progress, continue, press on, make headway.

forged *adj* fake, counterfeit, false, fraudulent, imitation, sham, bogus, spurious. OPPOSITE: genuine.

forgery *noun* fake, counterfeit, falsification, imitation, reproduction, sham, fraud, phoney (*inf*).

forget *verb* fail, fail to remember, overlook, neglect, disregard, ignore, omit, pass over, let slip. OPPOSITE: remember.

forget oneself misbehave, behave badly, misconduct oneself, act up (*inf*).

forgetful *adj* absentminded, abstracted, inattentive, negligent, neglectful, heedless, careless, oblivious, unmindful. OPPOSITE: mindful.

forgetfulness *noun* absentmindedness, abstraction, inattention, negligence, neglect, disregard, heedlessness, carelessness, obliviousness.

forgivable *adj* pardonable, excusable, slight, trifling, petty, venial. OPPOSITE: unforgivable.

forgive *verb* pardon, absolve, excuse, acquit, exonerate, remit, condone, overlook, let off (*inf*), let bygones be bygones, bury the hatchet. OPPOSITE: punish.

forgiveness *noun* pardon, absolution, exoneration, acquittal, remission, clemency, amnesty, mercy. OPPOSITE: punishment.

forgiving *adj* merciful, compassionate, lenient, humane, mild, clement, tolerant, forbearing, magnanimous. OPPOSITE: merciless.

forgo *verb* surrender, relinquish, give up, yield, sacrifice, hand over, renounce, abandon, waive, do without, go without, refrain from, abstain from, shun, abjure.

forgotten *adj* unremembered, past, gone, buried, left behind, bygone, lost, irretrievable, neglected, overlooked. OPPOSITE: remembered.

fork *verb* branch, branch off, bifurcate, divide, part, split, separate, diverge, go separate ways, divaricate. OPPOSITE: unite.
➤ *noun* bifurcation, divarication, separation, division, parting, parting of the ways, branch.

forked *adj* branching, diverging, branched, divided, split, separated, pronged, Y-shaped.

forlorn *adj* **1** (*he looked a forlorn figure*) miserable, wretched, sad, desolate, cheerless, comfortless, unhappy, woebegone, pathetic, pitiful, helpless, friendless, homeless, destitute, lost, abandoned. OPPOSITE: happy.
2 (*forlorn buildings*) desolate, deserted, abandoned, forsaken, neglected. **3** (*a forlorn hope*) desperate, hopeless, futile, vain, useless, irretrievable.

form *noun* **1** (*shadowy forms*) shape, configuration, figure, appearance, pattern, model, cut, structure, frame, outline, formation, cast, arrangement, construction, contour, build, body. **2** (*an early form of bicycle*) type, kind, sort, variety, style, design, description, nature, character, mode, manner, method, arrangement, system. **3** (*pour the mixture into a form*) mould, frame, cast, model, pattern, matrix. **4** (*fill in a form*) order, document, paper, application, sheet, blank. **5** (*know the form*) convention, etiquette, protocol, formula, style, formality, procedure, ritual, ceremony, practice, custom. **6** (*bad form*) conduct, manners, behaviour, the done thing (*inf*). **7** (*in good form*) condition, health, fitness, shape, trim, fettle. **8** (*go into the sixth form*) class, grade, group, stream, year. **9** (*sit on a form*) bench, seat.
➤ *verb* **1** (*formed from clay*) make, shape, mould, model, fashion, create, fabricate, build, construct, assemble, set up, produce. OPPOSITE: destroy. **2** (*form a proposal*) frame, devise, invent, conceive, formulate, think up, design, plan, concoct, develop, arrange, dispose, organize. **3** (*form the basis of the plan*) compose, make up, make, constitute, serve as, comprise. **4** (*ice began to form*) take shape, materialize, crystallize, appear, develop. OPPOSITE: vanish. **5** (*form a habit*) contract, acquire, develop, get, pick up, get into (*inf*). OPPOSITE: lose. **6** (*form a line*) arrange, assemble, line up, dispose, organize, range. **7** (*a mind formed by a classical education*) train, educate, instruct, teach, develop, drill, school, discipline.

formal *adj* **1** (*a formal statement*) conventional, customary, regular, standard, approved, official, set, fixed, methodical. OPPOSITE: unofficial. **2** (*a formal person*) strict, precise, exact, correct, punctilious, ceremonious, stiff, starched, prim, solemn, dignified, ceremonial, stately, pompous, aloof, remote, reserved. OPPOSITE: casual. **3** (*a formal garden*) symmetrical, methodical, ordered, arranged.

formality *noun* convention, form, custom, rule, usage, practice, procedure, red tape, ritual, ceremony, protocol, etiquette, decorum.

format *noun* design, layout, appearance, arrangement, organization, style, form, shape, order, pattern, composition, plan.

formation *noun* **1** (*the formation of a new government*) forming, making, creation, generation, production, manufacture, construction, setting up, inauguration, composition, constitution, make-up, establishment, development. OPPOSITE: destruction. **2** (*flying in formation*) arrangement, grouping, order, organization, configuration, pattern, design, layout, structure.

formative *adj* influential, lasting, controlling, dominant, shaping, determinative, important, significant.

former *adj* previous, earlier, prior, preceding, foregoing, antecedent, past, old, bygone, foregone, anterior, onetime, sometime, erstwhile, late. OPPOSITE: future.

formerly *adv* previously, in the past, at an earlier time, heretofore, hitherto, once, at one time.

formidable *adj* **1** (*a formidable prospect*) daunting, intimidating, alarming, terrifying, fearful, dreadful, frightful, menacing, threatening, horrible, awful, terrible, overwhelming, arduous, difficult. OPPOSITE: reassuring. **2** (*a formidable adversary*) tremendous, colossal, terrific, great, strong, powerful, mighty, considerable, impressive, redoubtable, indomitable.

formless *adj* amorphous, vague, indefinite, indeterminate, nebulous, shapeless, unformed, chaotic, disorganized.

formula *noun* rule, principle, code, expression, prescription, recipe, procedure, method, ritual, convention, blueprint, precept, formulary, equation.

formulate *verb* **1** (*formulate an idea*) define, specify, detail, set down, articulate, express, state, frame, itemize, particularize. **2** (*formulate a plan*) devise, draw up, invent, forge, coin, think up, work out, create, coin, conceive, plan.

fornication *noun* sexual intercourse, sex, sexual relations, lovemaking, copulation, coitus.

forsake *verb* **1** (*forsake one's family*) desert, leave, quit, abandon, cast off, jilt, leave in the lurch, give up, relinquish, forgo. **2** (*forsake comforts*) surrender, yield, forswear, renounce, have done with, turn one's back on. OPPOSITE: keep.

forsaken *adj* desolate, deserted, abandoned, neglected, forlorn, isolated, remote, godforsaken.

forswear *verb* abjure, renounce, reject, forgo, relinquish, give up, forsake, abandon, disavow, retract, deny, recant, repudiate, disown. OPPOSITE: retain.

fort *noun* fortress, stronghold, citadel, fastness, garrison, castle, defence, keep, tower, turret, battlement, fortification, donjon, redoubt.

forte *noun* strength, strong point, gift, skill, talent, métier, speciality, thing (*inf*). OPPOSITE: foible.

forth *adv* **1** (*from that time forth*) forward, forwards, onward, onwards. **2** (*stretch forth*) out, outside, away, off, abroad.

forthcoming *adj* **1** (*a forthcoming event*) future, prospective, coming, approaching, expected, imminent, impending. OPPOSITE: previous. **2** (*the money was not forthcoming*) available, ready, accessible, obtainable, on tap (*inf*). **3** (*teenagers who are not forthcoming*) communicative, open, sociable, expansive, chatty, unreserved, informative, talkative, responsive. OPPOSITE: reticent.

forthright *adj* direct, straightforward, plain, plainspoken, honest, candid, frank, blunt, outspoken. OPPOSITE: evasive.

forthwith *adv* directly, immediately, at once, instantly, straightaway, quickly, without delay, right away. OPPOSITE: presently.

fortification *noun* defence, bastion, rampart, battlement, barricade, parapet, bulwark, fort, stronghold, citadel, blockhouse, fastness.

fortify *verb* **1** (*fortify a city*) strengthen, reinforce,

stiffen, brace, buttress, support, protect, guard, cover, secure, defend, garrison. **2** (*fortified by a drink*) encourage, cheer, hearten, invigorate, revive, sustain, embolden, reassure, brace.

fortitude *noun* endurance, patience, forbearance, hardihood, courage, fearlessness, bravery, backbone, strength, grit, mettle, firmness, resolution, determination, tenacity, perseverance. OPPOSITE: weakness.

fortuitous *adj* accidental, unplanned, contingent, chance, unexpected, unforeseen, unanticipated, casual, random, haphazard, arbitrary, lucky, fortunate, fluky (*inf*). OPPOSITE: planned.

fortunate *adj* **1** (*a fortunate person*) lucky, happy, felicitous, fortuitous, blessed, favoured, prosperous, successful. OPPOSITE: unlucky. **2** (*a fortunate event*) auspicious, propitious, favourable, advantageous, promising, fortuitous, opportune, timely. OPPOSITE: unfortunate.

fortunately *adv* luckily, happily, providentially, by good luck, as luck would have it. OPPOSITE: unfortunately.

fortune *noun* **1** (*inherit a fortune*) wealth, riches, opulence, affluence, treasure, prosperity, substance, assets, possessions, property, estate. OPPOSITE: poverty. **2** (*earn a fortune*) king's ransom, mint, packet (*inf*), bomb (*inf*), pile (*inf*). **3** (*have the good fortune to be chosen*) luck, chance, accident, coincidence, providence, contingency, fortuity, fate, destiny, lot, portion, doom, kismet, future, prospect, expectation.

fortune-teller *noun* prophet, prophetess, soothsayer, seer, oracle, augur, diviner, sibyl, clairvoyant, psychic.

forum *noun* **1** (*provide a forum for public debate*) meeting, arena, assembly, discussion, debate. **2** (*an ancient Roman forum*) marketplace, market square, square.

forward *adj* **1** (*forward movement*) advancing, leading, progressing, progressive. **2** (*forward in development*) advanced, early, premature, precocious, progressive, onward. OPPOSITE: backward. **3** (*in a forward position*) front, leading, first, foremost, head, frontal, anterior, fore. OPPOSITE: back. **4** (*forward planning*) future, prospective, advance. **5** (*a forward young man*) bold, brazen, brash, cheeky, pert, impertinent, impudent, presumptuous, assuming, familiar, overfamiliar, fresh (*inf*), confident, overconfident, cocky (*inf*), pushy (*inf*). OPPOSITE: reserved.

➤ *adv* **1** (*move forward*) forwards, on, onward, onwards, forth, ahead. OPPOSITE: backward. **2** (*come forward*) out, into view, into the open, to the fore, into prominence.

➤ *verb* **1** (*forward her career*) advance, further, promote, foster, support, favour, back, aid, help, encourage, expedite, quicken, hasten, hurry, speed, speed up, accelerate, dispatch. OPPOSITE: hinder. **2** (*forward a letter*) send, transmit, dispatch, mail, post, deliver, ship, send on.

forward-looking *adj* progressive, forward-thinking, advanced, modern, enterprising, innovative, enlightened, go-ahead, avant-garde, radical.

forwardness *noun* boldness, brazenness, brashness, impertinence, impudence, presumption, familiarity, overfamiliarity, confidence, overconfidence, cheek (*inf*), pushiness (*inf*). OPPOSITE: reserve.

forwards *adv* forward, on, onwards, onward, forth, ahead. OPPOSITE: backwards.

fossil *noun* remains, remnant, ammonite, relic, coprolite, corralite.

foster *verb* **1** (*foster improved relationships*) promote, advance, further, encourage, stimulate, cultivate, support, help, aid, assist, maintain, cherish, nurture, back, facilitate, nurse, harbour, sustain, nourish. **2** (*foster a child*) raise, rear, bring up, take care of, look after.

foul *adj* **1** (*a foul smell*) disgusting, revolting, repulsive, nauseating, loathsome, putrid, fetid, stinking, dirty, filthy, soiled, unclean, impure, contaminated, polluted, tainted, sullied, offensive, rank, noisome. OPPOSITE: pure. **2** (*foul language*) filthy, vulgar, coarse, gross, obscene, ribald, scurrilous, profane, blasphemous, indelicate, dirty, blue, smutty. **3** (*in a foul mood*) bad, nasty, angry, unpleasant, disagreeable, furious. **4** (*foul play*) unfair, dishonourable, dishonest, unjust, fraudulent, crooked, underhand, unprincipled, unsportsmanlike, unscrupulous, shady (*inf*). OPPOSITE: fair. **5** (*foul weather*) nasty, dirty, unpleasant, disagreeable, rainy, wet, gloomy, murky, overcast, bad, stormy, rough, wild. OPPOSITE: fine. **6** (*foul deeds*) wicked, vile, ignoble, despicable, disgraceful, shameful, heinous, infamous, base, low, horrible, loathsome, revolting. OPPOSITE: noble.

≫ *verb* **1** (*dogs fouling the pavement*) soil, dirty, begrime, pollute, contaminate, taint, sully, stain, smear, besmear, defile. **2** (*a rope fouling a machine*) block, clog, jam, choke, snarl, entangle. OPPOSITE: clear.

found *verb* **1** (*found an organization*) establish, set up, institute, organize, originate, start, inaugurate, create, build, raise, erect. OPPOSITE: abolish. **2** (*founded on rock*) build, erect, construct, base, ground, root, fix, set, rest, place.

foundation *noun* **1** (*the foundation of the building*) base, basis, footing, groundwork, bottom, underpinning, understructure, substructure, substratum, root, bedrock. OPPOSITE: superstructure. **2** (*the foundation of an organization*) establishment, institution, organization, inauguration, endowment, settlement. **3** (*a solid foundation for his career*) basis, support, base, starting point, groundwork, bedrock, essence, core. **4** (*a story without foundation*) basis, proof, support, reasoning, backup.

founder[1] *verb* **1** (*the ship foundered*) sink, go down, submerge, run aground. **2** (*the horse foundered*) stumble, fall, collapse, trip, stagger. **3** (*the attempt foundered*) collapse, fail, abort, miscarry, fall through, break down, go wrong, misfire, come to nothing, fall, trip, stumble, stagger.

founder[2] *noun* (*the founder of an institution*) originator, creator, organizer, benefactor, architect, inventor, initiator, beginner, discoverer, designer, builder, constructor, author, father, mother.

foundling *noun* waif, orphan, stray, urchin, outcast.

fountain *noun* **1** (*a fountain of water*) jet, spout, spray, fount, spurt, spring, well, wellhead. **2** (*the fountain of all truth*) fountainhead, fount, source, origin, spring, wellspring, wellhead, rise, cause, derivation, beginning.

fowl *noun* bird, chicken, cock, hen, goose, duck, turkey, bantam.

foxy *adj* wily, artful, cunning, sly, crafty, devious, sharp, subtle, shrewd, astute, tricky, guileful, scheming. OPPOSITE: artless.

foyer *noun* entrance, entrance hall, lobby, vestibule, reception, reception area, anteroom.

fracas *noun* quarrel, row, brawl, fight, disturbance, fray, uproar, commotion, rumpus.

fraction *noun* part, piece, fragment, bit, portion, proportion, section, segment, division, subdivision. OPPOSITE: whole.

fractious *adj* **1** (*fractious children*) irritable, peevish, testy, touchy, captious, cross, bad-tempered, ill-humoured, sulky, snappish, waspish, crabby, petulant, fretful. OPPOSITE: affable. **2** (*the party's fractious members*) unruly, refractory, recalcitrant, rebellious, awkward, contrary, perverse. OPPOSITE: docile.

fracture *verb* break, crack, splinter, split, rupture, tear. OPPOSITE: mend.

≫ *noun* break, breakage, breaking, breach, crack, rift, division, split, splitting, fissure, cleft, aperture, opening, rupture, rent.

fragile *adj* **1** (*a fragile chair*) brittle, frangible, breakable, frail, delicate, dainty, flimsy, slight, fine, insubstantial. OPPOSITE: durable. **2** (*feel fragile being ill*) weak, feeble, infirm, unwell, ailing. OPPOSITE: strong.

fragility *noun* brittleness, frangibility, frailty, delicacy, flimsiness, weakness, fineness, insubstantiality, feebleness. OPPOSITE: strength.

fragment *noun* piece, portion, fraction, part, bit, particle, morsel, scrap, remnant, remainder, chip, splinter, sliver. OPPOSITE: whole.

≫ *verb* break, splinter, shatter, break up, disintegrate, collapse, come apart, fall apart.

fragmentary *adj* broken, disconnected, disjointed, bitty, incomplete, discontinuous, partial, sketchy, unfinished, scattered, piecemeal.

fragrance *noun* **1** (*the fragrance of the flowers*) scent, perfume, aroma, smell, odour, redolence, balm, bouquet. OPPOSITE: fetor. **2** (*soaps and fragrances*) perfume, toilet water, scent, eau de cologne, cologne.

fragrant *adj* perfumed, scented, ambrosial, balmy, aromatic, sweet-smelling, redolent, odoriferous. OPPOSITE: fetid.

frail *adj* **1** (*a frail person*) weak, feeble, infirm, vulnerable, delicate, ill. **2** (*a frail boat*) fragile, delicate, slight, slender, thin, dainty, flimsy. OPPOSITE: sturdy.

frailty *noun* **1** (*frailty from old age*) weakness, feebleness, infirmity, fragility, brittleness, delicacy, slenderness. OPPOSITE: sturdiness. **2** (*frailties in his character*) failing, faulty, defect, imperfection, foible, weakness, weak point, fallibility, vulnerability, susceptibility. OPPOSITE: strength.

frame *noun* **1** (*a picture frame*) border, setting, mount, case. **2** (*a bicycle frame*) structure, construction, framework, skeleton, shell, casing, support, substructure, scaffolding, form, shape, fabric, constitution, system.

3 (*her slight frame*) build, body, physique, shape, figure, size.
➤ *verb* **1** (*frame a picture*) enclose, surround, border, mount, encase. **2** (*frame a proposal*) make, form, construct, build, fashion, model, forge, fabricate, devise, invent, concoct, compose, draw up, formulate, draft, sketch, outline, map out, plan. **3** (*frame an innocent person*) trap, incriminate, conspire against, plot against, set up (*inf*), fit up (*inf*).

frame of mind condition, state, mood, temper, humour, disposition.

frame-up *noun* conspiracy, plot, trap, put-up job (*inf*), fit-up (*inf*).

framework *noun* **1** (*a framework of laws*) structure, system, order, arrangement, scheme, fabric. **2** (*the framework of a building*) structure, construction, frame, skeleton, shell, casing, support, substructure, scaffolding, form, shape, fabric, constitution, system.

franchise *noun* **1** (*universal franchise*) vote, suffrage, enfranchisement. **2** (*a franchise to sell the products*) right, privilege, licence, charter, warrant, warranty, authorization, prerogative, exemption, immunity, freedom.

frank *adj* **1** (*a frank answer*) honest, straightforward, direct, forthright, candid, outspoken, plain, plainspoken, unreserved, blunt, open, sincere, guileless, artless, ingenuous. OPPOSITE: devious. **2** (*with frank admiration*) undisguised, unconcealed, avowed, apparent, obvious, plain, clear, transparent. OPPOSITE: concealed.
➤ *verb* stamp, cancel, mark, postmark.

frankly *adv* candidly, bluntly, plainly, directly, honestly, openly, straight.

frantic *adj* frenzied, wild, mad, delirious, hysterical, panic-stricken, berserk, distraught, distracted, agitated, raging, furious, beside oneself, frenetic. OPPOSITE: calm.

fraternity *noun* **1** (*a university fraternity*) brotherhood, fellowship, association, society, league, guild, union, circle, set, clan, company. **2** (*a feeling of fraternity*) companionship, camaraderie, fellowship, friendship, closeness, affinity.

fraternize *verb* associate, league, unite, cooperate, sympathize, socialize, mix, mingle, go around, keep company, consort, hobnob, hang about (*inf*), hang around (*inf*).

fraud *noun* **1** (*jailed for fraud*) deception, deceit, trickery, swindling, cheating, fraudulence, sharp practice, double-dealing, imposture, duplicity, treachery. OPPOSITE: honesty. **2** (*the picture is a fraud*) trick, artifice, swindle, hoax, wile, deception, ruse, stratagem, con (*inf*), rip-off (*inf*), scam (*inf*). **3** (*he's a fraud*) impostor, charlatan, quack, sham, double-dealer, trickster, cheat, swindler, fake, phoney (*inf*), con artist (*inf*), conman (*inf*).

fraudulent *adj* deceitful, tricky, crafty, wily, knavish, treacherous, dishonest, cheating, swindling, double-dealing, duplicitous, unscrupulous, crooked (*inf*), false, shady (*inf*), counterfeit, fake. OPPOSITE: honest.

fraught *adj* **1** (*fraught with problems*) filled, full, charged, loaded, laden, replete, abounding, attended, accompanied. OPPOSITE: devoid. **2** (*a fraught silence*) anxious, tense, distraught, worried, stressed.

fray[1] *noun* (*join in the fray*) fight, battle, combat, conflict, quarrel, row, brawl, mêlée, riot, fracas. OPPOSITE: peace.

fray[2] *verb* **1** (*the rope is fraying*) wear, wear thin, unravel, shred, tatter, chafe, rub, fret. **2** (*their tempers frayed*) strain, stress, tax, overtax, irritate, vex.

freak *noun* **1** (*a freak of nature*) abnormality, aberration, anomaly, oddity, curiosity, mutant, teratism, malformation, deformity, abortion, monstrosity, monster. **2** (*a computer freak*) enthusiast, addict, fanatic, fan, buff (*inf*), fiend (*inf*). **3** (*think of him as a freak*) oddity, anomaly, curiosity, oddball (*inf*), weirdo (*inf*), nut (*inf*). **4** (*a freak of the mind*) whim, caprice, fancy, notion, vagary, crotchet, quirk, humour.
➤ *adj* odd, abnormal, anomalous, unnatural, curious, aberrant, strange, weird, exceptional, unpredictable, unexpected.

freakish *adj* **1** (*freakish behaviour*) abnormal, aberrant, unnatural, bizarre, weird, strange. OPPOSITE: normal. **2** (*freakish thoughts*) whimsical, capricious, fanciful, wayward, fitful, erratic, odd. OPPOSITE: consistent.

free *adj* **1** (*animals that are free to roam*) independent, unconfined, loose, on the loose, unattached, liberated, released, unfettered, unshackled, unrestrained, unrestricted, unbridled, at liberty, at large. OPPOSITE: confined. **2** (*a free country*) independent, sovereign, self-governing, self-ruling, autonomous, enfranchised, emancipated. **3** (*a free flow*) clear, unobstructed, unimpeded, unhampered, open, permitted, allowed. OPPOSITE: blocked. **4** (*the free end of the rope*) loose, unattached, unfastened. OPPOSITE: fixed. **5** (*a free lunch*) gratis, gratuitous, on the house (*inf*), complimentary, without charge, for nothing. **6** (*have free time*) idle, at leisure, unoccupied, vacant, empty, available, spare, time to spare. OPPOSITE: busy. **7** (*is this seat free?*) vacant, empty, available. OPPOSITE: taken. **8** (*a free manner*) informal, easy, relaxed, casual, easygoing, unceremonious, familiar, uninhibited, natural, open, frank, laid-back (*inf*). OPPOSITE: constrained. **9** (*a free translation*) rough, loose, general, broad, inexact, imprecise. OPPOSITE: literal. **10** (*free with his praises*) liberal, generous, lavish, openhanded, bountiful, bounteous, extravagant, prodigal, munificent. OPPOSITE: mean. **11** (*free will*) voluntary, unforced, willing, spontaneous, unbidden. OPPOSITE: forced.
➤ *verb* **1** (*free an animal*) liberate, release, loose, let go, set free, emancipate, unfetter, uncage, unleash, unchain, unbind, untie, manumit. OPPOSITE: bind. **2** (*freed them from the wreckage*) release, rescue, relieve, rid, clear, extricate, disentangle, disengage, deliver. OPPOSITE: embroil. **3** (*freed her from the responsibilities*) discharge, exempt, except, excuse, relieve, clear.

free from exempt from, immune from, devoid of, without, lacking, safe from, clear of, relieved from. OPPOSITE: liable to.

freebooter *noun* pirate, buccaneer, bandit, brigand, robber, raider, marauder, highway robber.

freedom *noun* **1** (*freedom for the prisoners*) liberty, emancipation, independence, liberation, release, deliverance. OPPOSITE: captivity. **2** (*countries seeking freedom*) independence, self-government, self-rule, autonomy, sovereignty, enfranchisement, emancipation, home rule. **3** (*freedom from paying tax*) exemption, exception, immunity, impunity, right, privilege. OPPOSITE: liability. **4** (*freedom of movement*) range, scope, play, latitude, leeway, licence, authority, flexibility, elbow room, free hand, free rein, carte blanche. OPPOSITE: restriction. **5** (*freedom of manner*) informality, unconstraint, ease, naturalness, spontaneity, familiarity, frankness, openness. OPPOSITE: constraint.

freely *adv* **1** (*speak freely*) unreservedly, plainly, openly, candidly, frankly, bluntly, without constraint. **2** (*give freely*) willingly, voluntarily, generously, liberally, lavishly, extravagantly. OPPOSITE: meanly.

freeze *verb* **1** (*water freezes*) solidify, congeal, harden, ice, ice up, refrigerate, chill, benumb. OPPOSITE: melt. **2** (*froze when he went on stage*) stop, stand still, stop dead, stop in one's tracks. **3** (*freeze prices*) hold, fix, peg, suspend.

freezing *adj* icy, bitter, biting, raw, wintry, chilling, chilly, frosty, piercing, cutting, numbing, Siberian, arctic, polar, glacial, frigid. OPPOSITE: hot.

freight *noun* **1** (*air freight*) transportation, conveyance, haulage, carriage, shipment. **2** (*carry freight by rail*) cargo, load, lading, burden, charge, consignment, goods, merchandise.

frenetic *adj* frantic, frenzied, wild, mad, uncontrolled, excited, demented, distraught. OPPOSITE: calm.

frenzied *adj* frantic, wild, mad, uncontrolled, excited, panic-stricken, distraught. OPPOSITE: calm.

frenzy *noun* agitation, excitement, fury, rage, passion, madness, derangement, wildness, distraction, aberration, hysteria, delirium, fit, spasm, paroxysm, outburst. OPPOSITE: composure.

frequency *noun* incidence, repetition, recurrence, prevalence, commonness.

frequent *adj* **1** (*frequent visits*) recurrent, repeated, incessant, continual, persistent, constant, many, numerous. OPPOSITE: rare. **2** (*a frequent correspondent*) common, everyday, familiar, customary, usual, constant, habitual. OPPOSITE: unusual.
» *verb* visit, attend, patronize, haunt, hang about in (*inf*).

frequenter *noun* customer, client, patron, regular, regular visitor, haunter, habitué.

frequently *adv* often, repeatedly, again and again, over and over, over and over again, many times, continually, constantly, regularly, commonly, usually, habitually. OPPOSITE: seldom.

fresh *adj* **1** (*fresh thinking*) new, recent, latest, modern, up-to-date, novel, original, innovative, newfangled, different, unfamiliar. OPPOSITE: old. **2** (*make fresh inquiries*) additional, extra, more, further, new, renewed, other. **3** (*fresh air*) cool, refreshing, invigorating, bracing, brisk, crisp, clear, clean, bright, pure, unpolluted, sweet. OPPOSITE: stale. **4** (*feel fresh after a holiday*) energetic, vigorous, lively, hearty. OPPOSITE: tired. **5** (*have a fresh complexion*) healthy, keen, alert, revived, refreshed, rested, strong, flourishing, blooming,

glowing, fair. **6** (*fresh fruit*) natural, unprocessed, uncured, raw, crude. OPPOSITE: processed. **7** (*a fresh white shirt*) clean, spruce, bright, clear, exciting. **8** (*fresh weather*) cold, windy, cool, chilly, brisk, bracing. **9** (*fresh recruits*) inexperienced, green, raw, callow, youthful, artless, unsophisticated, untrained. OPPOSITE: experienced. **10** (*get fresh with someone*) familiar, overfamiliar, forward, presumptuous, bold, cheeky, saucy, impertinent, impudent, disrespectful, cheeky (*inf*), saucy (*inf*).

freshen *verb* **1** (*freshen a room*) air, ventilate, clean, clear, purify, deodorize. **2** (*freshen the committee with new members*) refresh, invigorate, revive, revitalize, enliven, renew.

freshen up wash oneself, get washed, get shaved, tidy oneself up, spruce oneself up, get spruced up.

fret *verb* **1** (*don't fret*) worry, brood, agonize, grieve, pine. **2** (*the problem fretted him*) distress, torment, irritate, annoy, vex, trouble, disturb, upset, bother, ruffle, harass, provoke, goad. **3** (*the stone had fretted*) rub, chafe, wear, abrade, fray, erode, corrode, eat away.

fretful *adj* irritable, petulant, peevish, restless, troubled, waspish, cross, bad-tempered, captious, testy, touchy, fractious, querulous, edgy, anxious, distressed, uneasy.

friable *adj* crumbly, powdery, brittle. OPPOSITE: tough.

friction *noun* **1** (*friction against the rock*) attrition, abrasion, rubbing, grating, scraping, grinding, abrading, chafing, fretting. **2** (*friction between people*) disagreement, discord, dissension, dissent, disputation, dispute, quarrelling, conflict, strife, disharmony, hostility, antagonism, resentment, rivalry, bad blood, animosity. OPPOSITE: agreement.

friend *noun* **1** (*my best friend*) companion, intimate, confidant, confidante, familiar, comrade, ally, associate, partner, crony, chum (*inf*), buddy (*inf*), pal (*inf*), mate (*inf*). OPPOSITE: enemy. **2** (*become a friend of the local orchestra*) benefactor, patron, backer, supporter, angel (*inf*).

friendless *adj* alone, solitary, companionless, lonesome, unpopular, unloved, shunned, abandoned, deserted.

friendliness *noun* affability, kindness, amiability, geniality, approachability, sociability, companionableness, neighbourliness, mateyness (*inf*), chumminess (*inf*)

friendly *adj* **1** (*a friendly person*) amiable, affable, amicable, kind, kindly, benevolent, neighbourly, brotherly, sisterly, cordial, genial, sociable, outgoing, communicative, approachable, close, intimate, warm, convivial, hospitable, familiar, fond, affectionate, sympathetic, understanding, chummy (*inf*), matey (*inf*). OPPOSITE: unfriendly. **2** (*a friendly atmosphere*) favourable, benevolent, propitious, auspicious, advantageous, beneficial, helpful. OPPOSITE: hostile.

friendship *noun* amity, harmony, rapport, comradeship, companionship, friendliness, amicability, geniality, cordiality, kindness, benevolence, intimacy, familiarity, love, affection, fondness, affinity, compatibility, attachment, regard. OPPOSITE: enmity.

fright *noun* **1** (*jump with fright*) fear, alarm, scare, terror, shock, horror, panic, dismay, fearfulness, consternation, dread, trepidation, apprehension, jitters (*inf*), creeps (*inf*), willies (*inf*), heebie-jeebies (*inf*), blue funk (*inf*). OPPOSITE: reassurance. **2** (*gave me a fright*) scare, shock, start.

frighten *verb* alarm, scare, terrify, shock, startle, horrify, petrify, appal, dismay, daunt, intimidate, unnerve, make one's hair stand on end (*inf*), scare stiff (*inf*), scare out of one's wits (*inf*), scare the living daylights out of (*inf*), put the wind up (*inf*). OPPOSITE: reassure.

frightful *adj* **1** (*a frightful accident*) frightening, alarming, terrifying, fearsome, fearful, dreadful, terrible, awful, horrible, hideous, gruesome, ghastly, dire, grim, grisly, distressing, horrifying, shocking, appalling, abhorrent, repulsive, outrageous, monstrous. OPPOSITE: delightful. **2** (*in a frightful mess*) awful, dreadful, horrible, unpleasant, disagreeable, shocking, appalling.

frigid *adj* **1** (*frigid temperature*) cold, cool, chilly, icy, glacial, bitter, freezing, frozen, arctic, Siberian. OPPOSITE: hot. **2** (*a frigid politeness*) formal, stiff, rigid, prim, aloof, austere, unapproachable, forbidding, cool, chilly, cold, icy, unfriendly, unresponsive, unfeeling, passionless, passive, indifferent. OPPOSITE: warm.

frigidity *noun* coldness, coolness, formality, stiffness, aloofness, unapproachability, unfriendliness, impassivity, indifference, apathy. OPPOSITE: warmth.

frill *noun* **1** (*a frill on a skirt*) flounce, ruche, furbelow, ruff, ruffle, valance, purfle, border, trimming. **2** (*a presentation with no frills*) decoration, embellishment, ornamentation, trimming, extra, affectation, mannerism, ostentation, showiness, fuss, frippery.

fringe *noun* **1** (*the fringe of a curtain*) border, edging, trimming, edge. **2** (*on the fringe of society*) perimeter, periphery, outskirts, limits, border, margin, rim, verge. OPPOSITE: centre.
➤ *adj* experimental, unconventional, unofficial, unorthodox, avant-garde.
➤ *verb* edge, trim, border, skirt, surround, enclose.

frisk *verb* (*lambs frisking about*) frolic, gambol, caper, skip, jump, leap, dance, play, sport, romp, cavort. **2** (*frisked by a police officer*) search, body-search, inspect, check.

frisky *adj* bouncy, active, frolicsome, frolicking, sportive, playful, lively, full of beans (*inf*), coltish, high-spirited, animated, high (*inf*), hyper (*inf*). OPPOSITE: sedate.

fritter *verb* **1** (*fritter money*) waste, squander, spend, dissipate, misspend. OPPOSITE: save. **2** (*fritter away time*) waste, squander, idle away, dally away, while away.

frivolity *noun* frivolousness, levity, flippancy, lightheartedness, foolishness, silliness, puerility, childishness, triviality, superficiality. OPPOSITE: seriousness.

frivolous *adj* **1** (*a frivolous person*) foolish, silly, puerile, childish, flippant. OPPOSITE: serious. **2** (*a frivolous activity*) idle, light, trivial, petty, unimportant, paltry, superficial, shallow.

frolic *verb* gambol, caper, frisk, romp, cavort, play, sport.
➤ *noun* gambol, caper, romp, game, sport, lark, antic,

prank, fun, laughter, amusement, merriment, jollity, high jinks (*inf*).

frolicsome *adj* playful, sportive, frisky, sprightly, coltish, lively, merry. OPPOSITE: solemn.

front *noun* **1** (*the front of the building*) anterior, forepart, foreground, face, exterior, facade, frontage. OPPOSITE: back. **2** (*the front of a line*) fore, head, top, lead, vanguard, van, forefront, beginning. OPPOSITE: rear. **3** (*put on a brave face*) look, face, aspect, appearance, air, demeanour, bearing, mien, exterior, facade, mask, disguise, show. **4** (*a front for illegal activities*) cover, cover-up, facade, disguise, mask, pretext.
➤ *adj* foremost, leading, head, first, anterior, frontal, forward. OPPOSITE: back.
➤ *verb* face, be opposite, look out on, overlook, confront, encounter.
in front ahead, leading, first, before, in advance. OPPOSITE: behind.

frontier *noun* boundary, border, marches, limit, limits, confines, bounds, edge.

frost *noun* freeze, freeze-up, hoar, hoarfrost, rime, Jack Frost.

frosty *adj* **1** (*frosty weather*) icy, glacial, freezing, frigid, cold, chilly, wintry, rimy, arctic, nippy (*inf*), parky (*inf*). OPPOSITE: hot. **2** (*with a frosty stare*) unfriendly, unenthusiastic, indifferent, cool, frigid, distant, aloof, unwelcoming. OPPOSITE: warm.

froth *noun* **1** (*froth on the beer*) foam, spume, bubbles, effervescence, lather, suds, head, scum. **2** (*no substance, just froth*) triviality, emptiness, idle talk, superficiality, nonsense, humbug, flummery.
➤ *verb* foam, lather, spume, fizz, bubble, effervesce.

frothy *adj* **1** (*frothy surf*) foaming, foamy, fizzy, bubbly, effervescent, spumous, spumy, spumescent. **2** (*a frothy film*) trivial, empty, light, insubstantial, trifling, superficial. OPPOSITE: serious.

frown *verb* scowl, glower, glare, lower, pout, grimace, look daggers at, give someone a dirty look (*inf*). OPPOSITE: smile.
frown on disapprove of, dislike, discourage, disfavour, discountenance, take a dim view of. OPPOSITE: approve.

frowsy *adj* **1** (*frowsy in appearance*) unkempt, untidy, slovenly, slatternly, shabby, sloppy, frumpish, dirty. OPPOSITE: neat. **2** (*a frowsy room*) stale, musty, frowsty, fusty, ill-smelling.

frozen *adj* icy, frigid, arctic, glacial, Siberian, polar, chilled, frosted, hard, numb. OPPOSITE: hot.

frugal *adj* **1** (*lead a frugal life*) thrifty, sparing, economical, careful, provident, temperate, unwasteful, scrimping, abstemious, parsimonious, niggardly. OPPOSITE: extravagant. **2** (*a frugal meal*) meagre, scanty, inadequate, insufficient, insubstantial.

frugality *noun* thrift, economy, providence, temperance, parsimony, meagreness. OPPOSITE: extravagance.

fruit *noun* **1** (*the fruits of the field*) produce, crop, harvest, yield. **2** (*enjoy the fruits of your labour*) product, result, consequence, issue, effect, yield, outcome, return, profit, reward, benefit, advantage.

fruitful *adj* **1** (*fruitful land*) fruit-bearing, productive, prolific, fecund, fertile, rich, teeming, plentiful, plenteous, abundant, profuse, fructiferous. OPPOSITE: barren. **2** (*a fruitful meeting*) profitable, worthwhile, effective, successful, useful, productive, rewarding. OPPOSITE: fruitless.

fruition *noun* fulfilment, attainment, achievement, realization, completion, success, consummation, perfection, maturity, maturation, gratification, enjoyment. OPPOSITE: abortion.

fruitless *adj* futile, vain, useless, ineffective, ineffectual, unproductive, unprofitable, unsuccessful, abortive, idle, worthless, unavailing, unrewarding, bootless, barren, sterile. OPPOSITE: fruitful.

fruity *adj* **1** (*a fruity voice*) rich, mellow, deep, resonant, full. **2** (*a fruity story*) indecent, bawdy, suggestive, vulgar, blue, smutty, titillating, near the knuckle (*inf*), raunchy (*inf*).

frustrate *verb* **1** (*his illness frustrates him*) disappoint, discourage, dishearten, depress, upset, annoy, vex, irritate. OPPOSITE: gratify. **2** (*frustrate a plan*) thwart, foil, dash, balk, confound, baffle, defeat, undo, counter, impede, circumvent, check, block, stymie, hinder, prevent.

frustration *noun* **1** (*feel frustration in your work*) disappointment, dissatisfaction, discontentment, annoyance, anger, vexation, irritation. **2** (*frustration of their ambitions*) thwarting, balking, defeat, failure, circumvention, hindrance, prevention. OPPOSITE: gratification.

fuddled *adj* confused, muddled, stupefied, bemused, inebriated, intoxicated, drunk, tipsy. OPPOSITE: clear.

fuddy-duddy *noun* conservative, old fogey, stick-in-the-mud (*inf*), stuffed shirt (*inf*).

fudge *verb* avoid, evade, dodge, equivocate, stall.

fuel *noun* **1** (*burn fuel*) combustible, wood, coal, gas, oil, petrol. **2** (*fuel for the body*) food, nourishment, sustenance. **3** (*fuel to his fears*) incitement, provocation, stimulus, encouragement.

fugacious *adj* fleeting, transitory, transient, fugitive, brief, short-lived, passing, ephemeral, evanescent. OPPOSITE: permanent.

fugitive *noun* runaway, escapee, deserter, refugee. » *adj* **1** (*a fugitive slave*) runaway, escaping, deserting, refugee. **2** (*fugitive joys*) fleeting, transitory, transient, fugacious, brief, short-lived, passing, ephemeral, evanescent. OPPOSITE: permanent.

fulcrum *noun* pivot, support, prop.

fulfil *verb* **1** (*fulfil a task*) complete, do, carry out, accomplish, achieve, finish, conclude, realize, perfect, consummate, effect, effectuate, perform, execute, discharge. **2** (*fulfil the requirements*) satisfy, fill, meet, answer, comply with, obey, observe, keep.

fulfilled *adj* satisfied, happy, content, pleased, gratified. OPPOSITE: dissatisfied.

fulfilment *noun* **1** (*the fulfilment of a promise*) completion, accomplishment, achievement, realization, perfection, consummation, performance, execution, discharge, conclusion, observance. **2** (*feel a sense of fulfilment*) satisfaction, contentment, gratification, pleasure.

fuliginous *adj* sooty, smoky, dusky, dark.

full *adj* **1** (*a full box*) filled, brimming, packed, crowded, crammed, replete, sated, gorged, satiated, saturated, jam-packed (*inf*), chock-a-block (*inf*). OPPOSITE: empty. **2** (*stock the full range*) complete, entire, whole, intact, integral, unabridged, comprehensive, maximum. OPPOSITE: partial. **3** (*food full of flavour*) abundant, plentiful, plenteous, copious, ample, generous, capacious, voluminous, vast, extensive, large. OPPOSITE: restricted. **4** (*feel full after the meal*) satisfied, replete, gorged, sated, stuffed, bursting (*inf*). OPPOSITE: hungry. **5** (*at full speed*) greatest, maximum, highest, top. OPPOSITE: minimum. **6** (*lead a full life*) busy, active, lively, hectic, frantic. OPPOSITE: empty. **7** (*a full figure*) rounded, well-rounded, curvaceous, plump, buxom. **8** (*a full skirt*) wide, puffy, baggy, loose, loose-fitting. **9** (*a full sound*) resonant, rich, deep, loud, clear, distinct. OPPOSITE: muted. **10** (*the seats are full*) occupied, taken, in use. OPPOSITE: vacant.
» *adv* **1** (*struck him full in the face*) directly, straight, right, squarely, exactly, precisely, smack bang (*inf*). **2** (*with the lights full on*) completely, entirely, fully, wholly, quite, altogether. OPPOSITE: partly.
in full fully, completely, wholly, in total, in detail.
to the full fully, thoroughly, completely, to the utmost.

full-blooded *adj* committed, devoted, dedicated, wholehearted, enthusiastic. OPPOSITE: halfhearted.

full-grown *adj* adult, mature, grown-up, of age, fully developed, fully fledged.

fullness *noun* **1** (*fullness of joy*) abundance, ampleness, thoroughness, completeness, comprehensiveness, totality. **2** (*a feeling of fullness after the meal*) satisfaction, repleteness, satiation. **3** (*the fullness of her figure*) roundedness, plumpness, shapeliness, curvaceousness. **4** (*fullness of sound*) richness, resonance, depth, strength, body. **5** (*a fullness in the body*) swelling, growth, enlargement, distension, tumour, tumescence.
in the fullness of time eventually, finally, ultimately, in due course, in the end.

full-scale *adj* **1** (*a full-scale drawing*) full-size, full-sized, life-size, life-sized, big, unreduced. **2** (*a full-scale search*) complete, full, extensive, thorough, detailed, comprehensive, thoroughgoing, sweeping, wide-ranging.

fully *adv* **1** (*fully committed*) completely, entirely, wholly, totally, utterly, absolutely, altogether, quite, thoroughly, perfectly. OPPOSITE: partly. **2** (*dealt with fully*) sufficiently, adequately, enough, satisfactorily, amply, abundantly. OPPOSITE: inadequately.

fully-fledged *adj* developed, mature, full-blown, experienced, trained, qualified.

fulminate *verb* **1** (*fulminate against the councillors*) denounce, condemn, decry, rail, inveigh, roar, thunder, rage, fume, censure, upbraid, berate, animadvert, remonstrate, protest. OPPOSITE: extol. **2** (*gunpowder fulminating*) explode, detonate, blow up, burst.

fulmination *noun* **1** (*fulmination against the government*) denunciation, condemnation, censure, animadversion, tirade, diatribe, obloquy, philippic. OPPOSITE: eulogy.

2 (*fulmination of the chemicals*) explosion, detonation, blast.

fulsome *adj* excessive, extravagant, inordinate, overdone, adulatory, fawning, ingratiating, cloying, sycophantic, insincere, sickening, nauseating, over-the-top (*inf*). OPPOSITE: meagre.

fumble *verb* **1** (*fumbled with the lock*) grope, feel, scrabble, search, stumble. **2** (*fumbling his lines*) botch, bungle, muff.

fume *verb* **1** (*fuming over the reply*) rage, storm, rant, rave, seethe, boil, chafe, fret, hit the roof (*inf*), blow one's top (*inf*), blow one's cool (*inf*), rant and rave (*inf*), get hot under the collar (*inf*), foam at the mouth (*inf*). **2** (*chimneys fuming*) smoke, emit, exhale, reek.
➤ *noun* rage, storm, fury, passion, agitation, fret, stew (*inf*). OPPOSITE: calm.

fumes *pl noun* gas, vapour, smoke, exhaust, effluvium, exhalation, pollution, reek.

fumigate *verb* smoke, disinfect, purify, cleanse, sterilize, sanitize. OPPOSITE: infect.

fun *noun* amusement, entertainment, relaxation, diversion, recreation, sport, pleasure, good time, enjoyment, happiness, merriment, jollity, joy, high spirits, cheer, mirth. OPPOSITE: misery.
➤ *adj* **1** (*a fun party*) enjoyable, entertaining, amusing, pleasurable, diverting. **2** (*a fun person to be with*) amusing, lively, entertaining, engaging, charming, witty, sparkling.
for fun for a laugh, for kicks (*inf*), for the hell of it (*inf*).
fun and games horseplay, fooling about, pranks, capers, high jinks.
in fun as a joke, for a laugh, in jest.
make fun of ridicule, laugh at, mock, jeer, gibe, taunt, rag, deride, scoff at, satirize, lampoon, rib (*inf*), send up (*inf*), pull someone's leg (*inf*). OPPOSITE: respect.

function *noun* **1** (*the function of the machine*) purpose, use, part, role, province, duty, charge, task, job, office, position, business, mission, occupation. **2** (*speeches given at the function*) ceremony, party, reception, gathering, affair, do (*inf*).
➤ *verb* **1** (*the machine is functioning*) work, operate, act, run, go, perform. **2** (*functions as a noun*) serve, work, act, perform, operate, behave, play the part of.

functional *adj* **1** (*functional furniture*) useful, practical, utilitarian, serviceable, hard-wearing, plain. OPPOSITE: decorative. **2** (*the signals are now functional*) operational, working, in working order, running.

functionary *noun* official, officeholder, office bearer, bureaucrat, civil servant.

fund *noun* **1** (*the steeple restoration fund*) reserve, collection, treasury, kitty, endowment, foundation, capital. **2** (*a fund of stories*) stock, supply, store, reserve, accumulation, mass, hoard, reservoir, pool, treasury.
➤ *verb* finance, pay for, subsidize, support, back, endow, capitalize.

fundamental *adj* basic, foundational, rudimentary, primary, first, elementary, elemental, important, necessary, essential, principal, key, vital, indispensable, cardinal, underlying, organic, constitutional, integral. OPPOSITE: secondary.

fundamentally *adv* basically, essentially, primarily, at heart, at bottom, deep down.

fundamentals *pl noun* basics, rudiments, essentials, principles, rules, foundations, basis, crux, cornerstone, nitty-gritty (*inf*), nuts and bolts (*inf*).

funds *pl noun* cash, capital, assets, means, investment, savings, money, resources, finance, dough (*inf*), dosh (*inf*), lolly (*inf*), bread (*inf*), the ready (*inf*).

funeral *noun* burial, interment, inhumation, cremation, obsequies, exequies.

funereal *adj* mournful, dirgeful, gloomy, dismal, solemn, sorrowful, woeful, sombre, dark, dreary, lugubrious, grave. OPPOSITE: joyous.

funk *noun* fear, panic, terror, fright, alarm, dread, trepidation, nervousness. OPPOSITE: courage.
➤ *verb* flinch, recoil, quail, cower, take fright, chicken out (*inf*). OPPOSITE: face.

funny *adj* **1** (*tell a funny story*) amusing, comic, comical, humorous, droll, witty, facetious, entertaining, diverting, hilarious, hysterical, farcical, laughable, ridiculous, ludicrous, risible, killing (*inf*). OPPOSITE: serious. **2** (*what's that funny smell?*) odd, strange, weird, curious, bizarre, peculiar, mysterious, suspicious, dubious, queer. OPPOSITE: normal.

fur *noun* hair, coat, hide, skin, pelt.

furbish *verb* polish, rub, burnish, shine, brighten, clean up, renovate, restore. OPPOSITE: tarnish.

furcate *adj* forked, furcated, branched, divided, divaricate, bifurcate.

furious *adj* **1** (*furious at the news*) angry, enraged, fuming, indignant, livid, incensed, irate, infuriated, wrathful, raging, mad, frantic, frenzied, up in arms (*inf*), hot under the collar (*inf*), mad (*inf*), hopping mad (*inf*), foaming at the mouth (*inf*). **2** (*a furious storm*) wild, stormy, violent, agitated, turbulent, torrential, tempestuous, savage, fierce, intense, unrestrained. OPPOSITE: calm.

furl *verb* roll, wrap, fold, wind. OPPOSITE: unfurl.

furnish *verb* **1** (*furnish the apartment*) equip, rig, rig out, fit out, appoint, decorate. **2** (*furnished me with the information*) supply, provide, equip, give, grant, stock, afford, bestow, endow, invest.

furniture *noun* fixtures, appliances, fittings, movables, furnishings, appointments, effects, goods, belongings, possessions, chattels, things, apparatus, equipment, stuff (*inf*).

furore *noun* **1** (*a furore at the new plan*) outcry, uproar, commotion, stir, disturbance, hullabaloo, to-do, outburst, rage, fury, frenzy. OPPOSITE: apathy. **2** (*a furore for collecting stamps*) craze, mania, rage, enthusiasm, fad.

furrow *noun* **1** (*plough a furrow*) trench, trough, channel, rut, hollow, groove, flute. **2** (*furrows on her face*) wrinkle, crease, line, crow's-foot, seam.
➤ *verb* wrinkle, crease, knit, pucker.

further *adj* additional, more, extra, supplementary, new, fresh, other.
➤ *adv* **1** (*and further, the price is low*) furthermore, besides, moreover, in addition, additionally, what's more, also, yet. **2** (*further along the road*) farther, beyond, past, longer, more. OPPOSITE: nearer.

≫ *verb* advance, promote, forward, assist, help, aid, back, foster, encourage, support, facilitate, expedite, hasten. OPPOSITE: hinder.

furtherance *noun* advancement, promotion, boost, assistance, help, aid, encouragement, facilitating, support, backing. OPPOSITE: hindrance.

furthermore *adv* moreover, yet, in addition, besides, what's more, further, too, also, as well.

furthest *adj* farthest, utmost, outermost, outmost, uttermost, extreme, ultimate, remotest, most distant. OPPOSITE: nearest.

furtive *adj* secret, secretive, clandestine, hidden, covert, cloaked, sly, stealthy, surreptitious, sneaking, underhand. OPPOSITE: open.

fury *noun* **1** (*tremble with fury*) rage, anger, wrath, ire, passion, temper, frenzy, madness. **2** (*the fury of the storm*) violence, force, intensity, fierceness, ferocity, wildness, severity, vehemence, potency, tempestuousness, turbulence. OPPOSITE: calm. **3** (*his wife can be a fury*) shrew, vixen, termagant, virago, hellcat, spitfire.

fuse *verb* **1** (*to fuse the cells*) unite, join, combine, integrate, amalgamate, blend, mix, intermix, commingle, intermingle, merge, weld, coalesce. OPPOSITE: separate. **2** (*solids fusing*) melt, liquefy, smelt, weld, solder.

fusion *noun* union, amalgamation, coalescence, synthesis, blend, mixture, merger, amalgam, alloy.

fuss *noun* **1** (*what's all the fuss about?*) agitation, commotion, stir, to-do (*inf*), bustle, fluster, flurry, bother, ado, palaver, flap (*inf*), brouhaha, tizzy (*inf*), storm in a teacup (*inf*), excitement. OPPOSITE: peace. **2** (*kick up a fuss*) complaint, objection, difficulty, trouble. **3** (*a petty fuss outside the club*) argument, quarrel, dispute, row, altercation.
≫ *verb* bustle, fret, worry, flap (*inf*), make a song and

dance about (*inf*), get worked up (*inf*), take on, fidget, fume, gripe (*inf*), bother, pester.

fussy *adj* **1** (*a fussy person*) particular, overparticular, finicky, faddy, pernickety, choosy (*inf*), difficult, hard to please, fastidious, dainty, nit-picking, discriminating, exacting. OPPOSITE: easygoing. **2** (*fussy clothes*) ornate, elaborate, busy, cluttered, overdecorated, overelaborate, overdetailed. OPPOSITE: simple.

fustian *noun* bombast, rant, pomposity, grandiloquence, magniloquence, bluster.
≫ *adj* bombastic, pompous, high-flown, lofty, euphuistic. OPPOSITE: plain.

fusty *adj* **1** (*a fusty room*) musty, mouldy, mildewy, damp, frowsty, stale, rank, ill-smelling, stuffy. OPPOSITE: fresh. **2** (*fusty ideas*) old-fashioned, out-of-date, outmoded, antiquated, archaic, passé. OPPOSITE: modern.

futile *adj* **1** (*a futile attempt*) useless, vain, fruitless, ineffectual, unavailing, to no avail, idle, empty, profitless, worthless, abortive, unsuccessful, unproductive, pointless, bootless. OPPOSITE: fruitful. **2** (*futile remarks*) trifling, trivial, minor, insignificant, unimportant. OPPOSITE: important.

futility *noun* **1** (*the futility of life*) uselessness, vanity, fruitlessness, idleness, worthlessness, unproductiveness, pointlessness. OPPOSITE: usefulness. **2** (*the futility of the comments*) triviality, insignificance, unimportance. OPPOSITE: importance.

future *adj* forthcoming, coming, to come, prospective, expected, impending, approaching, eventual, ultimate, subsequent, later. OPPOSITE: past.
≫ *noun* prospect, outlook, expectation, anticipation, offing, hereafter.

fuzzy *adj* **1** (*fuzzy hair*) frizzy, fluffy, woolly, downy. OPPOSITE: smooth. **2** (*my thoughts are fuzzy*) blurred, blurry, indistinct, unclear, out of focus, unfocused, bleary, misty, shadowy, vague, obscure, distorted. OPPOSITE: sharp.

gab *verb* chatter, gossip, prattle, natter (*inf*), yak (*inf*), talk, blabber, blather, blether, babble, drivel, gibber, jabber, waffle (*inf*), jaw, prate.
➤ *noun* chat, conversation, talk, small talk, blab, blarney, chitchat, yak (*inf*), yackety-yak (*inf*), gossip, chatter, babble, prattle, tittle-tattle, waffle (*inf*), blather, tongue-wagging.

gabble *verb* jabber, gibber, spout, gush, chatter, babble, burble, blather, gaggle, gossip, prattle, rabbit (*inf*), rattle, waffle (*inf*), blab, blabber, blether, cackle, drivel, splutter, sputter.
➤ *noun* drivel, gibberish, chatter, babble, babbling, blather, cackling, prattle, gibbering, jargon, jabber, blabber, blethering, nonsense, twaddle, waffle (*inf*).

gad *verb* **gad about** gallivant, roam, rove, ramble, range, meander, traipse (*inf*), travel, wander, run around, flit about, stray.

gadabout *noun* gallivanter, pleasure-seeker, rambler, rover, runabout, globe-trotter, nomad, traveller, wanderer.

gadget *noun* device, contraption (*inf*), gizmo (*inf*), contrivance, appliance, gimmick, widget (*inf*), apparatus, tool, instrument, implement, mechanism, invention, doodah (*inf*), thingummy (*inf*), whatsit (*inf*), whatnot (*inf*), thing.

gaffe *noun* mistake, error, blunder, clanger (*inf*), howler (*inf*), boob (*inf*), boo-boo (*inf*), slip, indiscretion, bloomer (*inf*), brick (*inf*), faux pas, solecism, gaucherie.

gaffer *noun* **1** (*took their orders from the gaffer*) boss (*inf*), foreman, manager, supervisor, overseer, honcho (*inf*), ganger, superintendent. **2** (*soft spot for the old gaffer*) old boy (*inf*), old man, old bloke (*inf*), old fellow, old geezer (*inf*), granddad, old-timer (*inf*), greybeard.

gag¹ *verb* **1** (*they found her bound and gagged*) smother, muffle, muzzle, silence, stifle, block, stop up, plug, clog. **2** (*gagged by the law*) muzzle, muffle, stifle, smother, silence, quiet, still, suppress, check, curb, repress,

restrain, choke, throttle. **3** (*the sight of blood made him gag*) retch, heave, spew, vomit, throw up (*inf*), puke (*inf*).

gag² *noun* (*the old gags got the biggest laughs*) joke, quip, jest, one-liner, pun, witticism, crack (*inf*), wisecrack (*inf*), funny (*inf*), prank, trick, hoax.

gaiety *noun* **1** (*the gaiety of the party*) joy, joyousness, gayness, glee, cheerfulness, happiness, hilarity, mirth, jollity, joviality, joyousness, merriment, liveliness, animation, vivacity, buoyancy, exuberance, high spirits, delight, gladness, good humour, joi de vivre, elation, exhilaration, exultation, jubilation, lightheartedness, pleasure, effervescence, sprightliness, vivacity, blitheness, blithesomeness. OPPOSITE: sadness. **2** (*the announcement occasioned much gaiety*) merrymaking, festivity, revelry, revels, conviviality, celebration, frolics, fun, jollification. OPPOSITE: mourning. **3** (*the gaiety of the costumes*) flamboyance, colour, colourfulness, brightness, brilliance, gaudiness, garishness, show, showiness, sparkle, glitter. OPPOSITE: drabness.

gain *verb* **1** (*having gained the advantage*) acquire, procure, obtain, get, secure, attain, win, earn, capture, glean, gather, reap, harvest, procure, bag, score (*inf*). OPPOSITE: lose. **2** (*gained millions for the company*) profit, benefit, earn, make, yield, produce, net, clear, realize, bring in, gross. **3** (*gained the summit*) reach, arrive at, get to, come to, achieve, attain. **4** (*steadily gaining strength*) increase, pick up, gather, collect, add, build up, advance, progress, improve.
➤ *noun* **1** (*enormous financial gain*) profit, advantage, benefit, earnings, winnings, revenue, income, proceeds, return, reward, yield, pickings, takings, interest, dividend, emolument. OPPOSITE: loss. **2** (*gain in weight*) increase, growth, rise, addition, accumulation, increment, accretion, augmentation. OPPOSITE: decline. **3** (*proud of the gains she had made*) acquisition, achievement, acquirement, attainment. **4** (*gains on the battlefield*) advance, progress, headway, advancement, improvement.

gain on 1 (*gaining on the race leader*) catch up with, get nearer, approach, close with, close in on, narrow with, narrow the gap, come up to, level with, overtake. OPPOSITE: fall behind. **2** (*the race leader gaining on them*) draw away from, leave behind, outdistance, get away from, pull away, widen the gap between.

gain time delay, stall, procrastinate, dally, drag one's feet (*inf*), dilly-dally (*inf*), temporize.

gainful *adj* profitable, lucrative, remunerative, money-making, paying, rewarding, productive, fruitful, worthwhile, beneficial, advantageous, useful, fructuous. OPPOSITE: unprofitable.

gainsay *verb* deny, contradict, disagree with, dispute, challenge, oppose, contravene, rebut, controvert, disaffirm. OPPOSITE: affirm.

gait *noun* walk, step, pace, stride, tread, bearing, carriage.

gala *noun* celebration, festival, carnival, fête, jamboree, pageant, party, festivity, jubilee, fair, procession.
➤ *adj* festive, holiday, carnival, celebratory, convivial, merry, gay, joyous, joyful, jovial, diverting, entertaining, special, spectacular, showy, ceremonial, ceremonious, festal.

galaxy *noun* **1** (*far reaches of the galaxy*) stars, star system, solar system, Milky Way, the heavens, constellation, cluster, nebula. **2** (*a galaxy of famous names*) host, gathering, array, assemblage, assembly, collection, mass, bevy.

gale *noun* **1** (*blew down in a gale*) wind, hurricane, cyclone, tornado, typhoon, blast, squall, storm, tempest, mistral, sirocco. OPPOSITE: breeze. **2** (*gales of laughter*) burst, outburst, outbreak, peal, roar, eruption, explosion, blast, howl, ring, scream, shout, shriek, fit, wave.

gall[1] *noun* **1** (*had the gall to argue with her*) impudence, insolence, effrontery, impertinence, audacity, cheek (*inf*), nerve (*inf*), face (*inf*), presumption, presumptuousness, temerity, brazenness, brass (*inf*), sauce (*inf*), sauciness (*inf*), brass neck (*inf*), neck (*inf*), chutzpah (*inf*). OPPOSITE: reserve. **2** (*letters full of gall*) rancour, bitterness, sourness, spite, animosity, malice, resentment, acrimony, hostility, venom, bile, spleen, enmity, antipathy, malevolence, virulence, acerbity, asperity, bad blood, ill feeling, malignity, animus. OPPOSITE: charity.

gall[2] *noun* **1** (*accepted suffering without gall*) irritation, exasperation, vexation, annoyance, aggravation, nuisance, bother, botheration (*inf*), pest, harassment, irritant, provocation, plague, torment. OPPOSITE: appeasement. **2** (*a gall on the animal's leg*) sore, abrasion, scrape, scratch, graze, chafe, canker, ulceration, excoriation, raw spot, wound.
➤ *verb* irritate, exasperate, vex, annoy, aggravate, infuriate, irk, nettle, peeve (*inf*), rile, pique, bother, provoke, get to (*inf*), rub up the wrong way (*inf*), get in one's hair (*inf*), get on one's nerves (*inf*), embitter, piss one off (*sl*), harass, hassle (*inf*), nag, nark (*inf*), pester, plague, torment, fret, rankle, ruffle. OPPOSITE: appease.

gallant *adj* **1** (*a gallant deed*) brave, courageous, valiant, heroic, intrepid, bold, daring, fearless, plucky, audacious, dauntless, dashing, noble, honourable,

valorous, doughty, manly, manful, mettlesome. OPPOSITE: cowardly. **2** (*very gallant of him*) polite, courteous, chivalrous, gracious, gentlemanly, magnanimous, courtly, obliging, considerate, thoughtful, attentive, mannerly. OPPOSITE: churlish. **3** (*a gallant sight*) fine, noble, great, stately, dignified, majestic, elegant, august, imposing, grand, splendid, magnificent, glorious, lofty, regal.
➤ *noun* **1** (*accompanied by her new gallant*) beau, suitor, admirer, lover, boyfriend, escort, partner, paramour, wooer. **2** (*fancied himself as a bit of a gallant*) dandy, beau, fop, ladies' man, lady-killer, man about town, buck (*inf*), man of fashion.

gallantry *noun* **1** (*gallantry in the face of the enemy*) courage, bravery, braveness, valour, heroism, boldness, courageousness, fearlessness, audacity, intrepidity, mettle, spirit, daring, nerve, pluck, prowess, dauntlessness, doughtiness, manliness. OPPOSITE: cowardice. **2** (*behaved with great gallantry*) courtesy, politeness, chivalry, chivalrousness, graciousness, magnanimity, courteousness, courtliness, nobility, honour, gentlemanliness, attentiveness, thoughtfulness, consideration. OPPOSITE: churlishness.

gallery *noun* **1** (*three rooms opened off the gallery*) corridor, passage, hallway, landing, cloister, loggia, veranda, balcony. **2** (*on sale in the gallery*) art gallery, exhibition area, museum, arcade. **3** (*applause from the gallery*) balcony, circle, gods (*inf*).

gallivant *verb* gad about, rove, roam, range, wander, ramble, run around, travel, stray, traipse (*inf*), flit about.

gallop *verb* **1** (*the galloping horse*) canter, lope, frisk, prance. **2** (*he galloped towards the exit*) race, rush, run, dash, speed, sprint, hasten, hurry, fly, bolt, dart, career, scamper, scurry, scud, tear, zoom, shoot, barrel along (*inf*). OPPOSITE: amble.

gallows *noun* scaffold, gibbet.

galore *adv* lots of, loads of (*inf*), heaps of (*inf*), tons of (*inf*), stacks of (*inf*), aplenty, in plenty, in abundance, to spare, everywhere, oodles of (*inf*), in profusion, in numbers.

galvanize *verb* electrify, excite, stimulate, fire, arouse, rouse, stir, awaken, animate, invigorate, startle, shock, jolt, kick-start, move, prod, provoke, inspire, thrill, spur, urge, enliven, quicken, vitalize, dynamize, energize, wake, exhilarate. OPPOSITE: damp.

gambit *noun* ruse, ploy, stratagem, trick, artifice, device, manoeuvre, move, tactic, machination, wile.

gamble *verb* **1** (*gambling on the race*) bet, wager, game, back, stake, put money on, play for money, try one's luck, have a flutter (*inf*), take a punt (*inf*), chance one's arm. **2** (*to gamble on the market*) speculate, risk, chance, hazard, venture.
➤ *noun* **1** (*enjoyed the odd gamble on the horses*) bet, wager, flutter (*inf*), punt (*inf*). **2** (*the deal was a gamble*) risk, hazard, venture, speculation, chance, pot luck, lottery, toss-up, leap in the dark, uncertainty. OPPOSITE: certainty.

gambol *verb* frolic, frisk, romp, caper, cavort, dance, leap, hop, jump, trip, play, sport, skip, prance, bound, spring, curvet.

game[1] *noun* **1** (*a game all ages can play*) pastime, recreation, diversion, amusement, distraction, entertainment, sport, play, fun, frolic, merriment, romp. OPPOSITE: work. **2** (*the next game is on Friday*) match, contest, round, bout, confrontation, competition, tournament, meeting, event, fixture, head-to-head. **3** (*they played a little game on her*) trick, prank, ruse, joke, jest, lark (*inf*), hoax. **4** (*what game are you in?*) business, line, occupation, profession, trade, calling, industry, line of country (*inf*), activity, enterprise, adventure, undertaking. **5** (*like a hunter in search of game*) quarry, prey, spoils, chase, wild animals, wild fowl, gamebirds. **6** (*the game's afoot*) scheme, plan, plot, ploy, design, stratagem, strategy, tactic, device, ruse, trick, artifice, manoeuvre.

game^2 *adj* **1** (*he was a game fighter*) brave, courageous, valiant, plucky, resolute, dogged, spirited, bold, heroic, intrepid, daring, dashing, unflinching, unblenching, undaunted, dauntless, fearless, feisty (*inf*), persevering, persistent, unafraid, valiant, gallant, gritty, ballsy (*sl*), gutsy (*inf*), stouthearted, lionhearted. OPPOSITE: cowardly. **2** (*they were all game for the attempt*) ready, willing, eager, inclined, disposed, prepared, enthusiastic, interested, desirous. OPPOSITE: reluctant.

gamut *noun* compass, range, scale, scope, series, sequence, sweep, field, spectrum, area, variety, catalogue.

gang *noun* **1** (*surrounded by a gang of spectators*) band, group, pack, crowd, mob, horde, herd, gathering, company, party, ring, bevy. **2** (*the Friday night gang*) circle, set, coterie, clique, crew (*inf*), camp, club, lot, fraternity, sorority. **3** (*gang of dockers*) team, squad, troop, crew, shift, troupe, detachment, posse.

gangling *adj* lanky, gangly, gawky, spindly, skinny, stringy, angular, bony, awkward, ungainly, gauche, rangy, loose-jointed, tall, leggy.

gangster *noun* mobster, heavy (*inf*), hood (*inf*), hoodlum, crook (*inf*), racketeer, mafioso, bandit, criminal, brigand, robber, rough, ruffian, thug, tough, desperado, terrorist.

gap *noun* **1** (*the gap between the stones*) space, hole, opening, break, breach, cavity, aperture, void, rift, cleft, crack, fissure, fracture, crevice, chink, cranny, rent, divide, gulf, orifice, interstice. **2** (*they resumed after a gap*) break, interval, pause, hiatus, interruption, interlude, lull, intermission, recess, respite, rest. **3** (*huge gaps in her memory*) blank, hole, omission, void, vacuity, lacuna. **4** (*an unbridgeable gap between them*) breach, divide, chasm, difference, divergence, disparity, inconsistency.

gape *verb* **1** (*gaped in astonishment*) stare, gaze, gawk (*inf*), gawp (*inf*), goggle, rubberneck (*inf*), ogle, wonder. **2** (*the chasm gaped before them*) open, yawn, crack, part, split. OPPOSITE: close.

garb *noun* **1** (*the garb of a nun*) dress, attire, clothes, clothing, garments, wear, gear (*inf*), apparel, outfit, costume, getup (*inf*), togs (*inf*), rigout (*inf*), kit, habit, uniform, livery, robes, trappings, array, raiment, vestments, habiliment. **2** (*in the garb of a professional*) appearance, guise, look, cut, form, aspect, semblance, style, fashion, mode.
➤ *verb* clothe, dress, cover, robe, kit out (*inf*), rig out (*inf*), fit, outfit, array, attire, apparel.

garbage *noun* **1** (*collection of household garbage*) rubbish, refuse, waste, trash, litter. **2** (*the bin was full of garbage*) debris, scraps, remains, leftovers, junk, bits and pieces, odds and ends, slops, sweepings, swill, muck, filth, detritus, dross, scourings. **3** (*they were talking garbage*) nonsense, rubbish, gibberish, trash, crap (*sl*), balls (*sl*), bollocks (*sl*), bullshit (*sl*), bull (*sl*), shit (*sl*), claptrap (*inf*), cobblers (*inf*), bunk (*inf*), bunkum (*inf*), drivel, piffle (*inf*), bilge (*inf*), rot (*inf*), tripe, twaddle, balderdash, codswallop (*inf*), eyewash (*inf*), flapdoodle (*inf*), guff (*inf*), hogwash (*inf*), hokum (*inf*), poppycock (*inf*), stuff and nonsense, tommyrot (*inf*), foolishness, bosh (*inf*), tosh (*inf*), hot air (*inf*).

garble *verb* **1** (*his words were garbled*) confuse, mix up, muddle, jumble, scramble, misquote, misinterpret, mistranslate, misunderstand. OPPOSITE: clarify. **2** (*the truth had been deliberately garbled*) distort, twist, corrupt, slant, colour, spin, doctor, adulterate, misrepresent, misreport, misstate, falsify, mutilate, pervert, tamper with, warp.

gargantuan *adj* enormous, huge, immense, colossal, tremendous, prodigious, massive, mammoth, giant, gigantic, vast, humongous (*inf*), whopping (*inf*), monumental, titanic, towering, hulking, elephantine, leviathan, mountainous, monstrous, great, big, large. OPPOSITE: minute.

garish *adj* gaudy, flash (*inf*), flashy, showy, brash, flamboyant, glaring, lurid, brassy, glitzy (*inf*), glittering, loud, bold, meretricious, naff (*inf*), tacky (*inf*), tawdry, tasteless, vulgar, cheap, raffish. OPPOSITE: subdued.

garland *noun* wreath, festoon, coronal, coronet, chaplet, headband, crown, laurels, bays, honours, flowers, decoration.
➤ *verb* wreathe, festoon, crown, decorate, deck, adorn.

garments *pl noun* clothes, clothing, dress, wear, costume, garb, outfit, attire, apparel, array, habit, togs (*inf*), gear (*inf*), getup (*inf*), duds (*inf*), uniform, wardrobe, covering, vestments, raiments, habiliment.

garner *verb* gather, collect, accumulate, amass, assemble, heap, hoard, pile up, stack up, save, husband, preserve, store, lay in, lay up, put by, reserve, stockpile, stow away, cull, deposit. OPPOSITE: waste.

garnish *verb* decorate, adorn, ornament, deck, deck out, bedeck, beautify, embellish, festoon, trim, enhance, grace, prettify, set off. OPPOSITE: strip.
➤ *noun* decoration, adornment, ornament, ornamentation, embellishment, trim, trimming, beautification, enhancement, relish, garniture.

garret *noun* attic, loft, roof-space, mansard. OPPOSITE: basement.

garrison *noun* **1** (*called out the garrison*) armed force, detachment, troops, soldiers, unit, platoon, brigade, squadron, militia, command. **2** (*surrounded a heavily fortified garrison*) fort, fortress, fortification, stronghold, station, post, base, barracks, camp, encampment, blockhouse, citadel.
➤ *verb* **1** (*the port was garrisoned by French troops*) defend, protect, guard, man, occupy, fortify, preserve. **2** (*security men garrisoned in the park*) post, position, place, station, assign, mount, billet, furnish.

garrulous *adj* **1** (*a garrulous old woman*) talkative, loquacious, voluble, chattering, chatty, effusive, gabby (*inf*), prattling, babbling, gossipy, gushing, jabbering, mouthy (*inf*), prating. OPPOSITE: taciturn. **2** (*this garrulous version of events*) verbose, long-winded, windy, wordy, rambling, gassy (*inf*), prosy, diffuse, prolix.

gas *noun* vapour, fume, exhalation, effluvium, wind.

gash *noun* cut, incision, slash, slit, score, tear, rent, gouge, laceration, nick, split, cleft, wound.
➤ *verb* cut, slash, slit, score, lacerate, tear, rend, split, gouge, nick, incise, cleave, wound.

gasp *verb* pant, puff, blow, breathe, choke, wheeze, gulp, catch one's breath, draw in one's breath, fight for breath, heave.
➤ *noun* **1** (*with his last gasp*) breath, pant, puff, blow, wheeze, gulp, choke. **2** (*gasp of horror*) exclamation, ejaculation, gulp, intake.

gastric *adj* stomach, intestinal, abdominal, coeliac, enteric, stomachic.

gate *noun* **1** (*the gate swung open*) door, barrier, portal, wicket, postern. **2** (*the gates of heaven*) gateway, entrance, doorway, exit, access, egress, opening, passage.

gather *verb* **1** (*a crowd quickly gathered*) collect, come together, assemble, congregate, accumulate, meet, group, amass, hoard, cluster, flock together, crowd, mass, convene, muster, rally, foregather. OPPOSITE: disperse. **2** (*gather everyone together*) round up, call together, get together, assemble, collect, summon, convene, muster, marshal. **3** (*gathering information*) get together, collect, assemble, accumulate, amass, garner, hoard, store, stockpile, heap up, pile up, stack up, stash away. **4** (*I gather it is over*) understand, hear, conclude, assume, deduce, infer, surmise, believe, learn. **5** (*gather in the crops*) pick, pluck, glean, reap, harvest, crop, bring in, collect, cull, garner, select. **6** (*the storm gathered in strength*) increase, grow, swell, rise, build, expand, extend, enlarge, heighten, deepen, thicken, intensify, add, advance, progress, improve, develop, wax. OPPOSITE: decrease. **7** (*her skirt had been gathered at the hem*) pucker, ruffle, shirr, pleat, tuck, fold, crease, wrinkle, contract, knit.

gathering *noun* **1** (*gathering of the clans*) assembly, meeting, rally, muster, party, band, group, company, congregation, crowd, flock, get-together (*inf*), turn-out, round-up, horde, mass, mob, throng, knot, assemblage, collection, convention, conclave, congress, concourse, convocation. **2** (*the gathering of materials*) collection, accumulation, assemblage, aggregation, aggregate, mass, heap, hoard, pile, store, stock, stockpile, cluster, agglomeration, conglomeration, concentration. **3** (*information gathering*) collecting, accumulation, assembly, assembling, garnering, procuring. **4** (*gathering on the back of his finger*) pustule, abscess, ulcer, boil, carbuncle, pimple, spot, zit (*inf*), sore, ulcer, tumour.

gauche *adj* awkward, gawky, clumsy, bumbling, lumbering, shy, ungainly, inelegant, inept, ungraceful, unpolished, graceless, uncultured, unsophisticated, uncultivated, ignorant, ill-bred, ill-mannered, insensitive, tactless, maladroit. OPPOSITE: sophisticated.

gaudy *adj* bright, colourful, gay, brash, garish, flash (*inf*), flashy, showy, glitzy (*inf*), snazzy (*inf*), flamboyant, florid, ostentatious, glaring, loud, harsh, shrieking, stark,

brilliant, tinselly, multi-coloured, bold, meretricious, tawdry, tasteless, kitsch, cheap, tacky (*inf*), raffish, vulgar. OPPOSITE: muted.

gauge *verb* **1** (*she gauged the effect of her news*) assess, weigh, calculate, determine, evaluate, appraise, apprise, estimate, figure, guess, guesstimate (*inf*), judge, adjudge, rate, reckon. **2** (*gauged the depth*) measure, calculate, compute, determine, estimate, reckon, check, ascertain, count.
➤ *noun* **1** (*a gauge of their skill*) measure, standard, basis, model, pattern, norm, criterion, yardstick, bench mark, indicator, touchstone, guide, guideline, rule, par, criterion, example, exemplar, sample, test, meter. **2** (*tools with different gauges*) size, measure, magnitude, thickness, width, depth, height, area, extent, capacity, bore, span, degree, scope.

gaunt *adj* **1** (*he looked pale and gaunt*) thin, lean, lank, spare, meagre, skinny, scraggy, scrawny, spindly, drawn, emaciated, starved, shrivelled, underfed, wasted, withered, bony, angular, skeletal, cadaverous, pinched, haggard, hollow-eyed, hollow-cheeked, raw-boned, meagre, attenuated. OPPOSITE: plump. **2** (*the place had a gaunt aspect*) bleak, desolate, dismal, dreary, bare, barren, harsh, grim, forbidding, forlorn, stark, stern.

gawk *verb* gape, gawp (*inf*), goggle, stare, gaze, rubberneck (*inf*), ogle, look.

gawky *adj* awkward, ungainly, clumsy, gangling, lanky, gauche, lumbering, blundering, inept, graceless, uncoordinated, oafish, clodhopping, loutish, lumpish, clownish, doltish, maladroit. OPPOSITE: graceful.

gay *adj* **1** (*in a gay mood*) merry, jolly, jovial, cheerful, blithe, carefree, bright, gleeful, happy, joyful, joyous, glad, lighthearted, elated, in good spirits, in high spirits, mirthful, sunny, carefree, debonair, fun-loving, cock-a-hoop, exuberant, lively, animated, vivacious, sprightly, buoyant, effervescent, insouciant, playful, frolicsome. OPPOSITE: sad. **2** (*a gay time was had by all*) merry, festive, enjoyable, entertaining, convivial, amusing, hilarious. OPPOSITE: dull. **3** (*a gay costume*) bright, colourful, vivid, brilliant, sparkling, rich, multi-coloured, gaudy, garish, flashy, showy, flamboyant. OPPOSITE: sombre. **4** (*she told me he was gay*) homosexual, lesbian, queer (*inf*), bent (*inf*), camp (*inf*), poofy (*inf*), limp-wristed (*inf*), butch (*inf*). OPPOSITE: heterosexual.
➤ *noun* homosexual, lesbian, queer (*inf*), poof (*inf*), poofter (*inf*), homo (*inf*), woofter (*inf*), fag (*inf*), faggot (*inf*), dyke (*inf*), fairy (*inf*), pansy (*inf*), queen (*inf*), nancy (*inf*).

gaze *verb* stare, look, gape, gawk (*inf*), goggle, eye, eyeball (*inf*), stand agog, rubberneck (*inf*), contemplate, watch, regard, view, wonder. OPPOSITE: glance.
➤ *noun* stare, look, gape.

gazette *noun* journal, periodical, newspaper, paper, rag (*inf*), newssheet, organ, dispatch, notice.

gear *noun* **1** (*engaged the gear*) gearwheel, wheel, cog, cogwheel, gearing, ratchet. **2** (*problem with the rig's gear*) gears, mechanism, machinery, works. **3** (*all the technical gear*) equipment, apparatus, appurtenances, trappings, accessories, paraphernalia, tools, instruments, implements, appliances, kit, outfit, rig, supplies, utensils, material, harness, tackle, stuff (*inf*), accoutrements, contrivances. **4** (*came round with all his gear*) belongings, possessions, kit, baggage, luggage, effects, paraphernalia, stuff (*inf*), things (*inf*), goods and chattels, impedimenta. **5** (*told them to get their gear on*) clothes, clothing, wear, dress, attire, apparel, garments, togs (*inf*), getup (*inf*), rigout (*inf*), costume, garb, habit, vestments, array.

gelatinous *adj* viscous, glutinous, jelly-like, gooey (*inf*), gummy, gluey, sticky, congealed, rubbery, slimy, mucilaginous, viscid.

geld *verb* castrate, neuter, emasculate, unman, unsex, asexualize.

gelid *adj* icy, freezing, frozen, frigid, glacial, ice-cold, cold, frosty, wintry, snowy, bitter, chilly, arctic, polar. OPPOSITE: warm.

gem *noun* **1** (*dazzling display of gems*) gemstone, jewel, stone, precious stone, semiprecious stone, brilliant. **2** (*that book is a real gem*) jewel, treasure, prize, masterpiece, pick, flower, cream, crème de la crème, pearl.

genealogy *noun* pedigree, family tree, family history, ancestry, descent, extraction, derivation, line, lineage, bloodline, parentage, birth, family, dynasty, house, stock, roots, strain, breed, progeniture, heritage, stemma, stirps.

general *adj* **1** (*for general use*) universal, widespread, overall, extensive, common, public, collective, total, wide, popular, public, prevailing, prevalent, generic. OPPOSITE: specific. **2** (*the general procedure*) usual, regular, normal, standard, customary, habitual, common, ordinary, everyday, run-of-the-mill, typical, conventional, accepted, habitual. OPPOSITE: rare. **3** (*general knowledge*) universal, sweeping, wide-ranging, diverse, blanket, broad, across-the-board, all-inclusive, indiscriminate, comprehensive, encyclopedic, panoramic, catholic, miscellaneous, mixed, assorted, diversified, variegated. **4** (*you get the general idea*) vague, broad, rough, indefinite, approximate, unspecific, unspecified, ill-defined, inexact, imprecise, loose, undetailed. OPPOSITE: precise.
≫ *noun* commander, leader, chief, head.

generality *noun* **1** (*confined to generalities*) generalization, general statement, general principle, sweeping statement, loose statement, vague notion. **2** (*the generality of the description*) impreciseness, imprecision, indefiniteness, inexactitude, inexactness, lack of detail, looseness, roughness, approximation, vagueness. **3** (*the generality of the practice*) commonness, acceptedness, broadness, extensiveness, popularity, prevalence, universality. **4** (*the generality of opinion*) comprehensiveness, universality, all-inclusiveness, breadth, catholicity, miscellaneity, sweepingness, ecumenicity.

generally *adv* **1** (*it generally turns out all right*) usually, normally, in general, as a rule, almost always, by and large, on the whole, ordinarily, customarily, habitually, typically, regularly, mainly, mostly, in most cases, for the most part, chiefly, broadly, largely, conventionally, on average. **2** (*generally acknowledged*) commonly, widely, extensively, universally, comprehensively, publicly. **3** (*generally speaking*) in general, broadly,

loosely, approximately. OPPOSITE: specifically. **4** (*generally approved of*) predominantly, largely, mainly, mostly, for the most part, chiefly, principally, on the whole, in the main.

generate *verb* **1** (*generate heat*) produce, create, make, form. **2** (*generate a new species*) engender, breed, beget, sire, father, procreate, spawn, produce, propagate. **3** (*generate new ideas*) create, produce, cause, bring about, initiate, originate, give rise to, inspire, brainstorm, occasion, arouse, stir up, whip up, propagate. OPPOSITE: destroy.

generation *noun* **1** (*the generation of offspring*) production, creation, formation, propagation, procreation, breeding, reproduction, origination, genesis, begetting, siring, engendering, engenderment. OPPOSITE: destruction. **2** (*the generation of new initiatives*) creation, causing, inspiration, initiation, production, origination, inception, occasioning, propagation. **3** (*generations before today*) era, age, epoch, day, days, period, time, times. **4** (*with each passing generation*) lifetime, life span. **5** (*a lost generation*) age, age group, peer group.

generic *adj* **1** (*a generic name for numerous sub-species*) collective, general, common, sweeping, blanket, inclusive, all-inclusive, all-encompassing, comprehensive, universal, wide, nonspecific. OPPOSITE: specific. **2** (*generic goods*) unbranded, nonexclusive, nonregistered, nonproprietary, non-trademarked.

generosity *noun* **1** (*the generosity of the gift*) munificence, beneficence, benevolence, bounteousness, liberality, lavishness, open-handedness, charity, philanthropy, kindness, bounty, largess, hospitality, big-handedness. OPPOSITE: meanness. **2** (*great generosity of spirit*) magnanimity, unselfishness, selflessness, goodness, nobility, nobleness, high-mindedness, loftiness, altruism, disinterest, disinterestedness, honour, honourableness.

generous *adj* **1** (*proved a generous host*) hospitable, liberal, lavish, princely, prodigal, kind, open-handed, munificent, charitable, bountiful, bounteous, ungrudging, unstinting, free, free-handed. OPPOSITE: mean. **2** (*a generous nature*) magnanimous, noble, benevolent, beneficent, philanthropic, unselfish, selfless, kind, good, honourable, altruistic, high-minded, big (*inf*), bighearted, lofty, disinterested, unprejudiced, public-spirited. **3** (*a generous allowance*) abundant, plentiful, copious, rich, full, lavish, liberal, ample, overflowing, unstinting, superabundant. OPPOSITE: scanty.

genesis *noun* beginning, origin, birth, outset, start, root, source, creation, commencement, dawn, generation, foundation, founding, initiation, inception, engendering, formation, propagation. OPPOSITE: end.

genial *adj* hearty, cordial, congenial, warm, friendly, amiable, affable, jolly, jovial, happy, glad, joyous, cheerful, cheery, convivial, pleasant, agreeable, good-natured, warmhearted, merry, easygoing (*inf*), good-humoured, kind, kindly, benign, amicable, amenable, sociable, sunny, sympathetic. OPPOSITE: cold.

geniality *noun* cordiality, affability, amiability, friendliness, conviviality, congeniality, kindliness, kindness, warmheartedness, warmth, joviality, jollity, joy, joyousness, cheerfulness, happiness, gladness, cheeriness, good nature, good cheer, heartiness, mirth, agreeableness, pleasantness, amicableness, sociability, sunniness. OPPOSITE: unfriendliness.

genius noun 1 (*widely considered a genius*) prodigy, virtuoso, maestro, master, past master, mastermind, expert, adept, intellect, intellectual, Einstein (*inf*), egghead (*inf*), brain, brainbox (*inf*), brains (*inf*), boffin (*inf*), hotshot (*inf*), buff (*inf*), sage. OPPOSITE: dunce. 2 (*required a degree of genius*) brilliance, intelligence, intellect, brightness, cleverness, wisdom, brains (*inf*), grey matter (*inf*), little grey cells (*inf*). OPPOSITE: stupidity. 3 (*a genius for comedy*) gift, talent, aptitude, faculty, flair, forte, knack, ability, skill, power, inclination, bent, turn, propensity, capacity, capability, endowment.

genre noun category, class, school, style, type, sort, kind, brand, form, fashion, group, species, genus, character, stamp, strain, variety.

genteel adj 1 (*admired for his genteel manner*) polite, civil, courteous, well-mannered, gracious, decorous, courtly, polished, cultivated, mannerly, elegant, fashionable, stylish, urbane, formal, sophisticated. OPPOSITE: boorish. 2 (*hailed from a genteel background*) respectable, well-bred, aristocratic, noble, proper, gentlemanly, ladylike, well-born, blue-blooded, cultured, refined.

gentility noun 1 (*behaved with great gentility towards them*) politeness, civility, courtesy, respectability, breeding, good manners, mannerliness, propriety, decorum, refinement, graciousness, polish, elegance, stylishness, cultivation, sophistication, urbanity, courtliness, etiquette, formality. OPPOSITE: boorishness. 2 (*claimed links with the gentility*) aristocracy, nobility, good family, high birth, gentry, upper class, ruling class, rank, breeding, élite, blue blood.

gentle adj 1 (*a gentle soul*) tender, kind, kindly, compassionate, considerate, benign, merciful, indulgent, charitable, lenient, humane, sympathetic, tenderhearted, softhearted, sweet-tempered, amiable, clement, meek, mild, placid, calm, peaceful, quiet, serene, soft, still, tranquil, pacific, reposeful, bland. OPPOSITE: cruel. 2 (*her gentle caresses*) soft, light, soothing, smooth, stroking. OPPOSITE: rough. 3 (*a gentle climb*) gradual, easy, slow, light, slight, smooth, moderate, imperceptible, undemanding. OPPOSITE: steep. 4 (*a gentle breeze*) soft, soothing, mild, light, slight, calm, moderate, pleasant, temperate, balmy, clement, muted, placid, quiet, serene, smooth, tranquil. OPPOSITE: strong. 5 (*a gentle creature*) meek, tame, docile, placid, manageable, trained, schooled, broken, tractable, biddable. OPPOSITE: wild.

gentlemanly adj gentlemanlike, genteel, well-bred, courteous, polite, civil, mannerly, well-behaved, well-mannered, considerate, courtly, gallant, chivalrous, noble, honourable, reputable, polished, suave, urbane, debonair, refined, cultivated, cultured, civilized, accommodating, obliging. OPPOSITE: churlish.

gentry noun aristocracy, upper class, élite, nobility, nobles, gentility, gentlefolk, upper crust (*inf*).

genuine adj 1 (*the genuine article*) real, authentic, sterling, original, pure, natural, unadulterated, true, factual, veritable, actual, sound, valid, unalloyed, bona fide, legitimate, legal, lawful, pukka (*inf*), kosher (*inf*). OPPOSITE: fake. 2 (*their reassurances seemed genuine enough*) honest, sincere, earnest, unaffected, frank, candid, up-front (*inf*), heartfelt, truthful, open, unfeigned, undeceitful, artless, ingenuous, natural. OPPOSITE: insincere.

genus noun 1 (*plant of a different genus*) subdivision, subfamily, taxon. 2 (*another example of this genus*) order, class, species, breed, race, kind, sort, type, group, set, category, genre, division, variety.

germ noun 1 (*a new family of germs*) microbe, bacterium, bacillus, virus, microorganism, bug (*inf*). 2 (*germ of an idea*) beginning, start, commencement, inception, root, source, origin, spark, nucleus, cause, fountain. 3 (*the fertilized germ*) egg, ovum, ovule, seed, embryo, nucleus, bud, spore, sprout.

germane adj relevant, pertinent, connected, allied, related, akin, apposite, apropos, appropriate, fitting, to the point, to the purpose, suitable, suited, apt, applicable, material, proper, felicitous, cognate, analogous. OPPOSITE: irrelevant.

germinate verb 1 (*the plant will germinate in the spring*) sprout, shoot, grow, develop, vegetate, bud, take root, swell, spring up, burgeon, pullulate. OPPOSITE: wither. 2 (*the idea gradually germinated in his mind*) originate, grow, develop, take root, begin, start, commence.

gestation noun development, incubation, ripening, pregnancy, conception, evolution, planning, drafting, gravidity, maturation, parturiency.

gesticulate verb gesture, sign, signal, make a sign, motion, wave, beckon, indicate, nod.

gesture noun 1 (*with a gesture of his arm*) gesticulation, signal, sign, indication, action, motion, movement, wave, flourish. 2 (*a gesture of cooperation*) demonstration, action, deed, act.
» verb gesticulate, motion, signal, sign, make a sign, wave, beckon, indicate, point.

get verb 1 (*get a new computer*) obtain, acquire, procure, secure, gain, earn, buy, purchase, win, receive, come by, reap, glean, bring in, make, achieve, reach, find, attain, realize, clear, bag (*inf*), score (*inf*), inherit. OPPOSITE: lose. 2 (*she went to get her purse*) fetch, pick up, collect, bring, carry, go for, transport, convey. 3 (*got him at the third attempt*) catch, seize, capture, take, grab, lay hold of, grasp, collar, arrest, apprehend, trap, entrap, snare, hunt down, hit, kill, nab (*inf*), bag (*inf*), nick (*inf*), nail (*inf*). OPPOSITE: release. 4 (*it was getting late*) become, grow, turn, go, wax. 5 (*get a cold*) catch, contract, come down with, go down with, be afflicted with, fall victim to, pick up, develop, take. 6 (*get his secretary on the phone*) telephone, phone, contact, speak to, ring, radio, reach, communicate with, get in touch with. 7 (*how much he might get a week*) earn, receive, make, pocket, take home, bring in, gross, take, net. 8 (*I get your meaning*) understand, grasp, see, take in, perceive, hear, follow, fathom, twig (*inf*), work out, comprehend, apprehend, catch on (*inf*), suss out (*inf*). OPPOSITE: miss. 9 (*get them to join in*) persuade, induce, talk into, coax, prevail upon,

influence, urge, sway, convince, wheedle into, win over.
10 (*it will be dark by the time she gets here*) arrive, reach,
come, make it (*inf*), move, go. OPPOSITE: leave. **11** (*get to
see the match*) manage, arrange, succeed, fix, contrive,
organize, wangle (*inf*). **12** (*let's get lunch*) prepare, cook,
get ready, put out, put together, rustle up (*inf*), fix (*inf*).
13 (*we'll get them back for it*) get even with, pay someone
back, get back at (*inf*), take vengeance on, avenge
oneself, return like for like, give tit for tat, settle the
score with. **14** (*that film always gets me*) move, affect,
excite, stir, arouse, touch, grip, impress, stimulate, turn
one on (*inf*), send (*inf*). **15** (*that last question got me*)
stump, baffle, puzzle, perplex, mystify, confound,
nonplus, flummox, defeat. **16** (*such behaviour really gets
me*) irritate, annoy, provoke, bother, bug (*inf*),
exasperate, infuriate, nark (*inf*), nettle, pique, vex, get on
one's nerves, get one's goat (*inf*), anger, drive crazy (*inf*),
gall, irk, rile, upset, rub up the wrong way (*inf*).
get about move about, move around, travel.
get across communicate, put across, put over, get over,
make clear, make understood, bring home to, impart,
convey, transmit.
get ahead progress, advance, get on, make good, make
it (*inf*), do well, prosper, thrive, succeed, be successful,
flourish, rise, go places (*inf*), get somewhere (*inf*), make
the big time (*inf*), make one's mark (*inf*), go up in the
world (*inf*), cut it (*inf*).
get along 1 (*we just don't get along*) get on, hit it off
(*inf*), be on friendly terms, see eye to eye, agree,
harmonize. **2** (*getting along all right*) get on, do, manage,
cope, fare, get by (*inf*), survive, make out (*inf*), progress,
advance, develop.
get at 1 (*trying to get at the truth*) reach, attain, find, get
hold of, discover, identify, obtain. **2** (*stop getting at me*)
criticize, pick on, find fault with, hassle (*inf*), get on
one's back (*inf*), blame, carp, nag, attack, knock (*inf*),
slate (*inf*), slam (*inf*), pick holes in (*inf*), make fun of,
irritate, taunt. **3** (*she could not see what they were getting
at*) suggest, hint, imply, lead up to, intend, insinuate,
mean. **4** (*I think he's been got at*) bribe, buy off, corrupt,
influence, tamper with, suborn.
get away escape, get out, break away, break free, break
out, run away, flee, leave, depart, make good one's
escape, disappear, slope off (*inf*), abscond, decamp.
get back 1 (*get back to the house*) return, go back, come
back, arrive back, go home, come home, arrive home,
revert. **2** (*get back his clothing*) recover, retrieve, recoup,
regain, repossess. OPPOSITE: lose. **3** (*she swore to get her
back*) get, pay back, retaliate, get even with, hit back,
settle the score with, take vengeance on, avenge oneself
on, give tit for tat.
get by get along, cope, manage, fare, survive, make
ends meet (*inf*), make out (*inf*), scrape by (*inf*), hang on
(*inf*), keep one's head above water (*inf*), keep the wolf
from the door (*inf*), see it through (*inf*), weather the
storm (*inf*), exist, subsist.
get down 1 (*get down from a tree*) descend, get off,
climb down, step down, lower, alight, dismount,
disembark. **2** (*it gets me down*) depress, discourage,
dishearten, sadden, dispirit.
get off 1 (*get off a bus*) alight, disembark, dismount, get
down, get out, descend, climb off, leave, depart, exit.
OPPOSITE: embark. **2** (*get off scot free*) escape, avoid

punishment, evade punishment, be acquitted, be
cleared, be excused, be let off (*inf*), be let off the hook
(*inf*).
get on 1 (*time to get on the train*) board, climb on,
mount, ascend, get in, get into, embark. OPPOSITE:
disembark. **2** (*time will tell how he gets on*) get along,
manage, cope, make out (*inf*), fare, cut it (*inf*), prosper,
progress, proceed, advance, succeed. **3** (*they just don't get
on*) get along, agree, concur, hit it off (*inf*), harmonize.
get out 1 (*a last chance to get out*) escape, break out,
clear out (*inf*), clear off (*inf*), go away, be off, leave,
abscond, depart, quit (*inf*), withdraw, evacuate, decamp,
vacate, flee, vamoose (*inf*), extricate oneself, free oneself.
2 (*get out your books*) take out, produce. **3** (*if this ever gets
out*) circulate, spread, come out, leak out, become
known, become public, get abroad.
get out of avoid, dodge (*inf*), evade, escape, shirk, skive
(*inf*).
get over 1 (*took years to get over his injuries*) recover
from, recuperate from, get better, get well, come round,
mend, rally, pull through, respond to treatment, shake
off, revive, survive. **2** (*trying to get over her loss*) forget,
surmount, overcome, master, get round, defeat, deal
with, write off, come to terms with, get the better of,
shake off, complete. **3** (*get the facts over*) communicate,
get across, make clear, make understood, convey, put
across, put over, impart, explain.
get round 1 (*managed to get round the problem*)
circumvent, bypass, evade, avoid, skirt, outmanoeuvre,
edge. **2** (*I will get round her*) persuade, talk round, win
over, prevail upon, coax, cajole, induce, sway, wheedle,
convert.
get together 1 (*we must get together some time*) meet,
meet up, see one another, assemble, congregate, rally,
muster, join, unite, converge, foregather, collaborate.
2 (*get together the evidence*) collect, gather, accumulate,
assemble, compile, amass, organize.
get up 1 (*get up early*) rise, arise, wake up, waken,
awake, awaken, rouse, stir. **2** (*get up a hill*) mount,
ascend, climb, scale. **3** (*the wind is getting up*) increase,
become stronger, intensify, strengthen, escalate, swell.
getaway *noun* escape, breakout, break, flight,
absconding, decampment.
get-together *noun* meeting, party, gathering,
assembly, function, reception, knees-up (*inf*), do (*inf*),
bash (*inf*), thrash (*inf*), beanfeast (*inf*), social, soirée,
rally, reunion.
getup *noun* outfit, clothes, clothing, dress, gear (*inf*),
garb, garments, togs (*inf*), rigout (*inf*), apparel.
ghastly *adj* **1** (*met a ghastly end*) dreadful, frightful,
terrible, awful, shocking, appalling, hideous, horrible,
nasty, loathsome, repulsive, repellent, fearful,
frightening, terrifying, horrendous, horrid, grim, grisly,
gory, gruesome. OPPOSITE: pleasant. **2** (*you look ghastly*)
dreadful, awful, terrible, deathly pale, ill, sick, poorly,
rotten, lousy (*inf*), off colour (*inf*), unwell, ropy (*inf*),
under the weather (*inf*), god-awful (*inf*). **3** (*a ghastly
misunderstanding*) bad, serious, awful, dreadful, terrible,
frightful, appalling, grave, critical, unforgivable,
shocking, dangerous. **4** (*felt ghastly about it*) dreadful,
awful, terrible, ashamed, bad, shameful. **5** (*her skin went
a ghastly hue*) pale, ashen, cadaverous, deathly, livid,

spectral, pallid, colourless, wan, pasty, white. OPPOSITE: ruddy. **6** (*not that ghastly little boy*) dreadful, horrible, horrid, appalling, abominable, nasty, odious, loathsome, contemptible, foul, mean.

ghost *noun* **1** (*the ghost of an old lady*) spectre, phantom, spirit, soul, apparition, phantasm, wraith, spook (*inf*), ghoul, presence, shade, shadow, revenant. **2** (*the ghost of a chance*) glimmer, trace, shadow, suggestion, hint, impression, semblance, possibility.

ghostly *adj* eerie, creepy, weird, uncanny, unearthly, supernatural, spooky (*inf*), shadowy, haunted, spectral, illusory, insubstantial, phantom, phantasmal, phantasmic, ghostlike, wraithlike, otherworldly.

giant *noun* colossus, monster, ogre, titan, behemoth, leviathan. OPPOSITE: dwarf.
➤ *adj* gigantic, colossal, huge, immense, enormous, massive, vast, monstrous, monumental, mammoth, humongous (*inf*), jumbo (*inf*), whopping (*inf*), elephantine, gargantuan, prodigious, stupendous, titanic, cyclopean, king-size, industrial-size (*inf*), large, big. OPPOSITE: tiny.

gibber *verb* gabble, jabber, prattle, babble, chatter, blab, blabber, blather, cackle, cant, waffle (*inf*).

gibberish *noun* nonsense, rubbish, crap (*sl*), balls (*sl*), shit (*sl*), bull (*sl*), bullshit (*sl*), garbage (*inf*), jargon, twaddle, drivel, gobbledygook (*inf*), balderdash, hot air (*inf*), mumbo-jumbo, cobblers (*inf*), rot (*inf*), tosh (*inf*), tripe (*inf*), bilge (*inf*), bunkum (*inf*), hokum (*inf*), poppycock (*inf*), claptrap, bosh (*inf*), eyewash (*inf*), guff (*inf*), hogwash (*inf*), piffle (*inf*), tommyrot (*inf*), prattle, chatter, gabble, blather, humbug, yammer. OPPOSITE: sense.

gibe *noun* taunt, jeer, dig (*inf*), sneer, barb, crack (*inf*), mockery, ridicule, teasing, derision, scoff, poke, quip, sarcasm.
➤ *verb* jeer, scoff, mock, sneer, deride, taunt, tease, scorn, flout, laugh at, poke fun at, ridicule, make fun of, take the piss out of (*sl*), rib (*inf*), rag (*inf*). OPPOSITE: compliment.

giddy *adj* **1** (*the motion made him feel giddy*) dizzy, faint, light-headed, reeling, unsteady, woozy (*inf*), vertiginous. **2** (*she's a giddy little thing*) flighty, fickle, capricious, silly, volatile, scatterbrained, featherbrained, frivolous, skittish, impulsive, excitable, erratic, flippant, whimsical, mercurial, irresponsible, carefree, careless, thoughtless, insouciant, reckless, heedless, wild, frenzied, high (*inf*), changeable, unsteady, unstable, unbalanced, vacillating, inconstant. OPPOSITE: sensible.

gift *noun* **1** (*bought them both a small gift*) present, offering, donation, contribution, freebie (*inf*), handout, benefaction, bounty, largess, gratuity, tip, bonus, boon, grant, allowance, endowment, bequest, inheritance, legacy. **2** (*she had a gift for dancing*) talent, knack, genius, faculty, aptitude, flair, bent, facility, mind, skill, capacity, aptness, expertise, power, proficiency, ability, turn. OPPOSITE: inability.
➤ *verb* present, offer, give, contribute, donate, bestow, confer, proffer, endow, bequeath, leave, will.

gifted *adj* talented, accomplished, expert, masterly, adept, able, adroit, capable, proficient, skilful, skilled,

endowed, brilliant, clever, intelligent, bright, sharp, smart (*inf*), ingenious. OPPOSITE: inept.

gigantic *adj* giant, huge, enormous, immense, colossal, tremendous, vast, prodigious, gargantuan, monumental, monstrous, stupendous, titanic, elephantine, mammoth, jumbo (*inf*), king-size, humongous (*inf*), whopping (*inf*), great, big, large. OPPOSITE: minute.

giggle *verb* snigger, titter, laugh, cackle, chortle, chuckle, snicker.

gild *verb* **1** (*talk about gilding the lily*) adorn, decorate, embellish, beautify, enhance, enrich, brighten, ornament, deck, dress up, grace, festoon, garnish, array, bedeck. **2** (*that's what I call gilding the truth*) embroider, disguise, camouflage, window-dress.

gimcrack *adj* cheap, tacky (*inf*), shoddy, tatty (*inf*), kitsch, flimsy, jerry-built, tawdry, trashy, rubbishy, trumpery. OPPOSITE: well-made.

gimmick *noun* device, gadget, gizmo (*inf*), contrivance, attraction, stunt, manoeuvre, novelty, gambit, ploy, scheme, dodge, ruse, stratagem, trick.

gingerly *adj* cautiously, warily, carefully, daintily, delicately, tenderly, gently, hesitantly, reluctantly, timidly, tentatively, guardedly, suspiciously, watchfully, vigilantly, attentively, with caution, judiciously, prudently, cannily, heedfully, charily, fastidiously, squeamishly, timorously, circumspectly. OPPOSITE: boldly.

Gipsy *noun* Romany, Bohemian, traveller, roamer, wanderer, rover, rambler, nomad, transient, vagabond, vagrant, tinker, diddicoy, tzigane.

gird *verb* **1** (*girded themselves for the fight*) prepare, get ready, ready, brace, steel, fortify. **2** (*gird on his sword*) girdle, belt, strap, fasten, bind. **3** (*the warriors girded the hill*) encircle, surround, blockade, ring, encompass, compass, environ, hem in, enclose, enfold, confine, pen.

girdle *noun* corset, foundation, stays, belt, sash, cummerbund, waistband, truss, corselet, cincture, fillet.
➤ *verb* encircle, circle, surround, ring, encompass, enclose, environ, go round, bind, bound, hem, gird.

girl *noun* **1** (*a young girl*) maiden, maid, lass, lassie, miss, young lady, young woman, schoolgirl, wench, damsel, daughter, bird (*inf*), babe (*inf*), chick (*inf*). OPPOSITE: boy. **2** (*she's his girl*) girlfriend, sweetheart, lover, ladylove, date, mistress, significant other (*inf*), fiancée, inamorata.

girth *noun* **1** (*a girth of several metres*) circumference, perimeter, size, measure, bulk. **2** (*tightened the girth*) strap, band.

gist *noun* substance, essence, pith, marrow, matter, core, kernel, point, idea, meaning, significance, import, quintessence, sense, drift, direction, nucleus, nub, crux.

give *verb* **1** (*give me the hammer*) hand, pass, present, slip, offer, lend, grant, bestow, contribute, confer, donate, turn over, award, accord, leave, will, bequeath, make over, entrust, consign, vouchsafe. OPPOSITE: withhold. **2** (*give the wrong idea*) suggest, present, show, display, present, demonstrate, reveal, set forth, indicate, manifest, evidence. **3** (*will give you some help*) supply, provide, offer, proffer, accord, grant, permit, furnish. **4** (*give us all the latest*) communicate, give out, tell, utter, publish, transmit, impart, announce, declare, pronounce, convey, render, transfer, send. **5** (*give way at the junction*) yield, concede, cede, give in, give up, relinquish, surrender. **6** (*give them nightmares*) cause, create, make, give rise to, produce, provoke, occasion. **7** (*give everything to the company*) give up, sacrifice, devote, hand over, commit. OPPOSITE: retain. **8** (*give good results*) produce, yield, afford, result in. **9** (*give a celebratory dinner*) arrange, organize, stage, host, put on, lay on. **10** (*give a short cry*) let out, utter, issue, emit. **11** (*gave me to understand*) lead, make, cause, induce, move, force, dispose, incline, prompt. **12** (*the bridge may give*) collapse, give way, break, break down, fall apart, come apart, yield, bend, buckle, sag, sink, fall.

give away 1 (*don't give away our plans*) expose, divulge, reveal, disclose, let slip, let out, leak, uncover. **2** (*he gave them away*) betray, inform on, shop (*inf*), grass on (*inf*), rat on (*inf*), blow the whistle on (*inf*).

give in give up, surrender, yield, capitulate, submit, give way, concede, admit defeat, succumb, retreat, collapse, comply, quit (*inf*), throw in the towel (*inf*), throw in the sponge (*inf*), chuck it in (*inf*), pack it in (*inf*), jack it in (*inf*), call it a day (*inf*), show the white flag (*inf*).

give off emit, exude, exhale, give out, produce, send out, throw out, pour out, discharge, release, vent.

give out 1 (*aid workers giving out food*) distribute, hand out, dole out, share out, dish out (*inf*), allocate, allot, disperse, pass around, apportion, assign, deal, mete out. **2** (*giving out the news on the radio*) announce, communicate, declare, spread, circulate, disseminate, impart, make known, broadcast, publish, transmit, advertise, notify. **3** (*the oxygen supply will soon give out*) fail, run out, run dry, pack up (*inf*), come to an end, be exhausted, be depleted, stop working, break down, conk out (*inf*).

give up 1 (*promised to give up drinking*) stop, cease, renounce, forgo, forswear, desist, quit (*inf*), kick (*inf*), abandon, discontinue, chuck (*inf*), cut out (*inf*), leave off, relinquish, waive, sacrifice. OPPOSITE: continue. **2** (*give up to his opponent*) surrender, yield, give in, concede, capitulate, submit, quit (*inf*), resign, turn it in (*inf*), throw in the towel (*inf*). **3** (*sit down and give up*) despair, lose heart, abandon hope, give up hope.

given *adj* **1** (*given to practical jokes*) inclined, disposed, likely, apt, wont, liable, prone, addicted. **2** (*on any given date*) specified, specific, particular, stated, fixed, set, arranged, appointed, definite, individual, distinct.

giver *noun* donor, benefactor, patron, sponsor, backer, supporter, promoter, contributor, subscriber, provider, donator, grantor, subsidizer, philanthropist, helper, friend, well-wisher, fairy godmother (*inf*), angel (*inf*).

glacial *adj* **1** (*a glacial landscape*) icy, frozen, freezing, frigid, arctic, cold, polar, frosty, raw, bitter, biting, piercing, chill, chilly, Siberian, wintry, stiff, gelid. OPPOSITE: hot. **2** (*approached him with glacial reserve*) cold, icy, frigid, unfeeling, hostile, unfriendly, antagonistic, inimical. OPPOSITE: warm.

glad *adj* **1** (*I am glad to hear it*) happy, pleased, contented, gratified, delighted, elated, satisfied, overjoyed, chuffed (*inf*), thrilled, cheerful, over the moon (*inf*), tickled pink (*inf*). OPPOSITE: sad. **2** (*this is a glad day*) pleasing, gratifying, cheering, cheerful,

encouraging, welcome, pleasant, joyful, joyous, delightful, gladsome, merry, cheery, gay. OPPOSITE: gloomy. **3** (*glad to come aboard*) happy, pleased, delighted, eager, ready, keen, prepared, willing, inclined, disposed. OPPOSITE: reluctant.

gladden *verb* please, gratify, delight, elate, enliven, exhilarate, cheer, buoy up, encourage, hearten, brighten, make happy, animate, rejoice, buck up (*inf*). OPPOSITE: grieve.

gladly *adv* happily, cheerfully, gaily, freely, willingly, eagerly, readily, ungrudgingly, joyfully, joyously, gleefully, merrily, with good grace, with pleasure, fain. OPPOSITE: unwillingly.

glamorous *adj* **1** (*glamorous film star*) beautiful, fascinating, elegant, alluring, beguiling, lovely, gorgeous, sexy, smart, flashy (*inf*), attractive, captivating, bewitching, enchanting, entrancing, appealing, charming, irresistible, glossy, glitzy (*inf*), ritzy (*inf*), well-dressed, well-groomed. **2** (*a glamorous future*) exciting, thrilling, dazzling, glittering, glossy, glitzy (*inf*), ritzy (*inf*), high-profile, prestigious, stimulating, colourful. OPPOSITE: dull.

glamour *noun* **1** (*she oozed glamour*) beauty, elegance, loveliness, attractiveness, fascination, enchantment, allure, appeal, magnetism, charm, sex appeal, pizzazz (*inf*), excitement, glitter, glitz (*inf*), sparkle. **2** (*the glamour of working in television*) allure, attraction, charm, excitement, fascination, enchantment, captivation, thrill, magic, spell, prestige.

glance *verb* **1** (*glanced at him*) glimpse, peek, peep, look, check out (*inf*), sneak a look at (*inf*), view, clock (*inf*), take a dekko at (*inf*). OPPOSITE: stare. **2** (*glance at the headlines*) scan, skim, leaf, flip, flick, thumb, dip, cast an eye over, browse, riffle through, run through.
≫ *noun* glimpse, peek, peep, look, view, butchers (*inf*), dekko (*inf*), gander (*inf*), squint (*inf*), once-over (*inf*), shufti (*inf*).

glance off bounce off, rebound, fly off, ricochet, spring back.

glare *verb* **1** (*she glared at the intruder*) glower, scowl, frown, lower, glower, look daggers (*inf*), stare. OPPOSITE: smile. **2** (*searchlights glaring*) dazzle, blind, blaze, flame, flare, beam, shine.
≫ *noun* **1** (*shrank beneath his glare*) scowl, frown, glower, lower, stare, black look (*inf*), dirty look (*inf*). **2** (*the glare of the stage lights*) dazzle, blaze, brilliance, brightness, radiance, glow, flare, beam, flame. OPPOSITE: dullness.

glaring *adj* **1** (*glaring headlights*) dazzling, blazing, shining, bright, brilliant, blinding. **2** (*glaring errors*) conspicuous, prominent, obvious, manifest, patent, overt, blatant, flagrant, open, outrageous, audacious, gross, rank, lurid, undisguised, visible, egregious. OPPOSITE: concealed.

glass *noun* tumbler, wineglass, beaker, goblet, flute, schooner, balloon, chalice.

glasses *pl noun* spectacles, specs (*inf*), eyeglasses, bifocals, sunglasses.

glassy *adj* **1** (*the glassy surface of the water*) glasslike, shiny, smooth, polished, glossy, slick, mirrorlike, clear, crystal clear, crystalline, transparent, limpid, pellucid. **2** (*negotiating the glassy pavements*) icy, shiny, slippery, slick, treacherous. **3** (*strange, glassy expression*) blank, expressionless, vacant, empty, fixed, dazed, deadpan, glazed, vacuous, lifeless, dull, cold, motionless, unmoving.

glaze *verb* **1** (*to glaze pottery*) lacquer, varnish, gloss, enamel, coat, polish, burnish, furbish. **2** (*the cake is then glazed*) coat, cover, ice, frost. **3** (*glaze over*) become glazed, become glassy, become dull, mist over, cloud over, fade.
≫ *noun* **1** (*china with a brown glaze*) enamel, lacquer, varnish, coat, gloss, finish, lustre, shine, sheen, polish, patina. **2** (*pie glaze*) coating, icing, frosting.

gleam *noun* **1** (*cast a gleam of light*) glint, beam, flash, glow, shaft, ray, flare, flicker, shimmer. **2** (*the gleam of the moon*) glow, shine, lustre, gloss, sheen, brightness, brilliance, flash, coruscation. **3** (*a gleam of hope*) glimmer, flicker, ray, trace, suggestion, hint, inkling, grain, spark.
≫ *verb* glint, glisten, shine, radiate, coruscate, flare, flash, glow, glitter, beam, shimmer, glimmer, glance, sparkle, twinkle, scintillate.

glean *verb* gather, collect, find out, learn, pick up, select, cull, accumulate, harvest, reap, garner, amass. OPPOSITE: scatter.

glee *noun* delight, cheerfulness, pleasure, fun, joy, joyfulness, merriment, mirth, gladness, happiness, high spirits, liveliness, exhilaration, exuberance, elation, exultation, hilarity, jollity, joviality, joyousness, gaiety, sprightliness, verve, blitheness, cheer, gratification, jocularity, mirthfulness, triumph. OPPOSITE: sorrow.

gleeful *adj* delighted, pleased, cheerful, happy, chirpy (*inf*), over the moon (*inf*), beside oneself, merry, jolly, joyful, joyous, high-spirited, overjoyed, jubilant, jovial, cock-a-hoop (*inf*), gay, elated, exuberant, exhilarated, exultant, lively, blithe, mirthful, triumphant, gratified, rapt. OPPOSITE: sad.

glib *adj* smooth, slick, fluent, easy, facile, artful, quick, ready, talkative, plausible, insincere, slippery, suave, gabby (*inf*), garrulous, loquacious, voluble, gassy (*inf*), fast-talking, smooth-tongued, smooth-talking, sweet-talking, smooth-spoken, silver-tongued, unctuous. OPPOSITE: hesitant.

glide *verb* slide, slip, sail, skate, skim, fly, float, flow, drift, coast, roll, run, pass, soar.

glimmer *noun* **1** (*the first glimmer of dawn*) gleam, glint, flash, flicker, shimmer, shine, blink, twinkle, glitter, sparkle, glow, ray. **2** (*a faint glimmer of hope*) flicker, gleam, ray, hint, suggestion, inkling, trace, grain.
≫ *verb* gleam, glint, glisten, flash, flicker, shimmer, glitter, twinkle, sparkle, blink, wink, shine, glow.

glimpse *noun* glance, peep, peek, look, sight, sighting, squint, view, butchers (*inf*), gander (*inf*), shufti (*inf*). OPPOSITE: scrutiny.
≫ *verb* spot, catch sight of, sight, view, spy, clock (*inf*), espy, descry. OPPOSITE: scrutinize.

glint *verb* gleam, glimmer, flash, shine, glisten, glitter, sparkle, reflect, shimmer, twinkle, blink, dazzle, scintillate.
≫ *noun* gleam, glimmer, flash, shine, glistening, glitter, sparkle, reflection, shimmer, twinkle, twinkling, blink.

glisten *verb* shine, gleam, glint, glitter, flash, sparkle,

glance, twinkle, flicker, glimmer, shimmer, blink, wink, scintillate, coruscate.

glitter *verb* sparkle, twinkle, shimmer, spangle, gleam, glint, glimmer, glisten, flash, flicker, dazzle, blink, wink, scintillate, coruscate.
≫ *noun* **1** (*the glitter of sequins*) flash, beam, sparkle, gleam, glint, twinkle, shine, shimmer, glimmer, blink, flicker, winking, scintillation, coruscation. **2** (*the moon's glitter*) brilliance, brightness, sheen, lustre, shine, glare, radiance. OPPOSITE: dullness. **3** (*the glitter of Hollywood*) glamour, splendour, pageantry, tinsel, flashiness, gaudiness, glitz (*inf*), pizzazz (*inf*), razzmatazz (*inf*), razzle-dazzle (*inf*), ostentation, show, showiness.

gloat *verb* revel, exult, triumph, glory, crow, rejoice, delight, relish, boast, drool, rub it in (*inf*), vaunt.

global *adj* **1** (*dreams of global domination*) worldwide, world, international, universal, planetary. **2** (*with global application*) general, wide-ranging, extensive, comprehensive, all-inclusive, all-encompassing, exhaustive, unbounded, unlimited, thorough, encyclopedic, total, all-out, across-the-board. OPPOSITE: restricted.

globe *noun* **1** (*all round the globe*) world, earth, planet. **2** (*a series of globes*) sphere, orb, ball, round.

globule *noun* globulet, bead, ball, drop, droplet, bubble, pearl, pellet, particle, spherule, vesicle.

gloom *noun* **1** (*in the gathering gloom*) dark, darkness, blackness, shade, shadow, shadiness, obscurity, dimness, dullness, gloominess, murk, murkiness, cloud, cloudiness, dusk, duskiness, twilight. OPPOSITE: brightness. **2** (*sunk in gloom*) melancholy, depression, dejection, desolation, despondency, despair, sadness, sorrow, unhappiness, glumness, grief, misery, woe, hopelessness, downheartedness, low spirits, pessimism, blues (*inf*). OPPOSITE: cheerfulness.

gloomy *adj* **1** (*gloomy weather*) dull, cloudy, dark, overcast, murky, dismal, sunless, dreary, dim, shadowy. OPPOSITE: bright. **2** (*a gloomy cavern*) dark, shadowy, sombre, dismal, dreary, murky, dingy, unlit, black, obscure, crepuscular, tenebrous, stygian. OPPOSITE: light. **3** (*a gloomy prospect*) depressing, melancholy, cheerless, comfortless, joyless, hopeless, saddening, disheartening, discouraging, dispiriting, disappointing, distressing, sombre, dismal, pessimistic, sad, bad, black, funereal. OPPOSITE: encouraging. **4** (*the whole team looked gloomy*) depressed, despondent, disconsolate, desolate, dejected, blue (*inf*), low, crestfallen, melancholy, glum, down, down in the dumps (*inf*), down in the mouth (*inf*), saturnine, taciturn, downcast, dispirited, despairing, downhearted, sad, unhappy, in low spirits, miserable, moody, morose, sullen, sorrowful, pessimistic, woebegone, cheerless, chapfallen. OPPOSITE: cheerful.

glorify *verb* **1** (*glorify the Lord*) praise, exalt, honour, venerate, adore, revere, worship, extol, thank, bless, sanctify, magnify, laud, reverence, elevate, lift up, raise, ennoble, dignify, acclaim, applaud, celebrate. OPPOSITE: defame. **2** (*this film glorifies war*) celebrate, praise, romanticize, idealize, aggrandize, cry up, eulogize, idolize, magnify, hail, lionize, elevate, enshrine, immortalize, panegyrize.

glorious *adj* **1** (*boasted a glorious reputation*) illustrious, renowned, celebrated, great, famous, famed, noted, eminent, distinguished, honoured, noble, exalted, grand, supreme, excellent, splendid, magnificent, majestic, sublime, triumphant, victorious. OPPOSITE: humble. **2** (*a glorious summer's day*) beautiful, gorgeous, splendid, magnificent, superb, perfect, fine, sunny, radiant, brilliant, resplendent, bright, dazzling, glittering. OPPOSITE: dull. **3** (*a glorious prospect*) delightful, great (*inf*), wonderful, marvellous, splendid, resplendent, splendiferous (*inf*), superb, terrific (*inf*), enjoyable, pleasurable, agreeable, beautiful, dazzling, divine, heavenly, pleasant, pleasurable. OPPOSITE: awful.

glory *noun* **1** (*the glory of the regiment*) fame, honour, renown, illustriousness, greatness, prestige, reputation, credit, distinction, eminence, celebrity, recognition, acclaim, accolade, kudos (*inf*). OPPOSITE: shame. **2** (*the rose in all its glory*) magnificence, splendour, resplendence, grandeur, impressiveness, majesty, dignity, nobility, pomp, stateliness, pageantry, parade, triumph, success, radiance, brightness, brilliance, effulgence, lustre, beauty, sublimity. OPPOSITE: humility. **3** (*the glory of God*) praise, worship, adoration, exaltation, veneration, respect, homage, benediction, extolment, laudation, tribute, thanksgiving, blessing.
➤ *verb* triumph, exult, rejoice, revel, delight, relish, bask, boast, crow, drool, gloat, preen oneself.

gloss[1] *noun* **1** (*the gloss on his boots*) lustre, sheen, polish, burnish, shine, brightness, brilliance, gleam, glaze, varnish, shimmer, sparkle. OPPOSITE: dullness. **2** (*they put a good gloss on it*) appearance, facade, front, veneer, veil, show, disguise, camouflage, window-dressing, mask, semblance, surface.
➤ *verb* **1** (*busy glossing the tables*) polish, burnish, shine, buff up (*inf*). **2** (*learning to gloss china*) varnish, glaze, lacquer, japan.

gloss over disguise, mask, hide, conceal, camouflage, cover up, whitewash (*inf*), veil, smooth over, explain away, evade, avoid, ignore, dismiss. OPPOSITE: expose.

gloss[2] *noun* (*read the glosses carefully*) footnote, note, annotation, explanation, elucidation, explication, comment, commentary, definition, interpretation, translation, scholium.
➤ *verb* annotate, comment, define, explain, elucidate, expand, interpret, translate, construe.

glossy *adj* **1** (*a glossy finish*) shiny, shining, lustrous, bright, brilliant, glassy, sheeny, gleaming, polished, burnished, enamelled, glazed, shimmering, sparkling. OPPOSITE: matt. **2** (*the dog's glossy coat*) smooth, sleek, silky, silken, gleaming, shining.

glow *noun* **1** (*the glow of the streetlights*) light, luminosity, incandescence, phosphorescence, shine, lustre, brightness, brilliance, radiance, effulgence, lambency, blaze, gleam, glimmer. OPPOSITE: darkness. **2** (*the glow of his palette*) richness, vividness, brightness, brilliance, colourfulness, splendour. **3** (*felt a warm glow for him*) warmth, passion, ardour, fervour, eagerness, earnestness, enthusiasm, intensity, vehemence, impetuosity, excitement, thrill, contentment, happiness, satisfaction. OPPOSITE: apathy. **4** (*a pink glow suffused his cheeks*) blush, flush, bloom, burning, redness, pinkness, reddening, rosiness.
➤ *verb* **1** (*the fire glowed*) shine, radiate, gleam, glimmer,

burn, smoulder. **2** (*her cheeks glowed*) redden, blush, colour, flush, crimson, go scarlet, bloom.

glower *verb* glare, scowl, frown, lower, look daggers (*inf*), stare. OPPOSITE: smile.
➤ *noun* glare, scowl, frown, lower, stare, look, black look (*inf*), dirty look (*inf*).

glowing *adj* **1** (*a glowing fire*) aglow, smouldering, incandescent, luminous, phosphorescent, candescent, lambent. **2** (*glowing colours*) bright, vivid, brilliant, vibrant, rich, radiant, warm. **3** (*her glowing skin*) flushed, pink, red, ruddy, rosy, florid, flaming, suffused. **4** (*a glowing description*) complimentary, enthusiastic, favourable, flattering, rave (*inf*), ecstatic, rhapsodic, laudatory, eulogistic, adulatory, acclamatory, panegyrical.

glue *noun* adhesive, gum, paste, cement, fixative, mortar, size, mucilage.
➤ *verb* stick, paste, affix, cement, gum, fix, seal, adhere, bond.

glum *adj* gloomy, despondent, dejected, depressed, doleful, down (*inf*), downcast, downhearted, down in the dumps (*inf*), low (*inf*), crestfallen, dispirited, pessimistic, melancholy, morose, sullen, sulky, miserable, unhappy, forlorn, sad, unsmiling, moody, grumpy, surly, ill-humoured, crusty, gruff, huffy, sour, churlish, crabbed, saturnine, chapfallen. OPPOSITE: cheerful.

glut *noun* surfeit, excess, surplus, superfluity, overabundance, superabundance, plethora, overflow, oversupply, repletion, saturation. OPPOSITE: dearth.
➤ *verb* **1** (*glutted themselves at tea*) cram, gorge, stuff, fill, sate, satiate, surfeit. **2** (*glutted with refuse*) choke, clog, obstruct, stop up, dam up, cloy, flood, inundate, deluge, saturate, overload, oversupply.

glutinous *adj* sticky, gummy, gluey, treacly, pasty, tacky, adhesive, cohesive, mucilaginous, mucous, viscous, viscid.

glutton *noun* gourmand, gormandizer, gobbler, gannet (*inf*), gorger (*inf*), guzzler (*inf*), greedy guts (*inf*), pig (*inf*).

gluttonous *adj* greedy, voracious, insatiable, ravenous, piggish (*inf*), gluttonish, omnivorous, rapacious, gormandizing.

gluttony *noun* greed, greediness, voraciousness, voracity, insatiability, rapacity, piggishness (*inf*), gourmandism. OPPOSITE: temperance.

gnarled *adj* knotted, knotty, weather-beaten, wrinkled, rough, leathery, twisted, crooked, contorted, distorted, bent, lumpy, nodular, knurled, rugged.

gnash *verb* grind, rasp, grate, grit, scrape.

gnaw *verb* **1** (*the rat gnawed at the wood*) bite, nibble, chew, munch, crunch, masticate. **2** (*seas gnawing at the cliffs*) erode, corrode, wear, eat, consume, devour. **3** (*the question gnawed at him*) fret, worry, trouble, bother, nag, niggle, plague, prey, distress, torment, harass, haunt, harry.

go *verb* **1** (*let's get going*) move, proceed, advance, pass, progress, travel, journey, walk, make for, head, start, begin. OPPOSITE: stop. **2** (*don't go*) go away, set off, set out, leave, depart, decamp, quit (*inf*), withdraw, make tracks (*inf*), beat it (*inf*), scat (*inf*), scoot (*inf*), scram (*inf*), go away, retreat. **3** (*I wish this cold would go*) go away, vanish, disappear, melt away, cease, stop. **4** (*this car won't go*) work, operate, perform, function, run. OPPOSITE: fail. **5** (*tell us how things go*) turn out, develop, work out, end up, pan out (*inf*), progress, proceed, fare, result, happen, eventuate. **6** (*go mad*) become, grow, get, turn. **7** (*that piece should go here*) fit, belong, slot in, lie, stand. **8** (*that's as far as it will go*) extend, stretch, reach, run, spread, span, unfold, continue, lead to. **9** (*it should go bang*) emit, sound, resound, give off, send out, release. **10** (*how is the time going?*) elapse, slip away, pass, tick away, fly, go by, lapse, proceed, roll on, expire. **11** (*those clothes do not go*) match, blend, coordinate, belong, complement, suit, harmonize, chime, correspond, fit, accord. OPPOSITE: clash. **12** (*the two policies do not go*) fit, comply, conform, match, correspond. **13** (*feared she would go during the night*) die, pass away, expire, breathe one's last, decease, perish, kick the bucket (*inf*), give up the ghost (*inf*), buy it (*inf*), croak (*inf*), peg out (*inf*), check out (*inf*). **14** (*jobs will have to go*) be dismissed, be made redundant, be sacked (*inf*), be fired (*inf*), be axed (*inf*). **15** (*it only goes to show*) serve, contribute, help, tend, incline. **16** (*the building might go at any time*) collapse, break down, give way, fall down, cave in, crumble, disintegrate, fall to pieces.

➤ *noun* **1** (*had a go at everything*) try, attempt, essay, bid, stab (*inf*), shot (*inf*), crack (*inf*), whack (*inf*), whirl (*inf*), turn, endeavour, effort. **2** (*she has a lot of go*) drive, get-up-and-go (*inf*), energy, life, push (*inf*), vigour, verve, dynamism, spirit, determination, enterprise, force, oomph (*inf*), pep (*inf*), vim, vitality, vivacity, pizzazz (*inf*), animation, brio. OPPOSITE: lethargy.

go about 1 (*how to go about it*) set about, begin, approach, address, tackle, do, attend to, undertake, perform, engage in. **2** (*the story began to go about*) circulate, spread, go around, pass around.

go ahead go, proceed, advance, progress, move, continue, carry on, begin.

go along with 1 (*you can go along with me*) accompany, go with, join, escort, travel with. **2** (*let's go along with it*) comply with, acquiesce with, cooperate with, accept, agree with, obey, follow, support, abide by, assent to, concur with.

go around circulate, spread, go about, pass around.

go back on renege on, default on, deny, repudiate, forsake, retract, break one's promise, change one's mind.

go by 1 (*time goes by*) pass, elapse, lapse, move on, proceed, flow. **2** (*always go by the rules*) follow, observe, comply with, heed, obey, honour, respect.

go down 1 (*go down to the ground floor*) descend, sink, drop, fall, set. **2** (*shares will go down*) decrease, reduce, decline, plummet, deteriorate, degenerate. **3** (*may go down against such opposition*) submit, fail, founder, go under, collapse, fold (*inf*), lose, fail, come a cropper (*inf*). **4** (*the first ship to go down*) sink, founder, go under, submerge.

go for 1 (*worried she might go for him*) attack, assail, assault, rush at, set about, spring upon, lunge at. **2** (*I really go for blondes*) like, love, admire, enjoy, prefer, favour, choose, select, hold with, aim for.

go in for enter, take part in, go into, participate in, engage in, take up, embrace, adopt, undertake, practise, pursue, follow, espouse.

go into discuss, consider, probe, inquire into, look into, examine, investigate, research, study, analyse, scrutinize, delve into, dig into, work over, check out, review, dissect.

go off 1 (*go off into the woods*) leave, depart, go away, set out, move out, disappear, vanish, decamp, slope off, quit (*inf*), hook it (*inf*), abscond. **2** (*the bomb will go off in ten seconds*) explode, blow up, detonate, blast, burst, erupt, go bang (*inf*), ignite, fire. **3** (*all the food has gone off*) rot, go bad, turn, deteriorate, turn sour, go stale.

go on 1 (*how long will it go on?*) continue, carry on, proceed, persist, last, endure, abide, remain, stay. **2** (*the show goes on next week*) take place, happen, occur. **3** (*she goes on about it*) ramble, chatter, carry on, waffle (*inf*), prattle (*inf*), witter (*inf*), rabbit (*inf*), gab (*inf*), blether (*inf*), gas (*inf*).

go out 1 (*go out of the room*) exit, depart, leave, withdraw. **2** (*the fire has gone out*) extinguish, die out, expire, fade. **3** (*they are going out*) date (*inf*), go with, go together, go steady (*inf*), court, see one another, keep company.

go over examine, peruse, study, look over, inspect, scan, read, give the once-over (*inf*), discuss, think about, check, revise, review, list, repeat, rehearse.

go through 1 (*go through a terrible experience*) undergo, endure, suffer, experience, brave, bear, tolerate, stand, withstand, weather, brook. **2** (*go through them in detail*) investigate, examine, look through, check, explore, search, hunt, frisk (*inf*). **3** (*soon go through the supplies*) use up, consume, get through, exhaust, spend, squander.

go together 1 (*those clothes do not go together*) go, match, agree, harmonize, fit, suit, blend, coordinate, complement, accord. **2** (*they are still going together*) go out, date (*inf*), see one another, go steady (*inf*), court, keep company.

go under 1 (*the company has gone under*) collapse, close, close down, fold (*inf*), go out of business, flop (*inf*), go bust (*inf*), go to the wall (*inf*), founder, go bankrupt, go into receivership, fail, die, default. **2** (*fear the ship has gone under*) sink, founder, go down, submerge, drown, succumb.

go with 1 (*I shall go with you*) accompany, escort, take, usher. **2** (*it goes well with that dress*) match, harmonize, coordinate, blend, complement, suit, fit, agree, concur, correspond. **3** (*they are going with each other*) go out with, go together, see, date (*inf*), go steady (*inf*), court, keep company.

go without 1 (*go without cigarettes*) do without, abstain from, deny oneself, forgo, manage without, lack, want. **2** (*he will have to go without*) go short, go wanting.

goad *verb* spur, prick, prod, provoke, incite, induce, instigate, prompt, arouse, stimulate, inspire, motivate, impel, urge, push, drive, propel, egg on, exhort, jolt, hound, plague, annoy, irritate, hassle (*inf*), needle, sting, harass, nag, taunt, vex, worry, pressurize. OPPOSITE: deter.

➤ *noun* spur, incentive, prick, jolt, poke, stimulus, instigation, motivation, stimulation, impetus, inducement, urge, incitement, provocation, irritation, pressure. OPPOSITE: deterrent.

go-ahead *noun* permission, consent, authorization,

clearance, leave, sanction, approval, OK (*inf*), thumbs-up (*inf*), green light (*inf*), assent, agreement, confirmation, warranty. OPPOSITE: ban.

≫ *adj* ambitious, aspiring, enterprising, pioneering, progressive, dynamic, energetic, aggressive, vigorous, forward, forward-looking, opportunist, up-and-coming, pushy (*inf*), go-getting (*inf*).

goal *noun* aim, objective, mark, target, object, purpose, end, design, ambition, aspiration, destination, intent, intention.

gobble *verb* bolt, gulp, guzzle, wolf (*inf*), scoff (*inf*), pig out on (*inf*), swallow, devour, put away (*inf*), consume, gorge, cram, stuff.

gobbledygook *noun* gibberish (*inf*), babble, gabble, jargon, nonsense, rubbish, drivel, twaddle, balderdash, cant, double-talk, hocus-pocus, jabber, mumbo-jumbo, prattle, journalese, officialese, computerese, psychobabble, buzz words, circumlocution, verbiage.

go-between *noun* intermediary, mediator, middleman, third party, negotiator, arbiter, arbitrator, liaison, medium, messenger, contact, agent, broker, dealer, factor.

goblin *noun* imp, brownie, gnome, hobgoblin, dwarf, elf, gremlin, sprite, spirit, bogey, kelpie, kobold, fiend, demon.

god *noun* deity, divinity, goddess, spirit, genius, idol, image, icon. OPPOSITE: devil.

God *noun* Lord, Almighty, our Father, Supreme Being, Holy One, Deity, Divine Being, Creator, Maker, Godhead, Saviour, Jehovah, Yahweh, Allah, Brahma, Zeus. OPPOSITE: Satan.

godforsaken *adj* desolate, dismal, dreary, gloomy, remote, isolated, bleak, lonely, abandoned, forlorn, neglected, backward, deserted, miserable, wretched, depressing.

godless *adj* **1** (*a godless society*) pagan, heathen, atheistic, agnostic, faithless, sceptical, unbelieving. **2** (*godless behaviour*) ungodly, impious, profane, irreligious, unrighteous, unprincipled, depraved, sacrilegious, irreverent, sinful, bad, wicked, evil. OPPOSITE: godly.

godlike *adj* godly, divine, holy, heavenly, celestial, deific, exalted, saintly, sacred, sublime, superhuman, transcendent, perfect.

godly *adj* pious, devout, religious, holy, saintly, God-fearing, believing, pietistic, righteous, virtuous, pure, innocent, good, moral. OPPOSITE: godless.

godsend *noun* blessing, benediction, boon, bonanza, miracle, windfall, stroke of luck, benison.

goggle *verb* stare, ogle, gape, gaze, gawp (*inf*), gawk (*inf*), peer, rubberneck (*inf*), wonder.

goings-on *pl noun* happenings, events, activities, occurrences, affairs, scenes, business, funny business (*inf*), misbehaviour, mischief, misconduct, pranks, hanky-panky (*inf*), monkey business (*inf*).

gold *noun* **1** (*melt down the gold*) bullion, nugget, bar, ingot. **2** (*dreams of gold*) money, wealth, treasure, riches, fortune.

golden *adj* **1** (*golden skin*) gold, gold-coloured, gilded, gilt, yellow, flaxen, blond, blonde, fair, bright, gleaming, shining, resplendent, lustrous, dazzling, tow-coloured. **2** (*a golden chance*) precious, priceless, valuable, gilt-edged, unique, rare. **3** (*a golden era*) happy, joyful, blissful, glorious, prosperous, successful, flourishing, thriving, bright, brilliant, rich, great, classic, halcyon, palmy, treasured. **4** (*golden prospect*) favourable, propitious, excellent, auspicious, fortunate, timely, fine, superb, opportune, promising, rosy, advantageous, profitable, providential. OPPOSITE: unfavourable.

good *adj* **1** (*he was a good man*) virtuous, righteous, moral, upright, honest, honourable, admirable, trustworthy, worthy, praiseworthy, exemplary, high-minded, right-minded, ethical, noble, estimable. OPPOSITE: wicked. **2** (*have a good time*) nice, pleasant, pleasurable, enjoyable, agreeable, cheerful, convivial, congenial, sociable, amusing, pleasing, satisfying, gratifying, fine, excellent, cool (*inf*), great (*inf*), bad (*inf*), super (*inf*), crucial (*inf*), wicked (*inf*), marvellous, fantastic, terrific, first-rate, first-class, splendid, wonderful, capital, superb, tiptop (*inf*), exceptional, satisfactory, reasonable, desirable, acceptable, tolerable, passable, adequate. OPPOSITE: bad. **3** (*a good move*) beneficial, advantageous, profitable, worthwhile, useful, helpful, wholesome, healthy, salutary, salubrious, favourable, fortunate, lucky, propitious, opportune, auspicious, convenient. **4** (*good at that kind of thing*) proficient, competent, clever, brilliant, capable, able, skilful, skilled, efficient, dependable, reliable, adept, adroit, expert, accomplished, professional, dexterous, gifted, talented, first-class, first-rate, tip-top (*inf*), top-notch (*inf*). OPPOSITE: incompetent. **5** (*she was always good to me*) kind, kindly, kindhearted, considerate, friendly, benevolent, obliging, gracious, good-hearted, good-natured, sympathetic, humane, merciful, generous, well-disposed, benign, charitable, altruistic, philanthropic. OPPOSITE: unkind. **6** (*a good little boy*) well-behaved, well-mannered, polite, respectful, dutiful, obedient, mannerly, orderly, proper, seemly, decorous, tractable, malleable, compliant. OPPOSITE: naughty. **7** (*a good match*) suitable, appropriate, apt, fitting, proper, correct, right, sensible, sound, seemly. OPPOSITE: unsuitable. **8** (*our contacts are all good*) reliable, dependable, trustworthy, sound, secure. OPPOSITE: unreliable. **9** (*his claim was declared good*) authentic, bona fide, legitimate, real, valid, genuine, sound, true, proper, reliable, dependable, honest, trustworthy. **10** (*didn't feel too good*) well, fine, fit, healthy, robust, sound, strong, vigorous, hale and hearty. **11** (*exercise is good for you*) beneficial, healthy, health-giving, wholesome, healthful, salutary, nutritional. **12** (*a good amount*) sizeable, considerable, goodly, substantial, large, ample, tidy (*inf*), adequate, sufficient. OPPOSITE: small. **13** (*gone a good fifteen minutes*) whole, entire, full, complete, solid. **14** (*give the room a good dusting*) thorough, complete, exhaustive. **15** (*just good friends*) dear, close, intimate, bosom, loving, best, fast, valued, treasured. **16** (*expecting good weather*) fine, clear, calm, sunny, warm, mild, fair, bright, cloudless, sunshiny, balmy, clement, tranquil, halcyon.

≫ *interj* fine, all right, OK (*inf*), very well, right, perfect, agreed, indeed, just so, okeydoke (*inf*), okeydokey (*inf*).

≫ *noun* **1** (*for the good of everyone*) advantage, benefit, profit, gain, welfare, well-being, interest, behalf, sake, convenience, use, service, purpose, worth, merit, avail. OPPOSITE: harm. **2** (*a force for good*) virtue, right, righteousness, goodness, rectitude, ethics, morality, morals, integrity, uprightness, honesty, worth, honour, merit, excellence, probity. OPPOSITE: evil.

for good always, for ever, ever, evermore, for all time, for ever and a day, permanently, in perpetuity, finally, irrevocably, once and for all, eternally, till the end of time, till kingdom come (*inf*), till the cows come home (*inf*).

make good 1 (*make good the loss*) make up for, compensate for, put right, make amends for, make recompense for, make restitution for, pay for, reimburse for. **2** (*she finally made good*) succeed, go far, progress, get on, get on in the world, get to the top, get ahead, make it, set the world on fire (*inf*). **3** (*he made good his promise*) fulfil, realize, carry out, do, live up to, put into action, discharge, effect.

goodbye *interj* farewell, adieu, so long (*inf*), bye (*inf*), bye-bye (*inf*), cheerio (*inf*), cheers (*inf*), all the best (*inf*), ta-ta (*inf*), see you (*inf*), see you later (*inf*), see you around (*inf*), be seeing you (*inf*), take care (*inf*), mind how you go (*inf*), have a nice day (*inf*), toodle-oo (*inf*), au revoir, ciao (*inf*). OPPOSITE: hello.
» *noun* farewell, adieu, au revoir, leave-taking, parting, swan song, valediction.

good-for-nothing *adj* useless, worthless, lazy, idle, indolent, irresponsible, reprobate, no-good, profligate, slothful, feckless.
» *noun* ne'er-do-well, idler, layabout, lazybones (*inf*), loafer, waster, profligate, reprobate, bum (*inf*), wastrel, sluggard, skiver (*inf*), rapscallion, black sheep (*inf*).

good-humoured *adj* affable, amiable, friendly, cheerful, cheery, happy, jovial, genial, easygoing, congenial, pleasant, good-tempered, approachable. OPPOSITE: ill-humoured.

good-looking *adj* attractive, fair, comely, pretty, lovely, beautiful, handsome, personable, presentable, well-favoured. OPPOSITE: ugly.

goodly *adj* sizeable, considerable, substantial, large, ample, good, significant, sufficient, tidy (*inf*). OPPOSITE: small.

good natured *adj* kind, kindly, kindhearted, sympathetic, benevolent, generous, helpful, neighbourly, gentle, good-tempered, good-hearted, warmhearted, approachable, amiable, agreeable, friendly, well-disposed, charitable, tolerant, patient, accommodating. OPPOSITE: ill-natured.

goodness *noun* **1** (*famed for his goodness*) virtue, virtuousness, righteousness, good, rectitude, uprightness, honesty, integrity, probity, morality, honour, merit, nobility, altruism, helpfulness, worthiness. OPPOSITE: evil. **2** (*had the goodness to pay up*) kindness, benevolence, kindliness, kindheartedness, warmheartedness, compassion, thoughtfulness, generosity, graciousness, friendliness, unselfishness, humanity, mercy, charitableness, obligingness, beneficence, goodwill. OPPOSITE: unkindness. **3** (*enjoy the sheer goodness of life*) excellence, superiority, worth, quality, value, merit, advantage. OPPOSITE: inferiority.

4 (*bread full of goodness*) nourishment, nutrition, wholesomeness, benefit.

goods *pl noun* **1** (*goods and chattels*) belongings, possessions, effects, chattels, property, movables, trappings, furnishings, appurtenances, accoutrements, paraphernalia, things, gear (*inf*), stuff (*inf*). **2** (*goods in the warehouse*) merchandise, wares, stock, freight, lines, products, commodities, things.

goodwill *noun* benevolence, kindness, kindliness, compassion, goodness, generosity, graciousness, favour, friendliness, friendship, willingness, acquiescence, heartiness, zeal, amity. OPPOSITE: enmity.

gore *verb* pierce, stab, spear, stick, penetrate, impale, transfix, wound.
» *noun* blood, bloodshed, carnage, slaughter, butchery.

gorge *noun* ravine, canyon, crevice, cleft, fissure, defile, pass, rift, chasm, gap, gully, gulch, abyss.
» *verb* stuff, cram, fill, gormandize, feed, devour, bolt, wolf (*inf*), guzzle, gobble, gulp, swallow, glut, overeat, pig out (*inf*), sate, surfeit, overeat. OPPOSITE: fast.

gorgeous *adj* **1** (*a gorgeous woman*) beautiful, lovely, sexy (*inf*), stunning (*inf*), ravishing (*inf*), attractive, pretty, fine, sweet, glamorous, good-looking, handsome, pulchritudinous. OPPOSITE: plain. **2** (*a gorgeous scene*) magnificent, splendid, superb, fine, impressive, splendid, resplendent, sumptuous, rich, luxurious, exquisite, opulent, stately, imposing, beautiful, elegant, grand, glittering, glamorous, brilliant, dazzling, breathtaking, glorious, showy. **3** (*a gorgeous holiday*) good, marvellous, lovely, wonderful, terrific (*inf*), glorious, excellent, great, delightful, entertaining, pleasing, enjoyable. OPPOSITE: poor.

gory *adj* **1** (*a gory film*) bloodthirsty, grisly, bloody, sanguinary, brutal, horrific, savage, fierce, violent, murderous. **2** (*found a gory shirt*) bloodstained, blood-soaked, bloody, bloodied.

gospel *noun* **1** (*teachings of the gospel*) message of Christ, teaching of Christ, life of Christ, good news, New Testament. **2** (*take it as gospel*) truth, fact, certainty, verity. OPPOSITE: falsehood. **3** (*the gospel of scientific inquiry*) doctrine, creed, credo, belief, ethic, teaching, message, news, revelation, tidings, principle, tenet.

gossamer *adj* delicate, fine, flimsy, diaphanous, silky, gauzy, insubstantial, sheer, shimmering, airy, light, thin, cobwebby, transparent, see-through, translucent, frail, chiffony, feathery. OPPOSITE: heavy.

gossip *noun* **1** (*love a good gossip*) chat, talk, natter, chitchat (*inf*), chinwag (*inf*), small talk, idle talk, jaw (*inf*), prattle, tattle, tittle-tattle, yack (*inf*), scandal, mudslinging (*inf*), rumour, hearsay, dirt (*inf*), conversation, report, whisper. **2** (*she's a terrible gossip*) scandalmonger, gossipmonger, chatterbox, chatterer, telltale, prattler, tattler, busybody, babbler, nosy parker (*inf*), blabbermouth (*inf*), whisperer, quidnunc.
» *verb* chat, chatter, talk, natter, gabble, chinwag (*inf*), gab (*inf*), gas (*inf*), jabber (*inf*), jaw (*inf*), prate, prattle, rabbit (*inf*), tattle, waffle (*inf*), yack (*inf*), babble, blab, blether, blather, chew the fat (*inf*), tell tales, rumour, whisper.

gouge *verb* scratch, claw, scoop, dig, chisel, hack, cut, score, gash, slash, incise, groove, scoop, hollow, extract.

gourmet *noun* gastronome, connoisseur, foodie (*inf*), bon vivant, epicurean, epicure.

govern *verb* **1** (*govern the country*) rule, reign, hold office, direct, manage, administer, control, guide, lead, conduct, supervise, superintend, oversee, head, preside over, command, order, regulate, handle, steer, pilot, influence, sway. **2** (*govern his temper*) restrain, contain, constrain, arrest, check, curb, control, regulate, hold back, keep back, bridle, discipline, dominate, master, quell, rein in, subdue, tame.

government *noun* **1** (*the government of international affairs*) rule, sovereignty, dominion, direction, management, administration, control, guidance, conduct, regulation, supervision, superintendence, surveillance, command, charge, sway, leadership, authority, domination, power, law. **2** (*by order of the government*) state, parliament, executive, leadership, administration, cabinet, ministry, council, congress, authorities, Establishment, regime, powers that be (*inf*). **3** (*the government of his feelings*) control, restraint, constraint, discipline, checking, curbing, bridling.

governor *noun* ruler, president, director, manager, administrator, executive, head, chief, leader, master, commander, controller, comptroller, regulator, supervisor, overseer, superintendent, boss (*inf*), guide, president, viceroy, commissioner, warden.

gown *noun* dress, robe, frock, garment, garb (*inf*), habit, costume, dressing gown, evening gown, ball-gown, nightgown.

grab *verb* **1** (*she grabbed his arm*) grasp, grip, clutch, clasp, seize, snatch, pluck, take, take hold of, lay hold of, fasten upon, latch on to, catch. **2** (*they grabbed the gold*) seize, capture, snatch, steal, snap up, nab (*inf*), bag (*inf*), collar (*inf*), swipe (*inf*), nail (*inf*), commandeer, usurp, appropriate, annex.
⋙ *noun* clutch, grip, grasp, snatch, catch, capture.
up for grabs available, on offer, for sale, obtainable, at hand, for the asking (*inf*), to be had, accessible.

grace *noun* **1** (*admired for her grace*) gracefulness, elegance, ease, fluency, poise, ease, beauty, loveliness, attractiveness, charm, refinement, tastefulness, good taste, finesse, polish, smoothness, suaveness, cultivation, comeliness. OPPOSITE: clumsiness. **2** (*the grace of her movements*) gracefulness, elegance, fluidity, agility, suppleness, smoothness, ease. **3** (*the grace to admit guilt*) decency, courtesy, courteousness, manners, consideration, tact, tactfulness, etiquette, decorum, propriety, breeding. **4** (*fall from grace*) favour, prestige, goodwill, preferment. **5** (*a month's grace*) postponement, delay, deferment, deferral. **6** (*by the grace of God*) favour, goodwill, kindness, kindliness, benevolence, beneficence, goodness, generosity, compassion, indulgence, clemency, charity, leniency, lenity, mercy, pardon, forgiveness, consideration, virtue. OPPOSITE: unkindness. **7** (*the saying of grace*) blessing, benediction, thanks, thanksgiving, prayer.
⋙ *verb* **1** (*candles graced the cake*) adorn, beautify, prettify, embellish, decorate, ornament, set off, bedeck, deck, trim, garnish, enhance, enrich. OPPOSITE: mar. **2** (*graced us with his presence*) honour, favour, distinguish, dignify, elevate, glorify.

graceful *adj* **1** (*a graceful performer*) elegant, easy, smooth, flowing, fluid, supple, nimble, agile, deft, lithe, natural. OPPOSITE: clumsy. **2** (*a graceful woman*) elegant, refined, cultured, cultivated, tasteful, polished, suave, becoming, charming, appealing, pleasing, attractive, lovely, beautiful, comely, fine, slender.

graceless *adj* **1** (*graceless movements*) ungraceful, clumsy, awkward, unattractive, ungainly, forced, inelegant, gauche, gawky, untutored. OPPOSITE: graceful. **2** (*graceless behaviour*) uncouth, coarse, crude, boorish, ill-mannered, impolite, improper, unmannerly, unsophisticated, barbarous, indecorous, rough, rude, vulgar, shameless, unabashed.

gracious *adj* **1** (*a gracious act*) kind, kindly, kindhearted, warmhearted, benevolent, benign, beneficent, friendly, affable, pleasant, obliging, cordial, courteous, courtly, civil, polite, well-mannered, amiable, compassionate, considerate, sweet, gentle, mild, merciful, indulgent, accommodating, condescending, patronizing, charitable, generous, magnanimous, hospitable, chivalrous. OPPOSITE: churlish. **2** (*gracious surroundings*) elegant, tasteful, comfortable, refined, luxurious, sumptuous.

grade *noun* **1** (*reached the highest grade*) degree, level, stage, position, place, rank, standing, status, rung, order, station, echelon, quality, standard, condition, rating, mark, score, measure, size. **2** (*each sorted into a different grade*) category, class, classification, brand, group, type. **3** (*went up by grades*) stage, step, rung, notch. **4** (*clambered up a steep grade*) gradient, bank, hill, incline, rise, slope, acclivity, declivity.
⋙ *verb* arrange, sort, group, class, classify, categorize, pigeonhole, order, evaluate, assess, value, label, brand, mark, rate, range, rank, size, type, graduate.
make the grade come through, come up to scratch (*inf*), measure up, pass, pass muster, prove acceptable, qualify, succeed, get through, win through.

gradient *noun* slope, incline, bank, rise, grade, hill, ramp, acclivity, declivity.

gradual *adj* **1** (*making gradual progress*) slow, leisurely, unhurried, regular, step-by-step, steady, even, continuous, measured, progressive, successive, systematic, piecemeal. OPPOSITE: sudden. **2** (*a gradual rise*) gentle, moderate, easy. OPPOSITE: steep.

gradually *adv* little by little, bit by bit, step by step, by degrees, imperceptibly, unhurriedly, inch by inch, drop by drop, successively, continuously, constantly, progressively, piece by piece, piecemeal, slowly, gently, cautiously, gingerly, moderately, regularly, steadily, evenly.

graduate *verb* **1** (*graduate after three years*) qualify, pass. **2** (*graduate by degrees*) grade, mark off, divide, calibrate, regulate, measure out, proportion. **3** (*graduated into various groups*) arrange, sort, group, classify, categorize, grade, rank, order, range. **4** (*she graduated to senior nurse*) progress, move up, advance, move forward, make headway, go ahead, forge ahead.
⋙ *noun* bachelor, doctor, master, fellow, member, expert, specialist, consultant, professional, graduand, alumnus, valedictorian.

graft[1] *verb* join, unite, splice, engraft, implant, insert, attach, affix, transplant. OPPOSITE: separate.
➤ *noun* **1** (*a plant graft*) shoot, bud, sprout, growth, slip, splice, scion. **2** (*a skin graft*) implant, implantation, transplant.

graft[2] *noun* **1** (*succeeded through sheer graft*) effort, hard work, toil, industry, labour, work, sweat of one's brow (*inf*), slog (*inf*), dedication. **2** (*not above a bit of graft*) bribery, corruption, extortion, dishonesty, dirty tricks (*inf*), wheeling and dealing (*inf*), sharp practices (*inf*), shady business (*inf*), con tricks (*inf*), dirty dealings (*inf*), rip-off (*inf*), scam (*inf*), sting (*inf*), palm-greasing (*inf*).

grain *noun* **1** (*stores of grain*) cereal, corn, wheat, barley, oats, rye, maize, crops. **2** (*using only the grain*) seed, kernel, grist. **3** (*not a grain of truth*) particle, speck, granule, crumb, morsel, piece, bit, fragment, iota, mite, mote, atom, molecule, jot, ounce, scrap, trace, hint, suggestion, soupçon, suspicion, scintilla, modicum, whit. **4** (*the grain of the wood*) texture, pattern, marking, weave, nap, fibre, fabric, surface.

grand *adj* **1** (*a grand house*) impressive, great, large, imposing, majestic, august, lofty, exalted, illustrious, distinguished, lordly, noble, regal, princely, dignified, stately, glorious, opulent, splendid, magnificent, fine, striking, superb, sublime, sumptuous, lavish, luxurious, monumental, palatial. OPPOSITE: humble. **2** (*a grand gesture*) pompous, pretentious, ostentatious, showy, grandiose, imperious, lordly, haughty. **3** (*we had a grand holiday*) excellent, wonderful, marvellous, splendid, very good, first-class, first-rate, fantastic, great (*inf*), super (*inf*), superb, smashing (*inf*), cool (*inf*), mega (*inf*), wicked (*inf*), terrific (*inf*), outstanding, enjoyable, delightful, fine. OPPOSITE: poor. **4** (*he's the grand champion*) chief, principal, main, head, leading, supreme, arch, great, highest, senior, pre-eminent. OPPOSITE: minor. **5** (*the grand total*) total, final, complete, inclusive, all-inclusive, comprehensive, exhaustive, in full.

grandeur *noun* **1** (*the grandeur of the scene*) splendour, splendidness, magnificence, luxuriousness, luxury, sumptuousness, lavishness, opulence, augustness, glory, pomp, stateliness, majesty, dignity, greatness, impressiveness, importance, loftiness, sublimity. OPPOSITE: humility. **2** (*the grandeur of royalty*) greatness, eminence, nobility, illustriousness, prominence, fame, renown.

grandfather *noun* **1** (*visit my grandfather*) granddad (*inf*), granddaddy (*inf*), grandpa (*inf*), grandpapa (*inf*), gramps (*inf*), grandpop (*inf*). **2** (*honour our grandfathers*) forefather, forebear, ancestor, progenitor.

grandiloquent *adj* bombastic, pompous, pretentious, exaggerated, inflated, flowery, high-flown, high-sounding, rhetorical, wordy, orotund, swollen, turgid, periphrastic, euphuistic, fustian, magniloquent. OPPOSITE: simple.

grandiose *adj* **1** (*a grandiose project*) pretentious, extravagant, ostentatious, showy, flamboyant, pompous, affected, bombastic, high-flown, high-sounding, overambitious, over-the-top (*inf*), OTT (*inf*). OPPOSITE: plain. **2** (*such grandiose surroundings*) grand, impressive, imposing, magnificent, monumental,

splendid, striking, lofty, majestic, stately, ambitious. OPPOSITE: humble.

grandmother *noun* grandma (*inf*), granny (*inf*), gran (*inf*), nan (*inf*), nana (*inf*), nanna (*inf*), grandmama (*inf*).

grant *verb* **1** (*granted by parliament*) give, donate, bestow, award, present, confer, accord, impart, transmit, dispense, allot, allocate, assign, contribute, furnish, provide, supply, apportion. OPPOSITE: withhold. **2** (*I grant you that much*) admit, concede, acknowledge, cede, allow, permit, yield, accept, consent to, agree to, accede to, vouchsafe.
➤ *noun* award, gift, present, benefaction, annuity, bequest, bursary, scholarship, pension, honorarium, stipend, endowment, concession, allowance, allotment, donation, handout, contribution, subsidy, boon.

granule *noun* grain, particle, crumb, speck, fragment, piece, scrap, bead, iota, jot, atom, molecule, mite.

graph *noun* diagram, grid, chart, table, histogram, bar graph, bar chart, pie chart, scatter diagram.

graphic *adj* **1** (*a graphic account*) vivid, expressive, striking, telling, effective, descriptive, illustrative, well-drawn, picturesque, forcible, detailed, blow-by-blow, realistic, clear, lucid, cogent, explicit, lively. OPPOSITE: unclear. **2** (*in graphic form*) visual, pictorial, drawn, representational, diagrammatic, illustrative, delineative.

grapple *verb* **1** (*grappled with the rope*) grip, clasp, grasp, clench, seize, grab, clutch, snatch, hold, lay hold of, fasten on. OPPOSITE: release. **2** (*grappled with the problem all night*) contend, confront, face, address, tackle, attack, deal with, cope with, get to grips with, encounter, struggle, wrestle, tussle, battle, fight, combat, clash, engage, close.

grasp *verb* **1** (*he grasped the handlebars*) grip, clasp, hold, clutch, grapple, grab, seize, catch, snatch, clench, lay hold of, clinch. OPPOSITE: release. **2** (*could not grasp what she meant*) understand, comprehend, take in, realize, see, perceive, follow, apprehend, get (*inf*), get the picture (*inf*), get the drift (*inf*), catch on, latch on to, master.
➤ *noun* **1** (*escaped the witch's grasp*) grip, clasp, hold, clutches, embrace, possession. **2** (*beyond the grasp of the law*) reach, compass, scope, range, limits, extent, capacity, power, command, control, rule, dominion, sway, sweep, mastery. **3** (*a grasp of musical theory*) understanding, comprehension, apprehension, grip, realization, awareness, perception, ken, knowledge, familiarity, mastery.

grasping *adj* greedy, avaricious, covetous, acquisitive, rapacious, miserly, niggardly, parsimonious, mercenary, mean, selfish, tight-fisted, close-fisted, stingy, tight-arsed (*sl*), tight-assed (*sl*), penny-pinching, hoarding, grabby (*inf*), grabbing, usurious, venal. OPPOSITE: generous.

grate *verb* **1** (*grate the vegetables*) shred, grind, mince, pulverize, granulate, comminute, triturate. **2** (*the grate of metal on stone*) creak, rasp, rub, scrape, scratch. **3** (*that really grates with me*) annoy, irritate, exasperate, vex, irk, nark (*inf*), nettle, jar, aggravate, peeve (*inf*), get under one's skin (*inf*), get on one's nerves (*inf*), get one's goat (*inf*), get one down, set one's teeth on edge, rub one up the wrong way, rankle, gall, anger, chafe, fret, rile. OPPOSITE: soothe.

grateful *adj* **1** (*they were most grateful*) thankful, appreciative, obliged, obligated, beholden, indebted. OPPOSITE: ungrateful. **2** (*provided a grateful break*) pleasant, pleasing, agreeable, cheering, gratifying, satisfying, acceptable, welcome, refreshing, restful, pleasurable, nice, relaxing.

gratification *noun* satisfaction, fulfilment, indulgence, contentment, kick (*inf*), pleasure, enjoyment, relish, fun, glee, joy, delight, elation, thrill, reward. OPPOSITE: frustration.

gratify *verb* **1** (*gratified by your welcome*) please, delight, gladden, charm, cheer, thrill, satisfy. OPPOSITE: displease. **2** (*gratified his whim*) satisfy, fulfil, indulge, humour, favour, feed, requite, pamper, comply with, cater to, pander to, pacify, appease, give in to, placate, spoil, cosset.

grating *adj* **1** (*a grating sound*) harsh, strident, raucous, rasping, hoarse, scraping, scratching, grinding, creaking, jarring, squeaky, screeching, piercing, shrill, squawking, squeaky, croaky, discordant. **2** (*a grating manner*) irritating, annoying, vexatious, irksome, exasperating, galling, jarring, unpleasant, offensive, disagreeable.

gratis *adv* free, for free, free of charge, for nothing, at no cost, without charge, without payment, unpaid, complimentary, gratuitously, on the house (*inf*).

gratitude *noun* gratefulness, thankfulness, appreciation, obligation, indebtedness, thanks, acknowledgment, recognition. OPPOSITE: ingratitude.

gratuitous *adj* **1** (*on a gratuitous basis*) free, free of charge, gratis, for nothing, voluntary, spontaneous, complimentary, unpaid, unrewarded. **2** (*gratuitous violence*) groundless, baseless, unfounded, unwarranted, unjustified, uncalled-for, unasked-for, unnecessary, undeserved, unmerited, unprovoked, unsolicited, causeless, without cause, needless, superfluous, wanton, without reason, irrelevant.

gratuity *noun* tip, gift, present, reward, recompense, bonus, perk (*inf*), fringe benefit, perquisite, donation, benefaction, largess, bounty, boon, baksheesh.

grave[1] *adj* **1** (*a grave countenance*) serious, solemn, sombre, sober, severe, dignified, earnest, unsmiling, dour, gloomy, grim, grim-faced, long-faced, stone-faced, staid, sedate, subdued, restrained, thoughtful, preoccupied, pensive, muted, quiet, reserved, heavy, leaden. OPPOSITE: frivolous. **2** (*grave news*) significant, momentous, important, weighty, vital, crucial, critical, dangerous, hazardous, menacing, perilous, threatening, life-and-death, serious, urgent, pressing, acute, severe, pivotal, exigent. OPPOSITE: trivial.

grave[2] *noun* tomb, sepulchre, crypt, vault, mausoleum, burial place, burial site, resting-place, pit, barrow, cairn, tumulus.

graveyard *noun* cemetery, churchyard, burial ground, burial place, burial site, boneyard (*inf*), necropolis, charnel house, God's acre.

gravitate *verb* **1** (*gravitated towards each other*) incline, lean, tend, drift, move, be drawn. **2** (*gravitate towards the bottom*) descend, sink, drop, fall, precipitate, settle. OPPOSITE: rise.

gravity *noun* **1** (*with an air of gravity*) seriousness, solemnity, dignity, gravitas, sobriety, sombreness, dourness, thoughtfulness, pensiveness, sedateness, staidness, earnestness, grimness, gloominess, severity, reserve, restraint. OPPOSITE: frivolity. **2** (*the gravity of the news*) importance, weight, weightiness, moment, momentousness, seriousness, severity, enormity, significance, consequence, urgency, acuteness, danger, hazard, perilousness, exigency. OPPOSITE: triviality.

graze[1] *verb* (*animals grazing*) feed, browse, crop, pasture, ruminate.

graze[2] *verb* **1** (*the two vessels grazed one another*) brush, shave, touch, skim, clip, glance off, kiss. **2** (*grazed her elbow*) scrape, scratch, rub, skin, chafe, bark, bruise, abrade, contuse.
➤ *noun* scratch, scrape, abrasion, bruise, contusion.

greasy *adj* **1** (*a greasy surface*) oily, fatty, sebaceous, slimy, slippery, slippy, smeary, smooth, waxy, oleaginous, buttery, lardy, adipose. **2** (*a greasy salesman*) unctuous, oily, slimy, slippery, smooth, smooth-tongued, slick, glib, suave, smarmy (*inf*), fawning, ingratiating, grovelling, flattering, gushing, sycophantic, toadying.

great *adj* **1** (*the great plains*) big, large, huge, vast, immense, massive, enormous, bulky, colossal, tremendous, stupendous, gigantic, elephantine, mammoth, monstrous, humongous (*inf*), jumbo (*inf*), mega (*inf*), whopping (*inf*), ginormous (*inf*), impressive, extensive, boundless, unlimited, spacious, voluminous. OPPOSITE: small. **2** (*great attention to safety*) considerable, substantial, decided, pronounced, prodigious, sizeable, high, strong, exceptional, extravagant, extreme, excessive, inordinate. OPPOSITE: slight. **3** (*a great hero*) eminent, illustrious, distinguished, renowned, noted, famed, famous, celebrated, prominent, preeminent, noteworthy, notable, noted, outstanding, remarkable, noble, august. **4** (*a great house*) impressive, imposing, grand, august, majestic, noble, exalted, superior, sublime, magnificent, splendid, glorious, sumptuous, fine, heroic, lofty. OPPOSITE: lowly. **5** (*great changes*) important, significant, consequential, weighty, momentous, critical, crucial, essential, vital, paramount, major, serious, grave, salient, main, chief, principal, primary, leading. OPPOSITE: minor. **6** (*a great concert*) excellent, wonderful, marvellous, fine, good, first-rate, admirable, enjoyable, splendid, superb, tremendous, fabulous, fab (*inf*), brill (*inf*), cracking (*inf*), super (*inf*), smashing (*inf*), terrific (*inf*), fantastic (*inf*), cool (*inf*), crucial (*inf*), mega (*inf*), mean (*inf*), wicked (*inf*), ace (*inf*). OPPOSITE: awful. **7** (*a great waste*) absolute, utter, perfect, complete, total, thoroughgoing, out-and-out, positive, arrant, flagrant, downright, consummate, thundering (*inf*), unmitigated, unqualified, egregious. **8** (*a great performer*) expert, skilled, skilful, accomplished, masterly, excellent, brilliant, gifted, talented, able, adept, adroit, dexterous, proficient, virtuoso, experienced, practised, knowledgeable, professional, specialist, qualified, ace (*inf*), top-notch (*inf*), crack (*inf*). **9** (*a great walker*) keen, enthusiastic, eager, dedicated, devoted, zealous, active.

greatly *adv* much, very much, considerably, enormously, extremely, highly, immensely, vastly, noticeably, significantly, impressively, remarkably, notably, substantially, markedly, exceedingly, abundantly, tremendously, hugely, mightily, powerfully.

greatness *noun* **1** (*the greatness of his territories*) vastness, immensity, largeness, enormity, magnitude, bulk, mass, size, bigness, boundlessness, extensiveness, spaciousness, prodigiousness, length. OPPOSITE: smallness. **2** (*the greatness of the dynasty*) eminence, renown, fame, note, lustre, distinction, grandeur, majesty, pomp, splendour, nobility, dignity, magnificence, glory, gloriousness, sumptuousness, illustriousness, heroism. OPPOSITE: lowliness. **3** (*the greatness of this day*) importance, significance, gravity, seriousness, weight, momentousness, magnitude, power, intensity. OPPOSITE: triviality. **4** (*the greatness of his play*) talent, genius, expertise, skill, skilfulness, adeptness, excellence, proficiency.

greed *noun* **1** (*eyed the food with greed*) greediness, gluttony, gormandizing, voracity, voraciousness, hunger, ravenousness, insatiability, omnivorousness, piggishness (*inf*), hoggishness (*inf*), esurience, edacity. **2** (*a greed for glory*) desire, craving, longing, covetousness, avarice, selfishness, rapacity, acquisitiveness, cupidity, avidity, miserliness, parsimony, eagerness, enthusiasm, impatience. OPPOSITE: unselfishness.

greedy *adj* **1** (*a greedy boy*) hungry, gluttonous, voracious, insatiable, starving, ravenous, ravening, piggish (*inf*), hoggish (*inf*), omnivorous, esurient, edacious. **2** (*greedy politicians*) desirous, acquisitive, covetous, craving, avaricious, selfish, rapacious, grasping, grabbing, hoarding, miserly, niggardly, parsimonious, money-grubbing (*inf*), on the make (*inf*). OPPOSITE: unselfish. **3** (*greedy to hear the latest*) avid, eager, impatient.

green *adj* **1** (*green fields*) grassy, leafy, verdant, verdurous, grass-covered. **2** (*green shoots*) fresh, new, recent, raw, unripe, immature, unseasoned, young, healthy, vigorous, lush, budding, blooming, flourishing. OPPOSITE: decaying. **3** (*a green beginner*) inexperienced, callow, raw, unsophisticated, naive, ingenuous, gullible, credulous, simple, ignorant, inexpert, unqualified, unskilled, untrained, unversed, unpolished, wet behind the ears (*inf*), new, recent. OPPOSITE: experienced. **4** (*turned green with envy*) envious, jealous, covetous, grudging, resentful. **5** (*green issues*) ecological, environmental, environmentally friendly, environmentally aware, environmentally sound, eco-friendly, conservationist, non-polluting. **6** (*she went quite green*) wan, pale, pallid, ashen, sick, poorly, ill, nauseous, unhealthy. **7** (*green wood*) immature, pliable, supple, tender, undried, unseasoned, unfinished, young. ➤ *noun* lawn, grass, grassland, common, turf, field, meadow, sward, greensward, village green, lea, verdure.

greenhouse *noun* glasshouse, hothouse, conservatory.

greet *verb* **1** (*the two friends greeted one another*) hail, salute, address, acknowledge, accost, say hello to, kiss, wave to, nod to. OPPOSITE: ignore. **2** (*he greeted them at the entrance*) welcome, receive, meet.

greeting *noun* salutation, acknowledgment, address, hail, hello, salute, welcome, reception, nod, handshake, the time of day, seasonal greeting. OPPOSITE: farewell.

greetings *pl noun* respects, compliments, regards, best wishes, good wishes, congratulations, love, salutations.

gregarious *adj* sociable, social, outgoing, friendly, affable, companionable, genial, cordial, convivial, hospitable, extrovert, warm. OPPOSITE: reclusive.

grey *adj* **1** (*a grey dawn*) dull, drab, dismal, dreary, bleak, cheerless, gloomy, sombre, dim, dark, cloudy, misty, foggy, murky, sunless, overcast. OPPOSITE: bright. **2** (*a grey town*) gloomy, dismal, dreary, bleak, depressing, dull, cheerless, anonymous, uninteresting, characterless, colourless. **3** (*a grey countenance*) pale, pallid, colourless, neutral, ashen, wan, leaden, bloodless, anaemic, livid. **4** (*that's a grey area*) doubtful, arguable, debatable, uncertain, unclear, ambiguous, indistinct, mixed. **5** (*the grey vote*) old, aged, elderly, grey-haired, hoary, venerable, ancient. OPPOSITE: young.

grief *noun* sorrow, sadness, misery, unhappiness, woe, heartache, heartbreak, lamentation, mourning, mournfulness, bereavement, depression, dejection, desolation, despondency, despair, distress, anguish, affliction, agony, pain, suffering, trouble, hardship, trial, tribulation, regret, remorse. OPPOSITE: joy.

grievance *noun* **1** (*voiced their grievances*) complaint, grudge, moan, gripe (*inf*), grouse (*inf*), beef (*inf*), objection, protest, resentment, indignation, unhappiness. **2** (*suffered various grievances*) injury, damage, wrong, injustice, unfairness, offence, affliction, grief, trouble, hardship, trial, tribulation, affront, insult.

grieve *verb* **1** (*he grieved over her loss*) sorrow, lament, mourn, cry, sob, weep, wail, bewail, bemoan, deplore, rue, mope, brood, pine away, eat one's heart out, suffer, ache. OPPOSITE: rejoice. **2** (*this news grieves me*) sadden, afflict, dismay, distress, horrify, offend, shock, crush, upset, hurt, wound, pain, agonize. OPPOSITE: please.

grievous *adj* **1** (*a grievous wound*) serious, severe, grave, acute, sharp, injurious, wounding, hurtful, harmful, painful, agonizing, afflicting, sore, intense, damaging, appalling, dreadful, heavy. OPPOSITE: mild. **2** (*a grievous crime*) heinous, outrageous, monstrous, flagrant, glaring, grave, gross, dire, atrocious, appalling, iniquitous, shameful, shocking, dreadful, deplorable, lamentable, nefarious, egregious. OPPOSITE: commendable. **3** (*grievous news*) tragic, distressing, lamentable, sad, sorrowful, mournful, calamitous, disastrous, crushing, devastating, burdensome, unbearable, overwhelming.

grim *adj* **1** (*her grim father*) stern, severe, harsh, dour, formidable, forbidding, hard, cruel, ruthless, fierce, ferocious, threatening, menacing, merciless, gloomy, morose, sullen, sour, surly, sombre, ill-tempered, implacable, cross, churlish, crabbed, unattractive. OPPOSITE: benign. **2** (*grim news*) dire, dreadful, frightful, frightening, fearsome, terrible, horrible, horrid, hideous, horrendous, ghastly, grisly, gruesome, macabre, sinister, awful, unpleasant, appalling, harrowing, shocking, unspeakable. **3** (*grim determination*) resolute, firm, determined, decided, dogged, strong-willed, relentless, unrelenting, obstinate, persistent, adamant, stubborn, tenacious, inexorable, unflinching, unyielding, unwavering, unfaltering, unshakeable, inflexible, obdurate.

grimace *noun* frown, scowl, pout, sneer, smirk, face.

➤ *verb* frown, scowl, pout, lower, sneer, smirk, mouth, make a face, pull a face.

grime *noun* dirt, filth, muck, gunge (*inf*), crud (*inf*), yuck (*inf*), grot (*inf*), smut, soot, dust, mud.
➤ *verb* begrime, dirty, soil, befoul, sully, defile. OPPOSITE: cleanse.

grimy *adj* dirty, filthy, mucky (*inf*), gungy (*inf*), grubby, yucky (*inf*), cruddy (*inf*), soiled, stained, begrimed, besmirched, besmeared, dirt-encrusted, smutty, dusty, muddy, muddied, smudgy, sooty, foul, unclean. OPPOSITE: clean.

grin *verb* smile, beam, smirk, leer.

grind *verb* **1** (*to grind pepper*) pulverize, triturate, comminute, granulate, powder, crush, pound, mill, grate, crumble, mash, smash, kibble. **2** (*grind the knives*) sharpen, whet, sand, file, smooth, polish, rub, abrade. **3** (*gears grinding against each other*) rub, grate, rasp, grit, scrape, gnash, abrade.
➤ *noun* routine, toil, slog, labour, drudgery, chore, task, travail, exertion, hard work, slavery, sweat (*inf*).

grind down oppress, tyrannize, persecute, plague, afflict, crush, torment, harass, harry, hound, ill-treat, maltreat, scourge, trouble, torture, wear down, hold down.

grip *noun* **1** (*struggled to keep her grip*) hold, clasp, grasp, clutch, purchase, clench. **2** (*the stranger had a firm grip*) clasp, handclasp, handshake. **3** (*strengthened his grip on the army*) control, mastery, command, power, domination, dominion, clutches, hold, influence, rule, possession. **4** (*a firm grip of the subject*) grasp, understanding, comprehension, perception, awareness, apprehension. **5** (*picked up his grip*) bag, case, holdall, kitbag, shoulder bag, suitcase, valise, flight bag, overnight bag, travelling bag.
➤ *verb* **1** (*grip the ladder*) hold, clutch, clasp, grasp, grab, clench, latch on to, cling, seize, catch. OPPOSITE: release. **2** (*gripped by the show*) fascinate, engross, absorb, enthral, thrill, spellbind, mesmerize, hypnotize, entrance, rivet, hold, involve, engage, compel.

get to grips with deal with, tackle, handle, cope with, confront, face, face up to, meet head on, take on, grasp, grapple with, close with, undertake, take care of, look after.

gripe *verb* complain, moan, grumble, protest, groan, bleat, whinge (*inf*), whine (*inf*), bitch (*inf*), grouch (*inf*), grouse (*inf*), nag, carp (*inf*), beef (*inf*), bellyache (*inf*).
➤ *noun* complaint, grievance, groan, moan, grumble, whingeing (*inf*), bitch (*inf*), beef (*inf*), grouch (*inf*), grouse (*inf*), objection, protest.

gripping *adj* fascinating, exciting, thrilling, compelling, enthralling, entrancing, riveting, engrossing, absorbing, compulsive, spellbinding, suspenseful, unputdownable (*inf*).

grisly *adj* grim, gruesome, gory, macabre, spine-chilling, hideous, horrible, horrid, horrifying, dreadful, frightful, fearful, awful, ghastly, appalling, shocking, terrible, sickening, repugnant, repulsive, repellent, revolting, loathsome, abhorrent, odious, abominable, disgusting. OPPOSITE: pleasant.

grit *noun* **1** (*a lorryload of grit*) gravel, sand, pebbles, shingle, dust, dirt. **2** (*showed real grit*) courage, bravery,

balls (*sl*), nerve, pluck, mettle, valour, spirit, backbone (*inf*), bottle (*inf*), guts (*inf*), determination, fortitude, endurance, doggedness, perseverance, steadfastness, tenacity, resolution, resolve, toughness, hardiness, stamina, strength, gameness. OPPOSITE: weakness.
➤ *verb* clench, gnash, grate, grind, rasp, scrape.

gritty *adj* **1** (*a gritty mixture*) grainy, gravelly, pebbly, granular, bitty, powdery, sandy, shingly, dusty, rough, abrasive. OPPOSITE: smooth. **2** (*gritty determination*) determined, brave, courageous, ballsy (*sl*), feisty, plucky, resolute, hardy, tough, mettlesome, dogged, tenacious, enduring, steadfast, spirited, game, gutsy (*inf*), spunky (*inf*). OPPOSITE: cowardly.

grizzled *adj* grizzly, grey, greying, grey-haired, grey-headed, hoary, canescent.

groan *noun* **1** (*deep groans of pain*) moan, sigh, cry, murmur, whine, whimper, wail, lament. **2** (*a groan of protest*) complaint, grumble, moan, bitch (*inf*), whinge (*inf*), whine (*inf*), grievance, beef (*inf*), grouse (*inf*), grouch (*inf*), griping, objection, protest, outcry.
➤ *verb* **1** (*groan in distress*) moan, sigh, cry, murmur, whine, whimper, wail, lament. **2** (*groan in protest*) complain, grumble, bemoan, moan, bitch (*inf*), whinge (*inf*), whine (*inf*), grieve over, beef (*inf*), bellyache (*inf*), grouse (*inf*), grouch (*inf*), gripe, object, protest.

groggy *adj* dazed, stunned, confused, befuddled, bewildered, stupefied, weak, dopey, unsteady, wobbly, shaky, staggering, woozy (*inf*), punch-drunk, muzzy (*inf*), woolly-headed, dizzy, faint, reeling.

groom *verb* **1** (*groom oneself*) tidy, neaten, spruce up, smarten up, freshen up, turn out, smooth, preen, primp, clean, dress, brush, comb, adjust, arrange, do, fix, put in order. **2** (*groom the horses*) rub down, rub, brush, clean, curry, tend. **3** (*groomed for stardom*) prepare, prime, make ready, nurture, ready, train, coach, drill, school, teach, educate, instruct, tutor, drill, coach.
➤ *noun* **1** (*accompanied by the groom*) bridegroom, husband-to-be, husband, spouse, newlywed. **2** (*the grooms were already at work*) stableboy, stable lad, stableman, stable hand, stable worker, ostler.

groove *noun* **1** (*the grooves in the road*) furrow, channel, rut, track, canal, chamfer, gutter, trench, trough, hollow, gouge, indentation, cut, cutting, score, flute, rebate, slot. OPPOSITE: ridge. **2** (*stuck in the same old groove*) rut, routine, grind (*inf*), treadmill, habit.

grope *verb* **1** (*groping in the dark*) fumble, feel, scrabble, flounder, pick. **2** (*grope for his keys*) fumble, search, hunt, fish, finger, look, grabble, scrabble, probe, cast about.

gross *adj* **1** (*his gross frame*) big, large, great, fat, obese, bloated, corpulent, overweight, bulky, huge, colossal, immense, massive, heavy, hulking, lumpish, cumbersome, unwieldy. OPPOSITE: slight. **2** (*gross sense of humour*) coarse, vulgar, tasteless, crude, rude, improper, indecent, obscene, bawdy, lewd, blue (*inf*), smutty, pornographic, ribald, dirty, earthy, filthy, indelicate, offensive, risqué, impure. **3** (*I found him gross*) unsophisticated, unrefined, uncultured, uncultivated, loutish, oafish, yobbish (*inf*), vulgar, insensitive, tasteless, coarse, crass, boorish, ignorant, insensitive, dull, stupid. OPPOSITE: refined. **4** (*gross insult*) flagrant, glaring, blatant, obvious, arrant, shameful, shocking, outrageous, plain, apparent, manifest, sheer, utter, outright, rank, unmitigated, downright, egregious, serious, grievous. **5** (*gross takings*) before tax, before deductions, entire, comprehensive, inclusive, all-inclusive, total, complete, whole, aggregate. OPPOSITE: net.

≫ *verb* earn, make, take, bring in, fetch, rake in (*inf*), accumulate, total, aggregate.

grotesque *adj* bizarre, strange, weird, odd, peculiar, fantastic, whimsical, extravagant, fanciful, absurd, ludicrous, ridiculous, preposterous, freakish, monstrous, outlandish, incongruous, surreal, macabre, unnatural, deformed, malformed, misshapen, misproportioned, distorted, twisted, hideous, ugly, repugnant, unsightly. OPPOSITE: normal.

ground *noun* **1** (*sandy ground*) earth, soil, loam, dirt, dust, clod, sod, turf, clay, land, terrain. **2** (*landed safely on the ground*) earth, terra firma, floor, deck (*inf*), surface. **3** (*crowds at the ground*) stadium, arena, field, pitch, park (*inf*).

≫ *verb* **1** (*ground the flagpole*) base, found, establish, fix, set, settle. **2** (*well grounded in management skills*) instruct, inform, teach, educate, train, coach, drill, tutor, prepare, familiarize with, acquaint with, introduce, initiate.

groundless *adj* baseless, unfounded, unsubstantiated, unsupported, idle, empty, imaginary, illusory, false, unjustified, unjustifiable, unreasonable, without reason, unwarranted, unprovoked, uncalled-for, unauthorized, gratuitous, chimerical. OPPOSITE: justified.

grounds *pl noun* **1** (*the grounds of the hall*) estate, land, property, domain, territory, park, gardens, fields, acres, campus, surroundings, district, holding, plot, tract. **2** (*the allegations lack grounds*) basis, base, foundation, reason, motive, cause, inducement, occasion, call, excuse, justification, vindication, premise, pretext, rationale, argument. **3** (*grounds in the bottom of the cup*) dregs, sediment, residue, lees, deposit, settlings, scourings, precipitate.

groundwork *noun* foundation, basis, base, footing, cornerstone, underpinnings, bottom, basics, elements, essentials, fundamentals, preliminaries, preparation, research, homework, spadework, background.

group *noun* **1** (*split into groups*) grouping, category, bunch, batch, lot, set, class, classification, genus, species, family, school. **2** (*group of men*) party, company, body, band, gang, pack, flock, crowd, team, crew, congregation, gathering, troop, squad, detachment, contingent, unit, collection, clump, cluster, conglomeration, knot, bevy, posse, combination, assembly, assemblage. OPPOSITE: individual. **3** (*membership of the group*) club, society, association, guild, league, organization, party, company, set, camp, circle, clique, faction, coterie.

≫ *verb* **1** (*grouped up at the school*) collect, assemble, gather, cluster, clump, congregate, mass, bunch, huddle. OPPOSITE: separate. **2** (*group them in batches*) sort, classify, class, categorize, organize, arrange, range, dispose, marshal, line up, order, rank, grade, band, bracket, associate, link. OPPOSITE: disarrange.

grouse *verb* complain, grumble, moan, bemoan, bitch (*inf*), beef (*inf*), bellyache (*inf*), carp (*inf*), gripe (*inf*), grouch (*inf*), whinge (*inf*), whine (*inf*), bleat, find fault.

≫ *noun* complaint, grumble, moan, bitch (*inf*), beef (*inf*), bellyache (*inf*), gripe (*inf*), grouch (*inf*), whinge (*inf*), whine (*inf*), grievance, groan, objection, protest.

grove *noun* wood, copse, thicket, spinney, coppice, brake, covert, arbour, avenue, plantation, woodland.

grovel *verb* **1** (*grovel to the management*) crawl, creep, toady, fawn, cower, cringe, kowtow, bow and scrape, brown-nose (*sl*), butter up (*inf*), suck up (*inf*), kiss up (*inf*), kiss ass (*inf*), lick the boots of (*inf*), bootlick (*inf*), curry favour, flatter, pander, defer, abase oneself, humble oneself, ingratiate oneself, demean oneself. **2** (*grovel on the floor*) crawl, creep, cower, crouch, bow down, kneel, stoop, slither, prostrate oneself, lie down, fall on one's knees.

grovelling *adj* servile, obsequious, fawning, sycophantic, slavish, cringing, ingratiating, toadying, bootlicking, crawling, base, mean, low, abject.

grow *verb* **1** (*grow in stature*) lengthen, elongate, heighten, widen, broaden, thicken, deepen, increase, expand, enlarge, wax, swell, fill out, spread, extend, stretch, develop, multiply, escalate, mushroom, proliferate. OPPOSITE: shrink. **2** (*grew from this idea*) originate, arise, issue, stem, spring up. **3** (*flowers grow*) germinate, sprout, shoot, bud, blossom, flower, vegetate, mature, flourish, thrive, burgeon. OPPOSITE: decline. **4** (*the campaign should grow*) develop, thrive, flourish, prosper, succeed, burgeon, advance, progress, make headway, improve, expand. **5** (*grow dark*) become, turn, go, get, change, develop, wax. **6** (*grow vegetables*) cultivate, produce, raise, sow, plant, harvest, nurture, breed, propagate, farm.

growl *verb* snarl, rumble, roar, howl, snap, yap, yelp, bark.

grown-up *adj* adult, mature, full-grown, fully-grown, of age, fully-developed, fully-fledged. OPPOSITE: immature.

≫ *noun* adult, man, woman. OPPOSITE: child.

growth *noun* **1** (*growth of the empire*) increase, expansion, enlargement, extension, magnification, amplification, augmentation, deepening, development, spread, multiplication, proliferation, advance, advancement, evolution, headway, aggrandizement. OPPOSITE: decline. **2** (*growth in profits*) expansion, improvement, rise, advance, advancement, progress, prosperity, success. **3** (*the growth of plants*) germination, sprouting, springing, budding, shooting, flowering, vegetation, crop, produce, cultivation, burgeoning, development, maturation, pullulation. **4** (*a growth on her neck*) tumour, lump, swelling, excrescence, protuberance, outgrowth, intumescence, tumefaction.

grub *verb* **1** (*grub up roots*) dig, root, uproot, unearth, pull, tear, disinter, forage. **2** (*grub out the original documents*) search out, ferret out, rummage for, unearth, disinter, delve for, probe, search out, hunt for, scour, find, locate, uncover, retrieve.

≫ *noun* **1** (*grubs on the lettuces*) maggot, larva, caterpillar, worm, pupa, chrysalis. **2** (*grub on the table*) food, sustenance, nosh (*inf*), eats (*inf*), refreshment, victuals, rations, tuck (*inf*), meals, provision, nutrition.

grubby *adj* dirty, soiled, grimy, begrimed, besmeared,

filthy, messy, mucky (*inf*), gungy (*inf*), manky (*inf*), cruddy (*inf*), scuzzy (*inf*), unwashed, frowzy, scruffy, untidy, unkempt, shabby, slovenly, slatternly, seedy, squalid, smutty, sordid. OPPOSITE: clean.

grudge *noun* grievance, resentment, envy, jealousy, pique, spite, malice, malevolence, ill will, bitterness, rancour, hard feelings, bad feelings, animosity, antipathy, aversion, dislike, hate, hatred, enmity, antagonism, venom, animus.
➤ *verb* begrudge, resent, envy, covet, dislike, take exception to, object to, mind, hold back, stint.

gruelling *adj* arduous, strenuous, hard, difficult, fierce, harsh, severe, stiff, strenuous, tough, exhausting, draining, tiring, fatiguing, wearying, taxing, laborious, trying, demanding, punishing, backbreaking, brutal, crushing, grinding, inexorable, relentless, unsparing. OPPOSITE: easy.

gruesome *adj* grim, grisly, macabre, ghastly, hideous, loathsome, disgusting, repulsive, repellent, repugnant, revolting, sickening, odious, horrible, terrible, appalling, awful, fearful, frightful, horrific, horrifying, horrid, horrendous, dreadful, abhorrent, abominable, monstrous, shocking, spine-chilling. OPPOSITE: attractive.

gruff *adj* **1** (*a gruff manner*) surly, churlish, curt, brusque, abrupt, blunt, sour, sullen, grumpy, bad-tempered, ill-natured, ill-humoured, crotchety (*inf*), crabby, crabbed, cross, crusty, grouchy (*inf*), testy, tetchy, rough, rude, bearish, uncivil, ungracious, discourteous, impolite, unfriendly. OPPOSITE: affable. **2** (*his gruff voice*) throaty, guttural, harsh, rasping, raucous, husky, hoarse, croaking, rough, thick, low.

grumble *verb* **1** (*grumbles all day long*) complain, moan, grouse (*inf*), bleat, carp, groan, gripe (*inf*), grouch (*inf*), bellyache (*inf*), crab, beef (*inf*), whine (*inf*), whinge (*inf*), find fault, object, protest. **2** (*the volcano grumbled*) growl, rumble, gurgle, roar, murmur, mutter.
➤ *noun* **1** (*heard their grumbles*) complaint, grievance, protest, objection, moan, groan, grouse, bleat, bitch (*inf*), whinge (*inf*), whine (*inf*), grouch (*inf*), gripe (*inf*), beef (*inf*). **2** (*the grumble of the machinery*) growl, rumble, gurgle, roar, murmur, mutter.

grumpy *adj* grumbling, cantankerous, irascible, crabby, crabbed, crusty, huffy (*inf*), ratty (*inf*), testy, tetchy, snappy, surly, crotchety (*inf*), bad-tempered, ill-tempered, ill-natured, bearish, churlish, cross, irritable, grouchy (*inf*), edgy, peevish, petulant, querulous, sulky, sullen, liverish, discontented. OPPOSITE: contented.

guarantee *noun* **1** (*a one-year guarantee on the product*) warranty, warrant, insurance. **2** (*gave his guarantee*) pledge, promise, covenant, oath, bond, assurance, word, word of honour. **3** (*serve as guarantee*) security, collateral, surety, endorsement, testimonial, earnest.
➤ *verb* **1** (*guarantee the loan*) underwrite, vouch for, answer for, certify, back, support, assure, endorse, sponsor, ensure, secure, insure, protect. **2** (*they guarantee it will be on time*) pledge, promise, warrant, swear.

guarantor *noun* underwriter, guarantee, sponsor, supporter, backer, angel (*inf*), surety, warrantor, voucher, referee, covenanter.

guard *verb* **1** (*guard the base*) protect, watch over, defend, shield, screen, shelter, cover, save, conserve, preserve, secure, safeguard, patrol, police. OPPOSITE: neglect. **2** (*guard the president*) mind, watch over, supervise, look out for, take care of, escort, oversee. **3** (*guard against illness*) keep watch, take care, be alert, be on the alert, look out for, mind, beware.
➤ *noun* **1** (*safety guard*) protection, defence, shield, screen, bulwark, wall, fence, rampart, barrier, buffer, bumper, fender, pad, cushion, security, safeguard. **2** (*call out the guard*) sentry, sentinel, watch, watchman, nightwatchman, lookout, picket, garrison, warder, keeper, custodian, guardian, defender, protector, bodyguard, minder (*inf*), security. **3** (*accompanied by a guard*) escort, convoy, patrol. **4** (*keep a close guard*) watchfulness, vigilance, wariness, caution, care, heed, attention.
off one's guard careless, unprepared, unawares, unready, unwary, inattentive, unwatchful, unsuspecting, surprised, napping, cold (*inf*), red-handed (*inf*).
on one's guard alert, vigilant, attentive, watchful, careful, cautious, ready, prepared, on the lookout, on the alert, wary, wide awake, circumspect.

guarded *adj* careful, cautious, circumspect, watchful, wary, suspicious, prudent, discreet, reticent, noncommittal, reluctant, reserved, restrained, secretive, cagey (*inf*), chary. OPPOSITE: rash.

guardian *noun* protector, defender, champion, keeper, custodian, caretaker, steward, trustee, curator, warden, warder, guard, escort, attendant, preserver.

guerrilla *noun* freedom fighter, terrorist, resistance fighter, underground fighter, irregular, partisan, guerrillero, franc-tireur, bushwhacker.

guess *verb* **1** (*guess the answer*) estimate, guesstimate (*inf*), solve, work out, fathom, penetrate, hypothesize, postulate, predict, conjecture, surmise, hazard. **2** (*I guess so*) reckon, conjecture, surmise, speculate, judge, think, believe, consider, suspect, suppose, imagine, fancy, feel, dare say, divine, deem. OPPOSITE: know.
➤ *noun* conjecture, surmise, speculation, hypothesis, theory, estimate, guesstimate (*inf*), shot in the dark (*inf*), ball-park figure (*inf*), guesswork, reckoning, judgment, belief, feeling, idea, intuition, hunch, notion, opinion, assumption, prediction, supposition, suspicion, inference.

guesswork *noun* speculation, estimation, guesstimate (*inf*), conjecture, reckoning, prediction, supposition, presupposition, surmise, assumption, presumption, suspicion, intuition, theory, hypothesis.

guest *noun* visitor, caller, company, lodger, boarder, resident, patron, regular, visitant. OPPOSITE: host.

guidance *noun* **1** (*under my guidance*) direction, control, charge, leadership, handling, government, rule, management, instruction, teaching, conduct, auspices. **2** (*marriage guidance*) advice, counsel, counselling, assistance, help, direction, information, recommendation, suggestion, guideline, tip, hint, pointer, clue.

guide *verb* **1** (*guide the ship into port*) lead, direct, navigate, pilot, point, shepherd, steer, manoeuvre, conduct, usher, escort, show, accompany, attend, convoy. OPPOSITE: follow. **2** (*guide the conduct of the campaign*) control, regulate, handle, manage, direct, steer, govern, preside over, manipulate, oversee, supervise, superintend, command, rule. **3** (*guide the young*) advise, counsel, influence, sway, educate, teach, inform, instruct, train.

➤ *noun* **1** (*a tour guide*) leader, courier, conductor, usher, escort, attendant. OPPOSITE: follower. **2** (*his guide and mentor*) adviser, counsellor, mentor, confidant, confidante, teacher, instructor, tutor, guru. **3** (*the rock served as a guide to walkers*) pointer, sign, beacon, signal, landmark, mark, marker, signpost, lodestar, clue, hint, indication, key. **4** (*she opened the guide*) guidebook, tourist guide, travelogue, handbook, manual, instructions, catalogue, directory, key, ABC, vade mecum. **5** (*use the original as a guide*) guideline, model, pattern, example, exemplar, ideal, inspiration, archetype, prototype, par, paradigm, norm, precedent, benchmark, yardstick, gauge, standard, criterion, touchstone, measure.

guideline *noun* guiding principle, principle, standard, criterion, measure, gauge, benchmark, yardstick, touchstone, parameter, framework, instruction, recommendation, suggestion, direction, advice, information, indication, rule, regulation.

guild *noun* fellowship, fraternity, brotherhood, sisterhood, sorority, union, society, club, association, organization, alliance, federation, league, lodge, chapel, order, company, corporation, incorporation.

guile *noun* deceit, deception, fraud, duplicity, art, artfulness, craft, craftiness, cunning, deviousness, artifice, slyness, foxiness, wiles, wiliness, double-dealing, trickery, trickiness, treachery, underhandedness, gamesmanship, sharp practice, chicanery, skulduggery, knavery. OPPOSITE: honesty.

guileless *adj* artless, ingenuous, naive, trustful, trusting, innocent, unsophisticated, unworldly, sincere, candid, direct, frank, genuine, unreserved, natural, open, simple, straightforward, above-board, upfront (*inf*), transparent, honest, truthful, undesigning. OPPOSITE: deceitful.

guilt *noun* **1** (*his guilt was proved*) guiltiness, culpability, criminality, sin, sinfulness, delinquency, iniquity, misconduct, unlawfulness, wrong, wrongdoing, blame, blameworthiness, responsibility, censurableness. OPPOSITE: innocence. **2** (*overwhelmed by guilt*) remorse, shame, contrition, regret, repentance, penitence, self-reproach, self-accusation, self-condemnation, compunction, guilty conscience, conscience, disgrace, dishonour, infamy, stigma. OPPOSITE: impenitence.

guiltless *adj* innocent, blameless, unimpeachable, irreproachable, above reproach, sinless, clear, pure, spotless, faultless, immaculate, impeccable, stainless, unspotted, uncorrupted, unblemished, unsullied, untainted, untarnished, undefiled, clean (*inf*), inculpable. OPPOSITE: guilty.

guilty *adj* **1** (*found guilty*) culpable, criminal, convicted, condemned, at fault, blameworthy, blameable, censurable, reprehensible, reproachable, responsible, erring, errant, felonious, offending, delinquent, illegal, unlawful, iniquitous, wrong, evil, wicked, sinful, illicit. OPPOSITE: innocent. **2** (*felt very guilty*) guilt-ridden,

remorseful, contrite, bad, regretful, penitent, repentant, sorry, conscience-stricken, sheepish, ashamed, shamefaced, rueful, hangdog. OPPOSITE: impenitent.

guise *noun* **1** (*under the guise of offering assistance*) appearance, exterior, front, facade, face, semblance, pretence, show, behaviour, custom, air, aspect, mien, demeanour, form, shape, fashion, likeness, manner, mode, disguise, mask, screen, cover, blind. **2** (*donned her guise*) dress, costume, habit, outfit, style.

gulf *noun* **1** (*the shelter of the gulf*) bay, bight, basin, inlet, cove, sound. **2** (*a gulf yawned open*) chasm, abyss, rift, cleft, rent, fissure, gorge, gully, crevice, canyon, ravine, hole, hollow, pit, opening. **3** (*the gulf between the two friends*) chasm, abyss, breach, rift, split, difference, division, gap, void, separation.

gullet *noun* throat, craw, crop, maw, oesophagus, pharynx.

gullible *adj* credulous, suggestible, impressionable, unsuspecting, easily deceived, trustful, trusting, naive, unsophisticated, ingenuous, innocent, inexperienced, green, wet behind the ears (*inf*), born yesterday, simple, foolish.

gully *noun* channel, gutter, ditch, trench, watercourse, ravine, gorge, gulf, canyon, valley.

gulp *verb* **1** (*he gulped his drink*) swallow, swig, knock back (*inf*), quaff, swill, toss off. **2** (*they gulped the food*) guzzle, gobble, bolt, devour, stuff, wolf (*inf*), tuck into (*inf*). **3** (*she gulped back her tears*) choke, stifle, swallow, smother, fight, strangle, suppress.

➤ *noun* swallow, draught, mouthful, swig.

gum *noun* glue, adhesive, paste, cement, fixative, resin, mucilage.

➤ *verb* glue, stick, paste, fix, affix, cement, seal.

gum up **1** (*gummed up the tube*) block up, stop up, clog, obstruct, choke. **2** (*gum up the works*) hinder, impede, obstruct, halt, interfere with.

gumption *noun* common sense, initiative, enterprise, resourcefulness, sagacity, savvy (*inf*), nous (*inf*), horse sense (*inf*), get-up-and-go (*inf*), acumen, shrewdness, wit, ability, cleverness, astuteness, discernment, spirit.

gun *noun* pistol, revolver, handgun, rifle, shotgun, firearm, shooter (*inf*), shooting iron (*inf*), six-shooter, piece (*inf*), heater (*inf*), repeater, automatic, machine gun, carbine, flintlock, musket, blunderbuss.

gunman *noun* sniper, gunfighter, hit man (*inf*), hired gun (*inf*), liquidator (*inf*), assassin, murderer, terrorist, gunslinger, gangster, hood (*inf*), mobster, bandit, thug, killer, shootist.

gurgle *verb* **1** (*the brook gurgled*) babble, burble, murmur, bubble, ripple, lap, tinkle, splash, plash, purl. **2** (*a baby gurgling*) chuckle, laugh, burble, crow, babble.

➤ *noun* **1** (*the gurgle of the river*) babble, burbling, murmur, bubbling, ripple, lap, tinkling, splash. **2** (*the gurgle of her laughter*) chuckle, laugh, burbling, crowing, babbling.

guru *noun* maharishi, swami, mahatma, master, teacher, instructor, tutor, leader, mentor, guiding light, expert, authority, sage, luminary, pundit.

gush *verb* **1** (*oil gushed from the pipe*) flow, rush, pour, stream, run, surge, spurt, spout, burst, cascade, jet, flood, well, emanate, issue. OPPOSITE: drip. **2** (*she gushed about her new car*) enthuse, effuse, chatter, babble, go on (*inf*), jabber, wax lyrical, blather, prattle, gabble, drivel, effervesce, bubble over, fuss.

➣ *noun* flow, rush, outflow, outburst, spurt, spout, outpouring, stream, surge, torrent, cascade, flood, tide, burst, spate, jet.

gushing *adj* gushy, effusive, fulsome, demonstrative, emotional, saccharine, sentimental, cloying, sickly, mawkish, excessive, overdone, overenthusiastic. OPPOSITE: restrained.

gust *noun* **1** (*a sudden gust of wind*) blast, puff, flurry, blow, breeze, squall, gale, wind, storm, surge, rush, fit. **2** (*gusts of laughter*) outburst, burst, outbreak, eruption, explosion, paroxysm, fit, gale, storm, surge.

➣ *verb* blast, blow, puff, squall, bluster, breeze, rush, surge, burst out, erupt.

gusto *noun* relish, zest, enjoyment, pleasure, delight, zeal, appetite, savour, taste, enthusiasm, exhilaration, exuberance, energy, élan, brio, verve, fervour, appreciation, fondness, liking. OPPOSITE: apathy.

gusty *adj* blowy, squally, windy, blustery, blustering, breezy, stormy, tempestuous, inclement. OPPOSITE: calm.

gut *noun* **1** (*punched him in the gut*) stomach, belly, abdomen, paunch, solar plexus. **2** (*dissected the gut*) intestines, innards (*inf*), insides, bowels, entrails, vital organs, viscera.

➣ *verb* **1** (*gutted the fish*) disembowel, dress, clean, draw, eviscerate. **2** (*the building had been gutted*) strip, empty,

clear, ransack, plunder, rifle, loot, sack, rob, lay waste, destroy, devastate, ravage, despoil, clear out.

➣ *adj* instinctive, intuitive, involuntary, spontaneous, unthinking, natural, basic, deep-seated, emotional, visceral, heartfelt, innate, strong.

gutless *adj* cowardly, chicken (*inf*), yellow (*inf*), chickenhearted, chickenshit (*sl*), chicken-livered, lily-livered, spineless, feeble, weak, irresolute, timid, submissive, fainthearted, craven, abject. OPPOSITE: brave.

guts *pl noun* courage, bravery, daring, pluck, valour, boldness, forcefulness, audacity, grit (*inf*), tenacity, backbone (*inf*), bottle (*inf*), spunk (*inf*), nerve, fortitude, hardihood, toughness, mettle, spirit, gameness, willpower. OPPOSITE: weakness.

gutter *noun* channel, conduit, duct, pipe, tube, furrow, trough, trench, ditch, drain, culvert, sluice, sewer.

guttersnipe *noun* urchin, street urchin, street arab, waif, ragamuffin, mudlark, gamin.

guttural *adj* hoarse, husky, gruff, rasping, croaking, grating, gravelly, harsh, rough, throaty, thick, deep, low.

guy *noun* man, boy, lad, youth, fellow, chap (*inf*), person, bloke (*inf*), customer, individual, character.

guzzle *verb* **1** (*guzzled his food*) gobble, bolt, cram, stuff, pig out (*inf*), scoff (*inf*), wolf (*inf*), devour, gorge, polish off (*inf*), put away (*inf*), tuck into (*inf*), gormandize. **2** (*guzzled their drinks*) gulp, drink, swallow, quaff, swig, swill, knock back (*inf*), toss off, tope.

gyrate *verb* circle, revolve, rotate, turn, spiral, pirouette, spin, twirl, whirl, wheel, swirl, swivel.

gyration *noun* rotation, revolution, spin, spinning, whirl, swirl, swivel, wheel, whirling, pirouette, twirl, convolution, circle, spiral, turn.

habit *noun* **1** (*her usual habit of going for a swim after work*) practice, custom, usage, wont, procedure, routine, manner, way, style, pattern, mode, rule, convention, policy. **2** (*an unfortunate habit of spitting*) tendency, disposition, predisposition, propensity, inclination, bent, leaning, penchant, proclivity, practice, quirk, mannerism. **3** (*try to break the habit of smoking*) addiction, dependence, weakness, compulsion, obsession, fixation. **4** (*a methodical habit of mind*) disposition, nature, character, make-up, frame of mind, temper, temperament, humour. **5** (*put on his habit*) clothing, clothes, costume, dress, outfit, gear (*inf*), togs (*inf*), rags (*inf*), rigout (*inf*), garb, garments, attire, uniform, apparel, livery, robes, habiliments, vestments.

habitable *adj* inhabitable, fit to live in, livable-in, tenantable.

habitat *noun* **1** (*in their natural habitat*) environment, surroundings, territory, terrain, locality, element, home, domain, abode, haunt, home ground, stamping ground. **2** (*she returned to her habitat*) home, abode, residence, residency, dwelling, dwelling-place, habitation, location, situation, address.

habitation *noun* **1** (*unfit for human habitation*) occupation, occupancy, inhabitation, inhabitance, inhabitancy, residence, residency, tenancy, housing, lodging, lodgement, quartering, billeting, dwelling, living. **2** (*their remote habitation*) home, house, housing, rooms, dwelling, dwelling-place, abode, domicile, pad (*inf*), digs (*inf*), joint (*inf*), residence, residency, lodging, lodging-place, quarters, living quarters, accommodation.

habitual *adj* **1** (*began her habitual routine*) customary, usual, wonted, accustomed, recurrent, regular, fixed, set, established, standard, routine, traditional, common, ordinary, natural, normal, familiar. OPPOSITE: unusual. **2** (*an habitual drinker*) chronic, addicted, dependent, inveterate, ingrained, hardened, confirmed, established, frequent, persistent, obsessive. OPPOSITE: occasional.

3 (*habitual delays*) recurrent, frequent, repeated, persistent, constant, continual, continuous, perpetual, nonstop.

habituate *verb* accustom, familiarize, condition, acclimatize, make used to, adapt, condition, harden, inure, season, break in, train, school, tame, discipline.

habitué *noun* regular, patron, frequenter, denizen.

hack¹ *verb* **1** (*hacked at the logs*) cut, chop, fell, saw, hew, gash, slash, lacerate, mutilate, mangle. **2** (*hack a way through*) cut, slash, hew, clear.

hack² *noun* **1** (*worked for a time as a hack for the papers*) scribbler, penny-a-liner, journalist, writer. **2** (*a staff of hacks*) drudge, plodder, labourer, toiler, skivvy (*inf*), menial, slave, hireling, mercenary. **3** (*rode an old hack*) horse, nag (*inf*), workhorse, crock (*inf*), jade.

hackneyed *adj* banal, commonplace, hack, trite, clichéd, stale, tired, threadbare, worn-out, timeworn, overworked, overused, corny (*inf*), played-out (*inf*), run-of-the-mill (*inf*), unoriginal, pedestrian, stock, stereotyped, platitudinous, prosaic, uninspired, unimaginative, conventional, common. OPPOSITE: original.

hag *noun* crone, battle-axe (*inf*), old bat (*inf*), harridan, harpy, fury, virago, vixen, shrew, nag, scold, witch, gorgon, hellcat, termagant.

haggard *adj* gaunt, drawn, hollow-cheeked, careworn, worn, weary, pale, pallid, wan, ghastly, ghostlike, deathlike, cadaverous, pinched, peaked, emaciated, thin, wasted, drained, shrunken, wrinkled. OPPOSITE: fresh.

haggle *verb* **1** (*haggle with the shopkeeper*) bargain, barter, negotiate, beat down. **2** (*haggle over the issue*) wrangle, squabble, quarrel, argue, dispute, bicker, quibble. OPPOSITE: agree.

hail¹ *verb* **1** (*hailed his comrades*) greet, salute, address, welcome, receive, acknowledge, accost, smile at, nod to, wave to. **2** (*hail a passing ship*) signal, flag, flag down, accost, address, call, shout to, sing out to, halloo, wave down. **3** (*hailed the great victory*) acclaim, applaud, cheer, exalt, glorify, honour, praise, extol, laud. OPPOSITE: ignore.

hail from come from, originate from, have one's roots in.

hail² *noun* (*a hail of bullets*) shower, rain, storm, torrent, volley, barrage, bombardment, pelting.

➤ *verb* pelt, bombard, volley, shower, rain, pepper, batter, attack, assail.

hair *noun* **1** (*brush your hair*) locks, tresses, mop, shock. **2** (*made of animal hair*) mane, coat, fleece, fur, wool, pelt, hide.

let one's hair down let go, relax, chill out (*inf*), hang loose (*inf*), let off steam (*inf*), loosen up, let it all hang out (*inf*).

not turn a hair remain calm, keep one's cool (*inf*), keep one's hair on (*inf*), stay cool (*inf*).

split hairs find fault, nitpick (*inf*), quibble, niggle, cavil.

hair-raising *adj* frightening, scary, terrifying, horrifying, shocking, bloodcurdling, creepy (*inf*), eerie, spine-chilling, petrifying, alarming, startling, breathtaking, exciting, thrilling.

hairy *adj* **1** (*a hairy face*) hirsute, shaggy, bushy, furry, woolly, fleecy, fluffy, fuzzy, bearded, unshaven, bewhiskered, stubbly. OPPOSITE: hairless. **2** (*a hairy experience*) difficult, dangerous, hazardous, risky, perilous, exciting, frightening, scary (*inf*).

halcyon *adj* **1** (*a halcyon summer day*) peaceful, tranquil, serene, placid, calm, balmy, windless, pacific, still, quiet, undisturbed, unruffled, mild, gentle, moderate, temperate, pleasant. OPPOSITE: stormy. **2** (*a halcyon time*) happy, carefree, contented, joyful, joyous, palmy, blissful, golden, prosperous, flourishing, thriving.

hale *adj* healthy, hearty, robust, strong, sturdy, hardy, sound, well, able-bodied, fit, in fine fettle, in the pink, blooming, vigorous, energetic, athletic, lusty, flourishing, youthful. OPPOSITE: frail.

half *noun* fifty per cent, equal part, equal share, bisection, hemisphere, semicircle. OPPOSITE: whole.

➤ *adj* **1** (*a half measure*) halved, divided in two, equally divided, bisected, hemispherical, split. **2** (*a half wave*) partial, incomplete, limited, moderate, slight, inadequate, insufficient.

➤ *adv* partly, in part, partially, barely, incompletely, inadequately, insufficiently, moderately, slightly, nearly. OPPOSITE: completely.

by half very, considerably, excessively, far, too.

by halves incompletely, imperfectly, inadequately, insufficiently, scrappily, skimpily.

not half 1 (*not half as quick*) not nearly, not at all. **2** (*she didn't half hit him*) really, certainly, very, very much, indeed.

half-baked *adj* **1** (*another half-baked idea*) impractical, stupid, harebrained (*inf*), crackpot (*inf*), ill-conceived, unplanned, undeveloped, ill-judged, injudicious, shortsighted, premature, silly, crazy, foolish, senseless. **2** (*a half-baked individual*) foolish, stupid, silly, brainless, senseless, dim-witted (*inf*), half-witted (*inf*), dopey (*inf*), loopy (*inf*), ignorant, inexperienced, immature, callow, green, credulous.

halfhearted *adj* indifferent, uncaring, unconcerned, uninterested, apathetic, cool, lukewarm, neutral, dispassionate, unemotional, cool, unenthusiastic, spiritless, lacklustre, languid, listless, passive, tame, weak, half-arsed (*sl*), careless, perfunctory, cursory, superficial. OPPOSITE: enthusiastic.

halfway *adv* **1** (*halfway along*) midway, in the middle, centrally. **2** (*the job is not even halfway complete*) almost, nearly, just about, in part, partly, partially, part, in some measure, incompletely.

➤ *adj* central, equidistant, middle, mid, midway, intermediate, mean, median, medial.

meet someone halfway compromise, negotiate, accommodate, concede, make concessions, give and take, trade off, make a deal, go fifty-fifty with (*inf*), split the difference (*inf*).

halfwit *noun* fool, idiot, cretin, imbecile, dunce, blockhead, fathead, dimwit, simpleton, ignoramus, moron, buffoon, wally (*inf*), berk (*inf*), jerk (*inf*), nerd (*inf*), prat (*inf*), plonker (*inf*), pillock (*inf*), prick (*sl*), airhead (*inf*), charlie (*inf*), nincompoop (*inf*), ass (*inf*), birdbrain (*inf*), chump (*inf*), dipstick (*inf*), ninny (*inf*), clot (*inf*), dope (*inf*), dumbo (*inf*), numskull (*inf*), nitwit (*inf*), twit (*inf*), nit (*inf*), sucker (*inf*), mug (*inf*), twerp (*inf*).

half-witted *adj* simpleminded, simple, feebleminded, dim-witted (*inf*), dull-witted (*inf*), silly, foolish, idiotic, stupid, obtuse, dull, doltish, moronic, crazy, cracked (*inf*), crackbrained (*inf*), crackpot (*inf*), dotty (*inf*), potty (*inf*), nutty (*inf*), barmy (*inf*), batty (*inf*), dumb (*inf*), flaky (*inf*).

hall *noun* **1** (*he's waiting in the hall*) hallway, entrance-hall, vestibule, lobby, foyer, corridor, passage, passageway. **2** (*the hall was full that night*) concert-hall, conference hall, church hall, town hall, auditorium, amphitheatre, assembly room, chamber.

hallmark *noun* **1** (*a hallmark on silver cutlery*) assay mark, stamp of authenticity, authentication, endorsement, seal, sign. **2** (*the hallmark of his work*) mark, trademark, quality, feature, stamp, sign, indication, indicator, index, symbol, emblem, badge, device.

hallowed *adj* holy, sacred, sanctified, consecrated, dedicated, blessed, honoured, revered, sacrosanct, established, age-old. OPPOSITE: profane.

hallucinate *verb* dream, daydream, imagine, see things, fantasize, freak out (*inf*), trip (*inf*).

hallucination *noun* delusion, illusion, dream, daydream, fantasy, mirage, vision, apparition, phantasm, figment, figment of the imagination, imagining, delirium, phantasmagoria, trip (*inf*), freak-out (*inf*). OPPOSITE: reality.

halo *noun* circle of light, crown of light, ring of light, corona, nimbus, radiance, glory, aura, aureole, aureola, halation.

halt¹ *verb* **1** (*halt at the gate*) stop, pull up, draw up, pause, wait, stand still, stay. **2** (*halt for an hour*) cease, break off, stop, finish, rest, quit (*inf*), down tools, knock off (*inf*), desist, discontinue. **3** (*the process may halt*) stop, finish, cease, close down, come to an end. **4** (*halt the campaign*) hold back, stop, arrest, check, curb, stem, staunch, cut short, impede, block, obstruct, crush, frustrate, balk, nip in the bud, end, terminate. OPPOSITE: proceed.

➤ **noun 1** (*a halt in the conversation*) break, interruption, hiatus, stoppage, stop, rest, respite, impasse, pause, interval, intermission, breathing-space, breather (*inf*), arrest, discontinuance, discontinuation, standstill, close, end, termination, cessation. **2** (*come to a halt*) stop, standstill.

halt² *verb* **1** (*halting over his words*) hesitate, falter, stammer, stutter, stumble, flounder, fumble, haver, pause. **2** (*halted over his decision*) hesitate, waver, vacillate, dither.

halting *adj* **1** (*with a halting step*) limping, hobbling, stumbling, unsteady, awkward. **2** (*delivered with halting words*) hesitant, hesitating, faltering, fumbling, stumbling, stammering, stuttering, laboured, uncertain, broken, imperfect. OPPOSITE: fluent.

halve *verb* bisect, cut in half, divide in two, split in two, share equally, dichotomize.

hammer *verb* **1** (*hammer with his fists*) beat, pound, batter, strike, hit, slap, tap, knock, drive, drum, bang, bash, clobber (*inf*), wallop (*inf*), pummel, bludgeon, club. **2** (*hammer into shape*) beat out, forge, shape, form, fashion, make, mould, fabricate. **3** (*hammer the other party*) criticize, run down (*inf*), knock (*inf*), slam (*inf*), slate (*inf*), run rings round (*inf*), blow out of the water (*inf*), attack, condemn, blame, denigrate, decry, censure, lambaste. **4** (*we will hammer the remaining teams*) beat, defeat, slaughter (*inf*), thrash (*inf*), clobber (*inf*), lick (*inf*), trounce, annihilate, rout, outplay, overwhelm, overcome, drub, worst. **5** (*we tried to hammer it into him*) force, drum, drive home, din, drub, impress upon, instil. **6** (*hammer away at her work*) pound, persevere, keep at, persist, labour, work, slog, grind, plug, drudge, stick (*inf*), beaver (*inf*).

➤ **noun** claw hammer, sledgehammer, mallet, gavel.

hammer out thrash out, work out, sort out, negotiate, agree, resolve, settle, bring about, complete, accomplish, achieve, produce, effect, carry through.

hamper *verb* hinder, impede, slow down, hold up, retard, obstruct, block, encumber, embarrass, handicap, hamstring, shackle, inhibit, cramp, bind, bridle, fetter, shackle, restrain, restrict, confine, check, curb, prevent, stop, frustrate, balk, foil, thwart, stymie (*inf*). OPPOSITE: assist.

➤ **noun** basket, box, container, holder, pannier, creel.

hamstring *verb* **1** (*hamstring a player*) lame, cripple, injure, disable, incapacitate, hock. **2** (*hamstring their efforts*) hinder, impede, slow down, hold up, retard, stop, cramp, restrict, restrain, frustrate, ruin, balk, thwart, block, obstruct, check, curb, encumber, foil, cripple, paralyse, handicap, stymie (*inf*).

hand *noun* **1** (*held out her hand*) palm, fist, paw (*inf*), mitt (*inf*), meathook (*inf*), duke (*inf*). OPPOSITE: foot. **2** (*by my own hand*) agency, intervention. **3** (*I think he had a hand in it*) part, share, participation, influence. **4** (*we shall lend a hand*) help, aid, assistance, support, relief, succour. **5** (*try my hand at needlework*) ability, skill, craftsmanship, art, artistry. **6** (*the big hand on the clock*) pointer, indicator, needle, arrow, marker. **7** (*all hands on deck*) labourer, worker, workman, artisan, craftsman, craftswoman, craftsperson, operative, employee, assistant, helper, hireling, crew, crew member. **8** (*I would know her hand anywhere*) handwriting, writing, script, penmanship, fist (*inf*), calligraphy. **9** (*gave the entertainer a big hand*) ovation, clap, handclap, round of applause, acclaim.

➤ **verb** give, hand over, present, offer, submit, deliver, yield, pass, conduct, convey, transmit.

at hand 1 (*keep your torch at hand*) nearby, close, handy, to hand, on hand, within reach, accessible, on tap (*inf*), available, ready. **2** (*the hour is at hand*) close, coming, approaching, imminent, impending.

by hand manually, with one's hands.

from hand to mouth in poverty, on the breadline (*inf*), improvidently, meagrely, scantily, skimpily, precariously, dangerously, perilously, insecurely, uncertainly, from day to day.

hand down bequeath, will, transfer, pass on, pass down, leave, give, grant.

hand in glove closely, in partnership, in league, in collusion, in cahoots (*inf*), in collaboration, in close cooperation, in close association.

hand in hand 1 (*walked out hand in hand*) holding hands, clasping hands, with hands clasped. **2** (*hand in hand with this initiative*) together, side by side, associated, in association, in partnership, conjointly, concurrently, closely.

hand out distribute, dispense, give out, deal out, dole out, dish out (*inf*), share out, apportion, pass out, disburse, disseminate, mete. OPPOSITE: withhold.

hand over deliver, transfer, consign, give, donate, present, fork out (*inf*), pass, turn over, surrender, give up, yield, relinquish, release. OPPOSITE: retain.

in hand 1 (*everything is in hand*) under way, under control, in order, receiving attention, being attended to, being considered, being dealt with. **2** (*with resources in hand*) spare, in reserve, put by, ready, available.

to hand near, close, at hand, handy, accessible, available, ready, imminent.

try one's hand attempt, try, have a go (*inf*), have a stab (*inf*), have a shot (*inf*), have a crack (*inf*), seek, strive, essay.

handbill *noun* circular, leaflet, pamphlet, flier, brochure, notice, bulletin, announcement, advertisement, letter.

handbook *noun* manual, instruction book, instructions, directions, book of directions, directory, ABC, guide, guidebook, tourist guide, travel guide, companion, prospectus, vade mecum.

handcuff *verb* fetter, shackle, manacle, secure, tie, fasten.

handcuffs *pl noun* cuffs (*inf*), bracelets (*inf*), darbies (*inf*), wristlets, fetters, shackles, manacles.

handful *noun* **1** (*a handful of survivors*) few, small number, sprinkling, scattering, smattering. **2** (*those kids are a handful*) nuisance, pain (*inf*), pain in the neck (*inf*), thorn in the flesh (*inf*), headache, pest, bother, irritant.

handicap *noun* **1** (*born with a handicap*) disability, defect, disadvantage, abnormality, impairment. **2** (*her presence was a handicap*) hindrance, disadvantage, drawback, impediment, obstacle, stumbling-block,

obstruction, encumbrance, millstone, barrier, block, check, curb, constraint, restriction, limitation, penalty, shortcoming. OPPOSITE: advantage.
➤ *verb* hinder, hamper, impede, burden, check, block, obstruct, encumber, disadvantage, restrict, constrain, limit, hamstring, disable, impair, curb, bridle, hold back, retard. OPPOSITE: assist.

handicraft *noun* craft, art, skill, craftwork, handiwork, craftsmanship, artisanship, workmanship.

handiwork *noun* **1** (*the handiwork of a master criminal*) action, doing, deed, achievement, work, labour, creation, design, invention, product, production, result. **2** (*admired his handiwork*) craftsmanship, craftwork, craft, handicraft, workmanship, artisanship, art, skill.

handle *noun* knob, grip, stock, handgrip, haft, stock, hilt, shaft.
➤ *verb* **1** (*try not to handle the food*) feel, touch, finger, fondle, caress, stroke, pat, maul, paw (*inf*), poke, pick up, lift, hold, grasp, grip. **2** (*handle people carefully*) treat, deal with, cope with, manage, tackle. **3** (*handle all dealings*) control, conduct, direct, guide, supervise, operate, administer, manipulate. **4** (*handle the bike well*) operate, control, drive, steer, manoeuvre, ride. **5** (*handle drugs*) deal in, traffic in, sell, trade in, market, carry, stock.

handout *noun* **1** (*handouts to the poor*) charity, gifts, alms, dole, largess. **2** (*read this handout*) leaflet, pamphlet, circular, flier, bulletin, notice, statement, press release, brochure, literature.

handpicked *adj* choice, chosen, select, selected, elect, élite, picked, screened.

hands *pl noun* clutches, grasp, grip, possession, charge, supervision, keeping, management, custody, guardianship, care, responsibility, authority, jurisdiction, command, disposal, power, control.
hands down easily, effortlessly, without effort, no sweat (*inf*).

handsome *adj* **1** (*a handsome young man*) good-looking, attractive, personable, gorgeous, dishy (*inf*), hunky (*inf*). OPPOSITE: ugly. **2** (*she cut a handsome figure*) good-looking, attractive, fair, comely, well-proportioned, well-formed, elegant, graceful, fine, majestic, stately. **3** (*a handsome gift*) liberal, generous, lavish, ample, abundant, plentiful, bountiful, bounteous, large, considerable, sizeable, magnanimous, unstinting, unsparing, gracious, noble. OPPOSITE: stingy.

handwriting *noun* writing, script, hand, penmanship, scrawl (*inf*), scribble (*inf*), fist (*inf*), calligraphy.

handy *adj* **1** (*keep the tools handy*) nearby, near, close, at hand, on hand, to hand, within reach, available, ready, accessible, convenient. **2** (*a handy device*) convenient, useful, practical, practicable, helpful, functional, expedient, serviceable, neat. OPPOSITE: inconvenient. **3** (*handy at woodwork*) adroit, dexterous, skilful, skilled, deft, adept, nimble, nimble-fingered, practical, expert, proficient, clever. OPPOSITE: clumsy.

hang *verb* **1** (*let it hang over a chair*) drape, dangle, swing, droop, sag, drop, flop, sag, lean, incline, bend, fall, trail, hang down, loll. OPPOSITE: stand. **2** (*hang it up*) suspend, put up. **3** (*hang the wallpaper*) fasten, attach, stick, glue, paste, cement, fix, affix, append. **4** (*hang the room with paintings*) decorate, ornament, adorn, deck,

furnish. **5** (*hanging in the breeze*) hover, float, drift, waft, flit, flutter, linger, remain, cling. OPPOSITE: disperse. **6** (*they promised to hang the ringleader*) string up (*inf*), lynch, execute, put to death, kill.
get the hang of master, understand, grasp, comprehend, fathom, get the knack of, catch on (*inf*), twig (*inf*).
hang about 1 (*hang about with his mates*) hang around, linger, loiter, dawdle, dally, tarry, waste time, associate with, keep company with. **2** (*hang about some dodgy places*) frequent, haunt.
hang back hold back, stay back, hesitate, shy away, shrink back, recoil, stay behind, demur.
hang fire hold back, hang back, delay, procrastinate, stall, vacillate, hold on, stick, stop, wait.
hang on 1 (*hang on to the rail*) cling, cleave, stick, adhere, hold, hold fast, grip, grasp, clutch. **2** (*hang on to the end*) persevere, carry on, continue, go on, persist, hold out, endure, remain, stay, hold on, wait. **3** (*everything hangs on the decision*) depend on, hinge on, turn on, rest on.
hang over impend, loom, lean over, menace, threaten, approach, draw near.

hangdog *adj* abject, browbeaten, defeated, guilty, ashamed, shamefaced, embarrassed, cowed, intimidated, abashed, cringing, sheepish, downcast, crestfallen, abject, miserable, wretched, sneaking, furtive.

hanger-on *noun* follower, henchman, minion, lackey, retainer, toady, sycophant, fawner, parasite, leech, sponger (*inf*), freeloader (*inf*), groupie (*inf*), dependant, appendage.

hangover *noun* morning after (*inf*), aftereffects, crapulence.

hang-up *noun* inhibition, phobia, block, mental block, thing (*inf*), difficulty, problem, obsession, preoccupation, fixation, idée fixe.

hank *noun* coil, loop, twist, skein, length, roll, piece.

hanker *verb* long, yearn, yen (*inf*), pine, itch, hunger, thirst, crave, desire, hope, want, wish, covet, lust.

hankering *noun* longing, pining, yearning, yen (*inf*), itch, hunger, thirst, craving, hope, wish, want, desire, lust, urge. OPPOSITE: aversion.

haphazard *adj* **1** (*a series of haphazard events*) random, chance, arbitrary, accidental, fluky (*inf*). OPPOSITE: deliberate. **2** (*a haphazard approach*) careless, slipshod, slapdash, disorderly, disorganized, irregular, unmethodical, unsystematic, hit or miss (*inf*), indiscriminate, aimless, casual. OPPOSITE: orderly.

hapless *adj* unfortunate, unlucky, luckless, ill-fated, ill-starred, cursed, jinxed, star-crossed, forlorn, wretched, miserable, woebegone, unhappy. OPPOSITE: lucky.

happen *verb* **1** (*it may never happen*) occur, take place, come about, come to pass, chance, arise, crop up, transpire, appear, arrive, materialize, come off (*inf*), fall, result, develop, ensue, turn out, pan out (*inf*), eventuate. **2** (*what happened to them?*) become of, befall, betide.
happen on/upon chance on, chance upon, stumble on, encounter by chance, discover by chance, find unexpectedly, find suddenly, hit on, hit upon, light on.

happening *noun* event, occurrence, incident, event, eventuality, action, adventure, escapade, episode, occasion, eventuality, proceeding, affair, business, case, circumstance, chance, accident, experience, scene, phenomenon.

happily adv **1** (*playing happily*) gladly, joyfully, merrily, cheerfully, gaily, gleefully, blithely, heartily, delightedly, lightheartedly, contentedly, enthusiastically, willingly, joyously. **2** (*everything ended happily*) fortunately, favourably, successfully, felicitously, luckily, providentially, auspiciously, opportunely, propitiously, appropriately, fittingly, seasonably.

happiness noun joy, joyfulness, delight, bliss, blissfulness, ecstasy, elation, euphoria, exuberance, jubilation, glee, felicity, gladness, contentment, pleasure, enjoyment, gaiety, joviality, merriment, merriness, cheer, cheerfulness, cheeriness, lightheartedness, blitheness, high spirits, good spirits, well-being, satisfaction. OPPOSITE: sadness.

happy adj **1** (*in a happy mood*) joyful, joyous, delighted, overjoyed, thrilled, pleased, content, contented, satisfied, glad, gleeful, jovial, ecstatic, elated, euphoric, rapturous, exuberant, blissful, blithe, blithesome, cheerful, cheery, gay, smiling, radiant, buoyant, in good spirits, in high spirits, merry, jolly, lighthearted, over the moon, cock-a-hoop (*inf*), tickled pink (*inf*), on cloud nine (*inf*), in seventh heaven (*inf*), carefree, untroubled, unconcerned, unworried. OPPOSITE: sad. **2** (*very happy about it*) glad, pleased, delighted, contented, gratified, satisfied, thrilled. **3** (*a happy accident*) fortunate, lucky, favourable, felicitous, advantageous, helpful, beneficial, prosperous, successful, auspicious, propitious, convenient, seasonable, opportune, timely. OPPOSITE: unfortunate. **4** (*a happy choice*) appropriate, apt, fitting, fit, befitting, proper, good, right, seemly.

happy-go-lucky adj easygoing, free and easy, carefree, casual, blithe, nonchalant, cheerful, devil-may-care, lighthearted, insouciant, unconcerned, untroubled, unworried, reckless, heedless, irresponsible, improvident.

harangue noun address, speech, talk, oration, lecture, spiel (*inf*), sermon, declamation, exhortation, homily, tirade, diatribe, peroration, philippic.
   ≫ verb address, lecture, hold forth, rant, declaim, spout (*inf*), preach, exhort.

harass verb **1** (*harassed their teacher*) plague, torment, persecute, harry, pester, hassle (*inf*), molest, nag, hector, badger, hound, bother, trouble, worry, annoy, exasperate, fret, irritate, vex, disturb, agitate, provoke, antagonize, bedevil, bait, tease, tire, weary, stress, fatigue, wear out, exhaust, perplex. **2** (*harass the enemy*) harry, attack, raid, beleaguer.

harassed adj distraught, hassled (*inf*), stressed, stressed out (*inf*), uptight (*inf*), pressurized, pressured, under pressure, under stress, strained, distressed, troubled, worried, careworn, hounded, pestered, plagued, tormented, harried, agitated, vexed.

harbinger noun precursor, forerunner, herald, messenger, usher, announcer, warning, sign, indication, foretoken, omen, portent, augury.

harbour noun **1** (*ships in the harbour*) harbourage, port, anchorage, dock, wharf, mooring, marina, haven. **2** (*a*

safe harbour from all threats) haven, shelter, refuge, retreat, sanctuary, asylum.
   ≫ verb **1** (*harbour the killers*) protect, shelter, lodge, house, hide, conceal, shield, secrete, take in, put up, billet. OPPOSITE: expose. **2** (*harbour a grudge*) cherish, foster, nurture, nurse, hold on to, cling to, retain, maintain, entertain, believe, brood over.

hard adj **1** (*hard as steel*) solid, solidified, dense, compact, compacted, compressed, close-packed, condensed, firm, rigid, stiff, unyielding, inflexible, unmalleable, unpliable, resistant, impenetrable, strong, tough, stony, rocklike, steely. OPPOSITE: soft. **2** (*lots of hard work*) difficult, arduous, laborious, gruelling, uphill, strenuous, onerous, rigorous, formidable, tough, heavy, taxing, tiring, toilsome, exacting, exhausting, backbreaking, fatiguing. OPPOSITE: easy. **3** (*a hard task*) puzzling, baffling, perplexing, difficult, insoluble, incomprehensible, unfathomable, enigmatic, bewildering, intricate, complicated, complex, involved, knotty, thorny. OPPOSITE: simple. **4** (*he is a hard man*) harsh, severe, stern, strict, tyrannical, cruel, vicious, oppressive, ruthless, pitiless, merciless, implacable, unrelenting, unsparing, unyielding, obdurate, hardhearted, coldhearted, callous, unfeeling, unsympathetic, cold, unkind, unfair. OPPOSITE: tender. **5** (*a hard lesson to learn*) painful, distressing, unpleasant. **6** (*a hard childhood*) tough, harsh, severe, austere, grim, unpleasant, difficult, painful, disagreeable, bad, grievous, distressing, calamitous, disastrous, uncomfortable, unbearable, unendurable, intolerable, insupportable. OPPOSITE: pleasant. **7** (*a hard worker*) hardworking, industrious, diligent, persevering, persistent, unflagging, untiring, indefatigable, assiduous, earnest, conscientious, zealous, keen, enthusiastic, busy, energetic, sedulous. **8** (*a hard knock*) heavy, harsh, sharp, powerful, forceful, strong, intense, fierce, violent. **9** (*no hard feelings*) bitter, resentful, angry, rancorous, acrimonious, antagonistic. **10** (*a hard frost*) bitter, freezing, severe, cold, raw. **11** (*hard facts*) definite, real, actual, certain, verifiable, undeniable, indisputable, unquestionable, plain, bold, cold, bare, unvarnished, unembellished. **12** (*hard drugs*) addictive, habit-forming, narcotic, harmful, injurious, heavy, strong, potent.
   ≫ adv **1** (*working hard*) diligently, industriously, assiduously, conscientiously, enthusiastically, eagerly, keenly, determinedly, earnestly, intently, vigorously, energetically, strenuously, laboriously, steadily, persistently, busily, indefatigably, untiringly, sedulously. **2** (*hit hard*) violently, forcibly, forcefully, strongly, powerfully, vigorously, energetically, roughly, sharply, heavily, intensely, fiercely, severely, harshly, badly, painfully, agonizingly, distressingly. OPPOSITE: softly. **3** (*look hard*) closely, carefully, intently, sharply, keenly, attentively, painstakingly. **4** (*the trophy was hard won*) arduously, strenuously, laboriously, vigorously, with effort, painfully, bitterly, sorely, hardly. **5** (*raining hard*) heavily, severely, strongly, steadily, intensely.

hard-and-fast fixed, binding, definite, incontrovertible, incontestable, inflexible, invariable, rigid, set, strict, stringent, rigorous, unalterable, unchangeable, unchanging, immutable, uncompromising.

hard up poor, short, lacking, penniless, bankrupt, broke (*inf*), bust (*inf*), skint (*inf*), cleaned out (*inf*), strapped (*inf*), impoverished, impecunious, in the red, in difficulties. OPPOSITE: rich.

hard-bitten *adj* hardened, hard-boiled, hardheaded, hard-nosed, tough, toughened, case-hardened, callous, cynical, down-to-earth, inured, matter-of-fact, practical, realistic, ruthless, shrewd, unsentimental.

hard-boiled *adj* tough, cynical, hardened, hardheaded, hard-nosed, down-to-earth, world-weary, unsentimental.

hard-core *adj* **1** (*hard-core revolutionary*) steadfast, staunch, dedicated, diehard, dyed-in-the-wool, intransigent, rigid, uncompromising, obstinate, stubborn, extreme. **2** (*hard-core movies*) explicit, blatant, obscene, pornographic, blue (*inf*).

harden *verb* **1** (*the mixture will harden*) solidify, compact, set, stiffen, petrify, freeze, bake, cake, congeal, clot, coagulate, anneal. OPPOSITE: soften. **2** (*you must harden your heart*) strengthen, toughen, fortify, buttress, brace, steel, temper, reinforce, deaden, benumb, numb, nerve. OPPOSITE: weaken. **3** (*harden oneself to physical discomfort*) inure, season, habituate, accustom, acclimatize, break in, train, discipline.

hardened *adj* inveterate, confirmed, seasoned, toughened, inured, unfeeling, habitual, accustomed, habituated, chronic, shameless, reprobate, unregenerate, impenitent, incorrigible, irredeemable, obdurate, set, fixed.

hardheaded *adj* shrewd, astute, keen, sharp, sharp-witted, wise, levelheaded, coolheaded, clear-thinking, rational, businesslike, sensible, down-to-earth, realistic, practical, pragmatic, cool, unsentimental, hard-bitten, hard-boiled, hard-nosed, tough.

hardhearted *adj* cold, callous, hard, stony, stonyhearted, indifferent, insensitive, unmoved, obdurate, unfeeling, uncaring, unconcerned, insensible, unkind, uncompassionate, unsympathetic, coldhearted, heartless, cruel, inhuman, pitiless, merciless, intolerant, implacable. OPPOSITE: softhearted.

hard-hitting *adj* tough, uncompromising, unsparing, no-holds-barred (*inf*), condemnatory, critical, unsparing, bold, direct, blunt, frank, straight, straight-talking, vigorous, forceful.

hardihood *noun* **1** (*the hardihood of the early explorers*) courage, bravery, valour, heroism, guts (*inf*), pluck, mettle, nerve, spirit, intrepidity, boldness, audacity, daring, fearlessness, strength, firmness, hardiness, fortitude, determination, resolution. OPPOSITE: cowardice. **2** (*the hardihood of a mouse in challenging a lion*) audacity, effrontery, temerity, impudence, impertinence, impetuousness, rashness, recklessness, foolhardiness, assurance. OPPOSITE: caution.

hardiness *noun* robustness, toughness, ruggedness, sturdiness, healthiness, vigour, resilience.

hard-line *adj* uncompromising, strict, tough, extreme, immoderate, inflexible, intransigent, militant, unyielding, undeviating.

hardly *adv* scarcely, barely, narrowly, faintly, just, only just, not quite, not at all, by no means.

hardness *noun* **1** (*the hardness of the material*) solidity, firmness, rigidity, stiffness, resistance, strength, toughness. OPPOSITE: softness. **2** (*the hardness of the problem*) difficulty, arduousness, laboriousness, strenuousness, rigour, severity, complexity, intricacy. OPPOSITE: easiness. **3** (*showed hardness towards the inmates*) harshness, severity, strictness, sternness, firmness, rigidity, cruelty, inhumanity, pitilessness, callousness, insensitivity, coldness, unkindness. OPPOSITE: tenderness.

hard-pressed *adj* **1** (*hard-pressed by their attackers*) harried, hounded, pursued, under attack. **2** (*hard-pressed teachers*) hard-pushed, hard put, pushed (*inf*), harassed, under pressure, overburdened, overloaded, overtaxed, overworked, up against it (*inf*).

hardship *noun* trouble, difficulty, trial, tribulation, affliction, pain, suffering, torment, distress, misery, wretchedness, misfortune, adversity, privation, deprivation, want, need, poverty, destitution, austerity, burden, calamity, grievance, labour, travail, oppression, persecution. OPPOSITE: prosperity.

hard-wearing *adj* durable, lasting, resilient, well-made, strong, tough, stout, sturdy, rugged.

hard-working *adj* industrious, diligent, assiduous, sedulous, conscientious, enthusiastic, keen, zealous, busy, energetic, indefatigable.

hardy *adj* **1** (*they are hardy souls*) strong, tough, rugged, firm, sturdy, robust, hale, hearty, lusty, vigorous, sound, fit, healthy. OPPOSITE: weak. **2** (*hardy warriors*) courageous, brave, heroic, plucky, manly, mettlesome, valiant, valorous, intrepid, indomitable, fearless, feisty (*inf*), gritty, undaunted, daring, bold, audacious, determined, resolute, stalwart, stout, stouthearted, stoical. OPPOSITE: cowardly. **3** (*a hardy approach*) rash, audacious, reckless, foolhardy, headstrong, impetuous, impudent, daredevil, brazen. OPPOSITE: cautious.

harebrained *adj* **1** (*a harebrained idea*) daft, foolish, foolhardy, rash, reckless, ridiculous, crackpot (*inf*), mad, madcap, wild, half-baked, ill-conceived, ill-thought-out. **2** (*a harebrained young man*) foolish, silly, half-witted (*inf*), empty-headed, scatty (*inf*), scatterbrained, featherbrained, brainless, giddy, dizzy, whimsical, capricious, flighty, unstable.

hark *verb* listen, hear, give ear, hearken, pay attention, pay heed, note, notice, mark. OPPOSITE: ignore.

hark back recall, go back, turn back, look back, think back, remember, recollect, revert, retrovert, regress.

harlequin *noun* jester, fool, clown, joker, comic, buffoon, zany.

harlot *noun* prostitute, pro (*inf*), whore, call girl, streetwalker, tart (*inf*), hooker (*inf*), slag (*inf*), scrubber (*inf*), working girl (*inf*), hussy, trollop, strumpet, fallen woman (*inf*).

harm *verb* hurt, injure, wound, damage, destroy, ruin, impair, mar, spoil, blemish, deface, defile, maltreat, ill-treat, ill-use, abuse, molest. OPPOSITE: benefit.
➤ *noun* **1** (*cause others harm*) hurt, pain, injury, suffering, trauma, damage, defacement, defilement, impairment, destruction, loss, ruin, havoc, abuse, adversity, disservice, detriment, mischief, misfortune. **2** (*nursed a heart full of harm*) evil, ill, wrong,

wrongdoing, sin, sinfulness, immorality, iniquity, nefariousness, vice, wickedness, badness. OPPOSITE: good.

harmful adj **1** (*harmful results*) hurtful, injurious, wounding, dangerous, hazardous, damaging, destructive, deleterious, detrimental, disadvantageous, pernicious, noxious, poisonous, toxic, unhealthy, mischievous, baleful, baneful. OPPOSITE: beneficial. **2** (*a harmful presence*) evil, wicked, bad, malign, corrupting, subversive.

harmless adj **1** (*harmless chemicals*) safe, nontoxic, nonirritant, mild, innocuous, innoxious. **2** (*a harmless remark*) innocuous, inoffensive, unobjectionable, blameless, innocent, gentle, mild. OPPOSITE: pernicious.

harmonious adj **1** (*harmonious sounds*) harmonic, tuneful, melodious, euphonious, mellifluous, dulcet, mellow, musical, sweet-sounding, pleasant, harmonizing, symphonious, rhythmic. OPPOSITE: cacophonous. **2** (*harmonious colours*) matching, well-matched, coordinated, balanced, compatible, concordant, congruous, consistent, correspondent, consonant. **3** (*harmonious relations*) agreeable, amiable, amicable, friendly, compatible, congenial, cordial, fraternal, sympathetic, likeminded, peaceful, peaceable. OPPOSITE: discordant.

harmonize verb **1** (*the two parts harmonize*) agree, accord, correspond, go together, go well with, get on with, chime with, tally, reconcile, coincide, match, balance, coordinate, suit, fit in, tone, blend, mix. **2** (*a need to harmonize policies*) accommodate, adapt, arrange, compose, attune. OPPOSITE: differentiate.

harmony noun **1** (*the harmony of the tune*) tunefulness, tune, melody, melodiousness, mellifluousness, euphony, euphoniousness. **2** (*they were in harmony over the issue*) accord, concord, accordance, concordance, concurrence, agreement, consensus, assent, likemindedness, unison, unanimity, oneness, unity. **3** (*a natural harmony between the two parts*) affinity, balance, symmetry, blending, consonance, congruity, conformity, compatibility, correspondence, coordination, sympathy. **4** (*harmony between the two sides*) amity, amicability, friendliness, friendship, fellowship, comradeship, peace, understanding, cooperation, goodwill, rapport. OPPOSITE: discord.

harness noun tackle, tack, reins, straps, bridle, yoke, equipment, accoutrements, gear, trappings.
 » verb **1** (*harness a team of horses*) saddle, bridle, hitch up, couple, yoke. **2** (*harness the powers of nature*) control, utilize, exploit, channel, employ, apply, mobilize, free. **in harness** working, at work, employed, in action, active, busy.

harp verb **harp on** dwell, go on, repeat, nag, reiterate, labour, press, push, persist, insist.

harridan noun hag, virago, battleaxe (*inf*), old bag (*inf*), witch, dragon, harpy, vixen, nag, scold, fishwife, shrew, tartar, fury, gorgon, hellcat, spitfire, termagant.

harrowing adj distressing, disturbing, alarming, daunting, perturbing, upsetting, heartbreaking, heartrending, tormenting, afflicting, agonizing, excruciating, painful, wounding, traumatic, vexing,

frightening, terrifying, nerve-racking, unnerving, chilling, horrifying. OPPOSITE: soothing.

harry verb **1** (*raiders harrying the whole region*) ravage, devastate, raid, plunder, pillage, sack, rob, despoil, lay waste. **2** (*keep on harrying the council*) badger, pester, hassle (*inf*), nag, chivvy, harass, plague, torment, worry, fret, trouble, annoy, bother, exasperate, disturb, molest, vex, bedevil. OPPOSITE: appease.

harsh adj **1** (*a harsh whisper*) rough, coarse, gravelly, gruff, hoarse, croaking, guttural. **2** (*harsh sounds*) strident, shrill, ear-piercing, sharp, grating, rasping, grinding, cacophonous, dissonant, unharmonious, raucous, discordant, jarring, jangling, metallic, unpleasant. OPPOSITE: mellow. **3** (*harsh colours*) glaring, dazzling, bright, showy, loud, flashy, gaudy, garish, lurid, bold, crass, crude, vulgar. OPPOSITE: soft. **4** (*a harsh taste*) acrid, bitter, sharp, sour. **5** (*she got a harsh refusal*) curt, blunt, brusque, abrupt, short, concise, clipped, gruff, surly, discourteous, uncivil, ungracious. **6** (*a harsh regime*) severe, strict, stern, merciless, pitiless, unrelenting, ruthless, unfeeling, uncompassionate, brutal, cruel, despotic, tyrannical, draconian, hardhearted, inhuman, barbarous, savage. OPPOSITE: compassionate. **7** (*a harsh decision*) stern, severe, punitive, unforgiving, draconian. **8** (*harsh surroundings*) austere, barren, bleak, desolate, severe, stark, savage, bitter, grim, comfortless, inhospitable, wild, Spartan. **9** (*a harsh climate*) severe, extreme, hard, bitter, cold, freezing, arctic. OPPOSITE: mild. **10** (*harsh treatment*) hard, stern, cruel, unkind, pitiless, merciless, ruthless, unfeeling, brutal, abrasive, tough, acerbic, stringent, inhuman, unsympathetic. OPPOSITE: gentle.

harvest noun **1** (*a busy harvest*) harvesting, reaping, gathering-in. **2** (*a good harvest of fruit*) crop, yield, produce. **3** (*a hidden harvest of nuts*) store, stockpile, stock, hoard, cache, supply, accumulation. **4** (*the harvest of all her efforts*) result, consequence, outcome, issue, product, return, effect, fruits.
 » verb **1** (*harvest the crop*) gather, reap, mow, pick, pluck, glean. **2** (*too busy to harvest nuts*) garner, collect, amass, accumulate, hoard, stockpile. **3** (*harvest the rewards of all his work*) acquire, gain, obtain, get, secure, net, derive, procure.

hash noun mess, jumble, muddle, mix-up, screw-up (*inf*), confusion, medley, mishmash, hotchpotch, botch, bungle, mismanagement.

hassle noun **1** (*too much hassle for me*) trouble, inconvenience, bother, tribulation, nuisance, annoyance, difficulty, problem, struggle, harassment. **2** (*a bit of hassle after the match*) fighting, aggro (*inf*), argy-bargy (*inf*), squabbling, quarrelling, unpleasantness, disputing, bickering, altercation, disagreement, wrangling, tussling, struggling.
 » verb bother, bug (*inf*), pester, trouble, worry, annoy, badger, harass, plague, torment, hound, harry, chivvy.

haste noun **1** (*made haste to escape*) speed, rapidity, rapidness, swiftness, quickness, fastness, fleetness, celerity, velocity, dispatch, expedition, expeditiousness, promptitude, promptness, alacrity, briskness, nimbleness, urgency, immediateness. OPPOSITE: delay. **2** (*a decision made in haste*) hastiness, hurriedness, hurry, rush, bustle, hustle, precipitance, precipitateness, recklessness, rashness, foolhardiness, impetuosity, impulsiveness, carelessness, heedlessness. OPPOSITE: caution.

hasten *verb* **1** (*hasten the process*) quicken, hurry on, speed up, accelerate, advance, precipitate, expedite, dispatch, urge on, press on, push forward, goad, aid, boost, assist, help, facilitate, step up. OPPOSITE: retard. **2** (*hasten down the road*) make haste, hurry, rush, dash, race, fly, speed, run, sprint, hightail it (*inf*), hotfoot it (*inf*), bolt, beetle, scurry, scamper, scuttle, tear. OPPOSITE: dawdle.

hasty *adj* **1** (*a hasty escape*) quick, fast, rapid, speedy, swift, fleet, brisk, prompt, urgent, expeditious. OPPOSITE: slow. **2** (*a hasty check*) hurried, quick, rapid, rushed, superficial, cursory, perfunctory, transitory, fleeting, passing, brief, short, slight. OPPOSITE: thorough. **3** (*a hasty decision*) reckless, rash, hurried, rushed, impetuous, impulsive, precipitate, headlong, heedless, careless, thoughtless, ill-conceived, indiscreet, foolhardy, passionate. OPPOSITE: cautious. **4** (*a hasty character*) irascible, touchy, testy, short-tempered, quick-tempered, hotheaded, irritable, snappy, snappish, peevish, petulant, waspish, brusque, impatient, excitable, fiery, choleric, volatile. OPPOSITE: placid.

hatch *verb* **1** (*hatch a new clutch*) incubate, brood, sit on, breed, bring forth. **2** (*hatch a scheme for making a fortune*) contrive, devise, concoct, brew, conceive, think up, dream up (*inf*), cook up (*inf*), trump up (*inf*), invent, originate, formulate, manufacture, design, plot, plan, project, scheme.

hatchet *noun* axe, chopper, cleaver, battleaxe, tomahawk, pickaxe, machete, poleaxe.

hate *verb* **1** (*I hate her*) detest, despise, loathe, abhor, abominate, execrate, dislike, recoil from, shudder at. OPPOSITE: love. **2** (*I hate to disappoint you*) dislike, regret, apologize, be loath, be reluctant, flinch from, shrink from.
➤ *noun* hatred, detestation, loathing, abhorrence, odium, abomination, execration, aversion, dislike, antipathy, hostility, animosity, rancour, ill will, enmity, antagonism, resentment, bitterness, grudge. OPPOSITE: love.

hateful *adj* detestable, loathsome, abhorrent, abominable, odious, execrable, contemptible, despicable, horrible, horrid, obnoxious, vile, evil, heinous, foul, disgusting, offensive, nasty, repulsive, repellent, repugnant, revolting, disagreeable, unpleasant. OPPOSITE: delightful.

hatred *noun* hate, detestation, loathing, abhorrence, odium, abomination, execration, aversion, dislike, antipathy, hostility, enmity, animosity, rancour, ill will, antagonism, revulsion, repugnance, resentment, bitterness, grudge. OPPOSITE: love.

haughtiness *noun* arrogance, self-importance, hauteur, aloofness, loftiness, superciliousness, snobbishness, snootiness (*inf*), pomposity, airs, pride, conceit, contempt, contemptuousness, insolence, disdain. OPPOSITE: humility.

haughty *adj* arrogant, self-important, lofty, superior, vain, conceited, egotistical, swollen-headed, proud, presumptuous, supercilious, disdainful, condescending, patronizing, contemptuous, scornful, snobbish, snooty (*inf*), stuck-up (*inf*), hoity-toity (*inf*), high and mighty (*inf*), high-handed, overbearing, imperious, lordly, cavalier, aloof. OPPOSITE: humble.

haul *verb* **1** (*haul it out of the cave*) drag, lug, draw, pull, tow, tug, heave. OPPOSITE: push. **2** (*haul to the nearest town*) carry, convey, transport, ship, cart, move, hump (*inf*).
➤ *noun* catch, harvest, yield, gain, find, takings, spoils, booty, loot, plunder, swag (*inf*).

haunt *verb* **1** (*his spirit still haunts the castle*) roam, walk, visit, appear, materialize, possess. **2** (*haunt cheap bars*) frequent, visit, patronize, hang around (*inf*), repair, resort. **3** (*haunted by past failures*) obsess, possess, prey on, beset, harry, oppress, burden, weigh on, plague, torment, trouble, disturb, worry, recur, come back, stay with.
➤ *noun* retreat, resort, refuge, den, local (*inf*), meeting-place, rendezvous, stamping-ground, watering-hole (*inf*), hangout (*inf*).

haunted *adj* **1** (*haunted by a headless coachman*) possessed, cursed, spooky (*inf*), ghostly, eerie, hag-ridden, jinxed. **2** (*haunted by her past*) troubled, obsessed, preoccupied, worried, plagued, tormented.

haunting *adj* **1** (*a haunting theme*) evocative, nostalgic, atmospheric, poignant, wistful, disturbing, eerie, memorable. **2** (*haunting memories*) unforgettable, persistent, recurrent, recurring.

have *verb* **1** (*they have tickets for the show*) own, possess, hold, keep, retain. OPPOSITE: lack. **2** (*have a cigarette*) take, accept, receive, obtain, get, gain, acquire, procure. OPPOSITE: lose. **3** (*the module will have two parts*) comprise, consist of, include, contain, take in, embrace, incorporate, embody. **4** (*we have had problems*) experience, meet, encounter, find, undergo, go through, suffer, endure, submit to, tolerate, put up with. **5** (*have a good holiday*) enjoy, experience, go through. **6** (*he has a dream*) foster, entertain, nurse, cherish, harbour. **7** (*have a public debate*) arrange, organize, hold, participate in, take part in. **8** (*I shall have someone come round*) make, arrange, get, cause, oblige, require, persuade, induce, prevail upon, talk into, ask, tell, order, instruct, request, command, bid, force, compel, coerce. **9** (*have the cheek to protest*) show, display, manifest, demonstrate, exhibit, express. **10** (*have something with us*) eat, take, partake of, tuck into (*inf*), consume, swallow, devour, drink, down, knock back (*inf*), gulp, guzzle. **11** (*I just won't have it in my school*) put up with, take, stand, tolerate, bear, accept, allow, permit, abide, brook, entertain, consider. OPPOSITE: forbid. **12** (*they've been had*) cheat, swindle, deceive, dupe, take in (*inf*), fool, trick, con (*inf*), stiff (*inf*), diddle (*inf*), do (*inf*), outwit. **13** (*she had a girl*) bear, give birth to, bring into the world, bring forth, deliver, beget. **14** (*he said he had had her twice*) have sex with, make love to, copulate with, seduce, lay (*inf*), bed (*inf*).

have on 1 (*what did she have on?*) wear, be dressed in, be clothed in. **2** (*have a lot on tomorrow*) have arranged, have planned. **3** (*you're having me on*) tease, trick, kid (*inf*), joke with, wind up (*inf*), pull one's leg (*inf*).
have to must, ought to, should, be obliged to, be forced to, be compelled to.

haven *noun* **1** (*a haven for large ships*) harbour, harbourage, port, anchorage, moorage, dock, bay, cove. **2** (*a safe haven*) shelter, refuge, sanctuary, sanctum, asylum, retreat, oasis.

haversack *noun* backpack, rucksack, knapsack, kitbag, satchel.

havoc *noun* **1** (*the storm caused havoc*) damage, destruction, devastation, desolation, waste, wreck, wreckage, ruin, ruination, rack and ruin, carnage, slaughter, ravaging, despoliation. **2** (*created havoc in the office*) confusion, disorder, chaos, mayhem, shambles (*inf*), disruption, disorganization.

hawk *verb* peddle, sell, market, offer, vend, tout, cry, bark (*inf*).

hawker *noun* pedlar, door-to-door salesman, vendor, travelling salesman, touter, colporteur, huckster, crier.

haywire *adj* wrong, out of control, erratic, crazy, mad, wild, chaotic, confused, mixed up, disordered, disarranged, disorganized, tangled, shambolic (*inf*), topsy-turvy.

hazard *noun* **1** (*that constitutes a hazard*) danger, threat, menace, deathtrap, pitfall, risk, peril, jeopardy. **2** (*a game of hazard*) chance, luck, accident, fluke, gamble.
➢ *verb* **1** (*hazard a guess*) advance, venture, put forward, submit, offer, proffer, volunteer, dare, gamble, speculate, conjecture, stake, risk, chance. OPPOSITE: withdraw. **2** (*hazard the lives of the hostages*) risk, put at risk, endanger, imperil, jeopardize, expose.

hazardous *adj* **1** (*a hazardous route*) dangerous, risky, perilous, hairy (*inf*), dicey (*inf*), menacing, threatening, unsafe, insecure, precarious, fraught. OPPOSITE: safe. **2** (*a hazardous mission*) uncertain, unpredictable, random, haphazard, speculative, chancy (*inf*), risky. OPPOSITE: certain.

haze *noun* **1** (*a haze over the valley*) mist, mistiness, fog, fogginess, cloud, cloudiness, vapour, steam, smog, smoke, smokiness, film. **2** (*by the time she finished she was in a haze*) blur, confusion, bewilderment, uncertainty, befuddlement, muddle, vagueness, indistinctness, obscurity, dimness, haziness.

hazy *adj* **1** (*a hazy afternoon*) misty, foggy, cloudy, clouded, obscure, overcast, milky, smoky, smoggy, nebulous, filmy. OPPOSITE: clear. **2** (*a hazy recollection*) vague, indistinct, faint, fuzzy, blurry, blurred, muzzy, dim, veiled, unclear, obscure, ill-defined, indefinite, uncertain, muddled, confused, loose. OPPOSITE: definite.

head *noun* **1** (*put his hat on his head*) skull, cranium, pate (*inf*), nut (*inf*), noddle (*inf*), bonce (*inf*), conk (*inf*). OPPOSITE: foot. **2** (*use your head for once*) mind, brain, intellect, intelligence, reasoning, wit, wits, wisdom, sense, common sense, rationality, mentality, thought, understanding, genius, brains (*inf*), grey matter (*inf*), loaf (*inf*), noddle (*inf*). **3** (*a head for figures*) aptitude, flair, talent, faculty, ability, capacity, brain, mind. **4** (*the head of the organization*) leader, chief, controller, administrator, principal, headteacher, master, ruler, captain, commander, boss, director, manager, chairman, chairwoman, chair, chairperson, superintendent, supervisor, president, premier, prime minister, governor, chieftain. OPPOSITE: subordinate. **5** (*at the head of the company*) headship, top, command, leadership,
directorship, management, control, supervision, charge. **6** (*the head of the pass*) summit, top, apex, crown, crest, brow, peak, tip, vertex, acme, climax, zenith, height. OPPOSITE: base. **7** (*at the head of the column*) front, forefront, fore, vanguard, van, lead, beginning, start. OPPOSITE: end. **8** (*matters came to a head*) climax, culmination, crisis, turning point, crossroads, crunch (*inf*). **9** (*the head of the river*) source, fount, rise, spring, wellspring, wellhead, origin. **10** (*I like a head on my beer*) froth, foam, lather, suds, bubbles. **11** (*organized under different heads*) heading, section, subject, topic, branch, division, category, class, classification, department.
➢ *verb* **1** (*head the queue*) lead, go first, precede. OPPOSITE: follow. **2** (*head the country*) lead, command, direct, control, guide, steer, govern, rule, run, manage, administer, superintend, supervise, oversee.
➢ *adj* leading, first, chief, prime, principal, main, supreme, highest, premier, top, topmost, front, foremost, pre-eminent, dominant.

go to one's head 1 (*gin goes to his head*) intoxicate, inebriate, make drunk, befuddle. **2** (*success has gone to her head*) puff up (*inf*), excite, dizzy, intoxicate, overwhelm.

head for make for, steer for, turn for, aim for, direct towards, point towards, go towards, set out for, start out for.

head off intercept, intervene, divert, deflect, turn aside, avert, parry, fend off, ward off, forestall, prevent, stop, check, balk, block off, cut off.

head over heels completely, utterly, thoroughly, fully, wholeheartedly, uncontrollably, recklessly, madly (*inf*), intensely, passionately, fervently, fervidly, wildly.

keep one's head keep calm, keep cool, keep one's cool (*inf*), keep one's composure.

lose one's head panic, flap (*inf*), get excited, lose control, lose one's cool (*inf*), lose it (*inf*), blow one's top (*inf*), freak out (*inf*).

headache *noun* **1** (*gone to bed with a headache*) migraine, neuralgia, thick head (*inf*). **2** (*the children are a headache*) bother, pest, nuisance, pain (*inf*), pain in the neck (*inf*), problem, hassle (*inf*), trouble, inconvenience, worry, vexation, bane.

heading *noun* **1** (*read the headings under each picture*) title, rubric, caption, headline, name. **2** (*assembled under different headings*) section, division, head, category, class, classification, subject, topic, branch, department.

headland *noun* cape, head, promontory, foreland, spur, point, cliff, bluff.

headlong *adv* **1** (*ran headlong into the group of policemen*) headfirst, head-on. **2** (*dash headlong into a crisis*) hastily, hurriedly, precipitately, prematurely, pell-mell, helter-skelter, wildly, impetuously, impulsively, recklessly, rashly, impatiently, unrestrainedly, carelessly, heedlessly, thoughtlessly, without thinking. OPPOSITE: cautiously.
➢ *adj* hasty, rash, precipitate, reckless, careless, heedless, thoughtless, impetuous, impulsive, breakneck, foolhardy, dangerous. OPPOSITE: cautious.

head-on *adj* direct, full-frontal (*inf*), face-to-face, eyeball-to-eyeball (*inf*), straight-on, straight.

headquarters *pl noun* HQ, base, base camp, homebase,

command base, main branch, centre of operations, nerve centre, head office, main office.

headstrong adj **1** (*a headstrong character*) wilful, self-willed, obstinate, stubborn, mulish, stiff-necked, intractable, pigheaded, perverse, contrary, refractory, recalcitrant, intransigent, inflexible, unyielding, unruly, obdurate, ungovernable, wayward. OPPOSITE: tractable. **2** (*headstrong behaviour*) rash, reckless, imprudent, foolhardy, heedless. OPPOSITE: prudent.

headway noun progress, advance, ground, way, improvement, development, progression, movement, motion. OPPOSITE: regression.

heady adj **1** (*a heady brew*) intoxicating, strong, potent, inebriating. **2** (*a heady atmosphere*) exciting, thrilling, exhilarating, stimulating, rousing, arousing, invigorating, galvanizing, electrifying, intoxicating, overwhelming, overpowering, euphoric, ecstatic. **3** (*a heady nature*) rash, reckless, headlong, precipitate, hasty, impulsive, impetuous, wild, imprudent, incautious, foolhardy, heedless, thoughtless. OPPOSITE: cautious.

heal verb **1** (*the broken bone slowly healed*) mend, cure, remedy, treat, make well, get better, get well, recover, improve. **2** (*tried to heal the breach between them*) restore, repair, mend, put right, set right, reconcile, conciliate, patch up, make good, settle. OPPOSITE: aggravate. **3** (*in an attempt to heal her broken heart*) appease, assuage, soothe, comfort, soften, allay, alleviate, palliate, ameliorate, mitigate, salve.

healing adj curative, restorative, restoring, analeptic, remedial, medicinal, therapeutic, palliative, lenitive, soothing, comforting, gentle, mild. OPPOSITE: harmful.

health noun **1** (*a picture of health*) healthiness, fitness, well-being, soundness, robustness, haleness, strength, vigour. OPPOSITE: illness. **2** (*questions about his health*) condition, constitution, welfare, state, shape, form, tone, fettle.

healthy adj **1** (*I feel very healthy*) fit, fine, well, right as rain (*inf*), in the pink (*inf*), sound, robust, hale, hearty, hale and hearty, hardy (*inf*), sturdy, strong, vigorous, lusty, good, blooming, flourishing, thriving, able-bodied, active. OPPOSITE: ill. **2** (*a healthy diet*) healthful, health-giving, wholesome, nutritious, nourishing, good, sensible. **3** (*a healthy regime*) healthful, health-giving, beneficial, wholesome, good, bracing, invigorating, refreshing, stimulating, salubrious, salutary, hygienic, tonic. OPPOSITE: unhealthy.

heap noun **1** (*a heap of leaves*) pile, mound, mountain, stack, mass. **2** (*we've got heaps of time*) abundance, superabundance, plenty, quantities, great deal, lots, loads (*inf*), stacks (*inf*), lashings (*inf*), tons (*inf*), oodles (*inf*), pots (*inf*), millions (*inf*), scores (*inf*), oceans (*inf*), mass, hoard, stock, stockpile, store, supply, accumulation, assemblage, agglomeration, conglomeration, collection, bundle.
➤ verb **1** (*heap everything over there*) pile, stack, bank, build, amass, accumulate, gather, collect, assemble, hoard, store, stockpile, set aside, lay by. OPPOSITE: scatter. **2** (*heap praise upon them*) load, burden, shower, pour, lavish, supply, bestow, confer, assign, grant.

hear verb **1** (*hear what they were saying*) listen to, catch, make out, latch on to (*inf*), perceive, overhear,

eavesdrop, hark, hearken, heed, take in, attend. OPPOSITE: ignore. **2** (*I hear you're leaving*) learn, gather, understand, discover, find out, ascertain, hear tell, pick up, get wind of (*inf*), be informed, be told. **3** (*we shall hear the case next month*) try, pass judgment on, judge, adjudicate, examine, investigate, consider, inquire into.

hearing noun **1** (*test her hearing*) aural faculty, perception, ear. **2** (*adjourn the hearing*) audience, interview, examination, investigation, review, inquiry, inquest, inquisition, trial, tribunal, adjudication, judgment. **3** (*told everyone within hearing*) earshot, range, reach, sound.

hearsay noun rumour, gossip, word of mouth, common knowledge, talk, idle talk, report, buzz (*inf*), dirt (*inf*), grapevine (*inf*), tattle, tittle-tattle.

heart noun **1** (*heart of the matter*) core, centre, middle, kernel, nucleus, nub, hub, marrow, pith, root, essence, quintessence, substance, crux. OPPOSITE: surface. **2** (*have you no heart?*) tenderness, warmth, benevolence, compassion, concern, sympathy, empathy, pity, responsiveness, goodwill, humanity, humanitarianism, fellow feeling, kindness, kindliness, soul, spirit. **3** (*give it some heart*) passion, emotion, feeling, love, affection, warmth, soul, spirit, enthusiasm, liveliness. **4** (*showed great heart in battle*) courage, bravery, valour, fearlessness, heroism, guts (*inf*), balls (*sl*), fortitude, intrepidity, nerve, pluck, mettle, backbone, nerve, spirit, boldness, resolution, purpose, determination, stoutheartedness, eagerness, keenness, enthusiasm. OPPOSITE: cowardice.

at heart basically, actually, truly, in truth, really, in reality, fundamentally, at bottom, essentially, in essence, intrinsically, innately.

by heart by rote, parrot-fashion, pat, off pat, by memory, word for word, verbatim.

change of heart change of mind, change of tune, rethink, second thoughts.

from the bottom of one's heart deeply, sincerely, earnestly, heartily, passionately, profoundly, devoutly, fervently.

heart and soul eagerly, enthusiastically, completely, thoroughly, unreservedly, wholeheartedly, devotedly, gladly, heartily, zealously, absolutely, entirely.

set one's heart on wish for, long for, want, desire, yearn for, crave.

take heart cheer up, brighten up, buck up (*inf*), perk up (*inf*), rally, revive.

heartache noun distress, anguish, grief, sadness, sorrow, remorse, woe, misery, wretchedness, pain, agony, torment, torture, suffering, affliction, despair, bitterness, anxiety, worry, desolation, dejection, despondency, heartbreak. OPPOSITE: joy.

heartbreaking adj heartrending, distressing, sad, affecting, pitiful, tear-jerking, tragic, harrowing, agonizing, excruciating, grievous, bitter, harsh, painful, cruel, disappointing, poignant, desolating.

heartbroken adj brokenhearted, heartsick, sad, miserable, sorrowful, low, dismal, dejected, despondent, disheartened, dispirited, desolate, crushed, anguished, downcast, suffering, crestfallen, disappointed, grieving, grieved.

hearten *verb* cheer, cheer up, buoy up, buck up (*inf*), comfort, console, assure, reassure, encourage, boost, embolden, inspirit, inspire, animate, energize, rouse, incite, stimulate, pep up (*inf*), uplift, invigorate, elate, exhilarate, revitalize, revivify. OPPOSITE: depress.

heartfelt *adj* sincere, profound, deep, deepfelt, honest, genuine, unfeigned, hearty, cordial, kindly, warm, compassionate, earnest, ardent, devout, fervent, enthusiastic, eager, wholehearted. OPPOSITE: insincere.

heartily *adv* 1 (*praised them heartily*) warmly, cordially, feelingly, deeply, genuinely, profoundly, sincerely, wholeheartedly, gladly. 2 (*he worked heartily*) eagerly, enthusiastically, energetically, vigorously, earnestly, resolutely, zealously. 3 (*heartily fed up*) completely, absolutely, totally, thoroughly, very.

heartless *adj* cruel, unkind, unfeeling, uncaring, inconsiderate, uncompassionate, unsympathetic, unmoved, untouched, hard, hardhearted, cold, coldhearted, callous, harsh, stern, brutal, pitiless, merciless, ruthless, savage, cold-blooded, inhuman. OPPOSITE: kind.

heartrending *adj* heartbreaking, tear-jerking, harrowing, agonizing, painful, distressing, pitiful, piteous, pathetic, sad, tragic, affecting, moving, poignant.

heartsick *adj* sad, heartsore, heavyhearted, despondent, dejected, depressed, downcast, dispirited, disappointed, melancholy, glum, low.

heartwarming *adj* cheering, cheerful, heartening, warming, uplifting, gladdening, gratifying, satisfying, pleasing, encouraging, touching, moving, affecting, rewarding.

hearty *adj* 1 (*a hearty greeting*) genial, cordial, jovial, cheerful, amiable, affable, friendly, warm, warmhearted, ardent, earnest, unreserved, uninhibited, heartfelt, sincere, enthusiastic, eager, ebullient, effusive, exuberant. OPPOSITE: cool 2 (*a hearty dislike of the man*) profound, real, earnest, wholehearted, absolute, complete, total, thorough, genuine, unfeigned. 3 (*a hearty man*) strong, hale, healthy, well, robust, stalwart, sturdy, hardy, sound, vigorous, lusty, energetic, boisterous. OPPOSITE: feeble. 4 (*ate a hearty breakfast*) nourishing, nutritious, filling, substantial, generous, ample, abundant, large, sizeable, square, solid. OPPOSITE: meagre.

heat *noun* 1 (*the heat of summer*) warmth, warmness, hotness, high temperature, torridness, swelter, sultriness, closeness, calefaction. OPPOSITE: cold. 2 (*the heat of desire*) passion, warmth, zeal, ardour, earnestness, eagerness, enthusiasm, fervour, fervency, vehemence, intensity, violence, frenzy, rage, anger, fury, fieriness, excitement, agitation, animation, impetuosity. OPPOSITE: coolness.

➤ *verb* 1 (*heat in a warm oven*) warm, warm up, cook, heat up, reheat, make hot, boil, toast, microwave, bake, roast. OPPOSITE: chill. 2 (*heat the emotions*) excite, inflame, warm, stir, inspirit, rouse, arouse, stimulate, animate, impassion, anger, enrage, annoy. OPPOSITE: cool.

heated *adj* furious, angry, raging, passionate, impassioned, stormy, tempestuous, fiery, fierce, bitter, intense, vehement, violent, enraged, inflamed, excited, frenzied, animated, stirred, fired, stimulated, roused, worked-up (*inf*).

heathen *noun* pagan, infidel, unbeliever, disbeliever, idolater, idolatress, barbarian, savage, philistine, heretic, sceptic, atheist, agnostic.

➤ *adj* pagan, unbelieving, infidel, philistine, idolatrous, godless, ungodly, irreligious, heretical, barbarous, barbaric, savage, primitive, uncivilized, brutish, unenlightened. OPPOSITE: godly.

heave *verb* 1 (*heave the body over the side*) haul, drag, pull, tug, hoist, raise, lift, elevate, lever, hitch, heft (*inf*). 2 (*heave the ball into the air*) throw, chuck (*inf*), cast, fling, hurl, sling (*inf*), pitch, send, toss, let fly. 3 (*the ground heaved*) surge, swell, rise, expand, throb, billow, roll. 4 (*heave a sigh of relief*) pant, sigh, breathe, blow, gasp, groan, puff, sob, utter, give, let out, express. 5 (*the sight made him heave*) retch, gag, vomit, throw up (*inf*), spew (*inf*), chuck (*inf*).

heaven *noun* 1 (*the angels in heaven*) paradise, hereafter, afterworld, afterlife, life to come, life everlasting, next world, better place, kingdom of God, Elysium, elysian fields, Valhalla, Zion, happy hunting-ground, nirvana, utopia. OPPOSITE: hell. 2 (*I was in heaven*) ecstasy, rapture, bliss, happiness, felicity, joy, delight. OPPOSITE: torment.

heavenly *adj* 1 (*heavenly beings*) holy, angelic, seraphic, cherubic, saintly, godlike, blessed, beatific, divine, celestial, cosmic, extraterrestrial, immortal, supernatural, spiritual, unearthly, otherworldly. OPPOSITE: earthly. 2 (*a heavenly sight*) wonderful, marvellous, superb, delightful, lovely, beautiful, enchanting, entrancing, ravishing, alluring, exquisite, perfect, sublime, glorious, divine, blissful, rapturous, enjoyable, pleasurable, gratifying. OPPOSITE: abominable.

heavens *pl noun* sky, skies, ether, firmament.

heavily *adv* 1 (*breathing heavily*) hard, laboriously, painfully, ponderously, slowly, clumsily, awkwardly, with difficulty, sluggishly, weightily. 2 (*heavily ornamented*) compactly, densely, closely, solidly, thick, thickly. 3 (*heavily defeated*) utterly, decisively, absolutely, completely, thoroughly, roundly, soundly. 4 (*smoking heavily*) excessively, copiously, abundantly, considerably, to excess, too much, very much. OPPOSITE: lightly.

heaviness *noun* 1 (*struggled under the heaviness of his load*) weight, weightiness, heftiness, ponderousness, bulk, density, mass, solidity, thickness. OPPOSITE: lightness. 2 (*the heaviness of the sentence*) severity, harshness, oppressiveness, intensity. 3 (*an atmosphere of heaviness*) sadness, sorrow, dejection, depression, despondency, gloom, gloominess, melancholy. OPPOSITE: cheerfulness. 4 (*struggling against the heaviness she felt*) sluggishness, drowsiness, sleepiness, somnolence, languor, lassitude, listlessness, apathy, dullness, slowness, inactivity, inertia, deadness. OPPOSITE: activity.

heavy *adj* 1 (*a heavy bag*) weighty, hefty, bulky, big, massive, colossal, large, great, enormous, mighty, substantial, considerable, fat, stout, ponderous, cumbersome, burdensome, awkward, unmanageable, unwieldy. OPPOSITE: light. **2** (*heavy work*) laborious, arduous, tough, strenuous, difficult, troublesome, hard, harsh, grievous, oppressive, burdensome, demanding, taxing, exacting. OPPOSITE: slight. **3** (*a heavy responsibility*) weighty, burdensome, oppressive, onerous, taxing, exacting, crushing, difficult, troublesome, trying, wearisome, irksome, unbearable, intolerable. **4** (*a heavy knock*) hard, forceful, powerful, strong, severe, intense, sharp, stinging, penetrating, violent, grievous. **5** (*heavy fire*) intense, strong, violent, severe, excessive, immoderate, inordinate, extreme, great, serious, considerable, profuse. **6** (*with a heavy heart*) sad, sorrowful, downcast, crestfallen, discouraged, disheartened, downhearted, crushed, dejected, depressed, despondent, gloomy, grave, sombre, miserable, melancholy. OPPOSITE: cheerful. **7** (*proved heavy reading*) dull, boring, tedious, dry, uninteresting, wearisome, difficult. **8** (*too heavy for me*) profound, deep (*inf*), complex, critical, important, intense, sombre, grave. OPPOSITE: trivial. **9** (*the drug made him feel heavy*) sluggish, torpid, languid, listless, apathetic, indolent, drowsy, sleepy, dull, slow, stupid, inactive, inert. OPPOSITE: active. **10** (*he was a heavy man*) large, big, fat, bulky, stout, portly, tubby, paunchy, overweight, obese, corpulent, hulking, lumbering. **11** (*a heavy meal*) substantial, big, large, stodgy, filling, solid, indigestible, starchy. **12** (*the trolley was heavy with shopping*) burdened, laden, loaded, encumbered, weighted, groaning. **13** (*heavy skies*) overcast, cloudy, dull, gloomy, dreary, grey, dark, leaden, lowering. OPPOSITE: bright. **14** (*heavy seas*) stormy, rough, wild, tempestuous, turbulent, squally, violent, restless. **15** (*heavy fog*) dense, thick, solid, impenetrable.

heavy-handed *adj* **1** (*a heavy-handed approach to the staff*) clumsy, insensitive, tactless, thoughtless, unsubtle, inept. **2** (*heavy-handed with the china*) clumsy, awkward, blundering, ham-handed (*inf*), ham-fisted (*inf*), cack-handed (*inf*), unhandy, maladroit, bungling, inexpert, unskilful, ungraceful, graceless. **3** (*heavy-handed treatment of transgressors*) harsh, severe, stern, merciless, ruthless, hard, oppressive, overbearing, domineering, tyrannical, despotic, autocratic.

heckle *verb* interrupt, disrupt, shout down, boo, barrack (*inf*), taunt, jeer, bait, gibe, catcall, badger, hector, harass, pester.

hectic *adj* feverish, frenetic, frantic, frenzied, flurried, bustling, busy, fast, furious, excited, exciting, animated, heated, riotous, boisterous, rumbustious, tumultuous, turbulent, wild, chaotic, unruly. OPPOSITE: calm.

hector *verb* bully, browbeat, cow, coerce, intimidate, bulldoze (*inf*), steamroller, threaten, menace, torment, nag, provoke, plague, harass, badger, bait, chivvy, harry, worry.

hedge *noun* **1** (*a field surrounded by hedges*) hedgerow, fence, barrier, screen, windbreak, boundary. **2** (*a hedge against external threats*) safeguard, protection, shield, guard, cover, insurance.
➤ *verb* **1** (*hedge the garden*) surround, enclose, encircle, circle, border, edge, fence, skirt. **2** (*hedged in by political necessity*) hem in, confine, restrict, limit, obstruct, hinder, impede, block. **3** (*hedged when pressed by*

journalists) evade, dodge, sidestep, hum and haw, flannel (*inf*), duck the question (*inf*), stall, equivocate, prevaricate, quibble, fudge, waffle (*inf*), temporize. **4** (*hedge one's bets*) protect, guard, shield, safeguard, cover, insure, fortify. OPPOSITE: expose.

heed *verb* mind, attend, pay attention, listen, take notice, take into account, bear in mind, regard, consider, note, notice, mark, observe, obey, follow. OPPOSITE: ignore.
➤ *noun* attention, attentiveness, notice, note, regard, respect, mind, thought, consideration, care, caution, heedfulness, mindfulness, watchfulness, wariness, chariness. OPPOSITE: disregard.

heedful *adj* mindful, attentive, regardful, thoughtful, prudent, careful, circumspect, cautious, chary, wary, vigilant, watchful, alert, observant. OPPOSITE: heedless.

heedless *adj* unmindful, regardless, oblivious, unconcerned, thoughtless, unthinking, careless, inattentive, unobservant, unwatchful, unvigilant, neglectful, negligent, rash, reckless, precipitate, imprudent, foolhardy, unwary. OPPOSITE: heedful.

heel[1] *noun* **1** (*high heels*) stiletto, platform, wedge. **2** (*the heel of a cigar*) remnant, remainder, stub, stump, butt, rump, crust, end, tail end. **3** (*he's a heel*) scoundrel, blackguard, rat (*inf*), cad (*inf*), bounder (*inf*), rotter (*inf*), swine (*inf*).

heel[2] *verb* (*the ship heeled over in the storm*) lean, list, tilt, tip, cant, incline, keel over.

hefty *adj* **1** (*a hefty build*) heavy, bulky, big, large, huge, burly, hulking, stout, massive, beefy, muscular, solid, brawny, strapping, well-built, sturdy, robust, rugged, stalwart, strong, powerful. **2** (*a hefty punch*) heavy, weighty, powerful, forceful, hard, solid, mighty, vigorous. **3** (*a hefty package*) heavy, weighty, bulky, massive, big, large, colossal, huge, immense, tremendous, unwieldy, cumbersome, ponderous, awkward. **4** (*a hefty sum*) big, large, colossal, substantial, sizeable, considerable, expensive, pricey, overpriced, generous, ample.

height *noun* **1** (*at a considerable height*) altitude, elevation, highness, loftiness. OPPOSITE: depth. **2** (*drew himself up to his full height*) tallness, stature. **3** (*roaming the heights*) mountain, hill, summit, high ground, eminence, cliff, precipice. **4** (*scaled the mountain height*) top, summit, crest, crown, peak, pinnacle, apex, vertex, apogee. **5** (*at the height of her success*) climax, consummation, culmination, crowning point, high point, peak, zenith, apex. **6** (*the height of stupidity*) maximum, utmost, uttermost, ultimate, limit, extremity, extreme, acme.

heighten *verb* **1** (*heighten a building*) raise, elevate, uplift. **2** (*heightened the mood*) increase, augment, build up, amplify, magnify, intensify, sharpen, aggravate, enhance, enrich, improve, boost, strengthen. OPPOSITE: moderate. **3** (*heightened his reputation*) enhance, enrich, exalt, magnify, ennoble. OPPOSITE: lower.

heinous *adj* wicked, evil, nefarious, iniquitous, infamous, atrocious, scandalous, outrageous, shocking, flagrant, monstrous, villainous, vicious, awful, abominable, odious, loathsome, ghastly, hateful, hideous, deplorable, contemptible, despicable, detestable, execrable, revolting, abhorrent, unspeakable, reprehensible. OPPOSITE: admirable.

heir *noun* heiress, child, offspring, descendant, successor, scion, inheritor, inheritress, inheritrix, beneficiary, legatee.

helix *noun* spiral, screw, corkscrew, whorl, twist, coil, curl, loop.

hell *noun* **1** (*souls in hell*) underworld, perdition, inferno, infernal regions, bottomless pit, nether world, abyss, Hades, Gehenna. OPPOSITE: heaven. **2** (*she's gone through hell*) purgatory, torture, torment, anguish, agony, suffering, ordeal, affliction, trial, tribulation, misery, wretchedness, woe, nightmare. OPPOSITE: ecstasy.

hell for leather fast, quickly, rapidly, speedily, swiftly, at the double, hotfoot, posthaste, helter-skelter, full tilt, headlong, pell-mell, hurriedly, precipitately, recklessly, rashly, wildly.

raise hell object, protest, remonstrate, complain, kick up a fuss (*inf*), go ballistic (*inf*), go nuts (*inf*), hit the roof (*inf*), blow one's top (*inf*), raise Cain.

hellish *adj* **1** (*hellish demons*) infernal, diabolical, fiendish, satanic, demonic, demoniac, demoniacal, devilish. OPPOSITE: heavenly. **2** (*a hellish regime*) brutal, brutish, barbarous, barbaric, monstrous, savage, ferocious, vicious, ruthless, relentless, murderous, bloodthirsty, inhuman, cruel, wicked, evil, heinous, nefarious, damnable, accursed, detestable, abominable, atrocious, dreadful, execrable. **3** (*hellish weather*) appalling, nasty, unpleasant, awful (*inf*), dreadful, horrible (*inf*), horrid (*inf*).
» *adv* very, extremely, excessively, awfully (*inf*), jolly (*inf*), ever so (*inf*), unpleasantly.

helm *noun* rudder, wheel, tiller, steering gear.
at the helm in charge, in control, in command, in authority, leading, directing, in the driving seat, at the wheel, in the saddle, holding the reins.

help *verb* **1** (*help me with this*) assist, aid, lend a hand, guide, oblige. **2** (*help with the campaign*) assist, aid, back, support, stand by, rally round, encourage, boost, promote, abet, succour, nurse, contribute to, further, serve, cooperate with, collaborate with. OPPOSITE: hinder. **3** (*help environmental problems*) relieve, alleviate, mitigate, soothe, improve, ameliorate, assuage, ease, facilitate, further, cure, heal, remedy, restore. OPPOSITE: aggravate. **4** (*I cannot help it*) avoid, resist, withstand, refrain from, abstain, eschew, forbear, stop, prevent, control. **5** (*helped themselves to the cash*) steal, take, nick (*inf*), pinch (*inf*), make off with (*inf*), walk off with (*inf*), appropriate, commandeer.
» *noun* **1** (*offer help*) assistance, aid, helping hand, succour, backing, backup, support, boost, encouragement, advice, guidance, service, use, cooperation, collaboration. OPPOSITE: hindrance. **2** (*help for the discomfort*) relief, remedy, cure, healing, corrective, restorative, alleviation, amelioration, mitigation, improvement, balm, salve. OPPOSITE: aggravation. **3** (*advertise for a help*) helper, assistant, hired help, domestic help, servant, daily, maid, aider, abettor, mate, employee, hand, worker.

helper *noun* assistant, aider, aide, attendant, auxiliary,

help, supporter, backer, second, ally, accomplice, associate, colleague, co-worker, partner, mate, helpmate, sidekick (*inf*), collaborator, deputy, second-in-command, right-hand man, PA, subordinate, subsidiary, adjutant, employee, servant, maid, henchman. OPPOSITE: opponent.

helpful *adj* **1** (*a helpful suggestion*) useful, serviceable, timely, beneficial, advantageous, favourable, practical, constructive, worthwhile, productive, profitable, valuable. OPPOSITE: useless. **2** (*a helpful young man*) friendly, neighbourly, caring, sympathetic, considerate, kind, benevolent, beneficent, charitable, supportive, cooperative, obliging, accommodating. OPPOSITE: unfriendly.

helping *noun* serving, portion, plateful, bowlful, spoonful, dollop (*inf*), ration, share, amount, piece.

helpless *adj* **1** (*a helpless old woman*) infirm, invalid, bedridden, laid-up (*inf*), disabled, debilitated, dependent, feeble, incapable, incompetent, weak, unfit, impotent, powerless. OPPOSITE: strong. **2** (*helpless children*) unprotected, defenceless, vulnerable, exposed, abandoned, friendless, forsaken, forlorn.

helpmate *noun* helper, partner, assistant, associate, support, companion, helpmeet.

hem *noun* edge, border, margin, edging, fringe, frill, trim, trimming, flounce, valance.
» *verb* edge, border, skirt, fold, bind, trim, fringe.
hem in surround, encircle, environ, gird, enclose, confine, limit, restrict, constrain, shut in, close in, box in, hedge in, pen in, trap.

hence *adv* therefore, thus, for this reason, accordingly, consequently, on that account, ergo.

henceforth *adv* henceforward, hereafter, after this, subsequently, from now on, hence, in the future, hereinafter OPPOSITE: hitherto.

henchman *noun* attendant, servant, retainer, flunkey (*inf*), toady (*inf*), minion, follower, supporter, aide, associate, right-hand man, crony (*inf*), lackey, sidekick (*inf*), subordinate, underling, heavy (*inf*), hood (*inf*), bodyguard, minder (*inf*), satellite.

henpecked *adj* bullied, browbeaten, nagged, dominated, subjugated, intimidated, under the thumb (*inf*), criticized, harassed, pestered, badgered, tormented, cringing, cowering, meek, timid, docile.

herald *noun* **1** (*the king's herald*) messenger, courier, runner, announcer, usher, crier. **2** (*a herald of change*) harbinger, forerunner, precursor, sign, token, signal, indication, omen, portent, augury.
» *verb* **1** (*heralded the news*) announce, proclaim, trumpet, promote, promulgate, make known, make public, broadcast, advertise, publish. OPPOSITE: suppress. **2** (*herald a new era*) precede, usher in, show in, pave the way for (*inf*), portend, indicate, promise, presage, foreshadow, forebode, foretoken, augur.

herculean *adj* **1** (*a herculean effort*) laborious, arduous, backbreaking, strenuous, onerous, toilsome, heavy, hard, tough, difficult, formidable, daunting, gruelling, demanding, exacting, exhausting, uphill, great, tremendous, enormous, prodigious, colossal, gigantic, huge, large, mammoth, massive, powerful. OPPOSITE: easy. **2** (*a herculean build*) strong, mighty, powerful, stalwart, robust, rugged, strapping, sturdy, muscular, sinewy, brawny, athletic. OPPOSITE: puny.

herd noun **1** (*a herd of animals*) drove, pack, flock, swarm, cluster, collection. **2** (*a herd of sightseers*) horde, host, crowd, throng, multitude, mob, mass, crush, press, swarm. **3** (*the common herd*) mass, multitude, mob, rabble, riff-raff (*inf*), hoi polloi (*inf*), great unwashed (*inf*), populace.
> verb **1** (*herding the stock*) drive, round up, shepherd, lead, guide, goad, urge, force. OPPOSITE: disperse. **2** (*herd the guests together*) gather, get together, huddle, assemble, muster, flock, rally, congregate, collect.

here adv **1** (*put it here*) hereabouts, hither. **2** (*here's where I go home*) now, at this stage, at this point, at this time.

hereafter adv after this, hence, henceforth, henceforward, from now on, in the future, later, eventually.
> noun afterworld, afterlife, life after death, life to come, next world, the beyond, heaven, paradise, elysian fields.

hereditary adj **1** (*hereditary illness*) inheritable, hereditable, genetic, congenital, natural, inborn, inbred, innate, inherent, inherited, transmissible, transferable. OPPOSITE: acquired. **2** (*hereditary seat*) ancestral, family, traditional, inherited, bequeathed, handed down, willed, transmitted, transferred.

heresy noun unorthodoxy, heterodoxy, nonconformism, nonconformity, freethinking, dissidence, dissension, dissent, unbelief, blasphemy, impiety, schism, revisionism, recusancy, separatism, sectarianism, apostasy, iconoclasm, scepticism, atheism, agnosticism, paganism, idolatry. OPPOSITE: orthodoxy.

heretic noun dissenter, dissident, freethinker, apostate, nonconformist, revisionist, schismatic, recusant, unbeliever, sceptic, atheist, pagan, heathen, agnostic, separatist, sectarian.

heretical adj unorthodox, heterodox, freethinking, nonconformist, dissident, dissenting, revisionist, recusant, separatist, sectarian, schismatic, iconoclastic, unbelieving, atheistic, atheistical, agnostic, sceptical, impious, irreverent, blasphemous, idolatrous, heathen, pagan. OPPOSITE: orthodox.

heritage noun **1** (*our national heritage*) history, past, tradition, background, culture. **2** (*of royal heritage*) descent, birth, extraction, lineage, ancestry, family, dynasty, bloodline, heredity. **3** (*came to claim his heritage*) inheritance, birthright, due, lot, portion, share, legacy, bequest, endowment, estate, patrimony.

hermit noun recluse, loner, solitary, monk, anchorite, anchoress, ascetic, eremite, stylite.

hermitage noun retreat, refuge, hideaway, sanctum, sanctuary, cloister, shelter, haven, hiding-place, asylum, hideout.

hero noun **1** (*a national hero*) champion, figure, icon, idol, lion, celebrity, celeb (*inf*), conqueror, victor. **2** (*he became her hero*) heartthrob (*inf*), idol, ideal, paragon, god, star, superstar, pinup. **3** (*the hero of this tale*) protagonist, central character, lead, lead actor, leading actor.

heroic adj **1** (*heroic acts*) courageous, brave, valiant, valorous, intrepid, fearless, dauntless, undaunted,

determined, bold, adventurous, daring, gallant, noble, lionhearted, stouthearted, chivalrous, selfless. OPPOSITE: cowardly. **2** (*heroic mythology*) legendary, mythological, fabulous, classical, classic, Homeric. **3** (*written in the heroic style*) epic, grand, grandiose, bombastic, rhetorical, elevated, inflated, high-flown, high-sounding, exaggerated, extravagant, pretentious, orotund, magniloquent, turgid.

heroine noun **1** (*considered a heroine by her followers*) champion, victor, ideal, paragon, celebrity. **2** (*film heroine*) leading lady, leading actress, female lead, prima donna, diva, protagonist.

heroism noun courage, bravery, valour, courageousness, fortitude, intrepidity, fearlessness, dauntlessness, determination, boldness, stouteartedness, lionheartedness, doughtiness, daring, prowess, mettle, spirit, virility, gallantry, chivalry, selflessness. OPPOSITE: cowardice.

hero worship noun admiration, idolization, idealization, adoration, worship, veneration, exaltation, glorification, adulation, deification.

hesitancy noun **1** (*slight hesitancy in his manner*) uncertainty, unsureness, doubt, doubtfulness, indecision, indecisiveness, irresolution, vacillation, oscillation, shilly-shallying (*inf*), wavering, stalling, scepticism. **2** (*some hesitancy about getting involved*) reluctance, misgiving, reservation, unwillingness, disinclination, scruples, qualms, demurral.

hesitant adj **1** (*hesitant in her approach*) hesitating, uncertain, unsure, doubtful, doubting, dubious, indecisive, halfhearted, irresolute, vacillating, oscillating, shilly-shallying (*inf*), tentative, wavering, stalling, delaying, demurring, sceptical, halting, stammering, stuttering. **2** (*hesitant about seeing them*) reluctant, wary, unwilling, disinclined, diffident.

hesitate verb **1** (*hesitate before going in*) pause, wait, delay, hold back, hang back, waver, dither, shilly-shally (*inf*), dilly-dally (*inf*), dally, stall, temporize, vacillate, oscillate, doubt, be uncertain, demur. OPPOSITE: proceed. **2** (*hesitate about complaining*) shrink from, hang back from, be reluctant, scruple, think twice, demur from, balk at. **3** (*hesitating in his speech*) falter, stammer, stutter, stumble, fumble, hum and haw, halt.

hesitation noun **1** (*a hesitation in the process*) pause, delay, hesitancy, hanging back, holding back, waiting, wavering, vacillation, oscillation, stalling, temporizing, shilly-shallying (*inf*), dilly-dallying (*inf*), doubt, doubtfulness, dubiousness, uncertainty, unsureness, irresolution, indecision, indecisiveness, scepticism. **2** (*felt some hesitation about getting involved*) misgivings, qualms, scruples, reluctance, disinclination, unwillingness, demurral. OPPOSITE: decisiveness. **3** (*some hesitation in his speech*) faltering, stammering, stuttering, stumbling, fumbling, humming and hawing, halting.

heterodox adj unorthodox, heretical, dissident, dissenting, freethinking, revisionist, schismatic, iconoclastic, unsound. OPPOSITE: orthodox.

heterogeneous adj dissimilar, different, unlike, unrelated, disparate, discrepant, incongruous, unrelated, varied, diverse, diversified, divergent, contrasted, contrary, opposite, catholic, mixed, assorted, motley, miscellaneous, manifold, polymorphic. OPPOSITE: homogeneous.

hew *verb* **1** (*hew down the trees*) chop, chop down, hack down, axe, cut down, saw down, fell. **2** (*hew dead limbs off the tree*) lop, prune, trim, sever, chop off, cut off, hack off. **3** (*hew a figure out of the trunk*) carve, chip, whittle, chisel, hammer, sculpt, sculpture, shape, fashion, form, make, mould, model.

heyday *noun* prime, peak, pinnacle, flush, pink, bloom, flowering, culmination, crowning point, golden age, salad days, boom time.

hiatus *noun* **1** (*a hiatus in proceedings*) gap, break, interruption, lapse, lull, respite, pause, rest, suspension, interval. **2** (*a hiatus in the report*) break, blank, gap, discontinuity, interruption. **3** (*place a dressing over the hiatus*) opening, aperture, hole, cavity, fissure, rift, cleft, chasm, breach, space.

hidden *adj* **1** (*hidden documents*) concealed, covered, shrouded, unseen, unrevealed, masked, disguised, camouflaged, veiled, secret. OPPOSITE: visible. **2** (*hidden significance*) latent, covert, cryptic, secret, private, close, clandestine, ulterior, dark, indistinct, indefinite, unclear, obscure, vague, mysterious, unfathomable, inexplicable, occult, abstruse, arcane, recondite, mystical. OPPOSITE: obvious.

hide[1] *verb* **1** (*hide the truth*) conceal, cloak, shroud, cover, screen, mask, veil, dissemble, disguise, camouflage, obscure, suppress, hush up, blot out, withhold, bottle up (*inf*), sweep under the carpet (*inf*), keep under wraps (*inf*). **2** (*hide the bottles*) conceal, secrete, stash away (*inf*), cache, lock up, bury, store away, stow away. OPPOSITE: reveal. **3** (*hide the light*) shadow, obscure, eclipse, darken, cloud, block, obstruct. **4** (*hide in the barn*) take cover, conceal oneself, lie low, lie doggo (*inf*), go to ground, go into hiding, hole up (*inf*), keep a low profile (*inf*), go underground (*inf*), cover one's tracks, shelter, lurk.

hide[2] *noun* (*animal hides*) skin, pelt, fur, fleece, coat, leather.

hideaway *noun* hiding-place, hideout, hidey-hole (*inf*), retreat, refuge, shelter, haven, den, lair, nest, hole, nook, sanctuary, cloister, hermitage.

hidebound *adj* narrow-minded, narrow, intolerant, bigoted, prejudiced, uncompromising, reactionary, set, rigid, fixed, entrenched, intractable, straitlaced, conventional, orthodox, conservative, ultraconservative, fundamentalist.

hideous *adj* **1** (*a hideous scene*) ugly, grotesque, unsightly, repulsive, repellent, revolting, awful, ghastly, macabre, monstrous, gruesome, disgusting, grisly, grim. OPPOSITE: beautiful. **2** (*hideous cruelty*) horrible, horrid, frightful, dreadful, terrible, terrifying, horrific, horrifying, horrendous, appalling, shocking, outrageous, monstrous, heinous, odious, abominable, loathsome, contemptible, execrable, foul, vile, sickening.

hideout *noun* hiding-place, hideaway, retreat, refuge, sanctuary, shelter, haven, den, nest, lair, hole, cloister, hermitage.

hiding *noun* beating, thrashing, flogging, walloping (*inf*), whacking (*inf*), belting (*inf*), licking (*inf*), thumping, battering, whipping, caning, spanking, drubbing, tanning (*inf*).

hierarchy *noun* social order, class system, system, pecking order, ladder, ranking, grading, scale, series, strata, structure.

higgledy-piggledy *adv* disorderly, untidily, jumbled, confusedly, haphazardly, indiscriminately, topsy-turvy, anyhow. OPPOSITE: orderly.
➤ *adj* haphazard, indiscriminate, confused, disorganized, jumbled, muddled, untidy, helter-skelter, pell-mell, topsy-turvy.

high *adj* **1** (*a high spire*) tall, lofty, elevated, towering, soaring, steep. OPPOSITE: low. **2** (*at high speed*) great, extreme, excessive, intense, strong, powerful, vigorous, forceful. OPPOSITE: low. **3** (*high quality*) good, excellent, top, top-class, tiptop, fine, great, outstanding, select, choice, de luxe, classy (*inf*), gilt-edged, superior, superlative, surpassing, first-rate, first-class, perfect, unequalled, unparalleled. OPPOSITE: poor. **4** (*a high price*) expensive, dear, costly, excessive, exorbitant, extortionate, inflated, steep (*inf*), top. OPPOSITE: low. **5** (*high principles*) high-minded, noble, honourable, idealistic, virtuous, worthy, upright, moral, ethical, lofty. **6** (*a high note*) shrill, piercing, penetrating, acute, piping, high-pitched, tinny, soprano, treble, falsetto. OPPOSITE: deep. **7** (*a high representative*) high-ranking, top, senior, influential, leading, chief, ruling, eminent, prominent, important, powerful, exalted, distinguished, dignified, noble, notable, exalted, august. OPPOSITE: lowly. **8** (*adopted a high attitude*) haughty, arrogant, proud, high and mighty (*inf*), lordly, overbearing, domineering, supercilious, disdainful, contemptuous. **9** (*the thought made him high*) happy, cheerful, merry, jolly, joyful, elated, ebullient, excited, exhilarated, hyped up (*inf*), ecstatic, high-spirited, euphoric, boisterous, bouncy. OPPOSITE: depressed. **10** (*high on drugs*) drugged, doped (*inf*), wasted (*inf*), intoxicated, stoned (*inf*), bombed (*inf*), blitzed (*inf*), out of it (*inf*), spaced out (*inf*), turned on (*inf*), inebriated, delirious. **11** (*living the high life*) high-living, luxurious, lavish, extravagant, grand, rich, prodigal. **12** (*held in high esteem*) good, positive, favourable, complimentary, appreciative, approving, admiring, flattering. **13** (*that meat is high*) smelling, niffy (*inf*), whiffy (*inf*), gamy, rotting, bad, gone off, going off, off, tainted, rancid, putrid, decayed.
➤ *noun* **1** (*a record high*) level, figure, record, height, peak, summit, top, apex, zenith. **2** (*they were on a high*) euphoria, intoxication, trip (*inf*), delirium, ecstasy, transports.

high and dry abandoned, stranded, marooned, dumped (*inf*), ditched (*inf*), helpless, friendless, destitute, bereft.

high and mighty arrogant, conceited, haughty, proud, self-important, superior, egotistic, overbearing, overweening, condescending, patronizing, stuck-up (*inf*), highfalutin (*inf*), snobbish, disdainful, supercilious, cavalier, imperious.

highborn *adj* aristocratic, noble, gentle, wellborn, blue-blooded, patrician, thoroughbred.

highbrow *noun* intellectual, scholar, academic, aesthete, egghead (*inf*), boffin (*inf*), brains (*inf*),

brainbox (*inf*), genius, mastermind, bookworm (*inf*), know-it-all (*inf*), savant.
➤ *adj* intellectual, academic, scholarly, bookish, sophisticated, cultured, cultivated, educated, brainy (*inf*), deep, profound, serious.

high-class *adj* upper-class, top-class, top-drawer, A1 (*inf*), classy (*inf*), top-flight, tiptop (*inf*), up-market, high-quality, quality, de luxe, luxurious, superior, super (*inf*), posh (*inf*), ritzy (*inf*), swish (*inf*), excellent, first-rate, choice, select, exclusive, élite, elegant.

high-flown *adj* high-sounding, florid, flowery, exaggerated, extravagant, elaborate, flamboyant, ornate, ostentatious, pretentious, overdone, overblown, inflated, grandiose, bombastic, pompous, turgid, artificial, stilted, affected, la-di-da (*inf*), lofty, highfalutin, supercilious, grandiloquent.

high-handed *adj* bossy (*inf*), domineering, overbearing, peremptory, arrogant, haughty, imperious, lordly, tyrannical, dictatorial, despotic, autocratic, oppressive.

highland *noun* upland, plateau, tableland, height, mountain, hill, ridge, rise, mount, mound, elevation.

highlight *noun* climax, peak, cream, best, best part, high spot, high point, focal point, focus.
➤ *verb* stress, emphasize, play up, accent, accentuate, underline, point up, call attention to, bring to the fore, bring home, set off, spotlight, illuminate, show up, focus on, feature.

highly *adv* 1 (*highly likely*) extremely, very, very much, greatly, considerably, decidedly, certainly, hugely, immensely, vastly, tremendously, supremely, exceptionally, extraordinarily. 2 (*think very highly of her*) favourably, well, appreciatively, approvingly, enthusiastically, warmly, respectfully. OPPOSITE: badly.

highly-strung *adj* sensitive, temperamental, neurotic, nervous, nervy, jumpy, edgy, on edge, twitchy (*inf*), excitable, irritable, stressed, uptight (*inf*), overwrought, wound up (*inf*), tense, taut, restless.

high-minded *adj* noble, noble-minded, moral, ethical, principled, idealistic, lofty, elevated, pure, virtuous, upright, righteous, honourable, fair, good, worthy.

high-powered *adj* powerful, forceful, vigorous, aggressive, assertive, driving, insistent, pushy (*inf*), dynamic, ambitious, go-ahead (*inf*), go-getting (*inf*), enterprising, energetic.

high-priced *adj* overpriced, expensive, costly, dear, exorbitant, pricey, steep (*inf*), stiff (*inf*), high, unreasonable, excessive. OPPOSITE: cheap.

high-sounding *adj* grandiose, imposing, ostentatious, flamboyant, overblown, pompous, pretentious, florid, affected, artificial, bombastic, elaborate, extravagant, high-flown, grandiloquent, magniloquent, orotund.

high-spirited *adj* spirited, exuberant, boisterous, bouncy, buoyant, effervescent, full of beans (*inf*), full of life, full of vim, ebullient, cheerful, joyful, sparkling, sparky, frolicsome, animated, lively, active, vital, vigorous, vibrant, vivacious, dynamic, energetic, dashing, bold, daring.

high spirits *pl noun* spirit, exuberance, ebullience, boisterousness, animation, energy, dynamism,

exhilaration, vitality, liveliness, bounce (*inf*), bounciness, cheerfulness, joy, sparkle, good cheer, vivacity, hilarity, buoyancy, joie de vivre.

hijack *verb* commandeer, seize, take over, expropriate, skyjack.

hike *verb* 1 (*hike over the moors*) walk, tramp, trek, ramble, backpack, wander, march, trudge, plod, leg it (*inf*), hoof it (*inf*). 2 (*hiked up his socks*) hitch, pull, tug, hoist, jerk, jack, yank (*inf*), lift, raise. 3 (*hike up the cost*) increase, put, push (*inf*), jack (*inf*).
➤ *noun* walk, tramp, trek, ramble, wander, march, trudge.

hilarious *adj* 1 (*a hilarious story*) funny, amusing, comical, humorous, sidesplitting, hysterical (*inf*), killing (*inf*), farcical, laughable, risible, entertaining. 2 (*a hilarious evening*) uproarious, exuberant, noisy, animated, sparkling, vivacious, boisterous, riotous, rollicking, merry, amusing, entertaining, convivial, jolly, jovial, mirthful, cheerful, gay, joyful, joyous, happy, elated, exhilarated. OPPOSITE: serious.

hilarity *noun* merriment, jollity, mirth, laughter, fun, amusement, comedy, frivolity, gaiety, levity, conviviality, cheerfulness, glee, joviality, joy, exhilaration, exuberance, high spirits, boisterousness. OPPOSITE: despondency.

hill *noun* 1 (*a castle on a hill*) mound, knoll, hilltop, hillock, rise, foothill, mountain, mount, fell, tor, hummock, height, eminence, prominence, elevation. 2 (*struggle up the hill*) rise, incline, slope, gradient, ramp, ascent, acclivity, drop, descent, declivity. OPPOSITE: plain. 3 (*a hill of grain*) heap, mountain, pile, mound, stack, drift.

hillock *noun* mound, knoll, hummock, barrow, dune.

hilt *noun* handle, grip, handgrip, shaft, haft, hold.
to the hilt fully, all the way (*inf*), completely, totally, wholly, entirely, utterly, to the full, to the end, in every respect.

hind *adj* back, rear, posterior, hinder, after, tail. OPPOSITE: front.

hinder *verb* impede, obstruct, block, hamper, handicap, hamstring, encumber, thwart, foil, frustrate, baffle, balk, retard, delay, hold up, hold back, curb, slow down, check, stop, halt, forestall, stymie (*inf*), arrest, prevent, inhibit, deter, debar, interrupt, oppose, interfere with. OPPOSITE: help.

hindmost *adj* last, final, ultimate, concluding, rear, rearmost, tail, trailing, terminal, endmost, furthest, furthest back, farthest back, remotest.

hindrance *noun* impediment, encumbrance, handicap, obstacle, obstruction, block, stumbling block, deterrent, foil, barrier, bar, hitch, snag, drawback, difficulty, disadvantage, inconvenience, delay, holdup, stoppage, drag, check, curb, restriction, limitation, restraint, thwarting, interference, interruption. OPPOSITE: assistance.

hinge *verb* turn, hang, depend, rest, pivot, centre, revolve.

hint *noun* 1 (*she got the hint*) suggestion, intimation, implication, insinuation, innuendo, allusion, mention, inkling, clue, cue, reminder, indication, sign. 2 (*some*

useful hints) tip, pointer, advice, suggestion, help. **3** (a hint of scandal) trace, suspicion, suggestion, nuance, undertone, tinge, soupçon, sprinkling, dash, speck, touch, breath, whisper, taste, scent, whiff.
➤ *verb* suggest, intimate, imply, indicate, insinuate, allude, mention, tip off, signal, prompt.

hire *verb* **1** (hire a yacht) rent, charter, lease, let, book, commission. **2** (hire some help) employ, take on, sign up, contract, appoint, engage, enlist, retain.
➤ *noun* **1** (cars for hire) rental, rent, lease. **2** (worth their hire) fee, charge, pay, payment, salary, wage, cost, price.

hirsute *adj* hairy, shaggy, bristly, bearded, unshaven, bewhiskered. OPPOSITE: smooth.

hiss *verb* **1** (he hissed in his brother's ear) whistle, sibilate, shrill, rasp, wheeze. **2** (hissed off the stage) boo, hoot, catcall, jeer, mock, deride, scoff at, scorn, ridicule, revile, taunt, damn, decry, cry down, shout down. OPPOSITE: applaud.
➤ *noun* **1** (the hiss of escaping air) hissing, whistle, sibilance, sibilation, wheeze. **2** (a solitary hiss from the audience) boo, hoot, catcall, raspberry (inf), jeer, mockery, derision, contempt, scorn, scoffing, taunting. OPPOSITE: applause.

historian *noun* chronicler, chronologer, recorder, antiquarian, archivist, historiographer, narrator, biographer, diarist, annalist.

historic *adj* famous, famed, celebrated, noteworthy, notable, renowned, memorable, remarkable, extraordinary, outstanding, important, significant, consequential, red-letter (inf), momentous, epoch-making. OPPOSITE: inconsequential.

historical *adj* **1** (of historical importance) ancient, former, past, bygone, old, prior, of yore. **2** (historical fact) authentic, real, true, actual, factual, confirmed, verified, verifiable, attested, documented, chronicled, recorded, archival. OPPOSITE: legendary.

history *noun* **1** (a history of the royal family) chronicle, chronology, annal, archive, record, account, study, story, tale, saga, narration, narrative, recital, recapitulation, report, memoir, biography, life, autobiography. **2** (recorded history) antiquity, the past, former times, days of old, olden days, days of yore, bygone days, times gone by, yesteryear, yesterday. OPPOSITE: future. **3** (faced questions about her history) background, experience, record, circumstances, family, qualifications, credentials, education.

histrionic *adj* theatrical, melodramatic, dramatic, sensational, exaggerated, affected, forced, insincere, unnatural, false, artificial, bogus, ham, camp (inf).

hit *verb* **1** (hit him in the face) strike, knock, beat, batter, pound, smack, slap, tap, bat, whack (inf), punch, thump, box, cuff, bash (inf), belt (inf), clobber (inf), clout (inf), biff (inf), chin (inf), clip (inf), deck (inf), sock (inf), swat (inf), swipe (inf), wallop (inf), buffet, hammer, pummel, thrash. **2** (the car hit the wall) bump, bang, crash into, smash into, run into, plough into, collide with, clash with, meet head-on. OPPOSITE: miss. **3** (hit their target) reach, attain, accomplish, achieve, arrive at, gain, secure, strike. **4** (the news really hit her) affect, move, touch, influence, disturb, perturb, upset, trouble, hurt,

devastate, overwhelm, knock for six (inf). **5** (then it hit me) strike, occur to, dawn on, come to, come to mind.
➤ *noun* **1** (a hit on the chin) stroke, blow, knock, smack, slap, rap, tap, thump, punch, clout (inf), whack (inf), belt (inf), biff (inf), sock (inf), wallop (inf), cuff, box, bash, bump, shot, crash, smash, collision, clash, buffet, impact. **2** (the show is a hit) success, triumph, winner, sell-out (inf), sensation, smash (inf). OPPOSITE: failure.

hit it off get along, get on, become friends, warm to, grow to like, take to, relate well, be on the same wavelength (inf).

hit out lash out, strike out, assail, attack, rail, denounce, condemn, criticize, castigate, censure, vilify, revile, inveigh against.

hit upon find, discover, uncover, come upon, light upon, chance upon, happen upon, stumble upon, blunder upon, think of, dream up, arrive at, guess, realize.

hitch *verb* **1** (hitched the horse to the post) tie, fasten, make fast, attach, connect, join, unite, couple, yoke, bind, tether, moor, harness. OPPOSITE: loose. **2** (hitched up his socks) pull, tug, hoist, heave, hike, hoick, jerk, yank (inf).
➤ *noun* **1** (encountered a hitch) impediment, obstacle, obstruction, hindrance, barrier, stoppage, stumbling-block, block, problem, difficulty, drawback, snag, catch, setback, hiccup, mishap, trouble, delay, check, holdup. **2** (gave his socks a hitch) jerk, tug, pull.

hitherto *adv* up to now, until now, till now, so far, thus far, previously, before, beforehand, heretofore.

hit-or-miss *adj* random, haphazard, disorganized, indiscriminate, trial-and-error, aimless, undirected, unplanned, uneven, careless, casual, cursory, offhand, perfunctory, lackadaisical.

hoard *verb* gather, collect, amass, heap, pile up, stack up, accumulate, garner, store, stockpile, stock up, save, buy up, husband, keep, reserve, set aside, put away, put by, lay in, lay up, stash away (inf), deposit, squirrel away. OPPOSITE: squander.
➤ *noun* collection, store, stockpile, supply, reserve, reservoir, fund, cache, stash (inf), treasure trove, accumulation, aggregation, conglomeration, mass, heap, pile.

hoarder *noun* saver, collector, gather, miser, magpie, squirrel, tight-arse (sl).

hoarse *adj* husky, raucous, throaty, croaky, croaking, husky, guttural, gruff, gravelly, growling, raucous, harsh, cracked, rough, grating, rasping, discordant. OPPOSITE: mellow.

hoary *adj* **1** (a hoary beard) grey, silvery, frosty, white, grizzled, grizzly, grey-haired, white-haired. OPPOSITE: dark. **2** (a hoary old beggar) old, elderly, aged, ancient, venerable. **3** (a hoary old tale) old-hat (inf), hackneyed, trite, antiquated, antique, old, ancient, archaic.

hoax *noun* trick, practical joke, prank, leg-pull (inf), jest, deception, con (inf), scam (inf), fast one (inf), spoof (inf), put-up job (inf), frame-up (inf), ruse, fraud, imposture, bluff, fake, cheat, swindle, humbug.
➤ *verb* trick, deceive, take in, have on (inf), wind up (inf), take for a ride (inf), pull a fast one on (inf), pull the wool over (inf), delude, dupe, fool, hoodwink, double-

cross (*inf*), two-time (*inf*), bluff, gull, bamboozle (*inf*), cheat, swindle, con (*inf*).

hobble *verb* **1** (*he hobbled into the room*) limp, stumble, totter, reel, stagger, shamble, dodder, shuffle, falter, halt. OPPOSITE: run. **2** (*hobble the prisoner*) fetter, shackle, tie, bind, fasten, restrict, hamstring. OPPOSITE: unfetter.

hobby *noun* pastime, recreation, amusement, relaxation, diversion, interest, leisure activity, pursuit, entertainment, divertissement, game, sport, sideline. OPPOSITE: work.

hobgoblin *noun* goblin, elf, imp, gnome, dwarf, spirit, evil spirit, sprite, bogey, bogeyman.

hobnob *verb* fraternize, socialize, associate, mingle, mix, consort, keep company, hang about (*inf*), hang out (*inf*), go around.

hocus-pocus *noun* **1** (*suspected of hocus-pocus*) trickery, chicanery, deceit, deception, sleight of hand, legerdemain, artifice, hoax, sham, swindle, imposture, pretence, stratagem, delusion. **2** (*spouted a lot of hocus-pocus*) nonsense, gibberish, gobbledygook, jargon, cant, mumbo jumbo, humbug, rigmarole. **3** (*the wizard taught her a little hocus-pocus*) spell, magic, conjuring, abracadabra, charm, incantation, chant, invocation.

hog *noun* **1** (*kept three hogs*) pig, swine, porker, grunter, boar. **2** (*a hog at the table*) glutton, gourmand, big eater, wolf, pig (*inf*), gannet (*inf*).
➤ *verb* monopolize, corner, keep for oneself, control, take over, dominate. OPPOSITE: share.

hogwash *noun* rubbish, nonsense, gibberish, crap (*sl*), shit (*sl*), bullshit (*sl*), balls (*sl*), bollocks (*sl*), claptrap (*inf*), bunk (*inf*), bunkum (*inf*), cobblers (*inf*), drivel, trash, tripe, twaddle, balderdash (*inf*), gobbledygook (*inf*), bosh (*inf*), tosh (*inf*), rot (*inf*), tommyrot (*inf*), piffle (*inf*), bilge (*inf*), eyewash (*inf*), guff (*inf*), hot air (*inf*), hooey (*inf*), poppycock (*inf*).

hoi polloi *pl noun* masses, mob, common people, riff-raff (*inf*), rabble (*inf*), herd (*inf*), common herd, populace, proletariat, proles (*inf*), plebs (*inf*), peasants (*inf*), lower orders, third estate, underclass, great unwashed (*inf*).

hoist *verb* raise, upraise, lift, crane, winch, jack, elevate, uplift, heave, erect, rear. OPPOSITE: lower.
➤ *noun* jack, winch, crane, pulley, tackle, lift, elevator, capstan.

hold *verb* **1** (*hold this pencil*) grip, grasp, clutch, clasp, seize, clench, cling to, cleave to. OPPOSITE: drop. **2** (*hold the fort*) keep, retain, have, possess, own, occupy. **3** (*the tank holds ten litres*) carry, take, contain, accommodate. **4** (*the bridge should hold the weight*) support, sustain, bear, carry, take, prop up, brace, shoulder, suspend. **5** (*held him in detention*) detain, arrest, imprison, impound, confine, lock up, incarcerate, hold in custody, restrain, put behind bars. OPPOSITE: release. **6** (*hold the flow of water*) hold back, restrain, arrest, check, curb, stop, bar, impede, delay, prevent. **7** (*hold the post of secretary*) occupy, fill, take up, hold down, have, enjoy. **8** (*that should hold their interest*) engage, maintain, keep, occupy, involve, catch, arrest, absorb, engross, immerse, spellbind, fascinate, enthral, captivate, rivet, fill, monopolize. **9** (*it was once held that the earth was flat*) maintain, think, believe, consider, regard, view, judge, deem, suppose, reckon, assume, presume, entertain. **10** (*my argument still holds*) hold up, survive, apply, operate, remain, stay. **11** (*held the memory in her heart*) cherish, treasure, keep, harbour, prize, value, retain. **12** (*the joint should hold*) stick, adhere, cling. **13** (*she held him tight*) embrace, hug, enfold, hold on, clasp, cradle, fondle. **14** (*hopes his luck will hold*) last, endure, abide, remain, stay, persist, go on, continue, keep up, carry on, stand. **15** (*hold a meeting*) convene, summon, assemble, call, organize, conduct, run, officiate at, preside over, engage in, carry on.
➤ *noun* **1** (*lost his hold on the ladder*) grip, grasp, clasp, purchase, anchorage, footing, foothold. **2** (*had some kind of hold over her*) influence, control, power, clout (*inf*), pull (*inf*), authority, grip, sway, mastery, dominion, dominance, leverage, ascendancy.

hold back **1** (*hold back the crowd*) keep back, restrain, control, curb, check. **2** (*hold back tears*) smother, keep back, suppress, stifle. **3** (*hold back change*) repress, suppress, inhibit, retard, bar, restrain, hinder, impede, check, curb, rein, stop, delay, prevent, obstruct, control. **4** (*he held back from interfering*) hesitate, shrink, keep, refrain, desist, forbear, restrain oneself, refuse. **5** (*hold back the truth*) retain, withhold, suppress.

hold down **1** (*hold down two jobs*) keep, have, fill, occupy, continue in. **2** (*hold down the local resistance*) keep down, oppress, repress, dominate, tyrannize, suppress.

hold forth **1** (*holding forth his hand*) hold out, present, offer, extend, proffer. **2** (*hold forth on the subject of religion*) speak, talk, preach, lecture, sermonize, harangue, discourse, spout (*inf*), declaim, orate.

hold off **1** (*held off their attackers*) fend off, fight off, ward off, stave off, keep off, keep at bay, repel, rebuff. **2** (*hold off doing anything*) delay, postpone, defer, put off, put on hold, put on the back burner (*inf*), keep from, avoid, refrain from, wait.

hold on **1** (*hold on to the rail*) grasp, grip, clutch, clasp, seize, cling to. **2** (*she will hold on until we get there*) continue, endure, last, remain, persevere, carry on, hang on (*inf*), keep going, survive.

hold one's own hold out, stand one's ground, stand fast, stand firm, stay put, keep one's head above water (*inf*), resist, withstand, survive, keep pace.

hold out **1** (*hold out your hand*) offer, give, proffer, extend, present. **2** (*they can hold out until morning*) hang on (*inf*), carry on, last, last out, continue, endure, persist, persevere, resist, withstand, stand firm, stand fast.

hold over defer, put off, postpone, delay, suspend, shelve, adjourn, waive.

hold up **1** (*hold up the enemy's advance*) delay, retard, detain, set back, slow, slow down, hinder, impede, obstruct, prevent. OPPOSITE: advance. **2** (*will it hold up her weight?*) support, carry, hold, bear, sustain, brace, prop, shore up, buttress. **3** (*holding up a placard*) brandish, wave, flaunt, display, show, exhibit. **4** (*hold up the bank*) stick up (*inf*), mug (*inf*), waylay, rob, steal from, burgle, knock off (*inf*), knock over, break into, nobble (*inf*). **5** (*the theory does not hold up*) bear examination, hold water, ring true, convince.

hold with agree with, approve of, go along with, support, subscribe to, accept, countenance.

holder *noun* **1** (*replaced it in the holder*) container, case, cover, covering, rest, stand, sheath, housing, casing, receptacle. **2** (*the holders of the cup*) possessor, keeper, bearer, custodian, occupant, incumbent, owner, proprietor, purchaser.

holdup *noun* **1** (*there's been a holdup in events*) delay, wait, interruption, hitch, setback, snag, difficulty, problem, trouble, obstruction, stoppage, traffic jam, bottleneck. **2** (*a holdup at the bank*) stick-up (inf), robbery, break-in, heist (inf), raid, mugging (inf), burglary, theft.

hole *noun* **1** (*a hole in the keel*) aperture, opening, orifice, gap, space, break, breach, dent, dimple, recess, rift, cleft, fissure, cut, gash, incision, notch, slit, slot, split, tear, rent, vent, puncture, perforation. **2** (*a hole in the side of the hill*) hollow, dip, depression, excavation, cavity, concavity, scoop, pocket, pit, cave, cavern, chamber, chasm, crater, pothole, dugout, mine, shaft. **3** (*the rabbit returned to its hole*) burrow, den, nest, set, covert, lair, retreat, shelter. **4** (*an obvious hole in his logic*) fault, flaw, error, mistake, defect, crack, inconsistency, discrepancy, fallacy, weakness, loophole. **5** (*he's living in a right hole*) hovel, slum, dive (inf), dump (inf), pigsty (inf), tip (inf), shack. **6** (*he's in a bit of a hole*) predicament, difficulty, corner, tight corner, muddle, tangle, quandary, dilemma, plight, strait, fix (inf), mess (inf), jam (inf), spot (inf), tight spot (inf), pickle (inf), scrape (inf), hot water (inf), deep water (inf), pretty pass (inf).
≫ *verb* puncture, perforate, pierce, breach, break, crack, stab, spike, slit, lacerate, gash, rent.

hole up hide, hide out, take cover, lie low, lie up, go to ground, go to earth, go into hiding, conceal oneself, shelter, take refuge.

pick holes in criticize, rubbish (inf), run down (inf), put down (inf), knock (inf), slag off (inf), slate (inf), bad-mouth (inf), carp at, disparage, denigrate, nitpick (inf), find fault with, pull to pieces (inf), cavil at.

holiday *noun* **1** (*a holiday from work*) vacation, time off, leave, leave of absence, day off, break, rest, breathing-space, recess, sabbatical, furlough, trip. **2** (*a religious holiday*) festival, festivity, feast day, bank holiday, public holiday, holy day, saint's day, carnival, celebration, anniversary, gala, fête.

holier-than-thou *adj* sanctimonious, goody-goody (inf), self-righteous, self-satisfied, complacent, self-approving, smug, priggish, pietistic, pharisaical, pious, unctuous.

holiness *noun* piety, devoutness, religiousness, sacredness, spirituality, saintliness, godliness, sanctity, sanctitude, goodness, righteousness, virtuousness, blessedness, sinlessness, divineness, divinity, purity, virtue, consecration, dedication. OPPOSITE: profanity.

hollow *adj* **1** (*a hollow cylinder*) empty, vacant, void, unfilled. OPPOSITE: solid. **2** (*hollow cheeks*) sunken, deep, deep-set, indented, depressed, caved-in, concave, cavernous. **3** (*a hollow noise*) muffled, muted, low, deep, rumbling, echoing, reverberant, reverberating, flat, dull, dead, expressionless, toneless. **4** (*a hollow victory*) meaningless, pointless, insignificant, futile, empty, vain, specious, fruitless, profitless, unprofitable, unavailing, worthless, valueless, useless, pyrrhic. **5** (*hollow promises*) insincere, cynical, hypocritical, artificial, feigned, pretended, sham, false, counterfeit, deceitful, treacherous, two-faced, faithless, flimsy, spurious, untrue, unsound, dissembling. OPPOSITE: sincere.
≫ *noun* **1** (*a hollow at the foot of the hill*) depression, dip, basin, bowl, cup, cavity, concavity, pit, hole, well, groove, trough, crater, niche, nook, cranny, recess, cave, cavern, dent, dimple, indentation. **2** (*traversed the hollow*) valley, dale, glen, dell, ravine, gorge.
≫ *verb* dig out, excavate, scoop out, gouge out, burrow, furrow, tunnel, channel, groove, pit, indent, dent.

beat hollow annihilate, beat, defeat, devastate, hammer (inf), thrash (inf), lick (inf), slaughter (inf), trounce (inf), crush, rout, outdo, surpass, overwhelm, overcome, worst.

holocaust *noun* massacre, carnage, butchery, mass murder, genocide, ethnic cleansing, slaughter, annihilation, extermination, extinction, pogrom, sacrifice, ravaging, destruction, demolition, devastation, inferno, conflagration, flames.

holy *adj* **1** (*a holy man*) devout, pious, religious, saintly, godly, God-fearing, pietistic, good, virtuous, faithful, righteous, sinless, moral, pure, divine, spiritual, venerable, sublime. OPPOSITE: impious. **2** (*a holy site*) sacred, religious, spiritual, divine, hallowed, consecrated, revered, blessed, dedicated, sanctified, sacrosanct, venerated. OPPOSITE: profane.

homage *noun* **1** (*homage to the saints*) honour, respect, deference, praise, worship, adoration, adulation, veneration, reverence, esteem, admiration, awe, regard. OPPOSITE: disrespect. **2** (*owed homage to his master*) loyalty, allegiance, service, obeisance, constancy, devotion, fidelity, faithfulness, fealty, duty, tribute.

home *noun* **1** (*took them to her home*) house, abode, dwelling, dwelling place, residence, domicile, habitation, address, pad (inf), digs (inf). **2** (*home of many rare species*) habitat, territory, environment, natural element, stamping-ground, haunt, domain. **3** (*came from a respectable home*) family, household, background. **4** (*wandered away from home for many years*) birthplace, hometown, homeland, native land, native country, fatherland, motherland, mother country, country of origin, roots. **5** (*put her in a home*) residential home, retirement home, nursing home, convalescent home, old people's home, sheltered housing, children's home, institution, shelter, hospice, hostel, refuge, retreat, asylum. **6** (*the home of modern ballet*) birthplace, fount, source, cradle, place of origin.
≫ *adj* domestic, family, familiar, household, internal, interior, inland, national, local, native, central. OPPOSITE: foreign.

at home **1** (*made her feel at home*) comfortable, relaxed, at ease. **2** (*at home with such matters*) in one's element, on home ground, familiar, knowledgeable, experienced, used to, skilled, competent, proficient, conversant, au courant, well-versed, well up (inf), up on (inf).

bring home drive home, press home, impress, emphasize, stress, underline, highlight, make clear, instil, inculcate.

home in on aim at, focus on, concentrate on, zero in on, pinpoint.

nothing to write home about ordinary, mediocre,

dull, drab, boring, inferior, predictable, no great shakes (*inf*).

homeland *noun* native land, native country, country of origin, fatherland, motherland, mother country.

homeless *adj* of no fixed abode, itinerant, vagrant, travelling, nomadic, wandering, rootless, displaced, unsettled, dispossessed, evicted, exiled, outcast, abandoned, forsaken, destitute, down-and-out (*inf*), derelict.
➤ *noun* vagrants, tramps, squatters, travellers, vagabonds, down-and-outs (*inf*), dossers (*inf*), derelicts.

homely *adj* **1** (*a homely atmosphere*) homelike, homey, comfortable, comfy (*inf*), snug, cosy, welcoming, hospitable, informal, relaxed, friendly, familiar, intimate, cheerful. OPPOSITE: grand. **2** (*lived in homely surroundings*) simple, plain, modest, natural, unassuming, unaffected, unpretentious, unsophisticated, ordinary, everyday, familiar, domestic, homelike, homespun, folksy. **3** (*a homely face*) plain, plain-featured, plain-looking, unattractive, unlovely, ugly, unprepossessing.

homespun *adj* plain, simple, modest, uncomplicated, unpolished, unrefined, unsophisticated, natural, rustic, homely, folksy, home-made, rough, rude, crude, coarse, artless, inelegant, amateurish.

homicidal *adj* murderous, death-dealing, maniacal, lethal, deadly, violent, bloodthirsty, sanguinary.

homicide *noun* manslaughter, murder, assassination, killing, slaying, slaughter, bloodshed.

homily *noun* sermon, preaching, discourse, lecture, lesson, harangue, address, speech, talk, oration.

homogeneous *adj* uniform, consistent, unvaried, unvarying, identical, all one, alike, like, similar, akin, kindred, analogous, corresponding, parallel, cognate, correlative, comparable, compatible, harmonious. OPPOSITE: heterogeneous.

homogenize *verb* coalesce, fuse, unite, blend, merge, combine, amalgamate.

homosexual *noun* gay, lesbian, queer (*inf*), poof (*inf*), poofter (*inf*), fairy (*inf*), queen (*inf*), homo (*inf*), dyke (*inf*), faggot (*inf*), fag (*inf*), bent (*inf*), pansy (*inf*), nancy (*inf*), woofter (*inf*).
➤ *adj* gay, lesbian, queer (*inf*), bent (*inf*), camp (*inf*), butch (*inf*).

hone *verb* sharpen, point, edge, whet, strop, grind, file, polish. OPPOSITE: blunt.

honest *adj* **1** (*an honest politician*) trustworthy, trusty, reliable, dependable, loyal, upright, upstanding, reputable, respectable, law-abiding, righteous, virtuous, honourable, ethical, moral, good, worthy, just, fair, decent, high-minded, right-minded, principled, incorruptible, scrupulous, conscientious. OPPOSITE: dishonest. **2** (*give us your honest opinion*) truthful, sincere, candid, frank, blunt, up-front (*inf*), open, outspoken, direct, straightforward, straight, forthright, unequivocal, plain, simple, open, plain-speaking. **3** (*an honest decision*) fair, just, impartial, unprejudiced, unbiased, disinterested, objective, equitable, balanced, even-handed, lawful, legal, legitimate, above-board, fair and square (*inf*). **4** (*an honest mistake*) genuine, real, authentic, true, bona fide, proper.

honestly *adv* **1** (*honestly, I don't know anything about it*) to be honest, really, truthfully, sincerely, frankly, speaking frankly, candidly, directly, outright, openly, straight up (*inf*), truly, plainly. **2** (*came by it honestly*) legally, lawfully, legitimately, morally, ethically, fairly, justly, honourably, decently, on the level (*inf*), in good faith, legit (*inf*).

honesty *noun* **1** (*a reputation for honesty*) virtue, uprightness, honour, honourableness, worthiness, integrity, morality, morals, ethics, principles, righteousness, incorruptibility, reputability, scrupulousness, conscientiousness, trustworthiness, reliability, fidelity, faithfulness, genuineness, veracity, probity, goodness, rectitude, fairness. OPPOSITE: dishonesty. **2** (*the honesty of his response*) truthfulness, truth, sincerity, bluntness, frankness, candour, forthrightness, outspokenness, straightforwardness, explicitness, openness. **3** (*the honesty of the court*) fairness, legitimacy, legality, justice, justness, equitability, equity, objectivity, impartiality, balance, even-handedness.

honorarium *noun* fee, recompense, remuneration, pay, salary, reward, emolument.

honorary *adj* honorific, titular, nominal, in name only, complimentary, formal, ex officio, unofficial, unpaid.

honour *noun* **1** (*the honour of the regiment*) fame, glory, renown, repute, reputation, good name, illustriousness, esteem, distinction, eminence, pride, dignity, prestige, standing, credit, regard, respect, self-respect. OPPOSITE: disgrace. **2** (*a person of honour*) honesty, integrity, decency, fairness, justness, justice, probity, goodness, rectitude, righteousness, sincerity, trustworthiness, truthfulness, uprightness, worthiness, worth, virtue, morality, morals, ethics, principles, reliability, dependability, fidelity, faithfulness. OPPOSITE: dishonesty. **3** (*greeted him with due honour*) praise, acclaim, acclamation, applause, accolades, tribute, homage, reverence, veneration, adulation, lauding, worship, adoration, exaltation, glorification, admiration, respect, deference, compliments. OPPOSITE: contempt. **4** (*heaped honours upon the winner*) award, accolade, decoration, distinction, prize, reward, trophy, title, crown, laurel, commendation, tribute, acknowledgment, recognition. **5** (*an honour to be here*) privilege, pleasure, joy, pride, satisfaction. **6** (*feared for her honour*) virginity, chastity, purity, virtue, innocence, modesty.
➤ *verb* **1** (*honoured by all who knew him*) respect, esteem, appreciate, value, prize, admire, revere, reverence, venerate, worship, adore, idolize. OPPOSITE: despise. **2** (*a tribute to honour our leader*) praise, acclaim, applaud, celebrate, cheer, commemorate, commend, compliment, laud, eulogize, pay homage to, pay tribute to, acknowledge, recognize, glorify, dignify, exalt, ennoble, lionize, panegyrize. OPPOSITE: dishonour. **3** (*honour their word*) keep, observe, respect, live up to, discharge, fulfil, carry out, execute, perform. **4** (*honour the cheque*) pay, cash, clear, take, pass, accept, acknowledge.

honourable *adj* **1** (*an honourable man*) honest, upright, moral, ethical, principled, upstanding, good, decent, right, righteous, right-minded, proper, straight, virtuous, worthy, trustworthy, truthful, trusty, respectable, reputable, creditable, true, faithful, just, fair, reliable, dependable. OPPOSITE: dishonourable. **2** (*an honourable sacrifice*) noble, glorious, distinguished, creditable, illustrious, respected, notable, noted, eminent, great, venerable, esteemed, prestigious, renowned, famous. OPPOSITE: despised.

hood *noun* cowl, scarf, domino, capuche.

hoodlum *noun* **1** (*a Mafia hoodlum*) hood (*inf*), gangster, cutthroat, mobster (*inf*), heavy (*inf*), hatchet man, gunman, criminal, lawbreaker, felon, terrorist. **2** (*a mob of teenage hoodlums*) hooligan, lout, yob (*inf*), yobbo (*inf*), delinquent, vandal, thug, tough (*inf*), ruffian, rowdy, brute.

hoodwink *verb* dupe, deceive, delude, mislead, trick, hoax, fool, con (*inf*), take in, take for a ride (*inf*), have on (*inf*), outwit, bamboozle (*inf*), kid (*inf*), cheat, defraud, swindle, rook, gull, cozen.

hook *noun* **1** (*fastened with a hook*) hook-and-eye, hasp, clasp, catch, clip, fastener, link. **2** (*put her coat on a hook*) peg, holder. **3** (*working in the field with a hook*) billhook, sickle, scythe. **4** (*a hook in the road*) angle, crook, bend, turn, curve, twist, loop, elbow, bow, arc, dog-leg, oxbow. **5** (*a left hook to the jaw*) punch, blow, hit, stroke, box, thump, clout (*inf*), wallop (*inf*), cuff, clip, knock, rap. ➤ *verb* **1** (*hook a fish*) catch, capture, bag, grab, snare, ensnare, trap, entrap, enmesh, entangle. OPPOSITE: release. **2** (*helped to hook her necklace*) fasten, clasp, fix, secure, join, link, connect, hitch, close. OPPOSITE: unhook. **3** (*hooked the ball to the right*) curve, bend, curl. **off the hook** cleared, let off (*inf*), acquitted, exonerated, vindicated, in the clear.

hooked *adj* **1** (*a hooked nose*) hooklike, hook-shaped, bent, beaked, beaky, curved, crooked, bowed, angular, aquiline, barbed, curled. **2** (*hooked on drugs*) addicted, dependent. **3** (*hooked on her*) enamoured, obsessed, devoted.

hooligan *noun* lout, vandal, delinquent, yob (*inf*), yobbo (*inf*), ruffian, rowdy, hoodlum, mobster, thug, tough, rough.

hoop *noun* band, ring, circle, round, loop, wheel, girdle, circlet.

hoot *verb* **1** (*an owl hooted*) tu-whit tu-whoo, screech, shriek, call, cry, whoop, ululate. **2** (*a car hooting*) toot, beep. **3** (*hooting from the crowd below*) shriek, howl, yell, cry, shout, whoop, toot, boo, catcall, hiss, jeer, sneer, deride, mock, taunt. OPPOSITE: cheer. ➤ *noun* **1** (*the owl gave a single hoot*) tu-whit tu-whoo, screech, shriek, call, cry, toot, ululation. **2** (*the hoot of a car*) toot, beep. **3** (*the hoots of the crowd*) shriek, howl, yell, cry, shout, whoop, toot, boo, catcall, hiss, jeer, sneer, raspberry (*inf*), derision, taunt. OPPOSITE: cheer. **4** (*he's a real hoot*) clown, caution, card (*inf*), scream (*inf*), laugh (*inf*).

hop *verb* skip, caper, jump, leap, bound, spring, vault, frisk, prance, dance. ➤ *noun* **1** (*gave a hop of joy*) jump, leap, spring, bound, vault, bounce, step, skip, dance. **2** (*a short hop over the Channel*) flight, trip, journey, excursion, jaunt. **3** (*went with them to the hop*) dance, disco, social, knees-up (*inf*), party, rave (*inf*), shindig (*inf*).

hope *noun* hopefulness, optimism, ambition, dream, aspiration, expectation, expectancy, anticipation, longing, yearning, craving, desire, wish, prospect, promise, faith, trust, belief, conviction, assumption, confidence, assurance. OPPOSITE: despair. ➤ *verb* desire, long, yearn, crave, aspire, wish, expect, anticipate, contemplate, await, dream, look forward to, count on, reckon on, rely, trust, believe, assume.

hopeful *adj* **1** (*feeling very hopeful*) optimistic, sanguine, expectant, aspiring, positive, confident, assured, bullish (*inf*), buoyant, cheerful. OPPOSITE: despairing. **2** (*a hopeful development*) promising, encouraging, positive, optimistic, favourable, heartening, gladdening, reassuring, auspicious, propitious, bright, rosy, pleasant. OPPOSITE: discouraging.

hopefully *adv* **1** (*hopefully we will be on time*) with luck, if all goes well, all being well, it is hoped that, probably, conceivably, feasibly. **2** (*waiting hopefully*) expectantly, with anticipation, eagerly, optimistically, expectedly, confidently, buoyantly.

hopeless *adj* **1** (*dejected and hopeless*) despairing, desperate, despondent, downcast, downhearted, gloomy, demoralized, disconsolate, dejected, forlorn, wretched, woebegone, negative, pessimistic, defeatist, suicidal. OPPOSITE: hopeful. **2** (*a hopeless case*) lost, irretrievable, irredeemable, irreversible, irreparable, beyond repair, irremediable, beyond remedy, incurable, helpless, serious, grave, fatal, deadly, poor. OPPOSITE: promising. **3** (*in a hopeless condition*) impossible, impracticable, unattainable, unachievable, no-win (*inf*), vain, foolish, futile, useless, worthless, pointless, forlorn. OPPOSITE: worthwhile. **4** (*hopeless at art*) incompetent, lousy (*inf*), inadequate, bad, awful (*inf*), poor, inferior, weak, pathetic (*inf*), no good, ineffective, ineffectual. OPPOSITE: proficient.

horde *noun* crowd, multitude, throng, mass, mob, host, army, gang, pack, troop, band, crew, company, gathering, press, swarm, flock, herd, drove.

horizon *noun* **1** (*appeared over the horizon*) skyline, vista, prospect, range, field of view. **2** (*broaden her horizons*) scope, perspective, compass, sphere, realm, outlook, prospect, perception, ambit, ken, knowledge.

horizontal *adj* flat, level, levelled, plane, flush, smooth, prone, supine. OPPOSITE: vertical.

horrendous *adj* **1** (*a horrendous crime*) horrific, horrid, appalling, shocking, horrifying, terrifying, frightening, frightful, dreadful, terrible. **2** (*a horrendous personality*) nasty, unpleasant, disagreeable.

horrible *adj* **1** (*a horrible murder*) horrid, dreadful, frightful, frightening, fearful, awful, appalling, shocking, harrowing, bloodcurdling, terrible, terrifying, hair-raising, horrifying, horrific, horrendous, ghastly, grim, grisly, gruesome, heinous, hideous, loathsome, abominable, abhorrent, detestable, hateful, obscene, revolting, disgusting, repulsive. OPPOSITE: wonderful. **2** (*a horrible old man*) unpleasant, disagreeable, horrid, nasty, terrible, dreadful, frightful, awful, disgusting, beastly, hideous, loathsome, abominable, detestable, obnoxious, odious, offensive, ghastly, revolting, repulsive, mean, unkind.

horrid *adj* **1** (*a horrid woman*) horrible, awful, dreadful, unpleasant, disagreeable, nasty, obnoxious, mean, unkind, hateful, beastly (*inf*), cruel. OPPOSITE: pleasant. **2** (*a horrid crime*) horrific, horrifying, horrendous, ghastly, bloodcurdling, hair-raising, repulsive, revolting, grim, gruesome, hideous, harrowing, appalling, dreadful, abominable, awful, terrible, shocking, obscene, frightful, frightening, alarming, terrifying, offensive. OPPOSITE: wonderful.

horrific *adj* horrifying, horrendous, grisly, gruesome, frightening, alarming, terrifying, scary (*inf*), shocking, appalling, dreadful, ghastly, bloodcurdling, harrowing, awful, terrible, frightful. OPPOSITE: reassuring.

horrify *verb* **1** (*the conditions horrified us*) shock, appal, disgust, sicken, nauseate, dismay, distress, outrage, scandalize, offend, repel, revolt. OPPOSITE: reassure. **2** (*a story that will horrify you*) alarm, frighten, scare, terrify, petrify, terrorize, panic, startle, intimidate, scare to death (*inf*), scare stiff (*inf*), put the wind up (*inf*).

horror *noun* **1** (*eyes wide with horror*) terror, fear, fearfulness, panic, fright, alarm, shock, trepidation, nervousness, awe, dread, dismay, apprehension, apprehensiveness, uneasiness, consternation. OPPOSITE: reassurance. **2** (*fill with horror*) loathing, hatred, detestation, abomination, abhorrence, repugnance, repulsion, revulsion, outrage, disgust, distaste, hate, aversion. OPPOSITE: liking.

horse *noun* mount, steed, stallion, gelding, mare, filly, colt, foal, pony, hack, cob, nag, jade, dobbin, gee-gee (*inf*).

horseplay *noun* clowning, foolery, fooling, fooling around, tomfoolery, buffoonery, skylarking, pranks, high jinks, practical jokes, antics, capers, fun and games, rough-and-tumble, romping, monkey business (*inf*), shenanigans (*inf*).

horticulture *noun* gardening, cultivation, arboriculture, floriculture.

hose *noun* pipe, tube, tubing, channel, outlet, duct, conduit, siphon.

hosiery *noun* stockings, tights, leggings, socks, hose.

hospitable *adj* welcoming, friendly, neighbourly, genial, amicable, cordial, convivial, congenial, sociable, warm, warmhearted, kind, kindhearted, kindly, helpful, benevolent, generous, liberal, bountiful, openhanded, gracious, amenable, receptive, approachable, responsive, well-disposed. OPPOSITE: inhospitable.

hospital *noun* infirmary, medical centre, health centre, sanatorium, institute, hospice.

hospitality *noun* hospitableness, welcome, neighbourliness, friendliness, amicability, geniality, amenability, cheer, heartiness, cordiality, congeniality, conviviality, sociability, warmth, warmheartedness, kindness, kindheartedness, benevolence, generosity, liberality, bountifulness, openhandedness, helpfulness. OPPOSITE: unfriendliness.

host¹ *noun* **1** (*your host for the evening*) hostess, entertainer, master of ceremonies, MC, emcee (*inf*), compere, presenter, announcer, anchor, anchorman, anchorwoman, linkman. OPPOSITE: guest. **2** (*thank you, mine host*) proprietor, proprietress, publican, landlord, landlady, innkeeper, hotelier, hotel-keeper.

➤ *verb* **1** (*host the programme*) present, front (*inf*),

introduce, compere, emcee (*inf*). **2** (*host a party*) give, hold.

host² *noun* (*a host of friends*) throng, array, mass, multitude, myriad, army, legion, horde, crowd, mob, assembly, band, crush, drove, herd, troop, swarm, pack.

hostage *noun* prisoner, captive, pawn, surety, security, pledge.

hostile *adj* **1** (*a hostile attitude*) belligerent, bellicose, warlike, warring, militant, contrary, antagonistic, ill-disposed, malevolent, malicious, spiteful, inhospitable, unsympathetic, unfriendly, unkind, aggressive, rancorous, angry, wrathful. **2** (*hostile to the suggestion*) opposed, anti (*inf*), against, opposite, antagonistic, averse, ill-disposed, inimical. **3** (*a hostile environment*) adverse, unfavourable, unwelcoming, inhospitable, inauspicious, disadvantageous, unpropitious, contrary.

hostilities *pl noun* war, warfare, battle, strife, militancy, conflict, fighting, bloodshed, action. OPPOSITE: peace.

hostility *noun* **1** (*the changes provoked some hostility*) opposition, antagonism, enmity, hatred, ill will, unfriendliness, animosity, antipathy, aversion, inimicalness. **2** (*the hostility of his opponents*) belligerence, bellicosity, antagonism, aggression, militancy, unfriendliness, unkindness, malevolence, malice, spite, resentment, cruelty, anger, wrath. OPPOSITE: friendliness.

hot *adj* **1** (*hot drinks*) heated, warm, red hot, scalding, boiling, piping, steaming, sizzling, scorching, fiery, burning, flaming, blazing, roasting, searing. OPPOSITE: cold. **2** (*hot weather*) warm, scorching, scalding, blistering, blazing, boiling, baking, roasting, sizzling, searing, oven-like, parching, sweltering, torrid, tropical, sultry. **3** (*her skin feels hot*) feverish, fevered, delirious, febrile, burning, flushed, red. **4** (*a hot taste*) pungent, sharp, strong, acrid, fiery, biting, spicy, peppery, piquant. OPPOSITE: mild. **5** (*a hot temper*) fiery, fierce, ferocious, furious, enraged, raging, stormy, tempestuous, savage, angry, ardent, indignant, fervent, livid, fervid, passionate, heated, inflamed, infuriated, incensed, irascible, irate, touchy, impetuous, violent, wrathful, boiling, seething, fuming. OPPOSITE: calm. **6** (*hot competition*) intense, fierce, furious, keen, strong, cutthroat. **7** (*hot on the idea of going*) keen, enthusiastic, eager, earnest, zealous, ardent, fervent, fervid, excited, passionate, vehement, animated, warm. OPPOSITE: apathetic. **8** (*hot for her*) lustful, horny (*inf*), randy, lascivious, lecherous, libidinous. **9** (*hot news*) recent, latest, new, brand new, fresh, up-to-date, late, exciting. OPPOSITE: old. **10** (*handling hot cars*) stolen, wanted, smuggled, contraband, pilfered, ill-gotten. **11** (*brown is hot with designers this year*) popular, in (*inf*), in vogue, in demand, in favour, fashionable, approved, sought-after.

hot air nonsense, bullshit (*sl*), crap (*sl*), empty talk, rant, balderdash (*inf*), cobblers (*inf*), piffle (*inf*), bilge (*inf*), bosh (*inf*), bunk (*inf*), bunkum (*inf*), claptrap (*inf*), gas (*inf*), wind (*inf*), guff (*inf*), blather, blether, bluster, bombast, froth, verbiage.

hotbed *noun* breeding-ground, seedbed, forcing-house, cradle, nursery, school, den, hive, nest, womb.

hot-blooded *adj* **1** (*a hot-blooded embrace*) passionate, impassioned, ardent, sensual, lustful, lusty, randy (*inf*), horny (*inf*), libidinous. **2** (*a hot-blooded approach to life*) excitable, temperamental, fiery, ardent, heated, eager, spirited, high-spirited, impulsive, impetuous, precipitate, rash, fervent, bold, wild, quixotic.

hotel *noun* guesthouse, boarding house, inn, tavern, hostelry, public house, pub (*inf*), hostel, motel, pension.

hotfoot *adv* quickly, swiftly, speedily, at top speed, rapidly, promptly, without delay, hurriedly, in haste, hastily, posthaste, helter-skelter, pell-mell.

hotheaded *adj* hot-tempered, quick-tempered, short-tempered, excitable, volatile, explosive, fiery, volcanic, irascible, headstrong, impetuous, impulsive, hasty, precipitate, rash, foolhardy, reckless, unruly, wild. OPPOSITE: calm.

hothouse *noun* greenhouse, glasshouse, conservatory, orangery.

hound *verb* **1** (*hounded him over the moors*) chase, pursue, follow, dog, hunt, hunt down, stalk, track, trail, shadow, tail (*inf*). **2** (*they hounded her for an answer*) harry, harass, badger, nag, hassle (*inf*), bully, browbeat, persecute, provoke, impel, goad, prod, spur, pester, keep after, chivvy, drive, force, pressure, pressurize, urge.

house *noun* **1** (*a four-bedroomed house*) dwelling, abode, residence, domicile, home, homestead, habitation, pad (*inf*), building, edifice, cottage, bungalow, villa, mansion, semi (*inf*). **2** (*the whole house turned out*) household, family, family circle, ménage. **3** (*brought disgrace upon his house*) household, family, pedigree, lineage, line, ancestry, kindred, blood, strain, race, tribe, clan, dynasty. **4** (*a design house*) firm, business, company, partnership, concern, enterprise, establishment, organization, corporation, outfit (*inf*). **5** (*bring a measure before the house*) chamber, parliament, legislature, legislative body, assembly, congress, body. **6** (*played to a full house*) audience, auditorium, turnout, assembly, gathering, congregation, spectators, onlookers, listeners, viewers

➤ *verb* **1** (*house two families*) accommodate, put up, take in, domicile, lodge, board, quarter, billet, sleep, harbour, shelter. **2** (*the base houses the electrical circuits*) contain, hold, sheathe, store, shelter, guard, protect, cover.

on the house free, free of charge, for nothing, gratis, at no cost, without charge, without cost, without payment.

household *noun* family, family circle, menage, house, home, establishment, set-up.

➤ *adj* domestic, family, home, ordinary, plain, run-of-the-mill, common, usual, established, everyday, familiar, well-known.

householder *noun* homeowner, head of the household, freeholder, leaseholder, occupier, occupant, owner, proprietor, resident, tenant, landlord, landlady.

housekeeping *noun* domestic work, domestic matters, household management, housecraft, home economics, domestic science, homemaking, housewifery.

housing *noun* **1** (*housing for the poor*) accommodation, houses, homes, dwellings, habitation, shelter. **2** (*eased the device from its housing*) casing, case, container, holder, capsule, covering, guard, cover, sheath, jacket, protection, enclosure.

hovel *noun* hut, shack, shanty, cabin, shed, slum, dump (*inf*), hole (*inf*). OPPOSITE: palace.

hover *verb* **1** (*hover in the air*) hang, fly, float, drift, flap, flutter. **2** (*hovered nearby*) linger, hang about, lurk. **3** (*hovered over the decision*) pause, dither, falter, hesitate, waver, vacillate, fluctuate, alternate, oscillate, seesaw. OPPOSITE: decide.

however *adv* nevertheless, nonetheless, notwithstanding, regardless, but, still, yet, even so, though, anyhow, anyway, just the same, after all.

howl *verb* **1** (*a dog howled*) bay, yelp, yowl, ululate. **2** (*he howled with rage*) bellow, bawl, yell, wail, roar, cry, shout, shriek, scream, caterwaul, hoot, moan, groan.

➤ *noun* **1** (*the howl of a wild animal*) bay, yelp, yowl, ululation. **2** (*the howl of a stricken man*) bellow, yell, wail, roar, cry, shout, shriek, scream, caterwauling, hoot, moan, groan.

howler *noun* mistake, error, blunder, boob (*inf*), boo-boo (*inf*), bloomer (*inf*), clanger (*inf*), gaffe, solecism.

hub *noun* **1** (*the hub of a cartwheel*) pivot, axis. **2** (*the hub of the organization*) centre, middle, focus, focal point, core, heart, nerve.

hubbub *noun* noise, din, racket, uproar, tumult, commotion, disturbance, hullabaloo, brouhaha, clamour, hurly-burly, rumpus, riot, confusion, bedlam, chaos, pandemonium, disorder. OPPOSITE: quiet.

huddle *verb* **1** (*huddle into the room*) cluster, bunch, gather, congregate, converge, gravitate, meet, crowd, throng, herd, flock, cram, pack, press, squeeze. OPPOSITE: disperse. **2** (*huddle under the sheets*) nestle, cuddle, snuggle, curl up, crouch, hunch up.

➤ *noun* **1** (*a huddle of figures*) crowd, gathering, knot, throng, mass, cluster, bunch, pack. **2** (*a huddle of belongings*) heap, jumble, tangle, muddle, clump, confusion, disorder, mess. **3** (*the officials went into a huddle*) conclave, conference, discussion, consultation, powwow (*inf*), confab (*inf*), meeting.

hue[1] *noun* **1** (*a golden hue*) colour, shade, tint, tinge, tincture, tone, dye. **2** (*opinions of contrasting hue*) complexion, cast, aspect, light.

hue[2] *noun* **hue and cry** furore, uproar, commotion, fuss, hullabaloo, outcry, racket, rumpus, ruction (*inf*), brouhaha, clamour, to-do (*inf*).

huff *noun* temper, mood, bad mood, pique, sulks, rage, anger, passion, miff (*inf*), pet.

hug *verb* **1** (*hug each other*) embrace, cuddle, clasp, enfold, squeeze, press, hold, cling to, clutch, enclose. **2** (*hugs the road*) grip, hold, cling to, keep close to, follow closely. **3** (*hugged her dream*) cling to, hold on to, cherish, nurse, harbour, keep close, retain.

➤ *noun* embrace, cuddle, squeeze, clasp, hold, clinch (*inf*).

huge *adj* enormous, massive, tremendous, prodigious, stupendous, vast, immense, colossal, giant, gigantic, gargantuan, ginormous (*inf*), mega (*inf*), elephantine, mammoth, monstrous, monumental, mountainous, Herculean, titanic, great, big, large, jumbo (*inf*), extensive, bulky, heavy, unwieldy. OPPOSITE: tiny.

hulk *noun* **1** (*a rotting hulk*) wreck, shipwreck, derelict, ruin, remains, shell, skeleton, hull, frame. **2** (*an awkward hulk of a man*) lump, clod (*inf*), oaf, lout, lubber, lummox (*inf*).

hulking *adj* massive, bulky, gross, large, heavy, weighty, overgrown, cumbersome, awkward, clumsy, lumbering, lumpish, ponderous, ungainly.

hull[1] *noun* (*the hull of a boat*) body, skeleton, frame, framework, structure, casing, covering, shell.

hull[2] *noun* (*the hull of a fruit*) husk, peel, rind, skin, shell, pod, capsule, pericarp.
➤ *verb* peel, pare, husk, shell, strip, skin, trim, shuck.

hullabaloo *noun* noise, furore, hue and cry, din, fuss, racket, to-do (*inf*), bedlam, outcry, uproar, hubbub, clamour, brouhaha, commotion, disturbance, turmoil, tumult, upheaval, hurly-burly, palaver, rumpus (*inf*), ruction (*inf*), pandemonium, confusion. OPPOSITE: quiet.

hum *verb* **1** (*a fan humming*) buzz, whirr, purr, drone, murmur, thrum, throb, vibrate. **2** (*hum a tune*) sing, croon, murmur, mumble. **3** (*the place hums at weekends*) throb, pulsate, pulse, vibrate, bustle, buzz, stir.
➤ *noun* whirr, whirring, buzz, buzzing, purr, purring, thrum, throb, throbbing, drone, murmur, mumble, vibration, pulsation.

human *adj* **1** (*human in form*) anthropoid, manlike, mortal. **2** (*human weakness*) mortal, physical, bodily, fleshly, corporal, carnal. **3** (*perhaps he's human after all*) fallible, mortal, flesh and blood, vulnerable, susceptible, erring, weak, frail, natural. **4** (*revealed a human side to his nature*) kind, kindly, considerate, humane, sensitive, sympathetic, compassionate, understanding, approachable, accessible. OPPOSITE: inhuman.
➤ *noun* human being, homo sapiens, body (*inf*), person, individual, soul, mortal, man, woman, child. OPPOSITE: beast.

humane *adj* kind, kindhearted, kindly, benevolent, benign, good-natured, tender, loving, understanding, considerate, compassionate, sympathetic, merciful, forgiving, forbearing, magnanimous, generous, clement, lenient, mild, gentle, good, charitable, humanitarian. OPPOSITE: cruel.

humanitarian *adj* **1** (*humanitarian philosopher*) humane, benevolent, beneficent, kind, good, considerate, compassionate, sympathetic, understanding, merciful, lenient, gentle, generous, magnanimous, public-spirited, unselfish. **2** (*launched a humanitarian effort*) philanthropic, altruistic, charitable, welfare.
➤ *noun* philanthropist, altruist, benefactor, do-gooder (*inf*), Good Samaritan, social reformer.

humanity *noun* **1** (*a benefit to all humanity*) human race, man, mankind, humankind, womankind, homo sapiens, people, mortality, mortals, flesh. **2** (*a victim of her own humanity*) mortality, human nature, flesh and blood. **3** (*renowned for his humanity*) humaneness, kindness, kindheartedness, thoughtfulness, benevolence, benignity, tenderness, gentleness, compassion, sympathy, understanding, brotherly love, fellow feeling, mercy, mercifulness, pity, clemency, leniency, tolerance, generosity, magnanimity, goodwill, charity, philanthropy, goodness. OPPOSITE: inhumanity.

humanize *verb* civilize, tame, domesticate, educate, edify, enlighten, cultivate, refine, polish, improve, better, soften, mellow. OPPOSITE: brutalize.

humble *adj* **1** (*a humble leader*) modest, unassuming, unpretentious. OPPOSITE: haughty. **2** (*our humble abode*) modest, simple, plain, poor, inferior, mean, lowly, low, base, ordinary, common, commonplace, unassuming, unpretentious, unostentatious, undistinguished, unrefined, vulgar, insignificant, unimportant. **3** (*a humble attitude*) modest, meek, submissive, unassertive, unassuming, unpretentious, unostentatious, self-effacing, docile, servile, slavish, subservient, obsequious, sycophantic, deferential, respectful, polite, courteous.
➤ *verb* **1** (*the press sought to humble him*) humiliate, shame, discredit, disgrace, mortify, chagrin, chasten, abash, lower, reduce, bring down, bring low, break, degrade, abase, demean. OPPOSITE: exalt. **2** (*humbled by their kindness*) belittle, deflate, crush, subdue. **3** (*humbled his opponent*) subdue, conquer, vanquish, defeat, overwhelm, smash, crush, rout, trounce.

humbug *noun* **1** (*fooled by his humbug*) trick, trickery, deception, deceit, hoax, fraud, con (*inf*), imposture, pretence, delusion, sham, swindle, ruse, dodge, stratagem, wile. **2** (*nothing more than a humbug*) cheat, fraud, conman (*inf*), swindler, trickster, charlatan, rogue, bluffer, quack, fake, phoney (*inf*), sham, impostor. **3** (*that's just a lot of humbug*) nonsense, rubbish, balls (*sl*), bullshit (*sl*), crap (*sl*), shit (*sl*), bunkum (*inf*), hypocrisy, balderdash (*inf*), baloney (*inf*), bosh (*inf*), claptrap (*inf*), cobblers (*inf*), eyewash (*inf*), poppycock (*inf*), rot (*inf*), twaddle (*inf*).

humdrum *adj* monotonous, boring, tedious, tiresome, wearisome, dull, routine, repetitious, uninteresting, uneventful, unvaried, unvarying, prosaic, prosy, dry, dreary, mind-numbing, mundane, commonplace, ordinary, everyday, run-of-the-mill, banal. OPPOSITE: interesting.

humid *adj* damp, moist, wet, dank, soggy, misty, steamy, muggy, clammy, sticky, oppressive, close, sultry, heavy. OPPOSITE: dry.

humidity *noun* humidness, damp, dampness, moisture, moistness, dankness, mugginess, sultriness, steaminess, stickiness, closeness, heaviness, clamminess, wetness, sogginess, vaporousness, dew, mist.

humiliate *verb* mortify, chagrin, embarrass, abash, chasten, humble, deflate, shame, disgrace, discredit, discomfit, put down (*inf*), cut down to size (*inf*), abase, demean, degrade, bring low, lower, confound, break, crush, subdue. OPPOSITE: dignify.

humiliation *noun* **1** (*the last stage in his humiliation*) mortification, loss of face (*inf*), ignominy, chagrin, embarrassment, discomfiture, chastening, humbling, deflation, abashment, shame, disgrace, discredit, dishonour, abasement, debasement, degradation, lowering, confounding, crushing. OPPOSITE: dignity. **2** (*this latest humiliation*) indignity, snub, put-down (*inf*), rebuff, affront.

humility *noun* **1** (*noted for her humility*) humbleness, modesty, self-effacement, diffidence, lowliness, meekness, unassertiveness, unpretentiousness. OPPOSITE: arrogance. **2** (*behaved with humility towards his master*) submissiveness, subservience, deference, servility, sycophancy, obsequiousness.

hummock *noun* knoll, hillock, hump, mound, prominence, ridge, elevation, barrow.

humorist noun comic, comedian, comedienne, wit, joker, jokester, card (inf), wag, jester, clown, satirist, caricaturist, cartoonist.

humorous adj 1 (a humorous novel) funny, amusing, entertaining, comic, comical, droll, witty, facetious, farcical, laughable, hilarious, sidesplitting, rib-tickling, ludicrous, ridiculous, absurd, jocular, satirical. OPPOSITE: serious. 2 (a humorous companion) funny, amusing, entertaining, witty, waggish, comical, merry, playful, whimsical, jocular, jocose, facetious, zany (inf).

humour noun 1 (an evening of humour) comedy, wit, wittiness, drollery, amusement, fun, pleasantry, gags, jokes, joking, jesting, jests, wisecracks (inf), badinage, repartee, farce, satire, buffoonery, facetiousness, waggishness. OPPOSITE: seriousness. 2 (failed to see the humour of his predicament) funny side, funniness, comedy, comic side, laughableness, hilarity, farce, jocularity, ludicrousness, ridiculousness, absurdity, absurdness, drollness. 3 (he's in an odd humour this morning) mood, temper, frame of mind, state of mind, disposition, temperament, spirits, nature. 4 (an eccentric humour of hers) whim, whimsy, caprice, fancy, bent, bias, inclination, vagary, propensity, eccentricity, crotchet, quirk, kink, idiosyncrasy, freak.
➤ verb gratify, placate, mollify, soothe, satisfy, indulge, tolerate, suffer, pamper, coddle, cosset, spoil, pander to, flatter, favour, please, accommodate, comply with, go along with, acquiesce in.

hump noun 1 (a hump in the lawn) protuberance, bulge, swelling, lump, bump, mass, excrescence, intumescence, outgrowth, knob, projection, protrusion, prominence, mound, hunch. 2 (she's got the hump) annoyance, aggravation, irritation, vexation, exasperation, unhappiness, sadness, depression, gloom, dumps (inf), grumps (inf), mopes (inf), sulks (inf), blues (inf), doldrums (inf).
➤ verb 1 (humped her shoulders) arch, vault, hunch, tense, curve, crook, curl up. OPPOSITE: straighten. 2 (humped the basket across the road) carry, lug, heave, hoist, lift, shoulder.

hunch noun guess, intuition, sixth sense, feeling, impression, notion, idea, inkling, premonition, presentiment, suspicion.
➤ verb 1 (hunched his shoulders) hump, arch, bend, curve. OPPOSITE: straighten. 2 (hunched over their work) crouch, stoop, squat, huddle, bend.

hunger noun 1 (hunger and disease) hungriness, malnutrition, famine, starvation, emptiness, appetite, greed, greediness, ravenousness, voracity, esurience. 2 (a hunger for learning) longing, yearning, desire, want, need, craving, pining, hankering, lust, thirst, appetite, itch, yen (inf).
➤ verb long, yearn, desire, wish, want, need, crave, pine, hanker, lust, thirst, ache, itch, yen (inf).

hungry adj 1 (prepared to feed a dozen hungry guests) ravenous, peckish (inf), greedy, insatiable, voracious, starving, starved, half-starved, famished, hollow, empty, underfed, undernourished, malnourished. 2 (hungry to learn the truth) desirous, longing, yearning, craving, pining, needing, aching, greedy, thirsty, eager, avid, itching, hankering, covetous. OPPOSITE: contented.

hunk noun 1 (a hunk of bread) chunk, lump, dollop, gobbet, clod, block, wedge, slab, wodge (inf), piece, portion, slice, mass. 2 (he's a real hunk) he-man (inf), dreamboat (inf), beefcake (inf), Adonis.

hunt verb 1 (hunt a stag) chase, give chase, pursue, hound, dog, follow, shadow, stalk, trail, tail (inf), track. 2 (hunt for her passport) seek, search, look, scour, rummage, forage, fish, ferret. OPPOSITE: find.
➤ noun 1 (a hunt for wild animals) chase, pursuit, hunting, stalking, tracking, trailing, shadowing, tailing (inf). 2 (mounted a hunt for the lost ship) search, quest, rummage, investigation. OPPOSITE: discovery.

hurdle noun 1 (jumped the hurdle) barrier, bar, barricade, obstacle, fence, railing, rail, wall, hedge, hedgerow. 2 (placed hurdles in her way) impediment, hindrance, block, obstacle, obstruction, barrier, snag, complication, difficulty, problem, stumbling block, handicap.

hurl verb throw, toss, sling, fling, cast, pitch, heave, chuck (inf), catapult, project, shy, fire, launch, propel, let fly, send.

hurly-burly noun commotion, hubbub, disorder, disruption, unrest, uproar, bedlam, chaos, furore, pandemonium, upheaval, turmoil, tumult, turbulence, frenzy, distraction, agitation, confusion, trouble, hassle (inf), bustle, hustle, brouhaha.

hurricane noun gale, storm, tempest, cyclone, typhoon, tornado, whirlwind. OPPOSITE: breeze.

hurried adj 1 (a hurried movement) quick, swift, fast, rapid, speedy, hasty, precipitate, breakneck, posthaste. 2 (gave it a hurried skim-through) cursory, superficial, offhand, fleeting, passing, perfunctory, transitory, brief, short, hasty, hectic, quick, rapid, swift, rushed, slapdash, careless, shallow. OPPOSITE: thorough.

hurry verb 1 (hurry home) rush, hasten, make haste, press on, push on, race, dash, run, fly, scurry, scamper, bustle, lose no time, step on it (inf), hightail it (inf), hotfoot it (inf), cut and run (inf), barrel along (inf), get a move on (inf), get cracking (inf), go all out (inf), shake a leg (inf). OPPOSITE: dawdle. 2 (hurry the process) accelerate, quicken, speed up, hasten, precipitate, expedite, dispatch, drive, urge, push, goad, prod, hustle. OPPOSITE: retard.
➤ noun 1 (the hurry of the traffic) rush, haste, hustle, bustle, flurry, speed, fastness, quickness, rapidity, swiftness, celerity, dispatch, expedition, promptitude, precipitation. 2 (done in a great hurry) rush, haste, urgency. OPPOSITE: leisure.

hurt verb 1 (my hand hurts) ache, be sore, be painful, throb, smart, nip, burn, sting, tingle. 2 (he has hurt himself) harm, injure, damage, wound, cut, lacerate, scratch, bruise, burn, maim, mutilate, disable, incapacitate, debilitate. OPPOSITE: soothe. 3 (her cruelty hurts me) pain, afflict, grieve, wound, sting, distress, upset, offend, annoy, sadden, aggrieve, discompose. 4 (this may hurt the president's chances) damage, harm, impair, spoil, mar, blemish, blight.
➤ noun 1 (she complained of the hurt in her leg) pain, soreness, discomfort, ache, aching, burning, smart, smarting, stinging, pangs, throbbing, tingling, suffering. 2 (the nurse treated his hurt) wound, injury, sore, bruise, cut, laceration, scratch. 3 (his suicide caused her great hurt)

distress, anguish, misery, grief, upset, sorrow, sadness, suffering, pain, affliction. **4** (*hurt done to the company's profits*) harm, damage, injury, mischief, wrong, disadvantage, loss.

➤ *adj* **1** (*several people were hurt*) injured, wounded, harmed, cut, lacerated, bruised, grazed, scarred, maimed. **2** (*rubbed her hurt foot*) sore, painful, aching, throbbing, burning, tingling, smarting. **3** (*hurt by their attitude*) upset, wounded, distressed, anguished, sad, saddened, sorrowful, miserable, griefstricken, grieving, aggrieved, annoyed, miffed (*inf*), offended, piqued, affronted.

hurtful *adj* **1** (*several hurtful comments*) wounding, upsetting, distressing, mean, unkind, cruel, vicious, nasty, spiteful, malicious, mischievous, offensive, derogatory, catty, scathing, cutting. **2** (*hurtful to his chances*) injurious, damaging, destructive, ruinous, harmful, disadvantageous, detrimental, prejudicial, deleterious, pernicious, inimical. OPPOSITE: harmless.

hurtle *verb* rush, dash, tear, fly, race, shoot, speed, scoot, career, charge, plunge, dive, crash, stampede.

husband *noun* married man, hubby (*inf*), spouse, partner, mate, consort, bridegroom, groom, old man (*inf*), other half (*inf*), lord and master.

➤ *verb* conserve, save, economize, eke out, ration, budget, store, preserve, reserve, put aside, put by, save up, hoard. OPPOSITE: waste.

husbandry *noun* **1** (*skilled at husbandry*) agriculture, farming, tillage, cultivation, land management, farm management, agribusiness, agronomy, agronomics. **2** (*proud of her husbandry*) frugality, saving, thrift, thriftiness, economy, good housekeeping.

hush *verb* **1** (*plotted to hush his critics*) silence, quieten, shush, still, mute, muzzle, suppress. **2** (*tried to hush his mother's fears*) still, quieten, soothe, calm, allay, appease, assuage, pacify, mollify, compose, settle, subdue.

➤ *noun* quiet, quietness, silence, stillness, tranquillity, serenity, repose, calm, calmness, peace, peacefulness. OPPOSITE: noise.

➤ *interj* shush, quiet, silence, be quiet, shut up (*inf*), pipe down (*inf*), cut the cackle (*inf*), hold your tongue (*inf*), dry up (*inf*).

hush up suppress, smother, stifle, gag, squash, conceal, cover up, keep secret, keep dark, sit on (*inf*).

hush-hush *adj* secret, top secret, confidential, classified, restricted, under wraps (*inf*).

husk *noun* shell, hull, pod, capsule, shuck, chaff, peel, rind, skin, bark, covering, coating, case. OPPOSITE: kernel.

husky *adj* **1** (*a husky voice*) hoarse, guttural, gruff, gravelly, raucous, harsh, rough, coarse, thick, grating, rasping, croaky, croaking, throaty, low, deep. **2** (*a husky young man*) burly, brawny, muscular, hefty, beefy (*inf*), rugged, strapping, strong, sturdy, well-built, thickset, stocky. OPPOSITE: puny.

hustle *verb* **1** (*hustled the others aside*) push, shove, thrust, crowd, jog, jostle, elbow, nudge, shoulder. **2** (*had to hustle to get everything done*) bustle, hurry, make haste, hasten, dash, rush, speed, fly, get a move on (*inf*), step on it (*inf*), put one's foot down (*inf*). **3** (*hustle them into signing*) force, badger, coerce, pressure, pressurize, pester, prompt, impel, urge, spur, goad, prod, propel, egg on.

➤ *noun* bustle, hurly-burly, commotion, hubbub, fuss, activity, rush, rushing, haste, hurry, flurry, agitation, tumult, stir.

hut *noun* shed, cabin, hovel, lean-to, shanty, shack, shelter, booth. OPPOSITE: palace.

hybrid *noun* cross, crossbreed, mixed-breed, half-breed, half-blood, mongrel, mixture, amalgam, compound, composite, combination, conglomeration.

hygiene *noun* cleanliness, sanitariness, sanitation, sterility, purity, wholesomeness, disinfection.

hygienic *adj* clean, sanitary, sterile, sterilized, aseptic, germfree, disinfected, unpolluted, uncontaminated, pure, healthy, wholesome, salubrious. OPPOSITE: unhygienic.

hymn *noun* song of praise, psalm, anthem, song, chorus, carol, spiritual, plainsong, chant, offertory, paean.

hype *noun* publicity, promotion, advertising, advertisement, razzmatazz (*inf*), plugging (*inf*), puff, ballyhoo, brouhaha, build-up.

hyperbole *noun* exaggeration, overstatement, overkill, excess, extravagance, amplification, magnification.

hypercritical *adj* faultfinding, quibbling, niggling, nit-picking (*inf*), picky (*inf*), choosy (*inf*), hairsplitting, captious, carping, fussy, pernickety (*inf*), finicky, overscrupulous, censorious, overcritical, overexacting, overparticular, overstrict, cavilling, pedantic.

hypnotic *adj* mesmeric, mesmerizing, magnetic, fascinating, compelling, irresistible, entrancing, spellbinding, soporific, somniferous, sleep-inducing, sedative, numbing, stupefactive, narcotic.

hypnotize *verb* **1** (*hypnotized her on stage*) mesmerize, put under, put to sleep. **2** (*the scene hypnotized all present*) spellbind, bewitch, enchant, entrance, fascinate, captivate, beguile, absorb, magnetize.

hypochondria *noun* hypochondriasis, neurosis, valetudinarianism.

hypochondriac *adj* hypochondriacal, neurotic, valetudinarian.

hypocrisy *noun* insincerity, double-talk, double-dealing, two-facedness, dishonesty, duplicity, deceit, deceitfulness, deception, deceptiveness, falseness, falsity, speciousness, phoneyness (*inf*), pretence, imposture, lip service, dissembling, cant, sanctimoniousness, pharisaism. OPPOSITE: sincerity.

hypocrite *noun* fraud, impostor, phoney (*inf*), deceiver, charlatan, pretender, dissembler, mountebank, pharisee.

hypocritical *adj* insincere, double-dealing, fraudulent, phoney (*inf*), two-faced, spurious, duplicitous, dishonest, lying, untruthful, perfidious, deceptive, deceitful, false, specious, dissembling, hollow, canting, sanctimonious, self-righteous, pharisaical. OPPOSITE: sincere.

hypothesis *noun* theory, theorem, thesis, proposition, postulate, axiom, premise, premiss, assumption, supposition, presumption, conjecture, speculation. OPPOSITE: proof.

hypothetical *adj* theoretical, imaginary, imagined, supposed, assumed, presumed, proposed, conjectured, conjectural, speculative, putative, notional, academic. OPPOSITE: real.

hysteria *noun* hysterics, frenzy, panic, delirium, madness, mania, screaming habdabs (*inf*), neurosis, agitation.

hysterical *adj* **1** (*she became hysterical at the news*) mad, crazed, raving, delirious, demented, frenzied, beside oneself, wild, uncontrollable, out of control, berserk, frantic, distraught, distracted, agitated, overwrought, neurotic. OPPOSITE: calm. **2** (*the film was hysterical*) hilarious, sidesplitting, uproarious, priceless (*inf*), rich (*inf*), comical, very funny.

ice *noun* **1** (*a floating mass of ice*) frozen water, frost, rime, icicle, iceberg, floe, glacier. **2** (*gin and tonic with ice*) frozen water, ice cube, crushed ice, rocks (*inf*). **3** (*a choc ice*) ice cream, sorbet, water ice, ice lolly.
➤ *verb* **1** (*the river has iced over*) freeze, freeze over, solidify, harden, stiffen, frost, chill, refrigerate, cool, glaze. **2** (*ice a cake*) cover with icing, glaze, cover with frosting, decorate.
break the ice make the first move, start, begin, lead the way, relieve the tension, set the ball rolling (*inf*), take the plunge (*inf*).
put on ice delay, postpone, put off, shelve, put on the back burner (*inf*), keep in reserve, hold in abeyance.

icon *noun* idol, symbol, image, likeness, figure, representation, portrait, portrayal.

iconoclastic *adj* radical, nonconformist, irreverent, dissident, extremist, extreme, dissenting, rebellious, subversive, heretical, impious, denunciatory, sceptical, questioning, critical. OPPOSITE: conformist.

icy *adj* **1** (*icy winds*) cold, chilly, frosty, ice-cold, frozen, freezing, raw, bitter, arctic, glacial. OPPOSITE: hot. **2** (*icy roads*) frosty, frozen, freezing, glassy, slippery, slippy (*inf*), like a sheet of glass. **3** (*an icy greeting*) aloof, distant, hostile, unfriendly, stony, cold, frosty, cool, frigid, unwelcoming, unfeeling, indifferent, stiff, reserved. OPPOSITE: warm.

idea *noun* **1** (*that's a great idea*) plan, suggestion, thought, proposal, proposition, recommendation, brain wave, scheme, design. **2** (*his pretty strange ideas*) principle, belief, opinion, view, viewpoint, point of view, thought, concept, conception, notion, vision, theory, hypothesis, perception, abstraction, judgment. **3** (*have an idea of the cost*) estimation, understanding, approximation, guess, guesstimate (*inf*), surmise, supposition, conjecture. **4** (*the idea was to expand the business*) aim, intention, object, objective, purpose, reason, goal, target, end, point. **5** (*I had an idea she had moved*) impression, feeling, inkling, fancy, clue, hint, suspicion.

ideal *noun* **1** (*live up to high ideals*) perfection, epitome, archetype, model, exemplar, paragon, nonpareil, paradigm, example, pattern, standard, principle, benchmark, prototype. **2** (*attain my ideal*) aim, objective, goal, target.
➤ *adj* **1** (*he was her ideal man*) perfect, archetypal, exemplary, model, classic, consummate, complete, optimal, flawless, quintessential, supreme. OPPOSITE: imperfect. **2** (*an ideal world*) unreal, imaginary, romantic, fanciful, illusory, unattainable, utopian, impracticable, abstract, conceptual, mental, intellectual, theoretical, hypothetical, visionary, idealistic. OPPOSITE: real.

idealist *noun* perfectionist, visionary, dreamer, romantic, romanticist, optimist. OPPOSITE: realist.

idealistic *adj* perfectionist, utopian, visionary, dreamer, romantic, quixotic, starry-eyed, optimistic, unrealistic, impractical, airy-fairy (*inf*), impracticable. OPPOSITE: realistic.

ideally *adv* perfectly, in a perfect world, all things being equal, theoretically, in theory, hypothetically.

identical *adj* same, selfsame, one and the same, indistinguishable, like two peas in a pod (*inf*), matching, equal, corresponding, equivalent, like, alike, duplicate, twin, the dead spit of (*inf*), interchangeable, similar, congruous, tantamount. OPPOSITE: different.

identification *noun* **1** (*early identification of a disease*) recognition, detection, diagnosis, spotting, pinpointing, perception, differentiation, designation, naming, labelling. **2** (*the barman asked for identification*) credentials, ID, identity card, documents, badge. **3** (*identification with fellow sufferers*) empathy, association, sympathy, fellow feeling, rapport, relationship, connection, involvement.

identify *verb* **1** (*she identified him as the mugger*) recognize, spot, point out, know, finger (*inf*), pick out, pinpoint, name, put the finger on (*inf*), label, perceive, make out, discern, detect, single out, classify. **2** (*she could identify with the hero of the film*) relate to, associate with, sympathize, empathize, respond to, feel for. **3** (*he identified with the political radicals*) relate, associate, connect, ally, involve, align.

identity *noun* **1** (*a case of mistaken identity*) character, individuality, particularity, distinctiveness, singularity, uniqueness, personality, self, ego, name. **2** (*identity of reference*) sameness, oneness, likeness, similarity, closeness, unity, correspondence, equality, equivalence. OPPOSITE: difference.

ideology *noun* beliefs, ideas, tenets, principles, convictions, dogma, doctrine, creed, credo, teachings, philosophy, theory.

idiocy *noun* stupidity, senselessness, foolishness, asininity, folly, silliness, dopiness (*inf*), fatuity, imbecility, lunacy, craziness, insanity, absurdity, inanity. OPPOSITE: sanity.

idiom *noun* **1** (*adopt the common idiom*) language, jargon, patois, talk, speech, patter (*inf*), phraseology, parlance, vernacular, lingo (*inf*), argot, style, usage, locution. **2** (*a dictionary of contemporary idioms*) phrase, expression, set phrase, turn of phrase, colloquialism.

idiosyncrasy *noun* peculiarity, individuality, singularity, characteristic, mannerism, trait, speciality, affectation, quirk, eccentricity.

idiot *noun* fool, dope (*inf*), twit (*inf*), dimwit, ninny, twerp (*inf*), wally (*inf*), nit (*inf*), nitwit, clot (*inf*), mug (*inf*), half-wit, numskull (*inf*), simpleton, dunce, chump, nincompoop, dullard, ass, donkey, ignoramus, sucker (*inf*), dork (*inf*), nerd (*inf*), geek (*inf*), pillock (*inf*), plonker (*inf*), prat (*sl*), prick (*sl*), dingbat (*sl*), dunderhead, dolt, blockhead, dickhead (*sl*), imbecile, moron, cretin.

idiotic *adj* foolish, crazy, stupid, loopy (*inf*), asinine, half-witted, imbecilic, insane, lunatic, senseless, moronic, simple, witless, daft (*inf*), crackpot, dumb (*inf*), harebrained, fatuous, absurd, inane. OPPOSITE: sane.

idle *adj* **1** (*machinery standing idle*) inactive, unused, inoperative, not working, out of action, unemployed, jobless, redundant, in mothballs. OPPOSITE: active **2** (*an idle bunch of layabouts*) lazy, workshy, indolent, slothful, sluggish, lethargic, unoccupied, inert, shiftless. OPPOSITE: busy. **3** (*idle threats*) useless, vain, futile, ineffective, pointless, ineffectual, fruitless, empty, abortive, unprofitable, unproductive. OPPOSITE: fruitful. **4** (*idle chatter*) trivial, frivolous, superficial, unimportant, foolish, casual. OPPOSITE: meaningful.

> *verb* **1** (*idling away the hours*) laze, lounge, while, potter, do nothing, take it easy, drift, coast, mark time, loaf, arse around (*sl*), skive, shirk, bum around (*inf*), loiter, dawdle, sod about (*sl*), waste time, vegetate, veg out (*inf*). OPPOSITE: work. **2** (*the waiting taxi's engine idled*) tick over, run slowly.

idler *noun* loafer, layabout, lounger, lazybones, sluggard, sloth, laggard, dawdler, good-for-nothing, lounge lizard (*inf*), malingerer, shirker, dosser (*inf*), waster, time waster, skiver.

idol *noun* **1** (*he was her screen idol*) hero, heroine, favourite, pet, pinup (*inf*), darling, beloved, apple of one's eye (*inf*), blue-eyed boy (*inf*), golden girl (*inf*), star, superstar. **2** (*pagans worshipping their idols*) graven image, effigy, icon, god, deity, statue.

idolatrous *adj* adoring, adulatory, worshipping, worshipful, glorifying, idolizing, lionizing, hero-worshipping, reverential, uncritical, pagan, heretical, heathen.

idolatry *noun* worshipping, adulation, adoration, deification, exaltation, glorification, reverence, lionizing, hero-worshipping, doting, admiration, idolizing, idolism, paganism, heathenism, fetishism. OPPOSITE: vilification.

idolize *verb* worship, adore, love, exalt, glorify, hero-worship, lionize, deify, look up to, revere, put on a pedestal, reverence, venerate, admire. OPPOSITE: despise.

idyllic *adj* blissful, heavenly, perfect, out of this world, ideal, delightful, wonderful, charming, peaceful, picturesque, halcyon, pleasant, simple, pastoral, Arcadian, rustic, unspoiled. OPPOSITE: unpleasant.

if *conj* provided, providing, assuming, supposing, on condition that, allowing, granting, admitting, though, although, in case, whether, however, yet.

iffy *adj* uncertain, unsure, doubtful, undecided, unsettled, up in the air (*inf*), chancy (*inf*), dubious, dodgy (*inf*), unpredictable. OPPOSITE: certain.

ignite *verb* light, set fire to, set on fire, put a match to, set alight, torch (*inf*), catch fire, burn, burst into flames, flame up, inflame, fire. OPPOSITE: extinguish.

ignoble *adj* low, base, worthless, abject, unworthy, contemptible, despicable, dishonourable, ignominious, shameful, vile, disgraceful, heinous, infamous, mean, wretched, humble, common, vulgar, inferior. OPPOSITE: worthy.

ignominious *adj* shameful, disgraceful, dishonourable, degrading, humiliating, mortifying, contemptible, despicable, ignoble, unworthy, disreputable, infamous, vile, base, low, abject, mean, shabby. OPPOSITE: honourable.

ignominy *noun* dishonour, disgrace, shame, discredit, humiliation, mortification, disrepute, infamy, contempt, obloquy, opprobrium, odium, stigma. OPPOSITE: honour.

ignoramus *noun* dunce, duffer (*inf*), dimwit, fool, know-nothing (*inf*), simpleton, numskull, lowbrow, dummy (*inf*), donkey, ass, dullard, dolt, blockhead, bonehead (*inf*). OPPOSITE: intellectual.

ignorance *noun* unintelligence, illiteracy, unenlightenment, unawareness, inexperience, unfamiliarity, greenness, innocence. OPPOSITE: knowledge.

ignorant *adj* **1** (*ignorant about politics*) unaware, unenlightened, uninformed, green, in the dark, uneducated, unread, unschooled, untutored, unintelligent, dumb (*inf*), illiterate, thick (*inf*), dense (*inf*), unknowing, unwitting, blind, oblivious, innocent, inexperienced. OPPOSITE: knowledgeable. **2** (*annoyed by the noisy and ignorant louts*) ill-mannered, impolite, rude, crass, crude, coarse, inconsiderate, vulgar, gross, insensitive. OPPOSITE: polite.

ignore verb 1 (*ignore their petty gibes*) disregard, pay no attention to, take no notice of, turn a deaf ear to (*inf*), cut, snub, blank (*inf*), cold shoulder, send to Coventry (*inf*), shut one's eyes to. OPPOSITE: acknowledge. 2 (*she ignored the last part of the exam paper*) disregard, skip, pass over, omit, reject, neglect, overlook. OPPOSITE: observe.

ill adj 1 (*she resigned because of ill health*) sick, unwell, not very well, poorly (*inf*), out of sorts (*inf*), ailing, seedy (*inf*), off-colour, dicky (*inf*), under the weather (*inf*), laid up (*inf*), in a bad way, groggy (*inf*), diseased, at death's door (*inf*), infirm, unhealthy, indisposed. OPPOSITE: well. 2 (*ill effects*) adverse, unfavourable, unfortunate, unlucky, bad, harmful, hurtful, damaging, injurious, detrimental, evil, ominous, sinister, threatening, unpropitious, hostile, pernicious. OPPOSITE: favourable. 3 (*ill temper*) cross, fractious, crabby (*inf*), irritable, cantankerous, sullen, surly, snappish, waspish, irascible. OPPOSITE: good. 4 (*ill treatment*) harsh, unfriendly, unkind, hostile, acrimonious, antagonistic, resentful, rancorous, malevolent, malicious, belligerent. OPPOSITE: kind. 5 (*a man of ill repute*) bad, evil, wicked, vile, infamous, sinful, corrupt. OPPOSITE: good.
➤ adv 1 (*speak ill of the dead*) badly, unfavourably, unkindly, spitefully, adversely, improperly, disapprovingly. OPPOSITE: well. 2 (*they could ill afford a lottery ticket*) barely, scarcely, hardly, with difficulty, scantily. 3 (*it went ill with them*) poorly, badly, hard, adversely, unsuccessfully, unluckily, inauspiciously, unfortunately.
➤ noun 1 (*despite their past differences she wished him no ill*) harm, hurt, injury, affliction, pain, suffering, misery, mischief, misfortune, sorrow, trouble, disaster, calamity, evil. OPPOSITE: good. 2 (*bodily ills*) illness, ailment, complaint, disorder, sickness, disease, indisposition, malady, malaise.
ill at ease uncomfortable, uneasy, nervous, embarrassed, self-conscious, anxious, edgy, fidgety, apprehensive, on edge, twitchy (*inf*), unsure, unsettled, on tenterhooks.

ill-advised adj unwise, imprudent, foolish, foolhardy, hasty, rash, reckless, thoughtless, careless, inappropriate, injudicious, impolitic, misguided, ill-considered, ill-judged, incautious. OPPOSITE: wise.

ill-assorted adj mismatched, incompatible, unsuited, inharmonious, incongruous, uncongenial, discordant. OPPOSITE: well-matched.

ill-bred adj ill-mannered, rude, impolite, discourteous, uncivil, uncivilized, unmannerly, boorish, churlish, uncouth, vulgar, coarse, unrefined, unladylike, ungentlemanly. OPPOSITE: refined.

ill-defined adj indistinct, unclear, vague, nebulous, blurred, hazy, fuzzy, woolly, dim, shadowy. OPPOSITE: clear.

ill-disposed adj unfriendly, hostile, inimical, against, anti (*inf*), opposed, averse, antagonistic, uncooperative, unsympathetic, unwelcoming. OPPOSITE: well-disposed.

illegal adj unlawful, criminal, illicit, felonious, wrongful, prohibited, banned, forbidden, unauthorized, unlicensed, illegitimate, unofficial, unconstitutional, under-the-counter (*inf*), contraband, bootleg, black-market, fraudulent, outlawed, lawless. OPPOSITE: legal.

illegible adj unreadable, undecipherable, indecipherable, unclear, hieroglyphic, crabbed, obscure, scrawled, scrawly, scribbly. OPPOSITE: legible.

illegitimate adj 1 (*an illegitimate child*) natural, love, born out of wedlock, born on the wrong side of the blanket (*inf*), fatherless, bastard. OPPOSITE: legitimate. 2 (*illegitimate use of public money*) illegal, unlawful, illicit, unauthorized, lawless, forbidden, unsanctioned. OPPOSITE: lawful. 3 (*based on illegitimate principles*) illogical, invalid, unsound, incorrect, spurious.

ill-fated adj ill-starred, star-crossed, doomed, unfortunate, unlucky, blighted, luckless, hapless. OPPOSITE: lucky.

ill-favoured adj unattractive, ugly, hideous, repulsive, unsightly, plain, unprepossessing, offensive, objectionable. OPPOSITE: attractive.

ill feeling noun animosity, hostility, ill will, rancour, resentment, bad blood, bitterness, spite, malice, frustration, indignation, anger, wrath. OPPOSITE: goodwill.

ill-founded adj baseless, groundless, unsubstantiated, unproven, unconfirmed, unjustified. OPPOSITE: proven.

ill-humoured adj bad-tempered, cross, crabby (*inf*), irritable, grumpy, moody, morose, sullen, surly, testy, huffy, acrimonious, disagreeable, petulant, waspish, crotchety (*inf*), cantankerous. OPPOSITE: agreeable.

illiberal adj 1 (*illiberal views of some religions*) narrow-minded, intolerant, bigoted, prejudiced, hidebound, petty, reactionary. OPPOSITE: broad-minded. 2 (*illiberal terms of the pay deal*) miserly, mean, stingy, parsimonious, closefisted, tight (*inf*), tightfisted (*inf*), niggardly, close, near, ungenerous. OPPOSITE: generous.

illicit adj illegal, unlawful, criminal, unauthorized, unlicensed, unofficial, unconstitutional, illegitimate, prohibited, forbidden, banned, contraband, black-market, under the counter (*inf*), furtive, clandestine, secretive, improper, wrong, immoral. OPPOSITE: legal.

illimitable adj limitless, unlimited, inexhaustible, boundless, unbounded, bottomless, infinite, endless, unending, never-ending, eternal, vast, immense, immeasurable. OPPOSITE: limited.

illiterate adj ignorant, uneducated, untutored, untaught, unlearned, unlettered, uncultured, benighted. OPPOSITE: literate.

ill-judged adj unwise, foolish, ill-advised, foolhardy, misguided, ill-considered, hasty, rash, reckless, incautious, imprudent, injudicious, shortsighted. OPPOSITE: sensible.

ill-mannered adj bad-mannered, unmannerly, rude, impolite, ill-bred, discourteous, uncivil, uncouth, churlish, boorish, oafish. OPPOSITE: polite.

ill-natured adj bad-tempered, nasty, mean, spiteful, vindictive, crabbed, sullen, surly, sulky, disagreeable, unpleasant, unkind, cross, churlish, petulant, malicious, vicious, malignant. OPPOSITE: good-natured.

illness noun ailment, complaint, sickness, disease, disorder, condition, infirmity, affliction, lurgy (*inf*), indisposition, malady, malaise.

illogical adj unreasonable, irrational, unsound, invalid, faulty, fallacious, untenable, unscientific, inconsistent, absurd, senseless. OPPOSITE: logical.

ill-starred *adj* ill-fated, star-crossed, doomed, unfortunate, unlucky, blighted, luckless, hapless. OPPOSITE: lucky.

ill-tempered *adj* bad-tempered, annoyed, cross, irascible, grumpy, irritable, liverish, ratty (*inf*), sharp, curt, tetchy, touchy. OPPOSITE: good-tempered.

ill-timed *adj* inopportune, inconvenient, untimely, inappropriate, inept, unwelcome, awkward, unseasonable, at the wrong time, out of time. OPPOSITE: timely.

ill-treat *verb* abuse, mistreat, maltreat, misuse, ill-use, harm, damage, injure, batter, knock about, knock around, wrong, mishandle, persecute, oppress.

illuminate *verb* 1 (*the stadium was illuminated*) light, light up, shine a light on, floodlight, brighten. OPPOSITE: darken. 2 (*his notes helped to illuminate the lecture*) clarify, make clear, elucidate, explain, shed light on, enlighten, illustrate, instruct, inform. OPPOSITE: mystify. 3 (*illuminate the text using computer graphics*) decorate, adorn, ornament, embellish, illustrate.

illuminating *adj* instructive, informative, helpful, explanatory, enlightening, revealing. OPPOSITE: unhelpful.

illumination *noun* 1 (*poor illumination in the church hall*) light, lighting, lights, brightness, beam, ray, radiance. OPPOSITE: darkness. 2 (*clear illumination of the example*) clarification, instruction, revelation, insight, understanding, awareness, perception, enlightenment. 3 (*Blackpool illuminations*) decoration, adornment, ornamentation, embellishment.

illusion *noun* 1 (*be under no illusions*) misapprehension, false impression, misconception, deception, fallacy, error, notion, fancy. OPPOSITE: reality. 2 (*the haunted castle promised many illusions*) hallucination, mirage, vision, dream, fantasy, daydream, delusion, will o' the wisp, figment of the imagination, spectre, phantom, phantasm. OPPOSITE: reality.

illusory *adj* illusive, imaginary, unreal, fanciful, chimerical, deceptive, misleading, delusive, false, fallacious, sham, untrue. OPPOSITE real.

illustrate *verb* 1 (*two examples illustrated the problem*) exemplify, clarify, demonstrate, instance, explain, illuminate, exhibit, show. 2 (*she illustrated children's storybooks*) adorn, decorate, embellish, ornament, picture, draw, sketch, depict, illuminate.

illustration *noun* 1 (*figures for illustration purposes only*) example, instance, case, sample, specimen, analogy, explanation, clarification, elucidation, demonstration. 2 (*the manual contained clear illustrations*) picture, plate, figure, drawing, photograph, diagram, sketch, design, representation, ornamentation, decoration, embellishment.

illustrative *adj* descriptive, explanatory, representative, typical, exemplary, diagrammatic, graphic, pictorial.

illustrious *adj* famous, renowned, famed, well-known, acclaimed, prominent, celebrated, distinguished, noted, eminent, notable, great, noble, honoured, outstanding, brilliant, glorious, splendid. OPPOSITE: inglorious.

ill will *noun* hostility, enmity, antagonism, animosity, hard feelings, hate, hatred, dislike, spite, ill feeling, malice, rancour, venom, malevolence, acrimony, bitterness, bad blood, grudge, resentment, envy. OPPOSITE: goodwill.

image *noun* 1 (*conjures up an image*) idea, concept, notion, thought, mental picture, impression, vision, perception. 2 (*stick pins in waxen images*) likeness, representation, effigy, icon, picture, portrait, statue, figure, figurine, reflection, replica. 3 (*caught sight of her image in the glass*) reflection, reproduction, photograph, photo, picture, snapshot, appearance, facsimile, copy, duplicate. 4 (*she was the image of her father*) double, twin, spit (*inf*), spitting image (*inf*), dead ringer (*inf*), match, counterpart, doppelgänger, chip off the old block (*inf*). 5 (*images in poetry*) figure of speech, figurative expression, turn of phrase, simile, metaphor.

imaginable *adj* conceivable, thinkable, possible, believable, credible, probable, likely, feasible, plausible. OPPOSITE: inconceivable.

imaginary *adj* unreal, fanciful, fancied, illusory, illusive, fictitious, fictional, made-up, make-believe, invented, legendary, mythical, mythological, fantastic, hypothetical, supposed, notional, abstract, ideal, visionary, chimerical, shadowy, dreamlike, ghostly, spectral, unsubstantial, nonexistent. OPPOSITE: real.

imagination *noun* 1 (*stretches the imagination*) creativity, inventiveness, imaginativeness, ingenuity, resourcefulness, enterprise, inspiration, originality, vision, insight, perception. 2 (*it was only in my imagination*) conception, impression, idea, notion, fancy, mind's eye, unreality, dream, illusion, fantasy, chimera. OPPOSITE: reality.

imaginative *adj* creative, inventive, ingenious, resourceful, enterprising, inspired, clever, original, visionary, dreamy, whimsical, fanciful. OPPOSITE: unimaginative.

imagine *verb* 1 (*imagine you were on a desert island*) picture, visualize, envisage, conceive, conjure up, see in one's mind's eye, dream up, make believe, fancy, pretend, devise, plan, project, create, invent. 2 (*I imagine they were tired after the sales*) think, believe, fancy, guess, suppose, assume, reckon, presume, gather, surmise, take it, deduce, infer. OPPOSITE: know.

imbecile *noun* idiot, half-wit, fool, simpleton, dolt, dullard, thickhead, moron, cretin.
▷ *adj* imbecilic, feebleminded, idiotic, stupid, inane, simple, daft, foolish, barmy (*inf*), dopey (*inf*), thick (*inf*), witless, asinine, inane, fatuous, moronic. OPPOSITE: intelligent.

imbecility *noun* idiocy, feeblemindedness, stupidity, foolishness, incompetence, asininity, inanity, fatuity. OPPOSITE: sense.

imbibe *verb* 1 (*they had imbibed too much free ale*) drink, swallow, swig (*inf*), knock back (*inf*), tipple, consume, ingest, quaff. 2 (*imbibe radical ideas*) absorb, assimilate, take in, soak up, pick up, acquire, receive, gain.

imbroglio *noun* entanglement, complication, dilemma,

involvement, difficulty, misunderstanding, confusion, quandary, muddle.

imbue *verb* fill, instil, impregnate, inspire, infuse, pervade, inculcate, permeate, penetrate, steep, soak, bathe, saturate, dye, stain, colour, tint.

imitate *verb* **1** (*the comedian imitated the prime minister*) ape, copy, mimic, impersonate, do an impression of, caricature, send up (*inf*), take off (*inf*), spoof, parody, mock, echo, mirror, reflect. **2** (*imitate the Dutch artist's work*) copy, reproduce, replicate, duplicate, simulate, forge, fake, counterfeit. **3** (*imitate her teacher*) copy, emulate, follow, take after, follow in the footsteps of.

imitation *noun* **1** (*his imitation was really convincing*) mimicry, impersonation, impression, takeoff (*inf*), copy, mockery, burlesque, parody, travesty. **2** (*an imitation of a miniature masterpiece*) copy, reproduction, replica, duplicate, resemblance, likeness, sham, simulation, forgery, fake, counterfeit. OPPOSITE: original.
  ≫ *adj* simulated, artificial, synthetic, phoney (*inf*), repro, reproduction, man-made, ersatz, fake, spurious, counterfeit. OPPOSITE: genuine.

imitative *adj* mimicking, copying, copycat (*inf*), aping, parrot-like, simulated, mock, unoriginal, secondhand.

imitator *noun* mimic, impersonator, copycat (*inf*), impressionist, copier, parrot, carbon copy (*inf*).

immaculate *adj* **1** (*immaculate appearance*) clean, spotless, impeccable, unsoiled, clean as a new pin (*inf*), spick-and-span, neat, trim, pristine, spruce, squeaky-clean (*inf*), whiter than white (*inf*). OPPOSITE: unclean. **2** (*she was of immaculate character*) pure, sinless, virtuous, faultless, irreproachable, flawless, perfect, spotless, unspoilt, unblemished, uncontaminated, unpolluted, undefiled, unsullied. OPPOSITE: blemished.

immaterial *adj* irrelevant, insignificant, inconsequential, unimportant, of no account, trivial, trifling, minor. OPPOSITE: important.

immature *adj* **1** (*protect the immature saplings from the elements*) unripe, undeveloped, green, young, premature, raw, crude, unfinished, incomplete, unformed, rudimentary. OPPOSITE: ripe. **2** (*behave in an immature way*) inexperienced, callow, unsophisticated, young, adolescent, wet behind the ears (*inf*), youthful, puerile, jejune, childish, infantile. OPPOSITE: mature.

immaturity *noun* inexperience, greenness, unripeness, imperfection, incompleteness, crudity, rawness, youth, childishness, puerility. OPPOSITE: maturity.

immeasurable *adj* immense, vast, huge, unlimited, limitless, illimitable, boundless, unbounded, infinite, endless, never-ending, unfathomable, bottomless, countless, incalculable. OPPOSITE: limited.

immediate *adj* **1** (*for immediate dispatch*) instant, instantaneous, prompt, without delay, swift, speedy. OPPOSITE: delayed. **2** (*their immediate plans*) present, current, latest, actual, existing, urgent, pressing. OPPOSITE: future. **3** (*the immediate cause of death*) direct, primary, fundamental, basic, main, chief. **4** (*in the immediate vicinity*) near, next, next-door, adjacent, neighbouring, adjoining, contiguous. OPPOSITE: distant. **5** (*only the immediate family*) nearest, closest, nearest and dearest, kith and kin.

immediately *adv* instantly, that instant, at once, now, without delay, right away, this minute, straightaway, pronto (*inf*), like a shot (*inf*), on the nail (*inf*), forthwith, promptly, directly. OPPOSITE: later.

immemorial *adj* very old, ancient, age-old, olden, archaic, of yore, fixed, permanent, traditional, time-honoured. OPPOSITE: modern.

immense *adj* huge, enormous, colossal, vast, gigantic, giant, massive, mammoth, ginormous (*inf*), humongous (*inf*), elephantine, great, tremendous, mega (*inf*), prodigious, stupendous, extensive, immeasurable, boundless, unbounded, illimitable, limitless, unlimited. OPPOSITE: small.

immerse *verb* **1** (*immersed the skirt in black dye*) dip, plunge, duck, dunk, submerge, sink, douse, souse, bathe, baptize. **2** (*completely immersed in his studies*) engross, preoccupy, absorbed, occupy, involve, engage.

immersion *noun* **1** (*baptized by immersion in a tank of water*) dip, dipping, saturation, plunging, ducking, soaking, dousing, baptism, bathe. **2** (*complete immersion in his hobby*) absorption, preoccupation, concentration, involvement.

immigrant *noun* incomer, newcomer, settler, new arrival, expatriate, expat (*inf*). OPPOSITE: native.

imminent *adj* impending, forthcoming, coming, upcoming, approaching, just around the corner (*inf*), at hand, on the cards (*inf*), near, close, menacing, threatening, gathering, looming, brewing, in the offing, on the way, in the air. OPPOSITE: distant.

immobile *adj* unable to move, motionless, stationary, still, unmoving, static, at a standstill, like a statue, immovable, fixed, rooted, stiff, rigid, stable. OPPOSITE: mobile.

immobilize *verb* stop, bring to a standstill, freeze, paralyse, put out of action, transfix, cripple, disable. OPPOSITE: mobilize.

immoderate *adj* extreme, excessive, inordinate, unreasonable, unwarranted, undue, uncalled-for, exorbitant, over the top (*inf*), OTT (*inf*), intemperate, extravagant, unrestrained, unbridled, wanton. OPPOSITE: moderate.

immoderation *noun* excess, excessiveness, lack of restraint, unrestraint, exorbitance, intemperance, overindulgence. OPPOSITE: moderation.

immodest *adj* **1** (*the teenage girl's immodest behaviour*) bold, brazen, shameless, forward, pushy (*inf*), fresh (*inf*), cheeky (*inf*), saucy (*inf*). OPPOSITE: modest. **2** (*an immodest suggestion*) indecent, indecorous, improper, impure, unchaste, obscene, rude, coarse, gross, lewd, bawdy. OPPOSITE: proper.

immoral *adj* corrupt, depraved, degenerate, debauched, abandoned, dissolute, profligate, licentious, raunchy (*inf*), blue (*inf*), lewd, obscene, indecent, impure, sinful, wicked, bad, wrong, evil, unprincipled, dishonest, unscrupulous, unethical. OPPOSITE: virtuous.

immorality *noun* corruption, depravity, perversion, degeneracy, profligacy, licentiousness, obscenity, indecency, pornography, sin, wickedness, vice, evil, dishonesty, wrong, unscrupulousness. OPPOSITE: virtue.

immortal *adj* **1** (*the children believed Superman was immortal*) deathless, death-defying, undying,

imperishable, indestructible, eternal, everlasting, unfading, perennial, timeless, endless, ceaseless, lasting, enduring, abiding, perpetual, constant, permanent. OPPOSITE: perishable. **2** (*immortal words of the poet*) unforgettable, memorable, famous, well-known, distinguished, honoured.
➤ *noun* **1** (*the immortals enjoying eternal bliss*) god, deity, goddess, Olympian. **2** (*sporting immortals*) great, genius, hero.

immortality *noun* **1** (*millions long for immortality*) deathlessness, indestructibility, eternity, everlasting life, eternal life, endlessness, ceaselessness, perpetuity, constancy, permanence. OPPOSITE: death. **2** (*achieve immortality through my work*) fame, renown, celebrity, glory, greatness, honour, distinction.

immortalize *verb* commemorate, memorialize, eternalize, celebrate, glorify, exalt, enshrine, perpetuate.

immovable *adj* **1** (*despite their efforts the car was immovable*) jammed, rooted, set, fixed, immutable, riveted, fast, secure, firm, stable, immobile, stationary. OPPOSITE: mobile. **2** (*the committee was immovable on the appeal*) resolute, determined, steadfast, unalterable, unchangeable, unchanging, constant, staunch, inflexible, stubborn, dogged, unyielding, unshakeable, impassive. OPPOSITE: flexible.

immune *adj* exempt, free, not liable, excused, spared, absolved, safe, protected, resistant, proof, insusceptible, invulnerable, unaffected. OPPOSITE: susceptible.

immunity *noun* **1** (*tests showed he had an immunity to the disease*) protection, resistance, immunization, inoculation. **2** (*immunity to prosecution*) exemption, impunity, exoneration, freedom, release. OPPOSITE: liability. **3** (*diplomatic immunity*) privilege, indemnity, right, charter, permission, franchise, liberty.

immunize *verb* inoculate, vaccinate, inject, jab (*inf*), protect, safeguard.

immure *verb* imprison, incarcerate, confine, jail, enclose, shut in, wall up, cage.

immutable *adj* constant, invariable, unalterable, unchangeable, unchanging, changeless, inflexible, fixed, immovable, constant, steadfast, permanent, stable, enduring, abiding, ageless, perpetual. OPPOSITE: changeable.

imp *noun* **1** (*he dressed up as an imp*) sprite, goblin, hobgoblin, puck, demon, devil. OPPOSITE: cherub. **2** (*the toddler was a little imp*) scamp, rascal, urchin, brat, minx, pickle (*inf*).

impact *noun* **1** (*all passengers were killed on impact*) collision, crash, smash, bump, knock, jolt, bang, blow, shock, force, contact. **2** (*taxation had an adverse impact upon profits*) impression, effect, influence, bearing, burden, brunt, repercussions, consequences.
➤ *verb* hit, strike, collide, clash, crash.

impact on affect, influence, have an effect on, impinge on.

impair *verb* damage, injure, harm, weaken, debilitate, mar, spoil, lessen, reduce, enfeeble, enervate, vitiate, decrease, diminish, deteriorate. OPPOSITE: improve.

impale *verb* pierce, stick, spear, skewer, spike, spit, run through, transfix.

impalpable *adj* imperceptible, intangible, insubstantial, tenuous, shadowy, indistinct, airy, fine, delicate. OPPOSITE: palpable.

impart *verb* **1** (*they had great news to impart*) tell, communicate, make known, convey, relate, transmit, pass on, disclose, reveal, divulge. OPPOSITE: suppress. **2** (*he imparts such empathy to the role*) give, confer, grant, bestow, assign, afford, contribute. OPPOSITE: withhold.

impartial *adj* unbiased, unprejudiced, neutral, just, fair, equitable, open-minded, nonpartisan, disinterested, objective, detached, dispassionate. OPPOSITE: biased.

impartiality *noun* neutrality, lack of bias, evenhandedness, open-mindedness, nonpartisanship, detachment, dispassion, objectivity. OPPOSITE: bias.

impassable *adj* blocked, closed, obstructed, unnavigable, pathless, impenetrable, impervious, impermeable. OPPOSITE: passable.

impasse *noun* deadlock, stalemate, standoff, standstill, checkmate, blind alley (*inf*).

impassioned *adj* passionate, fervent, fervid, ardent, warm, inspired, intense, vehement, zealous, excited, fiery, enthusiastic, eager, animated, glowing, inflamed, forceful, vigorous. OPPOSITE: cool.

impassive *adj* emotionless, unemotional, unmoved, unfeeling, impassible, cool, aloof, reserved, inscrutable, poker-faced (*inf*), imperturbable, unruffled, composed, self-contained, serene, laid back (*inf*), indifferent, dispassionate, passionless, apathetic. OPPOSITE: emotional.

impatience *noun* **1** (*waiting with impatience*) restlessness, intolerance, agitation, edginess, fretfulness, keenness, eagerness, impetuosity. OPPOSITE: patience. **2** (*demanded with impatience*) abruptness, curtness, brusqueness, shortness, irritability, snappiness, intolerance.

impatient *adj* **1** (*impatient to start the race*) restless, fretful, jumpy, nervous, anxious, like a cat on a hot tin roof (*inf*), straining at the lease (*inf*), uneasy, excitable, eager, agog, impetuous, reckless, hasty, precipitate, headlong, vehement, violent. OPPOSITE: patient. **2** (*she gave an impatient retort*) irritable, testy, edgy, irascible, waspish, short-tempered, snappy, brusque, curt, abrupt, intolerant.

impeach *verb* **1** (*the senate impeached the president*) accuse, charge, indict, censure, denounce, blame, arraign, incriminate. OPPOSITE: vindicate. **2** (*the newspaper impeached his reputation*) call into question, question, impugn, discredit, disparage, malign, challenge.

impeccable *adj* excellent, perfect, exemplary, faultless, flawless, immaculate, spotless, unblemished, irreproachable, pure, innocent. OPPOSITE: imperfect.

impecunious *adj* poor, needy, penniless, poverty-stricken, hard up (*inf*), broke (*inf*), skint (*inf*), impoverished, destitute. OPPOSITE: wealthy.

impede *verb* hinder, block, obstruct, clog, encumber, hamper, hold up, delay, retard, thwart, disrupt, put a spanner in the works (*inf*), restrain, check, curb, prevent, stop. OPPOSITE: assist.

impediment *noun* **1** (*proceed without impediment*) obstruction, hindrance, block, obstacle, bar, barrier, encumbrance, defect, snag, difficulty, stumbling block. OPPOSITE: aid. **2** (*a hearing impediment*) handicap, defect, difficulty, problem.

impedimenta *pl noun* equipment, gear, belongings, possessions, effects, junk, things, stuff, odds and ends, paraphernalia, bits and pieces, luggage, baggage.

impel *verb* force, urge, drive, compel, press, constrain, oblige, spur, goad, incite, stimulate, motivate, move, push, inspire, influence, induce, persuade. OPPOSITE: deter.

impending *adj* approaching, imminent, coming, hovering, gathering, forthcoming, upcoming, brewing, looming, threatening, menacing, on the way. OPPOSITE: distant.

impenetrable *adj* **1** (*the fog closed in like an impenetrable blanket*) thick, dense, impervious, impermeable, solid, sealed, hermetic, impassable, pathless. OPPOSITE: penetrable. **2** (*the impenetrable assembly instructions*) incomprehensible, unintelligible, unfathomable, baffling, inexplicable, dark, obscure, abstruse, inscrutable, enigmatic, recondite. OPPOSITE: intelligible.

impenitent *adj* unrepentant, uncontrite, unremorseful, unabashed, hardened, obdurate, defiant, incorrigible, unreformed. OPPOSITE: penitent.

imperative *adj* **1** (*it was imperative that the operation went ahead*) vital, urgent, essential, pressing, important, crucial, necessary, exigent, compulsory, obligatory, binding. OPPOSITE: unimportant. **2** (*he spoke in imperative tones*) commanding, authoritative, dictatorial, domineering, peremptory, autocratic, imperious, lordly, magisterial.

imperceptible *adj* indiscernible, impalpable, inaudible, invisible, indistinguishable, microscopic, infinitesimal, tiny, minute, minuscule, slight, small, gradual, fine, subtle, faint, shadowy, unclear, vague, obscure. OPPOSITE: noticeable.

imperceptibly *adv* indiscernibly, unnoticeably, unobtrusively, inappreciably, invisibly, slowly, gradually, vaguely, subtly, little by little.

imperfect *adj* faulty, defective, deficient, flawed, impaired, damaged, broken, chipped, incomplete, unfinished, partial, undeveloped, rudimentary, inexact, crude. OPPOSITE: perfect.

imperfection *noun* fault, defect, flaw, blemish, blot, stain, scratch, scar, tear, crack, frailty, infirmity, weakness, weak point, weak link, failing, shortcoming, inadequacy, deficiency. OPPOSITE: perfection.

imperial *adj* sovereign, regal, royal, supreme, majestic, kingly, queenly, grand, imposing, stately, august, imperious, lordly, magisterial, lofty, noble, great, magnificent. OPPOSITE: lowly.

imperil *verb* endanger, jeopardize, risk, put in danger, put at risk, hazard, gamble, expose. OPPOSITE: protect.

imperious *adj* overbearing, domineering, dictatorial, despotic, tyrannical, autocratic, authoritative, commanding, high-handed, arrogant, haughty, lordly, magisterial. OPPOSITE: humble.

imperishable *adj* indestructible, everlasting, enduring, incorruptible, lasting, undying, unfading, eternal, immortal, abiding, perennial, permanent. OPPOSITE: perishable.

impermanent *adj* temporary, transient, transitory, passing, momentary, fleeting, brief, short-lived, fly by night (*inf*), mortal.

impersonal *adj* **1** (*large impersonal organizations*) objective, dispassionate, detached, remote, neutral, unprejudiced. OPPOSITE: personal **2** (*she didn't care for his impersonal manner*) cold, cool, aloof, formal, distant, clinical, wooden, stiff, rigid, stuffy, businesslike, unemotional. OPPOSITE: warm.

impersonate *verb* mimic, ape, imitate, do an impression of, pose as, copy, do (*inf*), send up (*inf*), mock, caricature, parody, burlesque, take off (*inf*), masquerade as.

impersonation *noun* imitation, mimicry, caricature, aping, impression, takeoff (*inf*), parody.

impertinence *noun* **1** (*the impertinence of the child*) impudence, insolence, rudeness, disrespect, impoliteness, effrontery, pertness, lip (*inf*), mouth (*inf*), sauce (*inf*), cheek (*inf*), nerve (*inf*), gall (*inf*), boldness, audacity, forwardness, assurance. OPPOSITE: politeness. **2** (*impertinence of the printed material*) irrelevance, inapplicability, inappropriateness, inappositeness. OPPOSITE: pertinence.

impertinent *adj* **1** (*her impertinent comment was ignored*) impudent, insolent, rude, impolite, disrespectful, pert, saucy, cheeky (*inf*), mouthy (*inf*), lippy (*inf*), bold, audacious, forward, presumptuous. OPPOSITE: polite. **2** (*the evidence was ruled as impertinent*) irrelevant, inapplicable, immaterial, inappropriate, inapposite. OPPOSITE: pertinent.

imperturbable *adj* calm, composed, collected, self-possessed, serene, placid, tranquil, unruffled, unfazed (*inf*), cool, unmoved, impassive, sedate. OPPOSITE: agitated.

impervious *adj* **1** (*impervious to criticism*) invulnerable, unreceptive, immune, insensitive, thick-skinned, unaffected by. OPPOSITE: vulnerable. **2** (*impervious to water*) impermeable, impenetrable, impassable, proof against, waterproof, heatproof, sealed, hermetic, resistant, tight. OPPOSITE: permeable.

impetuous *adj* hasty, precipitate, headlong, rash, reckless, impulsive, spontaneous, thoughtless, heedless, spur-of-the-moment, unplanned, unpremeditated, passionate, eager, vehement, violent, fierce, furious. OPPOSITE: cautious.

impetus *noun* force, energy, momentum, power, drive, push, spur, boost, goad, stimulus, incentive, motivation, impulse.

impiety *noun* irreverence, ungodliness, godlessness, unholiness, irreligion, profanity, blasphemy, sacrilege, disrespect, sin, iniquity, wickedness, vice. OPPOSITE: piety.

impinge *verb* **impinge on/upon 1** (*policies which impinge upon people's rights*) encroach on, infringe, trespass, intrude on, invade, violate, usurp. **2** (*impinged on his consciousness*) affect, influence, touch, impress upon. **3** (*huge hailstones impinged on their windows*) strike, hit, dash against, clash, smash, crash, collide with.

impious *adj* irreverent, ungodly, godless, unholy, irreligious, profane, blasphemous, sacrilegious, disrespectful, sinful, iniquitous, wicked, unrighteous. OPPOSITE: pious.

impish *adj* mischievous, naughty, elfin, elfish, rascally, roguish, devilish, puckish, waggish, arch. OPPOSITE: good.

implacable *adj* unbending, inflexible, unyielding, unappeasable, uncompromising, intractable, firm, adamant, inexorable, ruthless, relentless, unrelenting, pitiless, merciless, harsh, cruel, heartless, unforgiving. OPPOSITE: yielding.

implant *verb* **1** (*implant an idea*) instil, inculcate, introduce, inseminate, infix, infuse, imbue. **2** (*surgically implanted tissue*) graft, engraft, insert, place, put in place. **3** (*the tree supports were firmly implanted*) plant, embed, fix, root, sow.
≫ *noun* insert, insertion, graft, transplant.

implausible *adj* improbable, suspect, unlikely, unconvincing, dubious, doubtful, farfetched, questionable, incredible, flimsy, weak. OPPOSITE: likely.

implement *noun* tool, utensil, appliance, instrument, device, contrivance, gadget, equipment.
≫ *verb* execute, carry out, perform, do, enforce, put into effect, accomplish, fulfil, realize.

implementation *noun* execution, carrying out, performance, enforcement, completion, effecting, accomplishment, fulfilment, realization.

implicate *verb* incriminate, inculpate, involve, embroil, entangle, associate, include, tie in with, concern, compromise, affect, imply, stitch up (*inf*).

implication *noun* **1** (*the implications were obvious*) suggestion, insinuation, innuendo, inference, presumption, meaning, significance, connotation, overtone, ramification, conclusion. **2** (*the man's implication in the robbery*) incrimination, inculpation, entanglement, involvement, association, connection.

implicit *adj* **1** (*issued an implicit warning*) implied, inferred, suggested, insinuated, hinted, tacit, understood, unspoken, unexpressed, latent, inherent. OPPOSITE: explicit. **2** (*an implicit belief*) absolute, total, entire, utter, complete, full, wholehearted, unreserved, unconditional, unqualified, unquestioning, unhesitating, unshakeable. OPPOSITE: halfhearted.

implicitly *adv* absolutely, completely, totally, utterly, wholeheartedly, without reservation, unreservedly, unconditionally, unhesitatingly.

implied *adj* implicit, inferred, hinted at, suggested, insinuated, tacit, understood, unspoken, unstated. OPPOSITE: stated.

implore *verb* beg, beseech, entreat, supplicate, petition, solicit, conjure, plead, pray, crave, ask. OPPOSITE: demand.

imply *verb* suggest, insinuate, intimate, hint, give to understand, connote, signify, mean, indicate, denote, signal, point to, import, involve, entail. OPPOSITE: declare.

impolite *adj* rude, bad-mannered, unmannerly, ill-mannered, uncivil, discourteous, unrefined, ungentlemanly, unladylike, ungracious, impudent, impertinent, cheeky (*inf*), insolent, disrespectful, churlish, boorish, oafish, rough, coarse, crude, vulgar. OPPOSITE: polite.

impolitic *adj* unwise, ill-advised, ill-considered, injudicious, unsagacious, imprudent, indiscreet, undiplomatic, inexpedient, misguided. OPPOSITE: wise.

import *verb* **1** (*we import bananas*) bring in, introduce from abroad. OPPOSITE: export. **2** (*his tone imported there were problems*) mean, signify, indicate, denote, betoken, connote, imply.
≫ *noun* **1** (*imports and exports*) foreign produce, foreign commodity, imported goods. OPPOSITE: export. **2** (*people of import*) significance, importance, consequence, moment, weight, substance. OPPOSITE: insignificance. **3** (*the department understood the import of the news*) significance, meaning, magnitude, purport, sense, gist, nub, thrust, substance, intention, implication, connotation.

importance *noun* **1** (*the importance of the summit meeting*) significance, import, seriousness, graveness, urgency, consequence, momentousness, moment, weight, substance, concern, value, worth. OPPOSITE: unimportance. **2** (*an inflated sense of his own importance*) status, standing, prestige, prominence, eminence, notability, esteem, distinction, regard, influence, power, usefulness. OPPOSITE: insignificance.

important *adj* **1** (*a very important decision*) significant, consequential, momentous, far-reaching, weighty, material, critical, crucial, urgent, serious, grave, primary, essential, valuable, considerable. OPPOSITE: unimportant. **2** (*an important customer*) influential, powerful, prominent, eminent, prestigious, distinguished, esteemed, leading, foremost, valued, notable. OPPOSITE: powerless. **3** (*important points to remember*) salient, relevant, significant, principal, main, chief, major. OPPOSITE: irrelevant.

importunate *adj* persistent, insistent, dogged, demanding, exigent, exacting, pressing, urgent, clamorous, solicitous, troublesome, annoying.

importune *verb* harass, badger, pester, hound, plague, beset, dun, press, urge, cajole, beseech, entreat, beg, supplicate, solicit.

impose *verb* inflict, dictate, enforce, lay, place, set, put, establish, levy, exact, charge, prescribe, require, enjoin. OPPOSITE: lift.
impose on/upon intrude on, foist on, gate-crash (*inf*), take advantage of, inconvenience, bother, put out, take liberties, abuse, exploit.

imposing *adj* impressive, grand, majestic, stately, august, dignified, commanding, striking, effective. OPPOSITE: unimposing.

imposition *noun* **1** (*the imposition of a new tax*) burden, charge, duty, tax, levy, toll, tithe, constraint. **2** (*the imposition of martial law*) enforcement, infliction, institution, fixing, decree, exaction, prescription, injunction. **3** (*their unexpected arrival was a real imposition*) intrusion, liberty, cheek (*inf*), encroachment, presumption.

impossible *adj* **1** (*he said that delivery today was impossible*) impracticable, unattainable, unobtainable, unachievable, unthinkable. OPPOSITE: possible. **2** (*her lies* *were impossible to believe*) inconceivable, absurd, ludicrous, outrageous, preposterous, outlandish, illogical, unreasonable, inadmissible, unacceptable, out of the question. **3** (*an impossible situation*) unbearable, intolerable, unendurable, unacceptable, insoluble, unworkable, hopeless.

impostor *noun* fraud, charlatan, quack, phoney (*inf*), cheat, conman (*inf*), con artist, fake, deceiver, rogue, pretender, hypocrite, humbug, trickster, dissembler.

imposture *noun* deception, fraud, pretence, quackery, con (*inf*), con trick (*inf*), cheat, swindle, counterfeit, hoax, trick, ruse, wile, sting (*inf*), humbug, imposition, artifice. OPPOSITE: honesty.

impotence *noun* helplessness, uselessness, powerlessness, inability to act, ineffectiveness, inefficiency, inadequacy, incompetence, enervation, weakness, frailty, feebleness, infirmity. OPPOSITE: strength.

impotent *adj* powerless, helpless, weak, feeble, emasculated, frail, enervated, infirm, disabled, incapacitated, incapable, unable, crippled, paralysed, ineffective, incompetent, inept, inadequate. OPPOSITE: powerful.

impound *verb* **1** (*my car was impounded by the duty officer*) seize, confiscate, appropriate, expropriate, distrain, take away. **2** (*impound stray dogs*) confine, shut up, fence in, pen, enclose, cage, imprison, lock up, incarcerate. OPPOSITE: free.

impoverish *verb* **1** (*high taxes impoverish the economy*) beggar, ruin, bankrupt, pauperize, break (*inf*). **2** (*poor crop rotation impoverishes the soil*) exhaust, wear out, deplete, drain, sap, use up. OPPOSITE: enrich.

impoverished *adj* **1** (*a country impoverished by war*) indigent, destitute, poverty-stricken, ruined, bankrupt, poor, needy, penniless, skint (*inf*), strapped for cash (*inf*), distressed, down at heel, down and out, penurious, impecunious, broke (*inf*), hard up (*inf*). OPPOSITE: wealthy. **2** (*impoverished pastures*) exhausted, played out, worn out, depleted, spent, drained, empty, barren, sterile. OPPOSITE: rich.

impracticable *adj* **1** (*impracticable schemes*) impossible, unworkable, unattainable, unfeasible, unachievable, out of the question. OPPOSITE: possible. **2** (*the equipment is completely impracticable*) unsuitable, inconvenient, impractical, useless, unserviceable. OPPOSITE: serviceable.

impractical *adj* **1** (*an impractical budget plan*) impossible, inoperable, impracticable, unworkable, unserviceable, inapplicable. OPPOSITE: practical. **2** (*her strange ideas were impractical*) unrealistic, idealistic, airy-fairy (*inf*), romantic, starry-eyed, visionary, wild. OPPOSITE: realistic.

imprecation *noun* curse, malediction, execration, blasphemy, profanity, denunciation, bad language, slander, insult. OPPOSITE: blessing.

imprecise *adj* inexact, inaccurate, ill-defined, ambiguous, equivocal, indeterminable, estimated, indefinite, vague, hazy, blurred, approximate, rough, loose, woolly, inexplicit. OPPOSITE: precise.

impregnable *adj* invincible, unassailable, invulnerable, indestructible, impenetrable, inviolable,

unconquerable, strong, secure, unshakeable, irrefutable. OPPOSITE: weak.

impregnate *verb* **1** (*cloths impregnated with cleaning solution*) permeate, pervade, penetrate, suffuse, percolate, seep, saturate, imbue, infuse, soak, steep, fill. **2** (*impregnate the cow*) fertilize, fructify, make pregnant, inseminate, fecundate.

impresario *noun* manager, organizer, producer, director, promoter, entrepreneur, angel (*inf*).

impress *verb* **1** (*impress his parents with a good performance*) influence, sway, move, affect, touch, stir, strike, grab (*inf*). **2** (*impress a mark on the ceramic dish*) imprint, stamp, mark, print, engrave, emboss, indent.
impress on/upon stress, emphasize, instil, inculcate, fix.

impression *noun* **1** (*made an impression on her tutor*) effect, influence, impact, sway, power, control. **2** (*an impression where she had lain*) mark, stamp, imprint, indentation, brand, impress. **3** (*got the impression he was bored*) feeling, sensation, sense, idea, notion, fancy, suspicion, inkling, hunch, funny feeling, belief, concept, awareness, perception, recollection, remembrance. **4** (*his impression of the rock star*) impersonation, imitation, parody, takeoff (*inf*), send-up (*inf*). **5** (*the first impression sold well*) edition, issue, printing, print run.

impressionable *adj* susceptible, receptive, open, ingenuous, suggestible, gullible, sensitive, vulnerable.

impressive *adj* imposing, striking, commanding, awe-inspiring, moving, touching, stirring, powerful, dramatic. OPPOSITE: unimpressive.

imprint *noun* mark, impression, print, stamp, indentation.
➤ *verb* impress, stamp, emboss, print, engrave, etch, brand, fix, affix.

imprison *verb* jail, gaol, incarcerate, send down (*inf*), bang up (*inf*), confine, intern, lock up, put away, detain, constrain, put under lock and key, immure, detain. OPPOSITE: release.

imprisonment *noun* incarceration, confinement, internment, detention, doing bird (*inf*), porridge (*inf*), duress, custody, durance. OPPOSITE: freedom.

improbable *adj* unlikely, doubtful, uncertain, dubious, questionable, unconvincing, implausible, farfetched, incredible, preposterous, ridiculous, fantastic, unbelievable. OPPOSITE: likely.

improbity *noun* wickedness, villainy, knavery, dishonesty, fraud, falseness, crookedness (*inf*), unscrupulousness, immorality, lack of moral integrity. OPPOSITE: probity.

impromptu *adj* extempore, extemporaneous, extemporary, improvised, unrehearsed, unprepared, spontaneous, unpremeditated, off the cuff (*inf*), ad-lib, offhand. OPPOSITE: prepared.
➤ *adv* spontaneously, ad lib, without preparation, off the cuff (*inf*), off the top of one's head (*inf*), on the spur of the moment.

improper *adj* **1** (*improper behaviour*) unseemly, indecorous, unbecoming, impolite, indecent, rude, vulgar, shocking, risqué, obscene, offensive, indelicate, suggestive. OPPOSITE: proper. **2** (*improper practices*) illegal, dishonest, unlawful, wrong, irregular, abnormal, incorrect, inaccurate, erroneous, false. OPPOSITE: correct. **3** (*improper use of language*) unsuitable, inappropriate, unfit, inapt, uncalled-for, unwarranted, unseasonable, untimely, inapplicable, impractical. OPPOSITE: appropriate.

impropriety *noun* incorrectness, unseemliness, unfitness, indiscretion, indecency, immodesty, improper conduct, vulgarity, bad taste. OPPOSITE: propriety.

improve *verb* **1** (*the weather should soon improve*) get better, better, ameliorate, amend, mend, reform, correct, rectify, put right, restore. OPPOSITE: worsen. **2** (*improve one's language skills*) develop, progress, brush up (*inf*), touch up, polish, enhance.
OPPOSITE: impair. **3** (*her health soon improved*) get better, recover, rally, pick up, recuperate, be on the mend, convalesce, turn the corner, perk up. OPPOSITE: deteriorate. **4** (*with hard work his grade should improve*) increase, advance, rise, upgrade, progress, augment. OPPOSITE: decline.

improvement *noun* betterment, amelioration, amendment, change, alteration, correction, rectification, restoration, development, enhancement, progress, increase, rise, advancement, addition, rally, recovery. OPPOSITE: deterioration.

improvident *adj* wasteful, extravagant, lavish, prodigal, spendthrift, imprudent, incautious, thriftless, unthrifty, careless, heedless, reckless, rash. OPPOSITE: thrifty.

improvise *verb* **1** (*the stand-in had to improvise*) ad-lib, extemporize, play by ear (*inf*), wing it (*inf*), busk, vamp, speak off the cuff (*inf*). **2** (*improvise some form of shelter*) invent, devise, contrive, concoct, make do, throw together.

improvised *adj* impromptu, spontaneous, extempore, ad-lib, unrehearsed, off the cuff (*inf*), makeshift, devised, thrown together. OPPOSITE: rehearsed.

imprudent *adj* unwise, injudicious, incautious, rash, hasty, heedless, careless, thoughtless, irresponsible, indiscreet, impolitic, ill-advised, foolish. OPPOSITE: wise.

impudence *noun* rudeness, disrespect, impertinence, insolence, effrontery, audacity, boldness, shamelessness, assurance, presumption, cheek (*inf*), sauce (*inf*), lip (*inf*), mouth (*inf*), face (*inf*). OPPOSITE: politeness.

impudent *adj* rude, disrespectful, impertinent, insolent, impolite, audacious, bold, cocky, shameless, forward, presumptuous, pert, fresh (*inf*), cheeky (*inf*), saucy (*inf*). OPPOSITE: polite.

impugn *verb* dispute, challenge, question, call into question, cast aspersions upon, oppose, contradict, deny, criticize, attack, assail.

impulse *noun* **1** (*she had a sudden impulse to ring him*) urge, desire, yen (*inf*), wish, whim, caprice, notion, feeling, instinct, inclination, passion, drive. **2** (*the creative impulse*) impetus, thrust, boost, surge, force, momentum, push, spur, stimulus, stimulation, incitement, incentive, motive, motivation.

impulsive *adj* impetuous, rash, hasty, precipitate, madcap, headlong, heedless, thoughtless, ill-considered, passionate, emotional, spontaneous, unplanned,

unpremeditated, instinctive, natural, intuitive. OPPOSITE: deliberate.

impunity *noun* exemption, immunity, dispensation, licence, liberty, permission, privilege, security, exception.

impure *adj* **1** (*fears about impure products*) contaminated, polluted, infected, tainted, defiled, soiled, unclean, dirty, filthy, foul, poisoned, adulterated, mixed, unrefined, sullied. OPPOSITE: pure. **2** (*impure women*) unchaste, immodest, immoral, indecent, indelicate, shameless, wanton, promiscuous, depraved, corrupt, dissolute, lascivious, bawdy, sensual, carnal, coarse, gross. OPPOSITE: chaste. **3** (*impure thoughts*) vulgar, improper, risqué, smutty, lewd, lustful, lecherous, prurient, licentious, obscene, salacious, libidinous, unclean. OPPOSITE: decent.

impurity *noun* **1** (*fuels containing impurities*) contamination, pollution, infection, adulteration, contaminant, pollutant, adulterant, dirt, grime, filth, dross, scum, foreign body. **2** (*the impurity of some women*) immorality, immodesty, indecency, promiscuity, looseness, unchastity, wantonness. **3** (*impurity of pornography*) crudity, indecency, impropriety, smut, offensiveness, coarseness, obscenity, vulgarity, lewdness, licentiousness.

imputation *noun* ascription, attribution, accusation, charge, blame, censure, reproach, insinuation, defamation, aspersion, slander, slur, calumny.

impute *verb* ascribe, attribute, accredit, assign, accuse, charge, blame, put down to.

in *prep* within, inside, among, during, while, into.
» *adj* fashionable, stylish, chic, popular, trendy (*inf*), all the rage (*inf*), hip (*inf*), cool (*inf*), modish. OPPOSITE: unfashionable.

inability *noun* incapacity, incapability, impotence, powerlessness, inadequacy, incompetence, ineptitude. OPPOSITE: ability.

inaccessible *adj* remote, out of the way, isolated, unreachable, ungetatable (*inf*), out of reach, unattainable, impassable. OPPOSITE: accessible.

inaccuracy *noun* **1** (*the inaccuracy of the report*) incorrectness, inexactness, imprecision, erroneousness, unreliability, mistakenness. **2** (*full of inaccuracies*) error, mistake, slip-up (*inf*), howler (*inf*), blunder, boob (*inf*), gaffe, fault, defect, miscalculation, imprecision.

inaccurate *adj* incorrect, wrong, erroneous, inexact, imprecise, out, wide of the mark, way off beam (*inf*), mistaken, faulty, defective, unsound, unreliable. OPPOSITE: accurate.

inactive *adj* **1** (*the machinery lay inactive*) inert, immobile, still, idle, inanimate, stationary, dormant, quiescent, inoperative, unoccupied, unemployed, out of service, in abeyance. OPPOSITE: active. **2** (*inactive days of the unemployed*) indolent, slothful, lazy, lethargic, sluggish, torpid, slow, quiet, dull, passive, sedentary, sleepy, somnolent. OPPOSITE: busy.

inadequacy *noun* **1** (*inadequacy of child-care provision*) shortage, insufficiency, inadequateness, deficiency, meagreness, scarcity, paucity, lack, dearth. OPPOSITE: adequacy. **2** (*feelings of inadequacy*) inability, incompetence, unfitness, incapability, inefficiency, ineffectiveness, inaptness. **3** (*being aware of her own inadequacies*) shortcoming, failing, weakness, flaw, defect, fault, imperfection.

inadequate *adj* **1** (*the club had inadequate funds*) insufficient, deficient, lacking, scanty, meagre, skimpy, sparse, short, incomplete, imperfect, defective, faulty, pathetic, sketchy, unsatisfactory. OPPOSITE: adequate. **2** (*feel inadequate*) incompetent, incapable, inapt, inept, found wanting, not up to scratch (*inf*), unfit, unequal, substandard, unqualified. OPPOSITE: competent.

inadmissible *adj* immaterial, irrelevant, impertinent, unallowable, prohibited, precluded, inappropriate, inapposite, unacceptable. OPPOSITE: admissible.

inadvertence *noun* oversight, blunder, error, mistake, slip, omission, negligence, neglect, heedlessness, inattention, carelessness, thoughtlessness. OPPOSITE: attention.

inadvertent *adj* chance, accidental, unintentional, unpremeditated, involuntary, unwitting. OPPOSITE: deliberate.

inadvisable *adj* unwise, ill-advised, imprudent, injudicious, ill-considered, impolitic, inexpedient, foolish, silly. OPPOSITE: advisable.

inalienable *adj* absolute, sacrosanct, unviolable, unassailable, nonnegotiable, inherent, automatic, nontransferable, permanent. OPPOSITE: impermanent.

inane *adj* foolish, stupid, silly, fatuous, senseless, idiotic, asinine, absurd, unintelligent, puerile, mindless, frivolous, empty, vacuous, vain, futile, worthless. OPPOSITE: sensible.

inanimate *adj* **1** (*they examined the inanimate body*) lifeless, dead, extinct, defunct, inert, inactive, immobile, dormant, inorganic, mineral. OPPOSITE: living. **2** (*inanimate people*) lethargic, listless, apathetic, quiescent, sluggish, dull, vapid, soulless, spiritless. OPPOSITE: active.

inapplicable *adj* irrelevant, inapposite, impertinent, immaterial, inappropriate, unsuitable, inapt, unfit, unrelated. OPPOSITE: applicable.

inapposite *adj* inappropriate, unsuitable, out of place, unfit, inapt, inapplicable, irrelevant, impertinent. OPPOSITE: apposite.

inappreciable *adj* imperceptible, microscopic, infinitesimal, minuscule, minute, slight, insignificant, negligible. OPPOSITE: appreciable.

inappropriate *adj* unsuitable, inapt, unfit, ill-suited, unfitting, inapposite, incongruous, out of place, unseemly, indecorous, tasteless, unbecoming, improper, inapplicable, irrelevant, untimely, infelicitous. OPPOSITE: appropriate.

inapt *adj* **1** (*an inapt comment*) inappropriate, unsuitable, unfit, inapposite, unsuited, infelicitous. OPPOSITE: suitable. **2** (*an inapt worker*) inept, incompetent, incapable, maladroit, clumsy, awkward, gauche, dull, slow. OPPOSITE: clever.

inarticulate *adj* **1** (*inarticulate sounds*) incoherent, muffled, unclear, unintelligible, incomprehensible, blurred, indistinct. OPPOSITE: clear. **2** (*inarticulate emotions*) unspoken, speechless, voiceless, unuttered, soundless, wordless, dumb, mute, silent, tongue-tied

(*inf*). OPPOSITE: spoken. **3** (*the child was inarticulate*) faltering, hesitant, stammering, stumbling, stuttering, shaking, quavery, poorly spoken. OPPOSITE: eloquent.

inattention *noun* inattentiveness, absentmindedness, daydreaming, woolgathering, forgetfulness, oversight, inadvertence, negligence, neglect, carelessness, thoughtlessness, heedlessness, disregard, unconcern, indifference. OPPOSITE: care.

inattentive *adj* distracted, preoccupied, absentminded, dreamy, miles away (*inf*), unmindful, heedless, thoughtless, careless, slapdash, slipshod, remiss, regardless, unobservant, vague, neglectful. OPPOSITE: attentive.

inaudible *adj* imperceptible, silent, noiseless, quiet, muted, low, faint, indistinct, muffled, stifled, soft, whispered, murmured. OPPOSITE: audible.

inaugural *adj* first, initial, introductory, maiden, opening, launching, dedicatory.

inaugurate *verb* **1** (*inaugurate a magazine*) commence, begin, start, initiate, institute, originate, launch, get off the ground, open, introduce. **2** (*inaugurate the president*) induct, invest, install, ordain, instate. **3** (*the shelter for homeless people was inaugurated*) open, dedicate, commission, consecrate.

inauguration *noun* **1** (*the publisher gave an inauguration party*) commencement, beginning, start, setting up, initiation, institution, origination, launch, opening, introduction. **2** (*the president died within a month of his inauguration*) induction, investiture, installation, ordination.

inauspicious *adj* unpromising, discouraging, unpropitious, ill-starred, ominous, black, dark, ill-omened, unfavourable, bad, unlucky, unfortunate, untimely, untoward. OPPOSITE: auspicious.

inborn *adj* innate, congenital, inbred, inherent, natural, native, instinctive, intuitive, ingrained, inherited, hereditary, in one's blood. OPPOSITE: acquired.

inbred *adj* innate, natural, native, inherent, ingrained, deep-seated, constitutional. OPPOSITE: learned.

incalculable *adj* countless, innumerable, uncountable, numberless, inestimable, untold, incomputable, immeasurable, unfathomable, limitless, vast, enormous, immense, boundless, infinite. OPPOSITE: limited.

incandescent *adj* glowing, dazzling, gleaming, luminous, phosphorescent, dayglo, luminous, radiant, bright, brilliant, shining. OPPOSITE: dull.

incantation *noun* chant, charm, mantra, invocation, conjuration, spell, abracadabra, open sesame, hex, curse, magic, sorcery, witchcraft.

incapable *adj* unable, powerless, impotent, helpless, weak, feeble, inadequate, not up to scratch (*inf*), unequal, incompetent, ineffective, not up to it (*inf*), inept, unfit, unqualified. OPPOSITE: capable.

incapacitate *verb* weaken, debilitate, enfeeble, cripple, disable, put out of action, scupper (*inf*), enervate, immobilize, paralyse, disqualify. OPPOSITE: enable.

incapacitated *adj* crippled, disabled, immobilized, paralysed, out of action, scuppered (*inf*), indisposed, laid up (*inf*), unfit, disqualified. OPPOSITE: operative.

incapacity *noun* inability, incapability, unfitness,

powerlessness, uselessness, impotence, inadequacy, incompetence, ineffectiveness, feebleness, weakness, disqualification. OPPOSITE: ability.

incarcerate *verb* imprison, jail, gaol, send down (*inf*), bang up (*inf*), confine, intern, impound, immure, commit, detain, lock up, put away, restrain, put under lock and key, cage, pen, wall up. OPPOSITE: release.

incarceration *noun* imprisonment, jail, gaol, porridge (*inf*), stir (*inf*), detention, internment, custody, confinement, captivity, bondage, restraint.

incarnate *adj* human form, bodily form, embodied, corporeal, in the flesh, fleshly, made manifest, personified, typified.

incarnation *noun* embodiment, bodily form, archetype, personification, manifestation, exemplification, avatar.

incautious *adj* imprudent, unwise, ill-judged, injudicious, impolitic, unwary, ill-considered, careless, thoughtless, unthinking, heedless, impulsive, hasty, headlong, precipitate, rash, reckless, negligent, improvident, indiscreet. OPPOSITE: cautious.

incendiary *adj* **1** (*her incendiary remarks created havoc*) inflammatory, inciting, seditious, subversive, provocative, rabble-rousing, dissentious. OPPOSITE: calming. **2** (*an incendiary device*) combustible, flammable, fire-raising.
➤ *noun* **1** (*a group of incendiaries led the riot*) agitator, rabble-rouser, firebrand, insurgent, rebel, revolutionary, troublemaker. **2** (*he was charged with being an incendiary*) arsonist, pyromaniac, fire-raiser, firebug (*inf*).

incense[1] *verb* (*their bad behaviour incensed the teacher*) enrage, infuriate, madden, anger, make one see red (*inf*), rile, provoke, rouse, inflame, make one's blood boil (*inf*), irk, gall, aggravate, irritate, annoy, vex, exasperate, hassle (*inf*). OPPOSITE: pacify.

incense[2] *noun* (*sweet smell of the incense*) perfume, fragrance, balm, scent, aroma, redolence, bouquet.

incentive *noun* encouragement, inducement, enticement, bait, lure, carrot (*inf*), incitement, stimulant, stimulus, spur, goad, impetus, impulse, motivation, persuasion, sweetener (*inf*), motive, cause. OPPOSITE: deterrent.

inception *noun* beginning, start, commencement, inauguration, initiation, outset, kickoff (*inf*), birth, rise, dawn. OPPOSITE: end.

incessant *adj* unceasing, ceaseless, continual, continuous, unremitting, nonstop, uninterrupted, unbroken, perpetual, constant, persistent, relentless, eternal, everlasting, never-ending, unending, endless, interminable. OPPOSITE: intermittent.

inchoate *adj* **1** (*the project was at its inchoate stage*) incipient, inceptive, beginning, commencing, initial. OPPOSITE: advanced. **2** (*an inchoate draft*) elementary, rudimentary, embryonic, undeveloped, immature. OPPOSITE: mature.

incidence *noun* frequency, prevalence, extent, amount, degree, rate, occurrence.

incident *noun* **1** (*a major political incident*) occurrence, event, happening, occasion, circumstance, episode, scene, affair, matter, fact. **2** (*the sergeant prepared a report on the incident*) disturbance, commotion, encounter, confrontation, conflict, clash, mishap, skirmish, fight, brush, contretemps, fracas.

incidental *adj* **1** (*his part in the riot was quite incidental*) chance, accidental, unplanned, casual, fortuitous, random, odd. OPPOSITE: planned. **2** (*incidental expenses*) minor, unimportant, subsidiary, secondary, nonessential, occasional. OPPOSITE: essential. **3** (*training incidental to a job*) concomitant, related, attendant, accompanying, contingent. OPPOSITE: unrelated.

incidentally *adv* **1** (*incidentally, the roof has just been restored*) by the way, by the bye, in passing. **2** (*we met up again, quite incidentally*) by chance, coincidentally, unexpectedly, casually, fortuitously, accidentally, by accident.

incinerate *verb* burn, consume by fire, cremate, reduce to ashes, carbonize.

incipient *adj* inchoate, inceptive, beginning, commencing, starting, initial, nascent, developing, rudimentary, embryonic. OPPOSITE: complete.

incise *verb* cut, cut into, slit, gash, slash, notch, nick, etch, engrave, inscribe, carve, chisel, sculpt.

incision *noun* cut, gash, slit, slash, nick, notch, opening.

incisive *adj* sharp, keen, acute, piercing, penetrating, cutting, trenchant, mordant, biting, acid, caustic, stinging, sarcastic, satirical, sardonic. OPPOSITE: mild.

incite *verb* rouse, stir up, inflame, excite, whip up, egg on (*inf*), stimulate, animate, instigate, agitate, provoke, foment, prompt, put up to, goad, spur, prod, urge, drive, encourage, impel. OPPOSITE: restrain.

incitement *noun* rousing, stimulation, instigation, agitation, provocation, fomentation, prompting, goad, spur, encouragement, impulse, impetus, stimulus, motivation, motive, incentive, inducement.

incivility *noun* impoliteness, rudeness, bad manners, discourtesy, discourteousness, disrespect, unmannerliness, ill-breeding, boorishness, vulgarity, roughness. OPPOSITE: civility.

inclement *adj* **1** (*inclement weather conditions*) stormy, tempestuous, blustery, windy, rainy, squally, foul, bad, rough, intemperate, harsh, severe. OPPOSITE: mild. **2** (*masters treated their servants with inclemency*) cruel, unmerciful, merciless, pitiless, callous, hardhearted, unfeeling, harsh, severe, rigorous, tyrannical, draconian. OPPOSITE: kind.

inclination *noun* **1** (*he showed no inclination towards going home*) tendency, leaning, bent, proclivity, propensity, disposition, predisposition, penchant, partiality, predilection, bias, preference, liking, fondness, taste, desire, wish. OPPOSITE: aversion. **2** (*an inclination from the horizontal*) slope, slant, tilt, incline, leaning, gradient, angle, bend, pitch. **3** (*a slight inclination of the head*) bend, bow, bowing, nod.

incline *verb* **1** (*I incline to believe him*) tend, be disposed, predispose, sway, persuade, influence, bias, prejudice. **2** (*the path inclined steeply*) slope, slant, lean, tilt, cant. **3** (*he inclined his head*) bend, bow, lower, nod, stoop.
➤ *noun* inclination, slope, slant, gradient, rise, ramp, ascent, acclivity, dip, descent, declivity.

inclined *adj* disposed, predisposed, minded, of a mind (*inf*), prone, apt, likely, liable, given, willing. OPPOSITE: unlikely.

include *verb* **1** (*the price included service charges*) contain, comprise, take in, embrace, encompass, embody, incorporate, subsume, cover, involve. OPPOSITE: exclude. **2** (*make sure you include me*) count, number, add, insert, enter, introduce, incorporate, group, categorize. OPPOSITE: omit.

including *prep* as well as, with, together with, inclusive of, plus, counting, containing. OPPOSITE: excluding.

inclusion *noun* addition, insertion, incorporation, encompassing. OPPOSITE: exclusion.

inclusive *adj* comprehensive, all in, without exception, all-embracing, global, overall, blanket (*inf*), general, full, across-the-board. OPPOSITE: exclusive.

incognito *adj* disguised, in disguise, camouflaged, concealed, unrecognized, undercover, in secret, under an assumed name.

incognizant *adj* unaware, unconscious, unenlightened, ignorant, uninformed, unknowing, unsuspecting, unobservant.

incoherent *adj* unclear, confused, disjointed, unconnected, disconnected, uncoordinated, disordered, muddled, jumbled, wild, loose, wandering, rambling, discursive, inconsistent, illogical, unintelligible, inarticulate, stammering, stuttering. OPPOSITE: coherent.

incombustible *adj* fireproof, flameproof, nonflammable, noninflammable, noncombustible, fire-resistant, flame-resistant, flame-retardant. OPPOSITE: combustible.

income *noun* salary, pay, wages, earnings, remuneration, revenue, receipts, takings, proceeds, yield, return, gains, profits. OPPOSITE: expenditure.

incoming *adj* coming, arriving, entering, approaching, landing, returning, succeeding, new. OPPOSITE: outgoing.

incommensurate *adj* unequal, inequitable, disproportionate, insufficient, inadequate. OPPOSITE: commensurate.

incommode *verb* hinder, inconvenience, put out, bother, disturb, trouble, annoy, upset. OPPOSITE: assist.

incommodious *adj* inconvenient, awkward, cramped, restricted, confined, narrow. OPPOSITE: commodious.

incomparable *adj* matchless, peerless, unmatched, unequalled, unrivalled, unparalleled, paramount, transcendent, supreme, superlative, beyond compare, unique, inimitable. OPPOSITE: ordinary.

incomparably *adv* beyond compare, far and away, by far, easily, eminently, immeasurably, infinitely, supremely.

incompatible *adj* inharmonious, conflicting, discordant, clashing, jarring, contrary, antagonistic, antipathetic, irreconcilable, at odds, unsuited, mismatched, uncomplementary, incongruous, inconsistent, contradictory, dissentient. OPPOSITE: compatible.

incompetent *adj* **1** (*incompetent to do the work*) incapable, unfit, unable, unsuitable, unqualified, inadequate, insufficient, inefficient, unequal, useless, inept, ineffectual, ineffective. OPPOSITE: competent. **2** (*an incompetent tradesman*) inexpert, unskilful, inept, amateurish, bungling, botched, maladroit, clumsy, awkward, gauche. OPPOSITE: skilled.

incomplete *adj* **1** (*the artist's incomplete sketch*) unfinished, partial, undeveloped, unaccomplished, unperformed. OPPOSITE: finished. **2** (*an incomplete collection*) short, insufficient, inadequate, lacking, wanting, imperfect, broken, defective, fragmentary. OPPOSITE: complete. **3** (*incomplete text*) abridged, curtailed, shortened. OPPOSITE: complete.

incomprehensible *adj* **1** (*incomprehensible notes*) unintelligible, unreadable, indecipherable. OPPOSITE: legible. **2** (*incomprehensible actions*) beyond comprehension, unfathomable, impenetrable, opaque, obscure, enigmatic, inscrutable, mysterious, inexplicable, over one's head, baffling, puzzling, perplexing, complicated, deep, profound, inconceivable, unthinkable, unimaginable. OPPOSITE: understandable.

inconceivable *adj* unthinkable, unimaginable, incomprehensible, impossible, incredible, fantastic, unbelievable, unheard-of, mind-boggling (*inf*), staggering (*inf*), shocking, implausible, preposterous, outrageous, outlandish, out of the question, ridiculous, ludicrous, absurd. OPPOSITE: possible.

inconclusive *adj* indecisive, undecided, unsettled, uncertain, open, open to question, up in the air (*inf*), ambiguous, vague, indeterminate, unconvincing, unsatisfactory. OPPOSITE: conclusive.

incongruity *noun* incompatibility, inappropriateness, inaptness, disparity, discrepancy, anomaly, lack of harmony, inharmoniousness, discordancy, conflict, contradiction, inconsistency, unsuitability, inequality. OPPOSITE: congruity.

incongruous *adj* incompatible, inappropriate, inapt, improper, discrepant, discordant, conflicting, contradictory, contrary, at odds, irreconcilable, inconsistent, unsuitable, out of place, out of keeping, unbecoming, absurd. OPPOSITE: consistent.

inconsequential *adj* insignificant, unimportant, negligible, paltry, trifling, trivial, measly, petty, minor, piddling (*inf*), immaterial, irrelevant, incongruous. OPPOSITE: important.

inconsiderable *adj* unsubstantial, small, slight, light, minor, inconsequential, negligible, insignificant, small-time (*inf*), unimportant, immaterial, trivial, trifling, petty. OPPOSITE: considerable.

inconsiderate *adj* thoughtless, unconsidered, unkind, uncaring, uncharitable, unthinking, unmindful, careless, heedless, tactless, insensitive, intolerant, ungracious, rude, selfish, egotistic, self-centred. OPPOSITE: considerate.

inconsistent *adj* **1** (*inconsistent statements*) contradictory, conflicting, irreconcilable, incompatible, incongruous, contrary, discrepant, discordant, at odds, at variance, out of keeping. OPPOSITE: consistent. **2** (*she was criticized for being inconsistent*) inconstant, irregular, changeable, unpredictable, variable, unsteady, unstable, erratic, fickle, capricious. OPPOSITE: constant.

inconsolable *adj* brokenhearted, heartbroken, disconsolate, comfortless, forlorn, miserable, cheerless, melancholy, downcast, desolate, despairing, wretched, prostrate with grief, lost, hopeless. OPPOSITE: cheerful.

inconspicuous adj **1** (*inconspicuous dress*) unnoticeable, unobtrusive, indistinct, ordinary, unremarkable, plain, unostentatious, hidden, camouflaged. OPPOSITE: obvious. **2** (*she was shy and inconspicuous*) modest, quiet, muted, unassuming, retiring, low-key, in the background, insignificant. OPPOSITE: noticeable.

inconstant adj changeable, variable, vacillating, fluctuating, mutable, wavering, uncertain, unsteady, unstable, temperamental, unsettled, inconsistent, erratic, mercurial, volatile, fickle, capricious, wayward, undependable, unreliable. OPPOSITE: steady.

incontestable adj indisputable, incontrovertible, unquestionable, indubitable, unequivocal, undeniable, irrefutable, unassailable, unshakeable, evident, positive, certain, sure. OPPOSITE: dubious.

incontinent adj **1** (*an incontinent old man*) lacking bladder control, lacking bowel control. **2** (*incontinent passions*) unrestrained, uncontrolled, unchecked, unbridled, ungovernable, uncontrollable. OPPOSITE: controlled. **3** (*incontinent young people*) dissolute, debauched, licentious, lascivious, lecherous, lewd, lustful, wanton, profligate, promiscuous, unchaste, impure. OPPOSITE: chaste.

incontrovertible adj indisputable, beyond any doubt, incontestable, undeniable, irrefutable, unquestionable, indubitable, certain, sure, positive, evident, clear. OPPOSITE: questionable.

inconvenience noun **1** (*we apologized for the inconvenience caused*) trouble, bother, worry, disruption, hassle (*inf*). **2** (*a minor inconvenience*) nuisance, pain (*inf*), drag (*inf*), bore (*inf*), annoyance, vexation, disturbance, difficulty, drawback, disadvantage, bind, headache, hindrance.
‣ **verb** bother, trouble, put out, hassle (*inf*), upset, annoy, worry, disturb, disrupt, hinder, burden, impose upon.

inconvenient adj **1** (*an inconvenient moment*) awkward, embarrassing, troublesome, bothersome, annoying, inopportune, untimely, unseasonable, inappropriate, unsuitable, disadvantageous, difficult OPPOSITE: convenient. **2** (*the room was of an inconvenient size*) unsuitable, unwieldy, cumbersome, awkward, unmanageable, incommodious. OPPOSITE: manageable.

incorporate verb include, comprise, embody, embrace, take in, absorb, subsume, integrate, merge, blend, fuse, meld, mix, amalgamate, combine, unite, consolidate, coalesce, assimilate. OPPOSITE: separate.

incorporeal adj disembodied, bodiless, immaterial, insubstantial, metaphysical, spiritual. OPPOSITE: material.

incorrect adj **1** (*an incorrect spelling*) wrong, erroneous, false, untrue, inexact, inaccurate, out, off beam (*inf*), mistaken, wide of the mark (*inf*), faulty, unsound, flawed, fallacious. OPPOSITE: correct. **2** (*incorrect conduct*) improper, unbecoming, unseemly, inappropriate, unfitting, unsuitable. OPPOSITE: proper.

incorrigible adj hardened, inveterate, incurable, irremediable, irredeemable, beyond redemption, beyond

anything (*inf*), lost, hopeless, obdurate, intractable. OPPOSITE: reformable.

incorruptible adj **1** (*a reliable and incorruptible candidate*) honest, upright, honourable, trustworthy, high-minded, virtuous, moral, ethical, just, straight, as straight as a die (*inf*), unbribable, above suspicion. OPPOSITE: dishonest. **2** (*incorruptible materials*) imperishable, immortal, deathless, undying, everlasting, eternal, abiding, lasting, indestructible, nonbiodegradable, indissoluble. OPPOSITE: perishable.

increase verb **1** (*world population is increasing*) grow, enlarge, expand, advance, swell, extend, prolong, lengthen, add to, escalate, heighten, rise, spiral, climb, rocket, soar, build up, develop, spread, step up, mushroom, snowball, intensify, amplify, multiply, proliferate. OPPOSITE: shrink. **2** (*increase the cost of petrol*) raise, rise, add to, accrue, augment, boost, escalate, inflate, improve, bump up, heighten, spiral, rocket, hit the roof (*inf*), amplify, magnify. OPPOSITE: reduce.
‣ **noun** growth, rise, enlargement, expansion, extension, development, mushrooming, snowballing, augmentation, addition, gain, increment, escalation, upturn, intensification, boost, upsurge. OPPOSITE: reduction.

increasingly adv more and more, to a greater extent, to a higher degree, progressively, cumulatively.

incredible adj **1** (*the change in her looks is incredible*) unbelievable, beyond belief, inconceivable, unimaginable, unthinkable, preposterous, absurd, improbable, unlikely, impossible. OPPOSITE: believable. **2** (*it was an incredible performance*) extraordinary, marvellous, wonderful, astonishing, amazing, exceptional, sensational, fantastic, ace (*inf*), awesome (*inf*), fabulous, fab (*inf*), great, brilliant (*inf*), tremendous, terrific (*inf*), prodigious. OPPOSITE: ordinary.

incredulity noun disbelief, unbelief, scepticism, distrust, mistrust, doubt, incredulousness, stupefaction. OPPOSITE: belief.

incredulous adj disbelieving, unbelieving, sceptical, cynical, distrustful, mistrustful, doubtful, dubious, unconvinced, suspicious. OPPOSITE: credulous.

increment noun increase, addition, gain, augmentation, rise, growth, enlargement, step, accretion, accrual, supplement, step-up (*inf*). OPPOSITE: decrease.

incriminate verb accuse, charge, indict, arraign, impeach, blame, implicate, point the finger at (*inf*), inform against, grass (*inf*), involve, inculpate. OPPOSITE: vindicate.

inculcate verb instil, infuse, ingrain, implant, drum, din, drill, hammer (*inf*), impress, indoctrinate, teach.

inculpable adj innocent, guiltless, blameless, irreproachable, unimpeachable, above suspicion. OPPOSITE: guilty.

inculpate verb accuse, charge, incriminate, blame, cite, indict, arraign, impeach, censure, involve, implicate. OPPOSITE: exonerate.

incumbent adj **1** (*incumbent upon her to attend the jury service*) binding, obligatory, necessary, mandatory, compulsory. OPPOSITE: optional. **2** (*photographed

incumbent on the sofa) resting, reclining, lying, leaning, lounging, reposing. OPPOSITE: standing.
➤ *noun* office holder, official, officer, functionary, dignitary.

incur *verb* bring, bring upon oneself, sustain, suffer, lay oneself open to, arouse, draw, earn, gain, contract, experience, meet with, provoke. OPPOSITE: avoid.

incurable *adj* **1** (*an incurable disease*) fatal, terminal, inoperable, untreatable, irremediable, hopeless, unrecoverable. OPPOSITE: curable. **2** (*an incurable optimist*) incorrigible, inveterate, hardened, dyed-in-the-wool, hopeless, beyond redemption. OPPOSITE: redeemable.

incursion *noun* attack, raid, invasion, advance, onslaught, foray, sally, sortie, inroad, encroachment, infiltration, penetration. OPPOSITE: retreat.

indebted *adj* obliged, obligated, beholden, owing, grateful, thankful, appreciative. OPPOSITE: unappreciative.

indecency *noun* **1** (*the indecency of his comments*) immodesty, indelicacy, indecorum, impurity, suggestiveness, coarseness, crudity, grossness, tastelessness, smut, smuttiness, blueness, bawdiness, ribaldry, lewdness, obscenity, vulgarity, licentiousness. **2** (*the indecency of the pay rise they awarded to themselves*) impropriety, unseemliness, inappropriateness, unsuitableness, bad taste, tastelessness.

indecent *adj* **1** (*he made an indecent suggestion*) improper, immodest, impure, unchaste, indelicate, indecorous, unseemly, tasteless, offensive, obscene, shocking, outrageous, gross, crude, vulgar, coarse, smutty, lewd, salacious, pornographic, blue (*inf*), foul, dirty, filthy. OPPOSITE: decent. **2** (*arranged the funeral in indecent haste*) improper, unseemly, tasteless, inappropriate, unsuitable. OPPOSITE: proper.

indecipherable *adj* undecipherable, illegible, unreadable, unintelligible, crabbed, hieroglyphic, indistinguishable, inaudible. OPPOSITE: clear.

indecision *noun* indecisiveness, irresolution, tentativeness, hesitation, hesitancy, shilly-shallying (*inf*), vacillation, fluctuation, wavering, dithering, uncertainty, ambivalence, doubt. OPPOSITE: resolution.

indecisive *adj* **1** (*she was indecisive about the colour*) irresolute, hesitant, hesitating, in two minds (*inf*), sitting on the fence (*inf*), blowing hot and cold (*inf*), faltering, tentative, pussyfooting (*inf*), wavering, vacillating, undecided, wishy-washy (*inf*), shilly-shallying (*inf*), dithering, unresolved, uncertain, doubtful. OPPOSITE: decisive. **2** (*an indecisive result of the vote*) inconclusive, undecided, unsettled, indefinite, indeterminate, unclear, open. OPPOSITE: settled.

indecorous *adj* improper, unseemly, untoward, undignified, ill-bred, unbecoming, unfitting, unladylike, ungentlemanly, uncouth, uncivil, impolite, ill-mannered, boorish, rude, vulgar, coarse, indecent, immodest. OPPOSITE: proper.

indeed *adv* really, truly, in truth, in fact, in point of fact, surely, for sure, to be sure, without doubt, undoubtedly, doubtlessly, undeniably, certainly, positively, absolutely, actually, in reality, strictly, exactly.

indefatigable *adj* tireless, untiring, unwearied, unwearying, inexhaustible, unflagging, unfailing, indomitable, energetic, diligent, assiduous, sedulous, dogged, patient, persistent, persevering, stalwart, relentless, unremitting. OPPOSITE: tiring.

indefensible *adj* **1** (*indefensible conduct*) inexcusable, unjustifiable, unwarrantable, insupportable, unpardonable, unforgivable. OPPOSITE: justifiable. **2** (*morally indefensible*) untenable, weak, flawed, unsound, insupportable, unarguable, faulty, wrong. OPPOSITE: defensible. **3** (*an indefensible position*) defenceless, vulnerable, exposed, unprotected, unshielded, unguarded, unarmed. OPPOSITE: protected.

indefinable *adj* indescribable, inexpressible, indistinct, impalpable, obscure, vague, hazy, dim, nameless. OPPOSITE: definable.

indefinite *adj* **1** (*an indefinite ban*) unspecified, undefined, undetermined, unlimited, indeterminate, infinite, immeasurable, unbounded. OPPOSITE: limited. **2** (*she saw an indefinite form through the mist*) indistinct, unclear, vague, blurred, fuzzy, obscure. OPPOSITE: distinct. **3** (*an indefinite reply*) unclear, vague, loose, general, inexact, imprecise, ambiguous, equivocal, evasive, confused, unsettled, indecisive, uncertain, doubtful, unknown. OPPOSITE: definite.

indefinitely *adv* continually, for ever, endlessly, eternally, ad infinitum, till the cows come home (*inf*), sine die.

indelible *adj* permanent, unfading, lasting, enduring, ingrained, fixed, ineradicable, ineffaceable, indestructible. OPPOSITE: erasable.

indelicate *adj* indecent, embarrassing, coarse, crude, suggestive, blue (*inf*), risqué, rude, vulgar, gross, obscene, near the knuckle (*inf*), offensive, tasteless, improper, untoward, indecorous, unseemly, unbecoming, immodest. OPPOSITE: inoffensive.

indemnify *verb* **1** (*indemnified against future losses*) secure, guarantee, endorse, underwrite, insure, protect. **2** (*they couldn't indemnify all the pensioners in the fund*) compensate, reimburse, recompense, repay, pay, remunerate, repair, satisfy, requite.

indemnity *noun* **1** (*indemnity from prosecution*) insurance, assurance, protection, security, guarantee, safeguard. **2** (*they received an indemnity for their loss*) compensation, reimbursement, remuneration, reparation, restitution, atonement, repayment, satisfaction. **3** (*claimed indemnity for diplomatic reasons*) exemption, immunity, impunity, privilege, diplomatic immunity, right, prerogative, amnesty.

indent[1] *verb* (*the soldier indented for a new rifle*) ask for, order, request, requisition.

indent[2] *verb* **1** (*waves indenting the sea coast*) cut, nick, notch, score, mark, dent, serrate, scallop, pink. **2** (*the paragraphs were indented for clarity*) move away from the margin, move to the right, begin a new paragraph.

indentation *noun* notch, nick, cut, serration, dent, hollow, dimple, dip, depression, pit, groove, furrow.

indenture *noun* agreement, contract, compact, commitment, deal, settlement, certificate, deed, bond.

independence *noun* **1** (*small states wanted their own* *independence*) autonomy, freedom, liberty, home rule, self-rule, self-government, separation, sovereignty. OPPOSITE: subjection. **2** (*financial independence*) self-reliance, self-sufficiency, self-supporting, able to stand on one's own two feet (*inf*). OPPOSITE: dependence.

independent *adj* **1** (*independent nations*) autonomous, free, sovereign, self-governing, self-ruling, absolute. OPPOSITE: subject. **2** (*the teenager wanted to be independent*) free, self-reliant, self-sufficient, self-supporting, self-confident, unaided, individual. OPPOSITE: dependent. **3** (*independent component parts*) separate, unconnected, apart, self-contained, unattached, unrelated, freestanding. **4** (*arranged an independent enquiry*) unbiased, unprejudiced, impartial. OPPOSITE: biased. **5** (*an independent member*) neutral, nonaligned, freethinking, individualistic, unrestricted, unrestrained. OPPOSITE: aligned.

indescribable *adj* inexpressible, ineffable, indefinable, unutterable, beyond words, incredible, extraordinary. OPPOSITE: commonplace.

indestructible *adj* durable, unbreakable, imperishable, nonperishable, incorruptible, indelible, permanent, unfading, indissoluble, lasting, abiding, enduring, everlasting, eternal, immortal. OPPOSITE: perishable.

indeterminate *adj* **1** (*an indeterminate number*) indefinite, undetermined, unknown, ill-defined, uncertain, unspecified, unfixed, unsettled, uncalculated, inexact, imprecise, uncounted. OPPOSITE: definite. **2** (*he gave an indeterminate answer*) vague, unclear, obscure, general, loose, ambiguous, ambivalent, inexplicit, confused, equivocal. OPPOSITE: clear.

index *noun* **1** (*look in the book's index*) key, guide, list, table of contents, catalogue, directory, file. **2** (*the retail prices index*) guide, indication, hint, clue, sign, mark, token. **3** (*the index on the barometer*) pointer, needle, hand. **4** (*caught his index in the door*) forefinger, first finger, index finger.
▶ *verb* sort, tabulate, alphabetize, catalogue, arrange, rearrange, file, record.

indicate *verb* **1** (*a show of hands to indicate their interest*) show, mark, signify, signal, mean, suggest, imply, connote, represent, be symptomatic of, evince, manifest. OPPOSITE: conceal. **2** (*indicate one's true feelings*) express, tell, disclose, reveal, show, display, demonstrate, exhibit, make known, betray, register, record. OPPOSITE: hide. **3** (*indicate the position*) designate, point out, point to, show, specify.

indication *noun* sign, mark, symbol, signal, token, symptom, warning, omen, portent, forewarning, suggestion, intimation, hint, clue, evidence, record, explanation, manifestation.

indicative *adj* characteristic, significant, typical, symbolic, symptomatic, suggestive, indicatory, exhibitive, indicial.

indicator *noun* **1** (*the stock market indicator*) guide, index, sign, signal, mark, symbol, signpost. **2** (*fuel tank indicator lights*) gauge, meter, marker, pointer, needle, display, index.

indict *verb* charge, accuse, arraign, impeach, censure, rebuke, condemn, blame, incriminate, inculpate, prosecute, summon, serve with a summons. OPPOSITE: acquit.

indictment *noun* charge, accusation, allegation, arraignment, censure, impeachment, condemnation, blame, incrimination, prosecution, summons, inculpation. OPPOSITE: acquittal.

indifference *noun* coolness, coldness, aloofness, detachment, insensibility, insensitivity, callousness. OPPOSITE: concern.

indifferent *adj* **1** (*they were indifferent to her problems*) apathetic, unconcerned, uninterested, heedless, regardless, nonchalant, blasé, uncaring, cool, cold, aloof, distant, detached, impassive, insensitive, unmoved, unresponsive, unsympathetic, callous. OPPOSITE: concerned. **2** (*she was an indifferent hostess*) mediocre, fair, no great shakes (*inf*), passable, average, middling, so-so (*inf*), undistinguished, uninspired, moderate, ordinary. OPPOSITE: excellent.

indigenous *adj* **1** (*the kangaroo is indigenous to Australia*) native, original, home-grown, aboriginal, autochthonous. OPPOSITE: foreign. **2** (*an indigenous trait*) inherent, innate, congenital, inborn, inbred. OPPOSITE: acquired.

indigent *adj* poor, needy, destitute, penniless, on the breadline (*inf*), poverty-stricken, in dire straits, down and out, impoverished, impecunious, penurious, skint (*inf*), stony-broke (*inf*), on one's uppers (*inf*), on the rocks (*inf*), without two pennies to rub together (*inf*), necessitous. OPPOSITE: rich.

indigestion *noun* dyspepsia, heartburn, upset stomach, acidity, gastric upset, pyrosis, wind, flatulence, flatus.

indignant *adj* angry, irate, fuming (*inf*), seeing red (*inf*), incensed, wrathful, furious, livid, mad (*inf*), exasperated, miffed (*inf*), in a huff (*inf*), annoyed, hot under the collar (*inf*), riled, hacked off (*inf*), pissed off (*sl*), teed off (*inf*), irked, peeved (*inf*), shocked, resentful, disgruntled, fed up. OPPOSITE: pleased.

indignation *noun* anger, ire, wrath, rage, fury, exasperation, annoyance, vexation, pique, umbrage, resentment. OPPOSITE: composure.

indignity *noun* humiliation, embarrassment, insult, affront, slight, snub, slap in the face (*inf*), kick in the teeth (*inf*), abuse, injury, outrage, obloquy, aspersion, dishonour, disgrace, reproach, disrespect, opprobrium. OPPOSITE: respect.

indirect *adj* **1** (*an indirect route*) roundabout, circuitous, tortuous, long-drawn-out, meandering, curving, winding, zigzag, deviant, divergent, oblique, circumlocutory. OPPOSITE: direct. **2** (*indirect results of the cutbacks*) secondary, ancillary, subsidiary, subordinate, incidental, contingent. OPPOSITE: primary. **3** (*indirect references to her past*) underhand, insidious, surreptitious, backhanded, devious, deceitful, evasive. OPPOSITE: clear-cut.

indirectly *adv* in a roundabout way, secondhand, by implication, obliquely, circumlocutorily, deviously. OPPOSITE: directly.

indiscernible *adj* **1** (*indiscernible differences*) imperceptible, indistinguishable, unapparent, unnoticeable, hidden, inappreciable, impalpable, minuscule, microscopic, invisible, subtle, slight, inconsiderable. OPPOSITE: visible. **2** (*good indiscernible from evil*) imperceivable, indistinct, undetectable, indefinite, obscure, unclear, shadowy. OPPOSITE: apparent.

indiscreet *adj* **1** (*the indiscreet way she managed her affairs*) unwise, injudicious, imprudent, ill-judged, impolitic, incautious, ill-advised, heedless, rash, reckless, hasty, precipitate, ill-considered, naive, foolish, unthinking, inconsiderate, tactless, undiplomatic. OPPOSITE: cautious. **2** (*indiscreet behaviour*) unseemly, shameless, unashamed, brazen, bold, immodest, indelicate. OPPOSITE: seemly.

indiscretion *noun* **1** (*his indiscretion was out of character*) folly, imprudence, lack of diplomacy, heedlessness, rashness, recklessness, foolishness, carelessness, tactlessness, unseemliness, immodesty, indelicacy, indecency. OPPOSITE: caution. **2** (*the minister apologized for her unfortunate indiscretions*) gaffe, faux pas, breach of etiquette, blunder, slip, slip-up, bloomer (*inf*), boob (*inf*), oversight, lapse, error, mistake.

indiscriminate *adj* **1** (*indiscriminate bombing*) broad, wide, wholesale, general, unselective, random, haphazard, hit or miss (*inf*), aimless, careless, undiscriminating, unsystematic, unmethodical, sweeping. OPPOSITE: selective. **2** (*an indiscriminate mixture*) confused, chaotic, jumbled, higgledy-piggledy (*inf*), mixed, assorted, mongrel, miscellaneous, motley. OPPOSITE: ordered.

indispensable *adj* essential, vital, imperative, key, crucial, fundamental, basic, important, necessary, needed, required, requisite. OPPOSITE: nonessential.

indisposed *adj* **1** (*she was unable to attend as she was indisposed*) unwell, ill, sick, ailing, poorly (*inf*), incapacitated, laid up (*inf*), under the weather (*inf*), groggy (*inf*), out of sorts (*inf*), off sick, taking a sickie (*inf*). OPPOSITE: well. **2** (*they were indisposed to pay her expenses*) disinclined, unwilling, reluctant, hesitant, loath, averse. OPPOSITE: eager.

indisposition *noun* **1** (*not present because of sudden indisposition*) illness, ill health, disorder, complaint, disease, malady, ailment. **2** (*overcome an indisposition to move*) disinclination, reluctance, unwillingness, hesitation, aversion, dislike, distaste.

indisputable *adj* undeniable, irrefutable, unquestionable, indubitable, beyond doubt, incontrovertible, incontestable, unassailable, certain, sure, positive, absolute. OPPOSITE: doubtful.

indissoluble *adj* permanent, indestructible, imperishable, incorruptible, indivisible, unbreakable, inseparable, lasting, abiding, unfading, enduring, eternal, fixed, solid, binding. OPPOSITE: impermanent.

indistinct *adj* **1** (*indistinct shapes*) dim, faint, hazy, shadowy, misty, foggy, vague, blurred, out of focus, indefinite, undefined, ill-defined, obscure, confused, doubtful, unclear, ambiguous, indistinguishable, imperceptible, indiscernible. OPPOSITE: distinct. **2** (*indistinct sounds*) inaudible, incoherent, unintelligible, low, whispered, muted, muffled, mumbled, muttered. OPPOSITE: audible. **3** (*indistinct written material*) illegible, indecipherable, unreadable, faded, smudged. OPPOSITE: legible.

indistinguishable *adj* **1** (*forgeries indistinguishable from the real thing*) identical, twin, same, alike, like, like as two peas in a pod (*inf*), cut from the same cloth, similar. OPPOSITE: different. **2** (*an indistinguishable form in the fog*) indiscernible, imperceptible, indistinct, indefinite, obscure, invisible. OPPOSITE: conspicuous.

indite *verb* write, pen, compose, formulate, word, draft, frame.

individual *adj* separate, distinct, discrete, specific, respective, particular, peculiar, characteristic, typical, idiosyncratic, distinctive, singular, personal, own, lone, exclusive, personalized, original, unique, special, single, solitary, sole, isolated. OPPOSITE: general.
➤ *noun* person, party, being, creature, mortal, human, personage, soul, body, head, character, type, unit.

individualist *noun* independent, freethinker, nonconformist, free spirit, egoist, loner, lone wolf, maverick.

individualistic *adj* individual, independent, original, unique, special, distinctive, particular, characteristic, typical, idiosyncratic, egoistic, egocentric, self-reliant, unconventional. OPPOSITE: conventional.

individuality *noun* character, personality, disposition, uniqueness, originality, particularity, peculiarity, distinctiveness, distinction, separateness. OPPOSITE: sameness.

individually *adv* singly, independently, particularly, one at a time, one by one, severally, apart. OPPOSITE: together.

indoctrinate *verb* brainwash, drill, initiate, impress, imbue, inculcate, instil, infuse, school, instruct, teach, train, edify, enlighten, ground.

indolent *adj* idle, lazy, slothful, shiftless, workshy, sluggish, inactive, lackadaisical, lethargic, apathetic, torpid, languid, listless, slow, slack, inert, fainéant. OPPOSITE: diligent.

indomitable *adj* invincible, unconquerable, unbeatable, impregnable, unassailable, unyielding, irrepressible, undaunting, indefatigable, staunch, steadfast, unflinching, resolute, determined, firm, unwavering, bold, brave, courageous, valiant. OPPOSITE: feeble.

indubitable *adj* unquestionable, without question, beyond doubt, undoubted, indisputable, undeniable, irrefutable, incontrovertible, incontestable, unarguable, evident, obvious, open-and-shut, certain, sure, veritable. OPPOSITE: questionable.

induce *verb* **1** (*huge redundancy payments induced the employees to leave*) persuade, talk into, influence, move, encourage, urge, press, prevail upon, convince, impel, incite, prompt, spur, actuate, coax, entice. OPPOSITE: deter. **2** (*stress can induce health problems*) cause, bring about, occasion, give rise to, effect, produce, lead to, engender, instigate, generate, set in motion, set off. OPPOSITE: prevent.

inducement *noun* incentive, sweetener (*inf*), carrot (*inf*), enticement, lure, attraction, bait, reward, come-on (*inf*), motive, incitement, stimulus, impulse, spur, influence, encouragement, persuasion, consideration. OPPOSITE: deterrent.

induct *verb* inaugurate, install, swear in, invest, ordain, consecrate, enthrone, initiate, introduce.

induction *noun* **1** (*attended the premier's induction*) inauguration, investiture, swearing in, ordination, consecration, enthronement. **2** (*she completed her induction training*) introduction, initiation, installation. **3** (*his powers of induction*) reason, reasoning, inference, conclusion, deduction, judgment, generalization, conjecture, rationalization.

indulge *verb* **1** (*she liked to indulge her grandchildren*) give way to, pander to, pamper, cosset, coddle, pet, mollycoddle, spoil, gratify, satisfy, feed, satiate, yield to, cater to, humour. OPPOSITE: deny. **2** (*indulge one's love of chocolate*) bask in, luxuriate, revel, wallow in, treat, regale.

indulge oneself treat oneself, give oneself up to, go on a spree, go out on the town, paint the town red (*inf*), splurge (*inf*).

indulgence *noun* **1** (*a life full of indulgence*) self-indulgence, self-gratification, intemperance, dissipation, dissoluteness, immoderation, excess. OPPOSITE: temperance. **2** (*indulgence of one's natural desires*) gratification, satisfaction, fulfilment, satiation, appeasement. OPPOSITE: denial. **3** (*an occasional cigar was his one indulgence*) luxury, treat, extravagance. **4** (*they were permitted the indulgence of meeting the princess*) favour, privilege, courtesy, treat. **5** (*treated the inmates with indulgence*) kindness, leniency, tolerance, clemency, forbearance. OPPOSITE: severity. **6** (*he disapproved of the children's indulgence*) spoiling, mollycoddling, pampering, cosseting, coddling. OPPOSITE: strictness.

indulgent *adj* lenient, permissive, tolerant, liberal, forgiving, merciful, forbearing, clement, compassionate, sympathetic, understanding, patient, obliging, compliant, easygoing, gratifying, gentle, kind, tender, mild, fond, cosseting, spoiling, coddling, mollycoddling, pampering. OPPOSITE: strict.

indurate *verb* harden, toughen, strengthen, temper, inure, accustom, season, habituate. OPPOSITE: soften.

industrial *adj* business, commercial, trade, tradable, manufacturing, merchandisable.

industrialist *noun* manufacturer, producer, director, executive, boss, owner, capitalist, captain of industry, financier, magnate, baron, tycoon.

industrious *adj* hardworking, diligent, assiduous, sedulous, busy, active, energetic, vigorous, indefatigable, productive, purposeful, laborious, tireless, persistent, persevering, steady, conscientious, zealous. OPPOSITE: lazy.

industry *noun* **1** (*the motor industry*) business, commerce, commercial enterprise, trade, manufacture, production, service, line, field. **2** (*the farm labourers worked with great industry*) industriousness, diligence, assiduity, sedulity, work, toil, labour, effort, activity, energy, vigour, zeal, enthusiasm, application, concentration, intentness, determination, conscientiousness, tirelessness, dynamism, persistence, perseverance. OPPOSITE: idleness.

inebriated *adj* drunk, intoxicated, blind drunk, inebriate, crapulent, tight (*inf*), plastered (*inf*), well-oiled (*inf*), blotto (*inf*), merry, paralytic (*sl*), pie-eyed (*sl*), legless (*inf*), sloshed (*inf*), bombed (*inf*), boozed (*inf*), stewed (*inf*), tiddly (*inf*), canned (*inf*), squiffy (*inf*), pissed (*sl*), pissed as a newt (*sl*), smashed (*sl*), bevvied (*inf*), Brahms and Liszt (*sl*), drunk as a skunk (*sl*), cut (*inf*), half cut (*inf*), high (*inf*), sozzled (*inf*), tanked up (*inf*), the worse for drink, tipsy, under the influence (*inf*), three sheets to the wind (*inf*), loaded (*inf*), stoned (*inf*). OPPOSITE: sober.

inebriation *noun* drunkenness, intoxication, inebriety, insobriety, intemperance, crapulence, sottishness, alcoholism, dipsomania. OPPOSITE: sobriety.

inedible *adj* unfit to eat, not fit to eat, uneatable, unconsumable, unpalatable, unwholesome, bad, off, rotten, rancid, putrid, poisonous. OPPOSITE: edible.

ineffable *adj* indescribable, inexpressible, beyond words, incredible, unspeakable, indefinable, incommunicable. OPPOSITE: commonplace.

ineffective *adj* **1** (*ineffective medical treatment*) ineffectual, inefficacious, to no avail, useless, vain, futile, idle, inadequate, worthless, unsuccessful, abortive, fruitless, unproductive. OPPOSITE: effective. **2** (*an ineffective head teacher*) ineffectual, inept, unfit, unsuitable, incompetent, inefficient, impotent, powerless, feeble, lame, weak, pathetic, barren, sterile. OPPOSITE: efficient.

ineffectual *adj* **1** (*ineffectual attempts*) ineffective, inefficacious, unavailing, useless, futile, bootless, worthless, fruitless, unproductive, vain, idle, abortive. OPPOSITE: fruitful. **2** (*an ineffectual manager*) inept, impotent, powerless, inept, weak, effete, feeble, lame, pathetic, inadequate, inefficient, incompetent. OPPOSITE: effectual.

inefficacious *adj* ineffectual, ineffective, unavailing, useless, futile, bootless, worthless, fruitless, unproductive, barren, abortive, unsuccessful. OPPOSITE: efficacious.

inefficient *adj* competent, inept, inexpert, incapable, ineffectual, inefficacious, unprepared, disorganized, uneconomical, weak, wasteful, negligent, lax, slipshod, sloppy, careless. OPPOSITE: efficient.

inelegant *adj* unrefined, unpolished, unfinished, uncultured, unsophisticated, uncultivated, ill-bred, unattractive, ungraceful, graceless, uncourtly, uncouth, ungainly, gauche, clumsy, awkward, rough, coarse, crude, vulgar, rude. OPPOSITE: elegant.

ineligible *adj* unqualified, unsuitable, unfit, unfitted, unequipped, unacceptable, undesirable, disqualified, ruled out, incompetent, objectionable. OPPOSITE: eligible.

inept *adj* **1** (*an inept employee*) incompetent, inefficient, ineffectual, unskilful, unskilled, inexpert, clumsy, cack-handed (*inf*), awkward, gauche, clumsy, ham-fisted (*inf*), bungling, bumbling, maladroit, inadequate, unproductive. OPPOSITE: competent. **2** (*inept words*) inapt, inappropriate, unsuitable, unseemly, unfit, improper, out of place, naive, absurd, foolish, ridiculous, nonsensical, pointless, meaningless. OPPOSITE: apt.

inequality *noun* **1** (*inequality of pay scales*) disparity, imbalance, disproportion, unevenness, nonconformity, irregularity, difference, discrepancy, diversity, imparity. OPPOSITE: balance. **2** (*racial inequality*) bias, prejudice, discrimination, partiality, unfairness, injustice, unjustness, inequity. OPPOSITE: fairness.

inequitable adj unfair, unjust, biased, one-sided, prejudiced, partial, partisan, preferential, discriminatory, intolerant. OPPOSITE: equitable.

inequity noun unfairness, injustice, unjustness, prejudice, bias, partiality, discrimination.

inert adj **1** (an inert form) immobile, unmoving, motionless, static, still, stationary, quiescent, inactive, lifeless, passive, inanimate, unresponsive, leaden, dormant, dead. OPPOSITE: moving. **2** (inert associates of the club) idle, indolent, lazy, slothful, sluggish, slack, lethargic, sleeping, languid, listless, torpid, inactive, slow, dull, otiose. OPPOSITE: active.

inertia noun immobility, stillness, inactivity, deadness, lifelessness, quiescence, unresponsiveness, passivity, stagnation, idleness, indolence, laziness, sloth, sluggishness, apathy, lethargy, languor, lassitude, listlessness, torpor, stupor, dullness. OPPOSITE: activity.

inescapable adj unavoidable, inevitable, inexorable, unpreventable, destined, fated, assured, certain, bound to happen, sure to happen, ineluctable. OPPOSITE: preventable.

inessential adj unnecessary, superfluous, surplus, needless, redundant, extraneous, spare, uncalled-for, unasked-for, irrelevant, unimportant, dispensable, optional, extrinsic. OPPOSITE: essential.
➤ noun nonessential, extra, luxury, extravagance, superfluity, accessory, trimming, appendage. OPPOSITE: essential.

inestimable adj incalculable, immeasurable, measureless, infinite, prodigious, invaluable, priceless, worth a fortune, precious, mind-boggling (inf), immense, vast, untold. OPPOSITE: insignificant.

inevitable adj unavoidable, inescapable, ineluctable, definite, fated, certain, sure, destined, predestined, decreed, ordained, assured, fixed, settled, unpreventable, unalterable, irrevocable, inexorable. OPPOSITE: avoidable.

inexact adj inaccurate, incorrect, wrong, erroneous, false, fallacious, imprecise, approximate, indefinite, indeterminate, indistinct, fuzzy, loose, lax, muddled. OPPOSITE: exact.

inexcusable adj indefensible, unjustifiable, unwarrantable, unpardonable, unforgivable, intolerable, reprehensible, unacceptable, unatonable, inexpiable, blameworthy, outrageous. OPPOSITE: excusable.

inexhaustible adj **1** (an inexhaustible supply of fuel) unlimited, limitless, illimitable, boundless, infinite, endless, never-ending, unrestricted, bottomless, copious, measureless, abundant. OPPOSITE: limited. **2** (inexhaustible mountain climbers) tireless, unwearying, unwearied, untiring, indefatigable, undaunted, unflagging, unfailing, weariless, unfaltering, unwavering. OPPOSITE: tiring.

inexorable adj **1** (his seemingly inexorable decline) relentless, unrelenting, unavoidable, remorseless, inevitable, inescapable, unpreventable, unalterable, incessant, unavertable, irrevocable, fated, destined, certain, sure. OPPOSITE: relenting. **2** (an inexorable dictator) adamant, obdurate, inflexible, unbending, unyielding, immovable, intransigent, implacable, cruel,

ruthless, harsh, severe, draconian, strict, exacting, pitiless, unforgiving, uncompromising, merciless. OPPOSITE: indulgent.

inexpedient adj imprudent, injudicious, unwise, impolitic, ill-advised, ill-judged, inadvisable, ill-considered, misguided, indiscreet, foolish, thoughtless, unadvisable, undiplomatic, inappropriate, unsuitable, detrimental, disadvantageous. OPPOSITE: judicious.

inexpensive adj cheap, low-price, low-priced, economical, low-cost, reasonable priced, reasonable, modest, budget, bargain, marked-down, discounted, cut-rate, reduced. OPPOSITE: expensive.

inexperience noun inexpertness, ignorance, strangeness, unfamiliarity, greenness, freshness, newness, rawness, naiveness, naivety, immaturity, innocence. OPPOSITE: experience.

inexperienced adj inexpert, untrained, unqualified, untutored, unschooled, unpractised, unskilled, amateur, unversed, uninformed, ignorant, unfamiliar, unacquainted, unaccustomed, naive, untried, unseasoned, immature, green, raw, callow, fresh, new, wet behind the ears (inf). OPPOSITE: experienced.

inexpert adj untrained, unqualified, unpractised, unskilled, amateur, awkward, blundering, bungling, cack-handed. OPPOSITE: expert.

inexpiable adj unpardonable, unforgivable, inexcusable, unjustifiable, irremissible. OPPOSITE: pardonable.

inexplicable adj unexplainable, unintelligible, unaccountable, insoluble, unfathomable, incomprehensible, beyond comprehension, enigmatic, mysterious, strange, weird, incredible, unbelievable, miraculous, mystifying, puzzling, perplexing, bewildering, baffling. OPPOSITE: explicable.

inexpressible adj indescribable, undefinable, unutterable, incommunicable, unspeakable, beyond words, ineffable. OPPOSITE: commonplace.

inexpressive adj expressionless, blank, empty, vacant, dead, inanimate, lifeless, deadpan, poker-faced, inscrutable, impassive, emotionless, cold, stony. OPPOSITE: expressive.

inextinguishable adj unquenchable, ever-burning, indestructible, unsuppressible, unquellable, irrepressible, imperishable, enduring, lasting, undying, eternal, immortal. OPPOSITE: perishable.

inextricable adj **1** (culture and tradition are inextricable) inseparable, entangled, tangled, muddled, indivisible, indistinguishable, mixed-up, confused. OPPOSITE: separable. **2** (an inextricable issue) complicated, knotty, involved, intricate, convoluted, complex, puzzling, insoluble, indissoluble. OPPOSITE: solvable.

infallible adj **1** (humans are not infallible) faultless, unerring, error-free, unimpeachable, perfect. OPPOSITE: fallible. **2** (an infallible cure) unfailing, sure, certain, foolproof, fail-safe, surefire (inf), dependable, reliable. OPPOSITE: unsure.

infamous adj notorious, ignominious, ill-famed, disreputable, dishonourable, nefarious, shameful, disgraceful, shocking, scandalous, outrageous, hateful, egregious, villainous, heinous, vile, base, wicked, monstrous, atrocious, loathsome, detestable, abominable. OPPOSITE: illustrious.

infamy *noun* notoriety, ignominy, shame, disgrace, disrepute, obloquy, opprobrium, discredit, dishonour, scandal, wickedness, villainy, baseness. OPPOSITE: honour.

infancy *noun* **1** (*he first smiled early in his infancy*) babyhood, early childhood. OPPOSITE: adulthood. **2** (*her business was in its infancy*) beginning, start, commencement, outset, dawn, cradle, birth, origins, early stages, inception. OPPOSITE: end.

infant *noun* baby, babe, babe in arms, bairn, ankle-biter (*inf*), sprog (*inf*), rug rat (*inf*), suckling, toddler, tot, little one, child, minor. OPPOSITE: adult.
➤ *adj* newborn, baby, young, juvenile, dawning, emergent, nascent, developing, early, new. OPPOSITE: mature.

infantile *adj* babyish, childish, puerile, adolescent, immature, young, juvenile. OPPOSITE: mature.

infantry *noun* infantrymen, foot soldiers, rank and file, ranks, cannon fodder.

infatuated *adj* enamoured, besotted, mad (*inf*), in love, smitten (*inf*), crazy (*inf*), having a thing about (*inf*), sweet (*inf*), head over heels in love, enraptured, captivated, fascinated, bewitched, spellbound, under the spell of, beguiled, obsessed, possessed.

infatuation *noun* obsession, fixation, besottedness, craze, passion, love, crush (*inf*), puppy love (*inf*), thing (*inf*), madness, mania, folly, captivation, beguilement. OPPOSITE: indifference.

infect *verb* **1** (*infect the open sore*) contaminate, make septic, pollute, taint, mar, blight, corrupt, pervert, defile, vitiate, poison. OPPOSITE: sterilize. **2** (*infect everyone at work*) transmit infection to, pass on, spread to. **3** (*infect others with your excitement*) influence, affect, imbue, infuse, stimulate, inspire, excite, move.

infection *noun* **1** (*an infection in the ear*) contamination, poison, sepsis, septicity, germs, bacteria. **2** (*catch an infection*) disease, illness, contagion, germ, bug (*inf*), virus, complaint, condition. **3** (*an infection in the water supply*) contamination, pollution, defilement, tainting, taint, spoiling, fouling, blight, poison.

infectious *adj* **1** (*an infectious illness*) contagious, catching, spreading, communicable, transmittable, infective, septic, noxious, virulent, pestilent. **2** (*infectious laughter*) contagious, catching, spreading, compelling, irresistible.

infelicitous *adj* **1** (*an infelicitous circumstance*) unfortunate, unlucky, inauspicious, unfavourable, unhappy, sad, sorrowful, wretched, miserable. OPPOSITE: felicitous. **2** (*their arrival was infelicitous*) inapt, inappropriate, inopportune, untimely, unsuitable, unfitting, unfit, incongruous. OPPOSITE: appropriate.

infer *verb* **1** (*they inferred she was unwell*) conclude, deduce, reason, derive, gather, figure out (*inf*), understand, hypothesize, presume, surmise, suss (*inf*), guess, conjecture. **2** (*the defendant's demeanour inferred he was to blame*) indicate, point to, show, signal, demonstrate.

inference *noun* conclusion, deduction, corollary, presumption, assumption, surmise, guess, conjecture.

inferior *adj* **1** (*of inferior rank*) lower, lesser, subordinate, minor, junior, secondary, subsidiary, ancillary, insignificant, unimportant, lowly, humble, menial, subservient. OPPOSITE: superior. **2** (*inferior work*) substandard, mediocre, poor, bad, naff (*sl*), shoddy, crummy (*inf*), slipshod, ropy (*inf*), second-rate, second-class, low-quality, unsatisfactory, indifferent, imperfect, substandard. OPPOSITE: excellent.
➤ *noun* subordinate, junior, underling, minion, menial. OPPOSITE: superior.

inferiority *noun* **1** (*the inferiority of the workmanship*) inadequacy, second-rateness, imperfection, mediocrity, faultiness, poor quality, slovenliness, shoddiness, indifference. OPPOSITE: perfection. **2** (*a sense of inferiority*) inferior status, subordination, lowliness, humbleness, subservience. OPPOSITE: superiority.

infernal *adj* **1** (*the infernal powers of darkness*) demoniacal, demonic, devilish, diabolical, satanic, fiendish, hellish, damnable, accursed, Hadean. OPPOSITE: heavenly. **2** (*infernal behaviour*) atrocious, abominable, wicked, evil, vile, malevolent, execrable. **3** (*the infernal computer has crashed again*) damned, wretched, dratted (*inf*), darned (*inf*), blasted (*inf*), blooming (*inf*), flipping (*inf*), cursed, confounded, fiendish.

infertile *adj* sterile, barren, infecund, childless, unfruitful, unproductive, arid, parched. OPPOSITE: fertile.

infertility *noun* sterility, barrenness, infecundity, unfruitfulness, unproductiveness, aridity.

infest *verb* overrun, swarm, throng, crawl, pervade, penetrate, invade, beset, plague.

infidel *noun* pagan, heathen, unbeliever, disbeliever, atheist, heretic, sceptic, irreligionist, freethinker. OPPOSITE: believer.

infidelity *noun* **1** (*his infidelity destroyed their relationship*) unfaithfulness, adultery, playing around (*inf*), affair, cheating, liaison, faithlessness, disloyalty, treachery, betrayal, duplicity, perfidy. OPPOSITE: faithfulness. **2** (*religious infidelity*) disbelief, unbelief, scepticism, apostasy, irreligion. OPPOSITE: belief.

infiltrate *verb* penetrate, enter, insinuate oneself, intrude, invade, pervade, creep into, filter, seep, percolate, permeate.

infiltrator *noun* penetrator, intruder, insinuator, spy, subversive, seditionary.

infinite *adj* **1** (*infinite space*) limitless, unlimited, boundless, unbounded, endless, never-ending, eternal, everlasting, interminable, immeasurable, unfathomable, indeterminable, bottomless, inexhaustible, inestimable, vast, immense, all-embracing, total, absolute. OPPOSITE: limited. **2** (*an infinite number of errors*) incalculable, countless, numberless, innumerable, uncountable, immeasurable, untold, vast. OPPOSITE: calculable.

infinitesimal *adj* microscopic, minuscule, minute, tiny, teeny (*inf*), wee (*inf*), small, little, negligible, piddling (*inf*), trifling (*inf*), insignificant, inappreciable, inconsiderable, imperceptible. OPPOSITE: vast.

infinity *noun* eternity, perpetuity, limitlessness,

unlimitedness, endlessness, vastness, extensiveness, immensity. OPPOSITE: finiteness.

infirm *adj* **1** (*my infirm grandmother*) weak, feeble, frail, decrepit, debilitated, disabled, lame, enfeebled, doddering, doddery, shaky, unsteady, wobbly, unstable, unsound, insecure. OPPOSITE: strong. **2** (*infirm of purpose*) indecisive, irresolute, faltering, fluctuating, wavering, vacillating. OPPOSITE: resolute.

infirmity *noun* **1** (*the infirmity of the elderly*) weakness, feebleness, frailty, decrepitude, debility, ill health, disability, defect, failing. OPPOSITE: strength. **2** (*suffer from infirmities*) ailment, disorder, malady, illness, disease, sickness. OPPOSITE: health. **3** (*infirmity of purpose*) indecisiveness, irresoluteness, vacillation. OPPOSITE: resoluteness.

infix *verb* implant, engraft, fix, fasten, set, place, ingrain, impress, instil, infuse, inculcate.

inflame *verb* **1** (*inflame people's feelings*) arouse, excite, impassion, fire, kindle, stimulate, animate, incite, provoke, rouse, madden, enrage, stir up, whip up, rile, incense, infuriate, anger, exasperate. OPPOSITE: pacify. **2** (*inflame a quarrel*) aggravate, exacerbate, fan, increase, intensify. OPPOSITE: mitigate.

inflamed *adj* red, hot, sore, swollen, angry-looking, infected, septic, poisoned.

inflammable *verb* **1** (*inflammable furniture*) flammable, combustible, burnable, ignitable, incendiary. OPPOSITE: nonflammable. **2** (*an inflammable temper*) excitable, temperamental, volatile, fiery. OPPOSITE: placid.

inflammation *noun* heat, burning, redness, rash, swelling, pain, soreness, tenderness, infection, suppuration, septicity.

inflammatory *adj* **1** (*inflammatory comments*) provocative, rabble-rousing, fiery, explosive, inflaming, seditious, insurgent, intemperate, inciting, anarchic. OPPOSITE: calming. **2** (*an inflammatory condition*) sore, painful, allergic, festering, infected, septic.

inflate *verb* **1** (*inflate the beach ball*) expand, swell, blow up, puff up, bloat, dilate, distend, enlarge. OPPOSITE: deflate. **2** (*inflate prices*) increase, boost, amplify, raise, hike up (*inf*), escalate, augment. OPPOSITE: lower. **3** (*try not to inflate his ego*) add to, boost, magnify, aggrandize, overestimate, exaggerate, overstate.

inflated *adj* **1** (*inflated balloons*) puffed up, blown up, swollen, bloated, distended, tumid. OPPOSITE: deflated. **2** (*inflated prices*) increased, raised, extended, escalated. OPPOSITE: lowered. **3** (*inflated rhetoric*) pompous, conceited, high-flown, exaggerated, grandiloquent, magniloquent.

inflect *verb* **1** (*to inflect from a course*) curve, bend, flex, bow, crook, arch. OPPOSITE: straighten. **2** (*he inflected the tone of his voice*) modulate, intonate, intone.

inflection *noun* **1** (*inflections of the body*) angle, bend, curve, arc, arch, flexure, curvature. **2** (*an inflection in her voice*) modulation, intonation, change of tone, pitch, accent, stress. **3** (*inflections of verbs and nouns*) conjugation, declension, derivation, modification, word formation.

inflexible *adj* **1** (*inflexible material*) rigid, stiff, hard, firm, unyielding, unbendable, set,

inelastic, unsupple, unmalleable. **2** (*inflexible arrangements*) firm, unchangeable, unalterable, unadaptable, uncompromising. OPPOSITE: flexible. **3** (*inflexible people*) stubborn, obstinate, intractable, obdurate, adamant, implacable, immovable, unbending, fixed, hard and fast, unchangeable, unalterable, unadaptable, dyed-in-the-wool, inexorable, resolute, persevering, steely, dogged, steadfast. OPPOSITE: flexible.

inflict *verb* impose, enforce, apply, administer, mete out, deal out, wreak, exact, levy, visit. OPPOSITE: spare.

infliction *noun* **1** (*infliction of pain*) wreaking, dealing out, meting out, enforcement, perpetration, application, delivery, exaction. **2** (*suffer from an infliction*) suffering, trouble, worry, hurt, torment, punishment, penalty.

influence *noun* **1** (*have influence over your children*) power, sway, hold, control, authority, effect, weight, pressure, guidance, direction, rule, mastery, spell, magnetism. **2** (*have influence at head office*) connections, good offices, prestige, standing, importance, pull (*inf*), clout (*inf*).
➤ *verb* affect, modify, move, persuade, twist someone's arm (*inf*), induce, impress, carry weight (*inf*), control, guide, direct, lead, sway, pull strings (*inf*), incline, dispose, prompt, impel, incite, instigate.

influential *adj* powerful, potent, forceful, significant, dominant, forcible, effective, cogent, persuasive, moving, controlling, guiding, leading, authoritative, weighty, important, meaningful. OPPOSITE: insignificant.

influx *noun* inflow, inrush, flood, inundation, incursion, invasion, ingress, arrival.

inform *verb* **1** (*inform the police of the situation*) tell, apprise, fill in (*inf*), advise, let know, notify, tip off (*inf*), communicate, acquaint, keep posted (*inf*), enlighten, instruct, put in the picture (*inf*). **2** (*her experiences of homelessness inform her writing*) characterize, typify, brand, identify, distinguish, mark, permeate, pervade.

inform on betray, sell down the river (*inf*), denounce, grass on (*inf*), squeal (*inf*), tell (*inf*), rat on (*inf*), incriminate, blow the whistle on (*inf*), snitch (*inf*).

informal *adj* casual, unceremonious, easy, easygoing, relaxed, natural, simple, everyday, unpretentious, unofficial, familiar, colloquial, vernacular. OPPOSITE: formal.

informality *noun* unceremoniousness, lack of ceremony, unofficialness, casualness, ease, freedom, relaxation, naturalness, simplicity, unpretentiousness. OPPOSITE: formality.

informally *adv* unceremoniously, unofficially, off the record, casually, freely, simply, confidentially, on the quiet, privately. OPPOSITE: formally.

information *noun* knowledge, intelligence, facts, data, details, input, gen (*inf*), info (*inf*), tidings, news, bumf (*inf*), word, message, report, notice, bulletin, communiqué, briefing, advice, instruction, lowdown (*inf*), inside story (*inf*).

informative *adj* instructive, illuminating, enlightening, revealing, educational, helpful, constructive, chatty, newsy.

informed *adj* **1** (*an informed opinion*) authoritative, well-informed, expert, well-versed, well-read, well-researched, learned, erudite. **2** (*keep him informed*) acquainted, posted, briefed, up to date, abreast, conversant, familiar, au fait. OPPOSITE: unaware.

informer *noun* betrayer, informant, source, traitor, spy, mole (*inf*), grass (*inf*), whistle-blower (*inf*), squealer (*inf*), supergrass (*inf*), sneak, telltale, Judas, nark (*inf*), stool pigeon (*inf*).

infraction *noun* violation, breach, breaking, infringement, contravention, transgression, trespass, encroachment. OPPOSITE: observance.

infrequent *adj* occasional, rare, sporadic, intermittent, few, scarce, few and far between (*inf*), unusual, uncommon. OPPOSITE: frequent.

infringe *verb* violate, break, disobey, defy, flout, breach, contravene, infract, transgress, disregard. OPPOSITE: observe.
infringe on encroach on, trespass on, intrude on, impinge on.

infringement *noun* **1** (*infringement of the law*) violation, breach, breaking, contravention, infraction, transgression, trespass. OPPOSITE: observance.
2 (*infringement on his land*) encroachment, trespass, intrusion, impingement.

infuriate *verb* enrage, incense, madden, anger, make your blood boil (*inf*), provoke, bug (*inf*), exasperate, vex, needle (*inf*), nark (*sl*), piss off (*sl*), get one's goat (*inf*), get (*inf*), rub up the wrong way (*inf*), get on someone's nerves (*inf*), get up someone's nose (*sl*), irritate, rile. OPPOSITE: pacify.

infuriated *adj* furious, enraged, raging, flaming (*inf*), incensed, fuming, mad (*inf*), wrathful, irate, angry, beside oneself, vexed, irritated, indignant, exasperated, miffed (*inf*), peeved (*inf*). OPPOSITE: calm.

infuriating *adj* annoying, maddening, exasperating, vexatious, provoking, irritating, pesky (*inf*), galling, aggravating (*inf*).

infuse *verb* **1** (*infused with excitement*) instil, inculcate, ingrain, engraft, implant, infix, impart to, inspire, introduce, breathe into, imbue, pervade, permeate, saturate. **2** (*wait for the tea to infuse*) brew, steep, soak, macerate.

infusion *noun* **1** (*an infusion of hope*) instillation, inculcation, implantation, inspiration, introduction, saturation. **2** (*infusions of herbs*) soaking, maceration, brew.

ingenious *adj* clever, shrewd, astute, skilful, adroit, adept, dexterous, talented, gifted, masterly, brilliant, inventive, resourceful, on the ball (*inf*), innovative, creative, original, cunning, subtle, crafty, wily, sly. OPPOSITE: stupid.

ingenuity *noun* ingeniousness, cleverness, skill, dexterity, talent, flair, inventiveness, resourcefulness, innovativeness, creativity, imagination, shrewdness, genius, gift, knack. OPPOSITE: stupidity.

ingenuous *adj* artless, naive, unsophisticated, simple, innocent, guileless, trusting, direct, plain, open, sincere, honest, genuine, frank, candid, straightforward, on-the-level (*inf*).

ingenuousness *noun* artlessness, naivety, simplicity, innocence, guilelessness, openness, sincerity, honesty, genuineness, unreserve, frankness, forthrightness, candour. OPPOSITE: artfulness.

inglorious *adj* disgraceful, shameful, dishonourable, ignominious, infamous, ignoble, despicable, base, low, disreputable, discreditable, blameworthy, humiliating. OPPOSITE: glorious.

ingrain *verb* instil, impress, implant, root, entrench, embed, engraft, imprint, fix, imbue, infuse, dye, impregnate. OPPOSITE: eradicate.

ingrained *adj* fixed, ineradicable, rooted, implanted, deep-rooted, entrenched, deep-seated, inveterate, inbuilt, built-in, inherent, intrinsic, inborn, inbred, innate, fundamental.

ingratiate *verb* flatter, blandish, fawn, creep, crawl, grovel, brown-nose (*inf*), toady, curry favour, get into someone's good books (*inf*), suck up to (*inf*).

ingratiating *adj* flattering, servile, crawling, bootlicking (*inf*), obsequious, sycophantic, unctuous, toadying.

ingratitude *noun* ungratefulness, thanklessness, unappreciativeness, non-recognition.

ingredient *noun* constituent, component, part, element, factor, item. OPPOSITE: whole.

ingress *noun* entrance, entry, way in, admission, admittance, access, entrée. OPPOSITE: egress.

inhabit *verb* occupy, live in, dwell in, reside in, abide in, populate, people, colonize, make one's home in, tenant. OPPOSITE: vacate.

inhabitant *noun* resident, occupant, occupier, dweller, tenant, inmate, settler, citizen, denizen, native, aborigine, indigene. OPPOSITE: visitor.

inhale *verb* breathe in, respire, inspire, inbreathe, sniff, gulp, gasp, puff, take in, suck in, draw in. OPPOSITE: exhale.

inharmonious *adj* **1** (*inharmonious music*) discordant, cacophonous, unharmonious, unmelodious, unmusical, tuneless, atonal, clashing, jarring, grating, harsh, strident, raucous. OPPOSITE: harmonious.
2 (*inharmonious opinions*) incompatible, contradictory, dissonant, conflicting, irreconcilable, antagonistic, quarrelsome, unfriendly, stroppy (*inf*), perverse. OPPOSITE: harmonious.

inherent *adj* intrinsic, built-in, inborn, inbred, innate, immanent, ingrained, natural, native, congenital, hereditary, inherited, basic, fundamental. OPPOSITE: extraneous.

inherit *verb* come into, be left, be bequeathed, assume, succeed to, accede to, take over, receive, get, acquire. OPPOSITE: bequeath.

inheritance *noun* heritage, legacy, bequest, endowment, patrimony, birthright, accession, succession.

inhibit *verb* restrain, suppress, repress, constrain, curb, hold back, hinder, obstruct, frustrate, thwart, hamper, impede, prevent, stop, arrest, check, bridle, staunch, stem, discourage, interdict, prohibit, forbid, ban, bar. OPPOSITE: encourage.

inhibited *adj* repressed, self-conscious, shy, reticent, reserved, tongue-tied, embarrassed, uptight (*inf*), subdued, withdrawn, introverted. OPPOSITE: relaxed.

inhibition noun **1** (*forget your inhibitions*) repression, constraint, reserve, shyness, reticence, self-consciousness, hang-up (*inf*), embarrassment. OPPOSITE: openness. **2** (*inhibition of expansion of trade*) check, prohibition, ban, embargo, restraint, curb, hindrance, impediment, arrest, obstruction, hampering, thwarting. OPPOSITE: freedom.

inhospitable adj **1** (*an inhospitable greeting*) unfriendly, cool, cold, icy, unwelcoming, unreceptive, unsociable, hostile, aloof, uncongenial, ungracious, unkind, ill-disposed, ungenerous. OPPOSITE: friendly. **2** (*an inhospitable environment*) barren, sterile, desolate, bleak, uninviting, unwelcoming, lonely, empty, forbidding, unfavourable, uncongenial, uninhabitable, wild. OPPOSITE: hospitable.

inhuman adj **1** (*kept in inhuman conditions*) inhumane, unkind, cruel, brutal, fiendish, heartless, unfeeling, hardhearted, callous, pitiless, merciless, ruthless, implacable, remorseless, sadistic, animal, savage, barbarous, barbaric, cold-blooded. OPPOSITE: humane. **2** (*inhuman sounds*) nonhuman, nonmortal, strange, ghostly, animal.

inhumane adj unkind, insensitive, unfeeling, unforgiving, cold-blooded, coldhearted, heartless, hardhearted, pitiless, merciless, ruthless, brutal, cruel, harsh, savage, barbaric, diabolical. OPPOSITE: compassionate.

inhumanity noun unkindness, coldheartedness, hardheartedness, lack of feeling, mercilessness, pitilessness, ruthlessness, brutality, cruelty, harshness, savagery, barbarity, sadism, callousness.

inimical adj **1** (*inimical to their well-being*) harmful, injurious, pernicious, damaging, detrimental, deleterious, destructive. OPPOSITE: favourable. **2** (*an inimical climate*) hostile, antagonistic, adverse, unfavourable, opposed, contrary, unfriendly. OPPOSITE: friendly.

inimitable adj unique, peerless, superlative, faultless, perfect, unmatched, matchless, unparalleled, incomparable, consummate, unsurpassable, unequalled, unrivalled, unexampled. OPPOSITE: commonplace.

iniquitous adj evil, heinous, nefarious, wicked, unrighteous, immoral, unjust, atrocious, monstrous, awful, base, odious, dreadful, abominable, reprobate, infamous, lawless, criminal. OPPOSITE: virtuous.

iniquity noun sin, vice, wickedness, evil, heinousness, wrong, crime, offence, misdeed, transgression, infamy, wrongdoing, sinfulness, lawlessness, unrighteousness, injustice, unfairness, inequity. OPPOSITE: righteousness.

initial adj first, primary, opening, beginning, starting, commencing, early, original, introductory, foundational, elementary, inaugural, incipient, inceptive, inchoate. OPPOSITE: final.
➤ verb sign, endorse, countersign, undersign, put one's initials on.

initially adv at first, in the beginning, at the outset, firstly, in the early stages, primarily, originally, to start with. OPPOSITE: finally.

initiate verb **1** (*initiate the events*) begin, start, commence, kick start (*inf*), set the ball rolling (*inf*), get under way (*inf*), open, originate, inaugurate, institute,

found, set up, launch, get off the ground (*inf*), trigger, prompt, pioneer. OPPOSITE: close. **2** (*initiated into the mysteries of the institution*) teach, instruct, coach, tutor, school, train, drill, prime, ground, break in, indoctrinate, inculcate. **3** (*initiated into the club*) introduce, admit, let in, sign up, enrol, induct, instate, invest, ordain, install.
➤ noun member, recruit, entrant, newcomer, new boy, new girl, novice, rookie (*inf*), beginner, greenhorn (*inf*), convert, novitiate, neophyte, tenderfoot.

initiation noun **1** (*initiation of the new members*) admission, admittance, reception, entrance, debut, induction, introduction, ordination, investiture, inauguration, baptism. **2** (*initiation of the event*) beginning, start, origination, inception, commencement, launching, opening, inauguration.

initiative noun **1** (*take the initiative*) lead, first move, opening gambit, first step, beginning, commencement. **2** (*use one's initiative*) enterprise, originality, drive, ambition, dynamism, get-up-and-go (*inf*), resourcefulness, innovativeness, creativity, inventiveness. OPPOSITE: apathy.

inject verb **1** (*inject antibiotics*) immunize, inoculate, vaccinate, jab (*inf*), syringe, shoot (*sl*), shoot up (*sl*), mainline (*sl*). **2** (*inject a note of humour*) introduce, insert, infuse, instil, bring in, imbue.

injection noun **1** (*an injection of serum*) immunization, vaccination, inoculation, jab (*inf*), shot (*inf*), dose, fix (*sl*). **2** (*an injection of money*) introduction, infusion, insertion, instilling, imbuing.

injudicious adj imprudent, unwise, ill-judged, ill-advised, impolitic, inexpedient, indiscreet, rash, hasty, incautious, misguided, foolish. OPPOSITE: judicious.

injunction noun instruction, order, directive, command, dictum, dictate, mandate, ruling, precept, behest, exhortation, admonition.

injure verb **1** (*injured her back*) hurt, wound, damage, harm, maim, cripple, mutilate, disable, weaken, impair, enfeeble. OPPOSITE: heal. **2** (*injured his pride*) wrong, offend, abuse, maltreat, ill-treat, upset, vilify, defame, ruin, mar, spoil, deface, disfigure, besmirch, tarnish. OPPOSITE: benefit.

injured adj **1** (*her injured back*) hurt, harmed, wounded, damaged, broken, crippled, disabled, lame, maimed, sore. **2** (*the injured party*) wronged, maligned, offended, maltreated, ill-treated, vilified. **3** (*give an injured expression*) reproachful, insulted, cut to the quick, aggrieved, pained, put out, disgruntled.

injurious adj hurtful, damaging, harmful, pernicious, deleterious, detrimental, destructive, bad, noxious, baneful, mischievous, disadvantageous, unfavourable, adverse, ruinous, destructive, abusive, offensive, slanderous, libellous. OPPOSITE: beneficial.

injury noun **1** (*escape serious injury*) hurt, wound, harm, damage, impairment, ill, mischief, sore, bruise, gash, laceration, cut. **2** (*do an injury to others*) wrong, injustice, detriment, ill, grievance, abuse, offence, evil. OPPOSITE: reparation.

injustice noun unfairness, unjustness, inequity, inequality, discrimination, prejudice, bias, favouritism, partiality, one-sidedness, iniquity, offence, wrong, grievance, injury, ill-treatment. OPPOSITE: justice.

inkling *noun* intimation, suggestion, hint, insinuation, innuendo, clue, whisper, faintest (*inf*), suspicion, idea, notion, glimmering.

inky *adj* black, jet-black, pitch-black, coal-black, sooty, jet, ebony, sable, dark, dark-blue.

inlaid *adj* set, inset, veneered, enamelled, ornamented, tiled, tessellated, lined, studded.

inland *adj* internal, interior, up-country, home, domestic. OPPOSITE: foreign.

inlet *noun* bay, bight, cove, creek, arm, fiord, firth, opening, entrance, passage, sound.

inmate *noun* prisoner, jailbird, convict, detainee, patient, resident, inhabitant.

inmost *adj* innermost, deepest, central, private, intimate, dearest, personal, closest, confidential, secret, basic, fundamental, essential.

inn *noun* pub, local (*inf*), public house, tavern, bar, hostelry, hotel.

innards *pl noun* **1** (*the innards of an animal*) insides (*inf*), guts, intestines, entrails, offal, internal organs, viscera, vitals. **2** (*the innards of a computer*) inner workings, mechanism, works.

innate *adj* **1** (*an innate quality*) inborn, inbred, connate, congenital, native, natural, instinctive, intuitive, untaught, spontaneous, inherent, intrinsic, immanent, ingrained. OPPOSITE: acquired. **2** (*the innate defects of the scheme*) essential, fundamental, basic.

inner *adj* **1** (*an inner chamber*) interior, internal, inward, inside, innermost, central. **2** (*the Prime Minister's inner circle*) restricted, private, intimate, exclusive, secret, privileged, confidential. OPPOSITE: unrestricted. **3** (*a sense of inner peace*) spiritual, emotional, psychological, mental. **4** (*inner thoughts*) secret, hidden, unexpressed, unspoken, unrevealed, veiled. OPPOSITE: revealed.

innermost *adj* inmost, deepest, central, private, intimate, dearest, personal, closest, confidential, secret, basic, fundamental, essential. OPPOSITE: outermost.

innkeeper *noun* landlord, landlady, publican, barkeeper, host, hostess, mine host, hotelier, restaurateur.

innocence *noun* **1** (*innocence of the accused*) guiltlessness, blamelessness, unimpeachability, irreproachability, honesty, integrity, righteousness, impeccability, irreproachability, stainlessness, faultlessness. OPPOSITE: guilt. **2** (*innocence of the little children*) virtue, virtuousness, purity, chastity, spotlessness, virginity, morality. OPPOSITE: impurity. **3** (*innocence of their comments*) harmlessness, inoffensiveness, innocuousness, playfulness, lack of malice. OPPOSITE: harmfulness. **4** (*innocence of the novices*) naivety, artlessness, guilelessness, ingenuousness, inexperience, ignorance, frankness, simplicity, unsophistication, unworldliness, gullibility, credulity.

innocent *adj* **1** (*innocent of the crime*) guiltless, blameless, unimpeachable, inculpable, in the clear, clear, not guilty, above suspicion, irreproachable. OPPOSITE: guilty. **2** (*innocent children*) pure, chaste,

virginal, sinless, virtuous, upright, moral, decent, righteous, unsullied, spotless, immaculate, clean, faultless, uncorrupted, impeccable. OPPOSITE: impure. **3** (*an innocent prank*) harmless, innocuous, innoxious, inoffensive, unmalicious, safe, playful. OPPOSITE: injurious. **4** (*innocent young people*) naive, unsophisticated, artless, ingenuous, simple, guileless, gullible, credulous, trusting, inexperienced, green (*inf*), unworldly, wet behind the ears (*inf*). OPPOSITE: artful.
➤ *noun* beginner, novice, tenderfoot, ingenue, neophyte, greenhorn, babe, infant, child. OPPOSITE: expert.

innocuous *adj* harmless, innoxious, safe, innocent, inoffensive, unobjectionable, bland, mild. OPPOSITE: harmful.

innovation *noun* new method, new product, novelty, change, renovation, alteration, introduction, progress, reform, modernism. OPPOSITE: conservatism.

innovative *adj* original, fresh, new, imaginative, creative, enterprising, go-ahead, progressive, daring. OPPOSITE: conservative.

innuendo *noun* insinuation, allusion, slur, implication, suggestion, hint, intimation, whisper.

innumerable *adj* countless, untold, many, umpteen (*inf*), numberless, numerous, masses (*inf*), myriad, incalculable. OPPOSITE: few.

inoculate *verb* vaccinate, immunize, give a jab to (*inf*), protect, inject, imbue.

inoculation *noun* vaccination, immunization, jab (*inf*), shot (*inf*), protection, injection.

inoffensive *adj* unobjectionable, innocent, harmless, safe, innocuous, innoxious, mild, unobtrusive, retiring, quiet. OPPOSITE: offensive.

inoperable *adj* incurable, untreatable, irremovable, unremovable, fatal, deadly, terminal, hopeless. OPPOSITE: operable.

inoperative *adj* **1** (*an inoperative law*) ineffectual, ineffective, inefficacious, inefficient, useless, inadequate, worthless, valueless, futile. **2** (*an inoperative engine*) broken, not in operation, not working, defective, kaput (*int*), out of order, out of commission, knackered (*int*), buggered (*sl*), unserviceable, invalid, null and void. OPPOSITE: operative.

inopportune *adj* untimely, ill-timed, inconvenient, unsuitable, inappropriate, unseasonable, inauspicious, unfortunate, infelicitous, unfavourable. OPPOSITE: timely.

inordinate *adj* excessive, immoderate, outrageous, preposterous, extreme, exorbitant, disproportionate, unwarranted, undue, uncalled-for, unreasonable, extravagant, intemperate, unrestrained, unrestricted. OPPOSITE: moderate.

inorganic *adj* chemical, artificial, man-made, inanimate, mineral. OPPOSITE: organic.

inquest *noun* inquiry, inquisition, investigation, hearing, probe, examination, postmortem.

inquietude *noun* uneasiness, unease, anxiety, trepidation, worry, jumpiness, the jitters, nervousness, restlessness, disquiet, disquietude, discomposure. OPPOSITE: ease.

inquire *verb* **1** (*inquire into the exact circumstances*) investigate, research, look into, inspect, study, examine, scrutinize, probe, snoop (*inf*), explore. **2** (*inquire about his health*) ask, question, quiz, enquire, interrogate, grill (*inf*).

inquiring *adj* questioning, inquisitive, curious, interested, investigative, analytical, probing, nosy (*inf*), prying. OPPOSITE: incurious.

inquiry *noun* **1** (*an inquiry into the fire*) investigation, inquest, inquisition, hearing, study, examination, scrutiny, survey, research, probe, search, exploration, interrogation. **2** (*answer her inquiry*) enquiry, question, query.

inquisition *noun* interrogation, cross-examination, third degree (*inf*), examination, questioning, grilling (*inf*), quizzing, inquiry, inquest.

inquisitive *adj* inquiring, questioning, curious, probing, nosy (*inf*), prying, snooping, spying, intrusive, meddlesome, interfering. OPPOSITE: uninterested.

inroad *noun* incursion, advance, onslaught, raid, foray, irruption, invasion, intrusion, encroachment. OPPOSITE: retreat.
make inroads upon encroach upon, use up, eat up, eat away.

insalubrious *adj* unhealthy, unwholesome, noxious, insanitary, unhygienic, dirty, unclean. OPPOSITE: salubrious.

insane *adj* **1** (*a hospital for the insane*) mentally ill, mad, crazy (*inf*), deranged, out of one's mind, of unsound mind, not all there (*inf*), demented, lunatic (*inf*), unbalanced, unhinged, non compos mentis. OPPOSITE: sane. **2** (*he's insane to be out in the cold*) crazy, mad, foolish, nuts (*inf*), bonkers (*inf*), barmy (*inf*), crackers (*inf*), barking (*inf*), off one's trolley (*inf*), round the bend (*inf*), out of one's mind, potty (*inf*), batty (*inf*), bananas (*inf*), screwy (*inf*), mad as a hatter. OPPOSITE: sensible. **3** (*an insane plan*) foolish, daft (*inf*), stupid, crazy, mad, senseless, idiotic, off the wall (*inf*), irresponsible, irrational, absurd, ridiculous. OPPOSITE: sensible.

insanitary *adj* unsanitary, unhygienic, unhealthy, unclean, dirty, insalubrious, filthy, unsanitized, contaminated, polluted, infected, germy, infested. OPPOSITE: sanitary.

insanity *noun* **1** (*suffer from insanity*) madness, craziness (*inf*), lunacy, derangement, dementia, neurosis, mental disorder, mental illness, psychosis, aberration. OPPOSITE: sanity. **2** (*insanity of the plan*) folly, foolishness, daftness (*inf*), craziness, stupidity, idiocy, senselessness, lunacy, irresponsibility, absurdity. OPPOSITE: sense.

insatiable *adj* unquenchable, insatiate, unappeasable, rapacious, voracious, ravenous, greedy, gluttonous, immoderate, omnivorous.

inscribe *verb* **1** (*inscribed his name on a tree*) engrave, carve, cut, etch, incise, impress, imprint, stamp, brand, write, pen. OPPOSITE: erase. **2** (*inscribed his name in the book*) enter, record, register, enrol, enlist, engross, write. OPPOSITE: delete. **3** (*inscribed her new book*) sign, autograph, dedicate, address.

inscription *noun* engraving, etching, legend, words, writing, lettering, legend, epitaph, address, message, dedication, autograph.

inscrutable *adj* **1** (*an inscrutable look*) enigmatic, impenetrable, deadpan, unreadable, poker faced, sphinxlike, cryptic. OPPOSITE: expressive. **2** (*an inscrutable mystery*) inexplicable, unfathomable, incomprehensible, mysterious, unintelligible, puzzling, baffling, arcane. OPPOSITE: comprehensible.

insecure *adj* **1** (*feel insecure*) uncertain, unsure, diffident, hesitant, apprehensive, anxious, nervous, timid, fearful, afraid. OPPOSITE: confident. **2** (*an insecure position*) unsafe, risky, perilous, dangerous, hazardous, exposed, open to attack, vulnerable, unprotected, unshielded, unguarded, defenceless. OPPOSITE: safe. **3** (*an insecure building*) unstable, unsteady, shaky, wobbly, rickety, loose, infirm, jerry-built, insubstantial, unsound, flimsy, weak, frail. OPPOSITE: stable.

insecurity *noun* **1** (*emotional insecurity*) lack of confidence, timidity, diffidence, anxiety, worry, apprehension, nervousness, uneasiness, uncertainty. OPPOSITE: confidence. **2** (*insecurity of self-employment*) unsafety, hazard, peril, danger, vulnerability, defencelessness, unguardedness. OPPOSITE: security. **3** (*insecurity of the building*) unsteadiness, shakiness, wobbliness, looseness, infirmity, flimsiness, weakness, frailty. OPPOSITE: strength.

insensible *adj* **1** (*insensible of the risk*) unaware, oblivious, heedless, impervious, unconscious, unmindful, ignorant, blind, deaf. OPPOSITE: aware. **2** (*insensible to pain*) indifferent, insensitive, unaffected, impervious, oblivious, unmoved, untouched, unresponsive, inured. OPPOSITE: sensitive. **3** (*knocked insensible to the ground*) numb, unfeeling, unconscious, anaesthetized, zonked (*inf*), out for the count (*inf*), knocked out (*inf*), KO'd (*inf*), insensate, insentient, comatose. OPPOSITE: sentient.

insensitive *adj* **1** (*insensitive bureaucrats*) uncaring, unfeeling, uncompassionate, insensate, insensible, thick-skinned, heartless, callous, tactless. OPPOSITE: caring. **2** (*he is insensitive to women's rights*) insensible, indifferent, oblivious, unaffected, unmoved, unappreciative, unresponsive. OPPOSITE: sensitive. **3** (*insensitive to pain*) immune, proof, unsusceptible, impervious, unaffected, unreactive. OPPOSITE: sensitive.

inseparable *adj* **1** (*freedom and responsibility are inseparable*) indivisible, unseparable, undividable, inextricable, inseverable, indissoluble. OPPOSITE: separable. **2** (*the girl and her dog were inseparable friends*) devoted, intimate, constant, close, bosom.

insert *verb* introduce, place, stick in, push in, put in, enter, interpolate, intercalate, inject, interpose, interject, inset, implant, embed, infix, inlay. OPPOSITE: extract.
≫ *noun* insertion, inset, enclosure, circular, supplement, advertisement, ad (*inf*), notice.

insertion *noun* insert, entry, inclusion, addition, intercalation, inset, supplement.

inside *noun* interior, contents, centre, heart, guts (*inf*), middle. OPPOSITE: surface.
≫ *adj* **1** (*an inside part*) interior, inner, internal, innermost, inmost, inward. OPPOSITE: external. **2** (*get the inside story*) secret, classified, confidential, restricted, privileged, private, reserved. OPPOSITE: public.
≫ *adv* **1** (*go inside*) indoors, within. OPPOSITE: outside.

2 (*to feel happy inside*) internally, privately, secretly, emotionally, intuitively.

insider *noun* member, one of us (*inf*), participant, one of the in-crowd (*inf*), staff member.

insides *pl noun* innards (*inf*), guts, intestines, entrails, offal, stomach, tummy (*inf*), belly (*inf*), internal organs, viscera, vitals.

insidious *adj* stealthy, subtle, slick, crafty, sneaky, artful, sly, wily, cunning, guileful, tricky, crooked (*inf*), deceitful, deceptive, duplicitous, treacherous. OPPOSITE: straightforward.

insight *noun* **1** (*gain new insights*) awareness, eye-opener (*inf*), realization, understanding, comprehension, knowledge. **2** (*have insight into a complex matter*) penetration, perception, intuition, perspicacity, acumen, discernment, shrewdness, awareness, vision.

insightful *adj* perceptive, astute, observant, understanding, discerning, knowledgeable, sagacious, wise. OPPOSITE: superficial.

insignia *noun* badge, sign, emblem, crest, ribbon, decoration, mark, symbol, brand.

insignificant *adj* unimportant, trivial, trifling, piddling (*inf*), meagre, small, nugatory, immaterial, irrelevant, inconsiderable, negligible, minor, small-time (*inf*), small-fry (*inf*), paltry, petty, meaningless, of no account, not worth mentioning. OPPOSITE: significant.

insincere *adj* hypocritical, dissembling, two-faced, deceitful, mendacious, dishonest, underhand, untruthful, false, phoney (*inf*), untrue, hollow, empty, faithless, perfidious, disingenuous, evasive, shifty. OPPOSITE: sincere.

insinuate *verb* **1** (*she insinuated he was lying*) intimate, hint, suggest, imply, get at (*inf*), allude, refer. OPPOSITE: state. **2** (*tried to insinuate misgiving into their thoughts*) introduce, infuse, instil, infiltrate, implant, inject.
insinuate oneself ingratiate, fawn, curry favour, worm one's way, get in with.

insinuation *noun* **1** (*an insinuation that he did not know how to teach*) intimation, hint, suggestion, implication, innuendo, allusion. OPPOSITE: statement. **2** (*the insinuation of misgivings*) introduction, infusion, instillation, infiltration, implanting.

insipid *adj* bland, tasteless, flavourless, watery, wishy-washy (*inf*), colourless, anaemic, vapid, dull, boring, uninteresting, tedious, dry, flat, lifeless, spiritless, jejune, banal, trite, prosaic, stale, unimaginative, tame, characterless.

insist *verb* **1** (*the school insists that they wear uniform*) demand, require, command, urge, exhort, entreat. OPPOSITE: waive. **2** (*if they say no, you should insist*) stand one's ground, stand firm, be firm, put one's foot down, be determined, be resolute, not take no for an answer. **3** (*he insists that he didn't know*) maintain, assert, stress, emphasize, aver, vow, swear, declare, contend, claim. OPPOSITE: deny.

insistence *noun* **1** (*her insistence that they are punctual*) demand, requirement, command, urging, exhortation, entreaty. **2** (*his insistence that he is eighteen*) maintenance, assertion, aversion, avowal, declaration, stress, emphasis, contention.

insistent *adj* **1** (*she is insistent they keep to the paths*) emphatic, determined, unyielding, persistent, resolute, dogged, relentless, tenacious. **2** (*insistent calls on her time*) incessant, persistent, determined, compelling, pressing, coercive, demanding. **3** (*insistent tapping*) incessant, constant, repetitive, repeated, iterative.

insobriety *noun* drunkenness, intoxication, inebriety, intemperance, crapulence, tipsiness (*inf*). OPPOSITE: sobriety.

insolence *noun* impudence, impertinence, lip (*inf*), rudeness, sauce (*inf*), cheek (*inf*), backchat (*inf*), pertness, boldness, presumption, audacity, chutzpah (*inf*), effrontery, disrespect, contumely, arrogance. OPPOSITE: politeness.

insolent *adj* impudent, impertinent, rude, lippy (*inf*), mouthy (*inf*), saucy (*inf*), cheeky (*inf*), pert, fresh (*inf*), bold, audacious, brazen, disrespectful, ill-mannered, offensive, insulting, presumptuous, arrogant, contemptuous. OPPOSITE: deferential.

insoluble *adj* **1** (*the powder was insoluble*) indissoluble, not soluble. OPPOSITE: soluble. **2** (*the murder was insoluble*) insolvable, unfathomable, inexplicable, incomprehensible, inscrutable, indecipherable, intricate, mystifying, baffling, puzzling. OPPOSITE: soluble.

insolvency *noun* bankruptcy, liquidation, ruin, indebtedness, default, pennilessness, penury, impecuniosity, destitution. OPPOSITE: solvency.

insolvent *adj* bankrupt, in debt, liquidated, failed, gone under (*inf*), gone to the wall (*inf*), ruined, beggared, bust (*inf*), penniless, broke (*inf*), in queer street (*inf*), in the red (*inf*), skint (*inf*), destitute. OPPOSITE: rich.

insomnia *noun* sleeplessness, insomnolence, wakefulness, restlessness.

insouciant *adj* nonchalant, untroubled, unconcerned, heedless, carefree, easygoing, happy-go-lucky, frivolous, lighthearted, jaunty.

inspect *verb* examine, scrutinize, scan, peruse, study, check, audit, appraise, vet, investigate, view, review, observe, survey, supervise, oversee, visit, tour.

inspection *noun* examination, scrutiny, audit, perusal, dekko (*inf*), look-see (*inf*), check-up, once-over (*inf*), investigation, review, rec. (*inf*), survey, appraisal, supervision, tour.

inspector *noun* examiner, scrutinizer, censor, checker, critic, vetter, auditor, investigator, observer, supervisor, overseer, appraiser.

inspiration *noun* **1** (*she is an inspiration to us*) stimulation, stimulus, motivation, influence, muse, spur, incitement, incentive, encouragement, arousal. **2** (*his inspiration comes from classical music*) creativity, originality, genius, inventiveness, passion, enthusiasm, insight, afflatus. **3** (*suddenly have an inspiration*) brilliant thought, idea, bright idea, brain wave, stroke of genius, revelation, enlightenment, illumination.

inspire *verb* **1** (*inspired him to even greater success*) stimulate, provoke, motivate, encourage, animate, trigger, spark off, prompt, spur, goad, energize, galvanize. **2** (*she inspires confidence*) arouse, inflame, excite, ignite, kindle, bring about, give rise to.

inspired *adj* **1** (*an inspired speech*) brilliant, superlative, outstanding, out of this world (*inf*), enthralling, dazzling, marvellous, remarkable, memorable. OPPOSITE: dull. **2** (*an inspired guess*) instinctive, intuitive.

inspirit *verb* enliven, encourage, animate, invigorate, inspire, stimulate, arouse, move, incite, excite, stir, exhilarate, rouse, fire, cheer, gladden, hearten. OPPOSITE: depress.

instability *noun* **1** (*instability of her friendships*) inconstancy, temporariness, uncertainty, unreliability, unendurability, impermanence. OPPOSITE: constancy. **2** (*political instability*) uncertainty, insecurity, fluidity, unsteadiness, precariousness, shakiness, wobbliness, flimsiness. OPPOSITE: stability. **3** (*worried by his instability*) capriciousness, flightiness, fickleness, changeableness, variability, vacillation, wavering, volatility. OPPOSITE: stability.

install *verb* **1** (*install a new shower*) place, put in, put in place, situate, fix, lodge, station, locate. **2** (*install her as the new head teacher*) invest, induct, instate, introduce, institute, inaugurate, establish, initiate. OPPOSITE: oust. **3** (*installed themselves in the front row*) ensconce, settle, position, establish.

installation *noun* **1** (*installation of the new shower*) placing, positioning, fixing, situating, location, siting, establishment, fitting. **2** (*his installation as chairman*) investiture, induction, instatement, introduction, inauguration, initiation. OPPOSITE: ousting. **3** (*industrial installations*) plant, equipment, machinery. **4** (*a military installation*) base, post, camp, site, station, settlement, encampment, establishment, headquarters, HQ.

instalment *noun* **1** (*pay in instalments*) part payment, payment, repayment, hire purchase, HP. **2** (*listen to each instalment of the play on the radio*) episode, chapter, section, portion, part, segment.

instance *noun* **1** (*many instances of theft*) example, sample, case, illustration, occurrence, occasion, precedent, time, situation, place, stage, step. **2** (*she left at his instance*) request, demand, entreaty, urging, insistence, exhortation, solicitation, behest, suggestion, prompting, instigation.
  ➤ *verb* cite, quote, specify, name, adduce, mention, refer to.

instant *noun* moment, second, minute, tick (*inf*), twinkling, trice, two shakes of a lamb's tail (*inf*), flash, jiffy (*inf*).
  ➤ *adj* **1** (*an instant decision*) immediate, instantaneous, quick, prompt, direct. OPPOSITE: slow. **2** (*instant coffee*) pre-prepared, ready-prepared, ready-made, ready meal, quick to make, convenience. **3** (*at her instant request*) urgent, demanding, pressing, imperative, importunate, exigent, critical.

instantaneous *adj* instant, immediate, rapid, quick, prompt, direct, on-the-spot, sudden, abrupt. OPPOSITE: slow.

instantaneously *adv* straightaway, at once, immediately, promptly, quickly, pronto (*inf*), rapidly, in a trice, before you can say Jack Robinson (*inf*), in a twinkling, there and then, without delay. OPPOSITE: eventually.

instantly *adv* immediately, at once, now, pronto (*inf*),

without delay, forthwith, directly, straightaway, instantaneously. OPPOSITE: later.

instead *adv* alternatively, preferably, rather, in contrast, as a replacement, as a substitute.

instead of in lieu of, rather than, in preference to, in place of, as an alternative to, in contrast to.

instigate *verb* incite, provoke, spur, goad, egg on (*inf*), actuate, start, begin, initiate, bring about, prompt, urge, impel, encourage, influence, persuade, foment, rouse, stimulate, kindle, stir up. OPPOSITE: suppress.

instigation *noun* incitement, provocation, actuation, initiation, prompting, behest, urging, impulse, encouragement, influence, persuasion. OPPOSITE: suppression.

instigator *noun* prime mover, motivator, leader, ringleader, goad, agitator, troublemaker, agent provocateur, mischief-maker, fomenter.

instil *verb* infuse, imbue, insinuate, implant, engraft, inculcate, impress, infix, introduce, teach. OPPOSITE: eradicate.

instinct *noun* **1** (*he relied on instinct for survival*) intuition, feeling, hunch, sixth sense, gut feeling (*inf*), inner prompting, impulse, inclination, tendency, innate, proclivity, predisposition. OPPOSITE: reason. **2** (*have an instinct for music*) aptitude, ability, knack, flair, talent, gift, feel, bent, faculty.

instinctive *adj* intuitive, unlearned, unthinking, impulsive, automatic, spontaneous, involuntary, reflex, unpremeditated, natural, inherent, native, inborn, innate. OPPOSITE: rational.

institute *verb* **1** (*institute new rules*) found, establish, create, develop, set up, originate, initiate, introduce, organize, start, begin, enact, commence, inaugurate, launch, pioneer. OPPOSITE: terminate. **2** (*institute the new governor*) appoint, install, instate, invest, induct, initiate, ordain.
  ➤ *noun* **1** (*an institute for nuclear research*) institution, school, college, academy, seminary, conservatory, society, association, organization, foundation. **2** (*local institutes*) law, rule, regulation, decree, principle, tenet, custom, tradition.

institution *noun* **1** (*the institution of new working procedures*) introduction, initiation, starting, inauguration, origination, creation, setting-up, launch, commencement, appointment, installation, induction. OPPOSITE: termination. **2** (*a medical institution*) institute, school, college, hospital, asylum, home, establishment, organization, foundation, concern, business, company. **3** (*in an institution for life*) mental hospital, hospital, children's home, reformatory, prison. **4** (*regional institutions*) custom, tradition, ritual, usage, convention, rule, law, principle, practice. **5** (*the balloon-seller was an institution in town*) regular feature, familiar sight, prominent feature.

institutional *adj* **1** (*still retained an institutional approach*) bureaucratic, formal, organized, methodical, conventional, orthodox, accepted. OPPOSITE: unconventional. **2** (*only institutional food at the hostel*) regimented, uniform, unvarying, monotonous, dull, unchanging. OPPOSITE: individualistic. **3** (*less of an* *institutional atmosphere these days*) clinical, impersonal, formal, unwelcoming, forbidding, cold, cheerless. OPPOSITE: friendly.

instruct *verb* **1** (*instruct the child to be quiet*) tell, order, command, direct, bid, enjoin. **2** (*instruct the children in maths*) teach, educate, school, edify, prime, ground, enlighten, train, coach, drill, indoctrinate. **3** (*instruct them that there will be a delay*) inform, notify, tell, apprise, advise, acquaint, brief.

instruction *noun* **1** (*give the soldier an instruction*) order, command, mandate, direction, ruling, directive, requirement, briefing, recommendation, advice, guidance, guideline, rule. **2** (*give instruction in geography*) teaching, education, tuition, training, schooling, drilling, coaching, grounding, guidance, enlightenment, indoctrination.

instructions *pl noun* **1** (*his instructions were clear*) orders, commands, directions, requirements. **2** (*read the instructions*) directions, rules, guidebook, manual, handbook, guidelines, advice, legend, key.

instructive *adj* informative, educational, enlightening, illuminating, helpful, useful, edifying, uplifting, didactic, academic. OPPOSITE: uninformative.

instructor *noun* teacher, lecturer, tutor, pedagogue, schoolteacher, schoolmaster, schoolmistress, coach, trainer, adviser, mentor, guide, guru, demonstrator. OPPOSITE: pupil.

instrument *noun* **1** (*scientific instruments*) implement, tool, utensil, device, contraption (*inf*), contrivance, gadget, gizmo (*inf*), appliance, mechanism. **2** (*navigational instruments*) indicator, measure, gauge, meter, rule. **3** (*she became the instrument of peace*) agent, agency, vehicle, medium, channel, factor, way, means. **4** (*he was the instrument of the Prime Minister*) pawn, puppet, creature, minion, tool, dupe, stooge (*inf*), flunky.

instrumental *adj* helpful, serviceable, useful, contributory, conducive, important, significant, influential, active, involved. OPPOSITE: obstructive.

insubordinate *adj* recalcitrant, refractory, disobedient, contumacious, defiant, rebellious, mutinous, seditious, rude, insurgent, intractable, ungovernable, unruly, undisciplined, disorderly, riotous, turbulent. OPPOSITE: docile.

insubordination *noun* recalcitrance, disobedience, defiance, rebellion, mutiny, sedition, revolt, insurrection, disorder, riot, unruliness, ungovernability, indiscipline. OPPOSITE: compliance.

insubstantial *adj* **1** (*insubstantial evidence*) feeble, frail, weak, flimsy, tenuous, poor, insignificant, slight, inconsequential, thin. **2** (*insubstantial ghosts*) unreal, illusory, false, hallucinatory, fanciful, imaginary, immaterial, ephemeral, ghostlike, spectral.

insufferable *adj* unbearable, intolerable, unendurable, insupportable, too much, too much to bear, impossible, outrageous, shocking, detestable, loathsome, dreadful. OPPOSITE: tolerable.

insufficient *adj* inadequate, deficient, lacking, not enough, meagre, wanting, short, scanty, scarce, in short supply, at a premium, incapable, incompetent. OPPOSITE: sufficient.

insular *adj* **1** (*an insular outlook*) narrow-minded, narrow, illiberal, biased, bigoted, petty, parochial, provincial, inward-looking, blinkered, limited, restricted, parish-pump (*inf*), circumscribed. **2** (*to lead an insular life*) isolated, detached, separate, segregated, insulated, remote, aloof.

insulate *verb* **1** (*insulate children from the harshness of war*) isolate, separate, detach, cut off, sever, part, exclude, shield, cocoon, protect, shelter. **2** (*insulate the attic*) protect, shield, heatproof, soundproof, cover, wrap, envelop, pad, cushion.

insult *verb* abuse, affront, offend, hurt the feelings of, outrage, hurt, injure, wound, snub, slight, slander, slag off (*sl*), call names, mock, mortify, humiliate, disparage. OPPOSITE: flatter.
➤ *noun* abuse, affront, offence, outrage, rudeness, disrespect, insolence, snub, put-down (*inf*), gibe, barb, dig (*inf*), slight, slur, slander, aspersion, contumely, contempt, scorn, humiliation, indignity. OPPOSITE: compliment.

insulting *adj* abusive, affronting, offensive, rude, injurious, wounding, slighting, snubbing, slandering, mocking, mortifying, humiliating, disparaging. OPPOSITE: complimentary.

insuperable *adj* insurmountable, impassable, unconquerable, invincible, overpowering, overwhelming, formidable.

insupportable *adj* intolerable, unendurable, unbearable, insufferable, more than flesh and blood can bear, hateful, loathsome, detestable, unacceptable, indefensible, unjustifiable, untenable. OPPOSITE: tolerable.

insurance *noun* **1** (*car insurance*) assurance, protection, provision, cover, security, indemnity, guarantee, warranty, policy, premium. **2** (*use a padlock as extra insurance against theft*) safeguard, precaution, protection, prevention, provision.

insure *verb* protect, cover, indemnify, underwrite, guarantee, warrant, assure, safeguard. OPPOSITE: imperil.

insurer *noun* underwriter, protector, indemnifier, assurer, guarantor, warrantor.

insurgent *noun* rebel, revolutionary, insurrectionist, seditionist, rioter, mutineer, partisan, malcontent.
➤ *adj* rebellious, revolutionary, revolting, insurrectionary, riotous, mutinous, lawless, seditious, insubordinate, disobedient. OPPOSITE: obedient.

insurmountable *adj* insuperable, impassable, unconquerable, unassailable, invincible, overpowering, impossible, overwhelming, hopeless.

insurrection *noun* rebellion, revolt, uprising, rising, revolution, coup, coup d'état, putsch, mutiny, sedition, insurgency, insubordination, riot. OPPOSITE: subjugation.

insusceptible *adj* insensible, insensitive, indifferent, unmoved, unresponsive, immovable, proof against, immune, unimpressible. OPPOSITE: susceptible.

intact *adj* whole, entire, complete, integral, perfect, flawless, unbroken, sound, in one piece, unhurt, uninjured, unharmed, undamaged, unimpaired, unscathed, untouched, inviolate, unsullied. OPPOSITE: broken.

intangible *adj* impalpable, insubstantial, airy, vague, indefinite, shadowy, spectral, evanescent, incorporeal, unreal, imperceptible. OPPOSITE: tangible.

integral *adj* **1** (*to form an integral part of the team*) intrinsic, inherent, essential, requisite, indispensable, basic, fundamental, elemental, component, constituent. OPPOSITE: nonessential. **2** (*an integral collection of cricket books*) intact, integrated, whole, entire, complete, undivided, total. OPPOSITE: partial.

integrate *verb* incorporate, combine, consolidate, amalgamate, mix, intermix, mingle, blend, merge, fuse, knit, coalesce, unite, join, desegregate. OPPOSITE: segregate.

integrated *adj* incorporated, combined, consolidated, amalgamated, mixed, assimilated, mingled, blended, merged, harmonized, cohesive, fused, knitted, coalesced, joined.

integration *noun* unification, merger, incorporation, assimilation, amalgamation, consolidation, mix, fusion, harmony.

integrity *noun* **1** (*they think I lack integrity*) honesty, truthfulness, uprightness, rectitude, probity, sincerity, honour, decency, principle, morality, virtue, goodness, purity. OPPOSITE: dishonesty. **2** (*endanger the integrity of the kingdom*) unity, wholeness, completeness, entirety, totality, soundness, cohesion. OPPOSITE: incompleteness.

intellect *noun* **1** (*people of great intellect*) mind, intelligence, genius, brains, brain, brainpower, sense, reason, thought, understanding, comprehension, judgment. **2** (*one of the world's great intellects*) intellectual, thinker, mind (*inf*), brain (*inf*), egghead (*inf*), academic, boffin (*inf*), genius, mastermind.

intellectual *adj* **1** (*an intellectual student*) learned, erudite, academic, scholarly, donnish, highbrow, intelligent, bookish, studious, well-read, well-educated. **2** (*intellectual pursuits*) mental, cerebral, academic, logical, rational.
➤ *noun* scholar, academic, pedant, thinker, genius, mastermind, egghead (*inf*), bookworm, walking encyclopedia (*inf*). OPPOSITE: dunce.

intelligence *noun* **1** (*people of outstanding intelligence*) intellect, mind, brains, brainpower, grey matter (*inf*), aptitude, cleverness, understanding, comprehension, perception, acumen, discernment, quickness, alertness, brightness, sharpness, reason, sense, nous (*inf*). OPPOSITE: stupidity. **2** (*gather intelligence*) information, knowledge, gen (*inf*), facts, data, news, word, report, lowdown (*inf*), notification, tip-off (*inf*), warning, advice, dope (*inf*). **3** (*his work in intelligence*) espionage, surveillance, spying, observation, enemy investigation.

intelligent *adj* clever, brainy (*inf*), smart, using your loaf (*inf*), bright, knowing a thing or two (*inf*), quick, sharp, alert, astute, all there (*inf*), perceptive, discerning, perspicacious, knowledgeable, wise, sagacious, well-informed, educated, sensible, rational. OPPOSITE: stupid.

intelligentsia *noun* academics, eggheads (*inf*), literati, intellectuals, brains (*inf*), cognoscenti, illuminati.

intelligible *adj* comprehensible, understandable, clear, plain, distinct, explicit, legible, decipherable. OPPOSITE: unintelligible.

intemperate *adj* **1** (*intemperate language*) excessive, immoderate, inordinate, extreme, uncontrolled, unrestrained, incontinent, unbridled, uncurbed, extravagant, self-indulgent, profligate, wild, wanton. OPPOSITE: moderate. **2** (*the intemperate men left the pub*) drunken, intoxicated, boozy (*inf*), inebriated, plastered (*inf*), bibulous, crapulent, alcoholic. OPPOSITE: temperate.

intend *verb* **1** (*I intend to visit them*) mean, propose, have in mind, contemplate, plan, design, purpose, aim, expect, resolve. **2** (*stories intended for children*) mean, earmark, aim, design, destine, plan.

intended *adj* designated, planned, destined, future, designate, prospective, betrothed.
➤ *noun* betrothed, fiancé, fiancée, husband-to-be, wife-to-be.

intense *adj* **1** (*intense interest*) enthusiastic, eager, keen, ardent, burning, consuming, fervent, zealous, fanatical. OPPOSITE: apathetic. **2** (*intense cold*) acute, severe, extreme, concentrated, harsh, deep, profound, violent, fierce, intensive, consuming, great, strong, powerful, forceful, vigorous, energetic. OPPOSITE: mild. **3** (*he was an intense person*) earnest, serious, heavy, impassioned, emotional, tense, nervous. OPPOSITE: easygoing.

intensify *verb* heighten, enhance, deepen, strengthen, reinforce, sharpen, concentrate, magnify, increase, boost, step up, escalate, raise. OPPOSITE: moderate.

intensity *noun* **1** (*the intensity of his interest*) enthusiasm, eagerness, keenness, ardour, fervour, zeal, vehemence, fanaticism. **2** (*the intensity of the light*) fierceness, acuteness, greatness, extremity, harshness, concentration, depth, strength, power, potency, force, vigour, energy. OPPOSITE: mildness. **3** (*her intensity worried her parents*) seriousness, heaviness, emotion, tenseness, fraughtness, nervousness.

intensive *adj* thorough, concentrated, exhaustive, in-depth, comprehensive, detailed, all-out, intense. OPPOSITE: superficial.

intent *adj* steadfast, concentrated, focused, intense, eager, earnest, absorbed, engrossed, rapt, alert, attentive, preoccupied, occupied, wrapped up. OPPOSITE: indifferent.
➤ *noun* intention, aim, goal, object, point, end, purpose, design, plan.
intent on set on, determined to, resolute, bent on, hell-bent on (*inf*), eager to, committed to, keen on.
to all intents and purposes nearly, almost, virtually, practically, as good as, more or less, pretty much.

intention *noun* aim, goal, object, objective, target, end, intent, plan, design, purpose, meaning, ambition, aspiration.

intentional *adj* intended, premeditated, designed, planned, deliberate, meant, calculated, wilful, voluntary, conscious, studied, purposeful. OPPOSITE: accidental.

intentionally *adv* deliberately, by design, on purpose, wilfully, meaningly. OPPOSITE: accidentally.

intently *adv* attentively, keenly, closely, carefully, watchfully, staringly, fixedly.

inter *verb* bury, lay to rest, consign to the grave, inhume, entomb, sepulchre. OPPOSITE: exhume.

intercede *verb* mediate, arbitrate, intervene, interpose, step in, plead, entreat, advocate.

intercept *verb* interrupt, stop, check, arrest, impede, obstruct, thwart, delay, block, deflect, head off, cut off, catch, seize, commandeer.

intercession *noun* mediation, arbitration, intervention, advocacy, solicitation, plea, prayer, entreaty, petition, supplication.

interchange *verb* exchange, alternate, swap, trade, barter, replace, switch, substitute, change places, reciprocate.
➤ *noun* **1** (*the interchange of thoughts*) exchange, alternation, swap, trade, reciprocation, give and take, crossfire. **2** (*a motorway interchange*) junction, intersection, crossroads.

interchangeable *adj* exchangeable, transposable, equivalent, reciprocal, corresponding, similar, synonymous.

intercourse *noun* **1** (*social intercourse*) communication, dealings, commerce, trade, traffic, communion, association, liaison, contact correspondence. **2** (*sexual intercourse*) sex, it (*inf*), copulation, coitus, carnal knowledge, intimacy, lovemaking, making love, sleeping with someone (*inf*), nookie (*inf*), screw (*sl*), shag (*sl*), lay (*sl*), bonk (*sl*), bang (*sl*), fuck (*sl*).

interdict *verb* prohibit, embargo, ban, forbid, disallow, veto, rule out, bar, proscribe, outlaw. OPPOSITE: allow.
➤ *noun* interdiction, prohibition, embargo, ban, injunction, veto, bar, taboo, proscription. OPPOSITE: permission.

interest *noun* **1** (*the news was of interest*) concern, importance, consequence, moment, significance, consideration, magnitude, relevance, weight, note, urgency, gravity. OPPOSITE: indifference. **2** (*try to discourage her interest in boys*) curiosity, inquisitiveness, attention, concern, care, regard, notice, heed, appeal, fascination, involvement. OPPOSITE: boredom. **3** (*he had a wide range of interests*) hobby, pastime, diversion, activity, pursuit, amusement, recreation. **4** (*it would be in his best interests*) benefit, advantage, good, profit, gain. **5** (*business interests*) share, stake, stock, equity, investment, portion, part, right, claim, involvement, business, affair, concern, matter. **6** (*he should declare his interest in the matter*) involvement, favouritism, partiality, bias, prejudice, one-sidedness. **7** (*earn interest on savings*) premium, bonus, dividend, percentage, profit, gain, return, revenue. OPPOSITE: principal.
➤ *verb* engage, absorb, captivate, rivet, grip, fascinate, intrigue, attract, attract attention, amuse, move, excite, arouse, affect, concern, touch, involve. OPPOSITE: bore.
in the interests of for the sake of, in the furtherance of, for the sake of, for the benefit of.

interested *adj* **1** (*not interested in music*) curious, inquisitive, intrigued, attracted, drawn, attentive, held, engaged, absorbed, fascinated. OPPOSITE: uninterested. **2** (*all interested parties were contacted*) concerned, involved, affected, implicated. **3** (*no interested person can decide the outcome*) prejudiced, biased, partial, one-sided, partisan, involved. OPPOSITE: disinterested.

interesting *adj* intriguing, curious, engaging, absorbing, fascinating, amusing, entertaining, stimulating, thought-provoking, exciting, compelling, gripping, riveting, appealing, attractive, pleasing. OPPOSITE: boring.

interfere *verb* **1** (*interfere in matters that do not concern you*) interpose, intervene, meddle, stick one's oar in (*inf*), tamper, intrude, butt in, stick one's nose in (*inf*), pry. **2** (*interfere with the course of justice*) hinder, impede, hamper, block, obstruct, get in the way of (*inf*), inhibit, restrain, cramp, thwart, clash, conflict, oppose. **3** (*interfered with small children*) molest, assault, attack, abuse, sexually assault, rape.

interference *noun* **1** (*interference in other people's problems*) intervention, meddling, intrusion, prying, sticking one's oar in (*inf*). **2** (*industry should be free from government interference*) hindrance, impediment, handicap, hampering, obstruction, inhibition, conflict.

interim *noun* interval, meantime, meanwhile, interregnum.
➤ *adj* temporary, provisional, improvised, makeshift, stopgap, caretaker, acting.

interior *adj* **1** (*the interior walls were blue*) internal, inner, inside, inward. OPPOSITE: exterior. **2** (*interior affairs of state*) inland, central, upcountry, home, domestic, local, civil. **3** (*interior thoughts*) inner, mental, intimate, personal, secret, emotional, spiritual, involuntary, spontaneous, intuitive, instinctive.
➤ *noun* inside, contents, heart, core, centre. OPPOSITE: surface.

interject *verb* throw in, interpose, interpolate, intercalate, insert, put in, introduce.

interjection *noun* exclamation, ejaculation, cry, remark, interruption, interpolation, intercalation.

interlace *verb* interweave, twine, intertwine, plait, braid, interlock, twist, cross, reticulate. OPPOSITE: unravel.

interlock *verb* join, lock, interconnect, link, interlink, intertwine, interlace.

interlocution *noun* conversation, dialogue, colloquy, discussion, discourse, confabulation.

interloper *noun* intruder, trespasser, gate-crasher, unwanted visitor, encroacher, invader.

interlude *noun* interval, intermission, recess, break, pause, letup (*inf*), respite, breather (*inf*), breathing space, halt, hiatus, stoppage, delay.

intermediary *noun* negotiator, arbitrator, mediator, go-between, middleman, contact, third party, liaison, broker, agent.

intermediate *adj* intervening, transitional, intermediary, mean, middle, halfway, midway, in-between. OPPOSITE: extreme.

interment *noun* burial, burying, inhumation, sepulture, entombment, funeral, exequies, obsequy. OPPOSITE: exhumation.

interminable *adj* endless, seemingly endless, unending, never-ending, incessant, ceaseless, perpetual, eternal, everlasting, long, protracted, long-winded, wordy, monotonous, boring. OPPOSITE: limited.

intermingle *verb* intermix, mingle, mix, commingle,

commix, blend, merge, mix up, fuse, combine, amalgamate. OPPOSITE: separate.

intermission noun interlude, interval, entr'acte, break, pause, breathing-space, breather (inf), stop, let-up (inf), rest, respite, lull, recess, remission, suspension, interruption. OPPOSITE: continuance.

intermittent adj spasmodic, irregular, fitful, erratic, sporadic, periodic, cyclic, recurrent, occasional, broken, discontinuous, off and on, interrupted. OPPOSITE: continuous.

intern verb confine, hold in custody, jail, imprison, detain, hold. OPPOSITE: release.

internal adj 1 (internal doors) inner, interior, inside, inward. OPPOSITE: external. 2 (internal business affairs) domestic, home, civil, in-house, local. 3 (internal feelings in the mind) private, personal, intimate, spiritual, emotional, mental, psychological.

international adj global, worldwide, intercontinental, universal, cosmopolitan. OPPOSITE: national.

internecine adj 1 (internecine warfare) destructive, ruinous, violent, deadly, exterminating, mortal, bloody, sanguinary. 2 (internecine feuds in the ruling party) internal, civil, domestic.

interpolate verb insert, introduce, put in, interpose, interject, intercalate, add. OPPOSITE: delete.

interpolation noun insert, insertion, intercalation, injection, introduction, addition.

interpose verb 1 (when he paused, she interposed a question) insert, introduce, add, butt in, interpolate, intercalate, interject, intervene, muscle in (inf), intercede, come between, mediate, interfere, meddle, poke one's nose in (inf). 2 (interpose a barrier between the two rival gangs) place between, put between.

interpret verb 1 (interpret the meaning of dreams) explain, expound, elucidate, clarify, make clear, define, spell out, decode, decipher, read between the lines (inf), unravel, solve, render, translate, transcribe, paraphrase. OPPOSITE: mystify. 2 (interpret her actions as dissent) construe, take to mean, take, understand, read. 3 (actors interpreting the play) depict, portray, perform, enact.

interpretation noun 1 (interpretation of dreams) decoding, deciphering, translation, transcription, version, explanation, expounding, elucidation, clarification, exegesis. 2 (interpretation of her actions as consent) construing, understanding, meaning, reading. 3 (interpretation of the results) analysis, diagnosis, reading. 4 (the actors' interpretation of the play) depiction, rendition, portrayal, performance, enactment.

interpreter noun translator, linguist, annotator, elucidator, commentator.

interrogate verb question, catechize, quiz, grill (inf), give a roasting (inf), pump, cross-examine, give the third degree (inf), examine, debrief, ask, enquire.

interrogation noun questioning, catechization, quizzing, grilling (inf), roasting (inf), pumping, cross-examination, third degree (inf), going-over (inf), examination, inquisition, debrief.

interrogative adj questioning, catechistic, quizzical, grilling (inf), interrogatory, probing, inquisitive, curious.

interrupt verb 1 (interrupt someone while they are talking) intrude, break in, butt in, interpose, chip in (inf), interfere, disturb, heckle, obstruct. 2 (interrupt a process) discontinue, suspend, delay, postpone, stop, break off, halt, cease, cancel, end, sever, cut. OPPOSITE: continue. 3 (interrupt a view) hinder, obstruct, cut off, block, impede, disturb, interfere with.

interruption noun 1 (sleep without interruption) disturbance, disruption, interference, suspension, delay, intrusion, barging-in, cessation, discontinuance. 2 (interruptions were not welcome) interjection, question, remark, obstruction, obstacle, hitch. 3 (a short interruption in the conversation whilst coffee was served) break, pause, breather (inf), gap, interval, halt, stop, hiatus.

intersect verb divide, cut, cross, meet, crisscross.

intersection noun interchange, crossroads, junction, meeting, crossing.

intersperse verb scatter, sprinkle, pepper, dot, distribute, disperse, spread, interlard, intermix, diversify.

interstice noun gap, opening, chink, cranny, crevice, cleft, fissure, crack, space, interval.

intertwine verb twine, entwine, twist, intertwist, interweave, weave, interlace, interwind, reticulate, blend, mix. OPPOSITE: unravel.

interval noun 1 (have drinks in the interval) interlude, intermission, halftime, break, pause, breathing-space (inf), rest, hiatus, gap, lull, interim, meantime, period. 2 (the fence posts were placed at regular intervals) space, gap, interstice, space, interspace, opening, distance, time, period, spell, season.

intervene verb 1 (intervene in the quarrel) intercede, interpose, step in, involve oneself in (inf), mediate, negotiate, arbitrate, intrude, interfere. 2 (in the time that had intervened) happen, occur, take place, befall, elapse, pass, ensue.

intervention noun involvement, intrusion, interference, intercession, interruption, mediation, negotiation, arbitration, stepping-in.

interview noun meeting, dialogue, talk, discussion, conference, consultation, audience, exchange, assessment, appraisal, oral examination, viva.
≫ verb examine, question, interrogate, talk to, sound out, evaluate, vet.

interviewer noun evaluator, examiner, interrogator, inquisitor, questioner, reporter, correspondent, investigator.

interweave verb 1 (interweave different threads) inweave, interlace, intertwine, entwine, braid, plait. OPPOSITE: unravel. 2 (their histories were interwoven) intermingle, blend, mix, interlink, fuse, knit, connect. OPPOSITE: unravel.

intestinal adj abdominal, internal, visceral, enteric, stomachic, gastric, duodenal.

intestines pl noun bowels, guts, entrails, offal, viscera, innards (inf), insides (inf).

intimacy noun 1 (an unexpected lack of intimacy in their family life) close relationship, closeness, friendship, familiarity, confidentiality, privacy, confidence, amity, affection, love, warmth, understanding. 2 (intimacy took place on several occasions) sexual intercourse, sex, intimate relations, lovemaking, coitus, copulation, carnal knowledge.

intimate[1] *adj* **1** (*an intimate friendship*) close, cherished, dear, nearest and dearest, bosom, tight (*inf*), familiar, matey (*inf*). **2** (*an intimate occasion*) warm, snug, cosy, comfy (*inf*), friendly, affectionate. **3** (*spare us the intimate details*) confidential, personal, private, secret, privy. **4** (*intimate knowledge of philosophy*) deep, profound, thorough, exhaustive, detailed, personal, firsthand, direct. OPPOSITE: superficial.
   ≫ *noun* friend, confidant, confidante, familiar, crony, bosom friend, pal (*inf*), chum (*inf*), mucker (*inf*), buddy (*inf*).

intimate[2] *verb* (*he intimated that she already knew*) suggest, imply, tip someone the wink (*inf*), insinuate, hint, allude, indicate, signal, communicate, make known, declare, announce. OPPOSITE: conceal.

intimation *noun* suggestion, implication, insinuation, innuendo, hint, allusion, inkling, indication, signal, communication, notice, statement, reminder, warning.

intimidate *verb* frighten, scare, alarm, put the frighteners on (*inf*), appal, daunt, cow, overawe, lean on (*inf*), dismay, dishearten, dispirit, discourage, deter, bully, browbeat, compel, pressurize, coerce, warn off, threaten, get at (*inf*), blackmail, menace, terrorize. OPPOSITE: encourage.

intimidation *noun* frightening, threatening, tyrannization, terrorization, domineering, coercion, arm-twisting (*inf*), bullying, browbeating.

intolerable *adj* unbearable, insufferable, more than one can bear, unendurable, dreadful (*inf*), too much, the limit (*inf*), insupportable, impossible, the last straw (*inf*), the straw that broke the camel's back (*inf*), the end (*inf*). OPPOSITE: bearable.

intolerance *noun* **1** (*they showed intolerance to the newcomers*) impatience, prejudice, bias, discrimination, illiberalism, narrow-mindedness, small-mindedness, parochialism, bigotry, one-sidedness. **2** (*intolerance to aspirin*) allergy, sensitivity, hypersensitivity.

intolerant *adj* narrow-minded, illiberal, bigoted, biased, self-opinionated, small-minded, insular, prejudiced, racist, ageist, sexist, chauvinistic, dogmatic, fanatical, uncharitable. OPPOSITE: tolerant.

intonation *noun* modulation, tone, pitch, timbre, accentuation, cadence, inflection, lilt.

intone *verb* chant, intonate, recite, speak, enunciate, articulate, utter, voice, sing, croon.

intoxicate *noun* **1** (*the alcohol intoxicated them*) inebriate, make drunk, addle, fuddle, stupefy. **2** (*the news intoxicated them*) exhilarate, elate, excite, stimulate, invigorate.

intoxicated *adj* **1** (*intoxicated after drinking the cocktails*) inebriated, drunk, drunken, drunk as a lord (*inf*), under the influence, tipsy, merry, legless (*inf*), three sheets to the wind (*inf*), blotto (*inf*), sizzled (*inf*), stoned (*inf*), sloshed (*inf*), smashed (*sl*), sozzled (*inf*), tiddly (*inf*), tight (*inf*), plastered (*inf*), squiffy (*inf*), bevvied (*inf*), tanked up (*inf*), pissed (*sl*). OPPOSITE: sober. **2** (*intoxicated by the atmosphere*) excited, stimulated, exhilarated, moved, thrilled, carried away (*inf*), bowled over (*inf*), worked up.

intoxicating *adj* **1** (*the alcoholic punch was intoxicating*) inebriant, strong, alcoholic, spirituous. **2** (*the sunny weather was intoxicating*) exciting, elating, stimulating, thrilling, exhilarating, rousing, inspiring, moving, heady.

intoxication *noun* **1** (*his headache was the effect of intoxication*) drunkenness, inebriation, inebriety, insobriety, crapulence, alcoholism, dipsomania, tipsiness (*inf*). OPPOSITE: sobriety. **2** (*intoxication at the happy news*) euphoria, rapture, exhilaration, elation, pleasure, enthusiasm, excitement, delirium.

intractable *adj* stubborn, obstinate, unbending, obdurate, headstrong, wilful, undisciplined, intransigent, perverse, contrary, indocile, refractory, contumacious, insubordinate, unmanageable, ungovernable, unruly, wayward, wild, rowdy, awkward, difficult. OPPOSITE: amenable.

intransigent *adj* uncompromising, unbending, unyielding, intractable, unpersuadable, stubborn, obstinate, determined, obdurate, tough, rigid, immovable, implacable, hardline, determined. OPPOSITE: amenable.

intrepid *adj* fearless, dauntless, unafraid, gritty (*inf*), daring, brave, courageous, spunky (*inf*), valiant, audacious, valorous, bold, heroic, lionhearted, stouthearted, doughty, stalwart, indomitable, plucky, spirited, gutsy. OPPOSITE: cowardly.

intricate *adj* **1** (*intricate designs*) complex, ornate, fancy, labyrinthine, entangled, knotty, convoluted, circuitous. OPPOSITE: simple. **2** (*intricate issues*) involved, complicated, complex, obscure, enigmatic, mystifying, difficult, knotty, puzzling, thorny, perplexing, tortuous. OPPOSITE: simple.

intrigue *verb* **1** (*the plot intrigued her*) attract, interest, fascinate, captivate, rivet, charm, tantalize, arouse, stir, puzzle, baffle. OPPOSITE: bore. **2** (*intriguing to usurp the leader*) conspire, plot, scheme, connive, machinate, manoeuvre.
   ≫ *noun* **1** (*their intrigue was discovered*) conspiracy, plot, scheme, machination, cabal, ruse, dodge (*inf*), wile, stratagem, artifice, trickery, sharp practice (*inf*), double-dealing. **2** (*the private detective found evidence of the lovers' intrigue*) affair, liaison, amour, romance, intimacy.

intriguer *noun* collaborator, conniver, conspirator, plotter, schemer, wheeler-dealer (*inf*).

intriguing *adj* fascinating, captivating, absorbing, riveting, charming, beguiling, attractive, interesting, diverting, tantalizing. OPPOSITE: dull.

intrinsic *adj* inherent, essential, central, basic, fundamental, built-in, inborn, natural, native, indigenous, real, true, genuine. OPPOSITE: extrinsic.

introduce *verb* **1** (*they were introduced at the party*) present, acquaint, make known, familiarize, present formally, announce. **2** (*introduce a new assessment*) institute, begin, start, commence, initiate, inaugurate, launch, establish, found, originate, bring in, announce, herald, usher in, pioneer. OPPOSITE: end. **3** (*she introduced the lecture with a short synopsis*) preface, precede, lead into, start off, start, begin, commence. OPPOSITE: finish. **4** (*introduce a scheme*) propose, put forward, advance, set forth, submit, offer, moot, suggest, broach, bring up.

OPPOSITE: withdraw. **5** (*introduce a feeling of happiness*) insert, inject, interpose, interpolate, interject, instil, infuse, bring, add. OPPOSITE: remove.

introduction *noun* **1** (*she completed the formal introductions*) presentation, announcement, acquaintance, familiarization. **2** (*introduction of new working practices*) institution, start, beginning, commencement, initiation, inauguration, launch, establishment, development, debut. **3** (*the author's background was mentioned in the introduction*) preface, proem, foreword, intro (*inf*), preamble, prologue, preliminary, prelude, overture. OPPOSITE: epilogue. **4** (*an introduction to using computers*) fundamentals, basics, rudiments, first principles, essentials. **5** (*the introduction of an air of joyfulness*) insertion, injection, interposition, infusion, addition.

introductory *adj* preliminary, prefatory, preparatory, precursory, lead-in, opening, initial, starting, inaugural, commencing, early, elemental, rudimentary, basic, fundamental.

introspective *adj* inward-looking, self-analysing, introverted, withdrawn, reserved, reflective, meditative, contemplative, brooding, pensive, preoccupied.

introverted *adj* inward-looking, introspective, self-centred, inner-directed, self-examining, self-absorbed, withdrawn, reserved, reflective, meditative, contemplative, brooding, pensive, preoccupied. OPPOSITE: extroverted.

intrude *verb* obtrude, push in, butt in, break in, interrupt, chip in (*inf*), interpose, interfere, meddle, violate, gate-crash (*inf*), trespass, encroach, infringe. OPPOSITE: withdraw.

intruder *noun* trespasser, invader, raider, burglar, robber, thief, prowler, snooper (*inf*), interloper, unwelcome guest, gate-crasher (*inf*), infiltrator.

intrusion *noun* encroachment, infringement, invasion, trespass, violation, interruption, gate-crashing (*inf*), obtrusion, meddling, interference, interposition.

intrusive *adj* intruding, trespassing, invasive, unwelcome, pushy (*inf*), interrupting, interfering, meddlesome, nosy (*inf*), snooping (*inf*), inquisitive, forward, annoying, irritating, troublesome, disturbing. OPPOSITE: welcome.

intuition *noun* insight, instinct, clairvoyance, divination, sixth sense, presentiment, hunch, perception, discernment, feeling, inkling, gut feeling (*inf*). OPPOSITE: reason.

intuitive *adj* instinctive, intuitional, spontaneous, untaught, unlearned, innate, inborn, automatic, involuntary. OPPOSITE: learned.

intumescence *noun* swelling, tumefaction, turgescence, tumidity, turgidity, bloating, dilation, distension.

inundate *verb* flood, deluge, swamp, saturate, submerge, drown, engulf, bog down, overwhelm, overflow. OPPOSITE: drain.

inundation *noun* deluge, flood, torrent, tidal wave, overflow, spate, excess, surplus, tons (*inf*), heaps (*inf*).

inure *verb* harden, toughen, indurate, temper, season, accustom, make used to, habituate, familiarize, acclimatize.

invade *verb* **1** (*invade an island*) enter, penetrate, attack, assault, storm, raid, maraud, plunder, occupy, seize, march into, overrun, infest, pervade. OPPOSITE: evacuate. **2** (*invade his privacy*) intrude, encroach, infringe, trespass, violate, interrupt.

invader *noun* attacker, assailant, aggressor, raider, marauder, plunderer, intruder, trespasser, encroacher.

invalid[1] *noun* (*a bedridden invalid*) patient, convalescent, sufferer, valetudinarian.
➤ *adj* ill, unwell, sick, ailing, weak, feeble, frail, debilitated, infirm, bedridden, valetudinarian, disabled, handicapped. OPPOSITE: healthy.

invalid[2] *adj* **1** (*invalid reasons*) unsound, fallacious, untrue, false, incorrect, wrong, illogical, unscientific, irrational, baseless, groundless, unfounded, unjustified, erroneous, mistaken. OPPOSITE: valid. **2** (*the law is now invalid*) illegal, null, void, inoperative, null and void, worthless, cancelled, abolished, overturned, quashed, revoked. OPPOSITE: binding.

invalidate *verb* **1** (*invalidate a theory*) refute, rebut, disprove, undermine, discredit, weaken. OPPOSITE: validate. **2** (*invalidate a law*) annul, nullify, void, abrogate, veto, negate, repeal, rescind, quash, cancel. OPPOSITE: validate.

invaluable *adj* priceless, inestimable, precious, worth its weight in gold, valuable, costly, indispensable, useful. OPPOSITE: worthless.

invariable *adj* changeless, unchanging, unchangeable, immutable, unalterable, unvarying, constant, fixed, permanent, set, uniform, regular, consistent, stable, unfailing. OPPOSITE: variable.

invariably *adv* always, without exception, unfailingly, every time, inevitably, habitually, regularly, consistently, repeatedly, perpetually. OPPOSITE: sometimes.

invasion *noun* **1** (*invasion of the island*) attack, assault, raid, foray, irruption, inroad, incursion, aggression, offensive, onslaught, penetration, occupation. OPPOSITE: retreat. **2** (*invasion of their privacy*) interruption, intrusion, encroachment, infringement, trespass, violation, breach, infraction.

invective *noun* vituperation, revilement, censure, condemnation, denunciation, reproach, abuse, obloquy, diatribe, harangue, philippic, tirade, castigation, scolding, rebuke, reprimand, tongue-lashing, contumely, sarcasm. OPPOSITE: eulogy.

inveigh *verb* condemn, censure, blame, criticize, rail, vituperate, revile, denounce, abuse, reproach, scold, berate, lambaste, tongue-lash, expostulate, protest. OPPOSITE: praise.

inveigle *verb* beguile, coax, cajole, persuade, con (*inf*), entrap, bamboozle (*inf*), ensnare, entice, sweet-talk (*inf*), lure, tempt, wheedle, manipulate, manoeuvre.

invent *verb* **1** (*invent a new method*) originate, create, discover, design, think up, conceive, formulate, devise, contrive, coin, improvise, dream up, hit upon. **2** (*invent an alibi*) concoct, fabricate, make up, cook up (*inf*).

invention *noun* **1** (*the invention of the light bulb*) origination, formulation, creation, innovation, discovery, design, contriving, coining. **2** (*my latest invention*) creation, brainchild, design, innovation, development, discovery, machine, device, contrivance, gadget, concoction. **3** (*the tale was obviously an invention*) fabrication, deceit, lie, fib (*inf*), untruth, falsehood, sham, fiction, story, tall story (*inf*), fantasy, figment of one's imagination, romance. OPPOSITE: truth. **4** (*a man with powers of invention*) inventiveness, originality, resourcefulness, creativity, imagination, inspiration, genius, skill, talent, gift.

inventive *adj* creative, imaginative, original, innovative, inspired, artistic, gifted, clever, talented.

inventor *noun* discoverer, creator, designer, originator, innovator, developer, father, mother, architect, producer, engineer, author.

inventory *noun* list, listing, checklist, catalogue, enumeration, register, roll, record, description, account, schedule, tally.

inverse *noun* opposite, contrary, converse, flip side (*inf*), reverse, obverse.
  ➤ *adj* counter, opposite, other, reverse, converse, reversed, transposed, inverted.

inversion *noun* reversal, transposition, opposite, contrary, antithesis, reverse, converse.

invert *verb* reverse, transpose, turn upside down, upturn, overturn, upset, capsize, turn turtle, introvert, turn inside out.

invest *verb* **1** (*invest money in the company*) spend, lay out, put in, advance, fund, sink, subsidize. OPPOSITE: withdraw. **2** (*invest time in the project*) expend, put in, devote, give, contribute, donate, dedicate. **3** (*the authority invested in the governor*) endow, give, grant, bestow, confer, entrust, place. **4** (*invest the new president*) install, induct, instate, inaugurate, swear in, enthrone, ordain **5** (*the rebels invested the castle*) besiege, surround, lay siege to, blockade, encircle, beleaguer.

investigate *verb* explore, suss out (*inf*), examine, probe, sift, scrutinize, study, research, inspect, inquire into, look into, check out (*inf*), see which way the wind blows (*inf*). OPPOSITE: ignore.

investigation *noun* exploration, search, examination, probe, scrutiny, study, survey, review, analysis, inspection, fact-finding mission, inquiry, inquest, inquisition.

investigator *noun* explorer, searcher, examiner, analyst, prober, researcher, scrutineer, inquirer, inspector, detective, private detective, sleuth (*inf*), private eye (*inf*), gumshoe (*inf*).

investiture *noun* installation, admission, induction, instatement, inauguration, investment, enthronement, coronation, ordination.

investment *noun* **1** (*the company is not a secure investment*) risk, venture, speculation. **2** (*the investment amounted to £1,000*) stake, contribution, ante (*inf*).

inveterate *adj* **1** (*an inveterate smoker*) hardened, inured, chronic, habitual, confirmed, addicted, die-hard, dyed-in-the-wool. **2** (*inveterate hatred*) ingrained, deep-seated, deep-rooted, entrenched, incurable, established.

invidious *adj* unpleasant, unpopular, awkward, difficult, impossible, undesirable, hateful, repugnant, objectionable, offensive, slighting, odious, unfair, discriminating, prejudicial, deleterious.

invigorate *verb* enliven, animate, motivate, stimulate, quicken, brace, refresh, energize, fortify, strengthen, give a new lease of life to (*inf*), revitalize, pep up, rejuvenate, inspire, exhilarate. OPPOSITE: enervate.

invincible *adj* unconquerable, indomitable, unbeatable, invulnerable, impenetrable, unassailable, impregnable, insuperable, insurmountable, indestructible, unyielding. OPPOSITE: vulnerable.

inviolable *adj* inalienable, unalterable, untouchable, hallowed, sacrosanct, holy, sacred.

inviolate *adj* intact, whole, undamaged, unimpaired, unharmed, uninjured, unhurt, unsullied, undefiled, unspoiled, pure, virginal, untouched, undisturbed, stainless, unpolluted. OPPOSITE: defiled.

invisible *adj* unseen, hidden, concealed, disguised, out of sight, unobserved, unnoticed, imperceptible, indiscernible, unapparent, inconspicuous. OPPOSITE: visible.

invitation *noun* **1** (*accept the invitation to dinner*) summons, call, invite (*inf*), request, bidding, solicitation, proposition, offer. **2** (*unlocked doors are an open invitation to thieves*) attraction, allurement, lure, enticement, temptation, provocation, come-on (*inf*), encouragement, challenge. OPPOSITE: repulsion.

invite *verb* **1** (*invite in for a coffee*) ask, bid, summon. **2** (*invite applications*) request, ask for, call for, solicit, beg, seek, petition. **3** (*invite questions from the audience*) attract, welcome, encourage, court, tempt, entice, allure, foster, cause, provoke, induce, bring on. OPPOSITE: repel.

inviting *adj* attractive, pleasing, agreeable, welcoming, tempting, alluring, enticing, seductive, appealing, engaging, enchanting, beguiling, fascinating, captivating, winning, irresistible. OPPOSITE: repulsive.

invocation *noun* prayer, supplication, entreaty, solicitation, petition, appeal.

invoice *noun* bill, charges, statement, reckoning, list, schedule, record.

invoke *verb* **1** (*invoke the aid of his god*) call on, appeal to, implore, adjure, entreat, supplicate, beg, beseech, pray. **2** (*invoke a law*) implement, apply, use, put into effect, resort to. **3** (*invoke a spirit*) summon, call forth, conjure up, raise.

involuntary *adj* **1** (*an involuntary movement*) automatic, mechanical, reflex, spontaneous, instinctive, unintentional, unconscious, impulsive, unthinking, blind, uncontrolled. OPPOSITE: voluntary. **2** (*involuntary repatriation*) forced, compelled, coerced, reluctant, unwilling, compulsory, obligatory. OPPOSITE: willing.

involve *verb* **1** (*his job involves ordering supplies*) entail, require, imply, mean, necessitate, presuppose. OPPOSITE: exclude. **2** (*the changes will involve everyone*) include, contain, affect, incorporate, comprise, embrace, cover. OPPOSITE: exclude. **3** (*the joyrider involved his friends in the thefts*) implicate, incriminate, inculpate, connect, associate, embroil, entangle, complicate, confuse, mix up. OPPOSITE: extricate. **4** (*the book really involved her*) absorb, engross, preoccupy, engage, interest, occupy, hold, grip.

involved *adj* **1** (*an involved issue*) complex, complicated, difficult, confused, intricate, elaborate, tangled, jumbled, knotty. **2** (*involved in the situation*) associated, concerned, in on (*inf*), participating, mixed up, taking part, implicated.

involvement *noun* connection, association, participation, concern, interest, responsibility, commitment, implication, share, contribution.

invulnerable *adj* **1** (*invulnerable defences*) safe, secure, unassailable, invincible, impregnable, impenetrable, inviolable, indestructible. OPPOSITE: vulnerable. **2** (*her self-belief seemed to make her invulnerable*) unhurtable, unwoundable, insusceptible, indestructible, insensitive.

inward *adj* inner, internal, interior, inside, innermost, private, personal, intimate, confidential, secret, mental, spiritual. OPPOSITE: outward.

inwardly *adv* in one's heart, inside, deep down, within, privately, secretly, to oneself.

iota *noun* atom, jot, little, whit, bit, scrap, morsel, mite, grain, trace, glimmer, shadow, touch, hint, tad (*inf*).

irascible *adj* irritable, touchy, testy, hot-tempered, quick-tempered, short-tempered, cross, waspish, prickly (*inf*), edgy, snappish, peppery, cantankerous, crotchety, crabbed, peevish, petulant. OPPOSITE: affable.

irate *adj* angry, furious, incensed, mad (*inf*), worked up, enraged, livid, fuming, ireful, wrathful, indignant, annoyed, irritated, exasperated, riled, piqued. OPPOSITE: calm.

ire *noun* anger, rage, fury, choler, wrath, indignation, exasperation, annoyance, displeasure, irritation. OPPOSITE: composure.

iridescent *adj* shimmering, glittering, sparkling, pearly, nacreous, opalescent, opaline, multicoloured, polychromatic, prismatic, rainbow-like. OPPOSITE: dull.

irk *verb* irritate, annoy, vex, nettle, rile, anger, incense, provoke, rub up the wrong way (*inf*), put out, peeve (*inf*), miff (*inf*), aggravate, get one's goat (*inf*). OPPOSITE: please.

irksome *adj* tiresome, wearisome, annoying, irritating, infuriating, aggravating, vexatious, trying, troublesome, bothersome, disagreeable, tedious, boring, monotonous. OPPOSITE: pleasant.

iron *adj* inflexible, obdurate, unyielding, rigid, determined, adamant, firm, steady, strong, tough. OPPOSITE: flexible.
➤ *verb* press, flatten, smooth, remove the creases.

iron out clear up, resolve, sort out, put right, smooth over, reconcile, eradicate, get rid of, erase, eliminate.

ironic *adj* **1** (*an ironic comment*) ironical, sarcastic, sardonic, satirical, mocking, sneering, derisive, ridiculing, contemptuous. **2** (*ironic that he died on the last day of the war*) paradoxical, incongruous, coincidental.

irons *pl noun* chains, bonds, fetters, manacles, shackles.

irony *noun* **1** (*a hint of irony in his smile*) sarcasm, satire, ridicule, derision, mockery. **2** (*irony in the timing of his death*) paradox, incongruity, contrariness.

irradiate *verb* **1** (*the torch irradiated the path*) brighten, illuminate, illumine, light up, enlighten. OPPOSITE:

darken. **2** (*food is irradiated to prolong its shelf-life*) expose to radiation, treat with radiation, X-ray.

irrational *adj* **1** (*irrational behaviour*) illogical, unreasonable, absurd, preposterous, ridiculous, ludicrous, nonsensical, unwise, injudicious, foolish, crazy, senseless. OPPOSITE: rational. **2** (*an irrational person*) illogical, unthinking, idiotic, stupid, brainless, senseless, muddled, confused, insane, demented, raving. OPPOSITE: rational.

irreclaimable *adj* irrecoverable, irretrievable, lost, irredeemable, irremediable, irreparable, hopeless.

irreconcilable *adj* **1** (*irreconcilable beliefs*) incompatible, opposite, conflicting, at odds, opposed, at variance, incongruous, discordant. OPPOSITE: compatible. **2** (*irreconcilable foes*) unappeaseable, implacable, inexorable, uncompromising, intransigent, hard line, inflexible. OPPOSITE: appeaseable.

irrecoverable *adj* irretrievable, lost, unrecoverable, irreclaimable, unsavable, irredeemable, unsalvageable, irremediable. OPPOSITE: recoverable.

irrefutable *adj* incontrovertible, undeniable, incontestable, indisputable, unquestionable, irrefragable, unassailable, invincible, indubitable, conclusive, sure, certain, definite. OPPOSITE: questionable.

irregular *adj* **1** (*his face had irregular features*) uneven, rough, bumpy, craggy, pitted, lumpy, jagged, ragged, crooked, lopsided, unsymmetrical, asymmetric, unequal. OPPOSITE: smooth. **2** (*her heartbeat was irregular*) uneven, variable, fluctuating, erratic, fitful, spasmodic, sporadic, occasional, haphazard, random, aperiodic. OPPOSITE: regular. **3** (*irregular mealtimes*) erratic, sporadic, intermittent, random, variable, fluctuating, inconstant, unpunctual, occasional. OPPOSITE: regular. **4** (*accepting such payments is highly irregular*) dishonest, fraudulent, deceitful, false, cheating, against the rules, out of order, improper, unprincipled, indecent, unofficial. OPPOSITE: normal. **5** (*she had an irregular lifestyle*) unconventional, unorthodox, unusual, uncommon, peculiar, odd, eccentric, bizarre, strange, extraordinary, abnormal, deviant, lawless, dissolute, intemperate, immoral, licentious, improper. OPPOSITE: conventional. **6** (*he fought with an irregular army*) guerrilla, volunteer, resistance, partisan, mercenary.

irregularity *noun* **1** (*irregularity of her features*) unevenness, roughness, bumpiness, cragginess, jaggedness, raggedness, crookedness, lopsidedness, asymmetry. OPPOSITE: smoothness. **2** (*irregularity in his heartbeat*) unevenness, variability, fluctuation, fitfulness, occasionalness, haphazardness, unsteadiness. OPPOSITE: regularity. **3** (*irregularity of their attendance*) intermittence, randomness, variability, inconstancy, inconsistency, unpunctuality, patchiness. OPPOSITE: regularity. **4** (*irregularity of their actions*) dishonesty, fraudulence, deceit, cheating, abnormality, anomaly. OPPOSITE: normality. **5** (*irregularity of their lifestyle*) unconventionality, unorthodoxy, peculiarity, eccentricity, abnormality, deviation, freak, immorality. OPPOSITE: conventionality.

irrelevant *adj* inapplicable, impertinent, immaterial, inapposite, inappropriate, inapt, beside the point, unimportant, neither here nor there, unrelated, unconnected, foreign, extraneous. OPPOSITE: relevant.

irreligious *adj* **1** (*irreligious people*) godless, pagan, heathen, infidel, unbelieving, agnostic, atheistic. OPPOSITE: religious. **2** (*irreligious comments*) impious, ungodly, heretical, irreverent, blasphemous, sacrilegious, profane. OPPOSITE: reverent.

irremediable *adj* irreparable, remediless, irreversible, irredeemable, irrecoverable, incurable, hopeless, terminal, fatal. OPPOSITE: remediable.

irreparable *adj* irreclaimable, irretrievable, irrecoverable, irreversible, beyond repair, unrepairable, irremediable, incurable. OPPOSITE: reparable.

irreplaceable *adj* unique, matchless, peerless, precious, priceless, invaluable, indispensable, vital, essential. OPPOSITE: replaceable.

irrepressible *adj* uncontrollable, unstoppable, unrestrainable, uncontainable, insuppressible, uninhibited, animated, boisterous, bubbling over, vivacious, ebullient, buoyant. OPPOSITE: repressible.

irreproachable *adj* beyond reproach, irreprehensible, unimpeachable, inculpable, blameless, faultless, impeccable, immaculate, spotless, perfect, pure, innocent, guiltless. OPPOSITE: reproachable.

irresistible *adj* **1** (*irresistible temptation*) overwhelming, overpowering, compelling, powerful, forceful, imperative, indomitable, invincible, irrepressible, unsuppressible, uncontrollable, unavoidable, inescapable, ineluctable, inevitable. OPPOSITE: resistible. **2** (*she was irresistible*) tempting, seductive, alluring, tantalizing, fascinating, enchanting, charming, ravishing. OPPOSITE: repulsive.

irresolute *adj* undecided, unresolved, undetermined, uncertain, dubious, in two minds, ambivalent, indecisive, hesitant, vacillating, sitting on the fence (*inf*), wavering, tentative, faltering, unstable, fickle, inconstant, weak, feeble, halfhearted. OPPOSITE: resolute.

irrespective *adj* **irrespective of** regardless of, despite, in spite of, notwithstanding, apart from, setting aside, ignoring, discounting, independent of.

irresponsible *adj* **1** (*an irresponsible person*) unreliable, undependable, untrustworthy, careless, reckless, rash, flighty, scatterbrained, immature. OPPOSITE: responsible. **2** (*an irresponsible attitude*) thoughtless, unwise, ill-considered, injudicious, careless, devil-may-care, reckless. OPPOSITE: sensible.

irretrievable *adj* irrecoverable, irreclaimable, lost, unrecoverable, unsalvageable, irredeemable, irreparable. OPPOSITE: retrievable.

irreverent *adj* **1** (*an irreverent book about God*) impious, irreligious, godless, heretical, blasphemous, sacrilegious, profane. OPPOSITE: reverent. **2** (*teenagers are often irreverent to their parents*) disrespectful, discourteous, impolite, rude, impudent, impertinent, cheeky (*inf*), insolent. OPPOSITE: respectful.

irreversible *adj* unalterable, unchangeable, irrevocable, permanent, final, incurable, hopeless, irremediable, irreparable, unrectifiable. OPPOSITE: reversible.

irrevocable *adj* irreversible, unalterable, unchangeable, final, settled, immutable, irrecoverable, irretrievable. OPPOSITE: revocable.

irrigate *verb* water, wet, moisten, dampen, spray, soak, flood, wash, bathe. OPPOSITE: drain.

irritable *adj* touchy, shirty (*inf*), testy, irascible, waspish, snappish, peppery, peevish, stroppy (*inf*), petulant, impatient, short, short-tempered, quick-tempered, prickly, cross, ratty (*inf*), crabbed, crusty, crotchety (*inf*), grumpy, cantankerous, ill-humoured, bad-tempered. OPPOSITE: affable.

irritate *verb* **1** (*the loud music irritates the neighbours*) annoy, vex, nettle, needle, rattle, rile, get on one's nerves (*inf*), pique, aggravate, rub up the wrong way (*inf*), get (*inf*), exasperate, anger, enrage, incense, drive one up the wall (*inf*), infuriate, provoke, bother, bug (*inf*), pester, harass. OPPOSITE: please. **2** (*ointment irritating the skin*) inflame, hurt, rub, chafe, aggravate, exacerbate. OPPOSITE: soothe.

irritating *adj* annoying, aggravating, infuriating, bothersome, maddening, tiresome, pesky (*inf*), grating, disturbing, galling, vexing, provoking, trying. OPPOSITE: pleasing.

irritation *noun* **1** (*she showed her irritation*) annoyance, displeasure, irritability, impatience, pique, vexation, ill-temper, exasperation, crossness, anger, wrath, rage, ire. **2** (*the children were an irritation to him*) annoyance, source of annoyance, nuisance, bind (*inf*), bother, disturbance, pain (*inf*), pain in the neck (*inf*), pain in the arse (*sl*), pest, trouble, tease.

irruption *noun* invasion, incursion, inroad, raid, foray, sally. OPPOSITE: retreat.

island *noun* isle, islet, atoll, cay, key, ait, eyot.

isolate *verb* separate, set apart, segregate, sequester, quarantine, keep apart, insulate, cut off, maroon, detach, sever, divorce, disconnect, dissociate, ostracize, exclude, cold-shoulder. OPPOSITE: unite.

isolated *adj* **1** (*an isolated place*) solitary, alone, lonely, out-of-the-way, off-the-beaten-track (*inf*), remote, godforsaken, outlying, detached, separated, apart. **2** (*an isolated case*) unique, exceptional, uncommon, usual, abnormal, freak, untypical, single, solitary. OPPOSITE: common.

isolation *noun* **1** (*the sick child was in isolation*) separation, segregation, quarantine, insulation. **2** (*its geographical isolation meant the village was quiet*) remoteness, solitude, seclusion, exile, loneliness, desolation, detachment, disconnection, dissociation.

issue *noun* **1** (*discuss a topical issue*) topic, subject, point, question, problem, matter, affair, concern. **2** (*the next issue of the magazine is due*) edition, number, impression, version, copy, printing, instalment. **3** (*a new issue of bonds*) issuance, issuing, supply, delivery, distribution, circulation, sending out, dissemination, promulgation. **4** (*died without issue*) offspring, progeny, children, descendants, posterity, heirs. **5** (*the issue of all our activities*) result, decision, consequence, outcome, resolution, upshot, effect, end, conclusion, termination. **6** (*the issue of the brook*) outflow, discharge, effusion, outlet, egress, exit. OPPOSITE: influx.

➤ *verb* **1** (*issue a statement*) deliver, supply, give out, distribute, send out, circulate, disseminate, promulgate, publish, announce, proclaim, broadcast, put out, release. OPPOSITE: withhold. **2** (*her expertise issues from a love of art*) originate, spring, arise, stem, proceed, derive, result. **3** (*smoke issued from the building*) exude, come out, appear, emerge, emit, emanate, flow, pour forth, gush, ooze, seep.

at issue under discussion, being debated, in question, being discussed, to be decided.

take issue disagree, challenge, contest, dispute, argue, protest, fight, object, call into question.

itch *verb* **1** (*her foot itches*) tingle, prickle, tickle, crawl. **2** (*itch to start travelling*) yearn, long, ache, pine, crave, hunger, thirst, hanker, lust.
≫ *noun* **1** (*an itch on her leg*) itchiness, irritation, tingling, tickling, prickling. **2** (*have an itch for travelling*) yearning, longing, ache, craving, lust, hunger, thirst, hankering, yen (*inf*).

itching *adj* **1** (*an itching toe*) itchy, prickly, tingling, irritating. **2** (*they are itching to leave*) longing, hankering, dying, aching, craving, yearning, eager, raring, keen, impatient.

item *noun* **1** (*she bought four items*) article, thing, piece, object, component, ingredient, element. **2** (*an item in the newspaper*) story, bulletin, report, account, feature, article, dispatch, detail. **3** (*they broke up, so they are no longer an item*) couple, partners.

itemize *verb* detail, specify, record, list, document, inventory, register, instance, number.

iterate *verb* repeat, reiterate, dwell on, restate, recapitulate, stress, emphasize.

itinerant *adj* wandering, roving, roaming, strolling, travelling, peripatetic, nomadic, journeying, migratory, unsettled, vagrant.

itinerary *noun* **1** (*their itinerary took them through eight countries*) route, schedule, programme, timetable, plan, tour, circuit, course. **2** (*she wrote an itinerary of her travels*) journal, diary, logbook, log, record, guide, guidebook.

jab *verb* poke, prod, dig, nudge, elbow, stab, pierce, thrust, lunge, push, tap, punch.
➤ *noun* **1** (*a jab with his stick*) poke, prod, dig, nudge, stab, thrust, lunge, tap, punch. **2** (*a flu jab*) injection, shot.

jabber *verb* chatter, prattle, prate, babble, gibber, blather, gab (*inf*), ramble, witter (*inf*), rabbit (*inf*).

jack *verb* **jack up** **1** (*jack up the car*) lift, raise, hoist, elevate. **2** (*jack up prices*) increase, raise, put up, hike up, inflate. OPPOSITE: lower.

jacket *noun* **1** (*wearing a jacket*) coat, blazer, anorak, cardigan. **2** (*remove the protective jacket*) covering, cover, casing, case, wrapping, wrapper, sheath, envelope, shell, skin.

jackpot *noun* prize, winnings, first prize, main prize, bonanza, kitty, pool, pot, bank.

jaded *adj* **1** (*jaded after a day's work*) exhausted, weary, tired, fatigued, worn out, dead beat (*inf*), done in (*inf*), fagged (*inf*), pooped (*inf*), whacked (*inf*), bushed (*inf*), drained, spent. OPPOSITE: refreshed. **2** (*jaded appetites*) cloyed, sated, satiated, dulled, blunted, bored, fed up (*inf*).

jagged *adj* uneven, irregular, rough, ragged, notched, toothed, serrated, indented, ridged, craggy, broken, barbed, spiked. OPPOSITE: smooth.

jail *noun* gaol, prison, lockup, penitentiary, nick (*inf*), jug (*inf*), can (*inf*), clink (*inf*), quod (*inf*), cooler (*inf*), slammer (*inf*), stir (*inf*), inside (*inf*).
➤ *verb* gaol, imprison, lock up, incarcerate, immure, confine, intern, detain, send down, put away. OPPOSITE: release.

jailer *noun* gaoler, warder, warden, guard, screw (*sl*), keeper, captor.

jam¹ *verb* **1** (*jam the clothes into the drawer*) cram, stuff, pack, press, squeeze, squash, wedge, ram, force, push, thrust. **2** (*the roads were jammed*) block, obstruct, clog, congest, crowd. **3** (*the mechanism jammed*) stick, stall, stop.
➤ *noun* **1** (*a traffic jam*) stoppage, holdup, bottleneck, congestion, gridlock. **2** (*the jam at the turnstiles*) press, crush, crowd, mob, throng, multitude, horde, pack. **3** (*I'm in a bit of jam*) predicament, plight, trouble, dilemma, quandary, fix (*inf*), spot (*inf*), pickle (*inf*), hole (*inf*).

jam² *noun* (*strawberry jam*) preserve, conserve, jelly, marmalade.

jangle *verb* **1** (*the bells jangled*) clash, clang, clank, clink, jingle, rattle, clatter, chime. **2** (*jangling my nerves*) upset, disturb, bother, irritate, grate, jar.
➤ *noun* clash, clang, clank, clink, jingle, rattle, clatter, jarring, reverberation, clangour, din, racket, cacophony, dissonance, discord.

janitor *noun* caretaker, doorkeeper, concierge, porter.

jar¹ *noun* (*a jar of pickle*) pot, vessel, container, receptacle, vase, urn, jug, pitcher, flagon, flask.

jar² *verb* **1** (*she jarred his elbow*) jolt, jerk, jog, rattle, vibrate, shake, agitate. **2** (*jarring my nerves*) jangle, grate, rasp, irritate, annoy, bother, upset. **3** (*it jars with the overall design*) clash, conflict, be at variance, be at odds, disagree, quarrel. OPPOSITE: harmonize.

jargon *noun* vocabulary, phraseology, language, lingo (*inf*), usage, idiom, parlance, vernacular, cant, argot, slang, buzz words, journalese, computerspeak, psychobabble, mumbo jumbo, gobbledygook.

jaundiced *adj* cynical, sceptical, pessimistic, misanthropic, bitter, resentful, jealous, envious, bigoted, prejudiced, biased. OPPOSITE: optimistic.

jaunt *noun* excursion, outing, trip, ramble, stroll, airing, drive, ride, spin (*inf*).

jaunty *adj* **1** (*with a jaunty step*) brisk, sprightly, lively, perky, breezy, airy, buoyant, bouncy, blithe, carefree. **2** (*a jaunty outfit*) smart, spruce, trim, stylish, dapper, natty (*inf*). OPPOSITE: dowdy.

jaw *noun* mandible, maxilla, chap, chop.
➤ *verb* talk, chat, gossip, natter (*inf*), hold forth, lecture, drone on, go on (*inf*).

jaws *pl noun* mouth, maw, opening, aperture, orifice, entrance, threshold.

jazz *verb* **jazz up** brighten up, liven up, enliven, smarten up.

jealous *adj* **1** (*jealous of their success*) envious, covetous, grudging, begrudging, resentful, green, green-eyed, green with envy, discontented, dissatisfied. OPPOSITE: contented. **2** (*her jealous husband*) suspicious, distrustful, mistrustful, insecure, possessive. OPPOSITE: trusting. **3** (*we are jealous of our independence*) protective, attentive, watchful, vigilant, mindful, heedful. OPPOSITE: careless.

jealousy *noun* **1** (*couldn't hide their jealousy*) envy, enviousness, green-eyed monster, covetousness, desire, craving, grudge, resentment, bitterness, spite, discontent, dissatisfaction. OPPOSITE: contentment. **2** (*her husband's jealousy*) suspicion, distrust, mistrust, insecurity, possessiveness. OPPOSITE: trust. **3** (*guarding our independence with jealousy*) protectiveness, attentiveness, watchfulness, vigilance, care. OPPOSITE: negligence.

jeer *verb* scoff, mock, deride, scorn, contemn, sneer, taunt, gibe, heckle, barrack, boo, hiss. OPPOSITE: acclaim.
➤ *noun* mockery, derision, ridicule, sneer, taunt, gibe, catcall, boo, hiss. OPPOSITE: acclamation.

jejune *adj* **1** (*a jejune attitude*) naive, unsophisticated, inexperienced, simple, ignorant, uninformed, immature, callow, childish, puerile, juvenile, silly, inane. OPPOSITE: mature. **2** (*jejune writing*) dull, vapid, insipid, dry, arid, barren, tame, uninteresting, boring, trite, banal. OPPOSITE: exciting.

jeopardize *verb* endanger, imperil, risk, venture, gamble, hazard, chance, threaten, menace. OPPOSITE: protect.

jeopardy *noun* danger, peril, risk, hazard, vulnerability, precariousness, insecurity, threat, menace. OPPOSITE: safety.

jerk *verb* **1** (*the train jerked along the track*) jolt, jar, bump, bounce, lurch. **2** (*jerked it out of my hand*) pull, tug, yank, wrench, tweak, pluck. **3** (*jerking muscles*) twitch, convulse, shake, tremble.
➤ *noun* **1** (*stopped with a jerk*) jolt, jar, bump, bounce, lurch. **2** (*a quick jerk on the rope*) pull, tug, yank, tweak. **3** (*don't be a jerk!*) fool, idiot, twit (*inf*), dope (*inf*), wally (*sl*), prat (*sl*), nerd (*sl*).

jerky *adj* spasmodic, convulsive, twitchy, jumpy, shaky, tremulous, uncontrolled, uncoordinated, fitful, irregular, rough, bumpy, jolting, jarring. OPPOSITE: smooth.

jersey *noun* jumper, sweater, pullover, woolly (*inf*).

jest *noun* **1** (*one of his jests*) joke, quip, witticism, crack (*inf*), gag (*inf*), practical joke, prank, jape, lark, leg-pull (*inf*). **2** (*said it in jest*) fun, sport, play, banter, raillery.
➤ *verb* joke, quip, banter, chaff, tease, gibe, jeer, mock, trick, hoax, kid (*inf*), have on (*inf*), pull someone's leg (*inf*).

jester *noun* clown, harlequin, pantaloon, fool, buffoon, zany, joker, prankster, comic, comedian, wag, wit.

jet *noun* gush, stream, rush, flow, spout, spurt, squirt, spray, fountain, spring. OPPOSITE: trickle.
➤ *verb* gush, stream, rush, surge, pour, flow, shoot, spurt, squirt, spray. OPPOSITE: trickle.

jettison *verb* throw overboard, unload, offload, dump, eject, throw out, throw away, discard, get rid of, scrap. OPPOSITE: retain.

jetty *noun* breakwater, groyne, mole, pier, wharf, quay, dock, harbour.

jewel *noun* **1** (*stole her jewels*) gem, gemstone, precious stone, rock (*inf*), sparkler (*inf*), bauble, trinket, ornament. **2** (*the jewel of our collection*) pride, boast, flower, pearl, prize, treasure, pride and joy, showpiece, pièce de résistance.

jib *verb* **jib at** balk at, shrink from, recoil from, refuse, stop short of.

jiffy *noun* instant, moment, minute, second, tick, flash, trice, twinkling of an eye, two shakes of a lamb's tail (*inf*).

jilt *verb* abandon, forsake, desert, leave, throw over, chuck (*inf*), give the heave-ho (*inf*), give the brush-off (*inf*), discard, reject, cast aside, drop, dump (*inf*), ditch (*inf*).

jingle *verb* ring, tinkle, clink, chink, rattle, jangle, clang, chime.
➤ *noun* **1** (*the jingle of bells*) ringing, tintinnabulation, tinkle, clink, chink, rattle. **2** (*an advertising jingle*) song, tune, melody, chorus, chant, slogan, rhyme.

jingoism *noun* nationalism, patriotism, chauvinism, flag-waving.

jinx *noun* curse, spell, malediction, voodoo, black magic, evil eye, hex.
➤ *verb* curse, bewitch, hex.

jittery *adj* nervous, anxious, uneasy, agitated, in a state (*inf*), shaking, trembling, fidgety, jumpy, edgy. OPPOSITE: calm.

job *noun* **1** (*looking for a new job*) work, employment, position, situation, post, appointment, occupation, profession, calling, vocation, business, trade, craft, métier. **2** (*several jobs to do*) task, chore, assignment, errand, commission, project, venture, undertaking, enterprise. **3** (*it's your job to answer the phone*) duty, responsibility, charge, capacity, office, role, function, concern, affair, business. **4** (*had a job finding the keys*) difficulty, problem, trouble, bother, hard time.

jobless *adj* unemployed, out of work, on the dole, laid off, redundant, idle, unoccupied. OPPOSITE: employed.

jockey *noun* rider, horseman, horsewoman, equestrian.
➤ *verb* manoeuvre, manipulate, engineer, negotiate, cajole, wheedle, coax, finagle (*inf*).

jocose *adj* jocund, merry, jovial, jolly, blithe, cheerful, jocular, jesting, joking, playful, sportive, witty, droll, funny, humorous, comical. OPPOSITE: melancholy.

jocular *adj* jesting, joking, facetious, waggish, witty, droll, comical, funny, humorous, amusing, entertaining, jocose, merry, playful, sportive. OPPOSITE: serious.

jog *verb* **1** (*jogged his elbow*) jolt, jar, jerk, jostle, nudge, prod, shake, joggle, jiggle, bounce. **2** (*jogged my memory*) prompt, arouse, stir, stimulate, activate. **3** (*go jogging*) trot, run.

join *verb* **1** (*join the line to the rod*) attach, fasten, tie, bind, unite, conjoin, connect, link, couple, splice, knit, fuse, add, append. OPPOSITE: detach. **2** (*where the parts join*) unite, connect, meet, touch, abut, adjoin, border, verge. OPPOSITE: divide. **3** (*the companies have joined*) combine, merge, amalgamate, affiliate, ally, league, team up, join forces. OPPOSITE: split up. **4** (*join a club*) enrol, enlist, sign up, join up, become a member. OPPOSITE: leave.

join in contribute, participate, take part, lend a hand, pitch in, muck in (*inf*).

joint *noun* junction, connection, link, union, join, knot, seam, hinge, articulation, juncture, intersection.
» *adj* common, communal, shared, mutual, combined, collective, concerted, united, joined. OPPOSITE: individual.

joke *noun* **1** (*telling jokes*) jest, quip, witticism, pun, crack (*inf*), gag (*inf*), anecdote, yarn, funny story. **2** (*play a joke*) practical joke, prank, jape, lark, trick, hoax, leg-pull (*inf*).
» *verb* jest, quip, banter, chaff, tease, kid (*inf*), have on (*inf*), pull someone's leg (*inf*), fool, clown.

joker *noun* comedian, comic, wag, wit, humorist, clown, buffoon, fool, jester, trickster, prankster.

jollity *noun* fun, mirth, hilarity, merriment, gaiety, joviality, jocosity, jocundity, jocularity. OPPOSITE: melancholy.

jolly *adj* jovial, jocose, jocund, merry, happy, joyful, joyous, cheerful, cheery, blithe, playful, sportive, frolicsome, lively, spirited, genial, convivial, festive. OPPOSITE: sombre.

jolt *verb* **1** (*jolted by the movement of the train*) jar, jerk, jog, jostle, push, shove, bump, knock, shake, bounce, start, lurch. **2** (*jolted by the news*) shock, stun, stagger, astonish, startle, surprise, shake, upset, disturb, disconcert.
» *noun* **1** (*stopped with a jolt*) jerk, lurch, bump, knock, bang, impact. **2** (*the news came as a jolt*) surprise, blow, upset, shock, bombshell (*inf*), bolt from the blue (*inf*).

jostle *verb* push, shove, hustle, crowd, press, squeeze, force, elbow, shoulder, jolt, jog, bump, knock, shake.

jot *noun* iota, atom, bit, scrap, particle, grain, trace, mite, whit, tittle, smidgen (*inf*), tad (*inf*).
» *verb* write, scribble, note, record, list, register.

journal *noun* **1** (*a medical journal*) periodical, magazine, newspaper, paper, review, gazette, weekly, monthly. **2** (*keep a journal*) diary, log, chronicle, record, register, daybook.

journalism *noun* news, reporting, broadcasting, the press, the media, the fourth estate, Fleet Street.

journalist *noun* reporter, correspondent, columnist, feature writer, reviewer, newspaperman, newspaperwoman, hack (*inf*), editor, broadcaster, commentator, newshound, paparazzo, stringer.

journey *noun* voyage, trip, passage, expedition, trek, safari, odyssey, pilgrimage, cruise, excursion, jaunt, outing, tour, drive, ride, flight, sail.
» *verb* travel, voyage, go, proceed, roam, rove, ramble, wander, gallivant, peregrinate, trek, cruise, tour, drive, ride, fly, sail.

jovial *adj* jolly, genial, convivial, cordial, hearty, jocose, jocund, jocular, blithe, cheerful, cheery, merry, lively, animated. OPPOSITE: morose.

joy *noun* **1** (*squeals of joy*) happiness, gladness, glee, delight, rapture, ecstasy, bliss, felicity, elation, euphoria, exultation, jubilation, joyfulness, joyousness, gaiety, cheerfulness, enjoyment, pleasure, gratification. OPPOSITE: sorrow. **2** (*the car's a joy to drive*) treat, delight, thrill, pleasure. **3** (*had no joy with their search*) luck, success, satisfaction, achievement.

joyful *adj* **1** (*joyful children*) happy, pleased, glad, gleeful, delighted, overjoyed, elated, euphoric, exultant, jubilant, joyous, merry, jolly, jocose, jocund, cheerful, blithe, buoyant, on top of the world (*inf*), over the moon (*inf*), in seventh heaven (*inf*), on cloud nine (*inf*). OPPOSITE: unhappy. **2** (*joyful news*) good, pleasing, happy, glad, cheering, heartwarming, gratifying, reassuring. OPPOSITE: sad.

jubilant *adj* exultant, triumphant, rejoicing, joyful, joyous, overjoyed, thrilled, tickled pink (*inf*), elated, ecstatic, euphoric, walking on air (*inf*), over the moon (*inf*), on cloud nine (*inf*). OPPOSITE: despondent.

jubilation *noun* exultation, triumph, rejoicing, celebration, joy, elation, rapture, transport, ecstasy, euphoria. OPPOSITE: mourning.

judge *verb* **1** (*judge a competition*) adjudicate, referee, umpire, arbitrate, mediate. **2** (*judge a case in court*) try, hear evidence, sit in judgment, pass sentence, give a verdict, decree, rule. **3** (*judge how long it will take*) determine, ascertain, decide, calculate, reckon, gauge, estimate, guess. **4** (*judge the quality of their work*) assess, evaluate, appraise, weigh up, gauge, review, criticize. **5** (*judge him capable enough*) deem, consider, regard, think, believe, find, decide, conclude.
» *noun* **1** (*the judge passed sentence*) justice, magistrate, beak (*inf*), sheriff, coroner. **2** (*the judge's decision is final*) adjudicator, referee, umpire, arbiter, mediator, moderator, ombudsman. **3** (*I'm no judge of good wine*) assessor, evaluator, appraiser, authority, expert, connoisseur, critic, reviewer.

judgment *noun* **1** (*the judgment of the court*) verdict, finding, decision, conclusion, sentence, decree, ruling, order, award, adjudication, arbitration. OPPOSITE: pleading. **2** (*showing a lack of judgment*) discernment, perspicacity, discrimination, taste, perception, insight, penetration, understanding, sense, good sense, wisdom, sagacity, prudence, discretion, acumen, shrewdness, intelligence. OPPOSITE: folly. **3** (*her judgment of the situation*) assessment, evaluation, appraisal, diagnosis, estimation, view, opinion, belief. **4** (*the Day of Judgment*) damnation, doom, fate, retribution, punishment, sentence, conviction.

judicial *adj* judiciary, juridical, legal, forensic.

judicious *adj* wise, sagacious, prudent, provident, politic, discreet, diplomatic, careful, cautious, circumspect, sensible, rational, logical, sound, shrewd, astute, clever, intelligent, informed, enlightened. OPPOSITE: injudicious.

jug *verb* pitcher, ewer, urn, crock, carafe, decanter, flagon, flask, vessel, container, receptacle.

juggle *verb* manipulate, alter, change, rearrange, falsify, fake, tamper with, doctor (*inf*), rig, fix (*inf*).

juice *noun* liquid, fluid, extract, essence, secretion, sap, liquor, serum.

juicy *adj* **1** (*a juicy orange*) succulent, lush, moist, wet, flowing, dripping. OPPOSITE: dry. **2** (*a juicy story*) sensational, scandalous, racy, risqué, spicy, vivid, lurid, colourful, exciting, thrilling.

jumble *verb* disorder, disarrange, disorganize, throw into disarray, mix, mix up, muddle, confuse. OPPOSITE: arrange.

➤ *noun* disorder, disarray, muddle, confusion, chaos, mess, clutter, mixture, medley, miscellany, hotchpotch, mishmash (*inf*). OPPOSITE: order.

jumbo *adj* giant, extra-large, oversized, huge, enormous, immense, gigantic, colossal, mammoth.

jump *verb* **1** (*jump up and down*) leap, spring, bound, skip, hop, caper, prance, gambol, frolic, frisk, cavort. **2** (*jump the fence*) clear, vault, hurdle, jump over, leap over. **3** (*the noise made me jump*) start, jump out of one's skin (*inf*), wince, flinch, recoil, twitch, jerk, shake, quail. **4** (*jump a paragraph*) miss, omit, skip, leave out, cut out, pass over, disregard, ignore. OPPOSITE: include. **5** (*they jumped him from behind*) attack, assault, pounce on, swoop down on, fall on, set upon.

➤ *noun* **1** (*in a single jump*) leap, spring, bound, vault, skip, hop. **2** (*fell at the first jump*) hurdle, fence, obstacle, barrier, rail, gate, hedge. **3** (*woke with a jump*) start, jerk, jolt, lurch, wince, flinch, twitch, quiver. **4** (*a jump in prices*) rise, increase, escalation, hike (*inf*), upsurge, upturn, boost, advance. OPPOSITE: drop.

jump at grab, snatch, seize, leap at, pounce on.

jumper *noun* sweater, pullover, jersey, woolly (*inf*), top, sweatshirt.

jumpy *adj* nervous, anxious, fretful, agitated, jittery, twitchy, panicky, fidgety, restless, on edge, tense, apprehensive, uneasy. OPPOSITE: calm.

junction *noun* **1** (*the junction of the pipes*) joint, connection, link, coupling, join, seam, bond, union. **2** (*a road junction*) intersection, crossroads, crossing, interchange.

juncture *noun* point, stage, time, moment, minute, crux, crisis, emergency, exigency.

junior *adj* younger, minor, lesser, lower, inferior, subordinate, subsidiary, secondary. OPPOSITE: senior.

junk *noun* rubbish, refuse, trash, garbage, scrap, waste, litter, clutter, odds and ends, bric-à-brac.

jurisdiction *noun* **1** (*the territory under his jurisdiction*) power, authority, control, influence, sway, rule, dominion, sovereignty, mastery, leadership, administration, government. **2** (*matters outside her jurisdiction*) domain, province, realm, sphere, field, area, compass, range, scope.

just *adj* **1** (*just treatment*) fair, equitable, impartial, neutral, unbiased, unprejudiced, objective, dispassionate, disinterested, right, legal, legitimate, lawful, sound, valid. OPPOSITE: unjust. **2** (*a just ruler*) upright, honest, honourable, righteous, conscientious, good, virtuous, moral, ethical, principled. OPPOSITE: unscrupulous. **3** (*a just reward*) deserved, merited, justified, rightful, proper, reasonable, due, appropriate, apt, fitting, suitable, condign. OPPOSITE: unmerited. **4** (*a just description*) accurate, exact, precise, correct, truthful, factual, faithful, strict. OPPOSITE: inaccurate.

➤ *adv* **1** (*just right*) exactly, precisely, absolutely, completely, totally, perfectly. **2** (*we just got there in time*) barely, hardly, scarcely, only just, by a hair's breadth (*inf*), by the skin of one's teeth (*inf*). **3** (*he's just a boy*) only, merely, simply, no more than, nothing but. **4** (*she's just moved house*) recently, lately, not long ago, a short time ago, a moment ago.

just about almost, nearly, virtually, practically, well-nigh, as good as, to all intents and purposes.

justice *noun* **1** (*there's no justice in this world*) fairness, equity, justness, fair play, impartiality, neutrality, objectivity, dispassionateness, honour, integrity, honesty, righteousness, virtue, morality. OPPOSITE: injustice. **2** (*the justice of their claims*) propriety, legality, legitimacy, lawfulness, soundness, validity. **3** (*demanding justice*) amends, redress, compensation, recompense, reparation, requital, retribution.

justifiable *adj* excusable, defensible, warrantable, reasonable, acceptable, right, proper, fit, due, lawful, legitimate, valid, sound, tenable, plausible. OPPOSITE: unjustifiable.

justification *noun* **1** (*no justification for his conduct*) defence, plea, apology, excuse, explanation, reason, grounds, rationalization. **2** (*the justification of her allegations*) vindication, confirmation, verification, proof, substantiation.

justify *verb* excuse, explain, defend, support, uphold, maintain, substantiate, bear out, prove, verify, confirm, vindicate, warrant, rationalize.

jut *verb* project, protrude, stick out, overhang, beetle.

juvenile *adj* young, junior, minor, youthful, boyish, girlish, adolescent, immature, inexperienced, jejune, callow, puerile, infantile, childish. OPPOSITE: adult.

➤ *noun* minor, child, kid (*inf*), youth, adolescent, boy, girl. OPPOSITE: adult.

juxtaposition *noun* adjacency, contiguity, contact, proximity, nearness, closeness.

kaleidoscopic *adj* multicoloured, variegated, motley, psychedelic, changeable, variable, varying, ever-changing, protean, fluid, mobile, unstable.

keel *verb* **keel over 1** (*the boat keeled over*) overturn, turn over, capsize, turn turtle. **2** (*the bridegroom keeled over*) faint, collapse, lose consciousness, pass out, black out.

keen *adj* **1** (*a keen worker*) enthusiastic, ardent, fervent, fervid, zealous, earnest, eager, avid, diligent, assiduous, industrious, ambitious. OPPOSITE: apathetic. **2** (*keen to learn*) eager, impatient, itching, longing, yearning, hungry, thirsty. OPPOSITE: reluctant. **3** (*keen sarcasm*) sharp, acute, cutting, incisive, pointed, stinging, biting, caustic, trenchant, mordant, acid, acerbic, tart, pungent. OPPOSITE: blunt. **4** (*a keen wind*) penetrating, piercing, biting, bitter. OPPOSITE: mild. **5** (*keen eyesight*) sensitive, perceptive, sharp, acute, discerning, discriminating OPPOSITE: dull. **6** (*a keen mind*) shrewd, astute, quick, clever, smart, bright, perceptive, perspicacious, wise, sagacious. OPPOSITE: stupid. **7** (*a keen interest*) intense, strong, deep, profound. **8** (*keen competition*) fierce, intense, ruthless, cutthroat, dog-eat-dog (*inf*).
keen on fond of, liking, devoted to, loving.

keep *verb* **1** (*you can keep the change*) retain, keep hold of, hold on to, hang on to (*inf*), have, possess, own. OPPOSITE: discard. **2** (*keep trying*) continue, carry on, go on, keep on, persist, persevere. **3** (*keep it in the safe*) store, put, place, deposit, preserve, conserve. OPPOSITE: remove. **4** (*she keeps all the empty jars*) save, hoard, store, collect, amass, accumulate. OPPOSITE: use. **5** (*does the newsagent keep stationery?*) sell, deal in, stock, carry. **6** (*keeps the garden well*) tend, look after, mind, maintain, control. OPPOSITE: neglect. **7** (*with a family to keep*) sustain, support, maintain, subsidize, provide for, feed, clothe, board. **8** (*kept them from harm*) guard, protect, defend, shield, shelter. OPPOSITE: expose. **9** (*kept his promise*) fulfil, honour, observe, obey, comply with, abide by, keep to, stand by. OPPOSITE: break. **10** (*keep a tradition*) observe, keep up, respect, honour, celebrate, commemorate, solemnize, ritualize. **11** (*kept the truth from us*) hide, conceal, withhold, hold back, keep back, suppress, hush up. **12** (*don't let me keep you*) detain, delay, retard, hold back, keep back, restrain, check, curb, prevent, stop, hinder, hamper, obstruct, impede. **13** (*the fish won't keep*) stay fresh, last, endure. OPPOSITE: go off.
※ *noun* **1** (*pay for their keep*) board, subsistence, support, maintenance, upkeep, living, livelihood. **2** (*defending the keep*) tower, stronghold, citadel, fortress, castle, fort, dungeon, donjon.
for keeps for ever, for all time, for good.
keep back restrain, check, curb, hold back, suppress, stifle, bottle up, hide, conceal, hush up, censor.
keep off avoid, keep away from, stay away from, stay off, steer clear of, give a wide berth to (*inf*), shun, abstain from, refrain from.
keep on about dwell on, go on about, keep talking about, refer to again and again.
keep on at nag, go on at, badger, chivvy, harass, pester, plague.
keep up 1 (*if the rain keeps up*) continue, persist, go on, last. OPPOSITE: cease. **2** (*keep up the payments*) maintain, keep going, continue with, carry on with, go on with. **3** (*keep up with our rivals*) keep pace, keep abreast, compete, contend, vie. OPPOSITE: fall behind. **4** (*keep up with former colleagues*) stay in touch, keep in contact, remain acquainted.

keeper *noun* custodian, curator, conservator, caretaker, steward, superintendent, overseer, guard, sentry, warden, warder, jailer, guardian, escort, bodyguard, minder (*inf*).

keeping *noun* **1** (*documents in their keeping*) custody, charge, care, trust, hands, possession, retention, protection, safekeeping, guardianship, patronage, aegis, auspices. **2** (*in keeping with tradition*) conformity, accord, agreement, harmony, correspondence, consistency, congruity, compliance, observance.

keepsake *noun* memento, souvenir, reminder, remembrance, token, relic.

keg *noun* barrel, cask, vat, tun, butt, drum, firkin, hogshead.

ken *noun* knowledge, acquaintance, cognizance, perception, awareness, realization, comprehension, understanding, grasp, reach, range, scope.

kernel *noun* **1** (*the soft kernel of the nut*) seed, grain, core, nucleus, heart, centre. OPPOSITE: shell. **2** (*a kernel of truth in her story*) centre, heart, core, nucleus, nub, crux, pith, marrow, gist, substance, essence.

key *noun* **1** (*the key to the puzzle*) solution, answer, guide, pointer, clue, explanation, interpretation, translation, code, glossary, legend. **2** (*in a lower key*) tone, tonality, pitch, timbre, mood, vein, style, character.
➤ *adj* crucial, vital, essential, necessary, main, chief, principal, major, important, central, basic, fundamental. OPPOSITE: minor.

kick *verb* **1** (*kick the ball*) boot, punt, strike, hit, drive. **2** (*the gun may kick*) recoil, kick back. **3** (*kick the habit*) give up, abandon, stop, quit, leave off, desist from.
➤ *noun* **1** (*give the ball a kick*) boot, punt, blow. **2** (*put some kick into the company*) zest, vitality, energy, vigour, force, verve, sparkle, animation. **3** (*a drink with a bit less kick*) strength, potency, effect, punch (*inf*), bite (*inf*). **4** (*did it for kicks*) thrill, buzz (*inf*), excitement, pleasure, enjoyment, fun, amusement.

kick against oppose, resist, defy, rebel against, object to, protest about, complain about, grumble about. OPPOSITE: accept.

kick off start, begin, commence, get going, get under way, open, initiate, start the ball rolling (*inf*).

kick out eject, expel, evict, turn out, throw out, chuck out (*inf*), boot out (*inf*), give someone the boot (*inf*), show someone the door (*inf*), dismiss, discharge, fire (*inf*), sack (*inf*), give someone the sack (*inf*), get rid of, oust, remove.

kid *noun* child, offspring, daughter, son, baby, infant, toddler, boy, girl, youngster, youth, juvenile, adolescent, teenager. OPPOSITE: adult.
➤ *verb* joke, jest, fool around, tease, rib (*inf*), trick, dupe, deceive, delude, fool, have on (*inf*), pull someone's leg (*inf*).

kidnap *verb* abduct, carry off, seize, snatch, capture, take hostage, hold to ransom. OPPOSITE: free.

kill *verb* **1** (*kill the president*) slaughter, slay, murder, assassinate, execute, put to death, dispatch, do away with, do in (*inf*), bump off (*inf*), knock off (*inf*), top (*inf*), rub out (*sl*), waste (*sl*), destroy, annihilate, exterminate, liquidate, butcher, massacre, wipe out. **2** (*kill the sound*) deaden, dampen, stifle, smother, muffle, dull, negate, neutralize, cancel, suppress, quash, quell. **3** (*killing themselves with work*) exhaust, tire out, wear out, prostrate, overtire, overtax, strain. **4** (*killing time*) pass, spend, occupy, fill up, while away.

killing *noun* **1** (*the killing of innocent civilians*) slaughter, butchery, carnage, massacre, genocide, murder, manslaughter, homicide, assassination, execution, extermination, liquidation. **2** (*make a killing on the stock exchange*) coup, success, gain, profit, fortune, windfall, clean-up (*inf*).
➤ *adj* **1** (*the killing shot*) deadly, fatal, lethal, mortal, murderous, homicidal. OPPOSITE: harmless. **2** (*a killing workload*) tiring, exhausting, taxing, punishing, hard, arduous. OPPOSITE: light. **3** (*a killing joke*) hilarious, side-splitting, rib-tickling, uproarious, funny, comical, amusing.

killjoy *noun* spoilsport, damper, misery, wet blanket (*inf*), party-pooper (*inf*).

kin *noun* kindred, relations, relatives, family, kinsfolk, people, folks, connections, flesh and blood.

kind[1] *adj* benevolent, benign, kindly, charitable, philanthropic, beneficent, generous, bounteous, magnanimous, gracious, humane, gentle, tender, kind-hearted, warm, warm-hearted, affectionate, compassionate, sympathetic, understanding, indulgent, lenient, clement, mild, good, considerate, thoughtful, friendly, amiable, obliging, neighbourly. OPPOSITE: unkind.

kind[2] *noun* sort, type, class, group, order, genre, set, variety, species, genus, breed, race, family, ilk, style, nature, character, manner, make, brand, stamp, mould.

kindle *verb* **1** (*kindle a fire*) ignite, light, set alight, start, set fire to, set on fire. OPPOSITE: extinguish. **2** (*kindle a passion*) arouse, stimulate, excite, fire, touch off, activate, actuate, rouse, provoke, incite, inflame, fan, foment, agitate, stir. OPPOSITE: quell.

kindly *adj* kind, kind-hearted, warm, warm-hearted, sympathetic, compassionate, benevolent, benign, good, nice, pleasant, friendly, genial, cordial. OPPOSITE: cruel.
➤ *adv* benevolently, generously, magnanimously, graciously, humanely, gently, tenderly, warmly, compassionately, sympathetically, leniently, mildly, well, considerately, thoughtfully. OPPOSITE: unkindly.

kindness *noun* **1** (*the kindness of her friends*) benevolence, kindliness, charity, philanthropy, beneficence, generosity, magnanimity, graciousness, humanity, tenderness, warmth, affection, compassion, sympathy, understanding, indulgence, clemency, goodness, consideration, thoughtfulness. OPPOSITE: unkindness. **2** (*he did me a kindness*) favour, service, good deed, good turn, help, aid, assistance, help. OPPOSITE: disservice.

kindred *noun* **1** (*among her own kindred*) kin, relations, relatives, family, kinsfolk, people, folks, connections, flesh and blood. **2** (*claim kindred*) kinship, consanguinity, relationship, common ancestry.
➤ *adj* related, kin, consanguineous, akin, allied, cognate, similar, like, matching, corresponding. OPPOSITE: unrelated.

king *noun* **1** (*crowned him king*) monarch, ruler, sovereign, prince, emperor, lord, overlord, chief, chieftain. OPPOSITE: subject. **2** (*the king of jazz*) star, leader, supremo, greatest, leading light.

kingdom *noun* monarchy, sovereignty, principality, empire, realm, dominion, country, nation, state, land, territory, province, domain.

kingly *adj* royal, regal, sovereign, princely, imperial, majestic, stately, grand, imposing, dignified, august, noble, splendid. OPPOSITE: lowly.

kink *noun* **1** (*a kink in the line*) bend, curve, twist, curl, coil, corkscrew, crimp, wrinkle, knot, tangle. **2** (*a kink in*

the plan) flaw, fault, defect, imperfection, snag, hitch, glitch (*inf*). **3** (*a kink in her character*) quirk, eccentricity, idiosyncrasy, whim, caprice, vagary, crotchet, fetish, deviation, perversion, foible, failing, weakness.
≫ *verb* bend, curve, twist, curl, coil, crimp, frizz, wrinkle, knot. OPPOSITE: straighten.

kinky *adj* **1** (*kinky hair*) wavy, curly, frizzy, crimped, crinkled. OPPOSITE: straight. **2** (*a kinky wire*) bent, curved, twisted, coiled, tangled. **3** (*kinky practices*) deviant, perverted, warped, degenerate, depraved, unnatural, abnormal, unconventional, unorthodox, weird, bizarre, odd, strange, quirky, eccentric, idiosyncratic, whimsical, capricious. OPPOSITE: normal.

kinship *noun* **1** (*kinship with the emperor*) consanguinity, relationship, kindred, common ancestry, family, blood, extraction, descent, lineage. **2** (*kinship with contemporary writers*) connection, relationship, affinity, similarity, likeness, correspondence.

kiosk *noun* booth, stall, stand.

kismet *noun* destiny, fate, fortune, providence, portion, lot, karma, doom.

kiss *verb* **1** (*the lovers kissed*) embrace, osculate, peck (*inf*), neck (*inf*), snog (*inf*), smooch (*inf*), canoodle (*inf*). **2** (*the wind kissed the surface of the lake*) touch, caress, brush, graze, glance off.
≫ *noun* embrace, osculation, peck (*inf*), smacker (*inf*), snog (*inf*), smooch (*inf*).

kit *noun* **1** (*a repair kit*) set, parts, components, tools, implements, instruments, utensils, equipment, apparatus, gear, tackle, supplies, provisions. **2** (*in his football kit*) outfit, clothes, clothing, dress, rigout (*inf*), uniform, colours, strip (*inf*).
kit out equip, supply, provide, furnish, fit, fit out, outfit, cloth, dress, rig out, prepare, arm.

kitchen *noun* cookhouse, galley, scullery.

knack *noun* flair, talent, gift, faculty, aptitude, ability, capacity, skill, expertise, genius, facility, propensity, trick, hang (*inf*), dexterity, adroitness, proficiency, competence. OPPOSITE: inability.

knave *noun* rascal, rogue, scoundrel, blackguard, villain, miscreant, wrongdoer, reprobate, wretch, dastard, rotter (*inf*), bounder (*inf*).

knavery *noun* deceit, deception, duplicity, dishonesty, fraud, trickery, chicanery, villainy, roguery, rascality. OPPOSITE: honesty.

knavish *adj* rascally, roguish, villainous, dishonest, fraudulent, deceitful, tricky, dastardly, unscrupulous, unprincipled. OPPOSITE: honest.

knead *verb* work, ply, press, squeeze, manipulate, massage, rub, form, shape, mould.

kneel *verb* genuflect, bow, stoop, curtsy, kowtow.

knell *noun* toll, ring, chime, peal, sound.

knickers *pl noun* pants, panties, briefs, smalls (*inf*), bloomers, drawers (*inf*), underwear, lingerie, undies (*inf*).

knick-knack *noun* ornament, trinket, bauble, gewgaw, trifle, bagatelle.

knife *noun* blade, cutter, carver, scalpel, dagger, dirk, penknife, switchblade.
≫ *verb* stab, impale, transfix, pierce, cut, slash, lacerate.

knight *noun* horseman, equestrian, cavalier, cavalryman, soldier, warrior, lord, gallant, chevalier.

knit *verb* **1** (*knit the community together*) join, unite, bind, tie, link, connect, interlace, interweave, intertwine. OPPOSITE: separate. **2** (*the bones will knit*) heal, mend. **3** (*knitting his brows*) furrow, wrinkle, crease.

knob *noun* **1** (*knobs on the bark*) protuberance, projection, knurl, stud, boss, bump, lump, swelling, knot, node. **2** (*turn the knob*) handle, switch, button, control.

knock *verb* **1** (*knock on the window*) hit, strike, tap, rap, bang, bash, thump, pound, hammer. **2** (*knock against the wall*) bump, collide, crash, hit, strike, buffet, pound, hammer, beat, batter, dash, smash, smack, slap, clout (*inf*), wallop (*inf*). **3** (*knocking their efforts*) criticize, attack, run down (*inf*), belittle, deprecate, disparage, carp at, cavil at, find fault with, pick holes in (*inf*), censure, condemn, slate (*inf*), slam (*inf*), pan (*inf*). OPPOSITE: praise.
≫ *noun* blow, hit, tap, rap, bang, bump, collision, crash, thump, punch, smack, slap, clip (*inf*), clout (*inf*).
knock about beat, batter, abuse, maltreat, ill-treat, mistreat, manhandle, hurt, injure, damage.
knock down demolish, level, raze, fell, hew, floor. OPPOSITE: raise.
knock off **1** (*knock off work*) stop, finish, terminate, conclude, shut down, clock off, call it a day (*inf*). **2** (*knock off anybody who resists*) kill, slay, murder, assassinate, do away with, do in (*inf*), bump off (*inf*), rub out (*sl*), waste (*sl*). **3** (*knocked off a crate of whisky*) steal, filch, pilfer, purloin, pinch (*inf*), nick (*inf*), lift (*inf*).
knock out **1** (*knocked out the champion*) eliminate, defeat, beat, overcome, overthrow, overwhelm, floor, prostrate, KO (*inf*). **2** (*the effort knocked her out*) exhaust, tire out, wear out, do in (*inf*). **3** (*his performance knocked us out*) stun, amaze, astound, knock for six (*inf*), dazzle, impress, overwhelm, bowl over (*inf*), take someone's breath away (*inf*).
knock up **1** (*knock up a shelter*) improvise, put together, make, jerry-build. OPPOSITE: demolish. **2** (*knocked up 10,000 miles*) reach, achieve, attain, clock up (*inf*). **3** (*knocking up before the match*) warm up, practise.

knoll *noun* hill, hillock, hummock, mound.

knot *noun* **1** (*a knot in the rope*) tie, fastening, loop, bow, splice, hitch. **2** (*a knot of people*) bunch, clump, cluster, group, company, band, ring, circle, crowd, mob, throng, gathering, assemblage. **3** (*a knot in the wood*) protuberance, lump, swelling, knob, node, nodule, gnarl.
≫ *verb* tie, secure, tether, fasten, hitch, join, connect, splice, bind, lash, twist, loop, knit, entwine, entangle, ravel. OPPOSITE: untie.

knotty *adj* **1** (*a knotty problem*) complicated, complex, intricate, difficult, thorny, tricky, puzzling, perplexing, mystifying. OPPOSITE: simple. **2** (*a knotty surface*) gnarled, nodular, lumpy, bumpy, rough, coarse, rugged. OPPOSITE: smooth.

know *verb* **1** (*know what to do*) understand, comprehend, perceive, apprehend, realize, see, be aware, be conscious. **2** (*know the words of the song*) have learned, have memorized, be acquainted with, be familiar with, be conversant with, have at one's fingertips (*inf*). **3** (*do you know this man?*) be acquainted with, have met, be familiar with, recognize, identify, associate with, socialize with, fraternize with. **4** (*know right from wrong*) differentiate, distinguish, discriminate, discern, tell, identify. **5** (*she has known great suffering*) experience, undergo, go through.

knowing *adj* **1** (*with a knowing smile*) meaningful, significant, eloquent, expressive, perceptive, discerning, aware, wise, shrewd, astute, smart, clever, subtle, cunning. OPPOSITE: artless. **2** (*a knowing violation of the law*) deliberate, intentional, wilful, conscious. OPPOSITE: unconscious.

knowingly *adv* deliberately, intentionally, on purpose, wilfully, consciously, wittingly. OPPOSITE: unwittingly.

knowledge *noun* **1** (*study to acquire knowledge*) erudition, learning, scholarship, education, instruction, enlightenment, wisdom, judgment, discernment, information, intelligence, facts, data. OPPOSITE: ignorance. **2** (*knowledge of the language*) acquaintance, familiarity, cognizance, ken, understanding, comprehension, grasp, experience, proficiency, skill, expertise, know-how. **3** (*knowledge of the danger*) awareness, consciousness, realization, recognition, understanding, comprehension, grasp, perception, apprehension, cognition.

knowledgeable *adj* **1** (*a knowledgeable person*) erudite, learned, scholarly, educated, enlightened, informed, well-informed, well-read. OPPOSITE: ignorant. **2** (*knowledgeable about the subject*) expert, skilled, experienced, well-versed, acquainted, familiar, conversant.

kowtow *verb* **1** (*kowtowing to the emperor*) bow, kneel, genuflect, prostrate oneself. **2** (*kowtowing to the boss*) grovel, fawn, cringe, toady, suck up (*inf*), curry favour, bow and scrape (*inf*).

kudos *noun* prestige, glory, honour, fame, renown, acclaim, praise. OPPOSITE: disgrace.

label *noun* **1** (*a luggage label*) tag, ticket, docket, tab, sticker, marker. **2** (*sold under the shop's own label*) mark, brand, logo, trademark, trade name, proprietary name. **3** (*people given the 'unemployable' label*) epithet, name, title, description, identification, characterization, classification, categorization.
≫ *verb* **1** (*label the merchandise*) mark, stamp, tag, ticket, docket. **2** (*labelled her an intellectual*) call, name, term, dub, brand, describe, identify, characterize, class, classify, categorize.

laborious *adj* **1** (*a laborious task*) hard, arduous, strenuous, tiring, fatiguing, exhausting, wearisome, toilsome, burdensome, difficult, tough, uphill. OPPOSITE: easy. **2** (*laborious workers*) diligent, industrious, assiduous, sedulous, painstaking, thorough, hard-working, tireless, indefatigable, persevering. OPPOSITE: indolent.

labour *noun* **1** (*after three days' labour*) work, employment, toil, drudgery, sweat (*inf*), grind (*inf*), slog (*inf*), industry, effort, exertion, pains. OPPOSITE: idleness. **2** (*hiring labour for the new factory*) workers, labourers, hands, employees, staff, workforce. OPPOSITE: management. **3** (*the labours of Hercules*) job, task, chore, mission, assignment, undertaking. **4** (*his wife went into labour*) confinement, childbirth, parturition, delivery, contractions, travail.
≫ *verb* **1** (*labouring in the quarry*) work, toil, drudge, slave, work one's fingers to the bone. OPPOSITE: rest. **2** (*labour the point*) overdo, overemphasize, overstress, dwell on, overelaborate, belabour. OPPOSITE: play down. **3** (*laboured to meet the deadline*) struggle, strive, do one's best (*inf*), go all out (*inf*).

laboured *adj* strained, forced, stilted, stiff, unnatural, contrived, studied, overdone, heavy, ponderous. OPPOSITE: natural.

labourer *noun* worker, hand, workman, navvy, manual worker, unskilled worker, blue-collar worker, employee, hireling, drudge, menial.

labyrinth *noun* maze, warren, jungle, network, tangle, entanglement, puzzle, riddle.

labyrinthine *adj* mazelike, mazy, circuitous, tortuous, involved, intricate, complex, complicated, convoluted, tangled, knotty, confused, confusing, perplexing, puzzling. OPPOSITE: simple.

lace *noun* **1** (*skirts trimmed with lace*) netting, web, filigree, meshwork, openwork, tatting. **2** (*new laces for their shoes*) string, cord, thong, tie.
≫ *verb* **1** (*lacing her corset*) tie, fasten, lace up, do up, close, bind, thread, string. OPPOSITE: unlace. **2** (*lace the drink with brandy*) mix, blend, flavour, fortify, strengthen, spike (*inf*). **3** (*laced his fingers with mine*) interlace, interweave, intertwine.

lacerate *verb* tear, rip, rend, gash, slash, cut, mangle, mutilate, wound, injure, hurt, pain, harrow, afflict, distress. OPPOSITE: mend.

lack *noun* need, want, shortage, deficiency, insufficiency, dearth, scarcity, absence. OPPOSITE: abundance.
≫ *verb* need, want, require, be short of, be without. OPPOSITE: have.

lackadaisical *adj* lethargic, listless, apathetic, unenthusiastic, lukewarm, half-hearted, languid, idle, indolent, lazy. OPPOSITE: enthusiastic.

lackey *noun* **1** (*flattered by her lackeys*) sycophant, toady, fawner, yes-man (*inf*), parasite, hanger-on, minion, pawn, tool, instrument, puppet. **2** (*waited on by his lackeys*) servant, valet, attendant, flunkey, underling, menial. OPPOSITE: master.

lacking *adj* **1** (*financial support is lacking*) needed, required, missing, absent, deficient, inadequate, scarce, in short supply. OPPOSITE: abundant. **2** (*workers lacking motivation*) needing, wanting, short of, without, minus. OPPOSITE: having.

lacklustre *adj* uninteresting, boring, dull, unimaginative, uninspired, unimpressive, flat, dry, bland, vapid, ordinary, commonplace. OPPOSITE: brilliant.

laconic *adj* terse, succinct, concise, brief, short, pithy, crisp, curt, blunt, abrupt. OPPOSITE: verbose.

lad *noun* boy, youngster, kid (*inf*), youth, stripling, young man, fellow, chap (*inf*). OPPOSITE: lass.

laden *adj* loaded, burdened, encumbered, weighed down, full, charged. OPPOSITE: empty.

ladylike *adj* refined, polished, genteel, well-bred, elegant, dignified, proper, seemly, decorous, mannerly, courteous, polite. OPPOSITE: unseemly.

lag *verb* dawdle, saunter, loiter, linger, dally, idle, fall behind, trail, straggle, bring up the rear, hang back, tarry, delay, drag one's feet (*inf*). OPPOSITE: hurry.

laggard *noun* dawdler, loiterer, straggler, idler, loafer, sluggard, slowcoach (*inf*).

laid-back *adj* relaxed, at ease, casual, informal, easygoing (*inf*), nonchalant, carefree, leisurely, unhurried, calm, cool, imperturbable, unflappable (*inf*). OPPOSITE: uptight.

lair *noun* den, hole, cave, burrow, nest, haunt, hideaway, retreat, refuge.

lake *noun* pool, pond, reservoir, mere, tarn, loch, lough, lagoon, bayou.

lambaste *verb* scold, chide, reprimand, rebuke, castigate, upbraid, berate, attack, criticize, censure, hammer, drub, pitch into (*inf*).

lame *adj* **1** (*a lame horse*) crippled, disabled, handicapped, incapacitated, limping, hobbling, halting. OPPOSITE: able-bodied. **2** (*my lame leg*) defective, crippled, incapacitated, game, gammy (*inf*). **3** (*a lame excuse*) weak, feeble, flimsy, unconvincing, inadequate, unsatisfactory, poor, ineffectual. OPPOSITE: convincing. ➤ *verb* cripple, disable, handicap, incapacitate, injure, maim, hamstring.

lament *verb* mourn, bewail, bemoan, sorrow, grieve, cry, weep, wail, keen, moan, complain, regret, rue, deplore. OPPOSITE: rejoice. ➤ *noun* **1** (*heard their laments*) lamentation, cry, sob, wail, moan, complaint. **2** (*write a lament*) dirge, requiem, elegy, threnody, coronach.

lamentable *adj* deplorable, regrettable, unfortunate, pitiful, miserable, wretched, sorry, poor, sad, sorrowful, tragic, grievous, distressing.

lamentation *noun* lament, mourning, sorrow, grief, crying, weeping, wailing, ululation. OPPOSITE: rejoicing.

lamp *noun* light, lantern, torch, bulb.

lampoon *noun* satire, parody, travesty, burlesque, caricature, skit, spoof, send-up (*inf*). ➤ *verb* satirize, ridicule, mock, make fun of, parody, burlesque, caricature, send up (*inf*).

lance *noun* spear, pike, javelin, bayonet, harpoon. ➤ *verb* pierce, puncture, prick, stab, cut, incise.

land *noun* **1** (*back on land*) earth, ground, terra firma, soil, dirt, sod. **2** (*the owner of the land*) estate, property, realty, real estate, demesne, manor, grounds, acres. **3** (*my native land*) country, nation, state, province, region, area, territory, realm, empire. ➤ *verb* **1** (*we landed at Southampton*) arrive, end up, alight, disembark, dock, berth, touch down, put down.

OPPOSITE: depart. **2** (*the bird landed on its perch*) alight, come to rest, settle, come down. **3** (*land a part in the show*) get, obtain, acquire, secure, gain, win. **4** (*land us with a huge bill*) saddle, burden, encumber, weigh down.

landmark *noun* **1** (*few landmarks in the area*) monument, prominent feature, signpost, guidepost, marker, picket, beacon. **2** (*landmarks of history*) turning point, watershed, milestone, crisis, critical point.

landscape *noun* scene, panorama, view, prospect, vista, scenery, countryside.

landslide *noun* landslip, rockfall, avalanche.

lane *noun* track, path, course, way, road, passage, alley.

language *noun* **1** (*talking in different languages*) tongue, dialect, patois, idiom, parlance, vernacular, slang, argot, cant, lingo (*inf*), jargon, vocabulary, terminology. **2** (*couched in flowery language*) style, wording, phrasing, phraseology, expression, diction, rhetoric. **3** (*the acquisition of language*) speech, utterance, talk, conversation, discourse, interchange, communication.

languid *adj* weak, feeble, faint, limp, drooping, flagging, languishing, tired, weary, fatigued, enervated, debilitated, listless, lethargic, languorous, sluggish, torpid, inactive, inert, lazy, slothful, apathetic, spiritless, unenthusiastic, lukewarm, uninterested, indifferent. OPPOSITE: lively.

languish *verb* **1** (*languishing industries*) decline, deteriorate, go downhill (*inf*), weaken, flag, droop, fail, fade, wither, wilt, waste away, decay, rot. OPPOSITE: flourish. **2** (*languishing for his home and family*) pine, long, yearn, hanker, hunger, thirst, desire, want, sigh, mope, mourn, grieve.

languor *noun* **1** (*a feeling of languor*) weakness, feebleness, faintness, tiredness, weariness, fatigue, enervation, debility, listlessness, lassitude, lethargy, sluggishness, torpor, heaviness, sleepiness, drowsiness, inactivity, inertia, laziness, sloth, apathy. OPPOSITE: energy. **2** (*the languor of a summer afternoon*) stillness, tranquillity, calmness, calm, lull, silence.

lank *adj* limp, lifeless, dull, lustreless, straight, long.

lanky *adj* gangling, gawky, rangy, tall, thin, lean, skinny, scrawny, spindly, weedy (*inf*), bony, gaunt, angular. OPPOSITE: dumpy.

lap *noun* circuit, round, tour, loop, circle, orbit, stage, part, section, leg. ➤ *verb* fold, wrap, envelop, enfold, wind, swathe, swaddle, cover.

lapse *noun* **1** (*a minor lapse*) slip, error, mistake, fault, failing, oversight, omission, negligence. **2** (*a time lapse*) interval, gap, break, intermission, lull, pause, hiatus. OPPOSITE: continuation. **3** (*a lapse in standards*) drop, fall, downturn, decline, deterioration, degeneration. OPPOSITE: improvement. ➤ *verb* **1** (*standards seem to have lapsed*) drop, fall, sink, decline, deteriorate, degenerate, slip, slide, go downhill (*inf*). OPPOSITE: improve. **2** (*my visa has lapsed*) expire, become invalid, run out, terminate, discontinue, end, stop. OPPOSITE: continue. **3** (*as time lapsed*) pass, elapse, go by, slip away.

larceny *noun* theft, stealing, robbery, burglary.

large *adj* **1** (*a large expanse*) big, great, enormous, huge, massive, immense, colossal, gigantic, whopping (*inf*), ginormous (*inf*), vast, spacious, roomy, extensive, broad, wide, full, ample. OPPOSITE: small. **2** (*people of large build*) burly, strapping, bulky, hulking, thickset, heavy, stout. **3** (*a large sum of money*) considerable, substantial, abundant, copious, ample, generous.

at large **1** (*the rapist is still at large*) free, loose, at liberty, unconfined, fugitive, on the run. OPPOSITE: captive. **2** (*in the world at large*) as a whole, in general, generally, on the whole.

largely *adv* chiefly, mainly, principally, mostly, in general, on the whole, in the main, by and large, greatly, considerably. OPPOSITE: partly.

largess *noun* **1** (*the largess of his friends*) generosity, liberality, open-handedness, bounty, charity, philanthropy, beneficence, munificence. OPPOSITE: meanness. **2** (*grateful for her largess*) gift, present, donation, benefaction, contribution, handout, bequest, endowment.

lark *noun* prank, joke, trick, antic, escapade, caper, frolic, romp, play, sport, fun.
» *verb* play, sport, caper, cavort, frolic, gambol, romp.
lark about fool about, mess about, play, have fun.

lascivious *adj* **1** (*a lascivious look*) lecherous, lustful, lewd, libidinous, randy (*inf*), horny (*inf*), concupiscent, prurient, salacious, licentious, degenerate, depraved, dissolute, dissipated, voluptuous, sensual. OPPOSITE: chaste. **2** (*lascivious pictures*) obscene, indecent, pornographic, dirty, smutty (*inf*), blue (*inf*), ribald, bawdy, raunchy (*inf*), gross, crude, vulgar.

lash[1] *verb* **1** (*the culprit will be lashed*) beat, whip, flog, scourge, flail, flagellate, cane, birch. **2** (*rain lashed against the windows*) hit, strike, beat, pound, hammer, buffet, dash, smack. **3** (*the show was lashed by the reviewers*) attack, criticize, satirize, ridicule, castigate, scold, upbraid, berate, censure, condemn, denounce, flay, lambaste, lay into (*inf*). OPPOSITE: praise. **4** (*lashing their tails*) flick, whip, switch, wag.
» *noun* **1** (*beaten with a lash*) whip, scourge, horsewhip, bullwhip, cat-o'-nine-tails, cat. **2** (*sentenced to twenty lashes*) stroke, blow, hit, stripe.

lash[2] *verb* (*lashed to the post*) tie, bind, fasten, secure, make fast, tether, hitch, join, attach. OPPOSITE: untie.

lass *noun* girl, young woman, bird (*inf*), chick (*inf*), miss, maid, maiden, damsel. OPPOSITE: lad.

lassitude *noun* languor, lethargy, listlessness, apathy, tiredness, weariness, fatigue, enervation, debility, sluggishness, torpor, heaviness, sleepiness, drowsiness. OPPOSITE: vigour.

last[1] *adj* **1** (*the last page*) ultimate, final, closing, concluding, terminal. OPPOSITE: first. **2** (*the last person in the queue*) endmost, hindmost, rearmost, utmost, extreme. **3** (*last Monday*) latest, most recent, previous, preceding. OPPOSITE: next. **4** (*that's the last thing I expected*) least likely, most unlikely, least suitable, most unsuitable.
» *adv* at the end, in the rear, behind, after, ultimately, finally. OPPOSITE: first.
» *noun* end, finish, termination, conclusion, close. OPPOSITE: beginning.

at last finally, eventually, in the end, ultimately, in due course, at length.

last word **1** (*my last word on the subject*) ultimatum, final statement, final decision. **2** (*the last word in luxury*) latest, newest, dernier cri, best, finest, cream, epitome, quintessence, ne plus ultra.

last[2] *verb* **1** (*the rain lasted all night*) continue, carry on, go on, persist, remain, stay, abide. OPPOSITE: stop. **2** (*I can't last much longer without food*) survive, hold out, hold on, live, exist, subsist. **3** (*the paintwork won't last*) endure, stand up, wear, keep.

last-ditch *adj* desperate, frantic, frenzied, wild, final, last-minute, eleventh-hour (*inf*).

lasting *adj* abiding, enduring, continuing, persisting, long-term, perennial, lifelong, permanent, eternal, everlasting, immortal, never-ending, ceaseless, undying, constant, perpetual, deep-rooted, durable, strong, indestructible. OPPOSITE: transient.

lastly *adv* finally, ultimately, in conclusion, to sum up. OPPOSITE: firstly.

latch *noun* fastening, catch, lock, bolt, bar, hook, hasp.
» *verb* fasten, secure, lock, bolt, bar.
latch on understand, comprehend, realize, twig (*inf*).

late *adj* **1** (*the train was late*) unpunctual, delayed, tardy, belated, overdue, behind, behind schedule, behind time, slow. OPPOSITE: early. **2** (*late news*) recent, up-to-date, up-to-the-minute, current, fresh, new. OPPOSITE: old. **3** (*his late wife*) dead, deceased, departed, defunct. OPPOSITE: living. **4** (*the late prime minister*) former, ex-, previous, preceding, past, old. OPPOSITE: current.
» *adv* behind, behind schedule, behind time, unpunctually, tardily, belatedly. OPPOSITE: early.
of late lately, recently, latterly, in recent times.

lately *adv* recently, latterly, of late, in recent times.

latent *adj* potential, dormant, quiescent, inactive, unrealized, undeveloped, hidden, concealed, covert, secret, unseen, invisible, tacit, implicit. OPPOSITE: conspicuous.

later *adv* after, afterwards, subsequently, by and by, in a while. OPPOSITE: sooner.
» *adj* subsequent, succeeding, following, next. OPPOSITE: earlier.

lateral *adj* side, sideward, sideways, sidelong, indirect, oblique.

latest *adj* most recent, newest, current, up-to-date, up-to-the-minute, modern, fashionable, in (*inf*).

lather *noun* **1** (*rub the lather into the carpet*) suds, foam, froth, bubbles. **2** (*in a lather about the wedding*) fuss, fluster, dither, fever, state (*inf*), flap (*inf*), tizzy (*inf*).
» *verb* foam, froth.

latitude *noun* freedom, liberty, laxity, indulgence, licence, carte blanche, leeway, scope, range, room, space. OPPOSITE: restriction.

latter *adj* **1** (*the latter method is better*) second, last-mentioned. OPPOSITE: former. **2** (*during the latter part of her career*) later, final, last, closing, concluding, end. OPPOSITE: earlier. **3** (*in latter times*) latest, recent, modern. OPPOSITE: earliest.

latterly *adv* recently, lately, of late, in recent times. OPPOSITE: formerly.

lattice *noun* trellis, network, fretwork, openwork, tracery, mesh, web, grid, grille, grating.

laud *verb* praise, extol, eulogize, panegyrize, hail, acclaim, applaud, celebrate, honour, exalt, glorify, magnify, worship, revere, venerate. OPPOSITE: decry.

laudable *adj* praiseworthy, commendable, meritorious, deserving, admirable, estimable, creditable, worthy. OPPOSITE: blameworthy.

laugh *verb* giggle, chuckle, snigger, titter, chortle, guffaw, hoot, roar, split one's sides (*inf*), crease up (*inf*), be in stitches (*inf*), fall about (*inf*), be rolling in the aisles (*inf*). OPPOSITE: cry.
➤ *noun* **1** (*'OK,' she said with a laugh*) giggle, chuckle, snigger, titter, chortle, guffaw. OPPOSITE: sob. **2** (*he's such a laugh*) comic, comedian, joker, wag, wit, clown, hoot (*inf*), scream (*inf*), card (*inf*), caution (*inf*). **3** (*we did it for a laugh*) joke, jest, prank, trick, lark, fun, sport, play, mischief.

laugh at mock, ridicule, make fun of, poke fun at, deride, sneer at, jeer at, scoff at, taunt, tease.

laugh off belittle, minimize, play down, make light of, pooh-pooh (*inf*), shrug off, brush aside, ignore, disregard, discount, rule out.

laughable *adj* **1** (*their latest offer is laughable*) ludicrous, ridiculous, absurd, preposterous, outrageous, derisory, risible. OPPOSITE: reasonable. **2** (*the laughable antics of the clowns*) funny, amusing, comic, comical, droll, humorous, farcical, entertaining, hilarious, uproarious, side-splitting (*inf*). OPPOSITE: serious.

laughter *noun* laughing, giggling, chuckling, sniggering, tittering, chortling, mirth, merriment, hilarity, fun, amusement, entertainment. OPPOSITE: crying.

launch *verb* **1** (*launch a rocket*) propel, send off, dispatch, move, set in motion, set afloat, fire, discharge, hurl, cast, throw. **2** (*launch a campaign*) begin, start, commence, initiate, inaugurate, institute, establish, found. OPPOSITE: terminate.

launder *verb* wash, clean, dry-clean, iron, press.

laundry *noun* **1** (*sort the laundry*) wash, washing, clothes, linen, cleaning, dry-cleaning. **2** (*the local laundry*) launderette, washhouse, cleaner's, dry-cleaner's.

lavatory *noun* toilet, WC, loo (*inf*), bog (*inf*), bathroom, cloakroom, public convenience, ladies (*inf*), gents (*inf*), privy, latrine.

lavish *adj* **1** (*a lavish supply*) abundant, plentiful, profuse, copious, ample, prolific. OPPOSITE: scant. **2** (*a lavish display*) sumptuous, opulent, rich, lush, luxuriant, showy. **3** (*lavish in his spending*) extravagant, prodigal, wasteful, improvident, thriftless, wild, immoderate, intemperate, excessive. OPPOSITE: thrifty. **4** (*lavish with her praise*) generous, liberal, unstinting, open-handed, bountiful, munificent, free, effusive, fulsome. OPPOSITE: mean.
➤ *verb* shower, pour, heap, waste, squander, dissipate.

law *noun* **1** (*break the law*) statute, rule, regulation, decree, edict, enactment, ordinance, order, command, directive, direction, instruction, act, code, charter, constitution. **2** (*the laws of nature*) principle, formula, rule, canon, tenet, doctrine, precept, axiom, maxim, truth, standard, criterion. **3** (*a court of law*)

jurisprudence, legislation, litigation. **4** (*the law arrived on the scene*) police, cops (*inf*), fuzz (*inf*), bill (*inf*), filth (*sl*), pigs (*sl*).

law-abiding *adj* honest, upright, upstanding, good, virtuous, decent, righteous, honourable, obedient, dutiful, lawful, peaceful, orderly. OPPOSITE: criminal.

lawful *adj* legal, licit, legitimate, constitutional, rightful, right, proper, just, valid, permissible, allowable. OPPOSITE: unlawful.

lawless *adj* **1** (*a lawless state*) anarchic, ungoverned, unruly, disorderly, wild, chaotic, riotous, rebellious, insubordinate, revolutionary, mutinous, seditious, insurgent, insurrectionary. OPPOSITE: law-abiding. **2** (*lawless behaviour*) unlawful, illegal, illicit, illegitimate, criminal, felonious, wrong. OPPOSITE: lawful

lawsuit *noun* litigation, suit, action, case, proceedings, cause, dispute, prosecution, trial.

lawyer *noun* solicitor, barrister, counsel, advocate, attorney.

lax *adj* **1** (*lax about security*) loose, slack, negligent, neglectful, remiss, permissive, lenient, tolerant, indulgent, casual, laid-back (*inf*), easygoing (*inf*). OPPOSITE: strict. **2** (*lax ideas*) imprecise, inexact, inaccurate, broad, general, nonspecific, vague. OPPOSITE: precise. **3** (*lax muscles*) limp, flaccid, flabby, slack. OPPOSITE: firm.

laxative *noun* purgative, cathartic, aperient.

laxity *noun* laxness, looseness, slackness, negligence, neglect, freedom, latitude, permissiveness, indulgence, licence. OPPOSITE: strictness.

lay[1] *verb* **1** (*lay the rug on the floor*) put, place, set down, deposit, spread, rest, settle, lodge, plant. OPPOSITE: remove. **2** (*lay the cutlery on the table*) arrange, dispose, position, locate, set out, lay out. **3** (*laid charges against him*) present, put forward, advance, bring, submit, lodge. OPPOSITE: withdraw. **4** (*laid the blame on her*) attribute, ascribe, assign, allot, allocate, impute, charge. **5** (*a carefully laid plan*) prepare, devise, contrive, work out, hatch, concoct, design, make. **6** (*lay £50 on the favourite*) bet, wager, gamble, stake, risk, hazard. **7** (*lay their suspicions*) suppress, allay, assuage, ease, alleviate, quiet, still, calm, appease, pacify. OPPOSITE: arouse. **8** (*laid his friend's wife*) have sex with, make love to, copulate with, sleep with, go to bed with, bed (*inf*), shag (*sl*), bonk (*sl*), screw (*sl*), fuck (*sl*).

lay aside **1** (*laid the goods aside*) put aside, set aside, keep, save, store. **2** (*laid my fears aside*) cast aside, abandon, forsake, discard, reject, dismiss, forget.

lay bare uncover, expose, show, exhibit, reveal, disclose, divulge, unveil, unmask. OPPOSITE: conceal.

lay down **1** (*laid down our arms*) give up, surrender, relinquish, yield, hand over. OPPOSITE: take up. **2** (*laid down in the contract*) stipulate, set down, formulate, ordain, prescribe, state, assert.

lay in collect, amass, accumulate, store, hoard, stockpile.

lay into attack, assail, set about, set upon, pitch into, lambaste.

lay off **1** (*lay off staff*) discharge, dismiss, let go, make redundant, sack (*inf*), fire (*inf*). **2** (*lay off smoking*) stop, leave off, desist from, refrain from, give up, quit (*inf*).

lay on provide, supply, furnish, give, organize.

lay out 1 (*lay out the exhibits*) set out, arrange, dispose, plan, design, display, spread out. **2** (*lay out £100*) spend, pay, disburse, expend, contribute, shell out (*inf*), fork out (*inf*). **3** (*laid out with a single blow*) knock down, fell, floor, knock out, KO (*inf*).

lay waste destroy, raze, level, devastate, ravage, ruin, despoil, sack, pillage.

lay[2] *adj* **1** (*a lay preacher*) laic, laical, secular, nonclerical. OPPOSITE: ordained. **2** (*for the lay user*) amateur, nonprofessional, nonspecialist, dilettante. OPPOSITE: expert.

layabout *noun* good-for-nothing, ne'er-do-well, wastrel, idler, loafer, lounger, sluggard, skiver (*inf*).

layer *noun* **1** (*a layer of coal*) stratum, bed, seam, vein, band, ply, thickness, tier, row. **2** (*a layer of dust*) cover, covering, coat, coating, film, blanket.

laze *verb* idle, loaf, lounge, loll about, kill time, waste time. OPPOSITE: work.

lazy *adj* slothful, idle, indolent, slack, workshy, inactive, inert, sluggish, torpid, lethargic, slow, languid, languorous. OPPOSITE: industrious.

lead *verb* **1** (*led us to the exit*) guide, conduct, precede, show, escort, convoy, usher, marshal, pilot, steer. OPPOSITE: follow. **2** (*lead an organization*) head, rule, govern, preside over, command, direct, supervise, oversee. **3** (*led me to believe it was possible*) cause, move, prompt, influence, induce, persuade, incline, dispose. **4** (*lead the field*) outstrip, outrun, outdistance, outdo, surpass, excel, transcend, outshine, eclipse. **5** (*lead a lonely life*) pass, spend, live, have, experience, undergo.

lead on entice, lure, seduce, tempt, tantalize, beguile, deceive, delude, dupe, hoodwink, string along (*inf*).

lead to cause, produce, result in, bring on, provoke, contribute to.

‹ *noun* **1** (*in the lead*) first place, front, forefront, van, vanguard. OPPOSITE: rear. **2** (*take the lead*) priority, precedence, supremacy, edge, advantage, initiative. **3** (*follow their lead*) leadership, direction, guidance, example, model, pattern. **4** (*gave the police a few leads*) clue, hint, tip, suggestion, guide, indication, pointer, tip-off (*inf*). **5** (*playing the lead*) principal part, leading role, starring part, title role. **6** (*the dog's lead*) leash, rein, tether, chain.

‹ *adj* leading, principal, main, chief, primary, first, foremost. OPPOSITE: last.

leaden *adj* **1** (*leaden movements*) heavy, weighty, burdensome, laboured, stiff, wooden, sluggish, torpid, lifeless, spiritless. OPPOSITE: light. **2** (*under a leaden sky*) grey, dark, gloomy, dreary, overcast, cloudy, lowering, oppressive. OPPOSITE: bright.

leader *noun* **1** (*the leader of the party*) head, chief, ruler, governor, director, manager, boss (*inf*), commander, captain, skipper, principal, number one (*inf*). OPPOSITE: follower. **2** (*follow the leader*) guide, usher, escort, courier. **3** (*a leader in the field*) pioneer, trailblazer, groundbreaker, pathfinder, originator, innovator, front-runner, pacemaker.

leading *adj* principal, main, chief, primary, first, foremost, front, supreme, paramount, best, greatest,

highest, ruling, governing, directing, commanding. OPPOSITE: subordinate.

leaf *noun* **1** (*the leaves of a plant*) bract, frond, needle, pad. **2** (*the leaves of a book*) page, sheet, folio.

‹ *verb* flick, flip, skim, browse, thumb.

leaflet *noun* booklet, brochure, pamphlet, handout, handbill, circular, flyer.

league *noun* **1** (*join a league*) association, federation, confederation, confederacy, alliance, coalition, consortium, combine, syndicate, cartel, union, guild, fellowship, partnership, band, group. **2** (*in a different league from the rest*) class, category, group, level.

in league collaborating, cooperating, hand in glove (*inf*), in collusion, in cahoots (*inf*).

‹ *verb* associate, federate, confederate, ally, unite, amalgamate, combine, collaborate, join forces, band together. OPPOSITE: disband.

leak *verb* **1** (*petrol leaking from the tank*) seep, ooze, exude, drip, trickle, escape. **2** (*leak information*) divulge, disclose, reveal, expose, make public, pass on, give away, let slip. OPPOSITE: conceal.

‹ *noun* **1** (*a leak in the bucket*) crack, split, fissure, chink, opening, hole, puncture. **2** (*a gas leak*) leakage, seepage, oozing, drip, trickle, escape, discharge.

lean[1] *verb* **1** (*lean your head on my shoulder*) rest, recline, repose. **2** (*lean to the right*) bend, slant, slope, tilt, list, heel, incline, tend.

lean on depend on, rely on, count on, trust, have faith in.

lean[2] *adj* **1** (*a lean dog*) thin, slender, slim, spare, skinny, scrawny, scraggy, lanky, bony, angular, gaunt, emaciated. OPPOSITE: fat. **2** (*a lean harvest*) meagre, scanty, sparse, poor, barren, unproductive, unfruitful. OPPOSITE: rich.

leaning *noun* tendency, inclination, propensity, disposition, bent, bias, prejudice, partiality, liking, predilection, proclivity, penchant.

leap *verb* **1** (*leap for joy*) jump, bound, spring, bounce, hop, skip, caper, cavort, gambol, frisk, frolic. **2** (*leap the hurdle*) vault, clear, sail over, jump over, bound over, spring over. **3** (*prices have leapt*) surge, escalate, mount, soar, shoot up, rocket, skyrocket. OPPOSITE: plummet.

‹ *noun* **1** (*cleared the fence with a leap*) jump, bound, spring, vault, hop, skip, caper, frolic. **2** (*a leap in profits*) sudden rise, rapid increase, escalation, upsurge, upswing. OPPOSITE: dive.

by leaps and bounds rapidly, swiftly, quickly, speedily. OPPOSITE: gradually.

learn *verb* **1** (*learn a foreign language*) master, grasp, comprehend, understand, study, take in, absorb, assimilate, acquire, pick up, glean, gather. **2** (*learning their lines*) memorize, commit to memory, get off pat. OPPOSITE: forget. **3** (*he learned that she was leaving*) discover, find out, hear, get wind of, ascertain, determine, detect, perceive.

learned *adj* scholarly, erudite, lettered, literate, well-read, well-versed, well-informed, academic, intellectual, highbrow, bookish. OPPOSITE: ignorant.

learner *noun* novice, beginner, tyro, neophyte, apprentice, trainee, student, pupil. OPPOSITE: expert.

learning *noun* scholarship, erudition, letters, education, schooling, instruction, tuition, knowledge, information, lore, study, research. OPPOSITE: ignorance.

lease *verb* let, rent, hire, charter.

leash *noun* **1** (*a dog's leash*) lead, rein, tether, chain. **2** (*a tight leash on spending*) check, curb, control, restraint.

least *adj* smallest, slightest, lowest, fewest, minimum. OPPOSITE: most.

leave[1] *verb* **1** (*they left at noon*) depart, go, exit, quit (*inf*), make tracks (*inf*), push off (*inf*), shove off (*inf*), set out, set off, retire, withdraw, pull out, disappear, decamp, do a bunk (*inf*). OPPOSITE: arrive. **2** (*I'll never leave you*) abandon, desert, forsake, run out on, ditch (*inf*). **3** (*left her job*) renounce, relinquish, abandon, give up, quit (*inf*). OPPOSITE: keep. **4** (*left their homes*) vacate, evacuate, depart from. OPPOSITE: stay. **5** (*left his briefcase on the train*) leave behind, forget, mislay. OPPOSITE: remember. **6** (*leave money to charity*) bequeath, will, endow, make over, transfer, convey, devise. OPPOSITE: inherit. **7** (*leave the heavy work to us*) allot, consign, commit, entrust, hand over.

leave off stop, cease, discontinue, desist from, refrain from, quit (*inf*), give over (*inf*). OPPOSITE: continue.

leave out omit, exclude, except, miss out, overlook, ignore, disregard, reject. OPPOSITE: include.

leave[2] *noun* **1** (*leave to use the car*) permission, consent, sanction, authorization, dispensation, concession, indulgence, liberty, freedom, licence. OPPOSITE: prohibition. **2** (*three days' leave*) holiday, vacation, time off, break, furlough, sabbatical. OPPOSITE: work.

take one's leave say goodbye, say farewell, part, depart, retire, withdraw. OPPOSITE: greet.

leavings *pl noun* scraps, leftovers, remnants, remains, residue, dregs, dross, waste, refuse, rubbish.

lecherous *adj* lustful, lewd, lascivious, libidinous, randy (*inf*), horny (*inf*), concupiscent, prurient, salacious, licentious, degenerate, depraved, dissolute, dissipated, wanton, unchaste, promiscuous, voluptuous, sensual, carnal. OPPOSITE: chaste.

lecture *noun* **1** (*a lecture on industrial archaeology*) talk, speech, address, lesson, discourse, disquisition, harangue, sermon, homily. **2** (*gave me a lecture about borrowing money*) reprimand, rebuke, reproof, scolding, telling-off (*inf*), dressing-down (*inf*), tirade, diatribe.
➤ *verb* **1** (*lecturing at university*) teach, instruct, tutor. OPPOSITE: study. **2** (*lecturing on the environment*) talk, speak, discourse, hold forth, expound, spout (*inf*). **3** (*lectured us for misbehaving*) reprimand, rebuke, reprove, scold, chide, berate, upbraid, tell off (*inf*), haul over the coals (*inf*).

ledge *noun* shelf, mantelpiece, sill, step, ridge, projection, overhang.

lee *noun* shelter, protection, cover, refuge.

leech *noun* parasite, bloodsucker, hanger-on, freeloader (*inf*), sponger (*inf*), scrounger (*inf*).

leer *verb* stare, watch, eye, ogle, wink, smirk, grin.

lees *pl noun* dregs, residue, grounds, sediment, deposit, precipitate.

leeway *noun* scope, room, space, latitude, play, slack, margin.

left-handed *adj* **1** (*a left-handed person*) sinistral, cack-handed (*inf*), southpaw (*inf*). OPPOSITE: right-handed. **2** (*a left-handed compliment*) ambiguous, equivocal, double-edged, indirect, enigmatic, cryptic. OPPOSITE: direct.

leftover *adj* surplus, excess, remaining, unused, unwanted.

leg *noun* **1** (*insects have six legs*) limb, member. **2** (*he's broken his leg*) shank, pin (*inf*), stump (*inf*), peg (*inf*). **3** (*a stool with three legs*) upright, support, prop. **4** (*the next leg of the journey*) part, section, segment, portion, stage, lap, stretch.

a leg up help, assistance, aid, support, boost, advancement.

leg it walk, go on foot, hoof it (*inf*), run, hurry, hightail it (*inf*), hotfoot it (*inf*).

on one's last legs worn out, exhausted, all in (*inf*), failing, dying, at death's door (*inf*).

legacy *noun* bequest, inheritance, gift, endowment, devise, heritage, patrimony.

legal *adj* **1** (*legal practices*) lawful, licit, legitimate, constitutional, statutory, permissible, allowable, admissible, acceptable, authorized, sanctioned, above-board, legit (*inf*), proper, right, rightful, valid. OPPOSITE: illegal. **2** (*advised us on legal matters*) judicial, juridical, forensic.

legalize *verb* decriminalize, legitimize, legitimatize, legitimate, authorize, sanction, ratify, warrant, license, permit, allow, admit, accept. OPPOSITE: veto.

legate *noun* envoy, ambassador, emissary, nuncio, plenipotentiary, deputy, delegate, representative.

legation *noun* embassy, consulate, ministry, mission, deputation, delegation.

legend *noun* **1** (*African legends*) myth, tale, story, fable, romance, epic, saga. OPPOSITE: history. **2** (*the legend below the picture*) caption, inscription, motto, device, key, explanation.

legendary *adj* **1** (*the legendary exploits of the gods*) mythical, fictitious, fictional, fabled, storied, traditional, fabulous, fanciful, make-believe, story-book, romantic, heroic. OPPOSITE: historical. **2** (*legendary sporting figures*) famous, renowned, celebrated, illustrious, great, immortal. OPPOSITE: unknown.

legible *adj* readable, decipherable, clear, plain, neat, tidy. OPPOSITE: illegible.

legion *noun* **1** (*soldiers of the legion*) army, brigade, regiment, troop, division, unit. **2** (*legions of sightseers*) crowd, mob, throng, multitude, host, horde, mass, swarm, drove, myriad.
➤ *adj* numerous, many, myriad, countless, numberless, innumerable. OPPOSITE: few.

legislation *noun* **1** (*powers of legislation*) lawmaking, enactment, codification. **2** (*introduce new legislation*) law, statute, act, bill, rule, ruling, ordinance, decree, measure, code, charter, constitution.

legislature *noun* assembly, house, chamber, parliament, congress, senate.

legitimate *adj* **1** (*legitimate practices*) legal, lawful, licit, constitutional, statutory, authorized, sanctioned, permissible, allowable, admissible, acceptable, above-board, legit (*inf*). OPPOSITE: illegal. **2** (*the legitimate* *claimant*) genuine, authentic, real, true, proper, rightful, recognized, approved. OPPOSITE: illegitimate. **3** (*a legitimate deduction*) reasonable, logical, rational, sound, valid, justifiable, well-founded, plausible, correct. OPPOSITE: invalid.

leisure *noun* rest, ease, relaxation, recreation, freedom, liberty, free time, spare time, time off, holiday, vacation, break, respite, breathing space. OPPOSITE: work.
at one's leisure unhurriedly, at one's convenience, in one's spare time, when one gets round to it.

leisurely *adj* unhurried, slow, lingering, lazy, relaxed, comfortable, easy, gentle. OPPOSITE: hasty.

lend *verb* **1** (*lend money*) loan, advance. OPPOSITE: borrow. **2** (*lend force to the argument*) give, grant, bestow, impart, provide, supply, furnish, contribute, add. OPPOSITE: detract.
lend a hand help, help out, assist, aid, give a hand, pitch in (*inf*).
lend itself to be suitable for, be appropriate for, be adaptable to.

length *noun* **1** (*the length of the garden*) extent, reach, span, stretch, measure, distance. OPPOSITE: breadth. **2** (*for a considerable length of time*) span, stretch, period, term, duration. **3** (*a length of rope*) piece, portion, section, segment, measure.
at length 1 (*described it at length*) in detail, in depth, in full, fully, thoroughly, exhaustively. **2** (*spoke at length*) interminably, endlessly, on and on, for ages, for hours. OPPOSITE: briefly. **3** (*at length we persuaded her*) eventually, finally, ultimately, at last, in the end.

lengthen *verb* stretch, extend, elongate, prolong, protract, draw out, increase. OPPOSITE: shorten.

lengthy *adj* **1** (*after lengthy negotiations*) long, extended, prolonged, protracted, long-drawn-out. OPPOSITE: brief. **2** (*a lengthy account*) long-winded, verbose, wordy, prolix, diffuse, rambling, interminable, endless. OPPOSITE: short.

lenient *adj* tolerant, indulgent, forbearing, forgiving, clement, merciful, sparing, mild, gentle, moderate, kind, soft-hearted, tender, compassionate, generous, liberal, magnanimous. OPPOSITE: strict.

lenitive *adj* soothing, palliative, alleviating, assuaging, easing, emollient, balmy. OPPOSITE: irritant.

leper *noun* outcast, pariah, untouchable, undesirable, persona non grata.

lesbian *noun* homosexual, gay, lezzy (*inf*), dyke (*sl*), sapphist, tribade.
➤ *adj* homosexual, gay, butch (*inf*), dykey (*sl*), sapphic, tribadic.

lesion *noun* wound, injury, cut, scratch, abrasion, sore, trauma.

less *adj* smaller, slighter, fewer, lower, not as much. OPPOSITE: more.

lessen *verb* reduce, diminish, decrease, lower, abate, ease, moderate, subside, decline, dwindle, wane, ebb, shorten, curtail, abridge, contract, shrink, minimize. OPPOSITE: increase.

lesser *adj* smaller, lower, inferior, minor, secondary, subordinate. OPPOSITE: greater.

lesson *noun* **1** (*a biology lesson*) class, period, lecture, tutorial, seminar. **2** (*let that be a lesson to you*) example, model, deterrent, punishment, warning, admonition, reprimand, rebuke, reproof.

lessons *pl noun* **1** (*take dancing lessons*) teaching, instruction, tuition, coaching. **2** (*doing their lessons*) schoolwork, homework, assignments, exercises, drill, practice.

let[1] *verb* **1** (*let me borrow it*) permit, allow, grant, agree to, consent to, sanction, authorize, give the go-ahead to (*inf*), give the green light to (*inf*). OPPOSITE: forbid. **2** (*let the traffic flow more freely*) cause, make, enable. OPPOSITE: prevent. **3** (*let their house*) lease, rent, hire, charter.
let down disappoint, disenchant, disillusion, betray, fail, desert, forsake, abandon, leave in the lurch (*inf*). OPPOSITE: satisfy.
let in admit, allow to enter, give access to, accept, receive, welcome. OPPOSITE: bar.
let off 1 (*the culprit was let off*) excuse, exempt, pardon, forgive, absolve, exonerate, acquit, reprieve, discharge, release. OPPOSITE: punish. **2** (*let off fireworks*) set off, fire, detonate, explode.
let on 1 (*don't let on that you know*) reveal, divulge, make known, tell, let slip, give away, leak (*inf*), spill the beans (*inf*), let the cat out of the bag (*inf*). **2** (*I let on that I didn't care*) pretend, make out, feign, affect, simulate.
let out 1 (*let the animals out*) release, free, liberate, let go, set free, allow to leave. OPPOSITE: confine. **2** (*let out a scream*) utter, emit, produce, give vent to.
let up abate, subside, ease, lessen, diminish, moderate, die down. OPPOSITE: intensify.

let[2] *noun* (*without let or hindrance*) obstruction, obstacle, impediment, restriction, constraint, check.

lethal *adj* fatal, deadly, mortal, murderous, destructive, devastating, dangerous, hazardous, virulent, noxious, poisonous, toxic. OPPOSITE: safe.

lethargic *adj* sluggish, torpid, dull, slow, heavy, sleepy, drowsy, stupefied, inactive, inert, idle, lazy, apathetic, listless. OPPOSITE: energetic.

lethargy *noun* sluggishness, torpor, dullness, slowness, heaviness, sleepiness, drowsiness, somnolence, stupor, narcosis, inactivity, inertia, idleness, laziness, apathy, listlessness, lassitude, languor. OPPOSITE: vitality.

letter *noun* **1** (*a letter from my brother*) note, line, message, communication, dispatch, missive, epistle, reply, answer, acknowledgment. **2** (*in capital letters*) character, symbol, grapheme.
to the letter exactly, precisely, accurately, strictly, literally, verbatim, word for word.

lettered *adj* learned, scholarly, academic, erudite, educated, literate, cultivated, cultured, well-read, literary, intellectual, highbrow. OPPOSITE: ignorant.

letters *pl noun* learning, scholarship, erudition, education, cultivation, culture, literature, humanities, belles-lettres.

level *adj* **1** (*a level surface*) horizontal, plane, flat, even, smooth, uniform, flush, aligned. OPPOSITE: uneven. **2** (*the scores are level*) equal, even, balanced, level-pegging, on a par, neck and neck. OPPOSITE: unequal. **3** (*keep a level head*) cool, calm, collected, composed, self-possessed, serene, tranquil, unruffled, even, equable, balanced, steady, stable.

≫ *verb* **1** (*level the ground*) flatten, smooth, plane. **2** (*level the entire village*) raze, demolish, destroy, devastate, lay waste, knock down, pull down, tear down, bulldoze, flatten. OPPOSITE: build. **3** (*levelled the gun at his head*) direct, aim, point, focus, train. **4** (*I'll level with you*) be honest, be upfront (*inf*), be frank, speak plainly, tell the truth, keep nothing back, come clean (*inf*), put one's cards on the table (*inf*).
≫ *noun* **1** (*park on the level*) horizontal, flat. OPPOSITE: slope. **2** (*a higher level in the company*) position, rank, status, standing, degree, grade, stage, station. **3** (*a lower level of expenditure*) extent, degree, amount, quantity, size, magnitude. **4** (*at different levels*) height, altitude, elevation. **5** (*on different levels*) layer, plane, stratum, floor, storey.
on the level honest, above-board, genuine, bona fide, sincere, open, candid, upfront (*inf*).

lever *noun* **1** (*move the stone with a lever*) bar, crowbar, jemmy. **2** (*operate the machine with a lever*) handle, switch, joystick.
≫ *verb* prise, jemmy, force, move, shift, lift, raise.

leverage *noun* purchase, force, strength, power, weight, pull (*inf*), clout (*inf*).

levity *noun* flippancy, facetiousness, jocularity, fun, humour, light-heartedness, frivolity, triviality, silliness, skittishness, giddiness, flightiness, fickleness, inconstancy, instability, unreliability. OPPOSITE: seriousness.

levy *verb* impose, exact, demand, charge, raise, collect, gather. OPPOSITE: pay.
≫ *noun* **1** (*the levy of taxes*) imposition, exaction, collection, gathering. OPPOSITE: payment. **2** (*pay a levy*) charge, fee, tax, duty, excise, toll, tariff, imposition.

lewd *adj* **1** (*lewd behaviour*) lecherous, lustful, lascivious, libidinous, randy (*inf*), horny (*inf*), concupiscent, prurient, salacious, licentious, degenerate, depraved, dissolute, dissipated, wanton. OPPOSITE: decorous. **2** (*a lewd remark*) obscene, indecent, suggestive, dirty, smutty (*inf*), ribald, bawdy, raunchy (*inf*), gross, crude, vulgar. OPPOSITE: polite.

lexicon *noun* vocabulary, dictionary, wordbook, glossary.

liability *noun* **1** (*admit liability*) responsibility, answerability, accountability, fault, blame, culpability. OPPOSITE: unaccountability. **2** (*financial liabilities*) debt, due, obligation, responsibility, duty. OPPOSITE: asset. **3** (*she would be a liability on such an expedition*) handicap, hindrance, impediment, burden, encumbrance, millstone round one's neck (*inf*), nuisance, disadvantage, drawback, drag (*inf*). OPPOSITE: advantage. **4** (*a liability to leak*) tendency, disposition, inclination, proneness, aptness, likelihood.

liable *adj* **1** (*liable for his actions*) responsible, answerable, accountable, amenable, at fault, blameworthy, culpable. OPPOSITE: unaccountable. **2** (*liable to damage*) subject, susceptible, exposed, open, vulnerable, at risk, in danger. OPPOSITE: invulnerable. **3** (*the roof is liable to leak*) likely, apt, prone, inclined, disposed. OPPOSITE: unlikely.

liaise *verb* communicate, network, interface, collaborate, cooperate, interact.

liaison *noun* **1** (*liaison between departments*) communication, contact, interchange, exchange of information, collaboration, cooperation, connection, link, bond, tie. **2** (*a sexual liaison*) relationship, affair, romance, amour, intrigue, entanglement.

libel *noun* defamation, calumny, slander, traducement, aspersion, slur, obloquy, abuse, mudslinging (*inf*), disparagement, denigration, vilification, smear campaign, muckraking (*inf*). OPPOSITE: eulogy.
≫ *verb* defame, calumniate, slander, traduce, cast aspersions on, throw mud at (*inf*), revile, abuse, badmouth (*inf*), disparage, denigrate, vilify, malign, smear, drag someone's name through the mire (*inf*). OPPOSITE: praise.

libellous *adj* defamatory, calumniatory, slanderous, aspersive, abusive, scurrilous, malicious, false, misrepresentative, disparaging, denigratory. OPPOSITE: complimentary.

liberal *adj* **1** (*liberal attitudes*) progressive, forward-looking, reformist, radical, enlightened, broad-minded, permissive, tolerant, indulgent, open-minded, unbiased, unprejudiced, unbigoted, nonpartisan, catholic, general, wide-ranging, broad-based. OPPOSITE: narrow. **2** (*liberal with her money*) generous, open-handed, bounteous, bountiful, munificent, unstinting, unsparing, unselfish, altruistic, philanthropic, charitable, magnanimous, big-hearted. OPPOSITE: mean. **3** (*a liberal supply*) ample, abundant, plentiful, copious, profuse, lavish, rich, princely, handsome. OPPOSITE: meagre. **4** (*a liberal interpretation*) broad, loose, free, flexible, inexact, imprecise. OPPOSITE: strict.

liberate *verb* free, set free, loose, let go, emancipate, manumit, disenthral, unshackle, unfetter, unchain, release, discharge, deliver, rescue, ransom, redeem. OPPOSITE: confine.

liberation *noun* **1** (*the liberation of the slaves*) freeing, loosing, emancipation, manumission, release, discharge, deliverance, rescue. OPPOSITE: confinement. **2** (*the women's liberation movement*) emancipation, enfranchisement, equality, equal rights, freedom, liberty.

libertine *noun* profligate, debauchee, lecher, rake, roué, playboy, womanizer, philanderer, Don Juan, Casanova. OPPOSITE: ascetic.
≫ *adj* dissolute, profligate, debauched, depraved, corrupt, loose, wanton, abandoned, rakish, womanizing, philandering, licentious, unchaste, immoral. OPPOSITE: chaste.

liberty *noun* **1** (*restrictions on personal liberty*) freedom, independence, autonomy, self-determination. **2** (*gave the prisoners their liberty*) liberation, emancipation, manumission, release, discharge, deliverance. OPPOSITE: servitude. **3** (*have the liberty to do as we please*) right, privilege, dispensation, exemption, immunity, authorization, sanction, permission, leave, licence, latitude, carte blanche, choice, option, free will, volition. **4** (*taking liberties*) familiarity, impertinence, impudence, insolence, disrespect, impropriety, presumptuousness, presumption, forwardness, boldness, audacity. OPPOSITE: respect.
at liberty 1 (*the criminals are still at liberty*) free, loose,

at large, on the loose. OPPOSITE: imprisoned. **2** (*you are at liberty to change your mind*) entitled, allowed, permitted, free.

libidinous *adj* lecherous, lustful, lascivious, randy (*inf*), horny (*inf*), concupiscent, prurient, salacious, carnal, sensual, voluptuous, unchaste, impure, intemperate. OPPOSITE: chaste.

libido *noun* sex drive, sexual appetite, sexual desire, passion, ardour, lust, randiness (*inf*), horniness (*inf*).

licence *noun* **1** (*a pilot's licence*) certificate, permit, warrant, authority, charter, franchise. **2** (*licence to trade*) authorization, sanction, permission, leave, right, entitlement, prerogative, privilege, dispensation, exemption, immunity. OPPOSITE: prohibition. **3** (*giving greater licence to teachers*) liberty, freedom, independence, self-determination, latitude, carte blanche. OPPOSITE: restriction. **4** (*the licence of their behaviour*) abandon, unrestraint, self-indulgence, immoderation, excess, anarchy, unruliness, immorality, decadence, dissipation, debauchery, licentiousness. OPPOSITE: restraint.

license *verb* allow, permit, authorize, warrant, sanction, empower, commission, certify, accredit, charter, franchise. OPPOSITE: prohibit.

licentious *adj* dissolute, debauched, depraved, degenerate, decadent, profligate, abandoned, loose, wanton, promiscuous, unchaste, immoral, libidinous, lecherous, lustful, lascivious, lewd. OPPOSITE: chaste.

lick *verb* **1** (*licking the milk from her fingers*) tongue, wash, clean, taste, lap. **2** (*lick the stamp*) moisten, wet. **3** (*flames licked the branches*) touch, brush, play over, flicker over, dart over, ripple over. **4** (*licked the opposition*) beat, defeat, trounce, thrash (*inf*), hammer (*inf*), conquer, vanquish, overcome, overwhelm, rout.

licking *noun* **1** (*gave the home team a licking*) defeat, trouncing, drubbing, thrashing (*inf*), hammering (*inf*). **2** (*the culprits will get a licking*) beating, flogging, whipping, thrashing, spanking, hiding (*inf*).

lid *noun* top, cap, cover, stopper.

lie[1] *verb* (*lied about his age*) tell untruths, fib (*inf*), bear false witness, perjure oneself, fabricate, invent, dissemble, dissimulate, equivocate, prevaricate, falsify, misrepresent.
   » *noun* untruth, falsehood, fib (*inf*), whopper (*inf*), porky (*inf*), fiction, tale, tall tale (*inf*), story, cock-and-bull story (*inf*), fabrication, invention, dissimulation, equivocation, prevarication, mendacity. OPPOSITE: truth.
give the lie to disprove, contradict, negate, invalidate, refute, rebut. OPPOSITE: corroborate.

lie[2] *verb* **1** (*lie on the bed*) recline, be recumbent, be prostrate, stretch out, sprawl, rest, repose, lounge, loll, laze. OPPOSITE: stand. **2** (*the village lies close to the border*) be, be situated, be located, be found. **3** (*the machinery lay idle*) remain, stay, continue, be. **4** (*the problem lies in underfunding*) consist, inhere, reside, exist.
lie low hide, take cover, go to ground, hole up (*inf*), conceal oneself, keep a low profile, lurk, skulk.

liege *noun* lord, master, chief, leader, superior. OPPOSITE: vassal.

lieu *noun* **in lieu of** instead of, in place of, as an alternative to, as a substitute for.

life *noun* **1** (*loss of life*) being, existence, aliveness, viability, animation. OPPOSITE: death. **2** (*life on other planets*) living things, living beings, flora, fauna. **3** (*for the rest of my life*) lifetime, duration, course, span, days. **4** (*have an easy life*) lifestyle, way of life, existence, circumstances, situation. **5** (*wrote a life of Churchill*) biography, autobiography, memoir, memoirs, history, life story. **6** (*put some life into it*) energy, vigour, verve, animation, liveliness, vivacity, vitality, spirit, sparkle, élan, exuberance, enthusiasm, dynamism, oomph (*inf*), pep (*inf*), zip (*inf*). OPPOSITE: lethargy.

lifeless *adj* **1** (*their lifeless bodies*) dead, deceased, defunct, cold, inanimate, inorganic, inactive, inert. OPPOSITE: living. **2** (*a lifeless performance*) spiritless, dull, flat, insipid, lacklustre, stiff, wooden, lethargic, sluggish, torpid, listless. OPPOSITE: lively. **3** (*lifeless tracts of land*) barren, sterile, uncultivated, bare, empty, uninhabited, unoccupied.

lifelike *adj* realistic, true-to-life, vivid, graphic, photographic, exact, accurate, faithful, authentic.

lift *verb* **1** (*lift the rock*) raise, elevate, hoist, jack, pick up, hold up. OPPOSITE: drop. **2** (*lifted their spirits*) uplift, exalt, buoy up, boost, enhance, improve. OPPOSITE: lower. **3** (*lift the embargo*) revoke, rescind, countermand, annul, cancel, stop, terminate, remove, withdraw. OPPOSITE: impose. **4** (*lifted a paragraph from my article*) copy, crib (*inf*), pirate, plagiarize, borrow, steal, abstract, take. **5** (*the fog lifted*) rise, clear, disperse, dissipate, vanish, disappear. OPPOSITE: fall.
   » *noun* **1** (*go up in the lift*) elevator, hoist, paternoster. **2** (*offered her a lift to the station*) run, drive, ride, transportation. **3** (*the news gave me quite a lift*) boost, stimulus, fillip, pick-me-up, shot in the arm (*inf*).

ligature *noun* bond, tie, link, connection, ligament, band.

light[1] *noun* **1** (*the light of the sun*) illumination, luminosity, luminescence, incandescence, radiance, effulgence, brightness, brilliance, blaze, glare, ray, beam, shaft, glow, flash, glint. OPPOSITE: darkness. **2** (*extinguish the lights*) lamp, lantern, candle, torch, bulb, beacon. **3** (*the light began to fade*) daylight, sunshine, day, daytime. OPPOSITE: night. **4** (*they finally saw the light*) enlightenment, illumination, elucidation, understanding, comprehension, insight, knowledge, awareness. OPPOSITE: mystification. **5** (*a different light on the matter*) aspect, approach, viewpoint, angle, slant, dimension.
   » *adj* **1** (*not light enough to read*) bright, sunny, well-lit, illuminated, luminous, glowing. OPPOSITE: dark. **2** (*a light colour*) pale, pastel, whitish, faded, bleached, fair, blond. OPPOSITE: deep.
   » *verb* **1** (*light the fire*) ignite, kindle, set alight, set fire to. OPPOSITE: extinguish. **2** (*light the room with candles*) illuminate, brighten, lighten, light up. OPPOSITE: darken.
cast/shed/throw light on illuminate, elucidate, explain, clarify, clear up.
in the light of considering, taking into account, bearing in mind, in view of.

light[2] *adj* **1** (*light as a feather*) weightless, airy, buoyant. OPPOSITE: weighty. **2** (*light clothes*) thin, fine, flimsy, delicate, lightweight, insubstantial. OPPOSITE: thick. **3** (*light work*) easy, simple, effortless, undemanding.

OPPOSITE: hard. **4** (*light reading*) amusing, entertaining, diverting, pleasing, frivolous, superficial, trivial. OPPOSITE: serious. **5** (*a light wind*) gentle, soft, weak, faint. OPPOSITE: heavy. **6** (*a light punishment*) slight, inconsiderable, mild, moderate, small, trifling, petty, insignificant. OPPOSITE: severe. **7** (*light on his feet*) agile, nimble, sprightly, spry, lithe, supple, graceful, deft, dexterous. OPPOSITE: clumsy. **8** (*with a light heart*) cheerful, blithe, carefree, happy, joyful, merry, jolly. OPPOSITE: solemn.
➤ *verb* land, settle, alight.
light on come across, find, discover, stumble upon, happen upon, hit upon.

lighten[1] *verb* **1** (*lighten the sky*) illuminate, brighten, light, light up, shine, flash, glow. OPPOSITE: darken. **2** (*lightening the colours*) bleach, whiten, pale, fade. OPPOSITE: deepen.

lighten[2] *verb* **1** (*lighten your load*) lessen, reduce, ease, relieve, alleviate, assuage, disburden, disencumber, unload. OPPOSITE: increase. **2** (*lightened their spirits*) cheer, brighten, gladden, hearten, encourage, buoy up, uplift, revive, perk up. OPPOSITE: depress.

light-headed *adj* faint, dizzy, giddy, vertiginous, woozy (*inf*).

light-hearted *adj* cheerful, blithe, bright, merry, jolly, happy, joyful, carefree, happy-go-lucky, playful, frolicsome, amusing, entertaining. OPPOSITE: serious.

like[1] *adj* similar, alike, resembling, same, identical, allied, akin, related, cognate, corresponding, parallel, analogous, equivalent. OPPOSITE: different.
➤ *noun* equal, peer, match, counterpart, twin, mate, fellow.

like[2] *verb* **1** (*I like classical music*) enjoy, delight in, relish, appreciate, be partial to, care for, be keen on, be fond of, love, adore. OPPOSITE: dislike. **2** (*she seems to like him*) be fond of, have a soft spot for (*inf*), be keen on, fancy, love, adore, admire, esteem, prize, take to, care for, approve of. OPPOSITE: hate. **3** (*do what you like*) prefer, choose, select, wish, want, desire, care.
➤ *noun* liking, preference, partiality, predilection. OPPOSITE: dislike.

likeable *adj* nice, pleasant, agreeable, friendly, amiable, appealing, attractive, pleasing, charming. OPPOSITE: disagreeable.

likelihood *noun* likeliness, possibility, probability, prospect, chance. OPPOSITE: improbability.

likely *adj* **1** (*success seemed likely*) possible, probable, odds-on (*inf*), expected, anticipated, on the cards. OPPOSITE: improbable. **2** (*likely to fail*) liable, apt, inclined, disposed, prone. OPPOSITE: unlikely. **3** (*the most likely explanation*) plausible, convincing, credible, believable, feasible, reasonable, rational, logical, conceivable, imaginable. OPPOSITE: implausible. **4** (*a likely candidate*) promising, hopeful, appropriate, suitable, acceptable, pleasing, agreeable. OPPOSITE: unsuitable.

liken *verb* compare, equate, link, relate, associate, analogize, parallel, juxtapose.

likeness *noun* **1** (*her likeness to her mother*) similarity, resemblance, similitude, sameness, correspondence, analogy. OPPOSITE: dissimilarity. **2** (*a likeness of the emperor*) image, representation, study, picture, portrait, statue, effigy, copy, replica, facsimile, reproduction. **3** (*in the likeness of a bird*) semblance, guise, appearance, form, shape.

likewise *adv* **1** (*they did likewise*) similarly, the same, in like manner, in the same way. OPPOSITE: otherwise. **2** (*admired the house and likewise the garden*) moreover, furthermore, also, too, in addition, besides, into the bargain.

liking *noun* fondness, love, affection, attraction, affinity, partiality, preference, predilection, taste, relish, appreciation, admiration, fancy, inclination, tendency, propensity, weakness, soft spot (*inf*). OPPOSITE: aversion.

lilt *noun* rhythm, inflection, cadence.

limb *noun* **1** (*fractured limbs*) leg, arm, wing, member, appendage, extremity. **2** (*a limb of the tree*) bough, branch, projection, offshoot, spur, extension.
out on a limb isolated, alone, separate, segregated, sequestered, exposed, vulnerable.

limber *adj* lithe, lissom, supple, pliant, flexible, elastic. OPPOSITE: stiff.
➤ *verb* **limber up** warm up, loosen up, exercise, prepare, get ready.

limelight *noun* public eye, attention, notice, recognition, fame, renown, celebrity, stardom, prominence, glare of publicity, spotlight.

limit *noun* **1** (*the northern limit*) boundary, frontier, demarcation line, confine, bound, parameter, border, edge, rim, perimeter, end, termination, cut-off point. **2** (*stretched to the limit*) extreme, extremity, utmost, ultimate, maximum, greatest extent. **3** (*a limit on spending*) restriction, restraint, check, curb, limitation, maximum, ceiling.
➤ *verb* **1** (*limiting their movements*) restrict, restrain, curb, check, confine, control, hinder, hamper, impede. **2** (*limiting our territory*) delimit, demarcate, define, bound, circumscribe, encircle, encompass.

limitation *noun* **1** (*a limitation on the arms race*) restriction, restraint, control, curb, check, block, obstacle. **2** (*the idea has its limitations*) weakness, weak point, defect, flaw, drawback, snag, inadequacy, shortcoming. OPPOSITE: strength.

limited *adj* restricted, restrained, controlled, rationed, qualified, confined, cramped, scanty, meagre, minimal, small, finite, fixed. OPPOSITE: limitless.

limitless *adj* unlimited, illimitable, boundless, unbounded, infinite, endless, unending, never-ending, vast, immense, immeasurable, incalculable, inexhaustible. OPPOSITE: limited.

limp[1] *verb* hobble, shuffle, falter, stumble, stagger, totter.
➤ *noun* hobble, claudication, shuffle, lameness.

limp[2] *adj* flaccid, flabby, soft, flexible, pliant, slack, loose, lax, relaxed, drooping, weak. OPPOSITE: stiff.

limpid *adj* **1** (*limpid water*) clear, transparent, translucent, pellucid, glassy, crystalline. OPPOSITE: opaque. **2** (*limpid prose*) plain, lucid, clear, intelligible, comprehensible, unambiguous. OPPOSITE: incomprehensible. **3** (*a limpid summer's day*) calm, peaceful, serene, tranquil, still, quiet. OPPOSITE: stormy.

line noun **1** (*a line of people*) row, rank, file, queue, column, procession, series, sequence, succession. **2** (*draw a line*) stroke, rule, dash, streak, stripe, band, strip, bar. **3** (*lines on his face*) crease, wrinkle, furrow, groove. **4** (*pull on the line*) string, rope, cord, wire, cable, thread, filament. **5** (*cross the line*) limit, boundary, frontier, border, edge. **6** (*a car with elegant lines*) outline, contour, shape, configuration, silhouette, profile. **7** (*the line of flight*) course, path, track, trajectory, route, direction, way. **8** (*a line of action*) way, method, policy, procedure, system, practice, course, approach. **9** (*follow her line of thought*) direction, tack, drift, trend. **10** (*working in the same line*) occupation, job, business, trade, profession, calling, specialty, field, area, activity, pursuit. **11** (*a new line of toiletries*) brand, make, sort, type, kind, variety. **12** (*born of a noble line*) ancestry, descent, extraction, lineage, family, house, race, stock, breed.
➤ *verb* border, edge, fringe, bound, skirt.
line up 1 (*line up the pictures*) align, range, straighten, arrange, array, order, marshal. **2** (*line up outside the building*) file, queue up, fall in. **3** (*line up a speaker for the meeting*) organize, arrange, prepare, obtain, secure, lay on (*inf*).
on the line at risk, in danger, in jeopardy. OPPOSITE: safe.

lineage noun ancestry, descent, extraction, birth, parentage, family, house, line, race, stock, breed, pedigree, genealogy, offspring, progeny, succession.

lined adj **1** (*lined paper*) ruled, feint, scored, hatched. OPPOSITE: unlined. **2** (*their lined faces*) creased, wrinkled, furrowed. OPPOSITE: smooth.

linger verb **1** (*linger in the bar*) loiter, wait, remain, stay, hang around. OPPOSITE: leave. **2** (*linger over coffee*) lag, dally, dawdle, saunter, take one's time. OPPOSITE: rush. **3** (*we can't afford to linger*) delay, tarry, procrastinate. **4** (*lingering doubts*) persist, continue, endure, survive, remain.

lingerie noun underwear, underclothing, underclothes, undergarments, undies (*inf*), smalls (*inf*).

lingo noun language, tongue, speech, talk, idiom, vernacular, dialect, patois, argot, jargon, terminology.

link verb **1** (*computers linked to the network*) connect, join, couple, unite, tie, bind, fasten, attach, hook up. OPPOSITE: detach. **2** (*the events are not linked*) associate, relate, connect, join. OPPOSITE: separate.
➤ *noun* **1** (*strengthen the link*) connection, joint, coupling, union, tie, bond, fastening, attachment. **2** (*a link in the chain*) part, piece, member, element, constituent, component. **3** (*severed all links with the terrorists*) association, relationship, connection, liaison.

lion-hearted adj brave, courageous, bold, fearless, intrepid, daring, heroic, valiant, valorous, dauntless. OPPOSITE: cowardly.

lip noun **1** (*the lip of the crater*) edge, brim, rim, brink, verge, border, margin. **2** (*I've had enough of her lip!*) impudence, impertinence, insolence, effrontery, cheek (*inf*), sauce (*inf*), rudeness, disrespect, backchat (*inf*). OPPOSITE: politeness.

liquefy verb liquidize, liquesce, melt, thaw, fuse, dissolve, deliquesce. OPPOSITE: solidify.

liquid noun liquor, fluid, juice, solution. OPPOSITE: solid.
➤ *adj* **1** (*liquid wax*) fluid, flowing, running, runny, watery, wet, liquefied, molten, melted, thawed. OPPOSITE: solid. **2** (*liquid tones*) fluent, smooth, flowing, dulcet, mellifluous, sweet, pure, clear. OPPOSITE: harsh.

liquidate verb **1** (*liquidate a debt*) pay, settle, discharge, clear. **2** (*liquidate assets*) sell, cash, realize. **3** (*liquidate a company*) dissolve, break up, disband, terminate, close down, wind up. **4** (*liquidated their enemies*) kill, murder, assassinate, eliminate, do in (*inf*), bump off (*inf*), rub out (*inf*), exterminate, wipe out.

liquidize verb blend, process, purée, crush, pulverize.

list[1] noun (*a list of names*) catalogue, inventory, file, index, directory, roll, register, schedule, table, enumeration, series.
➤ *verb* enumerate, catalogue, file, index, tabulate, record, register, log, enter, write down.

list[2] verb (*the boat was listing*) lean, slant, slope, incline, tilt, tip, heel, cant.

listen verb hark, pay attention, concentrate, attend, hear, give ear, lend an ear, heed, mind, take notice. OPPOSITE: ignore.
listen in eavesdrop, overhear, monitor, tap, bug (*inf*).

listless adj lethargic, languid, languorous, sluggish, torpid, inactive, inert, tired, weary, enervated, debilitated, spiritless, unenthusiastic, apathetic, indifferent. OPPOSITE: energetic.

literal adj verbatim, word-for-word, strict, exact, precise, accurate, close, faithful, true, authentic, genuine, actual, unembellished, unvarnished, unexaggerated, undistorted. OPPOSITE: loose.

literally adv **1** (*translated literally*) verbatim, word for word, to the letter, strictly, exactly, closely, faithfully. OPPOSITE: loosely. **2** (*literally out of my mind with worry*) positively, absolutely, really, truly, actually.

literary adj scholarly, erudite, academic, learned, intellectual, highbrow, lettered, literate, well read.

literate adj educated, schooled, cultivated, cultured, learned, scholarly, erudite, well-read, knowledgeable. OPPOSITE: illiterate.

literature noun **1** (*nineteenth-century French literature*) literary works, books, novels, poetry, plays, essays, letters, writings, publications. **2** (*literature about the company*) printed matter, promotional material, brochures, leaflets, bumf (*inf*), information, data, facts.

lithe adj lissom, limber, supple, pliant, pliable, flexible, elastic, agile, nimble, graceful. OPPOSITE: stiff.

litigation noun lawsuit, action, case, proceedings, dispute, contest.

litigious adj quarrelsome, argumentative, disputatious, contentious, belligerent, pugnacious, combative. OPPOSITE: genial.

litter noun **1** (*throwing litter on the ground*) rubbish, refuse, waste, junk, trash, garbage, debris, detritus. **2** (*clear up the litter in your room*) clutter, mess, untidiness, disorder, disarray, jumble, confusion, shambles (*inf*). OPPOSITE: order. **3** (*a litter of puppies*) brood, young, progeny, offspring, family, issue. **4** (*litter for the animals*) bedding, straw, hay.
➤ *verb* strew, scatter, clutter, mess up, untidy, disarrange, disorder. OPPOSITE: tidy.

little adj **1** (*a little chair*) small, wee (*inf*), tiny, teeny (*inf*), minute, microscopic, short, slight, petite, diminutive, pint-sized (*inf*), miniature, lilliputian, dwarf, pygmy, baby. OPPOSITE: large. **2** (*when I was little*) young, small, baby. OPPOSITE: big. **3** (*in a little while*) short, brief, fleeting, passing, transitory, limited. OPPOSITE: long. **4** (*no little matter*) trivial, trifling, petty, paltry, inconsiderable, slight, minor, insignificant, unimportant, inconsequential. OPPOSITE: major. **5** (*little food*) insufficient, meagre, scant, skimpy, sparse. OPPOSITE: ample.
➤ adv **1** (*little known*) barely, scarcely, hardly, not much. OPPOSITE: much. **2** (*little used*) rarely, seldom, infrequently, not often. OPPOSITE: often.
➤ noun **1** (*add a little*) bit, dash, pinch, drop, spot, trace, hint, touch, trifle, modicum, tad (*inf*), smidgen (*inf*). OPPOSITE: lot. **2** (*wait a little*) moment, second, minute, bit. OPPOSITE: age.
little by little gradually, slowly, progressively, bit by bit, step by step, by degrees. OPPOSITE: rapidly.

liturgy noun service, ceremony, office, sacrament, celebration, observance, rite, ritual, form, usage.

live[1] verb **1** (*won't live much longer*) be, exist, be alive, breathe, survive, remain, endure, abide, persist, continue, last. OPPOSITE: die. **2** (*earn enough to live*) subsist, survive, stay alive, keep body and soul together, support oneself, make ends meet. **3** (*live next door*) reside, dwell, abide, occupy, inhabit, lodge, hang out (*inf*). **4** (*how you live your life*) pass, spend, lead.
live on feed on, eat, live off, subsist on.

live[2] adj **1** (*live animals*) alive, living, breathing, animate, existent, real. OPPOSITE: dead. **2** (*a live broadcast*) unrecorded, unedited. OPPOSITE: prerecorded. **3** (*this wire is live*) connected, charged. OPPOSITE: disconnected. **4** (*live coals*) burning, alight, ignited, glowing, aglow, hot. **5** (*a live bomb*) unexploded, explosive. OPPOSITE: defused. **6** (*debating live issues*) controversial, topical, current, active, important, vital, pressing, burning.

livelihood noun occupation, job, employment, work, living, income, keep, maintenance, support, subsistence, sustenance.

lively adj **1** (*a lively child*) active, energetic, dynamic, vivacious, animated, spirited, sparkling, bouncy, frisky, nimble, agile, spry, sprightly, alert, keen, eager, enthusiastic. OPPOSITE: lethargic. **2** (*a lively pace*) brisk, quick, swift, rapid, vigorous, invigorating. OPPOSITE: leisurely. **3** (*a lively place*) busy, bustling, astir, buzzing, teeming, swarming. OPPOSITE: quiet. **4** (*a lively debate*) animated, spirited, heated, stimulating, exciting, eventful. OPPOSITE: tedious. **5** (*a lively description*) vivid, graphic, colourful, bright, strong, striking, effective. OPPOSITE: dull.

liven verb enliven, animate, invigorate, vitalize, stimulate, rouse, brighten up, cheer up, perk up (*inf*), spice up, hot up (*inf*). OPPOSITE: dull.

livery noun uniform, costume, dress, attire, apparel, habit, garb, regalia, vestments.

livid adj **1** (*he'll be livid when he finds out*) angry, irate, furious, enraged, incensed, infuriated, raging, fuming, seething, beside oneself, mad (*inf*). OPPOSITE: calm. **2** (*their livid faces*) greyish, leaden, ashen, pale, pallid, wan, white, bloodless, ghastly. OPPOSITE: ruddy. **3** (*a livid patch on her arm*) discoloured, bruised, purple, black-and-blue.

living adj **1** (*living beings*) alive, live, breathing, animate, existent. OPPOSITE: dead. **2** (*a living language*) current, contemporary, active, operative, in use, extant, surviving. OPPOSITE: obsolete.
➤ noun keep, maintenance, support, subsistence, sustenance, income, livelihood, work, employment, job, occupation.

load noun **1** (*the ship's load*) cargo, freight, lading, shipment, consignment, burden, charge, contents. **2** (*a heavy load to bear*) burden, onus, encumbrance, weight, charge, duty, responsibility, trouble, worry, strain, pressure, affliction, oppression, cross, millstone. **3** (*a load of money*) lot, load (*inf*), heap (*inf*), pile (*inf*), stack (*inf*).
➤ verb **1** (*load the truck*) fill, pack, lade, freight, charge, heap, pile, stack, stuff, cram. OPPOSITE: empty. **2** (*load them with responsibility*) burden, encumber, weigh down, charge, tax, saddle, oppress, overwhelm. OPPOSITE: relieve. **3** (*load a rifle*) charge, prime. OPPOSITE: unload. **4** (*load the dice*) weight, bias, rig.

loaded adj **1** (*a loaded trolley*) full, filled, heaped, piled, stacked, stuffed, crammed, overflowing. OPPOSITE: empty. **2** (*a loaded rifle*) charged, primed. **3** (*loaded dice*) weighted, biased, rigged. **4** (*her parents are loaded*) rich, wealthy, affluent, well-off, well-heeled (*inf*), rolling in it (*inf*), flush (*inf*), in the money (*inf*). OPPOSITE: poor.

loaf[1] noun **1** (*a loaf of bread*) block, slab, cake, lump, mass. **2** (*use your loaf*) head, brain, mind, common sense, gumption (*inf*).

loaf[2] verb lounge, loll, idle, laze, loiter, hang around, mooch (*inf*), waste time, twiddle one's thumbs.

loafer noun idler, sluggard, lounger, shirker, skiver (*inf*), layabout, good-for-nothing, ne'er-do-well. OPPOSITE: worker.

loan noun advance, credit, lending, usury.
➤ verb lend, advance. OPPOSITE: borrow.

loath adj unwilling, reluctant, disinclined, indisposed, averse, opposed. OPPOSITE: eager.

loathe verb detest, abhor, abominate, execrate, hate, dislike. OPPOSITE: adore.

loathing noun detestation, abhorrence, abomination, execration, odium, hate, hatred, dislike, aversion, antipathy, repugnance, revulsion, disgust. OPPOSITE: love.

loathsome adj detestable, abhorrent, abominable, execrable, odious, hateful, repugnant, repulsive, disgusting, revolting, obnoxious, vile, nasty, offensive. OPPOSITE: delightful.

lob verb throw, fling, hurl, chuck (*inf*), toss, pitch, shy.

lobby noun **1** (*wait in the lobby*) vestibule, anteroom, foyer, entrance, hall, hallway, corridor, passage. **2** (*the anti-abortion lobby*) campaign, pressure group, interest group, ginger group.
➤ verb urge, press, pressure, influence, persuade.
lobby for campaign for, push for, call for, promote.

local adj **1** (*local government*) regional, provincial, parochial, municipal, neighbourhood, community.

OPPOSITE: national. **2** (*local inhabitants*) native, resident. **3** (*the local supermarket*) near, nearby, at hand. **4** (*a local infection*) limited, restricted, confined, contained, specific. OPPOSITE: general.

locality *noun* **1** (*in the locality*) neighbourhood, vicinity, surroundings, environment, district, area, region. **2** (*at a different locality*) location, place, spot, site.

localize *verb* **1** (*localize the rioting*) limit, restrict, contain, confine, circumscribe. **2** (*localize the fault*) locate, find, detect, identify, specify, pinpoint, zero in on.

locate *verb* **1** (*locate the cause of the problem*) find, discover, come across, unearth, ferret out, track down, detect, identify, pinpoint. **2** (*located on the coast*) situate, place, put, set, fix, establish, settle. OPPOSITE: remove.

location *noun* position, situation, whereabouts, place, spot, site, locality, locale, venue, scene, setting.

lock[1] *noun* (*fit locks on all the doors*) bolt, bar, latch, hasp, fastening, catch, padlock.
» *verb* **1** (*lock the gate*) fasten, secure, bolt, bar, latch, padlock. OPPOSITE: unlock. **2** (*firmly locked together*) join, unite, link, engage, interlock, mesh. **3** (*locked in his arms*) clasp, embrace, hug, hold, clutch.
lock up jail, imprison, incarcerate, confine, put behind bars, put under lock and key. OPPOSITE: release.

lock[2] *noun* (*a lock of hair*) tress, curl, ringlet, bunch, tuft, wisp, strand.

locomotion *noun* movement, motion, moving, progress, progression, headway, travel.

lodge *verb* **1** (*lodge with relatives*) live, reside, dwell, stay, sojourn, room, board, put up. **2** (*can't lodge all the students*) accommodate, house, billet, quarter, put up, board, take in, shelter, harbour, entertain. **3** (*lodge a complaint*) submit, put forward, register, file. OPPOSITE: withdraw. **4** (*lodged in her mind*) fix, implant, embed, stick, put, place, set, lay, deposit. OPPOSITE: remove.
» *noun* **1** (*living at the lodge*) gatehouse, cottage, hut, cabin, chalet. **2** (*a lodge of freemasons*) branch, chapter, group, society, association, club, fraternity, sorority. **3** (*animals in their lodges*) den, lair, retreat, shelter.

lodger *noun* boarder, paying guest, tenant. OPPOSITE: landlord.

lodgings *pl noun* accommodation, quarters, rooms, digs (*inf*), abode, residence, dwelling, habitation.

lofty *adj* **1** (*lofty buildings*) high, tall, towering, soaring, elevated, exalted. OPPOSITE: low. **2** (*lofty ideals*) elevated, exalted, noble, grand, imposing, stately, majestic, august, dignified, eminent, illustrious. OPPOSITE: lowly. **3** (*a lofty manner*) arrogant, proud, haughty, high-and-mighty (*inf*), lordly, overbearing, overweening, supercilious, disdainful, condescending, patronizing, snobbish, snooty (*inf*), stuck-up (*inf*), toffee-nosed (*inf*). OPPOSITE: humble.

log *noun* **1** (*burning logs*) branch, trunk, billet, piece, chunk. **2** (*the ship's log*) logbook, record, register, diary, journal, account, tally.
» *verb* **1** (*logging their progress*) record, register, write down, note down, book, chart, tabulate. **2** (*logged 150 miles that week*) cover, travel, do, achieve, attain.

loggerheads *pl noun* **at loggerheads** disagreeing, at variance, at odds, quarrelling, at each other's throats (*inf*), fighting, in conflict, at war, at daggers drawn (*inf*).

logic *noun* reasoning, argumentation, deduction, dialectics, rationale, reason, sense, judgment, coherence.

logical *adj* reasonable, rational, thinking, reasoning, sensible, wise, judicious, reasoned, sound, valid, clear, coherent, consistent. OPPOSITE: illogical.

logistics *pl noun* planning, organization, management, orchestration, coordination, strategy, tactics.

logo *noun* logotype, emblem, device, symbol, sign, trademark, badge, insignia.

loiter *verb* loaf, idle, hang around, skulk, tarry, delay, waste time, linger, dally, dilly-dally (*inf*), dawdle, saunter, lag. OPPOSITE: hurry.

loll *verb* **1** (*lolling on the sofa*) lounge, sprawl, slouch, slump, flop, lie, rest, recline, repose, lean. **2** (*with her head lolling*) hang, dangle, droop, sag, flop, flap.

lone *adj* **1** (*a lone figure*) isolated, separate, single, sole, only, solitary, unaccompanied, alone, lonely, by oneself, on one's own. **2** (*a lone parent*) single, unmarried, divorced, widowed, partnerless.

lonely *adj* **1** (*a lonely existence*) friendless, lonesome, alone, solitary, unaccompanied, by oneself, on one's own, isolated, withdrawn, sequestered, reclusive, abandoned, forsaken, forlorn, bereft, rejected, outcast. OPPOSITE: sociable. **2** (*a lonely beach*) remote, secluded, isolated, out-of-the-way, off the beaten track (*inf*), deserted, unfrequented, unoccupied, uninhabited. OPPOSITE: crowded.

loner *noun* individualist, lone wolf (*inf*), recluse, hermit, solitary.

long[1] *adj* **1** (*a long distance*) lengthy, extensive, extended, stretched, elongated. OPPOSITE: short. **2** (*a long wait*) protracted, prolonged, long-drawn-out, sustained, interminable, endless. OPPOSITE: brief.
before long soon, shortly, in a minute, in a moment, in the near future.

long[2] *verb* yearn, desire, wish, crave, hunger, thirst, pine, hanker, itch, hope, dream.

longing *noun* yearning, desire, wish, urge, lust, craving, hunger, thirst, hankering, itch, yen (*inf*), hope, dream, aspiration.
» *adj* yearning, desirous, wishful, covetous, craving, avid, eager, hopeful, wistful.

long-standing *adj* established, well-established, long-established, old, time-honoured, enduring, abiding, lasting, long-lasting, long-lived, continuing, long-running. OPPOSITE: short-lived.

long-suffering *adj* patient, forbearing, stoical, uncomplaining, resigned, tolerant, indulgent, easygoing (*inf*). OPPOSITE: impatient.

long-winded *adj* long, lengthy, overlong, long-drawn-out, interminable, endless, wordy, verbose, prolix, garrulous, discursive, diffuse, rambling. OPPOSITE: terse.

look *verb* **1** (*looking in our direction*) watch, observe, contemplate, survey, view, regard, see, scrutinize, study, examine, scan, gaze, stare, peer, gawp (*inf*), rubberneck (*inf*), glance, glimpse, peep, peek. **2** (*he looked upset*) seem, appear. **3** (*look in every cupboard*) search, hunt, rummage, forage.

> *noun* **1** (*have a look at the car*) observation, examination, inspection, scrutiny, view, sight, gaze, stare, glance, glimpse, peep, peek, squint (*inf*), shufti (*inf*), butcher's (*inf*), gander (*inf*), dekko (*inf*). **2** (*a look of embarrassment*) appearance, aspect, air, demeanour, manner, expression, face, countenance, features, guise, semblance, facade. **3** (*modelling the new look*) fashion, vogue, trend, style, design, fad, craze, rage.

look after mind, take care of, care for, attend to, tend, nurse, supervise, watch, keep an eye on, protect, guard. OPPOSITE: neglect.

look at watch, observe, eye, focus on, contemplate, study, examine, inspect, eyeball (*inf*), give the once-over (*inf*), get a load of (*inf*). OPPOSITE: ignore.

look back remember, recall, reminisce.

look down on despise, scorn, disdain, hold in contempt, look down one's nose at (*inf*). OPPOSITE: respect.

look for seek, search for, hunt for. OPPOSITE: find.

look forward to await, anticipate, expect, hope for, long for, be unable to wait for, count the days until.

look into investigate, explore, probe, examine, study, research, go into, inquire about, follow up, check out (*inf*).

look like resemble, remind one of, take after, favour (*inf*), be the spitting image of (*inf*), be a dead ringer for (*inf*).

look on regard, consider, think of, judge, deem, hold, count, see, take.

look out beware, watch out, be careful, pay attention.

look over inspect, examine, check, scan, glance at, cast an eye over.

look up 1 (*look up a reference*) search for, track down, find, locate, turn to, refer to, consult. **2** (*look me up when you're in the area*) visit, call on, go and see, drop in on (*inf*). **3** (*things are looking up*) improve, get better, ameliorate, pick up, advance, make progress, make headway. OPPOSITE: deteriorate.

look up to admire, esteem, respect, revere, venerate, worship, idolize, put on a pedestal. OPPOSITE: despise.

look-alike *noun* double, doppelgänger, twin, clone, duplicate, replica, image, spitting image (*inf*), dead ringer (*inf*).

lookout *noun* **1** (*on the lookout*) watch, guard, vigil, qui vive. **2** (*lookouts along the border*) guard, sentry, sentinel, watchtower, observation post. **3** (*it's her own lookout*) business, affair, concern, responsibility, problem, worry, pigeon (*inf*), funeral (*inf*).

loom *verb* **1** (*loomed in the distance*) appear, emerge, materialize, bulk, impend, be imminent, threaten, menace. OPPOSITE: recede. **2** (*looming above us*) tower, rise, soar, hover, overhang, hang over, overshadow, dominate.

loop *noun* circle, ring, hoop, noose, bend, curve, twist, kink, curl, coil, whorl, spiral.

> *verb* encircle, ring, surround, roll, wind, coil, spiral, curl, twist, turn, bend, curve.

loose *adj* **1** (*loose clothing*) baggy, sloppy, hanging, drooping, sagging, floppy, slack, lax, relaxed. OPPOSITE: tight. **2** (*the lions are loose*) free, unconfined, untethered, at large, at liberty, on the loose. OPPOSITE: confined. **3** (*the loose end of the rope*) untied, unfastened, undone,

detached, floating, hanging. OPPOSITE: fastened. **4** (*a loose connection*) insecure, movable, unsteady, wobbly. OPPOSITE: secure. **5** (*a loose description*) vague, indefinite, broad, general, imprecise, inexact. OPPOSITE: precise. **6** (*loose living*) dissolute, debauched, dissipated, degenerate, immoral, unchaste, wanton, abandoned, promiscuous, profligate, libertine, licentious. OPPOSITE: chaste.

> *verb* free, set free, release, let go, let loose, liberate, unleash, unchain, unfasten, untie, undo, detach, disengage, disconnect. OPPOSITE: secure.

at a loose end idle, unoccupied, at leisure, bored, twiddling one's thumbs (*inf*).

loosen *verb* **1** (*loosened my grip*) slacken, relax, ease, moderate, weaken, lessen, reduce, diminish. OPPOSITE: tighten. **2** (*loosened his clothing*) undo, unfasten, unbind, untie, unlace, unbuckle, slacken, let out.

loot *noun* spoils, booty, plunder, haul, swag (*inf*).

> *verb* pillage, plunder, sack, despoil, ravage, ransack, rifle, raid, maraud, rob, steal.

lop *verb* cut, chop, cut off, chop off, sever, detach, crop, dock, prune, clip, trim, truncate, shorten, curtail.

lope *verb* run, stride, spring, bound, lollop, canter, gallop.

lopsided *adj* asymmetrical, unbalanced, uneven, unequal, askew, skew-whiff (*inf*), crooked, awry, aslant, oblique. OPPOSITE: straight.

loquacious *adj* talkative, voluble, garrulous, wordy, verbose, chattering, babbling, gabby (*inf*), chatty, gossipy. OPPOSITE: taciturn.

loquacity *noun* talkativeness, volubility, garrulity, wordiness, verbosity, logorrhoea, verbal diarrhoea (*inf*), chattiness, gift of the gab (*inf*). OPPOSITE: taciturnity.

lord *noun* **1** (*her uncle is a lord*) peer, noble, nobleman, aristocrat, duke, viscount, earl, baron, count. OPPOSITE: commoner. **2** (*obeyed their lord*) master, ruler, governor, monarch, sovereign, king, prince, emperor, commander, leader, chief, superior. **3** (*praise the Lord*) God, Christ, Redeemer, Saviour.

lord it swagger, put on airs, be overbearing.

lord it over domineer, tyrannize, oppress, pull rank on, order around, boss around (*inf*).

lordly *adj* **1** (*a lordly attitude*) haughty, arrogant, proud, overbearing, domineering, bossy (*inf*), imperious, dictatorial, authoritarian, tyrannical, lofty, high-and-mighty (*inf*), condescending, patronizing, supercilious, snooty (*inf*), toffee-nosed (*inf*), stuck-up (*inf*). OPPOSITE: humble. **2** (*with lordly bearing*) noble, dignified, exalted, regal, kingly, princely, majestic, imperial, stately, grand. OPPOSITE: lowly.

lore *noun* knowledge, wisdom, learning, erudition, scholarship, teaching, traditions, beliefs, superstitions, sayings, stories, legends.

lorry *noun* truck, juggernaut, pantechnicon, artic (*inf*), van, pick-up.

lose *verb* **1** (*lose the key*) mislay, misplace, drop, forget. OPPOSITE: find. **2** (*lost my way*) stray from, wander from, depart from. **3** (*lost her chance*) miss, let pass, forfeit, sacrifice, pass up (*inf*). OPPOSITE: take. **4** (*losing valuable time*) waste, squander, dissipate, expend, use up, exhaust. OPPOSITE: gain. **5** (*lose credibility*) stop having, be deprived of, be divested of. **6** (*lost his pursuers*) elude, dodge, escape, evade, throw off, shake off, give the slip, outrun, outstrip, outdistance, leave behind. **7** (*always lose at cards*) be defeated, be beaten, fail, come to grief. OPPOSITE: win.

lose out suffer, miss out, be at a disadvantage, fail to benefit.

loser *noun* runner-up, also-ran, failure, flop (*inf*), nonstarter (*inf*), no-hoper (*inf*).

loss *noun* **1** (*loss of resources*) deprivation, privation, dispossession, forfeiture, sacrifice, waste, dissipation, depletion, exhaustion. OPPOSITE: gain. **2** (*suffered great loss*) disadvantage, detriment, harm, damage, destruction, ruin, death, bereavement. **3** (*losses in war*) casualty, fatality, dead, missing, wounded. **4** (*the team's first loss of the season*) failure, defeat. OPPOSITE: win. **5** (*business losses*) deficit, debit, debt, deficiency, shrinkage. OPPOSITE: profit.

at a loss puzzled, perplexed, baffled, mystified, bewildered, confused, helpless, lost.

lost *adj* **1** (*the lost key*) missing, mislaid, misplaced, disappeared, vanished, gone, irretrievable, irrecoverable. OPPOSITE: found. **2** (*lost time*) wasted, squandered, misused, misspent, forfeited, sacrificed, down the drain (*inf*). OPPOSITE: gained. **3** (*lost at sea*) wrecked, ruined, destroyed, dead, missing. OPPOSITE: saved. **4** (*lost civilizations*) extinct, bygone, past, forgotten. OPPOSITE: extant. **5** (*a lost cause*) hopeless, past hope, irredeemable, irreclaimable, irrecoverable, irretrievable, incorrigible, hardened, damned, fallen. OPPOSITE: recoverable. **6** (*lost in thought*) absorbed, preoccupied, engrossed, rapt, entranced, abstracted, absent, dreamy, faraway. **7** (*you look lost*) bewildered, confused, baffled, perplexed, puzzled, at a loss, disoriented, astray, adrift.

lot *noun* **1** (*a lot of money*) great deal, abundance, load (*inf*), heap (*inf*), pile (*inf*), stack (*inf*). OPPOSITE: bit. **2** (*another lot of letters*) collection, assortment, set, group, batch, bundle, consignment. **3** (*content with her lot*) fate, destiny, fortune, luck, doom. **4** (*decided by lot*) chance, hazard, gamble, lottery. **5** (*divided into lots*) share, portion, part, cut (*inf*), allowance, ration, quota. **6** (*a building lot*) plot, piece, patch, tract.

a lot often, frequently, much, a great deal. OPPOSITE: seldom.

lotion *noun* ointment, cream, balm, salve, emollient, unguent, embrocation, liniment.

lots *pl noun* a great deal, many, much, plenty, masses, loads (*inf*), heaps (*inf*), piles (*inf*), stacks (*inf*), oodles (*inf*), tons (*inf*), miles (*inf*), scores (*inf*). OPPOSITE: few.

lottery *noun* **1** (*win the lottery*) draw, raffle, sweepstake, tombola. **2** (*life is a lottery*) gamble, game of chance, hazard, risk, speculation, venture.

loud *adj* **1** (*a loud scream*) noisy, deafening, ear-splitting, booming, thundering, roaring, blaring, resounding, resonant, sonorous, stentorian, strident, piercing, shrill, raucous, clamorous, vociferous, rowdy, boisterous. OPPOSITE: quiet. **2** (*loud colours*) garish, glaring, gaudy, lurid, flashy, showy, ostentatious, flamboyant, tasteless, vulgar. OPPOSITE: subdued.

lounge *verb* rest, relax, repose, recline, lie, loll, sprawl, slump, loaf, idle, laze. OPPOSITE: work.

➤ *noun* living room, sitting room, drawing room, parlour.

lousy *adj* **1** (*a lousy effort*) poor, bad, inferior, second-rate, third-rate, unsatisfactory, inadequate, incompetent, no-good (*inf*), duff (*inf*), terrible (*inf*), rotten (*inf*), crap (*sl*). OPPOSITE: excellent. **2** (*a lousy trick*) mean, base, low, dirty, contemptible, despicable, rotten (*inf*). **3** (*I feel lousy*) ill, sick, poorly (*inf*), unwell, off colour, seedy, awful (*inf*). OPPOSITE: well.

lout *noun* boor, churl, oaf, dolt, slob (*inf*), brute, yahoo, barbarian, yob (*inf*), lubber, gawk, bumpkin, clodhopper (*inf*).

lovable *adj* adorable, endearing, winning, taking, charming, engaging, sweet, cute, cuddly, appealing, winsome, attractive, likeable. OPPOSITE: detestable.

love *verb* **1** (*I love you*) adore, cherish, hold dear, treasure, prize, be fond of, care for, like, desire, want, fancy (*inf*), be sweet on (*inf*), have a crush on (*inf*), lust after, have the hots for (*sl*), worship, idolize, dote on, think the world of. OPPOSITE: hate. **2** (*she loves skiing*) enjoy, like, adore, delight in, take pleasure in, relish, savour, appreciate, be partial to, have a thing about (*inf*), be mad on (*inf*). OPPOSITE: loathe.

➤ *noun* **1** (*their love for each other*) affection, attachment, fondness, liking, tenderness, warmth, intimacy, care, devotion, adoration, passion, infatuation, ardour, desire, lust. **2** (*his love of chocolate*) enjoyment, delight, relish, appreciation, taste, partiality, inclination, weakness, soft spot. OPPOSITE: hatred. **3** (*take care, my love*) dear, dearest, darling, sweetheart, beloved, pet, angel, treasure.

in love attracted, enamoured, devoted, infatuated, smitten, besotted.

make love have sex, copulate, go to bed, have it off (*sl*), have it away (*sl*), bonk (*sl*), shag (*sl*), screw (*sl*), fuck (*sl*).

lovely *adj* beautiful, attractive, pretty, comely, good-looking, handsome, sweet, charming, enchanting, adorable, exquisite, delightful, pleasing, agreeable, enjoyable, pleasant, nice. OPPOSITE: horrible.

lovemaking *noun* sexual intercourse, intercourse, sex, coition, coitus, copulation, carnal knowledge, having it off (*sl*), having it away (*sl*), nooky (*inf*), rumpy-pumpy (*inf*), bonking (*sl*), shagging (*sl*), intimacy, foreplay, courtship.

lover *noun* **1** (*living with her lover*) boyfriend, girlfriend, suitor, beau, sweetheart, fiancé, fiancée, partner, philanderer, gigolo, toy boy (*inf*), paramour, mistress, bit on the side (*inf*). **2** (*a lover of vintage cars*) admirer, fan, devotee, aficionado, enthusiast, buff (*inf*), freak (*inf*).

loving *adj* affectionate, tender, caring, solicitous, warm-hearted, kind, charitable, sympathetic, fond, devoted, adoring, doting, amorous, passionate.

low[1] *adj* **1** (*a low wall*) short, small, little, shallow, squat, stunted, dwarfish. OPPOSITE: high. **2** (*low land*) flat, low-lying, at sea level, depressed, sunken, deep. OPPOSITE: elevated. **3** (*a low income*) insufficient, inadequate, deficient, paltry, meagre, measly, trifling, scant, sparse. OPPOSITE: ample. **4** (*a low price*) cheap, inexpensive, modest, moderate, reasonable, reduced, cut, bargain, discount. OPPOSITE: exorbitant. **5** (*of low birth*) poor, inferior, lowly, humble, plebeian, lowborn, peasant, common, ordinary, simple, plain, modest, obscure. OPPOSITE: noble. **6** (*of low quality*) inferior, substandard, low-grade, second-rate, mediocre, deficient, lacking, inadequate. OPPOSITE: superior. **7** (*a low trick*) base, abject, mean, contemptible, despicable, vile, nasty, malicious, ignoble, dishonourable, unworthy. OPPOSITE: honourable. **8** (*low humour*) coarse, vulgar, rude, crude, unrefined, indelicate, improper, indecent, obscene, gross. OPPOSITE: refined. **9** (*a low moan*) quiet, soft, gentle, subdued, muted, muffled, hushed. OPPOSITE: loud. **10** (*a low note*) deep, bass, low-pitched, rich, sonorous. OPPOSITE: shrill. **11** (*I feel low*) depressed, blue (*inf*), low-spirited, down in the dumps (*inf*), dejected, despondent, downcast, gloomy, glum, miserable, sad, unhappy, melancholy. OPPOSITE: happy.

low² *verb* moo, bellow.

lowdown *noun* information, intelligence, data, facts, info (*inf*), gen (*inf*), dope (*inf*).

lower¹ *verb* **1** (*lower the curtain*) drop, let fall, let down, take down. OPPOSITE: raise. **2** (*lower the price*) reduce, decrease, diminish, lessen, cut, bring down. OPPOSITE: increase. **3** (*lower the volume*) soften, moderate, turn down, quieten, hush, muffle, mute. **4** (*the wind has lowered*) abate, subside, let up, die down, dwindle, decline. **5** (*I wouldn't lower myself*) abase, degrade, humble, humiliate, demean, belittle, debase, devalue, disgrace, dishonour.
➤ *adj* **1** (*of lower rank*) inferior, lesser, subordinate, secondary, minor, junior. OPPOSITE: superior. **2** (*the lower jaw*) under, nether, bottom. OPPOSITE: upper.

lower² *verb* **1** (*the sky lowered*) lour, darken, blacken, become overcast, threaten, menace. OPPOSITE: brighten. **2** (*he lowered at us*) frown, scowl, glower, glare, look daggers (*inf*), give black looks (*inf*), give dirty looks (*inf*). OPPOSITE: smile.

lowering *adj* louring, dark, black, grey, overcast, cloudy, murky, gloomy, threatening, menacing, ominous. OPPOSITE: bright.

low-key *adj* restrained, muted, subdued, subtle, understated, played down, quiet, soft, toned down.

lowly *adj* humble, lowborn, plebeian, poor, common, ordinary, simple, plain, unpretentious, modest, unassuming, meek, docile, submissive. OPPOSITE: lofty.

loyal *adj* faithful, true, devoted, dedicated, committed, patriotic, constant, unwavering, staunch, steadfast, trusty, dependable, reliable, trustworthy. OPPOSITE: perfidious.

loyalty *noun* allegiance, faithfulness, fidelity, fealty, devotion, duty, patriotism, constancy, staunchness, dependability, reliability. OPPOSITE: infidelity.

lubberly *adj* awkward, clumsy, gauche, maladroit, bungling, ungainly, gawky, clownish, oafish, doltish, loutish, churlish, boorish, uncouth. OPPOSITE: graceful.

lubricate *verb* oil, grease, moisturize, smooth.

lucid *adj* **1** (*a lucid explanation*) clear, plain, distinct, intelligible, comprehensible, understandable, simple, explicit, obvious, evident. OPPOSITE: unintelligible.
2 (*remained lucid right up to her death*) sane, rational, clear-headed, sensible, of sound mind, compos mentis, all there (*inf*). OPPOSITE: confused. **3** (*lucid stars*) bright, shining, radiant, luminous. OPPOSITE: dark. **4** (*lucid*

water) transparent, translucent, pellucid, clear, glassy, crystalline, limpid, pure. OPPOSITE: murky.

luck *noun* **1** (*leave it to luck*) chance, fortune, hazard, accident, fluke, fortuity, serendipity, providence, destiny, fate, lot. OPPOSITE: design. **2** (*wished him luck*) success, prosperity, good luck, good fortune, godsend, blessing, windfall, lucky break (*inf*). OPPOSITE: misfortune.

luckless *adj* unlucky, unfortunate, hapless, out of luck, unhappy, poor, wretched, miserable, unsuccessful, ill-fated, ill-starred, disastrous, calamitous, cursed, doomed, jinxed. OPPOSITE: lucky.

lucky *adj* **1** (*the lucky winner*) fortunate, happy, blessed, charmed, favoured, in luck, jammy (*inf*), successful, prosperous. OPPOSITE: unlucky. **2** (*a lucky omen*) favourable, advantageous, propitious, auspicious, promising, timely, opportune, fortuitous, providential.

lucrative *adj* paying, remunerative, well-paid, gainful, profitable, profit-making, rewarding, productive, fruitful, advantageous, worthwhile, economic, viable. OPPOSITE: unprofitable.

lucre *noun* wealth, riches, money, dosh (*inf*), dough (*inf*), bread (*inf*), profit, gain, yield, proceeds, spoils.

ludicrous *adj* absurd, ridiculous, silly, preposterous, comical, farcical, laughable, risible, droll, funny, humorous, zany, crazy, nonsensical, illogical, incongruous, eccentric, outlandish. OPPOSITE: serious.

lug *verb* **1** (*lugged the cart up the hill*) pull, drag, heave, tug, tow, haul. **2** (*lugging this bag all over town*) carry, bear, tote, hump (*inf*).

luggage *noun* baggage, bags, cases, suitcases, trunks, belongings, effects, things (*inf*), paraphernalia, impedimenta.

lugubrious *adj* mournful, doleful, sombre, funereal, gloomy, dismal, dreary, melancholy, sad, sorrowful, miserable, depressing. OPPOSITE: cheerful.

lukewarm *adj* **1** (*lukewarm water*) tepid, warm, cool, at room temperature. OPPOSITE: cold. **2** (*lukewarm about the idea*) indifferent, uninterested, unresponsive, apathetic, cool, unenthusiastic, half-hearted. OPPOSITE: enthusiastic.

lull *verb* **1** (*lulled our fears*) soothe, assuage, allay, alleviate, relieve, calm, still, quiet, hush, quell, appease, pacify. OPPOSITE: aggravate. **2** (*the storm has lulled*) abate, moderate, diminish, decrease, lessen, wane, ebb, subside, let up, die down, cease. OPPOSITE: increase.
➤ *noun* **1** (*the lull before the storm*) calm, peace, quiet, hush, stillness, tranquillity. **2** (*during a lull in the conversation*) pause, hiatus, break, respite, let-up (*inf*).

lumber¹ *verb* (*I was lumbered with the job*) burden, encumber, saddle, land (*inf*).
➤ *noun* jumble, rubbish, refuse, trash, junk, clutter, odds and ends.

lumber² *verb* (*lumbered along the road*) plod, trudge, stamp, stomp, stump, clump, shamble, shuffle.

lumbering *adj* awkward, clumsy, ungainly, lumpish, oafish, lubberly, clodhopping (*inf*), heavy, ponderous, unwieldy. OPPOSITE: dainty.

luminary *noun* star, leading light, celebrity, famous person, personality, personage, worthy, notable, VIP, bigwig (*inf*), big cheese (*inf*), big shot (*inf*). OPPOSITE: nobody.

luminous *adj* glowing, incandescent, luminescent, phosphorescent, fluorescent, bright, shining, brilliant, dazzling, radiant, effulgent, resplendent, lit, illuminated. OPPOSITE: dark.

lump *noun* **1** (*a lump of wax*) piece, chunk, hunk, ball, nugget, mass, cake, clod, clump, cluster, bunch. **2** (*a lump on his head*) bump, boss, swelling, growth, tumour, tumescence, protuberance, protrusion, bulge.
➤ *verb* collect, gather, cluster, mass, conglomerate, aggregate, accumulate, merge, fuse, coalesce, combine, unite, group, pool.

lumpish *adj* clumsy, awkward, ungainly, dull, obtuse, stupid, bovine, heavy, ponderous, stolid, elephantine, lumbering, oafish, doltish, loutish. OPPOSITE: dainty.

lumpy *adj* bumpy, knobbly, nodose, uneven, granular, clotted. OPPOSITE: smooth.

lunacy *noun* madness, craziness (*inf*), insanity, derangement, dementia, mania, psychosis, idiocy, stupidity, foolishness, folly, silliness, absurdity, senselessness. OPPOSITE: sanity.

lunatic *adj* mad, crazy (*inf*), insane, deranged, demented, manic, psychotic, idiotic, stupid, foolish, silly, absurd, irrational, illogical, senseless, foolhardy, daft (*inf*). OPPOSITE: sane.
➤ *noun* madman, madwoman, maniac, psychopath, nutter (*inf*), loony (*inf*), head case (*inf*), basket case (*inf*).

lunch *noun* luncheon, midday meal, dinner.

lunge *noun* **1** (*a lunge with his sword*) thrust, stab, jab, poke, pass, cut. **2** (*a lunge for the door*) spring, bound, leap, jump, dive, pounce, charge.
➤ *verb* **1** (*lunged at her attacker*) thrust, stab, jab, poke, lash out. **2** (*lunged for the door*) spring, bound, leap, jump, dive, pounce, charge.

lurch *verb* pitch, roll, toss, rock, sway, reel, swerve, veer, weave, stagger, totter.

lure *verb* tempt, entice, attract, draw, allure, decoy, seduce, beguile, inveigle. OPPOSITE: repel.
➤ *noun* temptation, enticement, attraction, draw, magnet, allurement, decoy, bait, carrot (*inf*), seduction, come-on (*inf*). OPPOSITE: repulsion.

lurid *adj* **1** (*a lurid account*) vivid, graphic, explicit, exaggerated, melodramatic, sensational, grisly, gory, gruesome, macabre, shocking, appalling. OPPOSITE: restrained. **2** (*lurid colours*) bright, brilliant, vivid, intense, dazzling, glaring, garish, gaudy. OPPOSITE: dull.

lurk *verb* skulk, prowl, sneak, slink, hide, lie low, lie in wait. OPPOSITE: emerge.

luscious *adj* delicious, delectable, scrumptious (*inf*), yummy (*inf*), tasty, appetizing, mouth-watering, succulent, juicy, fragrant, aromatic, delightful, attractive, beautiful, gorgeous, voluptuous, sensual. OPPOSITE: revolting.

lush *adj* **1** (*lush vegetation*) luxuriant, dense, prolific, rank, abundant, exuberant, flourishing, green, verdant. OPPOSITE: sparse. **2** (*lush furnishings*) luxurious, sumptuous, plush (*inf*), opulent, lavish, extravagant, grand. OPPOSITE: austere. **3** (*lush fruit*) soft, tender, fleshy, pulpy, succulent, juicy, moist, watery. OPPOSITE: dry.

lust *noun* **1** (*unable to satisfy his lust*) libido, sex drive, sexual appetite, sexual desire, passion, ardour, sexuality, sensuality, carnality, lechery, lasciviousness, lewdness, concupiscence, prurience, salacity, randiness (*inf*), horniness (*inf*). OPPOSITE: frigidity. **2** (*her lust for power*) desire, longing, yearning, craving, appetite, hunger, thirst, greed, covetousness, avidity, passion. OPPOSITE: indifference.
➤ *verb* desire, long, yearn, crave, hunger, thirst, covet.

lustful *adj* libidinous, lecherous, lascivious, randy (*inf*), horny (*inf*), concupiscent, prurient, salacious, carnal, sensual, voluptuous, unchaste, impure, intemperate, hot-blooded. OPPOSITE: frigid.

lustre *noun* **1** (*the lustre of the metal*) sheen, gloss, shine, gleam, sparkle, glitter, shimmer, glow, brightness, brilliance, radiance, effulgence, resplendence, splendour. OPPOSITE: dullness. **2** (*add lustre to her reputation*) glory, honour, distinction, credit, prestige, fame, renown, illustriousness.

lustrous *adj* shiny, glossy, polished, burnished, gleaming, sparkling, glittering, shimmering, glowing, bright, brilliant, radiant, effulgent, luminous. OPPOSITE: dull.

lusty *adj* **1** (*a lusty fellow*) strong, robust, sturdy, tough, hardy, healthy, hale, hearty, vigorous, energetic, stalwart, rugged, strapping, brawny. OPPOSITE: weak. **2** (*a lusty cry*) loud, hearty, vigorous, powerful, forceful. OPPOSITE: feeble.

luxuriant *adj* **1** (*a luxuriant head of hair*) lush, dense, thick, profuse, abundant, plentiful, prolific, rank, exuberant, riotous, overgrown. OPPOSITE: sparse. **2** (*luxuriant prose*) elaborate, ornate, fancy, flowery, rococo, baroque, flamboyant, ostentatious, showy. OPPOSITE: simple.

luxuriate *verb* **1** (*holidaymakers luxuriating in the sunshine*) bask, revel, wallow, indulge, enjoy, delight, relish, savour, appreciate, relax, take it easy. **2** (*plants luxuriating in the greenhouse*) flourish, thrive, prosper, sprout, burgeon, mushroom, boom. OPPOSITE: wither.

luxurious *adj* **1** (*luxurious furnishings*) sumptuous, opulent, rich, expensive, ritzy (*inf*), extravagant, lavish, plush (*inf*), grand, splendid, magnificent, comfortable, de luxe. OPPOSITE: austere. **2** (*luxurious habits*) voluptuous, sensual, self-indulgent, epicurean, hedonistic, sybaritic. OPPOSITE: ascetic.

luxury *noun* **1** (*the luxury of their surroundings*) luxuriousness, sumptuousness, opulence, richness, grandeur, splendour, magnificence. OPPOSITE: austerity. **2** (*a life of luxury*) affluence, comfort, ease, pleasure, delight, enjoyment, gratification, self-indulgence, voluptuousness, sensuality, hedonism. OPPOSITE: asceticism. **3** (*the luxury of central heating*) comfort, pleasure, delight, boon, advantage, benefit. OPPOSITE: drawback. **4** (*allowed myself a few luxuries*) indulgence, extravagance, treat, frill, extra. OPPOSITE: essential.

lying *noun* untruthfulness, mendacity, deceit, fibbing (*inf*), dishonesty, duplicity, falsity, perjury, dissimulation, equivocation, prevarication. OPPOSITE: honesty.

➢ *adj* untruthful, mendacious, deceitful, dishonest, false. OPPOSITE: truthful.

lynch *verb* hang, string up (*inf*), execute, put to death, kill, murder.

lyrical *adj* **1** (*a lyrical description*) poetic, expressive, passionate, songlike, musical, melodic. **2** (*waxed lyrical about the experience*) enthusiastic, rhapsodic, effusive, rapturous, ecstatic, euphoric, carried away. OPPOSITE: lukewarm.

lyrics *pl noun* words, libretto, text, book.

macabre *adj* gruesome, grim, grisly, gory, morbid, horrible, frightful, hideous, ghastly, eerie, ghostly, chilling, frightening, terrifying, horrifying, shocking, appalling.

mace *noun* staff, rod, stick, club, cudgel.

macerate *verb* soak, steep, soften, pulp, mash.

machiavellian *adj* crafty, artful, cunning, sly, wily, tricky, devious, shrewd, astute, deceitful, double-dealing, unscrupulous, opportunistic, scheming, designing, intriguing, conniving, treacherous, perfidious.

machinate *verb* plot, plan, scheme, devise, contrive, design, intrigue, connive, conspire.

machination *noun* plot, plan, scheme, device, design, intrigue, conspiracy, trick, ruse, ploy, stratagem, tactic, manoeuvre.

machine *noun* **1** (*a sewing machine*) instrument, tool, device, contrivance, contraption, gadget, mechanism, apparatus, appliance, engine, motor. **2** (*I'm a person, not a machine*) automaton, robot, puppet, zombie. **3** (*a propaganda machine*) agency, organization, structure, system, vehicle, organ.

machinery *noun* **1** (*repair the machinery*) mechanism, gear, tackle, equipment, apparatus, machines, instruments, hardware. **2** (*the machinery of government*) workings, organization, structure, set-up (*inf*), system, channels.

machismo *noun* maleness, masculinity, manliness, virility, toughness, aggressiveness, male chauvinism.

macho *adj* male, masculine, manly, virile, tough, aggressive, brave, strong, chauvinistic, sexist.

macrocosm *noun* universe, cosmos, solar system, creation, structure, totality, entirety. OPPOSITE: microcosm.

mad *adj* **1** (*the mad king was replaced by a regent*) insane, deranged, demented, unbalanced, unhinged, lunatic, manic, psychotic, non compos mentis, not all there

(*inf*), out of one's mind (*inf*), off one's head (*inf*), off one's rocker (*inf*), off one's trolley (*inf*), round the bend (*inf*), crazy (*inf*), daft (*inf*), bonkers (*inf*), crackers (*inf*), nuts (*inf*), barmy (*inf*), batty (*inf*), potty (*inf*), loopy (*inf*), mental (*inf*). OPPOSITE: sane. **2** (*a mad idea*) absurd, ridiculous, ludicrous, foolish, stupid, silly, idiotic, inane, senseless, irrational, illogical, foolhardy, reckless, madcap, imprudent, unwise, harebrained (*inf*). OPPOSITE: sensible. **3** (*a mad rush*) frenzied, frenetic, frantic, wild, unrestrained, uncontrolled, hysterical, delirious, excited. OPPOSITE: calm. **4** (*she'll go mad when she finds out*) angry, enraged, irate, wrathful, furious, incensed, raging, fuming, livid, berserk, ape (*inf*), infuriated, exasperated, irritated, annoyed. OPPOSITE: pleased. **5** (*mad about gardening*) ardent, fervent, impassioned, fanatical, zealous, enthusiastic, avid, eager, keen, infatuated, crazy (*inf*), wild (*inf*). OPPOSITE: indifferent.

like mad madly, wildly, fast, quickly, energetically, ardently, fervently, passionately, intensely, to distraction.

madcap *adj* foolhardy, rash, reckless, daredevil, hasty, impulsive, impetuous, hotheaded, thoughtless, heedless, imprudent, unwise, mad, wild, crazy (*inf*). OPPOSITE: sensible.

madden *verb* **1** (*maddened by their behaviour*) anger, enrage, incense, infuriate, exasperate, make someone's blood boil (*inf*), make someone see red (*inf*), irritate, annoy, aggravate (*inf*), vex, irk, bug (*inf*), inflame, provoke, get someone's back up (*inf*). OPPOSITE: please. **2** (*maddened by pain*) craze, derange, unbalance, unhinge, drive round the bend (*inf*).

madness *noun* **1** (*madness runs in the family*) insanity, derangement, lunacy, dementia, mania, psychosis, aberration, craziness (*inf*), frenzy, hysteria, delirium. OPPOSITE: sanity. **2** (*the madness of the scheme*) absurdity, foolishness, folly, stupidity, silliness, idiocy, inanity, senselessness, foolhardiness, recklessness, imprudence. OPPOSITE: sense. **3** (*her madness at his impertinence*) anger, rage, fury, ire, wrath, exasperation, irritation. OPPOSITE: composure.

maelstrom noun **1** (*sucked into the maelstrom*) whirlpool, vortex, eddy, Charybdis. **2** (*the maelstrom of conflict*) confusion, disorder, upheaval, tumult, turbulence, commotion, pandemonium, bedlam, chaos.

maestro noun master, expert, ace (*inf*), wizard (*inf*), virtuoso, genius.

magazine noun journal, periodical, review, paper, weekly, monthly, glossy (*inf*), publication, booklet, pamphlet, brochure.

magic noun **1** (*using magic to heal the sick*) sorcery, witchcraft, wizardry, necromancy, theurgy, thaumaturgy, the occult, the supernatural, black art, voodoo, enchantment, charm, spell, curse. **2** (*made it disappear by magic*) conjuring, prestidigitation, legerdemain, sleight of hand, illusion, deception, trickery, jiggery-pokery (*inf*). **3** (*the magic of show business*) charm, enchantment, fascination, allure, magnetism, glamour.
> *adj* **1** (*magic power*) magical, mystical, occult, supernatural, miraculous, enchanting, charming, bewitching, spellbinding, hypnotic, irresistible. **2** (*the magic forest*) enchanted, charmed, bewitched, spellbound. **3** (*the concert was magic*) wonderful, marvellous, excellent, great, smashing (*inf*), terrific (*inf*), fantastic (*inf*), brill (*inf*), ace (*inf*), mega (*sl*), wicked (*sl*). OPPOSITE: inferior.

magician noun **1** (*the magician put them under a spell*) sorcerer, wizard, warlock, sorceress, witch, enchantress, necromancer, thaumaturge, miracle-worker. **2** (*the magician at the children's party*) conjurer, illusionist.

magisterial adj authoritative, commanding, imperative, peremptory, bossy (*inf*), dictatorial, despotic, autocratic, authoritarian, domineering, overbearing, high-handed, imperious, lordly, lofty, haughty, arrogant, supercilious. OPPOSITE: humble.

magnanimity noun generosity, bounty, munificence, unselfishness, altruism, philanthropy, charity, kindness, benevolence, mercy, clemency, indulgence, tolerance, graciousness, nobility. OPPOSITE: meanness.

magnanimous adj generous, bountiful, munificent, liberal, open-handed, unselfish, selfless, altruistic, philanthropic, charitable, kind, benevolent, merciful, clement, lenient, indulgent, tolerant, forbearing, big, big-hearted, gracious, noble, high-minded. OPPOSITE: mean.

magnate noun tycoon, baron, mogul, industrialist, entrepreneur, financier, capitalist, fat cat (*inf*), captain of industry, chief, leader, notable, personage, VIP, big shot (*inf*), big wheel (*inf*). OPPOSITE: nobody.

magnetic adj charismatic, charming, enchanting, fascinating, entrancing, attractive, alluring, seductive, inviting, irresistible, compelling, hypnotic, mesmeric.

magnetism noun charisma, charm, fascination, attraction, allure, appeal, draw, pull.

magnificence noun grandeur, majesty, nobility, pomp, splendour, glory, excellence, opulence, luxury.

magnificent adj grand, stately, majestic, regal, noble, august, imposing, striking, impressive, splendid, superb, glorious, sublime, wonderful, marvellous, excellent, fine, exquisite, gorgeous, sumptuous, opulent, rich, lavish, luxurious. OPPOSITE: poor.

magnify verb **1** (*magnify the image*) enlarge, increase, amplify, boost, aggrandize, expand, dilate, inflate, blow up, extend, lengthen, widen, broaden. OPPOSITE: reduce. **2** (*magnify the problem*) intensify, deepen, heighten, exacerbate. **3** (*magnify the risks involved*) exaggerate, overstate, overemphasize, overstress, overplay, embroider, embellish, make a big thing of (*inf*), blow up out of all proportion (*inf*). OPPOSITE: understate.

magniloquence noun grandiloquence, loftiness, rhetoric, bombast, pomposity, fustian.

magniloquent adj grandiloquent, high-flown, lofty, declamatory, rhetorical, bombastic, pompous, fustian, orotund, turgid, overblown, stilted. OPPOSITE: simple.

magnitude noun **1** (*the magnitude of the problem*) greatness, immensity, importance, significance, consequence, weight, moment, note. OPPOSITE: triviality. **2** (*the magnitude of the network*) extent, size, vastness, hugeness, immensity, expanse, amplitude, dimensions, proportions. OPPOSITE: smallness. **3** (*an order of magnitude*) size, measure, proportion, extent, expanse, amplitude, amount, quantity, volume, mass.

maid noun servant, domestic, housemaid, maidservant.

maiden noun girl, lass, miss, wench, maid, young woman, young lady, damsel, virgin, spinster.
> *adj* **1** (*his maiden speech*) first, initial, inaugural, introductory. OPPOSITE: final. **2** (*a maiden aunt*) single, unmarried, unwed, celibate, virgin, spinster. OPPOSITE: married. **3** (*maiden land*) fresh, new, unused, untapped, untrodden, virgin.

maidenly adj modest, demure, decorous, seemly, pure, undefiled, chaste, virginal, vestal, virtuous, gentle, girlish, feminine.

mail noun post, correspondence, letters, packages, parcels.
> *verb* post, send, dispatch, forward.

maim verb disable, incapacitate, cripple, lame, put out of action, wound, injure, hurt, harm, mar, impair, mutilate, disfigure.

main adj **1** (*the main objective*) chief, principal, head, capital, leading, first, foremost, primary, supreme, paramount, pre-eminent, cardinal, prime, essential, vital, indispensable, critical, crucial, pivotal. OPPOSITE: minor. **2** (*by main strength*) sheer, pure, downright, utter, absolute, direct, brute.
> *noun* **1** (*the water main*) pipe, conduit, duct, channel, line, cable. **2** (*with might and main*) strength, might, power, force, energy, vigour. OPPOSITE: weakness.
in the main mainly, chiefly, mostly, for the most part, on the whole, by and large.

mainly adv chiefly, principally, primarily, predominantly, mostly, for the most part, in the main, on the whole, largely, essentially, generally, usually, as a rule. OPPOSITE: partly.

mainspring noun reason, motive, motivation, driving force, cause, source, origin.

mainstay noun prop, support, buttress, backbone, linchpin, anchor, foundation, base.

mainstream *adj* conventional, traditional, orthodox, standard, regular, normal, typical, established, accepted. OPPOSITE: alternative.

maintain *verb* **1** (*maintain a tradition*) keep, retain, conserve, preserve, keep up, continue, carry on, perpetuate, prolong, sustain. OPPOSITE: discontinue. **2** (*maintain the garden*) look after, tend, care for, take care of, keep in good condition, conserve, preserve. OPPOSITE: neglect. **3** (*with a family to maintain*) support, keep, provide for, sustain, feed, nourish, nurture. OPPOSITE: abandon. **4** (*maintained that it was possible*) state, assert, asseverate, aver, affirm, declare, insist, allege, contend, claim, profess, hold. OPPOSITE: deny. **5** (*maintaining their position*) defend, uphold, champion, advocate, back, support, stand by, fight for, justify, vindicate. OPPOSITE: attack.

maintenance *noun* **1** (*the maintenance of a tradition*) conservation, preservation, continuance, continuation, perpetuation, prolongation. OPPOSITE: discontinuation. **2** (*car maintenance*) upkeep, repairs, care, conservation, preservation. OPPOSITE: neglect. **3** (*paying maintenance to his ex-wife*) allowance, alimony, support, keep, subsistence, sustenance.

majestic *adj* regal, royal, kingly, queenly, princely, imperial, august, dignified, noble, lordly, lofty, exalted, grand, stately, magnificent, splendid, glorious, resplendent, impressive, imposing. OPPOSITE: lowly.

majesty *noun* regality, royalty, dignity, nobility, loftiness, grandeur, stateliness, pomp, magnificence, splendour, glory. OPPOSITE: humility.

major *adj* **1** (*the major part*) larger, bigger, greater, main, chief. OPPOSITE: minor. **2** (*a major role*) leading, prime, paramount, key, crucial, vital, important, significant, weighty. OPPOSITE: insignificant. **3** (*a major improvement*) great, considerable, notable, outstanding. OPPOSITE: slight. **4** (*one of our major players*) greatest, best, chief, leading, supreme, pre-eminent. **5** (*major surgery*) serious, complex, complicated, radical.

majority *noun* **1** (*the majority of the population*) bulk, mass, body, preponderance, greater part, greater number, more, most. OPPOSITE: minority. **2** (*until he reaches majority*) adulthood, maturity, seniority, manhood, womanhood, coming of age, age of consent.

make *verb* **1** (*made all the furniture*) create, fabricate, manufacture, produce, turn out, build, construct, assemble, put together, fashion, form, shape, mould, forge. OPPOSITE: destroy. **2** (*make plans*) devise, contrive, concoct, hatch, invent, originate, formulate, frame, write, compose, draw up, prepare. **3** (*make trouble*) cause, effect, bring about, occasion, generate, engender, produce, give rise to. OPPOSITE: undo. **4** (*made a rude gesture*) do, perform, execute, carry out, discharge, accomplish. **5** (*make them go*) force, oblige, require, compel, constrain, coerce, dragoon, drive, urge, impel, induce, prevail upon. OPPOSITE: prevent. **6** (*she was made president*) appoint, elect, nominate, designate, assign, invest, install, ordain. **7** (*making £500 a day*) earn, clear, net, gross, gain, get, obtain, acquire. OPPOSITE: spend. **8** (*two and two makes four*) amount to, add up to, total, come to. **9** (*what is it made of?*) constitute, compose, comprise, form. **10** (*it makes a good seat*) act as, serve as, function as, play the part of, be, represent.
≫ *noun* brand, marque, label, trademark, type, sort, kind, variety, shape, form, build, structure, construction, composition.

make believe pretend, play-act, imagine, dream, daydream, fantasize, romance.

make do cope, manage, get by, get along, survive, muddle through, improvise.

make for **1** (*make for the exit*) head for, aim for, proceed towards, be bound for. **2** (*doesn't make for good industrial relations*) lead to, be conducive to, contribute to, facilitate, favour, promote, advance, further.

make it arrive, get there, succeed, prosper, get on, survive, pull through.

make off run off, run away, clear off (*inf*), beat it (*inf*), flee, bolt, abscond, decamp, scarper (*inf*), skedaddle (*inf*), cut and run (*inf*).

make out **1** (*made out a ship on the horizon*) see, perceive, discern, descry, espy, detect, distinguish, recognize, pick out, notice, observe. **2** (*couldn't make out the name*) decipher, interpret, read, hear, perceive, distinguish. **3** (*trying to make out what had happened*) understand, comprehend, grasp, fathom, ascertain, work out, figure out. **4** (*made out that she was a beginner*) claim, allege, assert, aver, pretend, suggest, imply. **5** (*make out a cheque*) draw up, write out, fill in, fill out, complete. **6** (*how did you make out?*) fare, get on, get along, manage, do.

make up **1** (*make up an excuse*) invent, fabricate, manufacture, trump up (*inf*), concoct, hatch, cook up (*inf*). **2** (*make up a slogan*) compose, write, create, originate, coin, formulate. **3** (*a panel made up of professional people*) constitute, compose, comprise, form. **4** (*made up for his lack of experience*) recompense, make good, compensate, offset, requite, make amends, atone. **5** (*make up the deficit*) supply, provide, furnish, meet, complete, round off. **6** (*make up after a quarrel*) become reconciled, make peace, shake hands, bury the hatchet (*inf*), forgive and forget (*inf*).

make-believe *noun* pretence, play-acting, charade, imagination, dream, daydream, fantasy. OPPOSITE: reality.
≫ *adj* imaginary, fictitious, made-up, unreal, fantasy, dream, pretend (*inf*), mock, sham. OPPOSITE: real.

maker *noun* manufacturer, producer, builder, constructor, creator, fabricator, author, architect.

makeshift *adj* temporary, provisional, stopgap, make-do, improvised, rough-and-ready, cobbled together.

make-up *noun* **1** (*put on make-up*) cosmetics, maquillage, greasepaint, war paint (*inf*). **2** (*the make-up of the team*) constitution, composition, form, structure, formation, construction, assembly, organization. **3** (*it's not in my make-up*) character, personality, nature, disposition, temperament, style, stamp, mould.

making *noun* creation, fabrication, manufacture, production, construction. OPPOSITE: destruction.
in the making potential, developing, coming, nascent, budding, promising.

makings *pl noun* potential, capacity, capability, qualities, characteristics, essentials, materials, ingredients, beginnings.

maladjusted *adj* disturbed, unstable, neurotic, alienated, mixed-up (*inf*), screwed-up (*inf*). OPPOSITE: well-adjusted.

maladministration *noun* mismanagement, misgovernment, misrule, malpractice, malfeasance, corruption, inefficiency, incompetence, bungling.

maladroit *adj* clumsy, awkward, bungling, bumbling, ham-fisted (*inf*), cack-handed (*inf*), inept, inexpert, unskilful, incompetent, tactless, undiplomatic, insensitive, thoughtless. OPPOSITE: dexterous.

malady *noun* illness, sickness, ailment, complaint, disorder, disease, indisposition, affliction, infirmity. OPPOSITE: health.

malaise *noun* unease, discomfort, anxiety, angst, depression, ennui, weariness, listlessness, languor, lethargy, lassitude, weakness, feebleness, enervation, indisposition, illness, sickness. OPPOSITE: wellbeing.

malcontent *adj* discontented, disgruntled, dissatisfied, displeased, unhappy, grumbling, complaining, carping, uneasy, restive, factious, dissentious, rebellious, troublemaking. OPPOSITE: contented.
➤ *noun* grumbler, complainer, moaner, rebel, agitator, troublemaker, stirrer (*inf*).

male *noun* **1** (*an unmarried male*) man, gentleman, boy, lad. OPPOSITE: female. **2** (*the male has brighter plumage*) cock, buck, bull, ram, stag, stallion.
➤ *adj* masculine, virile, manly, gentlemanly. OPPOSITE: female.

malediction *noun* curse, anathema, imprecation, execration, damnation, denunciation, condemnation, slander, calumny. OPPOSITE: blessing.

malefactor *noun* criminal, felon, lawbreaker, crook (*inf*), offender, culprit, wrongdoer, miscreant, sinner, evildoer, villain.

malevolence *noun* ill will, animosity, hate, hatred, malignancy, malignity, spite, malice, bitterness, rancour, resentment, hostility. OPPOSITE: benevolence.

malevolent *adj* malignant, malign, ill-disposed, baleful, spiteful, malicious, vindictive, revengeful, bitter, rancorous, resentful, hostile, unfriendly, ill-natured. OPPOSITE: benevolent.

malfunction *verb* go wrong, break down, fail, pack up (*inf*), conk out (*sl*). OPPOSITE: work.
➤ *noun* breakdown, failure, fault, defect, flaw.

malice *noun* malevolence, malignancy, malignity, spite, vindictiveness, bitterness, rancour, resentment, grudge, spleen, venom, enmity, hostility, animosity, ill will. OPPOSITE: love.

malicious *adj* malevolent, malignant, malign, ill-disposed, spiteful, vindictive, bitter, rancorous, mischievous, injurious, hurtful, harmful, pernicious, vicious, venomous, bitchy (*inf*), catty (*inf*). OPPOSITE: kind.

malign *verb* defame, slander, calumniate, libel, traduce, vilify, denigrate, blacken, revile, disparage, derogate, run down (*inf*), bad-mouth (*inf*). OPPOSITE: praise.
➤ *adj* malignant, malevolent, evil, bad, harmful, injurious, pernicious, destructive. OPPOSITE: good.

malignant *adj* **1** (*a malignant expression*) malign, malevolent, spiteful, malicious, vindictive, bitter, rancorous, venomous, baleful, hostile. OPPOSITE: kindly. **2** (*a malignant condition*) deadly, fatal, incurable, terminal, uncontrollable, virulent, life-threatening, cancerous. OPPOSITE: benign.

malleable *adj* **1** (*a malleable metal*) plastic, pliant, flexible, workable, mouldable. **2** (*a malleable character*) impressionable, biddable, amenable, tractable, compliant.

malnutrition *noun* undernourishment, poor diet, hunger, starvation, famine.

malpractice *noun* misconduct, misbehaviour, malversation, malfeasance, negligence, dereliction, mismanagement, maladministration, wrongdoing, misdeed, offence, transgression.

maltreat *verb* mistreat, ill-treat, abuse, misuse, ill-use, injure, hurt, harm, mishandle, manhandle, bully.

mammoth *adj* enormous, huge, immense, colossal, vast, massive, gigantic, giant, king-size, jumbo (*inf*), gargantuan, Brobdingnagian, elephantine, herculean, titanic, mountainous, prodigious, tremendous, stupendous, monumental. OPPOSITE: tiny.

man *noun* **1** (*a man selling insurance*) male, gentleman, fellow, chap (*inf*), bloke (*inf*), guy (*inf*). OPPOSITE: woman. **2** (*all men are equal*) person, human, human being, mortal, adult, individual, body, soul. OPPOSITE: beast. **3** (*man's responsibility for the environment*) mankind, humankind, humanity, the human race, homo sapiens. **4** (*taking on several new men*) employee, worker, labourer, hand. OPPOSITE: employer. **5** (*the king's men*) soldier, servant, valet, page, attendant, follower, subject, dependant. OPPOSITE: master.
➤ *verb* staff, crew, work, operate.
to a man without exception, one and all, as one, unanimously.

manacle *verb* handcuff, shackle, fetter, chain, bind, restrain, confine, curb, check. OPPOSITE: free.
➤ *noun* handcuff, shackle, fetter, iron, chain, bond.

manage *verb* **1** (*managing the sales department*) administer, direct, run, conduct, control, be in charge of, supervise, superintend, oversee, head, lead, command, rule, govern. OPPOSITE: mismanage. **2** (*managed to persuade her*) contrive, succeed, engineer, manoeuvre, bring about, bring off, achieve, accomplish, effect. OPPOSITE: fail. **3** (*how will you manage on your own?*) cope, fare, get along, make do, survive. **4** (*can't manage the car on wet roads*) control, guide, steer, pilot, manipulate, handle, operate, wield, ply.

manageable *adj* **1** (*manageable children*) controllable, governable, tractable, amenable, docile, compliant, submissive. OPPOSITE: unmanageable. **2** (*a manageable size*) handy, convenient, easy, user-friendly. OPPOSITE: unwieldy. **3** (*a manageable task*) practicable, feasible, possible, doable. OPPOSITE: impracticable.

management *noun* **1** (*negotiating with management*) executive, administration, board, directorate, directors, managers, supervisors, employers, bosses (*inf*). OPPOSITE: labour. **2** (*problems caused by poor management*) administration, direction, running, control, regulation, supervision, command, rule, government. OPPOSITE: mismanagement. **3** (*management of our finances*) handling, conduct, care, charge.

manager *noun* administrator, executive, director, controller, supervisor, superintendent, overseer, governor, boss (*inf*), gaffer (*inf*). OPPOSITE: worker.

mandate *noun* command, order, bidding, direction, instruction, edict, decree, injunction, charge, commission, warrant, authority, authorization, sanction.

mandatory *adj* compulsory, obligatory, binding, necessary, requisite, essential, imperative. OPPOSITE: optional.

mangle *verb* **1** (*the mangled bodies of the victims*) mutilate, disfigure, maim, cripple, cut, lacerate, tear, maul, butcher, crush, destroy. **2** (*mangling my favourite piano sonata*) bungle, botch (*inf*), mess up (*inf*), mar, spoil, ruin, murder (*inf*).

manhandle *verb* **1** (*manhandled the rioters*) maltreat, mistreat, ill-treat, abuse, push, shove, maul, harm, damage, knock about (*inf*). **2** (*manhandled the trunk up the stairs*) heave, haul, push, shove, hump (*inf*), lug (*inf*).

manhood *noun* **1** (*when he reached manhood*) adulthood, maturity. OPPOSITE: boyhood. **2** (*a challenge to his manhood*) maleness, masculinity, virility, manliness, machismo, strength, fortitude, hardihood, stamina, bravery, courage, valour, determination, resolution. OPPOSITE: womanhood.

mania *noun* **1** (*symptoms of mania*) frenzy, wildness, hysteria, delirium, derangement, dementia, insanity, madness, lunacy. OPPOSITE: sanity. **2** (*a mania for collecting books*) passion, obsession, fixation, compulsion, fetish, craze, rage, fad, urge, desire, craving. OPPOSITE: phobia.

maniac *noun* **1** (*attacked by a maniac*) madman, madwoman, lunatic, psychopath, nutter (*inf*), loony (*inf*). **2** (*a football maniac*) enthusiast, fanatic, fiend (*inf*), freak (*inf*).

maniacal *adj* manic, frenzied, frantic, wild, raving, hysterical, delirious, mad, crazy (*inf*), lunatic, insane, deranged, demented, unbalanced. OPPOSITE: sane.

manifest *verb* show, exhibit, display, demonstrate, prove, indicate, evince, reveal, expose, make plain, declare, make known. OPPOSITE: hide.
≫ *adj* obvious, evident, plain, clear, visible, apparent, conspicuous, noticeable, unmistakable, glaring, blatant, palpable, patent, open, overt. OPPOSITE: unclear.

manifestation *noun* display, demonstration, show, exhibition, revelation, exposure, declaration, expression, profession, testimony, proof, evidence, sign, indication, token, mark. OPPOSITE: concealment.

manifesto *noun* statement, declaration, pronouncement, proclamation.

manifold *adj* numerous, many, multiple, several, various, diverse, sundry, varied, assorted, multifarious, multitudinous. OPPOSITE: few.

manipulate *verb* **1** (*manipulate a weapon*) handle, wield, ply, use, utilize, operate, work. **2** (*trying to manipulate the situation*) manage, control, influence, direct, guide, engineer, manoeuvre, exploit. **3** (*manipulated the data*) juggle, massage, falsify, rig, fiddle, cook (*inf*).

mankind *noun* man, humankind, humanity, the human race, homo sapiens, human beings, people, mortals.

manly *adj* virile, masculine, manful, macho (*inf*), strong, hardy, robust, tough, resolute, firm, brave, courageous, valiant, heroic, intrepid, gallant, chivalrous. OPPOSITE: womanly.

man-made *adj* synthetic, artificial, imitation, simulated, manufactured, ersatz. OPPOSITE: genuine.

manner *noun* **1** (*do it in the same manner*) way, method, system, technique, means, approach, style, fashion, mode, wont, custom, habit, practice, procedure, routine. **2** (*noticed nothing strange in his manner*) behaviour, conduct, bearing, carriage, deportment, demeanour, mien, air, aspect, appearance, guise, look. **3** (*what manner of woman is she?*) kind, sort, type, variety, make, brand, class, category.

mannered *adj* unnatural, artificial, stiff, stilted, affected, posed, pretentious, precious, stagy, theatrical. OPPOSITE: natural.

mannerism *noun* idiosyncrasy, characteristic, peculiarity, quirk, trait, habit, gesture.

mannerly *adj* polite, courteous, civil, respectful, deferential, well-mannered, well-behaved, well-bred, refined, polished, genteel, decorous, gentlemanly, ladylike. OPPOSITE: rude.

manners *pl noun* behaviour, conduct, comportment, politeness, courtesy, breeding, etiquette, protocol, decorum, propriety, the done thing (*inf*).

mannish *adj* unfeminine, unwomanly, unladylike, masculine, Amazonian, butch (*inf*). OPPOSITE: feminine.

manoeuvre *verb* **1** (*manoeuvred the car into the space*) steer, pilot, guide, direct, move, deploy, manage, manipulate, handle. **2** (*political manoeuvring*) plan, scheme, plot, intrigue, contrive, engineer, wangle (*inf*).
≫ *noun* **1** (*a series of manoeuvres to park the car*) move, movement, action, operation. **2** (*political manoeuvres*) plan, scheme, plot, intrigue, stratagem, tactic, gambit, ruse, artifice, trick, dodge, ploy. **3** (*military manoeuvres*) movement, deployment, action, operation, mission, strategy, tactic, drill, training, exercise.

manse *noun* vicarage, rectory, parsonage.

mansion *noun* palace, castle, villa, hall, manor house, stately home, country seat. OPPOSITE: hovel.

mantle *noun* **1** (*a mantle trimmed with fur*) cloak, cape, shawl, wrap. **2** (*a mantle of snow*) cover, covering, layer, blanket, pall, shroud, veil, curtain, screen, mask.
≫ *verb* cloak, wrap, envelop, cover, blanket, shroud, veil, curtain, screen, mask, disguise, conceal, hide.

manual *noun* handbook, instructions, guide, guidebook, vade mecum, companion, bible (*inf*).
≫ *adj* physical, labouring, human, hand-operated. OPPOSITE: automatic.

manufacture *verb* **1** (*manufacture electrical appliances*) make, produce, fabricate, build, construct, assemble, put together, turn out, mass-produce, process, form, shape. **2** (*manufacture an excuse*) invent, make up, think up, dream up, concoct, hatch, fabricate, formulate.
≫ *noun* making, production, fabrication, construction, assembly, mass-production, processing.

manufacturer *noun* maker, producer, fabricator, creator, industrialist.

manumission *noun* liberation, emancipation, enfranchisement, release, deliverance. OPPOSITE: servitude.

manumit *verb* liberate, free, set free, emancipate, enfranchise, release, deliver. OPPOSITE: enslave.

manure *noun* fertilizer, compost, dressing, dung, muck, excrement, ordure.

many *adj* numerous, manifold, multitudinous, myriad, countless, innumerable, umpteen (*inf*), scores of (*inf*), millions of (*inf*), abundant, copious, lots of (*inf*), loads of (*inf*), heaps of (*inf*), several, various, diverse, sundry. OPPOSITE: few.
➤ *noun* large numbers, a multitude, plenty, an abundance, hundreds, thousands, a lot (*inf*), lots (*inf*), loads (*inf*), piles (*inf*), heaps (*inf*), stacks (*inf*).

map *noun* chart, plan, diagram, guide, atlas, gazetteer.
➤ *verb* chart, plot, delineate, depict.
map out plan, draw up, set out, lay out.

mar *verb* spoil, damage, impair, taint, stain, sully, tarnish, blight, blemish, detract from, disfigure, deface, deform, mutilate, mangle, injure, hurt, harm, ruin, wreck. OPPOSITE: improve.

maraud *verb* raid, foray, forage, ransack, plunder, pillage, loot, sack, ravage, despoil.

marauder *noun* robber, bandit, brigand, raider, plunderer, pillager, looter, freebooter, pirate, corsair, buccaneer.

march *verb* walk, stride, step, pace, tramp, tread, trudge, hike, strut, stalk, parade, file, process, advance, proceed, progress. OPPOSITE: halt.
➤ *noun* **1** (*a protest march*) parade, procession, file, column, demonstration, demo (*inf*). **2** (*a full day's march*) walk, hike, trek, tramp. **3** (*a quick march*) step, pace, stride, gait. **4** (*the march of time*) advance, progression, headway, progress, development. OPPOSITE: retrogression.

margin *noun* **1** (*at the margin of the woods*) border, edge, periphery, perimeter, rim, lip, brim, brink, verge, bound, limit, boundary, frontier. **2** (*no margin for error*) allowance, extra, surplus, leeway, latitude, freedom, scope, space, room.

marginal *adj* **1** (*of marginal interest*) borderline, peripheral, fringe. OPPOSITE: central. **2** (*a marginal improvement*) slight, small, tiny, minute, minimal, negligible. OPPOSITE: major.

marijuana *noun* cannabis, hemp, hashish, ganja, bhang, grass (*inf*), pot (*inf*), hash (*inf*), mary jane (*inf*), kef (*inf*), kif (*inf*), dope (*inf*).

marinate *verb* marinade, soak, steep.

marine *adj* **1** (*marine organisms*) sea, oceanic, pelagic, thalassic, saltwater. OPPOSITE: land. **2** (*marine insurance*) nautical, naval, maritime, seafaring, ocean-going.

mariner *noun* sailor, seaman, seafarer, bluejacket, matelot (*inf*), tar (*inf*), salt (*inf*), sea dog (*inf*).

marital *adj* conjugal, connubial, matrimonial, nuptial, wedded, married. OPPOSITE: celibate.

maritime *adj* **1** (*maritime trade*) marine, nautical, naval, sea, oceanic, seafaring, ocean-going. **2** (*maritime regions*) coastal, littoral, seaside. OPPOSITE: inland.

mark *noun* **1** (*a mark on the paintwork*) spot, dot, speck, stain, blot, smear, smudge, blemish, bruise, dent, pit, scar, line, score, scratch. **2** (*left marks in the snow*) trace, track, trail, print, impression. **3** (*a mark of respect*) sign, indication, symbol, token, emblem, proof, evidence. **4** (*the company's mark*) brand, stamp, seal, badge, emblem, device, logo. **5** (*a punctuation mark*) symbol, sign, character. **6** (*a mark of a good wine*) characteristic, trait, feature, attribute, quality. **7** (*got a higher mark for her essay*) grade, score, percentage, assessment, evaluation. **8** (*falling below the mark*) point, level, stage, standard, criterion, yardstick, scale, measure. **9** (*missed the mark*) target, objective, goal, aim, purpose, intention. **10** (*nobody of mark was there*) note, distinction, eminence, prominence, fame, renown, celebrity, importance, significance, consequence, influence, prestige, rank, standing.
➤ *verb* **1** (*marked the paintwork*) spot, stain, blot, smear, smudge, blemish, bruise, dent, pit, scar, score, scratch. **2** (*mark it with your initials*) label, tag, name, identify, brand, stamp, characterize, distinguish, denote, designate, specify, indicate, flag. **3** (*mark my words*) note, heed, mind, pay attention to, take notice of, regard, observe. OPPOSITE: ignore. **4** (*marking exam papers*) correct, grade, assess, evaluate. **5** (*a party to mark the occasion*) celebrate, commemorate, remember, observe, recognize, honour, solemnize.
mark down reduce, decrease, lower, cut, slash, discount. OPPOSITE: increase.
mark out **1** (*mark out the playing area*) demarcate, delimit, measure out, mark off. **2** (*marked her out as a professional*) single out, set apart, separate, differentiate, distinguish.
mark up raise, increase, put up, jack up (*inf*). OPPOSITE: reduce.

marked *adj* obvious, evident, manifest, distinct, noticeable, conspicuous, blatant, glaring, pronounced, decided, prominent, salient, striking, outstanding, remarkable. OPPOSITE: imperceptible.

market *noun* **1** (*bought it at the market*) mart, bazaar, fair, exchange, shop, store, outlet, shopping centre, mall. **2** (*no market for these books*) demand, call, need, want, desire. **3** (*the market has picked up*) trade, commerce, business, buying, selling, dealing.
➤ *verb* sell, retail, vend, hawk, peddle, deal, trade, traffic. OPPOSITE: buy.

maroon *verb* abandon, desert, forsake, leave, strand, isolate, cut off.

marriage *noun* **1** (*her son's marriage*) wedlock, matrimony, match, union, wedding, nuptials. OPPOSITE: divorce. **2** (*a marriage of ideas*) alliance, union, merger, amalgamation, combination, association. OPPOSITE: separation.

marrow *noun* essence, substance, gist, pith, core, kernel, nucleus, heart, soul, spirit.

marry *verb* **1** (*they married in the spring*) wed, espouse, join in matrimony, become man and wife, get hitched (*inf*), get spliced (*inf*), tie the knot (*inf*). OPPOSITE: divorce. **2** (*marry the two designs*) join, link, connect, ally, unite, merge, amalgamate, combine, associate. OPPOSITE: separate.

marsh *noun* bog, swamp, fen, quagmire, morass, slough.

marshal *verb* **1** (*marshal the facts*) arrange, dispose, array, deploy, order, rank, line up, align, organize, assemble, muster, gather, collect. **2** (*marshal a group of sightseers*) lead, guide, conduct, usher, escort, shepherd.

marshy *adj* boggy, swampy, muddy, miry, squelchy, waterlogged. OPPOSITE: dry.

martial *adj* warlike, bellicose, belligerent, combative, militant, aggressive, military, soldierly, brave, courageous, heroic. OPPOSITE: pacific.

martyrdom *noun* death, persecution, torture, torment, ordeal, suffering, agony, anguish.

marvel *verb* wonder, gape, gaze, stare, goggle, be amazed.
➤ *noun* wonder, prodigy, miracle, phenomenon, spectacle, sensation.

marvellous *adj* **1** (*had a marvellous time*) wonderful, splendid, magnificent, excellent, superb, smashing (*inf*), super (*inf*), fantastic (*inf*), fabulous (*inf*), terrific (*inf*), brill (*inf*), magic (*inf*), awesome (*sl*), wicked (*sl*). OPPOSITE: dreadful. **2** (*a marvellous achievement*) wondrous, miraculous, incredible, unbelievable, astonishing, astounding, amazing, breathtaking, remarkable, extraordinary, phenomenal, stupendous, prodigious. OPPOSITE: ordinary.

masculine *adj* male, manlike, manly, virile, macho (*inf*), gallant, heroic, strong, muscular, strapping, rugged, mannish, butch (*inf*). OPPOSITE: feminine.

mash *verb* crush, pulp, purée, squash, pulverize, pound, beat, grind.
➤ *noun* mush, pulp, purée, paste, slush, pap.

mask *noun* disguise, camouflage, front, facade, guise, pretence, veil, cloak, blind, screen, cover, shield, protection.
➤ *verb* disguise, camouflage, hide, conceal, obscure, veil, cloak, screen, cover, shield, protect. OPPOSITE: expose.

masquerade *noun* **1** (*met him at a masquerade*) masque, masked ball, costume ball, fancy dress party. **2** (*kept up the masquerade for months*) pretence, subterfuge, dissimulation, imposture, deception, pose, front, facade, guise.
masquerade as impersonate, pose as, pass oneself off as, play, pretend to be, be disguised as.

mass *noun* **1** (*a mass of earth*) lump, chunk, block, piece, concretion. **2** (*a mass of wires*) bunch, cluster, collection, group, number, quantity, accumulation, conglomeration. **3** (*a mass of spectators*) crowd, throng, mob, horde, host, multitude. **4** (*a mass of colour*) expanse, sheet, sea. **5** (*calculate the mass of the object*) size, magnitude, dimensions, weight, bulk, volume. **6** (*the mass of the votes*) majority, body, bulk, preponderance, greater part, greater number. OPPOSITE: minority. **7** (*people in the mass*) whole, entirety, aggregate, total, sum.
➤ *adj* large-scale, widespread, extensive, wholesale, universal, general, popular. OPPOSITE: limited.
➤ *verb* collect, gather, assemble, muster, rally, crowd,

swarm, throng, cluster, amass, accumulate. OPPOSITE: disperse.

massacre *noun* killing, murder, slaughter, butchery, carnage, blood bath, extermination, genocide, ethnic cleansing, pogrom, holocaust.
➤ *verb* kill, slay, murder, slaughter, butcher, mow down, cut down, decimate, exterminate, annihilate, wipe out.

massage *verb* rub, knead, pummel, palpate, manipulate.
➤ *noun* rub, rubdown, rubbing, kneading, pummelling, palpation, manipulation, physiotherapy, acupressure, shiatsu, reflexology, aromatherapy.

masses *pl noun* **1** (*appeal to the masses*) populace, common people, proletariat, hoi polloi, plebs (*inf*), crowd, mob, herd, rabble, riff-raff (*inf*), the great unwashed (*inf*). OPPOSITE: élite. **2** (*masses of work to do*) a great deal, much, many, plenty, an abundance, lots (*inf*), loads (*inf*), heaps (*inf*), piles (*inf*), stacks (*inf*). OPPOSITE: little.

massive *adj* huge, enormous, colossal, immense, gigantic, vast, extensive, big, large, imposing, hulking, bulky, solid, substantial, heavy, hefty, weighty, ponderous. OPPOSITE: tiny.

master *noun* **1** (*obeyed their master*) lord, ruler, governor, director, manager, controller, chief, head, leader, commander, captain, owner, proprietor, holder, keeper, employer, boss (*inf*). OPPOSITE: servant. **2** (*learning from their master*) teacher, instructor, tutor, pedagogue, preceptor, guide, guru. OPPOSITE: pupil. **3** (*a master of the art*) expert, adept, past master, dab hand (*inf*), professional, pro (*inf*), genius, maestro, virtuoso, ace (*inf*), authority, pundit. OPPOSITE: novice
➤ *adj* **1** (*the master bedroom*) chief, principal, main, major, great, grand, leading, most important. OPPOSITE: minor. **2** (*a master builder*) expert, masterly, adept, proficient, skilled, skilful, practised, experienced, qualified, professional. OPPOSITE: amateur. **3** (*the master plan*) controlling, directing, commanding, ruling.
➤ *verb* **1** (*mastered her fear*) conquer, vanquish, defeat, beat, overpower, overcome, crush, quell, suppress, subdue, subjugate, control, dominate, rule, govern. **2** (*master a foreign language*) learn, grasp, get the hang of (*inf*), acquire, become proficient in.

masterful *adj* authoritative, dictatorial, despotic, tyrannical, autocratic, bossy (*inf*), controlling, dominating, domineering, overbearing, high-handed, imperious, peremptory, arrogant, haughty. OPPOSITE: meek.

masterly *adj* expert, skilful, skilled, adept, proficient, talented, gifted, excellent, first-rate, top-notch (*inf*), crack (*inf*), ace (*inf*), supreme, consummate, accomplished, polished. OPPOSITE: inept.

mastermind *noun* planner, organizer, director, prime mover, genius, intellect, brains (*inf*), originator, author, architect, engineer.
➤ *verb* plan, organize, direct, manage, originate, conceive, think up, devise, engineer.

masterpiece *noun* masterwork, chef d'oeuvre, magnum opus, work of art, pièce de résistance.

mastery *noun* **1** (*mastery over the rebels*) command, control, domination, upper hand, supremacy, ascendancy, sway, rule, dominion, sovereignty, power, authority, triumph, conquest, victory. OPPOSITE: servitude. **2** (*mastery of a foreign language*) knowledge, command, grasp, understanding, familiarity, proficiency, expertise, skill, ability, prowess, dexterity, virtuosity. OPPOSITE: incompetence.

masticate *verb* chew, munch, crunch, champ, chomp, eat.

masturbation *noun* autoeroticism, onanism, self-gratification, self-abuse, playing with oneself (*inf*), wanking (*sl*).

mat *noun* rug, carpet, pad, felt, coaster.
➤ *verb* tangle, entangle, ravel, interweave, interlace, intertwine, twist, knot, tousle. OPPOSITE: disentangle.

match *noun* **1** (*a cricket match*) game, competition, contest, tournament, test, trial, bout, meet, event. **2** (*met her match*) equal, peer, counterpart, equivalent, rival, competitor. **3** (*the match for this sock*) fellow, mate, companion, twin, counterpart, complement. **4** (*made the ideal match*) marriage, alliance, union, partnership.
➤ *verb* **1** (*it matches perfectly*) fit, suit, accord, agree, correspond, tally, harmonize, coordinate, team, blend, tone, go. OPPOSITE: clash. **2** (*match the nuts to the bolts*) join, unite, marry, mate, couple, pair. OPPOSITE: separate. **3** (*matched his strength against hers*) oppose, pit, set. **4** (*difficult to match such virtuosity*) equal, measure up to, rival, compete with, vie with, beat.

matching *adj* coordinating, harmonizing, toning, blending, complementary, corresponding, equivalent, parallel, analogous, comparable, similar, like, same, identical, twin, duplicate, double, paired, coupled. OPPOSITE: conflicting.

matchless *adj* peerless, unequalled, unrivalled, unmatched, unparalleled, incomparable, inimitable, unique, ideal, consummate, perfect. OPPOSITE: ordinary.

mate *noun* **1** (*looking for a mate*) spouse, husband, wife, partner, lover, significant other (*inf*). **2** (*a present from my mates*) friend, companion, comrade, pal (*inf*), chum (*inf*), buddy (*inf*), compeer, colleague, associate, fellow. **3** (*a plumber's mate*) assistant, helper, apprentice. **4** (*the mate of this glove*) match, fellow, companion, twin, counterpart, complement.
➤ *verb* pair, couple, copulate, breed.

material *noun* **1** (*a waxy material*) substance, matter, medium, stuff. **2** (*a length of dress material*) fabric, cloth, stuff, textile. **3** (*material for my article*) information, facts, data, details, particulars, notes, papers, documents.
➤ *adj* **1** (*material existence*) physical, corporeal, bodily, fleshly, worldly, earthly, temporal, concrete, substantial, tangible, palpable. OPPOSITE: spiritual. **2** (*facts that may be material*) relevant, applicable, pertinent, germane, important, significant, meaningful, essential, vital, key, momentous, weighty, grave, serious. OPPOSITE: immaterial.

materialize *verb* appear, become visible, take shape, come into being, emerge, show oneself, reveal oneself, turn up, happen, occur. OPPOSITE: disappear.

materially *adv* much, considerably, greatly, significantly, substantially, essentially, fundamentally, seriously. OPPOSITE: little.

maternal *adj* motherly, protective, caring, loving.

mathematical *adj* **1** (*mathematical equations*) numerical, arithmetical, algebraic, geometric, statistical. **2** (*with mathematical care*) exact, precise, accurate, strict, rigorous, meticulous, scrupulous.

matrimonial *adj* marital, nuptial, connubial, conjugal, married, wedded.

matrimony *noun* marriage, wedlock, wedding, nuptials.

matronly *adj* maternal, motherly, middle-aged, staid, sedate, dignified, portly, plump.

matter *verb* signify, be relevant, count, be important, carry weight, make a difference.
➤ *noun* **1** (*organic matter*) substance, material, medium, stuff. **2** (*the matter under discussion*) subject, topic, question, issue, business, affair, concern, thing, point, case, circumstance, situation, event, occurrence, incident. **3** (*what's the matter?*) trouble, problem, difficulty, distress, upset, worry. **4** (*of little matter*) importance, significance, consequence, note, moment, weight. **5** (*draining matter from the abscess*) pus, suppuration, purulence, sanies, discharge, secretion.
as a matter of fact in fact, in point of fact, actually, really, to tell the truth, in truth.
no matter never mind, it doesn't matter, it makes no difference, don't worry about it.

matter-of-fact *adj* down-to-earth, straightforward, unsentimental, unemotional, factual, literal, prosaic, pedestrian, flat, dry, deadpan, plain, mundane, unvarnished, unembellished.

mature *adj* **1** (*a mature woman*) grown-up, adult, of age, fully grown, fully developed. **2** (*a mature attitude*) responsible, sensible, wise, sagacious, shrewd, discriminating. OPPOSITE: immature. **3** (*mature cheese*) ripe, mellow, seasoned, aged, complete, perfect, ready.
➤ *verb* **1** (*let the cheese mature*) ripen, mellow, season, age. **2** (*as teenagers mature*) grow up, become adult, come of age, develop.

maudlin *adj* sentimental, emotional, tearful, lachrymose, weepy (*inf*), mawkish, soppy (*inf*), mushy (*inf*), slushy (*inf*).

maul *verb* **1** (*mauled by the tiger*) claw, lacerate, mutilate, mangle, wound, injure, attack, savage, tear to pieces. **2** (*mauling the merchandise*) paw, manhandle, maltreat, mistreat, damage, harm. **3** (*mauling the young women*) molest, paw, abuse, ill-treat, batter, beat, harm, hurt. **4** (*mauled by the critics*) censure, condemn, knock (*inf*), slate (*inf*), pan (*inf*), slam (*inf*), pull to pieces (*inf*), tear to shreds (*inf*). OPPOSITE: praise.

mausoleum *noun* tomb, vault, crypt, sepulchre, catacomb.

maverick *noun* individualist, nonconformist, rebel, dissenter, dissident.

mawkish *adj* sentimental, emotional, maudlin, soppy (*inf*), mushy (*inf*), slushy (*inf*), weak, feeble, nauseating, sickening, saccharine.

maxim *noun* saying, proverb, adage, aphorism, axiom, dictum.

maximum *noun* height, peak, pinnacle, top, summit,

acme, zenith, apogee, climax, limit, ceiling, extreme, extremity, utmost, uttermost. OPPOSITE: minimum.
➤ *adj* maximal, highest, top, greatest, most, utmost, supreme. OPPOSITE: minimal.

maybe *adv* perhaps, possibly, conceivably, perchance, peradventure, happen (*inf*). OPPOSITE: definitely.

mayhem *noun* chaos, havoc, confusion, disorder, commotion, tumult, uproar, bedlam, pandemonium, disturbance, trouble, disruption. OPPOSITE: order.

maze *noun* labyrinth, network, web, mesh, complex, jungle, tangle, confusion, imbroglio.

meadow *noun* field, paddock, grassland, pasture, lea.

meagre *adj* **1** (*meagre supplies*) scant, scanty, sparse, skimpy, short, deficient, inadequate, insufficient, small, little, slight, poor, paltry, miserly, niggardly, stingy (*inf*), measly (*inf*). OPPOSITE: ample. **2** (*their meagre bodies*) thin, lean, puny, skinny, scrawny, scraggy, bony, emaciated, underfed. OPPOSITE: fat.

meal *noun* repast, collation, snack, feast, banquet, blow-out (*inf*). OPPOSITE: fast.

mean[1] *verb* **1** (*what do these initials mean?*) signify, denote, betoken, represent, symbolize, stand for, indicate, portend, presage, augur, imply, suggest, connote, purport. **2** (*I didn't mean to offend you*) intend, aim, purpose, set out, contemplate, have in mind, propose, plan. **3** (*such things are meant to happen*) destine, fate, predestine, preordain. **4** (*it's meant for children*) design, make, intend. **5** (*this will mean extra expense*) cause, bring about, produce, result in, give rise to, involve, entail.

mean[2] *adj* **1** (*too mean to leave a tip*) miserly, niggardly, stingy (*inf*), parsimonious, penny-pinching (*inf*), close-fisted, tight-fisted, tight (*inf*), selfish, grasping, avaricious, ungenerous, illiberal, close, near. OPPOSITE: generous. **2** (*don't be mean to your sister*) unkind, nasty, unpleasant, disagreeable, spiteful, malicious, callous, cruel. OPPOSITE: kind. **3** (*a mean old man*) cross, irritable, irascible, bad-tempered, ill-humoured, crusty, crotchety (*inf*), cantankerous, grumpy, grouchy (*inf*). OPPOSITE: affable. **4** (*a mean trick*) base, low, despicable, contemptible, abject, shabby, shameful, disgraceful, dishonourable, ignoble, petty, small-minded. OPPOSITE: honourable. **5** (*a mean dwelling*) poor, lowly, humble, miserable, wretched, shabby, seedy, squalid, common, ordinary, inferior, second-rate. OPPOSITE: magnificent.

mean[3] *noun* average, norm, median, midpoint, middle, compromise, happy medium. OPPOSITE: extreme.
➤ *adj* medium, average, normal, middle, intermediate, median, medial. OPPOSITE: extreme.

meander *verb* **1** (*the river meandered*) wind, zigzag, snake, twist, turn, bend, curve. **2** (*the crowds meandered*) wander, ramble, rove, amble, stroll, drift, stray.

meandering *adj* **1** (*a meandering path*) winding, zigzag, snaking, serpentine, tortuous, twisting, turning. OPPOSITE: straight. **2** (*a meandering account*) wandering, rambling, roundabout, circuitous, indirect, tortuous, convoluted.

meaning *noun* **1** (*the meaning of the word*) sense, signification, significance, import, purport, connotation, implication, gist, drift, definition, interpretation, explanation, explication. **2** (*no mischievous meaning was*

apparent) aim, intention, idea, object, end, goal, purpose, plan, design. **3** (*life had lost its meaning*) value, worth, point, purpose, significance. **4** (*a glance full of meaning*) eloquence, meaningfulness, expressiveness, significance, suggestiveness, implication.

meaningful *adj* **1** (*a meaningful discussion*) significant, important, serious, worthwhile, useful, material, relevant. OPPOSITE: worthless. **2** (*a meaningful glance*) eloquent, expressive, significant, suggestive, pregnant.

meaningless *adj* **1** (*meaningless talk*) senseless, unintelligible, incomprehensible, nonsensical, absurd, trivial. OPPOSITE: meaningful. **2** (*a meaningless existence*) aimless, pointless, futile, worthless, empty, hollow. OPPOSITE: worthwhile.

means *pl noun* **1** (*a means of escape*) method, way, manner, mode, medium, vehicle, instrument, agency, course, avenue, channel, resource, measure, expedient, mechanism. OPPOSITE: end. **2** (*a woman of independent means*) resources, funds, finance, money, wherewithal, income, revenue, property, estate, capital, riches, wealth, fortune, substance. OPPOSITE: poverty.
by all means certainly, of course, definitely, absolutely.
by means of through, via, with, using.
by no means not at all, not in the least, certainly not, no way (*inf*).

meanwhile *adv* in the meantime, in the interim, for now, for the time being, at the same time, simultaneously.

measurable *adj* mensurable, fathomable, quantifiable, computable, assessable, estimable, perceptible, visible, noticeable, appreciable, significant.

measure *verb* quantify, weigh, survey, sound, fathom, size up, gauge, assess, estimate, rate, value, evaluate, appraise, calculate, compute, determine.
➤ *noun* **1** (*the measure of the land*) size, dimensions, proportions, magnitude, volume, capacity, weight, mass, quantity, amount, extent, area, scope, range. **2** (*a tape measure*) rule, ruler, gauge, meter, scale. **3** (*a measure of capacity*) unit, standard, norm, criterion. **4** (*a measure of their skill*) gauge, yardstick, touchstone, benchmark. **5** (*received our just measure*) portion, share, ration, quota, allocation, allotment, division, piece, part, cut (*inf*). **6** (*with a measure of sympathy*) amount, certain amount, degree, quantity. **7** (*arrogance beyond measure*) limits, bounds, limitation, control, restraint, moderation. **8** (*new measures to fight crime*) step, action, course, proceeding, procedure, resolution, act, bill, statute, law.
measure out distribute, dispense, administer, mete out, deal out, dole out, share out, allot, assign, allocate, apportion.
measure up pass muster, come up to standard, fit the bill, make the grade (*inf*), cut the mustard (*inf*).
measure up to match, meet, come up to, equal, fit.

measured *adj* **1** (*with measured steps*) slow, leisurely, unhurried, deliberate, steady, regular, even, rhythmical, uniform, regulated, precise, exact. OPPOSITE: hurried. **2** (*a measured response*) well-thought-out, carefully chosen, planned, premeditated, calculated, studied, considered, reasoned. OPPOSITE: hasty.

measureless *adj* immeasurable, unfathomable, incalculable, innumerable, limitless, unlimited, illimitable, boundless, unbounded, infinite, endless, interminable, vast, immense. OPPOSITE: finite.

measurement *noun* **1** (*the measurements of the crate*) dimension, length, breadth, width, height, depth, area, volume, capacity, weight, mass, size, magnitude, proportions, amount, quantity. **2** (*the measurement of time*) mensuration, quantification, assessment, estimation, evaluation, appraisal, calculation, computation.

mechanical *adj* **1** (*a mechanical system*) automatic, automated, mechanized, machine-operated, power-driven. OPPOSITE: manual. **2** (*a mechanical response*) involuntary, instinctive, automatic, unconscious, unthinking, habitual, routine, cold, unfeeling, impersonal, spiritless, lifeless. OPPOSITE: emotional.

mechanism *noun* **1** (*the mechanism of the clock*) works, workings, machinery, action, movement, operation, performance. **2** (*a mechanism for milling grain*) machine, appliance, motor, engine, device, contrivance, gadget, contraption, instrument, tool. **3** (*a mechanism for controlling prices*) means, method, system, technique, procedure, process.

meddle *verb* interfere, pry, snoop (*inf*), stick one's nose in (*inf*), interpose, intervene, intrude, butt in, put one's oar in (*inf*).

meddlesome *adj* meddling, interfering, intrusive, officious, inquisitive, prying, snooping (*inf*), nosy (*inf*).

medial *adj* middle, central, intermediate, median, average, mean, ordinary. OPPOSITE: extreme.

mediate *verb* arbitrate, referee, umpire, moderate, negotiate, intercede, intervene, interpose, reconcile, conciliate, make peace.

mediation *noun* arbitration, good offices, negotiation, intercession, intervention, reconciliation, conciliation, settlement, resolution.

mediator *noun* arbitrator, arbiter, judge, referee, umpire, moderator, negotiator, intermediary, go-between, honest broker, conciliator, peacemaker.

medicinal *adj* therapeutic, healing, curative, remedial, restorative, medical.

medicine *noun* **1** (*are you taking any medicines?*) medicament, medication, remedy, cure, drug. **2** (*study medicine*) medical science, the healing art.

mediocre *adj* average, middling, moderate, passable, tolerable, all right, OK (*inf*), so-so (*inf*), indifferent, unexceptional, undistinguished, nothing special (*inf*), ordinary, commonplace, run-of-the-mill (*inf*), inferior, second-rate, low-grade, not up to much (*inf*), no great shakes (*inf*), not much to write home about (*inf*). OPPOSITE: exceptional.

meditate *verb* **1** (*meditate on what she said*) reflect, ponder, muse, contemplate, brood, cogitate, ruminate, deliberate, consider, think. **2** (*meditate revenge*) plan, scheme, plot, project, intend, purpose, devise, contrive, design.

meditation *noun* reflection, contemplation, cogitation, rumination, deliberation, consideration, thought, cerebration, concentration, brown study.

medium *adj* average, middling, mean, medial, median, middle, intermediate. OPPOSITE: extreme.

▶ *noun* **1** (*the medium between extremes*) average, mean, midpoint, middle, compromise. OPPOSITE: extreme. **2** (*a medium of expression*) means, vehicle, agency, instrument, organ, channel, avenue, way. **3** (*a medium for growth*) element, habitat, environment, milieu, surroundings, setting, conditions. **4** (*the medium at the séance*) spiritualist, spiritist, psychic, clairvoyant, necromancer.

medley *noun* mixture, assortment, miscellany, mélange, mixed bag (*inf*), pot-pourri, hotchpotch, hodgepodge, mishmash, salmagundi, farrago, patchwork, omnium gatherum (*inf*), jumble, confusion.

meek *adj* mild, gentle, modest, unassuming, humble, lowly, deferential, compliant, submissive, yielding, docile, acquiescent, resigned, patient, long-suffering, forbearing, spiritless, spineless, timid, weak. OPPOSITE: assertive.

meet *verb* **1** (*I met her in the supermarket*) encounter, come across, happen upon, run into, bump into (*inf*), face, confront. OPPOSITE: miss. **2** (*where the lines meet*) join, converge, come together, touch, cross, intersect. OPPOSITE: diverge. **3** (*meet outside the town hall*) gather, collect, assemble, congregate, convene, muster, rally. OPPOSITE: disperse. **4** (*meet our requirements*) fulfil, satisfy, answer, match, comply with, measure up to. **5** (*she met her responsibilities*) discharge, carry out, perform, execute. OPPOSITE: avoid. **6** (*meet the challenge*) handle, cope with, deal with, manage. **7** (*his suggestion was met with enthusiasm*) answer, greet, treat, approach. **8** (*the English met the French at Agincourt*) oppose, encounter, face, confront, engage, join battle with, fight with. **9** (*prepared to meet death*) face, confront, encounter, experience, go through, undergo, endure, suffer.

meeting *noun* **1** (*at their first meeting*) encounter, confrontation, introduction, presentation, rendezvous, assignation, tryst, date. OPPOSITE: parting. **2** (*a meeting of the members*) gathering, assembly, congregation, convention, convocation, conference, conclave, concourse, rally, reunion, get-together (*inf*), session, meet. **3** (*at the meeting of the rivers*) union, convergence, confluence, junction, intersection, crossing. OPPOSITE: divergence.

melancholy *noun* melancholia, depression, dejection, despondency, glumness, gloominess, gloom, pessimism, low spirits, blues (*inf*), sadness, sorrow, unhappiness, misery, woe. OPPOSITE: elation.

▶ *adj* melancholic, depressed, dejected, disconsolate, despondent, glum, gloomy, pessimistic, downcast, downhearted, dispirited, low-spirited, down in the dumps (*inf*), blue (*inf*), doleful, dismal, mournful, sad, sorrowful, unhappy, miserable, woebegone. OPPOSITE: elated.

mêlée *noun* fight, brawl, struggle, scuffle, fray, affray, fracas, free-for-all, ruckus, rumpus, commotion, confusion. OPPOSITE: order.

mellifluous *adj* mellifluent, mellow, smooth, flowing, euphonious, melodious, harmonious, musical, soft, sweet, honeyed, dulcet, silvery. OPPOSITE: harsh.

mellow *adj* **1** (*mellow fruit*) ripe, mature, soft, tender, sweet, full-flavoured. OPPOSITE: unripe. **2** (*mellow sounds*) rich, full, resonant, well-rounded, mellifluous, mellifluent, smooth, euphonious, melodious, sweet, dulcet. OPPOSITE: harsh. **3** (*became more mellow in later life*) genial, affable, amiable, jovial, jolly, cheerful, good-natured, pleasant, placid, easygoing (*inf*). OPPOSITE: unpleasant.

   ➤ *verb* age, develop, improve, mature, season, ripen, soften, sweeten, temper, moderate.

melodious *adj* melodic, tuneful, musical, harmonious, euphonious, sweet, mellifluous, dulcet, silvery. OPPOSITE: discordant.

melodramatic *adj* histrionic, theatrical, stagy, overdramatic, hammy (*inf*), camp (*inf*), sensational, extravagant, exaggerated, overdone.

melody *noun* **1** (*hum the melody*) tune, music, theme, strain, air, song. **2** (*music that lacks melody*) melodiousness, tunefulness, musicality, harmony, euphony. OPPOSITE: discord.

melt *verb* **1** (*the wax melted*) liquefy, thaw, fuse, dissolve, deliquesce, soften. OPPOSITE: freeze. **2** (*her anger melted*) fade, disappear, vanish, evanesce, disperse, dissipate, dissolve, evaporate. **3** (*melted his heart*) touch, affect, move, soften, mollify, disarm. OPPOSITE: harden.

member *noun* **1** (*a member of the society*) adherent, associate, fellow, subscriber. **2** (*a member of the set*) part, component, constituent, element. **3** (*bandaged the injured member*) limb, arm, leg, organ, appendage, extremity.

membrane *noun* film, layer, sheet, skin, pellicle, integument.

memento *noun* keepsake, souvenir, reminder, memorial, remembrance, token, trophy, relic.

memoir *noun* record, account, narrative, history, chronicle, biography, life, essay, monograph.

memoirs *pl noun* reminiscences, recollections, memories, experiences, autobiography, life story, journal, diary.

memorable *adj* unforgettable, remarkable, outstanding, extraordinary, impressive, striking, distinctive, distinguished, noteworthy, notable, historic, significant, momentous, important, consequential, great, famous, illustrious, celebrated. OPPOSITE: insignificant.

memorandum *noun* memo, note, message, record, statement, minute, reminder, aide-mémoire.

memorial *noun* remembrance, memento, souvenir, monument, statue, shrine, plaque, inscription, commemoration.

memorize *verb* learn, learn by heart, commit to memory, get off pat, remember. OPPOSITE: forget.

memory *noun* **1** (*loss of memory*) recall, powers of recall, retention, recollection, remembrance. OPPOSITE: forgetfulness. **2** (*childhood memories*) recollection, remembrance, reminiscence, retrospection. **3** (*in memory of those who died*) commemoration, remembrance, observance, recognition, honour, tribute, glory.

menace *verb* **1** (*menaced by the gang*) threaten, intimidate, terrorize, bully, browbeat, alarm, scare, frighten, terrify. OPPOSITE: reassure. **2** (*dark clouds menaced*) lower, impend, loom.

   ➤ *noun* **1** (*demanding money with menaces*) threat,

intimidation, warning. OPPOSITE: reassurance. **2** (*a menace to society*) danger, peril, hazard, risk, jeopardy, threat. **3** (*the child is a menace*) nuisance, pest, bother, annoyance, vexation, plague, torment, pain (*inf*), thorn in one's flesh (*inf*).

menacing *adj* **1** (*a menacing gesture*) threatening, intimidating, intimidatory, minatory, minacious, alarming, frightening, sinister, dangerous, ominous, warning. OPPOSITE: reassuring. **2** (*a menacing storm*) lowering, impending, looming.

mend *verb* **1** (*good at mending things*) repair, fix, put back together, darn, patch, cobble, restore, renovate, renew, remedy, cure, heal. OPPOSITE: damage. **2** (*resolved to mend her ways*) correct, rectify, put right, amend, emend, reform, improve, ameliorate, better. **3** (*the patient began to mend*) recover, get better, recuperate, improve. OPPOSITE: deteriorate.

on the mend improving, getting better, recovering, recuperating, convalescent. OPPOSITE: deteriorating.

mendacious *adj* lying, untruthful, economical with the truth (*inf*), deceitful, dishonest, insincere, false, untrue, fictitious, fraudulent. OPPOSITE: honest.

mendacity *noun* lying, untruthfulness, deceit, dishonesty, insincerity, falsity, untruth, perjury, misrepresentation, deception, fraudulence. OPPOSITE: honesty.

mendicant *noun* beggar, vagrant, tramp, hobo (*inf*), bum (*inf*), cadger, scrounger (*inf*), sponger (*inf*).

menial *adj* **1** (*menial work*) humble, lowly, base, mean, ignoble, ignominious, degrading, demeaning, unskilled, routine, humdrum, boring, dull. **2** (*replied in menial tones*) servile, obsequious, sycophantic, fawning, slavish, subservient.

   ➤ *noun* servant, domestic, attendant, valet, lackey, flunkey, underling, slave, drudge, skivvy (*inf*). OPPOSITE: master.

menstruation *noun* menses, menstrual flow, menstrual cycle, period, curse (*inf*), monthlies (*inf*), time of the month (*inf*).

mensuration *noun* measurement, measuring, surveying, quantification, assessment, calculation, computation.

mental *adj* **1** (*mental activity*) intellectual, cerebral, abstract. OPPOSITE: physical. **2** (*mental illness*) psychological, psychiatric. **3** (*they thought he was mental*) insane, deranged, disturbed, unbalanced, psychotic, lunatic, mad, crazy (*inf*), off one's head (*inf*), bonkers (*inf*), nuts (*inf*). OPPOSITE: sane.

mentality *noun* **1** (*the criminal mentality*) frame of mind, way of thinking, mindset, psychology, attitude, outlook, character, temperament, disposition, nature, make-up. **2** (*of superior mentality*) intellect, intelligence, mind, brains, grey matter (*inf*), wit, understanding.

mention *verb* name, cite, quote, refer to, allude to, speak of, hint at, intimate, touch on, bring up, broach, point out, say, utter, declare, tell, communicate, disclose, divulge, reveal, make known, breathe a word of (*inf*). OPPOSITE: omit.

   ➤ *noun* **1** (*no mention of the incident*) reference, allusion, remark, observation, declaration, announcement. **2** (*a* *mention in dispatches*) tribute, citation, acknowledgment, recognition.

don't mention it not at all, it's a pleasure, forget it, don't worry, it doesn't matter, think nothing of it.

not to mention besides, in addition to, as well as, let alone, to say nothing of, not counting, not including.

mentor *noun* adviser, counsellor, therapist, confidant, guide, guru, master, teacher, instructor, tutor.

mercantile *adj* commercial, trade, trading, marketable, saleable.

mercenary *adj* **1** (*mercenary relatives hoping to inherit*) greedy, avaricious, covetous, grasping, acquisitive, money-grubbing (*inf*), materialistic, corrupt, venal. OPPOSITE: philanthropic. **2** (*mercenary soldiers*) hired, paid, bought, professional. OPPOSITE: voluntary.

merchandise *noun* goods, wares, commodities, stock, produce, cargo, freight.
➤ *verb* sell, deal in, trade in, distribute, market, promote, advertise, push (*inf*).

merchant *noun* trader, dealer, broker, trafficker, seller, vendor, distributor, wholesaler, retailer, shopkeeper, salesman, saleswoman.

merciful *adj* compassionate, sympathetic, soft-hearted, tender-hearted, forgiving, forbearing, sparing, clement, lenient, tolerant, indulgent, kind, benign, mild, humane, gracious, magnanimous, generous, liberal. OPPOSITE: merciless.

merciless *adj* unmerciful, pitiless, unforgiving, intolerant, unkind, harsh, hard, callous, heartless, unfeeling, unsympathetic, ruthless, relentless, unrelenting, implacable, cruel, inhuman, savage, barbarous. OPPOSITE: merciful.

mercurial *adj* volatile, capricious, fickle, changeable, variable, inconstant, erratic, unpredictable, impulsive, quicksilver, temperamental, flighty, lively, vivacious, active, energetic, spirited, irrepressible. OPPOSITE: steady.

mercy *noun* **1** (*pleading for mercy*) clemency, grace, pardon, forgiveness, forbearance, leniency, tolerance, indulgence, charity, pity, compassion, sympathy, tenderness, mildness, kindness, benevolence, humanity, magnanimity, generosity. OPPOSITE: cruelty. **2** (*it's a mercy that you remembered*) blessing, godsend, boon, favour, stroke of luck.

at the mercy of in the power of, in the control of, in the clutches of, defenceless against, prey to, exposed to, open to.

mere *adj* bare, sheer, stark, simple, plain, pure, unadulterated, unmitigated, utter, absolute, total, complete.

merely *adv* only, just, solely, simply, purely.

meretricious *adj* **1** (*meretricious glamour*) showy, flashy, gaudy, garish, tawdry, cheap. **2** (*a meretricious argument*) spurious, false, sham, bogus, counterfeit, insincere. OPPOSITE: genuine.

merge *verb* join, unite, meet, converge, combine, coalesce, amalgamate, incorporate, blend, mingle, mix, fuse. OPPOSITE: separate.

merger *noun* amalgamation, combination, incorporation, coalition, alliance, union. OPPOSITE: separation.

merit *verb* deserve, be worthy of, earn, incur, be entitled to, have a right to, warrant, justify.
➤ *noun* **1** (*literary merit*) excellence, goodness, quality, value, worth, worthiness. OPPOSITE: inferiority. **2** (*one of the merits of the scheme*) virtue, good point, strong point, asset, credit, plus (*inf*), advantage, benefit. OPPOSITE: fault. **3** (*received his merits*) desert, due, reward, recompense.

meritorious *adj* deserving, worthy, praiseworthy, commendable, creditable, admirable, exemplary, excellent, good, honourable, virtuous. OPPOSITE: despicable.

merriment *noun* mirth, hilarity, laughter, levity, jocundity, jollity, gaiety, high spirits, glee, joy, cheer, fun, amusement, pleasure, sport, revelry, merrymaking, festivity, conviviality. OPPOSITE: gloom.

merry *adj* **1** (*a merry party*) jolly, jovial, jocund, mirthful, gleeful, happy, joyful, cheerful, blithe, carefree, light-hearted, high-spirited, frolicsome, gay, festive, convivial. OPPOSITE: gloomy. **2** (*merry after a glass of champagne*) tipsy, tiddly (*inf*), squiffy (*inf*). OPPOSITE: sober.

make merry revel, carouse, party, celebrate, rejoice, have fun, have a good time, have a ball (*inf*).

mesh *noun* **1** (*wire mesh*) net, netting, network, lattice, trellis, web, reticulation, tracery. **2** (*caught in the mesh*) snare, trap, net, web, tangle, entanglement.
➤ *verb* **1** (*the gears meshed*) engage, interlock, fit together, dovetail. **2** (*the styles do not mesh*) coordinate, harmonize, match, go together. OPPOSITE: clash. **3** (*meshed in intrigue*) catch, snare, trap, net, entangle. OPPOSITE: free.

mesmerize *verb* hypnotize, magnetize, fascinate, captivate, enthral, grip, transfix, entrance, bewitch, spellbind.

mess *noun* **1** (*the mess in the garage*) untidiness, disorder, disarray, clutter, litter, jumble, muddle, confusion, chaos, shambles (*inf*), dirt, dirtiness, filth, squalor. OPPOSITE: order. **2** (*found myself in a mess*) difficulty, trouble, plight, predicament, quandary, dilemma, fix (*inf*), pickle (*inf*), jam (*inf*), hole (*inf*). **3** (*made a mess of the job*) botch, bungle, hash (*inf*), pig's ear (*inf*), dog's breakfast (*inf*), cock-up (*sl*), balls-up (*sl*), foul-up (*sl*).
➤ *verb* untidy, disorder, muddle, confuse, disarrange, tangle, dishevel, litter, dirty, pollute. OPPOSITE: clear.

mess about 1 (*messing about with the computer*) fool about, play about, muck about (*inf*), potter, tinker, fiddle, toy, tamper, interfere, meddle. **2** (*sorry to mess you about*) bother, trouble, inconvenience, upset.

mess up botch, bungle, spoil, ruin, make a mess of, make a hash of (*inf*), cock up (*sl*), screw up (*sl*), foul up (*sl*),

message *noun* **1** (*a message from the president*) communication, note, memorandum, memo (*inf*), letter, fax, e-mail, missive, dispatch, communiqué, bulletin, word, news. **2** (*the message of the film*) meaning, import, point, moral, theme, essence, gist, drift, idea. **3** (*sent her on a message*) errand, mission, commission, assignment, task, job.

get the message understand, comprehend, take the

hint, follow, see, get the picture (*inf*), get it (*inf*), catch on (*inf*), cotton on (*inf*).

messenger *noun* courier, runner, bearer, carrier, envoy, emissary, go-between, harbinger, herald.

messy *adj* untidy, disordered, cluttered, littered, dirty, grubby, slovenly, sloppy, unkempt, dishevelled, disarranged, disorganized, muddled, confused. OPPOSITE: neat.

metamorphosis *noun* change, alteration, modification, conversion, mutation, transmutation, transformation, transfiguration, transmogrification (*inf*).

metaphor *noun* allegory, image, symbol, image, figure of speech, trope, analogy.

metaphorical *adj* figurative, allegorical, symbolic, emblematic. OPPOSITE: literal.

metaphysical *adj* abstract, theoretical, intangible, immaterial, supernatural, transcendental, spiritual, intellectual, philosophical, ideal, speculative, abstruse, esoteric, recondite. OPPOSITE: material.

mete *verb* **mete out** dispense, administer, distribute, deal out, dole out, measure out, allot, assign, allocate, apportion. OPPOSITE: withhold.

meteoric *adj* rapid, swift, speedy, fast, quick, lightning, sudden, overnight, fleeting, momentary, brilliant, dazzling, spectacular. OPPOSITE: gradual.

method *noun* **1** (*try a different method*) way, manner, means, mode, fashion, style, technique, approach, procedure, process, system, routine, course, route, plan, scheme. **2** (*no method in the way they work*) order, orderliness, organization, planning, plan, design, structure, form, pattern, regularity. OPPOSITE: disorder.

methodical *adj* systematic, organized, well-ordered, orderly, neat, tidy, businesslike, efficient, structured, logical, planned, exact, precise, punctilious, meticulous. OPPOSITE: disorganized.

meticulous *adj* scrupulous, punctilious, fastidious, particular, exacting, fussy, finicky, conscientious, painstaking, careful, precise, exact, thorough, rigorous. OPPOSITE: slapdash.

metropolis *noun* capital, megalopolis, city.

mettle *noun* **1** (*of the same mettle*) character, disposition, temperament, nature, make-up, temper, humour, kind, sort, type. **2** (*proved her mettle*) spirit, vigour, energy, stamina, fortitude, hardihood, grit, backbone (*inf*), boldness, daring, bravery, courage, valour, pluck, nerve, guts (*inf*), bottle (*inf*).

miasma *noun* smell, odour, stench, reek, mephitis, effluvium.

microscopic *adj* minute, tiny, minuscule, infinitesimal, imperceptible, negligible. OPPOSITE: huge.

microcosm *noun* world, society, community, system, whole, entity. OPPOSITE: macrocosm.

midday *noun* noon, twelve, twelve o'clock, lunchtime.

middle *noun* **1** (*the middle of the line*) centre, midpoint, mean, median. OPPOSITE: end. **2** (*the middle of the forest*) heart, core, centre, midst, interior, inside. OPPOSITE: edge.
  ➤ *adj* central, midway, halfway, equidistant, intermediate, medium, mean, medial, median, inner, interior. OPPOSITE: extreme.

middleman *noun* broker, agent, factor, intermediary, go-between.

middling *adj* mediocre, average, medium, moderate, fair, passable, adequate, tolerable, so-so (*inf*), OK (*inf*). OPPOSITE: exceptional.

midget *noun* dwarf, pygmy, manikin, homunculus. OPPOSITE: giant.
  ➤ *adj* dwarf, pygmy, miniature, toy, pocket, baby, small, little, tiny, minute. OPPOSITE: giant.

midst *noun* middle, centre, heart, bosom, thick, depths. OPPOSITE: edge.

midway *adv* halfway, in the middle, in the centre.

mien *noun* bearing, carriage, deportment, demeanour, manner, air, appearance, look, aspect, aura.

miffed *adj* annoyed, vexed, irked, displeased, upset, aggrieved, hurt, offended, put out, piqued, peeved (*inf*), narked (*inf*).

might *noun* power, force, strength, vigour, energy, potency, forcefulness, mightiness, toughness, stamina. OPPOSITE: weakness.
  with might and main powerfully, forcefully, strongly, vigorously, full force, with all one's strength.

mighty *adj* **1** (*a mighty blow*) powerful, forceful, strong, vigorous, energetic, lusty, hearty. OPPOSITE: gentle. **2** (*his mighty opponent*) strong, tough, robust, hardy, sturdy, stalwart, strapping, muscular. OPPOSITE: weak. **3** (*the mighty mountain*) huge, enormous, immense, gigantic, colossal, massive, great, monumental, prodigious. OPPOSITE: tiny.
  ➤ *adv* very, extremely, exceedingly, greatly, highly, much.

migrant *adj* migratory, wandering, roving, nomadic, itinerant, peripatetic, travelling, on the move, displaced, unsettled.
  ➤ *noun* emigrant, immigrant, traveller, globetrotter, wanderer, rover, nomad, gypsy, itinerant, vagrant.

migrate *verb* move, relocate, resettle, emigrate, immigrate, travel, journey, wander, roam, rove. OPPOSITE: remain.

mild *adj* **1** (*a mild man*) gentle, tender, soft-hearted, warm-hearted, kind, compassionate, merciful, clement, lenient, tolerant, amiable, genial, good-natured, easygoing (*inf*), calm, placid, serene, tranquil, meek, docile. OPPOSITE: harsh. **2** (*a mild form of the disease*) moderate, light, slight, weak. OPPOSITE: severe. **3** (*mild weather*) warm, equable, temperate, balmy, clement, fair, pleasant. OPPOSITE: cold. **4** (*a mild flavour*) bland, mellow, smooth, subtle, insipid. OPPOSITE: strong.

mildew *noun* mould, fungus, blight, rust, blast, smut.

milieu *noun* environment, surroundings, setting, background, location, element, sphere.

militant *adj* aggressive, belligerent, bellicose, pugnacious, combative, assertive, vigorous, active, warring, fighting, embattled. OPPOSITE: peaceful.
  ➤ *noun* activist, combatant, fighter, warrior, belligerent, aggressor. OPPOSITE: pacifist.

military *adj* soldierly, armed, martial, warlike. OPPOSITE: civil.
  ➤ *noun* forces, services, armed forces, armed services, militia, army, navy, air force, marines.

militate *verb* **militate against** oppose, counter, conflict with, go against, act against, prejudice, damage, be detrimental to.

milky *adj* white, whitish, off-white, creamy, ivory, alabaster, pearly, cloudy, opaque.

mill *noun* **1** (*a cotton mill*) factory, plant, works. **2** (*a pepper mill*) grinder, crusher, roller.
 ➤ *verb* grind, pulverize, powder, comminute, triturate, crush, pound.
mill around crowd, throng, move about, wander, meander.

millstone *noun* burden, onus, weight, obligation, responsibility, duty, trouble, affliction, cross, albatross.

mime *noun* dumb show, pantomime, mummery, sign language.
 ➤ *verb* gesture, signal, indicate, act out.

mimic *verb* **1** (*mimicked her teacher*) imitate, ape, parrot, copy, impersonate, take off (*inf*), mock, ridicule, parody, caricature. **2** (*mimicking its surroundings*) simulate, mirror, echo, resemble.
 ➤ *noun* mimicker, imitator, ape, parrot, copycat (*inf*), impersonator, impressionist.

mince *verb* **1** (*mince meat*) chop, hash, dice, grind, crumble. **2** (*mincing along*) walk affectedly, pose, posture, attitudinize, put on airs.

mind *noun* **1** (*improving his mind*) intellect, intelligence, brain, grey matter (*inf*), mentality, wits, sense, understanding. **2** (*losing her mind*) sanity, head, wits, sense, reason, reasoning, rationality, understanding, judgment. **3** (*my mind wandered*) attention, thoughts, concentration, application. **4** (*it's all in the mind*) imagination, brain, head, psyche, subconscious. **5** (*it slipped my mind*) memory, recollection, remembrance. **6** (*of the same mind*) opinion, view, viewpoint, standpoint, attitude, way of thinking, feeling, sentiment, thought, belief, idea, judgment. **7** (*have a mind to refuse*) inclination, disposition, tendency, desire, wish, urge, notion, fancy, will, purpose, aim, intention. **8** (*one of the greatest minds of the century*) genius, intellectual, egghead (*inf*), thinker.
 ➤ *verb* **1** (*if they don't mind*) care, object, take offence, be bothered, be upset. **2** (*I mind having to move*) resent, disapprove of, dislike, object to. OPPOSITE: like. **3** (*mind what you're doing*) be careful, take care, pay attention to, concentrate on, beware, watch, look out. **4** (*didn't mind our warning*) heed, listen to, take notice of, mark, regard, note, observe, follow, obey, comply with. OPPOSITE: ignore. **5** (*mind you take your key*) be sure to, remember to, take care that, ensure that. **6** (*mind the children*) look after, take care of, have charge of, guard, watch over, keep an eye on (*inf*). OPPOSITE: neglect.
bear/keep in mind remember, note, consider, take into account.
in two minds unresolved, undecided, uncertain, unsure, hesitant, wavering, vacillating, dithering. OPPOSITE: resolved.

mindful *adj* aware, conscious, alert, attentive, regardful, heedful, thoughtful, careful, wary, chary, watchful. OPPOSITE: oblivious.

mindless *adj* **1** (*mindless of the danger*) heedless, inattentive, oblivious, careless, negligent, neglectful.

OPPOSITE: mindful. **2** (*mindless acts of vandalism*) foolish, stupid, unintelligent, witless, brainless, senseless, thoughtless, unthinking, barbarous, gratuitous. OPPOSITE: thoughtful. **3** (*a mindless job*) mechanical, automatic, routine, boring, tedious. OPPOSITE: interesting.

mine *noun* **1** (*coal from the mine*) pit, colliery, well, shaft, tunnel, excavation, quarry, vein, lode, seam, deposit. **2** (*a mine of information*) source, supply, reservoir, fund, reserve, store, repository, treasury, mint, wealth, abundance.
 ➤ *verb* **1** (*mine for coal*) dig, bore, excavate, quarry, extract, unearth. **2** (*mine the fortifications*) undermine, tunnel under, burrow under, sap, weaken.

mingle *verb* **1** (*the colours mingled*) mix, commingle, intermingle, intermix, merge, blend, fuse, coalesce, combine, amalgamate, join, unite. OPPOSITE: separate. **2** (*mingling with the other guests*) associate, fraternize, consort, hobnob, socialize, circulate.

miniature *adj* small, little, wee (*inf*), tiny, minute, diminutive, pint-sized (*inf*), mini, reduced, small-scale, pygmy, dwarf, midget, baby, toy, pocket. OPPOSITE: large.

minimal *adj* minimum, least, lowest, smallest, slightest. OPPOSITE: maximal.

minimize *verb* **1** (*minimize expenditure*) reduce, decrease, diminish, cut, slash, keep to a minimum. OPPOSITE: maximize. **2** (*minimize the problem*) play down, make light of, underestimate, underrate, belittle, deprecate, depreciate, disparage. OPPOSITE: exaggerate.

minimum *noun* least, lowest, bottom, nadir, depth. OPPOSITE: maximum.
 ➤ *adj* minimal, least, lowest, smallest, slightest. OPPOSITE: maximum.

minion *noun* underling, subordinate, hireling, menial, flunkey, lackey, sycophant, toady, bootlicker (*inf*), yes-man (*inf*), parasite, hanger-on, follower, favourite, pet, darling. OPPOSITE: master.

minister *noun* **1** (*a minister of religion*) cleric, clergyman, clergywoman, churchman, churchwoman, ecclesiastic, preacher, vicar, parson, pastor, rector, curate, priest, padre, chaplain. OPPOSITE: layperson. **2** (*a government minister*) politician, statesman, stateswoman, official, dignitary, administrator, executive, ambassador, diplomat, plenipotentiary, legate, emissary, envoy, agent, representative, secretary, servant.
minister to attend, serve, wait on, take care of, look after, tend, nurse, oblige, accommodate, cater to, pander to, help, aid, assist.

ministration *noun* help, aid, assistance, support, service, relief, care.

ministry *noun* **1** (*the ministry was his vocation*) church, clergy, priesthood, holy orders, religion. **2** (*the ministry of education*) government, cabinet, administration, executive, department, office, bureau, secretariat.

minor *adj* **1** (*a minor role*) lesser, smaller, secondary, subsidiary, subordinate, inferior, junior. OPPOSITE: major. **2** (*a minor problem*) slight, trivial, trifling, petty, insignificant, unimportant, inconsequential, small, inconsiderable, negligible. OPPOSITE: serious.

minstrel *noun* musician, singer, troubadour, bard, performer, entertainer.

mint *verb* **1** (*mint money*) coin, stamp, strike, punch, cast, forge, make, produce. **2** (*a newly minted expression*) formulate, think up, devise, invent, make up, create, fabricate, coin.
➤ *adj* perfect, pristine, brand-new, unused.
➤ *noun* **1** (*cost a mint*) fortune, king's ransom (*inf*), packet (*inf*), bundle (*inf*). **2** (*a mint of ideas*) source, supply, reservoir, mine, fund, treasury.

minus *adj* less, lacking, short of, without. OPPOSITE: plus.

minute[1] *noun* **1** (*wait a minute*) moment, second, instant, flash, twinkling, trice, tick (*inf*), jiffy (*inf*). OPPOSITE: age. **2** (*at the same minute*) instant, second, moment, time, point, stage, juncture.
in a minute soon, shortly, before long, in a tick (*inf*), in a jiffy (*inf*), in two shakes of a lamb's tail (*inf*), before you can say Jack Robinson (*inf*).

minute[2] *adj* **1** (*a minute fragment*) tiny, minuscule, microscopic, infinitesimal, small, little, fine, slight, negligible, inconsequential. OPPOSITE: huge. **2** (*a minute examination*) detailed, exact, accurate, precise, strict, close, meticulous, scrupulous, punctilious, painstaking, thorough, exhaustive. OPPOSITE: cursory.

minutely *adv* in detail, closely, meticulously, scrupulously, thoroughly, with a fine-tooth comb (*inf*).

minutes *pl noun* notes, record, transcript, proceedings, transactions.

minutiae *pl noun* details, particulars, niceties, subtleties, finer points, small print (*inf*), trivia, trifles.

miracle *noun* wonder, marvel, prodigy, phenomenon.

miraculous *adj* **1** (*a miraculous improvement*) wonderful, marvellous, fantastic (*inf*), prodigious, phenomenal, extraordinary, remarkable, amazing, astonishing, incredible, unbelievable. OPPOSITE: normal.
2 (*miraculous events*) inexplicable, unaccountable, supernatural, preternatural, superhuman, divine. OPPOSITE: natural.

mire *noun* **1** (*sinking into the mire*) marsh, bog, swamp, fen, quag, quagmire, morass, slough. **2** (*boots covered with mire*) mud, dirt, filth, muck (*inf*), slime, ooze.

mirror *noun* **1** (*look in the mirror*) glass, looking-glass, reflector. **2** (*art is the mirror of life*) reflection, copy, replica, model, pattern, representation, likeness, double, twin, clone, image.
➤ *verb* reflect, echo, imitate, copy, mimic, ape, simulate, represent, depict.

mirth *noun* merriment, jollity, levity, jocularity, hilarity, laughter, amusement, fun, sport, pleasure, happiness, glee, joy, cheerfulness, blitheness, gaiety, high spirits, revelry, festivity, merrymaking. OPPOSITE: melancholy.

mirthful *adj* merry, jolly, jovial, jocund, jocular, light-hearted, hilarious, amusing, fun-filled, enjoyable, happy, gleeful, joyful, cheerful, blithe, gay, festive, playful, sportive, frolicsome, high-spirited. OPPOSITE: gloomy.

misadventure *noun* misfortune, mischance, bad luck, ill fortune, mishap, reverse, setback, accident, calamity, disaster, catastrophe.

misanthropic *adj* cynical, unsociable, antisocial, reclusive, egoistic, narcissistic, selfish, surly, unsympathetic. OPPOSITE: philanthropic.

misapprehend *verb* misunderstand, misconceive, misconstrue, misinterpret, misread, mistake, get the wrong idea (*inf*), get hold of the wrong end of the stick (*inf*).

misapprehension *noun* misunderstanding, misconception, mistake, error, delusion, false impression.

misappropriate *verb* embezzle, peculate, defalcate, steal, thieve, pinch (*inf*), nick (*inf*).

misbegotten *adj* **1** (*a misbegotten scheme*) ill-conceived, abortive, ill-advised, harebrained (*inf*). **2** (*a misbegotten rogue*) dishonourable, contemptible, despicable, wretched.

misbehave *verb* behave badly, be naughty, get up to mischief, fool around, muck about (*inf*), play up (*inf*), act up (*inf*).

misbehaviour *noun* misconduct, naughtiness, mischief, insubordination, disobedience, impropriety, rudeness, misdemeanour, delinquency.

miscalculate *verb* misjudge, overestimate, underestimate, err, be wrong, make a mistake, slip up (*inf*).

miscarriage *noun* abortion, failure, breakdown, defeat, frustration, mismanagement, perversion. OPPOSITE: success.

miscarry *verb* abort, fail, go wrong, misfire, founder, come to grief, fall through, bite the dust (*inf*). OPPOSITE: succeed.

miscellaneous *adj* mixed, varied, assorted, diverse, sundry, various, heterogeneous, motley, multifarious.

miscellany *noun* mixture, assortment, collection, medley, mélange, mixed bag (*inf*), pot pourri, hotchpotch, hodgepodge, salmagundi, farrago, omnium-gatherum (*inf*), jumble, confusion.

mischance *noun* misfortune, misadventure, bad luck, ill fortune, mishap, accident, calamity, disaster.

mischief *noun* **1** (*children full of mischief*) naughtiness, misbehaviour, misconduct, wrongdoing, delinquency, roguery, rascality, impishness, devilment, pranks, tricks, monkey business (*inf*). **2** (*likely to cause mischief*) harm, hurt, injury, damage, annoyance, nuisance, trouble, upset, disruption, ill feeling.

mischievous *adj* **1** (*mischievous children*) naughty, roguish, rascally, impish, playful, frolicsome, badly behaved, delinquent, troublesome, annoying, exasperating. OPPOSITE: good. **2** (*a mischievous wink*) arch, playful, puckish, waggish, teasing. **3** (*mischievous gossip*) malicious, spiteful, malignant, vicious, bad, wicked, evil, harmful, hurtful, injurious, damaging, detrimental, pernicious.

misconception *noun* misunderstanding, misapprehension, misinterpretation, misconstruction, mistake, error, delusion, false impression, misjudgment, miscalculation.

misconduct *noun* misbehaviour, wrongdoing,

delinquency, malpractice, malfeasance, malversation, impropriety, mismanagement, maladministration.

misconstrue *verb* misinterpret, misread, take the wrong way, misunderstand, misapprehend, misconceive, mistake, misjudge, miscalculate.

miscreant *noun* wrongdoer, malefactor, criminal, villain, rogue, rascal, scoundrel, blackguard, wretch, reprobate, sinner.

misdeed *noun* misdemeanour, crime, felony, offence, wrong, fault, error, sin, transgression, trespass.

misdemeanour *noun* misdeed, offence, violation, infringement, peccadillo, transgression, trespass, fault, error.

miser *noun* niggard, skinflint, scrooge, cheeseparer, cheapskate (*inf*), penny-pincher (*inf*), money-grubber (*inf*), tightarse (*sl*). OPPOSITE: spendthrift.

miserable *adj* **1** (*she looked miserable*) unhappy, sad, sorrowful, forlorn, wretched, woebegone, doleful, mournful, melancholy, depressed, dejected, downcast, despondent, gloomy, glum, down in the dumps (*inf*), distressed, disconsolate, heartbroken. OPPOSITE: happy. **2** (*a miserable trick*) contemptible, despicable, ignominious, base, low, mean, abject. OPPOSITE: noble. **3** (*a miserable offer*) paltry, meagre, scanty, pathetic, low, poor, mean. OPPOSITE: generous. **4** (*living in miserable conditions*) sordid, squalid, seedy, shabby, dilapidated, wretched, sorry, pathetic, pitiful, pitiable. OPPOSITE: luxurious. **5** (*miserable beggars*) poor, penniless, impoverished, poverty-stricken, destitute, indigent, needy. OPPOSITE: rich. **6** (*a miserable November afternoon*) unpleasant, disagreeable, cheerless, joyless, gloomy, dismal, dreary. OPPOSITE: bright.

miserly *adj* mean, niggardly, stingy (*inf*), parsimonious, cheeseparing, penny-pinching (*inf*), money-grubbing (*inf*), close-fisted, tight-fisted, tight (*inf*), selfish, grasping, avaricious, covetous, ungenerous, illiberal, close, near. OPPOSITE: generous.

misery *noun* **1** (*a sigh of misery*) unhappiness, sadness, sorrow, grief, woe, wretchedness, melancholy, depression, dejection, despondency, gloom, distress, anguish, torment, torture, despair, desolation. OPPOSITE: joy. **2** (*living in misery*) poverty, need, want, deprivation, indigence, destitution, discomfort, hardship, suffering. OPPOSITE: affluence. **3** (*don't be such a misery!*) moaner, complainer, grouch (*inf*), pessimist, prophet of doom, damper, wet blanket (*inf*), spoilsport, killjoy, party-pooper (*inf*).

misfit *noun* eccentric, nonconformist, individualist, maverick, dropout, fish out of water (*inf*), square peg in a round hole (*inf*).

misfortune *noun* **1** (*suffer misfortune*) bad luck, ill luck, ill fortune, mischance, misadventure, adversity, affliction, hardship, trouble. **2** (*a series of misfortunes*) mishap, accident, blow, reverse, setback, calamity, disaster, catastrophe, trouble, trial, tribulation.

misgiving *noun* doubt, hesitation, uncertainty, suspicion, mistrust, distrust, qualm, scruple, reservation, anxiety, apprehension. OPPOSITE: assurance.

misguided *adj* misled, misinformed, deluded, imprudent, ill-advised, unwise, injudicious, foolish, erroneous, mistaken, wrong.

mishap *noun* accident, misfortune, misadventure, mischance, setback, reverse, contretemps, calamity, disaster, catastrophe.

mishmash *noun* hotchpotch, hodgepodge, jumble, confusion, mixture, assortment, miscellany, medley, pot-pourri, salmagundi, farrago, patchwork.

misinterpret *noun* misconstrue, misread, take the wrong way, distort, garble, misunderstand, misapprehend, misconceive, mistake, misjudge, miscalculate.

misjudge *verb* miscalculate, underestimate, underrate, overestimate, overrate, misinterpret, misunderstand.

mislay *verb* lose, misplace, miss, drop. OPPOSITE: find.

mislead *verb* misguide, misdirect, lead astray, throw off the scent (*inf*), send on a wild-goose chase (*inf*), misinform, deceive, delude, fool, trick, hoodwink, take for a ride (*inf*), pull the wool over someone's eyes (*inf*).

misleading *adj* deceptive, deceiving, delusive, illusory, fallacious, spurious, sophistical, casuistic, evasive, equivocal, ambiguous.

mismanage *verb* maladminister, misgovern, misdirect, misconduct, mishandle, botch, bungle, mess up, foul up (*sl*), cock up (*sl*), screw up (*sl*).

mismatched *adj* incompatible, unsuited, incongruous, ill-assorted, clashing, discordant. OPPOSITE: compatible.

misprint *noun* mistake, error, erratum, corrigendum, literal, typo (*inf*).

misquote *verb* misreport, misstate, misrepresent, distort, garble.

misrepresent *verb* falsify, distort, twist, pervert, garble, misinterpret, misstate, misquote.

misrule *noun* misgovernment, maladministration, mismanagement, anarchy, lawlessness, chaos, disorder, confusion, tumult, turmoil. OPPOSITE: order.

miss[1] *verb* **1** (*a plan that can't miss*) fail, miscarry, misfire. OPPOSITE: succeed. **2** (*missed his chance*) lose, let go, let slip, pass up. OPPOSITE: seize. **3** (*missed her piano lesson*) fail to attend, play truant from, skip, escape, evade, avoid, dodge. OPPOSITE: attend. **4** (*he misses his sister*) want, need, long for, pine for, yearn for. **5** (*you're missing the point*) misunderstand, overlook, disregard.
⯈ *noun* failure, mistake, error, slip, blunder, oversight, omission, loss. OPPOSITE: hit.

miss out skip, jump, pass over, omit, leave out, exclude, overlook, ignore, disregard. OPPOSITE: include.

miss[2] *noun* (*a clever little miss*) girl, lass, young woman, young lady, damsel, maiden.

misshapen *adj* deformed, malformed, twisted, bent, contorted, crooked, warped, distorted, unshapely, ill-proportioned, grotesque, ugly. OPPOSITE: shapely.

missile *noun* projectile, shot, bullet, arrow, bomb, rocket, torpedo, weapon.

missing *adj* lost, mislaid, misplaced, lacking, wanting, absent, gone, unaccounted for. OPPOSITE: present.

mission *noun* **1** (*their mission was to destroy the ship*) task, job, assignment, commission, duty, responsibility, charge, undertaking, errand, business, work, operation, campaign, quest, goal, objective, aim, purpose, raison d'être, vocation, calling. **2** (*a diplomatic mission*) embassy, commission, legation, delegation, deputation, ministry, task force.

missionary noun evangelist, proselytizer, preacher, campaigner, crusader, apostle, minister, champion.
➤ adj evangelical, evangelistic, campaigning, crusading, converting, reforming, enthusiastic, zealous.

missive noun letter, epistle, communication, message, memorandum, memo (inf), dispatch, bulletin, communiqué.

misspend verb misuse, misapply, squander, waste, dissipate, fritter away, throw away.

misstate verb misreport, misquote, misrepresent, falsify, distort, twist, pervert, garble.

mist noun haze, fog, cloud, vapour, steam, condensation, film, drizzle, spray.
mist up steam up, fog over, cloud over, blur, become hazy. OPPOSITE: clear.

mistake noun error, slip, inaccuracy, fault, blunder, gaffe, faux pas, boob (inf), booboo (inf), blooper (inf), solecism, howler (inf), clanger (inf), erratum, corrigendum, literal, typo (inf), oversight, omission, slip-up (inf), balls-up (sl), cock-up (sl), miscalculation, misunderstanding, misapprehension, misconception.
➤ verb 1 (mistook her meaning) misinterpret, misconstrue, misread, misjudge, misunderstand, misapprehend, get hold of the wrong end of the stick (inf). 2 (mistook the salt for sugar) confuse, mix up, get wrong.
make a mistake err, be wrong, slip up (inf), miscalculate, blunder, boob (inf).

mistaken adj wrong, erroneous, incorrect, inaccurate, inexact, imprecise, wide of the mark (inf), false, untrue, fallacious, unsound, faulty, in error, at fault, misguided, misled, misinformed, barking up the wrong tree (inf). OPPOSITE: correct.

mistakenly adv by mistake, in error, wrongly, erroneously, incorrectly, misguidedly. OPPOSITE: correctly.

mistreat verb maltreat, ill-treat, misuse, ill-use, abuse, molest, harm, injure, hurt, damage, mishandle, manhandle, batter, beat up (inf).

mistress noun 1 (her husband's mistress) lover, girlfriend, kept woman, bit on the side (inf), lady-love, inamorata, paramour, courtesan, concubine. OPPOSITE: wife. 2 (the mistress of the household) head, owner, proprietor, employer. OPPOSITE: servant. 3 (the chemistry mistress) teacher, instructor, tutor, governess. OPPOSITE: pupil.

mistrust verb distrust, doubt, lack faith in, suspect, disbelieve, be wary of, fear. OPPOSITE: trust.
➤ noun distrust, doubt, scepticism, suspicion, wariness, reservation, qualm, misgiving. OPPOSITE: confidence.

mistrustful adj distrustful, doubtful, dubious, sceptical, suspicious, wary, chary, cautious, hesitant. OPPOSITE: certain.

misty adj hazy, foggy, cloudy, murky, bleary, fuzzy, blurred, obscure, dim, vague, indistinct. OPPOSITE: clear.

misunderstand verb misapprehend, misinterpret, misconstrue, misconceive, get the wrong idea (inf), get hold of the wrong end of the stick (inf), mistake,

misread, mishear, misjudge, get one's wires crossed (inf). OPPOSITE: understand.

misunderstanding noun 1 (a misunderstanding of our instructions) misapprehension, misinterpretation, misconstruction, misconception, mistake, error, mix-up, crossed wires (inf). OPPOSITE: understanding. 2 (had a misunderstanding with her neighbour) disagreement, difference of opinion, quarrel, argument, dispute, tiff (inf), spat (inf), clash, conflict, breach, rift. OPPOSITE: agreement.

misuse noun 1 (misused her skills) misemploy, misapply, squander, waste, dissipate, profane, pervert, corrupt. 2 (misused by his employer) abuse, ill-use, mistreat, maltreat, ill-treat, exploit, harm, hurt.
➤ noun 1 (the misuse of money) misemployment, misapplication, wrong use, waste, dissipation, perversion, corruption. 2 (suffered years of misuse) abuse, ill-use, mistreatment, maltreatment, exploitation.

mitigate verb moderate, lessen, reduce, diminish, abate, alleviate, allay, assuage, ease, relieve, dull, blunt, subdue, temper, soften, lighten, extenuate, vindicate, calm, appease, mollify, pacify. OPPOSITE: aggravate.

mix verb 1 (mix the ingredients) combine, blend, mingle, intermingle, intermix, compound, alloy, merge, amalgamate, synthesize, homogenize, join, unite. OPPOSITE: separate. 2 (doesn't mix with the other children) associate, fraternize, consort, hobnob, socialize, mingle.
➤ noun mixture, combination, blend, compound, alloy, merger, amalgamation, synthesis, union.
mix up confuse, muddle, mistake, jumble, scramble, garble, complicate, involve.

mixed adj 1 (a mixed bunch) assorted, varied, diverse, motley, heterogeneous, miscellaneous. OPPOSITE: homogeneous. 2 (a dog of mixed breed) hybrid, crossbred, interbred, mongrel. OPPOSITE: pure. 3 (mixed feelings) ambivalent, conflicting, contradicting, equivocal, unsure, uncertain. 4 (a mixed school) multiracial, coeducational.
mixed up 1 (mixed up about the arrangements) confused, muddled, bewildered, puzzled, perplexed, disorientated, upset, disturbed, maladjusted. 2 (mixed up in a smuggling operation) involved, implicated, entangled, embroiled, incriminated.

mixer noun 1 (a food mixer) blender, liquidizer, processor. 2 (he's a good mixer) socializer, mingler, joiner, extrovert, life and soul of the party.

mixture noun 1 (a mixture of fear and excitement) combination, blend, amalgamation, synthesis, union, cross, hybrid. 2 (stir the mixture) blend, mix, brew, concoction, compound, alloy. 3 (a mixture of people) assortment, variety, mix, mélange, medley, miscellany, pot-pourri, hotchpotch, hodgepodge, jumble, mixed bag (inf).

moan verb 1 (moan about the delay) complain, grumble, whine, whinge (inf), bleat (inf), grouse, grouch, gripe (inf), bellyache (inf), beef (inf), bewail, bemoan, lament, mourn, grieve, deplore, carp, cavil, protest, make a fuss. OPPOSITE: rejoice. 2 (moaning in pain) groan, cry, wail, whine, howl, sigh.
➤ noun 1 (the moans of their customers) complaint, grumble, grievance, whine, whinge (inf), grouse, gripe

(*inf*), cavil, criticism, protest, objection. **2** (*the moans of the injured*) groan, cry, wail, whine, howl, sigh, lament, lamentation.

mob *noun* **1** (*a mob of sightseers*) crowd, throng, multitude, horde, host, herd, pack, flock, drove, swarm, gang, troop, company, body. OPPOSITE: individual. **2** (*appeal to the mob*) populace, commonalty, hoi polloi, plebs (*inf*), masses, rabble, riff-raff (*inf*). OPPOSITE: aristocracy.

mobile *adj* **1** (*a mobile library*) movable, portable, transportable, travelling, itinerant, peripatetic. OPPOSITE: stationary. **2** (*mobile features*) moving, motile, changeable, variable, lively, animated. OPPOSITE: immobile. **3** (*socially mobile*) flexible, adaptable, adjustable.

mobilize *verb* call up, muster, rally, marshal, assemble, organize, prepare, get ready.

mock *verb* **1** (*they mocked her when she began to sing*) ridicule, jeer at, scoff at, laugh at, make fun of, take the mickey out of (*inf*), take the piss out of (*sl*), tease, taunt, rag (*inf*), rib (*inf*), deride, scorn, sneer at. OPPOSITE: respect. **2** (*comedians who mock the government*) lampoon, parody, burlesque, satirize, send up (*inf*), mimic, ape, imitate, impersonate, take off (*inf*). **3** (*the weather mocked our attempts to leave*) thwart, frustrate, foil.
➤ *adj* imitation, simulated, synthetic, artificial, ersatz, dummy, false, counterfeit, fake, bogus, sham, feigned, pretended. OPPOSITE: genuine.

mockery *noun* **1** (*the mockery of his classmates*) ridicule, jeering, scoffing, gibe, taunt, sneer, scorn, contempt, derision. OPPOSITE: respect. **2** (*a mockery of established religion*) lampoon, parody, burlesque, satire, spoof, send-up (*inf*), imitation, impersonation, take-off (*inf*). **3** (*the trial was a mockery*) travesty, sham, pretence, joke, laugh, apology.

mode *noun* manner, way, method, means, approach, technique, style, fashion, form, custom, practice, convention.

model *noun* **1** (*the model on which it was based*) example, pattern, template, mould, standard, norm, archetype, prototype, original. **2** (*a model of efficiency*) exemplar, paragon, ideal, epitome, embodiment, acme. **3** (*a model of the building*) copy, replica, facsimile, representation, mock-up, dummy, imitation, miniature. **4** (*the latest model of the car*) version, mark, design, style, form, type, kind, sort, variety. **5** (*an artist's model*) sitter, poser, subject. **6** (*a fashion model*) mannequin, clothes-horse (*inf*).
➤ *verb* **1** (*modelled in clay*) make, mould, shape, form, fashion, sculpt, carve, cast, plan, design, base. **2** (*modelling the latest fashions*) wear, sport, show, display. **3** (*model for an artist*) sit, pose.
➤ *adj* **1** (*a model train*) small-scale, miniature, dummy, imitation, representative, illustrative. **2** (*a model pupil*) ideal, perfect.

moderate *adj* **1** (*moderate behaviour*) reasonable, restrained, controlled, steady, sober, middle-of-the-road. OPPOSITE: extreme. **2** (*a moderate climate*) temperate, equable, mild, calm. **3** (*of moderate ability*) average, medium, modest, mediocre, middling, fair, adequate, passable, so-so (*inf*).

➤ *verb* **1** (*moderated her anger*) control, regulate, temper, subdue, repress, restrain, curb, check. OPPOSITE: aggravate. **2** (*moderated the pain*) mitigate, ease, alleviate, allay, assuage, abate, reduce, lessen, diminish, lower, tone down, soften, lighten, appease, pacify, calm. OPPOSITE: intensify. **3** (*the wind has moderated*) decrease, reduce, lessen, diminish, abate, let up, die down. OPPOSITE: increase. **4** (*moderating the negotiations*) arbitrate, judge, umpire, referee, mediate, preside over, chair.

moderately *adv* rather, somewhat, fairly, quite, to a degree, to some extent, reasonably, tolerably, passably. OPPOSITE: extremely.

moderation *noun* **1** (*showing moderation in his behaviour*) control, regulation, temperance, restraint, self-control, self-restraint, calm, composure, equanimity. **2** (*the moderation of their demands*) decrease, reduction, diminution, lowering, mitigation, appeasement.
in moderation within reason, within limits, within bounds, moderately. OPPOSITE: to excess.

modern *adj* **1** (*modern times*) contemporary, current, existent, present, present-day. OPPOSITE: past. **2** (*modern technology*) recent, latest, up-to-date, up-to-the-minute, state-of-the-art, advanced, progressive, new, novel, fresh, innovative, newfangled (*inf*), modernistic, ultramodern, futuristic. OPPOSITE: out-of-date. **3** (*modern clothes*) stylish, fashionable, in fashion, in vogue, voguish, modish, trendy (*inf*). OPPOSITE: old-fashioned.

modernize *verb* update, upgrade, renew, refresh, rejuvenate, revamp, move with the times (*inf*).

modest *adj* **1** (*modest about his role in the affair*) humble, unassuming, unpretentious, self-effacing. OPPOSITE: boastful. **2** (*a modest young woman*) shy, bashful, coy, self-conscious, diffident, unassertive, reserved, reticent, retiring, quiet, demure, discreet, decent, seemly, decorous, chaste, virtuous. OPPOSITE: immodest. **3** (*a modest income*) moderate, average, medium, small, limited, unexceptional, adequate, acceptable, fair. OPPOSITE: exorbitant. **4** (*a modest apartment*) ordinary, simple, plain, humble, unpretentious, inexpensive. OPPOSITE: extravagant.

modicum *noun* bit, iota, jot, whit, atom, grain, pinch, drop, scrap, shred, ounce. OPPOSITE: lot.

modification *noun* **1** (*modification of the layout*) change, alteration, variation, adjustment, revision, refinement, improvement, transformation. **2** (*modification of their demands*) moderation, reduction, mitigation, limitation, restriction, qualification.

modify *verb* **1** (*modify the layout*) change, alter, vary, adjust, adapt, remodel, reshape, revise, recast, refine, improve, transform, convert. **2** (*modified their demands*) moderate, temper, lower, tone down, lessen, reduce, soften, mitigate, limit, restrict, qualify.

modulate *verb* adjust, regulate, tune, modify, change, alter, vary, inflect, temper, moderate.

modulation *noun* adjustment, regulation, balance, modification, change, alteration, variation, inflection, intonation, tone, accent.

mogul *noun* magnate, tycoon, baron, industrialist, entrepreneur, captain of industry, chief, lord, supremo,

VIP, bigwig (*inf*), big shot (*inf*), big cheese (*inf*). OPPOSITE: nobody.

moist *adj* damp, clammy, dank, humid, muggy, dewy, soggy, wet. OPPOSITE: dry.

moisten *verb* wet, damp, dampen, humidify, water, soak. OPPOSITE: dry.

moisture *noun* liquid, water, wet, wetness, damp, dampness, humidity, mugginess, clamminess, dankness, vapour, steam, condensation, dew, sweat, rain, drizzle. OPPOSITE: dryness.

mole[1] *noun* (*a mole on her arm*) blemish, blotch, spot, mark, freckle.

mole[2] *noun* (*waves crashing against the mole*) breakwater, groyne, pier, jetty, embankment, dyke.

mole[3] *noun* (*a mole in the organization*) infiltrator, spy, agent, secret agent, double agent.

molest *verb* **1** (*molesting young women*) accost, assault, attack, abuse, sexually assault, rape, mistreat, maltreat, hurt, injure. **2** (*molested by reporters*) pester, plague, harass, hassle (*inf*), badger, harry, worry, disturb, trouble, bother, annoy, irritate, bug (*inf*), torment, tease.

mollify *verb* **1** (*mollified the protesters*) calm, pacify, appease, placate, compose, soothe, tranquillize, still, quiet, mellow, sweeten. OPPOSITE: provoke. **2** (*mollifying his distress*) lessen, reduce, moderate, temper, allay, assuage, alleviate, ease, mitigate, soften. OPPOSITE: aggravate.

mollycoddle *verb* pamper, cosset, coddle, overprotect, spoil, ruin, indulge, pet, baby, featherbed, spoonfeed. OPPOSITE: discipline.

moment *noun* **1** (*just a moment*) minute, second, split second, instant, flash, twinkling, trice, tick (*inf*), jiffy (*inf*). OPPOSITE: age. **2** (*the moment she arrived*) instant, second, minute, time, point, stage, juncture. **3** (*a matter of great moment*) importance, significance, consequence, note, import, weight, gravity, seriousness, worth, value, interest, concern. OPPOSITE: insignificance.

in a moment soon, shortly, before long, in a second, in an instant, in a tick (*inf*), in a jiffy (*inf*), in two shakes of a lamb's tail (*inf*), before you can say Jack Robinson (*inf*).

momentarily *adv* briefly, fleetingly, for a moment, for a second, for an instant.

momentary *adj* brief, short, short-lived, transitory, transient, fleeting, passing, ephemeral, evanescent, temporary, impermanent. OPPOSITE: lengthy.

momentous *adj* important, significant, consequential, noteworthy, weighty, grave, serious, crucial, critical, vital, major, historic, epoch-making, earth-shattering (*inf*). OPPOSITE: trivial.

momentum *noun* impetus, impulse, force, thrust, drive, push, power, strength.

monarch *noun* ruler, sovereign, crowned head, king, queen, emperor, empress. OPPOSITE: subject.

monarchal *adj* monarchical, royal, regal, kingly, queenly, imperial

monastery *noun* friary, abbey, priory, cloister, charterhouse, religious community.

monastic *adj* reclusive, solitary, sequestered, cloistered, eremitic, anchoritic, ascetic, austere, celibate, contemplative, monkish, coenobitic, conventual. OPPOSITE: secular.

monetary *adj* financial, pecuniary, fiscal, budgetary, money, cash.

money *noun* **1** (*earning money*) currency, legal tender, coin, specie, cash, coins, banknotes, finance, funds, capital, wherewithal, resources, means, dosh (*sl*), bread (*sl*), lolly (*inf*), loot (*inf*), readies (*inf*), brass (*inf*), gelt (*sl*), spondulicks (*sl*), filthy lucre (*sl*). **2** (*a man of money*) wealth, riches, affluence, prosperity.

moneyed *adj* rich, wealthy, affluent, prosperous, well-off, well-heeled (*inf*), rolling in it (*inf*), flush (*inf*), loaded (*inf*), in the money (*inf*). OPPOSITE: poor.

money-making *adj* remunerative, lucrative, profitable, gainful, paying, commercial, economic, going, thriving, successful.

mongrel *noun* cross, crossbreed, mixed breed, hybrid.

monitor *noun* **1** (*seen on the monitor*) screen, VDU, recorder, scanner, detector, security camera, CCTV. **2** (*a monitor of standards*) observer, watchdog, invigilator, supervisor, overseer, prefect.
➤ *verb* check, observe, watch, keep under surveillance, supervise, oversee, record, plot, keep track of, follow, scan, survey.

monk *noun* friar, abbot, prior, brother, hermit, anchorite, coenobite.

monkey *noun* **1** (*the monkeys at the zoo*) simian, primate, baboon, gorilla, gibbon, orang-utan. **2** (*his sister's a little monkey*) imp, rascal, rogue, scamp, scallywag (*inf*), devil. OPPOSITE: angel.
➤ *verb* fool, play, fiddle, tinker, tamper, interfere, muck (*inf*), mess (*inf*).

monologue *noun* soliloquy, speech, address, oration, lecture, sermon. OPPOSITE: dialogue.

monomania *noun* fixation, obsession, idée fixe, bee in one's bonnet (*inf*).

monopolize *verb* appropriate, take over, control, dominate, corner, hog (*inf*), engross, absorb, occupy, tie up. OPPOSITE: share.

monopoly *noun* control, domination, exclusiveness, corner, sole rights. OPPOSITE: competition.

monotonous *adj* boring, tedious, dull, uninteresting, unexciting, uneventful, humdrum, repetitive, routine, soul-destroying, unvarying, unchanging, uniform, samey (*inf*), tiresome, wearisome, flat, colourless. OPPOSITE: interesting.

monotony *noun* boredom, tedium, dullness, repetition, routine, uniformity, sameness. OPPOSITE: variety.

monster *noun* **1** (*gave birth to a monster*) freak, mutant, teratism, monstrosity, miscreation, abortion. **2** (*stories about monsters*) mythical creature, fabulous beast, dragon, bogey. **3** (*my boss is a monster*) brute, beast, fiend, demon, devil, ogre, villain, savage, barbarian. **4** (*a monster of a marrow*) giant, colossus, titan, leviathan, behemoth. OPPOSITE: midget.
➤ *adj* giant, gigantic, colossal, titanic, jumbo, mammoth, huge, enormous, immense, massive, whopping (*inf*). OPPOSITE: tiny.

monstrosity *noun* **1** (*the building is a monstrosity*) eyesore, sight (*inf*), excrescence, carbuncle, blot on the landscape, horror, disgrace, scandal, outrage. **2** (*the monstrosity of the crime*) monstrousness, scandalousness, outrageousness, atrocity, heinousness, enormity, evil, viciousness, cruelty, inhumanity. **3** (*gave birth to a monstrosity*) monster, freak, mutant, teratism, miscreation, abortion.

monstrous *adj* **1** (*a monstrous crime*) dreadful, awful, frightful, terrible, horrible, horrendous, shocking, scandalous, outrageous, atrocious, heinous, vicious, cruel, barbaric, inhuman, fiendish, diabolical, satanic, abominable, odious, loathsome. OPPOSITE: wonderful. **2** (*a monstrous creature*) abnormal, unnatural, freakish, mutant, teratoid, deformed, misshapen, hideous, grotesque, gruesome. OPPOSITE: normal. **3** (*a monstrous ship*) huge, enormous, immense, massive, gigantic, colossal, titanic, gargantuan. OPPOSITE: tiny.

monument *noun* memorial, cenotaph, shrine, gravestone, tombstone, pillar, column, obelisk, cross, statue, commemoration, remembrance, reminder, memento, testament, witness, token.

monumental *adj* **1** (*a monumental failure*) great, huge, enormous, immense, massive, colossal, tremendous, prodigious, stupendous, staggering. OPPOSITE: slight. **2** (*a monumental contribution to medical science*) significant, important, momentous, major, historic, epoch-making, lasting, enduring, immortal, classic, memorable, unforgettable, grand, impressive, striking, awe-inspiring. OPPOSITE: minor. **3** (*a monumental inscription*) commemorative, memorial, lapidary.

mood *noun* **1** (*if she's in a good mood*) temper, humour, disposition, frame of mind, feeling, spirit, vein, tenor. **2** (*he's been in a mood all morning*) bad mood, bad temper, sulk, fit of pique, low spirits, the dumps (*inf*), the blues (*inf*).
in the mood disposed, inclined, willing, keen, eager.

moody *adj* **1** (*feeling moody and depressed*) glum, gloomy, morose, melancholy, broody, introspective, sullen, sulky, peevish, petulant, fretful, irritable, irascible, testy, touchy, bad-tempered, grumpy, grouchy (*inf*), crotchety (*inf*), hurt, offended, cross, angry. OPPOSITE: equable. **2** (*a moody child*) temperamental, unpredictable, changeable, mercurial, volatile, capricious, fickle, flighty, impulsive.

moor[1] *noun* moorland, heath, fell, upland.

moor[2] *verb* fasten, secure, tie up, berth, anchor. OPPOSITE: untie.

moot *adj* debatable, disputable, arguable, controversial, at issue, unresolved, unsettled, undecided, open to question, questionable, doubtful. OPPOSITE: indisputable.
➤ *verb* broach, bring up, introduce, submit, put forward, propose, mention, air, ventilate, discuss, debate.

mop *verb* swab, wash, clean, wipe, sponge, soak up, absorb, dry.
➤ *noun* **1** (*wiped it with the mop*) swab, sponge. **2** (*a mop of hair*) shock, mane, tangle, mat.

mope *verb* brood, fret, sulk, pout, be gloomy, be miserable, be dejected, grieve, pine, languish, droop, moon, mooch (*inf*).

moral *adj* **1** (*moral behaviour*) ethical, good, virtuous,

pure, chaste, decent, right, proper, just, fair, honest, upright, upstanding, righteous, honourable, noble, high-minded, principled. OPPOSITE: immoral. **2** (*moral support*) psychological, emotional, spiritual, mental.
➤ *noun* lesson, teaching, message, point, meaning, significance, maxim, adage.

morale *noun* confidence, spirit, heart, mood, humour, will, determination, resolve, hopefulness, optimism.

morality *noun* **1** (*the morality of the issue*) ethics, rights and wrongs. **2** (*questioned his morality*) morals, ethics, principles, goodness, virtue, purity, decency, propriety, justice, fairness, honesty, integrity, uprightness, righteousness, rectitude. OPPOSITE: immorality.

morals *pl noun* morality, moral code, ethics, principles, scruples, ideals, standards, mores, customs, habits, manners, behaviour, conduct.

morass *noun* **1** (*sinking into the morass*) swamp, marsh, bog, fen, quagmire, slough. **2** (*a morass of bureaucracy*) muddle, confusion, jumble, tangle.

moratorium *noun* postponement, deferral, suspension, adjournment, delay, respite, stay, halt, freeze, embargo, ban.

morbid *adj* **1** (*a morbid interest in death*) unhealthy, unwholesome, sick, ghoulish, macabre, gruesome, grisly, grim. OPPOSITE: healthy. **2** (*morbid thoughts about the future*) sombre, melancholy, lugubrious, morose, gloomy, pessimistic. **3** (*a morbid condition*) pathological, diseased, infected, unsound, unhealthy, sick, sickly.

mordant *adj* biting, caustic, cutting, trenchant, incisive, sarcastic, vitriolic, astringent, stinging, acid, acerbic, bitter, pungent, sharp. OPPOSITE: soothing.

more *adj* further, increased, additional, added, extra, fresh, new, other. OPPOSITE: fewer.
➤ *adv* further, longer, harder, again, besides, in addition. OPPOSITE: less.
➤ *noun* increase, addition, supplement, extra.

moreover *adv* furthermore, further, besides, in addition, too, as well, also, what is more, to boot.

morgue *noun* mortuary, funeral parlour, chapel of rest, charnel house.

moribund *adj* **1** (*the moribund patient*) dying, on one's deathbed, fading fast, in extremis, not long for this world (*inf*), with one foot in the grave (*inf*), on one's last legs (*inf*). OPPOSITE: nascent. **2** (*a moribund tradition*) declining, waning, crumbling, dying, obsolescent, on the way out (*inf*). OPPOSITE: flourishing.

morning *noun* daybreak, sunrise, dawn, morn, forenoon.

moron *noun* idiot, imbecile, cretin, halfwit (*inf*), dimwit (*inf*), fool, simpleton, dolt, nincompoop, blockhead, dunce, ignoramus, dope (*inf*), twit (*inf*), wally (*sl*), plonker (*sl*). OPPOSITE: genius.

morose *adj* gloomy, glum, melancholy, mournful, depressed, sombre, saturnine, dour, moody, sullen, sulky, sour, surly, gruff, crabbed, crusty, cross, ill-tempered. OPPOSITE: genial.

morsel *noun* bit, piece, fragment, crumb, scrap, grain, particle, bite, mouthful, titbit, nibble, taste.

mortal *adj* **1** (*mortal beings*) human, physical, corporeal, bodily, fleshly, worldly, earthly, temporal, passing,

transient, ephemeral. OPPOSITE: immortal. **2** (*a mortal injury*) deadly, fatal, lethal, destructive, murderous, killing. **3** (*mortal shame*) great, extreme, intense, terrible, awful, dire, severe, grave. OPPOSITE: mild. **4** (*mortal enemies*) sworn, bitter, irreconcilable, implacable, remorseless, unrelenting.
➤ *noun* human being, person, man, woman, individual, soul, body, earthling. OPPOSITE: god.

mortality *noun* **1** (*the mortality of our existence*) humanity, worldliness, earthliness, temporality, transience, ephemerality. OPPOSITE: immortality. **2** (*mortality on the roads*) death, loss of life, fatality, killing, slaughter, carnage.

mortification *noun* **1** (*mortification at their defeat*) humiliation, disgrace, dishonour, ignominy, shame, loss of face, chagrin, embarrassment, discomfiture, discomposure, annoyance, vexation, displeasure. OPPOSITE: pleasure. **2** (*mortification of the flesh*) discipline, control, restraint, asceticism. OPPOSITE: indulgence. **3** (*the mortification of tissues*) gangrene, necrosis, putrefaction, decay.

mortify *verb* **1** (*mortified by the criticism*) humiliate, humble, abase, degrade, take down a peg or two (*inf*), shame, abash, chagrin, embarrass, discomfit, discompose, confound, chasten, crush, deflate, annoy, vex, displease, hurt, wound, offend, affront. OPPOSITE: please. **2** (*mortify the flesh*) discipline, control, restrain, subdue, suppress, subjugate. OPPOSITE: indulge. **3** (*mortifying tissues*) fester, putrefy, necrose, become gangrenous, rot, decay.

mortuary *noun* morgue, funeral parlour, chapel of rest, charnel house.

most *adj* nearly all, greatest, highest, utmost, maximum. OPPOSITE: fewest.
➤ *adv* greatly, highly, very, extremely. OPPOSITE: somewhat.
➤ *pronoun* majority, greater part, greater number, nearly all, bulk, mass, lion's share (*inf*). OPPOSITE: least.

mostly *adv* **1** (*mostly children*) mainly, chiefly, principally, in the main, largely, predominantly, on the whole. **2** (*I mostly pay cash*) usually, normally, ordinarily, generally, as a rule.

mother *noun* **1** (*a mother's love for her children*) matriarch, materfamilias, mum (*inf*), mummy (*inf*), mom (*inf*), mama, ma (*inf*), mater. OPPOSITE: father. **2** (*suckled by its mother*) parent, progenitor, dam. **3** (*the mother of invention*) source, origin, spring, fount, cause, derivation, foundation, base.
➤ *verb* **1** (*she mothered triplets*) bear, give birth to, produce, bring forth, nurse, rear, raise. **2** (*she mothered her brothers*) look after, care for, foster, nurture, protect, pamper, indulge, spoil.

motherly *adj* maternal, kind, loving, tender, affectionate, caring, protective, gentle, warm, parental.

motion *noun* **1** (*the motion of the train*) movement, action, activity, mobility, motility, locomotion, travel, transit, passage, progress, course, flow, drift. OPPOSITE: rest. **2** (*made a beckoning motion*) gesture, gesticulation, movement, wave, nod, signal, sign. **3** (*vote on the motion*) proposal, proposition, suggestion, recommendation, idea, plan, scheme.
➤ *verb* signal, gesticulate, gesture, wave, beckon, nod.
in motion moving, astir, going, travelling, under way, running, working, operating, active. OPPOSITE: stationary.

motionless *adj* stationary, immobile, still, unmoving, paralysed, transfixed, stock-still, fixed, immovable, static, inert, inanimate. OPPOSITE: moving.

motivate *verb* prompt, incite, move, lead, spur, goad, impel, drive, stimulate, provoke, persuade, induce, cause, instigate, actuate, arouse, excite, inspire. OPPOSITE: deter.

motivation *noun* stimulus, inspiration, spur, goad, stimulation, incitement, inducement, incentive, motive, drive, ambition.

motive *noun* reason, rationale, cause, grounds, basis, object, purpose, intention, stimulus, inspiration, spur, incentive, inducement, motivation, drive, impulse, urge.

motley *adj* **1** (*a motley collection*) mixed, varied, diverse, assorted, miscellaneous, heterogeneous, dissimilar. OPPOSITE: uniform. **2** (*a motley fabric*) multicoloured, many-hued, polychromatic, kaleidoscopic, particoloured, variegated.

mottled *adj* speckled, dappled, pied, piebald, brindled, tabby, streaked, flecked, marbled, stippled, spotted, blotchy, motley, variegated.

motto *noun* slogan, watchword, saying, maxim, adage, proverb, aphorism, saw, axiom, dictum, precept, rule.

mould[1] *noun* **1** (*the mould used to make this part*) die, cast, form, matrix, pattern, frame, template. **2** (*the mould of the body*) shape, form, outline, contour, build, construction, structure, format, style, fashion, design, cut. **3** (*people of the same mould*) type, sort, kind, stamp, brand, calibre, nature, character.
➤ *verb* **1** (*moulded a figure of a horse*) shape, form, model, fashion, cast, forge, stamp, carve, sculpt, make, create. **2** (*moulding their minds*) influence, affect, direct, shape, form.

mould[2] *noun* (*mould on the bread*) mildew, fungus, blight, rot, mustiness, mouldiness.

moulder *verb* rot, decay, decompose, crumble, disintegrate, perish.

mouldy *adj* mildewed, blighted, musty, fusty, stale, rotting, decaying, rotten, bad. OPPOSITE: fresh.

mound *noun* **1** (*climbed up the mound*) hill, hillock, knoll, hummock, rise, elevation, dune, bank, ridge, embankment, rampart, bulwark, earthwork, barrow, tumulus. **2** (*a mound of clothes*) heap, pile, stack.

mount *verb* **1** (*mount the steps*) climb, ascend, go up, scale. OPPOSITE: descend. **2** (*mount the bus*) board, get on to. OPPOSITE: dismount. **3** (*tension was mounting*) increase, grow, intensify, escalate, multiply, accumulate, accrue, rise, soar. OPPOSITE: decrease. **4** (*mount a show*) produce, stage, put on, prepare, set up, organize, arrange, exhibit, display. **5** (*mount a gem*) frame, set.
➤ *noun* **1** (*a mount for the picture*) mounting, backing, setting, frame, stand, base, support. **2** (*sitting astride his mount*) horse, steed, charger.

mountain *noun* **1** (*climb a mountain*) fell, alp, mount, peak, pinnacle, height, elevation. **2** (*a mountain of paperwork*) heap, pile, stack, abundance, lot, mass.

mountainous *adj* highland, upland, hilly, steep, lofty, towering, huge, massive.

mountebank *noun* charlatan, quack, impostor, pretender, fraud, fake, cheat, trickster, conman (*inf*).

mourn *verb* lament, grieve, sorrow, bewail, bemoan, deplore, regret, miss, weep, wail, keen. OPPOSITE: rejoice.

mournful *adj* **1** (*looking mournful*) sad, sorrowful, unhappy, miserable, grief-stricken, woeful, gloomy, melancholy, depressed, downcast, heavy-hearted, doleful, disconsolate, heartbroken. OPPOSITE: happy. **2** (*a mournful sound*) funereal, elegaic, sombre, lugubrious, sad, sorrowful, piteous, plaintive, heartrending. OPPOSITE: merry. **3** (*mournful news*) depressing, distressing, tragic, grievous, lamentable, deplorable. OPPOSITE: cheerful.

mourning *noun* grief, sadness, sorrow, woe, lamentation, weeping, wailing.

mousy *adj* **1** (*a mousy person*) timorous, timid, shy, quiet, retiring, unassertive, self-effacing, unobtrusive. **2** (*mousy hair*) brownish-grey, greyish-brown, dun-coloured, dull, drab, neutral, colourless, lacklustre.

mouth *noun* **1** (*opened his mouth*) jaws, lips, maw, muzzle, gob (*inf*), trap (*inf*), kisser (*inf*). **2** (*the mouth of the cave*) orifice, opening, aperture, stoma, entrance, door, inlet, vent. **3** (*the mouth of the river*) outlet, estuary, delta. **4** (*she's all mouth*) boasting, bragging, braggadocio, empty talk, idle talk, hot air (*inf*). **5** (*I'll have less of your mouth!*) impudence, insolence, impertinence, rudeness, disrespect, cheek (*inf*), sauce (*inf*), lip (*inf*), backchat (*inf*).

mouthful *noun* bite, nibble, sip, gulp, taste, sample, bit, piece, morsel.

mouthpiece *noun* spokesperson, spokesman, spokeswoman, agent, representative, organ, publication, journal, periodical.

movable *adj* mobile, portable, transportable, transferable, adjustable, changeable. OPPOSITE: fixed.

move *verb* **1** (*don't move from that spot!*) stir, budge, shift. OPPOSITE: stand. **2** (*moving along the road*) go, advance, progress, proceed, pass. OPPOSITE: stop. **3** (*move the piano*) carry, transport, shift, transfer, transpose, switch, push, shove, shunt. OPPOSITE: fix. **4** (*move to Canada*) relocate, remove, migrate, leave, depart, go away. OPPOSITE: stay. **5** (*what moved him to do that?*) prompt, urge, drive, impel, induce, persuade, incite, provoke, actuate, activate, stimulate, motivate, inspire, cause, lead. OPPOSITE: deter. **6** (*moved by the speech*) touch, affect, impress, influence, stir, excite, rouse. **7** (*the government must move on this issue*) act, take action, do something. **8** (*I move that we refuse their offer*) propose, put forward, suggest, recommend, advocate, urge.
➤ *noun* **1** (*watched her every move*) movement, motion, gesture, action, activity. **2** (*a move to reduce crime*) act, action, step, measure, manoeuvre, stratagem, tactic. **3** (*a move to new premises*) relocation, removal, migration, transfer, change of address. **4** (*it's your move*) turn, go.
get a move on hurry up, make haste, speed up, step on it (*inf*), make it snappy (*inf*), get cracking (*inf*), shake a leg (*inf*). OPPOSITE: slow down.

on the move moving, in motion, going, travelling, under way, advancing, progressing. OPPOSITE: still.

movement *noun* **1** (*the movement of the branches*) motion, action, activity, stir. **2** (*the movement of furniture*) carriage, transportation, transfer, shifting, removal. **3** (*a movement of her head*) move, motion, gesture, action. **4** (*the feminist movement*) campaign, crusade, drive, faction, party, group, organization. **5** (*a movement towards self-sufficiency*) advance, progress, passage, course, drift, trend, swing. **6** (*little movement in the market*) shift, change, variation, fluctuation, development, improvement. **7** (*the second movement of the symphony*) part, section, division, passage. **8** (*the movement of the clock*) works, workings, mechanism, machinery.

moving *adj* **1** (*a moving performance*) touching, affecting, emotive, emotional, poignant, pathetic, stirring, rousing, stimulating, inspiring, impressive. **2** (*moving parts*) mobile, movable, dynamic, kinetic, active, in motion. OPPOSITE: still. **3** (*the moving force*) driving, impelling, motivating, leading.

mow *verb* cut, trim, clip, shear, scythe, prune, crop.
mow down slaughter, massacre, butcher.

much *adj* abundant, plentiful, ample, copious, great, considerable, substantial, extensive, a great deal of, a lot of (*inf*). OPPOSITE: little.
➤ *adv* **1** (*much improved*) greatly, considerably, a great deal, indeed. OPPOSITE: little. **2** (*I don't go there much*) often, frequently, a lot (*inf*). OPPOSITE: seldom. **3** (*much the same*) nearly, almost, practically, virtually.
➤ *noun* plenty, a great deal, a lot (*inf*), lots (*inf*), loads (*inf*), heaps (*inf*), lashings (*inf*).

mucilaginous *adj* sticky, gummy, viscous, viscid, glutinous, gelatinous, mucous, slimy.

muck *noun* **1** (*spread muck on the fields*) manure, dung, ordure, excrement, faeces, droppings, guano, sewage, slurry. **2** (*clean the muck off your boots*) dirt, filth, grime, mud, mire, sludge, crud (*inf*), gunge (*inf*).
muck about fool around, play around, mess about, clown around, lark around (*inf*).
muck up botch, bungle, spoil, ruin, make a muck of, make a mess of, cock up (*sl*), screw up (*sl*).

mucky *adj* dirty, filthy, grimy, grubby, soiled, muddy, messy. OPPOSITE: clean.

mud *noun* clay, soil, dirt, muck, sludge, mire, ooze.

muddle *verb* **1** (*muddled the papers*) confuse, mix up, jumble, scramble, disorder, disarrange, mess up. OPPOSITE: sort. **2** (*you're muddling me*) perplex, bewilder, confuse, confound, puzzle, baffle, disorientate, befuddle, daze. OPPOSITE: enlighten.
➤ *noun* **1** (*the muddle in her office*) confusion, mix-up, jumble, disorder, disarray, mess, clutter, chaos. OPPOSITE: order. **2** (*he's in a muddle*) perplexity, bewilderment, confusion, puzzlement, bafflement, disorientation, daze.

muddy *adj* **1** (*muddy ground*) boggy, swampy, marshy, quaggy, miry, sludgy, oozy, slushy. OPPOSITE: dry. **2** (*muddy boots*) mucky, dirty, filthy, grimy, grubby. OPPOSITE: clean. **3** (*muddy water*) cloudy, turbid, murky, opaque, dull, dingy. OPPOSITE: clear. **4** (*muddy thinking*) obscure, vague, woolly, jumbled, confused, muddled.

muffle *verb* **1** (*muffled the children up in scarves*) envelop, wrap, swathe, swaddle, cover, cloak. OPPOSITE: expose. **2** (*muffle the noise*) deaden, damp, mute, soften, dull, stifle, smother, gag, muzzle, silence, quieten, hush, suppress, conceal, mask. OPPOSITE: amplify.

muffled *adj* muted, subdued, stifled, smothered, suppressed, soft, dull, faint, indistinct. OPPOSITE: loud.

mug *noun* **1** (*a mug of coffee*) beaker, tankard, pot, cup, glass. **2** (*you must think I'm a mug*) fool, simpleton, sucker (*inf*), soft touch (*inf*).
≫ *verb* attack, assault, rob, beat up, rough up (*inf*), do over (*inf*).

muggy *adj* humid, clammy, sticky, damp, dank, moist, sultry, oppressive, close, airless, stuffy. OPPOSITE: fresh.

mulish *adj* stubborn, obstinate, headstrong, wilful, obdurate, intransigent, inflexible, intractable, refractory, recalcitrant, perverse, contrary. OPPOSITE: amenable.

mull *verb* **mull over** think about, reflect on, consider, weigh up, meditate on, ruminate on, contemplate, ponder, deliberate on, chew over.

multifarious *adj* many, numerous, manifold, multiple, multitudinous, myriad, legion, varied, diverse, assorted, miscellaneous, sundry, motley, variegated.

multiple *adj* several, many, numerous, manifold, various, diverse, multifarious. OPPOSITE: single.

multiply *verb* increase, augment, grow, build up, intensify, expand, extend, spread, proliferate, breed, reproduce, propagate. OPPOSITE: decrease.

multitude *noun* crowd, throng, mob, horde, host, flock, swarm, assembly, congregation, army, legion, myriad, mass, lot. OPPOSITE: few.

mum *adj* quiet, silent, dumb, mute, speechless, tight-lipped, secretive, uncommunicative, taciturn. OPPOSITE: talkative.

mumble *verb* mutter, murmur. OPPOSITE: exclaim.

munch *verb* chew, masticate, champ, chomp, crunch, eat.

mundane *adj* **1** (*mundane work*) banal, ordinary, everyday, commonplace, trite, hackneyed, humdrum, routine, regular, customary, normal, typical, usual. OPPOSITE: unusual. **2** (*mundane rather than spiritual issues*) worldly, earthly, terrestrial, temporal, secular, physical, material, carnal, fleshly. OPPOSITE: spiritual.

municipal *adj* civil, civic, urban, town, city, borough, local, public, community.

munificence *noun* generosity, bounty, largess, beneficence, magnanimity, charity, philanthropy. OPPOSITE: meanness.

munificent *adj* generous, bountiful, bounteous, open-handed, liberal, unstinting, lavish, beneficent, magnanimous, charitable, philanthropic. OPPOSITE: mean.

munitions *pl noun* ammunition, weapons, arms, matériel, stores, supplies, equipment, gear.

murder *verb* **1** (*murdered her husband*) kill, slay, assassinate, execute, dispatch, bump off (*inf*), knock off (*inf*), do in (*inf*), eliminate (*inf*), rub out (*sl*), waste (*sl*), slaughter, butcher, massacre, wipe out, destroy. **2** (*murdering my favourite song*) ruin, spoil, mar, mangle, mutilate, make a mess of.
≫ *noun* **1** (*guilty of murder*) homicide, manslaughter,

killing, assassination, hit (*inf*), slaughter, massacre, butchery, carnage, destruction. **2** (*it's murder trying to work in this heat*) trial, ordeal, nightmare, agony, torment, torture, hell (*inf*).

murderer *noun* killer, assassin, hitman (*inf*), slayer, cut-throat, slaughterer, butcher.

murderous *adj* **1** (*murderous deeds*) homicidal, deadly, lethal, fatal, mortal, savage, barbarous, cruel, brutal, ferocious, bloodthirsty, bloody, sanguinary. **2** (*a murderous drive*) difficult, arduous, rigorous, strenuous, exhausting, killing (*inf*), dangerous, perilous. OPPOSITE: easy.

murky *adj* **1** (*murky skies*) dark, gloomy, dismal, dreary, dull, dusky, dim, cloudy, overcast, grey, lowering, misty, foggy, obscure. OPPOSITE: bright. **2** (*murky water*) cloudy, turbid, muddy, dirty, dull, opaque. OPPOSITE: clear. **3** (*his murky past*) shady, dark, obscure, mysterious, secret, doubtful, questionable.

murmur *verb* **1** (*she murmured her acceptance*) mutter, mumble, whisper. OPPOSITE: shout. **2** (*the wind murmured in the trees*) whisper, sigh, rustle, babble. **3** (*murmuring against the government*) complain, moan, whine, whinge (*inf*), carp, grumble, grouse (*inf*), gripe (*inf*).
≫ *noun* **1** (*spoke in a murmur*) mutter, mumble, whisper, undertone. OPPOSITE: yell. **2** (*the murmur of distant traffic*) rumble, hum, drone, buzz. **3** (*murmurs about the tax increase*) complaint, moan, protest, objection, grumble, grouse (*inf*), gripe (*inf*).

muscle *noun* **1** (*pulled a muscle*) tendon, ligament, sinew, thew. **2** (*the organization lacks muscle*) power, force, potency, forcefulness, strength, might, influence, clout (*inf*).
muscle in interfere, intrude, encroach, push in, butt in (*inf*), force one's way in, elbow one's way in.

muscular *adj* brawny, sinewy, beefy (*inf*), husky (*inf*), strapping, burly, lusty, strong, robust, sturdy, stalwart, vigorous, energetic, athletic. OPPOSITE: puny.

muse *verb* ruminate, reflect, ponder, think, cogitate, consider, deliberate, meditate, ruminate, contemplate, brood, daydream.

mushroom *verb* spring up, shoot up, sprout, burgeon, flourish, prosper, thrive, grow, increase, expand, boom, snowball. OPPOSITE: decline.

music *noun* tune, melody, harmony, composition, opus, score.

musical *adj* tuneful, melodious, melodic, harmonious, euphonious, mellifluous, dulcet, lyrical. OPPOSITE: discordant.

musician *noun* player, instrumentalist, accompanist, performer, artist, minstrel.

must *noun* essential, necessity, requirement, requisite, sine qua non.

muster *verb* **1** (*muster an army*) marshal, rally, round up, summon, call up, mobilize, call together, convoke, bring together, assemble, gather. OPPOSITE: disperse. **2** (*we mustered outside the gates*) assemble, congregate, meet, come together, convene, rally, collect, gather.
≫ *noun* meeting, rally, assembly, congregation, gathering, collection, convention, convocation.

pass muster measure up, come up to scratch (*inf*), qualify, do, fit the bill, make the grade (*inf*).

musty *adj* mouldy, mildewy, stale, fusty, smelly, stuffy, airless, damp, dank. OPPOSITE: fresh.

mutable *adj* changeable, variable, alterable, convertible, changing, varying, inconstant, fickle, unstable, volatile, uncertain, irresolute, unsettled, vacillating, fluctuating, wavering. OPPOSITE: constant.

mutant *noun* mutation, deviant, anomaly, freak.

mutation *noun* change, alteration, modification, variation, transformation, metamorphosis.

mute *adj* silent, dumb, voiceless, speechless, mum (*inf*), taciturn, uncommunicative, quiet, wordless, unexpressed, unspoken. OPPOSITE: vocal.
➤ *verb* soften, quieten, lower, subdue, tone down, damp, deaden, muffle, stifle, smother, suppress.

muted *adj* soft, subdued, subtle, discreet, low-key, understated.

mutilate *verb* **1** (*their mutilated bodies*) maim, disable, cripple, disfigure, deface, injure, mangle, butcher, cut, hack, lacerate, dismember, amputate. **2** (*mutilate the text*) mar, spoil, ruin, damage, impair, distort, mangle, butcher, expurgate, bowdlerize.

mutinous *adj* rebellious, insurgent, revolutionary, seditious, subversive, riotous, unruly, disorderly, turbulent, insubordinate, disobedient, refractory, contumacious, ungovernable, unmanageable. OPPOSITE: obedient.

mutiny *noun* rebellion, insurrection, revolution, revolt, uprising, riot, insubordination, defiance, disobedience, sedition, resistance, protest, strike. OPPOSITE: obedience.
➤ *verb* rebel, revolt, rise up, defy, disobey, resist, protest, strike. OPPOSITE: obey.

mutter *verb* **1** (*muttering in his sleep*) mumble, murmur, talk under one's breath, talk to oneself. OPPOSITE: exclaim. **2** (*muttering about the price of fuel*) complain, carp, fuss, grumble, grouse (*inf*).

mutual *adj* reciprocal, interchangeable, interactive, joint, shared, common, communal, collective. OPPOSITE: individual.

muzzle *verb* gag, silence, censor, check, restrain, suppress, stifle.

myopic *adj* **1** (*spectacles for myopic people*) short-sighted, near-sighted. OPPOSITE: long-sighted. **2** (*their myopic attitude to the problem*) narrow-minded, short-sighted, unimaginative, ill-considered, insular, parochial, limited.

myriad *adj* innumerable, countless, untold, incalculable, many, numerous, multitudinous, manifold. OPPOSITE: few.
➤ *noun* multitude, host, army, legion, swarm, mass, sea, thousands (*inf*), millions (*inf*).

mysterious *adj* **1** (*mysterious phenomena*) unexplainable, inexplicable, unaccountable, enigmatic, inscrutable, cryptic, puzzling, baffling, mystifying, incomprehensible, unfathomable, strange, curious, bizarre, weird, uncanny, dark, obscure, veiled, hidden, abstruse, arcane, recondite. OPPOSITE: straightforward. **2** (*mysterious about their plans*) secretive, reticent, discreet, evasive, furtive, surreptitious. OPPOSITE: open.

mystery *noun* **1** (*it's a mystery*) enigma, riddle, conundrum, puzzle, question, secret. **2** (*shrouded in mystery*) secrecy, obscurity, vagueness, inexplicability, unscrutability, incomprehensibility.

mystical *adj* occult, esoteric, abstruse, arcane, recondite, supernatural, paranormal, metaphysical, transcendental, mysterious, enigmatic, cryptic.

mystify *verb* puzzle, baffle, perplex, stump (*inf*), nonplus, bewilder, confuse, confound. OPPOSITE: enlighten.

myth *noun* **1** (*Greek myths*) legend, saga, tale, story, fable, parable, allegory. OPPOSITE: history. **2** (*the myth that women are bad drivers*) lie, falsehood, untruth, fallacy, fabrication, fiction, fantasy, delusion. OPPOSITE: fact.

mythical *adj* **1** (*mythical heroes*) mythological, legendary, fabulous, fabled, storied, traditional, fairy-tale, storybook. OPPOSITE: historical. **2** (*her mythical new job*) fictitious, make-believe, invented, made-up, imaginary, fanciful, unreal, nonexistent, false, untrue. OPPOSITE: real.

mythology *noun* myths, legends, folklore.

nab *verb* arrest, catch, capture, seize, grab, snatch, collar (*inf*), nick (*inf*), nobble (*inf*). OPPOSITE: release.

nadir *noun* low point, lowest point, bottom, rock bottom, zero, depths, the pits (*inf*).

nag[1] *verb* **1** (*stop nagging me!*) find fault with, complain to, grumble at, moan at, criticize, scold, berate, henpeck, carp, cavil, pester, plague, badger, hector, harass, vex, irritate, go on at (*inf*), annoy, worry, bother, torment. **2** (*a doubt that keeps nagging me*) niggle, annoy, worry, bother, trouble, torment, bug (*inf*).
  ➤ *noun* shrew, termagant, virago, scold.

nag[2] *noun* (*ride a nag*) horse, hack, jade, plug (*inf*), Rosinante.

nagging *adj* **1** (*their constant nagging*) moaning, faultfinding, complaining, grumbling, criticizing, scolding, carping. **2** (*nagging fears*) upsetting, distressing, niggling, aching, painful, persistent, constant, continuous.

nail *noun* **1** (*fasten the wood with a nail*) pin, tack, brad, rivet, sprig, spike. **2** (*keep your nails cut short*) fingernail, toenail, nipper, pincer, claw, talon.
  ➤ *verb* **1** (*nail a sign to a tree*) fasten, tack, fix, hammer, pin, attach, secure. **2** (*nailed for robbery*) catch, arrest, capture, seize, nab (*inf*), collar (*inf*), nick (*inf*), pinch (*inf*). **3** (*nail rumours*) expose, uncover, detect, reveal, unearth, bare, unmask.

naive *adj* guileless, ingenuous, artless, unsophisticated, simple, innocent, trusting, childlike, unpretentious, unrealistic, unsuspicious, credulous, gullible, open, frank, candid, immature, raw, callow, wet behind the ears (*inf*). OPPOSITE: sophisticated.

naivety *noun* guilelessness, artlessness, simplicity, childishness, ingenuousness, innocence, inexperience, gullibility, credulousness, unworldliness. OPPOSITE: sophistication.

naked *adj* **1** (*a naked body*) nude, unclothed, undressed, uncovered, exposed, bare, au naturel, stripped, denuded, starkers (*inf*), in the altogether (*inf*), in the buff (*inf*), in one's birthday suit (*inf*), in the raw (*inf*). OPPOSITE: clothed. **2** (*a naked landscape*) barren, bare, exposed, stark, plain, stripped, grassless, treeless, denuded. **3** (*a naked light*) uncovered, exposed, unguarded, unprotected, unwrapped. OPPOSITE: covered. **4** (*the naked truth*) plain, stark, bald, evident, simple, open, obvious, apparent, blatant, flagrant, glaring, unveiled, undisguised, unqualified, unvarnished. OPPOSITE: veiled. **5** (*feel naked*) defenceless, unprotected, vulnerable, helpless, weak, exposed, powerless.

namby-pamby *adj* sentimental, oversentimental, weak, feeble, spineless, mawkish, maudlin, colourless, anaemic, insipid, womanish, effeminate, wet (*inf*), weedy, wimpish, effete, prim, prissy.

name *noun* **1** (*his name is Hugh Silvester*) appellation, denomination, designation, full name, first name, Christian name, middle name, surname, family name, last name, maiden name, title, term, style, label, epithet, cognomen, nickname, tag, pet name, pseudonym, alias, pen name, nom de plume, nom de guerre, assumed name, sobriquet, handle (*inf*), moniker (*inf*). **2** (*have a name for reliability*) reputation, character, credit, esteem, honour, distinction, note, fame, renown, repute, prominence, eminence, celebrity. **3** (*one of the biggest names in show business*) star, celebrity, leading light, luminary, VIP, dignitary, celeb (*inf*), big noise (*inf*), big shot (*inf*), bigwig (*inf*).
  ➤ *verb* **1** (*name a baby*) call, baptize, christen, dub, style, term, label, entitle, denominate. **2** (*name one's sources*) identify, state, mention, cite, specify, give. **3** (*name a new manager*) designate, nominate, appoint, select, choose, pick, specify, mention, cite.

nameless *adj* **1** (*nameless bureaucrats*) anonymous, unnamed, unidentified, unknown, obscure, unspecified, unlabelled. OPPOSITE: named. **2** (*nameless crimes*) inexpressible, unspeakable, indescribable, unmentionable, unutterable, unheard of.

namely *adv* that is to say, that is, i.e., viz., in other words, to wit.

nap[1] *noun* (*have a nap after lunch*) doze, catnap, snooze (*inf*), sleep, rest, lie-down, shut-eye, kip (*inf*), forty winks (*inf*).
≫ *verb* doze, catnap, slumber, drowse, snooze (*inf*), sleep, rest, lie down, nod off, drop off, get some shut-eye, kip (*inf*).

nap[2] *noun* (*the nap of the carpet*) pile, down, weave, surface, texture, grain, fibre, shag.

narcissism *noun* self-love, self-admiration, self-regard, self-conceit, vanity, egotism, egoism, egocentricity, self-centredness.

narcotic *noun* drug, opiate, sedative, tranquillizer, sleeping pill, soporific, anodyne, analgesic, painkiller, anaesthetic. OPPOSITE: stimulant.
≫ *adj* soporific, hypnotic, sedative, opiate, sleep-inducing, anaesthetic, tranquillizing, stupefying, calming, numbing, analgesic, somnolent.

narrate *verb* tell, relate, portray, recite, recount, rehearse, report, chronicle, detail, describe, repeat, set forth.

narration *noun* narrative, account, story, storytelling, tale, report, chronicle, history, recital, portrayal, sketch, description, relation.

narrative *noun* account, story, tale, report, statement, chronicle, history.

narrator *noun* storyteller, reporter, writer, author, chronicler, historian, annalist, describer, raconteur, recounter.

narrow *adj* **1** (*a narrow street*) thin, slender, slight, spare, attenuated, fine. OPPOSITE: wide. **2** (*be caught in a narrow space*) tight, cramped, pinched, constricted, close, squeezed, confined, restricted, limited, straitened, meagre, scanty. OPPOSITE: broad. **3** (*take a narrow view*) limited, narrow-minded, bigoted, prejudiced, small-minded, intolerant, straitlaced, insular, parochial, provincial. OPPOSITE: broad. **4** (*when the term is used in its narrow sense*) literal, strict, precise, faithful, exact, true, original, close. OPPOSITE: broad.
≫ *verb* taper, attenuate, constrict, confine, restrict, limit, straiten, tighten. OPPOSITE: broaden.

narrowly *adv* **1** (*narrowly escaped death*) scarcely, barely, just, only just, by a hair's breadth, by a whisker (*inf*). **2** (*watch someone narrowly*) carefully, closely, attentively, strictly, painstakingly.

narrow-minded *adj* biased, prejudiced, bigoted, illiberal, intolerant, insular, parochial, provincial, limited, conservative, hidebound, reactionary, dyed-in-the-wool, twisted, warped, small-minded, petty-minded. OPPOSITE: broad-minded.

nascent *adj* beginning, incipient, budding, developing, growing, burgeoning, evolving, young, embryonic. OPPOSITE: mature.

nasty *adj* **1** (*a nasty smell*) unpleasant, disagreeable, offensive, repulsive, revolting, disgusting, nauseating, odious, distasteful, unsavoury, loathsome, objectionable, obnoxious, horrible, vile, foul, polluted, squalid, grotty (*inf*), yucky (*inf*). OPPOSITE: pleasant. **2** (*nasty behaviour*) disagreeable, spiteful, malicious, mean, vicious, unkind, cruel, malevolent, ill-tempered, ill-natured, wicked, evil, villainous. OPPOSITE: kind. **3** (*nasty weather*) foul, awful, unpleasant, disagreeable, rainy, stormy. OPPOSITE: fine. **4** (*a nasty situation*) unpleasant, serious, critical, severe, worrying, threatening, alarming, tricky. **5** (*nasty jokes*) dirty, filthy, indecent, foul, pornographic, obscene, vulgar, blue.

nation *noun* country, land, realm, kingdom, republic, empire, commonwealth, state, people, race, population, society, community.

national *adj* civil, state, nationwide, countrywide, public, federal, general, domestic, internal. OPPOSITE: local.
≫ *noun* citizen, resident, inhabitant, subject.

nationalism *noun* patriotism, chauvinism, jingoism, allegiance, loyalty, xenophobia.

nationalistic *adj* patriotic, chauvinistic, jingoistic, loyal, xenophobic.

nationality *noun* nation, ethnic group, race, birth, clan, tribe.

nationwide *adj* national, countrywide, comprehensive, general, state, coast-to-coast, overall, extensive.

native *noun* inhabitant, resident, dweller, citizen, national, aborigine, autochthon, indigene. OPPOSITE: foreigner.
≫ *adj* **1** (*one's native language*) local, vernacular, domestic, home, mother, indigenous, aboriginal, autochthonous, original. OPPOSITE: foreign. **2** (*a native ability*) inborn, inbred, innate, connate, congenital, hereditary, natural, inherent, immanent, intrinsic. OPPOSITE: acquired.

nativity *noun* childbirth, birth, delivery, parturition.

natter *verb* chat, gossip, chatter, talk, blather, prattle, jabber, gabble, jaw (*inf*), witter (*inf*).
≫ *noun* chat, gossip, talk, conversation, chit-chat, gab, jabble, chin-wag.

natty *adj* smart, neat, trim, dapper, spruce, stylish, well-dressed, well-turned-out, snazzy (*inf*), trendy (*inf*), ritzy (*inf*).

natural *adj* **1** (*a natural reaction*) normal, typical, regular, usual, ordinary, common, run-of-the-mill, logical, reasonable. OPPOSITE: abnormal. **2** (*natural behaviour*) inborn, inbred, innate, congenital, inherent, ingrained, intrinsic, native, indigenous, basic, fundamental, instinctive, intuitive. OPPOSITE: acquired. **3** (*a natural smile*) genuine, artless, guileless, ingenuous, naive, unsophisticated, simple, frank, open, candid, sincere, unaffected, relaxed, spontaneous. OPPOSITE: contrived. **4** (*natural materials*) genuine, real, authentic, pure, unmixed, unprocessed, unpolished, whole, plain, raw, unrefined. OPPOSITE: artificial.

naturalist *noun* botanist, biologist, life scientist, plant scientist, ecologist.

naturalistic *adj* realistic, natural, lifelike, true-to-life, real-life, graphic, factual, representational.

naturalize *verb* habituate, familiarize, domesticate, accustom, acclimatize, adapt, adopt, take in, accept, assimilate, absorb, introduce, acclimate.

naturally *adv* **1** (*naturally, you'll want to discuss this with your wife*) of course, as a matter of course, obviously, certainly, no doubt, needless to say. **2** (*her hair is naturally blonde*) inherently, innately, genuinely, normally, typically. **3** (*speak naturally*) unaffectedly, spontaneously, simply, artlessly, sincerely, candidly.

nature *noun* **1** (*the nature of the difficulties*) essence, character, identity, constitution, make-up, quality, characteristic. **2** (*a problem of a personal nature*) kind, sort, type, class, category, style, description, species, brand, variety. **3** (*wonder at the beauties of nature*) creation, earth, world, universe, cosmos, environment. **4** (*I like her easygoing nature*) disposition, temper, humour, mood, temperament, character, personality.

naughty *adj* **1** (*naughty children*) bad, mischievous, disobedient, defiant, wayward, unmanageable, perverse, unruly, wicked, impish, roguish, vexatious, exasperating. OPPOSITE: good. **2** (*naughty books*) vulgar, rude, improper, indecent, bawdy, licentious, ribald, risqué, titillating, smutty, blue. OPPOSITE: decent.

nausea *noun* **1** (*nausea during pregnancy*) biliousness, queasiness, sickness, vomiting, gagging, retching, travel sickness, motion sickness, seasickness, airsickness, carsickness, throwing up (*inf*), puking (*inf*). **2** (*feel nausea listening to the enormity of the crimes*) disgust, revulsion, repugnance, loathing, aversion, dislike. OPPOSITE: relish.

nauseate *verb* sicken, disgust, revolt, turn one's stomach, repel, offend, appal.

nauseous *adj* **1** (*feel nauseous*) queasy, nauseating, sick, ill, unwell, off colour, travel sick, seasick, carsick, about to throw up (*inf*). **2** (*a nauseous smell*) nauseating, sickening, disgusting, revolting, repulsive, loathsome, offensive, distasteful. OPPOSITE: pleasant.

nautical *adj* naval, marine, maritime, seafaring, seagoing, sailing.

navigable *adj* passable, traversable, negotiable, unblocked, clear, unobstructed.

navigate *verb* **1** (*navigate a ship*) direct, guide, pilot, steer, drive, plot, plan, skipper. **2** (*navigate the Thames*) cross, sail, sail across, cruise, voyage.

navigator *noun* pilot, mariner, steerer, helmsman, seaman.

navvy *noun* labourer, worker, manual worker, workman, ganger.

navy *noun* fleet, flotilla, armada, marine.

near *adj* **1** (*on the near side*) close, nearby, neighbouring, within reach, adjacent, adjoining, contiguous, a stone's throw (*inf*). OPPOSITE: far. **2** (*in the near future*) imminent, impending, forthcoming, approaching, next, coming, in the offing, immediate. OPPOSITE: distant. **3** (*near relations*) dear, intimate, familiar, close, related, akin. OPPOSITE: remote. **4** (*near with his money*) close, mean, niggardly, parsimonious, stingy, miserly, tightfisted, closefisted, tight. OPPOSITE: generous.
➤ *adv* close, close by, nigh, nearby, at close quarters, within reach, within close range.
➤ *prep* nearby, close by, next to, within reach of, adjacent to, bordering on, in the neighbourhood of.
➤ *verb* approach, draw near, border on, move towards, come close to, come towards.

near miss near thing, narrow escape, close call, close shave (*inf*).

nearly *adv* almost, practically, all but, as good as, virtually, well-nigh, just about, close to, next to, approximately, roughly, more or less.

neat *adj* **1** (*a neat desk*) tidy, orderly, well-ordered, trim, smart, clean, spick-and-span, fastidious, methodical, in apple-pie order. OPPOSITE: untidy. **2** (*a neat person*) tidy, smart, spruce, trim, dapper, well-dressed, well-groomed, natty (*inf*). OPPOSITE: slovenly. **3** (*a neat solution*) clever, nice, convenient, ingenious, apt. **4** (*a neat movement*) nifty, clever, dexterous, adroit, deft, adept, apt, nimble, graceful, skilful, expert. OPPOSITE: clumsy. **5** (*I like my whisky neat*) straight, pure, unmixed, undiluted, unadulterated.

neaten *verb* tidy, tidy up, smarten, smarten up, straighten, spruce up, clean, clean up, groom, arrange, order. OPPOSITE: disarrange.

nebulous *adj* vague, indefinite, indeterminate, obscure, dim, shadowy, indistinct, hazy, misty, cloudy, shapeless, fuzzy, unformed, amorphous. OPPOSITE: clear.

necessarily *adv* automatically, certainly, definitely, by definition, of course, inevitably, unavoidably, undoubtedly, inescapably, incontrovertibly, perforce, willy-nilly.

necessary *adj* needed, required, needful, requisite, essential, vital, indispensable, imperative, compulsory, obligatory, mandatory, certain, unavoidable, inescapable, inevitable, inexorable. OPPOSITE: unnecessary.

necessitate *verb* cause, require, entail, demand, call for, oblige, force, compel, impel, exact, constrain, coerce.

necessitous *adj* needy, poor, disadvantaged, in need, in want, impoverished, poverty-stricken, indigent, impecunious, penurious, penniless, destitute, distressed. OPPOSITE: rich.

necessity *noun* **1** (*a car is a necessity for this job*) essential, fundamental, requisite, prerequisite, need, want, requirement, desideratum, sine qua non, demand, exigency. **2** (*the necessity for affordable houses*) indispensability, needfulness, compulsion, obligation, inevitability. **3** (*they were forced by necessity to steal*) poverty, indigence, penury, want, privation, destitution, need. OPPOSITE: wealth.

necromancy *noun* magic, black magic, spiritism, spiritualism, sorcery, witchcraft, wizardry, voodoo, divination, enchantment, thaumaturgy.

need *verb* **1** (*the machine needs mending*) lack, miss, be without, want, require, demand, call for, necessitate. **2** (*he needn't know*) must, have to, be obliged to, be compelled to.
➤ *noun* **1** (*their basic needs*) necessity, desideratum, essential, requisite, want, requirement. **2** (*in need of clothing*) want, lack, shortage. **3** (*the need for better safety procedures*) requirement, demand, requisite, obligation, want, exigency, urgency, emergency. **4** (*children in need*) poverty, indigence, penury, destitution, distress, extremity, deprivation, privation. OPPOSITE: wealth.

needful *adj* needed, necessary, required, requisite, essential, vital, indispensable. OPPOSITE: unnecessary.

needless *adj* unnecessary, gratuitous, redundant, superfluous, unwanted, useless, pointless, uncalled-for, excessive, dispensable, nonessential, expendable. OPPOSITE: necessary.

needy *adj* poor, necessitous, indigent, disadvantaged, impecunious, impoverished, poverty-stricken, penniless, destitute, deprived, underprivileged. OPPOSITE: wealthy.

nefarious *adj* wicked, evil, bad, sinful, iniquitous, heinous, flagitious, villainous, infamous, vile, odious, abominable, execrable, horrible, dreadful, atrocious, outrageous, scandalous, monstrous. OPPOSITE: admirable.

negate *verb* **1** (*pollution has negated the efforts to boost tourist trade*) nullify, annul, cancel, invalidate, revoke, repeal, rescind, abrogate, countermand. **2** (*does evolution negate the existence of God?*) repudiate, deny, contradict, gainsay, refute, disprove, dispute, oppose. OPPOSITE: affirm.

negation *noun* **1** (*a negation of our principles*) opposite, reverse, contrary, converse, antithesis. **2** (*negation of all our efforts*) nullification, annulment, cancellation, invalidation, abrogation. **3** (*negation of God's existence*) denial, contradiction, disavowal, disclaimer, retraction, repudiation, refusal, rejection, renunciation. OPPOSITE: affirmation. **4** (*is ignorance a negation?*) nothing, nullity, nonentity, void, vacuity, nothingness, nonexistence.

negative *adj* **1** (*a negative effect*) denying, contradictory, opposing, contrary, contradicting, nullifying, invalidating. OPPOSITE: positive. **2** (*negative attitudes*) pessimistic, cynical, unhelpful, unenthusiastic, defeatist, complaining, uncooperative, contrary, antagonistic. OPPOSITE: optimistic.
➤ *noun* contradiction, denial, negation, rejection, refusal, opposite, no.

neglect *verb* **1** (*neglected their children*) disregard, ignore, overlook, pass over, spurn, slight, abandon, forsake, leave alone. **2** (*neglect to do one's duty*) omit, miss, skip, forget, shirk, skimp.
➤ *noun* negligence, disregard, oversight, inattention, omission, remissness, forgetfulness, default, dereliction, carelessness, heedlessness, laxness, slight, spurning, laxity. OPPOSITE: attention.

neglectful *adj* negligent, remiss, careless, lax, heedless, regardless, disregardful, inattentive, unmindful, uncaring, thoughtless, forgetful. OPPOSITE: attentive.

negligence *noun* neglect, disregard, oversight, omission, dereliction, default, remissness, forgetfulness, inattention, carelessness, heedlessness, thoughtlessness, indifference, laxity, slackness. OPPOSITE: attention.

negligent *adj* neglectful, remiss, careless, heedless, inattentive, unmindful, uncaring, forgetful, slack, lax, indifferent, offhand, nonchalant. OPPOSITE: attentive.

negligible *adj* unimportant, insignificant, inconsequential, trifling, trivial, minor, petty, paltry, small, tiny, minute, imperceptible. OPPOSITE: important.

negotiable *adj* **1** (*is your price negotiable?*) questionable, open to discussion, open to question, arguable. **2** (*icy roads negotiable only with care*) traversable, passable, penetrable, navigable, unblocked, open, clear, unobstructed.

negotiate *verb* **1** (*negotiate a contract*) bargain, deal, debate, discuss, arrange, work out, mediate, arbitrate, conciliate, settle, complete, compromise, haggle, wheel

and deal, transact. **2** (*negotiate the narrow paths*) navigate, get through, get over, get round, surmount, clear, pass.

negotiation *noun* bargaining, discussion, arrangement, mediation, arbitration, conciliation, settlement, compromise, discussion, debate, consultation, haggling, wheeling and dealing, transaction.

negotiator *noun* bargainer, arbitrator, go-between, intermediary, middleman, moderator, broker, adjudicator, haggler, wheeler-dealer.

neighbourhood *noun* vicinity, environs, surroundings, district, area, quarter, locality, community, locale, neck of the woods (*inf*).
in the neighbourhood of near, about, almost, close to, nearby, next, adjacent to, bordering.

neighbouring *adj* adjoining, adjacent, contiguous, connecting, proximate, near, close, nearby, nigh. OPPOSITE: distant.

neighbourly *adj* sociable, friendly, amiable, affable, well-disposed, cordial, hospitable, kind, helpful, generous, obliging, attentive, civil. OPPOSITE: unfriendly.

nemesis *noun* punishment, retribution, vengeance, destruction, downfall, ruin, destiny, fate.

neologism *noun* new word, new expression, new phrase, new term, coinage, innovation, vogue word, buzzword.

neophyte *noun* novice, newcomer, initiate, beginner, tyro, learner, student, pupil, greenhorn, rookie (*inf*), apprentice, trainee, convert, proselyte. OPPOSITE: master.

nepotism *noun* favouritism, patronage, partiality, bias, preferential treatment, old-boy network, old-school tie, jobs for the boys (*inf*).

nerve *noun* **1** (*it takes a lot of nerve to give a lecture to a thousand people*) courage, bravery, valour, mettle, pluck, guts (*inf*), fortitude, endurance, will, firmness, determination, resolution, steadfastness, power, might, strength, vigour. OPPOSITE: weakness. **2** (*had the nerve to answer back*) audacity, boldness, effrontery, impudence, impertinence, insolence, gall, cheek (*inf*), face (*inf*), sauce (*inf*), brass (*inf*), brass neck (*inf*), lip (*inf*), mouth (*inf*), chutzpah (*inf*). OPPOSITE: timidity.
➤ *verb* steel, brace, strengthen, fortify, embolden, invigorate, hearten, encourage. OPPOSITE: weaken.

nerve-racking *adj* harrowing, tense, stressful, disquieting, distressing, worrying, anxious, trying, nail-biting (*inf*).

nerves *pl noun* nervousness, stress, tension, nervous tension, strain, worry, anxiety, apprehensiveness, the jitters (*inf*), butterflies in one's stomach (*inf*), the willies (*inf*), the shakes (*inf*), the heebie-jeebies (*inf*), the screaming habdabs (*inf*), the collywobbles (*inf*).

nervous *adj* excitable, highly strung, tense, agitated, shaky, anxious, worried, strained, apprehensive, fearful, fidgety, jumpy, fretful, uptight, panicky, jittery (*inf*), nervy (*inf*), funky (*inf*), edgy, on edge, on tenterhooks, uneasy, hesitant, timid. OPPOSITE: calm.

nervous breakdown *noun* mental breakdown, breakdown, crisis, depression, clinical depression, nervous collapse.

nervy *adj* tense, highly strung, anxious, worried,

strained, edgy, on edge, uptight, uneasy, restless, jittery (*inf*).

nest *noun* **1** (*a bird's nest*) den, breeding ground, lair, lodge, drey, burrow, form, set, eyrie, cote. **2** (*the criminals' nest*) retreat, hideaway, hideout, haunt, shelter, refuge, den.

nestle *verb* snuggle, cuddle, huddle, curl up, settle, lodge, shelter.

net[1] *noun* (*a fishing net*) mesh, meshwork, web, webbing, netting, network, latticework, openwork, drift, drag, driftnet, dragnet, seine, reticulum, lace.
≫ *verb* catch, capture, bag, trap, snare, ensnare, enmesh, entangle. OPPOSITE: release.

net[2] *adj* **1** (*a net salary*) take-home, after tax, after deductions, clear. OPPOSITE: gross. **2** (*a net result*) overall, actual, final, closing, ultimate, concluding.
≫ *verb* bring in, take home, clear, earn, gain, get, make, realize, pull in (*inf*), rake in (*inf*).

nether *adj* lower, under, bottom, inferior, underworld, hellish, infernal, stygian. OPPOSITE: upper.

nettle *verb* vex, annoy, irritate, irk, pique, chafe, provoke, ruffle, exasperate, bother, harass, incense, enrage, hassle (*inf*), bug (*inf*), get to (*inf*), rub up the wrong way (*inf*), get someone's back up (*inf*), get on someone's nerves (*inf*), get up someone's nose (*inf*), get under someone's skin (*inf*).

network *noun* **1** (*a network of wires*) grid, circuitry, mesh, meshwork, net, web, webbing, latticework, openwork, maze, labyrinth. **2** (*a network of business colleagues*) system, organization, complex, arrangement, structure, connections, contacts, grid, matrix, nexus, old school tie.

neurosis *noun* disorder, mental disorder, mental illness, disturbance, derangement, affliction, instability, deviation, fixation, obsession, phobia.

neurotic *adj* paranoid, mentally ill, disturbed, deranged, maladjusted, irrational, unstable, obsessive, compulsive, fixated, phobic.

neuter *verb* emasculate, castrate, geld, doctor, spay, do, fix, cut.

neutral *adj* **1** (*adopt a neutral position in an argument*) impartial, nonpartisan, unbiased, unprejudiced, open-minded, evenhanded, disinterested, indifferent, dispassionate, objective, aloof, uninvolved, uncommitted, nonaligned. OPPOSITE: partisan. **2** (*neutral language*) bland, dull, drab, ordinary, everyday, unremarkable, inoffensive, nondescript, colourless, insipid, expressionless, anodyne, achromatic, indeterminate, indistinguishable. **3** (*a neutral colour*) pale, colourless, uncoloured, achromatic, pastel, indistinct, grey, beige, light-brown, fawn.

neutralize *verb* counteract, balance, counterbalance, offset, compensate for, make up for, cancel, cancel out, negate, nullify, annul, undo. OPPOSITE: intensify.

never *adv* at no time, not at any time, not ever, not once, certainly not, not at all, under no circumstances, on no account, not on your life (*inf*), no way (*inf*), not in a month of Sundays (*inf*), not in a million years (*inf*), not on your nelly (*inf*), when hell freezes over (*sl*). OPPOSITE: always.

never-ending *adj* everlasting, eternal, endless, perpetual, unending, ceaseless, incessant, interminable, unremitting, unbroken, uninterrupted.

nevertheless *adv* nonetheless, however, yet, but, still, even so, be that as it may, notwithstanding.

new *adj* **1** (*a new invention*) latest, recent, modern, contemporary, present-day, up-to-the-minute, advanced, novel, original, creative, newfangled, state-of-the-art, futuristic, ultramodern, avant-garde, experimental, trendy (*inf*). OPPOSITE: old. **2** (*a new idea*) fresh, creative, innovative, novel, original, different, revolutionary, experimental, imaginative, unhackneyed, pioneering, unusual, unconventional. OPPOSITE: usual. **3** (*a new recipe*) improved, changed, altered, modernized, restored, redesigned, refreshed, renewed, regenerated. **4** (*add a new wing to the gallery*) additional, added, supplementary, extra, increased, further. **5** (*new to the company*) unfamiliar, unaccustomed, unknown, unacquainted, inexperienced, ignorant. OPPOSITE: familiar.

newcomer *noun* **1** (*a newcomer to the country*) immigrant, arrival, new arrival, settler, foreigner, alien, outsider, stranger, intruder. **2** (*a newcomer to the trade*) novice, learner, beginner, recruit, trainee, probationer, greenhorn (*inf*), rookie (*inf*).

newly *adv* recently, just, lately, of late.

news *noun* report, account, information, facts, data, bulletin, message, announcement, statement, newsflash, intelligence, word, advice, tidings, dispatch, communiqué, story, revelation, gen (*inf*), lowdown (*inf*), dope (*inf*).

newspaper *noun* paper, daily, journal, broadsheet, tabloid, gazette, weekly, monthly, rag (*inf*).

next *adj* **1** (*the next morning*) following, succeeding, subsequent, ensuing, later, consequent. OPPOSITE: last. **2** (*we can hear you in the next room*) neighbouring, adjacent, adjoining, nearest, bordering, closest, contiguous.
≫ *adv* later, then, afterwards, at a later time, thereafter, subsequently.

nibble *verb* bite, gnaw, peck at, eat, pick at.
≫ *noun* bite, morsel, titbit, mouthful, piece, snack, taste.

nice *adj* **1** (*that looks a nice place*) pleasant, agreeable, enjoyable, delightful, good, lovely, satisfying, appealing. OPPOSITE: unpleasant. **2** (*a nice person*) pleasant, agreeable, friendly, charming, attractive, pleasing, likeable, kind, kindly, good, amiable, understanding, sympathetic, polite, refined, courteous, civil, well-mannered, cultivated, polished. OPPOSITE: nasty. **3** (*a nice point of law*) fine, subtle, exact, precise, careful, accurate, strict, scrupulous, minute, delicate, fastidious, particular, discriminating.

nicely *adv* satisfactorily, properly, pleasantly, agreeably, delightfully, well, fine.

nicety *noun* **1** (*the niceties of correct behaviour*) delicacy, subtlety, refinement, detail, distinction, nuance. **2** (*lack the nicety of discrimination*) precision, accuracy, exactitude, exactness, rigour, fastidiousness, scrupulousness.

niche *noun* **1** (*a niche in a wall*) recess, alcove, nook, cranny, corner, cubbyhole. **2** (*find a niche in the market*) position, place, slot, specialist area.

nick *noun* notch, indentation, cut, chip, scratch, dent, groove.
➤ *verb* **1** (*nicked his skin*) notch, cut, chip, scratch, dent. **2** (*nicked some jewellery*) steal, take, pilfer, swipe (*inf*), pinch (*inf*), knock off (*inf*). **3** (*got nicked for speeding*) arrest, grab, catch, collar (*inf*), nab (*inf*), nobble (*inf*).

nickname *noun* pet name, familiar name, tag, diminutive, epithet.

nifty *adj* slick, clever, neat, nimble, smart, skilful, effective, fast, quick.

niggardly *adj* **1** (*a niggardly landlord*) penny-pinching, mean, miserly, stingy, parsimonious, closefisted, tight, tightfisted, ungenerous, frugal, sparing. OPPOSITE: generous. **2** (*a niggardly salary*) meagre, scanty, small, paltry, inadequate, insufficient. OPPOSITE: ample.

niggle *verb* **1** (*it's been niggling me all day*) bother, irritate, annoy, worry, trouble, nag, bug (*inf*). **2** (*stop niggling me!*) nag, find fault with, complain to, grumble at, moan at, criticize, scold, berate, carp.

nigh *adj* near, close, nearby, proximate, adjacent, next, imminent, impending. OPPOSITE: distant.
➤ *adv* nearly, almost, practically, about, approximately.

night *noun* dark, darkness, nighttime. OPPOSITE: day.

nightfall *noun* sunset, sundown, dusk, twilight, evening, gloaming, crepuscule. OPPOSITE: daybreak.

nightmare *noun* **1** (*I had this terrifying nightmare last night*) bad dream, frightening dream, incubus. **2** (*travelling across London is a real nightmare*) ordeal, trial, anguish, agony, horror, torment.

nihilism *noun* rejection, renunciation, denial, repudiation, negation, nothingness, nonexistence, void, pessimism, disorder, chaos, anarchy, lawlessness.

nil *noun* nothing, nought, zero, love, zilch (*inf*).

nimble *adj* **1** (*a nimble climber*) agile, sprightly, spry, active, lively, smart, quick, brisk, prompt, ready, deft, dexterous. OPPOSITE: clumsy. **2** (*have a nimble mind*) alert, clever, quick, quick-witted, quick-thinking. OPPOSITE: slow-witted.

nip[1] *verb* **1** (*nipped by a dog*) bite, pinch, squeeze, compress, tweak, snip, clip, catch, grip. **2** (*nip down the road*) pop, rush, hurry, go, fly, tear, dash.
nip in the bud stop, stem, check, halt, arrest, thwart, frustrate, block.

nip[2] *noun* (*a nip of alcohol*) dram, draught, drop, sip, swig (*inf*), shot (*inf*).

nipple *noun* teat, tit, mamilla, papilla, udder, dug, pap.

nippy *adj* chilly, cold, icy, raw, sharp.

nirvana *noun* enlightenment, knowledge, understanding, paradise, heaven, bliss, tranquillity, peace, joy.

nit-picking *adj* fussy, finicky, captious, fault-finding, pedantic, critical, overcritical, quibbling, carping, hairsplitting.

nitty-gritty *noun* essentials, basics, fundamentals, facts, essence, substance, gist, crux, brass tacks (*inf*), nuts and bolts (*inf*).

nitwit *noun* idiot, nit (*inf*), fool, dope (*inf*), twit (*inf*), dimwit, ninny, twerp (*inf*), wally (*inf*), clot (*inf*), mug (*inf*), halfwit, numskull (*inf*), simpleton, dunce, chump, nincompoop, dullard, ass, donkey, ignoramus, sucker (*inf*), dork (*inf*), nerd (*inf*), geek (*inf*), pillock (*inf*), plonker (*inf*), prat (*sl*), prick (*sl*), dingbat (*sl*), dunderhead, dolt, blockhead, dickhead (*sl*), imbecile, moron, cretin.

no *adv* not at all, certainly not, absolutely not, by no means, never, under no circumstances, no way (*inf*), nope (*inf*), not on your life (*inf*), not on your nelly (*inf*). OPPOSITE: yes.

nobble *verb* **1** (*attempt to nobble the jury*) bribe, influence, persuade, threaten, intimidate. **2** (*nobble a horse*) drug, dope, interfere with, disable, incapacitate, tamper with. **3** (*nobble plans*) thwart, frustrate, stop, halt. **4** (*got nobbled as he was stealing the loot*) catch, arrest, nab (*inf*), collar (*inf*), nick (*inf*).

nobility *noun* **1** (*marry into the nobility*) gentry, aristocracy, upper class, high society, peerage, lords, nobles. OPPOSITE: commonalty. **2** (*nobility of character*) nobleness, dignity, exaltation, eminence, loftiness, greatness, distinction, grandeur, magnificence, honour, virtue, goodness, integrity. OPPOSITE: lowliness.

noble *noun* aristocrat, nobleman, noblewoman, patrician, peer, peeress, lord, lady. OPPOSITE: commoner.
➤ *adj* **1** (*a noble family*) aristocratic, patrician, highborn, blue-blooded, titled, born with a silver spoon in one's mouth (*inf*). OPPOSITE: lowborn. **2** (*a noble person who was always ready to help others*) magnanimous, generous, worthy, honourable, self-sacrificing, unselfish. OPPOSITE: base. **3** (*a noble idea*) virtuous, good, great, dignified, distinguished, eminent, lofty, elevated, exalted, lordly, stately. **4** (*noble in stature*) grand, magnificent, impressive, superior, fine, excellent.

nobody *pronoun* no one, nonentity, nothing, cipher. OPPOSITE: somebody.

nocturnal *adj* night, nighttime, nightly, crepuscular. OPPOSITE: diurnal.

nod *verb* bow, dip, incline, acknowledge, agree, say yes to, approve, support, assent, indicate, show, signal, gesture, motion.
nod off fall asleep, drop off, doze off, doze, drowse, nap, sleep. OPPOSITE: wake.

node *noun* protuberance, nodule, knob, knot, growth, bulge, swelling, lump, bump.

noise *noun* sound, din, row, racket, clamour, outcry, uproar, hubbub, tumult, commotion, pandemonium, talk, cry. OPPOSITE: silence.

noiseless *adj* silent, inaudible, quiet, still, mute. OPPOSITE: loud.

noisome *adj* offensive, disgusting, repugnant, loathsome, detestable, foul, fetid, putrid, malodorous, mephitic, noxious, poisonous, pestilential, unhealthy, unwholesome, harmful, pernicious, deleterious, detrimental. OPPOSITE: wholesome.

noisy *adj* loud, clamorous, boisterous, rowdy, obstreperous, riotous, uproarious, turbulent, tumultuous, vociferous, cacophonous, strident, blaring, deafening, blasting, earsplitting. OPPOSITE: quiet.

nomad *noun* wanderer, vagrant, traveller, itinerant, migrant, roamer, rover.

nomadic *adj* wandering, roving, vagrant, travelling, itinerant, peripatetic, migrant, migratory.

nominal *adj* **1** (*the nominal leader*) titular, formal, theoretical, in name only, so-called, supposed, would-be, self-styled. OPPOSITE: actual. **2** (*a nominal price*) token, minimal, small, trivial, inconsiderable, insignificant. OPPOSITE: excessive.

nominate *verb* **1** (*nominate a candidate*) propose, put forward, suggest, present, name. **2** (*nominated as the official representative*) choose, select, elect, appoint, assign, designate.

nonaligned *adj* neutral, impartial, nonpartisan, uninvolved, uncommitted.

nonchalant *adj* unconcerned, dispassionate, indifferent, apathetic, careless, blasé, insouciant, carefree, cool, calm, easy, casual, offhand. OPPOSITE: concerned.

non compos mentis *adj* of unsound mind, mentally ill, deranged, unbalanced, mad, insane, crazy (*inf*).

nonconformist *adj* unconventional, dissident, rebel, individualist, radical, eccentric. OPPOSITE: conformist.
➤ *noun* dissident, rebel, individualist, radical, maverick, eccentric, fish out of water (*inf*), square peg in a round hole (*inf*), dropout (*inf*), oddball (*inf*).

nondescript *adj* unclassifiable, indefinite, indeterminate, unremarkable, unexceptional, characterless, dull, bland, ordinary, commonplace. OPPOSITE: distinctive.

none *pronoun* nobody, no one, not one, not any, not a single one, not a soul, zero. OPPOSITE: many.
➤ *adv* not at all, in no way, to no degree, to no extent.

nonentity *noun* nothing, nobody, cipher, lightweight (*inf*). OPPOSITE: somebody.

nonesuch *noun* paragon, nonpareil, ideal, exemplar, model, pattern.

nonetheless *adv* nevertheless, however, yet, still, but, even so, be that as it may, notwithstanding.

nonexistent *adj* unreal, imaginary, imagined, missing, insubstantial, hypothetical, fictitious, fanciful, fantasy, illusory, hallucinatory. OPPOSITE: real.

nonpareil *adj* peerless, matchless, unmatched, unequalled, unparalleled, incomparable, unique, unrivalled, supreme. OPPOSITE: ordinary.
➤ *noun* paragon, gem, jewel, ideal, exemplar.

nonplus *verb* confound, perplex, bewilder, confuse, puzzle, baffle, mystify, stump, stun, flabbergast, disconcert, take aback, dumbfound, astonish, astound, flummox (*inf*), faze (*inf*). OPPOSITE: enlighten.

nonsense *noun* rubbish, trash, rot, balderdash, humbug, twaddle, drivel, bosh (*inf*), gibberish, crap (*sl*), balls (*sl*), bullshit (*sl*), shit (*sl*), cobblers (*inf*), bunkum (*inf*), tosh (*inf*), tripe (*inf*), bilge (*inf*), claptrap (*inf*), waffle (*inf*), twaddle (*inf*), gobbledygook (*inf*), mumbo-jumbo (*inf*), eyewash (*inf*), hogwash (*inf*), poppycock (*inf*), senselessness, absurdity, silliness, stupidity, foolishness, folly, fatuity. OPPOSITE: sense.

nonsensical *adj* absurd, crazy, silly, foolish, senseless, meaningless, ridiculous, ludicrous, idiotic, preposterous, harebrained, crackpot (*inf*), dotty (*inf*), barmy, wacky (*inf*). OPPOSITE: sensible.

nonstop *adj* continuous, incessant, constant, ceaseless, unbroken, uninterrupted, endless, never-ending, interminable, persistent, relentless, unfaltering, unremitting.
➤ *adv* continuously, incessantly, constantly, ceaselessly, endlessly, interminably, relentlessly, unremittingly, without interruption.

nook *noun* corner, recess, niche, opening, alcove, cranny, cubbyhole, retreat.

noon *noun* midday, twelve noon, twelve o'clock, noonday, noontime, noontide.

norm *noun* average, mean, rule, usual, standard, gauge, scale, measure, pattern, criterion, yardstick, benchmark, type, model.

normal *adj* **1** (*under normal circumstances*) usual, common, general, ordinary, average, conventional, everyday, commonplace, customary, habitual, routine, regular, standard, typical, run of the mill. OPPOSITE: unusual. **2** (*a normal baby*) healthy, natural, rational, sane, balanced, well-adjusted. OPPOSITE: abnormal.

normality *noun* usualness, generality, ordinariness, commonness, regularity, typicality, routine, conventionality.

normally *adv* usually, commonly, in general, generally, ordinarily, as a rule, as a general rule, regularly, typically, characteristically, habitually, as a matter of routine.

nose *noun* **1** (*hit him on the nose*) bill, beak (*inf*), neb, snout (*inf*), hooter (*inf*), schnozzle (*inf*), conk (*inf*), snitch (*inf*), sniffer (*inf*). **2** (*develop a nose for getting a good bargain*) instinct, intuition, sixth sense, feel, sense, perception.

nose around search, pry, poke around, snoop (*inf*).

nose out uncover, detect, discover, search for, smell out, sniff out (*inf*).

nosedive *verb* plummet, fall suddenly, drop suddenly, dive, plunge, swoop.

nosegay *noun* posy, bouquet, bunch, spray, corsage.

nostalgia *noun* yearning, longing, pining, reminiscence, remembrance, wistfulness, regret, regretfulness, homesickness.

nostalgic *adj* yearning, longing, pining, wistful, reminiscing, remembering, sentimental, regretful, homesick.

nosy *adj* inquisitive, curious, prying, meddlesome, interfering, eavesdropping, intrusive, snooping (*inf*).

notable *adj* remarkable, noteworthy, special, significant, important, signal, noticeable, conspicuous, marked, outstanding, momentous, impressive, striking, memorable, uncommon, unusual, unforgettable, extraordinary, distinctive, pronounced, noted, distinguished, celebrated, famous, acclaimed, well-known, illustrious, pre-eminent, eminent. OPPOSITE: insignificant.
➤ *noun* personage, celebrity, VIP, dignitary, luminary, star, somebody, big name, big shot (*inf*), big noise (*inf*). OPPOSITE: nobody.

notably *adv* particularly, especially, noticeably,

significantly, importantly, conspicuously, markedly, memorably, impressively, remarkably, unusually, uncommonly, unforgettably.

notation *noun* symbols, signs, system, alphabet, code, characters, script, cipher, shorthand, hieroglyphics.

notch *noun* **1** (*cut a notch in the pole*) cut, nick, incision, indentation, groove, dent, gouge, mark, score. **2** (*move up one notch higher*) step, level, stage, rung, degree, grade, gradation.
➤ *verb* cut, nick, indent, serrate.

notch up score, gain, achieve, attain, register, chalk up (*inf*).

note *noun* **1** (*wrote a note to remind him*) memorandum, memo, record, report, minute, jotting, annotation, comment, remark, observation, message, letter, communication, missive, epistle. **2** (*artists of note*) fame, renown, celebrity, distinction, prestige, eminence, pre-eminence, greatness, regard, esteem, significance, importance, consequence. OPPOSITE: insignificance. **3** (*take special note*) care, heed, attention, regard, notice, observation. **4** (*a hundred pounds in notes*) banknote, bill, paper money. OPPOSITE: coin. **5** (*read the notes at the end of the chapter*) annotation, gloss, footnote, explanation, commentary, explication, marginalia. **6** (*detected a note of sadness in his voice*) quality, tone, indication, inflection, hint.
➤ *verb* **1** (*her success was noted*) notice, perceive, remark, observe, see, heed. OPPOSITE: ignore. **2** (*noted their names and addresses*) write down, log, mark, mark down, register, record, enter, jot down.

notebook *noun* memo book, notepad, jotter, exercise book, diary, journal, register, log book, personal organizer, Filofax®.

noted *adj* famous, renowned, celebrated, acclaimed, of note, notable, great, well-known, illustrious, distinguished, eminent, pre-eminent. OPPOSITE: unknown.

noteworthy *adj* remarkable, notable, outstanding, memorable, exceptional, unusual, extraordinary, important, significant, impressive, striking, signal. OPPOSITE: ordinary.

nothing *pronoun* nought, naught, nothing at all, nil, zero, cipher, zilch (*inf*), sweet Fanny Adams (*inf*), sod all (*sl*), bugger all (*sl*), fuck all (*sl*), sweet FA (*sl*). OPPOSITE: something.
➤ *noun* nonentity, nobody, cipher, void, nothingness, nihility, nullity, nonexistence. OPPOSITE: somebody.
for nothing **1** (*it's yours for nothing*) free, gratis, complimentary, without charge, on the house (*inf*). **2** (*travelled all that way for nothing*) in vain, to no purpose, unsuccessfully, needlessly, to no avail.

nothingness *noun* nothing, nihility, nullity, nonexistence, oblivion, void, emptiness.

notice *noun* **1** (*take notice of the warnings*) attention, observation, note, heed, regard, consideration, thought interest, respect, cognizance, vigilance, watchfulness. **2** (*give advance notice of the strike*) warning, information, notification, advice, instruction, order, announcement, declaration, intimation, news. **3** (*put up a notice on the board*) poster, placard, sign, bill, handbill, advertisement, pamphlet, leaflet, flyer. **4** (*gave their*

employees a month's notice) dismissal, discharge, the sack (*inf*), the push (*inf*) papers (*inf*), the boot (*inf*), marching orders (*inf*). **5** (*the film received brilliant notices in the press*) review, criticism, comment, critique, write-up.
➤ *verb* note, take notice of, take note of, perceive, remark, observe, see, detect, regard, mark, heed, take heed of, behold, descry. OPPOSITE: miss.

noticeable *adj* perceptible, appreciable, conspicuous, observable, discernible, distinguishable, distinct, clear, plain, evident, obvious, manifest, visible, apparent. OPPOSITE: inconspicuous.

notification *noun* announcement, declaration, notice, warning, advice, intimation, information, intelligence, statement, message, communication.

notify *verb* inform, tell, advise, warn, alert, acquaint, apprise, announce, communicate, declare, disclose, divulge, reveal. OPPOSITE: suppress.

notion *noun* **1** (*have only a vague notion of what happened*) idea, impression, concept, sentiment, thought, opinion, view, belief, conviction, theory, conception, apprehension, understanding, assumption, presumption. **2** (*took a notion to depart*) whim, impulse, desire, caprice, fancy, inclination.

notional *adj* theoretical, hypothetical, conceptual, suppositional, unreal, illusory, speculative. OPPOSITE: actual.

notoriety *noun* infamy, disrepute, disgrace, dishonour, opprobrium, obloquy. OPPOSITE: illustriousness.

notorious *adj* infamous, disreputable, ill-famed, ignominious, dishonourable, disgraceful, scandalous, opprobrious. OPPOSITE: illustrious.

notwithstanding *prep* despite, in spite of.
➤ *adv* though, nevertheless, however, even so, be that as it may, yet, nonetheless.

nought *noun* zero, nil, nothing, naught, love, zilch (*inf*), nothingness.

nourish *verb* **1** (*nourish a baby*) feed, sustain, nurture, nurse, bring up, rear, care for, tend. OPPOSITE: starve. **2** (*nourish a belief*) strengthen, maintain, support, advance, entertain, harbour, cherish, foster, encourage, promote.

nourishing *adj* nutritious, nutritive, healthy, wholesome, beneficial, alimentary, alimentative. OPPOSITE: unhealthy.

nourishment *noun* food, nutrition, nutriment, sustenance, subsistence, aliment, alimentation, grub (*inf*), tuck (*inf*), eats (*inf*), chow (*inf*), scoff (*inf*).

novel *adj* new, fresh, original, innovative, creative, different, uncommon, unusual, unfamiliar, unique, rare, strange. OPPOSITE: hackneyed.
➤ *noun* story, tale, book, narrative, romance, fiction.

novelist *noun* writer, creative writer, author, authoress.

novelty *noun* **1** (*the novelty of the new job soon wore off*) newness, freshness, originality, innovation, creativity, difference, unfamiliarity. **2** (*carnival and party novelties*) trifle, bagatelle, trinket, bauble, gimcrack, knick-knack, toy, gadget.

novice *noun* beginner, tyro, newcomer, neophyte, learner, pupil, student, apprentice, probationer, trainee, amateur, raw recruit. OPPOSITE: expert.

now *adv* **1** (*the price has now gone up to £100*) right now, just now, at present, at the moment, nowadays, today, currently. OPPOSITE: then. **2** (*please go now*) immediately, at once, straightaway, promptly, right away. OPPOSITE: later.

nowadays *adv* at present, at the present time, now, at the moment, today, in this day and age.

noxious *adj* poisonous, toxic, pernicious, harmful, hurtful, injurious, baleful, deleterious, detrimental, deadly, destructive, noisome, unwholesome, unhealthy, pestilential, foul. OPPOSITE: beneficial.

nuance *noun* shade, gradation, degree, distinction, subtlety, refinement, nicety, trace, touch, hint, suggestion.

nucleus *noun* centre, focus, core, kernel, heart, nub, pivot, essence, meat, pith, marrow.

nude *adj* naked, bare, unclothed, undressed, uncovered, exposed, starkers (*inf*), in the altogether (*inf*), au naturel, in the buff (*inf*), in one's birthday suit (*inf*), in the raw (*inf*). OPPOSITE: dressed.

nudge *verb* push, shove, poke, prod, dig, jab, elbow, jog.
» *noun* push, shove, poke, prod, dig, jab, elbow, jog.

nugatory *adj* worthless, trifling, frivolous, insignificant, ineffective, futile, useless, vain, bootless, unavailing. OPPOSITE: valuable.

nugget *noun* piece, lump, mass, chunk, wad, hunk, wodge.

nuisance *noun* annoyance, vexation, bother, trial, tribulation, pest, pain (*inf*), bore, trouble, inconvenience, burden, affliction, plague, hassle (*inf*), drag (*inf*), thorn in the flesh (*inf*), pain the arse (*sl*). OPPOSITE: pleasure.

null *adj* void, invalid, invalidated, powerless, worthless, useless, cancelled, annulled, repealed, rescinded, revoked, futile, ineffectual, characterless, nonexistent. OPPOSITE: valid.

nullify *verb* annul, abrogate, revoke, rescind, repeal, quash, invalidate, cancel, negate, abolish, dissolve, void, reverse, withdraw, renounce, repudiate.

numb *adj* dead, deadened, without feeling, dull, benumbed, insensible, insensate, frozen, paralysed, immobile, unfeeling, insensitive, torpid. OPPOSITE: sensitive.
» *verb* stun, daze, deaden, benumb, dull, freeze, chill, paralyse, immobilize, anaesthetize, drug.

number *noun* **1** (*the postcode consists of letters and numbers*) figure, numeral, digit, integer, symbol, character. **2** (*the number of incidents has risen*) sum, total, aggregate, collection, amount, tally, score. **3** (*the number of people here*) quantity, crowd, collection, multitude, amount, company, host, throng, many. **4** (*the last number of the magazine*) copy, issue, edition, printing.
» *verb* **1** (*number the pages*) count, total, add, add up, enumerate, calculate, compute, reckon. **2** (*my days are numbered*) limit, restrict, restrain.

numberless *adj* countless, innumerable, infinite, incalculable, immeasurable, untold, many, myriad, multitudinous. OPPOSITE: few.

numeral *noun* number, figure, digit, integer, cipher, character, symbol.

numerous *adj* many, manifold, several, lots of (*inf*), multiple, abundant, plentiful, innumerable, numberless, myriad. OPPOSITE: few.

nuncio *noun* envoy, representative, ambassador, legate.

nuptial *adj* conjugal, connubial, matrimonial, marital, bridal, wedding.

nuptials *pl noun* wedding, marriage, espousals.

nurse *verb* **1** (*nursed his sick mother*) tend, look after, care for, minister to, treat. OPPOSITE: neglect. **2** (*a mother nursing her baby*) suckle, feed, nurture, rear. **3** (*nurse a grudge*) harbour, preserve, keep, hold, have, entertain, cherish, foster, encourage, promote. OPPOSITE: banish.

nurture *verb* **1** (*nurture an infant*) nourish, feed, sustain, support, nurse, tend, rear, bring up, raise, train, discipline, educate, school, form, instruct. **2** (*nurture a plan*) cultivate, develop, encourage, promote, boost, forward, help, aid, assist, foster.
» *noun* care, encouragement, support, training, discipline, formation, education, instruction, cultivation.

nut *noun* **1** (*crack nuts*) kernel, pip, stone, seed. **2** (*a football nut*) fanatic, enthusiast, devotee, fan, buff (*inf*), freak (*inf*). **3** (*some nut shot the child*) madman, maniac, lunatic, psychopath, psycho (*inf*), weirdo (*inf*), crackpot (*inf*), headcase (*inf*).

nutrition *noun* nourishment, food, aliment, alimentation, sustenance, subsistence, nutriment, grub (*inf*), tuck (*inf*), eats (*inf*), chow (*inf*), scoff (*inf*).

nutritious *adj* nutritive, nourishing, good, wholesome, healthy, beneficial, alimentary, alimentative. OPPOSITE: unhealthy.

nuts *adj* **1** (*he's gone nuts*) mad, insane, crazy, wild, berserk, deranged, loony (*inf*), batty (*inf*), barmy (*inf*), out of one's mind (*inf*), off one's head (*inf*), off one's rocker (*inf*), out to lunch (*sl*), having a screw loose (*inf*). **2** (*nuts abut cars*) crazy, fanatical, enthusiastic, wild, passionate, devoted, mad (*inf*), daft (*inf*).

nuts and bolts basics, fundamentals, essentials, nitty-gritty (*inf*).

nuzzle *verb* snuggle, cuddle, nudge, nestle.

nymph *noun* sylph, dryad, naiad, oread, damsel, maiden, girl, lass.

oaf *noun* dolt, dunce, dullard, blockhead, idiot, fool, moron, bungler, numskull (*inf*), twit (*inf*), twerp (*inf*), wally (*inf*), simpleton, lout, clod, dickhead (*sl*), dingbat (*sl*).

oafish *adj* doltish, idiotic, stupid, foolish, moronic, half-witted, loopy (*inf*), dumb (*inf*).

oasis *noun* **1** (*an oasis in the middle of the desert*) watering hole, watering place. **2** (*an oasis of tranquillity*) refuge, retreat, hideaway, hideout, haven, sanctuary.

oath *noun* **1** (*swear an oath of loyalty to the monarch*) vow, pledge, promise, word, statement, bond, asseveration, affirmation, avowal, troth. **2** (*shout out loud oaths*) curse, imprecation, malediction, expletive, swearword, obscenity, blasphemy, four-letter word, bad language, foul language, profanity.

obdurate *adj* hard, hardhearted, cold, callous, unfeeling, insensitive, relentless, unrelenting, harsh, inflexible, unyielding, adamant, firm, stubborn, obstinate, mulish, pigheaded, headstrong, wilful, intractable, unshakeable, immovable. OPPOSITE: amenable.

obedient *adj* compliant, acquiescent, yielding, submissive, deferential, respectful, dutiful, law-abiding, docile, biddable, conforming, amenable, tractable, subservient. OPPOSITE: disobedient.

obeisance *noun* homage, deference, respect, reverence, honour, veneration, adoration, worship, salutation, bow, curtsy, genuflection, kowtow, stoop, salaam. OPPOSITE: disrespect.

obelisk *noun* pillar, column, monument, shaft, needle.

obese *adj* fat, stout, overweight, heavy, big, bulky, gross, corpulent, rotund, portly, plump, tubby, podgy, paunchy, fleshy. OPPOSITE: thin.

obey *verb* comply with, observe, keep, heed, mind, follow, abide by, conform to, submit to, yield to, adhere to, respect, discharge, fulfil, carry out, perform, execute. OPPOSITE: disobey.

obfuscate *verb* obscure, darken, cloud, hide, conceal, shadow, veil, befog, confuse, bewilder, blur, jumble, scramble, garble, muddle, perplex. OPPOSITE: clear.

object *noun* **1** (*a large metal object*) thing, article, something, item, device, entity, body. OPPOSITE: concept. **2** (*the object of the exercise*) aim, purpose, objective, goal, end, point, motive, intent, intention, ambition, design. **3** (*the object of their jokes*) butt, victim, focus, recipient, target.
➤ *verb* protest, disapprove, demur, mind, take exception, remonstrate, expostulate, oppose, complain, beg to differ. OPPOSITE: agree.

objection *noun* protest, disapproval, demur, demurral, opposition, dissent, argument, doubt, scruple, qualm, complaint, grievance, exception, remonstrance, expostulation. OPPOSITE: approval.

objectionable *adj* unpleasant, disagreeable, offensive, repulsive, repugnant, revolting, nauseating, obnoxious, abominable, loathsome, nasty, foul, abhorrent, contemptible, detestable, odious, vile, insufferable, intolerable, deplorable, unacceptable. OPPOSITE: agreeable.

objective *adj* impartial, unbiased, unprejudiced, nonpartisan, neutral, detached, uninvolved, disinterested, fair, just, equitable, dispassionate. OPPOSITE: subjective.
➤ *noun* aim, purpose, goal, end, target, object, point, idea, intention, intent, design, ambition, hope, desire, aspiration.

objurgate *verb* scold, chide, rebuke, reprove, reprimand, upbraid, berate. OPPOSITE: praise.

oblation *noun* offering, sacrifice, gift, present, donation, contribution.

obligate *verb* constrain, compel, make, require, necessitate, oblige, impel, force, press, coerce.

obligation *noun* duty, responsibility, charge, onus, liability, accountability, necessity, compulsion, requirement, function, pledge, contract, demand, bond, agreement, commitment, trust, debt.

obligatory *adj* compulsory, mandatory, binding, required, necessary, essential, prescriptive, requisite, imperative, unavoidable. OPPOSITE: optional.

oblige *verb* **1** (*otherwise we will be obliged to take further action*) compel, constrain, force, bind, necessitate, require, coerce, make, call for, press, pressurize, obligate. **2** (*I'll be glad to oblige*) accommodate, favour, do someone a favour, serve, help, please, indulge, gratify.

obliged *adj* indebted, grateful, thankful, appreciative, beholden.

obliging *adj* accommodating, amenable, willing, agreeable, kind, friendly, considerate, pleasant, cooperative, helpful, courteous, civil, polite, gracious.

oblique *adj* **1** (*an oblique line*) slanting, diagonal, angled, sloping, inclined, tilted. OPPOSITE: vertical. **2** (*an oblique statement*) indirect, evasive, devious, circuitous, roundabout, backhanded, furtive, sidelong. OPPOSITE: direct.
▶ *noun* diagonal, slant, slash, backslash, solidus.

obliterate *verb* eradicate, destroy, annihilate, wipe out, expunge, erase, rub out, cancel, remove, delete, cross out, strike out, efface, blot out. OPPOSITE: restore.

oblivion *noun* darkness, obscurity, extinction, abeyance, neglect, forgetfulness, disregard, carelessness, heedlessness, absentmindedness, obliviousness, blankness, unconsciousness. OPPOSITE: awareness.

oblivious *adj* unaware, unconscious, insensible, unmindful, blind, deaf, ignorant, unobservant, heedless, unheeding, neglectful, careless, forgetful, absentminded. OPPOSITE: aware.

obloquy *noun* censure, criticism, denunciation, upbraiding, invective, abuse, aspersion, defamation, vilification, slander, libel, calumny, reproach, reproof, blame, dishonour, discredit, scandal, shame, disgrace, infamy, ignominy, opprobrium. OPPOSITE: praise.

obnoxious *adj* objectionable, unpleasant, disagreeable, nasty, offensive, disgusting, revolting, repulsive, repugnant, odious, vile, horrid, hateful, abhorrent, despicable, loathsome, detestable, intolerable, reprehensible, insufferable. OPPOSITE: delightful.

obscene *adj* **1** (*obscene phone calls*) indecent, immoral, improper, offensive, disgusting, foul, dirty, filthy, smutty, blue, pornographic, salacious, lewd, bawdy, ribald, coarse, vulgar, rude, raunchy (*inf*), fruity (*inf*), erotic, sexy, gross, outrageous, shocking, shameless, immodest, impure, unchaste. OPPOSITE: decent. **2** (*an obscene waste of money*) shameless, offensive, shocking, atrocious, outrageous, scandalous, wicked, evil, sickening, revolting, nauseating.

obscenity *noun* **1** (*the obscenity of a brothel*) indecency, immorality, offensiveness, filthiness, salaciousness, lewdness, coarseness, vulgarity, rudeness, shamelessness. **2** (*shout out obscenities*) swearword, curse, expletive, profanity, four-letter word, malediction, bad language, foul language. **3** (*the obscenity of racial hatred*) atrocity, wickedness, evil, offence.

obscure *adj* **1** (*obscure writers*) unknown, inconspicuous, insignificant, undistinguished,

inglorious, unheard-of, little-known, unsung, nameless, minor, humble. OPPOSITE: famous. **2** (*written in obscure legal language*) unclear, indistinct, vague, indefinite, uncertain, doubtful, abstruse, arcane, recondite, hidden, concealed, cryptic, enigmatic, mysterious, impenetrable, unfathomable, incomprehensible, intricate, involved. OPPOSITE: clear. **3** (*an obscure form looming in the shadow*) faint, dim, hazy, vague, indistinct, blurred, dark, gloomy, murky, cloudy, shadowy. OPPOSITE: bright.
▶ *verb* **1** (*clouds obscuring the sun*) hide, conceal, cover, mask, screen, veil, shroud, eclipse, cloak, cloud, fog, befog, darken, dim, bedim, shade, shadow. **2** (*the discussion obscured the basic facts*) blur, confuse, muddle, hide, conceal, veil, cloak, mask, complicate, jumble, scramble, garble, obfuscate.

obscurity *noun* **1** (*the new president rose from relative obscurity*) insignificance, unimportance, inconspicuousness, humility, lowliness. OPPOSITE: fame. **2** (*the obscurity of technical terminology*) incomprehensibility, vagueness, abstruseness, impenetrability. OPPOSITE: clarity.

obsequies *pl noun* funeral ceremony, funeral service, funeral rites, funeral, burial rites.

obsequious *adj* servile, flattering, fawning, sycophantic, ingratiating, grovelling, unctuous, toadying, cringing, slavish, subservient, submissive, smarmy (*inf*), bootlicking (*inf*), arse-licking (*sl*).

observable *adj* noticeable, discernible, perceptible, visible, detectable, recognizable, perceivable, apparent, clear, plain, evident, obvious.

observance *noun* **1** (*observance of the rules*) keeping, obedience, honouring, adherence, compliance, discharge, fulfilment, performance, execution, attention, heed, regard, respect. OPPOSITE: disregard. **2** (*ceremonial observances*) rite, ritual, ceremony, ceremonial, service, celebration, custom, practice, convention, fashion, form, usage, tradition.

observant *adj* **1** (*being observant, he noticed she had been crying*) attentive, sharp, sharp-eyed, eagle-eyed, alert, vigilant, watchful, heedful, mindful, aware, perceptive, on the ball (*inf*). OPPOSITE: unobservant. **2** (*an observant Jew*) dutiful, orthodox, practising, committed, obedient, responsible.

observation *noun* **1** (*a detailed observation of plant life*) notice, attention, watch, examination, scrutiny, inspection, surveillance, study, monitoring, review, consideration, cognition. OPPOSITE: inattention. **2** (*wry observations about their behaviour*) comment, remark, statement, finding, discovery, pronouncement, utterance, declaration, note, annotation, reflection, thought, opinion, information, data.

observe *verb* **1** (*observe the suspect's movements*) watch, study, monitor, keep under surveillance, keep under scrutiny, review, check, contemplate, regard, look at, view, espy, witness, see, perceive, notice, note, catch sight, of, descry, discern, detect, discover, mark. OPPOSITE: miss. **2** ('*He looks worried about something,' she observed*) remark, comment, say, utter, state, declare, announce, mention, reflect. **3** (*observe a law*) keep, honour, heed, mind, follow, abide by, comply with, adhere to, conform to, fulfil, perform, discharge,

execute, respect, celebrate, mark, commemorate.
OPPOSITE: ignore.

observer *noun* watcher, viewer, spectator, onlooker,
looker-on, eyewitness, witness, bystander, reporter,
sightseer, beholder.

obsess *verb* preoccupy, dominate, rule, control,
consume, monopolize, possess, grip, prey on, torment,
hound, bedevil, plague, haunt.

obsession *noun* preoccupation, fixation, idée fixe,
passion, enthusiasm, mania, compulsion, fetish,
complex, phobia, thing (*inf*), hang-up (*inf*).

obsessive *adj* compulsive, excessive, gripping,
uncontrollable, overwhelming, tormenting, besetting.

obsolete *adj* discontinued, disused, outmoded,
outworn, antiquated, dated, passé, old-fashioned,
extinct, archaic, old, ancient, superannuated, old-hat
(*inf*), out of the ark (*inf*), past its sell-by date (*inf*).
OPPOSITE: modern.

obstacle *noun* barrier, bar, hurdle, obstruction,
barricade, block, impediment, hindrance, check, stop,
curb, snag, catch, difficulty, hitch, stumbling block, fly
in the ointment (*inf*), spanner in the works (*inf*).
OPPOSITE: advantage.

obstinate *adj* stubborn, mulish, pigheaded,
opinionated, headstrong, wilful, self-willed, dogged,
persistent, firm, adamant, unmanageable, immovable,
unshakeable, obdurate, inflexible, unyielding,
unbending, contrary, perverse, refractory, recalcitrant,
contumacious. OPPOSITE: amenable.

obstreperous *adj* boisterous, rowdy, uproarious,
clamorous, noisy, loud, rough, riotous, unruly,
disorderly, wild, undisciplined, tumultuous, turbulent,
uncontrolled, uncontrollable, unmanageable, out of
hand, bolshie (*inf*), stroppy (*inf*). OPPOSITE: quiet.

obstruct *verb* block, clog, choke, cut off, bar, barricade,
hinder, impede, hamper, prevent, stop, halt, limit,
restrict, arrest, check, curb, retard, inhibit, prohibit,
balk, frustrate, thwart, interrupt, interfere. OPPOSITE:
assist.

obstruction *noun* blockage, obstacle, barricade,
blockade, barrier, bar, hurdle, drawback, hindrance,
impediment, block, stop, check, snag, difficulty,
stumbling block. OPPOSITE: clearance.

obstructive *adj* unhelpful, awkward, uncooperative,
difficult, restrictive, delaying, interrupting, hindering.
OPPOSITE: helpful.

obtain *verb* **1** (*obtain planning permission*) get, acquire,
procure, come by, get hold of, take possession of, secure,
gain, win, earn, attain, achieve. OPPOSITE: lose. **2** (*this
situation no longer obtains*) prevail, exist, stand, rule, hold
sway, be in force, be the case, be effective.

obtainable *adj* available, attainable, achievable, at
hand, ready, on tap (*inf*).

obtrude *verb* push, thrust, impose, intrude, interfere.
OPPOSITE: withdraw.

obtrusive *adj* **1** (*satellite dishes thought to be obtrusive*)
conspicuous, obvious, noticeable, unmistakable, bold,
blatant, flagrant, prominent, protruding, protuberant.
OPPOSITE: unobtrusive. **2** (*his obtrusive manner*) intrusive,

interfering, officious, importunate, forward, prying,
meddling, nosy (*inf*), pushy (*inf*). OPPOSITE: retiring.

obtuse *adj* slow, slow-witted, dull, stupid, thick, dense,
unintelligent, dim (*inf*), dim-witted (*inf*), dumb (*inf*),
dopey (*inf*), stolid, insensitive, thick-skinned. OPPOSITE:
sharp.

obviate *verb* preclude, forestall, avert, prevent, counter,
get rid of, do away with. OPPOSITE: necessitate.

obvious *adj* evident, manifest, patent, clear, clear-cut,
plain, distinct, apparent, visible, discernible, noticeable,
perceptible, palpable, overt, unconcealed, conspicuous,
prominent, pronounced, unmistakable, staring one in
the face, right under one's nose, as plain as a pikestaff.
OPPOSITE: hidden.

obviously *adv* clearly, plainly, noticeably,
conspicuously, distinctly, unmistakably, evidently,
undoubtedly, of course.

occasion *noun* **1** (*they had met on an earlier occasion*)
time, occurrence, incident, instance, affair, event,
situation. **2** (*an engagement is a special occasion*) function,
affair, party, celebration, do (*inf*), get-together (*inf*).
3 (*an occasion for celebration*) opportunity, chance,
opening. **4** (*had occasion to doubt his story*) reason, cause,
motive, ground, grounds, call, excuse, justification.
➤ *verb* cause, bring about, prompt, elicit, provoke, lead
to, effect, give rise to, result in, generate, produce, create,
originate. OPPOSITE: prevent.

occasional *adj* intermittent, sporadic, irregular,
infrequent, rare, casual, periodic, incidental. OPPOSITE:
constant.

occasionally *adv* sometimes, periodically, at times,
intermittently, irregularly, rarely, seldom, now and
again, now and then, every so often, once in a while, off
and on, on and off, from time to time. OPPOSITE: often.

occult *adj* mystical, supernatural, magical, magic,
abstruse, arcane, esoteric, recondite, mysterious,
obscure, hidden, concealed, secret.
➤ *noun* magic, black magic, sorcery, witchcraft,
wizardry, devil worship, mysticism, supernatural,
supernaturalism.

occupancy *noun* occupation, tenure, tenancy,
possession, holding, residence.

occupant *noun* holder, owner, occupier, tenant,
leaseholder, resident, inhabitant, householder, dweller,
inmate, incumbent.

occupation *noun* **1** (*fill in one's occupation on the
application form*) job, profession, work, employment,
craft, trade, business, line of business, métier, vocation,
calling, career, activity, pursuit. **2** (*continued occupation of
the residence*) occupancy, tenure, tenancy, possession,
holding, residence. OPPOSITE: eviction. **3** (*occupation by a
foreign army*) conquest, defeat, seizure, invasion, control,
possession, capture, takeover, rule, subjection,
subjugation.

occupational *adj* professional, employment,
vocational, work, career, business.

occupy *verb* **1** (*occupied the flat upstairs*) inhabit, live in,
dwell in, reside in, own, possess. OPPOSITE: vacate.
2 (*computers occupy all his spare time*) fill, take up, use, use
up, utilize. **3** (*occupy a foreign country*) conquer, defeat,

seize, capture, invade, control, take over. **4** (*the children keep me occupied all day*) absorb, engross, preoccupy, engage, employ, busy, tie up, monopolize, entertain, amuse.

occur *verb* **1** (*the accident occurred in thick fog*) happen, take place, come about, chance, come to pass, turn up, befall, betide, transpire, supervene. **2** (*the disease occurs only in South America*) arise, result, appear, materialize, be present, exist.
occur to come to, strike, hit, dawn on, suggest itself to, come to mind.

occurrence *noun* **1** (*such expensive weddings are a rare occurrence*) happening, event, incident, circumstance, episode, occasion, instance, affair, proceeding. **2** (*the occurrence of cholera*) incidence, existence, appearance, manifestation, presence, materialization.

ocean *noun* sea, main, deep, briny (*inf*).

odd *adj* **1** (*he's an odd chap*) unusual, uncommon, strange, peculiar, funny, curious, queer, eccentric, unconventional, outlandish, idiosyncratic, weird, bizarre, singular, rare, remarkable, extraordinary, unique. OPPOSITE: ordinary. **2** (*do the odd bit of work*) occasional, incidental, casual, random, irregular, temporary, various, varied, sundry, diverse. OPPOSITE: regular. **3** (*odd socks*) unmatched, single, sole, solitary, lone, spare, surplus, leftover, uneven.
odd one out exception, nonconformist, odd man out, odd woman out, freak (*inf*), oddball (*inf*), fish out of water (*inf*), square peg in a round hole (*inf*).

oddity *noun* **1** (*the oddity of his manner*) peculiarity, strangeness, abnormality, uncommonness, rarity, idiosyncrasy. **2** (*he's a bit of an oddity*) curiosity, crank, eccentric, misfit, character (*inf*), freak (*inf*), fish out of water (*inf*).

oddment *noun* bit, piece, scrap, fragment, remnant, end, offcut, leftover.

odds *pl noun* **1** (*odds of one in a million*) probability, likelihood, chances. **2** (*the odds are in my favour*) advantage, lead, edge, superiority. **3** (*overcome enormous odds to win*) difference, disparity, inequality, dissimilarity, distinction.
at odds disagreeing, in disagreement, conflicting, in conflict, at loggerheads.
odds and ends bits and pieces, bits, pieces, scraps, fragments, leftovers, cuttings, offcuts, snippets, rubbish, odds and sods (*inf*).

odious *adj* obnoxious, objectionable, offensive, repugnant, repulsive, disgusting, abhorrent, revolting, disagreeable, contemptible, detestable, loathsome, abominable, execrable, hateful, horrid, nasty, unpleasant, vile. OPPOSITE: pleasant.

odium *noun* dislike, disfavour, hate, hatred, antipathy, loathing, detestation, abhorrence, repugnance, censure, shame, dishonour, obloquy, opprobrium. OPPOSITE: liking.

odour *noun* **1** (*the pleasant odour of roses*) smell, scent, aroma, fragrance, perfume, stench, redolence, stink, pong (*inf*), niff (*inf*), whiff (*inf*). **2** (*an odour of tolerance*) air, atmosphere, aura, spirit, quality, emanation, flavour.

odyssey *noun* journey, voyage, adventure, wandering, travels, pilgrimage, trek, peregrination.

off *adj* **1** (*the milk is off*) bad, rotten, sour, turned, mouldy, rancid, decomposed, high. **2** (*today's game is off*) cancelled, postponed, called off, shelved (*inf*). OPPOSITE: on. **3** (*why don't you take tomorrow off?*) absent, away, unavailable.
➤ *adv* **1** (*a long way off*) away, out, at a distance, apart, aside. **2** (*feel off today*) unwell, ill, sick, out of sorts, under the weather (*inf*).

off and on occasionally, sometimes, periodically, at times, intermittently, irregularly, rarely, seldom, now and again, now and then, every so often, once in a while, from time to time.

offbeat *adj* unconventional, unorthodox, unusual, untraditional, abnormal, weird, freakish, bizarre, wacky (*inf*), way-out (*inf*), off the wall (*inf*). OPPOSITE: orthodox.

off-colour *adj* **1** (*feel a bit off-colour today*) unwell, seedy, out of sorts, poorly, ill, below par, under the weather (*inf*), sick, queasy, nauseous. **2** (*an off-colour story*) risqué, indecent, dirty, rude, improper, vulgar, obscene, coarse, bawdy, blue, raunchy (*inf*), smutty (*inf*).

offence *noun* **1** (*commit a criminal offence*) violation, infringement, crime, breach of the law, misdemeanour, wrong, wrongdoing, fault, sin, trespass, transgression, misdeed, lapse, peccadillo. **2** (*an offence against the public*) affront, insult, snub, slight, injury, hurt, injustice, outrage, indignity. **3** (*his rudeness caused them great offence*) indignation, displeasure, annoyance, anger, resentment, umbrage, pique, huff. **4** (*a weapon of offence*) attack, assault, aggression, charge, invasion, offensive. OPPOSITE: defence.
take offence be offended, be upset, be hurt, resent, be angry, be indignant, be put out, feel resentment, take umbrage, take exception, be miffed (*inf*).

offend *verb* **1** (*I didn't mean to offend you*) upset, insult, hurt, wound, injure, wrong, affront, snub, slight, humiliate, outrage, displease, annoy, vex, irritate, anger, disgruntle, miff (*inf*), needle (*inf*), rile (*inf*), put someone's back up (*inf*), put someone's nose out of joint (*inf*), rub someone up the wrong way (*inf*). OPPOSITE: please. **2** (*offend the eye*) disgust, repel, revolt, sicken, nauseate, be disagreeable to, cause offence to. **3** (*criminals sometimes offend again*) break the law, do wrong, sin, transgress, trespass, err, go astray.

offender *noun* culprit, criminal, lawbreaker, miscreant, malefactor, wrongdoer, sinner, transgressor.

offensive *adj* **1** (*found his comments most offensive*) insulting, abusive, rude, disrespectful, insolent, impertinent, irritating, annoying, hurtful, wounding, affronting. OPPOSITE: kind. **2** (*the offensive smell of rotting food*) unpleasant, disagreeable, nasty, obnoxious, objectionable, repugnant, disgusting, revolting, vile, odious, loathsome, detestable, abominable, execrable. OPPOSITE: pleasant. **3** (*take up an offensive position*) aggressive, attacking, invading, assaulting, belligerent, warlike, on the warpath (*inf*). OPPOSITE: defensive.
➤ *noun* attack, assault, aggression, onset, drive, onslaught, invasion, incursion. OPPOSITE: defence.
go on the offensive attack, strike the first blow, make the first move, take strong action, take decisive action.

offer *verb* **1** (*offered her the job*) present, hold out, tender,

give, extend. OPPOSITE: withdraw. **2** (*offer a suggestion*) propose, make, give, suggest, put forward, submit, advance, bid, present, tender, proffer. **3** (*offered an excellent service*) provide, give, supply, present, afford, furnish. **4** (*offer oneself to help*) volunteer, make oneself available, come forward, be ready, be willing, show willing (*inf*). **5** (*offer goods for sale*) present, tender, put forward, provide. **6** (*offered them £100*) bid, tender, put in a bid of. **7** (*if the opportunity offers itself*) present, show, make known, happen, occur, appear. **8** (*offer a sacrifice*) make, give, offer up, present, consecrate. **9** (*offers excellent views of the harbour*) afford, provide, give, impart, yield, supply, furnish.
≫ *noun* **1** (*put in an offer for the house*) bid, tender, proposal, proposition, submission. **2** (*a shop's special offers*) reduction, discount, low price, cheapening. **3** (*an offer to help*) suggestion, proposal, proposition, advance, approach, overture.

offering *noun* **1** (*collect the offering in church*) present, gift, donation, contribution. **2** (*an offering on the altar*) sacrifice, oblation.

offhand *adv* impromptu, extempore, ad lib, off the cuff (*inf*), off the top of one's head (*inf*).
≫ *adj* casual, informal, unceremonious, abrupt, curt, brusque, rude, discourteous, cavalier, careless, nonchalant, cursory, perfunctory.

office *noun* **1** (*the manager's office*) room, place of business, firm, company, workplace, base, study, bureau. **2** (*the office of chairman*) post, position, situation, appointment, commission, role, capacity. **3** (*hold office in a government*) function, duty, responsibility, trust, charge, work, employment, service, place, station.

officer *noun* official, officeholder, office bearer, functionary, administrator, bureaucrat, executive, deputy, envoy, agent, representative.

offices *pl noun* support, help, aid, assistance, favour, backing, auspices, patronage, aegis, mediation, word, recommendation, referral.

official *adj* **1** (*an official statement*) authoritative, authorized, legitimate, approved, accredited, validated, endorsed, sanctioned, licensed, proper, authentic, bona fide. OPPOSITE: unofficial. **2** (*official activities*) formal, ceremonial, ritual, solemn. OPPOSITE: private.
≫ *noun* officer, officeholder, office bearer, functionary, administrator, bureaucrat, executive, deputy, agent, envoy, representative.

officiate *verb* preside, chair, conduct, run, direct, manage, oversee, supervise, take charge, be responsible.

officious *adj* obtrusive, importunate, interfering, meddlesome, intrusive, bustling, forward, pushy (*inf*), overzealous.

offing *noun* **in the offing** imminent, impending, forthcoming, coming, upcoming, approaching, just around the corner (*inf*), at hand, on the cards (*inf*), near, close, menacing, threatening, gathering, looming, brewing, on the way, in the air. OPPOSITE: distant.

offload *verb* unload, unburden, discharge, get rid of, dump (*inf*), jettison, deposit.

off-putting *adj* disconcerting, discouraging, disheartening, unnerving, unsettling, disturbing, discomfiting.

offset *verb* counterbalance, balance, balance out, make up for, compensate for, cancel out, counteract, neutralize, countervail.

offshoot *noun* branch, outgrowth, development, outcome, consequence, derivative, by-product, spin-off, subsidiary.

offspring *noun* child, children, young, family, progeny, issue, descendant, descendants, successor, successors, seed, posterity. OPPOSITE: parent.

often *adv* frequently, repeatedly, generally, regularly, time after time, again and again, time and time again, time and again, many times, many a time, oft. OPPOSITE: occasionally.

ogle *verb* eye, eye up, make eyes at, leer, stare, give someone the come-on.

ogre *noun* **1** (*the ogre in a fairy tale*) giant, monster, brute, beast, fiend, demon, devil, bogeyman, bogey, troll. **2** (*his uncle is a real ogre*) monster, brute, beast, savage.

oil *noun* grease, lubricant, ointment, lotion, cream, balm, unguent.
≫ *verb* lubricate, grease, anoint.

oily *adj* **1** (*an oily substance*) greasy, fatty, buttery, oleaginous. **2** (*an oily smile*) smooth, smooth-talking, fulsome, suave, urbane, unctuous, glib, flattering, servile, obsequious.

ointment *noun* balm, salve, gel, lotion, liniment, embrocation, cream, unguent.

OK *adj* okay, satisfactory, acceptable, reasonable, adequate, passable, tolerable, fair, all right, so-so (*inf*), not bad (*inf*), good, fine, correct, approved, permitted. OPPOSITE: unacceptable.
≫ *interj* okay, all right, fine, yes, right, very good, very well, agreed.
≫ *noun* okay, approval, authorization, agreement, permission, endorsement, consent, green light (*inf*), thumbs-up (*inf*).
≫ *verb* okay, approve, authorize, agree to, sanction, endorse, consent to, pass, give the green light to (*inf*), give the thumbs-up to (*inf*).

old *adj* **1** (*an old man*) aged, elderly, mature, older, getting on, past one's prime, not getting any younger, grey, grey-haired, hoary, senile, past it (*inf*), decrepit, ancient, long in the tooth (*inf*). OPPOSITE: young. **2** (*old traditions*) ancient, antique, early, primitive, age-old, bygone, primeval, prehistoric, primordial. **3** (*an old coat*) worn, worn-out, shabby, decayed, torn, ragged, tattered, cast-off. OPPOSITE: new. **4** (*old buildings*) broken-down, dilapidated, run-down, ramshackle, disintegrating, crumbling, tumbledown. **5** (*old furniture*) outdated, antiquated, obsolete, unfashionable, behind the times, passé, antediluvian, on the way out (*inf*), old hat (*inf*), past if (*inf*), past its sell-by date (*inf*), out of the ark (*inf*). OPPOSITE: modern. **6** (*he's an old friend*) long-standing, lasting, enduring, time-honoured, traditional. **7** (*an old soldier*) experienced, mature, sensible, wise, knowledgeable, skilled. **8** (*his old students*) former, earlier, previous, sometime, one-time, erstwhile, quondam. OPPOSITE: current.

old-fashioned *adj* outmoded, outdated, out-of-date, dated, unfashionable, passé, obsolete, former, bygone, démodé, old-time, antiquated, obsolescent, antediluvian, superannuated, old hat (*inf*). OPPOSITE: modern.

omen *noun* portent, sign, indication, token, foretoken, warning, premonition, harbinger, foreshadowing, presage, augury, prediction, prognostic, forecast, writing on the wall (*inf*).

ominous *adj* threatening, menacing, sinister, unpromising, unfavourable, unlucky, portentous, foreboding, unpropitious, inauspicious, premonitory.

omission *noun* **1** (*the omission of this fact is misleading*) exclusion, exception, gap, elimination, deletion, erasure. OPPOSITE: inclusion. **2** (*sins of omission*) forgetfulness, oversight, neglect, negligence, disregard, default, failure. OPPOSITE: commission.

omit *verb* **1** (*omitted his name deliberately*) exclude, leave out, drop, miss, miss out, except, delete, cross out, eliminate, skip, pass over, overlook, ignore, disregard. OPPOSITE: include. **2** (*omitted to mention she was already married*) neglect, forget, fail, overlook.

omnipotent *adj* almighty, all-powerful, supreme, sovereign, absolute, unlimited. OPPOSITE: powerless.

omnipresent *adj* all-present, present everywhere, universal, pervasive, infinite, ubiquitous.

omniscient *adj* all-knowing, all-wise, all-seeing. OPPOSITE: ignorant.

on *adv* **on and off** occasionally, sometimes, periodically, at times, intermittently, irregularly, rarely, seldom, now and again, now and then, every so often, once in a while, from time to time.

once *adv* formerly, previously, at one time, once upon a time, in the old days, long ago. OPPOSITE: now.
➤ *conj* when, after, as soon as.
at once 1 (*I must go at once*) immediately, instantly, straightaway, right away, right now, directly, forthwith, now. OPPOSITE: later. **2** (*all the problems happened at once*) together, simultaneously, at the same time, at the same moment.
once in a while occasionally, on occasion, sometimes, now and then, at times, infrequently, intermittently.

oncoming *adj* approaching, coming, advancing, nearing, upcoming, imminent.

one *adj* **1** (*one thing*) a, single, individual, lone, sole, only, unique. OPPOSITE: many. **2** (*we are all one*) united, unified, bound, like-minded, married, wedded, entire, whole, complete.

onerous *adj* burdensome, oppressive, heavy, weighty, strenuous, laborious, arduous, difficult, hard, taxing, crushing, backbreaking, toilsome. OPPOSITE: light.

oneself *pronoun* **by oneself 1** (*like to be by oneself*) alone, on one's own, lonely, lonesome, unaccompanied, on one's tod (*inf*). **2** (*do it all by oneself*) without help, unaided, unassisted, without assistance, independently, single-handed.

one-sided *adj* **1** (*a one-sided relationship*) uneven, unbalanced, unequal, one-way. OPPOSITE: balanced.
2 (*the report is very one-sided*) unfair, unjust, inequitable, partial, partisan, biased, prejudiced. OPPOSITE: impartial.

one-time *adj* former, earlier, previous, sometime, erstwhile, quondam. OPPOSITE: current.

ongoing *adj* continuing, developing, progressing, in progress, growing, current.

onlooker *noun* bystander, observer, spectator, watcher, viewer, witness, eyewitness.

only *adj* sole, solitary, lone, single, individual, exclusive, unique, one and only.
➤ *adv* just, merely, simply, purely, scarcely, barely, at most, not more than, no more than, alone.

onset *noun* **1** (*the onset of winter*) beginning, start, inception, commencement, outbreak. OPPOSITE: end.
2 (*the onset of the troops*) onslaught, onrush, attack, assault, charge. OPPOSITE: retreat.

onslaught *noun* attack, assault, charge, onrush, storming, raid, push, drive, blitz, bombardment.

onus *noun* burden, load, weight, responsibility, liability, charge, duty, obligation, encumbrance, millstone round one's neck, albatross.

onward *adv* onwards, forward, forwards, ahead, on. OPPOSITE: backward.

ooze *verb* seep, exude, percolate, filter, leak, escape, drip, trickle, drop, secrete, discharge, flow, pour out, pour forth, emit.
➤ *noun* sludge, slime, silt, mud, muck, mire, deposit, sediment.

opacity *noun* **1** (*degrees of opacity in paint*) cloudiness, haziness, murkiness, dirtiness, muddiness, filminess. OPPOSITE: transparency. **2** (*the opacity of his remarks*) obscurity, unintelligibility, incomprehensibility. OPPOSITE: clarity.

opalescent *adj* opaline, iridescent, pearly, nacreous, prismatic, multicoloured, kaleidoscopic.

opaque *adj* **1** (*opaque plastic sheeting*) cloudy, hazy, murky, dirty, muddy, turbid, dull, lustreless. OPPOSITE: transparent. **2** (*opaque texts*) obscure, unclear, unfathomable, abstruse, incomprehensible, unintelligible. OPPOSITE: clear. **3** (*an opaque person*) thick, dense, unintelligent, stupid, obtuse, dull. OPPOSITE: clever.

open *adj* **1** (*an open window*) unclosed, gaping, ajar, unlocked, unfastened, unsealed, unbolted, uncovered. OPPOSITE: closed. **2** (*open fields*) unenclosed, unsheltered, unfenced, extensive, sweeping, wide, broad. OPPOSITE: enclosed. **3** (*all roads are now open again*) unblocked, clear, unobstructed, free, unrestricted. OPPOSITE: blocked. **4** (*an open book*) unfolded, spread out, stretched out, unfurled. OPPOSITE: closed. **5** (*the competition is open to everyone*) public, accessible, general, available. **6** (*open admiration*) overt, plain, obvious, clear, noticeable, unhidden, evident, manifest, undisguised, unconcealed, apparent, visible. OPPOSITE: hidden. **7** (*the matter remains open*) undecided, unsettled, unresolved, arguable, debatable, moot. OPPOSITE: settled. **8** (*be open with each other*) frank, candid, unreserved, honest, direct, forthright, sincere, artless, ingenuous, natural. OPPOSITE: secretive. **9** (*be open to criticism*) liable, prone, susceptible, vulnerable, exposed, unprotected, undefended. OPPOSITE: safe. **10** (*open to fresh ideas*) receptive, open-minded, sensitive, responsive, willing, flexible, accommodating, alert, tolerant, catholic, broad-minded, liberal, unbiased, unprejudiced. **11** (*is the vacancy still open?*) vacant, free, available, unfilled, unoccupied. OPPOSITE: filled. **12** (*an open texture*) airy, holey, porous, openwork, cellular, honeycombed. OPPOSITE: close.

➤ *verb* **1** (*open a box*) unfasten, unlock, undo, unwrap, unbolt, unlatch, uncover, expose, unblock, clear. OPPOSITE: close. **2** (*the parachute failed to open*) spread, spread out, expand, extend, unfold, unfurl, split, part, separate. **3** (*the gap opened up*) split, break, separate, rupture. **4** (*the new business opens on Monday*) begin, start, launch, inaugurate, commence, kick off (*inf*), set the ball rolling (*inf*). OPPOSITE: end. **5** (*opened his heart to her*) disclose, reveal, show, lay bare, exhibit. OPPOSITE: hide.

open-air *adj* outdoor, outside, alfresco.

opening *noun* **1** (*an opening in the rocks*) gap, breach, aperture, orifice, hole, space, break, rupture, slot, vent, rent, cleft, split, rift, crack, fissure, crevice, chasm. **2** (*the opening of the cinema complex*) beginning, start, launch, inauguration, initiation, commencement, inception, birth, outset, onset, dawn. OPPOSITE: close. **3** (*an opening for me to express my opinion*) opportunity, chance, occasion, break (*inf*), lucky break (*inf*). **4** (*are there any openings for teachers?*) vacancy, place, job, position, opportunity.

➤ *adj* beginning, starting, commencing, first, initial, introductory, inaugural. OPPOSITE: closing.

openly *adv* **1** (*talked openly about her feelings*) frankly, candidly, honestly, sincerely, directly, forthrightly, naturally, unreservedly, with no holds barred (*inf*). OPPOSITE: secretively. **2** (*openly acknowledged his sexual orientation*) publicly, visibly, accessibly, overtly, unashamedly. OPPOSITE: secretly.

open-minded *adj* receptive, tolerant, catholic, broad-minded, liberal, fair, just, reasonable, unbiased, unprejudiced, impartial, dispassionate. OPPOSITE: bigoted.

operate *verb* **1** (*operate a business*) run, manage, make go, handle, be in charge of, employ, manipulate, manoeuvre. **2** (*the machine operates on solar energy*) run, function, work, act, perform, go.

operation *noun* **1** (*the operation of the machine*) running, using, performance, working, action, motion, handling, manipulation. **2** (*a rescue operation*) procedure, process, exercise, manoeuvre, task, job, affair, business, undertaking, enterprise, venture.

in operation in force, in action, operative, effective, running, working, functioning.

operational *adj* functioning, functional, in operation, going, running, working, active, in use. OPPOSITE: out of use.

operative *adj* **1** (*the processes that were operative then*) operational, in operation, functioning, working, active, in force, effective. OPPOSITE: inoperative. **2** (*'normally' is the operative word*) important, significant, key, crucial, relevant.

➤ *noun* **1** (*a cleaning operative*) worker, hand, employee, labourer, workman, artisan, mechanic, machinist, operator. **2** (*operative working in the intelligence service*) agent, secret agent, spy, double agent, mole (*inf*).

operator *noun* **1** (*a camera operator*) worker, employee, operative, machinist, technician. **2** (*a TV and cable operator*) contractor, trader, handler, manager. **3** (*he's a smooth operator*) manipulator, manoeuvrer, machinator, wheeler-dealer (*inf*).

opiate *noun* narcotic, drug, sedative, tranquillizer, soporific, anodyne. OPPOSITE: stimulant.

opine *verb* believe, think, feel, consider, reckon, judge, deem, suppose, conclude, say, declare.

opinion *noun* belief, judgment, view, point of view, viewpoint, standpoint, idea, notion, fancy, thought, impression, feeling, sentiment, theory, conjecture, estimation, assessment.

opinionated *adj* dogmatic, dictatorial, doctrinaire, overconfident, cocksure, arrogant, pompous, self-important, overbearing, pig-headed, stubborn, inflexible, obdurate, prejudiced, biased, bigoted. OPPOSITE: meek.

opponent *noun* adversary, antagonist, foe, enemy, rival, competitor, contestant, the opposition, dissenter, disputant, opposer. OPPOSITE: ally.

opportune *adj* timely, seasonable, convenient, advantageous, fortunate, appropriate, apt, suitable, fitting, fit, favourable, auspicious, propitious, happy, good, lucky, felicitous. OPPOSITE: inopportune.

opportunism *noun* exploitation, expediency, realism, pragmatism, unscrupulousness, making hay while the sun shines.

opportunity *noun* chance, occasion, time, moment, opening, break (*inf*), lucky break (*inf*).

oppose *verb* **1** (*oppose the plans to close the school*) resist, withstand, counter, fight, contest, disapprove of, dislike, stand against, stand up to, take issue with, combat, attack, face, confront, defy, hinder, obstruct, block, bar, check, prevent, thwart. OPPOSITE: aid. **2** (*oppose the present and the future*) contrast, compare, match, counterbalance, offset.

opposing *adj* contrary, different, contrasting, reverse, conflicting, contradictory, incompatible, irreconcilable, poles apart, clashing, antithetical, antagonistic, hostile.

opposite *adj* **1** (*on opposite sides of the street*) facing, corresponding, far. **2** (*hold the opposite view*) opposed, opposing, conflicting, antagonistic, hostile, inimical, contrary, reverse, contrasting, different, differing, antithetical, contradictory, incompatible, irreconcilable, poles apart. OPPOSITE: same.

➤ *noun* converse, inverse, reverse, contrary, contradiction, antithesis.

opposition *noun* **1** (*opposition to the policy*) antagonism, hostility, defiance, attack, resistance, counteraction, obstruction, hindrance, prevention, disapproval, dislike, conflict, competition, confrontation. OPPOSITE: agreement. **2** (*passed the ball to the opposition*) opponent, adversary, rival, competitor, contestant, other side, enemy, foe, antagonist.

oppress *verb* **1** (*oppress the poor*) subjugate, subdue, crush, suppress, persecute, overwhelm, overpower, tyrannize, enslave, maltreat, walk all over (*inf*), treat like dirt (*inf*). OPPOSITE: free. **2** (*oppressed by guilt*) burden, encumber, trouble, afflict, torment, weigh down, crush, discourage, sadden, depress. OPPOSITE: relieve.

oppressed *adj* crushed, tyrannized, persecuted,

subjugated, enslaved, suppressed, maltreated, downtrodden.

oppression *noun* tyranny, despotism, subjection, persecution, cruelty, severity, harshness, abuse, maltreatment, brutality, injustice, suffering, misery, hardship. OPPOSITE: liberty.

oppressive *adj* **1** (*an oppressive regime*) tyrannical, despotic, overbearing, harsh, severe, cruel, repressive, pitiless, merciless, ruthless, draconian, unjust. OPPOSITE: mild. **2** (*an oppressive climate*) sultry, stuffy, stifling, close, muggy, airless, uncomfortable, torrid. **3** (*an oppressive situation*) burdensome, onerous, heavy, overwhelming, overpowering.

oppressor *noun* tyrant, despot, dictator, persecutor, bully, torturer, tormentor, hard taskmaster, slave driver.

opprobrious *adj* **1** (*opprobrious language*) scornful, contemptuous, reproachful, derogatory, defamatory, vituperative, slanderous, calumniatory, unfavourable, offensive, insulting. OPPOSITE: laudatory. **2** (*opprobrious deeds*) shameful, disgraceful, dishonourable, infamous, ignominious, reprehensible, despicable, contemptible, odious, disreputable. OPPOSITE: honourable.

oppugn *verb* dispute, contest, question, call in question, oppose, resist, attack, assail.

opt *verb* **opt for** choose, select, decide on, elect, prefer, settle for, go for (*inf*).

optimism *noun* hopefulness, confidence, cheerfulness, idealism, expectancy. OPPOSITE: pessimism.

optimistic *adj* hopeful, confident, assured, sanguine, cheerful, positive, idealistic, bullish, buoyant, Panglossian, utopian. OPPOSITE: pessimistic.

optimum *adj* ideal, perfect, best, top, peak, exemplary, superlative, flawless, consummate.

option *noun* choice, alternative, selection, election, preference, wish, will, discretion.

optional *adj* voluntary, unforced, discretionary, elective. OPPOSITE: compulsory.

opulent *adj* **1** (*opulent people*) rich, wealthy, affluent, moneyed, prosperous, well-off, loaded (*sl*), rolling in it (*inf*). OPPOSITE: poor. **2** (*opulent hotels*) sumptuous, luxurious, lavish, plush (*inf*), ritzy (*inf*), exuberant, luxuriant, abundant, profuse, copious, plentiful. OPPOSITE: poor.

opus *noun* work, production, piece, creation, oeuvre.

oracle *noun* seer, prophet, soothsayer, sage, sibyl, augur.

oracular *adj* **1** (*an oracular statement*) prophetic, sibylline, vatic, fatidic, mantic, augural, divinatory, prognostic, predictive, wise, sage, venerable, grave, authoritative, positive, dogmatic, portentous, ominous, foreboding. **2** (*the remark's oracular terseness*) obscure, arcane, mysterious, cryptic, ambiguous.

oral *adj* verbal, spoken, vocal, unwritten, uttered. OPPOSITE: written.

oration *noun* speech, address, lecture, sermon, homily, spiel (*inf*), discourse, declamation, harangue.

orator *noun* speaker, lecturer, public speaker, demagogue, declaimer, rhetorician, rhetor, Cicero.

oratorical *adj* rhetorical, sonorous, high-flown, high-sounding, grandiose, grandiloquent, magniloquent, Ciceronian.

oratory *noun* rhetoric, eloquence, delivery, speech-making, declamation, grandiloquence, magniloquence.

orb *noun* ball, sphere, globe, circle, round.

orbit *noun* **1** (*the orbit of the Earth*) revolution, rotation, cycle, circle, circuit, track, path, course, trajectory. **2** (*not within the orbit of my authority*) range, scope, field, compass, sphere, domain.
➤ *verb* circle, encircle, revolve around, go round, move round.

orchestrate *verb* **1** (*orchestrate a complex plan*) arrange, organize, coordinate, manage, stage-manage, integrate, mastermind. **2** (*orchestrate a piece of music*) arrange, score.

ordain *verb* **1** (*ordain women as priests*) consecrate, anoint, frock, induct, invest, call, appoint. OPPOSITE: unfrock. **2** (*be ordained to fail*) destine, predestine, fate, doom, foreordain. **3** (*ordained by law*) order, command, decree, rule, enact, lay down, establish, bid, enjoin, prescribe.

ordeal *noun* trial, test, tribulation, trouble, affliction, suffering, hardship, anguish, torture, torment, nightmare.

order *noun* **1** (*in order of priority*) sequence, arrangement, disposition, progression, grouping, classification, structure, organization, system, layout. **2** (*put in an order for the food*) request, demand, commission, booking, application, reservation, requisition. **3** (*impose order on a state of confusion*) system, method, plan, organization, symmetry, neatness, tidiness, orderliness. OPPOSITE: chaos. **4** (*refuse to obey an order*) command, injunction, instruction, direction, decree, mandate, edict, ordinance, directive, dictate, stipulation, regulation, rule, law, precept. **5** (*the state of public order*) peace, quiet, calm, tranquillity, discipline, control, lawfulness, law and order. OPPOSITE: anarchy. **6** (*a religious order*) association, society, fraternity, brotherhood, sorority, sisterhood, community, fellowship, lodge, secret society, league, guild, sect, denomination. **7** (*botanical orders*) kind, sort, type, class, species, genus, family, rank, grade, level, degree.
➤ *verb* **1** (*he ordered them to leave immediately*) command, instruct, direct, bid, enjoin, decree, ordain, prescribe, demand, require. **2** (*order stationery*) request, book, reserve, apply for, send for, requisition. OPPOSITE: receive. **3** (*ordered according to size*) arrange, dispose, organize, systematize, catalogue, structure, marshal, classify, group, sort, sort out, neaten, tidy, tidy up. OPPOSITE: disarrange.

in order 1 (*kept his study in order*) tidy, neat, organized, trim, orderly, shipshape. **2** (*is it in order for me to reply?*) allowed, right, correct, acceptable, proper, suitable, OK (*inf*), done (*inf*).

out of order 1 (*the machine is out of order*) broken, inoperative, not working, kaput (*inf*), bust (*inf*), on the blink (*inf*). OPPOSITE: working. **2** (*such behaviour is out of order*) wrong, unseemly, indecorous, improper, not done.

orderly *adj* **1** (*an orderly arrangement of rules*) neat, tidy, shipshape, systematic, methodical, regular, well-organized. OPPOSITE: untidy. **2** (*walk in an orderly fashion*) well-behaved, disciplined, law-abiding, peaceable, quiet, restrained. OPPOSITE: disorderly.

ordinance *noun* **1** (*legal ordinances*) decree, edict, order, command, precept, rule, regulation, law, requisition, statute. **2** (*the ordinance of baptism*) ceremony, rite, ritual, sacrament, observance.

ordinarily *adv* usually, generally, in general, as a rule, normally, customarily, habitually, commonly.

ordinary *adj* common, commonplace, everyday, familiar, unexceptional, unremarkable, common or garden (*inf*), run-of-the-mill (*inf*), plain, simple, conventional, normal, standard, typical, usual, customary, habitual, wonted, accustomed, regular, routine, humdrum, average, medium, mediocre, indifferent. OPPOSITE: unusual.

out of the ordinary unusual, uncommon, exceptional, remarkable, outstanding, rare, surprising, striking, noteworthy, extraordinary, unique.

organ *noun* **1** (*internal organs of the body*) part, structure. **2** (*the organ of government*) mouthpiece, medium, voice, agency, forum.

organic *adj* **1** (*organic matter*) natural, biological, living, animate. OPPOSITE: inorganic. **2** (*has an organic simplicity*) basic, fundamental, structural, integral, constitutional, inherent, intrinsic. OPPOSITE: extraneous. **3** (*makes an organic unity*) systematic, methodical, organized, ordered, structured. OPPOSITE: unsystematic.

organism *noun* **1** (*living organisms in the soil*) creature, living thing, animal, plant, human. **2** (*a society is a complex organism*) system, organization, structure, unity, whole.

organization *noun* **1** (*a voluntary organization*) association, institution, society, firm, corporation, concern, company, group, league, guild, consortium, confederation, union, syndicate. **2** (*the organization of the department*) management, establishment, assembly, coordination, arrangement, order, classification, system, structure, construction, method, plan, design, constitution, composition.

organize *verb* coordinate, marshal, order, systematize, arrange, manage, run, take care of, be in charge of, dispose, classify, sort, categorize, shape, form, structure, mould, constitute, establish, found, create, set up. OPPOSITE: disrupt.

orgy *noun* drunken party, wild party, debauch, revel, carousal, bacchanalia, overindulgence, spree, binge (*inf*), splurge (*inf*).

orientate *verb* orient, direct, position, align, slant, angle, adjust, adapt, familiarize, acclimatize, accommodate, get one's bearings. OPPOSITE: disorientate.

orientation *noun* **1** (*political orientation*) inclination, leaning, tendency, views, beliefs, preferences. **2** (*the orientation of new recruits*) induction, introduction, initiation, adjustment, adaptation, familiarization, accommodation, acclimatization. **3** (*the orientation of the building*) location, position, direction, arrangement, alignment, bearings.

orifice *noun* opening, aperture, break, breach, hole, mouth, vent, rift, crevice, fissure.

origin *noun* **1** (*the origin of surnames*) source, root, fount, spring, cause, derivation, provenance, base, foundation. **2** (*the origins of the solar system*) beginning, start, commencement, birth, genesis, creation, dawn, foundation, inception, outset. OPPOSITE: end. **3** (*her country of origin*) ancestry, extraction, lineage, heritage, family, stock, pedigree, birth, descent.

original *adj* **1** (*back to its original shape*) first, initial, primary, earliest, early, primordial, primeval, primal, primitive, aboriginal, autochthonous. OPPOSITE: latest. **2** (*original designs*) fresh, new, novel, innovative, creative, inventive, different, imaginative, individual, unorthodox, unconventional. OPPOSITE: hackneyed. **3** (*in the original text*) real, genuine, authentic, master, prototypical, archetypal. OPPOSITE: copied.

≫ *noun* master, prototype, archetype, model, pattern, standard. OPPOSITE: copy.

originality *noun* freshness, novelty, innovativeness, creativity, inventiveness, imaginativeness, resourcefulness, individuality.

originally *adv* initially, to begin with, first, at first, at the start, at the outset.

originate *verb* **1** (*this style originated in the USA*) rise, spring, issue, proceed, result, arise, flow, emanate, come, derive, stem. OPPOSITE: end. **2** (*originate a procedure*) begin, start, initiate, inaugurate, commence, create, invent, set in motion, set up, formulate, conceive, discover, pioneer, launch, introduce, found, institute. OPPOSITE: abolish.

originator *noun* creator, founder, inventor, discoverer, author, initiator, architect, pioneer.

ornament *noun* **1** (*china ornaments*) adornment, decoration, embellishment, garnish, trimming, frill, accessory, bauble, trinket, knick-knack, gewgaw. **2** (*architecture rich in ornament*) decoration, embellishment, adornment.

≫ *verb* adorn, decorate, embellish, garnish, trim, deck, festoon, beautify, prettify. OPPOSITE: strip.

ornamental *adj* decorative, adorning, embellishing, ornate, attractive, showy, flowery. OPPOSITE: functional.

ornate *adj* elaborate, fancy, ostentatious, showy, baroque, rococo, florid, flowery, ornamented, beautiful, elegant, adorned, decorated, embellished. OPPOSITE: plain.

orotund *adj* **1** (*an orotund sound*) resonant, sonorous, rich, full, strong, clear, ringing, booming. OPPOSITE: soft. **2** (*orotund writing*) pompous, bombastic, grandiloquent, magniloquent, turgid, inflated. OPPOSITE: simple.

orthodox *adj* **1** (*orthodox methods*) conventional, conformist, accepted, approved, official, usual, proper, standard, regular, established, customary, traditional, sound, correct, true. OPPOSITE: unorthodox. **2** (*an orthodox person*) faithful, strict, true, devoted, devout, sound, traditional, conformist.

orthodoxy *noun* conformism, conventionality, traditionalism, soundness, correctness, properness.

oscillate *verb* swing, sway, vibrate, vacillate, move backwards and forwards, fluctuate, vary, waver, hesitate, falter.

ossify *verb* fossilize, petrify, solidify, harden, become hard, become rigid, become inflexible.

ostensible *adj* outward, superficial, pretended, alleged, supposed, professed, claimed, avowed, apparent, seeming, specious. OPPOSITE: real.

ostentation *noun* display, show, showiness, showing-off (*inf*), parade, pageantry, pomp, flourish, obtrusiveness, loudness, flamboyance, affectation, pretentiousness, window dressing, flashiness (*inf*), tinsel (*inf*). OPPOSITE: unpretentiousness.

ostentatious *adj* showy, flashy, flash (*inf*), flamboyant, obtrusive, loud, vulgar, affected, mannered, pretentious, pompous, vain, boastful, glitzy (*inf*), over the top (*inf*). OPPOSITE: subdued.

ostracize *verb* exclude, banish, exile, bar, expel, excommunicate, blacklist, blackball, reject, shun, cold-shoulder (*inf*), give someone the cold shoulder (*inf*), ignore, send to Coventry. OPPOSITE: accept.

other *adj* **1** (*using other words*) different, unlike, dissimilar, separate, distinct, variant, diverse. OPPOSITE: same. **2** (*we have other sizes in stock*) further, more, extra, additional, supplementary, spare, alternative.

otherwise *adv* **1** (*go now, otherwise you'll miss the train*) or, or else, if not. **2** (*dirty and depressed but otherwise none the worse*) apart from that, except for that, in other respects, in other ways. **3** (*think otherwise*) differently, in a different way.

ounce *noun* bit, piece, particle, iota, atom, trace, shred, speck.

oust *verb* eject, expel, throw out, evict, dispossess, dislodge, depose, unseat. OPPOSITE: install.

out *adv* **1** (*the headteacher is out at the moment*) away, absent, abroad, elsewhere, outside. OPPOSITE: in. **2** (*he was hit so hard he is now out cold*) unconscious, knocked out, KO. OPPOSITE: conscious. **3** (*the news is out*) exposed, revealed, disclosed, published, known, broadcast. **4** (*the flowers are out*) blooming, in bloom, in full bloom, blossoming, in flower. **5** (*long skirts are out*) unfashionable, passé, antiquated, dated, behind the times, old-fashioned. OPPOSITE: up to date. **6** (*the flames are out*) extinguished, dead, finished, exhausted, doused. **7** (*such behaviour is completely out*) forbidden, unacceptable, not allowed, excluded. OPPOSITE: allowed.

out-and-out *adj* absolute, thorough, complete, total, outright, utter, downright, arrant, unmitigated, unequivocal, unqualified, consummate, inveterate.

outbreak *noun* outburst, eruption, explosion, flare-up, start, burst, fit, rush, surge, rash, epidemic.

outburst *noun* outbreak, eruption, explosion, flare-up, tantrum, fit, spasm, attack, outpouring, burst.

outcast *noun* castaway, pariah, exile, expatriate, displaced person, refugee, wanderer, vagabond, leper.

outclass *verb* surpass, beat, defeat, top, excel, outdo, outrun, outdistance, outstrip, outrank, outrival, outshine, eclipse.

outcome *noun* consequence, result, issue, conclusion, upshot, sequel, aftereffect, aftermath. OPPOSITE: cause.

outcry *noun* protest, complaint, uproar, clamour, fuss, exclamation, shout, yell, hullabaloo, hue and cry, vociferation.

outdated *adj* old-fashioned, outmoded, out-of-date, dated, unfashionable, passé, obsolete, former, bygone, démodé, old-time, antiquated, obsolescent, superannuated, old hat (*inf*). OPPOSITE: modern.

outdistance *verb* surpass, outrun, outstrip, outpace, outrival, overtake, overhaul, leave behind, leave standing.

outdo *verb* surpass, exceed, beat, top, excel, get the better of, transcend, outshine, eclipse, outclass, outstrip, outdistance, outrun, outsmart, outwit.

outdoors *adv* outside, out, in the open air, alfresco.

outer *adj* **1** (*the outer covering*) external, exterior, outward, outside, outermost, peripheral, surface, superficial. OPPOSITE: inner. **2** (*in the outer suburbs*) remote, distant, outlying, perimeter, fringe.

outfit *noun* **1** (*wear a new outfit*) clothes, garb, ensemble, costume, dress, suit, getup (*inf*), rigout (*inf*), kit. **2** (*a tyre repair outfit*) set, gear, tools, apparatus, equipment, paraphernalia. **3** (*a small plant-hire outfit*) organization, group, team, company, firm, business.
➤ *verb* fit out, equip, supply, prepare, provide with, stock with, rig out, furnish.

outfitter *noun* tailor, costumier, costumer, dressmaker, clothier, haberdasher, modiste, couturier.

outflow *noun* discharge, rush, outrush, emergence, effluence, gush, spurt, issue, jet.

outgoing *adj* **1** (*the outgoing chairperson*) retiring, leaving, withdrawing, departing, past, last, ex-. OPPOSITE: incoming. **2** (*she has an outgoing personality*) extrovert, demonstrative, sociable, gregarious, affectionate, warm, friendly, approachable, cordial, affable, easy, easygoing, hail-fellow-well-met. OPPOSITE: reserved.

outgoings *pl noun* expenditure, outlay, expenses, costs, overheads, disbursement. OPPOSITE: income.

outing *noun* excursion, trip, tour, expedition, jaunt, airing.

outlandish *adj* unconventional, bizarre, curious, eccentric, weird, extraordinary, odd, peculiar, singular, strange, unknown, unfamiliar, unheard of, outré, exotic, foreign, alien, freakish, freaky (*inf*), wacky (*inf*), off the wall (*inf*), grotesque. OPPOSITE: conventional.

outlaw *noun* bandit, brigand, robber, villain, marauder, pirate, freebooter, fugitive, criminal, exile, outcast, pariah.
➤ *verb* ban, bar, exclude, prohibit, forbid, condemn, blacklist, embargo, excommunicate. OPPOSITE: allow.

outlay *noun* expenditure, costs, expense, spending, outgoings, disbursement. OPPOSITE: income.

outlet *noun* **1** (*an outlet for warm air*) vent, release, escape, exit, egress, valve, safety valve, way out, opening, channel. OPPOSITE: inlet. **2** (*a factory outlet*) market, marketplace, mart, store, shop. **3** (*an outlet for life's frustrations*) safety valve, release, release mechanism.

outline *noun* **1** (*an outline of my proposals*) draft, sketch, rough sketch, plan, skeleton, framework, drawing, tracing. **2** (*see the outline of the house through the mist*) contour, silhouette, shape, form, delineation, profile. **3** (*write an outline of the story first*) summary, synopsis, résumé, précis, recapitulation, thumbnail sketch.

➤ **verb 1** (*outline a plan*) draft, sketch, sketch out, trace, delineate, summarize, recapitulate. **2** (*on the map the area of our land is outlined in red*) trace, delineate, mark out, show, depict, indicate.

outlook *noun* **1** (*have a positive outlook on life*) attitude, viewpoint, point of view, perspective, frame of mind, slant, angle. **2** (*the outlook for next year*) prospect, expectation, future, forecast. **3** (*a house with a fine outlook over the meadows*) view, vista, panorama, prospect, scene.

outlying *adj* distant, remote, outer, outermost, peripheral, faraway, far-flung, isolated, inaccessible, out-of-the-way, off the beaten track. OPPOSITE: inner.

out-of-date *adj* outdated, old-fashioned, dated, unfashionable, passé, obsolete, démodé, old-time, obsolescent, antiquated, superannuated, old-hat (*inf*).

out-of-the-way *adj* outlying, distant, remote, outer, outermost, peripheral, faraway, far-flung, isolated, inaccessible, off the beaten track.

out-of-work *adj* unemployed, out of a job, jobless, workless, redundant, laid off, on the dole (*inf*).

outpouring *noun* flood, inundation, deluge, overflow, torrent, downpour, spate, flow, spurt, stream, effluence.

output *noun* productivity, production, manufacture, yield, return, harvest, fruits.

outrage *noun* **1** (*the latest terrorist attack is yet another outrage*) atrocity, enormity, crime, wrong, injury, harm, violation, desecration, abuse, horror, barbarism, offence, affront, insult, indignity. **2** (*a feeling of intense outrage*) anger, rage, fury, wrath, horror, indignation, shock.
➤ **verb** anger, enrage, infuriate, madden, offend, incense, annoy, insult, disgust, shock, horrify, abuse, injure, violate, desecrate.

outrageous *adj* **1** (*an outrageous lie*) shocking, scandalous, atrocious, abominable, unspeakable, vile, terrible, dreadful, hideous, horrible, monstrous, heinous, disgraceful, offensive, intolerable, insufferable. **2** (*protest against the outrageous charges*) immoderate, excessive, extravagant, extreme, unreasonable, preposterous. OPPOSITE: reasonable.

outré *adj* bizarre, eccentric, odd, unconventional, outlandish, extraordinary, strange, peculiar, wayout (*inf*), freaky (*inf*), off the wall (*inf*).

outright *adj* **1** (*outright condemnation*) total, complete, utter, absolute, sheer, perfect, consummate, thorough, thoroughgoing, unconditional, downright, unmitigated, unqualified, direct, straightforward. **2** (*an outright victory*) absolute, direct, unconditional, unqualified.
➤ **adv 1** (*accepted the offer outright*) totally, completely, utterly, absolutely, wholly, openly, unreservedly. **2** (*killed outright in the crash*) instantly, immediately, directly, at once, without delay, instantaneously.

outrun *verb* outstrip, outpace, outdistance, pass, overtake, escape, beat, surpass, excel, outdo.

outset *noun* start, beginning, commencement, birth, dawn, launch, opening, inauguration, inception. OPPOSITE: end.

outshine *verb* eclipse, overshadow, surpass, excel, transcend, tower above, outclass, outrival, outdo, be better than, outdistance, outstrip, put in the shade.

outside *noun* exterior, surface, edge, border, appearance, facade.
➤ **adj 1** (*an outside wall*) exterior, external, outer, outward, superficial, peripheral, extraneous. OPPOSITE: inside. **2** (*an outside chance that we will win*) distant, remote, unlikely, slim, vague, small, faint, negligible, marginal.
➤ **adv** outdoors, out, in the open air, alfresco.

outsider *noun* stranger, alien, foreigner, émigré, émigrée, immigrant, emigrant, newcomer, intruder, interloper, visitor, nonmember, gatecrasher (*inf*).

outskirts *pl noun* suburbs, environs, neighbourhood, precincts, periphery, purlieus, edge, border, boundary. OPPOSITE: centre.

outsmart *verb* trick, dupe, deceive, outwit, outfox, outmanoeuvre, get the better of, con (*inf*), kid (*inf*), run rings round (*inf*), take for a ride (*inf*).

outspoken *adj* candid, frank, blunt, explicit, open, free, unreserved, direct, plain, plainspoken, straightforward, forthright. OPPOSITE: reserved.

outspread *adj* outstretched, open, unfolded, unfurled, extended, expanded, spread out. OPPOSITE: closed.

outstanding *adj* **1** (*an outstanding cricketer*) excellent, superb, superior, exceptional, great, distinguished, eminent, pre-eminent, remarkable, notable, striking, impressive, prominent, well-known, famous, noticeable, conspicuous, memorable, salient, signal. OPPOSITE: insignificant. **2** (*outstanding invoices*) owing, due, unpaid, unsettled, remaining. OPPOSITE: paid.

outstretch *verb* outspread, extend, stretch out, expand, spread out, open, unfold, unfurl. OPPOSITE: close.

outstrip *verb* outrun, outpace, outdistance, outdo, surpass, exceed, excel, beat, outclass, outshine, eclipse.

outward *adj* outer, external, exterior, outside, superficial, apparent, visible, ostensible. OPPOSITE: inward.

outwardly *adv* on the surface, externally, superficially, apparently, seemingly, supposedly, on the face of it.

outweigh *verb* exceed, override, overcome, prevail over, surpass, be greater than, outbalance, overbalance, preponderate.

outwit *verb* cheat, defraud, trick, dupe, deceive, outjockey, outfox, outsmart (*inf*), pull a fast one on (*inf*), get the better of, outthink, overreach.

outworn *adj* old-fashioned, outmoded, outdated, obsolete, obsolescent, stale, hackneyed, antiquated, superannuated, behind the times.

oval *adj* eggshaped, ovoid, ovoidal, ovate, elliptical.

ovation *noun* applause, clapping, handclapping, cheers, cheering, accolade, acclaim, acclamation, praise, laudation, plaudits, bouquet (*inf*).

oven *noun* stove, cooker, microwave, kiln.

over *prep* **1** (*fly over the trees*) above, on, upon, on top of, higher than. OPPOSITE: under. **2** (*he's over 60*) exceeding, in excess of, more than, higher than, greater than. OPPOSITE: below. **3** (*travel over all of Australasia*) across, through.
➤ **adv 1** (*birds flying over*) above, overhead, out, beyond, on high, across, through. **2** (*have time over*) extra, surplus, remaining, left, left over, in excess, in addition.
➤ **adj** finished, ended, concluded, terminated, completed, done, gone, past.

over and above in addition to, plus, along with, as well as, added to, on top of, not to mention.

over and over over and over again, again and again, repeatedly, often, frequently, continually, time and time again, time and again.

overact verb exaggerate, lay it on (inf), lay it on thick (inf), ham it up (inf).

overall adj general, universal, global, comprehensive, all-embracing, inclusive, all-inclusive, complete, total, sweeping, blanket (inf).
≫ adv in general, generally speaking, generally, broadly, broadly speaking, on the whole.

overawe verb intimidate, cow, daunt, abash, disconcert, frighten, alarm, terrify, scare, domineer, browbeat. OPPOSITE: reassure.

overbalance verb lose one's balance, fall over, tumble, trip over, capsize, topple over, keel over, turn turtle.

overbearing adj domineering, imperious, lordly, high-handed, dogmatic, officious, haughty, arrogant, proud, supercilious, bossy (inf), snobby (inf), snooty (inf), too big for one's boots (inf), smart-arse (sl), autocratic, dictatorial, tyrannical, oppressive. OPPOSITE: humble.

overblown adj extravagant, overstated, excessive, pretentious, bombastic, overelaborate, high-flown, fustian, turgid, euphuistic, grandiloquent, magniloquent, over the top (inf).

overcast adj cloudy, grey, dull, sunless, gloomy, dreary, dismal, sombre, misty, hazy, murky, dark, darkened, threatening, lowering, leaden. OPPOSITE: clear.

overcharge verb 1 (overcharged by hundreds of pounds) surcharge, cheat, short-change, fleece (inf), swindle, rook (inf), rip off (inf), do (inf), diddle (inf). OPPOSITE: undercharge. 2 (hearts overcharged with gratitude) overload, overburden, strain, exaggerate, overstate, overdo, overtax.

overcome verb conquer, vanquish, defeat, beat, best, worst, overpower, overwhelm, overthrow, get the better of, crush, quash, trounce, quell, subdue, master, gain mastery over, surmount, triumph over, rise above, hammer (inf), clobber (inf), lick (inf), wipe the floor with (inf). OPPOSITE: submit.
≫ adj overwhelmed, speechless, lost for words, bowled over (inf), swept off one's feet (inf).

overcrowded adj packed out, crammed full, congested, swarming, teeming, jam-packed (inf), overloaded, overpopulated.

overdo verb exaggerate, go to extremes, go overboard (inf), overact, overplay, ham it up (inf), camp it up (inf), do to death (inf), stretch the point, pile it on (inf), lay it on (inf), lay it on thick (inf), lay it on with a trowel (inf), overstate, overindulge.

overdo it overwork, work too hard, do too much, overstretch oneself, strain oneself, burn oneself out, bite off more than one can chew (inf), burn the candle at both ends (inf).

overdone adj 1 (the beef is overdone) overcooked, burnt, overbaked, charred, spoilt, burnt to a crisp (inf). OPPOSITE: underdone. 2 (the sarcasm was overdone) exaggerated, excessive, too much, extreme, immoderate, inordinate, over the top (inf), OTT (inf).

overdue adj late, behind, behindhand, behind schedule, delayed, belated, tardy, owing, in arrears, due, payable. OPPOSITE: punctual.

overeat verb overindulge, eat too much, stuff oneself, gorge oneself, guzzle, gormandize, pig out (inf).

overestimate verb overrate, overvalue, overpraise, exaggerate, think too much of. OPPOSITE: underestimate.

overflow verb overrun, overspill, run over, flow over, brim over, spill over, surge, stream forth, pour forth, flood, inundate, deluge, swamp, overspread, cover, saturate, abound, teem. OPPOSITE: subside.
≫ noun excess, surplus, overspill, overabundance.
be overflowing with be full of, be full to the brim with, abound in, swarm with.

overhang verb jut out, stand out, stick out, protrude, extend, project, beetle.

overhaul verb 1 (overhaul the boiler) inspect, examine, check, check out, service, repair, recondition, revamp. 2 (one vehicle overhauling another) catch up, overtake, pass, get ahead of, outstrip.

overhead adv high, above, up, up above, on high. OPPOSITE: below.

overheads pl noun running costs, operating costs, expenditure, expenses, on-cost.

overindulge verb 1 (overindulge at Christmas) eat too much, drink too much, gorge, gormandize, guzzle, binge (inf), pig out (inf), make a pig of oneself (inf). 2 (overindulge the grandchildren) pamper, mollycoddle, spoil, coddle, cosset, pander to.

overjoyed adj delighted, ecstatic, elated, joyful, enraptured, in raptures, jubilant, thrilled, over the moon (inf), tickled pink (inf), in seventh heaven (inf), on cloud nine (inf). OPPOSITE: upset.

overlay verb cover, overspread, blanket, coat, carpet, varnish, veneer, laminate.

overload verb overcharge, overburden, strain, weigh down, overtax, oppress, burden, encumber. OPPOSITE: relieve.

overlook verb 1 (the hotel overlooks the lake) look on to, front on to, look over, command a view of. 2 (overlook a fact) miss, neglect, omit, leave out, skip, pass over, disregard, ignore, forget. OPPOSITE: note. 3 (overlook his faults) forgive, pardon, excuse, condone, take no notice of, blink at, wink at. OPPOSITE: punish.

overly adv very, too, very much, excessively, inordinately.

overpower verb 1 (overpowered the attacker) overwhelm, overcome, conquer, vanquish, defeat, beat, master, gain mastery over, gain the upper hand over, surmount, crush, quash, quell, subdue, best, worst. OPPOSITE: submit. 2 (a sense of guilt suddenly overpowered him) overcome, overwhelm, move, fill, touch, affect, stir, bowl over (inf), floor (inf), knock for six (inf).

overpowering adj overwhelming, strong, powerful, forceful, weighty, burdensome, irresistible, uncontrollable. OPPOSITE: weak.

overrate verb overestimate, overvalue, think too much of, overpraise, exaggerate. OPPOSITE: underrate.

overreach verb outwit, outsmart (inf), cheat, defraud, swindle, trick, dupe, deceive, con (inf), kid (inf), run rings round (*inf*), take for a ride (*inf*), outmanoeuvre, circumvent.

overreach oneself overstretch oneself, strain oneself, go too far, bite off more than one can chew (*inf*).

override *verb* **1** (*should the needs of parents override those of their children?*) be more important than, take precedence over, have priority over. **2** (*the headteacher overrode the teacher's decision*) overrule, disregard, ignore, supersede, outweigh, prevail over, quash, annul, reverse, cancel.

overriding *adj* most important, most significant, main, chief, first, major, prime, principal, central, focal, prevailing, paramount. OPPOSITE: irrelevant.

overrule *verb* **1** (*overrule the lower court's decision*) disallow, reject, override, supersede, annul, reverse, invalidate, rescind, abrogate, void, countermand, revoke, repeal, cancel, nullify. **2** (*the mind must overrule the body*) rule, govern, dominate, prevail over, influence, sway, control, direct.

overrun *verb* **1** (*a beauty spot overrun by tourists*) attack, invade, overwhelm, ravage, storm, devastate, infest, inundate, swarm, spread, overflow. **2** (*the meeting overran by half an hour*) exceed, go beyond, overshoot, overreach.

overseer *noun* supervisor, superintendent, master, manager, foreman, boss (*inf*), gaffer (*inf*), honcho (*inf*).

overshadow *verb* **1** (*he is overshadowed by his younger brother*) eclipse, outshine, outclass, surpass, excel, put in the shade, dwarf, dominate, tower over, rise above, upstage (*inf*). **2** (*his childhood was overshadowed by his father's suicide*) cloud, darken, dim, obscure, veil, spoil, blight, take the edge off.

oversight *noun* **1** (*through an oversight, I forgot to thank her*) omission, fault, lapse, slip, blunder, mistake, error, neglect, carelessness, inattention, dereliction. OPPOSITE: attention. **2** (*have oversight in a church*) supervision, surveillance, administration, management, direction, control, care, charge, custody.

overt *adj* plain, clear, manifest, patent, apparent, visible, observable, open, public, unconcealed, undisguised, conspicuous, blatant, deliberate. OPPOSITE: hidden.

overtake *verb* **1** (*overtake slower cars*) pass, go past, go faster than, leave behind, outrun, outstrip, catch up, overhaul. **2** (*disaster overtook them*) befall, happen to, come upon, surprise, catch unawares, take unawares.

overthrow *verb* oust, depose, topple, unseat, dethrone, conquer, vanquish, defeat, beat, overcome, overpower, subvert, overturn, crush, quash, quell, upset, bring down, demolish, raze, ruin, destroy, abolish. OPPOSITE: restore.
➤ *noun* defeat, fall, toppling, subversion, demolition, downfall, ruin, destruction, abolition, deposition, dethronement. OPPOSITE: restoration.

overtone *noun* suggestion, hint, implication, nuance, connotation, innuendo, insinuation.

overture *noun* **1** (*the overture to the musical*) introduction, prelude, opening, preface, prologue. OPPOSITE: finale. **2** (*rejected his overtures*) advance, approach, offer, proposal, suggestion, proposition, invitation.

overturn *verb* **1** (*the canoe overturned*) upset, capsize, overbalance, turn over, turn turtle, keel over, tip over, upend, invert, topple, spill. **2** (*overturn the lower court's ruling*) overrule, override, annul, reverse, cancel, veto, invalidate. **3** (*overturn the military regime*) overthrow, subvert, bring down, depose, topple, oust, unseat, destroy, abolish, reverse.

overused *adj* overworked, trite, hackneyed, banal, stereotyped, worn, commonplace. OPPOSITE: fresh.

overweening *adj* **1** (*his overweening vanity*) arrogant, haughty, supercilious, proud, conceited, presumptuous, vain, vainglorious, lordly, high and mighty (*inf*), pompous, opinionated, cocky, cocksure. OPPOSITE: meek. **2** (*overweening desires*) excessive, immoderate, extravagant, exaggerated.

overweight *adj* obese, fat, plump, stout, portly, heavy, large, big, broad, outsize, paunchy, podgy, ample, tubby, chubby, flabby, fleshy. OPPOSITE: skinny.

overwhelm *verb* **1** (*overwhelmed by grief*) overcome, move, fill, touch, affect, stir, shake, dumbfound, bowl over (*inf*), floor (*inf*), knock for six (*inf*). **2** (*overwhelmed with problems*) overcome, devastate, engulf, submerge, overburden, weigh down, snow under, inundate, flood, deluge, swamp, bury. **3** (*overwhelm the enemy*) overpower, overthrow, conquer, overcome, quell, vanquish, defeat, master, crush. OPPOSITE: submit.

overwhelming *adj* **1** (*the sheer numbers are overwhelming*) overpowering, strong, powerful, burdensome, staggering, irresistible, uncontrollable. **2** (*voted in by an overwhelming majority*) great, large, vast, massive, huge, immense.

overwork *verb* overdo it, work too hard, do too much, strain oneself, burn oneself out, bit off more than one can chew (*inf*), burn the candle at both ends (*inf*), work one's fingers to the bone (*inf*).

overworked *adj* overused, trite, hackneyed, banal, stereotyped, worn, commonplace. OPPOSITE: fresh.

overwrought *adj* **1** (*overwrought at the bad news*) distraught, excited, agitated, frantic, tense, on edge, keyed up, worked up (*inf*), in a tizzy (*inf*), wound up (*inf*), uptight (*inf*), overexcited. OPPOSITE: calm. **2** (*overwrought prose*) elaborate, fancy, ornate, flowery, contrived, overdone, overworked, overelaborate. OPPOSITE: plain.

owe *verb* be in debt to, be in arrears to, be indebted to, be under an obligation to, be beholden to.

owing *adj* due, unpaid, payable, owed, outstanding, unsettled, overdue, in arrears. OPPOSITE: paid.

own *adj* personal, private, individual, particular.
➤ *verb* possess, have, hold, keep, enjoy, retain.
on one's own alone, by oneself, singly, lonely, unaccompanied, independently, unaided, on one's tod (*inf*).

own up acknowledge, admit, confess, recognize, grant, concede, avow, come clean (*inf*), make a clean breast of it (*inf*). OPPOSITE: deny.

owner *noun* possessor, holder, keeper, proprietor, proprietress, master, mistress.

ownership *noun* possession, proprietorship, rights, title.

pace noun **1** (*three paces to the left*) step, stride, tread. **2** (*walk with an ungainly pace*) gait, walk, tread. **3** (*at a steady pace*) speed, lick (*inf*), clip (*inf*), velocity, rate, tempo, progress, quickness, rapidity, swiftness. **4** (*the pace of life*) tempo, momentum, measure.
➤ *verb* **1** (*pace up and down*) walk, stride, step, tramp, march, pound, patrol. **2** (*pace it out*) measure, mark out.

pacific adj **1** (*adopted a pacific stance*) conciliatory, placatory, appeasing, placating, mollifying, propitiatory, calming, mediatory, diplomatic, peacemaking, peaceable, peaceloving. OPPOSITE: belligerent. **2** (*pacific policies*) pacifist, peaceloving, peaceable, nonviolent, noncombative, nonbelligerent, nonaggressive, dovelike, mild, gentle, friendly. **3** (*a pacific scene*) peaceful, calm, serene, smooth, tranquil, placid, unruffled, undisturbed, quiet, still, motionless. OPPOSITE: turbulent.

pacifist noun peacemaker, peacelover, conscientious objector, conchy (*inf*), peacemonger, dove.

pacify verb appease, conciliate, propitiate, placate, mollify, calm, calm down, compose, lull, quiet, quieten, silence, soothe, tranquillize, still, allay, defuse, assuage, propitiate, moderate, mitigate, quell, crush, subdue, repress, put down, tame, soften. OPPOSITE: aggravate.

pack noun **1** (*pack of paper*) packet, bundle, package, parcel, carton, container, bale, load, burden. **2** (*a pack of animals*) herd, flock, drove, troop. **3** (*a pack of young men*) crowd, throng, mob, group, band, bunch, gang, company, troop, crew, clique. **4** (*a pack of lies*) mass, bunch, load, heap (*inf*), lot, set, collection, assortment. **5** (*picked up their packs*) bag, backpack, rucksack, haversack, knapsack, kitbag.
➤ *verb* **1** (*pack everything into the case*) cram, stuff, jam, wedge, press, ram, compact, compress, charge, fill, bundle, crowd, load. **2** (*pack the things away*) load, stow, store. **3** (*pack the valuables in cotton*) wrap, wrap up, tie up, parcel, package, box, crate, bundle, put in, cover, protect. **4** (*we all packed into the kitchen*) crowd, throng, mob, fill, cram, jam, press, squeeze.

pack in 1 (*pack in all his belongings*) crowd, cram, jam, stuff, squeeze, press, ram, wedge, fill, load, charge. **2** (*the show is packing them in*) draw in, pull in, attract. **3** (*let's pack in the whole idea*) give up, give over, chuck (*inf*), jack in (*inf*), throw in (*inf*), kick (*inf*), abandon, leave off, stop, end, desist, cease, resign.

pack off send, dismiss, dispatch, bundle off, send packing (*inf*), hustle out.

pack up 1 (*pack up one's things*) tidy up, tidy away, clear up, put away, store. **2** (*pack up trying*) cease, give up, throw up (*inf*), wrap up (*inf*), pack in (*inf*), jack in (*inf*), stop, finish, end, halt, call it a day (*inf*). **3** (*the engine packed up*) break down, fail, seize up (*inf*), stall, stop working, conk out (*inf*), malfunction.

package noun **1** (*handed over the package*) bundle, pack, parcel, packet, box, carton, container, bale, consignment. **2** (*part of a generous package*) deal, whole, unit, group, set, entity, amalgamation, combination.
➤ *verb* pack, box, wrap, parcel, batch.

packaging noun wrapping, wrapper, packet, packing, covering, container, box, presentation.

packed adj full, filled, crammed, jammed, jam-packed (*inf*), chock-a-block (*inf*), chock-full, crowded, thronged, congested, brimful, overflowing, overloaded.

packet noun **1** (*picked up the packet*) pack, package, parcel, box, carton, case, container, bag, receptacle, wrapper, wrapping, packing. **2** (*worth a packet*) lots, a lot, fortune, small fortune, bomb (*inf*), bundle (*inf*), mint (*inf*), pile (*inf*), pretty penny (*inf*), tidy sum (*inf*), megabucks (*inf*).

pact noun agreement, compact, covenant, concord, concordat, bond, contract, treaty, entente, understanding, convention, league, alliance, bargain, deal, settlement, arrangement, cartel, protocol.

pad[1] noun **1** (*protected by a foam-rubber pad*) cushion, pillow, bolster, wad, buffer, stuffing, padding, filling, wadding, stiffening, protection. **2** (*pad of paper*) writing-pad, block, jotter, notepad, notebook, tablet. **3** (*a bear's*

pad) paw, foot, sole, print, footprint. **4** (*a comfortable pad*) home, place, apartment, flat, rooms, room, quarters, penthouse.
➤ *verb* cushion, stuff, fill, pack, wad, wrap, line, protect.
pad out fill out, expand, inflate, flesh out, amplify, elaborate, increase, add to, lengthen, stretch out, spin out, eke out, augment, protract.

pad² *verb* (*a dog padding along the path*) tiptoe, creep, walk, move, step, run, tread, trudge, tramp, lope, plod, trek.

padding *noun* **1** (*put plenty of padding round the vase*) packing, filling, filler, stuffing, wadding, cushioning, lining, wrapping, protection. **2** (*too much padding in this essay*) verbosity, verboseness, verbiage, waffle (*inf*), wordiness, prolixity, bombast, hot air (*inf*).

paddle¹ *noun* **1** (*hold the paddles to row a boat*) oar, scull, sweep.
➤ *verb* row, pull, oar, scull, propel, pole, punt, steer.

paddle² *verb* **1** (*paddle in the sea*) wade, splash. **2** (*paddled her fingers in the basin*) splash, dabble, slop, plunge.

paddock *noun* field, meadow, enclosure, pen, fold, yard, pound, compound, stockade, corral.

padlock *noun* lock, latch, fastening, clasp, catch, bolt.

padre *noun* chaplain, pastor, minister, priest, cleric, vicar, reverend, father, parson, curate, rector, deacon, deaconess, clergyman, churchman.

paean *noun* **1** (*sing paeans to the Lord*) hymn, song of praise, psalm, anthem, exaltation, glorification, magnification. **2** (*offer paeans to his leadership*) praise, eulogy, bouquet, ovation, compliment, panegyric, encomium.

pagan *noun* heathen, unbeliever, nonbeliever, disbeliever, infidel, idolater, atheist, agnostic, pantheist. OPPOSITE: believer.
➤ *adj* heathen, idolatrous, irreligious, godless, atheistic, agnostic, infidel, pantheistic. OPPOSITE: believing.

page¹ *noun* **1** (*a page of writing*) leaf, sheet, folio, side, recto, verso. **2** (*a new page in history*) episode, chapter, period, time, phase, era, epoch, point, stage, event, incident.

page² *noun* (*work at the theatre as a page*) pageboy, bellboy, bellhop, servant, attendant, footman, messenger, squire.
➤ *verb* call, summon, bid, send for, ask for, announce.

pageant *noun* parade, procession, tableau, scene, spectacle, show, display, play, ritual, representation, exhibition, extravaganza, cavalcade.

pageantry *noun* pomp, ceremony, state, magnificence, splendour, glamour, grandeur, spectacle, parade, show, display, glitter, showiness, ostentation, theatricality, extravagance, flourish, melodrama, drama, pizzazz (*inf*).

pain *noun* **1** (*pain in both elbows*) hurt, discomfort, suffering, agony, ache, aching, throb, throbbing, cramp, pang, spasm, twinge, smart, smarting, stitch, soreness, tenderness, irritation. OPPOSITE: relief. **2** (*his attitude caused her pain*) distress, anguish, hurt, agony, suffering, trouble, tribulation, affliction, torment, torture, heartache, heartbreak, brokenheartedness, misery, unhappiness, sadness, sorrow, grief, woe, wretchedness,

desolation, anxiety, bitterness. OPPOSITE: joy. **3** (*he's a real pain*) pain in the neck (*inf*), pain in the backside (*inf*), pain in the arse (*sl*), nuisance, bother, pest, drag (*inf*), headache (*inf*), aggravation, annoyance, vexation, worry, bore (*inf*), burden.
➤ *verb* **1** (*my head pains me*) hurt, ache, throb, sting, smart, chafe, irritate, injure, wound, discomfort, ail. OPPOSITE: ease. **2** (*the news pains us*) distress, trouble, afflict, hurt, torment, torture, agonize, grieve, sadden, sorrow, disquiet, vex, rile, worry, annoy, exasperate, nark (*inf*), upset. OPPOSITE: comfort.

pained *adj* hurt, injured, wounded, stung, offended, miffed (*inf*), aggrieved, distressed, upset, worried, reproachful, unhappy, sad, saddened, grieved, vexed, piqued.

painful *adj* **1** (*nursed his painful foot*) sore, tender, hurting, aching, throbbing, cramped, stinging, smarting, inflamed, raw, agonizing, excruciating, stabbing, irritating. **2** (*a painful memory*) distressing, harrowing, unpleasant, nasty, disagreeable, upsetting, disturbing, disquieting, discomfiting, traumatic, grievous, humiliating, mortifying, wretched, miserable, unhappy, saddening, embarrassing, shameful, touchy (*inf*), disconcerting, uncomfortable. OPPOSITE: pleasant. **3** (*painful progress*) hard, difficult, tough, arduous, rigorous, severe, demanding, exacting, laborious, strenuous, tedious, toilsome, troublesome, trying, vexatious, awkward. OPPOSITE: easy.

painfully *adv* **1** (*her head ached painfully*) agonizingly, achingly, excruciatingly, intensely. **2** (*she looked painfully young*) distressingly, woefully, deplorably, pitifully, pitiably, alarmingly, worryingly, sadly, excessively, wretchedly, terribly (*inf*), awfully (*inf*), dreadfully (*inf*). **3** (*his inexperience was painfully obvious*) excessively, clearly, markedly, terribly (*inf*), woefully, uncomfortably, embarrassingly, disconcertingly.

painkiller *noun* anaesthetic, sedative, palliative, analgesic, anodyne, lenitive, drug, remedy.

painless *adj* **1** (*a painless operation*) pain-free. **2** (*painless work*) effortless, easy, trouble-free, simple, straightforward, undemanding, cushy (*inf*).

pains *pl noun* effort, bother, trouble, care, diligence, meticulousness, exactness, assiduousness.
be at pains be concerned, try hard, take care, be anxious, bother, go to great lengths, put oneself out.

painstaking *adj* **1** (*a painstaking search*) careful, scrupulous, punctilious, meticulous, assiduous, sedulous, searching, exacting, thorough, thoroughgoing. OPPOSITE: careless. **2** (*a painstaking worker*) careful, conscientious, scrupulous, dedicated, devoted, attentive, meticulous, punctilious, diligent, persevering, pertinacious, assiduous, earnest, thorough, industrious, hardworking.

paint *noun* colour, colouring, pigment, colourant, emulsion, gloss, distemper, whitewash, oil, stain, dye, tint.
➤ *verb* **1** (*paint the house*) colour, daub, smear, slap on (*inf*), wash, whitewash, tint, coat, cover, decorate, spray, plaster, dye, stain, lacquer, varnish, glaze. **2** (*had his portrait painted*) depict, portray, represent, sketch, draw, delineate. **3** (*his story painted a different picture*) depict,

portray, tell, recount, describe, unfold, reveal, conjure up, narrate, draw, sketch, picture, evoke, represent, delineate.

paint the town red celebrate, carouse, make merry, make whoopee (*inf*), go out, go on the razzle (*inf*), enjoy oneself, rejoice, revel, have fun, live it up (*inf*), whoop it up (*inf*), have a ball (*inf*), throw a party.

painter *noun* artist, illustrator, drawer, sketcher, dauber.

painting *noun* picture, portrait, watercolour, oil painting, oil, landscape, portrayal, representation, illustration, depiction, delineation, likeness, still life, miniature, fresco, mural, sketch, drawing.

pair *noun* couple, brace, two, twosome, twins, duo, doublet, set, combination.
  ≫ *verb* match, couple, link, mate, twin, team, partner, join, yoke, marry, unite, splice, wed, bracket, put together. OPPOSITE: separate.

pal *noun* friend, chum (*inf*), mate (*inf*), comrade, companion, partner, confidant, confidante, intimate, soul mate, buddy (*inf*), crony (*inf*), sidekick (*inf*).

palace *noun* castle, château, royal residence, stately home, mansion.

palatable *adj* **1** (*a palatable dish*) tasty, toothsome, savoury, delicious, appetizing, mouthwatering, flavourful, flavoursome, luscious, succulent, delectable, yummy (*inf*), scrumptious (*inf*), scrummy (*inf*), moreish (*inf*), edible, eatable. **2** (*a palatable prospect*) pleasant, pleasing, pleasurable, agreeable, acceptable, satisfactory, fair, attractive, enjoyable, nice. OPPOSITE: unpleasant.

palate *noun* **1** (*she had no palate for supper*) taste, appetite, stomach, heart. **2** (*a palate for modern poetry*) appreciation, liking, relish, zest, enjoyment, enthusiasm, gusto.

palatial *adj* grand, stately, majestic, regal, imposing, splendid, magnificent, sumptuous, plush (*inf*), posh (*inf*), ritzy (*inf*), luxurious, de luxe, opulent, grandiose, spacious. OPPOSITE: mean.

palaver *noun* **1** (*accompanied by a lot of palaver*) rigmarole, procedure, business (*inf*), performance (*inf*), bustle, commotion, activity, affair, fuss, song and dance (*inf*), carry-on (*inf*), flap (*inf*), flurry, fluster, agitation, stir. **2** (*what's all the palaver about?*) chatter, babble, prattle, natter, blather, blether, hubbub, tongue-wagging, yak (*inf*).

pale *adj* **1** (*a pale complexion*) colourless, whitish, white-faced, wan, waxen, waxy, anaemic, bloodless, drained, washed out, pallid, pasty, peaky, deathly, ashen, ashy, livid, sallow, chalky, white. OPPOSITE: dark. **2** (*pale colours*) bleached, faded, light, muted, pastel, colourless, washed-out. **3** (*a pale flicker*) dim, faint, feeble, weak, thin, poor, insipid, vapid.
  ≫ *verb* **1** (*he paled at the thought*) blanch, whiten, lose colour. **2** (*pale in comparison*) fade, dim, lessen, diminish, dwindle, decrease, melt, dull.

pall¹ *noun* **1** (*a pall of smoke*) covering, shroud, mantle, veil, cloak. **2** (*cast a pall over proceedings*) shadow, cloud, damper, gloom, melancholy, depression, sombreness, gravity.

pall² *verb* (*soon the novelty of living in a hotel began to pall*) cloy, bore, tire, weary, sicken, jade, wear off, satiate, glut, surfeit.

palliate *verb* **1** (*drugs designed to palliate the condition*) alleviate, mitigate, allay, assuage, soothe, ease, relieve, relax, temper, abate, dull, blunt, soften. OPPOSITE: aggravate. **2** (*palliate the insults given*) extenuate, make light of, lighten, excuse, minimize, lessen, diminish, moderate, mollify, tone down, play down, downplay, varnish, gloss over, paper over, whitewash (*inf*), conceal, cover up, cloak. OPPOSITE: expose.

palliative *noun* analgesic, anodyne, sedative, tranquillizer, painkiller, lenitive, calmative, demulcent.

pallid *adj* **1** (*a pallid countenance*) pale, wan, waxen, waxy, ashen, ashy, pasty, pasty-faced, whey-faced, cadaverous, peaky, sallow, sickly, anaemic, bloodless, drained, white, whitish, white-faced, colourless, deathly, ghostly, ghastly, lurid, green. **2** (*a pallid taste*) unexciting, dull, tedious, uninteresting, unimaginative, colourless, vapid, insipid, bland, sterile, boring, uninspired, tame, weak, lifeless, spiritless, tired.

pallor *noun* paleness, pallidness, pallidity, pastiness, peakiness, bloodlessness, chalkiness, sallowness, wanness, ghastliness, luridness, sickliness, whiteness, colourlessness. OPPOSITE: ruddiness.

palm *noun* hand, paw (*inf*), mitt (*inf*), meathook (*inf*).
palm off foist, fob off, offload, unload (*inf*), pass off, get rid of, impose, thrust.

palmist *noun* palm reader, fortune-teller, clairvoyant.

palmy *adj* prosperous, thriving, flourishing, carefree, halcyon, golden, glorious, luxurious, triumphant, successful, happy, fortunate, joyous. OPPOSITE: unfortunate.

palpable *adj* **1** (*a palpable change in his manner*) obvious, evident, manifest, patent, clear, plain, overt, blatant, glaring, perceptible, visible, apparent, conspicuous, definite, unmistakable. **2** (*palpable rewards*) tangible, real, concrete, solid, substantial, material, corporeal, touchable, feelable. OPPOSITE: impalpable.

palpitate *verb* **1** (*felt the bird's heart palpitating*) pulsate, pulse, beat, throb, pound, pump, thud, thump, flutter. **2** (*palpitating with terror*) tremble, quiver, quaver, shake, quake, vibrate.

paltry *adj* **1** (*paid him a paltry salary*) trivial, trifling, minor, petty, small, little, slight, insignificant, inconsiderable, meagre, negligible, poor, derisory, pitiful, beggarly, measly (*inf*), piddling (*inf*). **2** (*a paltry trick*) worthless, wretched, sorry, miserable, poor, contemptible, despicable, abject, puny, mean, base, low. OPPOSITE: considerable.

pamper *verb* indulge, overindulge, humour, gratify, spoil, ruin, coddle, mollycoddle, cosset, pander, baby, pet, fondle, spoonfeed. OPPOSITE: discipline.

pamphlet *noun* booklet, leaflet, brochure, circular, handout, notice, tract, treatise.

pan¹ *noun* (*pots and pans*) saucepan, pot, frying pan, skillet, casserole, wok, container, vessel, receptacle.
  ≫ *verb* criticize, censure, blast, lambaste, flay, find fault with, put down, hammer (*inf*), knock (*inf*), pull apart (*inf*), tear into (*inf*), roast (*inf*), rubbish (*inf*), slam (*inf*), slate (*inf*), slag (*inf*).

pan out work out, turn out, come out, fall out, result, happen, culminate, come to an end, eventuate, yield.

pan[2] *verb* (*the camera panned slowly across the stadium*) scan, sweep, follow, track, traverse, swing, circle, move, turn.

panacea *noun* cure-all, elixir, universal remedy, nostrum.

panache *noun* flamboyance, dash, flourish, ostentation, style, flair, swagger, élan, spirit, enthusiasm, zest, brio, pizzazz (*inf*), energy, verve, vigour.

pancake *noun* crêpe, waffle, flapjack, wafer, blini, griddle-cake, tortilla, bannock.

pandemic *adj* widespread, universal, pervasive, global, extensive, general, common, prevalent, far-reaching, rife, rampant.

pandemonium *noun* chaos, confusion, disorder, tumult, turmoil, turbulence, bedlam, riot, uproar, commotion, din, clamour, racket, rumpus, to-do (*inf*), hubbub, hullabaloo, hue and cry. OPPOSITE: peace.

pander *verb* humour, gratify, satisfy, fulfil, pamper, indulge, please, cater, provide.

panegyric *noun* eulogy, praise, homage, commendation, citation, accolade, tribute, encomium, paean. OPPOSITE: tirade.

panel *noun* **1** (*nail each panel*) sheet, board, plank, beam, timber, slab, section. **2** (*appeared before the panel*) board, council, committee, commission, trustees, directorate, jury, team.

pang *noun* **1** (*feel a pang in his neck*) pain, stab, sting, prick, twinge, spasm, throe, ache, stitch. **2** (*a pang of remorse*) twinge, qualm, scruple, spasm, stab, feeling, attack.

panic *noun* terror, alarm, fright, flap (*inf*), fear, horror, frenzy, hysteria, agitation, consternation, trepidation, nervousness, perturbation, dismay, confusion, turmoil, disquiet. OPPOSITE: composure.
➤ *verb* **1** (*do not panic*) be alarmed, overreact, go to pieces (*inf*), lose one's nerve (*inf*), lose one's head (*inf*), lose one's cool (*inf*), lose one's bottle (*inf*), get the shakes (*inf*), get the jitters (*inf*), get the wind up (*inf*). **2** (*panicked by the noise*) terrify, alarm, frighten, scare, petrify, unnerve, startle, agitate.

panic-stricken *adj* panicky, alarmed, fearful, scared, scared stiff, aghast, frightened, horrified, terrified, terror-stricken, horror-stricken, petrified, frantic, frenzied, hysterical, nervous, agitated, appalled, dismayed, disquietened, perturbed, thrown.

panoply *noun* array, display, trappings, show, regalia, splendour, dress, garb (*inf*), gear (*inf*), attire, getup (*inf*), raiment, equipment, insignia, armour.

panorama *noun* **1** (*the panorama from the hilltop*) view, vista, prospect, scenery, landscape, scene, spectacle. **2** (*offering a panorama of current affairs*) survey, appraisal, overview, perspective.

panoramic *adj* **1** (*panoramic views*) broad, extensive, wide, sweeping, far-reaching, bird's-eye, scenic. OPPOSITE: narrow. **2** (*panoramic knowledge*) wide, wide-ranging, all-embracing, widespread, sweeping, extensive, comprehensive, inclusive, overall, universal, general. OPPOSITE: limited.

pant *verb* **1** (*pant for breath*) puff, blow, gasp, wheeze, breathe, sigh, heave. **2** (*pant for success*) long, pine, yearn, desire, want, ache, thirst, hunger, lust, burn, covet, crave, hanker, sigh, yen (*inf*). **3** (*her heart was panting with excitement*) beat, pulsate, pulse, palpitate, pound, throb, thump.
➤ *noun* gasp, puff, huff, throb, wheeze.

pants *pl noun* **1** (*put his pants on under his trousers*) underpants, briefs, boxers, boxer shorts, Y-fronts. **2** (*pulled on his golfing pants*) trousers, slacks, jeans, strides (*inf*).

pap *noun* rubbish, crap (*sl*), drivel, trash, nonsense, gibberish, rot (*inf*), claptrap (*inf*), pulp, trivia.

paper *noun* **1** (*the daily paper*) newspaper, journal, gazette, daily, rag (*inf*), broadsheet, tabloid, weekly, periodical, magazine, organ. **2** (*obtain the paper for his release*) document, authorization, certificate, instrument, deed, assignment, record, paperwork. **3** (*write a paper on the subject*) article, study, work, report, monograph, treatise, essay, composition, dissertation, examination, thesis, analysis, critique.
➤ *verb* wallpaper, line, decorate, paste up, hang.

on paper 1 (*get it down on paper*) in writing, in black and white, written down, on the record. **2** (*looks good on paper*) in theory, theoretically, hypothetically.

paper over hide, conceal, cover up, gloss over, obscure, disguise, camouflage, veil, whitewash.

papers *pl noun* **1** (*signed the papers*) documents, certificates, certification. **2** (*the police examined her papers*) documents, identification documents, ID, identity card, credentials, accreditation.

papery *adj* papery, paper-thin, thin, ultra-thin, light, lightweight, flimsy, fragile, frail, delicate, insubstantial, translucent.

par *noun* **above par** excellent, first-rate, superior, exceptional, outstanding. OPPOSITE: inferior.

below par 1 (*his performance was below par*) substandard, below average, inferior, second-rate, poor, unsatisfactory, inadequate, lacking, wanting. OPPOSITE: excellent. **2** (*she felt a bit below par*) unwell, poorly, unfit, unhealthy, indisposed, under the weather (*inf*), sick, off colour, off form, out of sorts, tired.

on a par with equal to, equivalent to, the same as, as good as, well-matched. OPPOSITE: unequal.

par for the course average, typical, normal, ordinary, standard, usual, predictable, to be expected.

up to par acceptable, satisfactory, passable, adequate, good enough, up to scratch (*inf*), up to the mark, up to snuff (*inf*). OPPOSITE: unacceptable.

parable *noun* fable, allegory, tale, story, lesson.

parade *noun* **1** (*a parade in the street*) procession, train, column, file, review, march, progression, cavalcade, motorcade, ceremony. **2** (*fashion parade*) pageant, show, display, exhibition, demonstration, spectacle, array.
➤ *verb* **1** (*parade down the hill*) march, file, process. **2** (*parading the cup before their fans*) flaunt, vaunt, show off, display, exhibit, demonstrate, brandish, air. OPPOSITE: hide. **3** (*paraded through the town with her new husband*) swagger, strut.

paradigm *noun* pattern, model, ideal, standard, norm, gauge, example, original, criterion, prototype, archetype, exemplar, paragon, framework.

paradise *noun* **1** (*angels in paradise*) heaven, after life, hereafter, next world, life to come, happy hunting ground, Elysium, elysian fields, Eden, promised land. OPPOSITE: purgatory. **2** (*a paradise on earth*) utopia, fairyland, Shangri-la. **3** (*left him in a state of paradise*) bliss, ecstasy, rapture, happiness, delight, joy, felicity, seventh heaven (*inf*).

paradox *noun* contradiction, self-contradiction, incongruity, inconsistency, absurdity, anomaly, oxymoron, oddity, puzzle, riddle, enigma, mystery. OPPOSITE: truism.

paradoxical *adj* contradictory, self-contradictory, conflicting, inconsistent, incongruous, anomalous, absurd, illogical, improbable, impossible, enigmatic, mysterious, puzzling, baffling, confounding, equivocal.

paragon *noun* model, pattern, paradigm, ideal, epitome, quintessence, exemplar, archetype, prototype, nonpareil, standard, norm, criterion, apotheosis, acme.

paragraph *noun* **1** (*several paragraphs in the report*) section, part, portion, segment, subdivision, subsection, clause, passage. **2** (*the story rated a paragraph in the national press*) article, piece, item, notice, note.

parallel *adj* **1** (*parallel lines*) equidistant, aligned, side by side, alongside, collateral, coextensive. **2** (*a parallel experience*) corresponding, similar, like, akin, matching, analogous, homologous, comparable, complementary, equivalent, uniform, resembling. OPPOSITE: divergent.
» *noun* **1** (*this is the parallel of that*) counterpart, equivalent, equal, match, twin, duplicate, correspondent, analogue. OPPOSITE: converse. **2** (*draw a parallel between the two*) analogy, correspondence, similarity, likeness, equivalence, correlation, resemblance, comparison, symmetry. OPPOSITE: difference.
» *verb* **1** (*his experiences parallel my own*) equal, match, echo, correspond with, correlate with, agree with, conform with, compare with, resemble, chime with. OPPOSITE: differ. **2** (*no one is likely to parallel the feat*) match, equal, rival, emulate, surpass.

paralyse *verb* **1** (*paralysed her left side*) deaden, dull, numb, anaesthetize, freeze, immobilize, incapacitate, disable, debilitate, cripple, lame. **2** (*paralyse the government*) immobilize, cripple, halt, stop, disable. **3** (*paralysed with fear*) transfix, freeze, shock, stun, terrify, petrify, stupefy, unnerve.

paralysis *noun* **1** (*treatment for paralysis*) paraplegia, quadriplegia, palsy, incapacity, immobility, numbness, deadness, powerlessness. **2** (*paralysis of the government*) immobilization, standstill, halt, stoppage, stopping, shutdown, breakdown, arrest, stagnation.

paralytic *adj* **1** (*his paralytic arm*) paralysed, crippled, disabled, incapacitated, lame, immobilized, immobile, numb, palsied, quadriplegic, powerless, dead. **2** (*we got paralytic last night*) drunk, inebriated, intoxicated, legless (*inf*), plastered (*inf*), smashed (*inf*), sloshed (*inf*), pissed (*sl*), canned (*inf*), stoned (*inf*), blitzed (*inf*), wasted (*inf*), wrecked (*inf*), blotto (*inf*), pie-eyed (*inf*), stewed (*inf*), steaming (*inf*), out of it (*inf*), tired and emotional (*inf*).

parameter *noun* limit, limitation, boundary, restriction, constant, specification, criterion, guideline, indication, variable, framework.

paramount *adj* pre-eminent, supreme, superior, chief, capital, cardinal, main, principal, leading, outstanding, highest, topmost, uppermost, dominant, predominant, prime, primary, first, foremost. OPPOSITE: minor.

paranoia *noun* mania, obsession, delusions, psychosis, persecution complex, megalomania, monomania.

paranoid *adj* distrustful, mistrustful, suspicious, insecure, fearful, afraid, bewildered, confused, fazed.

parapet *noun* **1** (*the parapet of the bridge*) wall, fence, rail, railing, handrail, barrier, paling. **2** (*fighting on the parapet*) breastwork, rampart, barricade, battlement, fortification, defence, bulwark, bastion, embankment, bank.

paraphernalia *noun* **1** (*all the paraphernalia of the expedition*) stuff, gear, equipment, tools, implements, materials, apparatus, tackle, impedimenta, accoutrements, accessories, appurtenances, trappings, appointments, clobber (*inf*), bits and pieces (*inf*), odds and ends (*inf*). **2** (*got all her paraphernalia on board*) baggage, luggage, belongings, possessions, effects, things.

paraphrase *verb* reword, rephrase, restate, rehash, explain, render, translate, interpret, gloss.
» *noun* rewording, rephrasing, restatement, restating, rehash, explanation, interpretation, gloss, translation, rendering, rendition, version.

parasite *noun* **1** (*a parasite on the skin*) leech, bloodsucker. **2** (*a social parasite*) hanger-on, leech, sponger (*inf*), scrounger (*inf*), sycophant, freeloader (*inf*), drone, bum (*inf*), cadger (*inf*), toady, passenger.

parcel *noun* **1** (*carried the parcel to the door*) package, bundle, pack, packet, box, carton. **2** (*a parcel of goodies*) lot, batch, bunch, pack, deal, group, mass, heap (*inf*), load (*inf*), collection, assortment. **3** (*a small parcel of land*) piece, part, portion, plot, tract, patch, lot, allotment, area.
» *verb* package, wrap, gift-wrap, pack, tie up, do up, bundle, box. OPPOSITE: undo.

parcel out divide up, share out, apportion, allot, allocate, carve up, split up, mete out, dole out, deal out, hand out, distribute, dispense. OPPOSITE: withhold.

parched *adj* **1** (*a parched landscape*) dry, dried up, dried out, arid, dehydrated, desiccated, waterless, torrid, scorched, baked, burned, roasted, seared, blistered, withered, shrivelled. OPPOSITE: flooded. **2** (*I feel parched*) thirsty, dehydrated, dry (*inf*), gasping (*inf*).

pardon *verb* **1** (*pardon my bad manners*) forgive, excuse, condone, overlook. OPPOSITE: punish. **2** (*he was pardoned for his crime*) let off, acquit, clear, exonerate, reprieve, discharge, release, liberate, free, remit, absolve, exculpate, vindicate.
» *noun* **1** (*beg the pardon of all present*) forgiveness, mercy, grace, forbearance, clemency, indulgence, leniency, lenience, condonation. **2** (*received a full pardon*) acquittal, exoneration, discharge, release, reprieve, amnesty, absolution, exculpation, remission. OPPOSITE: punishment.

pardonable *adj* forgivable, excusable, allowable, permissible, justifiable, condonable, warrantable, understandable, slight, minor, venial. OPPOSITE: unpardonable.

pare *verb* peel, skin, shave, shear, clip, trim, cut, crop, prune, whittle, lop, dock, reduce, decrease, diminish, lessen.

parent noun **1** (*signed by both parents*) father, mother, old man (*inf*), old woman (*inf*), old lady (*inf*), guardian, foster parent, dam, sire, begetter, progenitor, procreator. **2** (*believed to be the parent of the project*) source, root, origin, cause, wellspring, fountain, originator, creator, author, architect, prototype, forerunner, begetter.
➤ verb bring into the world, create, produce, beget, procreate, nurture, rear, bring up, raise, foster, look after, take care of, educate, teach, train.

parentage noun ancestry, lineage, descent, extraction, derivation, birth, origin, family, line, race, source, stock, pedigree, heritage, paternity, affiliation, filiation.

pariah noun outcast, black sheep (*inf*), leper, untouchable, exile, castaway, outlaw, undesirable, persona non grata.

parish noun **1** (*greeted with consternation throughout the parish*) district, community, commune, village, town, canton. **2** (*attended by the whole parish*) parishioners, churchgoers, church, congregation, flock, fold.

parity noun equality, par, equivalence, parallelism, evenness, consistency, uniformity, unity, conformity, identity, affinity, sameness, likeness, similarity, similitude, resemblance, semblance, correspondence, agreement, congruence, congruity, consonance, analogy. OPPOSITE: disparity.

park noun **1** (*a band played in the park*) public park, municipal park, pleasure garden, public garden, amusement park, recreation ground, playground, play area. **2** (*the house was surrounded by a large park*) grounds, estate, parkland, woodland, grassland, lawns. **3** (*the park filled with fans*) ball park, ground, stadium, arena, field.
➤ verb **1** (*park the car nearby*) pull up, stop, station, leave. **2** (*park those things over there*) put, place, deposit, plonk (*inf*), position, set, leave.

parlance noun idiom, vernacular, jargon, language, tongue, lingo (*inf*), speech, talk, argot, cant, patter, diction, vocabulary, phraseology.

parley verb talk, discuss, negotiate, confer, converse, consult, confabulate, powwow (*inf*), deliberate, speak, get together.
➤ noun talk, discussion, meeting, conference, colloquy, dialogue, conversation, confabulation, confab (*inf*), powwow, palaver, congress, deliberation, tête-à-tête, council, seminar, get-together.

parliament noun legislature, assembly, council, congress, senate, house, chamber, diet, convocation.

parliamentary adj legislative, legislatorial, lawmaking, lawgiving, governmental, congressional, senatorial, democratic, representative, elected, popular, deliberative.

parlour noun **1** (*their guests took tea in the parlour*) front room, living-room, sitting-room, lounge, drawing-room. **2** (*a funeral parlour*) establishment, salon, shop, store.

parochial adj provincial, small-town, parish-pump, hick (*inf*), insular, small-minded, blinkered, narrow, narrow-minded, inward-looking, confined, restricted, limited, illiberal, petty.

parody noun **1** (*a humorous parody*) burlesque, lampoon, caricature, satire, spoof (*inf*), skit, send-up (*inf*), takeoff (*inf*), pastiche, mockery, mimicry. **2** (*a parody of fair play*) travesty, perversion, distortion, corruption, poor imitation, misrepresentation, apology.
➤ verb burlesque, lampoon, caricature, satirize, spoof (*inf*), send up (*inf*), take off (*inf*), ape, mock, mimic, imitate.

paroxysm noun fit, seizure, attack, spasm, convulsion, outburst, outbreak, eruption, flare-up, explosion.

parrot verb copy, repeat, imitate, mimic, ape, echo, rehearse, reiterate, take off.
➤ noun mimic, imitator, copycat, repeater, ape.

parry verb deflect, ward off, fend off, stave off, repulse, repel, rebuff, field, avert, block, avoid, evade, duck (*inf*), dodge (*inf*), steer clear of, sidestep, elude, turn aside, circumvent, keep at bay, ward off, shun.

parsimonious adj mean, stingy (*inf*), miserly, mingy (*inf*), penny-pinching (*inf*), money-grubbing, niggardly, close, closefisted, close-handed, tight (*inf*), tightfisted, tight-arsed (*sl*), ungenerous, grasping, frugal, sparing, stinting, scrimping, penurious, saving, near, cheeseparing, miserable. OPPOSITE: generous.

parsimony noun meanness, miserliness, stinginess (*inf*), tightness (*inf*), minginess (*inf*), frugality, tightfistedness, closeness, niggardliness, penny-pinching (*inf*).

parson noun clergyman, cleric, churchman, ecclesiastic, priest, minister, chaplain, rector, vicar, pastor, preacher, reverend (*inf*), man of the cloth, man of God, divine. OPPOSITE: layperson.

part noun **1** (*a small part of the cake*) piece, portion, share, section, division, proportion, percentage, segment, slice, fraction, fragment, bit, particle, scrap, chunk, wedge. **2** (*broken down into its separate parts*) ingredient, constituent, element, component, bit, factor, aspect, facet, dimension, module, unit. OPPOSITE: whole. **3** (*pain in various parts of her body*) limb, organ, member, wing, branch, department, sector. **4** (*travelled in remote parts*) region, area, territory, quarter, sector, neighbourhood, vicinity, section. **5** (*a series in five parts*) episode, chapter, instalment, section, volume, book, passage, scene, act. **6** (*he was quizzed about his part in the crime*) role, function, contribution, involvement, participation, interest, responsibility, task, duty, charge, job, work, office, place. **7** (*a man of many parts*) gift, talent, ability, skill, attribute, capability, capacity, accomplishment, faculty, endowment. **8** (*given the part of the hero*) role, character. **9** (*he promises to learn his part*) lines, script, words.
➤ verb **1** (*the clouds will part*) divide, separate, split, break, break up, sever, tear, disunite, come apart, disjoin, disconnect, detach, cleave, rend. OPPOSITE: join. **2** (*the time has come to part*) go, get going, depart, quit, leave, withdraw, retire, separate, say goodbye, take one's leave, head for home, split (*inf*), push off (*inf*), make tracks (*inf*), scarper (*inf*), clear off (*inf*), hit the road (*inf*), take off (*inf*). **3** (*I understand they parted years ago*) divorce, separate, break up, split up, part company.
➤ adj partial, half, unfinished, limited, restricted, imperfect, fragmentary.

for the most part on the whole, by and large, all in all, in the main, mainly, chiefly, principally, generally, usually, commonly, largely, mostly, to all intents and purposes.

in part partly, partially, up to a point, to some extent, to a certain extent, to some degree, to a certain degree, somewhat, moderately, slightly. OPPOSITE: entirely.

part with relinquish, give up, renounce, forgo, let go of, abandon, discard, jettison, sacrifice, surrender, yield, cede. OPPOSITE: retain.

take part in join in, participate in, engage in, play a part in, play a role in, share in, contribute to, associate oneself with, assist in, help with, have a hand in, partake in.

partake *verb* take part, participate, share, join, be involved, play a part, engage, enter, contribute.

partake of 1 (*partake of some refreshment*) eat, consume, drink, take, receive, share, have. **2** (*his actions partook of a generous character*) suggest, hint at, demonstrate, show, exhibit, evoke, evidence, evince, manifest.

partial *adj* **1** (*met with partial success*) incomplete, uncompleted, fragmentary, unfinished, imperfect, restricted, limited, part, in part. OPPOSITE: total. **2** (*the judge was partial*) biased, prejudiced, partisan, one-sided, unfair, unjust, discriminatory, coloured, preferential, predisposed, inequitable, affected, influenced, interested. OPPOSITE: impartial.

partial to liking, fond of, keen on, mad about (*inf*), crazy about (*inf*), loving, caring for, taken with. OPPOSITE: disliking.

partiality *noun* **1** (*a victim of the court's partiality*) bias, prejudice, partisanship, favouritism, preference, discrimination, unfairness, injustice, unjustness, inequity, inequitableness. **2** (*a partiality for cheese*) liking, fondness, love, inclination, penchant, preference, soft spot, affinity, predilection, predisposition, keenness, taste, weakness, proclivity.

partially *adv* incompletely, partly, in part, piecemeal, halfway, somewhat, to a certain degree, to some extent, in some measure, not fully, not wholly, moderately, slightly, fractionally.

participant *noun* entrant, competitor, contestant, contributor, participator, partaker, sharer, associate, partner, cooperator, helper, party, member.

participate *verb* share, partake, take part, play a part, play a role, be a party, join, engage, be involved, be associated, assist, help, enter, get in on, contribute, cooperate, have a hand.

participation *noun* part, involvement, sharing, taking part, partaking, partnership, cooperation, contribution, assistance, association.

particle *noun* **1** (*particles of dirt*) grain, speck, atom, molecule, bit, piece. **2** (*not a particle of evidence*) iota, whit, jot, atom, mite, morsel, tittle, hint, trace, touch, bit, scrap, shred, fragment, sliver, grain, crumb, drop, suggestion.

particular *adj* **1** (*this particular incident*) specific, precise, exact, certain, distinct, peculiar, separate, individual, single. OPPOSITE: general. **2** (*pay particular attention*) special, especial, close, express. **3** (*I remember one particular event*) notable, noteworthy, remarkable, marked, especial, exceptional, outstanding, singular,

peculiar, unusual, uncommon. OPPOSITE: ordinary. **4** (*she is a very particular woman*) fussy, finicky, fastidious, dainty, choosy (*inf*), picky (*inf*), pernickety (*inf*), discriminating, selective, critical, difficult, exacting, nice. **5** (*he made a particular record of the process*) careful, meticulous, exact, close, painstaking, thorough, precise, detailed, itemized, circumstantial, blow-by-blow, accurate, minute, punctilious, strict, faithful.
≫ *noun* particularity, detail, circumstance, specific, point, feature, item, fact.

in particular 1 (*I have one place in particular in mind*) specific, special, distinct. **2** (*this case in particular*) particularly, especially, specifically, to be specific, exactly, precisely, expressly, distinctly, in detail. OPPOSITE: generally.

particularize *verb* specify, stipulate, spell out, detail, itemize, individualize, enumerate, list, cite. OPPOSITE: generalize.

particularly *adv* **1** (*not particularly impressed*) especially, specially, exceptionally, unusually, uncommonly, singularly, distinctly, markedly, decidedly, notably, extraordinarily, remarkably, outstandingly, peculiarly, surprisingly. **2** (*particularly wanted to succeed*) in particular, expressly, specially, especially, specifically, explicitly, distinctly.

parting *noun* **1** (*felt sadness at their parting*) farewell, goodbye, adieu, valediction, leave-taking, departure, going, leaving, separation. **2** (*a parting in the clouds*) division, dividing, separation, separating, partition, cleavage, rift, split, splitting, break, breaking, rupture, severance, disunion, disjoining, detachment. OPPOSITE: union.
≫ *adj* farewell, goodbye, valedictory, departing, leaving, dying, closing, concluding, final, last. OPPOSITE: opening.

partisan *noun* **1** (*a socialist partisan*) adherent, follower, disciple, champion, supporter, backer, fan, upholder, enthusiast, stalwart, devotee, votary. **2** (*captured by partisans*) guerrilla, irregular, freedom fighter, resistance fighter, underground fighter.
≫ *adj* biased, prejudiced, coloured, partial, predisposed, interested, preferential, discriminatory, unfair, unjust, inequitable, one-sided, factional, sectarian. OPPOSITE: neutral.

partition *noun* **1** (*the partition of the nation*) division, dividing, subdivision, separation, segregation, parting, splitting-up, breaking-up, break-up, severance. OPPOSITE: union. **2** (*a partition divided the space into two rooms*) screen, barrier, wall, fence, panel, divider, separator.
≫ *verb* **1** (*planned to partition the country*) divide, divide up, separate, segregate, split, split up, break up, sever. **2** (*partition the space to make two rooms*) divide, divide up, subdivide, separate, screen off, wall off, fence off.

partly *adv* in part, partially, incompletely, half, halfway, not wholly, not fully, somewhat, up to a point, in some measure, to some extent, to a certain extent, to some degree, to a certain degree, a little, slightly, fractionally, moderately, relatively. OPPOSITE: wholly.

partner *noun* **1** (*his partner in the enterprise*) companion, comrade, ally, colleague, associate, copartner, cooperator, co-worker, confederate, collaborator, accomplice, helper, mate, teammate, accessory, sidekick (*inf*). OPPOSITE: rival. **2** (*accompanied by her partner*) spouse, husband, wife, other half (*inf*), significant other (*inf*), companion, consort, boyfriend, girlfriend, friend.

partnership *noun* **1** (*partnership between the government and the people*) association, collaboration, collusion, cooperation, sharing, participation, companionship, confederation, fellowship, fraternity, brotherhood, sisterhood, sorority, affiliation, combination, union, alliance. **2** (*form a business partnership*) company, firm, corporation, association, cooperative, combine, house, conglomerate, syndicate, society.

parturition *noun* childbirth, confinement, accouchement, labour, delivery.

party *noun* **1** (*held a wild party*) social, knees-up (*inf*), rave-up (*inf*), rave (*inf*), bash (*inf*), do (*inf*), shindig (*inf*), thrash (*inf*), celebration, festivity, function, gathering, get-together (*inf*), orgy, bacchanal, soirée, reception, at-home, reunion. **2** (*a party of workers*) group, band, gang, team, bunch (*inf*), crew, squad, troop, unit, body, company, contingent, detachment. **3** (*the fascist party*) faction, side, grouping, coterie, camp, set, clique, circle, ring, league, confederacy, alliance, association, affiliation, coalition, combination, caucus, cabal. **4** (*I could mention a certain party*) person, individual, character, someone, somebody. **5** (*a party to the suit*) participant, litigant, plaintiff, defendant.

pass[1] *verb* **1** (*pass through the exit*) go, move, proceed, progress, travel, roll, flow, course, run, drive, make one's way. OPPOSITE: stop. **2** (*pass over the bridge*) cross, go over, get over, get across, traverse, go through. **3** (*pass every car on the road*) go by, go past, drive past, overtake, overhaul, outdistance, outstrip, beat, lap, leave behind, pull ahead of. **4** (*pass the ball*) hand over, give, transfer, transmit, throw, kick. **5** (*the property will pass to the next in line*) go, devolve, transfer. **6** (*a nice way to pass the time*) spend, fill, occupy, employ, while away, take up, use up, devote. **7** (*the years pass quickly*) go by, go past, proceed, elapse, flow by, progress, advance, roll by, slip by, slip away, glide by, drag. **8** (*pass all previous attempts*) surpass, exceed, transcend, go beyond, outdo, outstrip. **9** (*pass the news to the office*) transmit, circulate, spread, transfer, exchange, convey. OPPOSITE: withhold. **10** (*I think I'll pass on that*) pass by, pass over, skip, leave, ignore, disregard, omit, overlook, miss, neglect. OPPOSITE: note. **11** (*first she must pass the exam*) succeed, get through, qualify, graduate, come up to scratch (*inf*), do, answer. OPPOSITE: fail. **12** (*the authorities passed his proposal*) approve, accept, let through. **13** (*pass a motion*) enact, legislate, sanction, approve, authorize, ratify, sanction, validate, vote for, accept, agree to, adopt, ordain, decree. OPPOSITE: reject. **14** (*the court passed judgment*) pronounce, utter, deliver, declare, express. **15** (*it came to pass*) happen, occur, come about, take place, arise, befall, transpire. **16** (*the crisis will pass*) depart, leave, go, end, finish, terminate, cease, die, pass on, pass away, fade, vanish, disappear, evaporate, blow over, dwindle, ebb, wane, melt away. OPPOSITE: remain. **17** (*pass from vapour to fluid*) change, become, develop, transfer, evolve, go, move, turn. **18** (*pass urine*) discharge, eliminate, void, evacuate, excrete, expel, emit, let out, release.

➤ *noun* **1** (*let me see your pass*) passport, visa, ticket, licence, warrant, permit, authorization, permission, identification, documents, papers, safe conduct. **2** (*he made a pass at her*) advance, approach, overture, play, suggestion, proposition. **3** (*made a pass at the ball*) move, thrust, push, lunge, swing, jab, kick. **4** (*she was awarded a pass in her exam*) success, victory. **5** (*a pretty pass*) plight, predicament, situation, condition, state of affairs, result, pickle (*inf*).

pass away pass on, die, decease, expire, kick the bucket (*inf*), give up the ghost (*inf*), pop off (*inf*), peg out (*inf*), croak (*inf*), snuff it (*inf*).

pass for be taken for, be mistaken for, be regarded as, appear to be.

pass off 1 (*everything passed off very well*) turn out, go off, happen, occur, take place. **2** (*the feeling passed off by the morning*) pass, fade, fade away, wear off, die down, ebb, disappear, vanish. **3** (*trying to pass it off as genuine*) palm off, feign, counterfeit, fake.

pass out 1 (*she passed out on the floor*) faint, collapse, swoon, black out, flake out (*inf*), keel over (*inf*), drop, lose consciousness. **2** (*pass out the goodies*) give out, hand out, share out, deal out, dole out, distribute, allocate, allot.

pass over 1 (*pass over his recent history*) ignore, gloss over, disregard, overlook, forget. **2** (*passed over for promotion*) overlook, disregard, ignore, omit, forget, neglect, miss.

pass up ignore, forgo, brush aside, miss, refuse, neglect, reject, decline, let slip, waive, abstain.

pass[2] *noun* (*a mountain pass*) gorge, ravine, canyon, defile, col, way, gap, passage.

passable *adj* **1** (*a passable effort*) fair, middling, all right, OK (*inf*), so-so (*inf*), acceptable, satisfactory, adequate, tolerable, admissible, allowable, ordinary, average, unexceptional, mediocre, indifferent, run-of-the-mill (*inf*), so-so (*inf*), moderate. OPPOSITE: excellent. **2** (*a passable route*) clear, unobstructed, unblocked, open, crossable, traversable, navigable. OPPOSITE: impassable.

passage *noun* **1** (*a passage through the trees*) route, course, path, track, trail, road, lane, alley, way, pass, thoroughfare, channel, avenue, conduit. **2** (*several rooms opened off the passage*) passageway, corridor, hall, hallway, entrance hall, lobby, vestibule, aisle. **3** (*sought passage to the kingdom*) access, admission, entry, safe conduct. **4** (*read the passage aloud*) section, piece, excerpt, extract, clause, paragraph, verse, quotation, citation, text. **5** (*a safe passage*) journey, voyage, trip, crossing, tour, trek. **6** (*looked for a passage to the sea*) waterway, strait, sound, neck. **7** (*to allow the passage of large crowds*) passing, course, flow, movement, progression, motion, progress, transit, advance. OPPOSITE: halt. **8** (*the story of his passage to manhood*) transition, transformation, change, metamorphosis, conversion, mutation, shift, switch, development, advance, progress, transfer, journey. **9** (*the smooth passage of the bill*) enactment, legislation, legalization, sanction, approval, acceptance, adoption, authorization, ratification, validation. OPPOSITE: rejection.

passé *adj* outdated, out-of-date, dated, outmoded, old-fashioned, unfashionable, obsolete, obsolescent, antiquated, archaic, old hat (*inf*), out (*inf*), outworn, square (*inf*), fuddy-duddy (*inf*).

passenger *noun* **1** (*the passengers in the train*) fare, fare-payer, rider, traveller, voyager, commuter, tourist. **2** (*too many passengers on this committee*) drone, parasite, freeloader (*inf*), sponger (*inf*), hanger-on, idler, bum (*inf*).

passer-by *noun* bystander, onlooker, looker-on, observer, spectator, witness, eyewitness, gawper (*inf*), rubberneck (*inf*).

passing *adj* **1** (*a passing fad for tall hats*) short-lived, temporary, transitory, transient, transitional, fleeting, momentary, ephemeral, brief, short. **2** (*gave it a passing look*) brief, hasty, hurried, quick, cursory, incidental, superficial, slight, casual, shallow.
➤ *noun* **1** (*the passing of the years*) passage, flow, course, progress, process, advance. **2** (*the passing of the bill*) enactment, acceptance, approval, adoption. **3** (*few mourned his passing*) death, demise, loss, perishing, passing away, expiration, expiry, decease, departure, end, finish, termination, disappearance.
in passing by the way, by the by (*inf*), en passant, incidentally, parenthetically.

passion *noun* **1** (*the passion of the crowd reached a height*) emotion, feeling, ardour, fervour, zeal, zest, enthusiasm, eagerness, excitement, animation, heat, warmth, fire, intensity, vehemence, spirit, rapture, joy, transport. OPPOSITE: apathy. **2** (*his passion for her knew no bounds*) desire, craving, lust, love, affection, attachment, fondness, adoration, ardour, infatuation. OPPOSITE: loathing. **3** (*at this he flew into a passion*) rage, fury, anger, resentment, wrath, indignation, ire, frenzy, temper, fit, paroxysm, tantrum, storm, outburst, explosion. OPPOSITE: composure. **4** (*model motor cars are his latest passion*) enthusiasm, infatuation, craze, mania, obsession, fixation, fascination, interest, fancy.

passionate *adj* **1** (*a passionate love of music*) vehement, impassioned, excited, animated, ardent, fervent, fervid, fanatical, warm, heartfelt, zealous, enthusiastic, eager, keen, avid, fierce, intense, strong. OPPOSITE: apathetic.
2 (*a passionate embrace*) loving, affectionate, amorous, ardent, aroused, lustful, desirous, erotic, sensual, sexy (*inf*), steamy (*inf*), sultry. OPPOSITE: frigid. **3** (*a passionate temper*) hot, fiery, inflamed, excitable, emotional, intense, temperamental, impulsive, impetuous, hotheaded, irritable, quick-tempered, peppery, stormy, tempestuous, violent, wild, frenzied, furious, irate, enraged, incensed. OPPOSITE: calm.

passionless *adj* **1** (*a passionless character*) cold, cold-blooded, coldhearted, frosty, icy, calm, emotionless, unemotional, frigid, passive, callous, indifferent, unfeeling, uncaring, unloving, unresponsive, undemonstrative, impassive, apathetic, withdrawn, restrained, unapproachable, aloof, detached, distant, dispassionate, insensible, remote, impartial, neutral. OPPOSITE: warm. **2** (*a passionless relationship*) emotionless, unemotional, spiritless, zestless, lifeless, flat, insipid, lacklustre, colourless, neutral, anaemic, vapid. OPPOSITE: intense.

passive *adj* **1** (*remained passive through it all*) submissive, unresisting, acquiescent, compliant, yielding, receptive, quiescent, unassertive, docile, patient, resigned, long-suffering, enduring. **2** (*looked at her with a passive expression*) impassive, unemotional, emotionless, unmoved, apathetic, dispassionate, undemonstrative, lifeless, indifferent, inert, still, detached, distant, remote, aloof. OPPOSITE: emotional. **3** (*played a passive role in proceedings*) inactive, inert, uninvolved, non-participating. OPPOSITE: active.

passport *noun* **1** (*holder of a current passport*) travel document, travel papers, travel permit, visa, pass, laissez-passer, identity card, ID. **2** (*the passport to a career in advertising*) key, entry, access, admission, admittance, door, doorway, avenue, path, way, route.

password *noun* watchword, signal, key word, word, open sesame, countersign, shibboleth.

past *adj* **1** (*the lesson of past challenges*) over, finished, ended, completed, done, accomplished. OPPOSITE: ahead. **2** (*in past times*) ancient, bygone, old, olden, former, erstwhile, previous, prior, foregoing, foregone, sometime, obsolete, early, gone, spent, extinct, elapsed, forgotten. OPPOSITE: future. **3** (*the past few days*) recent, preceding, late, latter, last.
➤ *noun* **1** (*a journey into the past*) history, antiquity, long ago, olden days, olden times, former times, yesteryear, yesterday, days gone by, days of yore, good old days. OPPOSITE: future. **2** (*a murky past*) life, background, record, history, track record, experience, youth, memories.
➤ *adv* by, on, beyond, over, across, ago.
➤ *prep* beyond, over, above, after, outside.

paste *noun* **1** (*stick with paste*) adhesive, glue, gum, cement, mucilage. **2** (*mixed to a paste*) pulp, mush, pap, blend, mixture, compound. **3** (*tomato paste*) puree, spread, pâté.
➤ *verb* stick, glue, gum, cement, fix, fasten.

pastel *adj* pale, soft, soft-hued, delicate, light, light-coloured, subtle, discreet, muted, subdued, faint, low-key.

pastiche *noun* assortment, collection, medley, variety, miscellany, blend, mix, mixture, mixed bag (*inf*), potpourri, mélange, mosaic, patchwork, conglomeration, hotchpotch, hodgepodge, confusion, jumble, farrago, mishmash (*inf*), gallimaufry, smorgasbord.

pastille *noun* lozenge, sweet, gumdrop, cough sweet, cough drop, drop, gum, tablet, pill, troche.

pastime *noun* hobby, recreation, activity, leisure activity, sport, game, entertainment, diversion, amusement, distraction, relaxation, play, fun. OPPOSITE: work.

pastor *noun* clergyman, clergywoman, member of the clergy, cleric, churchman, churchwoman, ecclesiastic, priest, minister, rector, parson, vicar, preacher, reverend (*inf*), canon, divine. OPPOSITE: layperson.

pastoral *adj* **1** (*a peaceful pastoral scene*) rural, rustic, country, agricultural, agrarian, simple, bucolic, idyllic, Arcadian. **2** (*neglected his pastoral duties*) clerical, ecclesiastical, ministerial, priestly.

pasture *noun* grazing, grassland, meadow, field, grass, paddock, pasturage, herbage.

pasty *adj* pasty-faced, pale, pallid, sallow, wan, whey-faced, anaemic, sickly, unhealthy.

pat *verb* tap, dab, hit, slap, clap, rap, stroke, pet, caress, touch, fondle.
> *noun* tap, dab, slap, clap, rap, touch, stroke, pet, caress.
> *adj* smooth, slick, glib, fluent, ready, automatic, easy, facile, simplistic.
> *adv* perfectly, faultlessly, flawlessly, fluently, exactly, precisely.
pat on the back congratulate, praise, compliment, commend, applaud, take one's hat off to (*inf*).

patch *noun* **1** (*a patch of material*) piece, scrap, bit, shred. **2** (*an eye patch*) cover, covering, pad, shield, protection, cloth. **3** (*a patch of land*) area, parcel, spot, tract, lot, plot, bed. **4** (*go through a bad patch*) phase, time, period, stretch, term, spell, interval.
> *verb* mend, repair, fix, reinforce, cover.

patchwork *noun* medley, jumble, blend, mixture, mishmash (*inf*), potpourri, mélange, miscellany, confusion, hash, hotchpotch, hodgepodge, pastiche, farrago, gallimaufry.

patchy *adj* sketchy, bitty, uneven, irregular, inconsistent, random, fitful, erratic, varying, variable.

patent *adj* obvious, plain, clear, manifest, evident, apparent, palpable, open, overt, unconcealed, undisguised, unmistakable, indisputable, unequivocal, manifest, conspicuous, blatant, flagrant, glaring, transparent, visible, downright. OPPOSITE: hidden.
> *noun* copyright, registered trademark, right, privilege, licence, certificate, grant, invention.

paternal *adj* fatherly, fatherlike, patriarchal, protective, solicitous, kindly, benevolent, concerned, vigilant.

path *noun* **1** (*a path through the woods*) footpath, pathway, footway, bridleway, walk, track, trail, towpath. **2** (*the path of the comet*) trajectory, track, course, orbit, circuit, route. **3** (*the path to success*) way, road, route, course, avenue. **4** (*it all depends on the path we adopt*) route, direction, approach, method, procedure, system, strategy.

pathetic *adj* **1** (*the old people were in a pathetic condition*) moving, touching, affecting, poignant, plaintive, piteous, pitiful, pitiable, poor, sorry, sad, dismal, miserable, distressing, harrowing, heartrending, heartbreaking, lamentable, mournful, woeful, wretched, tender, emotional. **2** (*I call that a pathetic apology*) feeble, contemptible, deplorable, derisory, miserable, worthless, useless, petty, puny, paltry, meagre, poor, measly, sorry, inadequate, unsatisfactory, pitiful, lamentable.

pathological *adj* irrational, compulsive, habitual, confirmed, chronic, inveterate, persistent, hardened, obsessive, addicted, dependent, unreasonable, illogical.

pathos *noun* poignancy, plaintiveness, pitifulness, pitiableness, piteousness, misery, sadness.

patience *noun* **1** (*this task will need a lot of patience*) tolerance, forbearance, calmness, cool (*inf*), composure, equilibrium, serenity, tranquillity, equanimity, even temper, imperturbability, unflappability (*inf*), self-control, self-possession, restraint, self-restraint, resignation, leniency. **2** (*endured the pain with great patience*) endurance, sufferance, stoicism, resignation, submission, perseverance, persistence, diligence, doggedness, tenacity, assiduity, constancy, fortitude, indefatigability. OPPOSITE: impatience.

patient *adj* **1** (*she was very patient with their questions*) tolerant, forbearing, clement, forgiving, lenient, indulgent, mild, understanding, accommodating, calm, composed, cool (*inf*), serene, quiet, tranquil, even-tempered, imperturbable, inexcitable, unflappable (*inf*), self-possessed, self-controlled, restrained. **2** (*remained patient during her long illness*) enduring, long-suffering, uncomplaining, stoical, philosophical, resigned, submissive, passive, persevering, persistent. OPPOSITE: impatient.
> *noun* invalid, sufferer, case, inmate, client.

patois *noun* dialect, vernacular, argot, cant, local parlance, local speech, lingua franca, lingo (*inf*), jargon, patter, slang.

patrician *noun* aristocrat, aristo (*inf*), noble, nobleman, lord, peer, gentleman, grandee, nob (*inf*). OPPOSITE: commoner.
> *adj* aristocratic, noble, lordly, high-born, well-born, high-class, blue-blooded, gentle. OPPOSITE: plebeian.

patrimony *noun* heritage, birthright, inheritance, legacy, bequest, portion, share, estate, property, revenue, possessions.

patriot *noun* nationalist, loyalist, flag-waver, jingoist, chauvinist.

patriotic *adj* nationalistic, nationalist, loyalist, loyal, flag-waving, jingoistic, chauvinistic.

patrol *verb* guard, keep guard, protect, defend, safeguard, police, keep watch, inspect, monitor, go the rounds, pound the beat, cruise.
> *noun* **1** (*out on patrol*) watch, guard, sentry duty, vigil, vigilance, surveillance, patrolling, policing, protection, defence, round, beat. **2** (*here comes the patrol*) guard, patrolman, patrolwoman, sentry, sentinel, garrison, watch, watchman, nightwatchman, security guard, police officer.

patron *noun* **1** (*the patrons of the hospital*) sponsor, promoter, backer, supporter, upholder, champion, sympathizer, advocate, benefactor, benefactress, philanthropist, guardian, guardian angel, angel (*inf*), fairy godmother (*inf*), protector, defender, helper, friend. **2** (*a regular patron of this establishment*) customer, client, regular (*inf*), frequenter, habitué, buyer, shopper, purchaser, subscriber.

patronage *noun* **1** (*could not survive without their patronage*) sponsorship, backing, funding, financing, promotion, championship, help, aid, assistance, encouragement, support, protection, benefaction. **2** (*I have considered removing my patronage from your shop*) trade, custom, business, commerce, buying, purchasing, shopping, subscription.

patronize *verb* **1** (*he has been known to patronize this bar*) frequent, shop at, buy from, deal with, trade with. **2** (*patronize various worthy causes*) sponsor, promote, champion, fund, finance, back, support, subscribe to, foster, maintain, help, assist, aid, befriend, encourage, protect. **3** (*don't patronize me*) condescend to, stoop, talk down to, look down on, despise, scorn, disparage, contemn, disdain. OPPOSITE: respect.

patronizing *adj* condescending, supercilious, superior, haughty, lofty, lordly, disdainful, scornful, contemptuous, stooping, snobbish, snooty (*inf*), stuck up (*inf*), high-and-mighty (*inf*), toffee-nosed (*inf*), hoity-toity (*inf*), uppity (*inf*).

patter[1] *verb* **1** (*raindrops pattered on his hat*) tap, pat, spatter, pitter-patter, pit-a-pat, rat-a-tat, drum, pound, beat, pelt. **2** (*a beetle pattering across the paper*) scuttle, scurry, trip, skip, tiptoe.
> *noun* pattering, tapping, drumming, pitter-patter, beating, pounding, pelting, rat-a-tat, pit-a-pat.

patter[2] *noun* (*sales patter*) chatter, gabble, jabber, nattering, prattle, line, pitch, spiel (*inf*), yak (*inf*), jargon, lingo (*inf*), harangue, monologue.

pattern *noun* **1** (*an intricate pattern*) design, style, motif, figure, device, decoration, ornamentation, ornament, marking. **2** (*patterns of work*) method, system, plan, arrangement, order, sequence. **3** (*a pattern of good behaviour*) model, exemplar, ideal, paragon, paradigm, par, criterion, standard, yardstick, norm, gauge, touchstone, benchmark, archetype, prototype, mould. **4** (*a knitting pattern*) model, stencil, template, guide, plan, diagram, blueprint, design, instruction, sample, swatch, specimen, original. OPPOSITE: copy.
> *verb* model, style, mould, shape, order, form, follow, imitate, match, stencil, emulate, copy.

patterned *adj* decorated, ornamented, figured, printed.

paucity *noun* dearth, lack, want, scarcity, scantiness, sparseness, sparsity, meagreness, paltriness, slenderness, slightness, smallness, fewness, rarity, shortage, deficiency, inadequacy, insufficiency, poverty. OPPOSITE: abundance.

paunch *noun* belly, pot, potbelly, beer belly (*inf*), beer gut, spare tyre (*inf*), stomach, abdomen.

pauper *noun* beggar, down-and-out, have-not, poor person, bankrupt, insolvent, indigent, mendicant.

pause *verb* stop, halt, cease, desist, break off, take a break, rest, take a rest, take a breather (*inf*), take five (*inf*), interrupt, discontinue, let up (*inf*), wait, delay, hold back, hesitate, waver, deliberate, adjourn. OPPOSITE: proceed.
> *noun* stop, stoppage, halt, cessation, suspension, discontinuation, break, rest, breather (*inf*), breathing space (*inf*), let-up (*inf*), lull, stay, respite, time out (*inf*), gap, interval, intermission, interlude, interruption, wait, delay, hesitation. OPPOSITE: continuance.

pave *verb* flag, cobble, tile, floor, concrete, asphalt, tar, tarmac, macadamize, surface, cover.

pave the way for prepare for, get ready for, make provision for, lead up to, introduce, take steps, take measures, clear the ground for, clear the way for, smooth the way for, lay the groundwork for, lay the foundations for, do the spadework for, set the scene for, facilitate, soften up. OPPOSITE: impede.

pavement *noun* footpath, path, footway, way, pedestrian walk, walkway, sidewalk, floor, bed, causeway.

paw *noun* foot, pad, forepaw, hind paw, hand.
> *verb* maul, touch, stroke, grab, manhandle, mishandle, molest, touch up (*inf*), goose (*inf*).

pawn[1] *verb* (*pawned his watch*) deposit, pledge, hock (*inf*), stake, wager, hazard, mortgage. OPPOSITE: redeem.

> *noun* deposit, pledge, security, collateral, surety, bond, gage, earnest, assurance, guarantee.

pawn[2] *noun* (*mere pawns in the hands of the dictator*) instrument, tool, stooge (*inf*), dupe, puppet, creature, toy, plaything, cat's-paw (*inf*).

pay *verb* **1** (*pay them for the work*) remunerate, reimburse, reward, refund, compensate, recompense, requite, indemnify. **2** (*pay her debt*) repay, pay back, pay off, pay in full, defray, settle, clear, discharge, liquidate, meet, satisfy, square, honour. OPPOSITE: owe. **3** (*pay huge amounts for the privilege*) spend, expend, disburse, pay out, lay out, outlay, fork out (*inf*), dish out (*inf*), shell out (*inf*), cough up (*inf*), stump up (*inf*), part with, hand over, render, remit, meet the cost of, foot the bill (*inf*), pick up the tab (*inf*), invest. **4** (*crime does not pay*) benefit, profit, yield profit, make a return, make money. **5** (*it might pay you to be careful*) repay, pay off, benefit, profit. **6** (*pay her a compliment*) give, offer, proffer, afford, bestow, render. OPPOSITE: withhold. **7** (*I fear he will pay for what he has done*) suffer, answer, atone, make amends.
> *noun* salary, wages, remuneration, reimbursement, earnings, payment, income, hire, fee, commission, stipend, honorarium, emoluments, reward, compensation, recompense.

pay back **1** (*pay back what he owed*) repay, pay off, give back, return, refund, recompense, settle, square, reimburse. **2** (*I intend to pay him back for that trick*) repay, punish, avenge oneself on, take revenge on, get one's own back, reciprocate, retaliate, hit back, get even with.

pay for **1** (*pay for the tickets*) foot the bill for, cough up for (*inf*), fork out for (*inf*), shell out for (*inf*), settle up for, defray the cost of. **2** (*pay for past crimes*) answer for, suffer for, atone for, pay the price for, make amends for, face the music (*inf*), compensate, cost dearly.

pay off **1** (*pay off what she owes*) pay, pay in full, discharge, settle, clear, meet, square, honour, liquidate. **2** (*pay off the staff at the end of the month*) dismiss, discharge, lay off, let go, make redundant, sack (*inf*), fire (*inf*). **3** (*all that planning paid off*) succeed, be successful, meet with success, be effective, work, get results, pay dividends.

pay out pay, spend, expend, lay out, dish out (*inf*), fork out (*inf*), cough up (*inf*), shell out (*inf*), part with, hand over, remit.

payable *adj* owed, owing, due, outstanding, unpaid, in arrears.

payment *noun* **1** (*payment of the bill*) settlement, discharge, liquidation, defrayal, clearance, squaring, remittance. **2** (*several easy payments*) instalment, amount, contribution, donation, advance, premium. **2** (*he will expect payment for the job*) recompense, compensation, reward, remuneration, fee, hire, fare, earnings, pay, salary, wages.

peace *noun* **1** (*peace between the two sides*) peacefulness, peaceableness, concord, harmony, harmoniousness, friendship, cordiality, amity, amicableness, goodwill, accord, agreement, pacification, conciliation, truce, ceasefire, armistice, nonaggression, nonviolence. OPPOSITE: war. **2** (*the peace of the mountains*) calm, calmness, tranquillity, serenity, restfulness, repose, quiet, quietness, silence, hush, still, stillness, peacefulness. OPPOSITE: disturbance. **3** (*a sense of peace crept over her*) contentment, peacefulness, calm, calmness, placidity, composure, repose, relaxation, rest, restfulness, serenity.

peaceable *adj* **1** (*have a peaceable nature*) pacific, pacifist, peaceloving, unwarlike, nonviolent, nonaggressive, nonbelligerent, noncombative, mild, easygoing, gentle, amiable, amicable, friendly, good-natured, peaceful, peacemaking, placid, even-tempered, irenic, dovish, conciliatory, placatory, inoffensive. OPPOSITE: warlike. **2** (*peaceable surroundings*) peaceful, quiet, restful, serene, tranquil, undisturbed, restful, balmy, harmonious, amicable, amiable, cordial, friendly, strife-free.

peaceful *adj* **1** (*a peaceful scene*) calm, tranquil, serene, quiet, still, restful, relaxing, placid, sleepy, reposeful, unruffled, undisturbed, untroubled. OPPOSITE: agitated. **2** (*peaceful relations*) peaceable, at peace, pacific, friendly, cordial, harmonious, on good terms, amicable, nonviolent, strife-free, peaceloving, peacemaking, irenic. OPPOSITE: belligerent.

peacemaker *noun* pacifist, pacifier, peacemonger, appeaser, conciliator, mediator, arbitrator, intercessor.

peak *noun* **1** (*the peak of the mountain*) top, summit, pinnacle, crest, tip, brow, crown. OPPOSITE: base. **2** (*no one has climbed those peaks*) mountain, mount, height, alp, hill, elevation. **3** (*activity reached a peak at noon*) climax, maximum, culmination, zenith, meridian, high point, apex, acme, apogee, heyday.
➤ *verb* climax, culminate, come to a head.

peaky *adj* pale, pallid, wan, pasty, whey-faced, white, drawn, drained, pinched, anaemic, ill, sick, sickly, poorly, unwell, under the weather (*inf*), washed-out (*inf*), off-colour.

peal *verb* **1** (*hear the bells peal*) ring, ring out, chime, toll, sound, resound, resonate, reverberate, clamour, tintinnabulate. **2** (*the thunder pealed*) roar, roll, thunder, boom, crash, crack, rumble, reverberate, resound.
➤ *noun* **1** (*a peal of bells*) chime, toll, knell, clang, clap, ring, ringing, sound, tintinnabulation, carillon. **2** (*a peal of thunder*) clap, rumble, roll, roar, boom, crash, crack, reverberation. **3** (*greeted with peals of laughter*) burst, outburst, explosion, roar, tinkle.

peasant *noun* **1** (*peasants in the fields*) countryman, countrywoman, rustic, agricultural worker, swain. **2** (*they're just a load of peasants*) country bumpkin, yokel, provincial, hick (*inf*), oaf, boor, lout, churl. OPPOSITE: citizen.

peccadillo *noun* error, fault, indiscretion, lapse, slip, slip-up (*inf*), boob (*inf*), misdeed, misdemeanour, petty offence, delinquency, infraction.

peck *verb* **1** (*a woodpecker pecking on a tree*) tap, rap, hit, strike, bite, nip, poke, jab, prick. **2** (*pecked his wife on the cheek*) kiss, plant a kiss. **3** (*pecked at his supper*) nibble, pick at, play with, toy with.

peculiar *adj* **1** (*a peculiar incident*) strange, odd, queer, curious, funny, droll, comical, weird, wacko (*inf*), offbeat, outlandish, bizarre, freakish, far-out (*inf*), off-the-wall (*inf*), way-out (*inf*), exotic, eccentric, abnormal, unconventional, offbeat, out-of-the-way, unusual, uncommon, rare, singular, exceptional, extraordinary,

quaint, grotesque. OPPOSITE: ordinary. **2** (*his own peculiar talents*) distinct, specific, particular, characteristic, conspicuous, distinctive, distinguishing, notable, remarkable, special, unique, individual, individualistic, idiosyncratic, personal, private. OPPOSITE: general. **3** (*feel very peculiar*) unwell, poorly, ill, sick, indisposed, out of sorts, strange, funny (*inf*), below par, under the weather (*inf*), dizzy.

peculiar to unique to, exclusive to, belonging to, characteristic of, representative of, typical of, indicative of.

peculiarity *noun* **1** (*the peculiarity of his manner*) strangeness, oddness, queerness, abnormality, eccentricity, curiosity, idiosyncrasy, individuality, particularity, singularity, unconventionality, bizarreness, weirdness, outlandishness, freakishness, grotesqueness, drollness. **2** (*he had several peculiarities*) eccentricity, foible, quirk, mannerism, idiosyncrasy, oddity. **3** (*a peculiarity of her style*) characteristic, trait, attribute, feature, speciality, mark, hallmark, stamp, property, quality.

pecuniary *adj* monetary, financial, fiscal, commercial.

pedagogue *noun* teacher, educator, educationalist, educationist, tutor, instructor, schoolmaster, schoolmistress, master, mistress, lecturer, don. OPPOSITE: pupil.

pedant *noun* **1** (*he is pedant when it comes to observing the rules*) perfectionist, purist, formalist, dogmatist, precisionist, literalist, quibbler, nit-picker (*inf*), sophist, casuist, hair-splitter, pettifogger. **2** (*attracted the attention of learned pedants*) intellectual, academic, scholar, egghead (*inf*), pedagogue, highbrow (*inf*), bluestocking.

pedantic *adj* **1** (*a pedantic attention to detail*) precise, precisionist, exact, perfectionist, meticulous, scrupulous, overscrupulous, punctilious, literalist, formalist, purist, overnice, fussy, picky (*inf*), finicky, finical, particular, dogmatic, hairsplitting (*inf*), nit-picking (*inf*), quibbling, priggish, pettifogging, casuistic, sophistical. **2** (*a florid, pedantic style*) stilted, pompous, bombastic, high-flown, highfalutin (*inf*), pretentious, rhetorical, sententious, grandiloquent, stuffy, formal, stiff, unimaginative, uninspired.

pedantry *noun* **1** (*her pedantry in checking the preparations*) perfectionism, punctiliousness, meticulousness, scrupulousness, overniceness, overnicety, quibbling, nit-picking (*inf*), hair-splitting, pettifogging, cavilling, dogmatism, literalism, casuistry, sophistry, formalism, precision, exactness. **2** (*the pedantry of his writing*) stuffiness, formality, stiffness, stiltedness, pomposity, pretentiousness, bombast, rhetoric, grandiloquence, euphuism.

peddle *verb* sell, hawk, vend, trade, market, traffic, push (*inf*), flog (*inf*), tout. OPPOSITE: buy.

pedestal *noun* plinth, pillar, column, mounting, platform, podium, base, stand, support, foundation, pier, foot.

put on a pedestal idolize, idealize, hero-worship, exalt, revere, glorify, admire, adulate, worship, deify.

pedestrian *noun* walker, foot-traveller, footslogger, hiker.
➤ *adj* plodding, dull, boring, flat, unimaginative,

uninspired, unexciting, prosaic, stodgy, turgid, uninteresting, humdrum, mundane, banal, ho-hum (*inf*), mediocre, run-of-the-mill, indifferent, commonplace, ordinary, no great shakes (*inf*). OPPOSITE: exciting.

pedigree *noun* descent, line, lineage, ancestry, parentage, family, extraction, race, stock, strain, breed, blood, stirps, genealogy, background, derivation.
➤ *adj* purebred, thoroughbred, pure-blooded, full-blooded, aristocratic. OPPOSITE: hybrid.

pedlar *noun* hawker, street-trader, vendor, seller, salesman, saleswoman, salesperson, dealer, peddler, pusher (*inf*). OPPOSITE: buyer.

peek *verb* peep, glance, glimpse, peer, spy, look, have a gander (*inf*), sneak a look (*inf*), have a look-see (*inf*).
➤ *noun* peep, glance, glimpse, look, blink, look-see (*inf*), gander (*inf*), dekko (*inf*), shufti (*inf*), butchers (*inf*).

peel *verb* **1** (*peel the skin from an apple*) pare, skin, strip, remove, take off, excoriate, decorticate. OPPOSITE: cover. **2** (*the child's skin began to peel*) scale off, flake off, skin.
➤ *noun* peeling, skin, rind, zest, covering, husk, epicarp, exocarp.
keep one's eyes peeled observe, watch closely, monitor, be alert, be on guard, keep one's eyes skinned, keep a lookout for.

peep[1] *verb* **1** (*peep round the corner*) peek, glimpse, glance, spy, peer, squint, look, take a butchers (*inf*). **2** (*spring flowers peep forth*) emerge, issue, appear, show, spring up, pop up.
➤ *noun* look, peek, glimpse, glance, squint, dekko (*inf*), look-see (*inf*), gander (*inf*), shufti (*inf*), butchers (*inf*).

peep[2] *verb* (*hear a bird peeping*) squeak, cheep, chirp, chirrup, chatter, tweet, twitter, pipe, warble.
➤ *noun* **1** (*the peep of a bird in the rafters*) chirp, cheep, chirrup, piping, tweet, chatter, twitter, warble, squeak. **2** (*she gave a peep of surprise*) cry, squeal, squeak. **3** (*didn't hear a peep from the baby*) noise, word, utterance, sound.

peephole *noun* spyhole, keyhole, hole, aperture, opening, interstice, slit, chink, crack, fissure, cleft, crevice.

peer[1] *noun* **1** (*a peer of the realm*) noble, nobleman, aristocrat, aristo (*inf*), lord, duke, marquess, marquis, earl, viscount, count, baron, patrician. OPPOSITE: commoner. **2** (*he had no peer*) equal, coequal, equivalent, match, like, counterpart, compeer, mate, fellow, confrère.

peer[2] *verb* (*peered closely at the small print*) squint, gaze, look, scan, scrutinize, examine, inspect, peep, peek, spy, snoop.

peerage *noun* aristocracy, nobility, lords and ladies, titled classes, upper crust (*inf*), top drawer (*inf*).

peerless *adj* matchless, unmatched, without equal, unequalled, unparalleled, unexcelled, unrivalled, unsurpassed, unbeatable, second to none (*inf*), nonpareil, superlative, supreme, paramount, outstanding, excellent, unique, incomparable, beyond compare. OPPOSITE: ordinary.

peeve *verb* annoy, irritate, exasperate, piss off (*sl*), bother, bug (*inf*), get (*inf*), irk, aggravate (*inf*), anger, provoke, upset, vex, pique, miff (*inf*), nark (*inf*), put out, hack off (*inf*), nettle, gall, rile (*inf*), rub up the wrong

way (*inf*), get under one's skin (*inf*), drive up the wall (*inf*).

peevish *adj* irritable, fretful, fractious, crotchety, cross, ratty (*inf*), touchy, testy, tetchy, crusty, short-tempered, waspish, snappish, petulant, crabbed, crabby, cantankerous, grumpy, huffy, complaining, whingeing (*inf*), sullen, sulky, petulant, moody, surly, ill-tempered, ill-natured, ill-humoured, churlish, childish, captious, querulous, splenetic, liverish, shrewish, pettish, sour, acrimonious. OPPOSITE: genial.

peg *noun* pin, nail, spike, skewer, dowel, bolt, screw, hook, knob, marker, post, stake.
➤ *verb* **1** (*peg the washing on the line*) pin, fasten, secure, fix, attach, join, make fast. **2** (*peg prices at a high level*) fix, set, freeze, stabilize, control, limit.
bring down a peg or two humble, humiliate, bring down, bring low, mortify, cut down to size, put someone in their place.
peg away persevere, persist, plug away, work away, apply oneself, beaver away (*inf*), plod along, keep going, keep at (*inf*), stick at (*inf*), stick with (*inf*), hang in (*inf*).

pejorative *adj* derogatory, deprecatory, depreciatory, disparaging, insulting, slighting, belittling, debasing, uncomplimentary, unflattering, unpleasant, negative, bad.

pellet *noun* **1** (*a pellet of dough*) ball, sphere. **2** (*taken in the form of a pellet*) pill, tablet, capsule, drop, lozenge. **3** (*air rifle pellets*) ball, shot, bullet, slug (*inf*), buckshot.

pell-mell *adv* **1** (*dogs running pell-mell out of the yard*) headlong, precipitously, helter-skelter (*inf*), hurry-scurry (*inf*), at full tilt, posthaste, rashly, recklessly, heedlessly, impetuously, feverishly, hastily, hurriedly. **2** (*his belongings lying pell-mell in the road*) in chaos, in disarray, in confusion, in disorder, in a muddle, in a mess, anyhow, untidily, haphazardly.

pellucid *adj* **1** (*pellucid streams*) transparent, translucent, clear, limpid, crystalline, glassy, bright. OPPOSITE: opaque. **2** (*pellucid writing*) clear, plain, straightforward, lucid, coherent, articulate, comprehensible, understandable, intelligible. OPPOSITE: unintelligible.

pelt[1] *verb* **1** (*pelt with snowballs*) bombard, pepper, shower, attack, assail, batter, pummel, beat, hit, strike, thrash, throw, hurl, cast, sling. **2** (*pelt down the road*) dash, race, run, sprint, rush, hurry, speed, shoot, career, hare, belt (*inf*), zip (*inf*), charge, tear. OPPOSITE: amble. **3** (*it's pelting down out there*) pour, teem, bucket, rain cats and dogs (*inf*). OPPOSITE: drizzle.

pelt[2] *noun* (*a fine buffalo pelt*) skin, hide, fur, fleece, coat, fell.

pen[1] *noun* (*write with a pen*) ballpoint, Biro®, felt-tip, fountain pen, marker, quill.
➤ *verb* write, write down, jot down, scribble, pencil, commit to paper, draft, compose, draw up.

pen[2] *noun* (*a sheep pen*) enclosure, compound, pound, corral, fold, sheepfold, stall, sty, cage, coop, hen-coop, hutch.
➤ *verb* enclose, confine, shut up, coop up, fence in, hem in, hedge, cage, coop. OPPOSITE: free.

penal *adj* punitive, penalizing, disciplinary, corrective, retributive, retaliatory, vindictive.

penalize *verb* **1** (*penalized for breaking the rules*) punish, discipline, correct, chastise, castigate, fine. OPPOSITE: reward. **2** (*society penalizes the disabled*) handicap, disadvantage.

penalty *noun* **1** (*suffered the penalty for his crime*) punishment, sentence, retribution, castigation, chastisement, penance, forfeiture, forfeit, fine, price, mulct. OPPOSITE: reward. **2** (*his blindness was a penalty*) handicap, disadvantage, drawback, obstacle, minus (*inf*), snag, downside (*inf*).

penance *noun* **1** (*a penance imposed by the court*) punishment, penalty. **2** (*underwent penance for her sins*) self-punishment, amends, atonement, reparation, contrition, self-abasement, mortification, humiliation, sackcloth and ashes.

penchant *noun* inclination, tendency, proclivity, propensity, leaning, bias, bent, liking, preference, predilection, predisposition, disposition, proneness, partiality, affinity, fondness, love, desire, passion, taste, fancy, whim, soft spot, weakness. OPPOSITE: aversion.

pendant *noun* locket, medallion, necklace.

pendent *adj* hanging, suspended, dangling, swinging, drooping, pendulous, overhanging, projecting, jutting out, beetling. OPPOSITE: erect.

pending *prep* **1** (*remain in prison pending a decision*) until, till, awaiting, waiting for. **2** (*stay abroad pending hostilities*) during, throughout, in the course of, while, whilst.
➤ *adj* **1** (*the matter is pending*) unsettled, undecided, unresolved, undetermined, uncertain, in abeyance, hanging fire, in the balance (*inf*), up in the air (*inf*), on the back burner (*inf*). **2** (*an announcement is pending*) imminent, impending, coming, forthcoming, approaching, near, close, on the way, in the offing, in the pipeline.

penetrable *adj* **1** (*penetrable material*) permeable, porous, pervious. **2** (*a penetrable defence*) vulnerable, flawed, weak. **3** (*written in penetrable prose*) comprehensible, understandable, intelligible, explicable, accessible, clear, open, fathomable. OPPOSITE: impenetrable.

penetrate *verb* **1** (*penetrate the lid*) pierce, puncture, perforate, stab, prick, spike, impale, bore. **2** (*penetrate the security cordon*) enter, get into, infiltrate, invade, make one's way, pass through. **3** (*the liquid had penetrated the seal*) permeate, saturate, seep, fill, imbue, suffuse, pervade, percolate, impregnate. **4** (*tried to penetrate his calculations*) decipher, crack (*inf*), unravel, understand, comprehend, suss (*inf*), apprehend, get to the bottom of (*inf*), grasp, fathom, make out, figure out, work out, resolve, solve, discern, perceive, see. **5** (*it took a long time for her words to penetrate his brain*) register, get through, come across, sink in, make an impression.

penetrating *adj* **1** (*a penetrating scream*) piercing, earpiercing, earsplitting, shrill, strident, loud, deafening, strong, carrying, harsh, intrusive. **2** (*penetrating cold*) sharp, acute, harsh, keen, biting, stinging, pervasive. **3** (*penetrating wit*) incisive, biting, keen, acute, sharp, quick, pungent, perceptive, percipient, perspicacious, discerning, observant, discriminating, intelligent, wise, clever, sagacious, profound, smart, shrewd, astute,

critical. OPPOSITE: dull. **4** (*subjected to a penetrating inquiry*) penetrative, searching, probing, deep, in-depth, incisive.

penetration *noun* **1** (*penetration of the plastic container*) piercing, puncturing, perforation, stabbing, pricking, incision. **2** (*penetration of the defences*) infiltration, invasion, entry. **3** (*the penetration of damp*) permeation, pervasion, suffusion. **4** (*a man of considerable penetration*) discernment, perception, perceptiveness, perspicacity, insight, discrimination, acumen, astuteness, incisiveness, sharpness, sharpwittedness, keenness, acuteness, acuity, shrewdness, wit, intelligence, cleverness, smartness. **5** (*penetration of the riddle was easy*) understanding, comprehension, apprehension, cracking (*inf*), fathoming, resolution.

penitence *noun* contrition, repentance, regret, remorse, remorsefulness, self-reproach, self-accusation, compunction, sorrow, shame, ruefulness. OPPOSITE: impenitence.

penitent *adj* contrite, repentant, conscience-stricken, regretful, remorseful, sorrowful, rueful, abject, humble, sorry, ashamed, shamefaced, apologetic. OPPOSITE: impenitent.

pen name *noun* pseudonym, alias, assumed name, false name, nom de plume, nom de guerre, stage name.

pennant *noun* flag, standard, banner, streamer, colours, ensign, jack, bunting.

penniless *adj* poor, impecunious, penurious, moneyless, short, broke (*inf*), stony-broke (*inf*), flat broke (*inf*), hard up (*inf*), bust (*inf*), skint (*inf*), strapped (*inf*), cleaned out (*inf*), bankrupt, ruined, down and out (*inf*), indigent, destitute, needy, necessitous, impoverished, poverty-stricken, on the breadline (*inf*), in reduced circumstances. OPPOSITE: rich.

penny-pinching *adj* mean, stingy (*inf*), mingy (*inf*), grasping, miserly, money-grubbing, tight, tightfisted, tight-arsed (*sl*), close, near, frugal, ungenerous, skimping, scrimping, parsimonious, niggardly, cheeseparing. OPPOSITE: generous.

pension *noun* annuity, allowance, benefit, grant, support, welfare.

pensioner *noun* old-age pensioner, OAP, senior citizen.

pensive *adj* thoughtful, reflective, contemplative, musing, meditative, ruminative, cogitative, absorbed, absentminded, dreamy, preoccupied, wistful, brooding, pondering, thinking, melancholy, mournful, sad, sober, solemn, serious, grave. OPPOSITE: carefree.

pent-up *adj* repressed, inhibited, suppressed, held back, held in, restrained, constrained, bridled, checked, curbed, confined, stifled, smothered, bottled up (*inf*). OPPOSITE: released.

penurious *adj* **1** (*a penurious old villain*) miserly, mean, stingy (*inf*), mingy (*inf*), skimping (*inf*), niggardly, cheeseparing, penny-pinching (*inf*), parsimonious, tight (*inf*), tightfisted, tight-arsed (*sl*), closefisted, close, frugal, grudging, ungenerous. OPPOSITE: generous. **2** (*in penurious circumstances*) poor, penniless, impecunious, impoverished, poverty-stricken, destitute, bankrupt, hard up, broke (*inf*), stony-broke (*inf*), bust (*inf*), skint (*inf*), strapped (*inf*), indigent, down and out, needy. OPPOSITE: rich.

penury *noun* poverty, destitution, impoverishment, impecuniousness, pennilessness, indigence, bankruptcy, insolvency, need, neediness, want, privation, dearth, beggary, beggarliness, pauperism. OPPOSITE: affluence.

people *noun* **1** (*hundreds of people*) persons, individuals, humans, human beings, human race, mortals, souls, men, women, children, mankind, humanity, humankind, folk. **2** (*a noble leader of his people*) nation, race, tribe, clan, community, society, population, inhabitants, public, folk. **3** (*surrender to the demands of the people*) populace, crowd, mob, general public, citizens, masses, multitude, commonalty, electorate, rank and file, rabble, herd, hoi polloi, riff-raff, plebs (*inf*). OPPOSITE: nobility. **4** (*come and meet my people*) family, folks (*inf*), kinsfolk, kin, kith and kin, parents, relations, relatives.
➤ *verb* populate, inhabit, occupy, settle, colonize.

pep *noun* energy, vigour, verve, vim, spirit, get-up-and-go (*inf*), sparkle, vitality, vivacity, animation, life, liveliness, exuberance, ebullience, effervescence, high spirits, pizzazz (*inf*), fire, dash, gusto, zest, brio, zip (*inf*).

pepper *verb* **1** (*he peppers all his food*) season, flavour, spice, spice up. **2** (*their bodies were peppered with bullets*) bombard, pelt, riddle, attack, assail, blitz. **3** (*peppered his essay with classical allusions*) sprinkle, intersperse, dot, shower, scatter, spatter, bespatter, strew, bestrew, fleck, stud, stipple.

peppery *adj* **1** (*a peppery taste*) hot, spicy, spiced, seasoned, pungent, piquant, sharp, fiery. OPPOSITE: mild. **2** (*a peppery temper*) irritable, irascible, quick-tempered, hot-tempered, fiery, choleric, testy, touchy (*inf*), snappish, grumpy, crabby, crabbed, splenetic, vitriolic, dyspeptic. OPPOSITE: affable. **3** (*made several peppery observations*) incisive, biting, stinging, sarcastic, acerbic, caustic, sharp, trenchant, astringent, waspish.

perceive *verb* **1** (*perceive a change in the landscape*) sense, feel, be aware of, see, view, witness, catch sight of, behold, glimpse, spot, descry, espy, spy out, observe, notice, note, remark, discern, discover, detect, make out, distinguish, recognize. **2** (*perceive the truth*) understand, comprehend, apprehend, suss (*inf*), grasp, gather, fathom, appreciate, realize, figure out, learn, know, conclude, deduce, see, sense, recognize.

perceptible *adj* perceivable, discernible, distinguishable, detectable, appreciable, recognizable, apparent, visible, noticeable, observable, distinct, clear, plain, evident, obvious, conspicuous, manifest, patent, palpable, tangible. OPPOSITE: imperceptible.

perception *noun* **1** (*showed acute perception of the threat posed*) awareness, consciousness, appreciation, discernment, recognition, cognizance, understanding, comprehension, apprehension, knowledge, grasp. **2** (*writings of great perception*) insight, intuition, feeling, sensitivity, responsiveness, awareness, discernment, discrimination, understanding, perspicacity, perceptiveness, percipience, observation, recognition. OPPOSITE: ignorance.

perceptive *adj* **1** (*the more perceptive among you will have noticed*) sharp, sharp-eyed, sharp-sighted, acute, keen, keen-sighted, alert, aware, observant, quick-witted, quick, vigilant. **2** (*a perceptive writer*) discerning, shrewd, discriminating, sensitive, responsive, perspicacious, percipient, understanding, intuitive. OPPOSITE: slow. **3** (*a perceptive essay*) shrewd, astute, discerning, penetrating, perspicacious, percipient.

perch *noun* pole, post, bar, rod, branch, roost, rest.
➤ *verb* alight, land, settle, rest, sit, roost, balance.

perchance *adv* **1** (*if perchance we win*) by chance, fortuitously. **2** (*perchance we will win*) perhaps, maybe, mayhap, possibly, feasibly, conceivably, probably, peradventure.

percipient *adj* **1** (*a percipient observer*) perceptive, perspicacious, astute, shrewd, sharp, discerning, discriminating, understanding, intuitive, knowing, intelligent, quick-witted, alert, responsive, sensitive, alive, aware. **2** (*a percipient account of the confrontation*) perceptive, penetrating, astute, shrewd, judicious, discerning, perspicacious.

percolate *verb* **1** (*water percolated through the soil*) strain, filter, filtrate, drip, drain, seep, ooze, exude, leach, trickle, leak, penetrate. **2** (*percolate the mixture through a sieve*) sieve, strain, filter, filtrate, sift. **3** (*the smell of coffee percolating*) brew, bubble. **4** (*news slowly percolated through the building*) permeate, pervade, spread, filter, pass.

percussion *noun* impact, crash, smash, collision, clash, knock, bump, bang, blow, jolt, thump, shock, concussion.

perdition *noun* damnation, destruction, ruin, ruination, annihilation, doom, downfall, hell, hellfire. OPPOSITE: salvation.

peregrination *noun* journey, voyage, tour, odyssey, trip, excursion, expedition, trek, trekking, exploration, travel, travelling, globetrotting, wandering, wayfaring, roaming, roving.

peremptory *adj* **1** (*a peremptory manner*) imperious, high-handed, overbearing, commanding, dogmatic, autocratic, authoritative, bossy (*inf*), dictatorial, domineering, arbitrary, tyrannical, despotic, intolerant, arrogant, assertive, overweening, supercilious, lordly. **2** (*issued peremptory instructions*) imperious, high-handed, imperative, urgent, pressing. **3** (*a peremptory decision*) incontrovertible, irreversible, binding, compelling, absolute, final, conclusive, decisive, definitive, categorical, irrefutable, obligatory, mandatory, undeniable.

perennial *adj* **1** (*of perennial fascination*) lasting, enduring, abiding, persisting, permanent, constant, perpetual, everlasting, eternal, immortal, undying, imperishable, unfailing, unchanging, endless, unending, never-ending, ceaseless. OPPOSITE: ephemeral. **2** (*a source of perennial irritation*) constant, continual, continuous, continuing, eternal, never-ending, incessant, ceaseless, uninterrupted, persistent, inveterate, recurrent, chronic.

perfect *adj* **1** (*a woman of perfect virtue*) pure, unblemished, flawless, immaculate, spotless, sinless, faultless, impeccable, blameless, exemplary. OPPOSITE: imperfect. **2** (*in perfect condition*) ideal, excellent, exemplary, superb, superlative, wonderful, spotless, flawless, faultless, clean, unblemished, unmarred, impeccable. **3** (*a perfect set*) complete, finished, consummate, entire, full, whole. OPPOSITE: incomplete.

4 (*the preparations are all perfect*) perfected, completed, finished. **5** (*a perfect idiot*) total, utter, absolute, sheer, complete, thorough, thoroughgoing, downright, out and out, unmitigated, unadulterated, unqualified. **6** (*a perfect copy*) accurate, precise, exact, correct, right, true, faithful, strict, unerring. OPPOSITE: inaccurate. **7** (*the perfect gift*) ideal, fitting, fit, suitable, appropriate, apt. **8** (*a perfect performer*) accomplished, practised, polished, adept, expert, experienced, ultimate, masterly, consummate, skilled, skilful. **9** (*a perfect performance*) faultless, flawless, finished, model, ideal, consummate, textbook, exemplary, excellent, marvellous, superb, superlative, terrific, fantastic, fabulous, wonderful.
≫ *verb* **1** (*perfect the job*) finish, complete, consummate, effect, fulfil, realize, perform, achieve, accomplish, carry out. **2** (*an opportunity to perfect his story*) polish, refine, cultivate, elaborate, hone, improve, better, ameliorate, rectify. OPPOSITE: spoil.

perfection *noun* **1** (*worked on the perfection of his plan*) improvement, polishing, refinement, completion, betterment, consummation, fulfilment, realization, achievement, accomplishment. **2** (*brought to a peak of perfection*) perfectness, purity, spotlessness, flawlessness, faultlessness, immaculateness, impeccability, excellence, superiority. OPPOSITE: imperfection. **3** (*the evening was perfection itself*) ideal, acme, model, crown, pinnacle, the tops (*inf*), paragon.

perfectionist *noun* stickler, purist, idealist, pedant, formalist, precisionist.

perfectly *adv* **1** (*the dress was perfectly ruined*) completely, totally, entirely, fully, altogether, quite, thoroughly, wholly, utterly, absolutely. OPPOSITE: partly. **2** (*they are perfectly suited*) flawlessly, faultlessly, superbly, superlatively, wonderfully, admirably, ideally, exactly, precisely, immaculately, correctly. OPPOSITE: badly.

perfidious *adj* treacherous, traitorous, false, faithless, unfaithful, disloyal, dishonest, deceitful, untrustworthy, untrue, two-faced, double-dealing, duplicitous, corrupt. OPPOSITE: loyal.

perfidy *noun* perfidiousness, treachery, betrayal, deceit, deceitfulness, dishonesty, falseness, falsity, faithlessness, unfaithfulness, infidelity, disloyalty, double-dealing, treason, duplicity, traitorousness. OPPOSITE: loyalty.

perforate *verb* hole, puncture, stab, pierce, gore, split, tear, penetrate, punch, bore, drill, prick, spike, burst, rupture.

perforce *adv* necessarily, by necessity, of necessity, unavoidably, inevitably, needs must, willy-nilly.

perform *verb* **1** (*perform the challenge*) do, carry out, discharge, execute, transact, effect, achieve, bring about, bring off, pull off, accomplish, complete, fulfil, conduct, comply with, satisfy, observe. OPPOSITE: fail. **2** (*perform a tragedy*) play, act, do, stage, put on, enact, present, represent, depict, render. **3** (*perform in a play*) act, appear, play. **4** (*the machine performs well*) work, act, function, operate, go, run, behave, produce.

performance *noun* **1** (*the third performance of the play*) staging, acting, playing, production, presentation, representation, showing, appearance. **2** (*a theatrical performance*) production, show, act, entertainment,

portrayal, interpretation, gig (*inf*), play, exhibition. **3** (*the performance of brave deeds*) accomplishment, achievement, completion, execution, discharge, act, deed, exploit, feat, doing, effecting, implementation, fulfilment, action, carrying out, conduct, conducting, consummation. **4** (*the performance of the new engine*) operation, functioning, running, working, going, conduct, behaviour, efficiency, practice. **5** (*she created a right performance*) fuss, bother, business, carry-on (*inf*), rigmarole, to-do.

performer *noun* **1** (*a popular performer*) entertainer, player, actor, actress, musician, singer, dancer, artist, artiste, trouper. **2** (*he's our star performer*) achiever, operator, doer, executor, worker, architect, author.

perfume *noun* **1** (*she wore expensive perfume*) scent, fragrance, essence, cologne, eau-de-Cologne, toilet water, eau de toilette, incense. **2** (*the perfume of fresh bread*) aroma, scent, fragrance, smell, niff (*inf*), bouquet, balminess, sweetness, redolence, odour. OPPOSITE: stench.

perfunctory *adj* cursory, superficial, desultory, brief, quick, fast, rapid, fleeting, sketchy, hurried, hasty, careless, slipshod, slovenly, automatic, mechanical, routine, wooden, indifferent, offhand, casual, negligent, heedless, inattentive, unconcerned, thoughtless, unthinking. OPPOSITE: thorough.

perhaps *adv* maybe, possibly, conceivably, feasibly, perchance, peradventure. OPPOSITE: definitely.

peril *noun* danger, jeopardy, risk, hazard, menace, threat, pitfall, vulnerability, exposure, insecurity, uncertainty. OPPOSITE: safety.

perilous *adj* dangerous, unsafe, risky, chancy (*inf*), hairy (*inf*), hazardous, fraught, menacing, threatening, dire, vulnerable, exposed, precarious, insecure, unsure. OPPOSITE: safe.

perimeter *noun* **1** (*the perimeter of a circle*) circumference, edge. OPPOSITE: centre. **2** (*terrorists have infiltrated the airport perimeter*) boundary, border, borderline, frontier, confines, limits, outer limits, edge, margin, periphery, fringe.

period *noun* **1** (*a period of time*) time, term, spell, space, span, interval, stretch, stint, shift, duration, season, session. **2** (*away for a period*) while, time, spell, stint. **3** (*periods of ancient history*) age, era, epoch, aeon, eon, time, days, years, generation, cycle, stage, phase, course. **4** (*that's my decision, period*) full stop, stop, end, finis, finish. **5** (*five periods before lunch*) lesson, class, lecture, seminar, tutorial, instruction. **6** (*put a period at the end of a sentence*) full stop, stop, point, full point. **7** (*her periods started late*) menstruation, menstrual flow, monthly flow, menses, the curse (*inf*).

periodic *adj* periodical, intermittent, recurrent, recurring, repeated, cyclic, cyclical, seasonal, regular, occasional, infrequent, sporadic, spasmodic, once in a while, every so often. OPPOSITE: continuous.

periodical *noun* magazine, review, journal, glossy (*inf*), paper, weekly, monthly, quarterly, serial, organ, publication.

peripatetic *adj* **1** (*a peripatetic lifestyle*) itinerant, wandering, journeying, roaming, roving, travelling, nomadic, migrant, migratory, ambulatory, vagabond, vagrant. **2** (*a peripatetic music teacher*) itinerant, travelling, mobile, supply.

peripheral *adj* **1** (*a peripheral part of the city*) outlying, outer, outermost, surrounding, neighbouring. OPPOSITE: central. **2** (*a peripheral issue*) secondary, subsidiary, marginal, borderline, incidental, lesser, minor, ancillary, surface, superficial, unimportant, unnecessary, inessential, tangential, irrelevant. OPPOSITE: major.

periphery *noun* **1** (*the periphery of the settlement*) boundary, outskirts, fringe, skirt, border, edge, limits, perimeter, outside. OPPOSITE: centre. **2** (*she was always on the periphery of our circle*) edge, fringe, margin, surface, brim, rim, rink, verge.

periphrastic *adj* circumlocutory, verbose, wordy, prolix, tautological, rambling, long drawn-out, discursive, circuitous, roundabout, indirect, oblique, tortuous, wandering. OPPOSITE: direct.

perish *verb* **1** (*only to perish at sea*) die, expire, decease, pass away, depart, lose one's life, breathe one's last, be killed, peg out (*inf*), pop off (*inf*), kick the bucket (*inf*), bite the dust (*inf*). **2** (*the fruit has perished*) go off, go bad, rot, spoil, decay, moulder, decompose, waste, wither. **3** (*their last hope perished*) disintegrate, collapse, crumble, wither, fade, die away, fail, decline, vanish, disappear, fall, come to an end, go under. OPPOSITE: last.

perishable *adj* destructible, decomposable, biodegradable, frail, fragile, unstable, shortlived, temporary, impermanent, transitory, fleeting. OPPOSITE: imperishable.

perjure *verb* **perjure oneself** commit perjury, lie, lie under oath, bear false witness, forswear oneself.

perjury *noun* false witness, falsification, false statement, false testimony, forswearing.

perk *noun* perquisite, fringe benefit, benefit, extra, freebie (*inf*), bonus, advantage, plus (*inf*), dividend, gratuity, tip, baksheesh.

perk up 1 (*perked up at the news*) cheer up, liven up, buck up (*inf*), pep up (*inf*), brighten up, take heart. **2** (*perked up after the doctor's visit*) rally, recover, recuperate, revive, improve, look up.

perky *adj* jaunty, sprightly, lively, vivacious, bouncy, buoyant, bubbly, upbeat (*inf*), effervescent, ebullient, animated, spirited, peppy, bright, cheerful, cheery, chirpy (*inf*), sunny, gay, sparkling. OPPOSITE: lethargic.

permanence *noun* stability, firmness, fixedness, imperishability, indestructibility, perpetuity, perpetualness, endlessness, everlastingness, immutability, constancy, endurance, steadfastness, persistence, durability. OPPOSITE: impermanence.

permanent *adj* **1** (*suffer permanent brain damage*) lasting, enduring, abiding, durable, imperishable, indestructible, unfading, everlasting, perpetual, eternal, lifelong, endless, unending, perennial, constant, persistent, steadfast, fixed, stable, changeless, unchanging, unchangeable, immutable, invariable, indelible. OPPOSITE: temporary. **2** (*a permanent post*) lasting, long-lasting, constant, fixed, unchanging, stable, established, sound, firm.

permanently *adv* always, constantly, continually, ceaselessly, unceasingly, incessantly, endlessly, unendingly, eternally, perpetually, in perpetuity, perennially, unremittingly, persistently, immutably, invariably, once and for all, indelibly, lastingly, everlastingly, evermore, for ever, for ever and ever, for all time, for keeps (*inf*), till the end of time, time without end, till the cows come home (*inf*), till hell freezes over (*inf*). OPPOSITE: temporarily.

permeable *adj* porous, absorbent, absorptive, spongy, pervious, penetrable, passable. OPPOSITE: impermeable.

permeate *verb* **1** (*damp had permeated the walls*) penetrate, soak through, seep through, leak through, infiltrate, percolate through, leach through, saturate, impregnate, spread through, filter through, pass through,. **2** (*fumes permeated the compartment*) spread through, pervade, fill, filter through, pass through, diffuse through, imbue, suffuse, penetrate, infiltrate, percolate through.

permissible *adj* allowable, allowed, permitted, lawful, legal, legitimate, authorized, sanctioned, right, proper, acceptable, admissible, tolerable, all right, OK (*inf*), kosher (*inf*). OPPOSITE: prohibited.

permission *noun* authorization, sanction, clearance, leave, approval, approbation, warrant, licence, permit, freedom, liberty, leave, consent, assent, acquiescence, agreement, allowance, tolerance, toleration, sufferance, dispensation, go-ahead, green light (*inf*), thumbs-up (*inf*). OPPOSITE: prohibition.

permissive *adj* liberal, broad-minded, open-minded, easygoing (*inf*), tolerant, indulgent, forbearing, lenient, overindulgent, lax, free, unrestricted, unprescriptive, latitudinarian. OPPOSITE: strict.

permit *verb* allow, let, sanction, approve of, authorize, give leave, endorse, warrant, license, enable, empower, consent, assent, agree to, admit, grant, tolerate, countenance, suffer, endure, brook. OPPOSITE: forbid. » *noun* permission, authorization, sanction, licence, warrant, pass, passport, visa.

permutation *noun* alteration, transformation, change, shift, variation, transposition, rearrangement, configuration, transmutation, commutation.

pernicious *adj* deadly, fatal, lethal, mortal, unhealthy, unwholesome, ruinous, destructive, injurious, hurtful, harmful, damaging, dangerous, deleterious, detrimental, malicious, bad, wicked, evil, malevolent, malignant, malign, baleful, noxious, toxic, poisonous, venomous, noisome, offensive, pestilent. OPPOSITE: beneficial.

pernickety *adj* fussy, choosy (*inf*), picky (*inf*), particular, overparticular, overprecise, finicky, exacting, difficult, carping, nit-picking (*inf*), hair-splitting (*inf*), nice, overnice, punctilious, fastidious, over-fastidious, painstaking.

peroration *noun* **1** (*he concluded with a peroration giving the main points*) summary, summing-up, conclusion, closing remarks, recapitulation, recapping (*inf*), reiteration. **2** (*they sat through their master's learned peroration*) speech, lecture, talk, address, oration, diatribe, harangue, declamation.

perpendicular *adj* **1** (*the mast was now perpendicular*) upright, vertical, straight, plumb, erect, standing, on end. OPPOSITE: horizontal. **2** (*a perpendicular cliff*) steep, sheer, precipitous, plumb, abrupt.

perpetrate *verb* commit, do, execute, perform, carry

out, pull off (*inf*), effect, effectuate, bring about, wreak, inflict.

perpetual *adj* **1** (*in a perpetual orbit around the sun*) eternal, everlasting, never-ending, endless, unending, undying, perennial, permanent, durable, lasting, abiding, enduring, persisting, constant, unchanging, unvarying, invariable, unfailing, infinite. OPPOSITE: temporary. **2** (*perpetual motion*) unceasing, incessant, ceaseless, unending, endless, non-stop, uninterrupted, unbroken, continuing, continuous, unremitting. **3** (*a source of perpetual irritation*) persistent, recurrent, repeated, interminable, continual, frequent.

perpetuate *verb* **1** (*perpetuate the tradition*) continue, keep up, keep going, maintain, sustain, preserve, conserve, keep alive. OPPOSITE: end. **2** (*composed an ode to perpetuate her memory*) immortalize, eternalize, eternize, commemorate, memorialize.

perpetuity *noun* eternity, time.
in perpetuity always, for ever, for ever and ever, evermore, for all time, for good, endlessly, eternally, everlastingly, perpetually, perennially, permanently.

perplex *verb* **1** (*perplexed by their questions*) puzzle, baffle, mystify, nonplus, stump, disconcert, dismay, dumbfound, flummox, bewilder, confuse, befuddle, bamboozle (*inf*), confound, muddle. OPPOSITE: enlighten. **2** (*tending to perplex matters further*) complicate, confuse, involve, embroil, encumber, entangle, tangle, jumble, muddle, mix up, snarl up, foul up (*inf*), thicken. OPPOSITE: simplify.

perplexing *adj* **1** (*his perplexing manner*) puzzling, baffling, mystifying, mysterious, enigmatic, bewildering, confusing, disconcerting, unaccountable, inexplicable, hard, strange, weird, amazing. **2** (*a perplexing issue*) complex, complicated, intricate, involved, difficult, paradoxical, knotty, thorny, taxing, trying, vexing, labyrinthine. OPPOSITE: simple.

perplexity *noun* **1** (*caused perplexity in his listeners*) bewilderment, confusion, puzzlement, bafflement, bamboozlement (*inf*), mystification, incomprehension, stupefaction, dismay, disconcertion, disconcertment. OPPOSITE: enlightenment. **2** (*the perplexity of the case*) complexity, intricacy, complication, involvement, entanglement, obscurity, puzzle, mystery, enigma, paradox, quandary, dilemma, difficulty, muddle.

perquisite *noun* perk (*inf*), freebie (*inf*), fringe benefit, benefit, extra, bonus, plus, advantage, dividend, gratuity, tip, baksheesh.

persecute *verb* **1** (*persecute their enemies*) torment, torture, martyr, crucify, maltreat, mistreat, ill-treat, abuse, victimize, oppress, tyrannize, afflict, distress. **2** (*persecuted by his creditors*) hassle (*inf*), harass, hound, hunt, pursue, pester, plague, badger, bother, molest, worry, vex, annoy.

perseverance *noun* persistence, stickability (*inf*), tenacity, dedication, commitment, diligence, patience, application, assiduity, sedulity, zeal, steadfastness, constancy, determination, resolution, resolve, purpose, purposefulness, doggedness, insistence, stamina, endurance, indefatigability, intransigence, pertinacity.

persevere *verb* persist, continue, remain, carry on, go on, keep going, keep on, keep at, pursue, maintain,

struggle on, soldier on, work, hammer away, plug away (*inf*), peg away (*inf*), hang in there (*inf*), hang on, endure, stand firm, stand fast, hold fast. OPPOSITE: waver.

persist *verb* **1** (*persist in her campaign*) continue, carry on, go on, keep on, keep at, keep going, persevere, soldier on, plug away (*inf*), stick at (*inf*), stand firm, stand fast, hold on, hang on, insist. OPPOSITE: desist. **2** (*these conditions are expected to persist*) last, linger, hold, endure, abide, remain, survive, continue, carry on, keep on. OPPOSITE: stop.

persistence *noun* tenacity, perseverance, determination, grit (*inf*), doggedness, resolution, pluck, purposefulness, insistence, intransigence, steadfastness, patience, application, diligence, pertinacity, assiduity, assiduousness, constancy, endurance, stamina, tirelessness, indefatigableness.

persistent *adj* **1** (*a persistent campaigner*) persevering, tenacious, diligent, patient, assiduous, steadfast, determined, resolute, dogged, purposeful, zealous, unflagging, tireless, indefatigable, intractable, pertinacious, stubborn, stiff-necked, obstinate, obdurate, unshakeable, immovable, fixed. OPPOSITE: wavering. **2** (*persistent rain*) constant, steady, unceasing, incessant, ceaseless, endless, never-ending, interminable, continual, continuous, continuing, unremitting, perpetual, repeated, frequent, lasting, enduring, unrelenting, relentless. OPPOSITE: intermittent.

person *noun* individual, body, soul, mortal, human, human being, being, man, woman, child, someone, somebody, creature, character, type.

persona *noun* character, personality, front, image, face, facade, mask, public face, role, part.

personable *adj* pleasant, pleasing, agreeable, likable, amiable, affable, warm, nice, attractive, presentable, good-looking, handsome, charming, winning, outgoing.

personage *noun* celebrity, notable, VIP (*inf*), worthy, dignitary, personality, person of note, luminary, name, celeb (*inf*), somebody (*inf*), public figure, household name, big shot (*inf*), big noise (*inf*), big gun (*inf*), bigwig (*inf*).

personal *adj* **1** (*details of her personal history*) private, individual, own, confidential, secret, intimate. OPPOSITE: communal. **2** (*a highly personal style*) personalized, individual, subjective, idiosyncratic, unique, peculiar, characteristic, distinctive. **3** (*give it my personal attention*) individual, special, particular, exclusive. **4** (*a number of personal comments*) insulting, rude, abusive, derogatory, critical, disparaging, offensive, upsetting, nasty, hurtful, wounding, slighting, disrespectful, pejorative.

personality *noun* **1** (*an attractive personality*) character, nature, make-up, disposition, temperament, temper, psyche, traits, individuality, identity. **2** (*he was distinctly lacking in personality*) charisma, magnetism, attraction, attractiveness, charm, likableness, dynamism. **3** (*a television personality*) personage, person of note, notable, dignitary, luminary, worthy, VIP (*inf*), public figure, celebrity, celeb (*inf*), star, famous person, famous name, household name.

personally *adv* **1** (*attend to it personally*) in person, in the flesh, individually, myself. **2** (*can I speak to you* *personally?*) privately, confidentially, exclusively, solely, alone, independently. **3** (*don't take it personally*) insultingly, offensively, as personal criticism.

personification *noun* embodiment, epitome, essence, quintessence, incarnation, manifestation, likeness, image, symbol, representation, portrayal, recreation, semblance.

personify *verb* embody, incarnate, exemplify, epitomize, represent, symbolize, typify, mirror.

personnel *noun* staff, employees, workers, workforce, labour force, helpers, crew, members, manpower, human resources, people.

perspective *noun* **1** (*see things from a different perspective*) viewpoint, point of view, vantage point, standpoint, stand, stance, outlook, angle, aspect, slant, attitude, context. **2** (*offering a fine perspective from the steeple*) view, vista, outlook, prospect, sweep, scene, panorama. **3** (*try to see things in perspective*) proportion, equilibrium, balance, context, relation.

perspicacious *adj* perceptive, observant, clear-sighted, percipient, sensitive, responsive, aware, alert, quick, quick-witted, astute, shrewd, sharp, sharp-witted, keen, acute, penetrating, discerning, discriminating, sagacious, judicious, wise, intelligent, clever, understanding, intuitive. OPPOSITE: dull.

perspicacity *noun* perception, perceptiveness, perspicaciousness, perspicuity, percipience, acuteness, alertness, astuteness, shrewdness, sharpness, keenness, penetration, discernment, discrimination, sensitivity, intuition, intuitiveness, insight, sagacity, acumen, sagaciousness, judiciousness, cleverness, intelligence, brains (*inf*), smartness, wisdom, wit, understanding. OPPOSITE: dullness.

perspicuity *noun* lucidity, clarity, clearness, transparency, plainness, straightforwardness, precision, distinctness, explicitness, intelligibility, comprehensibility, penetrability, limpidity. OPPOSITE: obscurity.

perspicuous *adj* lucid, clear, crystal-clear, limpid, transparent, plain, distinct, intelligible, comprehensible, understandable, explicit, unambiguous, straightforward, obvious, apparent, manifest, self-evident. OPPOSITE: obscure.

perspiration *noun* sweat, sweating, secretion, exudation, moisture, wetness, diaphoresis.

perspire *verb* sweat, secrete, exude, drip, swelter, glow.

persuade *verb* induce, bring round (*inf*), win over, convince, convert, move, urge, coerce, inveigle, impel, influence, lean on (*inf*), sway, prevail upon, incline, dispose, lead on, incite, prompt, entice, lure, allure, tempt, coax, talk into, sweet-talk (*inf*), soft-soap (*inf*), cajole, wheedle, lobby, advise, counsel. OPPOSITE: deter.

persuasion *noun* **1** (*they needed little persuasion*) persuading, convincing, inducement, enticement, temptation, cajolery, coercion, exhortation, prompting, urging, blandishment, inveiglement, sweet-talking (*inf*), soft-soaping (*inf*), arm-twisting (*inf*), wheedling, advice. OPPOSITE: dissuasion. **2** (*an argument of great persuasion*) persuasiveness, power, potency, force, cogency, influence, pull (*inf*). **3** (*others of the same persuasion*) belief, philosophy, faith, creed, credo, sect, cult,

denomination, school of thought, affiliation, camp, side, faction. **4** (*could not be altered in her persuasion*) opinion, belief, tenet, conviction, certitude, view, viewpoint.

persuasive *adj* convincing, credible, cogent, telling, effective, effectual, potent, forceful, pushy (*inf*), weighty, influential, impressive, logical, plausible, slick, sound, valid, compelling, winning, moving, touching. OPPOSITE: unconvincing.

pert *adj* **1** (*she's a pert little thing*) impudent, impertinent, insolent, rude, cheeky, cocky (*inf*), saucy, audacious, bold, brash, brazen, forward, fresh, flippant, flip (*inf*), presumptuous, bumptious. OPPOSITE: bashful. **2** (*a pert appearance*) jaunty, perky, lively, brisk, sprightly, smart, spruce, natty (*inf*), stylish, chic, trim, dapper.

pertain *verb* **1** (*this does not pertain to the matter in hand*) relate, apply, regard, concern, refer, bear on, have a bearing upon, appertain. **2** (*land pertaining to the property*) belong, go along with.

pertinacious *adj* tenacious, dogged, persistent, persevering, relentless, determined, resolute, purposeful, steadfast, constant, firm, unshakable, stubborn, insistent, obstinate, obdurate, mulish, pig-headed, bull-headed, self-willed, strong-willed, stiff-necked, inflexible, intransigent, intractable, uncompromising, unyielding, headstrong, wilful, refractory, perverse. OPPOSITE: irresolute.

pertinent *adj* relevant, germane, material, apposite, apropos, apt, appropriate, applicable, fit, fitting, suitable, proper, seemly, admissible, to the point, to the purpose. OPPOSITE: irrelevant.

perturb *verb* **1** (*it perturbs me*) trouble, disturb, upset, worry, disquiet, alarm, agitate, bother, discompose, faze, ruffle, fluster, unsettle, disconcert, discountenance, vex, harass. OPPOSITE: compose. **2** (*the system was perturbed by bad weather*) disorder, confuse, muddle, disorder, disarrange, jumble, unsettle.

perturbed *adj* disturbed, worried, troubled, anxious, upset, uncomfortable, uneasy, ill at ease, alarmed, fearful, nervous, shaken, restless, unsettled, discomposed, disconcerted, disquieted, agitated, flustered, flurried, ruffled, harassed, vexed.

perusal *noun* scrutiny, study, examination, inspection, check, browse, run-through, skim, read, look, glance.

peruse *verb* **1** (*peruse the birth certificate*) study, scrutinize, examine, inspect, read, pore over, scan, survey, look through, leaf through, work over, run through, check. **2** (*casually peruse the newspaper*) browse through, skim through, glance through, scan.

pervade *verb* permeate, spread through, pass through, diffuse, fill, charge, saturate, impregnate, penetrate, percolate, imbue, infuse, suffuse, infiltrate.

pervasive *adj* pervading, permeating, prevalent, widespread, ubiquitous, common, rife, extensive, universal, general, omnipresent, inescapable, diffuse, suffusive.

perverse *adj* **1** (*a perverse passion*) perverted, depraved, deviant, abnormal, unhealthy, improper. **2** (*a somewhat perverse character*) contrary, contradictory, bloody-minded, contumacious, disobedient, refractory, capricious, wayward, headstrong, wilful, stiff-necked, stubborn, obstinate, dogged, mulish, pig-headed, obdurate, pertinacious, intractable, intransigent, unyielding, awkward, difficult, troublesome, unruly, uncontrollable, unmanageable. OPPOSITE: docile. **3** (*he was in a perverse mood*) cantankerous, cross, peevish, petulant, ill-tempered, ill-natured, irascible, spiteful, fractious, crabbed, crabby, surly, churlish, stroppy (*inf*). OPPOSITE: affable.

perversion *noun* **1** (*sexual perversion*) corruption, depravity, debauchery, kinkiness (*inf*), immorality, vice, prostitution, wickedness, deviance, deviation, abnormality, unnaturalness, irregularity, aberration, kink (*inf*). **2** (*a perversion of what really happened*) distortion, deviation, misinterpretation, misconstruction, misrepresentation, twisting, travesty, falsification, misapplication, misuse.

perversity *noun* contrariness, contradictiveness, contradictoriness, wilfulness, intransigence, frowardness, disobedience, obstinacy, obduracy, pertinacity, stubbornness, pigheadedness, waywardness, awkwardness, cussedness (*inf*), wrong-headedness, contumacy, senselessness, unreasonableness, unruliness, unmanageableness, unmanageability, uncontrollability, rebelliousness, troublesomeness.

pervert *verb* **1** (*pervert an innocent soul*) corrupt, warp, deprave, debauch, abuse, lead astray, debase, degrade, vitiate. **2** (*pervert his master's words*) twist, warp, distort, misrepresent, falsify, misconstrue, misinterpret, garble, misuse, misapply. **3** (*pervert the course of justice*) subvert, deflect, divert, avert, turn aside, misdirect.
➤ *noun* deviant, perv (*inf*), degenerate, debauchee, deviate, weirdo (*inf*), offball (*inf*).

perverted *adj* corrupt, corrupted, depraved, debauched, debased, vitiated, deviant, bent (*inf*), kinky (*inf*), pervy (*inf*), abnormal, unnatural, aberrant, warped, twisted, distorted, unhealthy, sick, immoral, wicked, evil, vile.

pessimism *noun* hopelessness, defeatism, fatalism, cynicism, depression, dejection, despair, resignation, gloom, gloominess, glumness, despondency, melancholy, distrust, doubt, suspicion. OPPOSITE: optimism.

pessimist *noun* defeatist, fatalist, cynic, doubter, melancholic, misanthrope, worrier, alarmist, prophet of doom, doom merchant (*inf*), killjoy (*inf*), wet blanket (*inf*), doubting Thomas. OPPOSITE: optimist.

pessimistic *adj* negative, cynical, defeatist, fatalistic, alarmist, gloomy, glum, depressed, dejected, despondent, dismal, downhearted, morose, resigned, hopeless, despairing, bleak, distrustful, doubting, suspicious. OPPOSITE: optimistic.

pest *noun* nuisance, bother, irritation, irritant, aggravation, annoyance, vexation, worry, problem, trial, trouble, tribulation, inconvenience, bore, drag (*inf*), pain (*inf*), pain in the neck (*inf*), pain in the arse (*sl*), thorn in the flesh (*inf*). OPPOSITE: blessing.

pester *verb* plague, torment, bedevil, trouble, worry, provoke, bother, disturb, harass, hassle (*inf*), hound, badger, nag, get at (*inf*), pick on, annoy, bug (*inf*), irritate, aggravate (*inf*), vex, fret, irk.

pestilence *noun* **1** (*thousands fell victim to the pestilence*) plague, bubonic plague, Black Death, epidemic, pandemic, disease, sickness, contagion, infection, visitation, pest. **2** (*the pestilence of biting insects*) scourge, curse, bane, blight, canker, cancer, torment, affliction.

pestilential *adj* **1** (*pestilential interference in our lives*) annoying, irritating, infuriating, bothersome, vexatious, vexing, irksome, troublesome, tiresome. OPPOSITE: beneficial. **2** (*a pestilential effect upon the environment*) pernicious, dangerous, destructive, ruinous, deadly, fatal, malign, deleterious, virulent, detrimental, harmful, hazardous, injurious, noxious, toxic, poisonous, venomous, corrupting, foul, evil, unhealthy, insalubrious. OPPOSITE: pure.

pet[1] *noun* (*teacher's pet*) favourite, darling, idol, apple of one's eye (*inf*), blue-eyed boy (*inf*), treasure, jewel.
➤ *adj* **1** (*his pet cat*) tame, tamed, domestic, domesticated, house-trained, house-broken. OPPOSITE: wild. **2** (*her pet theory*) favourite, favoured, preferred, chosen, particular, special, personal, dearest, dear, beloved, cherished, prized, treasured.
➤ *verb* **1** (*don't pet the dog*) stroke, caress, pat, fondle. **2** (*teenagers petting on the bench*) kiss, embrace, cuddle, snog (*inf*), smooch (*inf*), neck (*inf*), canoodle (*inf*).
pet name nickname, diminutive, endearment, term of endearment.

pet[2] *noun* (*be in a pet*) mood, bad mood, temper, bad temper, ill humour, sulk, tantrum, pique, huff (*inf*), paddy (*inf*), hump (*inf*), grumps (*inf*).

peter *verb* **peter out** dwindle, fizzle out (*inf*), run out, die away, die out, melt away, evaporate, taper off, fade, wane, ebb, diminish, fail, fall through, cease, stop, come to an end, come to a halt, come to nothing.

petition *noun* **1** (*sign the petition*) appeal, protest, round robin. **2** (*sent their petition to the prime minister*) request, entreaty, plea, supplication, prayer, invocation, solicitation, application, suit.
➤ *verb* ask, request, appeal to, call upon, beg, implore, beseech, plead with, crave, entreat, bid, urge, press, supplicate, pray, solicit, apply to, sue.

petrify *verb* **1** (*the tree was petrified over the course of many centuries*) calcify, ossify, fossilize, harden, solidify, set, turn to stone. **2** (*petrified of the police*) stupefy, stun, daze, numb, paralyse, immobilize, transfix, dumbfound, stagger, astonish, astound, amaze, appal, horrify, frighten, panic, alarm, terrify. OPPOSITE: reassure.

petticoat *noun* slip, underskirt, undergarment.

pettish *adj* peevish, petulant, sulky, touchy, thin-skinned, testy, tetchy, snappish, waspish, cross, huffy (*inf*), bad-tempered, ill-humoured, irritable, ratty (*inf*), querulous, splenetic, liverish, fractious, fretful, grumpy. OPPOSITE: genial.

petty *adj* **1** (*sorted out the few remaining petty matters*) trivial, minor, lesser, secondary, subordinate, unimportant, inessential, insignificant, inconsequential, trifling, paltry, measly (*inf*), contemptible, piddling (*inf*), piffling (*inf*), slight, small, little, inconsiderable, negligible. OPPOSITE: important. **2** (*rather a petty attitude*) small-minded, narrow-minded, mean-minded, mean, stingy, niggardly, grudging, ungenerous, cheap, shabby, spiteful. OPPOSITE: generous.

petulant *adj* peevish, pettish, cross, grumpy, crotchety, crabby, crabbed, crusty, touchy, testy, ratty (*inf*), huffy (*inf*), browned off (*inf*), irascible, irritable, bad-tempered, ill-humoured, waspish, snappish, fretful, complaining, captious, querulous, impatient, sullen, sulky, moody, sour, ungracious. OPPOSITE: genial.

phantom *noun* ghost, spectre, apparition, spirit, spook (*inf*), wraith, phantasm, shade, revenant, chimera, illusion, figment, hallucination, vision.
➤ *adj* phantasmal, phantasmagoric, unreal, illusory, spectral, ghostly. OPPOSITE: real.

pharisaical *adj* pharisaic, sanctimonious, moralizing, canting, self-righteous, goody-goody (*inf*), holier-than-thou, pietistic, preachy, hypocritical, insincere.

phase *noun* **1** (*beginning a new phase in our history*) period, time, season, chapter, part, point, juncture, step. **2** (*going through an awkward phase*) spell, stage, period, time. **3** (*the phases of the moon*) aspect, facet, side, angle, stage, state, condition, position.
phase in introduce, incorporate, ease in, bring in, start, initiate.
phase out axe (*inf*), close, stop, terminate, wind down, wind up, run down, pull out, ease off, taper off, eliminate, deactivate, dispose of, get rid of, remove, withdraw.

phenomenal *adj* marvellous, wonderful, sensational, extraordinary, prodigious, stupendous, amazing, astonishing, astounding, mind-blowing (*inf*), mind-boggling (*inf*), breathtaking, remarkable, notable, exceptional, uncommon, unique, singular, outstanding, unparalleled, unprecedented, unheard-of, unbelievable, incredible, fantastic, fabulous, miraculous. OPPOSITE: ordinary.

phenomenon *noun* **1** (*no explanation for the phenomenon*) occurrence, event, happening, experience, incident, episode, fact, circumstance, sight, appearance. **2** (*he is a phenomenon*) marvel, wonder, prodigy, miracle, sensation, spectacle, rarity, curiosity.

philander *verb* flirt, womanize (*inf*), court, dally, trifle, play around, fool around, sleep around (*inf*).

philanderer *noun* womanizer, flirt, trifler, dallier, ladies' man, lady-killer (*inf*), libertine, playboy, stud (*inf*), wolf (*inf*), Casanova, Don Juan, lothario.

philanthropic *adj* **1** (*a philanthropic gesture*) humanitarian, humane, public-spirited, solicitous, altruistic, selfless, unselfish, kind, kindhearted, gracious. OPPOSITE: selfish. **2** (*a philanthropic organization*) charitable, almsgiving, benevolent, beneficent, munificent, benignant, benign, liberal, openhanded, generous, giving, bountiful, bounteous.

philanthropist *noun* **1** (*likes to be thought of as a philanthropist*) humanitarian, altruist. **2** (*we rely upon the support of philanthropists*) patron, backer, benefactor, sponsor, donor, contributor, giver, helper, almsgiver.

philanthropy *noun* **1** (*noted for his philanthropy*) humanitarianism, humanity, humaneness, public-spiritedness, social concern, social conscience, altruism, unselfishness, selflessness, kindheartedness. **2** (*an act of great philanthropy*) benevolence, beneficence, benignity, charity, charitableness, alms-giving, generosity, openhandedness, largess, kindness, liberality, munificence, bounty, bountifulness, bounteousness, patronage, sponsorship.

philippic *noun* diatribe, tirade, harangue, fulmination, denunciation, condemnation, criticism, attack, onslaught, reproof, reprimand, rebuke, abuse, insult, invective, obloquy, vituperation.

philistine *noun* boor, lout (*inf*), barbarian, lowbrow, ignoramus, bourgeois, yahoo, vulgarian. OPPOSITE: aesthete.
➤ *adj* uncultured, unrefined, uncultivated, uneducated, unlettered, unread, unenlightened, ignorant, boorish, barbaric, crass, loutish, lowbrow, bourgeois, tasteless. OPPOSITE: cultured.

philosopher *noun* philosophizer, thinker, theorist, theorizer, metaphysician, metaphysicist, logician, sage, guru, scholar, pundit, expert.

philosophical *adj* **1** (*wrote several philosophical works*) philosophic, wise, learned, erudite, thinking, thoughtful, pensive, contemplative, meditative, reflective, logical, rational, theoretical, metaphysical, analytical, abstract. **2** (*a philosophical attitude*) resigned, calm, composed, cool, collected, impassive, unruffled, self-possessed, dispassionate, tranquil, serene, stoic, stoical, patient, imperturbable, unperturbed, phlegmatic, rational, logical, realistic, practical. OPPOSITE: agitated.

philosophy *noun* **1** (*a degree in philosophy*) logic, reasoning, reason, metaphysics, aesthetics, knowledge, wisdom, thought, thinking. **2** (*she has a different philosophy upon life*) viewpoint, point of view, view, outlook, attitude, ideology, doctrine, beliefs, values, ideas, tenets, convictions, principles. **3** (*acted with philosophy in the face of danger*) resignation, calmness, calm, coolness, cool (*inf*), composure, equanimity, aplomb, self-possession, phlegm, serenity, tranquillity, stoicism, dispassion, imperturbability, patience, impassivity, logic, rationality, realism, practicality. OPPOSITE: agitation.

phlegmatic *adj* **1** (*a phlegmatic character*) calm, composed, cool, placid, impassive, dispassionate, imperturbable, serene, tranquil, philosophical, matter-of-fact, stoical. OPPOSITE: emotional. **2** (*received a phlegmatic reception*) apathetic, indifferent, uninterested, lethargic, languorous, sluggish, listless, indolent, stolid, bovine, unemotional, unfeeling, cold, frigid, dull, inert.

phobia *noun* fear, terror, neurosis, obsession, hang-up (*inf*), thing (*inf*), anxiety, horror, dread, dislike, distaste, aversion, hatred, loathing, detestation, revulsion, repulsion, antipathy. OPPOSITE: mania.

phone *noun* **1** (*pick up the phone*) telephone, blower (*inf*), receiver, handset, mobile phone, car phone, radio telephone. **2** (*give us a phone*) call, phone call, ring, buzz (*inf*), bell (*inf*), tinkle (*inf*).
➤ *verb* telephone, call, call up, ring, ring up, dial, contact, get in touch with, get on the phone, make a call, give a buzz (*inf*), give a bell (*inf*), give a tinkle (*inf*).

phoney *adj* **1** (*phoney money*) fake, bogus, sham, counterfeit, fraudulent, forged, feigned, false, trick, imitation. **2** (*a phoney welcome*) fake, feigned, bogus, sham, counterfeit, cod (*inf*), assumed, simulated, put-on,

affected, contrived, false, mock, make-believe, pseudo (*inf*), imitation, spurious, mock, ersatz.
➤ *noun* **1** (*the priest is a phoney*) impostor, pretender, fraud, fake, faker, sham, pseud (*inf*), quack (*inf*), humbug (*inf*), mountebank. **2** (*the necklace is a phoney*) fake, counterfeit, forgery, imitation, sham.

phosphorescent *adj* luminous, radiant, glowing, fluorescent, bright, luminescent.

photocopy *noun* copy, duplicate, Photostat®, Xerox®, facsimile, fax.
➤ *verb* copy, duplicate, Photostat®, print, run off, Xerox®, fax.

photograph *noun* picture, photo (*inf*), snapshot, shot, snap (*inf*), mug shot (*inf*), print, slide, still, transparency, image, likeness.
➤ *verb* take, snap (*inf*), shoot, film, video, tape, record.

photographic *adj* **1** (*a photographic record*) pictorial, filmic, cinematic, graphic. **2** (*a photographic memory*) detailed, accurate, exact, precise, vivid, faithful, lifelike, retentive.

phrase *noun* expression, locution, idiom, saying, remark, utterance, comment, clause, construction.
➤ *verb* express, put, word, style, couch, formulate, frame, say, utter, term, voice, deliver.

phraseology *noun* **1** (*study the author's phraseology*) style, syntax, phrasing, usage, idiom, language, parlance, speech, diction. **2** (*scientific phraseology*) phrasing, expression, language, wording, words, terminology, vocabulary.

physical *adj* **1** (*physical sensations*) bodily, corporeal, corporal. **2** (*leave behind the physical world*) earthly, material, unspiritual, corporeal, carnal, fleshly, fleshy, mortal. OPPOSITE: spiritual. **3** (*no physical trace of their presence*) material, solid, substantial, tangible, palpable, concrete, real, visible, actual.

physician *noun* doctor, doc (*inf*), quack (*inf*), healer, medic (*inf*), medico (*inf*), medical practitioner, general practitioner, GP, MD, specialist, consultant.

physiognomy *noun* features, face, mug (*inf*), clock (*inf*), dial (*inf*), countenance, visage, lineaments, look, aspect, appearance.

physique *noun* build, frame, figure, body, shape, form, constitution, make-up, structure.

pick *verb* **1** (*pick which one you want*) pick out, choose, select, elect, single out, mark out, decide on, go for, opt for, plump for (*inf*), sift out, sort out, settle on, fix on, prefer, favour. OPPOSITE: reject. **2** (*pick me some flowers*) pluck, gather, pull, cut, collect, take in, harvest, cull, glean. OPPOSITE: leave. **3** (*pick a safe*) open, crack, jemmy, prize open, force, break into, break open, rob, steal. **4** (*pick an argument*) provoke, incite, instigate, prompt, cause, start, begin, lead to, produce, give rise to, foment.
➤ *noun* **1** (*take your pick*) choice, choosing, selection, option, decision, favour, preference. **2** (*the pick of the bunch*) best, choicest, cream, flower, pride, prize, prime, élite, elect, choicest. OPPOSITE: reject.
pick at nibble at, peck at, play with, toy with, push round the plate.
pick off 1 (*pick off the sentries one by one*) shoot, shoot

down, gun down, fire at, hit, kill, take out. **2** (*pick off the buds*) remove, detach, pull off, pluck off, take away.
pick on bully, persecute, tease, torment, get at (*inf*), badger, nag, hector, bait, goad, needle (*inf*), criticize, blame, find fault with.
pick out 1 (*pick out a dress*) pick, choose, select, single out, handpick, separate out, sort out, cull. **2** (*pick out two figures in the dark*) distinguish, discriminate, tell apart, discern, perceive, recognize, notice, spot, make out.
pick up 1 (*pick up the bags*) lift, raise, hoist, take up. OPPOSITE: drop. **2** (*he'll pick you up on the way*) call for, collect, fetch, give a lift, give a ride. **3** (*things will pick up*) improve, perk up (*inf*), get better, mend, rally, recover, gain, advance, make progress, make headway, take a turn for the better. **4** (*see what you can pick up*) discover, unearth, gather, come across, chance upon, stumble across, happen upon, learn, hear, find, glean. **5** (*picked up by the police*) arrest, nick (*inf*), pinch (*inf*), nab (*inf*), collar (*inf*), apprehend, detain, take into custody, run in (*inf*), pull in (*inf*). **6** (*pick up where we left off*) resume, carry on, start again, begin again, continue, go on. **7** (*pick up a skill*) acquire, gain, obtain, grasp, master. **8** (*picked it up cheaply*) buy, purchase, acquire, get, obtain. **9** (*picked up a cold*) catch, get, go down with, come down with, contract. **10** (*pick up messages from outer space*) receive, detect, hear, get. **11** (*hope to pick up a girl*) take up with, fall in with, meet, get off with (*inf*).

picket *noun* **1** (*pickets prevented lorries entering the plant*) picketer, flying picket, striker, demonstrator, protester, objector, dissident, rebel. **2** (*post pickets round the perimeter*) guard, sentry, sentinel, patrol, watch, lookout, scout. **3** (*tied the goat to a picket*) post, stake, spike, peg, upright, pike, palisade, paling, pale, stanchion.
➤ *verb* **1** (*picket the plant*) blockade, boycott, demonstrate at, protest at. **2** (*picket the defences*) guard, patrol. **3** (*picket the meadow*) enclose, fence off, stake off, hedge in, pen in, rail in, corral, palisade, surround, box in, shut in, wall in. **4** (*picket the goat to a stake*) tie up, tether, fasten, secure.

pickle *noun* **1** (*cheese and pickle*) relish, chutney. **2** (*found themselves in a bit of a pickle*) mess, bind (*inf*), fix (*inf*), spot (*inf*), tight spot (*inf*), hot water (*inf*), jam (*inf*), pinch (*inf*), hole (*inf*), scrape (*inf*), predicament, plight, trouble, difficulty, quandary, dilemma, problem.
➤ *verb* marinade, souse, steep, preserve, conserve, cure, salt.

pick-me-up *noun* tonic, boost, shot in the arm (*inf*), bracer, restorative, restorer, refreshment, stimulant, stimulus.

pickpocket *noun* thief, purse-snatcher, dip (*inf*).

picnic *noun* **1** (*a family picnic*) outdoor meal, alfresco meal, outing, excursion. **2** (*the flight was no picnic*) easy task, pushover (*inf*), walkover (*inf*), piece of cake (*inf*), doddle (*inf*), breeze (*inf*), cinch (*inf*), child's play (*inf*).

pictorial *adj* illustrative, illustrated, representational, graphic, diagrammatic, schematic, photographic.

picture *noun* **1** (*a picture of a boat*) drawing, sketch, painting, canvas, etching, engraving, photograph, print, illustration, portrait, likeness, representation, image, semblance. **2** (*took several pictures of the view*) photograph, photo, shot, snapshot, snap, slide, print,

still. **3** (*he gave a fairly clear picture of what happened*) account, description, depiction, portrayal, impression, report, story, narrative, tale. **4** (*the picture of good health*) epitome, personification, embodiment, essence, quintessence, model, archetype, exemplar. **5** (*the very picture of his father*) image, spitting image (*inf*), spit (*inf*), dead ringer (*inf*), double, duplicate, twin, lookalike, replica, copy, carbon copy, likeness. **6** (*starred in several silent pictures*) film, movie, motion picture, flick (*inf*).
➤ **verb 1** (*I can picture them now*) imagine, envisage, envision, visualize, see, call to mind, conceive of. **2** (*the artist has pictured her in deep shadow*) depict, portray, draw, sketch, illustrate, represent, reproduce, show, delineate, render, paint, photograph.
put someone in the picture inform, explain, communicate, notify, tell, fill in (*inf*), clue up (*inf*), keep posted (*inf*), bring up to speed, bring up to date, update.

pictures *pl noun* cinema, movies, flicks (*inf*), picture house, picture palace, film theatre, multiplex.

picturesque *adj* **1** (*a picturesque scene*) scenic, quaint, attractive, beautiful, pretty, lovely, charming, delightful, idyllic, pleasant, pleasing. OPPOSITE: ugly. **2** (*picturesque language*) colourful, vivid, graphic, strong, striking, impressive.

piddling *adj* **1** (*a few piddling little jobs to do*) minor, small, piffling (*inf*), trifling, trivial, unimportant, insignificant, fiddling, petty, paltry, useless, worthless. **2** (*paid a piddling amount of money*) meagre, derisory, contemptible, measly (*inf*), piffling (*inf*), negligible, small, tiny, slight, trifling, paltry, poor, low, mean, miserable, wretched.

pie *noun* pastry, tart, tartlet.
pie in the sky fantasy, romance, illusion, delusion, mirage, daydream, dream, pipedream, castle in the air (*inf*), reverie, notion.

piebald *adj* pied, black and white, brown and white, dappled, flecked, mottled, speckled, brindled, spotted, variegated, skewbald, pinto.

piece *noun* **1** (*pick up every last piece*) bit, fragment, shred, scrap, shard, chip, splinter, crumb, morsel, flake, speck, fleck. **2** (*this must be the missing piece*) bit, part, segment, section, element, component, unit, constituent, division. OPPOSITE: whole. **3** (*a large piece of bread*) chunk, lump, hunk, block, slab, bar, slice, sliver, wedge, dollop, portion, morsel, bite, mouthful. **4** (*a piece of curtain fabric*) length, quantity, bit, scrap, snippet, remnant, offcut, sample. **5** (*a piece of the action*) share, cut, slice, portion, fraction, quantity, allotment, allocation, quota, percentage. **6** (*several fine pieces of porcelain*) example, specimen, sample. **7** (*write a piece for the local paper*) article, column, item, report, essay, review, story, paper. **8** (*a piece of music*) work, composition, creation, opus, production. **9** (*a piece of art*) work, painting, canvas, creation.
➤ **verb** join, unite, connect, put together, fit, fit together, assemble, fix, mend, repair, patch. OPPOSITE: separate.
all in one piece intact, unbroken, whole, complete, integral, entire, undamaged, sound, safe and sound, unharmed, unhurt, uninjured.
go to pieces break down, panic, lose control, lose one's

head, collapse, crumple, crack up (*inf*), fall apart, disintegrate.

pièce de résistance *noun* masterpiece, masterwork, showpiece, magnum opus, chef d'oeuvre, prize, jewel.

piecemeal *adv* piece by piece, bit by bit, little by little, gradually, by degrees, in stages, at intervals, in steps, in fits and starts, fitfully, intermittently.

pied *adj* piebald, mottled, dappled, speckled, brindled, spotted, flecked, streaked, skewbald, motley, variegated, multicoloured, parti-coloured. OPPOSITE: plain.

pier *noun* **1** (*steered the boat for the pier*) jetty, quay, wharf, dock, breakwater, landing, landing stage. **2** (*a platform supported by several piers*) support, upright, pillar, post, pile, piling, column, buttress.

pierce *verb* **1** (*the nail pierced his hand*) penetrate, enter, puncture, perforate, impale, transfix, spike, spear, skewer, stab, lance, prick, run through, stick into. **2** (*pierce the wood in three places*) hole, punch, perforate, bore, drill. **3** (*my heart was pierced by her remorse*) touch, move, affect, rouse, cut to the quick, pain, wound, hurt, stab, sting, prick. **4** (*the beam of a torch pierced through the fog*) penetrate, burst through, pass through, probe, light up, filter, percolate. **5** (*screams suddenly pierced the silence*) penetrate, pervade, permeate, fill, shatter.

piercing *adj* **1** (*a piercing scream*) shrill, high-pitched, earsplitting, earpiercing, loud, sharp, penetrating. **2** (*a man of piercing intelligence*) keen, sharp, sharp-witted, discerning, perceptive, percipient, perspicacious, shrewd, alert, astute, penetrating, probing, searching. **3** (*a piercing pain in the elbow*) fierce, sharp, intense, powerful, acute, extreme, severe, racking, stabbing, excruciating, exquisite, agonizing, painful, lacerating, penetrating, shooting. OPPOSITE: dull. **4** (*a piercing wind*) cold, freezing, frigid, arctic, wintry, frosty, nippy, raw, numbing, probing, searching, keen, sharp, biting, bitter, fierce, severe.

piety *noun* **1** (*a man of great piety*) piousness, devoutness, godliness, saintliness, holiness, sanctity, religion, religiousness, spirituality, faith, devotion, reverence, veneration. OPPOSITE: impiety. **2** (*filial piety*) respect, respectfulness, deference, obedience, dutifulness, duty.

pig *noun* **1** (*pigs on the farm*) hog, swine, sow, boar, piggy (*inf*), porker (*inf*). **2** (*her husband is a real pig*) beast, animal, brute, bastard (*inf*), monster, slob (*inf*), boor. **3** (*he's a pig at the table*) glutton, greedy guts (*inf*), hog (*inf*), guzzler (*inf*), gourmand, gormandizer.
➤ **verb** pig out, gorge, guzzle, stuff, wolf (*inf*).

pigeonhole *noun* **1** (*a letter in his pigeonhole*) cubbyhole, locker, cubicle, compartment, box, niche. **2** (*a tendency to put her friends in pigeonholes*) category, class, classification, compartment, section, slot (*inf*), niche.
➤ **verb 1** (*they should not pigeonhole people like that*) classify, categorize, label, tag, file, catalogue, compartmentalize, sort. **2** (*the project has been pigeonholed*) shelve, postpone, defer, put off, put on ice (*inf*), put on the back burner (*inf*).

pigheaded *adj* obstinate, stubborn, obdurate, perverse, self-willed, stiff-necked, inflexible, intractable, intransigent, contrary, mulish, dense, stupid, unyielding, uncompromising, headstrong, wilful, wrongheaded, bullheaded, adamant, dogged, tenacious, single-minded.

pigment *noun* colour, colouring, tint, tincture, hue, dye, paint, stain, colourant.

pile[1] *noun* **1** (*a pile of rubbish*) heap, mound, mountain, stack, mass, store, hoard, stockpile, bundle, accumulation, collection, assortment. **2** (*I have a pile of work to do*) load, lot, stack, heap, pack, ton, great deal, quantity, mountain, ocean, oodles, lashings. **3** (*they made a pile from the business*) fortune, bomb (*inf*), mint (*inf*), packet (*inf*), bundle (*inf*), wad (*inf*), heap, stash, riches, megabucks (*inf*), tidy sum (*inf*), pretty penny (*inf*). **4** (*inherited a huge Georgian pile*) mansion, building, edifice, structure.

➤ *verb* **1** (*pile the bricks over there*) heap, stack. OPPOSITE: scatter. **2** (*he piled up a mountain of tins over the years*) amass, mass, store up, stockpile, load, hoard, lay in, lay by, accumulate, build up, assemble, collect, gather. **3** (*hundreds of fans piled into the pub*) crowd, flock, jam, pack, crush, squeeze, flood, stream, tumble, rush, charge.

pile it on exaggerate, overemphasize, overplay, overstate, overdo, magnify, dramatize, overdramatize, lay it on (*inf*), blow up (*inf*).

pile up mount up, increase, grow, accumulate, multiply, escalate, soar.

pile[1] *noun* (*piles for the bridge were driven into the ground*) post, piling, pillar, column, support, foundation, pier, upright, buttress.

pile[2] *noun* **1** (*the deep pile of the carpet*) nap, shag, surface, texture. **2** (*the vacuum cleaner was blocked with pile*) fur, down, wool, fluff, fuzz, hair, fibre.

pile-up *noun* crash, smash (*inf*), smash-up (*inf*), prang (*inf*), collision, accident, bump, wreck.

pilfer *verb* steal, purloin, filch, pinch (*inf*), nick (*inf*), thieve, take, rob, shoplift, embezzle, misappropriate, walk off with, knock off (*inf*), swipe (*inf*), nobble (*inf*), lift (*inf*), snaffle (*inf*).

pilgrim *noun* crusader, traveller, wanderer, wayfarer, palmer, worshipper, devotee, hajji.

pilgrimage *noun* expedition, excursion, tour, journey, trip, voyage, peregrination, crusade, mission, hajj.

pill *noun* tablet, capsule, lozenge, pellet, bolus.

pillage *verb* ransack, rifle, rob, plunder, loot, maraud, raid, raze, sack, despoil, lay waste, strip, spoil, rape, ravage, vandalize.

➤ *noun* plunder, plundering, looting, pillaging, laying waste, sacking, ransacking, ravaging, marauding, raiding, harrying, depredation, spoliation, devastation, spoils, loot, booty.

pillar *noun* **1** (*a plinth supported by pillars*) column, shaft, post, pole, mast, pier, upright, stanchion, prop, pile, piling, pilaster, support. **2** (*a pillar of the community*) bastion, mainstay, upholder, backbone, support, rock, leading light (*inf*).

pillory *verb* brand, denounce, show up, stigmatize, ridicule, laugh at, mock, shame, pour scorn on, heap scorn on, cast a slur on.

pillow *noun* cushion, bolster, headrest, rest.

pilot *noun* **1** (*a fighter pilot*) captain, aviator, airman,

airwoman, aeronaut, flier. **2** (*a harbour pilot*) navigator, steerer, steersman, helmsman, guide.

➤ *verb* **1** (*pilot the aircraft*) fly, drive, operate, run, direct, control, handle, manage, manoeuvre. **2** (*pilot the vessel into harbour*) navigate, steer, guide, direct. **3** (*piloted her charges through the crowd*) guide, steer, direct, lead, conduct, shepherd, usher.

➤ *adj* trial, test, experimental, model.

pimple *noun* spot, zit (*inf*), blackhead, pustule, boil, swelling, eruption.

pin *verb* **1** (*pin the papers together*) staple, clip, fasten, secure, join, fix, attach. **2** (*pin the list on the wall*) attach, stick, fix, tack, fasten, nail. **3** (*tried to pin the blame on the others*) put, place, lay, attribute, ascribe, attach.

➤ *noun* peg, bolt, nail, tack, rivet, spike, dowel, clip, staple, brooch.

pin down 1 (*pinned down under the weight*) hold down, hold fast, constrain, force, press, pressurize, confine, restrain, bind, tie, immobilize. OPPOSITE: release. **2** (*we must try to pin down what it means*) pinpoint, nail down (*inf*), home in on, locate, identify, define, specify, determine. **3** (*you ought to pin them down until you get a decision*) pressure, pressurize, force, compel, constrain, nail down.

pinch *verb* **1** (*she pinched his leg*) nip, tweak, squeeze. **2** (*his shoes pinched his toes*) chafe, nip, hurt, crush, cramp, constrict, confine, press, compress. **3** (*my wallet's been pinched*) steal, take, rob, thieve, filch, snatch, pilfer, purloin, swipe (*inf*), nick (*inf*), knock off (*inf*), walk off with (*inf*), lift (*inf*), snaffle (*inf*), misappropriate, embezzle. OPPOSITE: return. **4** (*they've been pinched by the law*) arrest, run in (*inf*), pick up (*inf*), take into custody, pull in (*inf*), nick (*inf*), nab (*inf*), collar (*inf*), do (*inf*), bust (*inf*), book (*inf*), nail (*inf*), apprehend, detain, catch, capture, seize. **5** (*obliged to pinch and scrape to survive*) cut back, economize, save, stint, spare, scrimp, skimp, budget, tighten one's belt (*inf*).

➤ *noun* **1** (*gave her a little pinch*) squeeze, nip, tweak. **2** (*a pinch of salt*) bit, speck, mite, smidgen (*inf*), tad (*inf*), dash, jot, touch, trace, taste, soupçon. **3** (*might help in a pinch*) emergency, exigency, urgency, crisis, necessity, stress, pressure, oppression, difficulty, hardship, predicament, plight.

at a pinch if necessary, if need be, just possibly, in an emergency, with great difficulty.

pinched *adj* drawn, haggard, gaunt, careworn, worn, peaky, pale, thin, starved.

pine *verb* **1** (*pine for some excitement*) long, yearn, ache, thirst, hunger, hanker, crave, wish, desire, covet, sigh, lust. OPPOSITE: have. **2** (*she is slowly pining away*) languish, fret, droop, flag, wilt, wither, weaken, decline, fade, fail, waste, decay, sink, grieve, mourn. OPPOSITE: revive.

pinion *verb* **1** (*pinion the prisoner on the floor*) pin down, hold down, hold fast, press down, constrain, restrain, immobilize. **2** (*the convict's arms were pinioned*) fasten, bind, tie, chain, manacle, shackle, fetter, hobble.

pink[1] *adj* **1** (*pink in colour*) rose, reddish, pale red, salmon, shell, flesh. **2** (*a pink face*) rosy, roseate, blushing, flushed.

➤ *noun* perfection, best, flower, peak, summit, height, top, zenith, extreme, acme.

in the pink fit, fighting fit (*inf*), healthy, in perfect health, in rude health, hale and hearty, very well, in good shape, in fine fettle, right as rain (*inf*).

pink² *verb* 1 (*pink the canvas*) prick, pierce, perforate, punch, stab, bore, drill. 2 (*pink the edge of the fabric*) cut, notch, score, incise, serrate, scallop, crenellate.

pinnacle *noun* 1 (*the pinnacle of her fame*) peak, summit, height, eminence, crest, crown, top, cap, apex, apogee, acme, zenith, meridian, climax, culmination. OPPOSITE: base. 2 (*scaling alpine pinnacles*) mountain, peak, height, summit, top, crest. 3 (*the pinnacle of the church*) spire, steeple, belfry, turret, needle, pyramid, cone.

pinpoint *verb* identify, pin down, specify, define, discover, distinguish, determine, locate, place, spot, home in on, zero in on (*inf*), nail down (*inf*).

pioneer *noun* 1 (*a pioneer in the outback*) settler, colonist, colonizer, explorer, frontiersman, frontierswoman, trailblazer. 2 (*a pioneer in his field*) innovator, inventor, pathfinder, front-runner, ground-breaker, founder, founding father, architect, discoverer, developer, leader. ➤ *verb* launch, introduce, initiate, invent, discover, create, originate, instigate, start, begin, inaugurate, institute, found, establish, set up, open up, develop, prepare, lead the way, spearhead, blaze a trail, break new ground, pave the way (*inf*), set the ball rolling (*inf*).

pious *adj* 1 (*a pious priest*) devout, godly, God-fearing, faithful, saintly, sanctified, holy, spiritual, religious, reverent, good, righteous, virtuous, moral, dedicated, devoted, dutiful. 2 (*her pious attitude was irritating*) sanctimonious, self-righteous, holier-than-thou (*inf*), unctuous, pietistic, hypocritical, insincere, goody-goody (*inf*). OPPOSITE: impious.

pipe *noun* 1 (*pipes carrying water*) pipeline, piping, line, drainpipe, main, tube, tubing, cylinder, duct, flue, conduit, channel, passage, hose, overflow. 2 (*puffed on his pipe*) claypipe, clay, brier, meerschaum, hookah, hubble-bubble, peace pipe. 3 (*played three notes on his pipe*) whistle, penny whistle, flute, fife, recorder. ➤ *verb* 1 (*pipe hot water to the bathroom*) channel, funnel, siphon, bring, carry, take, convey, conduct, duct, transmit, deliver, supply. 2 (*a bird piping in the bush*) squeak, tweet, twitter, chirp, chirrup, cheep, peep, whistle, warble, tootle, trill, shrill, sing.

pipe down stop talking, shut up (*inf*), be quiet, quieten down, hush, belt up (*inf*).

pipe dream *noun* daydream, dream, delusion, mirage, castle in the air (*inf*), pie in the sky (*inf*), fantasy, reverie, romance, vagary.

pipeline *noun* pipe, main, tube, line, conduit, channel, passage, duct, conveyor.

in the pipeline under way, on the way, coming, brewing, imminent, in preparation, in production, planned.

piquancy *noun* 1 (*the piquancy of this dish*) pungency, spiciness, spice, tang, kick (*inf*), punch (*inf*), bite, edge, sharpness, tartness, zest, zing (*inf*), pepperiness, ginger, flavour. 2 (*the piquancy of their exchanges*) liveliness, vigour, vitality, spirit, pep (*inf*), pizzazz (*inf*), zest, zip (*inf*), colour, raciness, saltiness, provocativeness, edge

(*inf*), kick (*inf*), punch, excitement, interest, fascination, allurement.

piquant *adj* 1 (*a piquant recipe*) pungent, sharp, biting, stinging, tart, tangy, flavoursome, savoury, zesty, spicy, hot, peppery, seasoned. OPPOSITE: bland. 2 (*a piquant conversation*) lively, spirited, sparkling, scintillating, interesting, stimulating, provocative, intriguing, fascinating, colourful, juicy (*inf*), titillating, racy, salty. OPPOSITE: dull.

pique *verb* 1 (*he was piqued by her remarks*) wound, hurt, sting, offend, affront, get (*inf*), upset, put out, mortify, annoy, irritate, miff (*inf*), nettle (*inf*), peeve (*inf*), gall, irk, vex, displease, anger, incense, rile. OPPOSITE: please. 2 (*pique one's interest*) excite, arouse, awaken, kindle, galvanize, stimulate, provoke, stir, rouse, spur, goad, whet. ➤ *noun* offence, umbrage, resentment, indignation, annoyance, irritation, vexation, displeasure, gall, anger. OPPOSITE: pleasure.

piracy *noun* 1 (*a life of piracy at sea*) buccaneering, freebooting. 2 (*piracy of our designs*) plagiarism, hijacking, infringement, theft, stealing, robbery, bootlegging.

pirate *noun* 1 (*the galleon was seized by pirates*) corsair, buccaneer, rover, sea rover, freebooter, robber, brigand, raider, plunderer, marauder. 2 (*pirates selling bootleg videos*) plagiarist, plagiarizer, infringer. ➤ *verb* plagiarize, copy, reproduce, poach, crib (*inf*), lift (*inf*), nick (*inf*), steal, pinch, appropriate.

pit *noun* 1 (*a pit in the ground*) hole, cavity, crater, pothole, mine, coalmine, excavation, quarry, diggings, working, ditch, trench, shaft, well, abyss, chasm, gulf. 2 (*pits all over her face*) pockmark, pock, mark, scar, dimple, indentation, dent, depression, gouge, hollow. ➤ *verb* indent, dent, depress, dimple, pothole, pockmark, blemish, scar, mark, nick, notch.

pit against compete, match, oppose, set against.

pitch *verb* 1 (*pitch the ball*) hurl, fling, throw, chuck (*inf*), bung (*inf*), cast, launch, fire, toss, lob, bowl, sling, heave, aim, direct. OPPOSITE: catch. 2 (*pitch the tent*) erect, raise, put up, set up, establish, fix, settle, plant, locate, place, station. OPPOSITE: strike. 3 (*pitch headlong*) plunge, plummet, topple, tumble, dive, fall, drop. 4 (*the carriage pitched suddenly*) roll, reel, lurch, list, keel, sway, flounder, wallow, stagger. ➤ *noun* 1 (*tensions have now reached their highest pitch*) level, degree, grade, height, depth, point, extent, intensity. 2 (*the pitch of the slope*) gradient, slope, degree, incline, steepness, angle, tilt, slant, inclination, dip, cant. 3 (*the pitch of the vessel*) list, lurch, roll, reeling, swaying, rocking, keeling. 4 (*the pitch of her voice*) tone, timbre, sound, frequency, level, modulation. 5 (*the next pitch of the ball*) throw, chuck (*inf*), toss, lob, plunge, roll, fling, hurl. 6 (*the team walked onto the pitch*) field, sports field, playing-field, ground, park, arena, stadium. 7 (*sales pitch*) spiel (*inf*), patter, jargon, line, talk, chatter, gabble.

pitch in join in, muck in (*inf*), chip in (*inf*), do one's bit (*inf*), participate, contribute, help, assist, cooperate, collaborate, lend a hand.

pitch-black *adj* black, dark, pitch-dark, jet, jet-black, coal-black, ebony, inky, unlit, impenetrable, stygian.

pitcher *noun* jug, jar, ewer, urn, vessel, container, crock.

piteous *adj* pitiable, pitiful, pathetic, plaintive, mournful, sad, sorrowful, doleful, grievous, sorry, wretched, woeful, lamentable, deplorable, poignant, moving, touching, affecting, distressing, harrowing, heartrending, heartbreaking.

pitfall *noun* trap, snare, catch, hazard, danger, peril, snag, drawback, stumbling block, difficulty.

pith *noun* **1** (*the pith of his theory*) essence, quintessence, substance, gist, point, crux, nub, core, heart, kernel, meat, marrow. **2** (*his speech lacked pith*) importance, import, significance, consequence, moment, weight, depth, force, power, strength, vigour, cogency.

pithy *adj* terse, succinct, concise, compact, condensed, summary, brief, short, laconic, pointed, cogent, expressive, forceful, meaningful, weighty, incisive, trenchant, telling. OPPOSITE: verbose.

pitiable *adj* pitiful, pathetic, poor, sad, sorry, wretched, miserable, doleful, woeful, woesome, piteous, grievous, harrowing, lamentable, mournful, deplorable, distressing. OPPOSITE: enviable.

pitiful *adj* **1** (*a pitiful scene*) pathetic, pitiable, sorry, sad, wretched, doleful, mournful, miserable, piteous, affecting, emotional, emotive, moving, poignant, heartrending, heartbreaking, harrowing, distressing, poor, lamentable. **2** (*offered a pitiful pay increase*) deplorable, contemptible, miserable, lamentable, woeful, shabby, laughable, despicable, vile, low, base, mean, meagre, poor, pathetic, dismal, inadequate, worthless, paltry, insignificant. OPPOSITE: admirable.

pitiless *adj* merciless, unmerciful, unsparing, harsh, severe, hardhearted, callous, cold, coldhearted, cold-blooded, unfeeling, uncaring, unsympathetic, heartless, unkind, inhuman, inhumane, brutal, cruel, ruthless, relentless, unrelenting, unremitting, implacable, inexorable. OPPOSITE: compassionate.

pittance *noun* allowance, ration, modicum, trifle, peanuts (*inf*), chicken feed (*inf*).

pity *noun* **1** (*show pity for his victims*) compassion, tenderness, mercy, quarter, forgiveness, forbearance, clemency, grace, charity, humanity, understanding, kindness, sympathy, feeling, fellow feeling, emotion, commiseration, condolence, regret, sorrow, sadness, distress. OPPOSITE: cruelty. **2** (*it was a great pity*) disappointment, shame, crying shame (*inf*), regret, misfortune, bad luck, sin, crime (*inf*), bummer (*sl*).
➤ *verb* commiserate with, sympathize with, empathize with, feel for, feel sorry for, grieve for, weep for, bleed for.

take pity on forgive, pardon, show charity to, show mercy to, have mercy on, spare, reprieve, relent, melt, feel sorry for, feel for, commiserate with, sympathize with, empathize with, have compassion for.

pivot *noun* **1** (*hinged on a central pivot*) axis, fulcrum, axle, spindle, pin, hinge. **2** (*the pivot of all her hopes*) hub, centre, central point, focus, focal point, heart, raison d'être.
➤ *verb* **1** (*the arm pivots on this point*) revolve, rotate, spin, swing, turn, twirl. **2** (*everything pivots on the*

result of this match*) depend, hang, rely, hinge, turn, revolve around.

pixie *noun* elf, fairy, sprite, brownie, goblin, leprechaun.

placard *noun* notice, poster, advertisement, advert (*inf*), ad (*inf*), bill, sticker, sign, billboard.

placate *verb* pacify, appease, mollify, conciliate, soothe, lull, calm, calm down, quiet, assuage, propitiate, reconcile, win over. OPPOSITE: incense.

place *noun* **1** (*a place on the map*) spot, location, scene, site, position, situation, point, whereabouts, venue. **2** (*reports of riots in several places*) area, region, district, vicinity, locality, locale, neighbourhood, quarter, town, city, village, hamlet. **3** (*show me the place where it hurts*) spot, part, area, bit. **4** (*know one's place*) position, station, status, standing, rank, grade, role. **5** (*a place at court*) post, position, appointment, situation, office, berth, billet (*inf*), job, employment, role, niche. **6** (*not my place to interfere*) job, task, duty, responsibility, role, function, business, right, prerogative, affair, concern, charge. **7** (*in place of the cancelled programme*) lieu, stead, space. **8** (*she went back to his place*) house, flat, home, pad (*inf*), digs (*inf*), abode, dwelling, residence, property, domicile, accommodation, quarters, lodgings. **9** (*the diners took their places*) seat, position, space, post. **10** (*returned to its proper place*) position, location.
➤ *verb* **1** (*place everything within easy reach*) put, put down, lay, lay down, set, set down, deposit, dispose, plant, position, fix, locate, situate, station, settle, stand, lodge, stick, rest, leave. OPPOSITE: remove. **2** (*place the applicants according to their experience*) arrange, sort, order, group, rank, grade, class, classify, categorize, dispose, bracket. OPPOSITE: disarrange. **3** (*he could not place her at first*) identify, recognize, remember, know, pinpoint, categorize. **4** (*place your future in our hands*) entrust, put, lay, rest, set, consign, invest. **5** (*tried to place the children in good homes*) install, establish, accommodate, appoint, assign, allocate.

in place in position, arranged, set up, in order, all correct, working.

in place of instead of, in lieu of, in exchange for, as a replacement for, as an alternative to, as a substitute for, in someone's stead, taking the place of.

out of place 1 (*her things were all out of place*) disarranged, disordered, in disarray, in a mess, topsy-turvy, higgledy-piggledy (*inf*). **2** (*his comments were totally out of place*) inappropriate, unsuitable, unfitting, improper, tactless, unbecoming, unseemly, inapposite. **3** (*she felt out of place amidst such luxury*) uncomfortable, uneasy, ill at ease.

put someone in their place humble, humiliate, shame, mortify, crush, deflate, bring low, cut down to size (*inf*), take down a peg or two.

take place happen, occur, come about, come to pass, crop up, come off, befall, fall, betide, transpire, go on.

take the place of replace, substitute for, supersede, stand in for, cover for, act for.

placid *adj* **1** (*a placid nature*) calm, cool, coolheaded, serene, peaceful, peaceable, tranquil, quiet, undisturbed, unmoved, unruffled, unperturbed, untroubled, unfazed (*inf*), unexcitable, unflappable, even-tempered, unemotional, composed, collected, self-possessed, levelheaded, gentle, mild, easygoing, equable, imperturbable. OPPOSITE: excitable. **2** (*placid sea conditions*) calm, still, motionless, smooth, tranquil, halcyon, peaceful, pacific, restful, undisturbed, unruffled. OPPOSITE: stormy.

plagiarize *verb* pirate, borrow, rip off (*inf*), crib (*inf*), lift (*inf*), poach, steal, thieve, nick (*inf*), appropriate, copy, reproduce, imitate, forge, counterfeit.

plague *noun* **1** (*the plague killed millions*) epidemic, pandemic, pestilence, disease, sickness, infection, contagion. **2** (*a plague of flies*) infestation, swarm, host, multitude, invasion, influx. **3** (*the people suffered a series of plagues*) calamity, disaster, curse, bane, scourge, cancer, blight, affliction, visitation, evil, torment, trouble, trial, tribulation. **4** (*the press are a plague to me*) pest, nuisance, annoyance, irritant, vexation, aggravation (*inf*), bother, pain (*inf*), pain in the neck (*inf*), pain in the arse (*sl*), thorn in the flesh (*inf*), problem, trouble. OPPOSITE: blessing.
➤ *verb* **1** (*plagued by misfortune*) torment, torture, persecute, distress, trouble, afflict, bedevil, haunt. **2** (*plagued by photographers*) harass, harry, hassle (*inf*), badger, hound, dog, hamper, hinder, pester, bug (*inf*), tease, annoy, irritate, aggravate (*inf*), vex, irk, bother, molest, disturb, trouble, upset, worry.

plain *adj* **1** (*a plain difference*) clear, crystal-clear, clear-cut, distinct, obvious, apparent, transparent, visible, discernible, perceptible, noticeable, patent, pronounced, marked, striking, conspicuous, evident, manifest, open, overt, blatant, palpable, unmistakable. **2** (*plain instructions*) clear, straightforward, uncomplicated, simple, intelligible, understandable, comprehensible, accessible, lucid, unambiguous. OPPOSITE: obscure. **3** (*a plain style*) simple, unadorned, undecorated, unembellished, unornamented, unpatterned, unsophisticated, modest, restrained, muted, pure, basic, Spartan, austere, stark, unpretentious, ordinary, everyday, commonplace, workaday, homely. OPPOSITE: fancy. **4** (*she had rather a plain face*) ordinary, unattractive, unremarkable, ugly, unprepossessing, unlovely, ill-favoured. OPPOSITE: attractive. **5** (*a plain man*) ordinary, average, typical, simple, straightforward, forthright, downright, plain-spoken, outspoken, honest, sincere, upfront (*inf*), guileless, artless, unassuming, unaffected, unpretentious, ingenuous, frank, candid, open, blunt, direct. OPPOSITE: devious.
➤ *adv* completely, totally, utterly, thoroughly, downright, positively, unquestionably, undeniably, incontrovertibly, simply, quite.
➤ *noun* plateau, tableland, lowland, grassland, flat, prairie, steppe, pampas, savannah, tundra, mesa.

plain-spoken *adj* plain-speaking, candid, frank, blunt, direct, outspoken, straightforward, forthright, downright, upfront (*inf*), open, honest, truthful, unequivocal, unambiguous, explicit, outright. OPPOSITE: evasive.

plaintive *adj* mournful, doleful, sad, unhappy, disconsolate, melancholy, rueful, wistful, sorrowful, wretched, woeful, woebegone, piteous, pitiful, pathetic, heartrending, heartbroken, brokenhearted, grief-stricken. OPPOSITE: joyous.

plan *noun* **1** (*a plan to rob the bank*) plan of action, scheme, design, arrangement, programme, schedule,

project, idea, proposal, proposition, suggestion, plot, device, method, means, way, procedure, formula, system, strategy, tactics, contrivance. **2** (*it was his plan to go*) idea, intention, intent, aim, hope, ambition, aspiration, scheme, project, proposal. **3** (*a plan of the building*) diagram, chart, map, blueprint, layout, draft, drawing, sketch, illustration, representation, delineation.
➤ *verb* **1** (*plan to take the throne*) scheme, plot, design. **2** (*plan the day ahead*) arrange, organize, prepare, schedule, programme, line up, mastermind. **3** (*plan a building*) outline, draft, design, map out, sketch. **4** (*plan a way in*) devise, plot, formulate, work out, think of, think out, contrive, concoct, invent, frame, develop, shape. **5** (*plan to leave in the morning*) intend, purpose, propose, mean, aim, resolve, envisage, contemplate, foresee, want, wish, seek.

plane[1] *adj* (*a plane surface*) flat, level, even, flush, smooth, regular, uniform, plain, horizontal. OPPOSITE: uneven.
➤ *noun* **1** (*ensure the blocks are kept on a plane*) flat, level. **2** (*took us to a new plane of existence*) level, stratum, position, class, rank, rung, echelon, footing, condition, status, degree, stage.

plane[2] *noun* (*catch the last plane home*) aeroplane, airplane, aircraft, airliner.
➤ *verb* **1** (*plane through the air*) glide, fly, float, drift, sail, wing. **2** (*boats plane the bay*) glide, skim, skate.

plant *noun* **1** (*bought several plants at the nursery*) flower, vegetable, herb, shrub, bush, tree, weed. **2** (*industrial plant*) factory, mill, foundry, works, yard, workshop, shop. **3** (*installed the plant he needed*) machinery, equipment, apparatus, gear.
➤ *verb* **1** (*plant them in a rockery*) sow, seed, set out, scatter, bury, embed, root, implant, transplant. OPPOSITE: uproot. **2** (*plant that chair over there*) set, place, position, situate. **3** (*planted the idea in her head*) lodge, fix, settle, imbed, insert, establish. OPPOSITE: remove. **4** (*plant a secret camera in her room*) conceal, hide, secrete, disguise, place.

plaque *noun* plate, tablet, slab, panel, sign, shield, brass, medal, medallion, badge.

plaster *noun* **1** (*coat the walls with plaster*) plasterwork, mortar, cement, stucco, gypsum. **2** (*put a plaster on the scratch*) sticking-plaster, Elastoplast®, Band-aid®, dressing, bandage, patch.
➤ *verb* daub, bedaub, smear, spread, cover, coat, overlay.

plastic *adj* **1** (*plastic material*) soft, ductile, mouldable, malleable, shapeable, pliable, pliant, supple, tensile, flexible. **2** (*a plastic personality*) yielding, tractable, pliable, pliant, compliant, mouldable, receptive, responsive, impressionable, controllable, manageable, malleable, flexible, supple. **3** (*a plastic smile*) false, phoney (*inf*), sham, bogus, pseudo (*inf*), spurious, artificial, assumed, unnatural, synthetic, meretricious.

plate *noun* **1** (*food on a plate*) dish, platter, salver, trencher. **2** (*a plate of food*) plateful, serving, helping, portion, course, dish. **3** (*a plate of ice*) sheet, slab, layer, coating, pane, panel. **4** (*black-and-white photographic plates*) illustration, picture, print, photograph, lithograph. **5** (*a brass plate on the door*) plaque, sign, tablet, brass.

➤ *verb* coat, cover, face, overlay, laminate, veneer, galvanize, anodize, gild, silver, electroplate.

plateau *noun* **1** (*a mountain plateau*) highland, tableland, table, upland, plane, mesa. **2** (*business activity has reached a plateau*) lull, respite, break, let-up, flat period, level, levelling off, stability.

platform *noun* **1** (*spoke from the platform*) stage, dais, stand, podium, rostrum, soapbox (*inf*). **2** (*they fought on a free trade platform*) plan, programme, policy, manifesto, strategy, principles, objectives, aims, ideas, intentions, tenets, party line.

platitude *noun* truism, cliché, hackneyed statement, commonplace, stock expression, stereotype, trite phrase, overworked phrase, banality, inanity, chestnut (*inf*), bromide (*inf*).

platitudinous *adj* banal, clichéd, hack, hackneyed, overworked, stale, corny (*inf*), trite, stereotyped, well-worn, stock, commonplace, truistic, inane, tired, dull, flat, vapid.

platonic *adj* nonphysical, nonsexual, spiritual, romantic, incorporeal, intellectual, ideal, idealistic, transcendent.

platoon *noun* company, patrol, squad, squadron, battery, team, group, outfit (*inf*).

platter *noun* plate, dish, tray, salver, trencher, charger.

plaudits *pl noun* applause, clapping, hand (*inf*), ovation, acclaim, acclamation, accolade, cheers, congratulations, compliments, praise, bouquets (*inf*), commendation, approval, approbation. OPPOSITE: criticism.

plausible *adj* **1** (*a plausible excuse*) reasonable, likely, logical, probable, possible, imaginable, conceivable, credible, believable, persuasive, convincing, cogent. OPPOSITE: implausible. **2** (*a plausible manner*) smooth, smooth-talking, smooth-tongued, specious, glib.

play *verb* **1** (*watching the child play*) have fun, amuse oneself, enjoy oneself, occupy oneself, divert oneself, romp, frolic, frisk, gambol, sport, revel, caper, cavort, clown, fool. OPPOSITE: work. **2** (*play each other at tennis every day*) compete, contend, participate, take part, join in, challenge, oppose, take on, vie with, rival. **3** (*played the part of the king*) perform, act, portray, represent, impersonate. **4** (*don't play with your food*) toy, trifle, fiddle. **5** (*play the piano*) perform on, tinkle on (*inf*), hammer (*inf*), polish the ivories (*inf*). **6** (*play a deception on the others*) perform, accomplish, carry out, execute, do, engage in, act out. **7** (*moonlight playing on the water*) flicker, flit, dart, twinkle, flash, dance. **8** (*play the horses*) bet, wager, gamble, speculate, risk, chance.

➤ *noun* **1** (*all children enjoy play*) fun, revelry, amusement, merrymaking, enjoyment, entertainment, diversion, recreation, leisure, pastime, game, hobby, sport, caper, frolic, gambol, jest. OPPOSITE: work. **2** (*act in a play*) drama, comedy, tragedy, farce, melodrama, piece, entertainment, show, performance. **3** (*lots of play in the arm of the machine*) action, movement, freedom of movement, motion, flexibility, give (*inf*), slack, leeway, elbow-room, sweep, swing, margin. **4** (*give full play to his feelings*) scope, range, room, space, latitude, freedom,

liberty, free rein, licence, indulgence. **5** (*the play of political influences*) action, activity, function, operation, working, exercise, agency, interaction, interplay, transaction. **6** (*it was only in play*) jest, fun, joking, teasing, sport, foolery, kicks (*inf*), lark (*inf*), prank, laugh.

play around 1 (*don't play around with the controls*) interfere, meddle, tamper, fiddle, mess, toy, fidget. **2** (*his wife suspects he has been playing around*) womanize, philander, fool around, mess about (*inf*), flirt, trifle, dally.

play at pretend, make out, affect, put on an act, make like (*inf*), go through the motions (*inf*).

play down minimize, diminish, make light of, gloss over, soft-pedal (*inf*), downplay, underplay, understate, underrate, underestimate, undervalue, belittle, disparage. OPPOSITE: emphasize.

play on exploit, take advantage of, capitalize on, trade on, profit by, turn to account, utilize, impose on, milk, walk all over (*inf*), abuse, misuse.

play up 1 (*tried to play up their past record*) emphasize, stress, accentuate, talk up (*inf*), exaggerate, magnify, highlight, spotlight, underline, underscore, point up, call attention to, bring to the fore. **2** (*my stomach is playing up today*) give trouble, cause trouble, trouble, annoy, bother, irritate, hurt. **3** (*the children were playing her up*) misbehave, give trouble. **4** (*the generator is playing up*) malfunction, go wrong, go on the blink (*inf*).

play up to flatter, ingratiate oneself with, suck up to (*inf*), butter up (*inf*), brown-nose (*sl*), soft-soap (*inf*), bootlick (*inf*), lick one's boots (*inf*), curry favour with, kiss ass (*sl*), pander to, blandish, fawn over, toady to.

playboy *inf* philanderer, womanizer, ladies' man, lady-killer, rake, man-about-town (*inf*), socialite, libertine, roué, debauchee, stud (*sl*).

player *noun* **1** (*a player in the competition*) competitor, contestant, contender, participant, sportsman, sportswoman. **2** (*a player on the stage*) actor, actress, tragedian, comedian, trouper, performer, entertainer, artiste, artist, Thespian. **3** (*a player in the band*) musician, performer, instrumentalist, accompanist, virtuoso, artist, artiste.

playful *adj* **1** (*she was in a playful mood*) sportive, frolicsome, frisky, coltish, lively, spirited, high spirited, sprightly, rollicking, gay, fun-loving, merry, cheerful, jolly, coy, impish, kittenish, mischievous, puckish, skittish. **2** (*several playful comments*) humorous, joking, jesting, teasing, tongue-in-cheek, waggish, facetious, arch, roguish. OPPOSITE: serious.

playground *noun* play area, playing-field, adventure playground, amusement park, park, recreation ground, pleasure ground.

playwright *noun* dramatist, writer, dramaturge, dramaturgist, scriptwriter, screenwriter.

plea *noun* **1** (*a plea for clemency*) request, entreaty, appeal, petition, overture, suit, prayer, invocation, supplication, solicitation, intercession, imploration. **2** (*made several pleas concerning his behaviour*) excuse, explanation, pretext, apology, extenuation, vindication, justification, defence, claim. OPPOSITE: accusation. **3** (*the court heard the plea of the plaintiff in silence*) allegation, suit, case, claim, action.

plead verb **1** (*plead for mercy*) appeal to, entreat, beg, beseech, crave, implore, supplicate, petition, ask, request, solicit, supplicate, pray to, importune. **2** (*plead guilty*) declare, assert, state, allege, maintain, claim, put forward, present, argue, reason, adduce.

pleasant adj **1** (*a pleasant evening*) delightful, agreeable, enjoyable, pleasing, pleasurable, gratifying, entertaining, nice, lovely, charming, delectable, fine, refreshing, welcome, satisfactory, satisfying, acceptable, fair. **2** (*a pleasant couple*) charming, nice, lovely (*inf*), friendly, amiable, congenial, genial, likable, affable, cheerful, cheery, agreeable, good-humoured, courteous, engaging, winning, winsome. OPPOSITE: unpleasant.

pleasantry noun **1** (*exchanging a few pleasantries*) remark, comment. **2** (*related a few pleasantries to the president*) joke, jest, bon mot, quip, wisecrack (*inf*), witticism, sally, banter, badinage.

please verb **1** (*this should please them*) delight, gratify, humour, gladden, cheer, content, satisfy, fulfil, indulge, amuse, entertain, tickle, tickle pink (*inf*), divert, charm, captivate, attract, appeal to, suit. OPPOSITE: offend. **2** (*I will do as I please*) like, wish, want, desire, choose, opt, prefer, will, see fit, think fit.

pleased adj glad, happy, cheerful, contented, satisfied, fulfilled, gratified, delighted, thrilled, rapt, overjoyed, elated, tickled, chuffed (*inf*), euphoric, over the moon (*inf*), on cloud nine (*inf*), tickled pink (*inf*), pleased as punch (*inf*). OPPOSITE: upset.

pleasing adj **1** (*a pleasing sensation*) agreeable, pleasant, delightful, lovely (*inf*), nice, good, fine, welcome, acceptable, pleasurable, enjoyable, entertaining, amusing, satisfying, gratifying. **2** (*a pleasing young man*) pleasant, agreeable, nice, lovely (*inf*), delightful, attractive, charming, good-humoured, amiable, affable, likable, genial, engaging, winning. OPPOSITE: obnoxious.

pleasure noun **1** (*it gave her great pleasure*) gratification, fulfilment, contentment, satisfaction, enjoyment, delectation, delight, happiness, gladness, joy, comfort, solace. OPPOSITE: pain. **2** (*it is the king's pleasure to hear more*) choice, preference, wish, desire, mind, will, inclination, purpose, command. **3** (*a harmless pleasure*) amusement, recreation, diversion, entertainment, enjoyment, delight, joy, fun.

plebeian adj **1** (*a plebeian sense of taste*) common, vulgar, coarse, unrefined, uncultured, uncultivated, coarse, base, low, mean, ignoble. **2** (*a plebeian background*) working-class, lower-class, proletarian, low-born, peasant, mean. OPPOSITE: aristocratic.
➤ noun commoner, proletarian, worker, peasant, pleb (*inf*), prole (*inf*), man in the street. OPPOSITE: aristocrat.

pledge noun **1** (*gave them his pledge*) promise, vow, oath, bond, covenant, guarantee, warrant, agreement, undertaking, commitment, assurance, word, word of honour. **2** (*offer the house as a pledge for the loan*) surety, security, collateral, deposit, earnest, gage, pawn, bond, guarantee, warranty, bail. **3** (*take this as a pledge of my good faith*) token, symbol, sign, mark, proof, testimony, evidence. **4** (*let us drink a pledge to the future*) toast, health.
➤ verb **1** (*we pledge to remain faithful*) promise, plight, vow, give one's word, take an oath, swear, swear an oath, engage, bind, contract, guarantee, vouch. **2** (*pledged everything he owned on the outcome*) guarantee, mortgage, put up, pawn, plight. **3** (*pledge the happy couple*) toast, drink to.

plenary adj full, complete, entire, whole, thorough, sweeping, general, absolute, unqualified, open, unconditional, unrestricted, unlimited, integral. OPPOSITE: restricted.

plentiful adj abundant, plenteous, bountiful, bounteous, overflowing, copious, ample, profuse, lavish, generous, liberal, full, replete, inexhaustible, large, huge, infinite, bumper, prolific, fruitful, productive. OPPOSITE: scanty.

plenty noun abundance, bounty, profusion, wealth, substance, fortune, riches, fund, mine, store, mass, volume, mountains, oodles (*inf*), great deal, quantity, lot, enough, sufficiency, excess, superfluity, plethora, glut, copiousness, plentifulness, plenteousness, plenitude, amplitude, fullness, exuberance, fruitfulness, fertility, prosperity, affluence, opulence, luxury. OPPOSITE: lack.

plenty of enough, more than enough, sufficient, many, masses of, lots of (*inf*), heaps of (*inf*), piles of (*inf*), stacks of (*inf*).

plethora noun superfluity, excess, surplus, surfeit, glut, overabundance, superabundance. OPPOSITE: scarcity.

pliable adj **1** (*made of pliable material*) pliant, flexible, bendable, bendy (*inf*), elastic, supple, stretchable, lithe, limber, ductile, tensile, malleable, plastic. **2** (*a pliable young woman*) yielding, amenable, compliant, docile, biddable, controllable, governable, tractable, adaptable, flexible, accommodating, manageable, persuadable, responsive, receptive, impressionable, influenceable, susceptible.

pliant adj **1** (*pliant wooden panels*) pliable, flexible, bendable, bendy (*inf*), supple, lithe, ductile, tensile, malleable, plastic, mouldable. OPPOSITE: stiff. **2** (*a pliant personality*) yielding, compliant, docile, amenable, tractable, adaptable, accommodating, flexible, impressionable, susceptible, receptive, manageable, biddable, persuadable, influenceable, responsive. OPPOSITE: intractable.

plight[1] noun (*found himself in a terrible plight*) predicament, quandary, dilemma, fix (*inf*), jam (*inf*), hole (*inf*), scrape (*inf*), pickle (*inf*), hot water (*inf*), tight spot (*inf*), spot (*inf*), tight corner, extremity, difficulty, trouble, perplexity, straits, dire straits, state, case, condition, position, situation, circumstances.

plight[2] verb (*plight one's troth*) promise, vow, swear, pledge, engage, contract, covenant, guarantee, propose, affiance, vouch.

plod verb **1** (*plod through the snow*) trudge, tread, stump, stomp, tramp, clump, lumber, plough through. **2** (*plod on with the work*) drudge, toil, labour, slog, grind, grub, persevere, plug away (*inf*), peg away (*inf*), soldier on.

plot noun **1** (*a plot to overthrow the government*) plan, scheme, conspiracy, intrigue, cabal, machination, ruse, stratagem. **2** (*the plot of the opera*) story, storyline, narrative, theme, thread, action, scenario, outline, subject. **3** (*a plot of ground*) patch, allotment, parcel, tract, area, allotment, lot.

> *verb* **1** (*plot to kill the king*) plan, scheme, conspire, intrigue, cabal, collude, connive, machinate, contrive, design, devise, conceive, hatch, brew, cook up (*inf*), think up, dream up, concoct, frame, project, draft, lay. **2** (*plot the course on a map*) chart, map, map out, draw, locate, sketch, mark, outline, compute, calculate, follow, record.

plough *verb* till, work, dig, spade, ridge, cultivate, furrow, break up, turn up.

plough into crash into, smash into, drive into, run into, bump into, collide, hit, plunge into, lunge into, career into, bulldoze into, hurtle into.

plough through plod through, trudge through, clump through, press through, push one's way through, stagger through, wade through, flounder through, forge one's way through, cut through.

ploy *noun* manoeuvre, move, tactic, stratagem, scheme, gambit, contrivance, device, ruse, subterfuge, wile, artifice, dodge, game, trick.

pluck *verb* **1** (*pluck from the bunch*) draw, pick, extract, pull out, remove. **2** (*pluck a flower for his lapel*) pick, gather, collect, harvest, take in. **3** (*pluck nervously at his jacket*) tug, tweak, jerk, yank (*inf*), pull, clutch, catch, snatch. **4** (*pluck on a guitar*) pick, strum, thrum, plunk, twang, finger.

> *noun* courage, bravery, valour, mettle, spirit, balls (*sl*), nerve (*inf*), grit (*inf*), guts (*inf*), bottle (*inf*), gumption (*inf*), boldness, daring, audacity, fearlessness, heroism, fortitude, backbone, intrepidity, determination, resolution, heart. OPPOSITE: cowardice.

plucky *adj* courageous, brave, valiant, valorous, mettlesome, spirited, game (*inf*), bold, daring, audacious, heroic, intrepid, gutsy (*inf*), gritty (*inf*), ballsy (*inf*), fearless, undaunted, unflinching, doughty, feisty, mettlesome, determined. OPPOSITE: cowardly.

plug *noun* **1** (*put the plug back in the barrel*) bung, stopper, cork, seal. **2** (*give our product a plug on the programme*) publicity, promotion, mention, good word, advertisement, advert (*inf*), ad (*inf*), commercial, push (*inf*), puff, hype (*inf*), blurb. **3** (*cotton wool plug*) wad, ball.

> *verb* **1** (*plug the gap*) stop, close, block, clog, fill, pack, stuff, choke, obstruct, dam, bung, cork, seal. OPPOSITE: open. **2** (*plug our products*) publicize, promote, mention, write up, build up, advertise, market, tout, puff, hype (*inf*), push (*inf*).

plug away persevere, keep on, keep trying, plod on, slog away, peg away, grind away, toil away, labour at, soldier on.

plum *adj* prize, choice, cream, pick, best, first-class, excellent, cushy (*inf*).

plumb *adv* **1** (*fell plumb to the valley floor*) vertically, perpendicularly, straight up, straight down, sheer. **2** (*hit the target plumb in the centre*) exactly, precisely, spot on (*inf*), slap (*inf*), bang (*inf*), right, dead. OPPOSITE: obliquely.

> *verb* sound out, fathom, gauge, measure, probe, penetrate, delve into, go into, explore, search out, unravel, examine, investigate, inspect, scrutinize.

plumb the depths of reach rock bottom, hit the lowest point.

plummet *verb* plunge, crash, dive, nosedive, drop, fall, descend, go down, stoop, swoop, tumble, hurtle.

plump[1] *adj* (*a plump figure*) fat, obese, stout, portly, rotund, corpulent, round, rounded, well-rounded, fleshy, chubby, flabby (*inf*), gross (*inf*), podgy, tubby, beefy (*inf*), dumpy, buxom, well-upholstered (*inf*), full, ample. OPPOSITE: thin.

plump[2] *verb* **1** (*she plumped the bags down*) put down, set down, dump (*inf*), plonk (*inf*), deposit. **2** (*he plumped into a chair*) drop, fall, flop, slump, sink, collapse, descend.

plump for choose, pick, select, prefer, opt for, decide on, back, side with, vote for, back, support, favour.

plunder *verb* **1** (*plundered goods from the shop*) rob, steal, thieve, purloin, filch, snaffle (*inf*), walk off with (*inf*), make off with. **2** (*pirates plundered the region*) loot, pillage, rob, rifle, strip, ransack, fleece, sack, rape, despoil, ravage, lay waste, devastate, raid, maraud, harry, depredate.

> *noun* booty, spoils, pickings, loot, swag (*inf*), prize, pillage, rapine, sack.

plunge *verb* **1** (*plunge over the edge of the cliff*) dive, nosedive, fall, fall headlong, plummet, swoop, pitch, jump. **2** (*watched their profits plunge*) plummet, dive, nosedive, drop, fall, sink, tumble, descend, go down, decrease. OPPOSITE: soar. **3** (*plunge it in cold water*) immerse, submerge, dip, duck, douse. **4** (*plunge forward*) dash, rush, career, charge, lurch, race, tear, hurry, hurtle, tumble, hasten, precipitate. OPPOSITE: amble. **5** (*plunged the room into darkness*) throw, cast, pitch. **6** (*plunged the knife into his back*) stab, jab, thrust, push, drive, shove, stick, ram.

> *noun* **1** (*no one saw her last plunge into the pool*) dive, nosedive, jump, drop, fall, descent, swoop. **2** (*the alarming plunge of the train into the tunnel*) lurch, charge, rush, dash, career, hurtle. **3** (*a calamitous plunge in share prices*) plummet, fall, drop, dip, nosedive, tumble.

plus *prep* and, with, added to, in addition to, as well as, with, coupled with. OPPOSITE: minus.

> *noun* bonus, extra, perk (*inf*), perquisite, benefit, fringe benefit, advantage, gain, surplus, credit, asset.

plush *adj* luxurious, luxury, de luxe, lavish, sumptuous, gorgeous, palatial, opulent, rich, costly, affluent, stylish, glitzy (*inf*), ritzy (*inf*), classy (*inf*), posh (*inf*), swanky (*inf*).

ply[1] *verb* **1** (*ply one's trade*) practise, exercise, carry on, pursue, follow, work at, engage in. **2** (*ply the axe*) manipulate, handle, wield, apply, utilize, use, operate, employ. **3** (*ply the guests with refreshments*) provide, supply, furnish, lavish, shower, feed, load, heap. **4** (*ply the newcomers with questions*) bombard, assail, besiege, beset, hassle (*inf*), harass, importune, press, urge. **5** (*ply between the two ports*) travel, go, ferry, shuttle.

ply[2] *noun* (*two-ply timber*) layer, leaf, thickness, fold, sheet, strand.

poach *verb* **1** (*poaching on company property*) trespass, encroach, infringe, intrude. **2** (*poach books from the library*) steal, take, appropriate, misappropriate, plunder, pilfer, pirate, nick (*inf*), lift (*inf*), rip off (*inf*), borrow (*inf*).

pocket *noun* **1** (*a pocket in the case*) bag, pouch, sack, receptacle, compartment, envelope, cavity, hollow.

2 (*hard on the pocket*) finances, resources, funds, budget, means, money, capital, assets, wherewithal. **3** (*pocket of resistance*) patch, island, area, zone.

> *adj* small, little, miniature, mini (*inf*), pint-size (*inf*), abridged, potted, compact, concise, portable.

> *verb* take, appropriate, misappropriate, steal, thieve, purloin, filch, pilfer, nick (*inf*), pinch (*inf*), snaffle (*inf*), lift (*inf*), help oneself to, gain. OPPOSITE: return.

pod *noun* shell, husk, case, hull, shuck.

podgy *adj* fat, stout, chubby, tubby, dumpy, paunchy, plump, corpulent, fleshy, roly-poly, rotund, squat, chunky, stubby, stumpy.

podium *noun* platform, stage, stand, rostrum, dais.

poem *noun* verse, rhyme, ode, sonnet, lyric, ballad, lay, elegy, limerick, jingle, song.

poet *noun* versifier, verse-maker, rhymer, rhymester, rhymist, lyricist, sonneteer, balladeer, elegist, bard, minstrel, poetaster.

poetic *adj* **1** (*great poetic writing*) poetical, lyric, lyrical, elegaic, metrical, rhythmical, rhyming. OPPOSITE: prosaic. **2** (*a poetic style*) imaginative, creative, flowery, figurative, symbolic. **3** (*poetic movements*) aesthetic, artistic, beautiful, tasteful, graceful, flowing, elegant, expressive, sensitive.

poetry *noun* poems, poesy, verse, versification, lyrics, rhyme, rhyming. OPPOSITE: prose.

poignancy *noun* **1** (*the poignancy of their embrace*) tenderness, emotion, emotionalism, sentiment, feeling, intensity, pathos, plaintiveness, sadness, sorrowfulness, tearfulness, evocativeness. **2** (*the poignancy of her plight*) pathos, piquancy, pungency, piteousness, pitifulness, sadness, sorrow, misery, distress, wretchedness, pain, painfulness, bitterness, tragedy.

poignant *adj* **1** (*a poignant moment*) moving, touching, emotional, sentimental, affecting, heartfelt, tender, sad, sorrowful, tearful, evocative, intense. **2** (*a poignant scene*) moving, affecting, touching, distressing, upsetting, heart-rending, heartbreaking, harrowing, wretched, miserable, painful, agonizing, pitiful, pitiable, piteous, pathetic, plaintive, sad, sorrowful, mournful, tragic.

point *noun* **1** (*a point of light*) dot, mark, speck, spot. **2** (*a point in the courtyard*) spot, place, position, site, location, locality, area, situation. **3** (*at this point in proceedings*) stage, phase, period, time, moment, instant, juncture. **4** (*the noise reached such a point we had to complain*) degree, extent, stage, intensity. **5** (*the point of the spear*) tip, top, end, extremity, apex, spike, prong, nib, spur, tine. **6** (*the ship rounded the point*) cape, headland, head, bluff, promontory, bill, foreland. **7** (*on the point of breaking down*) verge, brink. **8** (*the whole point of the exercise*) aim, purpose, end, object, objective, goal, intent, intention, reason, motive, use. **9** (*the central point of the story*) gist, crux, nub, heart, core, essence, meat, marrow, pith, substance, question, matter, issue, subject, topic, thrust, meaning, significance, import, importance, keynote, theme, drift, vein, tenor, burden. **10** (*go through the points in turn*) detail, item, part, element, particular. **11** (*the new car has several innovative points*) detail, characteristic, feature, aspect, attribute, quality, trait, property, facet, component, constituent, ingredient. **12** (*put a point at the end of each sentence*) full

point, full stop, stop, period. **13** (*score a point for every blow*) mark, run, hit, goal.

> *verb* **1** (*point the gun at the target*) direct, aim, level, train, bring to bear. **2** (*point the way*) show, indicate, signal, gesture towards, point to, point at, designate, specify, point out, denote, signify, suggest. **3** (*point the blade of the axe*) sharpen, edge, whet, taper, barb. OPPOSITE: blunt.

beside the point irrelevant, immaterial, incidental, unrelated, unconnected, not to the point, not to the purpose, out of place, neither here nor there (*inf*), inconsequential.

in point of fact in fact, as a matter of fact, actually, really, in reality, truly, in truth.

point of view 1 (*we all know your point of view*) opinion, view, belief, judgment, attitude, feeling, sentiment, position, viewpoint. **2** (*look at it from a different point of view*) view, viewpoint, perspective, outlook, approach, angle, slant, aspect, stance, standpoint, position.

point out point to, indicate, draw attention to, call attention to, show, reveal, identify, specify, mention, bring up, allude to, remind.

point to indicate, show, suggest, evidence, signify, be evidence of.

point up emphasize, lay emphasis on, stress, lay stress on, play up, underline, underscore, accentuate, highlight, spotlight, bring to the fore, call attention to, draw attention to.

to the point relevant, related, pertinent, connected, germane, pithy, applicable, appropriate, apt, fitting, suitable, apropos, apposite.

up to a point to some extent, to some degree, slightly, in part, partly, somewhat.

point-blank *adv* **1** (*she refused point-blank to say where she had been*) outright, directly, forthrightly, straightforwardly, straight, bluntly, frankly, candidly, rudely, abruptly, brusquely, unequivocally, unreservedly, plainly, explicitly, openly, unambiguously. **2** (*fired point-blank at them*) at close range, close up, close to, touching.

pointed *adj* **1** (*he made several pointed observations*) sharp, incisive, cutting, biting, trenchant, pertinent, keen, acute, penetrating, cogent, forceful, striking, telling, significant, accurate. **2** (*she studied him with pointed indifference*) marked, obvious, conspicuous, evident, striking, unmistakable. **3** (*a pointed iron railing*) sharp, barbed, peaked, tapering, edged, cuspidate. OPPOSITE: blunt.

pointer *noun* **1** (*the pointer on the compass is broken*) hand, indicator, needle, arrow, guide. **2** (*gave the child a few pointers on his departure*) tip, hint, suggestion, recommendation, warning, caution, guideline, guide, advice, information. **3** (*picked up one or two pointers about what they were planning*) indicator, indication, clue, sign. **4** (*tapped the blackboard with his pointer*) stick, rod, can, pole.

pointless *adj* meaningless, irrelevant, inane, stupid, absurd, ridiculous, senseless, nonsensical, aimless, vain, fatuous, foolish, futile, useless, fruitless, unproductive, unprofitable, unavailing, ineffectual, insignificant, empty, valueless, worthless. OPPOSITE: worthwhile.

poise *noun* **1** (*she kept her poise despite the turmoil*)

composure, self-possession, self-control, aplomb, assurance, self-assurance, presence, presence of mind, confidence, cool (*inf*), coolness, sang-froid, imperturbability, calmness, equanimity, equilibrium, serenity, dignity, elegance, grace, gracefulness, suaveness. **2** (*a delicate poise between the two sides*) balance, equilibrium, steadiness, stability, control. OPPOSITE: instability.
➤ **verb 1** (*poised a coin on his nose*) balance, steady, position, support. **2** (*the acrobats poised in mid-air*) hover, hang, float, suspend. **3** (*poised to act*) ready, prepare, brace, steady.

poised *adj* **1** (*he remained poised under pressure*) composed, serene, self-possessed, assured, self-assured, self-controlled, calm, cool, together (*inf*), collected, dignified, nonchalant, imperturbable, unperturbed, unflappable (*inf*), unfazed (*inf*), unruffled, self-confident, graceful, suave, urbane, elegant, debonair. **2** (*poised for action*) ready, prepared, set, all set, standing by, waiting, expectant, on the brink.

poison *noun* **1** (*snake poison*) venom, toxin. **2** (*revealing the poison in political life today*) contagion, pollution, contamination, corruption, blight, canker, malignancy, virus, bane.
➤ **verb 1** (*the wound had become poisoned*) infect, contaminated, make septic. **2** (*the river was poisoned by chemicals*) pollute, contaminate, blight. OPPOSITE: cleanse. **3** (*poison innocent minds*) corrupt, taint, deprave, defile, debauch, pervert, subvert, undermine, warp, blight, spoil, vitiate.

poisonous *adj* **1** (*poisonous chemicals*) venomous, toxic, deadly, fatal, lethal, mortal. OPPOSITE: harmless. **2** (*he is a poisonous influence upon her*) pernicious, baleful, cancerous, evil, malignant, malevolent, malicious, spiteful, corrupting, harmful, virulent, infectious, contagious, pestiferous, pestilent, noxious.

poke *verb* **1** (*poked his brother in the ribs*) jab, prod, dig, nudge, elbow, butt, stab, punch. **2** (*poke a stick in the fire*) jab, push, thrust, stick, stab, shove.
➤ **noun 1** (*earned him a poke in the ribs*) prod, dig, jab, thrust, nudge, shove, butt, punch. **2** (*gave it a poke with his finger*) jab, push, thrust, shove.

poke around rummage around, forage, grope around, nose around, search for, look for, rake through, ransack.

poke fun at make fun of, laugh at, taunt, tease, ridicule, rib (*inf*), send up (*inf*), mock, jeer, deride, chaff, parody, take the mickey out of (*inf*), take the piss out of (*sl*).

poke one's nose into meddle in, interfere in, tamper with, pry into, snoop into (*inf*), butt into (*inf*), intrude on, stick one's oar in (*inf*).

poke out stick out, jut out, project, protrude, extend, overhang, beetle, extrude.

poky *adj* confined, cramped, narrow, tight, small, little, tiny, crowded, incommodious. OPPOSITE: spacious.

polar *adj* **1** (*the polar regions*) Arctic, Antarctic, frozen, freezing, cold, icy, glacial, Siberian, extreme. OPPOSITE: tropical. **2** (*polar extremes*) opposite, contradictory, contrary, conflicting, opposed, diametrically opposed, antagonistic, ambivalent, antipodal, antithetical.

polarity *noun* opposition, oppositeness, contradiction, conflict, contrariety, difference, separation, ambivalence, antagonism, duality, dichotomy, paradox, antithesis.

pole[1] *noun* (*a pole stuck in the sand*) shaft, post, upright, rod, stick, staff, mast, standard, pillar, prop, support, stanchion, stake, bar, spar.

pole[2] *noun* (*went from one pole to another*) extremity, extreme, limit.

poles apart worlds apart, miles apart, at opposite extremes, incompatible, irreconcilable, completely different, widely separated.

polemic *adj* polemical, controversial, disputatious, contentious, argumentative.
➤ **noun** controversy, debate, dispute, argument.

polemics *pl noun* debate, dispute, discussion, argument, argumentation, disputation, controversy, contention, wrangling.

police *noun* police force, cops (*inf*), coppers (*inf*), the law (*inf*), constabulary, the fuzz (*inf*), the Bill (*inf*), boys in blue, pigs (*inf*), rozzers (*inf*).
➤ **verb 1** (*police the base*) patrol, guard, protect, defend, make the rounds of, keep watch on, keep in order, keep the peace. **2** (*police the whole affair*) regulate, control, keep under control, monitor, check, watch, observe, oversee, supervise.

police officer *noun* policeman, policewoman, officer, constable, PC, WPC, cop (*inf*), copper (*inf*), bobby (*inf*), pig (*inf*), rozzer (*inf*), bogey (*inf*), flatfoot (*inf*), peeler (*inf*), bluebottle (*inf*), the fuzz (*inf*), the law (*inf*), Old Bill (*inf*).

policy *noun* plan, programme, scheme, strategy, theory, method, practice, custom, tactic, course, line, approach, stance, position, system, schedule, procedure, code, protocol, rule, guideline.

polish *verb* **1** (*polish the furniture*) buff, burnish, shine, rub up, wax, smooth, clean, brighten. OPPOSITE: tarnish. **2** (*polish up his technique*) refine, finish, perfect, improve, enhance, cultivate, correct, brush up, touch up.
➤ **noun 1** (*admired the polish of the metal*) shine, lustre, sheen, gloss, smoothness, finish, glaze, veneer, brilliance, brightness, sparkle, burnish. OPPOSITE: dullness. **2** (*rubbed in some polish*) wax, varnish. **3** (*the polish of his stage act*) refinement, sophistication, finesse, urbanity, suavity, elegance, grace, poise, style, class, breeding, cultivation. OPPOSITE: coarseness.

polish off 1 (*polish off the food*) finish, eat up, consume, devour, put away, shift (*inf*), dispose of, bolt, down, gobble, stuff, swill, wolf (*inf*). **2** (*polish off all his rivals*) murder, kill, dispose of, eliminate, blow away (*inf*), bump off (*inf*), do in (*inf*), take out (*inf*), knock off (*inf*), rub out (*inf*), liquidate (*inf*).

polished *adj* **1** (*polished mirrors*) shiny, shining, glossy, gleaming, lustrous, smooth, glassy, slippery, waxed, buffed, burnished, bright, brilliant. OPPOSITE: dull. **2** (*a polished manner*) refined, cultivated, sophisticated, elegant, graceful, suave, courtly, genteel, polite, well-mannered, well-bred, urbane, civilized. OPPOSITE: coarse. **3** (*a polished performance*) accomplished, masterly, adept, expert, professional, skilful, proficient, perfect, impeccable, faultless, flawless, consummate, excellent, fine, outstanding, remarkable, superlative, exquisite. OPPOSITE: incompetent.

polite *adj* **1** (*a polite child*) courteous, well-behaved, well-mannered, mannerly, civil, respectful, deferential, charming, gracious, obliging, thoughtful, considerate, gallant, chivalrous, tactful, diplomatic, gentlemanly, ladylike, well-bred. OPPOSITE: rude. **2** (*polite society*) genteel, refined, courtly, cultured, cultivated, polished, sophisticated, civilized, urbane, elegant, suave, well-bred, well-mannered.

politic *adj* **1** (*a politic move*) expedient, opportune, advisable, judicious, wise, prudent, shrewd, sensible, advantageous, tactful. OPPOSITE: rash. **2** (*a politic young woman*) wise, sagacious, judicious, prudent, discreet, diplomatic, tactful, shrewd, sensible, wary, cautious.

political *adj* **1** (*the political establishment*) civil, civic, public, state, governmental, parliamentary, constitutional, executive, ministerial, administrative, bureaucratic, judicial. **2** (*political loyalties*) party political, partisan, factional.

politics *pl noun* **1** (*long experience of politics*) government, affairs of state, public affairs, civic affairs, diplomacy, party politics. **2** (*the study of politics*) statecraft, statesmanship, political science. **3** (*petty office politics*) manoeuvring, wheeler-dealing (*inf*), machination, manipulation, machiavellianism, opportunism.

poll *noun* **1** (*lost when it came to the poll*) vote, voting, ballot, ballot-box, show of hands, head count, referendum, plebiscite. **2** (*a large poll in favour of change*) tally, count, enumeration, returns. **3** (*public opinion poll*) survey, canvass, sampling, census, market research. ➤ *verb* **1** (*the opposition polled the most votes*) win, get, gain, obtain, net, return, receive, record, register. **2** (*they polled the whole school for their views*) canvass, survey, sample, ballot, interview, question, solicit.

pollute *verb* **1** (*pollute the river*) contaminate, taint, adulterate, poison, infect, dirty, soil, foul, befoul. OPPOSITE: purify. **2** (*such films pollute innocent minds*) corrupt, warp, pervert, deprave, defile, debauch, poison. **3** (*pollute the reputation of the whole party*) besmirch, blacken, sully, taint, tarnish, stain, dishonour, debase, desecrate, profane, vitiate, mar, spoil.

pollution *noun* **1** (*pollution of the sea*) contamination, adulteration, infecting, poisoning, tainting, befouling, fouling, soiling, dirtying. **2** (*trying to clear the pollution off the beaches*) filth, oil, muck, grime, waste, rubbish, refuse, foulness, contamination, impurity. **3** (*the pollution of innocent minds*) corruption, corrupting, warping, perversion, depraving, depravity, defiling, debauching, poisoning. **4** (*the pollution of the party's reputation*) besmirching, blackening, sullying, tainting, tarnishing, staining, dishonouring, debasement, desecration, profaning, vitiating, marring, spoiling. **5** (*the pollution of widely-available pornography*) cancer, canker, poison, bane, blight, contagion, corruption, malignancy.

pomp *noun* **1** (*the pomp of a royal wedding*) show, display, state, ceremony, ceremonial, ceremoniousness, ritual, pageantry, pageant, parade, display, show, spectacle, flourish, grandeur, solemnity, formality,

splendour, magnificence, brilliance, glory, majesty, style. OPPOSITE: simplicity. **2** (*an occasion of unnecessary pomp*) ostentation, show, showiness, exhibitionism, pomposity, glitter (*inf*), grandiosity, vainglory.

pomposity *noun* **1** (*they behaved with great pomposity*) pompousness, vanity, arrogance, haughtiness, conceit, self-importance, egotism, pride, presumption, presumptuousness, affectation, pretension, pretentiousness, grandiosity, imperiousness, loftiness, uppishness (*inf*), superciliousness, patronization, condescension, airs. **2** (*the pomposity of his writing style*) pompousness, bombast, portentousness, grandiloquence, magniloquence, turgidity, euphuism, rhetoric, stuffiness, stiltedness, pedantry, preachiness, rant, fustian.

pompous *adj* **1** (*a pompous old fool*) pretentious, self-important, arrogant, boastful, conceited, haughty, proud, vain, vainglorious, puffed up, lofty, pontifical, presumptuous, overbearing, supercilious, condescending, patronizing, grandiose, uppity (*inf*), uppish (*inf*), imperious, magisterial, affected, snooty (*inf*), ostentatious. OPPOSITE: humble. **2** (*a pompous writing style*) bombastic, high-flown, high-sounding, overblown, inflated, windy, elaborate, flowery, ostentatious, showy, la-di-da (*inf*), grand, stilted, turgid, stuffy, pedantic, fustian, orotund, grandiloquent, magniloquent, preachy (*inf*), euphuistic.

pond *noun* millpond, duck pond, fish-pond, pool, puddle, lake, mere, tarn.

ponder *verb* **1** (*he pondered on his fate*) think about, reflect on, meditate on, mull over, consider, contemplate, dwell on, deliberate about, brood over, ruminate about, puzzle over, cogitate about, weigh up, analyse, study, examine, review. **2** (*let me ponder a while*) think, reflect, consider, contemplate, deliberate, meditate, ruminate, wonder, brood, cogitate.

ponderous *adj* **1** (*a ponderous load*) huge, massive, bulky, hefty, heavy, weighty, heavy-handed, cumbersome, lumbering, slow-moving, unwieldy, awkward, clumsy, graceless. OPPOSITE: light. **2** (*a ponderous writing style*) dull, boring, tedious, uninteresting, monotonous, dreary, dry, stodgy, humourless, serious, forced, laboured, laborious, lifeless, stilted, plodding, pedestrian, pedantic, long-winded, verbose.

pontificate *verb* hold forth, declaim, sound off, expound, pronounce, lay down the law (*inf*), preach, sermonize, lecture, harangue, moralize, dogmatize.

pool[1] *noun* **1** (*a pool of oil*) puddle, patch, splash. **2** (*the children have gone to the pool*) swimming-pool, swimming-bath, baths. **3** (*ducks on a pool*) pond, lake, mere, tarn.

pool[2] *noun* **1** (*pool of money*) fund, pot, accumulation, kitty, bank, purse, stakes. **2** (*a pool of wheelchairs for the use of patients*) supply, reserve. **3** (*a pool of local businesses*) syndicate, group, team, combine, consortium, trust, cartel, ring, collective. ➤ *verb* combine, merge, amalgamate, put together, contribute, chip in (*inf*), muck in (*inf*), share. OPPOSITE: distribute.

poor *adj* **1** (*a poor family*) needy, needful, in need, in want, penniless, impoverished, necessitous, bankrupt, penurious, impecunious, poverty-stricken, indigent, destitute, deprived, badly off, hard-up (*inf*), broke (*inf*), skint (*inf*), in the red, on the rocks (*inf*), down and out, exiguous. OPPOSITE: rich. **2** (*born into poor circumstances*) underprivileged, disadvantaged, reduced, humble, lowly, mean, modest, plain, miserable, wretched, distressed, needy, straitened. OPPOSITE: privileged. **3** (*a poor supply of food*) meagre, sparse, scanty, skimpy, measly, paltry, deficient, inadequate, insufficient, lacking, short, scant, depleted, exhausted, slight. OPPOSITE: ample. **4** (*a poor effort*) inferior, second-rate, third-rate, low-quality, low-grade, substandard, below par, shoddy, crappy (*sl*), ropy (*inf*), unsatisfactory, weak, feeble, rotten (*inf*), sorry, mediocre, naff (*inf*), pathetic (*inf*), bad, rubbishy, worthless, useless, faulty, imperfect, defective. OPPOSITE: good. **5** (*poor agricultural land*) barren, infertile, sterile, arid, unproductive, unyielding, unfruitful, uncultivatable, bare, depleted, impoverished. OPPOSITE: fertile. **6** (*poor chap*) luckless, unlucky, unfortunate, ill-fated, ill-starred, unhappy, hapless, wretched, miserable, sorry, pitiable, pitiful. OPPOSITE: fortunate. **7** (*a poor apology for a man*) miserable, wretched, abject, pathetic, sorry, sad, mean, low, base, disgraceful, despicable, contemptible.

poorly *adj* sick, sickly, ill, unwell, rotten (*inf*), off colour, under the weather (*inf*), out of sorts (*inf*), indisposed, ailing, below par, seedy (*inf*), groggy (*inf*).
➤ *adv* badly, inadequately, unsatisfactorily, unsuccessfully, faultily, incompetently, inexpertly, insufficiently, shabbily, shoddily, crudely, meanly, feebly.

pop *verb* **1** (*the balloon popped*) burst, explode, go off, detonate, bang, snap, crack. **2** (*pop it in your bag*) put, place, insert, slide, slip, drop, tuck, push, stick, shove, thrust. **3** (*pop round to the shops*) go, nip (*inf*), drop, stop by, visit.
➤ *noun* **1** (*burst with a loud pop*) burst, explosion, report, detonation, bang, boom, snap, crack. **2** (*offered the children some pop*) fizzy (*inf*), fizz (*inf*), soda, soft drink.
pop off die, perish, pass away, pass on, snuff it (*inf*), peg out (*inf*), kick the bucket (*inf*).
pop up crop up, turn up, show up, appear, occur, materialize, come along.

pope *noun* pontiff, His Holiness, Holy Father, Bishop of Rome, Vicar of Christ.

populace *noun* **1** (*the populace of the capital*) inhabitants, residents, occupants, natives, citizens, population. **2** (*the government made a direct appeal to the populace*) public, general public, people, folk, society, community, masses, multitude, rank and file, proletariat, common herd, rabble, throng, crowd, mob, plebs (*inf*), hoi polloi, commonalty.

popular *adj* **1** (*a popular product*) liked, well-liked, favourite, favoured, approved, admired, accepted. OPPOSITE: unpopular. **2** (*brown is the popular colour this year*) fashionable, cool (*inf*), trendy (*inf*), hip (*inf*), modish, in (*inf*), in vogue, in demand, in favour, wanted, desired, sought-after, well-received. **3** (*a popular star of stage and screen*) famous, well-known, renowned, celebrated, acclaimed, noted, idolized. **4** (*popular culture*) middle-of-the-road, middlebrow, lowbrow, accessible,

understandable, easy to understand, pop (*inf*). **5** (*popular reference*) general, nonspecialist, nontechnical, accessible, understandable, ordinary, mass-market. **6** (*of popular concern*) common, familiar, public, general, civic, universal. **7** (*the popular practice of buying matching sets*) prevailing, prevalent, widespread, ubiquitous, current, accepted, usual, conventional, standard, stock, customary. OPPOSITE: exclusive. **8** (*this is the less expensive popular range*) budget, low-budget, low-priced, moderately-priced, inexpensive, cheap, reasonable, down-market (*inf*).

popularity *noun* **1** (*the declining popularity of German wine*) favour, approval, acceptance, approbation, admiration. **2** (*the popularity of this design*) appeal, demand, fashionableness, vogue. **3** (*the theory has declined in popularity in recent years*) currency, recognition, prevalence, prevalency. **4** (*the company has gained in popularity recently*) fame, repute, reputation, renown, glory, regard, acclaim, esteem, adulation, adoration.

popularize *verb* **1** (*popularized the poetry of the Romantics*) familiarize, make accessible, simplify. **2** (*aimed to popularize monetary theory*) universalize, generalize, spread, propagate, disseminate, give currency to.

popularly *adv* commonly, generally, universally, widely, usually, regularly, customarily, ordinarily, conventionally, traditionally.

populate *verb* **1** (*this area is populated by rough types*) inhabit, occupy, people, live in, dwell in. **2** (*the first explorers to populate this region*) colonize, settle, people.

population *noun* inhabitants, residents, occupants, denizens, citizenry, natives, populace, people, folk, society, community.

populous *adj* crowded, overpopulated, densely populated, packed, teeming, swarming, crawling, thronged. OPPOSITE: deserted.

porch *noun* hall, hallway, entrance-hall, lobby, foyer, vestibule.

pore[1] *verb* **pore over** **1** (*pore over the papers*) study, examine, scrutinize, peruse, scan, read. **2** (*pored over his troubles*) brood over, dwell on, ponder, mull over, meditate on, reflect on, muse on, deliberate on, think about, contemplate, go over.

pore[2] *noun* (*pores in the skin*) opening, orifice, aperture, perforation, hole, outlet, vent, stoma.

pornographic *adj* obscene, indecent, smutty, dirty, filthy, risqué, coarse, bawdy, gross, lewd, salacious, blue, erotic, titillating, off-colour, prurient, x-rated.

pornography *noun* **1** (*his collection of pornography*) porn (*inf*), erotica, girlie magazines (*inf*). **2** (*too much pornography on television*) porn (*inf*), obscenity, indecency, sexploitation, smut, filth, dirt, salaciousness, grossness, bawdiness, lewdness, prurience.

porous *adj* **1** (*porous rock*) permeable, pervious, penetrable, absorbent. OPPOSITE: impermeable. **2** (*porous material*) spongy, spongelike, honeycombed, open.

port *noun* seaport, harbour, harbourage, dock, haven, anchorage, roadstead.

portable *adj* light, lightweight, compact, handy,

convenient, manageable, movable, transportable, conveyable. OPPOSITE: ponderous.

portend *verb* forebode, bode, foretoken, foretell, forecast, predict, prognosticate, foreshadow, promise, augur, harbinger, presage, indicate, point to, bespeak, betoken, signify, herald, threaten, warn of, forewarn, announce.

portent *noun* **1** (*a portent of disaster*) omen, sign, indication, token, harbinger, augury, precursor, forerunner, prognostication, foreshadowing, prophecy, prediction, presage, premonition, presentiment, foreboding, warning, threat. **2** (*a portent of modern science*) phenomenon, marvel, wonder, prodigy, miracle, spectacle.

portentous *adj* **1** (*a portentous sign of change*) ominous, foreboding, sinister, ill-omened, alarming, forbidding, minatory, threatening, menacing, inauspicious, unpropitious, momentous, fateful, weighty, consequential, significant, crucial, pivotal. OPPOSITE: insignificant. **2** (*a truly portentous feat of engineering*) phenomenal, prodigious, marvellous, spectacular, awe-inspiring, earth-shaking, epoch-making, miraculous, wondrous, remarkable, significant, important, extraordinary, amazing, astounding. OPPOSITE: ordinary. **3** (*a portentous manner*) pompous, ponderous, solemn, heavy, weighty, self-important, pontifical.

porter[1] *noun* (*a railway porter*) bearer, carrier, baggage-attendant, baggage-handler, baggage-carrier.

porter[2] *noun* (*the hotel porter*) doorman, doorkeeper, door attendant, concierge, gatekeeper, commissionaire, janitor, caretaker.

portion *noun* **1** (*you will all receive a portion*) share, division, segment, fraction, part, bit, piece, cut (*inf*), lot, measure, allotment, allocation, parcel, quota, percentage, ration. OPPOSITE: whole. **2** (*dished out several portions of rice*) helping, serving, piece, lot, quantity. **3** (*a portion of cheese*) slice, wedge, segment, piece, lump, chunk, hunk, scrap, morsel. **4** (*it seems to be her portion to suffer*) fate, lot, destiny, fortune, luck.
 ► *verb* apportion, allot, allocate, assign, share, divide, split, partition, carve up (*inf*), parcel out, distribute, deal out, hand out, dole out (*inf*), mete out.

portly *adj* stout, corpulent, round, rotund, fat, fleshy, plump, tubby (*inf*), obese, overweight, ample, burly, beefy (*inf*), stocky, well-built, large, heavy. OPPOSITE: slim.

portrait *noun* **1** (*a portrait of his wife hung on the wall*) picture, likeness, image, study, representation, characterization, portrayal, painting, canvas, drawing, sketch, caricature, miniature, icon. **2** (*kept a portrait of his children in his wallet*) photograph, photo, picture, snap, snapshot, shot, still, study. **3** (*a moving portrait of rural life*) portrayal, account, description, depiction, story, chronicle, sketch, vignette.

portray *verb* **1** (*portrayed several country scenes*) draw, illustrate, paint, sketch, depict, delineate. **2** (*portray life in an isolated mountain village*) depict, picture, represent, describe, characterize, evoke, illustrate. **3** (*she portrayed the heroine in his latest play*) act, play, perform, represent, impersonate, personify, characterize, render.

portrayal *noun* **1** (*a magnificent portrayal of the king on horseback*) portrait, picture, drawing, painting, sketch, depiction, representation, study, delineation. **2** (*gave an unrivalled portrayal of life in the gutter*) description, account, depiction, characterization, evocation, presentation. **3** (*his celebrated portrayal of the tragic hero*) interpretation, representation, impersonation, personification, characterization, performance, rendering, acting.

pose *verb* **1** (*pose for their picture*) model, sit. **2** (*pose the group*) arrange, dispose, place, position, locate, situate, stand, lay out, set out. **3** (*pose as an expert*) feign, pretend to be, impersonate, pass oneself off as, masquerade as, profess to be, act. **4** (*posturing and posing*) posture, attitudinize, show off, play-act, put on airs, affect, assume. **5** (*pose the question*) ask, put, put forward, propose, submit, set, posit, postulate, propound, advance, suggest, present, assert, state. **6** (*this could pose a problem*) create, produce, cause, give rise to, lead to, result in, present, threaten.
 ► *noun* **1** (*an arrogant pose*) posture, bearing, carriage, attitude, deportment, position, stance, air. **2** (*saw through her pose at once*) pretence, masquerade, act, play-acting, role, posture, sham, facade, front. **3** (*I am tired of her poses*) airs, affectation.

poser *noun* riddle, enigma, mystery, puzzle, problem, dilemma, conundrum, brain-teaser (*inf*).

poseur *noun* poser, posturer, exhibitionist, show-off, attitudinizer, play-actor, phoney (*inf*), sham, impostor, pseud (*inf*), charlatan.

posh *adj* **1** (*a posh neighbourhood*) smart, elegant, ornate, stylish, fancy, fashionable, exclusive, select, classy (*inf*), high-class, rich, opulent, luxurious, de luxe, luxury, up-market, top-drawer, grand, lavish, sumptuous, plush (*inf*), ritzy (*inf*), swanky (*inf*), swish (*inf*). OPPOSITE: vulgar. **2** (*he's really posh*) upper-class, upper-crust (*inf*), aristocratic, up-market, la-di-da (*inf*), fancy, genteel.

position *noun* **1** (*you can see a long way from this position*) place, situation, location, spot, area, point, site, setting, locality, locale, scene. **2** (*give the ship's position*) bearings, location, whereabouts. **3** (*adjusted his position in the chair*) posture, pose, stance, attitude, bearing. **4** (*what is the government's position on this?*) stance, standpoint, stand, opinion, point of view, viewpoint, view, angle, slant, outlook, attitude, feeling, belief. **5** (*they are in a serious position*) situation, case, state, state of affairs, condition, circumstances, pass, plight, predicament, background, factors. **6** (*a good position within the bank*) job, post, situation, appointment, place, office, role, function, capacity, occupation, employment, duty. **7** (*a respected position in society*) status, stature, standing, station, place. **8** (*hoping to improve their position in the league*) rank, ranking, class, grade, level.
 ► *verb* place, pose, arrange, dispose, array, lay out, deploy, station, put, fix, set, settle, stand, locate, situate, site, install, establish.

positive *adj* **1** (*we're positive about her guilt*) certain, sure, assured, confident, convinced. OPPOSITE: uncertain. **2** (*a positive difference*) clear, clear-cut, direct, precise, explicit, express, definite, categorical, firm, unequivocal, indisputable, undeniable, incontrovertible, incontestable, irrefutable, unmistakable, conclusive, decisive, emphatic. OPPOSITE: vague. **3** (*a positive force for good*) real, actual, concrete, substantial, true, genuine, veritable, absolute. **4** (*made several positive suggestions*) constructive, practical, helpful, useful, productive, beneficial. OPPOSITE: adverse. **5** (*a positive sign*) optimistic, encouraging, favourable, confident, hopeful, cheerful, heartening, promising, upbeat (*inf*). OPPOSITE: negative. **6** (*he's a positive idiot*) utter, complete, perfect, absolute, thorough, thoroughgoing, sheer, downright, outright, unmitigated, rank, out-and-out, veritable, consummate, unqualified.

positively *adv* **1** (*they assured us positively that the parcel would arrive today*) emphatically, definitely, certainly, assuredly, firmly, categorically, surely, absolutely, conclusively, confidently, expressly, dogmatically, unmistakably, unquestionably, incontrovertibly, incontestably, undeniably, indisputably, unequivocally. **2** (*she was positively incandescent with rage*) absolutely, extremely, really, very, indeed.

possess *verb* **1** (*longs to possess her own home*) own, have, hold, enjoy, acquire, gain, get. **2** (*possess the high ground*) take, take over, seize, occupy, obtain, acquire, get. **3** (*the urge to win possesses her*) consume, obsess, mesmerize, bewitch, haunt, enchant, infatuate, control, influence, dominate. OPPOSITE: lose. **4** (*possess good eyesight*) be endowed with, have, be gifted with.

possessed *adj* bewitched, enchanted, besotted, consumed, obsessed, infatuated, cursed, bedevilled, haunted, crazed, raving, mad, hag-ridden, maddened, demented, berserk, frenetic, frenzied.

possession *noun* **1** (*the goods are in my possession*) ownership, proprietorship, custody, control, hold, grip. **2** (*take possession of the house*) tenure, tenancy, occupancy, occupation, holding, title.

possessions *pl noun* belongings, property, effects, personal effects, things (*inf*), stuff (*inf*), gear (*inf*), wealth, riches, assets, accoutrements, appendages, paraphernalia, impedimenta, estate, goods, goods and chattels, movables, luggage, baggage.

possessive *adj* **1** (*possessive of their toys*) greedy, grasping, covetous, acquisitive, selfish. **2** (*a possessive attitude towards her children*) overprotective, clinging, controlling, domineering, dominating, jealous.

possibility *noun* **1** (*the possibility of success*) likelihood, liability, probability, odds, chance, prospect, risk, danger, hazard, hope, potentiality, practicability, feasibility, conceivability, attainability. **2** (*a future full of possibility*) promise, potential, potentiality, expectations, prospects, advantages, capabilities, talent. **3** (*marriage is one possibility*) option, alternative, recourse, choice, preference.

possible *adj* **1** (*one of several possible outcomes*) conceivable, imaginable, credible, likely, probable, potential, hypothetical, hopeful. **2** (*the project is not really possible*) feasible, practicable, attainable, achievable, realizable, on (*inf*), doable, viable, workable, deliverable, tenable. OPPOSITE: impossible.

possibly *adv* **1** (*you may possibly find it over there*) perhaps, maybe, perchance, peradventure, God willing. OPPOSITE: certainly. **2** (*we could not possibly get involved*) conceivably, by any means, at all, by any chance.

post[1] *noun* (*a post driven into the ground*) pole, shaft, stake, pale, palisade, banister, picket, prop, support, strut, leg, upright, standard, pillar, column, stanchion.
➤ *verb* **1** (*post the notice up on the wall*) affix, attach, put up, stick, stick up, pin, pin up, tack, tack up, hang, display. **2** (*post the news of his return*) announce, make known, publish, publicize, circulate, broadcast, report, advertise, promulgate.

post[2] *noun* (*moved to a new post within the organization*) position, situation, job, office, employment, assignment, appointment, vacancy, place, station, berth, beat.
➤ *verb* assign, appoint, second, station, place, position, put, locate, situate, transfer, move, send.

post[3] *noun* **1** (*the morning post*) mail, correspondence, letters, parcels, collection, delivery. **2** (*the post is not very reliable*) postal service, mail service, mail.
➤ *verb* **1** (*post the details to them*) mail, send, dispatch, forward, transmit. **2** (*post the results in the book*) enter, fill in, record, register, note, write up.
keep someone posted inform, notify, keep up to date, fill in (*inf*), brief, advise, keep in the picture (*inf*).

poster *noun* placard, bill, notice, advertisement, ad (*inf*), advert (*inf*), sticker, sign, bulletin, announcement.

posterior *noun* rear, behind, bottom, seat, haunches, hindquarters, rump, buttocks, backside, bum (*inf*).
➤ *adj* **1** (*the posterior part of the animal*) rear, rearward, back, hind, hinder. OPPOSITE: front. **2** (*at a posterior date*) after, later, latter, following, succeeding, ensuing, subsequent. OPPOSITE: anterior.

posterity *noun* descendants, successors, heirs, progeny, offspring, issue, seed, children, family, future generations. OPPOSITE: ancestry.

post-mortem *noun* **1** (*perform a post-mortem on the corpse*) autopsy, necropsy, dissection. **2** (*conduct a post-mortem on the match*) review, analysis, examination.

postpone *verb* delay, defer, shelve, hold over, table, suspend, adjourn, reschedule, procrastinate, put off, put back, put on ice (*inf*), put on the back burner (*inf*), pigeonhole, freeze. OPPOSITE: advance.

postponement *noun* deferment, deferral, delay, adjournment, suspension, moratorium, freeze, respite, stay.

postscript *noun* PS, addendum, afterthought, appendix, supplement, addition, epilogue, codicil. OPPOSITE: preface.

postulate *verb* assume, suppose, presume, presuppose, propose, advance, take for granted, posit, theorize, hypothesize, stipulate, predicate. OPPOSITE: prove.

posture *noun* **1** (*take up a relaxed posture*) position, attitude, pose. **2** (*she could work on her posture*) bearing, carriage, deportment, stance. **3** (*the board adopted a critical posture*) attitude, position, viewpoint, point of view, outlook, angle, slant, stand, standpoint, disposition, frame of mind, feeling, inclination, opinion.
➤ *verb* pose, strut, show off, strike an attitude, attitudinize, put on an act, play-act, put on airs, affect.

posy *noun* bouquet, nosegay, bunch, spray, buttonhole, corsage.

pot *noun* **1** (*poured something into the pot*) container, receptacle, vessel, pan, cauldron, casserole, bowl, basin, jar, urn, glass, mug, tankard, jug, teapot, coffee pot. **2** (*no more money in the pot*) kitty, purse, fund, reserve.

potency *noun* **1** (*the potency of the alcohol*) strength, power, powerfulness, effectiveness, efficacy, punch (*inf*), kick (*inf*), muscle (*inf*), headiness (*inf*). **2** (*the potency of her influence within government*) strength, power, powerfulness, force, forcefulness, might, mightiness, vigour, influence, dominance, potential, authority, authoritativeness, sway, capacity, energy. **3** (*no denying the potency of their argument*) persuasiveness, strength, power, powerfulness, force, forcefulness, cogency, effectiveness, impressiveness, conviction.

potent *adj* **1** (*a potent brew*) powerful, strong, effective, efficacious, intoxicating, heady (*inf*), pungent. **2** (*a potent force within the government*) strong, powerful, forceful, mighty, vigorous, influential, dominant, authoritative, commanding, dynamic, energetic. **3** (*a potent argument*) powerful, forceful, strong, cogent, eloquent, persuasive, convincing, compelling, telling, impressive, effective, efficacious, effectual, authoritative. OPPOSITE: weak.

potentate *noun* ruler, sovereign, monarch, emperor, empress, king, queen, prince, mogul, leader, overlord, chief, chieftain, despot, dictator, tyrant.

potential *adj* **1** (*a potential leader of the party*) possible, likely, probable, future, prospective, promising, budding, developing, embryonic, aspiring, would-be. **2** (*her potential skill*) undeveloped, unrealized, latent, dormant, hidden, concealed, inherent, embryonic. OPPOSITE: actual. **3** (*a potential husband*) possible, likely, probable.
➤ *noun* **1** (*she shows potential as a dancer*) promise, capacity, capability, ability, aptitude, talent, flair, gift, the makings (*inf*), wherewithal. **2** (*a situation full of potential*) potentiality, possibility, promise.

potion *noun* drink, beverage, draught, dose, brew, mixture, concoction, elixir, philtre, potation, medicine, tonic.

potter *verb* dawdle, amble, loiter, dally, dilly-dally (*inf*), toddle (*inf*).
potter about mess about (*inf*), muck about (*inf*), fool about, fiddle about, tinker about, play about, dabble, fritter.

pottery *noun* ceramics, earthenware, crockery, china, terracotta, stoneware.

pouch *noun* bag, sack, purse, wallet, satchel, pocket, container, receptacle.

pounce *verb* **1** (*the falcon pounced on a mouse*) swoop, dive, descend, drop, fall. **2** (*he pounced on the sentry*) swoop, spring, lunge, leap, jump, bound, surprise, take unawares, catch off guard, dash at, ambush, assault, attack, strike.
➤ *noun* swoop, spring, lunge, bound, jump, leap, grab, assault, attack.

pound[1] *verb* **1** (*pound on the door*) thump, bang, beat, drum, batter, pummel, pelt, hammer, strike, belabour, bash, smash. OPPOSITE: caress. **2** (*pound to dust*) pulverize, powder, crush, grind, granulate, comminute, triturate, beat, mash. **3** (*she could feel her heart pounding*) throb, pulsate, pulse, palpitate, pump, beat, thump, thud. **4** (*pound the streets*) walk, pace, tramp, plod, tread, trudge, stomp, clump.

pound[2] *noun* (*the pound in your pocket*) pound coin, pound sterling, quid (*inf*), nicker (*inf*), smacker (*inf*).

pound[3] *noun* (*took the strays to a pound*) compound, pen, yard, enclosure, corral, fold.

pour *verb* **1** (*water poured from the tap*) flow, stream, course, cascade, flood, run, rush, gush, spout, spurt, spew, jet, spill, splash, sprinkle. **2** (*people poured out of the stadium*) stream, flood, flow, leak, ooze, spill, crowd, swarm, throng, emerge, issue, come out, emit, discharge, disgorge. **3** (*pour everyone a drink*) serve, decant. **4** (*it is pouring out there*) rain, rain cats and dogs (*inf*), bucket down (*inf*), teem, pelt down, piss down (*inf*), sheet down, torrent down. OPPOSITE: drizzle.

pout *verb* frown, scowl, glower, lower, grimace, sulk, mope, brood. OPPOSITE: smile.

poverty *noun* **1** (*living in poverty*) want, need, impoverishment, indigence, destitution, beggary, pauperism, pennilessness, insolvency, bankruptcy, penury, impecuniousness, privation, deprivation, neediness, distress, hardship, lack, necessity. OPPOSITE: wealth. **2** (*the poverty of his imagination*) paucity, deficiency, inadequacy, insufficiency, meagreness, dearth, scarcity, shortage, depletion. **3** (*the poverty of agricultural land hereabouts*) barrenness, bareness, poorness, unproductiveness, unfruitfulness, sterility, infertility, aridity.

powder *noun* dust, grains, particles, triturate, pounce, talc.
➤ *verb* **1** (*powder the sugar*) pulverize, pound, crush, grind, granulate, beat, mash, comminute, triturate. **2** (*powder the bread with flour*) dust, dredge, sprinkle, scatter, strew, cover, coat.

powdery *adj* powdered, crumbly, friable, dry, fine, dusty, sandy, grainy, granular, granulated, ground, crushed, pulverized, chalky, floury, loose.

power *noun* **1** (*seize power*) control, command, authority, rule, sovereignty, mastery, dominion, domination, sway, ascendancy, supremacy. OPPOSITE: subjection. **2** (*I have you under my power*) control, command, authority, clutches, grip, influence. **3** (*the committee has little power*) authority, potency, effectiveness, clout (*inf*), muscle (*inf*), teeth (*inf*), pull (*inf*). **4** (*lose the power of speech*) ability, capability, capacity, potential, potentiality, aptitude, faculty, competence. OPPOSITE: inability. **5** (*the power of the impact*) powerfulness, force, forcefulness, strength, intensity, weight, energy, potency, might, vigour. OPPOSITE: weakness. **6** (*grant them the power to go ahead*) right, perogative, privilege, authority, authorization, warrant, licence. **7** (*the power of his words*) effectiveness, force, forcefulness, strength, powerfulness, potency, cogency, persuasiveness, eloquence, conviction.

powerful *adj* **1** (*a powerful physique*) strong, mighty, vigorous, robust, tough, sturdy, muscular, brawny, strapping, stalwart, burly, hardy, stout. OPPOSITE: weak. **2** (*a powerful figure in politics*) influential, authoritative, forceful, commanding, controlling, dominant, leading, high-powered, potent, supreme, prevailing. **3** (*made a* *powerful impression*) strong, forceful, telling, impressive, mighty, vigorous, intense, energetic, potent. **4** (*he made a powerful case for change*) strong, forceful, cogent, compelling, telling, persuasive, convincing, winning, overwhelming, effective. OPPOSITE: unconvincing.

powerless *adj* **1** (*the injury left him powerless*) helpless, incapable, paralysed, prostrate, disabled, incapacitated, debilitated, weak, feeble, frail, infirm, defenceless, vulnerable. **2** (*felt powerless against such opposition*) helpless, tied, impotent, ineffectual, ineffective, inadequate. OPPOSITE: powerful.

practicability *noun* feasibility, viability, possibility, workability, attainability, achievability, operability, practicality, use, usefulness, value.

practicable *adj* possible, feasible, practical, realistic, attainable, achievable, accomplishable, doable, workable, viable, performable. OPPOSITE: impracticable.

practical *adj* **1** (*they have practical knowledge of the problem*) actual, real, hands on, applied. **2** (*he is very practical when it comes to his work*) businesslike, efficient, down-to-earth, matter-of-fact, everyday, pragmatic, sensible, realistic, hard-headed, hard-nosed (*inf*). **3** (*a practical scientist rather than an academic*) experienced, trained, qualified, skilled, proficient, competent, accomplished, practised, experienced, seasoned, veteran. OPPOSITE: inexperienced. **4** (*a practical invention*) practicable, workable, utilitarian, functional, serviceable, workaday, useful, expedient, handy, realistic, feasible, sensible, commonsense. OPPOSITE: impractical. **5** (*sit in practical darkness*) virtual, effective, essential.

practically *adv* **1** (*practically unknown*) virtually, in effect, almost, nearly, well-nigh, pretty much (*inf*), pretty well (*inf*), all but, just about, close to, basically, essentially, fundamentally, to all intents and purposes. **2** (*approach the challenge practically*) realistically, pragmatically, matter-of-factly (*inf*), sensibly, reasonably, rationally.

practice *noun* **1** (*my usual practice is to have tea at this time*) custom, habit, routine, wont, rule. **2** (*a time-honoured practice*) tradition, convention, way, method, system, policy, procedure, usage, use. **3** (*have a practice on the pitch*) rehearsal, run-through, exercise, warm-up, work-out, drill, training, study, preparation, repetition. **4** (*put these ideas into practice*) effect, action, application, operation, use, performance. OPPOSITE: theory. **5** (*the practice of law*) profession, career, business, work, pursuit, following, occupation, employment, job, vocation. **6** (*the town's medical practice*) partnership, firm, business.

practise *verb* **1** (*practise self-discipline*) do, perform, carry out, undertake, execute, implement, apply, observe, follow, pursue, put into practice. **2** (*practise this piece on the piano*) rehearse, prepare, polish, refine, perfect, work at, work on, go over, go through, run through, repeat. **3** (*practise before the big game*) prepare, exercise, drill, train, warm up, work out, study. **4** (*practise law*) work at, engage in, ply, pursue, specialize in, carry on, undertake.

practised *adj* expert, masterly, proficient, able, adept, adroit, accomplished, consummate, finished, skilled, skilful, knowing, versed, knowledgeable, experienced,

seasoned, veteran, trained, qualified. OPPOSITE: inexperienced.

pragmatic *adj* practical, practicable, realistic, utilitarian, sensible, down-to-earth, matter-of-fact, businesslike, efficient, unsentimental, hard-headed, hard-nosed (*inf*).

praise *verb* **1** (*praise good practice*) commend, applaud, cheer, acclaim, hail, admire, approve, cry up, crack up (*inf*), rave over (*inf*), wax lyrical, congratulate, compliment, flatter, recognize, acknowledge, promote, extol, eulogize, panegyrize. OPPOSITE: censure. **2** (*praise the Lord*) worship, glorify, honour, exalt, hail, magnify, laud, adore.
➤ *noun* **1** (*a word of praise for the organizers*) commendation, tribute, accolade, laudation, eulogy, ovation, panegyric, testimonial, homage, encomium, applause, plaudits, cheering, cheers, acclaim, acclamation, congratulation, compliment, flattery, puff (*inf*), admiration, adulation, approval, recognition. **2** (*offer praise in church*) approbation, tribute, homage, thanks, thanksgiving, glory, honour, worship, exaltation, devotion, adoration. OPPOSITE: criticism.

praiseworthy *adj* commendable, laudable, honourable, meritorious, admirable, estimable, deserving, worthy, creditable, reputable, fine, excellent, exemplary, sterling. OPPOSITE: reprehensible.

prance *verb* **1** (*watched the foal prance about*) leap, spring, jump, skip, trip, bound, dance, gambol, frolic, caper, romp, frisk, cavort. **2** (*prance into the room*) swagger, strut, stalk, show off, swank (*inf*), parade, skip, cavort, curvet.

prank *noun* trick, practical joke, joke, caper, jape, lark (*inf*), skylarking (*inf*), hoax, stunt, frolic, mischief, antic, escapade.

prattle *verb* babble (*inf*), chat, chatter, jabber (*inf*), blather, blether, gab (*inf*), gabble, rattle, rabbit (*inf*), witter, twitter, patter, twaddle, drivel, gossip, prate.

pray *verb* **1** (*pray to the Lord*) commune with, offer prayers to, invoke, call on, praise, worship, adore, confess, thank. **2** (*pray for a second chance*) beg, plead, beseech, entreat, crave, solicit, implore, adjure, petition, supplicate, ask, request, urge, importune, sue.

prayer *noun* **1** (*prayers to the Lord*) communion, devotion, invocation, collect, litany, intercession. **2** (*a prayer for help*) appeal, plea, request, entreaty, petition, suit, solicitation, supplication, adjuration.

preach *verb* **1** (*preach to the congregation*) evangelize, spread the gospel, sermonize, moralize, pontificate, address, orate, lecture, harangue. **2** (*preach the truth as he saw it*) proclaim, declare, promulgate, disseminate, teach. **3** (*preach restraint*) recommend, advise, advocate, urge, exhort.

preacher *noun* **1** (*the preacher in church*) evangelist, missionary, clergyman, cleric, churchman, minister, parson, televangelist, revivalist. OPPOSITE: layman. **2** (*he likes to think of himself as a kind of preacher*) sermonizer, moralizer.

preamble *noun* introduction, lead-in, preface, prefatory remarks, prologue, foreword, prelude, front matter, preliminaries, prelims (*inf*). OPPOSITE: epilogue.

precarious *adj* **1** (*making a precarious living*) uncertain, unsure, unpredictable, insecure, doubtful, dubious, dodgy (*inf*), dicey (*inf*), iffy (*inf*), undependable, unreliable, unsettled, unstable, risky, chancy, vulnerable. **2** (*a precarious rope bridge*) unstable, shaky, wobbly, unsteady, insecure, unsafe, dangerous, treacherous, perilous, hazardous, risky, tricky, hairy (*inf*), dicey (*inf*). OPPOSITE: safe.

precaution *noun* **1** (*precautions against fire*) safeguard, safety measure, preventive measure, provision, protection, insurance, security. **2** (*approach the situation with precaution*) circumspection, caution, prudence, care, attentiveness, wariness, foresight, foresightedness, farsightedness, forethought, anticipation.

precede *verb* **1** (*the bishop will precede the queen*) go before, go ahead of, come first, lead, head, usher in. **2** (*calm precedes the storm*) go before, antecede, lead to, herald, usher in, pave the way, antedate, predate. **3** (*the meeting was preceded by introduction of the negotiators*) begin, open, launch, introduce, preface, prefix. OPPOSITE: follow.

precedence *noun* antecedence, precession, lead, priority, preference, rank, seniority, superiority, supremacy, primacy, pre-eminence, eminence, ascendancy, transcendence. OPPOSITE: subordination.
take precedence over come before, take priority over.

precedent *noun* antecedent, prototype, example, exemplar, instance, lead, case, model, pattern, parallel, standard, criterion, paradigm, yardstick, authority.

preceding *adj* **1** (*see preceding page*) previous, last, above, above-mentioned, foregoing, prior. OPPOSITE: subsequent. **2** (*on a preceding occasion*) prior, earlier, previous, past, former, aforesaid.

precept *noun* **1** (*live by the following precepts*) rule, principle, canon, guideline, instruction, direction, order, command, injunction, directive, charge, mandate, dictate, dictum, edict, tenet, decree, behest, ordinance, regulation, code, law, statute. **2** (*a favourite precept of hers*) maxim, saying, byword, adage, aphorism, saw, axiom, motto.

precinct *noun* centre, mall, gallery, zone, sector, district, quarter, area.

precincts *pl noun* environs, surrounds, bounds, boundary, ambit, confines, limits, purlieus, region, area, district, locality, vicinity, neighbourhood, milieu, close, enclosure, court.

precious *adj* **1** (*our precious daughter*) dear, dearest, darling, cherished, beloved, prized, treasured, favourite, beloved, loved, valued, esteemed, adored, idolized, revered, venerated. **2** (*a precious jewel*) valuable, expensive, costly, dear, high-priced, priceless, invaluable, inestimable, rare, fine, choice, exquisite. OPPOSITE: worthless. **3** (*I found her manner rather precious*) affected, pretentious, mannered, contrived, artificial, overrefined, simulated, flowery, effete, twee (*inf*).

precipice *noun* cliff, cliff face, bluff, crag, escarpment, height, drop.

precipitate *verb* **1** (*this should help precipitate action*) hasten, hurry, accelerate, quicken, speed up, advance, push forward, press, further, bring on, induce, trigger, expedite, dispatch, cause, occasion. OPPOSITE: retard. **2** (*the passengers were precipitated into the front seat*) throw, plunge, hurl, fling, cast, heave, propel, launch, send forth.
➤ *adj* **1** (*made a precipitate departure*) hurried, rapid, quick, speedy, swift, headlong, plunging, abrupt, brief, sudden, unexpected, breakneck, violent, precipitous. **2** (*regretted her precipitate decision*) hurried, hasty, rash, reckless, heedless, thoughtless, indiscreet, careless, ill-advised, abrupt, frantic, sudden, impetuous, impulsive, hare-brained, madcap, precipitous, hot-headed. OPPOSITE: cautious.

precipitous *adj* **1** (*peered over the precipitous drop*) steep, sheer, dizzy, perpendicular, vertical, abrupt, sudden, high, sharp. OPPOSITE: gradual. **2** (*made a precipitous departure*) hurried, rapid, precipitate, headlong. **3** (*avoid any precipitous movement*) hasty, rash, reckless, abrupt, sudden, violent. OPPOSITE: cautious.

précis *noun* summary, encapsulation, synopsis, abstract, résumé, digest, abridgement, condensation, contraction, abbreviation, epitome, outline, sketch, compendium, rundown, table.
➤ *verb* summarize, sum up, encapsulate, contract, compress, condense, synopsize, abridge, digest, shorten, outline, abstract, abbreviate, epitomize.

precise *adj* **1** (*a precise memory for detail*) exact, clear, clear-cut, accurate, detailed, minute, correct, distinct, explicit, unambiguous, unequivocal, definite, express, specific, strict, literal, faithful, actual. **2** (*he had a very precise manner*) particular, rigorous, finicky, nice, prim, meticulous, scrupulous, punctilious, fastidious, conscientious, methodical, rigid, severe, inflexible, fixed, formal, stiff, puritanical. OPPOSITE: vague. **3** (*the precise location*) exact, actual, very, specific, particular, distinct.

precisely *adv* **1** (*at noon precisely*) exactly, sharp, accurately, on the dot, dead, dead on (*inf*), plumb (*inf*), slap (*inf*), smack (*inf*), on the button (*inf*), bang on (*inf*), spot on (*inf*), square, squarely. **2** (*repeat precisely what she said*) exactly, absolutely, strictly, minutely, literally, correctly, verbatim, word for word.

precision *noun* **1** (*the precision of the operation*) exactitude, exactness, distinctness, explicitness, accuracy, detail, particularity, correctness, fidelity, faithfulness, strictness, rigour, nicety, care, carefulness, meticulousness, punctiliousness, scrupulousness, fastidiousness, conscientiousness, methodicalness. OPPOSITE: vagueness. **2** (*admire the precision of the stitching*) accuracy, exactness, reliability, regularity.

preclude *verb* **1** (*her health precludes any thoughts of a public appearance*) rule out, forestall, eliminate. **2** (*the law precludes children from drinking in a bar*) prohibit, debar, bar, block, exclude, prevent, obviate, stop, check, hinder, impede, inhibit, restrain. OPPOSITE: encourage.

precocious *adj* forward, advanced, bright, brilliant, clever, gifted, talented, smart, quick, fast, ahead, premature, early. OPPOSITE: backward.

preconception *noun* presupposition, presumption, assumption, preconceived idea, bias, prejudice, prejudgment, predetermination.

precondition *noun* prerequisite, condition, stipulation, requirement, must (*inf*), essential, necessity.

precursor *noun* **1** (*a precursor of change*) harbinger, forerunner, prelude, herald, messenger, usher, vanguard, trailblazer, curtain-raiser, sign, indication. **2** (*I remember your precursor here at the company*) predecessor, antecedent, forerunner. **3** (*this model incorporates the best features of its precursor*) predecessor, forerunner, ancestor, forebear, progenitor, originator, antecedent. OPPOSITE: follower.

precursory *adj* antecedent, preceding, previous, prior, anterior, preparatory, preliminary, introductory, prefatory, precursive, preambulatory. OPPOSITE: final.

predatory *adj* **1** (*the jungle is full of predatory creatures*) predacious, predative, rapacious, voracious, ravenous, carnivorous, hunting, preying. **2** (*the victim of predatory gangs*) plundering, pillaging, looting, robbing, thieving, ravaging, rapacious, marauding, despoiling. **3** (*a predatory attitude*) greedy, avaricious, rapacious, acquisitive, covetous, exploitative, vulturine, wolfish.

predecessor *noun* **1** (*the predecessor of what we use today*) forerunner, precursor, antecedent. **2** (*a portrait of a predecessor of his*) ancestor, forefather, forebear, progenitor, antecedent. OPPOSITE: successor.

predestination *noun* predetermination, preordination, foreordination, fate, destiny, lot, doom.

predestine *verb* destine, predestinate, fate, doom, mean, intend, foreordain, preordain, predetermine.

predetermined *adj* **1** (*their fate was predetermined*) predestined, ordained, preordained, foreordained, fated, destined, doomed. **2** (*a predetermined outcome*) prearranged, preplanned, arranged, agreed, set, settled, fixed, foregone, cut-and-dried (*inf*). OPPOSITE: open.

predicament *noun* plight, quandary, dilemma, impasse, crisis, pinch, fix (*inf*), jam (*inf*), pickle (*inf*), scrape (*inf*), spot (*inf*), tight spot (*inf*), corner (*inf*), tight corner (*inf*), hot water (*inf*), hole (*inf*), stew (*inf*), can of worms (*inf*), kettle of fish (*inf*), difficulty, trouble, mess, state, situation, extremity, emergency.

predicate *verb* assert, aver, asseverate, avow, affirm, maintain, proclaim, declare, state, contend, argue, postulate, posit. OPPOSITE: deny.

predict *verb* foretell, foresee, forecast, forewarn, prophesy, prognosticate, augur, divine, foreshadow, presage, portend, forebode.

predictable *adj* foreseeable, imaginable, expected, anticipated, probable, likely, certain, sure, reliable, dependable, on the cards (*inf*), odds-on (*inf*).

prediction *noun* prophecy, forecast, forewarning, prognostication, prognosis, augury, soothsaying, divination.

predilection *noun* inclination, leaning, tendency, bent, predisposition, affinity, proclivity, propensity, enthusiasm, bias, preference, partiality, proneness, liking, fondness, love, soft spot, weakness, taste, fancy, penchant. OPPOSITE: aversion.

predispose *verb* dispose, incline, prompt, induce, make, bias, prejudice, sway, move, influence, persuade, affect, prepare, prime.

predisposed *adj* disposed, inclined, liable, given to, prone, willing, biased, prejudiced, minded, prepared, ready, susceptible, agreeable, amenable, favourable.

predisposition *noun* **1** (*a predisposition towards heart problems*) susceptibility, proneness, inclination, tendency, vulnerability, liability, likelihood. **2** (*a predisposition towards violence*) predilection, proclivity, propensity, bias, inclination, leaning, bent, preference, penchant, proneness, willingness.

predominance *noun* **1** (*the predominance of the home side over their opponents*) dominance, dominion, control, ascendancy, mastery, supremacy, superiority, upper hand (*inf*), power, edge (*inf*), hold, influence, sway, weight, preponderance, leadership. **2** (*a predominance of women among the guests*) preponderance, dominance, prevalence, majority, bulk.

predominant *adj* **1** (*the predominant group within the party*) ruling, leading, sovereign, pre-eminent, dominant, ascendant, in the ascendancy, supreme, superior, controlling, in control, strong, principal, chief, main, primary, prime. **2** (*the predominant artistic style of the day*) prevailing, prevalent, preponderant, principal, chief, main, supreme, paramount. OPPOSITE: minor.

predominate *verb* **1** (*women predominate in the organization*) preponderate, be prevalent. **2** (*the left predominates in most cabinet meetings*) dominate, prevail, hold sway, hold the ascendancy, outweigh, outnumber, override, overrule, rule, rule the day, reign, overshadow, tell.

pre-eminence *noun* distinction, excellence, prestige, repute, eminence, prominence, importance, fame, renown, supremacy, superiority, predominance, transcendence, incomparability, matchlessness, peerlessness, paramountcy.

pre-eminent *adj* supreme, consummate, transcendent, paramount, outstanding, exceptional, leading, peerless, matchless, unequalled, unrivalled, unsurpassed, unmatched, incomparable, inimitable, superior, distinguished, excellent, superlative, predominant, prominent, eminent, important, famous, renowned, prevailing, foremost, main, chief, first. OPPOSITE: inferior.

pre-empt *verb* **1** (*try to pre-empt official action*) prevent, forestall, anticipate. **2** (*the authorities have pre-empted the whole area*) acquire, appropriate, assume, secure, commandeer, seize, take over, take possession of, occupy, usurp.

preen *verb* **1** (*the bird preened its feathers*) plume, clean, arrange, smooth, slick. **2** (*she spent hours preening herself to go out*) groom, array, deck out, doll up, dress up, tart up (*inf*), do up (*inf*), spruce up, trick out, trim, adorn, prettify, beautify, primp, prink, titivate.

preen oneself pat oneself on the back (*inf*), pride oneself, congratulate oneself, bask, exult, gloat.

preface *noun* introduction, foreword, prelude, prologue, preamble, frontmatter, preliminaries, prelims (*inf*). OPPOSITE: epilogue.
➤ *verb* introduce, open, begin, start, launch, prefix, precede, lead up to. OPPOSITE: close.

prefatory *adj* introductory, opening, preliminary, initial, preparatory, explanatory, precursory, preambulatory, antecedent. OPPOSITE: final.

prefer *verb* **1** (*she prefers the red dress*) favour, like better, choose, select, opt for, go for, plump for (*inf*), elect, pick, single out, fancy (*inf*), desire, want, wish. OPPOSITE:

reject. **2** (*expects to be preferred within the company fairly soon*) advance, promote, upgrade, elevate, raise, move up, favour, honour, aggrandize. OPPOSITE: downgrade. **3** (*we shall not prefer charges*) bring, press, lodge, file, tender, place, put forward, propose, proffer, offer, present. OPPOSITE: withdraw.

preferable *adj* better, superior, desirable, more desirable, more suitable, more eligible, worthier, nicer, preferred, favoured, chosen, advantageous, advisable, recommended.

preferably *adv* for preference, by preference, rather, much rather, sooner, much sooner, from choice, by choice, first.

preference *noun* **1** (*their preference is for coffee*) first choice, choice, option, wish, desire, selection, election, pick, favourite. **2** (*showed a preference for blue*) liking, fancy, inclination, leaning, bent, bias, predilection, partiality, discrimination, weakness. **3** (*accused of giving his friends preference*) priority, precedence, preferential treatment, favour, favouritism, partiality.

preferential *adj* special, superior, better, partial, partisan, biased, advantageous, favoured, favourable, privileged.

preferment *noun* advancement, promotion, upgrading, furtherance, improvement, betterment, aggrandizement, elevation, rise, moving up, exaltation, step up. OPPOSITE: demotion.

pregnancy *noun* gestation, gravidity, parturiency, impregnation.

pregnant *adj* **1** (*discovered she was pregnant*) expecting (*inf*), expectant, with child, preggers (*inf*), in the club (*inf*), in the family way (*inf*), up the spout (*inf*), up the duff (*inf*), with a bun in the oven (*inf*), parturient, gravid, enceinte. **2** (*a pregnant pause*) meaningful, significant, loaded, charged, weighty, pointed, eloquent, expressive, suggestive, telling, revealing. **3** (*a development pregnant with possibility*) fraught, full, rich, heavy, replete, abundant, teeming, prolific, productive, fruitful, fertile, fecund. OPPOSITE: barren.

prehistoric *adj* **1** (*prehistoric era*) primeval, primitive, primordial, earliest, early. **2** (*working with prehistoric equipment*) antiquated, ancient, archaic, old, old-fashioned, obsolete, superannuated, outmoded, out-of-date, antediluvian.

prejudice *noun* **1** (*showed prejudice towards his friends*) bias, favouritism, preference, partiality, one-sidedness, partisanship, predisposition, preconception, prejudgment, predetermination. **2** (*racial prejudice*) discrimination, bigotry, bias, intolerance, narrow-mindedness, unfairness, injustice, chauvinism, racism, sexism, ageism, xenophobia, anti-Semitism, misogyny, heterosexism, misanthropy. OPPOSITE: impartiality. **3** (*without prejudice towards any future claim*) harm, damage, impairment, hurt, injury, mischief, detriment, disadvantage, loss, ruin. OPPOSITE: benefit.
➤ *verb* **1** (*reports may prejudice the jury*) bias, colour, warp, distort, predispose, load, weight, sway, incline, slant, influence, dispose, jaundice, poison. **2** (*this may prejudice his future job prospects*) harm, damage, impair, ruin, wreck, hurt, injure, mar, spoil, hinder, undermine. OPPOSITE: aid.

prejudiced *adj* biased, warped, distorted, partial, one-sided, loaded, weighted, partisan, subjective, unfair, unjust, discriminatory, predisposed, jaundiced, influenced, conditioned, bigoted, blinkered, narrow-minded, chauvinist, chauvinistic, intolerant, racist, sexist, ageist, xenophobic, anti-Semitic. OPPOSITE: impartial.

prejudicial *adj* harmful, damaging, hurtful, injurious, mischievous, pernicious, detrimental, deleterious, counter-productive, disadvantageous, unfavourable, inimical, undermining. OPPOSITE: beneficial.

preliminary *adj* **1** (*made some preliminary comments*) introductory, beginning, opening, first, initial, initiatory, prior, precursory, preparatory, prefatory. OPPOSITE: final. **2** (*the team was knocked out in the preliminary round*) qualifying, eliminating, initial, inaugural, primary. **3** (*the government has made some preliminary approaches*) exploratory, test, trial, pilot, experimental, introductory, first, advance, early, earliest.
➤ *noun* preparation, groundwork, foundations, basics, introduction, opening, beginning, start, preface, foreword, preamble, prelims (*inf*), prelude, formalities.

prelude *noun* **1** (*a wonderful prelude to the evening*) preliminary, opening, opener, beginning, start, commencement, curtain-raiser, precursor, harbinger, herald, forerunner, preparation. OPPOSITE: finale. **2** (*write a prelude for the book*) introduction, intro (*inf*), preface, preamble, prologue, foreword. **3** (*composed his most famous prelude*) overture, voluntary.

premature *adj* **1** (*her premature death*) early, untimely, ill-timed, unseasonable, inopportune. **2** (*could be a premature decision*) hasty, over-hasty, precipitate, impulsive, impetuous, ill-considered, rash, previous (*inf*). OPPOSITE: late. **3** (*plans are still in a premature state*) incomplete, undeveloped, half-formed, embryonic, immature, unripe, green.

premeditated *adj* planned, preplanned, plotted, calculated, considered, studied, cold-blooded, conscious, intended, intentional, deliberate, wilful, prearranged, predetermined, contrived, predesigned. OPPOSITE: improvise.

premier *noun* head of government, prime minister, PM, chief minister, first minister, chancellor.
➤ *adj* principal, leading, prime, primary, first, cardinal, pre-eminent, foremost, supreme, chief, head, highest, top, top-ranking, main, arch.

première *noun* first performance, first showing, first night, opening, opening night, debut.

premise, premiss *noun* proposition, hypothesis, thesis, assumption, presumption, presupposition, supposition, assertion, postulation, argument, basis, ground.
➤ *verb* lay down, postulate, posit, predicate, stipulate, presuppose, assume, assert, state. OPPOSITE: conclude.

premises *pl noun* property, building, establishment, office, grounds, estate, site, place.

premium *noun* **1** (*pay a premium on the insurance policy*) instalment, payment. **2** (*receive a premium from the account*) bonus, bounty. **3** (*will pay a premium for work received early*) reward, recompense, remuneration, fee, perquisite, extra, tip, commission, perk (*inf*), percentage, prize.

at a premium costly, expensive, dear, in short supply, few and far between, scarce, rare, hard to come by, not to be had, in demand, like gold dust (*inf*).

put a premium on value, treasure, appreciate, favour, hold dear, regard highly, set great store by.

premonition *noun* **1** (*she had a premonition of disaster*) foreboding, presentiment, suspicion, idea, feeling, funny feeling (*inf*), gut feeling (*inf*), hunch, intuition, sixth sense, apprehension, worry, misgiving, anxiety, fear, presage. **2** (*the readings gave a premonition of the storm to come*) portent, omen, sign, indication, warning, forewarning.

preoccupation *noun* **1** (*lost in preoccupation*) abstraction, absorption, engrossment, absentmindedness, absence of mind, distraction, musing, pensiveness, concentration, reverie, brown study, deep thought, inattentiveness, heedlessness, obliviousness, oblivion, daydreaming, wool-gathering. **2** (*his chief preoccupation is music*) concern, interest, enthusiasm, hobby-horse, obsession, fixation, thing (*inf*), hang-up (*inf*), bee in one's bonnet (*inf*).

preoccupied *adj* engrossed, obsessed, absorbed, involved, taken up, wrapped up, lost, immersed, engaged, rapt, intent, abstracted, faraway, heedless, oblivious, unaware, distracted, distrait, inattentive, absentminded, daydreaming, pensive, deep in thought, lost in thought. OPPOSITE: attentive.

preoccupy *verb* occupy, absorb, engross, distract, engage, take up, involve, obsess.

preordain *verb* foreordain, destine, predestine, predetermine, fate, doom.

preparation *noun* **1** (*sort out the preparations for the expedition*) groundwork, spadework, preliminaries, basics, rudiments, foundation, provision, supply, equipping, plan, planning, arrangement, organization, assembling, assembly, development. **2** (*in a state of preparation for the attack*) readiness, preparedness, anticipation, expectation, precaution. **3** (*they have had a good preparation*) coaching, training, grooming, priming, education, study. **4** (*a preparation of herbs*) mixture, compound, concoction, composition, medicine, potion, lotion, tincture, application.

preparatory *adj* preparative, preliminary, introductory, initial, opening, prefatory, basic, rudimentary, elementary, fundamental, primary, precursory, prior. OPPOSITE: final.

preparatory to in preparation for, in advance of, in anticipation of, in expectation of, before, previous to, prior to, leading up to.

prepare *verb* **1** (*prepare a programme of events*) get ready, make ready, plan, draw up, map out, work out, arrange, organize, set up, develop, devise, put together, assemble, produce, compose, fashion, construct, concoct, draft, think up. OPPOSITE: destroy. **2** (*prepare for battle*) make preparations, get ready, make ready, arrange, make provision, get set, take steps, gear up for (*inf*), order, adjust, adapt, fit, rig, equip, provide, supply. **3** (*prepare for the test on Friday*) study, revise, swot (*inf*), mug up (*inf*). **4** (*prepare the team for the match*) train, coach, groom, prime, knock into shape (*inf*). **5** (*prepare for the race*) practise, train, warm up, exercise, get into shape.

6 (*prepare dinner*) make, put together, get ready, throw together, fix (*inf*), produce, concoct, assemble.

prepare oneself brace oneself, steel oneself, fortify oneself, ready oneself, gird oneself.

prepared *adj* **1** (*prepared for battle*) ready, in readiness, set, all set, arranged, organized, in order, primed, fixed, planned, fit. **2** (*prepared to consider it*) ready, willing, able, inclined, disposed, predisposed, of a mind, minded.

preponderance *noun* **1** (*a preponderance of women in the group*) predominance, dominance, prevalence, extensiveness, majority, bulk, mass. **2** (*the preponderance of radicals within the party*) dominance, predominance, domination, dominion, control, ascendancy, supremacy, superiority, upper hand, power, force, edge, sway, weight, mastery, leadership.

preponderate *verb* predominate, dominate, prevail, hold sway, outweigh, outnumber, override, overrule, rule, reign supreme.

prepossessing *adj* attractive, fetching, good-looking, beautiful, pretty, handsome, fair, charming, engaging, taking, winning, winsome, appealing, pleasing, agreeable, delightful, likeable, lovable, amiable, fascinating, magnetic, striking, captivating, taking, alluring, inviting, enchanting, bewitching. OPPOSITE: repulsive.

preposterous *adj* ridiculous, ludicrous, absurd, foolish, laughable, farcical, crazy, insane, irrational, illogical, unreasonable, senseless, asinine, nonsensical, outrageous, bizarre, astonishing, monstrous, shocking, unthinkable, intolerable, excessive, extravagant, incredible, unbelievable, impossible. OPPOSITE: reasonable.

prerequisite *noun* condition, precondition, proviso, qualification, requirement, requisite, imperative, necessity, essential, must (*inf*).
➤ *adj* indispensable, necessary, needed, needful, required, requisite, essential, vital, imperative, obligatory, mandatory, called for, fundamental.

prerogative *noun* privilege, right, birthright, liberty, choice, authority, sanction, licence, carte blanche, due, entitlement, claim, advantage, exemption, immunity.

presage *verb* **1** (*this news presages trouble*) indicate, point to, announce, herald, warn of, foreshadow, threaten, augur, bode, portend, bespeak, betoken, harbinger. **2** (*I presage disaster ahead*) predict, forecast, prophesy, prognosticate, foretell, forebode, forewarn, foresee, divine, feel, sense.

prescience *noun* foreknowledge, precognition, clairvoyance, prophecy, second sight, foresight, farsightedness.

prescribe *verb* **1** (*take the tablets prescribed by the doctor*) direct, specify, stipulate. **2** (*the law clearly prescribes*) lay down, require, stipulate, establish, define, direct, dictate, impose, specify, set, fix, ordain, decree, order, command, rule, enjoin. OPPOSITE: prohibit. **3** (*I prescribe caution in this matter*) advise, urge, recommend, commend, suggest.

prescription *noun* **1** (*wait while the doctor writes the prescription*) direction, instruction, order, recommendation. **2** (*please collect my prescription for me*) medicine, drug, preparation, mixture, remedy, treatment. **3** (*the prescription of restricted medicines*) prescribing, ordering, recommendation. **4** (*a prescription for financial disaster*) formula, recipe, guideline.

presence *noun* **1** (*to detect the presence of impurities*) being, existence. **2** (*her presence at the party*) attendance, company, companionship. OPPOSITE: absence. **3** (*in the presence of greatness*) company, proximity, vicinity, neighbourhood, nearness, closeness, propinquity. **4** (*an actor of great presence*) magnetism, attraction, charisma, aura, character, personality, poise, bearing, demeanour, carriage, comportment, dignity, self-confidence, self-assurance, self-possession. **5** (*a supernatural presence*) ghost, manifestation, spirit, apparition, phantom, spectre, wraith, shadow.

presence of mind aplomb, composure, poise, calm, cool (*inf*), coolness, level-headedness, sang-froid, phlegm, self-assurance, self-possession, imperturbability, unflappability (*inf*), alertness, quickness, quick-wittedness, wits.

present[1] *adj* **1** (*no drugs present in her blood*) existing, existent, extant. **2** (*at the present moment*) current, immediate, contemporary, present-day, existing. **3** (*I want a police officer present*) here, there, attending, in attendance, to hand, at hand, close at hand, available, ready, near, nearby. OPPOSITE: absent.

at present at the moment, for the moment, now, right now, at this time, at the present time, today, currently.
for the present for the moment, for the time being, for now, in the meantime, in the meanwhile, pro tem.
the present day now, nowadays, currently, today, modern times, this day and age. OPPOSITE: future.

present[2] *verb* **1** (*present the trophy*) give, donate, bestow, award, confer, grant, hand over, entrust, accord. OPPOSITE: withhold. **2** (*present a new idea*) introduce, submit, set forth, put forward, proffer, offer, tender, advance, suggest, declare, state, recount, relate, expound, pose. **3** (*presents his compliments*) extend, offer, tender, send, give. **4** (*presented his brother*) introduce, make known, acquaint with. **5** (*present their most recent paintings*) show, display, exhibit, demonstrate, introduce. **6** (*present a comedy*) stage, put on, produce, perform, mount, organize. **7** (*present the programme*) compère, host, introduce, announce, emcee (*inf*). **8** (*he was presented in a very bad light*) depict, portray, picture, represent, describe, characterize, delineate.

present oneself 1 (*she must present herself at the office next week*) be present, arrive, appear, attend, show up, turn up, pop up (*inf*). **2** (*should the chance present itself*) crop up, occur, arise, happen, transpire, materialize, come about, appear, emerge.

present[3] *noun* (*presents for all the children*) gift, pressie (*inf*), donation, offering, contribution, hand-out, gratuity, tip, freebie (*inf*), perk (*inf*), sweetener (*inf*), presentation, largess, award, grant, endowment, premium, benefaction.

presentable *adj* neat, tidy, smart, well-groomed, spruce, clean, respectable, decent, proper, becoming, acceptable, suitable, satisfactory, tolerable, passable, good enough, OK (*inf*).

presentation *noun* **1** (*the presentation of a knighthood*) presenting, giving, handing over, award, granting,

conferral, bestowal, investiture, donation, donating, according. **2** (*handed over the presentation*) gift, present, donation, offering, contribution, gratuity. **3** (*the presentation of new ideas*) introduction, submission, proffering, offering. **4** (*the presentation of the government's new manifesto*) launch, launching, introduction, demonstration, exhibition, display, show. **5** (*we enjoyed your presentation*) talk, address, speech, disquisition, lecture, seminar. **6** (*the presentation of his latest tragedy*) performance, production, mounting, staging, showing, rendition, representation, exhibition, appearance, delivery. **7** (*her presentation at court*) introduction, debut, launch, coming out. **8** (*the presentation of this research lacks a great deal*) appearance, arrangement, organization, ordering, disposition, layout, format, structure, scheme, system, form.

presentiment *noun* premonition, foreboding, intuition, hunch, feeling, suspicion, anticipation, expectation, apprehension, misgiving, bad vibes (*inf*), fear, forecast, foreknowledge, forethought, prescience.

presently *adv* **1** (*I shall be with you presently*) soon, shortly, pretty soon (*inf*), in a short time, in a short while, in a while, in a minute, in a moment, in a mo (*inf*), in a jiffy (*inf*), before long, by and by, later. **2** (*there is little enthusiasm for the plan presently*) at present, at the present time, now, currently, at the moment, these days, at this moment in time.

preservation *noun* **1** (*discovered in a good state of preservation*) conservation, keeping, protection, storage. **2** (*the preservation of good health*) maintenance, protection, defence, keeping, safekeeping, upkeep, safeguarding, guarding, shielding, perpetuation, continuation, retention, upholding, support. OPPOSITE: destruction. **3** (*the preservation of wealth*) conservation, maintenance, keeping, hoarding, saving, putting away.

preserve *verb* **1** (*preserve the environment*) protect, defend, shield, shelter, guard, safeguard, care for, look after, take care of, save, conserve. OPPOSITE: destroy. **2** (*preserve the old ways*) conserve, save, maintain, uphold, keep up, keep alive, keep going, secure, sustain, perpetuate, continue, prolong, retain. **3** (*a way to preserve one's wealth*) conserve, keep, retain, save, hoard, store, put away, put aside. **4** (*preserve all kinds of fruit*) store, keep, bottle, can, tin, pickle, cure, smoke, kipper, salt, dry, freeze.
▶ *noun* **1** (*fruit preserves*) jam, jelly, marmalade, conserve, confiture. **2** (*the preserve of the rich*) domain, sphere, realm, field, area, speciality. **3** (*animal preserve*) reservation, reserve, game reserve, safari park, sanctuary.

preside *verb* **1** (*preside over the meeting*) officiate, chair, conduct. **2** (*preside over the country*) lead, head, govern, rule, control, direct, run, manage, conduct, administer, supervise.

president *noun* **1** (*the presidents of three countries*) head of state, ruler. **2** (*president of the organization*) chief, boss (*inf*), head, leader, director, executive, principal, chairman, controller, captain.

press *verb* **1** (*press the switch*) push, depress, force down, bear down on. **2** (*a machine to press metal*) squeeze, compress, crush, pinch, mash. **3** (*the mob pressed round the gates*) crowd, flock, gather, throng, swarm, surge,

cluster, mill, jam, cram, push, stuff. **4** (*press this shirt*)
iron, smooth, smooth out. OPPOSITE: crumple. **5** (*press
flowers*) flatten, smooth out. **6** (*pressed the child against
her side*) hug, embrace, cuddle, clasp, clutch, grasp,
squeeze, crush, enfold. **7** (*he pressed her hand*) squeeze,
grip, clasp, clutch, grasp. **8** (*press them for a response*)
urge, beg, plead, implore, entreat, exhort, petition,
campaign, clamour for, importune, harass, worry, afflict,
plague, torment, trouble, besiege, demand, call for,
constrain, force, coerce, compel, pressurize, put pressure
on, insist on. **9** (*press the claim through the courts*) pursue,
push, pass, advance.
» *noun* **1** (*the press were waiting outside*) journalists,
reporters, hacks (*inf*), correspondents, photographers,
paparazzi, media, newspapers, papers, Fleet Street,
fourth estate, journalism. **2** (*the show enjoyed a good press*)
review, criticism, treatment, coverage, articles, write-
ups. **3** (*a press of angry people*) crowd, throng, multitude,
mob, horde, crush, swarm, cluster, pack, herd, flock,
push. **4** (*the press of city life*) hurry, hustle, bustle, hassle
(*inf*), urgency, demands, pressure, stress, strain.
press on press ahead, push on, persevere, go ahead, go
on, carry on, continue, proceed, advance, move, hasten,
hurry, rush.

pressed *adj* **1** (*pressed for cash*) short of, strapped (*inf*),
lacking, deficient in. **2** (*I'm very pressed at the moment*)
busy, pushed, preoccupied, hurried, rushed, harassed.

pressing *adj* urgent, crucial, pivotal, high-priority,
serious, critical, key, vital, essential, important,
imperative, burning, demanding, importunate, exigent.
OPPOSITE: trivial.

pressure *noun* **1** (*pressure on the foundations*) load,
weight, heaviness, stress, strain, force, power. **2** (*apply
pressure to the wound*) compression, squeezing. **3** (*put
pressure on them to comply*) constraint, duress,
compulsion, coercion, obligation, insistence, urgency,
force, power, influence. **4** (*the job brought a lot of pressure
with it*) stress, strain, tension, burden, load, weight,
harassment, oppression, hassle (*inf*), aggro (*inf*), trouble,
problems. OPPOSITE: relaxation.

pressurize *verb* pressure, press, force, compel,
constrain, oblige, coerce, bully, browbeat, lean on (*inf*),
put the screws on (*inf*), bulldoze, dragoon, drive.

prestige *noun* status, reputation, fame, esteem, renown,
celebrity, kudos, authority, influence, weight,
importance, eminence, distinction, standing, stature,
regard, honour, cachet, credit, superiority.

prestigious *adj* **1** (*a prestigious academic*) reputable,
respected, esteemed, exalted, eminent, prominent, high-
ranking, distinguished, notable, well-known, celebrated,
famous, illustrious, renowned, great, influential,
important. **2** (*a prestigious address*) impressive, imposing,
glamorous.

presumably *adv* in all probability, probably, in all
likelihood, most likely, very likely, as like as not (*inf*), all
things being equal, all things considered, no doubt,
doubtless, doubtlessly, apparently, seemingly, on the
face of it.

presume *verb* **1** (*I presume the post has arrived*) assume,
take for granted, take as read, take it, imagine, suppose,
presuppose, surmise, think, guess, conjecture,

hypothesize, postulate, believe, conclude, deduce, infer,
judge. OPPOSITE: know. **2** (*he presumed to ask directly*)
venture, dare, undertake, go so far as, make so bold as,
have the temerity, have the audacity, have the
effrontery.

presume on depend on, rely on, count on, bank on,
trust, take advantage of, exploit.

presumption *noun* **1** (*the presumption that he is guilty*)
assumption, supposition, presupposition, surmise,
guess, deduction, conjecture, belief, opinion,
hypothesis, inference, premiss. OPPOSITE: knowledge.
2 (*had the presumption to defy the king*)
presumptuousness, boldness, audacity, temerity,
effrontery, bumptiousness, impertinence, impudence,
insolence, cheek (*inf*), nerve (*inf*), gall (*inf*), brass (*inf*),
forwardness, assurance, confidence, arrogance, egotism.
OPPOSITE: modesty.

presumptive *adj* **1** (*we need presumptive evidence*)
believable, credible, plausible, feasible, reasonable,
conceivable, probable, likely. **2** (*the heir presumptive*)
designate, prospective, assumed, supposed, expected,
likely.

presumptuous *adj* bold, audacious, impertinent,
impudent, insolent, cheeky (*inf*), disrespectful, fresh
(*inf*), forward, brazen, assured, bumptious, pushy (*inf*),
overbearing, arrogant, haughty, big-headed (*inf*),
conceited, overconfident, ultraconfident, cocksure,
cocky (*inf*), too big for one's boots, foolhardy, rash.
OPPOSITE: modest.

presuppose *verb* assume, accept, take for granted, take
as read, take it, suppose, presume, postulate, posit,
imply.

presupposition *noun* assumption, presumption,
preconception, belief, supposition, theory, thesis,
hypothesis, premise, premiss.

pretence *noun* **1** (*a master of pretence*) make-believe,
acting, play-acting, shamming, faking, feigning,
dissembling, dissimulation, invention, imagination,
posturing. **2** (*not deceived by her pretence of concern*) show,
charade, semblance, masquerade, cloak, veil, mask,
veneer, cover, appearance, false front, guise, facade.
3 (*on the pretence that she was ill*) pretext, excuse, guise,
sham, ruse, wile, subterfuge, trickery, lie, falsehood,
fabrication, bluff, deception, deceit. OPPOSITE: truth.
4 (*make no pretence to expert knowledge*) claim, aspiration,
profession. **5** (*prepared food without any pretence*)
pretentiousness, ostentation, showiness, display,
affectation, flaunting, posturing, posing.

pretend *verb* **1** (*we think she's only pretending*) play-act,
put on an act, act, bluff, put it on, dissemble, fake, fake
it, feign, sham, dissimulate, make believe, posture, go
through the motions. **2** (*pretend you are a spaceman*)
make believe, imagine, suppose. **3** (*pretend ignorance*)
sham, fake, counterfeit, feign, simulate, put on, affect,
assume, make believe, dissemble, fabricate, invent.
4 (*pretend not to mind*) claim, profess, purport, allege.
5 (*pretend to the throne*) claim, aspire to, aim for.

pretended *adj* **1** (*pretended expertise in the subject*)
alleged, professed, purported, avowed, spurious,
insincere, bogus, sham, false, fake, faked, feigned,
counterfeit, phoney (*inf*), artificial, affected, put-on,

pseudo (*inf*), fictitious. **2** (*her pretended allies have deserted her*) pretend (*inf*), supposed, alleged, so-called, professed, ostensible, bogus, pseudo (*inf*).

pretender *noun* claimant, aspirant, candidate, claimer.

pretension *noun* **1** (*I cannot bear such pretension*) pretentiousness, pomposity, self-importance, airs, conceit, vanity, affectation, snobbishness, hypocrisy, show, showiness, flaunting, floweriness, flamboyance, ostentation, ostentatiousness. **2** (*make pretensions to be an expert*) claim, profession, demand, assertion, aspiration, ambition, pretence, assumption.

pretentious *adj* **1** (*a pretentious style of decoration*) ostentatious, showy, flamboyant, over-the-top (*inf*), OTT (*inf*), elaborate, theatrical, flowery, affected, extravagant, exaggerated, high-flown, ambitious, overambitious, grandiose, grandiloquent, magniloquent, highfalutin (*inf*), mannered, twee. **2** (*pretentious behaviour*) vain, conceited, affected, arrogant, puffed-up, self-immortant, immodest, pompous, bombastic, inflated, snobbish, vainglorious. OPPOSITE: unpretentious.

preternatural *adj* unnatural, anomalous, abnormal, irregular, unusual, exceptional, uncommon, extraordinary, out of the ordinary, singular, strange, odd, peculiar, weird, mysterious, inexplicable, unearthly, supernatural, paranormal. OPPOSITE: normal.

pretext *noun* excuse, reason, claim, allegation, pretence, guise, sham, semblance, simulation, appearance, show, cloak, mask, veil, cover, ploy, ruse, wile, red herring (*inf*).

pretty *adj* **1** (*a pretty girl*) attractive, good-looking, beautiful, fair, lovely, comely, personable, appealing, winning, winsome, cute, pleasing, delightful, prepossessing, charming, engaging, nice-looking, bonny, graceful. OPPOSITE: ugly. **2** (*a pretty dress*) lovely, attractive, delightful, nice, pleasant, pleasing, elegant, charming, dainty, delicate, neat, trim, fine, tasteful, bonny. **3** (*a pretty sum*) considerable, sizeable, large, substantial, tidy (*inf*), appreciable, fair, goodly, goodish, tolerable.
≫ *adv* **1** (*going pretty fast*) fairly, quite, moderately, reasonably, tolerably. **2** (*he was pretty annoyed*) quite, rather, fairly, somewhat, kind of (*inf*).

prevail *verb* **1** (*common sense prevailed eventually*) win, win through, win out, triumph, be victorious, succeed, conquer, overcome, rule, reign, gain ascendancy, gain mastery, carry the day (*inf*). OPPOSITE: lose. **2** (*according to prevailing conditions*) exist, abound, persist, obtain, predominate, preponderate, occur, hold sway.
prevail upon persuade, talk into, sweet-talk (*inf*), soft-soap (*inf*), incline, induce, dispose, prompt, influence, lean on (*inf*), urge, exhort, cajole, coax, sway, pull strings (*inf*), convince, win over, bring round, pressure, pressurize.

prevailing *adj* **1** (*the prevailing fashion for long hair*) prevalent, widespread, universal, general, common, usual, accepted, set, established, current, popular, mainstream, fashionable, in fashion, in vogue, in style. OPPOSITE: rare. **2** (*the prevailing side in the contest*) prevalent, predominant, predominating, dominant, preponderant, controlling, ruling, governing, superior,

ascendant, supreme, principal, chief, main, powerful. OPPOSITE: subordinate.

prevalence *noun* **1** (*the prevalence of illegal drug-taking*) frequency, regularity, popularity, fashionableness, commonness, profusion, pervasiveness, universality, acceptance, currency. **2** (*the prevalence of disease*) rifeness, frequency, ubiquity, ubiquitousness, extensiveness, universality, commonness. **3** (*the prevalence of such thinking*) predominance, dominance, preponderance, primacy, ascendancy, supremacy, rule, mastery, sway, hold.

prevalent *adj* **1** (*the prevalent mood in the high street*) prevailing, current, established, set, accepted, general, common, customary, habitual, everyday, usual, widespread, universal, popular, fashionable, frequent. **2** (*other prevalent diseases*) common, endemic, rife, rampant, widespread, ubiquitous, extensive, universal, usual, frequent. **3** (*the prevalent side in the contest*) prevailing, dominant, predominant, preponderant, superior, ascendant, ruling, governing.

prevaricate *verb* equivocate, evade, dodge (*inf*), hedge (*inf*), sidestep, shift, shuffle, quibble, waffle (*inf*), flannel (*inf*), beat about the bush (*inf*), sit on the fence (*inf*), hum and haw (*inf*), shilly-shally (*inf*), beg the question, cavil, lie, deceive, tergiversate.

prevarication *noun* evasion, evasiveness, equivocation, sidestepping, dodging (*inf*), hedging (*inf*), quibbling, shilly-shallying (*inf*), humming and hawing (*inf*), cavilling, pretence, lie, untruth, falsification, half-truth, misrepresentation.

prevent *verb* stop, halt, arrest, check, hold in check, preclude, hinder, impede, block, obstruct, intercept, hamper, deter, bar, restrain, hold back, inhibit, thwart, frustrate, foil, balk, forestall, keep from, anticipate, counteract, avert, avoid, ward off, fend off, stave off, head off, nip in the bud. OPPOSITE: aid.

prevention *noun* stoppage, halt, halting, arresting, check, checking, preclusion, hampering, foiling, frustration, forestalling, balking, hindrance, impediment, obstruction, obstacle, deterrence, determent, restraint, bar, barring, prohibition, inhibition, elimination, anticipation, avoidance, heading off, fending off, staving off, warding off. OPPOSITE: assistance.

preventive *adj* preventative, precautionary, protective, shielding, counteractive, inhibitory, obstructive, deterrent, pre-emptive, anticipatory, prophylactic.
≫ *noun* precautionary measure, prevention, protection, protective, safeguard, remedy, shield, deterrent, impediment, hindrance, block, obstruction, obstacle, prophylactic.

previous *adj* **1** (*the previous occupant*) former, preceding, foregoing, antecedent, precursory, past, erstwhile, sometime, one-time. **2** (*see previous page*) prior, preceding, foregoing, above, precursory, antecedent, anterior. OPPOSITE: later. **3** (*in previous years*) earlier, former, preceding, prior, erstwhile. **4** (*it was a bit previous of them*) premature, precipitate, untimely, hasty, overhasty, presumptuous, impetuous.

previously *adv* formerly, until now, hitherto,

heretofore, before, once, earlier, erstwhile, at one time, in the past, in years gone by.

prey *noun* quarry, game, kill, victim, target.

prey on 1 (*prey on small mammals*) hunt, seize, devour, eat, feed on, live off, live on, catch. **2** (*prey on the unsuspecting*) victimize, intimidate, bully, terrorize, exploit, take advantage of, dupe, con (*inf*), fleece (*inf*), bleed (*inf*), blackmail. **3** (*the thought preyed on his mind*) oppress, weigh down, weigh upon, burden, hang over, trouble, worry, distress, torment, plague, haunt.

price *noun* **1** (*the rising price of eggs*) cost, expense, fee, levy, toll, rate, bill, charge, value, worth, amount, sum, figure, expenditure, outlay, valuation, assessment, estimate, quotation, payment. **2** (*the price of defeat*) penalty, loss, forfeit, sacrifice, consequence, cost, result, punishment. **3** (*put a price on his head*) bounty, reward, premium, recompense, compensation.
≫ *verb* value, rate, cost, assess, estimate, appraise, evaluate.

at a price expensive, at a high price, at a high cost, at considerable cost.

at any price regardless, anyhow, at any cost, whatever it takes, whatever the cost, at whatever cost, no matter what it costs.

priceless *adj* **1** (*priceless antiques*) invaluable, valuable, inestimable, incalculable, beyond price, precious, prized, treasured, cherished, dear, expensive, costly, rich, unique, rare, incomparable, irreplaceable. OPPOSITE: cheap. **2** (*a priceless joke*) hilarious, riotous, side-splitting, rib-tickling, funny, amusing, comic, killing (*inf*), rich (*inf*).

prick *verb* **1** (*pricked her thumb*) pierce, puncture, perforate, punch, spike, jab, stab, impale, lance, jag, slit, gash, cut, nick, wound. **2** (*his skin pricked as though stung by a nettle*) prickle, sting, tingle, smart, itch, bite. **3** (*the story pricked her heart*) stab, move, touch, affect, grieve. **4** (*her fate pricked the king's conscience*) trouble, prompt, stir, distress, worry, goad, spur, prod, plague, prey on, gnaw at, harass, harry, incite.
≫ *noun* **1** (*gave her thumb a prick*) jab, stab, jag, nick, wound. **2** (*a tiny prick in the paper*) puncture, nick, perforation, pinhole, hole. **3** (*you'll feel just a tiny prick from the needle*) pricking, pang, spasm, twinge, tingle, tingling, pain. **4** (*mind the pricks on the stem*) prickle, thorn, spike, barb, spine.

prick up raise, erect, rise, stand up, point.

prickle *verb* **1** (*her skin prickled at the spider's touch*) tickle, tingle, twitch, itch, smart, creep, crawl. **2** (*he was prickled by the bush*) prick, jab, nick, nip, stick, sting.
≫ *noun* **1** (*the stem was covered in prickles*) thorn, spike, spine, barb, spur, point, needle. **2** (*the prickle of a jellyfish sting*) itching, smarting, stinging, sting, twinge, pang, tingle, tickle, pins and needles, goose-pimples. **3** (*a prickle of alarm*) sensation, feeling.

prickly *adj* **1** (*a prickly plant*) thorny, spiky, spiked, spiny, barbed, bristly, scratchy, rouch, brambly, pronged. **2** (*a prickly sensation*) prickling, tingling, itching, itchy, smarting, stinging, creeping, crawling. **3** (*a prickly temper*) irritable, irascible, fractious, stroppy (*inf*), ratty (*inf*), shirty (*inf*), crotchety (*inf*), tetchy, touchy, edgy, crabby (*inf*), grouchy (*inf*), grumpy, peevish, snappish, waspish, short-tempered, bad-

tempered, cantankerous. **4** (*a prickly topic*) thorny, complicated, complex, knotty, difficult, hard, tough, troublesome, tricky, ticklish, problematical, intricate, involved, trying, vexatious.

pride *noun* **1** (*the sin of pride*) vanity, conceit, egotism, self-love, boastfulness, big-headedness, self-praise, self-glorification, smugness, superciliousness, complacency, arrogance, disdain, haughtiness, hauteur, hubris, loftiness, self-importance, presumption, pretension, pretentiousness, snobbery. OPPOSITE: modesty. **2** (*he has no pride left*) dignity, self-respect, self-esteem, self-worth, ego, honour. OPPOSITE: shame. **3** (*the pride of the collection*) treasure, jewel, gem, prize, boast, cream, pick, élite. **4** (*takes great pride in his achievement*) pleasure, delight, joy, satisfaction, gratification.

pride oneself on congratulate oneself, flatter oneself, preen oneself on, take pride in, take satisfaction in, exult in, revel in, glory in, crow about, boast about, brag about, vaunt.

priest *noun* clergyman, clergywoman, cleric, ecclesiastic, divine, churchman, churchwoman, man of God, man of the cloth, minister, vicar, parson, rector, pastor, father, padre. OPPOSITE: layman.

priggish *adj* prim, strait-laced, prudish, narrow-minded, puritanical, smug, self-righteous, sanctimonious, goody-goody (*inf*), stiff, stuffy, starchy (*inf*), holier-than-thou (*inf*), pedantic.

prim *adj* formal, proper, demure, stiff, staid, stuffy, starchy (*inf*), strait-laced, priggish, prudish, puritanical, fussy, particular, fastidious, precise, prissy, fuddy-duddy (*inf*), old-maidish. OPPOSITE: easy-going.

primarily *adv* chiefly, principally, generally, largely, mainly, mostly, basically, first, firstly, first and foremost, fundamentally, especially, particularly, predominantly, predominately, essentially, in essence, in the main, on the whole, in the first place.

primary *adj* **1** (*their primary concern*) prime, principal, capital, cardinal, supreme, paramount, ultimate, foremost, highest, top, greatest, chief, main, leading, predominant, dominant. OPPOSITE: minor. **2** (*fuel is our primary requirement*) prime, basic, essential, fundamental, elementary, rudimentary. OPPOSITE: secondary. **3** (*the primary stages of the disease*) initial, first, early, opening, beginning, introductory. OPPOSITE: last. **4** (*the primary era of mankind's history*) earliest, first, original, primeval, prehistoric, primitive, aboriginal, primordial, primal.

prime *adj* **1** (*of prime importance*) primary, first, paramount, major, basic, principal, leading, chief, main, predominant. **2** (*the prime factor*) basic, fundamental, elemental, rudimentary, essential, primary. **3** (*a prime cut of meat*) first-rate, first-class, excellent, superior, choice, select, supreme, highest, best, top-quality, quality, top, top-grade, high-grade. OPPOSITE: inferior. **4** (*a prime example*) classic, typical, standard, characteristic, excellent, ideal.
≫ *noun* **1** (*at the prime of her powers*) zenith, peak, pinnacle, height, culmination, acme. OPPOSITE: decline. **2** (*jazz in its prime*) heyday, flower, bloom, maturity.
≫ *verb* **1** (*prime for use*) prepare, make ready, get ready, equip. **2** (*prime them with the details*) brief, inform, clue

up (*inf*), fill in (*inf*), gen up (*inf*), notify, tell. **3** (*prime the team with refreshments*) supply, provide, equip, furnish, provision.

primeval *adj* primordial, original, aboriginal, primitive, primal, primary, first, pristine, early, earliest, ancient, prehistoric, old. OPPOSITE: modern.

primitive *adj* **1** (*in primitive times*) primeval, primordial, primal, pristine, early, first, primary, original, ancient, archaic. OPPOSITE: modern. **2** (*using primitive weapons*) crude, rough, rudimentary, rude, simple, unsophisticated, undeveloped, unrefined. **3** (*primitive peoples*) uncivilized, uncultured, barbarian, barbaric, savage, wild. **4** (*primitive art*) unsophisticated, undeveloped, naive, childlike, simple, natural. OPPOSITE: sophisticated.

primordial *adj* primeval, primitive, primal, primary, first, earliest, pristine. OPPOSITE: modern.

prince *noun* ruler, lord, monarch, sovereign, potentate. OPPOSITE: subject.

princely *adj* **1** (*a princely sum*) generous, liberal, open-handed, bounteous, munificent, magnanimous, gracious, lavish, rich, ample, bountiful, sumptuous. OPPOSITE: mean. **2** (*a princely gesture*) noble, imperial, royal, regal, majestic, sovereign, stately, august, imposing, magnificent, grand, lofty, dignified. OPPOSITE: lowly.

principal *adj* chief, main, controlling, in charge, dominant, pre-eminent, leading, first, foremost, supreme, arch, highest, primary, prime, paramount, cardinal, major, key, essential. OPPOSITE: minor.
➤ *noun* **1** (*the principal of the company*) head, chief, leader, ruler, master, boss (*inf*), director, manager, controller, headmaster, headmistress, headteacher. OPPOSITE: subordinate. **2** (*paying interest on the principal*) capital, assets, funds, money, resources. **3** (*the principals in the play*) leading player, lead, star.

principally *adv* above all, mainly, mostly, largely, chiefly, primarily, especially, predominantly, particularly, for the most part, in the main, first and foremost.

principle *noun* **1** (*scientific principle*) rule, law, standard, criterion, formula, precept, theory, proposition, truth. OPPOSITE: practice. **2** (*the principle of bad driving out good*) rule, law, canon, tenet, code, doctrine, belief, credo, creed, dogma, philosophy, maxim, axiom, dictum, postulate, basis. **3** (*a man of principle*) morals, morality, ethics, standards, conscience, scruples, decency, honour, probity, integrity, virtue, goodness, honesty, uprightness, righteousness, rectitude. OPPOSITE: unscrupulousness.
in principle theoretically, in theory, ideally, in essence, in general.

print *verb* **1** (*print a hundred posters*) reproduce, copy, run off. **2** (*print the coins with the queen's head*) stamp, mark, impress, imprint, engrave, etch. **3** (*print a newspaper*) publish, issue.
➤ *noun* **1** (*the print of a foot*) impression, imprint, mark, indentation, footprint, fingerprint. **2** (*shocking to see it in print*) type, lettering, letters, typescript, newsprint, publication. **3** (*a thousand prints of the original*) reproduction, copy, replica, duplicate. **4** (*a photographic

print*) photograph, photo, snapshot, snap (*inf*), picture.
in print printed, published, out, in black and white, on paper, current, available, obtainable, in circulation, on the shelves, in the shops.

prior *adj* preceding, antecedent, earlier, anterior, previous, former, foregoing, aforementioned. OPPOSITE: subsequent.
prior to before, preceding, earlier than, until, up to.

priority *noun* **1** (*making money seems to be their priority*) prime concern, first concern, main thing, motivation, essential, requirement, interest. **2** (*this has priority*) precedence, more importance. **3** (*list in order of priority*) preference, urgency, antecedence. **4** (*her experience gives her priority*) superiority, supremacy, prerogative, seniority, rank, pre-eminence, right of way.

priory *noun* abbey, cloister, friary, monastery, religious house, convent, nunnery.

prise *verb* lever, force, jemmy, pry, raise, lift, hoist, dislodge, shift, yank (*inf*), pull, move, winkle.

prison *noun* **1** (*open day at the prison*) gaol, jail, lockup, nick (*inf*), inside (*inf*), can (*inf*), jug (*inf*), clink (*inf*), slammer (*inf*), cage (*inf*), cooler (*inf*), penitentiary, pen (*inf*), glasshouse (*inf*), cell, dungeon. **2** (*sentenced to prison*) imprisonment, confinement, detention, custody, stir (*inf*), porridge (*inf*).

prisoner *noun* **1** (*the prisoner was taken to the governor*) inmate, convict, con (*inf*), jailbird (*inf*), lag (*inf*), lifer (*inf*), detainee. **2** (*hundreds of soldiers became prisoners after the defeat*) captive, hostage, prisoner of war, POW, internee.

pristine *adj* **1** (*a pristine tablecloth*) perfect, immaculate, unblemished, unmarked, unspoilt, spotless, clean, fresh, in mint condition, pure, untouched, new, virgin, virginal, undefiled, uncorrupted, unsullied. OPPOSITE: defiled. **2** (*a pristine era in history*) original, early, earliest, ancient, first, initial, former, primary, primal, primeval, prehistoric, primordial. OPPOSITE: later.

privacy *noun* seclusion, privateness, retirement, retreat, solitude, isolation, sequestration, peace, quietness, secrecy, confidentiality, concealment. OPPOSITE: publicity.

private *adj* **1** (*whatever the judge's private opinions*) personal, intimate, individual, own, particular, special, exclusive. OPPOSITE: public. **2** (*private rooms*) exclusive, personal, particular, own, special, individual. OPPOSITE: communal. **3** (*press interest in her private life*) personal, confidential, intimate, innermost, secret, individual. **4** (*made a private approach to their rivals*) secret, confidential, classified, hush-hush (*inf*), privileged, unofficial, off the record. **5** (*a very private person*) reserved, quiet, uncommunicative, secretive, retiring, withdrawn, solitary, separate, self-contained, independent. **6** (*our private hideaway in the country*) secret, hidden, clandestine, secluded, undisturbed, quiet, out-of-the-way, sequestered, retired, solitary, isolated, remote. **7** (*tax from private industry*) privatized, independent, commercial, denationalized, self-governing.
➤ *noun* private soldier, enlisted man, squaddie (*inf*), infantryman.
in private privately, secretly, in secret, confidentially,

in confidence, in camera, behind closed doors, sub rosa, personally. OPPOSITE: publicly.

privation *noun* deprivation, want, need, neediness, necessity, lack, loss, hardship, misery, suffering, distress, disadvantage, poverty, penury, indigence, austerity, destitution, beggary, pauperism. OPPOSITE: wealth.

privilege *noun* **1** (*a privilege reserved for members*) right, birthright, prerogative, due, sanction, entitlement, benefit, advantage, claim, title. **2** (*granted privilege from prosecution*) immunity, exemption, dispensation, concession, freedom, liberty. **3** (*a life of privilege*) advantage, advantageousness, favour, indulgence. **4** (*it was my privilege to be of help*) honour, benefit, pleasure.

privileged *adj* **1** (*he hails from a privileged family*) favoured, advantaged, protected, sheltered, élite, titled, honoured, ruling, powerful, moneyed, indulgent, pampered, spoilt. **2** (*privileged from prosecution*) immune, exempted, exempt, empowered, allowed, sanctioned, licensed. **3** (*this is privileged information*) confidential, private, classified, secret, hush-hush (*inf*), unofficial, off the record, special.

privy *adj* private, personal, secret, confidential, off the record. OPPOSITE: public.

privy to informed about, acquainted with, aware of, wise to (*inf*), apprised of, cognizant of, in on (*inf*), hip to (*inf*), in the know about (*inf*), clued in on (*inf*), genned up on (*inf*).
➤ *noun* lavatory, toilet, loo (*inf*), bog (*inf*), public convenience, cloakroom, washroom, latrine, water closet, WC.

prize *noun* **1** (*first to win the million-dollar prize*) haul, stake, winnings, jackpot, purse, windfall. **2** (*won first prize at their third attempt*) trophy, medal, award, accolade, honour, palm, bays, laurels, reward, premium. **3** (*she was his prize*) goal, aim, ambition, desire, hope, conquest. **4** (*the prizes of war*) spoils, loot, booty, plunder, pillage, pickings, trophy, capture. OPPOSITE: penalty.
➤ *adj* best, top, choice, select, first-class, first-rate, excellent, outstanding, smashing (*inf*), terrific (*inf*), top-notch (*inf*), champion, winning, prize-winning, award-winning.
➤ *verb* value, appreciate, treasure, cherish, love, hold dear, esteem, revere, think highly of, hold in high regard, set great store by. OPPOSITE: underrate.

probability *noun* **1** (*a high probability that the match will be called off*) likelihood, likeliness, liability, expectation, prospect, chance, chances, odds, possibility. **2** (*have to face the probability of redundancy*) likelihood, prospect, possibility.

probable likely, expected, anticipated, odds-on (*inf*), presumable, presumed, predictable, foreseeable, apparent, seeming, ostensible, credible, believable, plausible, feasible, possible, reasonable. OPPOSITE: unlikely.

probably *adv* likely, most likely, as likely as not, doubtless, in all probability, in all likelihood, possibly, presumably, maybe, perhaps.

probation *noun* test, test period, trial, trial period, try-out, apprenticeship, supervision.

probe *verb* **1** (*probe the depths*) explore, search, sound,

plumb, penetrate, pierce, prod. **2** (*probe into the matter*) look into, go into, investigate, scrutinize, study, examine, analyse, sift, question, query, check, inquire, research, test.
➤ *noun* investigation, inquiry, scrutiny, scrutinization, examination, study, research, analysis, test, search, exploration.

probity *noun* integrity, uprightness, righteousness, rectitude, honesty, sincerity, truthfulness, fidelity, trustworthiness, honour, honourableness, worth, virtue, goodness, morality, principle, justice, equity, fairness. OPPOSITE: dishonesty.

problem *noun* **1** (*encounter a problem*) difficulty, complication, snag, hassle (*inf*), trouble, hole (*inf*), fix (*inf*), mess, predicament, plight, quandary, dilemma, pickle (*inf*), can of worms (*inf*). **2** (*several problems on her mind*) difficulty, complication, trouble, issue, matter. **3** (*they had a marital problems*) difficulty, dispute, disagreement. **4** (*a new problem to solve*) question, poser, riddle, enigma, puzzle, conundrum, teaser (*inf*). OPPOSITE: solution.
➤ *adj* troublesome, delinquent, unmanageable, unruly, disobedient, uncontrollable, intractable, intransigent, recalcitrant, nuisance.

problematic *adj* **1** (*a problematic turn of events*) problematical, difficult, fraught, troublesome, awkward, complicated, hard, puzzling, perplexing, intricate, involved, knotty, thorny, ticklish, tricky, dodgy (*inf*). **2** (*the eventual outcome is still problematic*) dubious, doubtful, questionable, debatable, arguable, moot, uncertain, unsettled, puzzling, enigmatic, chancy (*inf*). OPPOSITE: certain.

procedure *noun* **1** (*the procedure for getting permission*) process, method, methodology, system, course, technique, means, plan of action, modus operandi, policy, strategy, scheme, approach, way, custom, wont, practice, conduct, rule, formula, routine, rigmarole, operation, performance. **2** (*go through the necessary procedures*) step, action, process, measure, move, operation, transaction.

proceed *verb* **1** (*proceed down the road*) advance, progress, go, go ahead, go on, go forward, move on, press on, make one's way, continue, carry on. OPPOSITE: retreat. **2** (*proceed to unblock the drain*) take steps, take measures, take action, act, go ahead, move, progress, start, begin. **3** (*from this decision proceeded a whole chain of events*) arise, originate, spring, start, stem, emanate, issue, flow, derive, come, result, follow, ensue.

proceeding *noun* act, action, deed, action, course of action, procedure, process, step, measure, undertaking, venture, operation, transaction, move, manoeuvre.

proceedings *pl noun* **1** (*the proceedings kicked off with a speech*) activities, events, action, affairs, matters, doings, dealings, deeds, transactions, happenings, goings-on (*inf*), concerns, business. **2** (*consulted the proceedings of the society*) minutes, record, report, account, transactions, archives, annals. **3** (*launched proceedings against their employers*) legal proceedings, action, case, trial, lawsuit, process, litigation.

proceeds *pl noun* profit, gain, takings, receipts, returns, income, earnings, yield, produce, result. OPPOSITE: expenses.

process noun **1** (*the process of making tea*) operation, action, activity, procedure, practice, performance. **2** (*working on a new design process*) system, method, technique, means, manner, course, practice, procedure, way, mode, routine. **3** (*the ripening process*) development, evolution. **4** (*interrupt the process of the illness*) progress, progression, course, advance, movement, growth, development, formation. **5** (*the legal process got bogged down*) proceedings, action, case, lawsuit, trial.
➤ verb **1** (*process the order*) handle, deal with, dispose of, fulfil. **2** (*processed meat*) treat, prepare, refine, change, alter, convert, transform.
in the process of in the course of, in the middle of, in the midst of, in the performance of, in the making, in preparation, in the execution of, at the stage of.

procession noun **1** (*a procession in the street*) parade, march, column, file, train, cavalcade, cortège, motorcade. **2** (*a dreary procession of complaints*) stream, string, series, sequence, run, succession, course, cycle.

proclaim verb **1** (*proclaim the good news*) declare, announce, promulgate, pronounce, make known, notify, give out, enunciate, advertise, publish, broadcast, circulate, herald, blazon, blaze, cry, trumpet. OPPOSITE: suppress. **2** (*she was proclaimed queen*) pronounce, announce, declare, hail. **3** (*his hesitancy proclaimed his guilt*) reveal, indicate, show, prove, testify, affirm.

proclamation noun **1** (*a royal proclamation*) declaration, announcement, pronouncement, decree, edict, order, command, rule, manifesto. **2** (*the proclamation of the latest news*) announcement, declaration, pronouncement, publishing, publication, broadcasting, blazoning, circulation, promulgation, advertisement, notification, statement, notice.

proclivity noun bent, leaning, inclination, tendency, propensity, proneness, liability, disposition, predisposition, penchant, predilection, propensity, liking, fondness, partiality, bias, facility. OPPOSITE: aversion.

procrastinate verb defer, put off, postpone, adjourn, delay, stall, dally, dilly-dally (*inf*), play for time, drag one's feet, temporize, prolong, protract, retard. OPPOSITE: expedite.

procreate verb reproduce, beget, engender, propagate, breed, multiply, conceive, bring into being, sire, spawn, father, mother, generate, produce.

procure verb **1** (*procured everything they needed at the local shop*) obtain, get, acquire, appropriate, secure, gain, find, come by, pick up, lay hands on, get hold of, buy, purchase, earn, win. OPPOSITE: lose. **2** (*this procured the desired result*) effect, bring about, cause, fix (*inf*), contrive, manage, manipulate. **3** (*guilty of procuring prostitutes*) pimp, solicit, pander, importune.

prod verb **1** (*a prod in the ribs*) poke, jab, dig, elbow, nudge, push, shove (*inf*), butt, thrust. **2** (*prod the staff into working harder*) urge, goad, spur, prompt, stimulate, motivate, encourage, incite, egg on (*inf*), rouse, stir, impel, move.
➤ noun **1** (*gave his brother a prod*) poke, jab, dig, nudge, elbow, push, shove (*inf*). **2** (*use the cattle prod*) goad,

spike, stick. **3** (*she needs a prod to get her going*) prompt, prompting, reminder, cue, boost, stimulus, spur, goad, motivation, encouragement, incitement.

prodigal adj **1** (*he proved a prodigal spendthrift*) extravagant, wasteful, spendthrift, thriftless, unthrifty, improvident, imprudent, intemperate, squandering, reckless, wanton, profligate, excessive, immoderate. OPPOSITE: economical. **2** (*prodigal generosity to the poor*) generous, liberal, lavish, bountiful, bounteous, profuse, copious, unsparing, unstinting.

prodigious adj **1** (*a man of prodigious size*) huge, immense, massive, enormous, colossal, gigantic, giant, mammoth, monstrous, grotesque, vast, immeasurable, tremendous, stupendous, monumental, inordinate. OPPOSITE: small. **2** (*a prodigious feat*) wonderful, marvellous, fabulous (*inf*), fantastic (*inf*), phenomenal, miraculous, extraordinary, exceptional, unusual, abnormal, amazing, astounding, astonishing, startling, flabbergasting (*inf*), staggering, striking, impressive, remarkable, spectacular. OPPOSITE: ordinary.

prodigy noun **1** (*he was hailed as a prodigy while still a child*) genius, wonder child, wunderkind, virtuoso, mastermind, whiz kid (*inf*), Einstein (*inf*). OPPOSITE: dunce. **2** (*the bridge is a prodigy of modern engineering*) marvel, wonder, phenomenon, sensation, miracle. **3** (*she is a prodigy of goodness*) paragon, ideal, epitome, exemplar, example, paradigm.

produce verb **1** (*produce the desired result*) bring about, effect, result in, give rise to, yield, generate, engender, occasion, cause, create. OPPOSITE: withhold. **2** (*produce light machinery*) make, manufacture, create, construct, fabricate, build, fashion, put together, assemble, turn out. OPPOSITE: destroy. **3** (*produced his first great literary work*) compose, write, create, originate, frame, fashion, turn out. **4** (*produce the details of the affair*) present, set forth, set out, bring forward, bring forth, bring out, offer, proffer, advance, come up with, furnish, supply, provide, show, exhibit, demonstrate, disclose, reveal. **5** (*the policy may produce a backlash*) provoke, generate, cause, give rise to, bring about, occasion, engender, initiate, induce, evoke, spark off, start. **6** (*produce live young*) bear, breed, bring forth, deliver, beget, yield. **7** (*the farm produced a bumper crop*) yield, deliver, give, render, afford, grow. **8** (*produce another popular stage comedy*) show, exhibit, present, do, stage, mount, put on, perform, bring out, direct.
➤ noun product, yield, output, crop, harvest, fruit, vegetables, greens, food, foodstuffs.

producer noun **1** (*a major producer of fine textiles*) manufacturer, maker, creator. **2** (*a leading producer of soft fruit*) grower, farmer. **3** (*the producer of the film*) impresario, backer. **4** (*television producer*) director, manager.

product noun **1** (*salesmen pushing their company's own particular product*) commodity, merchandise, goods, wares, produce, production, output, article, item, artefact, concoction. **2** (*the product of their deliberations*) yield, produce, output, fruit, result, return, consequence, effect, outcome, issue, upshot, offshoot, spin-off, by-product, legacy. OPPOSITE: cause.

production noun **1** (*the production of fine china*) making, creation, fabrication, manufacture, manufacturing, producing, building, construction, assembly, preparation. OPPOSITE: destruction. **2** (*the production of new ideas*) creation, origination, preparation, formation, composition, development, framing, fashioning. **3** (*a worrying fall in production*) output, yield, harvest, fruit, return, productivity, manufacture, achievement, performance. **4** (*the production of secret letters*) disclosure, presentation, exhibition, offering, proffering. **5** (*the production of new ballets*) staging, mounting, performance, presentation, direction, management, organization. **6** (*I missed their latest production*) show, play, drama, concert, musical, opera, film, revue, piece, presentation, performance, creation.

productive *adj* **1** (*productive agricultural land*) fertile, fecund, rich, fruitful, high-yielding. **2** (*a productive effort*) profitable, rewarding, worthwhile, valuable, beneficial, gainful, fruitful, useful, constructive. OPPOSITE: unproductive. **3** (*a productive member of the team*) effective, efficient, prolific, creative, inventive, busy, energetic, vigorous.

productivity *noun* **1** (*the productivity of the land hereabouts*) productiveness, fertility, fecundity, fruitfulness, richness. **2** (*productivity at the factory has risen*) production, output, yield, capacity, work rate, efficiency.

profane *adj* **1** (*practices considered profane by the church*) blasphemous, sacrilegious, irreverent, disrespectful, irreligious, impious, ungodly, godless, wicked, heathen, pagan, idolatrous. OPPOSITE: reverent. **2** (*the church should not interfere in profane matters*) secular, lay, unconsecrated, unhallowed, unholy, unsanctified, worldly, temporal. OPPOSITE: sacred. **3** (*the use of profane language*) blasphemous, coarse, foul, obscene, abusive, crude, vulgar, filthy, unclean.
➤ *verb* abuse, desecrate, violate, misuse, misemploy, defile, debase, corrupt, pervert, pollute, contaminate, vitiate. OPPOSITE: hallow.

profanity *noun* **1** (*accused of profanity against the church*) blasphemy, profaneness, sacrilege, idolatry, irreverence, disrespect, disrespectfulness, irreligion, impiety, ungodliness, abuse. OPPOSITE: reverence. **2** (*mouthed several unrepeatable profanities*) swearword, four-letter word (*inf*), expletive, curse, obscenity, oath, execration, imprecation, malediction.

profess *verb* **1** (*profess complete ignorance of the crime*) claim, lay claim to, maintain, allege, make out, dissemble, pretend, sham, fake, feign. **2** (*profess his belief that she was dead*) assert, proclaim, declare, announce, affirm, confirm, certify, avow, aver, acknowledge, own, confess, admit. OPPOSITE: repudiate. **3** (*an offence to proclaim one's faith*) declare, avow, confess, confirm, acknowledge.

professed *adj* **1** (*a professed liar*) self-acknowledged, confessed, self-confessed, self-styled, confirmed, declared, certified, acknowledged, proclaimed, avowed. **2** (*a professed expert in such matters*) pretended, feigned, sham, fake, supposed, ostensible, apparent, alleged, claimed, purported, so-called, would-be.

profession *noun* **1** (*the law is a dubious profession*) business, trade, craft, occupation, calling, vocation, career, employment, line, walk of life, sphere, office, appointment, position, post, situation, job, métier. **2** (*made repeated professions of devotion*) declaration, announcement, assertion, claim, statement, affirmation, avowal, averment, acknowledgment, admission. **3** (*the profession of one's religious faith*) declaration, acknowledgement, attestation, confession, avowal, testimony. OPPOSITE: repudiation.

professional *adj* **1** (*a professional craftsman*) skilled, skilful, proficient, efficient, competent, businesslike, expert, masterly, adept, crack (*inf*), experienced, practised, trained, educated, qualified, licensed. **2** (*they did a very professional job*) polished, finished, refined, skilled, slick, expert, proficient. **3** (*a professional footballer*) paid, career. OPPOSITE: amateur.
➤ *noun* expert, master, past master, maestro, virtuoso, pro (*inf*), dab hand (*inf*), ace (*inf*), wizard (*inf*), buff (*inf*), specialist, authority.

proffer *verb* offer, tender, advance, extend, give, hold out, hand, present, propose, propound, submit, suggest, volunteer. OPPOSITE: withhold.

proficiency *noun* skill, skilfulness, expertise, adeptness, adroitness, deftness, experience, mastery, talent, knack, dexterity, facility, finesse, aptitude, accomplishment, capability, ability, competence, know-how (*inf*).

proficient *adj* skilled, skilful, expert, masterly, adept, adroit, deft, polished, practised, experienced, conversant, versed, capable, able, competent, apt, efficient, effective, trained, qualified, accomplished, gifted, talented, clever, good. OPPOSITE: incompetent.

profile *noun* **1** (*had himself drawn in profile*) side view, outline. **2** (*the profile of the cliff against the sky*) silhouette, outline, shape, form, contour, figure, lines. **3** (*drew up a profile of the company*) study, analysis, examination, survey, review. **4** (*put together a profile of the chief suspect*) biography, character sketch, characterization, curriculum vitae, CV, thumbnail sketch, portrait, sketch, vignette.

profit *noun* **1** (*we shall make a healthy profit this year*) gain, return, yield, proceeds, takings, earnings, winnings, income, revenue, dividend, interest, bonus, excess, surplus, rake-off (*inf*). OPPOSITE: loss. **2** (*you shall learn something to your profit*) advantage, benefit, good, avail, gain, use, value, worth, advancement, improvement.
➤ *verb* gain, make money, pay, serve, help, assist, aid, avail, promote, benefit, line one's pocket (*inf*), clean up (*inf*). OPPOSITE: lose.

profit from benefit from, take advantage of, turn to advantage, exploit, cash in on (*inf*), milk (*inf*), use, utilize, put to good use, capitalize on, reap the benefit of, learn from.

profitable *adj* **1** (*a profitable trade in ivory*) lucrative, paying, remunerative, gainful, cost-effective, economic, commercial, money-making, profit-making. OPPOSITE: unprofitable. **2** (*a profitable exercise for all concerned*) productive, fruitful, rewarding, successful, worthwhile, valuable, useful, beneficial, advantageous, serviceable, expedient.

profitless *adj* unprofitable, unremunerative, worthless, unproductive, fruitless, ineffective, ineffectual, unavailing, vain, useless, idle, futile, pointless, thankless, bootless. OPPOSITE: profitable.

profligacy noun 1 (the profligacy of this government) waste, wastefulness, extravagance, excess, unrestraint, lavishness, unthriftiness, recklessness, squandering, improvidence, prodigality. 2 (he was notorious for his profligacy) immorality, promiscuity, corruption, debauchery, degeneracy, depravity, libertinism, lechery, licentiousness, wantonness, dissipation, dissoluteness.

profligate adj 1 (a profligate young man) dissolute, dissipated, debauched, abandoned, loose, licentious, libertine, promiscuous, wanton, immoral, unmoral, degenerate, wicked, depraved, corrupt, reprobate, unprincipled, iniquitous, shameless. OPPOSITE: virtuous. 2 (the profligate lifestyles of the modern rich) extravagant, prodigal, wasteful, squandering, spendthrift, thriftless, reckless, immoderate, improvident, excessive. OPPOSITE: thrifty.
➤ noun 1 (widely regarded as a profligate) rake, roué, libertine, debauchee, degenerate, reprobate, lecher. 2 (a profligate with the public purse) wastrel, waster, spendthrift, squanderer, prodigal.

profound adj 1 (profound depths of the ocean) deep, bottomless, fathomless, abysmal, cavernous, yawning OPPOSITE: shallow. 2 (a profound thinker) sagacious, wise, learned, erudite, intellectual, knowledgeable, thoughtful, philosophical. 3 (profound insight) penetrating, discerning, abstruse, abstract, complex, difficult, impenetrable, recondite, esoteric, subtle, weighty, serious, deep (inf), joined-up (inf). OPPOSITE: superficial. 4 (it was with profound regret) deep, intense, keen, acute, great, extreme, heartfelt, sincere, hearty. OPPOSITE: mild. 5 (profound changes in society) radical, extensive, exhaustive, thorough, thoroughgoing, far-reaching 6 (a profound silence) deep, complete, utter, absolute, out-and-out, total, pronounced, consummate, unqualified.

profoundly adv deeply, intensely, seriously, extremely, greatly, very, thoroughly, acutely, keenly, sincerely, heartily.

profuse adj 1 (he gave profuse thanks to his colleagues) generous, liberal, unstinting, open-handed, lavish, fulsome, exuberant, rich, extravagant, excessive, immoderate, inordinate, prodigal. 2 (a profuse head of hair) abundant, copious, ample, full, plentiful, bountiful, luxuriant. OPPOSITE: scanty.

profusion noun plenty, wealth, multitude, plenitude, abundance, copiousness, bounty, exuberance, excess, surplus, superfluity, surfeit, glut, riot, plethora, cornucopia, quantities, loads (inf), heaps (inf), mountains (inf), stacks (inf), piles (inf), lots (inf), tons (inf), oodles (inf), lavishness, extravagance, prodigality, superabundance. OPPOSITE: lack.

progeny noun 1 (the elders of the tribe passed their knowledge to their progeny) descendants, issue, offspring, young, children, family. OPPOSITE: ancestry. 2 (the progeny of the last emperor) descendants, successors, posterity, breed, race, lineage, seed, stock, scions.

prognosis noun diagnosis, assessment, evaluation, prognostication, expectation, outlook, prospect, forecast, speculation, surmise, prediction, projection.

programme noun 1 (this is the programme for the week) schedule, timetable, agenda, calendar, syllabus, order of events, line-up, list, listing. 2 (programme of study) prospectus, curriculum, plan, scheme. 3 (radio programme) show, production, presentation, performance, episode, broadcast, transmission.
➤ verb 1 (these are the events programmed for the day) arrange, organize, plan, schedule, lay on, line up, list, map out, book, bill, prearrange. 2 (the computer is programmed to close down automatically) set, fix, arrange.

progress noun 1 (the progress of traffic) advance, advancement, movement, progression, headway, course, passage. 2 (the slow progress of the project worried him) advance, advancement, evolution, growth, development, improvement, amelioration, betterment, upgrading, furtherance, progression, promotion, headway, increase, breakthrough. OPPOSITE: retrogression.
➤ verb 1 (they progressed slowly up the hill) advance, proceed, continue, go forward, go on, move on, make headway, forge ahead, gain ground, travel. 2 (science and art progressing hand in hand) advance, move forward, make headway, make strides, grow, develop, mature, blossom, flourish, prosper, better, improve, ameliorate. OPPOSITE: retrogress.

in progress ongoing, going on, under way, in the pipeline (inf), on the stocks (inf), happening, occurring, continuing, proceeding, taking place.

progression noun 1 (smooth progression through the ranks) progress, passage, advancement, advance, furtherance, headway, development. 2 (we interviewed a progression of hopeful candidates) succession, stream, series, parade, string, chain, train, sequence, cycle.

progressive adj 1 (an interruption to the progressive movement of the crowd) advance, advancing, continuing, continuous, onward. 2 (a progressive climb in prices) growing, increasing, escalating, accelerating, intensifying, developing. 3 (a progressive style of management) forward-looking, forward-thinking, modern, avant-garde, advanced, enlightened, liberal, enterprising, go-ahead, dynamic, innovative. 4 (progressive politics) radical, reformist, revisionist, revolutionary, innovative.

prohibit verb 1 (prohibit the drinking of alcohol) forbid, disallow, ban, outlaw, proscribe, veto, debar, bar, interdict. OPPOSITE: permit. 2 (the outbreak of war prohibited further travel) stop, prevent, preclude, exclude, rule out, hinder, hamper, impede, obstruct, restrict, constrain.

prohibition noun 1 (the prohibition of dangerous drugs) forbidding, banning, barring, disallowing, proscription, vetoing, interdiction, outlawing. 2 (lift the prohibition on alcohol) ban, bar, interdict, veto, embargo, boycott, injunction, proscription, exclusion, restriction, prevention.

prohibitive adj 1 (a prohibitive attitude towards the use of firearms) restrictive, preventive, repressive, suppressive, proscriptive, prohibitory, forbidding, banning, barring, disallowing, vetoing. OPPOSITE: permissive. 2 (undeterred by the prohibitive cost) exorbitant, extortionate, excessive, steep (inf), sky-high (inf), preposterous, impossible.

project *noun* proposal, plan, programme, campaign, operation, scheme, design, purpose, idea, conception, enterprise, undertaking, venture, task, job, assignment, contract, activity, work, occupation. OPPOSITE: achievement.

➤ *verb* **1** (*project plans for the future*) propose, intend, plan, contemplate, map out, outline, scheme, devise, contrive, design, draft, frame. **2** (*project profits for the next five years*) calculate, estimate, gauge, reckon, extrapolate, predict, forecast. **3** (*project a stone into the air*) cast, throw, hurl, fling, propel, shoot, eject, launch, discharge. OPPOSITE: retain. **4** (*project out from the wall*) jut out, protrude, stick out, stand out, overhang, beetle, bulge, extend, obtrude.

projectile *noun* missile, rocket, shell, shot, grenade, bullet, ball.

projection *noun* **1** (*a projection from the cliff face*) protrusion, protuberance, bulge, overhang, prominence, extension, ledge, sill, shelf, ridge. **2** (*a projection for the firm's future development*) scheme, plan, programme, proposal, estimate, estimation, prediction, forecast, reckoning, expectation, extrapolation, calculation, blueprint, diagram, design, representation.

proletariat *noun* working class, workers, lower class, lower order, plebs (*inf*), proles (*inf*), commonalty, masses, mob, rabble, riff-raff (*inf*), rank and file, herd, hoi polloi, common people, great unwashed (*inf*). OPPOSITE: aristocracy.

proliferate *verb* increase, expand, extend, spread, reproduce, breed, multiply, build up, intensify, accelerate, escalate, burgeon, run riot, mushroom, snowball, rocket, flourish, thrive.

proliferation *noun* multiplication, increase, intensification, escalation, acceleration, expansion, spread, extension, growth, build-up, concentration, duplication, mushrooming, burgeoning, snowballing, rocketing.

prolific *adj* productive, fertile, fecund, fruitful, bountiful, copious, profuse, abundant, rank, luxuriant, teeming, rich. OPPOSITE: unproductive.

prolix *inf* verbose, wordy, long-winded, diffuse, rambling, discursive, digressive, lengthy, long, prolonged, protracted, long-drawn-out, spun out, tedious, tiresome, boring, prosaic, prosy. OPPOSITE: terse.

prologue *noun* introduction, preface, foreword, preamble, preliminary, prelude. OPPOSITE: epilogue.

prolong *verb* extend, lengthen, protract, draw out, spin out, drag out, stretch, elongate, delay, continue, sustain, perpetuate, carry on, keep up. OPPOSITE: curtail.

prominence *noun* **1** (*a prominence in the ground*) protuberance, projection, bulge, mound, rise, spur, bump, hump, lump, jutting, swelling, elevation, protrusion. **2** (*a prominence at the top of the cliff*) overhang, pinnacle, promontory, projection, crag, cliff, crest, height, headland. **3** (*the prominence of the building in the moonlight*) conspicuousness, obtrusiveness. **4** (*the story was given prominence by the press*) weight, importance, precedence, top billing, conspicuousness. **5** (*a figure of prominence among literary critics*) eminence, pre-eminence, illustriousness, importance, distinction, greatness, note, notability, prestige, rank, standing,

stature, fame, celebrity, renown, acclaim, reputation, name.

prominent *adj* **1** (*a prominent feature*) conspicuous, noticeable, marked, pronounced, striking, eye-catching, blatant, unmistakable, obvious, evident. OPPOSITE: inconspicuous. **2** (*a prominent member of the local community*) eminent, pre-eminent, outstanding, distinguished, respected, notable, noted, famous, celebrated, renowned, illustrious, well-known, popular, important, leading, foremost, top, chief, main. OPPOSITE: minor. **3** (*prominent eyebrows*) projecting, bulging, jutting, protruding, protuberant, protusive, obtrusive, standing out, sticking out.

promiscuity *noun* promiscuousness, dissoluteness, dissipation, licentiousness, looseness, laxity, profligacy, immorality, amorality, debauchery, depravity, lechery, abandon, wantonness, permissiveness.

promiscuous *adj* loose, wanton, abandoned, fast, licentious, libertine, profligate, dissolute, dissipated, immoral, debauched, unchaste. OPPOSITE: virtuous.

promise *verb* **1** (*promise to come back*) pledge, vow, swear, take an oath, give one's word, undertake, engage, contract, covenant, assure, guarantee, warrant, vouch. **2** (*the day promises well*) augur, presage, betoken, bespeak, denote, suggest, hint at, indicate, signify, look like, give hope of.

➤ *noun* **1** (*give me your promise*) pledge, vow, oath, word, word of honour, assurance, guarantee, engagement, commitment, undertaking, contract, covenant, bond, compact, agreement. **2** (*a performer of great promise*) potential, capacity, ability, capability, aptitude, talent, flair. **3** (*the promise of good weather ahead*) sign, hint, indication, suggestion, evidence.

promising *adj* **1** (*a promising prospect*) hopeful, likely, encouraging, reassuring, optimistic, bright, rosy, favourable, auspicious, propitious. OPPOSITE: hopeless. **2** (*a promising young player*) talented, able, gifted, budding, up-and-coming (*inf*).

promontory *noun* headland, head, cliff, precipice, height, foreland, bluff, cape, point, peninsula, projection, prominence, ridge, spur.

promote *verb* **1** (*promote the campaign for fresh food*) further, advance, forward, help, assist, aid, support, back, boost, encourage, espouse, urge, foster, nurture, cultivate, stimulate. OPPOSITE: hinder. **2** (*she was promoted last year*) upgrade, raise, elevate, advance, prefer, exalt, honour, aggrandize, move up, kick upstairs (*inf*). OPPOSITE: demote. **3** (*promote the product on television*) advertise, publicize, market, sell, push, plug (*inf*), hype (*inf*), puff up (*inf*), advocate, recommend, champion, popularize, endorse, sponsor.

promotion *noun* **1** (*his quick promotion through the ranks*) advancement, preferment, rise, elevation, move up, upgrading, ennoblement, aggrandizement, exaltation. OPPOSITE: demotion. **2** (*the promotion of new ideas*) advancement, advocacy, espousal, endorsement, championship, encouragement, recommendation, boosting, urging, fostering, contribution, furtherance, furthering, development, support, backing, sponsoring, assistance, aid, help. OPPOSITE: hindrance. **3** (*promotion of new products in the popular press*) publicity, advertising, hyping (*inf*), plugging (*inf*), pushing (*inf*), puffing up (*inf*), marketing, propaganda.

prompt *adj* **1** (*the situation demands prompt action*) immediate, instant, instantaneous, direct, quick, fast, swift, rapid, speedy, brisk, sharp, smart, punctual, timely, on time, early, expeditious, unhesitating. OPPOSITE: slow. **2** (*he is always prompt to help*) ready, eager, alert, willing, swift, rapid, speedy, fast, quick.
➤ *adv* promptly, punctually, sharp, exactly, precisely, to the minute, on the dot, dead (*inf*), dead on (*inf*), bang on (*inf*), spot on (*inf*).
➤ *verb* **1** (*we don't know what prompted her to do it*) cause, make, induce, impel, move, occasion, provoke, goad, spur, incite, stimulate, motivate, inspire, urge, encourage. OPPOSITE: deter. **2** (*prompt the actors*) cue, remind, assist, help, hint, prod, suggest.
➤ *noun* cue, reminder, help, prod, spur, stimulus, jolt, hint, encouragement, refresher.

promptly *adv* **1** (*the government reacted promptly*) immediately, instantly, instantaneously, at once, directly, unhesitatingly, quickly, fast, rapidly, speedily, swiftly, pronto (*inf*), expeditiously, hotfoot, forthwith. **2** (*she arrived promptly at noon*) punctually, on time, sharp, exactly, on the dot, to the minute, bang on (*inf*), spot on (*inf*), dead on (*inf*), on target, posthaste.

promptness *noun* **1** (*they responded with admirable promptness*) immediacy, immediateness, instantaneousness, rapidity, swiftness, quickness, fastness, speediness, expeditiousness, expedition, alacrity, punctuality, earliness. **2** (*the promptness of his contribution was appreciated*) rapidity, swiftness, speediness, alacrity, dispatch, briskness, haste, quickness, fastness, readiness, eagerness, willingness, alertness.

promulgate *verb* **1** (*promulgate the news*) make known, make public, publish, publicize, issue, divulge, announce, spread, communicate, disseminate, circulate, broadcast, advertise, promote. OPPOSITE: suppress. **2** (*promulgate the law*) proclaim, announce, decree, declare, herald, cry, trumpet, blazon.

prone *adj* **1** (*prone to change*) apt, inclined, disposed, predisposed, bent, liable, likely, given, subject, susceptible, vulnerable. OPPOSITE: unlikely. **2** (*lay prone on the grass*) prostrate, supine, full-length, face down, stretched, flat, horizontal, recumbent, procumbent. OPPOSITE: upright.

prong *noun* point, tip, spike, projection, spur, tine, fork.

pronounce *verb* **1** (*pronounce the words before him*) utter, articulate, enunciate, express, voice, vocalize, say, speak, sound, stress. **2** (*pronounce the unpalatable truth*) proclaim, declare, announce, deliver, decree, affirm, assert. OPPOSITE: suppress.

pronounced *adj* **1** (*talked with a pronounced accent*) marked, broad, thick, distinct, noticeable, conspicuous, obvious, evident, plain, striking, unmistakable. OPPOSITE: vague. **2** (*a pronounced opinion*) decided, definite, clear, strong, positive, distinct.

pronouncement *noun* declaration, announcement, proclamation, edict, decree, assertion, statement, judgment, notification, manifesto, promulgation, dictum.

pronunciation *noun* speech, diction, elocution, enunciation, inflection, articulation, saying, utterance, uttering, voicing, vocalization, sounding, delivery, accent, accentuation, stress, intonation, modulation.

proof *noun* **1** (*proof of ownership*) evidence, documentation, confirmation, substantiation, verification, validation, authentication, certification, corroboration, attestation, testimony, demonstration. OPPOSITE: conjecture. **2** (*the proofs of the finished novel*) page proof, galley, pull, print, impression.
➤ *adj* proofed, resistant, repellent, impervious, impenetrable, strong, tight, treated, waterproof, leakproof, fireproof, weatherproof, windproof, bombproof, bulletproof, childproof, tamperproof, soundproof.

prop *noun* **1** (*a prop holding up the roof*) support, brace, upright, buttress, bolster, shore, mainstay, stay, stanchion, truss, column, pillar, post, rod, pole, shaft, strut. **2** (*he was the main prop of the whole enterprise*) support, pillar, mainstay, anchor, rock, backbone, upholder, sustainer, supporter.
➤ *verb* lean, rest, stand, set, place, lay, balance, steady.

prop up **1** (*a post propped up the roof*) support, hold up, underpin, shore up, brace, bolster, buttress, reinforce, strengthen. **2** (*the government refused to prop up the company*) support, sustain, maintain, uphold, bolster up, shore up, subsidize, underwrite, fund, finance.

propaganda *noun* publicity, promotion, advertising, advertisement, hype (*inf*), ballyhoo (*inf*), information, disinformation, indoctrination, agitprop, brainwashing.

propagate *verb* **1** (*the population propagated rapidly*) reproduce, breed, procreate, spawn, increase, multiply, proliferate. **2** (*founded to propagate the theory*) disseminate, spread, diffuse, promulgate, circulate, proclaim, make known, publish, advertise, broadcast, communicate, transmit, distribute, publicize, promote. OPPOSITE: suppress.

propel *verb* drive, impel, urge, push, thrust, shove (*inf*), force, move, launch, start, project, shoot, throw, send. OPPOSITE: stop.

propensity *noun* tendency, disposition, bias, inclination, proneness, proclivity, bent, leaning, aptness, liability, susceptibility, weakness, foible, penchant, predisposition.

proper *adj* **1** (*the proper way to tie shoelaces*) correct, right, precise, accurate, exact, accepted, acceptable, established, usual, customary, conventional, orthodox, formal. OPPOSITE: wrong. **2** (*you will need proper tools*) appropriate, apt, suitable, right, fitting. **3** (*proper behaviour*) acceptable, seemly, becoming, fitting, decorous, decent, polite, respectable, genteel, gentlemanly, ladylike, refined, prim, prudish, formal, conventional, orthodox, punctilious, strict. OPPOSITE: improper. **4** (*each in its proper place*) correct, right, own, special, specific, respective, individual, particular, peculiar, personal, characteristic. **5** (*she needs a proper rest*) real, actual, genuine, true. **6** (*a proper disaster*) complete, total, utter, thorough, thoroughgoing, real.

property *noun* **1** (*those items are her property*) possessions, effects, gear (*inf*), belongings, things, paraphernalia, goods, chattels, assets, resources, means, capital, wealth, riches, fortune. **2** (*a fine property on the edge of town*) real estate, estate, land, house, building, freehold, holding, premises. **3** (*the magical properties of certain gems*) attribute, quality, virtue, ability, power, characteristic, feature, trait, quirk, peculiarity, idiosyncrasy, hallmark, mark.

prophecy *noun* prediction, forecast, prognostication, prognosis, augury, divination, clairvoyance, fortune-telling, soothsaying, second sight.

prophesy *verb* predict, foresee, foretell, divine, prognosticate, forecast, forewarn, augur, presage.

prophet *noun* soothsayer, diviner, clairvoyant, seer, fortune-teller, augur, oracle, sibyl, forecaster, prognosticator.

prophet of doom pessimist, doomwatcher, doomster (*inf*), doom merchant (*inf*), Jeremiah, Cassandra.

prophetic *adj* predictive, foretelling, forecasting, foreshadowing, prescient, prognostic, oracular, augural, divinatory, sibylline, portentous, ominous.

propinquity *noun* **1** (*the propinquity of the two villages*) nearness, closeness, proximity, vicinity, neighbourhood, contiguity, adjacency. OPPOSITE: distance. **2** (*the propinquity of husband and wife*) affinity, affiliation, kinship, kindred, tie, blood ties, consanguinity, relationship, connection.

propitiate *verb* pacify, placate, appease, mollify, soothe, satisfy, conciliate, reconcile. OPPOSITE: offend.

propitious *adj* auspicious, favourable, advantageous, beneficial, bright, rosy, promising, optimistic, encouraging, reassuring, timely, suitable, opportune, lucky, fortunate, happy. OPPOSITE: unfavourable.

proponent *noun* advocate, supporter, upholder, adherent, backer, subscriber, proposer, promoter, endorser, champion, defender, propounder, apologist, spokesman, spokeswoman, enthusiast, exponent, patron, sponsor, vindicator, partisan, friend, well-wisher.

proportion *noun* **1** (*the proportion of water to brandy*) ratio, relationship, quotient, distribution. **2** (*keep the two parts in proportion*) balance, symmetry, uniformity, harmony, agreement, correspondence, congruity, conformity. OPPOSITE: disproportion. **3** (*a small proportion of the funds*) share, portion, division, cut (*inf*), split (*inf*), whack (*inf*), lot, quota, ration, part, segment, fraction, amount, measure, percentage. OPPOSITE: whole. **4** (*the proportions of the room*) dimensions, measurements, size, magnitude, scale, scope, range, amplitude, extent, capacity, volume, bulk, mass, height, length, depth, breadth, width.
➣ *verb* adjust, arrange, regulate, balance, harmonize, fit.

proportional *adj* proportionate, relative, balanced, symmetrical, corresponding, analogous, comparable, consistent, commensurate, equivalent, even. OPPOSITE: disproportionate.

proposal *noun* proposition, presentation, suggestion, recommendation, offer, proffer, tender, terms, bid, motion, overture, plan, scheme, programme, manifesto, project, design, idea.

propose *verb* **1** (*propose the following course of action*) suggest, recommend, move, advance, put forward, submit, table, present, introduce, bring up, advocate,

offer, proffer, tender, propound. OPPOSITE: withdraw. **2** (*propose my colleague for chairman*) nominate, name, put up, recommend, suggest. **3** (*we propose to take the easier route*) plan, intend, purpose, aim, design, mean, have in mind. **4** (*proposed to her in the kitchen garden*) pop the question (*inf*), ask to marry, plight one's troth.

proposition *noun* **1** (*the board considered his proposition*) proposal, suggestion, theory, theorem, scheme, plan, project, programme, recommendation, manifesto, motion, bid, tender. **2** (*that climb is quite a proposition*) challenge, problem, undertaking, job, task, venture, activity. **3** (*the girl was shocked by his propositions to her*) advance, overture, approach, pass, suggestion, proposal, come-on (*inf*).
➣ *verb* accost, solicit, make a pass at (*inf*).

propound *verb* suggest, propose, present, put forward, set forth, lay down, advance, submit, offer, proffer, advocate, contend, postulate, state, declare.

proprietor *noun* owner, possessor, holder, landowner, freeholder, leaseholder, title-holder, master, mistress, landlord, landlady.

propriety *noun* correctness, rightness, seemliness, fitness, appropriateness, decorum, decency, etiquette, protocol, manners, good manners, courtesy, politeness, civility, breeding, gentility, respectability, refinement, modesty, delicacy, conventionality, orthodoxy, formality. OPPOSITE: impropriety.

propulsion *noun* drive, driving force, propelling force, momentum, impetus, impulse, impulsion, pressure, push, thrust, motive force, power.

prosaic *adj* prosy, dry, unimaginative, flat, tame, lifeless, spiritless, commonplace, ordinary, mundane, bland, routine, uninteresting, uninspiring, uninspired, vapid, dull, stale, tedious, boring, monotonous, pedestrian, everyday, workaday, trite, hackneyed, banal, vacuous, humdrum, matter-of-fact. OPPOSITE: imaginative.

proscribe *verb* **1** (*proscribe smoking within the shop*) condemn, denounce, censure, interdict, prohibit, forbid, ban, banish, bar, disallow, embargo, interdict, outlaw. **2** (*proscribed by the church*) outlaw, exile, banish, expel, deport, expatriate, excommunicate, exclude, boycott, reject, blackball, black, ostracize.

proscription *noun* **1** (*the proscription of soft drugs*) prohibition, prohibiting, forbidding, banning, barring. **2** (*lifted the proscription on the sale of tobacco*) bar, ban, prohibition, embargo, interdict. **3** (*the proscription of those found guilty of disloyalty*) expulsion, expelling, exiling, ejection, eviction, exclusion, deportation, expatriation, excommunication, outlawing, boycotting.

prosecute *verb* **1** (*shoplifters will be prosecuted*) sue, take to court, summon, litigate, prefer charges, charge, arraign, indict, accuse, try, put on trial. OPPOSITE: defend. **2** (*prosecute the campaign with complete ruthlessness*) pursue, organize, conduct, direct, manage, carry on, follow, proceed with, continue, persist with. OPPOSITE: abandon. **3** (*prosecute the business in hand*) accomplish, complete, finish, discharge, carry through, see through, bring to an end.

prospect *noun* **1** (*little prospect of an improvement*) chance, chances, possibility, probability, likelihood,

likeliness, odds. **2** (*the prospect of living rough worried him*) thought, idea, contemplation, outlook, expectation, hope, promise, anticipation. **3** (*offering a fine prospect of the mountains*) view, vista, scene, landscape, panorama, spectacle, vision, outlook, aspect, perspective.
» *verb* explore, examine, inspect, survey, search, look, seek, quest, check out, go after.

prospective *adj* **1** (*met his prospective in-laws for the first time*) future, intended, destined, expected, to-be, soon-to-be. **2** (*we must appeal to our prospective purchasers*) potential, likely, anticipated, awaited, would-be, hoped-for, looked-for, aspiring. **3** (*planning for his prospective appointment to the post*) imminent, impending, planned, intended, approaching, forthcoming, upcoming, coming, expected, anticipated, likely, probable, potential, possible, eventual.

prospectus *noun* syllabus, manifesto, outline, programme, plan, scheme, announcement, notice, list, catalogue, brochure, literature, pamphlet, leaflet.

prosper *verb* thrive, flourish, boom, succeed, make it (*inf*), get ahead (*inf*), get on, do well, fare well, make good, advance, progress, make headway, flower, bloom, burgeon. OPPOSITE: fail.

prosperity *noun* prosperousness, success, boom, fortune, good fortune, ease, well-being, plenty, luxury, affluence, wealth, riches, the good life (*inf*).

prosperous *adj* thriving, flourishing, blooming, successful, prospering, booming, lucky, fortunate, favourable, auspicious, promising, burgeoning, rich, wealthy, moneyed, affluent, well-off, well-heeled (*inf*), well-to-do. OPPOSITE: unsuccessful.

prostitute *noun* whore, harlot, fallen woman, strumpet, trollop, bawd, courtesan, call girl, streetwalker, pro (*inf*), tart (*inf*), hooker (*inf*), scrubber (*inf*), working girl (*inf*).
» *verb* devalue, cheapen, debase, degrade, demean, abuse, misuse, pervert, profane, misapply.

prostitution *noun* vice, the game (*inf*), the oldest profession (*inf*), whoredom, whoring, streetwalking, hustling (*inf*), harlotry.

prostrate *verb* **1** (*prostrate oneself before the king*) bow, kneel, abase oneself, kowtow, grovel, submit. **2** (*she was prostrated with grief*) overcome, overthrow, overpower, overwhelm, disarm, paralyse, crush, knock flat, flatten, level, lay low. **3** (*the soldiers were prostrated by suffering*) exhaust, wear out, weary, tire, tire out, drain, fatigue, sap, fag out (*inf*). OPPOSITE: restore.
» *adj* **1** (*the old man was found prostrate on the floor*) flat, horizontal, prone, lying down, stretched out, procumbent, recumbent, fallen, supine. OPPOSITE: erect. **2** (*prostrate with grief*) overcome, overwhelmed, overpowered, crushed, devastated, disarmed, paralysed, laid low, helpless, defenceless, impotent, powerless. OPPOSITE: powerful. **3** (*left prostrate after so much suffering*) exhausted, jaded, weary, tired, fatigued, spent, drained, all in (*inf*), fagged out (*inf*), bushed (*inf*), whacked (*inf*), disconsolate, desolate, dejected, depressed, heartbroken.

protagonist *noun* **1** (*the protagonist of the novel*) hero, heroine, principal, lead, leading character, central character, title role. **2** (*a protagonist of monetarism*)

supporter, backer, advocate, adherent, proponent, exponent, champion, promoter, standard-bearer, mainstay, upholder, defender, leader, prime mover, moving spirit.

protect *verb* **1** (*determined to protect his daughter*) defend, guard, safeguard, secure, keep safe, save, shield, preserve, shelter, escort, chaperone, watch over. OPPOSITE: expose. **2** (*a cloth to protect the surface*) screen, cover, preserve, conserve, shield, mask, conceal. **3** (*to protect the town from attack*) guard, safeguard, defend, secure, watch over, harbour, keep, keep safe, look after, care for, take care of.

protection *noun* **1** (*protection against the threat*) safety, safekeeping, shield, conservation, preservation, security, defence, precaution, insurance. OPPOSITE: exposure. **2** (*placed under international protection*) safekeeping, protectorship, guardianship, aegis, care, custody, charge, keeping, defence, support, aid. **3** (*protection against the elements*) shield, barrier, buffer, bulwark, screen, cover, defence, shelter, refuge, guard, safeguard.

protective *adj* **1** (*protective goggles*) defensive, protecting, safeguarding, shielding, covering, insulating. **2** (*protective parents*) paternal, maternal, fatherly, motherly, defensive, careful, wary, watchful, vigilant, possessive, over-protective, jealous, clinging.

protector *noun* **1** (*he considers himself her protector*) defender, champion, advocate, guard, guardian, bodyguard, minder, father-figure, patron, benefactor. **2** (*ear protectors*) pad, buffer, guard, safeguard, shield, cushion, bolster.

protégé *noun* pupil, student, ward, dependant, charge, discovery.

protest *verb* **1** (*he protested loudly about the decision*) object to, complain, gripe (*inf*), grouse (*inf*), whinge (*inf*), beef (*inf*), bitch (*inf*), speak out, oppose, take exception to, take issue, demur, expostulate, appeal, remonstrate, demonstrate, kick up a fuss (*inf*), disapprove, disagree, argue. OPPOSITE: agree. **2** (*they protest that what they saw was real*) maintain, contend, insist, profess, testify, argue, assert, avow, aver, asseverate, attest, affirm, declare, announce, proclaim. OPPOSITE: deny.
» *noun* **1** (*your protest has been noted*) objection, complaint, disapproval, opposition, demurral, dissent, exception, disagreement, protestation, appeal, expostulation, remonstration, remonstrance, outcry, fuss. OPPOSITE: agreement. **2** (*thousands turned out for the protest*) demonstration, demo (*inf*), march, riot, boycott. **3** (*they ignored her protests that she knew nothing about it*) protestation, profession, assertion, affirmation, attestation, assurance, avowal, contention, declaration, proclamation, announcement.

protestation *noun* **1** (*despite their protestations of innocence*) protest, declaration, profession, statement, announcement, assertion, affirmation, assurance, asseveration, avowal, expostulation, pledge, vow, oath. **2** (*made protestations against the decision*) protest, objection, opposition, exception, complaint, outcry, dissent, disagreement.

protester *noun* objector, demonstrator, agitator, striker, protest marcher, opposer, opponent, complainer, rebel, dissenter, dissident.

protocol *noun* procedure, etiquette, custom, convention, formalities, civilities, courtesies, manners, decorum, propriety, good form, politesse.

prototype *noun* original, model, mock-up, pattern, precedent, example, type, archetype, standard, norm, exemplar, ideal, paradigm. OPPOSITE: copy.

protract *verb* prolong, draw out, spin out, drag out (*inf*), extend, lengthen, elongate, stretch, make longer, continue, sustain, keep going. OPPOSITE: curtail.

protracted *adj* prolonged, extended, lengthy, lengthened, stretched out, spun out, drawn out, long, long-drawn-out, overlong, time-consuming, endless, never-ending, interminable.

protrude *verb* project, point, stick out, stand out, jut, jut out, poke out, extend, bulge, obtrude, beetle, thrust out.

protrusion *noun* lump, bump, hump, knob, projection, swelling, bulge, jut, protuberance, outgrowth, process.

protuberance *noun* bulge, swelling, lump, bump, knob, bulb, outgrowth, excrescence, protrusion, projection, prominence, process, tumour, wart, welt. OPPOSITE: cavity.

protuberant *adj* bulging, swelling, swollen, jutting, jutting out, prominent, proud, protruding, protrusive, extrusive, popping, beetling, bulbous.

proud *adj* **1** (*proud of her achievement*) satisfied, contented, content, gratified, pleased, happy, glad, delighted, thrilled, appreciative. **2** (*he is too proud to talk to us now*) conceited, self-satisfied, smug, complacent, vain, egotistic, self-important, boastful, big-headed (*inf*), pompous, arrogant, haughty, cocky, puffed up, imperious, high-handed, high and mighty (*inf*), lordly, overbearing, presumptuous, supercilious, stuck-up (*inf*), snooty (*inf*), toffee-nosed (*inf*), snobbish, jumped-up (*inf*), uppity (*inf*), disdainful, scornful. OPPOSITE: modest. **3** (*they remained proud even in defeat*) self-respecting, dignified, noble, high-minded, honourable. **4** (*a proud day for the school*) memorable, notable, red-letter (*inf*), glorious, marvellous, wonderful, splendid, happy, pleasing, gratifying, satisfying, rewarding. **5** (*they made a proud sight*) noble, majestic, stately, grand, magnificent, splendid, glorious, great, august, imposing, outstanding, exalted, eminent, distinguished, illustrious, honourable, worthy.

prove *verb* **1** (*we need the evidence to prove it*) demonstrate, show, manifest, document, verify, certify, attest, confirm, authenticate, corroborate, substantiate, justify, validate, bear out, uphold, sustain, establish, determine, ascertain. OPPOSITE: refute. **2** (*it proved all right in the end*) turn out, end up, come about, pan out (*inf*), transpire, eventuate. **3** (*prove a new product*) test, put to the test, try, assay, examine, analyse, check.

proverb *noun* saying, maxim, aphorism, adage, saw, precept, dictum, byword, apophthegm.

proverbial *adj* acknowledged, accepted, famous, famed, renowned, well-known, infamous, notorious, legendary, traditional, time-honoured, axiomatic, self-evident.

provide *verb* **1** (*they will provide the necessary tools*) supply, furnish, equip, contribute, provision, outfit, kit out, purvey, stock, bring. **2** (*provide an opportunity for*

some fun) give, lend, afford, render, impart, yield, produce, present. **3** (*provide for the future*) prepare, get ready, take precautions, anticipate, allow, make provision, plan, plan ahead, take steps, take measures, cater, arrange. **4** (*the agreement provides that the purchasers pay for all fees*) stipulate, specify, lay down, state, determine, require.

provide for maintain, support, sustain, keep, look after, care for, take care of, fend. OPPOSITE: neglect.

provided *conj* providing, given, on condition, on the understanding, on the assumption, subject to, with the proviso, as long as, so long as, contingent upon, if.

providence *noun* **1** (*providence guided our ship safely home*) fate, destiny, predestination, fortune, luck, lady luck, divine intervention, God's will. **2** (*act with providence*) prudence, wisdom, sagacity, judgment, discretion, shrewdness, circumspection, judiciousness, perspicacity, foresight, forethought, farsightedness, care, carefulness, caution, economy, frugality, thrift, thriftiness, canniness.

provident *adj* judicious, far-seeing, far-sighted, prudent, wise, sagacious, shrewd, circumspect, careful, cautious, wary, discreet, vigilant, economical, frugal, thrifty, canny, well-prepared. OPPOSITE: reckless.

providing *conj* provided, given, as long as, on condition, on the understanding, on the assumption, upon these terms, with the proviso, contingent upon, subject to, in the event, in case, if.

province *noun* **1** (*from a far-flung province*) region, territory, area, district, division, tract, zone, realm, domain, colony, dependency, county, shire, department. OPPOSITE: capital. **2** (*that lies outside my province*) field, area, patch, domain, turf (*inf*), sphere, orbit, line, charge, role, function, capacity, duty, concern, responsibility, business, office, pigeon (*inf*). **3** (*within the province of classical studies*) field, discipline, speciality, area.

provincial *adj* **1** (*provincial government*) regional, state, local. **2** (*a provincial upbringing*) rural, country, rustic. **3** (*a sadly provincial outlook*) parochial, insular, inward-looking, limited, unsophisticated, uninformed, home-grown, parish-pump, small-town, bigoted, prejudiced, intolerant, narrow, narrow-minded, small-minded.
≫ *noun* country bumpkin, country cousin, yokel, rustic, peasant.

provision *noun* **1** (*make provision for old age*) preparation, precaution, measure, step, arrangement, prearrangement, plan, allowance, concession. **2** (*the provision of groceries*) providing, supply, furnishing, giving, affording, equipping, outfitting, catering, victualling, accommodation. **3** (*inadequate provision for the disabled*) arrangements, facilities, amenities, services, recourses, concessions. **4** (*provisions to last three months*) food, foodstuff, sustenance, fare, eatables (*inf*), eats (*inf*), tack (*inf*), victuals, comestibles, groceries, rations, supplies, stocks, stores. **5** (*a provision of the will*) clause, term, requirement, stipulation, specification, condition, proviso, reservation, restriction, limitation, qualification, rider.

provisional *adj* temporary, interim, pro tem (*inf*),

stopgap, transitional, makeshift, conditional, contingent, provisory, tentative. OPPOSITE: absolute.

proviso *noun* clause, term, requirement, stipulation, specification, condition, provision, reservation, restriction, limitation, qualification, rider.

provocation *noun* **1** (*the children were engaged in provocation of the animals*) harassing, harassment, annoying, angering, aggravating (*inf*), aggravation (*inf*), incensing, enraging, maddening, infuriating, infuriation, irking, riling (*inf*), irritating, irritation, exasperating, exasperation, vexing. OPPOSITE: appeasement. **2** (*endure the provocations of the fans*) taunt, insult, affront, offence, injury, challenge. **3** (*claimed she acted under provocation from others*) incitement, inducement, goading, stimulation, stimulus, motivation, rousing, stirring. **4** (*the provocation of tears*) instigation, generation, occasioning, production, eliciting, kindling, evocation, inspiration, encouragement, promotion, precipitation, cause, grounds.

provocative *adj* **1** (*a provocative act*) provoking, inciting, stimulating, disturbing, offensive, insulting, abusive, annoying, irritating, aggravating (*inf*), infuriating, vexatious, exasperating, maddening, galling, outrageous. OPPOSITE: pacific. **2** (*she wore a provocative dress*) alluring, tempting, inviting, tantalizing, teasing, suggestive, seductive, sexy (*inf*), titillating, erotic, arousing, stimulating. OPPOSITE: repulsive.

provoke *verb* **1** (*you should not have provoked him*) anger, enrage, infuriate, aggravate (*inf*), incense, madden, exasperate, needle (*inf*), nark (*inf*), tease, taunt, vex, harass, hassle (*inf*), wind up (*inf*), irk, chafe, gall, rile, annoy, irritate, insult, affront, offend, nettle, pique, put out. OPPOSITE: appease. **2** (*tried to provoke a response*) incite, inspire, prompt, excite, rouse, instigate, foment, cause, occasion, bring about, evoke, elicit, induce, encourage, stimulate, produce, promote, agitate, goad, spur, prod, stir, inflame, move, motivate. **3** (*her surprise provoked laughter*) evoke, prompt, give rise to, cause, occasion, call forth, draw forth, instigate, elicit, induce, excite, inspire, kindle, generate, engender, produce, lead to, precipitate, promote. OPPOSITE: deter.

prow *noun* bow, bows, sharp end (*inf*), fore, stem, front, head, nose, forepart.

prowess *noun* **1** (*a marksman of some prowess*) skill, skilfulness, ability, expertise, mastery, command, genius, talent, dexterity, adroitness, adeptness, deftness, aptitude, facility, capability, competence, know-how, proficiency, accomplishment, attainment. OPPOSITE: incompetence. **2** (*the prowess of a true hero*) strength, might, bravery, heroism, mettle, pluck, grit (*inf*), guts (*inf*), bottle (*inf*), daring, audacity, boldness, valour, valiance, gallantry, courage, fearlessness, dauntlessness, intrepidity, fortitude, steadfastness, stoutness, sturdiness. OPPOSITE: cowardice.

prowl *verb* roam, rove, cruise, wander, range, steal, sneak, creep, slink, skulk, lurk, scavenge, forage, nose, snoop (*inf*), search, hunt, stalk, patrol.

proximity *noun* nearness, closeness, propinquity, vicinity, neighbourhood, contiguity, adjacency, juxtaposition. OPPOSITE: distance.

proxy *noun* substitute, agent, representative, delegate, deputy, surrogate, stand-in, factor.

prude *noun* prig, old maid, puritan, school-marm (*inf*), goody-goody (*inf*).

prudence *noun* **1** (*a ruler of great prudence*) wisdom, judgment, judiciousness, sagacity, shrewdness, common sense, good sense, sense, circumspection, farsightedness, foresight, forethought. **2** (*the need to show prudence in this case*) caution, cautiousness, discretion, care, carefulness, wariness, vigilance, planning, preparedness, heedfulness. **3** (*the modern theatre manager must learn prudence*) providence, thrift, thriftiness, good management, economy, saving, husbandry, frugality.

prudent *adj* **1** (*a prudent policy*) wise, shrewd, sagacious, well-judged, judicious, sage, sensible, circumspect, far-sighted, politic. OPPOSITE: rash. **2** (*a prudent observer*) cautious, careful, discreet, discerning, thoughtful, considerate, wary, vigilant, heedful. **3** (*the prudent shopper*) thrifty, economical, provident, frugal, sparing.

prudery *noun* prudishness, primness, squeamishness, overmodesty, strictness, stuffiness, starchiness, priggishness, prissiness, puritanism, puritanicalness, old-maidishness.

prudish *adj* prim, demure, modest, over-modest, strait-laced, starchy (*inf*), proper, priggish, stuffy, po-faced, up-tight (*inf*), prissy, puritanical, strict, narrow-minded, squeamish, old-maidish. OPPOSITE: broad-minded.

prune *verb* **1** (*prune the bushes*) trim, thin, thin out, cut, cut back, shape, clip, snip, lop, chop, dock, shorten, remove. **2** (*we must prune our budget*) cut, cut back, pare down, trim, curtail, reduce, adjust.

prurient *adj* lustful, lecherous, lewd, salacious, libidinous, lubricious, concupiscent, erotic, obscene, pornographic, blue (*inf*), indecent, dirty, smutty (*inf*), steamy (*inf*), voyeuristic. OPPOSITE: chaste.

pry *verb* meddle, interfere, intrude, question, inquire, nose, snoop (*inf*), ferret, dig, delve, spy, peep, peer.

prying *adj* meddlesome, meddling, interfering, intrusive, inquisitive, curious, nosy (*inf*), spying, peering, probing, snooping (*inf*), eavesdropping, impertinent.

psalm *noun* hymn, song, song of praise, religious song, canticle, chant, anthem, paean.

pseudo *adj* false, sham, phoney (*inf*), mock, pretended, imitation, simulated, fake, counterfeit, forged, fraudulent, feigned, bogus, quasi, artificial, spurious, ersatz.

pseudonym *noun* alias, incognito, assumed name, false name, pen name, nom de plume, nom de guerre, stage name, professional name, sobriquet, nickname.

psyche *noun* spirit, soul, mind, intellect, intelligence, understanding, consciousness, subconscious, anima, self, ego, awareness, personality, individuality.

psychiatrist *noun* analyst, therapist, psychoanalyst, psychotherapist, psychologist, psychoanalyser, shrink (*inf*), headshrinker (*inf*), head doctor (*inf*), trick cyclist (*inf*).

psychic *adj* **1** (*she claims to have psychic powers*) clairvoyant, telepathic, telekinetic, spiritualistic. **2** (*psychic phenomena*) supernatural, paranormal, preternatural, extrasensory, mystic, occult. OPPOSITE: natural. **3** (*a psychic disorder*) spiritual, psychological, mental, cognitive.

psychological *adj* **1** (*psychological analysis*) mental, cerebral, intellectual, psychic, psychical, cognitive. OPPOSITE: physical. **2** (*his symptoms are purely psychological*) pyschosomatic, subconscious, unconscious, unreal, imaginary, subjective, emotional, irrational, all in the mind.

psychology *noun* **1** (*a professor of psychology*) behaviourism, science of the mind, study of personality. **2** (*the psychology of a serial killer*) mindset, mind, mental processes, thought processes, behavioural characteristics, mental chemistry, make-up, way of thinking, attitudes.

psychopathic *adj* lunatic, mad, insane, maniacal, psychotic, sociopathic, deranged, mental (*inf*), unbalanced, mentally disturbed, disturbed, demented, certifiable.

pub *noun* public house, local (*inf*), boozer (*inf*), inn, tavern, alehouse, bar, hostelry (*inf*), watering-hole (*inf*), saloon.

puberty *noun* pubescence, sexual maturity, adolescence, teenage years, teens, youth, juvenescence.

public *adj* **1** (*intended for public use*) communal, common, general, universal, open, unrestricted, accessible. OPPOSITE: private. **2** (*public institutions*) state, government, national, nationalized, civic, civil, community, social, official, popular. **3** (*this is not public knowledge*) known, acknowledged, recognized, publicized, published, widespread, overt, plain, exposed, unconcealed, obvious, patent. OPPOSITE: secret. **4** (*the victory made her a public figure*) famous, well-known, celebrated, popular, prominent, eminent, prestigious, illustrious, important, influential, respected.
➤ *noun* **1** (*appeal to the public at large*) population, people, nation, country, community, society, populace, commonalty, ordinary people, mob, hoi polloi, multitude, masses, citizens, voters, electorate, everyone. **2** (*he likes to please his public*) clientele, patrons, customers, followers, following, supporters, fans, admirers, audience, spectators.
in public publicly, openly, in the open, overtly, for all to see, in full view.

publication *noun* **1** (*a landmark in newspaper publication*) publishing, printing, production. **2** (*this restricted the publication of the new rules*) publishing, publicizing, airing, reporting, distribution, circulation, dissemination, issue, issuance, announcement, declaration, communication, proclamation, advertisement, broadcasting, promulgation, revelation, disclosure, notification, divulgence, appearance. OPPOSITE: suppression. **2** (*their latest publication*) book, title, magazine, periodical, newspaper, journal, daily, weekly, monthly, quarterly, pamphlet, booklet, leaflet, brochure, handbill, edition, issue.

publicity *noun* **1** (*the new car was given plenty of publicity*) promotion, marketing, hype (*inf*), advertising, advertisement, plugging (*inf*), boosting, puffing, build-up (*inf*), ballyhoo (*inf*). **2** (*she was the subject of constant publicity*) public attention, media interest. OPPOSITE: obscurity.

publicize *verb* **1** (*publicize the latest developments*) make public, make known, announce, spotlight, blaze, write up, publish, broadcast, distribute, disseminate, circulate, spread about, promulgate. **2** (*publicize a new product*) promote, advertise, market, plug (*inf*), hype (*inf*), push (*inf*), puff, puff up, play up.

publish *verb* **1** (*they decided to publish her first novel*) print, produce, issue, release, bring out, put out. **2** (*publish news of this latest scientific breakthrough*) distribute, spread, circulate, disseminate, promulgate, announce, declare, proclaim, advertise, communicate, make public, publicize, broadcast, trumpet, blazon, disclose, reveal, divulge, leak, notify, report, expose, tell, impart. OPPOSITE: suppress

pucker *verb* **1** (*her blouse was puckered at the back*) gather, ruck, crumple, wrinkle, crinkle, crease, ruffle, pleat, corrugate. OPPOSITE: smooth. **2** (*the toddler's face puckered into a frown*) furrow, purse, pout, screw up, wrinkle, crinkle, crease, knit, tighten, contract.

pudding *noun* pud (*inf*), dessert, sweet, afters (*inf*), second course, last course, tart, pie, pastry.

puddle *noun* pool, splash.

puerile *adj* childish, babyish, infantile, juvenile, immature, adolescent, silly, foolish, irresponsible, inane, petty, trivial, ridiculous, frivolous. OPPOSITE: adult.

puff *noun* **1** (*a puff of wind*) gust, blast, whiff, breath, draught, waft, flurry. **2** (*took a puff on his pipe*) pull, drag, inhalation. **3** (*puff for the new product*) praise, commendation, good word, advertisement, publicity, promotion, marketing, plug (*inf*), push (*inf*), build-up (*inf*).
➤ *verb* **1** (*panting and puffing*) blow, pant, wheeze, gasp, gulp, breathe, exhale. **2** (*puff on a cigarette*) smoke, suck, draw, pull, drag (*inf*), inhale. **3** (*smoke puffed from the chimney*) waft, pour. **4** (*she puffed up the balloon*) swell, inflate, bloat, dilate, distend, puff up. OPPOSITE: deflate. **5** (*puffed the new show with all their energy*) praise, flatter, commend, advertise, promote, publicize, market, push (*inf*), plug (*inf*), hype (*inf*), crack up (*inf*). OPPOSITE: disparage.

puffy *adj* puffed up, inflated, swollen, inflamed, bloated, enlarged, dilated, distended, bulging.

pugnacious *adj* belligerent, hostile, bellicose, threatening, battling, combative, aggressive, irascible, irritable, bad-tempered, ill-tempered, hot-tempered, quarrelsome, argumentative, contentious, disputatious, antagonistic, petulant, choleric. OPPOSITE: peaceable.

pull *verb* **1** (*he pulled the desk over*) draw, drag, haul, tow, trail, tug, heave, jerk, yank (*inf*). OPPOSITE: push. **2** (*she was pulling up weeds in the garden*) pluck, pick, take out, draw out, root out, uproot, pull out, cull, gather, collect, extract, remove. **3** (*the show should really pull them in*) attract, draw, bring in, entice, tempt, lure. OPPOSITE: repel. **4** (*he thinks he has pulled a muscle*) dislocate, sprain, wrench, strain, damage, tear, rip, rend, stretch.
➤ *noun* **1** (*gave the rope a good pull*) drag, tow, haul, tug, yank (*inf*), jerk, twitch. OPPOSITE: push. **2** (*the pull of gravity*) power, force, forcefulness. **3** (*the pull of her beauty*) magnetism, attraction, lure, allurement, appeal,

draw, drawing power. **4** (*he has considerable pull in parliament*) influence, weight, leverage, clout (*inf*), muscle (*inf*).

pull apart 1 (*pull apart the package*) take to pieces, tear apart, dismantle, separate, part, break, dismember, demolish, destroy. **2** (*the film was pulled apart by the critics*) take apart, pull to pieces (*inf*), criticize, pick holes in (*inf*), blast, flay, slate (*inf*), pan (*inf*), slam (*inf*), run down (*inf*), attack.

pull back withdraw, fall back, draw back, back out, retreat, retire, disengage.

pull down take down, knock down, demolish, dismantle, level, raze to the ground, bulldoze, destroy.

pull in 1 (*pull in at the next service station*) pull up, stop, draw in, draw up, park. **2** (*the show is pulling in record audiences*) attract, draw, bring in, lure, entice. **3** (*the police have pulled in all the suspects*) arrest, apprehend, detain, take into custody, run in (*inf*), nick (*inf*), book (*inf*), bust (*inf*), collar (*inf*), nab (*inf*), capture, seize. **4** (*they say he will pull in a fortune*) make, clear, net, gross, rake in (*inf*), pocket, take home, earn, receive.

pull off 1 (*they managed to pull off the feat*) succeed, accomplish, execute, achieve, bring off, manage, carry off, carry out. OPPOSITE: fail. **2** (*pull off the doors*) detach, remove, separate, take off, tear off, rip off, wrench off, yank off (*inf*).

pull out 1 (*the man pulled out his wallet*) produce, withdraw, draw out, take out, bring out. **2** (*the unit pulled out of the town*) leave, depart, quit, withdraw, retreat from, move out, back out, evacuate, abandon, desert, give up. OPPOSITE: arrive.

pull through recover, come through, get over, rally, recuperate, get better, survive, weather.

pull up 1 (*pull up the dead plants*) uproot, dig out, raise, remove, extract. **2** (*the car pulled up at the crossroads*) stop, halt, park, draw up, pull in, pull over, brake. **3** (*the ref pulled them up for their language*) reprimand, rebuke, admonish, reprove, tell off (*inf*), bawl out (*inf*), scold, criticize, castigate, take to task, tick off (*inf*), dress down (*inf*), carpet (*inf*).

pulp *noun* **1** (*the pulp of the fruit*) flesh, marrow, soft part. **2** (*battered to a pulp*) paste, purée, mash, mush, pap, triturate.
➤ *verb* crush, squash, mash, pulverize, liquidize, purée.

pulpy *adj* fleshy, succulent, soft, squashy, mushy, sloppy, pappy, crushed. OPPOSITE: hard.

pulsate *verb* beat, throb, pulse, pound, thud, drum, hammer, thump, palpitate, vibrate, oscillate, quiver.

pulse *noun* beat, stroke, throb, thud, thump, rhythm, beating, throbbing, thudding, pounding, drumming, thumping, pulsation, vibration, oscillation.
➤ *verb* beat, throb, drum, thud, pound, pulsate, palpitate, vibrate.

pulverize *verb* **1** (*pulverize to dust*) powder, pound, crush, pulp, squash, mash, grind, crunch, mill, crumble, comminute, triturate. **2** (*he pulverized his rivals with his fists*) destroy, annihilate, demolish, flatten, wreck, crush, smash, thrash (*inf*), hammer (*inf*), defeat, vanquish, lick (*inf*), overwhelm, rout, trounce, blow out of the water (*inf*).

pummel *verb* batter, beat, thump, bang, pound,

hammer, hit, strike, knock, punch, belt (*inf*), clobber (*inf*), belabour, thrash.

pump *verb* **1** (*pumped water into the chamber*) drive, force, push, send, draw. **2** (*they pumped the witness for details*) interrogate, question, quiz, cross-examine, grill (*inf*), probe.

pump up pump, inflate, dilate, blow up, puff up, fill. OPPOSITE: deflate.

pun *noun* play on words, double entendre, witticism, quip.

punch[1] *verb* (*he punched the man on the chin*) strike, hit, box, thump, pummel, pound, batter, beat, cuff, slug, bash (*inf*), wallop (*inf*), sock (*inf*), clout (*inf*), thwack (*inf*), biff (*inf*), bop (*inf*), jab, knock.
➤ *noun* **1** (*received a punch on the jaw*) blow, hit, knock, thump, box, bash (*inf*), wallop (*inf*), sock (*inf*), slug (*inf*), clout (*inf*), thwack (*inf*), belt (*inf*), biff (*inf*), bop (*inf*), jab, cuff. **2** (*the story was told with plenty of punch*) strength, force, forcefulness, power, impact, effectiveness, drive, verve, vigour, bite (*inf*), panache, oomph (*inf*), pizzazz (*inf*).

punch[2] *verb* (*punch holes in the fabric*) pierce, puncture, perforate, prick, bore, hole, drill, stamp, pink, cut.

punctilious *adj* strict, exact, precise, correct, proper, formal, ceremonious, meticulous, scrupulous, conscientious, careful, particular, choosy (*inf*), fussy, finicky, picky (*inf*), nit-picking (*inf*), pernickety (*inf*), nice, minute. OPPOSITE: lax.

punctual *adj* prompt, on the dot (*inf*), on cue (*inf*), dead on time (*inf*), bang on time (*inf*), on time, in good time, timely, well-timed, early, seasonable, punctilious, exact, precise, regular. OPPOSITE: late.

punctuality *noun* promptness, promptitude, timeliness, earliness, regularity, readiness, strictness.

punctuate *verb* **1** (*the lecture was punctuated with jokes*) interrupt, interject, break, intersperse, sprinkle, pepper. **2** (*punctuated the rhythm by stamping on the floor*) emphasize, accentuate, underline, stress, point.

puncture *noun* **1** (*a tiny puncture in the material*) hole, perforation, cut, rupture, prick, nick, slit, opening, leak. **2** (*stopped the car to mend a puncture*) flat tyre, flat (*inf*), blow-out.
➤ *verb* **1** (*the child punctured the balloon*) burst, rupture, pierce, impale, penetrate, prick, spike, perforate, cut, nick, slit, punch, hole, bore. **2** (*this punctured her optimism*) deflate, prick, let down, put down (*inf*), flatten, humble, humiliate, disillusion, put a dent in (*inf*), discourage.

pundit *noun* authority, expert, master, buff (*inf*), maestro, guru, teacher, sage, savant, highbrow.

pungent *adj* **1** (*pungent smoke*) acrid, sharp, biting, stinging, burning, smarting, irritating. **2** (*a pungent taste*) strong, powerful, sharp, hot, peppery, fiery, spicy, highly-flavoured, piquant, seasoned, aromatic, bitter, biting, sour, tart, tangy, acid, caustic, harsh, keen, acute. OPPOSITE: mild. **3** (*he made some pungent comments about the president*) cutting, sharp, incisive, caustic, stinging, burning, acid, biting, barbed, pointed, acrimonious, sarcastic, trenchant, scathing, telling, acerbic, vitriolic, mordant, stringent, piercing, penetrating.

punish *verb* **1** (*punish the culprits*) discipline, penalize, sentence, correct, chastise, chasten, reprove, scold, castigate, spank, smack, beat, slap, cane, flog, whip, lash, scourge, execute, hang, crucify, imprison, fine. OPPOSITE: reward. **2** (*punish the opposition*) beat, defeat, trounce, batter, thump, pummel, hammer (*inf*), wallop (*inf*), thrash (*inf*), bash (*inf*), beat up, knock about, rough up (*inf*). **3** (*punish the engine*) misuse, abuse, maltreat, mistreat, damage, harm.

punishing *adj* arduous, demanding, strenuous, taxing, crippling, crushing, grinding, burdensome, hard, harsh, severe, cruel, gruelling, uphill, exhausting, backbreaking, fatiguing, tiring, wearying, wearing.

punishment *noun* **1** (*the punishment of offenders*) punishing, disciplining, discipline, correcting, correction, chastising, chastisement, penalizing, penalization, castigating, castigation, sentencing, retribution, smacking, slapping, beating, caning, flogging, whipping, lashing, scourging. **2** (*dishing out punishment with his fists*) battering, thrashing, bashing (*inf*), beating, thumping, walloping (*inf*), hammering (*inf*), pummelling, trouncing. **3** (*the engine has suffered considerable punishment*) abuse, misuse, mistreatment, maltreatment, rough treatment, manhandling, damage, harm.

punitive *adj* **1** (*modern punitive policy*) penal, disciplinary, corrective, castigatory, retaliatory, retributive, revengeful, vindictive. **2** (*a punitive climb*) punishing, crippling, crushing, hard, harsh, severe, cruel, savage, gruelling, demanding, taxing, stiff, burdensome.

puny *adj* **1** (*his puny frame*) weak, weakly, feeble, frail, delicate, slight, stunted, pint-sized (*inf*), undersized, underdeveloped, undeveloped, underfed, diminutive, dwarfish, pygmy, small, tiny, sickly. OPPOSITE: sturdy. **2** (*a puny contribution*) trivial, trifling, petty, paltry, measly (*inf*), piddling (*inf*), meagre, minor, inferior, insignificant, inconsequential.

pupil *noun* **1** (*the school has a thousand pupils*) student, scholar, schoolboy, schoolgirl, schoolchild, learner, beginner, novice, apprentice, trainee. OPPOSITE: master. **2** (*a pupil of the great philosopher*) protégée, disciple, follower.

puppet *noun* **1** (*a child's puppet*) glove puppet, marionette, dummy, doll. **2** (*a puppet of the king*) pawn, creature, dupe, stooge, poodle, cat's-paw, tool, instrument, mouthpiece, figurehead, quisling, gull.

purchase *verb* buy, pay for, shop for, procure, acquire, secure, gain, obtain, get, get hold of, pick up, snap up (*inf*), splash out on (*inf*), invest in. OPPOSITE: sell.
➤ *noun* **1** (*she made several purchases in town*) acquisition, buy, bargain, gain, deal, investment, holdings, asset, goods, possession, property. **2** (*lost his purchase on the ladder*) grasp, grip, hold, foothold, footing, toe-hold, leverage, advantage.

pure *adj* **1** (*pure alcohol*) undiluted, unadulterated, neat, straight, unmixed, unalloyed. **2** (*pure drinking water*) clear, fresh, clean, unpolluted, uncontaminated, untainted, uninfected, sterile, sterilized, disinfected, antiseptic, aseptic, germfree, hygienic, sanitary, wholesome. OPPOSITE: polluted. **3** (*a gem of pure quality*) real, authentic, genuine, true, natural, simple, perfect,

flawless, solid. OPPOSITE: impure. **4** (*a pure maiden*) chaste, virgin, virginal, maidenly, virtuous, immaculate, undefiled, unsullied. **5** (*a pure character*) moral, uncorrupted, unsullied, unblemished, impeccable, immaculate, virtuous, honourable, worthy, noble, righteous, pious, sinless, innocent, blameless, guileless, guiltless, stainless, spotless, honest, upright, decent, good. OPPOSITE: corrupt. **6** (*pure folly*) sheer, downright, utter, unmitigated, unqualified, outright, out-and-out, mere, perfect, thorough, absolute, complete, total. OPPOSITE: partial. **7** (*pure mathematics*) theoretical, conceptual, abstract, conjectural, academic, philosophical.

purely *adv* **1** (*purely theoretical*) only, solely, exclusively, merely, simply, just. **2** (*she was purely stunning*) completely, totally, entirely, wholly, plainly, utterly, thoroughly, absolutely.

purgative *noun* laxative, emetic, enema, purge, cathartic, aperient, evacuant.

purge *verb* **1** (*purge the soul*) cleanse, purify, clear, shrive. **2** (*purged of all charges*) absolve, clear, pardon, forgive, exonerate, expiate. **3** (*purge the company of dead wood*) rid, clear, empty, free, expel, eject, oust, depose, remove, eradicate, exterminate, root out, sweep out, weed out, eliminate, axe (*inf*), dismiss, wipe out, do away with, kill.
➤ *noun* **1** (*the doctors recommended a purge*) enema, purgative, laxative, cathartic, aperient, evacuant. **2** (*conducted another purge of his enemies*) witch hunt, rooting-out, weeding-out, ousting, eradication, elimination, extermination, liquidation, removal, ejection, disposal, expulsion, suppression, purgation, cleansing, purification.

purify *verb* **1** (*purify the water supply*) cleanse, clean, decontaminate, distil, filter, filtrate, clarify. **2** (*a system to purify the air*) clean, cleanse, freshen, deodorize, decontaminate, refine. OPPOSITE: befoul. **3** (*purify the operating theatre*) clean, cleanse, wash, decontaminate, disinfect, sanitize, sterilize, fumigate. **4** (*wished to purify his soul*) purge, redeem, sanctify, exculpate, cleanse, clear, absolve, shrive.

purist *noun* pedant, dogmatist, literalist, formalist, classicist, precisionist, stickler, quibbler, nitpicker (*inf*).

puritan *noun* moralist, disciplinarian, zealot, fanatic, pietist, prude, killjoy, spoilsport, goody-goody (*inf*).

puritanical *adj* puritan, prim, proper, strait-laced, moralistic, disciplinarian, strict, stern, forbidding, austere, ascetic, abstemious, severe, rigid, stiff, prudish, disapproving, bigoted, narrow-minded, stuffy, priggish, prissy, goody-goody (*inf*), fanatical, zealous. OPPOSITE: immoral.

purity *noun* **1** (*the purity of mountain air*) pureness, clearness, clarity, cleanness, cleanliness, freshness, untaintedness, wholesomeness. **2** (*diamonds of great purity*) perfection, spotlessness, flawlessness, authenticity, genuineness. OPPOSITE: impurity. **3** (*a fresh purity of style*) perfection, simplicity. **4** (*the duke boasted of the purity of his daughter*) pureness, chastity, chasteness, virginity, virtue, virtuousness, honour, innocence, blamelessness, guiltlessness, sinlessness. **5** (*praised for the purity of his soul*) pureness, righteousness, rectitude, morality, honesty, integrity, sincerity, honour, nobility, uprightness, virtue, virtuousness, worthiness, decency, goodness, piety. OPPOSITE: corruption.

purloin verb steal, pilfer, thieve, rob, pinch (inf), swipe (inf), nick (inf), lift (inf), knock off (inf), nobble (inf), pocket (inf), filch (inf), snaffle (inf), walk off with, embezzle, appropriate, take, remove. OPPOSITE: restore.

purport verb 1 (purport to know what the government thinks) claim, profess, seem, pretend, feign, pose as, allege, maintain, assert, declare, proclaim. 2 (the rumour purports that the end is near) mean, signify, indicate, denote, betoken, portend, show, imply, convey, suggest, express, state.
≫ noun 1 (the purport of her words) meaning, significance, signification, import, implication, drift, point, gist, idea, tenor, theme, thrust, spirit, tendency, bearing, direction, substance. 2 (his purport is to upset the opposing players) purpose, intent, intention, object, objective, aim, design, scheme, goal, plan.

purpose noun 1 (the purpose of her mission) point, reason, basis, motivation, motive, cause, justification, rationale. 2 (their ultimate purpose) aim, intention, intent, object, objective, end, goal, target, ambition, aspiration, desire, wish, hope, plan, design. 3 (he showed great purpose in the affair) resolution, resolve, determination, will, drive, firmness, persistence, perseverance, tenacity, doggedness, steadfastness, constancy, single-mindedness, devotion, dedication, zeal. OPPOSITE: indecision. 4 (it was all to no real purpose) avail, effect, result, good, use, usefulness, advantage, benefit, gain, profit, value, outcome.
≫ verb mean, intend, plan, design, propose, aim, aspire, resolve, settle, decide, determine, contemplate, meditate.
on purpose purposely, deliberately, intentionally, wilfully, wittingly, knowingly, consciously, by design. OPPOSITE: accidentally.

purposeful adj determined, decided, resolved, resolute, positive, deliberate, firm, set, fixed, constant, persistent, persevering, dogged, steadfast, tenacious, single-minded, strong-willed, immovable, unwavering, unfaltering. OPPOSITE: indecisive.

purposely adv on purpose, intentionally, with intent, deliberately, expressly, calculatedly, designedly, consciously, by design, wilfully, knowingly, wittingly, premeditatedly.

purse noun 1 (took some coins from her purse) wallet, money-bag, pouch. 2 (funds from the public purse) funds, finances, resources, coffers, treasury, exchequer, means, money, wealth, wherewithal. 3 (the winner gets a purse of several thousand pounds) prize, reward, award, present, gift.
≫ verb pucker, pout, wrinkle, press together, draw together, knit together, compress, contract, tighten, close.

pursue verb 1 (the police pursued the gang) follow, chase, give chase to, go after, run after, hunt, stalk, trail, track, shadow, tail (inf). 2 (they did not pursue the questioning) proceed with, chase up, continue with, carry on with, keep on with, persist with, see through, maintain, hold

to. 3 (pursue a career in education) follow, practise, engage in, conduct, prosecute, ply, work at, apply oneself to. OPPOSITE: abandon. 4 (pursue happiness) seek, search for, desire, aspire to, aim for, try for, strive for, strive towards, work towards. 5 (she pursued him tirelessly) chase after, run after, woo, court, make up to, pay suit to, set one's cap at, haunt, plague, dog, harass, harry, hound.

pursuit noun 1 (hundreds joined in the pursuit) chase, hunt, hue and cry, search. 2 (the pursuit of one's dreams) striving towards, following, search, quest, aim, goal, objective, aspiration. 3 (an absorbing pursuit) occupation, business, profession, trade, line, craft, vocation, speciality, hobby, pastime, activity, interest, recreation, pleasure. 4 (her pursuit of the ideal mate) hunting, search, chase, wooing, courting, suit.

purvey verb 1 (purvey fine foods) sell, provide, supply, stock, furnish, cater, provision, retail, deal in, trade in. 2 (purvey the latest news) transmit, spread, circulate, communicate, pass on, put about, make known, publicize, publish, broadcast, disseminate, propagate.

push verb 1 (push the crate over here) shove, thrust, drive, propel, move, force. OPPOSITE: pull. 2 (push the button) press, depress, squeeze, plunge, poke, prod, nudge, ram. 3 (journalists pushed round her) crowd, press, squash, cram, jostle, hustle, butt, jolt, elbow, shoulder, manhandle. 4 (pushed his wife to agree) press, urge, encourage, egg on (inf), incite, impel, spur, prod, goad, prompt, persuade, influence, pressurize, force, coerce, dragoon, bully. 5 (push their latest design) promote, boost, market, hype (inf), plug (inf), advertise, publicize. OPPOSITE: deter.
≫ noun 1 (gave the old man a push) shove, thrust, nudge, prod, poke, butt, knock, jolt, jostle. 2 (one last push to get the job done) effort, endeavour. 3 (the army was committed to a big push) attack, assault, offensive, onslaught, thrust, sortie, raid, foray, incursion, advance, charge, invasion. 4 (we need a manager with lots of push) drive, determination, force, forcefulness, ambition, enterprise, initiative, energy, dynamism, go (inf), get-up-and-go (inf), enthusiasm, verve, vigour, vitality, spirit, gumption (inf), pep (inf), pizzazz (inf).
push around bully, pick on, terrorize, torment, domineer, intimidate, victimize, trample on, tread on, browbeat, tyrannize.
push off go away, depart, leave, move, get out, push along (inf), shove off (inf), buzz off (inf), clear off (inf), beat it (inf), get lost (inf), slope off (inf), take off (inf), make tracks (inf), hit the road (inf), piss off (sl).

pushover noun 1 (the task was a pushover) child's play (inf), walkover (inf), picnic (inf), doddle (inf), piece of cake (inf), cinch (inf), breeze (inf). 2 (she's no pushover when it comes to money) walkover, soft touch (inf), easy touch (inf), sucker (inf), mug (inf), dupe, sap, fool.

pushy adj pushing, forward, bold, ambitious, enterprising, go-ahead, dynamic, forceful, assertive, self-assertive, presumptuous, assuming, arrogant, impertinent, brash, loud, over-confident, bumptious, aggressive, bossy (inf), officious, intrusive. OPPOSITE: meek.

pusillanimous adj timid, timorous, fearful, scared, cowardly, gutless (inf), faint-hearted, lily-livered, chicken (*inf*), chicken-hearted, spineless, yellow (*inf*), craven, wimpish (*inf*), weak, feeble. OPPOSITE: brave.

pustule *noun* abscess, ulcer, eruption, fester, gathering, blister, pimple, spot, zit (*inf*), boil, carbuncle.

put *verb* **1** (*put the table by the door*) place, set, set down, lay, lay down, dump (*inf*), plonk (*inf*), deposit, situate, locate, post, position, stand, station, install, plant, fix, settle, rest. OPPOSITE: remove. **2** (*put them in order of priority*) arrange, sort, place, class, classify, categorize, catalogue, bracket, group, rank, grade, rate, allocate to, consign to. **3** (*put a charge on parking*) place, lay, impose, inflict, levy, exact, demand, require, enjoin, apply, attach, fix. **4** (*put the blame on herself*) place, lay, pin, assign, attribute, ascribe, impute. **5** (*put to death*) condemn, sentence, consign, charge, commit, subject, doom, convict. **6** (*he put it very well*) say, speak, express, utter, voice, pronounce, word, phrase, formulate, state, declare, frame. **7** (*put the suggestion*) advance, put forward, set forth, propose, present, offer, proffer, submit, tender, couch, posit. OPPOSITE: withdraw. **8** (*put a lot of effort into the job*) sink, devote, dedicate, invest, spend, give, contribute. **9** (*put the men to work*) set, apply, use, employ, utilize, assign, allocate. **10** (*put his foot through the door*) thrust, kick, punch, smash, bash, force, drive, push, stick, plunge, lunge. **11** (*put in plain language*) translate, interpret, express, word, phrase, render, turn, convert, transcribe. **12** (*put all he had on the venture*) gamble, bet, wager, stake, risk, place, lay, chance, hazard. **13** (*her fortune is put at several million dollars*) value, evaluate, assess, calculate, estimate, reckon, guess, set, place.

put about tell, spread, make known, make public, circulate, publicize, broadcast, announce, disseminate, propagate, give out, bandy about.

put across communicate, get across, get over, put over, convey, make clear, clarify, make understood, explain, express, spell out.

put aside 1 (*put aside some money each week*) save, reserve, put by, lay by, set aside, lay aside, put away, salt away, stow away, squirrel away, deposit, hoard, stash (*inf*), stockpile, store, cache. **2** (*she put aside her plans*) set aside, lay aside, put to one side, cast aside, discard, dispense with, abandon, drop. **3** (*they put aside their quarrel*) set aside, lay aside, bury, disregard, ignore, forget.

put away 1 (*put away your things*) replace, put back, tidy up, tidy away, clear away, clear up. **2** (*put away part of her salary each month*) save, keep, retain, reserve, set aside, set by, put aside, put by, store, lay in, lay up, stockpile, stow. OPPOSITE: use. **3** (*he put away three helpings*) consume, devour, eat, drink, swallow, down, bolt, gobble, wolf (*inf*), guzzle (*inf*), scoff (*inf*), polish off (*inf*). **4** (*she put away all hopes of a reconciliation*) set aside, put aside, lay aside, cast aside, discard, forget, disregard, jettison. **5** (*they put him away for ten years*) imprison, gaol, jail, bang up (*inf*), lock up, shut up, shut away, send down (*inf*), confine, commit, incarcerate, certify, institutionalize. OPPOSITE: release.

put down 1 (*put it down in the book*) enter, log, record, register, list, jot down, note down, make a note of, take down, set down, write down, put in writing, inscribe, transcribe. **2** (*put down an uprising*) suppress, repress, quash, quell, defeat, crush, smash, stamp out, extinguish, stop, silence. **3** (*put down diseased cattle*) kill, destroy, put to sleep, put out of its misery, do away with. **4** (*put it down to her inexperience*) attribute, ascribe, impute, blame, mark down, set down, charge, lay. **5** (*he tried to put down his rival in public*) disparage, slight, belittle, criticize, deprecate, knock (*inf*), humiliate, humble, take down a peg (*inf*), snub, deflate, squash, mortify, crush, shame, condemn. OPPOSITE: praise.

put forward advance, suggest, recommend, nominate, propose, move, table, lay before, set before, introduce, present, submit, offer, proffer, tender.

put off 1 (*put off sending the letter*) postpone, defer, delay, put back, hold over, shelve, suspend, procrastinate, adjourn, reschedule, put on ice (*inf*), put on the back burner (*inf*). OPPOSITE: advance. **2** (*put off by her attitude*) deter, dissuade, discourage, dishearten, demoralize, daunt, intimidate, disconcert, distress, dismay, faze, unsettle, rattle (*inf*), throw (*inf*), distract, confuse, abash, discomfit, nonplus, repel, offend, disgust, revolt, sicken, nauseate. OPPOSITE: encourage. **3** (*a cough put him off his stroke*) distract, divert, sidetrack, deflect, turn away, turn aside.

put on 1 (*put on her best skirt*) don, change into, get into, slip into, throw on (*inf*), try on, wear, dress, clothe. **2** (*we think he's putting it on*) feign, fake, simulate, sham, pretend, play-act, assume, affect. **3** (*they are going to put on a comedy*) present, produce, mount, stage, perform, do, show. **4** (*put on the lights*) switch on, turn on, illuminate. **5** (*put on some refreshments*) organize, provide, supply, furnish, lay on. **6** (*put all he owned on the outcome*) wager, gamble, bet, lay, place.

put out 1 (*put out the flames*) extinguish, douse, quench, smother, snuff out, blow out, stamp out. OPPOSITE: light. **2** (*put out the news of her death*) announce, make known, make public, publish, publicize, broadcast, circulate, disclose, release, issue, bring out. **3** (*she was quite put out at his behaviour*) annoy, irritate, vex, irk, anger, exasperate, infuriate, provoke, confuse, faze (*inf*), disturb, perturb, disconcert, bother, harass, upset, agitate, unsettle, trouble, hurt, offend. **4** (*please don't put yourself out for us*) inconvenience, trouble, bother, discommode, incommode.

put up 1 (*put up a block of flats*) erect, build, construct, raise, assemble. OPPOSITE: demolish. **2** (*put up several guests*) accommodate, house, lodge, board, shelter, entertain. **3** (*put up interest rates*) raise, increase, bump up (*inf*), hike up (*inf*), jack up (*inf*), escalate. **4** (*put up the cash for the project*) provide, supply, offer, pledge, advance, pay, invest, give, donate, float. **5** (*we shall put up our own man for the committee*) put forward, propose, submit, present, recommend, nominate, suggest, choose.

put up with tolerate, endure, stand, suffer, lump (*inf*), bear, abide, take, accept, swallow, stomach, brook.

put upon impose upon, take advantage of, exploit, inconvenience, take for granted, saddle.

putative *adj* accepted, acknowledged, recognized, imputed, alleged, reputed, hypothetical, theoretical, suppositional, suppositious, conjectural, supposed, assumed, presumed. OPPOSITE: proven.

put-down *noun* snub, rebuff, slight, insult, gibe, dig

(*inf*), barb, affront, disparagement, sneer, humiliation.

putrefy *verb* rot, perish, decompose, decay, go bad, spoil, moulder, fester, corrupt, deteriorate, taint. OPPOSITE: preserve.

putrid *adj* rotten, decomposed, decayed, bad, off, rancid, addled, mouldy, fetid, rank, foul, offensive, corrupt, tainted, polluted, contaminated. OPPOSITE: fresh.

puzzle *verb* **1** (*he was puzzled by her absence*) perplex, baffle, mystify, confuse, confound, nonplus, bewilder, daze, dumbfound, flummox (*inf*), floor (*inf*), stump (*inf*), beat (*inf*), stagger. OPPOSITE: enlighten. **2** (*puzzle over the question*) ponder, study, reflect, deliberate, meditate, brood, mull, muse, consider, wonder, think.
  ➢ *noun* **1** (*try to solve the puzzle*) riddle, conundrum, enigma, mystery, poser, teaser, question, problem, brainteaser, paradox, dilemma. OPPOSITE: solution. **2** (*I was in a puzzle*) perplexity, bafflement, confusion, bewilderment. OPPOSITE: enlightenment.

puzzle out solve, resolve, work out, figure out, think out, think through, reason out, suss (*inf*), decipher, crack (*inf*), get (*inf*), decode, unravel, untangle, clear up, sort out, piece together.

puzzled *adj* baffled, perplexed, mystified, confounded, dumbfounded, at a loss, at sea (*inf*), stumped (*inf*), beaten, confused, bewildered, mixed up, flummoxed (*inf*), nonplussed (*inf*), lost, in a haze, in a fog.

puzzling *adj* baffling, perplexing, confusing, bewildering, mystifying, inexplicable, incomprehensible, unaccountable, unfathomable, impenetrable, intricate, involved, ambiguous, equivocal, mysterious, enigmatic, cryptic, unclear, abstruse, difficult, hard, mind-bending, mind-boggling, tortuous, knotty, labyrinthine, queer, curious, peculiar, strange, bizarre.

pygmy *noun* dwarf, midget, manikin, homunculus, shrimp (*inf*). OPPOSITE: giant.
adj miniature, diminutive, dwarfish, dwarf, midget, elfin, undersized, stunted, half-pint, pint-sized, small, little, tiny, minute, miniscule, pocket, toy, baby, Lilliputian. OPPOSITE: gigantic.

pyromaniac *noun* arsonist, incendiary, fire-raiser, firebug (*inf*).

quack *noun* **1** (*suspected he was a quack*) charlatan, fake, fraud, phoney (*inf*), impostor, pretender, mountebank, humbug, swindler, confidence trickster, con man (*inf*). **2** (*get a sick note from the quack*) doctor, doc (*inf*), physician, GP, medic (*inf*).
➣ *adj* fake, phoney (*inf*), bogus, counterfeit, fraudulent, pretended, sham, pseudo, false. OPPOSITE: genuine.

quaff *verb* drink, imbibe, sup, gulp, swig (*inf*), guzzle (*inf*), swallow, down.

quagmire *noun* **1** (*sink into the quagmire*) swamp, bog, marsh, mire, fen, morass, slough, quicksand. **2** (*an administrative quagmire*) muddle, tangle, imbroglio, difficulty, problem, predicament, quandary, dilemma, fix (*inf*), pickle (*inf*), impasse, stalemate.

quail *verb* shrink, recoil, get cold feet (*inf*), blanch, blench, flinch, cower, cringe, falter, waver, tremble, shake, quake, shudder.

quaint *adj* **1** (*a quaint village*) picturesque, charming, sweet, old-world, olde-worlde (*inf*), twee (*inf*), old-fashioned, antiquated. OPPOSITE: modern. **2** (*quaint ideas*) strange, unusual, uncommon, extraordinary, curious, odd, peculiar, bizarre, eccentric, offbeat, unconventional, outlandish, fantastic, fanciful, whimsical. OPPOSITE: ordinary.

quake *verb* tremble, shake, quiver, vibrate, shudder, shiver, quail, waver, falter, wobble, totter, rock, throb, pulsate, convulse.

qualification *noun* **1** (*academic qualifications*) certificate, diploma, licence, charter. **2** (*the right qualifications for the job*) accomplishment, achievement, attainment, skill, expertise, knowledge, know-how (*inf*), experience, competence, proficiency, ability, capability, capacity, aptitude, suitability, fitness, eligibility, attribute, quality, endowment, requirement, prerequisite. OPPOSITE: disqualification. **3** (*praised them without qualification*) restriction, limitation, reservation, caveat, modification, condition, proviso, stipulation, specification, exception, exemption.

qualified *adj* **1** (*a qualified nurse*) trained, certified, licensed, chartered, professional, experienced, practised, competent, proficient, expert, skilled, skilful, accomplished, knowledgeable, well-informed, talented, able, adept, capable, suitable, fit, eligible. OPPOSITE: unqualified. **2** (*qualified approval*) restricted, limited, reserved, guarded, equivocal, conditional, provisional, contingent, modified. OPPOSITE: unconditional.

qualify *verb* **1** (*qualify as an accountant*) train, pass, graduate, prepare, fit, equip, endow, capacitate, empower, permit, sanction, certify, license, charter. OPPOSITE: disqualify. **2** (*qualify a statement*) modify, alter, change, adapt, restrict, limit, regulate, control, restrain, moderate, mitigate, temper, reduce, diminish, soften, assuage.

quality *noun* **1** (*the qualities of a good teacher*) characteristic, property, attribute, feature, aspect, trait, peculiarity, idiosyncrasy. **2** (*the quality of her work*) character, nature, kind, sort, grade, rank, status, condition, standard, calibre, value, worth, merit. **3** (*a man of quality*) distinction, excellence, superiority, supremacy, eminence, nobility.

qualm *noun* **1** (*have no qualms about lying*) scruple, doubt, uncertainty, reluctance, hesitation, second thought, compunction, remorse, contrition, regret, twinge of conscience, misgiving, uneasiness, funny feeling (*inf*), apprehension, trepidation, anxiety, worry. OPPOSITE: ease. **2** (*qualms of seasickness*) pang, twinge, spasm, attack, nausea, queasiness.

quandary *noun* dilemma, cleft stick, doubt, uncertainty, puzzle, perplexity, predicament, difficulty, problem, trouble, plight, mess, fix (*inf*), spot (*inf*).

quantity *noun* amount, number, sum, total, aggregate, extent, measure, size, magnitude, volume, capacity, weight, mass, lot, portion, quota, proportion, part.

quarantine *noun* isolation, seclusion, segregation, separation.

quarrel *noun* argument, disagreement, dispute, squabble, tiff, spat (*inf*), row, altercation, wrangle, barney (*inf*), misunderstanding, difference of opinion, controversy, contention, clash, fight, feud, vendetta, brawl, scuffle, set-to (*inf*), scrap (*inf*), dust-up (*inf*), punch-up (*inf*), riot, fracas. OPPOSITE: agreement.
➤ *verb* argue, disagree, squabble, row, bicker, wrangle, altercate, dispute, be at loggerheads, differ, be at odds, feud, fall out (*inf*), contend, clash, fight, brawl, scrap (*inf*), spar. OPPOSITE: agree.

quarrel with object to, take exception to, carp at, cavil at, find fault with, pick holes in (*inf*), fault, criticize, disagree with, argue with, disapprove of, complain about.

quarrelsome *adj* argumentative, contentious, disputatious, dissident, combative, belligerent, bellicose, pugnacious, hostile, antagonistic, quick-tempered, choleric, irritable, irascible, peevish, petulant, querulous, testy, cross, bad-tempered. OPPOSITE: peaceable.

quarry[1] *noun* (*a slate quarry*) pit, mine, excavation.
➤ *verb* mine, extract, excavate, dig, obtain, get.

quarry[2] *noun* (*in pursuit of their quarry*) game, prey, victim, prize, object, aim, goal, target, mark.

quarter *noun* **1** (*one and a quarter*) fourth, fourth part, three months, thirteen weeks, ninety days, fifteen minutes. **2** (*the residential quarter*) district, region, area, zone, division, part, neighbourhood, vicinity, locality, location, place, province, territory, point, spot, direction, side. **3** (*gave the culprits no quarter*) mercy, pity, humanity, clemency, leniency, forgiveness, pardon, compassion, favour.
➤ *verb* accommodate, house, put up, lodge, board, billet, station, post, shelter.

quarters *noun* lodgings, digs (*inf*), accommodation, housing, residence, domicile, abode, dwelling, habitation, rooms, chambers, billet, barracks, station, post, cantonment, shelter.

quash *verb* **1** (*quash a rebellion*) suppress, subdue, squash, crush, put down, quell, overwhelm, repress, overthrow, defeat. **2** (*quash a conviction*) annul, nullify, void, invalidate, cancel, repeal, revoke, reverse, rescind, abolish, set aside, overrule, throw out, reject. OPPOSITE: vindicate.

quasi- *adv* supposedly, seemingly, apparently, partly, more or less, virtually, almost, to all intents and purposes, pseudo-, semi-.

quaver *verb* tremble, shake, quake, quiver, shiver, shudder, vibrate, flicker, flutter, waver, twitter, trill, warble.
➤ *noun* tremor, tremble, shake, quiver, vibration, wavering, trill, warble, break.

quay *noun* wharf, landing stage, jetty, pier, dock, harbour, marina.

queasy *adj* sick, bilious, nauseous, nauseated, squeamish, green about the gills (*inf*), ill, indisposed, unwell, out of sorts (*inf*) queer, groggy, dizzy, woozy (*inf*). OPPOSITE: well.

queen *noun* **1** (*queen of Spain*) monarch, ruler, sovereign, consort. **2** (*queen of the silver screen*) star, diva, prima donna, belle, idol, model, epitome, ideal.

queenly *adj* regal, royal, sovereign, majestic, stately, grand, imperial, noble.

queer *adj* **1** (*a queer noise*) odd, curious, strange, weird, funny, bizarre, uncanny, unusual, uncommon, extraordinary, remarkable, peculiar, singular, abnormal, anomalous, atypical, exceptional, freakish, eccentric, offbeat, outlandish, unorthodox, unconventional. OPPOSITE: normal. **2** (*a queer business*) dubious, doubtful, questionable, suspicious, suspect, irregular, shady (*inf*), fishy (*inf*), mysterious, puzzling. **3** (*feeling a bit queer*) dizzy, giddy, faint, groggy, woozy (*inf*), light-headed, unwell, ill, sick, queasy. OPPOSITE: well.
➤ *noun* homosexual, gay, lesbian.
➤ *verb* spoil, mar, ruin, wreck, thwart, frustrate, screw up (*sl*), bungle, botch, muff, jeopardize, endanger, imperil, threaten, impair, harm.

quell *verb* **1** (*quell a riot*) suppress, subdue, repress, put down, overwhelm, quash, crush, squelch, squash, stamp out, extinguish, conquer, vanquish, overcome, defeat. **2** (*quell our fears*) allay, assuage, mitigate, alleviate, moderate, soothe, mollify, dull, deaden, blunt, tranquillize, calm, pacify, quiet, silence. OPPOSITE: aggravate.

quench *verb* **1** (*quench his thirst*) slake, satisfy, sate, satiate, allay, appease. **2** (*quench a flame*) extinguish, douse, put out, snuff out, blow out. OPPOSITE: light. **3** (*quench her desires*) suppress, subdue, crush, quell, quash, smother, stifle, destroy, kill.

querulous *adj* peevish, petulant, whining, plaintive, grumbling, murmuring, complaining, carping, critical, censorious, fault-finding, fussy, pernickety (*inf*), hard to please, dissatisfied, discontented, fretful, irritable, fractious, grouchy, cranky, crabby, captious, grumpy, cross, irascible, ill-tempered, cantankerous, testy, touchy. OPPOSITE: contented.

query *noun* **1** (*answered their queries*) question, enquiry, problem, issue. **2** (*raised a query about his suitability*) doubt, uncertainty, scepticism, reservation, hesitation, objection. OPPOSITE: answer.
➤ *verb* question, dispute, challenge, doubt, disbelieve, mistrust, distrust, suspect, ask, enquire. OPPOSITE: accept.

quest *noun* search, seeking, hunt, pursuit, expedition, journey, crusade, mission, goal, objective, aim, target.

question *noun* **1** (*ask a question*) query, enquiry, interrogation, examination, investigation. OPPOSITE: answer. **2** (*the question of finance*) matter, issue, subject, topic, point, proposition, proposal, problem, difficulty. **3** (*is there any question about it?*) doubt, uncertainty, dispute, argument, debate, controversy. OPPOSITE: certainty.
➤ *verb* **1** (*question a suspect*) interrogate, examine, cross-examine, cross-question, interview, debrief, quiz, catechize, probe, sound out, grill (*inf*), pump (*inf*), give the third degree to (*inf*). **2** (*question her competence*) query, call into question, challenge, dispute, doubt, disbelieve, mistrust, distrust, suspect. OPPOSITE: accept.

beyond question beyond doubt, certain, indisputable, incontrovertible. OPPOSITE: debatable.

out of the question impossible, unacceptable, unthinkable, inconceivable, absurd. OPPOSITE: possible.

questionable *adj* debatable, disputable, dubious, doubtful, uncertain, moot, problematical, controversial, controvertible, arguable, equivocal, suspicious. OPPOSITE: indisputable.

questionnaire *noun* survey, opinion poll, quiz, test, form.

queue *noun* line, column, file, tailback, crocodile, train, string, chain, series, succession, sequence.

quibble *verb* **1** (*quibble about the details*) cavil, carp, split hairs, nit-pick (*inf*). **2** (*give me a straight answer and don't quibble!*) equivocate, prevaricate, hedge, fudge, avoid the issue, evade, beat about the bush (inf).
➤ *noun* **1** (*a few minor quibbles*) criticism, objection, complaint, protest, niggle, nicety, nit-picking (*inf*). **2** (*a bit less quibble and a bit more action*) equivocation, prevarication, evasion, avoidance.

quick *adj* **1** (*a quick journey*) fast, swift, rapid, speedy, nippy, express, fleet, nimble, agile. OPPOSITE: slow. **2** (*a quick reaction*) prompt, ready, sudden, expeditious, instant, instantaneous, immediate. OPPOSITE: delayed. **3** (*a quick glance*) hasty, hurried, cursory, perfunctory, brisk, brief, fleeting, momentary. OPPOSITE: leisurely. **4** (*quick thinking*) sharp, keen, acute, alert, quick-witted, shrewd, astute, smart, clever, intelligent, adroit, deft, dexterous, skilful. OPPOSITE: dull.

quicken *verb* **1** (*quicken the process*) accelerate, speed up, expedite, precipitate, hasten, hurry, dispatch. OPPOSITE: retard. **2** (*quicken their interest*) stimulate, rouse, kindle, inspire, whet, excite, animate, revive, revitalize, resuscitate, refresh, energize, enliven, vitalize, invigorate. OPPOSITE: deaden.

quickly *adv* **1** (*run quickly*) fast, swiftly, rapidly, speedily, at the double, like greased lightning (*inf*), hell for leather (*inf*), like a bat out of hell (*inf*), like the clappers (*inf*), posthaste, apace, at a rate of knots (*inf*). OPPOSITE: slowly. **2** (*act quickly*) promptly, immediately, instantly, forthwith, expeditiously. OPPOSITE: tardily. **3** (*read quickly*) hastily, hurriedly, briefly, cursorily, perfunctorily.

quick-tempered *adj* touchy, testy, irascible, irritable, hot-tempered, temperamental, waspish, snappy, peppery, petulant, choleric, impatient, excitable, fiery, explosive. OPPOSITE: affable.

quick-witted *adj* sharp, astute, keen, acute, alert, quick, quick on the uptake (*inf*), bright, intelligent, clever, smart, perceptive, discerning. OPPOSITE: stupid.

quiescent *adj* still, motionless, inactive, inert, dormant, latent, quiet, calm, tranquil, serene, placid, unruffled, peaceful, restful. OPPOSITE: active.

quiet *adj* **1** (*quiet machinery*) silent, noiseless, soundless, inaudible, hushed, low, soft, muffled, muted. OPPOSITE: noisy. **2** (*a quiet evening at home*) calm, serene, tranquil, peaceful, restful, untroubled, undisturbed, smooth, still, motionless. OPPOSITE: hectic. **3** (*a quiet person by nature*) reticent, reserved, shy, retiring, taciturn, uncommunicative, unforthcoming, introverted, withdrawn, mild, gentle, docile, placid, unruffled. OPPOSITE: talkative. **4** (*a quiet place*) private, secret, isolated, secluded, unfrequented, sleepy, lonely. OPPOSITE: public. **5** (*quiet colours*) subdued, sober, restrained, unobtrusive, understated, subtle. OPPOSITE: loud.
➤ *noun* quietness, silence, hush, noiselessness, soundlessness, peace, calm, calmness, tranquillity, serenity, rest, repose, ease. OPPOSITE: noise.

quieten *verb* quiet, silence, hush, shush, shut up (*inf*), muffle, mute, soften, deaden, stifle, still, calm, lull, tranquillize, soothe, pacify, appease, allay, assuage, mitigate, dull, blunt, quell, subdue. OPPOSITE: disturb.

quietly *adv* **1** (*move quietly*) silently, noiselessly, soundlessly, inaudibly. OPPOSITE: noisily. **2** (*speak quietly*) softly, low, in a whisper, in an undertone. OPPOSITE: loudly. **3** (*sleep quietly*) peacefully, calmly, serenely, placidly. **4** (*tell him quietly*) secretly, privately, confidentially, discreetly, unobtrusively.

quilt *noun* bedspread, coverlet, counterpane, eiderdown, duvet, continental quilt.

quintessence *noun* essence, quiddity, heart, core, kernel, pith, marrow, spirit, soul, embodiment, personification, exemplar.

quintessential *adj* ideal, perfect, consummate, archetypal, prototypical, definitive, ultimate, complete, entire, essential.

quip *noun* joke, jest, gag (*inf*), one-liner (*inf*), crack (*inf*), wisecrack (*inf*), witticism, bon mot, epigram, sally, riposte, retort, repartee, pleasantry, badinage.

quirk *noun* idiosyncrasy, peculiarity, characteristic, trait, mannerism, habit, oddity, eccentricity, whim, caprice, freak, vagary, foible, obsession, mania, fetish, kink.

quit *verb* **1** (*quit the habit*) stop, cease, desist from, leave off, discontinue, abandon, give up, pack in (*inf*), relinquish, surrender, renounce. OPPOSITE: start. **2** (*quit his job*) leave, depart, go, decamp, withdraw, retire, resign, abdicate. OPPOSITE: enter.

quite *adv* **1** (*quite certain*) completely, totally, entirely, wholly, fully, altogether, utterly, absolutely, positively, perfectly, thoroughly, exactly, really, truly, indeed. OPPOSITE: partly. **2** (*quite warm*) fairly, moderately, rather, pretty (*inf*), somewhat, to a degree. OPPOSITE: very.

quiver *verb* tremble, shake, quake, quaver, shiver, shudder, flicker, flutter, palpitate, vibrate, pulsate, oscillate.
➤ *noun* tremor, tremble, shake, shiver, shudder, vibration, palpitation, flutter, pulsation, convulsion, spasm.

quixotic *adj* impractical, impracticable, unrealistic, idealistic, utopian, fanciful, visionary, romantic, starry-eyed, fantastic, imaginary, wild, mad. OPPOSITE: practical.

quiz *noun* test, examination, questionnaire, survey, investigation, interrogation, questioning, cross-examination.
➤ *verb* interrogate, question, cross-question, examine, cross-examine, catechize, grill (*inf*), pump (*inf*).

quizzical *adj* puzzled, perplexed, mystified, baffled, questioning, enquiring, curious, teasing, mocking, satirical.

quondam *adj* former, one-time, past, previous, late, earlier. OPPOSITE: present.

quota *noun* share, portion, allotment, allocation, allowance, ration, part, slice, proportion, percentage, cut (*inf*), whack (*inf*).

quotation *noun* **1** (*quotations from Shakespeare*) citation, quote (*inf*), extract, excerpt, passage, piece, cutting, line, phrase, reference, allusion. **2** (*an insurance quotation*) estimate, quote (*inf*), tender, figure, cost, price, rate, charge.

quote *verb* cite, mention, refer to, name, give, instance, adduce, repeat, echo, recite, extract, excerpt.
➤ *noun* **1** (*get a quote for the repair*) estimate, quotation, tender, figure, cost, price, rate, charge. **2** (*biblical quotes*) citation, quotation, extract, excerpt, passage, piece, cutting, line, phrase, reference, allusion.

quotidian *adj* daily, diurnal, everyday, day-to-day, routine, regular, recurrent, habitual, customary, normal, common, commonplace, ordinary. OPPOSITE: unusual.

rabble *noun* **1** (*a rabble gathered at the entrance*) mob, crowd, throng, horde, swarm, herd. **2** (*the need to appease the rabble*) masses, common people, commonalty, populace, rank and file, proletariat, plebs (*inf*), peasantry, hoi polloi, riffraff (*inf*), great unwashed (*inf*), scum, mob, crowd, herd. OPPOSITE: aristocracy.

rabid *adj* **1** (*a rabid dog*) mad, hydrophobic. **2** (*a rabid desire for revenge*) wild, raging, raving, burning, ardent, frantic, frenetic, frenzied, hysterical, berserk, furious, ferocious, violent, maniacal, distracted. **3** (*a rabid reactionary*) fanatical, extreme, fervent, zealous, overzealous, overenthusiastic, unreasonable, irrational, intolerant, bigoted, narrow-minded, narrow. OPPOSITE: rational.

race[1] *noun* **1** (*runners in a race*) contest, competition, chase, pursuit, dash, sprint, relay, marathon, steeplechase. **2** (*the race for power*) contest, competition, quest, contention, rivalry. **3** (*a mill race*) flow, rush, stream, course, channel, sluice, waterway, watercourse.
➤ *verb* **1** (*race down the road*) run, dash, dart, bolt, sprint, tear, fly, gallop, hare, career, speed, accelerate, zoom. OPPOSITE: amble. **2** (*seven drivers raced for the prize*) compete, contend, run. **3** (*raced to reach the train*) hurry, rush, hasten, make haste, step on it (*inf*), get a move on (*inf*), get cracking (*inf*), put one's foot down (*inf*).

race[2] *noun* **1** (*a barbaric race*) people, nation, tribe, clan, folk, ethnic group. **2** (*prejudice based on race*) blood, bloodline, stock, breed, species, genus, family, kin, kindred, line, descent, extraction, strain, ancestry, parentage, lineage, house.

racial *adj* race-related, ethnic, ethnological, folk, tribal, national, genealogical, genetic.

racism *noun* racialism, discrimination, racial discrimination, prejudice, racial prejudice, racial bigotry, apartheid, bias, chauvinism, jingoism, xenophobia.

racist *noun* racialist, bigot, discriminator, chauvinist.
➤ *adj* racialist, discriminatory, prejudiced, bigoted, intolerant, illiberal.

rack *noun* stand, support, holder, frame, framework, trestle, structure, shelf.
on the rack tortured, in torment, in pain, in agony, anguished, afflicted, suffering, miserable.
➤ *verb* torture, torment, excruciate, agonize, pain, afflict, oppress, distress, persecute, plague, harass, crucify, convulse. OPPOSITE: soothe.

racket *noun* **1** (*listen to that racket*) din, noise, uproar, clamour, outcry, hubbub, hurly-burly, hullabaloo, commotion, pandemonium, tumult, turmoil, disturbance, row, fuss, shouting, yelling. OPPOSITE: quiet. **2** (*a money-laundering racket*) scheme, confidence trick, fraud, con (*inf*), swindle, fiddle, dodge. **3** (*he's in the media racket*) business, game (*inf*), line, job, occupation, profession.

racy *adj* **1** (*a comedian admired for his racy delivery*) lively, sparkling, spirited, animated, enthusiastic, energetic, vigorous, vivacious, boisterous, buoyant, dynamic, interesting, entertaining, dramatic, exciting, stimulating, fast-moving. OPPOSITE: dull. **2** (*telling racy jokes*) risqué, suggestive, bawdy, ribald, blue (*inf*), smutty, vulgar, coarse, crude, dirty, naughty, spicy (*inf*), off-colour, immodest, indecent, indelicate. **3** (*rather a racy flavour*) strong, piquant, pungent, sharp, spicy, tangy, peppery, tart, distinctive.

raddled *adj* haggard, gaunt, drawn, wasted, worn out, unkempt, dishevelled, dilapidated, broken-down, run-down.

radiance *noun* **1** (*the radiance of the sun*) light, brightness, brilliance, shine, glare, lustre, gleam, glow, luminosity, incandescence, radiation, sparkle, shimmer, glitter, effulgence. **2** (*the radiance of her smile*) resplendence, splendour. **3** (*laughter full of radiance*) joy, joyfulness, happiness, pleasure, delight, elation, ecstasy, gaiety, warmth, bliss, rapture.

radiant *adj* **1** (*a radiant moon*) bright, shining, brilliant, illuminated, resplendent, beaming, dazzling, effulgent, sparkling, glittering, gleaming, shiny, lustrous, glowing, luminous, luminescent, incandescent, irradiant, lambent. OPPOSITE: dark. **2** (*a radiant smile*) happy, joyful, delighted, gay, elated, ecstatic, blissful, overjoyed, pleased, over the moon (*inf*), on cloud nine (*inf*), on top of the world (*inf*), in raptures (*inf*). OPPOSITE: miserable. **3** (*she looked radiant*) beaming, glowing, sparkling, dazzling, vivid, glorious, magnificent, splendid, resplendent.

radiate *verb* **1** (*radiate heat*) give off, give out, send forth, send out, emit, emanate, diffuse, issue, shed, pour, disseminate, scatter, disperse, spread. **2** (*roads radiating*) diverge, branch out, spread out, divaricate. **3** (*radiate confidence*) show, demonstrate, exhibit, transmit, emanate.

radiation *noun* **1** (*the radiation of heat*) emanation, emission, transmission, propagation. **2** (*atomic radiation*) rays, waves.

radical *adj* **1** (*radical flaws in the design*) basic, fundamental, rudimentary, elementary, elemental, primary, constitutional, essential, inherent, innate, intrinsic, ingrained, deep-seated, profound, natural, native, organic. OPPOSITE: superficial. **2** (*a radical overhaul of the system*) complete, absolute, entire, utter, total, thorough, thoroughgoing, comprehensive, exhaustive, sweeping, far-reaching, profound, drastic, severe, extreme, excessive, violent. **3** (*radical politics*) fanatical, fanatic, revolutionary, rebel, rebellious, militant, extreme, extremist, immoderate, leftist, left-wing.
➤ *noun* extremist, fanatic, militant, revolutionary, rebel, fundamentalist, reformer, reformist. OPPOSITE: moderate.

raffle *noun* lottery, draw, sweepstake, sweep, tombola.

rag[1] *noun* **1** (*wiped his hands with a rag*) cloth, flannel, floorcloth, duster, towel. **2** (*her clothes were reduced to rags*) remnants, shreds, tatters.

rag[2] *verb* tease, badger, jeer, mock, send up (*inf*), ridicule, taunt, poke fun at, make fun of, kid (*inf*), rib (*inf*), torment, bait.

rage *noun* **1** (*incandescent with rage*) anger, fury, wrath, ire, passion, mania, raving, madness, vehemence. OPPOSITE: calmness. **2** (*fly into a rage*) fit, frenzy, temper, tantrum, paroxysm, rampage. **3** (*the rage of the sea*) turbulence, tumult, fury, violence.
➤ *verb* rant, rave, seethe, fume, storm, thunder, explode, rampage, raise hell (*inf*), see red (*inf*), go mad (*inf*), do one's nut (*inf*), fly off the handle (*inf*), foam at the mouth (*inf*), boil over (*inf*), lose one's temper (*inf*), lose one's cool (*inf*), blow one's cool (*inf*), blow a fuse (*inf*), blow a gasket (*inf*), blow one's top (*inf*), flip one's lid (*inf*), freak out (*inf*), hit the roof (*inf*), go up the wall (*inf*), lose one's rag, lose it (*inf*).

all the rage fashionable, popular, trendy (*inf*), stylish, in demand, in vogue, the craze.

ragged *adj* **1** (*ragged trousers*) tattered, ripped, torn, frayed, worn, worn-out, threadbare, in holes, holey, tatty, shabby, rent. **2** (*ragged appearance*) unkempt, untidy, scruffy, shabby, poor, destitute, down-at-heel, down and out, indigent. OPPOSITE: smart. **3** (*a ragged blade*) rough, uneven, jagged, notched, serrated, saw-toothed, indented, irregular, rugged, craggy. OPPOSITE:

smooth. **4** (*a ragged performance*) erratic, irregular, uneven, rough, crude, unpolished, unrefined, imperfect, faulty. **5** (*a ragged column of refugees*) fragmented, disorganized, straggling, straggly.

raging *adj* **1** (*a raging condemnation*) angry, furious, incensed, infuriated, enraged, frenzied, irate, wrathful, fuming, seething, ranting, raving, rabid, mad. **2** (*the raging wind*) wild, violent, stormy, turbulent, tempestuous, tumultuous, blustery, strong. OPPOSITE: calm. **3** (*a raging headache*) excruciating, painful, agonizing, throbbing, piercing, aching, sore.

raid *noun* **1** (*a guerrilla raid*) attack, assault, onslaught, charge, incursion, invasion, onset, inroad, foray, sortie, sally, thrust, strike, blitz. **2** (*a raid at the local post office*) robbery, break-in, hold-up, smash-and-grab (*inf*). **3** (*a raid by customs*) swoop, bust (*inf*), search.
➤ *verb* **1** (*raid the enemy camp*) attack, assault, assail, invade, descend upon, set upon, swoop on, rush, charge. **2** (*raid the larder*) plunder, pillage, loot, sack, ransack, steal from, rifle, forage, maraud. **3** (*raid the local newsagents*) rob, break into. **4** (*raided by the police*) bust (*inf*), search.

raider *noun* **1** (*a party of enemy raiders*) attacker, invader, looter, plunderer, pillager, sacker, ransacker, marauder. **2** (*the raiders wore balaclavas*) robber, thief, burglar, criminal, crook (*inf*), villain, pirate, brigand.

rail *verb* complain, criticize, denounce, declaim, fulminate, rage, arraign, inveigh, attack, censure, condemn, castigate, upbraid, vociferate, vituperate, revile, abuse, mock, ridicule, jeer, scoff, decry, protest.

railing *noun* fence, fencing, barrier, paling, palisade, rail, parapet, balustrade.

raillery *noun* banter, badinage, pleasantry, repartee, sport, persiflage, joking, jeering, jesting, teasing, kidding (*inf*), ribbing (*inf*), ragging (*inf*), satire, ridicule, mockery, invective, diatribe.

rain *noun* **1** (*play was interrupted by rain*) rainfall, raindrops, rainstorm, precipitation, drizzle, mizzle, shower, downpour, cloudburst, deluge, torrent, storm, thunderstorm, squall. **2** (*a rain of insults*) torrent, volley, shower, deluge, hail.
➤ *verb* **1** (*it started to rain*) drizzle, spit, fall, shower, precipitate, pour, teem, pelt, bucket (*inf*), come down in buckets (*inf*), come down in sheets (*inf*), come down in torrents (*inf*), piss down (*sl*). **2** (*stones rained down*) fall, pour, shower, drop, pelt. **3** (*rain invitations on them*) lavish, pour, give, bestow.

rainy *adj* wet, damp, showery, drizzly.

raise *verb* **1** (*raise the barrier*) lift, lift up, elevate, uplift, upthrust, hoist, heave up. OPPOSITE: lower. **2** (*raise the tent*) erect, set up, put up. **3** (*raise a new building on the site*) build, construct, erect. **4** (*raise the stakes*) put up, increase, jack up (*inf*), hike (*inf*), step up (*inf*), escalate. **5** (*raise the volume*) increase, augment, enhance, heighten, intensify, amplify, magnify, strengthen, boost. OPPOSITE: decrease. **6** (*raised to managing director*) promote, prefer, upgrade, advance, elevate, exalt, aggrandize. OPPOSITE: demote. **7** (*raise expectations*) arouse, awaken, stir, rouse, excite, provoke, whip up, evoke, stimulate, activate, cause, occasion, produce, create, engender, incite, instigate, kindle, foment, summon up. **8** (*raise a large family*) rear, bring up, nurture, educate. **9** (*raise new crops*) breed, cultivate, propagate, grow, farm, till, produce, develop. **10** (*this raises several questions*) bring up, broach, introduce, present, put forward, suggest, moot. **11** (*raise the necessary funds*) collect, gather, assemble, amass, muster, rally, recruit, levy, obtain, get, accumulate, scrape together (*inf*). **12** (*raised their embargo*) lift, remove, take away, get rid of, end, suspend. **13** (*tried to raise them on the phone*) call, reach, contact, get hold of, communicate with. **14** (*accused of raising the dead*) call up, call forth, summon up, conjure up.

rake¹ *verb* **1** (*rake the gravel*) scrape, scratch, hoe, graze, comb, level, even out, smooth, flatten. **2** (*rake some money together*) collect, gather, amass, accumulate, scrape. **3** (*raked through the documents*) search, comb, scour, hunt, ransack, rifle, rummage. **4** (*rake the street with machine-gun fire*) sweep, pepper, enfilade, search, shower.
rake in earn, receive, make, gather in, bring in (*inf*), pull in (*inf*), pile up, accumulate.
rake up bring up, drag up, call to mind, recollect, revive, raise, mention, remind, introduce.

rake² *noun* debauchee, degenerate, libertine, roué, dissolute, hedonist, sensualist, prodigal, profligate, playboy, womanizer (*inf*), lecher, spendthrift.

rakish *adj* stylish, snazzy (*inf*), natty (*inf*), sporty, smart, dapper, spruce, sharp, flamboyant, flashy, dashing, jaunty, breezy, debonair, nonchalant.

rally *verb* **1** (*rally to the cause*) come together, muster, assemble, unite, meet, gather, collect, congregate, group, regroup, band together, unite, convene. **2** (*rally the men*) muster, bring together, call together, get together, assemble, reassemble, mobilize, organize, round up, marshal, summon. OPPOSITE: disperse. **3** (*she rallied after treatment*) recover, recuperate, revive, improve, get better, get well, mend, pick up, perk up (*inf*), bounce back (*inf*), pull through, gain strength. OPPOSITE: deteriorate.
➤ *noun* **1** (*a peaceful rally*) gathering, meeting, assembly, mass meeting, march, demonstration, convention, conference, convocation, reunion, congregation. **2** (*a rally in their fortunes*) recovery, recuperation, rehabilitation, renewal, revival, improvement, comeback (*inf*), resurgence.

ram *verb* **1** (*he rammed his belongings into a case*) force, drive, thrust, cram, pack, stuff, crowd, jam, wedge, squeeze, compress, tamp. **2** (*ram pegs into the rock*) drive, hammer, pound, hit, strike, beat. **3** (*the boat rammed the lock gates*) hit, strike, run into, crash into, collide with, bump, smash into, dash against, slam into, butt.

ramble *verb* **1** (*rambling in the hills*) walk, hike, stroll, trek, tramp, amble, saunter, traipse, wander, roam, rove, range, meander, stray. **2** (*he rambled on for hours*) digress, drift, wander, expatiate, maunder, babble, gabble, rattle, chatter, waffle, blather, blether, gibber, witter (*inf*), rabbit (*inf*).
➤ *noun* walk, hike, stroll, saunter, wander, trek, roam, tramp, amble, traipse, jaunt, tour, trip, excursion.

rambler *noun* hiker, walker, stroller, traveller, rover, roamer, drifter, wanderer, saunterer, wayfarer.

rambling *adj* **1** (*a rambling privet hedge*) straggling, trailing. **2** (*the rambling medieval streets*) spreading, sprawling, unplanned, unsystematic. **3** (*a rambling discourse*) wandering, roundabout, circuitous, digressive, diffuse, periphrastic, errant, maundering, wordy, verbose, long-winded, long-drawn-out, disjointed, disconnected, incoherent.

ramification *noun* **1** (*the ramifications of this new policy*) development, consequence, upshot, outcome, result, issue, effect, sequel, aftermath, complication, implication. **2** (*a ramification of the main design*) branching, forking, divergence, divarication, branch, limb, offshoot, outgrowth, development, subdivision.

ramp *noun* slope, incline, gradient, rise, grade, acclivity, declivity.

rampage *verb* **1** (*students rampaging in the streets*) run riot, run wild, run amuck, run amok, charge, tear, rush. **2** (*the headteacher rampaged at the class*) rage, rave, rant, storm, go berserk.
➤ *noun* uproar, furore, rage, fury, frenzy, mayhem, turmoil, storm, violence, destruction.
on the rampage rampaging, running amok, going berserk, violent, destructive, frenzied, in a frenzy, out of control, wild.

rampant *adj* **1** (*rampant violence*) unrestrained, uncontrolled, out of control, uncontrollable, ungovernable, out of hand, unchecked, unbridled, excessive, wanton, riotous, widespread, prevalent, epidemic, pandemic. OPPOSITE: controlled. **2** (*rampant undergrowth*) luxuriant, lavish, profuse, exuberant, rife, rank. **3** (*a griffin rampant*) erect, upright, standing, rearing. OPPOSITE: couchant. **4** (*rampant nationalism*) violent, fanatical, radical, vehement, wild, aggressive.

rampart *noun* **1** (*storm the ramparts*) bulwark, fortification, embankment, bank, earthwork, breastwork, parapet, bastion, barricade, fence, wall, stronghold, fort. **2** (*a rampart against inflation*) shield, barrier, buffer, defence, guard, protection, security.

ramshackle *adj* tumbledown, dilapidated, broken-down, run-down, neglected, derelict, ruined, rickety, shaky, unsteady, flimsy, unsafe, decrepit, crumbling, tottering, jerry-built. OPPOSITE: sturdy.

rancid *adj* **1** (*rancid milk*) sour, off, stale, high, bad, rotten, overripe, tainted, turned, gamy, putrid. OPPOSITE: fresh. **2** (*a rancid odour*) rank, stale, sour, musty, stinking, fetid, foul, malodorous, offensive, obnoxious, noxious, noisome, unpleasant.

rancorous *adj* resentful, bitter, acerbic, acrimonious, hostile, spiteful, hateful, malignant, malevolent, splenetic, vindictive, venomous, vengeful, implacable, virulent.

rancour *noun* malice, spite, venom, vindictiveness, ill will, ill feeling, malignity, malevolence, animosity, antipathy, enmity, hostility, hatred, hate, resentment, resentfulness, acrimony, grudge, spleen, bitterness, animus. OPPOSITE: benevolence.

random *adj* haphazard, casual, hit or miss, arbitrary, accidental, chance, fortuitous, unsystematic, unmethodical, unplanned, unpremeditated, unarranged, indiscriminate, irregular, haphazard, sporadic, aimless, purposeless, stray, incidental, hit-or-miss (*inf*), spot, serendipitous. OPPOSITE: deliberate.

at random randomly, haphazardly, incidentally, fortuitously, arbitrarily, sporadically, irregularly, unsystematically, unmethodically, aimlessly, purposelessly, indiscriminately.

range *noun* **1** (*the range of the inquiry*) scope, reach, extent, sweep, spread, compass, limit, limits, bounds, confines, parameters, distance, span, scale, gamut, spectrum, radius, area, field, domain, province, sphere, orbit. **2** (*a range of huts*) line, row, rank, tier, file, string, chain, sequence, series, succession. **3** (*a range of products*) sort, kind, type, variety, array, assortment, selection, class, rank, order, species, genus. **4** (*pots on the range*) stove, cooker, oven, Aga®.
➤ *verb* **1** (*range the products in the window*) align, line up, draw up, order, place, position, dispose, array, arrange. **2** (*ranged according to their price*) rank, class, classify, file, categorize, catalogue, group, grade, bracket, compartmentalize, pigeonhole. **3** (*range from one extreme to another*) extend, stretch, reach, run, go, pass, cover, spread, vary, fluctuate. **4** (*range the countryside*) roam, rove, wander, stray, stroll, drift, meander, amble, ramble, traverse, travel.

rank[1] *noun* **1** (*a high rank within the company*) position, post, station, level, grade, gradation, echelon, mark, condition, stratum, tier. **2** (*a person of rank*) dignity, nobility, status, standing, class, caste, estate. **3** (*ranks of soldiers*) line, row, file, queue, column, string, train, tier, series, procession, succession, formation. **4** (*I don't want any stepping out of rank*) order, alignment, array, arrangement, organization.
➤ *verb* **1** (*how do you rank his achievement?*) rate, class, grade, classify, categorize. **2** (*rank the products by price*) sort, group, arrange, organize, marshal, place, position, align, order, line up, draw up, dispose, array.

rank and file 1 (*the rank and file of the army*) soldiers, private soldiers, ordinary soldiers, troops, men. **2** (*the government hoped for support from the rank and file within the party*) ordinary members, workers. **3** (*the news was not well received by the rank and file*) rabble, masses, populace, public, crowd, herd, mob, common people, riff-raff (*inf*), plebs (*inf*), proletariat, hoi polloi.

rank[2] *adj* **1** (*rank foliage*) exuberant, luxuriant, lush, dense, profuse, abundant, prolific, flourishing, rampant, vigorous, overgrown, spreading. OPPOSITE: scanty. **2** (*a rank odour*) foul, offensive, malodorous, acrid, stinking, smelly, evil-smelling, pungent, rancid, putrid, fetid, rotten, stale, disgusting, obnoxious, noxious, noisome, disagreeable, unpleasant, revolting, sickening, repulsive. OPPOSITE: fresh. **3** (*rank stupidity*) complete, utter, total, sheer, absolute, downright, thorough, thoroughgoing, unmitigated, unqualified, out-and-out, arrant, blatant, flagrant, glaring, gross. **4** (*these rank offences*) vile, outrageous, shocking, lurid, foul, filthy, nasty, coarse, vulgar, gross, immodest, indecorous, obscene, profane, smutty.

rankle *verb* fester, annoy, bug (*inf*), irritate, chafe, vex, peeve, irk, rile, gall, fret, nettle, embitter, anger.

ransack *verb* **1** (*ransacked their bags for drugs*) search, scour, comb, explore, rake, go through, look through, rummage through, rake through, turn inside out, turn

over, turn upside down. **2** (*ransacked the coastal region*) rifle, ravage, devastate, sack, loot, despoil, strip, fleece, raid, plunder, pillage, harry, maraud, rob.

ransom *noun* **1** (*the ransom of the hostages*) release, deliverance, rescue, redemption, restoration, freedom, liberation. **2** (*demand a ransom*) money, payment, pay-off, price.
➤ *verb* rescue, deliver, release, free, set free, liberate.

rant *verb* declaim, hold forth, shout, roar, cry, yell, bellow, bawl, bluster, spout (*inf*), rave, rant and rave, harangue, vociferate, tub-thump (*inf*).
➤ *noun* bombast, rhetoric, bluster, vociferation, declamation, oration, tirade, lecture, harangue, storm, diatribe, shouting, roaring, yelling, crying.

rap *verb* **1** (*the child rapped on the door*) tap, knock, thump, bang, hammer, batter. **2** (*rapped the boy on the knuckles*) hit, strike, clout, whack, tap, cuff, clip, crack. **3** (*the department was rapped for its mistakes*) reprove, rebuke, reprimand, criticize, knock (*inf*), slam (*inf*), slate (*inf*), censure, castigate, punish, blame, scold.
➤ *noun* **1** (*a rap on the door*) tap, knock, knocking, bang, thump, hammering, battering. **2** (*a rap on the knuckles*) tap, blow, hit, stroke, whack, clout, cuff, clip. **3** (*she will have to accept the rap*) blame, flak (*inf*), responsibility, accountability, slating (*inf*), slamming (*inf*), knocking (*inf*), stick (*inf*), rebuke, reprimand, censure, castigation, punishment, sentence, penalty.

rapacious *adj* **1** (*a rapacious old man*) greedy, grasping, avaricious, usurious, ravenous, ravening, voracious, wolfish, wolvish, vulturish, extortionate, insatiable, uncaring, preying, predatory, predacious. **2** (*rapacious pirates*) marauding, plundering, pillaging, looting, robbing.

rape *verb* **1** (*she was raped by her employer*) ravish, violate, assault, deflower, defile, molest, abuse, seduce. **2** (*the whole province was raped by hostile forces*) plunder, pillage, raid, ravage, forage, strip, despoil, spoliate, loot, rob, maraud, sack, ransack, devastate.
➤ *noun* **1** (*charged with the girl's rape*) ravishment, violation, molestation, assault, abuse. **2** (*the rape of the countryside*) plunder, plundering, pillage, pillaging, raiding, rapine, sack, sacking, ransacking, ravaging, marauding, foraging, stripping, looting, devastation, spoliation, despoliation, violation, defilement.

rapid *adj* fast, quick, swift, speedy, fleet, express, expeditious, hurried, hasty, precipitate, headlong, brisk, lively, prompt. OPPOSITE: slow.

rapidity *noun* rapidness, speed, speediness, velocity, quickness, swiftness, fleetness, haste, hurry, rush, dispatch, expedition, expeditiousness, briskness, precipitateness, promptness, promptitude, alacrity, celerity. OPPOSITE: slowness.

rapidly *adv* fast, quickly, speedily, at speed, swiftly, hastily, in haste, hotfoot, hurriedly, briskly, promptly, precipitately, expeditiously.

rapport *noun* sympathy, empathy, understanding, harmony, affinity, bond, link, tie, relationship.

rapt *adj* **1** (*rapt attention*) absorbed, engrossed, preoccupied, intent, lost, pensive, meditative. **2** (*a rapt expression crept over her face*) enthralled, entranced, captivated, fascinated, spellbound, transported, enchanted, bewitched, delighted, charmed, thrilled, enraptured, rapturous, blissful, ecstatic. OPPOSITE: bored.

rapture *noun* ecstasy, bliss, transport, ravishment, enchantment, euphoria, delight, rhapsody, elation, joy, happiness, delectation, felicity, exaltation, exhilaration, enthusiasm. OPPOSITE: sorrow.

rapturous *adj* ecstatic, blissful, transported, in transports, ravished, enchanted, euphoric, rhapsodic, elated, thrilled, enthusiastic, delighted, overjoyed, joyful, joyous, happy, on cloud nine (*inf*), in seventh heaven (*inf*), tickled pink (*inf*), over the moon (*inf*). OPPOSITE: sad.

rare *adj* **1** (*a rare occurrence*) uncommon, unusual, unfamiliar, unique, singular, remarkable, strange, phenomenal, exceptional, atypical, infrequent. **2** (*a rare plant*) uncommon, infrequent, scarce, sparse, scant, few. OPPOSITE: common. **3** (*furniture of rare quality*) excellent, exquisite, fine, choice, superior, superlative, outstanding, first-rate, top-notch (*inf*), incomparable, unparalleled, matchless, peerless, priceless, invaluable, precious, special. OPPOSITE: inferior.

rarely *adv* seldom, infrequently, occasionally, little, hardly, hardly ever, scarcely, scarcely ever, once in a blue moon (*inf*). OPPOSITE: often.

rarity *noun* **1** (*the rarity of such sightings*) infrequency, uncommonness, unusualness, scarcity, sparseness, shortage. **2** (*a collector of rarities*) curiosity, curio, gem, treasure, pearl, wonder, marvel, find, freak.

rascal *noun* **1** (*he has a reputation as a rascal*) scoundrel, rogue, rat (*inf*), good-for-nothing, ne'er-do-well, knave, blackguard, villain, cad, rotter (*inf*), bounder (*inf*), reprobate, wastrel, miscreant, wretch. **2** (*that dog's a little rascal*) imp, devil, scallywag, scamp, mischief.

rash[1] *adj* hasty, precipitate, reckless, thoughtless, heedless, careless, devil-may-care, incautious, imprudent, unguarded, indiscreet, unwary, impetuous, headstrong, hotheaded, harebrained, impulsive, foolhardy, madcap, headlong, precipitate, audacious, daredevil, brash. OPPOSITE: cautious.

rash[2] *noun* **1** (*a rash on her back*) eruption, outbreak, breaking out, hives, urticaria. **2** (*a rash of similar crimes*) outbreak, epidemic, plague, spate, flood, deluge, torrent, wave, series, run, rush, succession.

rasp *verb* **1** (*he rasped the blade against the stone*) scrape, scratch, rub, abrade, grate, grind, file, sand. **2** (*his constant jokes rasp my nerves*) grate, jar, irritate, irk, bug (*inf*), peeve (*inf*). **3** (*she rasped out her demands*) croak, squawk, screech, shrill.
➢ *noun* **1** (*the rasp of the saw*) scrape, scraping, scratch, scratching, grating, grinding. **2** (*hand me that rasp*) file, grater.

rate *noun* **1** (*slow the rate of decline*) speed, velocity, pace, motion, measure, tempo, stride, gait. **2** (*pay the proper rate for the job*) pay, payment, fee, amount, figure, remuneration, hire, charge, price, cost. **3** (*rate of interest*) ratio, proportion, percentage, grade, degree, standard.
➢ *verb* **1** (*the firm is rated very highly by most people*) regard, deem, consider, estimate, reckon, esteem, admire, value. **2** (*they were asked to rate each candidate*) judge, adjudge, value, evaluate, appraise, weigh up, assess, rank, grade, categorize, class, classify. **3** (*this book

rates a commendation at least*) deserve, merit, warrant, justify, be worthy of.

at any rate in any case, anyway, anyhow, nonetheless, nevertheless, regardless, no matter what, in any event, at all events.

rather *adv* **1** (*felt rather deflated*) somewhat, fairly, moderately, relatively, slightly, quite, pretty (*inf*), sort of (*inf*), kind of (*inf*), a bit, a little. OPPOSITE: very. **2** (*she would rather stay in tonight*) sooner, preferably, for preference, instead, from choice.

ratify *verb* authorize, sanction, warrant, approve, consent to, accept, agree to, endorse, confirm, affirm, corroborate, authenticate, validate, authorize, legalize, certify, substantiate, uphold, bear out, establish, settle, sign, countersign, seal, bind. OPPOSITE: repudiate.

rating *noun* **1** (*the rating of the ministry's performance*) assessment, appraisal, adjudging, evaluation, grading, ranking, scoring, marking, classification. **2** (*this confirms his rating among the top ten in the world*) ranking, rank, grading, grade, standing, status, position, placing, designation.

ratio *noun* proportion, symmetry, rate, percentage, fraction, quotient, relation, relationship, correspondence, correlation.

ration *noun* quota, allowance, share, portion, proportion, percentage, allocation, allotment, part, lot, measure, helping, amount.
➢ *verb* **1** (*they rationed out what little food there was*) distribute, issue, give out, hand out, dole out, parcel out, deal out, pass out, divide, share out, measure out, mete out, apportion, allot, allocate. OPPOSITE: withhold. **2** (*the decision to ration petrol*) restrict, limit, control, conserve, save, budget. OPPOSITE: squander.

rational *adj* **1** (*rational processes*) reasoning, thinking, cognitive, cerebral, mental, analytical, logical, conceptual. **2** (*a rational argument*) reasonable, logical, sensible, sound, practical, realistic, right, proper, wise, intelligent, sagacious, judicious, astute, shrewd, perceptive, prudent, discreet, circumspect, politic. **3** (*not in a rational frame of mind*) sane, sound, lucid, coherent, normal, well-balanced, clear-headed, compos mentis, reasoning, thinking. OPPOSITE: irrational.

rationale *noun* logic, reasoning, theory, hypothesis, thesis, principle, exposition, philosophy, reason, motive, motivation, basis, grounds.

rationalize *verb* **1** (*sought to rationalize the crime*) explain, explain away, account for, justify, excuse, make excuses for, make allowances for, vindicate. **2** (*rationalize official policy*) elucidate, clarify, think through, reason out. **3** (*the company is to rationalize its staff*) trim, cut back, streamline, reduce, economize, reorganize.

rations *pl noun* foodstuffs, food, provisions, supplies, stores, victuals.

rattle *verb* **1** (*the gate rattled*) clatter, knock, bang, clang, clank, jangle, clink. **2** (*he rattled the tin*) bang, knock, rap, clatter, clank, jingle, jiggle. **3** (*the train rattled over the points*) bounce, bump, jolt, jar, vibrate, shake. **4** (*the phone call rattled him*) disconcert, discompose, discountenance, confuse, unnerve, unsettle, fluster, faze (*inf*), put off, throw (*inf*), shake, disturb, perturb, upset, frighten, scare. OPPOSITE: reassure.

rattle off reel off, recite, list, run through, repeat.

rattle on chatter, babble, gabble, prattle, yak (*inf*), jabber, gibber, witter (*inf*), rabbit (*inf*), blather, blether, cackle, prate.

raucous *adj* hoarse, husky, harsh, jarring, discordant, dissonant, sharp, grating, rasping, scratching, rough, noisy, strident, shrill, piercing, ear-piercing, screeching. OPPOSITE: soft.

ravage *verb* spoil, mar, ruin, wreck, destroy, shatter, demolish, devastate, lay waste, damage, desolate, pillage, plunder, loot, sack, ransack, raze, level, harry, maraud, despoil. OPPOSITE: preserve.

ravages *pl noun* damage, ruin, havoc, destruction, demolition, devastation, desolation, ruination, wreckage, plunder, pillage, looting, ransacking, rape, rapine, spoliation.

rave *verb* **1** (*we found her raving*) ramble, babble, jabber, gibber, bellow, yell, cry. **2** (*she raved at the class for an hour*) rage, storm, thunder, roar, explode, rant, fume, fly off the handle (*inf*). **3** (*the critics raved about the show*) praise, extol, hail, gush, enthuse, rhapsodize, wax lyrical, acclaim, cry up, go wild, go mad.
» *adj* enthusiastic, rapturous, ecstatic, laudatory, praising, wonderful, favourable, excellent.
» *noun* **1** (*went to a rave last night*) rave-up (*inf*), party, disco, celebration, knees-up (*inf*), do (*inf*), bash (*inf*). **2** (*those colours are all the rave at the moment*) fashion, rage (*inf*), craze (*inf*), trend, vogue, fad.

ravenous *adj* **1** (*ravenous after the walk*) starving, famished, hungry. **2** (*ravenous children*) greedy, gluttonous, rapacious, voracious, insatiable, wolfish, ravening. OPPOSITE: sated.

ravine *noun* gorge, canyon, chasm, abyss, gully, gulf, gulch, defile, pass, gap.

raving *adj* mad, crazy (*inf*), crazed, insane, barmy (*inf*), batty (*inf*), loopy (*inf*), loony (*inf*), irrational, unbalanced, frantic, berserk, frenzied, deranged, demented, delirious, hysterical, raging, rabid, wild, furious. OPPOSITE: composed.

ravish *verb* **1** (*she was ravished by the demon*) rape, violate, assault, deflower, molest, abuse. **2** (*we were ravished by the scenery*) charm, delight, transport, enrapture, captivate, enchant, entrance, bewitch, spellbind, enthral, fascinate. OPPOSITE: repel.

ravishing *adj* charming, delightful, lovely, beautiful, stunning, radiant, gorgeous, alluring, seductive, bewitching, enchanting, entrancing, enthralling, captivating, fascinating, dazzling. OPPOSITE: repulsive.

raw *adj* **1** (*raw meat*) uncooked, fresh. OPPOSITE: cooked. **2** (*raw wheat*) natural, unprocessed, untreated, crude, coarse, unrefined, unfinished, unprepared, unmanufactured. OPPOSITE: processed. **3** (*raw recruits*) green, immature, callow, new, inexperienced, naive, unsophisticated, unseasoned, untested, untried, new, unskilled, untrained, unpractised, ignorant, untutored, unschooled, undisciplined, wet behind the ears (*inf*). OPPOSITE: experienced. **4** (*a raw spot on her leg*) tender, sore, painful, sensitive, scratched, bloody, grazed, abraded, chafed, skinned, excoriated, open, exposed. OPPOSITE: healed. **5** (*a raw wind*) bitter, biting, piercing, penetrating, freezing, cold, chill, chilling, chilly, nippy,

wet, damp, bleak. OPPOSITE: torrid. **6** (*raw talent*) unpolished, unrefined, unsophisticated, crude, rough. **7** (*a raw drama about the poor*) realistic, plain, naked, bare, brutal, blunt, frank, candid, forthright, straightforward, outspoken, unembellished, unvarnished.

ray *noun* **1** (*a ray of sunshine*) beam, shaft, streak, stream, flash, gleam, glint, glimmer, flicker, twinkle. **2** (*a ray of hope*) glimmer, flicker, spark, hint, trace, suggestion, indication.

raze *verb* **1** (*the town was razed to the ground*) demolish, destroy, level, fell, flatten, bulldoze, pull down, tear down, knock down, knock to pieces, take down, ruin, wreck. OPPOSITE: build. **2** (*his words were razed from the record*) erase, efface, obliterate, expunge, delete, strike out, extirpate, annihilate.

reach *verb* **1** (*reach for her hand*) stretch, stretch out, outstretch, hold out, extend, stick out, thrust out, project. **2** (*reach for a pencil*) touch, grasp, seize, get hold of, clutch at, grab at, catch at, strike out. **3** (*reach me down that box*) pass, hand, give. **4** (*reach a conclusion*) get to, arrive at, come to. **5** (*reach perfection*) attain, gain, achieve, accomplish, make, get to, amount to, hit (*inf*). **6** (*they could not reach her*) contact, get hold of, get onto, communicate with, get through to, get in touch with.
» *noun* **1** (*put everything within easy reach*) grasp, distance, stretch, spread, extension, extent, span. **2** (*beyond the reach of the law*) sweep, range, scope, sphere, compass, hold, command, control, influence, sway, authority, jurisdiction, orbit, ambit, territory, area, field, latitude.

react *verb* **1** (*she reacted in an unexpected way*) act, behave, cope, function, conduct oneself, proceed, operate, respond, reply, answer, acknowledge. **2** (*the children reacted against their parents' wishes*) rebel, rise up, oppose, defy, resist, retaliate.

reaction *noun* **1** (*his reaction surprised everyone*) response, reply, answer, acknowledgement, feedback (*inf*). **2** (*a reaction to rising inflation*) retaliation, backlash (*inf*), counteraction, counterbalance, counterpoise, reciprocation, reflex, repercussion, recoil, kickback (*inf*). **3** (*the forces of reaction*) conservatism, ultraconservatism, the right.

reactionary *adj* conservative, ultraconservative, right-wing, rightist, counter-revolutionary, traditional, die-hard, dyed-in-the-wool.
» *noun* conservative, ultraconservative, right-winger, rightist, counter-revolutionary, traditionalist, die-hard.

read *verb* **1** (*read the papers*) peruse, browse through, dip into (*inf*), scan, skim, pore over, look over, look through, look at, leaf through, thumb through, flick through, study, examine, scrutinize, wade through (*inf*). **2** (*he read her mood well*) interpret, decipher, decode, deduce, construe, understand, comprehend. **3** (*he read the essay to his tutor*) recite, deliver, present, declaim, utter, speak. **4** (*the clock read half-past three*) indicate, show, display, record, register, measure.
» *noun* perusal, study, look, scan, scanning, skimming, scrutiny, browse.

read into interpret, infer, deduce, construe, reason, assume, interpolate from, read between the lines (*inf*).

readable *adj* **1** (*readable instructions*) legible, decipherable, clear, intelligible, understandable, comprehensible. OPPOSITE: illegible. **2** (*an eminently readable novel*) interesting, entertaining, pleasant, enjoyable, absorbing, gripping, compulsive, unputdownable (*inf*), enthralling, captivating, stimulating. OPPOSITE: tedious.

readily *adv* **1** (*consented readily to their participation*) willingly, gladly, happily, cheerfully, eagerly, enthusiastically, with pleasure, unhesitatingly, without hesitation, freely, promptly, quickly, swiftly, rapidly, speedily, at once, right away. OPPOSITE: reluctantly. **2** (*the new car readily seats eight*) easily, with ease, effortlessly, smoothly, without difficulty.

readiness *noun* **1** (*the squad is at full readiness*) preparedness, fitness. **2** (*applaud their readiness to join in*) willingness, eagerness, keenness, inclination, gameness (*inf*), aptness. **3** (*the readiness of funds*) availability, accessibility, convenience, handiness. **4** (*the readiness of his replies*) promptness, rapidity, quickness, speed, speediness, swiftness, timeliness, punctuality. **5** (*famed for the readiness of his wit*) sharpness, alertness, keenness, acuteness, aptness, smartness, shrewdness, astuteness, discernment, intelligence, resourcefulness, cleverness, brightness, skill, skilfulness, dexterity, deftness, facility. **in readiness** ready, at the ready, prepared, in preparation, available, accessible, on hand, handy, on tap (*inf*), on standby (*inf*), on call (*inf*), on full alert (*inf*), primed.

reading *noun* **1** (*on her third reading of the article*) perusal, study, browsing, scan, scanning, scrutinization, scrutiny, examination, inspection. **2** (*our reading of the situation*) interpretation, deciphering, decoding, construction, deduction, understanding, comprehension, grasp, impression. **3** (*this is the preferred edition of his works*) version, rendering, rendition. **4** (*the reading in church*) lesson, passage, sermon, recital, recitation, lecture. **5** (*a man of extensive reading*) knowledge, learning, education, erudition, enlightenment, scholarship, attainment, edification. **6** (*make a note of the reading*) level, figure, measurement, indication, display.

ready *adj* **1** (*everything is ready*) prepared, set, all set, primed, fit, arranged, organized, done, completed, finished. **2** (*ready to lend a hand*) willing, agreeable, game (*inf*), eager, enthusiastic, anxious, keen, happy, cheerful, glad, inclined, disposed, predisposed, prone, given, minded, apt. OPPOSITE: reluctant. **3** (*a ready reply*) prompt, immediate, quick, rapid, swift, speedy, timely, punctual. OPPOSITE: slow. **4** (*a ready wit*) sharp, smart, acute, nimble, agile, deft, apt, adroit, skilful, clever, intelligent, bright, astute, keen, perceptive, shrewd, discerning, alert, easy, resourceful. **5** (*a ready supply of hankies*) handy, convenient, accessible, available, near, present, to hand, at hand, on hand, within reach, at one's fingertips (*inf*), on tap (*inf*). OPPOSITE: inaccessible. **6** (*ready to catch fire*) about, liable, likely, in danger of, on the brink of, on the verge of, on the point of.

real *adj* **1** (*in the real world*) actual, positive, factual, existent, existing, substantial, material, physical, tangible, concrete. **2** (*the painting is the real thing*) true,

genuine, authentic, veritable, legitimate, legal, valid, bona fide, official, rightful. OPPOSITE: false. **3** (*she spoke with real feeling*) sincere, earnest, fervent, genuine, heartfelt, honest, true, truthful, unaffected, unfeigned, unpretended, natural. **4** (*a real idiot*) complete, absolute, total, utter, thorough.

realistic *adj* **1** (*not a realistic proposal*) practical, pragmatic, down-to-earth, matter-of-fact, sensible, commonsensical, no-nonsense (*inf*), rational, businesslike, hard-headed, hard-boiled (*inf*), hard-nosed (*inf*), level-headed, clear-sighted, sober, objective, detached, unromantic, unsentimental. OPPOSITE: idealistic. **2** (*a realistic portrait*) natural, naturalistic, lifelike, true-to-life, faithful, close, graphic, vivid, real, authentic, genuine, truthful. OPPOSITE: unrealistic.

reality *noun* **1** (*brought back to reality with a bump*) real world, real life, actuality, existence, substantiality, corporeality, materiality, tangibility. OPPOSITE: imagination. **2** (*the reality of the situation*) truth, verity, fact, actuality. **3** (*the reality of the special effects*) realism, genuineness, authenticity, validity, verisimilitude.

realization *noun* **1** (*the realization that something was wrong*) awareness, appreciation, apprehension, comprehension, perception, discernment, recognition, consciousness, understanding, grasp, cognizance. **2** (*the realization of his dream*) accomplishment, fulfilment, achievement, consummation, fruition, effecting, implementation, actualization, performance. **3** (*the realization of massive profits*) earning, clearing, obtaining, gain, making, fetching.

realize *verb* **1** (*he quickly realized his mistake*) understand, comprehend, apprehend, be aware of, be conscious of, take in, catch on, grasp, learn, twig (*inf*), cotton on (*inf*), perceive, recognize, appreciate, conceive, discern, ascertain, discover, glean, know. OPPOSITE: misunderstand. **2** (*realize all her dreams*) fulfil, accomplish, achieve, carry out, perform, actualize, effect, effectuate, consummate, complete, bring about, bring off, bring to fruition, execute, make happen, implement. **3** (*realize a huge profit on the deal*) make, earn, clear, fetch, produce, net, sell for, bring in, get, obtain, acquire, gain.

really *adv* **1** (*this was not really accurate*) actually, in reality, in actuality, in fact, in truth, truly. **2** (*his arrest was really serious*) indeed, truly, surely, verily, genuinely, sincerely, certainly, assuredly, positively, absolutely, categorically, unquestionably, undoubtedly, without a doubt, indubitably. **3** (*a really bad idea*) very, extremely, exceptionally, remarkably, severely, highly, intensely, thoroughly, decidedly, truly.

realm *noun* **1** (*plague swept the realm*) kingdom, monarchy, country, land, empire, principality, state, domain, dominion, province, region, territory. **2** (*the realm of literature*) field, area, orbit, sphere, world, domain, zone, department, branch.

reap *verb* **1** (*reap this year's harvest*) cut, crop, harvest, mow, glean, gather in, bring in, take in, garner. OPPOSITE: sow. **2** (*reap the rewards of hard work*) get, obtain, acquire, secure, procure, receive, gain, win, collect, derive, realize.

rear *noun* **1** (*the rear of the bus*) back, back end, end, tail

end. OPPOSITE: front. **2** (*the animal's rear*) hind, hind part, tail, rump, behind, bottom, backside (*inf*), buttocks, posterior, stern.
➤ *adj* back, hind, hindmost, rearmost, last, tail-end.
➤ *verb* **1** (*rear a large family*) raise, bring up, nurse, nurture, look after, care for, foster, parent, train, instruct, educate. **2** (*rear organic pigs*) breed, keep, tend, grow, cultivate. **3** (*rear scaffolding against the tower*) put up, set up, stand up. **4** (*rear up buildings on all sides*) erect, build, construct, put up. OPPOSITE: demolish. **5** (*the horse reared its head*) raise, upraise, elevate, lift, hold up, hoist. OPPOSITE: lower. **6** (*the spire reared up against the sky*) rise, tower, loom, soar.

reason *noun* **1** (*she had a good reason to stay*) cause, ground, basis, motive, motivation, incentive, impetus, inducement, instigation. **2** (*they could give no reason for their failures*) excuse, justification, vindication, defence, explanation, argument, case, apology, rationale. **3** (*employ reason to solve the case*) intellect, intellectuality, mind, wit, brains (*inf*), gumption (*inf*), intelligence, understanding, apprehension, comprehension, sense, rationality, judgement, wisdom, sanity, reasoning, thought, logic. OPPOSITE: folly. **4** (*she has lost her reason*) sanity, mind, senses. **5** (*it stands to reason*) reasonableness, sense, common sense, practicability, practicality.
➤ *verb* **1** (*difficult to reason under such pressure*) think, ponder, consider, deliberate, cogitate, intellectualize, ratiocinate, analyse. **2** (*he reasoned that they must have already left*) conclude, deduce, infer, work out, reckon, solve, think, surmise. **3** (*no use reasoning with them*) argue, debate, dispute, discuss, talk over, prevail upon, plead, remonstrate, urge, persuade, dissuade, coax.
within reason in moderation, moderately, within limits, within bounds.

reasonable *adj* **1** (*a reasonable employer*) equitable, fair, just, impartial, unbiased, dispassionate, disinterested OPPOSITE: mad. **2** (*a reasonable course of action*) sensible, logical, practical, rational, sane, sober, wise, intelligent, sound, judicious, sagacious, advisable, well-advised, reasoned, justifiable, arguable, admissible, viable, credible, tenable, plausible, right, proper. **3** (*a reasonable price*) modest, inexpensive, cheap, low, low-priced, moderate. **4** (*we had a reasonable evening*) tolerable, passable, satisfactory, fair, acceptable, average, OK (*inf*). OPPOSITE: unreasonable.

reasoned *adj* clear, logical, sensible, sound, rational, judicious, methodical, systematic, organized, well-thought-out, well-expressed, well-presented.

reasoning *noun* **1** (*by process of reasoning*) reason, logic, deduction, analysis, interpretation, thought, thinking, rationalization, cerebration. **2** (*let's examine his reasoning*) theory, hypothesis, argument, supposition, interpretation, rationale, case.

reassure *verb* comfort, encourage, hearten, cheer, put at ease (*inf*), put one's mind at rest (*inf*), buoy up, brace, bolster, embolden, rally, inspirit. OPPOSITE: perturb.

rebate *noun* refund, repayment, discount, reduction, deduction, allowance, decrease. OPPOSITE: surcharge.

rebel *noun* **1** (*rebels have seized the capital*) revolutionary, revolutionist, insurrectionist, insurgent, agitator, revolter, mutineer, anarchist, seditionist, guerrilla, freedom fighter, traitor. **2** (*rebels within the church*) heretic, dissenter, nonconformist, apostate, schismatic, recusant.
➤ *verb* **1** (*rebel against their masters*) revolt, rise up, mutiny, riot, take to the streets. **2** (*rebel against her wishes*) resist, defy, disobey. **3** (*she rebelled at the idea of physical contact*) recoil from, shy away from, pull back from, shrink from, flinch from.
➤ *adj* **1** (*rebel forces*) revolutionary, insurgent, insurrectionary, mutinous, mutinying. **2** (*rebel factions within the party*) rebellious, disobedient, defiant, resistant, recalcitrant, malcontent.

rebellion *noun* **1** (*the rebellion spread quickly through the army*) revolt, revolution, insurgence, insurgency, insurrection, rising, uprising, coup, riot, mutiny, sedition, resistance. **2** (*rebellion against authority*) defiance, resistance, opposition, disobedience, insubordination, dissent, nonconformity, heresy, apostasy, schism, recusancy.

rebellious *adj* **1** (*rebellious factions within the navy*) revolutionary, rebel, rebelling, insurgent, insurrectionary, seditious, rioting, mutinous, mutinying. **2** (*rebellious behaviour in class*) unruly, defiant, insubordinate, disobedient, ungovernable, unmanageable, intractable, incorrigible, obstinate, refractory, recalcitrant, disorderly, turbulent, contumacious. OPPOSITE: submissive.

rebound *verb* **1** (*the ball rebounded off the wall*) bounce back, ricochet, recoil, spring back, return, boomerang, resound, reverberate. **2** (*their plan threatened to rebound on them*) backfire, misfire, come back, come home to roost (*int*).
➤ *noun* **1** (*caught the ball on the rebound*) bounce, ricochet, spring, recoil, return. **2** (*the rebound of the negative campaign ruined them all*) backfiring, misfiring, repercussion.

rebuff *verb* snub, reject, decline, repel, repudiate, repulse, check, resist, spurn, fend off, stave off, discourage, refuse, turn away, turn down, slight, cut, put down (*inf*), cold-shoulder (*inf*). OPPOSITE: accept.
➤ *noun* **1** (*the rebuff of all their suggestions*) rejection, refusal, repudiation, repulsion, spurning, discouragement, cold shouldering. (*Inf*) **2** (*he was hurt by her rebuffs*) snub, check, repulse, slight, cut, cold shoulder (*inf*), put-down (*inf*), brush-off (*inf*), slap in the face (*inf*), kick in the teeth (*inf*). OPPOSITE: acceptance.

rebuke *verb* scold, chide, upbraid, berate, castigate, reprove, reprehend, reproach, reprimand, admonish, tell off (*inf*), tick off (*inf*), bawl out (*inf*), take to task (*inf*), haul over the coals (*inf*), tear off a strip (*inf*), carpet (*inf*), lecture, censure, blame, lambaste, rate, remonstrate with. OPPOSITE: commend.
➤ *noun* scolding, dressing-down (*inf*), castigation, reproof, reproach, reproval, reprimand, admonition, telling-off (*inf*), ticking-off (*inf*), dressing-down (*inf*), bawling-out (*inf*), bollocking (*sl*), carpeting (*inf*), lecture, censure, blame, lambasting, remonstration. OPPOSITE: praise.

rebut *verb* refute, deny, disprove, negate, invalidate, discredit, confute, contradict, defeat, quash, overturn, explode (*inf*), give the lie to. OPPOSITE: support.

recalcitrant *adj* disobedient, insubordinate, refractory, contumacious, intractable, ungovernable, unmanageable, uncontrollable, unruly, defiant, rebellious, mutinous, uncooperative, headstrong, wilful, wayward, perverse, obstinate, stubborn, obdurate, contrary. OPPOSITE: amenable.

recall *verb* **1** (*I recall one particular incident*) remember, call to mind, recollect. OPPOSITE: forget. **2** (*happy hours recalling one's childhood*) reminisce about, look back on, think back to, hark back to. **3** (*such music recalls a simpler age*) evoke, call to mind, summon up. **4** (*he recalled the envoys*) summon, call back, order back, bring back. **5** (*her authority was recalled*) revoke, retract, withdraw, take back, repeal, rescind, countermand, overrule, veto, annul, nullify, invalidate, cancel, override, abrogate, recant, abjure.
➤ *noun* **1** (*times beyond recall*) memory, remembrance, recollection, reminiscence. **2** (*the recall of the order*) revocation, retraction, withdrawal, rescinding, repeal, countermanding, veto, vetoing, annulment, nullification, invalidation, cancellation, abrogation, recision.

recant *verb* withdraw, retract, revoke, recall, deny, disavow, disclaim, disown, repudiate, renege on, renounce, relinquish, abjure, forswear, take back, rescind, unsay, cancel, annul, repeal. OPPOSITE: maintain.

recapitulate *verb* restate, resay, repeat, reiterate, review, go over, run over, summarize, sum up, recount, recap (*inf*).

recede *verb* **1** (*the waters slowly receded*) retreat, withdraw, retire, return, go back, fall back, move back, move away, ebb, abate, sink, subside, slacken. OPPOSITE: advance. **2** (*the threat has now receded*) lessen, decrease, diminish, decline, dwindle, shrink, wane, fall off, drop, taper off, peter out, fade.

receipt *noun* **1** (*acknowledge receipt of the parcel*) delivery, acceptance, reception, receiving, recipience. **2** (*take the receipt back to the shop*) proof of purchase, sales slip, slip, counterfoil, stub, ticket, voucher, acknowledgement.

receipts *pl noun* takings, proceeds, profits, gains, income, turnover.

receive *verb* **1** (*received the money gratefully*) accept, take, be in receipt of, inherit. OPPOSITE: give. **2** (*receive permission from the authorities*) get, obtain, acquire, derive, come by, take, collect, gather. **3** (*they received the news with alarm*) hear, learn, find out about, gather, perceive, take, react to, respond to. **4** (*receive a severe beating*) suffer, undergo, sustain, experience, bear, endure, go through, meet with, encounter. **5** (*she received her guests at the door*) admit, greet, welcome, entertain. **6** (*this gun magazine will receive twenty bullets*) hold, accommodate, take, contain, admit.

recent *adj* modern, late, latest, latter, latter-day, new, novel, fresh, young, current, up-to-date, up-to-the-minute, contemporary, present-day. OPPOSITE: old.

recently *adv* newly, freshly, lately, of late, not long ago, a short time ago, a little while back.

receptacle *noun* container, vessel, holder, repository.

reception *noun* **1** (*reception of the letter that same day*) receipt, receiving, acceptance. **2** (*her announcement got a warm reception*) response, welcome, acknowledgement, recognition, reaction, treatment. **3** (*reception of the guests*) greeting, welcoming. **4** (*host a reception at the local hotel*) party, function, social, gathering, get-together, do (*inf*), bash (*inf*), shindig (*inf*), entertainment, soirée.

receptive *adj* open, open-minded, flexible, willing, amenable, accommodating, accessible, approachable, friendly, sympathetic, interested, perceptive, sensitive, responsive, alert, bright, quick, keen, suggestible, susceptible.

recess *noun* **1** (*a recess in the wall*) alcove, niche, nook, corner, bay, hollow, indentation, cavity. OPPOSITE: projection. **2** (*parliament is in recess*) break, interval, intermission, rest, respite, breather (*inf*), holiday, vacation, time off, time out (*inf*).

recesses *pl noun* depths, reaches, interior, innards (*inf*), bowels, heart, retreat, refuge, sanctum.

recession *noun* **1** (*economic recession*) depression, slump, decline, downturn, failure, collapse, crash, trough, slide, hard times (*inf*). **2** (*the recession of the waters*) retreat, receding, withdrawal, ebbing, abatement.

recipe *noun* **1** (*follow the recipe in the book*) directions, instructions, guide. **2** (*the recipe for success*) formula, prescription, method, process, procedure, way, means, technique, modus operandi, system, ingredients.

recipient *noun* receiver, beneficiary, legatee, assignee. OPPOSITE: donor.

reciprocal *adj* **1** (*a reciprocal gesture*) return, returned, requited, retaliated. **2** (*an atmosphere of reciprocal respect*) mutual, common, shared, exchanged, reciprocative, reciprocatory, interchangeable, alternate, alternating, complementary, corresponding, equivalent, correlative, give-and-take. OPPOSITE: one-sided.

reciprocate *verb* **1** (*reciprocate her generosity*) return, give back, give in return, requite, repay. **2** (*reciprocate memories*) exchange, swap, trade, barter, interchange, alternate, correspond, equal, match. **3** (*will the other side reciprocate?*) respond, respond in kind, reply, do the same.

recital *noun* **1** (*a recital of ancient church music*) performance, concert, solo, show. **2** (*the recital of blank verse*) recitation, speaking, saying, reading, rendering, rendition, declaiming, repetition. **3** (*offer a recital of the main points*) enumeration, detailing, itemizing, specification. **4** (*a recital of the bard's early life*) account, narration, narrative, report, record, description, relation, recapitulation, recounting, telling, chronicle, history, tale, story.

recitation *noun* **1** (*listen to the recitation of poetry*) recital, reciting, saying, narration, rendering, rendition, reading, declamation. **2** (*we enjoyed the recitations particularly*) reading, monologue, passage, piece, story, tale, poem, verse.

recite *verb* **1** (*recite extracts of the play*) repeat, rehearse, read aloud, speak, declaim, render, deliver, relate, tell, say, articulate, perform. **2** (*recite a long list of complaints*) narrate, recount, recapitulate, relate, detail, describe, enumerate, specify, particularize, itemize, list, reel off, rattle off.

reckless *adj* rash, heedless, unheeding, thoughtless,

careless, imprudent, incautious, inattentive, negligent, regardless, injudicious, ill-advised, unwise, foolish, harebrained, irresponsible, hasty, rash, impetuous, impulsive, foolhardy, madcap, daredevil, devil-may-care, headlong, wild, tearaway, irresponsible, precipitate, indiscreet. OPPOSITE: cautious.

reckon *verb* **1** (*we reckon it is over*) think, believe, imagine, fancy, suppose, assume, presume, guess, surmise, conjecture. **2** (*reckoned very highly by his colleagues*) consider, regard, look upon, deem, think of, judge, esteem, rate, estimate, value, evaluate, gauge, count, appraise, assess. **3** (*reckon the cost*) calculate, compute, work out, add up, total, tally, count, enumerate, number, figure. **4** (*he can reckon on a hot reception*) rely, depend, count, bank, trust, bargain, figure, expect, anticipate, plan, hope.

reckon with 1 (*we failed to reckon with a change in the weather*) anticipate, expect, foresee, bargain, take into account, take into consideration, take note of, allow for, plan for, bear in mind. **2** (*a new problem to reckon with*) cope with, deal with, contend with, handle, treat, face.

reckoning *noun* **1** (*the latest reckoning of the time this might take*) calculation, computation, working-out, addition, count, score, estimate, tally, total, summation. **2** (*the reckoning of all his debts*) settlement, payment, paying, discharging, squaring, clearance, defrayal. **3** (*bring us the reckoning*) account, bill, charge, tally, due, score, tab (*inf*), check (*inf*). **4** (*the day of reckoning for mankind*) doom, fate, judgment, settlement, retribution, punishment, damnation. **5** (*not the best in my reckoning*) opinion, view, estimation, assessment, evaluation, judgement, appraisal.

reclaim *verb* **1** (*they reclaimed their bags*) recover, retrieve, regain, get back, take back, claim back. **2** (*reclaim land for agriculture*) redeem, reinstate, retrieve, rescue, save, salvage, restore, recycle, convert. **3** (*a campaign to reclaim drug addicts*) save, redeem, rescue, reform, regenerate.

recline *verb* lean, lie, lie down, rest, repose, loll, lounge, sprawl, stretch out. OPPOSITE: stand.

recluse *noun* hermit, solitary, loner (*Inf*), anchorite, anchoress, eremite, ascetic, monk, nun.

recognition *noun* **1** (*recognition of her own parents*) identification, spotting, recollection, knowing. **2** (*recognition of the possibilities*) appreciation, realization, acknowledgement, perception, awareness, consciousness, understanding, knowledge. **3** (*finally won recognition of their rights*) acknowledgement, acceptance, admission, admittance, approval, validation, ratification, endorsement, sanctioning, granting. **4** (*she deserved greater recognition for her achievements*) acknowledgement, appreciation, respect, homage, applause, salute, salutation, reward, honour, bouquets (*inf*), gratitude, thankfulness.

recognize *verb* **1** (*recognize his old home*) identify, know, place, notice, spot, pick out, tell, remember, recall, recollect, call to mind. **2** (*recognize where we went wrong*) acknowledge, admit, own, grant, allow, concede, confess, accept, respect, see, perceive, discern, appreciate, realize, understand, apprehend. OPPOSITE: deny. **3** (*recognize their rights*) acknowledge, accept,

allow, admit, endorse, sanction, concede, grant, approve, validate, ratify, uphold. **4** (*his efforts should be recognized*) honour, respect, reward, salute, applaud, greet, appreciate, be thankful for. OPPOSITE: ignore.

recoil *verb* **1** (*the wire recoiled*) rebound, spring back, fly back. **2** (*she recoiled at the suggestion*) shy away, draw back, shrink, flinch, balk, quail, falter, start, hesitate, wince, cower. **3** (*his cunning has recoiled on him*) rebound, come back on, boomerang, backfire, misfire, go wrong. **4** (*the musket recoiled against his shoulder*) kick, kick back, jerk back, pull.
➤ *noun* **1** (*the recoil of the musket*) kick, kickback, pull. **2** (*the recoil from the campaign*) backlash, reaction, repercussion, consequence, rebound.

recollect *verb* remember, recall, reminisce, call to mind, cast one's mind back, think of, summon up, place. OPPOSITE: forget.

recollection *noun* memory, recall, remembrance, reminiscence, impression.

recommend *verb* **1** (*do as the doctor recommends*) advise, counsel, suggest, propose, put forward, advance, prescribe, urge, advocate, enjoin, exhort, guide. OPPOSITE: discourage. **2** (*we can recommend the restaurant on the corner*) praise, commend, promote, plug (*inf*), approve, endorse, vouch for. OPPOSITE: disapprove.

recommendation *noun* **1** (*recommendation of such procedures*) commendation, endorsement, sanction, advocacy. **2** (*at the recommendation of his advisers*) urging, advising, counselling. **3** (*the recommendations of the board of inquiry*) proposal, conclusion, advice, counsel, guidance, exhortation, enjoinder. **4** (*give me your recommendations for this week's films*) commendation, endorsement, tip, hint, suggestion, proposal, approval, praise, plug (*inf*), testimonial. **5** (*a property without a single recommendation to it*) advantage, good point, benefit, blessing, favourable aspect.

recompense *verb* pay, reward, remunerate, repay, reimburse, indemnify, compensate, redress, requite, satisfy, make amends.
➤ *noun* compensation, indemnity, indemnification, amends, damages, redress, reparation, restitution, requital, remuneration, reward, payment, repayment, reimbursement, satisfaction.

reconcile *verb* **1** (*reconcile the warring parties*) reunite, bring together, conciliate, propitiate, appease, mollify, pacify, placate, make peace between, bring to terms, shake hands (*inf*), make up (*inf*), forgive and forget (*inf*), bury the hatchet (*inf*). OPPOSITE: alienate. **2** (*reconcile their argument*) settle, resolve, square, adjust, attune, harmonize, accommodate, mend, patch up, remedy, heal, cure, put to rights, rectify. **3** (*reconciled to defeat*) accept, resign, submit, yield. OPPOSITE: oppose.

reconciliation *noun* **1** (*the reconciliation of the two parties*) reuniting, conciliation, bringing together, appeasement, rapprochement, pacification, placating, propitiation, mollification. **2** (*the reconciliation of their feud*) settling, settlement, squaring, resolving, resolution, mending, remedying, accommodation. **3** (*the war ended in reconciliation*) peace, harmony, agreement, compromise, concord, amity, end of hostilities.

recondite *adj* obscure, abstruse, abstract, esoteric,

profound, deep, mystical, hidden, concealed, secret, cryptic, occult, arcane, mysterious, dark, difficult, complex, complicated, intricate, involved, incomprehensible, inscrutable. OPPOSITE: patent.

reconnaissance *noun* recce (*inf*), reconnoitring, spying, scouting, search, survey, exploration, expedition, patrol, probe, investigation, examination, scrutiny, scan, inspection, observation.

reconnoitre *verb* recce (*inf*), survey, spy out, scout, patrol, explore, inspect, examine, investigate, scrutinize, view, observe, scan, case (*inf*), check out (*inf*), take stock of.

reconsider *verb* think over, rethink, review, revise, re-evaluate, re-examine, reassess, think better of, think twice, think again, have second thoughts.

reconstruct *verb* **1** (*reconstruct the shed*) rebuild, reassemble, remake, refashion, remodel, restore, renovate, recondition, revamp, regenerate. OPPOSITE: destroy. **2** (*reconstruct the situation*) recreate, re-enact, piece together. **3** (*reconstruct the government*) reorganize, rearrange, reform, shuffle, overhaul, redo, do over, make over.

record *noun* **1** (*consulted the official record*) journal, diary, history, chronicle, memoir, annals, archives, minutes, log, logbook, register, document, documentation, file, dossier, memorandum, note, account, report, entry, data. **2** (*a black spot on his record*) reputation, history, life history, background, career, curriculum vitae, past performance. **3** (*play this record*) recording, disc, CD, compact disc, album, LP, single, platter (*inf*), mini disc, vinyl, release. **4** (*a record of the occasion*) souvenir, token, memorial, memoir, remembrance, testimony, testimonial, witness, evidence, trace.
➤ *verb* **1** (*record everything on paper*) enter, note, write down, put in writing, inscribe, transcribe, put down, set down, take down, enter, register, enrol, log, list, catalogue, minute, document, file, chronicle, preserve, keep. **2** (*record the band live*) tape, video, videotape, cut. **3** (*this dial records air pressure*) register, read, indicate, show, display, express.
off the record confidential, in confidence, private, secret, sub rosa, unofficial, not for publication.
on record 1 (*the worst winter on record*) recorded, documented, noted. **2** (*her objections are on record*) noted, documented, registered, known.

recorder *noun* **1** (*switch on the recorder*) tape recorder, cassette recorder, video recorder, video. **2** (*the official recorder*) record keeper, registrar, archivist, annalist, clerk, stenographer, secretary, scribe. **3** (*a recorder of his age*) diarist, chronicler, chronologer, historian.

recording *noun* record, album, disc, gramophone record, vinyl, compact disc, CD, tape, tape recording, mini disc, DVD, video recording, video.

recount *verb* **1** (*recount the legend of the mountain*) narrate, relate, tell, communicate, impart, unfold, repeat. **2** (*recounted everything that had happened*) report, recite, cite, repeat, rehearse, detail, specify, enumerate, itemize, particularize, catalogue, list, describe, depict, portray.

recoup *verb* **1** (*try to recoup their belongings*) regain,

recover, retrieve, get back, win back, repossess, redeem, make good. **2** (*hoped to recoup them for their losses*) pay back, repay, refund, recompense, compensate, indemnify, reimburse.

recourse *noun* resort, refuge, way out, resource, choice, option, possibility, alternative, expedient, remedy.

recover *verb* **1** (*hoped to recover his fortune*) regain, recoup, get back, win back, retrieve, reclaim, repossess, recapture, redeem. OPPOSITE: lose. **2** (*she should recover quickly with treatment*) get better, get well, pull through, come round, improve, mend, heal, rally, revive, pick up, perk up (*inf*), bounce back, recuperate, convalesce, gain strength. OPPOSITE: deteriorate. **3** (*recover usable material from rubbish*) rescue, save, salvage, retrieve, reclaim, recycle, restore, redeem.

recovery *noun* **1** (*the recovery of the missing parts*) retrieval, reclamation, repossession, recapture, redemption, restoration. OPPOSITE: loss. **2** (*the patient is making a good recovery*) recuperation, convalescence, rally, revival, improvement, amelioration, cure, healing, rehabilitation. OPPOSITE: relapse. **3** (*a marked improvement in the balance of trade*) improvement, upturn, upswing, amelioration, betterment. **4** (*the recovery of plutonium from radioactive waste*) reclamation, retrieval, recycling, salvaging, rescue.

recreation *noun* **1** (*time devoted to recreation*) relaxation, refreshment, fun, play, sport, exercise, enjoyment, pleasure, entertainment, amusement, distraction, diversion, leisure, restoration. **2** (*includes mountaineering among his recreations*) hobby, pastime, amusement, diversion, distraction. OPPOSITE: work.

recrimination *noun* countercharge, counter-attack, retaliation, retort, retribution, reprisal, vengeance, accusation, counter-accusation.

recruit *verb* **1** (*recruit volunteers for the militia*) enlist, draft, call up, conscript, mobilize, levy, muster, round up, enrol, sign up, engage, take on, obtain, acquire, procure. OPPOSITE: dismiss. **2** (*the need to recruit a team of expert advisers*) put together, gather, assemble, muster, form, raise. **3** (*in an attempt to recruit the funds of the society*) renew, replenish, reinforce, strengthen, fortify, augment, increase, enlarge, add to, build up, shore up, beef up (*inf*), supply, furnish.
➤ *noun* **1** (*naval recruits*) conscript, enlistee, draftee, volunteer. **2** (*we must attract new recruits to the company*) newcomer, supporter, helper, novice, rookie (*inf*), beginner, initiate, learner, trainee, apprentice, neophyte. OPPOSITE: veteran.

rectify *verb* correct, right, put right, set right, redress, reform, remedy, fix, mend, repair, improve, ameliorate, better, make good, amend, emend, adjust, square, straighten, regulate.

rectitude *noun* **1** (*a man of moral rectitude*) uprightness, righteousness, virtue, goodness, decency, integrity, honesty, probity, incorruptibility, scrupulousness, morality, principle, honour, justice, equity. OPPOSITE: corruption. **2** (*the rectitude of this conclusion*) correctness, verity, accuracy, precision, exactitude, exactness, soundness.

rector *noun* cleric, clergyman, churchman, ecclesiastic, parson, vicar, minister, pastor. OPPOSITE: layman.

recumbent *adj* lying, reclining, leaning, resting, sprawling, prostrate, flat, horizontal, supine, prone. OPPOSITE: erect.

recuperate *verb* **1** (*time to recuperate from his wounds*) recover, convalesce, improve, get better, get well, mend, heal, pick up, perk up (*inf*), rally, revive, regain strength, pull through, bounce back. OPPOSITE: decline. **2** (*they hope to recuperate these losses in the long term*) recover, recoup, get back, regain, retrieve, reclaim, make good.

recur *verb* repeat, happen again, return, come back, reappear, persist, come and go.

recurrent *adj* recurring, repeated, repetitive, reiterative, frequent, regular, periodic, cyclical, intermittent, chronic, persistent, continual, habitual.

recycle *verb* reuse, reprocess, recover, reclaim, salvage, save.

red *adj* **1** (*red poppies*) reddish, crimson, cardinal, carmine, scarlet, ruby, cherry, rose, vermilion, maroon, wine, claret, auburn, russet, coral. **2** (*a red complexion*) rosy, ruddy, florid, glowing, blooming, blushing, flushed, bloodshot, inflamed, rubicund, roseate. OPPOSITE: pallid. **3** (*red hair*) ginger, flame-coloured, auburn, Titian, orange, sandy, foxy, chestnut, carroty. **4** (*the red faction within the party*) Communist, commie (*inf*), left-wing, leftist, lefty (*inf*), revolutionary, Bolshevik.
≫ *noun* **1** (*see how the artist has used lots of red*) crimson, scarlet, vermilion, maroon. **2** (*kick the reds out of the union*) Communist, commie (*inf*), socialist, left-winger, leftist, lefty (*inf*), revolutionary, Bolshevik.
in the red overdrawn, in debt, in debit, in arrears, owing money, insolvent, bankrupt, broke (*inf*), bust (*inf*), penniless, impoverished, on the rocks (*inf*).
see red go mad, lose one's temper, explode, boil over, seethe, blow one's top (*inf*), hit the roof (*inf*), fly off the handle (*inf*), lose one's rag (*inf*), lose one's cool (*inf*), lose it (*inf*).

redden *verb* go red, blush, flush, colour, crimson, suffuse.

redeem *verb* **1** (*plans to redeem his property tomorrow*) recover, regain, reclaim, get back, retrieve, repossess, recoup, recuperate, buy back, ransom. **2** (*a campaign to redeem sinners*) save, purge, absolve, convert, rehabilitate, reinstate. OPPOSITE: surrender. **3** (*his wish to redeem all political prisoners*) deliver, free, set free, liberate, emancipate, release, ransom, acquit, discharge, rescue, save. **4** (*this offer must be redeemed in person*) exchange, cash in, trade in, turn in, convert. **5** (*they should redeem their obligations*) discharge, fulfil, execute, perform, carry out, hold to, adhere to, abide by, make good, meet, satisfy, keep, obey. **6** (*this kindness redeemed his past cruelty to some extent*) expiate, make amends for, make up for, atone for, redress, offset, compensate for, outweigh.

redemption *noun* **1** (*the redemption of our luggage*) recovery, reclamation, retrieval, repossession. **2** (*the redemption of the prisoners*) freeing, emancipation, liberation, release, ransom, rescue, saving, salvation, deliverance, rehabilitation. **3** (*this goes some way towards the redemption of past sins*) expiation, atonement, reparation, redress, compensation, vindication. **4** (*he prayed for redemption*) deliverance, absolution, salvation.

5 (*the redemption of his promise*) fulfilment, discharge, making good, execution, adherence, meeting, satisfying.

redolent *adj* **1** (*a perfume redolent of pineapples*) fragrant, scented, perfumed, aromatic, odoriferous, smelling, sweet-smelling, reeking. OPPOSITE: malodorous. **2** (*tales redolent of a more innocent age*) reminiscent, remindful, suggestive, evocative.

redoubtable *adj* formidable, awe-inspiring, fearsome, strong, mighty, powerful, resolute, terrible, dreadful, awful, fearful. OPPOSITE: derisible.

redound *verb* **1** (*her kindness redounded to her good reputation*) conduce to, contribute to, lead to, tend to, result in, ensue in, affect. **2** (*his disloyalty will surely redound on him*) recoil on, rebound on, come back on.

redress *verb* **1** (*redress their mistake*) rectify, right, put right, set right, correct, remedy, make amends for, make up for, make restitution for, compensate for, recompense for, atone for, repair, fix. **2** (*redress the balance between the two sides*) amend, put right, correct, improve, adjust, regulate, even up.
≫ *noun* rectification, correction, remedy, remedying, putting right, cure, compensation, recompense, amends, amending, atonement, reparation, restitution, satisfaction, justice, relief, assistance, help, aid. OPPOSITE: wrong.

reduce *verb* **1** (*reduce the dimensions of the craft*) lessen, lower, diminish, decrease, shorten, cut, abridge, curtail, attenuate, contract, shrink, slim, abbreviate, moderate, alleviate, mitigate, abate. OPPOSITE: increase. **2** (*reduce the level of alcohol in the wine*) dilute, diminish, lower, deplete, weaken, impair. **3** (*reduced to penury*) bring to, drive to, force to. **4** (*reduced by the collapse in their business*) ruin, impoverish, bankrupt, break. **5** (*reduce to the ranks*) demote, downgrade, lower, degrade, debase, humble, humiliate. OPPOSITE: exalt. **6** (*reduce in price*) discount, lower, mark down, make cheaper, cheapen, cut, slash, knock down, put on sale. OPPOSITE: raise. **7** (*reduce the cities of their conquered enemy*) subdue, quell, crush, conquer, vanquish, overcome, overrun, overpower, overwhelm, master, subjugate.

reduction *noun* **1** (*a reduction in velocity*) lessening, lowering, diminution, decrease, drop, fall, decline, cut, cutback, abatement, moderation, alleviation, dilution, weakening, contraction, abbreviation, curtailment, restriction, limitation. **2** (*reduction to the ranks*) demotion, downgrading, lowering, humbling. **3** (*a big reduction in the price*) discount, cut, concession, deduction, devaluation, depreciation, allowance, rebate. **4** (*news of the reduction of their home town*) conquering, vanquishing, overpowering, overrunning, subjugation.

redundant *adj* **1** (*redundant information*) superfluous, unnecessary, inessential, de trop, surplus, unneeded, unwanted, supernumerary, extra, excessive. OPPOSITE: essential. **2** (*redundant workers crowded the job centre*) unemployed, laid off, out of work, jobless, on the dole (*inf*), idle, sacked (*inf*), fired (*inf*), dismissed. **3** (*a piece full of redundant description*) verbose, wordy, prolix, diffuse, padded, repetitious, tautological, periphrastic, unnecessary, inessential. OPPOSITE: terse.

reek *verb* smell, stink, pong (*inf*), hum (*inf*).

➤ *noun* smell, odour, stink, pong (*inf*), stench, fetor, effluvium. OPPOSITE: perfume.

reel *verb* **1** (*he reeled under a flurry of blows*) stagger, totter, falter, wobble, waver, stumble, lurch, pitch, rock, roll, sway. **2** (*the room seemed to reel about her*) go round, swim, spin, wheel, whirl, revolve, swirl, twirl, gyrate.

refer *verb* **1** (*he referred to this subject several times in his speech*) mention, allude, speak of, bring up, quote, cite, advert, touch on, hint at. **2** (*they referred me to this office*) direct, point, guide, send, pass, hand over, transfer, deliver, consign, commit, remit. **3** (*what does this letter refer to?*) relate, pertain, apply, belong, concern, mean, indicate, signify, suggest. **4** (*you must refer to a solicitor*) consult, turn, apply, appeal, have recourse, resort.

referee *noun* ref (*inf*), umpire, arbiter, judge, adjudicator, arbitrator.
➤ *verb* **1** (*referee the game*) umpire, judge, adjudicate. **2** (*referee the argument*) arbitrate, mediate, intercede.

reference *noun* **1** (*made two references to the incident*) mention, allusion, remark, hint, intimation, suggestion, insinuation. **2** (*with reference to the above matter*) regard, respect, consideration, concern, bearing, application, applicability, connection, relation, correlation, relevance, pertinence. **3** (*you will need two references for the job*) testimonial, character, recommendation, endorsement, credentials. **4** (*included the reference for the quote*) source, citation, quotation, authority, footnote, note, bibliography.

referendum *noun* poll, vote, public vote, popular vote, plebiscite.

refine *verb* **1** (*refine the mixture*) purify, rarefy, clarify, clear, cleanse, filter, sift, strain, distil, process, treat. OPPOSITE: pollute. **2** (*her manner was refined by her mother*) polish, cultivate, civilize, improve, ameliorate, hone, perfect, fine-tune. OPPOSITE: barbarize.

refined *adj* **1** (*refined behaviour*) cultivated, cultured, civilized, civil, polished, gracious, genteel, well-mannered, courtly, polite, well-bred, urbane, gentlemanly, ladylike, elegant, stylish, sophisticated. OPPOSITE: coarse. **2** (*a refined palate*) discriminating, discerning, sensitive, tasteful, sophisticated, fastidious, precise, exact, subtle, delicate, fine. **3** (*refined sugar*) pure, purified, clear, clarified, rarefied, clean, distilled, filtered, processed, treated. OPPOSITE: crude.

refinement *noun* **1** (*the refinement of sugar*) purification, processing. **2** (*his new girlfriend lacks refinement*) polish, finish, grace, graciousness, style, elegance, finesse, sophistication, cultivation, culture, civility, taste, discrimination, urbanity, good manners, courtliness, good breeding, politeness, politesse, gentility. **3** (*work on the refinements of the plot*) subtlety, nicety, nuance, fine point, detail. **4** (*the design is still in need of refinement*) modification, alteration, amendment, improvement, amelioration.

reflect *verb* **1** (*saw himself reflected in the water*) mirror, image. **2** (*the rays of the sun were reflected by the glass*) throw back, cast back, send back, return, give back, scatter, diffuse. **3** (*the sound of voices reflected by the valley walls*) echo, re-echo, bounce back, send back, imitate, copy, reproduce. **4** (*her attitude reflects her upbringing*) show, display, exhibit, demonstrate, manifest, reveal,

bear out, indicate, express, betray, bespeak, communicate, depict. OPPOSITE: conceal. **5** (*sit for hours reflecting upon the past*) meditate, contemplate, cogitate, ruminate, dwell, brood, ponder, muse, mull over, think, deliberate, consider, wonder. **6** (*their crimes reflect upon us all*) discredit, disgrace, detract from, tarnish, put in a bad light.

reflection *noun* **1** (*caught sight of her reflection*) image, echo, shadow, likeness. **2** (*a reflection of new confidence in the market*) expression, indication, sign, display, demonstration, manifestation, portrayal. **3** (*shared his reflections with his listeners*) thought, idea, opinion, view, impression, feeling, meditation, contemplation, cogitation, rumination, musing, deliberation, consideration, belief. **4** (*this crime is a poor reflection upon modern society*) censure, blame, criticism, reproach, aspersion, slur, imputation, discredit, disrepute, shame.

reflex *adj* automatic, mechanical, involuntary, uncontrollable, knee-jerk (*inf*), spontaneous, immediate. OPPOSITE: voluntary.

reform *verb* **1** (*a need to reform society*) improve, better, ameliorate, mend, repair, amend, emend, correct, rectify, change, revise, revolutionize, remodel, reorganize, reconstruct, rebuild, remake, restore, renovate, revamp, refashion, rehabilitate, reclaim, purge. OPPOSITE: deteriorate. **2** (*they say he has reformed his ways*) mend, amend, change, improve.
➤ *noun* reformation, improvement, amelioration, betterment, amendment, correction, rectification, change, revision, reorganization, progress, rebuilding, reconstruction, renovation, refashioning, remodelling, rehabilitation, reclamation. OPPOSITE: corruption.

refractory *adj* recalcitrant, contumacious, obstinate, stubborn, intractable, contrary, difficult, perverse, obdurate, wilful, mulish, headstrong, wayward, uncooperative, unruly, insubordinate, rebellious, mutinous, unmanageable, ungovernable, uncontrollable, disobedient, defiant, cantankerous, naughty. OPPOSITE: docile.

refrain¹ *verb* abstain, forbear, hold back, desist, stop, cease, give up, leave off, quit, renounce, forgo, do without, avoid, eschew. OPPOSITE: indulge.

refrain² *noun* chorus, response, strain, burden, melody, tune, song. OPPOSITE: verse.

refresh *verb* **1** (*this drink will refresh you*) freshen, cool, revive, revivify, reanimate, resuscitate, invigorate, revitalize, perk up (*inf*), brace, fortify, rejuvenate, exhilarate, cheer, enliven, inspirit, stimulate, energize, regenerate, renew, restore, repair, renovate. OPPOSITE: wear out. **2** (*let me refresh your memory*) jog, prompt, prod, rouse, arouse, stir, stimulate, activate, remind.

refreshing *adj* **1** (*a refreshing drink*) freshening, cooling, revitalizing, reviving, invigorating, bracing, stimulating, inspiring, exhilarating, energizing. **2** (*a refreshing new talent*) fresh, new, novel, original, different, unexpected.

refreshment *noun* **1** (*serve refreshments in the garden*) food, drink, sustenance, snacks, provisions, eats (*inf*), grub (*inf*), nosh (*inf*). **2** (*the refreshment of government policy*) freshening, energizing, exhilarating, revival, reanimation, invigoration, stimulation, revitalization, rejuvenation, regeneration, renewal, restoration. OPPOSITE: fatigue.

refrigerate *verb* cool, chill, freeze, keep cold. OPPOSITE: heat.

refuge *noun* **1** (*refuge from the storm*) shelter, protection, safety, security, sanctuary, asylum. OPPOSITE: exposure. **2** (*his refuge from the world*) haven, harbour, retreat, hideout, hideaway, bolthole, island. **3** (*going to the police offered a last refuge*) resort, recourse, expedient, tactic, stratagem, strategy, stopgap.

refugee *noun* displaced person, stateless person, exile, émigré, fugitive, escapee, runaway.

refund *verb* repay, pay back, return, give back, restore, reimburse, recompense, make good, replace. OPPOSITE: withhold.
➤ *noun* repayment, reimbursement, rebate, return.

refurbish *verb* renovate, do up (*inf*), make over, fix up (*inf*), redecorate, spruce up, revamp, overhaul, recondition, refit, re-equip, remodel, mend, repair.

refusal *noun* **1** (*the refusal of all requests*) denying, declining, rejecting, turning-down, spurning, withholding. **2** (*she has posted off her refusal of the invitation*) rebuff, demurral, regrets, non-acceptance, dissent, negation, no, thumbs down. **3** (*you still have first refusal*) option, choice, opportunity, consideration.

refuse¹ *verb* **1** (*refuse all invitations*) decline, turn down, reject, spurn, repudiate, deny, withhold, rebuff, repel, pass up (*inf*). OPPOSITE: accept. **2** (*refuse to contribute*) decline, avoid, resist, balk at, demur at, protest at.

refuse² *noun* rubbish, waste, garbage, trash, junk (*inf*), debris, litter, dregs, dross, scraps, sweepings, leavings, leftovers.

refute *verb* disprove, counter, rebut, negate, confute, deny, discredit, give the lie to. OPPOSITE: confirm.

regain *verb* **1** (*regain lost ground*) recover, get back, take back, retake, win back, retrieve, recoup, recapture, reclaim, recuperate, repossess, redeem. OPPOSITE: lose. **2** (*tried to regain the shore*) get back to, return to, reattain, reach.

regal *adj* royal, kingly, queenly, princely, imperial, sovereign, majestic, stately, august, noble, proud, magnificent, grand, sumptuous. OPPOSITE: lowly.

regale *verb* **1** (*he regaled them with anecdotes*) entertain, amuse, delight, divert, fascinate, captivate. **2** (*the company were regaled with food and drink*) feast, banquet, fête, treat, ply, refresh.

regard *verb* **1** (*regard the scene*) watch, look at, gaze at, stare at, observe, view, eye, keep an eye on, study, scrutinize, mark, behold. **2** (*regard this warning well*) heed, notice, note, remark, attend to, pay attention to, listen to, mind, take notice of, take into account, take into consideration. OPPOSITE: ignore. **3** (*regard the idea with misgiving*) consider, weigh up, think of, mull over, see, view, look upon, contemplate, reflect on, deliberate on. **4** (*her work is highly regarded*) esteem, estimate, value, honour, respect, hold, gauge, appraise, assess, account, deem, rate, judge, adjudge. **5** (*this regards future developments*) concern, relate to, pertain to, refer to, apply to, belong to, bear upon.
➤ *noun* **1** (*pay due regard to oncoming traffic*) notice, attention, heed, thought, mind, consideration, care, concern. OPPOSITE: neglect. **2** (*held in high regard*) esteem, respect, approval, approbation, estimation, appreciation, admiration, honour, deference, liking, fondness, affection, love, favour, sympathy. OPPOSITE: contempt. **3** (*with regard to the future*) reference, relation, relationship, relevance, pertinence, respect, concern, bearing, connection, application. **4** (*he shifted under her stony regard*) look, gaze, stare, observation, scrutiny. **5** (*we must agree to differ in this regard*) respect, aspect, matter, subject, point, particular, detail, feature, item.

regardful *adj* mindful, heedful, attentive, careful, thoughtful, considerate, watchful, vigilant, observant, noticing, circumspect, aware, respectful, dutiful. OPPOSITE: heedless.

regarding *prep* about, re, concerning, in connection with, respecting, with respect to, with regard to, in regard to, as regards, as to, with reference to, in relation to, apropos, on the subject of.

regardless *adj* heedless, mindless, unmindful, inattentive, reckless, careless, neglectful, negligent, disregarding, thoughtless, inconsiderate, indifferent, unconcerned. OPPOSITE: mindful.
➤ *adv* anyway, anyhow, in any case, at any price (*inf*), at any cost (*inf*), notwithstanding, despite everything, nevertheless, nonetheless, for all that, no matter what.

regards *pl noun* best wishes, good wishes, wishes, greetings, respects, compliments, salutations, remembrances.

regenerate *verb* **1** (*feel regenerated after a good rest*) renew, restore, refresh, revive, revivify, revitalize, reawaken, rekindle, energize, invigorate, stimulate, exhilarate, rejuvenate, uplift, inspirit. **2** (*regenerate the inner city*) reform, convert, change, amend, improve, reconstruct, remodel, reorganize, overhaul.

regime *noun* government, administration, establishment, system, reign, rule, control, command, direction, leadership, management.

region *noun* **1** (*this troubled region of the continent*) area, zone, territory, district, quarter, sector, province, department, country, land, tract, locality, part, section, division. **2** (*in the region of the performing arts*) realm, domain, sphere, orbit, ambit, field, range, scope, vicinity, neighbourhood, locality.
in the region of around, about, approximately, approaching, roughly, loosely, something like, more or less, give or take (*inf*), in the area of, in the neighbourhood of, in the vicinity of, or thereabouts, close to, not far off, nearly, just about, circa, in round numbers, rounded up, rounded down.

regional *adj* **1** (*regional differences in house prices*) geographical, topographical, territorial, zonal. **2** (*the regional quarter-finals*) local, district, provincial.

register *noun* **1** (*find his name on the register*) list, listing, roster, roll, catalogue, directory, index. **2** (*the parish register*) record, annals, archives, chronicle, journal, diary, log, ledger, schedule, minutes, files.
➤ *verb* **1** (*the death has been properly registered*) record, put on record, enter, write down, put in writing, inscribe, set down, take down, note, list, catalogue, chronicle, minute, mark. **2** (*you must register at the desk*)

check in, sign in, sign up, sign on, enrol, enlist. **3** (*the instrument registered a rise in temperature*) show, record, indicate, read, display. **4** (*his face registered fear*) express, show, manifest, display, exhibit, demonstrate, reveal, reflect, betray, evince, say. **5** (*the news did not seem to have registered with her*) get through, sink in, penetrate, make an impression, have an effect.

regress *verb* return, go back, retreat, ebb, recede, retrocede, retrogress, revert, relapse, lapse, backslide, degenerate, deteriorate, decline, wane, ebb, fall away, retrograde, recidivate. OPPOSITE: progress.
➤ *noun* regression, return, reversion, relapse, retrogression, retreat, retrocession, recession. OPPOSITE: progression.

regret *verb* **1** (*he regrets everything he has done*) rue, repent, feel remorse about. **2** (*she regrets this reversal in fortunes*) deplore, bemoan, bewail, lament, fret about, pine over, repine, mourn, grieve over, weep over, miss.
➤ *noun* **1** (*full of regret for her actions*) sorrow, grief, remorse, self-reproach, ruefulness, repentance, penitence, contrition, shame, compunction, lamentation. **2** (*felt regret at the end of the affair*) sorrow, disappointment, grief, lamentation, mourning, pining, bitterness. OPPOSITE: satisfaction.

regretful *adj* sorry, sorrowful, sad, apologetic, repentant, remorseful, ashamed, rueful, contrite, penitent, conscience-stricken, disappointed.

regrettable *adj* deplorable, reprehensible, lamentable, disgraceful, blameworthy, shameful, unfortunate, unlucky, unwelcome, distressing, upsetting, unhappy, sad, sorry, ill-advised, wrong.

regular *adj* **1** (*follow our regular routine*) normal, usual, customary, habitual, routine, typical, standard, familiar, conventional, ordinary, average, common, commonplace, everyday, daily, unvarying. OPPOSITE: abnormal. **2** (*this is the regular procedure*) formal, official, orthodox, conventional, usual, standard, established, fixed, stated, approved, proper, correct, bona fide, sanctioned, traditional, time-honoured, classic. **3** (*the regular beating of the drums*) rhythmic, steady, constant, unchanging, unvarying, recurrent, frequent, periodic. OPPOSITE: irregular. **4** (*guard towers at regular intervals*) fixed, set, consistent, even. **5** (*let's keep things regular*) orderly, well-organized, efficient, streamlined, smooth-running, methodical, systematic, uniform. **6** (*a regular finish*) level, smooth, flat, uniform, symmetrical. **7** (*she's a regular beauty*) real, absolute, complete, total, utter, thorough, genuine.

regulate *verb* **1** (*regulate the industry*) control, rule, govern, direct, manage, run, administer, supervise, superintend, oversee, monitor, handle, guide, arrange, settle, square, organize, conduct, establish, systematize, methodize, order. **2** (*regulate the timing*) adjust, fix, set, balance, synchronize, tune, moderate, modulate, control.

regulation *noun* **1** (*regulation of the project*) adjustment, control, rule, government, direction, guidance, management, administration, organization, handling, conducting, monitoring, superintendence, supervision. **2** (*rules and regulations*) rule, ruling, law, statute, act, ordinance, edict, decree, pronouncement, order,

command, commandment, directive, dictum, direction, requirement, precept, prescription. **3** (*regulation of the timing*) adjustment, fixing, balancing, synchronization, tuning, moderation, modulation, controlling.
➤ *adj* formal, official, orthodox, prescribed, statutory, obligatory, mandatory, required, fixed, set, accepted, standard, regular, usual, normal, customary. OPPOSITE: unorthodox.

regurgitate *verb* vomit, throw up (*inf*), spew, disgorge, bring up, puke (*inf*).

rehabilitate *verb* **1** (*rehabilitate long-term prisoners*) reintegrate, normalize, retrain, re-establish, reform, adjust, adapt, redeem, save. **2** (*the whole area has been rehabilitated*) restore, redevelop, reinstate, reconstitute, reclaim, renovate, recondition, fix up, refurbish, redecorate, renew, revive, reinvigorate, repair, mend, rebuild, reconstruct, improve.

rehearsal *noun* **1** (*dress rehearsal*) practice, practice session, drill, exercise, preparation, trial run, dry run (*inf*), dummy run (*inf*), run-through, going-over. **2** (*deliver a rehearsal of the main points*) list, listing, enumeration, itemization, catalogue.

rehearse *verb* **1** (*rehearse the next show*) practise, drill, exercise, train, prepare, run through, try out, go over. **2** (*she had rehearsed them to perfection*) drill, train, prepare. **3** (*rehearse tales of his childhood*) recount, relate, narrate, repeat, reiterate, recite, describe, depict, review, delineate, recapitulate, detail, list, enumerate.

reign *verb* **1** (*the Mafia reigned unchallenged for years*) rule, govern, command, hold sway. OPPOSITE: submit. **2** (*panic reigned*) hold sway, predominate, prevail, obtain.
➤ *noun* **1** (*the reign of the present queen*) monarchy, sovereignty, rule. **2** (*the reign of the bureaucrats*) rule, supremacy, ascendancy, government, administration, regime, command, control, sway, influence, power, charge, dominion.

reimburse *verb* repay, pay back, give back, return, restore, refund, remunerate, recompense, compensate, indemnify.

rein *noun* bridle, harness, curb, check, brake, restraint, constraint, restriction, limitation, control.
➤ *verb* restrain, restrict, limit, constrain, check, curb, bridle, hold back, slow down, stop, halt, arrest, control, guide. OPPOSITE: indulge.

reinforce *verb* **1** (*reinforce the south wall*) strengthen, fortify, support, brace, shore up, prop up, stay, consolidate, uphold, buttress, bolster, toughen, harden, stiffen, steel. **2** (*reinforce the team's attack*) augment, supplement, add to, increase, redouble. OPPOSITE: weaken.

reinforcement *noun* **1** (*the reinforcement of his main points*) strengthening, fortification, bolstering, propping up, supporting, stressing, emphasizing. **2** (*the reinforcement of front line troops*) augmentation, increasing, enlargement, supplementing, amplification. **3** (*quoted her words as a reinforcement of his position*) support, brace, prop, fortification, buttress, shore, stay, emphasis.

reinforcements *pl noun* auxiliaries, reserves, supplementaries, support, help, back-up.

reinstate *verb* restore, replace, reinstall, re-establish, recall, return, give back, rehabilitate, reappoint. OPPOSITE: remove.

reiterate *verb* repeat, go over, iterate, rehearse, restate, recapitulate, recap (*inf*), say again, retell, dwell on, harp on, emphasize, stress, hammer away at.

reject *verb* **1** (*they rejected the suggestion out of hand*) refuse, turn down, decline, pass up (*inf*), deny, disallow, veto, condemn, spurn, rebuff, repel, repudiate, despise. OPPOSITE: accept. **2** (*rejected by society*) cast aside, cast out, cast off, brush off (*inf*), set aside, discard, throw away, scrap, jettison, renounce, repudiate, jilt, abandon, forsake, eliminate, exclude, eject, expel.
➤ *noun* **1** (*they sell rejects at attractive prices*) discard, second. **2** (*a reject from college*) outcast, drop-out (*inf*), failure, derelict.

rejection *verb* **1** (*the rejection of this idea*) refusal, declining, denial, dismissal, turning down, spurning, repudiation. **2** (*rejection from society*) casting out, discarding, exclusion, elimination, renunciation, jettisoning. **3** (*a rejection of the offer arrived next day*) refusal, denial, non-acceptance, no, demurral, negation, dismissal, rebuff, veto, thumbs down, brush-off (*inf*).

rejoice *verb* exult, triumph, glory, revel, celebrate, make merry, feast, delight, take pleasure in, jump for joy (*inf*), whoop for joy (*inf*). OPPOSITE: mourn.

rejoicing *noun* happiness, gladness, pleasure, delight, elation, joy, jubilation, exultation, euphoria, glory, triumph, celebration, revelry, merry-making, festivity, feasting.

rejoinder *noun* reply, answer, response, riposte, quip, repartee, retort, comeback (*inf*).

relapse *verb* **1** (*the economy has relapsed*) revert, slip back, fall away, lapse, fail, backslide, regress, retrogress, retrograde, go backwards. **2** (*she relapsed into illness*) degenerate, deteriorate, worsen, decline, sink, weaken, sicken, suffer a relapse. OPPOSITE: improve.
➤ *noun* **1** (*the relapse of the industry*) reversion, lapse, regression, retrogression, backsliding. **2** (*she has suffered a relapse*) deterioration, setback. OPPOSITE: improvement.

relate *verb* **1** (*related the story of his birth*) narrate, tell, recount, recite, rehearse, describe, detail, delineate, report, chronicle, communicate, impart, present, set forth, mention. OPPOSITE: suppress. **2** (*you cannot relate the two things*) connect, link, associate, ally, couple, correlate, join. **3** (*this relates to her past*) refer, apply, regard, respect, concern, belong, bear, pertain, appertain. **4** (*she could not relate with his distress*) identify, sympathize, empathize, feel for, understand.

related *adj* **1** (*related matters*) connected, interconnected, interrelated, associated, linked, allied, affiliated, joint, mutual, correlated, accompanying, concomitant, relevant, akin. **2** (*I understand we are related*) connected, akin, kindred, cognate.

relation *noun* **1** (*explain the relation between the two issues*) relationship, connection, interconnection, link, linking, tie-in, bond, association, affiliation, correlation, interrelation, affinity, alliance, interdependence, similarity, propinquity. **2** (*she is a relation of mine*) relative, kinsman, kinswoman, kin, kindred. **3** (*with relation to the above*) reference, respect, regard, concern, bearing, relevance, pertinence, application, applicability. **4** (*the relation of his youth*) account, narrative, narration, narrating, telling, recounting, report, reporting, story, tale, recital, reciting, rehearsal, description.

relations *pl noun* **1** (*relations between the two countries*) contact, connections, dealings, affairs, terms, interaction, associations, communications, rapport, intercourse. **2** (*they admitted having had relations that night*) sex (*inf*), intercourse, sexual intercourse, sexual relationship, intimacy, coitus, carnal knowledge, liaison, affair. **3** (*surrounded by his friends and relations*) relatives, family, kin, kindred, kinsfolk, folks (*inf*).

relationship *noun* **1** (*the relationship between the two processes*) connection, association, link, bond, correlation, affinity, similarity, closeness, alliance, tie, tie-up, parallel, correspondence, conjunction, proportion, ratio. **2** (*they had a brief relationship as teenagers*) love affair, affair, romance, fling (*inf*), liaison, friendship.

relative *noun* relation, kinsman, kinswoman, kin, family.
➤ *adj* **1** (*a relative success considering the problems*) comparative, comparable, proportional, proportionate, in proportion to, in ratio to. OPPOSITE: absolute. **2** (*relative to the matter in hand*) relevant, related, interrelated, connected, pertinent, pertaining, germane, material, apropos, apposite, applicable, appropriate, appurtenant.

relatively *adv* **1** (*relatively good services for such a deprived area*) comparatively, in comparison, by comparison, proportionately. **2** (*she was relatively optimistic*) fairly, reasonably, quite, rather, somewhat.

relax *verb* **1** (*relax the belt a little*) loosen, slacken, untighten, ease. OPPOSITE: tighten. **2** (*we cannot relax our vigilance for a moment*) lessen, let up, ease off, slacken off, reduce, lower, decrease, diminish, abate, weaken. **3** (*the rules are relaxed at Christmas*) moderate, ease, soften. **4** (*time to relax after work*) unwind, wind down, chill out (*inf*), rest, laze, idle, take it easy (*inf*), put one's feet up (*inf*), hang loose (*inf*). **5** (*you need to relax a bit*) calm down, calm, tranquillize, sedate, pacify, soothe, ease up, unbend, loosen up.

relaxation *noun* **1** (*relaxation of the straps*) loosening, slackening, untightening, easing. **2** (*a relaxation in official vigilance*) lessening, letting-up, easing off, slackening off, reduction, lowering, decreasing, diminishing, abating, weakening. **3** (*relaxation of the rules*) moderation, easing, softening. **4** (*time for relaxation*) rest, leisure, refreshment, unwinding. OPPOSITE: work. **5** (*his relaxations include riding*) recreation, amusement, diversion, entertainment, hobby, pastime, fun, pleasure.

relay *noun* **1** (*work in relays*) relief, shift, stint, turn, period, spell. **2** (*pick up a news relay*) broadcast, transmission, programme, communication, message, dispatch.
➤ *verb* broadcast, transmit, send, communicate, spread, carry, supply, circulate, pass on, hand on.

release *verb* **1** (*release the animal from the box*) free, set free, loose, turn loose, set loose, let out, let go, drop,

liberate, deliver, emancipate. **2** (*release him from the handcuffs*) unshackle, free, set free, undo, unloose, loosen, untie, unbind, unfasten, unchain, unfetter, unleash. **3** (*I shall release you from your promise*) clear, absolve, acquit, discharge, let off, let go, excuse, exempt, exonerate. OPPOSITE: hold. **4** (*release a statement*) publish, make public, issue, circulate, broadcast, disseminate, distribute, spread, announce, make known, make available, put out, reveal, unveil, disclose, divulge, present, break. OPPOSITE: suppress.
➤ **noun 1** (*the release of all detainees*) freedom, liberation, emancipation, deliverance. OPPOSITE: imprisonment. **2** (*grateful for his release from the trap*) extrication, untying, unbinding, unchaining. **3** (*earned her release from any future obligation*) acquittal, let-off (*inf*), discharge, dispensation, excusing, absolution, exemption. **4** (*show me the latest press release*) announcement, bulletin, update, publication, proclamation, declaration, disclosure, revelation. **5** (*consternation followed the release of the decision*) publication, publishing, issue, circulation, broadcasting, dissemination, announcement, proclamation, declaration, divulging, breaking. **6** (*the band's latest release*) record, recording, CD, compact disc, disc, mini disc, album, single, book, publication, film, work.

relegate *verb* demote, send down, downgrade, degrade, reduce, banish, exile. OPPOSITE: promote.

relent *verb* **1** (*the authorities refused to relent*) unbend, yield, give way, give in, capitulate, soften, melt, come round, show mercy, give quarter. OPPOSITE: harden. **2** (*the rain fell all day without relenting*) let up, abate, die down, drop, fall off, ease, relax, slacken, weaken.

relentless *adj* **1** (*he proved a relentless taskmaster*) unrelenting, unyielding, implacable, inexorable, obdurate, remorseless, uncompromising, ruthless, strict, unbending, unflexible, unforgiving, hard, harsh, fierce, cruel, grim, merciless, pitiless, cold-hearted, uncompassionate. OPPOSITE: mild. **2** (*relentless pressure*) unrelenting, unremitting, unflagging, persevering, persistent, incessant, unbroken, unceasing, unabated, non-stop, unswerving, undeviating, unfaltering, unstoppable, punishing.

relevant *adj* pertinent, germane, apropos, applicable, admissible, to the point, to the purpose, apposite, material, significant, appropriate, apt, fitting, suitable, proper, related, congruous. OPPOSITE: irrelevant.

reliable *adj* **1** (*proved a reliable ally*) trustworthy, dependable, trusty, faithful, devoted, dutiful, conscientious, honest, unfailing, true, tried and true, tested, steadfast, steady, staunch, solid, stable, constant, sure, certain, infallible. OPPOSITE: unreliable. **2** (*a reliable contact*) trustworthy, dependable, sound, credible.

reliance *noun* **1** (*place great reliance upon her opinion*) trust, confidence, assurance, faith, belief, credit, conviction. **2** (*complete reliance upon his parents*) dependence, leaning.

relic *noun* **1** (*a relic of historical interest*) artefact, antique, heirloom. **2** (*her only relic of the affair*) keepsake, reminder, memento, token, souvenir, remembrance. **3** (*our political system is a relic of a former age*) survivor, survival, remnant, fragment, trace, vestige.

relics *pl noun* remains, artefacts, fragments, shards, scraps, reliquiae.

relief *noun* **1** (*the massage brought some relief of his back pain*) alleviation, lessening, reduction, mitigation, palliation, soothing, allaying, assuagement, easing, appeasement, abatement, release, remedy, cure. OPPOSITE: aggravation. **2** (*that is a great relief to me*) comfort, solace, consolation, reassurance, happiness, relaxation. **3** (*bring relief to the stranded survivors*) help, aid, assistance, support, succour, sustenance, rescue, deliverance. **4** (*he appreciated the relief from the constant pressure*) respite, rest, remission, breather (*inf*), let-up (*inf*), break, interruption, lull, diversion, variation, refreshment, relaxation. **5** (*we must arrange a relief to cover her absence*) replacement, substitute, stand-in, stand-by, fill-in, locum, proxy, surrogate, supply, temp (*inf*), understudy. **6** (*this puts the problem in sharp relief*) contrast, distinctness, vividness, intensity.

relieve *verb* **1** (*relieve his anxiety*) ease, alleviate, mitigate, palliate, appease, assuage, allay, soothe, soften, dull, reduce, diminish, lessen, abate, comfort, solace, console, reassure, cure, heal. OPPOSITE: aggravate. **2** (*efforts to relieve survivors of the disaster*) help, aid, assist, rescue, save, succour, support, sustain. **3** (*something to relieve the tedium*) break up, interrupt, punctuate, lighten, brighten, vary, relax. **4** (*they will relieve the present shift at midnight*) replace, take over from, stand in for, take the place of, substitute for. **5** (*relieve them of their responsibility*) free, set free, deliver, release, liberate, discharge, unburden, disburden, extricate, disencumber, disembarrass, excuse, exempt.

religious *adj* **1** (*discuss religious matters*) holy, sacred, divine, spiritual, scriptural, theological, doctrinal, devotional, sectarian, church. OPPOSITE: profane. **2** (*a religious woman*) pious, godly, God-fearing, devout, reverent, good, pure, righteous, saintly, holy, churchgoing, practising, committed. **3** (*religious attention to detail*) strict, rigid, rigorous, unswerving, undeviating, unfailing, exact, scrupulous, meticulous, conscientious, faithful, zealous. OPPOSITE: lax.

relinquish *verb* **1** (*relinquish the right to trial by jury*) abandon, give up, surrender, yield, cede, renounce, abdicate, resign, sign away, hand over. **2** (*he relinquished the place with regret*) quit, leave, pull out of, depart from, desert, vacate, abandon, forsake. **3** (*reluctant to relinquish his ambition*) repudiate, yield, waive, forgo, desist from, give up, abstain from, forbear from, discontinue, stop, cease, desist, drop, let go, release. OPPOSITE: retain.

relish *verb* **1** (*relish his opponent's discomfort*) enjoy, delight in, revel in, luxuriate in, savour, appreciate, like, love, adore. **2** (*relish the prospect*) look forward to, anticipate, fancy, savour. OPPOSITE: loath.
➤ **noun 1** (*watched the game with relish*) enjoyment, pleasure, delight, gusto, zest, liveliness, vivacity, vigour, satisfaction, gratification, liking, appreciation, fondness, fancy, partiality, predilection. OPPOSITE: aversion. **2** (*the sauce has a certain relish*) taste, flavour, savour, tang, spiciness, piquancy. OPPOSITE: insipidity. **3** (*put some relish on the side of my plate*) sauce, chutney, pickle, garnish, condiment, seasoning.

reluctance *noun* unwillingness, hesitancy, hesitance, lack of enthusiasm, backwardness, recalcitrance, disinclination, indisposition, loathing, loathness, repugnance, aversion, dislike, distaste, disrelish.

reluctant *adj* **1** (*a reluctant recruit*) unwilling, unenthusiastic, grudging, disinclined, hesitant. OPPOSITE: eager. **2** (*reluctant to disappoint his mother*) loath, unwilling, disinclined, indisposed, averse, slow, chary.

rely *verb* **1** (*he relies upon a change in policy*) depend, count, bank, reckon, trust, swear by, have confidence in, be sure of. OPPOSITE: distrust. **2** (*stop relying on me all the time*) depend on, lean on.

remain *verb* **1** (*few traces remain*) survive, last, abide, endure, persist, prevail, stand, be left. **2** (*remain at home*) stay, stay behind, stay put (*inf*), linger, tarry, wait, rest. OPPOSITE: go. **3** (*the news remains bad*) continue, stay.

remainder *noun* rest, remains, relics, remnants, vestiges, dregs, leftovers, leavings, residue, residuum, balance, surplus, excess, superfluity.

remains *pl noun* **1** (*the remains of a picnic*) remnants, remainder, rest, scraps, crumbs, leavings, leftovers, residue, dregs, fragments, oddments, vestiges, traces, debris, detritus. **2** (*archaeological remains*) relics, fragments, shards, reliquiae. **3** (*human remains*) corpse, body, carcass, cadaver, ashes.

remark *verb* **1** (*he remarked that she looked well*) comment, observe, mention, say, state, declare, pronounce, assert. **2** (*remarked the lack of safety barriers*) notice, note, see, perceive, observe, discern, regard, heed, mark. OPPOSITE: miss.
≫ *noun* **1** (*an uncalled-for remark*) comment, observation, reference, mention, utterance, statement, declaration, pronouncement, opinion, thought, reflection. **2** (*their contribution deserves remark*) attention, comment, heed, acknowledgement, recognition, regard, notice.

remarkable *adj* notable, noteworthy, memorable, outstanding, impressive, considerable, pre-eminent, prominent, striking, noticeable, conspicuous, distinctive, distinguished, extraordinary, unusual, uncommon, exceptional, rare, singular, signal, important, significant, momentous, peculiar, odd, strange, amazing, surprising, phenomenal, wonderful. OPPOSITE: ordinary.

remedy *noun* **1** (*a remedy for her skin condition*) cure, antidote, restorative, specific, treatment, medicine, medication, therapy, physic, nostrum, panacea. **2** (*offered no remedy for the problem*) solution, answer, corrective, countermeasure, relief, redress, panacea.
≫ *verb* **1** (*remedy the disease*) cure, heal, control, counteract, restore, treat, relieve, ease, alleviate, palliate, mitigate, assuage, soothe. **2** (*failed to remedy the situation*) rectify, correct, redress, put right, set to rights, sort out, fix, repair, improve, solve. OPPOSITE: aggravate.

remember *verb* **1** (*I cannot remember the incident*) recall, recollect, call to mind, place. **2** (*remember this warning*) bear in mind, keep in mind, memorize, commit to memory, learn, retain, hold onto. OPPOSITE: forget. **3** (*remember happier times*) recall, recollect, reminisce, look back on, think back on, hark back to, summon up. **4** (*the war dead are remembered by a new statue*) commemorate, honour, mark, celebrate. **5** (*remember me

to your wife*) send one's regards, send one's compliments, send greetings.

remembrance *noun* **1** (*her remembrance of childhood holidays*) memory, recollection, recalling, reminiscence. **2** (*keep this as a remembrance of this day*) souvenir, memento, keepsake, token, reminder, commemoration, memorial, relic. **3** (*pass on our remembrances to your father*) greetings, regards, compliments, best wishes.

remind *verb* **1** (*remind me to phone them*) prompt, nudge, jog the memory, refresh the memory. **2** (*this reminds me of last summer*) bring back, call up, evoke, put one in mind.

reminisce *verb* **1** (*spent the day reminiscing*) remember, recollect, think back, look back, hark back, dwell on the past. **2** (*reminisce about the war*) remember, recollect, recall, call to mind, review.

reminiscence *noun* memory, recall, recollection, remembrance, reflection, retrospection, review.

reminiscences *pl noun* memoirs, remembrances, anecdotes.

reminiscent *adj* evocative, suggestive, remindful, redolent, nostalgic.

remiss *adj* negligent, neglectful, careless, inattentive, heedless, thoughtless, casual, indifferent, unthinking, unmindful, forgetful, derelict, delinquent, culpable, dilatory, slack, lax, lackadaisical, slipshod, sloppy (*inf*), wayward, slow, tardy, indolent, slothful. OPPOSITE: diligent.

remission *noun* **1** (*remission of the sentence*) cancellation, repeal, annulment, rescinding, revocation, suspension, abrogation, discharge, acquittal, amnesty, reprieve, release. OPPOSITE: punishment. **2** (*sought remission for her sins*) forgiveness, pardon, absolution, indulgence, exoneration. **3** (*call for a remission in the campaign against speeding drivers*) respite, let-up (*inf*), relaxation, easing, diminution, reduction, lessening, moderation, abatement, ebb, decrease. OPPOSITE: increase. **4** (*greeted the remission of the wind*) easing, moderation, subsidence, abatement, slackening, weakening, dwindling, waning, wane, ebb, ebbing, lessening, decrease. **5** (*the remission of the parcel*) sending, dispatch, forwarding, transmission, posting, mailing.

remit *verb* **1** (*remit payment by return of post*) pay, settle, send, dispatch, mail, post, forward, transmit. **2** (*remit the bankruptcy order*) halt, stop, desist, forbear, reprieve, release, cancel, repeal, rescind, revoke, set aside, suspend. **3** (*the rain has remitted*) ease, relax, slacken, mitigate, alleviate, moderate, weaken, abate, ebb, wane, dwindle, subside, decrease, diminish, lessen, reduce, halt, stop. OPPOSITE: increase. **4** (*remit the hearing to later in the year*) postpone, defer, suspend, shelve, put off, hold off, delay, reschedule, prorogue. **5** (*remit the matter to a higher authority*) pass on, send on, refer, transfer, direct, hand on. **6** (*ask the priest to remit her sins*) pardon, forgive, excuse.

remittance *noun* payment, fee, allowance.

remnant *noun* **1** (*the last remnant of his mob*) remainder, rest, remains, vestiges, residue. **2** (*a small remnant of cloth*) scrap, shred, fragment, bit, piece, oddment, trace, vestige, leftover.

remonstrate *verb* **1** (*remonstrate with the crowd*) argue with, dispute with, take issue with, expostulate with. **2** (*remonstrate against blood sports*) argue against, protest against, complain about, gripe about, object to, take exception to, take a stand against, oppose, challenge. OPPOSITE: acquiesce.

remorse *noun* regret, sorrow, grief, contrition, penitence, repentance, ruefulness, self-reproach, guilt, shame, compunction. OPPOSITE: satisfaction.

remorseful *adj* sorry, apologetic, regretful, contrite, penitent, repentant, chastened, rueful, guilty, guilt-ridden, conscience-stricken, ashamed, sorrowful, sad. OPPOSITE: impenitent.

remorseless *adj* relentless, unrelenting, unremitting, inexorable, unstoppable, undeviating, implacable, unmerciful, merciless, pitiless, unforgiving, cruel, stern, hard, hard-hearted, harsh, callous, ruthless, savage, inhumane. OPPOSITE: merciful.

remote *adj* **1** (*a remote star*) distant, far, far-off, faraway, far-removed, removed. OPPOSITE: near. **2** (*a remote spot*) sequestered, secluded, isolated, lonely, godforsaken, inaccessible, outlying, out-of-the-way, off the beaten track (*inf*). **3** (*such considerations are remote from the matter in hand*) foreign, alien, extraneous, extrinsic, irrelevant, unassociated, unconnected, unrelated, immaterial, non-pertinent, inapposite, inappropriate, inapt. **4** (*a remote chance*) slight, slender, slim, small, meagre, poor, faint, inconsiderable, insignificant, negligible, outside, improbable, implausible, unlikely, doubtful, dubious. OPPOSITE: considerable. **5** (*a remote manner*) detached, reserved, stand-offish, distant, aloof, unapproachable, withdrawn, uncommunicative, indifferent, unconcerned, uninvolved, haughty, cool, frigid. OPPOSITE: friendly.

removal *noun* **1** (*the removal of their belongings*) moving, shifting, transfer, transporting, taking away, carrying away, conveying, conveyance. **2** (*his removal to a high-security prison*) transfer, relocation, move, departure, uprooting. **3** (*the removal of all objections*) withdrawal, removing, taking away, dismissal. **4** (*the removal of unnecessary adjectives*) deletion, elimination, erasure, obliteration, effacing, purging, extraction. **5** (*the removal of dissidents within the party*) uprooting, eradication, extirpation, destruction, extermination, annihilation, firing (*inf*), sacking (*inf*). **6** (*her removal from the list of candidates*) expulsion, ejection, ousting, dismissal, eviction, dislodgement, deposition. **7** (*the removal of his left leg*) amputation, cutting off, excision. **8** (*ordered the removal of his enemies*) killing, murder, assassination, liquidation, elimination, disposal.

remove *verb* **1** (*remove the bags from the car*) take, carry, move, shift, transport, transfer, convey. OPPOSITE: replace. **2** (*remove undesirable elements from the organization*) eliminate, eradicate, annihilate, get rid of, abolish, obliterate, efface, expunge, erase, delete, oust, cast out, throw out, thrust out, pull out, depose, unseat, dismiss, sack (*inf*), fire (*inf*), discharge, dislodge, displace, expel, eject, evict, relegate. **3** (*remove your hat*) take off, detach, doff, shed, pull off, strip. **4** (*the doctor removed the shattered limb*) cut off, chop off, amputate, lop off, take off, excise, detach. **5** (*remove the right to trial by jury*) take

away, abolish, do away with. **6** (*removed themselves to the next room*) withdraw, move, relocate, transfer.

remunerate *verb* pay, reward, recompense, reimburse, indemnify, repay, compensate, requite, redress.

remuneration *noun* payment, reward, recompense, reimbursement, remittance, profit, pay, wages, earnings, salary, income, emolument, stipend, fee, retainer, honorarium, indemnity, compensation.

remunerative *adj* profitable, moneymaking, gainful, lucrative, rewarding, paying, advantageous, worthwhile, fruitful, rich. OPPOSITE: unprofitable.

renaissance *noun* renascence, rebirth, revival, renewal, reappearance, resurgence, re-emergence, resurrection, awakening, reawakening, rejuvenation, regeneration, restoration.

rend *verb* tear, rip, cleave, sever, sunder, rive, split, divide, rupture, separate, fracture, break, crack, burst, splinter, smash, shatter, pierce, stab, lacerate. OPPOSITE: mend.

render *verb* **1** (*render assistance*) give, supply, provide, furnish, present, submit, offer, tender, deliver, yield. OPPOSITE: withhold. **2** (*render loyalty to his master*) show, exhibit, manifest, display, evince. **3** (*render the lead role in a new comedy*) perform, act, play, appear in, interpret, depict. **4** (*render a portrait in pastels*) represent, depict, portray, do, paint. **5** (*rendered her incapable of speaking*) make, cause to be, leave. **6** (*rendered into another language*) translate, transcribe, construe, interpret, explain, express, put, execute. **7** (*please render your account for payment*) present, hand over, send in, submit, tender, deliver, surrender, yield.

rendezvous *noun* **1** (*let's arrange a rendezvous*) meeting, appointment, engagement, date, assignation, tryst. **2** (*come to the rendezvous*) meeting-place, venue, place of assignation, haunt, resort.
⪢ *verb* come together, gather, gather together, meet, assemble, collect, convene, rally, converge, muster.

rendition *noun* rendering, performance, execution, presentation, delivery, arrangement, version, interpretation, depiction, portrayal, reading, construction, transcription, translation.

renegade *noun* traitor, apostate, backslider, recreant, dissenter, turncoat, defector, betrayer, deserter, runaway, rat (*inf*), mutineer, outlaw, rebel, revolutionary.

renege *verb* go back on, break one's promise, default, repudiate, back out, pull out, backslide, welsh (*inf*), cop out (*inf*).

renew *verb* **1** (*renew their efforts*) recommence, resume, restart, repeat, restate, reiterate, reaffirm, continue, extend, prolong. **2** (*renew the whole neighbourhood*) revive, restore, recreate, reconstitute, replenish, restock, refresh, regenerate, rejuvenate, reinvigorate, revitalize, resuscitate, repair, renovate, reform, transform, refurbish, refit, remodel, recondition, overhaul, modernize.

renounce *verb* **1** (*he renounced his previous policy of appeasement*) give up, forgo, abandon, forswear, eschew, forsake, desert, abdicate, resign, relinquish, let go, yield, surrender, cede. OPPOSITE: retain. **2** (*she renounced her family*) disown, disinherit, repudiate, cast off, discard, reject, spurn, shun. OPPOSITE: acknowledge. **3** (*he has renounced his faith*) abandon, deny, disclaim, recant, reject, give up, forsake, renege on, abjure.

renovate *verb* restore, renew, repair, do up (*inf*), fix up (*inf*), revamp, remodel, modernize, recondition, refurbish, redecorate, refit, rehabilitate, revive, refresh, overhaul, reform.

renown *noun* fame, celebrity, illustriousness, stardom, note, eminence, pre-eminence, prominence, mark, repute, reputation, consequence, distinction, prestige, honour, glory, acclaim, esteem. OPPOSITE: notoriety.

renowned *adj* famous, famed, well-known, celebrated, acclaimed, distinguished, illustrious, of repute, eminent, pre-eminent, prominent, notable, noted, of note, of consequence, prestigious.

rent[1] *verb* lease, let, hire, charter.
➤ *noun* rental, hire, lease, payment, tariff.

rent[2] *noun* tear, rip, slit, gash, slash, opening, gap, hole, perforation, crevice, cleft, chink, fissure, crack, split, rift, break, fracture, rupture, breach, division, schism.

renunciation *verb* **1** (*the renunciation of her rights*) surrender, waiving, giving up, abdication, resignation, relinquishment, abnegation. **2** (*the renunciation of her family*) repudiation, rejecting, rejection, discarding, disowning, disinheriting, spurning, shunning. **3** (*the renunciation of his faith*) abandonment, denial, forsaking, abjuration, reneging.

repair[1] *verb* **1** (*repair the car*) mend, fix, put right, service, refit, overhaul, maintain, correct, rectify, adjust, regulate, renovate, renew. OPPOSITE: damage. **2** (*repair relations between the two sides*) patch up, restore, redress, make good. **3** (*repair the hole in his sock*) mend, darn, patch, sew.
➤ *noun* **1** (*the car is in for repair*) mending, fixing, restoration, renovation, correction, adjustment, overhaul, servicing, service, refit. **2** (*the repair to his trousers*) mend, patch, darn. **3** (*the house is in a poor state of repair*) condition, maintenance, shape (*inf*), nick (*inf*), form, fettle, restoration, state.

repair[2] *verb* go, move, withdraw, leave for, remove, depart for, head for, resort, retire, have recourse, take off for, betake oneself.

reparation *noun* amends, atonement, redress, requital, restitution, satisfaction, recompense, compensation, indemnity, damages, repair, renewal, restoration. OPPOSITE: injury.

repartee *noun* banter, badinage, raillery, wordplay, exchange, persiflage, pleasantry, riposte, retort, rejoinder, jesting, quip, witticism.

repast *noun* meal, feast, banquet, food, nourishment, collation, spread (*inf*), feed (*inf*), snack, refection.

repay *verb* **1** (*they had to repay her everything they had received*) refund, return, pay back, give back, reimburse, requite, remunerate, recompense, indemnify, reward, square accounts with, settle up with. **2** (*I shall repay him for this insult*) get back at, hit back, get even with, reciprocate, retaliate against, settle the score with, revenge, avenge.

repeal *verb* rescind, revoke, abrogate, annul, nullify, void, abolish, quash, invalidate, countermand, overrule,

override, reverse, retract, withdraw, recall, cancel, set aside, abjure. OPPOSITE: enact.
➤ *noun* revocation, abrogation, annulment, nullification, voiding, abolition, reversal, cancellation, quashing, overruling, overriding, setting aside, countermanding, invalidation, retraction, withdrawal, recall, rescinding, rescission, abjuration.

repeat *verb* **1** (*repeat the question*) say again, restate, recapitulate, recap (*inf*), retell. **2** (*continually repeating the same old lies*) say again, restate, go over, reiterate, quote, reproduce, echo, copy, duplicate, parrot. **3** (*repeat the whole procedure*) redo, duplicate, renew. **4** (*repeat that bit of the video*) replay, rerun, reshow.
➤ *noun* **1** (*a repeat of the whole story*) repetition, recapitulation, recap (*inf*), retelling, restatement, reiteration. **2** (*a repeat of the first murder*) repetition, duplication, copy, reproduction, echo. **3** (*did you see the repeat of the first episode?*) replay, rerun, reshowing, rebroadcast.

repeated *adj* recurrent, recurring, persistent, frequent, regular, rhythmical, periodic, constant, continual, incessant, endless.

repeatedly *adv* frequently, often, again and again, over and over, time after time, time and time again.

repel *verb* **1** (*repel the first wave of invaders*) repulse, drive back, push back, beat back, force back, thrust back, fend off, ward off, hold off, stave off, foil, frustrate, check, resist, parry, keep at bay. **2** (*repel any suggestion of compromise*) reject, repulse, spurn, rebuff, decline, turn down. OPPOSITE: welcome. **3** (*repelled by the prospect*) disgust, nauseate, sicken, revolt, put off, offend, shock. OPPOSITE: attract.

repellent *adj* repulsive, disgusting, revolting, nauseating, sickening, repugnant, abhorrent, offensive, objectionable, distasteful, obnoxious, loathsome, vile, foul, off putting, nasty, odious, abominable, horrible, horrid, hateful, despicable, shocking, obscene, contemptible, reprehensible, heinous.

repent *verb* regret, rue, lament, sorrow, deplore, be penitent, be contrite, feel remorse, reproach oneself, recant, see the light (*inf*), do a U-turn (*inf*).

repentance *noun* penitence, contrition, contriteness, regret, ruefulness, remorse, self-reproach, compunction, sorrow, grief, guilt, shame, conscience. OPPOSITE: satisfaction.

repentant *adj* penitent, contrite, regretful, remorseful, rueful, conscience-stricken, guilt-ridden, sorry, sorrowful, chastened, apologetic, ashamed. OPPOSITE: unrepentant.

repercussion *noun* **1** (*the repercussions of this breakthrough*) result, consequence, effect, reverberation, aftermath, backlash (*inf*), ripple (*inf*), shock wave (*inf*). **2** (*the repercussion of artillery shelling*) reverberation, echo, recoil, rebound.

repetition *noun* **1** (*a repetition of the question*) restatement, retelling, recital, recapitulation, recap (*inf*), repeat, reiteration, iteration, rehearsal. **2** (*learnt through repetition*) repeating, restatement, echoing, parroting, quoting, copying. **3** (*by repetition of the same procedure*) duplication, reproduction, renewal, repeating, redoing. **4** (*too much repetition in style*) repetitiousness, tautology, redundancy, superfluity, recurrence. OPPOSITE: originality.

repetitive *adj* recurrent, unchanging, unvaried, undiversified, boring, tedious, monotonous, dull, mechanical, automatic, samey (*inf*).

replace *verb* **1** (*replace everything as it was*) put back, return, reinstate, restore. OPPOSITE: remove. **2** (*replace her in the post of minister*) supersede, take the place of, succeed, follow, oust, supplant, relieve, take over from, substitute for, stand in for, act for, fill in for, cover for, deputize for, understudy.

replacement *noun* substitute, stand-in, fill-in, reserve, understudy, locum, supply, proxy, surrogate, successor.

replenish *verb* **1** (*replenish your glasses*) refill, fill, top up, recharge, reload. **2** (*replenish supplies*) restock, stock up, fill up, make up, reload, replace, renew, stock, restore, supply, furnish, provide. OPPOSITE: exhaust.

replete *adj* **1** (*replete after the meal*) full, filled, gorged, glutted, sated, satiated, stuffed, bursting. **2** (*the report is replete with suggestions for improvements*) packed, jam-packed, crammed, full, well-stocked, well-provided, overflowing, brimming, brimful, chock-full (*inf*), teeming, abounding. OPPOSITE: empty.

replica *noun* copy, carbon copy, duplicate, reproduction, facsimile, model, imitation, clone. OPPOSITE: original.

reply *verb* **1** (*I must reply to that letter*) answer, acknowledge, respond to, write back. **2** (*she was not slow to reply*) answer, respond, counter, rejoin, retort, riposte, react, retaliate, return, echo. OPPOSITE: ask.
≫ *noun* answer, response, acknowledgement, reaction, rejoinder, comeback (*inf*), repartee, retort, retaliation, return, riposte, echo. OPPOSITE: question.

report *noun* **1** (*as detailed in the official government report*) account, statement, paper, study, record, minute, brief, file, dossier. **2** (*read the report in the paper*) account, article, item, story, tale, review, write-up, description, narrative, narration, relation, recital, announcement, declaration, news, tidings, word, communication, message, communiqué, dispatch, bulletin. **3** (*he is a rogue, according to local report*) rumour, gossip, talk, hearsay, tittle-tattle. **4** (*a worker of good report*) reputation, repute, fame, opinion, renown, standing, stature, credit, esteem, regard, name, honour, character, performance. **5** (*the report of the gun*) bang, crack, boom, shot, blast, explosion, crash, detonation, discharge, noise, sound, echo, reverberation, rumble.
≫ *verb* **1** (*report everything you hear*) tell, relate, recount, narrate, describe, delineate, detail, divulge, disclose, relay, pass on, communicate, announce, air, broadcast, circulate, publish, state, declare, proclaim, record, document, write up, set forth. OPPOSITE: suppress. **2** (*she reported him to the police*) inform on, tell on (*inf*), shop (*inf*), grass on (*inf*), squeal on (*inf*), split on (*inf*), rat on (*inf*), complain, accuse. **3** (*report to this office tomorrow*) present oneself, appear, come, arrive, show up (*inf*), turn up, clock in. **4** (*report the matter in full*) write up, write down, take down, chronicle, record, document, minute.

reporter *noun* journalist, correspondent, columnist, newspaperman, newspaperwoman, hack (*inf*), newshound (*inf*), newscaster, pressman, writer,

broadcaster, presenter, announcer, news commentator.

repose¹ *noun* **1** (*the weekend should be a time of repose*) rest, ease, respite, relaxation, time off, sleep, slumber, inactivity, idleness, inertia. OPPOSITE: activity. **2** (*the repose of the woods*) peace, peacefulness, quiet, quietness, silence, hush, tranquillity, serenity, calm, calmness, stillness. **3** (*keep one's repose in the face of danger*) composure, calmness, poise, aplomb, self-possession, equanimity, dignity. OPPOSITE: agitation.
≫ *verb* **1** (*repose after hard work*) rest, relax, laze (*inf*), sleep, slumber. OPPOSITE: work. **2** (*repose on cushions*) lie, lie down, lean, recline, stretch out, sprawl.

repose² *verb* (*repose great faith in her abilities*) place, put, set, store, lodge, deposit, entrust, confide, invest.

repository *noun* store, storehouse, storeroom, depository, depot, treasury, reservoir, bank, safe, vault, archive, cache, receptacle, container, magazine.

reprehensible *adj* blameworthy, censurable, culpable, blamable, disgraceful, reproachable, reprovable, shameful, unworthy, dishonourable, opprobrious, ignoble, discreditable, objectionable, odious, unpardonable, indefensible, inexcusable, unjustifiable, condemnable, erring, errant, delinquent, wrong, bad, remiss. OPPOSITE: commendable.

represent *verb* **1** (*this figure represents the present financial position*) indicate, correspond to, stand for, equal, symbolize, denote, mean, betoken. **2** (*this badge represents courage*) symbolize, stand for, epitomize, exemplify, typify, personify, amount to. **3** (*he represents the very ideal of elegance*) embody, exemplify, personify, typify, incorporate, constitute. **4** (*represent her likeness in paint*) express, illustrate, depict, picture, paint, draw, sketch, portray, describe, delineate, denote, reproduce, show, exhibit, display, evoke. **5** (*he represents the government*) act for, stand for, appear for, speak for, substitute for. **6** (*representing the central character in this new play*) portray, act, appear as, enact, perform, impersonate. **7** (*the company will represent two comedies*) present, produce, stage, perform, put on, show. **8** (*she represented herself as an expert*) pose as, pass off as, describe as, pretend to be. **9** (*the report represents a series of problems*) present, set forth, state, put forward.

representation *noun* **1** (*the representation of religious faith in modern art*) presentation, depiction, portrayal, portrait, description, delineation, illustration, picture, painting, drawing, sketch, image, model. **2** (*their representation of the drama*) performance, presentation, production, play, show, spectacle. **3** (*he will be our representation at the talks*) representative, spokesperson, spokesman, spokeswoman, agent, ambassador, envoy, delegate, delegation, deputy, deputation, proxy, stand-in, mouthpiece. **4** (*listen to their representations*) statement, request, account, report, declaration, allegation, argument, protest, protestation, complaint, remonstrance, remonstration, expostulation.

representative *noun* **1** (*the representative of his country*) agent, deputy, delegate, envoy, ambassador, commissioner, spokesperson, spokesman, spokeswoman, proxy, deputy, substitute, stand-in, mouthpiece. **2** (*a commercial representative called*) salesman, commercial traveller, travelling salesman, agent, rep (*inf*). **3** (*a representative of its type*) example, exemplar, exemplification, specimen, archetype, type, illustration, epitome, embodiment.

≫ *adj* **1** (*a representative work of art*) typical, usual, normal, archetypal, characteristic, exemplary, illustrative, indicative. **2** (*representative of the highest ideals*) symbolic, emblematic, evocative. **3** (*the representative bodies of each state*) elected, elective, delegated, nominated, appointed, commissioned, chosen, ambassadorial, authorized, accredited, official.

repress *verb* **1** (*repress the impulse to smile*) hold back, hold in, keep back, bite back, control, restrain, suppress, check, keep in check, curb, inhibit, bottle up, silence, muffle, stifle, smother. OPPOSITE: release. **2** (*repress the common people*) subjugate, oppress, intimidate, crush, conquer, vanquish, overpower, overcome, master, dominate, domineer, bully, tyrannize. **3** (*repressed the uprising with brutality*) put down, quell, quash, suppress, subdue, crush, squash, extinguish, stamp out, stop.

repressed *adj* **1** (*a repressed people*) oppressed, subjugated, tyrannized. **2** (*a repressed smile*) suppressed, restrained, muffled, smothered. **3** (*a repressed personality*) uptight (*inf*), introverted, frustrated, inhibited, withdrawn, self-restrained.

repression *noun* **1** (*repression of ethnic minorities*) oppression, subjugation, domination, tyrannicization. **2** (*the repression of the uprising was swift*) suppression, quelling, crushing, quashing. **3** (*living under intolerable repression*) oppression, tyranny, despotism, dictatorship, authoritarianism, domination, suppression, subjugation, coercion. **4** (*the repression of his true feelings*) suppression, inhibition, holding back, biting back, control, restraint, suffocation, gagging, stifling, muffling, smothering, censorship.

repressive *adj* oppressive, tyrannical, authoritarian, autocratic, despotic, dictatorial, totalitarian, dominating, coercive, suppressive, harsh, severe, absolute, strict, cruel, tough.

reprieve *verb* pardon, let off, acquit, spare, forgive, remit, postpone, relieve, allay, alleviate, mitigate, palliate.

≫ *noun* remission, stay of execution, suspension, deferment, pardon, let-off (*inf*), amnesty, respite, relief, alleviation, mitigation.

reprimand *verb* admonish, reprehend, scold, tell off (*inf*), tick off (*inf*), bawl out (*inf*), rebuke, reprove, reproach, chide, upbraid, berate, lecture, castigate, blame, censure, criticize, slate (*inf*), take to task, carpet (*inf*), haul over the coals (*inf*), rap over the knuckles (*inf*). OPPOSITE: commend.

≫ *noun* rebuke, reproof, reproach, admonition, lecture, reprehension, talking-to (*inf*), telling-off (*inf*), ticking-off (*inf*), dressing-down (*inf*), bawling-out (*inf*), wigging (*inf*), carpeting (*inf*), rocket (*inf*), scolding, tongue-lashing, chiding, castigation, berating, upbraiding, censure, blame. OPPOSITE: praise.

reprisal *noun* retaliation, retribution, requital, recrimination, counter-attack, redress, revenge, vengeance, tit for tat (*inf*).

reproach *verb* blame, censure, criticize, find fault with, rebuke, reprove, reprehend, reprimand, scold, chide,

upbraid, berate, castigate, defame, admonish, take to task, haul over the coals (*inf*), condemn, disparage, abuse. OPPOSITE: approve.

≫ *noun* **1** (*her speech was full of reproach*) blame, censure, criticism, disapproval, fault-finding, rebuke, reproof, reproval, reprimand, admonition, upbraiding, scolding, condemnation, abuse. OPPOSITE: approval. **2** (*this scandal is a reproach to the whole system*) shame, disgrace, dishonour, discredit, slur, stain, blemish, blot, smear, stigma. OPPOSITE: honour. **3** (*this betrayal brought reproach to the regiment*) disgrace, shame, dishonour, disrepute, discredit, ignominy, odium, opprobrium, obloquy, scorn, contempt, disrespect.

reproachful *adj* disapproving, critical, censorious, scolding, admonitory, disappointed, condemnatory, fault-finding, disparaging, reproving, castigatory, opprobrious, scornful, upbraiding.

reprobate *adj* corrupt, depraved, degenerate, dissolute, immoral, unprincipled, sinful, abandoned, shameless, profligate, irredeemable, incorrigible, hardened, damned, wicked, evil, vile, bad, base. OPPOSITE: virtuous.

≫ *noun* villain, degenerate, miscreant, wretch, vagabond, rogue, scoundrel, rascal, scamp, scallywag, profligate, ne'er-do-well, sinner, wrongdoer, evildoer, criminal, rake, roué. OPPOSITE: paragon.

reproduce *verb* **1** (*reproduce the document*) duplicate, replicate, photocopy, copy, print, Xerox®, Photostat®, transcribe, clone. **2** (*reproduce the conditions in the laboratory*) recreate, reconstruct, remake, replicate, copy, repeat, represent, emulate, imitate, match, ape, mimic, parallel, mirror, echo, follow. **3** (*the germs reproduce very rapidly*) propagate, multiply, breed, procreate, spawn, proliferate, produce, generate.

reproduction *noun* **1** (*reproduction of the species*) propagation, breeding, procreation, proliferation, multiplication, generation. **2** (*reproductions of the original painting*) duplicate, copy, replica, facsimile, print, imitation, photocopy, Xerox®. **3** (*the reproduction of official documents*) copying, printing, duplicating, duplication, photocopying.

reproof *noun* **1** (*earned the reproof of the board of inquiry*) reproval, disapproval, reproach, disapprobation, admonition, castigation, dressing-down (*inf*), telling-off (*inf*), ticking-off (*inf*), carpeting (*inf*), wigging (*inf*), criticism, censure, blame, condemnation. **2** (*tried to defend himself against the reproofs of the fans*) reproach, rebuke, reprimand, scolding, reprehension, lecture, admonition, castigation, censure, criticism, fault-finding, blame, chiding, berating, upbraiding. OPPOSITE: praise.

reprove *verb* rebuke, scold, tell off (*inf*), reproach, reprehend, reprimand, tick off (*inf*), bawl out (*inf*), admonish, reprove, lecture, chide, upbraid, berate, castigate, blame, censure, criticize, slate (*inf*), take to task, haul over the coals (*inf*), rap over the knuckles (*inf*), condemn. OPPOSITE: praise.

repudiate *verb* **1** (*they must repudiate any allegiance to the organization*) reject, renounce, denounce, disavow, abjure, disclaim, forsake, forswear, retract, revoke, rescind, deny, disown, abandon, desert, cast off, cut off, discard. OPPOSITE: acknowledge. **2** (*he categorically* *repudiated any responsibility*) deny, contradict, disclaim, disavow, gainsay.

repugnance *noun* repulsion, revulsion, horror, disgust, nausea, distaste, dislike, antipathy, loathing, abhorrence, aversion, hatred, reluctance, contempt, odium.

repugnant *adj* repellent, repulsive, revolting, disgusting, sickening, nauseating, offensive, despicable, reprehensible, contemptible, abominable, hateful, objectionable, distasteful, disagreeable, off-putting, horrible, horrid, nasty, obnoxious, odious, foul, ugly, loathsome, vile, abhorrent, heinous.

repulse *verb* repel, drive back, beat off, ward off, check, reject, refuse, rebuff, snub, spurn, turn down, disdain. OPPOSITE: welcome.

repulsive *adj* repellent, repugnant, revolting, disgusting, nauseating, sickening, offensive, objectionable, disagreeable, distasteful, off-putting, unpleasant, obnoxious, odious, loathsome, abhorrent, detestable, despicable, contemptible, reprehensible, hateful, abominable, hideous, ugly, foul, horrible, horrid, nasty, vile, heinous. OPPOSITE: delightful.

reputable *adj* respectable, respected, of good repute, of repute, well-thought-of, esteemed, estimable, worthy, upright, virtuous, good, creditable, reliable, dependable, conscientious, trustworthy, honourable, honest, irreproachable, above-board, legitimate, excellent, admirable.

reputation *noun* 1 (*they pride themselves on their reputation*) good name, name, good character, standing, good standing, respect, respectability, repute, stature, status, esteem, fame, celebrity, credit, renown. 2 (*a soldier of considerable reputation*) fame, renown, repute, name, character, standing, status, stature, respect, esteem, estimation, regard, celebrity, distinction, honour.

repute *noun* 1 (*an artist of repute*) good reputation, high standing, stature, good name, esteem, fame, renown, celebrity, distinction. 2 (*a house of ill repute*) reputation, name, character.

reputed *adj* supposed, putative, apparent, ostensible, seeming, alleged, believed, considered, thought, reckoned, judged, deemed, presumed, held, said, rumoured.

reputedly *adv* supposedly, allegedly, apparently, ostensibly, seemingly, reputatively.

request *verb* ask for, beg for, beseech, supplicate for, entreat, appeal, petition, implore, call for, plead for, pray for, sue for, seek, solicit, demand, require, desire, apply for, put in for.
➤ *noun* 1 (*at the request of the police*) entreaty, behest, supplication, application, solicitation, petitioning, asking, begging, pleading, imploration, desire. 2 (*her request fell on deaf ears*) appeal, entreaty, plea, petition, suit, call, behest, prayer, demand.

require *verb* 1 (*here is a list of what we require*) need, desire, want, wish, request, crave, lack, miss. 2 (*the task requires concentration*) need, necessitate, involve, take, call for, demand, ask for, entail, constrain. 3 (*he was required to surrender the policy*) order, command, oblige,

compel, force, make, enjoin, instruct, direct, bid, ask, call on, request.

required *adj* compulsory, obligatory, mandatory, set, prescribed, demanded, stipulated, recommended, essential, necessary, needed, requisite, vital.

requirement *noun* 1 (*the requirements of the refugees must be met*) need, necessity, necessary, want, lack. 2 (*the government has stipulated certain requirements*) condition, demand, must (*inf*), prerequisite, requisite, stipulation, precondition, proviso, specification, term, qualification, provision.

requisite *adj* required, prerequisite, needed, necessary, needful, essential, indispensable, vital, imperative, obligatory, compulsory, mandatory, prescribed, set, demanded, called-for. OPPOSITE: nonessential.
➤ *noun* 1 (*the requisites for a good party*) requirement, need, want. 2 (*the requisites for a successful application*) requirement, necessity, must (*inf*) essential, condition, precondition, prerequisite, stipulation, provision, specification, qualification.

requisition *noun* 1 (*fill out a requisition for more supplies*) application, order, request, claim, demand, call, summons. 2 (*the requisition of the cottage by the army*) confiscation, seizure, appropriation, commandeering, possession, occupation, takeover.
➤ *verb* 1 (*requisition for new uniforms*) put in for, apply for, order, request, claim, call for, demand. 2 (*the police requisitioned the property*) commandeer, appropriate, seize, confiscate, take, take over, take possession of, occupy.

requite *verb* repay, pay, remunerate, reciprocate, return, reimburse, recompense, compensate, redress, make good, reward, satisfy, retaliate, avenge.

rescind *verb* repeal, revoke, abrogate, reverse, retract, annul, nullify, negate, void, quash, overturn, invalidate, countermand, recall, cancel, set aside. OPPOSITE: confirm.

rescue *verb* save, deliver, redeem, ransom, free, set free, liberate, emancipate, relieve, loose, release, extricate, recover, salvage. OPPOSITE: endanger.
➤ *noun* rescuing, saving, salvation, deliverance, delivery, redemption, ransom, freeing, liberation, emancipation, extrication, relief, release, recovery, salvage.

research *noun* investigation, inquiry, study, analysis, probe, review, examination, exploration, inspection, scrutiny, assessment, testing, fact-finding, experiment, experimentation, groundwork, documentation.
➤ *verb* investigate, inquire into, look into, inspect, probe, search, assess, review, study, analyse, examine, explore, scrutinize, test, experiment with.

resemblance *noun* 1 (*a marked resemblance between the two men*) likeness, similarity, semblance, similitude, sameness, analogy, parity, uniformity, correspondence, comparison, comparability, parallelism, closeness, nearness, affinity, agreement, congruity, conformity, concurrence. OPPOSITE: dissimilarity. 2 (*a photographic resemblance of her grandmother*) image, representation, likeness, photograph, painting.

resemble *verb* look like, be like, bear resemblance to, be similar to, remind one of, take after, mirror, echo, parrot, duplicate, match, parallel.

resent *verb* begrudge, grudge, take offence at, take exception to, take umbrage at, take amiss, feel bitter about, grumble about, object to, dislike, envy.

resentful *adj* bitter, embittered, indignant, angry, irate, incensed, piqued, wrathful, miffed (*inf*), peeved (*inf*), huffy (*inf*), put out, displeased, grudging, jealous, envious, aggrieved, irritated, irked, annoyed, offended, hurt, wounded, vindictive, spiteful, malicious. OPPOSITE: contented.

resentment *noun* bitterness, ill will, animosity, hostility, hatred, malice, vindictiveness, spite, ill-feeling, indignation, offence, umbrage, pique, hurt, anger, rage, ire, annoyance, irritation, vexation, wrath, displeasure, grudge, jealousy, envy. OPPOSITE: satisfaction.

reservation *noun* **1** (*the reservation of fuel*) conservation, saving, putting aside, putting aside, retention, storing, storage. **2** (*confirm the reservation in writing*) booking, appointment, arrangement, prearrangement, engagement, order, charter, hire. **3** (*they accepted the deal without reservation*) qualification, limitation, condition, proviso, provision, stipulation, misgiving, qualm, scruple, demur, doubt, hesitation, hesitancy. **4** (*the ethnic population were confined to a reservation*) reserve, preserve, park, sanctuary, enclave, homeland, territory, area, plot, tract.

reserve *verb* **1** (*reserve some funds for a rainy day*) withhold, hold, keep, keep back, save, conserve, husband, retain, set aside, lay aside, put by, put away, store, hoard, stockpile, earmark. OPPOSITE: use. **2** (*we have reserved a table for you*) book, engage, secure, order, arrange, prearrange, retain, hire, charter. **3** (*reserve judgement*) withhold, postpone, put off, suspend, hold over, shelve, adjourn, defer, delay.
➤ *noun* **1** (*a plentiful reserve of tinned food*) stock, supply, store, stockpile, fund, reservoir, pool, bank, hoard, cache, accumulation, backlog. **2** (*the animals in the reserve are protected*) park, sanctuary, reservation, preserve, enclave, tract, territory, area. **3** (*he accepted the deal with some reserve*) reservation, doubt, reluctance, qualm, scruple, qualification, proviso, condition, limitation, stipulation. **4** (*overcome her natural reserve*) shyness, diffidence, reticence, detachment, distance, remoteness, aloofness, self-restraint, restraint, self-control, constraint, modesty, formality, coolness, coldness, frigidity, unapproachability, uncommunicativeness, unresponsiveness, secretiveness, taciturnity, silence. OPPOSITE: frankness.
➤ *adj* in reserve, substitute, auxiliary, spare, extra, additional, alternative.
in reserve available, at hand, to hand, obtainable, accessible, at one's disposal, on tap, unused, spare, stored.

reserved *adj* **1** (*reserved food*) conserved, stored, stockpiled. **2** (*his place is reserved*) booked, engaged, taken, spoken for, earmarked, designated, retained, arranged, kept, set aside, held, saved, chartered, hired. OPPOSITE: free. **3** (*she is a reserved character*) reticent, taciturn, silent, shy, retiring, unsociable, unfriendly, unapproachable, uncommunicative, undemonstrative, unresponsive, unforthcoming, secretive, aloof,

detached, distant, remote, standoffish, formal, restrained, self-restrained, cautious, prim, modest, demure, constrained, unemotional, cool, cold, frigid. OPPOSITE: frank.

reservoir *noun* **1** (*water from the local reservoir*) lake, loch, pool, pond. **2** (*time to top up the reservoir*) tank, cistern, receptacle, container, vat, holder, cask, bowl, basin. **3** (*a central reservoir of funds*) stock, supply, reserve, repository, store, fund, pool, stockpile, bank, cache, source, accumulation.

reside *verb* **1** (*they reside in a pleasant area*) live, dwell, abide, sojourn, stay, lodge, inhabit, occupy, settle. **2** (*the ambition residing in his soul*) lie, rest, exist, abide, dwell.

residence *noun* **1** (*a party at his country residence*) house, home, abode, dwelling, place, habitation, quarters, lodging, accommodation, domicile, seat, pad (*inf*), digs (*inf*). **2** (*began a residence of some ten years*) stay, sojourn, occupancy, occupation, habitation, inhabitancy, tenancy.

resident *noun* inhabitant, citizen, denizen, occupier, occupant, householder, tenant, local, dweller, sojourner, lodger, guest, inmate, patient, client. OPPOSITE: visitor.
➤ *adj* **1** (*a resident nurse*) live-in, living-in. **2** (*the resident population*) local, neighbourhood, inhabiting, dwelling, permanent, settled.

residue *noun* residuum, remainder, remains, rest, balance, difference, surplus, excess, extra, overflow, remnant, leavings, leftovers, dregs, lees.

resign *verb* **1** (*she has resigned from the company*) leave, quit (*inf*), give notice, hand in one's notice, retire, step down, stand down. **2** (*resign the throne*) abdicate, give up, leave, renounce, quit (*inf*), abandon, forsake, relinquish, vacate, hand over, surrender, yield, cede, waive. OPPOSITE: retain.

resignation *noun* **1** (*he has put in his resignation*) notice, letter of resignation. **2** (*the resignation of the prime minister*) retirement, standing-down, stepping-down, departure, quitting, vacating, leaving. **3** (*the resignation of all constitutional rights*) abdication, renunciation, relinquishment, surrender, waiving. **4** (*they listened in a mood of resignation*) acquiescence, submission, compliance, nonresistance, passivity, acceptance, endurance, patience, toleration, forbearance, sufferance, stoicism, reconciliation, defeatism. OPPOSITE: rebellion.

resigned *adj* **1** (*resigned to defeat*) reconciled, submitting, yielding, bowing, acceding, acquiescent. **2** (*he shot her a resigned glance*) compliant, unresisting, nonresistant, submissive, subdued, unprotesting, passive, docile, long-suffering, patient, tolerant, enduring, forbearing, stoical, philosophical, defeatist.

resilient *adj* **1** (*resilient material*) springy, bouncy, elastic, rubbery, flexible, whippy, pliable, pliant, supple, plastic. **2** (*he proved a resilient leader*) buoyant, irrepressible, tough, hardy, strong, adaptable.

resist *verb* **1** (*strong enough to resist the elements*) withstand, repel, repulse, rebuff. **2** (*resist change*) check, curb, restrain, stop, halt, block, stem, prevent, hinder, impede, inhibit, obstruct, thwart, frustrate. **3** (*resist attack*) fight, battle, combat, oppose, counter, counteract, withstand, defy, stand firm, stand up to, hold out against, face, confront, contend with, struggle against, weather. OPPOSITE: yield. **4** (*resist alcohol*) refrain from, abstain from, refuse, avoid, forgo, desist from, keep from, forbear from.

resistance *noun* **1** (*resistance to change*) curb, restraint, obstruction, prevention, hindrance, impedance, impediment, block. **2** (*resistance against attack*) fight, battle, combat, opposition, stand, defiance, confrontation, struggle, contention, avoidance, repulsion, withstanding.

resistant *adj* proof, impervious, unsusceptible, unaffected, invulnerable, immune, tough, strong.

resolute *adj* steadfast, firm, fixed, set, intent, determined, resolved, decided, earnest, staunch, stalwart, adamant, unwavering, unfaltering, unhesitating, unflinching, unswerving, inflexible, unyielding, stubborn, obstinate, obdurate, dogged, constant, steady, relentless, strong-willed, singleminded, persistent, persevering, dedicated, tenacious, serious, purposeful, deliberate, bold, courageous, undaunted, unshakable, unshaken. OPPOSITE: irresolute.

resolution *noun* **1** (*test the resolution of participants*) firmness, determination, resolve, resoluteness, steadfastness, intentness, constancy, perseverance, persistence, commitment, staunchness, tenacity, zeal, staying power, obstinacy, obduracy, doggedness, willpower, seriousness, earnestness, purposefulness, purpose, dedication, devotion, boldness, courage. OPPOSITE: irresolution. **2** (*their resolution is to continue*) decision, resolve, objective, object, intention, intent, aim, aspiration, plan, design, purpose. **3** (*the resolution of the board*) finding, verdict, motion, decree, judgement, declaration, statement, proposition. **4** (*the resolution of this difficulty*) solving, resolving, solution, answer, unravelling, disentangling, disentanglement, sorting out, working out, cracking.

resolve *verb* **1** (*he resolved to see it through to the end*) determine, decide, conclude, fix, settle, make up one's mind, intend, purpose, undertake. OPPOSITE: waver. **2** (*resolve a difficulty*) solve, explain, answer, fathom, sort out, work out, clear up, crack, unravel, disentangle. OPPOSITE: embroil. **3** (*resolve her last doubts*) dispel, remove, banish, clear up, answer, settle. **4** (*resolve the mixture*) break down, break up, reduce, dissolve, disintegrate, separate, divide, dissect, anatomize, analyse, convert.
➤ *noun* **1** (*our resolve must be to improve the situation*) decision, resolution, intention, intent, aim, purpose. **2** (*there is no questioning his resolve*) determination, resolution, resoluteness, firmness, steadfastness, staunchness, constancy, persistence, perseverance, doggedness, commitment, obstinacy, inflexibility, purposefulness, dedication, devotion, intentness, seriousness, earnestness, tenacity, zeal, boldness, courage, fortitude, willpower. OPPOSITE: irresolution.

resonant *adj* resounding, reverberant, reverberating, echoing, ringing, booming, loud, sonorous, strong, full, plummy, rich, vibrant, deep. OPPOSITE: quiet.

resort *verb* **1** (*resort to desperate measures*) fall back on, turn, have recourse to, use, make use, employ, utilize, exercise, avail oneself of, look. **2** (*visitors resort to the area*) go, head, repair, visit, frequent, haunt, patronize.

➤ *noun* **1** (*a popular holiday resort*) centre, spot, place, spa, retreat, refuge, haunt, rendezvous. **2** (*this is my last resort*) recourse, refuge, expedient, measure, step, alternative, choice, option, possibility, chance, hope.

resound *verb* resonate, reverberate, thunder, boom, ring, sound, echo, re-echo.

resounding *adj* **1** (*the resounding crash of the cannon*) resonating, resonant, reverberating, echoing, loud, ringing, booming, sonorous, thunderous, vibrant, full, rich. **2** (*a resounding victory*) decisive, great, remarkable, striking, notable, noteworthy, memorable, outstanding, impressive, emphatic, conclusive, thorough.

resource *noun* **1** (*a schemer of great resource*) ingenuity, enterprise, ability, capability, inventiveness, imagination, resourcefulness, initiative, cleverness, quick-wittedness, wit, talent. **2** (*he will employ any resource that is necessary*) device, contrivance, expedient, resort, recourse, course, way, means.

resourceful *adj* ingenious, inventive, innovative, original, enterprising, creative, imaginative, quick-witted, clever, bright, sharp, talented, gifted, able, capable, adroit, versatile.

resources *pl noun* wealth, capital, money, wherewithal, riches, funds, holdings, assets, materials, property, supplies, stores, stocks, reserves, means, hoard, stockpile, pool.

respect *verb* **1** (*children should respect their elders*) honour, praise, look up to, revere, venerate, esteem, admire, approve of, think highly of. OPPOSITE: despise. **2** (*I respect his opinion*) appreciate, prize, value, set store by. **3** (*we shall respect your decision*) heed, follow, observe, comply with, abide by, adhere to, obey, defer to, fulfil. **4** (*respect the privacy of others*) consider, take into consideration, show regard for, take into account, observe, pay heed to.
➤ *noun* **1** (*respect for the church*) reverence, veneration, praise, homage, obeisance, honour, regard, deference. OPPOSITE: disrespect. **2** (*his achievements should be treated with respect*) appreciation, consideration, recognition, attention, notice, esteem, admiration, approbation, approval, attentiveness, politeness, courtesy, civility. **3** (*it shows great respect for form and colour*) regard, heed, consideration, attention, notice. **4** (*a disappointment in all respects*) aspect, regard, particular, point, detail, matter, facet, feature, way, sense, characteristic. **5** (*with respect to the above*) reference, connection, relation, bearing, regard.

respectable *adj* **1** (*a respectable establishment*) respected, worthy, estimable, laudable, commendable, praiseworthy, admirable, honourable, dignified, venerable, reputable, trustworthy, honest, upright, proper, decent, decorous, virtuous, good, presentable. OPPOSITE: disreputable. **2** (*a respectable result*) acceptable, reasonable, appreciable, passable, tolerable, fair, adequate, satisfactory, all right, OK (*inf*). **3** (*she had put aside a respectable sum*) goodly, ample, considerable, sizable, substantial, reasonable, fair.

respectful *adj* courteous, courtly, polite, mannerly, well-mannered, civil, gracious, deferential, reverent, reverential, considerate, thoughtful, dutiful, obedient, submissive, subservient, humble. OPPOSITE: disrespectful.

respective *adj* individual, personal, separate, several, various, specific, particular, special, own, corresponding, relevant.

respects *pl noun* greetings, compliments, regards, best wishes, good wishes, remembrances, salutations.

respite *noun* **1** (*a respite in activity*) pause, lull, rest, break, interval, intermission, interruption, breather (*inf*), breathing space, let-up (*inf*), cessation, halt, gap, hiatus, relief, relaxation, recess. **2** (*the condemned man was granted a respite*) adjournment, postponement, suspension, deferment, delay, reprieve, remission, stay, stay of execution, moratorium.

resplendent *adj* splendid, glorious, bright, brilliant, radiant, irradiant, shining, dazzling, effulgent, gleaming, beaming, glittering, sparkling, lustrous, luminous. OPPOSITE: dull.

respond *verb* **1** (*respond to their inquiry*) reply, answer, acknowledge. **2** (*he responded to the insult immediately*) answer, reply, rejoin, retort, counter, riposte, come back, reciprocate, return.

response *noun* **1** (*she is still awaiting a response*) reply, answer, acknowledgement, rejoinder, retort, riposte, return, comeback (*inf*). **2** (*the programme provoked quite a response*) reaction, feedback, comeback (*inf*), reply.

responsibility *noun* **1** (*that is your responsibility*) duty, obligation, onus, role, task, affair, business, concern, baby (*inf*), burden, charge, care, trust. **2** (*he will have to accept responsibility*) accountability, answerability, liability, culpability, guilt, fault, blame. **3** (*she lacks responsibility*) maturity, common sense, sense, reliability, dependability, trustworthiness, stability, competence, conscientiousness. **4** (*the job brings with it considerable responsibility*) authority, power, influence, control.

responsible *adj* **1** (*responsible for the whole department*) in charge of, in control of, managing, controlling, leading, accountable, answerable, liable. **2** (*responsible for what happened*) accountable, answerable, culpable, at fault, guilty, blameworthy. **3** (*she proved herself to be very responsible*) mature, adult, dependable, reliable, competent, trustworthy, honest, conscientious, hard-working, industrious, upright, stable, steady, level-headed, sober, sound, sensible, rational, reasonable, sane. OPPOSITE: irresponsible. **4** (*he has a responsible post in government*) important, authoritative, powerful, senior, high-level (*inf*), executive.

responsive *adj* sensitive, receptive, susceptible, on the ball (*inf*), open, alert, alive, aware, awake, impressionable, sympathetic, forthcoming, perceptive, sharp, reactive, with it (*inf*). OPPOSITE: insensitive.

rest[1] *noun* **1** (*he is having a rest*) sleep, slumber, nap, doze, snooze (*inf*), forty winks (*inf*), lie-down (*inf*), siesta. **2** (*the weekend is a time for rest*) relaxation, inactivity, idleness, ease, leisure, repose. **3** (*a quick rest between sessions*) pause, lull, respite, break, breathing-space, breather (*inf*), time off, recess, holiday, vacation, interval, interlude, intermission, halt, cessation. OPPOSITE: continuation. **4** (*the sea was in a state of rest*) repose, quiet, quietness, calm, calmness, tranquillity, stillness, silence, hush, peace, peacefulness,

motionlessness, inertia, standstill. OPPOSITE: tumult. **5** (*book rest*) support, prop, brace, stand, base, holder, shelf.
➤ *verb* **1** (*no time to rest*) relax, take it easy (*inf*), laze, lounge, go to bed, sleep, slumber, nap, take a nap, catnap, doze, repose, recline, lie down, sit down, put one's feet up (*inf*). OPPOSITE: work. **2** (*the diggers rested from their efforts*) cease, desist, stop, halt, pause, stay. OPPOSITE: continue. **3** (*he rested the rifle on his knee*) support, prop, stand, place, position, lean, lay, lie, steady. **4** (*a lot rests on the outcome*) hinge, hang, depend, rely.

rest[2] *noun* (*the rest of the shipment was thrown away*) remainder, remains, residue, residuum, balance, surplus, excess, rump, remnants, leftovers, others.
➤ *verb* **1** (*please rest assured of our best attentions*) remain, stay, continue. **2** (*the final responsibility rests at his door*) lie, reside.

restful *adj* **1** (*restful music*) relaxing, calming, soothing, tranquillizing. **2** (*a restful scene*) calm, tranquil, serene, quiet, still, peaceful, placid, sleepy, languid, leisurely, unhurried, relaxed, undisturbed, comfortable. OPPOSITE: tumultuous.

restitution *noun* restoration, return, reparation, amends, damages, redress, atonement, requital, retribution, satisfaction, compensation, indemnity, indemnification, recompense, remuneration, repayment, refund, reimbursement. OPPOSITE: injury.

restive *adj* **1** (*the cattle were restive*) restless, unsettled, unquiet, uneasy, ill at ease, edgy, on edge, nervous, worked up, tense, uptight (*inf*), anxious, agitated, jumpy (*inf*), jittery (*inf*), fretful, impatient, fidgety. **2** (*a restive crowd of protestors*) refractory, recalcitrant, stubborn, obstinate, wilful, wayward, unruly, turbulent, unmanageable, uncontrollable. OPPOSITE: docile.

restless *adj* **1** (*she has been restless all day*) uneasy, ill at ease, restive, unquiet, fidgety, jittery (*inf*), jumpy (*inf*), edgy, on edge, fretful, nervous, anxious, worried, uptight (*inf*), agitated, unruly, troubled, turbulent, unsettled, impatient. **2** (*spent a restless night*) disturbed, broken, sleepless, wakeful, fitful, uncomfortable. OPPOSITE: restful. **3** (*the restless waves*) moving, active, unstable, changing, changeable, inconstant. OPPOSITE: still. **4** (*restless herds of zebra*) unsettled, wandering, roving, roaming, nomadic, itinerant, travelling, migrant, peripatetic.

restoration *noun* **1** (*restoration of the castle*) renovation, repair, reconstruction, rebuilding, refurbishment, reconditioning, rehabilitation, renewal. **2** (*the child's restoration to full health*) recovery, resuscitation, revival, refreshment, rejuvenation, revitalization. OPPOSITE: decline. **3** (*the restoration of her belongings*) return, restitution, replacement, reinstatement, recovery, compensation. OPPOSITE: removal. **4** (*the restoration of the monarchy*) reinstatement, reinstitution, reinstallation, reintroduction, re-establishment, reimposition.

restore *verb* **1** (*restore his belongings*) return, give back, hand back, send back, replace, put back, bring back. OPPOSITE: remove. **2** (*hope to restore parliamentary democracy*) reintroduce, reinstate, re-establish. **3** (*restore the whole palace to its original splendour*) renovate, redecorate, refurbish, repair, do up (*inf*), fix up (*inf*), touch up, mend, recondition, revamp, rebuild, reconstruct, remodel, rehabilitate, set to rights. **4** (*the patient is now fully restored*) renew, revive, revivify, resuscitate, revitalize, refresh, reinvigorate, strengthen, cure, build up. **5** (*restore the book to its proper place*) return, replace, put back, reinstate. **6** (*they restored the monarchy*) reinstate, reinstitute, reinstall, reintroduce, re-establish, reimpose.

restrain *verb* **1** (*restrain the angry mob*) hold back, curb, control, hold in check, subdue, keep within bounds. **2** (*restrain her impatience*) suppress, repress, control, check, bridle, moderate, smother, stifle, bottle up, contain, rein in. **3** (*restrain the horse from bolting*) prevent, stop, hold back, hinder, impede, obstruct, delay, inhibit. **4** (*restrain those suspects*) detain, arrest, lock up, imprison, confine, restrict, bind, tie up, chain up, fetter, manacle, pinnion. OPPOSITE: release.

restrained *adj* **1** (*she is very restrained for an actress*) controlled, self-controlled, self-restrained, unemotional, undemonstrative, uncommunicative, reticent, calm, steady, cool, aloof. **2** (*restrained shades*) muted, quiet, calm, mild, soft, subdued, subtle, discreet, understated, low-key, unobtrusive, tasteful, moderate.

restraint *noun* **1** (*an effective restraint on their enthusiasm*) constraint, check, curb, block, barrier, hindrance, impediment, deterrent, inhibition. **2** (*showed restraint under pressure*) self-restraint, self-control, self-discipline, moderation, judiciousness, prudence. **3** (*no place for restraint in her personal relationships*) self-restraint, self-control, self-possession, reserve, reticence, detachment, aloofness, coldness, formality, uncommunicativeness. **4** (*the suspects were placed under restraint*) restriction, confinement, detention, imprisonment, captivity, incarceration, duress, bondage. **5** (*a certain restraint in the decoration*) discrimination, subtlety, taste, tastefulness, discretion, understatedness, muteness.

restrict *verb* **1** (*restrict freedom of movement*) impede, hamper, hinder, handicap, retard, cramp. **2** (*restrict opening hours*) regulate, control, limit, moderate, keep within bounds, curtail. **3** (*restrict the suspects*) restrain, confine, lock up, imprison, wall up, hem in.

restricted *adj* **1** (*restricted leg-room*) cramped, confined, small, narrow, limited, tight. **2** (*restricted fuel consumption*) limited, controlled, regulated, moderate. **3** (*this area is restricted*) off limits, out of bounds, limited, secret, private.

restriction *noun* **1** (*restrictions on trade*) restraint, constraint, limitation, control, check, curb, ban, embargo, regulation, condition, provision, proviso, stipulation, qualification. OPPOSITE: freedom. **2** (*due to restriction of space*) confinement, constraint, crampedness. **3** (*the restriction of movement*) hindrance, impediment, handicap, cramping.

result *noun* **1** (*the result of all these efforts*) consequence, outcome, issue, effect, upshot, end, pay-off (*inf*), conclusion, termination, sequel, aftermath, repercussion, implication, reaction, event, product, end-product, by-product, side-effect, fruit, development.

OPPOSITE: cause. **2** (*the result of the calculation*) answer, solution.

➤ *verb* **1** (*a new policy resulted from these exchanges*) ensue, follow, eventuate, come about, issue, proceed, stem, flow, arise, emerge, emanate, spring, develop, evolve, occur, eventuate, happen. **2** (*result in the club's closure*) end, finish, culminate, terminate. OPPOSITE: begin.

resume *verb* **1** (*resume contact with her old friend*) renew, take up, recommence, restart, reopen, reinstitute. **2** (*resume what he had been doing before the fire*) continue, proceed, carry on, go on, reconvene. OPPOSITE: stop.

résumé *noun* summary, précis, abstract, synopsis, epitome, outline, sketch, digest, recapitulation, review, overview, breakdown, run-down, abridgement, compendium. OPPOSITE: amplification.

resurrect *verb* **1** (*resurrect from the dead*) raise, revive, restore. **2** (*resurrect the project*) revive, revitalize, renew, restore, resuscitate, breathe new life into, reactivate, bring back, reintroduce, re-establish, reinstall.

resurrection *noun* revival, revitalization, reappearance, comeback (*inf*), resuscitation, regeneration, rebirth, renaissance, resurgence, restoration, return, reintroduction, re-establishment, reinstallation. OPPOSITE: extinction.

resuscitate *verb* **1** (*resuscitate the child*) revive, bring round, save. **2** (*resuscitate the project*) revive, revivify, revitalize, restore, renew, reanimate, reinvigorate, resurrect, bring back, reintroduce, bring new life into.

retain *verb* **1** (*retain one's grip on reality*) keep, maintain, hold, keep hold of, grasp, grip, hang on to (*inf*). **2** (*retain the monarchy*) keep, hold, reserve, save, preserve, maintain. OPPOSITE: relinquish. **3** (*he retained every detail of the scene*) remember, recall, recollect, memorize, bear in mind, keep in mind, call to mind. OPPOSITE: forget. **4** (*retained for the season*) engage, employ, hire, pay, commission.

retainer *noun* **1** (*a family retainer*) servant, domestic, attendant, valet, lackey, footman, vassal, dependant, supporter. **2** (*pay a retainer*) fee, payment, deposit, advance.

retaliate *verb* return like for like (*inf*), repay, reciprocate, counter-attack, strike back, hit back, fight back, get back at, get one's own back (*inf*), get even with (*inf*), even the scores, settle a score, revenge, avenge, requite, exact retribution, pay someone back. OPPOSITE: forgive.

retard *verb* delay, slow down, slow up, brake, hold back, hold up, set back, detain, check, restrain, hinder, impede, hamper, obstruct, thwart, frustrate, interfere with, interrupt, restrict, handicap, incapacitate, arrest, halt, decelerate. OPPOSITE: accelerate.

retch *verb* gag, heave, reach, vomit, regurgitate, throw up (*inf*), puke (*inf*), spew, be sick, disgorge.

reticence *noun* reserve, restraint, shyness, diffidence, taciturnity, uncommunicativeness, secretiveness, quietness, silence, muteness.

reticent *adj* reserved, restrained, shy, diffident, taciturn, uncommunicative, unforthcoming, secretive, quiet, silent, tight-lipped, close-mouthed, mute, mum. OPPOSITE: garrulous.

retinue *noun* suite, followers, following, train, entourage, cortège, attendants, aides, servants, escort, bodyguard, personnel, staff.

retire *verb* **1** (*she retired from work last summer*) give up work, stop work, leave work, resign, bow out (*inf*), put out to grass (*inf*). **2** (*the generals retired to the next room*) withdraw, go away, go out, leave, depart, exit. **3** (*the mob retired from the square*) withdraw, retreat, pull back, fall back, give ground, decamp, recede, ebb. **4** (*time to retire for the night*) go to bed, turn in (*inf*), hit the hay (*inf*), hit the sack (*inf*), call it a day (*inf*).

retirement *noun* **1** (*the retirement of the royal party*) withdrawal, exit, departure. **2** (*the great man lives in retirement now*) seclusion, solitude, loneliness, retreat, privacy, obscurity.

retiring *adj* shy, reserved, reticent, quiet, diffident, bashful, timid, timorous, coy, modest, nervous, demure, meek, humble, unassuming, unassertive, self-effacing, shrinking. OPPOSITE: forward.

retort *verb* answer, reply, respond, riposte, retaliate, counter, return, rejoin.
➤ *noun* answer, reply, response, riposte, quip, repartee, rejoinder.

retract *verb* **1** (*retract the allegation*) recant, withdraw, take back, unsay, deny, abjure, disclaim, disavow, repudiate, disown, renounce, revoke, repeal, rescind, cancel, annul, recall, reverse, go back on, backtrack on, renege on, abrogate. OPPOSITE: confirm. **2** (*retract the aerial*) draw back, draw in, pull back, pull in, sheathe.

retreat *verb* **1** (*the enemy retreated*) retire, withdraw, depart, decamp, leave, pull back, fall back, back off, draw back, give ground, give way, recoil, shrink, turn tail (*inf*), quit (*inf*), flee, take flight. OPPOSITE: advance. **2** (*the water has retreated*) recede, ebb, go back.
➤ *noun* **1** (*the enemy are in retreat*) retirement, withdrawal, drawing back, pulling back, falling back, decamping, departure, evacuation, flight. **2** (*a country retreat*) refuge, haven, harbour, hideaway, hideout, resort, asylum, sanctuary, sanctum, shelter, den. **3** (*seeking retreat from all his cares*) retirement, sanctuary, privacy, seclusion, solitude.

retrench *verb* **1** (*the industry must retrench*) economize, save, cut back, slim down, reduce expenditure, husband resources. **2** (*the budget must be retrenched*) curtail, reduce, decrease, lessen, diminish, cut, shorten, abridge, abbreviate, crop, clip, trim, pare, prune, limit, restrict.

retribution *noun* punishment, reward, justice, just deserts (*inf*), nemesis, revenge, vengeance, retaliation, reckoning, reprisal, requital, repayment, payment, redress, satisfaction, reparation, restitution, recompense, compensation, measure for measure, tit for tat. OPPOSITE: pardon.

retrieve *verb* **1** (*retrieved her belongings*) recover, regain, get back, recoup, win back, redeem, reclaim, repossess, recapture, salvage, rescue, save, restore. OPPOSITE: lose. **2** (*retrieve the ball*) bring back, return, fetch, collect. **3** (*a plan to retrieve the situation*) remedy, repair, mend, set right, set to rights, put to rights, rectify, correct, redress, make good.

retrograde *adj* **1** (*a retrograde move*) backward, inverse, retreating, retrogressive, reverse. OPPOSITE: forward. **2** (*a retrograde condition*) declining, downward, waning, worsening, deteriorating, degenerate.

retrogress *verb* decline, deteriorate, worsen, wane, relapse, degenerate, regress, return, revert, retrograde, recede, drop, ebb, fall, sink, retrocede, withdraw, retire, retreat, backslide. OPPOSITE: progress.

retrospect *noun* review, survey, reminiscence, remembrance, recollection, hindsight, afterthought, reflection. OPPOSITE: speculation.

in retrospect retrospectively, on reflection, with hindsight, on looking back, on thinking back.

return *verb* **1** (*return to your homes*) go back, go home, revert, retreat. OPPOSITE: depart. **2** (*the bad weather has returned*) come back, come again, recur, reappear. **3** (*the spring will return on itself*) recoil, rebound, boomerang. **4** (*return the broom to the cupboard*) restore, replace, put back, reinstate, reinstall, take back, re-establish, carry back. OPPOSITE: remove. **5** (*please return his good wishes*) reciprocate, requite, repay, give back, send back, refund, remit, do the same (*inf*), exchange, match, equal, correspond. **6** (*the business is returning a good profit*) yield, earn, bring in, make, net. **7** (*he returned that he did not care*) retort, rejoin, riposte, answer, reply, respond, come back. **8** (*return the ball*) pass back, throw back, hit back, send back. **9** (*he was returned with a healthy majority*) elect, vote in, select, pick, choose. **10** (*the panel returned a gloomy verdict*) pronounce, deliver, bring in, announce, declare, submit.
➤ *noun* **1** (*we await her return*) homecoming, reappearance, arrival, turning up. **2** (*the return of the barrel*) recoil, rebound. **3** (*the return of the stolen items*) restoration, replacement, restitution, reinstatement, reinstallment. **4** (*in return for the favour*) exchange, response, reciprocation, repayment, requital, reparation, recompense. **5** (*expect a good return on the investment*) profit, gain, income, revenue, yield, interest, benefit, advantage. OPPOSITE: loss. **6** (*he got a sharp return*) retort, rejoinder, riposte, answer, reply, response, comeback (*inf*). **7** (*that tallies with the official returns*) statement, report, form, account, summary.

reveal *verb* **1** (*he opened the curtain to reveal the view*) show, exhibit, display, expose. OPPOSITE: conceal. **2** (*investigation revealed the seriousness of the flaw*) expose, uncover, unfold, bare, lay bare, unmask, unveil, unearth, bring to light. **3** (*she soon revealed the extent of her involvement*) disclose, divulge, make known, make public, tell, let out, let slip, let on, impart, communicate, broadcast, publish, publicize, proclaim, betray, leak, give away.

revel *verb* **1** (*she revelled in the thought*) wallow, bask, luxuriate, indulge, relish, savour, gloat over, rejoice, delight, take pleasure. **2** (*they revelled all night long*) party, whoop it up (*inf*), live it up (*inf*), rave (*inf*), carouse, make merry, celebrate, roister, paint the town red (*inf*), push the boat out (*inf*), go out on the town (*inf*), raise the roof (*inf*). OPPOSITE: mourn.
➤ *noun* carousal, spree, merrymaking, debauch, orgy, party, rave (*inf*), rave-up (*inf*), bash (*inf*), celebration, gala, festival, carnival, revelry, festivity, jollification.

revelation *noun* **1** (*the revelation of the view*) display, show, exhibition, exposure. **2** (*the revelation of terrible secrets*) uncovering, unearthing, bringing to light, discovery, disclosure, exposure, divulgence, publishing, publicizing, broadcasting, communication, proclamation, leaking, betrayal, exposition, manifestation, unmasking, confession, admission. OPPOSITE: concealment. **3** (*startling revelations in the press*) disclosure, divulgence, information, fact, detail, communication, announcement, proclamation, leak.

reveller *noun* party-goer, merrymaker, celebrator, raver, pleasure-seeker, carouser, roisterer, wassailer.

revelry *noun* celebrations, festivities, merriment, merrymaking, jollification, jollity, carousal, revels, debauchery, orgy, saturnalia. OPPOSITE: mourning.

revenge *noun* **1** (*sought revenge for this betrayal*) vengeance, retribution, reprisal, retaliation, requital, redress, satisfaction. OPPOSITE: forgiveness. **2** (*motivated by revenge*) vengefulness, spite, spitefulness, vindictiveness, malice, maliciousness, ill will, animosity, hostility, hate, hatred, venom, rancour, bitterness.
≫ *verb* avenge, requite, exact retribution for, get back at, hit back at, take reprisals for, settle a score (*inf*), get even with (*inf*), retaliate, fight back, return, repay, pay back. OPPOSITE: forgive.

revengeful *adj* vengeful, vindictive, malevolent, spiteful, malicious, malignant, bitter, resentful, unforgiving, merciless, unmerciful, pitiless, implacable, cruel, harsh. OPPOSITE: merciful.

revenue *noun* income, receipts, return, yield, profit, gain, proceeds, takings, rewards, interest. OPPOSITE: expenditure.

reverberate *verb* echo, re-echo, resonate, resound, ring, boom, vibrate.

revere *verb* reverence, venerate, honour, pay homage to, worship, adore, exalt, idolize, admire, respect, esteem, think highly of, look up to, defer to. OPPOSITE: despise.

reverence *noun* veneration, worship, honour, adoration, exaltation, admiration, devotion, homage, respect, esteem, deference, awe. OPPOSITE: contempt.
≫ *verb* revere, admire, respect, defer to, acknowledge, worship, venerate, adore, exalt, idolize.

reverent *adj* reverential, solemn, pious, devout, respectful, deferential, dutiful, humble, meek, submissive, awed, admiring, adoring, devoted, loving, worshipping. OPPOSITE: disrespectful.

reverie *noun* dream, fantasy, daydream, trance, abstraction, absentmindedness, inattention, musing, woolgathering, daydreaming, preoccupation, brown study. OPPOSITE: attention.

reversal *noun* **1** (*a reversal in official attitudes*) U-turn (*inf*), turn-round, turn-about, about-turn, about-face, volte-face, change of heart. **2** (*we experienced a reversal*) reverse, upset, blow, check, defeat, disappointment, setback, failure, misfortune, mishap, affliction, misadventure, adversity, hardship, difficulty, problem, vicissitude, delay. **3** (*the reversal of their roles*) exchange, change, swapping, trading, trade-off. **4** (*the reversal of the court's decision*) overturn, overthrow, revocation, repeal, countermanding, rescinding, annulment, cancellation, negation, invalidation, nullification.

reverse *verb* **1** (*reverse the vehicle*) back, back up, move backwards, retreat, backtrack, withdraw. OPPOSITE:

advance. **2** (*reverse the paper*) invert, transpose, turn round. **3** (*reverse the chair*) upend, upset, upturn, overturn, invert. OPPOSITE: right. **4** (*they reversed roles*) change, exchange, swap, trade. **5** (*the decision may be reversed by a higher court*) negate, invalidate, cancel, quash, overrule, countermand, set aside, revoke, annul, nullify, declare null and void, void, rescind, repeal, undo, upset, overturn, overthrow, alter, change.
≫ *noun* **1** (*the reverse is also true*) opposite, contrary, converse, inverse, antithesis. **2** (*write on the reverse of the paper*) back, rear, other side, flip side, underside. **3** (*the army experienced a series of reverses*) setback, reversal, check, delay, blow, defeat, failure, rout, disappointment, upset, misfortune, mishap, misadventure, mischance, adversity, hardship, trial, affliction, vicissitude, problem, difficulty. OPPOSITE: success.
≫ *adj* **1** (*a reverse opinion*) opposite, contrary, converse, inverse. **2** (*give the results in reverse order*) reversed, backwards, inverted, transposed.

revert *verb* return, go back, relapse, lapse, backslide, regress, resume.

review *noun* **1** (*a review of recent developments*) survey, report, study, analysis, assessment, inspection, examination, scrutiny, appraisal. **2** (*a thorough review of existing standards*) re-examination, reassessment, re-evaluation, reconsideration, reappraisal, recapitulation, revision, rethink (*inf*). **3** (*the play got a favourable review*) notice, criticism, critique, commentary, assessment, evaluation, judgment, rating, study. **4** (*publish a scientific review*) periodical, journal, magazine, newspaper. **5** (*we all attended the review of the navy*) parade, procession, display, inspection, march past.
≫ *verb* **1** (*let us review what we already know*) reconsider, size up (*inf*), take stock of, re-examine, reassess, recapitulate, recap (*inf*), re-evaluate, reappraise, revise, rethink. **2** (*review past glories*) recall, recollect, remember, reflect on, look back on, call to mind, summon up, evoke. **3** (*review current procedure*) inspect, examine, analyse, scrutinize, survey, study, assess, appraise. **4** (*she reviews the latest films*) criticize, assess, appraise, evaluate, judge, weigh up, discuss. **5** (*she reviews the army every summer*) inspect, view.

reviewer *noun* critic, commentator, judge, observer, connoisseur, arbiter.

revile *verb* abuse, scorn, vituperate, upbraid, reproach, vilify, asperse, smear, traduce, malign, denigrate, defame, slander, libel, calumniate. OPPOSITE: extol.

revise *noun* **1** (*we must revise accepted theory*) change, alter, reconsider, review, re-examine, reassess. **2** (*he revised his work extensively*) edit, rewrite, reword, redraft, correct, amend, emend, change, alter, modify, revamp, rework, recast, update. **3** (*revise for the exam*) study, cram (*inf*), mug up (*inf*), swot (*inf*), bone up on (*inf*), go over, run through, reread, learn, memorize.

revision *noun* **1** (*revision of the final draft*) correction, editing, rewriting, updating, alteration, amendment, emendation, modification, recasting. **2** (*the page was covered with revisions*) alteration, correction, amendation, emendation. **3** (*revision of current thinking*) alteration, amendment, changing, reconsideration, reconstruction, re-examination, review. **4** (*spend long hours on revision*) study, mugging up (*inf*), swotting (*inf*), rereading, memorizing, learning.

revival *noun* **1** (*the revival of the drowned man*) resuscitation, kiss of life. **2** (*the revival of a neglected tradition*) resurrection, restoration, reintroduction, re-establishment, reinstallation, rebirth, reawakening, resurgence, upsurge, resuscitation, revitalization, renewal, renaissance.

revive *verb* **1** (*attempt to revive the drowned man*) resuscitate, bring round, save. **2** (*the girl revived quickly from her faint*) recover, revive, recover consciousness, come round, wake up, rally. **3** (*a strong drink will revive you*) restore, refresh, cheer, hearten, revivify, reanimate, reinvigorate, invigorate, enliven, quicken, rouse, awaken, revitalize, rejuvenate, comfort. **4** (*this announcement should revive interest in the idea*) renew, restore, regenerate, rekindle, resuscitate, revitalize, re-establish.

revoke *verb* retract, withdraw, recant, take back, disavow, repudiate, rescind, renege, repeal, abrogate, annul, nullify, declare null and void, void, abolish, cancel, invalidate, overrule, override, quash, recall, reverse, countermand, set aside, abjure. OPPOSITE: confirm.

revolt *noun* rebellion, rising, uprising, insurrection, insurgence, mutiny, revolution, coup, coup d'état, putsch. OPPOSITE: loyalty.
≫ *verb* **1** (*the peasants revolted against their masters*) rebel, rise up, rise, riot, resist, mutiny, take up arms, take to the streets, defect, dissent. OPPOSITE: submit. **2** (*the idea revolts me*) disgust, repel, nauseate, sicken, make sick, put one off, turn one off (*inf*), turn one's stomach, offend, appal, shock, outrage, scandalize. OPPOSITE: attract.

revolting *adj* repulsive, repellent, repugnant, offensive, obnoxious, disgusting, nauseating, sickening, foul, distasteful, off putting, horrid, loathsome, abhorrent, despicable, contemptible, reprehensible, abominable, shocking, appalling, nasty, horrible, hateful, hideous, vile, odious, heinous, obscene. OPPOSITE: attractive.

revolution *noun* **1** (*the government was overthrown by a revolution*) revolt, rebellion, rising, uprising, insurrection, insurgence, mutiny, riot, sedition, putsch, coup, coup d'état. **2** (*a revolution in telecommunications*) transformation, metamorphosis, innovation, reformation, upheaval, upset, explosion, earthquake, cataclysm, sea change, change, alteration, shift. OPPOSITE: conservatism. **3** (*with each revolution of the sails*) rotation, turn, whirl, wheel, spin, circle, circuit, cycle, gyration, round, lap.

revolutionary *adj* **1** (*revolutionary factions within the army*) rebellious, rebel, mutinous, subversive, extremist, seditious, insurgent, insurrectionary, insurrectionist, insubordinate, anarchistic, factious. **2** (*a time of revolutionary change*) radical, complete, far-reaching, thoroughgoing, profound, drastic, progressive, innovative, new, novel, experimental.
≫ *noun* rebel, revolutionist, insurgent, anarchist, subversive, insurrectionist, mutineer.

revolve *verb* **1** (*the earth revolves in space*) go round, rotate, turn, wheel, whirl, spin, pivot, swivel, gyrate, circle, orbit. **2** (*his day revolves around his job*) centre on,

turn on, hinge on, hang on, focus on, concentrate on. **3** (*he revolved her words in his head*) turn over, mull over, consider, reflect upon, think over, think about, deliberate, meditate, ruminate, ponder, muse over.

revulsion *noun* repugnance, repulsion, disgust, nausea, loathing, hate, hatred, abomination, abhorrence, contempt, detestation, aversion, dislike, distaste, shrinking, recoil. OPPOSITE: attraction.

reward *noun* **1** (*he expects a reward for his help*) payment, recompense, return, requital, compensation, remuneration, pay, pay-off, gain, profit, return, benefit, prize, award, honour, medal, decoration, premium, cut (*inf*), bonus, bounty, present, gift, tip, gratuity. OPPOSITE: punishment. **2** (*they will get their just reward in the afterlife*) punishment, penalty, retribution, retaliation, requital, just deserts, deserts, comeuppance (*inf*).
≫ *verb* pay, recompense, repay, requite, compensate, remunerate, tip, honour, decorate. OPPOSITE: punish.

rewarding *adj* satisfying, pleasing, gratifying, worthwhile, fulfilling, enriching, edifying, advantageous, beneficial, profitable, lucrative, remunerative, productive, fruitful, valuable.

rhetoric *noun* **1** (*praised for his skill at rhetoric*) eloquence, oratory, delivery. **2** (*a speech full of empty rhetoric*) verbosity, wordiness, long-windedness, hyperbole, bombast, pomposity, grandiloquence, magniloquence, fustian, turgidity, prolixity.

rhetorical *adj* **1** (*demonstrate considerable rhetorical skill*) oratorical, verbal, stylistic, linguistic. **2** (*unimpressed by such rhetorical gestures*) flowery, florid, pretentious, pompous, magniloquent, grandiloquent, grand, hyperbolic, high-flown, high-sounding, ornate, ostentatious, extravagant, flamboyant, showy, bombastic, verbose, wordy, long-winded, periphrastic, turgid, prolix, orotund, declamatory, oratorical, artificial, insincere, empty. OPPOSITE: simple.

rhyme *noun* poetry, verse, poem, ode, limerick, jingle, song, ditty.

rhythm *noun* **1** (*the drums beat out a steady rhythm*) beat, pulse, tempo, cadence, measure, metre, lilt, throb. **2** (*the rhythm of the sonnet*) metre, cadence, accent, flow, swing. **3** (*interrupt the rhythm of the traffic*) flow, movement, pattern, regularity.

ribald *adj* bawdy, risqué, racy, naughty, suggestive, smutty, off-colour, dirty, filthy, rude, vulgar, obscene, blue (*inf*), indecent, indelicate, offensive, lewd, irreverent, foul-mouthed, licentious, salacious, scurrilous, gross, coarse, earthy, low, base, broad. OPPOSITE: pure.

rich *adj* **1** (*a rich businessman*) wealthy, affluent, opulent, moneyed, propertied, prosperous, well-off, well-to-do, well-heeled (*inf*), flush (*inf*), loaded (*inf*), rolling (*inf*). OPPOSITE: poor. **2** (*rich soil*) fertile, productive, fecund, fruitful. **3** (*a rich source of minerals*) prolific, ample, abundant, plentiful, plenteous, bountiful, copious, profuse. OPPOSITE: barren. **4** (*rich with opportunities*) well-provided, well-stocked, well-supplied, packed, steeped, abounding, overflowing, replete, full, filled, rife. **5** (*furnished with rich hangings*) valuable, precious, expensive, costly, priceless, dear, lavish, lush, sumptuous, luxurious, palatial, magnificent, splendid, resplendent, grand, gorgeous, superb, fine, elegant, exquisite, opulent, exuberant. OPPOSITE: cheap. **6** (*you must avoid rich food*) heavy, creamy, oily, spicy, fatty. **7** (*a rich taste*) savoury, tasty, juicy, succulent, luscious, delicious, piquant, full-bodied, full-flavoured. OPPOSITE: tasteless. **8** (*rich colours*) bright, vivid, brilliant, intense, strong, warm, vibrant, deep. **9** (*a rich tone*) deep, sonorous, resonant, full, mellifluous, mellow, dulcet, melodious. OPPOSITE: soft. **10** (*his attitude is somewhat rich*) ironic, outrageous, preposterous, ridiculous, laughable, risible.

riches *pl noun* **1** (*a chest full of riches*) treasure, gold, money, lucre (*inf*), capital, assets, funds, means, resources. **2** (*the riches of this organization*) wealth, affluence, opulence, prosperity, fortune, substance. OPPOSITE: poverty.

richly *adv* **1** (*this richly decorated style*) lavishly, expensively, luxuriously, gorgeously, ornately, exquisitely, sumptuously, palatially, splendidly, superbly, elegantly, magnificently, resplendently. **2** (*a fate richly deserved*) fully, thoroughly, completely, well, amply, strongly, utterly, appropriately, suitably, properly.

rickety *adj* shaky, unstable, insecure, unsteady, wobbly, tottering, flimsy, infirm, frail, feeble, weak, decrepit, ramshackle, derelict, dilapidated, broken-down, jerry-built. OPPOSITE: sturdy.

rid *verb* clear, free, relieve, unburden, disencumber, deliver, release, cleanse, purge, purify.
get rid of discard, throw away, throw out, chuck out (*inf*), ditch (*inf*), junk (*inf*), dispose of, do away with, remove, eject, expel, weed out, dump, jettison, scrap, unload, eliminate, abolish, dispense with. OPPOSITE: retain.

riddle *noun* puzzle, conundrum, enigma, mystery, problem, poser, brainteaser (*inf*). OPPOSITE: solution.

ride *verb* **1** (*ride a bicycle*) sit on, mount, bestride, control, handle, manage, propel, steer, drive. **2** (*ride on a train*) travel, go, journey, move, progress.
➤ *noun* journey, trip, excursion, jaunt, outing, drive, spin (*inf*), lift. OPPOSITE: walk.

ridge *noun* ledge, crest, summit, peak, mountain, hill, hummock, bank, escarpment, saddle, reef, range, spine.

ridicule *noun* mockery, derision, scorn, laughter, satire, sarcasm, irony, raillery, badinage, banter, chaff, taunting, teasing, kidding (*inf*), ribbing (*inf*), jeering, gibing. OPPOSITE: respect.
➤ *verb* mock, scorn, deride, burlesque, lampoon, parody, caricature, satirize, send up (*inf*), laugh at, make a fool of, make fun of, poke fun at, pull someone's leg (*inf*), pooh-pooh (*inf*), humiliate, scoff at, sneer, taunt, tease, kid (*inf*), rib (*inf*), jeer at, gibe at. OPPOSITE: admire.

ridiculous *adj* **1** (*a ridiculous story*) absurd, ludicrous, hilarious, laughable, risible, comical, farcical, funny, humorous, droll, facetious. OPPOSITE: serious. **2** (*a ridiculous plan*) nonsensical, senseless, foolish, stupid, mindless, fatuous, inane, pointless, silly, derisory. **3** (*the cost is ridiculous*) fantastic, unbelievable, incredible, unreasonable, shocking, outrageous, monstrous, preposterous.

rife *adj* **1** (*pessimism is rife*) prevalent, prevailing, common, current, rampant, raging, widespread, extensive, general, universal, ubiquitous, plentiful, abundant. OPPOSITE: rare. **2** (*the place is rife with vermin*) teeming, swarming, alive, overflowing, abounding.

riff-raff *noun* rabble, mob, hoi polloi, scum (*sl*), undesirables, dregs, commonality.

rifle *verb* **1** (*rifle through the papers*) ransack, rummage, rake, go, search. **2** (*the rooms had been rifled*) plunder, pillage, loot, sack, ransack, despoil, maraud, strip. **3** (*the contents of the cashbox had been rifled*) rob, steal, thieve, burgle.

rift *noun* **1** (*a rift in the cliff-face*) split, cleft, fault, fissure, fracture, crevice, chink, cranny, slit, crack, breach, break, gap, cavity, hole, aperture, opening, space. **2** (*a rift between friends*) difference, disagreement, quarrel, falling-out (*inf*), fight, conflict, row, feud, altercation, schism, split, breach, separation, division, alienation, estrangement. OPPOSITE: reconciliation.

rig *verb* **1** (*rig the expedition out*) equip, supply, furnish, provide, make ready. **2** (*all rigged out for the party*) kit out, fit, outfit, accoutre, attire, deck, bedeck, drape, array, clothe, dress, garb, robe, trim, turn out, trick out. **3** (*rig up a shelter*) put up, put together, throw together (*inf*), cobble together (*inf*), knock up (*inf*), erect, build, assemble, improvise, fit up, fix up. **4** (*rig the vote*) manipulate, falsify, fake, forge, trump up, doctor, pervert, tamper with, fix (*inf*), cook (*inf*), fiddle, distort, twist, engineer, arrange, manoeuvre, juggle, massage, misrepresent.
➤ *noun* gear, equipment, outfit, accoutrements, fittings, fixtures, apparatus, machinery, tackle, rigging, kit.

right *adj* **1** (*we believe it is the right thing to do*) just, fair, equitable, lawful, legal, good, virtuous, righteous, upright, moral, ethical, honourable, honest, principled, proper. OPPOSITE: wrong. **2** (*this is the right answer*) true, factual, actual, real, correct, accurate, precise, exact, valid, unerring, spot on (*inf*), bang on (*inf*). OPPOSITE: incorrect. **3** (*everything about this antique feels right*) authentic, genuine, legitimate, legit (*inf*), legal, lawful. **4** (*the way he treats her is not right*) proper, seemly, becoming, fit, fitting, apt, appropriate, suitable, desirable, preferable, ideal. OPPOSITE: inappropriate. **5** (*conditions are not right*) advantageous, convenient, suitable, appropriate, propitious, opportune, desirable, favourable. **6** (*not right in the head*) healthy, well, sound, normal, sane, rational, all there (*inf*), reasonable, lucid, sensible. **7** (*she feels right as rain now*) fine, well, healthy, fit, sound, normal, up to par, up to scratch (*inf*), in the pink (*inf*). **8** (*things are in a right muddle*) real, complete, absolute, total, thorough, thoroughgoing, utter, out-and-out. **9** (*a political swing to the right*) conservative, Tory, true-blue, reactionary.
➤ *adv* **1** (*it needs to be done right*) properly, correctly, well, satisfactorily. **2** (*it hit me right where it hurts*) precisely, exactly, accurately, squarely, just, bang, slap-bang (*inf*). **3** (*she went right there*) straight, directly, in a straight line, as the crow flies. **4** (*I'll be right with you*) immediately, instantly, promptly, quickly, directly, straightaway, without delay. **5** (*he's gone right over the top*) all the way, absolutely, totally, completely, entirely, wholly, utterly, quite. **6** (*we must do right by them*) properly, fairly, justly, honourably, honestly, morally,

ethically. **7** (*things will turn out right in the end*) well, favourably, advantageously, beneficially, for the better, for the best.

≫ *noun* **1** (*a right to privacy*) claim, title, privilege, prerogative, entitlement, birthright, authority, power, licence, freedom, opportunity, sanction, charter, warrant, due, permission. **2** (*right will triumph*) justice, fairness, equity, impartiality, legality, lawfulness, good, goodness, righteousness, virtue, virtuousness, rectitude, uprightness, honesty, truth, truthfulness, integrity, honour, honourableness, morality, ethics, propriety. OPPOSITE: wrong.

≫ *verb* **1** (*right the signpost*) set upright, stand up, adjust, erect. **2** (*try to right the situation*) straighten out, sort out, rectify, correct, redress, repair, fix, put right, put to rights, put in order, tidy up. **3** (*right ancient wrongs*) avenge, settle, set right, vindicate, redress, rectify, compensate for.

by right rightfully, rightly, correctly, in fairness, with justice, justly, justifiably, legally, lawfully, legitimately, properly.

put to rights right, set right, put right, sort out, fix, settle, straighten out, rectify, correct, put in order, repair, tidy up.

right away immediately, right now, now, straight away, straight off (*inf*), at once, this instant, instantly, directly, promptly, forthwith, without delay, without hesitation.

righteous *adj* **1** (*a righteous man*) good, virtuous, moral, ethical, upright, law-abiding, honest, honourable, incorrupt, worthy, god-fearing, holy, saintly, pure, innocent, faultless, blameless, guiltless, sinless, irreproachable, just, fair, equitable. OPPOSITE: wicked. **2** (*righteous anger*) justifiable, justified, rightful, proper, well-founded, supportable, excusable, defensible, admissible, explainable, allowable, warranted, reasonable, legitimate, valid, lawful, legal.

righteousness *noun* goodness, virtue, virtuousness, uprightness, innocence, blamelessness, purity, holiness, honesty, honour, honourableness, integrity, rectitude, morality, ethicalness, ethics, probity, faithfulness.

rightful *adj* legal, lawful, licit, legitimate, authorized, proper, suitable, correct, right, true, real, genuine, valid, just, fair, bona fide. OPPOSITE: wrongful.

rigid *adj* **1** (*rigid material*) stiff, hard, inflexible, unbending, unbendable, inelastic, unmalleable, taut, unyielding. OPPOSITE: flexible. **2** (*a rigid programme of study*) fixed, set, firm, hard and fast, invariable, unvarying, unalterable, unchangeable, inflexible. **3** (*he has a rigid faith in the death penalty*) strict, stern, rigorous, stringent, severe, harsh, austere, uncompromising, intransigent, unrelenting, tough, exact, precise, inflexible, unswerving.

rigorous *adj* **1** (*a rigorous training programme*) strict, stern, severe, hard, harsh, austere, tough, stringent, firm, rigid, inflexible, intransigent, uncompromising, exacting, demanding. **2** (*rigorous adherence to the rules*) exacting, meticulous, painstaking, laborious, conscientious, thorough, scrupulous, punctilious, nice, exact, precise, accurate. OPPOSITE: lax.

rigour *noun* **1** (*the rigours of a northern winter*) severity, hardship, harshness, adversity, privation, ordeal, trial,

suffering. **2** (*the rigour of the present rules*) strictness, firmness, sternness, severity, stringency, harshness, austerity, hardness, inflexibility, rigidity, intransigence. OPPOSITE: laxity. **3** (*he employed great rigour in completing the task*) accuracy, precision, preciseness, exactitude, exactness, meticulousness, punctiliousness, conscientiousness, scrupulousness, thoroughness.

rile *verb* annoy, irritate, vex, irk, nettle, peeve (*inf*), pique, put out, upset, bug (*inf*), exasperate, aggravate (*inf*), anger, incense. OPPOSITE: pacify.

rim *noun* **1** (*the rim of the cup*) edge, lip, brim, circumference. **2** (*the rim of the known world*) edge, margin, brink, verge, border, circumference. OPPOSITE: centre.

rind *noun* skin, peel, husk, shell, crust, epicarp.

ring[1] *noun* **1** (*the ring on her finger*) band, circle, round, loop, hoop. **2** (*a ring of light*) circle, halo, disc, round, band, girdle. **3** (*a ring of spectators*) band, knot, group, circle, gathering. **4** (*a gambling ring*) syndicate, combine, cartel, club, gang, mob, crew, clique, cell, coterie, fraternity, sorority, organization, league, alliance, society, association, trust, confederacy. **5** (*the boxers entered the ring*) arena, enclosure, area.

≫ *verb* encircle, surround, gird, girdle, circle, circumscribe, encompass, loop, enclose, fence in, hem in, cage in, seal off.

ring[2] *verb* **1** (*he heard a bell ring*) peal, chime, toll, knell, tinkle, jingle, clink, clang, ding, ding-dong, sound. **2** (*the building rang with laughter*) resound, resonate, reverberate, echo, re-echo. **3** (*her coronation rang in a new age*) herald, signal, usher in, announce, proclaim. **4** (*she says she will ring him*) phone, telephone, call, summon, give a bell (*inf*), give a buzz (*inf*), give a tinkle (*inf*), get in touch with, have a word with.

≫ *noun* **1** (*the ring of the great bell*) tolling, toll, ringing, peal, pealing, knell, chime, clang, ding-dong, tinkle, clink, jingle. **2** (*he gave them a ring*) call, telephone call, phone call (*inf*), buzz (*inf*), bell (*inf*), tinkle (*inf*).

rinse *verse* wash, clean, cleanse, bathe, dip, swill, flush, wet. OPPOSITE: dry.

riot *noun* **1** (*the army struggled to put down the riot*) rebellion, revolt, uprising, rising, insurrection, insurgence, disturbance, commotion, tumult, uproar, turbulence, scuffle, rumpus, row, brawl, mêlée, free-for-all, fray, fracas, anarchy, lawlessness, disorder, confusion. OPPOSITE: order. **2** (*the end of term is an excuse for riot among students*) revelry, partying, celebration, festivity, feasting, carousal, merrymaking, jollification, boisterousness, revels, debauchery, orgy, high jinks (*inf*). OPPOSITE: sobriety. **3** (*her dress was a riot of colour*) display, exhibition, show, splash, flourish, extravaganza.

≫ *verb* **1** (*the soldiers rioted at the news*) rebel, revolt, mutiny, rise up, rampage, go on the rampage, run riot, run amok, go berserk, take to the streets, fight, brawl. **2** (*hundreds of guest rioting at the party*) revel, celebrate, carouse, make merry, roister, paint the town red (*inf*).

run riot **1** (*students ran riot in the streets*) rampage, raise hell (*inf*), run amok, run wild, go wild, go berserk. **2** (*the weeds have been allowed to run riot*) spread, proliferate, run amok.

riotous *adj* **1** (*a riotous gathering*) rebellious, mutinous, insurrectionary, insubordinate, unruly, unrestrained, disorderly, uncontrollable, ungovernable, unmanageable, rowdy, wanton, wild, violent, brawling, lawless, anarchic. **2** (*a riotous evening*) boisterous, rowdy, uproarious, rollicking, tumultuous, orgiastic, loud, noisy.

rip *verb* tear, rend, split, burst, cut, lacerate, gash, rupture, slash, slit, hack, shred, separate. OPPOSITE: mend.

ripe *adj* **1** (*ripe fruit*) mature, seasoned, tempered, ripened, mellow, developed, fully developed, grown, fully grown, ready. OPPOSITE: unripe. **2** (*the time is ripe*) right, ready, ideal, favourable, advantageous, opportune, auspicious, suitable, fit, convenient. **3** (*ripe in years*) advanced, old, far on. **4** (*all is ripe for the big day*) prepared, arranged, set, ready, fit, full, perfect, finished, complete, developed.

ripen *verb* **1** (*grapes ripen quickly here*) grow ripe, develop, mature, mellow. **2** (*allow the cheese to ripen*) mature, season, age.

riposte *noun* retort, rejoinder, comeback (*inf*), reply, answer, response, return, repartee, quip, sally.
➤ *verb* retort, reciprocate, rejoin, come back, reply, answer, respond, return, quip.

ripple *verb* undulate, flow, lap, splash, babble, eddy, gurgle, purl, ruffle, crease, pucker, crumple, wrinkle.
➤ *noun* **1** (*a ripple in the water*) ripplet, wave, undulation, lapping, splash, babble, burble, eddy, gurgle, purl, disturbance. **2** (*his resignation caused ripples throughout the industry*) repercussion, shock wave (*inf*), effect, result, consequence, reverberation.

rise *verb* **1** (*rise from your chair*) arise, get up, stand up, jump up, leap up, spring up. **2** (*watch the moon rise in the sky*) arise, ascend, mount, climb, go up, move up. **3** (*the dome rises up above the rooftops*) soar, loom, tower, rear up. **4** (*demand for these products is rising*) go up, increase, grow, swell, intensify, escalate, soar, rocket. OPPOSITE: fall. **5** (*rise in quality*) advance, progress, go up, improve. **6** (*he always rises early*) get up, arise, wake up, get out of bed, surface (*inf*). **7** (*rise through the ranks*) advance, climb, progress, get on, prosper, thrive. **8** (*this court will rise*) adjourn, break off, pause, take a break, be suspended. **9** (*rise to the challenge*) respond, react, take, answer. **10** (*rise against their oppressors*) rebel, revolt, mutiny, riot, resist, take up arms, defect. OPPOSITE: submit. **11** (*this is where the water rises*) arise, appear, emerge, spring from, issue from, flow from, stem, emanate from, originate.
➤ *noun* **1** (*the rise of the moon*) ascent, rising. **2** (*a rise in popular interest*) increase, growth, intensification, upsurge, upswing, upturn. OPPOSITE: fall. **3** (*a rise in quality*) improvement, advance, upturn. **4** (*his meteoric rise through the ranks*) climb, progress, progression, passage, promotion, advancement, aggrandizement. **5** (*he climbed a gentle rise*) slope, incline, elevation, acclivity, hill, hillock. **6** (*the staff are demanding a rise*) raise, pay increase.

risible *adj* ridiculous, ludicrous, absurd, laughable, farcical, rib-tickling (*inf*), side-splitting (*inf*), comic, comical, funny, hilarious, amusing, humorous, droll. OPPOSITE: serious.

risk *noun* **1** (*at great risk to her personal safety*) hazard, threat, peril, danger, jeopardy. OPPOSITE: safety. **2** (*little risk of anything going wrong*) chance, possibility. **3** (*this investment is a risk*) gamble, speculation, uncertainty, venture.
➤ *verb* **1** (*he risked his life*) hazard, imperil, endanger, jeopardize, put in jeopardy. **2** (*we can't risk things going wrong*) chance, venture. **3** (*risk all her money on a horse race*) chance, venture, dare, gamble.

risky *adj* hazardous, perilous, dangerous, fraught, unsafe, precarious, uncertain, tricky, chancy (*inf*), dicey (*inf*), dodgy (*inf*), iffy (*inf*), touch-and-go. OPPOSITE: safe.

risqué *adj* indecent, improper, immodest, indelicate, off-colour, naughty, rude, suggestive, crude, coarse, earthy, lewd, smutty, bawdy, blue (*inf*), dirty, filthy, racy, spicy, salacious, licentious, ribald, adult (*inf*).

rite *noun* ritual, ceremony, ceremonial, service, sacrament, observance, worship, liturgy, office, ordinance, celebration, act, performance, practice, custom, form, formality, procedure, usage, tradition, convention.

ritual *noun* **1** (*church ritual*) rite, ceremony, ceremonial, service, sacrament, observance, solemnity, office, celebration, procedure, convention, practice, tradition, act. **2** (*go through the same ritual each morning*) ceremony, custom, habit, routine, wont, procedure, practice, tradition, convention, protocol, form, usage, formality. *adj* ceremonial, ceremonious, procedural, prescribed, formal, set, customary, conventional, traditional, routine, habitual.

rival *noun* **1** (*his rival in the competition*) competitor, opponent, opposition, antagonist, adversary, contender, contestant, challenger, vier. OPPOSITE: ally. **2** (*she has few rivals as an artist*) equal, match, peer, fellow, equivalent.
➤ *adj* competitive, competing, in competition, opposing, opposed, conflicting, in conflict, contending.
➤ *verb* compete with, vie with, contend with, oppose, challenge, equal, match, parallel, measure up to, compare with, bear comparison with, emulate.

rivalry *noun* competition, competitiveness, contention, conflict, opposition, strife, struggle, vying.

road *noun* **1** (*the road was blocked with traffic*) street, thoroughfare, highway, motorway, avenue, alley, lane, boulevard, track. **2** (*the road to success*) path, way, route, course, direction.

roam *verb* wander, rove, range, ramble, tramp, trek, drift, stray, meander, amble, stroll, saunter, prowl.

roar *verb* **1** (*the crowd roared*) bellow, yell, bawl, shout, scream, shriek, cry, bay, howl, growl, rumble, thunder. OPPOSITE: murmur. **2** (*roar with laughter*) guffaw, howl, hoot, fall about, crease up, break up.
➤ *noun* **1** (*the roar of the crowd*) bellow, yell, bawl, shout, howl, growl, rumble, shriek, scream, cry. **2** (*a roar of laughter from the audience*) guffaw, howl, hoot, explosion.

rob *verb* **1** (*rob the house*) burgle, burglarize, steal from, break into, loot, plunder, pillage, raid, rifle, ransack, sack. **2** (*he was robbed by two men*) hold up, mug (*inf*), jump (*inf*). **3** (*they have been robbed of their nest egg*) defraud, diddle (*inf*), do out of (*inf*), swindle, cheat, rip off (*inf*), do (*inf*), dispossess, strip, fleece. OPPOSITE: endow. **4** (*robbed of his self-respect*) deprive, dispossess.

robber *noun* burglar, housebreaker, thief, stealer, pilferer, mugger (*inf*), bandit, hijacker, brigand, pirate, highwayman, plunderer, looter, marauder, raider, swindler, embezzler, fraudster, con man (*inf*), cheat.

robbery *noun* **1** (*accused of robbery*) burglary, housebreaking, theft, stealing, pilfering, filching, thievery, larceny, embezzlement, fraud, swindling, misappropriation, piracy, plunder, pillage, rapine, spoliation. **2** (*a bank robbery*) hold-up, stick-up (*inf*), heist (*inf*), raid, break-in, mugging (*inf*), rip-off (*inf*).

robe *noun* **1** (*he donned his formal robes*) gown, vestment, habit, dress, costume, apparel, attire. **2** (*she wore a robe over her underwear*) bathrobe, dressing-gown, housecoat, wrap.
≫ *verb* clothe, dress, garb, attire, drape, vest. OPPOSITE: strip.

robot *noun* automaton, android, machine.

robust *adj* **1** (*a robust young man*) strong, powerful, muscular, sinewy, healthy, hale, hearty, sound, vigorous, energetic, athletic, fit, hardy, tough, rugged, brawny, well-built, strapping, lusty, sturdy, burly, stalwart, stout. OPPOSITE: delicate. **2** (*a robust manner*) forceful, hard-headed, strong, direct, straightforward, firm, practical, pragmatic, sensible, realistic, no-nonsense, down-to-earth. **3** (*a robust sense of humour*) lusty, coarse, boisterous, unrefined, earthy, crude, rough, raw, indecorous, ribald, risqué.

rock¹ *noun* **1** (*a large rock crowned the ridge*) stone, boulder, crag, outcrop, reef, pebble. **2** (*the rock on which the church was founded*) foundation, cornerstone, mainstay, support, prop. **3** (*he was the rock to which she clung*) anchor, tower of strength, bulwark, protection, security.

rock² *verb* **1** (*the vessel rocked from side to side*) sway, reel, roll, pitch, tilt, tip, lurch, swing, toss, undulate, oscillate, wobble, totter, stagger. **2** (*they were rocked by the announcement*) shock, stun, stagger, bewilder, astound, astonish, surprise, startle, take aback, amaze, dumbfound, daze, shake.

rocket *verb* **1** (*rocket into the sky*) take off, shoot up, soar, zoom. **2** (*inflation will rocket*) sky-rocket (*inf*), soar, escalate, increase, take off, go through the ceiling (*inf*).

rocky¹ *adj* rock-strewn, stony, craggy, pebbly, rugged, rough.

rocky² *adj* **1** (*she still feels rather rocky*) shaky, unsteady, wobbly, unstable, staggering, tottering, teetering. **2** (*a rocky partnership*) unstable, unsteady, iffy (*inf*), uncertain, unreliable, unsure, vulnerable, threatened, weak.

rod *noun* **1** (*he did not spare the rod*) stick, cane, switch, birch, staff, baton, wand, mace. **2** (*the rod holding the machine together*) bar, shaft, strut, pole, dowel, stick.

rogue *noun* **1** (*everyone knows he's a rogue*) crook (*inf*), villain, ne'er-do-well, good-for-nothing, reprobate, charlatan, fraud, fraudster, swindler, cheat, con man (*inf*), confidence trickster, deceiver, knave, mountebank, rascal, scoundrel, wretch, cad, bounder (*inf*), miscreant, blackguard. OPPOSITE: gentleman. **2** (*her children are little rogues*) rascal, scoundrel, scamp, imp, little devil, mischief.

roguish *adj* mischievous, cheeky, impish, rascally, knavish, puckish, waggish, arch, sportive, playful, frolicsome, coquettish.

role *noun* **1** (*she appeared in the leading role*) part, character, portrayal, representation, impersonation. **2** (*fulfilled his role as chief executioner*) function, purpose, use, job, task, duty, place, post, position, situation, capacity.

roll *verb* **1** (*the ball rolled over*) go round, revolve, rotate, turn, whirl, twirl, spin, gyrate, wheel, swing. **2** (*the river rolls on*) flow, run, go, move, pass, undulate, trundle. **3** (*roll it up in cotton wool*) wrap, enfold, envelop, swathe, wind, twist, curl, coil, furl, entwine. **4** (*roll the grass*) flatten, level, smooth, press, crush, even out. **5** (*the ship rolled on the waves*) rock, sway, reel, pitch, toss, lurch, wallow, stagger. **6** (*the thunder rolled*) rumble, thunder, roar, boom, resound, reverberate.
≫ *noun* **1** (*a single roll of the ball*) revolution, rotation, cycle, turn, twirl, spin, gyration. **2** (*a roll of wool*) cylinder, roller, drum, reel, spool, bobbin, ball, scroll. **3** (*we found his name on the roll of honour*) register, roster, list, file, inventory, catalogue, schedule, record, chronicle, annals, index, directory, census. **4** (*the roll of distant thunder*) rumble, thunder, roar, boom, resonance, reverberation. **5** (*butter the rolls for tea*) bun, bap, bread. **6** (*the roll of the boat*) rocking, tossing, pitching, undulation, swell, billowing, wave.

rollicking *adj* boisterous, spirited, exuberant, hearty, lively, noisy, playful, frisky, sprightly, sportive, romping, frolicsome, jolly, jovial, joyous, light-hearted, merry, gay, carefree, devil-may-care, swashbuckling. OPPOSITE: staid.

romance *noun* **1** (*they shared a brief romance*) love, passion, love affair, affair, relationship, liaison, intrigue, amour, courtship, attachment. **2** (*a celebrated medieval romance*) story, tale, fairy tale. **3** (*readers of popular romance*) romantic fiction, love story, tearjerker (*inf*), melodrama. **4** (*lost in the realms of romance*) fantasy, fancy, fiction, imagination, whimsy, idyll, make-believe, legend. OPPOSITE: fact. **5** (*his account of events is a romance*) invention, fabrication, exaggeration, falsehood, lie, tall story (*inf*), fairy tale.
≫ *verb* **1** (*no harm in the child romancing a little*) fantasize, daydream. **2** (*that is enough of your romancing*) lie, exaggerate. **3** (*dreamed of romancing the princess*) court, woo, date (*inf*), go out with (*inf*), go steady with (*inf*), see.

romantic *adj* **1** (*she has a romantic nature*) sentimental, soppy (*inf*), mushy (*inf*), sloppy (*inf*), tender, loving, fond, passionate, amorous. OPPOSITE: cold. **2** (*he cut a romantic figure*) glamorous, exotic, exciting, fascinating, mysterious, attractive. **3** (*a romantic version of events*) fanciful, idealistic, fantastic, unrealistic, starry-eyed, optimistic, utopian, imaginary, imaginative, visionary, quixotic, fictitious, improbable, unlikely, implausible, wild, exaggerated, extravagant, impractical. OPPOSITE: realistic.
≫ *noun* romanticist, idealist, dreamer, visionary, utopian.

romp *verb* frolic, caper, cavort, frisk, skip, gambol, sport, rollick, revel, carouse, make merry.

roof *noun* cover, top, ceiling, canopy, shelter. OPPOSITE: floor.

room *noun* **1** (*the room was empty*) chamber, apartment. **2** (*plenty of room for a piano*) space, volume, area, expanse, extent, range, territory. **3** (*room for future expansion*) scope, chance, opportunity, latitude, leeway, margin, play, capacity. OPPOSITE: restriction.

roomy *adj* spacious, capacious, commodious, voluminous, generous, ample, sizable, extensive, large, broad, wide. OPPOSITE: narrow.

root *noun* **1** (*the roots of the plant*) rhizome, tuber, stem. **2** (*the root of the trouble*) base, basis, foundation, source, origin, starting-point, fount, fountain-head, seat, derivation, cause, motive, motivation, occasion, reason, rationale, ground, bottom, germ, kernel, seed, nub, crux, heart, nucleus, essence.
➤ *verb* fix, plant, implant, embed, entrench, anchor, moor, ground, base, fasten, establish, set, stick. OPPOSITE: uproot.
root and branch completely, entirely, thoroughly, totally, wholly, utterly, radically, finally.
root around dig, delve, burrow, forage, rummage, shuffle, rifle, ransack, ferret, hunt, search, poke, pry, nose.
root out 1 (*root out traitors within the service*) unearth, uproot, weed out, remove, get rid of, do away with, eradicate, eliminate, destroy, erase, abolish, put an end to. **2** (*root out what went wrong*) discover, uncover, bring to light, unearth, dig up, turn up, dredge up, establish.

rooted *adj* fixed, set, firm, rigid, ingrained, entrenched, deep, deep-seated, inveterate, confirmed, radical, fundamental. OPPOSITE: superficial.

rope *noun* cable, cord, line, string, tether, halter, lanyard, painter, hawser.
➤ *verb* tie, bind, fasten, hitch, secure, moor, lash, tether, pinion. OPPOSITE: loose.
rope in enlist, engage, persuade, talk into, involve, inveigle.

roster *noun* rota, list, listing, roll, register, catalogue, index, table, schedule, calendar, agenda, directory.

rostrum *noun* platform, dais, podium, stage, stand, pulpit, lectern.

rosy *adj* **1** (*rosy cheeks*) pink, pinkish, rose, roseate, red, reddish, rubicund, ruddy, blushing, flushed, florid, blooming, glowing, fresh. OPPOSITE: pale. **2** (*a rosy prospect*) optimistic, hopeful, bright, cheerful, happy, encouraging, reassuring, promising, auspicious, favourable, sunny. OPPOSITE: hopeless.

rot *verb* **1** (*the wooden frame has rotted*) decay, decompose, crumble, disintegrate, perish, corrode, rust. **2** (*the apples may rot*) putrefy, go bad, go off (*inf*), spoil, moulder, fester, corrupt, taint. OPPOSITE: preserve.
➤ *noun* **1** (*how to prevent rot in stored fruit*) decay, decomposition, disintegration, putrefaction, mould, mildew, blight, corrosion, rust. **2** (*he talks a load of rot sometimes*) nonsense, rubbish, garbage, twaddle, drivel, crap (*sl*), balderdash, claptrap, bosh (*inf*), tosh (*inf*), codswallop (*inf*), hogwash (*inf*), tommy-rot (*inf*), poppycock (*inf*), guff (*inf*), piffle (*inf*), baloney (*inf*), bunkum (*inf*). OPPOSITE: sense.

rotary *adj* rotating, rotational, revolving, spinning, turning, gyrating, gyratory, whirling.

rotate *verb* **1** (*rotating gears*) go round, revolve, turn, twirl, whirl, spin, wheel, pivot, swivel, gyrate, reel, roll. **2** (*the guards rotate every hour*) alternate, take turns, interchange, switch.

rotation *noun* **1** (*with each rotation of the planet*) revolution, turn, spin, whirl, gyration, cycle, orbit. **2** (*he will see patients in strict rotation*) alternation, sequence, succession.

rotten *adj* **1** (*rotten fruit*) rotting, decayed, decaying, decomposed, decomposing, putrid, putrescent, festering, bad, off (*inf*), mouldy, mouldering, rancid, sour, rank, fetid, foul, tainted, spoiled. OPPOSITE: fresh. **2** (*rotten wood*) decomposed, decayed, corroded, crumbling, disintegrating, perishing. **3** (*he is a rotten swine*) despicable, contemptible, mean, low, crooked (*inf*), base, vile, vicious, nasty, unpleasant, wicked, villainous, evil, immoral, corrupt, debauched, degenerate, dissolute, dissipated, perverted, unprincipled, unscrupulous, dishonourable, dishonest, untrustworthy, iniquitous, wanton. **4** (*a rotten thing to say*) nasty, cruel, base, mean, beastly, uncalled-for, bad, dirty, filthy, foul, wicked, contemptible, despicable. **5** (*they have had a rotten time lately*) miserable, awful, unpleasant, disagreeable, unfortunate, unlucky, disappointing, regrettable. **6** (*I think it's a rotten plan*) bad, foolish, ill-advised, ill-considered, injudicious, stupid, silly. **7** (*the team turned in a rotten performance*) bad, poor, inadequate, inferior, lousy (*inf*), disappointing, lacklustre, substandard, unsatisfactory, unacceptable, wretched. **8** (*she says she feels rotten*) poorly (*inf*), sick, ill, unwell, unhealthy, below par, off colour, grotty (*inf*), ropy (*inf*), under the weather (*inf*), rough (*inf*).

rotter *noun* cad, bounder (*inf*), swine, scoundrel, blighter (*inf*), creep (*inf*), rat (*inf*), louse (*inf*), stinker (*inf*).

rotund *adj* **1** (*he slapped his rotund belly*) plump, corpulent, well-rounded, spherical, portly, stout, roly-poly, podgy, chubby, tubby, fleshy, heavy, fat, obese. OPPOSITE: slim. **2** (*rotund intonation*) full, rich, sonorous, resonant, mellow, orotund, round, magniloquent.

rough *adj* **1** (*a rough track*) uneven, irregular, bumpy, lumpy, stony, rugged, jagged, broken. **2** (*she stroked the animal's rough coat*) coarse, unkempt, bristly, unshaven, shaggy, hairy, bushy, fuzzy. OPPOSITE: smooth. **3** (*rough weather in store*) stormy, tempestuous, turbulent, squally, wintry, inclement, wild, violent, boisterous. OPPOSITE: calm. **4** (*the sea was too rough for sailing*) wild, choppy, agitated, tumultuous, turbulent, tempestuous. **5** (*indulged in some rough play*) rowdy, boisterous, raucous, noisy, lively, forceful, energetic, disorderly, wild, violent, savage. OPPOSITE: gentle. **6** (*criticized for his rough behaviour*) rude, impolite, discourteous, uncivil, unmannerly, ill-mannered, ill-bred, brutish, churlish, loutish, boorish, uncouth, coarse, crude, vulgar, unrefined, uncultured, insensitive, unsophisticated, brusque, blunt, curt. OPPOSITE: refined. **7** (*they had a rough time in prison*) hard, harsh, tough, nasty, difficult, severe, unpleasant, disagreeable, cruel, brutal, drastic, extreme, austere. **8** (*a rough finish*) crude, raw,

unfinished, unrefined, unprocessed, unpolished, undressed, uncut, incomplete. OPPOSITE: finished. **9** (*he had a rough unfriendly voice*) husky, gruff, hoarse, throaty, rasping, croaking, harsh, guttural, discordant, strident. **10** (*this will give you a rough idea*) preliminary, rudimentary, basic, brief, cursory, sketchy, general, vague, imprecise, hazy, crude, incomplete, approximate, inexact, hasty, quick. **11** (*this wine is a bit rough*) harsh, sharp, sour, unrefined. **12** (*he says he still feels a bit rough*) unwell, poorly (*inf*), rotten (*inf*), sick, ill, under the weather (*inf*), grotty (*inf*), ropy (*inf*), hung-over (*inf*), unhealthy, below par, off colour.
➤ *noun* **1** (*showed us a rough of his design*) draft, outline, sketch, mock-up, model. **2** (*roughs hanging about the docks*) ruffian, thug, yob (*inf*), bully, hooligan, tough (*inf*), roughneck (*inf*), bruiser (*inf*).
rough out draft, sketch out, outline, block out, mock up.
rough up beat up, knock about, do in (*inf*), batter, bash (*inf*), manhandle, maltreat, mistreat, abuse.

rough-and-tumble *noun* horseplay, scuffle, scrap (*inf*), struggle, fight, affray, brawl, fracas, rumpus, mêlée, dust-up (*inf*), punch-up (*inf*).

round *adj* **1** (*a round stone*) circular, annular, ring-shaped, hooplike, curved, convex, rounded, rotund, spherical, spheroid, globular, ball-shaped, discoid, cylindrical. OPPOSITE: angular. **2** (*he had a small round body*) chubby, stout, plump, portly, well-rounded, ample, rotund, tubby, corpulent, podgy, fat, obese. **3** (*a round total*) complete, entire, whole, full, ample. **4** (*a round accusation*) candid, frank, blunt, plain, direct, straightforward, outspoken. OPPOSITE: evasive. **5** (*a round figure*) rough, approximate, imprecise, estimated, ball-park (*inf*). OPPOSITE: exact. **6** (*she spoke in round tones*) full, rich, resonant, sonorous, mellow, flowing, orotund, plummy.
➤ *noun* **1** (*moulded into a round*) circle, disc, ring, band, hoop, sphere, ball, orb, globe, cylinder, disc. **2** (*a round of cutbacks*) cycle, series, succession, sequence, bout, period, session, turn. **3** (*doing the rounds of the wards*) circuit, lap, beat, ambit, course, route, path, routine, schedule, tour. **4** (*they went out in the first round*) heat, level, stage, lap, division, game, session. **5** (*put the rounds in the magazine*) bullet, cartridge, shell.
➤ *prep* around, about, surrounding, encircling.
➤ *adv* around, near, nearby, throughout.
➤ *verb* go round, travel round, circumnavigate, skirt, flank, bypass.
round off 1 (*a drink to round off the evening*) complete, finish, conclude, end, terminate, close, crown, cap, top off. OPPOSITE: begin. **2** (*round off any sharp edges*) plane, smooth, level, sand.
round on attack, turn on, set upon, criticize, abuse, lay into (*inf*), tear into (*inf*).
round up bring together, gather, collect, assemble, group, marshal, muster, rally, herd, drive. OPPOSITE: disperse.

roundabout *adj* **1** (*a roundabout route to the house*) indirect, winding, tortuous, circuitous, meandering. **2** (*a roundabout way of making his point*) indirect, circumlocutory, circuitous, long-winded, discursive, oblique, periphrastic, devious. OPPOSITE: direct.

rouse *verb* **1** (*rouse the volunteers*) wake, awaken, rise, get up, stir, arouse, call. **2** (*rouse the mob to riot*) stir, bestir, move, start, provoke, incite, induce, impel, foment, egg on, excite, agitate, disturb, stimulate, whip up, whet, animate, galvanize, enkindle, inflame. OPPOSITE: soothe. **3** (*this music rouses memories of my childhood*) kindle, stir up, evoke, provoke, conjure up, call up, touch off. **4** (*this action roused the middle classes*) anger, irritate, annoy, exasperate, infuriate, incense, work up.

rousing *adj* stimulating, inspiring, exciting, stirring, moving, exhilarating, electrifying, inflammatory, encouraging, vigorous, energetic, lively, brisk, spirited, inspiriting, enthusiastic, fervent.

rout *noun* **1** (*the rout of the enemy*) defeat, conquest, beating, thrashing (*inf*), licking (*inf*), pasting (*inf*), trouncing, drubbing, overthrow, subjugation, debacle. OPPOSITE: victory. **2** (*he put his opponents to rout*) flight, retreat, stampede.
➤ *verb* **1** (*rout the enemy cavalry*) drive off, scatter, chase, dispel. **2** (*rout all enemies*) defeat, vanquish, conquer, beat, overthrow, subjugate, overpower, crush, slaughter (*inf*), thrash (*inf*), drub, hammer (*inf*), trounce, worst.

route *noun* way, road, avenue, path, course, direction, journey, passage, itinerary, circuit, round, beat.

routine *noun* **1** (*she follows the same routine each day*) system, method, pattern, order, convention, custom, practice, habit, wont, procedure, order, programme, schedule, formula, course, way. **2** (*the comedian went through his routine*) act, spiel (*inf*), patter (*inf*), performance.
➤ *adj* **1** (*a routine inspection*) customary, habitual, wonted, regular, standard, scheduled, conventional, usual, normal, ordinary, common, typical, everyday, workaday. OPPOSITE: unusual. **2** (*just another routine day's work*) boring, dull, tedious, tiresome, humdrum, familiar, banal, run-of-the-mill, monotonous, predictable, hackneyed, unoriginal, unexciting, uninspiring.

rove *verb* wander, roam, range, stray, drift, cruise, meander, ramble, stroll, stray, traipse, gallivant, travel. OPPOSITE: settle.

rover *noun* wanderer, roamer, drifter, rambler, nomad, gypsy, itinerant, vagrant, gadabout (*inf*), traveller, transient.

row[1] *noun* **1** (*a row of soldiers*) file, column, queue, line, rank. **2** (*a row of disasters*) string, series, sequence, succession, chain. **3** (*a row of bottles*) line, rank, tier, bank, range.

row[2] *noun* **1** (*a family row*) quarrel, dispute, argument, disagreement, squabble, controversy, tiff, fight, conflict, altercation, brawl, free-for-all, scrap (*inf*), set-to (*inf*), dust-up (*inf*), fracas, scuffle, mêlée, wrangle, affray. OPPOSITE: harmony. **2** (*just listen to the row*) noise, din, racket, disturbance, commotion, fuss, tumult, turmoil, hubbub, clamour, rumpus, uproar, pandemonium. OPPOSITE: quiet.
➤ *verb* quarrel, argue, bicker, squabble, wrangle, scrap (*inf*), fight, brawl. OPPOSITE: agree.

rowdy *adj* noisy, loud, boisterous, obstreperous, wild, rough, unruly, disorderly, riotous, lawless, unrestrained. OPPOSITE: quiet.

royal *adj* **1** (*behaved with royal condescension*) regal, kingly, queenly, princely, imperial, sovereign, monarchical. **2** (*royal surroundings*) majestic, august, impressive, imposing, noble, stately, grand, glorious, magnificent, splendid, superb. OPPOSITE: lowly. **3** (*a right royal welcome*) marvellous, wonderful, excellent, fine, first-rate, first-class.

rub *verb* **1** (*the girl rubbed her knee*) knead, massage. **2** (*he rubbed her neck*) stroke, caress, fondle, pat, scratch. **3** (*rub off the rust*) polish, burnish, buff up, shine, smooth. **4** (*rub your face with the flannel*) wipe, clean, brush, scrub, scour. **5** (*rub grease into the joint*) apply, smear, spread, put on, work in. **6** (*he complained that he had rubbed his elbow against the table*) chafe, abrade, scrape, grate, graze, pinch.
➤ *noun* **1** (*give my back a rub*) massage, kneading, friction. **2** (*he gave her neck a rub*) stroke, caress. **3** (*give the car a rub*) polish, buffing, burnishing. **4** (*the window needs a quick rub*) clean, wipe, scrub, scour. **5** (*there's the rub*) difficulty, trouble, problem, obstacle, obstruction, impediment, hindrance, hitch, snag (*inf*), catch, drawback.

rub out **1** (*rub out what he had written*) erase, efface, wipe off, obliterate, expunge, remove, delete, cancel. **2** (*he rubbed out all his rivals*) kill, do in (*inf*), bump off (*inf*), murder, eliminate (*inf*), liquidate (*inf*), assassinate, put to death, do away with, finish off.

rubbish *noun* **1** (*take out the rubbish*) waste, refuse, garbage, litter, trash, sweepings, leavings, dregs, junk, lumber, rubble, scrap, debris, detritus, dross, flotsam and jetsam. **2** (*nothing but rubbish on television tonight*) nonsense, stuff and nonsense (*inf*), crap (*sl*), bullshit (*sl*), shit (*sl*), rot (*inf*), twaddle, gibberish, balderdash, humbug, bunk (*inf*), bunkum (*inf*), codswallop (*inf*), hogwash (*inf*), gobbledegook (*inf*), poppycock (*inf*), tosh (*inf*), bosh (*inf*), tripe (*inf*), piffle (*inf*), guff (*inf*), drivel, claptrap. OPPOSITE: sense.

ruddy *adj* red, reddish, rubicund, florid, glowing, blooming, flushed, blushing, pink, pinkish, rosy, rosy-cheeked, roseate, scarlet, crimson, sanguine, fresh, healthy. OPPOSITE: pale.

rude *adj* **1** (*he was very rude to his mother*) impolite, discourteous, uncivil, ill-mannered, bad-mannered, unmannerly, disrespectful, insolent, impudent, impertinent, churlish, cheeky (*inf*), saucy, curt, abrupt, short, brusque, blunt, sharp, offhand, insulting, abusive, offensive. OPPOSITE: polite. **2** (*life among the rude peasantry*) simple, oafish, loutish, boorish, barbarous, uncouth, unrefined, uncultured, artless, unpolished, uncivilized, untutored, uneducated, illiterate, ignorant, rough, coarse. OPPOSITE: refined. **3** (*fashion a rude aerial out of a coathanger*) crude, rudimentary, primitive, simple, rough, rough-and-ready, rough-hewn.
(*he told rude jokes all the way home*) crude, coarse, vulgar, obscene, smutty, dirty, filthy, blue (*inf*), indecent, indelicate, naughty, risqué, ribald, improper, bawdy, gross, licentious. **4** (*a rude shock*) nasty, violent, unexpected, sudden, abrupt, sharp, startling, disagreeable, unpleasant, harsh.

rudimentary *adj* **1** (*rudimentary health care*) rudimental, basic, fundamental, elementary, primary, initial, early, introductory. OPPOSITE: sophisticated. **2** (*using rudimentary tools*) crude, simple, primitive, rough. OPPOSITE: advanced. **3** (*a rudimentary thumb on her left hand*) undeveloped, immature, vestigial, incomplete, embryonic.

rudiments *pl noun* basics, fundamentals, essentials, principles, elements, foundations, beginnings.

rue *verb* regret, repent, feel remorse for, lament, deplore, bewail, bemoan, mourn, grieve, sorrow.

rueful *adj* regretful, remorseful, apologetic, sorry, sorrowful, sad, contrite, repentant, penitent, conscience-stricken, self-reproachful, lugubrious, woebegone, woeful, plaintive, mournful, doleful, melancholy, dismal, pitiable, pitiful, grievous.

ruffian *noun* thug, tough (*inf*), rough (*inf*), hooligan, yob (*inf*), hoodlum, bully, brute, bruiser, villain, scoundrel, rogue, roughneck, rascal, lout, wretch, miscreant. OPPOSITE: gentleman.

ruffle *verb* **1** (*ruffled his hair*) rumple, derange, disarrange, disorder, discompose, mess up, muss up (*inf*), tousle, tangle, dishevel, crease, crumple, wrinkle, ripple, pucker. OPPOSITE: smooth. **2** (*he was rather ruffled by her refusal*) agitate, disturb, upset, put out, rattle (*inf*), shake up (*inf*), unsettle, disconcert, discompose, fluster, perturb, confuse, worry, alarm, trouble, hassle (*inf*), harass, annoy, irritate, irk, vex, nettle, exasperate, aggravate (*inf*), bug (*inf*), rile, anger. OPPOSITE: compose.

rugged *adj* **1** (*a rugged mountain path*) rough, uneven, irregular, broken, bumpy, stony, rocky, craggy, jagged, ragged, precipitous. **2** (*the rugged features of the old sailor*) lined, wrinkled, gnarled, furrowed, leathery, weather-beaten, irregular. OPPOSITE: smooth. **3** (*the landscape has a rugged beauty*) stark, harsh, severe, stern, austere, crude, unrefined, unsophisticated, rude, uncouth. **4** (*a rugged adventurer*) tough, strong, sturdy, hardy, robust, vigorous, resolute, tenacious, determined, stalwart, husky (*inf*), beefy (*inf*), burly, brawny, muscular, sinewy, well-built, solid, mighty. **5** (*a rugged upbringing*) tough, hard, harsh, difficult, austere, stern, punishing, demanding, exacting, taxing, arduous, rigorous, strenuous, onerous, Spartan.

ruin *noun* **1** (*the castle is now a romantic ruin*) shell, wreck, skeleton, relic, remnant. **2** (*the house is in a state of ruin*) ruination, destruction, devastation, desolation, havoc, wreck, disrepair, dilapidation, decay, damage, demolition, deterioration, disintegration. OPPOSITE: restoration. **3** (*faced the ruin of all her plans*) defeat, conquest, overthrow, elimination, termination, end, collapse, failure, fall, downfall, undoing, thwarting, disappointment. **4** (*surrounded by the ruins of all his dreams*) wreckage, rubble, relics, remains, remnants, fragments, vestiges, traces, shambles, debris, detritus, chaos. **5** (*the whole industry faces ruin*) ruination, collapse, breakdown, disaster, failure, bankruptcy, insolvency, impoverishment, destitution, penury, indigence, deprivation. OPPOSITE: prosperity.
➤ *verb* **1** (*the royal palace was ruined*) destroy, devastate, desolate, lay waste, demolish, raze, wreck, shatter, break, smash, crush. OPPOSITE: restore. **2** (*all our plans are ruined*) spoil, mar, mess up, overthrow, overturn, overwhelm, cripple, defeat, wreck, damage. OPPOSITE:

fix. **3** (*the family were ruined when the market crashed*) bankrupt, impoverish, pauperize, cripple.

ruinous *adj* **1** (*a ruinous old mansion*) ruined, in ruins, derelict, ramshackle, decrepit, dilapidated, decaying, broken-down, in disrepair, wrecked, destroyed, devastated, shattered. **2** (*a ruinous defeat*) destructive, devastating, disastrous, calamitous, catastrophic, cataclysmic, pernicious, deleterious, baneful, mischievous, injurious, damaging, dire, baleful, noxious. OPPOSITE: beneficial. **3** (*the ruinous cost of the enterprise*) crippling, excessive, extortionate, exorbitant, unreasonable, immoderate.

rule *noun* **1** (*this rule must be observed*) ruling, regulation, statute, ordinance, law, by-law, tenet, canon, order, decree, command, commandment, directive, direction, restriction, instruction, guide, guideline. OPPOSITE: exception. **2** (*live by this one golden rule*) principle, precept, truth, truism, maxim, aphorism, standard, criterion, canon, motto. **3** (*the rule of foreign princes*) government, direction, reign, sovereignty, kingship, queenship, regime, dominion, administration, jurisdiction, domination, control, command, authority, ascendancy, sway, influence, mastery, leadership, supremacy, power. **4** (*we stay at home as a rule*) habit, routine, wont, custom, practice, form, procedure, convention, protocol, standard.
➤ *verb* **1** (*he ruled the country wisely*) govern, dominate, direct, guide, manage, administer, preside over, officiate, lead, command, control, regulate. OPPOSITE: submit. **2** (*the queen rules by the consent of her people*) reign, sit on the throne, wear the crown. **3** (*indulgence rules in modern society*) prevail, hold sway, predominate, preponderate, obtain, thrive. **4** (*the court ruled against her*) decree, judge, adjudge, adjudicate, decide, determine, resolve, settle, find, establish, pronounce, lay down, direct, order.
as a rule generally, in general, usually, ordinarily, normally, mainly, in the main, on the whole, for the most part, by and large. OPPOSITE: rarely.
rule out preclude, exclude, dismiss, disregard, ignore, reject, eliminate, ban, prevent, prohibit, forbid, disallow.

ruler *noun* **1** (*the ruler of this land*) monarch, sovereign, king, queen, emperor, empress, potentate, regent, head of state, head, president, overlord, lord, chief, chieftain, leader, commander, governor. OPPOSITE: subject. **2** (*measure it with a ruler*) measure, rule.

ruling *adj* **1** (*the ruling prince*) reigning, sovereign, regnant. **2** (*the ruling party*) governing, controlling, commanding, dominant, leading, supreme. OPPOSITE: subordinate. **3** (*the ruling school of thought*) prevailing, prevalent, leading, chief, principal, main, predominant, current, popular, widespread, general, universal.
➤ *noun* decree, judgment, adjudication, decision, resolution, finding, verdict, pronouncement.

rumble *verb* thunder, roll, roar, growl, resound, reverberate.

ruminate *verb* meditate, cogitate, muse, ponder, think, contemplate, deliberate, reflect, consider, brood, mull over, chew over.

rummage *verb* search, hunt, ransack, turn over, explore, examine, root, forage, rifle, delve, poke around, pry into.

rumour *noun* **1** (*according to local rumour*) gossip, hearsay, talk, grapevine (*inf*), bush telegraph (*inf*). **2** (*the latest rumour is that she has resigned*) word, whisper, speculation, scandal, report, story, information, news, tidings, buzz (*inf*). OPPOSITE: truth.
➤ *verb* circulate, spread, disseminate, publish, give out, put about, pass around, say, tell, report, gossip, noise abroad, hint, suggest, think.

rumple *verb* **1** (*my clothes are all rumpled*) crease, crumple, crush, scrunch up, crinkle, wrinkle, pucker. **2** (*he rumpled the child's hair*) ruffle, tousle, dishevel, disarrange, derange, disorder, mess up, muss up (*inf*). OPPOSITE: smooth.

rumpus *noun* commotion, uproar, confusion, disturbance, noise, row, ruction, brouhaha, kerfuffle (*inf*), furore, fuss, rout, row, tumult, fracas, mêlée, free-for-all, brawl, riot. OPPOSITE: peace.

run *verb* **1** (*he ran quickly across the grass*) sprint, race, charge, dash, dart, tear, bolt, career, hare (*inf*), speed, hasten, hurry, rush, scamper, scurry, scramble, scoot (*inf*), scuttle, gallop, lope, jog, trot, get a move on (*inf*), step on it (*inf*). OPPOSITE: saunter. **2** (*the traffic is running smoothly now*) go, proceed, flow, move, pass, progress, travel, issue, roll, glide, slide, course. OPPOSITE: stop. **3** (*the engine is running efficiently*) go, work, function, operate, perform. **4** (*blood ran from the wound*) flow, stream, spill, pour, gush, cascade, jet, spurt, issue, leak, drip, bleed, trickle. **5** (*wax ran down the candle*) melt, dissolve, liquefy. **6** (*try to run the country*) manage, administer, conduct, direct, operate, govern, control, regulate, command, lead, head, supervise, superintend, oversee, look after, organize, co-ordinate, carry on, own. **7** (*his property runs for miles*) spread, stretch, extend, reach, range. **8** (*the show will run for ever*) go on, continue, last. **9** (*run her over there in the car*) drive, take, convey, transport. **10** (*run supplies to the rebels*) convey, transport, ship, smuggle, traffic, deal in, bootleg. **11** (*he says he will run in the next presidential election*) compete, contend, challenge, stand, participate, take part in, enter. **12** (*she cannot afford to run a car*) drive, keep, use, maintain, possess, own, have. **13** (*the station refused to run the story*) broadcast, communicate, publish, print, carry, feature.
➤ *noun* **1** (*we go for a run each morning*) sprint, race, gallop, jog, canter. OPPOSITE: walk. **2** (*it was a pleasant run through the hills*) trip, journey, excursion, outing, jaunt, ride, drive, spin (*inf*), tootle (*inf*). **3** (*she flies the transatlantic run*) route, line, course, way, track, road. **4** (*a run of victories*) series, sequence, succession, string, cycle, chain, stream, course, round, spell, stretch, period. **5** (*a run on the market*) call, rush, pressure, demand, need, clamour. **6** (*outside the normal run of new products*) sort, kind, type, class, set, variety, category, order. **7** (*the birds are kept in a wire run*) coop, pen, pound, enclosure, fold, sty, paddock, yard. **8** (*found a run in her tights*) ladder, hole, snag, tear, split, slit, rip, cut, slash, gash.
in the long run eventually, ultimately, at last, in the end, at the end of the day (*inf*).
run across run into, meet, encounter, come across, chance upon, stumble upon, bump into (*inf*).

run away 1 (*the children ran away*) run off, make off, take flight, flee, bolt, clear off (*inf*), scarper (*inf*), abscond, escape, decamp, elope. OPPOSITE: return. **2** (*she cannot run away from this problem*) avoid, evade, ignore, disregard, brush aside (*inf*), overlook, neglect.

run away with 1 (*he ran away with a girl half his age*) run off with, elope with, make off with, abduct. **2** (*they ran away with the day's takings*) make off with, walk off with, pocket, steal, snatch, pinch (*inf*), nick (*inf*), swipe (*inf*), appropriate, purloin.

run down 1 (*she was run down by a delivery van*) run over, knock down, knock over, hit, strike. **2** (*the workforce will be slowly run down*) reduce, cut, cut back, pare down, trim, curtail, decrease. **3** (*he let the alarm run down*) halt, stop, cease. **4** (*output is slowly running down*) decline, dwindle, diminish, wane, drop, lose steam (*inf*). **5** (*he is continually running down his wife*) criticize, knock (*inf*), slag off (*inf*), slate (*inf*), rubbish (*inf*), attack, denounce, disparage, belittle, denigrate, defame, revile, vilify, decry. OPPOSITE: praise. **6** (*he ran her down in a small country vicarage*) track, run to earth, ferret out, find, locate, discover, hunt out, dredge up.

run in arrest, jail, apprehend, take into custody, nick (*inf*), bust (*inf*), collar (*inf*), nab (*inf*), pick up (*inf*), lift (*inf*).

run into 1 (*the train ran into the buffers*) bump into, crash into, collide with, knock into, strike, hit, ram. **2** (*guess who I ran into*) meet, encounter, bump into (*inf*), run across, chance on, happen upon.

run off 1 (*the intruder ran off*) run away, make off, scarper (*inf*), abscond, decamp, escape, flee, bolt, beat it (*inf*), clear out, skedaddle (*inf*). **2** (*she ran off several copies of the document*) copy, photocopy, duplicate, print, Photostat®, Xerox®.

run on go on, continue, carry on, keep going, extend, last.

run out finish, terminate, end, cease, close, expire, fail, give out, dry up, exhaust, consume, use up.

run out on desert, abandon, strand, maroon, forsake, jilt, chuck (*inf*), ditch (*inf*), dump (*inf*), walk out on (*inf*), rat on (*inf*), leave in the lurch (*inf*), leave high and dry (*inf*).

run over 1 (*he was run over by a lorry*) run down, knock down, hit, strike. **2** (*the tank started to run over*) overflow, spill over, overbrim. **3** (*run over the main points again*) run through, go over, go through, look over, recapitulate, recap (*inf*), repeat, review.

run through 1 (*run through the figures once more*) go through, go over, run over, look over, examine, survey, recapitulate, recap (*inf*), repeat, review. **2** (*she ran through a fortune in just a few days*) go through, spend, squander, fritter away, blow (*inf*), dissipate, waste, exhaust.

run to 1 (*the figure runs to millions*) amount, add up, come, extend, total. **2** (*they cannot run to a large wedding*) afford, fund.

runaway *noun* fugitive, refugee, deserter, escapee, absconder, truant.
➤ *adj* **1** (*two runaway piglets*) escaped, fugitive, loose, uncontrolled, wild. **2** (*a runaway success*) overnight, immediate, easy, effortless.

rundown *noun* **1** (*a rundown in economic activity*) slow-down, downturn, drop, reduction, decrease, decline,

curtailment, cut, cutback. **2** (*give the press a quick rundown of events*) summary, run-through, résumé, synopsis, review, recap (*inf*), analysis, briefing, brief, sketch, outline.

run-down *adj* **1** (*the suburbs are badly run-down*) dilapidated, neglected, dingy, seedy, shabby, ramshackle, tumbledown, broken-down, ruined, in ruins, decaying, decayed. **2** (*she complains of feeling very run-down*) weak, unhealthy, tired, weary, worn-out, exhausted, pooped (*inf*), fatigued, enervated, drained, debilitated, below par, grotty (*inf*), peaky (*inf*), seedy (*inf*), under the weather (*inf*).

runner *noun* **1** (*eight runners in the race*) racer, sprinter, athlete, competitor, participant, jogger. **2** (*a runner brought the bad news*) messenger, courier, bearer, dispatch rider. **3** (*trim the runners off the main plant*) shoot, offshoot, sprout, tendril, sprig, branch, stem.

running *noun* **1** (*he enjoys running*) racing, race, sprinting, sprint, jogging. **2** (*interfere in the running of the company*) administration, management, leadership, conduct, direction, charge, control, controlling, regulation, organization, supervision, coordination. **3** (*the smooth running of the engine*) operation, performance, working, functioning. **4** (*she is in the running for one of the medals*) contention, competition, contest.
➤ *adj* **1** (*a running fight*) continuous, constant, ceaseless, unceasing, incessant, unbroken, uninterrupted, perpetual. **2** (*she has not slept for three nights running*) in a row, in succession, successive, in sequence, consecutive, on the trot (*inf*).

run-of-the-mill *adj* ordinary, normal, common, commonplace, average, mediocre, middling, so-so (*inf*), everyday, unexceptional, undistinguished, unimpressive, unremarkable, tolerable, passable, acceptable, fair,

rupture *noun* **1** (*a rupture in the fuel tank*) fracture, fissure, break, burst, crack, split, breach, rift, cleft, tear, rent, puncture. **2** (*there has been a serious rupture between the two nations*) rift, bust-up (*inf*), break-up, quarrel, falling-out (*inf*), altercation, dispute, disagreement, feud, schism, breach, division, hostility, estrangement, alienation. OPPOSITE: reconciliation.
➤ *verb* break, burst, crack, split, fracture, breach, tear, rend, puncture, cleave, separate, divide, sever, cut off. OPPOSITE: mend.

rural *adj* country, countryside, rustic, bucolic, pastoral, agricultural, agrarian, Arcadian. OPPOSITE: urban.

ruse *noun* wile, trick, artifice, dodge (*inf*), stratagem, scheme, design, contrivance, device, subterfuge, blind, hoax, sham, deceit, deception, imposture, manoeuvre, ploy, plot, wile, tactic, machination.

rush *verb* **1** (*she rushed to the airport*) hurry, hasten, race, run, dash, bolt, dart, charge, stampede, career, speed, shoot, sprint, tear, fly, gallop, scurry, scamper, scramble, press, push, hustle, accelerate, quicken, dispatch, expedite. OPPOSITE: dawdle. **2** (*the squad rushed the defences*) charge, attack, assault, storm, take by storm, raid, seize, capture.
➤ *noun* **1** (*there was a rush for the doors*) dash, scramble, stampede, flood, stream, gush, surge. **2** (*a rush to get the

job done) bustle, urgency, hurry, haste, commotion, stir, activity, speed, quickness, swiftness, rapidity, dispatch, expedition. **3** (*he led the rush against the opposing team*) charge, attack, assault, onslaught, storm, strike, raid. **4** (*a rush on the latest model in the shops*) run, demand, clamour, call, need, pressure.

rushed *adj* hasty, hurried, brisk, speedy, swift, rapid, quick, fast, prompt, expeditious, busy.

rust *noun* corrosion, oxidation, verdigris, stain.
  ➤ *verb* corrode, oxidize, tarnish.

rustic *adj* **1** (*a rustic village scene*) rural, country, countryside, countrified, provincial, pastoral, agricultural, agrarian, bucolic, sylvan, Arcadian. OPPOSITE: urban. **2** (*admire this rustic bench*) simple, plain, homely, homespun, crude, unsophisticated. **3** (*the blacksmith and his rustic companions*) provincial, homely, homespun, clodhopping, oafish, unsophisticated, uncultured, unpolished, unrefined, artless, coarse, rough, uncouth, churlish, boorish, awkward, graceless, clumsy, blundering, lumbering, inept, loutish, plain, simple, naive, ingenuous, unassuming, guileless. OPPOSITE: sophisticated.
  ➤ *noun* peasant, countryman, countrywoman,

provincial, bumpkin, yokel, clodhopper, clod, boor, churl, oaf, hick (*inf*).

rustle *verb* whisper, sigh, swish, whoosh, susurrate, crinkle, crackle.
  ➤ *noun* rustling, whisper, swish, whoosh, susurration, crackle, crinkling.

rusty *adj* **1** (*a rusty nail*) rusted, rust-covered, corroded, tarnished, oxidized. **2** (*rusty hair*) rust-coloured, russet, copper, coppery, auburn, sandy, tawny, ginger, gingery, chestnut, brick-red, brick, reddish, reddish-brown. **3** (*her technique is rusty*) out of practice, unpractised, neglected, stale, stiff, creaking, outmoded, dated, old-fashioned, deficient, impaired, poor, below par, diminished, we

rut *noun* **1** (*a deep rut in the track*) groove, furrow, channel, gutter, trough, gouge, ditch, pothole, track, groove, hollow, indentation. **2** (*stuck in a rut*) daily grind, dead end, treadmill, routine, habit, pattern, system.

ruthless *adj* pitiless, unpitying, merciless, unmerciful, hard, harsh, severe, stern, cruel, brutal, barbarous, fierce, ferocious, savage, heartless, unfeeling, callous, hard-hearted, compassionless, relentless, unrelenting, unforgiving, unsparing, remorseless, heartless, implacable, inexorable OPPOSITE: compassionate.

sable *adj* black, jet, jet-black, pitch, pitch-black, coal-black, ink-black, inky, raven, ebony, dark, dusky, sombre. OPPOSITE: white.

sabotage *noun* **1** (*the sabotage of the company's computers*) vandalization, destruction, wrecking, damage, incapacitation, impairment. **2** (*the sabotage of all her dreams*) spoiling, thwarting, ruining, wrecking, fouling up (*inf*), disruption, subversion.
➤ *verb* **1** (*they sabotaged the railway line*) destroy, damage, disable, cripple, vandalize, wreck, incapacitate, impair. **2** (*they had sabotaged all her plans*) spoil, thwart, scupper, foul up (*inf*), wreck, ruin, destroy, undermine, disrupt, subvert, mar.

saccharine *adj* sweet, sugary, syrupy, sickly-sweet, oversweet, sentimental, schmaltzy (*inf*), mushy (*inf*), soppy (*inf*), sloppy (*inf*), gushy (*inf*), honeyed, cloying, maudlin, mawkish, sickly, nauseating.

sack[1] *noun* **1** (*a sack of oats*) bag, pack, pouch. **2** (*the workers were given the sack*) dismissal, discharge, boot (*inf*), push (*inf*), chop (*inf*), axe (*inf*), redundancy, notice, papers, P45 (*inf*), marching orders.
➤ *verb* dismiss, discharge, lay off, fire (*inf*), boot out (*inf*), kick out (*inf*), axe (*inf*), give the push (*inf*), give the chop (*inf*), give the elbow (*inf*) give someone their marching orders/their cards (*inf*). OPPOSITE: appoint.

sack[2] *verb* plunder, pillage, despoil, spoil, vandalize, ravage, raze, level, maraud, raid, ransack, rape, rob, loot, rifle, desecrate, strip, harry, demolish, devastate, lay waste, waste, forage, ruin, destroy.
➤ *noun* plunder, plundering, stripping, pillage, despoliation, ravaging, marauding, harrying, razing, levelling, rape, rapine, looting, vandalization, desecration, depredation, devastation, destruction, ruin, waste.

sacred *adj* **1** (*a sacred site*) holy, consecrated, dedicated, hallowed, sanctified, blessed, divine, heavenly. OPPOSITE: profane. **2** (*sacred song*) religious, church, devotional, ecclesiastical, spiritual. **3** (*a sacred entity*) divine, godly, deified, supreme, venerated. **4** (*his reputation is sacred*) venerable, revered, respected, sacrosanct, inviolable, inviolate, unimpeachable, untouchable, invulnerable, impregnable, secure, safe, protected, defended, unthreatened.

sacrifice *noun* **1** (*a sacrifice to the gods*) offering, gift, oblation, immolation, slaughter. **2** (*the sacrifice of her hopes*) surrender, renunciation, loss, destruction, forfeiture, relinquishment, abandonment, yielding, ceding, giving up. OPPOSITE: gain.
➤ *verb* **1** (*sacrifice two chickens on an altar*) offer, offer up, slaughter, immolate. **2** (*sacrifice his dream of becoming a footballer*) surrender, renounce, abandon, give up, forgo, let go, relinquish, yield, cede, forfeit, lose, destroy.

sacrilege *noun* desecration, profanation, violation, profanity, blasphemy, heresy, outrage, impiety, godlessness, irreverence, irreligion, disrespect, mockery. OPPOSITE: reverence.

sacrilegious *adj* blasphemous, profane, irreverent, impious, heretical, irreligious, disrespectful, godless, ungodly, unholy.

sad *adj* **1** (*the old lady looked sad*) unhappy, upset, sorrowful, downcast, dejected, depressed, despondent, low, low-spirited, heavy-hearted, dispirited, downhearted, down (*inf*), melancholy, doleful, disconsolate, glum, gloomy, blue (*inf*), mournful, long-faced, crestfallen, miserable, fed up (*inf*), cheerless, woebegone, wretched, heartbroken, broken-hearted, grief-stricken, grieving, tearful. OPPOSITE: happy. **2** (*sad news*) unhappy, distressing, depressing, upsetting, dispiriting, heartbreaking, heart-rending, tragic, miserable, sorry, regrettable, unfortunate, sorrowful, grievous, pitiful, pitiable, cheerless, dismal, sombre, serious, grave, calamitous, disastrous, painful, touching, poignant. OPPOSITE: joyful. **3** (*the house is in a sad state*) lamentable, deplorable, grievous, regrettable, unfortunate, sorry, pitiful, pitiable, pathetic (*inf*), wretched, shameful, disgraceful.

sadden *verb* upset, distress, grieve, deject, depress, dismay, cast down, dispirit, discourage, dishearten, downhearten, desolate. OPPOSITE: cheer.

saddle *verb* burden, encumber, load, charge, tax, impose, lumber (*inf*), land. OPPOSITE: relieve.

sadness *noun* unhappiness, misery, sorrow, sorrowfulness, distress, grief, heartache (*inf*), misfortune, melancholy, gloom, gloominess, woe, glumness, dejection, depression, despondency, desolation, cheerlessness, bleakness, wretchedness, joylessness, dolefulness, low spirits, dismalness, poignancy, sombreness, mournfulness, tearfulness, tragedy, pain, regret, pathos, lugubriousness.

safe *adj* **1** (*keep the money safe*) secure, protected, guarded, sheltered, defended, invulnerable, impregnable, immune, unassailable, out of harm's way (*inf*), in good hands (*inf*). OPPOSITE: exposed. **2** (*the hostages are safe*) all right, unhurt, unharmed, uninjured, well, alive and well, out of danger, undamaged, unscathed, sound, intact. **3** (*a safe pair of hands*) sure, certain, proven, dependable, reliable, trustworthy, tried and true, tested, sound, responsible, reputable, honest, honourable, upright. **4** (*he found their approach a bit too safe*) unadventurous, unenterprising, cautious, timid, circumspect, tame, prudent, conservative. OPPOSITE: risky. **5** (*safe chemicals*) harmless, innocuous, nonpoisonous, nontoxic, uncontaminated, wholesome. OPPOSITE: dangerous
» *noun* cash-box, safety-deposit box, safe-deposit box, strongbox, chest, coffer, repository, depository, locker, vault

safeguard *verb* protect, guard, defend, shield, screen, shelter, preserve, secure, look after, take care of, watch over. OPPOSITE: imperil.
» *noun* protection, guard, defence, shield, security, precaution, preventive, preventative, escort, convoy, bodyguard, guarantee, insurance, assurance, surety, cover.

safekeeping *noun* protection, care, charge, trust, keeping, custody, guardianship, trusteeship, wardship, supervision, surveillance.

safety *noun* **1** (*the safety of the investment*) safeness, security, secureness, immunity, protection, safeguard, soundness, impregnability, assailability. **2** (*they sought safety in the monastery*) shelter, sanctuary, refuge, cover. **3** (*they praised his safety as an adviser*) reliability, dependability, responsibility, trustworthiness, reputableness.

sag *verb* **1** (*the wall sagged dangerously*) bend, give, slump, subside, sink. **2** (*his trousers sagged*) droop, hang, bag. **3** (*expectations sagged as time passed*) fall, slump, flag, fail, flop, falter, dip, sink, drop, tumble, plummet, nose-dive, weaken, decline, fall off, decrease, languish, wilt. OPPOSITE: rise.

saga *noun* chronicle, epic, history, legend, romance, narrative, story, tale, yarn, soap opera, adventure.

sagacious *adj* wise, sage, judicious, shrewd, prudent, astute, sharp, acute, astute, discerning, penetrating, perceptive, percipient, perspicacious, insightful, clever, smart, intelligent, canny, wily, able, apt, quick, quick-witted, far-sighted, knowing, sapient, wary. OPPOSITE: stupid.

sage *noun* philosopher, thinker, savant, wise man, wise person, man of letters, guru, oracle, master, expert, authority, elder, pundit, teacher. OPPOSITE: fool.
» *adj* wise, judicious, politic, prudent, shrewd, sensible, intelligent, discerning, perspicacious, astute, acute, sagacious, canny, knowing, sapient, learned, knowledgeable. OPPOSITE: foolish.

sail *verb* **1** (*they sail north tomorrow*) set sail, put to sea, embark, hoist sail, weigh anchor, ship, shove off, put off, leave port, travel, journey. **2** (*he loves to sail*) boat, yacht. **3** (*leaves sailed by in the current*) drift, float, glide, plane, skim, sweep, slide, coast, cruise. **4** (*sail the ship into harbour*) pilot, steer, captain, skipper, navigate. **5** (*the kite sailed away on the breeze*) soar, fly, scud, wing.
» *noun* cruise, trip, journey, voyage, crossing.
sail into attack, assault, turn on, set about, tear into, lay into (*inf*), let fly, fall upon, belabour.
sail through romp through, walk (*inf*), breeze through (*inf*).

sailor *noun* seaman, seafarer, mariner, boatman, deckhand, rating, bluejacket, salt, tar (*inf*), Jack Tar (*inf*), matelot (*inf*), sea dog, yachtsman, oarsman.

saintly *adj* saintlike, godly, holy, pious, devout, reverent, God-fearing, religious, believing, spiritual, righteous, worthy, virtuous, moral, ethical, good, upright, pure, innocent, blameless, sinless, spotless, angelic, blessed. OPPOSITE: godless.

sake *noun* **1** (*do it for your father's sake*) account, interest, behalf, welfare, wellbeing, benefit, advantage, gain, profit, good, regard, concern, respect, consideration. **2** (*for the sake of glory*) purpose, reason, motive, cause, objective, object, goal, aim.

salacious *adj* **1** (*a salacious old man*) lecherous, lascivious, licentious, lewd, lustful, randy, horny, libidinous, concupiscent, prurient, loose, wanton, promiscuous. OPPOSITE: pure. **2** (*a salacious tale*) lewd, bawdy, ribald, crude, coarse, smutty (*inf*), filthy, dirty, blue (*inf*), obscene, scurrilous, raunchy, steamy (*inf*), erotic, pornographic, improper, indecent, indelicate.

salary *noun* pay, wage, remuneration, income, earnings, fee, emolument, honorarium, stipend.

sale *noun* **1** (*the sale of luxury items*) selling, marketing, vending, vendition, bargaining, trade, traffic, transaction, disposal. OPPOSITE: purchase. **2** (*the sale was completed yesterday*) deal, transaction, bargain. **3** (*a sale on all garments*) reduction, discount, clearance. **4** (*a heavy sale for industrial equipment*) market, demand, outlet.
for sale on sale, on offer, up for sale, on the market, up for grabs (*inf*), available, obtainable, purchasable.

salient *adj* **1** (*a salient feature*) prominent, striking, conspicuous, arresting, outstanding, noticeable, obvious, remarkable, signal, marked, pronounced, projecting, jutting, protruding. OPPOSITE: inconspicuous. **2** (*the salient points of his argument*) important, main, principal, chief, significant.

sallow *adj* yellow, yellowish, pale, pallid, wan, waxen, anaemic, colourless, jaundiced, pasty, pasty-faced, sickly, unhealthy. OPPOSITE: ruddy.

sally noun **1** (*a sally into enemy territory*) sortie, charge, thrust, foray, attack, offensive, raid, incursion, assault, onslaught, onset, drive, surge, dash, rush, onrush, outburst. **2** (*a sally to the local pub*) excursion, trip, visit, expedition, jaunt, outing, tour, wander. **3** (*they parted with a last sally*) retort, riposte, repartee, joke, jest, quip, barb, crack (*inf*), wisecrack (*inf*), witticism, bon mot.
➤ verb rush, surge, charge, storm, issue, erupt, venture.

salt noun **1** (*salt for the table*) sodium chloride, table salt, rock salt, sea salt. **2** (*his comments added salt to the discussion*) flavour, savour, taste, relish, seasoning, spice, spiciness, pungency, piquancy, smack, bite, punch, zest, zip (*inf*), zap (*inf*), zing (*inf*), liveliness, vigour, wit. **3** (*the bar was full of old salts*) sailor, seaman, seafarer, mariner, tar (*inf*), matelot (*inf*).
➤ adj salty, saline, salted, briny, brackish. OPPOSITE: sweet.
➤ verb preserve, cure, season, flavour.

salty adj **1** (*salty water*) salt, salted, saline, briny, brackish. **2** (*salty conversation*) lively, animated, exciting, vigorous, zestful, trenchant, pungent, biting, spicy, piquant, tangy, witty.

salubrious adj wholesome, healthy, healthful, health-giving, invigorating, bracing, refreshing, sanitary, hygienic, pleasant, beneficial, salutary. OPPOSITE: unhealthy.

salutary adj **1** (*a salutary lesson*) beneficial, advantageous, useful, helpful, valuable, profitable, good, timely, practical. OPPOSITE: harmful. **2** (*a salutary lifestyle*) healthy, healthful, health-giving, wholesome, sanitary, hygienic, salubrious, refreshing, invigorating.

salutation noun greeting, salute, homage, welcome, address, respects, reverence, obeisance.

salute verb **1** (*he saluted his friend across the street*) greet, hail, wave, bow, nod, address, accost, welcome, acknowledge, recognize, honour. OPPOSITE: ignore. **2** (*we must salute their contribution to the book*) acknowledge, celebrate, honour, mark, recognize, pay tribute to.
➤ noun **1** (*a salute of welcome*) greeting, salutation, address, welcome, wave, gesture, hail, handshake, nod, bow, acknowledgement, recognition. **2** (*accept the salute of the crowd*) homage, tribute, honour, testimonial, acknowledgement, recognition, celebration.

salvage verb save, preserve, conserve, rescue, redeem, reclaim, recover, retrieve, get back, retain, restore, repair. OPPOSITE: destroy.

salvation noun **1** (*the salvation of the damned*) saving, rescue, deliverance, redemption, liberation. **2** (*the salvation of threatened buildings*) restoration, preservation, lifeline, conservation, reclamation. OPPOSITE: destruction.

salve noun lotion, cream, remedy, cure, antidote, ointment, balm, liniment, embrocation, medication, preparation, application.

salvo noun fusillade, broadside, volley, outburst.

same adj **1** (*I had the same thought*) identical, selfsame. **2** (*they were wearing the same dress*) identical, twin, duplicate, indistinguishable, corresponding, matching, interchangeable, equal, equivalent, similar, like, alike, the very. OPPOSITE: different. **3** (*carry on in the same old routine*) changeless, unchanged, unchanging, unvarying, unvaried, invariable, unfailing, consistent, constant, uniform.

all the same 1 (*all the same, we have to talk*) nonetheless, nevertheless, notwithstanding, anyway, still, yet, however, even so, in any event, in any case, for all that, by any means, be that as it may. **2** (*it's all the same to me whatever they do*) immaterial, irrelevant, unimportant, inconsequential, of no consequence, regardless.

sameness noun consistency, invariability, uniformity, changelessness, monotony, tedium, tediousness, routine, predictability, repetition, resemblance, similarity, likeness, identicalness, identity, duplication, indistinguishability.

sample noun **1** (*a sample of fabric*) specimen, example, exemplification, instance, illustration, demonstration, model, pattern, type, representative, piece, swatch. **2** (*take a sample of public opinion*) sampling, test, cross-section.
➤ verb try, try out, test, inspect, examine, taste, sip, partake of, experience.
➤ adj **1** (*a sample reading*) representative, specimen, demonstrative, illustrative, typical. **2** (*a sample bottle*) dummy, trial, test, pilot.

sanctify verb **1** (*sanctify the new church*) consecrate, bless, dedicate, hallow, anoint. OPPOSITE: profane. **2** (*sanctify the guilty*) absolve, purify, cleanse. **3** (*an action sanctified by the courts*) sanction, authorize, ratify, approve, allow, permit, confirm, support, back, endorse, underwrite, accredit, warrant, license, legitimize, legitimatize.

sanctimonious adj self-righteous, self-satisfied, smug, superior, holier-than-thou, goody-goody (*inf*), priggish, pharisaical, pious, pietistic, moralizing, hypocritical, unctuous, mealy-mouthed.

sanction noun **1** (*they have the sanction of the king*) permission, consent, agreement, allowance, authorization, authority, warrant, licence, approval, seal of approval, approbation, accreditation, endorsement, backing, support, acceptance, ratification, OK (*inf*), go-ahead (*inf*), thumbs-up (*inf*), green light (*inf*). OPPOSITE: prohibition. **2** (*a sanction on foreign trade*) ban, embargo, restriction, prohibition, boycott. **3** (*the court has imposed certain sanctions*) penalty, deterrent, penance, penalization, punishment, sentence.
➤ verb permit, allow, authorize, warrant, license, approve, accept, countenance, endorse, underwrite, accredit, back, support, ratify, validate, confirm, legitimize, OK (*inf*). OPPOSITE: prohibit.

sanctity noun **1** (*the sanctity of the confessional*) holiness, sacredness, inviolability. OPPOSITE: profanity. **2** (*a man of sanctity*) saintliness, holiness, godliness, sanctitude, grace, piety, devoutness, devotion, righteousness, goodness, virtue, purity, spirituality, religiosity, religiousness, blessedness.

sanctuary noun **1** (*a holy sanctuary*) shrine, sanctum, church, temple, tabernacle, altar. **2** (*a sanctuary from the world*) refuge, asylum, haven, retreat, shelter, hide-out, hideaway, hiding-place. **3** (*he offered her sanctuary from her pursuers*) shelter, protection, security, safety, immunity. **4** (*a sanctuary for wild animals*) reserve, reservation, preserve, park, enclave.

sane *adj* **1** (*the court declared that he was sane*) rational, normal, compos mentis, lucid, well-balanced, of sound mind, all there (*inf*), the full shilling (*inf*). OPPOSITE: insane. **2** (*a sane decision*) sound, sober, prudent, wise, sensible, intelligent, rational, reasonable, responsible, judicious, advisable, balanced, level-headed.

sang-froid *noun* composure, calmness, coolness, self-possession, self-control, assurance, presence of mind, poise, aplomb, phlegm, nerve, nonchalance, cool (*inf*), indifference, equanimity, equilibrium, imperturbability, unflappability (*inf*). OPPOSITE: agitation.

sanguinary *adj* bloody, bloodied, gory, bloodthirsty, murderous, brutal, cruel, merciless, savage, ruthless, pitiless, grim.

sanguine *adj* **1** (*sanguine about her chances*) hopeful, optimistic, assured, confident, expectant, cheerful, buoyant, lively, ardent, spirited, animated. OPPOSITE: pessimistic. **2** (*a sanguine complexion*) ruddy, rosy, rubicund, reddish, red, flushed, pink, florid, fresh. OPPOSITE: pale.

sanitary *adj* hygienic, clean, germ-free, antiseptic, aseptic, sterile, disinfected, unpolluted, uncontaminated, pure, salubrious, healthy, wholesome. OPPOSITE: insanitary.

sanity *noun* **1** (*the pressure threatened his sanity*) saneness, mental health, soundness of mind, reason, sense, normality, rationality, lucidity, stability. OPPOSITE: insanity. **2** (*she doubted the sanity of the exercise*) wisdom, rationality, prudence, sagacity, judiciousness, soundness, common sense, sense, good sense, sensibleness, reasonableness, advisability.

sap[1] *noun* **1** (*the plant oozed sap*) juice, fluid. **2** (*he felt full of sap*) energy, vigour, oomph (*inf*), pep (*inf*), zip (*inf*), zest, vitality, vivacity, spirit, enthusiasm, lifeblood. **3** (*the poor sap got it in the neck*) fool, dupe, idiot, imbecile, simpleton, moron, nincompoop, ninny, jerk (*inf*), prat (*inf*), sucker (*inf*), nitwit (*inf*), twit (*inf*), clot (*inf*), drip (*inf*), wet (*inf*).

sap[2] *verb* **1** (*the effort sapped his strength*) weaken, undermine, enfeeble, debilitate, drain, bleed, enervate, devitalize, exhaust. OPPOSITE: strengthen. **2** (*the defeat sapped their confidence*) erode, wear away, wear down, reduce, deplete, diminish, impair, drain, bleed.

sapient *adj* wise, sagacious, sage, discerning, perspicacious, discriminating, judicious, knowing, intelligent, clever, shrewd, astute, sharp, keen, acute. OPPOSITE: stupid.

sarcasm *noun* irony, satire, cynicism, ridicule, mockery, scorn, derision, contempt, sneering, scoffing, taunting, gibing, acidity, acerbity, acrimony, asperity, mordancy, trenchancy, spitefulness, bitterness, resentment.

sarcastic *adj* ironical, ironic, sardonic, satirical, sarky (*inf*), cynical, snide, mocking, scornful, derisive, derisory, contemptuous, sneering, jeering, scathing, scoffing, taunting, disparaging, mordant, caustic, biting, cutting, incisive, trenchant, acerbic, bitter, spiteful, acrimonious.

sardonic *adj* sarcastic, ironical, ironic, cynical, scornful, mocking, sneering, jeering, scoffing, derisive, derisory,

contemptuous, dry, wry, bitter, malicious, malignant, malevolent, spiteful, cruel, heartless, biting, caustic, trenchant, mordant. OPPOSITE: pleasant.

satanic *adj* devilish, diabolic, diabolical, fiendish, demonic, demoniacal, hellish, infernal, accursed, damned, wicked, evil, iniquitous, malevolent, sinful, abominable, vile, foul, black, dark. OPPOSITE: angelic.

sate *verb* satisfy, gratify, fill, slake, satiate, saturate, surfeit, cloy, glut, overfill, stuff, gorge. OPPOSITE: starve.

satellite *noun* **1** (*a star with ten satellites*) moon, planet. **2** (*military satellites in space*) spacecraft, spaceship, space station, sputnik. **3** (*the president arrived with his band of satellites*) follower, adherent, disciple, minion, underling, subordinate, attendant, aide, dependant, retainer, vassal, lackey (*inf*), flunkey, sidekick, parasite, henchman, hanger-on, toady, sycophant, puppet (*inf*). OPPOSITE: leader. **4** (*a satellite of the parent state*) dependency, colony, dominion, protectorate.

satiate *verb* surfeit, cloy, glut, overfill, overfeed, stuff, gorge, engorge, sate, satisfy, fill, slake. OPPOSITE: starve.

satire *noun* **1** (*a master of satire*) irony, ridicule, sarcasm, mockery, piss-taking (*sl*). **2** (*a brilliant satire of contemporary society*) lampoon, burlesque, parody, caricature, travesty, skit, spoof (*inf*), send-up (*inf*), take-off (*inf*).

satirical *adj* ironical, ironic, sarcastic, sardonic, cynical, irreverent, burlesque, trenchant, acerbic, acrimonious, biting, cutting, mordant, pungent, stinging, caustic, bitter, incisive, mocking, taunting, ridiculing, derisive, critical, censorious.

satirize *verb* mock, deride, ridicule, lampoon, make fun of, poke fun at, burlesque, caricature, parody, travesty, send up (*inf*), take off (*inf*), criticize, take the piss out of (*sl*), take the mickey out of (*inf*), censure, attack.

satisfaction *noun* **1** (*the evening afforded her great satisfaction*) gratification, fulfilment, contentment, content, pleasure, happiness, enjoyment, delight, pride, smugness, comfort, ease. OPPOSITE: dissatisfaction. **2** (*he demanded satisfaction for the insult*) reparation, restitution, compensation, reimbursement, indemnification, indemnity, requital, recompense, amends, damages, atonement, redress, remuneration, settlement, payment. OPPOSITE: injury.

satisfactory *adj* adequate, sufficient, suitable, passable, average, acceptable, all right, OK (*inf*), fair, good, fine, competent, up to scratch, up to par, up to the mark, up to standard. OPPOSITE: unsatisfactory.

satisfied *adj* **1** (*his demands were satisfied*) fulfilled, gratified, sated, satiated, appeased, assuaged, full. **2** (*satisfied with the way things turned out*) happy, pleased, content, contented, smug. **3** (*satisfied by her explanation*) convinced, persuaded, reassured, sure, positive, certain, pacified.

satisfy *verb* **1** (*she tried to satisfy their needs*) meet, fulfil, gratify, indulge, appease, assuage, content, please, comply with, answer. OPPOSITE: dissatisfy. **2** (*satisfied her hunger*) sate, satiate, fill, slake, quench. **3** (*satisfy all debts*) discharge, settle, pay. **4** (*this should satisfy the fuel shortage*) answer, resolve, solve, match, suffice, serve. **5** (*we must satisfy the board of inquiry*) convince, persuade, assure, reassure, pacify. **6** (*satisfy an ancient* *insult*) atone for, requite, compensate for, recompense, indemnify, make reparation for.

satisfying *adj* **1** (*a satisfying evening*) gratifying, cheering, pleasing, pleasurable, fulfilling, enjoyable, refreshing. **2** (*a satisfying explanation*) satisfactory, persuasive, reassuring, reasonable, convincing.

saturate *verb* **1** (*our clothes were saturated*) soak, drench, waterlog, wet, wet through, douse, steep, souse, flood. **2** (*saturate the market*) sate, satiate, glut, surfeit, fill, overfill. **3** (*the whole place was saturated in light*) suffuse, imbue, pervade, permeate, infuse, bathe, impregnate. OPPOSITE: drain.

saturated *adj* wet through, soaked, soaking, drenched, waterlogged, steeped, flooded, sopping, dripping, wringing, sodden, soused.

saturnine *adj* gloomy, morose, glum, melancholy, moody, dismal, dull, sombre, grave, severe, austere, stern, phlegmatic, dour, heavy, taciturn, uncommunicative, unfriendly, withdrawn. OPPOSITE: jovial.

sauce *noun* **1** (*sauce for the meat*) condiment, relish, dip, dressing, ketchup, mayonnaise, seasoning, flavouring. **2** (*I've had enough of your sauce*) sauciness (*inf*), impertinence, impudence, insolence, rudeness, irreverence, disrespect, disrespectfulness, audacity, boldness, brashness, freshness, flippancy, brazenness, presumption, presumptuousness, temerity, gall, pertness, cheekiness, cheek (*inf*), brass (*inf*), nerve (*inf*), lip(*inf*), mouth (*inf*). OPPOSITE: respect.

saucy *adj* impertinent, pert, impudent, insolent, rude, disrespectful, irreverent, flippant, bold, brash, brazen, audacious, presumptuous, forward, fresh (*inf*), cheeky (*inf*), lippy (*inf*). OPPOSITE: respectful.

saunter *verb* stroll, walk, amble, promenade, ramble, roam, meander, wander, mooch (*inf*), mosey (*inf*), loiter, dawdle, dally, linger. OPPOSITE: hasten.
➤ *noun* stroll, walk, amble, promenade, ramble, roam, wander, meander, constitutional, turn, airing, mooch (*inf*), mosey (*inf*).

savage *adj* **1** (*a savage attack*) fierce, ferocious, vicious, beastly, cruel, brutal, brutish, inhuman, barbaric, barbarous, murderous, bloodthirsty, bloody, sadistic, diabolical, merciless, pitiless, ruthless, relentless, harsh, grim, terrible. OPPOSITE: gentle. **2** (*savage animals*) wild, untamed, undomesticated, feral, fierce, ferocious. **3** (*contact with savage tribesmen*) wild, uncivilized, uncultivated, barbarian, barbarous, barbaric, primitive, rough, rude. OPPOSITE: civilized.
➤ *noun* **1** (*one of the savages approached the fire*) barbarian, primitive, heathen, native, aborigine. **2** (*her husband is a savage*) barbarian, beast, brute, boor, monster, ogre, yahoo, churl.
➤ *verb* **1** (*the corpse had been savaged by wild animals*) maul, mangle, tear, tear to pieces, bite, claw, lacerate, attack. **2** (*he was savaged in the press*) criticize, denounce, run down (*inf*), slate (*inf*), slam (*inf*), knock (*inf*), take apart, tear to pieces (*inf*).

savant *noun* sage, philosopher, scholar, intellectual, man/woman of letters, master, expert, authority, mastermind, pundit, guru. OPPOSITE: fool.

save *verb* **1** (*all the passengers were saved*) rescue, free, set free, release, liberate, deliver, redeem, recover, reclaim, salvage. OPPOSITE: abandon. **2** (*save a little money*) keep, retain, reserve, conserve, hoard, store, stockpile, set aside, put aside, put by, put away, lay by, salt away, stash away (*inf*). OPPOSITE: squander. **3** (*the whole family needs to save*) budget, cut back, cut costs, cut expenditure, economize, practise economy, husband resources, tighten one's belt (*inf*). **4** (*she needs to be saved from herself*) protect, guard, safeguard, shield, screen, preserve, conserve, keep. OPPOSITE: expose. **5** (*that would save us from having to go ourselves*) spare, make unnecessary, forestall, prevent, obviate, preclude, rule out.

savings *pl noun* capital, investments, assets, reserves, resources, funds, nest-egg.

saviour *noun* redeemer, deliverer, liberator, emancipator, rescuer, protector, defender, guardian, champion.

savoir-faire *noun* expertise, skill, know-how (*inf*), savvy (*inf*), finesse, style, poise, aplomb, smoothness, adroitness, confidence, assurance, capability, ability, accomplishment, discretion, diplomacy, tact, tactfulness, suaveness, urbanity.

savour *noun* **1** (*the savour of real cream*) flavour, taste, relish, tang, piquancy, smack, zest, salt. **2** (*the savour of cut grass*) smell, odour, scent, aroma, fragrance, bouquet, perfume. **3** (*the affair had a savour of corruption*) suggestion, hint, trace, touch, tone, smattering, vein.
➤ *verb* **1** (*a prospect to savour*) relish, enjoy, appreciate, like, delight in, revel in, bask in, wallow in, luxuriate in. **2** (*their attitude savoured of prejudice*) smack, suggest, indicate, hint at, speak.

savoury *adj* **1** (*the savoury smell of cooked food*) mouth-watering, appetizing, fragrant, tasty, delicious, delectable, yummy (*inf*), scrumptious (*inf*), luscious, ambrosial, palatable, flavoursome, toothsome, pungent. **2** (*savoury snacks*) salty, spicy, piquant, tangy, tasty. OPPOSITE: insipid.

saw *noun* saying, adage, byword, dictum, proverb, axiom, maxim, aphorism, epigram, cliché, platitude, apophthegm.

say *verb* **1** (*say a few words*) utter, speak, pronounce, articulate, enunciate, voice, vocalize, mutter, grunt, drawl, exclaim, ejaculate. **2** (*he said he was happy*) state, declare, profess, allege, aver, avow, announce, answer, reply, respond, rejoin, retort, remark, observe, mention, affirm, assert, maintain. **3** (*say what you feel*) express, tell, put into words, phrase, articulate, communicate, reveal, disclose, divulge, convey. OPPOSITE: suppress. **4** (*say a few lines from the play*) recite, read, render, deliver, repeat, declaim, orate, perform, rehearse. **5** (*tell us what the readings say*) indicate, suggest, tell, specify, designate. **6** (*the papers say he is dead*) allege, claim, report, rumour, imply, suggest, signify, state. **7** (*I would say the fuel will last three days*) estimate, guess, reckon, judge, speculate, conjecture, predict, imagine, assume, suppose, presume, surmise.
➤ *noun* **1** (*everyone can have a say*) word, voice, turn, chance, vote, opinion, view. **2** (*she has little say in the final decision*) influence, weight, clout (*inf*), sway, power, authority, input, share, part.

that is to say that is, in other words, to put it another way.

saying *noun* saw, adage, dictum, proverb, axiom, maxim, epigram, slogan, motto, precept, catchphrase, quotation, statement, expression, aphorism, apophthegm, cliché, platitude.

scaffold *noun* **1** (*erect a scaffold around the statue*) scaffolding, frame, framework, platform, stage, gantry, tower. **2** (*the condemned man died on the scaffold*) gallows, gibbet.

scale[1] *noun* **1** (*fish scales*) plate, lamina, lamella, squama. **2** (*the pipe was covered in scale*) limescale, tartar, plaque, crust, incrustation, deposit, coating, coat, covering, layer, film. **3** (*scales of loose skin*) flake, scurf.

scale[2] *noun* **1** (*weigh it on the scale*) scales, balance, weighing machine.

scale[3] *noun* **1** (*on a scale of priority*) gradation, graduation, series, sequence, progression, succession, ranking, order, pecking order (*inf*), hierarchy, ladder. **2** (*on a different scale altogether*) level, range, reach, scope, spread, extent, compass, degree, spectrum, gamut. **3** (*the scale of the map*) ratio, proportion, measure.
➤ *verb* climb, mount, clamber, scramble, ascend, surmount, conquer, go up, shin up, escalate. OPPOSITE: descend.

scale down decrease, reduce, cut down, cut back, make less, lessen, lower, drop, contract, trim.

scaly *adj* flaky, rough, scurfy, scabby, scabrous.

scamp *noun* scallywag, rascal, rogue, monkey, whippersnapper (*inf*), tyke, mischief-maker, troublemaker, imp, devil, knave, blackguard, villain, wretch, miscreant, scapegrace.

scamper *verb* scurry, scoot (*inf*), scuttle, scramble, run, sprint, speed, race, hasten, hurry, dash, rush, dart, fly. OPPOSITE: amble.

scan *verb* **1** (*scan the horizon*) examine, scrutinize, inspect, study, investigate, search, scour, survey, sweep, check. **2** (*scan the report*) skim, browse, flick through, flip through, leaf through, thumb through, read through, look over, glance at, glance over, glance through, go over, run over, run one's eye over.

scandal *noun* **1** (*implicated in the scandal*) crime, sin, offence, transgression, impropriety, wrongdoing, misconduct. **2** (*the cost is a scandal*) outrage, disgrace, embarrassment. **3** (*a national scandal*) shame, disgrace, dishonour, blot, stain, disrepute, discredit, odium, opprobrium, obloquy, reproach, infamy, ignominy, pity. OPPOSITE: honour. **4** (*his allegations caused a scandal in the press*) outcry, furore, uproar. **5** (*their association was the subject of scandal*) gossip, rumour, talk, backbiting, muck-raking, dirt, defamation, slander, libel, calumny, slur, smear, aspersion, abuse, condemnation, censure.

scandalize *verb* horrify, appal, shock, outrage, offend, affront, insult, repel, revolt, disgust, dismay.

scandalous *adj* **1** (*a scandalous waste of money*) shocking, outrageous, monstrous, abominable, appalling, unspeakable, disgraceful, shameful, dishonourable, infamous, ignominious, opprobrious, atrocious, discreditable, disreputable, improper, unseemly, blatant, flagrant. OPPOSITE: creditable. **2** (*she made several scandalous allegations*) slanderous, libellous, scurrilous, defamatory, malicious.

scant *adj* little, sparse, measly (*inf*), limited, minimal, bare, insufficient, inadequate, deficient.

scanty *adj* meagre, skimpy, exiguous, scant, negligible, limited, restricted, insufficient, inadequate, deficient, short, little, small, narrow, thin, slender, sparse, bare, poor, paltry. OPPOSITE: ample.

scapegoat *noun* victim, fall guy (*inf*), sucker, whipping-boy, patsy (*inf*).

scar *noun* **1** (*a scar on his face*) mark, disfigurement, lesion, blemish, blotch, discolouration, cicatrix. **2** (*the incident left a scar on her psyche*) wound, injury, trauma, shock, damage, upset, suffering.
➤ *verb* **1** (*scarred by the flames*) mark, disfigure, deface, blemish, blotch, discolour. **2** (*the child was emotionally scarred*) traumatize, shock, damage, brand, stigmatize, injure, upset.

scarce *adj* rare, infrequent, uncommon, unusual, few, sparse, scanty, scant, in short supply, few and far between (*inf*), lacking, insufficient, deficient, inadequate, short, meagre, paltry. OPPOSITE: plentiful.

scarcely *adv* **1** (*she could scarcely hear them*) barely, hardly, only just. **2** (*that is scarcely a good reason to stay*) hardly, by no means, not, not at all, surely not, certainly not, definitely not, under no circumstances, on no account.

scarcity *noun* **1** (*a scarcity of food*) dearth, meagreness, paucity, lack, want, scantness, scantiness, shortage, sparseness, insufficiency, deficiency, inadequacy, undersupply. **2** (*the scarcity of these species is worrying*) rarity, rareness, infrequency, uncommonness, unusualness, sparseness. OPPOSITE: abundance.

scare *verb* frighten, affright, alarm, perturb, rattle (*inf*), put the wind up (*inf*), startle, shock, daunt, cow, awe, panic, terrify, terrorize, menace, threaten, petrify, horrify, appal, dismay, intimidate, unnerve. OPPOSITE: reassure.
➤ *noun* fright, alarm, start, shock, terror, horror, panic, hysteria, nervousness, fearfulness. OPPOSITE: reassurance.

scared *adj* frightened, afraid, fearful, terrified, terrorized, terror-stricken, petrified, horrified, nervous, anxious, alarmed, worried, shaken, startled, unnerved, cowed, panic-stricken, panicky, jittery, quivery.

scarf *noun* headscarf, muffler, neckerchief, kerchief, cravat, bandanna.

scary *adj* scaring, frightening, fearsome, alarming, disturbing, startling, nerve-racking, terrifying, petrifying, hair-raising, bloodcurdling, spine-chilling, chilling, creepy, spooky (*inf*), hairy (*inf*), eerie, intimidating, shocking, horrifying, appalling, daunting, forbidding, formidable.

scathing *adj* caustic, acid, vitriolic, mordant, stinging, biting, cutting, incisive, trenchant, virulent, critical, sarcastic, scornful, withering, unsparing, stern, severe, bitter, harsh, savage, fierce, ferocious, brutal. OPPOSITE: pleasant.

scatter *verb* **1** (*scatter the pieces everywhere*) sprinkle, sow, strew, broadcast, shower, disseminate, spread, diffuse, throw, fling, toss. OPPOSITE: gather. **2** (*the noise* *scattered the birds*) disperse, dispel, dissipate, disband, separate, break up, divide, disunite, dissolve, disintegrate. OPPOSITE: collect.

scatterbrained *adj* irresponsible, unreliable, forgetful, absentminded, scatty (*inf*), careless, carefree, inattentive, thoughtless, empty-headed, dreamy, wool-gathering, featherbrained, harebrained, brain like a sieve (*inf*), impulsive, frivolous, erratic, giddy.

scavenge *verb* forage, rummage, rake, search, look, hunt, scrounge.

scavenger *noun* forager, rummager, scrounger, raker.

scenario *noun* 1 (*the scenario of his new film*) outline, plot, script, text, screenplay, synopsis, rundown, summary, résumé, précis, storyline, scheme, plan, structure, projection, programme. 2 (*a worrying scenario*) situation, state of affairs, circumstances, scene, sequence of events.

scene *noun* 1 (*the scene of the crime*) place, spot, locality, locale, site, location, whereabouts, environment, position, setting, area. 2 (*against a scene of disorder*) background, backdrop, context. 3 (*the next scene of the story*) incident, episode, event, happening, proceeding, chapter, act, clip. 4 (*a pastoral scene*) view, vista, prospect, outlook, landscape, panorama, spectacle, tableau, pageant, picture, scenery. 5 (*she created quite a scene*) fuss, row, commotion, performance, drama, outburst, upset, furore, tantrum, to-do (*inf*), brouhaha, display, exhibition. 6 (*music is not her scene*) field, area, sphere, world, milieu, speciality, interest.

scenery *noun* 1 (*beautiful mountain scenery*) landscape, terrain, panorama, view, vista, prospect, outlook, scene, setting, surroundings. 2 (*scenery for the play*) set, setting, backdrop, mise en scène, background, flats.

scenic *adj* 1 (*a scenic part of the world*) picturesque, attractive, beautiful, pretty, pleasing, striking, impressive, grand, spectacular, breathtaking. 2 (*a scenic outlook*) panoramic, landscape.

scent *noun* 1 (*the scent of roses*) smell, odour, aroma, redolence, bouquet, perfume, fragrance, essence. 2 (*the dogs picked up the scent of a fox*) trail, track, trace, spoor. 3 (*she bought some expensive scent*) perfume, fragrance, essence, toilet water, eau de Cologne.
≫ *verb* 1 (*the old man scented food*) sniff, smell, nose out. 2 (*she scented trouble*) detect, discern, perceive, get wind of, sense, recognize.

scented *adj* perfumed, sweet-smelling, fragrant, aromatic.

sceptic *noun* 1 (*he found himself surrounded with sceptics*) doubter, disbeliever, dissenter, cynic, scoffer, questioner. 2 (*the church is full of sceptics*) doubter, doubting Thomas, agnostic, unbeliever, atheist.

sceptical *adj* doubting, doubtful, dubious, questioning, suspicious, distrustful, mistrustful, disbelieving, unbelieving, incredulous, unconvinced, hesitating, hesitant, cynical, scoffing, defeatist, pessimistic. OPPOSITE: credulous.

scepticism *noun* 1 (*he tried to overcome their scepticism*) doubt, doubtfulness, dubiety, hesitancy, suspicion, distrust, mistrust, disbelief, misbelief, incredulity, cynicism, scoffing, defeatism, pessimism. 2 (*religious scepticism*) unbelief, doubt, agnosticism. OPPOSITE: faith.

schedule *noun* 1 (*we must keep up to schedule*) plan, programme, timetable, scheme. 2 (*her schedule for the week*) agenda, itinerary, diary, calendar, list. 3 (*a schedule of plants in the collection*) list, inventory, catalogue, record, register, table.
≫ *verb* time, timetable, table, list, organize, arrange, programme, plan, appoint, book, assign.

scheme *noun* 1 (*a scheme to modernize the whole area*) plan, system, programme, schedule, procedure, tactic, project, design, proposal, proposition, suggestion, idea. 2 (*a scheme for the new building*) outline, draft, diagram, layout, blueprint, sketch, design, delineation, chart, map. 3 (*a scheme to defraud the taxman*) strategy, device, contrivance, wile, ruse, shift, racket (*inf*), game (*inf*), manoeuvre, machination, tactic, stratagem, subterfuge, ploy, plot, intrigue, conspiracy.
≫ *verb* plan, project, devise, contrive, formulate, frame, design, imagine, plot, intrigue, manoeuvre, machinate, conspire, collude, connive.

scheming *adj* calculating, designing, crafty, cunning, sly, tricky, artful, foxy, wily, conniving, unscrupulous, slippery, devious, underhand, deceitful, duplicitous, insidious, Machiavellian.

schism *noun* disunion, separation, division, split, break, breach, rift, rupture, detachment, severance, scission, discord, disagreement, estrangement. OPPOSITE: unity.

scholar *noun* 1 (*scholars going to their classes*) schoolboy, schoolgirl, schoolchild, student, pupil, learner. OPPOSITE: teacher. 2 (*a reputation as a scholar*) intellectual, academic, egghead (*inf*), highbrow (*inf*), don, bookworm (*inf*), man of letters, pundit, authority, expert, philosopher, mastermind, brainbox (*inf*), savant. OPPOSITE: dunce.

scholarly *adj* learned, erudite, academic, well-read, knowledgeable, intellectual, highbrow (*inf*), egghead (*inf*), brainy (*inf*), lettered, scholastic, literary, studious, bookish, scientific.

scholarship *noun* 1 (*a work of great scholarship*) erudition, learning, intelligence, knowledge, wisdom. 2 (*devoted his life to scholarship*) learning, letters, schooling, education, knowledge, lore, accomplishments, attainments, achievements. OPPOSITE: ignorance. 3 (*she won a scholarship to the college*) grant, bursary, fellowship, exhibition, award, endowment.

scholastic *adj* academic, educational, scholarly, learned, lettered, literary, bookish, pedagogic, analytical.

school *noun* 1 (*he did well at school*) college, academy, seminary, institute, institution, university. 2 (*the school of architecture*) faculty, department, discipline, division. 3 (*a more radical school of thought*) denomination, persuasion, belief, faith, credo, creed, doctrine, stamp, opinion, outlook, point of view. 4 (*he was one of a new school of writers*) movement, association, class, circle, set, group, sect, faction, clique, coterie, club, society, guild, league, company, followers, following, disciples, pupils, students, adherents, proponents, devotees, admirers, votaries.
≫ *verb* 1 (*she was schooled privately*) teach, educate, instruct, tutor. 2 (*the actors had been well schooled in their parts*) coach, train, instruct, indoctrinate, discipline, drill, direct, guide, prepare, prime, verse.

schooling *noun* **1** (*his schooling ended at sixteen*) education, tuition, teaching, instruction, learning, book-learning. **2** (*the schooling of actors*) coaching, training, instruction, preparation, grounding, guidance, indoctrination, drill, discipline.

schoolteacher *noun* teacher, schoolmaster, schoolmistress, schoolmarm, master, mistress, instructor, tutor, educator, pedagogue.

science *noun* **1** (*a degree in science*) physical science, physics, chemistry, biology, technology. **2** (*the science of kite-flying*) discipline, specialization, field of study. **3** (*the task demands a bit of science*) skill, expertise, expertness, proficiency, art, facility, technique, dexterity, deftness.

scientific *adj* **1** (*scientific data*) technical, technological. **2** (*undertake a scientific analysis*) logical, systematic, methodical, controlled, regulated, orderly, mathematical, analytical, accurate, exact, accurate, precise, thorough. OPPOSITE: unscientific.

scintillate *verb* sparkle, spark, twinkle, wink, gleam, coruscate, glitter, glint, glisten, flash, blaze, shine.

scintillating *adj* lively, stimulating, exhilarating, invigorating, spirited, animated, witty, vivacious, sparkling, shining, bright, brilliant, dazzling, glittering, flashing, exciting, effervescent, ebullient. OPPOSITE: dull.

scion *noun* **1** (*a scion of the royal house*) descendant, heir, successor, offspring, child, issue, progeny. **2** (*a scion of the parent plant*) offshoot, shoot, twig, branch, cutting, graft, sprout. OPPOSITE: stock.

scoff[1] *verb* (*scoffed at her comments*) mock, jeer, sneer, gibe, poke fun, make fun of, make a fool of, laugh, ridicule, belittle, disparage, deride, revile, taunt, tease, rib (*inf*), rag, scorn, despise, knock (*inf*), pooh-pooh (*inf*). OPPOSITE: respect.

scoff[2] *verb* (*scoffed all the cakes*) devour, eat, consume, wolf (*inf*), bolt, guzzle, gobble, cram, stuff, gorge, gulp down, put away (*inf*), finish off.

scold *verb* **1** (*scold the children*) upbraid, berate, reprimand, reprehend, admonish, rebuke, reprove, reproach, chide, remonstrate with, take to task, castigate, lecture, tell off (*inf*), tick off (*inf*), bawl out (*inf*), tear strips off (*inf*), blame, censure, carpet (*inf*), haul over the coals, rap over the knuckles. OPPOSITE: praise. **2** (*I wish she would stop scolding me*) nag, rail, go on (*inf*), carp, criticize, find fault, complain.

scolding *noun* telling-off (*inf*), talking-to (*inf*), ticking-off (*inf*), dressing-down (*inf*), rebuke, reproof, reprimand, chiding, reproach, castigation, upbraiding, lecture, carpeting (*inf*), bawling-out (*inf*), wigging (*inf*).

scoop *noun* **1** (*a scoop of butter*) ladle, spoon. **2** (*fit a new scoop on the digger*) bucket, shovel. **3** (*the press were pleased with the scoop*) exclusive, revelation, coup, sensation, inside story, exposé.
➤ *verb* **1** (*scoop out a hollow in the sand*) dig, excavate, hollow, gouge, scrape, empty, shovel. **2** (*scoop up their clothes*) gather, pick, lift.

scope *noun* **1** (*scope for some fun*) opportunity, freedom, liberty, latitude, leeway, capacity, space, room, elbow-room. **2** (*that lies outside the scope of our investigation*) range, extent, reach, compass, span, area, field, realm, sphere, ambit, orbit, sweep, breadth, limits, confines.

scorch *verb* **1** (*the wood was scorched*) burn, singe, char, blacken, sear, discolour. **2** (*the heat scorched the earth*) bake, parch, shrivel, wither, dry up, sear, toast, roast, brown, discolour, blister, scald.

scorching *adj* **1** (*scorching summer weather*) red-hot, roasting, sweltering, blistering, searing, boiling (*inf*), broiling (*inf*), baking (*inf*), sizzling (*inf*), burning, torrid, tropical. **2** (*he made several scorching observations*) scathing, caustic, stringent, biting, harsh, severe, trenchant, mordant.

score *noun* **1** (*the team notched up a huge score*) record, tally, reckoning, sum, total, points, marks, goals, runs, hits, tab (*inf*), bill. **2** (*the final score*) result, outcome. **3** (*a score of reasons*) twenty, lot, mass, multitude, myriad, swarm, shoal, drove, crowd, host, legion, army, hundred, thousand, million. **4** (*they were found wanting on several scores*) reason, cause, basis, grounds, account, count. **5** (*settle an old score*) grievance, grudge, wrong, injury, debt, obligation, complaint, dispute, quarrel, argument. **6** (*a score scratched on the wood*) notch, incision, scratch, line, groove, nick, slit, mark, scrape, cut, gash, gouge.
➤ *verb* **1** (*they scored a notable victory*) gain, achieve, attain, win, earn, get, make, chalk up (*inf*), notch up (*inf*), record, register. **2** (*she scores for the team*) keep a tally, keep count. **3** (*score a long scratch along the side of the car*) cut, incise, gouge, nick, slit, groove, notch, mark, scratch, scrape, graze, gash, slash, chip, indent, engrave.
score off get the better of, get one over on (*inf*), humiliate, make a fool of.
score out strike out, cross out, cancel, delete, remove, erase, efface, expunge, obliterate, put a line through.

scorn *noun* contempt, contemptuousness, disdain, disgust, scornfulness, derision, mockery, ridicule, sarcasm, sneering, disparagement, haughtiness, contumely. OPPOSITE: respect.
➤ *verb* **1** (*she scorned her critics*) despise, disdain, look down on, slight, disregard, deride, mock, laugh at, scoff at, sneer at, sniff at, hold in contempt, contemn. **2** (*scorn all offers of help*) refuse, reject, turn down, dismiss, spurn, shun.

scornful *adj* contemptuous, disdainful, disparaging, supercilious, haughty, arrogant, sneering, scoffing, jeering, derisive, mocking, sarcastic, sardonic, scathing, slighting, insulting, dismissive, contumelious. OPPOSITE: respectful.

scoundrel *noun* rogue, rascal, scamp, scallywag, rotter (*inf*), villain, vagabond, miscreant, ruffian, wretch, reprobate, cheat, wastrel, cad, bounder (*inf*), stinker (*inf*), louse (*inf*), rat (*inf*), swine (*inf*), ne'er-do-well, good-for-nothing, scapegrace, knave, blackguard. OPPOSITE: gentleman.

scour *verb* **1** (*scour the deck with brushes*) rub, abrade, scrub, clean, wash, wipe, polish, burnish, buff, cleanse, purge, clear, flush. OPPOSITE: soil. **2** (*scour the crime scene for clues*) search, hunt, ransack, forage, rummage, comb, rake, range, go over, drag.

scourge *noun* **1** (*the lash of the scourge*) whip, horsewhip, bullwhip, lash, cat o' nine tails, strap, thong, switch, flail, rod, birch. **2** (*it is the scourge of my existence*) punishment, penalty, torment, torture, plague, affliction, bane, curse, evil, menace, misfortune, trial, hardship, suffering, burden, pest, nuisance, visitation. OPPOSITE: blessing.

> *verb* **1** (*scourge the culprit*) whip, horsewhip, lash, beat, leather, flog, thrash, cane, belt (*inf*), strap, birch, wallop (*inf*). OPPOSITE: indulge. **2** (*scourged by doubt*) afflict, curse, plague, burden, torment, torture, punish, chastise, castigate, correct, discipline.

scout *noun* lookout, outrider, advance guard, vanguard, escort, spy.

> *verb* **1** (*scout out the land ahead*) reconnoitre, recce (*inf*), inspect, examine, study, investigate, check out (*inf*), explore, probe, spy out, survey, scan, case (*inf*), observe. **2** (*scout for talent*) search, look, hunt, seek, watch, ferret around, cast around.

scowl *verb* frown, glower, glare, grimace, lower, pout. OPPOSITE: smile.

> *noun* frown, glower, glare, grimace, dirty look, black look, pout.

scraggy *adj* scrawny, lean, thin, skinny, undernourished, emaciated, wasted, bony, angular, gaunt, spare, lanky. OPPOSITE: fat.

scramble *verb* **1** (*scramble up the slope*) clamber, climb, scale, crawl, grope, scrabble. **2** (*everyone scrambled to reach the gun*) struggle, jostle, tussle, strive, contend, compete, battle, vie, jockey, contest. **3** (*scramble out of the house*) hasten, hurry, rush, run, race, bustle, scurry, scamper. OPPOSITE: dawdle. **4** (*everything was scrambled in his head*) mix up, mix, blend, combine, jumble, tangle, disorder, confuse, disturb, disorganize.

> *noun* **1** (*a scramble for first place*) struggle, competition, tussle, jostle, battle, free-for-all. **2** (*a scramble in the hills*) trek, climb. **3** (*a scramble to finish by the deadline*) race, rush, hurry, dash. **4** (*everything was in a scramble*) muddle, mess, jumble, confusion, commotion.

scrap[1] *noun* **1** (*a scrap of paper*) piece, bit, fragment, remnant, tatter, snippet, part. **2** (*scraps of bread*) morsel, crumb, piece, bit, particle, mouthful, bite, shred, sliver, scraping. **3** (*without a scrap of evidence*) iota, mite, atom, particle, grain, trace, bit, vestige, whit. OPPOSITE: mass. **4** (*take the scrap away in a lorry*) waste, rubbish, junk, leftovers, remains, remnants, residue.

> *verb* discard, throw away, toss out, chuck out (*inf*), reject, abandon, jettison, junk (*inf*), ditch (*inf*), dump, shed, drop, get rid of, dispense with, write off, axe, demolish, cancel. OPPOSITE: keep.

scrap[2] *noun* (*had a scrap with his brother*) fight, scuffle, brawl, fracas, set-to (*inf*), punch-up (*inf*), run-in (*inf*), dust-up (*inf*), rumble (*inf*), ruck (*inf*), row, clash, quarrel, disagreement, argument, dispute, squabble, wrangle, tiff, barney (*inf*).

> *verb* fight, row, brawl, quarrel, argue, disagree, fall out (*inf*), squabble, bicker, wrangle.

scrape *verb* **1** (*scrape the paint off the metal*) file, rub, abrade, scrub, scour, sandpaper. **2** (*his spade scraped on stone*) grate, rasp, grind, scratch. **3** (*scrape the mud off her shoes*) clean, remove, erase. **4** (*the child had scraped his knee*) scratch, graze, skin, bark, scuff, cut, lacerate.

> *noun* **1** (*the scrape of her fingernail*) rasping, scratching, grating, grinding, squeaking, creaking. **2** (*he got away with just a scrape*) graze, scratch, abrasion, scuff, cut,

laceration, wound. **3** (*he's always getting into scrapes*) difficulty, predicament, plight, straits, dilemma, quandary, fix (*inf*), tight spot (*inf*), tight corner (*inf*), trouble, mischief, pickle (*inf*), muddle, mess.

scrape by manage, get by, scrimp, skimp, scrape a living, keep the wolf from the door.

scrape through manage, just pass, squeak through (*inf*).

scratch *verb* **1** (*she scratched her leg on the wire*) scrape, cut, lacerate, incise, gash, gouge, claw, tear, mark, score, nick, scuff, graze, skin, bark, rub, chafe. **2** (*scratch out the details*) erase, delete, cross out, strike out, eliminate, remove, expunge, obliterate.

> *noun* cut, laceration, gash, graze, abrasion, wound, scrape, scuff, mark, scar.

up to scratch up to par, up to standard, satisfactory, good enough, sufficient, adequate, acceptable, passable, tolerable, OK (*inf*), capable, competent, reasonable. OPPOSITE: unacceptable.

scrawl *verb* scribble, doodle, scratch, dash off, pen, jot down.

> *noun* scribble, squiggle, handwriting, writing, scratch.

scrawny *adj* scraggy, skinny, thin, lean, lanky, bony, angular, emaciated, undernourished, underfed.

scream *noun* **1** (*a scream of terror*) screech, shriek, cry, yell, shout, bawl, wail, yelp, squawk, squeal, howl, squall. OPPOSITE: whisper. **2** (*we all think he's a scream*) laugh, hoot (*inf*), caution (*inf*), riot (*inf*), character (*inf*), card (*inf*).

> *verb* screech, shriek, cry, call out, yell, shout, bawl, wail, yelp, squawk, squeal, howl, squall.

screech *noun* shriek, howl, shout, yell, yelp, squeal, squawk, call, cry, scream.

> *verb* shriek, howl, shout, cry, yelp, yell, squeal, scream.

screen *noun* **1** (*the room was divided by a screen*) partition, divider. **2** (*the door was fitted with a screen*) mesh, curtain, net, netting, shade, blind. **3** (*destroyers provided a screen against submarines*) cover, shelter, protection, guard, safeguard, shield, buffer. **4** (*a screen for their criminal activity*) cover, concealment, disguise, façade, front, mask, blind, camouflage, veil, cloak, shroud.

> *verb* **1** (*screen off a private area*) divide off, partition off, separate, conceal, hide. **2** (*screened by trees*) shelter, shade, cover, protect, guard, safeguard, shield, defend. **3** (*screened by fog*) hide, conceal, shroud, cloak, veil, mask, disguise, camouflage, cover. OPPOSITE: expose. **4** (*screen the material for impurities*) sieve, sift, filter, riddle, strain, process, sort. **5** (*screen the applicants one by one*) evaluate, examine, investigate, test, gauge, vet, scan, check, grade, pick, select.

screw *noun* **1** (*fastened with a screw*) bolt, pin, tack, nail, fastener. **2** (*with a screw of his head*) turn, twist, twirl.

> *verb* **1** (*screw it tight*) twist, wind, turn, fasten, tighten, clamp, fix. **2** (*she managed to screw the truth out of him*) force, extort, extract, wrench, wrest, squeeze, wring, bleed (*inf*), milk (*inf*).

put the screws on pressurize, press, force, coerce, compel, constrain, lean on (*inf*), dragoon.

screw up 1 (*the baby screwed up her face*) wrinkle,

pucker, twist, knit, distort, contort, crumple, contract, tighten. **2** (*they screwed up the whole project*) mess up, botch, spoil, ruin, bungle, cock up (*inf*), louse up (*inf*), mishandle, mismanage.

scribble *verb* scrawl, scratch, jot, dash off, write, pen, doodle.
➤ *noun* scrawl, squiggle, scratch, writing, handwriting.

scribe *noun* **1** (*work as a scribe to the great man*) copyist, amanuensis, transcriber, secretary, clerk. **2** (*a reputation as a scribe*) writer, author, pen-pusher, hack (*inf*).

scrimp *verb* stint, pinch, restrict, limit, straiten, reduce, economize, save, cut back, shorten, curtail, skimp. OPPOSITE: lavish.

script *noun* **1** (*the letters were written in a fine script*) hand, handwriting, writing, penmanship, pen, calligraphy. **2** (*the script for the play*) manuscript, text, lines, words, libretto, score, book, dialogue.

scripture *noun* bible, testament, word, word of God, holy writ, gospel.

scrounge *verb* forage, hunt, beg, cadge, borrow, sponge (*inf*), bum (*inf*), blag (*inf*).

scrounger *noun* sponger (*inf*), freeloader (*inf*), bum (*inf*), cadger, beggar, borrower, parasite.

scrub[1] *verb* **1** (*scrub the wall clean*) rub, brush, scour, wash, wipe, clean, cleanse. OPPOSITE: soil. **2** (*the trip was scrubbed*) cancel, call off, drop, discard, give up, do away with, scrap, abandon, delete, discontinue, axe (*inf*), abort.

scrub[2] *noun* scrubland, brushwood, brush, copse, coppice, thicket, undergrowth.

scruffy *adj* untidy, dishevelled, messy, bedraggled, unkempt, ungroomed, ill-groomed, sloppy (*inf*), disreputable, shabby, down-at-heel, run-down, worn-out, tattered, ragged, slovenly, seedy, squalid. OPPOSITE: smart.

scrumptious *adj* delicious, tasty, yummy (*inf*), scrummy (*inf*), appetising, mouth-watering, succulent, luscious, palatable, delectable, delightful, exquisite, morish (*inf*).

scrunch *verb* crumple, crush, squash, crunch, screw up, twist, chew, champ.

scruple *noun* **1** (*she had no scruples about deceiving her husband*) qualm, reservation, misgiving, conscience, compunction, difficulty, doubt, hesitation, uneasiness, reluctance. OPPOSITE: assurance. **2** (*a rogue without a scruple in his head*) moral, ethic, principle, standard.
➤ *verb* hesitate, falter, waver, vacillate, think twice, demur, doubt, shrink, recoil, balk, hold back, be loath.

scrupulous *adj* **1** (*scrupulous attention to detail*) punctilious, strict, exact, precise, meticulous, painstaking, rigorous, fastidious, minute, thorough, nice, careful, cautious, conscientious. OPPOSITE: lax. **2** (*scrupulous in his private life*) honest, honourable, upright, right-minded, righteous, moral, ethical, principled.

scrutinize *verb* examine, study, peruse, pore over, look over, look through, go over, go through, scan, survey, probe, explore, search, investigate, inspect, analyse, dissect, sift. OPPOSITE: ignore.

scrutiny *noun* examination, study, perusal, survey, scan, probe, exploration, search, investigation, inquiry, inspection, analysis, dissection.

scud *verb* run, race, speed, fly, sail, skim, shoot, dart, blow.

scuffle *verb* fight, struggle, come to blows, scrap (*inf*), contend, grapple, tussle, brawl, clash, row.
➤ *noun* fight, struggle, tussle, brawl, scrap (*inf*), set-to (*inf*), riot, fracas, affray, commotion, disturbance, melee, rumpus, brouhaha, row, quarrel, barney (*inf*), clash. OPPOSITE: peace.

sculpture *noun* statue, statuette, bust, head, figure, figurine, bronze, carving, bas-relief, cast.

scum *noun* **1** (*scum floating on the water*) froth, foam, film, layer, crust, rubbish. **2** (*the scum of society*) dregs, dross, riffraff, rabble, undesirables, rubbish, trash.

scupper *verb* **1** (*the captain scuppered the ship*) scuttle, sink, submerge, disable, destroy. **2** (*his campaign was scuppered*) wreck, smash, demolish, destroy, ruin, foil, defeat, overthrow, overwhelm.

scurrilous *adj* abusive, offensive, insulting, vituperative, defamatory, slanderous, libellous, disparaging, gross, foul, coarse, vulgar, rude, obscene, dirty, indecent, salacious, ribald, scandalous. OPPOSITE: complimentary.

scurry *verb* scamper, scuttle, scoot, scramble, dash, dart, run, race, sprint, trot, rush, hurry, hasten, make haste, bustle, fly, skim, scud. OPPOSITE: amble.
➤ *noun* rush, bustle, flurry, hurry, haste, racing, dashing, scuttling, scampering.

scurvy *adj* low, base, mean, bad, despicable, contemptible, pitiful, abject, vile, rotten, dirty, shabby, sorry, worthless, dishonourable, ignoble. OPPOSITE: honourable.

scuttle *verb* scamper, scurry, scramble, bustle, scoot, dash, dart, run, race, rush, hurry, hasten, fly, scud. OPPOSITE: amble.

sea *noun* **1** (*journey across the sea*) ocean, main, deep, briny (*inf*), drink (*inf*). OPPOSITE: land. **2** (*the boat was tossed on the sea*) swell, surge, waves, rollers, breakers, billows. **2** (*a sea of red and white*) profusion, mass, host, multitude, abundance, plethora, expanse, sheet.
at sea adrift, astray, lost, at a loss, disorientated, bewildered, baffled, perplexed, puzzled, confused, mystified.

seal *verb* **1** (*seal the bottle*) fasten, secure, close, shut, plug, cork, stop, stopper. OPPOSITE: open. **2** (*seal the agreement*) secure, settle, finalize, complete, clinch (*inf*), confirm, stamp, validate, sanction, endorse.
➤ *noun* **1** (*the royal seal*) insignia, signet, emblem, badge, crest, mark, symbol, stamp, monogram. **2** (*the seal of quality*) pledge, guarantee, proof, assurance, confirmation, attestation, ratification, authentication, warrant, warranty, cachet.
seal off close off, shut off, cut off, fence off, cordon off, block up, isolate, segregate, quarantine.

seam *noun* **1** (*a seam in the pipe*) joint, join, junction, weld, line, suture. **2** (*a seam of coal*) stratum, vein, layer, lode.

seaman *noun* sailor, mariner, seaman, seafarer,

bluejacket, tar (*inf*), Jack tar (*inf*), matelot (*inf*), seadog (*inf*).

seamy *adj* unpleasant, unattractive, disagreeable, nasty, repulsive, sordid, squalid, sleazy (*inf*), unsavoury, disreputable, dark, low, rough. OPPOSITE: pleasant.

sear *verb* burn, scorch, singe, char, fry, sizzle, cauterize, brand, brown, discolour, wither, wilt, dry, parch, desiccate.

search *verb* **1** (*search for an answer*) seek, look, hunt, cast around, scout out, ferret out, forage. **2** (*search through the ruins*) go, hunt, rummage, sift, comb, rifle, scour, probe, explore, ransack, turn upside down. **3** (*she searched her memory*) examine, scrutinize, study, survey, explore, probe, investigate, inspect. **4** (*search the suspects*) inspect, check, examine, frisk (*inf*).
≫ *noun* **1** (*a search for the missing items*) hunt, rummage, forage, ransacking. OPPOSITE: discovery. **2** (*a search for clues*) examination, scrutiny, exploration, probe, inspection, investigation, inquiry, research, pursuit, quest.

searching *adj* **1** (*a searching stare*) penetrating, piercing, keen, alert, observant, sharp, intent, discerning. **2** (*a searching inquiry*) thorough, close, inquiring, inquisitive, probing, penetrating, analytic, quizzical.

season *noun* time, period, spell, span, interval, term, quarter.
≫ *verb* **1** (*season with salt and pepper*) flavour, spice, salt. **2** (*the conversation was seasoned with a few jokes*) enliven, pep up (*inf*), leaven. **3** (*leave the wood to season*) age, mature, prepare, harden, toughen, mellow, ripen, prime, condition, treat, anneal, inure, habituate, accustom, acclimatize, train. **4** (*he has seasoned his opinion*) temper, moderate, qualify, mitigate, tone down.
in season ready, plentiful, available, obtainable, common, on the market.

seasonable *adj* opportune, timely, well-timed, suitable, appropriate, fit, fitting, apt, convenient, auspicious, providential, welcome. OPPOSITE: untimely.

seasoned *adj* experienced, mature, practised, well-versed, established, habituated, hardened, toughened, conditioned, veteran, old, long-serving, weathered.

seasoning *noun* flavouring, spice, salt, pepper, herbs, relish, condiment, sauce, dressing.

seat *noun* **1** (*pull up a seat*) chair, bench, stool, sofa, pew, stall, settle, throne, form. **2** (*a seat of learning*) place, centre, hub, heart, cradle, situation, site, location, axis. **3** (*he retired to his country seat*) residence, abode, house, mansion, stately home. **4** (*the seat of her worries*) cause, basis, root, source, origin, reason, grounds, base, foundation.
≫ *verb* **1** (*each carriage seats eight people*) accommodate, hold, contain, take. **2** (*seat the children near the door*) place, set, put, sit, install, establish, fix, settle, deposit.

seating *noun* seats, places, chairs, room, accommodation.

secede *verb* withdraw, retire, resign, leave, quit, pull out, drop out, break with, break away, split, separate, reject, repudiate, renounce. OPPOSITE: affiliate.

secluded *adj* isolated, remote, out-of-the-way, tucked-away, cut off, solitary, lonely, sequestered, cloistered, shut away, unfrequented, withdrawn, retired, sheltered,

private, hidden, concealed, screened. OPPOSITE: public.

seclusion *noun* privacy, solitude, isolation, retreat, retirement, withdrawal, sequestration, remoteness, concealment, shelter, hiding, secrecy.

second[1] *adj* **1** (*they were successful at the second attempt*) next, following, subsequent, succeeding. OPPOSITE: first. **2** (*she earned a second bonus*) further, extra, additional. **3** (*he had brought a second sample with him*) additional, extra, alternate, alternative, other, back-up, supplementary, substitute. **4** (*he was demoted to the second team*) secondary, subordinate, inferior, lower, lesser, minor. OPPOSITE: principal. **5** (*considered a second Picasso*) duplicate, double, twin, replicate, repeated, other.
≫ *noun* attendant, assistant, helper, supporter, backer, right-hand man. OPPOSITE: opponent.
≫ *verb* **1** (*seconded by a team of experts*) back, support, help, aid, assist. OPPOSITE: oppose. **2** (*she agreed to second the proposal*) endorse, back, back up, support, approve, agree with, promote, further, forward, advance, encourage.

second[2] *noun* instant, moment, minute, trice, twinkling, flash, jiffy (*inf*), jif (*inf*), sec (*inf*), mo (*inf*), tick (*inf*).

second[3] *verb* transfer, move, shift, relocate, assign, send, change.

secondary *adj* **1** (*a secondary detail*) subordinate, subsidiary, ancillary, auxiliary, extra, inferior, minor, lesser, lower, unimportant, non-essential. **2** (*a secondary source of power*) back-up, reserve, auxiliary, spare, supporting, second, alternative, extra, subsidiary. **3** (*a secondary effect of the decision*) resulting, resultant, derivative, derived, indirect. OPPOSITE: primary.

second-class *adj* second-rate, second-best, low-class, mediocre, indifferent, undistinguished, uninspired, uninspiring, inferior, lesser, unimportant.

second-hand *adj* hand-me-down (*inf*), reach-me-down (*inf*), used, worn, nearly-new, old.

second-in-command *noun* deputy, number two, assistant, substitute, subordinate, right-hand man, attendant.

second-rate *adj* inferior, second-class, second-best, sub-standard, mediocre, poor, poor-quality, low-quality, low-grade, tacky (*inf*), shoddy, cheap, rubbishy, tawdry, tinpot (*inf*), lousy (*inf*), uninspired, uninspiring, undistinguished.

secrecy *noun* **1** (*information communicated in the utmost secrecy*) confidentiality, confidence, privateness. **2** (*the secrecy of their activities*) furtiveness, covertness, stealth, stealthiness, surreptitiousness, clandestineness. **3** (*the secrecy of their honeymoon retreat*) privacy, seclusion, remoteness, sequestration, solitariness, retirement, concealment.

secret *adj* **1** (*a secret door*) hidden, concealed, disguised, camouflaged, invisible. **2** (*secret activity*) unseen, covert, surreptitious, clandestine, undercover, stealthy, furtive, conspiratorial, sly, underhand, cloak-and-dagger (*inf*), closet (*inf*). OPPOSITE: open. **3** (*secret papers*) private, classified, restricted, confidential, hush-hush (*inf*), sensitive, undisclosed, unpublished, unrevealed, untold, unknown. OPPOSITE: public. **4** (*a secret valley*) secluded,

solitary, lonely, remote, retired, isolated, cut off, out-of-the-way, cloistered, sequestered, unfrequented, private, sheltered, concealed, hidden. **5** (*secret occult knowledge*) hidden, mysterious, cryptic, occult, arcane, esoteric, recondite, abstruse. **6** (*he was very secret about his new job*) secretive, reticent, uncommunicative, discreet.
≫ **noun 1** (*a well-kept secret*) confidence, confidential matter. **2** (*a life full of secrets*) mystery, enigma, puzzle, riddle. **3** (*the secret of good cooking*) code, key, formula, recipe, solution, answer.
in secret 1 (*the deal must be done in secret*) secretly, confidentially, in confidence, in private, behind closed doors, in camera, quietly. **2** (*the organization operated in secret*) secretly, covertly, clandestinely, furtively, surreptitiously, stealthily, discreetly, privately.

secretary *noun* clerk, typist, scribe, amanuensis, assistant, aide, personal assistant, PA.

secrete *verb* **1** (*the battery has secreted acid*) discharge, emit, exude, excrete, emanate, give off, send out, produce, ooze, leak, leach. OPPOSITE: absorb. **2** (*secrete the gun under the floorboards*) hide, conceal, cover up, veil, screen, shroud, camouflage, disguise, stow, stash (*inf*), cache, bury, sequester. OPPOSITE: expose.

secretion *noun* discharge, release, emission, excretion, exudation, emanation, leakage, oozing.

secretive *adj* tight-lipped, reticent, close-mouthed, cagey (*inf*), close, uncommunicative, unforthcoming, reserved, withdrawn, taciturn, silent, quiet, intent, clamlike, secret.

secretly *adv* **1** (*negotiations continued secretly*) in secret, in private, privately, confidentially, in confidence, behind closed doors (*inf*), in camera, sub rosa, under cover, quietly. **2** (*he left the country secretly*) in secret, unobserved, clandestinely, surreptitiously, covertly, furtively, stealthily, on the sly, on the quiet. **3** (*she secretly wished she could go*) privately, in one's heart, to oneself.

sect *noun* **1** (*a religious sect*) cult, denomination, order. **2** (*different sects of the party*) faction, schism, group, splinter group, party, school, camp, wing, division, subdivision.

sectarian *adj* factional, denominational, partisan, bigoted, prejudiced, intolerant, insular, narrow-minded, narrow, limited, exclusive, parochial, hidebound, doctrinaire, rigid, dogmatic, fanatical, fanatic, extreme. OPPOSITE: broad-minded.

section *noun* **1** (*a section of the wing was missing*) part, segment, component, piece, bit, portion, slice, fragment, fraction, division, subdivision. OPPOSITE: whole. **2** (*a section of the organization*) part, division, department, branch. **3** (*the best section of the novel*) part, chapter, passage, paragraph, instalment, division, component.

sector *noun* **1** (*a sector of industry*) part, branch, field, division, area, category. **2** (*there has been trouble in this sector of the town*) area, district, zone, quarter, region.

secular *adj* lay, profane, temporal, worldly, earthly, state, civil, non-religious, non-spiritual. OPPOSITE: religious.

secure *adj* **1** (*secure from harm*) safe, protected, defended, fortified, sheltered, shielded, immune, invulnerable, impregnable, unharmed, undamaged.

OPPOSITE: vulnerable. **2** (*secure foundations*) firm, stable, fixed, immovable, steady, sturdy, strong, solid, sound, dependable, reliable, established, fast, tight. **3** (*she checked that the door was secure*) closed, shut, locked, fastened, sealed. **4** (*he felt secure in the prospect of victory*) confident, assured, reassured, sure, certain, settled, relaxed, safe, contented, happy. OPPOSITE: insecure.
≫ **verb 1** (*hope to secure a good job*) obtain, get, get hold of, gain, procure, acquire, come by (*inf*), land (*inf*). OPPOSITE: lose. **2** (*secure the rope*) tie, fix, attach, fasten, make fast, lash, bind, moor. OPPOSITE: release. **3** (*she secured the window*) fasten, close, shut, lock, padlock, bolt, latch, chain, seal, rivet, batten down. **4** (*secure the building*) defend, guard, safeguard, protect, fortify, strengthen. **5** (*they agreed to secure the loan*) guarantee, assure, ensure, insure, underwrite, cover, sponsor.

security *noun* **1** (*concern about the security of the data*) safety, protection, safe-keeping, shielding, invulnerability. **2** (*she was offered security from the mob*) asylum, shelter, safety, refuge, sanctuary, immunity, precaution, safeguard. OPPOSITE: danger. **3** (*her new wealth brought her security*) confidence, peace of mind, assurance, conviction, certainty, sureness, reliance. OPPOSITE: insecurity. **4** (*demand security for the loan*) collateral, guarantee, warranty, surety, pledge, gage, assurance, insurance.

sedate *adj* **1** (*a sedate demeanour*) calm, composed, cool, collected, serene, tranquil, placid, quiet, imperturbable, unruffled, unflappable, quiet, demure, staid, stiff, dignified, proper, decorous, sober, solemn, grave, earnest, serious. **2** (*he drove at a sedate speed*) slow, slow-moving, measured, leisurely, deliberate, dignified, staid.
≫ **verb** tranquillize, quieten down, calm, calm down, pacify, soothe, relax.

sedative *noun* tranquillizer, narcotic, opiate, barbiturate, sleeping pill, anodyne, calmative, downer (*inf*), depressant. OPPOSITE: stimulant.
≫ **adj** calming, soothing, soporific, narcotic, tranquillizing, assuaging, relaxing, anodyne, lenitive.

sedentary *adj* seated, sitting, inactive, motionless, immobile, unmoving, still, stationary, idle, desk bound. OPPOSITE: active.

sediment *noun* precipitate, dregs, lees, grounds, deposit, settlings, residue, residuum, dross, silt, scum.

sedition *noun* **1** (*tried on charges of sedition*) incitement, agitation, rabble-rousing, fomentation. **2** (*sedition spread through the colony*) rebellion, rioting, revolt, insurgence, uprising, insurrection, insubordination, disorder, mutiny, subversion, agitation, treason, treachery, disloyalty. OPPOSITE: loyalty.

seditious *adj* **1** (*a seditious influence*) seditionary, rabble-rousing, agitating, inciting, fomenting. **2** (*seditious junior officers*) rebellious, mutinous, insurgent, insurrectionary, insurrectionist, revolutionary, insubordinate, subversive, refractory, dissident, disloyal, treacherous, traitorous. OPPOSITE: obedient.

seduce *verb* **1** (*she was seduced by the squire*) corrupt, deprave, debauch, deflower, ravish, violate, dishonour, lead astray, ruin. **2** (*seduced from his intended path*) tempt, lure, lead astray, mislead, inveigle, ensnare, entice, beguile, attract, allure, charm, deceive. OPPOSITE: repel.

seductive *adj* **1** (*they made him a seductive offer*) tempting, tantalizing, enticing, beguiling, alluring, inviting, appealing, attractive, bewitching, captivating, irresistible. **2** (*a seductive dress*) provocative, sexy (*inf*), flirtatious, arousing, alluring, tempting, exciting, sultry, charming. OPPOSITE: repulsive.

sedulous *adj* assiduous, diligent, conscientious, scrupulous, painstaking, industrious, laborious, persevering, persistent, constant, unremitting, tireless, untiring, unflagging, energetic, active, busy, determined, resolved. OPPOSITE: idle.

see *verb* **1** (*you can see everything from up here*) make out, perceive, discern, descry, observe, view, spot, glimpse, notice, espy, identify, distinguish, recognize. OPPOSITE: miss. **2** (*see how they move together*) look at, behold, observe, regard, watch, witness, note, heed, mark, examine, inspect. **3** (*I see what you mean*) comprehend, understand, grasp, fathom, make out, take in, get, follow, know, feel, appreciate, realize, recognize. **4** (*you had better see what it's all about*) ascertain, determine, learn, find out, discover, investigate, ask, enquire. **5** (*she claims she can see the future*) predict, foresee, forecast, envisage, visualize, imagine, conceive, picture, anticipate. **6** (*let me see*) consider, deliberate, think, reflect, ponder. OPPOSITE: decide. **7** (*he saw his mother yesterday*) meet, encounter, receive, speak to. **8** (*he offered to see her home*) take, escort, accompany, usher, lead, show. **9** (*she is going to see her son's teacher*) visit, call on, consult, speak to, confer with, interview. **10** (*who is he seeing now?*) go out with, date (*inf*), take out, court, keep company with.

see about see to, deal with, arrange, organize, attend to, manage, cope with, sort out, look after, take care of, fix, repair.

see through 1 (*she saw through his lies*) penetrate, fathom, understand, comprehend. **2** (*they want to see the job through*) persevere, persist, continue, keep at, stick out (*inf*), hang in (*inf*).

see to arrange, organize, manage, mind, see about, attend to, cope with, deal with, take care of, look after, sort out, ensure.

seed *noun* **1** (*a seed from the plant*) germ, ovule, spore, grain, pip, stone, kernel, nucleus, sperm, ovum, egg, spawn, embryo. **2** (*the seeds of a new friendship*) source, origin, beginning, start, cause, root, grounds, basis, motivation, motive, reason. **3** (*the royal seed*) offspring, children, young, issue, family, progeny, descendants, successors, heirs, scions.

run to seed deteriorate, decay, degenerate, decline, go downhill (*inf*), go to the dogs (*inf*), go to pot (*inf*).

seedy *adj* **1** (*the building had a seedy appearance*) shabby, scruffy, unkempt, untidy, shoddy, rundown, dilapidated, dirty, squalid, sordid, sleazy (*inf*), grotty (*inf*), crummy (*inf*), decaying, mean, mangy, tatty. OPPOSITE: smart. **2** (*he says he feels pretty seedy*) ill, unwell, indisposed, ailing, poorly (*inf*), sick, sickly, groggy (*inf*), rough (*inf*), off-colour, out of sorts (*inf*), under the weather (*inf*). OPPOSITE: well.

seek *verb* **1** (*seek for her shoes*) hunt, look, search, pursue, follow. OPPOSITE: find. **2** (*seek to win*) try, attempt, endeavour, aim, aspire, strive. OPPOSITE: fail. **3** (*seek assistance*) want, desire, ask, beg, request, entreat, solicit.

seem *verb* look, appear, sound, feel, pretend, come across as. OPPOSITE: be.

seemingly *adv* apparently, ostensibly, allegedly, outwardly, superficially, on the surface, on the face of it. OPPOSITE: actually.

seemly *adv* proper, decent, nice, fit, fitting, befitting, suitable, suited, appropriate, apt, apposite, becoming, decorous, meet, attractive, handsome, comely. OPPOSITE: unseemly.

seep *verb* ooze, trickle, leak, drip, dribble, drain, percolate, leach, bleed, well, exude, permeate, soak.

seer *noun* prophet, soothsayer, augur, clairvoyant, sibyl.

seesaw *verb* swing, yo-yo (*inf*), alternate, fluctuate, oscillate, teeter, pitch.

seethe *verb* **1** (*the water seethed*) boil, bubble, foam, froth, effervesce, fizz, churn, ferment, surge, teem, swarm. **2** (*the king seethed with rage*) rage, rant, rave, fume, smoulder, simmer, be furious, explode (*inf*), boil over (*inf*).

segment *noun* section, portion, part, division, piece, bit, fragment, slice, wedge, component. OPPOSITE: whole.

segregate *verb* separate, dissociate, isolate, set apart, cut off, quarantine, ostracize, discriminate against, exclude, sequester. OPPOSITE: unite.

segregation *noun* separation, partition, isolation, dissociation, setting apart, discrimination, apartheid, sequestration.

seize *verb* **1** (*she seized his hand*) grab, snatch, take, grasp, grip, hold, clasp, clutch. OPPOSITE: drop. **2** (*the thieves were seized by the police*) capture, catch, apprehend, arrest, collar (*inf*), nab (*inf*). **3** (*customs seized the goods*) confiscate, impound, sequestrate, sequester, take, usurp, commandeer, appropriate. OPPOSITE: release. **4** (*terrorists seized the president*) kidnap, abduct, snatch, hijack.

seizure *noun* **1** (*the seizure of contraband goods*) confiscation, sequestration, commandeering, appropriation. **2** (*the seizure of the culprits*) capture, apprehension, arrest. OPPOSITE: release. **3** (*the seizure of hostages*) kidnapping, hijacking, taking, snatching, abduction. **4** (*the child suffered a seizure*) convulsion, fit, spasm, paroxysm, attack.

seldom *adv* rarely, infrequently, hardly ever, scarcely ever, occasionally, once in a blue moon (*inf*). OPPOSITE: often.

select *verb* pick, hand-pick, choose, single out, opt for, decide on, settle on, elect, prefer, favour.
➢ *adj* **1** (*a select choice of clothing*) selected, picked, hand-picked, preferred, choice, chosen, best, finest, prime, excellent, supreme, superb, first-class, first-rate, high-quality, top-quality, top. OPPOSITE: inferior. **2** (*a select hotel*) elite, exclusive, superior, privileged, posh (*inf*).

selection *noun* **1** (*a selection of items*) pick, choice, option, preference. **2** (*a selection of chocolates*) collection, assortment, potpourri, variety, range, choice, miscellany, medley, anthology.

selective *adj* particular, discerning, discriminating,

discriminatory, fastidious, choosy (*inf*), fussy, finicky (*inf*), picky (*inf*), pernickety (*inf*).

self-assurance *noun* assurance, self-confidence, confidence, self-possession, assertiveness, positiveness, aplomb, cockiness (*inf*).

self-centred *adj* egotistic, egotistical, egoistic, egocentric, narcissistic, selfish, self-absorbed, self-interested, self-seeking, self-serving.

self-confidence *noun* confidence, self-assurance, assurance, self-reliance, self-dependence, self-possession, aplomb, poise, composure, coolness.

self-conscious *adj* shy, bashful, coy, diffident, retiring, shrinking, self-effacing, timorous, timid, nervous, embarrassed, blushing, ill-at-ease, sheepish, shamefaced, awkward, uncomfortable.

self-control *noun* self-restraint, restraint, patience, self-discipline, self-denial, willpower, strength of will, composure, calmness, cool (*inf*).

self-denial *noun* self-discipline, abstinence, moderation, self-sacrifice, selflessness, unselfishness, altruism, asceticism, abstemiousness, temperance, self-abnegation, self-deprivation.

self-esteem *noun* self-respect, self-regard, self-assurance, self-confidence, ego, pride, dignity, amour-propre.

self-important *adj* conceited, arrogant, haughty, pompous, vain, proud, big-headed, swollen-headed, egoistic, egotistical, presumptuous, overbearing, overweening, strutting, swaggering, pushy (*inf*).

self-indulgence *noun* excess, extravagance, intemperance, immoderation, unrestraint, self-gratification, pleasure-seeking, sensualism, dissipation, profligacy, dissoluteness, hedonism.

selfish *adj* self-centred, self-absorbed, egotistic, egoistic, egotistical, egocentric, self-regarding, self-seeking, self-serving, self-interested, greedy, covetous, miserly, mean, ungenerous, inconsiderate, mercenary. OPPOSITE: altruistic.

selfless *adj* unselfish, generous, altruistic, self-denying, self-sacrificing, magnanimous, philanthropic, liberal, ungrudging.

self-possessed *adj* cool (*inf*), collected, calm, composed, unruffled, poised, self-assured, confident, together (*inf*), unflappable (*inf*), imperturbable. OPPOSITE: nervous.

self-respect *noun* self-esteem, self-regard, pride, self-belief, dignity, amour-propre.

self-righteous *adj* sanctimonious, holier-than-thou, superior, goody-goody (*inf*), pious, pietistic, priggish, unctuous, mealy-mouthed, pharisaic, smug, complacent.

self-sacrifice *noun* self-denial, selflessness, unselfishness, altruism, generosity, self-abnegation.

self-satisfied *adj* complacent, proud, smug, puffed up (*inf*), self-congratulatory, self-righteous, self-approving.

self-seeking *adj* self-serving, self-interested, selfish, self-loving, opportunistic, on the make (*inf*), ambitious, mercenary, calculating, fortune-hunting, gold-digging.

self-styled *adj* would-be, so-called, self-appointed, self-named, self-titled, pretended.

self-willed *adj* wilful, stubborn, obstinate, pig-headed, bloody-minded, contrary, mulish, perverse, headstrong, wayward, ungovernable, recalcitrant, refractory, intractable, stiff-necked, uncooperative, cussed (*inf*), self-opinionated, intransigent, difficult, disobedient.

sell *verb* **1** (*he must sell his car*) put up for sale, vend, dispose of, exchange, barter, trade, auction. OPPOSITE: buy. **2** (*she makes a living selling fancy goods*) trade in, traffic in, deal in, hawk, flog (*inf*), peddle, tout, handle, retail, market, merchandise, import, export, carry, stock. **3** (*they are trying to sell the idea of monetary union*) promote, advertise, push (*inf*), hype (*inf*), get across, win approval for.

sell out **1** (*the shop has sold out of flags*) run out of, have none left. **2** (*they were accused of selling out their friends*) betray, double-cross, rat on (*inf*), play false, sell down the river (*inf*), stab in the back (*inf*).

seller *noun* salesman, saleswoman, salesperson, vendor, trader, tradesman, merchant, dealer, retailer, shopkeeper, storekeeper, pedlar, supplier, stockist, wholesaler, agent, representative, rep (*inf*), commercial traveller.

selling *noun* **1** (*the selling of new products*) vending, trading, dealing, marketing, trafficking, promotion. **2** (*she got a job in selling*) marketing, merchandising, sales, salesmanship.

semblance *noun* appearance, look, aspect, air, demeanour, mien, guise, disguise, mask, cloak, camouflage, pretence, pretext, show, façade, front, veneer, likeness, similarity, resemblance, image.

seminary *noun* academy, college, institute, institution, school.

send *verb* **1** (*send a letter to the company*) forward, dispatch, get off, remit, address, mail, post, deliver, convey, consign. **2** (*send a report by radio*) transmit, broadcast, relay, beam, communicate, convey, radio, televise. OPPOSITE: retain. **3** (*the explosion sent ash into the air*) hurl, propel, project, emit, throw, fling, let fly, discharge, cast, shoot, fire, launch, drive, direct.

send for summon, call for, order, command, request.

send up take off (*inf*), take the piss out of (*sl*), lampoon, satirize, mock, ridicule, parody, caricature, mimic, imitate.

senile *adj* aged, old, doting, failing, doddering, decrepit, gaga (*inf*), confused. OPPOSITE: young.

senior *adj* **1** (*senior management*) superior, higher, high-ranking, chief. OPPOSITE: junior. **2** (*the senior generation*) older, elder.

sensation *noun* **1** (*a sensation of terror*) feeling, sense, impression, awareness, consciousness, perception. **2** (*the news caused a sensation*) commotion, fuss, furore, outrage, scandal, ado, agitation, excitement, thrill, stir. OPPOSITE: apathy. **3** (*the film proved a sensation*) triumph, hit (*inf*), smash (*inf*), winner (*inf*).

sensational *adj* **1** (*a sensational development*) exciting, stirring, thrilling, electrifying, hair-raising, shocking, dramatic, melodramatic, scandalous, melodramatic, lurid, amazing, startling, astounding, breathtaking, staggering. **2** (*a sensational performance*) marvellous, superb, wonderful, smashing (*inf*), fabulous (*inf*), fantastic (*inf*), terrific (*inf*), excellent, exceptional, remarkable, impressive, spectacular.

sense *noun* **1** (*the five senses*) feeling, sensation, sensibility, faculty. **2** (*a sense of sadness about the place*) feeling, atmosphere, aura, impression. **3** (*a sense of danger*) sensation, feeling, sentiment, awareness, consciousness, perception. **4** (*a question of good sense*) common sense, gumption (*inf*), wisdom, sagacity, prudence, reason, logic, sanity, understanding, intelligence, wit, cleverness, discernment, perception, discrimination, judgement, mind, intellect, brains. OPPOSITE: folly. **5** (*he failed to catch the sense of her words*) meaning, gist, drift, tenor, substance, point, import, purport, significance, signification, connotation, implication, nuance. **6** (*a strange sense of humour*) appreciation, awareness, understanding, comprehension.
➤ *verb* feel, suspect, perceive, discern, detect, observe, notice, grasp, pick up (*inf*), apprehend, understand, divine, appreciate, realize, recognize.

senseless *adj* **1** (*it was a senseless thing to do*) foolish, stupid, silly, idiotic, inane, asinine, crazy, mad, daft (*inf*), dotty (*inf*), batty (*inf*), brainless, mindless, moronic, imbecilic, unintelligent, unwise, ridiculous, nonsensical, absurd, ludicrous, fatuous, irrational, illogical, unreasonable, meaningless, pointless, futile. OPPOSITE: sensible. **2** (*he lay senseless on the floor*) unconscious, insensible, out cold, out, stunned, numb, numbed, deadened, insensate, unfeeling, anaesthetized. OPPOSITE: sensitive.

sensibilities *pl noun* feelings, susceptibilities, emotions, sentiments.

sensibility *noun* sensitivity, sensitiveness, susceptibility, delicacy, taste, discrimination, discernment, perceptiveness, insight, intuition, awareness, appreciation, responsiveness.

sensible *adj* **1** (*a sensible decision*) wise, sagacious, judicious, discerning, perceptive, far-sighted, prudent, well-advised, mature, sober, discreet, politic, sound, sane, level-headed, rational, logical, reasonable, commonsense, practical, realistic, down-to-earth, shrewd, sharp, intelligent, clever, brainy (*inf*). OPPOSITE: stupid. **2** (*sensible of the impact he was having*) aware, perceptive, alive to, sensitive to, responsive to, conscious, cognizant, mindful, observant. OPPOSITE: unconscious. **3** (*a sensible change in the atmosphere*) tangible, palpable, appreciable, perceptible, noticeable, discernible, observable, visible. OPPOSITE: imperceptible.

sensitive *adj* **1** (*sensitive to criticism*) receptive, responsive, aware, conscious of, sentient of, susceptible, impressionable, vulnerable. OPPOSITE: insensitive. **2** (*this will require sensitive handling*) sympathetic, empathetic, delicate, diplomatic, careful, considerate, responsive, receptive, perceptive, discerning, discriminatory. **3** (*sensitive skin*) tender, delicate, fine, soft. **4** (*a sensitive topic*) delicate, difficult, tricky, problematic, awkward, ticklish, controversial. **5** (*he's very sensitive about his bald patch*) touchy, irritable, thin-skinned, emotional, sensitized.

sensitivity *noun* **1** (*the sensitivity of the child's skin*) sensitiveness, tenderness, delicacy, fineness, softness,

fragility. **2** (*he showed great sensitivity towards their feelings*) sensitiveness, responsiveness, receptiveness, perceptiveness, awareness, discernment, discrimination, appreciation, sympathy. **3** (*her sensitivity about her weight*) over-sensitivity, touchiness, vulnerability.

sensual *adj* **1** (*an evening of sensual delight*) carnal, fleshly, voluptuous, bodily, physical, worldly, animal, lascivious, libidinous, lecherous, lustful, licentious, lewd, randy (*inf*), salacious. OPPOSITE: spiritual. **2** (*her sensual dancing*) sexy, voluptuous, erotic, sultry.

sensuous *adj* aesthetic, gratifying, pleasing, pleasant, pleasurable, voluptuous, sybaritic, rich, lush, sumptuous, luxurious.

sentence *noun* **1** (*the sentence of the court*) condemnation, judgement, ruling, decree, order, verdict, decision, pronouncement, punishment. **2** (*he served his sentence quietly*) prison term, time (*inf*), porridge (*inf*).
➤ *verb* **1** (*the court sentenced them*) condemn, doom, punish, penalize, pass judgement on, judge. OPPOSITE: acquit. **2** (*sentenced to live in poverty*) doom, condemn, punish, penalize.

sententious *adj* **1** (*he passed several sententious remarks*) pompous, canting, sanctimonious, moralistic, moralizing, judgemental. **2** (*deliver sententious comments from the bench*) terse, brief, short, pithy, succinct, concise, compact, pointed, laconic, aphoristic, epigrammatic, gnomic, axiomatic.

sentiment *noun* **1** (*he was full of sentiment towards her*) feeling, emotion, tenderness. **2** (*the script was weakened by its sentimentalism*) sentimentality, mawkishness, emotionalism, over-emotionalism, softness, softheartedness. OPPOSITE: reason. **3** (*an ugly sentiment*) thought, idea, judgement, notion, attitude, feeling, view, point of view, opinion, belief, persuasion.

sentimental *adj* **1** (*a sentimental child*) emotional, loving, tender, soft-hearted, affectionate, warm, nostalgic. **2** (*a sentimental movie*) romantic, emotional, over-emotional, touching, tear-jerking, pathetic, maudlin, mawkish, gushing, sugary, soppy (*inf*), sloppy (*inf*), mushy (*inf*), slushy (*inf*), weepy (*inf*), lovey-dovey (*inf*), schmaltzy (*inf*), corny (*inf*), sickly (*inf*). OPPOSITE: realistic.

sentimentality *noun* sentimentalism, emotionalism, over-emotionalism, romanticism, bathos, tenderness, mawkishness, soppiness, slushiness (*inf*), slush (*inf*), mush (*inf*), pulp (*inf*), schmaltz (*inf*), corniness (*inf*), nostalgia.

sentry *noun* guard, sentinel, picket, patrol, watch, lookout, watchman, guardian.

separate *verb* **1** (*separate the two halves*) divide, part, split, sunder, cleave, sever, detach, uncouple, disjoin, disconnect, dismantle, disunite. OPPOSITE: join. **2** (*his parents agreed to separate*) break up, split up, part, divorce, part company. **3** (*the gutter has separated from the wall*) come away from, come apart, break off, break up, part, diverge. **4** (*the police tried to separate the warring factions*) come between, divide, detach, segregate, keep apart, part, partition, split, isolate. OPPOSITE: mix. **5** (*separate the coins into different piles*) sort, sort out, divide, split, categorize, classify.

➤ *adj* **1** (*we met on two separate occasions*) individual, distinct, different, particular, independent, autonomous. **2** (*these are separate issues*) unconnected, disconnected, distinct, different, apart, isolated, unrelated, unattached, divided, disunited, disparate, discrete, sundry, detached, separated, divorced, single, alone. OPPOSITE: connected.

separately *adv* **1** (*they travelled separately*) independently, individually, singly, apart. **2** (*he considered each application separately*) independently, individually, singly, one by one, one at a time, severally, personally.

separation *noun* **1** (*the separation of the various parts*) division, partition, break, split, severance, cleavage, detachment, uncoupling, disengagement, disjunction, disunion, dissociation, disconnection, segregation, isolation. **2** (*his parents have announced their separation*) break-up, split-up, split, parting, parting of the ways, rift, estrangement, divorce.

septic *adj* infected, poisoned, festering, suppurating, putrid, putrefying, putrefactive.

sepulchral *adj* funereal, lugubrious, mournful, woeful, sombre, grave, morbid, sad, melancholy, dismal, solemn, cheerless, gloomy, hollow, deep. OPPOSITE: cheerful.

sepulchre *noun* tomb, grave, vault, mausoleum, burial place.

sequel *noun* development, continuation, follow-up, result, consequence, outcome, result, conclusion, upshot, issue, end, aftermath, pay-off. OPPOSITE: beginning.

sequence *noun* order, arrangement, pattern, series, set, progression, run, chain, string, succession, line, train, course, cycle, continuity. OPPOSITE: disorder.

sequestered *adj* withdrawn, retired, cloistered, private, reclusive, quiet, solitary, isolated, remote, out-of-the-way, secluded, lonely, unfrequented. OPPOSITE: public.

seraphic *adj* **1** (*decorated with seraphic figures*) angelic, cherubic, holy, divine, heavenly, celestial. OPPOSITE: diabolic. **2** (*a seraphic smile*) blissful, joyful, serene, rapt, beatific, innocent, pure, sublime.

serendipity *noun* chance, luck, fortuity, fortuitousness, good fortune, coincidence, accident.

serene *adj* **1** (*she remained serene*) tranquil, calm, peaceful, quiet, still, placid, cool, composed, unexcited, unruffled, undisturbed, untroubled, unperturbed, imperturbable, unflappable, unworried. OPPOSITE: agitated. **2** (*serene weather*) clear, cloudless, unclouded, bright, fair, sunny, halcyon. OPPOSITE: murky.

serenity *noun* **1** (*he admired her serenity*) composure, cool (*inf*), unflappability (*inf*), imperturbability, calm, calmness, tranquillity, peace, peacefulness, peace of mind, placidity, quietness, quiet, quietude, stillness. **2** (*the serenity of the weather*) clearness, cloudlessness, brightness, sunniness.

series *noun* sequence, succession, run, line, row, chain, stream, string, progression, course, cycle, train, set, arrangement, order, concatenation.

serious *adj* **1** (*she gave him a serious look*) grave, solemn, thoughtful, preoccupied, pensive, sombre, sober, sedate, stern, dour, grim, unsmiling, humourless, poker-faced, long-faced, earnest. OPPOSITE: jocose. **2** (*he is serious about what he says*) earnest, resolute, resolved, determined, firm, sincere, honest, genuine, fervent. **3** (*a serious setback*) important, significant, vital, crucial, critical, consequential, weighty, pressing, momentous, urgent, far-reaching, severe, dangerous, worrying. OPPOSITE: trivial. **4** (*he sustained a serious wound*) bad, grave, grievous, acute, critical, deep, dangerous, perilous, precarious, alarming.

seriously *adv* **1** (*he listened seriously to the child's complaint*) solemnly, gravely, earnestly, sincerely, thoughtfully, pensively, soberly, dourly, sombrely, unsmilingly, grimly, sternly. **2** (*the old man is seriously ill*) gravely, acutely, severely, critically, dangerously, perilously, grievously, distressingly, sorely, alarmingly, badly.

seriousness *noun* **1** (*no denying the seriousness of the situation*) severity, severeness, gravity, graveness, acuteness, grievousness, criticalness, badness, urgency, dangerousness, danger, perilousness, peril, significance, consequence, weightiness. **2** (*the seriousness of his manner alarmed her*) solemnity, gravity, graveness, gravitas, grimness, humourlessness, dourness, sternness, soberness, sobriety, sombreness, pensiveness, thoughtfulness, preoccupation. **3** (*he spoke with great seriousness*) earnestness, sincerity, genuineness, honesty, resolve, resolution, determination, firmness, fervour.

sermon *noun* **1** (*the vicar gives a good sermon*) oration, address, discourse, homily, speech, talk. **2** (*he gave her a lengthy sermon about her behaviour*) lecture, talking-to (*inf*), dressing-down (*inf*), rant, diatribe, harangue, reprimand, reproof, exhortation, remonstrance, castigation.

serpentine *adj* snaky, snakelike, snaking, sinuous, winding, meandering, twisting, tortuous, crooked, coiled, spiral. OPPOSITE: straight.

serrated *adj* notched, jagged, sawlike, saw-edged, saw-toothed, toothed, indented. OPPOSITE: smooth.

serried *adj* close, close-set, compact, dense, crowded, massed.

servant *noun* manservant, domestic, domestic help, help, home help, maid, housemaid, housekeeper, daily (*inf*), charwoman, charlady, char, cleaner, handyman, valet, steward, retainer, attendant, assistant, helper, hireling, menial, skivvy (*inf*), lackey, flunky, scullion, vassal, drudge, slave, serf. OPPOSITE: employer.

serve *verb* **1** (*he has served the company for more than 20 years*) work for, be in the service of. **2** (*serve the needs of others*) attend to, minister to, oblige, obey, succour, help, give help to, aid, assist, benefit, support, lend a hand to, fulfil, satisfy. OPPOSITE: command. **3** (*serve the children's meals first*) dish out, dish up, distribute, dole out, give out, provide, present, deliver, provide, supply. **4** (*this will serve for the purpose*) do (*inf*), suffice, suit, answer, function, perform, act. **5** (*serve each diner in turn*) wait on, attend to, look after, take care of, cater to.

service *noun* **1** (*he opted for service in the family firm*) employment, work, labour, duty, job, business. **2** (*it would do her a service to ignore her*) good turn, favour, help, aid, assistance, benefit, advantage. **3** (*the car needs*

a service) maintenance check, check, overhaul. **4** (*a church service*) ceremony, rite, ritual, sacrament, observance, worship.
➤ *verb* check, go over, maintain, overhaul, repair, recondition, tune.

serviceable *adj* **1** (*this bicycle looks like it might be serviceable*) usable, operative, functioning, repairable. **2** (*the new furniture is more serviceable than attractive*) practical, functional, utilitarian, convenient, sensible, simple, plain, useful, dependable, efficient, reliable, durable, tough, strong, hard-wearing.

services *pl noun* **1** (*extra money for the services*) forces, army, navy, air force, military. **2** (*the town offers a range of services*) amenities, facilities, resources, utilities.

servile *adj* **1** (*a servile attitude towards his bosses*) obsequious, slavish, menial, submissive, subservient, cringing, grovelling, bootlicking (*inf*), fawning, toadying, sycophantic, abject. OPPOSITE: independent. **2** (*servile jobs*) humble, low, lowly, menial, mean, base.

serving *noun* helping, portion, ration, share, bowlful, plateful, spoonful.

servitude *noun* bondage, bonds, shackles, chains, fetters, slavery, serfdom, captivity, enslavement, thraldom, thrall, subjection, subjugation, domination, vassalage, villeinage. OPPOSITE: command.

session *noun* **1** (*at the next session of the court*) meeting, sitting, gathering, assembly, conference, discussion. **2** (*a training session*) period, time, spell, stretch.

set *verb* **1** (*set that chair down over there*) place, put, put down, position, lay, lay down, locate, situate, station, plant, deposit, rest, stick (*inf*), lodge, plonk (*inf*), dump (*inf*). OPPOSITE: move. **2** (*set the flagpole upright*) fix, embed, lodge, insert, mount, establish, arrange, install. **3** (*set a time for the meeting*) arrange, stipulate, specify, determine, fix, establish, appoint, schedule, name, designate, select, choose, prescribe, assign, allocate, settle, decide, resolve, agree, decree, ordain, impose. OPPOSITE: change. **4** (*set her mind to the problem*) apply, address, direct, aim, focus, zero in on, concentrate, turn. **5** (*it set me to thinking*) start, begin, cause, occasion, prompt, trigger, motivate. **6** (*you can set your watch by her*) adjust, regulate, synchronize, calibrate, coordinate, harmonize. **7** (*set everything for the big day*) fix, prepare, make ready, arrange, organize. **8** (*set the table for four*) set out, lay, prepare, get ready, arrange. **9** (*the teacher set each child a task*) assign, allot, allocate, give, give out, distribute, dispense, deal out, dole out, mete out, prescribe. **10** (*set a new standard in efficiency*) establish, create, fix, institute, inaugurate. **11** (*the glue will take a few minutes to set*) solidify, harden, stiffen, congeal, coagulate, gel, jell, thicken, cake, crystallize. OPPOSITE: melt. **12** (*the sun set behind the hills*) sink, go down, dip, drop, decline, subside, disappear, vanish. OPPOSITE: rise.
➤ *noun* **1** (*a set of books*) collection, assortment, selection, arrangement, array, group, assemblage, succession, series, sequence, progression, batch, outfit, kit. **2** (*she has a strange set of friends*) circle, group, band, gang, crowd, company, crew (*inf*), party, faction, sect, clique, coterie. **3** (*the set of her shoulders told him everything*) bearing, carriage, posture, attitude, position, hang, cast, inclination, turn. **4** (*a theatrical set*) stage set,

setting, scene, scenery, flats, wings, backdrop, background, mise en scène.
➤ *adj* **1** (*follow a set procedure*) fixed, established, prescribed, specified, predetermined, determined, arranged, prearranged, ordained, appointed, agreed, decided, settled, scheduled. OPPOSITE: variable. **2** (*their set routine*) regular, usual, normal, everyday, common, habitual, customary, accustomed. **3** (*set in one's ways*) rigid, firm, fixed, entrenched, rooted, ingrained, hardened, inflexible, immovable, stubborn, hidebound, determined, resolute, intent. OPPOSITE: flexible. **4** (*he got a set reply from the minister*) standard, conventional, stock, stereotyped, routine, rehearsed, hackneyed, traditional. **5** (*everything is set*) ready, prepared, arranged, organized, completed, finished, primed, fit, equipped.

set about 1 (*set about the task*) start, begin, commence, embark on, lead off, wade into (*inf*), tackle, undertake, attack, get going, get cracking (*inf*), get weaving (*inf*), get down to (*inf*). OPPOSITE: finish. **2** (*he set about his assailants*) attack, assault, belabour, sail into (*inf*).

set apart differentiate, distinguish, characterize, mark off, single out, separate, demarcate.

set aside 1 (*set aside some funds for the project*) put aside, lay aside, lay by, put away, save, reserve, keep in reserve, keep, stockpile, store, hoard, stash away (*inf*), stow away, salt away, squirrel away, earmark. **2** (*she set aside what she was doing*) put aside, cast aside, abandon, discard, drop, dispense with. **3** (*you must set aside your personal feelings*) put aside, ignore, disregard, forget, discount. **4** (*the company applied to have the decision set aside*) overturn, overrule, annul, nullify, reverse, quash, dismiss, cancel, reject, repudiate, revoke, abrogate.

set back retard, slow down, delay, hold up, check, thwart, hinder, impede, obstruct. OPPOSITE: advance.

set down 1 (*set down everything on paper*) write down, write out, put in writing, commit to writing, note down, jot down, put down, mark down, record, register, catalogue. **2** (*as set down by the law*) lay down, stipulate, prescribe, assert, state, affirm, formulate. **3** (*I can only set it down to her naivety*) attribute, put down, ascribe, assign, charge.

set forth 1 (*set forth on the journey*) set out, start out, embark, depart, leave. **2** (*she set forth her grievance*) present, advance, submit, declare, state, explain, clarify, elucidate, explicate, expound, describe, detail, delineate.

set in arrive, come, begin, start, commence.

set off 1 (*set off for the shops*) set out, set forth, start out, begin, embark, leave, depart, go. OPPOSITE: arrive. **2** (*the intruder set off the alarm*) trigger, trip, touch off, activate. **3** (*the terrorists set off three bombs*) detonate, explode, blow up, trigger off, ignite, light. **4** (*this act set off a chain of events*) begin, start, inaugurate, initiate, commence, cause, set in motion, trigger, prompt, incite, encourage. **5** (*the foliage really sets off the red of the roses*) enhance, contrast, emphasize, intensify, show off, display, throw into relief, bring out, heighten, increase.

set out 1 (*set out for the shops*) set off, set forth, start out, begin, depart, leave, embark, hit the road (*inf*). **2** (*they set out to cause trouble*) intend, aim, mean, aspire. **3** (*she set out the food on a white cloth*) lay out, arrange, present, exhibit, display, dispose, array. **4** (*set out the history of his family*) present, set forth, detail, describe, explain.

set up 1 (*set up a monument*) build, erect, put up, construct, assemble, raise, elevate. **2** (*set up a new church*) establish, found, inaugurate, institute, introduce, create, form, start, begin, initiate, set going, get going. OPPOSITE: abolish. **3** (*set up a campaign*) prepare, arrange, organize, plan, devise. **4** (*the suspect claims he was set up*) frame, fit up (*inf*).

set upon set on, turn on, attack, assault, fall upon, pounce on, go for, fly at, beat up (*inf*), mug (*inf*).

setback *noun* reverse, reversal, check, delay, hold-up, hindrance, impediment, obstruction, hitch, problem, hiccup, snag (*inf*), upset, stumbling-block, blow (*inf*), misfortune, disappointment.

setting *noun* **1** (*a rural setting*) background, environment, surroundings, location, locale, place, site, context, milieu. **2** (*a theatrical setting*) set, scenery, scene, backdrop, mise en scène. **3** (*a ruby in a gold setting*) frame, mounting.

settle *verb* **1** (*settle things for the night*) arrange, organize, order, put in order, straighten out, regulate, adjust, clear up, resolve, reconcile, conclude. **2** (*they settled a time for the meeting*) appoint, arrange, set, fix, establish, determine, confirm, clinch (*inf*), agree on, decide, choose, select. **3** (*a bird settled on the roof*) land, alight, light, perch, lodge, repose, rest, come down, sink, drop, fall, descend, gravitate. **4** (*settle in the countryside*) set up home, dwell, live, reside, take up residence, put down roots, emigrate to. OPPOSITE: migrate. **5** (*the territory was settled by the Vikings*) populate, people, colonize, inhabit. **6** (*settle the debt in full*) pay, discharge, liquidate, clear, square. OPPOSITE: owe. **7** (*the panic has now settled*) subside, abate. OPPOSITE: rise. **8** (*his reassurances settled the old lady*) calm, calm down, quieten, quiet, soothe, relax, pacify, sedate, tranquillize, lull, quell. **9** (*they have settled their differences*) resolve, solve, clear up, patch up (*inf*), reconcile.

settle down calm down, quieten down, be quiet, still, soothe, compose, relax, make comfortable.

settlement *noun* **1** (*the settlement of their plans*) arrangement, ordering, organization, regulation, adjustment. **2** (*settlement of the argument*) reconciliation, resolution, conclusion, patching up (*inf*), agreement. **3** (*final settlement of the debt*) payment, discharge, clearance, clearing, satisfaction, liquidation, defrayal. **4** (*traces of a prehistoric settlement*) community, camp, encampment, plantation, hamlet, village, outpost, colony. **5** (*the settlement of uninhabited regions*) colonization, occupation, population, peopling, pioneering, founding, establishing.

settler *noun* colonist, colonizer, pioneer, frontiersman, frontierswoman, planter, immigrant, newcomer.

sever *verb* **1** (*sever the two halves*) part, divide, separate, cut, split, dissect, cleave, sunder, disjoin, detach, disunite. OPPOSITE: join. **2** (*sever a length of rope*) cut off, chop off, lop off, hack off, tear off, break off, amputate. **3** (*he severed his links with the firm*) dissociate, discontinue, break off, end, stop, cease, conclude, terminate, dissolve, suspend.

several *adj* **1** (*he put several coins on the table*) some, a few. **2** (*she left them to go their several ways*) sundry, various, assorted, different, diverse, divergent, separate,

disparate, distinct, own, individual, particular, specific, respective.

severe *adj* **1** (*a severe ruler*) strict, harsh, autocratic, tyrannical, despotic, draconian, rigid, unbending, inflexible, relentless, unrelenting, uncompromising, unsparing, merciless, pitiless, ruthless, unsympathetic, hard-hearted, iron-fisted, inexorable, implacable, cruel, tough, hard, stern, brutal, savage, inhuman, dour, grim, grave, sober. OPPOSITE: mild. **2** (*a severe climb*) hard, difficult, rigorous, arduous, tough, harsh, stringent, demanding, punishing, exacting, taxing, onerous, burdensome, unsparing. **3** (*severe criticism*) serious, extreme, sharp, painful, caustic, biting, cutting, scathing. **4** (*a severe style*) plain, simple, functional, bare, blank, unadorned, undecorated, unembellished, restrained, modest, austere, stark, ascetic, Spartan. **5** (*severe pain*) violent, fierce, intense, strong, powerful, forceful, extreme, bitter, acute. **6** (*a severe risk*) serious, extreme, acute, critical, dangerous, perilous, dire, grave. **7** (*he shot her a severe look*) stern, grim, cold, chilly, dour, grave, sombre, serious, disapproving, forbidding, austere, unsmiling, tight-lipped, sober. **8** (*severe weather*) extreme, harsh, inclement, rough, cold, freezing, frigid.

severely *adv* **1** (*his performance was severely impaired*) seriously, gravely, acutely, critically, dangerously. **2** (*he spoke severely to the children*) harshly, sternly, disapprovingly, sharply, coldly, grimly, unsparingly, unsympathetically, scathingly, caustically.

severity *noun* **1** (*the severity of his rule*) harshness, sternness, strictness, toughness, hardness, rigorousness, stringency, brutality, cruelty, pitilessness, savagery, relentlessness, ruthlessness, mercilessness, tyranny, despotism, inflexibility. **2** (*the severity of the judge's comments*) harshness, sternness, sharpness, stringency, rigorousness, gravity. **3** (*the storm increased in severity*) strength, intensity, violence, fierceness, forcefulness, harshness, extremity. **4** (*the severity of the style*) austerity, starkness, simplicity, plainness, bareness, restraint, rigour, asceticism, functionalism.

sew *verb* stitch, tack, hem, seam, embroider, darn, mend.

sex *noun* **1** (*details of age and sex*) gender, sexual identity. **2** (*sex brought them together*) sexuality, sex appeal, sexual attraction, sexual chemistry, sexual desire, sexual appetite, sex drive, libido. **3** (*children are taught about sex in school*) sexual reproduction, reproduction, facts of life, the birds and the bees (*inf*). **4** (*he wanted to have sex*) sexual intercourse, intercourse, sexual relations, coitus, union, copulation, fornication, carnal knowledge, intimate relations, intimacy, coupling, mating, lovemaking.

sexuality *noun* **1** (*sexuality should be irrelevant in the job market*) gender, sex. **2** (*his sexuality knew no bounds*) sexual appetite, sexual urge, sexual desire, lust, virility. **3** (*the overt sexuality of her performance on stage*) sexiness, sensuality, eroticism, voluptuousness.

sexy *adj* **1** (*a sexy young woman*) seductive, attractive, desirable, alluring, sensual, voluptuous, shapely, nubile, flirtatious, inviting. **2** (*a sexy book*) erotic, pornographic, salacious, raunchy (*inf*), provocative, titillating, suggestive, arousing, stimulating, exciting. **3** (*a sexy *nightie*) slinky, sensuous, seductive, provocative, titillating, arousing. **4** (*a sexy new car*) exciting, stylish, flashy (*inf*), desirable, trendy, fashionable.

shabby *adj* **1** (*shabby clothes*) ragged, frayed, tattered, tatty, worn, worn-out, threadbare, faded, moth-eaten, scruffy, dowdy, mangy (*inf*). OPPOSITE: smart. **2** (*shabby surroundings*) dilapidated, ramshackle, tatty, rundown, tumbledown, broken-down, scruffy, dingy, seedy, shoddy, tacky (*inf*), squalid, poky. **3** (*a shabby betrayal*) mean, base, low, cheap, dirty, rotten (*inf*), odious, low-down (*inf*), unfair, unworthy, ignoble, despicable, contemptible, dishonourable, shameful, disreputable. OPPOSITE: honourable.

shackle *verb* **1** (*the convicts were shackled together*) bind, tie, tether, chain, fetter, handcuff, manacle, secure, hobble. OPPOSITE: loose. **2** (*shackled by poverty*) restrict, limit, restrain, constrain, impede, hinder, hamper, obstruct, thwart, encumber, curb, deter. OPPOSITE: free.

shackles *pl noun* bonds, chains, fetters, manacles, handcuffs, cuffs (*inf*), bracelets (*inf*), darbies (*inf*), irons, gyves.

shade *noun* **1** (*a patch of shade from the sun*) shadiness, shadow, shadows, shadowiness, cover, shelter. **2** (*the gathering shade*) darkness, dark, dusk, twilight, gloaming, gloom, gloominess, dimness, murkiness, obscurity. OPPOSITE: light. **3** (*pull down the shade*) screen, shutter, blind, canopy, awning, curtain, veil, cover, shield, visor. **4** (*different shades of meaning*) degree, nuance, gradation. **5** (*an interesting shade of green*) colour, tone, hue, tint, tinge.
≫ *verb* **1** (*clouds shaded the sun*) shadow, eclipse, darken, dim, obscure, cloud. **2** (*he shaded his eyes from the glare*) screen, veil, cover, hide, conceal, shield, protect. OPPOSITE: expose.
a shade slightly, marginally, rather, a little, a bit, a trace, a touch, a dash, a trifle, a trace, a soupçon, a suspicion, a modicum.
put in the shade overshadow, eclipse, outshine, outclass, outstrip, outdo, cap, top, surpass, excel, transcend, put to shame, beat.

shadow *noun* **1** (*hidden in deep shadow*) shade, shadowiness. **2** (*lost in the gathering shadows*) darkness, dusk, twilight, gloaming, gloom, dimness, obscurity, cloud. OPPOSITE: brightness. **3** (*the shadow of a man*) outline, silhouette, shape, image. **4** (*without a shadow of doubt*) trace, touch, dash, vestige, remnant, hint, suggestion, suspicion, ghost, soupçon, shade, bit, modicum. **5** (*the news cast a shadow over the celebration*) cloud, gloom, gloominess, sadness, unhappiness, blight, foreboding. **6** (*she is his shadow everywhere he goes*) companion, intimate, follower, sidekick (*inf*).
≫ *verb* **1** (*the trees shadow the lawn*) overshadow, shade, overhang, eclipse, darken, screen, shield. OPPOSITE: expose. **2** (*he shadowed his quarry out of the town*) follow, trail, track, stalk, dog, hound, watch.

shadowy *adj* **1** (*a shadowy valley*) shady, shaded, dark, murky, gloomy, tenebrous, crepuscular, dim, obscure, indistinct, vague, bright. **2** (*a shadowy figure*) faint, indistinct, indefinite, ill-defined, vague, unclear, indeterminate, indistinguishable, hazy, nebulous, imaginary, illusory, dreamlike, unreal, unsubstantial,

impalpable, intangible, ethereal, mysterious, ghostly, phantom, spectral. OPPOSITE: real.

shady *adj* **1** (*a shady part of the terrace*) shaded, shadowy, dim, obscure, shrouded, clouded, veiled, dark, leafy, screened, shielded, covered, sheltered, protected. OPPOSITE: light. **2** (*he's a shady customer*) dubious, questionable, suspicious, suspect, shifty, slippery, disreputable, dishonest, dishonourable, untrustworthy, unscrupulous, unethical, unreliable, devious, tricky, underhand, crooked, iffy (*inf*), fishy (*inf*), slippery (*inf*). OPPOSITE: honest.

shaft *noun* **1** (*crank the shaft a couple of times*) handle, shank, stem, rod, pole, staff, bar, upright. **2** (*a shaft of sunshine*) ray, beam, dart, streak, pencil. **3** (*mine shaft*) tunnel, well, passage, flue, duct.

shaggy *adj* hairy, hirsute, long-haired, unkempt, untidy, dishevelled, tangled, matted, bushy, rough, coarse. OPPOSITE: smooth.

shake *verb* **1** (*the wind made the branches shake*) vibrate, tremble, quiver, quake, shudder, shiver, waver, vacillate, oscillate, swing, rock, roll, sway, swing, totter, bounce, wobble, convulse, heave, churn, rattle, jar, jerk, judder, joggle, jolt, bump. **2** (*he shook his rifle at his rival*) raise, brandish, wave, wield, swing, flourish. **3** (*she was shaken by their hostility*) stir, agitate, ruffle, disturb, perturb, upset, fluster, unsettle, unnerve, rattle (*inf*), faze (*inf*), discompose, disconcert, disquiet, confuse, muddle, frighten, shock, alarm, intimidate. **4** (*this may shake their confidence*) weaken, impair, harm, injure, hurt, undermine, lower, lessen, reduce, diminish.
≫ *noun* vibration, tremor, shudder, shiver, quiver, twitch, oscillation, convulsion, rattle, jolt, jerk, judder, bump, bounce, roll, wave, agitation.
shake off elude, lose, throw off, escape, leave behind, get away from, get rid of, give the slip, outdistance, outstrip, dislodge.
shake up 1 (*the news shook us all up*) shake, upset, shock, disturb, agitate, unsettle, rattle (*inf*), discompose, unnerve, alarm, distress. **2** (*engaged to shake up the company*) revitalize, rouse, stir up, reorganize, rearrange, reshuffle (*inf*).

shaky *adj* **1** (*a shaky grip*) shaking, trembling, tremulous, shivery, quivering, quivery, quavery, weak. OPPOSITE: firm. **2** (*she took a few shaky steps*) unstable, wobbly, tentative, tremulous, uncertain, unsteady, faltering, staggering, tottering, tottery, teetering, doddering. **3** (*the main supports are shaky*) unsound, unsupported, unsubstantial, unreliable, dubious, suspect, questionable, uncertain, rickety, precarious, wobbly, tottery, flimsy, weak. OPPOSITE: sound.

shallow *adj* superficial, empty, idle, meaningless, slight, unsubstantial, trivial, trifling, petty, unimportant, frivolous, silly, foolish, ignorant. OPPOSITE: deep.

sham *noun* **1** (*the antique bureau turned out to be a sham*) counterfeit, forgery, fake, copy, imitation, hoax. **2** (*his story was a complete sham*) pretence, fake, feint, counterfeit, imposture, simulation. **3** (*he was unmasked as a sham*) impostor, fraud, fake, phoney (*inf*), con man (*inf*), humbug (*inf*), pretender, charlatan, cheat, swindler, deceiver, dissembler.
≫ *adj* false, counterfeit, forged, fake, phoney (*inf*),

bogus, make-believe, spurious, insincere, mock, ersatz, artificial, synthetic, imitation, simulated, pretended, pretend, feigned, contrived, affected. OPPOSITE: genuine.
➤ *verb* pretend, feign, simulate, assume, affect, put on, fake, imitate, counterfeit, make believe.

shamble *verb* shuffle, falter, limp, dodder, totter, toddle, hobble.

shambles *pl noun* chaos, mess, muddle, confusion, disorder, havoc, disarray, wreck, disorganization, anarchy, bedlam.

shame *noun* **1** (*she flushed with shame*) mortification, humiliation, embarrassment, discomposure, abashment, chagrin, guilt, remorse. OPPOSITE: pride. **2** (*bring shame upon the family name*) disgrace, dishonour, scandal, ignominy, infamy, opprobrium, odium, discredit, disrepute, obloquy, reproach, stain. OPPOSITE: honour. **3** (*it's a real shame that he missed this evening*) pity, bad luck, ill luck, misfortune, disappointment.
➤ *verb* mortify, humiliate, humble, put to shame, show up, ridicule, embarrass, abash, confound, disgrace, discredit, dishonour, debase, degrade, reproach, stain, taint, sully.

put to shame put in the shade, show up, upstage, embarrass, disgrace, mortify, humiliate, humble, outshine, overshadow, eclipse, outclass, outstrip, surpass, excel.

shamefaced *adj* **1** (*she was shamefaced about her mistake*) ashamed, embarrassed, blushing, red-faced, humiliated, abashed, mortified, remorseful, regretful, contrite, penitent, apologetic, sorry, guilty, uncomfortable, conscience-stricken. **2** (*a shamefaced child*) shy, bashful, coy, shrinking, sheepish (*inf*), timid, timorous.

shameful *adj* **1** (*a shameful thing to do*) disgraceful, dishonourable, scandalous, ignominious, infamous, opprobrious, discreditable, disreputable, deplorable, despicable, contemptible, unworthy, unbecoming, heinous, abominable, atrocious, outrageous, shocking, nefarious, vile, wicked, reprehensible, mean, low, base. OPPOSITE: honourable. **2** (*a shameful admission*) shaming, embarrassing, humiliating, mortifying, ignominious.

shameless *adj* **1** (*she was quite shameless about it*) unabashed, unashamed, unrepentant, unregretful, unpenitent, impenitent, brazen, bold, audacious, defiant, incorrigible, impudent, insolent, brash, forward, barefaced, flagrant, blatant, immodest, indecent, improper, indecorous, unbecoming, unseemly, wanton, abandoned. OPPOSITE: ashamed. **2** (*shameless carryings-on*) immodest, improper, unbecoming, unseemly, indecorous, indecent, hardened, unprincipled, corrupt, depraved, dissolute, abandoned, wanton.

shanty *noun* shack, hut, cabin, shed, hovel, lean-to.

shape *noun* **1** (*the car has a new shape*) appearance, contour, profile, outline, silhouette, formation, configuration, design, format, build, structure. **2** (*appear in the shape of a priest*) guise, form, appearance, aspect, likeness, semblance, image, aspect, look. **3** (*a shape emerged from the shadows*) figure, form, outline, apparition, phantom. **4** (*he's in pretty good shape now*) form, condition, trim, state, fettle, health. **5** (*she has a shape to work from*) model, pattern, mould.

➤ *verb* mould, model, cast, forge, form, design, fashion, frame, make, produce, create, devise.

shape up take shape, come on, develop, make headway, progress, make progress, move forward.

shapeless *adj* amorphous, nebulous, unstructured, formless, unformed, undeveloped, unshaped, unfashioned, misshapen, irregular, asymmetrical, ill-proportioned, deformed.

shapely *adj* well-shaped, well-proportioned, well-formed, neat, trim, attractive, pretty, comely, elegant, graceful, curvaceous, curvy, voluptuous. OPPOSITE: ugly.

shard *noun* fragment, scrap, remnant, chip, piece, bit, part, particle, splinter, sliver, paring, shaving.

share *noun* portion, part, division, lot, measure, helping, serving, ration, quota, proportion, percentage, cut (*inf*), whack (*inf*), allocation, allotment, allowance, contribution. OPPOSITE: whole.
➤ *verb* **1** (*share the sweets between the children*) divide, split, apportion, allocate, distribute, allot, ration, give out, parcel out, deal out, dole out, hand out, assign. **2** (*share in the fun*) participate, take part, partake.

sharp *adj* **1** (*a sharp edge*) pointed, edged, razor-edged, keen, thin, fine, cutting, jagged, serrated. OPPOSITE: blunt. **2** (*a sharp eye for detail*) keen, acute. **3** (*a sharp change in the landscape*) sudden, abrupt, rapid, unexpected. **4** (*a sharp pain*) extreme, violent, fierce, intense, severe, acute, piercing, excruciating, stabbing, stinging, shooting. OPPOSITE: gentle. **5** (*sharp comments*) biting, cutting, incisive, barbed, caustic, sarcastic, sardonic, trenchant, bitter, acrimonious, acerbic, vitriolic, venomous, scathing, hurtful, hard, harsh, shrill, brusque, curt, malicious, unkind, cruel. OPPOSITE: mild. **6** (*a sharp taste*) tart, acrid, sour, vinegary, bitter, biting, piquant, pungent, burning, strong. **7** (*a sharp mind*) clever, intelligent, shrewd, astute, sharp-witted, quick-witted, quick, perceptive, perspicacious, discerning, penetrating, knowing, comprehending, smart, alert, bright, subtle, crafty, cunning, artful, sly. OPPOSITE: stupid.
➤ *adv* **1** (*the car stopped sharp*) suddenly, abruptly, unexpectedly, without warning. **2** (*pick me up at seven sharp*) punctually, promptly, exactly, precisely, on the dot, on the nose (*inf*).

sharpen *verb* file, hone, grind, strop, whet, edge, point. OPPOSITE: blunt.

shatter *verb* **1** (*the windscreen shattered*) break, smash, splinter, pulverize, fracture, shiver, split, crack, burst, crush. OPPOSITE: mend. **2** (*her dreams were shattered by the news*) dash, blight, blast, overturn, demolish, wreck, ruin, destroy, devastate. OPPOSITE: restore. **3** (*he was shattered by the rejection*) devastate, crush, overwhelm, upset, distress, dumbfound.

shave *verb* **1** (*he shaved off all his hair*) cut, snip, shear, trim, clip, crop, fleece, pare. **2** (*the car shaved the gatepost*) scrape, graze, brush, touch, skim, rub.

shear *verb* fleece, poll, clip, trim, cut, shave.

sheath *noun* **1** (*remove the sword from the sheath*) scabbard, case. **2** (*a sheath for the document*) sleeve, envelope, wrapping, wrapper, cover, covering, case. **3** (*take a sheath from the packet*) condom, contraceptive, prophylactic, rubber (*inf*).

shed[1] *noun* outhouse, lean-to, hut, shack, shelter.

shed[2] *verb* **1** (*shed water from the bucket*) spill, drop, discharge, exude, pour forth. **2** (*shed light upon the scene*) emit, radiate, diffuse, disperse, send forth, scatter, spread. **3** (*lizards shed their skins at regular intervals*) cast, slough, moult. **4** (*he shed his equipment as he ran*) drop, discard, remove, doff, strip off, take off, cast off, throw off, let fall, dispense with. OPPOSITE: retain.

sheen *noun* lustre, gloss, polish, burnish, patina, shine, gleam, shimmer, sparkle, brightness, brilliance. OPPOSITE: dullness.

sheepish *adj* abashed, ashamed, shamefaced, blushing, embarrassed, mortified, bashful, shy, chastened, timid, diffident, self-conscious, uncomfortable, silly, foolish.

sheer[1] *adj* **1** (*a sheer drop*) steep, precipitous, abrupt, sharp, perpendicular, vertical. OPPOSITE: gentle. **2** (*sheer madness*) utter, complete, out-and-out, downright, absolute, total, thorough, thoroughgoing, veritable, rank, unqualified, unmitigated, unadulterated, unalloyed, pure, simple. OPPOSITE: partial. **3** (*a sheer nightie*) thin, fine, light, transparent, translucent, see-through, diaphanous, gossamer, filmy, gauzy, flimsy, delicate. OPPOSITE: thick.

sheer[2] *verb* **1** (*the vehicle sheered to the right*) veer, swerve, slew, yaw, shift, drift, bend, turn. **2** (*sheer away from controversy*) avoid, dodge, evade, deviate, turn away.

sheet *noun* **1** (*the bed has clean sheets*) bed-linen, blanket. **2** (*a sheet of ice*) layer, covering, coating, coat, blanket, overlay, veneer, film, stratum. **3** (*a sheet of glass*) panel, plate, pane, slab, piece. **4** (*sheet of writing paper*) piece, page, folio, leaf. **5** (*a sheet of water*) expanse, stretch, span, sweep, reach, blanket, carpet.

shelf *noun* **1** (*a clock stood on the shelf*) mantelpiece, mantelshelf, ledge, bracket. **2** (*the wreck lay on a shelf*) sandbank, bank, sand bar, bar, reef, ledge, shoal, step.

shell *noun* **1** (*remove the nut from its shell*) case, casing, husk, pod. **2** (*the creature has a hard shell*) carapace, case, covering, crust. **3** (*artillery shell*) explosive, missile, shot, cartridge. **4** (*the shell of the building*) skeleton, framework, frame, structure, hull, chassis, body.
➤ *verb* **1** (*shell the nuts*) hull, husk, shuck, pod. **2** (*shell the enemy*) bomb, bombard, strafe, barrage, blitz, fire on.

shell out pay out, spend, expend, lay out, fork out (*inf*), cough up (*inf*), give, contribute, donate, disburse, squander.

shelter *noun* **1** (*a shelter for the homeless*) refuge, haven, harbour, sanctuary, asylum, retreat, covert. **2** (*seek shelter from the heat*) cover, shade, shadow, screen, shield, protection, safety, security, defence, guard.
➤ *verb* **1** (*the tree sheltered them from the glare*) cover, shade, shadow, shield, screen, shroud, protect, safeguard. **2** (*shelter the children from harm*) protect, defend, shield, screen, safeguard, guard, conceal, hide, harbour. OPPOSITE: expose.

sheltered *adj* secluded, withdrawn, retired, isolated, cloistered, protected, quiet, shady, shaded, screened, shielded, covered, cosy, snug, warm.

shelve *verb* postpone, defer, delay, put aside, lay aside, put off, suspend, put on ice (*inf*), put on the back-burner (*inf*), pigeonhole, mothball.

shepherd *verb* escort, conduct, convoy, usher, guide, steer, lead, marshall, herd.

shield *noun* **1** (*fight with sword and shield*) buckler, targe. **2** (*the family shield*) escutcheon, device, emblem, badge, crest. **3** (*a shield against inflation*) protection, defence, guard, safeguard, cover, shelter, screen, rampart, bulwark, support.
➤ *verb* protect, guard, safeguard, defend, shelter, screen, shade, cover, hide. OPPOSITE: expose.

shift *verb* **1** (*shift the chairs around a bit*) move, budge, carry, transfer, relocate, reposition, rearrange, switch, exchange, transpose. OPPOSITE: fix. **2** (*shift one's opinion*) change, alter, adjust, modify, vary, reverse. **3** (*we'll never shift these stains*) remove, get rid of, dislodge, budge. **4** (*they will have to shift for themselves*) manage, fend, get by, scrape by, get along, make do, contrive, devise.
➤ *noun* **1** (*he made a sudden shift to one side*) move, movement, removal, swerve, switch, relocation, repositioning, transposition. **2** (*a shift in popular thinking*) change, alteration, fluctuation, modification, variation, reversal, about-turn, U-turn (*inf*). **3** (*he did a shift at the coal face*) stint, period, spell, stretch, span, time. **4** (*any shift in an emergency*) device, contrivance, expedient, resort, resource, scheme, plan, stratagem, strategy, artifice, trick, wile, ruse, dodge, subterfuge, deception.

shiftless *adj* lazy, idle, indolent, slothful, aimless, directionless, unambitious, worthless, good-for-nothing, incompetent, ineffectual, inefficient, inept, irresponsible, ne'er-do-well, lackadaisical (*inf*).

shifty *adj* crafty, artful, wily, sly, tricky, slippery (*inf*), evasive, furtive, underhand, dishonest, crooked, shady (*inf*), iffy (*inf*), devious, deceitful, duplicitous, double-dealing, scheming, contriving, dubious, untrustworthy. OPPOSITE: honest.

shimmer *verb* glimmer, glisten, gleam, glint, glitter, flash, flicker, dance, shine, twinkle, sparkle, glow, scintillate, phosphoresce.
➤ *noun* glow, lustre, phosphorescence, incandescence, iridescence, lustre, shine, glimmer, glitter, glistening, gleam, glint, flicker, flash, twinkle, sparkle, scintillation. OPPOSITE: dullness.

shine *verb* **1** (*see how the puddles shine in the sun*) gleam, glint, beam, flash, glow, radiate, glisten, glimmer, sparkle, twinkle, flicker, glitter, shimmer, dazzle. **2** (*shine these shoes*) polish, burnish, buff, rub, wax, brush, gloss. **3** (*he shone at school*) excel, stand out, star.
➤ *noun* **1** (*the shine of new leather*) lustre, sheen, gloss, glaze, glow, polish, burnish, patina. OPPOSITE: dullness. **2** (*the shine of a thousand candles*) brightness, light, radiance, luminosity, luminescence, illumination, brilliance, beam, glare, dazzle, flash, gleam, glow, glint, glitter, glisten, sparkle, flicker, shimmer, twinkle, effulgence, splendour, resplendence.

shining *adj* **1** (*a shining bulb*) bright, luminous, radiant, glowing, gleaming, glinting, glistening, sparkling, twinkling, flickering, glittering, shimmering, flashing, dazzling, incandescent, phosphorescent, effulgent. **2** (*the child's shining face*) beaming, glowing, radiant, resplendent, blooming, healthy. **3** (*a shining performance*) outstanding, brilliant, splendid, magnificent, glorious, masterly, distinguished, illustrious, pre-eminent, eminent. **4** (*shining armour*) shiny, polished, gleaming, glossy, lustrous, burnished.

shiny *adj* bright, shining, radiant, gleaming, glistening, shimmering, glossy, sheeny, silky, sleek, lustrous, polished, burnished. OPPOSITE: dull.

ship *noun* vessel, craft, liner, steamer, boat, ferry, trawler, tanker, yacht.

shipshape *adj* neat, tidy, orderly, trim, spick and span, spruce, well-organized, well-planned, businesslike. OPPOSITE: untidy.

shirk *verb* evade, avoid, dodge, sidestep, shun, shrink from, funk (*inf*), duck (*inf*), slack, get out of, skive off (*inf*), play truant, malinger, neglect. OPPOSITE: discharge.
➤ *noun* shirker, idler, slacker, dodger, malingerer.

shirker *noun* dodger, slacker, idler, layabout, loafer, skiver (*inf*), quitter (*inf*), malingerer, truant, absentee.

shiver[1] *verb* shudder, tremble, shake, quiver, quaver, quake, flutter, palpitate, vibrate.
➤ *noun* shudder, tremor, twitch, start, tremble, quiver, quaver, shake, flutter, palpitation, vibration.

shiver[2] *noun* sliver, splinter, fragment, bit, piece, chip, shred, shard, shaving.
➤ *verb* shatter, splinter, smash, break, crack, split, fragment, explode. OPPOSITE: mend.

shivery *adj* feverish, trembly, trembling, fluttery, quivery, quivering, quavery, quaking, shaky, shaking, shuddering, cold, chilled, chilly, nervous.

shock *verb* horrify, appal, revolt, repel, disgust, offend, scandalize, traumatize, outrage, nauseate, sicken, disturb, perturb, unsettle, discompose, disquiet, distress, upset, stagger, amaze, stupefy, astound, astonish, dumbfound, dismay, stun, daze, numb, paralyse, bewilder, flabbergast, overwhelm, shake, agitate, jar, jolt. OPPOSITE: delight
➤ *noun* **1** (*the shock of the explosion*) impact, blow, bump, jolt, jar, jerk, shake, clash, collision, crash. **2** (*his dismissal was a huge shock*) upset, blow, disturbance, bombshell (*inf*), thunderbolt (*inf*), revelation, surprise, eye-opener. **3** (*she was in a state of shock*) trauma, collapse, stupefaction, stupor, astonishment, prostration, consternation, perturbation, horror, fright.

shocking *adj* horrifying, appalling, outrageous, scandalous, disgraceful, shameful, disgusting, sickening, nauseating, offensive, revolting, repulsive, repellent, repugnant, terrible, abominable, abhorrent, awful, frightful, dreadful, ghastly, grisly, monstrous, unspeakable, horrific, horrible, atrocious, hideous, loathsome, deplorable, odious, detestable, foul, vile, distressing, upsetting, disturbing, unsettling, perturbing, disquieting, agitating, stupefying, astonishing, amazing, bewildering, overwhelming. OPPOSITE: delightful.

shoe *noun* footwear, sandal, boot, clog, plimsoll, slipper.

shoot *verb* **1** (*shoot pellets at the target*) fire, discharge, propel, project, launch, let off, let fly, fling, hurl, lob, throw, aim, direct, send forth, emit. **2** (*he shot several wild birds*) bring down, gun down, pick off, hit, wound, kill, injure, bag, plug (*inf*), zap (*inf*), blast, bombard, snipe. OPPOSITE: miss. **3** (*shoot down the corridor*) dart, dash, tear, rush, hurry, hasten, run, race, speed, sprint, charge, scoot (*inf*), fly, hurtle, streak, bolt, flash, whisk,

spring, bound. OPPOSITE: amble. **4** (*the bulb has started to shoot*) germinate, sprout, bud, burgeon, spring up, appear, grow. **5** (*shoot the film on location*) film, photograph, video, record.
➤ *noun* sprout, bud, sucker, burgeon, offshoot, scion, branch, twig, sprig, graft, cutting.

shop *noun* store, supermarket, boutique, emporium, retail outlet, bricks and mortar, e-tailer.
➤ *verb* **1** (*shop for groceries*) buy, stock up on, get, purchase. **2** (*shop them to the authorities*) inform on, betray, tell on (*inf*), squeal (*inf*), grass on (*inf*), rat on (*inf*), split on (*inf*), blow the whistle on (*inf*), peach on (*inf*), impeach.

shore[1] *noun* (*swim to the shore*) seashore, foreshore, beach, strand, seaside, seaboard, waterfront, front, promenade, coast, bank, land.

shore[2] *noun* (*a shore for the roof*) support, prop, brace, buttress, strut, stay.
➤ *verb* support, prop, hold, strengthen, brace, reinforce, buttress, underpin. OPPOSITE: undermine.

short *adj* **1** (*a short man in a hat*) little, small, diminutive, petite, slight, tiny, pint-sized (*inf*), minuscule, dwarfish, dumpy, stubby, squat. OPPOSITE: tall. **2** (*a short round-up*) brief, concise, succinct, terse, laconic, crisp, pithy, to the point, compact, compressed, summary, summarized, sententious, condensed, abridged, abbreviated, curtailed, truncated. OPPOSITE: lengthy. **3** (*a short space of time*) fleeting, passing, momentary, transient, transitory, cursory, ephemeral, impermanent, temporary, short-lived, short-term, brief. OPPOSITE: long. **4** (*fuel is in short supply*) scant, scanty, scarce, deficient, insufficient, inadequate, lacking, wanting, meagre, sparse, tight (*inf*), poor, low, limited. OPPOSITE: ample. **5** (*he was quite short with her*) abrupt, curt, sharp, blunt, brusque, terse, gruff, snappy, tart, impolite, discourteous, rude, uncivil, surly, short-tempered, irascible, testy. OPPOSITE: affable.
➤ *adv* abruptly, unexpectedly, suddenly, all of a sudden, without warning, out of the blue.
fall short be insufficient, be inadequate, fail, disappoint.
in short in brief, briefly, in a word, in a few words, in a nutshell (*inf*), in essence, in conclusion.
short of lacking, wanting, missing, deficient in, in need of, low on, less than.

shortage *noun* dearth, shortfall, paucity, lack, want, need, scarcity, deficiency, deficit, insufficiency, inadequacy, absence, poverty. OPPOSITE: glut.

shortcoming *noun* defect, flaw, imperfection, fault, failing, weakness, weak point, infirmity, foible, frailty, drawback.

shorten *verb* cut, cut down, curtail, truncate, reduce, decrease, diminish, lessen, dock, trim, pare down, prune, abbreviate, abridge, condense, contract, compress. OPPOSITE: lengthen.

short-lived *adj* brief, momentary, temporary, fleeting, passing, impermanent, transient, transitory, ephemeral.

shortly *adv* **1** (*they should be with you shortly*) soon, presently, directly, by and by, before long, in a while, in a little while, in a short while. OPPOSITE: later. **2** (*he spoke shortly to them*) briefly, succinctly, concisely, tersely, abruptly, bluntly, brusquely, curtly, gruffly, rudely, impolitely, discourteously, uncivilly, sharply, surlily, testily, tartly.

short-sighted *adj* **1** (*short-sighted vision*) myopic, near-sighted. **2** (*a short-sighted policy*) rash, ill-considered, ill-advised, imprudent, improvident, unwise, injudicious, unwary, unthinking, thoughtless, heedless, careless, incautious, hasty.

short-tempered *adj* quick-tempered, bad-tempered, hot-tempered, irritable, irascible, impatient, ratty (*inf*), touchy (*inf*), testy (*inf*), crusty, fiery, peppery, choleric.

shot *noun* **1** (*the sound of a rifle shot*) report, blast, bang, crack, discharge, explosion. **2** (*load the gun with shot*) ball, pellet, bullet, slug (*inf*), projectile, missile, ammunition. **3** (*have another shot at it*) try, attempt, go (*inf*), crack (*inf*), stab (*inf*), bash (*inf*), whack (*inf*), effort, endeavour, essay, turn, guess. **4** (*the final shot of the game*) kick, hit, strike, throw, lob, fling, hurl. **5** (*he got a good shot with his camera*) photograph, photo, picture, snapshot, snap, print, image. **6** (*an anti-rabies shot*) vaccination, inoculation, injection, jab (*inf*), dose, immunization.

like a shot without hesitation, unhesitatingly, without delay, like a flash, instantly, immediately, willingly, eagerly, enthusiastically, right away, at once.

shoulder *verb* **1** (*shoulder responsibility for the work*) assume, accept, bear, carry, support, sustain, take on. **2** (*shoulder one's way through the crowd*) push, shove, elbow, jostle, thrust, force, press.

rub shoulders with fraternize with, associate with, meet with, socialize with, mix with, hobnob with (*inf*), consort with.

shoulder to shoulder together, as one, in cooperation, in partnership, in alliance, jointly, united, in unison, hand in hand, side by side, cheek by jowl, closely.

shout *verb* cry, call, yell, bellow, bawl, howl, bay, roar, scream, holler (*inf*), vociferate, exclaim. OPPOSITE: whisper.
➤ *noun* cry, call, yell, roar, howl, bawl, scream, shriek, holler (*inf*), vociferation, exclamation.

shove *verb* push, thrust, move, propel, drive, force, barge, jostle, jolt, shoulder, elbow, press, crowd. OPPOSITE: pull.
➤ *noun* push, thrust, jolt, jostle, shoulder, elbow.

shovel *noun* spade, scoop, bucket.
➤ *verb* dig, excavate, scoop, spade, dredge, heap, shift, clear.

show *verb* **1** (*show the latest finds from the tomb*) display, exhibit, present, produce, offer, set forth, demonstrate, reveal, uncover. **2** (*show his real feelings*) express, indicate, demonstrate, manifest, portray, disclose, divulge, register, reveal, betray, expose, make known, evince. OPPOSITE: conceal. **3** (*show them what to do*) demonstrate, explain, clarify, expound, elucidate, point out, teach, instruct. **4** (*show the old lady across the street*) usher, escort, conduct, accompany, attend, guide, lead, direct, steer. **5** (*show up clearly against the snow*) appear, be visible, stand out. **6** (*this shows we were right*) prove, evidence, mean, signify. **7** (*the speaker didn't show*) turn up, appear, put in an appearance, come, arrive.

➤ *noun* **1** (*the best stage show in town*) production, entertainment, extravaganza, spectacle, performance, showing, programme. **2** (*a modern art show*) display, exhibition, exposition, presentation, demonstration, parade, pageant, spectacle. **3** (*a show of public disapproval*) exhibition, demonstration, manifestation, representation, presentation, indication, sign. **4** (*no one believed his show of loyalty*) display, profession, pretence, semblance, guise, air, pose, appearance, façade, parade, front, exhibition. **5** (*more show than substance*) affectation, ostentation, illusion, display, window-dressing (*inf*) play-acting (*inf*). **6** (*the president has put her in charge of the whole show*) business, operation, organization, affair, enterprise, venture, proceeding, undertaking.

show off 1 (*show off the latest designs*) display, demonstrate, exhibit, advertise, parade, brandish, flaunt, strut. **2** (*the child is just showing off*) swagger, boast, brag, put on airs.

show up 1 (*the inspection showed up several failings*) reveal, give away, expose, lay bare, unmask, bring to light, highlight, pinpoint. **2** (*his wife really showed him up*) shame, put to shame, disgrace, embarrass, humiliate, mortify, let down, expose, outshine, upstage. **3** (*I'm sure she will show up eventually*) appear, make an appearance, turn up, materialize (*inf*), arrive, come. OPPOSITE: leave.

showdown *noun* confrontation, clash, crisis, climax, culmination, dénouement, face-off, moment of truth.

shower *noun* **1** (*a shower of rain*) fall, cloudburst, torrent, flurry, drizzle, sprinkling. **2** (*a shower of bullets*) barrage, fusillade, volley, hail. **3** (*a shower of offers*) flood, deluge, torrent, stream, profusion, abundance, plethora.
➤ *verb* **1** (*paint showered all over them*) rain, fall, spray, sprinkle, pour. **2** (*they showered her with invitations*) inundate, deluge, lavish, load, heap, overwhelm.

show-off *noun* exhibitionist, extrovert, poser, poseur, egotist, braggart, bragger, boaster, know-all (*inf*), swaggerer.

showy *adj* flamboyant, flashy, flash (*inf*), swanky (*inf*), fancy, ornate, elaborate, gaudy, garish, tawdry, loud, glittering, ostentatious, overdone, pretentious, pompous. OPPOSITE: subdued.

shred *noun* **1** (*a shred of cotton*) scrap, bit, fragment, piece, sliver, snippet, remnant, strip, ribbon, rag, tatter. OPPOSITE: whole. **2** (*not a shred of proof*) atom, iota, grain, particle, bit, scrap, jot, mite, whit, trace, speck, modicum.
➤ *verb* tear up, rip up, cut up, chop up, grate, slice.

shrew *noun* nag, scold, bitch (*inf*), termagant, virago, harridan, fury, harpy, dragon, vixen, spitfire. OPPOSITE: angel.

shrewd *adj* **1** (*a shrewd businessman*) astute, sharp, keen, acute, smart, clever, intelligent, wise, sagacious, quick-witted, alert, acute, discriminating, discerning, perspicacious, perceptive, observant, far-seeing, knowing, canny, artful, crafty, cunning, sly, wily, calculating. OPPOSITE: stupid. **2** (*a shrewd move*) wise, well-advised, judicious, calculated, astute, clever, far-sighted, crafty, wily, cunning, artful.

shrewdness *noun* astuteness, acumen, sharpness, alertness, quick-wittedness, cleverness, intelligence, smartness, discernment, perspicacity, perceptiveness, acuteness, penetration, wisdom, sagacity, cunning, craftiness, artfulness, wiliness, calculation.

shriek *verb* screech, scream, squeal, yell, cry, shout, wail, howl.

≫ *noun* screech, scream, squeal, yell, cry, shout, wail, howl.

shrill *adj* sharp, acute, piercing, ear-piercing, ear-splitting, penetrating, high, high-pitched, strident, screeching, shrieking. OPPOSITE: low.

shrine *noun* **1** (*worshippers flocked to the shrine*) temple, holy place, church, chapel, sanctuary, tabernacle. **2** (*a shrine to the fallen*) memorial, monument, cenotaph. **3** (*the shrine of a king*) tomb, burial chamber, sepulchre, reliquary.

shrink *verb* **1** (*we expect profits to shrink*) decrease, reduce, diminish, dwindle, decline, fall off, drop off, contract, shorten, narrow, shrivel, wither. OPPOSITE: expand. **2** (*he shrank from the prospect*) recoil, start back, draw back, pull back, shy away, flinch, wince, cringe, cower, balk, quail, withdraw, retreat, retire, shun. OPPOSITE: venture.

shrivel *verb* wither, wilt, wrinkle, shrink, dwindle, contract, pucker up, dry up, dehydrate, desiccate, parch, sear, frizzle, scorch. OPPOSITE: swell.

shrivelled *adj* withered, emaciated, wizened, wrinkled, puckered, shrunken, dried up, dry, desiccated, dehydrated.

shroud *noun* **1** (*the corpse was wrapped in a shroud*) winding sheet, burial clothes, cerecloth, cerement. **2** (*a shroud of fog*) mantle, cloud, blanket, cloak, pall, veil, screen, cover, covering.

≫ *verb* wrap, swathe, envelop, cover, hide, conceal, mask, veil, screen, cloak, blanket, cloud. OPPOSITE: expose.

shrug off *verb* disregard, brush off, ignore, dismiss, gloss over, minimize, play down, make light of.

shudder *verb* shiver, shake, tremble, quiver, quake, convulse, heave.

≫ *noun* shiver, tremor, tremble, quiver, quaver, shake, spasm, convulsion, heave.

shuffle *verb* **1** (*the old woman shuffled towards the door*) shamble, falter, limp, hobble, drag, doddle, toddle, scrape, scuffle. **2** (*shuffle the cards*) mix, intermix, jumble, muddle, confuse, disarrange, disorder, rearrange, reorganize, shift, switch. OPPOSITE: sort. **3** (*he shuffled awkwardly round the question*) equivocate, hedge, fence, parry, evade, dodge, quibble, cavil, prevaricate, beat about the bush, pussyfoot around (*inf*).

shun *verb* avoid, evade, elude, spurn, ignore, cold-shoulder (*inf*), ostracize, shirk, shrink from, shy away from, keep away from, eschew, steer clear of. OPPOSITE: court.

shut *verb* close, draw to, pull to, slam, lock, latch, bolt, bar, seal, secure, fasten. OPPOSITE: open.

≫ *adj* closed, locked, sealed, fastened. OPPOSITE: open.

shut down 1 (*shut down the machine*) stop, halt, close down, turn off, switch off, inactivate. **2** (*the strike shut down the factory*) close down, close.

shut in confine, imprison, lock in, restrain, immure,

enclose, hem in, box in, cage in, fence in, corral, keep in. OPPOSITE: release.

shut out 1 (*they shut out anyone with a prison record*) exclude, bar, debar, lock out, leave out, omit, blackball, ostracize, banish, exile, outlaw. OPPOSITE: admit. **2** (*a curtain shut out the light*) keep out, block out, mask, screen, veil, hide, conceal.

shut up 1 (*the prisoners were shut up in a cellar*) coop up, box in, cage, imprison, incarcerate, lock in, jail, confine, intern, immure. OPPOSITE: release. **2** (*tell the others to shut up*) be silent, keep silent, hush, be quiet, keep quiet, pipe down, clam up, keep mum. **3** (*I can't shut the baby up*) silence, hush, shush, quieten, quiet, gag.

shutter *noun* shade, blind, screen, louvre.

shuttle *verb* go to and fro, commute, alternate, seesaw, ply, shunt.

shy *adj* bashful, retiring, reserved, reticent, backward, diffident, self-effacing, shrinking, withdrawn, introverted, inhibited, coy, modest, demure, self-conscious, embarrassed, abashed, timid, timorous, nervous, fearful, hesitant, unconfident, wary, chary, cautious, distrustful, suspicious. OPPOSITE: bold.

fight shy of shy away from, avoid, shun, spurn, steer clear of, keep at arm's length (*inf*), eschew.

shy away avoid, recoil, shrink, flinch, back away, rear, buck, balk, quail, wince, swerve.

shyness *noun* bashfulness, reserve, reticence, diffidence, embarrassment, coyness, modesty, nervousness, timidity, timorousness, tearfulness, hesitancy, hesitation, wariness, suspicion, lack of confidence, self-consciousness, inhibition, constraint.

sibyl *noun* prophetess, oracle, fortune-teller, witch, sorceress, seer, wise woman.

sick *adj* **1** (*her mother is sick*) ill, unwell, ailing, poorly (*inf*), groggy (*inf*), rough (*inf*), indisposed, laid up (*inf*), weak, feeble, sickly, below par, off colour (*inf*), out of sorts (*inf*), under the weather (*inf*). OPPOSITE: well. **2** (*the motion made her feel sick*) queasy, bilious, nauseated. **3** (*sick of having no money*) tired, weary, bored, fed up (*inf*), jaded, satiated, surfeited, glutted. **4** (*a sick sense of humour*) morbid, sadistic, cruel, perverted, tasteless, vulgar, gross, ghoulish, gruesome, macabre, black. **5** (*they felt sick about their defeat*) fed up (*inf*), pissed off (*sl*), miserable, hacked off (*inf*), cheesed off (*inf*), browned off (*inf*), annoyed, angry, displeased, disgruntled, disgusted, distressed, upset.

sicken *verb* **1** (*the idea sickened her*) nauseate, disgust, revolt, repel, put off, shock, appal. OPPOSITE: please. **2** (*he began to sicken of the unchanging routine*) tire, weary. **3** (*the horse shows signs of sickening for something*) come down with (*inf*), go down with (*inf*), fall ill with, become ill, pick up, get, catch, contract, succumb to.

sickening *adj* nauseating, revolting, disgusting, repulsive, repellent, loathsome, offensive, off-putting, distasteful, vile, foul, stomach-turning, stomach-churning, nauseous, shocking, appalling.

sickly *adj* **1** (*a sickly child*) sick, ill, unhealthy, in poor health, delicate, infirm, weak, feeble, frail, puny, faint, ailing, languid, listless. **2** (*a sickly complexion*) pale, pallid, wan, peaky, washed-out (*inf*), anaemic, bloodless. OPPOSITE: healthy. **3** (*a sickly taste*) unpleasant, revolting, nauseating, insipid. **4** (*a rather sickly love story*) sentimental, soppy (*inf*), schmaltzy (*inf*), syrupy, cloying, mawkish, maudlin, slushy (*inf*), mushy (*inf*), gushy (*inf*).

sickness *noun* **1** (*suffering from an unidentifiable sickness*) illness, ailment, disorder, complaint, malady, affliction, indisposition, infirmity, ill-health, disease, bug (*inf*), virus (*inf*). OPPOSITE: health. **2** (*travel sickness*) nausea, queasiness, biliousness. **3** (*several of the pupils went down with sickness*) vomiting, retching, throwing up (*inf*), spewing up (*inf*), puking up (*inf*), stomach upset.

side *noun* **1** (*the side of the pool*) edge, border, boundary, fringe, margin, rim, brim, verge, brink, flank, skirt, periphery, bank, shore. OPPOSITE: centre. **2** (*a design on each side of the box*) face, facet, surface, end, profile. **3** (*he lives on the better side of town*) part, district, quarter, area, region, sector, zone, neighbourhood, section. **4** (*another side of the coin*) aspect, angle, facet, view, viewpoint, point of view, standpoint, opinion, slant, position. **5** (*he has come over to the government side*) team, party, wing, group, faction, sect, splinter, camp, interest, cause, caucus. **6** (*the whole side missed training*) team, squad, line-up.
➤ *adj* **1** (*execute a side attack*) lateral, wing, flanking. **2** (*a side issue*) minor, lesser, subordinate, secondary, subsidiary, incidental, unimportant, marginal, ancillary. OPPOSITE: main.
side by side alongside, together, close together, shoulder to shoulder, arm to arm, cheek by jowl.
side with agree with, support, back, favour, prefer, take the part of, team up with, ally with, join with, associate with. OPPOSITE: oppose.

sidelong *adj* sideways, sideward, indirect, oblique, covert.

sidestep *verb* avoid, evade, elude, dodge, skirt, bypass, circumvent, shirk, duck (*inf*).

sidetrack *verb* divert, deflect, head off, distract, lead away.

sideways *adv* **1** (*move sideways*) crabwise, to the side. **2** (*she entered the room sideways*) side first, edgewise, edgeways. **3** (*he looked sideways at her*) sidelong, askance, indirectly, obliquely.
➤ *adj* sidelong, sideward, indirect, oblique, slanted, lateral.

siege *noun* blockade, besiegement, encirclement.

siesta *noun* nap, catnap (*inf*), rest, relaxation, repose, doze, snooze (*inf*), forty winks (*inf*), sleep.

sieve *noun* colander, strainer, sifter, screen, riddle.
➤ *verb* **1** (*sieve the sand*) sift, strain, filter, screen, riddle. **2** (*sieve any bits from the mixture*) separate, sort, remove, winnow.

sift *verb* **1** (*sift the flour*) sieve, filter, riddle, screen, strain. **2** (*sift the seeds through the fingers*) sprinkle, shake, scatter, strew, distribute. **3** (*sift lumps from the mixture*) remove, separate, sort, winnow. **4** (*sift through the reports*) study, pore over, analyse, examine, scrutinize, look through, investigate, probe, screen.

sigh *verb* **1** (*she sighed deeply*) breathe, exhale, moan. **2** (*the wind sighed in the elms*) whisper, rustle, swish, crackle, susurrate. **3** (*the old man sighed for the old days*) lament, mourn, grieve, long, pine, weep, cry, yearn, languish.

sight *noun* **1** (*there is nothing wrong with his sight*) vision, eyesight, eyes, perception, observation, seeing. OPPOSITE: blindness. **2** (*they got a quick sight of the comet*) view, look, glimpse, glance, shot. **3** (*a sight to remember*) spectacle, scene, show, display, exhibition, appearance. **4** (*she looked a real sight*) mess, fright (*inf*), eyesore, monstrosity, spectacle. **5** (*they went to see the sights*) point of interest, feature, curiosity, wonder, marvel, splendour, beauty, amenity.
➤ *verb* see, look at, view, glimpse, catch sight of, perceive, observe, discern, make out, distinguish, notice, note, mark. OPPOSITE: miss.
catch sight of sight, glimpse, spot, see, perceive, observe, set eyes on, behold, discern, make out, notice, note, mark, descry, espy, identify.
set one's sights on aim for, aim at, intend, aspire to, strive after, strive towards, work towards, plan for, seek.

sign *noun* **1** (*a sign of better weather in the offing*) token, indication, manifestation, symptom, pointer, clue, hint, suggestion, evidence, proof. **2** (*she tried to decipher the signs on the paper*) symbol, mark, character, figure, cipher, code. **3** (*wait till he gives the sign*) password, countersign, signal, gesture, motion, movement, wave, gesticulation. **4** (*no sign of the missing car*) trace, vestige, hint, suggestion. **5** (*he considered it a bad sign*) omen, portent, augury, prognostication, harbinger, presage, warning, forewarning, foreboding. **6** (*road sign*) signpost, marker, board, notice, placard, indicator.
➤ *verb* **1** (*sign the document*) initial, autograph, countersign, endorse, subscribe, validate, authenticate, certify. **2** (*sign one's name*) autograph, write, inscribe. **3** (*he signed to the others to keep quiet*) signal, gesture, gesticulate, beckon, motion, indicate, wave, nod, wink.
sign on 1 (*sign on for the army*) sign up, enlist, enrol, register, join up, volunteer. OPPOSITE: leave. **2** (*sign on extra workers*) recruit, hire, employ, engage, appoint, take on. OPPOSITE: dismiss.
sign over make over, hand over, turn over, surrender, deliver, transfer, assign, consign, convey, entrust.

signal *noun* **1** (*give the signal to go*) sign, gesture, cue, indicator. **2** (*a signal of change*) indication, sign, symptom, pointer, token, evidence, hint. **3** (*he failed to register the signal*) sign, beacon, flag, siren, warning, alert, tip-off.
➤ *adj* conspicuous, noteworthy, remarkable, notable, memorable, significant, striking, outstanding, impressive, exceptional, extraordinary, eminent, distinguished, glorious, famous, important, momentous. OPPOSITE: ordinary.
➤ *verb* **1** (*signal to the train to advance*) gesture, gesticulate, motion, nod, wink, beckon, wave, sign, indicate. **2** (*feel the need to signal her annoyance*) communicate, express, show, indicate.

significance *noun* **1** (*the significance of his absence was not missed*) meaning, sense, point, message, gist, essence, import, purport, implications, signification. **2** (*a breakthrough of some significance*) importance, consequence, matter, moment, momentousness, solemnity, weight, weightiness, force, relevance, magnitude, impressiveness, seriousness.

significant adj **1** (*significant work in the theatre*) important, consequential, noteworthy, relevant, marked, weighty, momentous, memorable, impressive, considerable, appreciable, material, crucial, vital, key, fateful, serious, critical. OPPOSITE: trivial. **2** (*she shot him a significant look*) meaningful, suggestive, eloquent, indicative, expressive, telling, knowing, pregnant, ominous, symptomatic. OPPOSITE: meaningless.

signify verb **1** (*no one knows what the designs signify*) mean, denote, indicate, show, symbolize, represent, stand for. **2** (*what does this announcement signify?*) mean, denote, signal, betoken, augur, portend, imply, point to, suggest. **3** (*he has signified his consent to the deal*) impart, indicate, exhibit, show, convey, utter, express, communicate, intimate, tell, proclaim, announce, pronounce, declare. **2** (*it hardly signifies in the long run*) matter, count, be significant, be important, carry weight.

silence noun **1** (*silence descended*) quiet, quietness, hush, lull, peace, peacefulness, still, stillness, tranquillity, calm, calmness. OPPOSITE: noise. **2** (*the children were reduced to silence*) muteness, dumbness, speechlessness, wordlessness, voicelessness, soundlessness, uncommunicativeness, taciturnity, reticence. OPPOSITE: garrulity. **3** (*journalists pondered the official silence*) secrecy, secretiveness, reticence, reserve, uncommunicativeness, taciturnity, concealment.
≫ verb **1** (*try to silence the dog*) quieten, quiet, hush, mute, still, calm, pacify. **2** (*silence all protest*) quell, subdue, suppress, muffle, muzzle, gag, stifle, smother, extinguish, deaden, cut short, still, prevent.

silent adj **1** (*the house was silent*) quiet, still, hushed, calm, peaceful, tranquil, soundless, noiseless. **2** (*the prisoner remained silent under questioning*) dumb, mute, tight-lipped, tongue-tied, speechless, unspeaking, voiceless, wordless, mum (*inf*), taciturn, reticent, reserved, uncommunicative. OPPOSITE: talkative. **3** (*silent antagonism*) tacit, unspoken, mute, unsaid, unexpressed, unpronounced, unvoiced, wordless, understood, implicit, implied.

silhouette noun outline, contour, profile, shape, form, configuration, delineation, shadow.
≫ verb outline, profile, stand out, etch, delineate, configure.

silky adj silken, fine, velvety, satiny, soft, smooth, glossy, sleek, lustrous, diaphanous.

silly adj **1** (*a silly mistake*) stupid, daft (*inf*), crazy (*inf*), dotty (*inf*), absurd, ridiculous, ludicrous, laughable, farcical, preposterous, idiotic, foolish, nonsensical, senseless, mindless, unintelligent, childish, puerile, thoughtless, irresponsible, erratic, reckless, foolhardy, irrational, unreasonable, fatuous, asinine, unwise, imprudent, ill-considered, hare-brained, injudicious, inappropriate, misguided, inadvisable, pointless, meaningless. OPPOSITE: sensible. **2** (*the silly old fool*) stupid, mad, daft (*inf*), barmy (*inf*), crazy (*inf*), dotty (*inf*), nutty (*inf*), loopy (*inf*), foolish, unintelligent, idiotic, brainless, witless, insane, imprudent, giddy, scatter-brained, feather-brained, flighty, frivolous, foolhardy, reckless, irresponsible, indiscreet, naive, immature, childish, simple.

silt noun deposit, sediment, residue, ooze, sludge, mud, alluvium.

similar adj **1** (*the two bags are similar*) like, alike, much the same, comparable, equivalent, parallel, corresponding, analogous, approximate, kindred. **2** (*his thoughts were similar to hers*) resembling, like, akin, related, allied, corresponding, uniform, close. OPPOSITE: different.

similarity noun likeness, resemblance, sameness, comparability, compatibility, similitude, correspondence, equivalence, congruence, congruity, approximation, affinity, kinship, agreement, closeness, relation, parallel, parallelism, homogeneity, analogy, concordance, uniformity. OPPOSITE: difference.

similarly adv likewise, in like manner, correspondingly, uniformly, by the same token, by analogy, in the same way.

similitude noun similarity, resemblance, likeness, sameness, closeness, relation, comparability, compatability, affinity, uniformity, agreement, congruence, correspondence, equivalence, parallelism, analogy.

simmer verb **1** (*leave the soup simmering in the pot*) boil, seethe, bubble, cook, stew. **2** (*the policeman simmered with anger*) fume, rage, seethe, burn, smoulder, chafe, smart.
simmer down calm down, control oneself, collect oneself, cool off, subside.

simper verb smile, smirk, grimace, giggle, snigger, titter.

simple adj **1** (*a simple job*) easy, easy-peasy (*inf*), effortless, uncomplicated, uninvolved, straightforward, manageable, facile, elementary. **2** (*written in simple prose*) clear, plain, lucid, understandable, comprehensible, intelligible, elementary, uncomplicated, uninvolved, straightforward, direct. **3** (*made in a simple style*) plain, basic, ordinary, unpretentious, unfussy, uncluttered, restrained, pure, natural, unadorned, undecorated, unembellished, unelaborate, austere, bare, crude, stark, classic, homely, modest, rudimentary, humble, lowly, rustic, primitive. OPPOSITE: complex. **4** (*the simple fact of the matter is she lied*) plain, straightforward, bald, stark, blunt, frank, direct, candid, unambiguous, unvarnished, unqualified, unadorned, unembellished. **5** (*a simple son of the soil*) unsophisticated, artless, guileless, naive, gullible, ingenuous, unaffected, natural, open, direct, sincere. **6** (*a simple old man*) simple-minded, feeble-minded, slow-witted, dull-witted, backward, slow, retarded, witless, unintelligent, credulous, silly, foolish, stupid. OPPOSITE: clever.

simplicity noun **1** (*the simplicity of the idea*) simpleness, easiness, effortlessness, straightforwardness, elementariness, facility. **2** (*admire the simplicity of his poetry*) simpleness, plainness, clearness, clarity, purity, lucidity, lucidness, straightforwardness, directness, accessibility, intelligibility. **3** (*the breathtaking simplicity of the design*) simpleness, naturalness, plainness, unfussiness, unpretentiousness, informality, casualness, clean lines, restraint, austereness, starkness. **4** (*the simplicity of his explanation was disarming*) simpleness, plainness, frankness, straightforwardness, directness, openness, candour, candidness, honesty, sincerity, baldness, starkness.

simplify *verb* **1** (*simplify the booking form*) clarify, decipher, explain, translate, paraphrase, sort out, disentangle, untangle, unravel, shorten, reduce, abridge, condense. **2** (*a call to simplify the law*) make simple, streamline, reform.

simplistic *adj* oversimplified, simple, facile, superficial, shallow, naive, pat.

simply *adv* **1** (*he spoke simply for an hour*) plainly, straightforwardly, directly, clearly, intelligibly, lucidly. **2** (*the room was simply furnished*) unfussily, unpretentiously, naturally, casually, informally, unelaborately, modestly, humbly, austerely, starkly, spartanly, classically, with restraint. **3** (*this is simply the beginning*) merely, only, just, purely, solely. **4** (*she was simply stunning*) absolutely, utterly, completely, totally, wholly, certainly, positively, categorically, unreservedly, unconditionally, altogether, really, quite, undeniably, unquestionably.

simulate *verb* **1** (*simulate interest in the subject*) pretend, feign, sham, fake, affect, counterfeit, act, put on, assume. **2** (*the machine simulates the real thing*) reproduce, duplicate, imitate, mimic, parrot, echo, reflect, copy, parallel.

simultaneous *adj* concurrent, concomitant, coincident, coinciding, synchronous, parallel, contemporaneous, coexistent. OPPOSITE: separate.

sin *noun* **1** (*a sin against heaven*) trespass, transgression, error, lapse, fault, offence, crime, misdeed, misdemeanour, wrong. OPPOSITE: virtue. **2** (*sin became a way of life*) wrongdoing, wrong, iniquity, immorality, evil, evildoing, wickedness, badness, ungodliness, profanity, blasphemy, impiety, sacrilege, unrighteousness, irreverence, transgression, crime, error, vice, guilt.
➤ *verb* transgress, trespass, do wrong, go wrong, break the law, err, offend, lapse, stray, go astray, misbehave, fall from grace.

sincere *adj* **1** (*a sincere expression of regret*) honest, real, true, heartfelt, wholehearted, genuine, unfeigned, unadulterated, unaffected, bona fide, earnest, serious, fervent. OPPOSITE: insincere. **2** (*a sincere character*) genuine, honest, guileless, artless, trustworthy, above-board, truthful, frank, candid, open, up-front (*inf*), straightforward, direct, forthright, plain-dealing, earnest, wholehearted, plain, unaffected, natural.

sincerely *adv* **1** (*I sincerely hope so*) with all sincerity, earnestly, fervently, seriously, really, without reservation, wholeheartedly. **2** (*he was sincerely moved*) genuinely, really, truly, honestly.

sincerity *noun* **1** (*no doubting the sincerity of their grief*) genuineness, reality, wholeheartedness, earnestness, seriousness, fervour, honesty, truth. **2** (*he spoke with sincerity*) frankness, directness, candour, candidness, lack of deceit, genuineness, honesty, artlessness, guilelessness, ingenuousness, straightforwardness, openness, trustworthiness, integrity, probity, uprightness, honour.

sinewy *adj* strong, powerful, muscular, brawny, burly,

strapping, wiry, robust, sturdy, stalwart, vigorous, lusty, athletic. OPPOSITE: puny.

sinful *adj* **1** (*a sinful act*) bad, wicked, evil, wrong, wrongful, iniquitous, criminal, corrupt, immoral, profane, blasphemous, unrighteous, irreligious, impious, ungodly, sacrilegious, irreverent. **2** (*redeem sinful souls*) evil, wicked, bad, guilty, erring, criminal, immoral, corrupt, dissolute, depraved, fallen, unholy, ungodly, irreligious. OPPOSITE: virtuous.

sing *verb* **1** (*listen to the birds sing*) trill, warble, chirp. **2** (*the girls will sing for us later*) serenade, warble, vocalize, carol, quaver, croon, intone, pipe, chant, yodel. **3** (*the gang think he will sing to the authorities*) inform, tell tales, rat, grass (*inf*), squeal (*inf*), spill the beans (*inf*), blow the whistle (*inf*).

sing out cry out, call out, shout, yell, bellow, bawl, holler (*inf*).

singe *verb* burn, scorch, char, blacken, sear.

singer *noun* vocalist, soloist, songster, songstress, chorister, choirboy, choirgirl, crooner, warbler, chanteuse, diva, balladeer.

single *adj* **1** (*a single ticket*) sole, only, one, lone, solitary, isolated, separate, distinct, individual, particular, singular, unique, exclusive. OPPOSITE: numerous. **2** (*she's still single after all these years*) unmarried, unwed, unwedded, unattached, free, spouseless, available. OPPOSITE: married.

single out choose, select, pick, hand-pick, prefer, fix on, decide on, separate, set apart, isolate, highlight, pinpoint, distinguish, identify, cull, winnow. OPPOSITE: reject.

single-minded *adj* determined, resolute, purposeful, fixed, set, dogged, persevering, tireless, unwavering, unswerving, undeviating, steadfast, dedicated, devoted, committed, obsessive, monomaniacal.

singly *adv* one by one, one at a time, solely, independently, individually, separately, distinctly.

singular *adj* **1** (*a singular performance*) remarkable, outstanding, exceptional, unparalleled, noteworthy, notable, eminent, pre-eminent, striking, conspicuous, distinctive, rare, unusual, unique, extraordinary. **2** (*a singular occurrence*) odd, curious, peculiar, queer, bizarre, strange, eccentric, weird, abnormal, atypical, unusual, uncommon. OPPOSITE: ordinary.

sinister *adj* **1** (*a sinister development*) ominous, ill-omened, portentous, inauspicious, unlucky, disturbing, worrying, disquieting. **2** (*the sinister housekeeper*) menacing, threatening, frightening, terrifying, evil, wicked, bad, villainous, malign, malevolent, maleficent, vicious, baleful.

sink *verb* **1** (*he watched the water sink*) fall, drop, descend, go down, slip, slump, lower, subside, plunge, plummet, ebb, recede, disappear, vanish. **2** (*the boat will sink*) go down, go under, founder, capsize, submerge, dive. **3** (*the roof is sinking in the corner*) collapse, cave in, fall in, sag, droop. **4** (*he sank his body in the pool*) dip, immerse, submerge, engulf, plunge, dive, drown. **5** (*confidence in the bank is sinking*) abate, ebb, decrease, lessen, diminish, decline, deteriorate, degenerate, decay, fail, fade, weaken, flag, lapse, go downhill (*inf*). OPPOSITE: rise. **6** (*sink a well*) bore, drill, penetrate, dig, excavate, put

down, drive, embed, lay. **7** (*the news sank their last hopes*) ruin, destroy, wreck, demolish, devastate, foil, scuttle, scupper (*inf*). **8** (*he intends to sink a fortune in the computer business*) invest, put into, lay out, venture, risk, plough. **9** (*he did not understand the depths to which he would have to sink*) stoop, descend, go down, slump, plunge, succumb.
sink in penetrate, register (*inf*), be understood.

sinless *adj* innocent, guiltless, faultless, perfect, spotless, pure, immaculate, impeccable, undefiled, unblemished, uncorrupted, unsullied, unspotted, virtuous. OPPOSITE: sinful.

sinner *noun* transgressor, offender, trespasser, wrongdoer, evildoer, delinquent, miscreant, criminal, reprobate, malefactor. OPPOSITE: saint.

sinuous *adj* serpentine, meandering, winding, bending, turning, tortuous, flexuous, crooked, curved, curving, twisting, curling, coiling, wavy, undulating, convoluted, intricate, devious, supple, lithe, slinky. OPPOSITE: straight.

sip *verb* taste, sample, sup, drink.
➤ *noun* taste, sup, drink, swallow, drop, mouthful, spoonful, thimbleful.

siren *noun* **1** (*air raid siren*) alarm, alarm bell, burglar alarm, security alarm, warning bell, personal alarm, fire alarm, car alarm. **2** (*she was a real siren*) temptress, seductress, vamp (*inf*), femme fatale.

sit *verb* **1** (*sit at the table*) be seated, take a seat, settle down, squat. OPPOSITE: stand. **2** (*she sat the bags on the bench*) rest, perch, stand, place, lie, lay, deposit, position, situate, locate. **3** (*the bus sits forty passengers*) seat, accommodate, hold, contain. **4** (*the court will sit all weekend*) meet, assemble, convene, gather, deliberate.

site *noun* **1** (*the site of their last victory*) location, place, position, spot, situation, locality, setting, scene, station. **2** (*the site of the new house*) plot, lot, ground.
➤ *verb* place, locate, position, station, situate, set, put, install.

sitting *noun* meeting, session, hearing, assembly, period, spell.

situate *verb* place, locate, position, station, site, install, put, set.

situation *noun* **1** (*the house was in a pleasant situation*) position, place, location, seat, site, spot, locality, locale, environment, setting, scene. **2** (*her situation has improved since then*) circumstances, condition, case, state, state of affairs, plight, predicament. **3** (*a good situation in the City*) post, job, employment, place, position, office. **4** (*occupy a high situation in society*) status, station, rank, degree, position, standing, footing.

size *noun* dimensions, measurements, proportions, magnitude, bulk, area, mass, volume, greatness, bigness, largeness, vastness, immensity, height, length, extent, expanse, amount, range, scale, scope, amount.
size up gauge, estimate, rate, appraise, assess, weigh up, judge, evaluate.

skeleton *noun* **1** (*the skeleton of his ideas*) bones, bare bones, plan, blueprint, outline, sketch, draft. **2** (*the skeleton of the dome*) structure, framework, frame, support, shell, chassis.
➤ *adj* minimum, minimal, basic, essential.

sketch *noun* **1** (*a preliminary sketch for the painting*) drawing, outline, diagram, plan, delineation, representation, abstract, vignette. **2** (*they offered a quick sketch of the proposal*) summary, outline, précis, résumé, draft, plan, design, skeleton.
➤ *verb* **1** (*sketch in the main features first with a pencil*) draw, pencil, outline, rough out, draft, block out, delineate, represent, depict, portray. **2** (*briefly sketch out the whole campaign*) summarize, draft, outline, précis.

sketchy *adj* **1** (*his ideas remain sketchy*) unfinished, incomplete, unrefined, unpolished, rough, crude, preliminary, provisional. **2** (*sketchy coverage of the subject*) imperfect, vague, patchy, bitty, incomplete, slight, superficial, cursory, perfunctory, meagre, skimpy, scrappy, inadequate, insufficient, deficient, defective. OPPOSITE: thorough.

skilful *adj* **1** (*a skilful craftsman*) skilled, adept, proficient, expert, masterly, professional, adroit, deft, dexterous, gifted, talented, clever, smart, cunning, apt, able, competent, efficient, versed, experienced, practised, trained, accomplished, good, first-rate. OPPOSITE: clumsy.

skill *noun* skilfulness, proficiency, expertise, expertness, experience, training, professionalism, mastery, dexterity, facility, technique, efficiency, adroitness, adeptness, deftness, finesse, competence, gift, talent, faculty, ability, accomplishment, cleverness, intelligence, smartness, aptitude, art, technique, knack, address. OPPOSITE: ineptitude.

skilled *adj* **1** (*a skilled artist*) skilful, talented, gifted, accomplished, adept, competent, expert, masterly, proficient, efficient, able, capable, good. **2** (*skilled workers*) qualified, trained, schooled, professional, expert, experienced, practised.

skim *verb* **1** (*the bird skimmed over the water*) glide, coast, fly, skate, plane, float, graze, touch, brush. OPPOSITE: penetrate. **2** (*skim through the papers*) glance, scan, look, skip, flick, flip, leaf, thumb, browse, run, read. OPPOSITE: pore. **3** (*skim the cream from the milk*) cream, separate.

skimp *verb* economize, be economical, be frugal, scrimp, stint, limit, withhold, cut corners (*inf*), tighten one's belt (inf).

skimpy *adj* **1** (*a skimpy meal*) meagre, measly (*inf*), sparse, small, scanty, insubstantial, short, insufficient, inadequate, miserly, niggardly, beggarly, paltry. **2** (*a skimpy skirt*) short, brief, thin, tight, sketchy, insubstantial.

skin *adj* **1** (*a scratch on his skin*) epidermis, cuticle, integument, derma. **2** (*an animal skin*) hide, pelt, fleece, fell. **3** (*the skin of the fruit*) peel, rind, shell, husk, hull, pod, casing, outside. **4** (*a plastic skin*) covering, coating, layer, film, surface, membrane, crust.
➤ *verb* **1** (*skin fresh fruit*) peel, pare, hull, husk, strip. **2** (*the child skinned his knees*) graze, scrape, abrade, bark, excoriate.
by the skin of one's teeth by a hair's breadth, by a whisker (*inf*), narrowly, barely, only just.

skinny *adj* thin, lean, lank, scrawny, scraggy, gaunt, emaciated, undernourished, underfed, skeletal. OPPOSITE: plump.

skip *verb* **1** (*the lambs skipped over the grass*) hop, spring, jump, leap, bound, caper, frisk, cavort, gambol, prance, dance, bounce. **2** (*she skipped the next few passages*) omit, exclude, leave out, miss out, pass over, bypass, skim over. **3** (*skip from one subject to another*) leap, jump, bound, dart, race, rush, tear, zoom.

skirmish *noun* battle, fight, conflict, clash, contest, confrontation, tussle, scrap (*inf*), fray, fracas, combat, brush, encounter, engagement, dispute, altercation, quarrel, argument.
» *verb* fight, engage, combat, battle, clash, collide, come to blows, tussle, brawl, scuffle, contend, quarrel, argue, dispute, wrangle.

skirt *verb* **1** (*trees skirted the pool*) edge, border, flank, circle. **2** (*skirt enemy patrols*) avoid, evade, dodge, sidestep, circle, go round, move round, bypass, circumvent, circumnavigate.

skit *noun* burlesque, parody, caricature, travesty, take-off (*inf*), send-up (*inf*), spoof (*inf*), sketch, satire.

skittish *adj* nervous, jumpy, excitable, highly strung, restive, fidgety, lively, playful, fickle, frisky, sportive, fickle, capricious. OPPOSITE: steady.

skulk *verb* lurk, loiter, lie in wait, prowl, slink, sidle, sneak, steal, creep.

sky *noun* heaven, heavens, firmament, ether, azure, blue yonder, air, upper atmosphere, outer space. EARTH

slab *noun* block, piece, chunk, lump, hunk, brick, wedge, wodge (*inf*), slice, portion.

slack *adj* **1** (*a slack grip*) loose, lax, limp, relaxed, flaccid, flabby. OPPOSITE: taut. **2** (*slack clothing*) baggy, loose, sagging, flapping, limp, hanging. **3** (*a slack attitude*) negligent, neglectful, sloppy, slapdash, slipshod, remiss, careless, offhand, inattentive, lax, lazy, indolent, idle, dilatory, tardy. **4** (*a slack day on the market*) sluggish, slow, inactive, quiet. OPPOSITE: busy.
» *verb* shirk, skive (*inf*), dodge, evade, neglect, idle.
» *noun* **1** (*take up the slack in the rope*) looseness, play, give (*inf*). **2** (*little slack in the system*) room, leeway, surplus, excess.

slacken *verb* **1** (*slacken one's grip*) loosen, relax, ease. OPPOSITE: tighten. **2** (*the traffic slackened gradually*) lessen, moderate, abate, fall off, drop off, let up, reduce, diminish, decrease, dwindle, ebb, recede, wane, slow.

slacker *noun* idler, loafer, skiver (*inf*), shirker, dawdler, malingerer, layabout, good-for-nothing.

slake *verb* quench, satisfy, sate, satiate, relieve, extinguish, allay, assuage, mitigate, gratify.

slam *verb* **1** (*don't slam the door*) bang, crash, shut. **2** (*he slammed the coins down on the table*) bang, thump, slap, smash, dash, crash, hurl, fling, throw. **3** (*her performance was slammed by the reviewers*) criticize, slate (*inf*), blast (*inf*), rubbish (*inf*), pan (*inf*), denounce, damn, attack, pillory, villify, lambaste, tear to pieces (*inf*).

slander *noun* defamation, misrepresentation, detraction, obloquy, scandal, calumny, libel, abuse, aspersion, disparagement, denigration, vilification, slur, smear, backbiting. OPPOSITE: eulogy.
» *verb* defame, vilify, malign, disparage, denigrate, run down, badmouth (*inf*), decry, calumniate, libel, traduce, asperse, cast aspersions on, smear, blacken the name of, slur, abuse, backbite. OPPOSITE: praise.

slanderous *adj* defamatory, libellous, disparaging, insulting, denigrating, abusive, muck-raking, backbiting, calumniatory, calumnious, damaging, malicious.

slang *noun* **1** (*she dislikes the use of slang*) colloquialism, vulgarism. **2** (*technical slang*) jargon, gobbledygook (*inf*), mumbo-jumbo (*inf*), doublespeak, cant, argot, patter.

slant *verb* **1** (*the table slants to one side*) slope, incline, lean, dip, tilt, list, angle, shelve. **2** (*his account was slanted in his own favour*) angle, bias, twist, warp, distort, bend, colour, skew, weight.
» *noun* **1** (*the slant of the wall*) slope, tilt, dip, incline, inclination, lean, camber, ramp, gradient, pitch, angle, diagonal, shelving, list. **2** (*the government put its own slant on the announcement*) angle, bias, twist, distortion, prejudice, spin, emphasis, view.

slanting *adj* oblique, aslant, askew, sloping, slanted, inclined, leaning, angled, tilted, tilting, dipping, shelving, listing, diagonal. OPPOSITE: perpendicular.

slap *verb* **1** (*she slapped his cheek*) hit, strike, smack, bang, spank, punch, whack, wallop (*inf*), clout (*inf*), belt (*inf*), swipe (*inf*), sock (*inf*), cuff, clip (*inf*), clobber (*inf*), biff (*inf*). **2** (*he slapped the paper down on the table*) slam, bang, set down, stick, plonk, plop, plump, toss, throw, fling, hurl. **3** (*slap paint on the wall*) daub, dollop, plaster, spread, apply.
» *noun* blow, hit, smack, whack, wallop (*inf*), cuff, punch, clout (*inf*), belt (*inf*), swipe (*inf*), sock (*inf*), clip (*inf*), biff (*inf*), rap, bang, spank, thump.
» *adv* right, smack (*inf*), headlong, straight, bang (*inf*), slap-bang (*inf*), dead, plumb, directly, suddenly, exactly, precisely.

slap in the face insult, snub, rebuff, repulse, put down, humiliate.

slapdash *adj* slipshod, sloppy, careless, negligent, neglectful, remiss, offhand, untidy, messy, slovenly, disorganized, disorderly, hasty, rash, hurried, cursory, perfunctory, haphazard, thoughtless, heedless, clumsy.

slash *verb* **1** (*slash with a knife*) cut, gash, hack, score, slit, rip, rend, lacerate, knife. OPPOSITE: mend. **2** (*slash the size of the work force*) reduce, cut, drop, lower, decrease, mark down, prune, axe (*inf*). OPPOSITE: raise.
» *noun* cut, gash, slit, incision, laceration, score, rip, rent, tear.

slate *verb* criticize, blast, berate, censure, rebuke, reprimand, scold, blame, pan (*inf*), rubbish (*inf*), run down (*inf*), slam (*inf*), hammer (*inf*), lambaste, tear to pieces (*inf*).

slaughter *noun* killing, slaying, butchery, murder, liquidation, extermination, annihilation, bloodshed, carnage, massacre.
» *verb* **1** (*slaughter livestock*) kill, butcher. **2** (*they slaughtered the hostages*) kill, put to death, slay, butcher, massacre, murder, assassinate, liquidate, exterminate, destroy, annihilate.

slave *noun* **1** (*slaves on the plantations*) servant, bondservant, serf, vassal, villein, captive. **2** (*the slaves who do the cleaning*) drudge, skivvy (*inf*), menial (*inf*), lackey, labourer. OPPOSITE: master.
» *verb* toil, labour, work, slog, drudge, grind, sweat.

slaver *verb* slobber, drool, drivel, dribble.

slavery *noun* **1** (*slavery on the plantations*) bondage, thraldom, thrall, serfdom, servitude, enslavement, subjugation, captivity. OPPOSITE: freedom. **2** (*a life of domestic slavery*) toil, labour, slog, drudgery, grind.

slavish *adj* **1** (*slavish loyalty to his country*) servile, obsequious, submissive, subservient, sycophantic, deferential, fawning, grovelling, cringing, base, mean, low, menial, abject. OPPOSITE: independent. **2** (*a slavish copy of the original*) unoriginal, imitative, uninspired, unimaginative, literal.

slay *verb* kill, put to death, do away with, murder, rub out (*inf*), assassinate, execute, dispatch, slaughter, butcher, massacre, exterminate, eliminate, destroy. OPPOSITE: save.

sleek *adj* **1** (*a sleek coat*) smooth, shiny, glossy, lustrous, silky, silken, satiny, soft. OPPOSITE: rough. **2** (*he looked very sleek in his new suit*) well-groomed, stylish, slick, well-heeled (*inf*), thriving, prosperous.

sleep *verb* fall asleep, slumber, doze, drowse, nap, snooze (*inf*), kip (*inf*), nod off (*inf*), drop off (*inf*), flake out (*inf*), crash out (*inf*), drift off, go off, rest, repose, hibernate. OPPOSITE: wake.
➤ *noun* slumber, nap, catnap, doze, drowse, siesta, snooze (*inf*), forty winks (*inf*), shut-eye (*inf*), kip (*inf*), rest, repose, dormancy, hibernation. OPPOSITE: wakefulness.

sleepiness *noun* drowsiness, doziness, tiredness, somnolence, heaviness, lethargy, lassitude, torpor, torpidity, languor, languidness, sluggishness, inactivity.

sleepless *adj* **1** (*another sleepless night*) insomniac, wakeful, restless, disturbed. **2** (*sleepless vigilance*) watchful, vigilant, alert, awake.

sleeplessness *noun* insomnia, wakefulness.

sleepy *adj* **1** (*she felt sleepy after her long day*) drowsy, somnolent, tired, weary, lazy, sluggish, slow, heavy, torpid, languid, languorous, lethargic, dormant, inactive, comatose. OPPOSITE: alert. **2** (*a sleepy resort*) quiet, peaceful, dull, still, unfrequented, undisturbed.

slender *adj* **1** (*a slender figure*) slim, thin, lean, spare, willowy, svelte, graceful, trim, slight, narrow. **2** (*slender hope of success*) slim, inconsiderable, faint, remote, little, small, slight, trivial, frail, flimsy, fragile, weak, feeble. **3** (*slender resources*) meagre, scanty, scant, paltry, inadequate, insufficient, deficient, insubstantial, slight, negligible, trifling. OPPOSITE: ample.

sleuth *noun* detective, private detective, private eye (*inf*), private investigator, dick (*inf*), gumshoe (*inf*).

slice *noun* **1** (*a slice of bread*) piece, slab, chunk, hunk, wedge, sliver, rasher, wafer, portion, segment. **2** (*a slice of the action*) share, part, portion, helping, cut (*inf*), proportion, allotment, allocation.
➤ *verb* **1** (*slice the loaf*) cut, carve, chop, segment, sever. **2** (*slice the money up three ways*) split, divide.

slick *adj* **1** (*a slick performance*) smooth, polished, efficient, well-organized, streamlined, professional, masterly, skilful, dexterous, smart, sharp, shrewd, adroit, deft. **2** (*a slick manner of talking*) smooth, fluent, glib, plausible, specious. **3** (*a slick sales pitch*) smooth, smooth-talking, glib, insincere, smarmy, unctuous, easy, urbane, suave, polished, sophisticated. **4** (*slick hair*) smooth, sleek, glossy, shiny, oiled.

slide *verb* **1** (*slide across the ice*) slip, glide, skate, skim, slither, skid, plane, coast. **2** (*things have been allowed to slide*) deteriorate, decline, lapse, worsen, get worse, depreciate, drop, plummet, plunge, fall, lessen, decrease.

slight *adj* **1** (*a slight improvement in the weather*) small, little, tiny, minute, inconsiderable, imperceptible, inappreciable, modest, subtle. **2** (*a slight build*) slim, slender, spare, diminutive, petite, elfin, dainty, delicate, frail, feeble, weak, faint. **3** (*a slight shelter*) flimsy, rickety, fragile, frail. **4** (*a slight problem*) petty, insignificant, inconsiderable, unimportant, inconsequential, irrelevant, trivial, trifling, paltry, meagre, superficial, negligible, little, minor. OPPOSITE: considerable.
➤ *verb* snub, spurn, cut (*inf*), ignore, disregard, neglect, cold-shoulder (*inf*), rebuff, insult, affront, scorn, disdain, despise, disparage. OPPOSITE: acknowledge.
➤ *noun* snub, rebuff, cold shoulder (*inf*), disregard, indifference, inattention, neglect, scorn, disdain, contempt, insult, affront, discourtesy, disrespect, disparagement. OPPOSITE: respect.

slightly *adv* a little, a bit, somewhat, rather, quite, to some degree, to some extent.

slim *adj* **1** (*a slim young woman*) slender, thin, lean, trim, graceful, spare, willowy, svelte. OPPOSITE: fat. **2** (*only a slim chance of success*) slight, slender, remote, faint, small, little, scant, scanty, meagre, inconsiderable, insufficient, inadequate, feeble, flimsy, fragile, poor, tenuous.
➤ *verb* lose weight, diet, go on a diet.

slime *noun* mud, mire, ooze, sludge, muck, mess, goo (*inf*), yuck (*inf*).

slimy *adj* **1** (*slimy pavements*) muddy, sludgy, mucky, miry, greasy, oily, slippery, oozy, sticky, mucous, mucilaginous, viscous, glutinous. **2** (*a slimy lawyer*) oily, unctuous, servile, obsequious, toadying, sycophantic, ingratiating, grovelling, creeping, smarmy (*inf*).

sling *verb* **1** (*sling the bundle in the back*) throw, fling, hurl, catapult, toss, shy, cast, heave, pitch, lob, chuck (*inf*). **2** (*sling the ham from a beam*) suspend, hang, dangle, swing.
➤ *noun* bandage, strap, support, loop.

slink *verb* sneak, steal, creep, prowl, skulk, lurk, sidle, slip, slide.

slip¹ *verb* **1** (*she slipped on the polished floor*) slide, glide, slither, skid, skate, trip, fall, stumble, lose one's footing. **2** (*the plate slipped from his grasp*) fall, drop, slide. **3** (*the government has slipped up on this issue*) err, blunder, miscalculate, bungle, go wrong, screw up (*inf*). **4** (*slip away unnoticed*) sneak, steal, creep, slink, slide. **5** (*slip into some clean clothes*) put on, pull on, don, dress in, change into, get into, wear. **6** (*standards are slipping*) decline, deteriorate, degenerate, worsen, lapse, lessen, depreciate, fall, drop, sink, slump, decrease, plummet, plunge.
➤ *noun* **1** (*an unfortunate slip*) slip-up, error, mistake, blunder, boob (*inf*), bloomer (*inf*), howler (*inf*), clanger (*inf*), cock-up (*inf*), oversight, omission, indiscretion, fault, failure. **2** (*she wore a slip under the skirt*) petticoat, underskirt.

give the slip escape from, shake off, evade, elude,

dodge, duck, outwit, run away from, get away from, get rid of, flee from, break loose from.

let slip let out, disclose, reveal, divulge, tell, blurt out, come out with, leak, give away, betray.

slip[2] *noun* **1** (*a slip of paper*) paper, sheet, note, chit, card, coupon, voucher, certificate. **2** (*a slip from the best plant*) cutting, offshoot, sprout, sprig, twig, scion.

slippery *adj* **1** (*slippery steps*) slippy (*inf*), smooth, glassy, icy, greasy, slimy, oily, soapy, lubricated, wet, dangerous, perilous, unsafe. **2** (*a slippery customer*) treacherous, perfidious, faithless, unreliable, untrustworthy, shifty, foxy, tricky, sneaky, evasive, crafty, cunning, devious, deceitful, duplicitous, two-faced, dishonest, false, smarmy. OPPOSITE: trustworthy.

slipshod *adj* negligent, careless, lax, casual, slapdash, sloppy, disorderly, disorganized, unsystematic, unmethodical, untidy, messy, slovenly, slatternly. OPPOSITE: careful.

slit *verb* cut, slash, gash, slice, split, rip, tear, rend, pierce, lance, knife. OPPOSITE: mend.
≫ *noun* cut, incision, slash, gash, split, opening, rip, tear, rent, vent, fissure, aperture. OPPOSITE: seam.

slither *verb* slide, slip, skid, glide.

sliver *noun* flake, chip, splinter, fragment, scrap, shred, shard, bit, piece, slice, wafer, shaving, paring.

slobber *verb* slaver, drool, dribble, salivate, splutter, drivel.

slog *verb* **1** (*slog at the ball*) hit, strike, belt, thump, whack, bash (*inf*), slosh (*inf*), wallop (*inf*), slug (*inf*), sock (*inf*), hit for six (*inf*). **2** (*slog away at the task*) slave, persevere, labour, work, toil, plough, plod. **3** (*slog up the path*) trudge, tramp, trek, hike, plod, labour.
≫ *noun* **1** (*the task was a real slog*) struggle, effort, labour, grind, exertion. **2** (*a ten-hour slog over the moors*) hike, tramp, trek, plod, trudge.

slogan *noun* motto, jingle, rallying cry, war cry, battle-cry, catchphrase, watchword, logo.

slop *verb* splash, slosh, splatter, spatter, spill, overflow.

slope *verb* incline, angle, slant, pitch, lean, tilt, tip, list, skew, shelve, dip, drop, fall.
≫ *noun* **1** (*a slope in the road*) incline, inclination, ramp, gradient, pitch, angle, cant, slant, tilt, skew, acclivity, declivity, dip. OPPOSITE: level. **2** (*walk up the slope*) hill, hillside, mountain, hillock, bank, rise, climb, scarp.

slope off slip away, slink off, sneak off, steal away, go away, make oneself scarce (*inf*).

sloping *adj* oblique, slanting, slanted, angled, leaning, inclined, inclining, tilting, dipping, askew.

sloppy *adj* **1** (*sloppy mud*) wet, watery, runny, slushy, sludgy, soggy, muddy, splashy, liquid. OPPOSITE: dry. **2** (*sloppy writing*) careless, loose, offhand, slapdash, slipshod, slovenly, clumsy, amateurish, messy, untidy, disorganized, unmethodical, hasty, hurried. **3** (*a sloppy romance*) sentimental, emotional, mawkish, maudlin, banal, trite, gushing, gushy, slushy (*inf*), mushy (*inf*), soppy (*inf*), wet (*inf*), schmaltzy (*inf*), corny (*inf*), sickly (*inf*).

slot *noun* **1** (*put a coin in the slot*) opening, aperture, hole, slit, crack, groove, channel, notch, vent. **2** (*he was given the last slot in the programme*) place, position, spot,

gap, niche, window (*inf*), space, opening, vacancy, time.

sloth *noun* slothfulness, laziness, indolence, idleness, listlessness, inertia, inactivity, lethargy, languor, sluggishness, slackness, torpor, torpidity. OPPOSITE: industry.

slothful *adj* lazy, indolent, idle, workshy, skiving (*inf*), sluggardly, inert, slack, inactive, torpid, sluggish, lethargic, listless, languorous. OPPOSITE: industrious.

slouch *verb* stoop, droop, slump, hunch, bend, shuffle, shamble, lumber.

slovenly *adj* **1** (*a slovenly appearance*) scruffy, slatternly, sluttish, dirty, messy, unclean, untidy, unkempt, bedraggled, dishevelled, rumpled, tousled. **2** (*a slovenly approach to work*) sloppy (*inf*), careless, slipshod, slapdash, disorderly, disorganized, unmethodical, negligent.

slow *adj* **1** (*slow progress*) leisurely, unhurried, easy, gradual, deliberate, measured, ponderous, sluggish, lazy, dawdling, plodding, crawling, creeping, slack, inactive, protracted, lingering, lagging, loitering. OPPOSITE: fast. **2** (*slow to arrive*) late, behindhand, tardy, unpunctual, backward, dilatory, delayed. OPPOSITE: prompt. **3** (*a slow student*) unintelligent, stupid, thick (*inf*), dense, dumb (*inf*), dopey (*inf*), dull, dull-witted, daft, retarded, dim, obtuse, blockish, bovine. OPPOSITE: smart. **4** (*the film was very slow*) slow-moving, ponderous, long-drawn-out, tedious, monotonous, boring, uninteresting, dull, tiresome, wearisome, uninteresting, uneventful. OPPOSITE: lively. **5** (*slow to volunteer*) reluctant, hesitant, unwilling, averse, loath, disinclined, indisposed. **6** (*a slow kind of place*) sleepy, quiet, dull, stagnant, dead. **7** (*trade is slow at the moment*) slack, sluggish, quiet, dead.
≫ *verb* **1** (*the car slowed*) brake, decelerate, reduce speed, ease up. OPPOSITE: speed. **2** (*the conditions slowed us up*) delay, detain, restrain, retard, hold up, hold back, keep back, check, curb, handicap.

slowly *adv* unhurriedly, leisurely, lazily, steadily, gradually, ploddingly, ponderously, sluggishly.

sluggish *adj* **1** (*he felt sluggish all morning*) slow, torpid, apathetic, inert, inactive, lifeless, unresponsive, heavy, dull, lethargic, languid, languorous, listless, phlegmatic, lazy, slothful, indolent, idle, sleepy, drowsy, somnolent. OPPOSITE: quick. **2** (*trade is sluggish just now*) slow, slack, stagnant, inactive.

sluggishness *noun* **1** (*sluggishness brought on by too many late nights*) lethargy, listlessness, indolence, laziness, sloth, slothfulness, inactivity, inertia, heaviness, dullness, lifelessness, apathy, languidness, languor, lassitude, torpidity, torpor, phlegm, drowsiness, sleepiness, somnolence. **2** (*the sluggishness of the markets*) slowness, slackness, stagnation, inactivity.

slumber *noun* sleep, rest, repose, doze, drowse, nap, siesta, snooze (*inf*), shut-eye (*inf*), kip (*inf*), forty winks (*inf*).
≫ *verb* sleep, rest, repose, snooze (*inf*), nap, doze, drowse, hit the sack (*inf*), hit the hay (*inf*), snatch some zeds (*inf*).

slump *verb* **1** (*he slumped into a chair*) sink, fall, drop, collapse, subside, flop, sag, droop, bend, slouch, loll, lounge. **2** (*her confidence slumped*) plunge, plummet,

nosedive, drop, fall, slide, decrease, decline, collapse, crash, fail, deteriorate, degenerate. OPPOSITE: rise.
» *noun* recession, depression, depreciation, devaluation, stagnation, decline, decrease, slide, fall, drop, plunge, nosedive, downturn, downswing, trough, collapse, crash, failure. OPPOSITE: boom.

slur *noun* slight, insult, affront, aspersion, innuendo, insinuation, imputation, slander, libel, misrepresentation, calumny, stigma, brand, smear, stain, blot, disgrace, discredit.
» *verb* mumble, drawl, stumble over, splutter, stammer.

slush *noun* muck, mud, snow.

slut *noun* whore, tart (*inf*), hooker (*inf*), scrubber (*inf*), prostitute, harlot, trollop, hussy.

sly *adj* **1** (*he's a sly old fox*) artful, cunning, crafty, wily, foxy, tricky, subtle, shrewd, astute, sharp, clever, canny, smart, knowing, guileful, scheming, conniving, devious, underhand. OPPOSITE: artless. **2** (*a sly movement*) furtive, clandestine, surreptitious, stealthy, covert, secret, sneaky (*inf*), insidious. **3** (*a sly wink*) roguish, impish, arch, mischievous, playful, knowing.
on the sly secretly, in secret, privately, in private, furtively, sneakily, stealthily, surreptitiously, under cover, covertly, clandestinely.

smack[1] *noun* **1** (*the spices give a real smack to the dish*) flavour, taste, savour, piquancy, tang, relish, zest, smell, aroma. **2** (*just a smack of sauciness*) suggestion, trace, hint, impression, nuance, intimation, tinge, touch, dash, speck, whiff, air.
» *verb* resemble, seem like, suggest, bring to mind, hint, evoke, intimate, savour, smell.

smack[2] *verb* slap, spank, hit, strike, cuff, box, thump, punch, whack (*inf*), clout (*inf*), wallop (*inf*), belt (*inf*), biff (*inf*), clobber (*inf*), clap, bang, crash, thud, tap, pat.
» *noun* spank, blow, hit, slap, thump, cuff, box, punch, whack (*inf*), clout (*inf*), wallop (*inf*), belt (*inf*), biff (*inf*), clobber (*inf*), bang, crash, thud, tap, pat.
» *adv* slap, slap-bang, bang, headlong, straight, right, directly, plumb, exactly, precisely, suddenly.

small *adj* **1** (*a small man*) little, tiny, teeny, short, slight, under-sized, puny, diminutive, petite, miniature, minute, minuscule, compact, pocket-sized (*inf*), pint-sized (*inf*), microscopic. OPPOSITE: big. **2** (*of small importance*) insignificant, unimportant, inconsequential, inconsiderable, inappreciable, slight, minor, trifling, trivial, negligible, paltry. **3** (*evidence of a small mind*) petty, mean, small-minded, narrow, narrow-minded. **4** (*a small return on the investment*) limited, meagre, mean, paltry, scanty, insufficient, inadequate. OPPOSITE: ample. **5** (*a small start*) humble, modest, lowly, unpretentious, simple, low, base, inferior, poor. OPPOSITE: grand.

small-minded *adj* petty, mean, narrow-minded, bigoted, prejudiced, biased, intolerant, hidebound, insular, ungenerous, illiberal, rigid.

smart *adj* **1** (*a smart appearance*) spruce, trim, neat, presentable, tidy, dapper, natty (*inf*), well-dressed, well-groomed, well-turned-out, elegant, fashionable, cool (*inf*), snazzy (*inf*), chic, stylish, modish. OPPOSITE: untidy. **2** (*a smart operator*) bright, clever, intelligent, gifted, witty, shrewd, ingenious, astute, sharp, acute,

quick-witted, nimble-witted, ready, prompt, alert, apt, adept. **3** (*a smart movement*) quick, fast, swift, brisk, lively, spirited, vigorous, jaunty, energetic, active, agile. OPPOSITE: slow. **4** (*he made several smart remarks*) keen, sharp, poignant, stinging, painful, severe. OPPOSITE: dull.
» *verb* sting, prick, nip, bite, burn, tingle, twinge, throb, ache, pain, hurt.

smash *verb* **1** (*smash the bottle*) break, shatter, crack, splinter, shiver, dash, pulverize, crush, demolish, destroy, disintegrate, wreck, ruin, defeat. **2** (*the car smashed into the house*) crash, collide, wreck, bump, bang, thump, plough, drive, go, run, strike, knock, hit, bash.
» *noun* crash, collision, pile-up, accident, wreck, prang (*inf*), smash-up (*inf*), bump, shunt.

smashing *adj* marvellous, cool (*inf*), wicked (*inf*), ace (*inf*), mega (*inf*), great (*inf*), fantastic (*inf*), fabulous (*inf*), fab (*inf*), magnificent, tremendous, sensational, stupendous, super (*inf*), superb, superlative, terrific (*inf*), wonderful, excellent, first-rate, first-class.

smattering *noun* sprinkling, modicum, dash, bit, elements, basics, rudiments.

smear *verb* **1** (*smear mud on the walls*) besmear, daub, bedaub, rub, spread, plaster, slap, streak, coat, cover. OPPOSITE: scour. **2** (*the grease had smeared his shirt*) soil, dirty, smudge. **3** (*smear political rivals*) slander, libel, defame, defile, malign, badmouth (*inf*), calumniate, slur, vilify, sully, tarnish, stain, taint, blacken.
» *noun* **1** (*a smear of blood*) smudge, streak, patch, blotch, splodge, splotch, daub, spot, smear, blot. **2** (*smears in the press*) slander, libel, calumny, defamation, slur, taint, stain, blot, aspersion, vilification, obloquy, mudslinging (*inf*), muck-raking (*inf*).

smell *verb* **1** (*he could smell gas*) sniff, inhale, scent, detect. **2** (*the whole house smells of dogs*) stink, reek, pong (*inf*), hum (*inf*).
» *noun* odour, scent, aroma, perfume, fragrance, redolence, bouquet, whiff, stink, stench, reek, pong (*inf*), fetor.

smelly *adj* smelling, malodorous, whiffy (*inf*), pongy (*inf*), stinking, reeking, foul, bad, off, putrid, fetid, high, noisome, mephitic.

smile *noun* grin, beam, smirk, simper. OPPOSITE: frown.

smirk *verb* simper, grimace, grin, smile, leer, snigger, sneer.

smoke *noun* fumes, gas, exhaust, vapour, mist, fog, smog.
» *verb* **1** (*smoke a pipe*) puff, draw, inhale, exhale, light up. **2** (*they smoke all their own bacon*) cure, preserve, dry.

smoky *adj* **1** (*smoky buildings*) sooty, grimy, begrimed, black, grey, dark. **2** (*a smoky atmosphere*) murky, cloudy, hazy, foggy, smoggy.

smooth *adj* **1** (*a smooth surface*) level, even, flush, plane, horizontal, flat, uniform, regular. OPPOSITE: uneven. **2** (*a smooth coat*) glossy, shiny, polished, burnished, silky, silken, velvety, satiny, sleek. **3** (*they sailed over a smooth sea*) flat, glassy, mirrorlike, calm, still, peaceful, unruffled, serene, tranquil. OPPOSITE: rough. **4** (*a smooth way of talking*) fluent, easy, facile, glib, plausible, persuasive, slick, oily, smarmy (*inf*), unctuous,

ingratiating, fawning, suave, urbane, gracious, courteous, sophisticated. **5** (*the expedition made smooth progress*) easy, effortless, trouble-free, problem-free, simple. **6** (*the smooth rhythm of the propeller*) steady, even, regular, rhythmic, uniform, unbroken, uninterrupted, flowing, fluid.
➤ *verb* **1** (*smooth out the material*) level, plane, even, flatten, iron, roll, press, slick. **2** (*smooth public anxiety*) ease, calm, soothe, appease, pacify, tranquillize, assuage, allay, mitigate, alleviate, palliate. **3** (*his path to the top was smoothed by his patrons*) ease, facilitate, expediate, assist, aid, help.

smoothness *noun* **1** (*the smoothness of the surface*) flatness, evenness, levelness. **2** (*the smoothness of the rhythm*) regularity, steadiness, evenness, rhythm, unbrokenness, flow, fluidity. **3** (*the smoothness of the fabric*) glossiness, gloss, shine, shininess, polish, sleekness, silkiness, softness. **4** (*the smoothness of their progress*) ease, easiness, effortlessness, simplicity. **5** (*the smoothness of the sea*) flatness, calmness, stillness, tranquillity, serenity, glassiness.

smother *verb* **1** (*smothered by ash from the volcano*) suffocate, stifle, asphyxiate, choke, strangle, throttle. OPPOSITE: revive. **2** (*smother a sneeze*) suppress, repress, hold back, muffle, stifle, conceal, hide. **3** (*smothered in butter*) cover, heap with, pile with. **4** (*smother with blankets*) cover, wrap, envelop, shroud, cocoon, surround. **5** (*smother with kisses*) heap, shower, inundate, overwhelm. **6** (*smother the flames*) extinguish, snuff out, put out, stamp out, dampen, damp down.

smoulder *verb* **1** (*the fire smouldered*) burn, smoke, reek. **2** (*he smouldered with rage*) fume, rage, smart, simmer, seethe, fester, boil, foam.

smudge *verb* smear, blur, streak, daub, soil, dirty, blacken, besmirch, stain, blemish, mark, spot.
➤ *noun* smear, stain, spot, mark, blur, blot, blemish, spot, blotch, smut, streak.

smug *adj* complacent, self-satisfied, content, conceited, proud, superior, priggish, self-righteous, holier-than-thou.

smuggler *noun* bootlegger (*inf*), pirate, contrabandist, runner.

smutty *adj* dirty, filthy, obscene, indecent, improper, indelicate, risqué, racy, ribald, bawdy, suggestive, vulgar, ribald, crude, coarse, gross, earthy, blue (*inf*), pornographic, raunchy (*inf*), sleazy (*inf*), lewd, salacious, prurient. OPPOSITE: clean.

snack *noun* refreshments, light meal, bite, nibble, titbit, little something (*inf*).

snag *noun* drawback, disadvantage, difficulty, complication, problem, catch, hitch, setback, hindrance, impediment, obstacle, stumbling block, inconvenience. OPPOSITE: advantage.
➤ *verb* catch, rip, tear, hole, ladder.

snap *verb* **1** (*a branch snapped beneath his foot*) break, fracture, crack, crackle, pop, split, splinter, come apart, separate. **2** (*the dog snapped at the leash*) bite, nip. **3** (*the old man snapped at the nurses*) growl, bark, snarl, lash out at. **4** (*she snapped a few shots of the house*) photograph, take, shoot, film.
➤ *noun* **1** (*the snap of a breaking twig*) crack, crackle, pop,

click. **2** (*the snap of the creature's jaws*) bite, nip. **3** (*a cold snap is on the way*) spell, period, time, interval, stretch, span, stint. **4** (*we took a few snaps for the record*) snapshot, photograph, photo, shot, picture, print, still. **5** (*the snap on her handbag is broken*) catch, clasp, fastener.

snap up grab, grasp, snatch, seize, take, pick up, pluck, nab (*inf*), pounce on, swoop down on.

snappy *adj* **1** (*the boss is in a snappy mood*) snappish, waspish, testy, touchy, irritable, irascible, peevish, petulant, peppery, grumpy, crabbed, crotchety, grumpy, grouchy, crusty, edgy, cross, ill-tempered, bad-tempered, quick-tempered, ill-natured. OPPOSITE: affable. **2** (*they set off at a snappy pace*) brisk, lively, energetic, quick, hasty, sharp, abrupt, brusque, curt. **3** (*a snappy trouser suit*) smart, fashionable, chic, stylish, trendy (*inf*), snazzy (*inf*), natty (*inf*), elegant, dapper, modish, up-to-date, up-to-the-minute. OPPOSITE: shabby.

snare *noun* trap, gin, springe, wire, noose, net.
➤ *verb* catch, capture, seize, net, trap, entrap, ensnare. OPPOSITE: free.

snarl[1] *verb* growl, bark, snap, lash out at, threaten, grumble, complain. OPPOSITE: purr.

snarl[2] *verb* tangle, entangle, enmesh, entwine, twist, knot, ravel, confuse, muddle, jumble, complicate, embroil. OPPOSITE: disentangle.

snatch *verb* **1** (*snatch a book from the pile*) grab, seize, pluck, grasp, clutch, clasp, grip, take hold of, pounce on. **2** (*the thief snatched the money from the till*) grab, nab (*inf*), swipe (*inf*), steal, make off with, appropriate. **3** (*the child was snatched by two unknown women*) kidnap, abduct, seize, grab. OPPOSITE: release. **4** (*snatch a bargain*) secure, seize, gain, win, pluck, wrest, pull, take.
➤ *noun* **1** (*a snatch of music*) bit, piece, fragment, scrap, snippet, part. **2** (*grab a snatch of rest*) spell, period, fit, bout.

sneak *verb* **1** (*sneak around the house*) steal, creep, slip, sidle, slink, slide. **2** (*sneak round the back*) skulk, prowl, lurk, creep, pad. **3** (*she sneaked on the other children*) inform, grass (*inf*), squeal (*inf*), split (*inf*), rat (*inf*), tell (*inf*), tell tales, peach (*inf*), shop (*inf*), blow the whistle (*inf*).
➤ *noun* informer, tell-tale, grass (*inf*), squealer (*inf*), rat (*inf*), snitch (*inf*), whistle-blower (*inf*).
➤ *adj* secret, covert, clandestine, furtive, stealthy, surreptitious, quick, surprise.

sneer *verb* **1** (*he sneered unpleasantly*) smirk, snigger, snicker. **2** (*she sneered at all his suggestions*) jeer, scoff, gibe, taunt, insult, slight, mock, scorn, ridicule, deride, disdain, hold in contempt, look down on. OPPOSITE: admire.
➤ *noun* **1** (*a nasty sneer on the man's face*) smirk, snigger, snicker. **2** (*tired of the sneers of his betters*) jeer, gibe, insult, slight, taunt, mockery, ridicule, scorn, disdain, derision, contempt. OPPOSITE: respect.

sniff *verb* **1** (*the child sniffed through her tears*) snuffle, inhale, breathe in. **2** (*she sniffed at the perfume*) smell, scent, nose, whiff, get a whiff of.

sniff at scoff at, scorn, slight, mock, laugh at, sneer at, deride, disparage, disdain, look down on, turn one's nose up at, spurn, reject, refuse, shun, dismiss, disregard, overlook.

➤ *noun* smell, scent, whiff, hint, suggestion, impression, trace, intimation.

snigger *verb* laugh, titter, giggle, chuckle, chortle, smirk, sneer, snicker.

snip *verb* **1** (*snip a strand of hair*) cut, clip, trim, crop, dock, prune. **2** (*snip a length of cloth*) cut, incise, nick, slit, notch, snick.
➤ *noun* **1** (*a snip in the piece of paper*) cut, incision, nick, snick, slit, notch. **2** (*a snip of material*) bit, piece, scrap, shred, fragment, remnant, snippet, cutting, clipping, tatter. **3** (*a snip at the price*) bargain, good buy, giveaway (*inf*), steal (*inf*).

snippet *noun* bit, piece, scrap, clipping, cutting, fragment, shred, particle, snatch, part, portion, section, segment.

snivel *verb* **1** (*tell the child to stop snivelling*) grizzle, cry, weep, sob, bawl, blubber (*inf*), blub (*inf*), whine, whimper, moan. OPPOSITE: laugh. **2** (*the cold made her snivel*) sniff, sniffle, snuffle.

snobbery *noun* snobbishness, snootiness (*inf*), uppishness (*inf*), arrogance, haughtiness, superiority, loftiness, pride, pretension, airs, airs and graces, condescension, disdain, superciliousness.

snobbish *adj* snobby, condescending, patronizing, stuck-up (*inf*), snooty (*inf*), uppity (*inf*), toffee-nosed (*inf*), hoity-toity (*inf*), arrogant, haughty, proud, supercilious, disdainful, lofty, high and mighty. OPPOSITE: humble.

snoop *verb* spy, pry, nose, poke one's nose into (*inf*), interfere, meddle.
➤ *noun* **1** (*have a snoop around*) look, pry, poke, sneak, nose. **2** (*a snoop for the management*) snooper, spy, nosy Parker (*inf*), busybody, interferer, meddler.

snooze *verb* doze, drowse, nap, catnap, sleep, slumber, drop off, nod off, have a kip (*inf*), snatch some zeds (*inf*).
➤ *noun* doze, nap, catnap, sleep, slumber, repose, kip (*inf*), shut-eye (*inf*), forty winks (*inf*), siesta.

snub *verb* slight, cut (*inf*), cold-shoulder (*inf*), put down (*inf*), cut dead (*inf*), rebuff, repulse, brush off, spurn, shun, ignore, disregard, insult, affront, humiliate, shame, humble, mortify.
➤ *noun* slight, rebuff, repulse, brush-off (*inf*), put-down (*inf*), insult, affront, humiliation, mortification. OPPOSITE: flattery.

snug *adj* **1** (*a snug room*) cosy, comfortable, comfy (*inf*), intimate, friendly, homely, warm, sheltered, protected, safe, secure. OPPOSITE: exposed. **2** (*a snug fit*) small, compact, trim, neat, tight, close-fitting, skin-tight, figure-hugging.

snuggle *verb* nestle, cuddle, embrace, hug, nuzzle, curl up.

soak *verb* **1** (*the rain soaked his jacket*) wet, drench, saturate. OPPOSITE: dry. **2** (*leave them to soak overnight*) steep, immerse, souse, marinate, bathe. **3** (*the dye had soaked into the material*) permeate, infuse, penetrate, absorb.

soaking *adj* soaked, drenched, wet through, saturated, sodden, waterlogged, sopping, wringing, dripping, streaming.

soar *verb* **1** (*the plane soared over their heads*) rise, climb, mount, ascend, take off, tower, fly, wing. OPPOSITE: sink. **2** (*the cost of the building is soaring*) rise, climb, escalate, rocket, go up, increase, spiral.

sob *verb* cry, weep, blubber, boohoo (*inf*), bawl, howl, snivel. OPPOSITE: laugh.

sober *adj* **1** (*she's been sober for months*) teetotal, abstemious, on the wagon (*inf*), off the bottle (*inf*), dry (*inf*), abstinent, clear-headed, temperate, moderate. OPPOSITE: drunk. **2** (*a sober young man*) rational, reasonable, level-headed, practical, realistic, sound, calm, steady, composed, unruffled, unexcited, dispassionate, cool, staid, dignified, sedate, solemn, serious, thoughtful, grave, earnest, strict, puritanical. **3** (*the use of sober decoration*) sombre, staid, dark, drab, dull, subdued, restrained, plain, severe, austere, quiet, serene, cold.

sobriety *noun* **1** (*he abandoned his former life of sobriety*) temperance, moderation, self-restraint, abstinence, soberness, teetotalism. OPPOSITE: drunkenness. **2** (*she found their sobriety depressing*) seriousness, graveness, gravity, thoughtfulness, earnestness, solemnity, dispassionateness, objectivity, staidness, sedateness, restraint, steadiness, level-headedness, practicality, logicality, coolness, composure, calmness. **3** (*the sobriety of his dress*) sombreness, soberness, severity, austerity, drabness, darkness, restraint, quietness.

so-called *adj* **1** (*a so-called expert*) professed, self-styled. **2** (*his so-called contact turned out to be a cleaner*) alleged, supposed, would-be, pretended, ostensible.

sociability *noun* friendliness, affability, congeniality, conviviality, cordiality, neighbourliness, companionability, chumminess (*inf*), gregariousness.

sociable *adj* friendly, genial, cordial, convivial, neighbourly, amiable, familiar, warm, hospitable, affable, communicative, companionable, gregarious, outgoing, approachable, accessible, social. OPPOSITE: unsociable.

social *adj* **1** (*social amenities*) communal, community, group, collective, common, public, civil, civic. OPPOSITE: personal. **2** (*they are a social couple*) sociable, friendly, genial, amiable, affable, companionable, gregarious, cordial, convivial, communicative. OPPOSITE: asocial.

socialize *verb* mix, mingle, hobnob (*inf*), fraternize, get together, meet people, be sociable, keep company.

society *noun* **1** (*he was expelled from the society*) association, organization, club, circle, group, band, league, alliance, guild, federation, corporation, union, fraternity, brotherhood, sisterhood, sorority, fellowship, body, community. **2** (*seek some society*) company, companionship, fellowship, friendship, camaraderie. OPPOSITE: privacy. **3** (*a debt to society*) humanity, mankind, human race, community, public, general public, people, population, civilization, culture, world at large. **4** (*her debut in society*) high society, polite society, smart set, gentry, aristocracy, nobility, elite, beau monde, upper classes. OPPOSITE: commonalty.

sodden *adj* **1** (*sodden clothes*) soaked, soaking, saturated, drenched, waterlogged, sopping, wringing, dripping, wet. OPPOSITE: dry. **2** (*a sodden patch of land*) wet, saturated, soggy, waterlogged, sopping, flooded, boggy, marshy, swampy, miry.

soft *adj* **1** (*soft fruit*) squashy, mushy, gooey (*inf*), pulpy, spongy, squelchy, squishy (*inf*). **2** (*soft material*) yielding, elastic, pliable, pliant, supple, ductile, malleable, flexible, plastic. OPPOSITE: hard. **3** (*soft ground*) swampy, boggy, miry, quaggy, spongy. **4** (*soft skin*) silky, silken, smooth, velvety, satiny, fleecy, downy, furry, leathery. OPPOSITE: coarse. **5** (*soft lighting*) quiet, low, faint, dim, diffuse, muted, shaded, subdued. OPPOSITE: harsh. **6** (*soft colours*) light, pale, pastel, delicate, dull, subdued, muted, understated, restrained. **7** (*soft music*) low, mellow, melodious, mellifluous, pleasant, soothing, sweet, dulcet. **8** (*a soft breeze*) gentle, light, mild, moderate, temperate, balmy. **9** (*a soft manner*) gentle, docile, tender, kind, affectionate, warm, sweet, compassionate, loving, generous, soft-hearted, tender-hearted, easygoing (*inf*), sympathetic, sensitive, sentimental, romantic, soppy (*inf*), schmaltzy (*inf*). **10** (*the magistrate was too soft with them*) lenient, clement, indulgent, easygoing, forgiving, merciful, forbearing, permissive, tolerant, lax, liberal. OPPOSITE: severe. **11** (*living the soft life*) easy, cushy (*inf*), comfortable, cosy, pampered, privileged, successful, prosperous, luxurious.

soften *verb* **1** (*their opposition to her slowly softened*) moderate, tone down, modify, temper, melt, dissolve, mellow, relax, diminish, reduce, lessen, abate, die down. **2** (*her helmet softened the impact*) cushion, pad, ease, lessen, diminish, weaken, lighten, temper, mitigate, allay, assuage, muffle.
soften up work on, win over, persuade, disarm.

soggy *adj* wet, soaking, soaked, saturated, waterlogged, sodden, sopping, dripping, drenched, damp, moist, boggy, swampy, heavy, miry.

soil[1] *verb* dirty, begrime, besmirch, smudge, muddy, stain, spot, blot, sully, foul, defile, taint, pollute, tarnish, smear. OPPOSITE: clean.

soil[2] *noun* earth, ground, dirt, dust, clay, loam.

sojourn *verb* stay, stop, tarry, rest, abide, dwell, lodge, reside, visit. OPPOSITE: travel.
➤ *noun* stay, stop, visit, rest, holiday.

solace *noun* consolation, comfort, condolence, support, relief, cheer, succour. OPPOSITE: distress.
➤ *verb* console, comfort, cheer, relieve, support. OPPOSITE: afflict.

soldier *noun* warrior, fighter, mercenary, serviceman, infantryman, GI, trooper, private, rifleman, regular, conscript, recruit.
soldier on persevere, continue, persist, keep going, keep on, keep at it, hold on, hang on, plug away (*inf*), stick it out (*inf*).

sole *adj* only, single, singular, one, lone, alone, solitary, unique, exclusive, individual. OPPOSITE: numerous.

solecism *noun* **1** (*she found a number of solecisms in the article*) mistake, error, slip, lapse, gaffe, blunder, howler (*inf*), boob (*inf*), incongruity, absurdity. **2** (*an unforgivable solecism*) faux pas, impropriety, indiscretion, gaucherie.

solemn *adj* **1** (*a solemn expression*) serious, earnest, sincere, grave, sober, staid, sedate, sombre, glum, gloomy, grim, unsmiling, thoughtful, pensive, moody (*inf*). OPPOSITE: frivolous. **2** (*a solemn ceremony*) grand, stately, august, venerable, awe-inspiring, imposing, majestic, impressive, momentous, dignified, formal, ceremonial, ceremonious, ritual. OPPOSITE: informal. **3** (*solemn rites*) sacred, holy, religious, devotional. OPPOSITE: profane. **4** (*his solemn vow*) sincere, committed, wholehearted, genuine, earnest, grave, formal, honest.

solemnity *noun* **1** (*the solemnity of the ceremony*) solemness, graveness, gravity, formality, dignity, majesty, grandeur, stateliness, impressiveness, ceremoniousness. **2** (*the solemnity of his expression*) solemness, seriousness, gravity, sombreness, thoughtfulness, pensiveness. **3** (*the solemnity of his vow*) seriousness, sincerity, fervour, earnestness, formality, sanctity. **4** (*go through the necessary solemnities*) formality, ceremony, ceremonial, proceedings, rite, ritual, observance, celebration.

solemnize *verb* observe, keep, celebrate, commemorate, honour, dignify.

solicit *verb* ask for, request, apply for, seek, crave, beg, plead for, beseech, implore, entreat, pray, petition, canvass, urge, importune, sue, supplicate, accost.

solicitous *adj* concerned, caring, anxious, worried, uneasy, nervous, apprehensive, troubled, disturbed, careful, thoughtful, attentive, considerate. OPPOSITE: indifferent.

solicitude *noun* care, concern, regard, attentiveness, consideration, worry, anxiety, uneasiness, disquiet, nervousness, apprehensiveness, trouble.

solid *adj* **1** (*solid material*) hard, dense, compact, condensed, compressed, concrete, firm, thick, substantial. **2** (*a solid structure*) strong, sturdy, stable, substantial, durable, well-built, well-constructed. **3** (*solid ice*) solidified, frozen, congealed, set. **4** (*a solid defence*) reliable, dependable, stable, trustworthy, sure. **5** (*a solid argument*) reasonable, logical, sound, concrete, cogent, convincing, plausible, weighty, authoritative, valid, well-founded, well-grounded, sensible, level-headed. **6** (*solid gold*) genuine, real, pure, unalloyed, unmixed, unadulterated. **7** (*it came out in one solid piece*) complete, whole, united, undivided, uninterrupted, unbroken, continuous.

solidarity *noun* unity, unification, concordance, concord, harmony, accord, agreement, consensus, union, fellowship, camaraderie, team spirit, unanimity, stability. OPPOSITE: dissent.

solidify *verb* harden, set, congeal, coagulate, clot, cake, gel, jell, crystallize. OPPOSITE: melt.

solitary *adj* **1** (*a solitary figure*) alone, lone, sole, single, one, only, lonely, lonesome, friendless, companionless, separate, reclusive, unsociable, unsocial, antisocial, introverted. **2** (*a solitary cottage in the hills*) secluded, private, isolated, withdrawn, retired, lonely, remote, out-of-the-way, hidden, concealed, inaccessible, cloistered, separate, cut off, desolate, deserted, unfrequented, unvisited.

solitude *noun* loneliness, lonesomeness, isolation, remoteness, seclusion, privacy, retirement. OPPOSITE: society.

solution *noun* **1** (*the solution to the problem*) answer, result, explanation, key, remedy, elucidation, clarification, resolution, disentanglement. OPPOSITE: problem. 2 (*a chemical solution*) mixture, mix, compound, blend, emulsion, suspension.

solve *verb* answer, work out, figure out, puzzle out, resolve, decipher, crack (*inf*), unravel, disentangle, fathom (*inf*), interpret, clear up, clarify, explain, elucidate, unfold. OPPOSITE: complicate.

solvent *adj* financially sound, sound, creditworthy, in the black.

sombre *adj* **1** (*sombre colours*) dark, dull, dim, drab, dingy, gloomy, dismal, shady, shadowy. OPPOSITE: bright. **2** (*a sombre gathering*) dreary, dismal, gloomy, melancholy, depressed, doleful, sad, mournful, joyless, cheerless, lugubrious, funereal, sepulchral, sober, grave, serious.

somebody *noun* someone, personage, notable, dignitary, VIP, celebrity, bigwig (*inf*), big noise (*inf*), big shot (*inf*), big wheel (*inf*), star, superstar, luminary, household name, name, public figure, mogul, magnate. OPPOSITE: nobody.

sometimes *adv* occasionally, on occasion, at times, once in a while, now and then, now and again, on and off, from time to time, every so often. OPPOSITE: never.

somnolent *adj* drowsy, sleepy, dozy, half-awake, dopey (*inf*), slumberous, soporific, torpid. OPPOSITE: alert.

song *noun* carol, hymn, psalm, chant, anthem, ballad, lay, shanty, ditty, air, tune, melody, lyric, ode, sonnet, serenade.

sonorous *adj* resonant, resounding, sounding, reverberating, loud, deep, rich, full, full-throated, rounded, booming, ringing, orotund. OPPOSITE: soft.

soon *adv* shortly, in a short time, before long, anon, presently, any minute, in a minute, in a moment, in a twinkling, in a jiffy (*inf*), in a tick (*inf*), promptly, quickly, speedily, punctually, pronto (*inf*). OPPOSITE: later.

soothe *verb* **1** (*soothe the children*) calm, compose, still, quieten, quiet, hush, lull, pacify, tranquillize, mollify, settle, ease, relieve, comfort. **2** (*soothe the pain*) moderate, temper, mitigate, ease, assuage, allay, alleviate, relieve, palliate, appease, soften, lessen, reduce. OPPOSITE: irritate.

soothsayer *noun* prophet, foreteller, seer, augur, diviner, sibyl.

sophisticated *adj* **1** (*a sophisticated man*) refined, cultured, cultivated, educated, worldly-wise, worldly, cosmopolitan, urbane, suave, elegant, polished, stylish, jet-set, seasoned, experienced, blasé. OPPOSITE: uncouth. **2** (*a sophisticated civilization*) complex, complicated, intricate, elaborate, advanced, developed. OPPOSITE: primitive.

sophistication *noun* worldliness, experience, urbanity, urbaneness, suaveness, culture, refinement, finesse, poise, elegance, savoir faire.

sophistry *noun* quibbling, equivocation, sophism, casuistry, fallacy. OPPOSITE: truth.

soporific *adj* sleep-inducing, somnolent, sedative, narcotic, hypnotic, sleepy, somniferous. OPPOSITE: stimulant.

➤ *noun* sedative, sleeping pill, tranquillizer, narcotic, opiate, anaesthetic.

soppy *adj* sentimental, emotional, maudlin, mawkish, slushy (*inf*), mushy (*inf*), sloppy (*inf*), weepy (*inf*), schmaltzy (*inf*).

sorcerer *noun* magician, wizard, witch, warlock, necromancer, enchanter.

sorcery *noun* magic, black magic, witchcraft, wizardry, witchery, necromancy, enchantment, spell, charm, incantation.

sordid *adj* **1** (*the house was in a sordid state*) dirty, filthy, mucky, foul, unclean, grimy, soiled, stained, squalid, seedy, seamy, sleazy, slummy, poor. **2** (*a sordid occupation*) corrupt, immoral, degenerate, debauched, debased, shameful, disgraceful, despicable, dishonourable, disreputable, ignoble, abhorrent, base, low, shabby, wretched, foul, vile. OPPOSITE: respectable. **3** (*a sordid interest in money*) greedy, avaricious, covetous, grasping, selfish, self-seeking, mean, miserly, niggardly, parsimonious, stingy, ungenerous, mercenary, venal. OPPOSITE: generous.

sore *adj* **1** (*a sore spot on his arm*) tender, painful, raw, red, bruised, sensitive, inflamed, irritated, chafed, smarting, stinging, burning, hurting, aching, injured. **2** (*a sore point with him*) annoying, irritating, vexing, irksome, distressing, harrowing, grievous, afflictive, troublesome, sharp, acute, severe, dire. **3** (*he was pretty sore about it*) annoyed, vexed, irked, nettled, peeved (*inf*), irritated, bitter, aggrieved, afflicted, wounded, hurt, upset, distressed, angry, resentful, offended. OPPOSITE: pleased. **4** (*in sore need of attention*) dire, pressing, urgent, desperate, extreme, acute, critical.

➤ *noun* wound, injury, scrape, graze, abrasion, laceration, lesion, inflammation, swelling, ulcer, abscess, boil, gathering.

sorrow *noun* **1** (*she was overwhelmed with sorrow*) sadness, grief, woe, heartache, heartbreak, pain, misery, anguish, suffering, mourning, unhappiness, wretchedness, dejection, desolation, distress, regret, remorse. OPPOSITE: joy. **2** (*she has suffered many sorrows*) trouble, worry, misfortune, affliction, trial.

➤ *verb* **1** (*she sorrowed over his death*) mourn, grieve, weep, lament. **2** (*he was busy sorrowing over his losses*) lament, pine, weep, bemoan, bewail, despair. OPPOSITE: rejoice.

sorrowful *adj* **1** (*a sorrowful sight*) sorry, sad, miserable, pathetic, pitiful, affecting, moving, heart-rending, melancholy, wretched, lamentable, deplorable. **2** (*a sorrowful countenance*) unhappy, depressed, dejected, desolate, disconsolate, heartbroken, mournful, doleful, melancholy, lugubrious, weeping, tearful, sorry, miserable, wretched, woebegone. OPPOSITE: joyful.

sorry *adj* **1** (*a sorry child*) apologetic, penitent, repentant, contrite, remorseful, regretful, compunctious, conscience-stricken, guilt-ridden, sheepish, ashamed, shamefaced. OPPOSITE: impenitent. **2** (*sorry to hear what happened*) sad, upset, distressed, sorrowful, unhappy, moved, concerned, sympathetic. OPPOSITE: glad. **3** (*she met a sorry end*) wretched, dismal, miserable, sad, unhappy, grievous, heart-rending, pitiful, pitiable, piteous, pathetic, abject, poor, mean, shabby, paltry. OPPOSITE: splendid.

sort *noun* kind, class, category, order, group, set, genus, species, genre, ilk, variety, type, character, nature, description, denomination, make, brand, stamp, quality, style, breed, race, family.
➤ *verb* arrange, order, rank, categorize, classify, class, group, separate, segregate, distribute, divide, sort out, sift, screen, grade, select, assort, organize, systematize, catalogue, file. OPPOSITE: muddle.

out of sorts 1 (*he says he feels out of sorts*) unwell, sick, ill, poorly, seedy, groggy (*inf*), rough (*inf*), run down (*inf*), below par (*inf*), under the weather (*inf*), queasy, laid up, ailing, unhealthy. **2** (*she is always out of sorts these days*) irritable, cross, grumpy, ill-tempered, quick-tempered, touchy, testy, snappish, snappy, crotchety, crabby (*inf*), grouchy (*inf*), ratty (*inf*), stroppy (*inf*), fractious.

sort out 1 (*sort everything out into different boxes*) sort, arrange, organize, order, classify, class, categorize, grade. **2** (*sort out the best fruit for export*) separate out, pick out, select, sift, segregate, put to one side. **3** (*sort out the difficulty*) sort, resolve, solve, clear up, put right, put straight.

sortie *noun* foray, sally, raid, attack, assault, offensive, charge, rush, onrush, swoop, invasion.

soul *noun* **1** (*divide the soul from the body*) spirit, psyche, mind, reason, intellect, life, heart, essence, embodiment, character. **2** (*a dozen souls were lost overboard*) person, being, human being, individual, man, woman, body, mortal, creature. **3** (*she played with plenty of soul*) energy, vitality, animation, ardour, fervour, intensity, feeling, emotion, sensitivity, sympathy, compassion, tenderness, humanity, understanding. **4** (*she has been the soul of kindness*) personification, epitome, embodiment, incarnation, essence, model.

sound[1] *noun* **1** (*a small sound*) noise, report, din, racket, cry, utterance, resonance, reverberation. OPPOSITE: silence. **2** (*within the sound of the sea*) earshot, hearing, range.
➤ *verb* **1** (*sound each word clearly*) utter, say, voice, vocalize, pronounce, articulate, enunciate, declare, announce, express. **2** (*the foghorn sounded*) resound, echo, reverberate, resonate, go off, toll, ring, chime. **3** (*it sounds like an unlikely scenario*) seem, appear, look.

sound[2] *adj* **1** (*a sound body*) fit, healthy, hale, hearty, vigorous, robust, sturdy, firm, solid, strong, whole, intact, undamaged, unimpaired, uninjured, unhurt, unbroken, perfect. OPPOSITE: faulty. **2** (*a sound argument*) sensible, reasonable, logical, rational, valid, cogent, authoritative, weighty, well-founded, well-grounded, substantial, solid, good, convincing, plausible. **3** (*a sound investment*) reliable, dependable, trustworthy, proven, correct, right, true, secure, safe, proper, fair, wise, astute, shrewd, perceptive, sane, responsible, level-headed. OPPOSITE: unreliable.

sound[3] *verb* fathom, measure, plumb, probe, test, examine, inspect, investigate.
sound out investigate, examine, survey, canvass, research, question, explore, probe, look into, suss out (*inf*).

sound[4] *noun* channel, estuary, strait, passage, inlet, firth, fjord.

soundless *adj* noiseless, quiet, silent, still, inaudible, muffled. OPPOSITE: noisy.

sour *adj* **1** (*a sour taste*) tart, acid, acerbic, bitter, sharp, tangy, pungent, vinegary. OPPOSITE: sweet. **2** (*sour milk*) bad, rancid, curdled, turned, off (*inf*), unpleasant, offensive. **3** (*a sour character*) acrimonious, embittered, surly, churlish, ill-tempered, bad-tempered, ill-natured, cross, crusty, snappy, testy, touchy, peevish, petulant, resentful, waspish, sharp-tongued, crabbed, crotchety, grumpy, grouchy (*inf*), ratty (*inf*), sullen, morose, nasty, disagreeable, unpleasant. OPPOSITE: genial.
➤ *verb* **1** (*the quarrel soured their relationship*) spoil, embitter, envenom, disenchant, disillusion, exacerbate, alienate. **2** (*the milk has soured*) ferment, turn, curdle, go off.

source *noun* **1** (*the source of the legend*) origin, beginning, start, commencement, derivation, cause, root, rise, fountainhead, spring, wellspring. OPPOSITE: issue. **2** (*the source of the river*) rise, spring, fountainhead, wellspring, wellhead, headspring. **3** (*he refused to name his source*) informant, contact, authority, reference.

souse *verb* **1** (*souse the bundle in disinfectant*) plunge, immerse, submerge, plunge, douse, dip, sink, duck, dunk, drench, soak, saturate, steep. **2** (*fish soused in vinegar*) pickle, marinate, marinade, steep.

souvenir *noun* keepsake, memento, reminder, remembrance, token, relic, trophy, memorabilia.

sovereign *noun* ruler, monarch, king, queen, emperor, empress, tsar, autocrat, crowned head, potentate, lord. OPPOSITE: subject.
➤ *adj* **1** (*our sovereign master*) royal, regal, majestic, kingly, queenly, imperial. **2** (*sovereign parliament*) ruling, supreme, paramount, predominant, chief, dominant, principal. **3** (*a sovereign state*) independent, autonomous, self-ruling, self-governing. **4** (*a sovereign remedy for colds*) excellent, outstanding, unequalled, unrivalled, effectual, efficacious, efficient.

sovereignty *noun* **1** (*exercise sovereignty over the family*) supremacy, primacy, ascendancy, power, control, dominion, jurisdiction, sway. **2** (*the sovereignty of the state*) independence, autonomy.

sow *verb* **1** (*sow seeds in the earth*) plant, scatter, strew, bestrew, disperse, spread. OPPOSITE: reap. **2** (*sow dissension among the men*) spread, foment, foster, instigate, promote, broadcast, disseminate.

space *noun* **1** (*take up a lot of space*) room, area, expanse, extent, extension, capacity, volume. **2** (*little space for leisure activities*) scope, range, margin, leeway, latitude, play. **3** (*a few spaces left in the bus*) seat, place, berth, accommodation. **4** (*leave a space after each word*) gap, blank, break, omission. **5** (*there was a lull for brief space*) interval, period, spell, time, duration, span, stretch, shift, stint. **6** (*the search for alien life in space*) universe, galaxy, cosmos, solar system, sky, infinity. OPPOSITE: earth.
➤ *verb* **1** (*space the runners across the track*) arrange, order, put in order, dispose, array, line up, string out, range. **2** (*space out the sticks*) set apart, set at intervals.

spacious *adj* **1** (*spacious accommodation*) capacious, ample, roomy, commodious, sizeable. **2** (*a spacious park*) extensive, broad, wide, vast, immense, huge, big, large. OPPOSITE: small.

span *noun* **1** (*the span of the bridge*) length, distance, extent, stretch, reach, spread, compass. **2** (*a span of several hours*) space, interval, period, spell, term, duration, time.
≫ *verb* bridge, cross, traverse, bestride, extend, reach, vault, arch, cover.

spank *verb* smack, slap, beat, thrash, wallop (*inf*), belt (*inf*), whack (*inf*), tan (*inf*), slipper, cane.

spar *verb* argue, dispute, bicker, quarrel, squabble, wrangle, fall out (*inf*), fight, scrap (*inf*), contend, contest, skirmish, wrestle.

spare *verb* **1** (*he spared the prisoners*) pardon, reprieve, let off, release, free, forgive. OPPOSITE: punish. **2** (*their reputation spared them from the wrath of the mob*) protect, safeguard, save, rescue, defend. **3** (*he can spare the money*) afford, do without, manage without. **4** (*the authorities will not spare the money*) give, grant, allow, part with, dispense with, relinquish. OPPOSITE: keep.
≫ *adj* **1** (*a spare set of clothing*) extra, additional, supplementary, reserve, emergency. **2** (*spare to requirements*) superfluous, surplus, auxiliary, leftover, over, unwanted, remaining, unused. **3** (*spare time*) free, unoccupied, available, leisure. **4** (*a spare frame*) thin, slim, slender, lean, lank, gaunt, bony, wiry, skinny, scrawny, scraggy. **5** (*spare takings*) meagre, scanty, scant, modest, skimpy. OPPOSITE: ample. **6** (*a spare lifestyle*) frugal, sparing, economical.
to spare left over, surplus, superfluous.

sparing *adj* economical, thrifty, frugal, saving, careful, cautious, prudent, penurious, chary, mean, miserly, parsimonious, niggardly, tight-fisted, close-fisted, penny-pinching, stingy (*inf*), mingy (*inf*). OPPOSITE: lavish.

spark *noun* **1** (*a spark of light*) flash, sparkle, gleam, glint, flicker, flare. **2** (*a spark of hope*) flicker, gleam, glimmer, scintilla, trace, vestige, scrap, bit, hint, touch, suggestion, suspicion, atom, jot, whit, iota.
≫ *verb* excite, stimulate, kindle, animate, inspire, activate, stir, start.

spark off trigger off, set off, start off, touch off, precipitate, kindle, incite, inspire, stir up, cause, prompt, provoke, stimulate, occasion.

sparkle *verb* **1** (*the diamonds sparkled in the torchlight*) glitter, glisten, twinkle, shine, glow, gleam, glimmer, glint, beam, flash, flicker, coruscate, shimmer, scintillate, dance, blink, wink. **2** (*the champagne sparkled in her glass*) fizz, effervesce, bubble. **3** (*she sparkled at the party*) be vivacious, be lively, be animated, be spirited, be witty, be effervescent.
≫ *noun* **1** (*the sparkle of the lights on the water*) twinkle, spark, glint, gleam, glitter, flash, flicker, shimmer, coruscation, glow, shine, brilliance, radiance, dazzle. OPPOSITE: dullness. **2** (*her sparkle woke everyone up*) liveliness, vitality, vivacity, spirit, life, liveliness, elan, panache, energy, dash, pizzazz (*inf*), vim (*inf*), get-up-and-go (*inf*), gaiety, animation, ebullience, effervescence, enthusiasm.

sparse *adj* scattered, scanty, meagre, slight, thin, few, scarce, infrequent, sporadic. OPPOSITE: dense.

spartan *adj* austere, harsh, bleak, grim, strict, severe, rigorous, stringent, disciplined, ascetic, abstemious, self-denying, frugal, plain, simple. OPPOSITE: indulgent

spasm *noun* **1** (*spasms shook his body*) convulsion, contraction, twitch, tic, cramp. **2** (*a spasm of giggling*) outburst, burst, eruption, fit, frenzy, attack, bout, seizure, paroxysm, convulsion.

spasmodic *adj* fitful, irregular, erratic, periodic, sporadic, intermittent, occasional, jerky, convulsive. OPPOSITE: regular.

spate *noun* flood, flow, rush, deluge, torrent, outpouring, outbreak.

spatter *verb* splatter, bespatter, splash, splodge, sprinkle, besprinkle, shower, spray, speckle, spot, daub, bedaub, scatter, strew, bestrew.

speak *verb* **1** (*speak to her before she goes*) talk, chat (*inf*), chatter (*inf*), converse, have a word with (*inf*), communicate. **2** (*speak a few words*) say, utter, express, voice, articulate, enunciate, pronounce, declaim, declare, state, tell. **3** (*he spoke on a variety of subjects for three hours*) discourse, address, lecture, orate, hold forth, harangue, argue, discuss.

speak for represent, act for, stand for.

speak of talk about, refer to, make reference to, allude to, comment on, discuss, mention.

speak to rebuke, reprimand, scold, lecture, tell off (*inf*), tick off (*inf*), admonish, upbraid, dress down (*inf*), talk to (*inf*), carpet (*inf*), bring to book (*inf*), warn, accost, address.

speaker *noun* talker, lecturer, orator, declaimer, haranguer, tub-thumper (*inf*).

special *adj* **1** (*he had a special reason for wanting to go*) especial, specific, definite, express, particular, certain, precise. **2** (*a special day for us all*) memorable, momentous, important, significant, major, noteworthy, notable, red-letter (*inf*), singular, extraordinary, outstanding, distinguished, festive, gala. OPPOSITE: ordinary. **3** (*a special quality*) distinct, distinctive, characteristic, individual, unique, choice, exclusive, exceptional, remarkable, select, peculiar, particular, rare, singular, unusual, uncommon.

specialist *noun* expert, authority, master, professional, consultant, connoisseur.

speciality *noun* **1** (*dancing is his speciality*) strength, feature, forte, talent, gift, métier. **2** (*what is the professor's speciality?*), field of study, area of study.

species *noun* group, sort, class, kind, type, variety, category, genus, description, breed, genre.

specific *adj* **1** (*recruited for a specific task*) particular, specified, distinct, definite, fixed, set, determined. OPPOSITE: general. **2** (*he went against my specific orders*) explicit, express, detailed, exact, precise, unequivocal, unambiguous, clear-cut, well-defined.

specification *noun* **1** (*the specifications of the engine*) particulars, details, description. **2** (*he delivered his specifications for the job*) stipulation, requirement, condition, qualification.

specify *verb* state, name, cite, mention, itemize,

catalogue, enumerate, designate, indicate, detail, list, spell out, stipulate, particularize, describe, set out, delineate, define.

specimen *noun* sample, example, exemplar, exemplification, representative, illustration, case, instance, pattern, model, type.

specious *adj* misleading, deceptive, false, fallacious, unsound, untrue, sophistic, sophistical, casuistic, plausible.

speck *noun* **1** (*a speck of dirt*) spot, dot, mark, stain, blemish, smudge, fleck, speckle. **2** (*hardly a speck of food in the house*) bit, jot, iota, atom, piece, trace, shred, whit, tittle, mite, grain, particle.

speckled *adj* spotted, spotty, dotted, flecked, freckled, mottled, dappled, stippled, sprinkled, brindled.

spectacle *noun* **1** (*it was quite a spectacle*) sight, vision, picture, scene. **2** (*thousands took part in the spectacle*) show, display, exhibition, parade, pageant, extravaganza, performance. **3** (*a spectacle of the modern stage*) marvel, wonder, phenomenon, curiosity.

spectacles *pl noun* specs (*inf*), glasses, eye-glasses, bifocals.

spectacular *adj* impressive, picturesque, striking, stunning, breathtaking, staggering, amazing, astonishing, singular, outstanding, extraordinary, grand, glorious, splendid, resplendent, opulent, magnificent, remarkable, sensational, dramatic, dazzling, flamboyant, ostentatious, eye-catching, colourful. OPPOSITE: ordinary.
➤ *noun* spectacle, extravaganza, display, show, exhibition, pageant, performance.

spectator *noun* onlooker, looker-on, observer, bystander, passer-by, watcher, viewer, witness, eye-witness.

spectre *noun* ghost, apparition, phantom, spook (*inf*), spirit, wraith, revenant, shade, shadow, visitant, vision, presence.

speculate *verb* **1** (*speculate on the outcome*) conjecture, guess, surmise, suppose, theorize, hypothesize, consider, think, meditate, cogitate, reflect, deliberate, contemplate, ponder, muse, ruminate, wonder. OPPOSITE: know. **2** (*speculate on the market*) gamble, bet, risk, hazard, venture.

speculation *noun* **1** (*his speculation was proved correct*) conjecture, guess, guesswork, supposition, surmise, hypothesis, theory, opinion, view, thought, flight of fancy. OPPOSITE: reality. **2** (*speculation is rife*) conjecture, supposition, theorizing, guessing, surmising, musing, meditation, reflection, cogitation. **3** (*speculation in stocks and shares*) gamble, risk, hazard, venture, flutter (*inf*).

speculative *adj* **1** (*a speculative notion*) conjectural, theoretical, hypothetical, suppositional, notional, academic, unproven, tentative, vague, abstract, indefinite. **2** (*a speculative investment*) gambling, risky, iffy (*inf*), chancy (*inf*), dicey (*inf*), hazardous, uncertain, unpredictable.

speech *noun* **1** (*he delivered an entertaining speech*) talk, address, oration, lecture, discourse, patter, spiel (*inf*), monologue, soliloquy, tirade, diatribe, harangue,

sermon. **2** (*there was little speech between the two sides*) conversation, talk, discussion, dialogue, colloquy, communication. **3** (*study the speech of remote tribes*) language, lingo (*inf*), tongue, dialect, jargon, idiom, parlance, accent. **4** (*his speech was slurred*) diction, articulation, enunciation, pronunciation, elocution, utterance, delivery, voice.

speechless *adj* mute, dumb, silent, voiceless, inarticulate, tongue-tied, wordless, dumbfounded, dumbstruck, amazed, astounded, shocked, thunderstruck, aghast. OPPOSITE: talkative.

speed *noun* velocity, celerity, rapidity, swiftness, fastness, quickness, fleetness, promptness, alacrity, expeditiousness, expedition, haste, hurry, hurriedness, dispatch, rush, acceleration, momentum, pace, rate, tempo. OPPOSITE: slowness.
➤ *verb* **1** (*speed from one place to another*) hasten, make haste, hurry, scurry, scamper, rush, dash, charge, race, sprint, gallop, career, tear (*inf*), belt (*inf*), pelt (*inf*), hurtle (*inf*), zoom, bowl along. **2** (*speed up the delivery of aid*) accelerate, quicken, expedite, facilitate, advance, further, forward, boost, promote, aid, assist, stimulate. OPPOSITE: delay.

speedy *adj* **1** (*a speedy retreat*) hasty, hurried, precipitate, expeditious, fast, quick, rapid, swift, fleet, nimble, nippy (*inf*). OPPOSITE: slow. **2** (*he got a speedy response*) fast, rapid, quick, swift, express, prompt, early, immediate.

spell¹ *noun* **1** (*a magic spell*) charm, incantation, enchantment, bewitchment, magic, sorcery. **2** (*he fell victim to her spell*) influence, power, magnetism, allure, pull, draw, enticement, attraction, fascination, beguilement, charm, glamour.

spell² *noun* (*a spell of warm weather*) period, time, stretch, span, patch, interval, term, session, stint, bout, turn, course.

spell³ *verb* (*her withdrawal spells trouble ahead*) imply, indicate, amount to, add up to, signal, herald, suggest, mean, signify, denote, bespeak, promise, threaten, augur, portend, presage.

spell out clarify, make clear, make plain, explain, elucidate, emphasize, stipulate, specify, detail, set out, itemize, particularize.

spellbinding *adj* fascinating, riveting, gripping, entrancing, enthralling, enchanting, bewitching, captivating, mesmerizing, hypnotic, transfixing, charming.

spend *verb* **1** (*spend a lot of money*) disburse, pay out, expend, fork out (*inf*), splash out (*inf*), shell out (*inf*), blow (*inf*), splurge (*inf*), squander, dissipate, waste, fritter away, use up, consume, invest. OPPOSITE: save. **2** (*spend time on research*) employ, use, apply, devote, pass, fill, occupy, take up, put in, while away, kill (*inf*).

spendthrift *noun* wastrel, prodigal, profligate, squanderer, big spender (*inf*). OPPOSITE: miser.
➤ *adj* extravagant, prodigal, improvident, thriftless, wasteful, squandering. OPPOSITE: thrifty.

spent *adj* **1** (*the players were all utterly spent*) exhausted, worn out, weary, wearied, tired, drained, knackered (*inf*), shattered (*inf*), whacked (*inf*), fagged out (*inf*), dead beat (*inf*), bushed (*inf*), all in (*inf*), done in (*inf*). **2** (*our fuel* *supply is spent*) exhausted, consumed, used up, finished, expended, depleted, gone.

spew verb **1** (*the child spewed up in the car*) vomit, throw up (*inf*), puke (*inf*), regurgitate, retch, heave. **2** (*people spewed out of the exit*) pour, issue, gush, spurt, discharge, rush, spout.

sphere noun **1** (*a glass sphere*) ball, globe, orb, round, globule. OPPOSITE: cube. **2** (*little experience in this sphere*) field, area, domain, realm, province, department, discipline, speciality, territory, range, scope, compass, capacity, beat. **3** (*all her friends came from the same sphere of society*) order, rank, class, station.

spherical adj round, ball-shaped, globular, globe-shaped, orb-like, rotund.

spice noun **1** (*cooking with plenty of spice*) seasoning, flavouring, flavour, savour, relish, tang, piquancy, herbs. **2** (*add some spice to his humdrum existence*) excitement, life, interest, colour, gusto, kick (*inf*), pep (*inf*), piquancy, zest, zip (*inf*), zing (*inf*), zap (*inf*), pizzazz (*inf*).

spicy adj **1** (*a spicy dish*) piquant, pungent, aromatic, fragrant, tangy, tart, sharp, peppery, hot, seasoned, well-seasoned, savoury, flavoured, flavoursome. OPPOSITE: insipid. **2** (*a spicy tale*) racy, bawdy, ribald, indelicate, indecorous, indecent, risqué, suggestive, raunchy (*inf*), juicy (*inf*), blue (*inf*), adult (*inf*), improper, unseemly, scandalous, sensational.

spike noun point, projection, prong, spine, barb, tine, nail, pin, stake.
➤ verb **1** (*he spiked his finger*) prick, pierce, impale, spear, skewer, spit. **2** (*she had spiked the drink*) drug, adulterate, lace, contaminate.

spill verb upset, overturn, overflow, run over, brim over, pour out, slop over, tip, discharge, disgorge, shed, scatter.
➤ noun tumble, fall, overturn, upset, accident, header (*inf*), cropper (*inf*), nosedive (*inf*).
spill the beans inform, tell, rat (*inf*), split (*inf*), squeal (*inf*), blab (*inf*), grass (*inf*), let the cat out of the bag (*inf*).

spin verb **1** (*the coin spun in the air*) rotate, revolve, turn, twirl, twist, circle, whirl, wheel, pirouette, swivel, gyrate, reel. **2** (*spin a yarn*) tell, recount, relate, narrate, unfold, develop, concoct, invent, fabricate, dream up, make up.
➤ noun **1** (*go for a spin in the car*) ride, drive, run, jaunt, trip, journey, outing, whirl. **2** (*with each spin of the wheel*) turn, revolution, rotation, gyration, whirl, circle.
spin out protract, prolong, lengthen, extend, drag out, draw out, stretch out, amplify, pad out, fill out. OPPOSITE: abridge.

spine noun **1** (*a shiver ran down his spine*) backbone, vertebrae, vertebral column, spinal column. **2** (*the spines of a hedgehog*) point, spike, barb, quill, needle, prickle, thorn. **3** (*he showed a lot of spine*) courage, bravery, valour, pluck, guts (*inf*), bottle (*inf*), mettle, resolution, determination, fortitude, spirit.

spine-chilling adj blood-curdling, hair-raising, frightening, scary (*inf*), spooky (*inf*), eerie, horrifying, terrifying.

spineless adj weak, feeble, weak-willed, submissive, irresolute, indecisive, ineffective, timid, timorous, pusillanimous, cowardly, chicken (*inf*), yellow (*inf*), soft,

faint-hearted, lily-livered, spiritless, wimpish (*inf*). OPPOSITE: bold.

spinney noun copse, coppice, thicket, grove, wood.

spiral noun helix, coil, corkscrew, screw, twist, whorl, convolution.
➤ adj circular, coiled, winding, twisting, corkscrew, scrolled, whorled, helical. OPPOSITE: straight.
➤ verb **1** (*a leaf spiralled down*) twist, coil, wind, wreathe, circle, screw, gyrate, whorl. **2** (*the cost has spiralled*) soar, rocket, skyrocket, escalate, mount, climb, rise, go up, increase.

spire noun **1** (*the spire of the church*) steeple, belfry, tower. **2** (*the distant spires of the mountains*) peak, crest, pinnacle, summit, top, tip, point.

spirit noun **1** (*his spirit was reunited with his body*) soul, psyche, life, breath, mind, will, vital force. OPPOSITE: body. **2** (*get in the party spirit*) mood, frame of mind, state of mind, attitude, humour, temper, disposition, outlook, feeling, morale, temperament. **3** (*they argued with considerable spirit*) enthusiasm, zeal, fire, ardour, fervour, vigour, energy, enterprise, dash, zest, liveliness, vivacity, sparkle, animation. OPPOSITE: apathy. **4** (*he showed lots of spirit*) courage, bravery, valour, pluck, guts (*inf*), bottle (*inf*), mettle, backbone, determination, resolution, willpower, stoutheartedness, dauntlessness. **5** (*she understood the spirit behind his words*) essence, quintessence, substance, character, nature, sense, drift, gist, tenor, significance, meaning, purport, implication, intent. **6** (*the well is haunted by spirits*) ghost, spook (*inf*), apparition, spectre, phantom, wraith, revenant, visitant, shade, shadow, presence, fairy, sprite, imp, goblin, fiend, angel, demon, devil.
spirit away whisk away, carry off, make off with, remove, capture, snatch, seize, purloin, snaffle, steal away with.

spirited adj **1** (*a spirited performance*) lively, vivacious, animated, high-spirited, sparkling, active, energetic, vigorous, enthusiastic, ardent, zealous, fervent, fiery, passionate. OPPOSITE: apathetic. **2** (*a spirited attack*) courageous, brave, valiant, heroic, plucky, gritty, feisty (*inf*), mettlesome, determined, bold, resolute.

spiritless adj **1** (*a spiritless production*) listless, lacklustre, bland, insipid, indifferent, vapid, anaemic, prosaic, dull, colourless, wishy-washy (*inf*). OPPOSITE: spirited. **2** (*the defeat left the team spiritless*) unenthusiastic, apathetic, melancholic, depressed, dejected, dispirited, disconsolate, downcast, listless, lethargic, lifeless, sluggish, inert, torpid, weak.

spirits pl noun **1** (*the bar ran out of spirits*) liquor, strong liquor, hard stuff (*inf*), alcohol, moonshine, fire-water (*inf*). **2** (*her spirits were low*) feelings, emotions, mood, humour, temperament, temper, morale, attitude.

spiritual adj **1** (*the spiritual world*) incorporeal, immaterial, intangible, ethereal, ghostly, supernatural, unworldly, otherworldly. OPPOSITE: physical. **2** (*spiritual writings*) holy, sacred, heavenly, religious, ecclesiastical, divine, devotional, pious, devout, pure. OPPOSITE: profane.

spit verb **1** (*he spat on the floor*) expectorate, hawk. **2** (*the gun spat flame*) discharge, eject, issue. **3** (*the old man spat curses*) hiss, rasp, snort.

➤ *noun* spittle, saliva, phlegm, dribble, expectoration.

spitting image spit, dead spit (*inf*), dead ringer (*inf*), double, duplicate, twin, clone, likeness, lookalike, replica, image, picture.

spite *noun* spitefulness, malice, maliciousness, malevolence, malignity, venom, ill-will, bitterness, ill feeling, animosity, hostility, vindictiveness, vengeance, resentment, grudge, hate, gall, spleen, rancour, pique. OPPOSITE: benevolence.

➤ *verb* annoy, vex, offend, put out, pique, nettle, provoke, irritate, irk, gall, hurt, injure, wound, upset. OPPOSITE: please.

in spite of despite, notwithstanding, regardless of, in defiance of, against.

spiteful *adj* malicious, malevolent, malign, malignant, vengeful, vindictive, ill-natured, ill-disposed, nasty, poisonous, venomous, cruel, barbed, rancorous, hostile, bitchy (*inf*), bitter, resentful, grudging. OPPOSITE: benevolent.

splash *verb* **1** (*splashed with mud*) spatter, bespatter, splatter, daub, plaster, sprinkle, spray, shower, squirt, splodge, slosh, slop. **2** (*the water splashed against the quay*) dash, wash, beat, break, batter, surge, buffet. **3** (*the dog splashed about in the shallows*) paddle, bathe, dabble, wallow, wade. **4** (*his name was splashed in all the papers*) blaze, blazon, plaster, trumpet, broadcast, display, flaunt, exhibit, publicize, headline, show.

➤ *noun* **1** (*a splash of mud on her coat*) spot, splodge, splotch, stain, daub, smudge, smear, patch, dash, touch. **2** (*the subject of a big splash in the papers*) splurge, sensation, story. **3** (*a splash of colour*) burst, streak, patch, dash, touch, stain.

splash out lash out, invest in, splurge, spend, push the boat out (*inf*).

spleen *noun* spite, spitefulness, rancour, malice, maliciousness, hatred, hostility, vindictiveness, bitterness, acrimony, venom, gall, bile, biliousness, pique, peevishness, petulance, resentment, ill-will, irascibility, bad temper, ill-humour, anger, wrath. OPPOSITE: benevolence.

splendid *adj* **1** (*a splendid achievement*) brilliant, dazzling, glittering, radiant, superb, supreme, sublime, outstanding, remarkable, exceptional, admirable, excellent, first-class, marvellous, wonderful, super (*inf*), terrific (*inf*), renowned, celebrated. OPPOSITE: poor. **2** (*a splendid mansion*) great, imposing, impressive, magnificent, fine, grand, stately, lavish, gorgeous, opulent, sumptuous, rich, luxurious, showy, resplendent, glorious, illustrious, distinguished.

splendour *noun* **1** (*the splendour of the surroundings*) magnificence, grandeur, sumptuousness, opulence, luxury, luxuriousness, richness, lavishness, gloriousness, elegance. **2** (*the splendour of the occasion*) brilliance, resplendence, stateliness, majesty, glory, pomp, display, spectacle, parade, show, ceremony, solemnity.

splenetic *adj* spiteful, malicious, peevish, petulant, irritable, irascible, ratty (*inf*), bitchy (*inf*), bad-tempered, fretful, choleric, testy, touchy, acid, sour, angry, cross, surly, sullen, morose, crabby, crabbed, crusty, churlish, rancorous. OPPOSITE: genial.

splice *verb* join, fasten, unite, marry, connect, bind, tie,

braid, plait, graft, knit, mesh, interweave, entwine, intertwine, interlace. OPPOSITE: sever.

get spliced marry, get married, wed, get wed, get hitched (*inf*), tie the knot (*inf*), take the plunge (*inf*).

splinter *verb* shatter, smash, shiver, split, cleave, break up, fracture, disintegrate, crumble.

➤ *noun* piece, bit, fragment, flake, sliver, shiver, shard, chip, shred, shaving, paring.

split *verb* **1** (*split the loaf in half*) separate, divide, partition, halve, bisect. **2** (*the lightning split the rock*) break, sever, rend, part, chop, cleave, cut, slit, slash, crack, splinter, shiver, rupture, burst, rip, tear. OPPOSITE: unite. **3** (*the couple have agreed to split*) divorce, split up, break up, separate, part company, part, disband. **4** (*split the sweets between the children*) share, divide, separate, apportion, allocate, allot, parcel out, carve up (*inf*), hand out, dole out, distribute. **5** (*the road split at the top of the hill*) branch, fork. **6** (*he split on the rest of the gang*) inform, report, tell (*inf*), betray, shop (*inf*), grass (*inf*), rat (*inf*), squeal (*inf*), peach (*inf*).

➤ *noun* **1** (*a split in the wall*) crack, fissure, crevice, cleft, rift, rupture, break, breach, gap, cut, rip, rent, slash, slit, tear. **2** (*a split in the ranks*) rift, rupture, divergence, partition, schism, disunion, dissension, discord, break-up, separation, division, alienation, estrangement. OPPOSITE: union.

spoil *verb* **1** (*he spoiled her plans*) mess up (*inf*), louse up (*inf*), screw up (*inf*), ruin, wreck, destroy. **2** (*his haircut spoiled his whole appearance*) mar, harm, damage, injure, hurt, impair, disfigure, deface, blemish. OPPOSITE: improve. **3** (*that child has been spoiled*) indulge, overindulge, pamper, coddle, mollycoddle, cosset, baby. **4** (*the food spoiled in the heat*) decay, decompose, deteriorate, go bad, go off (*inf*), turn, curdle, sour, addle, taint, rot, putrefy.

spoil for thirst for, yearn for, long for.

spoils *pl noun* **1** (*the spoils of the robbery*) booty, loot, swag (*inf*), plunder, pillage, pickings (*inf*), haul, prize. **2** (*the spoils of seniority*) advantage, benefit, profit, gain.

sponge *verb* **1** (*sponge the surfaces dry*) wipe, mop, wash, rub, clean, rub out, efface, expunge. **2** (*sponge off his brother*) cadge, beg, scrounge (*inf*), bum (*sl*), freeload (*inf*), borrow, live off.

spongy *adj* porous, absorbent, soft, light, cushioned, yielding, squashy, elastic, springy, resilient.

sponsor *noun* patron, backer, supporter, promoter, guarantor, underwriter, angel (*inf*).

➤ *verb* back, support, finance, fund, bankroll, subsidize, patronize, promote, guarantee, underwrite.

spontaneous *adj* **1** (*spontaneous wit*) natural, instinctive, impulsive, unforced, off-the-cuff (*inf*). **2** (*a spontaneous act of generosity*) impetuous, free, voluntary, willing, unhesitating, unforced, unprompted, gratuitous, unpremeditated, unplanned, extempore, impromptu, unrehearsed, knee-jerk (*inf*), spur-of-the-moment (*inf*). OPPOSITE: studied.

sporadic *adj* irregular, uneven, random, occasional, intermittent, fitful, erratic, spasmodic, infrequent, scattered, dispersed, isolated, separate. OPPOSITE: continuous.

sport *noun* **1** (*sport makes you fit*) physical activity, games, exercise, athletics. **2** (*he likes to mix work and sport*) play, recreation, amusement, pleasure, enjoyment, diversion, entertainment, pastime, fun. OPPOSITE: work. **3** (*they had some good sport with him*) fun, jesting, joking, kidding (*inf*), mirth, humour, banter, badinage, raillery, mockery, ridicule.

➤ *verb* **1** (*they sported for hours in the field*) frolic, gambol, frisk, romp, caper, cavort, play, disport, amuse oneself, divert oneself. **2** (*he sported a new jacket*) wear, display, show off, exhibit.

sporting *adj* sportsmanlike, fair, just, reasonable, decent, modest, considerate, generous, respectable, honourable, gentlemanly, ladylike.

sportive *adj* playful, gamesome, frolicsome, high-spirited, frisky, coltish, kittenish, skittish, mischievous, lively, sprightly, prankish, gay, merry, jaunty, rollicking. OPPOSITE: sedate.

spot *noun* **1** (*a spot of paint*) mark, dot, speckle, fleck, speck, stain, smudge, blot, splodge, splotch, splash, daub, patch, blotch. **2** (*a black spot on his record*) blemish, flaw, defect, brand, taint, stain. **3** (*a spot on his nose*) pimple, blackhead, boil, pustule. **4** (*a pleasant spot*) place, site, point, locality, locale, location, position, situation, setting, scene, area. **5** (*they found themselves in a tight spot*) predicament, mess, trouble, plight, fix (*inf*), hole (*inf*), scrape (*inf*), jam (*inf*), pickle (*inf*), quandary, difficulty. **6** (*a spot of lunch*) bite, morsel, smidgen, little, bit. **7** (*each comedian was allowed a ten-minute spot*) slot, niche, place, position, opening, time.

➤ *verb* **1** (*they spotted a figure on the horizon*) discern, detect, notice, make out, catch sight of, observe, espy, descry, see, recognize, identify. OPPOSITE: miss. **2** (*she spotted the paper with ink*) mark, dot, speckle, fleck, stain, blot. OPPOSITE: clean. **3** (*the metal was spotted with rust*) tarnish, taint, blemish, soil, sully, dirty.

spotless *adj* **1** (*spotless sheets*) unspotted, unmarked, unstained, unblemished, unsullied, untainted, immaculate, clean, spick and span, white, gleaming, shining. **2** (*a spotless reputation*) pure, chaste, virginal, innocent, blameless, unsullied, untouched, unblemished, stainless, untarnished, perfect, faultless, flawless, irreproachable. OPPOSITE: impure.

spotlight *noun* limelight, public eye, publicity, attention, fame, notoriety, emphasis, interest.

➤ *verb* highlight, illuminate, point up, emphasize, underline, stress, accentuate, feature, focus on, zero in on.

spotted *adj* dotted, spotty, mottled, dappled, speckled, flecked, brindled, pied, piebald, polka-dot.

spotty *adj* **1** (*a spotty young man*) pimply, pimpled, acned, blotchy. **2** (*a spotty dog*) spotted, mottled, dappled, pied, piebald. **3** (*spotty pyjamas*) spotted, dotted, flecked, speckled, polka-dot. **4** (*rather spotty coverage*) patchy, bitty, uneven, irregular, erratic, incomplete, inconsistent.

spouse *noun* husband, wife, consort, companion, partner, mate, better half (*inf*), other half (*inf*), old man (*inf*), old woman (*inf*).

spout *verb* **1** (*water spouted from the pipe*) gush, spurt, squirt, jet, shoot, spray, surge, stream, flow, pour, spew, disgorge, discharge, erupt. **2** (*the speaker spouted on for

hours) hold forth, go on, waffle (*inf*), rabbit (*inf*), witter (*inf*), speechify, pontificate, rant, orate, declaim, sermonize.

sprain *verb* wrench, twist, strain, rick.

sprawl *verb* **1** (*he sprawled over the sofa*) loll (*inf*), recline, repose, lounge (*inf*), slouch, slump, flop, stretch. **2** (*the convoy sprawled for miles*) spread, straggle, stretch, ramble, trail.

spray^1 *noun* **1** (*a spray of rain*) mist, drizzle, spindrift, foam, froth, spume, shower, jet. **2** (*she came to borrow her mother's spray*) sprinkler, atomizer, aerosol, vaporizer.

➤ *verb* **1** (*the gardener sprayed the flowers*) sprinkle, shower, atomize. **2** (*mud sprayed from the car's tyres*) spatter, splash, jet, spout, gush, scatter.

spray^2 *noun* sprig, shoot, bough, branch, posy, nosegay, bouquet, garland, wreath, corsage.

spread *verb* **1** (*the stain spread rapidly*) stretch, extend, widen, broaden, expand, enlarge, sprawl, dilate, swell, mushroom, develop, increase, advance, escalate, proliferate. **2** (*spread the map out on the table*) unfold, unfurl, unroll, open out, lay out, arrange. OPPOSITE: fold. **3** (*spread the good news*) disseminate, distribute, circulate, broadcast, communicate, promulgate, propagate, publicize, publish, advertise, scatter, strew, sow, disperse, shed, radiate, diffuse. OPPOSITE: suppress. **4** (*spread plaster on the wall*) apply, daub, smear, plaster, coat, cover, lay, put.

➤ *noun* **1** (*the spread of his influence*) extent, expanse, stretch, reach, span, sweep, compass, range. **2** (*the spread of the rumour*) dissemination, dispersion, diffusion, radiation, transmission, broadcasting, communication, distribution, circulation, propagation. **3** (*the spread of the crisis*) escalation, development, advance, increase, growth, swelling, mushrooming, expansion, proliferation. **4** (*they put on a good spread*) feast, banquet, repast, meal, dinner, blow-out (*inf*).

spree *noun* fling, bout, revel, binge (*inf*), bender (*inf*), splurge (*inf*), orgy, debauch, carouse, romp, lark (*inf*).

sprig *noun* spray, twig, branch, bough, stem, shoot.

sprightly *adj* spry, agile, nimble, brisk, active, energetic, vital, jaunty, airy, lively, animated, spirited, vivacious, gay, buoyant, jocose, jolly, merry, blithe, perky (*inf*), cheerful, hearty, playful, light-hearted, frolicsome, sportive. OPPOSITE: lifeless.

spring *verb* **1** (*she sprang over the wall*) jump, leap, bound, vault, hop, skip. **2** (*all kinds of new ideas sprang from this discovery*) start, begin, commence, rise, arise, issue, appear, emanate, flow, emerge, proceed, grow, develop, originate, derive, stem, descend. OPPOSITE: end. **3** (*you shouldn't have sprung the news on her like that*) land, drop, reveal, tell.

➤ *noun* **1** (*a sudden spring in the air*) jump, leap, bound, bounce, vault, hop, skip. **2** (*the spring of the mattress*) elasticity, flexibility, resilience, springiness, bounce, bounciness, buoyancy, give (*inf*). **3** (*a spring in his step*) briskness, liveliness, spirit, energy, animation, cheerfulness, light-heartedness. **4** (*the spring of his inspiration*) well, fountainhead, wellspring, wellhead, fount, source, origin, root, basis, beginning, cause.

spring up appear, develop, sprout, proliferate,

mushroom, burgeon, shoot up, grow, develop. OPPOSITE: disappear.

springy *adj* bouncy, elastic, stretchy, rubbery, flexible, resilient, spongy, tensile.

sprinkle *verb* **1** (*he sprinkled water on the plant*) spray, shower, trickle, spatter, splash. **2** (*sprinkle flour on the bread*) scatter, strew, dust, powder, dredge, dot, pepper.

sprinkling *noun* **1** (*a sprinkling of snow*) sprinkle, scattering, dusting, smattering, touch, trace. **2** (*a sprinkling of spectators*) handful, trickle, few.

sprint *verb* race, run, rush, dash, fly, career, tear (*inf*), belt (*inf*), hare (*inf*), scoot (*inf*).

sprite *noun* elf, brownie, fairy, pixie, goblin, leprechaun, nymph, dryad, spirit.

sprout *verb* **1** (*the plant should sprout in the spring*) bud, burgeon, germinate, shoot. OPPOSITE: wither. **2** (*new rock groups sprouted up all over the place*) spring up, shoot up, appear, emerge, develop.

spruce *adj* smart, elegant, well-dressed, well-groomed, well-turned-out, trim, natty (*inf*), snazzy (*inf*), cool (*inf*), dapper, chic, neat, tidy. OPPOSITE: untidy.

spry *adj* brisk, nimble, agile, nippy (*inf*), active, lively, sprightly, energetic, quick, alert, ready. OPPOSITE: sluggish.

spur *noun* **1** (*he used his spurs on the horse*) goad, prick, prod. **2** (*a spur to do better*) stimulus, stimulant, motive, motivation, incentive, inducement, incitement, encouragement, impetus, prompt, urge. OPPOSITE: deterrent.
➤ *verb* **1** (*she spurred the horse on*) goad, prick, prod. **2** (*this news spurred him to act*) goad, prod, prick, poke, prompt, push, press, drive, propel, impel, stimulate, animate, incite, motivate, provoke, induce, urge, encourage. OPPOSITE: deter.
on the spur of the moment on impulse, impulsively, impetuously, spontaneously, impromptu, on the spot (*inf*), out of the blue (*inf*), all of a sudden, suddenly, unpremeditatedly, unexpectedly.

spurious *adj* false, unreal, counterfeit, fake, forged, fraudulent, deceitful, phoney (*inf*), bogus, fictitious, mock, sham, simulated, feigned, contrived, pretended, make-believe (*inf*), artificial, imitation, specious. OPPOSITE: genuine.

spurn *verb* reject, rebuff, repulse, repudiate, turn down, turn away, cold-shoulder (*inf*), ignore, disregard, snub, slight, scorn, despise, condemn, contemn, disdain. OPPOSITE: respect.

spurt *verb* gush, spout, squirt, spray, jet, shoot, issue, burst, erupt, surge, pour, stream, well.
➤ *noun* **1** (*a spurt of water*) gush, spout, squirt, spray, jet, stream, burst, surge, eruption, outpouring, welling. **2** (*a spurt of energy*) burst, outburst, rush, surge, spate, fit, increase, access.

spy *noun* agent, secret agent, double agent, fifth columnist, snooper, mole (*inf*), informer, detective, scout.
➤ *verb* watch, observe, see, espy, descry, discern, make out, spot, glimpse, detect, notice. OPPOSITE: miss.
spy on observe, watch, keep under surveillance, shadow, tail (*inf*), follow, keep an eye on, keep tabs on.

squabble *verb* quarrel, row, altercate, contend, bicker, wrangle, argue, dispute, clash, fight, scrap (*inf*), brawl. OPPOSITE: agree.
➤ *noun* quarrel, row, altercation, contention, disagreement, argument, dispute, barney (*inf*), wrangle, fight, tiff (*inf*), clash. OPPOSITE: agreement.

squad *noun* **1** (*a squad of workers*) band, gang, crew, team, group. **2** (*a squad of soldiers*) company, platoon, troop, unit, force.

squalid *adj* **1** (*the children were in a squalid state*) foul, filthy, unclean, dirty, mucky, grimy, grubby. OPPOSITE: clean. **2** (*squalid surroundings*) grotty (*inf*), sleazy (*inf*), sordid, dingy, seedy, run-down, broken-down, ramshackle, dilapidated, neglected, decayed, slovenly, untidy, unkempt. **3** (*a squalid tale*) disgusting, repulsive, nasty, sordid, obscene, offensive, unpleasant, vile, disgraceful, shameful.

squall *noun* gust, blast, blow, wind, gale, hurricane, storm, tempest.
➤ *verb* cry, bawl, yell, shriek, scream, howl, wail, yowl, moan, groan.

squalor *noun* squalidness, filthiness, filth, dirtiness, dirt, grime, griminess, grubbiness, grottiness (*inf*), muckiness, foulness, uncleanness, dinginess, sleaziness (*inf*), neglect, decay, meanness, wretchedness.

squander *verb* waste, dissipate, spend, blow (*inf*), fritter away, throw away, lavish, splurge, misuse, misspend. OPPOSITE: save.

square *noun* **1** (*the walls formed a square*) rectangle, quadrilateral, cube. OPPOSITE: circle. **2** (*the village square*) place, plaza, piazza, quadrangle, quad (*inf*).
➤ *adj* **1** (*a square block*) rectangular, quadrilateral, right-angled. **2** (*check the planks are square*) perpendicular, straight, true, level, even, equal, balanced. OPPOSITE: uneven. **3** (*her square opinion*) fair, just, honest, straightforward. OPPOSITE: dishonest. **4** (*a square taste in music*) conservative, traditionalist, conventional, strait-laced, old-fashioned, stuffy, fuddy-duddy (*inf*), bourgeois. OPPOSITE: avant-garde.
➤ *verb* **1** (*square the timber against the wall*) straighten, level, align, regulate, adjust. **2** (*difficult to square the two aims*) reconcile, tally, accommodate, balance, harmonize, conform, tailor, fit, adapt, accord, suit. **3** (*square their debts*) settle, pay, discharge, liquidate, satisfy.

squash *verb* **1** (*squash the oranges*) crush, squeeze, press, mash, pulp, compress, flatten, pulverize, trample, pound, grind. **2** (*squash any protests*) suppress, put down, quash, quell, crush, silence, humiliate.

squat *verb* crouch, kneel, stoop, hunch, bend, sit, cower. OPPOSITE: stand.
➤ *adj* short, squab, dumpy, stubby, chunky, stout, stocky, thickset, broad, tubby, fat. OPPOSITE: lanky.

squeak *verb* creak, whine, squeal, yelp, peep, cheep, pipe.
➤ *noun* creak, whine, squeal, yelp, peep, cheep, pipe.

squeal *verb* **1** (*she squealed with pain*) cry, shout, wail, yell, howl, squall, squeak, yelp, shriek, screech, scream. **2** (*he squealed to the authorities*) inform, tell tales, split (*inf*), rat (*inf*), snitch (*inf*), grass (*inf*).

➤ *noun* cry, shout, wail, yell, howl, squall, squeak, yelp, shriek, screech, scream.

squeamish *adj* queasy, nauseous, nauseated, sick, delicate, dainty, finicky, particular, fastidious, punctilious, scrupulous, prudish, strait-laced.

squeeze *verb* **1** (*squeeze the fruit*) press, compress, squash, crush, pulp, mash. **2** (*squeeze the water out of the towel*) wring, wrest, extract, force, press, twist. **3** (*she squeezed his arm*) pinch, nip, constrict, grip, clasp, clutch. **4** (*he squeezed her against him*) hug, embrace, enfold, cuddle. **4** (*the mob squeezed into the hall*) crowd, jam, wedge, pack, cram, crush, squash, stuff, ram, push, thrust, shove, force, jostle.
➤ *noun* **1** (*she gave the child a squeeze*) hug, embrace, cuddle. **2** (*he gave her hand a squeeze*) clasp, grip, clutch, grasp, hold. **3** (*it was a squeeze getting all the luggage in*) squash, crush, press, jam, crowd, congestion.

squirm *verb* writhe, wriggle, wiggle, fidget, squiggle, flounder, twist, turn, shift, move.

squirt *verb* spout, spray, spurt, gush, surge, jet, shoot, stream, well, pour, spew, emit, eject, expel, ejaculate, discharge, issue.
➤ *noun* spout, spray, spurt, gush, surge, jet, stream, discharge.

stab *verb* pierce, puncture, knife, spear, slash, bayonet, stick, skewer, run through, gore, transfix, cut, wound, hurt, injure, jab, thrust.
➤ *noun* ɪ (*he sustained a stab in the arm*) wound, injury, cut, incision, gash, slash, jab, puncture, thrust. **2** (*a stab of pain*) pang, twinge, prick, ache, throb, spasm. **3** (*let her have another stab at it*) try, attempt, endeavour, venture, effort, go (*inf*), bash (*inf*), crack (*inf*), shot (*inf*), whirl (*inf*).
stab in the back betray, double-cross, let down, sell out, sell down the river (*inf*), inform on, deceive, slander.

stability *noun* **1** (*the stability of the foundations*) secureness, soundness, firmness, solidity, strength, sturdiness, steadiness, fastness, stoutness. **2** (*the stability of his home life*) regularity, constancy, steadiness, unchangeability, uniformity, reliability, dependability, durability.

stable *adj* **1** (*a stable footing*) firm, steady, fast, fixed, anchored, immovable, sound, strong, sturdy, solid, secure, sure, reliable. **2** (*a stable relationship*) secure, steady, steadfast, solid, firm, sure, established, deep-rooted, well-founded, well-grounded, durable, enduring, abiding, permanent, lasting, long-lasting, long-lived, dependable, reliable, immutable, invariable, unwavering, unfaltering, unswerving, unalterable, perpetual. OPPOSITE: unstable. **3** (*the economy is in a stable condition*) constant, unchanging, steady, regular, uniform.

stack *noun* **1** (*a stack of clean laundry*) pile, heap, mound, mountain, mass, load, hoard, store, stockpile, accumulation, collection. **2** (*a stack of money*) load, lot, ton (*inf*), heap (*inf*), pile (*inf*), oodles (*inf*).
➤ *verb* pile, heap, load, amass, assemble, accumulate, hoard, gather, stockpile.

stadium *noun* sports ground, ground, arena, sports field, field, pitch, bowl, track, ring.

staff *noun* **1** (*the staff were given the day off*) employees, personnel, workers, workforce, teachers, officers, team, crew. **2** (*he carried a stout staff*) stick, cane, rod, pole, stave, club, crook, baton, wand, crutch, prop, support.
➤ *verb* man, people, work, operate, occupy, equip, furnish, fit out, provide, supply.

stage *noun* **1** (*at this late stage of the project*) point, juncture, period. **2** (*the next stage of the competition*) phase, lap, leg, step, level. **3** (*the speaker stood on a small stage*) platform, dais, rostrum, podium, stand, apron. **4** (*the stage was complete in time for the first production*) scene, setting, backdrop, background, arena.
➤ *verb* **1** (*stage a new play*) produce, present, give, do, put on, mount, perform, direct, put together, lay on. **2** (*stage a protest*) mount, arrange, organize, orchestrate, engineer.
the stage theatre, drama, dramatics, theatrics, the boards (*inf*), the footlights (*inf*), show business.

stagger *verb* **1** (*he staggered out of the house*) totter, wobble, reel, sway, lurch, pitch, teeter, rock, roll. **2** (*they were staggered by the scale of the building*) astound, astonish, amaze, flabbergast (*inf*), bowl over (*inf*), dumbfound, stupefy, surprise, nonplus (*inf*), confound, overwhelm, bewilder, stun, shake, shock, take aback.

stagnant *adj* **1** (*stagnant water*) brackish, foul, stale, filthy, smelly, putrid, putrefied, polluted, standing, static, inert, still, quiet, motionless. OPPOSITE: flowing. **2** (*a stagnant market*) quiet, dull, sluggish, slow, slow-moving, inactive, lethargic, torpid.

stagnate *verb* **1** (*the water in the pool had stagnated*) stand, vegetate, fester, putrefy, decay, rot. **2** (*industry is stagnating*) languish, die, dormant, deteriorate, decline, degenerate. **3** (*he stagnates all day in front of the telly*) languish, vegetate, idle, laze, loaf.

staid *adj* sedate, composed, calm, sober, serious, grave, solemn, quiet, settled, steady, demure, prim, proper, decorous, stiff, starchy, formal. OPPOSITE: frivolous.

stain *verb* **1** (*the ink stained the cloth*) mark, spot, discolour, soil, dirty, sully, blot, blotch. **2** (*stain the wood darker*) dye, tint, colour, tinge, paint, varnish. **3** (*the scandal stained his reputation*) smear, tarnish, blacken, blemish, taint, contaminate, defile, corrupt, disgrace, damage, injure.
➤ *noun* **1** (*a stain on the material*) mark, spot, blot, blotch, smear, smudge, splodge, discoloration. **2** (*she used a red stain on the curtains*) dye, tint. **3** (*a stain on her character*) blemish, taint, stigma, slur, smear, shame, disgrace, dishonour, damage, injury.

stake[1] *noun* (*tied to a stake*) pale, picket, palisade, stick, spike, post, pole, rod.
➤ *verb* **1** (*stake the rose to the wall*) tether, tie, fasten, secure, prop, support, brace. **2** (*stake a claim to the money*) lay claim to, declare, state, demand, establish.
stake out demarcate, mark out, outline, define, separate off, circumscribe, delimit.

stake[2] *noun* **1** (*a stake in the race*) bet, wager, ante (*inf*), pledge. **2** (*he staked everything he had on the outcome*) venture, risk, hazard, chance. **3** (*a large stake in the company*) interest, concern, share, involvement, investment.

➤ **verb** bet, wager, gamble, hazard, pledge, chance, risk, venture, imperil, jeopardize.

stakes pl noun **1** (*an entrant in the presidential stakes*) contest, race, competition. **2** (*play for high stakes*) prize, winnings, money, purse.

stale adj **1** (*stale cheese*) old, musty, fusty, hard, dry, flat, insipid, tasteless, mouldy, off (*inf*). OPPOSITE: fresh. **2** (*a stale joke*) trite, banal, insipid, hackneyed, clichéd, platitudinous, stock, run-of-the-mill (*inf*), stereotyped, overused, corny, tired, worn-out, jaded, commonplace, unoriginal, uninspired, dull, flat.

stalemate noun deadlock, impasse, standstill, halt, stand-off, draw, tie.

stalk verb **1** (*a fox stalking its prey*) hunt, track, trail, shadow, follow, pursue, chase. **2** (*he stalked angrily out of the court*) strut, stride, pace, march, walk, flounce. OPPOSITE: slink.

stall noun **1** (*market stall*) stand, booth, kiosk, table, counter. **2** (*a stall for animals*) cubicle, pen, coop, stable, enclosure, compartment.
➤ **verb** **1** (*the car stalled at the junction*) stop, halt, stick, get stuck. **2** (*she tried to stall the policeman's entrance*) delay, hold up, put off, postpone, hedge, equivocate, prevaricate, play for time, obstruct.

stalwart adj **1** (*a stalwart physique*) sturdy, stout, rugged, athletic, muscular, robust, strapping, lusty, brawny, burly, hardy, strong. OPPOSITE: weak. **2** (*he proved to be a stalwart ally*) staunch, trusty, faithful, devoted, committed, loyal, steadfast, steady, firm, reliable, dependable, resolute, determined, vigorous, brave, valiant, intrepid, indomitable, courageous, bold, daring.

stamina noun strength, vitality, energy, vigour, fortitude, grit (*inf*), endurance, resistance, resilience, indefatigability, power, force. OPPOSITE: weakness.

stammer verb stutter, splutter, falter, hesitate, pause, stumble, gibber, babble, mumble, lisp.
➤ **noun** stutter, speech impediment, speech defect.

stamp verb **1** (*the emperor stamped on the beetle*) tread, step, tramp, stomp (*inf*), trample, crush, squash, beat, pound, pulp, mash. **2** (*stamp the company logo on the product*) mark, brand, label, characterize, impress, imprint, print, inscribe, engrave, emboss. **3** (*he was stamped for life as a failure*) label, brand, fix, categorize, designate, characterize, identify, style, term, tag, name, dub.
➤ **noun** **1** (*the stamp of quality*) mark, brand, seal, label, tag, print, imprint, impression, hallmark, signature. **2** (*a different stamp of customer*) mould, cast, sort, kind, cut, type, variety, breed, character, description, form, fashion.

stamp out quell, suppress, crush, put down, eliminate, eradicate, extirpate, destroy, kill, quench, extinguish.

stampede noun rush, charge, flight, onrush, rout, scattering.
➤ **verb** charge, rush, fly, flee, take flight, race, dash, run, tear, shoot, sprint, gallop, scatter.

stance noun position, stand, standpoint, viewpoint, point of view, opinion, attitude, posture, bearing, deportment, carriage, policy, angle, slant, line.

stand verb **1** (*he stood up from the chair*) rise, get up, straighten up, be erect. **2** (*stand the broom in the corner*) place, put, position, set, up-end, erect. **3** (*the traffic was standing at the lights*) stop, halt, pause, rest, stay, abide. **4** (*he could stand the pain no longer*) bear, tolerate, endure, suffer, experience, abide, cope with, live with, brook, undergo, withstand, resist, put up with, stomach (*inf*). **5** (*the record stands*) hold, persist, continue, remain, prevail.
➤ **noun** **1** (*they took a principled stand*) standpoint, stance, attitude, position, opinion, viewpoint, point of view, policy, line. **2** (*the parade came to a stand*) stop, stoppage, halt, standstill, rest, stay. OPPOSITE: motion. **3** (*put the plate back on its stand*) base, frame, support, rack, shelf, pedestal, platform, stall, station, post, place. **4** (*put up a stand against prejudice*) opposition, resistance, defiance. OPPOSITE: submission.

stand by defend, side with, uphold, support, back, champion, stand up for (*inf*), stick up for (*inf*), stick by. OPPOSITE: abandon.

stand for 1 (*that badge stands for justice*) represent, symbolize, exemplify, betoken, denote, mean, indicate. **2** (*I will not stand for cruelty*) tolerate, bear, endure, brook, stomach (*inf*), put up with (*inf*), countenance, permit, allow. OPPOSITE: oppose.

stand in for substitute for, deputize for, understudy, replace, cover for, take the place of, hold the fort for (*inf*).

stand out 1 (*he really stands out from the others*) be prominent, be conspicuous, show, catch the eye (*inf*). **2** (*the mountain stood out on the horizon*) project, stick out, jut out, poke out, extend, project.

stand up hold up, hold water, stand, wash (*inf*).

stand up to defy, resist, withstand, endure, oppose, challenge, face up to, face, brave, confront.

standard noun **1** (*she set the standard we all have to follow*) model, pattern, example, exemplar, paradigm, sample, type, gauge, measure, criterion, yardstick, guide, guideline, benchmark, touchstone, scale, rule, principle, requirement, specification, norm, average. **2** (*he achieved a reasonable standard*) quality, level, grade. **3** (*follow the king's standard*) flag, banner, ensign, pennant, pennon, streamer, colours. **4** (*I have my standards*) principle, moral, scruple, ethic, ideal, code.
➤ **adj** **1** (*a standard procedure*) typical, average, regular, common, normal, usual, ordinary, customary, habitual, conventional, prevailing, stock, set, fixed, orthodox. OPPOSITE: irregular. **2** (*the standard work on the subject*) definitive, authoritative, classic, established, official, approved, accepted, recognized, basic, staple, universal.

standardize verb equalize, normalize, systematize, regulate, regularize, homogenize, stereotype, regiment.

stand-in noun deputy, second, substitute, understudy, proxy, delegate, representative, surrogate, locum.

standing noun **1** (*high standing in the community*) rank, ranking, status, seniority, eminence, position, place, station, footing, reputation, repute, credit, estimation, note. **2** (*a friendship of long standing*) duration, endurance, existence, continuance.
➤ **adj** **1** (*a standing stone*) upright, vertical, perpendicular, erect, up-ended. OPPOSITE: horizontal. **2** (*a standing army*) perpetual, permanent, regular, fixed,

constant. **3** (*pools of standing water*) static, still, motionless, stagnant.

standpoint *noun* viewpoint, point of view, opinion, perspective, vantage point, frame of reference, stance, position, station, angle, slant.

standstill *noun* stop, stoppage, dead stop, halt, stand, cessation, pause, lull, rest, hold-up, impasse, jam, log-jam, stalemate, deadlock.

staple *adj* basic, fundamental, standard, foremost, essential, important, indispensable, vital, necessary, principal, chief, key, main, chief, major, primary. OPPOSITE: minor.

star *noun* **1** (*the stars twinkled*) heavenly body, celestial body, sun, moon, planet, sphere, asteroid, satellite. **2** (*a star of the modern stage*) celebrity, personage, superstar, big name (*inf*), household name (*inf*), leading light (*inf*), luminary, idol. **3** (*the star of the film*) lead, leading man, leading woman, principal.
➤ *adj* celebrated, famous, well-known, renowned, distinguished, pre-eminent, eminent, prominent, brilliant, talented, gifted, great, illustrious, paramount, leading, principal, major, chief.

starchy *adj* stiff, formal, prim, stuffy, strait-laced, conventional, precise, punctilious. OPPOSITE: liberal.

stare *verb* **1** (*he stared at her*) gaze, gape, goggle, gawk (*inf*), gawp (*inf*), look, watch, glare. **2** (*the answer stared them in the face*) be blatant, be conspicuous, stick out a mile (*inf*), glare. OPPOSITE: ignore.
➤ *noun* gaze, goggle, gawk (*inf*), gawp (*inf*), look, glare.

stark *adj* **1** (*stark terror*) absolute, sheer, arrant, downright, out-and-out, thorough, utter, complete, total, unmitigated, unqualified, pure, mere, outright, flagrant, consummate. **2** (*stark reality*) plain, simple, blunt, bald, harsh, grim, severe, unembellished, unadorned, undecorated. **3** (*stark surroundings*) bare, barren, bleak, empty, desolate, forsaken, grim, dreary, gloomy, depressing, harsh, severe, austere.
➤ *adv* absolutely, utterly, quite, altogether, totally, entirely, completely, wholly, fully, clean. OPPOSITE: partially.

start *verb* **1** (*the programme starts at six*) begin, commence, get under way, kick off (*inf*). **2** (*she started for the station shortly after*) depart, set off, leave. **3** (*a new rebellion started*) appear, arise, issue, originate, crop up. **4** (*start a new initiative*) inaugurate, found, establish, set up, institute, initiate, activate, pioneer, open, launch, embark on, create, instigate, set in motion, turn on, trigger. OPPOSITE: finish. **5** (*the child started at the noise*) jump, flinch, wince, twitch, jerk, shy, shrink, recoil, leap.
➤ *noun* **1** (*the start of the project*) beginning, commencement, launch, opening, outset, onset, kick-off (*inf*), dawn, birth, inception, inauguration, origin, source, foundation, initiation, introduction, institution. OPPOSITE: end. **2** (*they have a good start on their rivals*) lead, advantage, head start. **3** (*a start in life*) chance, opportunity, break (*inf*), opening. **4** (*she gave a start at his appearance*) jump, leap, twitch, jerk, flinch, wince, spasm, convulsion, fit.

startle *verb* surprise, take aback, alarm, scare, frighten, shock, amaze, astound, astonish, agitate, disturb, perturb, unsettle, upset. OPPOSITE: compose.

startling *adj* surprising, remarkable, extraordinary, astonishing, astounding, shocking, disturbing, perturbing, staggering, electrifying, alarming, dramatic, sudden, unexpected, unforeseen.

starvation *noun* hunger, malnutrition, famine, fasting, undernourishment.

starve *verb* hunger, fast, be famished, be ravenous. OPPOSITE: gorge.

starving *adj* hungry, underfed, undernourished, famished, ravenous.

state *noun* **1** (*the present state of affairs*) condition, situation, position, juncture, circumstances, shape, form, case, plight, predicament, crisis. **2** (*his mother is in a real state*) panic, flap (*inf*), fluster (*inf*), tizzy (*inf*), bother, nerves. **3** (*the queen entered in state*) pomp, ceremony, grandeur, magnificence, splendour, glory, majesty, dignity. **4** (*an independent state*) nation, country, land, republic, commonwealth, realm, kingdom, territory, federation. **5** (*affairs of state*) government, parliament, administration, politics.
➤ *verb* say, tell, express, articulate, utter, voice, declare, communicate, assert, asseverate, aver, affirm, avow, maintain, profess, announce, proclaim, disclose, reveal, divulge, report, specify, set out, put. OPPOSITE: suppress.

stately *adj* pompous, grand, magnificent, splendid, elegant, graceful, glorious, august, dignified, solemn, imposing, impressive, lofty, majestic, regal, royal, imperial, noble. OPPOSITE: lowly.

statement *noun* declaration, announcement, proclamation, utterance, assertion, asseveration, averment, avowal, disclosure, divulgence, testimony, account, report, record, bulletin, communiqué, communication, presentation.

static *adj* stationary, still, motionless, unmoving, immobile, fixed, inert, resting, unchanging, changeless, unvarying, undeviating, constant, steady, stable.

station *noun* **1** (*bus station*) depot, terminus, stop, halt. **2** (*police station*) headquarters, base, post, office. **3** (*he took up his station on the wing*) place, post, position, location, situation, site. **4** (*one's station in life*) status, standing, position, level, rank, class, condition, grade, degree.
➤ *verb* post, assign, appoint, place, locate, fix, set, establish, install, garrison. OPPOSITE: move.

stationary *adj* motionless, still, unmoving, static, immobile, immovable, fixed, moored, parked.

statue *noun* sculpture, bronze, carving, figure, figurine, statuette, bust, head, effigy, idol, image, representation.

statuesque *adj* imposing, impressive, magnificent, dignified, stately, majestic, regal, noble, well-proportioned.

stature *noun* **1** (*of more than average stature*) height, tallness, elevation, loftiness, size. **2** (*a figure of some stature in contemporary music*) eminence, prominence, prestige, reputation, fame, renown, rank, standing, consequence, importance, weight.

status *noun* **1** (*he enjoys some status among his equals*) importance, consequence, weight, prestige, reputation, repute, eminence, distinction, standing. **2** (*she has been promoted to a higher status*) station, position, condition, rank, degree, level, grade, class.

statute *noun* decree, edict, act, enactment, law, ordinance, rule, regulation.

staunch *adj* loyal, faithful, devoted, committed, constant, true, trusty, trustworthy, reliable, dependable, steady, steadfast, firm, sound, sure, unwavering, unswerving, stout, hearty, resolute, strong. OPPOSITE: wavering.

stave off *verb* avert, evade, dodge, ward off, fend off, avoid, parry, foil, deflect, turn aside, repel, repulse, rebuff, keep at bay, keep back.

stay¹ *verb* **1** (*stay where you are*) remain, wait, stay put, keep, continue, abide, linger, loiter, pause, rest, delay, tarry, endure, persist, last. **2** (*we stayed in a hostel*) lodge, stop, put up, board, sojourn, rest, halt, visit, settle, live, reside, dwell. OPPOSITE: move. **3** (*the court stayed judgement*) defer, delay, suspend, postpone, put off, hold over, adjourn, reprieve, prorogue. OPPOSITE: hasten. **4** (*stay one's hand*) restrain, control, check, curb, arrest, halt, stop, prevent, block, obstruct, hinder, impede.
➤ *noun* **1** (*a brief stay at the seaside*) sojourn, visit, holiday, vacation, rest, stop, stopover, halt, pause. **2** (*a stay of execution*) postponement, deferment, remission, suspension, wait, delay, reprieve, adjournment.

stay² *noun* prop, support, brace, buttress, stanchion, reinforcement.

steadfast *adj* **1** (*a steadfast gaze*) steady, fixed, implacable, unflinching, intent, firm, unfaltering, unwavering, unswerving, persevering. OPPOSITE: wavering. **2** (*a steadfast ally*) resolute, constant, loyal, faithful, dedicated, staunch, stout-hearted, sturdy, dependable, reliable, stable, established.

steady *adj* **1** (*a steady grip*) sure, firm, solid, secure, safe, sound, unshaking, unwavering, unfaltering. **2** (*the ship remained steady at anchor*) motionless, unmoving, poised, fixed, immovable, balanced, well-balanced, stable. **3** (*a steady character*) stable, steadfast, level-headed, balanced, well-balanced, self-controlled, controlled, reliable, dependable, sensible, rational, serious, settled, down-to-earth, calm, imperturbable, sober, unexcitable, unflappable (*inf*), equable. OPPOSITE: unsteady. **4** (*a steady tread*) even, regular, rhythmic, uniform, consistent. OPPOSITE: irregular. **5** (*the steady drip of a tap*) constant, continual, continuous, perpetual, persistent, ceaseless, unceasing, endless, unending, unremitting, unchanging, changeless, unvarying, invariable, undeviating, unbroken.
➤ *verb* **1** (*he steadied himself against the motion*) brace, balance, stabilize, secure, fix, support. **2** (*she steadied her mount*) check, restrain, control, calm, settle, compose, subdue, still, tranquillize, soothe, relax.

steal *verb* **1** (*steal some money*) thieve, rob, take, snatch, swipe, pocket, pilfer, purloin, filch, shoplift, nick (*inf*), pinch (*inf*), knock off (*inf*), make off with (*inf*), run off with (*inf*), walk off with (*inf*), embezzle, peculate, appropriate, misappropriate, plagiarize, poach. OPPOSITE: return. **2** (*she stole into the children's room*) creep, tiptoe, slip, slide, slink, slither, sneak.

stealing *noun* **1** (*guilty of stealing from supermarkets*)

theft, thieving, pilfering, pinching (*inf*), nicking (*inf*), swiping (*inf*), filching (*inf*), robbery, shoplifting, burglary, larceny, embezzlement, misappropriation. **2** (*the stealing of another's idea*) plagiarism, plagiarizing, copying, lifting (*inf*), cribbing (*inf*), appropriation, misappropriation, poaching, piracy.

stealth *noun* stealthiness, furtiveness, surreptitiousness, covertness, unobtrusiveness, shadiness, secrecy, slyness, sneakiness, clandestineness.

stealthy *adj* furtive, sly, cunning, surreptitious, sneaky, shady, underhand, clandestine, unobtrusive, covert, undercover, secret, secretive, quiet. OPPOSITE: open.

steam *noun* **1** (*steam from the kettle*) vapour, mist, haze, fog, condensation, moisture, smoke, fume, exhalation. **2** (*the play ran out of steam towards the end*) energy, liveliness, vitality, vigour, activity, enthusiasm, eagerness, stamina, power, force.
steam up mist, mist up, fog up.
get steamed up lose one's cool (*inf*), boil over (*inf*), fly into a rage (*inf*), get angry, get agitated, get annoyed, get flustered, get excited.
under one's own steam independently, alone, by oneself, without help, unaided, unassisted.

steamy *adj* **1** (*steamy weather*) humid, muggy, sticky, steaming, close, damp, moist, sweaty, sultry, hot, boiling, sweltering, misty, hazy. **2** (*a steamy novel*) erotic, sexy (*inf*), raunchy (*inf*), blue (*inf*), passionate, tempestuous, sensuous, sensual, lustful, amorous, seductive.

steel *verb* brace, fortify, toughen, harden, nerve, prepare. OPPOSITE: relax.

steely *adj* **1** (*a steely grey colour*) grey, steel-coloured, steel-grey, iron-grey, blue-grey. **2** (*steely determination*) firm, resolute, strong, determined, hard, harsh, unwavering, unfaltering, unyielding, inflexible, pitiless, merciless, undaunted.

steep¹ *adj* **1** (*a steep drop*) sheer, abrupt, precipitous, vertical, perpendicular, headlong, sudden, sharp. OPPOSITE: gradual. **2** (*a steep price*) unreasonable, extreme, excessive, extortionate, inordinate, unwarranted, exorbitant, costly, dear, expensive, overpriced, high, stiff, uncalled-for, over the top (*inf*). OPPOSITE: moderate.

steep² *verb* **1** (*steep in brandy*) soak, marinate, pickle, macerate, souse, drench, immerse, submerge, saturate. OPPOSITE: dry. **2** (*a house steeped in history*) soak, drench, suffuse, immerse, imbue, impregnate, permeate, pervade, infuse, fill.

steeple *noun* spire, tower, belfry, campanile, turret, minaret.

steer *verb* pilot, guide, direct, control, conduct, navigate, cox, lead, usher, drive.
steer clear of shun, eschew, avoid, evade, dodge (*inf*), skirt, circumvent, bypass.

stem¹ *noun* stalk, trunk, branch, shaft, stock.
➤ *verb* arise, come, issue, emanate, flow, spring, originate, derive, develop.

stem² *verb* stop, halt, arrest, stay, check, curb, block, hold back, restrain, resist, oppose, contain, dam, staunch.

stench *noun* stink, smell, odour, whiff (*inf*), reek, pong (*inf*), niff (*inf*), fetor, mephitis, effluvium. OPPOSITE: perfume.

stentorian *adj* loud, strong, thundering, thunderous, booming, ringing, deafening, powerful, reverberating, resonant, sonorous, full, vibrant, strident. OPPOSITE: soft.

step *noun* **1** (*he took a step backwards*) pace, stride. **2** (*the step of a child outside the door*) footstep, footfall, footprint, track, gait, tread, tramp, walk. **3** (*the next step in the procedure*) phase, stage, move, action, act, deed, proceeding, process, progression, advance, measure, manoeuvre, development, movement, effort. **4** (*she walked down the steps*) stair, rung, tread. **5** (*he is one step above the others*) rank, degree, grade, level, stage, phase.
» *verb* move, walk, stride, pace, tread, stamp, advance, progress, proceed.
in step in harmony, in unison, in agreement, together.
out of step at odds, at loggerheads, in disagreement.
step by step bit by bit, gradually, progressively, slowly.
step down stand down, resign, withdraw, quit, abdicate, retire, leave.
step in intervene, interfere, interrupt, intrude, intercede, mediate, arbitrate, take a hand.
step up increase, raise, augment, build up, boost, escalate, accelerate, speed up, intensify. OPPOSITE: reduce.

stereotyped *adj* stereotypical, typecast, conventional, stock, unoriginal, standardized, standard, clichéd, platitudinous, hackneyed, corny, overused, stale, tired, threadbare, banal, trite.

sterile *adj* **1** (*a sterile landscape*) barren, infertile, unprolific, unfruitful, fruitless, unproductive, empty, bare, arid. **2** (*a sterile woman*) infertile, barren, infecund. **3** (*a sterile effort*) futile, unprofitable, abortive, ineffectual, pointless, useless. OPPOSITE: fruitful. **4** (*sterile medical instruments*) sterilized, disinfected, clean, germ-free, germless, antiseptic, aseptic, uncontaminated, pure.

sterility *noun* **1** (*she is receiving treatment for sterility*) infertility, barrenness, infecundity, impotence. **2** (*the sterility of government policy*) futility, uselessness, abortiveness, worthlessness, ineffectiveness, inefficacy, pointlessness, fruitlessness. **3** (*the sterility of the maternity ward*) cleanliness, purity, disinfection, sterileness, asepticism.

sterilize *noun* **1** (*sterilize the operating theatre*) disinfect, clean, cleanse, purify, fumigate. **2** (*the dog will be sterilized*) neuter, castrate, spay, fix (*inf*), doctor, geld, emasculate, vasectomize.

sterling *adj* **1** (*sterling quality*) genuine, true, real, sound, solid, pure, reliable, faithful, loyal, dependable, trustworthy. OPPOSITE: specious. **2** (*a sterling effort*) excellent, great, first-class, first-rate, superlative, outstanding, splendid, exceptional.

stern[1] *adj* **1** (*a stern attitude*) strict, severe, harsh, hard, rigid, firm, adamant, rigorous, stringent, exacting, demanding, inflexible, unyielding, uncompromising, relentless, inexorable, grim, cruel, relentless, unsparing, tyrannical, despotic, authoritarian. **2** (*he shot her a stern look*) forbidding, frowning, severe, dour, sombre, sober, austere, unsmiling, stark. OPPOSITE: lenient.

stern[2] *noun* poop, tail, tail end, rear, back.

stew *verb* **1** (*leave the meat to stew*) simmer, boil, braise, cook. **2** (*she decided to let him stew for a while*) fret, fuss, worry, agonize, seethe, sweat.
» *noun* **1** (*a beef stew*) casserole, goulash, ragout, fricassee. **2** (*he is in a bit of a stew about things*) bother, pother, flap (*inf*), tizzy (*inf*), panic, fluster, dither, worry, fret, agitation.

steward *noun* **1** (*air steward*) cabin attendant, attendant, air hostess. **2** (*the castle steward*) bailiff, agent, housekeeper, major-domo, butler, factor. **3** (*the club steward*) manager, caretaker, custodian, official, functionary, organizer.

stick[1] *noun* **1** (*he beat the boy with a stick*) rod, staff, wand, baton, pole, cane, switch, birch, club. **2** (*a bundle of sticks*) twig, branch. **3** (*he got a lot of stick in the press*) criticism, flak (*inf*), abuse, blame, reproof, punishment.

stick[2] *verb* **1** (*the lance stuck in his side*) stab, pierce, prick, puncture, penetrate, spear, transfix, impale, gore, jab, stab. **2** (*he stuck his finger in the hole*) poke, thrust, push. **3** (*stick the envelope down*) fasten, attach, join, fix, set, glue, gum, paste. **4** (*stick the two parts together*) cement, weld, solder, bond, fuse, adhere, fix, pin, tack, join, bind. OPPOSITE: separate. **5** (*stick the parcel over there*) put, place, position, set, site, locate, lay, plant, drop, deposit, plonk (*inf*). **6** (*stick around for a while*) stay, remain, linger, rest. **7** (*she could not stick it any longer*) stand, endure, tolerate, stomach (*inf*), bear, abide, put up with.
stick at 1 (*she says she'll stick at it a bit longer*) continue, carry on, keep at, persist, persevere, plug away (*inf*). **2** (*I stick at doing the work of two*) draw the line at (*inf*), demur at, balk at, scruple at, shrink from, hesitate at, recoil from.
stick by stick up for, stand up for, stand by, support, defend, champion, back, uphold, hold to, side with, adhere to.
stick it out persist, persevere, plug away (*inf*), keep at it (*inf*), hang in there (*inf*), continue.
stick out protrude, project, jut out, poke out, extend, bulge.
stick up for support, uphold, champion, defend, protect, fight for, stand by, stand up for, speak up for. OPPOSITE: oppose.

sticky *adj* **1** (*sticky tape*) adhesive, gummed, gummy, gluey, tacky. **2** (*sticky honey*) gluey, glutinous, treacly, gooey (*inf*), viscid, viscous. OPPOSITE: dry. **3** (*a sticky atmosphere*) muggy, clammy, close, oppressive, humid, sultry, sweltering. OPPOSITE: fresh. **4** (*a sticky moment*) difficult, awkward, embarrassing, tricky, hairy (*inf*), thorny, delicate, sensitive, ticklish, unpleasant.

stiff *adj* **1** (*stiff material*) rigid, inflexible, unbending, unyielding, inelastic, firm, hard, hardened, solid, solidified, thick, tight, taut, tense. OPPOSITE: limp. **2** (*a stiff penalty*) harsh, hard, severe, strict, stringent, tough, unsparing, pitiless, merciless, cruel, oppressive, rigorous, excessive, extreme, drastic. OPPOSITE: lenient. **3** (*a stiff climb*) difficult, hard, harsh, arduous, tiring, laborious, strenuous, fatiguing, exacting, demanding, challenging, rigorous, tough, trying. OPPOSITE: easy. **4** (*a stiff bearing*) formal, starchy (*inf*), strait-laced, reserved, prim, priggish, strict, precise, punctilious, ceremonious, ceremonial, pompous, chilly, cold, aloof, standoffish, constrained, unrelaxed, awkward, clumsy, graceless, inelegant. **5** (*a stiff wind*) strong, potent, forceful, powerful, vigorous, fresh, brisk, keen. OPPOSITE: light. **6** (*a stiff arm*) aching, tight, tense, arthritic, rheumatic. **7** (*a stiff drink*) strong, alcoholic, intoxicating.

stiffen *verb* **1** (*leave the mixture to stiffen*) set, harden, solidify, thicken, congeal, coagulate, jell, gel. **2** (*stiffen her determination*) strengthen, harden, brace, steel, reinforce, fortify.

stifle *verb* **1** (*he stifled his victims*) suffocate, asphyxiate, choke, smother, strangle. **2** (*dissent was stifled by the authorities*) restrain, crush, check, curb, suppress, repress, silence, hush, muffle, dampen, deaden, quell, subdue, smother, extinguish, quash, keep in, hold back.

stigma *noun* mark, spot, blot, stain, blemish, brand, slur, taint, defamation, shame, disgrace, dishonour.

still *adj* **1** (*he stood stock still*) motionless, unmoving, immobile, inert, stationary, sedentary, unstirring, inactive, lifeless, static. **2** (*a still night*) calm, tranquil, serene, sedate, restful, placid, peaceful, pacific, mild, unruffled, undisturbed, smooth, quiet, silent, hushed, noiseless. OPPOSITE: agitated.
➤ *noun* stillness, silence, quiet, quietness, hush, noiselessness, calm, tranquillity, serenity, peace, peacefulness. OPPOSITE: noise.
➤ *verb* **1** (*she stilled the children with reassurances*) hush, quiet, quieten, silence, lull, calm, tranquillize, appease, pacify, compose, soothe, allay, assuage, alleviate, settle. OPPOSITE: agitate. **2** (*activity was stilled for a moment*) subdue, check, stop, moderate, abate, slacken, smooth.
➤ *adv* **1** (*he is still working*) yet, even now, until now, up to this time. **2** (*still, it would be nice to go*) however, nevertheless, notwithstanding, though, although, even so, for all that, but.

stilted *adj* **1** (*a stilted conversation*) laboured, forced, stiff, wooden, artificial, formal. **2** (*stilted prose*) bombastic, pompous, turgid, inflated, high-flown, grandiloquent. OPPOSITE: simple.

stimulant *noun* tonic, restorative, pick-me-up (*inf*), bracer (*inf*), reviver, energizer.

stimulate *verb* arouse, rouse, excite, foment, fire, kindle, inflame, fan, whip up (*inf*), goad, spur, prick, prompt, urge, incite, instigate, provoke, trigger, motivate, animate, invigorate, inspire, inspirit, quicken, encourage, impel, induce. OPPOSITE: deter.

stimulating *adj* **1** (*a stimulating drink*) restoring, restorative, reviving, energizing, tonic. **2** (*a stimulating conversation*) stirring, exciting, interesting, thought-provoking, exhilarating, rousing, inspiring, provocative, provoking, intriguing.

stimulus *noun* incentive, fillip, provocation, motive, spur, goad, prod, impetus, drive, push, jolt, jog, impulse, urge, incitement, inducement, encouragement, shot in the arm (*inf*). OPPOSITE: deterrent.

sting *verb* **1** (*the child was stung by a wasp*) prick, bite, hurt, injure, wound. **2** (*my arm still stings*) burn, smart, tingle, irritate, hurt, pain. **3** (*he was stung by her remarks*) hurt, pain, injure, wound, distress, upset, annoy, offend, grieve, torment, torture, provoke, incense, needle, nettle, irritate, exasperate, vex, afflict, goad. OPPOSITE: soothe. **4** (*he was stung for a small fortune*) swindle, cheat,

defraud, rip off (*inf*), con (*inf*), trick, fiddle, fleece, deceive, take for a ride (*inf*).
➤ *noun* **1** (*the sting of a wasp*) prick, bite, nip, wound, injury. **2** (*the poultice took the sting out of his burns*) irritation, smarting, pain, hurt, tingling, tingle. **3** (*her column has lost its sting*) edge, bite, incisiveness, sharpness, pungency, causticness, causticity, sarcasm, spite, venom, malice, viciousness.

stingy *adj* **1** (*a stingy employer*) mean, parsimonious, niggardly, miserly, penurious, penny-pinching, tight (*inf*), tight-fisted, close-fisted, ungenerous, cheap (*inf*). OPPOSITE: generous. **2** (*stingy rations*) meagre, scanty, small, measly (*inf*), insufficient, inadequate. OPPOSITE: ample.

stink *noun* **1** smell, odour, stench, fetor, mephitis, effluvium, reek, pong (*inf*). OPPOSITE: perfume. **2** (*they kicked up quite a stink*) furore, uproar, row, fuss, song and dance (*inf*), hoo-ha (*inf*), brouhaha, to-do, commotion, stir, flap (*inf*), outcry, trouble, bother, fluster.
➤ *verb* reek, smell, pong (*inf*).

stint *verb* limit, restrict, confine, restrain, scrimp, pinch, economize, save, withhold, skimp (*inf*), begrudge. OPPOSITE: lavish.
➤ *noun* period, spell, stretch, time, shift, turn, bit, share, ration, quota.

stipend *noun* pay, salary, wages, remuneration, emolument, allowance, honorarium.

stipulate *verb* specify, set down, lay down, insist on, require, demand.

stipulation *noun* condition, specification, prerequisite, requirement, demand, provision, proviso, qualification, clause, term, obligation.

stir *verb* **1** (*do not stir from that spot*) move, budge, shift, go. OPPOSITE: stay. **2** (*stir the mixture*) mix, blend, beat, whip. **3** (*the grasses stirred in a slight breeze*) rustle, shake, twitch, quiver, tremble. **4** (*a breeze stirred the leaves*) disturb, agitate, rustle. **5** (*the reports stirred the government to action*) rouse, awaken, arouse, stimulate, provoke, spur, goad, drive, impel, incite, instigate, encourage, prompt, galvanize, electrify, inspire. **6** (*she was moved by his story*) affect, touch, move, excite, thrill, animate, inflame.
➤ *noun* excitement, commotion, disorder, confusion, ado, to-do (*inf*), flap (*inf*), fuss, bother, disturbance, uproar, tumult, activity, movement, hustle, bustle, flurry, agitation, ferment. OPPOSITE: tranquillity.

stirring *adj* rousing, stimulating, inspiring, moving, emotive, exciting, thrilling, exhilarating, intoxicating, heady, impassioned, dramatic, animated, spirited, lively, active, busy. OPPOSITE: dull.

stitch *verb* sew, tack, darn, embroider, hem, seam, mend, repair.

stock *noun* **1** (*a stock of stories*) store, supply, source, hoard, stockpile, cache, pile, heap, repertoire, reserve, reservoir, fund, inventory, accumulation, collection, assortment, range, selection, variety, quantity. **2** (*the shop was running low on stock*) goods, wares, merchandise, commodities. **3** (*the farmer has sold all his stock*) livestock, animals, cattle, sheep, horses, pigs. **4** (*the stock of the tree*) trunk, stalk, stem. **5** (*the stock of an axe*) shaft, butt, handle. **6** (*he comes of good stock*)

parentage, extraction, background, genealogy, lineage, line, descent, pedigree, ancestry, family, house, breed, blood, race, strain, type, species.
➤ *adj* **1** (*the fabric comes in stock widths*) standard, regular, average. **2** (*stock volumes in the school library*) staple, basic, essential, indispensable, fundamental, necessary, usual, normal, customary, common, regular. **3** (*a stock reply*) usual, routine, conventional, traditional, commonplace, stereotyped, hackneyed, clichéd, worn-out, overused, banal, trite, stale. OPPOSITE: novel.
➤ *verb* **1** (*the shop stocks most essentials*) keep, carry, deal in, sell, trade in, traffic in, handle, market, supply, provision. **2** (*stock the hut with emergency supplies*) equip, supply, provide, outfit, fit, kit out (*inf*), furnish, accoutre.
in stock available, on the shelves, for sale, on sale, on the market.
stock up 1 (*stock up on fuel for the journey*) store, amass, accumulate, lay in, hoard, stockpile, collect, gather, buy up, save, reserve, salt away (*inf*), squirrel away (*inf*), put away, put down, deposit. **2** (*stock up the shelves*) replenish, fill, load.
take stock assess, reassess, appraise, size up (*inf*), weigh up, review, evaluate, re-evaluate, re-examine, estimate, survey.

stockpile *verb* hoard, store, reserve, save, collect, gather, accumulate, amass, lay in, pile up, heap up, put aside, put away, stash away (*inf*), salt away (*inf*), squirrel away (*inf*), keep.

stocky *adj* thickset, chunky, sturdy, solid, squat, stubby, stumpy, dumpy, short, broad.

stoical *adj* philosophical, patient, long-suffering, uncomplaining, forbearing, accepting, resigned, indifferent, apathetic, impassive, dispassionate, unemotional, cool, calm, imperturbable, phlegmatic, unexcitable, unflappable, self-disciplined, self-controlled. OPPOSITE: excitable.

stoicism *noun* patience, long-suffering, fortitude, endurance, resignation, indifference, impassivity, unexcitability, dispassion, acceptance, forbearance, self-discipline, self-control, calmness, imperturbability, phlegm, fatalism, stolidity.

stolid *adj* dull, obtuse, bovine, dense, stupid, thick, slow, heavy, wooden, blockish, lumpish, indifferent, apathetic, impassive, uninterested, unemotional, phlegmatic, solemn, unimaginative, uninspiring.

stomach *noun* **1** (*a pain in the stomach*) abdomen, belly, tummy (*inf*), gut, paunch, inside. **2** (*no stomach for food*) appetite, hunger, desire, relish, taste, zest. **3** (*little stomach for the fight*) appetite, relish, taste, liking, desire, inclination, leaning, proclivity. OPPOSITE: aversion.
➤ *verb* tolerate, bear, endure, suffer, abide, brook, stand, put up with (*inf*), swallow.

stone *noun* **1** (*stones on a beach*) pebble, rock, boulder, cobble. **2** (*a precious stone*) gem, jewel. **3** (*remove the stones from the fruit*) seed, pip, nut, kernel. **4** (*she could not afford a stone for the grave*) gravestone, tombstone, headstone, slab.

stony *adj* **1** (*stony soil*) pebbly, rocky, shingly, gravelly, gritty. **2** (*a stony look*) hard, flinty, impenetrable, adamant, steely, unresponsive, unfeeling, indifferent,

callous, hostile, cold, icy, frosty, chilly, frigid, pitiless, heartless, merciless, cruel, severe, stern, unforgiving, rigid, inflexible, obdurate, inexorable, expressionless, deadpan, poker-faced, blank.

stoop *verb* **1** (*he stooped over the desk*) bend, lean, incline, lower, bow, slouch, droop. **2** (*he had to stoop to enter the cave*) hunch, crouch, squat, kneel, duck. **3** (*she refused to stoop so low*) condescend, deign, submit, yield, acquiesce, descend, sink, lower oneself, resort.
➤ *noun* **1** (*walk with a stoop*) hunch, droop, slouch, slump. **2** (*a stoop of his head*) bow, bending, inclination, ducking, lowering.

stop *verb* **1** (*stop doing that*) halt, pause, cease, discontinue, abandon, quit (*inf*), refrain, desist, kick (*inf*), pack in (*inf*), give over (*inf*), knock off (*inf*), finish, complete, conclude, end, bring to an end, terminate, arrest, suspend, interrupt. **2** (*she stopped him from getting involved*) prevent, obstruct, bar, frustrate, thwart, intercept, hinder, impede, block, check, curb, restrain, stall, delay, hinder, hamper, repress, suppress. **3** (*stop up the bottle*) stem, close, plug, bung, seal, block, stop up, staunch. **4** (*he stopped there for a couple of weeks*) stay, remain, rest, put up, tarry, wait, linger, visit, sojourn, reside, settle, lodge, board, live. OPPOSITE: depart.
➤ *noun* **1** (*work came to a stop*) halt, standstill, pause, break, interruption, intermission, cessation, end, finish, conclusion, termination, arrest, stoppage. OPPOSITE: continuation. **2** (*make an overnight stop*) stopover, stay, visit, sojourn, rest, break, pause. **3** (*several people were waiting at the stop*) halt, stopping-place, terminus, station.

stoppage *noun* **1** (*a stoppage in play*) stop, halt, standstill, interruption, cessation, discontinuation, arrest. **2** (*a stoppage on the line*) blockage, obstacle, obstruction, check, hindrance. **3** (*an industrial stoppage*) shutdown, closure, strike, industrial action, walk-out, sit-in. **4** (*his salary after stoppages*) deduction, reduction, subtraction, withdrawal, removal.

stopper *noun* bung, plug, seal, cork, cap, top.

store *verb* amass, accumulate, stockpile, stock up with, garner, save, reserve, put aside, lay by, lay in, lay down, lay up, salt away (*inf*), stash away (*inf*), hoard, gather, collect, keep, preserve, husband. OPPOSITE: consume.
➤ *noun* **1** (*a store of fuel*) stock, stockpile, supply, provision, fund, hoard, cache, reserve, reservoir, mine, accumulation, amassment, mass, heap, load, abundance, plenty, lot. **2** (*there were several customers in the store*) shop, supermarket, hypermarket, department store, retail outlet, emporium. **3** (*we will need to get the goods from the store*) warehouse, storehouse, storeroom, depot, depository, repository.
set store by value, admire, regard, esteem, appreciate, prize.

storm *noun* **1** (*the pier collapsed in a storm*) thunderstorm, tempest, squall, gale, hurricane, tornado, blizzard. OPPOSITE: calm. **2** (*organize a storm on the defences*) assault, attack, charge, raid, onslaught, offensive, onset, rush, raid, blitz. **3** (*a storm of protest*) outbreak, outburst, outcry, roar, clamour, tumult, furore, riot, rumpus (*inf*).
➤ *verb* **1** (*he stormed against the decision*) rage, roar, thunder, rant, rave, bellow, fume, seethe. **2** (*they stormed*

the castle during the night) assail, assault, attack, raid, charge, rush. **3** (*she stormed out of the theatre*) rush, charge, tear, stamp, stomp (*inf*), stalk, stride, flounce.

stormy *adj* tempestuous, wild, raging, furious, violent, rough, turbulent, squally, windy, gusty, rainy, choppy, blustery. OPPOSITE: still.

story *noun* **1** (*an adventure story*) tale, romance, novel, narrative, narration, account, record, recital, relation, history, chronicle, legend, myth, fable, anecdote, yarn (*inf*), fiction. OPPOSITE: fact. **2** (*she's been telling you stories*) lie, fib (*inf*), falsehood, untruth (*inf*). **3** (*according to the story in the papers*) article, report, feature, item.

stout *adj* **1** (*a stout build*) fat, obese, overweight, corpulent, portly, rotund, plump, fleshy, stocky, tubby, bulky, hulking, heavy, thickset, large, big, beefy, burly, brawny, strapping, athletic, muscular, rugged, tough, hardy, lusty. OPPOSITE: thin. **2** (*a stout box*) sturdy, strong, substantial, solid, tough, robust, durable. **3** (*he made a stout defence of his views*) brave, courageous, gutsy (*inf*), gritty (*inf*), heroic, gallant, valiant, bold, plucky, fearless, intrepid, dauntless, stout-hearted, resolute, determined, strong, forceful, firm, staunch, stalwart. OPPOSITE: weak.

stove *noun* oven, cooker, range, furnace.

stow *verb* pack, stuff, bundle, cram, load, store, hoard, stash (*inf*), put away, deposit, hide, secrete.

straggle *verb* **1** (*refugees straggled all along the route*) spread out, scatter, stray, digress, deviate, ramble, wander, roam, meander, rove, range, drift, amble. **2** (*the smallest children straggled behind the others*) lag, trail, fall, linger, loiter.

straight *adj* **1** (*a straight road*) direct, uncurving, undeviating, unswerving, unbending, unbent. **2** (*she put her hat straight*) level, even, flat, horizontal, vertical, upright, erect, right, true, aligned, symmetrical. OPPOSITE: crooked. **3** (*a straight approach to the subject*) straightforward, forthright, direct, blunt, outspoken, candid, frank, plain, unequivocal, unambiguous. **4** (*he's a straight guy*) honest, honourable, upright, decent, respectable, just, fair, reliable, faithful, sincere, trustworthy, upstanding. OPPOSITE: dishonest. **5** (*put the room straight*) neat, tidy, orderly, shipshape, spruce, arranged, organized. OPPOSITE: untidy. **6** (*three straight victories*) consecutive, successive, uninterrupted, unbroken, running, continuous, solid. **7** (*a straight whisky*) neat, undiluted, unmixed, pure, unadulterated.
➤ *adv* **1** (*he went straight home*) directly, at once, right away, without delay, pronto (*inf*), immediately, instantly, promptly. **2** (*he let them have it straight*) frankly, candidly, honestly, directly, bluntly, point-blank, forthrightly, straightforwardly, clearly, plainly.
straight away immediately, instantly, at once, right away, forthwith, directly, now, without delay, pronto (*inf*). OPPOSITE: later.

straighten *verb* **1** (*straighten bent wire*) unbend, align, flatten. **2** (*she straightened her dress*) put in order, order, adjust, arrange, put right, tidy, neaten.
straighten out put in order, order, put right, rectify, clear up, sort out, tidy up, settle, resolve, correct, realign, regularize, regulate, unsnarl, disentangle.

straighten up stand up, stand upright, stand erect, stand.

straightforward *adj* **1** (*a straightforward account of events*) frank, open, candid, forthright, plain, open, sincere, genuine, honest, truthful, direct, straight, outspoken, plain-speaking. OPPOSITE: deceitful. **2** (*a straightforward operation*) simple, easy, uncomplicated, routine, elementary, undemanding, unexacting. OPPOSITE: complicated.

strain[1] *verb* **1** (*strain on the rope*) pull, heave, tug, wrench. **2** (*he has strained a muscle*) wrench, sprain, twist, pull, rick, tear, injure, hurt. **3** (*the revelation strained her sense of loyalty*) exert, tax, overtax, force, drive, overexert, overtax, exhaust, fatigue, tire, weaken. **4** (*they strained to get the job done in time*) strive, struggle, labour, try, endeavour, go all out (*inf*). OPPOSITE: relax. **5** (*try not to strain the elastic*) tighten, stretch, elongate, extend, distend. **6** (*strain the mixture before cooking*) filter, percolate, screen, sieve, sift, riddle, separate, purify. **7** (*strain the water from the clothes*) drain, wring, squeeze.
➤ *noun* **1** (*put strain on the wire*) tension, tautness, stress, pressure. **2** (*the doctor diagnosed a strain of the wrist*) wrench, sprain, rick, twist, pull, injury. **3** (*the work involved a lot of strain*) effort, struggle, force, exertion, fatigue, exhaustion. OPPOSITE: relaxation. **4** (*she caved in under the strain*) tension, stress, pressure, anxiety, worry, duress, burden.

strain[2] *noun* **1** (*a different strain of the royal house*) family, race, stock, ancestry, descent, lineage, extraction, pedigree, breed. **2** (*a strain of cynicism*) trace, streak, vein, tendency, quality, characteristic, element, suggestion, suspicion, trait. **3** (*a strain of music*) tune, melody, air, theme, song, lay.

strained *adj* **1** (*a strained silence*) uneasy, awkward, embarrassed, uncomfortable, self-conscious. **2** (*a strained welcome*) stiff, wooden, tense, unrelaxed, laboured, forced, constrained, false, artificial, unnatural.

strait *noun* **1** (*the strait between the islands*) channel, sound, inlet, narrows. **2** (*he found himself in dire straits*) dilemma, quandary, predicament, plight, hole (*inf*), fix (*inf*), mess (*inf*), pickle (*inf*), difficulty, perplexity, emergency, problem, trouble, distress, extremity, hardship, poverty.

straitened *adj* distressed, embarrassed, pinched, reduced, limited, restricted, impoverished, poor, destitute.

strait-laced *adj* stuffy, starchy, prim, priggish, prudish, fuddy-duddy (*inf*), narrow-minded, narrow, puritanical, moralistic, proper, strict.

strand[1] *verb* maroon, cast away, shipwreck, beach, ground, run aground, abandon, desert, leave. OPPOSITE: rescue.
➤ *noun* shore, foreshore, seashore, coast, beach, front, waterfront.

strand[2] *noun* **1** (*a strand of cotton*) thread, fibre, filament, piece, length, string, hair, wire. **2** (*another strand in the story*) ingredient, element, component, theme, strain, feature, factor.

strange *adj* **1** (*a strange occurrence*) odd, peculiar, curious, queer, uncommon, unusual, rare, singular, exceptional, remarkable, extraordinary, fantastic, irregular, abnormal, surreal, weird, bizarre, eccentric, funny (*inf*), offbeat (*inf*), oddball (*inf*), unaccountable, inexplicable, uncanny, unexpected. OPPOSITE: normal. **2** (*travel to strange lands*) unfamiliar, unknown, exotic, foreign, alien, new, novel, unaccustomed, unacquainted, inexperienced, untried. OPPOSITE: familiar.

stranger *noun* alien, foreigner, visitor, guest, newcomer, outsider, incomer. OPPOSITE: acquaintance.

strangle *verb* **1** (*she was strangled by the intruder*) throttle, choke, suffocate, smother, asphyxiate, stifle. **2** (*the authorities sought to strangle public comment upon the affair*) stifle, smother, gag, repress, suppress, restrain, check, keep in, hold back, inhibit.

strap *noun* belt, thong, strip, band, tie, cord, leash.
➤ *verb* **1** (*they strapped him to the table*) tie, bind, truss, lash, fasten, secure, pinion. OPPOSITE: loose. **2** (*he was strapped by the headmaster*) beat, flog, whip, lash, scourge, belt.

stratagem *noun* ruse, artifice, trick, wile, scheme, plot, plan, ploy, intrigue, deception, dodge, gambit, tactic, manoeuvre, machination, device, subterfuge.

strategic *adj* **1** (*a strategic move*) tactical, calculated, planned, plotted, deliberate, diplomatic, politic, cunning, wily. **2** (*a strategic bridge*) key, vital, decisive, crucial, critical, important, essential.

strategy *noun* tactics, approach, policy, plan, plan of action, design, blueprint (*inf*), programme, scheme, schedule, procedure.

stratum *noun* **1** (*rock stratum*) layer, bed, seam, vein, lode. **2** (*a higher stratum of society*) level, grade, tier, degree, rank, status, station, class, caste, category.

stray *verb* **1** (*he strayed far into the desert*) wander, roam, rove, ramble, range, drift, straggle, meander, amble, saunter. **2** (*the speaker strayed from the topic*) digress, deviate, diverge. **3** (*she strayed from the straight and narrow*) swerve, go astray, err.
➤ *adj* **1** (*a stray dog*) lost, abandoned, homeless, vagrant, wandering, drifting, roaming. **2** (*a stray shot*) random, freak, accidental, erratic, chance, scattered, isolated.

streak *noun* **1** (*a streak of paint*) smear, smudge, daub, strip, stripe, line, band, bar, stroke, fleck, mark. **2** (*a streak of cruelty*) strain, vein, trace, dash, touch, element. **3** (*they're going through a bad streak*) spell, stretch, period, time, stint.
➤ *verb* **1** (*his trousers were streaked with mud*) smear, smudge, daub, fleck, slash, mark. **2** (*the animal streaked across the road*) rush, race, sprint, gallop, hurtle, speed, dart, dash, flash, tear, fly, scurry, whistle, zoom.

stream *noun* **1** (*a fast-flowing stream*) brook, beck, burn, river, freshet, rivulet, rill, tributary. **2** (*go with the general stream of things*) run, flow, current, race, drift, course, flow, tide. **3** (*a stream of hostile remarks*) rush, gush, torrent, cascade, burst, volley, jet, outpouring, surge, tide, flood, deluge.
➤ *verb* **1** (*blood streamed from the cut*) flow, issue, well, spill, pour, cascade, flood, run, course, rush, surge, gush, spout. OPPOSITE: halt. **2** (*her cloak streamed behind her*) trail, flap, flutter, flow, float, fly.

streamer *noun* pennon, pennant, flag, ensign, standard, banner, ribbon.

streamlined *adj* **1** (*a streamlined shape*) aerodynamic, sleek, smooth, elegant, graceful. **2** (*a streamlined organization*) efficient, professional, well-organized, slick, smooth-running, well-run, stripped-down.

street *noun* thoroughfare, road, avenue, boulevard, drive, terrace, row, crescent.

strength *noun* **1** (*physical strength*) power, might, force, vigour, clout (*inf*), energy, sinew, muscle, muscularity, brawn, fortitude, backbone, stamina, fitness, health. OPPOSITE: weakness. **2** (*this will test the strength of the structure*) toughness, solidity, soundness, resilience, firmness, robustness, sturdiness, durability, hardiness, stoutness, resistance, impregnability. **3** (*strength of will*) resolution, determination, firmness, persistence, assertiveness, forcefulness, fortitude, spirit, courage, bravery, pluck. **4** (*a performance of great strength*) intensity, vehemence, depth, passion, ardour, fervency, pungency, sharpness, vividness. **5** (*his argument had considerable strength*) power, force, forcefulness, potency, efficacy, effectiveness, weight, urgency, persuasiveness, cogency, validity, soundness. **6** (*his patience is one of his strengths*) strong point, gift, talent, asset, advantage, forte.

on the strength of based on, on the basis of, because of, on account of, on the grounds of, by virtue of.

strengthen *verb* **1** (*strengthen the wall*) fortify, reinforce, prop up, shore up, buttress, consolidate, stiffen, toughen, harden. OPPOSITE: weaken. **2** (*he was considerably strengthened by their support*) fortify, invigorate, energize, refresh, restore, rally, hearten, encourage, nerve, steel, brace, bolster, nourish. **3** (*strengthen calls for change*) support, back up, confirm, substantiate, corroborate, intensify, heighten, increase.

strenuous *adj* **1** (*he made a strenuous effort*) energetic, vigorous, active, forceful, ardent, zealous, spirited, persistent, tireless, determined, resolute, tenacious, eager, keen, earnest. OPPOSITE: feeble. **2** (*a strenuous climb*) uphill, arduous, hard, difficult, laborious, toilsome, heavy, gruelling, tough, tiring, exhausting, demanding, taxing.

stress *noun* **1** (*they lay stress on punctuality*) emphasis, accent, accentuation, weight, importance, significance, priority, urgency. **2** (*subject the structure to stress*) strain, tension, force, pressure, trauma. **3** (*suffering from stress*) worry, anxiety, distress, tension, strain, uneasiness, apprehension. OPPOSITE: relaxation.
➤ *verb* emphasize, accentuate, accent, highlight, spotlight, underline, underscore, point up, exaggerate, harp on, dwell on, belabour, repeat.

stretch *verb* **1** (*stretch the elastic*) extend, lengthen, elongate, pull, draw out, expand, distend, unroll, tighten, tauten, strain. OPPOSITE: contract. **2** (*stretch for the light switch*) reach, strain. **3** (*the kingdom stretches over a big area*) extend, spread, cover, range. **4** (*the task hardly stretched her*) challenge, test, tax, try, push, extend.
➤ *noun* **1** (*the stretch of his authority*) extent, spread, reach, range, scope, sweep, compass. **2** (*a stretch of water*) expanse, area, distance. **3** (*he was missing for a stretch*) space, spell, period, time, term.

stretch out 1 (*stretch out a hand*) reach out, hold out, put out, put forth, present, proffer, offer, extend. **2** (*she* *stretched out on the bed*) lie down, recline, sprawl, lounge, relax.

strew *verb* scatter, spread, diffuse, disperse, sow, sprinkle, bestrew, toss, litter, broadcast. OPPOSITE: gather.

stricken *adj* afflicted, smitten, affected, hit, struck, wounded, injured, laid low.

strict *adj* **1** (*a strict code of behaviour*) rigorous, stringent, harsh, hard, rigid, firm, inflexible, uncompromising, stern, severe, austere, tough, disciplinarian, authoritarian. OPPOSITE: lenient. **2** (*strict attention to detail*) exact, precise, accurate, faithful, true, close, careful, particular, punctilious, meticulous, scrupulous, conscientious, religious. OPPOSITE: loose. **3** (*strict observance of the rules*) complete, total, utter, absolute, thoroughgoing.

stricture *noun* **1** (*the strictures of the court*) censure, blame, criticism, flak (*inf*), rebuke, reproof, condemnation. OPPOSITE: praise. **2** (*trapped by the strictures of family life*) limitation, restriction, limit, confine, curb, check, bound, constraint, restraint, tightness.

stride *verb* pace, step, walk, march, tread, stalk.
≫ *noun* pace, step, walk, march, tread, stalk, progression, movement, advance.

strident *adj* harsh, rough, grating, raucous, jarring, rasping, discordant, clashing, jangling, unmusical, unmelodious, shrill, screeching, loud, thundering, roaring, booming, clamorous, vociferous, stridulant. OPPOSITE: soft.

strife *noun* conflict, discord, dissension, friction, animosity, hostility, ill-feeling, ill-will, disagreement, contention, controversy, quarrel, row, argument, dispute, bickering, wrangling, combat, warfare, brawl, battle, fight, struggle, contest, rivalry. OPPOSITE: peace.

strike *verb* **1** (*strike the drum*) hit, rap, tap, beat, bang, knock, pound, batter. **2** (*he refused to strike a woman*) punch, slap, smack, beat, clout (*inf*), clobber (*inf*), wallop (*inf*), whack (*inf*), swipe (*inf*), belt (*inf*), thump, box, buffet, cuff. OPPOSITE: caress. **3** (*the car struck the bollard*) collide with, crash into, smash into, hit, bump, touch, dash against. **4** (*we will strike the base at dawn*) attack, assail, assault, charge, storm, set upon, set about, pounce on, fall upon, raid, rush, ambush. **5** (*it struck her as strange*) impress, feel, seem, appear, look, sound, affect, touch. **6** (*the truth eventually struck him*) hit, dawn on, occur to, come to, register. **7** (*the staff have threatened to strike*) walk out, down tools, work to rule, mutiny, revolt. **8** (*a compromise was struck after several hours*) reach, agree, clinch (*inf*), secure, come to, arrive at, settle on, achieve. **9** (*strike oil*) find, reach, encounter, discover, locate, come upon, chance upon, happen upon, unearth, uncover. **10** (*strike an attitude*) assume, take on, adopt, feign, affect.
≫ *noun* **1** (*a firm strike of the bat*) blow, hit, stroke, wallop (*inf*), whack (*inf*), slap, belt (*inf*), biff (*inf*), smack, thump, thwack. **2** (*a strike deep into enemy territory*) attack, assault, raid, charge, rush. **3** (*the factory was closed by the strike*) walk-out, sit-in, go-slow, work-to-rule, industrial action, mutiny, revolt.

strike out delete, cross out, strike through, strike off, rub out, erase, efface, obliterate, remove, cancel.

strike up begin, start, commence, kick off (*inf*), introduce, instigate, initiate, establish.

striking *adj* **1** (*a striking appearance*) impressive, stunning (*inf*), dazzling, wonderful, extraordinary, outstanding, remarkable, astonishing, memorable, arresting, noticeable, conspicuous, distinct, visible, obvious, evident, salient. OPPOSITE: commonplace. **2** (*a striking woman*) handsome, good-looking, attractive, beautiful, stunning, glamorous, gorgeous, pretty.

string *noun* **1** (*a ball of string*) cord, twine, rope, thread, strand, yarn, cable, line. **2** (*a string of coincidences*) series, succession, sequence, chain, row, line, file, column, queue, procession, stream, train.
≫ *verb* **1** (*string lights on the tree*) hang, suspend, festoon, sling. **2** (*string the ribbons together*) thread, loop, join, link, tie, fasten.

string along deceive, fool, dupe, bluff, play false, hoax, humbug, mislead, take for a ride (*inf*), lead up the garden path (*inf*).

string out stretch, extend, lengthen, space out, spread out, fan out.

string up hang, lynch.

stringent *adj* **1** (*stringent rules*) strict, severe, harsh, tough, firm, rigorous, exacting, demanding, tight, rigid, inflexible, uncompromising. OPPOSITE: lax. **2** (*stringent conditions*) hard, harsh, difficult, tight, tough.

strings *pl noun* qualifications, conditions, provisos, prerequisites, requirements, restrictions, limitations, stipulations, obligations, catches.

stringy *adj* **1** (*stringy meat*) chewy, tough, gristly, leathery, fibrous. **2** (*a stringy youth*) spindly, wiry, skinny, lanky, gangling.

strip[1] *verb* **1** (*strip the husk away*) peel, skin, flay, excoriate, remove. **2** (*strip the body*) undress, unclothe, disrobe, denude, bare, uncover, expose. OPPOSITE: cover. **3** (*strip off those wet clothes*) take off, remove. **4** (*the house had been stripped*) rob, plunder, despoil, pillage, sack, loot, ransack, gut, clean out, clear, empty. **5** (*they were stripped of their titles*) deprive, divest, dispossess. **6** (*strip the engine*) take apart, take to pieces, pull apart, dismantle, disassemble, separate.

strip[2] *noun* piece, bit, slip, band, stripe, belt, ribbon, fillet, shred.

stripe *noun* band, bar, line, streak, fleck, flash, strip, belt, chevron.

striped *adj* stripy, streaky, banded, barred, striated, variegated.

stripling *noun* youth, youngster, lad, boy, fledgling, child, kid (*inf*), juvenile, minor, adolescent, teenager.

strive *verb* **1** (*we must strive to do better*) struggle, labour, work, toil, strain, try, attempt, exert, endeavour, aim, aspire. **2** (*the rivals strived with each other*) compete, vie, contend, engage, fight, battle, combat.

stroke *noun* **1** (*a single stroke of his fist*) blow, hit, knock, swipe, tap, rap, slap, cuff, thump, smack, wallop (*inf*), whack (*inf*), belt (*inf*), clobber (*inf*). **2** (*give the cat a stroke*) caress, rub, pat, fondle, pet. **3** (*a stroke of genius*) feat, accomplishment, achievement, action, coup. **4** (*with a stroke of the pen*) movement, flourish, sweep,

line. **5** (*suffer a stroke*) apoplexy, paralysis, attack, fit, spasm, seizure, thrombosis, collapse, shock.
≫ *verb* caress, rub, pat, fondle, pet.

stroll *verb* walk, amble, saunter, ramble, meander, dawdle, wander. OPPOSITE: run.
≫ *noun* walk, constitutional, promenade, amble, saunter, airing, excursion, ramble, turn.

strong *adj* **1** (*a strong build*) powerful, mighty, muscular, sinewy, brawny, beefy, burly, well-built, athletic, strapping, rugged, stalwart, lusty, hale, hearty, well, healthy, fit. OPPOSITE: weak. **2** (*strong material*) robust, hardy, tough, stout, sound, solid, sturdy, rugged, durable, long-lasting, hard-wearing, heavy-duty, resilient, substantial, firm. **3** (*a strong character*) resolute, determined, forceful, firm, formidable, strong-willed, strong-minded, single-minded, decisive, aggressive, assertive, positive. **4** (*strong colours*) intense, deep, bright, vivid. **5** (*strong emotion*) intense, deep, potent, powerful, fierce, violent, vehement, vigorous, fervent, passionate, ardent, zealous, eager, keen, enthusiastic, devoted, committed. **6** (*a strong flavour*) sharp, hot, spicy, piquant, pungent, biting, highly-flavoured, highly-seasoned. **7** (*a strong argument*) weighty, valid, sound, effective, efficacious, forceful, cogent, telling, potent, powerful, urgent, convincing, compelling, persuasive, plausible. **8** (*strong drink*) intoxicating, heady, alcoholic, potent.

stronghold *noun* fortress, fort, castle, citadel, bastion, bulwark, tower, keep, refuge.

structure *noun* **1** (*put up a new structure*) building, edifice, erection, construction. **2** (*the structure of the organization*) fabric, form, formation, shape, design, framework, construction, arrangement, organization, composition, make-up, set-up, constitution.
≫ *verb* construct, build, assemble, put together, form, shape, order, design, organize, arrange.

struggle *verb* **1** (*struggle to finish the job*) strive, labour, toil, endeavour, strain, try, work, exert oneself, do one's best, do one's utmost. **2** (*they struggled together for hours*) fight, battle, combat, contend, wrestle, grapple, engage, compete, contest, vie. OPPOSITE: yield.
≫ *noun* **1** (*he was injured in the struggle*) fight, battle, combat, skirmish, hostilities, scuffle, brawl, clash, conflict, strife, contention, contest, competition, encounter. OPPOSITE: peace. **2** (*the job involved a deal of struggle*) effort, exertion, strain, trouble, labour, toil, pain, work, endeavour.

strut *verb* swagger, prance, parade, stalk, flounce, swank (*inf*).

stub *noun* butt, end, tail, stump, remnant, fag-end (*inf*), dog-end (*inf*).

stubborn *adj* obstinate, difficult, mulish, pig-headed, stiff-necked, headstrong, wilful, self-willed, strong-willed, perverse, contrary, refractory, recalcitrant, contumacious, ungovernable, unmanageable, inflexible, rigid, unbending, uncompromising, unyielding, intractable, intransigent, persistent, dogged, tenacious, adamant, hidebound, obdurate. OPPOSITE: amenable.

stubby *adj* **1** (*a stubby figure*) short, squat, stumpy, dumpy, stocky, chunky, thickset. OPPOSITE: long. **2** (*a stubby chin*) rough, stubbly, bristly. OPPOSITE: smooth.

stuck *adj* **1** (*the vessel was stuck on the rocks*) fixed, fast, lodged, jammed, firm, embedded, rooted, immobile, unmovable. OPPOSITE: free. **2** (*stuck together with glue*) cemented, glued, joined, fastened. **3** (*she was stuck on the final problem*) baffled, mystified, stumped (*inf*), nonplussed, puzzled, perplexed, beaten.

get stuck into set about, get down to, tackle, embark on, start, begin.

stuck on fond of, obsessed with, infatuated with, keen on, enthusiastic about, wild about, crazy about, dotty about (*inf*), mad on (*inf*), nuts on (*inf*).

student *noun* pupil, schoolboy, schoolgirl, scholar, learner, apprentice, trainee, undergraduate. OPPOSITE: master.

studied *adj* deliberate, wilful, premeditated, purposeful, calculated, contrived, affected, forced, artificial, unnatural, planned, intentional, considered, conscious. OPPOSITE: spontaneous.

studious *adj* **1** (*a studious child*) scholarly, academic, intellectual, bookish, book-loving, serious, earnest, thoughtful, reflective. **2** (*a studious examination of the facts*) diligent, industrious, sedulous, assiduous, careful, painstaking, meticulous, punctilious, attentive, thorough. OPPOSITE: lazy.

study *verb* **1** (*study hard at school*) learn, swot (*inf*), cram, work, train, revise, mug up (*inf*), bone up (*inf*). **2** (*study the documents*) read, peruse, pore over, scan, survey, scrutinize, analyse, examine, investigate, research. **3** (*study the question at length*) consider, weigh, ponder, deliberate, meditate, muse, reflect, contemplate, cogitate, ruminate. OPPOSITE: ignore.
≫ *noun* **1** (*spent his days in study*) learning, reading, scholarship, education, swotting (*inf*), cramming (*inf*), revision, contemplation, meditation, thought. **2** (*a study of economic conditions*) examination, survey, investigation, inquiry, analysis, scrutiny, review. **3** (*come into my study*) office, studio, den (*inf*), library, workroom. **4** (*they agreed to publish the study*) report, essay, paper, thesis, monograph, review, survey, critique, work.

stuff *verb* **1** (*stuff the suitcase with clothes*) fill, pack, pad. **2** (*the box was stuffed with goodies*) pack, load, cram, crowd, jam. **3** (*stuff a rag into the hole*) thrust, shove (*inf*), ram, push, press, squeeze, force, wedge, compress. **4** (*he stuffed himself with chocolates*) gorge, fill, overindulge, satiate, sate.
≫ *noun* **1** (*a jacket of fine stuff*) cloth, fabric, material. **2** (*the stuff of his argument*) matter, substance, essence. **3** (*put your stuff in the back*) belongings, effects, things, objects, articles, items, gear (*inf*), clobber (*inf*), paraphernalia, kit, tackle, equipment, trappings, goods, luggage, chattels, possessions. **4** (*stuff and nonsense*) rubbish, nonsense, humbug, bunkum, balderdash, rot.

stuffing *noun* padding, packing, wadding, filling, quilting.

stuffy *adj* **1** (*a stuffy atmosphere*) close, muggy, airless, unventilated, sultry, suffocating, stifling, oppressive, heavy, musty, fusty, stale. OPPOSITE: fresh. **2** (*rather a stuffy attitude*) dull, dreary, uninteresting, stodgy, old-fashioned, stiff, starchy, fuddy-duddy (*inf*), square (*inf*), strait-laced, staid, prim, priggish, conservative, conventional, pompous.

stumble *verb* **1** (*she stumbled up the steps*) trip, fall, lurch, slip, stagger, reel, flounder, lumber, blunder. **2** (*he stumbled over his answer*) stammer, stutter, falter, hesitate.

stumble upon happen upon, chance upon, hit upon, light upon, come across, run across, find, discover, encounter. OPPOSITE: miss.

stump *noun* **1** (*the stump of the tree*) trunk, remains, remnant. **2** (*the stump of the cigarette*) remnant, remains, stub, butt, end, fag-end (*inf*), dog-end (*inf*).
➤ *verb* **1** (*the mystery stumped everyone*) baffle, mystify, nonplus (*inf*), puzzle, bewilder, dumbfound, perplex, outwit, confuse, confound, bamboozle (*inf*), flummox (*inf*), defeat, foil. OPPOSITE: enlighten. **2** (*he stumped up the stairs*) stamp, stomp (*inf*), trudge, plot, lumber, clump, clomp.

stump up pay up, pay out, fork out (*inf*), hand over, contribute, cough up (*inf*), shell out (*inf*), chip in (*inf*).

stun *verb* stupefy, daze, knock out (*inf*), bowl over (*inf*), shock, amaze, astound, astonish, overwhelm, overcome, overpower, flabbergast (*inf*), bowl over (*inf*), stagger, dumbfound, confound, confuse, bewilder.

stunning *adj* **1** (*a stunning breakthrough*) brilliant, striking, dazzling, impressive, imposing, wonderful, marvellous, splendid, great, sensational, spectacular, remarkable, extraordinary, amazing, astonishing, mind-blowing (*inf*), incredible, staggering. **2** (*a stunning young woman*) lovely, beautiful, gorgeous, ravishing, exquisite, sensational, smashing (*inf*), fabulous (*inf*).

stunt[1] *noun* feat, exploit, trick, turn, act, action, deed, enterprise, performance.

stunt[2] *verb* retard, check, restrict, curb, slow, hinder, hamper, impede, dwarf, stop, arrest.

stunted *adj* undersized, dwarfish, dwarfed, pygmy, diminutive, short, small, little, tiny. OPPOSITE: giant.

stupefy *verb* stun, daze, numb, benumb, bemuse, shock, amaze, astound, astonish, stagger, dumbfound, bowl over (*inf*), overwhelm, confound, confuse.

stupendous *adj* **1** (*a stupendous performance*) astounding, astonishing, amazing, staggering, stunning, wonderful, marvellous, extraordinary, phenomenal, fantastic (*inf*), fabulous, tremendous, prodigious, superb, breathtaking, overwhelming. OPPOSITE: ordinary. **2** (*of stupendous size*) immense, vast, colossal, prodigious, massive, enormous, huge, gigantic.

stupid *adj* **1** (*a stupid idiot*) unintelligent, dull, dull-witted, dumb (*inf*), slow, thick (*inf*), dense, gormless (*inf*), crass, fatuous, brainless, mindless, witless, half-witted, dim, dim-witted, simple, simple-minded, feeble-minded, foolish, silly, idiotic. OPPOSITE: intelligent. **2** (*a stupid thing to do*) silly, foolish, foolhardy, ill-advised, idiotic, moronic, imbecilic, childish, puerile, asinine, inane, absurd, ridiculous, ludicrous, mad, lunatic, senseless, pointless, meaningless, nonsensical, imprudent, unwise, rash, irresponsible. **3** (*the impact knocked him stupid*) stupefied, stunned, dazed, groggy, sluggish, semiconscious, torpid.

stupidity *noun* **1** (*a ruler renowned for his stupidity*) foolishness, thickness (*inf*), unintelligence, dimness (*inf*), denseness, dumbness (*inf*), mindlessness, brainlessness, dullness, dull-wittedness, doziness (*inf*), slowness, slow-wittedness, silliness. **2** (*an act of stupidity*) folly, foolishness, foolhardiness, silliness, idiocy, irresponsibility, brainlessness, senselessness, injudiciousness, absurdity, ludicrousness, ridiculousness, fatuousness, fatuity, asininity, futility, fruitlessness, pointlessness, meaninglessness, madness, craziness (*inf*), lunacy, insanity, imbecility.

stupor *noun* daze, trance, numbness, stupefaction, torpor, lethargy, inertia, sluggishness, oblivion, insensibility, coma, unconsciousness.

sturdy *adj* **1** (*a sturdy body*) strong, powerful, brawny, muscular, strapping, stalwart, robust, hardy, lusty, hale, hearty, healthy, vigorous, sound, solid, stout, tough, substantial, durable, firm. OPPOSITE: weak. **2** (*he encountered sturdy opposition from his rivals*) determined, strong, firm, vigorous, stalwart, tenacious, staunch, steadfast, unyielding, unwavering, uncompromising.

stutter *verb* stammer, splutter, hesitate, pause, falter, stumble, mumble.

style *noun* **1** (*a new style of doing things*) manner, mode, method, way, approach. **2** (*a skirt in the latest style*) fashion, design, cut, shape, form, kind, type, sort, tone, tenor. **3** (*she likes to dress in style*) vogue, mode, fashion, trend. **4** (*he has great style*) stylishness, elegance, flair, flamboyance, dash, panache, chic, smartness, polish, taste, refinement, culture, sophistication, suaveness, urbanity. **5** (*the emperor lived in style*) grandeur, comfort, luxury, affluence, wealth.
➤ *verb* **1** (*she has styled her hair differently*) design, fashion, cut, shape, tailor, adapt. **2** (*he styled himself president*) name, call, term, designate, denominate, dub, tag, label, address, title.

stylish *adj* **1** (*a stylish outfit*) fashionable, modish, modern, voguish, trendy (*inf*), natty (*inf*), snazzy (*inf*), chic, smart, elegant. OPPOSITE: dowdy. **2** (*a stylish rogue*) smart, elegant, classy (*inf*), suave, urbane, sophisticated.

suave *adj* urbane, sophisticated, debonair, smooth, polished, refined, polite, courteous, civil, civilized, agreeable, pleasant, charming, gracious, affable, bland, glib. OPPOSITE: rude.

subconscious *adj* inner, innermost, deep, hidden, latent, underlying, repressed, suppressed, unconscious, subliminal, instinctive, intuitive.

subdue *verb* conquer, vanquish, subjugate, subject, rout, crush, defeat, quash, overwhelm, overrun, overpower, overcome, master, control, discipline, humble, tame, break, master, quell, check, curb, restrain, suppress, repress, stifle, reduce, moderate, soften, quieten, tone down, mute, damp.

subject *noun* **1** (*the subject of the lecture*) topic, theme, substance, gist, text, thesis, point, object, matter, affair, issue, question. **2** (*the subject of the experiment*) patient, client, case, victim, guinea pig (*inf*). **3** (*a subject of this country*) dependant, subordinate, citizen, national. **4** (*she prefers arts subjects*) course, discipline, field.
➤ *adj* **1** (*subject to his control*) subordinate, dependent, subservient, inferior, subjugated, obedient, answerable, accountable. OPPOSITE: ruling. **2** (*subject to strong winds*) exposed, vulnerable, open, susceptible, liable, apt, prone. OPPOSITE: immune. **3** (*subject to conditions*

remaining favourable) conditional, dependent, depending, contingent.

➤ **verb 1** (*he was subjected to ill-treatment*) expose, lay open, put through, treat, submit. **2** (*they were subjected by the invaders*) subdue, subjugate, quell, conquer, vanquish, crush, master, subordinate.

subjection *noun* subjugation, mastery, domination, oppression, conquest, defeat, captivity, bondage, slavery, enslavement, servitude, subordination, dependence. OPPOSITE: independence.

subjective *adj* internal, mental, nonobjective, personal, individual, biased, prejudiced, bigoted, idiosyncratic, emotional. OPPOSITE: objective.

subjugate *verb* conquer, vanquish, rout, defeat, overwhelm, overthrow, overpower, overcome, master, crush, quell, reduce, subdue, humble, tame, discipline, subject, enslave, oppress, suppress. OPPOSITE: liberate.

sublimate *verb* **1** (*sublimate to a higher level*) refine, purify, exalt, uplift, heighten, elevate. OPPOSITE: degrade. **2** (*sublimate her energies*) divert, redirect, transfer, channel.

sublime *adj* **1** (*his sublime majesty*) exalted, noble, dignified, eminent, lofty, elevated, glorious, superb, magnificent, grand, august, stately, majestic, imposing. OPPOSITE: ridiculous. **2** (*sublime skill*) great, supreme, intense, extreme, complete, utter.

submerge *verb* **1** (*submerge in water*) submerse, immerse, plunge, dive, dip, duck, sink. OPPOSITE: surface. **2** (*the street was submerged by the flood*) drown, inundate, flood, deluge, engulf, swamp, overwhelm.

submission *noun* **1** (*submission to the enemy*) surrender, capitulation, yielding, resignation. **2** (*they demanded his submission to their rule*) submissiveness, surrender, capitulation, yielding, consent, compliance, deference, acceptance, acquiescence, agreement, assent. **3** (*we examined your submission with interest*) tender, proposal, offering, contribution, entry, suggestion, presentation.

submissive *adj* docile, tractable, malleable, biddable, yielding, unresisting, compliant, acquiescent, amenable, accommodating, obliging, uncomplaining, obedient, deferential, ingratiating, humble, meek, self-effacing, subdued, weak, patient, resigned, passive, subservient, servile, obsequious. OPPOSITE: obstinate.

submit *verb* **1** (*submit to their wishes*) yield, surrender, capitulate, succumb, accede, acquiesce, resign oneself, bow, bend, stoop, defer, obey, comply, conform. OPPOSITE: resist. **2** (*submit his resignation*) present, hand in, tender, offer, proffer, propose, advance, put forward, table, suggest. OPPOSITE: withdraw.

subordinate *adj* **1** (*a subordinate official*) inferior, junior, lesser, lower, subaltern, lowly. **2** (*of subordinate importance*) minor, lesser, dependent, secondary, subsidiary, ancillary, auxiliary, subservient. OPPOSITE: chief.

➤ **noun** inferior, junior, subaltern, hireling, underling (*inf*), assistant, second, deputy, aide, attendant, sidekick (*inf*), dependant, subject, menial, vassal. OPPOSITE: superior.

subscribe *verb* **1** (*subscribe to charity*) pledge, promise, pay, contribute, give, donate, chip in (*inf*), shell out (*inf*), fork out (*inf*). **2** (*subscribe to the same opinion*)

endorse, support, back, advocate, assent, consent, accede, agree, approve, countenance, underwrite.

subscription *noun* fee, dues, payment, donation, contribution, offering, membership.

subsequent *adj* succeeding, following, ensuing, future, successive, consequent, resulting, later, next. OPPOSITE: previous.

subsequently *adv* later, afterwards, after, consequently.

subservient *adj* **1** (*a subservient manner*) obsequious, servile, submissive, fawning, grovelling, toadying, deferential, slavish, sycophantic, unctuous, ingratiating. **2** (*subservient to the management*) subordinate, inferior, dependent, subject. OPPOSITE: independent.

subside *verb* **1** (*the noise subsided*) abate, let up, moderate, lessen, decrease, diminish, lull, quieten, wane, ebb, recede, dwindle, peter out, die down. OPPOSITE: increase. **2** (*the level subsided gradually*) sink, descend, decline, lower, settle, fall, drop, cave in, collapse. OPPOSITE: rise.

subsidence *noun* sinking, descent, settling, ebb, fall, decline, decrease, diminution, lessening, abatement, slackening.

subsidiary *adj* auxiliary, supplementary, additional, ancillary, supporting, contributory, accessory, aiding, assistant, helpful, instrumental, subservient, inferior, lesser, minor, secondary, subordinate. OPPOSITE: primary.

subsidize *verb* support, back, underwrite, sponsor, promote, endorse, fund, finance, invest in, aid, contribute to.

subsidy *noun* grant, allowance, assistance, aid, help, support, sponsorship, endorsement, investment, finance, funding, contribution.

subsist *verb* exist, be, live, survive, last, continue, endure, remain, maintain, keep going, cope, make ends meet. OPPOSITE: die.

subsistence *noun* **1** (*subsistence for the poor*) food, nourishment, sustenance, upkeep, maintenance, keep, support. **2** (*subsistence on government hand-outs*) living, existence, survival.

substance *noun* **1** (*a solid substance*) matter, material, stuff, fabric, body, element. **2** (*no substance in the rumour*) solidity, validity, truth, foundation, basis, ground, reality, actuality, substantiality. **3** (*the substance of the speech*) essence, gist, pith, burden, meaning, significance, sense, drift, import, point, subject, matter, topic, theme, text. **4** (*a woman of substance*) wealth, money, riches, affluence, means, prosperity, assets, resources, property, estate, power, influence.

substantial *adj* **1** (*a substantial property*) large, big, considerable, sizable, ample, generous, important, significant. OPPOSITE: small. **2** (*substantial material*) firm, strong, solid, stout, sturdy, sound, tough, durable, well-built. OPPOSITE: flimsy. **3** (*the substantial world*) real, actual, material, tangible, corporeal, existing, concrete. **4** (*it made a substantial difference*) real, actual, basic, fundamental, genuine, positive, meaningful. OPPOSITE: imaginary. **5** (*a substantial figure in business*) wealthy, rich, prosperous, affluent, moneyed, well-to-do, powerful, influential, successful. OPPOSITE: poor.

substantially *adv* **1** (*things have changed substantially*) significantly, considerably, markedly, greatly, to a great extent. **2** (*he is substantially correct*) essentially, basically, fundamentally, largely, mainly, in the main, materially, for the most part, to all intents and purposes.

substantiate *verb* prove, establish, confirm, uphold, support, back up, verify, validate, authenticate, corroborate, bear out. OPPOSITE: refute.

substitute *verb* **1** (*substitute the painting with a fake*) replace, exchange, change, interchange, swap (*inf*). **2** (*substitute for his superior*) deputize, stand in, cover, relieve, understudy, fill in (*inf*).
  ➤ *noun* replacement, relief, surrogate, agent, deputy, proxy, understudy, reserve, stand-in, supply, locum.
  ➤ *adj* acting, reserve, relief, deputy, surrogate, proxy, stand-by, stand-in, replacement, alternative, temporary.

subterfuge *noun* **1** (*a clever subterfuge to deceive the police*) artifice, stratagem, wile, ruse, trick, device, dodge, shift, manoeuvre, deception, excuse, pretext. **2** (*the use of subterfuge*) intrigue, duplicity, deception, deviousness, trickery, evasion.

subtle *adj* **1** (*a subtle aroma*) faint, delicate, slight, mild, indistinct, indefinite, elusive. OPPOSITE: obvious. **2** (*a subtle hint*) implied, indirect. **3** (*subtle decoration*) refined, sophisticated, tasteful, understated, low-key, fine. **4** (*a subtle mind*) astute, shrewd, keen, acute, penetrating, discerning, discriminating, deep, profound. OPPOSITE: stupid. **5** (*a subtle trick*) sly, cunning, crafty, wily, artful, designing, devious, Machiavellian, clever, smart. OPPOSITE: artless.

subtlety *noun* **1** (*the subtlety of the perfume*) faintness, delicacy, elusiveness, understatement. **2** (*the subtlety of his technique*) refinement, finesse, sophistication. **3** (*the subtlety of the contrast*) subtleness, fineness, slightness, nicety, indistinctness, indefiniteness. **4** (*he showed considerable subtlety in the matter*) sensitivity, perceptiveness, perception, discernment, discrimination, keenness, acuteness, shrewdness, astuteness, acumen, skill, sagacity. **5** (*he used subtlety to win the game*) cunning, guile, artfulness, wiliness, craftiness, slyness, deviousness, deception.

subtract *verb* deduct, take away, remove, detract, diminish, withdraw. OPPOSITE: add.

suburbs *pl noun* outskirts, environs, precincts, purlieus, neighbourhood, suburbia, edge, periphery. OPPOSITE: centre.

suburban *adj* provincial, insular, unsophisticated, parochial, bourgeois, middle-class, narrow-minded, narrow.

subversive *adj* revolutionary, insurrectionary, seditious, treacherous, traitorous, disruptive, troublemaking, inflammatory, incendiary, riotous, destructive, undermining, weakening.
  ➤ *noun* rebel, revolutionary, insurrectionary, saboteur, traitor, seditionary.

subvert *verb* **1** (*subvert the system*) overthrow, overturn, upset, disrupt, demolish, wreck, destroy, ruin, sabotage, undermine, invalidate. OPPOSITE: conserve. **2** (*subverted

by their evil influence) corrupt, deprave, pervert, demoralize, vitiate, contaminate, poison.

succeed *verb* **1** (*succeed in business*) thrive, prosper, flourish, make good, get on (*inf*), triumph, prevail, work. OPPOSITE: fail. **2** (*they succeeded in their mission*) bring off, pull off (*inf*), carry out, realize, accomplish, achieve, attain, arrive at, reach, complete, fulfil. **3** (*one thing succeeded another*) follow, ensue, supervene, come next, accede, replace, supersede, take over from. OPPOSITE: precede. **4** (*he succeeded to the property*) inherit, come into.

succeeding *adj* following, successive, coming, subsequent, next, ensuing.

success *noun* **1** (*the team enjoyed great success*) prosperity, luck, fortune, triumph, victory, achievement, attainment, accomplishment, fulfilment, realization, fame, eminence, happiness. **2** (*she proved a success on the stage*) celebrity, star, hit (*inf*), sensation, winner, VIP (*inf*), big name (*inf*), big shot (*inf*). OPPOSITE: failure.

successful *adj* **1** (*the successful side*) triumphant, victorious, winning. **2** (*a successful businessman*) prosperous, affluent, wealthy, thriving, flourishing, leading, top, famous, well-known, eminent. **3** (*a successful enterprise*) profitable, rewarding, paying, lucrative, booming, flourishing, thriving, fruitful. OPPOSITE: unsuccessful.

succession *noun* **1** (*a succession of setbacks*) chain, run, course, flow, train, string, series, procession, cycle, concatenation, sequence, progression, order. **2** (*succession to the throne*) accession, inheritance, elevation, assumption, promotion. **3** (*he can trace his succession through the centuries*) descent, posterity, lineage.
  in succession successively, consecutively, running, on the trot (*inf*), uninterruptedly, sequentially.

succinct *adj* brief, short, concise, terse, pithy, crisp, laconic, curt, compact, condensed, compendious, summary. OPPOSITE: prolix.

succour *noun* help, aid, assistance, support, relief, comfort.
  ➤ *verb* help, aid, assist, support, relieve, comfort, nurse, minister to.

succulent *adj* juicy, sappy, fleshy, moist, luscious, mouthwatering, lush, rich. OPPOSITE: dry.

succumb *verb* **1** (*succumb to the assault*) surrender, yield, give way, give in, submit, capitulate, fall. OPPOSITE: resist. **2** (*succumb to a cold*) go down with, catch, contract, pick up.

suck *verb* **1** (*suck in air*) draw in, take in, inhale. **2** (*suck up all the water*) absorb, blot up, soak up, drain.
  suck up to fawn on, toady to, curry favour with, flatter.

sudden *adj* abrupt, hasty, quick, fast, rapid, swift, prompt, hurried, rash, impetuous, impulsive, immediate, instantaneous, sharp, unexpected, unanticipated, unforeseen, surprising, startling, dramatic, brief, momentary. OPPOSITE: gradual.

suddenly *adv* all of a sudden, without warning, out of the blue (*inf*), abruptly, unexpectedly, quickly, sharply, immediately, instantaneously.

sue *verb* **1** (*sue for damages*) prosecute, summon, take to

court, prefer charges, indict, charge. OPPOSITE: defend.
2 (*sue for peace*) solicit, petition, appeal, beg, plead,
implore, entreat, beseech.

suffer *verb* **1** (*she suffered many misfortunes*) undergo,
experience, feel, endure, go through, meet with, sustain.
2 (*she will suffer his presence no longer*) bear, tolerate,
endure, abide, brook, stand, support, put up with (*inf*).
3 (*the animal is suffering*) ache, hurt, be in pain, grieve.

suffering *noun* **1** (*physical suffering*) pain, agony,
affliction, torment, torture, discomfort. **2** (*his death
caused much suffering*) distress, anguish, misery, grief,
wretchedness, hurt, pain, hardship. OPPOSITE: ease.

suffice *verb* do, satisfy, serve, content, answer, measure
up, fit the bill (*inf*), hit the spot (*inf*), be sufficient.

sufficient *adj* enough, adequate, ample, abundant,
plentiful, plenty (*inf*), satisfactory, decent (*inf*).
OPPOSITE: deficient.

suffocate *verb* asphyxiate, smother, stifle, choke,
strangle.

suffrage *noun* franchise, ballot, vote, voice.

suffuse *verb* cover, spread, overspread, colour, redden,
mantle, bathe, flood, imbue, permeate, pervade, infuse,
steep, transfuse. OPPOSITE: drain.

sugary *adj* sentimental, lovey-dovey (*inf*), emotional,
gushing, gushy (*inf*), maudlin, mawkish, touching,
syrupy, sloppy, soppy, slushy (*inf*), mushy (*inf*),
schmaltzy (*inf*), sickly (*inf*).

suggest *verb* **1** (*suggest a solution*) propose, submit, put
forward, float (*inf*), advance, advise, recommend. **2** (*his
absence suggests something is amiss*) hint, intimate, imply,
insinuate. **3** (*her voice suggested various memories*) evoke,
bring to mind.

suggestion *noun* **1** (*the suggestion was turned down*)
proposal, submission, proposition, motion, plan, idea,
advice, recommendation. **2** (*a suggestion of scandal*)
implication, insinuation, innuendo, intimation. **3** (*just
a suggestion of a foreign accent*) hint, trace, touch,
suspicion, intimation, indication.

suggestive *adj* **1** (*suggestive of her childhood*) evocative,
reminiscent, redolent, expressive. **2** (*a suggestive tale*)
ribald, bawdy, dirty, lewd, smutty, obscene, blue (*inf*),
off-colour, indecent, indelicate, improper, immodest,
risqué, provocative, racy, titillating, crude, vulgar.

suicide *noun* self-destruction, self-murder, hara-kiri.

suit *verb* **1** (*that colour suits you*) befit, become, flatter.
2 (*the job did not suit her lifestyle*) conform with,
harmonize with, complement, tally with, match, fit,
correspond with, accord with, agree with, answer,
satisfy, gratify, please. **3** (*the vehicle can be suited for most
needs*) adapt, fashion, proportion, adjust, accommodate,
fit.
➤ *noun* **1** (*he wore a grey suit*) outfit, ensemble, costume,
clothing. **2** (*the suit will have to go to court*) lawsuit, case,
action, trial, cause, proceeding, process, litigation,
prosecution, dispute, argument, contest. **3** (*he took his
suit to the king*) petition, appeal, plea, prayer, request,
entreaty, solicitation. **4** (*he paid his suit to the princess for
years*) addresses, courtship.

suitable *adj* **1** (*a suitable coat*) appropriate, apt,
apposite, fit, fitting, right. OPPOSITE: unsuitable. **2** (*he

greeted her with suitable respect*) seemly, fit, befitting,
proper, appropriate, apt, due, becoming, relevant,
pertinent. **3** (*agree a suitable date*) convenient,
opportune, acceptable, satisfactory, agreeable.

suitcase *noun* case, bag, overnight case, travel bag,
flight bag, holdall, portmanteau, grip, valise, trunk.

suite *noun* **1** (*a suite of rooms*) set of rooms, apartment.
2 (*a suite of officials*) retinue, train, entourage,
attendants, retainers, servants, followers, escort,
bodyguard.

suitor *noun* beau, gallant, admirer, lover, wooer,
follower.

sulk *verb* pout, mope, brood, grouse, be put out.
➤ *noun* mood, temper, huff (*inf*), miff (*inf*), pique.

sulky *adj* moody, brooding, moping, morose,
disgruntled, miffed (*inf*), put out, resentful, grudging,
grumpy, huffy (*inf*), out of sorts, cross, bad-tempered,
ratty (*inf*), sullen, unsociable, aloof.

sullen *adj* **1** (*a sullen child*) sulky, morose, glum,
gloomy, scowling, glowering, cross, peevish, petulant,
obstinate, stubborn, moody, surly, sour, bitter, resentful,
put out, silent, uncommunicative. OPPOSITE: cheerful.
2 (*a sullen sky*) dark, gloomy, sombre, leaden, heavy,
dull, dismal, cheerless.

sully *verb* soil, dirty, spot, stain, blemish, pollute,
contaminate, taint, tarnish, defile, disgrace, dishonour,
defame. OPPOSITE: clean.

sultry *adj* **1** (*sultry weather*) close, oppressive, muggy,
humid, hot, sticky, stuffy, stifling. OPPOSITE: cool. **2** (*a
sultry beauty*) voluptuous, sexy, sensual, seductive,
provocative, attractive, tempting, alluring, passionate.

sum *noun* **1** (*the sum of the day's takings*) total, aggregate,
tally, score, reckoning, result. **2** (*a tidy sum*) amount,
quantity, number. **3** (*consider the matter in its sum*)
whole, entirety, totality. OPPOSITE: part.
➤ *verb* add, add up, total, tot up, count, tally, reckon,
calculate.

sum up 1 (*she summed up the situation briefly*)
summarize, recapitulate, review. **2** (*this last failure
summed up the whole campaign*) epitomize, encapsulate,
exemplify, embody.

summarily *adv* immediately, instantly, promptly,
speedily, swiftly, expeditiously, forthwith, without
delay, right away, straight away, hastily, abruptly,
peremptorily, arbitrarily.

summarize *verb* sum up, epitomize, encapsulate,
outline, recapitulate, recap (*inf*), review, condense,
abridge, abbreviate, shorten, précis. OPPOSITE: amplify.

summary *noun* abstract, synopsis, précis, compendium,
conspectus, digest, condensation, epitome, outline,
résumé, rundown (*inf*), recapitulation, review,
abridgement. OPPOSITE: amplification.
➤ *adj* quick, rapid, speedy, swift, hasty, prompt,
immediate, instant, cursory, short, brief, concise,
succinct, pithy, terse, curt, peremptory, laconic,
condensed, compendious, compact. OPPOSITE: lengthy.

summit *noun* **1** (*the summit of the mountain*) top, crown,
cap, peak, pinnacle, apex, vertex, apogee. OPPOSITE: base.
2 (*at the summit of his success*) height, peak, pinnacle,
zenith, acme, climax, culmination.

summon *verb* **1** (*summoned to head office*) call, order, invite, beckon, bid, demand, send for, call for. **2** (*summon a meeting*) call, convene, muster, assemble, rally. OPPOSITE: dismiss.

summon up 1 (*summon up the courage to speak*) rouse, arouse, muster, collect, gather, mobilize, rally. **2** (*summon up the past*) evoke, recall, revive, conjure up, bring to mind, call to mind, call up. **3** (*summon up the devil*) conjure up, invoke, call up, rouse up.

sumptuous *adj* costly, expensive, dear, extravagant, lavish, luxurious, rich, opulent, magnificent, splendid, gorgeous, grand, superb, plush (*inf*), de luxe. OPPOSITE: poor.

sundry *adj* **1** (*sundry objects*) various, varied, diverse, assorted, miscellaneous. **2** (*on sundry occasions*) various, several, some, a few, different.

sunken *adj* **1** (*a sunken chamber*) buried, lower, lowered, submerged. **2** (*sunken eyes*) hollow, hollowed, depressed, concave, haggard, drawn.

sunless *adj* overcast, dark, black, grey, cloudy, murky, gloomy, dismal, bleak, sombre, dreary, depressing, cheerless. OPPOSITE: sunny.

sunny *adj* **1** (*sunny weather*) bright, sunshiny, sunlit, shining, radiant, clear, cloudless, fine, summery. OPPOSITE: dull. **2** (*a sunny disposition*) cheerful, cheery, merry, bubbly, blithe, jolly, genial, glad, happy, joyful, beaming, radiant, buoyant, optimistic. OPPOSITE: gloomy.

sunrise *noun* dawn, daybreak, daylight, first light, sun-up, cock-crow, morning.

sunset *noun* nightfall, dusk, twilight, gloaming, sundown, close of day.

super *adj* wonderful, marvellous, great, excellent, outstanding, glorious, magnificent, splendid, superb, sensational, smashing (*inf*), cool (*inf*), mega (*inf*), wicked (*inf*). OPPOSITE: awful.

superannuated *adj* old, elderly, aged, senile, decrepit, antiquated, passé, obsolete, past it (*inf*), moribund, retired, pensioned off.

superb *adj* **1** (*a superb evening*) excellent, great, first-rate, first-class, matchless, peerless, outstanding, remarkable, superior, superlative, marvellous, wonderful, magnificent, impressive, breathtaking, smashing (*inf*), ace (*inf*). OPPOSITE: poor. **2** (*superb costumes*) magnificent, splendid, glorious, gorgeous, sumptuous, fine, exquisite, grand, choice.

supercilious *adj* arrogant, haughty, insolent, contemptuous, scornful, disdainful, lofty, lordly, snooty (*inf*), snotty (*inf*), stuck-up (*inf*), proud, vain, domineering, overbearing, patronizing, condescending. OPPOSITE: humble.

superficial *adj* **1** (*superficial damage only*) surface, exterior, external, outer. **2** (*a superficial young man*) shallow, slight, trivial, frivolous, empty-headed. OPPOSITE: deep. **3** (*a superficial appearance of calm*) apparent, seeming, ostensible, outward. OPPOSITE: actual. **4** (*a superficial examination*) casual, hasty, cursory, sketchy, slapdash, careless, perfunctory. OPPOSITE: thorough.

superfluity *noun* superabundance, surfeit, surplus, excess, glut, plethora. OPPOSITE: lack.

superfluous *adj* **1** (*a superfluous amount of equipment*) superabundant, excessive, extra, surplus, redundant. OPPOSITE: deficient. **2** (*a superfluous gesture*) unnecessary, needless, uncalled-for, unwarranted.

superhuman *adj* **1** (*superhuman strength*) prodigious, stupendous, immense, great, herculean, phenomenal, miraculous. **2** (*of superhuman origin*) supernatural, preternatural, paranormal, divine. OPPOSITE: natural.

superintend *verb* supervise, manage, run, administer, oversee, inspect, direct, control, handle, steer.

superintendent *noun* supervisor, overseer, inspector, director, manager, administrator, chief, boss (*inf*), gaffer (*inf*).

superior *adj* **1** (*a superior model*) better, higher, greater, excellent, exclusive, first-rate, quality, exceptional, outstanding, superlative, supreme, matchless, unrivalled, peerless, choice, select, prize, fine. OPPOSITE: inferior. **2** (*a superior attitude to the less well-off*) haughty, arrogant, condescending, supercilious, disdainful, pretentious, patronizing, snobbish, snobby, snooty (*inf*), stuck-up (*inf*), toffee-nosed (*inf*), lofty, lordly.
➤ *noun* chief, boss (*inf*), manager, director, supervisor, senior. OPPOSITE: junior.

superiority *noun* supremacy, advantage, edge, lead, dominance, ascendancy, pre-eminence.

superlative *adj* supreme, best, greatest, highest, transcendent, superior, peerless, matchless, incomparable, unrivalled, unparalleled, excellent, first-class, first-rate, outstanding, ace (*inf*), brill (*inf*). OPPOSITE: poor.

supernatural *adj* **1** (*a supernatural presence*) ghostly, phantom, spectral, spiritual, mystical, magical, occult, otherworldly, unearthly, metaphysical, eerie. **2** (*she claims supernatural powers*) psychic, paranormal, uncanny, unnatural, extraordinary, abnormal, miraculous. OPPOSITE: normal.

supernumerary *adj* extra, superfluous, redundant, surplus, excess, excessive, spare, odd.

supersede *verb* **1** (*he superseded his father*) supplant, displace, oust, usurp, replace, succeed. **2** (*the former policy has been superseded*) discard, remove, set aside, override, overrule.

supervise *verb* **1** (*supervise the operation*) oversee, watch over, observe, inspect, guide. **2** (*supervise the group*) superintend, preside over, administer, direct, manage, run, handle, control, look after.

supervision *noun* **1** (*supervision of the campaign*) direction, management, administration, superintendence, control, charge, guidance. **2** (*under the supervision of the guards*) surveillance, inspection, oversight.

supervisor *noun* **1** (*the works supervisor*) superintendent, manager, foreman, overseer, director, administrator, controller, steward, chief, boss (*inf*). **2** (*the supervisor of the apprentices*) inspector, overseer, observer, guide.

supine *adj* **1** (*supine upon the bed*) recumbent, prostrate, prone, flat, horizontal. OPPOSITE: upright. **2** (*supine indifference*) lethargic, bored, apathetic, indifferent, sluggish, torpid, languid, listless, lifeless, inactive, inert, lazy, idle, indolent, slothful. OPPOSITE: energetic.

supper *noun* dinner, evening meal, tea.

supplant *verb* displace, replace, supersede, oust, usurp, remove, topple, overthrow, unseat.

supple *adj* **1** (*supple material*) pliable, pliant, flexible, elastic, plastic, yielding, bending. **2** (*a supple body*) lithe, lissom, limber. OPPOSITE: stiff.

supplement *noun* **1** (*a supplement to his usual diet*) addition, additive, add-on, extra, extension, complement. **2** (*a supplement to the main text*) addendum, appendix, postscript, codicil, rider.
≫ *verb* add to, augment, extend, top up, complement. OPPOSITE: reduce.

supplementary *adj* **1** (*a supplementary charge*) supplemental, additional, complementary, extra. **2** (*a supplementary article*) extra, appended, added, ancillary, auxiliary, secondary, subsidiary.

suppliant *adj* supplicant, supplicating, petitioning, entreating, beseeching, praying, imploring, importunate, asking, begging.

supplicate *verb* petition, solicit, beg, plead, crave, beseech, ask, pray, implore, invoke, entreat, importune. OPPOSITE: demand.

supplication *noun* petition, solicitation, invocation, prayer, plea, suit, entreaty, appeal, request.

supply *verb* **1** (*supply the team with equipment*) provide, furnish, equip, stock, replenish. **2** (*supply sufficient funds*) give, contribute, donate, fork out (*inf*), shell out (*inf*), afford, yield, grant, bestow. OPPOSITE: withhold. **3** (*supply his needs*) satisfy, meet, fulfil
≫ *noun* **1** (*undertake the supply of food*) provision, providing, supplying, furnishing. **2** (*a plentiful supply of oil*) stock, stockpile, store, hoard, reserve, reservoir, quantity, fund.

support *verb* **1** (*support the weight*) bear, carry, hold up, uphold, sustain, maintain, prop, brace, buttress, bolster, reinforce, strengthen. OPPOSITE: drop. **2** (*support the campaign*) back, second, further, forward, encourage, abet, help, assist, aid, promote, advocate, champion, defend, finance, subsidize, fund, foster, nurture. OPPOSITE: oppose. **3** (*evidence to support the claim*) endorse, verify, authenticate, validate, confirm, ratify, corroborate, substantiate, back up, bear out. OPPOSITE: refute. **4** (*she could support the idea no longer*) tolerate, put up with (*inf*), stomach, brook, bear, endure. **5** (*he supported her when she was down*) help, encourage, comfort, befriend, care for, be kind to, sympathize with, give strength to, motivate. **6** (*supported by the state*) maintain, keep, provide for, sustain, look after, take care of, feed, nourish.
≫ *noun* **1** (*the main supports of the structure*) prop, brace, buttress, stay, stanchion, upright, bolster, pillar, crutch, underpinning, substructure, base, foundation. **2** (*with the support of her friends*) help, encouragement, friendship, comfort, care, sympathy. **3** (*living on state support*) maintenance, keep, upkeep, sustenance, subsistence. **4** (*financial support*) finance, funding, sponsorship, patronage, subsidy, grant, donation, contribution. **5** (*support for the theory*) backing, evidence, confirmation, validation, ratification, substantiation,

authentication, verification. **6** (*support for the plan*) backing, encouragement, furtherance, help, assistance, aid, patronage, sponsorship. OPPOSITE: opposition.

supporter *noun* backer, patron, sponsor, advocate, champion, adherent, follower, admirer, fan, well-wisher, ally, colleague. OPPOSITE: opponent.

supportive *adj* encouraging, helpful, caring, comforting, reassuring, attentive, sympathetic, understanding.

suppose *verb* **1** (*I suppose that is the case*) presume, assume, postulate, surmise, conjecture, guess, suspect, imagine, fancy, believe, opine, think, conclude, judge, infer. OPPOSITE: know. **2** (*his theory supposes certain conditions*) assume, presume, presuppose, require, imply.

supposed *adj* hypothetical, assumed, presumed, accepted, so-called, professed, alleged, reputed, putative, believed.

supposition *noun* assumption, presumption, presupposition, postulate, postulation, hypothesis, theory, surmise, conjecture, guess, speculation, idea, notion. OPPOSITE: knowledge.

suppress *verb* **1** (*he suppressed a laugh*) restrain, rein in, curb, check, repress, smother, stifle, silence. **2** (*the rebellion was ruthlessly suppressed*) quash, quell, vanquish, subdue, crush, overpower, conquer, stamp out, extinguish, put out. **3** (*the story was suppressed by the government*) smother, stifle, strangle, muzzle, repress, conceal, withhold, cover up, censor.

suppression *noun* **1** (*the suppression of the uprising*) crushing, conquering, quelling, quashing, crackdown (*inf*), clampdown (*inf*), elimination, extinction **2** (*suppression of his laughter*) restraint, curbing, holding back, checking, inhibition. **3** (*official suppression of the story*) smothering, stifling, muzzling, withholding, concealment, censorship, cover-up.

supremacy *noun* **1** (*she established her supremacy over all rivals*) ascendancy, superiority, dominance, pre-eminence, primacy. **2** (*the supremacy of the crown*) sovereignty, rule, lordship, mastery, dominion, sway, ascendancy, power, authority. OPPOSITE: subjection.

supreme *adj* **1** (*the supreme champion*) greatest, best, superlative, unsurpassed, matchless, peerless, consummate, incomparable, top, paramount, transcendent, pre-eminent, predominant, prevailing, first, foremost, leading, principal, chief, main, sovereign. OPPOSITE: lowest. **2** (*an act of supreme bravery*) highest, greatest, utmost, uttermost, extreme, extraordinary, remarkable.

sure *adj* **1** (*he was quite sure about it*) certain, positive, definite, convinced, persuaded, satisfied, confident, assured, decided. OPPOSITE: doubtful. **2** (*a sure foundation*) reliable, dependable, trustworthy, trusty, guaranteed, unfailing, infallible, foolproof, unquestionable, indisputable, steady, firm, stable, secure, safe. OPPOSITE: precarious. **3** (*a sure disappointment*) inevitable, unavoidable, inescapable, bound, destined.

surely *adv* **1** (*she will surely succeed*) certainly, assuredly, definitely, undoubtedly, without doubt, doubtlessly, indubitably, without fail, unquestionably, incontestably, incontrovertibly, irrefutably, undeniably, inevitably, unavoidably, inexorably. **2** (*he climbed surely to the top of the ladder*) confidently, unhesitatingly, steadily, firmly.

surety *noun* **1** (*provide surety for the loan*) security, guarantee, warranty, indemnity, insurance, pledge, bond, bail, deposit. **2** (*act as surety*) guarantor, sponsor.

surface *noun* **1** (*the surface of the table*) exterior, outside, covering, coating, top. OPPOSITE: interior. **2** (*probe beneath the surface*) façade, veneer, appearance.
≫ *verb* **1** (*the swimmer surfaced*) come up, come to the top, arise, rise. **2** (*the scandal surfaced again after several years*) emerge, crop up, appear, reappear, materialize.
≫ *adj* superficial, apparent, outer, outside, outward, external, exterior.
on the surface superficially, externally, apparently, ostensibly, seemingly.

surfeit *noun* **1** (*a surfeit of materials*) excess, surplus, oversupply, glut, superabundance, superfluity, plethora. OPPOSITE: deficiency. **2** (*a surfeit of good things*) satiety, overindulgence.
≫ *verb* sate, satiate, glut, cloy, gorge, overfeed, fill, overfill, stuff, cram. OPPOSITE: starve.

surge *noun* **1** (*a surge of water*) rush, gush, stream, flow, outpouring. **2** (*a surge in interest*) upsurge, rise, escalation, increase, intensification, upswing. **3** (*the surge of the tide*) swell, eddy, billow, wave, breaker, roller.
≫ *verb* **1** (*the sea surged through the hole*) rush, gush, pour, flow, stream, sweep. **2** (*inflation surged*) rise, increase, escalate. **3** (*the water surged around them*) swell, swirl, eddy, billow, roll, heave, seethe, undulate.

surly *adj* sullen, sulky, cross, irritable, morose, grouchy, grumpy, testy, touchy, irascible, crabbed, crabby (*inf*), crotchety (*inf*), crusty, cantankerous, ill-tempered, ill-natured, bad-tempered, gruff, brusque, curt, churlish, uncivil, ungracious, rude. OPPOSITE: affable.

surmise *verb* infer, guess, conjecture, suppose, imagine, fancy, suspect, presume, assume, conclude, deduce, opine. OPPOSITE: know.
≫ *noun* inference, assumption, presumption, supposition, guess, conjecture, hypothesis, idea, thought. OPPOSITE: knowledge.

surmount *verb* overcome, conquer, vanquish, triumph over, get over, scale, climb, ascend, top. OPPOSITE: succumb.

surpass *verb* exceed, pass, transcend, excel, outstrip, outdo, beat, overshadow, outshine, eclipse.

surplus *noun* excess, surfeit, glut, superabundance, superfluity, plethora, residue, remainder, rest, balance. OPPOSITE: deficit.
≫ *adj* extra, spare, excess, superfluous, unused, remaining, left over, redundant.

surprise *verb* **1** (*he was surprised by her reaction*) amaze, astound, astonish, stun, stagger, bewilder, confuse, disconcert, flabbergast (*inf*), bowl over (*inf*), startle.
2 (*the thieves were surprised by the police*) catch unawares, catch in the act, catch red-handed, burst in on, unmask, expose.
≫ *noun* **1** (*his jaw dropped in surprise*) amazement, astonishment, incredulity, wonder, bewilderment, dismay. **2** (*a nasty surprise awaited her*) shock, bombshell

(*inf*), revelation, thunderbolt (*inf*), bolt from the blue, start.

surprising *adj* amazing, astounding, astonishing, stunning, staggering, startling, unexpected, unforeseen, incredible, extraordinary, remarkable, wonderful. OPPOSITE: ordinary.

surrender *verb* **1** (*he surrendered his post*) relinquish, part with, yield, hand over, give up, let go of, renounce, forgo, waive, resign, abdicate. OPPOSITE: hold. **2** (*they refused to surrender*) capitulate, submit, give in, concede, cede, quit (*inf*), succumb.
≫ *noun* capitulation, submission, yielding, waiving, relinquishment, renunciation, abandonment, abdication, resignation.

surreptitious *adj* clandestine, stealthy, covert, underhand, furtive, sneaky (*inf*), sly, secret, bidden, unauthorized. OPPOSITE: open.

surrogate *noun* substitute, replacement, stand-in, proxy, deputy, agent, representative.

surround *verb* encircle, circle, encompass, environ, enclose, envelop, confine, ring, gird, girdle, hem in, fence in, besiege.

surrounding *adj* bordering, neighbouring, nearby, adjoining, adjacent.

surroundings *pl noun* environment, milieu, scene, setting, background, environs, habitat, vicinity, neighbourhood, locality.

surveillance *noun* supervision, watch, observation, inspection, scrutiny, care, control, superintendence, direction. OPPOSITE: freedom.

survey *verb* **1** (*survey the landscape*) view, scan, scrutinize, observe, regard, look at, look over, contemplate, consider, review, study, research, examine, inspect. OPPOSITE: ignore. **2** (*survey the situation*) assess, appraise, evaluate, take stock of, size up (*inf*), estimate, calculate, measure, plan, plot, map, chart.
≫ *noun* review, study, examination, inspection, scrutiny, investigation, inquiry, appraisal, assessment.

survive *verb* **1** (*his work survived him*) outlive, outlast. **2** (*survive on a desert island*) live, subsist. OPPOSITE: die. **3** (*the old ways survive*) persist, last, continue, abide, remain, endure, hold out.

susceptibility *noun* **1** (*the susceptibility of a child*) impressionability, suggestibility, sensitivity, responsiveness, gullibility, credulity, credulousness, openness, vulnerability, defencelessness, emotionalism. **2** (*a susceptibility to hay fever*) liability, tendency, proneness, weakness, propensity, predisposition.

susceptible *adj* vulnerable, subject, given, liable, disposed, inclined, prone, open, receptive, responsive, sensitive, impressionable, gullible, suggestible, weak.

suspect *verb* **1** (*I suspect the truth of what she says*) doubt, mistrust, distrust, disbelieve. OPPOSITE: believe. **2** (*we suspect this is inevitable*) surmise, guess, conjecture, speculate, think, conclude, believe, imagine, fancy, suppose, assume, presume, infer. OPPOSITE: know.
≫ *adj* suspicious, questionable, doubtful, dubious, unreliable, debatable.

suspend *verb* **1** (*suspended the swing from a tree*) hang, dangle, swing. **2** (*the meeting was suspended*) postpone, defer, delay, put off, put on ice (*inf*), shelve, pigeonhole, adjourn, stop, stay, arrest, withhold, interrupt, discontinue, cease. OPPOSITE: continue. **3** (*she has been suspended from the party*) dismiss, debar, expel, exclude, remove, shut out.

suspense *noun* uncertainty, doubt, doubtfulness, indecision, irresolution, hesitation, vacillation, insecurity, anxiety, expectation, expectancy, anticipation, excitement.

suspension *noun* **1** (*he announced a suspension in negotiations*) break, interruption, adjournment, deferment, deferral, postponement, stay, delay, respite, remission, cessation, moratorium. **2** (*his suspension from his post*) dismissal, removal, expulsion, exclusion, debarment.

suspicion *noun* **1** (*he was filled with suspicion*) doubt, distrust, mistrust, scepticism, misgiving, qualm, wariness, caution, apprehension. OPPOSITE: trust. **2** (*he had a suspicion she was lying*) surmise, guess, conjecture, supposition, thought, idea, notion, belief, opinion, feeling, funny feeling (*inf*), hunch (*inf*), sixth sense (*inf*). **3** (*a suspicion of garlic*) trace, hint, touch, tinge, suggestion, soupçon, scintilla, shade, shadow, glimmer.

suspicious *adj* **1** (*suspicious of her motives*) distrustful, mistrustful, suspecting, sceptical, unbelieving, disbelieving, wary, chary, apprehensive, uneasy, unsure. OPPOSITE: trustful. **2** (*a suspicious character*) doubtful, dubious, questionable, dishonest, guilty, shifty, suspect, funny, odd, peculiar, shady (*inf*), dodgy (*inf*), iffy (*inf*), fishy (*inf*), strange, queer, irregular.

sustain *verb* **1** (*the weight was sustained by four pillars*) support, uphold, hold up, carry, bear. OPPOSITE: drop. **2** (*he sustained a serious injury*) suffer, undergo, experience, endure, withstand. **3** (*she sustained the pretence for months*) maintain, keep up, keep going, continue, prolong. **4** (*sustained by hot soup*) nurture, nourish, feed. **5** (*sustained by encouragement from her friends*) strengthen, foster, help, aid, assist, relieve, comfort, support. **6** (*the court sustained the decision*) uphold, endorse, verify, validate, justify, confirm, establish, ratify, sanction, approve. OPPOSITE: overrule.

sustained *adj* constant, unremitting, perpetual, prolonged, protracted, steady, continuous, continuing, long-drawn-out.

sustenance *noun* **1** (*provide sustenance for the refugees*) nourishment, nutrition, nutriment, food, fare, provisions, victuals. OPPOSITE: starvation. **2** (*rely on his family for sustenance*) support, maintenance, livelihood, living, upkeep, keep, subsistence.

swagger *verb* **1** (*he swaggered into the room*) strut, prance, parade. **2** (*he swaggered about with his latest acquisition*) show off (*inf*), swank (*inf*), vaunt, boast, brag, bluster.
   ➤ *noun* **1** (*she walked with a swagger*) strut, flourish. **2** (*they soon tired of his swagger*) boasting, bragging, showing-off (*inf*), swanking (*inf*).

swallow *verb* **1** (*she swallowed her tea quickly*) gulp, down (*inf*), knock back (*inf*), polish off (*inf*), guzzle (*inf*), eat, drink, consume, devour. OPPOSITE: vomit. **2** (*the village will be swallowed up in the suburbs*) absorb, assimilate, engulf, envelop, overwhelm, overrun. **3** (*they*

swallowed her story) believe, fall for (*inf*), buy (*inf*), accept. **4** (*she could not swallow the cruelty any more*) take, tolerate, suffer, endure, stand, stomach (*inf*), put up with, abide, bear. **5** (*he swallowed his rage*) suppress, repress, contain, hold back, smother, stifle.

swamp *noun* marsh, bog, morass, fen, slough, quagmire, quicksand.
   ➤ *verb* **1** (*the streets were swamped by the flood*) flood, inundate, deluge, drench, soak, saturate, waterlog. **2** (*they were swamped with replies*) overwhelm, engulf, inundate, deluge, flood, swallow up, submerge, besiege.

swampy *adj* boggy, marshy, miry, wet, soggy, squelchy, waterlogged, soft, spongy.

swap *verb* exchange, barter, trade, switch, transpose, substitute, interchange.

swarm *noun* throng, crowd, multitude, mob, horde, host, herd, drove, flock, bevy, shoal, mass, concourse.
   ➤ *verb* throng, crowd, cluster, flock, mass, teem, abound, crawl, overrun, infest, flood. OPPOSITE: scatter.

swarthy *adj* dark, dusky, dark-skinned, dark-complexioned, tanned, black, brown. OPPOSITE: pale.

swathe *verb* swaddle, bandage, bind, wrap, enwrap, envelop, fold, enfold, drape, clothe, cloak, shroud. OPPOSITE: unwrap.

sway *verb* **1** (*the tree swayed in the wind*) swing, rock, wave, totter, reel, lean, incline, wobble. **2** (*she swayed between the two choices*) fluctuate, vacillate, hesitate, waver, oscillate. **3** (*his contribution swayed the board*) influence, move, persuade, convince, win over, bring round. **4** (*swayed by greed*) control, guide, direct, govern, rule, dominate.
   ➤ *noun* influence, control, command, power, authority, dominion, rule, sovereignty, ascendancy. OPPOSITE: subjection.

swear *verb* **1** (*he swore that it was true*) affirm, avow, aver, asseverate, assert, insist, declare, vow, promise, pledge, testify, depose. OPPOSITE: deny. **2** (*she swore angrily at him*) blaspheme, curse, cuss (*inf*).

swear by believe in, have faith in, have confidence in, trust in, depend on, rely on.

sweat *verb* perspire, drip, exude, secrete.
   ➤ *noun* **1** (*sweat ran down his back*) perspiration, moisture, stickiness, diaphoresis, exudation, secretion. **2** (*he is in a sweat about his exams*) panic, fuss, fret, dither, flap (*inf*), tizzy (*inf*), stew (*inf*), lather (*inf*), fluster (*inf*), anxiety, agitation, worry. **3** (*the job was a real sweat*) chore, effort, labour, toil, drudgery.

sweaty *adj* sweating, perspiring, moist, damp, clammy, sticky.

sweep *verb* **1** (*sweep the yard*) brush, dust, clean, clear. **2** (*the car swept up the drive*) race, hurtle, streak, tear (*inf*), whip, whisk, skim, scud, glide, fly, sail, pass. **3** (*she swept aside the other children*) thrust, push, shove, elbow, jostle.
   ➤ *noun* **1** (*the sweep of his shot*) arc, curve, bend, stroke, swing. **2** (*a sweep of the hand*) stroke, gesture, wave, movement, move. **3** (*the sweep of his influence*) compass, scope, range, stretch, extent, reach, span, spread. **4** (*a sweep of water*) expanse, stretch, span, extent, vastness, immensity.

sweeping *adj* **1** (*this breakthrough will have sweeping application*) comprehensive, wide-ranging, all-inclusive, all-embracing, broad, wide, extensive, global, universal, general. **2** (*a sweeping generalization*) blanket (*inf*), indiscriminate, wholesale, oversimplified. OPPOSITE: specific.

sweet *adj* **1** (*a sweet taste*) sugary, sweetened, honeyed, saccharine, syrupy, tasty, toothsome, luscious, delicious. OPPOSITE: sour. **2** (*the room smells sweet now*) fragrant, aromatic, balmy, redolent, perfumed, scented, sweet-smelling, fresh, clean, pure, wholesome. OPPOSITE: foul. **3** (*sweet harmony*) dulcet, mellifluous, melodious, musical, tuneful, harmonious, euphonious, mellow, soft, silvery. OPPOSITE: discordant. **4** (*she is a sweet girl*) attractive, beautiful, pretty, lovely, appealing, charming, engaging, cute, pleasant, pleasing, delightful, agreeable, amiable, lovable, likeable, adorable, winsome, winning, affectionate, tender, kind, kindly, gentle, dear, beloved, darling, precious, treasured, cherished. OPPOSITE: nasty. **5** (*sweet water*) fresh, pure, clean, clear, wholesome.
➤ *noun* **1** (*ice cream for the sweet*) pudding, dessert, afters (*inf*). **2** (*a packet of sweets*) sweetie (*inf*), candy, confectionery, confection, bonbon.
sweet on fond on, keen of, infatuated with, taken with, crazy about (*inf*), mad about (*inf*).

sweeten *verb* **1** (*sweeten the mixture*) sugar, honey. **2** (*sweeten her master's temper*) mellow, soothe, mollify, appease, pacify, soften. **3** (*try to sweeten the blow*) soften, cushion, alleviate, ease, relieve, temper.

sweetheart *noun* love, lover, boyfriend, girlfriend, suitor, paramour, admirer, beau, beloved, betrothed, flame (*inf*).

swell *verb* **1** (*the balloon continued swelling*) expand, dilate, spread, extend, inflate, distend, bloat, puff up, bulge, billow, balloon. OPPOSITE: shrink. **2** (*the protests swelled*) enlarge, increase, augment, amplify, heighten, intensify, grow, proliferate, escalate, rise, mount, surge, skyrocket, mushroom, snowball, accelerate.
➤ *noun* **1** (*the boat tossed on the swell*) wave, billow, undulation. **2** (*a swell in public interest*) rise, surge, increase, escalation, acceleration, mushrooming, snowballing. **3** (*he was considered something of a swell*) dandy, fop, beau.
➤ *adj* grand, smart, luxurious, de luxe, flashy (*inf*), posh (*inf*), plush (*inf*), swanky (*inf*), ritzy (*inf*), expensive, exclusive, elegant, stylish, fashionable, great.

swelling *noun* bulge, bump, lump, protuberance, tumefaction, tumescence, distension, inflation, dilation, enlargement.

sweltering *adj* hot, boiling (*inf*), baking (*inf*), sizzling (*inf*), scorching, tropical, sultry, oppressive, torrid, stifling, suffocating, humid, sticky, clammy, muggy, steamy, close, stuffy, airless.

swerve *verb* turn, veer, stray, drift, wander, deviate, diverge, deflect, skew, sheer, twist.

swift *adj* **1** (*a swift mode of transport*) fast, rapid, quick, speedy, fleet, flying, express, expeditious, brisk, nimble, nippy (*inf*), prompt. OPPOSITE: slow. **2** (*a swift reversal*) sudden, abrupt, hurried, hasty.

swiftness *noun* **1** (*the swiftness of the horses*) speed, speediness, quickness, rapidity, rapidness, velocity, fastness, briskness, nippiness (*inf*), fleetness, expeditiousness, liveliness. **2** (*the swiftness of his*

departure surprised everyone*) rapidity, speed, abruptness, suddenness, hurriedness, haste, hastiness, promptness.

swill *verb* drink, imbibe, gulp down, knock back (*inf*), toss off (*inf*), swallow, swig, quaff, guzzle, drain, consume.
➤ *noun* **1** (*take a swill of wine*) swallow, swig (*inf*), gulp, drink. **2** (*swill for the animals*) pigswill, slop, waste, refuse, scourings.
swill out rinse, wash down, wash out, clean, cleanse, flush, sluice, drench.

swim *verb* bathe, take a dip, float.

swimmingly *adv* easily, effortlessly, smoothly, successfully, without difficulty, as planned, like clockwork.

swindle *verb* defraud, cheat, fleece, rook (*inf*), deceive, trick, dupe, overcharge, diddle (*inf*), do (*inf*), con (*inf*), rip off (*inf*).
➤ *noun* fraud, trickery, deception, sharp practice, fiddle, racket (*inf*), con trick (*inf*), rip-off (*inf*), scam (*inf*). OPPOSITE: honesty.

swindler *noun* fraud, fraudster, con man (*inf*), con artist (*inf*), crook (*inf*), trickster, cheat, sharper, impostor, charlatan, mountebank, rogue, scoundrel.

swing *verb* **1** (*the sign swung in the wind*) sway, wave, hang, dangle, spin, pivot, wheel, rotate. **2** (*the car swung from one side of the road to the other*) veer, swerve. **3** (*the road swung to the left*) turn, curve, bend, twist, wind, lean. **4** (*the vote may yet swing in their favour*) veer, change, waver, seesaw, fluctuate, oscillate. **5** (*we managed to swing an invite*) get, obtain, acquire, arrange, fix (*inf*), organize, achieve.
➤ *noun* **1** (*the swing of the rope*) swaying, oscillation. **2** (*a swing in public opinion*) change, shift, variation, fluctuation, vacillation, movement, move. **3** (*I like music with a swing*) rhythm, pulse, beat, rock.

swirl *verb* whirl, eddy, turn, gyrate, twist, spin, revolve, circulate, churn.

switch *noun* **1** (*a switch of willow*) twig, branch, shoot. **2** (*he thrashed the child with a switch*) rod, stick, cane, birch, lash, whip. **3** (*a switch in government policy*) change, shift, alteration, about-turn, reversal. **4** (*he suspected a switch of the two coats*) exchange, swap (*inf*), substitution, replacement, interchange.
➤ *verb* **1** (*switch emphasis*) change, shift. **2** (*they switched the two coins*) interchange, transpose, exchange, swap (*inf*), substitute, replace. **3** (*try to switch the attention of the press*) divert, deflect.

swivel *verb* turn, spin, pivot, gyrate, rotate, revolve, twirl, wheel, pirouette.

swollen *adj* expanded, dilated, inflated, bulging, bulbous, distended, bloated, blown-up, puffed-up, puffy, tumescent, tumid.

swoop *verb* descend, dive, plunge, sweep, rush, pounce, seize, snatch.
➤ *noun* descent, dive, plunge, rush, pounce, snatch.

sword *noun* blade, rapier, sabre, foil, scimitar, steel.
cross swords fight, clash, disagree, argue, quarrel, dispute, contend, wrangle, bicker.

sybaritic *adj* pleasure-loving, pleasure-seeking, easy, sensual, voluptuous, epicureal, hedonistic, dissolute, debauched, self-indulgent. OPPOSITE: ascetic.

sycophant *noun* flatterer, fawner, toady, yes man (*inf*), lickspittle, bootlicker (*inf*), cringer, groveller, parasite, sponger (*inf*), hanger-on.

sycophantic *adj* flattering, fawning, ingratiating, toadying, servile, subservient, obsequious, unctuous, slavish, grovelling, cringing, boot-licking (*inf*), arse-licking (*sl*). OPPOSITE: independent.

syllabus *noun* summary, synopsis, abstract, digest, conspectus, résumé, précis, outline, prospectus, curriculum.

symbol *noun* **1** (*a symbol of hope*) token, emblem, sign, badge, representation, image. **2** (*hieroglyphic symbols*) character, figure, letter, sign, mark. **3** (*the company symbol*) badge, logo, trademark, stamp, emblem, monogram.

symbolic *adj* **1** (*symbolic of hope*) representative, emblematic, typical. **2** (*a symbolic figure*) allegorical, figurative, metaphorical.

symbolize *verb* represent, stand for, signify, mean, denote, betoken, exemplify, typify, embody, personify.

symmetrical *adj* **1** (*a symmetrical design*) well-proportioned, proportional, regular, balanced, even, harmonious. **2** (*symmetrical lines*) uniform, consistent, regular, even, parallel.

symmetry *noun* **1** (*the symmetry of the design*) balance, proportion, harmony, congruity, regularity, evenness. OPPOSITE: asymmetry. **2** (*the symmetry of the lines*) regularity, evenness, uniformity, conformity, consistency, congruity, correspondence, agreement.

sympathetic *adj* **1** (*she took a sympathetic interest in his plight*) compassionate, affectionate, tender, kind, kindly, kind-hearted, warm, warm-hearted, caring, considerate, concerned, interested, solicitous, commiserating, commiserative, comforting, pitying, consoling, condoling, supportive, tolerant, understanding. OPPOSITE: unsympathetic. **2** (*a sympathetic companion*) pleasant, friendly, companionable, congenial, sociable, neighbourly, likeable, agreeable.

sympathize *verb* **1** (*he sympathized with her grief*) pity, feel for, commiserate, condole, console, comfort, understand, empathize. **2** (*they sympathize with the rebels*) side, identify, back, support, encourage, agree.

sympathizer *noun* **1** (*the loser was surrounded by sympathizers*) consoler, condoler, commiserator, comforter, empathizer, well-wisher. **2** (*government sympathizers*) supporter, backer, ally, adherent, advocate, partisan, admirer.

sympathy *noun* **1** (*sympathy for the poor*) compassion, concern, pity, commiseration, consolation, condolence, comfort, encouragement, support, tenderness, kindness, thoughtfulness, warmth, warm-heartedness, understanding, appreciation, empathy. OPPOSITE: indifference. **2** (*in sympathy with her views*) agreement, accord, harmony, correspondence, rapport, approval, approbation, affinity. OPPOSITE: antipathy.

symptom *noun* sign, indication, evidence, mark, symbol, token, signal, warning, feature, characteristic, note, expression, manifestation, display, demonstration.

symptomatic *adj* indicative, characteristic, typical, suggesting, suggestive, signalling, associated.

synchronous *adj* simultaneous, coincident, concurrent, contemporaneous.

syndicate *noun* trust, cartel, group, bloc, combination, combine, ring, alliance, federation, union, association.

synonymous *adj* equivalent, equal, corresponding, tantamount, similar, comparable, identical, interchangeable, substitutable. OPPOSITE: opposite.

synopsis *noun* outline, précis, résumé, abstract, sketch, digest, recapitulation, run-down (*inf*), epitome, condensation, abridgment, compendium, summary.

synthesis *noun* **1** (*a synthesis of factors*) combination, amalgamation, union, unification, fusion, welding, integration, coalescence. **2** (*a synthesis of the two chemicals*) combination, amalgam, compound, alloy, composite, blend, fusion, union, coalescence. OPPOSITE: analysis.

synthetic *verb* artificial, man-made, manufactured, imitation, mock, sham, ersatz, fake, bogus, simulated. OPPOSITE: genuine.

syrupy *adj* **1** (*a syrupy drink*) sweet, sweetened, honeyed, sticky, gooey (*inf*), sugary, saccharine. **2** (*a syrupy romantic novel*) sentimental, emotional, pathetic, sugary, mawkish, maudlin, gushing, gushy (*inf*), mushy (*inf*), slushy (*inf*), sloppy, soppy (*inf*), lovey-dovey (*inf*), schmaltzy (*inf*), sickly (*inf*).

system *noun* **1** (*a new system of doing things*) method, methodology, mode, procedure, process, technique, approach, way, means, practice, routine, line, attack. **2** (*transport system*) network, framework, organization, structure, set-up, arrangement. **3** (*no system behind his actions*) plan, planning, scheme, order, logic, systematization, methodicalness.

systematic *adj* methodical, efficient, businesslike, regular, orderly, ordered, well-ordered, organized, structured, planned, well-planned, logical, systematized. OPPOSITE: unsystematic.

tab *noun* loop, flap, tag, sticker, marker, label, ticket.

table *noun* **1** (*sit at the table*) board, slab, counter, bar, buffet, stand, bench, desk. **2** (*a table of figures*) chart, diagram, graph, plan, index, tabulation, inventory, list, catalogue, itemization, digest, record, register, schedule, timetable, programme.
➤ *verb* propose, submit, put forward, suggest, move, enter.

tableau *noun* **1** (*a tableau of figures*) arrangement, representation, portrayal, picture, illustration, diorama, vignette, spectacle, scene, pageant. **2** (*the tableau of the countryside below*) spectacle, scene, sight.

tablet *noun* **1** (*words carved on a tablet*) panel, slap, stone. **2** (*swallow one tablet every hour*) pill, capsule, lozenge. **3** (*a tablet of soap*) bar, block, cake.

taboo *noun* ban, prohibition, prescription, veto, restriction, interdiction, interdict, curse.
➤ *adj* prohibited, banned, proscribed, forbidden, ruled out, vetoed, unacceptable, unthinkable, frowned on, not allowed, outlawed, sacrosanct, unmentionable. OPPOSITE: permitted.

tabulate *verb* order, arrange, list, sort, class, classify, dispose, systematize, systemize, table, catalogue, categorize, group, grade, range, index, codify, tabularize.

tacit *adj* implied, implicit, understood, inferred, unspoken, unstated, unexpressed, undeclared, unvoiced, unmentioned, silent, wordless. OPPOSITE: avowed.

taciturn *adj* silent, quiet, reserved, reticent, withdrawn, unforthcoming, uncommunicative, unsociable, antisocial, untalkative, tight-lipped, close-mouthed, mum, mute, dumb, distant, detached, cold, aloof, dour, sullen. OPPOSITE: talkative.

tack *noun* **1** (*fastened with a tack*) nail, pin, drawing-pin, staple, rivet. **2** (*let's try a different tack*) direction, bearing, heading, course, line, way, path, approach, method, technique, plan, policy, strategy, tactic, procedure, process, attack.

➤ *verb* **1** (*tack the notice on the board*) nail, pin, staple, fasten, fix, attach, affix. **2** (*tack the sleeves of the dress*) stitch, sew. **3** (*tack it on at the end of the message*) append, annex, add, attach, affix, tag.

tackle *noun* gear, equipment, rig, outfit, apparatus, trappings, tools, implements, things (*inf*), stuff (*inf*), impedimenta, paraphernalia.
➤ *verb* **1** (*he says he will tackle the problem*) undertake, attempt, try, begin, set about, go about, embark on, turn one's hand to, attend to, deal with, handle, grasp, take on, grapple with, get to grips with, address, apply oneself to. **2** (*you must tackle her about it*) face, confront, challenge, accost, waylay, speak to. **3** (*he tried to tackle the burglar*) challenge, intercept, block, obstruct, halt, stop, deflect, seize, grab, catch, throw, bring down, take.

tacky[1] *adj* (*the paint is still tacky*) sticky, adhesive, gluey, gummy, gooey (*inf*).

tacky[2] *adj* (*tacky decorations*) tasteless, naff (*inf*), vulgar, gaudy, tawdry, kitsch, garish, crude, flashy, flash (*inf*).

tact *noun* diplomacy, discretion, sensitivity, perception, discernment, prudence, finesse, savoir faire, understanding, thoughtfulness, consideration, skill, dexterity, delicacy, subtlety, adroitness, judgement, judiciousness, sense, savvy (*inf*). OPPOSITE: tactlessness.

tactful *adj* diplomatic, discreet, prudent, politic, judicious, sensitive, perceptive, discerning, skilful, adroit, thoughtful, understanding, considerate, careful, delicate, subtle. OPPOSITE: tactless.

tactic *noun* manoeuvre, move, expedient, device, stratagem, trick, ruse, subterfuge, shift, scheme, plan, ploy, method, way, approach, tack, means, course of action.

tactical *adj* strategic, planned, calculated, cunning, shrewd, judicious, artful, adroit, skilful, clever, smart, prudent, politic.

tactics *pl noun* strategy, plan, scheme, method, approach, policy, line of attack, campaign, manoeuvres.

tactless *adj* undiplomatic, indiscreet, impolitic, injudicious, imprudent, undiscerning, gauche, awkward, blundering, maladroit, inappropriate, unskilful, clumsy, unsubtle, inept, bungling, careless, insensitive, unfeeling, thoughtless, inconsiderate, hurtful, unkind, indelicate, rude, impolite, discourteous, crude, rough. OPPOSITE: tactful.

tag *noun* **1** (*a tag with the owner's name*) label, sticker, ticket, docket, tab, note, slip, identification. **2** (*the tag has broken on my coat*) flap, tab, loop. **3** (*a collection of witty tags*) saying, proverb, expression, maxim, moral, motto, epithet, dictum, quotation, quote (*inf*), platitude, allusion, phrase, stock phrase, cliché.
➤ *verb* **1** (*tag each item*) label, mark. **2** (*they were tagged losers by the press*) name, christen, call, dub, term, designate, style, nickname, identify, title, entitle. **3** (*a note tagged to the end*) add, append, affix, fasten, attach, adjoin, tack, annex. **4** (*they tagged her as far as the park*) trail, tail, shadow, follow.
tag along go along with, go with, accompany, dog.

tail *noun* **1** (*the tail of the dog*) brush, dock. **2** (*the tail of the parade*) end, rear, back, extremity. OPPOSITE: head. **3** (*the tail of traffic*) queue, file, line, tailback, train. **4** (*the dog was hit on the tail*) bottom, backside, behind (*inf*), rear, rump, buttocks, posterior, arse (*sl*). **5** (*the tail of the hurricane*) tip, extremity, termination, conclusion, end, tail-end. **6** (*the police are on her tail*) track, trail, scent. **7** (*he soon shook off the tail*) shadow, detective, private detective, investigator, sleuth (*inf*), private eye (*inf*).
➤ *verb* follow, trail, track, shadow, stalk, dog.
tail off decrease, decline, drop off, fall away, fade, wane, die, dwindle, taper off, peter out, come to an end.
turn tail run away, flee, take off, bolt, retreat, cut and run, scarper (*inf*), skedaddle (*inf*), vamoose (*inf*).

tailor *noun* outfitter, dressmaker, couturier, costumier, seamstress, clothier.
➤ *verb* fit, cut, trim, suit, fashion, style, shape, mould, adapt, adjust, modify, convert, alter, accommodate.

taint *verb* **1** (*taint the water*) contaminate, infect, poison, pollute, adulterate, defile, befoul, spoil, begrime, dirty, soil, sully, blight. OPPOSITE: purify. **2** (*taint their reputation*) tarnish, stain, sully, besmirch, muddy, smear, ruin, damage, harm, injure, blemish, blacken, vitiate, corrupt, brand, stigmatize, shame, disgrace, dishonour.
➤ *noun* **1** (*the taint of the wine*) infection, contamination, contagion, pollution, corruption, adulteration. **2** (*a taint on his honour*) spot, stain, smear, blot, blemish, flaw, defect, fault, stigma, shame, disgrace, dishonour. **3** (*the slightest taint of corruption*) hint, suggestion, trace, touch.

take *verb* **1** (*take the knife*) grasp, grip, clasp, clutch, lay hold of, snatch. **2** (*we expect her to take the record*) get, obtain, acquire, secure, gain, procure, win, receive, come by. **3** (*they plan to take hostages*) seize, abduct, carry off, capture, catch, arrest, kidnap. **4** (*I take it you agree*) assume, presume, suppose, consider, gather, grasp, comprehend, apprehend, understand. **5** (*take a box at the theatre*) book, reserve, hire, engage, rent, lease, pay for, purchase, buy. **6** (*how many will your car take?*) hold, accommodate, contain, seat. **7** (*take any book you like*) pick, select, choose, opt for, decide on, settle on. OPPOSITE: leave. **8** (*take this figure from the total*) subtract, deduct, take away, remove. **9** (*he is accused of taking her bag*) steal, carry off, remove, make off with, appropriate, purloin, pinch (*inf*), nick (*inf*), pilfer (*inf*), swipe (*inf*), filch (*inf*), pocket. OPPOSITE: replace. **10** (*he took the train*) use, make use of. **11** (*take some tea with us*) have, eat, consume, swallow, drink. **12** (*I can't take it any more*) stand, put up with (*inf*), tolerate, stomach, brook, abide, bear, withstand, suffer, endure. **13** (*take this message to the king*) carry, bear, convey, transport, bring, fetch. **14** (*he says he will take her home*) escort, accompany, lead, conduct, guide, usher, shepherd, show. **15** (*it takes hard work to succeed in this business*) require, need, call for, demand, necessitate. **16** (*how do you think they will take the news?*) receive, cope with, deal with, handle, react to, respond to. **17** (*she clearly takes him for an idiot*) regard as, look upon as, consider as, reckon as, view as, suppose, believe. **18** (*you can take it from me*) accept, receive, adopt. **19** (*take readings of the pressure*) measure, determine, establish, ascertain, discover, find out. **20** (*they must take the blame*) accept, shoulder, bear, admit, undertake, acknowledge. **21** (*we were quite taken with him*) attract, charm, captivate, fascinate, enchant, delight, please, win over. OPPOSITE: repel. **22** (*she is taking four subjects at school*) study, learn, pursue, read, research.
➤ *noun* **1** (*a good take of fish*) catch, haul, bag. **2** (*carry the day's take to the bank*) proceeds, takings, returns, receipts, profits, earnings, winnings, pickings, gain, income, yield.

take after resemble, look like, be like, mirror, echo, favour, copy.

take against dislike, object to, disapprove of, despise, disfavour.

take back 1 (*she ordered him to take back what he had said*) retract, withdraw, disclaim, repudiate, recant, unsay, disavow, deny. **2** (*take back this parcel*) return, carry, bring, fetch, hand, give, send. **3** (*they offered to take back the goods*) swap, exchange, trade. **4** (*the general has vowed to take back the fort*) regain, repossess, reclaim, recapture.

take down 1 (*take down these figures*) write down, jot down, put down, set down, get down, note down, make a note of, record, put on record, document, minute, commit to paper, transcribe. **2** (*take down the wall*) demolish, tear down, remove, take apart, take to pieces, dismantle, disassemble, level, raze. **3** (*take down the flag*) pull down, lower, drop, haul down, let down. **4** (*take down a peg or two*) humble, humiliate, deflate, mortify, put down (*inf*).

take in 1 (*it was more than she could take in*) understand, comprehend, grasp, realize, appreciate, absorb, digest, assimilate. **2** (*the course takes in both practical and theoretical work*) include, incorporate, embrace, encompass, cover, comprise, contain. OPPOSITE: exclude. **3** (*take in lodgers*) accommodate, receive, welcome, lodge, board, admit, let in, shelter. **4** (*we were not taken in by the trick*) fool, deceive, con (*inf*), mislead, trick, dupe, cheat, defraud, swindle, hoodwink. **5** (*she took everything in*) observe, perceive, notice, note, take note of, see, regard.

take off 1 (*take the top off the tin*) remove, pull off, detach. **2** (*take off those wet things*) remove, strip off, peel off, shed, discard, throw off, doff. **3** (*watch the plane take* *off*) lift off, launch, leave the ground, depart. **4** (*the programme was taken off by the authorities*) cancel, withdraw, remove, terminate. **5** (*take the cost off the final figure*) subtract, deduct, take away, discount. **6** (*take off if you see anyone coming*) run away, do a runner (*inf*), split (*inf*), scarper (*inf*), skedaddle (*inf*), go, leave, depart, disappear, flee, decamp. **7** (*have you seen him take off the Prime Minister?*) impersonate, mimic, do, caricature, parody, satirize, send up (*inf*), spoof (*inf*), copy. **8** (*the campaign was quick to take off*) catch on, work, succeed, prosper, flourish, make it (*inf*).

take on 1 (*take on new employees*) employ, hire, engage, retain, enlist, enrol, recruit. OPPOSITE: dismiss. **2** (*it's a big job to take on*) undertake, accept, adopt, assume, tackle. **3** (*she must take on her strongest opponent yet*) face, challenge, contend with, compete with, oppose, fight.

take out 1 (*take out your appendix*) extract, remove, pull out, cut out, yank out. **2** (*he wants to take your daughter out*) invite out, go out with, date (*inf*), see, escort, accompany.

take over gain control of, take charge of, assume responsibility for.

take to 1 (*he's taken to walking in his sleep*) start, begin, commence, resort to. **2** (*they've taken to each other*) develop a liking for, like, get on with, appreciate. **3** (*she's really taken to dancing*) become good at, develop a liking for, enjoy, like.

take up 1 (*take up your backpacks*) lift up, raise, pick up. **2** (*cooking takes up too much time*) occupy, cover, fill, use up, consume, absorb. **3** (*he tried to take up where he had left off*) continue, carry on, go on, pick up, resume, recommence. **4** (*she ought to take up a new hobby*) start, begin, commence, pursue, embark on. OPPOSITE: stop. **5** (*I must decline to take up your kind offer*) accept, agree to, accede to, adopt.

take-off *noun* **1** (*report to the airport for take-off*) lift-off, departure, flight, ascent, climb. **2** (*we loved her take-off of the queen*) impersonation, send-up (*inf*), spoof (*inf*), imitation, parody, caricature, mimicry.

taking *adj* charming, captivating, enchanting, appealing, beguiling, bewitching, fascinating, intriguing, delightful, pleasing, engaging, compelling, attractive, alluring, winning, lovable, winsome, prepossessing, fetching (*inf*).

takings *pl noun* proceeds, receipts, returns, earnings, pickings, winnings, profit, gain, yield, income, revenue, gate money.

tale *noun* **1** (*he had a strange tale to tell*) story, yarn (*inf*), anecdote, narrative, narration, account, novel, romance, saga, epic, fable, myth, legend, allegory, parable. **2** (*you shouldn't tell tales*) lie, fib (*inf*), whopper (*inf*), porky (*inf*), story (*inf*), tall story (*inf*), untruth, fiction, fabrication, falsehood. **3** (*the tale is going about town*) rumour, gossip, hearsay.

talent *noun* gift, endowment, faculty, flair, aptitude, feel, knack, turn, bent, forte, genius, aptness, ability, capacity, skill, strength. OPPOSITE: inability.

talented *adj* gifted, brilliant, clever, accomplished, versatile, able, capable, apt, deft, adept, adroit, proficient, skilful, expert, artistic.

talk *verb* **1** (*that child never stops talking*) chat, chatter, speak, gossip, prattle, prate, jabber, natter (*inf*), rattle, babble, gabble, gibber, rabbit (*inf*), yak (*inf*), witter (*inf*). **2** (*she talked good sense*) utter, speak, articulate, express, say, voice, verbalize, pronounce, enunciate. **3** (*we must persuade the two sides to talk*) communicate, converse, confer, negotiate, haggle, parley, discuss, consult, confabulate, jaw (*inf*), rap (*inf*). **4** (*the police will keep him there until he talks*) confess, tell, reveal all, inform on, blab (*inf*), split (*inf*), grass (*inf*), sing (*inf*), spill the beans (*inf*), tell tales. **5** (*she is afraid the neighbours will talk*) gossip, pass comment, criticize. **6** (*he will talk to you on the subject of books*) speak, lecture, discourse.

≫ *noun* **1** (*a talk about politics*) speech, lecture, oration, address, discourse, seminar, symposium, harangue, disquisition, spiel (*inf*), sermon. **2** (*we had a long talk*) conversation, dialogue, confab (*inf*), chat, jaw (*inf*), rap (*inf*), confabulation, discussion, conference, chatter, natter (*inf*), chinwag (*inf*), prattle, gossip, tête-à-tête. **3** (*there is a lot of talk going about*) rumour, scandal, gossip, hearsay, tittle-tattle. **4** (*the talk of a foreign people*) speech, language, lingo (*inf*), dialect, jargon, cant, slang, idiom, utterance, words.

talk back answer back, retort, riposte, retaliate.

talk big boast, brag, bluster, exaggerate, crow, show off, swank, vaunt, blow one's own trumpet (*inf*).

talk down 1 (*a tendency to talk down to her employees*) patronize, look down on, condescend to, despise. **2** (*he talked down his opponents*) drown, silence, override, out-talk.

talk into persuade, coax, cajole, encourage, influence, sway, convince, win over, bring around.

talk out of dissuade from, discourage from, put off, deter from, stop, prevent.

talkative *adj* garrulous, loquacious, communicative, forthcoming, expansive, vocal, voluble, gabby (*inf*), gassy (*inf*), chatty, gossipy, conversational, verbose, gushing, effusive, longwinded, wordy, prolix. OPPOSITE: taciturn.

talker *noun* **1** (*an entertaining talker*) speaker, lecturer, narrator. **2** (*he's a real talker*) conversationalist, chatterbox (*inf*), gossip.

talking-to *noun* lecture, reprimand, reproof, row, telling-off, carpeting (*inf*), ticking-off (*inf*), read the riot act (*inf*).

tall *adj* **1** (*a tall building*) high, lofty, towering, soaring, elevated, sky-high. **2** (*tall for his age*) big, lanky, gangling, giant. OPPOSITE: short. **3** (*a tall story*) exaggerated, far-fetched, remarkable, absurd, preposterous, dubious, unlikely, unbelievable, incredible, improbable, implausible.

tall order difficult, demanding, challenging, trying, exacting, taxing, hard, unreasonable.

tally *noun* score, total, sum, count, enumeration, record, register, roll, reckoning, census.

≫ *verb* **1** (*this tallies with what she told us*) agree, correspond, accord, coincide, concur, match, harmonize, suit, fit, tie in, conform, square. OPPOSITE: clash. **2** (*tally up the score*) total, add, count, score, reckon, tot up, figure.

tame *adj* **1** (*a tame fox*) domesticated, broken, trained, fearless, unafraid. OPPOSITE: wild. **2** (*she's a tame little*

soul) gentle, docile, tractable, submissive, subdued, meek, obedient, compliant, amenable, biddable. **3** (*rather a tame piece of writing*) dull, flat, uninteresting, unexciting, uninspired, unadventurous, boring, humdrum, tedious, wearisome, prosaic, insipid, vapid, lifeless, spiritless, run-of-the-mill, mediocre, weak, feeble. OPPOSITE: exciting.
➢ *verb* **1** (*tried to tame a tiger*) domesticate, house-train, break, train. **2** (*she will soon tame this class*) discipline, master, curb, bridle, quell, control, bring to heel, subdue, subjugate, suppress, overcome, humble, moderate, soften, mellow, temper, calm, pacify.

tamper *verb* **1** (*don't tamper with the mechanism*) meddle, interfere, mess about, fool around (*inf*), monkey around (*inf*), muck about (*inf*), tinker, fiddle (*inf*). **2** (*the witnesses had been tampered with*) influence, corrupt, bribe, get at, fix (*inf*), manipulate, rig.

tan *adj* light brown, pale brown, brown, yellow-brown, yellowish, tawny.
➢ *verb* suntan, brown, go brown, bronze, darken, sunburn.

tang *noun* **1** (*a spicy tang*) flavour, taste, savour, relish, piquancy, pungency, sharpness, spice, odour, aroma, scent, smell, whiff, smack, bite (*inf*), edge (*inf*), kick (*inf*), punch (*inf*), pep (*inf*), zip (*inf*), zest. **2** (*a tang of lemon*) hint, trace, suggestion, touch, tinge, overtone.

tangible *adj* **1** (*tangible alterations*) palpable, tactile, touchable, visible, perceptible. **2** (*tangible improvements*) material, substantial, physical, corporeal, real, actual, positive, solid, concrete, hard, evident, clear, plain, distinct, discernible, unmistakable. OPPOSITE: intangible.

tangle *verb* entangle, ravel, snarl, mat, knot, twist, intertwine, intertwist, interlace, interweave. OPPOSITE: untangle.
➢ *noun* **1** (*a tangle of string*) knot, twist, coil, mesh, mat, web. **2** (*everything is in a tangle*) mess, jumble, muddle, confusion, snarl-up, complication, mix-up, imbroglio.

tangled *adj* **1** (*tangled weeds*) entangled, knotted, knotty, matted, tousled, twisted, tortuous, ravelled, snarled, dishevelled, messy. **2** (*a tangled affair*) complicated, involved, complex, confused, muddled, mixed-up, jumbled, convoluted, intricate, chaotic.

tank *noun* **1** (*water in the tank*) container, receptacle, reservoir, cistern, vat, aquarium. **2** (*an assault by tanks and infantry*) armoured car, armoured vehicle.

tantalize *verb* torment, torture, disappoint, frustrate, thwart, tease, bait, taunt, titillate, provoke, tempt, entice, allure, beguile, lead on. OPPOSITE: satisfy.

tantamount *adj* equivalent, equal, synonymous, commensurate, the same.

tantrum *noun* outburst, temper, rage, fit, paroxysm, fury, flare-up, scene, pet, paddy (*inf*).

tap *verb* rap, pat, touch, knock, hit, strike, beat, drum.
➢ *noun* rap, pat, touch, knock, blow, beat.

tap *noun* **1** (*water poured from the tap*) stopcock, spout, valve, spigot. **2** (*they wanted to put a tap on his telephone*) bug (*inf*), bugging device (*inf*), listening device, wire (*inf*).
on tap at hand, on hand, handy, ready, standing by, available, accessible, in reserve.
➢ *verb* **1** (*tap beer from a barrel*) siphon, draw off, drain,

bleed. **2** (*tap natural resources*) exploit, extract, obtain, mine, quarry, open up, explore, probe. **3** (*tap one's contacts for news*) exploit, utilize, use, make use of, draw on, milk. **4** (*they tapped her telephone*) bug (*inf*), wire (*inf*).

tape *noun* **1** (*repaired with tape*) adhesive tape, sticky tape, Sellotape®, parcel tape, masking tape, insulating tape. **2** (*a hat decorated with tapes*) ribbon, strip, string, band. **3** (*we've got the whole thing on tape*) audiotape, videotape, video, videocassette, audiocassette, cassette, magnetic tape, tape recording.
➢ *verb* **1** (*tape the parcel up*) fasten, tie, bind, stick, seal, secure, Sellotape®. **2** (*she taped the conversation*) record, video, video-record, tape-record.

taper *verb* **1** (*the blade tapered to a point*) narrow, thin. **2** (*business has tapered off*) diminish, decrease, dwindle, fade, lessen, reduce, subside, wane, ebb, thin out, die away, die off, tail off, slacken off, peter out, wind down.

tardy *adj* late, belated, overdue, delayed, procrastinating, behindhand, last-minute, retarded, backward, unpunctual, slow, leisurely, sluggish, slack, dilatory, dawdling, loitering. OPPOSITE: prompt.

target *noun* **1** (*the arrow hit the target*) mark, bull's eye. **2** (*this company has a new target*) objective, object, ambition, aim, goal, end, intention, purpose, destination. **3** (*the shooters had no shortage of targets*) prey, quarry, game. **4** (*the target of their practical joke*) victim, butt, scapegoat.

tariff *noun* **1** (*government tariffs on alcohol*) tax, duty, levy, excise, toll. **2** (*check the tariff in the window*) price list, list of charges, schedule, rate.

tarnish *verb* **1** (*the weather tarnished the metal*) discolour, rust, dull, dim, corrode. OPPOSITE: polish. **2** (*this scandal will tarnish his reputation*) stain, sully, soil, taint, blemish, spot, mar, blot, besmirch, befoul, blacken.
➢ *noun* **1** (*polish the tarnish away*) discoloration, rust, patina, oxidation. **2** (*a tarnish on the company's reputation*) stain, slur, blemish, blot, black mark, taint, stigma.

tarry *verb* linger, loiter, dally, dawdle, lag, delay, pause, remain, stay, sojourn, abide, bide, stop, rest, wait OPPOSITE: move.

tart *noun* **1** (*a plum tart*) pie, pastry, flan, tartlet, strudel. **2** (*spent all his money on tarts*) prostitute, hooker (*inf*), whore, harlot, streetwalker, call girl, scrubber (*inf*), fallen woman, woman of easy virtue. **3** (*he accused her of being a tart*) slut, loose woman, trollop, strumpet, wanton.
tart up 1 (*she got all tarted up*) doll up (*inf*), dress up, make up. **2** (*time to tart up the old place*) smarten up, renovate, decorate, redecorate, refurbish, modernize.

tart *adj* **1** (*a tart taste*) sour, acid, sharp, tangy, bitter, pungent, piquant, vinegary. OPPOSITE: sweet. **2** (*she made several tart comments*) biting, cutting, caustic, scathing, mordant, trenchant, incisive, piercing, acrimonious, sharp, barbed, stinging, astringent, acerbic, curt, waspish, testy, sarcastic, sardonic. OPPOSITE: mild.

task *noun* job, odd job, chore, duty, charge, burden, assignment, commission, exercise, mission, undertaking, engagement, errand, quest, work. OPPOSITE: leisure.
take to task rebuke, reprimand, tell off (*inf*), tick off

(*inf*), reprove, reproach, lecture, castigate, upbraid, berate, scold, blame, censure, criticize.

taste *noun* **1** (*this food has no taste*) flavour, savour, relish, tang, smack. **2** (*give the baby a taste*) bit, morsel, piece, mouthful, swallow, sample, titbit, bite, sip, drop, dash, touch, sample, spoonful, soupçon. **3** (*a taste for the good life*) liking, fondness, love, predilection, inclination, leaning, hankering, bent, partiality, preference, penchant, appetite, hunger, thirst, fancy, desire, longing, relish, palate. OPPOSITE: aversion. **4** (*a man of taste*) perception, discernment, discrimination, judgement, appreciation, culture, cultivation, refinement, polish, elegance, finesse, breeding, style, stylishness, grace. **5** (*her outfit lacked taste*) delicacy, propriety, decorum, etiquette, politeness, correctness, discretion, tact, tactfulness, diplomacy.
➤ *verb* **1** (*this sauce tastes of oranges*) smack, savour. **2** (*taste a little of this*) try, sample, test, sip, nibble. **3** (*can you taste the difference?*) tell, make out, discern, distinguish, perceive, differentiate. **4** (*they have tasted defeat*) experience, undergo, encounter, come up against, meet, know, feel.

tasteful *adj* **1** (*tasteful surroundings*) refined, polished, cultured, cultivated, elegant, graceful, stylish, smart, artistic, aesthetic, harmonious, restrained, pleasing, charming, exquisite, beautiful, pretty, handsome. OPPOSITE: tawdry. **2** (*tasteful manners*) polite, decorous, proper, seemly, correct, appropriate, fitting, fit, fastidious.

tasteless *adj* **1** (*tasteless food*) insipid, vapid, flavourless, unflavoured, unappetizing, bland, mild, flat, plain, stale, weak, thin, watery, watered-down, dull, tame, uninteresting, boring. OPPOSITE: tasty. **2** (*tasteless furnishings*) vulgar, tacky (*inf*), naff (*inf*), tawdry, cheap, kitsch, garish, gaudy, loud, flashy, showy, inelegant, graceless. **3** (*tasteless behaviour*) unseemly, improper, impolite, rude, unrefined, indecorous, incorrect, inappropriate, unfitting. **4** (*a tasteless joke*) improper, vulgar, rude, indelicate, coarse, crude, crass, gross, low, uncouth, tactless, indiscreet, undiplomatic. OPPOSITE: tasteful.

tasty *adj* savoury, flavoursome, flavourful, palatable, mouth-watering, toothsome, appetizing, delicious, delectable, luscious, succulent, scrumptious (*inf*), yummy (*inf*), spicy, piquant, pungent, sweet. OPPOSITE: insipid.

tattered *adj* ragged, frayed, threadbare, tatty, shabby, scruffy, torn, ripped, in shreds, in bits.

tattle *verb* gossip, tittle-tattle, gab (*inf*), chatter, prattle, prate, natter (*inf*), rabbit on (*inf*), witter on (*inf*), babble, blab, tell tales.

taunt *verb* tease, torment, provoke, goad, bait, mock, make fun of, poke fun at, rib (*inf*), jeer at, gibe at, sneer at, ridicule, deride, revile, insult, chaff. OPPOSITE: respect.
➤ *noun* gibe, jeer, sneer, catcall, insult, barb, brickbat (*inf*), dig (*inf*), put-down (*inf*), provocation, ridicule, derision, mockery, sarcasm.

taut *adj* **1** (*pull the rope taut*) tight, stretched, rigid, stiff. OPPOSITE: slack. **2** (*the taut muscles of a weightlifter*) tensed, flexed, contracted, tightened, unrelaxed. **3** (*the

teacher had a taut expression on her face) tense, strained, drawn, stressed, uptight (*inf*).

tautology *noun* repetition, repetitiousness, repetitiveness, iteration, reiteration, duplication, verbosity, wordiness, prolixity, redundancy, superfluity, pleonasm. OPPOSITE: conciseness.

tawdry *adj* flashy, showy, meretricious, loud, gaudy, garish, cheap, vulgar, tacky (*inf*), kitsch (*inf*), tasteless, shoddy, tatty (*inf*). OPPOSITE: tasteful.

tax *noun* **1** (*tax must be paid on these goods*) levy, duty, excise, customs, toll, rate, charge, tariff, contribution, tribute. **2** (*they are a tax upon local resources*) burden, load, weight, drain, strain, imposition, pressure, stress, encumbrance.
➤ *verb* **1** (*the government intends to tax these imports*) charge duty on, demand duty on, impose a toll on, exact payment on. **2** (*the challenge taxed his endurance*) load, burden, weigh down, encumber, strain, stretch, push, task, try, test, overload, overburden, wear out, exhaust, weary, tire, fatigue, enervate, weaken, sap, drain. OPPOSITE: relieve.

taxing *adj* demanding, exacting, burdensome, difficult, tough, hard, trying, onerous, punishing, heavy, tiring, exhausting, wearying, wearisome, draining, sapping, enervating, wearing, stressful.

teach *verb* **1** (*we need someone to teach our children*) educate, school, instruct, tutor, lecture, coach, train, ground, drill, discipline, verse, inform, enlighten, indoctrinate, edify, inculcate. **2** (*teach me how to do that*) explain, tell, show, demonstrate, advise, instruct, train, guide, direct.

teacher *noun* schoolteacher, schoolmaster, schoolmistress, master, mistress, tutor, lecturer, professor, don, educator, pedagogue, mentor, guru, instructor, coach, trainer.

team *noun* group, band, bunch, gang, company, troupe, set, stable, shift, party, crew, squad, side, line-up.
➤ *verb* join, unite, couple, combine, come together, get together, band together, work together, cooperate, ally with, collaborate, match, yoke.

tear *verb* **1** (*tear the shirt up*) rip, rend, split, divide, pull apart, break apart, pull to pieces, sever, sunder, rive, rupture, shred, ladder. OPPOSITE: mend. **2** (*the blade tore his hand*) lacerate, gash, slash, scratch, cut, claw, pierce, stab, hack, mutilate, mangle, injure, wound. **3** (*she tore the letter from his grasp*) snatch, seize, pluck, yank (*inf*), grab, pull, rip, wrench, wrest, extract. **4** (*he watched the men tear down the slope*) race, speed, sprint, run, charge, gallop, fly, rush, career, shoot, hurry, hasten, dash, dart, bolt, belt (*inf*), nip (*inf*), whizz (*inf*), zip (*inf*), zap (*inf*), zoom (*inf*). OPPOSITE: amble.
➤ *noun* **1** (*a tear in his trousers*) rip, rent, run, split, slit, rupture, hole. **2** (*a tear in the skin*) gash, slash, scratch, cut, laceration, injury, wound, mutilation.

tear *noun* drop, droplet, bead, globule.
in tears weeping, weepy (*inf*), crying, sobbing, blubbering, wailing, whimpering, tearful, upset, distressed, emotional, sad, sorrowful.

tearful *adj* **1** (*a tearful little girl*) weeping, crying, sobbing, wailing, in tears, lachrymose, weepy (*inf*), blubbering, blubbing (*inf*), whimpering, snivelling,

upset, distressed, emotional. **2** (*a tearful reunion*)
poignant, emotional, upsetting, pathetic, pitiful,
pitiable, piteous, maudlin, melancholy, sad, sorrowful,
lamentable, heartbreaking, heart-rending, distressing,
mournful, dolorous. OPPOSITE: happy.

tease *verb* torment, plague, harass, pester, badger,
bother, worry, annoy, irritate, aggravate (*inf*), vex,
provoke, goad, needle, tantalize, taunt, bait, rag (*inf*), rib
(*inf*), mock, ridicule, make fun of, poke fun at. OPPOSITE:
pacify.

technical *adj* **1** (*the technical details of the car*)
technological, mechanical, practical, scientific,
professional. **2** (*that's a bit technical for most of us*)
specialist, specialized, scientific.

technique *noun* **1** (*his usual technique*) manner, style,
mode, fashion, method, means, way, approach, system,
procedure, modus operandi, line, course. **2** (*he needs to
improve his technique*) skill, skilfulness, dexterity,
adroitness, deftness, performance, delivery, art, artistry,
craft, craftsmanship, facility, ability, capability, capacity,
knack, touch, know-how (*inf*), proficiency, mastery,
expertise, aptitude.

tedious *adj* boring, monotonous, dull, tiresome, tiring,
fatiguing, wearisome, wearying, soporific, long-drawn-
out, overlong, long-winded, prolix, prosaic, banal,
uninteresting, unexciting, lifeless, uninspired, unvaried,
drab, dreary, deadly, humdrum, run-of-the-mill,
routine, flat, insipid, vapid, laborious. OPPOSITE:
interesting.

tedium *noun* tediousness, boredom, ennui,
tiresomeness, wearisomeness, dullness, dreariness,
drabness, monotony, sameness, flatness, dryness,
lifelessness, banality, insipidity, vapidity, prolixity.

teeming *adj* swarming, bristling, crawling, seething,
brimming, alive, full, packed, chock-full (*inf*), chock-a-
block (*inf*), overflowing, bursting, prolific, abundant,
copious, replete, thick. OPPOSITE: empty.

teenage *adj* teenaged, adolescent, youthful, young,
juvenile, immature.

teenager *noun* teen (*inf*), adolescent, young person,
youth, juvenile, minor.

teeter *verb* **1** (*she teetered on the edge*) sway, rock, roll,
reel, lurch, pitch, stagger, stumble, totter, tremble,
wobble, balance, pivot, shake. **2** (*teeter between two
choices*) waver, hesitate, dither, vacillate, fluctuate,
oscillate, seesaw, shilly-shally.

teetotaller *noun* abstainer, non-drinker.

telepathy *noun* clairvoyance, mind-reading, sixth
sense, extrasensory perception, ESP, thought
transference, psychometry.

telephone *noun* phone, blower (*inf*), cellphone, cellular
telephone, mobile, cordless phone, car phone,
videophone.
➤ *verb* phone, call, ring, buzz (*inf*), dial, contact, get on
the blower (*inf*), give a bell (*inf*), give a tinkle (*inf*).

telescope *verb* **1** (*the vehicle had telescoped on impact*)
concertina, crush, squash, squeeze, compress, compact.
2 (*he telescoped the novel into a short story*) condense,
shrink, reduce, compress, compact, boil down,

consolidate, abbreviate, abridge, shorten, truncate, cut,
trim, curtail.

television *noun* TV (*inf*), telly (*inf*), set, box (*inf*),
gogglebox (*inf*), tube (*inf*), receiver.

tell *verb* **1** (*tell us one of your stories*) relate, narrate,
report, recount, recite, rehearse, describe, portray,
chronicle. **2** (*tell them the good news*) impart,
communicate, make known, announce, proclaim,
broadcast, disclose, reveal, divulge, publish, say, speak,
utter, voice, declare, state, mention, notify, let know,
inform, acquaint, apprise. OPPOSITE: suppress. **3** (*she'll go
mad, I tell you*) assure, guarantee, promise, warrant.
4 (*tell them what to do*) command, order, instruct, direct,
charge, require, call upon, bid, enjoin. **5** (*she threatened
to tell on him*) confess, blab (*inf*), betray, denounce, shop
(*inf*), inform, grass (*inf*), squeal (*inf*), blow the whistle
(*inf*), rat (*inf*), sing (*inf*), talk, give the game away. **6** (*can
you tell the difference?*) distinguish, discern, recognize,
perceive, see, identify, make out, discover, deduce,
understand, comprehend, tell apart, differentiate,
discriminate. **7** (*her absence told him everything*) reveal,
disclose, indicate, show, display, exhibit. **8** (*tell the votes
as they come in*) count, enumerate, number, reckon,
compute, calculate, tally, estimate to. **9** (*the strain is
beginning to tell*) take its toll, exhaust, drain, affect.
tell off reprimand, tick off (*inf*), scold, chide, berate,
upbraid, reprove, rebuke, reproach, censure, give a
talking-to (*inf*).

telling *adj* significant, striking, forceful, effective,
effectual, cogent, influential, important, substantial,
sizeable, considerable, powerful, potent, marked, solid,
weighty, decisive, impressive, revealing. OPPOSITE: weak.

temerity *noun* rashness, recklessness, foolhardiness,
heedlessness, boldness, audacity, nerve (*inf*), gall (*inf*),
cheek (*inf*), impudence, impertinence, brazenness,
effrontery, presumption. OPPOSITE: timidity.

temper *noun* **1** (*she has a gentle temper*) nature,
disposition, temperament, constitution, character,
stamp, humour, mood, frame of mind, cast of mind,
state of mind, attitude. **2** (*he flew into a temper at the
suggestion*) tantrum, paddy (*inf*), fit, rage, fury, storm,
anger, passion, bad mood. **3** (*he got the sharp edge of her
temper*) anger, fury, rage, ill humour, irritation,
annoyance, irritability, irascibility, peevishness,
petulance, surliness, resentment, churlishness. OPPOSITE:
calmness. **4** (*he never loses his temper*) calmness, calm,
composure, cool (*inf*), coolness, self-control,
equanimity, tranquillity, good humour. OPPOSITE: rage.
➤ *verb* **1** (*I wish he would temper his views*) moderate,
mitigate, modify, abate, lessen, reduce, palliate, allay,
assuage, alleviate, mollify, soften, calm, tone down,
qualify, weaken. OPPOSITE: intensify. **2** (*temper the steel*)
toughen, harden, fortify, strengthen, anneal, roughen.

temperament *noun* character, personality, nature,
disposition, make-up, temper, mood, humour, frame of
mind, cast of mind, attitude, stamp, outlook, tendency,
bent, spirit, constitution, complexion, mettle.

temperamental *adj* **1** (*he is very temperamental*)
excitable, emotional, fiery, passionate, volatile,
mercurial, capricious, highly-strung, sensitive, oversensitive, hyper-sensitive, neurotic, moody, hot-headed,

hot-blooded, irritable, explosive, touchy, petulant, impatient. OPPOSITE: placid. **2** (*this cooker is temperamental*) erratic, unpredictable, unreliable, inconsistent. OPPOSITE: reliable.

temperance *noun* teetotalism, abstinence, abstention, abstemiousness, sobriety.

temperate *adj* **1** (*a temperate climate*) mild, fair, moderate, clement, balmy, cool, calm, gentle, agreeable, pleasant. **2** (*known for his temperate lifestyle*) moderate, controlled, self-controlled, restrained, self-restrained, calm, even-tempered, composed, sensible, reasonable, self-denying, abstinent, abstemious, continent, sober, teetotal. OPPOSITE: intemperate.

tempest *noun* **1** (*the island suffered badly in the tempest*) storm, squall, hurricane, tornado, typhoon, cyclone, whirlwind, gale. OPPOSITE: calm. **2** (*a tempest of activity*) commotion, storm, furore, upheaval, uproar, tumult, turmoil, ferment, disturbance. OPPOSITE: peace.

tempestuous *adj* **1** (*battered by tempestuous weather*) stormy, squally, windy, blustery, gusty, breezy. **2** (*a tempestuous marriage*) stormy, turbulent, tumultuous, violent, wild, rough, intense, fierce, heated, feverish, passionate, impassioned, emotional, hysterical, frenetic, furious, boisterous, unrestrained, uncontrolled. OPPOSITE: calm.

temple *noun* place of worship, holy place, shrine, sanctuary, church, mosque, tabernacle, pagoda.

tempo *noun* **1** (*the tempo of the dance*) rhythm, beat, time, metre, pulse, pulsation, cadence. **2** (*the tempo of the times*) pace, rate, velocity, speed, measure.

temporal *adj* **1** (*the temporal world*) secular, lay, profane, mundane, earthly, worldly, terrestrial, mortal, carnal, fleshly, material. OPPOSITE: spiritual. **2** (*temporal existence*) passing, transient, transitory, fleeting, ephemeral, evanescent, momentary, temporary, impermanent. OPPOSITE: permanent.

temporarily *adv* **1** (*temporarily incapacitated*) for the moment, for the time being, for now, pro tem. **2** (*she was temporarily unable to respond*) briefly, fleetingly, momentarily, transiently, transitorily, for a short time, for a little while.

temporary *adj* **1** (*his depression was temporary*) impermanent, passing, transient, transitory, fleeting, fugitive, ephemeral, evanescent, brief, short, short-lived, momentary. OPPOSITE: lasting. **2** (*a temporary arrangement*) provisional, makeshift, stopgap, fill-in, interim, pro tem, short-term. OPPOSITE: permanent.

temporize *verb* delay, procrastinate, hang back, pause, fence, hedge, hum and haw (*inf*), equivocate, tergiversate, play for time, stall.

tempt *verb* **1** (*she was tempted by the prospect*) allure, lure, attract, captivate, entice, draw, seduce, woo, beguile, tantalize, invite, inveigle. OPPOSITE: repel. **2** (*they tried to tempt him*) persuade, coax, cajole, entice, court, incite, induce, urge, egg on, goad, provoke, bait, prompt, sway, influence.

temptation *noun* **1** (*a prey to temptation*) persuasion, cajolery, coaxing, urging, influence, enticement, incitement, inducement. **2** (*a prospect full of temptation*) attraction, appeal, allurement, lure, draw, pull,

enticement, inducement, invitation, come-on (*inf*), bait, snare.

tempting *adj* attractive, alluring, inviting, enticing, appealing, captivating, seductive, beguiling, fascinating, tantalizing, mouth-watering, appetizing. OPPOSITE: repulsive.

tenable *adj* sound, rational, reasonable, viable, plausible, arguable, believable, credible, maintainable, defensible, justifiable, supportable. OPPOSITE: untenable.

tenacious *adj* **1** (*he held the boy in a tenacious grip*) tight, firm, fast, secure, strong, iron, forceful, powerful, unshakeable. **2** (*his tenacious pursuit of the truth*) stubborn, obstinate, obdurate, dogged, persistent, pertinacious, determined, resolute, strong-willed, single-minded, purposeful, unshakeable, steadfast, relentless, unswerving, set, firm, adamant, intransigent, inflexible, inexorable, unyielding. **3** (*a tenacious memory*) retentive, remembering. **4** (*tenacious mud*) sticky, clinging, gluey, adhesive, cohesive.

tenacity *noun* **1** (*the tenacity of his grip*) tightness, firmness, fastness, security, strength, forcefulness, force, power. **2** (*he showed great tenacity in his research*) determination, resolution, resoluteness, resolve, firmness, steadfastness, single-mindedness, strength of purpose, purpose, purposefulness, persistence, pertinacity, doggedness, application, diligence, relentlessness, inexorability, staunchness, inflexibility, stubbornness, obstinacy, obduracy, intransigence. **3** (*the tenacity of the mud*) stickiness, adhesiveness, cohesiveness.

tenancy *noun* occupation, occupancy, residence, habitation, inhabitance, lease, leasing, renting, possession, holding, tenure, incumbency.

tenant *noun* lodger, renter, lessee, leaseholder, holder, possessor, occupant, occupier, resident, inhabitant, incumbent. OPPOSITE: landlord.

tend[1] *verb* **1** (*she tends towards the political left*) incline, lean, be inclined, be disposed. OPPOSITE: diverge. **2** (*inflation is tending upwards*) go, move, head, aim, point, bear, lead, gravitate.

tend[2] *verb* (*tend the garden*) care for, take care of, look after, attend to, see to, minister to, wait on, cater to, serve, watch over, keep an eye on, mind, protect, guard, nurse, nurture, cultivate, keep, maintain, handle, manage. OPPOSITE: neglect.

tendency *noun* **1** (*a tendency to jealousy*) leaning, bent, turn, inclination, disposition, predisposition, propensity, proclivity, penchant, partiality, predilection, liability, bias, proneness, aptness, susceptibility. OPPOSITE: aversion. **2** (*the downward tendency of the figures*) trend, movement, direction, bearing, heading, course, drift, bias, gravitation.

tender[1] *adj* **1** (*a tender plant*) soft, delicate, fragile, breakable, sensitive, slight, frail, feeble, weak. **2** (*she has a tender nature*) gentle, kind, kindly, humane, merciful, compassionate, sympathetic, caring, benevolent, generous, considerate, thoughtful, solicitous, tender-hearted, soft-hearted, sensitive, warm, affectionate, loving, fond, sentimental, emotional, amorous, romantic. OPPOSITE: harsh. **3** (*at the tender age of nine*) young, youthful, early, immature, inexperienced, callow, raw, green, impressionable, susceptible, vulnerable. **4** (*my knee still feels tender*) sore, painful, raw, sensitive, red, inflamed, irritated, aching, smarting, throbbing, bruised. **5** (*a tender cut of meat*) succulent, soft, fleshy, juicy. OPPOSITE: tough.

tender[2] *verb* proffer, offer, present, extend, give, propose, suggest, volunteer, advance, put forward, submit. OPPOSITE: withhold.
≫ *noun* **1** (*we have received two tenders for the job*) offer, bid, estimate, quotation, price, proposal, proposition, submission. **2** (*legal tender*) currency, money.

tenderness *noun* **1** (*the tenderness of this new growth*) fragility, frailty, frailness, delicacy, softness, sensitivity, sensitiveness, slightness, feebleness, weakness. **2** (*she showed great tenderness towards the children*) compassion, care, soft-heartedness, tender-heartedness, sweetness, kindness, kindliness, sympathy, pity, mercy, warmth, warm-heartedness, humaneness, humanity, gentleness, sensitivity, consideration, solicitousness, generosity, benevolence, sentimentality, emotionalism, affection, devotion, attachment, fondness, liking, love, amorousness. **3** (*the tenderness of youth*) youthfulness, immaturity, greenness, inexperience, callowness, vulnerability. **4** (*he complained about the tenderness of his neck*) soreness, painfulness, pain, aching, ache, smarting, throbbing, irritation, inflammation, rawness, redness, bruising.

tenet *noun* dogma, doctrine, principle, precept, presumption, maxim, rule, canon, creed, credo, belief, conviction, persuasion, opinion, teaching, view, theory, thesis, hypothesis, postulation.

tenor *noun* **1** (*the tenor of his words*) meaning, purport, intent, sense, essence, import, substance, theme, gist, drift, vein. **2** (*the general tenor of government policy*) aim, direction, movement, current, flow, drift, trend, course.

tense *adj* **1** (*tense muscles*) tight, taut, rigid, stiff, stretched, strained. OPPOSITE: slack. **2** (*she felt very tense*) nervous, keyed up, wound up (*inf*), uptight (*inf*), stressed out (*inf*), strung up (*inf*), on tenterhooks (*inf*), worked up, distraught, overwrought, strained, jumpy, edgy (*inf*), on edge, anxious, worried, apprehensive, agitated, restless, jittery, fidgety, uneasy. **3** (*it was a tense evening*) stressful, nerve-racking, nail-biting, fraught, worrying, uneasy, strained, exciting.
≫ *verb* brace, tighten, contract, strain, stiffen, stretch. OPPOSITE: relax.

tension *noun* **1** (*feel the tension in the rope*) tightness, tautness, rigidity, stiffness, stretch, strain, stress, pressure. **2** (*the tension before the race was unbearable*) suspense, apprehension, stress, stressfulness, strain, pressure, nervousness, apprehensiveness, jumpiness, nerves (*inf*), anxiety, distress, worry, unease, uneasiness, edginess, disquiet, agitation, restlessness, excitement. OPPOSITE: relaxation. **3** (*escalating tension in the border area*) unease, unrest, strain, antagonism, antipathy, hostility, ill feeling, ill-will, enmity, disagreement, dissension, contention, quarrel, dispute, discord, feud, friction, confrontation, clash, conflict, strife, opposition.

tentative *adj* **1** (*a tentative proposal*) experimental, exploratory, trial, test, pilot, untried, unproven, unconfirmed, indefinite, speculative, conjectural,

provisional. **2** (*she got a tentative reply*) hesitant, hesitating, cautious, unsure, doubtful, uncertain, faltering, wavering, undecided, diffident, timid. OPPOSITE: sure.

tenuous *adj* **1** (*a tenuous hold on reality*) flimsy, shaky, insubstantial, insignificant, slight, slender, weak, doubtful, dubious, questionable, hazy, nebulous, vague, indefinite. OPPOSITE: substantial. **2** (*a tenuous thread*) slender, slim, thin, fine, delicate.

tenure *noun* holding, possession, occupancy, occupation, habitation, proprietorship, residence, tenancy, incumbency, term, time.

tepid *adj* **1** (*tepid water*) lukewarm, warm, warmish, cool. **2** (*he got rather a tepid reception*) cool, lukewarm, half-hearted, apathetic, indifferent, unenthusiastic.

term *noun* **1** (*unable to understand the scientific term*) name, title, denomination, appellation, designation, word, phrase, expression, epithet. **2** (*a long term of imprisonment*) time, period, spell, space, span, interval, duration, stretch, season, session, course. **3** (*reach full term*) end, interval, conclusion, limit, finish, duration, period, culmination, close, bound, boundary, fruition, terminus.
≫ *verb* call, name, designate, denominate, style, dub, label, tag, christen, entitle, title.

terminal *adj* **1** (*a terminal illness*) mortal, incurable, fatal, lethal, deadly. **2** (*a terminal date*) boundary, bounding, limiting, closing, concluding, last, final, ultimate.
≫ *noun* **1** (*computer terminal*) workstation, console, monitor, visual display unit, VDU (*inf*), keyboard. **2** (*the bus stopped at the terminal*) depot, terminus. **3** (*the terminals of the property*) boundary, bound, limit, extremity, end, termination.

terminate *verb* **1** (*we must terminate this conversation*) end, bring to an end, conclude, complete, finish, close, stop, cease, discontinue, cut off, wind up (*inf*). OPPOSITE: begin. **2** (*the guarantee has terminated*) end, come to an end, cease, stop, expire, lapse, run out. **3** (*the talks terminated in agreement*) end, conclude, finish, result.

termination *noun* **1** (*the termination of the interview*) end, conclusion, completion, close, finish, ending, stopping, winding up. OPPOSITE: beginning. **2** (*the termination of the arrangement*) end, expiry, lapse, discontinuance, cessation, cancellation, demise. **3** (*the termination of these talks was a halt in hostilities*) end, conclusion, finish, issue, result, consequence, denouement.

terminology *noun* phraseology, vocabulary, language, lingo (*inf*), terms, expressions, jargon, cant, argot, nomenclature.

terminus *noun* terminal, depot, station, garage, end of the line.

terms *pl noun* **1** (*the terms of the agreement*) conditions, clauses, provisions, provisos, premises, stipulations, specifications, particulars, qualifications, points, details. **2** (*these are our terms*) prices, charges, costs, rates, fees, tariff. **3** (*terms of endearment*) phrases, words, expressions, language, terminology, phraseology. **4** (*we parted on good terms*) relations, relationship, footing, standing.

come to terms accept, come to accept, learn to live, reconcile oneself, resign oneself.

in terms of as regards, with regard to, in regard to, regarding, with reference to, as to, in respect of, in relation to.

terrestrial *adj* earthly, worldly, global, mundane, temporal. OPPOSITE: celestial.

terrible *adj* **1** (*he demonstrated his terrible strength*) extreme, great, severe, terrific, exceptional, intense. **2** (*a terrible fate*) awful (*inf*), appalling, dreadful (*inf*), dire, frightful (*inf*), fearful, frightening, terrifying, horrifying, horrific, shocking, horrible, horrendous, hideous, grim, gruesome, harrowing, unspeakable, unbearable, intolerable, insufferable, harsh. OPPOSITE: wonderful. **3** (*a terrible smell*) abominable, abhorrent, detestable, disagreeable, loathsome, odious, bad, foul, obnoxious, hateful, offensive, vile, nasty, unpleasant, repulsive, revolting, awful (*inf*), dreadful (*inf*), horrid, horrible. **4** (*he is a terrible dancer*) bad, poor, rotten (*inf*), useless, naff (*inf*), incompetent, talentless, crap (*sl*).

terribly *adv* very, much, extremely, exceedingly, greatly, decidedly, thoroughly, desperately, seriously, terrifically (*inf*), awfully (*inf*), dreadfully (*inf*), frightfully (*inf*).

terrific *adj* **1** (*a terrific noise*) extreme, great, huge, gigantic, considerable, intense, excessive, extraordinary, enormous, tremendous. **2** (*what terrific news*) great, excellent, superb, outstanding, marvellous, magnificent, remarkable, sensational, tremendous, wonderful, amazing, brilliant, brill (*inf*), smashing (*inf*), mega (*inf*), cool (*inf*), wicked (*inf*), fantastic (*inf*), awesome (*inf*), super (*inf*), fabulous (*inf*), fab (*inf*), neat (*inf*), ace (*inf*). OPPOSITE: ordinary.

terrified *adj* frightened, scared, scared stiff, scared to death (*inf*), petrified, paralysed, terror-stricken, terror-struck, terrorized, alarmed, panic-stricken, horrified, appalled, shocked, intimidated, awed, dismayed.

terrify *verb* frighten, scare, scare stiff, shock, horrify, appal, alarm, rattle (*inf*), panic, dismay, petrify, paralyse, numb, terrorize, intimidate, put the wind up (*inf*). OPPOSITE: reassure.

territory *noun* **1** (*far-flung territories of the empire*) country, domain, province, dependency, state, land. **2** (*a sparsely populated territory*) area, region, tract, terrain, zone, district. **3** (*that lies rather outside my territory of expertise*) area, field, province, realm, department, sector, jurisdiction, preserve. **4** (*a salesman's territory*) area, patch, beat, route.

terror *noun* **1** (*he was filled with terror at the thought*) fear, fright, horror, dread, trepidation, awe, panic, alarm, consternation, shock, dismay, intimidation. OPPOSITE: reassurance. **2** (*he was a little terror when he was young*) rascal, rogue, horror, monster, villain, ruffian, hooligan, tearaway, hoodlum. **3** (*pursued by nameless terrors*) monster, demon, fiend, devil, bogeyman.

terrorize *verb* **1** (*they were terrorized by local gangs*) frighten, terrify, petrify, scare, alarm. **2** (*he was terrorized into signing the contract*) intimidate, oppress, threaten, menace, bully, coerce, browbeat, bulldoze (*inf*), strong-arm (*inf*).

terse *adj* **1** (*a terse account of the latest developments*) concise, succinct, compact, condensed, pithy, crisp, incisive, brief, short, elliptical, epigrammatic. **2** (*a terse manner*) curt, abrupt, brusque, clipped, short, blunt, snappy, laconic. OPPOSITE: prolix.

test *verb* **1** (*this will test the system*) put to the test, put on trial, try, assay, check. **2** (*he tested each dish*) try out, sample, check, examine, study, investigate, analyse, assess, appraise, scrutinize, evaluate, screen, probe. **3** (*she's really testing my goodwill*) try, tax, strain, stretch, exact, burden, load, overload, encumber, tire, wear out, weary, drain, exhaust, sap, weaken.
➤ *noun* **1** (*hearing test*) check, check-up, assessment, evaluation, appraisal, investigation, inspection, analysis, scrutinization, scrutiny, study, probe, exploration. **2** (*let's give the car a test*) trial, try, try-out, experiment. **3** (*they all passed the test*) examination, exam, quiz, audition. **4** (*the test of a good beer*) proof, yardstick, model, pattern, standard, measure, touchstone.

testament *noun* testimony, evidence, proof, attestation, witness, tribute, demonstration, indication, exemplification.

testify *verb* **1** (*willing to testify in court*) give evidence, attest, bear witness. **2** (*he testified to the truth of what she said*) swear, state, depose, certify, assert, affirm, allege, attest, declare, avow, corroborate, substantiate, verify, support, back up, uphold, endorse, vouch for. OPPOSITE: deny. **3** (*these results testify to the efficacy of the drug*) bear out, prove, corroborate, confirm, show, demonstrate, indicate, establish.

testimonial *noun* **1** (*a testimonial from my ex-employer*) recommendation, commendation, reference, credential, endorsement. **2** (*he was given a testimonial to reward him for long service*) tribute, gift, trophy.

testimony *noun* **1** (*the prosecution tried to cast doubt on his testimony*) evidence, statement, attestation, deposition, affidavit. **2** (*he refused to change his testimony*) declaration, statement, affidavit, submission, allegation, assertion, asseveration, protestation. **3** (*a testimony to the strength of the material*) affirmation, demonstration, indication, manifestation, avowal, proof, evidence, witness, support, confirmation, corroboration, verification.

testy *adj* irritable, touchy (*inf*), tetchy (*inf*), crotchety (*inf*), irascible, petulant, sullen, peevish, waspish, peppery, snappish, snappy, grumpy, grouchy, cantankerous, crabbed, crabby, splenetic, cross, crusty, ratty (*inf*), stroppy (*inf*), shirty (*inf*), ill-tempered, quick-tempered, querulous, fretful, fractious, captious. OPPOSITE: genial.

tether *noun* rope, chain, cord, lead, leash, line, bond, fastening, restraint.
➤ *verb* tie, tie up, bind, fasten, secure, chain, lash, rope, restrain. OPPOSITE: loose.

text *noun* **1** (*consult the main text of the book*) contents, matter, body, words, wording. **2** (*she took the fall of man as her text*) subject, theme, matter, topic, motif, issue, point. **3** (*he read the text in church*) passage, verse, chapter. **4** (*this is now a set text*) book, textbook.

texture *noun* **1** (*the texture of the paint*) surface, feel, character, grain, appearance, consistency. **2** (*the texture *of the tapestry*) weave, fabric, structure, composition, constitution.

thank *verb* give thanks for, express thanks, appreciate, acknowledge, recognize, credit.

thankful *adj* **1** (*they were thankful to be rescued*) grateful, appreciative, pleased, relieved. **2** (*the old lady was thankful to them for their help*) grateful, obliged, indebted, beholden. OPPOSITE: ungrateful.

thankless *adj* **1** (*a thankless young man*) unthankful, ungrateful, unappreciative, unmannerly. OPPOSITE: grateful. **2** (*a thankless task*) unappreciated, unacknowledged, unrewarding, unrewarded, unrequited, unprofitable, fruitless, vain, useless. OPPOSITE: rewarding.

thanks *pl noun* gratitude, gratefulness, thankfulness, appreciation, acknowledgment, recognition, credit, thanksgiving. OPPOSITE: ingratitude.
» *interj* thank you, many thanks, ta (*inf*), cheers (*inf*), much obliged.

thanks to because of, as a result of, on account of, owing to, due to, through.

thaw *verb* **1** (*the ice-cap thawed*) melt, liquefy, dissolve, soften, defrost, unfreeze. OPPOSITE: freeze. **2** (*he thawed slowly in her presence*) relax, loosen up.

theatre *noun* **1** (*a new theatre opened last night*) playhouse, auditorium, hall. **2** (*a long career in the theatre*) show business, showbiz (*inf*), stage, drama, dramatics, the boards (*inf*).

theatrical *adj* **1** (*a theatrical entertainment*) dramatic, stage, thespian. **2** (*she made a theatrical entrance*) affected, exaggerated, showy, ostentatious, artificial, mannered, stilted, stagy, melodramatic, overdone, forced, histrionic, emotional, hammy (*inf*).

theft *noun* stealing, thieving, nicking (*inf*), pinching (*inf*), swiping (*inf*), nobbling (*inf*), pilfering, purloining, robbery, burglary, larceny, embezzlement, misappropriation, shoplifting, swindling, fraud.

theme *noun* **1** (*the theme of the programme*) subject, topic, matter, argument, gist, essence, burden, text, idea, thesis, thread, keynote. **2** (*the main theme of the symphony*) motif, leitmotif, melody, tune, air.

then *adv* **1** (*he gave up then*) at that time, at that point, at that moment, on that occasion, whereupon. **2** (*things were different then*) in those days, in those times. **3** (*then it was her turn*) next, after, after that, afterwards, subsequently, later. **4** (*and then there's the housework to do*) in addition, additionally, also, as well, too, besides, moreover, further, furthermore. **5** (*if that's what you think then you had better leave*) that being so, that being the case, in that case, under those circumstances, in which case. **6** (*the army then retreated*) therefore, thus, accordingly, consequently, as a result.

theological *adj* religious, ecclesiastical, divine, holy, doctrinal, scriptural, dogmatic.

theoretical *adj* **1** (*theoretical mathematics*) abstract, conceptual, impractical. OPPOSITE: practical. **2** (*a theoretical case*) hypothetical, conjectural, speculative, suppositional, notional, presumed, assumed, academic.

theorize *verb* form a theory, hypothesize, conjecture, speculate, propound, formulate, suppose.

theory *noun* hypothesis, conjecture, speculation, thesis, postulation, presumption, assumption, supposition, notion, surmise, guess, opinion, view, idea, abstraction.

therapeutic *adj* curative, curing, healing, medicinal, remedial, corrective, restorative, reparative, health-giving, ameliorative, beneficial, salutary, good, advantageous.

therapy *noun* **1** (*he offered therapy for her ailment*) treatment, remedy, cure, healing. **2** (*he's been in therapy for years*) psychotherapy, psychoanalysis.

thereabouts *adv* **1** (*by the door or thereabouts*) near there, around there, roundabouts, about there. **2** (*it took a minute or thereabouts*) approximately, roughly, about.

thereafter *adv* after that, afterwards, subsequently, then, next.

therefore *adv* consequently, as a result, hence, whence, thence, then, so, thus, ergo, accordingly.

thesaurus *noun* dictionary, lexicon, wordbook, vocabulary, encyclopedia, treasury, repository.

thesis *noun* **1** (*the university published her thesis*) dissertation, essay, treatise, disquisition, monograph, paper, composition. **2** (*this is his main thesis*) theory, hypothesis, idea, contention, postulation, premiss, supposition, proposal, proposition, argument, subject, theme, topic, idea, opinion, view.

thick *adj* **1** (*thick walls*) wide, broad, deep. **2** (*he had a thick neck*) broad, wide, large, big, bulky, solid, substantial, fat, beefy (*inf*), stout, chunky. **3** (*the dance floor was thick with people*) dense, close, crowded, packed, covered, bristling, brimming, teeming, crawling, swarming, bursting, alive, stiff, solid. OPPOSITE: sparse. **4** (*the air was thick with her perfume*) heavy, filled. **5** (*thick undergrowth*) dense, impenetrable, impassable, condensed, compact, concentrated. OPPOSITE: thin. **6** (*thick fog*) dense, heavy, murky, impenetrable, soupy, opaque, smoggy. **7** (*the boughs were thick with fruit*) abundant, abounding, overflowing, plentiful, numerous, full, packed. **8** (*too thick to get the message*) stupid, unintelligent, slow, slow-witted, dull, dull-witted, dumb, dense, stolid, obtuse, brainless, dim-witted (*inf*), boneheaded, gormless (*inf*), dopey (*inf*), doltish. OPPOSITE: clever. **9** (*a thick voice*) throaty, croaky, croaking, guttural, hoarse, rasping, gruff, husky, gravelly, rough, indistinct, muffled, unclear, inarticulate. OPPOSITE: clear. **10** (*a thick regional accent*) pronounced, marked, broad, rich, strong, distinct, obvious, decided, noticeable, striking. **11** (*he is very thick with her these days*) friendly, close, inseparable, devoted, familiar, intimate, matey (*inf*), pally (*inf*), chummy (*inf*). OPPOSITE: distant.

thicken *verb* **1** (*the paint had thickened*) set, solidify, congeal, gel, jell, stiffen, harden, coagulate, cake, clot, condense. OPPOSITE: thin. **2** (*the plot thickens*) deepen, intensify.

thicket *noun* coppice, copse, spinney, grove, wood. OPPOSITE: clearing.

thickness *noun* **1** (*the thickness of the paper*) width, depth, breadth, density, diameter, extent. **2** (*the thickness of his neck*) breadth, broadness, width, wideness, bigness, largeness, solidness, bulk, bulkiness, fatness, beefiness (*inf*). **3** (*a double thickness of paint*) layer, stratum, sheet, coat, film, lamina, ply, deposit, bed, vein, seam, band. **4** (*the thickness of the smoke*) denseness, impenetrability, murkiness, soupiness, opacity, opaqueness, heaviness. **5** (*the thickness of her accent*) broadness, strength, richness, markedness, obviousness.

thickset *adj* heavily built, well-built, heavy, solid, burly, bulky, strong, sturdy, stocky, brawny (*inf*), muscular, beefy (*inf*), powerful.

thick-skinned *adj* insensitive, tough, unfeeling, impervious, unsusceptible, invulnerable, hardened, case-hardened, hard-boiled (*inf*), hard-nosed (*inf*), callous, inured.

thief *noun* robber, burglar, pilferer, stealer, housebreaker, shoplifter, pickpocket, mugger (*inf*), swindler, fraudster, embezzler, crook (*inf*), kleptomaniac, bandit, larcenist.

thieve *verb* steal, rob, purloin, run off with, make off with, pilfer, filch, nick (*inf*), nobble (*inf*), pinch (*inf*), swipe (*inf*), lift (*inf*), knock off (*inf*), shoplift, embezzle, cheat, swindle, rip off (*inf*), misappropriate.

thin *adj* **1** (*a thin strip*) narrow, fine, attenuated. **2** (*a thin girl*) slim, slender, lean, slight, svelte, spare, skinny, scraggy, scrawny, lanky, underweight, emaciated, wasted, undernourished, anorexic, gaunt, bony, skeletal, shrunken, spindly. OPPOSITE: fat. **3** (*supplies are thin on the ground*) sparse, scattered, scarce, scant, scanty, deficient, poor, meagre, paltry. OPPOSITE: abundant. **4** (*thin cotton*) delicate, fine, gossamer, light, sheer, diaphanous, transparent, see-through, gauzy, filmy, translucent, flimsy, unsubstantial, weak. **5** (*thin hair*) sparse, skimpy, wispy, scanty, straggly. **6** (*a thin mixture*) watery, diluted, dilute, weak, wishy-washy (*inf*), runny. OPPOSITE: thick. **7** (*a thin whine*) weak, low, soft, quiet, small, feeble, faint. **8** (*they got a pretty thin response*) poor, inadequate, weak, feeble, lame, flimsy, unconvincing, inconclusive, unsubstantial, insufficient, deficient, shallow.
➤ *verb* **1** (*he was accused of thinning the beer*) water, water down, dilute, weaken. **2** (*thin out the applicants*) reduce, lessen, decrease, diminish, prune, trim, weed out. **3** (*the queues thinned to a trickle*) dwindle, decrease, diminish, fall.

thing *noun* **1** (*what is that thing?*) object, article, something, item, entity, thingy (*inf*), thingummy (*inf*), thingummybob (*inf*), thingummyjig (*inf*), whatsisname (*inf*), whatsit (*inf*), doodah (*inf*), what-d'you-call-it (*inf*). **2** (*then he did an amazing thing*) deed, act, action, feat, exploit, undertaking. **3** (*a surprising thing to suggest*) idea, notion, thought, concept, theory, conjecture. **4** (*stranger things have happened*) event, eventuality, occurrence, happening, episode, incident, phenomenon. **5** (*she does not listen to half the things he says*) statement, comment, remark, declaration, utterance, pronouncement. **6** (*she has a thing about spiders*) phobia, obsession, preoccupation, hang-up (*inf*), fixation, horror, fear, aversion, dislike. **7** (*he has a thing about her*) liking, love, fondness, affection, soft spot (*inf*), fancy, desire, affinity, predilection, penchant, preference, tendency, taste, appreciation, inclination, fixation, obsession, weakness. **8** (*the impressive thing about his performance*) quality, characteristic, attribute, property, trait, feature. **9** (*she's*

an odd little thing) creature, wretch, soul. **10** (*here's another weird thing*) fact, point, detail, particular, aspect, element. **11** (*the latest thing in music*) fashion, trend, style.

things *pl noun* **1** (*don't forget your things*) belongings, possessions, bits and pieces (*inf*), stuff (*inf*), clobber (*inf*), odds and ends (*inf*), bits and bobs (*inf*), oddments, paraphernalia, goods, effects, luggage, baggage. **2** (*give me your wet things*) clothes, clothing, garments, gear (*inf*), clobber (*inf*), togs (*inf*), attire, apparel. **3** (*I don't like the look of things*) conditions, circumstances, matters, affairs, state of affairs, relations, situation. **4** (*have you got all the things you will need?*) equipment, apparatus, implements, tools, gear, tackle.

think *verb* **1** (*I think things will improve soon*) believe, suppose, expect, anticipate, foresee, conceive, imagine, surmise, conjecture, fancy, guess, presume, maintain, feel, conclude, deduce, calculate. **2** (*we think she is very beautiful*) consider, judge, deem, regard, reckon, hold. **3** (*think about it and let me know*) ponder, meditate, deliberate, reason, reflect, muse, mull over, chew over, brood, cerebrate, cogitate, ruminate, weigh up, think over, review, contemplate, consider. **4** (*think of yourself swimming in that ocean*) imagine, picture, visualize, envisage, dream.
➤ *noun* consideration, contemplation, reflection, deliberation, meditation, cogitation, muse.

think better of reconsider, think twice about, rethink, have second thoughts about, decide against, change one's mind about, get cold feet about (*inf*).

think nothing of consider routine, consider normal, take in one's stride, dismiss.

think over contemplate, reflect upon, consider, deliberate about, weigh up, meditate, ponder, chew over, ruminate, mull over, muse over.

think up devise, contrive, invent, create, dream up, imagine, concoct, conceive, design, visualize, come up with.

thinker *noun* philosopher, intellect (*inf*), brain (*inf*), egghead (*inf*), mastermind, scholar, sage, theorist.

thinking *noun* reasoning, thought, judgement, opinion, view, outlook, meditation, rumination, contemplation, deliberation, assessment, appraisal, evaluation, reasoning.
➤ *adj* rational, reasoning, sensible, logical, intelligent, intellectual, cultured, sophisticated, philosophical, reflective, contemplative, meditative, thoughtful, analytic.

thin-skinned *adj* touchy (*inf*), temperamental, soft, vulnerable, tender, snappish, susceptible, sensitive, oversensitive, hypersensitive, supersensitive.

third-rate *adj* inferior, poor, poor-quality, low-quality, low-grade, bad, naff (*inf*), awful, mediocre, indifferent, unsatisfactory, slipshod, shoddy, ropy (*inf*), duff (*inf*).

thirst *noun* **1** (*sought to quench his thirst*) thirstiness, dryness, dehydration, parchedness, drought. **2** (*a thirst for adventure*) craving, desire, lust, hunger, appetite, yearning, longing, hankering, eagerness, keenness, passion, yen (*inf*), avidity, covetousness.
➤ *verb* crave, desire, hunger, yearn, long, hanker, lust, covet.

thirsty *adj* **1** (*he was thirsty after the journey*) dry (*inf*), dehydrated, parched (*inf*), gasping (*inf*), arid. **2** (*thirsty for success*) thirsting, eager, avid, keen, desirous, craving, longing, yearning, dying, burning, itching, greedy, hungry, covetous. OPPOSITE: satisfied.

thorn *noun* **1** (*pricked herself on a thorn*) prickle, spine, barb, point, spike, bristle, needle. **2** (*a thorn in his side*) nuisance, bother, vexation, irritation, annoyance, trouble, plague, scourge, curse.

thorny *adj* **1** (*the plant's thorny stem*) prickly, spiny, spined, barbed, spiky, bristly, pointed, sharp. OPPOSITE: smooth. **2** (*a thorny problem*) problematic, difficult, hard, tricky, complicated, complex, convoluted, knotty, involved, intricate, tough, trying, taxing, troublesome, bothersome, irksome, harassing, vexatious, worrying, upsetting, awkward, delicate, ticklish.

thorough *adj* **1** (*he is very thorough in his work*) meticulous, painstaking, methodical, scrupulous, punctilious, careful, conscientious, assiduous, efficient. **2** (*a thorough search*) exhaustive, extensive, intensive, in-depth, deep, detailed, comprehensive, all-inclusive, full, complete, all-embracing, sweeping, widespread. OPPOSITE: superficial. **3** (*a thorough nuisance*) complete, total, entire, perfect, downright, out-and-out, unmitigated, unqualified, absolute, pure, sheer, utter, thoroughgoing.

thoroughbred *adj* pedigree, pedigreed, pure, pure-bred, pure-blooded, full-blooded.

thoroughfare *noun* **1** (*the thoroughfare was blocked by an accident*) road, street, motorway, highway, freeway, way, avenue, concourse. **2** (*no thoroughfare for pedestrians*) access, passage, passageway, way.

thoroughly *adv* **1** (*search the room thoroughly*) exhaustively, fully, in detail, inside out, from top to bottom, carefully, completely, comprehensively, methodically, meticulously, painstakingly, scrupulously, conscientiously, intensively, extensively, assiduously, efficiently. **2** (*he was thoroughly fed up*) completely, totally, utterly, absolutely, entirely, perfectly, positively, unreservedly, downright, dead, quite.

though *conj* **1** (*he was happy though he lost*) although, albeit, notwithstanding that, despite the fact that. **2** (*he will pay though he thinks it is too much*) even if, allowing, admitting, granting.
➤ *adv* nevertheless, nonetheless, even so, still, yet, however, but, for all that, all the same (*inf*), be that as it may.

thought *noun* **1** (*she kept her thoughts to herself*) idea, concept, conception, fancy, notion, theory, opinion, view, belief. **2** (*deep in thought*) thinking, reasoning, brainwork, cerebration, concentration, reflection, cogitation, meditation, contemplation, pondering, speculation, consideration, deliberation, rumination, musing, mulling, introspection. **3** (*little thought of success*) hope, expectation, anticipation, prospect, dream, aspiration. **4** (*she had no thought of giving the money back*) plan, design, aim, intention, purpose. **5** (*tell me your thoughts on the matter*) sentiment, feeling, judgement, belief, opinion, assessment, appraisal, estimation, conclusion, conviction, point of view, position, stance, stand. **6** (*the task requires some thought*) care, carefulness, regard, scrutiny, attention, heed, consideration. **7** (*his preparations showed thought for his guests*) thoughtfulness, kindness, kindliness, compassion, concern, regard, consideration, solicitude, care, tenderness, sympathy. OPPOSITE: thoughtlessness.

thoughtful *adj* **1** (*a thoughtful touch*) considerate, caring, kind, kindly, compassionate, tender, regardful, concerned, attentive, solicitous, charitable, helpful, unselfish. OPPOSITE: thoughtless. **2** (*thoughtful about the possible consequences*) mindful, heedful, attentive, careful, cautious, wary, guarded, prudent, discreet, circumspect. **3** (*a thoughtful silence descended*) pensive, thinking, absorbed, abstracted, rapt, lost in thought, reflective, ruminative, contemplative, meditative, introspective, cogitative, wistful, dreamy, quiet. **4** (*a thoughtful piece of writing*) serious, deep, profound, considered, weighty, meaty, pithy, solemn.

thoughtless *adj* **1** (*a thoughtless thing to say*) inconsiderate, unkind, insensitive, careless, uncaring, tactless, undiplomatic, indiscreet, selfish, rude, impolite. **2** (*a thoughtless act*) unthinking, unmindful, mindless, heedless, careless, regardless, inattentive, absentminded, negligent, neglectful, remiss, rash, precipitate, reckless, foolish, imprudent, unwise, improvident, injudicious, ill-advised, ill-considered, stupid, silly. OPPOSITE: careful.

thrash *verb* **1** (*he thrashed the lad with a stick*) beat, whip, horsewhip, flog, lash, cane, birch, smack, spank, belt (*inf*), whack (*inf*), tan (*inf*), wallop (*inf*), scourge, punish, chastise. **2** (*they thrashed their opponents*) defeat, beat, crush, trounce, lick (*inf*), clobber (*inf*), hammer (*inf*), slaughter (*inf*), worst, conquer, overwhelm, vanquish, rout, drub, turn over (*inf*). **3** (*the fish thrashed around on the end of the line*) thresh, flail, jerk, writhe, squirm, toss, swish, twitch.

thrash out discuss, air, talk over, debate, negotiate, argue out, hammer out, settle, resolve.

thread *noun* **1** (*cotton thread*) yarn, cotton, fibre, filament, line, string, cord, strand. **2** (*the thread of the story*) theme, motif, plot, story line, train of thought, drift, course, direction, subject, tenor, motif.
➤ *verb* pass, ease, move, weave, wind, inch, meander, push, squeeze, shoulder, elbow.

threadbare *adj* **1** (*a threadbare jacket*) worn, worn out, ragged, holey, frayed, tatty (*inf*), tattered, scruffy, shabby, moth-eaten, old, thin, poor. OPPOSITE: new. **2** (*a threadbare argument*) trite, banal, hackneyed, clichéd, cliché-ridden, stereotyped, corny (*inf*), old-hat (*inf*), played-out (*inf*), overused, platitudinous, commonplace, conventional, stale, tired, worn-out, well-worn, stock.

threat *noun* **1** (*he made several dark threats*) warning, menace, ultimatum, intimidation. **2** (*the threat of disaster*) warning, menace, caution, danger, risk, omen, foreboding, portent, presage. **3** (*a threat to public health*) danger, peril, hazard, risk, menace.

threaten *verb* **1** (*he threatened his employees*) intimidate, menace, bully, cow, browbeat, lean on (*inf*), push around (*inf*), pressurize, terrorize, warn, caution, extort, blackmail. OPPOSITE: reassure. **2** (*a storm threatened*) impend, loom, hang over, foreshadow, approach. **3** (*the clouds threatened a change in the weather*) warn of, portend, forebode, foreshadow, augur, presage.

4 (*poverty threatened their happiness*) menace, endanger, jeopardize, put in jeopardy, imperil, put at risk.

threatening *adj* **1** (*guilty of threatening behaviour*) intimidatory, menacing, bullying, warning, cautionary. **2** (*a threatening sign of disaster*) foreboding, ominous, inauspicious, impending, looming, grim, sinister.

threesome *noun* trio, triple, triplet, triumvirate, triad, trinity, trilogy, triptych, troika.

threshold *noun* **1** (*she shall not cross the threshold of my home*) sill, door, doorstep, doorway, entrance. **2** (*we stand on the threshold of a new century*) start, beginning, commencement, outset, opening, debut, inception, brink, verge, dawn, kick-off (*inf*). OPPOSITE: end.

thrift *noun* economy, economizing, frugality, frugalness, thriftiness, husbandry, conservation, saving, scrimping, penny-pinching, carefulness, sparingness, prudence, parsimony, miserliness. OPPOSITE: extravagance.

thriftless *adj* extravagant, lavish, prodigal, wasteful, spendthrift, improvident, unthrifty, imprudent, profligate. OPPOSITE: thrifty.

thrifty *adj* economical, economizing, frugal, saving, sparing, scrimping, parsimonious, penny-pinching, provident, prudent, careful, miserly, mean. OPPOSITE: thriftless.

thrill *noun* **1** (*it gives me a thrill to be here*) excitement, stimulation, titillation, sensation, tingle, tremor, glow, kick (*inf*), charge (*inf*), buzz (*inf*). **2** (*a thrill of excitement ran through the crowd*) tremor, frisson, quiver, flutter, shudder, vibration, tremble, throb.
➤ *verb* excite, exhilarate, stimulate, galvanize, electrify, touch, move, stir, rouse, arouse, titillate, agitate. OPPOSITE: bore.

thrilling *adj* exciting, exhilarating, gripping, hair-raising (*inf*), electrifying, stirring, rousing, stimulating, moving, riveting, sensational. OPPOSITE: boring.

thrive *verb* prosper, succeed, do well, make good, advance, gain, increase, get on, flourish, boom, grow, wax, bloom, blossom. OPPOSITE: fail.

thriving *adj* prosperous, prospering, successful, advancing, progressing, flourishing, booming, burgeoning, growing, blooming, wealthy, rich, affluent.

throat *noun* gullet, oesophagus, windpipe, craw.

throb *verb* beat, pulsate, pulse, palpitate, pound, thump, drum, vibrate.
➤ *noun* beat, beating, pulse, pulsation, palpitation, throbbing, pounding, thumping, drumming, vibration.

throes *pl noun* **1** (*in the throes of childbirth*) pangs, pain, agony, anguish, excruciation, suffering, torture, distress. **2** (*in the throes of changing jobs*) upheaval, turmoil, disruption, chaos, confusion, pandemonium, hurly-burly.

throng *noun* crowd, multitude, mob, horde, host, mass, jam, press, gathering, congregation, assemblage, swarm, flock, pack, herd, drove.
➤ *verb* crowd, flock, swarm, troop, herd, pack, bunch, cram, jam, press, fill.

throttle *verb* **1** (*she tried to throttle the intruder*) strangle, strangulate, choke, suffocate, smother, asphyxiate.

2 (*dissent has been throttled*) gag, stifle, silence, suppress, restrain, check, inhibit, hold back, control.

through *prep* **1** (*walk through the wood*) across, from one end to the other. **2** (*through inattention to the task in hand*) because of, by, by virtue of, by way of, via, by means of, as a result of, as a consequence of, owing to, on account of, due to, thanks to. **3** (*they talked through the weekend*) during, throughout.
➤ *adj* **1** (*he will be through in a minute*) finished, done. **2** (*the work is through*) completed, finished, done, ended, terminated. **3** (*he's through with love*) finished, done, fed up, tired of.

through and through completely, utterly, thoroughly, totally, altogether, entirely, wholly, fully, unreservedly, out and out, from top to bottom.

throughout *prep* **1** (*panic throughout the nation*) all over, all round, in all parts of, in every part of, everywhere in. **2** (*he stayed with her throughout her illness*) through, all through, during, for the duration of.
➤ *adv* **1** (*make sure the meat is cooked throughout*) right through, all through, all over, everywhere, in every part. **2** (*she kept her eyes closed throughout*) all the time, until the end, from start to end, for the duration.

throw *verb* **1** (*throw the ball to me*) cast, fling, toss, hurl, sling, pitch, lob (*inf*), heave (*inf*), chuck (*inf*), shy, launch, catapult, propel, project, send, deliver. OPPOSITE: catch. **2** (*he threw himself into the work*) cast, fling, put, commit. **3** (*the moon threw a shadow*) cast, shed, project, send. **4** (*he threw his opponent*) floor, fell, bring down, prostrate, overturn, upset. **5** (*the horse threw its rider*) unseat, unsaddle, unhorse, dislodge, bring down. **6** (*his attitude threw his colleagues*) disconcert, disturb, put out, discomfit, confuse, confound, baffle, perplex, surprise, astonish, dumbfound, floor (*inf*), discountenance. **7** (*he threw the vehicle into reverse*) put, move, operate. **8** (*let's throw a party*) organize, put on, give, arrange, lay on, host.
➤ *noun* cast, fling, toss, sling, pitch, lob, shy, chuck (*inf*), heave (*inf*). OPPOSITE: catch.

throw away 1 (*throw away the wrapper*) throw out, discard, dispense with, reject, get rid of, scrap, dump (*inf*), ditch (*inf*), dispose of, waste, jettison. OPPOSITE: keep. **2** (*he threw away his chances*) waste, squander, blow (*inf*), fritter away, lose.

throw off 1 (*she threw off her coat*) cast off, discard, shed, drop, jettison, shake off, abandon. **2** (*he managed to throw off the pursuit*) shake off, evade, elude, lose, get away from, escape from, outdistance, outrun.

throw out 1 (*he was thrown out of the company*) expel, eject, evict, kick out (*inf*), turf out (*inf*), put out, dismiss. OPPOSITE: admit. **2** (*she threw out anything that was broken*) throw away, discard, dispose of, get rid of, scrap, jettison. **3** (*the whole plan was thrown out*) dismiss, discard, reject, turn down, dump (*inf*), ditch (*inf*). **4** (*the bulb threw out a bright light*) radiate, emit, emanate, exude, send out, give off, produce, disseminate, diffuse.

thrust *verb* **1** (*he thrust the man aside*) push, shove, drive, ram, propel, wedge. **2** (*he had responsibility for the whole campaign thrust upon him*) impose, urge, force, press, push, inflict, burden, saddle, foist, encumber. OPPOSITE: withdraw. **3** (*he thrust his spear at the lion*) push, poke, drive, stick, stab, jab, pierce, lunge, plunge, ram. **4** (*she* *thrust her way to the front*) push, shove, butt, force, press, shoulder, elbow, jostle.

➤ *noun* **1** (*a sudden thrust threw him backwards*) push, shove, drive, ram, poke, prod, press. **2** (*the thrust of the engine*) drive, force, pressure, impetus, momentum. **3** (*with one thrust of his sword*) lunge, stab, jab, poke, prod. **4** (*the general ordered a thrust into enemy territory*) attack, assault, offensive, onslaught, charge, raid, incursion, drive, advance, push. **5** (*the main thrust of government policy*) gist, drift, substance, message, point, theme, essence, tenor, subject, thesis.

thud *noun* thump, bang, bash, wallop (*inf*), knock, smack, crash, clonk, clunk, wham (*inf*).

➤ *verb* thump, bang, bash, wallop (*inf*), knock, smack, crash, clonk, clunk, wham (*inf*).

thug *noun* ruffian, hooligan, tough, rough, roughneck, heavy (*inf*), gangster, hoodlum, bandit, cut-throat, villain, robber, murderer, mugger (*inf*).

thumb *verb* leaf through, skim through, browse through, flick through, flip through, riffle through, peruse, scan, glance at.

thump *verb* **1** (*he thumped the burglar across the head*) hit, strike, knock, rap, slap, punch, smack, wallop (*inf*), whack (*inf*), belt (*inf*), clout (*inf*), beat, batter, box, cuff, cudgel, pummel, bang, crash, thrash. **2** (*she could feel her heart thumping*) palpitate, beat, pound, thud, throb, pulse, pulsate.

➤ *noun* **1** (*he felt a thump on his back*) blow, punch, rap, slap, smack, knock, wallop (*inf*), whack (*inf*), clout (*inf*), belt (*inf*). **2** (*a thump on the door*) knock, bang, rap, thud.

thunder *verb* resound, reverberate, rumble, roll, boom, clap, crash, bang, crack, blast, detonate, roar, bellow, bark.

➤ *noun* reverberation, rumble, rumbling, roll, boom, booming, roar, roaring, crash, crashing, bang, blast, crack, clap, peal, outburst, explosion.

thunderous *adj* booming, resounding, reverberating, rumbling, roaring, deafening, loud, noisy, ear-splitting, tumultuous.

thunderstruck *adj* stunned, startled, surprised, shocked, staggered, amazed, astonished, astounded, flabbergasted (*inf*), dazed, dumbfounded, struck dumb, speechless, open-mouthed, taken aback, paralysed, floored (*inf*), disconcerted, aghast, agape, bewildered, bowled over (*inf*), knocked for six (*inf*), flummoxed (*inf*), nonplussed (*inf*), gobsmacked (*inf*).

thus *adv* **1** (*he answered thus*) so, like so, in this way, like this, as follows. **2** (*he won and thus realized his dream*) therefore, consequently, accordingly, so, as a result, hence, ergo.

thwart *verb* frustrate, balk, foil, check, block, stop, cross, oppose, contravene, defeat, hinder, hamper, impede, obstruct, prevent, nobble, baffle, stymie. OPPOSITE: aid.

tic *noun* twitch, spasm, jerk.

tick *noun* **1** (*the tick of the clock*) tick-tock, ticking, click, stroke, tap, tapping, beat. **2** (*hold on a tick*) moment, instant, minute, sec (*inf*), second, flash, trice, jiffy (*inf*), half a mo (*inf*). **3** (*he put a tick against her name*) stroke, mark, line, dash.

➤ *verb* **1** (*the clock had stopped ticking*) tick-tock, click, tap, beat. **2** (*tick the names as I read them out*) mark, check, indicate.

tick off tell off (*inf*), scold, reprimand, reproach, reprove, rebuke, chide, lecture, censure, berate, upbraid, take to task, tear into (*inf*), tear off a strip (*inf*), carpet (*inf*). OPPOSITE: praise.

ticket *noun* **1** (*entry only with ticket*) pass, token, certificate, coupon, docket, voucher, card, stub, counterfoil. **2** (*look for the yellow price tickets*) slip, label, tag, sticker.

tickle *verb* **1** (*the dog likes to be tickled*) stroke, pet, touch. **2** (*the news really tickled him*) delight, gladden, amuse, entertain, captivate, divert, cheer, gratify, please, thrill, excite, stimulate, titillate, arouse.

ticklish *adj* sensitive, touchy, delicate, awkward, tricky, sticky (*inf*), dodgy (*inf*), difficult, problematic, complex, thorny, knotty, risky, unstable, unsteady, uncertain, precarious, hazardous.

tide *noun* **1** (*the tide comes in twice a day*) tidal flow, tidewater, tide race, ebb, flow, stream, current. **2** (*the general tide of opinion*) current, drift, trend, tendency, direction, run, movement, course, flow, flux.

tide over help, help out, assist, aid, keep going, see through.

tidings *pl noun* news, word, advice, information, info (*inf*), intelligence, gen (*inf*), dope (*inf*), low-down (*inf*), message, report, bulletin, notification, communication, greetings.

tidy *adj* **1** (*a tidy house*) neat, orderly, well-ordered, ordered, well-kept, uncluttered, trim, spruce, clean, shipshape, spick-and-span, immaculate. OPPOSITE: untidy. **2** (*a tidy worker*) neat, orderly, well-organized, organized, systematic, efficient, methodical, businesslike. **3** (*a tidy sum of money*) considerable, sizeable, good, goodly, large, largish, big, substantial, ample, generous, respectable, handsome, fair, decent, healthy. OPPOSITE: small.

➤ *verb* **1** (*go and tidy yourself up*) neaten, straighten, smarten, spruce up, brush down, clean, groom. **2** (*tell her to tidy her room*) straighten, straighten up, neaten, put to rights, arrange, put in order, order, clear up, clean, clean up. OPPOSITE: disorder.

tie *verb* **1** (*tie the rope*) bind, truss, knot, fasten, join, connect, unite, link, couple, attach, fix, secure, tether, moor, lash, rope, strap, chain. OPPOSITE: untie. **2** (*he was tied by his family commitments*) restrict, confine, limit, curb, restrain, constrain, cramp, tie up, shackle, hinder, hamper, impede. OPPOSITE: free.

➤ *noun* **1** (*secure the sapling with a tie*) bond, link, clip, tape, band, fastening, fastener. **2** (*the tie between husband and wife*) bond, connection, liaison, friendship, relationship, kinship, affiliation, allegiance. **3** (*the children are a tie*) obligation, commitment, duty, responsibility, restriction, limit, limitation, curb, restraint, constraint, hindrance, impediment, encumbrance. **4** (*he loosened the tie*) knot, bow, string, rope, fastening. **5** (*play ended in a tie*) draw, dead heat, deadlock, stalemate.

tie down tie, restrict, confine, constrain, curb, hamper, hinder, limit.

tie up 1 (*tie up the boat*) tether, secure, moor, rope, chain, attach, bind, fasten, connect. **2** (*tie up the bundle*) wrap, wrap up, do up, truss, bind. **3** (*he is tied up in a meeting*) occupy, engage, engross, keep busy. **4** (*we should tie up the whole business today*) conclude, complete, finish, finalize, settle, wind up (*inf*), wrap up (*inf*), terminate.

tier *noun* **1** (*a tier of seats*) row, rank, line, bank. **2** (*the cake has three tiers*) layer, level, stratum, stage, belt. **3** (*the hotel had two upper tiers*) floor, storey, level. **4** (*belonging to a different tier of society*) level, layer, rank, echelon.

tiff *noun* quarrel, row, dispute, squabble, words, disagreement, argument, set-to (*inf*), falling-out (*inf*), barney (*inf*), scrap (*inf*), spat (*inf*), difference. OPPOSITE: harmony.

tight *adj* **1** (*a tight hold on the ladder*) fixed, fast, secure, clenched. **2** (*a tight wire*) taut, stretched, strained, tense, stiff, rigid, firm, stable. **3** (*a tight sweater*) tight-fitting, close-fitting, close, figure-hugging, skin-tight, snug. **4** (*a tight mass of cables*) compact, compressed. OPPOSITE: loose. **5** (*how to fit everything into such a tight space*) cramped, restricted, constricted, limited. **6** (*the hull proved tight in the water*) watertight, impervious, impenetrable, sound, sealed, proof, hermetic, airtight. **7** (*he's very tight with his money*) mean, miserly, stingy, niggardly, tight-fisted (*inf*), close-fisted, parsimonious, penny-pinching. OPPOSITE: generous. **8** (*time is getting very tight*) short, limited, scant, sparse, inadequate, insufficient, in short supply. **9** (*we run a tight ship here*) efficient, strict, rigorous, exacting, uncompromising, inflexible, hard, rigid, stringent, tough. **10** (*they quickly realized they were in a tight spot*) precarious, dangerous, hazardous, perilous, difficult, awkward, problematic, sticky (*inf*), dodgy (*inf*), tricky, delicate, ticklish, worrying. **11** (*it was a tight contest*) close, even, evenly matched, well-matched, hard-fought, neck and neck (*inf*). **12** (*we all got pretty tight that night*) drunk, inebriated, intoxicated, pissed (*sl*), stoned (*inf*), tipsy (*inf*), tiddly (*inf*), blotto (*inf*), sloshed (*inf*), plastered (*inf*), tanked up (*inf*), paralytic (*inf*), smashed (*inf*), legless (*inf*), wasted (*inf*), wrecked (*inf*), sozzled (*inf*), pickled (*inf*), stewed (*inf*), well-oiled (*inf*), merry (*inf*), steaming (*inf*), off one's face (*inf*). OPPOSITE: sober.

tighten *verb* **1** (*he tightened his hold on the rail*) secure, make fast, squeeze. **2** (*the muscles in his arm tightened*) stiffen, tense, tauten, stretch. **3** (*tighten the hatches*) close, fasten, secure, fix, screw down. **4** (*the gap tightened*) narrow, close, contract, constrict, cramp.

till[1] *prep* **1** (*she waited till dark*) until, up to, to, as late as. **2** (*he didn't understand till then*) before, previous to, prior to, earlier than.

till[2] *verb* (*till the land*) farm, cultivate, work, dig, plough, turn over.

tilt *verb* slope, slant, incline, lean, tip, list, cant, pitch. OPPOSITE: straighten.
　➤ *noun* **1** (*with a tilt of the head*) slope, slant, incline, inclination, pitch, angle, cant. **2** (*the knights prepared for the tilt*) joust, tournament, tourney, lists, spar, contest, encounter, combat, fight, duel.
　at full tilt at full speed, at top speed, at full pelt, all out (*inf*), flat out (*inf*), headlong, very fast, very quickly.

timber *noun* **1** (*timber for the shed*) wood, plank, board, beam, spar, pole. **2** (*the slopes were covered by timber*) wood, forest, trees.

timbre *noun* tone, tonality, tone colour, tone quality, ring, resonance.

time *noun* **1** (*things remained quiet for a time*) duration, period, span, space, spell, stretch, while, term, interval, session. **2** (*at a distant time in the earth's history*) period, era, epoch, age, date. **3** (*it was the first time he had been late*) occasion, instance, point, juncture. **4** (*now is the time to act*) moment, instant, hour, season, point, stage. **5** (*I don't expect to see it in my time*) lifetime, life, lifespan, generation. **6** (*the band marched in strict time*) tempo, beat, rhythm, metre, measure.
　➤ *verb* **1** (*he was timed over a set distance*) count, measure, clock, regulate, calculate. **2** (*she timed the alarm to go off at seven*) adjust, set, synchronize, regulate. **3** (*the change will be timed to coincide with the new term*) fix, set, arrange, schedule, timetable, programme.
　all the time 1 (*the baby cried all the time*) throughout, for the duration, interminably. **2** (*she's away nearly all the time*) always, at all times, constantly, continually, continuously, incessantly, perpetually.
　at one time 1 (*they were in love at one time*) once, at one point, in times past, long ago, formerly, previously, hitherto. **2** (*trying to do two jobs at one time*) at once, at the same time, simultaneously, concurrently, together.
　at the same time 1 (*the bombs went off at the same time*) together, simultaneously, concurrently. **2** (*I agree, but at the same time I have my doubts*) just the same, even so, for all that, however, yet, still, but, nonetheless, nevertheless.
　at times sometimes, from time to time, now and then, now and again, occasionally, on occasion, periodically, every so often, off and on.
　behind the times old-fashioned, unfashionable, out of fashion, out of date, dated, outmoded, past, obsolete, passé, antiquated, old, fuddy-duddy (*inf*), old hat (*inf*).
　behind time behind, late, running late, behind schedule, delayed, overdue, unpunctual, tardy.
　for the time being for now, just now, right now, at the moment, for the moment, for the present, at present, temporarily, pro tem, in the meantime, meantime, meanwhile.
　from time to time now and then, now and again, every so often, once in a while, at times, sometimes, occasionally, on occasion, periodically, intermittently, sporadically, spasmodically.
　in good time on time, punctually, with time to spare, early, ahead of schedule, ahead of time.
　in time on time, in good time, punctually, early enough, on schedule.
　on time in good time, punctually, promptly, precisely, exactly, on the dot (*inf*), bang on (*inf*), spot on (*inf*), dead on (*inf*), sharp, early enough, in good time.
　time after time time and time again, time and again, again and again, over and over again, repeatedly, recurrently, frequently, often, on many occasions.

timeless *adj* ageless, immortal, undying, deathless, eternal, everlasting, enduring, lasting, permanent, abiding, endless, unending, ceaseless, changeless, unchanging, immutable, indestructible, imperishable.

timely *adj* opportune, seasonable, well-timed, prompt,

punctual, at the right time, propitious, auspicious, favourable, felicitous, convenient, suitable, appropriate. OPPOSITE: inopportune.

timetable *noun* schedule, programme, calendar, diary, agenda, list, listing, curriculum, rota, roster.
➤ *verb* schedule, programme, set, fix, arrange, list.

timid *adj* **1** (*a timid child*) timorous, shy, bashful, coy, nervous, diffident, modest, retiring, shrinking, unselfconfident, demure. **2** (*he was a timid footballer*) fearful, frightened, scared, afraid, wimpish (*inf*), yellow (*inf*), gutless (*inf*), lily-livered (*inf*), chicken (*inf*), fainthearted, pusillanimous, cowardly, spineless, apprehensive, irresolute, timorous. OPPOSITE: bold.

timorous *adj* **1** (*a timorous attitude to violence*) timid, fearful, scared, frightened, afraid, apprehensive, cowardly, chicken (*inf*). **2** (*a timorous child*) timid, shy, bashful, mousy (*inf*), diffident, retiring, modest, coy, reticent, tentative, trembling, nervous, shrinking, irresolute.

tinge *noun* **1** (*a tinge of yellow*) tint, tincture, shade, hue, tone, stain, wash, dye, colour. **2** (*a tinge of regret*) touch, trace, hint, suggestion, soupçon, bit, dash, drop, pinch, sprinkling, smattering, smack, tincture.
➤ *verb* **1** (*blue tinged with green*) tint, colour, shade, tincture, dye, stain. **2** (*her voice was tinged with sadness*) suffuse, imbue, colour, affect by, flavour.

tingle *verb* prickle, prick, sting, smart, itch, tickle, shiver, tremble, quiver, thrill, throb, vibrate.
➤ *noun* **1** (*a tingle at the back of her neck*) tingling, itch, itching, prickle, prickling, tickle, quiver, shiver, trembling, goosepimples, pins and needles (*inf*). **2** (*a tingle of anticipation*) quiver, tremor, thrill, throb.

tinker *verb* fiddle, play, toy, trifle, dabble, potter, meddle, tamper, fool about, fool around, mess about.

tinkle *verb* jingle, jangle, ring, peal, chime, clink.
➤ *noun* **1** (*the distant tinkle of a bell*) ring, jingle, jangle, ding, peal, chime, clink. **2** (*he gave them a tinkle last night*) call, phone call, telephone call, phone (*inf*), ring (*inf*), buzz (*inf*), bell (*inf*).

tint *noun* **1** (*a tint of gold in the sky*) colour, hue, shade, tone, tinge, touch, trace, cast, streak, tincture. **2** (*a blue tint in her hair*) dye, stain, rinse, wash, colouring, colourant.
➤ *verb* colour, stain, taint, dye, tinge, streak, tincture.

tiny *adj* minute, minuscule, infinitesimal, microscopic, miniature, mini, diminutive, pocket, pocket-sized, small, little, slight, petite, wee, teeny (*inf*), teeny-weeny (*inf*), itsy-bitsy (*inf*), pint-sized (*inf*), insignificant, inconsequential, trifling, negligible, dwarfish, midget, pygmy, Lilliputian. OPPOSITE: enormous.

tip[1] *noun* **1** (*the tip of the mountain*) point, head, top, apex, summit, peak, pinnacle, cap, crown. OPPOSITE: base. **2** (*the tip of the sword*) point, end, extremity.
➤ *verb* cap, crown, top, surmount.

tip[2] *verb* **1** (*the cart tipped to one side*) tilt, incline, lean, list, cant, slant. **2** (*he tipped over the bucket*) upset, upend, overturn, topple, capsize. **3** (*she tipped the contents onto the floor*) empty, pour, spill, dump, unload.
➤ *noun* rubbish dump, dump, refuse dump, rubbish heap, slag heap.

tip[3] *noun* **1** (*he left a tip for the waiter*) gratuity,

baksheesh, gift, bonus, present, reward. **2** (*let me give you a tip*) hint, suggestion, recommendation, clue, pointer, forecast, tip-off (*inf*), warning, advice, information.
➤ *verb* **1** (*tip the taxi driver*) reward, remunerate. **2** (*he tipped the grey for the next race*) recommend, back, suggest. **3** (*he tipped them off about the raid*) warn, forewarn, caution, advise, tell, inform.

tip-off *noun* warning, forewarning, hint, clue, suggestion, pointer, advice, information, notification.

tipple *verb* **1** (*tipple wine*) sip, swig (*inf*), bib, drink, quaff, imbibe. **2** (*he took to tippling excessively*) drink, booze (*inf*), indulge (*inf*).
➤ *noun* drink, alcohol, liquor, poison (*inf*), usual (*inf*).

tippler *noun* drinker, hard drinker, drunkard, drunk, inebriate, boozer (*inf*), soak (*inf*), sponge (*inf*), wino (*inf*), lush (*inf*), dipsomaniac, imbiber, bibber, sot, toper.

tipsy *adj* drunk, intoxicated, inebriated, tight (*inf*), squiffy (*inf*), tiddly (*inf*), happy (*inf*), merry (*inf*), mellow (*inf*), under the influence (*inf*), half-cut (*inf*). OPPOSITE: sober.

tirade *noun* diatribe, harangue, rant, lecture, invective, denunciation, censure, vilification, vituperation, outburst, abuse, obloquy, fulmination, upbraiding, philippic. OPPOSITE: eulogy.

tire *verb* **1** (*the climb tired her*) weary, wear out, fatigue, exhaust, drain, tax, strain, debilitate, enervate, jade, fag (*inf*), whack (*inf*). OPPOSITE: refresh. **2** (*her chatter quickly tired her audience*) bore, annoy, irritate, irk, exasperate, get to (*inf*), weary. **3** (*he tired with the incessant effort*) flag, droop, weaken, fail.

tired *adj* **1** (*tired after his day's work*) weary, wearied, fatigued, exhausted, drained, worn out, jaded, fagged (*inf*), fagged out (*inf*), done (*inf*), done in (*inf*), dead beat (*inf*), dog-tired (*inf*), knackered (*inf*), shattered (*inf*), all in (*inf*), whacked (*inf*), bushed (*inf*), pooped (*inf*), debilitated, enervated. OPPOSITE: refreshed. **2** (*she was tired after her late night*) sleepy, drowsy, weary. **3** (*tired of his job*) weary, wearied, bored, sick (*inf*), fed up (*inf*), irked, irritated, exasperated, annoyed. **4** (*the comedian's routine looked tired*) corny (*inf*), clichéd, stale, old, hackneyed, trite, banal, familiar, worn-out, well-worn, outworn, stock, platitudinous.

tireless *adj* untiring, unwearied, unflagging, indefatigable, energetic, diligent, industrious, vigorous, dogged, determined, resolute.

tiresome *adj* **1** (*a tiresome duty*) wearisome, wearing, laborious, fatiguing, boring, tedious, monotonous, humdrum, routine, dull, uninteresting, unexciting. OPPOSITE: pleasant. **2** (*his mother proved tiresome company*) annoying, irritating, irksome, vexatious, exasperating, trying, troublesome.

tiring *adj* wearying, wearisome, fatiguing, exhausting, draining, enervating, laborious, hard, difficult, tough, arduous, demanding, strenuous, exacting, taxing.

tissue *noun* **1** (*carefully wrapped in tissue*) tissue paper, gauze, gossamer. **2** (*a tissue of lies*) mesh, net, network, web, collection, set, series, chain, mass, accumulation, conglomeration. **3** (*a tissue to dry her tears*) paper handkerchief, paper hankie, disposable handkerchief, facial tissue, Kleenex.

titanic *adj* huge, gigantic, giant, colossal, enormous, massive, immense, mighty, vast, monumental, herculean, elephantine, jumbo, mammoth, monstrous, stupendous, towering, mountainous, prodigious. OPPOSITE: small.

titbit *noun* morsel, treat, goody (*inf*), snack, delicacy, dainty.

titillate *verb* tickle, excite, thrill, arouse, turn on (*inf*), stimulate, provoke, tease, tantalize, seduce, fascinate, captivate, intrigue, interest, please.

titillating *adj* exciting, arousing, stimulating, provocative, teasing, suggestive, seductive, sexy, erotic, lewd, lurid, thrilling, tantalizing, fascinating, captivating, intriguing, interesting.

titivate *verb* groom, smarten up, spruce up, doll up (*inf*), tart up (*inf*), do up (*inf*), touch up, refurbish, preen, make up, primp, prink.

title *noun* **1** (*he addressed his superior by his formal title*) name, handle (*inf*), form of address, appellation, denomination, designation, epithet, moniker (*inf*), sobriquet, rank, office, position, status. **2** (*the title of the book*) name, heading. **3** (*his name was given in the title below the photograph*) caption, legend, inscription, label, credit, heading, rubric. **4** (*he disowned his title to the property*) claim, right, due, privilege, entitlement, prerogative, ownership, possession, proprietorship. **5** (*the players expect to win the title*) championship, trophy, prize, laurels, crown.
➤ *verb* entitle, name, call, dub, style, term, designate, label, tag.

titter *noun* snigger, snicker, chuckle, chortle (*inf*), cackle, giggle, laugh.

titular *adj* nominal, token, puppet, so-called, self-styled, in name only, putative.

toast *verb* **1** (*she toasted the bread on the fire*) warm, heat. **2** (*they toasted the queen*) drink to, drink the health of, salute, pledge, honour.
➤ *noun* **1** (*he drank a toast to his son's future*) health, pledge, salute, tribute, salutation, best wishes, compliments, greetings. **2** (*they are the toast of the north-east tonight*) hero, heroine, darling, champion, favourite, celebrity.

today *noun* **1** (*I shall go there today*) this day, this very day. **2** (*things are different today*) now, nowadays, right now, just now, these days, at the present time, at this moment in time.

toddle *verb* **1** (*the child toddled towards the door*) totter, stagger, waddle, wobble, teeter, reel, lurch, sway, dodder, falter, waver, stumble, walk. **2** (*it's time for us to toddle off*) leave, go, depart.

together *adv* **1** (*let's do it together*) collectively, jointly, side by side, hand in hand, shoulder to shoulder, in concert, in conjunction, in cooperation, as a team, in unison. **2** (*they finished the race together*) as one, at the same time, at one time, simultaneously, concurrently, in unison, contemporaneously. OPPOSITE: separately. **3** (*he has now suffered three defeats together*) in a row, on the trot (*inf*), on end, back to back (*inf*), consecutively, in succession, successively, one after the other, continuously, without a break.
➤ *adj* composed, calm, cool (*inf*), level-headed, down-

to-earth, well-balanced, well-adjusted, well-organized, organized, efficient, stable, sensible.

toil *verb* **1** (*he toiled away for months*) work, labour, slog, strive, grind (*inf*), graft (*inf*), sweat (*inf*), plug away (*inf*), drudge, slave, persevere. OPPOSITE: relax. **2** (*the party toiled up the path*) labour, struggle, sweat (*inf*).
➤ *noun* hard work, donkey-work, labour, slog, striving, travail, grind (*inf*), graft (*inf*), elbow-grease (*inf*), drudgery, slavery, slaving, application, effort, exertion, industry. OPPOSITE: rest.

toilet *noun* lavatory, latrine, urinal, bathroom, washroom, powder room, cloakroom, water closet, WC, privy, public convenience, ladies, gents, loo (*inf*), bog (*inf*).

toilsome *adj* laborious, burdensome, arduous, hard, difficult, tough, severe, strenuous, taxing, tiring, fatiguing, exhausting, uphill, tiresome, wearisome, tedious, backbreaking, painful. OPPOSITE: easy.

token *noun* **1** (*a token of changing times*) symbol, sign, representation, emblem, badge, mark, indication, evidence, clue, proof, expression, demonstration, manifestation, recognition, index. **2** (*keep this as a token of our friendship*) reminder, remembrance, memorial, keepsake, souvenir, memento. **3** (*gift token*) voucher, coupon.
➤ *adj* nominal, minimal, superficial, slight, perfunctory, cosmetic, hollow, insincere, symbolic, emblematic.

tolerable *adj* **1** (*the pain was barely tolerable*) bearable, endurable, sufferable, supportable. OPPOSITE: intolerable. **2** (*such behaviour is not tolerable*) allowable, permissible, acceptable. **3** (*he achieved tolerable results*) passable, adequate, reasonable, satisfactory, good enough, fair, all right, indifferent, middling, mediocre, average, ordinary, run-of-the-mill, unexceptional, so-so (*inf*), OK (*inf*), not bad (*inf*). OPPOSITE: exceptional.

tolerance *noun* **1** (*preaching tolerance to his flock*) toleration, understanding, lenience, lenity, indulgence, permissiveness, forbearance, patience, open-mindedness, broad-mindedness, magnanimity, sympathy, liberalism, charity. **2** (*he showed tolerance in the face of the fiercest provocation*) toleration, resistance, resilience, toughness, fortitude, endurance, sufferance, stamina, hardiness.

tolerant *adj* broad-minded, open-minded, fair, liberal, catholic, unprejudiced, unbiased, unbigoted, patient, forbearing, long-suffering, benevolent, kind-hearted, magnanimous, sympathetic, understanding, indulgent, forgiving, lenient, permissive, compliant, lax, soft, free and easy, easy-going, complaisant, charitable. OPPOSITE: intolerant.

tolerate *verb* **1** (*the pain was more than he could tolerate*) endure, bear, take, suffer, brook, abide, stand, accept, put up with (*inf*), stomach (*inf*), swallow, submit to. **2** (*she will not tolerate interference*) permit, allow, admit, countenance, sanction, warrant, indulge, brook, condone.

toleration *noun* **1** (*show little toleration towards criminals*) tolerance, understanding, sympathy, patience, charity, forbearance, indulgence, leniency, lenity, broad-mindedness, open-mindedness, magnanimity, liberalism, permissiveness, laxness. **2** (*his toleration of stress*) tolerance, endurance, sufferance, resistance, resilience, toughness, fortitude, stamina, hardiness, acceptance.

toll[1] *verb* ring, knell, peal, clang, chime, sound, strike.

toll[2] *noun* **1** (*increase the toll on alcohol*) levy, tax, impost, duty, tariff, rate, fee, charge, payment, penalty. **2** (*the rising death toll*) loss, cost, damage.

tomb *noun* grave, burial place, vault, crypt, sepulchre, mausoleum, catacomb.

tombstone *noun* gravestone, stone, grave marker, headstone, memorial, monument.

tome *noun* volume, book, work, opus.

tomfoolery *noun* antics, pranks, capers, larks (*inf*), tricks, monkey tricks (*inf*), shenanigans (*inf*), mischief, horseplay, skylarking (*inf*), clowning, buffoonery, childishness, foolery, fooling, foolishness, folly, silliness, stupidity, idiocy, inanity, nonsense.

tone *noun* **1** (*the instrument has a mellifluous tone*) sound, noise, note, pitch, tonality, timbre, quality, colour. **2** (*they spoke in low tones*) intonation, inflection, modulation, cadence, accent, stress, emphasis, volume, expression. **3** (*painted in tones of grey and black*) colour, cast, tinge, tint, tincture, shade, hue. **4** (*the tone of his last album was very gloomy*) tenor, quality, character, feel, spirit, mood, temper, humour, vein, style, manner, attitude, approach, drift, gist, air. **5** (*trust him to lower the tone*) quality, style.
≫ *verb* harmonize, blend, go, co-ordinate, match, suit
tone down moderate, play down, modulate, temper, restrain, subdue, soften, soft-pedal (*inf*), dampen, assuage, mitigate, alleviate, reduce.

tongue *noun* language, lingo (*inf*), speech, discourse, talk, utterance, parlance, articulation, dialect, vernacular, idiom, jargon, slang, cant, argot, patois.

tonic *noun* **1** (*his granny gave him a tonic*) stimulant, cordial, restorative, bracer, refresher, pick-me-up (*inf*), analeptic. **2** (*the party was a tonic for everyone*) boost, shot in the arm (*inf*), stimulant, pick-me-up (*inf*), fillip.

too *adv* **1** (*she came too*) also, as well, in addition, besides, moreover, furthermore, likewise. **2** (*she found the work too hard*) excessively, inordinately, immoderately, unreasonably, ridiculously, unduly, over, overly, extremely, very.

tool *noun* **1** (*garden tools*) implement, instrument, gadget, gismo (*inf*), device, contraption, contrivance, aid, utensil, apparatus, appliance, machine, vehicle, means. **2** (*he is a tool of the government*) agent, pawn, creature, dupe, toady, lackey, flunkey, henchman, minion, stooge (*inf*), cat's-paw, puppet, hireling.
≫ *verb* work, machine, shape, cut, fashion, decorate, ornament, chase.

toothsome *adj* tasty, palatable, savoury, appetizing, delicious, flavoursome, mouth-watering, luscious, sweet, savoury, scrumptious (*inf*), yummy (*inf*), tempting, delectable, dainty, agreeable, attractive, nice. OPPOSITE: nasty.

top *noun* **1** (*the top of the mountain*) summit, peak, pinnacle, tip, crest, crown, apex, vertex, apogee. OPPOSITE: bottom. **2** (*he's at the top of his form*) height,
peak, pinnacle, high point, head, lead, crowning point, prime, acme, zenith, culmination, climax. **3** (*put the top back on the tin*) cap, lid, cover, cork, stopper. **4** (*take your top off if you are hot*) sweater, jumper, jersey, pullover, sweatshirt, shirt, blouse, smock.
≫ *adj* **1** (*the top shelf*) highest, topmost, uppermost, upper. OPPOSITE: lowest. **2** (*this is the top model in the range*) best, finest, excellent, supreme, quality, choicest, top-quality, top-grade. **3** (*he is the top man now*) principal, chief, main, leading, highest, first, foremost, dominant, ruling, commanding, sovereign. **4** (*she is the top performer of them all*) best, finest, greatest, foremost, leading, principal, pre-eminent. **5** (*working at top speed*) maximum, maximal, greatest, utmost.
≫ *verb* **1** (*the cake was topped with a cherry*) cap, crown, tip, cover, garnish, decorate, finish. **2** (*the achievement topped anything he had done before*) exceed, transcend, surpass, surmount, go beyond, excel, eclipse, outshine, outdo, outstrip, beat, better, best. **3** (*the band topped the charts*) head, lead.
over the top excessive, immoderate, inordinate, disproportionate, a bit much (*inf*), over the limit, exaggerated, extreme, too much, undue, uncalled-for, unreasonable, extravagant, exorbitant, OTT (*inf*).

topic *noun* subject, subject matter, matter, theme, issue, question, argument, point, thesis, text.

topical *adj* current, recent, up-to-date, up-to-the-minute, contemporary, newsworthy, popular, familiar.

topmost *adj* **1** (*the topmost shelf*) top, uppermost, upper, highest, loftiest. **2** (*the topmost expert in the field*) top, foremost, principal, pre-eminent, leading, supreme. **3** (*the topmost job in the cabinet*) chief, principal, highest, leading, dominant, paramount.

topple *verb* **1** (*the pile of dishes toppled over*) totter, overturn, overbalance, tip over, fall over, keel over, tumble, collapse, capsize. **2** (*he toppled his opponent*) upset, push over, tip over, knock over. **3** (*the government was toppled*) overthrow, overturn, bring down, displace, oust, unseat.

topsy-turvy *adj* upside down, inside out, disordered, disorderly, in disorder, chaotic, in chaos, confused, in confusion, messy, in a mess, muddled, in a muddle, untidy, disorganized, disarranged, mixed-up, jumbled, in a jumble, in disarray.

torment *noun* **1** (*the patient was in torment*) agony, pain, excruciation, suffering, anguish, distress, torture, affliction, misery, wretchedness, hell. OPPOSITE: relief. **2** (*the flies were a torment*) plague, scourge, curse, bane, vexation, affliction, annoyance, irritation, irritant, nuisance, bother, trouble, pest, harassment, provocation, thorn in the flesh (*inf*), pain in the neck (*inf*), worry.
≫ *verb* **1** (*her tooth was tormenting her*) torture, agonize, rack, excruciate, pain, persecute, distress, afflict, harrow, trouble. **2** (*stop tormenting the dog*) pester, bother, trouble, harass, harry, afflict, plague, badger, bedevil, annoy, vex, irritate, exasperate, provoke, tease, worry. OPPOSITE: soothe.

torn *adj* **1** (*the sheet was torn*) ripped, split, slit, cut, lacerated, rent, ragged, tattered. **2** (*he was torn between *the two*) split, divided, uncertain, undecided, unsure, irresolute, dithering, wavering, vacillating.

tornado *noun* cyclone, hurricane, typhoon, whirlwind, twister (*inf*), gale, squall, storm, tempest, monsoon. OPPOSITE: calm.

torpid *adj* sluggish, slow, slow-moving, lethargic, languid, languorous, dull, heavy, listless, apathetic, passive, lazy, indolent, slothful, dormant, somnolent, sleepy, supine, stagnant, inactive, inert, lifeless, dead, deadened, inanimate, insensible, nerveless, numb. OPPOSITE: active.

torpor *noun* torpidity, slowness, sluggishness, lethargy, indolence, drowsiness, laziness, sloth, slothfulness, somnolence, sleepiness, languor, languidness, listlessness, apathy, passivity, dullness, heaviness, inactivity, stagnation, inertia, inertness, numbness. OPPOSITE: activity.

torrent *noun* **1** (*a torrent of water*) flood, deluge, stream, current, spate, rush, cascade, inundation. OPPOSITE: trickle. **2** (*torrents of rain*) downpour, shower, deluge. **3** (*a torrent of applause*) outburst, outpouring, deluge, flood, flow, rush, spate, gush, barrage, battery, volley, storm.

torrid *adj* **1** (*torrid heat*) hot, scorching, boiling, blistering, roasting, sizzling, blazing, burning, fiery, sweltering, stifling, tropical, sultry, parched, scorched, arid, desert, dry, waterless. OPPOSITE: arctic. **2** (*a torrid love affair*) passionate, impassioned, ardent, fervent, fervid, erotic, lustful, amorous, steamy (*inf*).

tortuous *adj* **1** (*a tortuous route*) twisting, winding, snaking, snaky, coiling, sinuous, serpentine, zigzag, meandering, undulating, curved, curvy, spiralling, bent, crooked, twisted, mazy, convoluted, labyrinthine. OPPOSITE: straight. **2** (*a tortuous account of the crime*) involved, convoluted, complicated, indirect, circuitous, roundabout, unstraightforward, ambiguous.

torture *verb* **1** (*the prisoners were tortured*) persecute, torment, abuse, ill-treat, mistreat, work over (*inf*), punish. **2** (*he was tortured by her suffering*) torment, pain, distress, agonize, anguish, rack, excruciate, crucify, martyr, afflict, plague, harrow, trouble, worry. OPPOSITE: soothe.
➤ *noun* **1** (*her captors threatened torture*) persecution, abuse, ill-treatment, mistreatment, punishment, pain, torment, anguish, agony, suffering, martyrdom. OPPOSITE: ease. **2** (*he went through the torture of bankruptcy*) torment, agony, anguish, suffering, pain, excruciation, misery, distress, affliction.

toss *verb* **1** (*he tossed the coin in the air*) throw, pitch, fling, chuck (*inf*), cast, heave (*inf*), hurl, sling, lob, shy, launch, propel, project, flip. **2** (*the ball tossed about in the wake of the boat*) roll, rock, pitch, sway, heave, lurch, undulate. **3** (*he tossed and turned restlessly all night long*) thrash, heave, squirm, tumble, wriggle, writhe. **4** (*the pony tossed its head*) jerk, jolt, shake, throw back, throw up.
➤ *noun* throw, chuck (*inf*), fling, cast, pitch, flip.

tot *noun* **1** (*the nursery caters for a dozen tots*) infant, toddler, child, baby, mite, little one. **2** (*a tot of whisky*) measure, nip, dram, slug, shot (*inf*), finger (*inf*).

tot up add up, count, total, sum, reckon, tally, calculate, compute.

total *noun* sum, all, totality, entirety, whole, aggregate, lot. OPPOSITE: part.
➤ *adj* **1** (*look at the total picture*) complete, entire, full, whole, comprehensive, combined, integral, aggregate. **2** (*it was a total flop*) complete, absolute, utter, sheer, rank, thorough, thoroughgoing, out-and-out, all-out, outright, downright, perfect, consummate, unqualified, unmitigated, unconditional. OPPOSITE: partial.
➤ *verb* **1** (*the cost could total millions*) reach, make, add up to, amount to, come to, tot up to. **2** (*total up the takings*) sum up, add up, count up, reckon up, tot up.

totalitarian *adj* autocratic, authoritarian, dictatorial, undemocratic, monocratic, one-party, despotic, absolute, tyrannical, oppressive, fascist.

totality *noun* **1** (*the totality of her inheritance*) total, sum, whole, entirety, aggregate. **2** (*look at the project in its totality*) entirety, completeness, wholeness, fullness, inclusiveness.

totally *adv* completely, entirely, absolutely, thoroughly, utterly, perfectly, consummately, wholly, fully, comprehensively, wholeheartedly, unconditionally, undisputedly, quite.

totter *verb* **1** (*the drunk tottered towards the door*) stagger, stumble, waddle, reel, sway, rock, teeter, lurch, roll, wobble (*inf*). **2** (*the scaffolding tottered under the impact*) tremble, quiver, shake, shudder, judder, sway, lurch, rock.

touch *verb* **1** (*don't touch the display*) feel, finger, handle, hold, pick up, move, fiddle with, interfere with, play with, toy with. **2** (*he touched her on the cheek*) pat, fondle, caress, pet, stroke, brush, skim, graze, tickle. **3** (*the points must touch*) meet, contact, strike, come together, converge, abut, adjoin. **4** (*she hasn't touched her breakfast*) taste, eat, consume, take, partake of, drink. **5** (*he was touched by her vulnerability*) affect, influence, impress, inspire, involve, move, get to (*inf*), stir, concern, soften, melt, upset, disturb, sadden. **6** (*the car touched seventy miles per hour*) reach, attain, hit (*inf*), make, arrive at. **7** (*no one can touch her for sheer class*) match, equal, rival, parallel, better, approach, come near to, come close to, compare with, hold a candle to (*inf*). **8** (*the war barely touched the family*) affect, involve, concern, regard, relate to, pertain to, influence. **9** (*I wouldn't touch it with a barge pole*) handle, deal with, associate oneself.
➤ *noun* **1** (*she shrank from his touch*) caress, stroke, brush, pat, tap, blow. **2** (*the sense of touch*) feel, feeling, contact, tactility. **3** (*the leaf had a silky touch*) feel, surface, texture, grain, coating, weave. **4** (*there was a touch of desperation in his voice*) trace, hint, suggestion, suspicion, whiff (*inf*), soupçon, taste, dash, smack, tinge, tincture, spot, speck, drop, bit, pinch, jot. **5** (*stay in touch*) contact, communication, correspondence. **6** (*she has a deft touch*) technique, method, approach, style, manner. **7** (*he has not lost his touch*) skill, knack, flair, talent, virtuosity, expertise, ability, facility, dexterity, deftness, adroitness, art, artistry, craftsmanship, workmanship. **8** (*the set still needs a few finishing touches*) detail, adjustment, feature, point, nicety, addition, accessory.

touch off 1 (*touch off an explosion*) set off, trigger off, detonate, explode, ignite, set alight. **2** (*this suggestion touched off a barrage of complaints*) provoke, trigger off, spark off, set off, launch, instigate, start, begin, arouse, cause.

touch on deal with, cover, refer to, mention, speak of, allude to, broach.

touch up 1 (*he needs to touch up his technique*) brush up, polish up, enhance, improve, perfect. **2** (*high time the whole place was touched up*) retouch, patch up, fix up, repair, renovate, revamp, refurbish. **3** (*guilty of touching up women on public transport*) molest, fondle, interfere with.

touching *adj* moving, affecting, stirring, emotive, emotional, upsetting, sad, saddening, disturbing, tender, poignant, pathetic, pitiable, pitiful, piteous, heart-rending, heart-breaking.
≫ *prep* regarding, respecting, apropos, with reference to, concerning, about, relating to.

touchstone *noun* standard, criterion, norm, measure, gauge, guide, model, pattern, template, exemplar, yardstick, benchmark, test, proof.

touchy *adj* testy, tetchy, irritable, irascible, quick-tempered, petulant, prickly (*inf*), peevish, waspish, peppery, grumpy, bad-tempered, grouchy, surly, edgy (*inf*), cantankerous, splenetic, choleric, cross, crusty, crabbed, fractious, querulous, captious, sensitive, oversensitive, hypersensitive, thin-skinned. OPPOSITE: genial.

tough *adj* **1** (*a tough pair of boots*) strong, durable, resilient, resistant, sturdy, firm, solid, hard, rigid, stiff, inflexible. **2** (*a tough joint of meat*) chewy, rubbery, stringy, leathery, sinewy, fibrous, gristly. OPPOSITE: tender. **3** (*a tough old warrior*) hardy, sturdy, rugged, stalwart, robust, strong, strapping, vigorous, burly, brawny, muscular, fit. OPPOSITE: weak. **4** (*you have to be tough with young horses*) firm, stern, severe, harsh, adamant, determined, resolute, obstinate, stubborn, obdurate, tenacious, inflexible, unyielding, uncompromising. **5** (*he's a pretty tough customer*) rough, hardened, hard-boiled (*inf*), vicious, violent, callous, wild, unruly, disorderly. **6** (*it was a tough challenge*) difficult, hard, arduous, heavy, laborious, strenuous, uphill (*inf*), taxing, stressful, onerous, exacting, troublesome, thorny, knotty, ticklish, baffling, puzzling, perplexing. OPPOSITE: simple. **7** (*it was a tough life*) rough, hard, harsh, grim, dire, rugged, bleak, austere, exacting, taxing. **8** (*the decision was tough on the children*) hard, unpleasant, distressing, regrettable, unfortunate, unlucky.
≫ *noun* ruffian, thug, bruiser (*inf*), roughneck (*inf*), brute, hoodlum, lout, yob (*inf*), hooligan, bully.

toughen *verb* reinforce, strengthen, fortify, brace, harden, rigidify, stiffen, beef up (*inf*).

tour *noun* **1** (*a day tour*) trip, expedition, outing, jaunt, drive, ride, visit, voyage, journey, excursion, peregrination. **2** (*a tour of European capitals*) circuit, round, ambit, course. **3** (*let's skip the official tour*) guided tour, conducted tour, walk, inspection.
≫ *verb* **1** (*tour the country*) go round, travel round, ride round, journey through, explore. **2** (*they toured the historical district*) go round, wander, visit, sightsee (*inf*), inspect.

tourist *noun* holidaymaker, sightseer, traveller, voyager, visitor, tripper, globetrotter (*inf*), excursionist.

tournament *noun* **1** (*there are twelve teams in the tournament*) competition, contest, championship, match, meeting, meet, event. **2** (*a medieval tournament*) joust, jousting, lists (*inf*), tourney.

tousled *adj* ruffled, rumpled, tangled, dishevelled, untidy, unkempt, uncombed, messy, messed up, mussed up (*inf*), disarranged, disarrayed, disordered. OPPOSITE: groomed.

tout *verb* **1** (*tout one's wares*) sell, offer for sale, peddle, trade, hawk. **2** (*tout for custom*) solicit, petition, advertise, seek, hustle (*inf*), importune, approach, accost.

tow *verb* pull, draw, drag, haul, tug, lug, trail. OPPOSITE: push.
≫ *noun* pull, tug, haul, trail, lug.
in tow in attendance, accompanying, by one's side, following, in convoy.

towards *prep* **1** (*they drove towards the city*) to, for, in the direction of. **2** (*towards midnight*) nearly, near, almost, about, around, just before, shortly before, close to, coming to, getting on for, approaching, nearing. **3** (*her goodwill towards him*) respecting, with respect to, regarding, as regards, with regard to, in relation to, concerning, for, about, apropos, touching.

tower *noun* **1** (*church tower*) steeple, turret, spire, minaret, belfry, column, pillar, obelisk. **2** (*the attackers failed to take the tower*) citadel, fortress, fort, castle, stronghold, fortification, refuge, keep.
≫ *verb* **1** (*the mountain towers up over the village*) rise, ascend, soar, rear, mount. OPPOSITE: sink. **2** (*he towered above his contemporaries*) surpass, outshine, outclass, transcend, excel, exceed, cap, top, dominate, overshadow, overlook, loom, eclipse, put in the shade, run circles round (*inf*).

towering *adj* **1** (*towering cliffs*) high, tall, soaring, lofty, imposing, elevated, sky-high. **2** (*a towering rage*) passionate, intense, fierce, violent, frenzied, frantic, mighty, extreme. **3** (*a towering figure in modern sport*) outstanding, sublime, supreme, great, pre-eminent, extraordinary, superior, unrivalled, incomparable, peerless.

town *noun* township, burgh, borough, municipality, settlement, village, city, metropolis, conurbation.

toxic *adj* poisonous, venomous, pestilent, pernicious, virulent, noxious, harmful, unhealthy, deadly, lethal, baneful, dangerous. OPPOSITE: harmless.

toy *noun* **1** (*a toy for his birthday*) plaything, game. **2** (*she's his latest toy*) trifle, trinket, bauble, knick-knack.
≫ *verb* **1** (*he's just toying with her*) play, sport, trifle, dally, flirt, amuse. **2** (*he toyed with the controls*) tinker, fiddle, play around, fool around, mess about.

trace *noun* **1** (*little trace of this lost civilization*) mark, token, sign, indication, vestige, remains, remnant, relic, evidence, clue, record. **2** (*without a trace of regret*) hint, suggestion, suspicion, touch, tinge, tincture, soupçon, trifle, dash, pinch, bit, drop, spot, jot, iota, shadow, smack. **3** (*they were hot on their quarry's traces*) track, trail, spoor, scent, footprint, footmark, footstep.
≫ *verb* **1** (*he traced their footsteps*) follow, pursue, trail,

track, stalk, dog, shadow. **2** (*they could not trace any record of the inquiry*) hunt down, track down, run down (*inf*), find, discover, ascertain, detect, uncover, unearth, turn up, dig up, ferret out. **3** (*he traced out his plans*) sketch, draw, draft, rough out, outline, mark out, delineate, copy, depict, indicate, map, chart, record.

track *noun* **1** (*a track in the snow*) trail, trace, mark, print, imprint, impression, scent, spoor, footprint, footstep, footmark. **2** (*the track of the vessel*) wake, path, line, trail, route, course, way, orbit, trajectory. **3** (*the track is blocked*) road, rail, line, path, trail, route, way. ≫ *verb* trace, trail, tail, follow, shadow, stalk, dog, pursue, hunt, chase. OPPOSITE: catch.

keep track of keep up with, follow, check, watch, observe, keep an eye on, monitor, record.

track down find, discover, detect, trace, ferret out, nose out, sniff out, turn up, dig up, bring to light, hunt down, hunt out, run down (*inf*), run to earth, unearth, uncover, expose, catch, capture. OPPOSITE: miss.

tract[1] *noun* (*a tract of land*) area, region, stretch, expanse, extent, strip, patch, plot, lot, zone, district, quarter, territory.

tract[2] *noun* (*a religious tract*) treatise, dissertation, thesis, lecture, disquisition, essay, sermon, homily, discourse, monograph, pamphlet, booklet, leaflet, brochure.

tractable *adj* amenable, complaisant, compliant, biddable, persuadable, willing, yielding, submissive, docile, tame, dutiful, obedient, manageable, controllable, governable, workable, malleable, pliable, pliant, ductile. OPPOSITE: intractable.

trade *noun* **1** (*international trade*) business, commerce, e-commerce, e-tailing, dealing, buying, selling, merchandising, marketing, traffic, trafficking, transaction. **2** (*a trade of shirts*) barter, exchange, swap, switch. **3** (*he told us what trade he was in*) occupation, profession, calling, career, vocation, job, work, employment, line, craft, métier, skill. ≫ *verb* **1** (*trade in timber*) deal, transact, buy and sell, peddle, traffic, market, merchandise, bargain. **2** (*they traded stories*) barter, exchange, swap, switch.

trademark *noun* **1** (*the company's trademark*) trade name, brand name, brand, hallmark, proprietary mark, logo, symbol, label, stamp, sign, emblem, badge, crest, insignia. **2** (*their trademark is quick service*) hallmark, speciality, characteristic, feature, attribute, trait, penchant, peculiarity, idiosyncrasy, quirk.

trader *noun* merchant, dealer, buyer, seller, vendor, supplier, broker, tradesman, tradeswoman, wholesaler, retailer, merchandiser, marketeer, peddler, trafficker.

tradition *noun* **1** (*observe the ancient tradition*) custom, practice, routine, way, habit, convention, usage, ceremony, ritual, rite, observance, belief. **2** (*a society governed by tradition*) folklore, lore, unwritten law, oral history.

traditional *adj* **1** (*traditional beliefs*) folk, handed-down, oral, unwritten. **2** (*a traditional ceremony*) accustomed, customary, habitual, usual, wonted, routine, regular, set, fixed, old, age-old, time-honoured, historic, folk, ancestral, conventional, established, ritual, ritualistic.

traduce *verb* defame, slander, libel, misrepresent, malign, smear, vilify, abuse, insult, asperse, calumniate,

denigrate, revile, vituperate, decry, knock (*inf*), run down (*inf*), slag off (*inf*), denounce, disparage, deprecate, depreciate. OPPOSITE: eulogize.

traffic *noun* **1** (*little traffic on the road*) vehicles, cars. **2** (*traffic policy*) transport, transportation, shipping, freight. **3** (*traffic in illegal drugs*) trafficking, dealing, trade, trading, commerce, business, buying and selling, peddling, barter, exchange, smuggling. **4** (*she had little traffic with her husband after that*) contact, communication, dealings, relations, intercourse. ≫ *verb* deal, trade, peddle, buy, sell, bargain, barter, exchange, do business, smuggle.

tragedy *noun* disaster, catastrophe, calamity, adversity, blow, shock, affliction, misfortune, misadventure, unhappiness.

tragic *adj* **1** (*a tragic accident*) disastrous, catastrophic, calamitous, ill-fated, fatal, deadly, dreadful, terrible, awful, dire, shocking, appalling, miserable, wretched, unfortunate, unlucky. **2** (*a tragic story*) sad, sorrowful, melancholy, unhappy, miserable, doleful, mournful, gloomy, dismal, pathetic, pitiful, piteous, distressing, heart-breaking, disturbing, moving. OPPOSITE: comic. **3** (*a tragic waste of talent*) lamentable, deplorable, regrettable, terrible, dreadful, awful, dire.

trail *noun* **1** (*the trail of a wild animal*) track, trace, scent, spoor, footprint, footstep, footmark. **2** (*he set off down the trail*) path, footpath, pathway, way, track, road, route. **3** (*a long trail of refugees*) queue, procession, line, column, file, tail. **4** (*a trail of devastation*) wake, train, chain, series, sequence. ≫ *verb* **1** (*he trailed the sack behind him*) drag, draw, pull, haul, tow. **2** (*his cloak trailed behind him*) drag, sweep, dangle, hang, droop, extend, reach, stream. **3** (*she trailed after the others*) lag, linger, loiter, fall behind, straggle, dawdle, drag, trudge, plod. **4** (*he trailed his quarry through the woods*) track, trace, follow, pursue, stalk, tail, shadow, chase, dog, hunt. OPPOSITE: catch.

trail away fade away, fade out, fade, peter out, tail off, taper off, die away, melt away, disappear, vanish, diminish, decrease, shrink, lessen, dwindle, sink, subside, weaken.

train *noun* **1** (*a long train of soldiers*) line, file, column, convoy, procession, stream, caravan. **2** (*a train of great victories*) chain, series, succession, sequence, string, set, order, progression, trail. **3** (*he left great unhappiness in his train*) wake, wash, trail, track, path. **4** (*the queen entered with her train*) retinue, suite, entourage, cortège, attendance, staff, household, court, following, followers, attendants. ≫ *verb* **1** (*train the new recruits*) teach, instruct, school, educate, tutor, coach, drill, indoctrinate, inculcate, ground, prepare, guide, discipline. **2** (*she intends to train for the law*) study, prepare, read, qualify, learn. **3** (*the players need to train more often*) exercise, practise, work out, prepare, rehearse. **4** (*train your guns on the enemy*) direct, aim, point, focus, level, line up.

trainer *noun* coach, instructor, teacher, tutor, educator, handler.

training *noun* **1** (*the school offers training for the future*) teaching, instruction, coaching, education, lessons, schooling, learning, tuition, tutoring, drilling, discipline, preparation, grounding, guidance, indoctrination, inculcation. **2** (*the team are in training for the big match*) practice, preparation, exercise, working out.

trait *noun* characteristic, attribute, feature, property, quality, idiosyncrasy, peculiarity, quirk, mark.

traitor *noun* betrayer, deceiver, double-crosser, double-dealer, back-stabber (*inf*), two-timer (*inf*), snake in the grass (*inf*), Judas, quisling, informer, renegade, apostate, turncoat, defector, deserter, rebel, collaborator, fifth columnist. OPPOSITE: loyalist.

traitorous *adj* treacherous, treasonable, disloyal, faithless, unfaithful, false, false-hearted, double-dealing, double-crossing, back-stabbing, two-timing (*inf*), perfidious, seditious, untrue, dishonourable.

trajectory *noun* path, orbit, track, trail, line, route, course, flight, flight path.

trammel *noun* restraint, constraint, check, curb, block, obstacle, bar, barrier, hindrance, handicap, impediment, stumbling-block, fetter, bond, rein, shackle, drawback, snag. OPPOSITE: freedom.
» *verb* restrict, restrain, constrain, inhibit, curb, check, hinder, hamper, handicap, impede, block, clog, obstruct, thwart, frustrate, fetter, shackle, chain, tie, ensnare, entrap, enmesh, net, catch. OPPOSITE: release.

tramp *verb* **1** (*tramp through the snow*) trudge, plod, stump, stomp (*inf*), stamp, tread, trample. **2** (*tramp over the hills*) trek, hike, walk, slog, footslog, rove, range, ramble, roam, traipse (*inf*), wander.
» *noun* **1** (*he looked like a tramp*) vagrant, itinerant, vagabond, wanton, derelict, bum (*inf*), dosser (*inf*), drifter, down-and-out, hobo. **2** (*go for a tramp through the woods*) walk, ramble, hike, trek, march, footfall, tread, stamp. **3** (*everyone knows she's a tramp*) slut (*inf*), tart (*inf*), scrubber (*inf*), trollop, whore, prostitute.

trample *verb* **1** (*she trampled the fruit under her feet*) crush, squash, stamp, tread, tramp, flatten. **2** (*they knew their rights were being trampled upon*) disregard, encroach, infringe, violate, defy.

trance *noun* daze, stupor, dream, reverie, abstraction, spell, brown study, unconsciousness, coma, catalepsy, rapture, ecstasy.

tranquil *adj* **1** (*it was a tranquil night*) peaceful, calm, still, quiet, hushed, silent, restful, reposeful, undisturbed, serene, placid. OPPOSITE: agitated. **2** (*she is a tranquil soul*) calm, cool, placid, pacific, composed, laid-back (*inf*), serene, relaxed, imperturbable, even-tempered, unruffled, unmoved, unperturbed, untroubled, unexcited, unexcitable, unflappable (*inf*), sedate.

tranquillity *noun* **1** (*the tranquillity of the evening*) calm, calmness, stillness, peace, peacefulness, restfulness, repose, quiet, quietness, quietude, silence, hush, serenity, placidity. **2** (*there was little to disturb his tranquillity*) calm, calmness, composure, coolness, serenity, placidity, equanimity, imperturbability, unexcitability, unflappability.

tranquillize *verb* calm, calm down, compose, soothe, pacify, allay, quell, lull, still, hush, quiet, smooth, settle, relax, sedate. OPPOSITE: excite.

tranquillizer *noun* sedative, sleeping pill, calmative, narcotic, opiate, barbiturate, downer (*inf*).

transact *verb* conduct, carry out, carry on, do, perform, execute, prosecute, discharge, enact, accomplish, conclude, dispatch, negotiate, handle, manage, take care of, settle, see to.

transaction *noun* **1** (*the transaction took place behind closed doors*) deal, undertaking, bargain, business, negotiation, agreement, action, proceeding, matter, affair, deed. **2** (*the transaction of big deals*) performance, execution, discharge, enactment, conducting, conclusion, handling, settlement, negotiation, agreement.

transactions *pl noun* proceedings, dealings, doings (*inf*), goings-on (*inf*), records, minutes, annals, reports, affairs, concerns.

transcend *verb* **1** (*this transcends ordinary experience*) surpass, exceed, rise above, go beyond. **2** (*his achievement transcends all that went before*) surpass, excel, outrival, outrank, outstrip, outdo, eclipse, overshadow, put in the shade, outshine, leave behind, beat.

transcendent *adj* surpassing, unsurpassed, exceeding, excelling, matchless, peerless, unrivalled, unparalleled, unequalled, incomparable, predominant, pre-eminent, ascendant, paramount, supreme, superior, sublime, superlative, great, excellent, magnificent, consummate. OPPOSITE: ordinary.

transcendental *adj* mystic, mystical, abstract, metaphysical, spiritual, otherworldly, supernatural, preternatural.

transcribe *verb* **1** (*he will transcribe his jottings*) copy out, copy up, reproduce, write out, write up, rewrite, print out. **2** (*transcribed into English*) translate, render, interpret, transliterate.

transcript *noun* transcription, documentation, manuscript, copy, record, reproduction, duplicate, translation, transliteration.

transfer *verb* **1** (*the patient was transferred to hospital*) take, move, remove, transport, convey, carry, shift, transmit, relocate, transplant. **2** (*responsibility was transferred to the deputy*) hand over, hand on, hand down, pass on, turn over, make over, sign over, convey, devolve, assign, delegate, switch.
» *noun* move, shift, relocation, removal, displacement, transmission, change, handover, assignment, transference.

transfigure *verb* transform, change, alter, convert, translate, transmute, metamorphose, exalt, glorify, idealize, apotheosize.

transfix *verb* **1** (*we were transfixed by the sight*) rivet, stun, captivate, fascinate, hypnotize, mesmerize, spellbind, engross, hold, stun, astound, paralyse, petrify. **2** (*transfixed by a spear*) pierce, impale, perforate, penetrate, stab, spear, prick, stick, spike, skewer, run through.

transform *verb* change, convert, translate, transmogrify (*inf*), transmute, metamorphose, transfigure, alter, adapt, modify, remodel, rebuild, redo, reconstruct, reorganize, rearrange, renew, revolutionize.

transformation *noun* change, sea change, alteration,

conversion, transfiguration, mutation, transmutation, metamorphosis, revolution, reorganization, remodelling, reconstruction, renewal, transmogrification (*inf*).

transgress *verb* **1** (*he transgressed international rules*) break, disobey, violate, infringe, encroach, contravene, breach, defy, exceed, overstep, go beyond. **2** (*the child has transgressed*) sin, err, do wrong, trespass, lapse, go astray, offend, misbehave. OPPOSITE: obey.

transgression *noun* **1** (*guilty of serious transgressions*) offence, crime, sin, wrong, wrongdoing, fault, lapse, error, misdeed, misdemeanour, misbehaviour, trespass, iniquity, peccadillo. **2** (*transgression of the society's rules*) contravention, breach, breaking, infringement, infraction, violation, overstepping, defiance, disobedience.

transgressor *noun* sinner, wrongdoer, evil-doer, lawbreaker, trespasser, malefactor, miscreant, culprit, offender, delinquent, criminal, felon, villain, debtor.

transience *noun* impermanence, ephemerality, fleetingness, transitoriness, momentariness, temporariness, shortness, brevity, briefness, evanescence.

transient *adj* impermanent, ephemeral, transitory, fleeting, temporary, brief, short, passing, flying, momentary, short-lived, short-term, fugitive, mutable, evanescent, fugacious. OPPOSITE: permanent.

transit *noun* **1** (*the transit of goods*) passage, crossing, movement, motion, journeying, travel, change, transfer, transition. **2** (*the city's system of transit*) transport, transportation, conveyance, carriage, shipment, haulage.
in transit en route, on the way, on the road, travelling, on the journey, during transport.

transition *noun* change, change-over, conversion, development, evolution, gradation, transformation, transmutation, alteration, metamorphosis, passage, progress, progression, passing, movement, move, flux, shift, switch, jump, leap.

transitional *adj* **1** (*a transitional time for the company*) changing, evolutionary, developmental, intermediate, unsettled, fluid. **2** (*install a transitional administration*) provisional, temporary, passing.

transitory *adj* transient, temporary, impermanent, brief, short, ephemeral, evanescent, passing, fleeting, flying, momentary, short-lived, fugitive, fugacious. OPPOSITE: permanent.

translate *verb* **1** (*translate it into English*) render, interpret, construe, convert, transcribe, transliterate. **2** (*translated into plain words*) put, render, convert, reword, paraphrase, simplify, decode, decipher, explain, elucidate. **3** (*translate her ambitions into reality*) transform, transmute, convert, alter, realize, change, metamorphose, turn. **4** (*translate refugees from camps to their homes*) transfer, relocate, convey, transport, move, remove, shift.

translation *noun* **1** (*translation into a foreign language*) rendering, rendition, interpretation, construing, conversion, transcription, transliteration. **2** (*translation into everyday language*) rendering, rendition, conversion, rewording, paraphrasing, simplification, decoding,

deciphering, explanation, elucidation. **3** (*the translation of her ambitions into reality*) transformation, transmutation, conversion, realization, alteration, change, metamorphosis, turning. **4** (*the translation of the refugee population to safe areas*) transfer, transferral, conveying, transportation, moving, removal, shifting.

translucent *adj* transparent, clear, see-through, pellucid, diaphanous, limpid. OPPOSITE: opaque.

transmission *noun* **1** (*the transmission of the equipment*) transmittal, transmittance, conveyance, carriage, transport, shipment, dispatch, sending. OPPOSITE: reception. **2** (*the transmission of disease*) transfer, transferral, transference, spreading, dissemination, diffusion, passing on, communication, broadcasting, relaying. **3** (*a radio transmission*) broadcast, programme, show, signal.

transmit *verb* **1** (*your order has been transmitted by truck*) transfer, transport, carry, bear, take, convey, send, forward, dispatch, remit. OPPOSITE: receive. **2** (*transmit germs*) communicate, transfer, pass on, hand down, spread, diffuse, disseminate, carry, impart. **3** (*transmitting a strong signal*) broadcast, relay, send out, emit.

transmute *verb* change, transform, convert, translate, alter, remake, metamorphose, transfigure.

transparency *noun* **1** (*the transparency of the water*) clarity, clearness, translucency, limpidness, limpidity, lucidity. **2** (*the transparency of the fabric*) sheerness, gauziness, filminess, diaphanousness. **3** (*the transparency of their lies*) obviousness, plainness, clearness, apparency, patentness. **4** (*the transparency of this inquiry is vital*) openness, candidness, frankness, forthrightness, directness, lucidity, honesty, ingenuousness, artlessness. **5** (*a photographic transparency*) slide, photograph, photo, picture.

transparent *adj* **1** (*a transparent pool of water*) clear, translucent, limpid, pellucid, lucid, crystal-clear, crystalline, glassy. OPPOSITE: opaque. **2** (*she wore a transparent nightie*) diaphanous, sheer, see-through, gauzy, filmy. **3** (*a transparent lie*) obvious, patent, evident, apparent, clear, plain, distinct, visible, perceptible, discernible, recognizable, manifest, undisguised, unmistakable, noticeable. OPPOSITE: unclear. **4** (*the inquiry must be transparent*) open, candid, frank, forthright, direct, straight, artless, honest, ingenuous, straightforward.

transpire *verb* **1** (*it was all right as things transpired*) happen, occur, arise, chance, take place, come about, come to pass, turn out, befall, ensue. **2** (*it transpired that they had already left*) become known, become apparent, come to light, come out, emerge, appear, prove.

transplant *verb* move, remove, transfer, relocate, resettle, shift, displace, uproot.

transport *verb* **1** (*transport the bags by car*) convey, carry, bear, bring, fetch, ship, run, take, transfer, shift, move, haul, lug, cart, remove. **2** (*thieves were transported to the colonies*) banish, deport, exile, expatriate. **3** (*he was transported by her beauty*) entrance, enrapture, enchant, bewitch, enthral, captivate, spellbind, delight, overjoy, thrill, charm, ravish, fascinate, carry away. OPPOSITE: repel.

➤ **noun 1** (*the transport of cargo*) transportation, conveyance, carriage, shipment, shipping, haulage, transit. **2** (*send some transport for the rest of the party*) transportations, conveyance, vehicle, car, carriage. **3** (*she was in transports when she heard the news*) ecstasy, rapture, elation, exhilaration, happiness, joy, delight, exaltation, bliss, euphoria, enchantment, heaven, cloud nine (*inf*). OPPOSITE: anguish.

transpose *verb* interchange, exchange, switch, swap (*inf*), substitute, change, alter, convert, move, shift, transfer, rearrange, reorder, reverse, invert.

transverse *adj* crossways, crosswise, cross, athwart, oblique, diagonal. OPPOSITE: parallel.

trap *noun* **1** (*a poacher's trap*) snare, gin, net, mesh, noose. **2** (*they were caught in a trap*) snare, pitfall, ambush, prison, cage. **3** (*a trap to fool the innocent*) trick, ruse, wile, artifice, stratagem, device, deception, ploy, decoy, lure, bait.
➤ *verb* **1** (*he had trapped several birds*) catch, corner, net, snare, ensnare, entrap, enmesh. **2** (*he was trapped into revealing her name*) trick, take in, dupe, deceive, inveigle, beguile, lure. **3** (*the children were trapped by the fire*) corner, confine, cut off, imprison.

trappings *pl noun* appurtenances, accoutrements, gear, equipment, apparatus, adornments, appointments, trimmings, ornaments, ornamentation, livery, frippery, finery, fixtures, fittings, things (*inf*), paraphernalia, panoply.

trash *noun* **1** (*put the trash out*) rubbish, refuse, garbage, waste, litter, junk, sweepings, dregs. **2** (*that argument is a lot of trash*) nonsense, junk, balderdash, drivel, twaddle, bunkum, rubbish, garbage, gibberish, rot (*inf*), bullshit (*inf*), bilge (*inf*), bunk (*inf*), tripe (*inf*). OPPOSITE: sense. **3** (*poor white trash*) scum, vermin, rabble, riff-raff, undesirables, good-for-nothings.

trauma *noun* **1** (*her death was a trauma for everyone*) shock, blow, jolt, upset, disturbance, disorder, upheaval, ordeal, suffering, anguish, agony, torture, distress, pain, strain, stress. **2** (*suffered a major trauma to the head*) injury, wound, hurt, damage, lesion.

traumatic *adj* **1** (*the attack was a traumatic experience*) stressful, frightening, shocking, painful, agonizing, disturbing, upsetting, distressing, damaging, wounding, harmful, hurtful, injurious, scarring. **2** (*a traumatic day at the office*) disagreeable, unpleasant, distressing, troublesome, irksome, irritating, annoying, vexatious, wearying.

travel *verb* **1** (*she loves to travel abroad*) journey, take a trip, voyage, tour, sightsee. **2** (*they travelled across the desert by camel*) cross, traverse, journey, trek. **3** (*spend three years travelling the world*) roam, rove, ramble, trek, wander, wend, explore. OPPOSITE: settle. **4** (*the ball travelled quickly through the air*) go, move, proceed, progress, advance, carry.
➤ *noun* travelling, journeying, voyaging, touring, globetrotting (*inf*).

traveller *noun* **1** (*an international traveller*) voyager, wayfarer, passenger, excursionist, tourist, sightseer, holidaymaker, tourer, tripper (*inf*), explorer, wanderer, globetrotter (*inf*), commuter. **2** (*a commercial traveller*) salesman, representative, rep (*inf*), agent. **3** (*he joined a community of travellers*) nomad, gypsy, tinker, wanderer, wayfarer, itinerant, drifter, migrant, vagrant, tramp.

travelling *adj* **1** (*a travelling library*) mobile, peripatetic, moving, itinerant. **2** (*a travelling community*) nomadic, restless, unsettled, wandering, roaming, roving, itinerant, wayfaring, migrant, migratory, peripatetic, homeless, vagrant.

traverse *verb* **1** (*we must traverse the region in three days*) cross, pass over, travel over, journey over, range, roam, wander, negotiate. **2** (*a rope bridge traversed the canyon*) cross, lie across, stretch across, bridge, span, ford.

travesty *noun* parody, caricature, lampoon, satire, send-up (*inf*), spoof (*inf*), take-off (*inf*), wind-up (*inf*), burlesque, mockery, farce, sham, ridicule, distortion, misrepresentation, corruption, perversion, apology.

treacherous *adj* **1** (*a treacherous act of betrayal*) traitorous, perfidious, disloyal, double-crossing, double-dealing, two-timing (*inf*), back-stabbing, faithless, unfaithful, false, false-hearted, untrue, deceitful, duplicitous, dishonest, untrustworthy, unreliable, undependable, treasonable. OPPOSITE: loyal. **2** (*a treacherous path up the mountain*) dangerous, hazardous, perilous, risky, dicey (*inf*), unsafe, unreliable, unstable, precarious, deceptive, slippery, icy. OPPOSITE: safe.

treachery *noun* traitorousness, betrayal, deceit, deceitfulness, deception, perfidy, perfidiousness, treason, disloyalty, duplicity, faithlessness, unfaithfulness, infidelity, untrustworthiness, falseness, false-heartedness, two-timing (*inf*), double-crossing, double-dealing, back-stabbing, sabotage. OPPOSITE: loyalty.

tread *verb* **1** (*tread carefully round the glass*) walk, step, pace, go. **2** (*tread slowly up the hill*) walk, hike, trek, stride, march, tramp, trudge, plod, stump. **3** (*tread a beetle underfoot*) stamp, step on, trample, tramp, crush, squash, flatten, press.
➤ *noun* step, footstep, footprint, footmark, footfall, pace, walk, stride, tramp, gait.

treason *noun* treachery, betrayal, disloyalty, faithlessness, perfidy, sedition, subversion, mutiny, rebellion, insurrection. OPPOSITE: allegiance.

treasonable *adj* treacherous, traitorous, disloyal, false, unfaithful, faithless, perfidious, subversive, rebellious, mutinous, seditious.

treasure *noun* **1** (*pirate treasure*) riches, wealth, fortune, hoard, cache, cash, money, gold, silver, bullion, jewels, gems, valuables. OPPOSITE: rubbish. **2** (*she's a real treasure*) darling, jewel, gem, pearl, paragon, pride and joy, prize, find.
➤ *verb* **1** (*I treasure the memory*) prize, value, hold dear, esteem, cherish. OPPOSITE: scorn. **2** (*she is treasured by her grandparents*) dote on, cherish, prize, love, adore, idolize. **3** (*he treasured the paintings*) hoard, store, lay by, stow away, stash away (*inf*), salt away, save, collect, accumulate.

treat *noun* **1** (*she had arranged a special treat*) party, entertainment, diversion, amusement, celebration, excursion, outing, surprise, indulgence, feast, banquet. **2** (*the child received several birthday treats*) present, gift, goodie (*inf*). **3** (*the whole show was a real treat*) delight, joy, pleasure, gratification, thrill, fun.

➤ *verb* **1** (*they treated her with kindness*) handle, deal with, cope with, contend with, act towards, behave towards, use, manage. **2** (*we must treat the reports with suspicion*) regard, view, look upon, consider. **3** (*she treats injured animals*) care for, look after, attend to, tend, minister to, nurse, doctor, medicate, cure, heal. OPPOSITE: neglect. **4** (*he treated them to a great evening*) entertain, amuse, delight, cheer, divert, gratify, regale, feast, wine and dine. **5** (*he treated the company to a round of drinks*) pay for, buy, stand (*inf*). **6** (*treat the wound with ointments*) apply, put on, lay on, spread on, cover with, smear, rub, paint, use on, ply with. **7** (*he treats the subject in his last book*) discuss, deal with, go into, touch upon, analyse, study, consider, review. **8** (*they refused to treat with their enemies*) negotiate, discuss terms, talk, confer, parley, bargain.

treatise *noun* discourse, exposition, disquisition, dissertation, essay, tract, work, thesis, study, paper, monograph, article, pamphlet.

treatment *noun* **1** (*he could not complain of harsh treatment*) handling, use, usage, manipulation, dealing, management, conduct, action, behaviour. **2** (*they are receiving treatment for their wounds*) care, ministration, nursing, doctoring, medication, medicament, first aid, therapy, cure, healing, remedy, drugs, therapeutics.

treaty *noun* agreement, compact, covenant, bargain, deal, contract, pact, bond, pledge, convention, concordat, entente, alliance.

trek *verb* travel, journey, tramp, trudge, plod, slog, footslog, march, walk, hike, ramble, roam, rove, traipse (*inf*).
➤ *noun* journey, voyage, expedition, trip, odyssey, march, walk, hike, ramble, roam, safari, slog, footslog, trudge, tramp.

tremble *verb* **1** (*the leaves trembled in the wind*) shake, quiver, quaver, quake, shiver, twitch, wiggle. **2** (*the earth trembled beneath their feet*) shudder, judder, shake, vibrate, oscillate, rock, wobble, teeter, totter.
➤ *noun* tremor, shake, quiver, quake, shiver, shudder, judder, vibration, wobble, oscillation.

tremendous *adj* **1** (*a rock of tremendous size*) huge, great, vast, immense, massive, enormous, colossal, giant, gigantic, prodigious, stupendous, monstrous, mammoth, gargantuan, titanic, whopping (*inf*), formidable, awful, terrible, dreadful. OPPOSITE: small. **2** (*a tremendous feat*) wonderful, marvellous, remarkable, sensational, spectacular, extraordinary, exceptional, amazing, great, incredible, fantastic (*inf*), fabulous (*inf*), terrific (*inf*), smashing (*inf*), super (*inf*), fab (*inf*), wicked (*inf*). OPPOSITE: ordinary. **3** (*a tremendous improvement in standards*) great, huge, vast, immense, enormous, massive, colossal, gigantic, towering, prodigious, stupendous, formidable, profound.

tremor *noun* **1** (*a tremor went through him*) shudder, shiver, quiver, quaver, tremble, trembling, shake, shaking, judder, spasm, twitch, paroxysm, vibration, oscillation, wobble, agitation, palpitation. **2** (*an earth tremor*) earthquake, quake (*inf*), shock.

tremulous *adj* **1** (*a tremulous whisper*) trembling, trembly, shaky, shaking, wavering, quavering, quaking, quivering, vibrating, shivering, shuddering, nervous,

agitated. OPPOSITE: steady. **2** (*a tremulous grip*) trembling, shaky, shaking, shuddering, juddering, jerky, quivery, jumpy, jittery (*inf*), twitchy, twitching, unsteady, spasmodic. **3** (*a tremulous approach to life*) timid, shy, diffident, fearful, frightened, apprehensive, timorous, scared, afraid, anxious, nervous, alarmed, cowardly.

trench *noun* furrow, ditch, drain, cut, channel, conduit, duct, gutter, pit, trough, entrenchment, excavation, earthwork, moat, fosse, waterway.

trenchant *adj* **1** (*a trenchant wit*) keen, acute, astute, sharp, pointed, piercing, penetrating, incisive, cutting, caustic, biting, scathing, pungent, mordant, acrid, acid, tart, bitter, astringent, acerbic, sarcastic, severe. OPPOSITE: mild. **2** (*a trenchant argument*) clear, effective, effectual, vigorous, energetic, powerful, potent, forceful, strong, forthright, emphatic, blunt, terse. OPPOSITE: ineffectual.

trend *noun* **1** (*a trend in opinion*) tendency, course, drift, inclination, bias, leaning, bent, swing, bearing, current, direction, flow. **2** (*the latest trend*) fashion, fad (*inf*), vogue, mode, style, look, craze, rage (*inf*).
➤ *verb* tend, lean, incline, drift, veer, swing, turn, head, shift, move, go.

trepidation *noun* fear, fearfulness, terror, panic, fright, alarm, perturbation, consternation, dismay, dread, apprehension, apprehensiveness, anxiety, worry, nervousness, cold feet (*inf*), willies (*inf*), qualms, misgivings, uneasiness, disquiet, discomposure, unrest, agitation, jitters (*inf*), jumpiness, trembling, shaking, quaking, quivering, tremor. OPPOSITE: composure.

trespass *verb* **1** (*do not trespass on this property*) intrude, invade, encroach, infringe, poach, violate. **2** (*he has trespassed upon their kindness*) exploit, abuse, take advantage of, impose upon. **3** (*as a youth he trespassed many times*) err, sin, do wrong, go astray, offend, transgress.
➤ *noun* **1** (*they staged a mass trespass*) unlawful entry, intrusion, invasion, encroachment, infringement, contravention, violation, poaching. **2** (*he was punished for his trespasses*) sin, offence, wrong, wrongdoing, transgression, infraction, crime, misdemeanour, misdeed, malefaction, error.

trespasser *noun* **1** (*a trespasser on his land*) intruder, invader, interloper, encroacher, infringer, gate-crasher (*inf*), poacher. **2** (*the judge was stern upon trespassers brought before him*) wrongdoer, offender, transgressor, criminal, evildoer, sinner, delinquent, malefactor.

trial *noun* **1** (*the computer system underwent extensive trials*) test, testing, test run, dry run (*inf*), dummy run, check, try-out, practice, rehearsal, experiment, examination, assay. **2** (*each candidate must pass the trial*) test, test period, audition, probation, analysis, examination, selection. **3** (*the court has set a date for the trial*) case, lawsuit, hearing, inquiry, tribunal, litigation, examination, appeal, retrial. **4** (*she is a real trial to her husband*) nuisance, pain in the neck (*inf*), hassle (*inf*), bother, pest (*inf*), worry, vexation, annoyance, irritation, irritant, bane, curse, affliction, burden, cross to bear, thorn in the flesh (*inf*), plague (*inf*). **5** (*he survived many trials*) suffering, distress, misery, wretchedness, unhappiness, sadness, woe, grief, pain, hardship, trouble, adversity, tribulation, affliction, blow, ordeal, worry, anxiety, vexation, burden, load, cross to bear. OPPOSITE: relief. **6** (*she succeeded at the third trial*) try, attempt, effort, endeavour, go (*inf*), shot (*inf*), stab (*inf*), crack (*inf*), venture.

⯈ *adj* testing, test, experimental, exploratory, pilot, dry (*inf*), dummy, probationary, provisional, tentative.

tribe *noun* group, ethnic group, people, nation, race, clan, family, house, caste, dynasty, blood, stock, class, branch, division, posse (*inf*), sept.

tribulation *noun* trial, care, hardship, adversity, ordeal, trouble, travail, pain, distress, heartache, suffering, affliction, vexation, anxiety, worry, grief, misery, sadness, sorrow, woe, wretchedness, unhappiness, misfortune, bad luck, curse, blow, load, burden. OPPOSITE: joy.

tribunal *noun* **1** (*she was called before the tribunal*) court, bar, bench, board, judicature, committee, forum. **2** (*the tribunal will take place in the summer*) trial, case, hearing, examination, inquisition, assizes, session.

tribute *noun* **1** (*tributes poured in on the announcement of his death*) accolade, testimonial, acclaim, acclamation, applause, recognition, acknowledgment, congratulation, compliments, bouquets (*inf*), honour, homage, praise, exaltation, commendation, eulogy, panegyric, glorification, paean. OPPOSITE: censure. **2** (*each district offered tributes to the king*) homage, payment, gift, present, offering, donation, contribution, impost, duty, tax, levy, tariff, toll, charge, customs, excise.

trice *noun* moment, second, minute, instant, twinkling, flash, jiffy (*inf*), sec (*inf*), shake (*inf*), tick (*inf*). OPPOSITE: age.

trick *noun* **1** (*no one suspected the trick*) wile, stratagem, ploy, artifice, ruse, deceit, deception, feint, dodge, contrivance, device, manoeuvre, subterfuge, trap, hoax, fraud, imposture, swindle, con (*inf*), scam (*inf*), rip-off (*inf*), diddle (*inf*). **2** (*he played a cruel trick on his wife*) caper, prank, practical joke, joke, jest, leg-pull (*inf*), fast one (*inf*), jape, stunt, gag, antic, frolic. **3** (*she practises her tricks for hours at a time*) sleight of hand, legerdemain, juggling. **4** (*he has the trick of making people feel at ease*) knack, talent, technique, expertise, art, flair, craft, gift, ability, capability, faculty, facility, skill, know-how (*inf*), hang (*inf*). **5** (*a trick of the light*) illusion, apparition, mirage, fantasy. **6** (*she has a trick of tossing her head*) trait, characteristic, idiosyncrasy, eccentricity, quirk, peculiarity, foible, mannerism, habit, practice.

⯈ *verb* dupe, cheat, defraud, trap, deceive, delude, mislead, fool, outwit, hoodwink, beguile, bluff, hoax, bamboozle (*inf*), take in (*inf*), take for a ride (*inf*), lead up the garden path (*inf*), have on (*inf*), do (*inf*), overreach, swindle, diddle, con (*inf*), pull a fast one (*inf*).

trick out decorate, embellish, ornament, dress up, deck out, bedeck, spruce up, do up (*inf*), doll up (*inf*), tart up (*inf*), array, attire, adorn.

trickery *noun* deceit, deception, cheating, fraud, swindling, guile, artifice, wiliness, cunning, subterfuge, craft, craftiness, chicanery, dishonesty, duplicity, imposture, pretence, double-dealing, monkey business (*inf*), shenanigans (*inf*), hanky-panky (*inf*), hocus-pocus (*inf*), jiggery-pokery (*inf*).

trickle *verb* drip, drop, dribble, run, leak, ooze, seep, exude, filter, percolate. OPPOSITE: gush.

trickster *noun* cheat, swindler, fraud, fraudster, con man (*inf*), confidence man, deceiver, dissembler, deluder, hoodwinker, hoaxer, impostor, pretender, phoney, charlatan.

tricky *adj* **1** (*a tricky task*) difficult, problematic, sticky (*inf*), dodgy (*inf*), complicated, knotty, thorny, awkward, delicate, sensitive, touchy, ticklish, risky, precarious, uncertain. OPPOSITE: simple. **2** (*he's a tricky devil*) crafty, cunning, artful, scheming, sly, wily, foxy, subtle, slippery, clever, devious, deceitful, deceptive, dishonest, dodgy (*inf*). OPPOSITE: artless.

trifle *noun* **1** (*he brought trifles for all the family*) toy, plaything, bauble, trinket, knick-knack, doodah, whatnot. **2** (*I try not to waste time on trifles*) triviality, trivia, inessential, bagatelle, nothing. **3** (*give her just a trifle of food*) bit, drop, spot, dash, pinch, touch, trace, jot, little, iota, particle.

⯈ *verb* **1** (*he should not trifle with her*) toy, play, dally, dabble, flirt, sport. **2** (*she spent the morning trifling around the house*) tinker, fiddle, meddle, fritter, potter, fool, mess, hang, loiter, idle, waste.

trifling *adj* **1** (*a trifling sum of money*) trivial, inconsiderable, insignificant, small, tiny, minuscule, negligible, nominal, paltry, piddling (*inf*), infinitesimal, valueless, worthless. **2** (*a trifling question*) unimportant, insignificant, inconsequential, petty, trivial, superficial, shallow, worthless, valueless, empty, frivolous, idle, foolish, silly. OPPOSITE: important.

trigger *verb* set off, spark off, set in motion, activate, give rise to, generate, produce, bring about, cause, start, initiate, prompt, provoke, elicit.

trim *adj* **1** (*a trim appearance*) neat, spruce, spick-and-span, tidy, orderly, shipshape, smart, well-groomed, well-dressed, well-turned-out, dapper, natty (*inf*), cool (*inf*), elegant, presentable. OPPOSITE: disorderly. **2** (*she looked fit and trim*) slim, slender, lean, lissom, sleek, streamlined, svelte, willowy, shapely, compact, fit.

⯈ *verb* **1** (*trim the hedge*) clip, prune, snip, cut, chop, hack, crop, pare, shave, shear, dock, lop, shorten, curtail, neaten, tidy up, shape. **2** (*trim the dress with ribbons*) decorate, adorn, ornament, embellish, garnish, festoon, deck, trick out, beautify, embroider, border, fringe, edge, pipe. OPPOSITE: strip. **3** (*trim government spending*) reduce, cut back, scale down, decrease, diminish, curtail, dock.

⯈ *noun* **1** (*the animals are in good trim*) order, condition, state, shape, form, health, fitness, fettle. **2** (*attach the trim to the dress*) trimming, decoration, adornment, ornamentation, embellishment, garnish, frill, fringe, edging, piping, border, braid, embroidery.

trimmings *pl noun* **1** (*a wedding with all the trimmings*) frills, extras, trappings, accompaniments, accessories, accoutrements, adornments, paraphernalia. **2** (*they swept up the trimmings*) clippings, cuttings, shavings, parings, ends.

trinket *noun* bauble, trifle, bagatelle, gewgaw, knick-knack, ornament, jewel.

trio *noun* threesome, triple, triumvirate, triad, trinity, trilogy, triptych, troika, triplets.

trip *noun* **1** (*she's away on a trip*) journey, excursion,

tour, jaunt, outing, run, ride, drive, expedition, voyage, foray. **2** (*the broken pavement caused his trip*) stumble, fall, tumble, slip, spill. **3** (*they made a bit of a trip there*) blunder, mistake, error, gaffe, slip, slip-up (*inf*), lapse, oversight, inaccuracy, howler (*inf*), bloomer (*inf*), clanger (*inf*), booboo (*inf*), boob (*inf*).
➤ *verb* **1** (*he tripped over the carpet*) stumble, fall, tumble, slip, stagger, totter. **2** (*they tripped up over the figures*) slip, slip up (*inf*), err, lapse, go wrong, blunder, bungle. **3** (*the prosecution tried to trip him up*) catch out, wrongfoot (*inf*), throw (*inf*), trick, trap, snare, ensnare, ambush, outwit, outsmart, confuse, unsettle, disconcert, discountenance, surprise. **4** (*the child tripped lightly round the room*) hop, skip, dance, gambol, caper, bound, frisk, cavort, prance, spring, waltz.

triple *adj* threefold, treble, triplicate.
➤ *noun* threesome, trio, triumvirate, triad, trinity, troika, trilogy, triplet.

tripper *noun* tourist, holidaymaker, traveller, sightseer, voyager, journeyer, excursionist.

trite *adj* hackneyed, corny (*inf*), stale, tired, worn, worn-out, thin, threadbare, old, unoriginal, unimaginative, uninspired, stock, clichéd, stereotyped, overused, overdone, common, commonplace, ordinary, dull, pedestrian, routine, run-of-the-mill, humdrum, banal, platitudinous. OPPOSITE: original.

triumph *noun* **1** (*they were delighted with their triumph*) victory, win, conquest, walk-over (*inf*), hit (*inf*), sensation, masterstroke, coup, feat, accomplishment, achievement, attainment, success, mastery, ascendancy. OPPOSITE: failure. **2** (*her face was full of triumph*) jubilation, exultation, elation, rejoicing, joy, joyfulness, celebration, pride. OPPOSITE: regret.
➤ *verb* **1** (*he triumphed in the competition*) win, prevail, conquer, vanquish, succeed, prosper, carry the day. OPPOSITE: lose. **2** (*the team triumphed over the opposition*) conquer, beat, defeat, overcome, overpower, overwhelm, vanquish, best, worst, prevail against, dominate. **3** (*they triumphed all night long*) rejoice, jubilate, exult, glory, celebrate, revel, gloat, swagger, brag, boast, crow. OPPOSITE: lament.

triumphant *adj* **1** (*they emerged triumphant*) winning, conquering, victorious, successful, prize-winning, trophy-winning, unbeaten, undefeated. OPPOSITE: beaten. **2** (*triumphant fans thronged the streets*) exultant, jubilant, elated, celebratory, rejoicing, joyful, joyous, proud, gloating, boastful, swaggering, cock-a-hoop (*inf*).

trivia *pl noun* trivialities, trifles, technicalities, minutiae, details.

trivial *adj* trifling, unimportant, insignificant, inconsequential, insubstantial, piddling (*inf*), measly (*inf*), negligible, inconsiderable, small, little, minor, immaterial, meaningless, paltry, petty, frivolous, banal, trite, foolish, worthless. OPPOSITE: important.

triviality *noun* **1** (*he brushed aside these trivialities*) detail, trifle, technicality. **2** (*the triviality of her chatter*) insignificance, inconsequentiality, pettiness, foolishness, frivolity, worthlessness, insubstantiality, flimsiness, paltriness. **3** (*the triviality of young girls today*) frivolity, frivolousness, giddiness, silliness, small-mindedness.

troop *noun* group, band, company, contingent, unit, crew (*inf*), posse (*inf*),team, squad, gang (*inf*), bunch, crowd, host, mob, throng, multitude, horde, herd, flock, drove, pack, stream, swarm, assemblage, body, gathering.
➤ *verb* flock, gather, collect, muster, throng, crowd, mill, surge, swarm, stream, go, march, parade, trudge. OPPOSITE: disperse.

troops *pl noun* soldiers, soldiery, army, armed forces, military, servicemen, servicewomen, fighting men, men.

trophy *noun* **1** (*the team won the trophy*) cup, prize, award, medal, laurels, bays. **2** (*trophies of his days in the colonies*) spoils, booty, souvenir, keepsake, reminder, memento, relic.

tropical *adj* hot, torrid, sultry, sweltering, stifling, boiling, humid, sticky, steamy.

trot *verb* canter, lope, run, jog, pace, scuttle, scurry, bustle, scamper.

trouble *noun* **1** (*her family have caused her a lot of trouble*) worry, concern, anxiety, disquiet, unease, agitation, distress, unhappiness, heartache, torment, woe, suffering, pain, grief, anguish, hardship, adversity, misfortune, trial, tribulation, affliction, burden, difficulty, problem, nuisance, pest, bother, inconvenience, hassle (*inf*), harassment, headache (*inf*), vexation, irritation, annoyance. OPPOSITE: relief. **2** (*trouble in the streets*) unrest, disturbance, disorder, commotion, upheaval, tumult, turbulence, strife, conflict, fighting, rowing, law-breaking, anarchy, mischief. OPPOSITE: order. **3** (*he went to a great deal of trouble*) bother, fuss, hassle (*inf*), ado, inconvenience, disturbance, effort, exertion, pains, labour, work, care, attention, thought, thoughtfulness. **4** (*she has heart trouble*) ailment, illness, disorder, disease, complaint, dysfunction, defect.
➤ *verb* **1** (*she was troubled by his coldness towards her*) worry, bother, agitate, alarm, concern, upset, distress, disturb, perturb, discompose, confuse, perplex, pester, annoy, irk, fret, irritate, torment, plague, harass, hassle (*inf*), vex, sadden. OPPOSITE: soothe. **2** (*the wound troubled him*) afflict, pain, incapacitate, worry, nag at, burden, weigh down, oppress, grieve. **3** (*sorry to trouble you*) bother, inconvenience, put out, disturb, impose upon, discommode.

troublemaker *noun* mischief-maker, agitator, rabble-rouser, agent provocateur, instigator, incendiary, inciter, stirrer, ringleader, demagogue.

troublesome *adj* annoying, irritating, irksome, upsetting, vexatious, bothersome, tiresome, wearisome, inconvenient, worrying, worrisome, distressing, disturbing, perturbing, harassing, nagging, burdensome, oppressive, difficult, hard, awkward, problematic, tricky, thorny, demanding, exacting, laborious, taxing, arduous. OPPOSITE: easy.

trough *noun* ditch, trench, channel, conduit, duct, drain, culvert, gutter, furrow, groove, gully, depression.

trounce *verb* defeat, thrash, beat, rout, overwhelm, crush, paste, punish, drub, best, slaughter (*inf*), wallop (*inf*), hammer (*inf*), clobber (*inf*), lick (*inf*), walk all over (*inf*), wipe the floor with (*inf*).

troupe *noun* company, band, troop, group, set, cast.

trousers *pl noun* pants, slacks, jeans, denims, flannels, shorts, bottoms (*inf*), breeches.

truancy *noun* absenteeism, absence, shirking, skiving (*inf*), bunking-off (*inf*), malingering, French leave.

truant *noun* absentee, dodger, shirker, skiver (*inf*), idler, malingerer, deserter, runaway.
➤ *adj* absent, missing, runaway, AWOL, skiving (*inf*). OPPOSITE: present.
➤ *verb* play truant, dodge, shirk, skive (*inf*), malinger, bunk off (*inf*), go AWOL (*inf*), play hooky (*inf*), desert.

truce *noun* armistice, ceasefire, peace, rest, break, intermission, interval, lull, let-up (*inf*), respite, stay, suspension, treaty, pact, moratorium. OPPOSITE: war.

truck[1] *noun* (*he drives a truck*) lorry, articulated lorry, artic (*inf*), heavy goods vehicle, HGV (*inf*), pantechnicon, van, wagon.

truck[2] *noun* (*we will have no truck with terrorists*) dealings, business, commerce, trade, traffic, relations, association, contact, communication, intercourse, connection.

truculent *adj* aggressive, hostile, antagonistic, contentious, obstreperous, quarrelsome, argumentative, pugnacious, belligerent, bellicose, combative, disobedient, defiant, fierce, ferocious, violent, cruel, brutal, savage, grim, sullen, surly, bad-tempered, ill-tempered, cross, discourteous, disrespectful, rude. OPPOSITE: gentle.

trudge *verb* plod, tramp, stump, clump, lumber, shuffle, slog, footslog, toil, labour, traipse (*inf*), march, walk, hike, trek.

true *adj* **1** (*which version of events is true?*) accurate, truthful, genuine, faithful, correct, right, valid, factual, actual, real, veritable, exact, precise, reliable, veracious, honest. **2** (*this is the true article*) authentic, genuine, real, actual, valid, sincere, legitimate, bona fide, rightful, proper. OPPOSITE: false. **3** (*they proved a true ally*) faithful, loyal, dutiful, devoted, dedicated, sincere, staunch, supportive, constant, unswerving, unwavering, firm, steadfast, steady, fast, trusty, trustworthy, reliable, dependable. OPPOSITE: faithless.
➤ *adv* **1** (*he loved her true*) truly, sincerely, truthfully, faithfully, candidly, honestly, veraciously. **2** (*he banged the nail in true*) accurately, exactly, precisely, correctly, unerringly, spot on (*inf*), on target, unswervingly.

truism *noun* platitude, commonplace, cliché, bromide, axiom, truth. OPPOSITE: paradox.

truly *adv* **1** (*this is truly what happened*) really, in reality, indeed, in truth, in fact, actually, certainly, definitely, surely, assuredly, decidedly, absolutely, positively, undoubtedly, beyond doubt, indubitably, unquestionably, beyond question, genuinely, sincerely. **2** (*truly remarkable*) very, really, extremely, exceptionally. **3** (*is that truly your opinion?*) honestly, truthfully, frankly, candidly, openly. **4** (*truly, I did not take the money*) honestly, truthfully, really, indeed, veritably, genuinely. **5** (*he loved her truly*) faithfully, devotedly, sincerely, dutifully, loyally, firmly, constantly, unswervingly, reliably. **6** (*the past is truly recreated in the film*) accurately, faithfully, exactly, closely, precisely, correctly.

trump up *verb* invent, make up, fabricate, create, devise, concoct, cook up (*inf*), contrive, hatch, fake.

trumpery *adj* rubbishy, trashy, worthless, useless, valueless, tawdry, shabby, shoddy, flashy, flash (*inf*), showy, cheap, grotty (*inf*), nasty, meretricious, trivial, trifling. OPPOSITE: valuable.

trumpet *noun* bugle, horn, clarion.
➤ *verb* **1** (*the papers trumpeted the announcement*) proclaim, announce, broadcast, herald, promulgate, advertise. OPPOSITE: suppress. **2** (*the elephant trumpeted its call*) roar, bellow, blare, blast, yell, shout, call out.

truncate *verb* shorten, curtail, cut, lop, clip, crop, prune, trim, dock, abbreviate, reduce, decrease, diminish.

truncheon *noun* club, cudgel, baton, staff, cosh, stick.

trunk *noun* **1** (*tree trunk*) stem, stalk, stock, bole. **2** (*the headless trunk of a body*) body, torso, frame. **3** (*put the letters back in the trunk*) chest, coffer, box, crate, portmanteau, suitcase, case. **4** (*an elephant's trunk*) snout, nose, proboscis.

truss *verb* tie up, bind, fasten, secure, strap, tether, chain up, pinion. OPPOSITE: loose.
➤ *noun* **1** (*an arch supported by trusses*) support, prop, brace, buttress, strut, stay, joist, shore. **2** (*each player wore a truss*) support, pad, binding.

trust *noun* **1** (*we have complete trust in her*) faith, belief, confidence, conviction, certainty, certitude, credence, assurance, reliance, dependence, hope, expectation, credit. **2** (*the children were placed in his trust*) trusteeship, guardianship, charge, custody, care, protection, safekeeping. **3** (*a position of considerable trust*) duty, responsibility, obligation, commitment.
➤ *verb* **1** (*they trust in the president*) believe, have faith in, have confidence in, swear by. OPPOSITE: doubt. **2** (*can we trust in the weather to stay calm?*) rely on, depend on, bank on, count on. **3** (*I trust you will be there*) presume, assume, suppose, imagine, surmise, hope, expect, believe. **4** (*he trusted the project to his deputy*) commit, entrust, consign, turn over, assign, delegate, give, confide.

trustworthy *adj* trusty, dependable, reliable, loyal, faithful, devoted, committed, true, constant, stable, staunch, steadfast, firm, honest, truthful, honourable, righteous, ethical, principled, virtuous, upright, sensible, responsible, level headed. OPPOSITE: unreliable.

trusty *adj* trustworthy, dependable, reliable, firm, steady, staunch, strong, supportive, honest, upright, faithful, loyal, responsible, straightforward, true.

truth *noun* **1** (*the truth will out*) reality, actuality, verity, fact. **2** (*he doubted the truth of what she told him*) veracity, verity, truthfulness, accuracy, correctness, rightness, validity, fidelity, legitimacy, authenticity, genuineness, honesty, factualness, factuality. OPPOSITE: deceit. **3** (*this paper prides itself on the truth of its reports*) truthfulness, honesty, integrity, honour, honourableness, sincerity, uprightness, righteousness, candour, frankness, precision, exactness, correctness. OPPOSITE: falseness. **4** (*he was reminded of an old truth*) truism, home truth, platitude, proverb, adage, aphorism, saying, saw, axiom, maxim, principle, law.

truthful *adj* **1** (*a truthful child*) honest, veracious, sincere, frank, candid, straightforward, forthright, straight, open, trustworthy, reliable. OPPOSITE: deceitful.

2 (*a truthful account of the crime*) accurate, exact, precise, correct, right, genuine, valid, reliable, honest, veracious, faithful, literal, realistic, factual, true. OPPOSITE: false.

try *verb* **1** (*try to reach the handle*) attempt, endeavour, essay, undertake, venture, seek, aim, strive, struggle, have a go (*inf*), have a bash at (*inf*), have a shot at (*inf*), have a stab at (*inf*), have a crack at (*inf*), make an effort, exert oneself. **2** (*try this new drink*) test, assay, experience, taste, experiment with, prove, examine, inspect, investigate, assess, appraise, analyse, sample, evaluate. **3** (*they are trying her goodwill*) tire, wear out, weary, strain, stress, tax, sap, drain, exhaust, weaken, stretch. **4** (*don't try your mother*) bother, pester, nag, trouble, plague, torment, annoy, harass, afflict, irritate, vex, irk. **5** (*try the charges in court*) hear, examine, judge, adjudicate, adjudge.
➤ *noun* **1** (*have a try*) attempt, endeavour, effort, go (*inf*), bash (*inf*), shot (*inf*), crack (*inf*), stab (*inf*). **2** (*give it a try*) trial, test, evaluation, appraisal, experiment, sample, taste.

try out try, test, put to the test, experiment with, check out, evaluate, appraise, inspect, sample, taste.

trying *adj* **1** (*a trying experience*) hard, difficult, arduous, tough, taxing, demanding, stressful, upsetting, tiring, fatiguing, exhausting. OPPOSITE: easy. **2** (*a trying turn of events*) annoying, exasperating, infuriating, irksome, irritating, aggravating (*inf*), vexatious, troublesome, bothersome, tiresome, wearisome.

tube *noun* pipe, hose, line, cylinder, passage, channel, spout, conduit, duct, shaft.

tuck *verb* **1** (*he tucked the socks back in the drawer*) stuff, cram, push, thrust, put, insert. **2** (*tuck the hem of the dress*) fold, pleat, gather, crease, pucker, ruffle, ruck.
➤ *noun* **1** (*a tuck in the sleeve*) fold, crease, pleat, ruck, ruffle, pucker, gather. **2** (*the boys had hoarded some tuck*) food, snacks, grub (*inf*), eats (*inf*), nosh (*inf*), scoff (*inf*), victuals, comestibles.

tuck away stash away, stow away, save up, store, hoard, hide, conceal, secrete.

tuck in tuck up, put to bed, make comfortable, cover up, wrap up.

tuck into eat up, dine, feast, devour, gobble up (*inf*), gorge, scoff (*inf*), wolf down (*inf*), get stuck into (*inf*).

tuft *noun* bunch, clump, cluster, knot, truss, wisp, crest, beard.

tug *verb* **1** (*he tugged on the rope*) pull, jerk, wrench, yank (*inf*), heave, pluck. **2** (*the locomotive tugged the carriage away*) pull, haul, drag, draw, tow, trail, lug. OPPOSITE: push.
➤ *noun* pull, tow, haul, jerk, yank (*inf*), heave, wrench, pluck.

tuition *noun* instruction, teaching, schooling, education, training, coaching, lessons, drill, direction, guidance.

tumble *verb* **1** (*the child tumbled down the stairs*) fall, topple, slip, trip, stumble, stagger, sprawl, pitch. **2** (*viewing figures have tumbled*) plummet, drop, fall, plunge, dive, nosedive, slump, slide, collapse, flop, decline, decrease. **3** (*the boat tumbled about on the water*) toss, roll, lurch, pitch, reel, sway, heave.
➤ *noun* **1** (*he took a tumble down the steps*) fall, header

(*inf*), nosedive (*inf*), spill, trip, stumble. **2** (*prices have taken a tumble*) dive, nosedive (*inf*), plunge, plummet, drop, fall, collapse, failure, decline. **3** (*the whole house is in a tumble*) mess, chaos, disorder, clutter, jumble, confusion, disarray.

tumble to understand, comprehend, grasp, realize, latch on to (*inf*), suss (*inf*), twig (*inf*), apprehend, perceive, cotton on to (*inf*).

tumbledown *adj* ramshackle, dilapidated, ruined, broken-down, crumbling, crumbly, disintegrating, decrepit, ruined, ruinous, in ruins, rickety, shaky, unstable, unsteady, unsafe, tottering, teetering.

tumid *adj* **1** (*a tumid corpse*) swollen, puffy, puffed up, distended, bloated, inflated, turgid, tumescent, bulging, bulbous, protuberant. OPPOSITE: shrunken. **2** (*a tumid style*) pompous, affected, stilted, bombastic, orotund, fustian, pretentious, magniloquent, grandiloquent, grandiose, turgid, rhetorical, inflated, overblown, high-flown, fulsome, flowery.

tumour *noun* swelling, lump, growth, protuberance, tumefaction, intumescence, malignancy, cancer, sarcoma.

tumult *noun* **1** (*the tumult was deafening*) uproar, commotion, racket, pandemonium, bedlam, din, noise, clamour, shouting, yelling, hubbub, hullabaloo. **2** (*the class was in tumult*) disorder, disarray, chaos, confusion, upheaval, unrest, uproar. OPPOSITE: peace. **3** (*a tumult in the street*) riot, insurrection, rebellion, brawl, free-for-all (*inf*), row, altercation, fight, strife, affray, fracas, brouhaha, disturbance, agitation, protest, quarrel, rumpus. **4** (*her feelings were in tumult*) confusion, turmoil, turbulence, ferment, upheaval.

tumultuous *adj* **1** (*tumultuous noise*) noisy, loud, blaring, deafening, clamorous, ear-shattering, ear-piercing, uproarious, boisterous, unrestrained. **2** (*he got a tumultuous reception*) noisy, vociferous, vehement, fervent, passionate, raging, wild, turbulent, stormy, tempestuous, violent, fierce, rowdy, unruly, disorderly, boisterous, obstreperous, riotous, excited, frenzied, restless, agitated, disturbed, uncontrolled, unrestrained. OPPOSITE: quiet.

tune *noun* melody, air, song, strain, theme, motif. OPPOSITE: discord.
➤ *verb* adjust, adapt, set, regulate, temper, pitch, harmonize, attune, synchronize.

change one's tune change one's mind, change one's opinion, backtrack, switch horses (*inf*).

in tune with in agreement with, in accord with, in accordance with, in sympathy with, in harmony with, in correspondence with, in conformity with, in congruence with.

tuneful *adj* melodious, melodic, lyrical, harmonious, euphonious, musical, sweet, dulcet, mellifluous, mellow, pleasant, agreeable, catchy (*inf*). OPPOSITE: discordant.

tunnel *noun* **1** (*a tunnel under the house*) passage, passageway, underpass, subway, shaft, mine, gallery. **2** (*a tunnel made by animals*) burrow, passage, hole.
➤ *verb* dig, excavate, burrow, mine, bore, undermine, sap.

turbid *adj* muddy, cloudy, clouded, murky, dim, opaque, unclear, foul, impure, thick, dense, foggy, fuzzy,

hazy, muddled, confused, unsettled, turbulent.
OPPOSITE: clear.

turbulence noun **1** (*the turbulence of the water*)
tempestuousness, storminess, roughness, choppiness,
boiling, agitation. **2** (*the turbulence of her feelings*)
turmoil, agitation, confusion, commotion, chaos,
instability, upheaval, disruption, disorder. **3** (*the
turbulence of the animals*) restlessness, unrest, agitation,
turmoil, tumult, instability, unruliness, disorderliness,
rowdiness.

turbulent adj **1** (*a turbulent mass of animals*) agitated,
disturbed, restless, confused, disordered, tumultuous,
wild, unruly, disorderly, undisciplined, boisterous,
noisy, clamorous, uproarious, rebellious, riotous,
obstreperous, furious, violent. **2** (*turbulent water*)
agitated, choppy, blustery, rough, stormy, tempestuous,
raging, foaming. OPPOSITE: calm. **3** (*at the mercy of his
turbulent feelings*) agitated, confused, disordered,
troubled, disturbed, unsettled, unstable, distraught.

turf noun grass, lawn, sward, green.

turf out **1** (*she turfed out the old furniture*) throw out,
chuck out (*inf*), dump (*inf*), discard, scrap, fling out,
dispose of, get rid of. **2** (*he was turfed out of the house*)
throw out, chuck out (*inf*), kick out (*inf*), fling out, turn
out, eject, expel, evict, banish, oust, dismiss, discharge,
bounce (*inf*), elbow (*inf*), sack (*inf*), fire (*inf*).

turgid adj **1** (*turgid joints*) swollen, puffy, puffed up,
distended, bloated, inflated, enlarged, tumid, tumescent,
bulging, protuberant. OPPOSITE: shrunken. **2** (*a turgid
style*) pompous, bombastic, orotund, fustian,
extravagant, magniloquent, grandiloquent, grandiose,
pretentious, ostentatious, affected, stilted, oratorical,
rhetorical, inflated, overblown, high-flown, high-
sounding, fulsome, flowery.

turmoil noun tumult, turbulence, uproar, commotion,
noise, din, racket, clamour, hubbub, bustle, flurry, stir,
unrest, agitation, ferment, disturbance, chaos, disorder,
disarray, upheaval, confusion, pandemonium, bedlam,
fuss, ado, trouble. OPPOSITE: peace.

turn verb **1** (*the planet turns slowly in space*) rotate,
revolve, spin, roll, spiral, twirl, wheel, whirl, reel, pivot,
swivel, gyrate, circle, go round. **2** (*the car turned right*) go,
veer, swerve, swing, wheel, diverge. **3** (*turn the picture
over*) flip over, reverse, invert. **4** (*his mood turned to anger*)
change, alter, modify, convert, transform,
metamorphose, mutate. **5** (*the men turned their guns on
their officers*) aim, direct, level, train, focus. **6** (*let us turn
to the next question*) move on, attend to, set about,
undertake, take up, concentrate on. **7** (*she turned greedy
on seeing the money*) become, go, grow, get. **8** (*the milk
has turned*) curdle, sour, go off (*inf*), go bad, spoil, taint.
9 (*he managed to turn the ball*) bend, curve, twist. **10** (*he
can turn his hand to anything*) adjust, adapt, fit, suit,
apply, shape, form, use. **11** (*everything turns on her
decision*) hinge, hang, rest, depend. **12** (*he turned a perfect
wooden bowl*) fashion, form, model, carve, shape, mould,
cast, construct.

➤ noun **1** (*closer with each turn of the wheel*) rotation,
revolution, circle, cycle, round, gyration, spin, twirl,
swivel. **2** (*a turn in the road*) bend, curve, corner, twist,
turning, winding. **3** (*the car did a quick turn*) swerve, veer,
deviation, divergence. **4** (*a turn for the worse*) change,

alteration, variation, vicissitude, shift, adjustment,
deviation, divergence, difference. **5** (*the general turn of
events*) tendency, trend, bias, leaning, drift, direction.
6 (*an analytical turn of mind*) inclination, tendency, bent,
propensity, aptitude, flair, gift, talent, knack, genius,
faculty. OPPOSITE: disinclination. **7** (*it's your turn at the
tiller*) shift, stint, spell, time, period. **8** (*whose turn is it?*)
move, go (*inf*), try, attempt, shot (*inf*), chance,
opportunity, occasion. **9** (*one good turn deserves another*)
deed, act, action, gesture, service, favour. **10** (*I will go for
a turn in the garden later*) stroll, saunter, walk,
promenade, amble, drive, ride, spin (*inf*), outing,
excursion, airing, jaunt, constitutional. **11** (*the sudden
noise gave him quite a turn*) surprise, shock, start, scare,
fright. **12** (*a music hall turn*) routine, act, performance.

turn against **1** (*she turned against her parents*) take a
dislike to, fall out with, rebel against. **2** (*they turned him
against his friends*) set against, influence against,
prejudice against.

turn away turn aside, avert, deflect, send away, reject,
repel, rebuff, cold-shoulder (*inf*).

turn down **1** (*turn down the volume*) lower, reduce,
lessen, diminish, decrease, soften, quieten, muffle, mute.
OPPOSITE: raise. **2** (*she turned down the invitation*) reject,
refuse, decline, spurn, rebuff, repudiate, veto. OPPOSITE:
accept.

turn in **1** (*all officers must turn in their guns*) hand in,
hand over, give in, give back, return, deliver, submit,
tender, surrender. **2** (*turn in for the night*) go to bed, go to
sleep, retire, call it a day, hit the hay (*inf*), hit the sack
(*inf*).

turn off **1** (*turn off the light*) switch off, turn out, put
off, shut off, shut down, flick off, unplug, disconnect,
stop, extinguish. **2** (*he turned off the motorway*) leave, quit
(*inf*), depart from, deviate from, divert from, branch off
from. **3** (*she was turned off by the prospect*) put off,
alienate, repel, displease, disenchant, discourage,
disgust, offend, sicken, nauseate.

turn on **1** (*she turned on the light*) switch on, put on,
start, flick on, plug in, connect, activate, operate. **2** (*that
really turns me on*) arouse, excite, stimulate, thrill,
titillate, attract, please. **3** (*his father turned on him*) attack,
round on, set upon, fall on, lay into (*inf*), tear into (*inf*).
4 (*a lot turns on this result*) depend on, rest on, hinge on,
pivot on, hang on.

turn out **1** (*they were turned out into the street*) expel, put
out, throw out, chuck out (*inf*), turf out (*inf*), kick out,
eject, evict, oust. OPPOSITE: admit. **2** (*he was turned out of
the company*) eject, dismiss, discharge, axe, drum out, fire
(*inf*), boot out (*inf*), kick out (*inf*), sack (*inf*). **3** (*they turn
out thousands of units per week*) make, manufacture,
fabricate, produce, process, bring out, put out, churn out
(*inf*). **4** (*turn out the lights*) switch off, turn off, put off,
put out, shut off, flick off, unplug, disconnect. **5** (*turn
out your pockets*) empty, clear out, clean out. **6** (*things
turned out very well*) result, ensue, transpire, pan out (*inf*),
happen, occur, come about, end up, develop, emerge,
eventuate. OPPOSITE: begin. **7** (*the whole family turned out
for the funeral*) turn up, show up (*inf*), come, go, arrive,
appear, put in an appearance, present oneself, assemble,
gather, attend.

turn over **1** (*the dinghy turned over*) overturn, capsize,
keel over, turn turtle, upturn, topple. **2** (*her elbow turned*

the lamp over) upset, overturn, upturn, upend, invert, reverse. **3** (*they were instructed to turn over all documentation*) hand over, surrender, deliver, transfer, assign, consign. **4** (*she turned the problem over in her mind*) consider, ponder, deliberate, mull over, muse on, think about, think over, reflect on, contemplate, ruminate about, examine.

turn up 1 (*hundreds of people turned up*) turn out, arrive, appear, put in an appearance, show up (*inf*), attend, present oneself, come. **2** (*turn up the sound*) raise, increase, amplify, intensify. OPPOSITE: lower. **3** (*some new facts have been turned up*) discover, find, dig up, unearth, uncover, expose, disclose, reveal, hit upon, bring to light, ferret out, root out. **4** (*something will turn up*) crop up, pop up, arise, come to light, transpire, manifest itself.

turning-point *noun* crossroads, critical period, crux, crisis, crisis point, critical point, decisive point, watershed, moment of truth.

turnout *noun* **1** (*a big turnout at the match*) attendance, gate, audience, crowd, gathering, number, congregation, assembly, assemblage. **2** (*his turnout was very smart*) appearance, outfit, dress, clothes, costume, rig-out (*inf*), get-up (*inf*), gear (*inf*), clobber (*inf*), togs (*inf*), ensemble, attire, array.

turnover *noun* **1** (*the company's turnover has doubled*) output, yield, volume, income, profits, revenue, business, productivity, production, sales. **2** (*a fast turnover of managers*) change, flow, replacement, movement.

turpitude *noun* baseness, vileness, wickedness, evil, corruption, depravity, degeneracy, foulness, sin, sinfulness, iniquity, immorality, criminality, villainy, viciousness, vice. OPPOSITE: nobility.

tussle *noun* fight, battle, conflict, contest, skirmish, scramble, scuffle, struggle, wrestle, bout, brawl, set-to (*inf*), scrap (*inf*), punch-up (*inf*), dust-up (*inf*), fracas, fray, affray.

tutelage *noun* guardianship, charge, care, custody, wardship, patronage, protection, supervision, vigilance, aegis, guidance, instruction, tuition, schooling, teaching, education, preparation.

tutor *noun* teacher, instructor, coach, preceptor, schoolmaster, schoolmistress, professor, lecturer, educator, supervisor, guide, guru, mentor. OPPOSITE: pupil.
» *verb* teach, instruct, coach, train, educate, school, discipline, drill, direct, guide.

TV *noun* television, telly (*inf*), small screen, receiver, set, box (*inf*), tube (*inf*).

twaddle *noun* nonsense, rubbish, garbage, trash, balls (*sl*), rot, drivel, balderdash, bunkum, humbug, babble, prattle, chatter, gibberish, guff, claptrap, hogwash (*inf*), blather, blether, gabble, tattle, gossip, waffle (*inf*), bunk (*inf*), piffle (*inf*), poppycock (*inf*). OPPOSITE: sense.

tweak *verb* pinch, nip, squeeze, twist, twitch, pull, tug, jerk.

twiddle *verb* fiddle, finger, adjust, wiggle, play, toy, twirl, twist, swivel, turn.

twig *noun* stick, stem, branch, shoot, offshoot, spray, sprig, whip. OPPOSITE: log.

twilight *noun* **1** (*they waited until twilight*) dusk, gloaming, sunset, early evening. **2** (*she could barely see the man in the twilight*) gloom, dimness, semi-darkness, half-light, shadow. **3** (*in the twilight of his life*) closing years, decline, ebb, waning.

twin *noun* **1** (*this chair should have a twin*) fellow, mate, match, counterpart, equivalent, complement. **2** (*she is an exact twin for the famous actress*) double, duplicate, look-alike, likeness, spitting image (*inf*), spit (*inf*), dead spit (*inf*), ringer (*inf*), dead ringer (*inf*), clone.
» *adj* similar, like, corresponding, parallel, symmetrical, double, dual, duplicate, twofold, paired, matching, identical. OPPOSITE: single.
» *verb* join, pair, link, couple, yoke, match.

twine *noun* string, rope, cord, yarn, thread, cotton.
» *verb* **1** (*the snake twined round his leg*) twist, wind, turn, weave, wrap, curl, meander, wreathe, coil, spiral, encircle, surround. **2** (*the ribbons were twined together*) interlace, interweave, weave, entwine, twist, knit, splice, braid, plait, tangle. OPPOSITE: unravel.

twinge *noun* pang, spasm, twitch, tweak, tic, throb, ache, cramp, stitch, pain, stab, pinch, prick, tingle.

twinkle *verb* sparkle, shimmer, glimmer, shine, dazzle, glisten, glitter, glint, gleam, flash, coruscate, scintillate, flicker, blink, wink.
» *noun* **1** (*the twinkle of the streetlights*) twinkling, sparkle, shimmer, shine, shining, glimmer, glitter, glint, gleam, flash, dazzle, flicker, coruscation, scintillation, blink, wink. **2** (*he'll be with you in a twinkle*) twinkling, instant, moment, mo (*inf*), second, sec (*inf*), flash, trice, jiffy (*inf*), tick (*inf*), shake (*inf*).

twinkling *noun* **1** (*the twinkling of a thousand candles*) twinkle, sparkling, shimmering, shining, glistening, glimmering, glittering, glinting, gleaming, flashing, dazzling, flickering, coruscation, scintillation, blinking, winking. **2** (*it will be ready in a twinkling*) twinkle, instant, moment, mo (*inf*), second, sec (*inf*), flash, trice, jiffy (*inf*), tick (*inf*), shake (*inf*).

twirl *verb* **1** (*the skaters twirled over the ice*) spin, wheel, whirl, gyrate, pirouette, pivot, swivel, twist, turn, revolve, rotate. **2** (*he twirled the wire into a loop*) twist, curl, coil, wind.
» *noun* **1** (*the skater performed several twirls on the ice*) turn, spin, whirl, pirouette, gyration, rotation, revolution. **2** (*a twirl of hair*) twist, curl, coil, spiral, whorl.

twist *verb* **1** (*ivy had twisted round the trunk*) coil, curl, twine, entwine, wind, weave, wrap. **2** (*he twisted the wire until it broke*) wrench, bend, warp, contort, distort, deform, wring, wrest. **3** (*he had twisted his ankle*) sprain, strain, turn, wrench, rick. **4** (*his face twisted into a scowl*) contort, screw up. **5** (*they twisted the truth*) distort, warp, pervert, garble, alter, change, falsify, misrepresent, misinterpret, misquote, misreport. **6** (*he twisted the thread round his fingers*) twine, intertwine, twirl, coil, curl, weave, plait, braid, entangle. **7** (*the procession twisted its way through the streets*) wind, meander, snake, worm, curve, bend, twine, zigzag. **8** (*the fish twisted on the end of the line*) writhe, wriggle, squirm, skew. **9** (*the boy twisted round in his seat*) turn, rotate, revolve, swivel, spin, pivot.

➤ *noun* **1** (*he gave the rope a twist*) wrench, screw, turn, contortion, pull, jerk, yank. **2** (*a twist in the rail*) warp, distortion, kink, defect, flaw, imperfection, deformity, aberration. **3** (*another twist in the path*) turn, bend, curve, wind, meander, zigzag. **4** (*a twist of wire*) coil, curl, twirl, loop, spiral, roll, convolution, tangle. **5** (*a severe twist of the ankle*) sprain, wrench, rick, strain. **6** (*there were several twists in the story*) surprise, turnabout, variation, break, turn, change.

twit *noun* idiot, fool, simpleton, halfwit (*inf*), nincompoop (*inf*), clown, ass, blockhead, chump (*inf*), dope (*inf*), clot (*inf*), twerp (*inf*), nitwit (*inf*).

twitch *verb* **1** (*the dog twitched in its sleep*) jerk, jump, start, quaver, quiver, shiver, shake. **2** (*his eyelid twitched uncontrollably*) flutter, tremble, blink, jump. **3** (*she twitched nervously at her skirt*) snatch, pluck, pull, tug, tweak, jerk, yank (*inf*).
➤ *noun* **1** (*his hand gave a twitch*) jerk, jump, start, spasm, convulsion, shiver, tremor, quaver, quiver, shake. **2** (*an uncontrollable twitch in her eye*) flutter, tremble, blink, jump, tic, tremor, twinge, spasm. **3** (*a twitch on the fishing line*) jerk, tug, pull, yank (*inf*).

twitter *verb* **1** (*hear the birds twitter*) chirp, chirrup, cheep, tweet, warble, trill, sing, whistle. **2** (*the children twittered happily*) chatter, prattle, jabber, babble, gabble, witter, blather, blether, gossip.
➤ *noun* **1** (*the twitter of small birds*) tweeting, trilling, warbling, chirruping, chirping, cheeping, song, cry, chatter, whistle. **2** (*all of a twitter*) flutter, flurry, tizzy (*inf*), dither (*inf*), state (*inf*).

two-faced *adj* deceitful, deceiving, hypocritical, insincere, false, lying, untrustworthy, treacherous, duplicitous, double-dealing, perfidious, dissembling.

tycoon *noun* magnate, industrialist, capitalist, entrepreneur, mogul, baron, fat cat (*inf*), big noise (*inf*), big cheese (*inf*).

type *noun* **1** (*a different type of animal*) class, classification, order, genre, species, genus, breed, form, variety, kind, sort, set, group, category, ilk (*inf*), strain, stamp, mark, style, designation, description. **2** (*the very type of a city businessman*) specimen, sample, example, exemplar, model, pattern, standard, essence, quintessence, personification, embodiment, archetype, prototype, epitome, paradigm. **3** (*set in type*) print, face, font, fount, characters, lettering, letters.

typhoon *noun* tropical storm, cyclone, tornado, whirlwind, twister (*inf*), hurricane, squall, tempest.

typical *adj* **1** (*a typical example of his work*) representative, illustrative, classic, archetypal, true, exemplary, characteristic, indicative, symbolic, emblematic, quintessential, standard, orthodox, stock. **2** (*a typical day's work*) normal, ordinary, average, regular, general, usual, habitual, routine, customary, conventional, run-of-the-mill. OPPOSITE: abnormal.

typify *verb* **1** (*she typifies the modern girl*) represent, exemplify, epitomize, embody, incarnate, encapsulate, personify, sum up, characterize, symbolize. **2** (*an attempt to typify levels of achievement*) denote, indicate, represent, illustrate.

tyrannical *adj* tyrannous, autocratic, despotic, dictatorial, arbitrary, absolute, domineering, overpowering, overbearing, bullying, high-handed, authoritarian, totalitarian, imperious, magisterial, oppressive, repressive, coercive, harsh, ruthless, unjust, unreasonable, strict, severe, cruel, brutal, savage, inhuman. OPPOSITE: democratic.

tyrannize *verb* oppress, suppress, repress, crush, intimidate, terrorize, bully, subjugate, dictate, dominate, domineer, browbeat, coerce.

tyranny *noun* **1** (*he ruled by tyranny*) dictatorship, despotism, autocracy, absolutism, authoritarianism, totalitarianism. OPPOSITE: democracy. **2** (*the tyranny of their rule*) despotism, authoritarianism, absolutism, arbitrariness, imperiousness, high-handedness, oppressiveness, oppression, bullying, coercion, ruthlessness, harshness, strictness, severity, brutality, cruelty, inhumanity, injustice, unjustness, unreasonableness.

tyrant *noun* dictator, despot, autocrat, absolutist, authoritarian, oppressor, bully, martinet, slave-driver, taskmaster.

ubiquitous *adj* omnipresent, everywhere, all over the place, universal, global, ever-present, common, frequent. OPPOSITE: rare.

ugly *adj* **1** (*an ugly building*) unsightly, unattractive, plain, unlovely, unprepossessing, ill-favoured, hideous, revolting, repulsive, grotesque, monstrous. OPPOSITE: beautiful. **2** (*an ugly disposition*) unpleasant, disagreeable, nasty, horrible, objectionable, offensive, disgusting, revolting, repulsive, loathsome, obnoxious, vile. OPPOSITE: pleasant. **3** (*the crowd turned ugly*) menacing, threatening, ominous, sinister, dangerous, hostile, nasty, unpleasant, ill-natured, spiteful, angry, bad-tempered, malevolent, evil. OPPOSITE: friendly.

ulcer *noun* sore, abscess, boil, pustule, fester, gathering, ulceration.

ulterior *adj* hidden, concealed, covert, undisclosed, unrevealed, undivulged, unexpressed, secret, private, personal. OPPOSITE: overt.

ultimate *adj* **1** (*their ultimate destination*) final, last, terminal, endmost, furthest, extreme, conclusive, decisive, eventual. OPPOSITE: first. **2** (*the ultimate sacrifice*) utmost, extreme, maximum, most, supreme, paramount, greatest, highest, top. OPPOSITE: least. **3** (*ultimate reality*) basic, fundamental, elementary, primary.
➤ *noun* utmost, extreme, height, peak, summit, culmination, last word (*inf*), consummation, perfection, epitome, nonpareil.

ultimately *adv* **1** (*they will ultimately succeed*) finally, in the end, at last, eventually, in the long run, sooner or later. **2** (*it is ultimately a question of money*) basically, fundamentally, primarily, at heart, deep down.

ultra *adj* extreme, radical, immoderate, inordinate, excessive, fanatical. OPPOSITE: moderate.

umbrage *noun* (*take umbrage*) take offence, be insulted, be piqued, be miffed (*inf*), be indignant, get in a huff (*inf*), take exception, resent, begrudge, be upset, be put

out, be displeased, be annoyed, be angry, be in high dudgeon.

umpire *noun* referee, ref (*inf*), adjudicator, judge, arbiter, arbitrator, moderator, mediator.
➤ *verb* referee, ref (*inf*), adjudicate, judge, arbitrate, moderate, mediate.

umpteen *adj* numerous, very many, thousands, millions, countless, innumerable. OPPOSITE: few.

unabashed *adj* unashamed, unembarrassed, unblushing, brazen, bold, undaunted, undismayed, confident. OPPOSITE: abashed.

unable *adj* incapable, powerless, impotent, ineffectual, incompetent, unqualified, unfit, not equal to, not up to (*inf*). OPPOSITE: able.

unabridged *adj* complete, full, whole, entire, intact, uncut, unexpurgated, unshortened, uncondensed. OPPOSITE: abridged.

unacceptable *adj* intolerable, insupportable, objectionable, offensive, disagreeable, undesirable, unwelcome, unpopular, inadmissible, unsuitable, improper, unsatisfactory, inadequate. OPPOSITE: acceptable.

unaccommodating *adj* unobliging, uncooperative, inflexible, unbending, intransigent, uncompromising, awkward, difficult, stubborn, obstinate. OPPOSITE: obliging.

unaccompanied *adj* solitary, alone, on one's own, by oneself, lone, solo, unattended, unescorted. OPPOSITE: accompanied.

unaccountable *adj* inexplicable, unexplainable, incomprehensible, unfathomable, insoluble, puzzling, baffling, mysterious, odd, peculiar, strange, curious, extraordinary, remarkable. OPPOSITE: understandable.

unaccustomed *adj* **1** (*unaccustomed to driving in heavy traffic*) unused, unfamiliar, unacquainted, inexperienced, unpractised, unversed. OPPOSITE: used. **2** (*unaccustomed behaviour*) unusual, uncommon, out of the ordinary, extraordinary, remarkable, strange, unfamiliar, uncharacteristic, unexpected, unprecedented, new, different. OPPOSITE: usual.

unadorned *adj* plain, simple, stark, unvarnished, unembellished, unornamented, undecorated. OPPOSITE: ornate.

unadulterated *adj* pure, unmixed, undiluted, real, genuine. OPPOSITE: mixed.

unaffected *adj* 1 (*an unaffected manner*) natural, unpretentious, simple, plain, unsophisticated, artless, guileless, ingenuous, naive, sincere, honest, genuine, true, real, unfeigned, unpretended. OPPOSITE: artificial. 2 (*unaffected by what had happened*) unchanged, unaltered, untouched, unmoved, unconcerned, indifferent, unresponsive, unfeeling, impervious, proof. OPPOSITE: changed.

unafraid *adj* fearless, brave, courageous, intrepid, dauntless, undaunted, bold, confident. OPPOSITE: frightened.

unaided *adj* unassisted, single handed, solo, alone, on one's own, by oneself. OPPOSITE: assisted.

unanimity *noun* agreement, concurrence, like-mindedness, accord, consensus, unity, unison, concert, harmony, concord. OPPOSITE: dissent.

unanimous *adj* agreed, agreeing, like-minded, accordant, concordant, harmonious, in harmony, concerted, united, solid, uniform, consistent. OPPOSITE: disagreeing.

unanimously *adv* without exception, as one, in concert, of one mind, with one voice, by common consent, nem con, unopposed, without opposition.

unanswerable *adj* 1 (*an unanswerable case*) irrefutable, incontestable, undeniable, unarguable, incontrovertible, indisputable, conclusive, absolute. OPPOSITE: disputable. 2 (*an unanswerable question*) insoluble, unsolvable, unexplainable, inexplicable. OPPOSITE: solvable.

unappetizing *adj* unappealing, uninviting, unattractive, off-putting, unpleasant, disagreeable, unsavoury, unpalatable, tasteless, insipid, vapid, uninteresting. OPPOSITE: appetizing.

unapproachable *adj* 1 (*her father was unapproachable*) aloof, standoffish, distant, remote, reserved, withdrawn, uncommunicative, unresponsive, cold, chilly, unsociable, unfriendly. OPPOSITE: friendly. 2 (*living in unapproachable places*) remote, distant, inaccessible, out-of-the-way, off the beaten track (*inf*), out of reach, ungetatable (*inf*). OPPOSITE: accessible.

unarmed *adj* weaponless, defenceless, unprotected, unguarded, vulnerable, pregnable, exposed, open, helpless, weak. OPPOSITE: armed.

unasked *adj* uninvited, unbidden, unsolicited, unrequested, unwanted, voluntary, spontaneous. OPPOSITE: requested.

unassailable *adj* 1 (*an unassailable position*) impregnable, invulnerable, invincible, inviolable, strong, secure. OPPOSITE: vulnerable. 2 (*unassailable evidence*) undeniable, irrefutable, indisputable, unquestionable, incontestable, incontrovertible, absolute, certain, sure, positive. OPPOSITE: questionable.

unassuming *adj* modest, self-effacing, humble, meek,

retiring, reticent, reserved, shy, bashful, diffident, unassertive, backward in coming forward (*inf*), unobtrusive, unostentatious, demure, unpretentious, unaffected, natural, simple. OPPOSITE: bold.

unattached *adj* 1 (*an unattached line*) loose, detached, separate, free, at liberty. OPPOSITE: fastened. 2 (*invited a few unattached males*) single, unmarried, unwed, partnerless, available, free, footloose and fancy-free, uncommitted, independent, autonomous. OPPOSITE: attached.

unattended *adj* 1 (*unattended children*) unaccompanied, unescorted, unsupervised, alone, solitary, on one's own, by oneself. OPPOSITE: accompanied. 2 (*an unattended garden*) neglected, untended, ignored, disregarded, forsaken, abandoned. OPPOSITE: looked after. 3 (*unattended baggage*) unwatched, unguarded, unsupervised, abandoned, forsaken, forgotten, left alone, by itself. OPPOSITE: attended.

unattractive *adj* unappealing, uninviting, off-putting, plain, unprepossessing, unlovely, ill-favoured, ugly, unsightly, unappetizing, unsavoury, undesirable, unwelcome, unpleasant, disagreeable. OPPOSITE: attractive.

unauthorized *adj* unofficial, illegal, unlawful, illicit, illegitimate, unlicensed, uncertified, unaccredited, unapproved, unsanctioned, unwarranted, prohibited, forbidden. OPPOSITE: authorized.

unavailing *adj* vain, futile, useless, pointless, ineffectual, ineffective, fruitless, unproductive, abortive, failed, unsuccessful. OPPOSITE: successful.

unavoidable *adj* inevitable, inescapable, ineluctable, inexorable, necessary, required, compulsory, obligatory, mandatory, fated, destined, certain, sure. OPPOSITE: avoidable.

unaware *adj* ignorant, unknowing, unacquainted, unfamiliar, unenlightened, uninformed, in the dark (*inf*), unconscious, oblivious, unmindful, heedless, blind, deaf, unsuspecting, unprepared. OPPOSITE: aware.

unawares *adv* 1 (*caught her unawares*) unexpectedly, by surprise, off guard, unprepared, on the hop (*inf*), with one's trousers down (*inf*), suddenly, abruptly, without warning. 2 (*landed unawares on enemy territory*) accidentally, unintentionally, by mistake, inadvertently, unwittingly, unknowingly, unconsciously, without noticing. OPPOSITE: deliberately.

unbalanced *adj* 1 (*an unbalanced display*) asymmetrical, lopsided, unstable, uneven, unequal, disproportionate. OPPOSITE: even. 2 (*his mind was unbalanced*) unsound, irrational, unhinged, deranged, disturbed, demented, insane, lunatic, mad, crazed, crazy (*inf*), barmy (*inf*), round the bend (*inf*). OPPOSITE: sane. 3 (*unbalanced reporting*) biased, prejudiced, bigoted, one-sided, partial, partisan, unfair, unjust. OPPOSITE: unbiased.

unbearable *adj* insufferable, insupportable, intolerable, unacceptable, unendurable, excruciating, too much (*inf*), more than flesh and blood can stand (*inf*), the limit (*inf*), the last straw (*inf*). OPPOSITE: bearable.

unbeatable *adj* invincible, unconquerable, indomitable, unsurpassable, matchless.

unbecoming *adj* 1 (*unbecoming behaviour*) unseemly,

indecorous, improper, indelicate, inappropriate, unsuitable, unfit, unfitting, unbefitting, ungentlemanly, unladylike, **2** (*an unbecoming hat*) unattractive, unflattering, unsightly. OPPOSITE: becoming.

unbelief *noun* nonbelief, disbelief, incredulity, doubt, scepticism, distrust, mistrust, agnosticism, atheism. OPPOSITE: belief.

unbelievable *adj* incredible, beyond belief, far-fetched, implausible, unconvincing, unlikely, improbable, impossible, inconceivable, unthinkable, amazing, astonishing, astounding, staggering. OPPOSITE: credible.

unbend *verb* relax, unwind, loosen up, let one's hair down (*inf*).

unbending *adj* inflexible, stiff, rigid, unyielding, firm, resolute, intractable, intransigent, formal, severe, strict, stern, harsh, tough, uncompromising, unrelenting. OPPOSITE: flexible.

unbiased *adj* unprejudiced, unbigoted, impartial, disinterested, dispassionate, objective, neutral, nonpartisan, fair, just, equitable, even-handed. OPPOSITE: biased.

unbidden *adj* **1** (*unbidden assistance*) spontaneous, voluntary, willing, free, unforced, uncompelled. OPPOSITE: forced. **2** (*unbidden criticism*) uninvited, unasked, unwelcome, unwanted, unsolicited, unrequested. OPPOSITE: welcome.

unbind *verb* loose, free, release, let go, untie, unfetter, unchain, unshackle, unfasten, undo. OPPOSITE: bind.

unblemished *adj* perfect, flawless, faultless, immaculate, spotless, clean, pure, unsullied, untarnished, unspotted, stainless, unimpeachable, irreproachable. OPPOSITE: flawed.

unblinking *adj* fearless, unafraid, unflinching, unshrinking, steady, unfaltering, unwavering, cool, calm, composed, unemotional, impassive. OPPOSITE: fearful.

unblushing *adj* shameless, immodest, bold, brazen, unashamed, unabashed, unembarrassed. OPPOSITE: ashamed.

unborn *adj* embryonic, in utero, expected, awaited, future, to come, subsequent, succeeding.

unbosom *verb* unburden, lay bare, reveal, disclose, divulge, let out, pour out, tell all (*inf*), confess, make a clean breast of it (*inf*), admit, confide. OPPOSITE: suppress.

unbounded *adj* boundless, unlimited, limitless, illimitable, vast, immense, immeasurable, infinite, interminable, endless, unrestricted, unconfined, unrestrained, uncontrolled, unchecked, unbridled, immoderate. OPPOSITE: limited.

unbreakable *adj* indestructible, infrangible, shatterproof, toughened, durable. OPPOSITE: fragile.

unbridled *adj* unrestrained, uncontrolled, unchecked, uninhibited, wild, unruly, rampant, immoderate, intemperate, wanton, profligate. OPPOSITE: restrained.

unbroken *adj* **1** (*an unbroken plate*) intact, sound, undamaged, unharmed, whole, complete, entire, integral. OPPOSITE: broken. **2** (*unbroken sleep*) uninterrupted, continuous, endless, unending, nonstop, ceaseless, unceasing, incessant, constant, unremitting.

OPPOSITE: interrupted. **3** (*an unbroken record*) unbeaten, unsurpassed, unrivalled, unequalled, unmatched. OPPOSITE: beaten. **4** (*an unbroken horse*) untamed, wild. OPPOSITE: tame.

unburden *verb* unload, disencumber, unbosom, lay bare, expose, open, reveal, disclose, divulge, tell all (*inf*), confess, come clean (*inf*), admit, acknowledge, confide. OPPOSITE: suppress.

uncalled-for *adj* unnecessary, needless, gratuitous, unjustified, unwarranted, unmerited, undeserved, unfair, unjust, unprovoked, unprompted, unsolicited, unsought, unasked, uninvited, unwelcome, unwanted. OPPOSITE: necessary.

uncanny *adj* **1** (*an uncanny sound*) strange, mysterious, odd, weird, queer, bizarre, eerie, creepy (*inf*), ghostly, spooky (*inf*), unnatural, supernatural, unearthly. **2** (*an uncanny coincidence*) extraordinary, remarkable, striking, exceptional, astounding, astonishing, amazing, incredible. OPPOSITE: ordinary.

uncaring *adj* indifferent, unconcerned, unmoved, unfeeling, cold, callous, unsympathetic. OPPOSITE: compassionate.

unceasing *adj* ceaseless, incessant, constant, unremitting, continuous, uninterrupted, nonstop, endless, unending, never-ending, interminable, continual, perpetual, eternal, everlasting. OPPOSITE: intermittent.

unceremonious *adj* **1** (*an unceremonious gathering*) informal, casual, natural, simple, relaxed, easy, laid back (*inf*). OPPOSITE: formal. **2** (*her unceremonious dismissal*) sudden, hasty, hurried, undignified, abrupt, brusque, curt, rude, impolite, discourteous, unmannerly.

uncertain *adj* **1** (*uncertain what to do*) doubtful, dubious, unsure, irresolute, undecided, unresolved, ambivalent, in two minds (*inf*), hesitant, wavering, vacillating, unclear, vague, hazy. OPPOSITE: decided. **2** (*the future is uncertain*) undecided, unresolved, unsettled, undetermined, pending, in the balance, up in the air (*inf*), unpredictable, unforeseeable, in the lap of the gods (*inf*), indefinite, unconfirmed, speculative, conjectural, unknown. OPPOSITE: settled. **3** (*an uncertain method*) risky, chancy, iffy (*inf*), precarious, questionable, unreliable, unpredictable, erratic, capricious, changeable, variable, fitful, inconstant. OPPOSITE: sure.

uncertainty *noun* **1** (*expressed his uncertainty*) doubt, misgiving, qualm, scepticism, doubtfulness, unsureness, lack of confidence, irresolution, indecision, ambivalence, hesitancy, vagueness. OPPOSITE: certainty. **2** (*the uncertainty of the method*) riskiness, chanciness, unreliability, unpredictability, capriciousness, changeability, variability, inconstancy. OPPOSITE: reliability.

unchangeable *adj* unalterable, invariable, immutable, changeless, fixed, established, firm, stable, steady, permanent, enduring, abiding, lasting, eternal. OPPOSITE: changeable.

unchanging *adj* lasting, abiding, enduring, eternal, perpetual, constant, same, unvarying, changeless, unchangeable. OPPOSITE: transitory.

uncharitable *adj* unkind, unfeeling, insensitive,

unchristian, mean, ungenerous, selfish, cruel, ruthless, harsh, severe, stern, hard, unforgiving, merciless, unsympathetic, uncompassionate. OPPOSITE: charitable.

uncharted *adj* unmapped, unsurveyed, unexplored, unknown, unfamiliar, strange, foreign, alien.

unchaste *adj* impure, defiled, loose, wanton, promiscuous, indecent, immoral, depraved, dissolute, lewd, lascivious, licentious. OPPOSITE: chaste.

uncivil *adj* rude, discourteous, impolite, unmannerly, ill-mannered, ill-bred, impudent, impertinent, disrespectful, ungracious, surly, brusque, curt, gruff, boorish, churlish, uncouth. OPPOSITE: civil.

uncivilized *adj* uncouth, vulgar, coarse, rough, unrefined, unpolished, uncultured, uncultivated, uneducated, unenlightened, unsophisticated, philistine, primitive, barbaric, barbarian, barbarous, brutish, savage, wild. OPPOSITE: civilized.

unclean *adj* **1** (*unclean water*) dirty, filthy, soiled, foul, sullied, defiled, contaminated, polluted, tainted, adulterated, impure. OPPOSITE: clean. **2** (*unclean thoughts*) immoral, impure, unchaste, corrupt, depraved, degenerate, lewd, lascivious, licentious, sinful, bad, wicked, evil. OPPOSITE: pure.

unclear *adj* vague, indistinct, hazy, foggy, dim, obscure, indefinite, ambiguous, equivocal, uncertain, unsure. OPPOSITE: clear.

uncomfortable *adj* **1** (*felt uncomfortable about it*) uneasy, ill-at-ease, awkward, embarrassed, disturbed, troubled, distressed, upset, anxious, worried, nervous, tense, on edge (*inf*). OPPOSITE: relaxed. **2** (*working in uncomfortable conditions*) disagreeable, unpleasant, hard, rough, cramped, ill-fitting, painful, irritating. OPPOSITE: comfortable.

uncommon *adj* unusual, out of the ordinary, unfamiliar, strange, odd, curious, queer, rare, infrequent, scarce, few and far between (*inf*), thin on the ground (*inf*), unique, singular, extraordinary, remarkable, striking, exceptional, noteworthy, notable, outstanding. OPPOSITE: common.

uncommonly *adv* exceptionally, remarkably, singularly, peculiarly, unusually, particularly, extremely.

uncommunicative *adj* reserved, reticent, shy, quiet, silent, taciturn, tight-lipped, secretive, close, unforthcoming, unresponsive, withdrawn, retiring, unsociable, distant, remote, aloof, standoffish. OPPOSITE: talkative.

uncompromising *adj* inflexible, unyielding, unbending, rigid, stiff, firm, obstinate, stubborn, obdurate, intransigent, inexorable, implacable, determined, resolute, dogged, tenacious. OPPOSITE: flexible.

unconcerned *adj* indifferent, uninterested, apathetic, uninvolved, dispassionate, detached, remote, aloof, uncaring, unsympathetic, unmoved, unaffected, untroubled, unworried, oblivious, nonchalant, insouciant, carefree, blithe. OPPOSITE: concerned.

unconditional *adj* total, complete, full, utter, downright, out-and-out, thoroughgoing, absolute, categorical, definite, positive, unqualified, unreserved, unrestricted, unlimited. OPPOSITE: conditional.

unconnected *adj* **1** (*the two incidents are unconnnected*) separate, detached, independent, unrelated, unassociated. OPPOSITE: connected. **2** (*an unconnected style of writing*) disconnected, disjointed, incoherent, rambling, diffuse. OPPOSITE: coherent.

unconquerable *adj* invincible, indomitable, insuperable, insurmountable, overpowering, overwhelming, unbeatable, undefeatable. OPPOSITE: weak.

unconscionable *adj* **1** (*an unconscionable villain*) unscrupulous, unprincipled, amoral, immoral, unethical, dishonourable. OPPOSITE: principled. **2** (*an unconscionable number of defects*) unreasonable, excessive, immoderate, inordinate, extreme, outrageous, preposterous, unpardonable, inexcusable, unwarrantable, unjustifiable. OPPOSITE: reasonable.

unconscious *adj* **1** (*lying unconscious on the floor*) insensible, senseless, knocked out, out (*inf*), out cold (*inf*), comatose, asleep, dead to the world (*inf*), stunned, dazed, concussed. OPPOSITE: conscious. **2** (*unconscious of our presence*) unaware, oblivious, blind, deaf, insensitive, unmindful, heedless, ignorant, unknowing, incognizant. OPPOSITE: aware. **3** (*an unconscious reaction*) automatic, involuntary, reflex, instinctive. OPPOSITE: voluntary. **4** (*an unconscious desire*) subliminal, subconscious, latent, repressed, innate, inherent. **5** (*an unconscious insult*) unintentional, unintended, accidental, inadvertent, unwitting, unthinking. OPPOSITE: deliberate.

uncontrollable *adj* ungovernable, unmanageable, wild, unruly, disorderly, intractable, recalcitrant, refractory, irrepressible, mad, frantic, raging, violent. OPPOSITE: controllable.

unconventional *adj* unorthodox, unusual, uncommon, unfamiliar, unwonted, abnormal, atypical, irregular, informal, original, individual, singular, peculiar, eccentric, bizarre, odd, offbeat (*inf*), way-out (*sl*), alternative, fringe, nonconformist, bohemian, avant-garde, experimental. OPPOSITE: conventional.

unconvincing *adj* weak, feeble, flimsy, lame, dubious, doubtful, suspect, questionable, inconclusive, improbable, unlikely, implausible. OPPOSITE: convincing.

uncoordinated *adj* clumsy, awkward, maladroit, gauche, inept, bungling, bumbling, all thumbs (*inf*), butter-fingered (*inf*), ungainly, graceless, inelegant, lumbering, clodhopping, blundering, like a bull in a china shop (*inf*). OPPOSITE: graceful.

uncouth *adj* crude, coarse, vulgar, rude, rough, rugged, loutish, oafish, boorish, churlish, impolite, discourteous, uncivil, ill-bred, ill-mannered, uncivilized, uncultivated, uncultured, unrefined, unpolished, unsophisticated, provincial. OPPOSITE: refined.

uncover *verb* bare, strip, unwrap, open, expose, show, reveal, disclose, divulge, unveil, unmask, unearth, discover, bring to light. OPPOSITE: cover.

unction *noun* unguent, oil, lotion, ointment, salve, balm.

unctuous *adj* **1** (*unctuous praise*) insincere, gushing, effusive, smooth, glib, suave, urbane, sycophantic, servile, fawning, ingratiating, flattering. OPPOSITE:

sincere. **2** (*an unctuous substance*) oily, oleaginous, greasy, fatty.

undaunted *adj* undismayed, undeterred, unbowed, unflinching, unshrinking, unfaltering, unwavering, steadfast, resolute, intrepid, bold, brave, courageous, indomitable, dauntless, fearless, unafraid. OPPOSITE: afraid.

undeceive *verb* correct, put right, set straight, enlighten, disabuse, disillusion, disenchant. OPPOSITE: deceive.

undecided *adj* **1** (*undecided about her career*) uncertain, unsure, doubtful, dubious, irresolute, indecisive, hesitant, wavering, vacillating, unresolved, ambivalent, torn, in two minds (*inf*). OPPOSITE: sure. **2** (*the matter was left undecided*) unsettled, unresolved, pending, in the balance, up in the air (*inf*), open, moot, undetermined, indefinite. OPPOSITE: settled.

undefiled *adj* pure, chaste, virginal, clean, immaculate, spotless, unspotted, stainless, untarnished, unblemished, flawless, clear, unsullied, unpolluted, uncontaminated. OPPOSITE: defiled.

undefined *adj* shadowy, formless, indefinite, ill-defined, vague, nebulous, hazy, blurred, imprecise, inexact, indistinct, dim, unclear, obscure, indeterminate, unspecified, nonspecific. OPPOSITE: clear.

undemonstrative *adj* restrained, reserved, reticent, unemotional, unaffected, formal, stiff, distant, remote, aloof, unresponsive, uncommunicative. OPPOSITE: demonstrative.

undeniable *adj* unquestionable, indisputable, incontestable, incontrovertible, irrefutable, indubitable, definite, positive, certain, sure, proven, obvious, evident, manifest, patent. OPPOSITE: questionable.

under *prep* **1** (*under the table*) underneath, beneath, below, lower than. OPPOSITE: over. **2** (*working under the general manager*) below, lower than, inferior to, subordinate to, junior to, reporting to, subject to, controlled by. OPPOSITE: above. **3** (*at temperatures under 20 degrees*) lower than, below, less than, smaller than. **4** (*living under martial law*) subject to, liable to, bound by, governed by, controlled by.
➤ *adv* down, downwards, underneath, beneath, below.
➤ *adj* subordinate, junior, secondary, auxiliary, deputy, vice.

underclothes *pl noun* underwear, undergarments, underclothing, underlinen, lingerie, undies (*inf*), smalls (*inf*), unmentionables (*inf*).

undercover *adj* secret, hush-hush (*inf*), hidden, concealed, private, confidential, covert, surreptitious, furtive, clandestine, underground. OPPOSITE: public.

undercurrent *noun* **1** (*an undercurrent in the river*) undertow, underflow. **2** (*undercurrents of dissatisfaction*) undertone, overtone, hint, suggestion, murmur, whisper, feeling, sense, aura, atmosphere, trend, drift.

underdog *noun* loser, victim, scapegoat, fall guy (*inf*).

underestimate *verb* miscalculate, misjudge, underrate, undervalue, misprize, hold cheap, sell short (*inf*), disparage, deprecate, belittle, minimize, play down. OPPOSITE: overestimate.

undergo *verb* suffer, endure, bear, stand, tolerate, sustain, withstand, experience, go through, submit to, be subjected to, put up with.

underground *adj* **1** (*an underground passage*) subterranean, buried, sunken, below ground. **2** (*an underground organization*) secret, clandestine, undercover, covert, surreptitious, subversive, revolutionary, radical, unofficial, unorthodox, illegal.
➤ *adv* below ground, into hiding.
➤ *noun* **1** (*travel by underground*) metro, subway, tube (*inf*). **2** (*members of the underground*) resistance, opposition.

undergrowth *noun* thicket, brush, scrub, ground cover, underwood, brushwood, underbrush.

underhand *adj* underhanded, sly, crafty, cunning, scheming, devious, sneaky, stealthy, surreptitious, furtive, unscrupulous, unethical, immoral, dishonourable, dirty, unfair, below the belt (*inf*), fraudulent, dishonest, crooked (*inf*), shady (*inf*). OPPOSITE: above-board.

underline *verb* underscore, italicize, stress, emphasize, accent, accentuate, point up, highlight. OPPOSITE: play down.

underling *noun* menial, lackey, flunky, minion, servant, hireling, subordinate, junior, inferior, nobody, nonentity. OPPOSITE: master.

underlying *adj* basic, fundamental, elementary, primary, root, latent, hidden, concealed.

undermine *verb* **1** (*undermine morale*) sap, weaken, impair, damage, erode, wear away, subvert, sabotage, ruin. OPPOSITE: strengthen. **2** (*undermine the fortifications*) tunnel under, burrow under, dig, excavate, mine.

underneath *prep* under, beneath, below, lower than. OPPOSITE: above.
➤ *noun* bottom, underside. OPPOSITE: top.

undernourished *adj* malnourished, underfed, half-starved, underweight, anorexic.

underprivileged *adj* deprived, disadvantaged, poor, needy, impoverished, destitute. OPPOSITE: wealthy.

underrate *verb* underestimate, undervalue, misprize, disparage, belittle. OPPOSITE: overrate.

undersized *adj* stunted, atrophied, underdeveloped, underweight, puny, runtish, dwarf, miniature, small, little, tiny, minute. OPPOSITE: oversized.

understand *verb* **1** (*didn't understand the instructions*) comprehend, apprehend, fathom, penetrate, figure out, make out, grasp, catch on (*inf*), cotton on (*inf*), twig (*inf*), follow, get (*inf*), tumble to (*inf*), perceive, discern, see, learn, take in, assimilate, get one's head round (*inf*). **2** (*I understand your concern*) appreciate, realize, recognize, acknowledge, accept, sympathize with, empathize with, commiserate with, pity. **3** (*I understand you wish to leave*) believe, hear, gather, conclude, suppose, assume, presume.

understanding *noun* **1** (*an understanding of how it works*) comprehension, apprehension, grasp, knowledge, awareness, perception. OPPOSITE: ignorance. **2** (*matters beyond our understanding*) intelligence, intellect, mind, brains, reason, sense, knowledge, wisdom, perception, discernment, insight, appreciation, realization. **3** (*my understanding of the situation*) interpretation, judgement, opinion, view, belief, idea, impression, feeling. **4** (*we have an understanding*) agreement, bargain, pact, arrangement.

➤ *adj* sympathetic, compassionate, tender, kind, considerate, thoughtful, patient, tolerant, forbearing, forgiving. OPPOSITE: intolerant.

understate *verb* minimize, make light of, play down. OPPOSITE: overstate.

undertake *verb* **1** (*undertake the task*) take on, shoulder, assume, embark on, begin, start, commence, set about, tackle. OPPOSITE: achieve. **2** (*undertake to pay the running costs*) agree, promise, pledge, vow, swear, guarantee, engage, contract, covenant.

undertaker *noun* funeral director, mortician.

undertaking *noun* **1** (*a dangerous undertaking*) venture, project, enterprise, affair, business, task, mission, campaign, effort, endeavour. **2** (*an undertaking not to mention his name*) agreement, promise, pledge, vow, word, assurance, guarantee.

undertone *noun* **1** (*remarked in an undertone*) murmur, whisper, low voice. OPPOSITE: shout. **2** (*with sarcastic undertones*) undercurrent, connotation, nuance, overtone, hint, intimation, suggestion, insinuation, trace, touch, tinge, flavour, aura, atmosphere.

undervalue *verb* underestimate, underrate, misprize, set little store by, hold cheap, sell short (*inf*), disparage, deprecate, belittle, minimize. OPPOSITE: overestimate.

underwater *adj* subaquatic, subaqueous, submarine, undersea, submerged, immersed.

underwear *noun* underclothes, underclothing, undergarments, underlinen, lingerie, undies (*inf*), smalls (*inf*), unmentionables (*inf*).

underwrite *verb* **1** (*underwrite a document*) endorse, sign, countersign, initial. **2** (*underwrite a project*) approve, sanction, authorize, endorse, guarantee, insure, back, support, sponsor, fund, finance, subsidize, subscribe to, contribute to.

undesirable *adj* unwelcome, unwanted, unenviable, unattractive, uninviting, unappetizing, unsavoury, unpleasant, disagreeable, nasty, offensive, objectionable, obnoxious, unacceptable, unsuitable, inappropriate. OPPOSITE: desirable.

undeveloped *adj* developing, immature, embryonic, inchoate, rudimentary, unformed, potential, latent, underdeveloped. OPPOSITE: mature.

undignified *adj* unseemly, unbecoming, indecorous, improper, inelegant, ungainly, inappropriate, unsuitable, infra dig (*inf*). OPPOSITE: dignified.

undisciplined *adj* wild, unruly, disorderly, wilful, wayward, obstreperous, recalcitrant, refractory, untrained, unschooled, unrestrained, uncontrolled, disorganized, unsystematic. OPPOSITE: disciplined.

undisguised *adj* open, overt, evident, obvious, plain, manifest, patent, unconcealed, transparent, naked, unadorned, genuine, sincere. OPPOSITE: veiled.

undisputed *adj* unchallenged, uncontested, undoubted, unquestioned, recognized, acknowledged, accepted, certain, sure, indisputable, unquestionable, incontrovertible, undeniable. OPPOSITE: debatable.

undistinguished *adj* ordinary, commonplace,

everyday, run-of-the-mill, unexceptional, unremarkable, nothing special (*inf*), nothing to write home about (*inf*), indifferent, mediocre, so-so (*inf*), unimpressive, not up to much (*inf*), not much cop (*inf*). OPPOSITE: exceptional.

undisturbed *adj* calm, tranquil, serene, placid, composed, collected, unruffled, unperturbed, untroubled. OPPOSITE: agitated.

undivided *adj* full, complete, total, entire, whole, intact, unbroken, solid, united, unanimous, wholehearted, exclusive, dedicated, concentrated. OPPOSITE: divided.

undo *verb* **1** (*undo the package*) untie, open, unwrap, free, release, loose, unwind, unravel, disentangle, disengage, unlock, unscrew. OPPOSITE: do up. **2** (*undoing her skirt*) unfasten, unbutton, unhook, unzip, unbuckle, unlace. OPPOSITE: fasten. **3** (*can't undo the mistake*) reverse, neutralize, counteract, cancel, invalidate, nullify, annul, repeal, rescind, revoke. **4** (*undoing a lifetime's work*) ruin, wreck, destroy, shatter, crush, annihilate, obliterate.

undoing *noun* ruin, ruination, destruction, downfall, collapse, defeat, overthrow.

undoubted *adj* certain, sure, obvious, evident, undisputed, unchallenged, unquestioned, indubitable, indisputable, unquestionable, incontrovertible, undeniable, accepted, acknowledged. OPPOSITE: dubious.

undoubtedly *adv* doubtless, without doubt, certainly, surely, assuredly, indubitably, definitely, of course. OPPOSITE: perhaps.

undress *verb* disrobe, unclothe, divest, strip. OPPOSITE: dress.

➤ *noun* nakedness, nudity, deshabille.

undue *adj* excessive, immoderate, inordinate, extreme, disproportionate, unnecessary, uncalled-for, unwarranted, unjustified, undeserved, unmerited, unreasonable, inappropriate, unseemly, improper. OPPOSITE: moderate.

undulate *verb* roll, ripple, heave, surge, swell, billow.

unduly *adv* excessively, immoderately, inordinately, disproportionately, overmuch, overly, unnecessarily, unreasonably. OPPOSITE: moderately.

undying *adj* immortal, deathless, eternal, everlasting, unending, endless, imperishable, indestructible, permanent, lasting, abiding, enduring, unfading, undiminished. OPPOSITE: transient.

unearth *verb* excavate, dig up, exhume, disinter, find, discover, uncover, expose, reveal, disclose. OPPOSITE: bury.

unearthly *adj* **1** (*unearthly beings*) weird, strange, eerie, uncanny, ghostly, spectral, spooky (*inf*), supernatural, preternatural, extraterrestrial, otherworldly. OPPOSITE: earthly. **2** (*at an unearthly hour*) unreasonable, ungodly (*inf*), unholy (*inf*), outrageous, preposterous, ridiculous, absurd, unheard-of. OPPOSITE: reasonable.

uneasy *adj* **1** (*felt uneasy in his presence*) uncomfortable, ill-at-ease, awkward, constrained, strained, tense, keyed up (*inf*), edgy, on edge (*inf*), nervous, anxious, worried, apprehensive, upset, troubled, agitated, disturbed, perturbed, restless, restive. OPPOSITE: relaxed. **2** (*an* *uneasy truce*) precarious, insecure, unstable. OPPOSITE: stable.

uneconomic *adj* unprofitable, unremunerative, uncommercial, lossmaking, nonprofitmaking. OPPOSITE: viable.

uneducated *adj* ignorant, illiterate, unschooled, untaught, untutored, uncultured, uncultivated, unenlightened, benighted, unlettered, unread. OPPOSITE: educated.

unemotional *adj* cool, cold, frigid, unfeeling, unresponsive, impassive, unmoved, detached, phlegmatic, undemonstrative, reserved, restrained, self-controlled. OPPOSITE: emotional.

unemployed *adj* jobless, out of work, unwaged, on the dole (*inf*), laid off, redundant, idle, unoccupied. OPPOSITE: employed.

unending *adj* endless, interminable, never-ending, nonstop, unceasing, ceaseless, incessant, continuous, uninterrupted, unremitting, relentless, continual, constant, perpetual, eternal, everlasting. OPPOSITE: brief.

unenthusiastic *adj* apathetic, half-hearted, lukewarm, unmoved, unimpressed, bored, uninterested, indifferent, neutral. OPPOSITE: enthusiastic.

unenviable *adj* undesirable, unpleasant, disagreeable, nasty, difficult, dangerous, thankless. OPPOSITE: pleasant.

unequal *adj* **1** (*unequal amounts*) uneven, unbalanced, asymmetrical, lopsided, disproportionate, unmatched, different, disparate, unlike, dissimilar. OPPOSITE: even. **2** (*unequal treatment*) unfair, unjust, inequitable, discriminatory, biased, prejudiced. OPPOSITE: equal. **3** (*unequal to the task*) incapable, unable, inadequate, insufficient, found wanting, not up to (*inf*), unfit, unsuitable, not cut out for (*inf*). OPPOSITE: adequate.

unequalled *adj* peerless, matchless, unmatched, unparalleled, unrivalled, unsurpassed, inimitable, incomparable, unique, transcendent, supreme, paramount. OPPOSITE: inferior.

unequivocal *adj* unambiguous, explicit, clear, clear-cut, crystal-clear, plain, unmistakable, obvious, evident, manifest, patent, unquestionable, indisputable, indubitable, undeniable, sure, certain, positive, categorical, absolute, unqualified, direct, straightforward, point-blank. OPPOSITE: ambiguous.

unerring *adj* sure, certain, exact, accurate, precise, true, perfect, faultless, unfailing, infallible. OPPOSITE: faulty.

unethical *adj* immoral, unprofessional, unscrupulous, unprincipled, dishonourable, dirty, unfair, underhand, dishonest, corrupt, bad, wrong, sinful, evil. OPPOSITE: ethical.

uneven *adj* **1** (*uneven ground*) rough, rugged, lumpy, bumpy, hilly, undulating. OPPOSITE: flat. **2** (*uneven columns*) unequal, odd, unbalanced, asymmetrical, lopsided, disproportionate, different, disparate. OPPOSITE: even. **3** (*an uneven contest*) unfair, unjust, inequitable, ill-matched, unequal, one-sided. OPPOSITE: equal. **4** (*an uneven performance*) irregular, inconsistent, variable, varying, fluctuating, fitful, spasmodic, erratic, patchy. OPPOSITE: consistent.

uneventful *adj* ordinary, commonplace, dull, boring, monotonous, tedious, routine, humdrum, unexciting, uninteresting, unexceptional, unremarkable, unmemorable, normal, average. OPPOSITE: eventful.

unexpected *adj* unanticipated, unforeseen, unlooked-for, sudden, abrupt, startling, surprising, unpredictable, chance, fortuitous. OPPOSITE: expected.

unexpectedly *adv* suddenly, abruptly, surprising, unpredictably, by chance, out of the blue.

unfailing *adj* certain, sure, reliable, dependable, constant, staunch, steadfast, unflagging, inexhaustible, limitless, infallible, unerring. OPPOSITE: unreliable.

unfair *adj* **1** (*unfair treatment*) unjust, inequitable, uneven, unequal, unbalanced, one-sided, biased, prejudiced, discriminatory, partial, partisan. OPPOSITE: fair. **2** (*unfair to blame him*) undue, unwarranted, unjustified, unreasonable, undeserved, unmerited, uncalled-for. OPPOSITE: reasonable. **3** (*using unfair tactics*) dishonest, unethical, unscrupulous, dishonourable, unsporting, foul, dirty, below the belt (*inf*).

unfaithful *adj* **1** (*unfaithful friends*) faithless, disloyal, false, untrue, perfidious, traitorous, treacherous, unreliable, untrustworthy, deceitful, insincere. OPPOSITE: loyal. **2** (*unfaithful to her lover*) adulterous, fickle, inconstant, cheating (*inf*), two-timing (*inf*). OPPOSITE: faithful. **3** (*an unfaithful account*) inaccurate, inexact, imprecise, incorrect, wrong, erroneous, faulty, imperfect. OPPOSITE: accurate.

unfaithfulness *noun* **1** (*unfaithfulness to their leader*) faithlessness, disloyalty, falseness, perfidy, treachery. OPPOSITE: loyalty. **2** (*his wife's unfaithfulness*) adultery, infidelity, inconstancy, two-timing (*inf*). OPPOSITE: fidelity.

unfaltering *adj* unflagging, untiring, tireless, indefatigable, unswerving, unwavering, steady, constant, unfailing, staunch, steadfast, resolute, firm, determined, resolved. OPPOSITE: wavering.

unfamiliar *adj* **1** (*an unfamiliar sight*) unusual, uncommon, unaccustomed, unknown, strange, odd, alien, foreign, new, novel. OPPOSITE: familiar. **2** (*unfamiliar with this software*) unacquainted, unconversant, unversed, unskilled, inexperienced, unpractised, unaccustomed, unused. OPPOSITE: acquainted.

unfashionable *adj* out-of-date, old-fashioned, dated, outdated, outmoded, démodé, passé, old hat (*inf*), obsolete, archaic, antiquated. OPPOSITE: fashionable.

unfasten *adj* undo, untie, untether, unbind, let go, unlock, unbolt, open, unbutton, unzip, unlace, uncouple, disconnect, detach, separate. OPPOSITE: fasten.

unfathomable *adj* **1** (*an unfathomable gulf*) deep, bottomless, unplumbed, immeasurable. OPPOSITE: shallow. **2** (*unfathomable mysteries*) incomprehensible, inexplicable, baffling, impenetrable, inscrutable, deep, profound, abstruse, recondite, esoteric. OPPOSITE: comprehensible.

unfavourable *adj* adverse, contrary, hostile, inimical, bad, negative, disadvantageous, detrimental, unpromising, discouraging, inauspicious, unpropitious, threatening, ominous, untimely, unseasonable, unlucky, unfortunate, unhappy. OPPOSITE: favourable.

unfeeling *adj* cold, callous, hard-hearted, stony-hearted, unsympathetic, insensitive, uncaring, heartless, harsh, cruel, pitiless, inhuman. OPPOSITE: compassionate.

unfeigned *adj* genuine, true, real, sincere, honest, heartfelt, wholehearted, pure, natural, unaffected, spontaneous, unforced. OPPOSITE: feigned.

unfettered *adj* free, unconfined, unrestrained, unchecked, unbridled, uninhibited, unconstrained, unshackled, unbound, unhampered, unhindered. OPPOSITE: restrained.

unfinished *adj* incomplete, lacking, wanting, deficient, imperfect, sketchy, rough, raw, crude, unaccomplished, undone. OPPOSITE: finished.

unfit *adj* **1** (*unfit for the job*) unsuitable, inappropriate, inadequate, unequal, unqualified, ineligible, ill-equipped, unprepared, incompetent, incapable, ineffectual, inept, useless, no good. OPPOSITE: suitable. **2** (*exercises for unfit people*) weak, feeble, frail, delicate, unhealthy, out of condition. OPPOSITE: fit.

unflagging *adj* indefatigable, tireless, untiring, unfailing, unwavering, unfaltering, constant, steady, persistent, unceasing. OPPOSITE: faltering.

unflappable *adj* cool, calm, collected, composed, level-headed, equable, phlegmatic, impassive, imperturbable, unexcitable. OPPOSITE: temperamental.

unflattering *adj* **1** (*an unflattering remark*) uncomplimentary, critical, blunt, frank, unfavourable, disparaging. OPPOSITE: flattering. **2** (*an unflattering dress*) unbecoming, unprepossessing, unattractive, unsightly.

unfledged *adj* undeveloped, immature, raw, green, callow, inexperienced. OPPOSITE: experienced.

unflinching *adj* unshrinking, unfaltering, unwavering, unblinking, steady, sure, firm, resolute, brave, fearless, bold, dauntless, undaunted, unshaken. OPPOSITE: afraid.

unfold *verb* **1** (*unfolding its wings*) open, unfurl, unroll, undo, spread out, flatten, straighten, stretch out, extend, expand, display, show. OPPOSITE: fold. **2** (*she had dark secrets to unfold*) tell, recount, relate, narrate, reveal, disclose, divulge, make known, explain, elaborate. **3** (*as his career unfolded*) develop, evolve, grow, mature, blossom.

unforeseen *adj* unexpected, unanticipated, unpredicted, unlooked-for, sudden, abrupt, surprising, startling. OPPOSITE: expected.

unforgettable *adj* memorable, striking, remarkable, exceptional, extraordinary, historic, momentous, special, distinctive. OPPOSITE: unmemorable.

unforgivable *adj* inexcusable, unpardonable, unjustifiable, unwarrantable, indefensible, reprehensible, deplorable, disgraceful, shameful, despicable, contemptible. OPPOSITE: forgivable.

unfortunate *adj* **1** (*their unfortunate children*) unlucky, luckless, hapless, poor, wretched, miserable, unhappy, ill-fated, ill-starred, cursed, doomed. OPPOSITE: fortunate. **2** (*the unfortunate result*) unfavourable, untoward, adverse, disadvantageous, disastrous, calamitous, tragic, regrettable, lamentable, deplorable. OPPOSITE: favourable. **3** (*an unfortunate choice of words*) inappropriate, unsuitable, tactless, unhappy, ill-advised,

injudicious, regrettable, deplorable. OPPOSITE: appropriate.

unfortunately *adv* unluckily, unhappily, sadly, regrettably, alas. OPPOSITE: fortunately.

unfounded *adj* baseless, groundless, idle, vain, unproven, unsubstantiated, speculative, conjectural, spurious, false. OPPOSITE: proven.

unfrequented *adj* deserted, uninhabited, remote, isolated, secluded, solitary, lonely, godforsaken. OPPOSITE: populous.

unfriendly *adj* hostile, antagonistic, inimical, aggressive, unsociable, uncongenial, inhospitable, unwelcoming, unneighbourly, aloof, standoffish, unapproachable, distant, remote, cool, chilly, cold, frosty, surly, sour, unpleasant, disagreeable. OPPOSITE: friendly.

unfruitful *adj* fruitless, unproductive, barren, sterile, infertile, infecund, unprofitable, unrewarding. OPPOSITE: fruitful.

unfurl *verb* open, unroll, unfold, spread out. OPPOSITE: furl.

ungainly *adj* awkward, clumsy, gauche, maladroit, ungraceful, inelegant, gangling, gawky, uncoordinated, lumbering, hulking, unwieldy. OPPOSITE: graceful.

ungenerous *adj* mean, illiberal, niggardly, stingy (*inf*), parsimonious, tight-fisted, cheeseparing, penny-pinching (*inf*), uncharitable, selfish. OPPOSITE: generous.

ungodly *adj* **1** (*ungodly practices*) impious, irreverent, irreligious, godless, profane, sacrilegious, wicked, sinful, corrupt, depraved, immoral, evil. OPPOSITE: pious. **2** (*at this ungodly hour*) unreasonable, unearthly (*inf*), unholy (*inf*), outrageous, preposterous, ridiculous, absurd, unheard-of. OPPOSITE: reasonable.

ungovernable *adj* refractory, recalcitrant, intractable, uncontrollable, unmanageable, wild, unruly, disorderly. OPPOSITE: meek.

ungracious *adj* discourteous, impolite, uncivil, rude, unmannerly, ill-bred, churlish. OPPOSITE: gracious.

ungrateful *adj* unthankful, unappreciative, rude, impolite. OPPOSITE: grateful.

unguarded *adj* **1** (*the castle was left unguarded*) unprotected, undefended, defenceless, vulnerable, exposed, open to attack. OPPOSITE: protected. **2** (*an unguarded remark*) careless, incautious, unthinking, thoughtless, undiplomatic, indiscreet, ill-advised, imprudent, foolhardy, rash. OPPOSITE: cautious. **3** (*in an unguarded moment*) unwary, off guard, inattentive, unmindful, heedless, distracted, absent-minded.

unhappy *adj* **1** (*he looked so unhappy*) miserable, sad, depressed, dispirited, dejected, despondent, disconsolate, downcast, crestfallen, glum, down in the dumps (*inf*), sorrowful, mournful, woebegone, melancholy, blue (*inf*). OPPOSITE: happy. **2** (*unhappy with the results*) displeased, disappointed, dissatisfied, discontented. OPPOSITE: pleased. **3** (*in unhappy circumstances*) wretched, miserable, adverse, unfavourable, unfortunate, unlucky, luckless, hapless, ill-fated, ill-starred. OPPOSITE: fortunate. **4** (*an unhappy choice of words*) inappropriate, unsuitable, tactless, unfortunate, ill-advised, injudicious, regrettable, deplorable. OPPOSITE: appropriate.

unharmed *adj* safe, sound, unhurt, uninjured, unscathed, undamaged, whole, intact. OPPOSITE: harmed.

unhealthy *adj* **1** (*an unhealthy child*) unwell, ailing, indisposed, sick, ill, poorly (*inf*), sickly, delicate, frail, feeble, weak, infirm, invalid, unsound, diseased. OPPOSITE: healthy. **2** (*an unhealthy atmosphere*) unwholesome, insalubrious, unhygienic, insanitary, noxious, detrimental, deleterious. OPPOSITE: salubrious. **3** (*an unhealthy interest in death*) morbid, unwholesome, unnatural, undesirable.

unheard-of *adj* **1** (*an unheard-of actor*) unknown, undiscovered, unfamiliar, obscure, little-known, unsung. OPPOSITE: famous. **2** (*achieving unheard-of results*) unprecedented, unexampled, new, novel, unmatched, unparalleled, unique, exceptional, extraordinary, incredible, unbelievable, undreamt-of, unimaginable, inconceivable, unthinkable. OPPOSITE: ordinary.

unheeded *adj* ignored, disregarded, overlooked, neglected, unobserved, unnoticed. OPPOSITE: heeded.

unheralded *adj* unannounced, unproclaimed, unpublicized, unadvertised, surprise, unexpected.

unhesitating *adj* unwavering, unfaltering, unshrinking, unquestioning, unreserved, unqualified, wholehearted, spontaneous, immediate, instant, instantaneous, ready, prompt. OPPOSITE: hesitant.

unhinge *verb* derange, unbalance, craze, madden, confuse, discompose, unsettle, disorder.

unholy *adj* **1** (*the unholy people of the town*) impious, irreligious, ungodly, godless, irreverent, sacrilegious, profane, wicked, sinful, iniquitous, evil. OPPOSITE: devout. **2** (*an unholy racket*) outrageous, preposterous, shocking, appalling, dreadful, awful.

unhurried *adj* slow, leisurely, easy, sedate, deliberate, relaxed, easygoing (*inf*), laid back (*inf*). OPPOSITE: hasty.

unhurt *adj* uninjured, unscathed, safe, sound, unharmed, undamaged, whole, intact. OPPOSITE: hurt.

unhygienic *adj* insanitary, insalubrious, unwholesome, unhealthy, dirty, unclean, impure, contaminated, polluted, infected, infested. OPPOSITE: hygienic.

unidentified *adj* anonymous, unnamed, nameless, unmarked, unclassified, unknown, unfamiliar, unrecognized, incognito, strange, mysterious. OPPOSITE: identified.

unification *noun* union, combination, merger, amalgamation, confederation, coalition, alliance. OPPOSITE: division.

uniform *noun* outfit, costume, dress, garb, livery, regalia, habit, suit.
➤ *adj* regular, even, equal, equable, unvarying, unchanging, steady, stable, constant, consistent, homogeneous, same, identical, similar, alike. OPPOSITE: irregular.

uniformity *noun* **1** (*uniformity of temperature*) regularity, evenness, steadiness, stability, constancy, consistency, homogeneity. OPPOSITE: variation. **2** (*the uniformity of her existence*) sameness, similarity, monotony, tedium. OPPOSITE: variety.

unify *verb* unite, join, combine, merge, amalgamate, consolidate, fuse, coalesce. OPPOSITE: separate.

unimaginable *adj* inconceivable, unthinkable, unheard-of, incredible, unbelievable, staggering, mind-boggling (*inf*), undreamt-of, beyond one's wildest dreams (*inf*), unlikely, improbable, impossible. OPPOSITE: conceivable.

unimaginative *adj* uninspired, uncreative, unoriginal, derivative, ordinary, everyday, mundane, commonplace, trite, banal, pedestrian, prosaic, stale, hackneyed, dull, boring, monotonous, dry, barren, uninteresting, uninspiring, unexciting, tame, bland, insipid. OPPOSITE: imaginative.

unimpaired *adj* undamaged, unharmed, unhurt, uninjured, unscathed, sound. OPPOSITE: impaired.

unimpeachable *adj* blameless, irreproachable, above reproach, perfect, impeccable, faultless, unblemished, spotless, immaculate, unquestionable, unassailable, unexceptionable. OPPOSITE: blameworthy.

unimportant *adj* insignificant, inconsequential, inconsiderable, insubstantial, slight, little, no big deal (*inf*), trivial, trifling, nugatory, petty, minor, marginal, peripheral, incidental, immaterial, irrelevant, not worth mentioning (*inf*). OPPOSITE: important.

uninhabited *adj* deserted, empty, vacant, unoccupied, untenanted, unpopulated, unpeopled, unsettled, unfrequented, abandoned, forsaken. OPPOSITE: inhabited.

uninhibited *adj* free, unconstrained, unrepressed, unselfconscious, natural, spontaneous, uncontrolled, unchecked, unrestrained, unbridled, unreserved, outspoken, open, frank, candid, informal, casual, relaxed. OPPOSITE: inhibited.

unintelligent *adj* stupid, foolish, dumb (*inf*), dull, slow, brainless, empty-headed, gormless (*inf*), thick (*inf*), dense, obtuse, unthinking, unreasoning. OPPOSITE: intelligent.

unintelligible *adj* incomprehensible, unfathomable, impenetrable, meaningless, incoherent, inarticulate, confused, muddled, garbled, scrambled, indecipherable, illegible. OPPOSITE: clear.

unintentional *adj* accidental, inadvertent, unintended, unpremeditated, unplanned, uncalculated, involuntary, unconscious, unwitting, chance, fortuitous. OPPOSITE: intentional.

uninterested *adj* indifferent, unconcerned, unresponsive, incurious, blasé, bored, apathetic, unenthusiastic, aloof, distant, detached, uninvolved. OPPOSITE: fascinated.

uninteresting *adj* boring, tedious, monotonous, dull, dreary, humdrum, unexciting, uneventful, wearisome, tiresome, flat, stale, prosaic, pedestrian. OPPOSITE: exciting.

uninterrupted *adj* unbroken, continuous, endless, unending, never-ending, nonstop, interminable, ceaseless, incessant, continual, perpetual, constant, steady, sustained, unremitting. OPPOSITE: broken.

uninviting *adj* unappealing, undesirable, unattractive, unwelcoming, unpleasant, disagreeable, unappetizing, unpalatable, repulsive, revolting, off-putting (*inf*). OPPOSITE: inviting.

union *noun* **1** (*the union of the parts*) joining, fusion, combination, amalgamation, merger, blend, mixture, synthesis, junction, connection. OPPOSITE: separation. **2** (*join a union*) league, alliance, coalition, confederacy, confederation, federation, association, society, guild. **3** (*failed to reach union*) agreement, concurrence, accord, concord, harmony, unison, consensus, unanimity, unity, concert. OPPOSITE: discord. **4** (*blessed their union*) marriage, matrimony, wedlock, wedding. OPPOSITE: divorce. **5** (*sexual union*) intercourse, copulation, coupling, coitus.

unique *adj* **1** (*a unique design*) single, sole, only, solitary, lone, exclusive, one-off. OPPOSITE: common. **2** (*a unique opportunity*) matchless, unmatched, peerless, unequalled, unparalleled, unexampled, unprecedented, incomparable, inimitable, unrivalled, second to none, exceptional, singular, rare. OPPOSITE: frequent.

unison *noun* agreement, harmony, accord, concord, unity, concert, consensus, unanimity. OPPOSITE: discord.

unit *noun* **1** (*considered as a unit*) whole, entity, one, group. **2** (*divided into units*) part, component, element, constituent, piece, portion, segment, section, module, item, member. **3** (*metric units*) measurement, measure, quantity.

unite *verb* **1** (*unite the parts*) join, unify, combine, blend, mix, fuse, weld, bind, connect, link, marry, wed, amalgamate, merge. OPPOSITE: separate. **2** (*unite to fight oppression*) ally, associate, league, band, team up, join forces, pool resources, cooperate, pull together (*inf*). OPPOSITE: disband.

united *adj* **1** (*a united effort*) combined, collective, joint, concerted, cooperative. OPPOSITE: individual. **2** (*a united organization*) corporate, amalgamated, allied, confederate, federal. OPPOSITE: separate. **3** (*a united front*) agreed, in agreement, like-minded, unanimous. OPPOSITE: divided.

unity *noun* **1** (*the unity of the design*) wholeness, integrity, oneness, singleness. **2** (*striving for political unity*) agreement, accord, concord, harmony, union, consensus, unanimity, unison, concert, togetherness, solidarity. OPPOSITE: discord.

universal *adj* general, comprehensive, all-embracing, all-inclusive, across-the-board, widespread, worldwide, global, ecumenical, catholic, total, whole, entire. OPPOSITE: narrow.

universe *noun* cosmos, macrocosm, creation, nature, world, humanity.

unjust *adj* **1** (*an unjust law*) unfair, inequitable, biased, prejudiced, discriminatory, partial, one-sided. OPPOSITE: just. **2** (*unjust criticism*) wrongful, wrong, undue, unreasonable, unwarranted, uncalled-for, unmerited, undeserved. OPPOSITE: reasonable.

unjustifiable *adj* indefensible, unwarrantable, inexcusable, unforgivable, unpardonable, wrong, culpable, unacceptable, unreasonable, undue, uncalled-for. OPPOSITE: justifiable.

unkempt *adj* dishevelled, tousled, rumpled, uncombed, ungroomed, disordered, disarranged, messy, untidy, slovenly, slatternly, scruffy, sloppy (*inf*). OPPOSITE: tidy.

unkind *adj* cruel, nasty, uncharitable, unchristian, unfriendly, unneighbourly, mean, spiteful, malicious, bitchy (*inf*), unfeeling, insensitive, callous, hard-hearted, unsympathetic, thoughtless, inconsiderate. OPPOSITE: kind.

unknown *adj* **1** (*entering unknown territory*) unfamiliar, strange, new, novel, unexplored, undiscovered. OPPOSITE: familiar. **2** (*an unknown benefactor*) anonymous, nameless, unnamed, unidentified, unrevealed, undisclosed, secret, hidden, concealed. OPPOSITE: known. **3** (*by an unknown author*) unheard-of, obscure, little-known, unsung. OPPOSITE: well-known.

unlawful *adj* illegal, illicit, illegitimate, against the law, criminal, felonious, prohibited, forbidden, banned, outlawed, proscribed, unauthorized, unlicensed. OPPOSITE: lawful.

unleash *verb* loose, unloose, let loose, free, release. OPPOSITE: restrain.

unlike *adj* different, dissimilar, like chalk and cheese (*inf*), diverse, divergent, disparate, distinct, opposed, contrasted, incompatible, incongruous, unequal. OPPOSITE: similar.
  prep different from, dissimilar to, as opposed to, in contrast to. OPPOSITE: like.

unlikely *adj* improbable, doubtful, dubious, questionable, implausible, unconvincing, incredible, unbelievable, inconceivable, unimaginable. OPPOSITE: likely.

unlimited *adj* **1** (*unlimited resources*) infinite, limitless, illimitable, boundless, unbounded, unrestricted, immense, vast, great, immeasurable, incalculable, countless, untold, endless, never-ending. OPPOSITE: limited. **2** (*unlimited power*) absolute, full, total, unconditional, unqualified, unrestricted, unconstrained, unchecked, uncontrolled, unimpeded, unfettered, untrammelled. OPPOSITE: restricted.

unload *verb* discharge, disburden, unburden, unlade, empty, unpack, relieve, disencumber. OPPOSITE: load.

unlock *verb* open, unlatch, unbolt, unfasten, undo, free, release. OPPOSITE: lock.

unlooked-for *adj* unexpected, unforeseen, unpredicted, unanticipated, unhoped-for, undreamt-of, sudden, surprising. OPPOSITE: expected.

unloved *adj* unpopular, disliked, hated, detested, loathed, uncared-for, neglected, forsaken, unwanted, spurned, rejected, loveless. OPPOSITE: loved.

unlucky *adj* **1** (*the unlucky victim*) unfortunate, luckless, hapless, cursed, doomed, jinxed, ill-fated, ill-starred, poor, wretched, miserable. OPPOSITE: lucky. **2** (*an unlucky omen*) unfavourable, adverse, untoward, disadvantageous, inauspicious, unpropitious, unpromising, ominous. OPPOSITE: favourable.

unman *verb* demoralize, dishearten, discourage, dispirit, weaken, enfeeble, enervate, unnerve, daunt, intimidate.

unmanageable *adj* **1** (*an unmanageable child*) uncontrollable, ungovernable, wild, unruly, disorderly, difficult, intractable, refractory, recalcitrant, obstreperous, stroppy (*inf*). OPPOSITE: docile. **2** (*an unmanageable load*) unwieldy, unmanoeuvrable, inconvenient, unhandy, incommodious, awkward, cumbersome, bulky. OPPOSITE: handy.

unmanly *adj* effeminate, womanish, sissy (*inf*), soft, namby-pamby, weak, feeble, weedy, wet (*inf*), cowardly, yellow (*inf*), timorous, wimpish (*inf*). OPPOSITE: manly.

unmannerly *adj* rude, impolite, discourteous, uncivil, ungracious, bad-mannered, ill-bred, uncouth, boorish, churlish. OPPOSITE: polite.

unmarried *adj* single, unwed, unattached, celibate, bachelor, spinster. OPPOSITE: married.

unmask *verb* expose, uncover, unveil, uncloak, show, reveal, disclose, discover. OPPOSITE: mask.

unmatched *adj* matchless, peerless, unequalled, unparalleled, unrivalled, unsurpassed, incomparable, paramount, supreme, consummate. OPPOSITE: inferior.

unmentionable *adj* unspeakable, unutterable, disgraceful, shameful, scandalous, shocking, embarrassing, unpleasant, indecent, immodest.

unmerciful *adj* merciless, pitiless, unpitying, unsparing, cruel, brutal, inhuman, sadistic, harsh, hard, callous, heartless, relentless, unrelenting, inexorable, implacable, ruthless, remorseless. OPPOSITE: merciful.

unmethodical *adj* unsystematic, disorganized, unorganized, confused, muddled, disorderly, desultory, haphazard, random, irregular, illogical. OPPOSITE: methodical.

unmindful *adj* oblivious, unaware, unconscious, blind, deaf, inattentive, heedless, unheeding, mindless, unthinking, careless, negligent, neglectful, remiss, lax. OPPOSITE: mindful.

unmistakable *adj* clear, distinct, plain, obvious, evident, manifest, patent, clear-cut, well-defined, pronounced, conspicuous, striking, glaring, blatant, palpable, unquestionable, indisputable, indubitable, certain, sure, positive, definite, unequivocal, unambiguous. OPPOSITE: doubtful.

unmitigated *adj* **1** (*an unmitigated failure*) absolute, categorical, unqualified, unconditional, veritable, sheer, perfect, consummate, thorough, utter, complete, total, downright, out-and-out. OPPOSITE: partial. **2** (*unmitigated suffering*) undiminished, unmodified, unalleviated, intense, severe, harsh, oppressive, relentless, unrelenting.

unmoved *adj* **1** (*unmoved by our tale of woe*) unaffected, untouched, uncaring, indifferent, impassive, dispassionate, unfeeling, cold, dry-eyed, impervious. OPPOSITE: moved. **2** (*unmoved in their demands*) unshaken, unwavering, unswerving, staunch, steadfast, firm, adamant, resolute, determined. OPPOSITE: shaken.

unnatural *adj* **1** (*an unnatural reaction*) abnormal, irregular, unusual, anomalous, aberrant, deviant, odd, strange, bizarre, extraordinary. OPPOSITE: normal. **2** (*an unnatural style*) artificial, forced, laboured, stilted, stiff, affected, mannered, theatrical, stagy, studied, contrived, self-conscious, assumed, feigned, false, insincere. OPPOSITE: spontaneous.

unnecessary *adj* needless, unneeded, nonessential, inessential, expendable, dispensable, useless, wasted, superfluous, redundant, unwanted, uncalled-for, gratuitous. OPPOSITE: necessary.

unnerve *verb* daunt, dismay, intimidate, unman, discourage, dishearten, dispirit, demoralize, disconcert, discompose, disquiet, fluster, shake, rattle (*inf*), upset, unsettle, throw off balance. OPPOSITE: embolden.

unnoticed *adj* unseen, unobserved, unheeded, ignored, disregarded, overlooked.

unobtrusive *adj* inconspicuous, unostentatious, unpretentious, unassuming, restrained, subdued, low-key, humble, meek, self-effacing, modest, quiet, simple, reserved, retiring, low-profile. OPPOSITE: pretentious.

unoccupied *adj* **1** (*an unoccupied building*) empty, vacant, deserted, uninhabited, untenanted. OPPOSITE: occupied. **2** (*while you are unoccupied*) idle, inactive, at leisure, unemployed. OPPOSITE: busy.

unofficial *adj* **1** (*an unofficial experiment*) unauthorized, unsanctioned, unaccredited, unlicensed. OPPOSITE: authorized. **2** (*an unofficial visit*) informal, casual, secret, undeclared. OPPOSITE: formal. **3** (*an unofficial report*) unconfirmed, unsubstantiated, uncorroborated. **4** (*unofficial remarks*) off-the-record, confidential, private.

unorthodox *adj* unconventional, unusual, uncommon, uncustomary, abnormal, irregular, anomalous, aberrant, nonconformist, uncanonical, heterodox, heretical, alternative, fringe. OPPOSITE: orthodox.

unpaid *adj* **1** (*an unpaid invoice*) due, overdue, outstanding, unsettled, owing, payable. OPPOSITE: paid. **2** (*unpaid work*) voluntary, honorary, unwaged, unsalaried, unremunerative. OPPOSITE: remunerative.

unpalatable *adj* unsavoury, unappetizing, inedible, uneatable, unpleasant, disagreeable, nasty, distasteful, disgusting, revolting, offensive, repulsive, repellent, repugnant. OPPOSITE: palatable.

unparalleled *adj* peerless, unequalled, matchless, unmatched, unrivalled, unsurpassed, inimitable, incomparable, beyond compare, unprecedented, unexampled, unique, singular, superlative, supreme, consummate. OPPOSITE: ordinary.

unpardonable *adj* unforgivable, inexcusable, unjustifiable, indefensible, reprehensible, deplorable, disgraceful, shameful, shocking, scandalous. OPPOSITE: forgivable.

unperturbed *adj* cool, calm, collected, composed, serene, tranquil, placid, unruffled, unflustered, untroubled, unworried, poised, self-possessed, imperturbable, unflappable (*inf*). OPPOSITE: agitated.

unpleasant *adj* **1** (*an unpleasant odour*) offensive, obnoxious, foul, disgusting, revolting, repulsive, repugnant, unsavoury, unpalatable, nauseating, sickening. OPPOSITE: pleasant. **2** (*unpleasant weather*) disagreeable, nasty, bad, unattractive, horrible, hateful, detestable, undesirable, annoying, irksome, vexatious, troublesome. OPPOSITE: nice. **3** (*unpleasant neighbours*) nasty, offensive, disagreeable, obnoxious, objectionable, unlikeable, unlovable, ill-natured, bad-tempered, rude, surly, mean, unkind, spiteful, unfriendly. OPPOSITE: agreeable.

unpleasantness *noun* **1** (*the unpleasantness of their surroundings*) unattractiveness, undesirability, disagreeableness, nastiness, offensiveness, repugnance.

OPPOSITE: pleasantness. **2** (*hoping to avoid unpleasantness*) nastiness, ill-feeling, trouble, bother, fuss, upset.

unpolished *adj* rough, coarse, rude, crude, rough and ready, sketchy, unfinished, unrefined, uncultured, uncultivated, uncivilized, unsophisticated, uncouth, vulgar. OPPOSITE: polished.

unpopular *adj* disliked, unloved, hated, detested, unattractive, objectionable, unwelcome, undesirable, unsought-after, unwanted, rejected, shunned, friendless, out of favour, ignored, cold-shouldered, sent to Coventry (*inf*). OPPOSITE: popular.

unprecedented *adj* new, novel, unheard-of, unexampled, unparalleled, unequalled, unmatched, exceptional, remarkable, extraordinary, out of the ordinary, uncommon, unusual, unconventional, original, unique, atypical, abnormal, anomalous, freakish. OPPOSITE: usual.

unpredictable *adj* **1** (*an unpredictable outcome*) unforeseeable, chance, accidental, uncertain, unsure, doubtful, dubious, in the balance, up in the air (*inf*), in the lap of the gods (*inf*). OPPOSITE: predictable. **2** (*unpredictable behaviour*) erratic, capricious, whimsical, fickle, mercurial, volatile, unstable, inconstant, changeable, variable, unreliable, undependable. OPPOSITE: constant.

unprejudiced *adj* unbiased, impartial, nonpartisan, neutral, disinterested, objective, dispassionate, detached, open-minded, fair, just, equitable, even-handed, balanced. OPPOSITE: prejudiced.

unpremeditated *adj* unplanned, spontaneous, impulsive, spur-of-the-moment (*inf*), unprepared, impromptu, extempore, ad lib, off the cuff (*inf*). OPPOSITE: deliberate.

unprepared *adj* unready, unsuspecting, ill-equipped, unfinished, incomplete, unplanned, unrehearsed, spontaneous, impromptu. OPPOSITE: ready.

unprepossessing *adj* unattractive, unlovely, plain, unbecoming, ugly, unsightly. OPPOSITE: attractive.

unpretentious *adj* modest, humble, simple, plain, ordinary, homely, unaffected, natural, straightforward, unassuming, unostentatious, unobtrusive. OPPOSITE: pretentious.

unprincipled *adj* unscrupulous, dishonest, deceitful, crooked (*inf*), unethical, unprofessional, amoral, immoral, unconscionable, dishonourable, corrupt, wicked, evil. OPPOSITE: honest.

unproductive *adj* fruitless, unfruitful, sterile, barren, unprofitable, unremunerative, unrewarding, worthless, useless, futile, vain, unavailing, ineffective, ineffectual, inefficacious, unsuccessful, abortive. OPPOSITE: productive.

unprofessional *adj* **1** (*unprofessional behaviour*) unethical, unprincipled, unscrupulous, improper, unseemly. OPPOSITE: professional. **2** (*unprofessional work*) amateur, amateurish, lax, negligent, sloppy (*inf*), incompetent, inexpert, unskilled, unqualified, untrained.

unprofitable *adj* unremunerative, unrewarding, worthless, valueless, unproductive, fruitless, useless, vain, unavailing, unsuccessful. OPPOSITE: profitable.

unpromising *adj* unfavourable, adverse, unpropitious, inauspicious, gloomy, black, ominous, discouraging, dispiriting, doubtful, dubious. OPPOSITE: promising.

unprotected *adj* unguarded, unattended, unarmed, unfortified, undefended, defenceless, vulnerable, open, exposed, unsheltered, naked, bare, uncovered. OPPOSITE: safe.

unqualified *adj* **1** (*unqualified staff*) unlicensed, untrained, amateur, lay. OPPOSITE: qualified. **2** (*I am unqualified to judge*) unable, incapable, incompetent, ineligible, unfit, unsuited, unprepared, ill-equipped. OPPOSITE: eligible. **3** (*their unqualified approval*) unconditional, unreserved, wholehearted, categorical, unequivocal, positive, absolute, utter, complete, total, thorough, downright, outright, out-and-out, unmitigated, perfect, consummate. OPPOSITE: partial.

unquestionable *adj* indisputable, uncontestable, incontrovertible, beyond question, indubitable, undoubted, beyond doubt, irrefutable, undeniable, certain, sure, clear, plain, evident, obvious, patent, manifest, conclusive, definite, positive. OPPOSITE: questionable.

unravel *verb* **1** (*unravel the rope*) untangle, disentangle, unsnarl, unknot, undo, untwist, unwind, disengage, separate out. OPPOSITE: entangle. **2** (*unravel the mystery*) solve, puzzle out, work out, figure out (*inf*), penetrated, fathom, get to the bottom of (*inf*), resolve, clear up, straighten out, explain, decipher, interpret. OPPOSITE: complicate.

unreal *adj* imaginary, fanciful, illusory, visionary, chimerical, intangible, insubstantial, immaterial, nonexistent, hypothetical, fictitious, legendary, mythical, fantastic, fabulous, make-believe, pretend (*inf*), false, artificial, synthetic, mock. OPPOSITE: real.

unrealistic *adj* impractical, impracticable, unworkable, idealistic, quixotic, unreasonable, irrational, illogical, foolish, absurd, improbable, impossible. OPPOSITE: realistic.

unreasonable *adj* **1** (*under unreasonable pressure*) excessive, immoderate, inordinate, unconscionable, undue, unfair, unjust, uncalled-for, unjustified, unwarranted. OPPOSITE: reasonable. **2** (*an unreasonable price*) exorbitant, extortionate, high, steep (*inf*). OPPOSITE: low. **3** (*unreasonable behaviour*) irrational, illogical, senseless, foolish, stupid, silly, mad, crazy, absurd, ridiculous, ludicrous, preposterous. OPPOSITE: sensible. **4** (*don't be so unreasonable*) awkward, obstinate, obdurate, headstrong, wilful, opinionated, blinkered, narrow-minded. OPPOSITE: accommodating.

unrefined *adj* **1** (*unrefined oil*) raw, crude, unprocessed, untreated, unpurified, unfinished, unpolished, rough, coarse. OPPOSITE: refined. **2** (*unrefined manners*) uncultured, uncultivated, uncivilized, unsophisticated, uncouth, boorish, loutish, rude, coarse, vulgar. OPPOSITE: cultured.

unrelenting *adj* **1** (*an unrelenting taskmaster*) relentless, implacable, inexorable, merciless, pitiless, cruel, ruthless, remorseless, unsparing. OPPOSITE: merciful **2** (*unrelenting rain*) continuous, unbroken, continual, constant, perpetual, unremitting, unabating, incessant, ceaseless, unceasing, endless, unending, never-ending, nonstop. OPPOSITE: intermittent.

unreliable *adj* undependable, untrustworthy, irresponsible, fickle, changeable, capricious, erratic, uncertain, doubtful, suspect, questionable, unsound, implausible, unconvincing. OPPOSITE: reliable.

unremitting *adj* incessant, ceaseless, unceasing, perpetual, constant, continual, continuous, unrelenting, relentless, assiduous, diligent, tireless.

unrepentant *adj* impenitent, unremorseful, unapologetic, unashamed, shameless, abandoned, unregenerate, unreformed, incorrigible, inveterate, hardened. OPPOSITE: repentant.

unreserved *adj* **1** (*with unreserved enthusiasm*) unqualified, unconditional, unrestricted, unlimited, unrestrained, wholehearted, categorical, unequivocal, absolute, positive, outright, utter, total, entire, full. OPPOSITE: qualified. **2** (*an unreserved person*) uninhibited, unconstrained, demonstrative, outgoing, extrovert, communicative, open, frank, candid, direct, outspoken. OPPOSITE: reserved. **3** (*an unreserved seat*) unbooked, free, vacant, available. OPPOSITE: booked.

unresolved *adj* unsettled, undecided, pending, in the balance, up in the air (*inf*), open, moot, undetermined, indefinite, vague, unsolved, unanswered. OPPOSITE: settled.

unrest *noun* rebellion, strife, discord, dissension, protest, discontent, dissatisfaction, disquiet, unease, worry, anxiety, restlessness, agitation, turmoil, turbulence, disorder, commotion. OPPOSITE: peace.

unrestrained *adj* unchecked, unbridled, uncontrolled, unrestricted, unlimited, unhindered, unimpeded, free, uninhibited, unrepressed, wild, immoderate. OPPOSITE: restrained.

unrestricted *adj* unlimited, limitless, unbounded, boundless, free, open, unhindered, unhampered, unimpeded, unobstructed, unrestrained, unchecked. OPPOSITE: restricted.

unripe *adj* unripened, green, immature, undeveloped, unready. OPPOSITE: ripe.

unrivalled *adj* matchless, unmatched, peerless, nonpareil, unequalled, without equal, unparalleled, inimitable, incomparable, beyond compare, unsurpassed, supreme. OPPOSITE: inferior.

unroll *verb* open, unfold, unfurl, unwind. OPPOSITE: roll.

unruffled *adj* **1** (*she remained unruffled*) cool, calm, collected, composed, poised, self-possessed, unmoved, unperturbed, imperturbable, unflappable (*inf*), placid, serene, tranquil. OPPOSITE: agitated. **2** (*the unruffled surface of the lake*) flat, smooth, level, even, calm, peaceful, tranquil.

unruly *adj* ungovernable, unmanageable, intractable, uncontrollable, restive, wild, wayward, wilful, headstrong, obstreperous, refractory, recalcitrant, disobedient, insubordinate, rebellious, mutinous, riotous, rowdy, disorderly, turbulent, lawless. OPPOSITE: orderly.

unsafe *adj* dangerous, hazardous, perilous, treacherous, risky, hairy (*inf*), chancy, dicey (*inf*), uncertain,

unsound, unreliable, precarious, insecure, vulnerable, exposed. OPPOSITE: safe.

unsaid *adj* unspoken, unuttered, unvoiced, unmentioned, unstated, tacit, implicit, understood.

unsatisfactory *adj* unacceptable, not good enough, inadequate, insufficient, deficient, defective, faulty, poor, inferior, mediocre, weak, disappointing, dissatisfying, unsatisfying. OPPOSITE: excellent.

unsavoury *adj* unpleasant, disagreeable, objectionable, offensive, obnoxious, repulsive, repellent, repugnant, revolting, disgusting, nauseating, nasty, unpalatable, unappetizing, distasteful, sordid, squalid, seamy, disreputable. OPPOSITE: pleasant.

unscathed *adj* unhurt, uninjured, unharmed, undamaged, unimpaired, safe, sound, whole, intact. OPPOSITE: hurt.

unscrupulous *adj* unprincipled, unethical, amoral, immoral, unconscionable, shameless, corrupt, dishonest, crooked (*inf*), dishonourable, bad, wicked. OPPOSITE: honest.

unseasonable *adj* untimely, ill-timed, inopportune, inappropriate, unsuitable. OPPOSITE: seasonable.

unseat *verb* **1** (*the horse unseated its rider*) unsaddle, unhorse, throw. **2** (*trying to unseat the president*) depose, dethrone, oust, remove, dismiss, discharge, overthrow, topple.

unseemly *adj* unbecoming, undignified, improper, indecorous, indecent, unbefitting, unfitting, unsuitable, inappropriate, indelicate, tasteless, crass. OPPOSITE: proper.

unseen *adj* unnoticed, unobserved, undetected, hidden, concealed, invisible. OPPOSITE: visible.

unselfish *adj* altruistic, selfless, self-sacrificing, self-denying, charitable, philanthropic, public-spirited, magnanimous, gracious, generous, liberal, unsparing, unstinting. OPPOSITE: selfish.

unsettle *verb* upset, perturb, trouble, disturb, bother, fluster, ruffle, agitate, rattle (*inf*), disconcert, confuse, throw (*inf*), destabilize, unbalance, derange, disorganize, disarrange, disorder. OPPOSITE: calm.

unsettled *adj* **1** (*unsettled weather*) changeable, variable, inconstant, erratic, unpredictable, unreliable, undependable. OPPOSITE: settled. **2** (*living in unsettled times*) unstable, insecure, disorderly, disorganized. OPPOSITE: stable. **3** (*I felt unsettled*) uneasy, tense, nervous, anxious, on edge (*inf*), restless, fidgety, agitated, troubled, perturbed, flustered, ruffled, discomfited, confused, disoriented. OPPOSITE: calm. **4** (*the question remains unsettled*) unresolved, undecided, pending, in the balance, up in the air (*inf*), open, moot, undetermined. OPPOSITE: resolved. **5** (*unsettled accounts*) unpaid, payable, owing, due, outstanding, in arrears. OPPOSITE: paid. **6** (*unsettled lands*) uninhabited, unoccupied, deserted, unpopulated, unpeopled, uncolonized. OPPOSITE: inhabited.

unshakeable *adj* firm, resolute, determined, staunch, steadfast, constant, unwavering, unswerving, fixed, sure.

unsightly *adj* ugly, hideous, repulsive, unattractive, unprepossessing, unpleasant, disagreeable. OPPOSITE: beautiful.

unskilful *adj* clumsy, awkward, gauche, maladroit, unhandy, inexpert, amateurish, unprofessional, inept, incompetent, bungling. OPPOSITE: skilful.

unskilled *adj* untrained, unqualified, inexperienced, amateur, lay, inexpert, amateurish, unprofessional. OPPOSITE: skilled.

unsociable *adj* unfriendly, uncongenial, unneighbourly, inhospitable, hostile, uncommunicative, unforthcoming, reticent, retiring, withdrawn, introverted, reclusive, aloof, standoffish, distant, remote. OPPOSITE: sociable.

unsolicited *adj* unsought, unrequested, unasked, uninvited, unwanted, unwelcome, voluntary, spontaneous, gratuitous, free. OPPOSITE: requested.

unsophisticated **1** (*an unsophisticated young woman*) innocent, childlike, naive, unworldly, inexperienced, guileless, artless, ingenuous, natural, simple, unaffected, genuine, unrefined, unpolished, uncultured, uncultivated. OPPOSITE: sophisticated. **2** (*an unsophisticated system*) simple, uncomplicated, straightforward, plain, basic, rudimentary, primitive, crude, unrefined. OPPOSITE: complex.

unsound *adj* **1** (*an unsound constitution*) weak, feeble, frail, delicate, infirm, unhealthy, unfit, unwell, ailing, sickly, diseased. OPPOSITE: healthy. **2** (*of unsound mind*) deranged, unhinged, unbalanced, impaired, imperfect, defective. OPPOSITE: sane. **3** (*an unsound argument*) faulty, flawed, defective, illogical, irrational, false, specious, fallacious, erroneous, wrong, invalid, untenable, ill-founded. OPPOSITE: valid. **4** (*the foundations are unsound*) unstable, shaky, rickety, wobbly, unsteady, insecure, unsafe, dangerous, flimsy, insubstantial, damaged, impaired, broken-down, rotten, decayed. OPPOSITE: stable.

unsparing *adj* **1** (*unsparing with their praise*) generous, liberal, open-handed, munificent, unstinting, ungrudging, bountiful, lavish, profuse, abundant. OPPOSITE: mean. **2** (*our captors were unsparing*) merciless, unmerciful, pitiless, unpitying, relentless, unrelenting, inexorable, implacable, ruthless, cruel, harsh, severe, stern, unforgiving. OPPOSITE: merciful.

unspeakable *adj* **1** (*unspeakable surprise*) unutterable, ineffable, inexpressible, indescribable, unimaginable, inconceivable, unthinkable, unbelievable, incredible, unheard-of, extreme, overwhelming. **2** (*unspeakable crimes*) unmentionable, horrible, awful, dreadful, terrible, loathsome, detestable, odious, abominable, execrable, heinous, monstrous, villainous, atrocious, deplorable, shocking, appalling, despicable, contemptible.

unspectacular *adj* unimpressive, unremarkable, unmemorable, unexceptional, ordinary, average, unexciting, uninteresting, dull, boring. OPPOSITE: spectacular.

unspoilt *adj* perfect, intact, unharmed, undamaged, unimpaired, preserved, unchanged, untouched, unaffected, simple, natural, pure, uncorrupted, undefiled.

unspoken *adj* tacit, understood, assumed, implied, implicit, unstated, unexpressed, unsaid, unuttered, silent, mute, wordless, voiceless, unvoiced, unpronounced. OPPOSITE: stated.

unstable *adj* **1** (*the structure is unstable*) unsteady, insecure, unsound, shaky, rickety, wobbly, unsafe, dangerous, precarious, risky. OPPOSITE: steady. **2** (*an unstable market*) unpredictable, changeable, variable, inconstant, vacillating, fluctuating, volatile, erratic, fitful, irregular. OPPOSITE: stable. **3** (*an unstable personality*) unbalanced, deranged, unhinged, unsound, irrational, moody, mercurial, volatile, capricious, fickle, unreliable, unpredictable. OPPOSITE: balanced.

unsteady *adj* **1** (*unsteady on his feet*) shaky, wobbly, tottering, staggering, doddering, unstable, insecure, unsound, unsafe, precarious. OPPOSITE: steady. **2** (*an unsteady pulse*) irregular, erratic, inconstant, wavering, vacillating, fluctuating, changeable, variable. OPPOSITE: constant.

unstinting *adj* generous, liberal, open-handed, munificent, unsparing, ungrudging, prodigal, bountiful, lavish, profuse, abundant, plentiful. OPPOSITE: mean

unstudied *adj* natural, unaffected, unpretentious, unrehearsed, spontaneous, impulsive, impromptu, casual, informal. OPPOSITE: affected.

unsubstantial *adj* insubstantial, fanciful, imaginary, unreal, visionary, illusory, airy, light, slight, thin, frail, fragile, flimsy, weak, tenuous, unsound. OPPOSITE: solid.

unsubstantiated *adj* uncorroborated, unsupported, unconfirmed, unverified, unproven, questionable, disputable, debatable. OPPOSITE: proven.

unsuccessful *adj* **1** (*an unsuccessful mission*) useless, futile, vain, unavailing, ineffectual, ineffective, worthless, fruitless, unproductive, unprofitable, failed, abortive, foiled, frustrated, thwarted. OPPOSITE: successful. **2** (*the unsuccessful candidate*) losing, defeated, beaten, disappointed, unfortunate, unlucky, luckless, hapless, ill-fated, ill-starred. OPPOSITE: victorious

unsuitable *adj* inappropriate, inapt, inapposite, unfitting, unfit, unsuited, incompatible, incongruous, out of place, out of keeping, impractical, unacceptable, unseemly, unbecoming, unbefitting, indecorous, improper. OPPOSITE: suitable.

unsullied *adj* clean, pure, spotless, unspotted, immaculate, unsoiled, unblemished, stainless, unstained, untarnished, untainted, unpolluted, uncontaminated, unspoilt, untouched, undefiled, uncorrupted. OPPOSITE: sullied.

unsung *adj* unacclaimed, uncelebrated, unacknowledged, unrecognized, unhonoured, unrenowned, disregarded, ignored, overlooked, neglected, anonymous, nameless, unnamed, unknown. OPPOSITE: famous.

unsure *adj* **1** (*unsure where to go*) uncertain, doubtful, irresolute, undecided, unresolved, ambivalent, in two minds (*inf*), hesitant, wavering, vacillating, unclear. OPPOSITE: sure. **2** (*unsure of their loyalty*) doubtful, dubious, sceptical, suspicious, distrustful, uncertain, unconvinced, unpersuaded. OPPOSITE: convinced. **3** (*unsure of herself*) hesitant, insecure, lacking confidence, lacking assurance. OPPOSITE: confident.

unsurpassed *adj* supreme, paramount, transcendent, unbeaten, unexcelled, unrivalled, unparalleled, unmatched, matchless, unequalled, peerless, nonpareil, incomparable, inimitable. OPPOSITE: inferior.

unsuspecting adj unsuspicious, trusting, trustful, credulous, gullible, naive, ingenuous, unwary, off guard. OPPOSITE: suspicious.

unswerving adj straight, direct, undeviating, single-minded, devoted, dedicated, committed, constant, staunch, steadfast, unfaltering, unwavering, untiring, unflagging.

unsympathetic adj unpitying, unmoved, untouched, unconcerned, indifferent, uncaring, unfeeling, insensitive, callous, heartless, hard-hearted, stony-hearted, cold, cruel, unkind, inconsiderate. OPPOSITE: sympathetic.

unsystematic adj unmethodical, unorganized, disorganized, disorderly, confused, muddled, chaotic, shambolic (inf), random, haphazard, indiscriminate, irregular. OPPOSITE: systematic.

untamed adj wild, feral, undomesticated, savage, barbarous. OPPOSITE: tame.

untangle verb disentangle, unsnarl, unknot, unravel, straighten out, sort out, clear up, free, extricate.

untarnished adj 1 (untarnished metal) clean, bright, shining, gleaming, polished, burnished. OPPOSITE: tarnished. 2 (an untarnished reputation) unsullied, spotless, unspotted, immaculate, stainless, unstained, unblemished, untainted. OPPOSITE: sullied.

untenable adj indefensible, insupportable, unsound, weak, flawed, faulty, fallacious, specious, ill-founded, unfounded, groundless, baseless, unreasonable, irrational, illogical, unacceptable, inadmissible. OPPOSITE: sound.

unthinkable adj unimaginable, inconceivable, unheard-of, incredible, unbelievable, beyond belief, unlikely, improbable, implausible, absurd, preposterous, outrageous, impossible, out of the question, not on (inf). OPPOSITE: conceivable.

unthinking adj 1 (an unthinking remark) thoughtless, inconsiderate, insensitive, crass, tactless, undiplomatic, indiscreet, rude, impolite. OPPOSITE: thoughtful. 2 (an unthinking gesture) automatic, mechanical, involuntary, instinctive, impulsive, rash, careless, neglectful, negligent, unmindful, mindless, heedless, inadvertent, unintentional.

untidy adj 1 (an untidy room) cluttered, littered, messy, disorderly, disorganized, disordered, disarranged, muddled, jumbled, chaotic, shambolic (inf), topsy-turvy, higgledy-piggledy (inf). OPPOSITE: tidy. 2 (her untidy appearance) slovenly, slatternly, unkempt, dishevelled, scruffy, bedraggled. OPPOSITE: neat. 3 (untidy work) messy, careless, slipshod, sloppy (inf). OPPOSITE: careful.

untie verb undo, unfasten, unknot, unlace, unbind, untether, unhitch, release, loose, free, let go. OPPOSITE: tie.

untimely adj 1 (her untimely death) premature, early. 2 (an untimely frost) unseasonable, ill-timed, inopportune, inconvenient, awkward, inappropriate, unsuitable. OPPOSITE: timely.

untiring adj tireless, indefatigable, unflagging, unwearying, unfaltering, unwavering, unfailing,

unremitting, unceasing, incessant, steady, constant, persistent, persevering, tenacious, dogged, determined, resolute. OPPOSITE: wavering.

untold adj 1 (causing untold suffering) unspeakable, unutterable, ineffable, inexpressible, indescribable, unimaginable, inconceivable, unthinkable, unbelievable, incredible, unheard-of, extreme. 2 (untold wealth) incalculable, immeasurable, measureless, countless, innumerable, numberless, myriad, infinite, inexhaustible. 3 (the untold truth) secret, private, confidential, unknown, hidden, concealed, unrevealed, undisclosed, undivulged, unpublished, unreported, unrelated, unmentioned, unstated, unspoken.

untouched adj 1 (an untouched landscape) unchanged, unaltered, unspoilt, pristine, intact, whole, undamaged, unharmed, unhurt, uninjured, unscathed. OPPOSITE: spoilt. 2 (untouched by the tragedy) unmoved, unaffected, dry-eyed, indifferent, unconcerned, apathetic. OPPOSITE: moved. 3 (three untouched boxes) unused, new, brand-new, unopened, complete, full. 4 (his breakfast remained untouched) uneaten, unconsumed.

untoward adj 1 (untoward events) adverse, unfavourable, contrary, hostile, unfortunate, unlucky, inauspicious, unpropitious, inopportune, untimely, ill-timed, unseasonable, awkward, inconvenient, annoying, vexatious. 2 (untoward behaviour) unseemly, unbecoming, indecorous, improper, unsuitable, inappropriate. OPPOSITE: seemly. 3 (didn't notice anything untoward) unexpected, unusual, uncommon, out of the ordinary, out of place, atypical, abnormal. OPPOSITE: normal.

untried adj untested, unproved, unproven, experimental, exploratory, new, novel, innovative, innovatory. OPPOSITE: tested.

untroubled adj cool, calm, collected, composed, poised, self-possessed, unworried, unconcerned, unruffled, unperturbed, undisturbed, placid, tranquil, serene. OPPOSITE: agitated.

untrue adj 1 (the rumours are untrue) false, untruthful, fabricated, made-up (inf), trumped-up (inf), wrong, mistaken, erroneous, fallacious, incorrect, inaccurate, inexact, imprecise, wide of the mark, deceptive, misleading. OPPOSITE: true. 2 (his friends were untrue) unfaithful, faithless, disloyal, traitorous, treacherous, perfidious, false, deceitful, double-dealing, hypocritical, insincere, two-faced (inf), untrustworthy, unreliable. OPPOSITE: faithful.

untrustworthy adj unreliable, undependable, slippery (inf), dishonest, deceitful, duplicitous, double-dealing, false, untrue, disloyal, faithless, unfaithful, inconstant, fickle, treacherous, perfidious. OPPOSITE: trustworthy.

untruth noun 1 (telling untruths) falsehood, lie, fib (inf), whopper (inf), porky (inf), fabrication, fiction, tale, story, cock-and-bull story (inf). OPPOSITE: truth. 2 (full of untruth) lying, mendacity, untruthfulness, falsity, deceit, deceitfulness, fabrication, fiction, inaccuracy, terminological inexactitude (inf). OPPOSITE: truthfulness.

untruthful adj 1 (an untruthful person) lying, mendacious, economical with the truth (inf), deceitful, dishonest, insincere, hypocritical, two-faced (inf). OPPOSITE: truthful. 2 (an untruthful story) false, untrue, fabricated, invented, wrong, erroneous, incorrect, inaccurate. OPPOSITE: true.

unused *adj* **1** (*unused goods*) new, brand-new, pristine, untouched, intact, leftover, surplus. OPPOSITE: used. **2** (*unused to such hard work*) unaccustomed, unfamiliar, unacquainted, inexperienced, unpractised. OPPOSITE: accustomed.

unusual *adj* uncommon, out of the ordinary, exceptional, extraordinary, remarkable, unexpected, surprising, singular, peculiar, odd, strange, curious, queer, weird, offbeat (*inf*), unconventional, unorthodox, irregular, abnormal, atypical, different, unfamiliar, unwonted, infrequent, rare. OPPOSITE: usual.

unutterable *adj* ineffable, unspeakable, inexpressible, indescribable, beyond words.

unvarnished *adj* plain, simple, bare, naked, undisguised, unembellished, unadorned, pure, sheer, stark, direct, straightforward, honest, frank, candid. OPPOSITE: embellished.

unvarying *adj* unchanging, changeless, constant, perpetual, steady, stable, uniform, same, invariable, unchangeable. OPPOSITE: changing.

unveil *verb* reveal, expose, uncover, lay bare, unmask, disclose, divulge, make known. OPPOSITE: veil.

unwanted *adj* unsolicited, unsought, unasked, uninvited, unwelcome, undesirable, uncalled-for, unneeded, unnecessary, surplus, superfluous, redundant, rejected. OPPOSITE: wanted.

unwarranted *adj* unjustified, uncalled-for, gratuitous, unprovoked, undeserved, unmerited, unreasonable, undue, wrong, unjust, unfair, unjustifiable, unwarrantable, indefensible, inexcusable, unforgivable, unpardonable. OPPOSITE: justified.

unwary *adj* incautious, unguarded, off guard, careless, heedless, thoughtless, unthinking, hasty, rash, reckless, indiscreet, imprudent, unwise. OPPOSITE: wary.

unwavering *adj* unfaltering, unswerving, undeviating, unhesitating, unquestioning, firm, unshakeable, constant, staunch, steadfast, unflagging, untiring, determined, resolute, resolved, single-minded. OPPOSITE: wavering.

unwelcome *adj* unwanted, uninvited, unpopular, rejected, unacceptable, undesirable, unpleasant, disagreeable. OPPOSITE: welcome.

unwell *adj* ill, sick, ailing, indisposed, poorly (*inf*), under the weather (*inf*), off colour, below par, out of sorts (*inf*), unhealthy, unfit, run down. OPPOSITE: well.

unwieldy *adj* bulky, large, heavy, hefty, weighty, ponderous, cumbersome, ungainly, clumsy, awkward, unmanageable, unhandy, inconvenient. OPPOSITE: handy.

unwilling *adj* reluctant, averse, loath, indisposed, disinclined, opposed, resistant, hesitant, unenthusiastic, grudging. OPPOSITE: willing.

unwind *verb* **1** (*unwind the tape*) unroll, unreel, uncoil, undo, untwist, untwine, unravel. OPPOSITE: wind. **2** (*unwind at the end of the day*) relax, calm down, wind down, slow down, take it easy (*inf*), put one's feet up (*inf*), chill out (*sl*), hang loose (*sl*).

unwise *adj* imprudent, incautious, indiscreet, impolitic, inadvisable, ill-advised, injudicious, ill-judged, ill-considered, foolhardy, rash, reckless, irresponsible, silly, foolish, stupid, senseless, unintelligent. OPPOSITE: wise.

unwitting *adj* **1** (*an unwitting accomplice*) unknowing, ignorant, unaware, unconscious, oblivious, involuntary, unsuspecting, unthinking. OPPOSITE: aware. **2** (*an unwitting mistake*) accidental, chance, inadvertent, unintentional, unintended, unconscious, involuntary. OPPOSITE: deliberate.

unwonted *adj* unusual, uncommon, rare, unfamiliar, unaccustomed, uncustomary, atypical, abnormal, out of the ordinary, extraordinary, exceptional, unheard-of. OPPOSITE: usual.

unworldly *adj* **1** (*unworldly phenomena*) spiritual, metaphysical, unearthly, supernatural, otherworldly, extraterrestrial. OPPOSITE: material. **2** (*an unworldly young man*) unsophisticated, inexperienced, raw, green (*inf*), naive, guileless, artless, ingenuous, innocent, childlike, trusting, credulous, gullible, natural, simple, unaffected, romantic, visionary, idealistic. OPPOSITE: worldly.

unworthy *adj* **1** (*behaviour unworthy of an officer*) unseemly, unbecoming, unbefitting, unsuitable, inappropriate, unfitting, incompatible, incongruous, out of keeping, out of character, out of place, discreditable, dishonourable, ignoble, reprehensible, contemptible, despicable, base. OPPOSITE: worthy. **2** (*unworthy of the award*) undeserving, ineligible, unqualified. **3** (*an unworthy offering*) inferior, second-rate, poor, paltry.

unwrap *verb* undo, open, uncover. OPPOSITE: wrap.

unwritten *adj* oral, verbal, word-of-mouth, unrecorded, understood, accepted, conventional, traditional.

unyielding *adj* inflexible, unbending, stiff, rigid, firm, hard, solid, immovable, staunch, steadfast, resolute, determined, adamant, intransigent, uncompromising, obstinate, stubborn, obdurate, intractable. OPPOSITE: flexible.

up-and-coming *adj* promising, ambitious, enterprising, assertive, go-getting (*inf*), pushy (*inf*).

upbeat *adj* optimistic, hopeful, positive, bullish (*inf*), cheerful, buoyant, bright, rosy, promising, encouraging, heartening. OPPOSITE: downbeat.

upbraid *verb* scold, chide, reprimand, reprove, reproach, rebuke, castigate, berate, tell off (*inf*), criticize, censure, blame, condemn. OPPOSITE: praise.

upbringing *adj* raising, rearing, bringing up, breeding, parenting, care, nurture, instruction, training, education.

update *verb* modernize, upgrade, renew, refresh, revise, amend.

upgrade *verb* **1** (*upgrade the system*) improve, better, ameliorate, enhance, update, modernize. OPPOSITE: downgrade. **2** (*upgraded to manager*) promote, advance, elevate, raise. OPPOSITE: demote.

upheaval *noun* disruption, disturbance, disorder, confusion, turmoil, chaos, upset, shake-up (*inf*), revolution, cataclysm.

uphill *adj* **1** (*an uphill task*) hard, difficult, strenuous, arduous, laborious, tiring, wearisome, exhausting, gruelling, punishing, taxing, tough, Herculean,

Sisyphean. OPPOSITE: easy. **2** (*an uphill slope*) rising, ascending, upward, climbing, mounting. OPPOSITE: downhill.

uphold *verb* sustain, maintain, support, back, endorse, advocate, promote, champion, defend. OPPOSITE: oppose.

upkeep *noun* maintenance, conservation, preservation, support, subsistence, sustenance, expenses, costs, overheads, expenditure, outlay.

uplift *verb* **1** (*uplifted by the explosion*) lift, lift up, raise, elevate, hoist. OPPOSITE: lower. **2** (*uplift their morale*) exalt, raise, elevate, edify, enrich, enhance, improve, ameliorate, better. **3** (*uplifted by the news*) cheer, gladden, hearten, buoy up, elate, exhilarate, inspirit, inspire. OPPOSITE: depress.

upper *adj* higher, superior, loftier, greater, senior, high, elevated, exalted, top, topmost, uppermost. OPPOSITE: lower.

upper-class *adj* aristocratic, noble, highborn, patrician, blue-blooded, high-class, exclusive, élite, top-drawer (*inf*), posh (*inf*). OPPOSITE: plebeian.

upright *adj* **1** (*an upright post*) vertical, perpendicular, straight, erect, on end. OPPOSITE: horizontal. **2** (*an upright citizen*) righteous, virtuous, good, worthy, decent, respectable, honourable, reputable, upstanding, honest, law-abiding, moral, ethical, principled, high-minded, just, fair. OPPOSITE: dishonest.

uprising *noun* rebellion, revolt, revolution, insurrection, insurgence, riot, mutiny, coup, putsch.

uproar *noun* turmoil, tumult, turbulence, disturbance, disorder, riot, pandemonium, mayhem, bedlam, din, racket, noise, commotion, clamour, brouhaha, hubbub, outcry, furore, fracas, brawl, rumpus, ruction. OPPOSITE: peace.

uproarious *adj* **1** (*an uproarious gathering*) tumultuous, turbulent, disorderly, riotous, noisy, clamorous, rowdy, wild, boisterous. OPPOSITE: quiet. **2** (*an uproarious performance*) very funny, hilarious, hysterical, side-splitting, rib-tickling, killing (*inf*).

uproot *verb* pull up, deracinate, extirpate, root out, displace, remove, destroy, eliminate, eradicate, wipe out.

upset *verb* **1** (*upset the boat*) overturn, knock over, tip over, spill, capsize, upend, topple, destabilize. OPPOSITE: right. **2** (*upset his mother*) distress, sadden, grieve, hurt, dismay, frighten, alarm, worry, agitate, trouble, bother, anger, annoy, put out, disturb, perturb, ruffle, discompose, disconcert, fluster. OPPOSITE: reassure. **3** (*upset the system*) disrupt, spoil, mess up, confuse, muddle, jumble, mix up, disorganize, disarrange, turn upside down.
➤ *adj* distressed, sad, unhappy, hurt, sorry, dismayed, frightened, alarmed, worried, agitated, troubled, bothered, angry, annoyed, put out, disturbed, perturbed, ruffled, discomposed, disconcerted, flustered, in a state (*inf*). OPPOSITE: calm.
➤ *noun* **1** (*causing a lot of upset*) distress, sorrow, grief, dismay, alarm, worry, agitation, trouble, bother, disturbance, disruption. **2** (*a stomach upset*) ailment, illness, sickness, bug (*inf*), disorder, disturbance, complaint.

upshot *noun* result, consequence, outcome, issue, effect, end, conclusion. OPPOSITE: beginning.

upside down *adj* **1** (*the picture is upside down*) inverted, wrong way up, wrong side up, upended, overturned, capsized, upset. **2** (*the office was upside down for weeks*) untidy, in disorder, in disarray, topsy-turvy, chaotic, in a mess, in a muddle, jumbled up.

upstart *noun* parvenu, arriviste, nouveau riche, social climber, wannabe (*inf*).

up-to-date *adj* modern, contemporary, fashionable, in vogue, trendy (*inf*), cool (*inf*), all the rage (*inf*), current, prevailing, recent, new, latest, up-to-the-minute, state-of-the-art (*inf*), present-day, now (*inf*). OPPOSITE: old-fashioned.

upturn *noun* upswing, improvement, recovery, revival, rise, increase, upsurge, boost. OPPOSITE: downturn.

urban *adj* civic, municipal, metropolitan, town, city, oppidan, built-up. OPPOSITE: rural.

urbane *adj* elegant, refined, polished, suave, debonair, gracious, charming, courteous, polite, civil, well-mannered, sophisticated, worldly, civilized, cultured, cultivated. OPPOSITE: uncouth.

urbanity *noun* elegance, refinement, suavity, charm, courtesy, politeness, civility, sophistication, worldliness, culture, cultivation.

urchin *noun* kid, brat, ragamuffin, guttersnipe, gamin, imp, waif, stray.

urge *verb* **1** (*urging them on*) push, drive, propel, impel, force, constrain, incite, provoke, goad, spur, encourage, egg on (*inf*), prompt, stimulate, induce, persuade. OPPOSITE: deter. **2** (*she urged us to reconsider*) beg, implore, beseech, entreat, exhort, plead with, supplicate, appeal to, petition. **3** (*urge restraint*) advise, counsel, recommend, suggest, advocate, endorse.
➤ *noun* desire, wish, itch (*inf*), yearning, longing, yen (*inf*), impulse, fancy, drive, need, compulsion.

urgency *noun* importance, seriousness, gravity, exigency, extremity, emergency, priority, hurry, haste.

urgent *adj* **1** (*more urgent matters*) pressing, instant, immediate, important, high-priority, serious, grave, imperative, exigent, crucial, critical, vital, essential. OPPOSITE: unimportant. **2** (*urgent requests*) insistent, importunate, earnest, persistent.

urinate *verb* pass water, micturate, wee (*inf*), wee-wee (*inf*), pee (*inf*), piss (*sl*), piddle (*inf*), widdle (*inf*), tinkle (*inf*), spend a penny (*inf*), have a leak (*inf*), have a slash (*inf*).

usable *adj* utilizable, exploitable, available, functional, operational, serviceable.

usage *noun* **1** (*an age-old usage*) custom, practice, habit, tradition, convention, form, method, procedure, routine, rule, etiquette, fashion, mode. **2** (*with careful usage*) use, employment, application, treatment, handling, management, operation, running, control.

use *verb* **1** (*use force*) utilize, employ, make use of, avail oneself of, resort to, have recourse to, apply, exercise, operate, wield, ply, practise. **2** (*badly used by her employers*) treat, deal with, handle, manipulate, exploit, take advantage of, impose on, walk all over (*inf*), abuse,

misuse. **3** (*use too much fuel*) consume, spend, expend, get through, use up, exhaust, drain, deplete, waste, squander, fritter away. OPPOSITE: save.
➣ *noun* **1** (*the use of machinery*) utilization, employment, exploitation, application, exercise, operation, practice. **2** (*with careful use*) treatment, handling, manipulation, usage. **3** (*years of constant use*) usage, wear, wear and tear. OPPOSITE: disuse. **4** (*of little use*) utility, usefulness, advantage, benefit, good, profit, value, worth, help, assistance, avail, service. OPPOSITE: uselessness. **5** (*I have no use for it*) need, necessity, call, demand, cause, occasion, purpose, reason, point. **6** (*established by use*) custom, practice, habit, usage.

used *adj* secondhand, pre-owned, cast-off, hand-me-down (*inf*). OPPOSITE: new.

used to accustomed to, familiar with, no stranger to (*inf*), at home with (*inf*), acclimatized to, habituated to, inured to, hardened to.

useful *adj* helpful, serviceable, advantageous, beneficial, profitable, valuable, worthwhile, fruitful, productive, effective, efficacious, practical, functional, utilitarian, handy, convenient, labour-saving, versatile, all-purpose. OPPOSITE: useless.

useless *adj* futile, vain, idle, unavailing, ineffective, inefficacious, fruitless, unproductive, abortive, unsuccessful, worthless, unusable, impractical, no good (*inf*). OPPOSITE: useful.

usher *noun* guide, escort, attendant, doorkeeper.
➣ *verb* guide, escort, pilot, steer, lead, direct, conduct, show.

usher in herald, announce, precede, pave the way for, introduce, bring in, launch, get under way.

usual *adj* customary, accustomed, habitual, wonted, routine, regular, set, established, normal, typical, average, general, stock, standard, conventional, familiar, common, ordinary, everyday, run-of-the-mill. OPPOSITE: unusual.

usually *adv* normally, typically, generally, ordinarily, as a rule, by and large, nine times out of ten (*inf*), mainly, chiefly, mostly, on the whole. OPPOSITE: rarely.

usurp *verb* seize, take over, commandeer, appropriate, expropriate, arrogate, assume, infringe, encroach.

utensil *noun* implement, instrument, tool, device, contrivance, apparatus, appliance, gadget.

utilitarian *adj* practical, functional, useful, serviceable, sensible, plain.

utility *noun* usefulness, helpfulness, serviceability, practicality, convenience, use, help, service, avail, advantage, benefit, profit. OPPOSITE: futility.

utilize *verb* use, employ, make use of, avail oneself of, put to use, exploit, take advantage of, turn to account.

utmost *adj* **1** (*the utmost faith in their ability*) maximum, most, greatest, highest, supreme, paramount. OPPOSITE: minimum. **2** (*the utmost limit*) extreme, uttermost, farthest, furthest, last, final, ultimate.
➣ *noun* maximum, most, best, top, peak, pinnacle, uttermost.

utopian *adj* ideal, perfect, dream, paradisiacal, elysian, idealistic, visionary, quixotic, impractical, unworkable.

utter[1] *verb* say, speak, express, voice, vocalize, verbalize, pronounce, articulate, enunciate, declare, proclaim, announce, promulgate. OPPOSITE: suppress.

utter[2] *adj* complete, total, thorough, absolute, downright, out-and-out, sheer, arrant, unmitigated, unqualified, unconditional, categorical. OPPOSITE: partial.

utterance *noun* **1** (*ignoring his utterances*) remark, comment, statement, declaration, proclamation, announcement. **2** (*gave utterance to her intentions*) expression, voice, vocalization, verbalization, articulation, enunciation.

utterly *adv* completely, totally, thoroughly, absolutely, downright, perfectly, unconditionally. OPPOSITE: somewhat.

vacancy *noun* **1** (*a vacancy in the company*) opportunity, opening, job, post, position, place, situation, slot. **2** (*the hotel had a vacancy*) room, space. **3** (*a vacancy between the walls*) void, gap, space. **4** (*the vacancy of his expression*) vacuousness, expressionlessness, emotionlessness, blankness, emptiness.

vacant *adj* **1** (*a vacant chair*) empty, void, unfilled, unoccupied, free, not in use, available. OPPOSITE: occupied. **2** (*a vacant expression*) blank, expressionless, deadpan, impassive, vacuous, inane, thoughtless, unthinking.

vacate *verb* evacuate, abandon, desert, quit, leave, depart, withdraw.

vacation *noun* holiday, trip, rest, leave, furlough, time off, break, recess.

vaccinate *verb* inoculate, immunize, protect.

vacillate *verb* fluctuate, oscillate, waver, falter, hesitate, dither, be indecisive, sway, shilly-shally (*inf*), rock.

vacillating *adj* indecisive, irresolute, uncertain, wavering, dithering, hesitant, fickle. OPPOSITE: firm.

vacuous *adj* **1** (*a vacuous look*) blank, vacant, expressionless, deadpan. **2** (*a vacuous pupil*) vacant, stupid, unintelligent, mindless, brainless. OPPOSITE: intelligent.

vacuum *noun* void, emptiness, vacuity, space, gap, chasm.

vagabond *noun* vagrant, tramp, beggar, nomad, itinerant, migrant, wayfarer, wanderer, rogue, rascal, down-and-out, beachcomber, outcast.

vagary *noun* whim, whimsy, fancy, humour, caprice, quirk, notion.

vagrancy *noun* nomadism, itineracy, wandering, roving, roaming, travelling, drifting, homelessness, rootlessness.

vagrant *noun* tramp, vagabond, down-and-out, beggar, nomad, itinerant, drifter, wanderer.
 ⮞ *adj* nomadic, itinerant, peripatetic, wandering,

vagabond, roaming, roving, shiftless, rootless, unsettled, homeless, down-and-out. OPPOSITE: settled.

vague *adj* **1** (*a vague outline*) indistinct, indeterminate, ill-defined, unclear, obscure, nebulous, shadowy, hazy, misty, foggy, fuzzy, blurred, blurry, bleary, unfocused, out of focus, dim, faint. OPPOSITE: clear. **2** (*a vague explanation*) imprecise, ambiguous, hazy, woolly, unclear, indefinite, inexact, generalized, rough, loose, evasive, lax. **3** (*he was vague about what happened*) uncertain, unsure, doubtful, confused.

vaguely *adv* **1** (*the face is vaguely familiar*) dimly, obscurely, distantly, remotely, somehow. **2** (*he nodded vaguely in reply*) absent-mindedly, absently, vacantly, vacuously, abstractedly. **3** (*gesture vaguely towards the north*) roughly, imprecisely, approximately.

vain *adj* **1** (*a vain young woman*) conceited, boastful, proud, arrogant, haughty, self-important, self-satisfied, stuck-up (*inf*), snooty (*inf*), overweening, cocky, egotistical, big-headed (*inf*), swollen-headed (*inf*), full of him/herself (*inf*), inflated, affected, pretentious, ostentatious. OPPOSITE: modest. **2** (*a vain attempt*) futile, idle, hollow, empty, useless, pointless, unavailing, ineffective, ineffectual, fruitless, unproductive, unprofitable, bootless, abortive, worthless, trivial, unimportant. OPPOSITE: worthwhile.

in vain vainly, to no avail, uselessly, ineffectually, fruitlessly, unsuccessfully.

valediction *noun* farewell, goodbye, adieu, leave-taking. OPPOSITE: greeting.

valedictory *adj* farewell, parting, departing, last, final.

valiant *adj* valorous, brave, courageous, heroic, intrepid, fearless, dauntless, undaunted, bold, daring, gallant, plucky, doughty, indomitable. OPPOSITE: cowardly.

valid *adj* **1** (*a valid reason*) sound, good, well-founded, well-grounded, logical, reasonable, cogent, telling, convincing, credible, powerful, forceful, substantial, weighty, efficacious, conclusive, justifiable, just. OPPOSITE: weak. **2** (*a valid passport*) official, legal, lawful, legitimate, genuine, proper, authentic, bona fide, real, true, binding, effective. OPPOSITE: invalid.

validate *verb* **1** (*validate the document*) ratify, certify, sanction, endorse, authorize, legalize, legitimize, license, approve. **2** (*validate the claim*) substantiate, confirm, corroborate, authenticate, verify, justify, prove.

valley *noun* dale, dell, vale, glen, hollow, depression. OPPOSITE: hill.

valour *noun* bravery, courage, heroism, intrepidity, fearlessness, dauntlessness, fortitude, boldness, daring, gallantry, pluck, spirit, mettle. OPPOSITE: cowardice.

valuable *adj* **1** (*a valuable painting*) precious, costly, expensive, dear, priceless, rare. OPPOSITE: worthless. **2** (*valuable experience*) helpful, important, advantageous, beneficial, instructive, profitable, useful, worthy, worthwhile.

value *noun* **1** (*the value of this discovery*) worth, merit, importance, significance, use, usefulness, utility, advantage, benefit, profit, good, gain, avail, desirability. **2** (*the value of the jewellery*) cost, price, worth, valuation, assessment.
≫ *verb* **1** (*he was valued by all his friends*) prize, esteem, admire, appreciate, respect, cherish, hold dear, treasure. OPPOSITE: scorn. **2** (*he valued the collection for them*) evaluate, assess, appraise, estimate, rate, price, survey.

values *pl noun* morals, principles, ethics, standards.

van *noun* lorry, truck, pantechnicon, wagon, trailer, carriage.

vandalism *noun* destruction, ruin, damage, mutilation.

vanguard *noun* fore, forefront, front rank, front line, firing line, advance guard, spearhead, van, trendsetter.

vanish *verb* **1** (*the figure vanished*) disappear, fade, evanesce, dissolve, melt away, evaporate, dissipate, disperse, go away, depart, leave, recede, withdraw. OPPOSITE: appear. **2** (*his doubts had vanished by morning*) pass away, die out, end.

vanity *noun* **1** (*the idea appealed to her vanity*) conceit, egotism, self-love, self-satisfaction, self-glorification, narcissism, pride, arrogance, haughtiness, snootiness (*inf*), boastfulness, big-headedness (*inf*), swollen-headedness (*inf*), high-headedness. OPPOSITE: modesty. **2** (*the vanity of the endeavour*) futility, worthlessness, emptiness, hollowness, uselessness, idleness, pointlessness, fruitlessness, frivolity, triviality, unreality, insignificance, unimportance.

vanquish *verb* defeat, conquer, subjugate, subdue, humble, rout, overwhelm, overcome, overpower, overthrow, crush, quell, repress, beat, master, confound, turn over (*inf*), trounce, thrash. OPPOSITE: surrender.

vapid *adj* insipid, flat, limp, lifeless, colourless, flavourless, tasteless, watery, wishy-washy, bland, banal, tame, dull, boring, tedious, tiresome, grey, uninteresting, stale, trite.

vapour *noun* steam, smoke, fog, mist, haze, fumes, breath, exhalation.

variable *adj* changeable, mutable, vacillating, wavering, fluctuating, capricious, mercurial, fickle, inconstant,

fitful, uneven, unsteady, unstable, shifting, protean. OPPOSITE: constant.

variance *noun* variation, discrepancy, disparity, divergence, difference, disagreement, inconsistency.
at variance in disagreement, in conflict, in opposition, at odds, in dispute. OPPOSITE: agreement.

variant *noun* variation, alternative, development, modification, deviant.
≫ *adj* alternative, divergent, different, derived, modified, deviant.

variation *noun* **1** (*variations of the original design*) alteration, modification, variant, change, innovation, novelty. **2** (*some variation between the two samples*) diversity, variety, difference, discrepancy, deviation, divergence, diversification, fluctuation, vacillation.

varied *adj* various, assorted, mixed, diverse, multifarious, wide-ranging, different, miscellaneous, heterogeneous, sundry, motley.

variegated *adj* mottled, speckled, dappled, pied, motley, marbled, streaked, varicoloured, multicoloured. OPPOSITE: plain.

variety *noun* **1** (*observe the variety between the two species*) difference, dissimilarity, discrepancy, disparity, variation, change, diversity, multiplicity. OPPOSITE: uniformity. **2** (*a variety of models*) miscellany, assortment, mixture, medley, pot-pourri, collection, range. **3** (*identify the variety of butterfly*) class, classification, kind, type, sort, order, group, species, brand, make, strain.

various *adj* **1** (*choose between various colours*) varying, different, diverse, assorted, miscellaneous, mixed, motley, dissimilar, disparate. OPPOSITE: identical. **2** (*at various times of the day*) varied, sundry, many, numerous, several, manifold.

varnish *noun* glaze, gloss, lacquer, polish, resin, enamel, shellac, veneer, coating.
≫ *verb* glaze, lacquer, polish, gloss, coat, enamel.

vary *verb* **1** (*vary the pitch*) change, alter, modify, modulate, diversify, transform, permutate, alternate. **2** (*his confession varied from the truth*) deviate, diverge, swerve, depart, differ, disagree, clash, fluctuate. **3** (*their opinions varied*) be at odds, disagree, be in conflict, differ, be in opposition, be in disagreement.

vast *adj* **1** (*a vast ocean*) immense, broad, wide, extensive, expansive, boundless, unbounded, limitless, illimitable, immeasurable, measureless, infinite. **2** (*a vast building*) massive, huge, bulky, hulking (*inf*), immense, enormous, great, tremendous, monumental, prodigious, colossal, gigantic, mammoth, elephantine. OPPOSITE: tiny.

vault[1] *noun* **1** (*the vault of the ceiling*) arch, span, roof. **2** (*the vault beneath the castle*) cellar, basement, chamber, cavern. **3** (*bank vault*) strongroom, repository, depository. **4** (*laid to rest in the vault*) tomb, crypt, mausoleum.

vault[2] *verb* leap, spring, jump, leap-frog, bound, hurdle, clear.

vaunt *verb* boast, brag, crow, trumpet, parade, flaunt, show off (*inf*), swank (*inf*). OPPOSITE: belittle.

veer *verb* change, swing, shift, turn, sheer, tack, swerve, wheel, deviate, diverge.

vegetate *verb* **1** (*the plant should vegetate within days*) sprout, grow, shoot, burgeon, germinate, swell. OPPOSITE: wither. **2** (*she vegetated in her room*) languish, idle, do nothing, waste time, laze, hang out (*inf*), loaf, lounge about, stagnate. OPPOSITE: work.

vegetation *noun* foliage, greenery, flora, herbage, plants, trees, flowers.

vehemence *noun* passion, spirit, fervour, fervency, ardour, energy, vigour, verve, enthusiasm, zeal, keenness, eagerness, earnestness, strength, power, force, forcefulness, intensity, emphasis, gusto, urgency, impetuosity, animation, violence, warmth, heat.

vehement *adj* ardent, fervent, impassioned, passionate, spirited, earnest, enthusiastic, eager, keen, intense, urgent, forceful, forcible, emphatic, furious, vigorous, violent, burning, heated, fierce, strong, powerful. OPPOSITE: subdued.

vehicle *noun* **1** (*we need a vehicle to take us there*) conveyance, transportation, car, bus, means of transport. **2** (*a vehicle for his frustration*) means, agency, instrument, medium, organ, channel.

veil *noun* cover, screen, cloak, mantle, curtain, blanket, shroud, mask, disguise, blind.
➤ *verb* cover, screen, cloak, blanket, muffle, dim, obscure, conceal, hide, mask, disguise, camouflage, shield. OPPOSITE: expose.

vein *noun* **1** (*a vein of gold*) seam, stratum, lode. **2** (*a vein of white*) streak, stripe, line. **3** (*a dark vein of pessimism*) strain, streak, hint, dash. **4** (*he was in optimistic vein*) frame of mind, mood, humour, disposition, bent, tendency, character, tenor, tone, attitude. **5** (*the veins in his arm showed*) blood vessel, artery.

velocity *noun* speed, rate, swiftness, rapidity, quickness, impetus, celerity. OPPOSITE: slowness.

velvety *adj* velvet, smooth, soft. OPPOSITE: coarse.

venal *adj* corrupt, corruptible, bribable, bent (*inf*), mercenary, avaricious, grasping, rapacious, sordid. OPPOSITE: incorruptible.

vendetta *noun* feud, rivalry, war, quarrel, enmity, bad blood, bitterness.

vendor *noun* seller, merchant, trader, dealer, supplier, stockist, salesperson, e-tailer.

veneer *noun* **1** (*this table has an ebony veneer*) layer, coat, coating, covering, surface, facing, finish. **2** (*a veneer of respectability*) front, façade, show, appearance, pretence, guise, mask, semblance.

venerable *adj* venerated, revered, reverenced, respected, honoured, esteemed, worshipped, hallowed, august, grave, wise.

venerate *verb* revere, reverence, honour, esteem, adore, worship. OPPOSITE: despise.

vengeance *noun* revenge, retribution, requital, retaliation, reprisal, tit for tat (*inf*). OPPOSITE: forgiveness.
with a vengeance 1 (*the fire burned with a vengeance*) furiously, vehemently, violently, forcefully, energetically, wildly. **2** (*he set to with a vengeance*) flat

out, all out, at full pelt, to the utmost, to the full, full tilt (*inf*).

vengeful *adj* revengeful, vindictive, spiteful, unforgiving, avenging, retaliatory, retributive. OPPOSITE: forgiving.

venial *adj* excusable, pardonable, forgivable, allowable, slight, minor, insignificant, trivial, trifling. OPPOSITE: unforgivable.

venom *noun* **1** (*snake venom*) poison, toxin. **2** (*she spoke with venom*) rancour, spite, spitefulness, ill will, bitterness, resentment, acrimony, malice, malignity, malevolence, hate, hostility, enmity, animosity, gall, spleen, grudge. OPPOSITE: benevolence.

venomous *adj* **1** (*a venomous snake*) poisonous, deadly, lethal, toxic, envenomed, noxious, harmful, virulent. OPPOSITE: harmless. **2** (*a venomous remark*) spiteful, malicious, vindictive, vicious, hostile, malevolent, malignant, baleful, rancorous, bitter. OPPOSITE: benevolent.

vent *noun* hole, aperture, opening, outlet, spiracle, orifice, passage, duct.
➤ *verb* air, express, utter, voice, emit, let out, pour out, discharge, release.

ventilate *verb* **1** (*ventilate the house*) air, aerate, oxygenate, fan, air-condition, cool, freshen, purify. **2** (*he needed to ventilate his ideas*) express, discuss, talk about, debate, go over, review, examine, scrutinize, broadcast, air, make known.

venture *verb* **1** (*venture a fortune*) risk, hazard, endanger, imperil, jeopardize, speculate, stake, wager, chance. **2** (*he ventured to suggest a way out*) dare, presume. **3** (*may I venture a suggestion?*) advance, put forward, volunteer.
➤ *noun* **1** (*a new business venture*) undertaking, enterprise, project, operation, endeavour, speculation, gamble, risk, hazard. **2** (*an exciting venture into the unknown*) adventure, mission, exploit, journey.

venturesome *adj* daring, bold, adventurous, enterprising, brave, courageous, doughty, dauntless, daredevil (*inf*), fearless, intrepid, plucky, spirited, reckless, foolhardy. OPPOSITE: cowardly.

veracious *adj* **1** (*a veracious witness*) truthful, honest, frank, sincere, virtuous, candid, trustworthy, decent, upright, upstanding, honourable, reliable. OPPOSITE: dishonest. **2** (*a veracious account of events*) true, truthful, factual, literal, accurate, precise, exact, realistic.

verbal *adj* spoken, oral, vocal, unwritten, said, uttered, verbatim, literal, word-of-mouth. OPPOSITE: written.

verbatim *adv* word-for-word, literally, to the letter, faithfully, exactly, precisely, closely.

verbiage *noun* verbosity, prolixity, wordiness, long-windedness, waffle, loquacity, circumlocution, periphrasis, tautology, repetition, redundancy. OPPOSITE: terseness.

verbose *adj* prolix, wordy, windy, long-winded, diffuse, loquacious, garrulous, talkative, circumlocutory, roundabout, periphrastic, tautological. OPPOSITE: terse.

verbosity *noun* verboseness, long-windedness, windiness, wordiness, garrulity, loquaciousness, loquacity, prolixity.

verdant *adj* green, grassy, leafy, fresh, lush.

verdict *noun* decision, judgement, adjudication, conclusion, finding, ruling, opinion, sentence.

verge *noun* **1** (*the verge of the road*) edge, border, margin, lip, rim, brim, brink, limit, boundary. **2** (*on the verge of a breakthrough*) brink, threshold, point.
➤ *verb* approach, border on, incline, tend, bear, lean.

verification *noun* confirmation, proof, authentication, validation, ratification, corroboration, substantiation, endorsement, attestation, checking.

verify *verb* confirm, substantiate, corroborate, endorse, ratify, bear out, prove, establish, attest, testify, affirm, authenticate, validate, accredit. OPPOSITE: refute.

verisimilitude *noun* probability, likelihood, likeliness, credibility, plausibility, realism, authenticity, semblance, resemblance. OPPOSITE: improbability.

veritable *adj* real, actual, genuine, authentic, positive, absolute.

verity *noun* truth, truthfulness, reality, actuality, fact, factuality, validity, veracity, authenticity, soundness. OPPOSITE: falsity.

vernacular *adj* native, indigenous, local, informal, colloquial, popular, common, vulgar. OPPOSITE: foreign.
➤ *noun* native language, speech, mother tongue, parlance, dialect, patois, idiom, cant, jargon, slang.

versatile *adj* **1** (*a versatile performer*) adaptable, all-round, multifaceted, many-sided, flexible, resourceful, clever. **2** (*a versatile vehicle*) all-purpose, general-purpose, multipurpose, adaptable, adjustable, handy, functional.

verse *noun* **1** (*she read some verse*) poetry, rhyme, ode, sonnet, limerick, lyric, song, ballad, ditty, doggerel. **2** (*a poem with six verses*) stanza, canto, couplet, part.

versed *adj* skilled, proficient, accomplished, practised, experienced, acquainted, familiar, conversant, knowledgeable. OPPOSITE: inexperienced.

version *noun* **1** (*a new version of the play*) rendering, adaptation, interpretation, account, translation, reading. **2** (*the latest version of the car*) type, model, style, design, kind, form, variant.

vertex *noun* apex, apogee, peak, summit, point, tip, top, crown, acme, zenith, pinnacle, height. OPPOSITE: base.

vertical *adj* upright, perpendicular, erect, upstanding, on end. OPPOSITE: horizontal.

vertigo *noun* giddiness, dizziness, light-headedness, wooziness (*inf*).

verve *noun* vigour, energy, force, enthusiasm, spirit, passion, fervour, life, dash, sparkle, élan, vitality, vivacity, liveliness, animation, relish, gusto, pizzazz (*inf*), zip (*inf*). OPPOSITE: apathy.

very *adv* extremely, exceedingly, terribly (*inf*), awfully (*inf*), dreadfully (*inf*), jolly (*inf*), remarkably, excessively, exceptionally, unusually, uncommonly, highly, deeply, greatly, really, absolutely, quite, pretty (*inf*), truly, acutely, particularly, noticeably, incredibly, unbelievably. OPPOSITE: slightly.
➤ *adj* **1** (*this is the very hat he wore*) actual, exact, precise, real, selfsame, same, identical, true, genuine. **2** (*that is the very thing I need*) perfect, ideal, exact, right, fitting, appropriate, suitable. **3** (*the very cheek of it*) sheer, utter, pure, plain, simple, bare, mere.

vessel *noun* **1** (*board the vessel*) boat, ship, craft. **2** (*fill the vessel with water*) container, receptacle, holder, jar, jug, pot, bowl.

vest *verb* give, grant, endow, bestow, confer, invest, supply, sanction, authorize.

vestibule *noun* lobby, foyer, anteroom, antechamber, hall, entrance hall, entranceway, porch.

vestige *noun* **1** (*few vestiges of their presence*) trace, mark, sign, indication, impression. **2** (*the last vestiges of the city*) relics, remains, evidence. **3** (*not a vestige of blame*) hint, touch, tinge, scrap, dash, jot, iota, whiff (*inf*), suggestion, suspicion, inkling, soupçon, glimmer.

vestigial *adj* **1** (*a vestigial limb*) undeveloped, rudimentary, functionless, incomplete, reduced. **2** (*vestigial relics of the past*) remaining, surviving.

vet *verb* check, inspect, scrutinize, appraise, survey, review, scan, investigate, examine.

veteran *noun* old hand, old-timer, old stager, past master, master, expert. OPPOSITE: novice.
➤ *adj* experienced, practised, expert, proficient, adept, seasoned, long-serving, old, battle-scarred (*inf*).

veto *noun* prohibition, proscription, interdiction, ban, embargo, refusal, rejection, thumbs-down (*inf*). OPPOSITE: approval.
➤ *verb* reject, turn down, prohibit, proscribe, forbid, disallow, ban, rule out. OPPOSITE: consent.

vex *verb* annoy, irritate, provoke, pique, nettle, chafe, exasperate, infuriate, irk, anger, bother, pester, harass, hassle (*inf*), bug (*inf*), put out (*inf*), torment, tease, plague, trouble, worry, fret. OPPOSITE: soothe.

vexation *noun* **1** (*she wept with vexation*) annoyance, irritation, displeasure, exasperation, pique, provocation, perturbation, worry, discomposure, agitation, anger, rage, fury. **2** (*the job proved a vexation*) pain (*inf*), bother, nuisance, irritant, pest, problem, trouble, worry.

vexatious *adj* annoying, irritating, exasperating, aggravating (*inf*), infuriating, irksome, nagging, bothersome, burdensome, troublesome, trying, worrying, worrisome, provoking, tormenting, teasing, upsetting, distressing, disappointing, disagreeable, unpleasant.

vexed *adj* **1** (*she was exceedingly vexed*) annoyed, irritated, aggravated (*inf*), exasperated, nettled (*inf*), peeved (*inf*), provoked, angry, irate, incensed, infuriated, bothered, confused, perplexed, harassed, hassled (*inf*), ruffled, riled, agitated, put out, disturbed, troubled, worried, flustered, distressed, upset, displeased. **2** (*a vexed question*) difficult, controversial, contested, debated, disputed, moot.

viable *adj* practicable, feasible, workable, sound, usable, possible, achievable, sustainable, operable, applicable.

vibrant *adj* **1** (*a vibrant young performer*) energetic, dynamic, vigorous, lively, spirited, animated, vivacious, sparkling, electrifying, electric, thrilling, sensitive, responsive. **2** (*vibrant orange*) bright, brilliant, vivid, strong, striking, colourful.

vibrate *verb* **1** (*the wire vibrated*) oscillate, shake, tremble, quiver, shiver, swing, sway, wave, undulate. **2** (*music vibrated through the house*) palpitate, pulse, pulsate, throb, resonate, resound, reverberate, ring, echo.

vibration *noun* **1** (*the vibration of the machine*) shake, shaking, shudder, shuddering, judder (*inf*), juddering (*inf*), throb, throbbing, pulsating, trembling, tremble, quivering, quiver, quaver, shiver, shivering, tremor. **2** (*the vibration of loud music*) throb, throbbing, pulse, pulsation, resonance, reverberation, ringing, echoing.

vicar *noun* minister, parson, chaplain, pastor, rector, clergyman, clergywoman, cleric, priest, ecclesiastic, churchman.

vicarious *adj* indirect, second-hand, sympathetic, empathetic, surrogate, substitutive, delegated, deputed, acting, commissioned. OPPOSITE: personal.

vice *noun* **1** (*a reputation for vice of all kinds*) sin, wickedness, wrong, wrongdoing, iniquity, evil, evil-doing, immorality, corruption, depravity, degeneracy, profligacy. OPPOSITE: virtue. **2** (*smoking is her only vice*) weakness, foible, fault, flaw, imperfection, defect, failing, shortcoming.

vice versa *adv* conversely, inversely, reciprocally, oppositely, the other way round, contrariwise.

vicinity *noun* **1** (*in the vicinity of the capital*) neighbourhood, area, district, locality, precincts, environs, purlieus. **2** (*she was worried about the vicinity of the prison*) closeness, nearness, proximity, propinquity. OPPOSITE: distance.

vicious *adj* **1** (*vicious wild animals*) savage, ferocious, fierce, dangerous, hostile. **2** (*a vicious attack on the old man*) savage, violent, ferocious, fierce, brutal, cruel, sadistic, barbarous, atrocious, inhuman, monstrous, fiendish, diabolical. **3** (*vicious condemnation in the press*) spiteful, malicious, malevolent, malignant, vindictive, bitter, rancorous, venomous, caustic, harsh, severe, defamatory, slanderous, nasty, bitchy (*inf*), catty (*inf*). **4** (*a gang of vicious criminals*) wicked, evil, bad, sinful, immoral, unscrupulous, disreputable, unprincipled, corrupt, depraved, degenerate, dissolute, dissipated, debauched, profligate, infamous, notorious, vile. OPPOSITE: kind.

vicissitude *noun* variation, change, mutation, shift, turn, alteration, alternation, fluctuation, divergence, deviation. OPPOSITE: stability.

victim *noun* **1** (*a victim of the plague*) sufferer, casualty. **2** (*the victim of their jokes*) target, butt, fall guy (*inf*), dupe, sucker (*inf*), scapegoat, prey, quarry. **3** (*a sacrificial victim*) sacrifice, martyr.

victimize *verb* **1** (*he was victimized at school*) persecute, discriminate against, pick on. **2** (*loan sharks victimize the poor*) exploit, prey on, use, deceive, fool, dupe, swindle, cheat, trick, hoodwink, defraud.

victor *noun* winner, champion, champ (*inf*), conqueror, vanquisher, hero. OPPOSITE: loser.

victorious *adj* triumphant, successful, winning, conquering, prize-winning, unbeaten, champion, first, top. OPPOSITE: losing.

victory *noun* win, conquest, triumph, success, superiority, mastery, subjugation. OPPOSITE: defeat.

victuals *pl noun* food, provisions, supplies, stores, rations, viands, eatables (*inf*), edibles, comestibles, sustenance, grub (*inf*), nosh (*inf*).

vie *verb* strive, struggle, compete, contend, contest, rival, fight.

view *noun* **1** (*a boat came into view*) sight, vision, eyeshot. **2** (*the factory ruined the view*) scene, spectacle, vista, prospect, aspect, outlook, perspective, panorama, landscape, seascape. **3** (*an overall view of the economy*) survey, review, examination, inspection, scrutiny, study, assessment, observation, contemplation. **4** (*it is a mistake in my view*) opinion, judgement, belief, way of thinking, thinking, thought, viewpoint, impression, idea, notion, conviction, persuasion, estimation, sentiment, feeling, attitude. **5** (*with a view to finishing next week*) aim, intention, purpose, design, object, end. ➤ *verb* **1** (*view events as they happen*) watch, observe, see, behold, look at, regard, survey, scan, examine, inspect, scrutinize, eye. OPPOSITE: ignore. **2** (*she viewed his proposal with suspicion*) consider, contemplate, think about, regard, deem, judge.
in view of considering, bearing in mind, in the light of, taking into account, taking into consideration.

viewer *noun* spectator, onlooker, watcher, observer.

viewpoint *noun* standpoint, stance, point of view, perspective, slant, attitude, angle, position.

vigilance *noun* watchfulness, alertness, wakefulness, attention, attentiveness, carefulness, caution, circumspection, observation, guardedness, wariness.

vigilant *adj* watchful, observant, attentive, awake, alert, wide-awake, aware, sleepless, unsleeping, wary, cautious, careful, circumspect. OPPOSITE: careless.

vigorous *adj* **1** (*vigorous exercise*) energetic, strenuous, brisk, intense. **2** (*a vigorous performance*) dynamic, full-blooded, lively, energetic, vital, vivacious, sparkling, animated, spirited, sprightly. **3** (*a vigorous young man*) strong, robust, lusty, hardy, hale, hearty, sound, sturdy, tough, fit, flourishing. OPPOSITE: weak. **4** (*a vigorous defence of their position*) powerful, forceful, strong, stout, cogent, effective.

vigorously *adv* energetically, strenuously, lustily, heartily, eagerly, enthusiastically, forcefully, powerfully, strongly, briskly, hard, all out.

vigour *noun* energy, vitality, dynamism, activity, liveliness, vivacity, strength, power, force, forcefulness, might, potency, stamina, health, robustness, sturdiness, toughness, resilience, spirit, verve, gusto, vehemence, intensity. OPPOSITE: weakness.

vile *adj* **1** (*a vile rogue*) base, low, mean, bad, wicked, evil, sinful, immoral, depraved, corrupt, ignoble, villainous, heinous, nefarious, vicious, contemptible, despicable, loathsome, wretched, miserable, worthless. **2** (*a vile smell*) foul, odious, loathsome, disgusting, repulsive, revolting, repugnant, nauseating, sickening, nasty, horrible, horrid, offensive, obnoxious, objectionable, unpleasant, disagreeable, distasteful. OPPOSITE: good.

vilify *verb* defame, denigrate, denounce, revile, malign, slander, libel, berate, calumniate, traduce, vituperate, asperse, slur, smear, disparage, criticize, slam (*inf*), slate (*inf*), decry, abuse, badmouth (*inf*). OPPOSITE: praise.

villain *noun* scoundrel, blackguard, knave, reprobate, wretch, rogue, rascal, miscreant, malefactor, criminal, wrongdoer, evildoer, baddy (*inf*). OPPOSITE: hero.

villainous *adj* wicked, evil, sinful, bad, vile, base, debased, mean, ignoble, nefarious, heinous, infamous, notorious, vicious, cruel, criminal, depraved, degenerate. OPPOSITE: good.

villainy *noun* wickedness, evil, vice, sin, viciousness, badness, iniquity, wrongdoing, crime, criminality, offence, misdeed, delinquency, rascality, roguery, knavery, atrocity, baseness, depravity, degeneracy, turpitude.

vindicate *verb* **1** (*he was vindicated by the court*) clear, acquit, exculpate, exonerate, absolve, excuse, rehabilitate. **2** (*his protest was vindicated*) justify, defend, champion, support, back, uphold, corroborate, confirm, verify, warrant, maintain, sustain, assert, establish, advocate.

vindictive *adj* vengeful, revengeful, spiteful, malicious, rancorous, venomous, malevolent, malignant, unforgiving, resentful, implacable, relentless, unrelenting. OPPOSITE: forgiving.

vintage *noun* **1** (*looking forward to this year's vintage*) crop, harvest, gathering. **2** (*such ideas belong in a different vintage*) era, epoch, period, time.
➤ *adj* **1** (*vintage wine*) choice, fine, select, superior, supreme, quality, high-quality, prime, best, rare. **2** (*a vintage play*) classic, enduring, ageless, venerable.

violate *verb* **1** (*violate the laws of society*) break, flout, contravene, transgress, infringe, breach, disobey, disregard, ignore. OPPOSITE: observe. **2** (*she claimed she was violated by her attacker*) rape, ravish, debauch, seduce, molest, abuse. **3** (*violate the sanctity of the church*) profane, desecrate, defile, dishonour, disturb, disrupt, invade. OPPOSITE: respect.

violence *noun* **1** (*the violence of the blow*) power, strength, force, forcefulness, might. **2** (*the violence of their hatred*) intensity, vehemence, passion, ferocity, fierceness. **3** (*the storm increased in violence*) strength, intensity, ferocity, fierceness, severity, wildness, turbulence. **4** (*violence on the streets*) fighting, hostilities, bloodshed, aggression, brutality, savagery, roughness, wildness, fury, destructiveness.

violent *adj* **1** (*a violent impact*) strong, powerful, forceful, mighty, intense, ferocious, brutal, savage, damaging, ruinous, destructive, devastating. OPPOSITE: gentle. **2** (*violent pirates*) savage, fierce, ferocious, brutal, cruel, bloodthirsty, murderous, vicious, aggressive, wild. **3** (*a violent storm*) wild, uncontrollable, boisterous, blustery, turbulent, stormy, tempestuous, tumultuous, raging, furious, fierce. **4** (*a violent passion*) vehement, ardent, fervent, strong, intense, great, impassioned, passionate, fiery, hot, extreme, excessive, inordinate, uncontrolled, unbridled, unrestrained, uncontrollable, ungovernable, impetuous. **5** (*a violent headache*) intense, excruciating, agonizing, painful, severe, harsh, acute, sharp, biting.

virago *noun* shrew, termagant, harridan, battle-axe (*inf*), fury, vixen, scold, nag. OPPOSITE: angel.

virgin *noun* maid, maiden, girl, celibate, virgo intacta.
➤ *adj* **1** (*a virgin bride*) virginal, chaste, pure, immaculate, intact, maidenly, celibate, virtuous, modest, uncorrupted. **2** (*virgin snow*) new, fresh, pure, untouched, undefiled, unspoilt, unsullied, untarnished, untainted, unblemished, spotless, stainless, pristine.

virginal *adj* virgin, pure, chaste, maidenly, vestal, celibate, virtuous, immaculate, spotless, untouched, undefiled, uncorrupted.

virile *adj* **1** (*a virile hero*) manly, masculine, all-male, macho (*inf*). OPPOSITE: effeminate. **2** (*a virile physique*) powerful, forceful, strong, muscular, rugged, robust, strapping, sturdy, hardy, vigorous, lusty.

virility *noun* **1** (*an insult to his virility*) manliness, masculinity, manhood, machismo (*inf*). **2** (*he liked to show off his virility*) strength, muscularity, vigour, robustness, ruggedness, huskiness.

virtual *adj* **1** (*a virtual disaster*) practical, essential, effective, in effect. **2** (*the virtual leader of the expedition*) implied, implicit, in all but name, potential. OPPOSITE: actual.

virtually *adv* practically, as good as, in essence, in effect, effectively, almost, nearly, more or less. OPPOSITE: actually.

virtue *noun* **1** (*a man of great virtue*) goodness, righteousness, morality, rectitude, uprightness, worthiness, probity, integrity, excellence, honesty, honour, incorruptibility. OPPOSITE: vice. **2** (*the virtue of this new arrangement*) advantage, benefit, strength, asset, quality, credit, merit, worth. **3** (*no one dared to question the girl's virtue*) chastity, purity, virginity.
by virtue of because of, owing to, on account of, thanks to, by means of, by reason of, as a result of, with the help of, by way of, by dint of.

virtuosity *noun* skill, skilfulness, mastery, prowess, expertise, excellence, artistry, craftsmanship, brilliance, polish, finish, finesse, flair, panache, éclat, bravura, wizardry.

virtuoso *noun* master, expert, maestro, genius, connoisseur.
➤ *adj* masterly, skilful, expert, excellent, brilliant, dazzling, impressive, outstanding.

virtuous *adj* **1** (*a virtuous character*) good, righteous, moral, ethical, honest, honourable, incorruptible, upright, upstanding, decent, respectable, excellent, exemplary, blameless, worthy, trustworthy. OPPOSITE: wicked. **2** (*a virtuous maiden*) pure, chaste, virginal, innocent, celibate, modest.

virulent *adj* **1** (*a virulent poison*) poisonous, venomous, toxic, infective, deadly, lethal, fatal, noxious, pernicious. OPPOSITE: harmless. **2** (*virulent hatred of their enemies*) bitter, acrimonious, hostile, resentful, spiteful, malicious, malevolent, malignant, vitriolic, rancorous, vicious. OPPOSITE: mild.

viscous *adj* sticky, adhesive, gluey, tacky, mucilaginous, glutinous, thick, syrupy, treacly, gelatinous, gummy, gooey (*inf*).

visible *adj* **1** (*a ship was visible in the distance*) perceptible, detectable, perceivable, discernible. OPPOSITE: invisible. **2** (*a visible improvement in conditions*) apparent, evident, noticeable, detectable, recognizable, observable, manifest, unmistakable, clear, plain, obvious, exposed, open, overt, patent, palpable, conspicuous, distinct, distinguishable, undisguised, unconcealed.

vision *noun* **1** (*the old man's vision is not good*) sight, eyesight, perception, discernment, seeing. **2** (*a vision of the future*) view, foresight, insight, far-sightedness, perception, penetration, intuition. OPPOSITE: blindness. **3** (*a vision manifested before him*) apparition, spectre, phantom, ghost, wraith, phantasm. **4** (*he had a vision of the event*) dream, daydream, fantasy, mirage, hallucination, illusion, delusion, chimera, image, figment of the imagination.

visionary *adj* **1** (*a visionary nature*) romantic, idealistic, quixotic, utopian, impractical, impracticable, unrealistic, dreaming, dreamy. **2** (*visionary images*) unreal, imaginary, illusory, fanciful, chimerical, spectral, ghostly, phantasmal, phantasmagoric. OPPOSITE: real. **3** (*a visionary leader*) far-seeing, far-sighted, discerning, perceptive, intuitive, wise. **4** (*a visionary idea*) unworkable, unrealistic, impractical, unfeasible, theoretical, hypothetical.
➤ *noun* **1** (*many writers are visionaries*) romantic, romanticist, idealist, dreamer, daydreamer, fantasist, utopian. OPPOSITE: cynic. **2** (*the words of a visionary*) seer, prophet, mystic.

visit *verb* **1** (*she visited her mother*) call on, look up, see, stop by, drop in on (*inf*), drop by (*inf*), pop in (*inf*), stay with. **2** (*the prince will visit the plant*) inspect, examine. **3** (*the whole country was visited by disease*) assail, attack, afflict, inflict, plague, curse, trouble, punish.
➤ *noun* **1** (*a visit to the shops*) call, trip. **2** (*their visit lasted three days*) stay, stop, sojourn. **3** (*an official visit*) inspection, examination, visitation.

visitation *noun* **1** (*a visitation by government inspectors*) visit, inspection, examination. **2** (*the visitation of disease*) affliction, infliction, scourge, blight, plague, pestilence. **3** (*a lamentable visitation*) disaster, ordeal, calamity, tragedy, catastrophe, cataclysm.

visitor *noun* **1** (*a visitor to the house*) caller, guest, visitant. **2** (*many visitors in the resort*) tourist, holidaymaker, traveller, pilgrim.

vista *noun* view, scene, prospect, outlook, panorama.

visual *adj* visible, discernible, perceivable, perceptible, seeable, observable.

visualize *verb* picture, conjure up, envisage, envision, imagine, conceive.

vital *adj* **1** (*a vital issue*) critical, crucial, key, important, essential, requisite, necessary, indispensable, fundamental, imperative, urgent, decisive. OPPOSITE: unimportant. **2** (*a vital organism*) living, alive, animate. OPPOSITE: dead. **3** (*a vital personality*) lively, spirited, vivacious, vibrant, dynamic, energetic, animated, zestful, forceful.

vitality *noun* vigour, energy, life, animation, dynamism, strength, power, forcefulness, stamina, spirit, spiritedness, liveliness, vivacity, vibrancy, sparkle, exuberance, zest, zestfulness. OPPOSITE: weakness.

vitiate *verb* impair, harm, mar, spoil, blight, debase, corrupt, deprave, pervert, defile, pollute, contaminate, adulterate, deteriorate. OPPOSITE: improve.

vitriolic *adj* caustic, biting, acrimonious, acerbic, acid, acrid, astringent, mordant, vituperative, trenchant, virulent, spiteful, bitter, abusive, vicious, venomous, malicious, sardonic, scathing, destructive.

vituperate *verb* censure, reproach, reprove, slam (*inf*), slate (*inf*), condemn, denounce, revile, blame, rail against, berate, upbraid, vilify, denigrate, slander, abuse. OPPOSITE: praise.

vivacious *adj* lively, animated, spirited, high-spirited, sprightly, gay, merry, cheerful, jolly, sportive, bubbly (*inf*), sparkling, ebullient, effervescent. OPPOSITE: torpid.

vivacity *noun* liveliness, vitality, animation, high spirits, spirit, gaiety, energy, quickness, vigour, ebullience, effervescence. OPPOSITE: torpor.

vivid *adj* **1** (*vivid colours*) bright, strong, rich, intense, brilliant, dazzling, glowing, glaring, lurid, flamboyant, dynamic, colourful, vibrant, vigorous, lively, spirited. OPPOSITE: dull. **2** (*a vivid account*) powerful, graphic, striking, telling, dramatic, realistic, true to life, lifelike, clear, distinct, memorable.

vocal *adj* **1** (*a vocal record*) oral, spoken, said, uttered, voiced, expressed. **2** (*he was very vocal about it*) noisy, vociferous, forthright, outspoken, plain-spoken, articulate, eloquent. OPPOSITE: silent.

vocation *noun* calling, career, profession, occupation, métier, trade, work, business, job, craft, employment, pursuit.

vociferate *verb* shout, yell, bellow, bawl, scream, cry, roar, clamour. OPPOSITE: whisper.

vociferous *adj* noisy, vocal, loud, strident, clamorous, uproarious, loud-mouthed (*inf*), obstreperous, insistent, vehement. OPPOSITE: quiet.

vogue *noun* **1** (*the latest vogue*) fashion, mode, style, trend, fad (*inf*), rage, craze. **2** (*it was in vogue a few years ago*) favour, popularity, prevalence, currency, custom, practice, usage, use.

voice *noun* **1** (*she gave voice to her frustration*) expression, utterance, airing, vocalization, verbalization. OPPOSITE: silence. **2** (*a distinctive voice*) speech, language, sound, tone, accent, articulation. **3** (*she wanted them to pay attention to her voice*) wish, view, opinion, desire. **4** (*they demanded a voice in the debate*) vote, say, preference, choice, option.
➤ *verb* express, state, utter, say, declare, proclaim, air, ventilate. OPPOSITE: suppress.

void *adj* **1** (*the safe was void*) empty, unfilled, vacant, unoccupied, blank, clear, free. OPPOSITE: full. **2** (*void of inspiration*) devoid, destitute, lacking, wanting, without. **3** (*his passport was declared void*) invalid, null, ineffectual, ineffective, inoperative, cancelled, worthless, useless, vain, nugatory. OPPOSITE: valid.
➤ *noun* **1** (*a void in her life*) emptiness, vacuity, vacuum, blankness. **2** (*a void between the walls*) space, blank, gap, hole, hollow, chasm, abyss, opening.
➤ *verb* **1** (*void the account*) cancel, invalidate, nullify, annul, disallow, revoke, rescind, quash. **2** (*void the chamber*) empty, evacuate.

volatile *adj* changeable, variable, fickle, inconstant, erratic, capricious, whimsical, flighty, mercurial, restless, unstable, unsteady, giddy, frivolous. OPPOSITE: stable.

volition *noun* will, free will, discretion, determination, purpose, resolution, decision, choice, option, election, preference, wish. OPPOSITE: compulsion.

volley *noun* barrage, bombardment, fusillade,

cannonade, salvo, report, discharge, explosion, blast, shower, hail, storm, emission.

voluble *adj* fluent, glib, talkative, loquacious, garrulous, chatty (*inf*), articulate, forthcoming. OPPOSITE: taciturn.

volume *noun* **1** (*the volume of the canister*) bulk, capacity, size, dimensions. **2** (*the volume of the contents*) quantity, amount, mass, total. **3** (*return the volume to the shelf*) tome, book, publication. **4** (*turn down the volume*) loudness, sound, amplification.

voluminous *adj* spacious, roomy, capacious, big, large, bulky, vast, ample, copious. OPPOSITE: small.

voluntarily *adv* willingly, freely, of one's own free will, by choice, by preference, intentionally, spontaneously, consciously, deliberately, purposely.

voluntary *adj* **1** (*a voluntary contribution*) free, gratuitous, unasked, unsolicited, unconstrained, willing, unforced, optional, spontaneous. OPPOSITE: compulsory. **2** (*a voluntary act*) intentional, intended, conscious, deliberate, purposeful, optional, unpaid.

volunteer *verb* offer, proffer, tender, present, give, propose, put forward, step forward. OPPOSITE: withhold.

voluptuous *adj* **1** (*a voluptuous lifestyle*) sensual, carnal, fleshly, licentious, hedonistic, self-indulgent, sybaritic, voluptuary. OPPOSITE: ascetic. **2** (*a voluptuous woman*) seductive, provocative, erotic, sexy (*inf*), buxom, well-endowed, shapely, curvaceous (*inf*).

vomit *verb* disgorge, spew (*inf*), regurgitate, puke (*inf*), bring up, throw up (*inf*), be sick, heave, retch.

voracious *adj* greedy, ravenous, gluttonous, omnivorous, insatiable, rapacious, avid, hungry.

vortex *noun* whirlpool, maelstrom, eddy, whirlwind.

votary *noun* devotee, adherent, disciple, follower, zealot, fanatic, enthusiast, aficionado.

vote *noun* **1** (*the result of the vote*) ballot, poll, election, referendum. **2** (*women fought for their vote*) suffrage, franchise, voice, say.
≫ *verb* ballot, elect, appoint, opt, choose, plump for.

vouch *verb* guarantee, assure, asseverate, attest, affirm, assert, certify, confirm, uphold, support, back, answer for. OPPOSITE: repudiate

voucher *noun* receipt, chit, slip, note, document, paper, coupon, token, ticket.

vouchsafe *verb* grant, give, confer, accord, deign, condescend, yield, concede. OPPOSITE: refuse.

vow *noun* promise, pledge, word, oath.
≫ *verb* promise, pledge, undertake, swear, dedicate, devote, consecrate.

voyage *noun* journey, trip, expedition, cruise, passage, crossing.
≫ *verb* journey, travel, go, tour.

vulgar *adj* **1** (*a vulgar manner*) coarse, rough, crude, rude, boorish, uncouth, unmannerly, ill-bred, unrefined, unsophisticated, uncultivated, indecorous, indecent, obscene, dirty, tasteless, common, low, base. OPPOSITE: refined **2** (*vulgar humanity*) ordinary, general, popular, common. **3** (*vulgar speech*) colloquial, vernacular. **4** (*vulgar decoration*) loud, gaudy, garish, tasteless, flashy, showy, ostentatious, kitsch, tacky (*inf*).

vulgarity *noun* **1** (*his speech was full of vulgarity*) coarseness, rudeness, crudity, crudeness, indecency, ribaldry, suggestiveness, dirtiness. **2** (*the vulgarity of her new outfit*) tastelessness, gaudiness, garishness, showiness.

vulnerable *adj* unprotected, assailable, defenceless, unguarded, exposed, insecure, weak, powerless, helpless, tender, sensitive, susceptible, open. OPPOSITE: tough.

wad *noun* **1** (*a wad of cotton wool*) lump, mass, ball, hunk, chunk, block, plug. **2** (*a wad of money*) roll, bundle, wodge (*inf*).

wadding *noun* packing, padding, stuffing, filling, filler, lining, insulation.

waddle *verb* shuffle, toddle, totter, wobble, sway, rock.

wade *verb* **1** (*wade the river*) cross, ford, traverse, negotiate. **2** (*she waded in the surf*) paddle, splash, flounder, wallow.

wade in pitch in, launch in, buckle down, get cracking (*inf*), get stuck in (*inf*), set to, set to work, go to it.

wade through plough, trawl, labour, toil away, work one's way, plug away, peg away.

waffle *noun* padding, equivocation, verbiage, prattle, babbling, blather, jabbering, wittering (*inf*), nonsense, rubbish.
➤ *verb* ramble, prattle, jabber, babble, blather, witter (*inf*), rabbit (*inf*).

waft *verb* **1** (*the smoke wafted on the breeze*) drift, float, glide, blow, puff. **2** (*the tide wafted the debris to the shore*) carry, bear, convey, transport, transmit.

wag[1] *verb* **1** (*the dog wagged its tail*) wave, swing, sway, shake, twitch, quiver, vibrate, flutter. **2** (*she wagged her finger at the child*) wiggle, waggle, wave, shake. **3** (*he wagged his head*) nod, bob, shake.

wag[2] *noun* humorist, comic, comedian, comedienne, wit, joker, jokester, wisecracker, jester, clown, fool, droll.

wage *noun* pay, salary, earnings, remuneration, emolument, compensation, hire, fee, stipend, payment, recompense, returns, reward, allowance.
➤ *verb* engage in, carry on, pursue, undertake, execute, conduct, practise.

wager *noun* bet, gamble, flutter (*inf*), stake, pledge, punt, hazard, speculation, venture.
➤ *verb* bet, gamble, put money on, lay odds, stake, pledge, punt, risk, chance, hazard, speculate, venture.

waggish *adj* impish, puckish, roguish, mischievous, arch, playful, sportive, frolicsome, witty, amusing, entertaining, droll, humorous, comical, funny, whimsical, facetious, jocular, jocose, joking, jesting, merry, risible, bantering. OPPOSITE: serious.

waggle *verb* wag, wiggle, jiggle, wobble, shake, wave, sway, flutter, quiver, oscillate.

waif *noun* stray, orphan, foundling.

wail *verb* cry, moan, lament, bewail, bemoan, mourn, weep, keen, ululate, howl, yowl, whine, sob. OPPOSITE: rejoice.
➤ *noun* cry, moan, groan, lament, lamentation, weeping, ululation, howl, yowl, whine.

wait *verb* **1** (*wait over there a while*) stay, remain, abide, rest, linger, tarry. **2** (*wait before going in*) pause, hesitate, delay. OPPOSITE: proceed. **3** (*wait until we call for you*) stand by, hold back, hang on (*inf*), be patient, mark time, sit tight (*inf*), hang fire (*inf*).
➤ *noun* delay, hesitation, stay, stop, halt, pause, rest, interval, hold-up.

wait for await, expect, anticipate, look forward to, be ready for, be in store for.

wait on serve, attend to, tend to, minister to, look after, take care of.

waiter *noun* attendant, servant, server, host, hostess, steward, stewardess, maid, waitress.

waive *verb* **1** (*he waived his rights to the money*) renounce, relinquish, resign, give up, abandon, surrender, yield, cede. OPPOSITE: assert. **2** (*waive the formalities*) forgo, do without, set aside, ignore, disregard, dispense with. **3** (*waive the decision until another day*) defer, postpone, put off, shelve, delay.

wake[1] *verb* **1** (*wake from deep sleep*) waken, awake, awaken, get up, come to, come round, rouse, stir, arise, rise. **2** (*that should wake up the audience a bit*) arouse, stir up, animate, stimulate, activate, enliven, galvanize, provoke, spur, goad, prod. **3** (*wake dormant fears*) awaken, rouse, stir, kindle, rekindle, reignite, fire, excite,

quicken, resuscitate, revive, evoke, conjure up, call up. **4** (*wake to the danger*) become aware of, become conscious of, become alert, become alive to.
➤ *noun* vigil, watch, funeral, death-watch.

wake[2] *noun* (*the wake of the boat*) wash, backwash, path, trail, track, aftermath, train.

wakeful *adj* **1** (*they spent a wakeful night*) sleepless, unsleeping, restless, insomniac. OPPOSITE: asleep. **2** (*he kept a wakeful look-out*) alert, watchful, vigilant, heedful, wary, attentive, observant. OPPOSITE: unwary.

waken *verb* **1** (*she wakened from a deep sleep*) wake, awake, awaken, get up, come to, stir, rise, rouse. **2** (*the picture awakened old emotions*) wake, awaken, arouse, stir, animate, stimulate, revive, activate, kindle, rekindle, excite, call up, evoke.

walk *verb* **1** (*walk a little slower*) step, stride, pace, pad, march, promenade, perambulate, saunter, amble, stroll, strut, ramble, hike, trek, tramp, plod, trudge, go, move, advance, proceed. OPPOSITE: run. **2** (*let me walk you home*) escort, accompany, convoy, guide, conduct, lead, usher, shepherd.
➤ *noun* **1** (*he went for a walk*) stroll, amble, saunter, promenade, ramble, hike, tramp, traipse, march, perambulation, constitutional, airing. OPPOSITE: ride. **2** (*she has a funny walk*) gait, carriage, step, stride, pace. **3** (*a shaded walk*) walkway, way, path, footpath, pathway, pavement, street, esplanade, promenade, track, trail, drive, lane, alley, road, avenue. **4** (*he followed his regular walk*) route, round, beat, circuit, run.

walk of life occupation, line of work, line, trade, profession, career, pursuit, vocation, job, craft, avocation, area, arena, field, sphere.

walk off with walk away with, make off with, go off with, run off with, carry off, steal, nick (*inf*), pocket, snatch, filch, pinch (*inf*), pilfer, embezzle.

walk out 1 (*he walked out in a rage*) storm out, flounce out, take off (*inf*). **2** (*the staff have walked out*) stop work, down tools, strike, go on strike, take industrial action.

walk out on desert, leave, abandon, forsake, run out on (*inf*), chuck (*inf*), dump (*inf*), jilt, throw over.

walker *noun* pedestrian, rambler, hiker, wayfarer, footslogger.

walk-out *noun* industrial action, strike, stoppage.

walk-over *noun* pushover (*inf*), doddle (*inf*), cinch (*inf*), child's play (*inf*), piece of cake (*inf*).

wall *noun* **1** (*an interior wall*) partition, divider. **2** (*a garden wall*) screen, fence. **3** (*the attackers scaled the wall*) parapet, embankment, rampart, stockade, fortification, bulwark, breastwork, barricade, palisade, paling. **4** (*tried to erect walls against official investigation*) barrier, block, obstacle, obstruction, impediment.

wallet *noun* pocket book, notecase, purse.

wallow *verb* **1** (*the elephant wallowed in the pool*) loll, roll, lie, splash, flounder, wade, stagger, lurch. **2** (*he wallowed in his victory*) bask, luxuriate, indulge, revel, delight, enjoy, glory, relish, savour.

wan *adj* **1** (*a wan complexion*) pale, pallid, ashen, colourless, sallow, pasty, waxen, whey-faced, white, anaemic, bloodless, ghastly, sickly, peaky, haggard, gaunt, tired, washed out, weary, worn. OPPOSITE: ruddy.

2 (*the wan light of the moon*) pale, weak, faint, feeble, dim.

wand *noun* stick, twig, sprig, rod, baton, staff, mace, sceptre.

wander *verb* **1** (*she wandered the streets for hours*) stray, roam, rove, traipse (*inf*), drift, meander, straggle, range, drift, ramble, amble, saunter, stroll, prowl, peregrinate. OPPOSITE: settle. **2** (*we are wandering off the main point*) depart, deviate, swerve, diverge, veer, stray, go astray, digress, err. **3** (*the patient is wandering*) rave, ramble, babble, gibber.
➤ *noun* saunter, stroll, ramble, amble, cruise, meander, prowl, excursion.

wanderer *noun* drifter, itinerant, wayfarer, voyager, traveller, rambler, stroller, rover, ranger, roamer, nomad, gypsy, migrant, tramp, vagabond, vagrant, straggler, stray, hobo (*inf*).

wandering *adj* roaming, roving, rambling, strolling, drifting, itinerant, rootless, homeless, peripatetic, migrant, migratory, nomadic, vagrant, vagabond, gypsy, wayfaring, voyaging, travelling, transient. OPPOSITE: settled.

wane *verb* diminish, decline, decrease, lessen, ebb, subside, abate, taper off, fade, peter out, wind down, die out, dwindle, vanish, shrink, contract, deteriorate, degenerate, wither, fail, weaken, dim, droop, drop, sink. OPPOSITE: wax.
➤ *noun* diminution, decline, decrease, lessening, dwindling, tapering off, ebb, subsidence, abatement, contraction, drop, fall, failure, deteriorating, degenerating, decay, fading, weakening, vanishing, sinking.

wangle *verb* fix, fiddle (*inf*), arrange, contrive, scheme, engineer, manoeuvre, manage, manipulate, bring off, pull off.

want *verb* **1** (*she wants a drink*) need, require, demand, wish for, hope for, desire, fancy, have a yen for (*inf*), long for, yearn for, pine for, lust after, hanker after, covet, crave, hunger for, thirst for, feel like. OPPOSITE: possess. **2** (*the set wants several pieces*) lack, miss, need, require, demand, call for.
➤ *noun* **1** (*tell us your wants*) need, necessity, requirement, demand, wish, desire, longing, yearning, craving, coveting, hankering, fancy, lust, yen (*inf*), appetite, hunger, thirst. OPPOSITE: possession. **2** (*cried for want of attention*) lack, absence, dearth, default, deficiency, inadequacy, insufficiency, shortage, paucity, scarcity, scarceness, scantiness. OPPOSITE: abundance. **3** (*millions living in want*) poverty, privation, indigence, penury, destitution, need, neediness. OPPOSITE: wealth.

wanting *adj* **1** (*something was still wanting*) missing, absent, lacking, short. **2** (*wanting in quality*) short, lacking, deficient, insufficient, inadequate, imperfect, substandard, defective, faulty, flawed, unsound, inferior, second-rate, poor, patchy, sketchy, disappointing, unsatisfactory, unacceptable.

wanton *adj* **1** (*a wanton young woman*) lewd, lecherous, lascivious, libidinous, lustful, prurient, licentious, fast, loose, abandoned, debauched, degenerate, dissolute, dissipated, libertine, promiscuous, impure, immoral, immodest, mindless, shameless, unchaste, unvirtuous.

OPPOSITE: chaste. **2** (*a wanton act of vandalism*) needless, unnecessary, motiveless, unmotivated, groundless, unjustifiable, unjustified, gratuitous, uncalled-for, unprovoked, senseless, pointless, purposeless, wilful, deliberate, arbitrary, cruel, vicious, malicious, malevolent, spiteful, evil, wicked. **3** (*a wanton breeze*) playful, sportive, capricious, impulsive, irresponsible, rash, reckless, careless, heedless. **4** (*the grass grew in wanton abandon*) unrestrained, uncontrolled, wild, abundant, profuse, lavish, extravagant, luxuriant, immoderate.

➤ *noun* whore, prostitute, loose woman, tart (*inf*), hussy, slut, harlot, trollop, strumpet, profligate, debauchee, lecher, libertine, rake, roué, voluptuary.

war *noun* **1** (*the day war broke out*) warfare, hostilities, fighting, combat, conflict, strife, bloodshed, contention, contest, confrontation, struggle, battle, skirmish, clash. OPPOSITE: peace. **2** (*the war against drugs*) campaign, fight, battle, crusade.

➤ *verb* wage war, make war, fight, battle, contend, combat, take up arms, cross swords, quarrel.

warble *verb* trill, sing, chirp, chirrup, twitter, quaver, pipe.

ward *noun* **1** (*representing a ward of the city*) district, precinct, division, zone, quarter, area. **2** (*ten patients in each hospital ward*) room, apartment. **3** (*he was made a ward of his uncle*) charge, protégé, pupil, dependant, minor. OPPOSITE: guardian.

ward off *verb* **1** (*tried to ward off the blows*) avert, deflect, parry, fend off, stave off, turn aside, rebuff, keep at bay, foil. **2** (*they warded off several attacks*) drive off, drive back, beat off, beat back, repel, repulse, rout, put to flight, send packing (*inf*), disperse, scatter.

warden *noun* **1** (*he's a warden at the museum*) curator, guardian, keeper, custodian, protector, janitor, caretaker. **2** (*a warden at the prison*) guard, warder, prison officer, turnkey, screw (*inf*). **3** (*traffic warden*) superintendent, supervisor, overseer, attendant.

warder *noun* prison officer, guard, gaoler, jailer, warden, screw (*inf*), custodian.

wardrobe *noun* **1** (*dresses hanging in the wardrobe*) cupboard, closet. **2** (*an extensive wardrobe of designer outfits*) clothes, apparel, garments, gear (*inf*), togs (*inf*), raiment.

warehouse *noun* depot, depository, store, storehouse, storeroom, stockroom, repository.

wares *pl noun* goods, products, commodities, merchandise, produce, stock, lines, stuff.

warfare *noun* war, hostilities, fighting, combat, strife, struggle, conflict, contention, discord, blows, confrontation, contest, battle. OPPOSITE: peace.

warily *adv* **1** (*he looked around warily*) cautiously, carefully, guardedly, hesitantly, gingerly, watchfully, circumspectly, vigilantly, on the alert. **2** (*she regarded him warily*) suspiciously, cautiously, distrustfully, mistrustfully, apprehensively, uneasily, cagily (*inf*), charily.

wariness *noun* **1** (*proceed with wariness*) caution, care, carefulness, vigilance, watchfulness, heedfulness, mindfulness, alertness, attention, circumspection, discretion, foresight, apprehension. **2** (*treat his claims*

with wariness) suspicion, distrust, mistrust, unease, caution, circumspection, prudence.

warlike *adj* belligerent, bellicose, pugnacious, combative, hostile, unfriendly, militant, aggressive, bloodthirsty, martial, militaristic, war-mongering. OPPOSITE: pacific.

warlock *noun* sorcerer, wizard, magician, conjurer, necromancer.

warm *adj* **1** (*warm water*) tepid, lukewarm, heated, hot, thermal. OPPOSITE: cool. **2** (*warm weather*) fine, sunny, summery, balmy, close, temperate. **3** (*he got a warm reception*) enthusiastic, eager, effusive, animated, lively, energetic, hearty, genial, cordial, vigorous, ardent, fervent, vehement, passionate, intense, emotional, earnest, sincere, heartfelt. OPPOSITE: apathetic. **4** (*a warm personality*) friendly, affable, cordial, genial, hearty, amiable, loving, caring, affectionate, tender, kind, kindly, hospitable, warm-hearted, sympathetic, charitable, genuine, sincere, zealous. OPPOSITE: cold.

➤ *verb* heat, reheat. OPPOSITE: cool.

warm up 1 (*this should warm up the party*) animate, enliven, liven, rouse, stir, stimulate, awaken. **2** (*the players need to warm up*) exercise, prepare, loosen up, limber up, practise, train, stretch.

warmth *noun* **1** (*the warmth of the fire*) heat, hotness, warmness. OPPOSITE: coolness. **2** (*the warmth of his reception*) effusiveness, heartiness, cordiality, geniality, friendliness, hospitality, ardour, fervour, vehemence, passion, intensity, zeal, sincerity, enthusiasm, eagerness. OPPOSITE: apathy. **3** (*the warmth of her personality*) friendliness, affability, amiability, cordiality, geniality, affection, love, tenderness, care, kindness, kindliness, sympathy, charity, sincerity, genuineness. OPPOSITE: coldness.

warn *verb* **1** (*warn him about the risks*) caution, alert, forewarn, advise, counsel, exhort, urge. **2** (*he warned them about the changes*) advise, notify, inform, tell, acquaint, alert, apprise, forewarn, give notice, tip off (*inf*). **3** (*warned by the judge*) admonish, rebuke, reprimand, reprove, caution, tell off, remonstrate with.

warning *noun* **1** (*a warning to guard against over-optimism*) caution, advise, exhortation, counselling. **2** (*a warning from the gods*) omen, portent, premonition, augury, foretoken, token, sign, signal. **3** (*he had advance warning of the visit*) advice, alert, alarm, notice, notification, information, forewarning, tip, tip-off (*inf*), word, threat. **4** (*earned a warning from the referee*) admonition, rebuke, reprimand, remonstrance.

warp *verb* twist, bend, turn, contort, misshape, deform, distort, kink, pervert, bias, deviate, corrupt. OPPOSITE: straighten.

warrant *noun* authorization, authority, validation, permission, permit, sanction, consent, licence, carte blanche, commission, warranty, guarantee, pledge, security.

➤ *verb* **1** (*he warrants that the story is true*) guarantee, pledge, swear, assure, certify, testify, declare, affirm, vouch for, answer for, endorse, support, back, stand by, uphold, underwrite. OPPOSITE: repudiate. **2** (*the situation warrants radical action*) require, call for, necessitate. **3** (*the rules warrant expulsion*) authorize, sanction, approve, permit, allow, entitle, empower, commission, license. **4** (*her rudeness was not warranted*) justify, excuse, vindicate, support.

warrantable *adj* permissible, allowable, lawful, legal, acceptable, justifiable, defensible, excusable, explicable, explainable, reasonable, supportable, accountable, right, proper. OPPOSITE: unjustifiable.

warring *adj* at war, conflicting, fighting, hostile, belligerent, combatant, opposing, opposed, rival, clashing, contending, embattled.

warrior *noun* fighter, soldier, fighting man, combatant, champion, warhorse.

wary *adj* **1** (*she was wary when travelling alone*) cautious, careful, chary, circumspect, prudent, heedful, guarded, watchful, vigilant, observant, attentive, alert, on one's toes (*inf*). OPPOSITE: rash. **2** (*he was wary of her motives*) suspicious, distrustful, mistrustful, cautious, careful, cagey, chary.

wash *verb* **1** (*wash oneself before going to bed*) bath, bathe, shower, freshen up, clean, cleanse, scrub, rinse, sponge. OPPOSITE: soil. **2** (*wash down all the surfaces*) clean, cleanse, scrub, rinse, swill, soak, sponge, wipe, mop, swab down. **3** (*wash this garment by hand*) launder, clean. **4** (*she's staying in to wash her hair*) shampoo, clean. **5** (*the tide washed up against the jetty*) splash, swell, flow, beat, break, dash. **6** (*the house was washed away in the flood*) sweep, bear, carry off. **7** (*their explanation does not wash*) hold up, stand up, stick (*inf*), bear scrutiny, bear examination, pass muster.
➤ *noun* **1** (*he is just having a quick wash*) bath, bathe, shower, clean, ablution. **2** (*put that shirt in the wash*) washing, laundry. **3** (*give the floor a wash*) clean, cleansing, scrub, rinse, mop, wipe. **4** (*the wash of the tide*) surge, swell, sweep, flow, splash, roll. **5** (*a wash of paint*) coat, coating, layer, film, stain, rinse.

washed out *adj* **1** (*her face looked washed out*) pale, pallid, wan, anaemic, bloodless, white, colourless, drawn, haggard, etiolated. **2** (*washed-out colours*) pale, flat, lacklustre, lifeless, faded, bleached. **3** (*by the time he got home he was washed out*) exhausted, tired out, dog-tired (*inf*), knackered (*inf*), worn out, fatigued, weary, spent, drained, all in (*inf*), done in (*inf*), pooped (*inf*).

waspish *adj* irritable, irascible, cross, short-tempered, bad-tempered, ill-tempered, snappish, cantankerous, splenetic, peppery, crabbed (*inf*), crabby (*inf*), crotchety (*inf*), grumpy, grouchy (*inf*), peevish, bitchy (*inf*), petulant, querulous, captious, prickly (*inf*), touchy, testy, critical. OPPOSITE: genial.

waste *verb* **1** (*try not to waste any paper*) squander, fritter away, misspend, misuse, dissipate, lose, use up, consume, go through, get through, run through, throw away, blow (*inf*), lavish, splurge (*inf*). OPPOSITE: save. **2** (*she just wasted away*) wither, shrivel, shrink, atrophy. **3** (*famine had wasted their bodies*) consume, emaciate, gnaw, eat away, erode, weaken, enfeeble, debilitate, sap, exhaust, drain. **4** (*the company is just wasting away*) decline, decay, wear, wilt, wane, fade, dwindle, shrink, decrease, diminish. OPPOSITE: flourish. **5** (*bandits wasted the province*) devastate, desolate, ravage, destroy, plunder, pillage, sack, spoil, despoil, loot, ruin, raze, maraud, harry, rape.

➤ *noun* **1** (*reduce waste in modern industry*) dissipation, prodigality, misuse, squandering, frittering away, consumption, loss, extravagance, wastefulness, unthriftiness. OPPOSITE: economy. **2** (*the council will collect the waste*) rubbish, refuse, trash, garbage, leftovers, leavings, scraps, slops, litter, dross, dregs, debris. **3** (*the wastes of the steppe*) wasteland, desert, wilderness, wild, barrenness, vastness, emptiness.
➤ *adj* **1** (*the process produces little waste material*) useless, worthless, extra, superfluous, supernumerary, leftover, unused, unwanted. **2** (*waste land*) desolate, uncultivated, unproductive, desert, wild, barren, bare, arid, uninhabited, unpopulated, deserted, empty, void, solitary, lonely, dismal, dreary, cheerless, bleak. OPPOSITE: cultivated.

wasted *adj* **1** (*his efforts were wasted*) squandered, lost, thrown away, misapplied, useless, unrewarded, unnecessary, needless, unrequired. **2** (*a wasted afternoon*) squandered, thrown away, lost, misspent, misused. **3** (*wasted bodies*) shrivelled, shrunken, emaciated, withered, weakened, weak, atrophied.

wasteful *adj* extravagant, prodigal, profligate, lavish, spendthrift, thriftless, unthrifty, improvident, uneconomical. OPPOSITE: economical.

watch *verb* **1** (*watch what happens*) observe, view, eye, see, behold, regard, monitor, stare at, peer at, gape at, gaze at, look at, look on, survey, scan, inspect, scrutinize, examine, contemplate, notice, note, mark. OPPOSITE: ignore. **2** (*he watched the house while we were away*) guard, protect, keep, mind, tend, look after, supervise, superintend, take care of, keep an eye on (*inf*), keep tabs on (*inf*). OPPOSITE: neglect. **3** (*watch for any tricks*) watch out, look out, be careful, pay attention, take care, take heed.
➤ *noun* **1** (*he checked the time on his watch*) wristwatch, pocket watch, timepiece, chronometer, clock. **2** (*keep a watch on the house*) vigil, guard, observation, lookout, vigilance, watchfulness, attention, alertness, surveillance.

watch out 1 (*watch out for the hole*) look out, mind out, pay attention, be careful, take care, have a care, take heed, be vigilant, be wary, keep your eyes peeled (*inf*). **2** (*watch out for your mother*) look out for, keep an eye open for (*inf*), wait for.

watch over look after, guard, stand guard over, mind, protect, defend, shield, shelter, preserve, tend, take care of.

watchdog *noun* guardian, custodian, protector, monitor, inspector, vigilante, scrutineer.

watcher *noun* spectator, observer, looker-on, onlooker, viewer, witness, lookout, spy.

watchful *adj* vigilant, alert, attentive, observant, guarded, on one's guard, cautious, chary, wary, suspicious, heedful, careful, circumspect, sharp-eyed. OPPOSITE: heedless.

watchman *noun* security guard, guard, caretaker, custodian, janitor.

watchword *noun* **1** (*courtesy is our watchword*) slogan, motto, maxim, byword, catchword, catchphrase, battle-cry, mission statement. **2** (*you must give the correct watchword*) password, countersign, signal.

water *noun* sea, ocean, lake, pool, loch, reservoir, river, stream, rivulet, current, torrent.
⟩ *verb* damp, dampen, moisten, wet, sprinkle, spray, hose, douse, irrigate, soak, drench, saturate, sodden, flood. OPPOSITE: parch.

water down 1 (*accused of watering down the beer*) dilute, weaken, thin, adulterate, mix. **2** (*they are trying to water down the significance of the decision*) tone down, play down, downplay, soft-pedal (*inf*), soften, understate, underemphasize, mitigate, qualify, disguise.

waterfall *noun* fall, cascade, cataract, torrent, chute.

watertight *adj* **1** (*a watertight compartment*) waterproof, sound. **2** (*the suspect had a watertight alibi*) foolproof, airtight, unassailable, impregnable, indisputable, incontrovertible, firm, sound, flawless.

watery *adj* **1** (*a watery patch of ground*) wet, damp, moist, boggy, soggy, sodden, saturated, waterlogged, squelchy, miry, marshy, swampy. OPPOSITE: dry. **2** (*a watery concoction*) liquid, liquefied, fluid, aqueous, hydrous. **3** (*watery broth*) thin, runny, weak, diluted, dilute, adulterated, watered down, insipid, tasteless, flavourless, wishy-washy (*inf*).

wave *verb* **1** (*the flag waved in the wind*) flap, flutter, waft, wag, waggle, shake, quiver, stir, ripple, undulate, sway, rock, swing, oscillate. **2** (*he waved the book in the air*) flourish, brandish, shake, wag. **3** (*she waved to them to join her*) beckon, gesture, gesticulate, indicate, signal, sign.
⟩ *noun* **1** (*he watched the waves roll in*) breaker, roller, billow, comber, white horse (*inf*), white cap, ripple, wavelet, surf, swell, foam, froth. **2** (*a wave of enthusiasm*) surge, upsurge, sweep, rush, rash, outbreak, swell, ground-swell, welling up, flood, flow, stream. **3** (*waves of light*) undulation, ripple, vibration, oscillation.

wave aside brush aside, set aside, reject, spurn, dismiss, shelve, disregard, ignore.

waver *verb* **1** (*the light wavered*) flicker, quiver, wobble, shake, tremble, fluctuate, oscillate. **2** (*she wavered about going*) hesitate, dither, vacillate, shilly-shally (*inf*), falter, equivocate, seesaw, hem and haw (*inf*). OPPOSITE: decide. **3** (*the woman wavered on the edge of the cliff*) stagger, wobble, sway, rock, teeter, totter, reel, weave.

wavy *adj* undulating, rippled, ridged, curvy, curving, winding, curling, curly, sinuous, squiggly, zigzag.

wax *verb* grow, increase, develop, enlarge, expand, swell, extend, spread, widen, broaden, magnify, mushroom, fill out, mount, rise. OPPOSITE: wane.

way *noun* **1** (*a new way of doing things*) method, manner, fashion, mode, means, procedure, process, system, technique, scheme, plan, approach, strategy. **2** (*that is the way to town*) direction, route, course, road. **3** (*the way was blocked with traffic*) road, roadway, street, highway, thoroughfare, passage, path, track, lane, avenue, alley, drive. **4** (*him and his funny ways*) custom, practice, wont, usage, habit, trait, mannerism, peculiarity, idiosyncrasy, characteristic, attribute, manner, style, conduct, behaviour, nature, character, personality, disposition, temper, temperament. **5** (*a long way home*) distance, journey, stretch, length. **6** (*it is good news in one way*) respect, sense, particular, aspect, point, feature, detail.

by the way incidentally, in passing, en passant, by the by.

give way 1 (*the ceiling might give way*) collapse, cave in, fall in, subside, give, break, disintegrate. **2** (*they gave way to his demands*) give in, yield, acquiesce, accede, concede, submit, surrender, capitulate, cave in, back down.

under way moving, in motion, going, in progress, begun, started, afoot.

wayfarer *noun* traveller, wanderer, journeyer, walker, hiker, rambler, roamer, rover, trekker, nomad, itinerant, vagrant, vagabond, gypsy.

wayfaring *adj* travelling, wandering, journeying, walking, hiking, rambling, roaming, roving, trekking, nomadic, itinerant, peripatetic, drifting.

waylay *verb* **1** (*they were waylaid by robbers*) ambush, hold up, set upon, attack, surprise, seize. **2** (*she was waylaid by a customer*) buttonhole, accost, intercept, stop, catch.

wayward *adj* **1** (*a wayward teenager*) wilful, self-willed, perverse, contrary, uncooperative, refractory, recalcitrant, contumacious, headstrong, stubborn, obstinate, obdurate, difficult, fractious, disobedient, insubordinate, rebellious, unruly, intractable, incorrigible, ungovernable, unmanageable. **2** (*her wayward husband*) capricious, fickle, flighty, unpredictable, unstable, erratic, volatile, whimsical, mercurial, inconstant, changeable, variable. OPPOSITE: docile.

weak *adj* **1** (*he felt old and weak*) feeble, frail, fragile, delicate, faint, flimsy, shaky, puny, weedy (*inf*), enervated, tired, exhausted, spent, fatigued, worn out, sickly, unhealthy, debilitated, incapacitated, indisposed, ailing, infirm, decrepit. OPPOSITE: strong. **2** (*her husband was too weak to stand up to her*) powerless, impotent, ineffectual, inept, effete, useless, timorous, timid, spineless, cowardly, pusillanimous, yellow (*inf*), irresolute, indecisive, soft. OPPOSITE: powerful. **3** (*a weak performance*) poor, inadequate, imperfect, substandard, lame, deficient, lacking, wanting, unconvincing, inconclusive, faulty, defective. **4** (*the defenders occupied a weak position*) vulnerable, unprotected, unguarded, defenceless, exposed. **5** (*a weak flicker of light*) faint, imperceptible, dim, pale, wan, dull, soft, slight, small. **6** (*a weak voice*) faint, low, muted, muffled, stifled. **7** (*a weak brew*) watery, dilute, diluted, thin, thinned down, adulterated, understrength, runny, insipid, tasteless, flavourless, wishy-washy (*inf*).

weaken *verb* **1** (*weakened by loss of blood*) enervate, debilitate, disable, enfeeble, incapacitate, cripple, paralyse, exhaust, tire, weary, wear out, sap. OPPOSITE: strengthen. **2** (*weaken the mixture with water*) dilute, water down, thin, adulterate. **3** (*this weakened the impact considerably*) diminish, lessen, reduce, lower, moderate, mitigate, temper, soften, sap, undermine, impair, invalidate. **4** (*the wind has weakened*) abate, dwindle, diminish, lessen, decrease, ease up, let up, die down.

weakling *noun* wimp (*inf*), weed (*inf*), wet (*inf*), drip (*inf*), sissy (*inf*), doormat (*inf*), coward, mouse, milksop.

weakness *noun* **1** (*weakness confined him to the house*) feebleness, frailty, puniness, fragility, delicacy, delicateness, debility, decrepitude, infirmity,

indisposition, incapacity, fatigue. OPPOSITE: strength.
2 (*they scorned him for his weakness*) ineffectuality,
ineptness, impotence, powerlessness, vulnerability,
cowardliness, timidity, spinelessness. **3** (*a weakness in the
design*) fault, flaw, defect, deficiency, imperfection,
blemish, shortcoming, failing, foible, Achilles' heel. **4** (*a
weakness for pretty blondes*) liking, fondness, love,
passion, soft spot, partiality, preference, predilection,
predisposition, proneness, proclivity, inclination,
leaning, penchant. OPPOSITE: aversion.

wealth *noun* **1** (*he has sufficient wealth to last his
retirement*) money, cash, capital, wherewithal (*inf*),
dough (*inf*), bread (*inf*), readies (*inf*), funds, riches,
treasure, assets, resources, means, fortune, property,
goods, possessions, estate. **2** (*a lavish display of wealth*)
affluence, opulence, prosperity, richness, substance.
OPPOSITE: poverty. **3** (*a wealth of opportunity*) abundance,
mass, plenty, profusion, bounty, cornucopia, plenitude,
amplitude, copiousness. OPPOSITE: scarcity.

wealthy *adj* rich, prosperous, affluent, well-off, well-to-
do, well-heeled (*inf*), rolling (*inf*), moneyed, loaded (*inf*),
flush (*inf*), comfortable. OPPOSITE: poor.

wear *verb* **1** (*wear the blue skirt*) put on, dress in, don,
have on, sport. **2** (*he wore a worried look*) have, show,
display, exhibit, present, assume. **3** (*the rubber is wearing
away*) erode, waste, consume, eat away, corrode, abrade,
rub, grind, fray, impair, deteriorate. OPPOSITE: reinforce.
4 (*this jacket has worn well*) last, endure, survive, hold up,
bear up. **5** (*the job is wearing her out*) tire, weary, fatigue,
exhaust. OPPOSITE: invigorate. **6** (*he finds her company
very wearing*) irritate, annoy, bore, tax, enervate, sap.
» *noun* **1** (*these gloves have survived a lifetime's wear*) use,
employment, utility, service. **2** (*suitable wear for rainy
weather*) clothes, clothing, attire, dress, garb, outfit,
garments, apparel, gear (*inf*), clobber (*inf*). **3** (*little wear
on the tyres*) wear and tear, deterioration, degeneration,
damage, erosion, corrosion, abrasion, friction.
wear down 1 (*the heels have worn down*) wear away, rub
down, grind down, erode, corrode, abrade. **2** (*he slowly
wore down her resistance*) overcome, erode, grind down,
undermine, reduce, diminish, lessen.
wear off 1 (*the label has worn off*) rub away, fade,
efface. **2** (*public interest in the scandal will soon wear off*)
fade, dwindle, subside, ebb, wane, weaken, peter out,
decrease, diminish, disappear, abate, lessen.
wear on pass, go on, go by, elapse, move on, roll on.
wear out 1 (*training just wears the players out*) exhaust,
weary, tire, fatigue, knacker (*inf*), frazzle (*inf*), drain, sap,
stress, strain, weaken, enfeeble, prostrate, enervate.
2 (*those shoes will wear out if you run in them*) deteriorate,
erode, fray.

weariness *noun* fatigue, tiredness, exhaustion,
lassitude, lethargy, listlessness, languor, drowsiness,
sleepiness, enervation.

wearing *adj* fatiguing, tiring, tiresome, wearying,
wearisome, taxing, trying, exhausting, draining,
stressful, oppressive, exasperating, irksome.

wearisome *adj* tiring, fatiguing, wearing, exhausting,
draining, trying, tiresome, troublesome, bothersome,
burdensome, boring, tedious, irksome, annoying,
vexatious, monotonous, dull, flat, dreary, humdrum,
routine, uninteresting. OPPOSITE: exciting.

weary *adj* **1** (*she complained of feeling weary*) wearied,
tired, fatigued, worn out, exhausted, drained, spent,
jaded, fagged (*inf*), all in (*inf*), done in (*inf*), dog-tired
(*inf*), dead beat (*inf*), fagged out (*inf*), knackered (*inf*),
bushed (*inf*), whacked (*inf*), pooped (*inf*), sleepy.
OPPOSITE: refreshed. **2** (*a weary task*) wearing, wearisome,
trying, taxing, irksome, tiresome, boring, tedious, dull,
arduous, laborious, exhausting, tiring, fatiguing. **3** (*her
complaints made him weary*) fed up, sick and tired (*inf*),
browned off (*inf*), brassed off (*inf*), cheesed off (*inf*),
discontented, jaded, bored, uninterested, listless,
lethargic.
» *verb* **1** (*the effort wearied them*) tire, fatigue, exhaust,
knacker (*inf*), wear out, sap, drain, tax. OPPOSITE: refresh.
2 (*her nagging wearied him*) bore, jade, annoy, irritate,
exasperate, irk, vex.

weather *noun* climate, conditions, temperature,
forecast, outlook.
» *verb* **1** (*constant wind has weathered the surface*) erode,
wear, bleach, colour, stain. **2** (*weather disaster*) endure,
withstand, stand, resist, brave, bear up, survive, come
through, pull through, get through, surmount,
overcome, rise above, ride out, stick out (*inf*). OPPOSITE:
succumb.
under the weather unwell, sick, ill, poorly (*inf*),
groggy (*inf*), seedy (*inf*), nauseous, off colour, below par,
out of sorts, queer, indisposed, ailing.

weave *verb* **1** (*she sat weaving the coloured threads*)
interlace, lace, intertwine, twine, interweave, braid,
plait, knit, spin, join. OPPOSITE: unravel. **2** (*she weaves a
web of lies*) make, create, compose, build, construct,
fabricate, contrive, invent, spin, put together. OPPOSITE:
destroy. **3** (*the car was seen weaving across the road*)
zigzag, criss-cross, wind, swerve.

web *noun* **1** (*a web of lines*) cobweb, mesh, net, netting,
network, webbing, lattice, latticework, interlacing. **2** (*a
web of lies*) network, knot, tangle, complex, tissue.

wed *verb* **1** (*they are to wed next month*) marry, espouse,
tie the knot, get hitched (*inf*). OPPOSITE: divorce.
2 (*the two pieces of furniture had been wedded together*)
join, unite, unify, fuse, blend, combine, amalgamate,
link, ally, merge. **3** (*she is wedded to her career*) devote,
dedicate.

wedding *noun* marriage, nuptials, matrimony, wedlock,
union. OPPOSITE: divorce.

wedge *noun* lump, chunk, block, piece, wodge (*inf*).
» *verb* **1** (*she wedged the door open*) jam, lodge, prop.
2 (*he wedged more food into his mouth*) cram, ram, pack,
squeeze, stuff, push, jam, thrust, force, lodge, fit.

weed *verb* remove, eliminate, eradicate, purge,
extirpate, get rid of, root out, separate out, dispense
with.

weekly *adv* every week, once a week, by the week,
hebdomadal.

weep *verb* cry, shed tears, bawl, sob, blub (*inf*), blubber
(*inf*), wail, snivel, whimper, whine, moan, mourn,
lament, grieve, keen. OPPOSITE: rejoice.

weepy *adj* tearful, lachrymose, crying, sobbing,
blubbering, upset.

weigh *verb* **1** (*weigh one thing against another*) measure,
balance, compare, evaluate. **2** (*weigh up the likelihood of*

failure) consider, contemplate, mull over, brood over, muse on, ponder, deliberate, reflect upon, meditate on, examine, think over, think about. **3** (*her past record will weigh with the judges*) tell, count, carry weight, have influence. **4** (*the knowledge weighed on his mind*) weigh down, encumber, burden, bear down, oppress, prey. OPPOSITE: relieve.

weigh down 1 (*her car was weighed down with technical gear*) load, overload, burden, overburden. **2** (*the thought weighed down on her*) press down, oppress, bear down, burden, prey on, trouble, afflict, worry, depress, get one down (*inf*).

weight *noun* **1** (*the weight of the sack*) heaviness, load, mass, gravity, pressure. **2** (*that's a weight off my mind*) burden, load, trouble, worry, strain, millstone, encumbrance, responsibility, duty, onus. **3** (*his opinion carries a lot of weight*) influence, importance, consequence, significance, moment, value, substance, power, force, clout (*inf*), authority, effect, impact.
➤ *verb* load, weigh down, burden, oppress.

weighty *adj* **1** (*a weighty parcel*) heavy, hefty (*inf*), bulky, substantial, ponderous, massive, cumbersome. OPPOSITE: light. **2** (*a weighty responsibility*) burdensome, onerous, oppressive, demanding, taxing, exacting, troublesome, stressful, worrisome, vexatious. **3** (*a weighty consideration*) important, significant, consequential, influential, momentous, grave, solemn, serious, crucial, critical, vital, potent, cogent, persuasive. OPPOSITE: trivial.

weird *adj* **1** (*a weird coincidence*) strange, queer, uncanny, eerie, unnatural, supernatural, preternatural, unearthly, ghostly, spooky (*inf*), creepy (*inf*), mysterious, mystifying, unnerving. **2** (*weird behaviour*) strange, bizarre, odd, way-out (*inf*), far-out (*inf*), queer, peculiar, freakish, eccentric, grotesque, outlandish, off the wall (*inf*). OPPOSITE: ordinary.

welcome *adj* agreeable, delightful, pleasant, pleasing, gratifying, cheering, desirable, popular, acceptable, refreshing. OPPOSITE: unwelcome.
➤ *noun* greeting, salutation, reception, acceptance, hospitality.
➤ *verb* greet, salute, hail, receive, meet.

welfare *noun* **1** (*concerned for her welfare*) well-being, prosperity, health, soundness, happiness, comfort, security, advantage, benefit, good, interest, fortune. **2** (*living on welfare*) benefit, income support, social security, state aid, the dole (*inf*).

well¹ *noun* **1** (*water from a well*) spring, fountainhead, fount, waterhole. **2** (*a well of experience*) fount, reservoir, pool, well-spring, well-head, source, mine.
➤ *verb* flow, gush, run, stream, trickle, ooze, seep, spring, surge, pour, rush, spout, spurt, jet, issue, swell, brim over.

well² *adv* **1** (*everything went well*) satisfactorily, adequately, fine, nicely, properly, correctly, rightly, suitably, fittingly, smoothly. OPPOSITE: badly. **2** (*she did well in her exams*) excellently, splendidly, admirably, successfully, competently. **3** (*he gets on well with her family*) happily, agreeably, pleasantly, smoothly, comfortably, capitally (*inf*), famously (*inf*). **4** (*the team played well enough*) adequately, sufficiently, effectively, competently, skilfully, proficiently, ably, expertly, adeptly. **5** (*if a thing's worth doing, it's worth doing well*) properly, thoroughly, fully, completely, efficiently, effectively, carefully, conscientiously, industriously. **6** (*they treated the children well*) kindly, generously, hospitably, genially, civilly, politely. **7** (*I know him well*) personally, intimately, thoroughly, deeply, profoundly, fully. **8** (*well over the limit*) considerably, far, very much, greatly, markedly, substantially. **9** (*listen well*) carefully, closely, attentively, conscientiously. **10** (*that may well be so*) probably, possibly, conceivably, likely, undoubtedly, certainly, unquestionably. **11** (*he spoke well of you*) highly, admiringly, warmly, glowingly, with praise, approvingly, favourably. **12** (*we all like to live well*) comfortably, in comfort, in luxury. **13** (*I expect things to turn out well*) fortunately, luckily, auspiciously, propitiously.
➤ *adj* **1** (*he says he feels very well*) healthy, in good health, fit, able-bodied, sound, hale, hearty, robust, strong. OPPOSITE: ill. **2** (*everything is well at this end*) satisfactory, all right, OK (*inf*), good, fine, thriving, flourishing. OPPOSITE: bad. **3** (*it is well to revise for the exam*) advisable, sensible, prudent, wise.

as well also, too, in addition, furthermore, moreover, besides, to boot, into the bargain (*inf*).

as well as in addition to, together with, besides, along with, including, over and above.

well-advised *adj* sensible, wise, reasonable, prudent, shrewd, sagacious, sound, judicious, circumspect, far-sighted, long-sighted.

well-balanced *adj* **1** (*a well-balanced young man*) sensible, rational, reasonable, well-adjusted, level-headed, together (*inf*), sound, stable, practical, discerning, logical, sane, sober. **2** (*a well-balanced composition*) balanced, symmetrical, even, well-proportioned, proportional, harmonious, well-ordered, well-arranged, graceful, elegant.

well-being *noun* welfare, health, good health, happiness, good, comfort, prosperity, security.

well-bred *adj* well-mannered, mannerly, well-brought-up, civil, polite, courteous, gentlemanly, ladylike, refined, cultivated, cultured, debonair, urbane, polished, genteel, gallant, chivalrous. OPPOSITE: ill-bred.

well-built *adj* strong, muscular, sturdy, robust, hulking (*inf*), hefty (*inf*), beefy (*inf*), strapping, burly, husky (*inf*), brawny, stout, big.

well-groomed *adj* neat, tidy, smart, trim, dapper, natty (*inf*), spruce, well-dressed, well-turned-out.

well-known *adj* **1** (*a well-known practice*) known, familiar, everyday, common, usual. **2** (*the well-known actor*) famous, famed, celebrated, renowned, illustrious, eminent, notable, noted. OPPOSITE: unknown.

well-nigh *adv* virtually, practically, almost, nearly, more or less, all but, just about, to all intents and purposes.

well off *adj* **1** (*her family are very well off*) wealthy, rich, affluent, well-to-do, prosperous, moneyed, well-heeled (*inf*), loaded (*inf*), flush (*inf*), rolling in it (*inf*), on easy street (*inf*). **2** (*compared to them we are well off*) fortunate, lucky, comfortable, successful, flourishing, thriving.

well-read *adj* educated, well-educated, knowledgeable, erudite, well-informed, literate, lettered, cultured.

well-spoken *adj* articulate, clear, coherent, well-expressed, fluent, eloquent, silver-tongued, smooth-talking.

well-thought-of *adj* highly thought-of, highly regarded, looked up to, respected, esteemed, admired, acclaimed, honoured, revered, venerated.

well-to-do *adj* wealthy, rich, well off, well-heeled (*inf*), loaded (*inf*), flush (*inf*), rolling in it (*inf*), affluent, moneyed, prosperous.

welter *noun* jumble, muddle, tangle, confusion, hotchpotch, mish-mash (*inf*), mess, web.

wend *verb* go, move, proceed, travel, progress, walk, hike, trudge, plod, wander, meander.

wet *adj* **1** (*a wet towel*) damp, dampened, moist, moistened, soaked, soaking, drenched, saturated, dripping, sopping, sodden, soggy, waterlogged, wringing. OPPOSITE: dry. **2** (*wet weather*) rainy, raining, pouring, teeming, showery, drizzling, misty, damp, dank, humid, clammy. OPPOSITE: fine. **3** (*tell the child not to be so wet*) weak, feeble, weedy (*inf*), spineless, cowardly, timid, timorous, irresolute, soft, namby-pamby (*inf*), effete, ineffective, ineffectual, inept.
➤ *noun* **1** (*the wet has seeped through the wall*) wetness, moisture, moistness, damp, dampness, condensation, humidity, clamminess. **2** (*come in out of the wet*) rain, drizzle, damp. **3** (*we all think he's a bit of a wet*) weakling, wimp (*inf*), weed (*inf*), drip (*inf*), softy, namby-pamby (*inf*), milksop.
➤ *verb* **1** (*wet the flannel*) damp, dampen, moisten, soak, drench, saturate, steep, douse, dip. OPPOSITE: dry. **2** (*wet the plant*) water, spray, sprinkle, irrigate, douse, splash.

wharf *noun* dock, quay, quayside, pier, jetty, landing stage.

wheedle *verb* cajole, coax, inveigle, beguile, charm, persuade, talk into, win over, entice, induce, entreat, implore, flatter, butter up (*inf*), humour, court, influence.

wheel *noun* **1** (*a set of wheels*) disc, round, circle, ring, hoop, caster. **2** (*with a wheel of his arm*) turn, pivot, gyration, twirl, whirl, spin, rotation, roll, revolution.
➤ *verb* **1** (*he wheeled round at the noise*) spin, circle, gyrate, rotate, revolve, turn. **2** (*the regiment wheeled to the right*) pivot, swivel, revolve, twirl, whirl, roll, swing.

at the wheel **1** (*his wife was at the wheel of the car*) in the driving seat, driving, steering, in control. **2** (*at the wheel of the company*) at the helm (*inf*), in the driving seat (*inf*), in control, in charge, in command, heading up (*inf*), directing, responsible.

wheeze *verb* gasp, pant, rasp, hiss, whistle, cough.
➤ *noun* **1** (*the cold left him with a wheeze*) gasp, pant, rasp, hiss, whistle, cough. **2** (*a clever wheeze*) idea, notion, scheme, plan, ruse, ploy, trick, stunt, prank, joke, gag.

whereabouts *noun* location, place, position, site, vicinity, situation.

wherewithal *noun* means, resources, supplies, reserves, funds, cash, money, readies (*inf*), loot (*inf*), dough (*inf*), bread (*inf*), finance, capital, necessary.

whet *verb* **1** (*whet the edge of the knife*) sharpen, hone, edge, strop, file, grind, rasp. OPPOSITE: blunt. **2** (*whet her curiosity*) stimulate, arouse, rouse, stir, awaken, kindle, quicken, excite, provoke, tempt, incite, increase, titillate.

whiff *noun* **1** (*a whiff of fresh air*) breath, puff, gust, blast, draught. **2** (*a whiff of danger*) trace, hint, suggestion, suspicion, soupçon, touch. **3** (*a whiff of perfume*) smell, scent, aroma, odour, sniff, reek, stink, stench.
➤ *verb* waft, blow, puff, breathe, inhale, sniff, smell.

while *noun* time, period, spell, season, stretch, interval, span.

while away *verb* pass, spend, use up, occupy.

whim *noun* fancy, notion, idea, impulse, urge, inclination, humour, quirk, caprice, vagary.

whimper *verb* cry, snivel, sniffle, sob, weep, blubber, grizzle (*inf*), whine, whinge (*inf*), moan, groan, wail. OPPOSITE: laugh.
➤ *noun* whine, sob, cry, snivel, moan, groan, wail.

whimsical *adj* fanciful, fantastical, quirky, capricious, impulsive, unpredictable, playful, mischievous, freakish, eccentric, dotty (*inf*), weird, odd, peculiar, queer, bizarre, curious, unusual, quaint, funny, droll, waggish.

whine *verb* **1** (*the dog whined*) whimper, cry, sob, wail, groan, grizzle (*inf*). **2** (*the children whined all the way there*) whinge (*inf*), moan, groan, complain, carp, grumble, go on (*inf*), grouch (*inf*), grouse (*inf*), gripe (*inf*), beef (*inf*), bellyache (*inf*).
➤ *noun* **1** (*the whine of a dog*) cry, sob, whimper, wail, moan. **2** (*ignore the whines of the children*) complaint, grumble, moan, groan, grouse (*inf*), grouch (*inf*), gripe (*inf*), bellyache (*inf*), whinging (*inf*), beefing (*inf*).

whip *verb* **1** (*he was sentenced to be whipped*) beat, lash, flog, scourge, flagellate, birch, strap, cane, spank, belt (*inf*), tan (*inf*), clout (*inf*), whack (*inf*), wallop (*inf*), leather, thrash, strike, punish, castigate, discipline, chastise. OPPOSITE: caress. **2** (*he whipped a gun from under his coat*) pull, jerk, yank (*inf*), whisk, snatch, flash, produce. **3** (*he whipped the crowd into a frenzy*) drive, push, spur, goad, prod, rouse, stir up, prompt, provoke, incite, instigate, urge, agitate, encourage. **4** (*whip the cream for me*) beat, whisk, stir, mix.
➤ *noun* lash, scourge, horsewhip, bull whip, cat-o'-nine-tails, birch, cane, crop, switch.

whip up stir up, rouse, provoke, work up, excite, inflame, kindle, incite, instigate, agitate, foment, psych up (*inf*).

whipping *noun* **1** (*he was given a whipping as a punishment*) lashing, flogging, scourging, flagellation, birching, caning, thrashing, belting (*inf*), walloping (*inf*), hiding (*inf*), beating, spanking, leathering, tanning (*inf*), castigation, punishment. **2** (*the other team got a real whipping*) thrashing, beating, trouncing, routing, walloping (*inf*).

whirl *verb* **1** (*she whirled round*) spin, twirl, pivot, pirouette, gyrate, reel, rotate, revolve, circle, turn, wheel, swirl. **2** (*his mind whirled*) reel, spin, go round.
➤ *noun* **1** (*the whirl of a spinning top*) spin, rotation, revolution, pivot, turn, twirl, twist, circle, wheel, reel, swirl, gyration, pirouette. **2** (*I'll give it a whirl*) try, go (*inf*), shot (*inf*), crack (*inf*), bash (*inf*), stab (*inf*), attempt.

3 (*the next few hours passed in a whirl*) daze, jumble, muddle, spin, confusion, dither. **4** (*a whirl of events*) sequence, succession, progression, round, series, string, chain, cycle, flurry. **5** (*she entered the social whirl*) merry-go-round, hurly-burly, bustle, tumult, hubbub, commotion, uproar, to-do.

whirlpool *noun* vortex, maelstrom.

whirlwind *noun* tornado, cyclone, vortex.
➤ *adj* headlong, impulsive, impetuous, hasty, rash, speedy, rapid, swift, quick, lightning.

whisk *verb* **1** (*whisk the mixture*) beat, whip, mix, stir. **2** (*the animal whisked its tail*) flick, twitch, wave, brandish. **3** (*he whisked the flies away*) flap, flick, brush, sweep. **4** (*she whisked the drinks away*) whip, whirl, snatch, jerk, yank (*inf*), remove, pull. **5** (*he whisked down the corridor*) dart, dash, dodge, shoot, tear, dive, fly, bolt, whip, race, rush, hasten, hurry, speed, zoom. OPPOSITE: amble.
➤ *noun* **1** (*with a whisk of her hand*) flick, wave, brandish. **2** (*a few whisks of a duster*) brush, sweep, wipe.

whisper *verb* **1** (*he whispered under his breath*) murmur, mutter, mumble, breathe, sigh, hiss. OPPOSITE: shout. **2** (*the leaves whispered in the breeze*) rustle, murmur, sigh, swish, hiss.
➤ *noun* **1** (*his voice dropped to a whisper*) undertone, murmur, mutter, mumble. **2** (*the whisper of leaves*) rustle, murmur, sigh, swish, hiss. **3** (*have you heard the latest whisper?*) rumour, scandal, gossip, report, revelation, insinuation, innuendo, intimation, disclosure, divulgence, hint, suggestion. **4** (*a whisper of scandal*) breath, whiff, trace, tinge, hint, suggestion, suspicion, soupçon.

whit *noun* iota, jot, trifle, tittle, particle, crumb, bit, scrap, shred, grain, speck, pinch, dash, mite, fragment, piece, atom, trace, scintilla, modicum.

white *adj* **1** (*her face was white*) pale, pallid, wan, ashen, waxen, chalky, pasty, peaky, anaemic, bloodless, colourless, whey-faced. OPPOSITE: ruddy. **2** (*he smoothed down his white hair*) snowy, silver, silvery, grizzled, hoary, grey, light. OPPOSITE: dark. **3** (*a white reputation*) pure, clean, spotless, immaculate, unsullied, undefiled, stainless. OPPOSITE: foul.

white-collar *adj* professional, clerical, executive.

whiten *verb* bleach, blanch, fade, blench, pale, wash out, whitewash, etiolate. OPPOSITE: colour.

whitewash *noun* cover-up, camouflage, mask, concealment, deception.
➤ *verb* cover up, conceal, hide, camouflage, gloss over, suppress, soft-pedal, downplay, minimize, make light of.

whittle *verb* **1** (*whittling figures from a block of wood*) cut, carve, model, hew, shave, pare, trim. **2** (*his inheritance was soon whittled away*) eat away, consume, erode, use up, wear away, undermine. **3** (*the government continues to whittle away at subsidies*) reduce, cut back, lessen, decrease, diminish.

whole *adj* **1** (*the whole evening was a disaster*) entire, complete, total, full, integral, undivided, uncut, unabridged. OPPOSITE: partial. **2** (*nothing was left whole*) perfect, flawless, intact, sound, unbroken, in one piece, unimpaired, undamaged, unharmed, unhurt, uninjured, unmutilated, unscathed. OPPOSITE: imperfect. **3** (*he feels whole again*) fit, well, healthy, recovered, sound, strong.
➤ *noun* aggregate, total, sum total, all, entirety, totality, fullness, ensemble, entity, unit, lot. OPPOSITE: part.

on the whole 1 (*on the whole everything is going well*) all in all, all things considered, by and large. **2** (*we stay in to eat on the whole*) as a rule, mostly, for the most part, in the main, generally, generally speaking, in general, as a general rule.

wholehearted *adj* **1** (*a wholehearted performance*) heartfelt, passionate, warm, sincere, committed, genuine, unfeigned, real, true, hearty, emphatic, unstinting, unreserved, unqualified, complete. OPPOSITE: half-hearted. **2** (*a wholehearted supporter of the party*) earnest, eager, zealous, keen, enthusiastic, committed, dedicated, devoted, serious.

wholesale *adj* indiscriminate, mass, comprehensive, extensive, wide-ranging, far-reaching, sweeping, broad, all-inclusive, total, outright.
➤ *adv* indiscriminately, totally, comprehensively, extensively, all at once, in a mass, en bloc, without exception, on a large scale.

wholesome *adj* **1** (*a wholesome diet*) healthy, healthful, health-giving, nourishing, nutritious, good, sanitary, hygienic. **2** (*wholesome exercise*) beneficial, good, bracing, invigorating, refreshing, stimulating, salutary, salubrious. OPPOSITE: deleterious. **3** (*a wholesome family show*) decent, respectable, moral, ethical, clean, pure, virtuous, proper, righteous, uplifting, improving, edifying, beneficial, helpful, prudent.

wholly *adv* **1** (*I am wholly in agreement*) entirely, purely, completely, totally, fully, unreservedly, perfectly, altogether, thoroughly, utterly, absolutely, comprehensively, enthusiastically. OPPOSITE: partly. **2** (*this must be wholly her decision*) exclusively, purely, solely.

whoop *noun* shout, yell, cry, call, scream, shriek, roar, hoot, cheer, hurrah.
➤ *verb* shout, yell, cry, call, scream, shriek, roar, hoot, cheer.

whore *noun* prostitute, streetwalker, tart (*inf*), hooker (*inf*), call girl, harlot, fallen woman, strumpet, trollop, courtesan.

wicked *adj* **1** (*a wicked ruler*) evil, bad, wrong, sinful, iniquitous, vile, villainous, black-hearted, base, vicious, heinous, nefarious, flagitious, atrocious, abominable, criminal, lawless, dishonourable, unprincipled, unethical, godless, ungodly, unholy, impious, irreligious, devilish, profane, unrighteous, immoral, amoral, abandoned, depraved, debauched, perverted, dissolute, corrupt, reprobate, degenerate, dissipated. OPPOSITE: virtuous. **2** (*it was a wicked thing to do*) bad, unpleasant, nasty, mean, cruel, abominable, abhorrent, loathsome, detestable, reprehensible, hateful, awful, terrible, dreadful, dire, grim, gruesome, horrible, hideous, atrocious, dastardly, damnable, monstrous, infamous, harmful, foul, base, offensive, gross, odious, obnoxious, scandalous, shameful, ignoble, ignominious, dishonourable, disgraceful, nefarious, iniquitous, sinful, vile, villainous, worthless, wrong, illicit, illegal, unlawful, lawless, unholy, ungodly, godless, impious, impure, profane, blasphemous, irreverent, irreligious.

3 (*you wicked child*) naughty, mischievous, impish, roguish, rascally, arch. OPPOSITE: good. **4** (*a wicked pair of trainers*) excellent, cool (*inf*), brill (*inf*), brilliant, great (*inf*), admirable, superior, superlative, outstanding.

wide *adj* **1** (*a wide expanse of grass*) broad, extensive, sweeping, vast, immense, ample, spacious, roomy, capacious. **2** (*she had a wide frame*) broad, large, thick, ample, full. **3** (*wide experience of the tropics*) comprehensive, catholic, encyclopedic, all-embracing, inclusive, compendious, general, immense, expansive, extensive, far-ranging, wide-ranging, sweeping, vast, broad, ample. OPPOSITE: narrow. **4** (*the first shot went wide*) off-course, off-target, off the mark.
➤ *adv* **1** (*the door gaped wide*) fully, completely, to the full extent, all the way. **2** (*she went wide on her next attempt*) astray, off target, off course, off the mark.

wide-awake *adj* **1** (*he was wide awake before dawn*) awake, conscious, roused, open-eyed. **2** (*the sentries must remain wide awake*) alert, on the alert, sharp, keen, aware, vigilant, wary, observant, watchful, attentive, heedful, quick-witted, on the ball (*inf*).

widen *verb* broaden, extend, expand, spread, stretch, enlarge, augment, supplement, increase, add to, open. OPPOSITE: narrow.

wide open *adj* **1** (*her eyes were wide open*) open wide, dilated, gaping. **2** (*she welcomed him with arms wide open*) open wide, outspread, outstretched, extended, splayed open. **3** (*the town is wide open to attack*) vulnerable, at risk, in danger, exposed, susceptible, defenceless, unprotected, unguarded, unfortified.

widespread *adj* rife, prevalent, pervasive, common, extensive, general, universal, sweeping, far-reaching, far-flung, wide-ranging, broad, unlimited, wholesale, epidemic. OPPOSITE: restricted.

width *noun* **1** (*the width of the plank*) breadth, thickness, broadness, diameter, span, girth. **2** (*the width of their ambition*) breadth, reach, scope, range, span, compass, extent, extensiveness, vastness, expansiveness, immensity, immenseness, comprehensiveness, measure.

wield *verb* **1** (*wield the brush with skill*) handle, manipulate, brandish, flourish, shake, wave, swing, control, manage, hold, have, use, put to use, employ, ply. **2** (*wield supreme power*) exercise, employ, exert, have, hold, possess, command, control, maintain.

wife *noun* spouse, other half (*inf*), better half (*inf*), old woman (*inf*), little woman (*inf*), missis (*inf*), 'er indoors (*inf*), bride, mate, companion, consort, woman, helpmate, squaw.

wild *adj* **1** (*wild animals*) untamed, undomesticated, unbroken, feral, savage, ferocious, fierce. OPPOSITE: tame. **2** (*wild jungle tribesmen*) barbarous, barbaric, savage, fierce, ferocious, brutish, primitive, uncivilized, ignorant. **3** (*a wild region*) uncultivated, uncivilized, desolate, isolated, forsaken, waste, desert, empty, barren, rugged, inhospitable, uninhabited, unpopulated, unsettled, unfrequented. **4** (*a wild storm*) violent, furious, raging, stormy, tempestuous, turbulent, blustery, choppy, rough, howling. **5** (*a wild party*) riotous, boisterous, rowdy, noisy, rough, lawless, excited, unruly, frantic, turbulent, violent, undisciplined, intractable, unmanageable, unbridled,

unchecked, uncontrolled, out of control, unrestrained, unconstrained, uncurbed. OPPOSITE: restrained. **6** (*a wild plan to climb the mountain*) rash, reckless, impulsive, madcap, foolhardy, unwise, ill-advised, ill-considered, imprudent, foolish, outrageous, preposterous, extravagant, fantastical, impracticable. OPPOSITE: sensible. **7** (*he had a wild appearance*) disorderly, disarranged, untidy, messy, dishevelled, tousled, unkempt. OPPOSITE: tidy. **8** (*the audience went wild*) berserk, mad, frantic, frenzied, hysterical, crazy (*inf*), bonkers (*inf*), bananas (*inf*), demented. **9** (*the noise drove her wild*) mad (*inf*), crazy (*inf*), angry, infuriated, incensed, exasperated, seething, nuts (*inf*), nutty (*inf*). **10** (*he's wild about dinosaurs*) enthusiastic, eager, keen, passionate, crazy (*inf*), mad (*inf*), nuts (*inf*), daft (*inf*), potty (*inf*), obsessed.

wilderness *noun* **1** (*they were lost in the wilderness*) wilds, wasteland, desert, jungle. **2** (*a wilderness of streets*) confusion, muddle, labyrinth, maze, clutter, jumble, tangle, hotchpotch, miscellany.

wile *noun* (*his use of wile to fool the enemy*) cunning, artfulness, slyness, craft, craftiness, guile, trickery, chicanery, deceit, deception, cheating, fraud. OPPOSITE: artlessness.

wiles *pl noun* stratagem, artifice, device, contrivance, subterfuge, trick, ruse, dodge (*inf*), manoeuvre, ploy, lure.

wilful *adj* **1** (*a wilful child*) headstrong, obstinate, stubborn, intransigent, mulish, pig-headed, obdurate, adamant, inflexible, unyielding, uncompromising, intractable, refractory, recalcitrant, perverse, contrary, disobedient, wayward, self-willed, strong-willed, dogged, persistent, determined. OPPOSITE: docile. **2** (*a wilful act of vandalism*) intentional, intended, deliberate, premeditated, planned, calculated, on purpose, conscious, purposeful, voluntary. OPPOSITE: accidental.

will *noun* **1** (*the right to free will*) volition, option, preference, choice, discretion, decision. **2** (*it is his will to go*) wish, desire, fancy, mind, inclination, preference, pleasure, disposition. **3** (*the will to succeed*) purpose, purposefulness, determination, resolution, resolve, pluck, mettle, nerve, doggedness, commitment, single-mindedness, firmness, willpower. **4** (*it is the will of the emperor*) command, order, decree, ordinance, dictate, decision, wish. **5** (*he made his will*) testament, deed, bequest.
➤ *verb* **1** (*as willed by the court*) ordain, decree, order, command, direct, bid, desire, wish. **2** (*do what you will*) choose, prefer, elect, decide, determine, see fit, think fit, please, want, wish, desire. **3** (*she willed the house to her son*) leave, give, transfer, bequeath, pass on, hand down.

willing *adj* **1** (*willing to have a go*) prepared, disposed, inclined, ready, consenting, amenable, compliant, game (*inf*), content, happy, glad, desirous, nothing loath. **2** (*a willing volunteer*) eager, enthusiastic, keen, ready, avid. **3** (*a willing disposition*) cheerful, agreeable, obliging, accommodating, cooperative, biddable. OPPOSITE: reluctant.

willingly *adv* **1** (*they paid up willingly*) freely, voluntarily, by choice, spontaneously. **2** (*she'll go along with the idea willingly*) happily, gladly, cheerfully, readily, eagerly, ungrudgingly, with pleasure, without hesitation. OPPOSITE: reluctantly.

willingness noun **1** (*her willingness to join in*) eagerness, readiness, keenness, enthusiasm, wish, desire. **2** (*their willingness to accept the proposal*) readiness, preparedness, inclination, disposition, consent, agreeableness, amenability.

willpower noun will, strength of will, resolution, resolve, determination, firmness, purposefulness, doggedness, persistence, drive, commitment, single-mindedness, self-discipline, self-control, pluck, nerve, mettle, grit (*inf*).

wilt verb **1** (*the flowers are wilting*) wither, shrivel, droop, sag, flop. OPPOSITE: thrive. **2** (*his enthusiasm is wilting*) fade, flag, dwindle, ebb, wane, melt away, diminish, lessen, fail, weaken, grow less, languish.

wily adj artful, crafty, cunning, sly, guileful, subtle, shrewd, sharp, astute, tricky, shifty, scheming, intriguing, designing, underhand, crooked (*inf*), foxy, deceitful, deceptive, cheating, fraudulent. OPPOSITE: artless.

win verb **1** (*who will win in this contest?*) triumph, succeed. OPPOSITE: lose. **2** (*he will win against all his enemies*) conquer, vanquish, prevail, win the day (*inf*), carry the day, overcome, come first. **3** (*win a reward*) get, gain, obtain, receive, acquire, procure, collect, pick up, secure, attain, earn, take, catch, net, bag (*inf*), achieve, accomplish.
➤ noun victory, triumph, success, conquest, mastery. OPPOSITE: defeat.

win over persuade, convince, sway, influence, convert, carry, bring round, talk round, prevail upon, induce, charm, allure, attract.

wince verb flinch, start, jump, jerk, blench, cower, quail, shrink, recoil, draw back, cringe, grimace, squirm.
➤ noun flinch, start, jump, jerk, cringe, grimace.

wind[1] noun **1** (*a wind had sprung up*) breeze, gale, storm, hurricane, typhoon, tornado, cyclone, blast, gust, draught, air, zephyr, puff, breath. **2** (*he is often troubled by wind*) gas, flatulence. **3** (*the staff got wind of the changes*) hint, suggestion, intimation, inkling, intelligence, news, report, rumour, gossip.
in the wind in the offing, on the way, approaching, impending, looming, close at hand, about to happen, coming near, expected, likely, probable, on the cards (*inf*).

wind[2] verb **1** (*the fog winding among the trees*) coil, curl, twist, spiral, roll, wreathe, furl, snake, twine. **2** (*the path winds along the coast*) twist, turn, loop, bend, curve, spiral, zigzag, meander, ramble, snake.
➤ noun winding, bend, curve, twist, turn, loop, convolution, coil, whorl, zigzag.

wind down 1 (*she likes to wind down with a drink*) unwind, relax, ease up, calm down, quieten down, cool off. **2** (*production is expected to wind down*) slow down, slacken off, ease up, taper off, dwindle, diminish, lessen, reduce, decline, subside, stop, bring to an end, come to an end, come to a close.

wind up 1 (*her colleagues really wind her up sometimes*) agitate, fluster, disconcert, discompose, strain, work up, put on edge. **2** (*don't wind the children up*) tease, make

fun of, chaff, kid (*inf*), annoy, irritate. **3** (*wind up the evening with a song*) end, close, conclude, finish, terminate, wrap up (*inf*). **4** (*wind up the company*) close down, liquidate, dissolve. **5** (*we should wind up at the river*) end, finish, fetch, find oneself.

winded adj breathless, out of breath, panting, puffed out (*inf*), gasping for breath.

windfall noun stroke of luck, piece of luck, godsend, jackpot, bonanza, find.

winding adj twisting, turning, bending, curving, looping, sinuous, snaking, serpentine, tortuous, circuitous, indirect, roundabout, meandering, rambling, zigzagging, spiralling, crooked, convoluted. OPPOSITE: straight.

window noun pane, opening, skylight, casement, light.

windy adj **1** (*windy weather*) breezy, blowy, blustery, blustering, gusty, gusting, stormy, squally, windswept, boisterous, tempestuous, turbulent, wild. OPPOSITE: still. **2** (*a windy address to the audience*) long-winded, verbose, wordy, garrulous, rambling, meandering, diffuse, prolix, loquacious, bombastic, pompous, turgid, empty.

wing noun **1** (*the organization's political wing*) arm, branch, group, grouping, set, section, faction, circle, side, segment. **2** (*a ghost in the west wing*) extension, annexe.
➤ verb **1** (*wing through the clouds*) fly, glide, soar. **2** (*she winged through the village on her bicycle*) fly, flit, hurry, hasten, race, speed, zoom, travel. **3** (*winged by a bullet*) wound, hit, clip, nick.

wink verb **1** (*he winked at her*) blink, flutter, bat. **2** (*the lamp winked over the water*) twinkle, sparkle, flash, flicker, gleam, glitter, glimmer, glint.
➤ noun **1** (*with a wink of her eye*) blink, flutter, bat. **2** (*the wink of aircraft lights*) twinkle, sparkle, flash, flicker, gleam, glitter, glimmering, glint. **3** (*I'll be finished in a couple of winks*) instant, moment, minute, second, in a tick (*inf*), sec (*inf*), flash, mo (*inf*), jiffy (*inf*).

wink at ignore, disregard, overlook, neglect, tolerate, let pass, pass over, condone, connive at, turn a blind eye to (*inf*).

winkle verb extricate, extract, draw, prise, worm.

winner noun victor, champion, champ (*inf*), conqueror, vanquisher, prizewinner. OPPOSITE: loser.

winning adj **1** (*the winning army*) victorious, conquering, vanquishing, unbeaten, undefeated, triumphant, successful. **2** (*he has a winning way about him*) captivating, charming, enchanting, taking, engaging, endearing, beguiling, bewitching, disarming, winsome, attractive, alluring, fetching, pleasing, amiable, delightful, sweet, lovely, darling.

winnings pl noun proceeds, gains, takings, spoils, profits, booty, jackpot, prize.

winnow verb separate, divide, part, sort out, sift.

winsome adj winning, engaging, charming, pleasing, amiable, delightful, agreeable, sweet, pretty, lovely, comely, attractive, prepossessing, fetching (*inf*), alluring, endearing, captivating, fascinating, enchanting, bewitching, beguiling. OPPOSITE: repulsive.

wintry adj **1** (*wintry weather*) cold, freezing, frozen, arctic, glacial, icy, snowy, frosty, chilly, biting, piercing, raw, nippy, hibernal, bleak, desolate, cheerless, dismal, harsh. OPPOSITE: summery. **2** (*he got a wintry reception*) cold, chilly, frosty, icy, cool, unfriendly, hostile, harsh, unwelcoming, distant, remote, bleak, cheerless, desolate.

wipe *verb* **1** (*wipe the glass clean*) rub, clean, mop, sponge, swab, dust, brush, dry. **2** (*wipe the blood away*) remove, efface, erase, get rid of, rub off, clean off, sponge off, mop up, brush off, take away, take off.
➣ *noun* mop, sponge, swab, clean, rub, brush, dry, dust.
wipe out destroy, demolish, raze, obliterate, erase, blot out, eradicate, exterminate, extinguish, eliminate, expunge, abolish, extirpate, annihilate, massacre.

wiry *adj* **1** (*a wiry young man*) lean, spare, sinewy, muscular, tough, strong. **2** (*wiry hair*) coarse, rough, wavy, strong, stiff, rigid, bristly, prickly, thorny.

wisdom *noun* **1** (*the wisdom of the ancients*) understanding, comprehension, sagacity, sapience, discernment, perception, insight, penetration, sense, commonsense, intelligence, cleverness, reason, knowledge, learning, erudition, acumen, enlightenment, philosophy. **2** (*the wisdom of this policy*) soundness, sense, commonsense, reasonableness, smartness, prudence, judiciousness, judgement, perspicacity, astuteness, shrewdness, circumspection, foresight, logic. OPPOSITE: folly.

wise *adj* **1** (*a wise adviser*) sage, sagacious, sapient, perceptive, discerning, intelligent, clever, smart, shrewd, astute, erudite, knowledgeable, learned, educated, well-read, informed, enlightened, philosophic, experienced, aware. **2** (*a wise policy*) sensible, sound, judicious, well-advised, far-sighted, long-sighted, circumspect, prudent, shrewd, smart, astute, politic, reasonable, rational, logical. OPPOSITE: foolish.

wish *verb* **1** (*wish for good news*) desire, want, long, yearn, pine, sigh, hanker after (*inf*), covet, crave, hunger, thirst, prefer, fancy, lust after. **2** (*you will do as I wish*) desire, bid, demand, ask, order, command, direct, instruct, require.
➣ *noun* **1** (*the nation's wish for change*) desire, want, longing, yearning, hope, aspiration, inclination, hankering (*inf*), yen (*inf*), urge, craving, hunger, thirst, lust, liking, fondness, fancy, whim, preference. **2** (*tell me your wishes*) desire, want, demand, instruction, requirement, bidding, request, command, order, direction, will.

wishy-washy *adj* **1** (*the colours are rather wishy-washy*) weak, pale, wan, pallid, sickly. **2** (*a wishy-washy approach to life*) feeble, weak, puny, namby-pamby (*inf*), irresolute, ineffectual, effete, spineless. **3** (*wishy-washy food*) insipid, vapid, tasteless, flavourless, bland, flat, weak, watery, thin, diluted.

wistful *adj* **1** (*her mood was wistful*) pensive, thoughtful, reflective, contemplative, meditative, musing, dreaming, dreamy, daydreaming. **2** (*a wistful song*) melancholy, sad, disconsolate, forlorn, mournful, longing, yearning.

wit *noun* **1** (*a biting wit*) humour, drollery, facetiousness, wittiness, waggishness, funniness, repartee, jocularity, levity, badinage, banter, raillery. **2** (*a playwright and wit*) humorist, comic, comedian, wag, jokester, satirist, card (*inf*). **3** (*has he sufficient wit for the*

job?) intelligence, intellect, reason, brains (*inf*), gumption (*inf*), understanding, comprehension, wisdom, sagacity, discernment, acumen, sharpness, shrewdness, astuteness, insight, perception, percipience, perspicacity, judgement, sense, commonsense, cleverness, ingenuity. OPPOSITE: stupidity.

witch *noun* sorceress, enchantress, hag, necromancer, magician, soothsayer, occultist.

witchcraft *noun* sorcery, witchery, black magic, magic, enchantment, divination, necromancy, wizardry, occultism, conjuration, sortilege.

withdraw *verb* **1** (*that item has been withdrawn from the sale*) remove, pull out, take back, take away, extract, recall. **2** (*withdraw from the competition*) back out, retire, retreat, pull out, secede, drop out. **3** (*she withdrew from the room*) leave, depart, go, retire, retreat. OPPOSITE: remain. **4** (*he was asked to withdraw the allegation*) take back, retract, recant, rescind, disavow, unsay, disclaim, revoke, cancel, annul, rescind. OPPOSITE: present. **5** (*the patient has withdrawn into himself*) recoil, recede, retreat, retire, draw back, pull back, fall back, shrink back.

withdrawal *noun* **1** (*the withdrawal of all expletives*) removal, extraction, taking away, expurgation. **2** (*the withdrawal of all charges*) retraction, repudiation, recantation, recall, revocation, rescinding, disavowal, disclaimer, nullification. **3** (*the withdrawal of peacekeeping forces*) retreat, falling back, drawing back, pulling back, retirement, evacuation, disengagement, departure, exit, exodus, leaving.

withdrawn *adj* **1** (*a withdrawn child*) shy, bashful, reserved, retiring, diffident, shrinking, timid, timorous, private, introverted, self-contained, detached, aloof, distant, quiet, silent, taciturn, unsociable, uncommunicative, unforthcoming. OPPOSITE: extrovert. **2** (*a withdrawn cottage in the hills*) remote, secluded, solitary, private, isolated, distant, hidden, out-of-the-way.

wither *verb* **1** (*the plants withered without water*) shrivel, shrink, droop, wilt, waste, dry up, die. OPPOSITE: flourish. **2** (*hope withered as time passed*) fade, wane, ebb, languish, wilt, falter, die, perish.

withering *adj* scornful, contemptuous, scathing, wounding, humiliating, mortifying, destructive, devastating, deadly.

withhold *verb* **1** (*he could not withhold his impatience*) restrain, check, curb, control, suppress, repress, hide, conceal, retain, keep, keep back, hold back, reserve, refrain. OPPOSITE: give. **2** (*the council withheld the promised funds*) keep back, retain, reserve, deduct, refuse, decline.

without *prep* **1** (*she played without boots*) lacking, wanting, requiring, short of, deprived of. OPPOSITE: with. **2** (*without tax*) free from, excluding, exclusive of, not including.

withstand *verb* oppose, resist, fight, combat, take on, hold off, stand up to, stand firm against, hold out against, defy, thwart, confront, face, brave, weather, survive, take, bear, endure, stand, tolerate, put up with, cope with, last out. OPPOSITE: yield.

witness *noun* **1** (*there were several witnesses to the crime*) eyewitness, onlooker, looker-on, spectator, viewer, observer, watcher, beholder, bystander. **2** (*she was called as a witness in the case*) testifier, deponent, attestant. **3** (*his appearance bore witness to his inner turmoil*) testimony, attestation, deposition, statement, evidence, confirmation, proof, corroboration.

➤ *verb* **1** (*she witnessed the turn of two centuries*) see, observe, view, perceive, watch, look on, behold, mark, note, notice, attend. OPPOSITE: miss. **2** (*her demeanour witnessed to her innocence*) testify, bear witness, give evidence, depose, confirm, prove, corroborate, attest, bear out, support. **3** (*the deed had to be witnessed by two people*) endorse, countersign, sign, verify.

witticism *noun* quip, riposte, bon mot, pun, joke, jest, sally, epigram, repartee, pleasantry, wisecrack, gag (*inf*), one-liner (*inf*).

witty *adj* humorous, comic, droll, whimsical, fanciful, facetious, funny, amusing, waggish, jocular, clever, brilliant, ingenious, original, lively, sparkling, scintillating. OPPOSITE: dull.

wizard *noun* **1** (*break the wizard's spell*) sorcerer, warlock, witch, necromancer, magician, enchanter, conjurer, occultist, magus. **2** (*he's a wizard at cards*) expert, adept, ace (*inf*), hotshot (*inf*), master, maestro, virtuoso, genius, prodigy, star, dab hand (*inf*).

wizened *adj* shrivelled, shrunken, dried-up, withered, wasted, worn, gnarled, wrinkled, lined.

wobble *verb* **1** (*the ladder wobbled*) rock, totter, teeter, sway, shake, tremble, quake, quiver, vibrate, see-saw, oscillate. **2** (*he wobbled off down the path*) stagger, teeter, totter, dodder, waddle. **3** (*she wobbled between the two choices*) waver, vacillate, hesitate, dither, shilly-shally (*inf*), fluctuate.

➤ *noun* **1** (*the wobble of the chair*) rocking, swaying, teetering, shaking, tremble, vibration, oscillation. **2** (*he walks with a distinct wobble*) stagger, teeter, totter. **3** (*he spoke with a wobble in his voice*) shake, tremble, tremor, quake, quiver, quaver.

woe *noun* **1** (*his heart was heavy with woe*) grief, misery, sorrow, sadness, unhappiness, wretchedness, agony, pain, torment, heartache, heartbreak, depression, gloom, melancholy, dejection, despondency, desolation, anguish, distress, suffering, affliction, misfortune, disaster. **2** (*they have suffered a series of woes*) adversity, hardship, misfortune, trouble, trial, tribulation, curse, ordeal, burden, suffering, affliction, disaster, calamity, catastrophe. OPPOSITE: joy.

woebegone *adj* miserable, wretched, woeful, unhappy, sad, sorrowful, sorrowing, grief-stricken, blue (*inf*), disconsolate, mournful, gloomy, forlorn, downcast, despondent, long-faced, downhearted, dejected, crestfallen, doleful, lugubrious, desolate, depressed, dispirited, despairing, tearful, troubled.

woeful *adj* **1** (*he looked very woeful*) woebegone, sad, unhappy, sorrowful, miserable, wretched, dismal, doleful, gloomy, depressed, dejected, disconsolate, despondent, mournful, plaintive, anguished. OPPOSITE: joyful. **2** (*she met a woeful end*) sad, saddening, unhappy, sorry, miserable, wretched, dismal, doleful, gloomy, tragic, dreadful, terrible, piteous, pitiable, pitiful, pathetic, agonizing, heart-rending, heartbreaking, grievous, distressing, lamentable, disastrous, calamitous,

catastrophic, ruinous, cruel, harsh. **3** (*a woeful effort*) deplorable, lamentable, poor, bad, mean, inadequate, hopeless, sub-standard, disgraceful, paltry, pathetic, wretched, feeble, disappointing, awful, dreadful, rotten (*inf*), terrible (*inf*), lousy (*inf*), appalling (*inf*), shocking (*inf*).

wolf *verb* devour, bolt, gobble, gulp, stuff, cram, eat, gorge, scoff (*inf*), put away (*inf*), pack away (*inf*).

woman *noun* **1** (*a beautiful woman*) female, lady, girl, lass, miss, maid, maiden, bird (*inf*), dame (*inf*), chick (*inf*). OPPOSITE: man. **2** (*my woman will see you to your room*) maid, maidservant, domestic, housekeeper, charwoman, char (*inf*), lady-in-waiting.

womanhood *noun* womankind, womenkind, women, woman, womenfolk, sisterhood (*inf*), sorority.

womanizer *noun* lady-killer, ladies' man, philanderer, seducer, lecher, wolf (*inf*), Casanova, Romeo, Don Juan, Lothario.

womanly *adj* feminine, female, gentle, soft, tender, kind, warm, motherly, matronly, ladylike, womanlike, womanish, effeminate.

wonder *noun* **1** (*we all gasped with wonder*) awe, wonderment, admiration, amazement, astonishment, surprise, bewilderment, stupefaction, curiosity, fascination. OPPOSITE: indifference. **2** (*a wonder of the modern age*) marvel, phenomenon, miracle, prodigy, curiosity, rarity, sight, spectacle, nonpareil.

➤ *verb* **1** (*it makes you wonder*) meditate, ponder, reflect, muse, deliberate, think, speculate, conjecture, doubt, question, query, inquire, puzzle, ask oneself. **2** (*the child wondered at the sight*) marvel, gape, stare, stand in awe, goggle, look agog, boggle (*inf*).

wonderful *adj* **1** (*a wonderful achievement*) marvellous, extraordinary, remarkable, prodigious, phenomenal, amazing, astonishing, astounding, startling, surprising, wondrous, awesome, awe-inspiring, staggering, incredible, miraculous, fantastic, unprecedented, unheard-of, unparalleled. **2** (*we had a wonderful day out*) fantastic (*inf*), marvellous, super (*inf*), splendid, magnificent, sensational, outstanding, stupendous, superb, brilliant, brill (*inf*), cool (*inf*), ace (*inf*), wicked (*inf*), excellent, first-rate, terrific, tremendous, fabulous (*inf*), great (*inf*), smashing (*inf*), admirable. OPPOSITE: ordinary.

wont *noun* habit, routine, practice, custom, use, rule, way, convention.

➤ *adj* accustomed, used, in the habit, given, inclined, habituated.

wonted *adj* habitual, customary, familiar, common, usual, normal, routine, regular, accustomed, conventional, frequent. OPPOSITE: unusual.

woo *verb* **1** (*he wooed her for months*) court, seek the hand of, pursue, chase after, make love to. **2** (*woo consumers with reduced prices*) chase, pursue, attract, seek, importune, solicit, coax, press, urge, cultivate.

wood *noun* **1** (*there are wild animals in the wood*) forest, woodland, thicket, copse, coppice, spinney, grove, plantation, trees. OPPOSITE: clearing. **2** (*exports of wood*) timber, planks, lumber.

wooded *adj* woody, forested, timbered, tree-covered, tree-clad, sylvan.

wooden *adj* **1** (*a wooden cabin*) wood, timber. **2** (*a wooden expression*) expressionless, blank, deadpan, inexpressive, vacant, empty, vacuous, glassy, impassive, unresponsive, lifeless, spiritless, unanimated, emotionless, unemotional. **3** (*the wooden delivery of the speech*) stilted, stiff, leaden, rigid, expressionless, lifeless, spiritless, stodgy, stolid, graceless, inelegant, awkward, clumsy, ungainly, gauche, maladroit.

wool *noun* fleece, hair, down, coat.

woolly *adj* **1** (*a woolly jumper*) woollen, fluffy, fleecy, furry, frizzy, shaggy, hairy. **2** (*woolly television reception*) unclear, ill-defined, indistinct, blurred, hazy, fuzzy, foggy, cloudy. **3** (*she gave a woolly version of events*) muddled, confused, disorganized, vague, hazy, indefinite.

word *noun* **1** (*find the word in the dictionary*) term, name, expression. **2** (*she said a word or two before leaving*) remark, comment, statement, utterance, declaration, expression, observation. **3** (*we had a quick word*) chat, chit-chat (*inf*), talk, discussion, conversation, consultation, tête-à-tête, confab (*inf*). **4** (*let me give you the latest word from the authorities*) news, tidings, communication, report, account, notice, message, communiqué, dispatch, bulletin, information, intelligence, gen (*inf*), low-down (*inf*), dope (*inf*), intimation. **5** (*he gave me his word*) promise, pledge, assurance, guarantee, oath, vow, undertaking. **6** (*just give us the word and we'll get down to business*) command, order, instruction, signal, go-ahead, green light (*inf*), thumbs-up (*inf*). **7** (*the word on the street*) rumour, gossip, talk, hearsay, whisper, speculation, scandal.
≫ *verb* phrase, put, express, couch, utter, say, state, explain, write.
in a word briefly, in brief, to be brief, in short, in a nutshell (*inf*), to sum up, concisely, succinctly.
word for word verbatim, literally, accurately, closely, faithfully, exactly, precisely, strictly.

words *pl noun* lyrics, libretto, book, text, script.

wordy *adj* verbose, prolix, garrulous, loquacious, voluble, windy, long-winded, rambling, digressive, protracted, discursive, diffuse. OPPOSITE: terse.

work *noun* **1** (*the task requires a lot of work*) toil, labour, slog (*inf*), sweat, elbow-grease (*inf*), effort, exertion, drudgery, graft (*inf*), grind (*inf*), industry, travail, trouble. OPPOSITE: idleness. **2** (*the work needs to be done by tomorrow*) task, job, chore, undertaking, charge, duty, assignment, commission, mission. **3** (*what line of work is she in?*) occupation, employment, job, business, profession, vocation, calling, career, line, livelihood, field, trade, craft, pursuit. **4** (*a work of genius*) product, creation, opus, composition, piece, oeuvre, production, achievement, accomplishment, deed, feat. **5** (*observe the work in the details of this painting*) workmanship, skill, craft, art.
≫ *verb* **1** (*he works hard*) toil, labour, drudge, slog (*inf*), plug away (*inf*), peg away (*inf*), slave, exert oneself, be busy. OPPOSITE: rest. **2** (*work as a salesman*) be employed, have a job, hold down a job, earn a living, ply one's trade, do business. **3** (*that till does not work properly*) operate, function, go, run, perform, act. OPPOSITE: fail. **4** (*he worked the digger with ease*) handle, manipulate, manoeuvre, wield, ply, use, manage, direct, control,

drive, operate, run. **5** (*he worked miracles at that school*) accomplish, do, achieve, pull off (*inf*), effect, implement, execute, cause, bring about, create, contrive, produce, perform, carry out. **6** (*it is doubtful that the ruse will work*) succeed, have effect, be effective, go well, prosper. **7** (*work the land*) till, cultivate, farm, dig. **8** (*he worked the situation to his own advantage*) arrange, engineer, handle, manipulate, manoeuvre, fix (*inf*), fiddle (*inf*), wangle (*inf*), swing (*inf*), contrive, bring off, carry off, pull off. **9** (*work the dough*) knead, shape, manipulate, mould, form, fashion, model, process. **10** (*work your way to the front*) make, force, push, elbow, manoeuvre, penetrate, move, progress.

work out **1** (*work out the following sums*) solve, resolve, clear up, figure, calculate, puzzle, sort. **2** (*we must work out a plan*) plan, arrange, organize, devise, invent, contrive, construct, put together, formulate, develop, evolve, elaborate. **3** (*I hope things will work out*) succeed, go well, prosper, be effective, be effectual, go as planned, go as arranged. **4** (*let's see how the evening works out*) turn out, pan out (*inf*), come out, go, result, develop, evolve. **5** (*she works out regularly*) exercise, train, drill, keep fit, warm up, practise.

work up **1** (*the crowd were really worked up by now*) agitate, rouse, excite, inflame, stir, move, stimulate, animate. **2** (*he knows how to work up an audience*) arouse, move, stir up, generate, kindle, incite, spur, foment, wind up (*inf*). **3** (*the run had worked up a thirst in her*) build up, whet, cause, create, generate, stimulate, arouse.

workable *adj* practical, practicable, viable, feasible, doable, possible, realistic.

workaday *adj* ordinary, everyday, common, commonplace, familiar, mundane, routine, humdrum, run-of-the-mill (*inf*), average, dull, prosaic.

worker *noun* employee, workman, workwoman, working man, working woman, labourer, hand, tradesman, operative, artisan, craftsman, craftswoman, proletarian, wage-earner, breadwinner.

working *adj* **1** (*a working man*) in work, employed, waged, active. **2** (*in working order*) running, functioning, operating, operative, going.
≫ *noun* functioning, operation, running, routine, process, method, action, system.

workings *pl noun* diggings, excavations, mine, pit, quarry, shaft.

workmanship *noun* skill, technique, craftsmanship, craft, artistry, art, handicraft, handiwork, expertise, execution, finish, work.

workout *noun* training session, training, practice, drill, warm-up, physical exercise, exercise, physical jerks, aerobics, gymnastics, isometrics, callisthenics, eurhythmics.

works *pl noun* **1** (*an industrial works*) factory, mill, plant, workshop, foundry, shop. **2** (*examine the works of the engine*) machinery, mechanism, movement, action, workings, parts, innards (*inf*), insides (*inf*), guts (*inf*). **3** (*famed for his good works*) actions, acts, doings, deeds.

workshop *noun* **1** (*his last day at the workshop*) works, workroom, factory, shop, plant, mill, garage, studio. **2** (*a theatre workshop*) seminar, symposium, study group, discussion group, class.

world *noun* **1** (*all the peoples of the world*) earth, globe. **2** (*life on another world*) planet, star, moon, satellite, heavenly body. **3** (*who cares what the world thinks?*) humankind, humanity, human race, people, mankind, man, public, general public, everybody, everyone. **4** (*she did not belong in his world*) sphere, realm, kingdom, domain, province, field, area, department. **5** (*the classical world*) epoch, era, age, period, time. **6** (*a world of difference*) great deal (*inf*), immensity (*inf*), ocean.

worldly *adj* **1** (*let us turn to worldly matters*) temporal, earthly, terrestrial, mundane, physical, fleshly, corporeal, carnal, material, secular, profane, human. OPPOSITE: spiritual. **2** (*he turned out to be very worldly*) materialistic, greedy, grasping, avaricious, covetous, selfish, ambitious. **3** (*a worldly lifestyle*) cosmopolitan, urbane, streetwise (*inf*), sophisticated, knowing, worldly-wise, experienced. OPPOSITE: unsophisticated.

worldwide *adj* universal, international, global, general, ubiquitous, widespread, pandemic, extensive, far-reaching, wide-ranging.

worn *adj* **1** (*worn material*) worn out, threadbare, tatty, tattered, in tatters, ragged, frayed, shabby, shiny. **2** (*worn by years of hard labour*) worn out, exhausted, wearied, weary, spent, fatigued, tired out, dog-tired, overtired, knackered (*inf*), bushed (*inf*), pooped (*inf*), all in (*inf*), done in (*inf*). **3** (*he looked tired and worn*) haggard, drawn, jaded, strained, careworn.

worn out 1 (*that jacket is worn out*) worn, used, threadbare, tatty, tattered, in tatters, ragged, frayed, shabby, shiny. **2** (*I feel totally worn out*) exhausted, wearied, weary, spent, fatigued, tired out, dog-tired, overtired, knackered (*inf*), bushed (*inf*), pooped (*inf*), all in (*inf*), done in (*inf*).

worried *adj* anxious, troubled, bothered, concerned, distressed, disturbed, perturbed, upset, distraught, uneasy, ill at ease, disquieted, tense, uptight (*inf*), edgy, on edge, overwrought, worked-up, nervous, dismayed, apprehensive, fretful, agitated, distracted, fearful, afraid, frightened. OPPOSITE: calm.

worry *verb* **1** (*don't worry about it*) fret, be anxious, agonize, brood. **2** (*the noise worried her*) disturb, bother, trouble, concern, distress, disquiet, discompose, agitate, unsettle, fret. OPPOSITE: reassure. **3** (*you shouldn't worry the cat*) harass, hassle (*inf*), harry, plague, torment, persecute, tease, aggravate (*inf*), bug (*inf*), pester, nag, badger, importune, vex, irritate, annoy, upset. **4** (*the carcass had been worried by hyenas*) bite, savage, tear at, gnaw at, lacerate, pull at, shake, attack, go for.
≫ *noun* **1** (*he was seized with worry*) anxiety, uneasiness, unease, misgiving, disquiet, disquietude, agitation, edginess, fretfulness, upset, disturbance, concern, trouble, care, distress, anguish, misery, tenseness, tension, stress, strain, nervousness, apprehension, perturbation, fear, fearfulness. OPPOSITE: delight. **2** (*the press are a worry to the government*) annoyance, vexation, irritation, irritant, bother, nuisance, pest, plague, torment, trouble, problem, trial, concern, burden, responsibility.

worsen *verb* **1** (*the weather slowly worsened*) deteriorate, degenerate, decline, sink, slip, slide, get worse, retrogress. OPPOSITE: improve. **2** (*her comments only worsened the situation*) aggravate, exacerbate, intensify, heighten, increase, weaken.

worship *verb* **1** (*we worship the same God*) venerate, revere, reverence, honour, adore, praise, exalt, glorify, laud, extol. **2** (*he worships the ground she walks on*) adore, love, cherish, treasure, esteem, idolize, lionize, dote, adulate, admire, respect. OPPOSITE: scorn.
≫ *noun* **1** (*religious worship*) veneration, reverence, homage, devotion, praise, prayer, adoration, respect, regard, love, honour, glory, glorification, exaltation, laudation, extolment. **2** (*her worship of her husband knew no bounds*) esteem, adulation, adoration, admiration, idolization, hero-worship, devotion. OPPOSITE: contempt.

worst *verb* defeat, beat, conquer, vanquish, master, best, crush, subdue, subjugate, thrash, whip, drub, overcome, overpower, overthrow, overwhelm, rout, trounce.

worth *noun* **1** (*a man of great worth*) worthiness, merit, quality, virtue, credit, value, excellence, importance, significance, eminence, estimation. **2** (*her advice proved to be of little worth*) value, usefulness, use, utility, service, advantage, benefit, good, help, aid, assistance, gain, profit, avail. **3** (*paintings of great worth*) cost, price, value.

worthless *adj* **1** (*a worthless property*) valueless, cheap, poor, trashy, rubbishy. **2** (*a worthless bit of advice*) valueless, useless, futile, pointless, ineffectual, ineffective, nugatory, meaningless, trivial, insignificant, unimportant, paltry, unavailing, vain. **3** (*a worthless individual*) useless, good-for-nothing, base, low, abject, vile, corrupt, depraved, contemptible, despicable. OPPOSITE: worthy.

worthwhile *adj* valuable, useful, beneficial, good, worthy, advantageous, helpful, profitable, gainful, constructive, productive, justifiable.

worthy *adj* **1** (*a worthy cause*) good, deserving, worthwhile, commendable, creditable, laudable, praiseworthy, meritorious, noble, excellent, exemplary, admirable, estimable. **2** (*a worthy pillar of the local community*) respectable, reputable, decent, honest, honourable, moral, upright, blameless, irreproachable, unimpeachable, virtuous, righteous, trustworthy, reliable. OPPOSITE: worthless. **3** (*worthy of serious attention*) deserving, meriting.
≫ *noun* dignitary, VIP (*inf*), notable, celebrity, bigwig (*inf*), big noise (*inf*), big gun (*inf*), personage, name, luminary, official.

wound *noun* **1** (*he sustained a wound in the fight*) injury, hurt, harm, damage, cut, graze, scratch, gash, laceration, slash, lesion, tear, puncture, scar. **2** (*it was a wound from which she never recovered*) hurt, blow, injury, trauma, shock, insult, slight, offence, affront, grief, pain, pang, ache, distress, anguish, torment, torture.
≫ *verb* **1** (*he was wounded in the attack*) injure, hurt, harm, damage, cut, gash, graze, scratch, lacerate, slash, tear, puncture, pierce, stab. OPPOSITE: heal. **2** (*his words wounded her deeply*) hurt, grieve, mortify, distress, upset, offend, affront, injure, pain, shock, traumatize, insult, slight.

wraith *noun* ghost, spirit, spectre, phantom, phantasm, spook (*inf*), apparition, shade, vision.

wrangle *noun* argument, quarrel, squabble, altercation, tiff, row, fight, contest, dust-up (*inf*), barney (*inf*), spat (*inf*), set-to (*inf*), bickering, brawl, rumpus, dispute, disagreement, controversy, tussle. OPPOSITE: agreement.
➤ *verb* argue, quarrel, bicker, squabble, row, fight, scrap, spar, clash, contend, brawl, differ, disagree, dispute, fall out (*inf*). OPPOSITE: agree.

wrap *verb* **1** (*the chips were wrapped in newspaper*) envelop, enfold, encase, surround, sheathe, enclose, roll up, bundle up, cocoon, cover, shroud, cloak, muffle. OPPOSITE: unwrap. **2** (*wrap a bandage round the cut*) bind, swathe, wind, fold. **3** (*wrap several gifts in paper*) wrap up, gift-wrap, do up, parcel up, package, tie up.
➤ *noun* shawl, cloak, stole, cape, mantle, robe.

wrap up 1 (*wrap up all the presents*) wrap, gift-wrap, do up, parcel up, package, pack up, tie up. **2** (*wrap up the party with a song*) conclude, complete, finish, wind up, round off, end, bring to an end, bring to a close, terminate. **3** (*I wish the old man would wrap up*) shut up (*inf*), be quiet, be silent, belt up (*inf*), dry up (*inf*), pipe down (*inf*), give it a rest (*inf*), put a sock in it (*inf*).

wrapper *noun* **1** (*dispose of this wrapper carefully*) wrapping, packaging, covering, paper, cover. **2** (*remove the wrapper from the monitor*) cover, covering, sleeve, sheath, jacket, case, casing.

wrath *noun* anger, ire, ill humour, rage, fury, passion, indignation, displeasure, bitterness, high dudgeon, resentment, exasperation, irascibility, irritation, annoyance. OPPOSITE: composure.

wrathful *adj* angry, irate, ireful, incensed, enraged, infuriated, raging, furious, fuming, ranting, raving, passionate, bitter, indignant, cross, displeased, exasperated, irritated, irascible, bad-tempered, hopping mad (*inf*), ill-humoured. OPPOSITE: pleased.

wreak *verb* inflict, execute, carry out, cause, bring about, perpetrate, create, vent, unleash, indulge, gratify.

wreath *noun* **1** (*a laurel wreath*) garland, chaplet, circlet, coronet, crown, band, diadem, festoon, coronal. **2** (*a wreath of smoke*) ring, loop, circle.

wreathe *verb* **1** (*wreathed with flowers*) festoon, garland, decorate, adorn, crown, envelop, shroud, cover. **2** (*fog wreathed round the trees*) twist, wind, coil, curl, spiral, twine, entwine, encircle, surround, envelop, enfold, wrap.

wreck *verb* **1** (*they wrecked the house*) ruin, destroy, demolish, devastate, smash, damage, break, ravage, write off (*inf*). OPPOSITE: build. **2** (*their plans for the future were wrecked*) destroy, devastate, smash, shatter, ruin, demolish, spoil, disrupt, undo, mar, upset, play havoc with. **3** (*the storm wrecked three ships*) shipwreck, capsize, sink, run aground.
➤ *noun* **1** (*the wreck of the train*) wreckage, debris, remains, fragments, pieces, relics, detritus, rubble, ruins, remains, shards, remnants. **2** (*she lamented the wreck of her ambitions*) wreckage, wrecking, ruin, ruination, destruction, devastation, desolation, demolition, smashing, shattering, breaking, disintegration, disruption, undoing, loss.

wreckage *noun* **1** (*locate the wreckage of the aeroplane*) wreck, debris, remains, fragments, pieces, relics, detritus, rubble, ruins, remains, shards, remnants. **2** (*the wreckage of the enterprise was total*) wreck, wrecking, ruin, ruination, destruction, devastation, desolation, demolition, smashing, shattering, breaking, disintegration, disruption, undoing, loss.

wrench *verb* **1** (*he wrenched his wrist in the fall*) strain, sprain, rick, twist. **2** (*wrench the door open*) jerk, pull, tug, yank (*inf*), force, rip, tear, wrest, twist.
➤ *noun* **1** (*he took the door off with a single wrench*) jerk, pull, tug, yank (*inf*), twist. **2** (*you will need a wrench to undo that*) spanner, monkey wrench. **3** (*she has given her shoulder a wrench*) strain, sprain, rick, twist. **4** (*it was a wrench to leave the family*) sadness, sorrow, trauma, distress, anguish, blow, pang, pain, ache.

wrest *verb* seize, take, pull, twist, wrench, wring, grasp, force, snatch, extract, remove.

wrestle *verb* fight, grapple, scuffle, tussle, vie, battle, strive, struggle, contend, contest, combat.

wretch *noun* **1** (*the wretches even stole the child's piggy-bank*) scoundrel, villain, rogue, rascal, criminal, blackguard, ruffian, miscreant, reprobate, delinquent, louse (*inf*), rat (*inf*), swine (*inf*), worm (*inf*), creep (*inf*), rotter (*inf*). **2** (*a starving wretch*) unfortunate, outcast, beggar.

wretched *adj* **1** (*she feels wretched about her loss*) miserable, unhappy, sad, sorrowful, sorry, disconsolate, down, downcast, downhearted, broken-hearted, distressed, dejected, depressed, crestfallen, woebegone, melancholy, forlorn, gloomy, mournful, cheerless, doleful, abject. OPPOSITE: happy. **2** (*she had a wretched childhood*) miserable, unhappy, sorry, poor, hard, harsh, grim, difficult, unfortunate. **3** (*his cold makes him feel wretched*) awful, unwell, ill, sick, sickly, below par, ailing, under the weather (*inf*), out of sorts (*inf*). **4** (*the wretched victims of the famine*) unfortunate, unlucky, miserable, poor, pathetic, pitiable, piteous, hapless, forlorn, woebegone, sad, unhappy, sorry, abject, tragic. **5** (*he is a wretched swine*) contemptible, despicable, shameful, mean, base, vile, worthless, low. **6** (*it was a wretched meal*) bad, poor, awful, terrible, low-quality, substandard, inferior, paltry, inadequate, appalling, horrible, dreadful, deplorable, outrageous, shocking.

wriggle *verb* squirm, writhe, twist, wiggle, jerk, jiggle, worm, snake, slink, crawl, sidle.
➤ *noun* squirm, writhe, wiggle, twist, jiggle, jerk, twitch.

wring *verb* **1** (*wring water from the towel*) squeeze, extract, twist, screw, mangle. **2** (*wring the truth out of the suspect*) wrench, wrest, extract, force, screw, extort, exact, coerce. **3** (*his tale wrung her heart*) pierce, rend, stab, wound, harrow, rack, distress, pain, hurt, torture, tear, lacerate.

wrinkle *verb* crease, fold, crumple, crinkle, rumple, pucker, gather, line, furrow, corrugate. OPPOSITE: smooth.
➤ *noun* crease, fold, crumple, rumple, crinkle, pucker, gather, line, ridge, furrow, corrugation.

writ *noun* court order, summons, subpoena, decree.

write *verb* **1** (*write with your other hand*) pen, inscribe, transcribe, scribble, scrawl, note, record, register, jot down, set down, take down, put down, put in writing.

2 (*write a new novel*) draft, compose, create, pen, dash off (*inf*), draw up.

write off 1 (*he wrote off his new car*) wreck, destroy, smash, crash, demolish. **2** (*write off the debt*) wipe out, cross out, score out, delete, cancel, annul, nullify, disregard, forget about. **3** (*they wrote off the possibility*) disregard, dismiss, ignore.

writer *noun* author, scribbler (*inf*), pen-pusher (*inf*), scribe, novelist, biographer, chronicler, essayist, playwright, dramatist, poet, scriptwriter, journalist, correspondent, columnist, diarist.

writhe *verb* wriggle, squirm, twist, coil, roll, turn, jerk, flail, toss, struggle, thrash, thresh, contort, distort.

writing *noun* **1** (*illegible writing*) handwriting, hand, penmanship, script, text, print, calligraphy, scribble, scrawl. **2** (*his collected writing*) book, publication, volume, opus, work, composition, document, letter.

wrong *adj* **1** (*a wrong reply*) incorrect, inaccurate, imprecise, inexact, erroneous, in error, mistaken, false, untrue, faulty, unsound, off target, off beam (*inf*), wide of the mark (*inf*). OPPOSITE: correct. **2** (*it is wrong to say such things*) bad, sinful, iniquitous, reprehensible, corrupt, unethical, immoral, wicked, evil, wrongful, unlawful, illegal, illicit, criminal, felonious, delinquent, crooked (*inf*), dishonest, dishonourable, unfair. OPPOSITE: good. **3** (*quite the wrong thing to do*) inappropriate, unsuitable, inapt, inapposite, improper, unseemly, unfitting, unconventional, incongruous, indecorous, infelicitous, undesirable, unacceptable. OPPOSITE: right. **4** (*something's wrong with the car*) faulty, defective, amiss, awry, not right, out of order, up the spout (*inf*).
➤ *adv* **1** (*where did I go wrong?*) astray, amiss, awry, badly. **2** (*he was dressed wrong*) wrongly, incorrectly, improperly, faultily, inappropriately, erroneously, inaccurately, mistakenly, inexactly, imprecisely, falsely. OPPOSITE: properly.
➤ *noun* **1** (*he committed many wrongs*) sin, misdeed, trespass, transgression, offence, crime, infringement, infraction, injustice, grievance, outrage, atrocity, error, mistake. **2** (*we must fight wrong*) wickedness, evil, badness, sin, sinfulness, iniquity, crime, unlawfulness, wrongdoing, immorality, abuse, unfairness, injustice, dishonour, dishonesty, crookedness (*inf*). OPPOSITE: right.
➤ *verb* **1** (*he was wronged by his employers*) abuse, mistreat, maltreat, ill-treat, oppress, exploit, cheat, hurt, harm, injure. **2** (*they wrong her memory by repeating those lies*) insult, malign, defame, slander, libel, discredit, dishonour, misrepresent, impugn, vilify, denigrate.

go wrong 1 (*the printer has gone wrong*) break down, pack up (*inf*), seize up (*inf*), conk out (*inf*), fail, malfunction, stop working. **2** (*I just know that everything will go wrong*) fail, collapse, flop (*inf*), go badly, go astray, go amiss, go awry, miscarry, misfire, come to grief, come to nothing, come a cropper (*inf*).

in the wrong at fault, in error, mistaken, guilty, culpable, blameworthy, to blame.

wrongdoer *noun* offender, lawbreaker, criminal, felon, villain, culprit, delinquent, miscreant, evildoer, sinner, trespasser, transgressor, malefactor.

wrongful *adj* unjust, unfair, unjustified, unwarranted, reprehensible, illegal, unlawful, criminal, illegitimate, illicit, immoral, improper, unethical, dishonest, dishonourable, blameworthy, wrong, wicked, evil. OPPOSITE: rightful.

wry *adj* **1** (*pull a wry face*) awry, askew, crooked, lopsided, uneven, twisted, distorted, contorted, deformed, warped. OPPOSITE: straight. **2** (*a wry observation*) droll, witty, humorous, dry, ironic, sardonic, sarcastic, mocking. OPPOSITE: serious.

Xerox® *verb* photocopy, copy, duplicate, reproduce, Photostat®, run off, print.
➤ *noun* photocopy, copy, duplicate, facsimile, reproduction, Photostat®, print.

Xmas *noun* Christmas, Noël, Yule, Yuletide.

x-ray *noun* radiograph, radiogram, roentgenogram.

yank *verb* pull, jerk, tug, haul, heave, wrench, snatch.
➤ *noun* pull, jerk, tug, wrench, snatch.

yap *verb* **1** (*the dog yapped*) yelp, bark. **2** (*that woman never stops yapping*) chatter, jabber, prattle, babble, gossip, jaw (*inf*), gab (*inf*), gabble, gibber, clack, yammer (*inf*).

yard *noun* quadrangle, quad (*inf*), courtyard, court, enclosure, compound, backyard, garden.

yardstick *noun* measure, gauge, scale, standard, rule, rules, pattern, model, comparison, guide, guideline, criterion, touchstone, benchmark.

yarn *noun* **1** (*he tells a good yarn*) tale, story, anecdote, fable, tall story (*inf*). **2** (*a length of yarn*) thread, fibre, strand.

yawning *adj* wide open, wide, gaping, cavernous, huge, vast.

yearly *adj* annual, per annum, once a year, every year, perennial.
➤ *adv* annually, per annum, once a year, every year, perennially.

yearn *verb* desire, long for, pine, hanker after, yen (*inf*), want, wish, covet, fancy, crave, hunger, thirst, lust, ache, itch.

yearning *noun* longing, pining, craving, desire, wish, want, hankering, fancy, yen (*inf*), hunger, thirst, ache, burning, lust.

yell *verb* shout, scream, cry, shriek, screech, squeal, bellow, holler (*inf*), roar, howl, bawl, yelp, yowl, whoop. OPPOSITE: whisper.
➤ *noun* shout, scream, cry, shriek, screech, squeal, bellow, holler (*inf*), roar, howl, bawl, yelp, yowl, whoop.

yelp *verb* yap, bark, cry, yell, bay, yowl, squeal.

yen *noun* yearning, hankering, longing, want, wish, craving, fancy, desire, lust, passion, hunger, thirst, itch.

yes *adv* right, all right, righto (*inf*), yeah (*inf*), yep (*inf*), aye, sure, certainly, quite, absolutely, of course, by all means.

yet *adv* **1** (*the situation is bad yet not hopeless*) still, but, nevertheless, nonetheless, notwithstanding, however, for all that, despite that, just the same. **2** (*no change yet*) so far, thus far, hitherto, heretofore, until now, up to now, up till now, as yet. **3** (*yet more to sort out*) still, even, also, as well, too, to boot, in addition, additionally, further, furthermore, besides, into the bargain (*inf*), moreover.

yield *verb* **1** (*that tree always yields a good crop*) produce, bear, bring forth, give, supply, provide. **2** (*yield a profit*) return, give, bring in, earn, net, gross, generate, produce, fetch, pay, furnish, provide. **3** (*yield first place to his opponent*) surrender, give up, abandon, part with, relinquish, deliver up, give over, turn over, forgo, abdicate, renounce, resign, remit, cede. **4** (*he called upon his rival to yield*) surrender, submit, capitulate, quit, give in, give up, give way, admit defeat, concede, succumb, abdicate, throw in the towel (*inf*), throw in the sponge (*inf*). **5** (*yield to her wishes*) submit, bow, cave in (*inf*), knuckle under, comply with, acquiesce, accede, agree, consent, go along with. OPPOSITE: resist.
➤ *noun* **1** (*the farmers expect a good yield this year*) crop, produce, harvest, output. **2** (*a poor yield on the investment*) profit, return, revenue, income, earnings, takings, proceeds, haul.

yielding *adj* **1** (*she was yielding in his arms*) submissive, docile, tractable, obedient, manageable, compliant, amenable, biddable, obliging, complaisant, acquiescent, accommodating, unresisting. OPPOSITE: stubborn. **2** (*a yielding material*) flexible, pliant, pliable, supple, soft, elastic, spongy, springy, resilient. OPPOSITE: rigid.

yoke *noun* **1** (*put a yoke on the ox*) collar, harness, coupling. **2** (*the yoke of marriage*) link, tie, bond. **3** (*the yoke of tyranny*) oppression, servitude, subjugation, slavery, enslavement, bondage, burden, thrall. OPPOSITE: freedom.
➤ *verb* **1** (*yoke the horse to the cart*) couple, hitch, harness. **2** (*yoke the two together*) couple, link, unite, join,

tie, bond, connect, fasten, hitch, harness, bracket. OPPOSITE: release.

yokel *noun* rustic, peasant, bumpkin, clodhopper (*inf*), provincial, countryman, countrywoman, country cousin, hick, hillbilly (*inf*), bucolic, boor.

young *adj* **1** (*young children*) youthful, adolescent, juvenile, junior, childish, childlike, immature, small, little, baby, infant, kid (*inf*), teenage. OPPOSITE: old. **2** (*a young industry*) new, recent, fledgling, unfledged, undeveloped, growing, fresh, early, green, callow, inexperienced.
➤ *noun* offspring, progeny, family, children, issue, brood, litter, babies, little ones.

youngster *noun* child, kid (*inf*), toddler, boy, lad, girl, lass, youth, nipper (*inf*), adolescent, juvenile, teenager. OPPOSITE: adult.

youth *noun* **1** (*he remembered the days of his youth*) childhood, boyhood, girlhood, early life, adolescence, teens, immaturity. OPPOSITE: age. **2** (*a gang of youths*) adolescent, teenager, youngster, juvenile, kid (*inf*), boy, lad, girl, stripling. OPPOSITE: man.

youthful *adj* **1** (*a youthful star of stage and screen*) young, juvenile, boyish, girlish, childish, immature. OPPOSITE: old. **2** (*the old man gave a surprisingly youthful performance*) young, fresh, vigorous, active, lively, sprightly, spry.

zany *adj* comical, funny, droll, amusing, clownish, crazy, loony (*inf*), eccentric, peculiar, odd, weird (*inf*), wacky (*inf*), screwy (*inf*), ridiculous, absurd, daft (*inf*). OPPOSITE: serious.

zap *verb* kill, murder, put to death, destroy, slay, liquidate, finish off, do in (*inf*), rub out (*inf*), knock off (*inf*), bump off (*inf*), wipe out (*inf*).

zeal *noun* **1** (*the child attacked the meal with zeal*) fervour, fervency, ardour, spirit, passion, fire, warmth, enthusiasm, eagerness, keenness, earnestness, intensity, vigour, energy, verve, zest, gusto, vehemence. OPPOSITE: apathy. **2** (*the zeal of a true fanatic*) zealotry, dedication, devotion, commitment, fanaticism, extremism.

zealot *noun* fanatic, enthusiast, fiend (*inf*), partisan, bigot, radical, militant, extremist.

zealous *adj* ardent, passionate, impassioned, fervent, fervid, enthusiastic, eager, keen, committed, dedicated, earnest, burning, fiery, intense, vehement, energetic, vigorous, spirited, zestful, devoted, fanatical. OPPOSITE: apathetic.

zenith *noun* height, high point, crowning point, peak, summit, pinnacle, apex, meridian, vertex, apogee, top, acme, climax, culmination, prime. OPPOSITE: nadir.

zero *noun* **1** (*a score of zero*) nought, nothing, nil, love. **2** (*his confidence had hit zero*) lowest point, rock bottom, bottom, nadir.

zero in on focus on, aim for, train on, level at, direct at, concentrate on, home in on, converge on, centre on, pinpoint.

zest *noun* **1** (*a recipe with plenty of zest*) relish, spice, tang, savour, flavour, taste, interest, pungency, piquancy, kick (*inf*), zing (*inf*), oomph (*inf*). OPPOSITE: insipidity. **2** (*a zest for adventure*) gusto, relish, appetite, enjoyment, joy, keenness, enthusiasm, zeal, eagerness, energy, vigour, liveliness.

zigzag *adj* crooked, tortuous, serpentine, sinuous, meandering, twisting, winding. OPPOSITE: straight.

zing *noun* gusto, zest, pep, punch, sparkle, energy, vim, spirit, animation, zeal, enthusiasm, eagerness, life, liveliness, vitality, vivacity, vigour, élan, brio, oomph (*inf*), go (*inf*), dash (*inf*), zip (*inf*), pizzazz (*inf*).

zip *noun* zest, enthusiasm, eagerness, gusto, drive, life, liveliness, vitality, vivacity, spirit, animation, zeal, sparkle, pep, punch, vigour, élan, brio, oomph (*inf*), go (*inf*), dash (*inf*), zip (*inf*), pizzazz (*inf*).
➤ *verb* fly, dash, rush, race, tear, shoot, hurry, hasten, pelt, scurry, speed, flash, hare (*inf*), zoom (*inf*), whizz (*inf*).

zone *noun* area, region, district, belt, section, sector, province, territory, tract, domain, sphere.

zoom *verb* shoot, fly, hurtle, streak, speed, race, hurry, hasten, rush, dash, tear, scurry, pelt, hare (*inf*), whizz (*inf*), zip (*inf*).

Appendices

Collective Nouns

Actors	COMPANY, TRIPOD	Buffalo	HERD, GANG
Aeroplanes	FLIGHT, SQUADRON	Bureaucrats	PLANNING
Agreements	PACT	Buses	GARAGE
Ale	YARD	Candidates	SLATE
Allegations	CAMP	Cardinals	CONCLAVE
Angels	FLIGHT, THRONG	Cards	HOUSE, PACK
Anglers	CASK	Carollers	WASSAIL
Apes	SHREWDNESS	Cars	FLEET, GARAGE
Architects	VAULT	Casinos	GAMBLE
Arguments	GIST	Catholics	MASS
Arms	STAND	Cats	CLOWDER
Artillery	PARK	Cattle	HERD, DROVE
Artists	PALETTE	Cavalry	CHARGE, SQUADRON
Asses	PACE, HERD	Chairmen	COMPANY
Athletes	STRADDLE	Change	WIND
Authorities	BODY, CONSPIRACY	Chickens	BROOD
Badgers	CETE	Choristers	CHOIR
Baptists	SPLASH	Choughs	CHATTERING
Barbers	BABBLE	Church-bells	TOLLING
Barflies	BUZZ	Clergy	SYNOD
Barons	TRUTH	Clerics	CURACY
Bartenders	BLARNEY	Clocks	STRIKING
Bats	FLITTER	Coal	SACK, SCUTTLE
Bayonets	STAB	Colts	NAG, RAG
Bears	SLOTH	Comedian	GIGGLE
Beauty	GALAXY	Compasses	BOXING
Beer	CASK, DRAUGHT	Concubines	HAREM
Bees	HIVE, SWARM, DRIFT, BIKE	Consumption	METER
Beggars	FIGHTING, POVERTY	Convicts	SENTENCING
Birds	FLOCK, FLIGHT	Cookery	NOOK
Bishops	BENCH	Cooking	SAVOUR
Boars	SINGULAR	Cooks	HASTINESS
Books	LIBRARY	Coots	COVERT
Boyfriends	INFIDELITY	Corn	SHEAF
Boys	BLUSH	Corporations	BODY
Brewers	FEAST	Cranes	HERD
Bricks	LOAD	Crooks	GANG
Briefs	BOREDOM	Crows	HOVER
Brooks	BABBLE	Curiosities	CABINET

Curlew	HERD	Hunters	BLAST
Currencies	BASKET	Husbands	HENPECK
Curs	COWARDICE	Indexes	ALPHABET
Dancers	CAPER	Influence	ZONE
Daubers	SQUAT	Information	DISC
Decimals	POINT	Initials	CONFUSION
Deer	HERD, MOB	Insurgents	HORDE
Delights	BOX	Interest	FIELD
Dignitaries	BUMBLE	Interests	ALLIANCE
Diocese	SEA	Investments	RANGE
Disgrace	PIT	Kangaroos	MOB, TROOP
Distance	MILE	Kine	DROVE
Doctors	CURE	Kittens	KINDLE
Dogs	PACK, KENNEL, DOGDOM	Knights	ROUTE
Doves	FLIGHT	Ladies	BEVY
Drinks	BOTTLE	Lambs	GAMBLE
Drunks	BELCHING	Larks	EXALTATION
Ducks (in flight)	TEAM	Lawyers	ELOQUENCE
Ducks (on water)	RAFT, BUNCH, PADDLING, DABBLING	Leopards	LEAP
		Life-styles	SYMBIOSIS
Dunces	BLOCKHEAD	Light	SPECTRUM
Eagles	CONCOVATION	Lions	PRIDE
Eggs	HATCHING	Liquids	TANK
Elephants	HERD	Lovers	LEAP
Elks	GANG	Machine-guns	NEST
Entanglements	KNOT	Mail	BAG, BATCH
Entries	CHARGE	Majors	MORBIDITY
Errors	COMEDY	Makers	MELODY
Events	SEQUENCE, RECORD	Mallards	SORD, SUTE
Exchequers	BUDGET	Martens	RICHNESS
Explosions	BLAST	Medals	HATFUL
Ferrets	BUSINESS, FESNYING	Meetings	MOTION
Finches	CHARM	Millers	FRAUNCH
Firemen	BRIGADE	Miners	PIT
Fish	SHOAL, TAKE	Ministers	CABINET
Fishers	DRIFT	Mites	BITE
Flies	CLOUD, BUSINESS	Moles	LABOUR
Foxes	SKULK	Money	BANK
Garbage	LITTER	Monkeys	TROOP
Geese	GAGGLE	Mules	BARREN
Geese (flying)	SKEIN, WEDGE, TEAM	Music	CONCERT
Giraffe	HERD	Nails	BED
Goats	TRIBE, TRIP, FLOCK, HERD	Nations	ALLIANCE, LEAGUE
Goldfinches	CHARM	Naturists	NUDITY
Gossip	COLUMN	Nightingales	WATCH
Grass	LAWN, TUFT	Organizations	ACRONYM
Grouse	PACK, COVEY	Ostlers	LAUGHTER
Guards	BRIGADE	Oxen	TEAM
Gulls	COLONY	Paper	QUIRE, REAM
Guns	BATTERY	Papers	BUDGET
Handymen	BLACKSLACK	Pardoners	LYING
Hares	DOWN	Partridges	COVEY
Harpers	MELODY	Patients	WARD
Harpists	TWANGING	Peacocks	MUSTER
Hawks	CAST	Pearls	ROPE
Hay	BALE, TRUSS, BOTTLE	Peers	BURKE
Hens	BROOD	Penguins	ROOKERY
Herons	SEDGE, SIEGE	People	CROWD, DRUCK
Highlanders	FOLD	Pheasants	NYE
Holes	BERRY	Phones	EXCHANGE
Horsemen	CAVALCADE	Pickpockets	NEST
Horses	TEAM, HARRAS	Pigeons (flying together)	KIT
Hounds	PACK, KENNEL, CRY	Pigs	HERD

Pipers	POVERTY	Soldiers	REGIMENT
Players	TEAM	Songs	CAVALCADE, MELODY
Pleasure craft	MARINA	Space	YARD
Plots	HATCHING	Spheres	ORBIT
Plovers	CONGREGATION, STAND, WING	Stallions	STUD
		Starlings	MURMURATION
Police	POSSE	Stars	GALAXY, CLUSTER
Policies	SAFEGUARD	Steppes	FLATNESS
Politics	SPECTRUM	Stocks	EXCHANGE
Popcorn	PECK	Stones	RUCK
Popes	PAPACY	Strawberries	PUNNET
Porpoises	SCHOOL	Supporters	ROLE
Porters	SAFEGUARD	Surfaces	AREA
Potage	MESS	Surroundings	GEOGRAPHY
Priests	DISCRETION	Swallows	FLIGHT
Princes	STATE	Swans	LAMENTATION, UPPING, GAME, HERD
Principles	LACK		
Pugilists	FIGHTING	Swine	SOUNDER, HERD
Pups	LITTER	Tame swine	DOYLT
Quail	BEVY, DRIFT	Tea	BREAK
Rabbits	BIRTHRATE, NEST	Teal	COIL, SPRING
Racehorses	STRING	The clans	GATHERING
Rams	BATTERING	Thieves	GANG
Ranks	CASTE	Threshers	THRAVE
Ravens	UNKINDNESS	Thrushes	MUTATION
Recipes	PALATE	Toms	PEEPING
Redundancies	SACK	Traffic	JAM
Regulations	CHAOS	Trains	TERMINUS
Religions	CASTE	Trees	CLUMP
Remembrances	HISTORY	Troubles	SEA
Reserves	BANK	Tuners	DISCORD
Roes	BEVY	Tunes	MEDLEY
Rooks	BUILDING, PARLIAMENT	Turtles	DULE
Ruffs	HILL	Typists	POOL
Saints	COMMUNITY	Uncertainties	WINDS
Savages	HORDE, POSSE	Unitarians	SOLE
Scandals	TABLOID	Verse	ANTHOLOGY
Schoolgirls	GIGGLE	Viols	CONSORT
Scots	TARTAN	Wages	SCALE
Seals	POD, HERD, ROCKERY	Warships	FLEET
Seamen	CREW	Wasps	STINGING
Sea-speeds	KNOT	Waterfowl	BUNCH, KNOB
Sergeants	SHOUTING, SUBTILNE	Whales	SCHOOL, HERD, POD, GAM
Sewers	CREDENCE	Wheat	SHEAF
Sex	SPECTRUM	Whelps	LITTER
Shares	PORTFOLIO	Widgeon	COMPANY, TRIP
Sheep	FLOCK, HERD	Wild duck	KNOB
Sheldrake	DOPPING	Wildfowl	PLUMP
Ships	CONVOY, YARD	Wines	CELLAR
Silk	SKEIN	Wives	IMPATIENCE
Sins	CONFESSION	Wolves	PACK, ROUT
Situations	GEOGRAPHY	Women	GAGGLE, REGIMENT
Smoke	BELCHING	Woodcock	FALL
Snakes	TROGLE	Wool	SKEIN
Snipe	WISP	Worms	CLAT
Snuff	PINCH	Wrens	HERD
Societies	CASTE	Writers	WORSHIP

Foreign Phrases

Fr. *French* Gr. *Greek*
Ger. *German* It. *Italian*
L. *Latin* Sp. *Spanish*

à bas (Fr.) down, down with
ab extra (L.) from without
ab incunabilis (L.) from the cradle
ab initio (L.) from the beginning
ab intra (L.) from within
à bon marche (Fr.) cheap, a good bargain
à bras ouverts (Fr.) with open arms
absente reo (L.) the accused being absent
absit invidia (L.) let there be no ill-will; envy apart
ab uno disce omnes (L.) from one specimen judge of all the
　rest; from a single instance infer the whole
ab urbe condîtâ (L.) from the building of the city; i.e.
　Rome
a capite ad calcem (L.) from head to heel
à chaque saint sa chandelle (Fr.) to each saint his candle;
　honour where honour is due
à cheval (Fr.) on horseback
à compte (Fr.) on account; in part payment
à corps perdu (Fr.) with might and main
à couvert (Fr.) undercover, protected; sheltered
ad astra (L.) to the stars
ad calendas Græcas (L.) at the Greek calends; i.e. never, as
　the Greeks had no calends in their mode of reckoning
à demi (Fr.) by halves; half-way
a Deo et rege (L.) from God and the king
ad hoc (L.) arranged for this purpose; special
ad hominem (L.) to the man; to an individual's interests or
　passion; personal
adhoc sub judice lis est (L.) the case has not yet been
　decided
a die (L.) from that day
à droit (Fr.) to the right
ad infinitum (L.) to infinity
ad interim (L.) in the meantime
ad libitum (L.) at pleasure
ad modum (L.) after the manner of
ad nauseam (L.) to disgust or satiety
ad referendum (L.) for further consideration
ad rem (L.) to the purpose; to the point

ad valorem (L.) to the purpose; to the point
affaire d'amour (Fr.) a love affair
affaire d'honneur (Fr.) an affair of honour; a duel
affaire de cœur (Fr.) an affair of the heart
a fortiori (L.) with stronger reason
à gauche (Fr.) to the left
à genoux (Fr.) on the knees
à haute voix (Fr.) aloud
à huis clos (Fr.) with closed doors; secretly
à belle étoile (Fr.) under the stars; in the open air
à la bonne heure (Fr.) well timed; all right; very well; as
　you please
à l'abri (Fr.) under shelter
à la mode (Fr.) according to the custom or fashion
à la Tartuffe (Fr.) like Tartuffe, the hero of a celebrated
　comedy by Molière; hypocritically
al fresco (It.) in the open air; out-of-doors
al più (It.) at most
alter ego (L.) another self
à merveille (Fr.) to a wonder; marvellously
amor patriæ (L.) love of coutnry
amour-propre (Fr.) self-love, vanity
ancien régime (Fr.) the ancient or former order of things
anguis in herba (L.) a snake in the grass
anno Christi (L.) in the year of Christ
anno Domini (L.) in the year of our Lord
anno mundi (L.) in the year of the world
annus mirabilis (L.) year of wonders; wonderful year
ante bellum (L.) before the war
ante lucem (L.) before light
ante meridiem (L.) before noon
à outrance (Fr.) to the utmost; to extremes; without
　sparing
à pied (Fr.) on foot
à point (Fr.) to a point, just in time, exactly right
a posse ad esse (L.) from possibility to reality
ariston metron (Gr.) the middle course is the best; the
　golden mean
arrière-pensé (Fr.) hidden thought; mental reservation

au courant (Fr.) fully acquainted with

audi alteram partem (L.) hear the other side

au fait (Fr.) well acquainted with; expert

au fond (Fr.) at bottom

auf Wiedersehen! (Ger.) till we meet again

au pis aller (Fr.) at the worst

au revoir (Fr.) adieu; till we meet again

aut vincere aut mori (L.) either to conquer or to die; death or victory

a verbis ad verbera (L.) from words to blows

a vinculo matrimonii (L.) from the bond of matrimony

à volonte (Fr.) at pleasure

a vostra salute (It.) to your health

à votre santé (Fr.) to your health

a vuestra salud (Sp.) to your health

bas bleu (Fr.) a blue-stocking; a literary woman

beau monde (Fr.) the world of fashion

beaux esprits (Fr.) men of wit, gay spirits

beaux yeux (Fr.) fine eyes; good looks

ben trovato (It.) well or cleverly invented

bête noire (Fr.) a black beast; a bugbear

bon gré mal gré (Fr.) with good or ill grace; willing or unwilling

bonhomie (Fr.) good-nature; artlessness

bonne bouche (Fr.) a delicate or tasty morsel

bon vivant (Fr.) a good liver; a gourmand

brutum fulmen (L.) a harmless thunderbolt

canaille (Fr.) rabble

candida Pax (L.) white-robed Peace

casus belli (L.) that which causes or justifies war

causa sine qua non (L.) an indispensable cause or condition

caveat emptor (L.) let the buyer beware (or look after his own interest)

cela va sans dire (Fr.) that goes without saying, needless to say

ceteris paribus (L.) other things being equal

chacun à son goût (Fr.) every one to his taste

cogito, ergo sum (L.) I think, therefore I am

comme il faut (Fr.) as it should be

compos mentis (L.) sound of mind; quite sane

compte rendu (Fr.) an account rendered; a report or statement drawn up

conditio sine qua non (L.) a necessary condition

conseil de famille (Fr.) a family consultation

consensus facit legem (L.) consent makes the law

consilio et animis (L.) by wisdom and courage

consilio et prudentia (L.) by wisdom and prudence

constantia et virtute (L.) by constancy and virtue

contra bonos mores (L.) good manners

contretemps (Fr.) an unlucky accident; a hitch

cordon bleu (Fr.) blue ribbon; a cook of the highest class

cordon sanitaire (Fr.) a line of guards to prevent the spreading of contagion or pestilence

corpus delicti (L.) the body or substance of a crime or offence

corrigenda (L.) things to be corrected

coup de grâce (Fr.) a sudden decisive blow in politics; a stroke of policy

coup de soleil (Fr.) sunstroke

cucullus non facit monachum (L.) the cowl does not make the friar

cui bono? (L.) for whose advantage is it? to what end?

culpam poena premit comes (L.) punishment follows hard upon crime

cum grano salis (L.) with a grain of salt; with some allowance

cum privilegio (L.) with privilege

currente calamo (L.) with a fluent pen

da locum melioribus (L.) give place to your betters

damnant quod non intelligunt (L.) they condemn what they do not comprehend

data et accepta (L.) expenditures and receipts

de bon augure (Fr.) of good augury or omen

de bonne grâce (Fr.) with good grace; willingly

de die in diem (L.) from day to day

de facto (L.) in point of fact; actual or actually

dei gratia (L.) by God's grace

de jure (L.) from the law; by right

de mal en pis (Fr.) from bad to worse

de novo (L.) anew

deo volente (L.) God willing; by God's will

de profundis (L.) out of the depths

dernier ressort (Fr.) a last resource

deus ex machina (L.) one who puts matters right at a critical moment; providential intervention

dies non (L.) a day on which judges do not sit

distingué (Fr.) distinguished; of genteel or elegant appearance

dolce far niente (It.) a sweet doing-nothing; sweet idleness

double entendre (Fr.) double meaning; a play on words

dramatis personae (L.) characters of the drama or play

dum spiro, spero (L.) while I breathe, I hope

ecce homo! (L.) behold the man!

eheu! fugaces labuntur anni (L.) alas! the fleeting years glide by

einmal ist keinmal (Ger.) just once doesn't count

en avant (Fr.) forward

en badinant (Fr.) in sport; in jest

en déshabillé (Fr.) in a state of undress

en famille (Fr.) with one's family; in a domestic state

enfant terrible (Fr.) a terrible child, or one that makes disconcerting remarks

enfin (Fr.) in short; at last; finally

en passant (Fr.) in passing; by the way

en plein jour (Fr.) in broad daylight

en rapport (Fr.) in harmony; in agreement; in relation

en règle (Fr.) according to the rules; in order

entente cordiale (Fr.) cordial understanding, especially between two states

entre nous (Fr.) between ourselves

en vérite (Fr.) in truth; verily

e pluribus unum (L.) one out of many; one composed of many

esprit de corps (Fr.) the animating spirit of a collective body, as a regiment, learned profession or the like

et sequentes, et sequentia (L.) and those that follow

et tu, Brute! (L.) and thou also, Brutus!

ex animo (L.) heartily; sincerely

ex capite (L.) from the head; from memory

ex cathedra (L.) from the chair or seat of authority, with high authority

exceptio probat regulam (L.) the exception proves the rule

ex curia (L.) out of court

ex dono (L.) by the gift

exeunt omnes (L.) all go out or leave the stage

exit (L.) he goes out

ex mero mota (L.) from his own impulse, from his own free will

ex nihilo nihil fit (L.) out of nothing, nothing comes; nothing will come of nothing

ex officio (L.) in virtue of his office

ex post facto (L.) after the deed is done; retrospective

face à face (Fr.) face to face

façon de parler (Fr.) manner of speaking

faire bonne mine (Fr.) to put a good face upon the matter

fait accompli (Fr.) a thing already done

fama clamosa (L.) a current scandal; a prevailing report

faute de mieux (Fr.) for want of better

faux pas (Fr.) a false step; a slip in behaviour

festina lente (L.) hasten slowly

fiat justitia, ruat cœlum (L.) let justice be done though heavens should fall

fiat lux (L.) let there be light

fide et amore (L.) by faith and love

fide et ficuciâ (L.) by fidelity and confidence

fide et fortitudine (L.) with faith and fortitude

fidei defensor (L.) defender of the faith

fide non armis (L.) by faith, not by arms

fide, sed cui vide (L.) trust, but see whom

fides et justitia (L.) fidelity and justice

fides Punica (L.) Punic faith; treachery

filius nullius (L.) a son of nobody; a bastard

finis coronat opus (L.) the end crowns the work

flagrante bello (L.) during hostilities

flagrante delicto (L.) in the commission of the crime

floreat (L.) let it flourish

fons et origo (L.) the source and the origin

force majeure (Fr.) irresistible compulsion; superior force

forensis strepitus (L.) the clamour of the forum

fortuna facet fortibus (L.) fortune favours the bold

functus officio (L.) having performed one's office or duty; hence, out of the office

gaudeamus igitur (L.) so let us be joyful!

genius loci (L.) the genius or guardian spirit of a place

gradu diverso, via una (L.) the same road by different steps

grande toilette (Fr.) full or ceremonial dress

guerra al cuchillo (Sp.) war to the knife

Hannibal ante portas (L.) Hannibal before the gates; the enemy close at hand

hiatus valde deflendus (L.) a chasm or deficiency much to be regretted

hic et nunc (L.) here and now

hic et ubique (L.) here and everywhere

hic jacet (L.) here lies

hic labor, hoc opus est (L.) this is a labour, this is a toil

hic sepultus (L.) here buried

hoc genus omne (L.) all of this sort or class

hoi polloi (Gr.) the many; the vulgar; the rabble

hominis est errare (L.) to err is human

homme de robe (Fr.) a man in civil office

homme d'affair (Fr.) a man of business

homme d'esprit (Fr.) a man of wit or genius

honi soit qui mal y pense (Old Fr.) evil to him who evil thinks

honores mutant mores (L.) honours change men's manners or characters

hors de combat (L.) out of condition to fight

hors de propos (Fr.) not to the point or purpose

ich dien (Ger.) I serve

idée fixe (Fr.) a fixed idea

id est (L.) that is

il a diable au corps (Fr.) the devil is in him

Ilias malorum (L.) an Iliad of ills; a host of evils

il penseroso (It.) the pensive man

il sent le fagot (Fr.) he smells of the faggot; he is suspected of heresy

imperium in imperio (L.) a state within a state; a government within another

in actu (L.) in act or reality

in articulo mortis (L.) at the point of death; in the last struggle

in capite (L.) in chief

in curia (L.) in court

in esse (L.) in being; in actuality

in extenso (L.) at full length

in extremis (L.) at the point of death

in memoriam (L.) to the memory of; in memory

in nubibus (L.) in the clouds

in petto (It.) (my) breast; to one's self

in re (L.) in the matter of

in sano sensu (L.) in a proper sense

in situ (L.) in its original situation

in vino veritas (L.) there is truth in wine; truth is told under the influence of wine

ipse dixit (L.) he himself said it; a dogmatic saying or assertion

ipsissima verba (L.) the very words

ipso facto (L.) in the fact itself

ipso jure (L.) by the law itself

jacta est alea (L.) the die is cast

je ne sais quoi (Fr.) I know not what; an indescribable something

joci causa (L.) for the sake of a joke

labor omnia vincit (L.) labour/work conquers everything

l'allegro (It.) the merry man

lapsus linguæ (L.) a slip of the tongue

lares et penates (L.) household goods

laus Deo (L.) praise to God

le beau monde (Fr.) the fashionable world

lector benevole (L.) kind or gentle reader

le jeun n'en vaut pas la chandelle (Fr.) the game is not worth the candle; the object is not worth the trouble

le mot de l'énigme (Fr.) the key to the mystery

le mot juste (Fr.) the exact word; precise expression

le point de jour (Fr.) daybreak

lèse-majesté (Fr.) high-treason

lettre de cachet (Fr.) a sealed letter containing private orders; a royal warrant

lex loci (L.) the law or custom of the place

lex non scripta (L.) unwritten law; common law

lex scripta (L.) written law; statue law

locum tenens (L.) a deputy

lucri causa (L.) for the sake of gain

magnum opus (L.) a great work, masterpiece

mala fide (L.) with bad faith; treacherously

mal à propos (Fr.) ill-timed; out of place

malgré nous (Fr.) in spite of us

malheur ne vient jamais seul (Fr.) misfortunes never come singly

malum in se (L.) evil or an evil in itself

mardi gras (Fr.) Shrove Tuesday

mariage de convenance (Fr.) marriage from motives of interest rather than of love

mauvais goût (Fr.) bad taste

mauvais honte (Fr.) false modesty

mea culpa (L.) my fault; by my fault

me judice (L.) I being judge; in my opinion

mens agitat molem (L.) mind moves matter

mens legis (L.) the spirit of the law

mens sana in corpore sano (L.) a sound mind in a sound body

meo periculo (L.) at my own risk

meo voto (L.) according to my wish

mise en scène (Fr.) stage setting; surrounding of an event

modus operandi (L.) manner of working

more suo (L.) in his own way

motu proprio (L.) of his own accord

multum in parvo (L.) much in little

mutatis mutandis (L.) with suitable or necessary alteration

nervus probandi (L.) the sinews of the argument; chief argument

nihil ad rem (L.) irrelevant

nil desperandum (L.) there is no reason to despair

noblesse oblige (Fr.) rank imposes obligations; much is expected from one good position

nolens volens (L.) willing or unwilling

nom de guerre (Fr.) a false or assumed name

non compos mentis (L.) not of sound mind

non sequitur (L.) it does not follow

nosce te impsum (L.) know thyself

nota bene (L.) (abbr. *NB*) mark well

nudis verbis (L.) in plain words

obiter dictum (L.) a thing said by the way

omnia vincit amor (L.) love conquers all things

ora pro nobis (L.) pray for us

O tempora! O mores! (L.) O the times! O the manners (or morals)!

oui-dire (Fr.) hearsay

padrone (It.) a master; a landlord

par excellence (Fr.) above all

pari passu (L.) at an equal pace or rate of progress

particeps criminis (L.) an accomplice in a crime

pas de quoi (Fr. abbr. *Il n'y a pas de quoi*) don't mention it

passim (L.) everywhere; in all parts of the book, chapter etc.

pâté de foie gras (Fr.) goose-liver pâté

pater patriæ (L.) father of his country

patres conscipti (L.) the conscript fathers; Roman senators

pax robiscum (L.) peace be with you

per ardua ad astra (L.) through rough ways to the stars; through suffering to renown

per capita (L.) by the head or poll

per contra (It.) contrariwise

per diem (L.) by the day; daily

per se (L.) by itself; considered apart

pied-à-terre (Fr.) a resting-place; a temporary lodging

pis aller (Fr.) the worst or last shift

plebs (L.) the common people

poco a poco (It.) little by little

prima facie (L.) at first view or consideration

primus inter pares (L.) first among equals

pro forma (L.) for the sake of form

pro patria (L.) for our country

pro tanto (L.) for so much; for as far as it goes

pro tempore (L.) for the time being

quid pro quo (L.) one thing for another; tit for tat; an equivalent

qui m'aime, aime mon chien (Fr.) love me, love my dog

qui tacet consentit (L.) he who is silent gives consent

quod erat demonstrandum (L.) (abbr. *Q.E.D.*) which was to be proved or demonstrated

quod erat faciendum (L.) which was to be done

quod vide (L.) (abbr. *q.v.*) which see; refer to the word just mentioned

quo jure? (L.) by what right?

raison d'être (Fr.) the reason for a thing's existence

re (L.) in the matter or affair of

reculer pour mieux sauter (Fr.) to draw back in order to leap better; await a better opportunity

reductio ad absurdum (L.) the reducing of a position to a logical absurdity

requiescat in pace (L.) may he (or she) rest in peace

respice finem (L.) look to the end

respublica (L.) the commonwealth

revenons à nos moutons (Fr.) let us return to our sheep; let us return to our subject

re vera (L.) in truth

sans peur et sans reproche (Fr.) without fear and without reproach

sans rime ni raison (Fr.) without rhyme or reason

sans souci (Fr.) without a care

sartor resartus (L.) the botcher repatched; the tailor patched or mended

sauve qui peut (Fr.) let him save himself who can

savoir-faire (Fr.) the knowing how to act; tact

savoir-vivre (Fr.) good-breeding; refined manners

semper idem (L.) always the same

seriatim (L.) in a series; one by one

sic passim (L.) so here and there throughout; so everywhere

sicut ante (L.) as before

sine die (L.) without a day being appointed

sine mora (L.) without delay

sine qua non (L.) without which, not; indispensable condition

sotto voce (It.) in an undertone

spirituel (Fr.) intellectual; witty

stet (L.) let it stand; do not delete

sub judice (L.) under consideration

sub pœna (L.) under a penalty

sub rosa (L.) under the rose; privately

sub voce (L.) under such or such a word

sui generis (L.) of its own or of a particular kind

summum bonum (L.) the chief good

tableau vivant (Fr.) a living picture; the representation of some scene by a group of persons

tant mieux (Fr.) so much the better

tant pis (Fr.) so much the worse

tempora mutantur, nos et mutamur in illis (L.) the times are changing and we with them

tempus fugit (L.) time flies

tête-à-tête (Fr.) head to head; a private conversation

tiers état (Fr.) the third estate; the commons

tour de force (Fr.) a feat of strength or skill

tout à fait (Fr.) wholly; entirely

tout à l'heure (Fr.) instantly

toute de suite (Fr.) immediately

tu quoque (L.) thou also
ubique (L.) everywhere
ubi supra (L.) as above stated
vade in pace (L.) go in peace
variæ lectiones (L.) various readings
variorum notæ (L.) the notes of various commentators
vede et crede (L.) see and believe
veni, vidi, vici (L.) I came, I saw, I conquered
verbatim et literatim (L.) word for word and letter for letter
verbum sat sapienti (L.) a word is enough for a wise man
ver non semper vivet (L.) spring is not always green
rexata quæstio (L.) a disputed question
via media (L.) a middle course
via trita, via tuta (L.) the beaten path is the safe path

vice versa (L.) the terms of the case being reversed
videlicet (L.) that is to say; namely
vi et armis (L.) by force of arms; my main force; by violence
vigilante et orate (L.) watch and pray
vita brevis, ars longa (L.) life is short; art is long
viva regina! (L.) long live the queen!
vivat rex (L.) long live the king!
viva voce (L.) by the living voice; orally
voilà (Fr.) behold; there is; there are
voilà tout (Fr.) that's all
volo, non valeo (L.) I am willing, but unable
vox populi, vox Dei (L.) the voice of the people is the voice of God